FREE MONEY TO CHANGE YOUR LIFE

First Edition

by

MATTHEW LESKO

with

Andrew Naprawa

and

Mary Ann Martello

Editors:
Andrew Naprawa
Mary Ann Martello

Copy Editor: Martha Hess

Contributing Writer: Kurt Samson

Researchers:
Mercedes Sundeen, Caroline Pharmer
Daniel Meeks, Jr.; Michelle McNabb
Diana Webster; Margret Miller
Lynda Burns; Terry Plas
Elaine Sikorski; Denise Burek
Jenny Robinson

Publicity: Debbie Samson

Marketing Director: Kim McCoy

Production Coordinator: Pam Schultz

Production: Meserve Associates, Inc.

Production Designer: Beth Meserve

Production Assistant: Peggy Yates

Cover Design: John Koehler

Cover Photo: Bruno Joachim

Illustrations: Martha Murphy

FIRST EDITION

Library of Congress Cataloging-in-Publication Data

Lesko, Matthew.

Naprawa, Andrew

Martello, Mary Ann

ISBN #1-878346-40-7 (paperback)

Other books written by Matthew Lesko:

Lesko's Info-Power III

Government Giveaways for Entrepreneurs III

Info-Fobia: How To Survive In An Information Society

Free Legal Help

Free Health Care

Everything You Need To Run A Business At Home

Gobs and Gobs of Free Stuff

Discounts For Seniors

Free Stuff For Seniors

Expert Health Advice

Seniors' Yellow Pages

Free Stuff For Busy Moms

Free Stuff For Women's Health, Fitness and Nutrition

Free College Money And Training For Women

Free Money And Help For Women Entrepreneurs

Free Money to Change Your Life CD-ROM

For ordering information on any of Matthew Lesko's publications, call 1-800-UNCLE-SAM, or contact his web site at www.lesko.com.

Most books by Matthew Lesko are available at special quantity discounts for bulk purchases for sales promotions, premiums, fund-raising or educational use. Special books or book excerpts also can be created to fit specific needs.

For details, write Information USA, Special Markets, Attention: Kim McCoy, P.O. Box E, Kensington, MD 20895; or 1-800-797-7811, Marketing; {www.lesko.com}.

Table of Contents

Table of Contents

Table of Contents

Table of Contents

Matthew Lesko, Information USA, Inc., 12081 Nebel Street, Rockville, MD 20852 • 1-800-955-7693 • www.lesko.com

Table of Contents

Warning: This Book Is Out Of Date

In our fast changing information oriented society, as soon as something is published it is bound to be out of date. As self publishers, we do make corrections each time we print books, but it is still impossible to keep up with change in a printed book. So, if you happen to encounter a source whose telephone number, email or address is no longer valid, it does not mean that this organization or program is no longer available. Contact the information operator for the city listed to locate a new listing. We apologize for any inconvenience this may cause you.

Introduction

Matthew Lesko, Information USA, Inc., 12081 Nebel Street, Rockville, MD 20852 • 1-800-955-7693 • www.lesko.com

Isn't It About Time?

Hate your job? Feel as though your life is at a standstill? Want more time with your family? Need more money? Or simply feel unfulfilled? Don't just complain about your life. Do something about it. You can even get **free money to change your life**.

Sounds unbelievable, doesn't it? Like those late night infomercials who find some garbage collector in Cincinnati who read some book and became a millionaire overnight.

Don't worry, this isn't television. This is about real life. Because the government is certainly real and that's what I'm talking about. The government is where all this money comes from. And it's not just happening to one person in Cincinnati. It's happening to over 20 million people each and every year. Rich people, poor people, young people, and even old people are all eligible for programs that the government offers to help change your life.

There are over 5,000 government money programs where you can find opportunities like:

- $50,000 to Open Up a Coffee House
- $30,000 to Go to School in Hawaii
- $43,000 to Become a French Chef
- $100,000 to Open a Country Inn
- $30,000 to Become a Grizzly Bear Tagger
- $70,000 to Study Arts Management
- $50,000 to Edit Science Magazines at Home
- $2,000 to Study Storytelling
- $20,000 to Produce a TV Show For Kids
- $12,000 to Attend a Cowboy Festival in Australia
- $5,000 to Start a Street Hockey Equipment Distributorship
- $75,000 to Renovate an Old House
- $100,000 to Start a Day Care Center

These are programs which give out billions in taxpayers money each year but never spend a dime in letting people know that they're available.

Most of us only dream about getting money to make changes in our lives. We dream of winning the lottery or inheriting a bundle from some long lost relative. Or we may be wishing for a giant raise that will somehow solve all our problems. But none of these dreams seem to come true and we continue to languish through life in varying states of unhappiness. To change takes effort, and for some of us, it seems easier to complain about our lot in life than to stir things up by taking a new direction.

What most of us are totally unaware of, is that on the other side of a telephone line is over $350 billion worth of taxpayers funds that you can use to help make your dreams come true.

Next year you could be one of the:

- 1,000,000 entrepreneurs who will get money from the government to start or grow a business, or
- 4,000,000 people who will get money to invest in real estate, or
- 6,000,000 people who will get money to go to college, or
- 10,000,000 people who will get free help and training for a better job, or

- the tens of thousands of people who will get free money to help them travel around the world, work on their invention, change their neighborhood, or start their own nonprofit, or
- one of the many who have gotten money to become an artist, a writer, a talk show host, or cowboy.

Is there a catch? Yes, there is. The catch is that getting the money is going to take effort on your part. You won't have to invest thousands of dollars in high priced seminars, consultants, or experts, but you will have to invest some of your time. In our information driven society, it's information that is the tool for success. This book gives you all the tools you need to change your life because it's loaded with all kinds of valuable information. But it has to be <u>you</u> that puts it all to use. Changing your life isn't like adding a room to your house, where you can hire a contractor to do all the work. You have to take an active role in order to change your life, and here are the tools to help you do it.

Being Prepared For Change

We are living in a society with a very high misery index. I don't mean the official misery index that the economists refer to as a combination of current inflation and unemployment statistics. The misery I'm talking about is the fact that very few people seem to be happy. There are very few people who truly enjoy their jobs, or even their lives in general. Most people would rather be somewhere else, or seem to live in constant fear that the job they really don't enjoy anyway will be taken away from them.

The only way to deal with this anxiety is to learn how to deal with the changes that are happening in our society. But to do this people have to change themselves. We all know that the only people who really like change are busy cashiers and babies with wet diapers!.

Change is moving like a freight train through our society, and successful people are the ones who will learn how to deal with it and change their lives to accommodate it. Those who are anxious about our changing society as well as those who are already victims of it both fall into the trap of feeling that they can still wait until they have to do anything serious with their own lives in order to deal with our changing society.

If you are one of those who is not quite sure about the impact change is having on our society, these facts should make it all a little clearer for you.

- From about 1979 to 1994, Fortune 500 companies eliminated over 47 million jobs. That's about 25% of the entire U.S. workforce. Recent layoffs include 85,000 at IBM, 83,500 at AT&T, and 74,000 at General Motors.

- From 1979 to 1993, all age groups of men saw their wages go down or stay the same, except men over 65.

- A 30-year old man today makes 20% less than a 30-year old made 25 years ago. For the first time since WWII a generation of men in their late forties and early 50's have suffered a decline in wages.

- Wages declined at the same time when corporations experienced record breaking profits, executives' salaries have gone through the roof, and the Dow Jones Industrial index has gotten so high that it gave investors nose bleeds!

- The number of people who consider themselves self-employed has almost doubled since 1977.

- In 1992, temporary jobs accounted for two out of every three new private sector jobs. Temporary, contract, and part time workers now make up more than 25 percent of the U.S. workforce.

- More people now work for Manpower Inc., a temporary worker firm than, for IBM or General Motors.

- The average person now works 180 more hours per year than they did a generation ago.

- In 1978, the average person with a college degree earned 38% more than a person with only a high school diploma. By 1990, college grads earned 80% more than high school grads.

- 70% of all the new jobs created in our country have been managerial, professional, and other positions that require higher education, but only about 25% of the workforce has a college degree.

- In 1980, United States Steel, America's largest integrated steel company, employed 120,000 people in steel production. Ten years later, it employed only 20,000 people in steel production, and yet produced almost the same steel tonnage.

- There are more people on campuses today who are over 35 than there are 18 and 19 year olds.

- In the 1980's, 45% of those laid off got their jobs back, but in the 1990's, only 15 to 20% of those laid off get their same jobs back.

- Almost 70% of those laid off workers will earn less than they did before being laid off.

- You have a 50% greater chance of being laid off than you have of being a victim of crime.

- Even the newspaper comic strip character Spider Man announced that he couldn't make enough money with his spider powers so he was changing careers and joining a circus.

Have you had enough?

How To Change In A Changing Society

Nothing that worked for you yesterday is likely to work for you tomorrow. The only thing that will remain constant is change. If you don't change yourself, someone else is going to do it for you and you may be less than ready for it. Change is the code word for survival in the new economy. Both organizations and individuals who want to thrive or hope to survive are those that learn how to continually reinvent themselves.

You can no longer get a job with a big company and look forward to 30 years of work with full health insurance and a retirement plan. Those kinds of jobs that used to be available in our transportation and manufacturing industries and paid $50,000 a year with only a high school diploma are quickly disappearing with each merger or downsizing.

Workers have become disposable, and the only workers that become valuable are those that have skills for the new jobs that are being created and skills for the old ones that are disappearing. We're leaving the industrial age and entering the age of information and services. We're now living at a time where muscles are no longer needed but where brain power is all important. Over 70% of all the new jobs are knowledge based. Almost all new high paying jobs require analytical and information oriented training.

Getting Trained and Retrained

Both the doctor who is trying to keep up on the latest cures to cancer and the typist who is trying to keep up on the latest in word processing programs know that they have to keep learning in order to service their clients to the best of their abilities. Those who don't learn something new will be destined to watch the world pass them by. And those who don't enter the workforce with the latest skills will likely find themselves on the bottom rungs of the ladder for a long, long time.

In our society there is no reason <u>not</u> to get the education and training you need to get ahead in our highly specialized economy. There are hundreds of programs worth tens of billions of dollars for people of all ages and all economic backgrounds just waiting to be used. And these programs are not going to go away due to budget cuts because voters want to keep them. Right before the 96 elections, 67% of the electorate said that education and training is the most effective way to improve things economically, and only 36% said the same thing about tax cuts.

Here are the kinds of programs you can take advantage of in order to get trained or retrained in our fast changing society:

- Free College Tuition If You're Over 55
- Free Tutoring If You're a Woman Having Trouble in Math and Science
- Free Training and Expense Money If You're a High School Dropout
- Grants To Go To College If You Make Over $100,000 Per Year
- Free Training If You're a Woman Who Wants a Job in the Construction Industry
- $6,500 for College If You Lost Your Job Because of Imports
- $10/hour for a Part Time Job To Help Pay For Your College Tuition
- $3,000 for a New Employer To Hire and Train You
- $63,000 To Cover All Your College Expenses

Change For A Wealthier, Healthier, and Fun Life

Getting a job you really like or simply getting out of one you dislike is not only a faster way to a wealthier life, it's also a faster way to a healthier life and one that holds a lot more fun for the individual. It will not only be healthier and more fun for you, it will also be healthier and more fun for your loved ones and those around you who will obviously benefit from your increased optimism and sense of fulfillment.

Researchers at the University of Pennsylvania found that parents who have control over how, when, and where their work gets done have fewer behavior problems with children than those parents who have less control over their lives. They also found that the amount of time parents spend working isn't linked to their children's behavior, But what does seem to have an impact on children is how much parents' work tensions affect home life.

Another group of researchers at the University of California, Irvine, has found that parents with more stimulating, challenging jobs are warmer, less harsh, and more responsive in their parenting.

Accomplishing career goals is also a major factor in our mental health and well-being. A sociologist at the University of Wisconsin at Madison interviewed 3,052 women at age 35 to see what kind of career goals they set for themselves. The researcher then interviewed them again at age 53 to see how well they were doing. She found that those who fell short of their career goals had lower levels of psychological well being and higher levels of depression compared with women who had attained their career goals.

I recently interviewed a group of gerontologists and leaders of organizations who work with the elderly, and to a person, they each preach that the key to a long and healthy life is staying engaged in meaningful activity. Searching for that career that you enjoy most is the best way to stay involved in stimulating activity for the longest possible time.

And if you are looking for real fun in life, you might find it in the struggle to find out what you really want to do in life. So many people believe that fun is sitting around doing nothing or doing something that requires no effort. It's no fun to play someone in a game that is at a level that is way beneath your ability. Beating them by an overwhelming score quickly loses its sense of fun. We have the most fun when we play someone who is a little bit better than we are and are successful in figuring out a way to beat them. Fun is derived when we achieve something that is unexpected because that is when we experience true growth.

Fun is doing something whether we get paid for it or not. And when we are engaged in that kind of fun, time becomes unimportant, our worries seem to disappear, and we are able to share the joy and happiness of life with others.

So why be stuck doing something when you would rather be doing something else? Here are 10,000 programs worth over $350 billion dollars to help you do the things you always wanted to do with your life.

This Book Takes Work

You can't expect to pay for the book, place it on your shelf, and have your life magically changed. You also can't expect your life to change even after you buy the book and sit down and read it. In order for the book to be valuable to you, it is going to require a lot of hard work on your part.

You are the one who is going to have to make the telephone call in order to get the book to work for you. You are the one who is going to have to read the application forms, fill out these forms, and maybe even fill them out again.

It's going to take a lot of effort. It's even going to take a lot of time. It could take six weeks, or even six months, or longer. That's simply the way the world works. Even if it takes you 16 months, if it means a lifetime of satisfaction, then it's well worth your efforts.

It's also important to know that you just can't apply to one program, or just one office. That would be like looking for a job and asking only one employer if they will hire you today. If that employer says no to you, it certainly doesn't mean that there aren't any jobs in the world. So if one office says that there is no money for your idea, that doesn't mean that it's true everywhere. There are thousands of offices and each year millions of people will be getting money through hundreds of programs.

It's All Not In The Book

It's impossible for this book to have every imaginable program there is in the universe. Organizations are adding programs every day, and no matter how good our research staff is, it is still possible that we missed some programs when we were compiling this book. So with this in mind, as you are contacting offices in this book for information about their programs, be sure to inquire if they know of any other programs that may be relevant to your search. It is very likely that people working in a given field may know what other programs are available in their field. It never hurts to ask, and that holds true for the sources listed in this book.

How To Treat The People Who Are Going To Give You Money

The key to getting what you need from the sources in this book is how you treat these people when you first call them. Remember, most of these people will get paid the same salary if they hang up on you right after you say hello, or if they work for you for free for two weeks. We have no control over their salary. Even though your tax dollars go toward paying their salary, you have no control over how much they get or even if they get it all. But how much help they give you about the inside information on getting the money in their program or help in filling out their forms or directing you to other programs depends a great deal on how well you treat them. This also goes for everyone else in our society: the teller at your bank or the customer representative at your insurance company. Sure, they all want to help you, because it's their job. But you have to help create an environment in which they want to help you as much as they possibly can. And the only way you can accomplish this is by using your personality.

Another problem is that many people believe that government employees are all lazy and shiftless people, so they don't deserve our best and most courteous behavior. It does you no good at all to believe this. Because if you do, they will feel this from you and will be less inclined to help you. These people have the money and help you need to change your life, so you should be doing all you can to make it easy for them to help you.

Here are some simple things to keep in mind when dealing with the people in this book. Remember, getting help and information is a people business, and how much help and information you get depends on how well you treat the people who have the information that you want.

Ten Basic Telephone Tips

1) **Introduce Yourself Cheerfully**

   The way you open the conversation will set the tone for the entire interview. Your greeting and initial comment should be cordial and cheerful. Your telephone attitude should give the feeling that this is not going to be just another telephone call, but a pleasant interlude in someone's day.

2) **Be Open and Candid**

   You should be as candid as possible with your source since you are asking the same of him. If you are evasive or deceitful in explaining your needs or motives, your source will be reluctant to provide you with information.

3) **Be Optimistic**

   Throughout the entire conversation you should exude a sense of confidence. If you call and say "You probably aren't the right person" or "You don't have any information, do you?" it makes it easy for the person to say "You're right, I can't help you." A positive attitude will encourage your source to stretch his mind to see what information he might have that could possibly help you and maybe even save you some money.

4) **Be Humble and Courteous**

   You can be optimistic and still be humble. Remember the old adage that you can catch more flies with honey than you can with vinegar. People in general, and experts in particular, love to tell others what they know, as long as their position of authority is not questioned or threatened. In fact, if they are made to feel like an expert by the way you treat them, chances arc that they will give you more information than they originally intended to give.

5) **Be Concise**

   State your problem simply. A long-winded explanation may bore your contact and reduce your chances for getting a thorough response.

6) **Don't Be a "Gimme"**

   A "gimme" is someone who says "give me this" or "give me that," and has little consideration for the other person's time or feelings. Remember to "ask" for information or a particular document that you're interested in.

7) **Be Complimentary**

   This goes hand in hand with being humble. A well placed compliment about your source's expertise or insight about a particular topic will serve you well. In searching for information in large organizations, you are apt to talk to many colleagues of your source, so it wouldn't hurt to convey some respect for your source's abilities. A good example of a favorable comment might be, "Everyone I spoke to said you are the person I must talk with." It is reassuring for anyone to know that they have the respect of their peers.

8) **Be Conversational**

   Avoid spending the entire time talking about the information you need. Briefly mention a few irrelevant topics such as the weather, the Washington Redskins, or the latest political campaign. The more social you are without being too chatty, the more likely that your source will open up to you.

9) **Return the Favor**

You might share with your source information or even gossip you have picked up elsewhere. However, be certain not to betray the trust of another source. If you do not have any relevant information to share at the moment, it would still be a good idea to call back when you are further along in your research when you might have information of value to offer to an especially helpful source.

10) **Send Thank You Notes**

A short note, typed or handwritten, will help ensure that your source will be just as cooperative in the future, should you need their help.

Lesko's Lessons
On Life

Matthew Lesko, Information USA, Inc., 12081 Nebel Street, Rockville, MD 20852 • 1-800-955-7693 • www.lesko.com

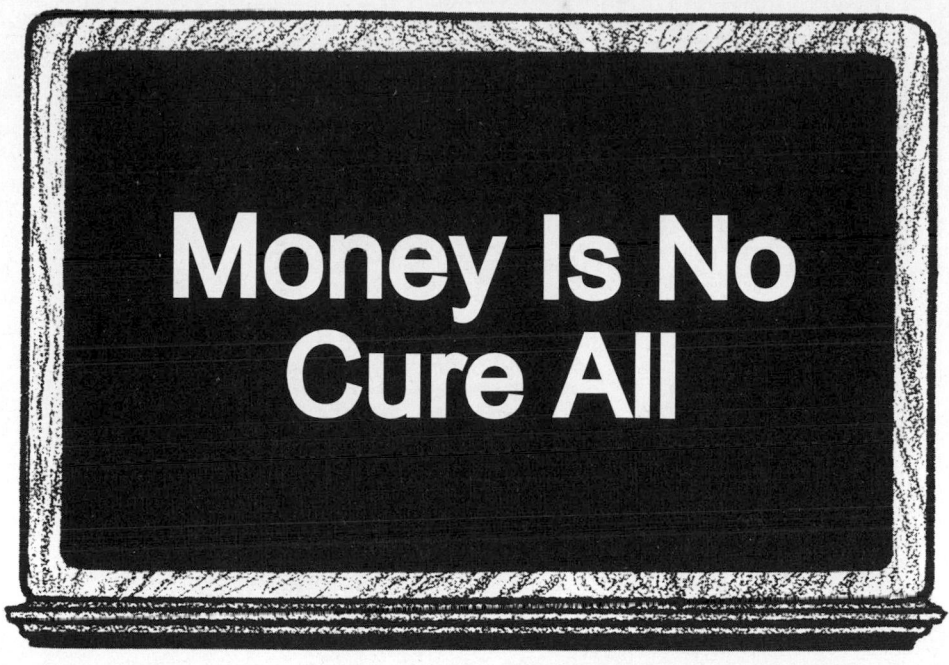

Money Is No Cure All

Many of us still believe that money will solve all of our problems. We say to ourselves: 'If I only had the money, I'd start my own business; I'd go back to school and become an art teacher; or be like Mother Teresa, and spend the rest of my life doing something meaningful.'

Money was probably your motive for buying this book.

I'm promising you free money to change your life — and I can deliver — but stop for a minute and think about it. Isn't this the same finger we point at our elected representatives in Washington? Congress tries to solve the country's problems by throwing more and more money at them, we say. In our hearts, we know money won't cure the nation, yet in our own lives, we think it will.

But that doesn't makes us hypocrites. We have been raised to strive toward success, and to equate success with a fat bank account. Not so. Money isn't going to solve our problems. In fact, it often creates more problems than it solves. Ask any big lottery winner. We all think about ways to make money doing the kind of work that we <u>want</u> to do — something fun and exciting, and certainly not what we're doing now. We yearn to escape the humdrum everyday kind of life and instead, do something that makes us really want to get out of bed every morning.

While many of us use money as an excuse for not chasing our dream, success takes a lot more than ready cash. It takes a strong will, perseverance, and, above all, a commitment to the chase. These are the important ingredients, and none of them requires a nickel.

ML

You Can't Buy Someone Else's Magic

Money will not solve your problems. It seems that it will, but ask anyone who has made a lot of cash, quick. There's always some motivational talk show person with a monetary cyclone to offer that promises to make millionaires of us all. They dangle dollars as bait. An inspiring author, a stimulating seminar, or a self help guru to guide you along is usually part of the deal, too. We tell ourselves this person has figured out the mysteries of success, and if we read a book or attend a seminar, some of it will rub off, and all of our problems will suddenly disappear. That's precisely what all of these fast talkers hope for. The more people who fall for their line, the more money they pull in. All the while, they're busy developing their next "get rich" scheme to hype to anyone willing to listen. Their ideas for success are like puffy clouds that suddenly materialize, quickly change form, and just as suddenly disappear.

Things don't work that way. You can't buy someone else's magic, you have to find your own — then nourish it with your actions. We all have our own unique magic, we just have to tap into it so that we can share it with the world in our own special way.

Many of these self-help gurus are magicians all right, because they have a magical way of getting people to part with their money. Even the good ones, those who really do have something to offer, can only give you a few tools that you might be able to use to build your own success in life. Changing your life is not like putting in a new bathroom — it's not redecorating. You can't hire a contractor to build a new life, it's got to be a do-it-yourself project. And it usually takes some time, a lot of hard work, and maybe even a little luck.

   Matthew Lesko, Information USA, Inc., 12081 Nebel Street, Rockville, MD 20852 • 1-800-955-7693 • www.lesko.com

Strive For Failure

My fear of failure was one of the biggest obstacles I had to overcome to achieve something worthwhile with my life. By being so afraid of failing, I did everything on the safe side. I followed the rules I'd learned in school, or the advice of one expert after another. But none of it worked, and as a consequence, my first two businesses were crashing failures. I'm probably the only person who had a computer software business back in the mid 1970s that failed, and I honestly believe one of the reasons was because I had an MBA in Computer Science. I ran my businesses like I had been taught to back in school, thinking that it would guarantee my success. Boy was I wrong! I followed the book instead of following my instincts, and it took two failed businesses to unlearn everything I'd been taught.

But now I can say that these failures were the best thing that ever happened to me. They taught me that the world did not end when my efforts failed, and the experience forced me to think harder about how to launch my next business. I concluded that my first two businesses went bust because I'd followed the advice of too many other people. I listened to their recommendations for success instead of following my own heart and, as a result, I didn't have any fun running the show. And certainly one of the biggest reasons that we all dream of having our own business is to have a little fun.

The third time, I said to myself, "I'm going to do this the way I think it should be done, not how everyone else says it should".

I figured that the worst thing that could happen was another failure, and having already experienced two, I knew it wasn't all that painful and that I would survive. This time, I told myself, at least I'll have some fun failing. Sure enough, that's when I had my first success, and success is a whole lot more fun than failure, take it from someone who has had both experiences.

I believe that you have to fail to succeed at anything — it's the only way most of us learn the important lessons in life. Without risking failure, you can't get anywhere in life. So it's important to prepare yourself to handle failure, because it's probably going to happen more than once before you succeed at something. Look at children learning to walk, or a kid on his or her first bike. It's the same process when we begin any new adventure on the road to success. Falling down, brushing ourselves off, and getting up to try again is all part of the learning process — whether you're two years old or 62!

When my kids first started to walk they would hold on to the edge of the coffee table for security. Then they would take one step by themselves and then fall on their butts. Then they would crawl back to the coffee table, grab the edge, pull themselves up, and try it again. But sure enough they would fall again. And this would go on for days, until they finally made it all the way to the kitchen without falling. They learned perseverance through this process, and gained confidence in themselves when they finally succeeded.

This is also true of anything new that you're going to do in life. You try. Then you fail. You try again. And then you fail again. You keep doing it until you get it right.

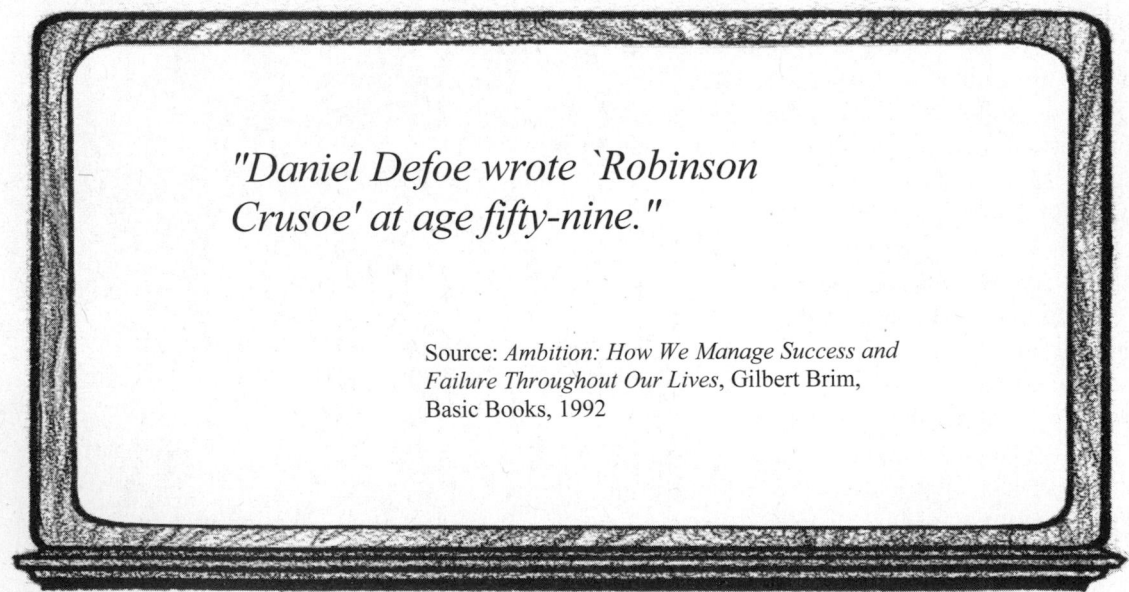

"Daniel Defoe wrote `Robinson Crusoe' at age fifty-nine."

Source: *Ambition: How We Manage Success and Failure Throughout Our Lives*, Gilbert Brim, Basic Books, 1992

Your Fears Are Wrong

We all have fears. Some of these fears are real, but often, they are simply imagined fears that have no real basis. The problem is that often unreal fears stop us from doing the things we really want to do.

Here's an example. The average taxpayer is consumed with the fear of an IRS audit. It's a fear that rules much of our lives, especially around tax time. But do you know your real chances of being audited are only about 9 out of 1,000. So why do we worry so about being audited? Probably because of an even bigger fear — the fear of being audited and the government finding out that we have somehow cheated and we'll end up in jail. Well, the chances of that happening to you is about 1.6 out of 100,000.

Your chances of being injured in a car accident are far greater than your chances of going to jail for cheating on your taxes. Yet, we all seem to fear the tax man much more than the driver next to us on the highway. It's a fear with no basis in fact, but a true fear, nonetheless.

Every day when we want to go somewhere, we get into our cars and never worry about the dangers involved. We just get into the car

Matthew Lesko, Information USA, Inc., 12081 Nebel Street, Rockville, MD 20852 • 1-800-955-7693 • www.lesko.com

17

and go. But when we want to go somewhere new with our life, we sit down and think about the fears of going down this new path, for example:

- we may lose our home
- we may wind up on welfare
- we may become a bag lady, homeless, or
- we may even starve to death

We're intelligent and we don't want these bad things to happen. So we stop, and we don't take the chance of going in a new direction. We limit ourselves to the safe path — the 9 to 5 job, the minuscule raise each year — instead of venturing out and testing the unknown path.

Don't let unrealistic fears stop you from doing what you really want to do in life. Listed below are a number of fears along with an estimate of your chances of these predicaments happening to you.

- Your chances of dying in a plane are 1 in 300,256
- Your chances of starving are 1 in 1,061,399
- Your chances of getting hit by a car are 1 in 40,471
- Your chances of dying in an auto accident are 1 in 6,157
- Your chances of dying from a snake bite are 1 in 28,657,778
- Your chances of dying from excessive cold are 1 in 402,371
- Your chances of dying due to a volcano or earthquake are 1 in 15,171,765
- Your chances of dying from being struck by lightning are 1 in 4,524,912
- Your chances of dying from a falling object are 1 in 361,232

Goals Are A Trap

Maybe it was having parents who lived through the Depression or seven years of business school that made me believe that I always had to have quantitative goals or a plan of where I wanted to be in five years. When I got out of the Navy, my goal was to have a million dollar business. But after having two businesses that failed, this goal was beginning to look about as likely as me playing tennis at Wimbledon. But lo and behold, my third business made it. We were doing over a million and a half dollars of business within about three years. When I reached the million dollar mark, I got on the phone and called everyone I could think of to tell them the news. And when that was over, big deal. I had to go to work the next day and think of another goal to strive for.

I remember another big goal of mine that was even more disappointing. I always wanted to be a guest on one of the big morning TV talk shows, like The Today Show or Good Morning America. It was back in 1981 when I finally got my big break and was invited to be on Good Morning America. I was so excited, thinking that this was my big break. I had this fantasy of being on the show, being terrific, and then getting a call from some fat cat smoking a cigar in Hollywood who was going to make me some kind of big star. I saw lots of movies like that, so naturally I thought it should also happen to me. Well, of course it didn't happen that way. I was great on the show, or at least that's what the producers told me. The telephone did ring off the hook at ABC with people wanting more information about the book, and that was good. But no one called to make me a star, and I had to go to work the next day. Just like every other day.

Now I think that quantifiable goals are a big trap. You reach them and then what do you do? The real goal is to be doing what you want to be doing every single day of your life. Because that's what life really is, living every day. And if you are doing what you want, then every day is a pleasure, not just a day closer to reaching some goal. The process of what you are doing becomes the goal, not some artificial yardstick that you are forever trying to grasp.

I also found that goals made me do things that I was sometimes not very proud of. Being bright, I found myself looking for short cuts that would get me to my goal faster — like not being completely truthful, or withholding selective information to make myself look better, or working with people I disliked just for the money. It didn't make me feel the best, but I thought I had to do things like that to reach my goals.

Now life is different, I try to enjoy my work every day of my life, and not just on the days when I achieve some artificial goal. That's why I believe that goals can trap you into doing things you don't enjoy doing every day. And that can be a wasted life.

Credentials Don't Count

Growing up in the 50s, I believed like most people that you had to go to Harvard or some other top notch school in order to write a book in this country. I also believed that you had to be an A student and have at least an MBA to be a success in business. Well, I certainly don't believe that anymore. I got a D in English at Marquette University and I've written over 50 books, and two of them have been New York Times Best Sellers. I finally got my MBA, and my first two businesses still failed. Now no one ever asks if I have an MBA or not.

Life is full of examples of people who accomplish so much in a given field without having the proper credentials. Look at the two people who started Apple Computer, Steve Jobs and Steve Wozniak. When they started their business they did not even have the credentials to get a job at IBM. They never even finished college, but they went into their garage and started an entire new computer industry. The same with the people who started Ben and Jerry's. One never finished college and the other was trying to get into medical school but couldn't. When they started the business, they didn't even know how to make ice cream! My understanding is that they took a $5 government correspondence course from the Cooperative Extension Service to show them how to do it. And the rest is history.

And if you think that grades are so important, do you realize that:

- over 50% of all the CEOs for Fortune 500 companies had C or C- averages in college
- 65% of all U.S. senators come from the bottom half of their school classes
- 75% of U.S. presidents were in the Lower-Half Club in school
- over 50% of millionaire entrepreneurs never finished college.

(Source: *If It Ain't Broke..Break It!*, Robert J. Kriegel and Louis Patler, Warner Books, 1991)

It is pure and simple desire that overcomes credentials and even the lack of talent. In my own case, my first successful business was doing term papers for Fortune 500 clients. I did market studies for merger and acquisition clients. When you look at my background I should have never been doing it, let alone be successful at that kind of work. Besides not passing English in college, I also never even did a term paper in college. Every time one was due, I would look for someone to do it for me or I'd buy one. So why was I successful at something I had no previous aptitude or training for? It's just one word...desire.

It's well known to sports fans that Joe Montana was the best quarterback of his time, even though he couldn't throw as hard or as fast as most of the other NFL quarterbacks he played against. Or that basketball's Larry Bird was considered one of the best, even though he couldn't run as fast or jump as high as most NBA players.

It's not having perfect abilities, it's having enough drive and determination. We have become such a credential oriented society when, in fact, credentials really don't mean that much. What has happened is that the lack of credentials has become a handicap or roadblock for us in doing the things that we really want to do. I used to say, "I can't start my own business because I don't have an MBA". Well, I finally got the MBA, and my first two businesses failed. I now feel that I would have been a lot more successful, a lot sooner, without that MBA.

It's Never Too Late

In 1996, the first of the baby boomers turned 50 years old. This means that there are tens of thousands of people going to work realizing that they have spent the last 20 years of their lives in a profession or job that they never really liked. They wound up there because of money, family, greed, insecurity, or just plain ignorance. I will bet that 20 or 30 years ago, all they were thinking about was 1) how to get a job that would feed them and, 2) sex. By 50, most of these boomers have seen some of the world, their interests are more varied, and they've figured out, at least MOST, of the two major problems they were thinking about in their twenties. Knowing what they know now, they probably would have chosen a different career path, but they figure it's too late now...or is it?

It's never too late to change. It's never too late to make your life even more worthwhile. By the time you reach 50 or 60, you have a good chance of making it to 80 and even 90 years of age. For a 50 year old, that can mean 40 more years of life. And you might as well be doing what you really want to be doing in the last 40 years of your life if you didn't have the chance to do it in the first part of your life.

Boomers also grew up with the mind set that people in their 50's and 60's were old, over the hill, like their grandmothers or grandfathers. When the boomers were kids, their grandparents looked old at 50 or 60 and didn't live very long after that. And they were told that life was for the young people, the Pepsi Generation. Advertisers, anxious to tap into the bulk of the U.S. market made up of all those boomers, told us that 50 was ancient.

Now that all those young baby boomers are in their 50's, the advertisers are starting to tell us that life is for seniors, the Depends Generation.

Thoughts of being too old are just old tapes rewinding and replaying in our head. They're not based on fact, but rather on perception and pop culture. So, you have to change those tapes. And it's not just 50 year olds who believe it's too late to change — 30 year olds believe it, 40 year olds believe it, and even 70 year olds believe it. Consider this:

There are more people on college campuses today over 35 than there are 18 and 19 year olds. There are more than 1200 women, aged 50 to 64, that are in school today getting their first professional degree in law, dentistry, pharmacy, and even divinity.

> *"Most people in the Age of Integrity (over 65) will continue to work in one way or another part time, or as consultants, contract teachers, community volunteers, or self-employed entrepreneurs — not only because they want to feel a sense of purpose or self-worth but because they will have to be prepared to support themselves for greatly elongated later lives."*
>
> Source: *New Passages*, Gail Sheehy, Random House, 1995

Matthew Lesko, Information USA, Inc., 12081 Nebel Street, Rockville, MD 20852 • 1-800-955-7693 • www.lesko.com

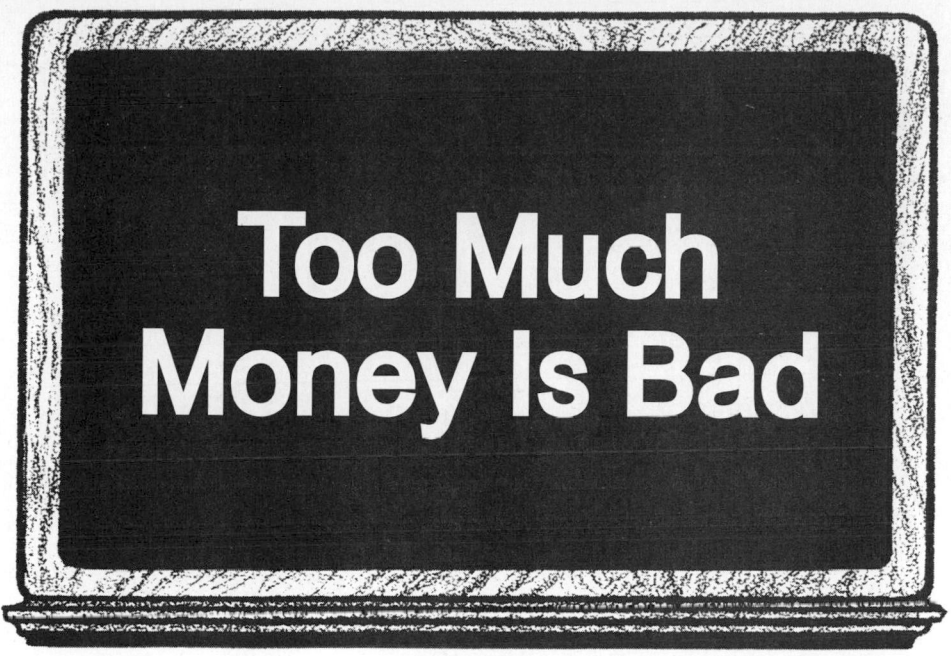

Too Much Money Is Bad

In a capitalist society this really sounds dumb. But I truly believe it. Remember one thing: anybody can do anything if they have a lot of money. The trick is to do what you want with as little money as possible. The people who need a lot of money to do things are the weak people, not the strong people. The strong ones are those who do what they want on a little bit of money. And in a weak economy, it's always the strong that survive.

If you had a million dollars to start your own business it would be a snap, and it would also be bad. Why? Because you would teach yourself how to do business when times are good but not when times are bad. And sooner or later, times will always turn bad. If you don't know how to handle bad times, you'll go out of business. That's why during downturns in the economy, it's the weak businesses, the ones who don't know how to operate lean and mean, that quickly close up shop. They only know how to operate with a lot of money. If you start your business with as little money as possible, you'll learn, right from the beginning, how to operate in a lean and mean fashion. So, when the good times come you'll make a whole lot of money, and when the bad times inevitably occur, you'll be ready for them.

Not having a lot of money is also an excuse for not doing the things that we want to do. I hear it all the time. People saying, "I can't go back to school because I don't have enough money. Or I can't change careers because I don't have a lot of money." What we're doing in times like this is trying to solve all of our problems with money. But in our hearts, we know that it's nonsense. We keep yelling at our elected officials about this same issue. We complain that they are always trying to solve the country's problems by throwing money at those problems. We know you can't solve a problem by throwing money at it, but it becomes a comfortable excuse for not changing our own lives.

Too Much Education

I always believed that unless I had an MBA (Master in Business Administration), I wouldn't be able to get anywhere in life. I finally earned one at age 27, and after that, it took me two failed businesses to unlearn everything they had taught me in business school. Most of the courses for this graduate degree involved training students to run huge companies like General Motors. If You Need Money, Go To The Bank, we were taught. Also, Conduct A Cost Benefit Analysis Before Making Any Major Decision. As a young entrepreneur trying to get a business going, I quickly learned that banks were not interested in people like me, long on solid money-making ideas, but short on cash. In school they also taught us that if we wanted to succeed, we needed to hire lawyers and accountants to help us build the right financial and legal structure for our companies. Because that image was supposed to be an important ingredient to success, we would need the power desk, the power business cards, even power drapes for our offices.

When my first two businesses failed, I looked around and couldn't help but notice that my accountants, lawyers, even the people I'd bought my power drapes and furniture from were all making money hand over fist. They all got paid before I went out of business, but I felt like the biggest loser on the block. So when I started my next business, I threw away that line of thinking, along with almost everything else that I'd learned in business school.

I figured out that as an entrepreneur, I had to concentrate on what I considered the critical success factors of my new business, the most essential of which was attracting customers.

26   *Matthew Lesko, Information USA, Inc., 12081 Nebel Street, Rockville, MD 20852 • 1-800-955-7693 • www.lesko.com*

Potential clients weren't concerned about my legal or financial structure, and even less worried about the color of my drapes. It seemed to me that the more time I spent meeting with accountants, lawyers, or picking out office furniture, the less time I would have for what was most critical for my success — finding new customers. I even decided not to bother with government forms, except for taxes. Government forms were just another waste of my time, and my time was too important. I was starting a business! Creating new jobs! I also figured it would take the government at least three years to discover my oversight, and by then I'd either be out of business again or making enough money to painlessly pay an extra $50 to $100 in late filing fees. What I needed to get started was the time to find clients, not recordkeeping chores.

Higher education can knock the creativity out of you. It's true. The more you jump through the bureaucratic hoops of higher learning, the more you get programmed into being just like everyone else. It's what the system's looking for, and what it needs least. Solving today's real problems means coming up with unique ideas, because the old ones just don't work anymore.

Don't get me wrong, I'm not totally against school. We are entering an age where the average job is going to require more and more brain power and training. A college degree is now worth up to a million dollars more in lifetime earning power. So it's not all bad. But I know the more you learn in the structured bureaucracy of a college classroom, the more you will have to fight to regain your creative problem solving power later, as you attempt to start a business.

I also believe that the more formal education you have, the easier it is to talk yourself out of taking risks and doing what really interests you in life. Many of the fun things in life are not intellectual decisions, but rather emotional choices. Take having children, for instance. I was close to 40 years old before I had my first child, because when I first considered starting a family, I approached the issue analytically. Just as I had been taught in school, I made lists about the pros and cons. When I realized all the problems that having kids might bring into my life, I'd ask myself, "Why would I do something to myself that had so many possible bad consequences?" So I put it off. Then, when I had a child that wasn't planned — that wasn't the result of a cost-benefit analysis — I discovered it was the greatest thing that ever happened to me.

Having a book on the New York Times Best Seller List: I found that by the time you get there, it's no big deal. Another example is creating a million dollar business. By the time you do that, there's no real payoff. But having your first child. Wow, that's success.

The good decisions in life are made from the gut, not the brain. It's far too easy to talk yourself out of doing anything worthwhile if you think it over for too long. Learn to follow your gut and go with your feelings. You'll rarely be disappointed.

The Best information Is Free

Most of us grew up hearing that the best things in life are free, and we were skeptical until we fell in love or helped another person solve a problem and realized it felt pretty good. Still, our society bombards us with the message that money equals happiness, and all too often we believe it.

But where do these images are coming from? That's simple: from people who want to sell you something. No wonder people believe they need a lot of money to have the good things in life. You're never going to see an advertisement showing people having fun at a party, and the ad is sponsored by say, the Bosnian Peace Cooperative.

Our information society bolsters the money myth. The best lawyers cost millions, as we've seen at the OJ trial. The top investment advisors are the most expensive. We've seen them on the money shows. The best medical care comes from the most expensive doctors, otherwise they couldn't drive fancy cars and belong to exclusive clubs.

Again, it isn't true. This is the Information Age, and believe it or not, the most comprehensive information on almost any subject is available free from the government.

Matthew Lesko, Information USA, Inc., 12081 Nebel Street, Rockville, MD 20852 • 1-800-955-7693 • www.lesko.com

Whether it's law, medicine, or money, the best advice comes from the most knowledgeable experts, those who are ahead of the information curve. And many of those people work for the government as strategists and scientists, economists and tax experts, and in hundreds of other positions where they are privy to the latest information. These experts are at the forefront of breaking developments in their respective fields, months and even years before the general public is made aware.

If you learn how to use the system — and it isn't difficult — their expertise is yours. Remember, they already work for you.

Sure you can hire expensive experts to solve your problems, and many of these specialists are probably good. That's fine if you have money to burn. But thinking that you have to have money to get the information you need to get ahead is roadblock thinking. It's another barrier that keeps you from doing whatever it is you want to do with your life, from not solving problems when the answers are right at your fingertips.

Even if you have the money to hire an expensive specialist, you still have to do your homework to make sure you're getting your money's worth from that person. Why not skip a step and do it yourself? It's just sound business sense.

If you learn how to use the government, you can get better, more timely, information than anyone else. The government is the largest source of information and expertise in the world, and it's all available for free or next to nothing. The government represents approximately 37 percent of the entire U.S. economy, and that's a powerful demographic. Ask anyone in business.

In the 1990 census, the government spent over $3 billion to count all the noses and toilets in the country. And they spent plenty on the year 2000 Census. Even General Motors can't afford what amounts to a $3 billion dollar market study! But you can get all of the information that you need with one phone call.

The government spends over $10 billion each year generating free medical information. Why ask a doctor about the latest remedies for back pain when you can call the National Institutes of Health and talk to a back pain expert, someone who is part of a multimillion dollar research effort.

Unlike most doctors who have barely enough time to scan The New England Journal of Medicine each week, NH experts can often tell you what will be in The New England Journal next week or even next year. They're doing the research today, and they're way ahead of the cure curve.

What about free legal help? Most laws are written and enforced by the government, and they constantly change from day to day. Courts around the country constantly interpret and reinterpret them. Keeping up with these changes is, to a large degree, what attorneys get paid for, usually by the hour.

But, again, you can do it yourself by calling the government.

For example, if you're interested in buying a franchise, you can go out and hire a franchise attorney and pay $200 an hour for them to research current franchise laws. Or you can call the Federal Trade Commission and talk to someone who actually helped write the law — and they won't charge you a dime. It's their job to give you the information that you're looking for, and most government experts are eager to talk to anyone about their area of expertise.

The same is true if you need investment information. Investment advisors are sales reps, nothing more. Their goal is to get you to spend money so they can take their commission. So instead of listening to a biased broker pitch biotechnology futures, you can call one of dozens of government biotechnology experts and ask their opinion. They know which companies are making the most progress, and where the next medical breakthrough is likely to be made. They know who is researching what, and how far along the studies are.

But perhaps best of all, from an investment standpoint, they know the early research findings long before they appear in professional medical journals. These experts know which drugs hold promise and which companies hold a piece of the pie, so they can tell you what will be in the Wall Street Journal next week, next month, or even next year. This isn't insider trading remember — it's just smart investing based on the most up to date information available.

Here's a little known fact about the government as the largest source of information in this country. Each year, commercial U.S. publishers release a total of 50,000 new titles. Yet just one government agency — the National Technical Information Service — publishes over 100,000 titles each year, on almost every technical subject imaginable. And most people have never even heard of this service, let alone used it.

The government also has more computer databases than all the commercial online services combined. The Internet wouldn't even exist were it not for the government, because it is supported by a telecommunications network developed by the U.S. Department of Defense.

Of course this information really isn't free. After all, you pay for it with your tax dollars. But that's all the more reason to use it. If you've already paid for it, why pay twice?

Plan For The Worst

Maybe it was my Navy training or my guilt ridden Catholic upbringing, but I've always expected and planned for the worst. It has been a great motivation for trying to do exactly what I've really wanted to do with my life, and not necessarily sticking to the "safe bets" in life.

In the early days of my business, I would sit in front of my telephone and try to get up the nerve to make calls and ask perfect strangers to toss some work my way. I wondered why it was so difficult to make each call — what was I afraid of? Then I'd ask myself, "What's the worst thing that can happen if I make this call? Will the person reach through the wires, grab me by the throat and start squeezing?"

I knew this kind of phone assault was fiction, science fiction, even. The worst anyone could do was say no and hang up. Big deal. I didn't have their business in the first place, so what had I lost? Nothing.

But I also came to realize that if I did make that telephone call, I might just get some business. If they said yes, I'd be that much closer to my dream of financial independence as an entrepreneur. But there was absolutely NO CHANCE of getting their business if I didn't ask for it — so I picked up the phone, over and over again.

Guess what? It worked.

It's natural to try to avoid discomfort and embarrassment. Not everyone's born to sell — let alone to sell themselves. Pride's at stake, but you have to push yourself past pride to get ahead. Failure makes you better, not worse, as long as you get back up and try again. That's the only way you build confidence. With any luck at all, you'll get to do those things in life you really dream of doing if you just open yourself up to the risk of failure.

A few years ago, I did an undercover survey that found 94 percent of all U.S. doctors didn't know that there were money programs available for their patients that could help them locate free prescription drugs, free hospitalization, and even free treatment by the best doctors in the world.

I felt the best way to dramatize my findings was to go public with each physician's name. I agonized over this decision for days, fearing a huge backlash from the medical community and, of course, a stack of lawsuits. Still, the truth was there, and I felt I had to publish their names. I even sat down with my family and discussed my dilemma. They too would be affected by my actions, should I take the names public. We are not rich, but live in a nice home in the Washington, D.C. suburbs. I tried to explain to my family how important I felt it was that doctors didn't know about programs that could help their less fortunate patients.

Then I asked them for the worst possible scenario, the worst thing that might happen to us if I released the survey results and named doctors.

I envisioned a monster lawsuit in which we'd lose everything and have to start over again from scratch.

Then I realized that it would not be a dead end. I would still have my family and my work. I could still support them, even if it meant eating bologna casseroles six nights a week. We would still be together, wouldn't we? And we'd still have fun. Besides, like I teach my kids, we need to tell the truth. So that's what I did.

And you know what happened? Nothing. I published the list of names and received broad press coverage, but only two of the doctors contacted me and their only complaint was that in their opinion, my survey was unscientific. In the end — much sweat, but no big deal. And I learned another big lesson.

If you really want to push yourself to do the things you want to do in life, just consider what I learned, and how I learned it. Tell yourself that the worst that can happen is a dead end, and what the heck, life has a serious punctuation mark at the end, even if you don't take chances. You shouldn't let fear of failure — like having to move to a rundown condo 10 miles outside of town — stop you from trying. Life's not that cheap, and success is well worth the worry.

Loved Ones Can Be Your Worst Enemy

People who love you can be the biggest obstacle from pursuing your dream. They want to protect you from failure, and not incidentally, protect themselves.

They'll warn you that starting a small business is too risky. "Don't you know that three out of four businesses fail?" Or, "You can't quit your job, what about your pension, what about our health insurance?"

Friends and colleagues do it too, but their words of caution often come from simple jealousy rather than concern for your well being. You're willing to put everything on the line to buck the status quo, but they aren't. Inside, many of them wish that they had your nerve. At least you're willing to try, while they probably feel that they can't even risk trying something new.

Socrates said that if you love someone, you help them do whatever they want to do — not make them do what YOU want them to do. For all others, like neighbors or fellow citizens, your job is not necessarily to help them get what they want, just to stay out of their way as they pursue their goals. It would probably also be helpful not to play the doomsayer to their dreams, and instead, encourage them as much as possible.

I'm not one to argue with Socrates, and I've come to learn the wisdom of his words. How better can we show our appreciation for loved ones than by supporting them as they strive for greater happiness and fulfillment in life? It sounds like a good living to me.

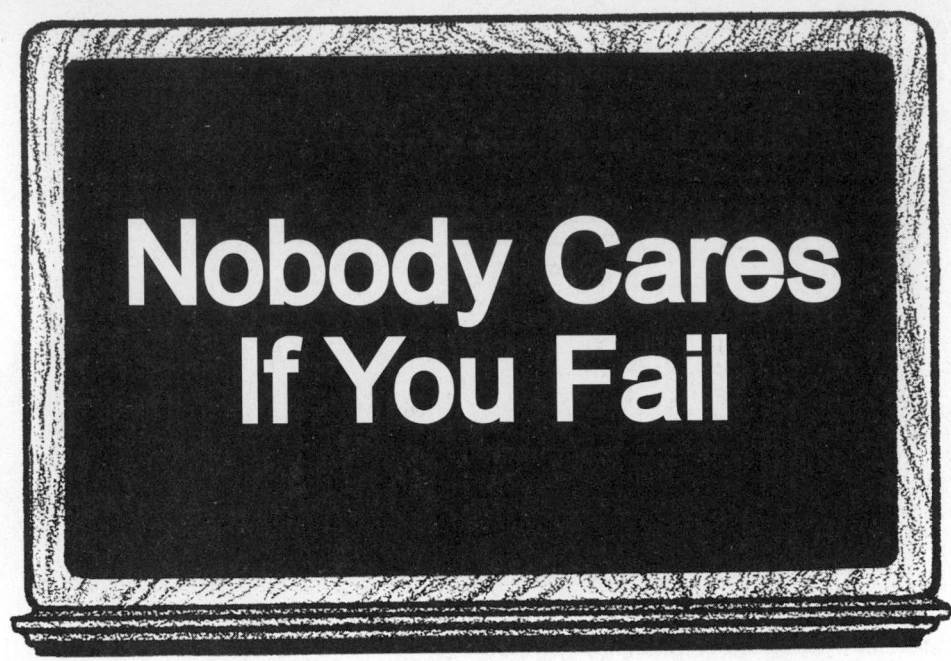

Nobody Cares
If You Fail

I used to think that if I failed at something, I would be left walking around with a big, red F stamped on my forehead. Everybody would be whispering behind my back, and I'd be the laughing stock of the city.

But the first time a business of mine failed, I found most people didn't really care. Even my family stopped talking about it after a relatively short period of time. This taught me that most people are so wrapped up in their own lives, they really don't have time to worry about anyone else's trials and tribulations. There's no room left on their emotional disk for much else than what they are struggling with each day.

Friends and acquaintances offered their condolences and asked sympathetic questions, listened for a few minutes, and even offered advice (even though many had never taken a business risk in their lives). Much to my amazement, I found that their interest passed quickly and the subject never came up again. If anything, they were interested and even eager to hear about my next business venture. I think they felt that at least I was having some fun trying something new, while they plodded along with their own boring jobs.

So why stop yourself from doing what you really want to do in life? Because you're afraid of what others might think or say if you fail? Guess what? The truth is they don't really care.

 Matthew Lesko, Information USA, Inc., 12081 Nebel Street, Rockville, MD 20852 • 1-800-955-7693 • www.lesko.com

Retirement Is Passe

Being raised in the 50's, I was brought up to believe that at 65 you retired and moved somewhere sunny to play golf for the rest of your days. That's the way it used to be, but times have changed. Now that I'm getting close to that age, the idea seems dreadful for many reasons.

1) We're living too long

Back in the 50s, retiring at 65 and relaxing for the rest of your life meant 5 to 10 "Golden Years" of golf, bridge, bird watching, fishing, or playing mah jong. Then, if you were lucky, a short stop at the nursing home before your Big Exit.

That's just not true anymore. Here are some data taken from Gail Sheehy's recent book, New Passages (Random House, New York City, 1995). "During most of human history only one in ten people lived to the age of 65. In contemporary America, eight in ten people sail past their sixty-fifth birthday,' and that `already the average healthy man who is 65 today — an age now reached by the majority of the U.S. population — can expect to live until 81." Sheehy writes 'A woman who reaches 50 today — and remains free of cancer and heart disease — can expect to see her 92nd birthday.'

Matthew Lesko, Information USA, Inc., 12081 Nebel Street, Rockville, MD 20852 • 1-800-955-7693 • www.lesko.com

So why would anyone 'retire' with 20 or 30 more years to finally do what they've dreamed of doing? That's enough time to launch a new life or at least a whole new career.

2) You'll Need The Money

In the old days, planning for retirement was easy. Social Security was there, most people had a company pension plan, and through 40 years of work, most people were able to save a little nest egg for their retirement.

But financially, it's a whole new world out there. The health of the Social Security system is in question, and even if there is a check in the mail, it won't cover next month's rent. Organizations are cutting back on retirement plans, health insurance, and other benefits for retirees, and the cost of living just keeps rising. It's also nearly impossible to save enough money to live on comfortably for a period of 30 or more years. Never has been, probably never will be.

Who wants to spend half a life chasing a little white ball around a golf course, even if the weather is perfect? Most people need to succeed at something other than a card game or catching a big fish. Anyone who has spent 40 years in any profession has skills to market, and running your own business leaves you room for recreation. You call your own shots, set your own hours, take three day weekends when you want to. Plus, you stay active and engaged in life which, research shows, will help you live even longer.

So take your retirement worries and throw them out the window. If you're tired of working at 65, take some time off. Maybe play a little golf. Then start planning your post-retirement career doing something you always wanted to try, but never found the time for.

3) You Can Do What You Like

I think that most people look forward to retirement, and doing nothing all day, because they hate their jobs. But this wouldn't be the case if you love your work. People stay in jobs they hate for millions of reasons, and some are legitimate. Yet many people stay because they are afraid of change. Retirement is a golden opportunity for charting a new life course, for getting excited about yourself and what you can contribute. You know that you've got talent and skills, and most of these qualities can be applied regardless of the nature of the work you choose to perform in retirement.

The greatest satisfaction has never been found in retiring from a useful life, but from continuing to make a difference in the lives of others by contributing our talents and skills where they matter, are recognized, and appreciated.

Most of us want to help others, to make a difference in the community — and getting older is no obstacle. Does anyone ever ask Mother Teresa to stop serving the sick and poor? Did anyone tell the late George Burns he was too old to make people laugh? Of course not.

There are many people (though not enough) who have found bliss in their work, and they are paid for doing what they love. They don't think of it as work. It's something they'll do until they die, paid or not, because they feel they are contributing their best to society. Imagine feeling that way about what you do every day. You too can find this kind of satisfaction once you find your life's true calling. When you do, you won't think about retirement anymore. When you die you can rest forever, but while you're here make yourself useful — especially to others.

4) New Jobs Are Suited For Seniors

It used to be that Americans worked in factories and in jobs that required hard physical labor. As people aged, they were unable to continue such strenuous work, and there were few other opportunities available. Now jobs requiring physical labor are fast disappearing. More people work for the government than in manufacturing, a trend that seems sure to continue. Our economy is quickly shifting from one based on manufacturing to one driven by information and services, and the better paying jobs are all going to require brain power, not muscle power. At age 60 or 70, the body can't take running a blast furnace in a steel factory, but it certainly can handle a computer keyboard or analyzing data from financial statements. Even starting a small pet-sitting business and walking peoples' dogs every day can earn you enough money for a comfortable living.

5) Demographics Are In Your Favor

Baby boomers represent the largest segment of our population, and the first wave is just hitting retirement age. Who's going to do all the work once they're gone? Who's going to keep the Social Security System solvent? It used to be that seniors left the workforce to make way for younger workers, but now there are fewer newcomers. Where seniors in the past were encouraged by companies to leave, more often than not, employers in the future will encourage them to stay on — even in a part time capacity or as consultants. Either way, the future looks pretty bright for retirement-aged people who want to keep right on working, and even find the time to play a little golf now and then.

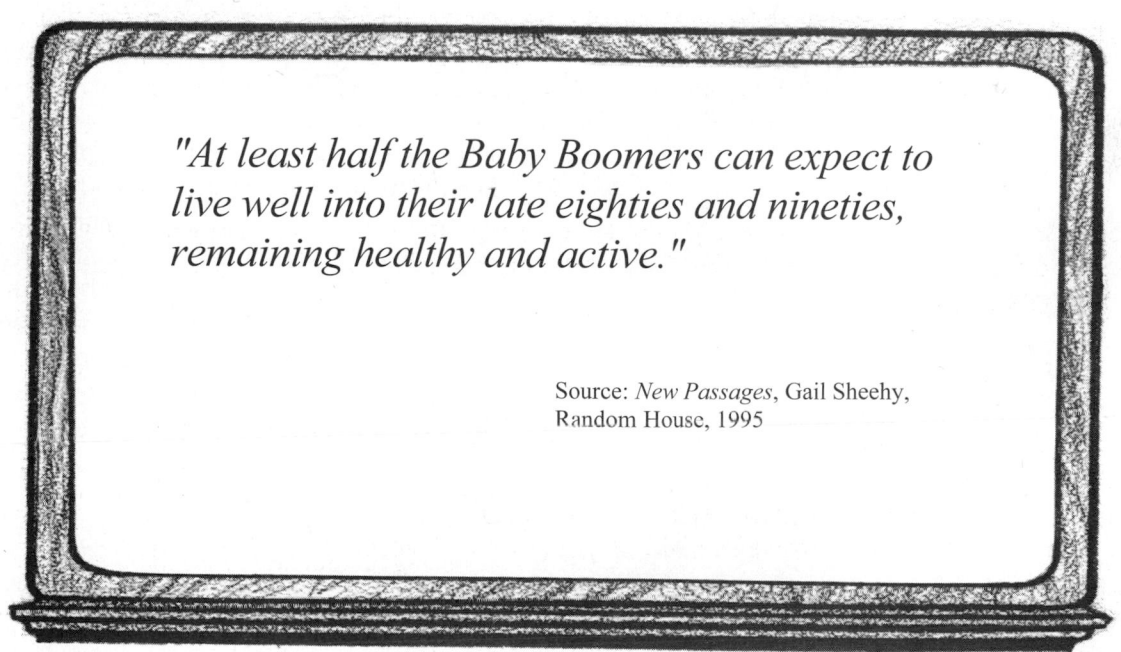

"At least half the Baby Boomers can expect to live well into their late eighties and nineties, remaining healthy and active."

Source: *New Passages*, Gail Sheehy, Random House, 1995

Be Your Own Hero

As a kid I had a lot of heroes: Superman, Batman, Mickey Mantle, and more. But as I grew older, they stopped serving as role models as I became aware of the more human qualities of each hero. Batman and Superman turned out be nothing more than ink, and Mickey Mantle became a full blown alcoholic. It didn't matter much to me, I long ago stopped reading comic books and was never good at baseball anyway. But I had trouble finding heroes to replace them.

The media always jumps on the shortcomings of anyone who has the remotest chance of becoming one of our heroes. Dig up the dirt, editors tell their reporters, find the skeletons. Maybe none of us can accept that nobody's perfect. But who ever said heroes are perfect? Every hero, in myth or in real life, has had faults - it's what has always made them human and someone that we were able to identify with. From Hercules to Dr. Martin Luther King, this is the real lesson of heroes. They teach us that we don't need to be perfect to demonstrate valor, stamina, and courage in the face of seemingly unbeatable odds.

My way out of the hero dilemma was to work toward becoming one myself. Instead of being continually disappointed by the world around me, and by people I didn't know, I began putting all of my efforts into making myself a better person by helping others in any way that I could. I quit fantasizing about watching someone else's movie and started trying to be the action hero of my own life. And I believe you can do it too.

Matthew Lesko, Information USA, Inc., 12081 Nebel Street, Rockville, MD 20852 • 1-800-955-7693 • www.lesko.com

We're all on a separate pathway in life. We have guidebooks and mentors, but in the end we make our own decisions and have to find our own unique trail. It might not suit everyone, but if we're successful, it will suit us.

When making decisions, I often ask myself a question. If I were watching myself in a movie, what would the hero do? I think long and hard about it, then usually choose the more difficult route. Like giving up money for the sake of principle, or choosing paths that others say are too difficult, too stupid, or simply can't be followed.

For each of us this is the real test, the real challenge. By nature, most of us want to take the safe and easy road through life — a road that is well paved, with bright lights and stepping stones to follow. Business school might train you to make tough decisions, but not heroic ones. And our society doesn't exactly encourage any of us to break out of the pack and do something different. We're constantly being pointed in the easiest, safest, and surest direction to get anything and everything we want. But these are shortcuts that lead nowhere worthwhile. Sooner or later the trail doubles back on itself, and many travelers get lost along the way.

If you are interested in reading more about the path of the hero, dig into Joseph Campbell's work. He devoted his life to studying those myths that are common among cultures throughout the world, and the similarities all of our heroes have shared down through the ages. Campbell's wonderful books help explain our reason for being alive. If you are unfamiliar with Campbell's work, it's best to begin with *The Power of Myth*, a PBS television feature narrated by Bill Moyers. You can ask your local book store to locate the audio and book versions for you, or call the PBS affiliate in your city or check your local library.

Campbell found that the legends of heroes are remarkably similar in almost every culture around the world. First the hero is forced out into the world to make his own way. He then enters a dangerous place — in Western lore, often an uncharted forest. There the hero must find his way out, cutting his own path through, and along the way encountering — and overcoming — many challenges and obstacles, monsters, and mysteries. These victories provide the hero with new wisdom and strength. And these are passed along to his people, once the hero returns.

In the Star Wars films, George Lucas relied on Campbell's work to insure that this cross-cultural heroic dynamic was central to the plot of each movie. But the truth is, we don't need blockbuster movies to show us the way. We can become heroes ourselves on a daily basis, getting better all the time.

Three Cheers For Mediocrity

...Or as some others have put it, 'Perfection Is The Enemy Of The Good'. Trying to get things perfect used to keep me from doing a lot of things in life. I didn't think I could start my own business unless I had an MBA. Or I couldn't write a book, because I didn't have an English degree from Harvard. Perfection kept me from deciding what kind of business I wanted to start in the first place. I couldn't start a consulting business because I lacked the information, expertise and money of Booz, Allen & Hamilton, at the time probably the largest consulting group in the world.

Then this need for perfection started undermining my ability to finish projects. There was always something more I could add to make it better, always some additional information I needed to improve my product. Trying to get things perfect was stopping me from getting anything done at all, perfect or otherwise.

One day, I began looking at the things I was spending money on — clothes, appliances, books, etc. None of them were perfect by any stretch of the imagination, but I bought and used them anyway. That was when I realized that my work projects didn't have to be perfect either. The important thing was getting them done — people would only buy a finished product — and making each one as good as possible under the circumstances.

Matthew Lesko, Information USA, Inc., 12081 Nebel Street, Rockville, MD 20852 • 1-800-955-7693 • www.lesko.com

We all work under constraints, mostly money, time, or talent. These keep us from doing a perfect job every time, but it shouldn't keep us from marketing our best efforts. I've found that people will need your goods and services, even if they aren't perfect.

Don't get me wrong, I believe in good products. But it's more important to finish — to contribute something — than to let perfection slow you down or stop you outright.

Every quarterback can't be Joe Montana, but all football teams need a quarterback. Not every artist is a Picasso, but walls need pictures. And while we're all not Einstein, major scientific discoveries are being made each year by researchers who see Einstein as a role model. Genius inspires, but it's not a prerequisite for making a sincere effort to contribute your best in any field.

One of my sons recently reminded me of this. When my older boy was in sixth grade, he wanted to enter a statewide science competition. He's a good student, mind you, but I knew there were hundreds of other kids out there who were probably better at science than he is, and they were ready to compete against him. No one in our family is especially gifted in science, but my son liked the teacher in charge of the science fair and convinced us to let him try.

He worked on a Rube Goldberg-type of contraception for weeks — you know, like the game Mousetrap. Balls fell into cups that dropped on pulleys to set other balls rolling down chutes. It was OK, in my eyes, but nothing brilliant — it didn't even work that well. Still, he took it to the state competition and won first prize.

It wasn't that his invention was necessarily mediocre, but I was expecting some kid's project on advanced particle physics or recombinant DNA mass spectroscopy to take top honors, or at least something to do with fruit flies. In other words, just because we might view a work product as less than perfect, doesn't always mean that it's not good enough. Sometimes it's better than good — it wins first prize! I was wrong, and my son taught me a lesson I'll never forget.

Life Is A Smorgasbord

I used to think that life was something like a fancy restaurant, where you wait politely until someone comes to take your order. I don't see it that way anymore. I now know life is more like a smorgasbord or an all you can eat salad bar. You can't wait for opportunities to fall into your lap, you have to get up from the table and grab them yourself. No one is going to wait on you anymore. They're all too busy tending to their own needs. So speak up, get up, and take what you need to make life worthwhile for you.

Matthew Lesko, Information USA, Inc., 12081 Nebel Street, Rockville, MD 20852 • 1-800-955-7693 • www.lesko.com

Control Your Life Or Someone Else Will

You can play the good sailor and float through life, being pulled here and there by others who will use you to fulfill their own dreams. Or you can decide what YOUR dreams are, and start figuring out what YOU must do to make them come true. Try being the master of your own destiny by exercising some control over what you work at in life. Later, when you look upon your accomplishments with pride, you'll be glad that you exerted yourself.

The Experts Are Wrong

It used to be that experts could predict the future by looking to the past. History repeats itself, they said. But that was before our present age of rapid change, before our country became much more susceptible to external forces rather than internal ones.

At one time, we only had to worry about what was going on here at home, but now the actions of people half a world away can have a bigger impact on our welfare. This seemed to start with the oil embargo in 1973, when one country in the Middle East stopped our economy cold. At that point it became almost impossible for experts to forecast the future and predict trends correctly.

The fellow who started Federal Express proposed the delivery service as a project while he was a student at Yale. His professor gave him a D. I'll bet that professor regrets not having a few original shares of his student's dumb idea now.

Or why couldn't all the experts at IBM see the coming of the micro computer age? It took two college dropouts to show them the way. What about David Bobert, who was told he was stupid for trying to market a coin operated machine that dispensed air for filling tires? Air is free, they laughed. Nobody laughs now that Air-Vend is a $5 million dollar business[1]. And during the early stages of the 1994 presidential campaign, none of the talking heads on the Sunday TV talk shows believed that Bill Clinton had a prayer of winning the election.

---

[1] *If It Ain't Broke...Break It!*, Robert J: Kriegel, Warner Books, New York City 1991

I recently heard that the inventor of Post-It Notes also was told the idea wouldn't work. Experts at the 3M Company spent a lot of time and money researching the market, and concluded that nobody would buy sticky little notepads. Now they're everywhere and people wonder what they ever did without them.

Remember the fallibility of experts when you are trying to do what you want in life. Most of us, when we have an idea, instinctively ask an expert, or worse yet, friends and relatives. We need the feedback, and that's fine. But remember that they are very likely to be wrong, not only your friends and relatives, but the experts too. They don't know you well enough to know you can make your idea succeed. Experts are best at telling you what has worked in the past, and they'll steer you towards the more traditional concepts that have worked before.

This kind of advice might keep you from making obvious mistakes, but that's about all. Remember, the remarks and comments of experts and even friends and relatives can be detrimental to your future success. More often than not, they'll discourage any bold new ideas you might have about your life or the life around you. And unfortunately it's bold new ideas that we need. This world is changing fast, and what worked yesterday won't necessarily work tomorrow. That's why IBM, the steel companies, and even the auto manufacturers got into trouble over the past 20 years.

Even if your idea has proved a failure in the past, that does not mean you cannot make it happen. Your individuality is the most important ingredient for turning your idea into a success. Each of us brings something new to the marketplace. Your uniqueness means you will do things differently than anyone has in the past, and that could be all that's needed to make your plan succeed. Remember, all great innovations in the past started with some pretty crazy ideas — even the wheel.

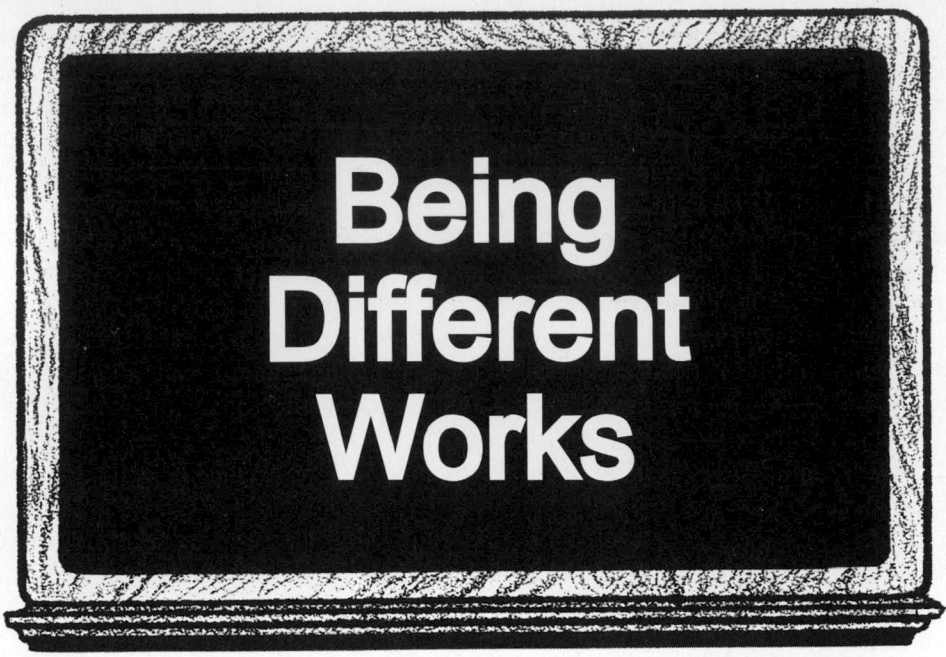

Being Different Works

In the section called "The Experts Are Wrong", I talked about the importance of finding and expressing your uniqueness when it comes to getting what you want out of life. There's a tendency among all of us — especially experts — to try to imitate success rather than to look for new solutions. Most markets are big enough to handle more than one supplier or service, but when you play follow-the-leader you may be giving up the truly unique quality that you have to offer the world. It already has all the other stuff, so why give it more of the same?

Do you think the world is good the way it is, and that we need more of the same? I don't think so. We need different solutions. We are all unique and capable of coming up with novel answers, but we are hardly ever encouraged to do so. In school, we're told there's only one right answer, and we'd better know it. And most organizations also expect workers to do things the company way, the way things have always been done before. The longer you are in situations like these, the harder it will be to regain your creativity when you go out on your own. People who don't want to follow all of the rules are not often welcomed by corporations, or even by schools. That notion of having to "go along" to get ahead stifles creativity in all of us, and just plain kills it in some people.

 Matthew Lesko, Information USA, Inc., 12081 Nebel Street, Rockville, MD 20852 • 1-800-955-7693 • www.lesko.com

The Microsofts of the world understand the uniqueness of the individual, and they encourage creativity rather than conformity. Why do you think they're making so much money? Because they're allowing freedom on the part of their employees to conduct business in a different way — more open and creative, with less emphasis on corporate politics.

What works well for someone else won't work as well for you, because you're different. You have to find what is unique and special about you and share it with the world. That's when the magic begins, and the experts will start advising others how to imitate you.

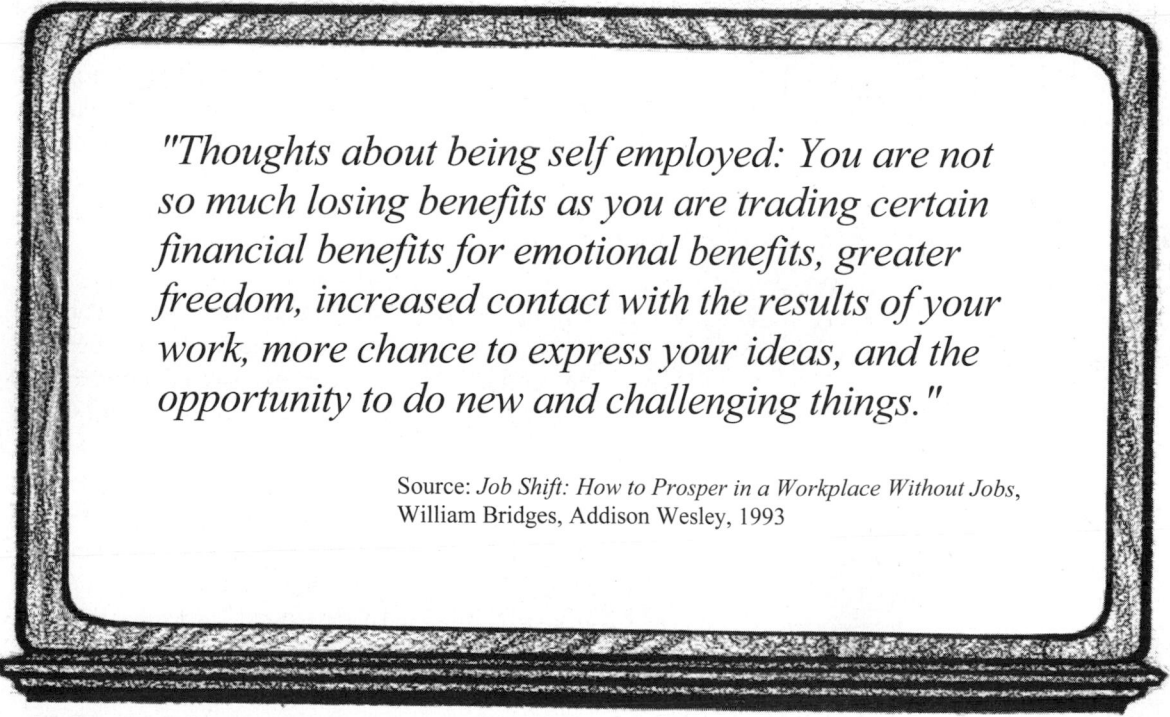

"Thoughts about being self employed: You are not so much losing benefits as you are trading certain financial benefits for emotional benefits, greater freedom, increased contact with the results of your work, more chance to express your ideas, and the opportunity to do new and challenging things."

Source: *Job Shift: How to Prosper in a Workplace Without Jobs*, William Bridges, Addison Wesley, 1993

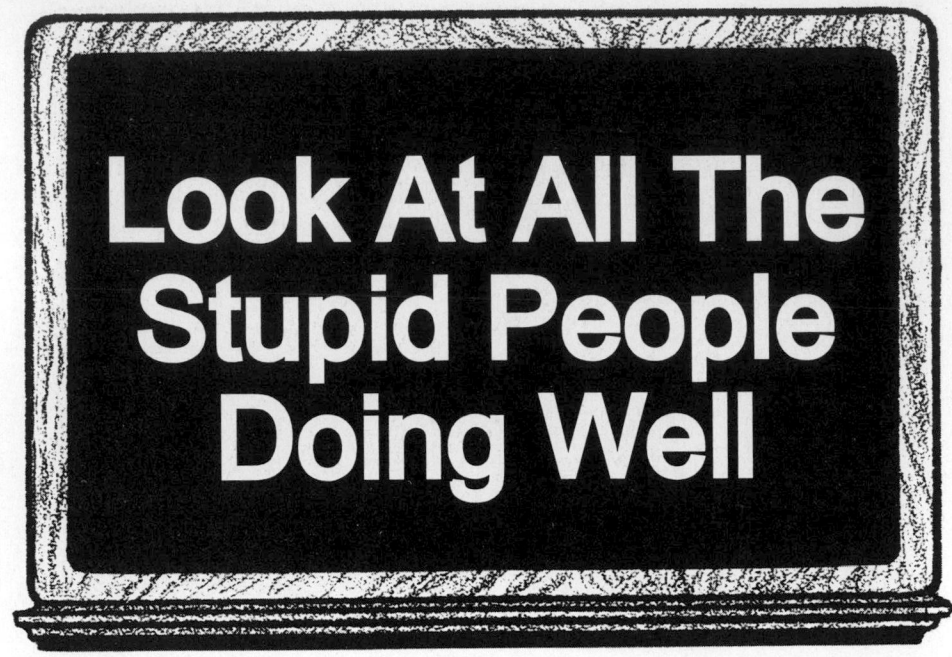

Look At All The Stupid People Doing Well

Every time I was on someone else's payroll, it would usually take less than six months before I realized that my boss wasn't making the right decisions. There were times I would think he was pretty dumb. Sometimes I'd get so frustrated that I'd mumble dirty words about him behind his back.

I don't think this is unique to me. I've heard friends, relatives, neighbors and even perfect strangers criticize their employers. This is because bosses DO make dumb decisions. We all do. It's part of being human. It doesn't take a genius to become a boss, or even the head of an organization. Take a moment and think about all the dummies you've ever worked for.

I figure about 98 percent of the people who run things in this country got where they are because of connections, drive or maybe pure chance — but not brain power. So you don't have to waste your time and energy whispering about your boss when, instead, you can be in charge and have other people wasting their time whispering behind your back. It's a lot more fun.

 Matthew Lesko, Information USA, Inc., 12081 Nebel Street, Rockville, MD 20852 • 1-800-955-7693 • www.lesko.com

Giving Is Selfish

I used to think that in order to run my own business, I had to be a tough, hardnosed son-of-a-gun. I couldn't give anything away, and always had to look out for number one. But after my first two businesses failed, I took another look at this approach. In my third business, I started being more myself — less selfish and self-protective, and more giving. I discovered that giving things away for free helped my business more than anything I'd done before.

At first, I tried selling research services to business clients by placing small advertisements in newspapers and cold-calling potential customers. But I was getting nowhere. It wasn't until I started publishing a free newsletter on information giveaways that my business finally began taking off. I would put every source of free information that I could find into my newsletter, and even though it seemed like I was giving away the store, it worked. Potential clients thought I was smart because I had one or two sources in my newsletter that they didn't know about. But of course I knew more than they did; I was spending much more time looking for free information than they were. I also think that giving the information away somehow increased the comfort level for many potential clients. Showing them that I was free and open with my sources, rather than close mouthed and secretive, seemed to make it easier for them to want to hire me. The bottom line is that this free newsletter launched my business, and my phone has not stopped ringing since.

I now believe that giving is a selfish act — not bad selfish, but good. In business, as well in your personal life, I've learned that you have to give in order to receive. The more you help others, the more comes back to you. It's like a boomerang. So giving must be selfish, right? It feels good to give, but it also does wonders for business. The problem most of us have is finding someone who deserves our help. But this same problem can work in your favor. When you give things away to potential clients, you look like a very deserving person — someone they can feel good about and trust with a business project.

There is another side to giving that I would like to share, and it has to do with interfering with others' gift giving. As a young adult, I used to be very hot-headed and independent. I didn't want to take anything from anyone, not even gifts from friends and relatives. I didn't want anyone's help. But after I got a little older, and understood more about the joy of giving, I changed my mind about accepting gifts. Now I graciously accept them, not so much because I'm greedier, but because I now know that by not accepting presents I'm denying people the opportunity to feel good — nice-selfish — about themselves. And who am I to deprive them of that pleasure?

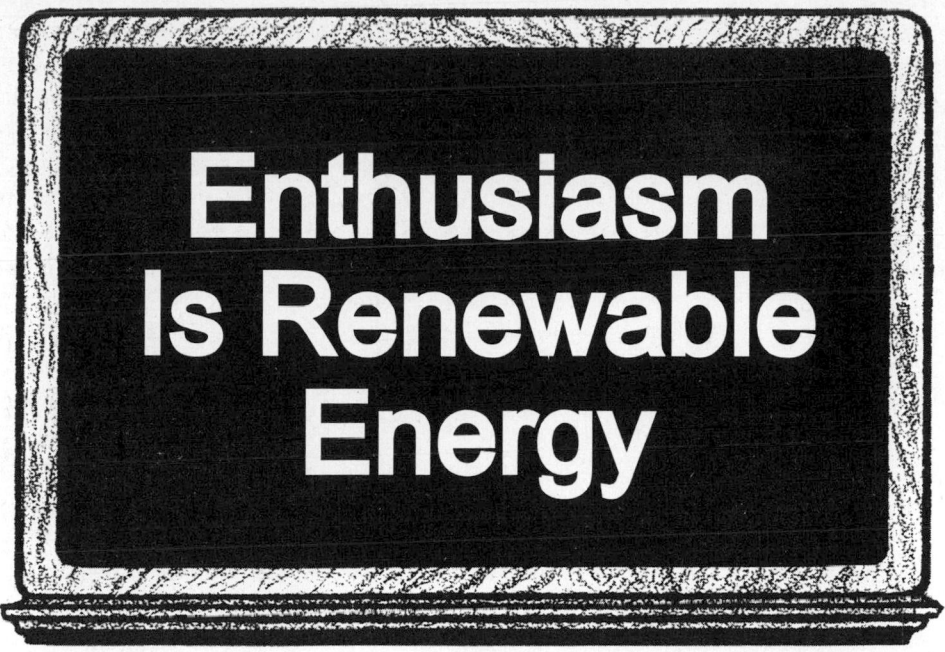

Enthusiasm Is Renewable Energy

Before I started working on my own dreams, I used to get tired every afternoon at 3 o'clock. It was like clockwork. I'd get tired and start daydreaming about other things I'd rather be doing, like playing golf or traveling to exotic places around the globe. Now that I'm doing something I really love, I don't get tired at 3 o'clock anymore. In fact, there are days when I don't even need sleep.

A few years back I put together a publicity trip called INFO-VAN. My whole family and I packed up a big truck loaded with free stuff you can get from the government. We went to 17 cities in 17 days. I dressed like Uncle Sam and sat in each town square, handing out free items from Washington, and there were days when I functioned perfectly well on just a few hours of sleep. We spent all day handing out stuff, and then drove all night to get to the next city on time. It was exhilarating. I was fulfilling a dream, and seemed to have all the energy in the world. And I still find this to be true. Recently I appeared on the Home Shopping Network. I spent about 11 hours one day on live TV, selling my books, and telling people where to get free help from the government. I lived on only two or three hours of sleep, but it was so exhilarating that I did it for two days in a row. And I was 52 years of age.

So forget all of these pep pills and oriental extracts that profess to increase your energy. I believe most people lose energy — not because they need snake oil or coffee — but because they're not doing what they want in life. I've found that when you are, not only do you get renewed energy, but many of life's other little annoyances disappear. For example, when I worked for other people and traveled around the country, I would be really angry when my plane was late or I got a bad seat — or if my hotel bed sagged in the middle. Now when I travel, I don't care if I have to travel by camel and sleep in a tent (at least most of the time). Doing what I want now makes all the difference. How I reach a destination has become a minor detail, when it used to be the entire focus of my efforts, back before I realized the energy and freedom of working for myself.

You can do it too. Recharge yourself — and get rid of many of life's little annoyances — by pursuing something you really care about.

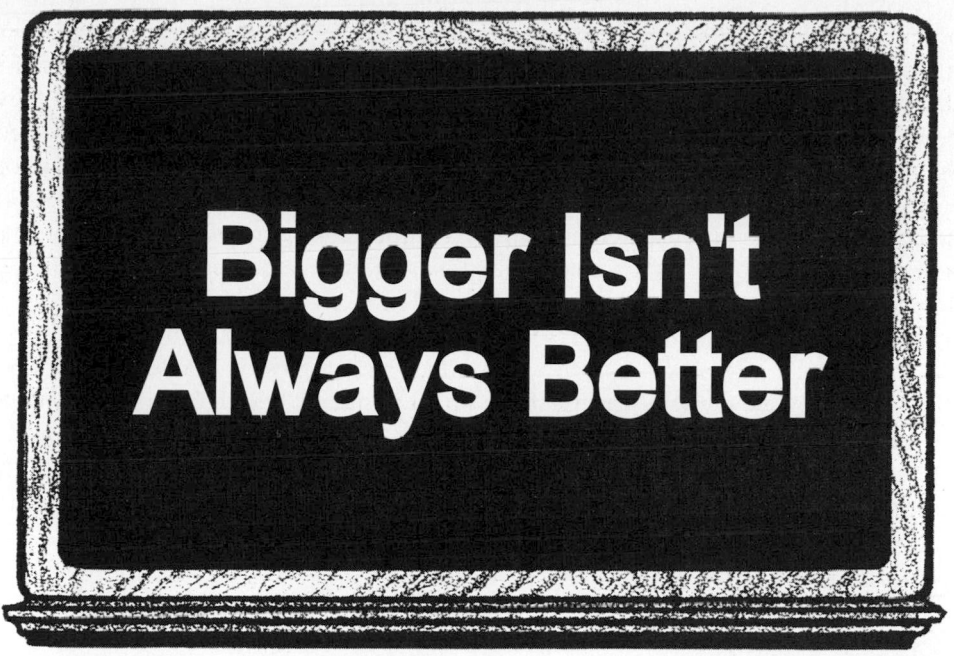

Bigger Isn't Always Better

Most of us grew up believing that in business, the larger your company grew, the better for all concerned. It still seems to be the prevailing sentiment among the business community, despite thousands of examples of companies that have grown too fast, too soon — then failed. When I first started my business, I wanted it to grow, and grow fast. At first it was just me, a telephone, and a desk in a one bedroom apartment. I was overjoyed when my business grew to over 30 employees in just three years. It was great for my ego, I found, but bad for my soul.

One of the main reasons I always wanted my own business was because I hated top-heavy organizations that made me follow inflexible rules. Personnel manuals, vacation schedules, and long, boring meetings drove me nuts. I hated how I found myself playing office politics, and doing things like coming in on Saturday mornings just to impress my boss.

If I had my own company, I told myself, I'd let people work intuitively. They'd be able to go to lunch when they were hungry, take a vacation when they needed it, and I'd assume everyone was bright enough to get things done without sitting through endless meetings. But once I had 30 people working for me, I discovered that the easiest way to get things done was by using the same old bureaucratic tools that I'd hated ... meetings, manuals, and office politics as usual. What a disappointment, I was creating the same kind of workplace that I'd run from not so many years ago.

Another reason I always wanted my own business was that I wanted the freedom of working for myself, and not having to answer to the boss. I wanted to be the boss, plain and simple. It sounded nice in theory, but once I had 30 employees, reality set in — in an upside down sort of way. I found that I no longer had just one boss — I had 30. I was working for my employees, trying to make payroll every week so they could keep their jobs. Before, when I used to come in on Saturdays to impress the boss, I now found myself coming in on Saturdays to set an example for my employees. It may have been a backwards sort of pressure, but it was still the same kind of pressure.

So I eventually started listening more to my soul and less to my ego, and began scaling back the size of my company. I now work out of my house and while I have employees, they too work at home and I don't have to be there to manage them. I'm at home with my family, don't have to put up with on-site employees, and also lose no time commuting. When my kids come home from school, I can walk up and meet them at the bus stop. We spend some time having cookies and milk in the kitchen. Believe me, it's much more rewarding than talking football around the water cooler.

Make Something Bigger Than Yourself

One day you'll probably be able to quit working. How boring! I believe we're put here to do more than relax, even after 30 years of hard work and paying taxes. Sitting around is no reward, but I've found out what really works, at least for me. The real pleasure in my life comes from contributing to others. I've found that helping others has benefits that far exceed putting money in the bank — it's an energy booster each and every time you do it. And what most of us want after we've made enough money to live comfortably isn't more time to take naps; it's more energy to enjoy life! I guarantee that once you begin contributing to others, you'll have more energy. Even if you haven't made enough money yet — maybe you're just starting out — helping others will ensure that you won't have to figure out what to do with you life once you have some money in the bank. You'll already be doing something worthwhile and reaping the benefits of this renewed energy and enthusiasm.

Also, making decisions is easier if you know your work helps others. For one thing, your ego won't get in the way of the value of your work because you are making a contribution to society — making a difference. When I first started doing television shows to sell books, I found the attention of the spotlight was as intoxicating as it was addictive. The more I appeared on TV, the more I wanted to be on. It was sick, I've come to realize. I was doing things I normally wouldn't, just to get on the tube and satisfy my ego as a talk-show personality. It's something that happens to most people who get close to the business of television and feel how persuasive it can be in selling a product or a personality.

In my heart, I knew that television helped sell my books, and that my books helped people. So I learned to remove my personal self from the fickle decision making that drives the media business, and instead concentrated on selling books to help others. It was like a light bulb went off over my head. Instead of feeling defensive or apologetic about my zany TV personality, I accepted that it was just another tool to sell my books to people who needed the information to get their own lives jump-started. I provide the booster cables, and television reaches a far larger audience than direct mail or taking out an ad in a magazine. Oh, yes, I make money. But more importantly, my books help others.

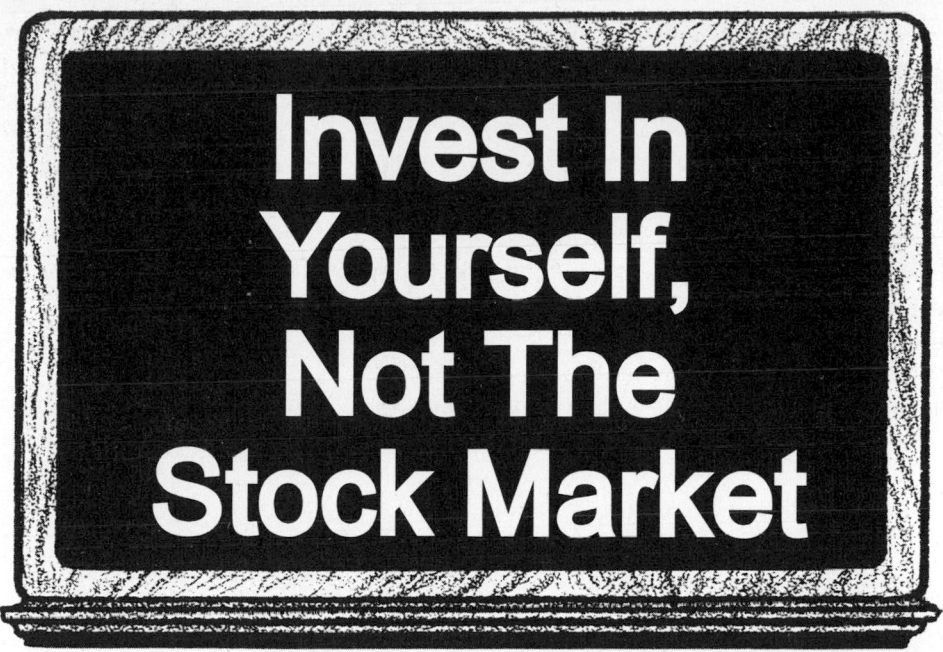

Invest In Yourself, Not The Stock Market

It amazes me that people give so much of their money to stockbrokers and investment advisors — these people get all the fun of playing with your money, yet take none of the risk. All you get as an investor is the worry, and if you are lucky, a dividend check. Sure, some people make a killing on pork bellies, but most investors wind up eating Rolaids for breakfast.

Money should be used to get all you can out of life. I don't believe that you can do that by turning your money and investment decisions over to someone else. Many of us are unhappy with the way the world is, yet we give our money to those people running it in the same old way. If you have an idea — something you believe would make the world a better place — put your money in it. Forget the investors, invest in yourself.

You are your best asset, not blue chip stocks or profit-sharing plans. You should continually be investing in yourself to make sure that you continue to grow. Why invest money in someone else? They're only trying to make their own money and increase their own investments. Learn how to make your own money yourself. Then you'll find real security, and a sense of a job well done — a sense of self worth.

I see rich people fall into the investment trap all the time. On a nice sunny day, stand in front of any big name brokerage office in New York or Chicago. You'll witness a very interesting phenomenon — wealthy people pull up in their limousines, go inside, and give their money to someone who came to work by subway, bus or bike.

Go figure.

If these rich people spent the money themselves — investing in projects that they believed in — they would probably not make as much. But they would earn, learn, and get a much better return out of their investment. They might even learn to behave creatively with a little bit of that money, and find out how exciting investing can be.

> *"Taking out the bottom 10% where money matters a great deal to those who do not have enough to live on — the relationship between income and happiness for the rest of the population is not of real importance. Rich people are virtually no happier. Even national surveys of young American children ages 7-11 show that their self reported happiness is not related to their parents' income levels."*
>
> Source: *Ambition: How We Manage Success and Failure Throughout Our Lives*, Gilbert Brim, Basic Books, 1992

   Matthew Lesko, Information USA, Inc., 12081 Nebel Street, Rockville, MD 20852 • 1-800-955-7693 • www.lesko.com

Don't Put The Hurdles Too High

If you want to learn to play the piano, don't set your sights on Carnegie Hall after one lesson. Sure you're excited, but your goals have to be realistic and achievable. Otherwise you'll be playing frustration and hopelessness, not Chopin. Do something that allows you to contribute to the best of your abilities. If you don't feel you've got the talent to play major concert halls around the country, but you're the best piano teacher in town, think it through. There are hundreds of children who will love you for teaching them, and love is far better than applause. It usually lasts a lot longer, too.

We set our own goals, but too often put our hurdles too high. It's best to put them just high enough to be a struggle, but not too high that we can't get over any of them. Raise or lower them as you go through life. What feels right for this year may not be right for the next. Professional men and women on the fast-track wake up one day with little children and the next day they are living with teenagers. And then they're gone. Miss anything?

Many professionals with children are opting out of the fast lane, shifting their focus from becoming a partner at a high-powered law firm or advertising agency to working from home — managing 4 or 5 clients — and eating cookies with the kids after school. Tell me who gets the real bonus out of that kind of an arrangement.

Trying to become a partner at a law firm requires putting in 60 to 70 hours each week, but handling 4 or 5 clients might take

20 hours. If you try to make partner while raising young children, you will probably fail at both tasks. Time, energy, and frustration will sap your drive, and too often you'll be forced to give one up. These are both full time jobs. Supermom is a super myth, a marketing angle for the sellers of microwave breakfasts, pre-packaged lunches and carryout dinners. By lowering your sites in your professional life, you can create an atmosphere where both jobs, professional and personal, can get done pretty well.

I recently read a book called "Ambition: How we Manage Success and Failure Through Our Lives" by Gilbert Brim. In the beginning of the book, the author tells a wonderful story that addresses this topic. Brim talks about his father, who retired as a college professor and bought an abandoned farm of several hundred acres. His father had always longed to return to the life he had as a boy, growing up on a farm. When he finally was able to buy the place, he first cleaned the woods, put up fences, roamed the hillside and mountaintops, and trimmed the trees and brush along the drive. As he grew older, his father's legs and back began tiring earlier and earlier in the day, until he had to hire a young man to help him. As he grew older still, the upper part of the mountain behind the farm became too hard to reach, and his father stayed closer to home.

Brim's father lived to be 103, and every few years there was less and less that he could do around the place. But he always found something within his capabilities. At 100, he couldn't even tend the little garden in front of the house, so he constantly worked on four outdoor window boxes of flowers. They were waist high, so he didn't have to bend down to cultivate the flowers. There is a giant lesson here for all of us.

Find something that will challenge your abilities, even as your abilities may lessen. Set realistic and achievable goals every day, but don't set them in concrete. Make them flexible and attainable, and perhaps you too will live to be 103.

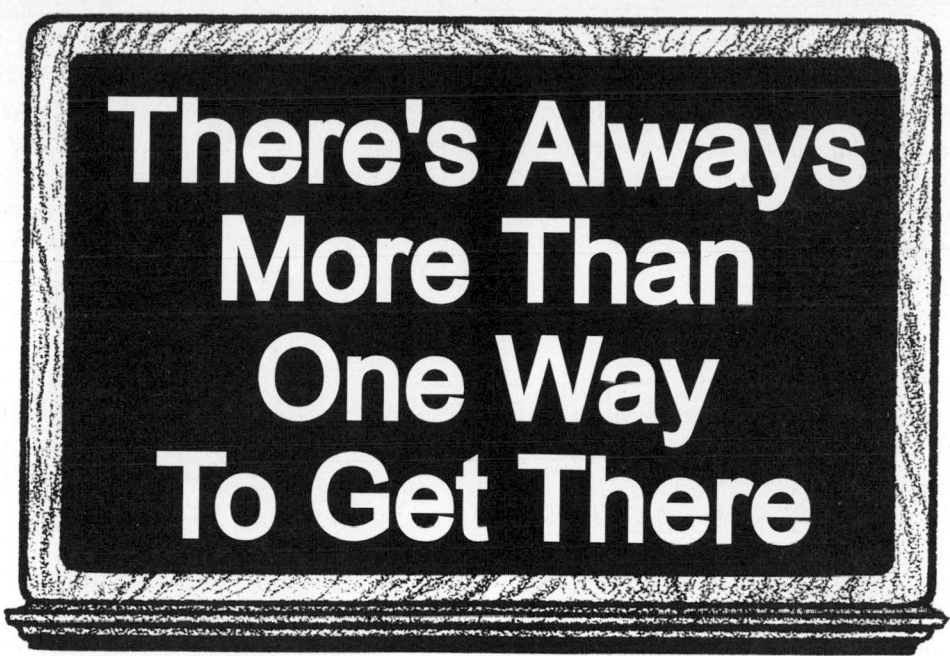

There's Always More Than One Way To Get There

We often have to figure out more than one way to get where we're going, whether it's due to a traffic jam or a vacation threatened by bad weather. The same is true in launching a successful business.

If you want to open a store in your local shopping mall but don't have the $100,000 it will take to start one, consider a different route — become a vendor with a push cart, or perhaps open a booth in the same mall, for a lot less money. All of these business ideas will only cost a few hundred dollars to get started, but it's a start. Or maybe you want to make a living on the professional golf tour, but you know your game is a little shaky — your 18 point handicap won't even get you into the qualifying school. So what? Think about all the other opportunities there are on the circuit. You could get a job with the PGA Tour selling flowers or catering, or become a saleswomen calling on pro shops with a line of golf clothing.

The point is — avoid tunnel vision. View the big picture, and don't let society or any of your own pre-conceived notions lock you out of an area where you want to make a living. The world is full

of possibilities, but sometimes you have to create them for yourself. Even if your first step is small, and not where you envision yourself being, at least you're making progress. And that progress can build on itself and turn into real momentum. You're moving toward what you want — and if you have the stamina and drive — you'll get there.

Few people know exactly what they want in life, and often, by the time they get there, their goals and outlook have changed considerably — or the world has. It's a waste of time waiting around for that perfect job or perfect circumstance. Just start doing what you want to do and keep moving in that direction. Nothing worthwhile happens overnight. It always starts a little imperfect and evolves into something better.

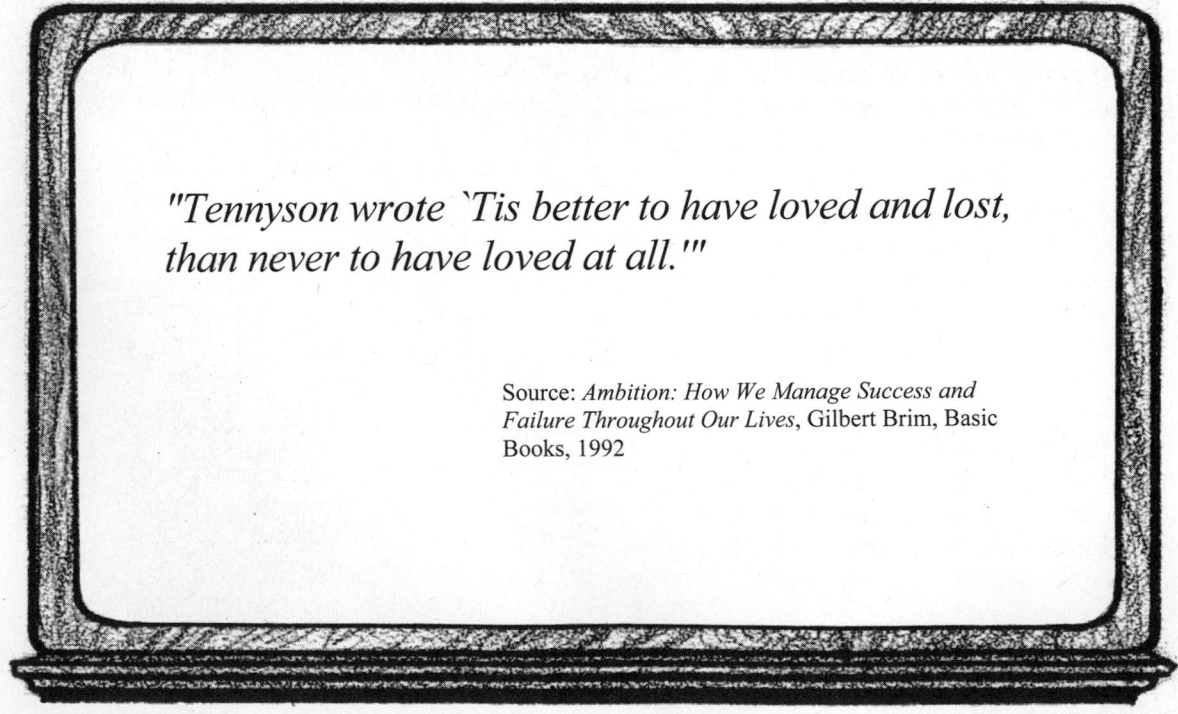

"Tennyson wrote `Tis better to have loved and lost, than never to have loved at all.'"

Source: *Ambition: How We Manage Success and Failure Throughout Our Lives*, Gilbert Brim, Basic Books, 1992

Leisure Is Boring When Your Work Is Fun

I covered some of this earlier when I talked about retirement being passe. Still, it's important to mention it again in another context. Many of us have been conditioned to believe that work stinks, and that being able to sit on our butts for the rest of our lives would be heaven. We also seem programmed into believing that the easier the work is, the better. What a joke! Even though we are sometimes burnt out from our daily labors, the reality is that the harder we work, the better we feel. Even if we're tired at the end of the day — if we've worked hard we feel like we've accomplished something. It's human nature to want to work hard, to push ourselves to the limit. Plus you sleep better at night when you're happily exhausted from what you've been doing all day.

So why do so many people try to find the easy way out of work? Why do they call in sick when they're feeling OK? It's because most people don't like what they are doing and try to do as little of it as possible. That's human nature too.

When people find work with meaning — something that interests them and gives them personal satisfaction — they suddenly start loving their jobs and willingly work longer hours. Then they find leisure time is no longer engaging or nearly as enjoyable as a hard day's work and a good night's sleep.

I'm not talking about workaholics who feel they have to work 70 hours a week to just keep up or get ahead. I mean people who work 12 hour days just because they love doing it! The key is not resigning yourself to a job that you hate instead of taking the risks of changing careers or looking for a more meaningful job.

But I have bills, bills, bills, people argue. Of course — we all do. But isn't it better to take risks and succeed than to spend your days hating your job and longing for a couch and a TV to escape into? That's not living, it's resignation! And if you're going to resign from life, find more challenging work and resign from your current job.

Then you'll bounce out of bed in the morning, raring to go, instead of dragging yourself through another dreary workday, just waiting for it to be over. Because one day it will, and then what will you do?

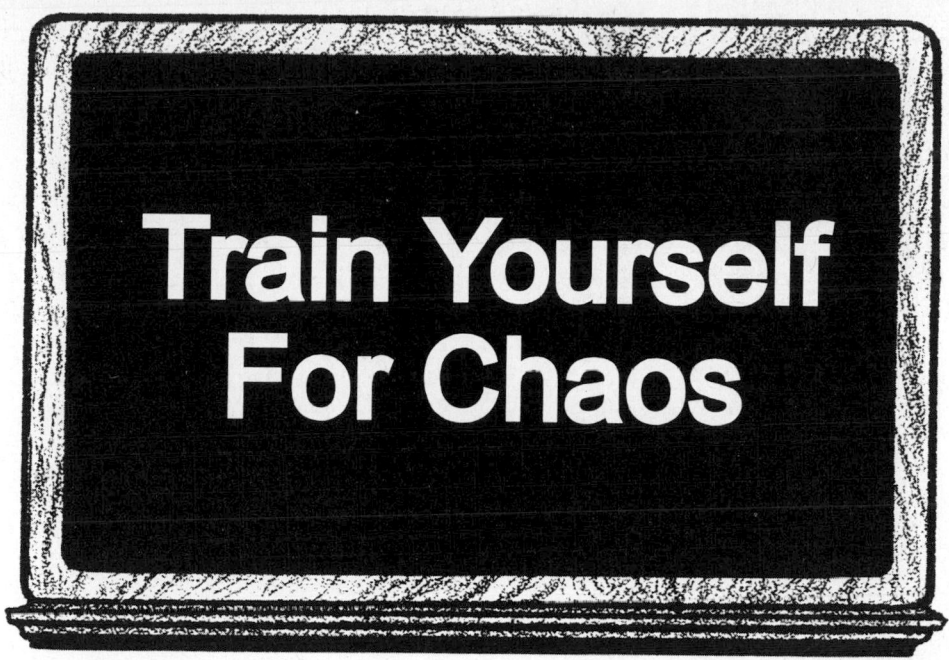

Train Yourself For Chaos

When I began starting businesses, I used to try to get everything to run smoothly. That's what I was trained to do in seven years of business school. Their educational mission was to teach us to get everyone and everything to work perfectly in business. Nice concept on paper.

In real life, nothing ever runs perfectly. Once I was in the real business world, something or someone was always going wrong. People would screw up. Materials wouldn't be delivered on time. Customers wouldn't pay their bills. Nothing seemed to work smoothly — the way I thought they would if I worked at it hard enough. I spent all my time putting out fires and frustrated myself to no end. Eventually, I quit trying to train myself to handle things perfectly, because perfection so rarely happened.

Instead, I began training myself to cope with chaos. Now I plan for what will go wrong when I step into the office tomorrow. What will I do when I don't get my money on time? What will I do when my materials don't come in on time, or bills aren't paid?

In a perfect world, we wouldn't need business schools. Businesses would run themselves, turning handsome profits each quarter. Perfection handles itself, it needs no fine tuning. But perfection rarely happens in life or in business — so I recommend chaos training. Everyone needs a crash course in it before starting a new business. Think of it as business boot camp for the coming millennium.

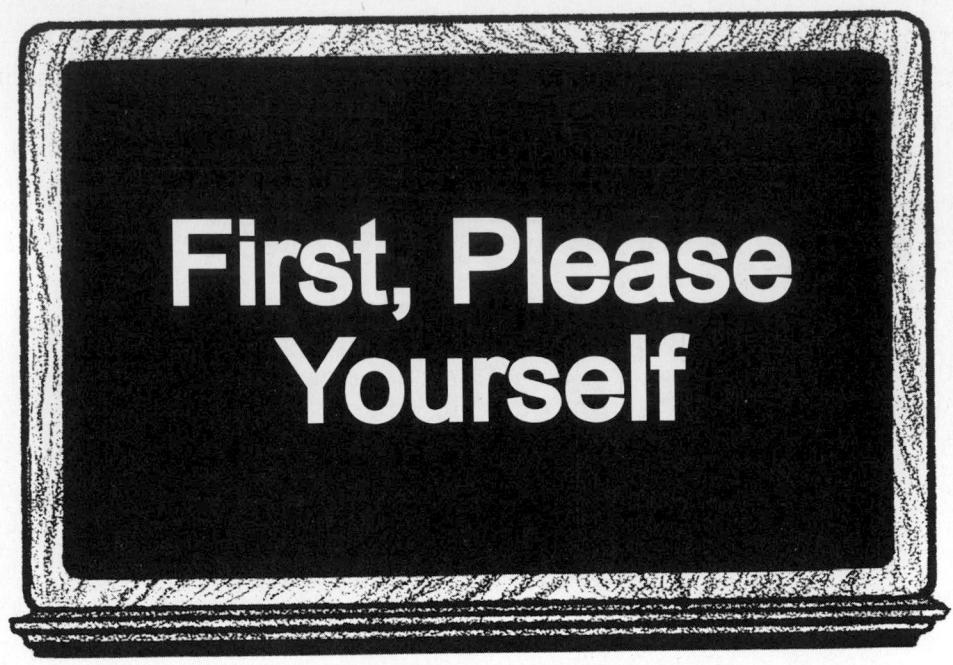

First, Please Yourself

So many of us grow up with the Judeo-Christian ethic of self sacrifice and putting others first, that we don't know where to draw the line in our own lives. This may sound like heretical Me Generation propaganda, but it's true. Just because you help yourself doesn't mean you forget everyone else — you just put yourself in the picture, too.

I believe in helping others, but I also know there are times when trying to please others hurts you — and indirectly them, in the long run. It's like a boomerang. You have to throw it, it won't throw itself. You have to be the nicest to yourself first in order to be nice to others. If I'm not happy in what I'm doing, I can't be joyful and helpful to others around me.

When I had my first child, I started having all kinds of anxieties about my finances. Believe me, I sweated bullets! I'd need a big house in a great neighborhood and an even bigger bank account to afford college. I worried for months and months — I didn't have any of these things. Where would they come from?

Then I started spending all my time trying to figure out how to make more money just to alleviate my anxiety. I began making most decisions not because I thought they were right and I wanted to do them, but more because I thought they would make more money.

Matthew Lesko, Information USA, Inc., 12081 Nebel Street, Rockville, MD 20852 • 1-800-955-7693 • www.lesko.com

Soon work was less fun — I wasn't making enough to live up to my expectations of a bright future for my kid. As a result, life was less fun, and I became less able to bring joy and laughter to those around me.

Then one day I began thinking about what I remembered most about my father. It was never the house he provided, or money for college — it was the upbeat attitude and love we shared around the house that had the greatest impact on my life.

Right then and there I changed directions completely. I realized that my major duty to my children would not be to have the biggest house on the block, the nicest car, or a fat bank account. Instead, I decided to do work that I felt was important and meaningful, so that I could come home happy and share this with my family. They would remember me as the kind of father that was always around, trying new things, and staying curious about life.

I think this "me first" boomerang approach also works with almost all other personal relationships in life. If you do not take care of your happiness and self-fulfillment first, you cannot be genuinely generous and caring with others. You simply won't have the capacity or energy to give graciously of yourself. And that won't help anyone.

Don't Worry If You Can't Fix It

We waste too much time worrying about the things we can't control. Does my boss like me? Will my company downsize and put me on the streets? Are terrorists stealing nukes? Will the airplane crash? Are antibiotic resistant diseases about to create the Mother of all Plagues? Will Aunt Lila like my gift? On and on it goes…

Usually there's little we can do to influence these events. If someone doesn't like you, it's usually because of a personality conflict. How can you change that and remain true to yourself? Impossible! If you wind up on welfare, it's the economy, stupid. Don't worry, be resourceful — plan for economic chaos and you won't be left out in the cold. Nuclear black market and terrorists? What does that have to do with you? Write your elected representatives and express your concern — then let it go. Unless you're the pilot, you have absolutely no control of the airplane — whether its gets to your destination on time or falls out of the sky. Listen to the flight attendant and notice the emergency procedures — and then relax — you have no control.

Sure, there are little things we can do that may influence such events, but I believe the amount of your worry should be proportionate to your ability to control the outcome.

It pays to be prepared, to be somewhat cautious and definitely concerned about

 Matthew Lesko, Information USA, Inc., 12081 Nebel Street, Rockville, MD 20852 • 1-800-955-7693 • www.lesko.com

threatening issues. But when all is said and done, the only real control you have is over your own decisions in life. Make good ones, and the rest of your worries fall into the proper perspective.

If you are worried about money, remember Howard Hughes. He was brilliant, good looking, rich and famous — smart as a whip. He dined with movie stars, presidents, and kings. Then he started worrying. He worried about germs and microbes, and wound up a wasted hermit living in an airtight penthouse in Las Vegas with the drapes drawn shut to keep the bugs away. Guess what? He died anyway.

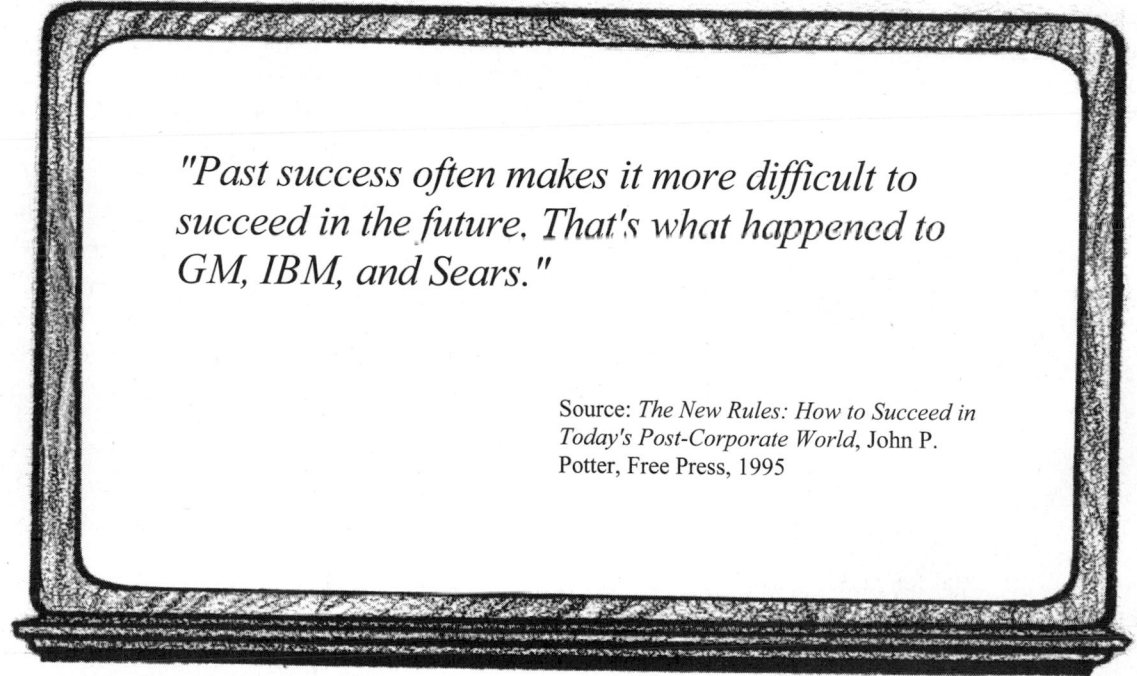

"Past success often makes it more difficult to succeed in the future. That's what happened to GM, IBM, and Sears."

Source: *The New Rules: How to Succeed in Today's Post-Corporate World,* John P. Potter, Free Press, 1995

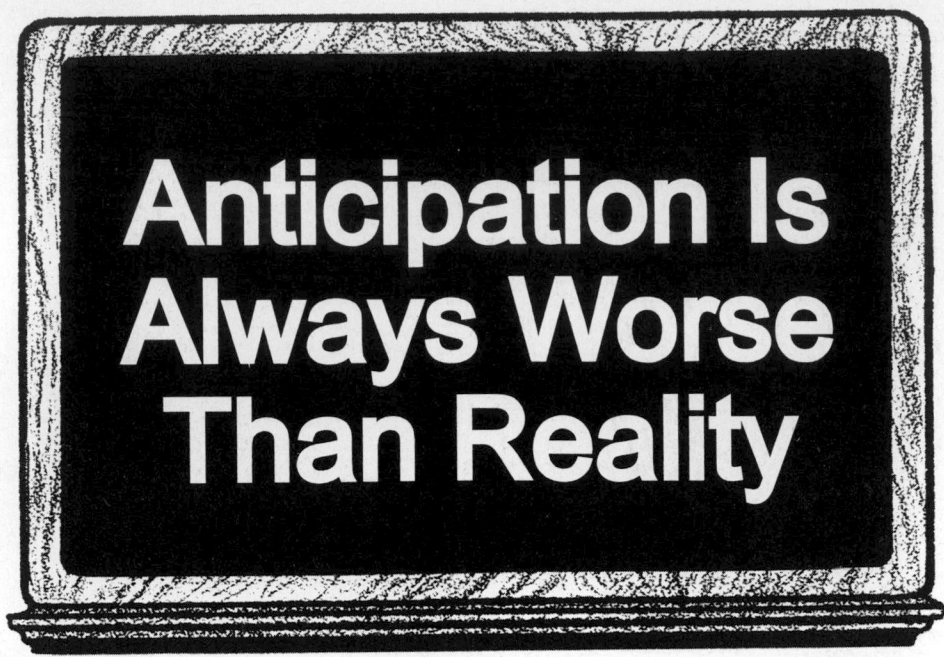

Anticipation Is Always Worse Than Reality

It never fails. Every time I worry about doing some unpleasant task like confronting someone who owes me money, or firing an employee who has been with me for a long time, I realize that thinking about what's going to happen is always worse than the actual event itself. I usually worry about the confrontation so much that my stomach will ache, and then, when I finally make the call or have the meeting, it's never as bad as I expected. So now I try to get any potentially stressful situation over as fast as possible. Procrastinating only makes things worse, I know that now. The sooner I get it over with, the better I'll feel, and the actual event is never as bad as I imagine it will be.

Now my stomach doesn't hurt when I've got bad news to deliver or a confrontation to face. I visualize a positive outcome — what it will be like afterwards. People appreciate the honesty and directness of such an approach, and so do I.

 Matthew Lesko, Information USA, Inc., 12081 Nebel Street, Rockville, MD 20852 • 1-800-955-7693 • www.lesko.com

Technology Won't Pass You By

In our fast changing society, too many people are afraid that if they're not using the latest technology they'll be left in the dust — selling apples on street corners instead of making a killing by staying up with the virtual pack.

In a consumer society like ours, this fear is absurd. The truth is, the longer you hold out on acquiring some new technological whiz-bang product, the better off you'll be when you finally do buy the next generation of products. Save your time, worry and aggravation, and let new technology pass you by for awhile. Then, when you're ready, the products will be better, cheaper, easier to use — and you'll be fresh and excited about them — not jaded and cynical like the others who feel burnt because last year's hot software isn't worth a slice of toast anymore.

The problem is, we never get any encouragement to wait and not act impulsively. Everyone tells us to buy now — or life will pass us by. This has been going on in our country ever since the first car was offered to consumers. Earlier, really. For farmers, it was the steam combine; for tailors, the foot-pedal sewing machine.

But the car was the first big piece of technology that truly revolutionized the world. When the first automobiles appeared, slick salesmen told people how life was going to pass them by if they didn't own one. A lot of people were fooled into believing that their life was better with a car, but it wasn't. They were buying the sizzle and not the steak. Those early cars were complicated to run, and required special tools and skills. And they were even a lot slower than the existing mode of transportation, the horse. Most importantly, there was no "software" for the first cars — no roads to ride on. Because of this, some of those early car owners weren't even able to try out this new gadget that was supposed to revolutionize their lives.

Still, there were people who just had to have a car.

And what eventually happened? After everyone who just had to have the first cars had one, the manufacturers started figuring out how to make them cheaper, easier to use, and more useful. The next models were a lot better, as were subsequent generations of cars.

The same is true of computers. I remember in the early 1980s, when personal computers were first introduced. Salesmen told us our lives and businesses would fail if we didn't run out and buy the latest personal computers — at the time selling for around $5,000! They told us that we could balance our checkbook on the computer! Keep recipes! If our children didn't know computers, they'd never get into college!

Well, if you never balanced your checkbook by hand, you would probably never do it by computer. It would take longer. A $5,000 piece of machinery to store recipes? Great idea! And the college gambit is as old as the encyclopedia salesman. The only thing a student could do on a computer back then was word processing. And if they had to write a report, a $200 typewriter would still do the job just fine.

The longer you waited to buy a computer, the cheaper they became and the more problems they could solve in less time. Fifteen years have passed, and it's finally getting easier to balance your checkbook by computer, but only if you write a lot of checks. You see — it pays to wait.

I see the same thing happening with the Internet. In early 1994 when I first started playing with the Internet, it was a little expensive for a commercial connection and very difficult to use. The information available there was also questionable as to it's value. But by late 1995, it became a whole lot easier to use, and the price keeps dropping. There is a lot more information available, but I still question its usefulness in real time. If you're not on the Internet yet, don't fret, and don't believe those that imply that you're one of the only ones not online. It won't hurt to keep waiting, and when you do sign on, it will be with a much better service than it was — well, yesterday.

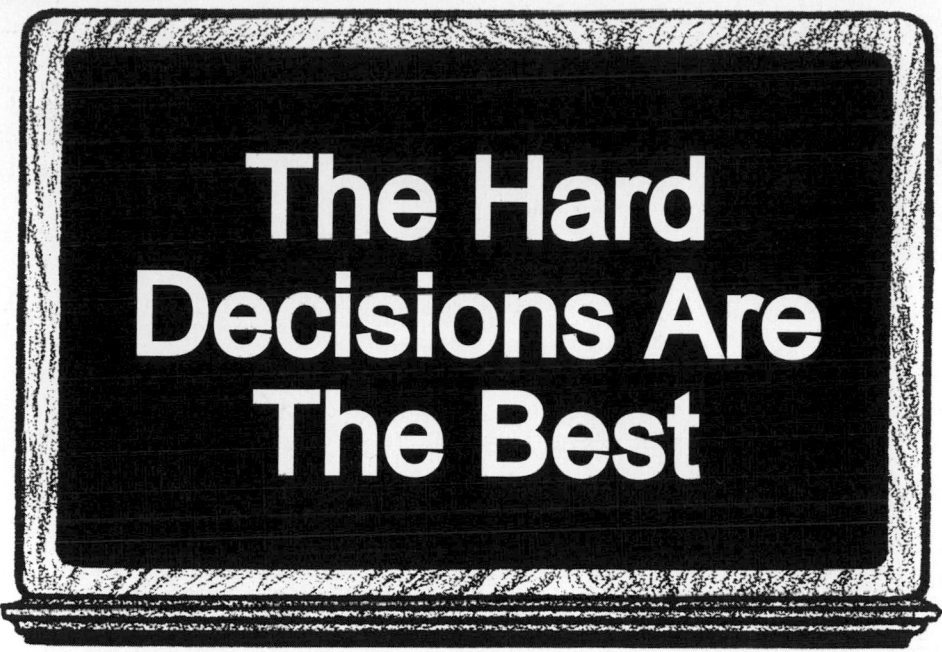

The Hard Decisions Are The Best

It's human nature to try and avoid making hard decisions, but I say the toughest ones are some of the best moments in life. Every time I've ever had to make a hard decision, I've always chosen the most difficult path. And these moments have become some of the most important and best turning points in my life. They made my life far richer than I could ever have dreamed, and were responsible for quantum jumps in my self confidence and inner security.

So now I look for those hard decisions — in fact, I'm eager to take them on. They don't come around very often, but when they do, try to appreciate them for the opportunities they can offer. The problem with tough decisions is that your intellect — as well as your friends and hired experts — will always caution you to go one way, while your heart tells you to pick another way. These decisions are usually choices between money and an idea or project that you believe in — even changing your career or spending your vacation building houses for the poor. Trust your heart — that's what it's there for.

Assets Are A Trap

You pay for your assets twice. Once in cold cash, and again in the limitations they place on your ability to make decisions to change your life.

We are all conditioned to believe that the game of life is won by the person who has the most assets when they finally bite the dust. "He Who Dies With the Most Toys Wins" — you've seen the bumper sticker, but nothing could be further from the truth. I find assets are a burden to life. The more assets I have, the more time I spend worrying about losing them, and the less time I spend having fun with my life — doing what I really want to do.

I'm not advocating taking a vow of poverty — I'm just saying be careful about accumulating too many assets or getting trapped in the "gimme more" mind set. You don't want to find yourself working just to add new toys to the playground — most of the time, you'd be too busy to enjoy those toys, anyway. If you can't afford to lose those material things, don't bother accumulating them in the first place.

 Matthew Lesko, Information USA, Inc., 12081 Nebel Street, Rockville, MD 20852 • 1-800-955-7693 • www.lesko.com

Don't Trust Me

I deeply believe in what I've written in these past 36 philosophical vignettes, but don't trust me. What works for me might not work for you — you've got to find out for yourself. This goes for anyone you turn to for advice — whether it's your mother, your stock broker, your barber or your therapist. Face it, we're all different, and each of us must create our own unique mosaic of what works and, even more importantly, what doesn't work.

I don't actually follow everything I'm professing here each and every day — I'd love to, but I don't. Sometimes I give in to my own personal weaknesses or to outside influences and can't live up to my own expectations of myself. But I try and I keep trying, continually learning from my mistakes.

That's what has been so wonderful about writing this book. It's given me an opportunity to put what I really believe in down on paper — an itemized account of my values and beliefs, what's important in life and what isn't, at least to me. It's taken me a lot of years of experiencing both success and failure to arrive at what I feel is important to me in life. And I'm sure that those beliefs will continue to change as I keep on learning from my life.

Use this book like a philosophical lazy susan or salad bar. Pick and chose — help yourself. In the end, you'll have your own unique mix of principles that work best — different from mine and different from the person right beside you. And that's empowering.

"The Emptiness of Success
First, the amount of time and effort required to achieve a given goal may be so great that it causes failure in other important areas of life. Life becomes unbalanced. A second reason is described as `fear of failing.' When the success is seen as the result of luck or other external causes rather than one's own effort, problems may arise. A third reason why winning may not bring happiness is we may be wrong about the value of the goal."

Source: *Ambition: How We Manage Success and Failure Throughout Our Lives*, Gilbert Brim, Basic Books, 1992

I Wanna Go To School

Matthew Lesko, Information USA, Inc., 12081 Nebel Street, Rockville, MD 20852 • 1-800-955-7693 • www.lesko.com

66 Federal Money Programs
Worth $30 Billion

Most people have heard of the federal government's largest money programs for students like the Pell Grant Program and the Guaranteed Student Loan program. But did you know that the federal government is the single largest source of money for students — whether they show financial need or not? It's true, but very few people are aware of the many grant programs in place and just waiting to give money to those students smart enough to find out about them. These little known programs provide students with:

- $15,000 to do graduate studies in housing related topics for the Department of Housing and Urban Development
- Money to finance a graduate degree in criminal justice from the Department of Justice
- $14,000 to get a graduate degree in foreign languages from the Department of Education
- $8,800 plus tuition and expenses to be a nurse from the Department of Health and Human Services

How To Apply

Requirements and application procedures vary widely from program to program. Some programs accept applications once a year, while others award money on a year round basis. Some programs require you to apply directly to the main funding office in Washington, DC, while other programs distribute the money to local organizations, which then distribute funds to individuals. Many of the programs give the money directly to the schools, and then the schools distribute it. For those, you need to request a listing of the schools that receive the funds.

All these federal programs are listed in the *Catalogue of Federal Domestic Assistance*, which is available in most libraries. This catalogue lists all the government grant and loan programs available. The program name and number in parenthesis refer to this publication.

* Money To Study Food

(Food and Agricultural Science National Needs Graduate Fellowship Grants 10.210)
Grants Program Manager
Office of Higher Education Programs
CSREES, U.S. Department of Agriculture
Room 3912, South Building
Washington, DC 20250   202-720-7854
www.reeusda.gov/serd/hep/index.htm

The program awards grants to colleges and universities that have superior teaching and research competencies in the food and agricultural sciences. These grants are to be used to encourage outstanding students to pursue and complete a graduate degree in an area of the food and agricultural sciences for which there is a national need for development of scientific expertise. Money can be used to support a student completing a graduate, masters, or doctorate degree. Students must apply to those institutions that received the money. For a listing of institutions that received money, contact the office listed above. Money available: $2,873,280.

* Money To Help Math Students and Summer Scientists

(Independent Education and Science Projects and Programs 11.449)
Tony Tafoya
NOAA/OAR
Building 22, 325 Broadway
Boulder, CO 80303   303-497-6731
www.noaa.gov

This program objective is to increase the number of minority students enrolling in college and majoring in math, science and engineering. Another objective is to recruit scientists and engineers from the Boulder county area to serve as science/math tutors. Money can be used to help high school and middle school students who are part of the Math, Engineering, Science Achievement (MESA) Program in Colorado. It is also for students pursuing a course of study related to oceanic and atmospheric sciences and who are interested in a summer hands-on experience in a laboratory setting. Money can be used for transportation, housing and stipends for students during the summer months where students learn about the laboratories mission and perform hands-on assignments. Money available: $75,000.

* Opportunity To Receive College Tuition From NSA

(Mathematical Sciences Grants Program 12.901)
National Security Agency
Manager, Undergraduate Training Program
Attn: R51A
9800 Savage Rd., Suite 6840
Ft. Meade, MD 20755-6840   301-688-0400
www.nsa.gov

National Security Agency (NSA) will consider any student who meets the requirements below and who chooses a full-time college major in either computer science, electrical or computer engineering, languages or mathematics. Requirements consist of having a minimum SAT score of 1100 and a minimum composite ACT score of 25. Chosen students can receive college tuition, reimbursement for books, year-round salary, summer work and have a guaranteed job with the NSA after graduation. Students must work for NSA for one and a half times their length of study, which is usually about five years. Money available: $2,600,000.

* Money To Study Community Planning and Development

(Community Development Work-Study Program 14.512)
U.S. Department of Housing and Urban Development
Community Planning and Development
Office of University Partnerships
451 7th St., SW, Room 8106   202-708-3061
Washington, DC 20410   800-245-2691
www.hud.gov/progdesc/cdwsp.cfm

The Community Development Work-Study Program makes grants to institutions of higher education to provide assistance to economically disadvantaged and minority students. Students take part in community development work-study programs while they are enrolled full-time in graduate or undergraduate programs with that major. Grants are given to encourage minority and economically disadvantaged students to develop careers in community and economic development, community planning, and community management. Related fields include public administration, urban management, and urban planning. Student assistance is in the form of work stipends, tuition support, and additional support to cover books and travel related to conferences and seminars. Students must apply to those institutions that received the money. For a listing of institutions that received money, contact the office listed above. Money available: $3,000,000. Average grant per student is $30,000.

* Money To Study Housing Issues

(Doctoral Dissertation Research Grant Program 14.516)
Armand Carriere
Office of University Partnerships
U.S. Department of Housing and Urban Development
451 7th St., SW, Room 8106
Washington, DC 20410   202-708-3061
www.huduser.org

The program objective is to encourage doctoral candidates to engage in policy related housing and urban development research and to assist them in its timely completion. Money can used to support Ph.D candidates while they complete work towards their degree. Students must have a fully developed and approved dissertation proposal that addresses the purpose of this program. Students can request an application package from the address listed above or by calling HUD USER at 800-245-2691. Each student is eligible for up to $25,000 per year.

* Money For Members Of Indian Tribes To Go To College

(Indian Education-Higher Education Grant Program 15.114)
Bureau of Indian Affairs
Office of Indian Education Programs
Room MS-3512-MIB
U.S. Department of the Interior
1849 C St., NW
Washington, DC 20240   202-208-3478
www.oiep.bia.edu

The program objective is to provide financial aid to eligible Indian students to enable them to attend accredited institutions of higher education. Members of an Indian tribe may be eligible for these grants to supplement the total financial aid package prepared by their college financial aid officer. Once you have been accepted by a college and have completed their financial aid application, you may request a grant application form from your tribal group. Money available: $25,267,060. The amount of assistance per student ranges from $300-$5000 per year.

* Money For Criminal Justice Majors

(Criminal Justice Research and Development - Grant Research Fellowships 16.562)
National Institute of Justice
633 Indiana Ave., SW
Washington, DC 20531   202-307-2942
www.ncjrs.org

The program objective is to improve the quality and quantity of knowledge about crime and the criminal justice system. Additionally, the program seeks to increase the number of persons who are qualified to teach in collegiate criminal justice programs, to conduct research related to criminal justice issues, and to perform more effectively within the criminal justice system. Students can receive a fellowship for a year, plus, two to three months to visit the National Institute of Justice to work with staff as an intern. This competitive program provides fellowship stipends, major project costs and certain university fees, round trip travel expenses to the Institute, and housing costs. Detailed information can be received by requesting the NIJ Research Plan from the National Criminal Justice Reference Service, Box 6000, Rockville, MD 20850; 800-851-3420. Money available: $120,000. Maximum grant per student $15,000.

* Money To Study The Break Up Of The USSR

(Russian, Eurasian, and East European Research and Training 19.300)
Eurasian and East European Research and Training Program
INR/RES
U.S. Department of State
2201 C St., NW, Room 2251
Washington, DC 20520   202-736-4572
www.state.gov/www/regions/mis/grants

The program is designed to sustain and strengthen American expertise on the Commonwealth of Independent States, Georgia, the Baltic countries, and countries of Eastern Europe by supporting graduate training; advanced research; public dissemination of research data, methods, and findings; contact and collaboration among government and private specialists; and first hand experience of the (former) Soviet Union and Eastern European countries by American specialists, including on site conduct of advanced training and research. Graduate students interested in conducting research on the Commonwealth of Independent States, Georgia, the Baltic countries, and the countries of Eastern Europe can receive fellowships which can support a student while conducting research or training. Funds are given to nonprofit organizations and institutions of higher learning who act as intermediaries for the federal funds by conducting their own competitions to make the awards. Grants in the past include grants for onsite independent short term research; individual exchange fellowships for American graduate students to pursue research in the region; and advanced in-country language training fellowships in Russian, Ukrainian, Hungarian, Polish, and more. Students must apply to those institutions that received the money. For a listing of institutions that received money, contact the office listed above. Money available: $5,000,000.

* $3,000 A Year To Be A Merchant Marine

(State Marine Schools 20.806)
Office of Maritime Labor and Training
Maritime Administration
U.S. Department of Transportation
400 7th St., SW
Washington, DC 20590   202-366-5755
www.marad.dot.gov

The program objective is to train merchant marine officers in State Marine Schools. You can receive $3,000 per year to train to be a merchant marine officer at a designated State Marine School. In exchange for this incentive payment program, you must commit yourself to a minimum of five years duty to the Maritime Administration, which can be satisfied by: serving as a merchant marine officer aboard vessels; as an employee in a U.S. maritime related industry, profession or marine science; or as a commissioned officer on active duty in an armed force of the U.S. or in the National Oceanic and Atmospheric Administration. You must also remain in a reserve unit of an armed force for a minimum of eight years. Students need to apply to one of the State Marine Schools. Money available: $7,457,000.

* All Expenses Plus $558 A Month To Be A Merchant Marine

(U.S. Merchant Marine Academy – Kings Point 20.807)
Office of Maritime Labor and Training
Maritime Administration
U.S. Department of Transportation
400 Seventh St., SW
Washington, DC 20590   202-366-5755
www.marad.dot.gov

This program trains merchant marine officers while they attend the Merchant Marine Academy in Kings Point, NY. Students receive training, subsistence, books, quarters, uniforms, medical care, and program travel without cost. In addition, the student will receive a monthly wage from their steamship company employer. Money available: $47,822,000. An allowance is prescribed for all personnel for uniforms and textbooks. During the sea year a midshipman will earn $600 per month from the steamship employer.

* Part-Time Jobs In The Government

(Student Temporary Employment Program 27.003)
Employment Service
Office of Personnel Management
1900 E St., NW
Washington, DC 20415   202-606-0830
www.usajobs.opm.gov

The program gives students 16 years of age and older an opportunity for part time temporary employment with federal agencies in order to allow them to continue their education without interruptions caused by financial pressures. The money can be used to pay expenses while attending school. Apply for this program through the youth division of the local office of the State Employment Service. Look in the government section of your phone book to find an office near you, or contact the Main State Employment Service office for referral to a local office.

* Internships For Graduate Students To Work AT 54 Government Agencies

(Presidential Management Intern Program 27.013)
U.S. Office of Personnel Management
Philadelphia Service Center
Federal Building
600 Arch St.   215-597-7136
Philadelphia, PA 19106   215-597-1920
www.usajobs.opm.gov

The PMI Program is a two-year entry-level employment and career development program designed to attract to the federal civil service men and women with graduate degrees from diverse cultural and academic backgrounds. Interns will have demonstrated academic excellence, possess management and leadership potential, and have a commitment to and a clear interest in a public service career. Nominees for the PMI Program undergo a rigorous, competitive screening process. Being selected as a PMI Finalist is a first step, but does not guarantee a job. Agencies designate positions for the PMIs and each establishes its own procedures for considering and hiring PMIs. Once hired by agencies, PMIs are encouraged to work with their agencies to establish an "individual development plan." PMIs participate in training conferences, seminars, and congressional briefings. Money can be used to pay for expenses. An application form and more information can be requested by contacting the Career America Hotline at 912-757-3000.

* $30,000 To Study The Humanities

(Promotion of the Humanities - Fellowships and Stipends 45.160)
Fellowships and Stipends
Division of Research and Education
National Endowment for the Humanities
1100 Pennsylvania Ave., Room 318
Washington, DC 20506   202-606-8200
www.neh.gov

Fellowships and Summer Stipends provide support for scholars to undertake full-time independent research and writing in the humanities. Grants are available for 6 to 12-month fellowships and two months of summer study. Projects may contribute to scholarly knowledge or to the general public's understanding of the humanities. The proposed study or research may be completed during the grant period or it may be part of a longer project. Contact the office listed above for application information. Money available: $7,000,000. Stipends are $5,000 for summer; $24,000 for 6-8 months; and $40,000 for 9-12 months.

* Money For Social, Behavioral, And Economic Sciences Students

(Social, Behavioral, and Economic Sciences 47.075)
Assistant Director
Social, Behavioral, and Economic Research
National Science Foundation
4201 Wilson Blvd., Suite 935
Arlington, VA 22230   703-292-8710
www.nsf.gov

The program objective is to promote the progress of the social, behavioral, and economic science; to facilitate cooperative research activities with foreign scientists, engineers, and institutions and to support understanding of the resources invested in science and engineering in the U.S. Funds are provided for U.S. scientists and engineers to carry out studies abroad, to conduct research, to engage in joint research projects with foreign counterpart organizations, and to support international scientific workshops in the U.S. and abroad. Money can be used for paying associated costs necessary to conduct research or studies for doctorate students; and more. Students must contact the office listed above for application information. Money available: $168,790,000.

* Money For Disabled Veterans To Go To College

(Vocational Rehabilitation For Disabled Veterans 64.116)
Department of Veterans Affairs
Veterans Benefits Administration   202-273-7419
Washington, DC 20420   800-827-1000
www.va.gov

The program objective is to provide all services and assistance necessary to enable service-disabled veterans and service persons hospitalized pending discharge to achieve maximum independence in daily living and, to the maximum extent possible, to become employable and to obtain and maintain suitable employment. The fund provides for the entire cost of tuition, books, fees, supplies, and other services to help the veteran live with a reduced dependency on others while staying in their homes and communities. The veteran also receives a monthly allowance, a work-study allowance, and more. Enrollment can be in a trade, business, or technical schools, colleges, apprenticeship programs, cooperative farming, special rehabilitation facilities, or at home when necessary. Students must obtain an application from any Veterans Affairs office or regional office. Money available: Direct payments: $436,638,000; Loan advances: $2,726,000. Monthly full time allowances per student range from $448 for a single veteran to $655 for a veteran with two dependents, plus $47.76 for each dependent in excess of two.

* Money For Spouses And Children Of Deceased Or Disabled Veterans To Go To School

(Survivors and Dependents Educational Assistance 64.117)
Department of Veterans Affairs
Central Office   202-273-7132
Washington, DC 20420   800-827-1000
www.va.gov

The program provides partial support to those seeking to advance their education who are qualifying spouses, surviving spouses, or children of deceased or disabled veterans who, as a result of their military service, have a permanent and total (100 percent) service connected disability, or a service personnel who have been listed for a total of more than 90 days as currently Missing in Action, or as Prisoners of War. Spouse, surviving spouse, or child of a deceased or disabled veteran can receive monthly payments to be used for tuition, books, subsistence, for courses, training, or college. Financial assistance is $485 per month, and there is tutorial assistance, vocational counseling and testing, and a work-study allowance. Benefits may be awarded for pursuit of associate, bachelor, or graduate degrees at colleges and universities, as well as study at business, technical, or vocational schools. Information on the program and application forms are available from your local or regional Veterans Affairs office. Money available: $179,043,000.

* Money For Vietnam Veterans To Go To School

(Post-Vietnam Era Veterans' Educational Assistance 64.120)
Department of Veterans Affairs
Central Office   202-273-7132
Washington, DC 20420   800-827-1000
www.va.gov

Post-Vietnam veterans who entered the Armed Services between 1977 and 1985 may be eligible for funds to obtain a college degree or vocational training. Through this program, the government matches $2 for every $1 the serviceman contributes. Some contribution to the fund must have been made prior to April 1, 1987. Contact your local or regional Veterans Affairs office for additional information or application materials. Money available: $15,151,000. Up to a maximum of $8,100 of basic benefits is available per student, as well as a work-study allowance of minimum wage and tutorial assistance up to a maximum of $1,200.

* Money For Retired Veterans To Go To School

(All-Volunteer Force Educational Assistance 64.124)
Department of Veterans Affairs
Central Office   202-273-7132
Washington, DC 20420   800-827-1000
www.gibill.va.gov

This program helps servicemen readjust to civilian life after their separation from military service, assists in the recruitment and retention of highly qualified personnel in the active and reserve components in the Armed Forces, and extends the benefits of a higher education to those who may not otherwise be able to afford it. Honorably discharged veterans can take advantage of the Montgomery GI Bill Active Duty benefits, which provides funds to pursue professional or vocational education, and even covers correspondence courses. Veterans can receive a monthly stipend while attending school, with the amount varying depending upon date of entry into the service and length of service. Additional information and application materials are available through any regional Veterans Affairs office. Money available: $1,376,127,000. A maximum allowance of $28,800 as basic assistance is available per student, as well as a work-study allowance, and up to $1,200 in tutorial assistance.

* Money For Minority Students At Junior Colleges Who Are Energy Majors

(Minority Technical Education Program 81.082)
Office of Economic Impact and Diversity

U.S. Department of Energy, ED-1
Forrestal Building, 5B-110
Washington, DC 20585   202-586-8383
www.hr.doe.gov/ed/OMEI/Omei.htm

The program objective is to provide scholarship funding to financially needy minority honor students pursuing training in energy related technologies and to develop linkages with energy industries. Scholarship funds are available to defray costs of tuition, books, tools, transportation, and laboratory fees for minority students attending junior colleges and majoring in energy related field. The students must apply to those institutions that received the money. For a listing of those institutions contact the office listed below. Money available: $500,000.

* $15,000 For Graduate Students To Study Overseas

(Educational Exchange - Graduate Students 19.400)
Institute of International Education
809 United Nations Plaza   212-883-8200
New York, NY 10017   Fax: 212-984-5452
www.iie.org

Graduate students who would like to spend a year studying overseas can apply for the Fulbright Program, where if accepted, they will receive round trip transportation, tuition, books, maintenance for one academic year in one country, and health insurance. Students apply through the Fulbright program adviser located at their college or university, or they can apply as an at-large applicant by contacting the New York office of the Institute of International Education. Money available: $14,500,000. The average award per student is $21,000, but awards can range anywhere from $1,200 to $35,000.

* $4,000 Grants For Students Having Trouble Paying Tuition

(Federal Supplemental Education Opportunity Grants 84.007)
Student Financial Assistance Program
Office of the Assistant Secretary for Post-Secondary Education
U.S. Department of Education   800-USA-LEARN
400 Maryland Ave., SW   TTY: 800-437-0833
Washington, DC 20202   Fax: 202-401-0689
www.ed.gov/offices/OSFAP

If you are working towards your first undergraduate baccalaureate degree and are having trouble paying the bills, you may qualify for money through the Federal Supplemental Educational Opportunity Grants (FSEOG) program. Grants are for undergraduate study and range from $100 to $4000 per academic year, with the student eligible to receive a FSEOG for the time it takes to complete their first degree. Students should contact the Financial Aid office of the school they attend or plan to attend for information regarding application. A student *Financial Aid Handbook* is available, as is a list of grantee institutions by contacting the Federal Student Aid Information Center, P.O. Box 84, Washington, DC 20044; 800-433-3243. Money available: $725,000,000. Estimated average award is $748.

* Money For a Foreign Language Degree

(National Resource Centers and Fellowships Program for Language and Area or Language and International Studies 84.015)
Higher Education Programs
U.S. Department of Education
1990 K Street, NW
Washington, DC 20006   202-502-7700
www.ed.gov/offices/OPE/HEP/iegps/flasf.html

In this glob}al world, foreign languages and international studies are becoming increasingly important. The Department of Education has funds to support centers that promote instruction in foreign language and international studies at colleges and universities. In addition, there are graduate fellowships to pursue this course of study in order to develop a pool of international experts to meet our nation's needs. Funds for centers may be used for instructional costs of language and area and international studies programs, administration, lectures and conferences, library resources and staff, and travel. Grants for fellowships include tuition, fees, and a basic subsistence allowance. Students must apply to those institutions that received the money. For a listing of institutions that received money, contact the office listed below. Students can contact these institutions directly. Money available: Grants: $27,500,000.

* Money For Students And Teachers To Travel Overseas

(Fulbright-Hays Training Grants - Group Projects Abroad 84.021)
Higher Education Programs
U.S. Department of Education
Office of Post-Secondary Education

1990 K Street, NW, 6th Floor
Washington, DC 20006   202-502-7700
www.ed.gov/offices/OPE/HEP/iegps/gpa.html

The program objective is to help educational institutions improve their programs in modern foreign language and area studies through overseas study/travel seminar group research, advanced foreign language training, and curriculum development. Funds are available to support overseas study/travel seminar group research and advanced foreign language training. Grant funds may be used for international travel, maintenance allowances, rental of instructional facilities in the country of study, and more. Money available: $2,326,000.

* Money For Ph.D. Students To Do Research Overseas

(Fulbright-Hays Training Grants - Doctoral Dissertation Research Abroad 84.022)
Karla Ver Bryck Block
Advanced Training and Research Team
Center for International Education
Office of Assistant Secretary for Post-Secondary Education
U.S. Department of Education
400 Maryland Ave., SW
Washington, DC 20202   202-502-7632
www.ed.gov/offices/OPE/HEP/iegps/ddrap.html

Graduate students now have the opportunity to engage in full time dissertation research abroad in modern foreign language and area studies. This program is designed to develop research knowledge and capability in world areas not widely included in American curricula. The grant includes a basic stipend, round trip airfare, baggage allowance, tuition payments, local travel, and more. Candidates apply directly to the institutions at which they are enrolled. Money available: $4,150,000.

* Loans To Go To School

(Federal Family Education Loans 84.032)
Office of Student Financial Assistance
U.S. Department of Education
Washington, DC 20202   800-4FED-AID
www.ifap.ed.gov

Guaranteed loans for educational expenses are available from eligible lenders such as banks, credit unions, savings and loan association, pension funds, insurance companies, and schools to vocational, undergraduate, and graduate students enrolled at eligible institutions. Loans can be used to pay the costs associated with obtaining a college education. The PLUS program is also available, which allows parents to borrow for their dependent student. More information is available by contacting the lending institution regarding the loans available and the application procedure. Money available: $35,000,000,000.

* Work-Study Program Pays For School

(Federal Work-Study Program 84.033)
Division of Policy Development
Student Financial Assistance Programs
Office of Assistant Secretary for Postsecondary Education
400 Maryland Ave., SW
Washington, DC 20202   800-443-3243
www.ed.gov/offices/OSFAP/Students

Part-time employment is available to students to help meet education expenses. This program pays an hourly wage to undergraduates. Graduate students may be paid by the hour or may receive a salary. There are Federal Work-Study jobs both on and off campus. Money can be used to help defray the costs of higher education. Students should contact the educational institution they attend or plan to attend to find out about application procedures. A Student Financial Aid Handbook is available, as is a list of grantee institutions, by contacting Federal Student Aid Information Center, P.O. Box 84, Washington, DC 20044; 800-433-3243. Money available: $1,011,000,000. Average Award: $1,252.

* Low-Interest Student Loans

(Federal Perkins Loan Program 84.038)
Division of Policy Development
Student Financial Assistance Programs
Office of Assistant Secretary for Postsecondary Education
U.S. Department of Education
400 Maryland Ave., SW
Washington, DC 20202-5446   800-443-3242
www.ed.gov/offices/OSFAP/Students

Low-interest loans are available to eligible post-secondary students with demonstrated financial need to help meet educational expenses. Students can borrow money to meet the costs of school. These loans are for students with exceptional financial need. To apply, contact the Financial Aid office of the school you attend or plan to attend. A student Financial Aid Handbook is available, as well as a list of grantee institutions by contacting the Federal Student Aid Information Center, P.O. Box 84, Washington, DC 20044; 800-433-3242; TTY: 800-730-8913. Money available: $100,000,000.

* Get Help To Study

(TRIO Upward Bound 84.047)
Margaret Wingfield
Federal Trio Programs
College and University Preparation and Support Team
Office of Postsecondary Education
U.S. Department of Education
400 Maryland Ave., SW
Washington, DC 20202-5249   202-502-7600
www.ed.gov/offices/OPE/OHEP/trio

This program generates skills and motivation necessary for success in education beyond high school among low income and potential first-generation college students and veterans. The goal of the program is to increase the academic performance and motivational levels of eligible enrollees so that they have a better chance of completing secondary school and successfully pursuing postsecondary educational programs. Eligible students must have completed the eighth grade and be between the ages of 13 and 19, enrolled in high school, and need such services to achieve their goal of college. The program provides instruction in reading, writing, study skills, and mathematics. They can provide academic, financial, or personal counseling, tutorial services, information on student financial assistance, assistance with college and financial aid applications, and more. Contact your local Upward Bound project to find out more about this program. For a listing of institutions that received money contact the office listed below. Money available: $264,000,000.

* $2,700 Grants To Go To School

(Federal Pell Grant Program 84.063)
Division of Policy Development
Office of Student Financial Assistance
U.S. Department of Education
400 Maryland Ave., SW
Washington, DC 20202   800-433-3243
www.ed.gov/offices/OSFAP/Students

Grants are available to students with financial need to help meet education expenses. Grants may not exceed $2,700 per year, and must be used for student's first bachelor's or other professional degree. Once an application is completed, the student's financial eligibility for assistance is calculated and the agency then notifies the student of eligibility. A Free Application for Federal Student Aid is available from the Federal Student Aid Information Center, P.O. Box 84, Washington, DC 20044; 800-433-3243. Money available: $8,756,000,000. Average Award: $2,057.

* Money For Students Interested In Helping People With Disabilities

(Rehabilitation Training 84.129)
Tim Morris
Rehabilitation Services Administration
Office of Special Education and Rehabilitation Services
U.S. Department of Education
400 Maryland Ave., SW
Washington, DC 20202   202-205-8926
www.ed.gov/offices/OSERS/RSA/PGMS/RT/scholrsp.html

This program supports projects that provide new personnel and improve the skills of existing personnel trained in providing vocational rehabilitation services to individuals with disabilities in areas targeted as having personnel shortages. Training grants are provided in fields directly related to the vocational and independent living rehabilitation of individuals with disabilities, such as rehabilitation counseling, independent living, rehabilitation medicine, physical and occupational therapy, speech-language, pathology and audiology, and more. Projects include residency scholarships in physical medicine and rehabilitation; teaching and graduate scholarships in rehabilitation counseling; and more. Students must apply to those institutions that have received the program money. A catalogue of projects is available that provides address, phone number, contact person, and an abstract for each grant awarded. Money available: $25,000,000.

* Aid For Students Who Want To Help The Deaf

(Training Interpreters For Individuals Who Are Deaf and Individuals Who Are Deaf-Blind 84.160)
Mary Lovley
Office of Special Education and Rehabilitation Services
U.S. Department of Education

400 Maryland Ave., SW   202-205-9393
Washington, DC 20202   TTY: 202-401-3664
www.ed.gov/offices/OSERS/RSA/PGMS/RT/scholrsp.html

This program supports projects that train new interpreters and improve the skills of manual, oral, and cued speech interpreters already providing services to individuals who are deaf and individuals who are deaf-blind. Grants are awarded for training, classroom instruction, workshops, seminars, and field placements. Ten grants are awarded to colleges and universities that have ongoing sign language/oral interpreter training programs of proven merit. Programs include training courses connected to degree programs in interpreting; short term practical training leading to interpreter certification; and workshops, seminars, and practices. Students must apply to those institutions that have received the program money. For a listing of institutions that received money contact the office listed below. Money available: $2,100,000.

* $25,400 Per Year For Graduate Study

(Jacob K. Javits Fellowships 84.170)
Carolyn Proctor
Higher Education Programs
Office of Postsecondary Education
U.S. Department of Education
1990 K Street, NW, 6th Floor
Washington, DC 20006   202-502-7567
www.ed.gov/offices/OPE/HEP/iegps/javits.html

This program provides fellowships to individuals of superior ability for graduate study in the fields within the arts, humanities, and social sciences. Money can be used to support a student while he or she attends an institution of higher education. To apply for these fellowships contact the Federal Student Aid Information Center, P.O. Box 84, Washington, DC 20044; 800-4-FED-AID. Money available: $10,800,000.

* $1,500 Per Year For College

(Robert C. Byrd Honors Scholarships 84.185)
U.S. Department of Education
Office of Student Financial Assistance
Office of the Assistant Secretary for Postsecondary Education
Division of Higher Education Incentive Programs
400 Maryland Ave., SW
Washington, DC 20024   202-502-7700
www.ed.gov/offices/OPE/HEP/idues/byrd.html
Contac: Argelia Velez-Rodrigues   202-502-7582

Scholarships are available to exceptionally able students who show promise of continued academic achievement. Scholarships for up to four years to study at any institution of higher education are available through grants to the states. The scholarships are awarded on the basis of merit and are renewable. To apply for this grant award, interested applicants must contact their state educational agency, which administers this program. Money available: $41,001,000.

* Money For Graduate Study

(Graduate Assistance In Areas Of National Need 84.200)
International Education and Graduate Programs Service
Office of Postsecondary Education
U.S. Department of Education
400 Maryland Ave., SW
Washington, DC 20202   202-502-7600
www.ed.gov/offices/OPE/HEP/iegps/gaann.html
Contact: Brandy Silverman   202-502-7886

Fellowships are available through graduate academic departments to graduate students of superior ability who demonstrate financial need and are able to enhance the capacity to teach and conduct research in areas of national need. Designated academic areas change each year and are currently biology, chemistry, engineering, foreign languages, mathematics, and physics. Money can be used to support a student completing a graduate degree program. Students must apply to those institutions that have received the money. For a listing of institutions that received money contact the office listed below. Money available: $31,000,000.

* Grants For Those Who Have Trouble Paying Tuition

(Ronald E. McNair Post Baccalaureate Achievement 84.217)
U.S. Department of Education
Federal Trio Programs
College and University Support Team
Office of Postsecondary Education
400 Maryland Ave., SW
Washington, DC 20202   202-502-7600
www.ed.gov/offices/OPE/HEP/trio/mcnair.html

This program provides grants to institutions of higher education to prepare low income, first-generation college students and students underrepresented in graduate education for graduate study. Money can be used to pay the costs for research and other scholarly activities, summer internships, seminars, tutoring, academic counseling, and securing admission and financial assistance for graduate study. Students must apply to those institutions that have received the money. For a listing of institutions that received money contact the office listed below. Money available: $36,856,000.

* Get Loans Directly From Your School

(Federal Direct Loan 84.268)
U.S. Department of Education
Direct Loan Payment Center
P.O. Box 746000
Atlanta, GA 30374   800-557-7394
www.ed.gov/DirectLoan/

The Direct Loan Program was begun to provide loans directly to students through schools, rather than through private lenders. Borrowers complete an application, the Free Application for Federal Student Aid (FAFSA), for all Department student financial aid programs. Schools receive the funds and then disburse them to students. There are four different direct loans: Federal Direct Stafford/Ford Loans are for students who demonstrate financial need; Federal Direct Unsubsidized Stafford/Ford Loans are for students regardless of financial need; Federal Direct PLUS Loans are for parents to pay for their children's education; and Federal Direct Consolidation Loans help combine one or more federal education loans into one loan. The amount one can borrow depends upon dependent/independent status of student and year in school. There are several different repayment options including income contingent repayment plan. Interest rates for loans vary each year. For your Free Application for Federal Student Aid, contact Federal Student Aid Information Center, P.O. Box 84, Washington, DC 20044; 800-433-3243.

* Money For Public Service Students

(Harry S. Truman Scholarship Program 85.001)
Louis Blair, Executive Secretary
Truman Scholarship Foundation
712 Jackson Place, NW
Washington, DC 20006   202-395-4831
www.truman.gov

A special scholarship program for college juniors has been established to encourage students to pursue careers in public service. Money can be used to support a student completing his or her undergraduate and graduate studies. A faculty representative is appointed for each school and is responsible for publicizing the scholarship program; soliciting recommendations on students with significant potential for leadership; conducting a competition on campus; and forwarding the institution's official nomination to the Truman Scholarship Review committee. For more information write to the Foundation listed above. Money available: $3,187,000.

* Health Professions Scholarships For American Indians

(Health Professions Pregraduate Scholarship Program for Indians 93.123)
Indian Health Service
Scholarship Program
801 Thompson Ave., Suite 120
Rockville, MD 20852   301-443-6197
www.ihs.gov

The program objective is to provide scholarships to American Indians and Alaskan Natives for the purpose of completing pregraduate education leading to baccalaureate degree in the areas of pre-medicine or pre-dentistry. Money can be used to support a student while completing their degree. Contact the Indian Health Service for application information. Money available: $2,004,879. Awards range from $18,913 to $27,217.

* Money To Train To Become A Nurse Anesthetist

(Nurse Anesthetist Traineeships 93.124)
Karen Breeden
Division of Nursing
Bureau of Health Professions
Health Resources and Services Administration
Public Health Service
U.S. Department of Health and Human Services
Room 9-36, 5600 Fishers Lane
Rockville, MD 20857   301-443-5787
http://bhpr.hrsa.gov

Registered nurses can receive money to become nurse anesthetists through this program that provides funds for a maximum 18-month period of full-time study. Nurses must complete 12 months of study in a nurse anesthetist

program. Money can be used to support a student while completing the training program. Students need to apply to those institutions that have received the money. For a listing of institutions that received money contact the office listed below. Student stipend is usually $8,800 plus tuition and other expenses. Money available: $3,036,158.

* Money For Minorities Pursuing a Health Professions Education

(Programs of Excellence In Health Professions Education For Minorities 93.157)
Division of Disadvantaged Assistance
Bureau of Health Professions
Health Resources and Services Administration
Public Health Service
U.S. Department of Health and Human Services
Room 8A-09, Parklawn Building
5600 Fishers Lane
Rockville, MD 20857   301-443-2100
http://bhpr.hrsa.gov

The program helps health professions schools train minority health professionals. These funds can be used to recruit and retain faculty, improve the facilities and information resources, and improve student performance, student recruitment, and student research. Students must apply to those institutions that have received the money. For a listing of institutions that received money contact the office listed below. Money available: $32,637,570.

* Money To Repay Loans

(National Health Service Corps Loan Repayment 93.162)
National Health Service Corps Scholarships
Division of Scholarships and Loan Repayments
Bureau of Primary Health Care
Health Resources and Services Administration
Public Health Service
U.S. Department of Health and Human Services
4350 East-West Hwy., 10th Floor   301-594-4400
Bethesda, MD 20814   800-435-6464
www.nhsc.bhpr.hrsa.gov

The National Health Service Corps provides for the repayment of educational loans for health professionals who agree to serve in a health manpower shortage area. Priority is given to primary care physicians, dentists, certified nurse midwives, certified nurse practitioners, and physicians' assistants. Money can be used to repay student loans. The amount of money available per professional is up to $25,000 a year during the first two years of practice and $35,000 for each year after that. Health professionals also receive a very competitive salary and benefits package. Money available: $49,820,000.

* Get Your Loans Paid Through Indian Health Service

(Indian Health Service Loan Repayment Program 93.164)
Indian Health Service
Loan Repayment Program
801 Thompson Ave., Suite 120
Rockville, MD 20852   301-443-3369
www.ihs.gov

To ensure that there are enough trained health professionals, the Indian Health Service provides for the repayment of loans to those professionals who agree to serve in an Indian Health Service Facility. Money can be used for the repayment of student loans. An application is available by contacting the office listed above. Money available: $16,923,500. The minimum period of participation is two years, and the maximum loan payment is $20,000 per year.

* Money For Disadvantaged Students To Study Nursing

(Nursing Education Opportunities For Individuals From Disadvantaged Backgrounds 93.178)
Division of Nursing
Bureau of Health Professions
Health Resources and Services Administration
Public Health Services
U.S. Department of Health and Human Services
Room 8C-26, Parklawn Building
5600 Fishers Lane
Rockville, MD 20857   301-443-6880
http://bhpr.hrsa.gov

Schools of nursing can receive financial assistance to meet the costs of projects that increase nursing education opportunities for individuals from disadvantaged backgrounds. Money can be used for counseling, preliminary education of students, and to support a student while completing a nursing degree. Students must apply to those institutions that have received the money. For a listing of institutions that received money contact the office listed above. Money available: $6,173,000.

* Grants For Pediatric Training

(Grants For Pediatric Primary Care Residency Training 93.181)
Division of Medicine
Bureau of Health Professions
Health Resources and Services Administration
Public Health Service
U.S. Department of Health and Human Services
Room 8C-26, Parklawn Building
5600 Fishers Lane
Rockville, MD 20857   301-443-6880
http://bhpr.hrsa.gov

Hospitals and schools of pediatric medicine can receive money to support residency programs for primary care pediatric practice. Funds can be used to cover the development and establishment of Pediatric Primary Care Residency programs and to provide resident stipends for those planning to specialize in pediatric primary care. Money can be used to support a resident while he or she completes his or her pediatric primary care residency. Students must apply to those institutions that have received the money. For a listing of institutions that received money, contact the office listed above. Money available: $770,000.

* Money For Health Care Training In Rural Areas

(Interdisciplinary Training For Health Care For Rural Areas 93.192)
Division of Associated, Dental and Public Health Professions
Bureau of Health Professions
Health Resources and Services Administration
Room 8C-26, Parklawn Building
5600 Fishers Lane
Rockville, MD 20857   301-443-6867
http://bhpr.hrsa.gov/interdisciplinary/rural.html

This program is designed to help fulfill the health care needs of people living in rural areas. Money is set aside to recruit and retain health care professionals in rural health care settings. Funds can be used for student stipends, postdoctoral fellowships, faculty training, and the purchase or rental of necessary transportation and telecommunication equipment. Money can be used to support health profession students while they complete their degree or training. Students must apply to those institutions that have received the money. For a listing of institutions that received money, contact the office listed above. Money available: $6,081,419.

* Money For Job Safety and Health Training

(Occupational Safety and Health - Training Grants 93.263)
National Institute for Occupational Safety and Health (NIOSH)
Centers for Disease Control and Prevention
Public Health Service
U.S. Department of Health and Human Services
1600 Clifton Rd.
Atlanta, GA 30333   404-498-2537
www.cdc.gov/niosh

The program objective is to develop specialized professional and paraprofessional personnel in the occupational safety and health field with training in occupational medicine, occupational health nursing, industrial hygiene, and occupational safety. Money can be used to pay for long and short-term training and educational resource centers. Students must apply to those institutions that have received the money. For a listing of institutions that received money contact the office listed above. Money available: $18,379,866.

* Scholarships For National Health Service Corps

(National Health Service Corps Scholarship Program 93.288)
National Health Service Corps Scholarships
Division of Scholarships and Loan Repayments
Bureau of Primary Health Care
Health Resources and Services Administration
Public Health Service
U.S. Department of Health and Human Services
4350 East-West Hwy., 10th Floor
Bethesda, MD 20814   301-594-4410
www.bphc.hrsa.dhhs.gov/nhsc   800-638-0824

The program objective is to provide service-conditioned scholarships to health professions students to assure an adequate supply of physicians, dentists, certified nurse midwives, certified nurse practitioners, and physician assistants in Health Professional Shortage Areas. The scholarship pays for tuition and required fees, books, supplies, and equipment for the year, plus a monthly stipend to students ($1065 per month), and a single annual payment to cover the cost of all other reasonable educational expenses. Each year of support incurs one year of service, with a two-year minimum service obligation required. Service sites are selected from those listed by the National Health Service Corps one year prior to service in federally designated Health Professional Shortage Areas. Money available: $39,600,000.

* Money for Health Profession Students

(Health Professions Student Loans 93.342)
Mary Farrington
Division of Health Careers, Diversity and Development
Bureau of Health Professions
Health Resources and Services Administration
Public Health Service
U.S. Department of Health and Human Services Administration
Parklawn Building, Room 8-34
5600 Fishers Lane
Rockville, MD 20857   301-443-4776
http://bhpr.hrsa.gov/dsa/

The Health Professions Student Loan Program provides long-term, low interest rate loans to full-time financially needy students pursuing a degree in dentistry, optometry, pharmacy, pediatric medicine, or veterinary medicine. Under this program, funds are made available to schools for the establishment of revolving student loan funds. To apply for this loan, contact the student financial aid office at the school where you intend to apply for admission or where you are enrolled. Loans can not exceed tuition. The interest rate is 5%. A Health Professions Student Loan Fact Sheet is available from the office listed above. Money available: $14,000,000.

* Money For Primary Care Students

(Health Professions Student Loans, Including Primary Care Loans 93.342)
Mary Farrington
Bureau of Health Professions
Health Resources and Services Administration
Public Health Service
U.S. Department of Health and Human Services Administration
Parklawn Building, Room 8-34
5600 Fishers Lane
Rockville, MD 20857   301-443-4776
http://bhpr.hrsa.gov/dsa/

The Primary Care Loan Program provides long-term low interest rate loans to full-time financially needy students pursuing a degree in allopathic or osteopathic medicine. Under this program, funds are made to schools to establish revolving student loan funds. Students must agree to enter and complete residency training in primary care and to practice in primary care until the loan is paid in full. To apply for this loan, contact the student financial aid office at the school where you intend to apply for admission or where you are enrolled. Loans cannot exceed tuition. Money available: $14,000,000.

* Loans For Disadvantaged Health Profession Students

(Loans for Disadvantaged Students 93.342)
Mary Farrington
Bureau of Health Professions
Health Resources and Services Administration
Public Health Service
U.S. Department of Health and Human Services Administration
Parklawn Building, Room 8-34
5600 Fishers Lane
Rockville, MD 20857   301-443-4776
http://bhpr.hrsa.gov/dsa/

Loans for Disadvantaged Students Program provides funding to eligible health professions schools for the purpose of providing long-term, low-interest loans to assist full-time, financially needy, disadvantaged students to pursue a career in allopathic or osteopathic medicine, dentistry, optometry, podiatry, pharmacy, or veterinary medicine. To apply for this loan, contact the student financial aid office at the school where you intend to apply for admission or where you are enrolled. *Loans For Disadvantaged Students Fact Sheet* is available from the office listed above. Money available: $5,000,000.

* Money To Train To Be A Professional Nurse

(Professional Nurse Traineeships 93.358)
Division of Nursing

Bureau of Health Professions
Health Resources and Services Administration
Public Health Service
U.S. Department of Health and Human Services
5600 Fishers Lane, Room 9-35
Rockville, MD 20857   301-443-6333
http://bhpr.hrsa.gov

The program objective is to prepare individuals who have completed basic nursing preparation as nurse educators, public health nurses, nurse midwives, and nurse practitioners, or as other clinical nursing specialists. Money can be used to support a student while they complete the professional nurse traineeships. Students must apply to those institutions that have received the program money. A fact sheet is available entitled *Program Guide for Professional Nurse Traineeship Program*. For a listing of institutions that received money contact the office listed below. Money available: $18,547,184. Students may receive stipends up to $8,800 plus tuition and other expenses.

* Money For Nursing Students

(Nursing Student Loans 93.364)
Mary Farrington
Division of Health Careers, Diversity and Development
Bureau of Health Professions
Health Resources and Services Administration
Public Health Service
U.S. Department of Health and Human Services Administration
Parklawn Building, Room 8-34
5600 Fishers Lane
Rockville, MD 20857   301-443-4776
http://bhpr.hrsa.gov/dsa/

The Nursing Student Loan program provides for long-term, low-interest loans to full-time and half-time financially needy students pursuing a course of study leading to a diploma, associate, baccalaureate or graduate degree in nursing. Federal funds for this program are allocated to accredited public or nonprofit nursing schools. These schools are responsible for selecting the recipients of loans and for determining the amount of assistance a student requires. To apply for this loan, contact the student financial aid office at the school where you intend to apply for admission or where you are enrolled. Interest rate is 5%. Money available: $4,500,000.

* Health Careers Opportunity Program

(Health Careers Opportunity Program 93.822)
Division of Health Careers, Diversity and Development
Bureau of Health Professions
Health Resources and Services Administration
Public Health Services
U.S. Department of Health and Human Services
Room 8A-09, 5600 Fishers Lane
Rockville, MD 20857   301-443-2100
http://bhpr.hrsa.gov/dhpd/hcophome1.htm

The Health Careers Opportunity Program provides assistance to individuals from disadvantaged backgrounds to obtain a health or allied health profession degree. Grants can be used to identify, recruit, and select individuals from minority and disadvantaged backgrounds for education and training in a health or allied health professions school; facilitate entry of eligible students into such schools; provide counseling or other services designed to assist such individuals in successfully completing their education and training; provide preliminary education for a period prior to entry into the regular course of health or allied health professions education, designed to assist students in successfully completing regular courses of education, or refer the appropriate individuals to institutions providing preliminary education; and provide disadvantaged students with information on financial aid resources. For a listing of institutions that received money contact the office listed below. Money available: $34,795,000.

* Money For Dental Students For Advanced Residency Training

(Residency Training And Advanced Education in General Practice Of Dentistry 93.897)
Public Health and Dental Education Branch
Division of Public Health and Allied Health
Bureau of Health Professions
Health Resources and Services Administration
Public Health Service
U.S. Department of Health and Human Services
5600 Fishers Lane, Room 8C-26
Rockville, MD 20857   301-443-6880
http://bhpr.hrsa.gov/dadphp/dadphp.htm

The program objective is to assist schools of dentistry or dental training to institute residency training and advanced educational programs in the general practice of dentistry. The grant can be used to support personnel, residents or trainees who are in need of financial assistance, to purchase equipment, and for other expenses necessary to conduct the program. Money can be used to support a student while he or she completes a dental training program or residency. Students must apply to those institutions that have received the money. For a listing of institutions that received money, contact the office listed above. Money available: $3,500,000.

* Money For Nursing Students To Repay Their Loans

(Nursing Education Loan Repayment Agreements For Registered Nurses Entering Employment At Eligible Health Facilities 93.908)
Chief
Diversity and Basic Nurse Education Branch
Division of Nursing
Bureau of Health Professionals
Health Resources and Services Administration
5600 Fishers Lane, Room 9-36   301-443-3232
Rockville, MD 20857   866-813-3753
http://bphc.hrsa.gov/nursing/

As an incentive for registered nurses to enter into full time employment at health facilities with nursing shortages, this program assists in the repayment of their nursing education loans. The program is designed to increase the number of registered nurses serving designated nurse shortage areas. Nurses can use the money to pay off nursing student loans. An Applicant Information Bulletin For Registered Nurses is available at the address listed below. Money available: $15,000,000.

* Money For Faculty Loan Repayments

(Disadvantaged Health Professions Faculty Loan Repayment Program 93.923)
Mary Farrington
Division of Health Careers, Diversity and Development
Bureau of Health Professions
Health Resources and Services Administration
Public Health Service
U.S. Department of Health and Human Services Administration
Parklawn Building, Room 8-34
5600 Fishers Lane   301-443-4776
Rockville, MD 20857   888-275-4772
http://bhpr.hrsa.gov/DSA/flrp/index.htm

The Faculty Loan Repayment Program provides a financial incentive for degree-trained health professionals from disadvantaged backgrounds to pursue an academic career. The health professional must agree to serve as a member of a faculty of a health professions school, providing teaching services for a minimum of two years, faculty for schools of medicine, nursing, osteopathic medicine, dentistry, pharmacy, pediatric medicine, optometry, veterinary medicine, public health, or a school that offers a graduate program in clinical psychology. The federal government, in turn, agrees to pay as much as $20,000 of the outstanding principal and interest on the individual's educational loans. To participate in the program, an individual must be from a disadvantaged background, must not have been a member of a faculty of any school at any time during the 18 month period preceding the date on which the program application is received, must have a degree or be enrolled as a full-time student in the final year of training leading to a degree in one of the eligible disciplines, and must have entered into a contract with an eligible health professions school to serve as a full-time faculty member for a minimum of two years. Money available: $1,003,000.

* Scholarships For Disadvantaged Health Profession Students

(Scholarships For Health Profession Students From Disadvantaged Backgrounds 93.925)
Mary Farrington
Bureau of Health Professions
Health Resources and Services Administration
Public Health Service
U.S. Department of Health and Human Services Administration
Parklawn Building, Room 8-34
5600 Fishers Lane
Rockville, MD 20857   301-443-4776
http://bhpr.hrsa.gov/dsa/

The Scholarships For Disadvantaged Students program provides funds to eligible schools for the purpose of providing scholarships to full-time financially needy students from disadvantaged backgrounds enrolled in health professions and nursing programs. Under this program, funds are awarded to accredited schools of medicine, osteopathic medicine, dentistry, optometry, pharmacy, podiatric medicine, veterinary medicine, nursing (diploma, associate, baccalaureate, and graduate degree), public health, allied health (baccalaureate and graduate degree programs of dental hygiene, medical laboratory technology, occupational therapy, physical therapy, radiologic technology), and graduate programs in clinical psychology. The schools are responsible for selecting recipients, making reasonable determinations of need and disadvantaged student status, and providing scholarships that cannot exceed the student's financial need. To apply for this scholarship, contact the student financial aid office at the school where you intend to apply for admission or where you are enrolled. Money available: $46,000,000.

* Money For Health Professionals Who Want To Be In Public Health

(Public Health Traineeships 93.964)
Division of Associated, Dental, and Public Health Professions
Bureau of Health Professions
Health Resources and Services Administration
Public Health Service
Parklawn Bldg., Room 8C-09
5600 Fishers Lane
Rockville, MD 20857   301-443-6896
http://bhpr.hrsa.gov

The program objective is to help support graduate students who are studying in the field of public health. Grants are given to colleges and universities offering graduate or specialized training in the public health field. Support is limited to the fields of biostatistics, epidemiology, environmental health, toxicology, public health nutrition, and maternal and child health. Money can be used to support a student completing a public health degree, and includes a stipend, tuition, and fees, and a transportation allowance. Students must apply to those institutions that have received the money. For a listing of institutions that received money contact the office listed above. Money available: $1,822,000.

* Money For American Indians Who Want To Be Health Care Professionals

(Health Professions Recruitment Program For Indians 93.970)
Indian Health Service
Division of Health Professions Support
801 Thompson Ave., Suite 120
Rockville, MD 20852   301-443-4242
www.ihs.gov

The program objective is to increase the number of American Indians and Alaskan Natives who become health professionals and money has been set aside to help identify students interested in the field and to assist them in enrolling schools. Some of the projects funded include the recruitment of American Indians into health care programs, a variety of retention services once students have enrolled, and scholarship support. Students should contact their school directly for assistance. Money available: $2,881-321.

* Money For American Indians Who Need Extra Studies For Health Care Program

(Health Professions Preparatory Scholarship Program for Indians 93.971)
Indian Health Service
Scholarship Program
801 Thompson Ave., Suite 120
Rockville, MD 20852   301-443-6197
www.ihs.gov

The program objective is to make scholarship available to American Indians and Alaskan Natives who need to take some extra courses in order to qualify for enrollment or re-enrollment in a health profession school. Money can be used for up to two years of scholarship support, and the funds can cover tuition, stipends, and books. Students must apply to the Indian Health Service Office for application information. Money available: $1,024,584. Grants range from $17,000 to $26,019.

* Scholarships For Health Care Professionals

(Health Professions Scholarship Program 93.972)
Indian Health Service
Scholarship Program
801 Thompson Ave., Suite 120
Rockville, MD 20852   301-443-6197
www.ihs.gov

This program objective is to provide scholarships to American Indians and Alaskan natives attending health professions schools and who are interested in serving other Indians. Upon completion, scholarship recipients are obligated to serve in the Indian Health Service one year for each year of scholarship support, with a minimum of two years. The health professions needed are listed annually in the Federal Register. The money can be used to support a student completing a health profession degree. Money available: $8,469,000. Grants range from $24,128 to $38,222.

* Volunteer And Earn Money To Pay For School

(AmeriCorps 94.006)
Corporation for National and Community Service
1201 New York Ave., NW
Washington, DC 20525   202-606-5000, ext. 474
www.americorps.org

AmericCorps is an initiative designed to achieve direct results in addressing the nation's critical education, human, public safety, and environmental needs at the community level. The program provides meaningful opportunities for people to serve their country in organized efforts, fostering citizen responsibility, building their community, and providing education opportunities for those who make a serious commitment to service. Stipends can be used to support the person while they volunteer. Health care and childcare benefits may also be provided. Participants will also receive an education award, which may be used to pay for higher education or for vocational training, and may also be used to repay any existing student loans. Contact the Corporation for National Service to locate programs in your area or to apply for programs at the national level. Money available: $233,395,000.

Over $3 Billion In State Aid For Students

After checking out what money programs are available from the Federal government, your next task is to find out what's available at the state level. There are close to 400 programs worth almost $3 billion dollars in financial aid available through all 50 states. Just because you or your parents don't have the money to pay for college, that doesn't mean your dream of a college degree will never happen. Even if you do have the money, financial assistance from one of these programs could make things a little easier for all concerned.

Did you know that there are state money programs which:

- Pay for a singing degree?
- Give you money to study wildlife?
- Give you $2000 to go to vocational school?
- Pay for your nursing, teaching, or law degree?
- Give you $7,000 to study marine sciences?

The advantage of many of these programs is that most people don't even know they exist, so your competition will be less. Each state has different requirements for their various programs, so you may need to do some checking on what specific programs might fit your needs. Some programs are exclusive to residents of a particular state, whereas others have no limitations. In addition, some programs will award money to a student, and put no limitation on what school the student chooses to attend. In some cases, for teachers or health professionals a service requirement may exist which says that the student will practice in a particular state after graduation for a certain period of time.

What follows is a concise and comprehensive state-by-state listing of available programs. It will allow you to shop around for the best program to suit your individual needs. By remaining flexible and adjusting your educational goals to fit the program that most appeals to you, chances are you might find yourself pursuing the college education that you always thought was beyond your reach. Using this information might be an important first step in building a successful future for yourself.

Alabama

Alabama Commission on Higher Education
P.O. Box 30200   334-242-2271
Montgomery, AL 36130-2000   Fax: 334-242-0268
www.ache.state.al.us
General requirements: Resident of Alabama and attending an in-state school.
Programs Available:
Grants To Students Who Can't Afford Tuition (Alabama Student Assistance Program)
Grants To Students Attending Private Colleges (Alabama Student Grant Program)
Join The National Guard And Get $1,000 A Year For College (Alabama National Guard Assistance Program)
Scholarships and Loans To Nursing Students (Alabama Nursing Scholarships)
Tuition, Fees, And Books To Spouses and Children Of Veterans (Alabama GI Dependents Educational Benefit Program)
Grants To Children And Grandchildren Of Veterans (American Legion Scholarship and American Legion Auxiliary Scholarship Programs)
Free Tuition If You're Over 60 (Senior Adult Scholarships)
Money For Jocks Going To Junior College (Junior And Community College Athletic Scholarships)
Money For Dancers, Singers, and Actors Attending Junior College (Junior and Community College Performing Arts Scholarships)
Grants To Children Of The Blind (Alabama Scholarships For Dependents of Blind Parents)
Grants For Dependents Of Fire Fighters And Police Officers Killed In The Line Of Duty (Police Officers and Fire Fighters Survivor's Educational Assistance Program)
Loans That Guarantee The Price Of Your Future Tuition (Prepaid College Tuition Program)

Tuition And Fees, For Teachers To Take Technology Classes (Technology Scholarship Program For Alabama)
Money For Tuition And Books To Smart Students Attending A Two-Year College (Two-Year College Academic Scholarship)

Alaska

Alaska Commission on Postsecondary Education
3030 Vintage Boulevard   907-465-2962
Juneau, AK 99801-7109   800-441-2962
www.state.ak.us/acpe/home.html   Fax: 907-465-5316
General requirements: Alaska resident and attending an in-state or out-of-state school.
Programs Available:
Free Money To Go To School If You Work In Law Enforcement (Michael Murphy Memorial Scholarship Loan)
Money For 8 Years Of College If You Study Food Or Wildlife (A.W. "Winn" Brindle Memorial Scholarship Loan)
$7,500 A Year and Travel Money If You Study To Be A Teacher In A Small Town (Teacher Scholarship Loan Program)
Alaska Residents Get Special Tuition Rate At Select Out-Of-State Colleges (Western Undergraduate Exchange Program)
Reduced Tuition Rates In Select Masters and Doctoral Programs At Colleges In 14 Western States (Western Regional Graduate Program)
Receive Residential Tuition Rate At University Of Washington School Of Medicine And Return To Alaska And Practice Medicine (WWAMI Medical Education Program)

Arizona

Arizona Commission for Postsecondary Education
2020 North Central, Suite 275   602-229-2591

Matthew Lesko, Information USA, Inc., 12081 Nebel Street, Rockville, MD 20852 • 1-800-955-7693 • www.lesko.com

Phoenix, AZ 85004-4503   Fax: 602-229-2599
www.acpe.asu.edu

General requirements: Students should contact the financial aid office at the college they plan to attend for applicable scholarship, grant, and loan information. State residency is required for the programs listed.

Programs Available:

$2,500 Grants For Students Having Trouble Paying Tuition (Leveraging Education's Assistance Partnership (LEAP))

$1,500 A Year For Full-Time Study At A Private School In A Baccalaureate Degree-Granting Program (Arizona Private Postsecondary Education Student Financial Assistance Program (PFAP))

Money To Students Who Honored Their Pledge To The ASPIRE Program (ASPIRE)

Arkansas

Arkansas Department of Higher Education
114 East Capitol   501-371-2000
Little Rock, AR 72201   Fax: 501-371-2001
www.adhe.arknet.edu

General Requirements: Applicants must be current residents of Arkansas.

Programs Available:

$600 Per Year On First-Come, First-Served Basis (Student Assistance Grants)

$4,000 For High School Graduates With At Least 3.6 Averages (Governor's Scholars)

$2,500 For High School Graduates with At Least 2.5 Averages (Arkansas Academic Challenge Scholarship)

$1,000 Stipends for Freshman and Sophomore Minorities to Enroll in Teaching Programs (Freshman/Sophomore Minority Grant Program)

Tuition Reimbursement for Teachers and Administrators to Continue Their Education (Teacher and Administrator Grant Program)

Free Money For School If You Become a Math, Science, or Special Education Teacher, or a Guidance Counselor (Emergency Secondary Education Loan)

Up To $5,000 Per Year for African-American, Asian American, and Hispanic College Juniors and Seniors When They Agree to Teach in Arkansas (Minority Teacher Scholarship)

$1,000 To Top Ten GED Scorers (Second Effort Scholarship)

Up To $7,500 for Minorities to Enter a Master's Program in Mathematics, the Sciences, or Foreign Language (Minority Masters Fellows Program)

Grants To Dependents Of Law Enforcement Officers, Firemen, and Game Officers Killed Or Totally Disabled In The Line Of Duty (Law Enforcement Officer's Dependents Scholarship)

California

California Student Aid Commission
P.O. Box 419026   916-526-7590
Rancho Cordova, CA 95741-9026   Fax: 916-526-8002
www.csac.ca.gov

General requirements: Applicants must be residents of California.

Programs Available:

Grants For Tuition, Living Expenses, and Vocational Training (Cal Grants A, B, and C)

Help To Work Your Way Through College (State Work-Study Program)

$8,000 To Become A Teacher (Assumption Program of Loans for Education (APLE))

Grants To Dependents Of Fire Fighters, Police Officers, and Correctional Officials Killed Or Totally Disabled In The Line Of Duty (Law Enforcement Personnel Dependents Scholarship)

Up To $6,000 Loan Assumption to Become a full-time Faculty Member (Graduate Assumption Program of Loans for Education)

Money for High School Graduates and Community College Transfer Students in Financial Need (California Student Opportunity and Access Program)

Colorado

Colorado Commission on Higher Education
1300 Broadway, 2nd Floor
Denver, CO 80203   303-866-2723
www.state.co.us/cche_dir/hecche.html

General requirements: Applicants must be resident of Colorado.

Programs Available:

Grants To Students From Families Who Don't Normally Go To College (Colorado Diversity Grants)

Grants To Students Who Are Having Trouble Paying For Tuition (Colorado Student Incentive Grants (CSIG))

More Grants To Students Who Are Having Trouble Paying For Tuition (Colorado Student Grants (CSG))

Money For Students Going To College Part Time (Colorado Part Time Grants)

State Jobs For Students Having Trouble Paying Tuition (Colorado Work-Study)

Money For Smart Students Going To College In Colorado (Undergraduate Merit Awards)

Money For Graduates Who Have Trouble Paying Tuition (Colorado Graduate Grants)

Money For Smart Graduate Students (Colorado Graduate Fellowships)

Grants To Dependents Of POW/MIA's or Fire Fighters, Police Officers, and Correctional Officials Killed Or Totally Disabled In The Line Of Duty (Law Enforcement/POW-MIA Dependents Tuition Assistance)

Money To Be A Nurse And Practice In Colorado (Colorado Nursing Scholarship)

Receive Up To 75% of Tuition To Become A Colorado National Guard (Colorado National Guard Tuition Assistance)

Connecticut

Department of Higher Education
61 Woodland Street   860-947-1800
Hartford, CT 06105   Fax: 860-947-1310
http://ctdhe.commnet.edu

General requirements: Applicants must be Connecticut residents for in-state and out-of-state schools programs.

Programs Available:

$2,000 A Year If You Are In Top 20% Of Your High School Class (Capitol Scholarship)

$7,777 A Year To Attend A Private College (Connecticut Independent College Student Grant)

Money For Students Who Need Help Paying Tuition At A Public University (Connecticut Aid for Public College Students)

Up To $5,000 A Year For Minority Juniors Or Seniors To Become Teachers In The Connecticut Public School System. (Connecticut Minority Teacher Incentive Program)

Money For Students Who Need Help Paying For College (Tuition Set Aside Aid)

Delaware

Commission on Higher Education
Carvel State Office Building   800-292-7935
820 N. French St   302-577-3240
Wilmington, DE 19801   Fax: 302-577-6765
www.doe.state.de.us/high-ed

General requirements: Applicants must be Delaware residents for in-state or out-of-state colleges.

Programs Available:

Money To Be A Teacher In Delaware (Christa McAuliffe Teacher Scholarship Loan)

$1250 A Year For Undergraduate Students (Diamond State Scholarship)

Full Tuition, Room and Board To Smart High School Seniors (B. Bradford Barnes Scholarship)

$3,000 A Year To Be A Registered Or Practical Nurse And Practice In A State-Owned Hospital (Delaware Nursing Incentive Scholarship Loan)

Money For Students From Delaware To Study Optometry In Pennsylvania (Delaware Optometric Institutional Aid)

Money Towards Education For Children Of Deceased Veterans Or State Officers, and Prisoners Of War or MIA's (Educational Benefits For Children Of Deceased Veterans)

Up To $1,000 Per Year For Part-Time Students Who Work Part-Time (Governor's Workforce Development Grant)

Money For Full-Time Students in Undergraduate Or Graduate Program in Financial Need (Scholarship Incentive Program)

Tuition, Fees, and Room and Board At Delaware State University For Smart High School Seniors in Financial Need (Holloway Scholarship)

$20,000 Per Year for Medical Training To Practice In Delaware (DIMER Loan Program)

Money For Smart and Needy Students To Become A Librarian In Delaware (Librarian Incentive Scholarship Program)

Money For A Master's in Speech/Language Pathology To Be Used For Service In Delaware Public Schools (Speech/Language Pathologist Incentive Program)

District of Columbia

Office of Postsecondary Education
2100 Martin Luther Kings, Jr., Avenue, SE
Washington, DC 20020   202-727-3688
www.dhs.washington.dc.us/Prog_Cit_Service/OPERA/opera.htm

General requirements: Applicants must be District of Columbia.

Programs Available:

Money For Students In Great Need (D.C. Leveraging Educational Assistance Program)

Florida

Florida Office of Students Financial Assistance
255 Collins Building
325 West Gaines Street   850-488-4095
Tallahassee, FL 32399 0400   Fax: 850-488-3612
www.firn.edu/doe/bin00065/home0065.htm

General requirements: Applicants must be Florida residents for in-state or out-of-state school programs.

Programs Available:

Money For Excellent High School Graduates (Florida Bright Futures Scholarship Program)

Money For Students Who Have Trouble Paying Their Tuition (Florida Student Assistance Grants (FSAG))

Up To $4,000 To Study To Be An Occupational Therapist, A Physical Therapist, or An Assistant And Work In Florida Public Schools (Occupational Therapist And Physical Therapist Scholarship Loan Program)

$2,000 For Hispanic Americans Who Want To Go To College (Jose Marti Scholarship Challenge Grant Fund)

Up To $4,000 To Descendants Of African American Rosewood Families In Need (Rosewood Family Scholarship Fund)

Money For Dependents Of Deceased Or Disabled Veterans And POW/MIA's (Scholarships For Children Of Deceased Or Disabled Veterans)

Money For Smart High School Graduates Who Want To Be Teachers In Florida ("Chappie" James Most Promising Teacher Scholarship)

Free College Money If You Teach In Florida Public Schools (Critical Teacher Shortage (CTS) Forgivable Loans)

Grants For American Indians To Go To College (Seminole/Miccosukee Indian Scholarship)

Money To Become A Nurse And Work In An Underserved Area Of Florida For One Year (Nursing Scholarship Program)

Tuition Assistance To Students At Private Non-Profit Colleges (William L. Boyd, IV, Florida Resident Access Grant)

50% Of Tuition A Year For Community College Graduates, Or State Student Transfers To Enroll In Limited Access Programs At A Private College (Limited Access Competitive Grant)

Money To Community College And Private College Students (Ethics In Business Scholarship Program)

Jobs Related To Educational Goals For Students In Financial Need (Florida Work Experience Program)

$3,000 A Year To Smart High School Graduates (Mary McLeod Bethune Scholarship)

Georgia

Student Finance Commission
2082 East Exchange Place
Tucker, GA 30084
www.gsfc.org

800-776-6878
770-414-3000
Fax: 770-724-9089

General requirements: Must be a resident for Georgia for in-state or out-of-state programs.

Programs Available:

$1,000 Per Year To Attend A Public In-State College Within 50 Miles Of The Border, Or An Independent Out-Of-State College (Tuition Equalization Grant)

Up To $1,575 Per Year For High School Valedictorian, Salutatorian or STAR Students (Governor's Scholarship Program)

$3,000 Per Year To Become An Engineer In Georgia (Scholarship for Engineering Education)

$2,000 Per Year For Children of Georgia Officers, Firefighters, and Prison Guards Permanently Disabled Or Killed In The Line Of Duty (Law Enforcement Personnel Dependents)

Money To Children Of Officers, Firefighters, EMT's, Correction Officers and Prison Guards Permanently Disabled Or Killed In The Line Of Duty (Public Safety Memorial Grant)

$1,500 Per Year To Participate In The ROTC Program At N.G.A. College and State University (North Georgia College ROTC Grant)

Full Scholarship For Outstanding Students To N.G.A. College and State University and To Join Georgia's Army National Guard (North Georgia College Military Scholarship)

Smart Students Receive a Full Scholarship To Georgia Military College and Then Join the Georgia National Guard (Georgia Military College State Service Scholarship)

$10,000 Per Year To Become A Primary Care Physician And Practice In Underserved Areas Of Georgia (Osteopathic Medical Loan)

Up To $5,000 per Year To Students Having Trouble Paying For College-Must Apply For The Federal Pell Grant Also (Student Incentive Grant)

Funds For College To Former Georgia Peach Corps Member (Georgia Peach CORPS Grant)

Get Financial Aid For College If You Work At Jobs On Campus (Work Incentive For Student Education)

Hawaii

Systems Group
641-18th Avenue, V201
Honolulu, HI 96816

808-733-9124

General requirements: Applicants must be Hawaii residents.

Programs Available:

Money To High School Graduates With A 3.5 GPA (Regents Scholarship for Academic Excellence)

Money For Students Planning To Study Pacific/Asian Studies (Pacific Asian Scholarships)

Idaho

Office of the State Board of Education
P.O. Box 83720
Boise, ID 83720-0037
www.idahoboardofed.org

208-334-2270

General requirements: Applicants must be Idaho residents.

Programs Available:

$2,750 To Study In Idaho (Idaho Scholarship Program)

Disadvantaged High School Students Can Get $3,000 To Go To College (Idaho Minority and "At-Risk"Student Scholarship)

Free Money For Students Studying To Be Teachers Or Nurses (Education Incentive Loan Forgiveness)

Up To $5,000 For Students In Need To Attend A Public Or Private School In Idaho (Idaho Student Incentive Grant)

Illinois

Illinois Student Assistance Commission
1775 Lake Cook Drive
Deerfield, IL 60015
www.isac-online.org

847-948-8550 ext. 3503
Fax: 847-831-8519

General requirements: Applicants must be Illinois residents.

Programs Available:

Grants Up To $4,120 No Matter What Your Grades Are (Monetary Award Program)

$1,000 For Students In The Top 5% Of Their Class (Illinois Merit Recognition Scholarship Program)

Join The National Guard For Free Tuition For Graduate Or Undergraduate Studies (National Guard Grant Program)

Veterans Living In Illinois Can Get Free Tuition and Fees (Illinois Veteran Grant Program)

Grants To Dependents Of Fire Fighters Or Police Officers Killed Or Permanently Disabled In The Line Of Duty (Grant Program For Dependents Of Police Officer Or Fire Officers)

Grants To Dependents Of Correctional Officers Killed Or Disabled In The Line Of Duty (Correctional Officer Grant Program)

Money For Freshman Students In Great Financial Need (Illinois Incentive For Access Program)

Money To Holders Of Illinois College Savings Bonds When They Mature (Bonus Incentive Grant)

Up To $5,000 Per Year For African-Americans, Hispanic-Americans, Asian-Americans, Or Native Americans To Become Teachers In Illinois (Minority Teachers Of Illinois Scholarship Program)

Up To $5,000 For Talented Minority Students To Teach In Designated Areas Of Illinois (David A. DeBolt Teacher Shortage Scholarship Program)

Talented Students Receive Free Tuition To Become Special Education Teachers (Illinois Special Education Teacher Tuition Waiver Program)

Indiana

State Student Assistance Commission of Indiana
150 West Market Street, Suite 500
Indianapolis, IN 46204
www.state.in.us/ssaci

317-232-2350
Fax: 317-232-3260

General requirements: Applicants must be Indiana residents.

Programs Available:

Indiana College Students Who Have Trouble Paying Tuition (Indiana Higher Education Grant Program)

Four Years Of Tuition To 8th Graders Who Pledge Good Citizenship To The State Twenty-first Century Scholars Program)

Money To Nursing Students Who Will Work As A Nurse In Indiana For 2 Years (Nursing Scholarship)

Money to Black Or Hispanic Students To Become A Teacher, Special Education Teacher, Or Occupational or Physical Therapist And Work In Indiana (Minority Teacher/Special Education Scholarship)

Iowa

Iowa College Student Aid Commission
200 Tenth Street, 4th Floor
Des Moines, IA 50309-2036
www.state.ia.us/collegeaid

515-281-3501

General requirements: Applicants must be Iowa residents.

Programs Available:

Money For High School Graduates In The Top 15% Of Their Class (State of Iowa Scholarship Program)

Grants To Pay For Tuition At Private Colleges (Iowa Tuition Grants)

$600 To Take A Vocational Education Course (Iowa Vocational-Technical Tuition Grants)

Grants To Students Who Need Money For Education (Iowa Grants)

Kansas

Kansas Board of Regents
700 SW Harrison, Suite 1410   785-296-3421
Topeka, KS 66603   Fax: 785-296-0983
www.ukans.edu/~kbor
General requirements: Applicants must be Kansas's residents.

Programs Available:
$1,500 A Year For Minority Students (Ethnic Minority Scholarships)
$500 To Take A Vocational training Course (Vocational Scholarship)
$5,000 A Year If You Study To Be A Teacher In Kansas (Kansas Teacher Scholarship)
$3,500 A Year To Be A Nurse (Kansas Nursing Scholarship)
$1,000 To High School Graduates Who Have Trouble Paying Tuition (Kansas State Scholarship)
Money For Students At Public Or Private School Who Need Financial Help (Kansas Comprehensive Grants)
Up To $15,000 Per Year At Osteopathy School To Practice In Kansas (Kansas Osteopathy Scholarship)
Get Residence Tuition Rate To Attend An Out-Of-State School Of Optometry And Practice In Kansas (Kansas Optometry Scholarship)
Pay In-State Tuition Rate At University Of Missouri-Kansas City To Study Dentistry (Kansas Dentistry Assistance)
Stipends From $1,000 To $ $8,000 To Study Abroad (James B Pearson Fellowship)
Tuition And Fee Reimbursement To Continue Graduate Studies At A Kansas Public University Kansas Distinguished Scholarship Program)
Up To $8,000 A Year To Ethnic Minority Students For Enrollment In Kansas Graduate Programs (Kansas Ethnic Minority Fellowship)

Kentucky

Kentucky Higher Education Assistance Authority
1050 U.S. 127 South, Suite 102   800-928-8926
Frankfort, KY 40601-4323   502-564-7990
www.kheaa.com
General requirements: Applicants must be residents of Kentucky.

Programs Available:
Grants To Financially Needy Full-Time And Part-Time Students (College Access Program Grants (CAP))
Up To $1,500 To Needy Students Attending Private Colleges (Kentucky Tuition Grant (KTG))
Money To Smart High School Graduates Going To College (Kentucky Educational Excellence Scholarship)
Money To Smart, Financially Needy Students Studying To Be A Teacher (KHEAA Teacher Scholarship)
Reduced Tuition Rate At Pikeville College School of Osteopathic Medicine (Osteopathic Medicine Scholarship)
Students Attending School At Least Half-Time Work AT Career Related Jobs (KHEAA Work-Study)

Louisiana

Office of Student Financial Assistance
P.O. Box 91202   225-922-1011
Baton Rouge, LA 70821-9202   Fax: 225-922-0790
www.osfa.state.la.us
General Requirements: Applicants must be Louisiana residents.

Programs Available:
Maximum $7,000 Grant To Study Forestry Or Marine Sciences (Louisiana Rockefeller State Wildlife Scholarship)
Free Tuition For Smart Students (Louisiana Tuition Opportunity Program (TOPS))
Up To $2,000 For High School Graduates Having Trouble Paying For College. Must Also Apply For The Federal Pell Grant (State Student Incentive Grant)

Maine

Finance Authority of Maine (FAME)
83 Western Avenue   TDD: 207-626-2717
P.O. Box 949   207-632-3263
Augusta, ME 04332-0949   Fax: 207-623-0095
www.famemaine.com
General requirements: Applicants must be Maine residents.

Programs Available:
Money For Students From Maine To Study In New England States, Alaska, Delaware, DC, Maryland, and Pennsylvania (Maine Student Incentive Scholarship Program (MSISP))
Money For Students In The Upper 1/4 Of Their Class Who Want To Be Teachers (Teachers for Maine)
Money For Dependents Of Veterans Killed Or Disabled In Military Service (State Veterans Benefits)
Aid To Needy Students Studying In Fields Of Medicine, Dentistry, Optometry and Veterinary Science (Medical Education Program)
Access To Seats AT Out-Of-State Medical Schools (Maine Access To Medical Education Program)

Maryland

Maryland Higher Education Commission
State Scholarship Administration
The Jefferey Building
16 Francis Street, Suite 209   410-974-5370
Annapolis, MD 21401-1781   Fax: 410-974-5994
www.mhec.state.md.us
General requirements: Applicants must be Maryland residents, unless specified for in-state or out-of-state schools.

Programs Available:
$2,000 To Full- Or Part-Time Students (Senatorial Scholarship Program)
$200 To Full-Time Or Part-Time Students (Delegate Scholarship Program)
$1,500 To Take A Vocational Education Course (Tolbert Grant)
$3,000 A Year For Smart Students (Distinguished Scholar Program)
$4,800 To Get A Degree In Nursing (Maryland State Nursing Scholarship)
$3,000 A Year To Become A Teacher In Maryland (Teacher Education Distinguished Scholar Program)
Grants To Dependents of POW's, Fire Fighters, Police Officers, and Safety Personnel Killed Or Disabled In The Line OF Duty (Edward Conroy Grant)
Grants to Study Physical Therapy (Physical and Occupational Therapists and Assistants Scholarships)
$7,500 A Year To Study Family Practice Medicine (Family Practice Medical Scholarship)
Grants To Study Law, Dentistry, Medicine, Nursing, Or Pharmacy (Professional School Scholarship)
Tuition, Fees, Room and Board To Become A Teacher (Sharon Christa McAuliffe Critical Shortage Teacher Scholarship)
$2,000 To Study Child Care, Full Or Part-Time (Child Care Provider Scholarship)
Free Tuition To Fire Fighters, and Rescue Squad Members Who Want To Study Full Or Part-Time (Reimbursement of Fire Fighters, Ambulance, and Rescue Squad Members)
Student Loans If You Work For A Non-Profit (Loan Assistance Repayment Program (LARP))
Up To $8,300 Per Year To Students In Extreme Financial Need (Guaranteed Access Grant)
Up To $3,000 Per Year For Students From Low Or Moderate Income Families (Educational Assistance Grant)
Money Towards Tuition And Fees To Study And Practice To Be A Nurse In Maryland (State Nursing Scholarship and Living Expenses)
Tuition Reimbursement To Medical Residents and Physicians Specializing In Primary Care Who Work In Undeserved Areas of Maryland (Loan Assistance Repayment Program in Primary Care Services)
Non-resident Nursing Students Pay Resident Rate At Maryland Public Colleges (Health Manpower Shortage Program Tuition Reduction for Non-resident Nursing Student)

Massachusetts

Board of Higher Education
Office of Student Financial Assistance
330 Stuart Street, Suite 304   617-727-9420
Boston, MA 02116   Fax: 617-727-0667
www.osfa.mass.edu
General requirements: Applicants must be Massachusetts's residents.

Programs Available:
Maximum $2,500 For Full-Time Students (MASSGrant)
Money To MASSGrant Smart Students Who Are In Financial Need (Performance Bonus Grant)
Grants To Residents Attending An Independent School Full-Time (Gilbert Grant)
Money To Undergraduates Attending Public Colleges Or Universities (Tuition Waiver/Cash Grant)
Aid To Children And Spouses Of Deceased Fire, Police Or Corrections Officers, Or Children Of POW/MIA (Public Service Scholarship)
Money To Part-Time Students In Public Colleges Who Are In Financial Need (Part-Time Grant)
Up To 50% Of The Cost Of College For High School Students With Severe Personal Problems, Medical Problems, Or Have Overcome A Hardship (Christian A. Herter Memorial Scholarship)
No Interest Loan Program (NIL)

Michigan

Michigan Department of Treasury
Higher Education Assistance Authority
1st Floor, Hannah Building
608 West Allegan   888-447-2687
Lansing, MI 48901   517 447-2687
www.treas.state.mi.us/college/mheaa.htm
General requirements: Applicants must be Michigan residents.

Programs Available:

Money For Smart Kids Who Have Trouble Paying Tuition (Competitive Scholarships)

Money For Students Attending Private Colleges (Tuition Grants)

Minnesota

Minnesota Higher Education Programs
Capitol Square Building
Suite 400
550 Cedar Street   800-657-3866
St. Paul, MN 55101   612-296-3974
www.heso.state.mn.us

General requirements: Applicants must be residents of Minnesota, unless otherwise specified.

Programs Available:

Money To Pay Half Your College Expenses (State Grant Program)

Money To Help Pay For Child Care While You Go To School (Child Care Grant Program)

Money To High School Students Who High On The Advanced Placement or International Baccalaureate Tests (Advanced Placement and International Baccalaureate Scholarships)

Up To $4,000 Per Year For Minority Students To Become A RN (Nursing Grants For Persons Of Color)

Up To $1,850 For Indian Students In Financial Need That Will Benefit From College (Minnesota Indian Scholarship Program)

$1,000 For High School Students To Take Summer Courses At A College (Summer Scholarships For Academic Enrichment)

Part or Full-Time Work On Or Off Campus For Students With A Financial Need (State Work-Study Program)

Money To Dependents of POW's And MIA's (State Veterans' Dependents Assistance Program)

Tuition And/Or Stipends To Veterans And Children Of Deceased Veterans (Educational assistance For War Orphans And Veterans)

Tuition And Fees For Children And Spouses Of Public Safety Officers Killed In The Line Of Duty After 1973 (Safety Officers' Program)

Minnesota Students Pay Reduced Tuition Rate At Selected Out Of State Colleges (Reciprocity Programs)

Aid To Dislocated Workers For Training Programs (Grants For Dislocated Workers)

Tuition To High School Students That Have Excelled At English/Creative Writing, Fine Arts, Foreign Language, Math Science Or Social Science (Minnesota Academic Excellence Scholarship)

Tuition Assistance To High School Students That Graduated In The Top 10% Of Their Class That Are Attending The College of Agriculture, Food and Environmental Sciences (Farm Families Scholarships)

Mississippi

Mississippi Institution of Higher Learning
Office of State Student Financial Aid
3825 Ridgewood Road
Jackson, MS 39211-6453   601-982-6663

General requirements: Applicants must be residents of Mississippi.

Programs Available:

Stipend/Apprenticeship Program To Study Psychology During The Summer (Apprenticeship Program)

Money To Students In A Speech Pathology, Psychology or Occupation Therapy Program Who Will Serve

In A State-Operated Health Hospital (Health Education Programs)

Money To Registered Nurses Who Want To Become Nursing Teachers In Mississippi (Nursing Teacher Stipend Program)

$4,000 A Year To Attend The University of Mississippi School of Dentistry And Practice In A Needed Area (State Dental education Loan/Scholarship Program)

$6,000 A Year To Study Family Medicine, Internal Medicine, Pediatrics or Obstetrics/Gynecology At The University of Mississippi School of Medicine (State medical Education Loan/Scholarship Program)

$6,000 A Year For Minority Students To Study At The Mississippi State University College of Veterinary Medicine (Veterinary Medicine Minority Loan/Scholarship Program)

Full Tuition For Financially Needy Students To Pursue A Baccalaureate Or First Associate Undergraduate Degree (Higher Education Legislative Plan For Needy Students (HELP))

Up To $2,500 To Smart First-Time Freshmen (Mississippi Eminent Scholars Grant (MESG))

Money To Residents To Attend Public or Private Schools In Mississippi (Mississippi Resident Tuition Assistance Grant (MTAG))

Grants To Minority Students To Study At The Gulf Coast Research Laboratory During The Summer (Gulf Coast Research Laboratory Minority Summer Grant Program)

Tuition, Room And Fees To Spouses and Children Of Firefighters And Law Enforcement Officers That Were Totally Disabled Or Killed (Mississippi Law Enforcement Officers and Firemen Scholarship Program)

Grants To Full-Time Students Who Have Trouble Paying For Tuition (State Student Incentive Grant)

Tuition, Room And Meals, Books And Fees To Students Studying For A Class "A" Standard Teacher Education License Who Will Teach In Mississippi (Critical Needs Teacher Loan/Scholarship Program (CNTP))

Up To $8,000 To Smart Students Who Get A Class "A" Standard Teacher Educator License And Teach In Mississippi Public Schools (William Winter Teacher Scholar Loan Program (WWTS))

Aid To Teachers To Pursue A First Master's Degree And A Class "AA" Standard Teacher Education License (Graduate Teacher Summer Loan/Scholarship (GTS))

Financial Aid To Teachers From An Area With A Shortage Of Teachers To Study For A Masters Or Educational Specialist Degree (Mississippi Teacher Fellowship)

Money To Minority Students To Study For A Ph.D Degree In Science, Math, Math or Science Education, And Engineering. (Southern Regional Education Board (STEB) Doctoral Scholars)

Students Studying For A Graduate Degree In Criminal Justice, Public Administration, or Public Policy Can Work For State Or Local Agencies And Offices (Mississippi Public Management Graduate Intern Program)

Money To Pursue Health Related Degrees In Another State That Are Not Offered In Mississippi (Out Of State Programs)

Assistance To Residents To Attend Designated Out Of State Schools of Optometry or Osteopathic Medicine (Southern Regional Education Bard (SREB) Loan/Scholarship Program)

Nursing Education Loans/Scholarship Program:

$1,500 A Year For RN's Going To School To Get A BSN Degree Who Will Be A Nurse In Mississippi (RN To BSN Program)

Up To $4,000 For Nursing Students To Get A BSN Degree (BSN Program)

$3,000 Per Year To Study Full-Time For A MSN Degree (MSN Program)

$5,000 Per Year For To Get A DSN Degree And Work In Mississippi For One Year (DSN Program)

Missouri

Missouri Department of Higher Education
P.O. Box 1438
3515 Amazonas Drive   573-751-2361
Jefferson City, MO 65109-5717   Fax: 573-751-6635
www.mocbhe.gov

General requirements: Applicants must be Missouri residents.

Programs Available:

$2,000 A Year To Students With ACT Scores In The Top 3% (Missouri Higher Education Academic Scholarship Program)

Grants To Full-Time Students In Financial Need (Charles Gallagher Student Financial Assistance Program)

Tuition For Dependents Of Public Safety Officers Or Department Of Highway Officers Who Were Killed In The Line Of Duty (Public Service Officer or Employee's Child Survivor Grant Program)

Help Paying Tuition For Part-Time Students Who Work (Marguerite Ross Barnett Memorial Scholarship)

Tuition For Child Or Spouse of Deceased Vietnam Veteran (Vietnam Veterans Survivors Grant Program)

Money For College For Top Undergraduates and Graduates (Higher Education Scholarship Program

Reduced Tuition For Designated Programs At A College In Kansas, Michigan, Minnesota or Nebraska (Midwest Student Exchange Program)

Montana

Office of the Commissioner of Higher Education
P.O. Box 203101   406-444-6570
Helena, MT 59620-3101   Fax: 406-444-1469
www.montana.edu/wwwoche

General requirements: Applicants must be Montana residents.

Programs Available:

Grants To Students Who Can't Afford Tuition (Leveraging Education Assistance Partnership Program)

Money For Students Who Are Semifinalists In The National Merit Scholarship Competition (Honor Scholarship for National Merit Scholarship Semifinalists)

$1350 To Top Ranking High School Seniors (High School and Community College Honor Scholarships)

Free Tuition For Senior Citizens, Veterans, War Orphans, Etc. (Fee Waivers)

Money For Students Who Work To Help Pay For College (Montana Tuition Assistance Program)

Nebraska

Nebraska Coordinating Commission
For Postsecondary Education
140 North Eighth Street, Suite 300
P.O. Box 95005   402-471-2847

Lincoln, NE 68509-5005   Fax: 402-471-2886
http://nol.org/NEpostsecondaryed

General requirements: Nebraska has a de-centralized grant program. Students should apply for grants through the financial aid office of the college or university that they plan to attend. The school distributes the aid to the specific student. State residency is required.

Nevada

Nevada Department of Education
Student Incentive Grant Program
700 East 5th Street
Carson City, NV 89701-9050   775-687-9200

General requirements: Nevada has no state scholarships. Students should contact the financial aid office at the college they plan to attend for further information. State residency is required.

Programs Available:

Up To $2,500 For Undergraduate and Graduate Students In Financial Need (Access Grant)

Up To $5,200 A Year To Students That Offer Leadership And Service To Their School (Grants-in-Aid)

Grants To Students Who Need Help Paying For School (Leveraging Educational Assistance Program)

New Hampshire

New Hampshire Postsecondary Education Commission
2 Industrial Park Drive   603-271-2555
Concord, NH 03301-8512   TDD:800-735-2964
www.state.nh.us/postsecondary   Fax: 603-271-2696

General requirements: Applicants must be New Hampshire residents for programs involving colleges in and out of state.

Programs Available:

Grants To Attend Colleges In The New England States (New Hampshire Incentive Program)

Money For Dependents Of Veterans Who Died In Service (War Orphans Scholarship)

Grants For Nurses Who Agree To Practice In New Hampshire (New Hampshire Nursing Scholarship Program)

Aid For Students Who Enroll In Programs That Are In Need Of Trained Employees (Career Incentive Program)

New Jersey

New Jersey Department of Higher Education
Office of Student Assistance
4 Quakerbridge Plaza, CN 540
Trenton, NJ 08625   609-588-3288
www.state.nj.us/treasury/osa

General requirements: Applicant must be a New Jersey resident.

Programs Available:

$6050 A Year In Grants To Full-Time Students (Tuition Aid Grants)

Grants, Tutoring, and Counseling To Students On Limited Income (Educational Opportunity Fund Grants (EOF))

Grants To Students With High SAT Scores (Edward J. Bloustein Distinguished Scholar Program)

Grants To Smart High School Juniors (Garden State Scholars Program)

Tuition to Disadvantaged/Minority Students In A Program Leading Toward A Medical Degree At University of Medicine and Dentistry of New Jersey (Martin Luther King Jr. Physician-Dentist Scholarship)

Tuition, Fees, Room and Board To Disadvantaged/ Ethnic Minority Students In The Minority Student Program at Rutgers University School for Law (C.Clyde Ferguson Law Scholarship)

$1,000 Per Year To Top 10% Of Class From An Urban Area (Urban Scholars)

Tuition For Spouses And Children Of Emergency Service Personnel And Law Enforcement Officers Killed In The Line Of Duty (Public Tuition Benefits Program)

Up To $70,000 Student Loan Redemption For Physicians and Dentist Located In Needy Areas Of New Jersey (Physician and Dentist Loan Redemption Program)

Attend A Veterinarian School Out-Of-State (Veterinary Medicine Scholarship)

New Mexico

New Mexico Commission On Higher Education
1068 Cerrillos Road
Santa Fe, NM 87501   505-827-7383
www.nmche.org   Fax: 505-827-7392

General requirements: Applicants must be New Mexico residents, unless otherwise stated.

Programs Available:

Free Tuition To Students with "Good Moral Character" (Three Percent Scholarship Program)

Tuition, Books, and Fees For High School Students In Top 5% Of Class (New Mexico Scholars Program)

Part-Time Jobs To Undergraduate and Graduate Students (New Mexico Work-Study Program)

Money For Osteopathic Students Willing To Practice In New Mexico (Osteopathic Medical Student Loan Program)

Grants To Half-Time and Full-Time Students In Financial Need (New Mexico Student Incentive Grant)

Tuition, Books, And Fees To Vietnam Veterans (Vietnam Veterans' Scholarship Program)

Money For Students Attending Private Colleges (Student Choice)

Money Applied Towards Tuition and Fees For Athletes (Athletic Scholarships)

Financial Aid To Students With Children (Child Care Grants)

Children Of Military Personnel, Members Of New Mexico National Guard, and New Mexico State Police Killed On Active Duty (Children Of Deceased Military and State Police Personnel Scholarship)

Smart Out-Of-State Students Pay Resident Rate At A Public New Mexico College (Competitive Scholarships)

Money To High School Seniors Going Directly Into College Full-Time (Lottery Success Scholarships)

Up To $2,500 For Students In Financial Need To Attend College Full-Time (Legislative Endowment Scholarships)

Reduced Tuition For New Mexico's Senior Citizens (Senior Citizens Reduced Tuition Act)

Money For Osteopathic Students Willing To Practice In New Mexico (Osteopathic Medical Student Loan For Service Program)

$12,000 For Nursing Students Willing To Practice In New Mexico (Nursing Student Loan For Service Program)

Money For Medical Students Willing To Practice In New Mexico (Medical Student Loan for Service Program)

Money For Women And Minority Ph.D. Students (Minority Doctoral Assistance Loan for Service Program)

Students Of Allied Health Programs That Will Practice In Designated Areas Of New Mexico (Allied Health Professional Loan For Service Program)

Loan Reimbursement To Health Professionals That Practice In Specified Areas of New Mexico (Health Professional Loan Repayment Program)

New York

New York Higher Education Services Corporation
Grants and Scholarship Information
99 Washington Avenue   888-NYSHESC
Albany, NY 12255   518-474-1137
www.hesc.com

General requirements; Applicants must be residents of New York. Amounts awarded are determined by the type of school your are planning to attend, your financial state (net taxable income), year in which the award is received, and amount of tuition.

Programs Available:

Grants For Full-Time Students (Tuition Assistance Program (TAP))

Grants For Part-Time Students (Aid For Part-Time Study (APTS)

Money For Accounting, Veterinary, and Students Pursuing 19 Other Professional Careers (New York Regents Professional Opportunity Scholarships)

Money For Students Studying Medicine Or Dentistry (New York Regents Health Care Opportunity Scholarships)

Money For Native Americans To Attend College (State Aid To Native Americans)

Grants To Dependents Of Deceased Or Disabled Veterans (Regents Award For Child Of Veteran)

Grants To Dependents Of Deceased Correction Officer (Child Of Correction Officer)

Tuition And Fees For Dependents Of Deceased Police Officers And Fire Fighters (Memorial Scholarships For Children Of Deceased Police Officers And Fire Fighters)

$1,000 Per Semester For Vietnam Veterans (Vietnam Veterans Tuition Awards)

Outstanding High School Seniors Receive Up To $1,500 A Year (Scholarships For Academic Excellence)

Up To $15,000 For A Career As A Midwife, Nurse Practitioner, Or Physician Assistant (New York State Primary Care Service Corps)

Up To $1,000 Per Semester For Persian Gulf Veterans (Persian Gulf Veterans Tuition Awards)

$4,725 For Full-Time AmeriCorp Members (AmeriCorps Education Award)

Up To $3,400 A Year In Tuition For Members Of State Military Forces (National Guard-NYS Educational Incentive Program)

North Carolina

North Carolina State Education Assistance Authority
P.O. Box 2688   919-549-8614
Chapel Hill, NC 27515-2688   Fax: 919-549-8481
www.ncseaa.edu

General requirements: Applicants must be residents of North Carolina.

Programs Available:

Grants For Full-Time And Part-Time Students (Appropriated Grants)

$3,000 For Smart High School Students Active In Public Service (Incentive Scholarship Program)

Grants For Minorities Studying Part Time Or Full Time (Minority Presence Grant Program)

Grants For Minorities Studying Law, Veterinary Medicine, Or Working On A Ph.D. (Minority Presence Grant Program: Doctoral/Law/Veterinary Medicine Program)

Grants For Students Going Part Time To Junior Colleges (North Carolina Community College Scholarship Program)

Grants Given By State Legislators To Students Who Don't Even Need The Money (North Carolina Legislative Tuition Grant Program, Private College)

$8,500 A Year For Undergraduate Or Graduate Students In Health, Science, Or Mathematics (North Carolina Student Loan Program For Health, Science, and Mathematics)

$5,000 A Year To Students Who Want To Be Teachers (North Carolina Teaching Fellows Scholarship Program)

Grants To Dependents Of Deceased Or Disabled Veterans Or POW/MIA's (North Carolina Veteran Scholarship)

Grants To Full-Time Or Part--Time Native American Students (Incentive Scholarship and Grant Program)

Money For Students In 2-Year Or 4-Year Nursing Programs (Nurse Education Scholarship Loan Program)

$5,000 A Year For Nursing Students Willing To Practice In North Carolina (Nurse Scholars Program)

$5,000 Plus Tuition And Fees For Dental Students (Board of Governors Dental Scholarship)

$5,000 Plus Tuition And Fees For Medical Students (Board of Governors Medical Scholarship Program)

Free Loans For Studying Psychology, Counseling, Or Speech (Prospective Teacher Scholarship Loans)

Grants To Part-Time Or Full-Time Students Attending Private Colleges (State Contractual Scholarship Program, Private Colleges)

Tuition, Fees, And Day Care For The Physically Or Mentally Disabled (Vocational Rehabilitation Program)

$6,000 A Year Towards A Master's Degree For Nurses Who Will Teach In North Carolina (North Carolina Master's Nurse Scholar Program)

Up To $4,000 A Year For Active Members Of The North Carolina Army Or Air National Guard To Attend School (North Carolina National Guard Tuition Assistance Program (TAP))

Money For College To Vietnam Veterans Or Their Families

Four-Year Scholarships To Students Who Are Going To Enroll In The ROTC Program (Reserve Officer's Training Corps Scholarships (ROTC))

Tuition, Fees, And Books For The Freshman Year Of College At Select Universities In North Carolina (Freshman Scholars Program)

$3,000 To Native American Freshmen Who Graduated In The Top 1/2 Of Their Class And Active In Public Service (AMBUCS Scholarships For Therapists Merit Based Scholarship)

$2,500 A Year For Students In Academic Health Science Programs To Study Substance Abuse (North Carolina Governor's Institute On Alcohol And Substance Abuse Public Policy Scholars Program)

$20,000 A Year For Full-Time Study To Become Part of The Administration In Public Schools (Principal Fellows Program)

$1,200 A Year For Teacher Assistants To Attend Community College (Teacher Assistant Scholarship Loan Two-Year Program)

Tuition, Fees, Books and Supplies, and Reader Services To Full-Time Visually Impaired Students With Financial Need (Rehabilitation Assistance For Visually Handicapped)

North Dakota

University Systems
600 East Boulevard
Bismarck, ND 58505-0230   701-328-4114
General requirements: Applicants must be residents of North Dakota.
Programs Available:
Money for Students In Financial Need (State Grant Student Incentive Program)

Tuition Aid For Students In The Upper 5% Of Their Class (North Dakota Scholars Program)

Ohio

Ohio Board of Regents
State Grants and Scholarship Department   888-833-1133
P.O. Box 182452   614-466-7420
Columbus, OH 43218-2452   Fax: 614-752-5903
www.regents.state.oh.us
General requirements: Applicants must be residents of Ohio.
Programs Available:
Grants For Low To Moderate Income Families To Pay Tuition (Ohio Instructional Grants)

Grants To Pay Tuition At Private Colleges (Ohio Student Choice Grant Program)

Grants To Dependents Of Deceased Or Disabled Veterans (Ohio War Orphans Scholarship Program)

$2,000 A Year To Smart High School Students Who Attend Ohio Colleges (Ohio Academic Scholarship Program)

$3,500 A Year For Smart Graduate Students (Regents Graduate/Professional Fellowship Program)

Tuition Assistance To Dependents Of Fire Fighters And Police Officers Killed In The Line Of Duty (Ohio Safety Officers College Memorial Fund)

Money For Students Who Need Financial Help To Attend School Part-Time (Part-Time Student Instructional Grant Program)

$3,000 Per Year For Students Enrolled in A Nurse Education Program (Nurse Education Assistance Loan Program)

Oklahoma

Oklahoma State Regents for Higher Education
500 Education Building
State Capitol Complex   405-524-9100
Oklahoma City, OK 73105   Fax: 405-524-9230
www.okhighered.org
General requirements: Applicants must be Oklahoma residents.
Programs Available:
Money For Students Having Trouble Paying Tuition (Oklahoma Tuition Aid Grant Program)

Grants To Top 15% High School Students Who want To Be Teachers (Future Teachers Scholarship Program)

Money To Smart Students Going To Public Or Private Colleges (Academic Scholars Program)

Money For Members And Enlistees Of The National Guard Going To School To Earn A Bachelor's Degree (National Guard Tuition Waiver)

Aid For Smart, Well Behaved High School Students With Financial Need (Must Apply During 9th and 10th Grade) (Oklahoma Higher Learning Access Program)

Tuition, Fees, Room and Board, and Required Books For Smart Students At 10 Participating Universities In Oklahoma (Regional University Baccalaureate Scholarship)

Money For Full-Time Undergraduates Who Need Help To Pay For School (William P. Willis Scholarship)

Money To Minority Graduate Students Who Agree To Teach At Oklahoma Colleges Or Universities After Graduating With A Doctor's Degree (Doctoral Study Grant Program)

$4,000 A Year And A Fee Waiver To Minorities To Study In The Field Of Medicine, Dentistry, Law, Optometry, Pharmacy, And Veterinary Medicine (Professional Study Grant)

Tuition, Special Fees, Books, and Room And Board To Dependent Children Of Victims Of The Bombing Of The Alfred P. Murrah Federal Building (Heartland Scholarship Fund)

Money To Study In A Specialized Field Of Chiropractic Medicine (Chiropractic Education Assistance Program)

Oregon

Oregon State Scholarship Commission
1500 Valley River Drive, Suite 100   800-452-8807
Eugene, OR 97401   503-687-7400
www.ossc.state.or.us
General requirements: Applicants must be residents of Oregon.
Programs Available:
Grants To College Students In Financial Need; Must Apply For FASA Too (Need Grants)

Tuition And Fees For Children Of Firefighters, Police Officers, Correction and Investigators That Are In Financial Need (Deceased Or Disabled Public Safety Officer)

$600 For Full-Time Attendance At Hair Stylist, Cosmetology Or Manicure School; Must Also Apply For FASA (Oregon Barbers And Hairdressers Grant Program)

Student Loans Forgiven If You Become A Nurse In A Needed Area Of Oregon (Oregon Nursing Loan Program)

Pennsylvania

Pennsylvania Higher Education Assistance Agency
1200 North 7th Street   TTY: 800-654-5988
Harrisburg, PA 17102   717-720-2850
www.pheaa.org   Fax: 717-720-3907
General requirements: Applicants must be Pennsylvania residents for in-state schools, unless otherwise specified.
Programs Available:
80% Of Tuition And Fees For Financially Needy Students (Pennsylvania State Grants)

Students Provided With Employment Opportunities In High-Technology And Community Service Positions (Pennsylvania State Work-Study Program)

$2,900 For Veterans Who Want To Go To School (Financial Aid For Veterans)

Tuition, Fees and Room And Board Waiver For The Children Of Police Officers, Firefighters, Rescue And Ambulance Squad Members, Correction Employees and National Guard Members Who Died In The Line Of Duty (The Postsecondary Educational Gratuity Program)

Rhode Island

Rhode Island Higher Education Assistance Authority
560 Jefferson Boulevard   401-736-1100
Warwick, RI 02886   Fax: 401-732-3541
www.riheaa.org   TDD: 401-222-6195

General requirements: Applicants must be residents of Rhode Island.

Programs Available:

Money For Students Who Need Help Paying For College (State Grant Program)

Students In Financial Need Can Get Work At Non-Profit Agencies In Rhode Island; Must Be Receiving The Rhode Island State Grant Program (Community Service Initiative)

Work-Study Awards To Students That Work For Specific Rhode Island Employers (College Allocation Program (CAP))

South Carolina

South Carolina Commission on Higher Education
1333 Main Street, Suite 200   803-737-2260
Columbia, SC 29201   Fax: 803-737-1426
www.state.sc.us/tuitiongrants

General requirements: Applicants must be residents of South Carolina.

Programs Available:

$3,320 For Students In Financial Need (South Carolina Tuition Grants)

$5,000 For High School Seniors With High Test Scores (Palmetto Fellows Scholarship)

Up To $2,500 To Students In Extreme Financial Need (Need Based Grant)

$2,000 A Year For Smart Students (Legislative Incentive For Future Excellence (LIFE))

Money To High School Students Who Graduated With A STAR Diploma (Superior Scholars For Today and Tomorrow (STAR) Scholarship)

South Dakota

South Dakota Department of Education And Cultural Affairs
Office of the Secretary
7000 Governors Drive
Pierre, SD 57051   605-773-3134

Currently, there are no state aided financial aid programs available. South Dakota assigns state general funds to support public higher education schools. General state funds are rarely awarded directly to student aid.

Tennessee

Tennessee Student Assistance Corporation
404 James Robertson Parkway, Suite 1950   615-741-6101
Nashville, TN 37243-0820   Fax: 615-741-6101
www.state.tn.us/tsac

General requirements: Applicants must be residents of Tennessee.

Programs Available:

$5,000 A Year For Minorities In The Top 25% Of Class To Become Teachers (Minority Teaching Fellows Program)

$1,626 For Financially Needy Students (Tennessee Student Assistance Award Program (TSAA))

$6,000 A Year For Very Smart High School Graduates Entering College (Ned McWherter Scholars Program)

Up To $3,000 Of Student Loan Forgiven For College Juniors, Seniors And Post Baccalaureate Students Who Will Teach In Tennessee Public Schools (Tennessee teaching Scholars program)

Money To Smart Full-Time Students In A Teacher Education Program (Christa McAuliffe Scholarship Program)

Financial Aid For Children Of Law Enforcement Officers, Firemen, Or Emergency Medical Technicians Killed In The Line Of Duty (Dependent Children's Scholarship Program)

Grants To Tennessee Residents With A Physical, Mental or Emotional Disability (Vocational Rehabilitation Grants)

Texas

Texas Higher Education Coordinating Board
Box 12788, Capitol Station
Austin, TX 78711-2788   512-483-6100
www.thecb.state.tx.us/start/stu

General requirements: Applicants must be residents of Texas, unless otherwise specified.

Programs Available:

Money To Attend Public Colleges In Texas (Texas Public Education Grant)

Money To Attend Private Colleges In Texas (Tuition Equalization Grant)

$1,250 For Half Time Or Full Time Students (Student Incentive Grant)

Grants to Financially Needy Students (Texas Tuition Assistance Grant)

Money To Study To Be A Nurse

Tuition And Fees For Blind Or Deaf Students

Money For Dependents Of Disabled Or Deceased Firemen, Peace Officers, Custodial Employees of the Department Of Corrections, Or Game Wardens

Money For Dependents Of POW/MIAs (Children Of Prisoners Of War Or Persons Missing In Action)

Tuition And Fees For Fire Fighters To Take Science Courses (Fire Fighters Enrolled in Fire Science Courses)

Free Tuition And Fees For Veterans (Veterans and Dependents (The Hazelwood Act))

Money For The smartest High School Students (High Ranking High School Graduate)

Money For Foreign Students From Central America (Students from Other Nations of the American Hemisphere (Good Neighbor Scholarship))

Aid To Students Who Graduate In No More Than 36 Months (Early High School Graduation Scholarship)

Tuition and Fees For At Least Half-Time (Texas New Horizons Scholarship Program)

Money To Students that Have Completed 120 Hours Of College Work That Want To Be Accountants (Fifth-Year Accounting Student Scholarship Program)

Residents Or Non-Residents With Financial Need (License Plate Insignia Scholarship)

Aid To Students Who Practice Primary Health Care In Designated Communities After Graduation (Community Scholarship program)

Stipends Of Up To $15,000 A Year To Primary Care Residents To Practice In Medically Under-Served Areas (Texas Health Service Corps Repayment Program)

Money To Students Who Are Studying For A Degree In Specified Primary Care Areas And Agree To Serve In Areas With Severe Shortages (Texas Health Service Corps Scholarship Program)

Forgiveness Loans For Top Students To Work In Their Community After Graduation (Outstanding Rural Scholarship Program)

Up To 5 Years Of Loan Repayment for Physicians In Specialized Areas (Physician Education Loan Repayment Program)

Up To $5,000 In Loan Repayment For Physician Assistants Who Have Practiced In Specified Area (Rural Physician Assistant Loan Reimbursement)

Hours Of Part-time Work For Students In Financial Need (Texas College Work-Study Program)

Fees and Tuition For Disabled Peace Officers (Disabled Peace Officers)

Tuition and Fees For Students That Have Been In Foster Care (Foster Care Students)

Exemption From Tuition For Up To 6 Semester Credit Hours Per Semester (Senior Citizens)

Exemption From Fees and Tuition For Up To 1 Year For High School Seniors That Received Financial Assistance. (Assistance For Needy Families)

ROTC Students receive Tuition, Fees And Partial Exemption From Room and Board (Reserve Officer's Training Corps/National Guard Students)

Money To Currently Employed Certified Educational Aides In Financial Need (Certified Educational Aides)

Special Tuition Rate For Graduate Students To Out-Of-State College When The Degree Is Not Offered In Texas (Academic Common Market)

Utah

Utah System of Higher Education
3 Triad Center, Suite 550
Salt Lake City, UT 84180-1205   801-321-7101
www.state.ut.us/html/education.htm

General requirements: Applicants must be residents of Utah.

Programs Available:

Grants For Students In Financial Need (State Student Incentive Grant Program)

Money To Go To School In Utah (Utah Centennial Opportunity Program For Education Grant)

Tuition and General Fees For Outstanding Students To Teach In Utah (Terrel H. Bell Teaching Incentive Loan)

Vermont

Vermont Student Assistance Corporation
P.O. Box 2000
Champlain Mill- 4th Floor   800 798-8722
Winooski, VT 05404   802-655-4050
www.vsac.org

General requirements: Applicants must be Vermont residents, unless otherwise stated.

Programs Available:

Grants For Students In Financial Need (Vermont Incentive Grants)

Grants For Part Time Students (Vermont Part Time Student Grants)

$500 Per Course If You're NOT Working Toward A Degree (Vermont Non-Degree Student Grant Program)

Virginia

Virginia State Council of Higher Education
Office of Financial Aid
James Monroe Building   804-225-2137
101 North 14th Street, 9th Floor   TDD: 804-371-8017
Richmond, VA 23219   Fax: 804-225-2604
www.schev.edu

General requirements: Applicants must be Virginia residents.

Programs Available:

$3,000 For Students In Financial Need (Virginia College Assistance Program (CSAP))

Grants For Students Even Though They Don't NEED The Money (Virginia Tuition Assistance Grant Program (TAG))

Free Tuition For White Students To Attend Black Colleges (Virginia Transfer Grant Program (VTGP))

Grants To Black Undergraduate Students (Last Dollar Program)

Nursing Students Receive $100 A Month For Every Month They Agree To Work In Virginia (Medical Scholarship Program)

$2,500 To Dental Students Who Agree To Work In Small Virginia Towns (Rural Dental Scholarships)

$3,000 A Year For Teaching Students For Every Year They Agree To Work In Virginia (Virginia Teaching Scholarship)

Free Tuition, Fees, And Room and Board For State Cadets (State Cadetships)

Free Tuition For Dependents Of Disabled Veterans (Virginia War Orphan Education Act)

Free Tuition And Fees For Students Who Want To Study Soil Science (Soil Scientist Program)

Free Tuition For Students Over 60 (Senior Citizens Tuition Waiver)

Money To Needy Students Attending AT Least Half Time (Commonwealth Awards)

Money For Smart Students Going To School Full Time (Graduate and Undergraduate Program)

Money To High School Graduates Who Need Help Paying For College (Virginia Guaranteed Assistance Program (VGAP))

Virginia Army National Guard Members Receive Tuition Assistance (Virginia National Guard)

Financial Aid For Visually Handicapped Students; Must Also Apply For Additional Funding (Virginia Assistance For The Visually Handicapped)

Vocational Rehabilitation To Residents With A Disability; Must Also Apply for Additional Aid Virginia Department of Rehabilitative Services College Program)

In-State Tuition Rate For Students Who Study A Selected Program At One Of 13 Southern State Schools (Academic Common Market)

Aid To Northhampton Or Accomack Juniors And Seniors Who Commute To The University of Maryland-Eastern Shore or Salisbury State University (Eastern Shore Tuition Assistance Program)

Tuition Assistance To Study Library Science, Optometry, Forensic Science and Paper and Pulp Technology At Specified Out-Of-State Schools (Regional Contract Programs)

Washington

Higher Education Coordinating Board
917 Lakeridge Way
P.O. Box 43430   360-753-7809
Olympia, WA 98504-3430   TTY: 360-753-7809
www.hecb.wa.gov   Fax: 360-753-7808

General requirements: Applicants must be Washington residents for in-state or out-of-state programs, when specified.

Programs Available:

College Students Who Have Trouble Paying For Tuition (Washington State Need Grant Program)

Part-Time Employment To Students Who Need Money (Washington State Work Study Program)

Grants To Financially Needy Placebound Students To Finish Their Education (Educational Opportunity Grant)

Money To Students Who Will Practice Primary Care In Needed Areas After Graduating (Health Professional Scholarship)

Grants To Teachers, Principals, and School District Administrators For Part-Time Study At University of Washington (Christa Mc Auliffe Award For Excellence)

Money To High School Students In The Top 1% (Washington Scholars Program)

Money To Outstanding Vocational-Technical Students (Washington Award For Vocational Excellence (WAVE))

Financial Aid For American Indian Students In Need (American Indian Endowed Scholarship)

Up To $200 To Blind Students For Reimbursement Of Special Equipment, Services And Supplies (Aid To Blind Students)

Money To Study Optometry In Other States And Practice In Washington (Western Interstate Commission

For Higher Education (WICHE) Professional Student Exchange Program)

Money To Get A Master's Or Ph.D. In Out-Of-State Schools (Western Interstate Commission For Higher Education(WICHE) Regional Graduate Program)

Free Tuition And Fees To Financially Needy Students (Tuition Waiver Program)

West Virginia

State College and University Systems
1018 Kanawha Boulevard, East, Suite 700   304-558-2101
Charleston, WV 25301   Fax: 304-558-0259
www.scusco.wvnet.edu

General requirements: Applicants must be residents of West Virginia.

Programs Available:

Money For Financially Needy Students (West Virginia Higher Education Grant)

Money To Study Teaching At The Graduate Or Undergraduate Level (Underwood-Smith Teacher Scholarship Program

Money For Medical Students To Practice In West Virginia For A Time (Medical Student Loan Program)

Wisconsin

State of Wisconsin Higher Education Aids Board
P.O. Box 7885   608-267-2206
Madison, WI 53707-7885   Fax: 608-267-2808
http://heab.state.wi.us

General requirements: Applicants must be residents of Wisconsin. Students should contact the Financial Aid Office of the College they plan on attending for applications.

Programs Available:

Grants To College Or Vocational Students (Wisconsin Higher Education Grant)

Grants To Students Attending Private Colleges In Wisconsin (Wisconsin Tuition Grant)

Grants To Blacks, Hispanics, Native Americans, And Former Citizens Of Laos, Vietnam, and Cambodia (Minority Retention Grant)

Grants To Non-Traditional Students (Talent Incentive Program)

Cheap Tuition For Attending Minnesota University (Minnesota-Wisconsin Reciprocity Program)

$2,250 A Year To High School Seniors Who Have The Highest GPA In Their School (Academic Excellence Scholarships)

Up To $1,800 A Year To Severely Visually Or Hearing Impaired Students To Go To College In Or Out-Of-State (Handicapped Student Grant)

$2,500 Per Year For Minority College Juniors Or Seniors Who Become Teachers In Wisconsin (Minority Teacher Loan Program)

$2,000 For Students In Programs At The Milwaukee Teacher Education Center Who Agree To Teach In Wisconsin (Teacher Education Loan Program)

Wyoming

Wyoming Department of Higher Education
Hathaway Building
2300 Capitol Avenue
Cheyenne, WY 82002   307-777-6213

General Requirements: Wyoming offers the Leveraging Educational Assistance Program (LEAP). Applicants must be Wyoming residents and college freshmen and sophomores in financial need. The individual schools handle these programs and should be contacted for information and applications.

I Wanna Write A Book

Matthew Lesko, Information USA, Inc., 12081 Nebel Street, Rockville, MD 20852 • 1-800-955-7693 • www.lesko.com

I Wanna Write A Book

Yes, you can make money writing a book. Sometimes you can even make a <u>lot</u> of money. I've made a bundle, and I even got a D in college English. So, if I can do it, there is no reason why you can't.

There are a number of ways you can make money writing a book:
1) You can get a grant from the government or a nonprofit organization
2) You can go directly to publishers
3) You can find a literary agent who will contact publishers for you
4) You can publish the book yourself

What Kind Of Money Is Available

The government money that's available is in the form of a grant. That's money you don't have to pay back, so of course, there's no better money than that. The money you might get from a publisher will usually be in the form of an advance towards future royalties. That means they will give you a certain amount of money when you sign the contract. Sometimes this money will be spread out in payments, some you could receive at the signing and some when you turn in the manuscript. This advance will be deducted from the royalties you earn when the book sells. If the book sells more than what the publisher gave you in the advance, you will receive more money. If the book sells less than the advance figure, the publisher loses.

Using the government or a publisher will usually mean **you get money up front**. Publishing yourself means **you put up your own money**. There is more risk, but it can also mean more reward. I've published about 12 books with New York publishers, but in the last five years I've been publishing myself. And to tell you the truth, I'm a lot happier now.

What You Need To Start

So many people believe that you have to have the entire book completed in order to get anyone interested in your project. Not so. All you usually need to have completed is a chapter or two along with an outline to get someone interested. I believe that it is important not to write the entire book, especially for the commercial market. If your idea is of any value, people are going to give you ideas on how to make it better. More importantly, they will tell you what they want to see in the book in order for them to publish it. And a bigger issue today is that no one has time to read a complete manuscript. They are more likely to review your book if you give them as little to do as possible. Most people want to see the basic concept of a book in progress, and nothing more.

Government Grants To Publish Your Books

This can be the most difficult way to get published mainly because so few books are published this way each year. Approximately 50,000 books are published annually by commercial publishers, while the government only publishes a few hundred titles. However, the odds of getting a grant from the government are probably a lot better than getting money from private sources. You have about a one in eight chance of getting a government grant for your book, which as odds go, isn't bad at all. Many of the government programs have now stopped giving money directly to individuals and only give money to organizations who in turn pass it on to the individuals who have applied for it.

The point is to ignore what I just said, because if you want to change your life you have to try everything, and I mean **everything!**. Listed below are the sources of government grants for writers. When you call the organizations listed below, be thorough in your questioning of the person on the other end of the line — have they told you about every program available that might be able to give you some money? Also look in the Freelance Writers chapter to learn how to get a job writing for the government.

National Endowment for the Arts
1100 Pennsylvania Ave., NW
Washington, DC 20506   202-682-5400
www.nea.gov

National Endowment for the Humanities
1100 Pennsylvania Ave., NW
Washington, DC 20506   202-606-8400
www.neh.fed.us

Going Directly To Publishers

This seems to be the most obvious method and it works for many people. The world of publishing is very big and there is probably an editor at some publishing house who would be interested in your idea. Life, like so many things, is a numbers game. So the more publishers you call, the more editors you talk with, and the more likely you are to find someone interested in your book idea.

Listed below are the sources that identify publishers in the United States. You can find these sources in most local libraries.

Literary Marketplace, Reed Reference Publishing Co., New Providence, NJ
Literary Agents of North America, The Associates, New York, NY
Insider's Guide to Book Editors, Publishers, and Literary Agents, Prima Publishing, Rocklin, GA
Literary Agents: A Writer's Guide, Adam Begley, Penguin, New York, NY

Publishing Your Own Book

With a successful book, you'll make a lot more money publishing it yourself. What profits a publishing company would have made will end up being yours to keep. But you'll need money up front to publish your own book. How much? That depends on the kind of book.

There are three major issues involved in publishing your own book: printing, distribution and marketing. The most expensive part of it can be printing. There are ways of getting the other two necessities for free, but you need to have books to sell first. The first book is the most expensive to produce. If you print 5,000 to 10,000 copies of a 300 page book you may be able to have them printed for about $2 each. But printing only 300 books can cost you $30 each. If you are going to sell your book for $20, you're in big trouble if you only print 300 copies. But if you print 5000 copies, it's going to cost you $10,000 before you make even one sale. A $10,000 advance from a publisher may start to look a lot better after adding up these numbers.

If you are publishing a self help book, you can consider other alternatives. You can make single copies of books at a local copy store, or your home computer and put it into a three ring binder. You can also charge more for the book in this kind of format. This could work well for books like: How To Fix Your Credit, How To Get Free Legal Advice, How To Travel Cheap, Make Money On The Internet, etc.

Distribution is an important element in anything you produce in this country. Getting your book in bookstores can be a major problem. You can find distributors who will do it for you and charge you a commission for doing so, or you can contact the bookstore chains directly. Either way it's hard, but not impossible. The bigger problem for a self publisher is that bookstores work on consignment. That means if they sell your book, you get the money. If they don't, you get the book back and get no money. And it may take three to six months to find out which of these two events actually occur.

When I first started publishing my own books, I decided that I couldn't afford to be in bookstores. If every bookstore purchased 10 copies of my book, I'd be out of business. If there are 5,000 book stores, that would mean 50,000 books at $2 each. I would have to put up $100,000 to cover printing costs and have no idea if and when I'd get anything back. So I decided on distributing my publications through mail order. If someone sent me the money, I would send them the book.

Nothing happens without successful marketing. You can have production and distribution all figured out but if you don't know how to sell your book, you're sunk. I use talk shows. I was on talk shows when I was writing for New York publishers, so I knew how the system works (you make hundreds of telephone calls and try to convince the producers you have something interesting to say.) But this time when I got on the shows, instead of saying the book was in book stores, I'd say the book was only available by calling 1-800-UNCLE-SAM.

If you want to sell your own book, you'll find the way that works best for you.

Using A Literary Agent

This may be the most productive method for someone trying to get their first book published. Using a middle man, in this case a literary agent, can save you time in finding a publisher. Also, most big publishers would rather deal with an agent who knows the business rather than dealing directly with you. They don't want to spend time explaining contracts and educating you about the process. The agent performs this role for them.

Every literary agent has her area of expertise, collection of publishers, and editors within those companies, whom they are close to and know the kinds of books for which they are looking. So instead of contacting hundreds of publishers and editors directly, you can now concentrate on just dozens of agents. To contact an agent, write a brief letter describing your work, list any prior publications, and include a self-addressed stamped envelope (SASE) to receive a reply. The cost? They will normally ask you for 10% to 15% of what they get for you from the publisher. Some particularly successful agents are in such demand for their time that they charge a flat fee just to read your book outline or sample chapters.

Listed below is a small collection of literary agents around the country who do not charge reading fees. For additional information on literary agents contact: Association of Authors' Representatives (AAR), P.O. Box 237201, Ansonia Station, New York, NY 10003, {www.aar-online.org}. The AAR will send you a list of 22 suggested questions to ask, the AAR's *Canon of Ethics*, and a listing of agents who are members for $5, plus postage and handling.

Literary Agents

California

Linda Allen Literary Agency
1949 Green St. #5   415-921-6437
San Francisco, CA 94123   Fax: 415-921-3733
Email: linda@lallenlitagency.com
This agency handles fiction and non-fiction. For non-fiction send a proposal. For fiction, send a synopsis and the first 20-40 pages.

Atchity Editorial/Entertainment International Literary, Inc.
Management and Film Production
9601 Wilshire Blvd., Box 1202   323-933-0407
Beverly Hills, CA 90212   Fax: 323-933-0321
www.aeionline.com
Subjects this agency is most interested in include: fiction; mainstream that can also be made into television or feature films, screenplays (especially true stories with television potential). Non-fiction: entrepreneurial business books, heroic and true stories, general interest, and reference books. Screenplays; heroic true stories, action, thrillers, romance, comedy, or science fiction. Submit query letter and 25 sample pages. Include an SASE.

Castiglia Literary Agency
1155 Camino del Mar   858-755-8761
Del Mar, CA 92014   Fax: 858-755-7063
Email: jaclagency@aol.com
This agency will look at query letters, synopsis, and two chapters but will return unread unsolicited complete manuscripts. They represent fiction and non-fiction. In non-fiction: science, business, finance, health, spiritual, women's issues, biography, and niche books. In fiction: ethnic, mainstream, literary, and some genre.

Sandra Dijkstra Literary Agency
1155 Camino del Mar, Suite 515   858-755-3115
Del Mar, CA 92014   Fax: 858-794-2822
Email: sdla@dijkstraagency.com
This agency requires the first 50 pages with synopsis or outline along with an SASE. They specialize in literary and commercial fiction and non-fiction.

Epstein-Wakefield & Associates
280 South Beverly Dr., #400   310-278-7222
Beverly Hills, CA 90212   Fax: 310-278-4640
This agency handles television, books, and film scripts. Submit a query letter with SASE.

Peter Fleming Agency
P.O. Box 458
Pacific Palisades, CA 90272   310-454-1373
The Agency handles adult non-fiction, specializing in innovative, professional, business, and pro-free market topics. Submit query letter first with an SASE.

Samuel French, Inc.
7623 Sunset Blvd.   323-876-0570
Hollywood, CA 90046   Fax: 323-876-0570
www.samuelfrench.com
Stage plays for publication and representation are handled by this agency. A variety of subject areas are considered such as comedy, contemporary issues, crime, ethnic, experimental, fantasy, horror, mystery, religious, and thrillers. Submit a query letter or manuscript and include an SASE.

The Charlotte Gusay Literary Agency
10532 Blythe, Suite 211   310-559-0831
Los Angeles, CA 90064   Fax: 310-559-2639
www.mediastudio.com/gusay
Both fiction and non-fiction are handled. Prefers commercial, mainstream, quality material (especially books that can be marketed as film material). Projects on children's books are limited. They like material that is innovative, unusual, eclectic, and nonsexist. The agency will consider literary fiction with crossover potential. No unsolicited manuscripts are accepted, submit a succinct and clear query letter with an SASE.

Reece Halsey Agency
8733 Sunset Blvd., Suite 101   310-652-2409
Los Angeles, CA 90210   Fax: 310-652-7595
This agency specializes in literary fiction, writing they feel is exceptional in its field. Submit a query letter with one or two sample chapters and an SASE.

Frederick Hill Associates
1842 Union St.   415-921-2910
San Francisco, CA 94123   Fax: 415-921-2802
Submit query first along with an SASE. This agency handles fiction and non-fiction. They do not accept westerns, romance, or science fiction.

Michael Larsen/Elizabeth Pomada Literary Agents
1029 Jones St.
San Francisco, CA 94109-5023   415-673-0939
www.larsen-pomada.com
This agency handles fiction and non-fiction. For fiction, send the first 30 pages and a synopsis and an SASE. For non-fiction, contact the agency.

The Maureen Lasher Agency
Attn: Ann Cashman
P.O. Box 46370   323-654-5288
Los Angeles, CA 90046   Fax: 323-654-5388
Send written inquiry, synopsis, 50 pages, and include an SASE. No telephone or fax inquiries are accepted. The agency handles general fiction and non-fiction, and it does not handle science fiction or romance novels.

Julie Popkin, Literary Agent
15340 Albright St., #204   310-459-2834
Pacific Palisades, CA 90272   Fax: 310-459-4128
This agency handles fiction, literary and popular including mysteries; non-fiction, especially social issues. Film rights only for clients whose books are under contract. Queries accepted if by mail with SASE only. No phone or fax inquiries.

The Angela Rinaldi Literary Agency
P.O. Box 7877   310-842-7665
Beverly Hills, CA 90212-7877   Fax: 310-837-8143
Email: amr@RinaldiLiterary.com
The agency is interested in fiction and non-fiction submissions. Prefers non-fiction topics that appeal to a wide audience, such as women's issues, pop culture, current issues, biography, popular reference, business, popular science and books written by academics, doctors, and therapists based on their research. Queries only by mail, no phone or fax. If you are sending a novel, send a synopsis, the first 100 pages, and a chapter outline with an SASE. For non-fiction, send a draft of your proposal which includes an outline and a sample chapter, but a detailed query letter which includes a brief synopsis and outline is acceptable. Include an SASE.

Ken Sherman & Associates
9507 Santa Monica Blvd., Suite 211   310-273-8840
Beverly Hills, CA 90210   Fax: 310-271-2875
Email: ksassociates@earthlink.net
This agency does not accept unsolicited material. All material must come through a referral only from either a client, producer or writer who they already know who has read the material and can vouch for the quality. They handle film television, fiction and non-fiction writers.

Spieler Agency/West
4096 Piedmont Ave.   510-985-1422
Oakland, CA 94611   Fax: 310-985-1323
Email: spielerlit@aol.com
Literary non-fiction areas include history, social issues, the environment, economics, and business. Literary fiction is also handled. Reports on queries in 2 weeks, reports on manuscripts in 5 weeks. Manuscripts without an SASE or sufficient money to cover postage will not be returned.

Susan Travis Literary Agency
1317 N. San Fernando Blvd., Suite 175   818-557-6538
Burbank, CA 91504   Fax: 818-557-6549
This agency is currently looking for submissions of fiction and non-fiction. Fiction interests include mainstream and literary fiction, romance, mystery, historical, and thrillers. Non-fiction should be for the general trade market, including but not limited to business, health, parenting, cookbooks, and reference. Fiction submissions should be in the form of a query letter with a one page synopsis. You may attach the first 15-20 pages and indicate the page length of your manuscript. Non-fiction submissions should be in the form of a query letter giving a brief overview, the target audience/market, your credentials, and indicate whether you have written a proposal or have completed the entire manuscript. Always include an SASE.

The Turtle Agency
77209B El Camino Real #125
Carlsbad, CA 92009
The Turtle Agency specializes in the areas of television, film, interactive, and books. It is best to be recommended to the agency through industry contact, but you may submit query letter and/or manuscript. Include an SASE if you want material returned.

Annette Van Duren Agency
11684 Ventura Blvd., #235   818-752-6000
Studio City, CA 91604   Fax: 818-752-6985

Television and film writers, writer/directors, or writer/producers are represented. No unsolicited manuscripts will be accepted. Submit query with SASE.

Waterside Productions, Inc.
The Waterside Building
2191 San Elijo Ave. 760-632-9190
Cardiff-by-the-Sea, CA 92007-1839 Fax: 760-632-9295
CompuServe address: 75720,410
www.waterside.com

This agency specializes in computer books. Other areas of strength include business, education, health, biography, sports, psychology, spiritual/self-help, how-to, and science book placement. Submit query letter or request the submission guidelines for non-fiction.

West Coast Literary Associates
Attn: Acquisitions
395 S. Hwy. 65, Suite 395A
Lincoln, CA 94648 916-408-1473

The agency represents authors of book length fiction (literary, mainstream, all genres) and book length non-fiction. Submit a one page synopsis and the first 25 manuscript pages for preliminary review and evaluation. Include an SASE.

Colorado

Jody Rein Books, Inc.
7741 S. Ash Court 303-694-4430
Littleton, CO 80122 Fax: 303-694-0687
www.jodyreinbooks.com

This agency sells primarily very commercial non-fiction. Unsolicited manuscripts are not accepted. Send query letter with SASE.

Connecticut

New England Publishing Associates
P.O. Box 5 860-345-READ
Chester, CT 06412 Fax: 860-345-3660
Email: nepa@nepa.com
www.nepa.com

New England Publishing Associates provides editorial guidance, representation, and manuscript development for book projects with a focus on general interest non-fiction for the adult market, particularly reference, science, health, crime, biography, women's issues, current events, history and politics. They do accept unsolicited manuscripts which should include a proposal, outline and sample chapter (guidelines available upon request).

District of Columbia

Goldfarb and Graybill Law Offices
1501 M St., NW 202-466-3030
Washington, DC 20005 Fax: 202-293-3187
Email: rglawlit@aol.com

A large part of the firm's work is book, television and movie agentry. Manuscripts are accepted on an exclusive basis only and they try to respond within 6-8 weeks. They want to know if the material has been seen and rejected by any other agents or publishers. Any writer may submit a proposal by sending it to the address above. An SASE is required.

Literary and Creative Artists Agency, Inc.
3543 Albemarie St., N.W. 202-362-4688
Washington, DC 20008 Fax: 202-362-8875
www.lcadc.com

The agency considers general non-fiction by credentialed authors and both literary and commercial fiction. Send query letter with a synopsis or outline, 3 sample chapters, and an author biography, including publication and representation history. Include SASE. Unsolicited manuscripts are not accepted. If a full manuscript is requested, allow review period of two weeks.

Florida

The Westchester Literary Agency, Inc.
2533 Egret Lake Dr. 561-642-2908
West Palm Beach, FL 33413 Fax: 561-439-2228

Most genres of fiction and non-fiction are acceptable. Preference for fiction is for mainstream/literary but important genres that approach mainstream appeal will be considered. Protocol Sheets for preparing and submitting manuscripts are available at no cost, but an SASE is required.

Georgia

The Knight Agency
2407 Matthews St. 404-816-9620
Atlanta, GA 30319 Fax: 404-237-3439

Email: Deidre@aol.com
www.knightagency.net

No unsolicited manuscripts are accepted. For fiction send query letter, synopsis or outline (no more than 3 pages), the first three chapters of your completed manuscript, and an SASE. For non-fiction, send the same as for fiction, but add a bibliography and a summary of your qualifications.

Talent Source Agency
107 East Hall St.
P.O. Box 14120 912-232-9390
Savannah, GA 31416 Fax: 912-232-8213
www.talentsource.com

Work handled includes feature film, all types, especially character driven dramas, comedies, and children's films. Submit query letter with synopsis and SASE. Allow 4-6 weeks for responses.

Illinois

Jane Jordan Browne
Multimedia Product Development, Inc.
410 South Michigan Ave., Suite 724 312-922-3063
Chicago, IL 60605 Fax: 312-922-1905
www.mpdinc.net

Submit a 1-3 page query letter along with an SASE. No unsolicited materials are accepted. The agency is interested in commercial, overnight sellers in the areas of mainstream fiction and non-fiction. For fiction: mainstream, women's fiction, mystery/suspense, romances and thrillers. For non-fiction: biography, business, current events, gardening, health/medicine, how-to, humor, parenting, pop culture, psychology, reference, science, and true crime.

Maryland

The Sagalyn Literary Agency
7201 Wisconsin Ave., Suite 675 301-718-6440
Bethesda, MD 20814 Fax: 301-718-6444
www.sagalyn.com

This agency asks that people who are submitting send a query letter first and be sure to include an SASE. They will only accept submissions through the mail. They handle adult fiction and non-fiction.

Massachusetts

The Doe Coover Agency
P.O. Box 668 781-721-6000
Winchester, MA 01890 Fax: 781-721-6727

No unsolicited manuscripts are accepted. Send query letter and sample manuscript along with an SASE. The agency handles non-fiction and fiction, specializing in literary and commercial fiction, social sciences, journalism, science, biography, and cookbooks.

The Palmer & Dodge Agency
One Beacon St. 617-573-0100
Boston, MA 02108 Fax: 617-227-4420

This agency handles general non-fiction and fiction for adults, film and television rights for books and life stories. No screenplays or treatments. No unsolicited manuscripts are accepted. Send query letter first with outline, sample chapter, author biography and SASE.

Alison J. Picard
Literary Agent
P.O. Box 2000
Cotuit, MA 02635 508-477-7192

This agent represents mainstream and literary fiction, contemporary and historical romances, non-fiction, mysteries and thrillers, juvenile and young adult books. Preferences are toward commercial non-fiction, romances, and mysteries/suspense/thrillers. Submit query letter with SASE.

Helen Rees Literary Agency
123 N. Washington St., 5th Floor
Boston, MA 02114 617-723-5232
Email: wwhelen@aol.com

This agency handles business books, literary fiction, biography, women's issues and current political issues. Do not submit short stories, poetry, cookbooks, children's literature, science fiction or sports. Submit query letter with a brief outline and an SASE.

Michigan

Joseph S. Ajlouny
Literary Agent-Attorney at Law
29205 Greening Blvd. 810-932-0090
Farmington Hills, MI 48334-2945 Fax: 810-932-8763

This agency specializes in humor (joke books), and also selectively represents book length projects in the areas of popular culture, popular reference, and other light non-fiction topics. They do not accept novels, poetry, children's stories, articles or screenplays. Submissions via regular mail should include a cover letter; a brief biography of the author; an outline, table of contents or other description of the scope and organization of the book; sample illustrations if any; and an explanation of why your book is salable. Please address all correspondence to Gwen Foss, editor, and allow up to two months for a reply.

Minnesota

The Lazear Agency
Editorial Board
860 Washington Ave., N, Suite 660   612-332-8640
Minneapolis, MN 55401   Fax: 612-332-4648

This is a full service agency assisting clients in all phases of the publication process. They handle fiction and non-fiction. Submit a 1-2 page query letter, including a synopsis of the work you would like considered, and any relevant writing experience, such as previously published works along with an SASE. Allow 4-6 weeks for a response.

Sebastian Agency
172 Sixth St. E, Suite 2005   651-224-6670
St. Paul, MN 55101   Fax: 651-224-6855
www.sebastianagency.com

No new fiction authors are being accepted at this time. New clients, mainly on referral, are being accepted in the areas of business, biographies (no family memoirs), consumer reference, health/nutrition, psychology/ self-help, gift/inspirational, popular culture; social issues/current affairs, humor, and sports. Send query explaining project, telling about the author and why you are doing this book. Submit proposal, outline or synopsis and sample chapter with SASE.

New Jersey

Reid Boates Literary Agency
274 Cooks Crossroad   908-730-8523
Pittstown, NJ 08867   Fax: 908-730-8931
Email: boatesliterary@att.net

This agency deals with non-fiction, adult general interest areas such as biography and autobiography, investigative journalism, current affairs, spirituality and personal enrichment, health and self-help. Query first with SASE.

March Tenth, Inc.
4 Myrtle St.   201-387-6551
Haworth, NJ 07641   Fax: 201-387-6552

The subjects this agency is most interested in representing are popular culture, music, general non-fiction, biography, and fiction. Submit a query letter describing the project in a concise way, state credentials, and include an SASE.

Puddingstone Literary, Authors' Agents
11 Mabro Dr.
Denville, NJ 07834   973-366-3622

This agency handles general trade and mass market fiction and non-fiction, motion picture scripts and teleplays. Submit query letter first with SASE. If interested, you will be notified to send outline and sample chapters.

New York

Michael Amato Agency
1650 Broadway   212-247-4456/4457
New York, NY 10019   Fax: 212-664-0641

This agency handles movie and television scripts. Most new clients are through recommendations but queries are welcome. Material will not be returned.

Marcia Amsterdam Agency
41 West 82nd St.
New York, NY 10024   212-873-4945

Mostly fiction, mainstream non-fiction, young adult, television and movie scripts are handled by this agency. Submit query letter with an SASE. No unsolicited manuscripts are accepted.

Malaga Baldi Literary Agency
201 W. 84 St., Suite 3-C   212-579-5075
New York, NY 10024   Fax: 212-579-5078
Email: mbaldi@aol.com

This agency handles literary fiction and non-fiction, no children or young adult. No unsolicited manuscripts or phone calls, submit query letter with an SASE. Allow 10 weeks minimum for response.

Pam Bernstein & Associates Inc.
790 Madison Ave.   212-288-1700
New York, NY 10021   Fax: 212-288-3054
Email: pbernassoc@aol.com

A query letter (not a full manuscript) with an SASE is requested as a first step. If interested in further materials, such as sample chapters or an entire manuscript, they will contact the author. They handle fiction and non-fiction.

Georges Borchardt, Inc.
Literary Agency
136 West 57th St.   212-753-5785
New York, NY 10022   Fax: 212-838-6518

This agency does not consider unsolicited manuscripts, but does consider new writers who come recommended by authors and/or editors whom they know and trust. They handle literary fiction and high quality non-fiction.

Brandt & Hochman Literary Agents, Inc.
1501 Broadway   212-840-5760
New York, NY 10036   Fax: 212-840-5776

The agency does not accept unsolicited manuscripts, but they will respond to a letter about the author and the work in question. They are a general literary agency, but do not handle poetry or film scripts.

Patricia Breinin Literary Services
212 Inwood Rd.
Scarsdale, NY 10583   914-472-6417

The Service handles quality fiction and non-fiction (no children or young adult books). They prefer to have new clients referred to them by publishers, editors, or authors known to the agent.

Marie Brown Associates
412 W 154 St.   212-939-9725
New York, NY 10032   Fax: 212-939-9728
Email: mbrownlit@aol.com

Unsolicited query letters are accepted, (does not review unsolicited manuscripts), multiple submissions, encourages unpublished/unproduced writers, enclose an SASE for all correspondence. They specialize in commercial fiction, contemporary fiction, erotica, gay/lesbian fiction, juveniles picture books and 6-8 year old and 9-12 year old literary fiction, mainstream fiction, novella, novel length fiction, poetry collections, professional books, quality fiction, self-help, screen plays, short stories, short story collections, trade non-fiction, translations, women's fiction, young adult fiction and non-fiction.

Knox Burger Associates, Ltd.
425 Madison Ave.   212-759-8600
New York, NY 10012   Fax: 212-759-9428

Fiction and non-fiction, excluding romance, fantasy, science fiction, poetry and juvenile are handled by this agency. No phone queries or unsolicited manuscripts are accepted. They will consider and respond to letters of inquiry, provided they are accompanied by an SASE.

Sheree Bykofsky Associates, Inc.
16 W 36th St., 13th Floor.
New York, NY 10018   212-244-4144
www.shereebee.com

Subjects and categories the agent is most enthusiastic about representing include popular reference, adult non-fiction, and quality fiction. Submit a query letter with an SASE.

Clausen, Mays & Tahan Literary Agency
249 W 34th St.   212-239-4343
New York, NY 10001   Fax: 212-239-5248
Email: cmtassist@aol.com

This agency handles mostly non-fiction: memoirs, biography, true stories, medical, health and nutrition, psychology, how-to, financial, women's issues, spirituality, true crime, fashion/beauty, style, and humor. Submit a query letter or proposal, including an SASE.

Don Congdon Associates, inc.
156 Fifth Ave., Suite 625   212-645-1229
New York, NY 10010-7002   Fax: 212-727-2688
Email: dca@doncongdon.com

Submit a query letter with an SASE as a first step. The agency handles fiction and non-fiction.

Richard Curtis Associates, Inc.
Authors' Representatives
171 East 74th St.   212-772-7363
New York, NY 10021   Fax: 212-772-7393
www.curtisagency.com

Authors are requested to send a query letter with an SASE for a reply. Do not send manuscripts or outlines until or unless requested to do so. The agency handles popular fiction and non-fiction in all fields.

Elaine Davie Literary Agency
620 Park Ave.
Rochester, NY 14607 716-442-0830
Specializes in popular commercial fiction. Looking for well written novels on a wide variety of topics, including women's fiction, particularly romance. Send the first 80-100 pages and be sure to include a synopsis. To confirm receipt of your manuscript, enclose a stamped, self addressed postcard (allow a few weeks for the return of your postcard). Also include an SASE with proper postage and an envelope large enough to accommodate your manuscript.

Donadio & Olson Inc.
Literary Representatives
121 West 27th St., Suite 704 212-691-8077
New York, NY 10001 Fax: 212-633-2837
www.donadioandolson.com
No unsolicited manuscripts are accepted. The agency handles fiction and non-fiction. Submit a query letter with an SASE.

Nicholas Ellison, Inc.
5 Fifth Ave. 212-206-6050
New York, NY 10003 Fax: 212-463-8718
www.greenburger.com
No unsolicited manuscripts will be accepted. Submit query first and include sample chapters. Fiction and non-fiction (all subjects) are accepted.

Ann Elmo Agency, Inc.
60 East 42nd St. 212-661-2880/2881
New York, NY 10165 Fax: 212-661-2883
The Ann Elmo Agency handles non-fiction and fiction (romance, suspense and juvenile). No unsolicited manuscripts are accepted. Submit query letter with an SASE.

Farber Literary Agency
14 East 75th St., Apt #2 212-861-7075
New York, NY 10021 Fax: 212-861-7076
Email: farberlit@aol.com
The agency handles both fiction and non-fiction, including young adult and children's works. They also handle stage plays. Prospective clients should submit a proposal and approximately three chapters and should include an SASE if the material is to be returned.

Samuel French, Inc.
45 West 25th St. 212-206-8990
New York, NY 10010 Fax: 212-206-1429
www.samuelfrench.com
The agency handles stage plays for publication and representation. A variety of subject areas are considered such as comedy, contemporary issues, crime, ethnic, experimental, fantasy, horror, mystery, religious, and thrillers. Submit query or manuscript with an SASE.

Max Gartenberg, Literary Agent
521 Fifth Ave., Suite 1700 212-292-4354
New York, NY 10175 Fax: 212-535-5033
Email: gartenbook@att.net
This agent handles adult fiction and non-fiction. Unsolicited manuscripts are not accepted. Writers must send a query letter first, enclosing an SASE and receive an explicit invitation to submit material.

Gelfman Schneider Literary Agents, Inc.
250 West 57th St. 212-245-1993
New York, NY 10107 Fax: 212-245-8678
Email: mail@gelfmanschneider.com
This agency does not accept unsolicited manuscripts. Anyone seeking representation should send a query letter detailing the work they have written and mention any previous publishing experience. The agency specializes in literary and mystery novels as well as business and political non-fiction. They do not typically represent science fiction, romance, or children's books.

Richard Henshaw Group
Authors Representatives
127 W. 24th St. 212-414-1172
New York, NY 10011 Fax: 212-417-5208
Email: RHGAGENTS@aol.com
www.richh.addr.com
Areas of specialty are mainstream novels and genre fiction including mystery, thriller, suspense, crime, science fiction, fantasy, horror, historical, young adult and literary. In non-fiction, the group is open to a wide variety of areas including popular reference, business, popular science, parenting, health, humor, popular culture, how-to, celebrity biography, and true crime. Writers of fiction should submit a query letter and the opening 50 pages, along with an SASE. Writers of non-fiction should send a query letter and an SASE. Any writer may send a query letter to the Email address, provided the letter does not exceed one page.

The Jeff Herman Agency, Inc.
332 Bleecker St. 212-941-0540
New York, NY 10014 Fax: 212-941-0614
www.jeffherman.com
Subjects handled include all areas of commercial non-fiction, with particular interest shown in business, investigative, spiritual, self-help, history, humor, popular culture, and computers. Submit a query letter and include an SASE.

Susan Herner Rights Agency, Inc.
P.O. Box 303 914-725-8967
Scarsdale, NY 10583 Fax: 914-725-8769
Twosues@worldnet.att.net
The agency handles adult fiction and non-fiction. No unsolicited manuscripts are accepted. Submit query letter with first three chapters along with an SASE.

International Creative Management, Inc.
40 West 57th St. 212-556-5600
New York, NY 10019 Fax: 212-556-5665
www.icmtalent.com
This agency handles film and television rights. Send query letter briefly describing yourself and the project. You may include a two page outline of your work, or enclose the first one or two pages. Also enclose an SASE and allow one or two months for a response.

IMG Literary
22 East 71st St. 212-772-8900
New York, NY 10021 Fax: 212-772-2617
www.imgworld.com
IMG represents a wide range of fiction and non-fiction titles. Potential authors must send in a query letter with an SASE before a manuscript will be reviewed.

Janklow & Nesbit Associates
598 Madison Ave. 212-421-1700
New York, NY 10022 Fax: 212-980-3671
At this time, the agency is only taking work referred to them by authors known to Janklow & Nesbit.

Harvey Klinger, Inc.
301 West 53rd St. 212-581-7068
New York, NY 10019 Fax: 212-315-3823
www.harveyklinger.com
Type of work handled includes broad based commercial fiction and non-fiction. Submit a query letter first and include an SASE. Queries by fax are not accepted.

Triden Media Group
Ellen Levine Literary Agency, Inc.
15 East 26th St., Suite 1801 212-889-0620
New York, NY 10010-1505 Fax: 212-725-4501
www.ellenlevineagency.com
Submit a query letter with an SASE. This agency handles literary and commercial fiction and non-fiction, and some children's books.

Levine Greenberg Literary Agency
307 Seventh Ave., Suite 1906 212-337-0934
New York, NY 10001 Fax: 212-337-0948
Email: LevineJA@aol.com
www.levinegreenberg.com
For non-fiction books send proposal including contents, summary, and information about the author. For novels, send a 50 page excerpt, plus a synopsis of no more than 10 pages. Enclose an SASE to have material returned. For more complete instructions, request a copy of "The JLC Kit," which contains information about the agency, including services, practices, and book proposals.

The Literary Group International
270 Lafayette St., Suite 1505 212-274-1616
New York, NY 10012 Fax: 212-274-9876
www.theliterarygroup.com
This agency prefers that authors submit a complete novel and for non-fiction projects a thorough proposal is sufficient. All submissions require an SASE. The Literary Group is a full service agency and handles all general trade titles.

Nancy Love Literary Agency
250 East 65th St., Suite 4A 212-980-3499
New York, NY 10021 Fax: 212-308-6405
For novels submit a query letter and synopsis; for non-fiction submit a query letter and proposal. This agency is interested in: fiction - mysteries, thrillers, multi-cultural; non-fiction - current affairs, biography, health, and medicine (including alternative), true crime, psychology, self-help, social issues, women's issues, nature, spiritual and inspirational.

Donald Maass Literary Agency
160 W. 95th St., Suite B   212-866-8200
New York, NY 10025   Fax: 212-866-8181
The Donald Maass literary agency specializes in handling commercial novels, with an emphasis on genre fiction; mystery, suspense, science fiction, fantasy, and romance. For initial contact, send a typed, one page query letter, with an SASE for reply.

Manus & Associates Literary Agency, Inc.
445 Park Ave.   212-644-8020
New York, NY 10022   Fax: 212-644-3374
www.manuslit.com
Prospective clients should send a query letter and, if they wish, sample chapters, with an SASE for a reply. Never submit a full manuscript unsolicited. The agency handles both fiction and non-fiction, particularly mystery/thrillers, true crime, and commercial fiction.

Helen Merril Ltd.
295 Lafeyette St., Suite 915   212-226-5015
New York, NY 10012   Fax: 212-226-5079
This agency handles fiction, non-fiction and theater. No unsolicited manuscripts accepted. Submit query letter with resume and one page synopsis. Include an SASE for a reply.

Henry Morrison Inc.
P.O. Box 235   914-666-3500
Bedford Hills, NY 10507   Fax: 914-241-7846
This agency represents a large range of books, from international thrillers to general novels, women's fiction, mystery and science fiction, and the occasional non-fiction book on contemporary subjects. Prospective clients should write a letter outlining in some detail what the book is about and include an SASE.

Ruth Nathan
141 E. 33rd St.
New York, NY 10016   Phone/Fax: 212-889-2696
This agent handles mostly fiction and specializes in illustrated books, fine art, decorative art, theater, film, show business, biography, and true crime. No unsolicited manuscripts are accepted. Submit query letter with an SASE.

Fifi Oscard Agency, Ltd.
110 West 40th St., 17th Floor   212-764-1100
New York, NY 10018   Fax: 212-840-5019
This agency covers all areas of fiction and non-fiction. Do not send unsolicited manuscripts. Submit a query letter with an SASE.

The Richard Parks Agency
138 East 16th St., #58
New York, NY 10003   212-254-9067
This agency handles general trade fiction and non-fiction. Fiction is read only by referral. Writers of non-fiction book proposals may submit a query letter provided that it is accompanied by an SASE. Unsolicited manuscripts and fax queries are not accepted.

Perkins Associates
5800 Arlington Ave.   718-543-5344
Riverdale, NY 10471   212-304-1602
   Fax: 718-543-5355
   Fax: 212-569-8188
Perkins Associates specializes in horror, dark thrillers, literary fiction, pop culture, science fiction, fantasy, mysteries, history, and journalistic non-fiction. Submit query or manuscript and include an SASE. Reports immediately on queries, 8-12 weeks on manuscripts.

Arthur Pine Associates, Inc.
250 West 57th St., Suite 417   212-265-7330
New York, NY 10019   Fax: 212-265-4650
Email: info@arthurpine.com
Represents authors in all fields (book publishing, motion pictures, and TV production, etc.). No unsolicited manuscripts are accepted, nor are manuscripts that have previously been submitted to other agencies or simultaneous submissions. A proposal of the manuscript with SASE should be sent first.

Aaron Priest Literary Agency
708 Third Ave., 23rd Floor   212-818-0344
New York, NY 10017   Fax: 212-573-9417
Submit query letter and proposal/synopsis along with an SASE. The agency handles mainstream fiction and some non-fiction. Do not submit screenplays, plays, or poetry.

RLR Associates, Ltd.
7 West 51st St.   212-541-8641
New York, NY 10019   Fax: 212-262-7084

www.rlrassociates.net
RLR handles a broad range of fiction and non-fiction. The agency is not taking new children's book clients. Submit query letter first with an SASE.

The Robbins Office, Inc.
405 Park Ave.   212-223-0790
New York, NY 10022   Fax: 212-223-2535
The type of work handled by this agency include general, literary fiction and non-fiction, television and motion picture rights. No unsolicited manuscripts, query first by referral only; submit proposal or outline (non-fiction) or outline and sample chapters (fiction).

Russel & Volkening, Inc.
50 West 29th St., Apt. 7E   212-684-6050
New York, NY 10001   Fax: 212-889-3026
Any writer who would like to submit information about a project should do so with a query letter describing the project and information about the author, along with an SASE. This agency handles literary fiction, non-fiction, and children's books.

Victoria Sanders Literary Agency
241 Avenue of the Americas, Suite 11H   212-633-8811
New York, NY 10014   Fax: 212-633-0525
www.victoriasanders.com
The agency handles fiction, both literary and commercial, African American, Latino and Asian. Of special interest: women's biography, history, autobiography, psychology, women's studies, gay studies, and politics. Submit query letter first along with an SASE.

Susan Schulman Literary Agency
454 West 44th St.   212-713-1633
New York, NY 10036   Fax: 212-581-8830
www.susanschulmanagency.com
Submit a query letter with an SASE. This agency specializes in non-fiction books by and about women and family issues. Emphasis on popular psychology, self-help, wisdom, spirituality, alternative spirituality and the social sciences, literary memoir, and biography.

The Shepard Agency
Pawlings Savings Bank
Route 22   914-279-2900
Brewster, NY 10509   Fax: 914-279-3239
http://home.mindspring.com/~shepardagcy
The Sheppard Agency specializes in adult, children, general trade fiction and non-fiction, professional, reference and business titles. Submit query letter first, including an SASE.

Spectrum Literary Agency
320 Central Park W., Suite D   212-362-4323
New York, NY 10025   Fax: 212-362-4562
www.spectrumliteraryagency.com
Submit query letter first with an SASE. The agency handles commercial fiction and non-fiction.

Spieler Agency
154 West 57th St., Room 135   212-757-4439
New York, NY 10019   Fax: 212-233-2019
Spielerlit@aol.com
This agency handles non-fiction, most notably in the areas of history, social issues, the environment, economics and business; and literary fiction. Reports on queries in two weeks, reports on manuscripts in five weeks. Manuscripts without an SASE or sufficient money to cover return postage will not be returned.

Wieser & Wieser Inc.
25 East 21st St.   212-260-0860
New York, NY 10010   Fax: 212-505-7186
Submit query first with outline and sample chapters along with an SASE. The agency specializes in trade and mass market adult fiction and non-fiction books.

Witherspoon Associates
235 East 31st St.   212-889-8626
New York, NY 10016   Fax: 212-595-5843
This agency deals in both fiction and non-fiction. Submit query letter first, including an SASE.

Ann Wright Representatives
165 46th St.   212-764-6770
New York, NY 10036-2501   Fax: 212-764-5125
Clients include screen writers, authors, television writers, and playwrights. Novels and movie scripts with themes that have film potential are handled. Writers should send letter with SASE giving information about themselves and their material. If the agency is interested in your work, you will receive a response.

Writers House Inc.
21 West 26th St.   212-685-2400
New York, NY 10010   Fax: 212-685-1781

Writers House is interested in trade books of all types, fiction and non-fiction. Unsolicited manuscripts are accepted, but you must first submit a query letter with an SASE.

Susan Zeckendorf Associates, Inc.
171 West 57th St., Suite 118
New York, NY 10010   212-245-2928

Type of material handled includes literary fiction, commercial fiction, thrillers, mysteries, and women's fiction. Non-fiction areas are science, music, biography, self-help, sports, parenting, and psychology. Send a brief query letter with an SASE.

Oregon

First Books, Inc.
6750 SW Franklin St., Suite A   503-968-6777
Portland, OR 97223   Fax: 503-968-6779
www.firstbooks.com

First Books will accept unsolicited manuscripts for book length fiction and non-fiction for adults and children. Be sure to include SASE with sufficient postage.

Pennsylvania

Toad Hall, Inc.
Sharon Jarvis & Company Literary Agency
R.R. 2, Box 16B   570-869-2942
Laceyville, PA 18623   Fax: 570-869-1031
Email: toad-hall@Prodigy.com
www.laceyville.com/Toad-Hall

Submit a query letter describing yourself and your project. Include a synopsis or a table of contents of not more than three pages, a biography or curriculum vitae, the length of the book, and any pertinent information. They are currently interested in popular non-fiction of all types, and are also interested in New Age, occult, paranormal, UFO's, etc.

Texas

DHS Literary, Inc.
2528 Elm St., Suite 350   214-363-4422
Dallas, TX 75206   Fax: 214-363-4423
www.dhsliterary.com

DHS offers representation to a broad range of fiction and non-fiction literary properties. The agency handles work by published and unpublished writers. It seeks to maintain a diverse mix of projects, including literary and mainstream fiction; category fiction such as mystery, historical, horror and romance; as well as quality commercial non-fiction. Submit query letter with SASE. You may also request a copy of the agency's submission guidelines.

The Fogleman Literary Agency
7515 Greenville Ave., Suite 712
                                         214-361-9956

Dallas, TX 75231   Fax: 214-361-9553
www.fogleman.com

This agency is interested in women's fiction (both category and mainstream, including romance and mysteries), popular business, psychological self-help; non-fiction geared for the women's market; political biography; author biography. Submit query letter or call. If calling, be prepared to give a short synopsis of your book, including what category it falls into, and the word count.

Utah

Executive Excellence   800-304-9782
1366 East 1120 South   801-375-4060
Provo, UT 84606   Fax: 801-377-5960
www.eep.com

The agency works with authors of non-fiction trade books in the areas of business, management, and personal development/self-help. The agency also offers assisted self-publishing services, including editorial, design, and printing. Please query by phone, fax, or letter first. After initial query, submit outline/proposal with approximately 20-40 pages of sample material.

Washington

The Catalog
Literary Agency & Book Publicity
P.O. Box 2964
Vancouver, WA 98668   360-694-8531

The agency is currently looking for manuscripts in almost all subjects, especially business, health, psychology, money, science, how-to, self help and women's interest. Also considered are text books, professional books, juvenile fiction and non-fiction, and adult mainstream fiction. Query with an outline, sample chapters, and an SASE.

Levant & Wales Literary Agency, Inc.
108 Hayes St.   206-284-7114
Seattle, WA 98109   Fax: 206-284-0190

This agency is particularly interested in works of narrative non-fiction, often called "creative non-fiction" or "literary journalism", especially if the work espouses a progressive cultural or political view, projects a new voice, or, simply shares an important, compelling story. The agency looks for talented story tellers in fiction or non-fiction with a special interest in writers from the northwest, Alaska, the West Coast, and Pacific Rim countries. Send a query letter, including a brief description of the book project, as well as a writing sample from the project. Include an SASE.

Wisconsin

Daniel P. King Literary Agent
5125 North Cumberland Blvd.
Whitefish Bay, WI 53217   414-964-2903
                                    Fax: 414-964-6860

This agency seeks novel, novellas, short stories, story collections, scripts and non-fiction materials from published authors. Special interests in fiction are mystery, crime, science fiction romance, and mainstream. Submit a query letter with a synopsis, two chapters, and the author's vitae including previous publication credits. Include SASE.

Writer's Organizations

Writing can be a lonely and isolating profession. Writer's organizations are there to assist you with networking and to provide you with some added inspiration when you most need it. Membership entitles you to a variety of services such as newsletters, job information, workshops, and other types of support services. Associations typically focus on a specific genre (i.e. mystery writing, science writing), and membership fees or dues are usually required. The list that follows provides information on a variety of organizations to get you started on finding your place among fellow writers.

American Medical Writers Association (AMWA)
40 W. Gude Dr., Suite 101   301-294-5303
Rockville, MD 20850   Fax: 301-294-9006
Email: amwa@amwa.org

Since 1940, AMWA has served an interdisciplinary membership of medical writers, editors, public relations specialists, audiovisual experts, and other professionals with varied roles in biocommunications. Benefits of membership in AMWA include: professional identification as a communicator; meetings, workshops, and Core Curriculum program; and professional development. Membership fee is $75.

American Society of Journalists and Authors, Inc. (ASJA)
1501 Broadway, Suite 302   212-997-0947
New York, NY 10036   Fax: 212-768-7414
www.asja.org

ASJA membership is open only to professional freelance writers of non-fiction for general audiences, produced over a substantial period of time. ASJA provides its members with an array of professional supports including: monthly newsletter, membership directory, and an ongoing survey of payment rates. A $25 application fee will be applied to the $100 initiation fee upon acceptance. Annual membership dues are $165.

American Translators Association (ATA)
225 Reinekers Lane, Suite 590   703-683-6100
Alexandria, VA 22314   Fax: 703-683-6122
www.atanet.org

The ATA is the largest professional association of translators and interpreters in the US. Their primary goals include fostering and supporting professional development for translators and interpreters and promoting the translation profession. ATA membership is open to anyone with an interest in translation as a profession or as a scholarly pursuit. Benefits of membership include: networking opportunities, subscription to the ATA Chronicle, job information, and a copy of the ATA Membership Directory. Membership fees are $50 for students, $95 for Associate Member, $120 for Institutional Membership, and $175 for Corporate Membership.

The Associated Writing Programs (AWP)
Tallwood House, Mail Stop 1E3
George Mason University   703-993-4301
Fairfax, VA 22030   Fax: 703-993-4302
Email: awp@gmu.edu
www.awpwriter.org

For 29 years, writers and teachers have joined the AWP for community and support, for information and inspiration, for contacts and new ideas. The $50 membership fee includes six issues of AWP Chronicle, seven issues of AWP Job List, a 33% discount to enter Award Series, and an 18% discount on annual conferences.

The Authors Guild, Inc.
31 East 28th St., 10th Floor   212-563-5904
New York, NY 10016   Fax: 212-564-8363
www.authorsguild.org

The Authors Guild is the nation's oldest, largest, and most prestigious professional society of published authors. A few benefits of membership include the quarterly Bulletin; symposia and seminars; online services; business advice on problems that arise with publishers, agents, booksellers, or editors, as well as legal and accounting advice. There is no initiation fee. First year dues are $90. After the first year of membership the dues are based on an individual's annual writing income.

The Dramatists Guild, Inc.
1501 Broadway, Suite 701   212-398-9366
New York, NY 10036-3909   Fax: 212-944-0420
www.dramaguild.com

The Guild works to protect and promote the professional interests and rights of writers of dramatic and musical works. Membership privileges include Dramatists Guild production contracts, business advice, marketing information, royalty collection, publications, free Guild symposia, and access to health and dental insurance programs. Categories of membership and dues are: Active members who have had a theater production, $125; Associate members are all other theater writers, $75; Estate members services are available to the estate of any playwright, composer, bookwriter, or lyricist, $125; Student members must be currently enrolled in an accredited writing degree program, $35.

Editorial Freelancers Association (EFA)   866-929-5400 (toll free)
71 West 23rd St., Suite 1504   212-929-5400
New York, NY 10010   Fax: 212-929-5439
www.the-efa.org

Any full or part time freelancer may apply for membership. All EFA members receive: bimonthly newsletter, annual membership directory, Business Practices Survey; admission to all meetings and events; reduced tuition for courses; and eligibility for medical, dental, and disability insurance. Annual membership is $95 for resident members living in the greater New York City metropolitan area, and $75 for non-resident members.

Educational Writers Association (EWA)
2122 P St., NW, #201   202-452-9830
Washington, DC 20037   Fax: 202-452-9837
Email: EWAoffice@aol.com
http://www.ewa.org

Members include over 800 education reporters from newspapers, television and radio; and education writers and public information officers from organizations, school districts and colleges. Membership brings free copies of all EWA publications, the bimonthly newsletter Education Reporter, useful referral and source information by phone, Email, and through mailings, and study opportunities. Annual membership fees are $50.

Horror Writers Association (HWA)
P.O. Box 50577
Palo Alto, CA 94303
http://www.horror.org

The HWA is devoted to helping writers at every point in their career. Whether you're an aspiring writer or trying to make that first sale, or a seasoned novelist with a dozen books to your name, the HWA has something for you. Benefits include publicity information, agent database, networking, regional chapters, Internet connections, grievance committee and worldwide organizations. Annual dues are $55.

International Association of Crime Writers (IACW)
(North American Branch)
JAF Box 1500
New York, NY 10116   Phone/Fax: 212-243-8966
Email: mfrisque@apc.org

IACW is an organization of professional published writers whose primary goal is to promote communication among writers of all nationalities and to promote crime writing as an influential and significant art form. IACW sponsors a number of conferences and an annual celebration. The North American branch publishes a newsletter, sponsors social events, and has created several anthologies of international crime writing. Membership dues are $50.

Media Communications Association International
1000 Executive Pkwy, #220   314-514-9995
St. Louis, MO 63141   Fax: 314-576-7989
www.mca-i.org

MCA-I is the only association dedicated to serving the needs of video professionals in nonbroadcast video production. The association has worked to advance the video profession and to promote the growth and quality of video related media through providing relevant member services. Membership offers you: career advancement, networking, special services, discounts, industry leadership, and periodicals. Annual fee is $150.

The International Women's Writing Guild
Box 810, Gracie Station   212-737-7536
New York, NY 10028   Fax: 212-737-9469
Email: iwwg@iwwg.com
http://www.iwwg.com

The Guild is a worldwide nonprofit organization open to all women, regardless of portfolio, which offers its members services including: annual subscription to NETWORK newsletter, membership listing, list of 35 agents and other writing services, health plans, opportunities to participate in regional and national writing conferences, and various online services. Annual dues are $35.

Mystery Writers of America
17 East 47th St.   212-888-8171
New York, NY 10017   Fax: 212-888-8107
www.mysterywriters.org

This is a nonprofit professional organization of mystery and crime writers in all categories. Benefits of membership include: mystery writing courses, the Edgar Allan Poe Awards Banquet, monthly meetings, local bulletins, the Third Degree, which is published 10 times a year, and the MWA Anthology, which is published annually. There is no initiation fee and dues for all categories of memberships are $65 per year.

National Association of Science Writers (NASW)
P.O. Box 890   304-754-5077
Hedgesville, WV 25427   Fax: 304-754-5076
www.nasw.org

The NASW sponsors directly or works closely with regional science writing groups and around the country where members gather for workshops, meetings, and field trips. Members receive the newsletter, ScienceWriters, which provides timely, incisive reports on professional issues. To join, you must show evidence of science writing ability and be sponsored by at least two active NASW members. Membership dues are $15 for Student, $60 for Associate, and $60 for Active membership.

The National League of American Pen Women, Inc.
Pen Arts Building
1300 17th St.
Washington, DC 20036-1973   202-785-1997
www.americanpenwomen.org

The League offers its members association with creative professional women, workshops, discussion groups and lectures. The Pen Woman, the official publication of The League, is published six times a year and features news, accomplishments, and works of its members. Membership requires the submission of at least three sample chapters and proof of sale. Authors who are self published (not vanity published) shall submit copies to be evaluated by the Branch.

The National Writers Association
3140 S. Peoria St., #295PMB   303-841-0246
Aurora, CO 80014   Fax: 303-841-0247
www.nationalwriters.com

It doesn't matter if you're a new writer needing to know proper manuscript format, or a professional needing contract suggestions and assistance, the Association offers help with searching out competent and reliable agents, assistance in writing a good synopsis, and professional advice about self publishing. Membership fees are $50 for General member and $60 for Professional member (credits required).

National Writers Union
(East Coast Office)
113 University Place, 6th Floor   212-254-0279
New York, NY 10003   Fax: 212-254-0673

(West Coast Office)
337 17th St., Suite 101   510-839-6092
Oakland, CA 94612   Fax: 510-839-6097
www.nwu.org

The National Writers Union is an innovative labor union committed to improving the working conditions of freelance writers through the collective strength of its members. The Union welcomes all writers whether you write for money or publication. Dues are based on one's annual writing income. The National Writers unions also has a Supporter's Circle open to individuals who are not writers, but advocate on their behalf.

The PEN American Center
568 Broadway   212-334-1660
New York, NY 10012-3225   Fax: 212-334-2181
www.pen.org

PEN American Center, the largest of the 124 centers worldwide that compose International PEN, is a membership association of prominent literary writers and editors. The 2,800 members are poets, playwrights, essayists, editors, and novelists, as well as literary translators and those agents who have made a substantial contribution to the literary community. Among the activities,

programs, and services are public literary events, literary awards, outreach projects, and assistance to writers in financial need. Members of American PEN are elected by the Membership Committee. Dues are paid annually.

Poets and Writers, Inc.
72 Spring St.   212-226-3586
New York, NY 10012   Fax: 212-226-3963
www.pw.org

Poets and Writers is a central source of practical information for the Literary community. Their Information Center keeps track of addresses for over 7,000 poets and fiction writers and compiles a Directory of American Poets and Fiction Writers. The Reading/Workshops Program provides matching fees for readings and workshops given by emerging and established writers. The Writers Exchange is a national program that introduces emerging writers to literary communities outside their home state. Poets and Writers is not a membership organization, and therefore, anyone can use their services.

Poetry Society of America (PSA)
15 Grammercy Park
New York, NY 10003   212-254-9628
www.poetrysociety.org

The PSA is the nation's oldest poetry organization reaching more people daily with poetry than any other literary organization. Membership is open to everyone. Members are entitled to: enter all PSA contests, discount admission to PSA readings, workshops, the PSA newsletter, program calendars and invitations to readings and events, discounts on book purchases, and vote in PSA elections. Membership fees are tax deductible and range from $25 Student, $40 Member, and can go as high as $1000.

Romance Writers of America (RWA)
3707 FM 1960 West, Suite 555   281-440-6885
Houston, TX 77068   Fax: 281-440-7510
www.rwanational.org

RWA is dedicated to promoting excellence in romantic fiction. General membership is open to all writers actively pursuing a career in romantic fiction. Associate membership is open to all editors, agents, booksellers, and other industry professionals. Published members are invited to join the Published Authors Network (PAN) for an additional $20 a year. Membership benefits include workshops; networking opportunities with authors, editors, agents and industry professionals; awards; and RWA publications. There is a $10 processing fee for new applicants and annual dues are $60.

Science-Fiction and Fantasy Writers of
America, Inc. (SFWA)
P.O. Box 877
Chestertown, MD 21620
www.sfwa.org

The SFWA has brought together the most successful and daring writers of speculative fiction throughout the world, and has grown in numbers and influence and is now recognized as one of the most effective nonprofit writers' organizations in existence. Over 1200 SF/Fantasy writers, artists, editors, and allied professionals are members. The SFWA Bulletin, published quarterly, is subscribed to by many non-members. Beginning writers might be particularly interested in its informative market reports and articles about the business of writing and selling science fiction and fantasy. Dues are collected annually.

Society of American Travel Writers
1500 Sunday Dr., Suite 102   919-861-5586
Raleigh, NC 27607   Fax: 919-787-4916
www.satw.org

The Society of American Travel Writers is a nonprofit, public service organization dedicated to serving the interest of the traveling public, to promote international understanding and good will, and to further promote unbiased, objective reporting of information on travel topics. Membership in the Society is by invitation. Applicants must be sponsored by two members. The initiation fee for Active members is $200 (yearly dues $120), for Associate members $400 (yearly dues $240). A nonrefundable $50 application fee will be applied toward the initiation fee of accepted members.

Society of Children's Book Writers and
Illustrators (SCBWI)
8721 Beverly Blvd.   323-782-1010
Los Angeles, CA 90048   Fax: 323-782-1892
www.scbwi.org

The SCBWI acts as a network for the exchange of knowledge between writers, illustrators, editors, publishers, agents, librarians, educators, bookstore personnel, and others involved with literature for young people. Membership is open to anyone with an active interest in children's literature. Membership dues are $50 per year.

Society of Professional Journalists (SPJ)
3909 N. Meridian St.   317-927-8000
Indianapolis, IN 46208   Fax: 317-920-4789

www.spj.org
SPJ membership offers many benefits, including: continuing professional education, career services and support, and journalism advocacy. Membership dues range from $33 to $85.

Washington Independent Writers (WIW)
220 Woodward Building
733 Fifteenth St., NW   202-737-9500
Washington, DC 20005   Fax: 202-638-7800
www.washwriter.org
WIW's membership includes recognized writers, writers with a growing number of credits and those who are just beginning their careers in the freelance profession. Membership benefits include: WIW's newsletter , the Independent Writer; the Job Bank; access to Small Groups based on areas of mutual interest; and the availability of a group health insurance plan and a legal services program. Dues are: Students-1yr $55 & 2yr $100; Dual-new members 1yr $160 & 2yr $285; renewing members-1yr $130 & 2yr $240; Full and Associate-new members 1yr $95 & 2yr $1700, current renewing members, 1yr $80 & 2yr $145.

Western Writers of America
209 E. Iowa
Cheyenne, WY 82009
www.westernwriters.org
Western Writers of America (WWA) is an association of professional writers dedicated to preserving and celebrating the heritage of the American West, past and present. For over 40 years, WWA has served both fiction and non-fiction writers recognized for their work in all types of books, periodicals, screenplays, and other media. To be eligible for membership in WWA, you must be published. A subscription to Roundup Magazine is included with membership dues or if you are interested in subscribing to the Roundup Magazine, the cost is six issues a year for $30.

Writers Guild of America-East
555 West 57th St.   212-767-7800
New York, NY 10019   Fax: 212-582-1909
www.wgaeast.org

Writers Guild Of America-West
7000 West 3rd St.
Los Angeles, CA 90048   323-951-4000
www.wga.org
Writers Guild of America is a labor union representing professional writers in motion pictures, television, and radio. Membership can be acquired only through the sale of literary material or employment for writing services in one of these areas. There is an initiation fee of $1,500 for new members, basic dues of $100 paid in quarterly installments of $25, and an assessment of 1-11/2 on earnings from the sale of material or from employment as a writer in motion pictures, television, or radio. The Guild also provides a registration service for literary material. Writers are advised to register their material before showing it to a producer or agent.

"Five of the best-selling books of this century were first rejected by more than a dozen publishers: Dr. Seuss's **And To Think That I Saw It On Mulberry Street** *(rejected by twenty-three publishers), Richard Hooker's* **M*A*S*H** *(rejected twenty-one times),* **Kon-Tiki***, by Thor Heyerdahl (twenty rejections)* **Jonathan Livingston Seagull***, by Richard Bach (eighteen rejections), and Patrick Dennis's* **Auntie Mame** *(rejected by seventeen publishers)."*

Source: *Ambition: How We Manage Success and Failure Throughout Our Lives*, Gilbert Brim, Basic Books, 1992

I Wanna Travel

Matthew Lesko, Information USA, Inc., 12081 Nebel Street, Rockville, MD 20852 • 1-800-955-7693 • www.lesko.com

I Wanna Travel

If your dream is to become an international jet setter, don't let a little problem like money stand in your way. The Federal government has over 60 programs devoted to travel within the U.S. and abroad, spending over 65 million dollars a year to send you packing. They will even pay to have foreign relatives come and study here. No matter if you are 16 or 65, there is something in these programs for everyone.

You can be like:

- Ryan Louis from California, a Fulbright fellow who conducted research in biochemistry in Japan.
- Mark Door, who conducted workshops in criminal law in Tirana, Albania.
- AmeriCorps members that restored a polluted swamp into a natural lake.
- Laura DeLuca herded cattle and worked on crops in Tanzania.
- Rudolph Ware, who studied Lived Histories of Islamic Education and the State in Senegal.
- Laurel Anderson, who cut marks as evidence of pre-Columbia human sacrifice and postmortem bone modification on the North Coast of Peru.
- Dwayne Ball, who spent 10 weeks in Portugal lecturing.
- An American Fulbrighter, who studied molecular biology in Morocco.
- Cowboy artists from the Western Folklife Center of Elko, NV who shared their lore at a festival in Melbourne, Australia with a grant from the National Endowment for the Arts.
- Nancy Friese of Cranston, RI who went to Japan for six months to explore relationships between natural and man-made environments in Japanese landscape gardens through the United States/Japan Artist Exchange Program at the Japan/US Friendship Commission.
- Carl A. Chase, a steel drum maker and tuner from Brooksville, MA who was able to visit Trinidad and Tobago for a residency with one of the islands' foremost steel drum makers through the Travel Grants Program at the National Endowment for the Arts.
- William Ulfelder who spent a year studying the rainforest in Costa Rica as a Fulbright Scholar.
- A police officer from Los Angeles who helped in the creation of D.A.R.E. (Drug Awareness Resistance Education) in several Latin American countries through the U. S. Thematic Programs.
- Piano/violin duo Susan Keith and Laura Kobayashi who toured Latin America and the Caribbean together as Artistic Ambassadors for the U.S. Information Agency.
- Tamara Astor from Northfield, IL who spent a year teaching grades 1-3 in London, England through the Fulbright Teacher Exchange Program at the U.S. Information Agency.
- Central Washington University who sent thirteen K-12 teachers from the state of Washington to Chile for a four-week seminar on the country through the Fulbright-Hays Group Projects Abroad through the U.S. Department of Education.
- Columbia University in New York City acting as the host of seven different humanities seminars for college teachers with grants from the National Endowment for the Humanities.
- Maria Marotti from Santa Barbara, CA who was awarded a $3,000 grant from the National Endowment for the Humanities to study Italian feminism.

* High School Students And Teachers Can Visit Russia
(Secondary School Partnership Program)
Youth Programs Division
Office of Citizen Exchanges
Bureau of Educational and Cultural Affairs
301 4th St., SW, Room 568
Washington, DC 20547
202-619-6299
Fax: 202-619-5311
http://exchanges.state.gov/education/citizens/students
The program objective is to sponsor the exchange of high school students and teachers between the U.S. and the former Soviet Union through grants to private not-for-profit organizations and public institutions. Grants are awarded to fund projects in two program areas: academic year in the U.S., and short-term exchanges of groups of students and teachers between linked schools. The total amount of money available is $15 million. Contact the office listed above for information on organizations to which you need to apply or for more information on the programs available.

* Spend A Year In Europe On A Mid-Career Break
(Hubert Humphrey Fellowship)
Hubert H. Humphrey Fellowship Program
Humphrey Fellowships and Institutional Linkage Branch (ECA/A/S/U)
Institute of International Education
U.S. Department of State
SA-44, 301 4th Street, SW
202-619-5289
202-326-7701

Washington, DC 20547   Fax: 202-326-7702
http://exchanges.state.gov/education/hhh
www.iie.org/template.cfm?&Template=/programs/hhh/default.htm

The program provides opportunities for accomplished mid-career professionals from designated countries of Africa, Asia, Latin America, the Caribbean, the Middle East, and Eurasia, to come to the United States for a year of study and related practical professional experiences. The program provides a basis for establishing lasting ties between citizens of the United States and their professional counterparts in other countries, fostering an exchange of knowledge and mutual understanding throughout the world. Fellows are placed in groups at selected U.S. universities and design individualized programs of academic coursework and professional development activities. The total amount of money available is $5 million. Applications must be submitted in the candidates' home countries to the United States Embassy, Public Affairs Section or Fulbright Commissions. Applicants must have an undergraduate degree, five years of substantial professional experience, demonstrated leadership qualities, and fluency in English. Contact the office listed above for more information on the application process.

* Money For Artists, Filmmakers, Playwrights, And Museum Professionals To Go Overseas

(Creative Arts Exchange Program)
Cultural Programs Division
Bureau of Educational and Cultural Affairs
U.S. Department of State, SA-44
301 4th St., SW, Suite 568   202-205-2209
Washington, DC 20547   Fax: 202-619-6315
http://exchanges.state.gov/education/citizens/culture/creative.htm

The program supports projects by U.S. nonprofit organizations for exchanges of professionals in the arts and museum fields. Priority is given to institutionally-based projects involving artists in the creation of their particular art forms and projects which will lead to institutional linkages. Two way exchanges are encouraged and cost sharing is required. This exchange program is designed to introduce American and foreign participants to each other's cultural and artistic life and traditions. It also supports international projects in the United States or overseas involving composers, choreographers, filmmakers, playwrights, theater designers, writers and poets, visual artists, museum professionals, and more. The program operates through biannual Federal Register requests for proposals. For more information on the application process and program eligibility, contact the office listed above.

* Money For Students, Teachers, Bankers, Lawyers, And Journalists To Travel Overseas

(Fulbright Scholar Program)
Council for International Exchange of Scholars
3007 Tilden St., NW, Suite 5L   202-686-4000
Washington, DC 20008-3009   Fax: 202-362-3442
www.iie.org/cies

The program provides grants to U.S. students, teachers, and scholars to study, teach, lecture, and conduct research overseas, and to foreign nationals to engage in similar activities in the United States to increase mutual understanding and peaceful relations between the people of the United States and the people of other countries. Fields of study and subjects taught include the arts and humanities, social sciences, and physical sciences. In addition to the exchange of students and scholars, the program includes professional exchanges in journalism, law, management, banking, and public administration. Participants take part in degree programs, nondegree and self-study courses, internships, and professional seminars. The total amount of money available is $119 million. Contact the office listed above for application information.

* Money For English, Law, And Journalism Professionals To Go Abroad

(Professional Exchanges)
Office of Citizen Exchanges
Bureau of Educational and Cultural Affairs
U.S. Department of State, SA-44
301 4th St., SW, Room 238   202-619-5348
Washington, DC 20547   Fax: 202-619-4350
http://exchanges.state.gov/education/citizens/professionals

This program sends Americans overseas to aid foreign institutions seeking professional assistance in such academic disciplines as English teaching, law, and journalism. Experts on the United States can consult with academic and professionals at foreign educational or other relevant institutions about special issues, or to conduct seminars/workshops for professional personnel. The total amount of money available is $2 million. Contact the office listed above for guidelines and application information.

* Foreign High School Teachers Can Spend Six Weeks In The U.S.

(Fulbright American Studies Institutes — Study Of The United States)
Study of the US Branch
U.S. Department of State
301 4th St., SW, Room 252   202-619-4557
Washington, DC 20547   Fax: 202-619-6790
http://exchanges.state.gov/education/amstudy/fasi.htm

This program provides grants to foreign secondary and postsecondary school educators for a 4 to 6 week program of academic workshops in U.S. history, culture, and institutions to enhance and update the content of what is taught about the United States abroad. The total amount of money available is $1.6 million. Contact the office listed above for guidelines and application information.

* Exchange Program For English Teachers

(English Language Specialist Program)
Office of English Language Programs
U.S. Department of State, Annex #44
301 4th St., SW, Room 304   202-619-5869
Washington, DC 20547   Fax: 202-401-1250
http://exchanges.state.gov/education/engteaching

The program promotes the study and teaching of English abroad, in host country institutions, and through American educational and binational centers in 41 countries. TEFL/TESL English teaching programs concentrate on training teachers through seminars, exchanges of foreign and American English specialists, and the development and distribution of curricula and materials for teaching the English language and American culture. The total amount of money available is $300,000. Contact the office listed above for application information.

* Teach School Overseas

(Dependent Schools)
U.S. Department of Defense
Teacher Recruitment Section
4040 N. Fairfax Dr.   703-696-3067
Arlington, VA 22203-1634   Fax: 703-696-2699
www.odedodea.edu

The U.S. Department of Defense is responsible for providing schooling to dependent children of military personnel. There are employment positions for elementary and secondary teachers, as well as those that can provide support services. The schools are located in 14 countries around the world, with an enrollment of approximately 106,000 students, and are staffed with about 8,800 teachers. Contact the office listed above for an application and program information.

* Volunteer In The U.S.

(Corporation for National and Community Service
AMERICORPS - 94.006)
Corporation for National Service
1201 New York Ave. NW   800-942-2677
Washington, DC 20525   202-606-5000
http://www.cns.gov

The objective of this program is to supplement efforts of private, nonprofit organizations and federal, state, and local government agencies to eliminate poverty and poverty-related problems by enabling persons from all walks of life and all age groups to perform meaningful and constructive service as volunteers throughout the U.S. AmeriCorps volunteers receive a modest subsistence allowance, an end-of-service stipend, health insurance, and money for college. The total amount of money available is $284,000,000. Applications are available through AmeriCorps State Offices or contact the office listed above for additional information.

* $30,000 To Study Farming Internationally

(Scientific Cooperation and Research — 10.961)
U.S. Department of Agriculture
International Collaborative Research Program
USDA/FAS/ICD/RSED
Ag Box 4314
Room 3230 South Building
14th and Independence Ave., SW
Washington, DC 20250-1084   202-690-4872
www.fas.usda.gov/icd/grants/scrp.htm

This program enables American scientists to work with foreign researchers to help solve critical problems that are affecting the food systems, agriculture, fisheries, forestry and the environment in the U.S. and the collaborating country. Contact the office listed above for an application form. U.S. researchers from USDA agencies, universities, and private nonprofit agricultural research institutions are eligible. A maximum of $45,000 is available for each 3-year research project.

* Your Friends In The Ukraine Can Come To The U.S. To Learn Free Enterprise

(Special American Business Internship Training Program (SABIT)
11.114)
U.S. Department of Commerce
Special American Business Internship Training Program
1401 Constitution Ave., NW
FCB-4th Floor-410 W
Washington, DC 20230   202-482-0073
http://www.mac.doc.gov/sabit/snw/index.htm

This program awards internships in U.S. firms to business managers and scientific workers from the newly independent states of the former Soviet Union. SABIT provides the intern with a hands-on training program in the business skills necessary to operate in a market economy. A counselor is provided to help with cultural adjustments. Companies provide medical insurance, housing, and any other living expenses beyond those covered by the daily stipend provided by the U.S. The amount of money available varies, but averages $18,000. Apply to the program through the U.S. Department of Commerce which considers applications through a competitive process. A SABIT fact sheet is also available.

* Money For Students And Teachers To Travel Together Overseas

(International: Overseas Group Projects Abroad — 84.021)
International Studies Team
International Education and Grants Programs Service
Office of Postsecondary Education
U.S. Department of Education
400 Maryland Ave. SW   202-502-7633
Washington, DC 20202-5332   Fax: 202-205-9489
http://www.ed.gov/offices/OPE/OHEP/iegps/gpa.html

This program is designed to contribute to the development and improvement of the study of modern foreign languages and area studies in the United States, and provide opportunities for American teachers, advanced students, and faculty to study in foreign countries. Grants allow groups to conduct overseas group projects in research, training, and curriculum development. Money can be used for international travel, maintenance allowances, rent of instructional materials in the country of study, and more. The total amount of money available is $4,415,000. Contact the office listed above for application information.

* Finish Your Doctorate Research Abroad

(Fulbright-Hays Doctoral Dissertation Research Abroad 84.022)
Higher Education Programs
U.S. Department of Education
1990 K St., NW
Washington, DC 20006   202-502-7700
http://www.ed.gov/offices/OPE/OHEP/iegps/ddrap.html

This program is designed to provide opportunities for graduate students to engage in full-time dissertation research abroad in modern foreign language and area studies with the exception of Western Europe. This program is designed to develop research knowledge and capability in world areas not widely included in American curricula. Money can be used for a basic stipend, round trip air fare, baggage allowance, tuition payments, local travel, and more. The total amount of money available is $3.1 million. Candidates apply directly to the institutions at which they are enrolled in a Ph.D. program.

* Money For College Teachers To Do Research Overseas

(Fulbright-Hays Faculty Research Abroad - 84.019)
Higher Education Programs
U.S. Department of Education
1990 K St., NW, 6th Floor
Washington, DC 20006   202-502-7700
http://www.ed.gov/offices/OPE/OHEP/iegps.fra.html

This program is designed to help develop modern foreign language and area studies in U.S. higher educational institutions. This program enables faculty members to maintain expertise in specialized fields through support of research in the non-Western areas of the world. Fellowships of 3 to 12 months are available. The total amount of money available is $1,580,000. Candidates should apply directly to their institution. More information is available on this program through the office listed above.

* Money For Teachers To Take A Sabbatical Overseas

(Fulbright-Hays Seminars Abroad - 84.018)
Higher Education Programs
U.S. Department of Education
1990 K St., NW

Washington, DC 20006   202-502-7700
http://www.ed.gov

This program is designed to improve understanding and knowledge of people and culture of a different country. There are 7 to 10 seminars that last 4 to 6 weeks held in countries outside of Western Europe. Eligible persons are teachers in social sciences and humanities, administrators, and curriculum specialists of state and local education agencies, college faculty, librarians and museum teachers who are primarily responsible for teaching undergraduates in the social sciences, humanities, and area studies. The total amount of money available is $1,580,000. Contact the office listed above for application information, as well as a listing of the seminars available.

* Grants To College Teachers Who Want To Create Programs In International Business

(Business And International Education - 84.153)
Higher Education Programs
U.S. Department of Education
1990 K St., NW, 6th Floor
Washington, DC 20006   202-502-7626
http://www.ed.gov/offices/OPE/OHEP/iegps/bie.html

This program is designed to promote innovation and improvement in international business education curricula at institutions of higher education and promote linkages between these institutions and the business community. Institutions must enter into an agreement with a business enterprise, trade organization, or association engaged in international economic activity, or a combination or consortium of the named entities. The total amount of money available is $4,720,000. Contact the office listed above for application information.

* Conduct Cancer Research In a Different Country

(Short-Term Scientist Exchange Program)
National Cancer Institute
Office of International Affairs
6130 Executive Boulevard, Suite 100
Bethesda, MD 20892-7301   301-496-4761
www.cancer.gov/about_nci/oia

This program is designed to promote collaborative research between established U.S. and foreign scientists by supporting exchange visits to each country's laboratories. Visits may last from one week to six months time. Candidates must have at least three years postdoctoral experience in cancer research and an invitation from a qualified sponsor. Contact the office listed above for application forms including instructions and other requirements.

* Visit The U.S. To Do Health Research

NIH Visiting Program)
International Services Branch
Office of Research Services
National Institutes of Health (NIH)
13 South Dr., MSC 5774
Bethesda, MD 20892   301-496-6166
www.nih.gov/od/ors/dirs/isb/isb.htm

This program provides talented scientists throughout the world with the opportunity to participate in the varied research activities of the National Institutes of Health. There are two categories of Visiting Program participants: Visiting Fellows and Visiting Scientists. Each participant works closely with a senior NIH investigator who serves as supervisor or sponsor during the period of award or appointment. The Visiting Fellow award is for obtaining research training experience. Fellows must have a doctoral degree, not more than 3 years of relevant postdoctoral research experience, and cannot be U.S. citizens. Visiting Scientists are appointed to conduct health-related research and are considered employees of NIH, and receive a salary and benefits. Individuals interested in a Visiting Program fellowship award or appointment should write to NIH senior scientists working in the same research field, enclosing a resume and brief description of his/her particular research area. Information about the research being conducted by NIH scientists and their names may be obtained from the NIH's Scientific Directory and Annual Bibliography, which can be obtained from the office listed above.

* New U.S. Researchers Can Continue Research In Developing Countries

(International Research Scientist Development Award-IRSDA)
International Research Scientists Development Award
Fogarty International Center
Division of International Training and Research
National Institutes of Health
Building 31, Room B2C39
31 Center Drive, MSC 2220   301-496-8733
Bethesda, MD 20892-2220   Fax: 301-402-0779

www.fic.nih.gov/programs/irsda.html
This program provides opportunities for foreign postdoctoral biomedical or behavioral scientists who are in the formative stages of their career to extend their research experience in a laboratory in the United States. The total amount of money available is $4.4 million. To learn more about the requirements and application process, contact the office listed above.

* Conduct Medical Research With Foreign Scientists

(Fogarty International Research Collaboration Award)
Division of International Research and Training
Fogarty International Center
Building 31, Room B2C39
31 Center Drive, MSC 2220   301-496-1653
Bethesda, MD 20892-2220   Fax: 301-402-0779
www.fic.nih.gov/programs/firca.html

This program provides for collaborative research between U.S. biomedical scientists and investigators in foreign countries. These awards are made for research projects that, for the most part, will be carried out at the foreign research site. Its purpose is to promote discovery and reduce global health disparities. The foreign countries involved are Africa, Asia, Latin America, the Caribbean Region, the Former Soviet Union, and Central and Eastern Europe. Information and application instructions are available from the office listed above.

* Research Internationally

(International Training and Research Program in Emerging Infective Disease-ITREID)
Division of International Training and Research
Fogarty International Center
National Institutes of Health
Building 31, Room B2C39
31 Center Drive, MSC 2220   301-496-7614
Bethesda, MD 20892-2220   Fax: 301-402-0779
www.fic.nih.gov/programs/erid.html

This program provides the opportunity for research and training needs in emerging and re-emerging infectious diseases in developing countries. ITREID is designed to, among other things, train laboratory scientists and public health workers in developing countries and the U.S. in research, control and prevention strategies, and their implementation and evaluation related to these diseases. For a list of program directors, refer to the address above.

* Money To Study In Japan

Japan-U.S. Friendship Commission
1110 Vermont Ave., NW, Suite 800
Washington, DC 20005   202-418-9800
http://www.jusfc.gov   Fax: 202-418-9802

This program provides grants to institutions and associations to support American studies in Japan, Japanese studies in the United States, exchange programs in the arts, policy-oriented research, and public affairs, and education. In addition, the Commission is interested in sponsoring research on Japan-US economic relations and activities in Asia, with priority given to Japanese investment in Asia and its effect on Japan-US economic, trade and political relations. The total amount of money available is $2.9 million. Contact the office listed above for more information about the various grant programs, as well as a biennial report which lists previous grants recipients and their projects.

* Money For Artists and Performers To Travel Overseas

(Fund For U.S. Artists)
Arts International
251 Park Ave. S, 5th Floor
New York, NY 10010   212-674-9744
http://www.artsinternational.org/programs/the_fund/index.htm   Fax: 212-674-9092

This program provides grants to assist individual U.S. performers and organizations who have been invited to international festivals abroad, and who need additional support to make their performances possible. Travel, per diem, international communications, shipping, and salary expense related to participation in the international festival are among eligible costs supported through the Fund. The Fund is particularly interested in receiving proposals which reflect the cultural and regional diversity of the United States and which involve events in areas of the world where U.S. work is rarely performed. The average amount of money available ranges from $1,000 to $5,000, but it does not exceed $25,000. Contact the office listed above for guidelines and an application packet.

* Go To Japan For 6 Months

(United States/Japan Creative Artists' Program)
Japan-U.S. Friendship Commission
1110 Vermont Ave., NW, Suite 800   202-418-9800
Washington, DC 20005   Fax: 202-418-9802
http://www.jusfc.gov/

The program is designed to allow artists who create original work to pursue their individual artistic goals and interests by living in Japan for six months, observing developments in their field, and meeting with their professional counterparts in Japan. The total amount of money available is $200,000. Contact the office listed above for guidelines and an application packet.

* Money For Artists To Work With the Newly Independent States

(Artslink)
CEC International Partners
12 West 31st St., Suite 400   212-643-1985
New York, NY 10001-4415   Fax: 212-643-1996
http://godai.comset.net/cecip

Artslink encourages artistic exchange with the newly independent states in Central and Eastern Europe, the former Soviet Union, and Eurasia by offering three categories of support: Artslink Projects, which provides funding to U.S. artists to work on mutually beneficial projects with counterparts abroad; Artslink Residencies, which supports U.S. arts organizations wishing to host a visiting artist or arts manager for a five-week residency; and Independent Projects, where artists and art managers can work on projects in the U.S. The total amount of money available varies. Contact the office listed above for guidelines and an application packet.

* Artists Can Travel To Improve Their Art

(Fund for U.S. Artists at International Festivals and Exhibitions)
Cultural Programs Division
Bureau of Educational and Cultural Affairs
U.S. Department of State
SA-44, 301 4th St., SW, Suite 568   202-619-4794
Washington, DC 20547   Fax: 202-619-6315
http://exchanges.state.gov/education/citizens/culture/perffest.htm

This program is designed to enable U.S. artists to pursue opportunities abroad that further their artistic development. Grant decisions will be based on artistic excellence, the applicant's reasons for wanting to travel to a particular country, as well as his or her sensitivity to the culture and country to which he or she wants to travel. The grants will support artists pursuing a wide variety of activities abroad including the development or expansion of relationships with artists and arts organizations and the exploration of significant developments in their field. The total amount of money available is $100,000. Contact the office listed above for guidelines and an application packet.

* Summer Seminars For Teachers

(Promotion of the Humanities – Seminars and Institutes – 45.161)
Summer Seminars and Institutes Programs
Division of Education Programs
National Endowment for the Humanities
1100 Pennsylvania Ave., NW, Room 302
Washington, DC 20506   202-606-8463
www.neh.gov/grants/guidelines/seminars.html
Email: research@neh.fed.us

Schoolteachers, college and university teachers, along with selected foreign secondary teachers, can engage in intensive study of basic humanities texts and documents and work closely with outstanding scholars for 4 to 6 weeks at colleges, universities, and other appropriate sites, some of which may be located in a foreign country. Contact the office listed above for a list of seminar offerings, as well as an application packet.

* Money For Teachers To Study

(Promotion of the Humanities – Fellowships and Stipends - 45.160)
Fellowships and Stipends
Division of Research
National Endowment for the Humanities
1100 Pennsylvania Ave., NW, Room 318   202-606-8200
Washington, DC 20506   Fax: 202-606-8204
http://www.neh.gov/grants/guidelines/stipends.html
Email: research@neh.gov

Grants provide support for college and university teachers; individuals employed by schools, museums, libraries, etc.; and others to undertake full-time independent study and research in the humanities for two consecutive summer months. Recipients must work full-time on their projects during the two-month period. Contact the office listed above for guidelines and an application packet.

* $40,000 To Study And Conduct Research

(Fellowship Programs at Independent Research Institutions)
Division of Research
National Endowment for the Humanities
1100 Pennsylvania Ave., NW, Room 318   202-606-8200
Washington, DC 20506   Fax: 202-606-8204
www.neh.gov/grants/guidelines/fpiri.html
Email: research@neh.fed.us

Grants provide support for fellowship programs for post doctorates and independent scholars. It is administered by one of two groups: Independent centers for advanced studies, libraries, and museums in the U.S., or American overseas research centers and other organizations that have expertise in promoting research on foreign cultures. Programs that provide long-term fellowships, four months or longer, are given priority. Individuals looking to pursue research at the centers should apply directly to that center. The maximum amount of the stipend is $40,000.

* Become A Humanities Fellow

(Fellowships)
Division of Research Programs
National Endowment for the Humanities
1100 Pennsylvania Ave., NW, Room 318   202-606-8200
Washington, DC 20506   Fax: 202-606-8204
http://www.neh.fed.us
Email: research@neh.fed.us

Grants support postdoctoral fellowship programs at independent centers for advanced study which offer scholars opportunities to pursue independent research in the humanities while benefiting from collegial association with scholars in other areas or disciplines of study. Fellowships in this program are awarded and administered by the centers themselves. Tenure of the fellowships may run from six to twelve consecutive months, and stipends vary at the different centers. Eligibility also varies from center to center, but neither candidates for degrees nor persons seeking support for work toward degrees are eligible to apply. Contact the office listed above for more information on theses programs, as well as a list of centers which accept applications.

* Scientific Collaboration

(International Opportunities for Scientists and Engineers)
International Programs Division
National Science Foundation
4201 Wilson Blvd., Room 935
Arlington, VA 22230   703-292-5111
http://www.nsf.gov/sbe/int
Email: info@nsf.gov

This program is designed to advance and benefit U.S. interests by enabling U.S. scientists and engineers to avail themselves of research opportunities in other countries. The Division of International Programs supports efforts to initiate international cooperation involving new foreign collaborators, or new types of activities with established partners. Contact the office listed above for guidelines and application information.

* Research In The Tropics

(Short-Term Fellowships)
Office of Fellowships
Smithsonian Institution
955 L'Enfant Plaza, Suite 7302   202-287-3271
Washington, DC 20560   Fax: 202-287-3691
www.stri.org/What_we_do/Fellowship_Opportunities.html
Email: fellow@tivoli.si.edu

The objective of this program is to enable selected candidates to work in the tropics and explore research possibilities at the Smithsonian Tropical Research Institute. Fellowships are primarily for graduate students, but awards are made occasionally to undergraduate and postdoctoral candidates. Contact the office listed above for guidelines and application procedures.

* Teachers Can Study Abroad

(Fulbright Teacher and Administrator Exchange Program)
Fulbright Teacher Exchange Program
ATTN: NSL   202-314-3520
600 Maryland Ave., SW, Suite 320   800-726-0479
Washington, DC 20024-2520   Fax: 202-479-6806
http://grad.usda.gov/International

The program is designed to promote mutual understanding between citizens of the United States and other countries through educational and cultural exchanges. It is open to teachers and administrators from the elementary through the postsecondary levels, allowing for classroom-to-classroom exchange of teaching positions between U.S. teachers and counterpart teachers from selected countries worldwide. Exchange grants may include full or partial travel grants and cost of living supplements, depending on the country. The total amount of money available is $527,000. Contact the office listed above for guidelines and an application packet.

* Money To Attend Workshops Overseas

(Citizens Exchanges)
Office of Citizen Exchanges
Bureau of Educational and Cultural Affairs
U.S. Department of State, SA-44
301 Fourth St., SW   202-619-5348
Washington, DC 20547   Fax: 202-619-4350
http://exchanges.state.gov/education/citizens

This program awards grants to U.S. nonprofit organizations for projects that link their international exchange interests with counterpart institutions/groups in other countries. Subject areas include environmental protection, trade unionism, education administration and curriculum reform, protection, small business development and management training, and more. Programs are normally multi-phase and extend over more than one fiscal year. Programs usually consist of sending American specialists on 2-3 week visits to a country for workshops and meetings, followed by a visit to the U.S. by foreign counterparts. The total amount of money available is $2 million. The Office of Citizen Exchanges develops a series of Requests for Proposals (RFPs) during the course of the fiscal year. Specific application and review guidelines are available upon written request to the office listed above. RFPs are also published in the Federal Register.

* Spend Six Weeks In A Foreign Country Working With Art Colleagues

(American Cultural Specialists)
Cultural Programs Division
Bureau of Educational and Cultural Affairs
U.S. Department of State, SA-44
301 4th St., SW, Room 567   202-619-4779
Washington, DC 20547   Fax: 202-619-6315
http://exchanges.state.gov/education/citizens

Participants in this program spend two to six weeks in one country working with foreign colleagues. Among other activities, they may conduct workshops or master classes, direct a play, rehearse a ballet, or advise on arts management. Specialists are provided with economy international travel and a honorarium of $200 per day plus limited allowances for educational and miscellaneous expenses by the Department of State. The U.S. embassy and/or the local co-sponsor provide per diem domestic travel and all local program costs. The total amount of money available is $380,000. This is not a grant program from which individuals can request financial assistance for overseas projects, but as a response to a specific request from embassies abroad. To learn more on how to your resume reviewed so your name can be placed on the Cultural Specialist roster, contact the office listed above.

* Eight Week Foreign Tours For Jazz Musicians And Bands

(Jazz Ambassador Program)
Cultural Programs Division
Bureau of Educational and Cultural Affairs
U.S. Department of State, SA-44
301 4th St., SW, Room 568   202-619-4800
Washington, DC 20547   Fax: 202-619-6315
http://exchanges.state.gov

This program is designed to use the wealth of often undiscovered musical talent in the U.S. to enhance the mission of promoting cross-cultural understanding. Jazz Ambassadors travel to four or five countries for a period of four to eight weeks. In addition to public performances, they may conduct workshops and master classes. The total amount of money available is $169,000. Nominations of classical musicians in various categories are sought from music schools, conservatories, colleges and universities throughout the U.S. Artistic Ambassadors may not be under management and are selected through live auditions on the basis of their musical ability and suitability as "goodwill ambassadors." To learn more about the application process, contact the office listed above.

* Foreign Leaders Can Study In The U.S.

(International Visitors Program – 19.402)
Office of International Visitors
U.S. Department of State
301 4th St., SW, Room 266   866-283-9090
ECA/PE/V/C/P   202-619-5217
Washington, DC 20547   Fax: 202-205-0792
http://exchanges.state.gov/education/ivp

This office arranges programs for foreign leaders and potential leaders designed to develop and foster professional contacts with their colleagues in the United States and provide a broader exposure to American social, cultural, and political institutions. Areas of expertise government, politics, media, education, science, labor relations, the arts, and other fields. The total amount of money available is $10,250,000. Participants are nominated by U.S. embassies. For more information on the program contact the office listed above.

* Do Your Part To Help The World

(Peace Corps)
Peace Corps
1111 20th St., NW   800-424-8580
Washington, DC 20526   Fax: 202-606-9410
http://www.peacecorps.gov

The program objective is to promote world peace and friendship, to help other countries in meeting their needs for trained manpower, and to help promote understanding between the American people and other peoples served by the Peace Corps. Volunteers serve for a period of 2 years, living among the people with whom they work. Volunteers are expected to become a part of the community and to demonstrate, through their voluntary service, that people can be an important impetus for change. Volunteers receive a stipend and health insurance. Contact the office listed above for information on how to become a Peace Corps volunteer.

* Money For Engineering Students To Travel The Country Visiting DOE Laboratories

(Faculty and Student Teams Program)
Science Education Programs
Office of Science Education
U.S. Department of Energy   202-586-0987/7174
Washington, DC 20585   Fax: 202-586-0019
www.scied.science.doe.gov/scied/fast/about.html

The program objective is to provide college and university science and engineering faculty and students with energy-related training and research experience in areas of energy research at Department of Energy research facilities. Funds can be used to conduct energy research at one of the DOE research facilities. Students can also participate in energy-related workshops and conferences. Successful candidates receive a stipend of $800 per week for each week at the lab, as well as travel and housing expenses. Students must apply to a participating laboratory or university. Contact the office listed above for information on laboratories and universities that take part in this program.

* Community College Students Can Intern at Energy Laboratories

(Community College Institutes)
Science Education Programs
Office of Science Education   202-586-7174
U.S. Department of Energy   202-586-0987
Washington, DC 20585   Fax: 202-586-0019
www.scied.science.doe.gov/scied/CCI/about.html

The objective of this program is to give community college students the opportunity to participate in hands-on research at the cutting edge of science at the Department of Energy Laboratories, and to provide training and experience in the operation of sophisticated state-of-the-art equipment and instruments. College students who are majoring in an energy-related field can spend a semester using some of the Federal government's equipment and instruments at many of the Department of Energy's labs. The energy research must be in an area of the laboratory's ongoing research. Students receive a weekly stipend of $400, complimentary housing or a housing allowance, and a round-trip ticket to the lab. Applications may be obtained by writing to the address above.

* The Military Could Be Your Ticket Overseas

(U.S. Department of Defense)
U.S. Air Force Recruiting Service
550 D St., W, Suite 1   800-423-USAF
Randolph Air Force Base, TX 78150-4527   210-652-5993
www.airforce.com/

Commander
Naval Recruiting Command
4015 Wilson Blvd.
Arlington, VA 22203   800-USA-NAVY
www.navyjobs.com/

Commanding General
Marine Corps Recruiting Command
2 Navy Annex
Washington, DC 20380-1775   800-MARINES
www.usmc.mil/

Army Opportunities

1307 Third Avenue
Fort Knox, KY 40121-2726   800-USA-ARMY
www.goarmy.com/

U.S. Coast Guard Information Center
4200 Wilson Blvd., Suite 450
Arlington, VA 22203   800-GET-USCG
http://www.uscg.mil

The Army, Navy, Marine Corps, Air Force, and the Coast Guard (part of U.S. Department of Transportation) are responsible for protecting the security of the U.S. There are 2.87 million men and women on active duty, with over 600,000 serving outside the United States. Length of service does vary, as does pay and types of jobs available. You can even earn the chance to go to college. The military has bases all around the country and the world, and your local recruiter can answer all your questions about the opportunities they have to offer.

* Join The Foreign Service

(Foreign Service with the Department of State)
Recruitment Branch
Employment Division
U.S. Department of State
HR/REE, SA-1
2401 E St., NW, Room H-518
Washington, DC 20522   202-261-8888
http://www.state.gov

Professionals in the Foreign Service advance and protect the national interests and security of the United States, both overseas and at home. Foreign Service Officers are generalists who perform administrative, consular, economic and political functions. Foreign Service Specialists perform vital technical, support, and administrative services overseas and in the United States. You must be a U.S. citizen, between the ages of 20 and 59, a high school graduate, and be available for assignment anywhere in the world. Contact the office listed above for information and application procedures.

* Thousands Of Government Jobs In Foreign Countries

(Office of Personnel Management)
Federal Job Information Center
Office of Personnel Management
1900 E St., NW
Washington, DC 20415   202-606-1800
http://www.usajobs.opm.gov

The Federal government hires personnel to do everything from typing to spying, and there are posts all around the world. Those interested in jobs overseas can contact the Office of Personnel Management to learn current job openings and the skills required. Other government agencies also hire for jobs abroad, and you could contact them directly for information on employment opportunities. Contact the office listed above for more information, or you may contact the Career America Connection at 912-757-3000. Other agencies that hire for overseas employment include:

Agency For International Development
Recruitment Division
M/HR/POD/SP, 2.08 RRB
Washington, DC 20523   202-712-5043
http://www.info.usaid.gov

U.S. Customs Service
1300 Pennsylvania Avenue, NW
Washington, DC 20229   202-927-1250
www.customs.treas.gov

Central Intelligence Agency   703-482-1100
Office of Personnel   800-562-7242
McLean, VA 22209-8727   Fax: 703-482-7814
www.cia.gov

U.S. Department of Commerce
Human Resources Management Office
U.S. and Foreign Commercial Service
1401 Constitution Ave., NW
Room 5001   202-482-4938
Washington, DC 20230   Fax: 202-482-0249
www.doc.gov

U.S. Department of Agriculture
Foreign Agricultural Service
Personnel Division
1400 Independence Ave., SW
Washington, DC 20250   703-812-6339
www.fas.usda.gov

* Sell Your Goods Overseas

(U.S. Department of Commerce)
Trade Information Center
U.S. Department of Commerce
Washington, DC 20230   800-USA-TRADE
www.trade.gov/td/tic

The Trade Information Center is a comprehensive "one-stop-shop" for information on U.S. government programs and activities that support exporting efforts. This hotline is staffed by trade specialists who can provide information on seminars and conferences, overseas buyers and representatives, overseas events, export financing, technical assistance, and export counseling. They also have access to the National Trade Data Bank. They offer trade missions to help you find local agents, representatives, distributors, or direct sales. Their Trade Shows promote U.S. products with high export potential. The Agent/ Distributor Service will locate, screen, and assess agents, distributors, representatives, and other foreign partners for your business. Matchmaker Trade Delegations prescreen prospects interested in your product and assist with meetings. If you cannot afford the cost of traveling overseas, the Trade Information Center can refer you to several programs that offer loans to help you start exporting. You can also receive assistance from your own state's Department of Economic Development. Contact the office listed above for more information on exporting in general, and for more specific information on your product or service.

* Work On Assignment for U.S. Embassies

(English Language Specialists)
Office of English Language Programs
U.S. Department of State, Annex #44
301 4th Street, SW, Room 304
Washington, DC 20547   202-619-5869
http://exchanges.state.gov/education/engteaching/specialists.htm

This program recruits American academics in the fields of TEF:/TES: and Applied Linguistics to complete assignments needed by overseas American Embassies. These assignments may include curriculum projects, teacher training seminars, textbook development, English for Specific Purposes and program evaluation. If a candidate is not specified by the Embassy, one will be recruited by the Office of English Language Programs. Eligible Specialists will hold a MA or Ph.D., and have overseas and teacher training experience. Benefits include an honorarium of $200 per day, round-trip airfare, materials allowance, and basic health insurance. To find out how to become a Specialist, contact the office above.

* U.S. and Chinese Students Work Together

(U.S.-China Youth Exchange Initiative)
Youth Program Division
U.S. Department of State, SA-44
301 4th Street, SW, Room 568
Washington, DC 20547   202-619-6299
http://exchange.state.gov/education/citizens/students/eap.htm

This program is for secondary school students in the US and China so that they may develop an understanding of their counterpart's community life. Students and educators at selected schools work on Internet-based projects. The top seven partnerships are then involved in a 3 or 4-week exchange. For more information, contact the office above.

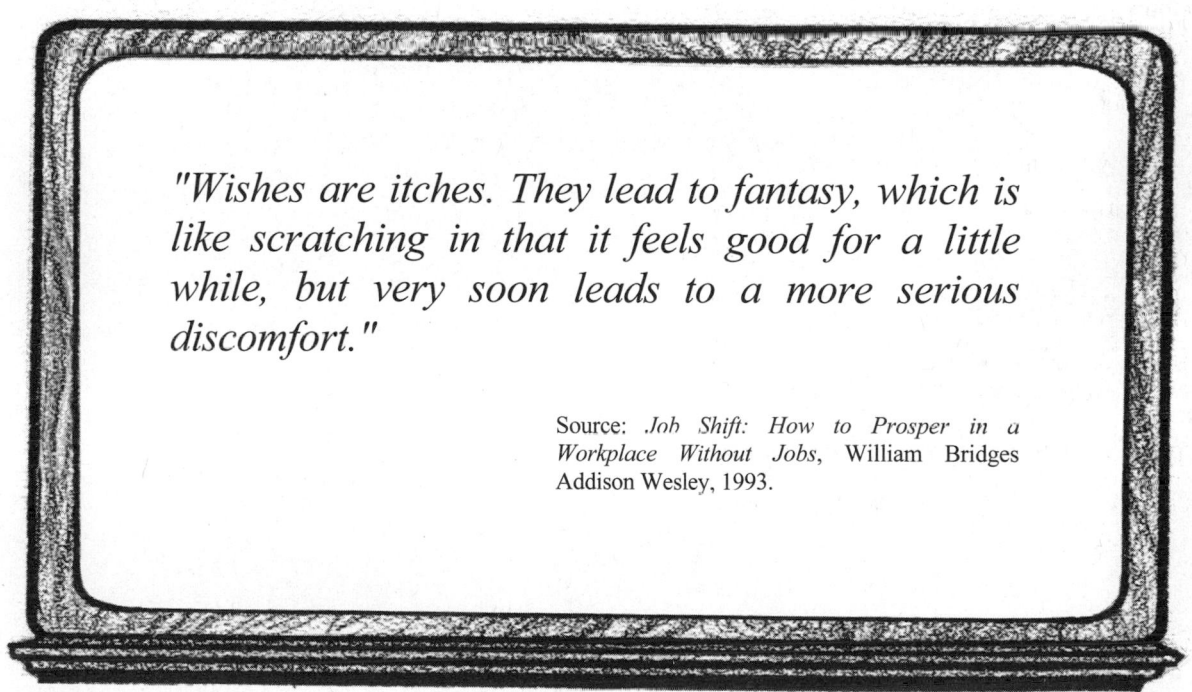

"Wishes are itches. They lead to fantasy, which is like scratching in that it feels good for a little while, but very soon leads to a more serious discomfort."

Source: *Job Shift: How to Prosper in a Workplace Without Jobs*, William Bridges Addison Wesley, 1993.

I Wanna Be an Artist Singer, Dancer, Writer, Photographer

The Words "Poor and Starving" Don't Have To Apply To Artists Any Longer!

National Endowment for the Arts Grants to Organizations

The National Endowment for the Arts (NEA) is an independent agency of the Federal government that was created to encourage and support American art and artists who are actively creating art in various mediums. The Endowment does this by awarding grants to nonprofit arts organizations in all fields, as well as through its own leadership activities. The agency does not direct the creative activities of individual artists or arts organizations but acts as a catalyst and as a partner with others who support the arts. The NEA helps to enhance the quality of life for Americans through a breathtaking array of cultural activity: from the best in theaters and touring dance companies to folk festivals and music concerts; from museums and orchestras to arts programs in our nation's schools that reach millions of students each year who might otherwise lack exposure to the arts.

The Endowment awards grants to nonprofit organizations in three areas: Grants for Arts Projects, Leadership Initiatives and Partnership Agreements. In addition, individual fellowships in literature and honorary fellowships in jazz and the folk and traditional arts are awarded. Forty percent of Endowment funds are awarded to state and regional arts organizations. For more information, contact National Endowment for the Arts, 1100 Pennsylvania Avenue, NW, Washington, DC 20506; 202-682-5482; Fax: 202-682-5626; {www.nea.gov}.

* Grants for Arts Projects

Grants for Arts Projects support exemplary projects in dance, design, folk and traditional arts, literature, media arts, museums, music, musical theater, opera, theater, visual arts and multidisciplinary forms. Grants are awarded on the basis of artistic excellence and merit, including such factors as the project's potential influences and the applicant's ability to carry out the project. Grants are awarded to organizations in the following areas:

Artistic Creativity and Preservation
- **Creativity**: To support the creation and preservation of artistically excellent and significant work.
- **Heritage and Preservation**: To preserve those forms of artistic expression and practice that reflects our nation's many cultural traditions.
- **Services to Arts Organizations and Artists**: To help arts organizations and artists become more effective in realizing their artistic and public service goals.

Challenge America: Access to the Arts: To provide communities throughout the country greater access to the arts.

Learning in the Arts for Children and Youth: To increase the availability of arts education.

* Leadership Initiatives

The Endowment takes an active role in developing and carrying out hallmark projects of national significance in the arts. Such projects reach communities in all 50 states, promote international exchanges or link the arts in new ways with non-arts fields. In addition, the Endowment currently maintains over 25 collaborative partnerships with other federal agencies including the Department of Education and the Department of Justice.

* Partnership Agreements

Each year 40 percent of the Endowments monies are directed to state, jurisdictional and regional arts organizations. These organizations then make grants and offer services to their communities. The Partnership Agreement for the state arts agencies includes an arts education, arts in underserved communities and Challenge America components.

* Fellowships & Awards

The Endowment recognizes individual achievements through the *American Jazz Masters Fellowship, National Heritage Fellowship* and the *National Medal of Arts*. Published creative writers and translators in poetry and prose are recognized by the Endowment through their *Literature Fellowships*.

Attention Artists!
Over $180,000,000 Available From State Governments

How do most struggling artists perfect their craft? By working alongside masters in their specific craft, and believe it or not, there are money programs administered on the state level to help you do just that. If you are working with an arts group, there are state grants to assist you in organizing special productions, grants that will allow you the resources to travel around the state to represent your art organization, or grants that would allow you to hire people with special capabilities to enhance your productions.

Here's just a sampling of what some states can provide:

- $2,000 to study music, dance, or storytelling (Alaska)
- $2,500 for choreographers (California)
- Money for architects to help school children (Georgia)
- $5,000 to work with a master artist in their studio (Idaho)
- $10,000 for creative writers (Idaho)
- $10,000 for photographers (Illinois)
- $1,000 for poets (Iowa)
- $2,000 for art teachers to attend a workshop (Maine)
- $150 a day for artists who can spend two days a week at a local school (Massachusetts)
- $10,000 to put on a program of poetry readings (Nebraska)
- $8,000 for dancers (North Carolina)
- $500 for writers to attend a workshop (North Carolina)
- $10,000 for art critics (North Dakota)
- $2,000 to put on an arts festival (Oklahoma)
- $5,000 for printmakers (Texas)
- $500 to writers on a first-come first-served basis (Virginia)

Eligibility Requirements

Almost every state requires that you be a state resident to receive money through these programs. The exceptions to this rule are often found in those programs where the state will pay an artist from another state to come to work with school children within their state. Eligibility requirements for all programs vary greatly. Some states, like Pennsylvania, require that you have lived in the state for two years and have three years of professional experience. States like Rhode Island require that you are at least 18 years of age and have resided in the state for at least one year. With residency requirements being as minimal as one year, it may be worth looking for a state that has some specific programs that interest you, and to establish residency there.

What Are Your Chances?

Remember, you have to play to win, and your chances of winning and receiving these funds will be slightly different for each of the programs listed. For instance, Virginia has a program that gives out money on a first-come first-served basis. So, if your application is the first received, your chances of success are 100 percent. Vermont, on the other hand, has one of the more competitive programs that awards funds to only approximately 5% of their applicants. Whatever your chances, remember that each year the money has to be awarded to someone, and your chances will be just plain zero if you don't apply!

How To Work With Arts Organizations

A lot of the state money programs are awarded to art organizations. Therefore, if you have trouble getting money as an individual it may be worth your time to find an art organization to collaborate with or perhaps become your own art organization. Your state arts council can help you locate organizations that may be willing (and even eager) to work with you in order to be awarded this grant money. Talk to your local community college, community group, or even your church about joining together to win funding. You might make an arrangement where you share the proceeds of the program if you win, and both you and the community group lose nothing if your efforts are unsuccessful.

Some of the money given to organizations requires matching grants in order to receive the funding. A matching grant requires that the recipient raise funds in some proportion to the amount awarded. This may not be as difficult as it sounds because oftentimes, in-kind goods and services may be used as matching grants. An in-kind contribution of goods is an offering of any tangible, useable item that the organization would have otherwise had to purchase. An in-kind contribution of a service includes intangible contributions such as donations of volunteer time, or the use of facilities or equipment.

Alabama

Alabama State Council on the Arts
201 Monroe St., Suite 110   334-242-4076
Montgomery, AL 36104   334-240-3269
www.arts.state.al.us
Eligibility requirements: For individual artist programs state residency is required, unless otherwise specified. Grants to organizations must be matched by at least an equal amount from other sources located by the applicant.
Programs Available:
$5,000 To Art Administrators (Fellowship in Arts Administration)
$10,000 For Artists, Craftsmen, Photographers (Artists Fellowships)
$1,000 To Develop Administrative Skills (Technical Assistance)
Money To Be An Artist In Residence (Artist Residences)
$5,000 For Master Folk Artists (Folk Art Apprenticeships)
Money For Schools To Hire Artists (Arts in Education Projects)
$500 For Folk Artists (Folklife Program)
$1,000 For Community Arts Projects (Project Assistance Programs)
Awards To Master Folk Artists (Folk Heritage Awards)
Money For Artists To Perform At Rural Schools (Rural Touring School Program)

Alaska

Alaska State Council on the Arts
411 W. 4th Ave., Suite 1E   907-269-6610
Anchorage, AK 99501-2343   Fax: 907-269-6601
www.eed.state.ak.us/aksca
Eligibility requirements: State residency is required for individual grants to artists. The Council awards funds only to Alaskan nonprofit organizations, schools, or government agencies.
Programs Available:
$2,500 For Artists To Develop New Works (Individual Artist Fellowships)
$2,000 To Study With a Master Craftsperson, Musician, Dancer, or Storyteller (Master Arts and Apprentice Grants in Traditional Native Arts)
Money For Local Art Agencies (Grants to Local Arts Agencies)
Money To Support a Local Art Project (Project Grants)
Money To Pay Artists To Speak At Workshops (Workshop Grants)
Money For Schools To Have An Artist Program (Artist In Schools)
Money To Support Short-term Projects Of Professional Artists In Visual, Literary, Media, Performing or Folk And Traditional Arts (Career Opportunity Grants)
$2,000 To Non-profit Art Groups And Organizations (Community Art Development Grants)
Money To Cover The Production Costs Of Activities Of Art Organizations (Operating Support Grants)
$1,000 For Artists To Train And Speak At Workshops (AIE Incentive Grants)

Arizona

Arizona Commission on the Arts
417 W. Roosevelt St.   602-255-5882
Phoenix, AZ 85003   Fax: 602-256-0282
www.arizonaarts.org
Eligibility requirements: Individual Artist Fellowships require state residency. Priority for organizational funding is given to projects in rural areas of the state and projects coordinated by ethnic-run organizations or those that primarily serve ethnic communities.
Programs Available:
$5,000 For Artists To Use For Research And Travel (Artist Projects)
Money For Schools To Have Artists In Residence Programs (Artists in Residence)
Money For Schools With New Ideas In Art (Education Initiatives)
$5,000 For Artists And Writers (Fellowships)
Over $50,000 In Grants To Support Administrative Expenses Of Art Organizations (General Operating Grants)
Grants To Artists And Organizations To Support Special Art Projects (Project And Development Grants)
Money For Local Art Agencies (Grants To Local Agencies)

Arkansas

Arkansas Arts Council
1500 Tower Bldg.
323 Center St.   501-324-9766
Little Rock, AR 72201   Fax: 501-324-9207
www.arkansasarts.com
Eligibility requirements: State residency is required for individual artist programs. Individuals must be at least 25-years old. Funds awarded to nonprofit organizations and educational institutions must be at least equally matched by the applicant organization with cash from sources other than the Council or National Endowment for the Arts (NEA).
Programs Available:
$5,000 For Craftspersons and Artists (Individual Artist Fellowship Program)
$50,000 To Arts Organizations (General Operating Support Grants)
Grants To Put On Art Shows For The Public (Program Support Grants)
Money For Schools Or Communities To Have An Artist In Residence (Arts-in-Education)
More Money For Schools Or Communities To Have An Artist In Residence (Artists In Residence)
Grants To Support New And Emerging Organizations (Major Arts Partners)
$1,000 For Emergency Arts Funding (Assistance Mini-grants)
Money To Support Community Arts Activities (Arts On Tour Program)

California

California Arts Council
13001 I Street, Suite 930   916-332-6555
Sacramento, CA 95814   Fax: 916-332-6575
www.cac.ca.gov
Eligibility requirements: State residency is required for individual artists programs.

Programs Available:
Based on reduction to the agency's budget, all grant programs have been suspended. Contact the California Arts Council for updated information on grants programs.

Colorado

Colorado Council on the Arts (CCAH)
1380 Lawrence St., Suite 1200   303-866-2723
Denver, CO 80204-2059   Fax: 303-866-4266
www.coloarts.state.co.us

Eligibility requirements: For individual artist programs, state residency is required, unless otherwise specified. Money available: $220,000.

Programs Available:
Colorado currently has only one grants program available. The *Grants to Artists and Organizations* is a broad based program that funds: collaborations between schools and artists, increased cultural participation, community building through the arts, folk or traditional arts, technical assistance services and professional development. Matching grants amounts range from $2,000 to a maximum of 3.5% of the total grants funding pool.

Connecticut

Connecticut Commission on the Arts
1 Financial Program
775 Main Street   860-566-4770
Hartford, CT 06103   Fax: 860-566-6462
www.ctarts.org

Eligibility requirements: Individual Artist Programs: State residency is required, unless otherwise specified.

Programs Available:
$2,500 For Visual Artists (Artist Fellowship)
Money For Organizations To Hire An Artist In Residence
    (Artists Residencies)
Money For Organizations To Conduct Public Art Programs (Organizational
    Support Program)
$1,000 For Organizations To Engage In Professional Development Activities
    (Arts Management Technical Assistance Program)
Matching Grants For Organizations And Local Art Agencies To Culturally
    Improve The Community (Arts Partnerships For Stronger
    Communities)
$1,000 To Performing Artists (Arts Presentation Grants)
Grants To Assist In The Long-term Stabilization Of The State's Arts Industry
    (Connecticut Arts Endowment Fund)
$2,500 to Arts Administrator (Elizabeth L. Mahaffey Arts Administration
    Fellowship)

Delaware

Delaware Division of the Arts
Carvell State Office Building
820 North French St.   302-577-8278
Wilmington, DE 19801   Fax: 302-577-6561
www.artsdel.org

Eligibility requirements: Individual artist programs require state residency, unless otherwise specified.

Programs Available:
Money For New Or Established Artists (Individual Artist Fellowships)
Money For Operating Expenses (General Operating Support Grants)
Money For Schools To Have An Artist In Residence (Arts in Education
    Residencies)
Money For The Professional Development Of Organizations (Technical
    Assistance Grants)
More Money To Support Art Organizations (Delaware Arts Stabilization
    Fund)
$750 For Art Organizations (Opportunity Grants)
Money To Support Art Programs In Schools (Education Partnership Planning
    Grants)

District of Columbia

District of Columbia Commission on Arts and Humanities
410 Eight St., NW, 5th Floor
Stables Art Center   202-724-5613
Washington, DC 20004   Fax: 202-727-4135
http://dcarts.dc.gov

Eligibility requirements: Individual artist programs require residency in the District of Columbia for at least one year prior to application deadline and the applicant must maintain residency during the grant period. Individuals and arts organizations may apply in one of the following disciplines: crafts, dance, interdisciplinary/performance art (individuals only), literature, media, multi-disciplinary, music, theater, and the visual arts.

Programs Available:
$1,000 To Individual Artists And Organizations (Small Projects Program)
$2,500 To Professional Artists (Individual Artist Fellowship Program)
Money For Artists To Promote Art In Local Communities (City Arts Project)
To Provide Funds For Art Projects, Workshops, Performance And
    Residencies In Schools (Arts Education Program)
$2,500 to Young Artists For Innovative Projects (Young Artist Program)

Florida

Florida Arts Council
Division of Cultural Affairs
1001 DeSoto Park Drive   850-245-6470
Tallahassee, FL 32301   Fax: 850-245-6492
www.florida-arts.org

Eligibility requirements: Individual Artist Programs: State residency is required, unless otherwise specified.

Programs Available:
$5,000 To Professional Artists (Individual Artist Fellowship Program)
Grants To Schools And Organizations Involved In Lifelong Art Education
    Projects (Arts In Education)
Money For Special Projects (Challenge Grant Program)
Money For Local Arts Agencies (Local Arts Agency/State Service
    Organization Program)
$1,500 For Professional Development In Art Organizations (Quarterly Grant
    Assistance Program)
Technical Assistance For Art Organizations In Rural Communities
    (Underserved Arts Communities Assistance Program)
Grants To Sponsoring Organizations To Cover Project Costs (State Touring
    Program)
Money To Support Programming That Fosters Diversity In Art (Cultural
    Support Grants)
Money For Organizations Involved In International Exchange Projects
    (International Cultural Exchange)

Georgia

Georgia Council for Arts
260 14th St., NW, Suite 40   404-685-2787
Atlanta, GA 30318   Fax: 404-685-6788
www.web_dept.com/gca

Eligibility requirements: In general, grant categories include: architecture/environmental arts, dance, arts-related education, film-making, folk arts/heritage arts and crafts, arts-related historic preservation, literary arts, multi-media, museums, music, photography, public radio and television, theater and visual arts. No individual funding is available. Money available: $2,300,000.

Programs Available:
Grants For Art Groups To Tour (Georgia Touring Grants)
$1000 To Hire An Arts Consultant (Technical Assistance Grants)
Money To Support Art Organizations (General Operating Support)
$20,000 For Art Related Activities (Specific Project Support)
Up To $100,000 For Organizations (Challenge Grant Program)
Money For Schools To Have An Artist In Residence
    (Artists Residencies)
$30,000 For Curriculum-Based Arts Education Programs
    (The Georgia Challenge)
$5,000 To Support Traditional Arts (Folklife Grant Program)
Grants For Students To Learn From Master Folk Artists
    (Traditional Arts Apprenticeship Program)

Hawaii

Hawaii State Foundation on Culture and Arts (SFCA)
250 South Hotel St., 2nd Floor   808-586-0300
Honolulu, HI 96813   Fax: 808-586-0308
www.state.hi.us/sfca

Eligibility requirements: State residency is required for individual artist programs. Money available: $1,432,000.

Programs Available:
$5,000 To Talented Visual And Performing Artists (Individual Artists
    Fellowship Program)
Money For Schools To Promote Art Education (Arts In Education Program)
Grants To Individuals And Organizations To Preserve Folk Arts In Hawaii
    (Folk Arts Program)
$3,000 For Artists To Study As An Apprentice (Folk Arts Apprenticeship
    Awards)
Money For Arts In Public Places Program

Idaho

Idaho Commission on Arts
P.O. Box 83720   800-334-2488

2410 North Old Penitentiary Road
Boise, ID 83720-0008
208-334-2119
Fax: 208-334-2488
www2.state.id.us/arts

Eligibility requirements: Individual artist programs require state residency, unless otherwise specified.

Programs Available:
Money For An Arts Group (General Operating Support)
Money To Build A Cultural Facility (Cultural Facilities Grants)
Money For Schools Or Nursing Homes To Have An Artist In Residence (Artists in Residence)
$3,500 For Artists, Dancers, Designers, and Craftspersons (Fellowship Awards)
$8,000 To Be A Writer In Residence (Writer In Residence Award)
Money To Fund Art Activities (Quick Art$ Program)
$2,000 To Study With A Master Craftsperson (Traditional Arts Apprenticeship Program)

Illinois

Illinois Arts Council
State Of Illinois Center
100 West Randolph
Suite 10-500
Chicago, IL 60601
312-814-6750
Fax: 312-814-1471
www.state.il.us/agency/iac

Eligibility requirements: Individual artist programs require state residency, unless otherwise specified. In addition to the programs detailed, grants are funded for choral music and opera, dance, ethnic and folk arts, symphonies and ensemble, theater, and visual arts programs.

Programs Available:
$7,000 for Artists, Photographers, Writers, and Poets (Fellowships)
Grants To Artists To Study As Apprentices (Apprenticeship Program)
Money For Writers And Nonprofit Magazines (Literary Awards)
Money To Provide Art To Communities Normally Deprived Of Art (Access Program)
Money For Touring Art Groups (ArtsTour)
Special Money For Arts Programs and Projects (Special Assistance Grants)
Money For Schools Or Other Organizations To Have An Artist In Residence (Artists in Residence)
Grants For Schools To Develop Special Art Classes (Arts Resource)
Grants For Art Organizations To Solve Technical Or Administrative Problems (Technical Assistance Program)

Indiana

Indiana Arts Commission
150 West Market St., #618
Indianapolis, IN 46204
317-232-1268
Fax: 317-252-5595
www.state.in.us/iac

Eligibility requirements: Individual Artist Programs: State residency is required, unless otherwise specified. Grants are awarded in 16 categories: dance, design arts, education, expansion arts, folk arts, literature, local arts agencies, media arts, multi-arts, museums, music, presenters, statewide arts service organizations, theater, and visual arts.

Programs Available:
Grants To Arts Organizations (General Operating Support)
Grants To Local Arts Organizations (State and Local Partnership)
Grants To Run Special Art Projects (Arts Projects and Series)
Money For Artists In Residence Programs (Arts in Education Grants)
Money For Art Administrators To Attend Workshops (Technical Assistance)

Iowa

Iowa Arts Council
Capitol Complex
600 Locust
Des Moines, IA 50319-0290
515-281-6412
Fax: 515-242-6498
www.iowaartscouncil.org

Eligibility requirements: Individual artist programs require state residency, unless otherwise specified.

Programs Available:
Cash Matching Grants For Non-Profit Organizations To Develop Art Projects (Organization Projects)
Grants To Individual Artists (Artists Projects)
Money For Schools To Have An Artist In Residence (Arts In Education/Residencies)
Annual Monetary Awards For Art Organizations (Operational Support Grant Program)
$1,000 To High School Seniors Who Are Involved In The Arts (Iowa Scholarship For The Arts)
$3,000 For Elementary Schools To Plan For Art (Art Partners for Achievement)
$200 For Schools To Be Trained In Character Counts! (Character Counts

Through the Arts!)
Money To Participate In Significant Arts-Related Programs (Conference, Workshop & Forum Grants and Mini-Grants)
Matching Grants For Folk and Traditional Arts Projects (Folk & Traditional Arts Projects Grants and Mini-Grants

Kansas

Kansas Arts Commission
Jayhawk Tower
700 Jackson, Suite 1004
Topeka, KS 66603-3761
785-296-3335
Fax: 785-296-4989
http://arts.state.ks.us

Eligibility requirements: Individual Art programs require state residency. The Commission provides direct or indirect funding to artists, schools, government units, and cultural, social and educational organizations as well as nonprofit organizations. Major grants are awarded each May for the following fiscal year. Money available: $1,432,123.

Programs Available:
$5,000 For Artists And Writers (Fellowships in the Performing Arts)
$500 For Artists Creating Original Work (Artist Mini-Fellowship)
Grants To Produce Art Publications, Workshops, Exhibits, and Performances (Project Support)
Money For Schools and Organizations To Have An Artist In Residence (Artist in Residency and Visiting Artist Grants)
Matching Grants For Programming and Administrative Costs (Operational Support for Arts & Cultural Organizations)
$7,500 To Help Pay For Performance Fees (Kansas Touring Program)
$1,200 To Develop New Public Exhibitions of Kansas Artists (Kansas Visual Arts Program)
$2,000 4:1 Matching Grant For Rural, Multicultural, Culturally Specific and Emerging Organizations (Grassroots Grants)
$2,000 2:1 Matching Grant For Rural, Multicultural, Culturally Specific Emerging Organizations and Arts & Cultural Organizations (Technical Assistance)

Kentucky

Kentucky Arts Council
300 West Broad
Frankfort, KY 40601
502-564-3757
Fax: 502-564-2839
www.kyarts.org

Eligibility requirements: Matching grants from the Council are available to Kentucky nonprofit organizations committed to providing arts programs and services to the public. Grant amounts vary from year to year and depend upon the availability of funds. Non-matching fellowships are available to Kentucky artists. Interim Grants are available in all program areas to provide one-time funding for emergencies or for unexpected and outstanding opportunities in the arts.

Programs Available:
Grants To Arts Organizations (Challenge Grants)
Money To Help Pay Artists And Art Administrators (Arts Development Grants)
Money For Schools To Have An Artist In Residence (Artists in Residence Grants)
Grants For Teachers To Put Art In Their Classrooms (Teacher Incentive Project Grants)
$7,500 For The Professional Development Of Individual Kentucky Artists (Artist Fellowships)
$500 To Fund Activities That Help Artists Develop Their Careers (Individual Artist Professional Development Program)
$7,500 To Fund Public Performing Arts Events (Kentucky Arts On Tour)
$3,000 For Master Artists To Teach Students (Folk And Traditional Arts Apprenticeship)
$3,000 To Spend On Art Projects (Folk Arts Project And Tour)
$3,000 For Organizations To Enhance Art Programs (Project Grant Program)
Up To $5,000 To Establish Art Organizations (Community Arts Development Grants)
Money For Operating Expenses For Arts and Cultural Organizations (General Operating Support Grants I and II)
$5,000 To encourage Partnerships That Contribute To The Cultural, Social and Economic Growth Of The Community (Arts Build Community Grants)
$1,050 To Bring Professional Artists Into Early Childhood/Preschool Facilities (ArtStart! Grants Program)

Louisiana

Louisiana State
Division of the Arts
P.O. Box 44247
Baton Rouge, LA 70804
220-342-8180
Fax: 225-342-8173
www.crt.state.la.us/arts

Eligibility requirements: Individual artist programs require state residency.
Programs Available:
$5,000 For Artists To Work With A Master (Folklife Apprenticeships)
$20,000 For Art Organizations (Project Assistance Program)
$20,000 To Support Arts In Education (Arts In Education Program)
Up To $250,000 For Art Groups (General Operating Support Program)
Up To $250,000 For Local Art Agencies (Local Arts Agency Program)
Grants For Specific Art Activities (Individual Artist Mini-Grant Program)
Money For Artists, Craftspersons, Designers And Musicians (Artist
Fellowships)

Maine

Maine Arts Commission
State House Station 25   207-287-2724
Augusta, ME 04333   Fax: 207-287-2335
www.mainearts.com

Eligibility requirements: Individual artist programs require state residency. Maine offers an Institutional Support Program which provides two-year funding for established professional, nonprofit cultural organizations, schools, and other organizations for specific local arts projects and programs.
Programs Available:
$3,000 To Artists (Fellowships)
Up To $20,000 For Special Art Programs (Project Support)
$4,000 For School Teachers To Go To Art Seminars (Professional
Development for Teachers)
$5,000 To Support Art Projects (Public Art Grants)
Money For Students To Learn From Master Artists (Traditional Arts
Apprenticeships)
$1,000 For Artist Ideas And Improvement (Good Idea Grant)
$7,500 To Assist Art Organizations Collaborate With The Community (Artist
In Maine Communities Program)

Maryland

Maryland State Arts Council
175 West Ostend St., Suite E   410-767-6555
Baltimore, MD 21230   Fax: 410-333-1062
www.msac.org

Eligibility requirements: The Council provides direct grants to individual artists, offers professional advice, and initiates projects that provide services and opportunities for Maryland artists. State residency is required for participation. The Council's Community Arts Development program supports county arts council organizations in each of the 23 counties of Maryland and Baltimore City. Funds are used in each county to regrant to local arts organizations, support various arts programs, assist local arts groups with fund raising, publicity, promotion and planning, and to support the operating expenses of the county arts council.
Programs Available:
$6,000 For Creative Artists (Individual Artist Awards)
Money For Large Arts Organizations (Grants to Major Institutions)
Help For Those Interested In Maryland Folklife (Maryland Folklife Program)
Money For Poets, Artists, and Performers To Be At Schools (Artists in
Education Program)
Grants For Organizations To Support One-Time Public Activities (Arts
Project Grants)
$1,000 For Individuals To Develop Their Artwork (Individual Artist Mini-
Grant Program)
Money For Technical Assistance (Grant For Organizations)
Money To Help Underserved Audiences (Arts in Communities)
Help For Local Arts Councils (Community Arts Development Grants)
Assist Schools Obtain Quality Performers (Visiting Performers Program)

Massachusetts

Massachusetts Cultural Council
10 St. James Avenue, 3rd Floor   617-727-3668
Boston, MA 02116   Fax: 617-727-0044
www.massculturalcouncil.org

Eligibility requirements: Individual artist programs require state residency, unless otherwise specified. Programs are open to individuals, organizations and schools.
Programs Available:
Money For Arts Organizations (Organizational Support Grant)
Funds To Provide Art To Children (Creative Schools Program)
$5,000 Awarded To Individual Artists (Artist Fellowship Grants)
Money For Artists To Work In Schools (Local Cultural Council Program)
$6,000 To Support The Teaching Of Traditional Arts (Traditional Arts
Apprenticeship)
Funds To Subsidize The Cost Of Field Trips (PASS Program)
Money To Help Youth In Need By Providing Arts Related Activities
(YouthReach Initiative)

Michigan

Michigan Council for the Arts
702 West Kalamazoo Street
P.O. Box 30705   517-241-4011
Lansing, MI 48909   Fax: 517-241-3979
www.michigan.gov/hal

Any nonprofit organization or institution, artist, local government, school or community group in Michigan is eligible to apply for MCA grant funds. All funded activities must take place within the state and comply with Equal Opportunity Standards. Contact the Council for specific program guidelines.
Programs Available:
Money For Artists To Teach In Schools (Arts And Learning Program)
Grants For Schools To Have An Artist In Residence (Artists In Schools
Program (AIS))
Grants To Organizations For Art Projects And Programs (Anchor
Organization Program)
Grants To Small Organizations (Arts Organization Development Program
(AOD))
Money For Regional Cultural Projects (Cultural Projects Program)
Grants To Community Based Organizations (Art Agencies Services Program)
$4,000-$10,000 To Support the Arts, Culture, Heritage, and History of 39
Identified Counties (Rural Arts and Cultural Program)
$4,000 Matching Grants for locally Developed Art and Cultural Programs
(Mini-Grant Regional Regranting Program)
$100,000 Matching Grant to Improve Facilities (Capital Improvements
Program)
Grant Money To Improve Curriculum (The Big Culture Lesson)
$30,000 2:1 Match For Non-Profit Organizations Fund Arts Projects (Arts
Project Program)

Minnesota

Minnesota State Arts Board
400 Sibley St., Suite 200   651-215-1600
St. Paul, MN 55101   Fax: 651-215-1602
www.arts.state.mn.us

Eligibility requirements: Individual artist programs require state residency, unless otherwise specified.
Programs Available:
Money For Schools To Have An Artist In Residence (School Support Grants)
$6,000 For Community-Based Projects By Artists Or Organizations (Cultural
Collaborations)
Grants To Art Organizations (Institutional Support)
Money To Display Art In Public Places (Percent For Art In Public Places
Program)
$2,000-$6,000 Awarded To Artists At Various Stages Of Their Careers
(Artist Initiative Grants)

Mississippi

Mississippi Arts Commission
239 North Lamar St., Suite 207   601-359-6030
Jackson, MS 39201   Fax: 601-359-6008
www.arts.state.mo.us

Eligibility requirements: Individual artist programs require state residency.
Programs Available:
$5,000 For Writers, Composers, Video Producers (Artist Fellowships)
$25,000 For Arts And Cultural Organizations
(General Operating Support)
$7,500 For Local Schools To Improve Their Art Programs (Arts In
Education)
$7,500 For New Artists (Project Grants)
$2,000 To Fund Community Based Traditional Art Forms (Folk Art
Apprenticeship Program)
$500 Mini-Grants (Mini-Grants For Artists)

Missouri

Missouri Arts Council
Wainwright Office Complex
111 N. 7th St., Suite 105   314-340-6845
St. Louis, MO 63101-2188   Fax: 314-340-7215
www.missouriartscouncil.org

Eligibility requirements: The Council offers financial assistance through seven art areas: dance, literature, media, multi-discipline, music, theater, and visual arts. A program administrator supervises applications in each area.
Programs Available:
Money For Smaller Arts Organizations (Community Arts Program (CAP))
Money For Arts Groups Serving The Entire State (Statewide Arts Service
Organizations)
Money For Art Organizations To Perform Outside Their Home Areas
(Missouri Touring Program)

Money To Incorporate Arts Education Programs Into School Curricula
(Missouri Alliance For Arts Education)
$2,500 To Help Nonprofit Develop Skills (Organizational Development
Program)
$30,000 To Fund A Variety Of Arts Activities (Discipline Program
Assistance)
Money For Folklife Festivals (Folk Arts Program)
Funds For A Three-Year Period (Mid-Sized Arts Organizations Operating and
Program Support)
Money For Non-Traditional Arts Venues (Minority Arts Program)

Montana
Montana Arts Council
316 N. Park Ave., Suite 252
P.O. Box 202201
Helena, MT 59620-2201
www.art.state.mt.us
406-444-6430
Fax: 406-444-6548
Eligibility requirements: Individual artist programs require state residency.
Programs Available:
Grants For Arts Preservation, Media Arts, Archaeology, and Folklore
(Cultural and Aesthetic Project Grants)
Biennial Grants To Art Organizations (Organizational Excellence Grants)
Grants To Community Based And Traditional Artists
(Folk Arts Program)
$1,000 To Artists And Organizations For Opportunities Or Emergencies
(Opportunity Grants)
Money To Help Non Profit Organizations Hire Artists (Artists in Schools &
Communities)
Funds Targeted For Use With Rural or Underserved Communities For Arts
Programs (Building Arts Participation)
$500 Matching Fee Support For Touring Companies (Fee Support for
Touring Companies)

Nebraska
Nebraska Arts Council
Jocelyn Castle Carriage House
3838 Davenport St.
Omaha, NE 68131-2329
www.nebraskaartscouncil.org
402-595-2122
Fax: 402-595-2334
Eligibility requirements: Individual artist programs require state residency.
Programs Available:
Money For Writers, Artists, and Performers
(Individual Artist Fellowships)
Grants To Arts Organizations (Basic Support Grant)
Over $2,500 To Pay For Artists' Residencies In Schools (Artists In
Residency)
Grants To Support Art Projects In Schools (Impact: Arts Education Program)
Money To Support Organizations That Sponsor Collaborative Arts Projects
(Impact: Collaborative Arts)
Money To Pay For Programs Of Cultural Organizations (Multi-Cultural
Assistance Program)
Grants For People Of Color In Existing Or New Arts Programming
(Multi-Cultural Organization)
Money For Touring Exhibits And Programs (Nebraska Touring And Exhibits
Sponsor Grant)
Grants To Organizations For Professional Development, Emergencies And
New Ventures (Special Opportunity Support)

Nevada
Nevada Arts Council
716 North Carson St., Suite A
Carson City, NV 89701
http://dmla.clan.lib.nv.us/docs/arts
775-687-6680
Fax: 775-687-6688
Eligibility requirements: Individual artist programs require state residency.
Money available: $600,000.
Programs Available:
$5,000 For Artists To Create New Works (Artists Fellowships)
$2,500 For Master Folk Artists To Teach Apprentices
(Folk Arts Apprenticeships)
Money For Schools To Have An Artist In Residence
(Artist in Residence Program)
Money to Stimulate Local Cultural Activity (Nevada Touring Initiative)
$3,000 For Commissioned Artwork (Governor's Arts Awards)
Money For Art Education For Youths At Risk (YouthReach Nevada)
Grants For Arts Education Workshops For Educators (Professional
Development Grants)
$2,500 For Innovative Arts Education Programs (Special Project Grants For
Schools and Organizations)

New Hampshire
New Hampshire Division of Arts
Council of the Arts
2 1/2 Beacon Street, 2nd Floor
Concord, NH 03301-4974
www.state.nh.us/nharts
603-271-2789
Fax: 603-271-3584
Eligibility requirements: Individual artist programs require state residency,
unless otherwise specified.
Programs Available:
$5,000 For Individual Artists (Individual Artist Fellowships)
$5,000 For Special Projects And Developing Artists (Exploration/New Works
Grant)
$3,000 To Learn From An Experienced Artist (Traditional Arts
Apprenticeships)
$10,000 To Support Cultural Organizations
(Operating Grant)
$3,500 For Schools To Bring In Artists (Artists In Residence)
$2,500 For Arts Education In Schools (Arts Link Initiative)
$3,500 To Support Art Projects In Communities
(Community Arts Project Grant)
$1,000 More For Arts In Communities (Mini-Grants Program)
$500 Matching Grants For Consultations (Peer Mentorship Program)
$5,000 Matching Grants For Artists To Serve As Resources For Teachers
(AIE Leadership Grant)

New Jersey
New Jersey State Council on the Arts
225 West State St.
P.O. Box 306
Trenton, NJ 08625
www.njartscouncil.org
609-292-6130
Fax: 609-989-1440
Eligibility requirements: Individual artist programs require state residency,
unless otherwise specified.
Programs Available:
Grants For Artists, Mimes, Sculptors, Poets, and Opera Singers (Fellowships)
Money For Regional and State-Wide Organizations (General Operating
Support)
Grants To Support Special Art Projects (Special Project Support)
Money For Art Programs In Local Schools
(Projects Serving Artist Grants)
Funding For Arts Organizations (Support Grants)
Money For Public Or Parochial School Art Programs (Educational Funding:
Arts in Education Programs (AIE))
Money For Jazz, Folk, And Theater Artists In Residence (Artists in Education
Programs)
Grants For A Consortium of Community Organizations (Community Arts
Collaboration Grants)
Money For Grants and Regrants in 21 Counties (Local Arts Program)
Support For County Arts Agencies To Increase Permanent Arts Staff (Local
Arts Staffing Initiative)
Funds To Support The Passing On Of Folk Arts (Folk Arts Apprenticeship)

New Mexico
New Mexico Arts
P.O. Box 1450
Santa Fe, NM 87504-1450
www.nmarts.org
505-827-6490
Fax: 505-827-6043
Eligibility requirements: The New Mexico Art Division is unable to fund
fellowships to individuals. It strongly encourages applicant organizations to
involve resident New Mexico artists. However, the Division does support
local sponsorship of out-of-state artists or organizations to enrich a resident
group or when the services fill a need that is not being met locally.
Organizational Funding: New Mexico administers awards to nonprofit
organizations. Generally, award applicants must provide at least a one-to-one
cash match.
Programs Available:
Grants For Community Based Organizations (Organizations For The Arts
Program)
Grants To Organizations That Produce Performing Arts Exhibits And
Outreach (Arts Organizations Touring And Outreach)
Money For Folk Artists In Communities (Rural Arts Economic Development
Initiative)
Money For Students To Learn From Master Artists (Folk Arts Program)
Grants For Preserving Folk Arts (Folk Arts Program)
Grants For Schools To Have Artists In Residence (Artists Residencies)
Money For Art Projects In Schools (Arts In Education Program)

New York
New York State Council on the Arts
175 Varick Street
212-627-4455

New York, NY 10014   Fax: 212-387-7164
www.nysca.org
Eligibility requirements: Individual artist programs require state residency. Nonprofit organizations can obtain support in 17 areas including: architecture, planning and design, arts in education, capital funding initiative, dance, electronic media and film, folk arts, individual artists, literature, museum, music, musical instrument revolving loan fund, presenting operations, special arts services, state local partnership, theater, and the visual arts.
Programs Available:
Money For Artists (Individual Artist Programs)
Grants For Arts Organizations (General Operating Support)
Money For School Art Programs In Music, Theater, and Media (Arts in Education)
$5,000 For Local Art Groups (State And Local Partnership Program)
Grants To Support Professional And Ethnic Art Activities (Special Arts Services)
Grants To Support Traditional Art In Communities (Folk Arts Program)
Support Excellence In Design And Planning in the Public Realm (Architecture Planning & Design)

North Carolina

North Carolina Arts Council
Department of Cultural Resources   919-733-2111
Raleigh, NC 27699-4632   Fax: 919-733-4834
www.ncarts.org
Eligibility requirements: Individual artist programs require state residency. Money for arts organizations is in eight categories: community development, dance, folklife, literature, music, theater, touring/presenting, and the visual arts. Support includes funding for program support, interdisciplinary/ special projects, and organizational development grants.
Programs Available:
$8,000 For Artists, Dancers, Musicians, and Writers (Fellowships)
Grants To Schools For Art Projects (Arts in Education)
Grants To Visual Artists And Writers For Residencies (Residency Center Opportunities)
Money For Artists And Organizations That Document Folk Art (Folklife Documentary Program)
Money For Public Folk Art Awareness Projects (Folklife Projects)
Grants To Support Art Organizations (General Support Grant)
Money For Local Arts Program (Grassroots Arts Program)
Money For Organizations To Learn About Management (Technical Assistance)
Money For Individual Art Projects (Regional Artist Project Grants)
$15,000 Support Over Three Years To Improve Arts Education (Arts In Education Rural Development)
$20,000 For Artists Residencies (Arts In Education Artist Residencies)
$5,000 Grants For Communities To Develop Public Art Design (Creating Place: Community Public Art and Design Development)
$5,000 Matching Grants For Communities To Carry Out Their Public Art Design (Creating Place: Community Public Art and Design Implementation)
$10,000 Matching Grants to Commission New Work (Literary, Performing and Visual Arts Program Support)
Money To Develop and Sustain Organizations That Serve Multicultural and People With Disabilities (Outreach)
$35,000 Matching Grants For Organizations That Provide Arts Services On A State Or Regional Basis (Statewide Service Organizations)
$10,000 Matching Grants For Artist Fees, Travel, Marketing and Project Related Costs (Touring/Presenting)

North Dakota

North Dakota Council On Arts
1600 East Century Avenue, Suite 6   701-328-7590
Bismarck, ND 58503   Fax: 701-328-7595
www.state.nd.us/arts
Eligibility requirements: Individual artist programs require state residency, unless otherwise specified.
Programs Available:
Money For Artists, Dancers, Opera Singers, Photographers, and Writers (Artists Fellowships Program)
Money For Schools To Have An Artist In Residence (Artists in Residence)
$2,000 For Students To Learn From Master Artists (Traditional Arts Apprenticeship Program)
$500 For Artists To Improve Their Skills (Professional Development)
$1,000 For Performances, Exhibitions And Special Events (Institutional Support Program)
$2,000 For Organizations To Serve Rural Communities (Access Programs)
$600 For New Projects And Touring Events (Special Project Grants)

$300 To Teachers To Explore New and Creative Ways To Incorporate the Arts into Non-Arts Curriculum (Teacher Initiative)
$3,000 To Communities For Performances, Exhibitions, Murals and Special Events (Lewis and Clark Community Grant)

Ohio

Ohio Council on Arts
727 East Main St.   614-466-2613
Columbus, OH 43205   Fax: 614-466-4494
www.oac.state.oh.us
Eligibility requirements: State residency is required, unless otherwise specified.
Programs Available:
$10,000 For Artists And Art Critics (Individual Artist Fellowships)
$1,000 For Artists To Attend Workshops (Professional Development Assistance)
$2,000 For An Artist To Work With A Master (Traditional and Ethnic Arts Apprenticeship Program)
Grants To Arts Organizations (Major Institution Support)
Money To Support Special Projects (Project Support)
Money For Administrative Expenses (Operating Support)
$2,000 For Special Art Opportunities (Sudden Opportunity Grants)
Grants For Specific Projects (Artists Projects Program)
Grants For Activities That Promote Art In Education (Arts In Education Program)
Grants To Organizations For Community Art Projects (Arts Education Partnership)
Grants To Have Professional Artists in Residency (Artists in Residence Program)
Money To Support Out-of-School Arts Opportunities For At Risk Youth (YouthReach Ohio)
$2,000 To Assist Artists, Art Organizations and Citizens In 29 Appalachian Counties (Appalachian Arts Program)

Oklahoma

State Arts Council of Oklahoma
2101 N. Lincoln Blvd.
P.O. Box 52001-2001   405-521-2931
Oklahoma City, OK 73152-2001   Fax: 405-521-6418
www.oklaosf.state.ok.us/~arts/
Eligibility requirements: The Council is unable to fund individuals. Applications are accepted from non-religious, nonprofit, tax exempt organizations. Colleges, schools, and universities which receive funding through the State Regents for Higher Education or substantial private sources, are a lower funding priority, except in areas where the university or college is the sole source of arts events in a community. Money available: $1,600,000. All funding for the Advanced Request, Over $4,000 and Under $4,000 Project Assistance categories must be matched dollar for dollar by the applicant. Fifty percent of the matching funds must be cash. The Council will fund personnel or administrative costs associated with a project. The Council does not fund general administrative expenses or general organizational support.
Programs Available:
Grants For Community Arts Celebrations (Fairs and Festival Funding)
Money For An Artist In Residence In Schools Or Community Groups (Artists in Residences Program).
Money For Artists To Tour (Oklahoma Touring Program)
Grants For Students To Learn From Professional Folk Artists (Master Apprenticeship Program)
Grants To Schools For Arts Activities (ArtsPower Education Grant)
Money For Arts Projects (Project Assistance)
Funds For Community Arts Projects and Events (MiniGrant)
Grants For DHS Childcare Centers For Quality Arts Based Projects (Youth Arts Program)

Oregon

Oregon Arts Commission
775 Summer St., NE   503-986-0082
Salem, OR 97301   Fax: 503-986-0260
www.oregonartscommission.org
Eligibility requirements: Individual artist programs require state residency, unless otherwise specified.
Programs Available:
Money To Be An Artist In Residence (Artist Residencies)
Money For Arts Programs In Oregon Communities (Arts Build Communities Grants)
More Money For Arts Programs In Schools (Regional Arts Education Partnerships)
Grants To Small Arts Groups And Artists (Regional Arts Partnerships)
Grants To Folk Artists And Organizations

(Oregon Folklife Program)
Grants For Oregon Schools (Oregon Arts Education Network Grants)
Matching Funds To Support Projects Advancing the Commission's Arts
Education Goals (Arts Education Leadership Grants)
Money To Support Projects That Demonstrate the Connection Between the
Arts, Landscape, Outdoor Recreation and Trail Corridors (Arts and
Trails)

Pennsylvania

Pennsylvania Council on the Arts
Room 216, Finance Bldg.   717-787-6883
Harrisburg, PA 17120   Fax: 717-783-2538
www.arts.net.org/pca

Eligibility requirements: For individual artist programs, applicants must have
lived in Pennsylvania for two years prior to applying for funding and should
have had a minimum of three years professional experience in their field.
Organizational funding programs require that organizations must be
nonprofit, tax exempt corporations that provide arts programming and/or
services to Pennsylvania. Categories include: broadcast of the arts, crafts,
interdisciplinary arts, dance, literature, local arts services, local government,
media arts, museums, music, presenting organizations, theater, and visual arts.
Nonprofit organizations may apply on behalf of an unincorporated arts group.
In this capacity, the organization becomes a "conduit" for grant funds and is
financially, administratively, and programmatically responsible for a grant.
Programs Available:
Grants To Artists Who Work In Schools (Arts In Residence)
Grants To Teach Literary, Performing Or Visual Arts
(Arts In Education Projects)
Grants To Arts Organizations And Artists
(Local Government Grants)
Grants To Underserved Artists (Pennsylvania Partners In The Arts)
Grants To Cultural Arts Groups (Preserving Diverse Cultures)
Money To Hire A Consultant For Your Art Group (Professional Development
And Consulting)
$10,000 To Dancers, Jazz Composers, Writers And Artists (Fellowships)
Money For New Arts Organizations And Projects (Entry Track)
Money For Regular Arts Organizations And Programs (AOAP Track)

Rhode Island

RI State Council on The Arts
83 Park Street, 6th Floor   401-222-3880
Providence, RI 02903   Fax: 401-222-3018
www.arts.ri.gov

Eligibility requirements: Applicants for the individual artist programs must be
eighteen years of age or older and have lived in the state for at least one year
prior to application. Minimum grants awarded to organizations is $100 and
funds must be expended during the fiscal year of the award. Program grants,
with the exception of general operating support, are divided into two
categories. Level I grants range from $100 to $2,000. Level II grants range
from $2,001 to $5,000. A dollar for dollar cash match is required.
Programs Available:
$3,000 For Artists, Choreographers, Designers, and Printmakers
(Fellowships)
$2,000 For Folk Art Apprenticeships (Folk Arts Apprenticeships)
Grants To Art Organizations (Expansion Grants)
Money For Operating Expenses (General Operating Support)

South Carolina

South Carolina Arts Commission
1800 Gervais St.   803-734-8696
Columbia, SC 29201   Fax: 803-934-8526
www.state.sc.us/arts

Eligibility requirements: Individual artist programs require state residency.
Programs Available:
$5,000 For Artists, Performers, Writers, And Craftsmen
(Fellowships)
$1,000 To Be Used For Professional Development
(Quarterly Grants)
Up To $500,000 To Arts Groups (General Support Grants)
Money To Bring Art Programs To Schools (Arts in the Basic Curriculum)
Money For Schools To Have An Artist In Residence (Arts in Education)
Grants To Non-Profit Organizations To Present Performances Of South
Carolina Artists (Community Tour)
Money For Organizations To Utilize Artistic and Cultural Resources (Cultural
Visions For Underserved Communities Grant)
$7,500 To Support Programs That Promote Traditional Art Forms (Folklife
and Traditional Arts Program)
$2,000 For Qualified Master Artists To Instruct an Apprentice (Folklife and
Traditional Arts Apprenticeship Initiative)
Up To $3,000 To Support the Creation of a Five-Year Arts Education

Program (AIE Comprehensive Planning Grant)
Up To $20,000 To Help School Districts Create Arts Curriculum Coordinator
Positions (AIE District Arts Coordinator Initiative Grant)

South Dakota

South Dakota Arts Council
800 Governors Dr.   605-773-3131
Pierre, SD 57501   Fax: 605-773-6962
www.state.sd.us/deca/sdarts

Eligibility requirements: Individual artist programs require state residency.
Applicant organizations and individuals are funded up to 50% of projected
costs. Funding is available in the following arts disciplines: dance, music,
opera/music theater, theater, visual arts, design arts, crafts, photography,
media arts, literature, and folk arts.
Programs Available:
$500 For Arts Groups To Hire Consultants   (Technical Assistance)
$500 For Art Group Managers To Improve Their Skills
(Professional Development)
Money For Touring Art Groups (Touring Arts)
Money For Schools To Have An Artist In Residence
(Artists in Schools)
Grants To Arts Institutions (Arts Challenge Grants)
Money To Present Music Programs In Native American Communities (Music
Residency Program)
$3,000 For Artists To Work On Specific Projects
(Artist Project Grants)
Money To Bring In Musicians Into Communities (Importation of Musicians)
Matching Funds To Transport Students To Programs In Another Town
(Excursion Program)
Grants To Encourage Multi-State Collaboration (Artist Collaboration Grants)
Funds Provide Master Artists the Opportunity to Teach Qualified
Apprenticeships (Traditional Arts Apprenticeship Grants)

Tennessee

Tennessee Art Commission
401 Charlotte Ave.   615-741-1701
Nashville, TN 37243-0780   Fax: 615-741-8559
www.arts.state.tn.us

Eligibility requirements: Individual artist programs require state residency.
Programs Available:
$2,500 For Artists, Musicians, Writers, And Dancers
(Individual Artists Fellowships)
Grants For Arts Organizations (Arts Build Communities)
$6,000 For Special Art Projects (Arts Projects)
Grants To Operate An Arts Organizations (General Operating Support)
$2,500 To Hire Out-Of-Town Consultants
(Technical Assistance Program)
$10,000 For A Nonprofit Agency To Have An Artist In Residence
(Artists Residencies)
Grants To Art Organizations Of Color (Advancement And Expansion)
Grants For Established Large Arts Organizations
(Major Cultural Institutions)
Grants For Activities In Rural Areas (Rural Arts Projects Support)

Texas

Texas Commission on the Arts
920 Colorado, Suite 501
P.O. Box 13406
Capitol Station   512-463-5535
Austin, TX 78711-3406   Fax: 512-475-2699
www.arts.state.tx.us

Eligibility requirements: Texas does not offer direct funding to individuals.
Individual artists are funded indirectly through the Arts in Education and the
Touring Programs. In addition, individual artists may apply to the
Commission under the umbrella of a nonprofit organization or government
entity.
Programs Available:
$25,000 To Support Projects Demonstration Artistic Merit and "Best
Practices" in Arts Education (Arts Education)
$2,000 Funding For Strategic Development in Arts Education (Arts Education
Team Building)
$35,000 Support For Organizations To Present, Promote and Produce Artistic
Programs (Core Support Organizations and Local Arts Agencies)
$3,000 To Encourage Non-Profit Organizations, Governments and Schools in
Rural Areas To Expand the Arts (County Arts Expansion Program)
$2,000 Mini-Grants To Enhance the Growth of the Arts Industry (Cultural
Connections)
$15,000 To Ethnically-Specific/Minority Organizations That Serve
Ethnically-Specific/Minority Communities (Development Assistance
To Minority Organizations)

$7,500 To Prepare Art Exhibits (Exhibit Preparation To Tour)
$15,000 For Project Assistance (Project Support)
$35,000 For Administrative Support (Statewide Services)
$2,500 For 8th to 12th Graders to Attend Arts Programs (Young Masters Program)

Utah

Utah Arts Council
617 E. South Temple   801-236-7555
Salt Lake City, UT 84102   Fax: 801-236-7556
http://arts.utah.gov
Eligibility requirements: Individual artist programs require state residency, unless otherwise specified.
Programs Available:
$5,000 For Artists, Printmakers, Photographers, and Video Artists (Visual Artist Fellowships)
$5,000 For Creative Writers (Creative Writing Award)
$2,000 For An Artist To Learn From A Master (Folk Arts Apprenticeship Program)
Money For Schools To Have An Artist In Residence (Artist In Residence)
$2,000 For Teachers In The Arts (Professional Development)
$12,000 For Arts Organizations And Museums (Community Arts Program)
Grants For Arts Organizations (General Operating Support)
$12,000 For Artists Who Work In Underserved Communities (AIE Underserved Communities)

Vermont

Vermont Council on Arts
136 State St., Dr 33   802-828-3291
Montpelier, VT 05633-6001   Fax: 802-828-3363
www.vermontartscouncil.org
Eligibility requirements: Individual artist programs require state residency.
Money available: $600,000.
Programs Available:
$15,000 For Arts Groups (Operating Grants)
Grants To Develop Art-Related Courses (Development Grants)
$500 For Artists To Attend Classes And Workshops (Development Grants)
$5,000 For Art Projects (Standard Project And Program)
$750 For New Art Projects (Incentive Project And Program)
$750 For Arts In Communities (Technical Assistance)
$7,000 To Arts Organizations (Opportunity Grants)
Money For Arts In Schools (Arts In Education Initiative)

Virginia

Virginia Commission for the Arts
Lewis House
223 Governor St.   804-225-3132
Richmond, VA 23219-2010   Fax: 804-225-4327
www.arts.state.va.us
Eligibility requirements: Individual artist programs require state residency.
Programs Available:
$5,000 For Professional Artists To Advance Their Careers (Project Grants)
$15,000 To Run An Arts Organization (General Operating Support)
$750 To Hire Management Consultants (Technical Assistance Grants)
$5,000 To Help Local Governments Support The Arts (Local Government Challenge Grants)
Money For Artists To Tour The State (Touring Assistance Programs)
Money For Schools To Have An Artist In Residence (Artist in Education Residencies)
Grants For Community Colleges To Have An Artist In Residence (Community College Artist Residencies)
Funding For Workshops and Consultants In Arts Education (Arts in Education Development Grants)
$300 For Teachers To Develop Innovative Art Programs (Teacher Incentive Grant Program)
Money To Hire Consultants Or Attend Conferences In Arts Education (Arts In Education Technical Assistance)

Washington

Washington State Arts Commission
234 E. 8th Ave.
P.O. Box 42675   360-753-3860
Olympia, WA 98504-2675   Fax: 360-586-5351
www.arts.wa.gov
Eligibility requirements: Individual artist programs require state residency.
Programs Available:

$5,000 To Professional Literary, Performing, and Two-Dimensional Artists (Artist Fellowship Awards)
Grants To Ethnic Heritage Artists (Governor's Ethnic Heritage Awards)
$2,000 For Short-Term Art Projects (Project Support)
$10,000 For Arts Organizations (Organizational Support)
Money To Support Arts Organizations (Institutional Support Program)
Money For Schools To Have An Artist In Residence (Artists in Residence Program (AIR))
Money For Communities To Build Strong Arts Programs (Arts Education Community Consortium Grant)
$500 To Attend Workshops (Professional Development Assistance Program)
Funds For Master Artists To Instruct Students (Apprenticeship Program)

West Virginia

Arts and Humanities Division
Division of Culture and History
Cultural Center
1900 Kanawha Blvd. East   304-558-0240
Charleston, WV 25305-0300   Fax: 304-558-2779
www.wvculture.org/arts
Money available: $2,431,110.
Programs Available:
Money For Individual Artists (Individual Artist Programs)
Money For The Professional Development Of Artists (Support for Artists Program)
$15,000 For An Art Exhibition (Presenting West Virginia Artists Program)
$125,000 For Art Organizations (Major Institutions Support Grant)
$25,000 For Theaters, Galleries, and Museums (Support for Arts Institutions/Arts Organizations)
Money To Fund Art Programs (Touring Program)
Money To Support New Works Of Composers, Playwrights, Writers, and Choreographers (Performing Arts)
Money to Develop Special Art Programs For Schools (Arts in Education)
Funds For Music, Theater and Dance Groups To Support Unique Production Costs With New Works (Support For New Productions)
Funds For Traditional Arts, Ethnic, Folk or Culturally Diverse Arts Festivals (Support The Festivals)
Grants For the Presentation of Arts Events Which Involve People With Disabilities (Access)
$1,000 To Present West Virginia Artists in Performances, Workshops and Other Projects (Mini-Grant Program)
Money For Special Educational Projects (Arts In Education: Special Projects)
Funding For Art Organizations To Expand Their "Arts Services" (Cultural Facilities and Capital Resources Grant)

Wisconsin

Wisconsin Arts Board
101 E. Wilson St., Suite 301   608-266-0190
Madison, WI 53702   Fax: 608-267-0380
www.arts.state.wi.us
Eligibility requirements: Individual artist programs require state residency. For most programs, recipients must match state awards with cash or donated services.
Programs Available:
$8,000 For Artists, Writers, and Folk Artists (Fellowships)
$3,000 For Small Groups And Individual Artists (Small Organization Support)
Grants To Community Art Programs (Community Arts Program)
Support For The Performing Arts Network (Performing Arts Network (PAN)-Wisconsin)
Money For Organizations To Bring In Professional Touring Artists (Wisconsin Touring Program)
$5,000 For Folk Artists (Folk Arts Opportunity Grants)
Grants For Culturally Diverse Art Projects (Cultural Diversity Initiative)
Money For Schools To Have An Artist In Residence (Artists in Education Residency)
Money For Schools To Bring Artists Into The Classroom (Educational Opportunity Grants)
$3,000 To Encourage Collaborative Projects Between Artists and Their Communities (Artist and Community Collaboration)
Money To Provide Artistic, Program and Operational Support To Nonprofit Arts Institutes (Artistic Program Support)
Assistance To Arts Organizations To Leverage Income From Private Sources (Arts Challenge Initiative)

Wyoming

Wyoming Arts Council
2320 Capitol Ave.   307-777-7742
Cheyenne, WY 82002   Fax: 307-777-5499
http://wyoarts.state.wy.us

Eligibility requirements: Individual fellowships require state residency. For educational funding, grants require a one-to-one cash match.

Programs Available:
Grants For Arts Organizations (Organizational Funding)
Grants To Strengthen An Arts Organization (Technical Assistance)
Grants To Schools And Organizations To Plan Arts Programs (Art is Essential Grant)
Grants For Schools To Have An Artist In Residence (Artist In Residence Grants)

Money To Develop Art Courses In Schools (Project Grants)
$3,000 For Writers (Literary Awards)
$1,000 For Arts Projects (Community Services Program)
$500 For Arts Programs And Events (Open Door Grants)
$300 For Artists To Work In Communities (Arts Across Wyoming)
Money For Arts Organizations And Artists (Art Access)
$2,500 For Performers (Fellowship)

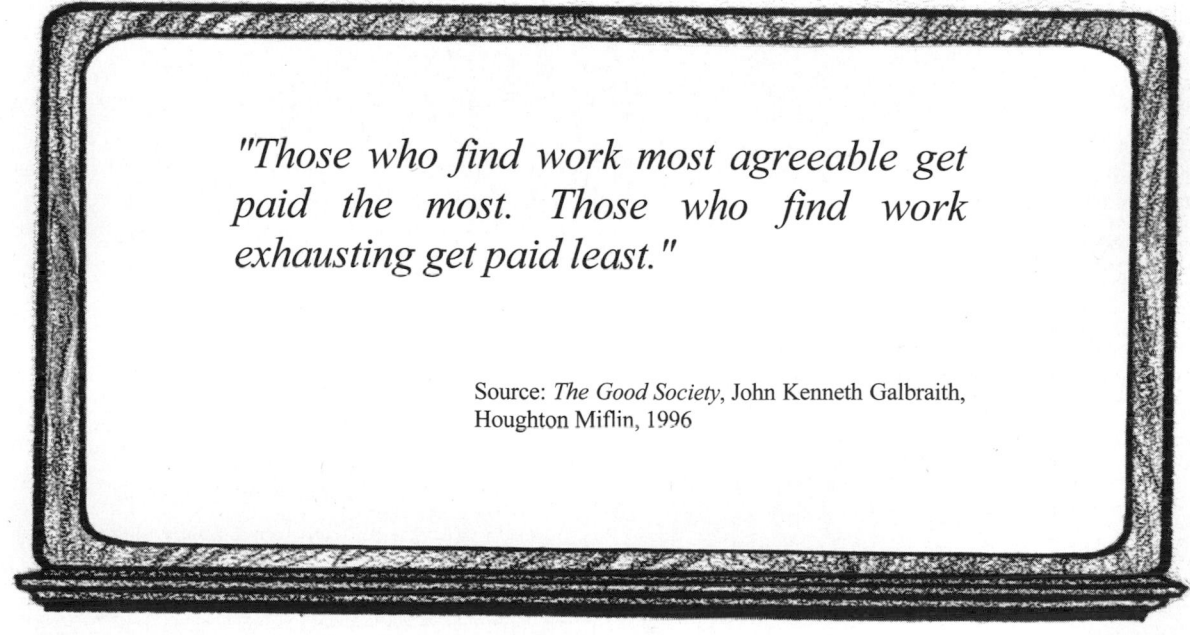

"Those who find work most agreeable get paid the most. Those who find work exhausting get paid least."

Source: *The Good Society*, John Kenneth Galbraith, Houghton Miflin, 1996

Matthew Lesko, Information USA, Inc., 12081 Nebel Street, Rockville, MD 20852 • 1-800-955-7693 • www.lesko.com

I Wanna Be a Freelancer

The Joys of Freelancing:
Starting a Business Without Money

More and more people are realizing that there are many benefits to freelancing. In fact, every day more data show that the demand for freelancing is growing. Some analysts estimate that 25% of the nation's workforce is now working on a freelance basis, which includes part time, temporary, and contractual workers[1]. In the last five years, the number of temporary agencies that supply these kinds of workers increased from 3,500 to 7,000[2]. Manpower, one of these temporary agencies, now employs more than General Motors or IBM. Peter F. Drucker predicts that by 2010 50% of Americans will be self-employed in one way or another[3].

We've heard the terms in recent years: downsizing, rightsizing, restructuring, streamlining, reinventing, and now outsourcing. All this boils down to more and more companies becoming less and less interested in providing for the long term wellbeing of its employees. It's a trend that's likely to continue at an even greater pace.

Companies want to be lean and mean. They want to be flexible and don't want to take on the responsibility and financial burden of full time employees. This may be bad for employees, but it's great for the world of freelancing. And don't think of freelancing as losing benefits: think of it as an exchange of benefits. Your personal freedom and control over your life are worth more than your health and retirement benefits and the security of your job, all of which are disappearing fast anyway. The new status symbol of the new millenium won't be doing your own thing, it will be controlling your own time.[4]

Here are some advantages to being a freelancer:

- You can be still looking for a full time job while you are pretending to look for freelancing or consulting work.
- You can give yourself a title while you are out of work, such as an independent consultant, freelance wordprocessor, etc.
- You can take more tax deductions around the home and at play, such as the part of your house and car you use for business. Even some of your meals and entertainment expenses may fall into this category.
- You can have more control over your hours, take vacations when you want, or only work certain days.
- It's ideal for a household member that is only interested in a part time job while staying at home with the kids. A freelance artist can easily work 20 hours a week at home and still be with the children.

And here are some advantages from the employer's eyes. You may even want to include some of these points in your sales letter:

- They don't have to commit to you forever, and then worry about firing you when they want to downsize.
- They don't have to pay you benefits, overhead, supplies, etc.
- They can show their bosses that they are getting more work done with less people because freelancers are not counted as employees, and are often paid from a different budget than that of full time employees.

- They can get a project done and not worry about keeping those people busy once the project is completed.
- They can get more value for their money by hiring more qualified people for a shorter period of time.
- They have less liability from the potential harmful effects of employee protection laws like Equal Employment Opportunity Laws.

What Do You Need To Be A Freelancer?

The only thing you really need is a customer. And this is basically true for any business. If you have a customer or a client, you're in business. The tools that will make getting a customer easier are a phone, a desk, and business cards. And the next level of tools you will find helpful are a resume, a brochure, or samples of your work. If you think you need a lot of expensive equipment you may want to rethink being a freelancer. The beauty of freelancing is that you can start a business without any money. All your money should be invested in getting business, not in equipment. Even if you think you need to buy a lot of equipment to do the work you want to do, for heaven's sake don't go out and buy it. Nothing can put you out of business faster than having a lot of equipment around that is not being used because you don't have a lot of business. Rent the equipment only when you need it, or use someone else's equipment at night. Believe me, all your resources should be spent in getting customers. Once you have a steady flow of customers, then you should look into buying your own equipment. Sure it would be nice to have all the fancy equipment you need, right in your house, but in the beginning that can be a ticket to failure. The most important part of being a successful freelancer is staying in business long enough to reap the rewards of all the seeding that you are planting in your "garden of opportunity." What you plant today will come back to you next year, and what you plant next year will come back to you the year after. The trick is to be around a few years from now so that you can enjoy the benefits of what you planted today. Buying all the equipment you need will just run you out of money faster, so that you will have less of a chance of being around and in business next year. It's a game of beat the clock. You have to figure out how to get all the customers you need before you run out of money.

How To Get Free Legal, Marketing, and Tax Advice

What stops many people from starting their own freelancing career is misinformation. Here's the kind of thinking that can go through your head when you think about freelancing. "Gee. I'm going to start a business at home. If something goes wrong, somebody will sue me and I'll lose my house. I wonder if incorporating as a business will protect me?" Now that the "what ifs" got you, you're smart enough to know that this sounds like a legal question and you'd better talk to an attorney. So you call a friend of a friend who is an attorney and they tell you it will cost you $500 to $1000 to help you solve this problem. You don't have an extra $500 to $1000, so you figure you will put off starting your new career until you get the extra money. **You don't have to do that.** You can get free legal advice on this or any other subject if you just contact one of the local Small Business Development Centers that are located in almost every city in the country. (See the chapter entitled "I Wanna Start My Own Business" for a state-by-state listing for Small Business Development Centers.)

These centers will sit down with you for free and help you figure out any kind of legal, management, financial, or even tax problem you are having in trying to start and develop a business. They will even help you get the business you need. They can help you identify potential clients and will work with you to devise a plan for getting development money. You just can't beat that.

The Government Will Buy Your Freelancing Services

The government buys more freelancing services than anyone else in the world. They buy typing services, legal services, accounting services, and landscaping services, to name just a few. One year the government even spent $30,000 for the services of a freelance priest. And you don't have to be living in Washington, DC to get the work. Only about 20% of all government business is done in Washington, DC. The rest is done all over the country and all over the world.

Freelancing can be your first step to a multimillion dollar business. The time is right and you can do it without any money of your own.

Sources:
[1] When Workers Lives Are Contingent On Employers' Whims, Sue Shellenbager, The Wall Street Journal, Page B1, February 1, 1995.
[2] The Network Society, Peter Drucker, The Wall Street Journal, Page A12, March 29, 1995.
[3] www.freelancerworld.com.
[4] Job Shock, Harry S. Dent, Jr., St. Martin's Press, New York, NY.

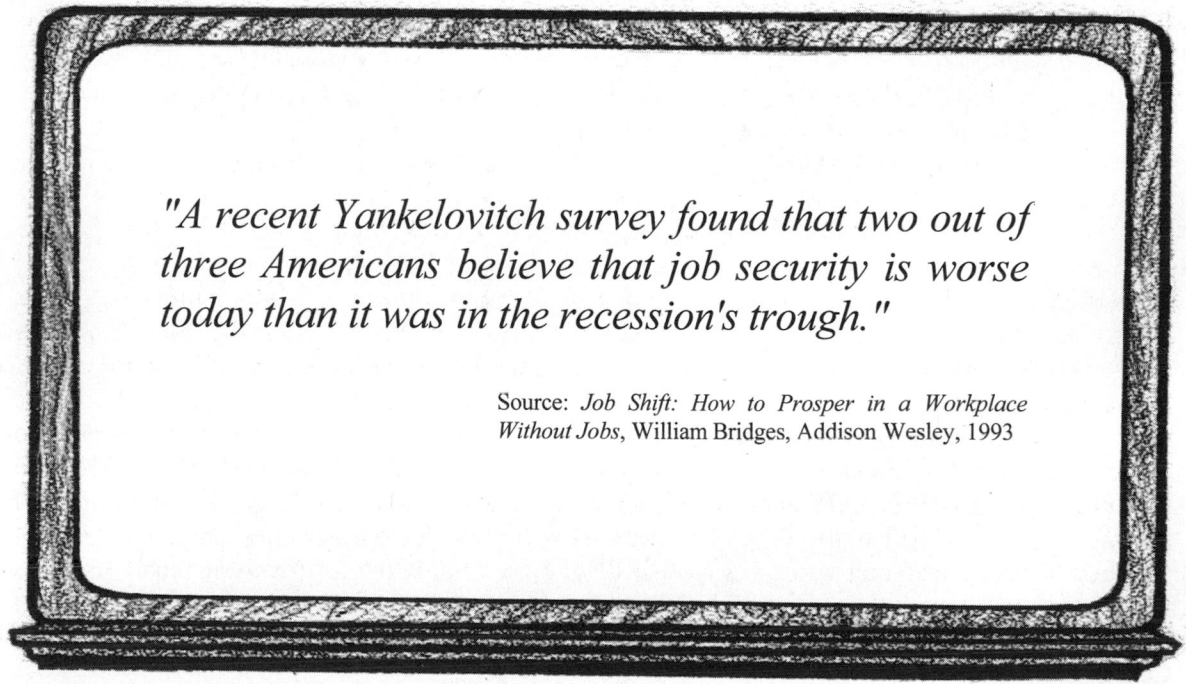

"A recent Yankelovitch survey found that two out of three Americans believe that job security is worse today than it was in the recession's trough."

Source: *Job Shift: How to Prosper in a Workplace Without Jobs*, William Bridges, Addison Wesley, 1993

How Artists, Designers, and Photographers Can Get Freelance Government Contracts

The Federal government spends millions of dollars each year for the services of artists, graphic designers, illustrators, painters, calligraphers, photographers, computer graphics specialists, and other art-related specialists. Because the government is involved, many artists might shy away from finding out how they can get in on these worthwhile opportunities. The following listing is put together to help you get in contact — often in just one phone call — with the people who hire artists like yourself. Don't forget to check the general section on freelancing, as well as checking out state contracts.

It's difficult to get a clear estimate of the amount of government contracts that go to artists. If you count prime contracts as well as subcontracts, the figure could be as high as $20 to $30 million dollars. Here are what some of the major agencies spend each year:

Spending By Major Agencies On Artists

Department of Agriculture	$186,000	Food and Drug Administration	$200,000
National Science Foundation	$187,500	Federal Emergency Management Agency	$ 25,000
Labor	$400,000	U. S. Customs Service	$ 40,000
Postal Service	$378,000	National Park Service	$1,900,000
U. S. Geological Survey	$100,000		

Here are some examples of artists who have landed art contracts with the government:

Artists Who Received Government Contracts

Jacob Lawrence received **$95,000** to create a ceramic tile wall mosaic to be placed in the Joseph P. Addabbo Federal Building in Queens, NY. GSA, 1989.

Linda Sherman Design, Inc., of Gaithersburg, MD, received **$432,000** to provide graphic art and editorial support services to NASA in 1990.

Manuel Neri received **$100,000** to create a marble sculpture entitled "Ventana al Pacifico" that was placed outside the Gus J. Solomon Courthouse in Portland, Oregon. GSA, 1989.

Gerald Farrar and Associates, Inc., of Tulsa, OK, received **$3,540** to provide graphic art services to the Department of Energy in 1991.

Lehman-Scaffa Photo and Art of Silver Spring, MD, received **$12,000** to provide graphic arts services to the National Science Foundation, including viewgraphs, slides, charts, maps, mechanical and conceptual drawings, page layouts, publication covers, signs, typesetting, posters, prints, negatives, and exhibit materials.

Hugh Moore and Associates of Alexandria, VA, received **$35,000** from the National Science Foundation to provide graphic art support services, including designing educational pieces for a national science program.

Inkwell, Inc., of Washington, D.C., received **$10,000** from the USDA to provide graphic art support services.

Douglass Harding Group of Washington, D.C., received **$32,000** from the USDA to provide graphic art support services in 1990.

Thomas Baldwin, Inc., of Alexandria, VA, received **$138,000** from the Forest Service to design the interior of the Service's National Visitors Center.

Standsbury Ronsaville Wood Inc., of Annapolis, MD, landed a contract from the National Park Service worth **$16,000** to provide graphic design services, including illustrations, layout, exhibit production, publication design, and more in 1991.

Nelson/Hendrickson of Purcellville, VA, landed a contract from the National Park Service worth **$72,948** to provide production-ready wayside exhibit plan packages.

Maria Alquilar received **$19,000** to create a high fired clay sculpture for the General Services Administration that was placed in the Main Border Station in San Luis, AZ.

Caleb Bach received **$18,000** to produce two paintings entitled "The Effects of Good and Bad Government" that were placed in the Seattle Courthouse.

Robert Brooks received **$4,000** to create a photographic mural that was placed in the U.S. Border Station in Fort Kent, ME. GSA, 1984.

Houston Conwill received **$49,000** to create a bronze sculpture on a granite platform that was placed in the Joseph P. Addabbo Federal Building in Queens, NY.

The painter, **Blue Sky**, received **$12,600** to create an oil painting entitled "Moonlight on the Great Pee Dee" which was placed in the J.M. McMillan Federal Building in Florence, SC. GSA, 1978.

Frank Smith received **$20,000** to create a ceramic tile wall mural for the Joseph P. Addabbo Federal Building in Queens, NY. GSA, 1989.

Another Color, Inc., received **$422,000** to provide graphic art and editorial support services to NASA in 1990.

Creative Service, Inc., received **$200,000** to provide graphic art and editorial support services to NASA in 1990.

Artists Who Received Money from the National Park Service in a Recent Year:

Lloyd Townsend	$ 6,663	Chris White Design	$ 50,974
Hugh Brown	$ 14,721	Dorothy Novick	$ 4,056
Robert Hynes	$ 4,020	G.S. Images	$236,294
Louis Glanzman	$ 9,362	General Graphics	$268,363
Glenn Moy	$ 9,511	G.S. Images	$ 86,643
Charles Hazard	$ 3,528	Specialty Graphics	$103,932
Steven Patricia	$ 7,020	General Graphics	$ 17,246
Robert Hynes	$ 8,786	Scribing Graphics	$100,167

Freelance opportunities are everywhere throughout the federal government. Plan on taking some time to get to know the system and to market yourself, your product and services. Your time will be well worth the effort when you receive a government contract.

When To Apply

Keep in mind that because new contracts are awarded at the beginning of the government's fiscal year in October, you should make sure that an agency you're interested in working for has seen your portfolio by late spring or early summer-this will give them enough time to consider you and the services that you offer for the current fiscal year. Otherwise you may have to wait an entire year before you get any work, especially the larger contracts.

Know The Rules

If you are going to do business with the government, you must know how play the game. The federal government's procurement system has many laws, rules and regulations. Each agency must follow these rules to procure any goods or services. You will be ahead of the game if you know how this system works. You can view the regulations online at {www.arnet.gov/far}.

Identify Your Product or Service

The government uses the North American Industry Classification System to identify many products and services. Many government product and service listings and future procurements are identified by these codes. You can search web sites for the codes that correspond to the products and services you have to offer and then go after those contracts. You can view the codes at {www.census.gov/epcd/www/naics.html} or at {www.fpdc.gov}.

Get Registered

The Federal Acquisition Regulation requires contract registration with the Central Contract Registration (CCR). The CCR is the government database for many contracting opportunities. The CCR is the primary vendor database for the Department of Defense, NASA, Department of Transportation and Department of Treasury. They offer a Dynamic Small Business Database to showcase those businesses interested in doing business with the federal government. You can register your business at {www.ccr.gov}. In order to register with the CCR, you must first have a DUNS Number. You can obtain one online at {www.dnb.com}.

US General Service Administration

The US General Service Administration provides a procurement vehicle for vendors interested in selling to the federal government. This "contract vehicle" is a procurement vehicle where federal agencies can place orders. GSA Schedule contracts are an important vehicle for businesses in the federal procurement process. Because of the GSA Schedules ease of use, many federal agencies choose a GSA Schedule Contractor to fill a product or service need within their agency. In addition, GSA offers classes on "How to Contract with the Federal Government" throughout the country. You can find them at {www.gsa.gov}.

Get Certified As a Small Business

If you are a freelancer, you are a small business. You can find assistance with a number of organizations, starting with the Small Business Administration. If you qualify with the SBA as a specially identified business, you may be eligible for opportunities not available for larger businesses. Their web site

"Government Contracting" {www.sba.gov/GC} lists programs to help businesses which include: *Small Disadvantaged Business,Very Small Business Program, Assistance for Women Business Owners (CAWBO), 8(a) Business, Veterans* and others.

BiZMatch Tool is an automated online database of minority businesses operated by the Department of Commerce's Minority Business Development Agency (MBDA). This database is used by Federal, state and local governments to locate minority enterprises to meet their procurement needs. You must register with the MBDA to be included in this database. {http://www.mbda.gov/index.php?section_id=4}

Procurement Levels

Now that you know something about the Federal government procurement procedures you must look for procurement opportunities. There are many "vehicles" or ways to win a government contracts. The way a Federal agency will contract will partially depend on the dollar amount threshold for each contract. Each agency conducts their procurement procedure slightly differently so you should contact that agency directly.

- *Micro-Purchases*: Purchases under $2,500, which can be made at the sole discretion of the Contracting Officer or purchasing official to either large or small businesses with no competition.
- *Simplified Acquisition Procedure*: All purchase between $2,500 and $100,000 are reserved exclusively for small businesses providing that the Contracting Officer expects to obtain offers from at least two small businesses.
- *Formal Contracting Procedures*: Over $100,000

Get Assistance

All you need to do is ask. There are many organizations that are prepared to help you get a contract with the Federal government.

- The Small Business Administration can answer many of you questions. {www.sba.gov}
- Federal Procurement Technical Assistance Offices (listed in this book)
- Office of Small and Disadvantaged Business Utilization (listed in this book)
- State Procurement Offices (listed in this book)
- Each Federal agency's Procurement Office (listed in this book)

Find Current Procurement Opportunities

The federal government has developed a single point-of-entry for procurement opportunities over $25,000. Government buyers publicize their business opportunities by posting them on {www.FedBizOpps.gov}. You can monitor and retrieve opportunities by the entire Federal contracting community.

Check Out The Past And Look Into The Future

You can check out past winning contracts to get an understanding of what is purchased and what makes a successful bid contract. Through the Freedom of Information Act Request from the agency in question, you can get copies of winning bids from previous years. Remember, the competition is very high but most freelancers don't know about this information to give them an edge in the procurement process.

You can also look into the future of each agency. By law, each agency must publish their procurement forecast for the coming year. This information can help you prepare for what each agency will need in the future. You can contact the agency directly or check AcqNet at {www.acqnet.gov} to see the current forecasts.

Subcontracting

Federal prime contractors are required by law to subcontract with small businesses whenever possible. So you can get a contract with a company that has done all of the work to get a Federal contract. A small business can contact the prime contractor directly or a Federal agency directly. You can get a listing of prime contractors at {www.acq.osd.mil/sadbu/publications/subdir/index.html}. The Small Business Administration also maintains a site devoted to subcontracting at {http://web.sba.gov/subnet/}.

Market, Market, Market

After you have identified your customers, researched their requirements and familiarized yourself with procurement regulations and strategies it is time to market your product or service. Here are some things to remember:

- You must network to be successful.
- Remember to be competitive, persistent and patient.
- Attend conferences and workshops
- Attend Trade Shows
- Check out the SBA calendar of events {www.sba.gov/calendar}
- Maintain a one-to-one contact with the Contract Officer or Contracting Specialist.

Federal Department Procurement Offices

* Agriculture Department
1400 Independence Avenue, SW
Mail Stop 9303
Washington, DC 20250
202-720-7527
Fax: 202-720-8972
www.usda.gov/procurement
The United States Department of Agriculture procurement office has prepared a kit, *Doing Business With USDA*. This kit is available online to assist businesses that are interested in selling their products or services to the USDA.

* Commerce Department
Office of Acquisition Management
14th and Constitution Avenue, NW
Washington, DC 20230
202-482-4248
http://oamweb.osec.doc.gov
The Department of Commerce has a great web site to provide information about the Acquisition Management Office and what it can do for you. Listed below are the divisions of the Department of Commerce and their procurement offices.

National Institute of Standards and Technology (NIST)
Acquisition Office
100 Bureau Drive, Stop 3460
Gaithersburg, ND 20899-3460
301-975-NIST
www.nist.gov/admin/od/contract/contract.htm
The National Institute of Standards and Technology relies on contractors and vendors to supply many goods and services necessary to fulfill their mission. Every year NIST buys millions of dollars worth of supplies and services. Check out their web site to see if some of the millions could be for your work.

National Oceanic and Atmospheric Administration
Acquisition Management Division
1305 East West Highway, 7th Floor
Silver Springs, MD 20910
301-713-0325
www.ofa.noaa.gov/%7Eago/index.html

Patent and Trademark Office
USPTO Contact Center
Crystal Plaza 3, Room 2C02
P.O. Box 1450
Alexandria, VA 22313-1450
800-786-9199
703-308-4357
www.uspto.gov/web/offices/ac/comp/proc/

U.S. Census Bureau
Acquisition Management Office
4700 Silver Hill Road
Washington, DC 20233-0001
301-763-3342
www.census.gov/procur/www/
Even the Census Department buys goods and services from freelancers. Check their web site for information on how to get a contract with the Census Bureau.

* Education Department
400 Maryland Avenue, SW
Washington, DC 20202
202-401-2000
Fax: 202-401-0689
www.ed.gov/fund/contract/about/booklet1.html
The Department of Education publishes Doing Business With the Department of Education. You can view a copy online at the above web address.

* Energy Department
Office of Procurement and Assistance Management
1000 Independence Ave., SW
Washington, DC 20585
800-dial-DOE

202-586-5575
Fax: 202-586-4403
www.pr.doe.gov

The Department of Energy's e-center site is a one-stop information center for all of your contracting needs. You can browse opportunities online 24 hours a day. They provide information on the procurement process, competing for awards, sealed bid purchases, small business programs and other issues. The Department of Energy even provides a DVD titled "Doing Business with the Department of Energy" that you can download onto your computer. http://ipvideo.lbl.gov:554/ramgen/DoingBusinessWithDoe.rm

* US Environmental Protection Agency

Ariel Rios Building
Office of Acquisition Management
1200 Pennsylvania Avenue, N.W.
Mail Code 3801R
Washington, D.C. 20460
202-564-4310
www.epa.gov/oam/

* Federal Communications Commission

Office of Procurement
445 12th Street SW
Washington, DC 20554
202-418-1952
Fax: 202-418-0237
www.fcc.gov/omd/contracts/

This office is responsible for the nationwide procurement needs for the Federal Communications Commission.

* Federal Emergency Management Administration

Financial & Acquisitions Management
500 C Street, SW
Washington, DC 20472
202-646-4006
www.fema.gov/ofm/toc.shtm

The Federal Emergency Management Administration publishes a guide Doing Business with FEMA to assist firms develop marketing strategies and help answer questions to those new to government contracting. The publication is a wealth of information. You may also call FEMA for information concerning small business matters, solicitations or disaster contracting. When an award exceeds $25,000 it will be published in the Commerce Business Daily.

* Food and Drug Administration

Office of Facilities, Acquisitions and Central Services
Room 2074, HFA 230
5600 Fishers Lane
Rockville, MD 20857
301-827-7211
Fax: 301-827-7228
www.fda.gov/oc/ofacs/contracts/

The Food and Drug Administration (FDA) post its solicitations on the FedBizOpps web site at www.fedbizopps.gov. In addition, the FDA web site lists the FDA programs and the contract coordinator to contact if you want to do business with the FDA. The FDA publishes a magazine called the FDA Consumer that has very limited writing freelance opportunities for writers with a record of successful translation of scientific and medical material into easy-to-read articles. Explore the web site at www.fda.gov/fdac to determine if you may qualify. If you think you can contribute you will need to send a resume and samples of your work to the FDA.

* Forest Service

USDA Forest Service Acquisition Management
1621 North Kent Street, Suite 707 RP-E
Arlington, VA 22209-2131
703-605-4744
Fax: 703-605-5100
www.fs.fed.us/business

The Forest Service Acquisition Management office can help you if you are interested in freelancing for the Forest Service. This is the office you should contact if you are interested in a radio contract.

* General Services Administration Headquarters

1800 F Street NW
Washington, DC 20405-0001
202-501-0445
Fax: 202-208-5938
www.gsa.gov
Serving the United States

To become a GSA Schedule contractor, you must first submit an offer in response to the applicable GSA Schedule solicitation. GSA awards contracts

to that offer commercial items falling within the generic descriptions in the GSA Schedule solicitations. They offer a publication Doing Business with General Services that can be viewed on their web site. GSA offers many free workshops on how to obtain GSA Schedules contracts.

Sheron Snyder
General Services Administration Regional Office
400 15th SW
Auburn, WA 98001-6599
253-931-7956
Fax: 253-804-4887
Sheron.snyder@gsa.gov
Serving: Alaska, Idaho, Oregon, and Washington

Lori Falkenstrom
General Service Administration Regional Office
450 Golden Gate Avenue, Room 5-6535
San Francisco, CA 94102-3434
415-522-2700
Fax: 415-522-2705
Lori.falkenstrom@gsa.gov
Serving: Arizona, California, Hawaii, and Nevada

Willie Heath
General Services Administration Regional Office
819 Taylor Street
Fort Worth, TX 76102
817-978-0800
Fax: 817-978-0440
Willie.heath@gsa.gov
Serving: Arkansas, Louisiana, New Mexico, Oklahoma, and Texas

Shirley Hopkins
General Services Administration Regional Office
Federal Center #41, Room 240
P.O. Box 25006
Denver, CO 80225
303-236-7408
Fax: 303-236-7403
Shiley.Hopkins@gsa.gov
Serving: Colorado, Montana, North Dakota, South Dakota, Utah and Wyoming

France Lopez
General Services Administration Regional Office
Thomas P. O'Neill Jr. Federal Building
10 Causeway Street
Boston, MA 02222-1047
617-565-8100
Fax: 617-565-8101
France.lopez@gsa.gov
Serving: Connecticut, Massachusetts, Maine, New Hampshire, Rhode Island, and Vermont

Angela Ditommaso
General Services Administration Regional Office
20 North Eighth Street, 9th Floor
Philadelphia, PA 19107-3191
215-446-4918
Fax: 215-446-5133
Angela.ditommaso@gsa.gov
Serving: Delaware, Maryland, Pennsylvania, Virginia, and West Virginia

Colleen Pappas
General Services Administration Regional Office
18-130
26 Federal Plaza
New York-Manhattan, NY 10278-0000
212-264-1236
Fax: 212-264-2760
Colleen.pappas@gsa.gov
Serving: New York and New Jersey

Rebecca Vanover
General Services Administration Regional Office
77 Forsyth Street, Room 600
Atlanta, GA 30303-0000
404-331-3374
Fax: 404-331-1721
Rebecca.vanover@gsa.gov
Serving: Alabama, Florida, Georgia, Kentucky, Mississippi, North Carolina, South Carolina, and Tennessee

Beverly Coley
General Services Administration Regional Office
230 S Dearborn Street, Room 3718
Chicago, IL 60604
312-353-1100
Fax: 312-886-9893
Beverly.coley@gsa.gov
Serving: Indiana, Illinois, Michigan, Minnesota, Ohio, and Wisconsin

Ruby Rice
General Services Administration Regional Office
1500 E. Bannister Road
Kansas City, MO 64131-3009
816-926-7203
Fax: 816-823-1167
Ruby.rice@gsa.gov
Serving: Iowa, Kansas, Missouri, and Nebraska

Public Buildings Service

Design Excellence Program
1800 F Street NW
Washington, DC 20405-0001
202-501-2635
www.gsa.gov

This program is part of General Service Administration. They seek the finest architects and artists to commission their work for public buildings throughout the United States.

* Health and Human Services

Office of Acquisition Management
Room 517-D, Hubert H. Humphrey Building
200 Independence Avenue, SW
Washington, DC 20201
202-401-6103
Fax: 202-690-6902
www.hhs.gov/ogam/oam

The Office of Acquisition Management (OAM) provides information and training to help understand the acquisition process. The web site lists contracting opportunities in a variety of areas. To view the Health and Human Services Contracting Opportunities Forecasts go to www.hhs.gov/osdbu/publications/forecast.html .

* US Department of Homeland Security

1800 G Street NW, 10th Floor
Washington, DC 20528
202-786-0036
www.dhs.gov/dhspublic/display?theme=37

Listed below are the divisions of the US Department of Homeland Security (DHS) and their procurement offices. Their web site contains business and contracting forms to help you do business with the DHS. They also publish a handbook How to do Business with the Department of Homeland Security that is a valuable resource.

US Customs Service

1300 Pennsylvania Avenue, NW, Suite 1310
Washington, DC 20229
202-927-1229
Fax: 202-927-1190
www.customs.gov/xp/cgov/toolbox/contracting/

US Coast Guard

2100 2nd Street, SW, Room 2606
Washington, DC 20593
202-267-1146
Fax: 202-267-4011
www.uscg.mil/ccs/cfp/cpm/index.html

* Department of Housing and Urban Development

451 7th Street S.W.
Washington, DC 20410
202-708-1112
www.hud.gov/offices/cpo/contract.cfm

The Department of Housing and Urban Development offers their procurement forecast, Guide to Contracting With HUD, and a list of current competitive procurements to help your business win bids with HUD.

* Department of Interior

1849 C Street, NW
Washington, DC 20240
202-208-3100
www.doi.gov/pam/dave.html

The Department of Interior's acquisition office provides information on how to get contracts with their department. Listed below are the divisions of the Department of Interior and their procurement offices.

Bureau of Land Management

National Business Center Acquisition Division
P.O. Box 25047, MS BC660
Denver, CO 80225-0047
303-236-0226
Fax: 303-236-9470
www.blm.gov/natacq/

The Bureau of Land Management hires arts/graphics designers, film/video production services as well as, general photographic services. Check out their web site for information on how to get work with the BLM.

Bureau of Reclamation

Acquisition and Assistance Management Division
P.O. Box 25007
Denver, CO 80225-0007
303-445-2783
www.usbr.gov/pmts/acquisitions/

The Bureau of Reclamation publishes an Acquisition Handbook to guide prospective freelancers through the contracting process.

US Fish and Wildlife Service

Division of Contracting and Facilities Management
4401 N. Fairfax Drive, Suite 212
Arlington, VA 22203
703-358-2225
Fax: 703-358-2264
http://contracts.fws.gov

The Division of Contracting and Facilities Management supports the acquisitions of the Fish and Wildlife Service. The Washington Office supports nationwide and headquarter acquisitions with Regional Contracting Offices supporting regional and local requirements. They offer assistance to vendors and contractors interested in doing business with the Fish and Wildlife Service. All vendors interested in doing business must be registered in the Central Contractor Registration (CCR) prior to being awarded a contract.

U.S. Geological Survey Headquarters

Business Utilization and Development Specialist
12201 Sunrise Valley Drive
Mail Stop 205P
Reston, Virginia 20192
703-648-7346
www.usgs.gov/contracts

U.S. Geological Survey-Central Region

Business Utilization and Development Specialist
Box 25046 Denver Fed. Center
Denver, Colorado 80225
303-236-9331
Serving: Arkansas, Colorado, Iowa, Kansas, Louisiana, Montana, Minnesota, Missouri, Nebraska, New Mexico, North Dakota, Oklahoma, South Dakota, Texas and Wyoming.

U.S. Geological Survey-Western Region

Business Utilization and Development Specialist
345 Middlefield Road
Mail Stop 285
Menlo Park, California 94025
650-329-4162
Serving: Washington, Idaho, Oregon, California, Nevada, Arizona, Utah, Alaska, and Hawaii.

U.S. Geological Survey-Eastern Region

Business Utilization and Development Specialist
12201 Sunrise Valley Drive
Mail Stop 152
Reston, Virginia 20192
703-648-7375
Serving Connecticut, Illinois, Indiana, Kentucky, Maine, Maryland, Delaware, Massachusetts, Michigan, New Hampshire, New Jersey, New York, Ohio, Pennsylvania, Vermont, Virginia, West Virginia, Wisconsin. Southeast states: Alabama, Florida, Georgia, Mississippi, North Carolina, Caribbean, South Carolina, South Carolina, and Tennessee.

All of these U.S. Geological Survey offices can assist you in contracting opportunities. The web site has the departments acquisition forecast so you can see if they will need your services in the future.

Office of Surface Mining
1951 Constitution Avenue, NW
Washington, DC 20240
202-208-2719
www.osmre.gov/business.htm

Minerals Management Service
381 Elden Street
Herndon, VA 20170
703-787-1358
Fax: 703-787-1009
www.mms.gov/adm/procure.htm

National Park Service
Business and Economic Development Office
P.O. Box 37127 Mail Stop 3130
Washington, DC 20013-7127
http://www.nps.gov/legacy/business.html
The National Park service offers a limited number of freelance opportunities. They do contract for architectural services, audio-visual arts and other arts related work. Contact the National Park Service or go directly to the office you want consideration.

Artist-in-Residence Program
National Park Service
1849 C Street NW
Washington, DC 20240
202-208-6843
www.nps.gov/volunteer/air.htm
The National Park Service offers opportunities for two-dimensional visual artists, photographers, sculptors, performers, writers, composers and craft artists to live and work in the parks. Currently, there are 27 parks participating in the Artist-in-Residence program. Check the web site for current programs.

* Justice Department
950 Pennsylvania Avenue, NW
Washington, DC 20530-0001
202-307-0608
Fax: 202-307-0086
www.usdoj.gov/07business
The Department of Justice's web site Doing Business with DOJ provides information to people seeking business opportunities with the Department of Justice. Listed below are the divisions of the Department of Justice and their procurement offices.

Bureau of Alcohol, Tobacco, Firearms and Explosives
Acquisitions and Business Opportunities
650 Massachusetts Avenue, NW, Room 8290
Washington, DC 20226
202-927-8332
Fax: 202-927-7311
www.atf.gov/acquisition/

Bureau of Prisons
320 First Street, N.W.
Washington, DC 20534
202-307-3067
Fax: 202-514-4418
www.bop.gov/contract.html
The Bureau of Prisons publishes an online publication How To Do Business With the Bureau of Prisons to help freelancers. If you are interested in work for the Bureau of Prisons monitor their web site for the most up-to-date acquisition information.

Drug Enforcement Administration
Office of Acquisition Management
2401 Jefferson Davis Highway
Alexandria, VA 22301
202-353-9505 Acquisition Management
202-307-4921 Small Business Specialist
http://128.121.209.186
The Drug Enforcement Administration (DEA) buys the products and services it needs to through the Office of Acquisition Management. The DEA conducts the majority of its procurements as full and open competitive or small and small disadvantaged business set-aside, including 8(a)'s. This office supports acquisitions at the simplified acquisition threshold of $2500-$100,000.

Federal Bureau of Investigation
Procurement and Management Section
J. Edgar Hoover Building, Room 6823

935 Pennsylvania Avenue, NW
Washington, DC 20535
202-324-2143
Fax: 202-324-1172
www.fbi.gov/business/business.htm
The Federal Bureau of Investigation encourages the participation of small, Women-owned, Disadvantaged Business owners in their contracting activities. Their web site lists products and services purchased by the FBI as well as procurement procedures.

Justice Management Division
1331 Pennsylvania Avenue, NW, Suite 1000
NPB 1000
Washington, DC 20530
202-307-2000
Fax: 202-307-1933
www.usdoj.gov/jmd/pss/
The Procurement Services Staff (PSS) provides acquisition support to litigation components. In 2002, contracts totaled approximately $1 billion. Of this amount, about 23% was awarded to small businesses and 2.5% to small and disadvantaged businesses.

United States Marshals Service
National Procurement & Acquisition Office
CS-3, Room 1124
600 Army-Navy Drive
Arlington, VA 22202
202-307-8640
Fax: 202-307-9695
www.usdoj.gov/marshals/doing.html
If you've always wanted to work with a Marshal, this may be the department for you. The United States Marshal Service buys services from video production to graphic design.

* Labor Department
U.S. Department of Labor
Frances Perkins Building
200 Constitution Avenue, NW
Washington, DC 20210
202-219-4631
Fax: 202-219-6853
www.dol.gov/dol/business.htm
The Department of Labor's web site Doing Business With the Department of Labor, is a wealth of information for all kinds of contracting options. The Office of the Assistant Secretary for Administration and Management through the Department's Procurement Executive is responsible for the Department's procurement programs.

* National Aeronautics and Space Administration
Headquarters Information Center
Washington, DC 20546-0001
202-358-0000
Fax: 202-358-3251
http://www.hq.nasa.gov/office/procurement/
There are many business opportunities at NASA. Their web site offers information on NASA acquisition forecasts, financial and contractual status of active procurements, marketing to NASA and how to prepare and submit unsolicited proposals. NASA's Acquisition Internet Service Business Opportunities (NAIS) gives entrepreneurs on-line access to contract opportunities at NASA, a procurement reference library and other procurement information. You can search freelance contract opportunities in its database and also be notified by e-mail when procurement announcements are made. Procurement opportunities are available throughout the country at individual NASA centers so don't forget to check them out too when looking for freelance work.

NASA Procurement Sites

NASA, Ames Research Center
Mail Stop 241-1/T.Kolis
Moffett Field, CA 94035-1000
650-604-4690
Fax: 650-604-4646
http://server-mpo.arc.nasa.gov/Services/Proc/home.tml
www.arc.nasa.gov

Dryden Flight Research Center
P.O. Box 273
Edwards, CA 93523-0273
661-258-3311
www.dfrc.nasa.gov/Business/Procurement/index.html

Glenn Research Center
Mail Stop 500-313
21000 Brookpark Road
Cleveland, OH 44135-3191
216-433-4000
www.grc.nasa.gov/WWW/Procure/home.htm

Goddard Space Flight Center
Code 200
Greenbelt, MD 20771-0001
301-286-3596
Fax: 301-286-0237
http://genesis.gsfc.nasa.gov/procure.htm

Jet Propulsion Laboratory Acquisition Division
4800 Oak Grove Drive
Pasadena, CA 91109
818-354-6190
http://acquisition.jpl.nasa.gov/
The Jet Propulsion Laboratory (JPL) is a government-owned, Federally Funded Research and Development Center. JPL procurements are California Institute of Technology contracts, not government-direct contracts. Contractors should contact Caltech/JPL to become familiar with how JPL contracts are awarded.

NASA-Johnson Space Center
Mailcode BA
Houston, TX 77058
281-244-2100
http://jsc-web-pub.jsc.nasa.gov/bd01/

Kennedy Space Center
Code OP
Kennedy Space Center, FL 32899
321-867-5000
www.ksc.nasa.gov/procurement

NASA Langley Research Center
100 NASA Road
Mail Stop 134
Hampton, VA 23681-2199
757-864-1000
http://procurement.larc.nasa.gov/

Marshall Space Flight Center
Code PS01
Marshall Space Flight Center, AL 35812
256-544-2121
http://ec.msfc.nasa.gov/msfc/home.shtml

Stennis Space Center
Code DA00
Stennis Space Center, MS 39529-6000
228-688-3341
www.ssc.nasa.gov/~procure/scripts/welcome.cgi

* The National Science Foundation

4201 Wilson Boulevard
Arlington, VA 22230
703-292-5111
800-877-8339
www.nsf.gov/home/about/contracting/
The National Science Service offers composition and printing contracts, which are listed on their web site. If you are interested in working for the NSF contact them at the office listed above.

* Office of Personnel Management

1900 E Street NW
Washington, DC 20415-1000
202-606-1800
www.opm.gov/procure/index.asp
The Office of Personnel Management publishes a guide titled Contracting Opportunities. Check their web site for your next freelance contract.

* US Government Printing Office

Printing Procurement Department
Room C-899
North Capitol & H Streets, N.W.
Washington, D.C. 20401
202-512-0327
Fax: 202-512-1745
www.access.gpo.gov/procurement/index.html

* US Postal Service

Services Purchasing
475 L'Enfant Plaza West, SW
Washington, DC 20260-6237
202-268-2826
www.usps.com/purchasing
Although the Postal Service is a government agency, it is also an independent program under the executive branch of the United States. They are therefore exempt from laws that usually apply to US government agencies. To view their regulations you can view their publication, Purchasing Manual, online.

* Social Security Administration

Office of Acquisition and Grants
1710 Gwynn Oak Avenue
Baltimore, MD 21207-5279
www.ssa.gov/oag/
The Social Security Administration can assist you in the acquisition process.

* US Department of State

2201 C Street NW
Washington, DC 20520
202-647-4000
www.statebuy.gov/home.htm
The State Department provides community training and counseling about doing business with the Department of State.

* U.S. Department of Transportation

Acquisition and Grants
400 7th Street, S.W., Room 9414
Washington, DC 20590
800-532-1169
202-366-1930
Fax: 202-366-7538
www.dot.gov/ost/m60/index.html
The Department of Transportation (DOT) offers a publication on the web site, Contracting with the DOT, to help anyone interested in doing business with the DOT. The publication offers a wealth of information, DOT contacts and links to many useful services. You can also get a procurement forecast at http://osdbuweb.dot.gov/business/procurement/forecast.html to see if the DOT is planning on using a service you would be able to provide.

* Department of Treasury

1500 Pennsylvania Avenue, NW
Washington, DC 20220
202-622-2000
www.ustreas.gov/offices/management/dcfo/procurement/
Listed below are the bureaus of the Department of Treasury and their procurement offices.

Bureau of Engraving and Printing

Contract Administration Division
14th and C Streets, S.W., Room 705A
Washington, DC 20228
202-874-2065
www.moneyfactory.com/procurement/index.cfm/113
The Bureau of Engraving and Printing provides a yearly forecast document that can be viewed on the web site. The Bureau of Engraving Contract Division administers all contracts awarded in the Office of Procurement.

Financial Management Service

Acquisition Management
401 14th Street, SW
Room 110, Liberty Center
Washington, DC 20227
202-874-6910
http://fms.treas.gov/aboutfms/business.html

Department of Internal Revenue

Office of Procurement Operations
Room 700, Constellation Centre
6009 Oxon Hill Road
Oxen Hill, MD 20745
202-283-1610
Fax: 202-283-1514
www.procurement.irs.treas.gov/

Bureau of Public Debt
Bureau of the Public Debt
Division of Procurement
200 Third Street, UNB 4th Floor
Parkersburg, WV 26101-5312
304-480-7137
www.publicdebt.treas.gov/oa/oaprocr.htm

* Department of Veterans Affairs
Office of Acquisition and Materiél Management
810 Vermont Avenue, NW
Washington, DC 20420
202-273-6029
Fax: 202-273-6163
www.appc1.va.gov/oamm/index.htm

Matthew Lesko, Information USA, Inc., 12081 Nebel Street, Rockville, MD 20852 • 1-800-955-7693 • www.lesko.com

I Wanna Start My Own Business

Matthew Lesko, Information USA, Inc., 12081 Nebel Street, Rockville, MD 20852 • 1-800-955-7693 • www.lesko.com

Small Business Development Centers

Small Business Development Centers (SBDCs) could be the best deal the government has to offer to entrepreneurs and inventors, and a lot of people don't even know about them! Where else in the world can you have access to a $150 an hour consultant for free? There are over 700 of these offices all over the country and they offer free (or very low cost) consulting services on most aspects of business including:

- how to write a business plan
- how to get financing
- how to protect your invention
- how to sell your idea
- how to license your product
- how to comply with the laws
- how to write a contract
- how to sell overseas
- how to get government contracts
- how to help you buy the right equipment

You don't even have to know how to spell ENTREPRENEUR to contact these offices. They cater to both the dreamer, who doesn't even know where to start, as well as to the experienced small business that is trying to grow to the next stage of development. In other words, the complete novice or the experienced professional can find help through these centers.

Why spend money on a consultant, a lawyer, an accountant, or one of those invention companies when you can get it all for free at your local SBDC?

Recently, I spoke with some entrepreneurs who used a California SBDC and each of them had nothing but praise for the services. A young man who dropped out of college to start an executive cleaning business said he received over $8,000 worth of free legal advice from the center and said it was instrumental in getting his business off the ground. A woman who worked in a bank started her gourmet cookie business by using the SBDC to help her get the money and technical assistance needed to get her venture up and running. And a man who was a gymnast raved about how the SBDC helped him get his personal trainer business off the ground. All kinds of businesses being started, and all kinds of compliments for the SBDC's role in assisting these entrepreneurs, in whatever they are attempting. It sounds like a solid recommendation to me.

Can something that is free be so good? Of course it can. Because most of the people who work there are not volunteers, they are paid for by tax dollars. So it's really not free to us as a country, but it is free to you as an entrepreneur. And if you don't believe me that the SBDCs are so good, would you take the word of Professor James J. Chrisman from the University of Calgary in Calgary, Alberta, Canada? He was commissioned to do an independent study of SBDCs and found that 82% of the people who used their services found them beneficial. And the businesses who used SBDCs had average growth rates of up to 400% greater than all the other businesses in their area. Not bad. Compare this to the Fortune 500 companies who use the most expensive consulting firms in the country and only experience growth rates of 5% or less. So, who says you get what you pay for?

To locate the nearest Small Business Development Center, contact your lead SBDC from the list below, contact the Small Business Administration Answer Desk at 800-8-ASK-SBA, or go online at {www.sba.gov/services}.

Small Business Development Centers

Alabama

Lead Center:
John Sandefur
Office of State Director
Alabama Small Business Development
Consortium
University of Alabama at Birmingham
2800 Milan Court, Suite 124
Birmingham, AL 35211-6908
205-943-6750
Fax: 205-943-6752
www.asbdc.org
Email: sandefur@uab.edu

Auburn University
Small Business Development Center
415 West Magnolia
Room 108B Lowder
Auburn University, AL 36849-5243
334-844-4220
Fax: 334-844-4268
Email: dipofja@auburn.edu

University of Alabama at Birmingham
Small Business Development Center
901 South 15th Street, Room 201
Birmingham, AL 35924-2060
205-934-6760
Fax: 205-934-0538
www.business.uab.edu/sbdc
Email: sbdc@uab.edu

University of North Alabama
Small Business Development Center
UNA Box 5159
Keller Hall, Room 135
Florence, AL 35632-0001
256-765-4629
Fax: 256-765-4813
www.una.edu/sbdc/index.html
Email: clong@unanov.una.edu

North East Alabama Regional
Small Business Development Center
225 Church Street, NW
Huntsville, AL 35801
256-535-2061
Fax: 256-535-2050
www.hsvchamber.org
Email: egarcia@hsvchamber.org

Jacksonville State University
Small Business Development Center
700 Pelham Road
114 Merrill Hall
Jacksonville, AL 36265
256-782-5271
Fax: 256-782-5179
www.jsu.edu/depart/sbdc
Email: klowe@jsucc.jsu.edu

University of Alabama
Small Business Development Center
Station 35
Livingston, AL 35470
205-652-3665
Fax: 205-652-3516
http://sbdc.uwa.edu
Email: kdoggette@uwa.edu

University of South Alabama
Small Business Development Center
Mitchell College of Business
MCOB, Room 118
Mobile, AL 36688
251-460-6004
Fax: 251-460-6246

www.southalabama.edu/sbdc
Email: sbdc@usouthal.edu

Alabama State University
Small Business Development Center
915 South Jackson Street
Montgomery, AL 36104
334-229-4138
Fax: 334-269-1102
www.cobanetwork.com/sbdc
Email: lpatrick@asunet.alasu.edu

Troy State University
Small Business Development Center
102 Bibb Graves
Troy, AL 36082-0001
334-670-3771
Fax: 334-670-3636
http://spectrum.troyst.edu/~sbdc/index.htm
Email: jkervin@troyst.edu

Culverhouse College of Commerce &
Business Administration
University of Alabama
P.O. Box 87037
Tuscaloosa, AL 35487-0396
205-348-7011
Fax: 205-348-6974
http://sbdc.cba.ua.edu
Email: kdavidso@cba.us.edu

Alaska

Lead Center:
Jan Fredericks
University of Alaska
Small Business Development Center
430 West 7th Avenue, Suite 110
Anchorage, AK 99501-3550
907-274-7232
800-478-7232 (Outside Anchorage)
Fax: 907-274-9524
www.aksbdc.org
Email: anjaf@uaa.alaska.edu

University of Alaska-Anchorage
Small Business Development Center
Rural Outreach Program
430 West 7th Avenue, Suite 110
Anchorage, AK 99501
907-274-7232
800-478-7232 (Outside Anchorage)
Fax: 907-274-9524
Email: anbas2@uaa.alaska.edu

University of Alaska-Fairbanks
Small Business Development Center
613 Cushman Street, Suite 209
Fairbanks, AK 99701
907-456-7232
800-478-1701 (Outside Fairbanks)
Fax: 907-456-7233
www.tvc.uaf.edu/sbdc.html
Email: fnsts@uaf.edu

Southeast Alaska
Small Business Development Center
3100 Channel Drive, Suite 306
Juneau, AK 99801
907-463-3789
Fax: 907-463-3489
Email: anjas3@uaa.alaska.edu

Ketchikan Area
Small Business Development Center
306 Main Street, Suite 325
Ketchikan, AK 99901
907-225-1388

Fax: 907-225-1385
Email: analc2@uaa.alaska.edu

Matanuska-Susitna Borough
Small Business Development Center
P.O. Box 3029
201 North Lucielle Street, Suite 2A
Wasilla, AK 99654
907-373-7232
Fax: 907-373-7234
Email: anamp@uaa.alaska.edu

Kenai Peninsula SBDC
43335 Kalifornsky Beach Road, Suite 16
Soldotna, AK 99669
907-262-7497
Fax: 907-262-6762
Email: inmeg@uaa.alaska.edu

Arizona

Lead Center:
Michael York
Arizona Small Business Development Center
2411 West 14th Street
Tempe, AZ 85281
480-731-8720
Fax: 480-731-8729
www.dist.maricopa.edu/sbdc
Email: mike.york@domail.maricopa.edu

Central Arizona College
Small Business Development Center
1015 East Florence Boulevard, Suite B
Casa Grande, AZ 85222
520-426-4341
Fax: 520-876-5966
www.cac.cc.az.us/biz

Coconino Community College
Small Business Development Center
3000 North 4th Street
Flagstaff, AZ 86004
928-526-7654
Fax: 928-526-8693
www.coconino.edu/sbdc

Northland Pioneer College
Small Business Development Center
P.O. Box 610
Holbrook, AZ 86025
1001 West Deuce of Clubs
Show Low, AZ 85901
928-532-6170
Fax: 928-532-6171
http://206.207.18.37/SBM/default.htm
Email: npcsbdc@cybertrails.com

Mojave Community College
Small Business Development Center
1971 Jagerson Avenue
Kingman, AZ 86401
928-757-0895
Fax: 928-757-0836
www.mohave.edu/pages/245.asp

Maricopa Community Colleges
Small Business Development Center
2400 North Central Avenue, Suite 104
Phoenix, AZ 85004
602-784-0590
Fax: 602-230-7989
www.dist.Maricopa.edu/mccdsbdc
Email: rich.senopole@domail.maricopa.edu

Yavapai College
Small Business Development Center
115 South McCormick Street, Suite 4

Prescott, AZ 86301
928-541-1405
Fax: 928-541-1406
www.yavapai.cc.az.us/sbdc.nsf

Cochise College
Small Business Development Center
901 North Colombo, Room 308
Sierra Vista, AZ 85635
520-515-5478
Fax: 520-515-5437
800-966-7943 ext. 5478
www.cochise.cc.az.us
Email: hollism@cochise.edu

Eastern Arizona College
Small Business Development Center
622 College Avenue
Thatcher, AZ 85552-0769
928-428-8590
Fax: 928-428-8591

Pima Community College
Small Business Development Center
401 North Bonita Avenue
Tucson, AZ 85709-1260
520-206-6404
Fax: 520-206-6550
http://cc.pima.edu/sbdc
Email: sbdc@pima.edu

Arizona Western College
Small Business Development Center
281 West 24th Street
Yuma, AZ 85364
928-341-1650
Fax: 928-726-3626
www.yumasbdc.com

Arkansas

Lead Center:
Janet Roderick, State Director
Arkansas Small Business Development
Center
University of Arkansas at Little Rock
Little Rock Technology Center Building
2801 S. University
Little Rock, AR 72204
501-324-9043
800-862-2040 (outside Pulaski)
Fax: 501-324-9049
http://asbdc.ualr.edu
Email: jmroderick@ualr.edu

Henderson State University
Small Business Development Center
P.O. Box 7624
Arkadelphia, AR 71999
870-230-5224
Fax: 870-230-5236
www.hsu.edu/dept/sbdc.index.html
Email: jacksol@hsu.edu

University of Arkansas at Fayetteville
Small Business Development Center
140 Reynolds Center
Fayetteville, AR 72701
479 -575-5148
Fax: 479 -575-4013
http://sbdc.waltoncollege.uark.edu/default.asp
Email: lsexton@walton.uark.edu

University of Arkansas-Fort Smith
Small Business Development Center
Fort Smith, AR 72903
479-788-7755
Fax: 479-788-7780
http://asbdc.ualr.edu/fortsmith
Email: vvanzant@uafortsmith.edu

Southern Arkansas University
Small Business Development Center

P.O. Box 9192
Magnolia, AR 71754-9379
870-235-5033
www.saumag.edu/sbd
Email: tpconsidine@saumag.edu

Arkansas State University
Small Business Development Center
P.O. Box 2650
State University, AR 72467
870-972-3517
Fax: 870-972-3678
http://business.astate.edu/sbdc
Email: asusbdc@astate.edu

University of Arkansas-Monticello
College of The-McGehee
1609 East Ash
P.O. Box 747
McGehee, AR 71654
870-222-4900
Fax: 870-222-4900
www.greatriverstech.org/SBDC/SBDChome
.htm
Email: peacock@uamont.edu

California

Lead Center:
Nelson Chan, State Director
California Small Business Development
Center
California Technology, Trade & Commerce
1102 Q Street, Suite 6000
Sacramento, CA 95814
916-324-5511
916-323-0459
Help Line: 800-303-6600
Fax: 916-324-5791
www.commerce.ca.gov/state/ttca/ttca_htmldi
splay.jsp
Email: nchan@commerce.ca.gov

Central Coast Small Business Development
Center
c/o Cabrillo College
6500 Soquel Drive
Aptos, CA 95003
831-479-6136
Fax: 831-479-6166
www.businessonline.org
Email:sbdc@businessonline.org

Sierra College
Small Business Development Center
560 Wall Street, Suite J
Auburn, CA 95603
530-885-5488
Fax: 530-823-2831
www.sbdcsierra.org
Email: sbdcinfo@sbdcsierra.org

Weill Institute
Small Business Development Center
2100 Chester Avenue
Bakersfield, CA 93301
661-395-4126
Fax: 661-395-4134
www.weill-sbdc.com

Butte College
Small Business Development Center
19 Williamsburg Lane
Chico, CA 95926
530-895-9017
Fax: 530-566-9851
www.bcsbdc.org
Email: konuwaso@butte.cc.ca.us

Southwestern College
Small Business Development Center
International Trade Center
900 Otay Lakes Road

Building 1600
Chula Vista, CA 91910
619-482-6391
Fax: 619-482-6402
www.sbditc.com
Email: support@sbditc.org

Outreach Center
Commerce Small Business Development
Center
500 Citadel Drive, Suite 213
Commerce, CA 90040
323-887-9627
Fax: 323-887-9670
www.riohondo.edu/ecd/sbdc

Contra Costa Small Business Development
Center
2425 Bisso Lane, Suite 200
Concord, CA 94520
925-646-5377
Fax: 925-646-5299
www.contracostasbdc.com
Email: bhamile@ContraCostaSBDC.com

Imperial Valley Small Business
Development Center
El Centro, CA 92243
760-312-9800
Fax: 760-312-9838
www.ivsbdc.org

North Coast Small Business Development
Center
520 E Street
Eureka, CA 95503
707-445-9720
Fax: 707-445-9652
www.northcoastsbdc.org
Email: email@northcoastsbdc.org

Central California Small Business
Development Center
3419 West Shaw Avenue, Suite 102
Fresno, CA 93711
559-275-1223
800-974-0064
Fax: 559-275-1499
www.ccsbdc.org
Email: Dennisw@ccsbdc.org

Gavilan College
Small Business Development Center
8351 Church Street, Building E
Gilroy, CA 95020
408-847-0373
800-847-0373
Fax: 408-847-0393
www.gavilansbdc.org
Email: shannonbishop@verizon.net

Satellite Operation
Glendale Small Business Development
Center
330 North Brand Boulevard, Suite 190
Glendale, CA 91203
818-552-3254
Fax: 818-552-3322
www.sfvsbdc.org
Email: sbdcgln@ibm.net

Outreach Center
Amador Small Business Development
Center
P.O. Box 1077
1500 S Highway 49
Jackson, CA 95642
209-223-0351
Fax: 209-223-2261
www.amador-edc.org

Yuba College Small Business Development
Center
330 9th Street

P.O. Box 262
Marysville, CA 95901
530-749-0153
Fax: 530-749-0155
Email: phpd@aol.com

Satellite Operation
Valley Sierra
Small Business Development Center
2000 M Street
Merced, CA 95340
209-567-4910
800-323-2623
Fax: 209-383-4959
www.sbdcvalleysierra.org
Email: msoaza@inreach.com

Valley Sierra Small Business Development
Center
1013 11th Street
Modesto, CA 95354
209-567-4910
Fax: 209-567-4955
www.sbdcvalleysierra.org
Email: bearden@scedo.org

Napa Valley College
Small Business Development Center
1556 First Street, Suite 103
Napa, CA 94559
707-253-3210
Fax: 707-253-3068
www.napasbdc.org
Email: nvcsbdc@napasbdc.org

East Bay Small Business Development
Center
519 17th Street, Suite 210
Oakland, CA 94612
510-893-4114
Fax: 510-893-5532
www.ebsbdc.org
Email: info@ebsbdc.org

North San Diego County Small Business
Development Center
1823 Mission Avenue
Oceanside, CA 92054
760-795-8740
Fax: 760-795-8728
www.sandiegosmallbiz.com
Email: centerinfor@miracosta.edu

Satellite Operation
SFV Financial Development Corporation
12502 Van Nuys Boulevard, Suite 119
Pacoima, CA 91331
818-834-9860
Fax: 818-897-8007
www.sfvsbdc.org
Email: nevsbdc@vedc.org

Satellite Operation
Coachella Valley Small Business
Development Center
Palm Springs Satellite Center
500 South Palm Canyon Drive, Suite 222
Palm Springs, CA 92264
760-864-1311
Fax: 760-864-1319

Eastern Los Angeles County
Small Business Development Center
300 West Second Street, Suite 203
Pomona, CA 91766-1634
909-629-2247
800-450-72323
Fax: 909-629-8310
http://vclass.mtsac.edu/sbdc

Cascade Small Business Development
Center
737 Auditorium Drive, Suite A
Redding, CA 96001

530-225-2770
Fax: 530-225-2769
www.cascadesbdc.org
Email: nheubeck@scedd.org

Inland Empire Small Business Development
Center
1201 Research Park Drive
Riverside, CA 92507
909-781-2345
Fax: 909-781-2353
www.iesbdc.org

Greater Sacramento Small Business
Development Center
1410 Ethan Way
Sacramento, CA 958125
916-563-3210
Fax: 916-563-3266
www.sbdc.net
Email: info@sbdc.net

Satellite Operation
Inland Empire Business Incubator
155 South Memorial Drive, Suite B
San Bernardino, CA 92408
909-382-0065
Fax: 909-382-8543

San Francisco Small Business Development
Center
455 Market Street, 6th Floor
San Francisco, CA 94105
415-908-7501
Fax: 415-974-6035
www.sfsbdc.org
Email: info@sfsbdc.org

Silicon Valley
Small Business Development Center
84 West Santa Clara, Suite 100
San Jose, CA 95113-1815
408-494-0240
888-726-2712
Fax: 408-494-0245
www.siliconvalley-sbdc.org
Email: sbdc@siliconvalley-sbdc.org

South Central Coast Small Business
Development Center
3566 South Higuerea Street, Suite 100
San Luis Obispo, CA 93401
805-549-0401
877-549-8349
Fax: 805-543-5198
www.smallbusinessinfo.org
Email: sccsbdc@smallbusinessinfo.org

Orange County Small Business Development
Center
900 North Broadway, 8th Floor
Santa Ana, CA 92701
714-564-5200
Fax: 714-647-1168
www.ocsbdc.com
Email: roessler_michael@rsccd.org

Satellite Operation
Westside Small Business Development
Center
3233 Donald Douglas
Loop South
Santa Monica, CA 90405
310-398-8883
Fax: 310-398-3024
www.sfvsbdc.org

Redwood Empire Small Business
Development Center
606 Healdsburg Avenue
Santa Rosa, CA 95401
707-524-1770
888-346-7232
Fax: 707-524-1772

www.santarosa.edu/sbdc
Email: sbdc@santarosa.edu

San Joaquin Delta College
Small Business Development Center
445 North San Joaquin Street
Stockton, CA 95202
209-943-5089
Fax: 209-943-8325
http://sbdc.deltacollege.org
Email: gmurphy@deltacollege.edu

Solano County Small Business Development
Center
424 Executive Court North, Suite C
Suisun, CA 94534-4019
707-864-3382
Fax: 707-864-8025
www.solanosbdc.org/index.html
Email: epratt@solano.cc.ca.us

North Los Angeles County SBDC
5121 Van Nuys Boulevard
Van Nuys, CA 91403-2100
818-907-9922
Fax: 818-907-9890
www.sfvsbdc.org
Email: vnsbdc@vedc.org

Satellite Operation
Gold Coast Small Business Development
Center
5700 Ralston Street, Suite 310
Ventura, CA 93003
805-658-2688
Fax: 805-658-2252
www.sfvsbdc.org
Email: gcsbdc@vedc.org

Satellite Operation
Victorville Satellite Center
15490 Civic Drive, Suite 102
Victorville, CA 92392
760-951-1592
Fax: 760-951-8929
www.iesbdc.org
Email: iensbdc@earthlink.net

Satellite Operation
Central California Small Business
Development Center
720 West Mineral King Avenue
Visalia, CA 93279
P.O. Box 787
Visalia, CA 93279-0787
559-625-3051
Fax: 559-625-3053
www.ccsbdc.org
Email: wendi@ccsbdc.org

Outreach Location
EDC of Tuolumne County
39 North Washington Street
Sonora, CA 95370
Contact the Modesto SBDC 209-567-4910
or the EDC 209-588-0128

Outreach Location
Job Connection Mariposa
5078 Bullion St.
Mariposa, CA 95338
Contact the Merced SBDC 209-388-9659
or Job Connection 209-966-6700

Northeast Los Angeles SBDC
1576 1/2 Colorado Boulevard
Eagle Rock, CA 90041
323-340-1525
Fax: 323-340-1925
www.sfvsbdc.org

Desert Communities Empowerment Zone
Enterprise Way, Suite 6
Coachella, CA 92236

760-398-7405
Fax: 760-398-5774
www.iesbdc.org
Email: ezsbdc@earthlink.net

Inland Empire West
Ontario Office
4141 Inland Empire Boulevard, Suite 231
Ontario, CA 91764
909-466-6244
Fax: 909-466-6274
www.iesbdc.org
Email: iewsbdc@earthlink.net

Central Los Angeles County SBDC
3375 South Hoover Street, Suite 201
Los Angeles, CA 90007
213-821-2100
Fax: 213-746-4587

Eastern Los Angeles County SBDC
300 West Second Street, Suite 203
Pomona, CA 91766
909-629-2244
Fax: 909-629-8310
http://vclass.mtsac.edu/sbdc
Email: sbdcpom@attglobal.net

Colorado

Lead Center:
Kelly Manning, Director
Colorado Small Business Development
Center
Office of Economic Development
1625 Broadway, Suite 1710
Denver, CO 80202
303-892-3840
Fax: 302-892-3848
www.state.co.us/oed/sbdc.
Email: kelly.manning@state.co.us

Alamosa Small Business Development
Center
Adams State College
208 Edgemont Street
Alamosa, CO 81102
719-587-7372
Fax: 719-587-7603
http://sbdc.adams.edu
Email: mchoffman@adams.edu

Aurora Small Business Development Center
Community College of Aurora
9915 East Colfax
Aurora, CO 80010-2119
303-361-0847
Fax: 303-361-2953
www.ci.aurora.co.us/
Email: businessdev@auroragov.org

Boulder Small Business Development Center
Boulder Chamber of Commerce
2440 Pearl Street
P.O. Box 73
Boulder, CO 80302
303-442-1044
Fax: 303-938-8837
www.boulderchamber.com/chamber/sbdc.asp
Email: Sean@boulderchamber.com

Canon City Small Business Development
Center
51320 West Highway, 50
Canon City, CO 81212
719-296-6119
Fax: 719-296-8936
Email: allan.mconnell@pcc.cccoes.edu

Colorado Springs Small Business
Development Center
815 Eagle Rock Road, Building 202
P.O. Box 7150

Colorado Springs, CO 80933
719-272-7232
Fax: 719-262-3878
http://web.uccs.edu/sbdc
Email: sbdc@uccs.edu

Craig Small Business Development Center
Colorado Northwestern Community College
601 Yampa Ave.
Craig, CO 81625
970-824-7078
Fax: 970-824-5004
Email: nwsbdcfdb@springsips.com

Delta Small Business Development Center
Delta Montrose Vocational Center
1765 U.S. Highway 50
Delta, CO 81416
970-874-7671
Fax: 970-874-8796
www.dmavtc.tec.co.us
Email: info@dmavtc.co.us

Denver Small Business Development Center
Community College of Denver/Greater
Denver Chamber of Commerce
1445 Market Street
Denver, CO 80202
303-620-8076
Fax: 303-534-2145
www.coloradosbdc.com
Email: susan.widhalm@den-chamber.org

Durango Small Business Development
Center
Fort Lewis College
1000 Rim Drive
140 Education Business Hall
Durango, CO 81301-3999
970-247-7009
Fax: 970-247-7205
http://soba.fortlewis.edu/sbdc
Email: sbdc@fortlewis.edu

Fort Collins Small Business Development
Center
125 South Howes Street, Suite 150
Key Tower Building
Fort Collins, CO 80521
970-498-9295
Fax: 970-498-8924
Email: SBDC@frii.com

Fort Morgan Small Business Development
Center
Morgan Community College
300 Main Street
Fort Morgan, CO 80701
970-542-3263
800-622-0216 ext. 3263
Fax: 970-867-3352
www.mcc.cccoes.edu/Educational/SBDC/sbdc.htm
Email: merle.rhoades@MorganCC.edu

Glenwood Springs Small Business
Development Center
Colorado Mountain College
817 Colorado Avenue, Suite 306
Glenwood Springs, CO 81602
800-621-1647
970-928-0120
Fax: 970-947-8324
www.ColoradoSBDC.com
Email: jlivingston@coloradomtn.edu

Lakewood Small Business Development
Center
1667 Cole Boulevard
Building 19, Suite 400
Golden, CO 80401
303-277-1840
Fax: 303-277-1899
Email: sbdcrrcc@rmi.net

Grand Junction Small Business Development
Center
Mesa State College
Western Co. Business Development
2591 B 3/4 Road
Grand Junction, CO 81503
970-243-5242
Fax: 970-241-0771
www.gjincubator.org
Email: jmorey@giincubator.org

Greeley Small Business Development Center
Aims Community College/Greeley and Weld
Chamber of Commerce
902 7th Avenue
Greeely, CO 80631
970-352-3661
Fax: 970-352-3572
Email: dcabbott@aims.edu

Lamar Small Business Development Center
South Eastern C. Enterprise Development
2401 South Main Street
Lamar, CO 81052
719-336-1586
Fax: 719-336-2448
www.ColoradoSBDC.com
Email: Cheryl.sanchez@lcc.cccoes.edu

Pueblo Small Business Development Center
Pueblo Community College
900 West Orman Avenue
Academic Building, Room 154
Pueblo, CO 81004
719-549-3224
Fax: 719-549-3139
www.pueblocc.edu/sbdc
Email: Allan_McConnell@pueblocc.edu

Trinidad Small Business Development
Center
Trinidad State Junior College
136 West Main Street
Trinidad, CO 81082
719-846-3644
Fax: 719-846-4550
www.tsjc.cccoes.edu/sbdc/sbdc.htm

Westminster Small Business Development
Center
Front Range Community College
3645 West 112th Avenue
Campus Box 6
Westminster, CO 80031
303-460-1032
Fax: 303-469-7143
http://frcc.cc.co.us/pub_index.cfm?cid=2797
Email: peter.miller@frontrange.edu

South Metro SBDC
South Metro Denver Chamber of Commerce
6840 South University Boulevard
Centennial, CO 80122
303-540-5300
Fax: 303-795-7520
Email: skristel@bestchamber.com

LaJunta Small Business Development Center
1802 Colorado Avenue
Humanities Building, Room 108
LaJunta, CO 81050
719-384-6969
www.ColoradoSBDC.com
Email: sbdc@ojc.cccoes.edu

Connecticut

Lead Center:
Connecticut Small Business Development
Center
University of Connecticut
School of Business Administration
2100 Hillside Rd., Unit 1094

Storrs, CT 06269
860-486-4135
Fax: 806-486-1576
www.business.uconn.edu/csbdc
Email: CSBDCInformation@business.
uconn.edu

Small Business Development Center
10 Middle Street, 1st Floor
Bridgeport, CT 06604-4229
203-330-4813
Fax: 203-335-1297
Email: BridgeportCSBDC@business.
uconn.edu

The Greater Danbury Chamber of
Commerce
Small Business Development Center
39 West Street
Danbury, CT 06810
203-743-5565
Fax: 203-794-1439
Email: DanburyCSBDC@business.
uconn.edu

Quinebaug Valley Community & Technical
College
Small Business Development Center
742 Upper Maple Street
Danielson, CT 06239-1440
860-774-1133. ext. 457
Fax: 860-774-6737
www.qvctc.comment.edu/cpl/2SB.htm
Email: danielsonCSBDC@business.
uconn.edu

Asnuntuck Community College Continuing
Education
Small Business Development Center
170 Elm Street
Enfield, CT 06082
860-253-3125
Fax: 860-253-3067
Email: enfieldCSBDC@business. uconn.edu

University of Connecticut
Small Business Development Center
Administration Building, Room 104
1084 Shennecossett Road
Groton, CT 06340-6097
860-405-9002
Fax: 860-405-9041
Email: grotonCSBDC@business. uconn.edu

Middlesex County Chamber of Commerce
Small Business Development Center
393 Main Street
Middletown, CT 06457
860-344-2158
Fax: 860-346-1043
Email: middletownCSBDC@business.
uconn.edu

New Haven Small Business Development
Center
Greater New Haven Chamber of Commerce
900 Chapel Street, 10th Floor
New Haven, CT 06510
203-782-4390
Fax: 203-782-4329
Email: newhavenCSBDC@business.
uconn.edu

Stamford Small Business Development
Center
c/o Southwestern Area Commerce and
Industry Association
One Landmark Square
Stamford, CT 06901
203-359-3220, ext. 302
Fax: 203-967-8294
Email: stamfordCSBDC@business.
uconn.edu

Greater Hartford Area Small Business
Development Center
1800 Asylum Avenue
West Hartford, CT 06117-2659
860-570-9109
Fax: 860-570-9170
Email: WestHartfordCSBDC@business.
uconn.edu

Eastern Connecticut State University
Small Business Development Center
83 Windham Street
Willmantic, CT 06226-2295
860-465-5349
Fax: 960-465-5143
Email: willmanticCSBDC@business.
uconn.edu

CTSBDC
University of Connecticut
1st Floor, 99 East Main Street
Waterbury, CT 06702
203-236-9933
Fax: 203-236-9949
Email: WaterburyCSBDC@business.
uconn.edu

Delaware

Lead Center:
Clinton Tymes, State Director
Delaware Small Business Development
Center
Delaware Technology Park
One Innovation Way, Suite 301
Newark, DE 19711
302-831-1555
Fax: 302-831-1423
www.delawaresbdc.org
Email: tymesc@udel.edu

Delaware State University
1200 North Dupont Highway, Suite 108
Dover, DE 19901
302-678-1555
Fax: 302-857-6950
www.dsc.edu/som/entrepreneur/ENTMAIN.
HTM
Email: dover@delawaresbdc.org

Delaware Technical Community College
Small Business Development Center
103 West Pine Street
Georgetown, DE 19947
302-856-1555
Fax: 302-854-6979
www.dtcc.edu/owens/ccp/Pages/sbdc1.html
Email: georgetown@delawaresbdc.org

New Castle County Center
University of Delaware SBDC
1318 North Market Street
Wilmington, DE 19801
302-571-1555
Fax: 302-571-5222

District of Columbia

Lead Center:
Henry Turner, Executive Director
Howard University
Small Business Development Center
2600 6th Street, NW, Room 128
Washington, DC 20059
202-806-1550
Fax: 202-806-1777
www.bschool.howard.edu/SBDC
Email: sbdc@bschool.howard.edu

Center for Urban Progress/Office of Latino
Affairs
2000 14th Street, NW, Suite 330 North

Washington, DC 20002
202-671-2828
Fax: 202-671-2597

UDC David Clarke School of Law
Small Business Development Center
4200 Connecticut Avenue, NW
Building 38, 2nd Floor
Washington, DC 20008
202-274-7363
Fax: 202-274-7363
www.law.udc.edu/clinics/commdev/index.html

Anacostia Economic Development Center
Southeastern University, SBDC
2021 MLK Avenue, SE
Washington, DC 20020
202-889-5090
Fax: 202-889-9508
www.anacostiacdc.com

Howard University at Environmental
Protection Agency
Office of Small Disadvantaged Business
Utilization Outreach Center
1200 Pennsylvania Ave., NW, Suite 1230A
Washington, DC 20020
202-564-4584
Fax: 202-501-0756

Florida

Lead Center:
Jerry Cartwright, State Director
Florida Small Business Development Center
University of West Florida
Downtown Center
401 East Chase, Suite 100
Pensacola, FL 32502
850-595-6060
Fax: 850-595-6070
www.fsbdc.com
Email: fsbdc@uwf.edu

Central Florida Development Council
Small & Minority Business Development
Center
300 West Church Street, Suite 130-A
Bartow, FL 33830
863-534-5943/5941
Fax: 863-534-7521
www.cfdc.org/smb
Email: mstan@cfdc.org

Florida Atlantic University
Small Business Development Center
777 Glades Road
Building T-9
P.O. Box 3091
Boca Raton, FL 33431
561-297-1140
Fax: 561-297-1141
www.fausbdc.com
Email: sbdc@fau.edu

Daytona Beach Community College
Small Business Development Center
Center for Business & Industry
1200 West International Speedway
Boulevard
P.O. Box 2811
Daytona Beach, FL 32120-2811
904-947-5463
Fax: 904-254-4465
htttp://go.dbcc.edu/sbdc/default.html
Email: burgwil@dbcc.edu

Indian River Community College
Small Business Development Center
3209 Virginia Avenue
Fort Pierce, FL 34981-5599
772-462-4794
866-866-4722

http://www.ircc.cc.fl.us/atircc/progrcs/workf
orce/bdc/bdc.html
Email: bdc@ircc.edu

Okaloosa-Walton
University of West Florida
Small Business Development Center
1170 Martin Luther King Boulevard
Fort Walton Beach, FL 32547
850-863-6543
Fax: 850-863-6564
www.sbdc.uwf.com
Email: jbriere@uwf.edu

Gainesville SBDC
Gainesville Technology Enterprise Center
2153 S.E. Hawthorne Road, Suite 126
Gainesville, FL 32641
352-334-7230
Fax: 352-334-7233
www.sbdc.unf.edu
Email: tll-sbdc@atlantic.net

University of North Florida
Small Business Development Center
College of Business
12000 Alumni Drive
Jacksonville, FL 32224-2678
904-620-2476
Fax: 904-620-2567
www.sbdc.unf.edu
Email: smallbiz@unf.edu

Gulf Coast Community College
Small Business Development Center
2500 Minnesota Avenue
Lynn Haven, FL 32444
850-271-1108
800-542-7232
Fax: 850-271-1109
www.northfloridabiz.com
Email: gcccsbdc@knology.net

Brevard Community College
Small Business Development Center
3865 North Wickham Road
Melbourne, FL 32935
321-632-111 ext. 32760
888-747-2802
www.brevardcc.edu/cpe/pages/melbourne_h
ome.html
Email: peakev@brevard.cc.fl.us

Small Business Development Center
110 East Silver Springs Boulevard
Ocala, FL 34470
352-622-8763
Fax: 352-351-1031
www.sbdc.unf.edu
Email: sbdcoca@atlantic.net

University of Central Florida
Small Business Development Center
College of Business Administration
315 E. Robinson Street, Suite 100
Orlando, FL 32801
407-420-4850
Fax: 407-420-4862
www.bus.ucf.edu/sbdc
Email: karen.ruiz@bus.ucf.edu

Seminole Community College
Small Business Development Center
1445 Dolgner Place
Sanford, FL 32771
407-321-3495
Fax: 407-321-4184
http://sbdc.scc-fl.edu
Email: templetr@scc-fl.edu

Florida A&M University
Small Business Development Center
1363 East Lafayette Street
Tallahassee, FL 32301

850-599-3407
Fax: 850-561-2049
www.mckayw.com/SBDC
Email: patricia.mcgowan@famu.edu

University of South Florida
Small Business Development Center
1101 Channelside Drive, Suite 210
Tampa, FL 33602
813-905-5800
Fax: 813-905-5801
www.sbdc.usf.edu

Escambia/Santa Rosa Counties
University of West Florida
401 E. Chase Street
Pensacola, FL 32501
850-595-5480
Fax: 850-595-5487
www.sbdc.uwf.com
Email: lstrain@uwf.edu

Kissimmee Chamber of Commerce
1425 E. Vine St.
Kissimmee, FL 34744
407-847-2452
Fax: 407-847-5971
www.bus.ucf.edu/sbdc
Email: kiss.sbdc@bus.ucf.edu

Largo SBDC
Young-Rainey STAR Center
7887 Bryan Dairy Road, Suite 118
Largo, FL 33777
727-549-6393
Fax: 727-549-6394

Manatee Community College
Small Business Development Center
8000 South Tamiami Trail
Venice, FL 34293
941-408-1413
Fax: 941-480-3156
www.mccfl.edu/academ/WorkDep/CorTrain.
htm

Florida Gulf Coast University
Small Business Development Center
12751 Westlinks Drive, Building III, Unit 7
Fort Meyers, FL 33913
239-225-4220
Fax: 239-225-4221

Georgia

Lead Center:
Hank Logan, State Director
Georgia Small Business Development Center
University of Georgia
Chicopee Complex
1180 East Broad Street
Athens, GA 30602-5412
706-542-6762
Fax: 706-542-6776
www.sbdc.uga.edu
Email: hlogan@sbdc.uga.edu

Small Business Development Center
University of Georgia Business Outreach
Center
230 South Jackson Street, Suite 333
Albany, GA 31701-2885
www.sbdc.uga.edu

Small Business Development Center
University of Georgia
Chicopee Complex
1180 East Broad Street
Athens, GA 30602-5412
706-542-7436
Fax: 706-542-6803
www.sbdc.uga.edu

Small Business Development Center
University of Georgia Business Outreach
Center
University Plaza, Box 874
Atlanta, GA 30303-3083
404-651-3550
Fax: 404-651-1035
www.gsu.edu/`wwwspd
Email: sbdrec@langate.gsu.edu

Small Business Development Center
University of Georgia Business Outreach
Center
1054 Claussen Road, Suite 301
Augusta, GA 30907-3215
706-737-1790
Fax: 706-731-7937
www.sbdc.uga.edu

Small Business Development Center
University of Georgia Business Outreach
Center
501 Gloucester Street, Suite 200
Brunswick, GA 31520
912-264-7343
Fax: 912-262-3095
www.sbdc.uga.edu

State University of West Georgia
Small Business Development Center
Room 130 Cobb Hall
Carrollton, GA 30118
770-838-3082
Fax: 770-838-3083
www.westga.edu/~busn/sbdc/sbdc.html
Email: sbdcinfo@westga.edu

Small Business Development Center
University of Georgia Business Outreach
Center
1030 First Avenue
Columbus, GA 31901-2402
706-649-7433
Fax: 706-649-1928
www.sbdc.uga.edu

Small Business Development Center
University of Georgia Business Outreach
Center
Technical Building, Room 112
213 North College Drive
Dalton, GA 30260
706-272-2700
Fax: 706-272-2701
www.sbdc.uga.edu

DeKalb Chamber of Commerce
Small Business Development Center
750 Commerce Drive
Decatur, GA 30030 2622
404-371-7399
Fax: 404-371-7484
www.sbdc.uga.edu

Small Business Development Center
University of Georgia Business Outreach
Center
604 Washington Street, NW, Suite B-2
Gainesville, GA 30501
770-531-5681
Fax: 770-531-5684
www.sbdc.uga.edu
Email: resimmon@sbdc.uga.edu

Small Business Development Center
University of Georgia Business Outreach
Center
401 Cherry Street, Suite 701
Macon, GA 31201-6592
478-751-6592
Fax: 478-751-6607
www.sbdc.uga.edu

Kennesaw State University
Small Business Development Center
Busbee Drive
1000 Chastain Rd. #0409
Kennesaw, GA 30144-5591
770-423-6450
Fax: 770-423-6564
http://coles.kennesaw.edu/sbdc
Email: Lydia_Jones@coles2.kennesaw.edu

Clayton College and State University
Small Business Development Center
P.O. Box 285
Morrow, GA 30260
770-961-3440
Fax: 770-961-3428
www.sbdc.uga.edu

Floyd College Small Business Development
Center
P.O. Box 1864
Rome, GA 30720
706-295-6326
Fax: 706-295-6732
www.floyd.edu/sbdc
Email: matthews@floyd.edu

Small Business Development Center
University of Georgia Business Outreach
Center
111 East Liberty Street, Suite 200
Savannah, GA 31401
912-651-3200
Fax: 912-651-3209
www.sbdc.uga.edu

Small Business Development Center
University of Georgia Business Outreach
Center
College of Business Administration
P.O. Box 8156
Statesboro, GA30460-8156
912-681-5194
Fax: 912-681-0648
www2.gasou.edu/coba/centers/sbdc
Email: sbdc@ggasou.edu

Valdosta State University
Small Business Development Center
Thaxton Hall, Room 100
Valdosta, GA 31698
229-245-3738
Fax: 229-245-3741
www.valdosta.edu/sbdc
Email: sbarnett@valdosta.edu

Georgia Southwestern University SBDC
School of Business
800 Wheatley Street
Americus, GA 31709
229-931-6918
Fax: 229-931-6917

The University of Georgia Business
Outreach Services/SBDC
1000 University Center Lane
Building A, Suite 1520
Lawrenceville, GA 30043
678-407-5385
Fax: 678-407-5386

Georgia Southern University
SBDC Satellite Office
1200 Bellevue Avenue
P.O. Box 818
Dublin, GA 31040
479-274-2496
Fax: 478-275-0811

Clark Atlanta University SBDC
School of Business Administration
223 James P. Brawley Drive, S.W.
Atlanta, GA 30314
404-880-8483

Hawaii

Lead Center:
Darryl Mleynek, State Director
Hawaii Small Business Development Center
University of Hawaii at Hilo
308 Kamehameha Avenue, Suite 201
Hilo, HI 96720-4091
808-974-7515
Fax: 808-974-7683
www.hawaii-sbdc.org
Email: darryl_mleynek@hawaii-sbdc.org

Small Business Development Park
Maui Research and Technology Center
590 Liposa Parkway
Kihei, HI 96753-6900
808-875-2402
Fax: 808-875-2452
www.hawaii-sbdc.org/maui.htm
Email: david_fisher@hawaii-sbdc.org

Small Business Development Center
Kauai Community College
308 Kamehameha Avenue, Suite 201
Lihue, HI 96766-9591
808-246-1748
Fax: 808-245-5102
www.hawaii-sbdc.org/kauai.htm
Email: darryl_mleynek@hawaii-sbdc.org

East Hawaii Center
100 Pauahi Street, Suite 109
Hilo, HI 96720
808-933-0776
Fax: 808-933-0778
www.hawaii-sbdc.org/
Email: constance_cate@hawaii-sbdc.org

Small Business Development Center
O'ahu Center
1041 Nuuanu Avenue, Suite A
Honolulu, HI 96817
808-522-8131
Fax: 808-522-7494
www.hawaii-sbdc.org/
Email: laura_noda@hawaii-sbdc.org

Idaho

Lead Center:
James Hogge, State Director
Idaho State Business Development Center
Boise State University
1910 University Drive
Boise, ID 83725
208-426-1640
800-225-3815
Fax: 208-426-3877
www.idahosbdc.org
Email: info@idahosbdc.org

Boise State University
Small Business Development Center
1021 Manitou Ave
Boise, ID 83725
208-426-1640
Fax: 208-426-3877
www.idahosbdc.org
Email: cchamber@boisestate.edu

Idaho State University
Small Business Development Center
2300 North Yellowstone
Idaho Falls, ID 83401
208-523-1087
Fax: 208-528-7127
Email: woodrhon@isu.edu
Email: cappmary@isu.edu

Lewis-Clark State College
Small Business Development Center
500 8th Avenue

Lewiston, ID 83501
208-799-2465
800-933-5272
Fax: 208-799-2878
www.lcsc.edu/isbdc.edu
Email: mfmatson@lcsc.edu

Boise Satellite Office
Small Business Development Center
P.O. box 1901
McCall, ID 83638
208-634-2883
Email: klabrum@boisestate.edu

Idaho State University
Small Business Development Center
1651 Alvin Ricken Drive
Pocatello, ID 83201
208-232-4921
Fax: 208-282-4813
www.isu.edu/departments/respark/bizdev/sbdc.html
Email: smallbus@isu.edu

North Idaho College
Small Business Development Center
525 West Clearwater Loop
Post Falls, ID 83854
208-666-8009
Fax: 208-769-3223
www.nic.edu/wft/default.htm

College of Southern Idaho
Small Business Development Center
Evergreen Building, Room C78
315 Falls Avenue
P.O. Box 1238
Twin Falls, ID 83303-1238
208-733-9554
800-6800-CSI (Idaho & Nevada)
Fax: 208-733-9316
www.csi.edu/support/isbdc/SBDC.html
Email: info@csi.edu

Illinois

Lead Center:
Mark Petrelli
Illinois Small Business Development Center
Department of Commerce
620 East Adams Street
Springfield, IL 62701-1696
800-252-3998
www.illinoisbiz.biz/bus/sba.html
Email: sagnew@illinoisbiz.biz
Email: mpetrill@commerce.state.il.us

Waubonsee Community College
Small Business Development Center
5 East Galena Boulevard
Aurora, IL
630-906-4143
Fax: 630-892-4668
www.wcc.cc.il.us/business_org/sbdc.php
Email: sbdc@waubonsee.edu

Southern Illinois University-Carbondale
Dunn Richard Small Business Development
Center
150 East Pleasant Hill Road
Carbondale, IL 62901-6702
618-536-2424
Fax: 618-453-5040
www.siuc.edu/~sbdc
Email: sbdc@siu.edu

Kaskaskia College
Small Business Development Center
27210 College Road
Centralia, IL 62801-7878
618-532-2049
Fax: 618-532-4983

Small Business Development Centers

Asian American Alliance
222 West Cermak, Suite 303
Chicago, IL 60616-1986
312-326-2200
Fax: 312-326-0399
www.asianamericanalliance.com
Email:
megnakano@asianamericanalliance.com

Back of the Yards Neighborhood Council
Small Business Development Center
1751 West 47th Street, 2nd Floor
Chicago, IL 60609-3889
773-523-4419
Fax: 773-254-3525
www.bync.org/small_business/index.cfm
Email: sbdc@bync.org

Chicago State University
Greater Southside Small Business
Development Center
9501 South King Drive, BHS 601
Chicago, IL 60628-1598
773-995-4487
Fax: 773-995-2269
www.csu.edu/CollegeofBusiness
Email: I_conda@csu.edu

Greater North Pulaski Development
Corporation
Small Business Development Center
4054 West North Avenue, 2nd Floor
Chicago, IL 60639
773-384-2262
Fax: 773-384-3850
www.gnpdc.org/sbdc.htm
Email: sbdc@gnpdc.org

North Side Uptown Center Hull House
4520 North Beacon
Chicago, IL 60640
773-561-3500
Fax: 773-561-3507
www.hullhouse.org
Email: jsierecki@hullhouse.org

South Side Parkway Community House
500 East 67th Street
Chicago, IL 60637
773-955-8027
Fax: 773-955-8028
www.hullhouse.org
Email: krobbins@hullhouse.org

North Business and Industrial Council
5353 West Armstrong Avenue
Chicago, IL 60646-6509
773-594-9292
www.norbic.org
Email: info@norbic.org

Women's Business Development Center
Small Business Development Center
8 South Michigan, Suite 400
Chicago, IL 60603
312-853-3477
Fax: 312-853-0145
www.wbdc.org
Email: wbdc@wbdc.org

Industrial Council of NW Chicago
Small Business Development Center
2023 West Carroll Avenue
Chicago, IL 60612
312-421-3941
Fax: 312-421-1871
www.industrygroup.com/icnc/index.html
Email: icnc@industrygroup.com

Latin American Chamber of Commerce
Small Business Development Center
3512 West Fullerton Avenue
Chicago, IL 60647
773-252-5211

Fax: 773-252-7065
www.laccl.com/sbdc.html
Email: gbula@yahoo.com

Eighteenth Street Development Corporation
Small Business Development Center
1839 South Carpenter
Chicago, IL 60608-3347
312-733-2287
Fax: 312-733-8242

Chicago Loop Small Business Development
Center
DCCA/James R. Thompson Center
100 West Randolph, Suite 3-400
Chicago, IL 60601-3219
312-814-6111
Fax: 312-814-5247

McHenry County College
Small Business Development Center
8900 U.S. Highway 14
Crystal Lake, IL 60012-2761
815-455-6098
Fax: 815-455-9319
www.ccedtraining.mchenry.edu/sbdc.asp
Email: SBDC@mchenry.edu

Danville Area Community College
Small Business Development Center
28 West North Street, 1st Floor
Danville, IL 61832-5729
217-442-7232
Fax: 217-442-6228
www.dacc.edu/sbdc
Email: sbdc@dacc.edu

Cooperative Extension Service
Small Business Development Center
2525 East Federal Drive, Suite 1105
Decatur, IL 62526-2184
217-875-8284
Fax: 217-875-8288
web.extension.uiuc.edu/cie/offices/index-
t.cfm?oid=228
Email: uie-sbdc@extension.uiuc.edu

Sauk Valley College
Small Business Development Center
173 Illinois Route #2
Dixon, IL 61021-3188
815-288-5511 ext. 320
Fax: 815-288-5958
Email: sbdc@svcc.edu

Black Hawk College
Small Business Development Center
301 42nd Avenue
East Moline, IL 61244-4038
309-755-2200 ext. 211
Fax: 309-755-9847
Email: scalfd@outrol.bhc.edu

East St. Louis Small Business Development
Center
601 J. R. Thompson Drive, Room 2090
East St. Louis, IL 62201-2955
618-482-3833
Fax: 618-482-8341
www.siue.edu/ESL/small_business/small_bu
siness.htm
Email:; tmeehan@siue.edu

Southern Illinois University-Edwardsville
Small Business Development Center
Campus Box 1107
Edwardsville, IL 62026-0001
618-650-2929
Fax: 618-650-2607
www.siue.edu/SBA/
Email: jbagent@siue.edu

Elgin Community College
Small Business Development Center

1700 Spartan Drive, BCC-115
Elgin, IL 60123
847-214-7488
Fax: 847-931-3911
http://elgin.edu/smallbusiness
Email: BusinessResourceCenter@elgin.edu

The Technology Innovation Center
Small Business Development Center
1840 Oak Avenue
Evanston, IL 60201-3670
847-866-1817
Fax: 847-866-1808
www.theincubator.com/html_docs/sbdc.html
Email: sbdcrch@ponymail.com

College of DuPage
Small Business Development Center
425 Fawell Blvd.
Glen Ellyn, IL 60137-6599
630-942-2771
Fax: 630-942-3789
www.cod.edu/BPI/SBDC.htm
Email: gaydav@cdnet.cod.edu

College of Lake County
Small Business Development Center
19351 West Washington Street, Room B201
Grayslake, IL 60030-1198
847-543-2033
Fax: 847-223-9371
www.clcillinois.edu/ddd/dept/sbd.asp
ecd384@clcillinois.edu

Southeastern Illinois College
Harrisburg, IL 62946-2125
618-252-5001
Fax: 618-252-0210
www.sic.cc.il.us/web2001/business/sbdc/ind
ex.htm
Email: becky.williams@sic.edu

Rend Lake College
Small Business Development Center
Student Center, 2nd Floor
Ina, IL 62846-9801
618-437-5321 ext. 335
Fax: 618-437-5677
www.rlc.edu/Academic_Programs/Communi
ty_Services/BusCenter/small_business_cente
r.htm

Joliet Junior College
Small Business Development Center
Renaissance Center
214 North Ottawa Street
Joliet, IL 60432
815-280-1400
Fax: 815-722-1895
Email: sbdc@jjc.cc.il.us

Kankakee Community College
Small Business Development Center
Box 888 River Road
Kankakee, IL 60901-7878
815-933-0376
Fax: 815-933-0217
www.kcc.cc.il.us
Email: kcrite@kcc.cc.il.us

Western Illinois University
Small Business Development Center
214 Seal Hall
Macomb, IL 61455
309-298-2211
TDD: 309-292-4444
Fax: 309-298-2520
www.wiusbdc.org
Email: sb-center@wiu.edu

Maple City Business and Technology
Small Business Development Center
620 South Main Street
Monmouth, IL 61462-2688

309-734-4664
Fax: 309-734-8579

Illinois Valley Community College
Small Business Development Center
815 North Orlando Smith Avenue
Oglesby, IL 61348-9692
815-224-2720 Ext.212
Fax: 815-224-3033
www.ivcc.edu/conted/Small_Business_Deve
lopment_Center/index.html
Email: bpalmer@ivcc.edu

Illinois Eastern Community College SBDC
702 West High Street
Olney, IL 62450-2119
618-395-3011
Fax: 618-395-1922
www.ieccsbdc.com
Email: sbdc@iecc.edu

Moraine Valley College
Small Business Development Center
10900 South 88th Avenue
Palos Hills, IL 60465-0937
708-974-5468
708-974-8412
www.morainevalley.edu/SBDC/default.htm
Email: sbdc@morainevalley.edu

Bradley University
Small Business Development Center
141 North Jobst Hall 1st Floor
1501 West Bradley Avenue
Peroria, IL 61625-0001
309-677-2992
Fax: 309-677-3386
www.bradley.edu/turnercenter/sbdc.html
Email: sbdc@bradley.edu

Triton College
2000 Fifth Avenue
River Grove, IL 60171-1995
708-456-0300 ext. 3593
www.triton.edu/community/cbpd/sbdc.html
Email: gbarnes@triton.cc.il.us

Rock Valley College
Small Business Development Center
3301 N. Mulford Rd, Room 277
Rockford, IL 61101
815-921-2081
Fax: 815-921-2057
http://www.rockvalleycollege.edu/show
Email: C.Klotz@rvc.cc.il.us

Lincoln Land Community College
Small Business Development Center
1300 South 9th
Springfield, IL 62703-1002
217-789-1017
Fax: 217-522-3512
www.llcc.cc.il.us/bti/sbdc
Email: sbdc@llcc.cc.il.us

Shawnee College
Small Business Development Center
8364 Shawnee College Road
Ullin, IL 62992-2206
618-634-9618
1-800-481-2242 ext. 3284
Fax: 618-634-9028.
www.shawneecc.edu/communit/sbdc.asp
Email: benm@shawneecc.edu

Governors State University
Small Business Development Center
1 University Parkway
University Park, IL 60466
708-534-4929
Fax: 708-534-1646
www.centerpointgsu.com
Email: h_gereg@govst.edu

Cooperative Extension Service
Small Business Development Center
1817 South Neil Street, Suite 201
Champaign, IL 61820
217-378-8535
Fax: 217-359-1809
web.extension.uiuc.edu/cie/offices/index-
t.cfm?oid=228
Email: uie-sbdc@extension.uiuc.edu

The Chicagoland Entrepreneurial Center
330 N. Wabash, Suite 2800
Chicago, Illinois 60611-3605
312-494-6777
www.wehaveanswers.org/
Email: dweinstein@chicagolandchamber.org

University of Illinois at Chicago
Small Business Development Center
College of Business Administration
601 South Morgan Street, Suite B4UH
Chicago, IL 60607
312-413-8130
Fax: 312-355-3604
Email: freidac@uic.edu

Illinois Hispanic Chamber of Commerce
Westside Technical Institute SBDC
2800 South Western Avenue
Chicago, IL 60608
773-843-4500

Kishwaukee College
Small Business Development Center
21193 Malta Road
Malta, IL 60150-9699
815-825-2086 ext. 205
kish.cc.il.us/bid/small-business.shtml
Email: bid@kougars.kish.cc.il.us

Black Hawk College
Small Business Development Center
4703 16th Street, Suite G
Moline, IL 61265
309-764-2213
Fax: 309-797-9344
Email: scalfd@bhc1.bhc.edu

1200 West Algonquin Road
Palatine, IL 60067-7398
847-925-6000/2969
www.harpercollege.edu/learning/ce/program
/pd/sb.shtml
Email: brichter@harper.cc.il.us

Kaskaskia College
Small Business Development Center
206 West Main
Salem, IL 62881
618-548-9001
618-548-9007
http://www.kc.cc.il.us/BusinessServiceCente
r/SmallBusinessDevelopmentCenter.asp
Email: dcsbdc@kaskaskia.edu

Indiana

Lead Center:
Debbie Bishop-Trocha
Indiana Small Business Development Center
Small Business Development Center
Corporation
One North Capitol, Suite 900
Indianapolis, IN 46204
317-234-2082
888-ISBD-244
Fax: 317-232-8872
www.isbdc.org
Email: dbishop@isbdc.org

South Central Indiana Small Business
Development Center
216 Allen Street

Bloomington, IN 47403
812-339-8937
Fax: 812-335-7352
www.sbdcbiz.com
Email: southcentral@isbdc.org

Columbus Satellite Office
Columbus Enterprise Development Center
4920 North Warren Drive
Columbus, IN 47203
800-282-7232

Southwestern Indiana Small Business
Development Center
Evansville Chamber of Commerce
100 NW Second Street, Suite 200
Evansville, IN 47708
812-425-7232
Fax: 812-421-5883
Email: southwestern@isbdc.org

Northeastern Indiana Small Business
Development Center
1830 Wayne Trace
Fort Wayne, IN 46803
260-426-0040
877-676-6160
Fax: 260-424-0024
www.neisbdc.org
Email: neisbdc@isbdc.org

Small Business Development Center
212 North Main St.
Kokomo, IN 46901
765-454-7922
www.wdsi.org/SBDC_home.htm
Email: sstreet@isbdc.org

Greater Lafayette Area Small Business
Development Center
337 Columbia Street
PO Box 311
Lafayette, IN 47902-0311
765-742-2394
Fax: 765-742-6276
www.glpi.org/sbdc.asp
Email: grlafayette@isbdc.org

Southeastern Small Business Development
Center
975 Industrial Drive
Madison, IN 47250
812-265-3127
800-595-3127
Fax: 812-265-5544
www.madisonchamber.org/sbdc.html
Email: southeastern@isbdc.org

Northwest Indiana Small Business
Development Center
6100 Southport Road
Portage, IN 46368
219-762-1696
Fax: 219-763-2653
www.nwisbdc.org
Email: northwest@isbdc.org

East Central Indiana Small Business
Development Center
33 South 7th Street, Suite 3
Richmond, IN 47374-5462
765-962-2887
Fax: 765-966-0882
www.rwchamber.org/chamber_programs.ht
m
Email: eastcentral@isbdc.org

Indiana State University/Wabash Valley
Small Business Development Center
School of Business
Ninth & Sycamore Streets
Terre Haute, IN 47809-5402
812-237-7676
800-227-7232

Fax: 812-237-7675
www.indstate.edu/schbus/sbdc
Email: SBDC@indstate.edu

Merrillville Small Business Development
Center
1919 West 81st Avenue
Merrillville, IN 46410
219-762-1696 (Portage Office contact)
Fax: 219-763-2653
www.nwisbdc.org

Michigan City Small Business Development
Center
200 East Michigan Boulevard
Michigan City, IN 46360
219-874-6221
www.nwisbdc.org

Valparaiso Small Business Development
Center
150 Lincolnway
Valparasio, IN 46383
219-462-1105
www.nwisbdc.org

Satellite Office
Tri-State University
1 University Avenue
Angola, IN 46703
877-676-6160

Bedford Satellite Office
1116 16th Street
Bedford, IN 47421
812-275-4493

Satellite Office
Wells County Chamber of Commerce
WorkOne Office
3156 E. State Rd 124
Buffton, IN. 46714
877-676-6160

Southern Indiana SBDC
1613 E. Eighth St.
Jeffersonville, IN 47130
812-288-645
Fax: 812-284-8315
southern@isbdc.org

Satellite Office
Kendallville Chamber of Commerce
122 S. Main Street
Kendallville, IN 46755
877-676-6160

Linton Satellite Office
159 1st Street NW
Linton, IN 47441
812-847-4846

Central Indiana SBDC
One North Capitol, Suite 900
Indianapolis, IN 46204
317-233-SBDC
Fax: 317-232-8872
www.isbdc.org
centralindiana@isbdc.org

Nashville Satellite Office
37 W. Main St.
Nashville, IN 47448
812-988-6647

South Bend Area SBDC
401 East Colfax Avenue, Suite 120
South Bend, IN 46617
574-282-4350
Fax: 574-236-1056
southbend@isbdc.org

Spencer Satellite Office
205 East Morgan Street, Suite D

Spencer, IN 47460
812-829-3245

Iowa

Lead Center:
Ronald Manning
Iowa Small Business Development Center
Iowa State University
College of Business Administration
Chamblynn Building
137 Lynn Avenue
Ames, IA 50014-7126
515-292-6351
800-373-7232
Fax: 515-292-0020
www.iabusnet.org/sbdc/index
Email: jonryan@iastate.edu

Iowa State University
Small Business Development Center
2501 North Loop Drive
Building 1, Suite 1615
Ames, IA 50010-8283
515-296-7828
Fax: 515-296-6714
www.iabusnet.org

Des Moines Area Community College
Small Business Development Center
Circle West Incubator
P.O. Box 204
Lot 3, Industrial Park
Audubon, IA 50025
712-563-2301
Fax: 712-563-2301
www.iabusnet.org
Email: circlew@netins.net

Eastern Iowa Community College District
Small Business Development Center
320 W. 3rd St
Davenport, IA 52801
563-336-3401
800-462-3255, ext. 3401
Fax: 563-336-3479
www.eicc.edu/proser/biznind.html
Email: eiccdinfo@eicc.edu

Drake University
Small Business Development Center
Drake Business Center
2507 University Avenue
Des Moines, IA 50311-4505
515-271-2655
Fax: 515-271-1899
www.cbpa.drake.edu/aspx/SBDC/default.aspx
Email: drakesbdc@drake.edu

Northeast Iowa Community College
Small Business Development Center
300 Main Street, Suite 200
Dubuque, IA 52001
563-588-3350
Fax: 563-557-1591
www.dubuquechamber.com/Public/Business
_Assistance.cfm
Email: tsullivan@neiasbdc.org

Iowa Central Community College
Small Business Development Center
330 Avenue M
VocTech - Room 302
Fort Dodge, IA 50501
515-576-5090
800-362-2793 ext. 2732
Fax: 515-576-0826
www.iccc.cc.ia.us/btech

University of Iowa-Oakdale Campus
Small Business Development Center
108 Pappajohn Business Administration
Building, Suite S-160

Iowa City, IA 52242-1000
319-335-3742
Fax: 319-335-2445
www.iowajpec.org/entreps/smallbus.html
Email: paul-heath@uiowa.edu

Kirkwood Community College
Small Business Development Center
3375 Armar Drive
Marion, IA 52302
319-377-8256
Fax: 319-398-5698
www.iabusnet.org
Email: sspragu@kirkwood.cc.ia.us

North Iowa Area Community College
Small Business Development Center
500 College Drive
Mason City, IA 50401
614-422-4342
888-GO NIACC ext. 4342
Fax: 614-422-4129
www.niacc.cc.ia.us/pappajohn/smbusdev.ht
ml
Email: peterric@niacc.cc.ia.us

Indian Hills Community College
Small Business Development Center
623 Indian Hills Drive, Building 12
Ottumwa, IA 52501
614-683-5127
800-726-2585 ext. 5127
Fax: 614-683-5263
www.ihcc.cc.ia.us/ihbirc/sbdc.asp
Email: bziegler@ihcc.cc.ia.us

Western Iowa Tech Community College
Small Business Development Center
4647 Stone Avenue, Building B
P.O. Box 5199
Sioux City, IA 51102-5119
712-274-6418
Fax: 712-274-6429
www.iabusnet.org

Iowa Lakes Community College
Small Business Development Center
1900 North Grand Avenue, Suite 8
Spencer, IA 51301
712-262-4213
Fax: 712-262-4047
www.iabusnet.org
Email: kmccarty@ilcc.cc.ia.us

University of Northern Iowa
Small Business Development Center
212 East 4th Street
Waterloo, IA 50703
319-236-8123
Fax: 319-236-8240
www.uni.cdu/rbc
Email: info@unirbc.org

Southeastern Community College
Small Business Development Center
P.O. Box 180
1500 West Agency Road
West Burlington, IA 52655-0180
319-752-2731 ext. 8103
Fax: 319-752-3407
www.secc.cc.ia.us/workforce/smallbus.html
Email: jclover@secc.cc.ia.us

Kansas

Lead Center:
Wally Kearns
Kansas Small Business Development Center
Fort Hays State University
214 SW 6th Street, Suite 301
Topeka, KS 66603-3719
785-296-6514
Fax: 785-291-3261

www.fhsu.edu/ksbdc
Email: ksbdc.wkearns@fhsu.edu

Colby Community College
Small Business Development Center
1255 South Range
Colby, KS 67701
785-462-3984 ext. 239
www.fhsu.edu/sbdc
Email: bob@Katie.colby.cc.ks.us

Emporia State University
Small Business Development Center
1320 Cof E Drive
Emporia, KS 66801
620-341-5308
Fax: 620-341-5418
www.emporia.edu/sbdc
Email: brumbaul@emporia.edu

Garden City Community College
Small Business Development Center
801 Campus Drive
Garden City, KS 67846
620-276-9632
Fax: 620-275-3249
www.westernkansas.net/sbdc
Email: sbdc@gcnet.com

Barton County Community College
Small Business Development Center
245 NE 30th Road
Great Bend, KS 67530
316-792-9214
www.fhsu.edu/sbdc
Email: simmonse@barton.cc.ks.us

Fort Hays State University
Small Business Development Center
109 West 10th Street
Hays, KS 67601
785-628-6786
Fax: 785-628-0533
Email: sbdc@fhsu.edu

University of Kansas
Small Business Development Center
734 Vermont, Suite 104
Lawrence, KS 66044
785-843-8844
Fax: 785-843-8878
www.kusbdc.net
Email: office@kusbdc.net

Johnson County Community College
Small Business Development Center
12345 College Boulevard
Carlsen Center, Room 223
Overland Park, KS 66210-1299
913-469-3878
Fax: 913-469-2547
www.centerforbusiness.org/program.asp?ksbdc
Email: cstreet@jcc.net

Pittsburg State University
Small Business Development Center
Shirk Hall
1501 South Joplin
Pittsburg, KS 66762
620-235-4920
Fax: 620-235-4919
www.pittstate.edu/bti
Email: drichard@pittstate.edu

Salina Area Chamber of Commerce
Small Business Development Center
120 West Ash
Salina, KS 67401
785-827-9301
Fax: 785-827-9758
www.salinakansas.org/SBDC/Sbdc.htm
Email: gaines@informatics.net

Washburn University
Small Business Development Center
120 SE 6th Street, Suite 1100
Topeka, KS 66603
785-234-3235
Fax: 785-234-8656
www.washburn.edu/sbdc/index.html
Email: sbdc@wasburn.edu

WSU CCCC Outreach Center
Small Business Development Center
Cloud County Community College
2221 Campus Drive
P.O. Box 1002
Concordia, KS 66901
785-243-1435 ext. 324
800-729-5101 ext.324
www.webs.wichita.edu/ksbdc
Email: lsutton@cloud.edu

WU MACC Outreach Center SBDC
Manhattan Area Chamber of Commerce
(MACC)
501 Poyntz Avenue
Manhattan KS 66502-6605
785-587-9917
Email: susie.pryor@washburn.edu

Wichita State University
Small Business Development Center
1845 Fairmount, Campus Box 248
Wichita, KS 67260-0148
316-978-3193
Fax: 316-978-3647
www.webs.wichita.edu/ksbdc
Email: wsusbdc@wichita.edu

Kentucky

Lead Center:
Becky Naugle
Kentucky Small Business Development
Center
University of Kentucky
225 Gatton College of Business and
Economics
Lexington, KY 40506-0034
859-257-7668
888-475-SBDC
Fax: 859-323-1907
www.ksbdc.org
Email: lrnaugo@uky.edu

Ahsland Small Business Development
Center
Moorehead State University
1401 Winchester Avenue, Suite 305
Ashland, KY 41101
606-329-8011
Fax: 606-324-4570
www.morehead-st.edu/sbdc
Email: k.jenkin@moorehead-st.edu

Bowling Green Small Business Development
Center
Western Kentucky University
2355 Nashville road
Bowling Green, KY 42101
270-745-1905
Fax: 270-745-1931
www.wku.edu/Dept/Support/AcadAffairs/IED/SBDC
Email: rick.horn@wku.edu

Elizabethtown Small Business Development
Center
1105 Julianna Court, #6
Elizabethtown, KY 42701
270-765-6737
Fax: 270-769-5095
www.ksbdc.org
Email: pksbdc@kvnet.org

North Kentucky Small Business
Development Center
Northern Kentucky University
BEP Center, Room 463
Highland Heights, KY 41009-0506
859-572-6524
Fax: 859-572-6177
www.nku.edu/~sbdc
Email: landrys@nku.edu

Hopkinsville Small Business Development
Center
Murray State University
5221 Ft. Campbell Boulevard
Hopkinsville, KY 42240
270-886-8666
Fax: 270-886-3211
www.ksbdc.org
Email: mike.carter@murraystate.edu

Lexington Areas Small Business
Development Center
4th Floor Central Library Building
140 East Main Street
Lexington, KY 40507-1376
859-257-7666
Fax: 859-257-1751
www.ksbdc.org
Email: dharbut@uky.edu

Greater Louisville Small Business
Development Center
123 East Main Street
Lousiveille, KY 40202
502-625-0123
Fax: 502.625.1181
www.louisvillesmallbiz.org/site/home.asp
Email: SBDCInfo@greaterlouisville.com

Southeast Kentucky Small Business
Development Center
Southeast Community College-Bell County
Campus
1300 Chichester Avenue
Middlesboro, KY 40965-2265
606-242-2145 ext. 2021
888-225-7232
Fax: 606-242-4514
www.secc.kctcs.edu/cbdc/sbdc
Email: John.Moore@kctcs.net

Moorehead Small Business Development
Center
Moorehead State University
203 Combs Building
Moorehead, KY 40351
606-783-2895
Fax: 606-783-5020
www.morehead-st.edu/sbdc

West Kentucky Small Business
Development Center
Murray State University
Business Building South, Room 253
Murray, KY 42071
270-762-2856
Fax: 270-762-3049
www.ksbdc.org
Email: rosemary.miller@murraystate.edu

Owensboro Small Business Development
Center
Murray State University
3860 U.S. Highway 60 West
Owensboro, KY 42301
270-926-8085
Fax: 270-684-0714
www.ksbdc.org
Email: mickeyjohnson@gradd.com

West Kentucky Small Business
Development Center
MSU-Harry L. Crisp Sr. Regional Higher Ed
Campus

3000 Irvin Cobb
Paduch, KY 42001
270-442-3897
Fax: 270-762-5473
www.ksbdc.org
Email: loretta.daniel@murraystate.edu

Pikeville Small Business Development
Center
Moorehead State University
3455 North Mayo Trail #4
Pikeville, KY 41501
606-432-5848
Fax: 606-432-8924
www.morehead-st.edu/sbdc
Email: m.morley@moorehead-st.edu

South Central Small Business Development
Center
Eastern Kentucky University
The Center for Rural Development
2292 South Highway 27, Suite 260
Somerset, KY 42501
606 677-6120
859-622-1384 (Richmond)
877-EKU-SBDC
Fax: 859-622-1413
www.centertech.com
Email: kmoats@centertech.com

Paintsville SBDC
340 Main Street Suite #200
Paintsville, KY 41240
www.morehead-st.edu/sbdc

Louisiana

Lead Center:
Mary Lynn Wilkerson
Louisiana Small Business Development
Center
University of Louisiana at Monroe
College of Business Administration
Room 2-57
Monroe, LA 71209-6435
318-342-5506
Fax: 318-342-5510
www.lsbdc.org/index.htm
Email: brwilkerson@ulm.edu

Capital Small Business Development Center
1933 Wooddale Boulevard
Baton Rouge, LA 70806
225-922-0998
Fax: 225-922-0024
Email: grspa@yahoo.com

Louis State University
Small Business Development Center
South Stadium Drive
Baton Rouge, LA 70803 6100
225-578-4842
Fax: 225-578-3975
www.bus.lsu.edu/lbtc
Email: lsu-sbdc@lsu.edu

Southeastern Louisiana University
Small Business Development Center
College of Business
SLU 10522
Hammond, LA 70402
985-549-3831
Fax: 985-549-2127
www.selu.edu/Academics/Business/SBDC
Email: sbdc@selu.edu

University of Louisiana at Lafayette
Acadiana Small Business Development
Center
P.O. Box 43732
Lafayette, LA 70504
337-262-5344
Fax: 337-262-5296

www.louisiana.edu/Research/SBDC
Email: sbdc@louisiana.edu

McNeese State University
Small Business Development Center
Burton Business Center, Room 423
P.O. Box 90508
Lake Charles, LA 70609
318-475-5529
Fax: 318-475-5528
www.mcneese.edu/colleges/bus/sbdc/sbdc.htm
Email: msusbdc@mail.mcneesc.edu

University of Louisiana at Monroe
College of Business Administration
Monroe, LA 71209
318-342-1224
Fax: 318-342-1209
ele.ulm.edu/esc/sbdc.htm
Email: esc@ulm.edu

Northwestern State University
Small Business Development Center
Russell Hall, Room 114A
Natchitoches, LA 71497
318-357-5611
Fax: 318-357-6810
www.nsula.edu/nsusbdc
Email: sbdc@alpna.nsula.edu

University of New Orleans
Small Business Development Center
LA International Trade
2926 World Trade Center
New Orleans, LA 70130
504-568-8222
Fax: 504-568-8228
www.uno.edu/~litc
Email: litc@uno.edu

Loyola University
Small Business Development Center
Box 134
New Orleans, LA 70118
504-864-7942
Fax: 504-864-7070
www.cba.loyno.edu
Email: sbdc@loyno.edu

Southern University
Small Business Development Center
College of Business Administration
Room 114
New Orleans, LA 70126
504-286-5308
Fax: 504-284-5512
www.suno.edu/college_bus/program%20info
.htm
Email: ktousant@suno.edu

University of New Orleans
Small Business Development Center
UNO Technology Enterprise Center
1600 Canal Street, Suite 620
New Orleans, LA 70112
504-539-9292
Fax: 504-539-9295
www.uno.edu/~coba/sbdc

Louisiana Tech University
Small Business Development Center
College of Administration and Business
Box 10318, Tech Station
Ruston, LA 71272
318-257-3537
Fax: 318-257-4253
www.cab.latech.edu/public/DEPTS/sbdc/ind
ex.htm
Email: sbdc@latech.edu

Louisiana State University Shreveport
Small Business Development Center
One University Place
Business/Education Building, Room 103

Shreveport, LA 71115
318-797-5144
Fax: 318-797-5208
www.lsus.edu/sbdc
sbdc@pilot.lsus.edu

Nicholls State University
Small Business Development Center
105 White Hall
P.O. Box 2015
Thibodaux, LA 70310
985-448-4242
Fax: 985-448-4922
www.nich.edu/sbdc
Email: sbdc@nicholls.edu

Maine

Lead Center:
John Massaua
Maine Small Business Development Center
University of Southern Maine
68 High Street, 2nd Floor
Mail: 96 Falmouth Street
       P.O. Box 9300
Portland, ME 04104-9300
207-780-4420
TTY: 207-780-5646
Fax: 207-780-4810
www.mainesbdc.org
Email: mainesbdc@usm.maine.edu

Androscoggin Valley Council of
Governments (AVCOG)
Small Business Development Center
125 Manley Road
Auburn, ME 04210
207-783-9186
Fax: 207-783-5211
www.avcog.org/business_home.php
Email: mdubois@avcog.org

Coastal Enterprises, Inc
Small Business Development Center
Weston Building
7 North Chestnut Street
Augusta, ME 04330
207-621-0245
Fax: 207-622-9739
www.ceimaine.org/business.htm/msbdc/hom
e.htm
Email: wbs@ceimaine.org

Eastern Maine Development Corporation
Small Business Development Center
One Cumberland Place, Suite 300
P.O. Box 2579
Bangor, ME 04401
207-942-6389
800-339-6389
Fax: 207-942-3548
www.emdc.org
Email: tgallant@emdc.org

Satellite Operation
Brunswick Small Business Development
Center
11 Cumberland Street
Brunswick, ME 04011-1903
207-373-0851
Email: jburbank@gwi.net

MidCoast Council for Business
Development & Planning
49 Pleasant Street
Brunswick, ME 04011
207-729-0144
Fax: 207-725-0989
www.mcbdp.org/sbdc.htm
Email: sgill@mcbdp.org

Satellite Operation
Calais Small Business Development Center

Washington County Technical College
RR1, Box 22C, River Road
Calais, ME 04619
207-454-1066
Email: srichard@emdc.org

Northern Maine Regional Planning
Commission
Small Business Development Center
11 West Presque Isle Road
P.O. Box 779
Caribou, ME 04736
207-498-8736
800-427-8736
Fax: 207-493-3108
www.nmdc.org/bus/sbdchome.html
Email: rthompson@nmdc.org

Satellite Operation
Dover-Foxcroft Small Business
Development Center
Penquis Higher Education Center
50 Mayo Street
Dover-Foxcroft, ME 04426
800-339-6389
207-942-1744
Fax: 207-942-3548
Email: srichard@emdc.org

Satellite Operation
East Millinocket Small Business
Development Center
KATEC Center
1 Industrial Drive
East Millinocket, ME 04430
800-339-6389 (ME)
207-942-1744
Fax: 207-942-3548
Email: mballesteros@emdc.org

Fairfield Small Business Development
Center
Kennebec Valley Council of Governments
17 Main Street
Fairfield, ME 04937
207-453-4258 ext. 16
Fax: 207-453-4264
www.ceimaine.org/business/msbdc/home.htm
Email: trw@ceimaine.org

Satellite Operation
Fort Kent Small Business Development
Center
Aroostook County Register of Deeds
2 Hall Street Suite 201
Fort Kent, ME 04743
207-498-8736
800-427-8736 (ME)
Fax: 207-493-3108
Email: dspooner@nmdc.org

Satellite Operation
Houlton Small Business Development
Center
39 Bangor Street
Houlton, ME 04730
207-498-8736
800-427-8736 (ME)
Fax: 207-493-3108
Email: rthompson@nmdc.org

Satellite Operation
Kittery Small Business Development Center
Gateway of Maine Chamber of Commerce
306 US Route 1
Kittery, ME 03904
207-439-7545

Satellite Operation
Lewiston Small Business Development
Center
Lewiston Career Center
5 Mollison Way
Lewiston, ME 04240

207-783-9186 (Auburn Office)
Fax: 207- 783-5211
Email: ggould@avcog.org

Satellite Operation
Machias Small Business Development
Center
Career Center
15 Prescott Drive, Suite 2
Machias, ME 04654
800-339-6389 (ME)
207-255-1919
Fax: 207-255-4778
Email: srichard@emdc.org

Small Business Development Center
University of Southern Maine
68 High St, 2nd Floor
P.O. Box 9300
Portland, ME 04104-9300
207-780-4949
Fax: 207-780-4810
www.usm.maine.edu/sbdc
Email: entwstle@maine.edu

Satellite Operation
Portland Small Business Development
Center
Portland Resource Hub
441 Congress Street
Portland, ME 04101
207-756-8180
Fax: 207-780-4810
Email: burwell@usm.maine.edu

Satellite Operation
Rockland Small Business Development
Center
Key Bank of Maine
331 Main Street
Rockland, ME 04841
207-882-4340 (Wiscasset Office)
207-882-4456
Email: cfm@ceimaine.org

Satellite Operation
Biddeford-Saco Small Business
Development Center
Biddeford-Saco Chamber of Commerce
110 Main Street
Saco, ME 04072
207-282-1567
Fax: 207-282-3149
Email: gplatt@usm.maine.edu

Southern Maine Regional Planning
Commission
Small Business Development Center
21 Bradeen Street, Suite 304
Springvale, ME 04083
207-324-0316
Fax: 207-324-2958
www.smrpc.org/businesseconomicframeset.
htm
Email: gplatt@usm.maine.edu

Coastal Enterprises, Inc.
Small Business Development Center
36 Water Street, Box 268
Wiscasset, ME 04578
207-882-4340
Fax: 207-882-4456
www.ceimaine.org/business.htm/msbdc/hom
e.htm
Email: drhill@ceimaine.org

Satellite Operation
York Small Business Development Center
York Chamber of Commerce
449 Route 1
York, ME 03909
207-363-4422
Fax: 207-324-2958

Maine Small Business Development Center
Outreach Office
Hutchinson Center
80 Belmont Avenue
Belfast, ME 04915
207-621-0245
Fax: 207-622-9739
Email: drhill@ceimaine.org

Bingham SBDC Outreach Office
Municipal Building, Town of Bingham
13 Murray Street
P.O. Box 652
Bingham, ME 04920-0652
207-453-4258 ext. 16
207-672-5519
Email: trw@ceimaine.org

Ellsworth SBDC Outreach Office
248 State Street, Suite 3A
Ellsworth, ME 04605
207-664-2317
Fax: 207-667-4789
Email: srichard@emdc.org

Coastal Aracadia Economic Development
Small Business Development Center
217 High Street
P.O. Box 554
Ellsworth, Maine 04605
207-664-7457
Fax: 207-664-0902
www.acadia.net/cadc
Email: cdavisems@yahoo.com

The Thomas M. Teaque Biotechnology
Center of Maine
Maine's Applied Technology Development
Centers
P.O. Box 149
50 Eskelund Drive
Fairfield, ME 04537
207-423-4283 ext.16
Fax: 207-453-4264
Email: trw@ceimaine.org

Franklin SBDC Outreach Office
Aquaculture and Marine Science
33 Salmon Farm Road
Franklin, ME 04634
207-664-7457
207-460-4467
Email: cdavisems@yahoo.com

Maine Technology Institute
Small Business Development Center
2E Mechanic Street Above the Log Cabin
Fuel Building
Gardiner, ME 04345
207-582-4790
Fax: 207-582-4772
www.mainetechnology.org
Email: meriby@usm.maine.edu

Limestone SBDC Outreach Office
Loring Applied Technology Center
191 Development Drive
Limestone, ME 04750
207-498-8736
Email: rthompson@nmdc.org

Orono SBDC Outreach Office
Maine Aquaculture Incubators
Maine Aquaculture Innovation Center
5717 Corbett Hall, Room 438
Orono, ME 04469
207-882-4340
Fax: 207-882-4456
Email: drhill@ceimaine.org

Orono SBDC Outreach Office
Target Technology Center
20 Godfrey Drive
Orono, ME 04473

207-942-1744
Fax: 207-942-3548
Email: dneuman@emdc.org

Rumford SBDC Outreach Office
River Valley Business Resource Center
34 River Street
Rumford, ME 04276
207-363-0062
Fax: 207-363-0062
Email: bkasputes@avcog.org

Outreach Office
River Valley Precision Manufacturing
Incubator
P.O. Box 559
60 Lowell Street
Rumford, ME 04276
207-781-9186
Fax: 207-783-5211
Email: bkasputes@avcog.org

Sanford Outreach Office
P.O. Box 508
60 Community Drive
Sanford, ME 04073
207-324-0316
Fax: 207-324-2958
Email: gplatt@usm.maine.edu

South Paris SBDC Outreach Office
218 Main Street
South Paris, ME 04281
207-743-5297
Fax: 207-783-5211
Email: clogan@avcog.org

Wilton SBDC Outreach Office
862 US Route 2E
Wilton, ME 04234
207-645-5824
Fax: 207-783-5211
Email: ggould@avcog.org

Maryland

Lead Center:
Renee Sprow
University of Maryland
Small Business Development Ctr.
Administrative Offices
7100 Baltimore Avenue, Suite 401
College Park, MD 20740-3627
301-403-8300
877-787-SBDC
Fax: 301-403-8303
www.mdsbdc.umd.edu
Email: rsprow@sbdc.umd.edu

Central Small Business Development Center
3 West Baltimore Street #170
Baltimore, MD 21201
888-898-2073

Charles County Community College
Southern Region Small Business
Development Center
P.O. Box 910
Mitchell Road
LaPlate, MD 20646-0910
301-934-7583
800-762-7232
Fax: 301-934-7681
www.sbdchelp.com

Satellite Operation
Calvert County Department of Economic
Development
Small Business Development Center
Courthouse Annex, Suite 101
175 Main Street
Prince Frederick, MD 20678

301-934-7583 (appointments)
www.sbdchelp.com

Eastern Shore Small Business Development
Sub-Center
Salisbury State University
PP171
Salisbury, MD 21801
410-548-3991
800-999-7232
Fax: 410-548-5389
www.salisbury.edu/community/sbdc

Towson University
Small Business Development Center
8000 York Road
Towson, MD 21252-0001
877-421-0830
410-704-5001
Fax: 410-704-5009
wwwnew.towson.edu/sbdc/aboutsbdc.asp
Email: SBDC@towson.edu

Satellite Operation
Small Business Development Center
Wye Mills Campus
PO Box 8
1000 College Drive
Wye Mills, MD 21679
888-852-6712
www.salisbury.edu/community/sbdc

St. Mary's SBDC Satellite
CSM Training Center
21795-D1 North Shangi-La Drive
Lexington Park, MD 20653
301-866-1923
Fax: 301-934-7681
www.sbdc.help.com

Satellite Operation
Dorchester County Chamber of Commerce
Cambridge, MA
410-228-3715
www.salisbury.edu/community/sbdc

SBDC - Western Region, Inc
957 National Highway Suite 3
LaVale, MD 21502-7328
301-729-2400
800-457-7232
Fax: 301-729-8700
www.hagerstownmd.org/html/small_busines
s.html

Massachusetts

Lead Center:
Georgiana Parkin
Massachusetts Small Business Development
Center
University of Massachusetts Amherst
227 Isenberg School of Management
121 Presidents Drive
Amherst, MA 01003-9310
413-545-6301
Fax: 413-545-1273
http://msbdc.som.umass.edu
Email: gep@msbdc.umass.edu

Procurement Technical Assistance Center
Small Business Development Center
University of Massachusetts Amherst
227 Isenberg School of Management
121 Presidents Drive
Amherst, MA 01003
413-545-6303
Fax: 413-545-1273
msbdc.som.umass.edu/ptac
Email: info@msbdc.umass.edu

Satellite Operation
Massachusetts Export Center

State Transportation Building
10 Park Plaza, Suite 4510
Boston, MA 02116
617-973-8664
Fax: 617-973-8681
www.state.ma.us/export
Email: pmurphy@massport.com

Satellite Operation
Minority Business Assistance Center
Small Business Development Center
100 Morrissey Boulevard
Boston, MA 02125-3393
617-287-7750
Fax: 617-287-7767
www.sbdc.umb.edu

Boston College
Small Business Development Center
142 Beacon Street
Chestnut Hill, MA 02467
617-552-4091
Fax: 617-552-2730
www.bc.edu/centers/sbdc
Email: sbdcmail@bc.edu

University of Massachusetts at Dartmouth
Southeastern Massachusetts Regional Small
Business Development Center
200 Pocasset Street
Fall River, MA 02772
508-673-9783
Fax: 508-674-1929
www.umassd.edu/sbdc
Email: cornwell@msbdc.umass.edu

Satellite Operation
Chamber of Commerce of the Berkshires
Small Business Development Center
75 N Street, Suite 360
Pittsfiled, MA 01201
413-499-0933
Fax: 413-499-0933

Salem State College
Northeast Region Small Business
Development Center
Enterprise Center
121 Loring Avenue, Suite 310
Salem, MA 01970
978-542-6343
Fax: 978-542-6345
www.salemsbdc.org

University of Massachusetts
Western Regional Small Business
Development Center
One Federal Street
Springfield, MA 01105-1160
413-737-6712
Fax: 413-737-2312
msbdc.som.umass.edu/wmass
Email: ddoherty@msbdc.umass.edu

Clark University
Small Business Development Center
5 Maywood Place
Worcester, MA 01610
508-793-7615
Fax: 508-793-8890
www.clarku.edu/offices/sbdc
Email: lmarsh@clarku.edu

Michigan

Lead Center:
Carol Lopucki
Michigan Small Business and Technology
Development Centers
Seidman School of Business
Grand Valley State University
510 W. Fulton
Grand Rapids, MI 49504

616-331-7480
Fax: 616-331-7485
www.misbdc.org
Email: sbtdchq@gvsu.edu

Satellite Operation
Lenaweee County Chamber of Commerce
Small Business Development Center
128 E. Maumee Street
Adrian, MI 49221
517-266-1488
Fax: 517-265-2432
www.misbtdc.org/region12
Email: spin@wccnet.org

Satellite Operation
Ottawa County Economic Development
Office, Inc.
Small Business Development Center
6676 Lake Michigan Drive
P.O. Box 539
Allendale, MI 49401-0539
616-892-4120
Fax: 616-895-6670
www.misbtdc.org/region7
Email: ken@ocedo.org

Alpena Community College
666 Johnson Street
Alpena, MI 49707
989-358-7383
Fax: 989-358-7554
www.misbtdc.org-region3
Email: bourdelc@alpena.cc.mi.us

Satellite Operation
Huron County Economic Development
Center
Small Business Development Center
Huron County Building, Suite 303
250 East Huron
Bad Axe, MI 48413
989 -269-6431
Fax: 989 -269-7221
www.misbtdc.org/region6
Email: carl@huroncounty.com

Satellite Operation
Mecosta County Area Chamber of
Commerce
246 North State Street, Suite B
Big Rapids, MI 49307
231-796-7649
Fax: 231-796-1625
www.misbtdc.org/region4
Email: anja@mecostacounty.com

Satellite Operation
Tuscola County Economic Development
Small Business Development Center
157 North State Street
Caro, MI 48723
989-673-2849
Fax: 989-673-2517
www.misbtdc.org/region6

Metropolitan Center for High Technology
Small Business Development Center
2727 Second Avenue, Suite 113
Detroit, MI 48201
313-967-9295
Fax: 313-967-9296
www.misbtdc.org/region9
Email: emu.sbdc@emich.edu

1st Step, Inc.
Small Business Development Center
2415 14th Avenue, S
Escanaba, MI 49829
906-786-9234
Fax: 906-786-4442

Grand Valley State University
MI-SBTDC Region 7

401 West Fulton Street, 4th Floor
DeVos Center, 318C
Grand Rapids, MI 49504
616-331-7370
Fax: 616-331-7195
www.misbtdc.org/region7
Email: sbtdcinfo@gvsu.edu

Satellite Operation
Oceana Economic Development Corporation
Small Business Development Center
P.O. Box 168, 314 State Street
Hart, MI 49420-0168
231-873-7141
Fax: 231-873-5056
www.misbtdc.org/region4
Email: edcoceana1@chartermi.net

Satellite Operation
Jackson Business Development Center
414 North Jackson Street
Jackson, MI 49201
517-787-0442
Fax: 517-787-3960
www.misbtdc.org/region12
Email: vweaver@enterprisegroup.org

Kalamazoo College
Small Business Development Center
MI-SBTDC Region 11
Stryker Center
1327 Academy Street
Kalamazoo, MI 49006
269-337-7350
Fax: 269-337-7352
www.misbtdc.org/region11
Email: sbdc@kzoo.edu

Lansing Community College
Small Business Development Center
MI-SBTDC Region 8
P.O. Box 40010
520 Seymour Street
Lansing, MI 48901
517-483-1921
Fax: 517-483-1675
www.misbtdc.org/region8
Email; sbtdc@email.lcc.edu

Satellite Operation
Lapeer Development Corporation
Small Business Development Center
449 McCormick Drive
Lapeer, MI 48446
810-667-0080
Fax: 810-667-3541
www.misbtdc.org/region6

Satellite Operation
Midland Economic Development Council
Small Business Development Center
300 Rodd Street, Suite 201
Midland, MI 48640
989-839-0340
Fax: 989-839-7372
www.misbdtc.org/region5
Email: kat@midlandedc.org

Satellite Operation
Monroe County IDC
PO Box 926
2929 E. Front Street
Monroe, MI 48161
734-241-8754
Fax: 734-241-0813
www.misbtdc.org/region9
Email: mail@monroecountyidc.com

MI-Regional Small Business Technology
and Development Center
1 South Main Street, 7th Floor
Mt. Clemens, MI 48043
586 -469-5118
Fax: 586 -469-6787

www.co.macomb.mi.us/planning/economic_
development.htm
www.misbtdc.org/region10
Email; SBDC@co.macomb.mi.us

Satellite Operation
Ontonagon County Economic Development
Corporation
725 Greenland Road
Ontonagon, MI 49953
906-884-4188
Fax: 906-884-6788
www.misbtdc.org/region1
Email: ontcoedc@jamadots.com

Satellite Operation
Economic Development Alliance of St. Clair
Shores
Small Business Development Center
735 Erie Street, Suite 250
Port Huron, MI 48060
810-982-9511
Fax: 810-982-9531
www.misbtdc.org/region10
Email: sbtdc@edaofstclaircounty.com

Satellite Operation
Saginaw County Minority Business
Development Center
PO Box 1993
Saginaw, MI 48605-1993
989-755-7630
www.misbtdc.org/region5
Email: katw@concentric.net

Satellite Operation
Saginaw Future, Inc.
Small Business Development Center
301 East Genessee, Suite 300
Saginaw, MI 48607
989-754-8222
Fax: 989-754-1715
www.misbtdc.org/region5
Email: info@saginawfuture.com

Satellite Operation
Downriver Community Conference
15100 Northline Road
Southgate, MI 48195
734-362-3477
Fax: 734-281-0276
www.misbtdc.org/region9
Email: paulab@dccw.org

Satellite Operation
Sterling Heights Chamber of Commerce
12900 Hall Road, Suite 110
Sterling Heights, MI 48313
586-731-5400
Fax: 586-731-3521
www.misbtdc.org/region10
Email: ladams@suscc.com

Satellite Operation
Northwestern Michigan College
1701 East Front Street
Traverse City, MI 49686
231-946-1596
Fax: 231-946-2565
www.misbtdc.org/region2
Email: tbedc@gtii.com
Email: info@tcchamber.org

Travers Bay Economic Development
Corporation
Traverse City Small Business Development
Center
202 East Grandview Parkway
Traverse City, MI 49684
231-995-2023
Fax: 231-995-2022
www.misbtdc.org/region2
Email: khornburg@nmc.edu

Northwest Michigan Council of Governments
1209 South Garfield Avenue, Suite C
P.O. Box 506
Traverse City, MI 49685-0506
231-922-3780
Fax: 231-929-5042
www.nwm.org/business/sbtdc
Email: bpalladi@nwm.cog.mi.us

Satellite Operation
Warren/Centerline/Sterling Heights Chamber of Commerce
30500 Van Dyke Avenue, Suite 118
Warren, MI 48093
586-751-3939
Fax: 586-751-3995
www.misbdtc.org/region10
Email: jmillhench@wcschamber.com

MI-SBTDC Regional Center
Small Business Development Center
301 West Michigan Avenue, Suite 101
Ypsilanti, MI 48197
734-547-9170
Fax: 734-547-9178
www.misbtdc.org/region12
Email: sbtdc@wccnet.org

Albion Economic Development Corporation
309 N. Superior St.
PO Box 725
Albion, MI 49224
517-629-3926
Fax: 517-629-3929
www.misbtdc.org/region 11
Email: psindt@albionedc.org

Allegan County Economic Alliance
2891 116th Avenue, M-222 East
PO Box 2777
Allegan, MI 49010
269-673-8442
Fax: 269-686-2232
www.misbtdc.org/region11
Email: aeeda.aeen.org

USDA Rural Development-Lake County, Baldwin
P.O. Box 220
Baldwin, MI 49304
231-745-8364
Fax: 231-745-8493
www.misbtdc.org/region4
Email: reggie.magee@mi.usda.gov

Keweenaw Bay Indian Community
Baraga Village Office
100 Hemlock Street
Baraga, MI 49908
906-353-6237
Fax: 906-353-6100

Battle Creek Area Chamber of Commerce
77 E. Michigan Avenue, Suite 200
Battle Creek, MI 49017
269-962-8996
Fax: 269-962-3692
www.misbtdc.org/region11
Email: Larry@battlecreek.org

MI-SBTDC Region 11
Lake Michigan College
M-TEC
400 Klock Road
Benton Harbor, MI 49022
269-926-4047
Fax: 269-926-1956
www.misbtdc.org/region11

Northern Lakes Economic Alliance
PO Box 8
1313 Boyne Avenue
Boyne City, MI 49712

231-582-6482
Fax: 231-582-3213
www.misbtdc.org/region2
Email: tom@northernlakes.net

Glen Oaks Community College Center for Business Services
62249 Shimmel Rd.
Centreville, MI 49072
269-467-9945 ext.296
Fax: 269-467-7912
www.misbtdc.org/region11
Email: showell@glenoaks.cc.mi.us

Branch County Economic Growth Alliance
20 Division St.
Coldwater, MI 49036
517-278-4146
Fax: 517-279-8936
www.misbtdc.org/region11
Email: bcega@bcega.com

Iron County EDC
2 South 6th Street, Suite 8
Crystal Falls, MI 49920
906-875-6688
Fax: 906-875-0657
Email: edc@iron.org

Michigan SBTDC - East Detroit
Jefferson East Business Association
14628 E. Jefferson
Detroit, MI 48215
313-331-7939
Fax: 313-331-0311
www.misbtdc.org/region9
Email: Dinist@aol.com

MI-SBTDC Region 6
University of Michigan, Flint
432 North Saginaw Street, Suite 805
Flint, MI 48502-1950
810-767-7373
Fax: 810-767-7183
www.misbtdc.org/region6
Email: hblecker@umflint.edu

Newaygo County EDC, Fremont
4747 W. 48th Street, Suite 108
Fremont, MI 49412
231-924-8890
Fax: 231-924-9250
www.misbtdc.org/region4
Email: alofgren@ncisd.net

Otsego County Economic Alliance
225 West Main Street, Room 209
Gaylord, MI 49735
989-732-6484 ext. 337
Fax: 989-732-7764
www.misbtdc.org/region3
Email: ratclifj@msue.msu.edu

Business Information Center
233 East Fulton Street, Suite 101
Grand Rapids, MI 49503
616-771-6880
Fax: 616-771-8021
www.misbtdc.org/region7
Email: garnere@kamls.org

Grayling Regional Chamber of Commerce
P.O. Box 406
City Park/213 North James Street
Grayling, MI 49738
989-348-2921
Fax: 989-348-7315
www.misbtdc.org/region3
Email: visitor@grayling-mi.com

Finlandia University
601 Quincy Street
Hancock, MI 49930
906-487-7344

Fax: 906-487-7290
Email: Joanne.macinnes@finlandia.edu

Hastings Industrial Incubator
1035 E. State Street
Hastings, MI 49058
269-945-2468
Fax: 269-962-6309
www.misbtdc.org/region11

Mid Michigan Community College
M-TEC Building
1375 South Clare Avenue
Harrison, MI 48625
989-802-0993
Fax: 989-802-0971
www.misbtdc.org/region4
Email: melliott@midmich.edu

Holland Area Chamber of Commerce
272 East 8th Street
Holland, MI 49432
616-392-9719
www.misbtdc.org/region7
Email: sbdc@chamber-holland.org

Houghton Lake Chamber of Commerce
1625 West Houghton Lake Drive
Houghton Lake, MI 48629
989-366-5644
Fax: 989-366-9472
www.misbtdc.org/region3
Email: hlcc@iserve.net

Satellite Office
Lansing Community College
Howell Center
1600 Pinckney Rd
Howell, MI 49943
517-545-3522
Fax: 517-545-3525
www.misbtdc.org/region8
Email: dennisw@brightoncoc.org

Dickinson Area Partnership
600 South Stephenson Avenue
Iron Mountain, MI 49801
906-774-2002
Fax: 906-774-2004

Greater Gratiot Development, Inc., Ithaca
136 South Main
Ithaca, MI 48847
989-875-2083
Fax: 989-875-2990
www.misbtdc.org/region4
Email: don.schurr@gratiot.org

Michigan SBTDC
Western Wayne Co.
Schoolcraft College
18600 Haggerty
Livonia, MI 48152
734-462-4438
Fax: 734-462-4439
www.misbtdc.org/region9
Email: vmathur@schoolcraft.cc.mi.us

Manistee Economic Council & Chamber Alliance
50 Filer Street, Suite 224
Manistee, MI 49660
231-723-4325
Fax: 231-723-1515
Email: tkubanek@manistee.com

Schoolcraft County EDC
PO Box 277
Manistique, MI 49854
906-341-5126
Fax: 906-341-5555

Lake Superior Community Partnership
501 South Front Street

Marquette, MI 49855
906-226-6591
Fax: 906-226-2099

Marshall Chamber of Commerce
424 E. Michigan Ave.
Marshall, MI 49068
269-781-5163
Fax: 269-781-6570
www.misbtdc.org/region11
Email: mea@voyager.net

River Cities Regional Chamber of
Commerce
1005 Tenth Avenue
Menominee, MI 49858
906-863-2679
Fax: 906-863-3288

Mid Michigan Community College, Mt.
Pleasant Campus
5805 E. Pickard Street
Mt. Pleasant, MI 48858
989-773-6622
Fax: 989-772-2386
www.misbtdc.org/region4
Email: pfairchi@midmich.edu

Muskegon Area Chamber of Commerce
900 Third Street, Suite 200
Muskegon, MI 49440
231-722-3751
Fax: 231-728-7251
www.misbtdc.org/region7
Email: sbdcinfo@gvsu.edu

Luce County EDC
401 W. Harrie Street
Newberry, MI 49868
906-293-5982
Fax: 906-293-2904
Email: mclaren@up.net

Southwestern Michigan College
Business Development
2229 US 12 East
Niles, MI 49120
269-687-5640
Fax: 269-687-5655
www.misbtdc.org/region11
Email: jcousins@skyenet.net

Alpena Community College/Huron Shores
Campus
5800 Skeel Avenue
Oscoda, MI 48750
989-358-7375
Fax: 989-358-7554
www.misbtdc.org-region3
Email: mehargk@alpenacc.edu

MSU Extension Center - Van Buren
226 East Michigan Ave.
Paw Paw, MI 49079
269-655-8308
Fax: 268-655-8307
www.misbtdc.org/region11
Email: thomasm@msue.msu.edu

Michigan SBTDC - Northern Oakland Co.
Oakland University, School of Business
Administration
238H Elliott Hall
Rochester, MI 48309-4493
248-370-2726
Fax: 248-370-4963
www.misbtdc.org/region9
Email: oaklanduniversity.sbdc@emich.edu

Presque Isle County EDC
658 South Bradley Highway
Rogers City, MI 49779
989-734-8446
Fax: 989-734-2577

www.misbtdc.org/region3
Email: heidemam@msue.msu.edu

Higgins Lake-Roscommon Chamber of
Commerce
P.O. Box 486
701 Lake Street
Roscommon, MI 48653
989-275-8760
Fax: 989-275-2029
www.misbtdc.org/region3
Email: hlrcc@voyager.net

MI-SBTDC Region 5
Delta College Corporate Services
310 Johnson Street, Suite 245
Saginaw, MI 48607
989-686-9597
Fax: 989-667-2222
www.misbtdc.org/region5
Email: sbtdc@corpserv.delta.edu

Biz Resource Center
Michigan Works! Service Center
3875 Bay Road, Suite 7
Saginaw, MI 48603
989-249-5232
www.misbtdc.org/region5

Sault Area Chamber of Commerce
2581 I-75 Business Spur
Sault Ste. Marie, MI 49783
906-632-3301
Fax: 906-632-2331
Email: saultchamber@30below.com

Mackinac County EDC
100 South Marley
St. Ignace, MI 49781
906-643-0356
Fax: 906-643-6581
Email: edc@mackinaccounty.net

Ogemaw County EDC
205 South Eight Street
West Branch, MI 48661
989-345-0692
Fax: 989-345-1284
www.misbtdc.org-region3
Email: zoiay@msue.msu.edu

MI-SBTDC Regional Center
Eastern Michigan University
306 Gary M. Owen Building
300 West Michigan Avenue
Ypsilanti, MI 48197
734-487-0355
734-481-3354
www.misbtdc.org/region9
Email: emu.sbdc@emich.edu

Minnesota

Lead Center:
Mary Kruger
Minnesota Small Business Development
Center
Department of Trade and Economic
Development
500 Metro Square Building
121 7th Place East
St. Paul, MN 55101-2146
612-297-5773
Fax: 612-296-1290
www.dted.state.mn.us
Email: mary.kruger@state.mn.us

Central Lakes College
Small Business Development
501 West College Drive
Brainerd, MN 56401
218-855-8142
Fax: 218-855-8141

www.clcmn.edu/smallbusiness
Email: gbergman@clcmn.edu

University of Minnesota at Duluth
Small Business Development Center
11 East Superior Street, Suite 210
Duluth, MN 55802
218-726-6192
888 387 4594
Fax: 218-726-6338
www.umdced.com
Email: lbujold@umdced.com

Vermillion Community College
Small Business Development Sub-Center
1900 East Camp Street, Room PE 140
Ely, MN 55731
218 365 7295
Fax: 218 365 2248
www.umdced.com
Email: jzigich@umdced.com

Itasca Development Corporation
Small Business Development Sub-Center
12 NW 3rd Street
Grand Rapids, MN 55744
218-327-2241
Fax: 218-327-2242
www.umdced.com
Email: mikea@itascadv.org

Hibbing Community College
Small Business Development Sub-Center
1515 East 25th Street
Hibbing, MN 55746
218-262-6703
Fax: 218-262-6717
www.umdced.com
Email: jtolan@umdced.com

Small Business Development Center
Rainy River Community College
1501 Highway 71
International Falls, MN 56649
218-285-2255
Fax: 218-285-2239
www.umdced.com

Region Nine Development Commission
Small Business Development Center
P.O. Box 3367
410 Jackson Street
Mankato, MN 56002-3367
507-387-5643
800-450-5643
Fax: 507-387-7105
www.rndc.org/programs/sbdc

Southwest State University
Small Business Development Center
ST #105
1505 State Street
Marshall, MN 56258
507-537-7386
Fax: 507-537-6094
www.southwest.msus.edu
Email: struve@ssu.southwest.msus.edu

University of St. Thomas
Small Business Development Center
Graduate School of Business
1000 LaSalle Avenue, TMH #100LL
Minneapolis, MN 55403
651-962-4500
800-328-6819 ext. 2-4500
Fax: 651-962-4508
www.stthomas.edu/sbdc
Email: smallbus@stthomas.edu

Moorhead State University
Small Business Development Center
Box 132
1104 7th Avenue South
Moorhead, MN 56563

www.mnstate.edu/cbi
Email: sliwoski@mnstate.edu

Pine Technical College
Small Business Development Sub-Center
1000 4th Street
Pine City, MN 55063
320-629-7340
Fax: 320-629-7603

Rochester Community and Technical
College
Small Business Development Center
Riverland Hall
851 30th Avenue, SE
Rochester, NN 55904
507-285-7536
Fax: 507-280-5502
www.roch.edu/rctc/workforce/CEWEDIndex
/business.html
Email: michelle.pyfferoen@roch.edu

St. Cloud State University
Small Business Development Center
Business Resource Center
720 4th Avenue, South
St. Cloud, MN 56301-3761
320-255-4842
Fax: 612-255-4957
Email: djensen@stcloudstate.edu

North Shore Business Enterprise Center
Small Business Development Sub-Center
1313 Fairgrounds Road
P.O. Box 240
Two Harbors, MN 55616
218-834-3494
888-387-4594
www.umdced.com
Email: hhelgen@umdced.com

Bemidji State University
Center for Research and Innovation
3801 Bemidji Avenue North
Bemidji, MN 56601
218-755-4900
www.cri-bsu.org/SBDC/index.html
Email: cfalk@bemidjistate.edu

University of Minnesota Duluth
Center for Economic Development
Natural Resources Research Institute
5013 Miller Trunk Highway
Hermantown, MN 55611
218-726-7298
888-387-4594
Fax: 218-726-6338
Email: www.umdced.com

Mesabi Range Community & Technical
College
1001 Chestnut Street West
Virginia, MN 55792
218-749-7752
888-387-4594
www.umdced.com
Email: rbraun@umdced.com

Mississippi

Lead Center:
Walter Gurley, Jr.
Mississippi Small Business Development
Center
University of Mississippi
P.O. Box 1848
B19 Jeanette Phillips Drive
University, MS 38677-1848
662-915-5001
800-725-7232 (MS)
Fax: 662-915-5650
www.olemiss.edu/depts/mssbdc
Email: msbdc@olemiss.edu

Northeast Mississippi Community College
Small Business Development Center
Holliday Hall 303
Cunningham Boulevard
Booneville, MS 38829
662-720-7448
Fax: 662-720-7464

Delta State University
Small Business Development Center
P.O. Box 3235 DSU
Cleveland, MS 38733
662-846-4236
Fax: 662-846-4235
www.deltastate.edu/sbdc/online
Email: dsusbdc@deltastate.edu

East Central Community College
Small Business Development Center
P.O. Box 129
275 Broad Street
Decatur, MS 39327
601-635-2111 ext. 297
Fax: 601-635-4031
www.eccc.edu/PROGRAMS/onestop/#F
Email: rwestbrook@eccc

Jones Jr. College
Small Business Development Center
900 Court Street
Ellisville, MS 39437
601-477-4235
Fax: 601-477-4166
www.jcjc.cc.ms.us/depts/crc/sbdc.html
Email: greg.butler@jcjc.cc.ms.us

Mississippi Gulf Coast Community College
Small Business Development Center
P.O. Box 100
2300 Highway 90
Gautier, MS 39553
228-497-7723
Fax: 228-497-7788
Email: janice.mabry@mgccc.cc.ms.us

Delta Community College
Small Business Development Center
P.O. Box 5607
1656 East Union
Greenville, MS 38704-5607
662-378-8183
Fax: 662-378-5349
Email: mdccsbdc@tecinfo.com

Pearl River Community College
Small Business Development Center
Highway 49 South
Forrest County Center, Building 1
Hattiesburg, MS 39401
601-544-5533
Fax: 601-544-5549
www.prcc.cdu/fcc/smallbusiness.htm
Email: sbdc@prcc.cc.ms.us

Jackson State University
JSU Small Business Development Center
JSU Mississippi E-Center
1230 Raymond Road, Box 500
Jackson, MS 39204
601-979-2795
Email: hthomas@jsums.edu

University of Southern Mississippi
Small Business Development Center
136 Beach Park Place
Long Beach, MS 39560
228-865-4578
Fax: 228-865-4581
www.gp.usm.edu/sbdc/index.html
Email: Jill.Scafide@usm.edu

Alcorn State University
Small Business Development Center
1000 ASU Drive #90

Alcorn State, MS 39096-7500
601-877-3901
601-877-6450
Fax: 601-877-3900
www.alcorn.edu/Outreach/Sbdc.htm
Email: gpurohit@lorman.alcorn.edu

Co-Lin Community College
Small Business Development Center
11 Co-Lin Circle
Natchez, MS 39120
601-445-5254
Fax: 601-446-1221
www.colin.edu/communityservi/Workforce_
Dev_Center/small_business_development_c
ente.htm
Email: RobertRuss@colin.edu

Hinds Community College
Small Business Development Center
International Trade Center
PMB 11263
1500 Raymond Lake Road, 3rd Floor
PO Box 1100
Raymond, MS 39154-1100
601-857-3536
Fax: 601-857-3474
www.hindscc.edu/Departments/RCU/Small_
Business_Development_Center
Email: mhwall@hindscc.edu

Mississippi State University
Small Business Development Center
Mississippi Research & Technology Park
The Technology Center, Suite 201
Starkville, MS 39760
662-325-8684
Fax: 662-325-4016
www.cbi.msstate.edu/cobi/sbdc/sbdc.html
Email: sfisher@cobilan.msstate.edu

Southwest MS Community College
Small Business Development Center
College Drive
Summit, MS 39666
601-276-3890
Fax: 601-276-3883
www.smcc.cc.ms.us/support/ccenter/webdoc
6.htm
Email: waller@smcc.cc.ms.us

University of Mississippi
Small Business Development Center
P.O. Box 1848
B19 Jeanette Phillips Drive
University, MS 38677-1848
662-234-2120
662-951-1291
Fax: 662-951-5650
www.olemiss.edu/depts/umsbdc
Email: sbdc@olemiss.edu

Greenville Higher Education Center
Small Business Development Center
DSU Office Suite 332
2900 A Hwy 1 South
Greenville, MS 38701
662-378-8589
www.deltastate.edu/sbdc/online
Email: dsusbdc@deltastate.edu

Missouri

Lead Center:
Max Summers
Missouri Small Business Development
Center
University of Missouri-System
1205 University Avenue, Suite 300
Columbia, MO 65211
573-882-0344
Fax: 573-884-4297

www.mo-sbdc.org
Email: sbdcmso@missouri.edu

Southeast Missouri State University
Small Business Development Center
Rovert A Dempster Hall
One University Plaza MS-5925
Cape Girardeau, MO 63701
573-986-6084
Fax: 573-986-6083
www2.semo.edu/sesbdc/homepage.html
Email: c402sbi@semovm.semo.edu

Satellite Operation
Small Business Development Center
Chillicothe City Hall
715 Washington Street
Chillicothe, MO 64601-2229
660-646-6920
Fax: 660-646-6811
Email: lkturner@greenhills.net

University of Missouri at Columbia
Small Business Development Center
306 Cornell Hall
 Columbia, MO 65211
573-882-7096
Fax: 573-882-9931
http://business.missouri.edu/sbdc/
Email: eastinb@missouri.edu

Missouri Southern State College
Small Business Development Center
3950 Newman Road
Joplin, MO 64801-1595
417-625-3128
Fax 417-625-9782
www.msscsbdc.com
Email: krudwig-j@mssu.edu

Truman State University
Small Business Development Center
100 East Normal
Kirksville, MO 63501-4221
660-785-4307
www.sbdc.truman.edu
Email: sbdck@missouri.edu

Northwest Missouri State University
Small Business Development Center
McKmey Center for Lifelong Learning
800 University Drive
Maryville, MO 64468
660-562-1701
Fax: 660-562-1890
www.nwmissouri.edu/sbdc
Email: sbdcm@missouri.edu

Southwest Missouri State University
Small Business Development Center
Center for Business Research
901 South National
Springfiled, MO 65804-0089
417-836-5685
Fax: 417-836-7666
www.sbdc.smsu.edu
Email: sbdcs@missouri.edu

Satellite Operation
St. Joseph Satellite Center
3003 Frederick Avenue
St. Joseph, MO 64506
816-232-4461
Fax: 816-364-4873
www.nwmissouri.edu/sbdc
darnellsbdc@saintjoseph.com

St. Louis Enterprise Center
315 Lemay Ferry Road, Suite 131
St. Louis, MO 63125
314-631-5327
Fax: 314-631-7996
http://mo-sbdc.org/stlouis/index.html
Email: RichteA@missouri.edu

Central Missouri State University
Small Business Development Center
Dockery Suite 102
Warrensburg, MO 64093-5037
660-543-4402
Fax: 660-543-8159
www.cmsu.edu/sbdc
Email: sbdc@cmsu1.cmsu.edu

Southwestern Missouri State University-
West Plains
Small Business Development Center
128 Garfield
West Plains, MO 65775-2715
417-255-7966
Email: sbdc@wp.smsu.edu

University of Missouri-Kansas City
Small Business Development Center
4747 Troost, Suite 113B
Kansas City, MO 64110
816-235-6063
Fax: 816-235-5754
www.bloch.umkc.edu/sbdc/index.htm
Email: sbdckc@missouri.edu

Kansas City Satellite Center
1901 NE 48th Street
Kansas City, MO 64118
816-792-7720
Email: reuben.siverling@rockhurst.edu

SBA St. Louis District Office
200 N Broadway, Suite 1500
St. Louis, MO 63102
314-539-6600 ext. 227
Fax: 314-539-3785
www.mo-sbdc.org/stlouis/index.html
Email: JakubovskisA@missouri.edu

St. Louis Empowerment Zone
100 N Tucker Blvd, Suite 530
St. Louis, MO 63101
314-241-1511
Fax: 314-241-4099
http://www.mo-sbdc.org/stlouis/index.html
 Email: williamsand@missouri.edu

5988 Mid Rivers Mall Drive
St. Charles, MO 63304-7119
636-928-7714
www.mo-sbdc.org/stlouis/index.html
Email: muellerrf@missouri.edu

Montana

Lead Center:
Ann Desch
Montana Small Business Development
Center
Department of Commerce
301 S. Park Ave.
Helena, MT 59620
406-841-2747
Fax: 406-841-2728
http://commerce.state.mt.us/brd/brd_sbdc.html

Billings Small Business Development Center
Big Sky Economic Development Authority
222 North 32nd Street
Billings, MT 59101
406-256-6871
Fax: 406-256-6877
www.bigskyeda.org/SBDC/index.htm
Email: langman@bigskyeda.org

Bozeman Small Business Development
Center
Gallatin Development corporation
222 East Main, Suite 102
Bozeman, MT 59715
406-587-3113

Fax: 406-587-9565
www.bozeman.org/cgi-
bin/gdc/small_biz_dev_center
Email: askus@bozeman.org

Butte Small Business Development Center
Headquarters RC&D
305 West Mercury, Suite 211
Butte, MT 59701
406-782-7333
Fax: 406-782-9675
http://hosts4.in-
tch.com/www.headwatersrcd.org/redisbdc.htm
Email: jdonovan@headwatersrcd.org

Colstrip Small Business Development Center
Southeastern Montana Development
Corporation
P.O. Box 1935
6200 main Street
Colstrip, MT 59323
406-748-2990
Fax: 406-748-2990
www.semdc.org
Email: semdc.org@mcn.net

Great Falls Small Business Development
Center
High Plains Development Authority
710 1st Avenue North
P.O. Box 2568
Great Falls, MT 59403-2568
406-453-8834
Fax: 406-454-2995
www.gfdevelopment.org/smallbiz.htm
Email: suzie@gfdevelopment.org

Havre Small Business Development Center
Bear Paw Development Corporation
P.O. Box 170
48 2nd Avenue
Havre, MT 59501
406-265-4945
Fax: 406-265-5602
www.bearpaw.org/
small_business_development_center.htm
Email: tjette@bearpaw.org

Helena Small Business Development Center
Gateway Economic Development
Corporation
225 Cruise Ave
Helena, MT 59601
406-447-1512
Fax: 406-447-1514
www.gatewayedc.org/sbdc.htm
Email: hlnsbdc@mt.net

Kalispell Area Chamber of Commerce
Small Business Development Center
15 Depot Park
Kalispell, MT 59901
406-758-2802
Fax: 406-758-2805
www.kalispellsmallbusiness.com
Email: kalsbdc@centrurytel.net

Missoula Community Development
Corporation
Small Business Development Center
110 East Broadway, Second Floor
Missoula, MT 59802
406-728-9234
fax: 406-542-6671
www.mtcdc.org/sbdc.html
Email: mcdc@mtcdc.org

Wolf Point Small Business Development
Center
233 Cascade Street
Wolf Point, MT 59201
406-653-2590
Fax: 406-653-1840
www.gndc.org/sbdc.htm

Small Business Development Centers

Nebraska

Lead Center:
Robert Bernier
Nebraska Business Development Center
University of Nebraska at Omaha
College of Business Administration
Roskens Hall, Room 415
Omaha, NE 68182
402-554-2521
Fax: 402-554-3473
http://nbdc.unomaha.edu
Email: robert_bernier@unomaha.edu

University of Nebraska at Kearney
Nebraska Business Development Center
1917 W. 24th Street
West Center Bldg, Room 135
Kearney, NE 68849-3035
308-865-8344
Fax: 308-865-8153
www.unk.edu/departments/NBDC
Email: ingersollo@unk.edu

Nebraska Business Development Center
1135 M Street, Suite 200
Lincoln, NE 68508
402-472-3358
Fax: 402-472-3363
NBDCLincolnNE@aol.com

Northeast Community College
Lifelong Learning Center
801 East Benjamin Avenue
Norfolk, NE 68702-0469
402-844-7234
Email: rheld@mail.unomaha.edu

Nebraska Business Development Center
Mid Plains Voc. Tech. Campus
1101 Halligan Drive, Room 409B
North Platte, NE 69101
308-534-5115
Email: dkurth@mail.unomaha.edu

Entrepreneur Shop
10868 West Dodge Road
Omaha, NE 68154
402-595-1158
Fax: 402-595-1194

Nebraska Business Development Center
Omaha Business and Technology Center
2505 North 24th Street, Suite 101
Omaha, NE 68110
402-595-3511
MaryGraffNEPTAC@netscape.net

Nebraska Business Development Center
Peter Kiewit Conference Center
1313 Farnam, PKCC Suite 230
Omaha, NE 68182-0164
402-595-2381
Fax: 402-595-2385
Email: dmuellerfichepain@mail.unomaha.edu

Nebraska Business Development Center
US Bank Building
1620 Broadway, Room 201
Scottsbluff, NE 69361
308-635-7513

Wayne State College
Nebraska Business Development Center
Gardner Hall
1111 Main Street
Wayne, NE 68787
402-375-7575
Fax: 402-375-7574
www.wsc.edu/nbdc
Email: nbdc@wsc.edu

Nevada

Lead Center:
Sam Males
Nevada Small Business Development Center
University of Nevada Reno
College of Business Administration
Business Building, Room 411
Reno, NV 89577-0100
702-784-1717
Fax: 702-784-4337
www.nsbdc.org
Email: nsbdc@unr.nevada.edu

Great Basin College
Small Business Development Center
723 Railroad St
Elko, NV 89801
775-753-2245
Fax: 775-753-2242
www.nsbdc.org/offices/elko
Email: judye@gbcnv.edu

University of Nevada at Las Vegas
Small Business Development Center
851 E Tropicana, Building 700
Mailing Address:
    UNLV, 4505 Maryland Parkway
    Box 456011 (mail)
Las Vegas, NV 89154
www.nsbdc.org/offices/lasvegas
Email: nsbdc@nevada.edu

Carson City Chamber of Commerce
Small Business Development Center
1900 South Carson Street, #100
Carson City, NV 89701
775-882-1565
Fax: 775-882-4179
www.nbdc.org/offices/carson_city
Email: ccchamber@semp.net

Ely Small Business Development Center
Rural Nevada Development Corporation
740 Park Avenue
Ely, NV 89301
775-289-8519
www.nsbdc.org/offices/ely
Email: rbart@idsely.com

Fallon Small Business Development Center
Churchill County Economic Development
Authority
448 West Williams Street
Fallon, NV 89406
775-423-8587
Fax: 775-423-0381
www.nsbdc.org/offices/fallon
Email: rlattin@sci-nevada.com

Carson Valley Small Business Development
Center
Carson Valley Chamber of Commerce
1512 Highway 395 North, Suite 1
Gardnerville, NV 89410
775-782-8144
Fax: 775-782-1025
www.nsbdc.org/offices/carson_valley
Email: rhalbard@prodigy.net

Henderson Small Business Development
Center
112 Water Street
Henderson, NV 89015
702-992-7208
Fax: 702-992-7245
www.nsbdc.org/offices/henderson
Email: bernief@nevada.edu

Hi-Desert Economic Development Authority
Small Business Development Center
90 West Fourth Street
P.O. Box 820
Winnemucca, NV 89445

www.nsbdc.org/offices/winnemucca
Email: sbdc@desertlink.com

Safety and Environmental Assistance
Business Environmental Program
PO Box 15225
Las Vegas, NV 89114
702-866-5962
Fax: 702-866-6800
http://nsbdcbep.org

Safety and Environmental assistance
Business Environmental Program
Sierra Pacific Power Company
6100 Neil Road, Suite 400
Reno, NV 89511
775-689-6688
800-882-3233
Fax: 775-689-6689
http://nsbdcbep.org

New Hampshire

Lead Center:
Mary Collins
New Hampshire Small Business
Development Center
University of New Hampshire
The Whittemore School of Business
108 McConnell Hall
15 College Road
Durham, NH 03824-3593
603-862-2200
Fax: 603-862-4876
www.nhsbdc.org
Email: mary.collins@unh.edu

Keene State College
Small Business Development Center
Mail Stop 2101
Keene, NH 03435-2101
603-358-2602
Fax: 603-358-2612
www.nhsbdc.org/keene.htm
Email: gchabot@keene.edu

Small Business Development Center
120 Main Street
Littleton, NH 03561
603-444-1053
Fax: 603-444-5463
www.nhsbdc.org/littleto.hmt
Email: eaward@ncia.net

Small Business Development Center
670 N. Commercial Street
4th Floor, Suite 1
Manchester, NH 03101
603-634-2000
Fax: 603-647-4410
www.nhsbdc.org/manchest.htm
Email: bob.ebberson@verizonesg.net

Plymouth State College
Small Business Development Center
101 Samuel Read Hall
Plymouth, NH 03264-1595
603-535-2526
Fax: 603-535-2850
www.nhsbdc.org/plymouth.htm
Emaill: eburt@mail.plymouth.edu

Small Business Development Center
Rivier College, Sylvia Trottier Hall
420 Main St.
Nashua, NH 03060
603-897-8588
Fax: 603-897-8884
www.nhsbdc.org/nashua.htm
Email: dnelson@rivier.edu

International Trade Resource Center
17 New Hampshire Avenue

Peace International Tradeport
Portsmouth, MH 03801-2838
603-334-6074
Fax: 603-334-6110
www.nhsbdc.org/itrc.htm
Email: nh.sbdc@unh.edu

New Hampshire Small Business
Development Center
c/o Rochester Chamber of Commerce
18 South Main Street, Suite 2A
Rochester, NH 03867
603-330-1929
Fax: 603-330-1948
www.nhsbdc.org/rocheste.htm
Email: wdaniel@cisunix.unh.edu

Seacoast Satellite Office
Pease Tradeport
320 Corporate Drive
Portsmouth, NH 03801
603-330-1929
www.nhsbdc.org/rocheste.htm

New Jersey

Lead Center:
Brenda Hopper
New Jersey Small Business Development
Center
Rutgers Business School
49 Bleeker Street
Newark, NJ 07102-1993
973-353-1927
800-432-1565
Fax: 973-353-1110
www.njsbdc.com
Email: bhopper@njsbdc.com

Rutgers University Campus at Camden
Small Business Development Center
School of Business
325 Cooper Street, 3rd Floor, Room 334
Camden, NJ 08102
856-225-6221
Fax: 856-225-6621
http://camden-sbc.rutgers.edu/rsbdc
Email: hcharles@camden.rutgers.edu

Brookdale Community College
Small Business Development Center
765 Newman Springs Road
Lincroft, NJ 07738
732-224-2751
www.brookdale.cc.nj.us/staff/sbdc

Rutgers University Campus at Newark
Small Business Development Center
University Heights
Bleeker Street
Newark, NJ 07102
973-353-5950
Fax: 973-353-1030
www.njsbdc.com/newark
Email: tndoro@njsbdc.com

Paterson Small Business Development
Center
131 Ellison Street
Paterson, NJ 07505
973-754-8695
Fax: 973-754-9153

Kean University
Small Business Development Center
East Campus, Room 242
Union, NJ 07083
908-737-5950
Fax: 908-527-2960
Email: mkostak@kean.edu

Warren County Community College
Skylands Small Business Development
Center

475 Route 57 West
Washington, NJ 07882
908-689-9620
Fax: 908-689-2247
www.warren.edu/ssbdc/aboutus.html
Email: sbdc@warren.edu

Small Business Development Center
5100 Harding Highway
Mays Landing, NJ 08330
609-909-5339
Fax: 609-909-9671
Email: jmolineaux@njsbdc.com

Bergen Community College
Small Business Development Center
Ciarco Learning Center
355 Main Street
Hackensack, NJ
201-489-8670
www.bergen.edu/SBDC
Email: jtenuto@bergen.edu

Raritan Valley Community College
Small Business Development Center
Route 28 & Lamington Road
Information Center, South Building
Mailing address:
    Corporate and Continuing Education
    P.O. Box 3300
    Somerville, NJ 08876-1265
Regional
    North Branch, NJ 08876
908-526-1200 ext.8515
Fax: 908-725-9687
www.sbdcrvcc.com
Email: sjohnson@raritanval.edu

New Jersey City University
SBDC
20 College Street
Jersey City, NJ 07301
201-200-2156
Fax: 201-200-3404
Email: boneal@njcu.edu

Ocean County College
SBDC
Center For Lifelong Learning
College Drive
Toms River, NJ 08754
732-255-0468
www.ocean.edu/conted/small_business_deve
lopment_center.htm
Email: jpeterson@ocean.edu

Mercer/Middlesex Small Business
Development Center
36 South Broad Street
Trenton, NJ 08608
609-989-5232
Fax: 609-989-7638
Email: lallen@tcnj.edu

William Paterson University
Small Business Development Center
300 Pompton Road
Wayne, NJ 07470
Email: mirabeaul@wpunj.edu

New Mexico

Lead Center:
J. Roy Miller
New Mexico Small Business Development
Center
Santa Fe Community College
6401 Richards Avenue
Santa Fe, NM 87508
505-428-1362
800-281-7232
Fax: 505-438-1469

www.nmsbdc.org
Email: info@nmshbdc.org

New Mexico State University at
Alamogordo
Small Business Development Center
2230 Lawrence Boulevard
Alamogrodo, NM 88310
505-434-5272
Fax: 505-434-1432
www.alamosbdc.org
Email: director@alamosbdc.org

South Valley Small Business Development
Center
700 4th Street, SW
Albuquerque, NM 87102
505-248-0132
Fax: 505-248-0127
Email: svsbdc.org@abq.com

New Mexico State University at Carlsbad
Small Business Development Center
221 South Canyon Street
Carlsbad, NM 88220
505-885-9531
Fax: 505-885-1515
Email: lcoalson@cavern.nmsu.edu

Clovis Community College
Small Business Development Center
417 Schepps Boulevard
Clovis, NM 88101
505-769-4136
Fax: 505-769-4135
www.clovis.cc.nm.us/BusinessCommunity/S
BDC/index.asp
Email: sbdc@clovis.edu

Northern New Mexico Community College
Small Business Development Center
921 Paseo de Onate
Espanola, NM 87532
505-747-2235/2236/2237
Fax: 505-747-2234
http://nnmcc.edu/www/pages/sbdc.htm
Email: rprather@nnmcc.edu

San Juan College
Small Business Development Center
5101 College Blvd
Farmington, NM 87402
505-566-3528
Fax: 505566-3698
www.sjc.cc.nm.us/qcb/sbdc.html
Email: armstrongl@sanjuancollege.edu

University of New Mexico at Gallup
Small Business Development Center
103 West Highway 66
Gallup, NM 87301
505-722-2220
Fax: 505-863-6006
Email: sbdc@gallup.unm.edu

New Mexico State University at Grants
Small Business Development Center
709 East Roosevelt
Grants, NM 87020
505-287-8221
Fax: 505-287-2125
www.grants.nmsu.edu/gr_general/sbdc.html
Email: sbdcgrant@7cities.net

New Mexico Junior College
Small Business Development Center
5317 Lovington Highway
Hobbs, NM 88240
505-392-5603 ext. 651
Fax: 505-492-1493
www.nmjc.edu/sbdc

Dona Ana Branch Community College
Small Business Development Center

Small Business Development Centers

Box 30001, Department 3DA
2345 East Nevada Street
Las Cruces, NM 88003-8001
505-527-7601
505-527-7676/7606
Fax: 505-528-7432
http://dabcc-www.nmsu.edu/comm/sbdc
Email: fowensby@nmsu.edu

Luna Community College
Small Business Development Center
P.O. Box 1510
Las Vegas, NM 87701
505-454-2582
800-588-7232 ext. 1759
Fax: 505-454-5326
www.nmsbdc.org/lasvegas
Email: lvtisbdc@nmhu.campus.mci.net

University of New Mexico at Los Alamos
Small Business Development Center
P.O. Box 715
190 Central Park Square
Los Alamos, NM 87544
505-622-0001
Fax: 505-662-0099
www.losalamos.org/lacdc/unmla.html
Email: sbdc@losalamos.org

University of New Mexico at Valencia
Small Business Development Center
280 La Entrada
Los Lunas, NM 87031
505-925-8980
Fax: 505-925-8981
www.unm.edu/loslunas

Eastern New Mexico University at Roswell
Small Business Development Center
20 West Mathis
P.O. Box 6000
Roswell, NM 88201-6000
505-624-7133
Fax: 505-624-7132
www.nmsbdc.org/roswell
Email: eugene.simmons@roswell.enmu.edu

Santa Fe Community College
Small Business Development Center
6401 Richards Road
Santa Fe, NM 87505
505-428-1343
Fax: 505-428-1469
www.nmsbdc.org/santafe

Western New Mexico University
Southwest Small Business Development
Center
P.O. Box 2672
Silver City, NM 88062
505-538-6320
Fax: 505-538-6341

Mesalands Community College
Small Business Development Center
911 South 10th
Tucumcari, NM 88401
505-461-4413 ext. 133 or 140
Fax: 505-461-1901/4318
www.nmsbdc.org/Tucumcari
Email: sbdc@mesalands.edu

Albuquerque SBDC
TVI Workforce Training Center
5600 Eagle Rock Ave NE, Suite 201
Albuquerque NM 87113
505-224-5250
Fax: 505-224-5256
http://planet.tvi.cc.nm.us/wtc/abqsbdc
Email: sbdc@tvi.edu

Taos Satellite Office
1332 Gusdorf Road Suite B

Taos, NM 87571
505-737-5651

New York

Lead Center:
James L. King
New York Small Business Development
Center
State University Plaza
41 State Street
Albany, NY 12246-0001
518-443-5398
800-732-7232
Fax: 518-443-5275
www.nyssbdc.org
Email: kingjl@nyssbdc.org

State University of New York at Albany
(SUNY)
Small Business Development Center
1 Pinnacle Place, Suite 218
Albany, NY 12203-3439
518-453-9567
Fax: 518-453-9572
Email: albsbdc@nycap.rr.com

Binghamton University
Small Business Development Center
Binghamton, NY 13902-6000
607-777-4024
Fax: 607-777-4029
http://sbdc.binghamton.edu
Email: sbdc@binghamton.edu

State University College at Brockport
Small Business Development Center
350 New Campus Drive
Morgan III, Room 3205
Brockport, NY 14420
585-395-2334
Fax: 585-395-2467
http://cc.brockport.edu/~smallbus/index.html
Email: sbdc@brockport.edu

Lehman College
Bronx Small Business Development Center
250 Bedford Park Boulevard, West
Bronx, NY 10468
718-960-8806
Email: bxsbdc@binc.org

Boricua College
9 Graham Avenue
Brooklyn, NY 11206
718-963-4112
718-960-8697
Fax: 718-963-2031
Email: boricuasbdc@mindspring.com

Buffalo State College
Small Business Development Center
Buffalo State College , GC206
Buffalo, NY 14222
716-878-4030
Fax: 716-878-4067
www.nyssbdc.org
Email: buffalosbdc@yahoo.com

SUNY Canton
Canton Small Business Development Center
Faculty Office Building, Room 202
Cornell Drive
Canton, NY 13617
315-386-7312
Fax: 315-379-3814
www.nyssbdc.org

Corning Community College
Small Business Development Center
24 Denison Parkway West
Corning, NY 14830-2607
607-962-9461

Fax: 607-936-6642
www.nyssbdc.org
Email: gestwicki@corning-cc.edu

Mercy College Outreach Center
Small Business Development Center
555 Broadway
Dobbs Ferry, NY 10522-1189
914-674-7845
Fax: 914-693-4996
www.nyssbdc.org/centers/centers.cfm?centid=16

SUNY Geneseo
Small Business Development Outreach
Center
South Hall 111
1 College Circle
Geneseo, NY 14454
716-245-5429
Fax: 716-245-5430
www.sunyniagara.cc.ny.us/sbdc/index.html
Email: SBDC@uno.cc.geneseo.edu

EOC Hempstead Outreach Center
Small Business Development Center
269 Fulton Avenue
Hempstead, NY 11550
516-564-8672
Fax: 516-564-1895
www.nyssbdc.org/centers/centers.cfm?centid=17
Email: schwarjf@farmingdale.edu

York College, The City University of New
York
Small Business Development Center
94-20 Guy R. Brewer Blvd
Jamaica, NY 11451
718-262-2880
Fax: 718-262-2881
www.nyssbdc.org/centers/centers.cfm?centid=22
Email: atitone@york.cuny.edu

Jamestown Community College
Small Business Development Center
Community Services Center
525 Falconer Street
Jamestown, NY 14701
716-665-5754
800-522-7232
Fax: 716-665-6733
www.sunyjcc.edu/sbdc/sbdc.html
Email: dobiesia@jccw22.cc.sunyjcc.edu

Mid-Huron Small Business Development
Center
Business Resource Center
1 Development Court
Kingston, NY 12401
845-339-0025
Fax: 845-339-1631
www.nyssbdc.org/centers/centers.cfm?centid=15
Email: hardingf@sunyulster.edu

Midtown Outreach Center
Small Business Development Center
Baruch College
Field Center
55 Lexington Avenue
New York, NY 10010
646-312-4790
Fax: 646-312-4781
www.nyssbdc.org/centers/centers.cfm?centid=24
Email: patrice_tombline@baruch.cuny.edu

Pace University
Small Business Development Center
163 William Street, 16th Floor
New York, NY 10038
212-346-1900

Fax: 212-346-1613
www.nyssbdc.org/centers/centers.cfm?centid
=21
Email: sbdc@pace.edu

International Trade Center
Niagara Falls Small Business Development
Center
Niagara Office Building
345 Third Street
Niagara, Falls, NY 14303-117
716-285-4793
Fax: 716-285-4797
www.sunyniagara.cc.ny.us/sbdc/index.html
Email: sbdc@niagaracc.suny.edu

Plattsburgh State University of New York
Small Business Development Center
Ward Hall 118
101 Broad Street
Plattsburgh, NY 12901
518-564-2042
Fax: 518-564-2043
www.nyssbdc.org/centers/centers.cfm?centid
=8
Email: SBDC@plattsburgh.edu

Small Business Development Outreach
Center-SUNY Brockport
55 St. Paul St., Riverside Entrance
Rochester, NY 14604
716-232-7310
Fax: 716-232-7274
http://cc.brockport.edu/~smallbus/index.html

Niagara County Community College at
Sanborn
Small Business Development Center
3111 Saunders Settlement Road
Sanborn, NY 14132
716-614-6480
Fax: 716-614-6825
www.sunyniagara.cc.ny.us/sbdc/index.html

Southampton Outreach Small Business
Development Center
Long Island University
Abney Peak, Montauk Highway
Southhampton, NY 11968
631-287-0059
Fax: 631-287-8287
http://naples.cc.sunysb.edu/CEAS/smallbusi
ness.nsf

The College of Staten Island
Small Business Development Center
2800 Victory Boulevard
Building 2A
Staten Island, NY 10314
718-982-2560
Fax: 718-982-2323
www.nyssbdc.org/centers/centers.cfm?centid
=23
Email: schwartzm@postbox.csi.cuny.edu

SUNY at Stony Brook
Small Business Development Center
Harriman Hall, Room 101
Stony Brook, NY 11794-3775
516-632-9070
Fax: 516-632-7176
http://naples.cc.sunysb.edu/CEAS/smallbusi
ness.nsf

Onondaga Community College at Syracuse
Small Business Development Center
Whitney Applied Technology Center, Suite
106
Syracuse, NY 13215-2099
315-498-6070
Fax: 315-492-3704
www.nyssbdc.org/centers/centers.cfm?centid
=6
Email: SBDC@SUNYOCC.EDU

Brookhaven National Laboratory
Small Business Development Outreach
Center
Building 179B, Bell Avenue
Upton, NY 11973
631-344-2393
Fax: 631-344-3543

SUNY Institute of Technology at
Utica/Rome
Small Business Development Center
Route 12 North
P.O. Box 3050
Utica, NY 13504-3050
315-792-7547
Fax: 315-792-7554
www.sbdc.sunyit.edu
Email: sbdc@sunyit.edu

Jefferson Community College
Small Business Development Center
Coffeen Street
Watertown, NY 13601
315-782-9262
Fax: 315-782-0901
www.nyssbdc.org/centers/centers.cfm?centid
=4
Email: sbdc@sunyjefferson.edu

The Small Business Resource Center
Small Business Development Center
222 Bloomingdale Road, Suite 400
White Plains, NY 10605-1500
914-948-4349/4450
www.nyssbdc.org/centers/centers.cfm?centid
=16

Outreach Office
Centro Civico of Amsterdam Inc.
143-145 East Main Street
Amsterdam, NY 12010
518-842-3762

36 South Street
Auburn, NY 13021
315-498-6070

Madison County Industrial Development
Agency
Canastota Business Center
Canastota, NY 13032
315-697-9817

Delaware County Chamber of Commerce
97 East Main Street
Delhi, NY 13753
607-746-2281

Outreach Office
Jamestown Community College
10807 Bennett Road
Dunkirk, NY 14048
800-522-7232

Cortland County Chamber of Commerce
34 Tompkins Street
Cortland, NY 13045
607-756-2814

Farmingdale State University of New York
Campus Commons
Farmingdale, NY 11735-1006
631-420-2765
631-370-8888
Fax: 631-370-8895
www.nyssbdc.org/centers/centers.cfm?centid
=17
wesnofl@farmingdale.edu

Marist College Extension
400 Westage Business Center
Fishkill, NY 12524-2947
845-897-3945
Fax: 845-897-4653

Outreach Office
5 Warren Street
Glens Falls, NY 12801-2801
518-453-9567

LI Business and Technology Center
3500 Sunrise Highway
Great River, NY 11739
631-859-8929
Fax: 631-859-8929

Herkimer County Community College
Offices of Community Education
Herkimer, NY 13350
315-866-0300

Outreach Office
Akwesasne Mohawk Reservation
412 State Route 37
Hogansburg, NY 13655-3109
315-386-7312
Fax: 315-379-3814

Essex City Business Council
216 Main Street at Lake Placid Visitor's
Bureau
Lake Placid, NY 12946
518-523-4906
518-564-2042

8015 Oswego Road
(Rte. 57)
Liverpool, NY 13090
315-498-6070

LaGuardia Community College SBDC
29-10 Thomson Avenue, 9th Floor
Long Island City, NY 11101
718-482-5303
www.nyssbdc.org/centers/centers.cfm?centid
=95
Email: sbdc@lagcc.cuny.edu

Outreach Office
LCIDA
7642 State Street, Box 106
Lowville , NY, 13367
315-782-9262

One Work Source Center
158 Finney Blvd.
Malone, NY 12953
518-481-5755
518-564-2042

SUNY Canton Education Center
St. Lawrence Centre Mall
Massena , NY, 13662
315-386-7312
315-764-5321
Fax: 315-379-3814

IBIG
Orange County Community College
Middletown, NY 10940-6437
845-341-4771
Fax: 845-341-4921

Sullivan Co. Comm. Coll.
196 Broadway
Monticello, NY, 12701-9998
845-791-8338
Fax: 845-791-5287

Outreach Office
Stewart Airport
33 Airport Center Drive
New Windsor, NY 12553
845-567-2702
Fax: 845-567-6085

Chenango County Chamber of Commerce
The Eaton Center
19 Eaton Avenue

Norwich, NY 13815
607-334-1400

Otsego County Chamber of Commerce
12 Carbon Street
Oneonta, NY 13820
607-432-4500

Tioga County Chamber of Commerce
188 Front Street
Owego, NY 13827
607-687-2020

Outreach Office
Oswego State University
100 Sheldon Hall
Oswego , NY 13126-3599
315-312-5696
Fax: 315-312-3374

BOSS Project Incubator
32 Front Street
Port Jervis, NY 12771
845-856-3830
845-856-2169

Chamber of Commerce
One Civic Center Plaza
Poughkeepsie , NY, 12601-3117
845-454-1700
Fax: 845-454-1702

Rome Industrial Development Corporation
139 West Dominick Street
Rome, NY 13440
315-337-6360
www.sbdc.sunyit.edu

Outreach Office
28 Clinton Street
Saratoga Springs, NY 12866-2866
518-453-9567

1201 East Fayette Street
Syracuse, NY 13210-1953
315-498-6070

PRIDE of Ticonderoga, Inc
111 Montcalm Street, Suite 2
Ticonderoga, NY 12883
518-585-6366
518-564-2042

Outreach Office
The Rice Building
216 River Street
Troy, NY 12180
518-453-9567
Email: albsbdc@nycap.rr.com

Outreach Office
257 Ranger School Road
Wanakena, NY 13695-0048
315-386-7312

Mercy College Small Business Development
Center
Westchester 1
Park Building 3
Yonkers, NY 10701-2752
914-375-2107
Fax: 914-375-9276
www.nyssbdc.org/centers/centers.cfm?centid
=16
Email: tmorley@mercy.edu

North Carolina

Lead Center:
Scott Daugherty
North Carolina Small Business and
Technology Development Center
5 W. Hargett St., Suite 600

Raleigh, NC 27601
919-715-7272
800-258-0862
Fax: 919-715-7777
www.sbtdc.org
Email: info@sbtdc.org

Asheville Office
Western Region Small Business and
Technology Development Center
P.O. Box 2510
Bank of America Building
68 Patton Avenue, Suite 1
Asheville, NC 28801
828-251-6025
Fax: 828-232-5126

Appalachian State University
Small Business and Technology
Development Center
Walker College of Business
P.O. Box 32114
Boone, NC 28608
828-262-2492
Fax: 828-262-2027

Small Business and Technology
Development Center
608 Airport Road, Suite B
Chapel Hill, NC 27514
919-962-0389
800-815-8906
Fax: 919-962-3291

Small Business and Technology
Development Center
The Ben Craig Center
8701 Mallard Creek Road
Charlotte, NC 28262
704-548-1090
Fax: 704-548-9050

Western Region Small Business and
Technology Development Center
Western Carolina University
WCU School of Business
204 Forsyth Building
Cullowhee, NC 28723
828-227-3504
Fax: 828-227-7422

Elizabeth City State University
Small Business and Technology
Development Center
Northeastern Region
K.E. White Graduate Center
Box 874
Elizabeth City, NC 27909
252-335-3247
800-258-0862
Fax: 252-335-3648

Fayetteville State University
Small Business and Technology
Development Center
Continuing Education Center
P.O. Box 1334
Fayetteville, NC 28302
910-672-1727
Fax: 910-672-1949

NC A&T University/
Small Business and Technology
Development Center
2007 Yanceyville Street, Suite 300
Greensboro, NC 27405
336-334-7005
Fax: 336-334-7073

East Carolina University
Small Business and Technology
Development Center
300 1st Street
Greenville, NC 27858-4353

252-328-6157
Fax: 252-328-6992

Appalachian-Foothills Small Business and
Technology Development Center
905 Highway 321 NW, Suite 354
Hickory, NC 28601
828-345-1110
Fax: 828-326-9117

University of North Carolina at Pembroke
P.O. Box 1510
Pembroke, NC 28272-1510
910-521-6611
Fax: 910-521-6550
www.uncp.edu/rc/sbtdc

University of North Carolina at Wilmington
Small Business and Technology
Development Center
5051 New Centre Drive, Suite 122
Wilmington, NC 28403
910-962-3744
Fax: 910-962-3014
www.uncw.edu/dpscs/sbtdc
Email: llanger@sbtdc.org

Winston-Salem University
Small Business and Technology
Development Center
Northern Piedmont Region
P.O. Box 19483
Winston-Salem, NC 27110
306-750-2030
Fax: 306-750-2031

Durham SBTDC
School of Business
15 Alexander-Dunn Building
North Carolina Central University
Durham, NC 27707
919.530.7386

Raleigh SBTDC
5 West Hargett Street, Suite 212
Raleigh, NC 27601-1348
919-715-0520

Rocky Mount SBTDC
100 Coastline Street, Suite 309
Rocky Mount, NC 27804-0100
252-467-0338

North Dakota

Lead Center:
Christine Martin
North Dakota Small Business Development
Center
University of North Dakota
118 Gamble Hall
P.O. Box 7308
Grand Forks, ND 58202-7308
701-777-3700
800-445-7232
Fax: 701-777-3225
www.ndsbdc.org
Email: ndsbc@und.edu

Small Business Development Center
Bismarck Regional Center
700 East Main Avenue, 2nd Floor
Bismarck, ND 58502
701-328-5865
800-596-6622
Fax: 701-250-4304
Email: rnewman@minotstateu.edu

Small Business Development Center
Minot Regional Center
1925 South Broadway
Minot, ND 58701
701-852-8861

Fax: 701-839-3889
Email: anderson@minotstateu.edu
Email: votava@minotstateu.edu

Willston Regional Center
Small Business Development Center
Box 1326, Creighton Building
Williston, ND 58802-1326
701-774-4235
Fax: 701-774-4201
Email: gsukat@minotstateu.edu

Small Business Development Center
Devils Lake Regional Center
417 5th Street
Devils Lake, ND 58301
701-662-8131
Fax: 701-662-8132
Email: denisencpc@stellarnet.com

Small Business Development Center
Fargo Regional Center
51 Broadway, Suite 505
Fargo, ND 58102
701-235-1495
800-698-5726
Fax: 701-237-9734
Email: linda_liebert_hall@und.edu

Small Business Development Center
Grand Forks Regional Center
1501 28th Avenue South
Grand Forks, ND 58201
701-795-3734
Fax: 701-772-9238
Email: dwadholm@state.nd.us

Small Business Development Center
Grafton Regional Center
516 Cooper Avenue, Suite 101
Grafton, ND 58237
701-352-3550
Fax: 701-352-3015
Email: dkeeley@state.nd.us

Small Business Development Center
Jamestown Regional Center
210 10th Street SE
Jamestown, ND 58402
701-252-8060
Fax: 701-252-4930
Email: scdrc@csicable.net
Email: sbdc@csicable.net

Ohio

Lead Center:
Ohio Small Business Development Center
77 South High Street, 28th Floor
Columbus, OH 43216-0101
616-466-2711
800-848-1300
Fax: 614-644-5167
www.odod.state.oh.us/edd/osb/sbdc/
Email: sbdc@odod.state.oh.us

Greater Akron Chamber of Commerce
Akron Regional Development Board
Small Business Development Center
One Cascade Plaza, 17th Floor
Akron, OH 44308-1192
330-237-1258
800-621-8001
Fax: 330-379-3164
www.greaterakronchamber.org/cgi-
bin/content/content.pl?id=25

Southeast Ohio SBDC
Ohio University
Small Business Development Center
Enterprise & Technology Building
20 East Circle Drive, Suite 174
Athens, OH 45701

740-593-1797
Fax: 740-593-1795
www.voinovichcenter.ohio.edu
Email: abdella@voinovichcenter.ohio.edu

Small Business Development Center
Bowling Green State University
40 College Park
Bowling Green, OH 43403
419-372-9536
877-650-8165
Fax: 419-372-8667

Kent State University Geagua Campus
14111 Claridon-Troy Road
Burton, OH 44021
440-834-4187
Fax: 440-834-8846
www.geauga.kent.edu
Email: smarshall@geauga.kent.edu

Kent Stark Small Business Development
Center
Office of Corporate and Community
Services
6000 Frank Avenue, NW
Canton, OH 44720
330-244-3279
Fax: 330-494-6121
http://yourcorporateu.kent.edu/BusinessDeve
lopment/index.cfm
Email: sbdc@stark.kent.edu

Wright State University Lake Campus
Small Business Development Center
7600 State Route 703
Celina, OH 45822
419-586-0355
800-237-1477 ext. 8355
Fax: 419-586-0358
www.wright.edu/lake/webpages/sbdc.html

Cincinnati Small Business Development
Center
University of Cincinnati
7162 Reading Road, Suite 725
Cincinnati, OH 45237-3844
513-556-2072
Fax: 513-556-2074
www.cba.uc.edu/cbainfo/sbdc
Email: kennesn@email.uc.edu

Greater Cleveland Growth Association
Small Business Development Center
200 Tower City
50 Public Square
Cleveland, OH 44113-2291
216-621-3300
Fax: 216-621-6013
www.clevelandgrowth.com
Email: jkroeger@clevegrowth.com

Columbus Ohio ITAC
Columbus Chamber of Commerce
37 North High Street
Columbus, OH 43215-3065
614-225-6949
Fax: 614-469-8250
www.columbus-chamber.org/sbdc.html
Email: mercedes_moore@columbus.org

Ohio Small Business Development Center at
Wright State University
College of Business
120 Rike Hall
3640 Colonel Glenn Highway
Dayton, OH 45435
937-775-3503
Fax: 937-775-3545
www.sbdcwsu.org
Email: michael.bodey@wright.edu

Maumee Valley Planning Organization
Northwest Small Business Development
Center
197-2-B1 Park Island Avenue

Defiance, OH 43512
419-782-6270
Fax: 419-782-6273
Email: nwsbdc@defiance-county.com

Small Business Development Center
Fremont Office
Terra Community College
2830 Napoleon Road
Freemont, OH 43420-9967
419-334-8400
800-826-2431
Fax: 419-334-9414
Email: baxter@terra.cc.oh.us

Greater Hamilton Chamber of Commerce
Small Business Development Center
201 Dayton Street
Hamilton, OH 45011
513-844-1500
Fax: 513-844-1999
www.hamiltonohio.org/chamber/sbdc.asp

Satellite Small Business Development
Center
36 West Walnut Street
Jefferson, OH 44047
216-576-9134
Fax: 216-576-5003

The Ohio Manufacturing, Defense, &
Technology SBDC
Kent State University
NEOH Manufacturing Small Business
Development Center
Van Deusen Hall
School of Technology
P.O. Box 5190
Kent, OH 44242-0001
330-672-2892
Fax: 330-672-2894
www.tech.kent.edu/pages/outreach.asp
Email: tsouthards@tech.kent.edu

Kent-Portage Small Business Development
Center
Kent State University Partnership
College of Business Administration, Room
300A
Kent, OH 44242
330-672-1279, ext. 21279
Fax: 330-672-9338
http://business.kent.edu/SBDC/index.htm
Email: lyost@bsa3.kent.edu

Dayton PTAC Supersite
Edison Materials Technology Center
3155 Research Park, Suite 206
Kettering, OH 45420
937-259-1321
Fax: 937-252-9314
Email: dwallace@emtec.org

Region 3 Lead Center
The Ohio SBDC at Rhodes State College
Small Business Development Center
545 West Market Street, Suite 305
Lima, OH 45801-4717
419-224-0396
Fax: 419-229-5424
Email: hyter.j@rhodesstate.edu

Lorain County Chamber of Commerce
Small Business Development Center
6100 South Broadway, Suite 201
Lorain, OH 44053
440-233-6500
Fax: 440-246-4050
www.lorcham.org/sbdc
Email: djones@lorcham.org

Mid-Miami Valley
Small Business Development Center
1500 Central Avenue

Middletown, OH 45044
513-422-4551
Fax: 513-422-6831
www.mmvchamber.org/SBDC.htm
craig@mmvchamber.org

Lake Erie College
Lake County Economic Development Center
391 West Washington Street
Painesville, OH 44077
440-357-2293
Fax: 440-357-2296
www.lcedc.org/sbdc/Default.htm
Email: lcedc@lcedc.org

East Central Region SBDC
Kent State University Tuscarawas Campus
Small Business Development Center
300 University Drive, NE
New Philadelphia, OH 44663-9447
330-308-7479
Fax: 330-339-2637
www.tusc.kent.edu/ServicesforBusiness/small_business.cfm
Email: pcomanitz@tusc.kent.edu

Lawrence EDC
Small Business Development Center
P.O. Box 488
216 Collins Avenue
Southpoint, OH 45680
800-408-1334
Email: klawhorn@zoomnet.net

Springfield Small Business Development
Center
300 East Auburn Avenue
Springfield, OH 45505
937-322-7821
Fax: 937-322-7824
www.smbusdev.org
Email: smichaels@smbusdev.org

Toledo Chamber of Commerce
Small Business Development Center
Enterprise Suite 200
300 Madison Avenue
Toledo, OH 43604-1575
419-243-8191
Fax: 419-241-8302
www.toledochamber.com/small_business_development_center.htm
Email: joinus@toledochamber.com

Small Business Development Center
241 Federal Plaza West
Youngstown, OH 44503
330-746-3350
Fax: 330-746-3324
www.ohiosbdc-ysu.com

Akron MCBAP
Safe Harbor Incubator
1046 South Arlington Street
Akron, OH 44306
330-773-2598
Email: IKUMAH1@aol.com

Region 6 Lead Center
The Ohio SBDC at Ashland University
19 West Main Street, Suite 9
Ashland, OH 44805
877-289-1468
Email: msynorac@ashland.edu

Satellite Office
4536 Main Avenue
Ashtabula, OH 44004
440-998-6998
800-487-GROW (4769)
Fax: 440-992-8216
www.ohiosbdc-ysu.com

PTAC of Ohio at Bowling Green State
University/Toledo

Jerome Library, Room 140B
Bowling Green, OH 43403
419-372-9257
Email: rarcher@bgnet.bgsu.edu

The Ohio SBDC at Ohio Mid-Eastern
Government Association
326 Highland Avenue
P.O. Box 130
Cambridge, OH 43725
740-439-4471
www.omega-ldd.org/page4.htm
Email: cvoorhies@omega-ldd.org

The Ohio Manufacturing, Defense &
Technology SBDC at TechSolve
6705 Steger Drive
Cincinnati, OH 45237
800-345-4482
513-948-2064
www.techsolve.org
Email: jacobson@techsolve.org

Cincinnati MCBAP
Cincinnati B.D.S., Inc.
7165 Reading Road, Suite 630
Cincinnati, OH 45237
513-631-7666
Email: omartin@ohiostatewidembdc.org

Cleveland MCBAP
David N. Myers University
112 Prospect Avenue
Cleveland, OH 44115
216-523-1190
Email: csbaemcap@aol.com

Region 1 Lead Center
The Ohio SBDC at the Greater Columbus
Chamber of Commerce
37 N. High Street
Columbus, OH 43215
614-225-6910
www.columbus-chamber.org/a/services/sbdc.htm
Email: michael_bowers@columbus.org

Central Ohio ITAC
Greater Columbus Chamber of Commerce
37 North High Street
Columbus, OH 43215
614-225-6949
Email: mercedes_moore@columbus.org

The Ohio Manufacturing, Defense, &
Technology SBDC at Central Ohio
1214 Kinnear Road
Columbus, OH 43212
614-688-4018
Email: jshick@stcc.org

Columbus MCBAP
Central Ohio Minority Business Association
1000 East Main Street
Columbus, OH 43205
614-252-8005
Email: kimknights@comba.com

Central Ohio PTAC Supersite
1214 Kinnear Road
Columbus, OH 43212
614-365-3200
Email: coptac@netwalk.com

Dayton MCBAP
City of Dayton MCBAP
201 Riverside Drive, Suite 1E
Dayton, OH 45405
937-223-2164
Email: mcbaphrc@dayton.net

PTAC of Ohio at KRBA, Inc.
Kent State University
College of Business Administration, Room
300

Kent, OH 44242
330-672-9448
Email: ktarbett@bsa3.kent.edu

The Ohio Manufacutring, Defense &
Technology SBDC at Wright State
University
3155 Research Boulevard, Suite 106
Kettering, OH 45420
937-259-1307
Email: cbaumhauer@emtec.org

Dayton PTAC Supersite
Edison Materials Technology Center
3155 Research Boulevard, Suite 106
Kettering, OH 45420
937-259-1321
Email: dwallace@emtec.org

The Ohio SBDC at Washington State
Community College
710 Colgate Drive
Marietta, OH 45750
740-374-8716
Fax: 740-376-0257
www.wscc.edu/workforce/default.htm
Email: sberry@wcss.edu

The Ohio SBDC at Clermont County
Chamber of Commerce
553 Chamber Drive
Milford, OH 45150
513-576-5000
www.clermontchamber.com
Email: john.melvin@clermontchamber.com

North Coast ITAC & PTAC Supersite
Lake County Economic Development Center
391 West Washington Street
Painesville, OH 44077
440-357-2290 Ext. 29
www.lcedc.org
Email: itac@lcedc.org

Region 7 Lead Center
Ohio SBDC at The Ohio State University
South Center Enterprise Center
1864 Shyville Road
Piketon, OH 45661
800-860-7232
740-289-3727
www.sbdc.osu.edu
Email: fox.264@osu.edu

The Ohio Manufacturing, Defense, &
Technology SBDC at The Ohio State
University Enterprise Center
1864 Shyville Road
Piketon, OH 45661
800-297-2072
740-289-2071
www.sbdc.osu.edu
Email: boulay.1@osu.edu

Portsmouth MCBAP
Portsmouth Inner City Development
Corporation
P.O. Box 847
1206 Waller Street
Portsmouth, OH 45662
740-354-6626
Email: pidc@zoominternet.net

PTAC of Ohio at South Point
Lawrence Economic Development
Corporation
P.O. Box 488
South Point, OH 45680
800-408-1334
Email: klawhorn@zoominternet.net

The Ohio Manufacturing, Defense, &
Technology SBDC at Edison Industrial
Systems Center

2600 Dorr Street
Toledo, Ohio 43607
877-668-3472
419-535-6000
Email: greg.stewart@eisc.org

Northwest ITAC
Toledo Area Chamber of Commerce
300 Madison Avenue, Suite 200
Toledo, Ohio 43604
419-243-8191
Email: joe.loeffler@toledochamber.com

Toledo MCBAP
Economic Opportunity Planning Association
505 Hamilton Street
Toledo, Ohio 43602
419-242-7304
Email: jpowell@eopa.org

Youngstown/Warren Satellite
418 South Main Avenue
Warren, OH 44481
330-841-2566
Fax: 330-841-2738
www.ohiosbdc-ysu.com

Oklahoma

Lead Center:
Dr. Grady Pennington
Oklahoma Small Business Development
Center
Southeastern Oklahoma State University
1405 N. 4th Ave. PMB 2584
Durant, OK 74701
580-745-7577
800-522-6154
Fax: 580-745-7471
www.osbdc.org/osbdc.html
Email: gpennington@sosu.edu

East Central State University
Small Business Development Center
1036 East 10th St.
Ada, OK 74820
580-436-3190
Fax: 580-436-3190
www.ecok.edu/dept/osbdcecu
Email: aritter@mailclerk.ecok.edu

Northwestern State University
Small Business Development Center
709 Oklahoma Boulevard
Alva, OK 73717
580-327-8608
Fax: 580-327-8408
www.nwosu.edu/osbdc/index.html
Email: BWGregory@nwosu.edu

Southeastern State University
Small Business Development Center
517 University
Durant, OK 74701
580-745-7577
Fax: 580-745-7471
www.osbdc.org
Email: hmanning@sosu.edu

Northwestern State University
Enid Satellite Center
2929 East Randolph
Enid, OK 73701
580-213-3197
Fax: 580-213-3196
www.nwosu.edu/osbdc/index.html
Email: BWGregory@nwosu.edu

Northwestern State University
Goodwell Satellite
Small Business Development Center
301 Sewell Hall
Goodwell, OK 73939

580-349-2611
Fax: 580-349-2302
Email: osbdc@opsu.edu

Lawton Satellite Center
Small Business Development Center
711 SW "D", Suite 203
Lawton, OK 73501
580-248-4946
Fax: 580-357-4964
Email: jveal@sbcglobal.net

Northeastern State University
Miami Satellite
NEO A&M College
Dyer Hall, Room 306
Miami, OK 74354-0985
918-540-0575
Fax: 918-540-0575
Email: clcox@neoam.cc.ok.us

Rose State College
Procurement Specialty Center
6420 SE 15th Street
Midwest City, OK 73110
405-733-7348
Fax: 405-733-7495
www.rose.edu/commfriend/bizdev
Email: sbdc@rose.edu

University of Central Oklahoma
Small Business Development Center
115 Park Avenue
Oklahoma City, OK 73102
405-232-1968
Fax: 405-232-1967
www.osbdc.org
Email: osbdc@osbdc.org

Langton University
Minority Assistance Center
4205 North Lincoln Boulevard
Oklahoma City, OK 73105
405-962-1628
Fax: 405-962-1639
Email: jmbowers@lunet.edu

Eastern Central University
Poteau Satellite Center
Small Business Development Center
1507 South McKenns
Poteau, OK 74953
918-647-4019
Fax: 918-647-4019
Email: dqualls@casc.cc.ok.us

Northeastern State University
Tulsa Satellite
Small Business Development Center
Williams Towers II, Suite 150
2 West 2nd St.
Tulsa, OK 74103
918-5813-2600
Fax: 918-599-6173
Email: johnblue@tulsachamber.com

Southwestern State University
Small Business Development Center
100 Campus Drive
Weatherford, OK 73096
580-774-7095
Fax: 580-774-7096
Email: balchs@swosu.edu

Oregon

Lead Center:
Edward Cutler
Oregon Small Business Development Center
99 W. 10th Ave., Suite 390
Eugene, OR 97401
541-463-5250
Fax: 541-345-6006

www.bizcenter.org
E-mail: carterb@lanecc.edu

Linn-Benton Community College
Small Business Development Center
6500 Pacific Boulevard SW
Albany, OR 97321
541-917-4923
Fax: 541-917-4445
www.lbcc.cc.or.us/bdc
Email: albany@bizcenter.org

Central Oregon Community College
Small Business Development Center
The Welcome Center
The Center for Business and Industry
2600 NW College Way
Bend, OR 97701
541-383-7290
Fax: 541-317-3445
http://daedalus.cocc.edu/cbi/
Email: cbi@cocc.edu

Lane Community College
Small Business Development Center
1445 Williamette Street, Suite 1
Eugene, OR 97401-4087
541-463-5255
Fax: 541-686-0096
www.lanecc.edu/cc_gen/bdc/busdc.htm
Email: scheideckerj@lanecc.edu

Rogue Community College
Small Business Development Center
214 SW 4th Street
Grants Pass, OR 97526
541-956-7494

Mount Hood Community College
Small Business Development Center
323 NE Roberts Street
Gresham, OR 97030
503-491-7658
Fax: 503-666-1140
www.mhcc.cc.or.us/center/bizcenter/main.htm
Email: loomisd@mhcc.edu

Oregon Institute of Technology
Small Business Development Center
3201 Campus Drive, Boivin Hall 119
Klamath Falls, OR 97601-8801
541-885-1760
Fax: 541-885-1761
www.oit.edu//sbdc
Email: sbdc@oit.edu

LaGrande Small Business Development
Center
Eastern Oregon University
One University Boulevard
LaGrande, OR 97850
541-962-1532
www.eoni.com/sbdc
Email; sbdc@eoni.com

Small Business Development Center
Oregon Coast Community College
North County Center
1206 SE 48th Street
Lincoln City, OR 97367
541-994-4166
Fax: 541-996-4958
www.occc.cc.or.us/sbdc/index.html
Email: gfaust@occc.cc.or.us

Small Business Development Center
322 West 6th Street
Medford, OR 97501
541-772-3478
Fax: 503-776-2224
www.sou.edu/business/SBDC.htm

Clackamas Community College
Small Business Development Center

7736 SE Harmony Road
Milwaukie, OR 97222
503-656-4447
Fax: 503-650-7358
depts.clackamas.cc.or.us/bdc
Email: bizcenter@clackamas.edu

Treasure Valley Community College
Small Business Development Center
650 College Road
Ontario, OR 97914
541-881-8822, ext. 256
Fax: 541-881-2743
www.tvcc.or.us/del/page38.htm
Email: ontario@bizcenter.org

Blue Mountain Community College
Small Business Development Center
2411 N.W. Carden Avenue
Morrow Hall Room M-11
Pendelton, OR 97801
541-276-6233
888-441-7232
Fax: 541-276-6819
www.bluecc.edu/programs/sbdc/index.html
Email: Pendelton@bizcenter.org

Portland Community College
Small Business Development Center
2025 Lloyd Center Mall
Portland, OR 97232
503-978-5080
Fax: 503-288-1366
www.pcc.edu/pcc/pro/sbdc/default.htm
Email: yjohnson@pcc.edu

Umpqua Community College
Small Business Development Center
2555 NE Diamond Lake Boulevard
Roseburg, OR 97470
541-672-2535
Fax: 541-672-3679
www.umpqua.cc.or.us/commed/sbdc.htm
Email: swagert@umpqua.edu

Chemeketa Community College
Small Business Development Center
365 Ferry Street, SE
Salem, OR 97301
503-399-5088
Fax: 503-581-6017
Email: salem@bizcenter.org

Columbia Gorge Community College
Small Business Development Center
400 East Scenic Drive, Suite 257
The Dalles, OR 97058
541-298-3118
Fax: 541-298-3119
www.cgcc.cc.or.us/SBDC/SBDC.htm
Email: sbdc@cgcc.or.us

Tillamook Bay Community College Service
District
Small Business Development Center
401 B Main Street
Tillamook, OR 97141
503-842-8222 ext. 101
Fax: 503-842-2555
www.tbcc.cc.or.us/prgms/sbdc.html
Email: tillamook@bizcenter.org

Southwestern Oregon Community College
The Brookings BizCenter
420 Alder Street
Brookings, OR
541-469-5017
Email: Brookings@bizcente.org

The Coos Bay/North Bend BizCenter
2455 Maple Leaf Lane
North Bend, OR 97459
541-756-6866
Email: coosbay@bizcenter.org

The Seaside BizCenter
1761 North Holladay Drive
Seaside, OR 97138
503-738-3347
Email: seaside@bizcenter.org

Pennsylvania

Lead Center:
Pennsylvania Small Business Development
Center
University of Pennsylvania
The Wharton School
409 Vance Hall, 4th Floor
3733 Spruce Street
Philadelphia, PA 19104-6374
215-898-1219
Fax: 215-573-2135
www.pasbdc.org
Email: pasbdc@wharton.upenn.edu

Lehigh University
Small Business Development Center
Rauch Business Center
621 Taylor Street, Room 390
Bethlehem, PA 18015-3117
610-758-3980
Fax: 610-758-5205
www.leigh.edu/~insbdc
Email: insbdc@lehigh.edu

Clarion University of Pennsylvania
Small Business Development Center
102 Dana Still Business Administration
Bldg.
Clarion, PA 16214-1232
814-393-2060
Fax: 814-393-2636
www.clarion.edu/sbdc/index.html
Email: yearney@clarion.edu

Gannon University
Small Business Development Center
120 West 9th Street
Erie, PA 16501
814-871-7232
877-258-6648
Fax: 814-871-7383
www.gannon.edu/resource/other/org/sbdc
Email: gusbdc@gannon.edu

Kutztown University
Small Business Development Center
Dixon University Center SSHE
2917 North Front Street
Harrisburg, PA 17110
717-346-2029
Fax: 717-346-2038
www.kutztownsbdc.org/default1.htm
Email: mckowen@kutztown.edu

St. Vincent College
Small Business Development Center
Center for Global Competitiveness
300 Fraser Purchase Road
First Floor, Benedict Hall
Latrobe, PA 15650
724-537-4572
866-SBDC-CGC (Toll free)
Fax: 724-537-0919
http://sbdc.stvincent.edu
Email: sbdc@stvincent.edu

Bucknell University
Small Business Development Center
125 Dana Engineering building
Lewisburg, PA 17837
570-577-1249
866-275-6010
Fax: 570-577-1768
www.departments.bucknell.edu/sbdc
Email: sbdc@bucknell.edu

Lock Haven University of Pennsylvania
Small Business Development Center
105 Annex Building
Lock Haven, PA 17745
570-893-2589
www.lhup.edu/sbdc

St. Francis College
Small Business Development Center
117 Evergreen Drive
Loretto, PA 15940
814-472-3200
Fax: 814-472-3202
www.sfcpa.edu/sbdc
Email: brc@francis.edu

Temple University
Small Business Development Center
1510 Cecil B. Moore Avenue
Philadelphia, PA 191221
215-204-7282
Fax: 215-204-4554
www.temple.edu/sbdc
Email: sbdc@sbm.temple.edu

University of Pennsylvania
Small Business Development Center
The Wharton School, Vance Hall
3733 Spruce Street
Philadelphia, PA 19104-6374
215-898-4861
Fax: 215-898-1063
http://whartonsbdc.wharton.upenn.edu
Email: mail@sbdc.wharton.upenn.edu

Chrysler Corporation Small Business
Development Center
Duquesne University
108 Rockwell Hall
600 Forbes Avenue
Pittsburgh, PA 15282-0103
412-396-6233
Fax: 412-396-5884
http://srv02a.sbdc.business.duq.edu/sbdc/def
ault.ofm
Email: duqsbdc@duq.edu

University of Pittsburgh
Small Business Development Center
First Floor, Wesley W. Posvar Hall
Pittsburgh, PA 15620
412-648-1542
Fax: 412-648-1636
http://iee.katz.pitt.edu/sbdc
Email: ieeinfo@katz.pitt.edu

University of Scranton
Small Business Development Center
Fl 2, Estate Building
200 Monroe Ave
Scranton, PA 18510-4639
570-941-7588
800-829-7232
Fax: 570-941-4053
http://sbdc.scranton.edu
Email: sbdc@scranton.edu

Pennsylvania State University
Small Business Development Center
117 Technology Center
University Park, PA 16802-7000
814-863-4293
www.research.psu.edu/sbdc
Email: sbdc@psu.edu

Wilkes College
Small Business Development Center
Hollenback Hall
192 South Franklin Street
Wilkes-Barre, PA 18766
570-408-4340
800-945-5378 ext. 4340
Fax: 570-824-2245
www.sbdc.wilkes.edu

Outreach Center
Small Business Development Center
McDade Trust & Transit Centre
100 West 3rd Street
Willliamsport, PA 17701
570-326-1971
www.lhup.edu/sbdc

Rhode Island

Lead Center:
Robert Hamlin
Rhode Island Small Business Development
Center
Bryant College
1150 Douglas Pike
Smithfield, RI 02917-1284
401-232-6111
Fax: 401-232-6933
www.risbdc.org
Email: rhamlin@risbdc.org

Northern Rhode Island Chamber of
Commerce
Small Business Development Center
6 Blackstone Valley Place, Suite 301
Lincoln, RI 02865-1105
401-334-1000
Fax: 401-334-1009
Email: djobling@bryant.edu

East Bay Office
Small Business Development Center
Newport County Chamber of Commerce
45 Valley Road
Middletown, RI 02842-6377
401-849-6900
Fax: 401-841-0570
www.newportchamber.com
Email: dcotham@bryant.edu

Rhode Island Small Business Development
Center
Enterprise Community Office
550 Broad Street
Providence, RI 02907-1445
401-272-1083
Fax: 401-272-1186
www.risbdc.org
Email: mencucci@bryant.edu

Bryant College
Small Business Development Center
30 Exchange Terrace, 4th Floor
Providence, RI 02903-1793
401-831-1330
Fax: 401-454-2819
www.bryant.edu/BUSINESS.HTM
Email: djobling@bryant.edu

Verizon Telecommunications Center
Small Business Development Center
Bryant College Koffler Technology Center
1150 Douglas Pike
Smithfield, RI 02917-1284
401-232-0220
Fax: 401-232-0242
www.risbdc.org
Email: sbrigido@bryant.edu

Export Assistance Center
Bryant Colllege EAC
1150 Douglas Pike
Smithfield, RI 02917-1284
401-232-6407
Fax: 401-232-6416
www.rieac.org
Email: postoffice@rieac.org

East Bay Chamber of Commerce
654 Metacom Avenue, Suite 2
Warren, RI 02885-0250

401-245-0750
Fax: 401-245-0110

Central Rhode Island Chamber of Commerce
3288 Post Road
Warwick, RI 02886-7151
401-732-1101
Fax: 401-732-1107
Email: dfournar@bryant.edu

Center for Women and Enterprise Office
55 Claverick Street
Providence, RI 02903
401-277-0800
Fax: 401-277-1122

South Carolina

Lead Center:
John Lenti
South Carolina Small Business Development
Center
The Frank L. Roddey SBDC of South
Carolina
University of South Carolina
Moore School of Business
1705 College Street
Columbia, SC 29208
803-777-4907
Fax: 803-777-4403
http://scsbdc.moore.sc.edu
Email: sbdc@moore.sc.edu

University of South Carolina-Aiken
Small Business Development Center
471 University Parkway, Box 9
School of Business
Aiken, SC 29801
803-641-3646
Fax: 803-641-3647
www.usca.edu/sbdc
Email: sbdc@usca.edu

University of South Carolina at Beaufort
Small Business Development Center
801 Carteret Street
Beaufort, SC 29902
843-521-4143

Clemson University
Small Business Development Center
425 Sirrine Hall
Clemson, SC 29634-1392
864-656-3227
Fax: 864-656-4869
http://business.clemson.edu/sbdc
Email: jillb@clemson.edu

University of South Carolina
Small Business Development Center
Moore School of Business
Columbia, SC 29208
803-777-5118
Fax: 803-777-4403
http://scsbdc.moore.sc.edu

Columbia Manufacturing Field Office
1136 Washington Street, Suite 300
Columbia, SC 29201
803-252-6976 ext. 237

Coastal Carolina University
Small Business Development Center
School of Business Administration
P.O. Box 261954
Wall Building, Suite 111
Conway, SC 29528-6054
843-349-2170
Fax: 803-349-2445
http://cba.winthrop.edu/sbdc
Email: sbdcweb.badm.sc.edu

Florence/Darlington Technical College
Small Business Development Center
P.O. Box 100548
Florence, SC 29501-0548
843-661-8256
Fax: 843-661-8041
http://cba.winthrop.edu/sbdc
Email: lowdert@flo.tec.sc.us

Upper Savannah Area Small Business
Development Center
600 Monument Street, Suite 106
Greenwood, SC 29648
864-943-8028
Fax: 864-942-8592
http://business.clemson.edu/sbdc

University of South Carolina at Hilton Head
Small Business Development Center
1 College Center Drive
Hilton Head Island, SC 29928
843-785-3995
Fax: 843-785-7730
Email: Pcameron@sc.edu

Charleston Area Small Business
Development Center
5900 Core Drive, Suite 104
North Charleston, SC 29406
843-740-6160
Fax: 843-740-1607
Email: Lenr@Infoave.net

South Carolina State College
Small Business Development Center
School of Business
Algernon S. Belcher Hall
300 College Street
Campus Box 7176
Orangeburg, SC 29117
803-536-8445
Fax: 803-536-8066
www.sbdc.scsu.edu
Email: zs_sthomas@scsu.edu

Winthrop University
Small Business Development Center
118 Thurmond Building
Rock Hill, SC 29733
803-323-2283
Fax: 803-323-4281
http://cba.winthrop.edu/sbdc
Email: sbdctech@winthrop.edu

Spartanburg Office
Small Business Development Center
142 South Dean Street, Suite 216
P.O. Box 5626
Spartanburg, SC 29304-5626
864-316-9162
864-586-3602
http://business.clemson.edu/sbdc
Email: Dtinsel@clemson.edu

Sumter Area Small Business Development
Center
University of South Carolina at Sumter
200 Miller Road
Sumter, SC 29150-2498
803-938-3833
Email: Leron@uscsumter.uscsu.sc.edu

Greenville Office
1200 Woodruff Road, Suite C-38
Greenville, SC 29607
864-297-1016
Fax: 864-329-0453
http://business.clemson.edu/sbdc

Conway Area SBDC
Myrtle Square Mall #11
2501 North Kings Hwy.
Myrtle Beach, SC 29577
843-913-7883

843-913-7884
Fax: 843-913-7888
http://cba.winthrop.edu/sbdc
Email: nniles@coastal.edu

South Dakota

Lead Center:
Belinda Engelhart and Mark Slade, Acting
co-State Directors
South Dakota Small Business Development
Center
University of South Dakota
414 East Clark
Vermillion, SD 57069-2390
605-677-5287
Fax: 605-677-5427
www.sdsbdc.org
Email: sbdc@dailypost.com

Aberdeen Small Business Development Ctr.
416 Production Street North
Aberdeen, SD 57401
605-626-2565
Fax: 605-626-2667
Email: kweaver@midco.net

Pierre Small Business Development Center
221 South Central
Pierre, SD 57501
605-945-1661
Fax: 605-224-8320
Email: hughsobolik@csded.org

Small Business Development Center
444 North Mount Rushmore Rd., Room 204
Rapid City, SD 57701
605-394-5311
Fax: 605-394-6140
Email: bmadden@tie.net

Small Business Development Center
1000 North West Avenue, #230
Sioux Falls, SD 57104
605-367-5757
Fax: 605-367-5755
Email: mslade@usd.edu

Watertown Small Business Development
Center
124 First Avenue, NW
P.O. Box 1207
Watertown, SD 57201
605-882-5115
Fax: 605-882-5049
Email: sbdc@dailypost.com

Yankton Small Business Development
Center
1808 Summit Avenue
P.O. Box 687
Yankton, SD 57078
605-665-0751
Fax: 605-665-0303
www.districtiii.org/SBDC.html
Email: sbdc@districtiii.org

Tennessee

Lead Center:
Albert Laabs
State University and Community College
Tennessee Small Business Development
Center
1415 Murfreesboro Rd, Suite 350
Nashville, TN 37217
615-366-3900
877-898-3900
Fax: 615-366-4464

www.tsbdc.org
Email: alaabs@mail.tsbdc.org

Chattanooga State Technical Community
College
Small Business Development Center
100 Cherokee Boulevard, Suite 202
Chattanooga, TN 37405
423-756-8668
Fax: 423-756-6195
www.chattanoogastate.edu/TSBDC/default.h
tm
Email: rtawil@mail.tsbdc.org

Cleveland State Community College
Small Business Development Center
P.O. Box 3570
Cleveland, TN 37320-3570
423-614-8707
Fax: 423-478-6251
www.clscc.cc.tn.us/sbdc/SbdcPage/
Email: rplatz@clevelandstatecc.edu

Small Business Development Center
Maury County Alliance
106 West Sixth Street
P.O. Box 8069
Columbia, TN 38402
931-388-5674
Fax: 931-867-3344
Email: gosekowsky@mail.tsbdc.org

Tennessee Technological University
Small Business Development Center
College of Business Administration
P.O. Box 5023
Cookeville, TN 38505-0001
931-372-3638
Fax: 931-372-6534
Email: mreel@mail.tsbdc.org

Dyersburg Community College
Small Business Development Center
1510 Lake Road
Dyersburg, TN 38024
731-286-3201
Fax: 731-286-3271
Email: jfrakes@mail.tsbdc.org

Four Lakes Regional Industrial Development
Authority
Small Business Development Center
P.O. Box 63
Hartsville, TN 37074-0063
615-374-4607
Fax: 615-374-4608

Jackson State Community College
Small Business Development Center
210 East Chester Street
Jackson, TN 38301-3797
731-424-5389
800-355-5722 ext. 627
Fax: 731-425-2641
http://conted.jscc.edu/sbdc.htm
Email: croth@jscc.cc.tn.us

East Tennessee State University
Small Business Development Center
College of Business
2109 West Market Street
Johnson City, TN 37604
423-439-8505
Fax: 423-461-7080
http://business.etsu.edu/Tsbdc
Email: bjustice@mail.tsbdc.org

Kingsport Small Business Development
Center
1501 University Boulevard
Kingsport, TN 37660
432-392-8017
http://business.etsu.edu/Tsbdc
Email: rgraham@mail.tsbdc.org

International Trade Center
601 West Summit Hill Drive
Knoxville, TN 37915
423-632-2990
Fax: 423-521-6367
www.tsbdc.org/itm.htm

Pellissippi State Technical Community
College
Small Business Development Center
601 West Summit Hill Drive, Suite 300
Knoxville, TN 37902-2011
865-632-2980
Fax: 865-971-4439
www.pst.no.cc.tn.us/bcs/TNsbdc.html

Small Business Development Center
320 South Dudley Street
Memphis, TN 38101-3206
901-527-1041
Fax: 901-527-1047
www.tsbdc.memphis.edu

University of Memphis
Small Business Development Center
976 W. Park Loop, Room 101
Memphis, TN 38152
901-678-4041
Fax: 901-678-4072
Email: jmalloy@mail.tsbdc.org

Middle Tennessee State University
Small Business Development Center
Chamber of Commerce Building
501 Memorial Boulevard
Murfreesboro, TN 37129
615-898-2745
Fax: 615-893-7089
www.tsbdc.org/mtsu/sbdc.html
Email: pgeho@mail.tsbdc.org

Tennessee State University
Small Business Development Center
330 10th Avenue, North
Nashville, TN 37203-3401
615-963-7179
Fax: 615-963-7160
www.tnstate.edu/
Email: wlatham@tnstate.edu

Austin Peay State University
420B Madison Street, Suite 2
Clarksville, TN 37044
931-647-2331 ext. 261
931-221-1370
Fax: 931-503-0984
www.apsu.edu/ext_ed/small_business/
Email: tsbdc@apsu.edu

Satellite Office of MTSU
149 Public Square
Lebanon, TN 37087
615-444-5503
Fax: 615-443-0596

Satellite Office of University of Memphis
Business Information Center
555 Beale Street
Memphis, TN 38103
901-526-9300
Fax: 901-525-2357

Satellite Office of PSTCC
201 South Washington Street
Maryville, TN 37804
865-983-2241

Technology 2020 Office
Affiliate Office of PSTCC
1020 Commerce Park Drive
Oak Ridge, TN 37830-8026
865-483-2668
Fax: 865-220-2030
Email: dcollier@mail.tsbdc.org

Satellite- Rogersville Chamber of Commerce
107 E. Main Street, Suite 100
USBANK Building
Rogersville, TN 37857
423-439-8505
Email: bjustice@mail.tsbdc.org

Satellite Office
1227 Ninth Avenue North
Nashville, TN 37208
615-963-7179 (TN State contact)
www.tnstate.edu

Texas

Lead Centers:
North Texas Small Business Development
Center
Dallas County Community College
1402 Corinth Street
Dallas, TX 75215
214-860-5835
800-350-7232
Fax: 214-860-5813
www.tded.state.tx.us/guide
www.ntsbdc.org
ntsbdc@dcccd.edu

Texas Economic Development
Office of Small Business Assistance
1700 North Congress Avenue
Austin, TX 78711
512-936-0297
Fax: 512-936-0440
www.tded.state.tx.us/SmallBusiness

Small Business Development Center
500 Chestnut, Suite 601
Albilene, TX 79602
325-670-0300
www.abilene-sbdc.org/
Email: b.Anderson@nwtsbdc.org

Small Business Development Center
2300 North Western
Amarillo, TX 79124
806-372-5151
Fax: 806-372-5261
http://www.amarillo-sbdc.org/
Email: ppronger@mail.wtamu.edu

Coastal Plains SBDC
2200 7th Street, Suite 300
Bay City, TX 77414
979-244-8466
Fax: 979-244-8463
Email: sbdc@wcnet.net

Best Southwest SBDC
207 N. Cannady Drive
Cedar Hill, TX 75104
972-860-7894
Fax: 972-291-1320
Email: bswcvcc@airmail.net

The Government Contracting SBDC
1402 Corinth Street
Dallas, TX 75215
214-860-5889
www.ntsbdc.org/NTGovernment.htm
Email: cpw9421@dcccd

Denton Chamber of Commerce Bldg.
414 Parkway
Denton, TX 76201
940-380-1849
Fax: 940-382-0040
www.nctc.cc.tx.us/Continuing_education/sb
dc.html
Email: nctcsbdc@denton-chamber.org

Kingsville Chamber of Commerce
635 E King

Kingsville, TX 78363
361-592-6438
Fax: 361-661-1119
www.delmar.edu/sbdc
Email: ruralsbdc@sdcglobal.net

University of Houston
Small Business Development Center
2302 Fannin, Suite 200
Houston, TX 77002
713-752-8444
www.sbdc.uh.edu/offices.html
Email: rskebo@uh.edu

San Jacinto College District
5800 Uvalde, S209C
Houston, TX 77049
281-459-7643
Fax 281-459-7694
www.sjcd.edu/sbdc

Small Business Development Center
4901 East University Boulevard
Odessa, TX 79762
915-552-2455
Fax: 915-552-3455
http://www.midland-odessa-sbdc.org/
Email: Connor_a@utpb.edu

San Jacinto College District
2006 East Broadway, Suite 101
Pearland, TX 77581
281-485-5214
Fax: 281-485-6978
www.sjcd.edu/sbdc

Austin Community College SBDC
202 North C M Allen Parkway
San Marcos, TX 78666
512-393-5912

Small Business Development Center
Box T-0650
Stephenville, TX 76402
254-968-9330
Fax: 254-968-9329
www.stephenville-sbdc.org
Email: beck@tarleton.edu

North Harris Montgomery Community
College
5000 Research Forest Drive
The Woodlands, TX 77381-4399
832-813-6674
Fax: 832-813-6662
http://www.cbed.org/sbdc/

Middle Rio Grande Development Council
209 North Getty Street
Uvalde, TX 78801
830-758-5025
Fax: 830-278-2929

Small Business Development Center
3410 Taft Boulevard
Wichita Falls, TX 76308
940-397-4373
Fax: 940-397-4374
www.wichita-falls-sbdc.org
Email: jeannie.hilbers@mwsu.edu

Texas Gulf Coast Small Business
Development Center
University of Houston
2302 Fannin
Houston, TX 77002
713-752-8444
Fax: 713-756-1500
www.sbdc.uh.edu
Email: gshelton@uh.edu

Northwest Texas Small Business
Development Center
2579 South Loop 289, Suite 210

Lubbock, TX 79423
806-745-3973
800-992-7232
Fax: 806-745-6207
http://nwtsbdc.org
Email: SBDCweb@nwtsbdc.org

South Texas Border Small Business
Development Center
University of Texas at San Antonio
Downtown
Institute for Economic Development
UT San Antonio SBDC
145 Duncan Drive Suite 200
San Antonio, TX 78226
210-458-2460
Fax: 210-458-2464
www.iedtexas.org
Email: MWOODS@UTSA.EDU

SUL Ross State University
Big Bend Region Minority and Small
Business Development Center
Room 319, Briscoe Administration Building
P.O. Box C-47
Alpine, TX 79832
432-837-8694
Fax: 432-837-8104
www.sulross.edu/~sbdc
Email: lgarcia@sulross.edu

Trinity Valley Small Business Development
Center
100 Cardinal Drive
Athens, TX 73751
903-675-7403
Fax: 903-675-5199
www.ntsbdc.org
Email: jloden@tvcc.edu

Lee College
Small Business Development Center
P.O. Box 818
Baytown, TX 77522-0818
281-425-6309
Fax 281-425-6307
www.lee.edu/sbdc
Email: thatthawa@lee.edu

John Gray Institute/Lamar University
Small Business Development Center
855 Florida Avenue, Suite 101
Beaumont, TX 77705
409-880-2367
800-722-3443
Fax: 409-880-2201
http://hal.lamar.edu/~sbdc
Email: arnolde@hal.lamar.edu

Blinn College
Small Business Development Center
902 College Avenue
Brenham, TX 77833
409-830-4137
Fax: 409-830-4135
www.blinn.edu/sbdc
Email: sbdc@blinncol.edu

Brazos Valley Small Business Development
Center
4001 East 29th Street, Suite 175
Bryan, TX 77802
979-260-5222
Fax: 979-260-5229
www.bvsbdc.org

Del Mar College, East Campus
Small Business Development Center
101 Baldwin Boulevard
Corpus Christi, TX 78404-3897
361-698-1021
888-698-6111
Fax: 361-698-1024

www.delmar.edu/sbdc
Email: lfarr@delmar.edu

Navarro Small Business Development
Center
120 North 12th Street
Corsicanna, TX 75110
903-874-0658
Fax: 903-874-4187
www.ntsbdc.org
Email: torte@nav.cc.tx.us

Dallas Small Business Development Center
1402 Corinth
Dallas, TX 75215
214-860-5865
Fax: 214-860-5867
www.ntsbdc.org/dallas.htm
Email: dsbdc@dcccd.edu

International Small Business Development
Center
2050 Stemmons Freeway
World Trade Center, Suite 156A
P.O. Box 20451
Dallas, TX 75342
214-747-1300
800-337-7232
Fax: 214-748-5774
www.iexportimport.com
Email: information@iExportImport.com

Grayson Small Business Development Ctr
6101 Grayson Drive
Denison, TX 75020
903-463-8787
Fax: 903-463-5437
www.ntsbdc.org
Email: stidhamk@grayson.edu

University of Texas/Pan American
Small Business Development Center
2412 S. Closner
Edinburg, TX 78539-2999
956-316-2610
Fax. 956-316-2612
http://coserve1.panam.edu/sbdc/location.html
Email: sbdc@panam.edu

El Paso Community College
Small Business Development Center
1359 Lomaland Drive, Suite 535
El Paso, TX 79902-1423
Fax: 915-831-7734
www.elpasosbdc.biz
dannyn@epcc.edu
Email: roques@epcc.edu

Small Business Development Center for
Excellence, ARRI
7300 Jack Newell Boulevard
Fort Worth, TX 76118
817-272-5930
Fax: 817-272-5952
http://arri.uta.edu/sbdc/home.htm
Email: jweddle@arri.uta.edu

Tarrant Small Business Development Center
1150 South Freeway, Suite 229
Fort Worth, TX 76104
817-871-6028
Fax: 817-332-6417
web.tccd.net/ce/ce_sbdc.asp
Email: tcc_sbdc@fwbac.com

North Central Texas Small Business
Development Center
1525 West California
Gainesville, TX 76240
940-668-4220
Fax: 940-668-6049
www2.nctc.cc.tx.us/user/continuing_educati
on/SBDC/index.html
Email: nctc_sbdc@lists.nctc.edu

Galveston College
Small Business Development Center
4015 Avenue Q
Galveston, TX 77550
409-762-7380
888-743-7380
Fax: 409-762-7898

Sam Houston State University
Small Business Development Center
College of business Administration
2424 Sam Houston Avenue
Huntsville, TX 77340
936-294-3737
Fax: 936-294-3738
www.shsu.edu/~sbd_www
Email: sbd_rab@shsu.edu

Brazosport College
Small Business Development Center
500 College Drive, Room K-201
Lake Jackson, TX 77566
979-230-3380
Fax: 979-230-3482
www.brazosport.cc.tx.us/~sbdc

Laredo Development Foundation
Small Business Development Center
616 Leal Street
Laredo, TX 78041
956-722-0563
800-820-0564
Fax: 956-722-6247
www.laredo-ldf.com/page6.html
Email: lozano@laredo_ldf.com

Kilgore College
Small Business Development Center
911 Loop 281, Ste. 209
Longview, TX 75604
903-757-5857
Fax: 903-753-7920
www.kilgore.edu/sbdc.html
Email: bradbunt@aol.com

Texas Tech University
Small Business Development Center
2579 South Loop 289
Lubbock, TX 79423
806-745-1637
Fax: 806-745-6717
www.lubbock-sbdc.org
Email: s.caldwell@nwtsbdc.org

Angelina Community College
Small Business Development Center
3500 South First Street
P.O. Box 1768
Lufkin, TX 75902
936-633-5400
Fax: 936-633-5478
www.angelina.cc.tx.us/
SBDC/CS%20SBDC%20.INDEX.htm
Email: dbrowning@agelina.edu

Northeast/Texarkana Small Business
Development Center
P.O. Box 1307
Mt. Pleasant, TX 75455
903-897-2956
800-357-7232
Fax: 903-897-1106
www.bizcoach.org
Email: sbdcnetcc@aol.com

Paris Small Business Development Center
2400 Clarksville Street
Paris, TX 75460
903-782-0224
Fax: 903-782-0219
www.paris.cc.tx.us/sbdc
Email: pbell@paris.cc.tx.us

San Jacinto College District
Small Business Development Center
8060 Spencer Highway B105E

Pasadena, TX 77501
281-542-2024
Fax: 281-478-3610
www.sjcd.edu/sbdc

Collin County Small Business Development
Center
Courtyard Center for Professional and
Economic Development
4800 Preston Park Boulevard
Suite A126
Plano, TX 75093
972-985-3770
Fax: 972-985-3775
www.cccd.edu/sbdc
Email: sbdc@cccd.edu

Lamar State College
Small Business Development Center
1401 Proctor Street
Port Arthur, TX 77640
409-984-6531
Fax 409-984-6063
www.portarthur.com/sbdc/main.htm
Email: Linda.Tait@lamarpa.edu

Angelo State University
Small Business Development Center
P.O. Box 10910, ASU Station
San Angelo, TX 76909
325-942-2098
Fax: 325-942-2096
www.angelo.edu/services/sbdc
Email: SBDC@angelo.edu

Kelly Small Business Assistance Center
1222 North Main, Suite 450
San Antonio, TX 78212
210-458-2470
Fax: 210-458-2464

Tyler Small Business Development Center
1530 South SW Loop 323, Suite 100
Tyler, TX 75701
903-510-2975
903-510-2972
www.tjc.edu/sbdc/
Email: dpro@tjc.tyler.cc.tx.us

University of Houston-Victoria
Small Business Development Center
700 Main Center, Suite 102
Victoria, TX 77901
512-575-8944
Fax: 512-575-8852
www.vic.uh.edu/sbdc
Email: parksc@viptx.net

McLennan Small Business Development
Center
401 Franklin
Waco, TX 76701
254-714-0077
Fax: 254-714-1668
http://mcweb.mcc.cc.tx.us/sbdc/sbdc.html

Utah

Lead Center:
Mike Finnerty
Salt Lake Community College
Small Business Development Center
1623 South State Street
Salt Lake City, UT 84115
801-957-3493
Fax: 801-957-3488
www.slcc.edu/sbdc
Email: holtlu@slcc.edu

College of Eastern Utah
Small Business Development Center
639 West 100 South
Blanding, UT 84511

435-678-2201 ext. 173
Fax: 435-678-2220
Email: Bill_olderog@sanjuan.ceu.edu

Southern Utah University
Small Business Development Center
351 West Center
Cedar City, UT 84720
435-586-5400
Fax: 435-586-5493
www.suu.edu/business/sbdc/

Snow College
Small Business Development Center
345 West 100 North
Ephraim, UT 84627
435-283-7372
Fax: 435-283-6913
Email: wheelwright@snow.edu

Utah State University
Small Business Development Center
East Campus Building, Room 24
1330 East 700 North
Logan, UT 84322-8330
435-797-2277
Fax: 435-797-3317
Email: fprante@ext.usu.edu

Moab Higher Education Center
125 West 200 South
Moab, UT 84532
435-259-3622
Email: BrianD@ext.usu.edu

Weber State University
Small Business Development Center
School of Business and Economics
3806 University Circle
Ogden, UT 84408-3806
801-626-7051
Fax: 801-626-7423
http://community.weber.edu/sbdc
Email: sbdc@weber.edu

College of Eastern Utah
Utah Valley State College
800 West University Parkway
Orem, UT 84058
801-222-8230
801-764-7071
http://www.uvsc.edu/sbdc/
riggsle@uvsc.edu

Small Business Development Center
375 East Carbon Avenue
Price, UT 84501
435-637-5444
Fax: 435-637-7336
www.seualg.dst.ut.us/econdev/sbdc/sbdc.htm
Email: dpaletta@seualg.dst.ut.us

Salt Lake Community College
9750 South 300 West Suite 205
Sandy, UT 84070-3264
801-957-5200
Fax: 801-957-5333
Email: bartleba@slcc.edu

Salt Lake Community College
1623 South State Street
Salt Lake City, UT 84115
801-957-3480
Fax: 801-957-3489
Email: huntpa@slcc.edu

Dixie College
Small Business Development Center
225 South 700 East
St. George, UT 84770
435-652-7741
Fax: 435-652-7870
www.dixiebusinessalliance.com/sbdc.htm
Email: carter@dixie.edu

Utah State University Extension
Small Business Development Center
1680 West Highway 40
Vernal, UT 84078
435-789-6100
Fax: 435-789-3916
Email: markh@ext.usu.edu

Vermont

Lead Center:
Don Kelpinski
Vermont Small Business Development
Center
Vermont Tech. College
P.O. Box 188
Randolph, VT 05061-0188
802-728-9101
800-464-7232 (in Vermont)
Fax: 802-728-3026
www.vtsbdc.org
Email: dkelpins@vtsbdc.org

Greater Burlington Industrial Corporation
P.O. Box 786
60 Main Street
NW VT SBDC
Burlington, VT 05402-0786
802-658-9228 ext. 13
Fax: 802-860-1899
Email: dcohen@vtsbdc.org

Brattleboro Dev. Credit Corp.
Small Business Development Center
76 Cotton Mill Hill, C-1
Brattleboro, VT 05301-1177
802-257-7731
Fax: 802-258-3886
Email: scasabon@vtsbdc.org

Addison Co. Econ. Dev. Corp
Small Business Development Center
RD#4, Box 1309A
Middlebury, VT 05753
802-388-7953
Fax: 802-388-8066
www.addisoncountyedc.org/index.html
Email: spaddock@vtsbdc.org

Central VT Econ. Dev. Center
Small Business Development Center
P.O. Box 1439
Montpelier, VT 05601-1439
802-223-4654
Fax: 802-223-4655
www.central-vt.com/cvedc/sbdc.htm
Email: ptravers@vtsbdc.org

Lamoille Econ. Dev. Center
Small Business Development Center
P.O. Box 455
Morrisville, VT 05661-0455
802-888-4542
Fax: 802-888-5640
Email: mjohnson@vtsbdc.org

Bennington Co. Industrial Corp.
Small Business Development Center
P.O. Box 357
No. Bennington, VT 05257
802-442-8975
Fax: 802-442-1101
Email: wmook@vtsbdc.org

Lake Champlain Islands
Chamber of Commerce SBDC
P.O. Box 213
North Hero, VT 25474-0213
802-372-5683
802-372-8400 ext. 12
Fax: 802-372-6104
Email: sbourgeois@vtsbdc.org

Franklin County Industrial Dev. Corp.
Small Business Development Center
P.O. Box 1099
St. Albans, VT 05478-1099
802-524-2194
Fax: 802-527-5258
www.fcidc.com/sbdc.htm

Northeastern VT Dev. Assn.
Small Business Development Center
P.O. Box 630
St. Johnsbury, VT 05819
802-748-1014
Fax: 802-748-1223
www.nvda.net/NVDAasRDC/sbdc.html
Email: jfreeman@vtsbdc.org

Rutland Economic Development
Corporation
110 Merchants Row
4th Floor, Suite 3
Rutland, VT 05701
802-773-9147
www.rutlandeconomy.com/key_assoc.asp
Email: wwilton@vtsbdc.org

Springfield Regional Development
Corporation
14 Clinton Square, Suite 7
Springfield, VT 05156
802-257-7731
www.springfielddevelopment.org/srdcmore.
htm
Email: scasabon@vtsbdc.org

Virginia

Lead Center:
Bob Wilburn
Department of Business Assistance
Virginia Small Business Development
Center
4031 University Drive, Suite 200
Fairfax, Virginia 22030
703-277-7700
Fax: 703-277-7730
www.virginiasbdc.org
Email: jkeenan@gmu.edu

VA Highland Community College
Small Business Development Center
P.O. Box 828
Abingdon, VA 24212
276-739-2474
www.vhcc.edu/cbi

Alexandria Small Business Development
Center
801 N. Fairfax Street, Suite 402
Alexandria, VA 22314
703-778-1292
Fax: 703-778-1293
www.alexandriasbdc.org
Email: info@alexandriasbdc.org

Community Business Partnership
Northern VA SBDC
6911 Richmond Highway, Suite 290
Alexandria, VA 22306
703-768-1440
www.cbponline.org
aschrief@gmu.edu

George Mason University/Arlington Campus
Small Business Development Center
3401 N. Fairfax Drive, Room #224
Arlington, VA 22201
703-993-8128
Fax: 703-993-8130
www.arlingtonsbdc.org
Email: mail@arlingtonsbdc.org

Mountain Empire Community College
Small Business Development Center
PO Drawer 700, Route 23S
Big Stone Gap, VA 24219
276-523-6529
Fax: 276-523-8139
www.me.cc.va.us/dept/sbdc
Email: tblankenbecler@me.vccs.edu

Central Virginia Small Business
Development Center
308 East Market Street
Charlottesville, VA 22902
434-295-8198
Fax: 434-295-7066
http://avenue.org/sbdc
Email: sbdc@cstone.net

Fairfax Small Business Development Center
4031 University Drive
Fairfax, VA 22030
703-277-7700
Fax: 703-277-7730
www.sbdc.org
Email: info@sbdc.org

Longwood Small Business Development Ctr.
515 Main Street
Farmville, VA 23909
434-395-2086
Fax: 434-395-2359
www.longwood.edu/sbdc
Email: kcopelan@longwood.edu

Rappahannock Region Small Business
Development Center
The James Monroe Center
121 University Boulevard
Fredericksburg, VA 22406
540-286-8060
Fax: 540-286-8042
www.jmc.mwc.edu/sbdc
Email: rrsbdc@mwc.edu

Small Business Development Center
600 Butler Farm Road, Suite A1105
Hampton, VA 23666
757-865-3127/3128
Fax: 757-865-5885
www.hrsbdc.org
Email: jcarroll@hrccva.com

James Madison University
Small Business Development Center
College of Business
1598 South Main Street
MSC 5502
Harrisonburg, VA 22807
276-632-4462
Fax: 276-632-5059
www.jmu.edu/sbdcenter
Email: sbdc@jmu.edu

Lynchburg Regional Small Business
Development Center
147 Mill Ridge Road
Lynchburg, VA 24502
434-582-6170
800-876-7232
Fax: 434-582-6106
www.lbdc.com
Email: sbdcinfo@lbdc.com

Martinsville Small Business Development
Center
115 Broad Street
Martinsville, VA 24114
540-632-4462
Fax: 540-632-5059
www.longwood.edu/sbdc
Email: jtberry@neocomm.net

Crater Small Business Development Center
1964 Wakefield Street

Petersburg, VA 23805
804-518-2003
Fax: 804-518-2004
Email: dhowerton@cpd.state.va.us

Radford University
Business Assistance Center
P.O. Box 6953
Radford, VA 24142
540-831-6056
http://btp.radford.edu/ba/sbdc.html
Email: bac@radford.edu

Southwest Virginia Community College
Small Business Development Center
P.O. Box SVCC
Richlands, VA 24641
540-964-7345
Fax: 540-964-7575
www.sw.vccs.edu/sbdc/svccsbdc.htm
Email: Jim.boyd@sw.cc.va.us

Greater Richmond Small Business
Development Center
201 East Franklin Street
Richmond, VA 23241-2280
804-648-1234
Fax: 804-783-9366
www.grsbdc.com
Email: mike.leonard@grcc.com

Regional Chamber Small Business
Development Center
212 South Jefferson Street
Roanoke, VA 24011
540-983-0717
Fax: 540-983-0723
www.rrsbdc.org

South Boston Small Business Development
Center
820 Bruce Street
South Boston, VA 24592
434-572-5484
Fax: 434-572-5462
www.longwood.edu/sbdc
Email: lharris@longwood.edu

Loudoun County Small Business
Development Center
21145 Whitfield Place, Suite 104
Sterling VA 20165
703-430-7222
Fax: 703-430-7258
www.loudounsbdc.org
Email: sbdc@loudounsbdc.org

Lord Fairfax Small Business Development
Center
6480 College Street
Warrenton, VA 20187
540-351-1595
Fax: 540-351-1597
www.lfsbdc.org/fauquier/index.html
Email: bpoffenberger@lfsbdc.org

Warsaw Small Business Development Ctr
P.O. Box 490
479 Main Street
Warsaw, VA 22572
804-333-0286
800-524-8915
http://homepages.sylvaninfo.net/sbdcwar
Email: sbdcwarsaw@sylvaninfo.net

Wytheville SBDC
300 Gordondale Road
Atkins, VVA 24311
276-783-1777
Fax: 276-783-8335
www.wcc.vccs.edu/sbdc
Email: wcedwar@wcc.vccs.edu

Hampton Roads Chamber of Commerce
400 Volvo Parkway
Chesapeake, VA 23320
757-664-2592
Fax: 757-548-1835
www.hrsbdc.org

Dan River Small Business Development
Center
300 Ringgold Industrial Parkway
Danville, VA 24540
434-793-9100
Fax: 434-793-9200
www.danriversbdc.org/contact.html
Email: dfunkhouser@danriverincubator.com

Eastern Shore SBDC - Hampton Roads
SBDC
P.O. Box 133
Melfa, VA 23410-0133
757-789-3418
Fax: 757-787-7579
www.hrsbdc.org/contact/eshore.html
Email: sbdc@esva.net

Lord Fairfax Small Business Development
Center
173 Skirmisher Lane, Suite 317
Lord Fairfax Community College
Middletown, VA 22645
540-868-7093
Fax: 540-868-7095
www.lfsbdc.org/lord_fairfax/
Email: bsirbaugh@lfsbdc.org

Blue Ridge Community College
Box 80
Weyers Cave, VA 24486
540-213-7037
540-941-3757
888-750-2722 (VA)
www.jmu.edu/sbdcenter/SBDC/home.html
Email: sbdc@br.vccs.edu

Williamsburg SBDC
T.N.C.C Historic Triangle Office
161-C John Jefferson Place
Williamsburg, VA 23185
757-253-4322
Fax: 757-253-4335
www.hrsbdc.org/contact/williamsburg.html
Email: rileys@tncc.vccs.edu

Washington

Lead Center:
Jim Kraft
Washington Small Business Development
Center
Washington State University
601 West First Ave.
Spokane, WA 99201-3899
509-358-7765
Fax: 509-358-7764
www.wsbdc.org
Email: kraft@wsu.edu

Bellevue Community College North Campus
Small Business Development Center
10700 Northup Way, Bellevue, WA
Bellevue, WA 98007-6484
Mailing:
    3000 Landerholm Circle SE
    Bellevue, WA 98007-6484
425-564-2888
Fax: 425-564-4023
www.conted.bcc.ctc.edu/sbdc/sbdc.asp
Email: wsbdc@bcc.ctc.edu

Western Washington University
Small Business Development Center
College of Business and Economics
119 North Commercial Street, Suite 195

Bellingham, WA 98225
360-733-4014
Fax: 360-733-5092
www.cbe.www.edu/SBDC
Email: sbdc@www.edu

Edmonds Community College
Small Business Development Center
728 134th Street SW, Suite 128
Everett, WA 98204
425-640-1435
Fax: 425-640-1371
www.btc.edcc.edu/sbdc
Email: rbattles@edcc.edu

Big Bend Community College
Small Business Development Center
7662 Chanute Street
Building 1500
Moses Lake, WA 98837-3299
509-762-5351 ext. 906
Fax: 509-762-6289
Email: stephani@bbcc.ctc.edu

Skagit Valley College
Small Business Development Center
204 W. Montgomery
P.O. Box 40
Mt. Vernon, WA 98273
360-336-6114
Fax: 360-336-6116
Email: ryan@skagit.org

South Puget Sound Community College
Small Business Development Center
665 Woodland Square Loop SE
Suite 201
Lacey, WA 98503
360-753-5616
Fax: 360-586-5493
Email: DouglasHammel@olywa.net

Port Angeles Small Business Development
Center
102 East Front Street
P.O. Box 1085
Port Angeles, WA 98362
360-417-5657
Fax: 360-452-9618
Email: kpurdy@clallam.org

Seattle Small Business Development Center
Parkplace Building
1200 6th Avenue, Suite 1700
Seattle, WA 98101
206-553-7328
Fax: 206-553-7044
Email: mfranz@connectexpress.com

Community College of Spokane
Small Business Development Center
SIRTI Building
665 North Riverpoint Boulevard, Suite 201
Spokane, WA 99202
509-358-7890
Fax: 509-358-7896
ccs.spokane.cc.wa.us/TECC/small_business.
htm
Email: spokesbdc@wsu.edu

Washington State University
Small Business Development Center
12000 NE 95th Avenue, Suite 504
Vancouver, WA 98682
360-260-6372
Fax: 360-260-6369
www.columbian.com/SBDC/sbdc.html
Email: harte@vancouver.wsu.edu

Yakima Valley Community College
Small Business Development Center
P.O. Box 1647
113 South 14th Avenue
Yakima, WA 98902

509-574-4935
Fax: 509-574-4943
www.yvcc.edu/academics/WorkforceEd/busin
ess%20development%20center/smallbus.asp
Email: arice@yakima.edu

Columbia Basin College
Tri-Cities Small Business Development
Center
901 North Colorado
Kennewick, WA 9936
509-735-6222
Fax: 509-735-6609
www.cbc2.org/instruct/bus/sbdc.htm
Email: BlakesCafe@3-cities.com

Walla Walla Community College
Small Business Development Center
500 Tausick Way
Walla Walla, WA 99362
509-527-4681
Fax: 509-525-3101
www.portwallawalla.com/smbcenter/info.htm
Email: rm@portwallawalla.com

Green River Community College
108 South Division St. Suite A
Auburn, WA 98001
253-333-1600
Fax: 253-333-8635
www.greenriver.edu/businesscenter
Email: dburnett@grcc.ctc.edu

Small Business Development Center
1611 North National Avenue
Chehalis, WA 98532
360-748-0114
Fax: 360-748-1238
Email: dbaria@localaccess.com

Highland Community College
Small Business Development Center
PO Box 98000 M/S Omni 3-3
Des Moines, WA 98198
206 878-3710 ext. 5151
Fax: 209- 870-5915
http://flightline.highline.edu/cel/sbdc.htm
Email: jshelton@highline.edu

Enumclaw Small Business Assistance Center
1414 Griffin Avenue
Enumclaw, WA 98022
253-288-3400
www.greenriver.edu/businesscenter

Okanogan County SBDC
P.O. Box 626
320 Omak Avenue #400
Omak, WA 98841
509-826-5107
Fax: 50-826-7425
Email: blakeney@methow.com

Olympic Peninsula SBDC
Port Townsend Office
540 Water Street
P.O. Box 1849
Port Townsend, WA 98368
360-344-3078
Fax: 360-344-3079
Email: kpurdy@clallam.org

Community Capital Development
SBDC
PO Box 22283
1437 S Jackson
Seattle, WA 98122
206-324-4330 ext. 107
Fax: 206-324-4322
www.seattleccd.com/sbdc/index.htm
Email: lindak@seattleccd.com

Seattle SBDC
3600 -15th Avenue West, Suite 303

Seattle, WA 98119
206-298-4402
Fax: 206-298-4423
Email: wwong@wolfenet.com

Tacoma SBDC
Bates Technical College
1101 South Yakima Avenue
Room M-123
Tacoma, WA 98405
253-680-7768
Fax: 253-680-7771
Email: dyoung@bates.ctc.edu

Small Business Development Center
Columbia Station, 3rd Floor
300 S. Columbia
Wenatchee, WA 98801
509-662-8016
509-662-3256
Email: SBDC@wenatchee.org

West Virginia

Lead Center:
Conley Salyer
West Virginia Small Business Development
Center
West Virginia Development Office
1900 Kanawha Boulevard East
Building 6 Room 652
Charleston, WV 25305
304-558-2960
888-WVA-SBDC
Fax: 304-558-0127
www.sbdcwv.org
Email: csalyer@wvsbdc.org

Charleston Small Business Development Sub
Center
State Capitol Complex
1900 Kanawha Blvd. East
Building 6, Room 652
Charleston, WV 25305
304-558-2960
Fax: 304-558-0127
www.sbdcwv.org

Elkins Satellite Small Business Development
Center
1 Station Square
Room 202 Railroad Avenue
Elkins, WV 26241
304-637-7205
Fax: 304-637-4902
Email: jrjm@westvirginia.com

Fairmont State College
Small Business Development Center
3000 Technology Drive, Suite 200
Fairmont, WV 26554
304-367-2712
Fax: 304-367-2717
www.fscwv.edu/fsctc/sbdc
Email: mgamble1@mail.fscwv.edu

Marshall University
Small Business Development Center
2000 Seventh Avenue
Cabell Hall, Suite 304
Huntington, WV 25703-1527
304-696-6246
Fax: 304-696-4835
www.marshall.edu/ibd/sbdc.htmlx
Email: emcclain@marshall.edu

Eastern WV Community and Technical
College
Small Business Development Center
HC 65, Box 402
Moorefield, WV 26836
304-434-8000
Fax: 304-434-7003

www.eastern.wvnet.edu/sbdc.htm
Email: kellyj@eastern.wvnet.edu

West Virginia University
Small Business Development Center
3040 University Ave. Suite 2008
Morgantown, WV 26505
304-293-5839
Fax: 304-293-8905

West Virginia University at Parkersburg
Small Business Development Center
300 Campus Drive
Parkersburg, WV 26101
304-424-8277
Fax: 304-424-8266
www.wvup.wvnet.edu/www/BIDS/Sbdc.htm
Email: greg.hill@mail.wvu.edu

Flatwoods Outlet Mall, Suite 249
Small Business Development Center
249 Skidmore Lane
Sutton, WV 26601-9272
304-765-7300
Fax: 304-765-7724
Email: cook@glenville.wvnet.edu

West Virginia Northern Community College
Small Business Development Center
1704 Market Street
Wheeling, WV 26003
304-233-5900 ext. 4355
Fax: 304-232-3819
http://techctr1.northern.wvnet.edu/northern/
CBDS_sbdc.htm
Email: daberegg@northern.wvnet.edu

Region I Workforce SBDC - Beckley
921 W. Neville Street, Suite 200
Beckley, West Virginia 25801
304-55-4022
800-766-4556
Fax: 304-252-9584
Email: tparrish@r1workforcewv.org

Southern WV Community & Technical
College
300 Main Street
Logan, WV 25601
304-792-7234 ext. 27
Fax: 304-792-7239
www.southern.wvnet.edu/wd/EconDev/Main
default.htm
Email: raye@southern.wvnet.edu

Community & Technical College of
Shepherd
400 West Stephen Street
Martinsburg, WV 25401
304-260-4385
Fax: 304-260-4384
www.shepherd.edu/sbdcweb
Email: clundberg@shepherd.edu

Region I Workforce SBDC - Summersville
812 Northside Drive, Suite 7J
Summersville, WV 26651
304-872-0020
Fax: 304-872-0020
Email: jepling@r1workforcewv.org

Wisconsin

Lead Center:
Erica Kauten
Wisconsin Small Business Development
Center
University of Wisconsin
432 North Lake Street
Room 423
Madison, WI 53706
608-263-7794
800-940-SBDC

Fax: 608-263-7830
www.wisconsinsbdc.org

University of Wisconsin at Eau Claire
Small Business Development Center
P.O. Box 4004
210 Water Street
Eau Claire, WI 54702-4004
715-836-5811
866-UWEC4CE
Fax: 715-836-5263
Email: ce@uwec.edu

University of Wisconsin at Green Bay
Small Business Development Center
835 Potts Ave
Green Bay, WI 54304
920-496-2115
Fax: 920-496-6009
www.uwgb.edu/outreach/sbdc
Email: dgjerde@titletown.org

Kenosha County Small Business
Development Center
c/o Job Center/Human Services Building
8600 Sheidan
Kenosha, WI 53141
262-697-4525
Fax: 262-697-4563
http://oldweb.uwp.edu/admin/community.par
tnerships/sbdc
Email: dschacht@co.kenosha.wi.us

University of Wisconsin at LaCrosse
Small Business Development Center
120 W. Carl Wimberly Hall
La Crosse, WI 54601
608-785-8782
Fax: 608-785-6919
www.uwlax.edu/sbdc
Email: gallaghe.jani@uwlax.edu

University of Wisconsin at Madison
Small Business Development Center
School of Business
975 University Avenue, Room 3260
Madison, WI 53706
608-263-7680
Fax: 608-263-0818
www.uwsbdc.org
Email: sbdc@bus.wisc.edu

University of Wisconsin at Milwaukee
Small Business Development Center
161 West Wisconsin Avenue, Suite 6752
Milwaukee, WI 53203
414-227-3142
http://cfprod.imt.uwm.edu/sce/dci.cfm?id=15
Email: lucyh@csd.uwm.edu

University of Wisconsin at Oshkosh
Small Business Development Center
347 Park Plaza
Oshkosh, WI 54901
920-424-1453
800-232-8939
Fax: 920-424-2005
www.ccp.uwosh.edu/services/
services_smallbusiness.html
Email: nigl@uwosh.edu

University of Wisconsin at Platteville
Southwest Wisconsin Small Business
Development Center
Room 710/711 Pioneer Tower Building
UW-Platteville
Plateville, WI 53818
608-342-1038
Fax: 608-342-1599
www.uwplatt.edu/~swsbdc/index.html
Email: swsbdc@uwplatt.edu

University of Wisconsin at River Falls
Small Business Development Center

410 South Third Street, 128 SH
River Falls, WI 54022
715-425-0620
Fax: 715-425-0707
www.uwrf.edu/cbe/sbdc
Email: Kathy.bartelt@uwrf.edu

University of Wisconsin at Stevens Point
Small Business Development Center
2100 Main Street
103 Main Building
Stevens Point, WI 54481
715-346-3838
800-898-9472
Fax: 715-346-4045
www.uwsp.edu/extension/sbdc
Email: vloberme@uwsp.edu

University of Wisconsin at Superior
Small Business Development Center
Belknap & Catlin
P.O. Box 2000
Superior, WI 54880-2898
715-394-8351
Fax: 715-394-8592
www2.uwsuper.edu/bdc/index.htm
Email: mpekklal@staff.uwsuper.edu

University of Wisconsin at Whitewater
Small Business Development Center
2000 Carlson Hall
Whitewater, WI 53190
262-472-3217
800-621-7235
Fax: 262-472-5692
www.uww.edu/sbdc

2320 Renaissance Boulevard
Sturtevant, WI 53177
262-898-7414
Fax: 262-898-7401
www.racine-sbdc.com
Email: info@racine-sbdc.com

Wyoming

Lead Center:
Diane Wolverton
University of Wyoming
Small Business Development Ctr.
P.O. Box 3922
Laramie, WY 82071-3922
307-766-3505
800-348-5194
Fax: 307-766-3406
http://uwadmnweb.uwyo.edu/sbdc
Email: ddw@uwyo.edu

Wyoming Small Business Development
Center
300 South Wolcott, Suite 300
Casper, WY 82601
307-234-6683
800-348-5207
Fax: 307-577-7014
Email: sbdc@trib.com

Laramie County Community College
Small Business Development Center
1400 East College Drive
Cheyenne, WY 82007-3298
307-632-6141
800-348-5208
Fax: 307-632-6061
Email: sewsbdc@wyoming.com

Region 5 Small Business Development
Center
First Interstate Bank Building
222 South Gillette Avenue, Suite 402
Gillette, WY 82716
307-682-5232
888-956-6060

Fax: 307-686-5792
Email: sbdc@vcn.com

Region 2 Small Business Development
Center
143 South Bent Street, Suite A
Powell, WY 82435
307-754-2139
800-383-0371
Fax: 307-754-0368
Email: director@wir.net

Fremont County Satellite Office
Riverton Branch Public Library

1330 West Park Avenue
Riverton, WY 82501-1790
307-857-1174
Fax: 307-1175
Email: wsbdc@tcinc.net

Region 1 Small Business Development
Center
1400 Dewar Drive, Suite #205
Rock Springs, WY 82901
307-352-6894
800-348-5205
Fax: 307-352-6876
Email: bellis@uwyo.edu

Microenterprise:
When You Need Just A Little Money
To Start A Big New Business

A recent survey showed that approximately 33% of the top 500 fastest growing small businesses in the U.S. started with less than $10,000. It doesn't take much money to start a business in today's information age and service economy. We're no longer in the manufacturing age, when you needed a lot of money to start a business because you needed to buy an expensive plant and costly equipment. Today, many businesses are started with nothing more than a phone, a desk, and business cards. Traditional government money programs required entrepreneurs to ask for at least $50,000 to $100,000. Now the government has set up Microenterprise Programs where you can ask for just a little amount of money to make that big change in your life.

A Growing Unknown Resource

These programs are continually growing. They seem so successful that policy makers are finding new ways to help them grow. But this growth and success seems to be causing as many problems as the opportunities they are creating. On one hand, the SBA programs recently increased the number of banks that participate in its microloan program from 100 to 200 and also added a subcategory of lenders to include for profit and nonprofit organizations. Grants under this program will increase from $45 million in 1995 to $98 million in 1997, and direct loans will increase from $120 million to $250 million during the same period. But, on the other hand I read that programs like the one at the U.S. Department of Housing and Urban Development fell short of quota by $1.5 billion because not enough people applied. This means that the poor bureaucrat administering the program couldn't give out all their money because not enough people applied. I even got a personal call from a local organization who had $50,000 of this money for someone to open up a bakery, and no one applied for it.

66% Chance of Being a Microloan Winner

Each year thousands of people will be getting microloans to start or expand their businesses. Although data is not available for every program, one of the major microloan lenders estimates that 66% of the people who apply for money, get it. Here are a few examples of recent recipients:

- $5,000 to Street Smart, Inc., a street-hockey equipment distributor in Southeastern Pennsylvania

- $25,000 to Med-Ex Medical Express, a courier service that specializes in the health care field

- $15,000 to Jeannette Saunders and Pamela Marshall of Sacramento, CA to start P&J Word Processing Service

* Up To $10,000 For Refugees

ORR/Division of Community Resettlement
370 L'Enfant Promenade, SW Sixth Floor — 202-401-9250
Washington, DC 20447 — Fax: 202-401-5487

Refugees can receive technical assistance, training, or loans of up to $10,000 through a program called the Micro-Enterprise Development Project. The program allows states and public or private, nonprofit organizations and institutions to apply to receive grants to develop and administer micro-enterprise programs consisting of small-scale financing ($10,000) available through microloans to refugees. It also includes funding for technical assistance and support to these refugee entrepreneurs. For information on organizations which were awarded grants, contact the office listed above.

* Your State Can Get You Money

Community Connections Information Center
Office of Community Planning and Development — 800-998-9999
P.O. Box 7189 — TDD: 800-483-2209
Gaithersburg, MD 20898-7189 — Fax: 301-519-5027/5622

This is the second largest component of the Community Development Block Grant (CDBG) program and aids communities that do not qualify for assistance under the CDBG entitlement program. The grants assist communities in carrying out a wide range of community development activities directed toward neighborhood revitalization, economic development, and the provision of improved community facilities and services. Funds can also be used to provide assistance to public and private organizations, agencies, and other entities (including nonprofits and for profits to facilitate economic development in supporting micro-enterprise).

Funds can be used to establish credit (direct loans and loan guarantees, revolving loan funds, and more) for the stabilization and expansion of microenterprises; provide technical assistance, advice, and business support services to owners of micro-enterprises; and provide general support to owners of micro-enterprises and organizations developing micro-enterprises.

If you are an interested citizen, you should contact your local officials for more information. If your local government or state officials cannot answer your questions, you may wish to contact the HUD Field Office that services your area (look for the office closest to you from the list later in this chapter). Be aware that the state administers the program and determines which local projects receive funding.

You can also contact: Community Connections, Information Center, Office of Community Planning and Development, P.O. Box 7189, Gaithersburg, MD 20898-7189; 800-998-9999.

* Public Housing Entrepreneurs

U.S. Department of Housing and Urban Development
Deputy Director of Resident Initiatives
451 Seventh Street, SW — 202-705-1112
Washington, DC 20410 — TTY: 202-708-1455

Call yourself a handyman and get money to fix up your neighborhood. Money is set aside to give to public housing residents to modernize existing public housing projects. The money can also be used to provide residents with on-the-job training in construction and contractor related trades. It's called the Comprehensive Grant Program, and is available to Public Housing Agencies of 250 housing units or more, which includes 897 public housing agencies nationwide. Contact your local Public Housing Authority for more information or you may contact the office listed above.

* State Microloan Programs

Contact the State Office of Economic Development listed in your state capital

or

See the chapter, State Money and Help For Your Business, page 216

In addition to the federal programs, many state governments are also putting their money into microloan opportunities. Here are a few microloan programs that are currently available at the state level:

Iowa - Self Employment Loan Program ($5,000 for low income)

Maine - Job Start Program ($10,000)

New York - Micro Loan Program - NY Job Development

North Dakota - Micro Business Loans

Ohio - Ohio Mini-Loan Program

South Carolina - Micro Enterprise Loan Program

Texas - Rural Microenterprise Loan Program

New programs are being added all the time, so be sure to contact your state capital for the most current information.

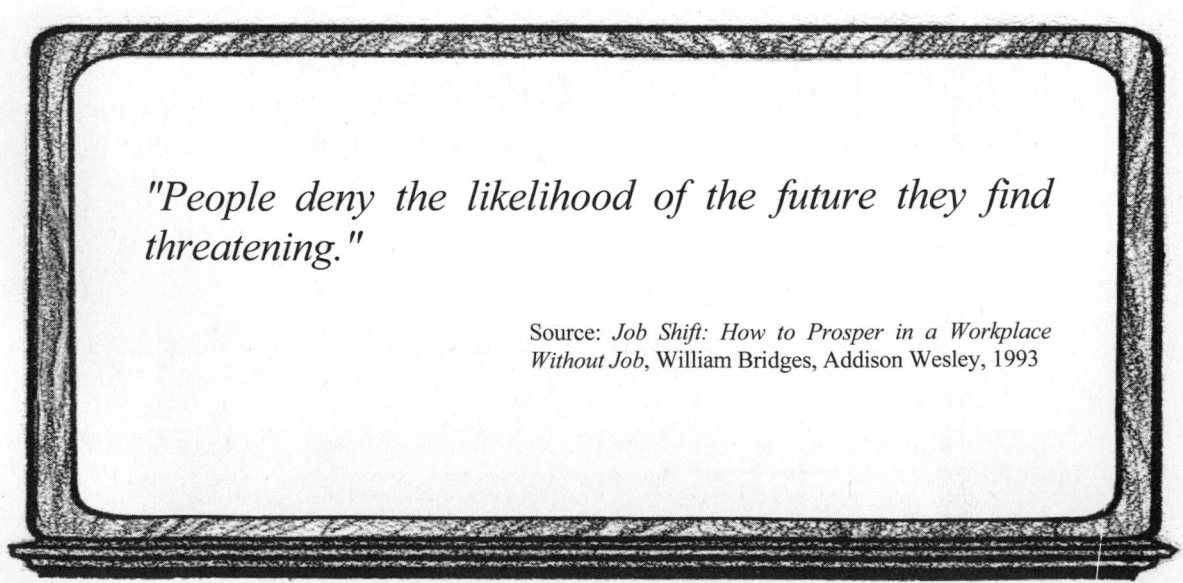

"People deny the likelihood of the future they find threatening."

Source: *Job Shift: How to Prosper in a Workplace Without Job*, William Bridges, Addison Wesley, 1993

Money To Start A Business In A Small Town

The Intermediary Relending Program (IRP) is a rural development program administered by the Rural Business-Cooperative Service (RBS). The purpose is to provide loans for the establishment of new businesses, expansion of existing businesses, creation of new employment opportunities, saving of existing jobs, and funds to recipients for business facilities or community development projects in rural areas.

Loans are made to intermediaries who relend funds to recipients for business facilities or community development. You can borrow up to $150,000 with a maximum term of 30 years and an interest rate of one percent per annum.

For information, copies of regulations, and forms, contact any USDA, Rural Development State Office or write to the RBS National Office at USDA, Rural Business-Cooperative Service, 1400 Independence Avenue, SW, Room 5050 South Building, Washington, DC 20250; 202-720-1019; {www.rurdev.usda.gov/rbs/oa/oadir.htm} For state office locations, see the next listing.

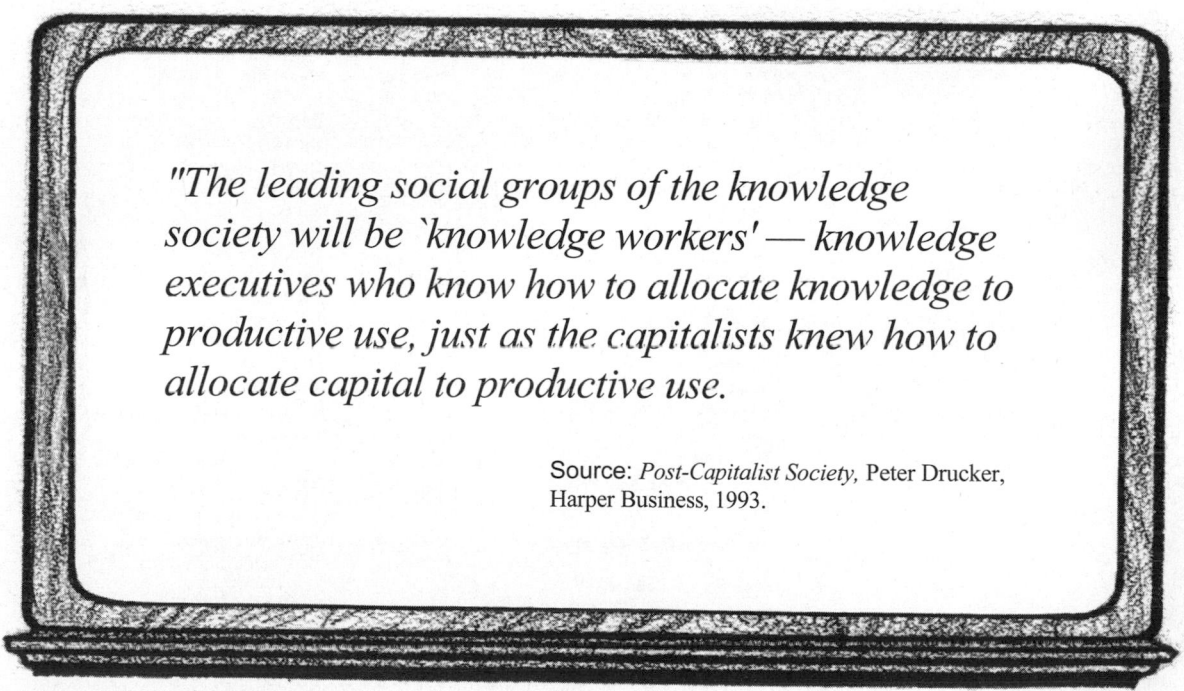

"The leading social groups of the knowledge society will be `knowledge workers' — knowledge executives who know how to allocate knowledge to productive use, just as the capitalists knew how to allocate capital to productive use.

Source: *Post-Capitalist Society,* Peter Drucker, Harper Business, 1993.

Rural Business Grants

The Rural Business Enterprise Grant Program (RBEG) is administered by the Rural Business-Cooperative Service (RBS), and provides grant funds to a local or regional intermediary which, in turn, lends funds in a flexible manner to local businesses. Funds are designed to facilitate the development of small and emerging private business, industry, and related employment.

Money can be used for the acquisition and development of land, and the construction of buildings, plants, equipment, access streets and roads, parking areas, utility and service extensions, refinancing, fees, technical assistance, startup operating cost, working capital, providing financial assistance to a third party, production of television programs to provide information to rural residents; and to create, expand, and operate rural distance learning networks. Grant applications are available from any USDA Rural Development State Office.

For more information, contact the U.S. Department of Agriculture, Rural Business-Cooperative Service, 1400 Independence Avenue, SW, Room 5050 South Building, Washington, DC 20250; 202-720-1400.

U.S. Department Of Agriculture Rural Development State Offices

Alabama
USDA Rural Development
Steve Pelham
4121 Carmichael Road
Sterling Center, Suite 601
Montgomery, AL 36106-3683
334-279-3400
Fax: 334-279-3404
Email: steve.pelham@al.usda.gov
www.rurdev.usda.gov/al

Alaska
USDA Rural Development
Bill Allen
800 West Evergreen, Suite 201
Palmer, AK 99645
907-761-7705
Fax: 907-761-7783
Email: bill.allen@ak.usda.gov
www.rurdev.usda.gov/ak

Arizona
USDA Rural Development
Eddie Browning
3003 N. Central Ave., Suite 900
Phoenix, AZ 85012
602-280-8701
Fax: 602-280-8770
Email: eddie.browning@az.usda.gov
www.rurdev.usda.gov/az

Arkansas
USDA Rural Development
Shirley Tucker
Federal Building, Room 3416
700 W. Capitol Avenue
Little Rock, AR 72201-3225
501-301-3280
Fax: 501-301-3294
Email: shirley.tucker@ar.usda.gov
www.rurdev.usda.gov/ar

California
USDA Rural Development
Charles Clendenin
430 G Street
Agency 4169
Davis, CA 95616
530-792-5800
Fax: 530-792-5838
TDD: 530-792-5848
Email: chuck.clendenin@ca.usda.gov
www.rurdev.usda.gov/ca

Colorado
USDA Rural Development
Leroy W. Cruz
655 Parfet Street
Room E100
Lakewood, CO 80215
720-544-2903
TTY: 720-544-2976
Email: leroy.cruz@co.usda.gov
www.rurdev.usda.gov/co

Delaware/Maryland
USDA Rural Development
James E. Waters
4607 South DuPont Highway
P.O. Box 400
Camden, DE 19934
302-697-4324
TTY: 302-697-4303
Fax: 302-697-4388
Email: jim.waters@de.usda.gov
www.rurdev.usda.gov/de

Florida
USDA Rural Development
Joseph M. Mueller
4440 NW 25th Place
Gainesville, FL 32606
352-338-3482
Fax: 352-338-3450
Email: joe.mueller@fl.usda.gov
www.rurdev.usda.gov/fl

Georgia
USDA Rural Development
Howard W. Franklin
Stephens Federal Building
335 E. Hancock Ave.
Athens, GA 30601-2768
706-546-2154
Fax: 706-546-2135
Email: howard.franklin@ga.usda.gov
www.rurdev.usda.gov/ga

Hawaii
USDA Rural Development
Steven Chapman
Room 311, Federal Building
154 Waianuenue Avenue
Hilo, HI 96720
808-933-8317
Fax: 808-933-8327
TDD: 808-933-8321
Email: steven.chapman@hi.usda.gov
www.rurdev.usda.gov/hi

Idaho
USDA Rural Development
Daryl G. Moser
9173 West Barnes Street
Suite A1
Boise, ID 83709
208-378-5623
Fax: 208-378-5643
TDD: 208-378-5644
Email: daryl.moser@id.usda.gov
www.rurdev.usda.gov/id

Illinois
USDA Rural Development
Gerald Townsend
2118 West Park Ct., Suite A
Champaign, IL 61821
217-403-6209
Fax: 217-403-6215
Email: gerald.townsend@il.usda.gov
www.rurdev.usda.gov/il

Indiana
USDA Rural Development
Joseph Steele
5975 Lakeside Boulevard
Indianapolis, IN 46278
317-290-3100
Fax: 317-290-3127
Email: joseph.steele@in.usda.gov
www.rurdev.usda.gov/in

Matthew Lesko, Information USA, Inc., 12081 Nebel Street, Rockville, MD 20852 • 1-800-955-7693 • www.lesko.com

Iowa

USDA Rural Development
Randy Frescoln
210 Walnut Street, Room 873
Des Moines, IA 50309-2196
515-284-4663
Fax: 515-284-4821
Email: randy.frescoln@ia.usda.gov
www.rurdev.usda.gov/ia

Kansas

USDA Rural Development
Gary Smith
1303 SW First American Place
Suite 100
Topeka, KS 66604
785-271-2730
Fax: 785-271-2708
Email: gsmith@rdasun2.rurdev.usda.gov
www.rurdev.usda.gov/ks

Kentucky

USDA Rural Development
Vernon Brown
771 Corporate Drive, Suite 200
Lexington, KY 40503
859-224-7336
Fax: 859-224-7344
Email: vernon.brown@ky.usda.gov
www.rurdev.usda.gov/ky

Louisiana

USDA Rural Development
John Broussard
3727 Government Street
Alexandria, LA 71302
318-473-7960
TYY/TDD: 318-473-7655/7697
Fax: 318-473-7829
Email: john.broussard@la.usda.gov
www.rurdev.usda.gov/la

Maine

USDA Rural Development
Janice Kremin
967 Illinois Avenue
P.O. Box 405
Bangor, ME 04402-0405
207-990-9100
Fax: 207-990-9129
Email: jan.kremin@me.usda.gov
www.rurdev.usda.gov/me

Massachusetts/Connecticut/ Rhode Island

USDA Rural Development
Daniel R. Beaudette
451 West Street
Amherst, MA 01002-2999
413-253-4318
Fax: 413-253-4347
Email: dbeaudet@rurdcv.usda.gov
www.rurdev.usda.gov/ma

Michigan

USDA Rural Development
Lee Bambusch
3001 Coolidge Road, Suite 200
East Lansing, MI 48823
517-324-5220
TDD: 517-337-6906
Fax: 517-324-5225
Email: lee.bambusch@mi.usda.gov
www.rurdev.usda.gov/mi

Minnesota

USDA Rural Development
John J. Melbo
410 Farm Credit Service Bldg.
375 Jackson Street
St.Paul, MN 55101-1853
651-602-7814

Fax: 651-602-7824
Email: john.melbo@mn.usda.gov
www.rurdev.usda.gov/mn

Mississippi

USDA Rural Development
Charlie Joiner
Suite 831, Federal Building
100 West Capital St.
Jackson, MS 39269
601-965-5457
Fax: 601-965-4566
Email: charlie.joiner@ms.usda.gov
www.rurdev.usda.gov/ms

Missouri

USDA Rural Development
Clark Thomas
601 Business Loop 70 West
Park Aid Center, Suite 235
Columbia, MO 65203
573-876-0995
TDD: 573-876-9480
Fax: 573-876-0984
Email: clark.thomas@mo.usda.gov
www.rurdev.usda.gov/mo

Montana

USDA Rural Development
John D. Guthmiller
P.O. Box 850
Bozeman, MT 59771
406-585-2540
TDD: 406-585-0819
Fax: 406-585-2565
Email: john.guthmiller@mt.usda.gov
www.rurdev.usda.gov/mt

Nebraska

USDA Rural Development
Deborah D. Drhal
Room 152 Federal Building
100 Centennial Mall North
Lincoln, NE 68508
402-437-5558
TDD: 402-437-5093
Fax: 402-437-5408
Email: deborah.drbal@ne.usda.gov
www.rurdev.usda.gov/ne

Nevada

USDA Rural Development
Virginia Fleming
1390 South Curry Street
Carson City, NV 89703
775-887-1222 ext. 24
Fax: 775-885-0841
TDD: 775-885-0633
Email: gini.fleming@nv.usda.gov
www.rurdev.usda.gov/nv

New Hampshire

USDA Rural Development
Rob McCarthy
10 Ferry St., Suite 218
Box 317
Concord, NH 03301-5004
603-223-6045
Fax: 603-223-6061
Email: rob.mccarthy@nh.usda.gov
www.rurdev.usda.gov/nh

New Jersey

USDA Rural Development
Michael P. Kelsey
8000 Midatlantic Dr., Suite 500
Mt. Laurel, NJ 08054
856-787-7750
Fax: 856-787-7783
TDD: 856-787-7784
Email: michael.kelsey@nj.usda.gov
www.rurdev.usda.gov/nj

New Mexico

USDA Rural Development
Mike McDow
6200 Jefferson, NE, Room 255
Albuquerque, NM 87109
505-761-4949
TTY: 505-761-4938
Fax: 505-761-4976
Email: mike.mcdow@nm.usda.gov
www.rurdev.usda.gov/nm

New York

USDA Rural Development
Lowell Gibson
The Galleries of Syracuse
441 South Salina Street
Suite 357, 5th Floor
Syracuse, NY 13202-2425
315-477-6425
Fax: 315-477-6448
Email: lowell.gibson@ny.usda.gov
www.rurdev.usda.gov/ny

North Carolina

USDA Rural Development
Thurman Burnette
4405 Bland Road
Raleigh, NC 27609
919-873-2041
Fax: 919-873-2075
Email: thurman.burnette@nc.usda.gov
www.rurdev.usda.gov/nc

North Dakota

USDA Rural Development
Clare Carlson
220 East Rosser Avenue
P.O. Box 1737
Bismarck, ND 58502
701-530-2037
Fax: 703-530-2108
Email: clare.carlson@nd.usda.gov
www.rurdev.usda.gov/nd

Ohio

USDA Rural Development
James Cogan
200 North High Street, Room 507
Columbus, OH 43215
614-255-2420
Email: jim.cogan@oh.usda.gov
www.rurdev.usda.gov/oh

Oklahoma

USDA Rural Development
Michael Schrammel
100 USDA, Suite 108
Stillwater, OK 74074
405-742-1060
TTY/TDD: 405-742-1007
Fax: 405-742-1005
Email: michael.schrammel@ok.usda.gov
www.rurdev.usda.gov/ok

Oregon

USDA Rural Development
Bud Fischer
101 SW Main, Suite 1410
Portland, OR 97204-3222
503-414-3366
Fax: 503-414-3398
Email: bud.fischer@or.usda.gov
www.rurdev.usda.gov/or

Pennsylvania

USDA Rural Development
Linda Hager
Suite 330, One Credit Union Place
Harrisburg, PA 17110-2996
717-237-2289
Fax: 717-237-2196
TTY: 717-237-2261

Email: linda.hager@pa.usda.gov
www.rurdev.usda.gov/pa

South Carolina

USDA Rural Development
Mike Hucks
Strom Thurmond Federal Building
1835 Assembly St., Room 1007
Columbia, SC 29201
803-253-3183
Fax: 803-765-5910
Email: mike.hucks@sc.usda.gov
www.rurdev.usda.gov/sc

South Dakota

USDA Rural Development
Robert R. Bothwell
200 4th Street SW
Federal Building, Room 210
Huron, SD 57350
605-352-1142
Fax: 605-352-1146
Email: bob.bothwell@sd.usda.gov
www.rurdev.usda.gov/sd

Tennessee

USDA Rural Development
Dan Beasley
3322 West End Ave., Suite 300
Nashville, TN 37203
615-783-1341
800-342-3149
Fax: 615-783-1301
Email: dan.beasley@tn.usda.gov
www.rurdev.usda.gov/tn

Texas

USDA Rural Development
Pat Liles

101 S. Main, Suite 102
Temple, TX 76501
254-742-9780
Fax: 254-742-9709
Email: pat.liles@tx.usda.gov
www.rurdev.usda.gov/tx

Utah

USDA Rural Development
Richard Carrig
125 State, Room 4431
Salt Lake City, UT 84138
801-524-4322
Fax: 801-524-4406
Email: richard.carrig@ut.usda.gov
www.rurdev.usda.gov/ut

Vermont

USDA Rural Development
David Robinson
89 Main Street, 3rd Floor
City Center
Montpelier, VT 05602
802-828-6010
Fax: 802-828-6076
Email: david.robinson@vt.usda.gov
www.rurdev.usda.gov/vt

Virginia

USDA Rural Development
Reginald Rountree
Culpeper Building
Suite 238
1606 Santa Rosa Road
Richmond, VA 23229-5014
804-287-1557
Fax: 804-287-1786
Email: reginald.rountree@va.usda.gov
www.rurdev.usda.gov/va

Washington

USDA Rural Development
Chris Cassidy
1835 Black Lake Boulevard SW
Suite B
Olympia, WA 98501
360-704-7740
Fax: 360-704-7742
Email: chris.cassidy@wa.usda.gov
www.rurdev.usda.gov/wa

West Virginia

USDA Rural Development
Jerry Teter
75 High Street, Room 320
Morgantown, WV 26505
304-284-4860
Fax: 304-284-4893
Email: jerry.teter@wv.usda.gov
www.rurdev.usda.gov/wv

Wisconsin

USDA Rural Development
4949 Krischling Court
Stevens Point, WI 54481
715-345-7615
Fax: 715-345-7669
www.rurdev.usda.gov/wi

Wyoming

USDA Rural Development
Jerry Tamlin
100 East B Street, Room 1005
Casper, WY 82601
307-261-6319
Fax: 307-261-6339
TDD: 307-261-6333
Email: jerry.tamlin@wy.usda.gov
www.rurdev.usda.gov/wy

Welfare Moms Can Start Their Own Business

If you're getting help from Temporary Assistance for Needy Families (TANF), you may be able to get free training on how to become an entrepreneur, along with money to help you become your own boss. The program is called Job Opportunities for Low-Income Individuals (JOLI) program, which seeks to enhance the capacity and self-sufficiency of participating individuals.

JOLI aims to help TANF recipients and others whose income falls below the federal poverty guidelines become self-sufficient by starting their own micro-enterprises or through employment in newly created permanent jobs. The program is designed to demonstrate and evaluate ways of creating new employment and business opportunities for certain low income individuals through the provision of technical and financial assistance to private employers in the community, self-employment/micro-enterprise programs, and/or new business development programs. JOLI awards grants to nonprofit organizations to develop these projects.

For information on programs in your area or application information, contact U.S. Department of Health and Human Services, Office Community Services, 370 L'Enfant Promenade, SW Fifth Floor, Washington, DC 20447; 202-401-5282; {www.acf.dhhs.gov/programs/joli/welcome.htm}.

Job Opportunities for Low-Income Individuals

Alaska
Fairbanks Native Association (FNA)
Annetta Freiberger, Executive Director
201 First Avenue, Suite 200
Fairbanks, AK 99701-4892
907-452-1648
Fax: 907-456-4148
Email: afreiburge@fairbanksnative.org

California
Valley Economic Development Center, Inc.
Roberto E. Barragan, President
5121 Van Nuys Boulevard, 3rd Floor
Van Nuys, CA 91403
818-907-9977
Fax: 818-907-9720
Email: Roberto@vedc.org

Hawaii
Parents and Children Together (PACT)
Ruthann Quitiquit, Executive Director
1505 Dillingham Boulevard, Suite 208
Honolulu, HI 96819
808-847-3285
Fax: 808-841-1485
Email: adminrquitiquit@pacthawaii.org

Illinois
Community and Economic Development
Association of Cook County, Inc.
Robert Wharton, President/CEO
208 S. LaSalle, Suite 1900

Chicago, IL 60604
312-795-8983
Fax: 312-795-0240

Women's Self-Employment Project
Wanda White, President
11 South LaSalle, Suite 1850
Chicago, IL 60603
312-606-8255
Fax: 312-606-9215
Email: wwhite@wsep.com

Massachusetts
Jewish Vocational Service
Barbara S. Rosenbaum, Executive Director
105 Chauncy Street
Boston, MA 02111
617-451-8147
Fax: 617-451-9973
Email: brosenbaum@jvs-boston.org

Nebraska
Industrialization Center, Inc.
Dr. Bernice Dodd, President/CEO
2724 North 24th Street
Omaha, NE 68110
302-457-4222
Fax: 402-457-6635

Pennsylvania
Northside Leadership Conference
Dana Jara, Executive Director

415 East Ohio Street, Suite 300
Pittsburgh, PA 15212
412-231-4714
Fax: 412-231-5306
Email: dana@nslconf.org

Puerto Rico
Centros Sor Isolina Ferre, Inc.
Allan Cintron, Director
P.O. Box 34360
Ponce, PR 00734-4360
787-844-7743
Fax: 787-843-2347

Tennessee
YMCA of Greater Memphis
Mary Cole Nichols, Executive Director
766 S. Highland
Memphis, TN 38111
901-323-2211
Fax: 901-458-3784
Email: mary.cole.nichols@memphisywca.org

Texas
George Gervin Youth Center, Inc.
Barbara D. Hawkins
Executive Director
6903 Sunbelt Drive South
San Antonio, TX 78218
210-804-1786
Fax: 210-804-1469
Email: gervinc@txdirect.net

Grants To Towns
That Will Lend You Business Money

Cities can get grants that can be used to lend you money to start a small business. The Entitlement Grants is the largest component of the Community Development Block Grant Program and provides annual grants to entitled cities (population 50,000) and counties (population 200, 000) to develop viable urban communities by providing decent housing and suitable living environments, and by expanding economic opportunities, principally for low and moderate income persons.

The program provides funds to carry out a wide range of community development activities directed toward neighborhood revitalization, economic development, improved community facilities and services, and micro-enterprise. Funds can be used to establish credit (direct loans and loan guarantees, revolving loan funds, and more) for the stabilization and expansion of micro-enterprise; provide technical assistance, advice, and business support services to owners of micro-enterprises; and provide general support to owners of micro-enterprises and organizations developing micro-enterprises.

To learn if your community received funds and the person to contact in your area for more information, contact Community Connections, Information Center, Office of Community Planning and Development, P.O. Box 7189, Gaithersburg, MD 20898-7189; 800-998-9999; TDD: 800-983-2209; Fax: 301-519-5027/5622; {www.comcon.org}. You may also contact the HUD office nearest you (listed below).

HUD Offices

New England

Boston Region
Kevin Keogh, Regional Director
HUD-Boston Office
10 Causeway Street
Room 301
Boston, MA 0222-1092
617-994-8200
Fax: 617-565-6558

Burlington Region
Michael McNamara
Field Office Director
HUD-Burlington Office
159 Bank Street, 2nd Floor
Burlington, VT 05401
802-951-6290
Fax; 802-951-6298

Manchester Region
David B. Harrity
Field Office Director
HUD-Manchester Office
Norris Cotton Federal Building
275 Chestnut Street
Manchester, NH 03103-2487
603-666-7682
Fax: 603-666-7667

Bangor Region
Loren W. Cole
Field Office Director
HUD-Bangor Office
202 Harlow Street
Chase Building, Suite 101
P.O. Box 1384
Bangor, ME 04402-1384
207-945-0468
Fax: 207-945-0533

Rhode Island Region
Nancy D. Smith
Field Office Director
HUD-Providence Office
10 Weybosset Street, 6th Floor
Providence, RI 02903-2808
401-528-5352
Fax: 401-528-5097

Hartford Region
Julie Fagan, Field Office Director
HUD-Hartford Office
One Corporate Center
Hartford, CT 06106-3220
860-240-4844
Fax 860-240-4850

New York/New Jersey

New York Region
Marisel Morales, Regional Director
HUD-New York Office
26 Federal Plaza, Suite 3541
New York, NY 10278-0068
212-264-1161
Fax: 212-264-3068

Albany Region
Vacant
Field Office Director
HUD-Albany Office
52 Corporate Circle
Albany, NY 12203-5121
518-464-4200
Fax: 518-464-4300

Buffalo Region
Stephen Banko, Field Office Director
HUD-Buffalo Office
5th Floor, Lafayette Court

465 Main Street
Buffalo, NY 14203-1780
716-551-5733
Fax: 716-551-5752

Camden Region
Vacant
Field Office Director
HUD-Camden Office
800 Hudson Square, 2nd Floor
Camden, NJ 08102-1156
609-757-5081
Fax: 609-757-5373

Syracuse Region
Stephen Banko, Field Office Director
HUD-Syracuse Office
128 Jefferson Street
Syracuse, NY 13202
315-477-0616
Fax: 315-477-0196

New Jersey Region
Diane Johnson, Field Office Director
HUD-Newark Office
13th Floor, One Network Center
Newark, NJ 07102-5260
973-622-7619
Fax: 973-645-2323

Midatlantic Area

Pennsylvania Region
Milton Pratt, Regional Director
HUD-Philadelphia Office
The Wanamaker Building
100 Pennsylvania Square, E
Philadelphia, PA 19107-3380
215-656-0606
Fax: 215-656-3445

Charleston Region
George Rodriguez, Field Office Director
HUD-Charleston Office
405 Capitol Street, Suite 708
Charleston, WV 25301-1795
304-347-7000
Fax: 304-347-7050

Pittsburgh Region
Richard M. Nemoytin
Field Office Director
HUD-Pittsburgh Office
339 6th Avenue, 6th Floor
Pittsburgh, PA 15222-2515
412-644-5945
Fax: 412-644-4240

Richmond Office
MaryAnn Wilson, Field Office Director
HUD-Richmond Office
600 East Broad Street
Richmond, VA 23219-4920
804-771-2100
Fax: 804-771-2090

District of Columbia Region
Lorraine Richardson
Acting Field Office Director
HUD-Washington, DC Office
820 1st Street, NE, Suite 300
Washington, DC 20002-4205
202-275-9200
Fax: 202-275-9212

Delaware Region
Diane Lello, Acting Field Office Director
HUD-Wilmington Office
920 King Street, Suite 404
Wilmington, DE 19801-3016
302-573-6300
Fax: 302-573-6259

Maryland Region
Harold D. Young, Field Office Director
HUD-Baltimore Office, 5th Floor
10 South Howard Street
Baltimore, MD 21201-2505
410-962-2520
Fax: 410-962-1849

Southeast Area

Atlanta Region
Jay Chaplin, Regional Director
HUD-Atlanta Office
40 Marietta Street
Five Points Plaza
Atlanta, GA 30303-2806
404-331-4111
Fax: 404-730-2392

Birmingham Region
Cynthia Yarbrough, Field Office Director
HUD-Birmingham Office
950 22nd Street North, Suite 900
Birmingham, AL 35203-2617
205-731-2630
Fax: 205-290-7593

Caribbean Region
Michael A. Colon, Field Office Director
HUD-Puerto Rico Office
171 Carlos E. Chardon Avenue
San Juan, PR 00918-0903
787-766-5201
Fax: 787-766-5995

Columbia Region
Dudley Gregorie
HUD-Columbia Office
1835 Assembly Street
Columbia, SC 29201-2480
803-765-5592
Fax: 803-253-3040

Greensboro Region
Deborah Holston, Field Office Director
2306 West Meadowview Road
Greensboro, NC 27401-3707
910-547-4001
Fax: 910-547-4138

Jackson Region
Reba Cook, Field Office Director
HUD-Jackson Office
100 W. Capitol St., Room 910
Jackson, MS 39269-1096
601-965-4700
Fax: 601-965-4773

Jacksonville Region
Dwight Peterson, Field Office Director
HUD-Jacksonville Office
301 West Bay Street, Suite 2200
Jacksonville, FL 32202-5121
904-232-2627
Fax: 904-232-3759

Knoxville Region
Mark Brezina, Field Office Director
HUD-Knoxville Office
710 Locust Street, SW
Knoxville, TN 37902-2526
423-545-4384
Fax: 423-545-4569

Louisville Region
Ben Cook, Field Office Director
HUD-Louisville Office
601 West Broadway
Louisville, KY 40202
502-582-5251
Fax: 502-582-6074

Memphis Region
Yvonne Leander, Field Office Director
HUD-Memphis Office
One Memphis Place
200 Jefferson Avenue, Suite 1200
Memphis, TN 38103-2335
901-544-3367
Fax: 901-544-3697

Miami Region
Orlando Lorie, Field Office Director
HUD_Miami Office
909 SE First Avenue
Miami, FL 33131
305-536-5678
Fax: 305-536-5765

Nashville Region
Edward Pringle
Field Office Director
HUD-Nashville Office
235 Cumberland Bend Dr.
Suite 200
Nashville, TN 37228-1803
615-736-5213
Fax: 615-736-2018

Orlando Region
Michael Daly
Acting Field Office Director
HUD-Orlando Office
3751 Maguire Blvd., Room 270
Orlando, FL 32803-3032
407-648-6441
Fax: 407-648-6310

Tampa Region
Karen Jackson Sims
Acting Field Office Director
HUD-Tampa Office
500 Zack Street, Suite 402
Tampa, FL 33602-3945
813-228-2026
Fax: 813-228-2431

Midwest Area

Chicago Region
Joseph Galvan, Regional Director
HUD-Chicago Office
Ralph Metcalfe Federal Building
77 West Jackson Boulevard
Chicago, IL 60604-3507
312-353-5680
Fax: 312-886-2729

Cincinnati Region
James Cunningham, Field Office Director
HUD-Cincinnati Office
15 E. Seventh Street
Cincinnati, OH 45202-2401
513-684-3451
Fax: 513-684-6224

Cleveland Region
Douglas W. Shelby
Acting Field Office Director
HUD-Cleveland Office
1350 Euclid Avenue, Suite 500
Cleveland, OH 44115-1815
216-522-4058
Fax: 216-522-4067

Columbus Region
Thomas Leach, Field Office Director
HUD-Columbus Office
200 North High Street
Columbus, OH 43215-2499
614-469-2540
Fax: 614-469-2432

Detroit Region
Vacant
Field Office Director
HUD-Detroit Office
477 Michigan Avenue
Detroit, MI 48226-2592
313-226-7900
Fax: 313-226-5611

Grand Rapids Region
Louis K. Berra, Field Office Director
HUD-Grand Rapids Office
Trade Center Building
50 Louis Street, NW
Grand Rapids, MI 49503-2633
616-456-2100
Fax: 616-456-2114

Flint Region
Vacant
Field Office Director
HUD-Flint Office
1101 S. Saginaw St.
Flint, MI 48502-1953
517-766-5110
Fax: 517-766-5122

Indianapolis Region
William K. Fattic, Field Office Director
HUD-Indianapolis Office
151 N. Delaware St., Suite 1200
Indianapolis, IN 46204-2526
317-226-6303
Fax: 317-226-6317

Wisconsin State
Delbert Reynolds, Field Office Director
HUD-Milwaukee Office
Henry S. Reuss Federal Plaza
310 W. Wisconsin Ave.
Room 1380
Milwaukee, WI 53203-2289
414-297-3214
Fax: 414-297-3947

Minneapolis Region
Thomas Feeney, Field Office Director
HUD-Minneapolis Office
220 Second Street, South

Minneapolis, MN 55401-2195
612-370-3000
Fax: 612-370-3220

Springfield Region
Anthony Randolph, Field Office Director
HUD-Springfield Office
320 W. Washington, 7th Floor
Springfield, IL 62707
217-492-4120
Fax: 217-492-4154

Southwest

New Mexico State
Michael R. Griego, Field Office Director
HUD-Albuquerque Office
625 Silver Avenue, SW
Albuquerque, NM 87102
505-262-6463
Fax: 505-262-6704

Dallas Area
James Slater, Field Office Director
HUD-Dallas Office
Room 860
525 Griffin Street
Dallas, TX 75202-5007
214-767-8300
Fax: 214-767-8973

Arkansas State Office
Bessie Jackson, Field Office Director
HUD-Little Rock Office
425 W. Capitol Ave., Suite 900
Little Rock, AR 72201-3488
501-324-5401
Fax: 501-324-6142

Lubbock Area Office
Miguel C. Rincon, Jr., Field Office Director
HUD-Lubbock Office
1205 Texas Avenue
Lubbock, TX 79401-4093
806-472-7265
Fax: 806-472-7275

Texas State
Cynthia Leon, Regional Director
HUD-Ft. Worth Office
801 Cherry Street
P.O. Box 2905
Ft. Worth, TX 76113-2905
817-978-5980
Fax: 817-978-5567

Louisiana State Office
Patricia Hoban-Moore
HUD-New Orleans Office
Hale Boggs Building
501 Magazine Street, 9th Floor
New Orleans, LA 70130-3099
504-589-7201
Fax: 504-589-6619

Oklahoma State Office
Kevin McNeely, Field Office Director
HUD-Oklahoma City Office
500 West Main Street, Suite 400
Oklahoma City, OK 73102-2233
405-553-7500
Fax: 405-553-7588

San Antonio Area Office
Luz Day, Field Office Director
HUD-San Antonio Office
800 Dolorosa Street
San Antonio, TX 78207-4563
210-475-6806
Fax: 210-472-6804

Shreveport Region
Martha Sakre, Field Office Director
401 Edwards Street, Room 1510
Shreveport, LA 71101-3289

318-676-3440
Fax: 318-676-3407

Tulsa Region
James Colgan, Field Office Director
HUD-Tulsa Office
1516 S. Boston Ave., Suite 100
Tulsa, OK 74119-4030
918-581-7496
Fax: 918-581-7440

Great Plains Area

Missouri State
Macie Houston, Regional Director
HUD-Kansas City Office
400 State Avenue, Room 200
Kansas City, KS 66101-2406
913-551-5462
Fax: 913-551-5469

Iowa State
William McNarney, Field Office Director
HUD-Des Moines Office
210 Walnut Street, Room 239
Des Moines, IA 50309-2155
515-284-4573
Fax: 515-284-4743

St. Louis Region
Roy Pierce, Field Office Director
HUD-St. Louis Office
1222 Spruce Street, #3207
St. Louis, MO 63103-2836
314-539-6560
Fax: 314-539-6384

Nebraska State Office
Stan Quy, Field Office Director
HUD-Omaha Office
10909 Mill Valley Road
Omaha, NE 68514-3955
402-492-3103
Fax: 402-492-3150

Rocky Mountain Area
Colorado State Region
John Carson, Regional Director
HUD-Denver Office
633 17th Street, 14th Floor
Denver, CO 80202-3607
303-672-5440
Fax: 303-672-5004

Wyoming State
Vacant
Field Office Director
100 East B Street, Room 1010
P.O. Box 120
Casper, WY 82601-1969
307-261-6251
Fax: 307-261-6245

North Dakota State Region
Joel Manske, Field Office Director
HUD-Fargo Office
Federal Building
657 2nd Avenue, North, Room 366
P.O. Box 2483
Fargo, ND 58108
701-239-5040
Fax: 701-239-5249

Montana State Region
Richard Brinck, Field Office Director
HUD-Helena Office
7 W. 6th Avenue
Helena, MT 59601
406-449-5050
Fax: 406-449-5052

Utah State Region
Russell Beckley, Field Office Director
HUD-Salt Lake City Office
257 East 200 South, Room 550

Salt Lake City, UT 84111-2072
801-524-6070
Fax: 801-524-3439

South Dakota State Region
Sheryl Miller, Field Office Director
2400 W. 49th St., Room I-201
Sioux Falls, SD 57105-6558
605-330-4223
Fax: 605-330-4428

Pacific/Hawaii

California State Region
Lilly Lee, Acting Regional Director
HUD-San Francisco Office
450 Golden Gate Avenue
P.O. Box 36003
San Francisco, CA 94102-3448
415-436-6560
Fax: 415-436-6446

Fresno Region
Ann Marie Sudduth
Field Office Director
HUD-Fresno Office
2135 Fresno Street, Suite 100
Fresno, CA 93721-1718
559-487-5032
Fax: 559-487-5191

Hawaii State Region
Gordon Y. Furutani, Field Office Director
HUD-Honolulu Office
500 Ala Moana Boulevard
Suite 3A
Honolulu, HI 96813-4918
808-522-8175
Fax: 808-522-8194

Nevada State Region
Ken Lobene, Field Office Director
HUD-Las Vegas Office
333 North Rancho Drive
Atrium Building, Suite 700
Las Vegas, NV 89106-3714
702-388-6500/6208
Fax: 702-388-6244

Arizona State Region
Rebecca Flanagan, Field Office Director
HUD-Phoenix Office
One Central Avenue, Suite 600
Phoenix, AZ 85004
602-379-7100
Fax: 602-379-3985

Reno Region
Wayne Waite, Acting Field Office Director
HUD-Reno Office
3702 S. Virginia Street
Reno, NV 89502-6581
775-784-5356
Fax: 775-784-5066

Sacramento Region
William L. Bolton
Field Office Director
HUD-Sacramento Office
925 "L" Street
Sacramento, CA 95814
916-498-5220
Fax: 916-498-5262

San Diego Region
Charles Wilson, Field Office Director
HUD-San Diego Office
750 B Street, Suite 1600
San Diego, CA 92101-8131
619-557-5310
Fax: 619-557-5312

Santa Ana Region
Theresa Camiling
Field Office Director

HUD-Santa Ana Office
1600 N. Broadway, Suite 101
Santa Ana, CA 92706-3927
714-796-5577
Fax: 714-796-1285

Los Angeles Region
Jason Coughenour, Field Office Director
HUD-Los Angeles Office
611 West 6th, Suite 800
Los Angeles, CA 90017
213-894-8007
Fax: 213-894-8110

Tucson Region
Sharon Atwell, Field Office Director
HUD-Tucson Office
160 North Stone Avenue
Suite 100
Tucson, AZ 85701-1467
602-670-6000
Fax: 602-670-6207

Northwest Alaska Area
Washington State Region
John Meyers, Regional Director
HUD-Seattle Office
909 First Avenue, Suite 200
Seattle, WA 98104-1000
206-220-5101
Fax: 206-220-5108

Alaska State Region
Colleen Bickford
Field Office Director
HUD-Anchorage Office
949 East 36th Avenue, Suite 401
Anchorage, AK 99508-4399
907-271-4170
Fax: 907-271-3778

Idaho State Region
Constance Hogland
Field Office Director
HUD-Boise Office

Plaza IV, Suite 220
800 Park Boulevard
Boise, ID 83712-7743
208-334-1900
Fax: 208-334-9648

Oregon State Region
Thomas C. Cusack
Field Office Director
HUD-Portland Office
400 SW 6th Avenue #700
Portland, OR 97204-1632
503-326-2568

Spokane Region
Arlene Patton, Field Office Director
HUD-Spokane Office
US Courthouse Bldg.
920 W. Riverside, Suite 588
Spokane, WA 99201-1010
509-353-0674
Fax: 509-353-0682

> *"Most modern complex societies are rich in possible sources of support when we are making a change. There has been an unprecedented emergence of social groups designed to provide support to those who are seeking change. Over 15,000,000 Americans of all kinds are involved in nearly 500,000 organized groups of this nature."*
>
> Source: *Ambition: How We Manage Success and Failure Throughout Our Lives*, Gilbert Brim, Basic Books, 1992

Microloans

The U.S. Small Business Administration's (SBA) Microloan Program was developed for those times when just a small loan can make the real difference between success and failure. Under this program, loans range from less than $100 to a maximum of $35,000.

SBA has made these funds available to nonprofit organizations for the purpose of lending to small businesses. These organizations can also provide intense management and technical assistance. A microloan must be repaid on the shortest term possible — no longer than six years, depending on the earnings of the business. The interest rates on these loans will be competitive and based on the cost of money to the intermediary lender.

This program is currently available in 44 states. To learn which nonprofit organizations in your area offer this program, contact U.S. Small Business Administration, 409 3rd St., SW, Suite 8300, Washington, DC 20416; 800-8-ASK-SBA; 202-205-6490; {www.sba.gov}.

Participating Intermediary Lenders and Non-Lending Technical Assistance Providers

Intermediary Lenders
Alabama
Community Equity Investments, Inc.
302 N. Barcelona St.
Pensacola, FL 32501
850-595-6234
888-605-2505
Fax: 850-595-6264
Email: bigdanfla@aol.com
www.ceii.pensacola.com
Executive Director: Dan Horvath
Microloan Contact: Elbert Jones
Service Area: Baldwin, Mobile, Washington, Clarke, Monroe, Escambia, Conecuh, Covington, Geneva, Coffee, Dale, Henry, and Houston counties

Birmingham Business Resource Center
110 12th Street North
Birmingham, AL 35203
205-250-6380
Fax: 205-250-6384
Email: BBRC@Inlinenet.net
www.bbrc.biz/
Executive Director: Robert Dickinson, Jr.
Microloan Contact: Rodney E. Evans
Service Area: Jefferson County

Southeast Community Capital
1020 Commerce Park Drive
Oak Ridge, TN 37830
865-220-2020
Fax: 865-220-2030
Email: hortonw@tech2020.org
http://www.tech2020.org
Executive Director: Don Welty
Microloan Contact: David Bradshaw
Service Area: Bibb, Blount, Calhoun, Chambers, Chilton, Colbert, Coosa, Cullman, De Kalb, Elmore, Etowah, Fayette, Franklin, Hale, Jackson, Lauderdale, Lawrence, Limestone, Macon, Madison, Marion, Marshall, Morgan, Pickens, Randolph, St. Clair, Shelby, Talladega, Tallapoosa, Tuscaloosa, Walker, and Winston

Alaska
Alaska Village Initiatives
1577 C St., Suite 104
Anchorage, AK 99501

907-274-5400
Fax: 907-263-9971
Email: avi@ruralak.org
www.akvillage.com/index.html
Executive Director: Tom Harris
Microloan Contact: Tom Harris
Service Area: State of Alaska.

Arizona
Prestamos CDFI, LLC
1112 E. Buckeye Rd.
Phoenix, AZ 85034-4043
602-252-0483
Fax: 602-252-0484
Executive Director: Pete Garcia
Microloan Contact: Joe Martinez
www.cplc.org
Service Area: Urban Maricopa and Pima counties, Graham and Gila counties (including Point of Pines Reservation and the Southwestern area of Fort Apache Reservation), Coconino and Mohave counties (including the Kaibab, Havasupai, and Hualapai Reservations and western portions of the Navajo and Hopi Reservations), Yavapai and LaPaz counties

PPEP Housing Development Co.
Micro Ind. Credit Rural Org.
802 E. 46th St.
Tucson, AZ 85713
520-806-9513
Fax: 520-806-9515
Email: gballesteros@ppepruralinst.org
www.ppep.org
Exec. Director: Frank Ballesteros
Microloan Contact: Frank Ballesteros
Service Area: Cochise, Santa Cruz, Pinal, Yuma, rural Pima, and rural Maricopa counties including the Fort McDowell, Gila River, Maricopa, Papago, Salt River, and San Xavier Indian Reservations.

Self-Employment Loan Fund, Inc.
1601 North 7th St., Suite 340
Phoenix, AZ 85006
602-340-8834
Fax: 602-340-8953
Email: self@uswest.net
www.selfloanfund.org

Executive Director: Caroline Newsom
Microloan Contact: Caroline Newsom
Service Area: Maricopa County

Arizona Council for Economic Conversion
10 East Broadway, Suite 210
P.O. Box 42108
Tucson, AZ 85701
520-620-1241
Email: bmurphy@acec-az.org
Pimawbe.vstone.com/
Executive Director: Rosalyn Boxer
Microloan Contact: Bart T. Murphy
Service Area: Tucson, and Pima Counties

Arkansas
White River Planning and Development District, Inc.
1652 White Drive
P.O. Box 2396
Batesville, AR 72501
870-793-5233
Fax: 870-793-4035
Email: billray@wrpdd.org
www.arkplan.org/WRPDD.html
Executive Director: Van C. Thomas
Microloan Contact: Bill Ray
Service Area: Cleburne, Fulton, Independence, Izard, Jackson, Sharp, Stone, Van Buren, White, and Woodruff counties

Southern Financial Partners
605 Main Street
Pine Bluff, AR 71923
870-246-9739
Fax: 870-246-2182
Email: slinn@ehbt.com
www.southernfinancialpartners.org
Executive Director: Penny Penrose
Microloan Contact: William Matthews or Sandy Linn
Service Area: Southern and extreme northeast areas of the State including Arkansas, Ashley, Bradley, Calhoun, Chicot, Clark, Clay, Cleveland, Columbia, Craighead, Dallas, Desha, Drew, Garland, Grant, Greene, Hempstead, Hot Spring, Howard, Jefferson Lafayette, Lawrence, Lincoln, Little River, Lonoke, Miller, Mississippi, Montgomery, Nevada, Ouachita, Phillips, Pike, Poinsett,

Polk, Prairie, Pulaski, Randolph, Saline, Sevier, and Union Counties

Forge-Financing Ozarks Rural Growth and Economy
208 East Main P.O. Box 1138
Huntsville, AR 72740
501-738-1585
Fax: 501-738-6288
Email: forgein@madisoncounty.net
Executive Director: Alva C. West
Microloan Contact: Charlie Stockton
Service Area: Crawford, Baxter, Yell, Perry, Conway, Boone, Madison, Marion, Carroll, Franklin, Pope, Benton, Washington, Searcy, and Newton

California

Arcata Economic Development Corporation
100 Ericson Court, Suite 100
Arcata, CA 95521
707-822-4616
Fax: 707-822-8982
Email: arianek@reninet.com
www.aedc1.org
Executive Director: Jim Kimbrell
Microloan Contact: Arianne Knoeller or Kelly Denny
Service Area: Del Norte, Humboldt, Lake, Mendocino, Siskiyou, and Trinity counties

California Coastal Rural Development Corporation
221 Main St., Suite 300
P.O. Box 479
Salinas, CA 93906
831-424-1099
Fax: 831-424-1094
Email: rey_hidalgo@calcoastal.org
www.calcoastal.org/
Executive Director: Herb Aarons
Microloan Contact: Ray Hidalgo
Service Area: Santa Cruz, Monterey, San Benito, San Luis Obispo, Santa Barbara, and Ventura

Southeast Asian Community Center
875 O'Farrell St.
San Francisco, CA 94109
415-885-2743
Fax: 415-885-3253
Email: seaccphilip@juno.com
Executive Director: Philip Tuong Duy Nguyen
Microloan Contact: Victor Hsi
Service Area: Alameda, Contra Costa, Marin, Merced, Sacramento, San Francisco, San Joaquin, San Mateo, Santa Clara, and Stanislaus counties

Valley Small Business Development Corporation
3417 W. Shaw, Suite 100
Fresno, CA 93711
559-438-9680
Fax: 559-438-9690
Email: valleysb@psnw.com
www.vsbdc.com/
Executive Director: Michael E. Foley
Microloan Contact: Lee Takikawa
Service Area: Fresno, Kings, Kern, Stanislaus, Madera, Mariposa, Merced, Tuolumne, and Tulare counties

CDC Small Business Finance Corp.
925 Ft. Stockton Dr.
San Diego, CA 92110
619-291-3594
Fax: 619-291-6954
Email: arobinson@cdcloans.com
www.cdcloans.com/
President: Kurt Chilcott
Microloan Contact: Alex Robinson
Service Area: San Diego

Oakland Business Development Corporation
519 17th Street Suite 100
Oakland, CA 94612
510-763-4297
Fax: 510-763-1273
Email: mike@obdc.com robert@obdc.com
www.obdc.com/
Executive Director: Micheal McPherson
Microloan Contact: Robert Gebauer
Service Area: Alameda and Contra Costa counties

PCR Small Business Development
3255 Wilshire Blvd.
Los Angeles, CA 90010
213-739-2999, ext. 222
Fax: 213-739-0639
Email: mark.robertson@pcrcorp.org
www.pcrcorp.org/
President: R. D. Lottie, Jr.,
Microloan Contact: Mark Robertson, Jr.
Service Area: South Los Angeles County

Sierra Economic Development District
560 Wall Street Suite F
Auburn, CA 95603
530-823-4703
Fax: 530-823-4142
Email: betty@sedd.org dille@sedd.org
www.sedd.org/
Executive Director: Betty Riley
Microloan Contact: Tom Dille
Service Area: Modoc, El Dorado, Lassen, Nevada, Plumas, Sierra, and Placer counties

Valley Economic Development Corp.
5121 Van Nuys Blvd. 3rd Floor
Van Nuys, CA 91403
818-907-9977
Fax: 818-907-9720
Email: roberto@vedc.org
www.vedc.org
Executive Director: Roberto Barragan
Microloan Contact: Rebecca Haas
Service Area: Los Angeles and Orange County

Colorado

Colorado Enterprise Fund
1888 Sherman St. Suite 530
P.O. Box 2135
Denver, CO 80203
303-860-0242
Fax: 303-860-0409
Email: microloans@coloradoenterprisefund.org
www.coloradoenterprisefund.org
Executive Director: Cecilia H. Prinster
Microloan Contact: Angela Valdez
Service Area: City of Denver, and Adams, Arapahoe, Boulder, Denver, and Jefferson counties

Region 10 LEAP for Economic Development
P.O. Box 849
300 N. Cascade St., Suite 1
Montrose, CO 81401
970-249-2436
Fax: 970-249-2488
Email: region10@rmii.com
www.region10.net
Executive Director: Leslie Jones
Microloan Contact: Bob Bolt
Service Area: West Central area including Delta, Gunnison, Hinsdale, Montrose, Ouray, and San Miguel counties

Connecticut

Community Economic Development Fund
50-G Weston Street
Hartford, CT 06120
860-249-3800
Fax: 860-249-2500
Email: donnwertenbach@cedf.org
www.cedf.com/

Executive Director: Donna Wertenbach
Microloan Contact: Thomas Holloway
Service Area: Statewide

Connecticut Community Investment Corp.
100 Crown St.
New Haven, CT 06510
203-776-6172
Fax: 203-776-6837
Email: mcousineau@ctcic.org
Email: bmcmanus@ctcic.org
www.ctcic.org
Executive Director: Salvatore J. Brancati, Jr.
Microloan Contact: Mark Cousineau
Service Area: Statewide

Delaware

Wilmington Economic Development Corporation
100 W. 10th St., Suite 706
Wilmington, DE 19801
302-571-9088
Fax: 302-652-5679
Email: wedco@wedcode.org
www.wedco.org/
Executive Director: Constance McCarthy
Microloan Contact: Constance McCarthy
Service Area: New Castle county, in the cities of Wilmington, Newark, New Castle, Middletown, Odessa, and Townsend

District of Columbia

ARCH Development Corporation
1227 Good Hope Rd., SE
Washington, DC 20020
202-889-5023
Fax: 202-889-5035
Executive Director: Duane Gautier
Microloan Contact: Teina Linthicum
Service Area: Portions of the District of Columbia commonly referred to as Adams Morgan, Mount Pleasant, and Anacostia, Congress Heights, Columbia Heights, and 14th Street Corridor

H Street Development Corp.
501 H Street, NE
Washington, DC 20002
202-544-8353
Fax: 202-544-3051
Email: yulonda.queen@hstreetcdc.org
www.cdsc.org/404.html
Executive Director: William Barrow
Microloan Contact: Yulonda Queen
Service Area: West-the Anacostia River; East-7th Street, NW; North-Benning Road to K Street; and South-the Southeast/ Southwest Freeway: Servicing Capitol Hill, H Street, NE, Lincoln Park, Mt. Vernon Square, Judiciary Square, Benning Road-West of the Anacostia River, Union Station, Stadium Armory, and Lower North Capitol. Eastern border of North Capitol to Rhode Island to 7th Street NW; West-Anacostia River; North-Eastern Avenue to North Capitol; and Southeast/Southwest Freeway: Servicing Eckington, Catholic University, Michigan Park, Edgewood, Brookland, Ft. Lincoln, New York Avenue, Florida Avenue, Brentwood-DC, Woodridge, Trinidad, and NE Rhode Island Avenue, Silver Springs, Takoma Park, Hyattsville, Riverdale, Bladensburg, Seat Pleasant, Capitol Heights, District Heights, Cheverly, Landover, Suitland, Hillcrest Heights, Marlow Heights, Oxon Hill, Mt. Ranier, and Coral Hills.

East of the River Community Development Corporation
3101 Martin Luther King, Jr. Ave., SE
Washington, DC 20032
202-561-4974
Fax: 202-561-4978
Email: gilliam@ercdc.org
www.ercdc.org/

Exec. Director: W. Retta Gilliam
Microloan Contact: W. Retta Gilliam
Service Area: Portion of southeast Washington DC commonly known as Ward 8. Westernmost boundary of the Anacostia River; Oxon Creek, Oxon Run Drive to Southern Avenue, SE; Northeast to Naylor Road, SE; Southwest of Altamont Place, SE; Pearson Street, SE to Erie Street, SE; West of Erie to Morris Street, SE; North of Chicago Street, SE to Interstate 295; North of Interstate 295 to the 11th Street bridge southeast to the Anacostia River

Florida

Community Equity Investments, Inc.
302 North Barcelona St.
Pensacola, FL 32501
850-595-6234
Fax: 850-595-6264
Email: bigdanfla@aol.com
www.ceii.pensacola.com/
Executive Director: Dan Horvath
Microloan Contact: Elbert Jones
Service Area: Florida Panhandle including Bay, Calhoun, Escambia, Gadsden, Gulf, Jackson, Holmes, Liberty, Leon, Franklin, Wakulla, Walton, Wasington, Okaloosa, and Santa Rosa counties

United Gainesville Community Dev. Corp., Inc.
505 NW 2nd Avenue
P.O. Box 2518
Gainesville, FL 32602
352-334-0943
Fax: 352-334-0947
Email: vian@ugcdc.org
Email: lyndah@ugcdc.org
Executive Director: Appie L. Graham
Microloan Contact: Appie L. Graham
Service Area: Alachua and Marion counties

Central Florida Community Development Corporation
P.O. Box 15065
Daytona Beach, FL 32115
368-258-7520
Fax: 368-238-3428
Email: geraldc@n-jcenter.com
www.cfcdc.com/
Executive Director:
Microloan Contact: Gerald O. Chester
Service Area: Brevard county

Clearwater Neighborhood Housing Services, Inc.
608 North Garden Avenue
Clearwater, FL 33755
727-442-4155
Fax: 727-446-4911
Executive Director: Isay M. Gulley
Microloan Contact: John J. Moloney
Service Area: City of Clearwater and Pinellas County

Minority/Women Business Enterprise Alliance, Inc.
625 E. Colonial Drive
Orlando, FL 32803
407-428-5860
Fax: 407-428-5869
www.allianceflorida.com/
Executive Director: Geovanny Sepulveda
Microloan Contact: Geovanny Sepulveda
Service Area: Orange, Osceola, Lake, Seminole, Polk, Hillsborough, Sumter, Brevard, Volusia, and Marion counties

Partners for Self-Employment, Inc./
d.b.a./Micro-Business, USA
3000 Biscayne Boulevard Suite 102
Miami, FL 33137
877-722-4505

Fax: 305-438-1411
www.microbusinessusa.org/
Executive Director: Diane Silverman
Microloan Contact: Diane Silverman
Service Area: Miami-Dade, Broward, Palm Beach and Pinellas counties

Tampa Bay Economic Development Corporation
2105 N. Nebraska Avenue 2nd Floor
Tampa, FL 33602
813-274-7969
Fax: 813-274-7551
www.tampagov.net/dept_TEDCO/
Executive Director:
Microloan Contact: George Guida
Service Area: Hillsborough county

The Business Loan Fund of the Palm Beaches, Inc.
1016 North Dixie Highway, 2nd Floor
West Palm Beach, FL 33401
561-838-9027
Fax: 561-838-9029
Email: blfpb@evcom.net
www.businessloanfund.org/index.html
Executive Director: John B. Brown
Microloan Contact: John B. Brown
Service Area: Palm Beach County, Hendry, Indian River, Martin, Palm Beach County Development Regions and St. Lucie

Georgia

Enterprise Funding Corp/GRASP Enterprises
241 Peachtree Street, Suite 200
Atlanta, GA 30303
404-659-5955
Fax: 404-880-9561
Email: tscott@graspnet.org
www.grasp.net
Executive Director: Maurice Coakley
Microloan Contact: Tim Scott
Service Area: Fulton, Dekalb, Cobb, Gwinnett, Fayette, Clayton, Henry, Douglas, and Rockdale counties

Small Business Assistance Corporation
111 E. Liberty St., Suite 100
P.O. Box 10750
Savannah, GA 31412-0716
912-232-4700
Fax: 912-232-0385
Email: toreilly@sbacsav.com
www.sbacsav.com/
Executive Director: Tony O'Reilly
Microloan Contact: Tony O'Reilly/Stephen George
Service Area: Appling, Atkinson, Brooks, Bacon, Berrien, Ben Hill, Bryan, Bulloch, Bleekly, Brantley, Coffee, Charlton, Camden, Clinch, Candler, Cook, Chatham, Dodge, Emanuel, Echols, Effingham, Evans, Glynn, Irwin, Johnson, Jeff Davis, Laurens, Liberty, Long, Lowndes, Lanier, McIntosh, Montgomery, Pierce, Tift, Turner, Telfair, Truetlen, Toombs, Tattnall, Ware, Wilcox, Wayne, and Wheeler counties

Southeast Community Capital
1020 Commerce Park Drive
Oak Ridge, TN 37830
865-220-2020
Fax: 865-220-2030
Email: hortonw@tech2020.org
Executive Director: Don Welty
Microloan Contact: David Bradshaw
Service Area: Barrow, Bartow, Carroll, Cherokee, Dade, Elbert, Fannin, Floyd, Franklin, Gordon, Gwinnett, Hall, Hart, Heard, Paulding, Pickens, Polk, Stephens, Union, Walker, and Whitfield

Hawaii

Pacific Gateway Center

720 N. King St.
Honolulu, HI 96817
808-845-3918
Fax: 808-842-1962
Email: pgcmyaing@hotmail.com
www.pacificgateway.org
Exec. Dir.: Tin Myaing Thein
Microloan Contact:
Service Area: Statewide

Idaho

Sage Community Resources
10624 W. Executive Dr.
Boise, ID 83713
208-322-7033
Fax: 208-322-3569
Email: pmchoate@ida-ore.com
www.sageidaho.com/
Executive Director: Robert Barber
Microloan Contact: Bob Richards
Service Area: Payette, Washington, Adams, Valley, Gem, Boise, Elmore, Ada, Canyon and Owhyee counties

Panhandle Area Council
11100 Airport Dr.
Hayden, ID 83835-9743
208-772-0584
Fax: 208-772-6196
Email: pacbus@nidlink.com or ksmith@pacni.org
www.pacni.org/
Exec. Dir.: James Deffenbaugh
Microloan Contact: kay Kitchel
Service Area: Northern Panhandle including Benewah, Bonner, Boundary, Kotenai, and Shoshone counties

Illinois

Accion Chicago, Inc.
3245 W. 26th
Chicago, IL 60623
773-376-9004
Fax: 773-376-9048
Email: lpacheco@accionchicago.org
www.accionchicago.org/
President: F. Leroy Pacheco
Microloan Contact: Jonathan Brereton
Service Area: Cook County (including parts of Chicago), Lake, McHenry, Dekalb, Kane, Dupage, Kendall, Grundy, Kankanee, Will, and Lasalle counties

Justine Petersen Housing & Reinvestment Corporation
5031 Northrup Avenue
St. Louis, MO 63110
314-664-5051 ext. 117
Fax: 314-644-5364
Email: sflanigan@justinepetersen.org
http://justinepetersen.org/
Executive Director: Robert Boyle
Microloan Contact: Sheri Fannigan-Vasquez
Service Area: Clinton, Jersey, Madison, and St. Clair counties

Neighborhood Inst./Women's Self Employment Project
11 South LaSalle Street, Suite 1850
Chicago, IL 60603
312-606-8255
Fax: 312-606-9215
Email: wsepaa@wsep.com
www.wsep.net
Executive Director: Wanda White
Microloan Contact: Wanda White
Service Area: Portions of the City of Chicago

Indiana

Seed-Corp
216 W. Allen Street
Bloomington, IN 47403
812-323-7827

Fax: 812-335-7352
Email: tbrown@thestarcenter.com
www.seed-corp.org
Executive Director: Terri Brown
Microloan Contact: Charlotte Zietlow, Beth Kuebler
Service Area: Morgan, Owen, Greene, Lawrence, Monroe, Brown, and Jackson Bartholomew, Decatur, Jennings counties

Iowa

Siouxland Economic Development Corporation
428 Insurance Center
507 7th St.
P.O. Box 447
Sioux City, IA 51102
712-279-6286
Fax: 712-279-6920
Email: glenda@simpco.org
www.siouxlandedc.com
Executive Director: Ken Beekley
Microloan Contact:
Service Area: Cherokee, Ida Monona, Plymouth, Sioux, and Woodbury counties

Kansas

South Central Kansas Economic Development District, Inc.
209 East William Street, Suite 300
Wichita, KS 67214
316-262-7035
Fax: 316-262-7062
www.sckedd.org/
Exec. Dir.: William Bolin
Microloan Contact: Christie Henry
Service Area: Butler, Chautauqua, Cowley, Elk, Greenwood, Harper, Harvey, Kingman, Marion, McPherson, Reno, Rice, Sedgwick, and Sumner counties

Growth Opportunity Connection (Go Connection)
4747 Troost Ave.
Kansas City, MO 64110
816-235-6146
Fax: 816-756-1530
Email: info@goconnection.org
www.goconnection.org
Executive Director: Alan Corbet
Microloan Contact: Rebecca Gubbels
Service Area: Wyandotte, Johnson, Douglas, and Leavenworth counties

Kentucky

Community Ventures Corporation
1450 N. Broadway
Lexington, KY 40505
816-231-0054
Fax: 816-231-0261
Email: cvccorp@prodigy.net
www.cvcky.org/
Executive Director: Kevin Smith
Microloan Contact: Tyrone Tyra/David Collins
Service Area: Anderson, Bourbon, Boyle, Clark, Estill, Fayette, Franklin, Garrard, Harrison, Jessamine, Lincoln, Madison, Mercer, Nicholas, Powell, Scott, and Woodford counties

Kentucky Highlands Investment Corporation
362 Whitley Rd.
P.O. Box 1738
London, KY 40743-1738
606-864-5175
Fax: 606-864-5194
Email: cbowles@khic.org
www.khic.org/default.htm
Executive Director: Jerry Rickett
Microloan Contact: Edgar Davis/Cindy Bowles
Service Area: Bell, Clay, Clinton, Harlan,

Jackson, McCreary, Rockcastle, Wayne, and Whitley counties

Louisville Central Development Corporation/Business Plus
1407 W. Jefferson St., Suite 200
Louisville, KY 40203
502-583-8821
Fax: 502-583-8824
Email: swatkins@louisvillecentralcenters.org
www.lcccnews.org
Executive Director: Sam Watkins Jr.
Microloan Contact: Kirk Bright
Service Area: Jefferson County/Primary focus Enterprise Empowerment Zone

Purchase Area Development District
1002 Medical Drive
P.O. Box 588
Mayfield, KY 42066
502-247-7171
Fax: 502-251-6110
Email: henry.hodges@mail.state.ky.uw
www.purchaseadd.org/
Executive Director: Henry Hodges
Microloan Contact: Norma Reed-Drouin
Service Area: Ballard, Calloway, Carlisle, Fulton, Graves, Hickman, McCracken and Marshall counties

Louisiana

NewCorp Business Assistance Center
1600 Canal Street, Suite 601
New Orleans, LA 70112
504-539-9340
Fax: 504-539-9343
Email: newcorpinfo@newcorpbac.net
URL: www.newcorpbac.net
Executive Director: Vaughn R. Fauria
Microloan Contact: Romona D. Summers
Service Area: State of Louisiana

Maine

Coastal Enterprises, Inc.
P.O. Box 268
36 Water Street
Wiscasset, ME 04578
207-882-7552
Fax: 207-882-7308
Email: efg@cei.maine.org or
jgs@cei.maine.org
www.ceimaine.org/
Executive Director: Ronald Phillips
Microloan Contact: Ellen Golden
Service Area: Statewide excluding Aroostock, Piscataquis, Washington, Oxford, Penobscot and Hancock counties

Northern Maine Development Commission
302 S. Main St.
P.O. Box 779
Caribou, ME 04736
207-498-8736
Fax: 207-493-3108
Email: rclark@nmdc.org
www.nmdc.org/indexv1.cfm
Executive Director: Robert Clark
Microloan Contact: Duane Walton
Service Area: Aroostook
 In consortium with
 Eastern Maine Development Corporation
 One Cumberland Pl., Suite 300
 Bangor, ME 04401
 207-942-6389
 Fax: 207-942-3548
 Email: dmetzler@emdc.org
 Executive Director: David Cole
 Microloan Contact: Debbie Metzler
 Service Area: Hancock, Penobscot, Piscataquis, and Washington counties

Community Concepts, Inc.
19 Market Sq.
P.O. Box 278

South Paris, ME 04281
207-743-7716
Fax: 207-743-6513
Email: wriseman@community-concepts.org
www.community-concepts.org/
Executive Director: Charleen Chase
Microloan Contact: Walter Riseman
Service Area: Oxford county

Androscoggin Valley Council of Government
125 Manley Road
Auburn, ME 04210
207-783-9186
Fax: 207-783-5211
Email: gwhitney@avcog.org
www.avcog.org/
Executive Director: Robert J. Thompson
Microloan Contact: Julie Sherman
Service Area: Androscoggin, Franklin and Oxford counties

Maryland

The Development Credit Fund
2526 N. Charles St. Suite 200
Baltimore, MD 21218
410-235-8100
Fax: 410-235-5899
Email: ejohnson@developmentcredit.net
www.developmentcredit.com/
Executive Director: Acknell M. Muldrow, II
Microloan Contact: Erik Johnson
Service Area: Statewide Maryland excluding Montgomery and Prince Georges counties

H Street Community Development Corporation
501 H Street, NE
Washington, DC 20002
202-544-8353
Fax: 202-544-3051
Email: oomhscdc@aol.com
www.hstreetcdc.org/
Exec. Director: William Barrow
Microloan Contact: Yulonda Queen
Service Area: Montgomery and Prince George's counties

Massachusetts

Economic Development Industrial Corp. of Lynn
37 Central Square, 3rd Floor
Lynn, MA 01901
617-581-9399
Fax: 617-581-9731
Email: pdeveau@shore.net
Exec. Director: Peter M. DeVeau
Microloan Contact: Peter M. DeVeau/Mary Smalley
Service Area: City of Lynn

Jewish Vocational Service, Inc.
105 Chauncy St., 6th Floor
Boston, MA 02111
617-451-8147
Fax: 617-451-9973
Email: ckorsh@jvs-boston.org
www.jvs-bosten.org/
Exec. Dir.: Barbara Rosenbaum
Microloan Contact: Erik Korsh
Service Area: Greater Boston with special emphasis on businesses in the Boston Enterprise Zone/Boston Empowerment Zone, and businesses in Mattapan, Dorchester, Roxbury, Hyde Park, and Jamaica Plain

Jobs for Fall River, Inc.
One Government Center
Fall River, MA 02722
508-324-2620
Fax: 508-677-2840
Email: kenfiolajn@aol.com
Executive Director: Kenneth Fiola
Microloan Contact: Stephen Parr
Service Area: City of Fall River

Greater Springfield Entrepreneurial Fund
1176 Main St.
Springfield, MA 01103
413-781-6900
Fax: 413-736-0650
Email: hcetc@javanet.com
Executive Director: Jim Krzytofik
Microloan Contact: James Asselin
Service Area: Hampden County excluding the
towns of Chester and Chicopes.

Western Massachusetts Enterprise Fund
P.O. Box 1077
Greenfield, MA 01302
413-774-4033
Fax: 413-773-3673
Email: info@wmef.org
www.wmef.org/
Exec. Director: Christopher Sikes
Microloan Contact: Moon Morgan
Service Area: Berkshire, Franklin counties, the
towns of Chester and Chicopes within
Hampden county, the towns of Athol,
Petersham, Phillipston and Royalston within
Worcester county, and Hampshire county.

Community Development Transportation
Lending Services
1341 G Street, NW, Suite 600
Washington, DC 20005
202-661-0210
Fax: 202-737-9197
Email: Kellogg@ctaa.org
www.ctaa.org/transitfunding/
Executive Director: Dale J. Marsico
Microloan Contact: Patrick Kellogg
Service Area: North Central Massachusetts -
county subdivisions of Athol, Winchendon,
Gardner, Templeton, Phillipston, Orange,
Erving, Wendell, Montague, Gill, and
Greenfield counties

South Eastern Economic Development
Corp/SEED
80 Dean Street
Taunton, MA 02780
508-822-1020
Fax: 508-880-7869
Email: SEEDCORP@aol.com
www.seedcorp.com/
Executive Director: Maria Gooch-Smith
Microloan Contact: Janice Johnson Plumer
Service Area: SE Massachusetts – Norfolk,
Bristol, Plymouth,Barnstable, Dukes, and
Nantucket counties

Michigan
Center for Empowerment and Economic
Development (CEED)
2002 Hogback Rd., Suite 12
Ann Arbor, MI 48105
734-677-1400
Fax: 734-677-1465
Email: mrichards@wwnet.net
www.miceed.org/
Exec. Director: Michelle Richards
Microloan Contact: Michelle Richards
Service Area: Washtenaw, Oakland, Wayne
and Livingston counties.

Community Capital Development Corp.
The Walter Reuther Center
316 W. Water St.
Flint, MI 48503
810-239-5847
Fax: 810-239-5575
Email: ccdc@tir.com
Executive Director: Harold Hill
Microloan Contact: Jarasha Washington
Service Area: Genesee county

Northern Economic Initiatives Corp.
228 West Washington St.
Marquette, MI 49855

906-226-1662
800-254-2156
Fax: 906-228-5572
Email: todd_horton@northernminits.com
www.northerninitiatives.com
Microloan Contact: Todd Horton
Service Area: Upper Peninsula of Michigan.

Rural Michigan Intermediary Relending
Program, Inc.
121 East Front Street Suite 201
Traverse City, MI 49686
231-941-5858
Fax: 231-941-4616
Email: mhaddad@timbc.com
Executive Director: Michael Haddad
Microloan Contact: Stephen Spencer
Service Area: Emmet, Charlevoix, Antrim,
Leelanau, Benzie, Grand, Traverse, Kalkaska,
Manistee, Wexford, Missaukee, Cheboygan,
Presque Isle, Otsego, Montmorency, Alpena,
Crawford, Oscoda, Alcona, Roscommon,
Ogemaw, Iosco, Osceola, Mason, Lake
counties

Saginaw Economic Development Corporation
301 E. Genesee, 3rd Floor
Saginaw, MI 48607
989-759-1395
Fax: 989-754-1715
Email: SEDCLW@aol.com
www.saginawfuture.com/
Executive Director: Leslie Weaver
Microloan Contact: Leslie Weaver
Service Area: Saginaw county

Minnesota
Northeast Entrepreneur Fund, Inc.
8355 Unity Drive, Suite 100
Virginia, MN 55792
218-749-4191
800-422-0374
Fax: 218-741-4249
Email: info@necfund.org
www.entrepreneurfund.org
Exec. Director: Mary Mathews
Microloan Contact: Alison Beauregard
Service Area: Koochiching, Itasca, St. Louis,
Aitkin, Carlton, Cook Cass, Pine and Lake
counties

Women Venture
2324 University Ave., Suite 200
St. Paul, MN 55112
651-646-3808
Fax: 651-291-2597
Email: sbaker@womenventure.org
www.womenventure.org
Exec. Director: Tene Heidelberg
Microloan Contact: Jan Jordet
Service Area: Cities of Minneapolis and St.
Paul, and Anoka, Carver, Chisago, Dakota,
Hennepin, Isanti, Ramsey, Scott, Steele,
Washington, and Wright counties

Minneapolis Consortium of Community
Developers
2308 Central Ave. NE
Minneapolis, MN 55418
612-789-7337
Fax: 612-789-8448
Email: jroth@cando.org
www.mccdmn.org/
Executive Director: Jim Roth
Microloan Contact: Jim Roth
Service Area: Portions of the City of
Minneapolis

Northwest Minnesota Foundation
4225 Technology Drive, NW
Bemidji, MN 56601
218-759-2057
Fax: 218-759-2328
Email: timw@nwmf.org

www.nwmf.org
Executive Director: John Ostem
Microloan Contact: Tim Wang
Service Area: Beltrami, Clearwater, Hubbard,
Kittsson, Lake of the Woods, Mahnomen,
Marshall, Norman, Pennington, Polk, Red
Lake, and Rousseau counties

Southern Minnesota Initiative Foundation
525 Florence Avenue
P.O. Box 695
Owatonna, MN 55060
507-455-3215
Fax: 507-455-2098
Email: patricks@smifoundation.org
www.smifoundation.org/
Executive Director: Patrick T. Stallman
Microloan Contact: Patrick T. Stallman
Service Area: Sibley, Nicollett, LeSueur, Rice,
Wabasha, Brown, Watonwan, Blue Earth,
Waseca, Dodge, Olmsted, Winona, Martin,
Faribault, Freeborn, Mower, Fillmore, and
Houston

Southwest Minnesota Foundation
1390 HWY 15 South
P.O. Box 428
Hutchinson, MN 55350
320-587-4848
Fax: 320-587-3838
Email: bernyb@swmnfoundation.com
www.swmnfoundation.org/
Executive Director: Sherry Ristau
Microloan Contact: Bernadette Berger
Service Area: 18 counties of Southwest, MN
(Big Stone, Chippewa, Cottonwood, Jackson,
Kandiyphi, Lac qui Parle, Lincoln, Lyon,
McLeod, Meeker, Murray, Nobles, Pipestone,
Renville, Rock, Swift, and Yellow Medicine)

Mississippi
Delta Foundation
819 Main St.
Greenville, MS 38701
662-335-5291
Fax: 662-335-5295
Email: fdn@tecinfo.com
Executive Director: Harry Bowie
Microloan Contact: Lucille Dean
Service Area: Statewide excluding Issaquena,
Sharkey, Humphreys, Madison, Leake,
Kemper, Copiah, Hinds, Rankin, Newton,
Smith, Jasper, Clarke, Jones, Wayne, and
Greene counties

Friends of Children of Mississippi, Inc.
939 North President St.
Jackson, MS 39202
601-353-3264
Fax: 601-714-4278
Executive Director: Marvin Hogan
Microloan Contact: Brenetta Walker
Service Area: Statewide

Missouri
Growth Opportunity Connection (Go
Connection)
4747 Troost Ave.
Kansas City, MO 64110
816-561-8567
Fax: 816-756-1530
Email: acorbet@kc-cbi.org
www.goconnection.org/
Executive Director: Alan Corbet
Microloan Contact: Alan Corbet
Service Area: Platte, Jackson, Clay and Cass
counties.

Justine Petersen Housing & Reinvestment
Corporation
5031 Northrup Avenue
St. Louis, MO 63110
314-664-5051 ext. 117

Fax: 314-664-5364
Email: sflanigan@justinepetersen.org
www.justinepetersen.org/
Executive Director: Robert Boyle
Microloan Contact: Sheri Fanigan-Vazquez
Service Area: Counties of Franklin, Jefferson,
Lincoln, St. Charles, St. Louis, Warren, and
the City of St. Louis

Rural Missouri, Incorporated
1014 Northeast Drive
Jefferson City, MO 65109
573-635-0136
Fax: 573-635-5636
Email: zola@rmiinc.org
kluke45@mailexcel.com
www.rminc.org
Executive Director: Ken Lueckenotte
Microloan Contact: Zola Finch
Service Area: Statewide excluding Platte,
Jackson, Clay and Cass counties

Montana

Capital Opportunities/District IX HRDC, Inc.
321 E. Main St., Suite 300
Bozeman, MT 59715
406-587-5444
Fax: 406-585-3538
Executive Director: Jeff Rupp
Microloan Contact: Kittie Bowen
Service Area: Gallatin, Park and Meagher
counties

Montana Community Development Corp.
110 East Broadway, 2nd Floor
Missoula, MT 59802
406-728-9234
Fax: 406-542-6671
Email: mcdc@mtcdc.org
www.mtcdc.org/
Executive Director: Rosalie Cates
Microloan Contact: Mica Nioleyczik
Service Area: Lake, Mineral, Missoula,
Ravalli, and Sanders counties

Nebraska

Rural Enterprise Assistance Project
Center for Rural Affairs
101 S. Tallman St.
P.O. Box 406
Walthill, NE 68067
402-846-5428
Fax: 402-846-5420
Email: gerardr@cfra.org or
Jeffr@alltel.net
www.cfra.org/reap
Executive Director: Chuck Hassebrook
Microloan Contact: Jeff Reynolds/Gerard Ras
Service Area: Adams, Antelope, Banner,
Blaine, Boone, Box Butte, Boyd, Brown,
Burralo, Burt, Butler, Cass, Cedar, Cherry,
Cheyenne, Clay, Colfax, Cuming, Custer,
Dakota, Dawes, Deuel, Dixon, Dodge,
Fillmore, Franklin, Gage, Garden, Garfield,
Greeley, Hall, Hamilton, Harlan, Holt,
Howard, Jefferson, Johnson, Kearney, Keya
Paha, Kimball, Knox, Lancaster, Loup,
Madison, McPherson, Merrick, Morrill,
Nance, Nemaha, Nuckolls, Otoe, Pawnee,
Phelps, Pierce, Platte, Polk, Richardson, Rock,
Saline, Saunders, Seward, Sheridan, Sherman,
Sioux, Scottsbluff, Stanton, Thayer, Thurston,
Valley, Washington, Wayne, Webster,
Wheeler and York counties

West Central Nebraska Development District,
Inc.
201 East 2nd Street, Suite C
P.O. Box 599
Ogailala, NE 69153
308-284-6077
Fax: 308-284-6070
Email: mowcndd@lakemac.net
Executive Director: Martin O'Haus
Microloan Contact: Paul Rausch

Service Area: Arthur, Chase, Dawson, Dundy,
Frontier, Furnas, Gosper, Grant, Hayes,
Hitchcock, Hooker, Keith, Lincoln, Logan,
MacPherson, Perkins, Red Willow, and
Thomas counties

Nevada

Nevada Microenterprise Initiative
113 West Plumb Lane
Reno, NV 89509
702-734-3555
Fax: 702-734-3530
Email: asiefert@earthlink.net
www.nmimicro.org/
Executive Director: Nancy Erends Bahr
Microloan Contact: Anna Siefert
Service Area: Statewide

New Hampshire

Northern Community Investment Corp.
347 Portland St.
P.O. Box 904
St. Johnsbury, VT 05819
802-748-5101
Fax: 802-748-1884
Email: carol@ncic.org
www.ncic.org
Executive Director:
Microloan Contact: Carol Walker
Service Area: Grafton, Carol and Coos
counties

New Jersey

Trenton Business Assistance Corp.
209 E. Front St.
Trenton, NJ 08608
609-396-8271
Fax: 609-396-0559
Email: info@tbacloan.com
www.tbacloan.com
Executive Director: Deborah Osgood
Microloan Contact: Russ Haas
Service Area: Portions of the City of Trenton,
Hunterdon, Mercer, Burlington, and Warren
counties

Greater Newark Business Development
Consortium
774 Broad St., 26th Floor
Newark, NJ 07102-5265
973-242-4134
Fax: 973-242-0485
www.gnbdc.org/
Executive Director: David Means
Microloan Contact: David Means
Service Area: Bergen, Essex, Hudson,
Middlesex, Monmouth, Morris, Passaic,
Sussex and Ocean counties.

Union County Economic Development Corp.
Liberty Hall Corporate Center
1085 Morris Ave., Suite 531
Union, NJ 07083
908-527-1166
Fax: 908-527-1207
Email: afarrah@ucedc.com
www.ucedc.com
Executive Director: Maureen Tinen
Microloan Contact: Carlos N. Sanchez
Service Area: Union and Somerset counties

Community Lending and Investment Corp. of
Jersey City
30 Montgomery Street
Jersey City, NJ 07302
201-333-7797
Fax: 201-946-9367
www.jcedc.org/clic.shtml
Executive Director: Thomas Ahern
Microloan Contact: John Rodgers
Service Area: City of Jersey City

Cooperative Business Assistance Corporation
328 Market St.
2nd Floor, Suite 201
Camden, NJ 08102
856-966-8181
Fax: 856-966-0036
Email: hstonecbac2000@aol.com
www.cbaclenders.com/home.html
Executive Director: R. Michael Diemer
Microloan Contact: R. Michael Diemer
Service Area: Camden, Gloucester, Atlantic,
Cape May, Cumberland, and Salem counties

New Mexico

Women's Economic Self Sufficiency Team
414 Silver SW
Albuquerque, NM 87102-3239
505-241-4670
Fax: 505-241-4766
Email: agnes@swcp.com or dbaca@swcp.com
www.wesst.org/
Executive Director: Agnes Noonan
Microloan Contact: Debbie Baca
Service Area: Statewide

New York

Adirondack Economic Development
Corporation
60 Main St., Suite 200
P.O. Box 747
Saranac Lake, NY 12983
518-891-5523
Fax: 518-891-9820
Email: beverly@aedconline.com
www.aedconline.com/
Executive Director: Ernest Hohmeyer
Microloan Contact: Beverly Desot
Service Area: Clinton, Essex, Franklin, Fulton,
Hamilton, Herkimer, Jefferson, Lewis, Oneida,
Oswego, St. Lawrence, Saratoga, Warren and
Washington counties

Hudson Development Company
444 Warren St.
Hudson, NY 12534-2415
518-828-4718
Fax: 518-828-0901
Email: jgalvin@mhcable.com
Executive Director: Bernadina C. Torrye
Microloan Contact: John Galvin
Service Area: Columbia and Green counties

Manhattan Borough Development Corp.
55 Johns St., 17th Floor
New York, NY 10038
212-791-3660
Fax: 212-571-0873
Email: ochapman@mbdc.org
www.mbdc.org/
Executive Director: Ollie Chapman
Microloan Contact: Marta Gomez
Service Area: The borough of Manhattan

Rural Opportunities Enterprise Center, Inc.
400 East Avenue
Rochester, NY 14607
585-340-3387
Fax: 585-340-3326
Email: jdallis@ruralinc.org
www.ruralinc.org
Executive Director: Lee Beaulac
Microloan Contact: John Bell
Service Area: Allegheny, Cattaraugua,
Cayuga, Chatauqua, Erie, Genessee,
Livingston, Niagara, Ontario, Orleans, Seneca,
Steuben, Wayne, Wyoming, Ulster, Onandaga,
Monroe, Schuyler, Duchess, Chemung,
Greene, Orange, Putnam, Sullivan, and Yates
counties

Alternatives Federal Credit Union
125 N. Fulton St.
Ithaca, NY 14850
607-273-3582

Fax: 607-277-6391
Email: jhalleron@alternatives.org
www.alternatives.org/
Executive Director: William Myers
Microloan Contact: John Halleron
Service Area: Schuyler, Tompkins, Tioga,
Cortland, Chemung, and Broome counties

Buffalo Economic Renaissance Corp. (BERC)
617 Main Street
Buffalo, NY 14203
716-842-6923
Fax: 716-842-6942
Email: mcurrie@berc.org
www.growbfo.org/
Executive Director: Marie F. Curie
Microloan Contact: Marie F. Curie
Service Area: City of Buffalo

Buffalo and Erie County Industrial Land
Development Corp.
275 Oak Street
Buffalo, NY 14203
716-856-6525
Fax: 716-856-6754
Email: dkerchof@ecidany.com
www.ecidany.com/
Executive Director: David Kerchoff
Microloan Contact: David Kerchoff
Service Area: Erie County

Community Development Corporation of
Long Island
2100 Middle Country Rd
Suite 300
Centereach, NY 11720
631-471-1215
Fax: 631-471-1210
Email: tdavis@cdcli.org
www.cdcli.org
Executive Director: Wilbur Klatsky
Microloan Contact: Trevor Davis
Service Area: Suffolk and Nassau counties

Albany-Colonie Regional Chamber of
Commerce
1 Computer Drive South
Albany, NY 12205
518-453-5223
Fax: 518-453-5220
Email: walterb@ac-chamber.org
www.ac-chamber.org/
Executive Director: Madeline Taylor
Microloan Contact: Walter Burke
Service Area: Albany, Rensselaer, Saratoga,
Schenectady, Schoharie, Greene, Fulton, and
Montgomery counties

NY Assoc. for New Americans, Inc.
17 Battery Place
New York, NY 10004
212-425-5051
Fax: 212-425-7260
Email: mhandelm@nyana.org
www.nyana.org/
Executive Director: Mark Handelman
Microloan Contact: Maya Crawford
Service Area: The borough of Queens,
Manhattan, the Bronx, Brooklyn, and Staten
Island.

Renaissance Economic Development
Corporation
1 Pike Street
New York, NY 10002
212-964-6002
Fax: 212-964-6181
Email: benjamin@renaissance-ny.org
www.renaissance-ny.org/
Executive Director: Benjamin Warnke
Microloan Contact: Susan Yee
Service Area: The boroughs of Brooklyn,
Manhattan, and Queens

North Carolina
Self-Help Ventures Fund
301 W. Main St.
P.O. Box 3619
Durham, NC 27701
919-956-4400
Fax: 919-956-4600
Email: bob@self-help.org
www.self-help.com
Executive Director: Martin Eakes
Microloan Contact: Bob Schall/Carolyn
Walker
Service Area: Statewide, excluding Watauga,
Avery, Mitchell and Yancey counties

W.A.M.Y. Community Action
152 Southgate Dr., Suite 2
Box 2688
Boone, NC 28607
828-264-2421
Fax: 828-264-0952
Email: wamyloan@boone.net
Executive Director: Dr. James Jordan
Microloan Contact: Dave Lindsley
Service Area: Watauga, Avery, Mitchell, and
Yancey counties

Neuse River Development Authority, Inc.
233 Middle Street 2rd Floor
New Bern, NC 28563
252-638-6724 Ext. 3032
Fax: 252-638-1819
Email: bbrown@nrda.org
www.nrda.org/
Executive Director: Donald T. Stewart
Microloan Contact: Barbara Brown
Service Area: Carteret, Craven, Duplin,
Greene, Jones, Johnston, Lenoir, Onslow,
Pamlico and Wayne counties

North Dakota
Lake Agassiz Regional Development
Corporation
417 Main Ave.
Fargo, ND 58103
701-235-1197
Fax: 701-235-6706
Email: darin@lakeagassiz.com
Executive Director: Irvin Rustad
Microloan Contact: Darin Bullinger
Service Area: Griggs, Bismarck, Mandan,
Jamestown, and Valley City

Dakota Certified Development Corporation
51 Broadway Suite 500
Fargo, ND 58102
701-293-8892
Fax: 701-293-7819
Email: toby@fedc.com or
wendy@dakotacdc.com
www.dakotacdc.com/
Executive Director: Toby Sticka
Microloan Contact: Wendy Simek
Service Area: Grand Forks, Devils Lake,
Minot, Williston, and Dickinson counties

Ohio
Enterprise Development Corporation
9030 Hocking Hills Dr.
The Plains, OH 45780-1209
740-797-9646
Fax: 740-797-9659
Email: llathan@edcseo.org or
gseeley@edcseo.org
www.edcseo.org/
Executive Director: Gary Seeley
Microloan Contact: Lisa Latham
Service Area: Adams, Ashland, Athens,
Belmont, Brown, Carrol, Columbiana,
Coshocton, Gallia, Guernsey, Harrison,
Highland, Hocking, Holmes, Jackson,
Jefferson, Knox, Lawrence, Meigs, Monroe,

Morgan, Muskingum, Noble, Perry, Pike,
Ross, Scioto, Tuscarawas, Vinton and
Washington counties

Community Capital Development Corporation
900 Michigan Ave.
Columbus, OH 43215-1165
614-645-6171
800-756-CCDC
Fax: 614-645-8588
Email: fvincent@columbus.rr.com or
bshimp@ccdcorp.org
www.ccdcorp.org/
Executive Director: Brad Shrimp
Microloan Contact: Kendra Krebs-Vincenty
Service Area: Franklin, Delaware, Fairfield,
Licking, Union, Pickaway, Fayette, and
Madison counties

Hamilton County Development Co., Inc.
1776 Mentor Ave.
Cincinnati, OH 45212
513-631-8292
Fax: 513-631-4887
Email: lawalden@hcdc.com
www.hcdc.com/
Executive Director: David Main
Microloan Contact: Lou Ann Walden
Service Area: City of Cincinnati, Adams,
Brown, Butler, Clermont, Clinton, Hamilton,
Highland, and Warren counties

Women's Organization for Mentoring,
Entrepreneurship, and Networking
526 S. Main St., Suite 235
Akron, OH 44311-1058
330-379-9280
Fax: 330-379-3454
Email: women@ald.net
www.womennet.org/
Executive Director: Janice Robinson
Microloan Contact: Janice Robinson
Service Area:Cuyahoga, Lake, Lorain,
Mahoning, Medina, Stark, Summit, and
Wayne counties.

County Corp Development
40 W. Fourth St. Ste. 1600
Dayton, OH 45402
937-225-6328
Fax: 937-225-5089
Email: ed@countycorp.com
www.countycorp.com/
Executive Director: Marni Flagle
Microloan Contact: Tracy Shultz
Service Area: Miami, Montgomery, and
Greene county

Kent Regional Business Alliance
College of Business #300-A, KSU
Kent, OH 44242
330-672-1275
Fax: 330-672-9338
Email: lyost@bsa3.kent.edu
www.business.kent.edu/dean/krba.htm
Executive Director: Linda Yost
Microloan Contact:
Service Area: Ashtabula, Geauga, Trumbull,
Portage, Columbiana, Carroll, Holmes,
Coshocton, Tuscarawas, Stark, and Harrison
counties

Working for Empowerment through
Community Organizing (WECO)
2700 E. 79th Street, 4th Street
Cleveland, OH 44104
216-881-9650
Fax: 216-881-9704
Email: judi@wecofund.com
www.wecofund.com/
Executive Director: Judith W. Miles
Microloan Contact:
Service Area: Cuyahoga county

Microenterprise Loans

Oklahoma

Rural Enterprises, Inc.
2912 Enterprise Blvd.
P.O. Box 1335
Durant, OK 74702
580-924-5094
Fax: 580-920-2745
Email: veazie@ruralenterprises.com or debbiep@ruralenterprises.com
www.ruralenterprises.com/
Executive Director: Tom Smith
Microloan Contact: Ray Veazie/Debbie Partin
Service Area: Statewide excluding Adair, Canadian, Cherokee, Cleveland, Craig, Creek, Delaware, Haskell, Hayes, Hughes, Kay, Latimer, Leflore, Lincoln, Logan, McIntosh, Muskogee, Noble, Nowata, Okfuskee, Oklahoma, Okmulgee, Osage, Ottawa, Pawnee, Payne, Pittsburgh, Pottawatomie, Rogers, Seminole, Sequoyah, Wagoner, Washington, and Wayne counties including the city of Tulsa.

Tulsa Economic Development Corporation
907 S. Detroit Ave., Suite 1001
Tulsa, OK 74120
918-585-8332
Fax: 918-585-2473
Email: tmartin@tulsaecondevcorp.com
Executive Director: Rose Washington-Rentie
Microloan Contact: Tara Martin
Service Area: Adair, Canadian, Cherokee, Cleveland, Craig, Creek, Delaware, Haskell, Hayes, Hughes, Kay, Latimer, Leflore, Lincoln, Logan, McIntosh, Muskogee, Noble, Nowata, Okfuskee, Oklahoma, Okmulgee, Osage, Ottawa, Pawnee, Payne, Pittsburg, Pottawatomie, Rogers, Seminole, Sequoyah, Wagoner, Washington, and Wayne counties including the city of Tulsa

Greenwood Community Development
131 N. Greenwood Ave, 2nd Floor
Tulsa, OK 74120
918-585-2084
Fax: 918-585-9268
Email: rgant@tulsacoxmail.com/rking@tulsacoxmail.com
Executive Director: Reuben Gant
Microloan Contact: Reuben Gant
Service Area: Northwest Tulsa county

Little Dixie Community Action
502 West Duke St.
Hugo, OK 74743
580-326-3351
Fax: 580-326-2305
Email: jpool@littledixie.org
www.littledixiecaa.homestead.com/
Executive Director: Jerry Pool
Microloan Contact: Clarke LaForce 580-326-6441
Service Area: Choctaw, McCurtain, and Pushmataha counties

Tulsa Economic Development Corporation
907 S. Detroit Ave., Suite 1001
Tulsa, OK 74120
918-585-8332
Fax: 918-585-2473
Email: tmartin@tulsaecondevcorp.com
Executive Director: Rose Washington-Rentie
Microloan Contact: Tara Martin
Service Area: Adair, Canadian, Cherokee, Cleveland, Craig, Creek, Delaware, Haskell, Hayes, Hughes, Kay, Latimer, Leflore, Lincoln, Logan, McIntosh, Muskogee, Noble, Nowata, Okfuskee, Oklahoma, Okmulgee, Osage, Ottawa, Pawnee, Payne, Pittsburg, Pottawatomie, Rogers, Seminole, Sequoyah,

Wagoner, Washington, and Wayne counties including the city of Tulsa

Oregon

Cascades West Financial Services, Inc.
1400 Queen Ave., SE, Suite 205C
P.O. Box 686
Albany, OR 97321
541-924-8480
Fax: 541-967-4651
Email: dsearle@ocwcog.org
www.cascadeswest.com/
Executive Director: Mary Merriman Smith
Microloan Contact: Diane Searle
Service Area: Benton, Clackamas, Hood River, Jefferson, Lane, Lincoln, Linn, Marion, Multnomah, Polk, Tillamook, Wasco, Washington, and Yamhill

Ida-Ore Planning and Development Association, Inc.
10624 W. Executive Dr.
Boise, ID 83713
208-322-7033
Fax: 208-322-3569
Email: pmchoate@ida-ore.com
www.sageidaho.com/
Executive Director: Phillip Choate
Microloan Contact: Bob Richards
Service Area: Harney and Malheur counties

Southern Oregon Women's Access to Credit, Inc.
33 North Central #209
Medford, OR 97501
541-779-3992
Fax: 541-779-5195
Email: dpdavis@sowac.org
www.sowac.org/
Executive Director: Helen Wallace
Microloan Contact: Dennis Davis
Service Area: Jackson, Josephine, Klamath, and Lake counties

Oregon Association of Minority Entrepreneurs Credit Corporation
4134 N. Vancouver Avenue
Portland, OR 97217
503-249-7744
Fax: 503-249-2027
Executive Director: Samuel Brooks
Microloan Contact: Samuel Brooks
Service Area: Multnomah, Washington, Clackamas, Columbia, Tillamook, Clatsop, and Hood Counties

Umpqua Community Development Corporation
738 SE Kane Street
Roseburg, OR 97470
541-673-4909
Fax: 541-673-5023
Email: btamm@mcsi.net/ or rault@mcsi.net
www.umpquacdc.org/
Executive Director: Betty Tamm
Microloan Contact: Bob Ault
Service Area: Coos, Curry and Douglas Counties

Pennsylvania

The Ben Franklin Tech. Center of SE Pennsylvania
11 Penn Center
1835 Market St., Suite 1100
Philadelphia, PA 19103
215-972-6700
Fax: 215-972-5588
Email: bftc@benfranklin.org
www.sep.benfranklin.org/seed/cel.html
Executive Director: Rose Ann Rosenthal
Microloan Contact: Dieter Littles
Service Area: Bucks, Chester, Delaware, Montgomery, and Philadelphia counties

The Washington County Council on Economic Development
40 S. Main Street, Lower Level
Washington, PA 15301
724-228-8223
Fax: 724-250-8202
Email: wcced@cobweb.net
www.washingtoncountypa.org
Exec. Director: Malcolm Morgan
Microloan Contact: Alan A. Hill
Service Area: Southwestern area of Pennsylvania including Greene, Fayette, Washington, and Westmoreland counties

Aliquippa Alliance for Unity and Development
392 Franklin Ave
Aliquippa, PA 15001
724-378-7422
Fax: 724-378-9976
Email: pkribbs@aaud.org
www.aaud.org/
Executive Director: Roseanne Stead
Microloan Contact: Patricia Kribbs
Service Area: Beaver, Butler, and Lawrence counties

Community First Fund
44 N Queen Street P. O. Box 524
Lancaster, PA 17608-0524
866-822-3863
Fax: 717-393-1757
Email: dbetancourt@commfirstfund.org
gmachia@commfirstfund.org
URL: http://www.commfirstfund.org
Executive Director: Dan Betancourt
Microloan Contact: Glenda Machia
Service Area: Lancaster, York, Berks, Dauphin, Lebanon, Cumberland, Perry, and Adams counties

Community Loan Fund of Southwestern PA, Inc.
1920 Gulf Towers
707 Grant Street
Pittsburgh, PA 15219
412-201-2450
Fax: 412-201-2451
Email: mpeterson@clfund.com
mbevan@clfund.com
URL: http://www.clfund.com
Executive Director: Mark Peterson
Microloan Contact: Laura Swiss
Service Area: Allegheny, Armstrong, Beaver, Butler and Indiana counties

Northeastern Pennsylvania Alliance (aka: NEPA)
1151 Oak St.
Pittston, PA 18640-3795
570-655-5581
Fax: 570-654-5137
Email: tompel@nepa-alliance.org
www.nepa-alliance.org/
Executive Director: Cameron Moore
Microloan Contact: Tom Pellegrini
Service Area: Carbon, Lackawanna, Luzerne, Monroe, Pike, Schuylkill, and Wayne counties

MetroAction, Inc.
222 Mulberry Street
P.O. Box 4731
Scranton, PA 18501-0431
570-342-7711
Fax: 570-347-6262
Email: kfrench@scrantonchamber.com
www.scrantonchamber.com
Executive Director: John Kokinchak
Microloan Contact: Kristine French
Service Area: Luzerne, Lackawanna, and Monroe counties

North Central PA Regional Planning & Dev.

Commission
651 Montmorenci Avenue
Ridgway, PA 15853
814-773-3162
Fax: 814-772-7045
Email: jfoys@ncentral.com
Executive Director: Ronald W. Kuleck
Microloan Contact: Jill Foys
Service Area: Cameron, Clearfield, Elk,
Jefferson, McKean and Potter counties

Northwest Pennsylvania Regional Planning &
Dev. Commission
395 Seneca Street
Oil City, PA 16301
814-677-4800
Fax: 814-677-7663
Email: dalem@nwplan.org
www.nwcommission.org/
Executive Director: William Steiner
Microloan Contact: Dale F. Massie
Service Area: Clarion, Crawford, Erie, Forest,
Lawrence, Mercer, Warren and Venango
counties

Philadelphia Commercial Development
Corporation
1315 Walnut Street Suite 600
Philadelphia, PA 19107
215-790-2210
Fax: 215-790-2222
Email: econpcdc@aol.com
URL: www.philadelphiacommercial.com
Executive Director: Curtis Jones, Jr.
Microloan Contact: Rick Dean/Linda House
Service Area: Philadelphia

SEDA-Council of Governments
RR #1, Box 372
Lewisburg, PA 17837
570-524-9190
Fax: 570-524-4491
Email: venditti@seda-cog.org
www.seda-cog.org/
Executive Director: Dennis E. Robinson
Microloan Contact: Thomas J. Venditti
Service Area: Centre, Clinton, Columbia,
Juniata, Lycoming, Mifflin, Montour,
Northumberland, Perry, Snyder, and Union
counties.

Southern Alleghenies Planning &
Development Commission
541 58th Street
Altoona, PA 16602
814-949-6545
Fax: 814-949-6505
Email: sapdc@sapdc.org
URL: www.sapdc.org
Executive Director: Edward M. Silvetti
Microloan Contact: Michael Mignogna
Service Area: Bedford, Blair, Cambria, Fulton,
Huntingdon, and Somerset counties

Puerto Rico
Economic Development Corporation of San
Juan (COFECC)
1103 Avenida Munoz Rivera
P.O. Box 191791
Rio Piedras, PR 00926
787-756-5080
Fax: 787-753-8960
Email: cofecc@worldnet.att.net
www.cofecc.net/
Exec. Director: Giovanna Piovanetti
Microloan Contact: Giovanna Piovanetti
Service Area: Territory wide

Rhode Island
Rhode Island Coalition for Minority
Investment
216 Weybosset Street 2nd Floor
Providence, RI 02903
401-351-2999

Fax: 401-351-0990
Email: dbarge.midc@
efortress.com/allawi@prodigy.net
www.midcri.com
Executive Director: Denise Barge
Microloan Contact: Henry Reid
Service Area: Statewide

South Carolina
Charleston Citywide Local Development
Corporation
75 Calhoun St., 3rd Floor
Charleston, SC 29403
803-724-3796
Fax: 803-724-7354
Email: brennans@ci.charleston.sc.us
www.ci.charleston.sc.us/ldc.htm
Executive Director: Sharon Brennan
Microloan Contact: Michelle Ingle/Dwayne
Jubar
Service Area: City of Charleston

Santee-Lynches Regional Development Corp.
36 West Liberty St.
P.O. Box 1837
Sumter, SC 29150
803-775-7381
Fax: 803-773-6902
Email: slrdc@slcog.org
www.slcog.state.sc.us/
Exec. Director: James Darby, Jr.
Microloan Contact: Walter Dunlap
Service Area: Clarendon, Kershaw, Lee and
Sumter counties

Carolina Capital Investment Corporation
P. O. Box 8327
Columbia, SC 29202
803-461-3800
Fax: 803-461-3826
Email: mgaylor@businesscarolina.net
Executive Director: Elliott E. Franks, III
Microloan Contact: Melissa Gaylor
Service Area: Abbeville, Aiken, Allendale,
Anderson, Bamberg, Barnwell, Beaufort,
Berkeley, Calhoun, Charleston, Cherokee,
Chester, Chesterfield, Colleton, Darlington,
Dillon, Dorchester, Edgefield, Fairfield,
Florence, Georgetown, Greenville,
Greenwood, Hampton, Horry, Jasper,
Lancaster, Laurens, Lexington, Marion,
Marlboro, McCormick, Newberry, Oconee,
Orangeburg, Pickens, Richland, Saluda,
Spartanburg, Union, and York counties

South Dakota
Lakota Fund
Trade Center
P.O. Box 340
Kyle, SD 57752
605-455-2500
Fax: 605-455-2585
Email: monica@rapidnet.com
www.lakotafund.org/
Exec. Dir.: Elsie Meeks
Microloan Contact: Monica Perkildsen
Service Area: Bennett county, Pine Ridge
Indian Reservation, and areas of Shannon and
Jackson counties which are surrounded by
Indian Lands, and exclusive of Northern
Jackson county

Tennessee
Economic Ventures, Inc.
P.O. Box 3550
Knoxville, TN 37927-3550
865-594-8762
Fax: 865-594-8659
Email: kbell@cityofknoxville.org
Executive Director:
Microloan Contact:
Service Area: Anderson, Blount, Campbell,
Clairborne, Cocke, Grainger, Hamblen,

Jefferson, Knox, Loudon, Monroe, Morgan
Roane, Scott, Sevier, Union, Greene, Hancock,
Hawkins, Sullivan, Washington, Johnson,
Carter, and Unicoi counties

LeMoyne-Owen College Community
Development Corporation
802 Walker Avenue, Suite 5
Memphis, TN 38126
901-942-6265
Fax: 901-942-6448
Email: jeffrey_higgs@nile.lemoyne-
owen.edu/austin.emeagwai@nile.lemoyne-
owen.edu
www.loccdc.org
Executive Director: Jeffrey T. Higgs
Microloan Contact: Austin Emeagwai
Service Area: Memphis and Shelby county

Southeast Community Capital
1020 Commerce Park Drive
Oak Ridge, TN 37830
865-220-2025
Fax: 865-220-2030
Email: hortonw@tech2020.org
URL: http://www.tech2020.org
Executive Director: Don Welty
Microloan Contact: Louanne Horton-White
Service Area: Statewide

Woodbine Community Organization
222 Oriel Avenue
Nashville, TN 37210
615-833-9580
Fax: 615-833-9727
Email: oliverdent2001@cs.com
Executive Director: Oliver Dent
Microloan Contact: Oliver Dent
Service Area: Cheatham, Davidson, Dickson,
Robertson, Rutherford, Sumner, Williamson,
and Wilson counties

Texas
Business Resource Center Incubator
401 Franklin
Waco, TX 76701
254-754-8898
Fax: 254-756-0776
Email: john@brc_waco.com
Executive Director: John Dosher
Microloan Contact: John Dosher
Service Area: Bell, Bosque, Coryell, Falls,
Hill, and McLennan counties

The Corporation for Economic Development
of Harris County, Inc.
118-3 1@ 1 East Tex Freeway
Houston, TX 77027
281-590-5600
Fax: 281-590-5605
Email: jacklyngriffen@cedhc.com
www.cedhc.com/
Executive Director: Jacklyn Griffin
Microloan Contact: Janis Fowler
Service Area: Brazoria, Chambers, Fort Bend,
Galveston, Harris, Liberty, Montgomery, and
Waller counties

San Antonio Local Development Company
215 S. San Saba, Room 107
San Antonio, TX 78207
210-207-3932
Fax: 210-207-8151
Email: roberta@sanantonio.gov
www.saldc.com/
Executive Director: Ramire Cavazos
Microloan Contact: Robert Ayala
Service Area: Atascosa, Bandera, Bexar,
Comal, Frio, Gillespie, Guadalupe, Karnes,
Kendall, Kerr, Medina, San Antonio, and
Wilson counties

Southern Dallas Development Corporation

351 West Blvd., Suite 800
Dallas, TX 75208
214-428-7332
Fax: 214-948-8104
Email: velmore@sbdc.org
Executive Director: Jim Reid
Microloan Contact: Victor Elmore
Service Area: Portions of the City of Dallas

ACCION Texas, Inc.
2014 S. Hackberry Street
San Antonio, TX 78210
210-226-3664
Fax: 210-226-2940
Email: info@acciontexas.org
www.acciontexas.org/
Executive Director: Janie Barrera
Microloan Contact: Elizabeth Montoya
Service Area: Arkansas, Atascosa, Austin,
Bandera, Bastrop, Bee, Bexar, Blanco,
Brewster, Brooks, Brownsville, Burnet,
Carmeron, Caldwell, Calhoun, Comal,
Concho, Corpus Christi, Crockett, Culberson,
Dallas,DeWitt, Dimmit, Duval, Edwards, El
Paso,Fayette, Fort Worth, Frio, Gillespie,
Goliad, Gonzales, Green, Guadalupe, Harris,
Hays, Houston, Hidalgo, Hudspeth, Irion,
Jackson, Jeff Davis, Jim Hogg, Jim Wells,
Karnes, Kendall, Kenedy, Kerr, Kimble,
Kinney, Kleberg, Lampasas, Laredo, LaSalle,
Lavaca, Lee, Live Oak, Llano, Loving, Mason,
Maverick, Medina, McAllen, McCulloch,
McMullen, Menard, Midland/Odessa, Nueces,
Pecos, Presidio, Real, Reeves, Real, Reeves,
Refugio, San Antonio, San Patricio, San Saba,
Schleicher, Starr, Sutton, Tarrant, Tom Green,
Travis, Uvalde, Val Verde, Victoria , Webb,
Willacy, Zapata and Zavala counties

BIG - Businesses Invest In Growth
4100 Ed Bluestein , Suite 207
Austin, TX 78741
512-928-8010
Fax: 512-926-2997
Email: Melissa@big.org
www.bigaustin.org/
Executive Director: Jeannette Peten
Microloan Contact: Jeannette Peten
Service Area: Travis, Williamson, Hays,
Bastrop, Blanco, Burnet, Burleson, Milam,
Gillespie, Lampasas, Lee, Llano, Mason,
Mcculloch, and SanSaba counties

Neighborhood Housing Services of Dimmitt
County, Inc.
301 Pena Street
Carrizo Springs, TX 78834
830-876-5295
Fax: 830-876-4136
Email: nhsdc@brushco.net
Executive Director: Manuel Estrada, Jr.
Microloan Contact: Manuel Estrada, Jr.
Service Area: Dimmit, La Salle, Zavala
Edwards, Kinney, Real, Uvalde, Val Verde
and Maverick counties

Rural Development and Finance Corporation
711 Navarro Street Suite 350
San Antonio, TX 78207
210-212-4552
Fax: 210-212-9159
Email: RDFC@DCCI.COM
www.rdfc.org/
Executive Director: Gloria Guerrero
Microloan Contact: Lucy Brooks
Service Area: Cameron, El Paso, Starr,
Hidalgo, Willacy, Maverick, Dimmit, Webb,
Zapata, and Zavala counties

Vermont
Economic Development Council of Northern
Vermont, Inc.
155 Lake St.
St. Albans, VT 05478

802-524-4546
Fax: 802-527-1081
Email: edcnv@together.net
Executive Director: Connie Stanley-Little
Microloan Contact: William Farr
Service Area: Chittenden, Franklin, Grand
Isle, Lamoille, and Washington counties

Northern Community Investments Corporation
347 Portland Street
P.O. Box 904
St. Johnsbury, VT 05819
802-748-5101
Fax: 802-748-1884
Email: carol@ncic.org
www.ncic.org
Executive Director:
Microloan Contact: Carol Walker
Service Area: Caledonia, Essex, and Orleans
counties

Vermont Development Credit Union
18 Pearl Street
Burlington, VT 05401
802-865-3404
Fax: 802-862-8971
www.vdcu.org/
Executive Director: Caryl J. Stewart
Microloan Contact: Jeff Smith
Service Area: Addison, Bennington, Orange,
Rutland, Windham, and Windsor counties

Virginia
Group Enterprise Development
1038 S. Highland St.
Arlington, VA 22204
703-685-0510
Fax: 703-685-0529
Email: belay.embaye@ecdcinternational.org
www.ecdcinternational.org/
Exec. Director: Tschaye Teferra
Microloan Contact: Haddish Weldaly
Service Area: Prince William, Arlington and
Fairfax counties and the cities of Alexandria
and Falls Church

Business Development Centre, Inc.
147 Mill Ridge Road
Lynchburg, VA 24502
434-582-6100
Fax: 434-582-6106
Email: rich@lbdc.com
www.lbdc.com
Executive Director: Catherine McFaden
Microloan Contact: Rich Stallings
Service Area: Amherst, Appomattox, Bedford,
Campell counties, cities of Lynchburg and
Bedford, and the Town of Amherst and
Altavista

People Incorporated of Southwest Virginia
1173 W. Main St.
Abingdon, VA 24210
276-619-2239
Fax: 276-628-2931
Email: afortner@naxs.com
www.businesstart.org
Executive Director: Robert G. Goldsmith
Microloan Contact: Amanda Fortner/Phillip
Black
Service Area: Buchanan, Carroll, Dickenson,
Grayson, Lee, Russell, Scott, Smythe,
Tazewell, Wythe, Washington, Wise counties
and the cities of Bristol and Norton

Center for Community Development
440 High Street Suite 204
Portsmouth, VA 23704
757-399-0925
Fax: 757-399-2642
Email: profitl@infi.net
www.ccdi-va.net
Executive Director: Bruce Asberry

Microloan Contact: Monique Harrell
Service Area: Chesapeake, Hampton, Newport
News, Norfolk, Portsmouth, Suffolk, and
Virginia Beach

Lightstone Community Development Corp.
HC 63, Box 73
Moyers, WV 26815
304-249-5200
Fax: 304-249-5310
Email: tony@lightstone.org
www.lightstone.org/
Executive Director: Anthony E. Smith
Microloan Contact: Anthony E. Smith
Service Area: Bath and Highland counties

Richmond Economic Development
Corporation
501 E. Franklin St. Suite 358
Richmond, VA 23219
804-780-3013
Fax: 804-788-4310
Email: sjschley@aol.com
www.reacfinance.org
Executive Director: Stephen Schley
Microloan Contact: Brenda Lewis
Service Area: City of Richmond

Total Action Against Poverty
145 Campbell Avenue, S.W. Suite 303
P.O. Box 2868
Roanoke, VA 24011-2868
540-345-6781
Fax: 540-343-9892
Email: chris.scott@taproanoke.org
www.taproanoke.org/
Executive Director: Ted Edlich
Microloan Contact: Chris Scott
Service Area: Alleghany, Bath, Botetourt,
Craig, and Roanoke counties including the
City of Clifton Forge, Covington, Roanoke,
and Salem

Community Development Loan Fund
1624 Hull Street
Richmond, VA 23224
804-233-2014
Fax: 804-233-2158
Email: JFraitesvcdlf@earthlink.net
URL: http://www.vcdlf.org
Executive Director: Tim Hayes
Microloan Contact: Janice Fraites
Service Area: The counties of Henrico,
Chesterfield, Goochland, Hanover, Powatan,
and the cities of Petersburg and Hopewell

Washington
Tri-Cities Enterprise Association
124 W. Kennewick Ave.
Kennewick, WA 99336
509-582-9440
Fax: 509-582-9720
Email: kfast@enterprisecenter.net
www.enterprisecenter.net/
Executive Director: Wilfred Henderson
Microloan Contact: Katie Fast
Service Area: Benton, Franklin, Columbia,
Garfield, Asotin, Whitman, and Spokane
counties

Community Capital Development
1437 South Jackson, Suite 201
Seattle, WA 98144
206-324-4330 ext. 104
Email: artm@seattleccd.com
URL: http://www.seattleccd.com/
Executive Director: Jim Thomas
Microloan Contact: Art Mickel
Service Area: Adams, Chelan, Douglas, Grant,
Kittitas, Klickitat, Okanogan, Yakima, King,
Pierce, Skagit, San Juan, Snohomish, Island,
Kitsap and Whatcom

Oregon Association of Minority Entrepreneurs
Credit Corporation
4134 N. Vancouver Avenue
Portland, OR 97217
503-249-7744
Fax: 503-249-2027
Executive Director: Samuel Brooks
Microloan Contact: Samuel Brooks
Service Area: Clark county

Washington Assn. for Minority Entrepreneurs/
Rural Community Development
Resources(RCDR)
24 South 3rd Avenue
Yakima, WA 98902
509-453-5133
Fax: 509-453-5165
Email: delnorte@nwinfo.net
Executive Director: Luz Bazan Gutierrez
Microloan Contact: Luz Bazan Gutierrez
Service Area: Mattawa and Othello in Grant
County; Moses Lake and Royal City in Adams
County; Walla Walla County; and Pasco in
Franklin County; Yakima County

Washington CASH (Community Alliance for
Self-Help)
1912 East Madison St.
Seattle, WA 98122
206-352-1945
Fax: 206-352-1899
Email: washcash@nwlink.com
URL: http://www.washingtoncash.org
Executive Director: Kathy Gilman
Microloan Contact: Kathy Gilman
Service Area: Clark, Cowlitz, Island, King,
Kitsap, Lewis, San Juan, Skagit, Snohomish,
Thurston, and Whatcom counties

Rural Community Development Resources,
Inc.
24 South 3rd Avenue
Yakima, WA 98902
509-453-5133
Fax: 509-453-5165
Email: delnorte@nwinfo.net
President & CEO: Luz Bazan Gutierrez
Service Area: Mattawa and Othello in Grant
County; Moses Lake and Royal City in Adams
County; Walla Walla County; and Pasco in
Franklin County

West Virginia
The Washington County Council on Economic
Development
100 West Beau Street, Suite 703
Washington, PA 15301-4432
724-228-6949
Fax: 724-250-6502
Email: waced@cobweb.net
www.washingtoncountypa.org
Executive Director: Malcolm L. Morgan
Microloan Contact: Ray Grudi
Service Area: Monongalia county

Lightstone Community Development Corp.
HC 63, Box 73
Moyers, WV 26815
304-249-5200
Fax: 304-249-5310
Email:tony@lightstone.org
www.lightstone.org/
Executive Director: Anthony E. Smith
Microloan Contact: Anthony E. Smith
Service Area: Statewide

Mountain CAP of West Virginia, Inc.
105 Jerry Burton Drive
Sutton, WV 26601
304-765-7738
Fax: 304-765-7308
Email: mtcapt@rtol.net or
kctmountaincap@neumedia.net
www.mountaincap.com/

Executive Director: Mary Chipps
Microloan Contact: Tara Rexroad
Service Area: Barbour, Braxton, Clay, Fayette,
Gilmer, Lewis, Nicholas, Randolph, Roane,
Upshur Raleigh, Harrison, and Webster
Counties

Wisconsin
Advocap, Inc.
19 W. 1st St.
P.O. Box 1108
Fond du Lac, WI 54935
920-922-7760
Fax: 920-922-7214
Email: morta@advocap.org
www.advocap.org/
Executive Director: Michael Bonertz
Microloan Contact: Mort Gazerwitz
Service Area: Fond du Lac, Green Lake, and
Winnebago counties

Impact Seven, Inc.
147 Lake Almena Dr.
Almena, WI 54805
715-357-3334
Fax: 715-357-6233
Email: impact7@execpc.com
www.impactseven.org/
Executive Director: William Bay
Microloan Contact: Inger Sanderud
Service Area: Statewide with the exceptions of
Fond du Lac, Green Lake, Kenosha,
Milwaukee, Oasukee, Racine, Walworth,
Waukesha, Washington, and Winnebago
counties and inner city Milwaukee

Wisconsin Women's Business Initiative
Corporation
2745 N. Dr. Martin Luther King Jr. Dr.
Milwaukee, WI 53212
414-263-5450
Fax: 414-263-5456
Email: info@wwbic.com
www.wwbic.com/
Executive Director: Wendy Werkmeister
Microloan Contact: Carol N. Maria
Service Area: Brown, Dane, Dodge, Jefferson,
Kenosha, Milwaukee, Ozaukee, Racine,
Walworth, Washington and Waukesha
counties

Lincoln Neighborhood Redevelopment Corp.
2266 S. 13th St.
Milwaukee, WI 53215
414-671-5619
Fax: 414-385-3270
Email: LNRC@cbgmail.com
Executive Director: Michael Gapinski
Microloan Contact: Matthew Maigatter
Area Served: Greater Milwaukee SMSA

Northeast Entrepreneur Fund, Inc.
1225 Town Avenue
Superior, WI 54880
800-422-0374
Fax: 715-392-6131
Email: info@neefund.org
www.entrepreneurfund.org/
Executive Director: Mary Mathews
Microloan Contact: Robert Voss
Service Area: Douglas County

Wyoming
Wyoming Women's Business Center
13th and Lewis Streets P.O. Box 3661
Laramie, WY 82071
307-766-3083
Fax: 307-766-3085
Email: wwbc@uwyo.edu
www.wyomingwomen.com/
Executive Director: Rosemary Bratton
Microloan Contact: Rosemary Bratton
Service Area: State Wyoming

Technical Assistance Grant Recipients
Alaska
Juneau Economic Development Council
612 W. Willoughby, Suite A
Juneau, AK 99801-1732
907-463-3662
Fax: 907-463-3929
Email: jedc@ptialaska.net or
kflanders@ptialaska.net
www.jedc.org/
Executive Director: Charles Northrip
Microloan Contact: Kirk Flanders
Service Area: Through SBDCs, the Alaska
Panhandle

California
Women's Initiative for Self Employment
1390 Market St., Suite 113
San Francisco, CA 94102
415-247-9473
Fax: 415-247-9471
Email: wils@igc.org
www.womensinitiative.org/
Executive Director: Barbara Johnson
Microloan Contact: Corinne Florek
Service Area: defined sectors of San Francisco
Bay Area

Connecticut
Woman's Business Development Center
400 W. Main St., Suite 500
Stamford, CT 06902
203-353-1750
Fax: 203-353-1084
Email: sharonwbdc@ferg.lib.ct.us
Executive Director: Fran Pastore
Microloan Contact: Sharon Dubinsky
Service Area: SW corner including Ansonia,
Beacon Falls, Bethel, Bridgeport, Bridgewater,
Brookfield, Danbury, Darien, Derby, Easton,
Fairfield, Greenwich, Milford, Monroe, New
Canaan, New Fairfield, New Milford, Newtown,
Norwalk, Oxford, Redding, Ridgefield,
Seymour, Shelton, Sherman, Stamford, Stratford,
Trumbull, Weston, Westport, and Wilton
counties

Florida
Lee County Employment and Economic Dev.
Corp.
2774 First Street
Fort Myers, FL 33916
239-337-2300
Fax: 239-337-4558
Executive Director: Roy Kennix
Microloan Contact: Roy Kennix
Service Area: Community Redevelopment areas
of Lee County including Charleston Park,
Dunbar, Harlem Heights, North Fort Myers, and
State Road 80

Illinois
Women's Business Development Center
8 South Michigan Ave., Suite 400
Chicago, IL 60603
312-853-3477
Fax: 312-853-0145
Email: wbdc@aol.com
www.wbdc.org/
Executive Director: Hedy Ratner
Microloan Contact: Carol Dougal
Service Area: Boone, Cook, DeKalb, DuPage,
Kane, Kankakee, Kendall, Lake, McHenry, Will,
and Winnebago counties

Indiana
Community Action of Southern Indiana
1613 E. 8th
P.O. Box 843
Jeffersonville, IN 47130
812-288-6451, ext. 111

Fax: 812-284-8314
www.casijeff.net/
Executive Director: Fred Mitchell
Microloan Contact: Leatha Jackson
Service Area: Clark, Floyd, and Harrison counties

Iowa

Institute for Social and Economic Development
910 23rd Avenue
Coralville, IA 52241
319-338-2331
Fax: 319-338-5824
Email: cpigsley@ised.org
www.ised.org/
Executive Director: Christine Pigsley
Microloan Contact: Christine Pigsley
Service Area: Statewide

Kansas

Great Plains Development, Inc.
100 Military Plaza, Suite 128
P.O. Box 1116
Dodge City, KS 67801
316-227-6406
Fax: 316-225-6051
Exec. Director: Patty Richardson
Microloan Contact: Patty Richardson
Service Area: Statewide

Michigan

Cornerstone Alliance
38 W. Wall St.
P.O. Box 428
Benton Harbor, MI 49023-0428
616-925-6100
Fax: 616-925-4471
Email: gvaughn@ cstonealliance.org
www.cstonealliance.org/
Executive Director: Jeff Noel
Microloan Contact: Gregory Vaughn
Service Area: Berrien County and City of Benton Harbor

Minnesota

Neighborhood Development Center, Inc.
651½ University Ave.
St. Paul, MN 55104
651-291-2480
Fax: 651-291-2597
Email: windndc@mtn.org
www.windndc.org/
Executive Director: Mihailo Temali
Microloan Contact: Mara O'Neil
Service Area: Districts 3, 5, 6, 8, 9, and 16 of the City of St. Paul

Missouri

Community Development Corporation of Kansas City
2420 E. Linwood Blvd., Suite 110

Kansas City, MO 64109
816-924-5800
Fax: 816-921-3350
Exec. Director: William Threatt, Jr.
Microloan Contact: William Dayton
Service Area: Cass, Clay, Platte, Ray and Jackson counties

Montana

Montana Department of Commerce
SBDC Division
1424 9th Ave.
P.O. Box 200505
Helena, MT 59620-0505
406-444-4325
Fax: 406-444-1872
Email: adesch@state.mt.us
http://commerce.state.mt.us/
Executive Director: Ann Desch
Microloan Contact: Robyn Hampton
Service Area: Through SBDCs, Cascade, Chouteau, Fergus, Glacier, Golden Valley, Judity Basin, Musselshell, Petroleum, Pondera, Teton, Toole, and Wheatland counties, and the Blackfeet, Flathead, and Fort Peck Reservations, and the Crow, Fort Belknap, Northern Cheyenne and Rocky Boys Reservations and their Trust Lands

New Mexico

New Mexico Community Development Loan Fund
700 4th Street, SW
P.O. Box 705
Albuquerque, NM 87103-0705
505-243-3196
Fax: 505-243-8803
Email: vgnmcdfl@aol.com
www.nmcdlf.org/
Executive Director: Vangie Gabaldon
Microloan Contact: Rockling Todea
Service Area: Statewide

New York

Brooklyn Economic Development Corporation
175 Remsen Street, Suite 350
Brooklyn, NY 11201
718-522-4600
Fax: 718-797-9286
Email: info@bedc.org or mad@bedc.org
www.bedc.org/
Executive Director: Joan Bartolomeo
Microloan Contact: Hector Rivera
Service Area: The five boroughs of New York City

North Carolina

North Carolina Rural Economic Development Center, Inc.
4021 Carya Dr.
Raleigh, NC 27610

919-250-4314
Fax: 919-250-4325
Email: pblack@mindspring.com
www.ncruralcenter.org/
Executive Director: Billy Ray Hall
Microloan Contact: Phil Black
Service Area: Statewide

Pennsylvania

Women's Opportunities Resource Center
1930 Chestnut Street, Suite 1600
Philadelphia, PA 19103
215-564-5500
Fax: 215-564-0933
Email: worc-pa@erols.com
www.worc-pa.com/
Executive Director: Lynne Cutler
Microloan Contact: Lynne Cutler
Service Area: Bucks, Montgomery, Philadelphia, Chester, and Delaware counties

Texas

Corpus Christi Chamber of Commerce
1201 N. Shoreline
Corpus Christi, TX 78401
361-881-1850
Fax: 361-882-5627
Email: jestell@theccchamber.org
www.corpuschristichamber.org/
Executive Director: Tom Niskala
Microloan Contact: Jerry Estell
Service Area: Nueces and San Patricio counties

Vermont

Champlain Valley Office of Economic Opportunity, Inc.
431 Pine Street, #2
Burlington, VT 05401
802-860-1417
Fax: 802-860-1387
Email: mbdp@together.net
www.cvoro.org/
Executive Director: Jim White
Microloan Contact: Dale Lane
Service Area: Statewide

Virginia

VA SBDC Business Assistance Network
Division of Virginia Department of Business Assistance
P.O. Box 446
Richmond, VA 23218
804-371-6280
Fax: 804-225-3384
Email: seure@dba.state.va.us
www.dba.state.va.us/smdev/
Executive Director: Vicky Humphreys
Microloan Contact:
Service Area: Through SBDCs, statewide

Small Business Help

Need help writing a business plan or completing a loan application? The SBA has Technical Assistance Grant Recipients who can offer a helping hand and other guidance while you pursue your dream of owning your own business. The services offered vary from place to place, so contact the one nearest you to learn more about what is offered in your area. To find the office nearest you, contact U.S. Small Business Administration (SBA), 409 Third St., SW, Suite 8300, Washington, DC 20416; 202-205-6490.

Technical Assistance Grant Recipients

Alaska
Juneau Economic Development Council
612 W. Willoughby
Juneau, AK 99801-1724
907-463-3662
Fax: 907-463-3929
Email: jedc@ptialaska.net or
kflanders@ptialaska.net
Executive Director: Charles Northrip
Microloan Contact: Kirk Flanders
Service Area: Through SBDCs, the Alaska Panhandle

California
Women's Initiative for Self Employment
1390 Market St., Suite 113
San Francisco, CA 94105
415-247-9473
Fax: 415-247-9471
Email: frontdesk@womensinitiative.org
Executive Director: Julie Abrams
Microloan Contact: Laura Hoover
Service Area: defined sectors of San Francisco Bay Area

Connecticut
Women's Business Development Center
400 Main Street, Suite 500
Stamford, CT 06902
203-353-1756
Executive Director: Fran Pastore
Service Area: SW corner including Ansonia, Beacon Falls, Bethel, Bridgeport, Bridgewater, Brookfield, Danbury, Darien, Derby, Easton, Fairfield, Greenwich, Milford, Monroe, New Canaan, New Fairfield, New Milford, Newtown, Norwalk, Oxford, Redding, Ridgefield, Seymour, Shelton, Sherman, Stamford, Stratford, Trumbull, Weston, Westport, and Wilton counties

Florida
Lee County Employment and Economic Dev. Corporation
2774 First Street
Fort Myers, FL 33916
239-337-2300
Fax: 239-337-4558
Executive Director: Roy Kennix
Microloan Contact: Roy Kennix
Service Area: Community Redevelopment areas of Lee County including Charleston Park, Dunbar, Harlem Heights, North Fort Myers, and State Road 80

Illinois
Women's Business Development Center
8 South Michigan Ave., Suite 400

Chicago, IL 60603
312-853-3477
Fax: 312-853-0145
Email: wbdc@aol.com
Executive Director: Hedy Ratner
Microloan Contact: Carol Dougal
Service Area: Boone, Cook, DeKalb, DuPage, Kane, Kankakee, Kendall, Lake, McHenry, Will, and Winnebago counties

Indiana
Hoosier Valley Economic Development Corp.
1613 E. 8th
P.O. Box 843
Jeffersonville, IN 47130
812-288-6451
Fax: 812-284-8314
Executive Director: Robert Moore
Microloan Contact: Darnell Jackson
Service Area: Clark, Crawford, Floyd, Harrison, Orange, Scott, and Washington counties

Iowa
Institute for Social and Economic Development
910 23rd Avenue
Coralville, IA 52241
319-338-2331
800-888-4733
Fax: 319-338-5824
Email: jfriedman@ised.org
Executive Director: Jason Friedman
Microloan Contact: Jason Friedman
Service Area: Statewide

Kansas
Great Plains Development, Inc.
100 Military Plaza, Suite 128
P.O. Box 1116
Dodge City, KS 67801
316-227-6406
Fax: 316-225-6051
Exec. Director: Patty Richardson
Microloan Contact: Patty Richardson
Service Area: Statewide

Michigan
Cornerstone Alliance
38 W. Wall St.
P.O. Box 428
Benton Harbor, MI 49023-0428
616-925-6100
Fax: 616-925-4471
Email: gvaughn@ cstonealliance.org
Executive Director: Jeff Noel
Microloan Contact: Gregory Vaughn
Service Area: Berrien County and City of Benton Harbor

Minnesota
Neighborhood Development Center, Inc.
651½ University Ave.
St. Paul, MN 55104
651-291-2480
Fax: 651-291-2597
Email: windndc@mtn.org
Executive Director: Mihailo Temali
Microloan Contact: Mara O'Neil
Service Area: Districts 3, 5, 6, 8, 9, and 16 of the City of St. Paul

Missouri
Community Development Corporation of Kansas City
2420 E. Linwood Blvd., Suite 400
Kansas City, MO 64130
816-924-5800
Fax: 816-921-3350
Email: cdckcl@aol.com
Exec. Director: Donald Maxwell
Microloan Contact: Terrance Hendricks
Service Area: Cass, Clay, Platte, Ray and Jackson counties

Montana
Montana Department of Commerce
SBDC Division
1424 9th Ave.
P.O. Box 200501
Helena, MT 59620-0501
406-444-4780
Fax: 406-444-1872
Email: Rkloser@mt.gov
Executive Director: Gene Marcille
Service Area: Through SBDCs, Cascade, Chouteau, Fergus, Glacier, Golden Valley, Judith Basin, Musselshell, Petroleum, Pondera, Teton, Toole, and Wheatland counties, and the Blackfeet, Flathead, and Fort Peck Reservations, and the Crow, Fort Belknap, Northern Cheyenne and Rocky Boys Reservations and their Trust Lands

New Mexico
New Mexico Community Development Loan Fund
P.O. Box 705
Albuquerque, NM 87102-0705
505-243-3196
Fax: 505-243-8803
Exec. Director: Vangie Gabaldon
Microloan Contact: Rockling Todea
Service Area: Statewide

New York
Brooklyn Economic Development Corporation
175 Remsen Street, Suite 350
Brooklyn, NY 11201

Matthew Lesko, Information USA, Inc., 12081 Nebel Street, Rockville, MD 20852 • 1-800-955-7693 • www.lesko.com

718-522-4600
Fax: 718-797-9286
Email: info@bedc.org or mad@bedc.org
Exec. Director: Joan Bartolomeo
Microloan Contact: Madeline Marquez
Service Area: The five boroughs of New York
City

North Carolina

North Carolina Rural Economic Dev. Center,
Inc.
4021 Carya Dr.
Raleigh, NC 27610
919-250-4314
Fax: 919-250-4325
Email: pblack@mindspring.com
Executive Director: Billy Ray Hall
Microloan Contact: Phil Black
Service Area: Statewide

Pennsylvania

Women's Opportunities Resource Center
1930 Chestnut Street, Suite 1600
Philadelphia, PA 19103
215-564-5500
Fax: 215-564-0933
Executive Director: Lynne Cutler
Microloan Contact: Lynne Cutler
Service Area: Bucks, Montgomery,
Philadelphia, Chester, and Delaware counties

Texas

Greater Corpus Christi Business Alliance
1201 N. Shoreline
P.O. Box 640
Corpus Christi, TX 78403
361-881-1850
Fax: 361-888-5627
Email: rortiz@cctexas.org
Executive Director: Tom Niskala
Microloan Contact: Jerry Estell
Service Area: Nueces and San Patricio
counties

Vermont

Champlain Valley Office of Economic
Opportunity, Inc.
95 North Ave.
Burlington, VT 05401 or
P.O. Box 1603
Burlington, VT 05402
802-860-1417
Fax: 802-860-1387
Email: mbdp@together.net
Executive Director: Jim White
Microloan Contact: Dale Lane
Service Area: Statewide

Virginia

Virginia Microbusiness Development Plan
VA SBDC Network
P.O. Box 446
Richmond, VA 23218
804-371-6280
Fax: 804-225-3384
Email: lroberts@dba.state.va.us
Executive Director: Vicky Humphreys
Microloan Contact: Vicky Humphreys
Service Area: Through SBDCs, statewide

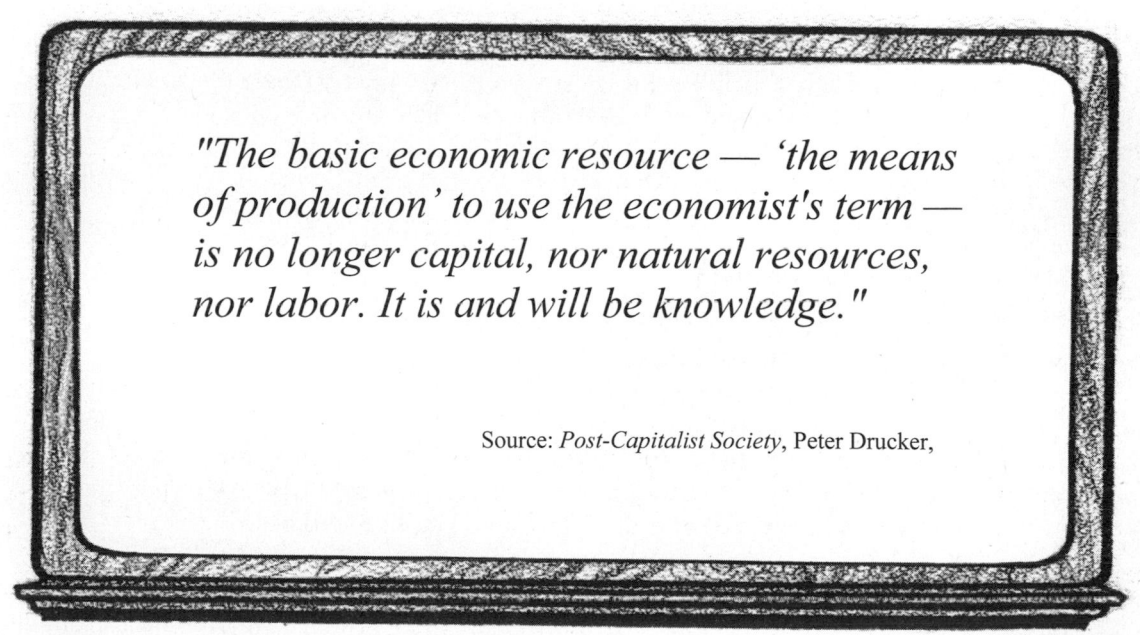

"The basic economic resource — 'the means of production' to use the economist's term — is no longer capital, nor natural resources, nor labor. It is and will be knowledge."

Source: *Post-Capitalist Society*, Peter Drucker,

State Money and Help For Your Business

Who Can Use State Money?

All states require that funds be used solely by state residents. But that shouldn't limit you to exploring possibilities only in the state in which you currently reside. If you reside in Maine, but Massachusetts agrees to give you $100,000 to start your own business, it would be worth your while to consider moving to Massachusetts. Shop around for the best deal.

Types Of State Money And Help Available

Each state has different kinds and amounts of money and assistance programs available, but these sources of financial and counseling help are constantly being changed. What may not be available this year may very well be available next. Therefore, in the course of your exploration, you might want to check in with the people who operate the business "hotlines" to discover if anything new has been added to the states' offerings.

Described below are the major kinds of programs which are offered by most of the states.

Information

Hotlines or One-Stop Shops are available in many states through a toll-free number that hooks you up with someone who will either tell you what you need to know or refer you to someone who can. These hotlines are invaluable — offering information on everything from business permit regulations to obscure financing programs. Most states also offer some kind of booklet that tells you to how to start-up a business in that state. Ask for it. It will probably be free.

Small Business Advocates operate in all fifty states and are part of a national organization (the National Association of State Small Business Advocates) devoted to helping small business people function efficiently with their state governments. They are a good source for help in cutting through bureaucratic red tape.

Funding Programs

Free Money can come in the form of grants, and works the same as free money from the federal government. You do not have to pay it back.

Loans from state governments work in the same way as those from the federal government -- they are given directly to entrepreneurs. Loans are usually at interest rates below the rates charged at commercial institutions and are also set aside for those companies which have trouble getting a loan elsewhere. This makes them an ideal source for riskier kinds of ventures.

Loan Guarantees are similar to those offered by the federal government. For this program, the state government will go to the bank with you and co-sign your loan. This, too, is ideal for high risk ventures which normally would not get a loan.

Interest Subsidies On Loans is a unique concept not used by the federal government. In this case, the state will subsidize the interest rate you are charged by a bank. For example, if the bank gives

Matthew Lesko, Information USA, Inc., 12081 Nebel Street, Rockville, MD 20852 • 1-800-955-7693 • www.lesko.com

you a loan for $50,000 at 10 percent per year interest, your interest payments will be $5,000 per year. With an interest subsidy you might have to pay only $2,500 since the state will pay the other half. This is like getting the loan at 5 percent instead of 10 percent.

Industrial Revenue Bonds Or General Obligation Bonds are a type of financing that can be used to purchase only fixed assets, such as a factory or equipment. In the case of Industrial Revenue Bonds the state will raise money from the general public to buy your equipment. Because the state acts as the middleman, the people who lend you the money do not have to pay federal taxes on the interest they charge you. As a result, you get the money cheaper because they get a tax break. If the state issues General Obligation Bonds to buy your equipment, the arrangement will be similar to that for an Industrial Revenue Bond except that the state promises to repay the loan if you cannot.

Matching Grants supplement and abet federal grant programs. These kinds of grants could make an under-capitalized project go forward. Awards usually hinge on the usefulness of the project to its surrounding locality.

Loans To Agricultural Businesses are offered in states with large rural, farming populations. They are available solely to farmers and/or agribusiness entrepreneurs.

Loans To Exporters are available in some states as a kind of gap financing to cover the expenses involved in fulfilling a contract.

Energy Conservation Loans are made to small businesses to finance the installation of energy-saving equipment or devices.

Special Regional Loans are ear-marked for specific areas in a state that may have been hard hit economically or suffer from under-development. If you live in one of these regions, you may be eligible for special funds.

High Tech Loans help fledgling companies develop or introduce new products into the marketplace.

Loans To Inventors help the entrepreneur develop or market new products.

Local Government Loans are used for start-up and expansion of businesses within the designated locality.

Childcare Facilities Loans help businesses establish on-site daycare facilities.

Loans To Women And/Or Minorities are available in almost every state from funds specifically reserved for economically disadvantaged groups.

Many federally funded programs are administered by state governments. Among them are the following programs:

The SBA 7(A) Guaranteed and ***Direct Loan*** program can guarantee up to 90 percent of a loan made through a private lender (up to $750,000), or make direct loans of up to $150,000.

The SBA 504 establishes Certified Development Companies whose debentures are guaranteed by the SBA. Equity participation of the borrower must be at least 10 percent, private financing 60 percent and CDC participation at a maximum of 40 percent, up to $750,000.

Small Business Innovative Research Grants (SBIR) award between $20,000 to $50,000 to entrepreneurs to support six months of research on a technical innovation. They are then eligible for up to $500,000 to develop the innovation.

Small Business Investment Companies (SBIC) license, regulate and provide financial assistance in the form of equity financing, long-term loans, and management services.

Community Development Block Grants are available to cities and counties for the commercial rehabilitation of existing buildings or structures used for business, commercial, or industrial purposes. Grants of up to $500,000 can be made. Every $15,000 of grant funds invested must create at least one full-time job, and at least 51 percent of the jobs created must be for low and moderate income families.

Farmers Home Administration (FmHA) Emergency Disaster Loans are available in counties where natural disaster has substantially affected farming, ranching or aquaculture production.

FmHA Farm Loan Guarantees are made to family farmers and ranchers to enable them to obtain funds from private lenders. Funds must be used for farm ownership, improvements, and operating purposes.

FmHA Farm Operating Loans to meet operating expenses, finance recreational and nonagricultural enterprises, to add to family income, and to pay for mandated safety and pollution control changes are available at variable interest rates. Limits are $200,000 for an insured farm operating loan and $400,000 for a guaranteed loan.

FmHA Farm Ownership Loans can be used for a wide range of farm improvement projects. Limits are $200,000 for an insured loan and $300,000 for a guaranteed loan.

FmHA Soil And Water Loans must be used by individual farmers and ranchers to develop, conserve, and properly use their land and water resources and to help abate pollution. Interest rates are variable; each loan must be secured by real estate.

FmHA Youth Project Loans enable young people to borrow for income-producing projects sponsored by a school or 4H club.

Assistance Programs

Management Training is offered by many states in subjects ranging from bookkeeping to energy conservation.

Business Consulting is offered on almost any subject. Small Business Development Centers are the best source for this kind of assistance.

Market Studies to help you sell your goods or services within or outside the state are offered by many states. They all also have State Data Centers which not only collect demographic and other information about markets within the state, but also have access to federal data which can pinpoint national markets. Many states also provide the services of graduate business students at local universities to do the legwork and analysis for you.

Business Site Selection is done by specialists in every state who will identify the best place to locate a business.

Licensing, Regulation, and Permits information is available from most states through "one-stop shop" centers by calling a toll-free number. There you'll get help in finding your way through the confusion of registering a new business.

Employee Training Programs offer on-site training and continuing education opportunities.

Research And Development assistance for entrepreneurs is a form of assistance that is rapidly increasing as more and more states try to attract high technology-related companies. Many states are even setting up clearing houses so that small businesses can have one place to turn to find expertise throughout a statewide university system.

Procurement Programs have been established in some states to help you sell products to state, federal, and local governments.

Export Assistance is offered to identify overseas markets. Some states even have overseas offices to drum up business prospects for you.

Assistance In Finding Funding is offered in every state, particularly through regional Small Business Development Centers. They will not only identify funding sources in the state and federal governments but will also lead you through the complicated application process.

Special Help For Minorities And Women is available in almost every state to help boost the participation of women and minorities in small business ventures. They offer special funding programs and, often, one-on-one counseling to assure a start-up success.

Venture Capital Networking is achieved through computer databases that hook up entrepreneurs and venture capitalists. This service is usually free of charge. In fact, the demand for small business investment opportunities is so great that some states require the investor to pay to be listed.

Inventors Associations have been established to encourage and assist inventors in developing and patenting their products.

Annual Governors' Conferences give small business people the chance to air their problems with representatives from state agencies and the legislature.

Small Business Development Centers (SBDCs), funded jointly by the federal and state governments, are usually associated with the state university system. SBDCs are a god-send to small business people. They will not only help you figure out if your business project is feasible, but also help you draw up a sensible business plan, apply for funding, and check in with you frequency once your business is up and running to make sure it stays that way.

Tourism programs are prominent in states whose revenues are heavily dependent on the tourist trade. They are specifically aimed at businesses in the tourist industries.

Small Business Institutes at local colleges use senior level business students as consultants to help develop business plans or plan expansions.

Technology Assistance Centers help high tech companies and entrepreneurs establish new businesses and plan business expansions.

On-Site Energy Audits are offered free of charge by many states to help control energy costs and improve energy efficiency for small businesses. Some states also conduct workshops to encourage energy conservation measures.

Minority Business Development Centers offer a wide range of services from initial counseling on how to start a business to more complex issues of planning and growth.

Business Information Centers (BICs) provide the latest in high-tech hardware, software, and telecommunications to help small businesses get started. BIC is a place where business owners and aspiring business owners can go to use hardware/software, hard copy books, and publications to plan their business, expand an existing business, or venture into new business areas. Also, on-site counseling is available.

U.S. Small Business Administration (SBA) Programs

The SBA offices listed under each state can provide you with detailed information on the following programs:

Small Business Innovative Research Grants (SBIR): Phase I awards between $20,000 to $50,000 to entrepreneurs to support six months of research on a technical innovation. Phase II grants are an additional $500,000 for development. Private sector investment funds must follow.

International Trade Loans: Guaranteed long-term loans through private lenders to develop or expand export markets, or to recover from the effects of import competition. Maximum guaranteed loan is $1,000,000 for fixed assets and an additional $250,000 for working capital and/or export revolving line of credit.

Contract Loan: Short-term loans are available to small businesses to finance the costs of labor and materials on contracts for which the proceeds are assignable. Program guarantees up to 90 percent of loans not in excess of $750,000. Qualifying small businesses must be in business for at least 12 calendar months prior to the date of the loan application.

General Contractor Loans: Small general construction contractors may obtain short-term loans or loan guarantees for residential or commercial construction or rehabilitation of property to be sold. The SBA will guarantee up to 90 percent of qualifying loans made by private lenders up to a maximum of $750,000. Direct loans can be up to $150,000.

7(a) Loan Guaranty Program: This program is used to fund the varied long-term needs of small businesses. It is designed to promote small business formation and growth by guaranteeing long-term loans to qualified firms. Can guarantee up to $750,000, generally between 70%-90% of the loan value, at an interest rate not to exceed 2.75 over the prime lending rate. Maturities are up to 10 years for working capital; up to 25 years for fixed assets.

7(a) Loan Guaranty Program
Low Documentation Loan Program (LowDoc): Purpose is to reduce the paperwork involved in loan requests of $100,000 or less. A one-page application is used and it relies on the strength of the individual applicant's character and credit history.

7(a) Loan Guaranty Program
GreenLine Program: Intended to finance short-term, working-capital needs of small businesses. Loan advances are usually made against a borrower's certified level of inventory and accounts payable.

7(a) Loan Guaranty Program
Vietnam-Era and Disabled Veteran Loan Program: Assists disabled veterans of any era who can't secure business financing from private sector or other guaranty loan sources. Veterans can

apply for loans to establish a small business or expand an existing small business. The maximum is $150,000.

7(a) Loan Guaranty Program

Handicapped Assistance Loans: Assists individuals with disabilities and public/private nonprofit organizations for the employment of the handicapped. Financing is available for starting/acquiring or operating a small business. There are 2 programs of assistance: HAL-1 and HAL-2.

> **HAL-1:** Financial assistance is available to state and federal-chartered organizations that operate in the interest of disabled individuals. Applicants must provide evidence that the business is operated in the interest of handicapped individuals.

> **HAL-2:** Financial assistance is provided to handicapped persons who provide evidence that their business is a for-profit operation, qualifies as a small business, is 100% owned by 1 or more handicapped individuals, and the handicapped owner(s) must actively participate in managing the business.

7(a) Loan Guaranty Program

Women's Prequalification Loan Program: Provides women business owners a pre-authorized loan guaranty commitment. It provides a quick response to loan requests of $250,000 or less.

7(a) Loan Guaranty Program

Secondary Market: Lenders who hold business loans guaranteed by the SBA may improve profitability and liquidity by selling the guaranteed portions of those loans in the secondary market. Banks, savings and loan companies/ credit unions and pension funds, and insurance companies are frequent buyers.

8(a) Participant Loan Programs: Makes financial assistance available to 8(a) certified firms. Applicants must be participants in the 8(a) Program and eligible for contractual assistance. Loans can be made directly or through lending institutions under the agency's immediate participation or guaranty programs. Loans may be used for facilities/equipment or working capital.

7(m) MicroLoan Demonstration Program: Aimed at small businesses needing small-scale financing/technical assistance for start-up or expansion. Short-term loans of up to $25,000 are made to small businesses for the purchase of machinery and equipment, furniture and fixtures, inventory, supplies and working capital.

502 Local Development Company Program: Provides long-term, fixed asset financing through certified development companies. Proceeds are provided as follows: 50% by an unguaranteed bank loan, 40% by an SBA guaranteed debenture, 10% by the small business customer. The maximum SBA debenture is $1 million.

504 Certified Development Company Program: Provides long-term, fixed asset financing through certified development companies. Proceeds are provided as follows: 50% by an unguaranteed bank loan, 40% by an SBA guaranteed debenture, 10% by the small business customer. The maximum SBA debenture is $1 million.

Surety Bond Program

Prior Approval Program: Aimed at small construction/ service contractors; surety/insurance companies; minority/ women's groups; federal/state agencies; state insurance departments; federal/state and other procurement officials.

Surety Bond Program

Preferred Surety Bond (PSB) Program: Aimed at small construction and service contractors; surety/insurance companies; minority and women's groups; federal/state agencies; state insurance departments; federal and state and other procurement officials. The decision to issue a surety bond guarantee is made by participating sureties. There are participating sureties authorized by SBA to issue/monitor and service bonds without prior SBA approval. SBA guarantees surety bonds for construction, service/supply contracts up to $1.25 million.

Export Working Capital Program (EWCP): Replaces the Export Revolving Line of Credit Program. EWCP will allow up to a 90% guarantee on private-sector loans of up to $750,000 for working capital. Loans can be for single or multiple export sales and can be extended for pre-shipment working capital and post-shipment exposure coverage.

Disaster Assistance Loan Program: A disaster-assistance loan program for nonagricultural victims. Eligibility is based on financial criteria. Interest rates fluctuate according to statutory formulas. There is a lower rate available to applicants without credit available elsewhere, not to exceed 4%, and a higher interest rate for those with credit available elsewhere, not to exceed 8%.

Disaster Assistance to Businesses

Loans for Physical Damage: Available to qualified businesses for uninsured losses up to $1.5 million for businesses of any size to repair/replace business property to pre-disaster conditions. Loans may be used to replace/repair equipment, fixtures, inventory, and leasehold improvements.

Disaster Assistance to Businesses

Economic Injury Disaster Loan (EIDL): For businesses that sustain economic injury as a result of a disaster. Working capital loans are made to help businesses pay ordinary/necessary expenses which would have been payable barring disaster. Maximum loan amounts is $1.5 million EIDL and physical damage loans combined unless the business meets the criteria for major source of employment.

Disaster Assistance to Businesses

Loan for Major Source of Employment (MSE): For business, large and small, and nonprofit organizations. The $1.5 million limit may be waived for businesses that employ 250 or more in an affected area.

Disaster Assistance to Individual Homeowners and Renters:

Real Property: Loans available to qualified homeowner/ renter applicants for uninsured losses up to $200,000 to repair/ restore a primary residence to pre-disaster condition. Homeowners may apply for an additional 20% for disaster mitigation. This is a long-term program for individual disaster losses.

Disaster Assistance to Individuals Homeowners and Renters:

Personal Property: Loans available to qualified homeowner/ renter applicants for uninsured losses up to $40,000 to repair/replace personal property such as clothing, furniture, cars, etc.

Government Contracting

Certificate of Competency: Helps small businesses to receive government contracts by providing an appeal process to low-bidder businesses denied government contracts by contracting officers for perceived lack of ability to satisfactorily perform.

Government Contracting

Prime Contract: Program increases small business opportunities in the federal acquisition process through initiation of small business set-asides, identification of new small business sources, counseling small businesses on how to do business with the federal government, and assessment of compliance with the Small Business Act through surveillance reviews.

Government Contracting
Breakout Program: Promotes/influences and enhances the break-out of historically sole-source items for full and open competition in order to effect significant savings to the federal government.

Government Contracting
Natural Resources Sales Assistance Program:

Timber Sales: Set-aside program maintains small businesses in the forest products industry by providing them with preferential bidding opportunities for purchasing timber offered by the federal government. Joint operation of the SBA and federal timber-selling agencies throughout the U.S.

National Small Business Tree Planting Program: Allocates grants to the states/trust territories for the purpose of contracting with small businesses to plant trees on land owned and controlled by state/local governments. Federal dollars are matched by community funds.

Government Contracting
Procurement Automated Source System (PASS): A computerized database of small businesses nationwide which are interested in federal procurement opportunities. Information on each company includes a summary of capabilities, ownership and qualifications.

Small Business Technology Transfer Program (STTR) Pilot Program: This is similar in philosophy and objectives to the SBIR program. It has a requirement that the small firm competing for the Small Business Technology Transfer Program (STTR) Research and Development (R&D) project must collaborate with a nonprofit research institution. This is a joint venture project from the initial bid submission to project completion. Available to small high-tech R&D firms.

Alabama

* Alabama Development Office
401 Adams Avenue, Suite 670   800-248-0033
Montgomery, AL 36130-4106   334-242-0400
www.ado.state.al.us/finance1.htm   Fax: 334-242-2414
Alabama offers a variety of financial options aimed at starting and growing your business. They offer one-stop support and incentives that will tailor programs to meet individual companies needs. The Alabama Development Office administers the following programs: *Industrial Revenue Bonds, Industrial Development Grants, Linked Deposits, Revolving Loan Funds, Infrastructure Grant Program, Appalachian Regional Grant Program, Commercial Lending Sources, Tennessee Valley Authority Economic Development Loan Fund, Alabama Industrial Access Road and Bridge Program.*

* Rural Development
USDA Rural Development
4121 Carmichael Road, Suite 601   334-279-3400
Montgomery, AL 36106-3683   Fax: 334-279-3403
www.rurdev.usda.gov/al
There are many forms of grants and loans provided by the Alabama Rural Development Office. Funds are available in the form of guaranteed loans through a local lender, and direct loans and grants directly from the U.S. Treasury, they include *Rural Business Enterprise Grants, Rural Business Opportunity Grants, Business and Industry Direct Loan Program, Business and Industry Guaranteed Loan Program, Intermediary Relending Program, Rural Economic Development Zero Interest Loans, Rural Economic Development Grants and Rural Cooperative Development Grants.* Contact your state office for additional information.

* Alabama Department of Revenue
P.O. Box 327001   334-242-1170
Montgomery, AL 36132-7001   Fax: 334-242-0550
www.ador.state.al.us
The Alabama Department of Revenue administers several tax incentives for existing, expanding and new industries. They are a one-stop office for tax forms, filing information, laws and tax publications.

* Alabama Technology Network
500 Beacon Parkway West   205-943-4808
Birmingham, AL 35209   Fax: 205-943-4813
www.atn.org
The Alabama Technology Network helps manufacturers in Alabama improve their global competitiveness through technical assistance, workforce training and technology transfer. They provide ten network centers that will provide assistance to Alabama's existing industries.

* Department of Agriculture and Industry
P.O. Box 3336
Montgomery, AL 36109   334-240-7100
agri-ind.state.al.us
Supplies both information and technical support to farmers, businesses and consumers.

* Alabama Industrial Development and Training
One Technology Court
Montgomery, AL 36116   334-242-4158
www.aidt.edu

Offers recruiting, assessing and training potential employees; developing and producing training materials, and locating facilities; and, delivering customized services.

* Alabama International Trade Center

University of Alabama
Box 870396
Tuscaloosa, AL 35498-0396   205-348-7621
www.aitc.ua.edu

Services offered include foreign market research, strategic planning and consulting, implementation recommendations, training seminars and general information.

* Office of Minority Business Enterprise

401 Adams Ave.   334-242-2224
Montgomery, AL 36130   800-447-4191
www.adeca.alabama.gov/content/dir/dir_ombe.aspx

Assists minorities in achieving effective and equitable participation in the American free enterprise system and in overcoming social and economic disadvantages that have limited their participation in the past. Management and technical assistance is provided to minority firms on request.

* State Treasurer's Office

Linked Deposits
Room S-106
The State Capitol Building
Montgomery, AL 36130   334-242-7500
www.treasury.state.al.us

The Alabama State Treasury administers the *Linked Deposit Program*, which provides low interest loans to small business owners and farmers starting new businesses or maintaining existing ones.

* Small Business Administration

801 Tom Martin Drive   205-290-7101
Birmingham, AL 35211   Fax: 205-290-7404
http://www.sba.gov/al/

The Alabama SBA provides counseling and training along with a start-up kit to help you as you begin your own business. Their services include a Women's Business Ownership Representative to assist women business owners, an International Trade Specialist is to assist businesses interested in exporting and a Veterans Affairs Program.

* Certified Development Corporations

Alabama Community Development Corporation, (ALACOM Finance)
Diane Roehrig, President
117 Southcrest Drive, Suite 100   205-942-3360
Homewood, AL 35209   Fax: 205-942-5984
Email: alacom@worldnet.att.net
http://www.alacom.com
Area of Operation: State of Alabama except Sumter, Choctaw and Washington Counties

Birmingham Citywide Local Development Company
Bob Dickerson, Executive Director
110 - 12th Street, North   205-250-6380
Birmingham, AL 35203   Fax: 205-250-6384
Email: bbrc@inlinenet.net
www.bbrconline.com
Area of Operation: Citywide Birmingham; Jefferson and Shelby Counties of Alabama

Greater Mobile Development Corporation
Teresa Sands, Economic Development Coordinator
Business Innovation Center
1301 Azalea Road, Suite 201   251-650-0826
Mobile, AL 36693   Fax: 251-650-0827
Mailing address:
P.O. Box 1827
Mobile, AL 36633
Email: sands@ci.mobile.al.us
www.cityofmobile.org
Area of Operation: Baldwin and Mobile Counties of Alabama

Southern Development Council
Tamara Y. Lee, Executive Director   334-244-1801
8132 Old Federal Road   1-800-499-3034
Montgomery, AL 36117-8007   Fax: 334-244-1421
Email: sdci@sdcinc.org

http://www.sdcinc.org
Area of Operation: State of Alabama

The 504 Certified Development Company (CDC) Program provides growing businesses with long-term, fixed-rate financing for major fixed assets, such as land and buildings. A Certified Development Company is a nonprofit corporation set up to contribute to the economic development of its community or region. CDC's work with the Small Business Administration and private-sector lenders to provide up to 90% financing to small businesses. There are about 270 CDC's nationwide, each covering a specific region.

* Small Business Investment Companies

FJC Growth Capital Corp
William B. Noojin, Manager
165 West Park Loop   256-922-2918
Huntsville, AL 35807   Fax: 256-922-2909
Email: jharper@fjcgrowth.com

Hickory Venture Capital Corp
J. Thomas Noojin, President
301 Washington Street, NW, Suite 100 256-539-1931
Huntsville, AL 35801   Fax: 256-539-5130
Email: jbise@hvcc.com

TD Javelin Capital Fun
Lyle Honke, Manager
2850 Cahaba Road, Suite 240   203-629-8700
Birmingham, AL 35223   Fax: 203-629-9293
Email: jceliberti@tullisdickerson.com

Harbinger Mezzanine Partners, L.P.
John Harrison
One Riverchase Parkway South   615-301-6400
Birmingham, AL 35244   Fax: 615-301-6401
Email: nhartin@harbert.net

The SBA licenses, regulates, and provides financial assistance to privately owned and operated Small Business Investment Companies. SBICs make venture or risk investments by supplying capital and extending unsecured loans and loans not fully collateralized to small enterprises which meet their investment criteria. Financing is made by direct loans and by equity investments.

Alaska

* Department of Community and Economic Development

P.O. Box 11080   907-465-2017
Juneau, AK 99811   Fax: 907-465-3767
www.dced.state.ak.us

The Department of Community and Economic Development should be your first stop in starting your own business in Alaska. They oversee many agencies critical to your businesses success including: Community and Business Development, International Trade and Market Development, Industrial Development and Export Authority and many more.

* Rural Development

800 W. Evergreen, Suite 201   907-761-7705
Palmer, AK 99645   Fax: 907-761-7783
www.rurdev.usda.gov/ak

The Rural Development Team of Alaska is dedicated to providing rural Alaskans with a wide variety of programs designed to assist community and businesses. Loans and grants are available to entrepreneurs to develop and maintain local business and industry.

* Alaska Department of Revenue

Tax Division
P.O. Box 110420   907-465-2320
Juneau, AK 99811-0420   Fax: 907-465-2375
www.revenue.state.ak.us

Although Alaska has no state income tax or sales tax, the Department of Revenue can provide the entrepreneur with information on regulations and other tax issues concerning their business.

* International Trade and Market Development

P.O. Box 110804   907-465-2017
Juneau, AK 99811-0804   Fax: 907-465-3767
www.dced.state.ak.us/trade

The International Trade and Market Development, a division of the Community and Economic Development Office provides representatives to help promote Alaska's products and services by providing information and access to markets overseas, including government-to-government relations.

Small Business Administration

510 L Street, Suite 310   907-271-4022
Anchorage, AK 99501-1952   800-755-7034
www.sba.gov/ak   Fax: 907-271-4545

The Alaska SBA's goal is to assist entrepreneurs in many aspects of business. They provide counseling and training along with a start-up kit to help you as you begin your own business.

Certified Development Corporations

Evergreen Community Development Association
900 Fourth Avenue Suite 2900   206-622-3731
Seattle, WA 98201   800-878-6613
www.ecda.org

The 504 Certified Development Company (CDC) Program provides growing businesses with long-term, fixed-rate financing for major fixed assets, such as land and buildings. A Certified Development Company is a nonprofit corporation set up to contribute to the economic development of its community or region. CDC's work with the Small Business Administration and private-sector lenders to provide up to 90% financing to small businesses. There are about 270 CDC's nationwide, each covering a specific region.

* Buy Alaska

University of Alaska
Small Business Development Center
430 W. 7th Avenue, Suite 110   907-274-7232
Anchorage, AK 99501   800-478-7232
www.buyalaska.com

The Buy Alaska Program's mission is to assist businesses, consumers, and government entities in finding competitive Alaskan sources for goods and services with the goal of keeping more dollars in Alaska. The Buy Alaska Program offers the free service of researching buying needs and "matching" buyers with sellers. Businesses and consumers seeking to buy competitively-priced goods and services can get help from Buy Alaska in identifying local Alaskan vendors and providers from which to make their purchases.

* Alaska Science and Technology Foundation

4500 Diplomacy Drive, Suite 515   907-272-4333
Anchorage, AK 99508   Fax: 907-274-6228
www.dced.state.ak.us/astf/index.cfm

The mission of the Alaska Science and Technology Foundation is to enhance the development and application of science and technology for the benefit of Alaskans. The Foundation provides grants in five areas: *Major Individual Grants, Small Grants, Group Project Grants, Direct Grants to Teachers,* and *Small Business Innovation Research Bridging Grants.*

* Alaska Growth Capital

3900 C Street, Suite 302   907-339-6760
Anchorage, AK 99507   888-315-4904
www.akgrowth.com   Fax: 907-339-6771

This is a commercial financial institution, licensed and regulated by the State of Alaska. It is not regulated as a bank, but rather as a Business and Industrial Development Corporation (BIDCO). BIDCOs do not accept deposits and do not provide consumer lending. BIDCOs focus exclusively on financing businesses.

* Power Project Fund

Alaska Energy Authority
813 W. Northern Lights Blvd.   907-269-3000
Anchorage, AK 99503   Fax: 907-269-3004
www.aidea.org/powerloan.htm

Provides loans to local utilities, local governments or independent power producers for the development or upgrade of electric power facilities, including conservation, bulk fuel storage and waste energy conservation, or potable water supply projects. Loan term is related to the life of the project.

* The Polaris Fund

Jim Yarmon
c/o Yarmon Investments
840 K Street, #201

Anchorage, AK 99501   907-276-4466
www.alaska.net/~jimyarm/polhome.htm

The purpose of the Polaris Fund is to finance young companies with potential to achieve profitable sales by providing equity capital. Ideal companies should have an experienced management team, an innovative, distinctive product with a $100-$500 million growing market and a well-defined channel for sales. Polaris investments are usually in the $100,000 to $500,000 range, and favor companies that align Polaris closely with management.

* Business Incentive Program

Bill Paulick
Division of Trade & Development
P.O. Box 110804
Juneau, AK 99811-0804   907-465-3961
Email: Bill_Paulick@commerce.state.ak.us

Under this program companies will be reimbursed (rather than be paid up front) for designated portions of relocation costs, site development costs, special employee training not covered by other programs, and special analysis of sites in Alaska. The program was passed into law in April 1998 and is limited to $3 million annually.

* Small Business Economic Development Revolving Loan Fund

Alaska Department of Commerce and Economic Development
Division of Investments
P.O. Box 34159   800-478-LOAN
Juneau, AK 99803   907-465-2510
www.dced.state.ak.us/investments

This program was established in 1987 in conjunction with the U.S. Department of Commerce, Economic Development Administration (EDA). The purpose of the program is to provide private sector employment in the areas designated by EDA. The maximum loan amount is $300,000. Applicants are required to obtain additional private, non-public financing of approximately twice the amount requested. The interest rate of prime minus 4 points is set by the Loan Administration Board consisting of three members from the existing divisional loan committee and two members from the private sector. The board is responsible for setting loan policy and for making all major loan decisions.

* Commercial Fishing Revolving Loan Fund

Alaska Department of Community and Economic Development
Division of Investments
P.O. Box 34159
Juneau, AK 99803   907-465-2510
www.dced.state.ak.us/investments

Commercial fishing loans are available for various purposes at prime plus two percent (up to a maximum of 10.5%) for a 15-year term. All loans must be secured by adequate collateral.

* Alaska Employment Service

Work Opportunity Tax Credit Coordinator
P.O. Box 25509   907-465-5953
Juneau, AK 99802   Fax: 907-465-8753

Work Opportunity Tax Credit (WOTC): Offers employers tax credits as an incentive to hire people from seven target groups including Alaska Temporary Assistance Program (ATAP) and Aid for Families with Dependent Children (AFDC) recipients, food stamp recipients, veterans, vocational rehabilitation recipients, ex-felons, and high risk youth. The credit amount is 40% of up to $6,000 in qualified first year wages with a maximum credit of $2,400.

Welfare-to-Work Tax Credit (W2W): The W2W tax credit is available for hiring long-term ATAP and AFDC clients. The W2W tax credit is 35% of the first $10,000 in wages paid the first year, and 50% of the first $10,000 paid for the second year. The maximum tax credit is $3,500 the first year and $5,000 the second year for a total of $8,500.

* Exploration Incentive

Department of Natural Resources
Division of Oil and Gas
550 West 7th Ave., Suite 800
Anchorage, AK 99501   907-269-8900
www.dog.dnr.state.ak.us/oil/programs/incentives/incentives.htm

Up to $30 million in qualifying costs can be credited against future state corporate income tax, mining license tax and production royalties. Geophysical and geochemical surveys, trenching, bulk sampling, drilling, metallurgical testing and underground exploration are included as qualifying costs. Unused credit can be retained for 15 years and may be assigned to successors in interest.

* Alaska Industrial Development and Export Authority (AIDEA)

813 West Northern Lights	907-269-3000
Anchorage, AK 99503-6690	800-300-8534
http://www.aidea.org/	Fax: 907-269-3044

The Alaska Industrial Development and Export Authority's (AIDEA) mission is to encourage economic growth and diversification in Alaska. AIDEA finances businesses, helping to diversify the economy of Alaska and creating jobs for Alaskans. AIDEA also oversees the Alaska Energy Authority. The AIDEA has many programs; contact them directly to see if they have one to fit your business needs.

Loan Participation Program: provides long-term financing to Alaska businesses for new or existing projects, or for the refinancing of existing loans. This program has helped diversify the Alaskan economy by providing financing for a large variety of commercial facilities ranging from office buildings, warehouses and retail establishments to hotels, fishing vessels and manufacturing facilities. Financing is available for up to 15 years for personal property and up to 25 years for real property.

Business and Export Assistance Loan Guarantee: the program is designed to assist small to medium sized Alaskan businesses. The guarantee is applied to loans made to eligible Alaska business enterprises for real property, tangible personal property, working capital and export transactions. Through the program AIDEA is authorized to guarantee up to 80% of a loan, not to exceed $1 million, originated by eligible financial institutions. A part of this program, aimed at small businesses in rural areas, provides a streamlined application process for secured and unsecured loan guarantees up to $100,000.

Conduit Revenue Bond Program: Manufactures can apply for tax-exempt financing through small-issue manufacturing bonds. The bonds can be used to finance a manufacturing facility.

* Alaska Department of Natural Resources

Division of Agriculture

1800 Glenn Hwy, Suite 12	907-745-7200
Palmer, AK 99645-6736	Fax: 907-745-7242
www.dnr.state.ak.us/ag/ag_arlf.htm	

Agricultural Revolving Loan Fund: Available to individual farmers, ranchers, homesteaders, partnerships or corporations who are Alaska residents and can demonstrate experience in the farming business. Provides direct short term loans (1-year) up to $200,000. Product processing and land clearing loans up to $250,000, farm development loans up to $1 million. Interest rates at 5 percent with varying pay back periods.

* Division of Energy

Alaska Energy Authority/AIDEA

813 West Northern Lights Blvd.	907-269-3036
Anchorage, AK 99503	Fax: 907-269-3044
www.aidea.org/loanfund.htm	

Bulk Fuel Revolving Loan Fund: Assists communities in purchasing bulk fuel oil. A private individual who has a written endorsement from the government body of the community is eligible. Loan amount may not exceed 90 percent of the wholesale price of the fuel being purchased. Maximum loan amount is $200,000. Loan must be repaid within one year.

* Fisheries Research and Development Grants

National Oceanic and Atmospheric Administration
National Marine Fisheries Services

P.O. Box 21668	907-586-7221
Juneau, AK 99802-1668	Fax: 907-586-7249
www.fakr.noaa.gov/omi/grants	

The Grants Program Office of the National Marine Fisheries Service, Alaska Region administers a broad range of financial assistance and programs. The programs provide financial assistance for research and development projects to benefit the U.S. fishing industry.

* Alaska Commercial Fishing and Agriculture Bank (CFAB)

P.O. Box 92070	
Anchorage, AK 99509	907-276-2007
www.cfabalaska.com	

Established by Alaska Statute, CFAB is a private lending cooperative in which borrowers become members. Loans may be made for harvesting, marketing, or processing of fish or agriculture products. Interest rates are determined by the periodic sale of Farm Credit bonds in the national market.

* State Conservationist

USDA - Natural Resources Conservation Service

800 W. Evergreen Avenue, Suite 100	907-761-7760
Palmer, AK 99645	Fax: 907-761-7790
http://www.ak.nrcs.usda.gov/programs/index.html	

The Natural Resources Conservation Service assists owners of America's private land conserve their soil, water and other natural resources. They offer many programs to achieve harmony between people and the land. The voluntary program *Environmental Quality Incentives Program (EQIP)* is for Alaskan farmers and ranchers that are concerned about environmental quality. EQIP offers financial and technical help to assist eligible participants install and implement conservation programs.

* Conservation Grants

Alaska Conservation Foundation

441 West 5th Avenue, Suite 502	907-276-1917
Anchorage, AK 99501	Fax: 907-274-4145
www.akcf.org	

The Alaska Conservation Foundation is a foundation committed to the environment that receives and awards grants to protect the Alaska ecosystems and sustainable communities for the Alaskan people. The Foundation provides a number of grants for a variety of needs including: *General Grantmaking, Rapid Response Grants, Sustainable Community Development Grants, Watchable Wildlife Conservation Trust Grants* and more.

* Alaska Economic Development Resource Guide

Division of Community and Business Development
Department of Community and Economic Development

550 W 7th, Suite 770	907-269-4580
Anchorage, AK 99501	Fax: 907-269-4539
http://www.dced.state.ak.us/cbd/edrg/EDRG.htm	

This publication describes more than 120 assistance programs for Alaskan individuals and businesses. It is available for $7 for a hard copy or you can obtain a free copy at the above web site.

* Alaska Product Preference and Forest Product Preference Programs

Department of Community and Economic Development
Division of Community and Business Development

550 W 7th, Suite 1770	907-269-8110
Anchorage, AK 99507	Fax: 907-269-8125
http://www.dced.state.ak.us/cbd/prodpref/prodpref.htm	

These programs provide incentives for Alaska businesses responding to bids or proposals for state contracts by giving them preferential consideration. The Alaska Product Preference Program and the Alaska Forest Product Preference Program can provide a cost preference of up to 7%.

Arizona

* Arizona Department of Commerce

Executive Tower, Suite 600

1700 W. Washington	800-528-8421
Phoenix, AZ 85007	602-771-1100
www.azcommerce.com	

If you are thinking about starting a business or already have a business in Arizona, you should get to know the Department of Commerce. They provide a wealth of information about all aspects of business including financial options.

Arizona Business Connection: A resource center for information, referrals and advice for every stage of small business development. Representatives are available to answer questions and provide a free custom packet.

Small Business Advocate: Works with chambers of commerce and other groups to develop policies and programs that will address fundamental statewide issues of concern to all small businesses.
- Develops customized packets of information and licenses required for small business start-up, expansion, and relocation.
- Provides the booklet *Guide To Establishing and Operating a Business In Arizona* which includes an extensive directory and resources for referrals and networking opportunities.

- Provides coordination and publicity for programs and services that assist minority and women business owners, and assists state agencies in certification of minority and women owned businesses.
- Conducts seminars to help local companies procure goods and services from qualified firms.
- Assists entrepreneurs in resolving matters involving state government offices.
- The High Technology Division aids and assists the growth of high technology companies in Arizona.

The Community Planning Staff: Provides technical assistance on development-related issues, such as community-strategic planning, land-use planning, design review, zoning and infrastructure development, and financing. Provides direct assistance to rural communities in organizing an economic development program or effort, and evaluating community resources. Provides assistance with downtown revitalization projects. Provides support for rural community tourism development efforts. This program helps organizations responsible for retention and expansion develop a program to retain and encourage expansion of existing businesses.

Arizona's Work Force Recruitment and Job Training Program: Provides job training assistance to businesses creating net new jobs in Arizona. The program is designed to provide companies with a well equipped work force while ensuring maximum leverage of state and federal training funds.

Strategic Finance Division: Offers a wide range of loan and grant programs which provide economic development resources for companies relocating to or expanding in Arizona including the following:
- *Commerce & Economic Development Commission (CEDC)*: A low-interest rate loan program funded by proceeds from the Arizona Lottery. The CEDC's activities include:
  - *Direct Assistance To Arizona Business*: to provide expansion capital to existing companies.
  - *Technology Sector Capital*: financing that supports the development and growth of high-tech industries.
  - *Intermediary Participation Program*: partnerships with other groups that provide economic development loans.
  - A CEDC loan can be used to purchase fixed assets. A grant component tied to specific wage levels may also be available. In general, projects are weighted based on job creation, the presence of other investors and projected tax revenues. Final loan approval is determined by a six-member commission appointed by the Governor of Arizona. Attractive terms and a fixed interest rate are available.

Revolving Energy Loans for Arizona (RELA): A loan fund to promote and assist energy-related projects and companies. Arizona non-profit entities, political subdivisions or companies that purchase energy-conserving products for use in their own facilities are eligible. In addition, manufacturers of energy-conserving products may apply. Loan requests may range from $10,000 to $500,000 up to a maximum of 60% of total project costs. The RELA program offers a 5% interest rate and variable terms depending on energy payback.

Economic Strength Projects (ESP) offers grants for road construction. This is a very competitive program based on the economic impact of applicant projects in the community in which it will be located. Applications are submitted by a town, city or county.

The Enterprise Zones Program: Offers income tax credits and property tax reclassification for eligible companies meeting employment and industry requirements. Benefits are based on net new job creation, employment of economically disadvantaged or dislocated workers and location in an enterprise zone.

Minority/Women-Owned Business Enterprises Office: Acts as a resource and advocate for women and minority small businesses. Services include: a statewide directory of women/minority-owned businesses, Professional Women's conference sponsorship, newsletter containing calendar of events and relevant articles, marketing to state agencies and businesses, and certification seminars.

* Arizona Rural Business Program
Arizona Rural Development Office
3003 North Central, Suite 900   602-280-8701
Phoenix, AZ 85012-2906   Fax: 602-280-8708
http://www.rurdev.usda.gov/az/RBuss.htm
The Arizona Rural Business Program is committed to the creation of viable new and improved business and cooperatives in rural Arizona. The program delivers a variety of assistance to businesses including: *Business and Industry Guaranteed Loans, Intermediary Relending Program, Rural Business Enterprise Grants* and *Rural Cooperative Development Grants.*

* Arizona Department of Revenue
3191 N. Washington
Chandler, AZ 85225   602-225-2060
http://www.revenue.state.az.us
The Arizona Department of Revenue doesn't just collect taxes; it also offers a variety of information for the small business owner. They offer the guides *A-Z Taxes for Small Business Program* and *Business Basics: A Guide to Taxes for Arizona.* In addition they will provide Business Seminars, Education Classes and Tax Credit information.

* Small Business Administration (SBA)
2828 N. Central Ave., #800   602-745-7200
Phoenix, AZ 85004-1093   Fax: 602-745-7210
www.sba.gov/az
The Arizona District Small Business Administration Office delivers a variety of programs and services, such as startup and operational assistance through small business training and counseling, financial assistance for startup's, operational and disaster help, business opportunities, such as government contracting, subcontracting, procurement, and much more.

* Small Business Investment Companies
Grayhawk Venture Fund I, L.P.
Sherman Chu, Contact
5050 North 40th Street, Suite 310   602-956-8700
Phoenix, AZ 85018   Fax: 602-956-8080
Email: schu@gvp.us

Magnet Capital, L.P.
Gregory Mischel/Michael Shields, Contact
3550 North Central Ave., Suite 1400   602-222-4801
Phoenix, AZ 85012   Fax: 602-222-4807
Email: info@magnetcapital.com
The SBA licenses, regulates, and provides financial assistance to privately owned and operated Small Business Investment Companies. SBICs make venture or risk investments by supplying capital and extending unsecured loans and loans not fully collateralized to small enterprises which meet their investment criteria. Financing is made by direct loans and by equity investments.

* Certified Development Corporations
Business Development Finance Corporation
Richard Jeffrey, Vice President
2200 E. Camelback, Suite 215   602-381-6292
Phoenix, AZ 85016   Fax: 602-381-8012
Area of Operation: Counties of Cochise, Graham, Greenlee, Pima, Pinal, and Santa Cruz. Cities of Chandler, Mesa, Tempe in Maricopa County.

Southwestern Business Financing Corporation
Robert D. McGee, President
3200 North Central Avenue, 27th Floor   602-495-6495
Phoenix AZ 85012   Fax: 602-230-0945
Area of Operation: City wide Phoenix

The 504 Certified Development Company (CDC) Program provides growing businesses with long-term, fixed-rate financing for major fixed assets, such as land and buildings. A Certified Development Company is a nonprofit corporation set up to contribute to the economic development of its community or region. CDCs work with the Small Business Administration and private-sector lenders to provide financing to small businesses.

Arkansas

* Arkansas Department of Economic Development
1 State Capitol Mall   501-682-1121
Little Rock, AR 72201   800-ARKANSAS
www.aedc.state.ar.us   Fax: 501-682-7394
Existing Workforce Training Program (EWTP): Provides financial assistance to Arkansas manufacturing industries for upgrading the skills of their existing workforce. Secondary objectives are to build the capacity within their state-supported institutions to supply the ongoing training needs of Arkansas industries and to increase industry participation in the state's School-to-Work initiative.

ScrapMatch: A program designed to help Arkansas manufacturers find markets for their industrial scrap materials, thereby lowering the cost of doing business. ScrapMatch uses an electronic data management system to match industrial waste generators with secondary material markets.

Industrial Waste Minimization Program and Resource Recovery: Reduction, reuse, and recycling of industrial waste is the Industrial Waste Minimization Program's focus. By-product and surplus asset marketing assistance are also provided. The program provides on-site waste reduction audits and technical assistance to industry.

Customized Training Incentive Program: Provides intensive pre-employment training for Arkansas workers to meet the increasing technical employment needs of the state's new and expanding businesses. Additionally, financial assistance to manufacturing industries for upgrading the skills of their existing workforce is also available.

Bond Guaranty Programs: For companies that have a financial history but are unable to sell industrial revenue bonds to the public, the Arkansas Economic Development Commission (AEDC) can assure bond holders of repayment by guaranteeing up to $4 million of a bond issue. The state's guaranty allows the bonds to be sold at a higher credit rating, therefore lowering the effective interest rate for the company. The AEDC charges a 5% fee for guaranteeing issues of this type.

Economic Development District Revolving Funds: Several planning and development districts in Arkansas have revolving loan funds for economic development purposes. The loans are limited to $100,000 per business, must involve specific levels of job creation, and must be matched by a bank loan.

Create Rebate Program: Companies hiring specified net new full-time permanent employees within 24 months after completion of an approved expansion and/or new location project can be eligible to receive a financial incentive to be used for a specific purpose. This incentive ranges from 3.9% to 5% in areas with an unemployment rate in excess of 10%, or more than 3% above the state's average unemployment rate for the preceding calendar year.

Industrial Revenue Bonds: Provide manufacturers with below-market financing. Interest on tax exempt issues is normally 80% of prime, but this may vary depending on terms of the issue. For real estate loans, 15 years is the most common term. The primary goal of this financing program is to enable manufacturers to purchase land, buildings, and equipment to expand their operations.

Arkansas Economic Development Act (AEDA): To utilize the AEDA program, companies must sign a financial agreement prior to construction outlining the terms of the incentives and stipulations. There are two basic incentives provided: A state corporate income tax credit up to 100% of the total amount of annual debt service paid to the lender financing a project; Refund of sales and use taxes on construction materials, machinery, and equipment associated with a project during the period specified by the financial agreement.

Advantage Arkansas Program: A job tax credit program for qualifying new and expanding companies which provides corporate income tax credits and sales and use tax refunds to companies locating or expanding in Arkansas.

Free Port Law: No tax on goods in transit or raw materials and finished goods destined for out-of-state sales; no sales tax on manufacturing equipment, pollution control facilities, or raw materials; no property tax on textile mills.

Day Care Facility Incentive Program: Companies can receive a sales and use tax refund on the initial cost of construction materials and furnishings purchased to build and equip an approved child care facility. Additionally, a corporate income tax credit of 3.9% of the total annual payroll of the workers employed exclusively to provide childcare service, or a $5,000 income tax credit for the first year the business provides its employees with a day care facility is also available.

Tourism Development: Provides state sales tax credits up to 10% of approved project costs for the creation or expansion of eligible tourist attractions exceeding $500,000, and 25% of project costs exceeding $1,000,000.

Recycling Equipment Tax Credit: Allows taxpayers to receive a tax credit for the purchase of equipment used exclusively for reduction, reuse, or recycling of solid waste material for commercial purposes, whether or not for profit, and the cost of installation of such equipment by outside contractors. The amount of the credit shall equal 30% of the cost of eligible equipment and installation costs.

Motion Picture Incentive Act: Qualifying motion picture production companies spending in excess of $500,000 within six months, or $1 million within 12 months may receive a refund of state sales and use taxes paid on qualified expenditures incurred in conjunction with a film, telefilm, music video, documentary, episodic television show, or commercial advertisement.

Biotechnology Development and Training Act: Offers three different income tax credits to taxpayers furthering biotechnical business development. The first credit is a 5% income tax credit applied to costs to build and equip eligible biotechnical facilities. The second credit allows a 30% income tax credit both for eligible employee training costs and for contract with state-supported institutions for higher education to conduct qualified cooperative research projects. The third credit allows an income tax credit for qualified research in biotechnology, including but not limited to the cost of purchasing, licensing, developing, or protecting intellectual property. This credit is equal to 20% of the amount the cost of qualified research exceeds the cost of such resource in the base year.

The *Arkansas Economic Development Commission's (AEDC)* international offices assist Arkansas companies in exporting their products and services by arranging personalized meetings with potential distributors, sales representatives or end users in the countries targeted for AEDC's export promotion efforts. In addition to this service, they also offer the following:
- Market research
- Assisting companies exhibiting in international trade fairs
- Planning and coordinating trade missions
- Obtaining trade leads
- Representing and/or advising companies on export transactions
- Accompanying company representatives on export sales trips
- Promoting companies in meetings with prospective buyers

* USDA Rural Development

Shirley Tucker
Director for Rural Business Cooperative Programs
700 West Capitol, Room 3416   501-301-3280
Little Rock, AR 72201-3225   Fax: 501-301-3294
www.rurdev.usda.gov/ar

The Rural Business-Cooperative Service provides loans to help develop emerging businesses that will bring employment opportunities to rural areas. Grants are available for public bodies and private non-profit corporations to facilitate development of small emerging private business enterprises in rural areas. They offer the following assistance: *Business and Industry Guaranteed Loans, Intermediary Relending Program, Rural Business Enterprise and Opportunity Grants* and *Rural and Economic Development Loans and Grants*.

* Environmental Permitting Services

Arkansas Department of Environmental Quality
8001 National Dr.
Little Rock, AR 72219   501-682-0821
www.adez.state.ar.us/custsvs/businessasst.htm

The Arkansas Department of Environmental Quality works in a pro-business manner with companies looking to locate or expand operations in Arkansas. The agency recognizes the need for business growth in Arkansas while maintaining their state's positive environmental quality.

* Arkansas Capital Corporation

2005 S. Commerce St.   501-374-9247
Little Rock, AR 72201   800-216-7237
http://acc.arccapital.com

A privately-owned, nonprofit organization established in 1957 to serve as an alternative source of financing for companies in Arkansas. Its main goal is to improve the economic climate in the state by providing long-term, fixed-rate loans to Arkansas companies. As a preferred lender for the Small Business Administration, ACC makes loans to existing operations and business start-ups for everything from new construction and equipment to working capital. ACC loans may be used in combination with bank loans, municipal bond issues, or other sources of financing.

* ASTA Investment Fund

Arkansas Science and Technology Authority
100 Main St., Suite 450
Little Rock, AR 72201   501-324-8755
www.accessarkansasscience.org/seed.html

The Arkansas Science and Technology Authority (ASTA) administers a special Investment Fund of $2.9 million which can provide seed capital for new and developing technology-based companies through loans, royalty agreements, and limited stock purchases.

* Arkansas Development Finance Authority (ADFA)

P.O. Box 8023
423 Main Street, Suite 500   501-682-5905

Little Rock, AR 72203   Fax: 501-682-5859
www.accessarkansas.org/adfa

Industrial Development Bond Guaranty Program: Offers taxable and tax exempt bond financing to both small and large businesses. Umbrella bonds, available to small businesses, spread the costs of the bond issue among all of the borrowers. ADFA also can provide interim financing for approved projects awaiting bond issuance. Available to manufacturing facilities.

Export Finance: Short-term loans to businesses based on export transactions. Financing is provided through the exporter's local bank which funds 10 percent of the loan value.

Beginning Farmer Loan Program: assists beginning farmers acquire agricultural property at lower interest rates.

Speculative Building Loan Program: provides a source of financing to Industrial Development Corps. interested in building spec. industrial facilities.

Capital Access Program: creates a method for making slightly higher risk loans more attractive to participating lending institutions.

Waste Water Revolving Loan Fund: provides low interest rate financing to municipalities wishing to improve their waste water treatment facilities.

Cooperative Revolving Loan Fund: provides low interest rate loans to agricultural cooperatives who are producing/marketing fruit & vegetable products.

Disadvantaged Business Enterprise Program: provides banks with working capital guarantees for disadvantaged business enterprise contractors.

Intermediary Relending Loan Program: $3 million Federal loan to ADFA which can be relended to businesses and communities in rural Arkansas.

Port Facilities Revolving Loan Program: supports investment in port facilities for Arkansas' navigable waterways.

Aquaculture Program: coordinates the aquaculture industry in Arkansas.

Farm Mediation Program: provides a forum for farmers and lenders to resolve loan debt service payment problems.

Farm Link Program: a listing service that links up retiring farmers with aspiring farmers.

Crop and Livestock Loan Program: provides a 50% guarantee to a commercial lender making a loan to a 4-H or FFA member.

* Arkansas Science and Technology Authority

423 Main St., Suite 200   501-683-4400
Little Rock, AR 72201   Fax: 501-683-4420
www.accessarkansasscience.org

Promotes science and technology in both the public and private sectors and works to support scientific research and job creating technology development. The following is a listing of some of the programs offered.

Applied Research Grant Programs: For companies in need of research and development and would welcome working with an Arkansas college or university to have this work completed on a cost-sharing basis.

The Technology Development Program: provides assistance in development and commercialization of new technology-based products and processes through innovative technology development projects.

Seed Capital Investment Program: Program seeks to invest in innovative Arkansas companies that utilize new products or processes in their businesses. Does not fund entire projects, just the initial working capital portion of the financing package.

* Small Business Administration (SBA)

2120 Riverfront Dr., #100   501-324-5871
Little Rock, AR 72202-1794   Fax: 501-324-5199
www.sba.gov/ar

The Arkansas District Small Business Administration Office delivers a variety of programs and services, such as startup and operational assistance through small business training and counseling, financial assistance for startup's, operational and disaster help, business opportunities, such as government contracting, subcontracting, procurement, and much more.

* Arkansas Capital Corporation

Arkansas Capital Corporation	800-216-7237
200 S. Commerce	501-374-9247
Little Rock, AR 72201	Fax: 501-374-9425

Arkansas Capital Corporation	800-705-9295
700 Research Center Blvd., Suite 1608	479-444-8881
Fayetteville, AR 72701	Fax: 479-444-8882

Arkansas Capital Corporation	
P.O. Box 1403	
2905 King Street	870-923-8002
Jonesboro, AR 72403	888-726-9229
Contact: Mike Taylor	Fax: (870) 932-0135

Arkansas Capital Corporation	
The Chamber Building	870-352-2853
119 W. 3rd Street	888-870-8685
Fordyce, AR 71742	Fax: 870-352-5126
Contact: Ms. Bryn Bagwell	
www.arcapital.com	

A private, non-profit corporation that provides fixed-rate financing for projects which do not meet the requirements for conventional bank loans. Projects must increase or maintain employment, and major portion of loan must be used for fixed assets.

* Small Business Investment Companies

Small Business Investment Capital, Inc.
Jerry W. Davis, President
12103 Interstate 30
Mail: P.O. Box 3627   501-455-6599
Little Rock, AR 72203   Fax: 501-455-6556
Email: lmartinez@afslr.com

Diamond State Ventures, L.P.
Joe T. Hays, Contact
200 South Commerce Street, Suite 400   501-374-9247
Little Rock, AR 72201-1728   Fax: 501-374-9425
Email: jhays@arcapital.com

The Small Business Investment Company (SBIC) program. SBICs, licensed by the Small Business Administration, are privately organized and privately managed investment firms. They are participants in a vital partnership between government and the private sector economy. With their own capital and with funds borrowed at favorable rates through the Federal Government, SBICs provide venture capital to small independent businesses, both new and already established.

* Certified Development Companies

Arkansas Certified Development Corporation
200 South Commerce
Little Rock, AR 72201   501-374-9247
Area of Operation: Entire state of Arkansas

West Central Arkansas Planning and Development District, Inc.
825 Central Avenue
P.O. Box 1558
Hot Springs, AR 71901   501-624-1036
Area of Operation: Clark, Conway, Garland, Hot Springs, Johnson, Montgomery, Perry Pike, Pope & Yell.

Ark-Tex Regional Development
P.O. Box 5307
Texarkana, TX 75505   903-832-8636
Area of Operation: Miller County

The 504 Certified Development Company (CDC) Program provides growing businesses with long-term, fixed-rate financing for major fixed assets, such as land and buildings. A Certified Development Company is a nonprofit corporation set up to contribute to the economic development of its community or region. CDCs work with the Small Business Administration and private-sector lenders to provide financing to small businesses.

California

* California Trade and Commerce Agency

1102 Q Street, Suite 6000   800-303-6000
Sacramento, CA 95814   916-322-1394
http://commerce.ca.gov/state/ttca/ttca_homepage.jsp

California's business resources are many and varied with many local and regional programs. The following is not all-inclusive:

Office of Small Business: Offers workshops, seminars, individual counseling, and publications for those interested in small businesses. They have information and expertise in dealing with state, federal, and local agencies.

The Loan Guarantee Program: Assists small businesses that cannot qualify for bank loans. Normally, 80% of the loan amount, with the guaranteed portion of the loan not exceeding $350,000 is offered. Microloans, up to $25,000, are fully guaranteed.

Fishing Vessel: Direct loans to finance commercial fishing vessel equipment and modifications that result in fuel savings. Loans are from $10,000 to $25,000.

Hazardous Waste: Direct loans to finance equipment or a production practice that reduces waste or lessens hazardous properties. The minimum loan is $20,000. The maximum loan is $150,000.

Small Corporate Offering Registration Network: Raise up to $1 million by issuing shares directly to investors through a state-registered public offering.

Sudden and Severe Economic Dislocation (SSED): The California Trade and Commerce Agency provides gap financing to businesses in areas of the state affected by plant and military base closures, defense downsizing, industry layoffs, presidentially declared disasters and other economic problems which have contributed to job loss in California.

Old Growth Diversification Revolving Loan Fund: The California Trade and Commerce Agency provides low cost capital to businesses that create jobs in targeted timber-dependent areas. Businesses may borrow from $5,000 to $150,000 at a reduced interest rate to purchase machinery and equipment or for working capital.

Net Operating Loss Carryover: Allows businesses that experience a loss for the year to carry this loss forward to the next year in order to offset income in the following year.

Enterprise Zone Program: Encourages business development in 39 designated areas through numerous special zone incentives.

Local Agency Military Base Recovery Area: Designations which are similar to enterprise zones allowing communities to extend the aforementioned California tax credits to companies locating in a LAMBRA zone.

International Trade and Investment: Acts as a catalyst to create jobs in California through vigorous and sustained promotion of exports to global markets and foreign investment into the Golden State. They have offices in California and ten foreign locations. They offer promotion of California products and companies abroad through the Office of Export Development, current information on foreign market opportunities, the Special American Business Internship Training Program, and assistance with attracting foreign investment through the California Office of Foreign Investment. They also provide exporting financial assistance for going global through several economic development programs provided by the California Export Finance Office, a division of California's Trade and Commerce Agency. The maximum guarantee amount is $750,000. That is 90% of an $833,000 loan.

* Rural Development Authority

Charles Clendenin, Program Director
Rural Business-Cooperative Service
430 G Street, Agcy. 4169   530-792-5800
Davis, CA 95616   Fax: 530-792-5837
www.rurdev.usda.gov/ca

This service is responsible for business development programs including guaranteed loans to rural business and industries, grants to facilitate development of small and emerging private business enterprises in rural areas, and revolving loan programs that finance rural businesses. The RBS administers programs directed toward increasing rural job opportunities, facilitating development of small and emerging private business enterprises, and improving the economic and environmental climate of rural communities.

California State Treasurer's Office

915 Capitol Mall
Sacramento, CA 95814
Mailing address:
Post Office Box 942809
915 Capitol Mall C-15
Sacramento, CA 94209-0001   916-653-2995
http://www.treasurer.ca.gov/

The California Treasurer's Office has information on a variety of bonds for businesses and offers publications on many business topics.

* Energy Technology Export Program

California Energy Commission
1516 Ninth St., MS-45
Sacramento, CA 95814   916-654-4528
www.energy.ca.gov

The California Energy Commission assists California companies through several energy export programs.

* California Capital Access Program

California Pollution Control Financing Authority
Attention: SBAF Program Manager
915 Capitol Mall, Room 466
Sacramento, CA 95814   916-654-5610
www.treasurer.ca.gov/cpcfa/cpcfa.htm

The California Pollution Control Financing Authority (CPCFA) provides a form of loan portfolio insurance which provides up to 100% coverage on certain loan defaults, encouraging banks and other financial institutions to make loans to small businesses that fall just outside of most banks' conventional underwriting standards. The maximum loan amount is $2.5 million. The maximum premium CPCFA will pay is $100,000 (per loan).

* California Industrial Development Financing Advisory Commission (CEDFAC)

California Industrial Development Financing Advisory Commission
915 Capitol Mall
Sacramento, CA 95814   916-653-3843
www.treasurer.ca.gov/CIDFAC/cidfac.htm

The Treasurer's office assists California manufacturing businesses in funding capital expenditures for acquisitions or expansions. Allows a business to borrow funds at competitive rates through the issuance of tax-exempt bonds enhanced by a letter of credit. The maximum face amount of an IDB bond issue is $10 million per applicant per public jurisdiction.

* Small Business Administration (SBA)

Los Angeles District Office
330 N. Brand, Suite 1200   818-552-3210
Glendale, CA 91203   Fax: 818-552-3260

Mark Quinn
Small Business Administration (SBA)
455 Market, 6th Floor   415-744-6820
San Francisco, CA 94105-2420   Fax: 415-744-6812
www.sba.gov/ca

Local Offices
Fresno   559-487-5791
                                         Fax: 559-487-5636
Sacramento   916-930-3700
                                         Fax: 916-930-3737
San Diego   619-557-7250
                                         619-557-5894
Santa Ana   714-550-7420
                                         714-550-0191

The California Small Business Administration Office delivers a variety of programs and services, such as startup and operational assistance through small business training and counseling, financial assistance for startup's, operational and disaster help, business opportunities, such as government contracting, subcontracting, procurement, and much more.

* Small Business Investment Companies

AltoTech II, L.P.
Walter Lee, Contact
707 Menlo Avenue, Suite 120   650-330-0881
Menlo Park, CA 94025   Fax: 650-330-0885
Email: wlee@altotechventures.com

American River Ventures, L.P.
Corley Phillips, Contact
2270 Douglas Blvd., Suite 212   916-780-2828
Roseville, CA 95661   Fax: 916-780-5443
Email: plans@arventures.com

Aspen Ventures III, L.P.
Alex Cilento, Thaddeus Whalen, Contacts
1000 Fremont Avenue, Suite 200   650-917-5670

Los Altos, CA 94024
Email: DSchilling@AspenVentures.com
Fax: 650-917-5677

Aspen Ventures West II, L.P.
Alexander Cilento & David Crocket, Mgrs.
1000 Fremont Avenue, Suite V
Los Altos, CA 94024
Email: DSchilling@AspenVentures.com
650-917-5670
Fax: 650-917-5677

AVI Capital, L.P.
P. Wolken, B. Weinman & B. Grossi, Mgrs.
One First Street, Suite 12
Los Altos, CA 94022
Email: wang@avicapital.com
650-949-9862
Fax: 650-949-8510

Bank of America Ventures
Carla Perumean, Senior Vice President
950 Tower Lane, Suite 700
Foster City, CA 94404
Email: carla.s.perumean@bankofamerica.com
650-378-6000
Fax: 650-378-6040

Bay Partners L.S. Fund, L.P.
John Freidenrich, Marcella Yano
10600 N. DeAnza Boulevard, Suite 100
Cupertino, CA 95014
Email: avallen@baypartners.com
408-725-2444
Fax: 408-446-4502

Bay Partners SBIC II, L.P.
John Friedenrich & Neal Dempsey, Mgrs.
10600 N. DeAnza Boulevard, Suite 100
Cupertino, CA 95014
Email: avallen@baypartners.com
408-725-2444
Fax: 408-446-4502

Bay Partners SBIC, L.P.
John Freidenrich & Neal Dempsey, Mgrs.
10600 North De Anza Blvd., Suite 100
Cupertino, CA 95014
Email: avallen@baypartners.com
408-725-2444
Fax: 408-446-4502

Bentley Capital
John Hung, President
592 Vallejo Street, Suite #2
San Francisco, CA 94133
Email: bc8081@aol.com
415-362-2868
Fax: 415-398-8209

Canaan SBIC, L.P.
Eric Young, Manager
2884 Sand Hill Road
Menlo Park, CA 94025
415-854-8082
Fax: 415-854-8127

Celerity Partners SBIC, L.P.
Clifford A. Lyon, Contact
11111 Santa Monica Blvd., Suite 1127
Los Angeles, CA 90025
Email: kraus@celeritypartners.com
Fax: 310-268-1712

Charterway Investment Corporation
Edmund C. Lau, Chairman
9660 Flair Dr., Suite 328
El Monte, CA 91731
Email: toysanaba@aol.com
626-279-1189
Fax: 626-279-9062

Chase Venture Capital Associates
101 California Street, 27th Floor
San Francisco, CA 94111
415-393-1283
Fax: 415-393-1205

CVP SBIC, L.P.
Christopher J. Hadsell, Contact
873 Santa Cruz Avenue, Suite 206
Menlo Park, CA 94025
Email: derek@cardinalvc.com
650-614-4860
Fax: 650-614-4865

DB Capital Partners SBIC, L.P.
300 South Grand Avenue
Los Angeles, CA 90071

Draper Associates, a California LP
Timothy C. Draper, President
400 Seaport Court, Suite 250
Redwood City, CA 94063
Email: karen@dfj.com
650-599-9000
Fax: 650-599-9726

Draper-Richards L.P.
William Draper III, President

50 California Street, Suite 2925
San Francisco, CA 94111
Email: clam@draperintl.com
415-616-4050
Fax: 415-616-4060

East Gate Private Equity Fund III, L.P.
Ken Choi, Contact
514 High Street, Suite #5
Palo Alto, CA 94301
Email: bcbrant@eg-group.com
650-325-5077
Fax: 650-325-5072

Far East Capital Corp.
Daniel Michener
350 S. Grand Ave., Suite 4100
Los Angeles, CA 90071
Email: donald.kim@fareastnationalbank.com
213-830-2435
Fax: 213-617-7939

Fulcrum Venture Capital Corporation
Brian Argrett, President
300 Corporate Pointe, Suite 380
Culver City, CA 90230
Email: brian@fulcrumventures.com
310-645-1271
Fax: 310-645-1272

GKM SBIC, L.P.
Jonathan R. Bloch, Contact
11150 Santa Monica Blvd., Suite 825
Los Angeles, CA 90025
Email: jbloch@gkm.com
310-268-2623
Fax: 310-268-0870

Hall, Morris & Drufva II, L.P.
Ronald J. Hall, Managing Director
26161 La Paz Road, Suite E
Mission Viejo, CA 92691
714-707-5096
Fax: 714-707-5121

Hamilton Apex Technology Ventures, L.P.
Richard Crosby, Contact
12526 High Bluff Drive, Suite 260
San Diego, CA 92130
Email: rcrosby@hamiltonventures.com
858-314-2350
Fax: 858-314-2355

Housatonic Equity Investors SBIC, L.P.
Barry Reynolds, Michael Thorndike
44 Montgomery Street, Suite 4010
San Francisco, CA 94104
Email: breynolds@housatoincpartners.com
415-955-9020
Fax: 415-981-0617

Huntington Capital, L.P.
Morgan Miller and Barry Wilson, Contacts
11988 El Camino Real, Suite 160
San Diego, CA 92130
Email: susan@huntingtoncapital.com
858-259-7654
Fax: 858-259-0074

Inglewood Ventures, L.P.
Dr. M. Blake Ingle, Daniel Wood
12526 High Bluff Drive, Suite 300
San Diego, CA 92130
Email: danwood@ix.netcom.com
858-792-3579
Fax: 858-792-3417

J.P. Morgan Partners (SBIC), LLC
101 California Street, 27th Floor
San Francisco, CA 94111
415-393-1283
Fax: 415-393-1205

Kline Hawkes California SBIC, L.P.
Frank R. Kline, Manager
11726 San Vicente Blvd., Suite 300
Los Angeles, CA 90049
Email: kmagnin@klinehawkes.com
310-442-4700
Fax: 310-442-4707

LaiLai Capital Corp.
Danny Ku, President
18249-2 Valley Blvd.
City of Industry, CA 91744
Email: lailaicapital@aol.com
626-333-5420
Fax: 626-934-9699

Magna Pacific Investments
Cynthia Jopanda, President
330 North Brand Boulevard, Suite 670
Glendale, CA 91203
Email: Magnapacific@cs.com
818-547-0809
Fax: 818-547-9303

Marwit Capital Company, L.P.
Matthew Witte, President
180 Newport Center Drive, Suite 200
Newport Beach, CA 92660
Email: mckay@marwit.com
949-640-6234
Fax: 949-720-8077

Milepost Ventures, L.P.
Christine Cordaro, Contact
One Embarcadero Center, Suite 3250
San Francisco, CA 94104
Email: cindy@milepostventures.com
415-391-8950
Fax: 415-391-8937

Montreux Equity Partners II SBIC, L.P.
Daniel K. Turner III, Contact
2500 Sand Hill Road, Suite 215
Menlo, CA 94025
Email: dturner@montreuxequity.com
650-234-1200
Fax: 650-234-1250

New Vista Capital Fund, L.P.
Roger Barry & Frank Greene, Managers
540 Cowper St, Suite 200
Palo Alto, CA 94301
Email: rbarry@nvcap.com
650-328-9434
Fax: 650-329-6889

NewVista Capital Fund, II, L.P.
Dr. Frank Green, Contact
540 Cowper St., Suite 200
Palto Alto, CA 94300
Email: rbarry@nvcap.com
650-857-0799
Fax: 650-857-0773

Novus Ventures, L.P.
Daniel D. Tompkins, Manager
20111 Stevens Creek Boulevard, Suite 130
Cupertino, CA 95014
Email: ddthompkins@novusventures.com
408-252-3900
Fax: 408-252-1713

Opportunity Capital Corporation
J. Peter Thompson, President
2201 Walnut Avenue, Suite 210
Fremont, CA 94538
Email: rcg@ocpcapital.com
510-795-7000
Fax: 510-494-5439

Opportunity Capital Partners II, L.P.
J. Peter Thompson, General Partner
2201 Walnut Avenue, Suite 210
Fremont, CA 94538
Email: rcg@ocpcapital.com
510-795-7000
Fax: 510-494-5439

Outlook Ventures III, L.P.
Carl Nichols, Contact
135 Main Street, Suite 1350
San Francisco, CA 94105
Email: carl@iminds.com
415-547-0000
Fax: 415-547-0010

Pacific Mezzanine Fund, L.P.
Nathan W. Bell, General Partner
2200 Powell St., Suite 1250
Emeryville, CA 94608
Email: esl@pacmezz.com
510-595-9800
Fax: 510-595-9801

Peninsula Equity Partners SBIC, L.P.
Gregory C. Ennis, Contact
3000 Sand Hill Road
Building 3, Suite 125
Menlo Park, CA 94025
Email: ennis@peninsulaequity.com
650-854-0314
Fax: 650-854-0670

Pinecreek Capital Partners, L.P.
Randall F. Zurbach, President
24 Corporate Plaza, Suite 160
Newport Beach, CA 92660
Email: tmorgan@pinecreekcap.com
949-720-4620
Fax: 949-720-4629

Positive Enterprises, Inc.
Kwok Szeto, President
1489 Webster Street, Suite 228
San Francisco, CA 94115
Email: pei-sba@pei-sba.com
415-885-6600
Fax: 415-928-6363

Red Rock Ventures II, L.P.
Robert Todd, Jr., Curtis K. Meyers
180 Lytton Avenue
Palo Alto, CA 94301
Email: carol@redrockventures.com
650-325-3111
Fax: 650-853-7044

Rocket Ventures II SBIC, L.P.
David Adams
3000 Sand Hill Road, Building 1, Suite 170
Menlo Park, CA 94025
Email: david@rocketventures.com
650-561-9100
Fax: 650-561-9183

Seacoast Capital Partners, L.P.
Jeff Holland
One Sansome Street, Suite 2100
San Francisco, CA 94104
415-956-1400
Fax: 415-956-1459

Selby Venture Partners, L.P.
Robert Marshall & James Marshall, Mgrs.
3500 Alameda De Las Pulgas, 2nd Floor
Menlo Park, CA 94025
Email: paul@selbyventures.com
650-854-7399
Fax: 650-854-7039

Shepherd Ventures II, L.P.
George C. Kenney, Contact
12250 El Camino Real, Suite 116
San Diego, CA 92130
Email: olga@shepherdventures.com
858-509-4744
Fax: 858-509-3662

Smart Technology Ventures III SBIC, L.P.
Joseph Marks, Contact
1801 Century Park West, 5th Floor
Los Angeles, CA 90067
Email: sbic@smarttechnologyventures.com
310-203-3800
Fax: 310-203-3801

Sorrento Growth Partners I, L.P.
Robert Jaffe, Manager
4370 La Jolla Village Drive, Suite 1040
San Diego, CA 92122
Email: cbarberio@sorrentoventures.com
858-452-3100
Fax: 858-452-7607

St. Cloud Capital Partners, L.P.
Terrence Ng, Contact
10866 Wilshire Blvd., Suite 1450
Los Angeles, CA 90024-
Email: TNg@stcloudcapital.com
310-475-2700
Fax: 310-475-0550

Stone Canyon Venture Partners, L.P.
Kenneth R. Kilroy, Contact
2121 Avenue of the Stars, Suite 2800
Los Angeles, CA 90067
Email: kkilroy@ix.netcom.com
310-551-2210
Fax: 310-556-0547

Tangent Growth Fund, L.P.
Alexander H. Schilling, Manager
180 Geary St., Suite 500
San Francisco, CA 94108
Email: lwang@tangentfund.com
415-392-9228
Fax: 415-392-1928

TeleSoft Partners IA L.P.
Arjun Gupta, Manager
1450 Fashion Island Boulevard, Suite 610
San Mateo, CA 94404
Email: telesoft@telesoftvc.com
650-358-2500
Fax: 650-358-2501

UnionBanCal Venture Corporation
Robert S. Clarke, President
445 South Figueroa Street, Suite 2100
P.O. Box 3100
Los Angeles, CA 90071
Email: Terri.Lang@UBOC.com
213-236-6566
Fax: 213-236-7619

Utah Ventures II L.P.
Allan Wolfe
32511 Sea Island Drive
Dana Pt., CA 92629
949-661-2861

Walden-SBIC, L.P.
Arthur S. Berliner, Manager
750 Battery Street, 7th Floor
San Francisco, CA 94111
Email: angela@waldenvc.com
415-391-7225
Fax: 415-391-7262

Wells Fargo SBIC, Inc.
Steven W. Burge, Managing Director
333 South Grand Avenue, Suite 1150
Los Angeles, CA 90071
213-253-3671
Fax: 213-621-2623

Wells Fargo SBIC, Inc.
Richard R. Green, Managing Director
One Montgomery Street
West Tower #2530
San Francisco, CA 94104
415-222-1800
Fax: 415-765-1569

Western General Capital Corporation
Alan Thian, President

13701 Riverside Drive, Suite 610
Sherman Oaks, CA 91423
818-907-8272
Fax: 818-905-9220

Woodside Fund III SBIC, L.P.
Vincent Occhipinti & Frank Mendicino
350 Marine Parkway, Suite 300
Redwood Shores, CA 94065
650-610-8050
Fax: 650-610-8051
Email: garyt@woodsidefund.com

The Small Business Administration (SBA) licenses, regulates, and provides financial assistance to privately owned and operated Small Business Investment Companies. SBICs make venture or risk investments by supplying capital and extending unsecured loans and loans not fully collateralized to small enterprises which meet their investment criteria. Financing is made by direct loans and by equity investments.

* Certified Development Corporations

California Coastal Rural Development Corporation
Wendy Dodson, SBA 504 Manager
221 Main Street, Suite 301
P.O. Box 479
Salinas, CA 93901
831-424-1099 ext. 222
Fax: 831-424-1094
Email: wendy_dodson@calcoastal.org
Area of Operation: Monterey and Santa Cruz counties

Central Coast Development Corporation
Coast Business Finance
Brian Kearns, Senior Loan Officer
930 S. Broadway, Suite 101
Santa Maria, CA 93454
805-739-1665
Fax: 805-739-9257
Email: ccdc@impulse.net
Area of Operation: Counties of San Luis Obispo, Santa Barbara and Ventura

Fresno Certified Development Corporation
Robert R. Garcia, Executive Director
906 N Street, Suite 100
Fresno, CA 93721
559-485-5735
Fax: 559-485-5302
Email: rgarcia@fresnocdc.com
Area of Operation: Fresno and Kings Counties

Mid State Development Corporation
Keith Brice
4800 Easton Drive, Suite 111
Bakersfield, CA 93309
661-322-4241
Fax: 661-322-0536
Mailing address:
P.O. Box 302
Bakersfield, CA 93302
Email: president@midstatedevelopment.com
Area of Operation: Kern County

Stanislaus County Economic Development Corporation
Susan Martin, Vice President, Fin.
1012 I Street, 2nd Floor
Modesto, CA 95354-0808
209-521-9333
Fax: 209-521-9373
Email: suem@scedco.org
Area of Operation: Stanislaus County

Business Finance Center of Tulare County
Lisa Hollingshead, Director of Financial Services
205 E. San Joaquin Street
Tulare, CA 93274
559-688-6666
Fax: 559-688-6899
Email: lisa@edctulare.com
Area of Operation: Tulare County

Business Finance Center
Raymond K. Sakaida, General Manager
6055 E. Washington Blvd., Suite 414
Commerce, CA 90040
213-278-9600
Fax: 213-278-4898
Area of Operation: Los Angeles County

Enterprise Funding Corporation
Jeffery C. Sceranka
101 E. Redlands Blvd., Suite 219
Redlands, CA 92373
909-792-3803
Fax: 909-792-3813
Area of Operation: San Bernardino County

Long Beach Area Certified Development Corporation
Regina Grant Peterson, Executive Director
11 Golden Shore, Suite 630
Long Beach, CA 90802
310-983-7450
Fax: 310-983-7453
Area of Operation: Cities of Long Beach, Signal Hill and Southern Los Angeles County

Amador Economic Development Corporation
Ron Mittelbrunn, Executive Director
22 North Highway 49
Jackson, CA 95642
209-223-0351
Fax: 209-223-2261
Mailing address:
P.O. Box 1077
Jackson, CA 95642
Area of Operation: County of Amador

Economic Development Foundation of Sacramento, Inc.
Frank Dinsmore, Executive Director
7509 Madison Avenue, Suite 111
Citrus Heights, CA 95610
916-962-3669
Fax: 916-962-1822
Area of Operation: Counties of El Dorado, Nevada, Placer, Sacramento, San Joaquin, Sierra, Sutter, Yolo and Yuba

Greater Sacramento Certified Development Corporation
Raymond Sebastian, Executive Director
5428 Watt Avenue
Sacramento, CA 95660-4945
916-339-1096
Area of Operation: Sacramento, El Dorado, Placer and Yolo Counties

Tracy/San Joaquian County Certified Development Corporation
Roger Birdsall
1151 W. Robinhood Drive, Suite B-4
Stockton, CA 95207
209-951-0801
Fax: 209-951-0999
http://www.sjcdc.com
Area of Operation: San Joaquin County

La Habra Local Development Company, Inc.
A. Edwards Evans, Executive Director
441 East Whittier Boulevard, Suite C
La Habra, CA 90631
562-690-6400
Fax: 562-690-6300
Area of Operation: Los Angeles and Orange Counties

Southland Economic Development Corporation
James R. Davis, President
2000 E. Fourth Street, Suite 206
Santa Ana, CA 92705
714-647-1143
Fax: 714-953-0944
Area of Operation: Orange and San Bernardino Counties

CDC Small Business Finance Corporation
Kurt Chilcott, President and CEO
925 Fort Stockton Drive
San Diego, CA 92103
619-291-3594
Fax: 619-291-6954
Mailing address:
P.O. Box 882228
San Diego, CA 92108
Area of Operation: Imperial, San Diego, Riverside and Orange Counties

Arcata Economic Development Corporation
Kathleen E. Moxon, Executive Director
100 Ericson Court, Suite 100
Arcata, CA 95521
707-822-4616
Fax: 707-822-8982
Area of Operation: Humboldt and Del Norte Counties

Bay Area Employment Development Company
James Baird, Executive Director
1801 Oakland Boulevard, Suite 300
Walnut Creek, CA 94596
925-926-1020
Fax: 225-926-1021
Area of Operation: San Francisco, San Mateo, Santa Clara, Alameda, Contra Costa, Solano, Napa, Sonoma and Marin Counties

California Statewide Certified Development Corporation
Barbara A. Vohryzek, Executive Director
426 "D" Street
Davis, CA 95616
530-756-9310
800-348-6258
Fax: 530-756-7519
Email: vohryzek@aol.com
Area of Operation: Statewide

Capital Business Group, Inc. dba Capital Access Group
Jacklyn Jordan, President / Kelly McAuliffe, Marketing Director
300 Beale St., Suite 101
San Francisco, CA 94105
415-284-1460
Fax: 415-284-1590
Area of Operation: California counties of Alemeda, Contra Costa, Marin, Napa, San Francisco, San Mateo, Santa Clara, Solano and Sonoma

The Mortgage Capital Development Corporation
Barbara Morrison, President/CEO
611 Front Street
San Francisco, CA 94111
415-989-8855
Fax: 415-989-3382
Area of Operation: California counties of Alameda, Contra, Costa, Marin, Napa, San Francisco, San Mateo, Santa Clara, Solano and Sonoma

Economic Development Corporation of Shasta County
Jimce Zanhu, General Manager
410 Hemsted Drive, Suite 220   530-224-4920
Redding, CA 96002   Fax: 530-224-4921
Area of Operation: Shasta, Trinity, Siskiyou and Modoc counties

Los Medanos Fund, A Local Development Company
Tom LaFleur, Executive V.P.
329 Railroad Avenue   510-439-1056
Pittsburgh, CA 94565   Fax: 510-439-0831
Mailing address:
P.O. Box 1397
Pittsburgh, CA 94565
Area of Operation: City of Pittsburg; Alameda, Contra Costra, Marin, Napa, San Francisco, San Mateo, Santa Clara, Solano and Sonoma Counties

The 504 Certified Development Company (CDC) Program provides growing businesses with long-term, fixed-rate financing for major fixed assets, such as land and buildings. A Certified Development Company is a nonprofit corporation set up to contribute to the economic development of its community or region. CDC's work with the Small Business Administration and private-sector lenders to provide up to 90% financing to small businesses. There are about 270 CDC's nationwide, each covering a specific region.

Colorado

* Office of Economic Development and International Trade

1625 Broadway, Suite 1710   303-892-3840
Denver, CO 80202   800-592-5920
www.state.co.us /oed/index.cfm   Fax: 303-892-3848
       TDD: 800-659-2656

The Office of Economic Development (OED) works with companies starting, expanding or relocating in Colorado. OED offers a wide range of services to assist new and existing businesses of every size.

Colorado Business Assistance Center: Acting as the first point of contact for the Colorado Small Business Development Center Network, the Colorado Business Assistance Center (BAC) is a one-stop shop for new and existing business owners for information regarding all of their federal, state and local licensing requirements. The BAC provides referrals to other state assistance programs around the state. The BAC distributes the *Colorado Business Resource Guide*, a comprehensive guide to starting and operating a business in Colorado.

Revolving Loan Fund Programs (RLFs): Administered locally in 14 geographic regions covering the rural areas of the state. RLFs have considerable flexibility to make small loans of two or three thousand dollars up to $250,000. Applicants can be existing or startup businesses.

Larger Business Loans: Between $100,000 and $250,000 are provided by OBD through the Community Development Block Grant Business Loans Program when the local government is willing to assume the risk on the loan in order to create or retain jobs. Larger loans may be considered on a case by case basis.

Economic Development Commission: Will provide interest rate write-downs, low interest rate loans or subsidies to companies interested in relocating to or expanding in Colorado.

Private Activity Bonds (PABs): Provide a tax-exempt financing vehicle for facilities and equipment used in the manufacture or production of tangible personal property.

Sales Tax Exemptions: For purchases over $500 on machinery and machine tools purchased for use in manufacturing; Purchases of electricity, coal, gas, or fuel oil for use in processing, manufacturing, and all industrial uses; Sale of tangible personal property for testing, modification, inspection, or similar types of activities in Colorado; Interstate long distance telephone charges.

Local Governments: May provide incentive payments or property tax credits based on the amount of increased property taxes for qualifying new business activity in their jurisdictions.

Colorado International Trade Office (ITO): Responsible for assisting Colorado companies with all aspects of exporting, including counseling, protocol, leading trade missions, and conducting trade shows abroad. By promoting Colorado exports and attracting foreign investment, the ITO helps to build Colorado's identity as an international business center, encouraging foreign buyers to look to Colorado for products and services. The ITO is open to the public and most services are rendered at no cost.

Women's Business Office: Strives to keep the women entrepreneurs of Colorado informed about pertinent issues through all modes of communication.

Office of Economic Development Minority Business Office: Acts as a clearinghouse to disseminate information to the minority business community. Promotes economic development for minority businesses in cooperation with the state economic development activities. Establishes networks between majority and minority business sectors. Promotes minority participation in state procurement. Assists Colorado in achieving its Minority Procurement Goals of 17%. Works with the Minority Business Advisory Council and the minority community in promoting minority business development.

* USDA Rural Development

Community & Business Programs Assistant
April Dahlager
655 Parfet Street, Room E-100   720-544-2909
Lakewood, CO 80215   Fax: 720-544-2972
www.rurdev.usda.gov/co
Areas of operation: Chaffe, Clear Creek, Eagle, Garfield, Gilpin, Grand, Jackson, Lake, Moffat, Park, Rio Blanco, Routt and Summit Counties

Community & Business Programs Specialist/ Cooperative Services
Dolores Sanchez-Maes
655 Parfet Street, Room E-100   720-544-2927
Lakewood, CO 80215   Fax: 720-544-2972
www.rurdev.usda.gov/co
Areas of operation :Cheyenne, Crowley, Elbert, El Paso, Fremont, Kiowa, Kit Carson, Lincoln, Pueblo and Teller Counties.

Community & Business Programs Specialist
Linda Sundine
655 Parfet Street, Room E-100   720-544-2929
Lakewood, CO 80215   Fax: 720-544-2972
www.rurdev.usda.gov/co
Areas of operations: Adams, Araphaoe, Broomfield, Boulder, Denver, Douglas, Jefferson, Larimer, Logan, Morgan, Phillips, Sedgwick, Washington, Weld and Yuma counties.

Community and Business Program Loan Specialist
Fred Eanes
422 1st Street   719-846-3681
Trinidad, CO 81082   Fax: 719-846-0525
www.rurdev.usda.gov/co
Area of operation: Alamosa, Baca, Bent, Conejos, Costilla, Custer, Huerfano, Las Animas, Mineral, Otero, Prowers, Rio Grande and Saguache counties.

Community and Business Program Loan Specialist
Sue McWilliams
628 West 5th Street   970-565-8416, ext. 4
Cortez, CO 81321   Fax: 970-565-8797
www.rurdev.usda.gov/co
Areas of operation: Archuleta, Delta, Dolores, Gunnison, Hinsdale, La Plata, Mesa, Montezuma, Montrose, Ouray, Pitkin, San Juan and San Miguel counties.

The Colorado Rural Business Programs are designed to aide in the improvement, development, and financing of rural communities by enhancing the economic climate or rural businesses. Rural Business assistance is delivered through several programs: *Business and Industry Loans, Rural Business Opportunity and Enterprise Grants, Intermediary Relending Program, Rural Economic Development Loan and Grant Programs* and *Biobased Products and Bioenergy.*

* Colorado Housing and Finance Authority (CHFA)

1981 Blake St.   303-297-2432
Denver, CO 80202   1-800-877-2432 in Colorado
www.colohfa.org
The Colorado Housing and Finance Authority (CHFA) is a public enterprise working to finance affordable housing, business and economic growth opportunities for Colorado. CHFA's Business Finance Division provides a wide variety of programs, including loan programs specific to businesses located in rural communities, women- and minority-owned businesses, manufacturers in the state, and nonprofit organizations committed to better serving the needs of Colorado citizens.

ACCESS Program (SBA 504 Program): A first mortgage program for established small businesses acquiring land, buildings, and equipment, which generally requires 10% equity on the part of the borrower. CHFA may participate with a local lender or may directly originate the first mortgage while SBA provides a second mortgage generally resulting in a 90% loan to value. {www.colohfa.org/bf_access.shtml}

Business & Industry Loan Program: Targeted for businesses located in communities with populations under 50,000, the loan may be used to finance real estate, equipment and machinery. The loan offers a fixed rate on fully amortized terms of 3 to 25 years and is partially guaranteed by Rural Business Cooperative Service, a division of the U.S. Department of Agriculture. {www.colohfa.org/bf_B&I_1.shtml}

QAL Program: This program provides land, equipment and machinery financing to farm and ranch operations. The financing is made available through local banks and participation with Rural Business Cooperative Services. Loans are made at below market interest rates for terms up to 30 years. {www.colohfa.org/bf_qal.shtml}

CHFA Direct Real Estate Program: real estate financing program where CHFA originates a direct loan for up to 85% of the project cost, and provides a fixed rate for the entire term of the transaction. Allows for financing of machinery and equipment, as long as it is part of the real estate transaction.

Nonprofit Real Estate Program: CHFA provides affordable financing of real estate for nonprofits.

The Rural Development Loan Program: provides financing for businesses located in rural areas. CHFA makes direct loans up to $150,000.

Quality Investment Capital (QIC) Program: CHFA purchases the guaranteed portion of the SBA 7(a) loans, and the borrower is able to take advantage of a long-term fixed rate loan.

Manufacturing Revenue Bond Program: Tax-exempt Private Activity Bond financing targeted to small manufacturers. Provides financing of real estate, machinery, and equipment associated with expansion.

Brownsfields Revolving Loan Fund: Fund used to finance cleanup of environmentally contaminated commercial properties for future reuse or redevelopment.

* Colorado Agricultural Development Authority (CADA)

700 Kipling, #4000   303-239-4114
Lakewood, CO 80215   Fax: 303-239-4125
www.ag.state.co.us/mkt/cada.html

Colorado Value-Added Feasibility Grant Program: May be used only for the development of a report or study that analyzes the feasibility of processing an agricultural commodity produced in Colorado. Maximum award s $15,000. Grants must be equally matched with a cash or in-kind contribution by applicant. Businesses need the approval of the local government where the proposed project is to be located.

Specialty Crops Program: Provides $10,000-$25,000 for developing solutions to agricultural production problems for specialty crops.

Beginning Farmer Loan Program: May borrow up to $250,000 for agricultural property; $250,000 for farm equipment; $62,500 for breeding cattle and used equipment. Must be beginning farmer. Can be used in conjunction with the Farm Service Agency Beginning Farmer Program.

* Small Business Administration (SBA)

721 19th St., Suite 426   303-844-2607
Denver, CO 80202-2517   Fax: 303-844-6468
www.sba.gov/co

The Colorado Small Business Administration Office delivers a variety of programs and services, such as startup and operational assistance through small business training and counseling, financial assistance for startup's, business opportunities and much more.

* Small Business Investment Companies

CapEx L.P.
Jeffrey Ross, Manager
518 Seventeenth Street, 17th Floor   303-869-4700
Denver, CO 80202   Fax: 303-869-4602
Email: grace@capexsbic.com

Cornerstone Ventures, L.P.
John R. Ord, Contact
11001 West 120th Avenue, Suite 310   303-410-2500
Broomfield, CO 80021   Fax: 303-469-6370
Email: jord@cornerstoneventures.com

Hanifen Imhoff Mezzanine Fund, L.P.
Edward C. Brown, Manager
1125 17th St., Suite 2260   303-297-1701
Denver, CO 80202   Fax: 303-297-1702
Email: rpesicka@rockycapital.com

NewWest Mezzanine Fund, L.P.
David Henry, Chester Winter, Contacts
1700 Lincoln Street
Suite 1800   303-764-9677
Denver, CO 80203   Fax: 303-832-6154
Email: dhenry@mezzcap.com

Rocky Mountain Mezzanine Fund II, L.P.
Edward Brown & Paul Lyons, Mgrs.
1125 17th Street, Suite 2260   303-297-1701
Denver, CO 80202   Fax: 303-297-1702
Email: rpesicka@rockycapital.com

Roser Partnership III, SBIC, L.P. (The)
James Roser and Christopher Roser, Mgrs.
1105 Spruce Street   303-443-6436
Boulder, CO 80302   Fax: 303-443-1885
Email: avalenti@roserventures.com

Vista Ventures Advantage, L.P.
Catharine M. Merigold, Contact
215 West Oak Street, 10th Floor   303-410-2509
Fort Collins, CO 80521   Fax: 303-466-9316
Email: catharine@vistavc.com

Wolf Venture Fund III, L.P.
David Wolf, Elliott Husney, Contacts
1600 Stout St., Suite 1510   303-321-4800
Denver, CO 80202   Fax: 303-321-4848
Email: bkelly@wolfventures.com

The SBA licenses, regulates, and provides financial assistance to privately owned and operated Small Business Investment Companies. SBICs make venture or risk investments by supplying capital and extending unsecured loans and loans not fully collateralized to small enterprises which meet their investment criteria. Financing is made by direct loans and by equity investments.

* Certified Development Companies

Community Economic Development Company of Colorado
Accredited Lender Program
Small Business Finance Corporation
1111 Osage Street, Suite 110   303-893-8989
Denver, CO 80204   Fax: 303-892-8398
Email: bill@cedco.org
Area of Operation: Statewide

Denver Urban Economic Development Corporation
1905 Sherman Street, Suite 200   303-861-4100
Denver, CO 80203   Fax: 303-861-9456
Email: stephanieg@duedc.org
Area of Operation: Adams, Arapahoe, Boulder, Denver, Douglas, and Jefferson Counties

Front Range Regional Economic Development Corporation
Preferred Certified Lender
Colorado Lending Source Program
7000 North Broadway, Suite 215   303-657-0010
Denver, CO 80221   Fax: 303-657-0140
Email: mike@coloradolendingsource.org
Area of Operations: Adams, Arapahoe, Boulder, Denver, Douglas, Jefferson, Larimer, Morgan, and Weld Counties

Pikes Peak Regional Development Corporation
228 North Cascade Avenue, Suite 208   719-471-2044
Colorado Springs, CO 80903   Fax: 719-471-2042
Email: doug@pprdc.com
Area of Operations: El Paso County

SCEDD Development Company
1104 North Main   719-545-8680
Pueblo, CO 81003   Fax: 719-545-9908
Email: tomkins.scedd@worldnet.att.net
Area of Operations: Alamosa, Archuleta, Baca, Bent, Chaffee, Conejos, Costilla, Crowley, Custer, Dolores, Fremont, Huerfano, Kiowa, Lake, LaPlata, Las Animas, Mineral, Montezuma, Otero, Prowers, Pueblo, RioGrande, Saguache, San Juan Counties

Associate Development Company (ADC)
Economic Development District of Southwest Colorado
295A Girard Street   970-247-9621
Durango, CO 81301   Fax: 970-247-9513
Email: region9edd@frontier.net
Area of Operation: Archuleta, Dolores, La Plata, Montezuma, and San Juan Counties
Associated with SCEDD Development Company, Pueblo, Colorado

The 504 Certified Development Company (CDC) Program provides growing businesses with long-term, fixed-rate financing for major fixed assets, such as land and buildings. A Certified Development Company is a nonprofit corporation set up to contribute to the economic development of its community or region. CDC's work with the Small Business Administration and private-sector lenders to provide up to 90% financing to small businesses. There are about 270 CDC's nationwide, each covering a specific region.

* Colorado Department of Local Affairs

Division of Grants and Financial Assistance
1313 Sherman St., Room 500   303-866-2771
Denver, CO 80203   Fax: 303-866-4819
www.dola.state.co.us
The Colorado Department of Local Affairs mission is to help local governments deal with the financial assistance and technical assistance needs of businesses on a community level. The Department of Grants and Financial Assistance provide a variety of help to the residents of Colorado including the *Community Development and Service Block Grants* and *The Conservation Trust Fund*.

* Colorado Venture Management

2575 Park Lane, Suite 200   303-440-4055
Lafayette, CO 80026   Fax: 303-440-4636
www.coloradovca.org
Email: ewetherbee@cvmequity.com
CVM Equity Fund: Provides equity financing for start-up businesses in the state through private venture capital partnerships. CVM will run the seed capital fund. Focus is on start-up and early stage investments in service and technology-based businesses. Investments will be considered in the range of $25,000 to $300,000.

Connecticut

* Economic Resource Center

Connecticut Department of Economic and
  Community Development   860-571-7136
805 Brooks St., Bldg. 4   800-392-2122
Rocky Hill, CT 06067-3405   Fax: 860-571-7150
www.cerc.com
One Stop Centers: Authorized to enable businesses to obtain many necessary permits and licenses in one location.

Connecticut Economic Resource Center (CERC): A non-profit private-sector organization formed and managed through a unique partnership of utility/telecommunication companies and state government. The CERC coordinates Connecticut's business-to-business marketing and recruitment efforts on behalf of the state. As a one-stop gateway to the state's programs and services for business, the CERC helps businesses obtain quick and accurate information in the areas of financing, export assistance, licensing, manufacturing programs, job training, utility, telecommunications and real estate help, all at no cost.

Business Resource Index: The Connecticut Economic Resource Center's website {www.cerc.com}offers a large and comprehensive database of programs and services for businesses. The database contains information from the public and private sectors on federal, state and local levels including license and permit information. The *Business Resource Index* is divided into three major sections, each of which can be searched individually or collectively. The sections include *Resources By Agency*, *Licensing*, and *Helpful Fact Sheets*. Available business resources are often divided by city or region. Listings are extensive. To illustrate, a search with the keyword "Small Business" yielded 119 documents including loans, technical assistance, consulting services, grants, and economic development assistance among others. As an example, the Entrepreneurial Loan Program offers loans up to $100,000 insured by the Connecticut Development Authority, for the benefit of start-up and early stage business anywhere in Connecticut. The website also features a real estate search engine enabling the user to input parameters such as size of building and desired location to aid with business site selection.

Technology Extension Program: Provides direct technical assistance to small and mid-sized manufacturing firms.

Institute for Industrial and Engineering Technology: Offers assistance with process improvement, technical training, procurement, human resources, business incubators, and others.

Program Finder: A comprehensive computer database of available commercial and industrial properties.

Demographic and Economic Analysis: Services include industry profiles, competitive intelligence, regional analysis, survey research, bench marking and evaluation.

* Connecticut Development Authority

999 West St.
Rocky Hill, CT 06067   860-258-7800
www.cda.state.ct.us/
The Connecticut Development Authority works to ensure that Connecticut businesses have access to capital to accelerate business formation and expansion and to create and retain jobs. The CDA works with private lending and business professionals to provide loan guarantees and direct loans for working capital, equipment and real estate. The CDA offers the following financing programs:

URBANK: Loans up to $500,000 for any small business enterprise in targeted communities that are unable to obtain conventional financing.

Business Loans: Up to $10 million for medium size enterprises.

Industrial Revenue Bonds: Low rate, tax exempt financing for manufacturers, utilities, certain non-profits and others.

Job Training Finance Program: Pays up to 25% of the cost of improving skills of manufacturing workers.

Custom Job Training Program: Department of Labor will pay up to 50% for eligible training expenses.

Guaranteed and Participating Loans: For Connecticut companies to accelerate business formation and expansion and retain and create jobs.

Brownsfields Grants and Financing: Grants up to $10,000 for redevelopment and productive use of Brownfield sites.

Information Technology Grants and Loans: Loans and grants as incentives to developers of new projects in high technology, information technology, research, biosciences, and pharmaceuticals.

Equity-Equivalent Investment: Equity and subordinated capital to accelerate business formation and expansion.

Direct Loans: CDA has a direct loan program that strives to stimulate economic development. Eligible businesses can apply for funds up to $5 million.

SBA 504: This program provides long-term, low cost financing for fixed assets. There is a 10% equity investment requirement for businesses applying for the up to $2,500,000 loan.

* Department of Economic and Community Development

State of Connecticut
Department of Economic and Community Development
505 Hudson Street
Hartford, CT 06106-7107   860-270-8000
www.ct.gov/ecd
Economic and Manufacturing Assistance Fund: Program includes loans, defense diversification project funding, tax credits and funding for new machinery and equipment.

Naugatuck Valley Loan Fund: Fund can be used to purchase land or buildings, construction, renovation, rehabilitation, and/or the purchase and installation of machinery and equipment. Maximum loan is $200,000.

* Rural Development Offices

Norwich Service Center
238 West Town Street   860-859-5218 ext. 3004

Norwich, CT 06360 Fax: 860-859-5223
Serving Windham and New London Counties

Windsor Service Center
100 Northfield Drive, 4th Floor 860-688-7725 ext. 4
Windsor, CT 06095-4729 Fax: 860-688-7979
www.rurdev.usda.gov/ma
Serving Tolland, Middlesex, Hartford, Litchfield, New Haven and Fairfield Counties.

The Southern New England Office administers the USDA Rural Development Program in Connecticut with service centers in Windsor and Norwich. They offer Business Development Programs that are available in rural areas, which are outside the boundary of a city or town of 50,000 or more inhabitants and are immediately adjacent urbanized area. They offer the following programs to assist businesses: *Business & Industry Loans, Rural Business Enterprise Grants* and *Intermediary Relending Program Loans.*

* State of Connecticut Department of Revenue Services

25 Sigourney Street 860-297-5962
Hartford, CT 06106 800-382-9463 (In-state)
www.drs.state.ct.us Fax: 860-297-5698
When you start your new business the Department of Revenue Services has some help for you. They publish a pamphlet called *Getting Started in Business* to guide you through many of your tax questions. They also offer other assistance for entrepreneurs, call to see how they can help your business.

* Community Economic Development Fund

50-G Weston St. 800-656-4613
Hartford, CT 06120 860-249-3800
www.cedf.com
CEDF provides loans to start-up and existing businesses who have difficulty obtaining traditional financing or need flexible terms. Programs include:

Standard Loan Program: Loans from $5,000-$250,000 for start-up or existing businesses.

Grow Your Business Loan: Businesses three years old or more can qualify for loans up to $250,000.

SBA Microloan Program: For loans up to $35,000.

Microloan Guarantee Program for Women and Minority Owned Businesses: Helps women and minority owned businesses obtain flexible financing with loans from $5,000-$50,000.

CT Inner City Business Loan Guarantee Program: Guarantees for small business loans in designated industry clusters in Waterbury, Hartford, new Britain, Bridgeport, and New Haven. Loans are for $50,000-$250,000.

* Connecticut Venture Group

1895-B Post Rd.
Fairfield, CT 06430 203-256-5955
www.ct-venture.org
Connecticut Venture Group: A non-profit membership organization that brings entrepreneurs and investors together.

Innovations Technology Financing: Offers a wide range of support from research assistance to financing for product development and marketing.

* Minority and Small Business Contractors Set-Aside Program

Department of Economic and Community Development
Attn: Set Aside Unit
505 Hudson St.
Hartford, CT 06106 860-270-8025
www.ct.gov/ecd
Procurement Program: Set-Aside Program requires state agencies and political subdivisions to set aside 25% of their budget for construction, housing rehabilitation and the purchasing of supplies. These services are awarded to certified small business contractors, minority businesses, enterprises, non-profit corporations and individuals with a disability. 25% of this amount is to be awarded to certified minority owned firms.

Minority Supplier Development Council: A non-profit organization whose mission is to foster business relationships between corporations and certified minority businesses. Services include training seminars, matchmaking activities, bid notifications, networking functions and a large trade expo.

* Connecticut Innovation, Inc. (CII)

999 West St. 860-563-5851
Rocky Hill, CT 06067 Fax: 860-563-4877
www.ctinnovations.com
Connecticut Innovations is the state's corporation dedicated to technology development, making risk capital investments in high technology companies throughout the state. They offer a wide range of support from research assistance to financing for product development and marketing. Connecticut Innovations offers the following programs:

Yankee Ingenuity Technology Competition: The Yankee Ingenuity Technology Competition provides royalty-based, market driven funding for applied high technology research and development projects that lead to marketable products of processes. The purpose of this initiative is to encourage collaborations between Connecticut colleges and universities and Connecticut business and industry for the development and commercialization of products or processes with high potential to contribute to long-term, sustainable economic growth in Connecticut.

Connecticut Innovations Resource Center: The Connecticut Innovations Resource Center is a high-tech information clearinghouse and a gateway to resources available from Connecticut Innovations. The Center maintains a complete listing of educational programs and services and state and federal resources to assist in converting ideas into products. The Center offers: Access to business planning materials; Guidelines for Connecticut Innovations' programs; Directories and databases of high-tech companies in Connecticut, to assist in the identification of growth industries, companies and localities, and the identification of export companies; Information on federal R & D grant programs and state assistance programs; and Sources of private and public financing.

Eli Whitney Fund: Focuses on information technology, bioscience, photonics, and energy and environmental systems. Investments range from $500,000 to $2 million.

Connecticut BioSeed Fund: Helps accelerate the growth of early stage biotech enterprises. Up to $500,000 for young Connecticut companies.

Technology Test Bed Program: State agency or facility can serve as a demonstration site for one of Connecticut Innovations companies and can receive support to defray costs.

Next Generation Ventures: Venture capital to support entrepreneurial high tech companies.

Bioscience Facilities Fund: A $55 million fund to support the expansion of biotechnology laboratory space in Connecticut. Funding may be offered in the form of lease or loan guarantee and/or direct investments.

Connecticut Clean Energy Fund: Promotes investment in renewable energy resources, e.g. fuel cells, landfill gas, and tidal, wind and solar power.

* Small Business Administration (SBA)

330 Main St. 860-240-4700
Hartford, CT 06106 Fax: 860-240-4659
www.sba.gov/ct
The Connecticut Small Business Administration Office delivers a variety of programs and services, such as startup and operational assistance through small business training and counseling, financial assistance for startup's, business opportunities and much more.

* Small Business Investment Companies

AB SBIC, Inc.
Adam J. Bozzuto, President
275 School House Road 203-272-0203
Cheshire, CT 06410 Fax: 203-250-2954
Email: jsantoli@bozzutos.com

Bon Secours Community Investment Fund, L.P.
Leo Mellow, Vice President
c/o Smith Whiley & Company
242 Trumbull Street, 8th Floor 860-548-2513
Hartford, CT 06103 Fax: 860-548-2518
Email: mellowl@smithwhiley.com

Brookside Pecks Capital Partners, L.P.
80 Field Point Road, Third Floor
Greenwich, CT 06830
203-618-0202
Fax: 203-618-0984

Canaan SBIC, LP
Gregory Kopchinsky, Manager
105 Rowayton Ave.
Rowayton, CT 06853
203-855-0400
Fax: 203-854-9117
Email: grusso@caanaan.com

Cygnet Capital Partners L.P. SBIC
Owen S. Crihfield, Contact
281 Tresser Boulevard, 4th Floor
Stamford, CT 06901
203-602-0011
Fax: 203-602-2206
Email: osc@hrco.com

FieldPoint Partners SBIC, L.P.
Ian Michel, Contact
80 Field Point Road
Greenwich, CT 06830
203-869-5444
Fax: 203-869-6345
Email: imichel@aol.com

First New England Capital, LP
Richard C. Klaffky, President
100 Pearl St.
Hartford, CT 06103
860-293-3333
Fax: 860-293-3338
Email: rklaffky@firstnewenglandcapital.com

First New England Capital 2, L.P.
Richard Klaffky, Manager
100 Pearl Street
Hartford, CT 06103
860-293-3333
Fax: 860-293-3338
Email: rklaffky@firstnewenglandcapital.com

GreenLeaf Capital, L.P.
Jon Atkeson, Contact
177 Broad Street
Stamford, CT 06901
203-973-1670
Fax: 203-973-1422
Email: jatkeson@jhwhitney.com

GreenLeaf Mezzanine Capital, L.P.
Peter Denious, Contact
177 Broad Street
Stamford, CT 06901
203-973-1400
Fax: 203-973-1422
Email: pdenious@jhwhitney.com

Imprimis SB, LP
Charles Davidson, Joseph Jacobs, Mgrs.
411 West Putnam Avenue
Greenwich, CT 06830
203-862-7074
Fax: 203-862-7374
Email: pjacob@wexford.com

Ironbridge Mezzanine Fund, L.P.
Marc Reich, President, Contact
200 Fisher Drive
c/o Ironwood Capital Advisors LLC
Avon, CT 06001
860-409-2101
Fax: 860-409-2120
Email: reich@ironwoodcap.com

Marketing 1 to 1 Ventures, L.P.
Bruce Blasnik, Contact
One Landmark Square
Stamford, CT 06901
203-325-4000
Fax: 203-325-8900
Email: blasnik@1to1ventures.com

MSR I SBIC, L.P.
Daniel A. Levinson
8 Wright Street
Westport, CT 06880
203-227-5320
Fax: 203-227-5312
Email: kc@mainstreet-resources.com

RFE Capital Partners, LP
Robert M. Williams, Managing Partner
36 Grove Street
New Canaan, CT 06840
203-966-2800
Fax: 203-966-3109
Email: DAJNOVA@aol.com

RFE Investment Partners V, LP
James A. Parsons, General Partner
36 Grove St.
New Canaan, CT 06840
203-966-2800
Fax: 203-966-3109
Email: DAJNOVA@aol.com

RFE VI SBIC, L.P.
James Parsons & Robert Williams, Mgrs.
36 Grove Street
New Canaan, CT 06840
203-966-2800
Fax: 203-966-3109
Email: DAJNOVA@aol.com

Saugatuck Capital Company, L.P. IV, SBIC
Frank Hawley, Thomas Berardino
One Canterbury Green
Stamford, CT 06901
203-324-6669
Fax: 203-324-6995
Email: otharrington@saugatuckcapital.com

TD Javelin Capital Fund, L.P.
Joan Neuscheler, General Partner
Two Greenwich Plaza
Greenwich, CT 06830
203-629-8700

Valentis SB, L.P.
Paul M. Jacobi
411 West Putnam Avenue
Greenwich, CT 06830
203-862-7074
Fax: 203-862-7374
Email: pjacob@wexford.com

The SBA licenses, regulates, and provides financial assistance to privately owned and operated Small Business Investment Companies. SBICs make venture or risk investments by supplying capital and extending unsecured loans and loans not fully collateralized to small enterprises which meet their investment criteria. Financing is made by direct loans and by equity investments.

* Certified Development Corporations

Commercial Loan Partners, INC
20 Tower Lane
Avon, CT 06001
860-667-1004
Fax: 860-667-1047
www.commercialloanpartners.com
Service Area: New Haven, Hartford, Middlesex, New London, Tolland, and Windham Counties

Connecticut Business Development Corporation
999 West Street
Rocky Hill, CT 06067
860-258-7855
Fax: 860-257-7582
Service Area: Statewide

Connecticut Community Investment Corporation, LDC
100 Crown Street
New Haven, CT 06510
203-776-6172, ext. 25
Fax: 203-776-6837
www.ctcic.org
Service Area: Hartford, Middlesex, New Haven, New London, Tolland, and Windham Counties

Housatonic Industrial Development Corporation
57 North Street, Suite 407
Danbury, CT 06810
203-743-0306
Fax: 203-744-0915
Service Area: Fairfield, Hartford (West of Conn. River), Litchfield, Middlesex, (West of Conn River) and New Haven Counties

The 504 Certified Development Company (CDC) Program provides growing businesses with long-term, fixed-rate financing for major fixed assets, such as land and buildings. A Certified Development Company is a nonprofit corporation set up to contribute to the economic development of its community or region. CDCs work with the Small Business Administration and private-sector lenders to provide financing to small businesses.

Delaware

* Delaware Economic Development Office

John S. Riley
99 Kings Highway
P.O. Box 1401
Dover, DE 19903
302-739-4271
Fax: 302-739-5749
www.state.de.us/dedo/index.htm
Offers referrals to appropriate state agencies and other organizations. Free tabloid, *Small Business Start-Up Guide* is available. Provides support for new businesses and coordinates the efforts of organizations statewide that assist small businesses.

Workforce Development Section: Works to ensure the availability of a skilled, multilevel workforce for new and existing Delaware businesses. Helps employers obtain, upgrade and retain suitable workers, by helping Delawareans gain the education and training to get and keep quality jobs and steady employment. {www.delawareworkforce.com}

Business Research Section: Collects, analyzes and distributes statistical data on the state's economy and business climate and develops research regarding the economic vitality of the State of Delaware

Delaware Tourism Office: Assists the tourism industry.

The State Data Center: Provides economic and demographic data for Delaware.

Business Magazine: Maintained by the Delaware State Chamber of Commerce (DSCC), it is the state's central location for listing business-related events.

Green Industries Initiative: Targets specific businesses for receipt of financial and technical assistance to further the goals of Governor Castle's Executive Order #82 and Delaware's Pollution Prevention Program. The State of Delaware provides corporate income tax credits and/or gross receipts tax reductions for existing Delaware firms and those choosing Delaware as a location for new operations. The type of financial assistance is dependent upon the category under which assistance is requested.

Industrial Revenue Bonds: Statewide financial assistance to new or expanding businesses through the issuance of bonds (IRBs). The maximum for IRBs issued annually in Delaware is $150 million.

Economic Development Loan Program: Assists Delaware businesses to finance projects when 100% financing cannot be obtained through a bank. The program does require 70% bank financing. The remaining 30% is financed through the program up to a maximum of $450,000. In most cases the interest rate for monies loaned through the Economic Development Loan Program is 60% of the prime lending interest rate.

The Delaware Access Program: Designed to give banks a flexible and extremely non-bureaucratic tool to make business loans that are somewhat riskier than a conventional bank loan, in a manner consistent with safety and soundness. It is designed to use a small amount of public resources to generate a large amount of private bank financing, thus providing access to bank financing for many Delaware businesses that might otherwise not be able to obtain such access. The program sets minimum and maximum limits for the borrower's payment. At a minimum, it must be at least 1-1/2% of the loan amount. The maximum is 3-1/2%. (The premium payment, and other up-front expenses, may be financed as part of the loan.)

Small Business Innovation Research (SBIR): Bridge grant assistance to encourage Delaware businesses to participate in the federal Small Business Innovation Research (SBIR) grant program. The SBIR program requires that 1.25% of all federal research dollars be made available to small businesses. Phase I awardees are granted up to $100,000 by the federal government.

The Delaware Innovation Fund: Assists in the initial capitalization of pre-seed and seed stage enterprises within the State of Delaware. The Fund provides financial and technical assistance to Delaware based businesses which have the potential to launch innovative products and processes into national markets, to create new jobs, and to make a significant contribution to the economic diversity and the technology base of Delaware's communities.

Demonstration Funding: Limited one-time availability, provides $10,000 to $25,000 to aid in establishing patents, business plans and proof of concept issues.

Commercialization Funding: Ranging from $25,000 to $250,000, this funding is used to begin the commercialization process of early-stage businesses and may be available in multiple years.

Venture Capital Funds: Three funds — Anthem Capital, L.P., Triad Investors Corporation, and Blue Rock Capital — have the ability to fund a variety of seed stage, early stage, and later stage companies in both technology-related and non-technology fields. The investment focus of each fund varies. Investments can range from $150,000 for seed stage companies up to $2,000,000 or more for later stage companies.

Export Trading Company Exemption: Delaware exporters who qualify as an Export Trading Company can receive exemption from Delaware income and mercantile taxes.

* USDA/Rural Development

4607 South DuPont Highway	302-697-4300
Post Office Box 400	TTY: 302-697-4303
Camden, DE 19934	Fax: 302-697-4390
www.rurdev.usda.gov/de	

The Community & Business Programs Division consists of the Rural Utilities Service (RUS) and the Rural Business & Cooperative Service

(RBS). RUS programs assist rural America in building infrastructure by providing loans and grants for water and wastewater disposal systems, solid waste disposal systems, storm drainage systems and advanced telecommunications. RBS programs help provide financial as well as technical assistance to businesses, non-profit organizations, educational institutions and cooperatives. The financial assistance is provided in the form of loans, guaranteed loans and grants.

* State of Delaware Department of Finance

Division of Business Revenue	302-577-8205
820 N. French Street	800-292-7826 (Delaware only)
Wilmington, DE 19801	Fax: 302-577-8202
http://www.state.de.us/revenue/	

The Office of Business Taxes provide businesses information on registering a business, obtaining a license and doing business in Delaware.

* Advanced Technology Centers (ATCs)

Delaware Economic Development Office	
820 French St.	
Wilmington, DE 19801	302-577-8496
www.state.de.us	

Public/private partnerships designed to bolster Delaware's technology base and to create and retain quality high-tech jobs. The State of Delaware has committed $11 million to date in grants to establish five Centers. Funding for the program comes from the state's 21st Century Fund. Amounts are not available without a specific inquiry.

* Wilmington Economic Development Corporation

100 W. 10th St., Suite 706	
Wilmington, DE 19801	302-571-9088
www.wedco.org	

Projects located within the city limits of Wilmington may also apply for financing through the Wilmington Economic Development Corporation (WEDCO). Financing programs offered include SBA Section 504 Loans, Revolving Loan Funds, and other special purpose financing.

* Sussex County Office of Economic Development

P.O. Box 589	
9 S. Dupont Hwy.	
Georgetown, DE 19947	302-855-7770
www.sussexcounty.net/depts/econdev/index.html	

Operates an Industrial Revenue Bond program with a cap of $15 million each year for industrial projects in the County. Project review requires a letter of commitment for placement of the bond before a project recommendation is made by the Industrial Revenue Bond Review Committee to Sussex County Council (political jurisdiction). The Industrial Revenue Bond process may require as little as five weeks from inception to bond closing.

* Minority Business Programs

Office of Minority and Women Business Enterprise (M/WBE)	
Mary Schreiber, Director	
Department of Administrative Service	
410 Federal Street	
Margaret O'Neill Bldg.	
Dover, DE 19901	302-739-7830
www.state.de.us/omwbe/	

The office sponsors activities ranging from training workshops for agencies, regional workshops for minority and women-owned businesses to orientation sessions for newly certified minority-owned business enterprises. They assist government agencies to use certified minority and women-owned businesses when purchasing and contracting for the state.

* International Trade Section

Delaware Economic Development Office	
820 French St.	
Carvel State Office Bldg., 10th Floor	
Wilmington, DE 19801	302-577-8464
www.state.de.us	

A one-stop resource for exporter assistance and international trade information in Delaware.

* Small Business Administration (SBA)

824 N. Market St.	302-573-6294
Wilmington, DE 19801-3011	Fax: 302-573-6060

www.sba.gov/de

The Delaware Small Business Administration Office delivers a variety of programs and services, such as startup and operational assistance through small business training and counseling, financial assistance for startup's, business opportunities and much more.

* Small Business Investment Companies

Blue Rock Capital, L.P.
Virginia Bonker & Paul Collison, Mgrs.
5700 Kennett Pike, Second Floor   302-426-0981
Wilmington, DE 19807-1135   Fax: 302-426-0982
Email: Koneill@pfadmin.com

Inflection Point Ventures II, L.P.
Jeffrey A. Davison, Contact
Delaware Technology Park
15 Innovation Way, Suite 280   302-452-1120
Newark, DE 19711   Fax: 302-452-1101
Email: jdavison@inflectpoint.com

The Small Business Investment Company (SBIC) program. SBICs, licensed by the Small Business Administration, are privately organized and privately manage investment firms. They are participants in a vital partnership between government and the private sector economy. With their own capital and with funds borrowed at favorable rates through the Federal Government, SBICs provide venture capital to small independent businesses, both new and already established.

* Certified Development Companies

Wilmington Economic Development Corporation (WEDCO)
Constance C. McCarthy, Executive Director
605-A Market Street Mall   302-571-9093
Wilmington, DE 19801   Fax: 302-652-5679
Area of Operation: New Castle County only.

Mid-Atlantic Business Finance Company
Paula Klepper, President
Two Hopkins Plaza, Suite 901   410-539-2449
Baltimore MD 21201-2911   Fax: 410-539-7110
Area of Operation: Kent and Sussex Counties only.

The 504 Certified Development Company (CDC) Program provides growing businesses with long-term, fixed-rate financing for major fixed assets, such as land and buildings. A Certified Development Company is a nonprofit corporation set up to contribute to the economic development of its community or region. CDCs work with the SBA and private-sector lenders to provide financing to small businesses.

District of Columbia

* Office of Economic Development

John A. Wilson Building
1350 Pennsylvania Ave., NW, Suite 317
Washington, DC 20004   202-727-6365
www.dcbiz.dc.gov/main.shtm

Welcome To Washington D.C. Online: A useful website with links to business & finance opportunities in the district.

The DC Office of International Business: OIB was created to support the District of Columbia's development and expansion of local business through international trade and joint-venture partnerships, and to attract outside investment to the District of Columbia. Programs offered include:
- *International Trade Counseling and Technical Program*: OIB offers counseling and assistance on all aspects of international business to firms, organizations and residents of the District of Columbia.
- *Resource Center for International Trade Information*: Offers country market profiles, current export licensing regulations, information on trade and financing, a comprehensive database of trade resources and a directory of Washington-based international firms.
- *Trade and Investment Program*: Offers a database of local, small and medium sized businesses, using criteria and categories useful for the analysis of the local market; match making potential for local small business, and investment needs; facilitates trade and investment leads; identifies overseas markets for local goods and services; supports trade and investment missions; hosts foreign buying delegations; works in tandem with its sister agencies in devising strategies and marketing activities to attract foreign investment and business entities to the District of Columbia; establishes regular and close relationships with the diplomatic community, chambers of commerce and other

regional and state agencies to identify export and investment opportunities for local and area businesses.
- *OIB Seminar Series*: Provides hands-on training through an eight week course designed to provide concise, nuts-and-bolts instructions on how to conduct import, export, and joint venture transactions. Topics cover every aspect of international trade with emphasis on small business involvement. Upon successful completion of the course, participants receive a "Certificate of Achievement."
- *OIB Internship Program*: OIB offers a high school and college internship program that provides local youth with on-the-job training, skill development and an orientation to international trade.
- *reSTORE DC Main Streets*: designated local Main Street programs receive technical assistance, training and more. Non-profits may apply for $80,000 grant.
- *reSTORE DC Commercial Development Technical Assistance Program*: awards technical assistance and grants to assist commercial revitalization activities that enhance neighborhood business districts. Non-profits are eligible for grants from $500-$25,000.
- *reSTORE DC Commercial Property Acquisition and Development Program*: awards grants to assist in acquiring or developing commercial real estate projects that enhance neighborhood business districts. Non-profits may apply for $10,000 to $250,000.

* Transferable Development Rights

Local Business Development
441 4th St., NW, Suite 970N
Washington, DC 20001   202-727-3900
http://olbd.washingtondc.gov

Permits businesses to purchase the right to develop at higher densities in designated TDR "receiving zones."

* Business Location Assistance

D.C. Chamber of Commerce
1213 K Street, NW
Washington, DC 20005   202-347-7201
www.dcchamber.org

D.C. Building Industry Association
5100 Wisconsin Ave., NW, Suite 301
Washington, DC 20016   202-966-8665
www.dcbia.org

* Bond Financing and General Information

D.C. Enterprise and Revenue Bond Program
1350 Pennsylvania Avenue, NW, Suite 317
Washington, DC 20004   202-727-6365
www.dcbiz.dc.gov/info/rb.shtm

Qualified businesses located in the Enterprise Zone, nonprofit and manufacturing businesses throughout the city can apply for below market rate loans. The funds can be used for a variety of capital projects.

* Local and Minority Business Development

DC Department of Local Business Development
DC Department of Human Rights and
Minority Business Development
441 4th Street, NW, Suite 970   202-727-3900
Washington, DC 20001   Fax: 202-724-3786
www.oibd.dc.gov

Minority Business Opportunity Commission: Promotes equal opportunity in all aspects of District life and fosters minority business development through:
- *Business Marketing Directory*: listing of Local, Small, Disadvantaged and Minority Business Enterprises.
- *Minority Business Certification Program*
- *Technical Assistance Program*: Aids minority business enterprises through workshops, contracting conferences, referrals and the MBOC Directory to bid and compete on District Government contracts.
- *Bonding Assistance Program*: Establishes a financial assurance pool to serve as limited collateral for surety bonds on public construction projects awarded by the DC government.

* Department of Housing and Community Development

801 N. Capitol St., NE, 8th Floor   202-442-7200
Washington, DC 20002   Fax: 202-442-8391
www.dhcd.dcgov.org

Apartment Improvement Program: provides technical assistance to owners of rental housing for property improvements.

Construction Assistance Program: helps non-profit land trusts acquire land and buildings for development of low-income housing.

Community Land Acquisition Program: helps non-profit land trusts acquire land and buildings for development.

Distressed Properties Improvement Program: provides tax relief and other financial incentives to property owners if they are willing to make repairs.

Housing Finance for Elderly, Dependent, and Disabled: provides financing to commercial and non-profit applicants to develop community-based residential facilities that house individuals with special needs.

Housing Production Trust Fund: provides financial assistance to non-profit and commercial developers to plan and build low to moderate-income housing and related facilities.

Low Income Housing Tax Credit Program: available to developers that provide new or rehabilitated rental housing.

Community Based Services: supports non-profit organizations that provide comprehensive housing counseling services.

Emergency Shelter Grant Program: improves the quality of existing emergency shelters for the homeless.

Enterprise Community Program: provides residents in enterprise communities with the resources and training needed to achieve upward mobility.

Multi-Family Housing Rehabilitation Loan Program: low-cost interim construction financing and permanent financing for the rehabilitation of residential properties that contain five or more units.

Neighborhood Development Assistance Program: provides administrative support to Community Development Corporations for neighborhood development projects and neighborhood revitalization activities.

Tenant Purchase Technical Assistance Program: provides technical service assistance to non-profit organizations that provide legal counseling, loan packaging, and other services to low and moderate-income tenant groups that try to purchase their existing housing units.

* Employment Training Tax Credits

DC Department of Employment Services
609 H St., NE
Washington, DC 20002 — 202-724-7000
http://does.dc.gov

The Department of Employment Services helps develop Washington's workforce through training and education.

Customized Training Program: employers are reimbursed for funds spent to train District residents as skilled employees.

Enterprise Zone Employment Tax Credit: annual employment tax credit for 20% of wages paid to DC resident employees (up to $3,000 per employee).

Work Opportunity Credit: annual employment tax credit of up to $2,400 per employee in tax credits for employees that meet eligibility criteria.

Welfare to Work Program: Up to $8,500 per employee in tax credits for employees that meet eligibility criteria ($5,000 for year one).

Metro Tech Program: cost of training/certification of information technology professionals is borne by Metro Tech.

* Office of Banking & Financial Institutions

1400 L Street, NW, Suite 400
Washington, DC 20005 — 202-727-1563
http://dbfi.dc.gov/main.shtm

The general mission of the office is to promote a climate in which financial institutions will organize to do business in the District of Columbia and contribute to the economic development of the District through the increased availability of capital and credit and to expand advantageous financial services to the public in a nondiscriminatory manner.

* Washington District Small Business Administration

1110 Vermont Ave. NW, 9th Floor — 202-606-4000
Washington, DC 20005 — Fax: 202-606-4225
www.sba.gov/dc

The District of Columbia Small Business Administration Office delivers a variety of programs and services, such as startup and operational assistance through small business training and counseling, financial assistance for startup's, business opportunities and much more.

* Certified Development Companies

Community First, Inc.
Tim Walter, President
One Dupont Circle, NW, Suite 700 — 202-265-4569
Washington, DC 20037-7121 — Fax: 202-265-4598
Area Of Operation: Washington, D.C.

Virginia Asset Financing Service Corporation
Sally Robertson, Executive Director — 703-352-0504
4165 Chain Bridge Road — 800-305-0504
Fairfax VA 22030 — Fax: 703-352-9100
Area Of Operation: State of Virginia except for those counties covered by other Virginia CDCs.

Prince George's County Financial Services Corporation
Shelly Gross-Wade, Executive Director
4640 Forbes Blvd., Suite 200 — 301-429-3044
Lanham, MD 20706 — Fax: 301-429-8762
Area Of Operation: Prince George's County

Mid-Atlantic Certified Development Company
Paula Klepper, President
1410 North Crain Highway, Suites 5B — 800-730-0017
Glen Burnie MD 21061 — Fax: 410-863-7446
Area Of Operation: State of Maryland

The 504 Certified Development Company (CDC) Program provides growing businesses with long-term, fixed-rate financing for major fixed assets, such as land and buildings. A Certified Development Company is a nonprofit corporation set up to contribute to the economic development of its community or region. CDC's work with the Small Business Administration and private-sector lenders to provide up to 90% financing to small businesses. There are about 270 CDC's nationwide, each covering a specific region.

* Small Business Investment Companies

Allied Investment Corporation
Kelly Anderson, Controller
1919 Pennsylvania Ave., NW — 202-973-6328
Washington, DC 20006-3434 — Fax: 202-973-6328
Email: Anderson@alliedcapital.com

Broadcast Capital, Inc.
John E. Oxendine, President
1001 Connecticut Ave., Suite 705 — 202-496-9250
Washington, DC 20006 — Fax: 202-496-9259
Email: broadcap@aol.com.

Core Capital Partners, L.P.
William Dunbar, Jonathan Silver, Contact
901 15th Street, Suite 950 — 202-589-0090
Washington, DC 20005 — Fax: 202-589-0091
Email: mwright@core-capital.com

Grosvenor Special Ventures IV, L.P.
Bruce B. Dunnan
1808 Eye Street, NW, Suite 900 — 202-861-5650
Washington, DC 20006 — Fax: 202-861-5653
Email: bbd@grosvenorfund.com

The SBA licenses, regulates, and provides financial assistance to privately owned and operated Small Business Investment Companies. SBICs make venture or risk investments by supplying capital and extending unsecured loans and loans not fully collateralized to small enterprises which meet their investment criteria. Financing is made by direct loans and by equity investments.

* DC Marketing Center/DC Business Connections

1213 K St., NW
Washington, DC 20005 — 202-638-7333
www.dcmarketingcenter.com/business

A public/private partnership between the District of Columbia 's Office of the Deputy Mayor for Planning and Economic Development and private sector sponsors. Through DC Business Connections, participating Washington based companies have the opportunity to establish a unique communication forum with the Government of the District of Columbia to address important issues associated with conducting business in the District.

Florida

* Florida Economic Development Council

P.O. Box 3186   850-201-FEDC
Tallahassee, FL 32315   Fax: 850-201-3330
www.fedc.net

or

Enterprise Florida
390 North Orange Avenue, Suite 1300   407-316-4600
Orlando, FL 32801   Fax: 407-316-4599
www.eflorida.com

Enterprise Florida: Offers information and referral services for current and potential small business owners. Also serves as ombudsman to small businesses to help resolve problems being experienced with state agencies. They sponsor workshops and business forums and an annual Small Business Development Workshop that brings together local, state, and federal agency representatives. Distributes and publishes the *Florida New Business Guide Checklist* for small businesses.

Innovation and Commercialization Centers: Sponsored by Enterprise Florida, Technology Development Corporation provides services and assistance designed to help entrepreneurs and emerging technology-based companies grow, launch new products and succeed in the marketplace. Services include business planning, market development, technology access, commercialization assistance, financial expertise and additional services.
- *Vendor Bid System*: An online computer service allowing searches for state bids that fit a particular business.
- *Quick Response Training*: Up to 18 months of employee training for businesses that produce exportable goods or services, create new jobs and employ Florida workers who require customized entry-level skills training.
- *Info-bid*: Helps businesses locate bid opportunities to sell to federal, state and local government agencies, as well as some commercial firms.

The Economic Development Transportation Fund: Commonly referred to as the "Road Fund," provides funding to units of local government for the elimination of transportation problems that adversely impact a specific company's location or expansion decision. Up to $2,000,000 may be provided to a local government to implement the improvements.

The Florida Recycling Loan Program: Provides funding for machinery and equipment for manufacturing, processing, or conversion systems utilizing materials which have been or will be recycled; collection systems are not eligible. Direct Loans — Maximum to $200,000; minimum of $20,000. Maximum amount for leveraged loans will be $200,000, or 40% of total eligible costs, whichever is less. {www.ffcfc.com}

Florida Export Finance Corporation: Makes available pre- and post-shipment working capital to small and medium size Florida exporters. Programs include state-supported direct loans and guarantees as well as packaging services that provide access to EXIM Bank and SBA export finance and working capital guaranty programs. Direct loans for the lesser of 90% of the product cost or $50,000. Loan guarantees for the lesser of 90% of a loan provided by a lender or $500,000. No minimum size. {www.dos.state.fk.us/fefc}

Rural Revolving Loan Program: Designed to provide gap funding for economic development projects in rural counties. Loan size to $200,000 or 10% of the project being assisted, whichever is less.

Florida Venture Finance Directory: Acts as a "wholesaler" in providing information to assist in the guidance of financing searches, Capital Development developed and published *The Florida Venture Finance Directory*. The *Directory* serves as an effective tool for economic development organizations (primary distributors) to assist local businesses in their fund raising efforts. 407-316-4646

Venture Capital Network Development: Financial support, within budget limitations, is provided to a limited number of venture capital conferences at which Florida entrepreneurs have opportunity to present their ventures to members of the venture capital community. Enterprise Florida also is specifically interested in supporting initiatives leading to increased participation of private individual investors in Florida business ventures.

The Technology Investment Fund: Makes co-investments with Florida companies in promising technology-related projects with near-term commercial potential. Investments fall within a range of $25,000 to $250,000, depending upon the project's scope, commercial potential,

matching funds, leveraged funds, the number and quality of other proposals received and the amount of funding requested in the highest ranked proposals.

Minority Business Development Centers: Offers existing and potential minority entrepreneurs a wide range of free services, from initial counseling on how to start a business to the more complex issues of planning and growth.

Office of Supplier Diversity: Responsible for certifying minority business enterprises to do business with state agencies.

Black Business Venture Corporation: A vehicle for initiating business acquisitions and engaging in real estate development. Serves a twofold purpose: to provide real and/or commercial office space for Black businesses; and to address the larger community needs such as local employment and retail centers.

Manufacturing Facility Bond Pool: This allows manufacturing land acquisition, new facility construction, and new equipment purchases with low-cost financing

Florida First Business Bond Pool: Funding for job creation projects that address air or water quality or solid waste management issues.

Front Porch Microcredit Loan Program: This program involves both technical training and a loan for qualified businesses in the Front Porch Community. The loan portion provides capital to small business entrepreneurs that may not have otherwise qualified for conventional financing. Up to $15,000 of funding can be used for startups of cottage industries and micro-enterprises.

Urban Incentives: Businesses located in many urban areas may be eligible for incentive awards and lower wage qualification thresholds.

* Florida Rural Development Office

4440 NW, 25th Place   352-338-3402
Gainesville, FL 32606   Fax: 352-338-3405
www.rurdev.usda.gov/fl

The Rural Development Office in Florida offers a variety of opportunities to businesses in rural areas. The Rural Business-Cooperative Service offers the following programs: Business & Industry Guaranteed Loans, Business and Industry Direct Loans, Intermediary Relending Loans, Rural Business Enterprise Grants, Rural Economic Development Loans and Grants, Cooperative Development Services, and Rural Business Opportunity Grants.

* State of Florida Department of Revenue

5050 W. Tennessee Street   850-488-6800
Tallahassee, FL 32399-0100   800-352-3671 (Florida only)
www.myflorida.com/dor/businesses/

The Department of Revenue provides information to new business owner and publishes a New Business Owner's Guide.

* Division of International Trade

Enterprise Florida, Inc.
2801 Ponce de Leon Blvd., Suite 700   305-569-2650
Miami, Florida 33134   Fax: 305-569-2686
www.eflorida.com

Enterprise Florida, Inc. is a partnership between Florida's government and business leaders and is the principal economic development organization for the State of Florida. Enterprise Florida's mission is to increase economic opportunities for all Floridians, by supporting the creation of quality jobs and globally competitive businesses. It pursues this mission in cooperation with its statewide network of economic development partners.

Export Counseling: Enterprise Florida's Division of International Trade provides an export counseling service for Florida manufacturers and service companies whose interest in and commitment to exporting is genuine. Export counseling sessions normally take the form of one-on-one meetings at the business location or an EFI office. Contact: Manny Mencia Enterprise Florida International Trade Division, Coral Gables, 305-569-2650

Enterprise Florida's Division of International Trade offers small and medium-sized Florida businesses interested in doing business internationally the opportunity to participate in overseas trade events and marketing missions. Open to all businesses registered in the state of Florida interested in doing business internationally, Enterprise Florida market-site trade events are professionally planned missions that feature one-on-one, prearranged appointments with business executives interested in the specific product lines or services of participants. Contact: Enterprise Florida International Trade Division, Coral Gables, 305-569-2650

* The Economic Development Commission

Mr. Darrell Kelley, President & CEO
Mr. Michael Bobroff, Executive Vice President
Economic Development Commission of Mid-Florida, Inc.
301 East Pine Street, Suite 900   407-422-7159
Orlando, FL 32801-1992   Fax: 407-843-9514
Email: bobroff@business-orlando.org
http://www.business-orlando.org
Serving the counties of Lake, Orange, Osceola, and Seminole

Mr. W.D. Higginbotham, Jr.
Director of Economic Development
2009 NW 67 Place, Suite A   352-955-2200
Gainesville, FL 32653-1603   Fax: 352-955-2209
Email: higginbotham@ncfrpc.org
http://www.originalflorida.org
Serving the counties of Alachua, Bradford, Columbia, Dixie, Gilchrist, Hamilton, Lafayette, Madison, Suwannee, Taylor, and Union

Ms. Betty Neale, Executive Director
P.O. Box 1196
5813 Olive Road   863-385-4900
Sebring, FL 33872-6041   Fax: 863-385-4808
Email: bnc@strato.net
www.fhredi.com
Serving the counties of DeSoto, Glades, Hardee, Hendry, Highlands, and Okeechobee

Mr. Stuart Rogel, Executive Director
Mr. Mike Evans, Business Development
4300 West Cypress Street   813-878-2208, ext. 23
Tampa, FL 33607   Fax: 813-872-9356
Email: srogel@tampabay.org
Email: mevans@tampabay.org
www.tampabay.org
Serving the counties of Hernando, Hillsborough, Manatee, Pasco, Pinellas, Sarasota, and Polk

The Economic Development Commission (EDC) is an organization that helps business. They are dedicated to meeting the needs of today's industries and creating a competitive economic climate where businesses can thrive. To meet this goal, the EDC provides key services and support, which range from relocation and expansion expertise to export counsel to long-term planning with our community partners.

* Florida Black Business Investment Board

1711 S. Gadsen St.
Tallahassee, FL 32301   850-487-4850
www.fbbib.com

Oversees the state's investment in black business investment corporations, which provide technical assistance and loans to black-owned businesses.

Black Business Investment Corporations: Provides loans, loan guarantees, joint ventures, limited partnerships or any combination thereof.

* Office of Supplier Diversity

Florida Department of Management Services
4050 Esplanade Way, Suite 360
Tallahassee, FL 32399-0950   850-487-0915
http://mbaao.fdles.state.fl.us

The Office of Supplier Diversity (OSD) is responsible for certifying minority business enterprises to do business with state agencies. Develops statewide initiative to help minority and women-owned business prosper in Florida and the global marketplace.

* Florida Export Finance Corporation

10400 NW 33 Street, Suite 200   786-845-0400
Miami, FL 33172-5092   Fax: 786-845-0404
www.dos.state.fl.us/fefc

The Florida Export Finance Corporation Loans and Guarantees are available for exporters in Florida that have been turned down by at least one potential lender. They will guarantee a revolving line of credit up to $50,000. Businesses can also benefit from information, technical and counseling assistance.

* Florida Manufacturing Extension Partnership

1180 Celebration Blvd.
Celebration, Fl 34747   321-939-4000
www.floridamep.org

Services are available to small, and medium sized manufactures in the Florida. Businesses can obtain help in the following areas: plant layout, health and safety issues, marketing and business development, technology transfer/processing improvements and access to workforce training and capital services.

* Economic Development and Commercial Revitalization

Bureau of Community Assistance
2555 Shumard Oak Blvd.   850-487-3644
Tallahassee, FL 32399-2100   Fax: 850-922-5609
www.dca.state.fk.us/fhcd.programs/cdbgp/index.htm

Small City Community Development Block Grant (CDBG): Available to cities populations of 50,000 or less or counties with populations of less than 200,000. Designed to address and resolve specific community and economic development needs for low and moderate income families. The state sets aside CDBG funds to assist private entities for the purpose of creating or retaining jobs for low and moderate income persons. Funds can be used for the acquisition, construction, rehabilitation, or installation of commercial or industrial buildings, structures and other real property and for public and private improvements.

* Small Business Administration (SBA)

Small Business Administration (SBA)
7825 Baymeadows Way, Suite 100B   904-443-1900
Jacksonville, FL 32256   Fax: 904-443-1980
www.sba.gov/fl/north

Small Business Administration (SBA)
100 S. Biscayne Blvd., 7th Floor   305-536-5521
Miami, FL 33131   Fax: 305-536-5058
www.sba.gov/

The Florida Small Business Administration Office delivers a variety of programs and services, such as startup and operational assistance through small business training and counseling, financial assistance for startups, business opportunities and much more.

* Small Business Investment Companies

BOCF, LLC
Steven Lux, Stephen Bennett
777 S. Harbour Island Blvd., Suite 375   813-223-3825
Tampa, FL 33602   Fax: 813-221-6453
Email: jmbordonak@stonehengecapital.com

Crossbow Venture Partners LP
Stephen J. Warner, Contact
One North Clematis Street, Suite 510   561-838-9005
West Palm Beach, FL 33401-5523   Fax: 561-838-4105
Email: rsoto@cb-ventures.com

Market Capital Corp.
Eugene C. Langford, President
1715 W. Cleveland Street   813-251-6055
Tampa, FL 33606   Fax: 813-251-1900
Email: pcaskey@langfordhill.com

Power Equities, Inc.
Maureen Beavers
50 N. Laura Street, 9th Floor
FL9-001-09-03   904-791-7601
Jacksonville, FL 32202   Fax: 904-791-7516

The SBA licenses, regulates, and provides financial assistance to privately owned and operated Small Business Investment Companies. SBICs make venture or risk investments by supplying capital and extending unsecured loans and loans not fully collateralized to small enterprises which meet their investment criteria. Financing is made by direct loans and by equity investments.

* Certified Development Corporations (CDCs)

Alabama Community Development Corporation   205-870-3360
117 Southcrest Drive, Suite 100   800-239-5909
Birmingham, AL 35209   Fax: 205 - 942 - 5984
www.ululcom.com

Area of Operation: Bay, Calhoun, Escambia, Franklin, Gadsden, Gulf, Holmes, Jackson, Leon, Liberty, Okaloosa, Santa Rosa, Wakulla, Walton and Washington Counties

Business Development Corporation of Northeast FL
9143 Phillips Highway, Suite 350 904-363-6350
Jacksonville, FL 32256 Fax: 904 - 363 - 6356
Area of Operation: Baker, Clay, Flagler, Lake, Nassau, St. Johns, Seminole, Putnam and Volusia Counties

Florida Business Development Corporation
6801 Lake Worth Road, Suite 209 561-433-0233
Lake Worth, FL 33467 Fax: 561-433-8545
or
780 NW LeJune Rd., Suite 520 305-567-2646
Miami, FL 33126 Fax: 305-567-0735
Area of Operation: Brevard, Broward, Charlotte, Collier, Dade, Indian River, Lee, Manatee, Martin, Orange, Osceola, Palm Beach, Polk, St. Lucie and Sarasota Counties

Florida First Capital Finance Corporation, Inc.
P.O. Box 4166 850-681-3601
Tallahassee, FL 32315 – 4166 Fax: 850-681-3699
www.ffcfc.com
Area of Operation: Baker, Bay, Bradford, Brevard, Broward, Calhoun, Charlotte, Clay, Citrus, Collier, Columbia, DeSoto, Escambia, Franklin, Gadsden, Glades, Gilchrist, Gulf, Hamilton, Hardee, Hendry, Hernando, Highland, Holmes, Indian River, Jackson, Jefferson, Lafayette, Lake, Lee, Leon, Levy, Liberty, Madison, Manatee, Marion, Martin, Monroe, Nassau, Okaloosa, Okeechobee, Orange, Osceola, Palm Beach, Polk, Pasco, St. Lucie, Santa Rosa, Sarasota, Seminole, Sumter, Suwannee, Taylor, Union, Volusia, Wakulla, Walton, and Washington Counties

Jacksonville Economic Development Company, Inc. (JEDCO)
1300 Riverplace Blvd., Suite 105 904-398-9411
Jacksonville, FL 32207 Fax: 904-398-4995
www.jedco.net
Area of Operation: Duval County

North Central Florida Areawide Development Co., Inc.
2009 Northwest 67th Place, Suite A 352-955-2199 ext. 107
Gainesville, FL 32653 – 1603 Fax: 352-955-2209
Area of Operation: Alachua, Bradford, Columbia, Dixie, Gilchrist, Hamilton, Lafayette, Levy, Madison, Marion, Suwannee, Taylor and Union Counties

Southern Development Council
8132 Old Federal Road 334-244-1801
Montgomery, AL 36116 Fax: 334-244-1421
Area of Operation: Bay, Calhoun, Escambia, Franklin, Gadsden, Gulf, Holmes, Jackson, Leon, Liberty, Okaloosa, Santa Rosa, Wakulla, Walton and Washington Counties

Florida First Capital Finance Corporation, Inc.
1351 North Gadsden Street 850-681-3601
Tallahassee, FL 32301 Fax: 850-681-3699
Area of Operation: Bay, Brevard, Broward, Calhoun, Charlotte, Citrus, Collier, DeSoto, Escambia, Franklin, Gadsden, Glades, Gulf, Hardee, Hendry, Hernando, Highlands, Hillsborough, Holmes, Indian River, Jackson, Jefferson, Lake, Lee, Leon, Levy, Liberty, Manatee, Marion, Martin, Monroe, Okaloosa, Okeechobee, Orange, Oceola, Palm Beach, Pasco, Polk, Santa Rosa, Sarasota, Seminole, Saint Lucie, Sumter, Wakulla, Walton, Washington and Volusia Counties

St. Petersburg Certified Development Corporation
dba Gulf Coast CDC
227 Second Avenue North 727-895 - 2504
St. Petersburg, FL 33731 Fax: 727-822 - 2504
Area of Operation: Manatee, Pasco, Pinellas and Sarasota Counties

Southwest Florida Regional Development Corporation
4980 Bayline Drive, 4th Floor 941-656-7726
North Fort Myers, FL 33917 Fax: 941-656-7724
Area of Operation: Charlotte, Collier, DeSoto, Glades, Hardee, Hendry, Lee, Polk and Sarasota Counties

Tampa-Bay Economic Development Corporation
2105 North Nebraska Avenue 813-274-7971
Tampa, FL 33602 Fax: 813-274-7551
Area of Operation: Hillsborough County

Certified Development Corporations are nonprofit organizations licensed by the Small Business Administration to administer small business loan

programs for new or expanding businesses for the purpose of promoting economic growth in a particular area. Contact one in your area.

Georgia

* Office of Economic Development
Georgia Department of Community Affairs
60 Executive Park South, NE, Suite 250 404-679-4940
Atlanta, GA 30329-2231 Fax: 800-736-1155
www.dca.state.ga.us
Georgia Department of Community Affairs (DCA): Responsible for state administration of many incentive programs as well as providing technical assistance in the area of economic development to local governments, development authorities, and private for-profit entities. Provides information on financing programs and other services offered by the state government.

DCA maintains a highly skilled and extremely dedicated graphics and editorial staff to ensure that the information it gathers is effectively digested and promptly disseminated. Some of the department's many publications include:
- *Small Business Resource Guide*: Manual for small business owners with useful instruction, organization addresses and telephone numbers and resources.
- *Georgia's Communities-Planning, Growing, Achieving*: Publication contains information about various federal, state, and local financing programs that benefit businesses located in Georgia.
- *Economic Development Financing Packet*
- *Regional Development Center Listing*: List of Georgia's 16 RDCs with addresses and telephone numbers.

One-Stop Environmental Permitting: Georgia offers one-stop environmental permitting through its Department of Natural Resources, Environmental Protection Division. The state has the full authority of the U.S. Environmental Protection Agency (EPA) to issue permits that meet Federal standards, thus allowing a single permit to meet all requirements.

Industrial Revenue Bonds: Taxable and tax-exempt industrial revenue bond financing is available through the state or local development authorities at competitive, below-prime rates.

Supplier Choice Power: Georgia companies with electricity demands of 900 kilowatts or higher may choose among competing suppliers, taking advantage of a competitive market. This cost-saving option has been available to Georgia consumers long before deregulation of the industry was even contemplated.

The Employment Incentive Program: A financing program that may be used in conjunction with traditional private financing to carry out economic development projects which will result in employment of moderate and low income persons. Amounts not available.

Community Home Investment Program (CHIP): Created by the National Affordable Housing Act of 1990, the Home Investment Partnerships (HOME) Program is the first federally funded block grant designed to address state and local affordable housing concerns with a maximum amount awarded per local government applicant of $200,000.

Immediate Threat and Danger Program: Funds community development, having a particular urgency because existing conditions pose a serious and immediate threat to the health or welfare of the community. The maximum amount an applicant may receive is $50,000, which shall not exceed half of total project cost.

Local Development Fund: A state funded grant program that provides local governments with matching funds for community improvement projects. The maximum grant amount is $10,000 for single community projects and $20,000 for multi-community projects.

Appalachian Regional Commission (ARC): An economic development program providing matching grant funds to eligible applicants for projects that will benefit the entire 35-county area of Appalachian Georgia.

Appalachian Region Business Development Revolving Loan Fund: A $2.2 million pool that can be used in the Appalachian Region for loans to projects that create or save jobs. The maximum loan amount is $200,000 per qualifying business, or 50% of total project cost, whichever is less. There is no maximum project cost and no minimum loan amount.

Regional Assistance Program (RAP): Grants are available on a competitive basis to local governments, development authorities, and regional development centers for regional industrial parks and similar facilities, regional water and sewer treatment facilities, regional transportation and communication facilities, regional marketing and recruitment programs, and other projects important to regional economic development. Grants will be available up to $250,000 per multi-county or regional economic development implementation project with no minimum match required.

Business Retention and Expansion Process: Provides a process for local governments, chambers and/or development authorities to survey existing industries and identify the perceptions and potential problems of private sector firms concerning issues like future plans, international trade, labor and manpower, local government services, energy requirements, and community linkages.

Surety Bond Guarantee Program: Enables small contractors to obtain the surety bonds necessary to compete for government and non-government contracts.

Industrial Enterprise Zones: The City of Atlanta, as authorized under a special provision of Georgia law, has designated two industrial parks as industrial enterprise zones. Companies in both the Atlanta and Southside industrial parks receive 100% freeport on all three classes of inventory and may receive real property tax reduction for up to 25 years. All buildings constructed in these enterprise zones are exempted from local property taxes at levels that begin at 100%. These exemptions decrease in increments of 20% every five years. New businesses in both parks are eligible for a $2,500-per job tax credit for a payroll of ten or more persons.

Bond Allocation Program: Businesses that are looking to construct or improve manufacturing facilities, single and multi-family housing projects can benefit from this program. Economic development projects must keep or create one job for every $125,000 of funding.

Industrial Development Bond Financing: Long-term, low-rate financing for businesses looking to improve or construct manufacturing facilities. Up to $10 million is available per project.

The Redevelopment Fund Program: The Redevelopment Fund provides flexible financial assistance to local governments to assist them in implementing challenging economic and community development projects that cannot be undertaken with existing public sector grant and loan programs.

Downtown Development Revolving loan Fund (DDRLF): The Downtown Development Revolving Loan Fund is designed to assist non-entitlement cities and counties in implementing quality downtown development projects. Loans may be used for a variety of public or private projects that involve infrastructure improvements, real estate development or redevelopment, and, in some cases, purchase or lease of equipment.

Georgia Academy for Economic Development: The Academy is a consortium of public and private economic development organizations providing economic development training throughout Georgia. These professionals serve as the Academy's program leaders and resource experts.

* Rural Development Administration

Community and Business Programs Division
Georgia State Office
335 East Hancock Ave.   706-546-2162
Athens, GA 30610   Fax: 706-546-2152
www.rurdev.usda.gov/ga
Special Grant Programs
Recycling and Waste Reduction Grants: Objectives are to reduce or eliminate pollution of water resources and improve planning and management of solid waste sites. Grants may be used to evaluate current landfill conditions to determine threats to water resources; provide technical assistance and/or training to enhance operator skills in the maintenance and operations of active landfills; provide technical assistance and/or training to help communities reduce the solid waste stream; and provide technical assistance and/or training for operators of landfills which are closed or will be closed in the near future.

Value-Added Agricultural Producer Grants: The Value-Added Agricultural Producer Grants program is designed to encourage independent producers of agricultural commodities to process their raw products into marketable goods, thereby increasing farm income. There are four entities that may apply for funds. They are: Independent Producer, Farm or Ranch Cooperative, Agricultural Producer Groups and Majority-Controlled Producer Based Business Ventures. Funds for eligible products may be used for planning and working capital. Contact Craig Scroggs at 333 Phillips Dr. McDonough, GA 30253 or by email at craig.scroggs@ga.usda.gov

Rural Business Enterprise Grants: This grant program supports the development of small emerging private business enterprises in rural areas. Small or emerging businesses generally employ 50 or fewer employees and

have less than $1,000,000 in projected gross revenues. The grants may be used to acquire and develop land, construct or make repairs to buildings/equipment, technical assistance, providing financial assistance and other business purposes. Contact the office or web site for a complete listing.

State Historic Preservation Tax Incentives: Designed to encourage rehabilitation of both residential and commercial historic buildings that might otherwise be neglected. The law provides an owner of historic property which has undergone substantial rehabilitation an eight-year freeze on property tax assessments. For the ninth year, the assessment increases by 50% of the difference between the recorded first year value and the current fair market value. In the tenth and following years the tax assessment will then be based on the current fair market value. The rehabilitation project must meet a rehabilitation test. If the property is: *Residential* (owner occupied C rehabilitation must increase the fair market value of the building by at least 50%. *Mixed-use* (primarily residential and partially income-producing property) C rehabilitation must increase the fair market value of the building by at least 75%. *Commercial and Professional Use* (income producing property) C rehabilitation must increase the fair market value of the building by at least 100%.

Business and Industry Loans: This Direct Loan Program provides loans to private parties, who can't obtain credit elsewhere and to public bodies. This assistance is available in areas outside of the city with a population of 50,000 or less. Loans can be used for improving, developing or financing business and industry, employment and to improve the economic and environmental rural community, including pollution control. The maximum loan available is $10 million.

Renewable Energy System and Energy Efficiency Improvement Program: This grant, loan and loan guarantee program is available to farmers, ranchers and rural small businesses to purchase renewable energy systems and for making energy efficiency improvements. Grants for Renewable Energy Systems are limited to $500,000. Grants for Energy Efficiency Improvements are limited to $250,000.

* The Phoenix Fund

Atlanta Development Authority
86 Pryor St., Suite 300   404-880-4100
Atlanta, GA 30303   Fax: 404-880-9333
www.atlantada.com
A program created to assist small and medium-sized businesses providing loan amounts from $10,000-$100,000 for construction or renovation of privately-owned commercial buildings, equipment purchases needed to operate a business, and, in some cases, working capital.

* The Georgia Procurement Assistance Center

Georgia Tech Economic Development Institute
760 Spring Street, Suite 330   404-953-3155
Atlanta, GA 30332-0640   Fax: 404-953-3169
www.edi.gatech.edu/gtpac
Assists firms in their efforts to do business with the federal government. The Center helps firms solicit bids and locate procurement opportunities with the Department of Defense and area military facilities seeking certain goods and services. Although assistance is given upon request to any firm, the majority of clients are small and disadvantaged businesses.

* Atlanta Regional Export Assistance Center

285 Peachtree Center Avenue   404-657-1961
Atlanta, GA 30303   Fax: 404-657-1970
www.dtae.org/econdev/gitdn.html
The Atlanta Export Assistance Center offers the following resources: Marketing Assistance, Resource Center, Financial Assistance, The Atlanta Export Assistance Center combines the export promotion and finance resources of the following eight agencies: U.S. Department of Commerce, U.S. Small Business Administration, The Georgia Department of Agriculture, The Georgia Department of Industry, Trade & Tourism, The Georgia Housing and Finance Authority, Georgia's Institute of Technology's Center for International Standards and Quality, and the Service Corps of Retired Executives.

The *Atlanta Region* houses consulates, trade offices, and Chambers of Commerce for 44 countries. These organizations provide assistance with foreign exporting, importing and investing.

International Trade Data Network (ITDN): A not-for-profit data multiplier, GDITT provides the business community with the timely, detailed market intelligence needed to be competitive in the global arena.

* Minority Small Business Resource Organizations

Atlanta Business League
PO Box 92363
931 Martin Luther King Dr.   404-584-8126
Atlanta, GA 30314   Fax: 404-584-0445
www.theabl.org

Atlanta Public Schools
Contract Compliance Office
130 Trinity Avenue, SW, 4th Floor
Atlanta, GA 30303   404-827-2436
www.atlanta.k12.ga.us/inside_aps/finance/contractsw/default.htm

Business Development Center – NAACP
2034 Metropolitan Parkway, SW
Atlanta, GA 30315   404-761-1266
www.atlantanaacp.org

Department of Commerce
Minority Business Development Agency (MBDA)
Summit Building, Room 1715
401 West Peachtree Street, NW   404-730-3300
Atlanta, GA 30308   Fax: 404-730-3313

Small Business Administration
Minority Small Business Division
233 Peachtree Road, NW, Suite 1900
Atlanta, GA 30303   404-331-0100
www.sba.gov/ga

These organizations provide a variety of technical counseling and financial assistance to minority small businesses:

* Department of Administrative Services

Governor's Small Business Center
200 Piedmont Ave., SE
West Tower, Suite 1804   800-495-0053
Atlanta, GA 30334-9010   404-656-6315
www.doas.state.ga.us

The mission of the Governor's Small Business Center is to contribute to Georgia's economic growth by increasing opportunities for new, emerging and established Georgia-based small and minority businesses to improve their operations, build business alliances, develop joint ventures and promote their businesses.

New Vendor Orientation: these monthly sessions provide general information on how to become a registered vendor with the state, marketing strategies and more. These sessions are also offered online at {http://www2.state.ga.us/departments/doas/gsbc/newvendor.html}.

Small and Minority Business Coordinators: this program is designed to inform you of procurement opportunities with their specific agencies. In addition, they provide state purchasing agencies with a vendor list to increase bid opportunities to small and minority businesses.

Governor's Mentor-Protégé Program: The Governor's Mentor-Protégé Program pairs leading Georgia companies with emerging businesses for mentoring relationships that can increase their odds of success.

* First Stop Business Information Center

Suite 315, West Tower   404-656-7061
2 Martin Luther King, Jr. Drive   800-656-4558
Atlanta, GA 30334   Fax: 404-657-6380
Email: firststop@sos.state.ga.us
www.sos.state.ga.us/firststop

The First Stop Business Information Center provides the small business owner and the prospective entrepreneur with a central point of information and contacts for state regulatory requirements for operating a small business. The primary objective of this center is to facilitate sustainable small business development in Georgia by offering a central location for determination of what licenses and permits must be obtained and maintained by individuals and businesses conducting their enterprises in our great state.

* Small Business Assistance Program

Georgia Department of Natural Resources
Georgia Environmental Protection Division
4244 International Parkway   404-362-4842
Suite 120   888-373-5947
Atlanta, GA 30354   877-427-6255
www.gasmallbiz.org   Fax: 404-651-5778
Georgia Department of Natural Resources created a Small Business

Assistance Program (SBAP) in 1993. The goal of the SBAP is to help small businesses comply with clean air requirements in Georgia. Air quality regulations require many small businesses to obtain permits, install pollution control equipment, and maintain extensive records on emissions.

* Office of Adult Literacy Programs

GEA Office
1800 Century Place, NE   404-679-1644
Atlanta, GA 30345   Fax: 404-679-4911
State Office of Adult Literacy   404-679-1625
www.dtae.org/adultlit.html   Fax: 404-679-1630
Georgia Department of Technical and Adult Education
Georgia Department of Revenue
Georgia Tax Credit for Adult Basic Skills Education: Designed to encourage businesses to provide or sponsor basic skills education programs for their employees. The program provides tax credits under Article 2 of Chapter 7 of Title 48 of the Official Code of Georgia Annotated, 48-7-41. The amount of tax credit shall be equal to one-third of the costs of education per full-time equivalent student, or $150 per full-time equivalent student, whichever is less, for each employee who has successfully completed an approved adult basic skills education program. The tax credit granted to any employer pursuant to the Code shall not exceed the amount of the taxpayer's income liability for the taxable year as computed without regard to this Code section.

* Georgia Department of Technical and Adult Education

Michael Jones, Manager
1800 Century Pl., Suite 300   404-679-1700
Atlanta, GA 30345-4304   Fax: 404-679-1710
www.dtae.org

Quick Start: The State of Georgia's internationally known training program for new and expanding business and industries. Quick Start directly provides a full range of high quality customized training services at no cost to client companies. These services cover not only job specific skills but also automation, productivity enhancement and human resource development training. Examples: Statistical Process Control, Programmable Logic Controller, and Team Skills training. Also provides comprehensive training for office operations such as corporate headquarters, billing and remittance centers, and telecommunications operations such as customer service centers.

* Georgia Department of Labor

Assistant Commissioner
Job Training Division
148 International Blvd., NE, Suite 650   404-232-3775
Atlanta, GA 30303   Fax: 404-651-9377
www.dol.state.ga.us

The Department of Labor is responsible for implementing the federal Workforce Investment Act (WIA). There are over 45 One-Stop service locations throughout the state to assist in job training for both the employee and employer.

* The Community Investment Services Department

Federal Home Loan Bank
1475 Peachtree St., NE   404-888-8000
Atlanta, GA 30309-3037   800-536-9650
www.fhlbatl.com

Federal Home Loan Bank
Community Investment Services: The fund provides long-term funds to its member institutions for lending in their communities. Funds may be used to assist first-time home buyers, for loans to small businesses, for the rehabilitation of historic districts, for community redevelopment programs, and for home mortgages for low- and moderate-income families. The maturities offered are up to 20 years at fixed rates.

* Georgia Environmental Facilities Authority

Paul Burks, Executive Director
2090 Equitable Bldg.
100 Peachtree St.   404-656-0938
Atlanta, GA 30303   Fax: 404-656-6416
www.gefa.org

The Georgia Environmental Facilities Authority will responsively and responsibly provide environmental and energy efficiency financing, coordination and education to governmental units and non-profit organizations so that they can use available resources in an environmentally sensitive manner for all Georgians.

Recycling And Waste Reduction Grants: The purpose of this grant program is to assist local governments in planning, expanding, improving and implementing waste reduction programs in Georgia. The grants are designed to provide much needed technical and financial assistance to Georgia local governments for recycling and waste reduction infrastructure. The goal of the grants is to help local governments foster an integrated approach to waste reduction through waste minimization, recycling, composting and other innovative programs.

Clean Water State Revolving Loan Fund (CWSRF): This federally funded program is administered by the Environmental Facilities Authority for waste water projects. Low interest loans are available for a variety of water quality and wastewater treatment projects that include: construction of new wastewater treatment plants, installing sewer lines, purchasing street and storm sewer cleaning equipment and others.

Drinking Water State Revolving Loan Fund (DWSRF): This federally funded program is administered by the Environmental Facilities Authority for drinking water projects. Low interest loans are available for a variety of public health related water supply projects that include: replacing aging infrastructure, installing or upgrading treatment facilities to improve drinking water quality, maintain compliance and many others.

Georgia Fund Loans through this state bond funded program finance all types of water and sewer projects including water and sewer lines, treatment plants, pumping stations, and water storage tanks. Loans from this program range from $20,000 to $3 million. Over 70% of communities receiving Georgia Fund are in rural areas. Contact Dan Clarke for additional information at (404) 656-0940 .

Environmental Emergency Loans: Environmental emergency loans are available at any time for projects needed to protect community health or safety. The interest rate is only 2.0%. The maximum loan amount is $200,000, but this can be combined with other GEFA loan programs to fully finance projects that cost more than $100,000. Contact James Thompson for more information at (404) 656-4046 .

Construction Loans: GEFA offers up to $1,000,000 in interim financing for applicants with a known source of permanent financing, such as Special Purpose Local Option Sales Taxes (SPLOST), a United States Department of Agriculture loan, etc.

Solid Waste Facility Financing: GEFA offers low interest loans of up to $1 million for solid waste capital projects that serve local governments. Also, to help minimize their waste streams, cities and counties can purchase facilities and equipment for new recycling or waste reduction programs through GEFA recycling and waste reduction grant funds.

GEFA / ENERGY: As the State Energy Office, the GEFA Division of Energy Resources is the primary agency for energy programs, grants, and educational materials. Through a broad array of programs ranging from Home Energy Clinics for the residential sector and the installation of weatherization materials in low income homes to assisting fleets to use clean alternative fuels, GEFA annually assists thousands of citizens throughout the state.

* Small Business Administration (SBA)

Small Business Administration
233 Peachtree St., NE, Suite 1900   404-331-0100
Atlanta, GA 30303   Fax: 404-331-0101
www.sba.gov/ga

The Georgia Small Business Administration Office delivers a variety of programs and services, such as startup and operational assistance through small business training and counseling, financial assistance for startup's, business opportunities and much more

* Small Business Investment Companies

Cordova Enhanced Fund, L.P.
Paul DiBella & Ralph Wright, Managers
2500 North Winds Parkway, Suite 475   678-942-0300
Alpharetta, GA 30004   Fax: 678-942-0301
Email: bl@cordovaventures.com

EGL/NatWest Ventures USA, L.P.
Salvatore Massaro, Manager
3495 Piedmont Road
Building Ten, Suite 412
Atlanta, GA 30305   404-949-8300
Email: samassaro@eglholdings.com   Fax: 404-949-8311

First Growth Capital, Inc.
Vijay K. Patel, President

P.O. Box 815
I-75 and GA 42
Best Western Plaza   912-994-9260
Forsyth, GA 31029   Fax: 912-994-1280
Email: vkpfgc@aol.com

Global Capital Funding Group, L.P.
Brad A. Thompson, Contact
106 Colony Park Drive, Suite 900   678-947-0028
Cumming, GA 30040   Fax: 678-947-6499
bthompson@gcaltd.com

The SBA licenses, regulates, and provides financial assistance to privately owned and operated Small Business Investment Companies. SBICs make venture or risk investment by supplying capital and extending unsecured loans and loans not fully collateralized to small enterprises which meet their investment criteria. Financing is made by direct loans and by equity investments.

* Georgia Development Authority

Agricultural Loan Division
2082 E. Exchange Pl., Suite 102   770-414-3400
Tucker, GA 30084   Fax: 770-414-3407
www.gda.georgia.gov

Georgia business owners have a fast, convenient way to register their business with the State of Georgia. By visiting www.georgia.gov and clicking the Online Business Registration Section, business owners will be able to register for a state sales tax identification number and a provisional Federal Employee Identification Number (FEIN). Obtaining a state sales tax identification number and a provisional Federal Employee Identification Number (FEIN) used to take several days.

* Local or Certified Development Corporations

The Business Growth Corporation of Georgia
1450 S. Johnson Ferry Road   404-475-6002
Atlanta, GA 30319   Fax: 404-475-6016

Coastal Area District Development Authority
501 Gloucester Street, Suite 201   912-261-2500
Brunswick, GA 31520   Fax: 912-261-0032

or

#1 Bull Street, Suite 301   912-236-9566
Savannah, GA 31401   Fax: 912-236-9562

CSRA Local Development Corporation
3023 Riverwatch Parkway, Suite A   706-210-2010
Augusta, GA 30907-2016   Fax: 706-210-2006

Economic Devel. Corp. Of Fulton County
141 Pryor St., Suite 5001   404-836-7731 Fulton county only
Atlanta, GA 30303   Fax: 404-836-7712

Uptown Columbus, Inc.
P.O. Box 1237   706-596-0111
Columbus, GA 31902   Fax: 706-596-0012

North Georgia Certified Development Corporation
503 West Waugh St.   706-272-2300
Dalton, GA 30720   Fax: 703-272-2253

Georgia Mountains Regional Economic Development Corporation
460 Enota Dr.   770-536-7839
Gainsville, GA 30503   Fax: 770-536-9026

Development Corporation of Middle Georgia
175 C Emery Hwy.   478-751-6160
Macon, GA 31201   Fax: 478-751-6517

Small Business Assistance Corp.
111 E. Liberty St., Suite 100   912-232-4700
Savannah, GA 31401   Fax: 912-232-0385

South Georgia Regional Development Corporation
327 West Savannah Ave.
P.O. Box 1223   229-333-5281
Valdosta, GA 31601   Fax: 229-333-5312

Georgia Certified Development Corporation
3353 Peachtree Road, NE, Suite 1155   404-442-2480
Atlanta, GA 30326   Fax: 404-442-2481

These corporations offer some local or SBA Section 502/503/7(u) loan funding for qualified small businesses in Georgia. Contact one of the above for further information.

* Intellectual Capital Partnership Program

Office of Economic Development
University System of Georgia
270 Washington Street, SW   404-656-2275
Atlanta, GA 30334   Fax: 404-657-1489
www.icapp.org

The Intellectual Capital Partnership Program provides one-stop entry to the intellectual capital of the University of Georgia, which includes educational programs, facility expertise, and research and development facilities.

* Coastal Venture Investment Forum

210 Technology Circle
Savannah, GA 31407   912-681-0213
www.coastalvif.org/

The Coastal Venture Forum is designed to promote the development of promising businesses located within the coastal region of Georgia. VIF assists by reviewing business plans to determine if private investment is warranted.

* The Business Improvement Loan Fund Program

Atlanta Development Authority
86 Pryor Street, Suite 300   404-880-4100
Atlanta, GA 30303   Fax: 404-880-9333
www.atlantada.com

The Business Improvement Loan Fund Program is designed to encourage the revitalization of targeted business districts in Atlanta, and to support commercial /industrial development in other eligible areas. District loans and loan participation up to $50,000 are available to businesses that are not able to obtain a market rate loan.

* GRASP Enterprises

241 Peachtree Street, NE, Suite 200   404-659-5955
Atlanta, GA 30303   Fax: 404-880-9561
www.graspnet.org

GRASP Enterprises, Inc. is a non-profit business development agency providing business programs and support services to metro Atlanta's small business community. Their mission is to enable aspiring entrepreneurs and existing small businesses achieve a stronger competitive position, larger market share, and greater chance of long term survival by providing a comprehensive and complete business solution. The organization's services include: Atlanta Women's Business Center, Business Training, Business Consulting, Business Financing, and Incubator Services.

Hawaii

* Department of Business, Economic Development and Tourism

P.O. Box 2359
Honolulu, HI 96804
No. 1 Capitol District Bldg.
250 S. Hotel Street   808-586-2423
Honolulu, HI 96813   Fax: 808-587-2790
www.hawaii.gov/dbedt/index.html

Small Business Information Service: Responsible for providing referrals and information on government licenses, permits and procurement, funding source, and entrepreneurship training.

Business Services Division: Helps new and existing businesses with direct business loans, community development projects, information programs, licensing and permit information and referral, and business advocacy.

Hawaii Small Business Innovation Research Grant Program: Its purpose is to expand science and technology-based economic development in Hawaii, increase revenues and quality job opportunities in the State. {www.htdc.org/sbir}
- Federal SBIR Program: Phase I awards determine the feasibility of a new technology and are valued up to $100,000. Phase II awards are a continuation of successful Phase I efforts. Phase II awards typically involve developing a prototype and are valued up to $750,000
- Hawaii SBIR Matching Grant Program: To encourage Hawaii companies to participate in the program, the High Technology Development Corporation provides a matching grant of up to $25,000 to Hawaii companies that receive Phase I awards

State of Hawaii Government: May finance exports through its Department of Business, Economic Development & Tourism's Hawaii Capital Loan Program (HCLP). The loan program's objective is to provide standard commercial loans to small businesses unable to get financing from private lenders. With an average loan award amount of $250,000 (maximum $1 million) for terms of up to 20 years, HCLP is available to all SBA- defined small businesses with two bank turndowns. The interest rate is set at a very attractive prime rate minus 1%, which is not to exceed 7.5%.

U.S. Department of Commerce-Commercial Service (Honolulu District office): The trade specialist at the Honolulu District office assists U.S. companies seeking to expand into export markets. The Honolulu District office provides companies with trade leads, foreign market research, and information on trade events, seminars, and conferences.

Local Chambers of Commerce: Provide exporters with copies of and instructions for completing a general Certificate of Origin. This certificate is a notarized statement authenticating the country of origin of an export good.

Thai Trade Representative Office: Focuses primarily on the promotion of Thailand products in Hawaii.

Research and Economic Analysis Division: This division provides accurate timely statistical and economic information for Hawaii businesses, including access to information and services available from other government sources in the State of Hawaii, nationally and internationally. There are 15,000 titles relating to business, government and economic development in the State of Hawaii with an emphasis on statistical information.

* Rural Development

U.S. Department of Agriculture
Rural Development
Room 311, Federal Building
154 Waianuenue Avenue   808-933-8380
Hilo, HI 96720   Fax: 808-933-8327
www.rurdev.usda.gov/hi

Business And Industry Guarantee And Direct Loans: The guaranteed B&I program provides financial assistance to rural businesses by offering guarantees to lenders as an incentive to extend credit in rural areas. If credit is not available elsewhere, Rural Development may provide direct loans to rural borrowers. Loan funds may be used to support the establishment or expansion of businesses, for working capital, machinery and equipment, buildings and real estate, and certain types of debt refinancing. Businesses involved in forestry, aquaculture, growing of hydroponics and mushrooms and commercial nurseries are eligible for assistance in addition to businesses involved in producing value-added products. The primary purpose is to create and maintain employment and improve the economic climate in rural communities.

Intermediary Relending Program: The Intermediary Relending Program allows an eligible intermediary organization to borrow funds directly from Rural Development at a one percent interest rate for the purpose of establishing a revolving fund. The revolving fund is used to provide a source of funds to businesses located in rural areas for business and community development purposes that would not otherwise qualify for commercial loans.

Rural Business Enterprise Grant (RBEG): Rural Business Enterprise Grants are used to finance and facilitate development of private business enterprises. The purpose of the grant is to assist public bodies and non-profit corporations finance and facilitate development of small and emerging private business enterprises located in areas outside the boundary of a city of 50,000 or more and its immediate adjacent urbanized area. RBEGs are awarded on a competing basis.

Rural Business Opportunity Grant (RBOG): Rural Business Opportunity Grant funds provide for technical assistance, training, and planning activities that improve economic conditions in rural areas. Applicants must be located in rural areas (this includes all areas other than cities of more than 10,000 people). Nonprofit corporations and public bodies are eligible. Funding is available to be distributed on a national competition basis. The RBOG program can be used to promote sustainable economic development in rural communities with exceptional needs. Making grants to organizations to provide for economic development planning, technical assistance, or training accomplishes this.

Hawaii Capital Loan Program: This loan provides loans to small businesses for financing construction, land acquisition, machinery, supplies or working capital for business owners unable to secure financing from conventional sources.

Native Hawaiian Revolving Loan Fund: This lending program is for Native Hawaiians to increase sustainable Native Hawaiian-owned businesses by providing economic independence, commitment and fiscal responsibility through entrepreneurial/job development.

* Employment and Training Fund Program

Oahu Branch
Honolulu Office
830 Punchbowl Street, Room 112   808-586-8715
Honolulu, HI 96813   Fax: 808-586-8724

Hawaii Branch
Hilo Office
180 Kinoole Street, Room 205   808-974-4126
Hilo, HI 96720   Fax: 808-974-4125

Kona Office
74-5565 Luhia Street   808-327-4770
Kailua-Kona, HI 96740   Fax: 808-327-4774

Kauai Branch
Kauai Office
3100 Kuhio Hwy., C-9   808-274-3056
Lihue, HI 96766   Fax: 808-274-3059

Maui Branch
Maui Office
2064 Wells Street, Room 108   808-984-2091
Wailuku, HI 96793   Fax: 808-984-2090

Molokai Office
75 Makaena Street   808-553-1755
Kaunakakai, HI 96748   Fax: 808-553-1754

This program provides business specific training, upgrade training, new occupational skills training, management skills training, and other similar activities are available to both employers and individuals. {http://dlir.state.hi.us}.

* The Honolulu Minority Business Development Center

1088 Bishop Street, Suite 2506   808-521-6221
Honolulu, HI 96813   Fax: 808-524-3313
www.mbdc-honolulu.com

The objectives of the Honolulu Minority Business Development Center are to 1) promote the creation and/or expansion of viable and competitive minority-owned businesses, 2) increase contracting opportunities from public and private sources for minority-owned businesses, and 3) provide management and technical assistance to qualified minority individuals and firms in the areas of planning, finance, construction assistance and general management to improve the overall performance, profit and net worth of minority firms.

* Business Action Center

State Department of Business
Economic Development and Tourism
1130 N. Nimitz Hwy., Suite A-220
Honolulu, HI 96817   808-586-2545
www.hawaii.gov/dbedt/br26.html

Provides Hawaii's entrepreneurs with the information, business forms, licenses and permits they need to make their small business dreams a reality.

* Pacific Business Center Program

College of Business Administration
University of Hawaii at Manoa
2404 Maile Way, A413   808-956-6286
Honolulu, HI 96822   Fax: 808-956-6278
www.hawaii.edu/pbcp

The Pacific Business Center matches faculty, students, and facilities at the University of Hawaii at Manoa with requests for assistance from businesses and community development organizations in Hawaii and the U.S. territories in the Pacific Islands. Consultation with program staff is free of charge, and after that clients may be assessed a modest consulting fee to pay faculty and students working on individual projects.

* Alu Like, Inc.

Career Education
458 Keawe St.
Honolulu, HI 96813   808-535-6700
www.alulike.org

Alu-Like, Inc. offers a wide range of office support services and technical assistance to all individuals regardless of race. The organization charges a nominal fee, and has several sites.

* Hawaii Island Economic Development Board

PMB-281
200 Kanoelehua Ave.   808-966-5416
Hilo, HI 96720   Fax: 808-966-6792
www.hiedb.org

HIEDB's mission is to facilitate federal resource programs and implement appropriate economic development projects. HIEDB provides valuable information and contacts for area businesses and industries, as well as key liaison to federal, state, county and private sector resources in financing, business planning, permitting, legal advice and other business services.

* High Technology Development Corporation

2800 Woodlawn Dr., Suite 100   888-677-4292
Honolulu, HI 96822   808-539-3806
www.htdc.org

Promotes the growth of commercial high-technology industry and assists in promoting hi-tech products and software.

* Hawaii Department Of Agriculture

Agricultural Loan Division
1428 S. King St.
Honolulu, HI 96814   808-973-9460
www.hawaiiag.org/hdoa/

The Agricultural Loan Program is intended to provide financing to "Qualified Farmers" and "New Farmers" engaged in agricultural production of food, feed and fiber. Loans can be made to qualifying sole proprietorships, corporations, partnerships and cooperatives. In addition, qualifying corporations and cooperatives can obtain funding for enterprises engaged in marketing, purchasing, processing and for those who provide certain farm business services.

Aquaculture Loan Program: Aquaculture means the production of aquatic plant and animal life in a controlled salt, brackish, or freshwater environment situated on real property. Loans can be made to "Qualified Aquaculturists" organized as sole proprietorships, corporations, cooperatives and partnerships.

* Hawaii Strategic Development Corporation

No. 1 Capitol District Building
250 South Hotel Street, Suite 503
P.O. Box 2359   808-587-3829
Honolulu, HI 96804   Fax: 808-587-3832
www.htdc.org/hsdc

The Hawaii Strategic Development Corporation (HSDC) is a state agency designed to provide capital, mainly to technology-oriented businesses, from public and private sources. The HSDC provides both seed and venture capital through limited partnerships.

* Maui Research & Technology Center

590 Lipoa Parkway
Kihei, HI 96753   808-875-2320
www.mrtc.org

The Maui Research & Technology Center operated by the Maui Economic Development Board under a grant from the State of Hawaii's High Technology Development Corporation. This two building complex houses incubator space for start-up businesses, a video conferencing facility, a multi-media production facility, an entry-level computer lab operated by Maui Community College, a small business and technology library, the offices of the UH Hilo Small Business Development Center, and the UH Manoa Office of Technology Transfer and Economic Development.

* The Office of Technology Transfer (OTTED)

Mark J. Andrews, Associate Director
University of Hawaii/OTTED
2800 Woodlawn Dr., Suite 280   808-539-3817
Honolulu, HI 96822   Fax: 808-539-3833
www.mic.hawaii.edu

OTTED represents a link to the scientific, technical, and business development resources of the University of Hawaii. These resources include the University's unique research facilities and faculty expertise which may be used to assist individuals, organizations or businesses with scientific or technical problems.

* Manoa Innovation Center

The High Technology Development Corporation (HTDC)
2800 Woodlawn Drive Suite 100

Honolulu, Hawaii 96822
Executive Office: 808-539-3600
Technology Outreach: 808-539-3814
www.htdc.org/mic/

The High Technology Development Corporation's (HTDC) mission is to facilitate the development and growth of commercial high technology industry in Hawaii. HTDC actively markets and promotes Hawaii as a site for high-technology applications and gives advice on policy and planning. HTDC serves as an advocate for start-up and existing high-technology companies doing business in Hawaii and is a source of information on high technology activity in the State.

* Agribusiness Development Corporation
State Office Tower
235 S. South Beretania St. Room 205 808-586-0186
Honolulu, HI 96813 Fax: 808-586-0189
www.hawaiiag.org/hdoa/adc.htm

The mission of the Agribusiness Development Corporation (ADC) is to provide leadership and advocacy for the conversion of agribusiness into a dynamic growth industry through the use of financial and other tools enabled by the founding legislation for the pursuit of specific projects to achieve the legislative objectives.

* Office of Hawaiian Affairs
711 Kapiolani Boulevard, Suite 500 808-594-1888
Honolulu, HI 96813 Fax: 808-594-1865
www.oha.org

Native Hawaiian Revolving Loan Fund: The Native Hawaiian Revolving Loan Fund (NHRLF) is a lending program for Native Hawaiians whose mission is to increase sustainable, Native Hawaiian-owned businesses by fostering economic independence, commitment and fiscal responsibility through entrepreneurial development.

* Small Business Administration (SBA)
Room 2235, Box 50207
300 Ala Moana Blvd. 808-541-2990
Honolulu, HI 96850-4981 Fax: 808-541-2976
www.sba.gov/hi

The Hawaii Small Business Administration Office delivers a variety of programs and services, such as startup and operational assistance through small business training and counseling, financial assistance for startup's, business opportunities and much more

* Small Business Investment Companies
HMS Hawaii
Richard Grey, Contact
Davies Pacific Center
841 Bishop Street, Suite 860 650-906-0488
Honolulu, HI 96813 Fax: 650-856-9864
Email: dick@hmsgroup.com

Pacific Century SBIC, Inc.
Darlene Blakeney, Manager
130 Merchant St., 12th Floor
Mailing Address:
PO Box 2900
Honolulu, HI 96846-6000 808-537-8088
Honolulu, HI 96813 Fax: 808-521-7602
Email: dblakeney@boh.com

Pacific Venture Capital, Ltd.
Dexter J. Taniguchi, President
222 S Vineyard St., PH.1 808-521-6502
Honolulu, HI 96813 Fax: 808-521-6541
Email: FrankT@lava.net

The SBA licenses, regulates, and provides financial assistance to privately owned and operated Small Business Investment Companies. SBICs make venture or risk investments by supplying capital and extending unsecured loans and loans not fully collateralized to small enterprises which meet their investment criteria. Financing is made by direct loans and by equity investments.

* Certified Development Corporations
HEDCO Local Development Corporation
222 South Vineyard Street, Penthouse – 1 808-521-6502
Honolulu HI 96813-2445 Fax: 808-521-6541
Area of Operation: Statewide and American Samoa

Lokahi Pacific Rural Development, Inc.
Jo-Ann Ridao, Managing Director
1935 Main Street 808-244-2200
Wailuku, HI 96793 Fax: 808-244-2057
Area of Operation: Counties of Maui and Hawaii

The 504 Certified Development Company (CDC) Program provides growing businesses with long-term, fixed-rate financing for major fixed assets, such as land and buildings. A Certified Development Company is a nonprofit corporation set up to contribute to the economic development of its community or region. CDC's work with the Small Business Administration and private-sector lenders to provide up to 90% financing to small businesses. There are about 270 CDC's nationwide, each covering a specific region.

Idaho

* Idaho Department of Commerce
700 West State Street
P.O. Box 83720 208-334-2470
Boise, ID 83720-0093 Fax: 208-334-2631
www.idoc.state.id.us/

Economic Development Division: This office can provide information and expertise in dealing with state, federal, and local agencies. They also have information on financing programs and other services offered by the state government.

Idaho Business Network (IBN): Operated by the Idaho Department of Commerce to help Idaho companies bid on federal, state and large corporation contracts.
- *Opportunity Notices*: Every day bid notices on federal, state and private contracts are entered into the Idaho Business Network computer. These bidding opportunities are matched with the capabilities of Idaho businesses participating in the IBN. When a match occurs the client company is notified with a printed or e-mail version "opportunity notice" alerting them to the opportunity and providing information needed to obtain the bid package.
- *Military and Federal Standards*: Federal bid packages often reference military and federal specifications by name or number without providing the actual documents. The Idaho Business Network maintains a CD-ROM library of all military and federal standards and specifications. Printed copies of required specifications and standards are provided at no charge to businesses participating in the IBN.
- *Federal Acquisition Regulations (F.A.R.)*: Contains the rules and regulations used by federal agencies to purchase products and services. Bid packages often refer to F.A.R. clauses by name or number without providing the text of the document. The IBN maintains the F.A.R. on CD-ROM, and provides printed copies of needed clauses to participating companies at no charge.
- *Trade Missions*: All IBN clients are welcome to attend periodic trade missions to visit large corporations, military sites, and other government agencies. Businesses attending the trade missions have the opportunity to meet with buyers to market their products and services.
- *Workshops and Seminars*: The IBN holds workshops statewide on topics such as selling to Mountain Home Air Force Base, selling to the INEEL, how to package for the military, quality assurance, etc.
- *The Governor's Business Opportunity Conference*: Annually, the IBN hosts the Governor's Business Opportunity Conference with over 60 large private corporations and government agencies sending buyers to meet with representatives of Idaho businesses. Concurrent training workshops are also held during the conference on a wide range of topics, such as introduction to procurement and marketing strategies for small businesses.
- *Electronic Bulletin Board*: Provides computer and modem access to all bid notices obtained by the IBN for the most current ten days.
- *CAGE Code*: All companies wishing to do business with the U.S. Department of Defense must have an identification number known as a Commercial and Government Entity Code, or CAGE Code. Companies applying for a CAGE Code must be sponsored by a government agency. The Idaho Business Network provides CAGE Code application forms and sponsors participating Idaho business applications
- *New Industry Training Program*: Provides customized job training for new and expanding industries.
- *Work Force Training*: Funds are available to provide skilled workers for specific economic opportunities and industrial expansion initiatives.

Industrial Revenue Bonds: Idaho cities and counties are able to form public corporations for the purpose of issuing industrial revenue bonds (IRBs). The IRB program provides for loans of up to $10 million, at tax-exempt interest rates, to finance the improvement or purchase of land, buildings, and machinery or equipment used in manufacturing, production, processing, or assembly.

Rural Economic and Community Development Administration: Offers guarantees up to 90% of loans between $500,000 and $10 million made to small businesses located in areas not within the boundaries of a city of 50,000 or more. Loan proceeds can be used for the purchase, development or improvement of land, buildings and equipment, or a start-up and working capital.

Nonbusiness-Related Contributions: Corporations are allowed credit for certain nonbusiness-related contributions, e.g., education and rehabilitation. Net operating loss carrybacks are limited to $100,000 per tax year. The $100,000 loss limit may be carried back three years and if it is not absorbed by the income in those three years, the rest of the loss may be carried forward 15 years. Instead of carrying a loss back, a taxpayer may choose to carry the loss forward for up to 15 years or until it has been completely absorbed.

The Idaho Department of Commerce's Division of International Business: Provides a variety of services and assistance to all Idaho firms interested in doing business overseas, with special programs for small- and medium-sized firms.

Idaho International Business Development Center (IIBDC): Seeks to coordinate efforts statewide to promote Idaho in the global marketplace. The division, in partnership with the Boise Branch Office of the U.S. Department of Commerce, maintains regular contact with importers, distributors, wholesalers, and retailers in foreign countries and can supply market data and information on foreign packaging, labeling requirements, language barriers, consumer preferences, and other trade factors.

Idaho Department of Agriculture: Offers a broad range of assistance to Idaho companies which export Idaho agricultural commodities and processed and specialty food products. The Department of Agriculture sponsors many special agricultural trade events and participates with the Department of Commerce in joint seminars, workshops, and trade shows.

* Rural Development

Rural Business-Cooperative Service (RBS)
9173 West Barnes, Suite A1
Boise, ID 83709   208-378-5623
www.rurdev.usda.gov/id

The Rural Business-Cooperative Service (RBS) administers programs directed toward increasing rural job opportunities, facilitating development of small and emerging private business enterprises, and improving the economic and environmental climate of rural communities. This service is committed to assisting with economic growth and diversification by providing the following programs to rural businesses:
- Business loans to local private parties and public agencies B&I Direct Loan Program
- Business loan guarantees B&I Guaranteed Loan Program
- Business development grants to public agencies non-profit corporations Rural Business Enterprise Grants
- Business and community development revolving loan fund loans Intermediary Relending Program
- Helps rural residents form new cooperative businesses and improves the operations of existing cooperatives
- Cooperative Services Technical Assistance
- Business and community development loans and grants to RUS electric/telephone borrowers Rural Economic
- Development Loan and Grant Program

* Idaho State Department of Agriculture

Division of Marketing and Support Services
P.O. Box 790
2270 Old Penitentiary Road
Boise, ID 83712   208-332-8530
    Fax: 208-334-2879
www.agri.state.id.us/marketing.export.htm

Services include technical assistance, business workshops, and publications for value-added food processing, specialty foods, traditional and specialty crops, organic production, and ranch recreation; international trade assistance for food and agriculture products; domestic marketing promotions; and start-up and rural rehabilitation.

* Idaho Department of Environmental Quality

Pollution Prevention/Environmental Education
1410 N Hilton   208-373-0502
Boise, ID 83706-1255   Fax: 209-373-0417

www.deq.state.id.us

The Environmental Education section provides assistance to businesses and the public interested in reducing wastes at the source.

* Workforce Development Training

Larry Hertling or Leandra Burns
Idaho Department of Labor
317 Main St.   208-334-6298
Boise, ID 83735   208-334-6158

Regional Economic Development Specialists
Idaho Department of Commerce
P.O. Box 83720
Boise, ID 83720-0093   208-334-2470

Dick Winn
Idaho State Division of Vocational Education
P.O. Box 83720
Boise, ID 83720-0095   208-334-3216

If your company is considering locating or expanding in Idaho, the Workforce Development Training Fund (WDTF) can help. Through the WDTF, your company may be able to receive funds to train new employees or upgrade the skills of current workers who are at risk of being permanently laid off. For information regarding the WDTF program, contact any of the people listed below. Potential applicants are encouraged to seek information and technical assistance on allowable activities prior to submitting a proposal. {www.labor.state.id.us}

* Small Business Administration (SBA)

1020 Main St., Suite 290   208-334-1696
Boise, ID 83702-5745   Fax: 208-334-9353
www.sba.gov/id

The Idaho Small Business Administration Office delivers a variety of programs and services, such as startup and operational assistance through small business training and counseling, financial assistance for startup's, business opportunities and much more

* Certified Development Corporations

Capital Matrix, Inc.
1471 Shoreline Drive, Suite 123   208-383-3473
Boise, ID 83702   Fax: 208-383-9404
Email: Capmatrx@Capitalmatrix.com
Area of Operation: Idaho Counties of Ada, Adams, Boise, Canyon, Elmore, Gem, Owyhee, Payette, Valley and Washington; Oregon Counties of Harney and Malheur

East-Central Idaho Development Company
310 N. 2nd E., Suite 115   208-356-4524
Rexburg ID 83440   Fax: 208-356-4544
Email: david.ogden@ecipda.org
www.ecidc.org
Area of Operation: Bonneville, Butte, Clark, Custer, Fremont, Jefferson, Lemi, Madison and Tenton Counties

Eastern Idaho Development Corporation
1651 Alvin Ricken Drive   208-234-7541
Pocatello ID 83201   Fax: 208-282-4813
Email: coxpaul@isu.edu
Area of Operation: Bannock, Power, Bear Lake, Bingham, Caribou, Franklin and Oneida Counties

Region IV Development Corporation, Inc.
315 Falls Avenue
P.O. Box 5079   208-732-5730
Twin Falls, ID 83303   Fax: 208-732-5454
Email: Rparrish@cdi.edu
www.rivdco.org
Area of Operation: Blaine, Camas, Cassia, Gooding, Jerome, Lincoln, Minidoka and Twin Falls Counties

Panhandle Area Council, Inc.
11100 Airport Drive   208-772-0584
Hayden ID 83835   Fax: 208-772-6196
Area of Operation: 5 Northern Counties of Idaho - Benewah, Bonner, Boundary, Kootenai and Shoshone

Greater Eastern Oregon Development Corporation
P.O. Box 1041   541-276-6745
Pendleton, OR 97801   Fax: 541-276-6071
Email: gmdavis@OregonVOS.net

Area of Operation: Gilliam, Grant, Morrow, Umatilla, Wheeler, Union, Baker and Wallowa Counties

Oregon Certified Business Development Corporation
2363 SW Glacier Place   541-548-8163
Redmond OR 97756-8120   Fax: 541-923-3416
Email: mackinnon@coic.org

Area of Operation: Crook, Deschutes, Harney, Jefferson, Klamath, Lake and Malheur Counties

The 504 Certified Development Company (CDC) Program provides growing businesses with long-term, fixed-rate financing for major fixed assets, such as land and buildings. A Certified Development Company is a nonprofit corporation set up to contribute to the economic development of its community or region. CDC's work with the Small Business Administration and private-sector lenders to provide up to 90% financing to small businesses. There are about 270 CDC's nationwide, each covering a specific region.

* Energy Resources Division

Idaho Department of Water Resources
1301 North Orchard   208-327-7900
Boise, ID 83706   1-800-334-SAVE (7283) in ID
www.idwr.state.id.us/energy   Fax: 208-327-7866

Energy Conservation Loans: Loans to businesses for energy conservation improvements to existing buildings, or new construction. Energy savings must have simple payback of less than 10 years. Interest rate of 4 percent term of 5 years.

* Association of Idaho Cities

3314 Grace   208-344-8594
Boise, ID 83703   Fax: 208-344-8677
www.idahocities.org

Tax Increment Financing: Tax exempt bonds for community development in designated areas. Amount of funding dependent upon increased property values within revenue allocation area. Only available within incorporated cities.

In addition to the government sponsored programs, there are many other financial loan and grant programs available through private institutions and private investors that you may wish to consider. You can obtain details on individual private assistance programs currently being offered by contacting the institutions directly.

Illinois

* Illinois Department of Commerce and Economic Opportunity

Department of Commerce and Economic Opportunity
620 E. Adams   217-782-7500
Springfield, IL 62701   Fax: 217-524-3701
www.illinoisbiz.biz

100 West Randolph St., Suite 3-400   312-814-7179
Chicago, IL 60601   Fax: 312-814-2370

Department of Commerce and Economic Opportunity: Provides information, assistance and advocacy to facilitate and advance the economic development process in partnership with Illinois' communities, businesses, and their network of public and private sector providers.

Small Business Division: Responsible for an environment that supports small business success resulting in increased employment opportunities and prosperous communities throughout Illinois. Provides advocacy, business assistance, training and information resources to help entrepreneurs, small companies and their partners enhance their competitiveness in a global economy. Serves customers through a dynamic, integrated small business assistance delivery system that matches the diversity of their customers' current and future needs.

Workforce Development & Manufacturing Technology Assistance: Provides programs to assist manufacturers to improve employee job skills and manufacturing efficiency. Labor-Management programs are also available.

First Stop Business Information Center: 800-252-2923
Provides individuals with comprehensive information on state business permits and licenses, business startup assistance, regulatory guidance, demographic and census data. Guides them through permitting, licensing and regulatory processes.

Procurement Technical Assistance Centers (PTAC): Provide one-on-one counseling, technical information, marketing assistance and training to existing Illinois businesses that are interested in selling their products and/or services to local, state or federal government agencies. The services are offered through PTACs located at community colleges, universities, chambers of commerce and business development organizations.

Small Business Innovation Research Centers (SBIRC): Provide counseling, technical information and training to Illinois entrepreneurs and small businesses interested in pursuing research and development opportunities available to them through various federal and state programs. These programs provide small businesses with a means of developing new and marketable technologies and innovations and also for enhancing existing products and services.

Participation Loan Program: Through these loan participation programs, the Illinois Department of Commerce and Community Affairs (DCCA) helps small businesses obtain financing through Illinois banks, development corporations, and lending institutions for business start-up, expansion, modernization and competitiveness improvement. Generally, the Department may provide subordinated small business loans up to 25% of the total amount of a project, but not less than $10,000 or more than $750,000.

Title IX Revolving Loan Fund: Provides low-cost supplemental financing to small and medium-sized manufacturers located in areas declared eligible for assistance. Proceeds may be used for the acquisition of land, buildings, machinery and equipment, building construction or renovations, and leasehold improvements.

Rural Development Loan Program: Assists businesses in communities with populations less than 25,000. Proceeds may be used to purchase land, construct or renovate buildings and purchase machinery and equipment.

State Treasurer's Economic Program: Provides companies with access to affordable capital to expand their operations and retain or create jobs in the state. For each permanent full-time job that is created or retained, the Treasurer can deposit $25,000 at well below market rates into the borrower's financial institution. That institution will then lend the money at below prevailing interest rates to the borrower.

Enterprise Zone Financing Program: Designed to encourage businesses to locate within an Illinois Enterprise Zone. DCCA may participate in an eligible loan for no less than $10,000, nor more than $750,000. In no case shall the amount of DCCA's subordinated participation exceed 25% of the total project. Ineligible uses of funds are debt refinancing and contingency funding.

Development Corporation Participation Loan Program: Provides financial assistance through a Development Corporation to small businesses that provide jobs to workers in the region served by the Development Corporation. The state will participate in loans up to 2% of the total amount of a project but not less than $10,000 nor more than $750,000.

Capital Access Program (CAP): Designed to encourage lending institutions to make loans to businesses that do not qualify for conventional financing. CAP is based on a portfolio insurance concept where the borrower and DCCA each contribute a percentage of the loan amount into a reserve fund located at the lender's bank. This reserve fund enables the financial institution to make loans beyond its conventional risk threshold and is available to draw upon to recover losses on loans made under the program.

Technology Venture Investment Program (TVIP): Provides investment capital for young or growing Illinois businesses in cooperation with private investment companies or investors. Program investments will be used for businesses seeking funding for any new process, technique, product or technical device commercially exploitable by Illinois businesses in fields such as health care and biomedical products, information and telecommunications, computing and electronic equipment, manufacturing technology, materials, transportation and aerospace, geoscience, financial and service industries, and agriculture and biotechnology. Program funds shall be used for such costs including, but not limited to, research and development costs, acquisition of assets, working capital, purchase or lease of machinery and/or equipment, and the acquisition and/or improvement or rehabilitation of land and buildings.

Affordable Financing of Public Infrastructure Program: Provides financial assistance to or on behalf of local governments, public entities, medical facilities and public health clinics.

Community Services Block Grant Loan Program: Provides long-term, fixed-rate financing to new or expanding businesses that create jobs and employment opportunities for low-income individuals.

Industrial Training Program: Assists companies in training new workers or upgrading the skills of their existing workers. Grants may be awarded to individual companies, multi-company efforts and intermediary organizations offering multi-company training.

Industrial Revenue Bonds: IDFA issues tax-exempt bonds on behalf of manufacturing companies to finance the acquisition of fixed assets such as land, buildings and equipment. Proceeds may also be used for new construction or renovation.

International Trade Centers/NAFTA Opportunity Centers (ITC/NOC): Provide information, counseling and training to existing, new-to-export Illinois companies interested in pursuing international trade opportunities. The NOCs provide specialized assistance to those firms seeking to take advantage of the trade opportunities in Mexico and Canada made possible by the North American Free Trade Agreement.

Surety Bond Guaranty Program: Designed to provide Illinois' small, minority and women contractors technical assistance, help them receive experience in the industry and assist in obtaining bid, performance and payment bonds for government, public utility and private contracts.

Minority, Women and Disabled Participation Loan Program: The Minority, Women and Disabled Participation Loan Program guidelines differ, in that the program funding may not exceed 50% of the project, subject to a maximum of $50,000.

Community Development Assistance Program (CDAP): CDAP assists smaller Illinois local governments in financing public facilities, housing rehabilitation projects or other economic development needs. Grants are made to governments and may be loaned to businesses for projects that will create and retain jobs in the community. The program is limited to communities with less than 50,000 people.

Employer Training Investment Program (ETIP): The Employer Training Investment Program assists companies in training new workers or upgrading the skills of their existing workers.

Illinois Technology Enterprise Center Program (ITEC): The Illinois Technology Enterprise Centers assist entrepreneurs to locate pre-seed and early stage financing, help entrepreneurs in high growth, high technology fields and assist with new product development and marketing.

Illinois Small Business Energy Program: This program offers energy conservation and energy efficiency information and technical assistance to Illinois businesses.

Illinois Small Business Environmental Assistance Program: The Environmental Assistance Program helps small businesses understand and comply with state and federal pollution regulations. This service is free and confidential.

* Rural Development

2118 West Park Court, Suite A   217-403-6202
Champaign, IL 61821   Fax: 217-403-6243
www.rurdeve.usda.gov/il

The USDA Rural Development in Illinois operates Federal loan programs designed to strengthen rural businesses, finance new and improved rural housing, develop community facilities, and maintain and create rural employment. Direct and/or guaranteed loans are available for housing, water and waste, rural businesses, community facilities, telecommunications and much more.

Direct Rural and Guaranteed Rental Housing Loans: These loans, with rates as low as 1 percent, are available to developers of affordable housing.
Housing Preservation Grants: Housing Preservation Grants provide grants for non-profit and public organizations to help very low- and low-income homeowners repair and rehabilitate their homes. Rental property owners can use them to repair and rehabilitate their units if they agree to make such units available to low- and very low-income families.

Community Development Programs: These programs help assist rural communities in financing construction, enlargement or improvement of essential community facilities. Programs include: Direct and Guaranteed Community Facility Loans, Community Facilities Grants, Water and Waste Disposal Loans, Technical Assistance and Training, Solid Waste Management Grants, Distance Learning and Telemedicine Loan and Grant Funds and Rural Community Development Initiative Funds.

Business Development Programs: The Rural Development Programs of Illinois promote a dynamic business environment in rural America. They work in partnership with the private sector and community-based organizations to provide financial assistance and business planning. In

addition, they provide technical assistance to rural businesses and cooperatives, conduct research into rural economic issues, and provide cooperative education material to the public. The Business and Industry Programs help fund projects that create or preserve quality jobs and/or promote a clean rural environment. The financial resources of Rural Development are often leveraged with those of other public and private credit source lenders to meet business and credit needs in under-served areas. Recipients of these programs may include individuals, corporations, partnerships, cooperatives, public bodies, non-profit corporations, and private companies. Programs include: Business & Industrial Guaranteed Loans, Intermediary Relending Program, Rural Cooperative Development Grants, Rural Business Enterprise Grants, Rural Economic Development Loans and Grants Rural Business Opportunity Grants and Cooperative Development Technical Assistance.

* The Illinois Coalition

One East Wacker, Suite 2410
Chicago, IL 60601   312-229-1970
www.ilcoalition.org

The Illinois Coalition is a nonprofit organization of leaders in business, government, academia and labor dedicated to encouraging technology-based economic development. Founded in 1989, the Illinois Coalition seeks to leverage public and private sector support for research and development, to facilitate technology transfer, to foster the commercialization of new technologies, and to advance the deployment of technology modernization services. The Illinois Coalition is responsible for overseeing the affiliate network of private sector experts, comprised of approximately 50 CEO's of technology companies, partners in venture capital and professional service firms, and R&D heads, that reviews applications for financing under the Technology Development Bridge. It makes investment recommendations to the Authority and assists all companies not receiving investment.

* Illinois Development Finance Authority

Technology Development Bridge Program provides seed stage equity financing to small technology companies. The goal is to help the businesses access capital in order to grow and create jobs.
{http://www.idfa.com/products/vc/vc.html}

Chicago office: 312-627-1434
Springfield office: 217-524-1567
Peoria office: 309-495-5959
Carbondale office: 618-453-5566

* Small Business Administration (SBA)

500 West Madison, Suite 1250   312-353-4528
Chicago, IL 60661-2511   Fax: 312-886-5688
www.sba.gov/il

The Illinois Small Business Administration Office delivers a variety of programs and services, such as startup and operational assistance through small business training and counseling, financial assistance for startup's, business opportunities and much more

* Small Business Investment Companies

ABN AMRO Capital (USA) Inc.
Paul Widuch, Chairman
135 South LaSalle Street   312-904-6445
Chicago, IL 60674   Fax: 312-904-6376
Email: aamir.khan@abnamro.com

Alpha Capital III SBIC, L.P.
122 South Michigan Avenue, Suite 1700   312-322-9800
Chicago, IL 60603   Fax: 312-322-9808
Email: AmyColeman@earthlink.net

Banc One Equity Capital SBIC Fund II, L.L.C
55 West Monroe Street, 16th Floor   312-732-9825
Chicago, IL 60670   Fax: 312-732-7495
Email: susan_klaus@bankone.com

BancAmerica Capital Investors SBIC II, L.P.
Dennis McCrary, Robert Perille
231 South LaSalle Street, 7th Floor   312-828-1781
Chicago, IL 60697   Fax: 312-828-6298
Email: Janice.Erickson@BankofAmerica.com

BMO Nesbitt Burns Equity Investments, Inc.
William C. Morro, President
111 West Monroe Street, 20th Floor   312-461-2021
Chicago, IL 60603   Fax: 312-765-8000
Email: helen.schubbe@bmonesbittburns.com

Cardinal Growth, L.P.
311 South Wacker Drive, Suite 5500 312-913-1000
Chicago, IL 60606 Fax: 312-913-1001
Email: mphelan@cardinalgrowth.com

CFB Venture Fund I, Inc.
120 S. Riverside, Suite 2160 312-466-9276
Chicago, IL 60606 Fax: 312-466-9278

Channel Medical Partners, L.P.
5750 Old Orchard Road, Suite 310 847-779-1550
Skokie, IL 60077 Fax: 847-779-1535
Email: gshearer@chanmed.com

Chicago Venture Partners, L.P.
John Fife, Manager
303 East Wacker Drive, Suite 311 312-297-7000
Chicago, IL 60601 Fax: 312-819-9701
Email: general@chicagoventure.com

CIVC Partners Fund, LLC
Christopher Perry, Marcus Wedner
231 South LaSalle Street, Seventy Floor 312-828-6570
Chicago, IL 60697 Fax: 312-987-0763
Email: christopher.perry@bankofamerica.com

Continental Illinois Venture Corporation
Christopher J. Perry, President
209 South LaSalle St.
Mailing Address
231 South LaSalle St. 312-828-8023
Chicago, IL 60697 Fax: (312)987-0887
Email: christopher.perry@bankofamerica.com

DNJ Leasing II, L.P.
150 N. Wacker Drive, Suite 3025 312-629-2877
Chicago, IL 60606 Fax: 312-629-2874
Email: jpfeffer@dnjcapital.com

First Chicago Equity Corporation
David J. Vitale, President
Three First National Plaza, Suite 1330 312-895-1000
Chicago, IL 60670 Fax: 312-895-1001
Email: deborah.morrin@em.fcnbd.com

High Street Capital III SBIC, L.P.
11 South LaSalle Street, 5th Floor 312-423-2650
Chicago, IL 60603 Fax: 312-423-2655
Email: Jkatcha@Highsr.com

Mercantile Capital Partners I, L.P.
Steven Edelson, Contact
1372 Shermer Road 847-509-3711
Northbrook, IL 60062 Fax: 847-509-3715
Email: Isedelson@MercantilePartners.com

Midwest Mezzanine Fund II, L.P.
135 South LaSalle Street, 20th Floor 312-992-4580
Chicago, IL 60603 Fax: 312-992-4595
Email: Allan.Kayler@ABNAMRO.com

Open Prairie Ventures I, L.P.
Dennis D. Spice, Contact
115 North Neil Street, Suite 209 217-351-7000
Champaign, IL 61820 Fax: 217-351-7051
Email: dspice@openprairie.com

Peterson Finance and Investment Company
James S. Rhee, President
3300 West Peterson Avenue, Suite A 773-539-0502
Chicago, IL 60659 Fax: 773-583-6714
Email: jsrhee@aol.com

Prairie Capital II, L.P.
C. Bryan Daniels, Contact
300 South Wacker Drive, Suite 1050 312-360-1133
Chicago, IL 60606 Fax: 312-360-1193
Email: bdaniels@prairie-capital.com

Prairie Capital Mezzanine Fund, L.P.
Bryan Daniels & Stephen King, Partners
300 S. Wacker Drive, Suite 2400 312-360-1133
Chicago, IL 60606 Fax: 312-360-1193
Email: hlane@prairie-capital.com

Prism Opportunity Fund SBIC, L.P.
444 N. Michigan Avenue, Suite 1910 312-464-7900
Chicago, IL 60611 Fax: 312-464-7915
Email: steve@prismfund.com
Email: alan_keaton@sbk.com

SvoCo, L.P.
John Svoboda, Michelle Collins, Contacts
1 North Franklin St. 312-759-7850
Chicago, IL 60606 Fax: 312-759-7855
Email: jas@svoco.com

USHCC Private Equity, L.P.
311 South Wacker Drive 312-697-4590
Chicago, IL 60606 Fax: 312-697-0145
Email: vmaruri@duffllc.com

The SBA licenses, regulates, and provides financial assistance to privately owned and operated Small Business Investment Companies. SBICs make venture or risk investments by supplying capital and extending unsecured loans and loans not fully collateralized to small enterprises which meet their investment criteria. Financing is made by direct loans and by equity investments.

* Certified Development Companies

Illinois Business Financial Services
124 Southwest Adams Street, Suite 300 309-676-0755
Peoria IL 61602 Fax: 309-676-7534
Area of Operation: Citywide in Peoria; Counties of Peoria, Tazewell and Woodford

Illinois Small Business Growth Corporation
2921 Greenbriar Drive, Suite C 217-787-7557
Springfield, IL 62704 Fax: 217-787-2872
Area of Operation: Statewide

Rockford Local Development Corporation
515 North Court Street 815-987-8127
Rockford IL 61103 Fax: 815-987-8122
Area of Operation: City of Rockford

Somercor 504, Inc.
2 East 8th Street, Suite 200 312-360-3163
Chicago IL 60605 Fax: 312-360-9177
Area of Operation: Cook Dupage, Lane Kane, McHenry and Will Counties

South Central Illinois Regional Planning & Development Comm.
120 Delmar Avenue, Suite A 618-548-4234
Salem IL 62881-2006 Fax: 618-548-4236
Area of Operation: Counties of Effingham, Fayette and Marion; also Cities of Centralia and Wamac

CenterPoint 504, Inc.
Governors State University 708-534-4924
University Park IL 60466 Fax: 708-534-8457
Area of Operation: South Suburban Cook and Eastern Will Counties

The 504 Certified Development Company (CDC) Program provides growing businesses with long-term, fixed-rate financing for major fixed assets, such as land and buildings. A Certified Development Company is a nonprofit corporation set up to contribute to the economic development of its community or region. CDC's work with the Small Business Administration and private-sector lenders to provide up to 90% financing to small businesses. There are about 270 CDC's nationwide, each covering a specific region.

Indiana

* Indiana Department of Commerce

One North Capitol 317-232-8888
Suite 700 800-463-8081
Indianapolis, IN 46204 Fax: 317-233-5123
www.in.gov/doc

Indiana Department of Commerce: This office can provide information and expertise in dealing with state, federal, and local agencies. They also have information on financing programs and other services offered by the state government.

Energy and Recycling Office: A wide range of assistance in energy efficiency, alternative energy and recycling market development programs.

Enterprise Advisory Group: Counsels emerging and mature businesses.

Government Marketing Assistance Group: Helps companies that wish to sell to federal, state or local governments.

Office of Regulatory Ombudsman: Acts as a mediator, expediter and problem-solver in areas affecting business.

Trade Show Assistance Program (TSAP): Provides reimbursement for a portion of the costs incurred while companies exhibit their products at overseas trade shows.

Loans:

Product Development/Commercialization Funding: Provides loans for businesses in need of financing to support research and development projects, or to support commercialization of new technology. Loan amounts vary.

Capital Access Program (CAP): Helps financial institutions lend money to Indiana businesses that don't qualify for loans under conventional lending policies. CAP loans may be of any amount

Industrial Development Loan Fund: Revolving loans for industrial growth. Loans up to $1 million are available.

Industrial Energy Efficiency Fund: The Energy Policy Division provides loans for improving energy efficiency in industrial processes. The maximum amount available per applicant is $250,000 or 50% of the total eligible project costs, whichever is less.

Loan Guaranty Programs: Financing for land or building acquisition or improvements, structures, machinery, equipment, facilities and working capital. Loan guaranties are available up to $300,000.

Recycling Promotion and Assistance Fund: Loans to enhance the development of markets for recyclable materials.

Small Business Investment Company Program: Long-term and/or venture capital for small firms.

Certified Development Companies: Loans 1% over Treasury-bond rate for 10 to 20 years for financing fixed-assets including; land, buildings, machinery, equipment and renovations.

Grants:

Industrial Energy Efficiency Fund: The Energy Policy Division provides grant to manufacturers to study energy use in their facilities and recommend ways to reduce energy use and energy costs. Maximum amount available per applicant is $250,000.

Alternative Energy Systems Program: The Energy Policy Division offers grants to businesses to fund eligible alternative-fuel technologies and infrastructure development. The maximum amount available per project is $10,000.

Industrial Development Grant Fund: Grants for non-profits and local units of government for off-site infrastructure projects in support of new business development. The grant amount is determined based on project needs. However, the program is designed to supplement local funding sources.

National Industrial Competitiveness Through Energy, Environment and Economics Grant: The Energy Policy Division has information about Federal grants, with possible state matching funds, to improve energy efficiency, promote a cleaner production process and improve the competitiveness of industry. The maximum amount of federal grant available per applicant is $500,000.

Tire Market Development Research and Prototype Grant Program: Provides grant to support research on new products or machinery for handling scrap tire recycling. Grant range from $5,000 to $50,000.

Tire-Derived Fuel Testing Grant Program: Provides grants to develop fuel uses for scrap tires. Amount based on project needs.

Trade Show Assistance Program (TSAP): Provides reimbursement for a portion of the costs incurred while companies exhibit their products at overseas trade shows. Reimbursement includes 100% of exhibit space rental or $5,000, whichever is less.

Bonds:

Twenty-First Century Scholars Program Support Fund Credit: Credit for contributions to the fund. A maximum credit of the lesser of (a) $1,000; (b) 50% of the contribution made, or (c) 10% of the adjusted gross income tax is available.

Maternity Home Credit: Credit for maternity-home owners who provide a temporary residence for a pregnant woman (women).

Prison Credit: Credit for investments in Indiana prisons to create jobs for prisoners. The amount is limited to 50% of the inventory in a qualified project plus 25% of the wages paid to the inmates. The maximum credit a taxpayer may claim is $100,000 per year.

Real-Property Abatement Calculation: Real-property abatement is a declining percentage of the increase in assessed value of the improvement based on one of the three following time periods and percentages as determined by the local governing body.

Enterprise Zones: The purpose of the enterprise zone program in the state of Indiana is to stimulate local community and business redevelopment in distressed areas. An enterprise zone may consist of up to three contiguous square miles. There are 18 enterprise zones in Indiana. In order to stimulate reinvestment and create jobs within the zones, businesses located within an enterprise zone are eligible for certain tax benefits. These tax benefits include:
- A credit equal to 100% of property-tax liability on inventory.
- Exemption from Indiana Gross Income Tax on the increase in receipts from the base year.
- State Investment Cost Credit (up to 30% of purchase price) for individuals purchasing an ownership interest in an enterprise zone business.
- State Loan Interest Credit on lender interest income (5%) from qualified loans made in an enterprise zone.
- State Employment Expense Credit based on wages paid to qualified zone-resident employees. The credit is the lesser of 10% of the increase in wages paid over the base year, or $1,500 per qualified employee.
- Tax deduction to qualified zone-resident employees equal to the lesser of 50% of their adjusted gross income or $7,500.

Industrial Recovery Site (Dinosaur Building): Much like the dinosaurs, many large buildings that were once used for mills, foundries and large manufacturers are obsolete for today's new production methods and technologies. Because of this, these buildings now stand vacant. This program offers special tax benefits to offset the cost of adaptive reuse.

Economic Development for a Growing Economy (EDGE): Provides tax credits based on payroll. Individual income tax withholdings for the company's employees can be credited against the company's corporate income tax. Excess withholdings shall be refunded to the company.

Skills Enhancement Fund: Grants are reimbursement of up to 50% of eligible training costs. Awards for retraining have a maximum ceiling of $200,000.

The TECH Fund: Training activities for reimbursement resulting in full-time, Indiana-resident employee receiving certification in systems administration, systems engineering, or software development. Up to 50% of eligible training costs with a maximum of $50,000 or $2,500 per employee, whichever is less.

Incumbent Worker Training Fund (IWTF): Incumbent Worker grants are designed to provide financial assistance to companies committed to expanding the skills of their existing workforce. There are no maximum grant amounts; however, funds are limited. Most grants do not exceed $200,000 and there is no minimum.

Skills Trades Apprenticeship (STA): The STA grants are designed to provide financial assistance to companies expanding the skills of their existing workers through training programs that result in industry-recognized credentials. The maximum grant award is $200,000.

Brownsfields Grant and Loan Fund: This grant program assists in the environmental and remediation of brownsfield sites throughout Indiana. Grants of up to $50,000 per applicant per round are available for environmental site assessment; low-interest loans of up to 10% of the Brownsfield Fund are available for remediation/demolition; and grants of up to $250,000 per applicant per round are available for petroleum remediation.

The Distributed Generation Grant Program (DGGP): The Distributed Generation Grant Program offers grants of up to $30,000 or up to 30% of eligible costs and is designed to enable businesses and institutions to install and study alternatives to central generation such as fuel cells, micro turbines, cogeneration, combined heat & power and renewable energy sources.

Indiana Biomass Grant Program: This program was developed to assist in the research and implementation of Indiana biomass energy systems. Biomass is any organic matter available on a renewable basis for conversion to energy. Eligibility for this program is limited to individuals, businesses, universities or institutions that operate in the state of Indiana.

Indiana Coal Research Grant Program: This program was created to assist businesses in undertaking coal research projects and further develop competitive communities with secure jobs in Indiana. Eligible research projects must use Indiana coal or have direct application to Indiana coal for funding consideration.

Waste Tire Recycling-Civil Engineering Field Reuse: grants for waste tire utilization in an IDEM approved civil engineering reuse project.

Waste Tire Recycling-Recreational Field Reuse: grants for waste tire utilization in an IDEM approved recreational facility beneficial reuse project.

* Indiana Business Modernization and Technology Corporation

10 W. Market St., Suite 450	800-877-5182
Indianapolis, IN 46204	317-635-3058
www.bmtadvantage.org	

BMT provides services that include comprehensive business assessments and recommendations, development of action plans and access to cost-effective resources to help you implement your action plans. BMT also helps companies address industry-level concerns such as quality, workforce strategies and technology access through industry-specific programs and company alliances. BMT's can result in increased sales, reduced costs, improved cash flow and access to working capital.

Indiana Micro-Electronics Center (IMC): Assists businesses in using Application Specific Integrated Circuits (ASICs).

The Indiana Quality Initiative: Quality-awareness education, assessments and information

Regional Manufacturing Extension Centers (RMEC): Helps small and medium-sized businesses assess and solve problems related to technology, training, marketing and financing.

* USDA Rural Development

5975 Lakeside Boulevard	317-290-3100, ext. 400
Indianapolis, IN 46278	Fax: 317-290-3095
www.rurdev.usda.gov/in	

Program assistance is provided in many ways, including direct or guaranteed loans, grants, technical assistance, research and educational materials. To accomplish its mission, USDA Rural Development often works in partnership with state, local and tribal governments, as well as rural businesses, cooperatives and nonprofit agencies. The Rural Business-Cooperative Service (RBS) provides help to rural areas that need to develop new job opportunities, allowing businesses and cooperatives to remain viable in a changing economy.

Business Program Guaranteed Loans are used to improve, develop, or finance business, industry, and employment, and improve the economic and environmental climate in rural communities, including pollution abatement and control. This objective is achieved through bolstering the existing private credit structure with guarantees of quality loans, which will provide lasting community benefits. This type of assistance is available to business located in rural communities with a population of less than 50,000.

Intermediary Relending Program finances business facilities and community development projects in rural communities with a population of less than 25,000. This is achieved through loans made by USDA to intermediaries that provide loans to ultimate recipients for business facilities and community development in a rural area.

Rural Cooperative Development Grants establish and operate centers for rural technology or cooperative development to carry out activities and generate information useful to rural industries, cooperatives, businesses, and others in the development and commercialization of new products, processes, or services.

Rural Economic Development Loans and Grants make zero interest loans and grants available to rural electric and telephone borrowers to promote rural economic development and job creation projects.

Rural Business Enterprise Grants assist public bodies and nonprofit corporations finance and facilitate development of small and emerging private businesses located in rural areas.

Rural Business Opportunity Grants to promote sustainable economic development in rural communities with exceptional needs. Making grants to organizations to provide for economic development planning, technical assistance, or training accomplishes this.

* Indiana Development Finance Authority (IDFA)

One N. Capitol, Suite 900	317-233-4332
Indianapolis, IN 46204	Fax: 317-232-6786
www.in.gov/idfa	

Helps Indiana businesses obtain financial assistance through loan guaranty programs, tax-exempt private activity bonds for industrial development, Ex-Im Bank loan guarantees, insurance and direct loans for export products and flexible lending through case reserve accounts.

* Indiana Economic Development Association (IEDA)

233 McCrea St., Suite 400	317-269-6283
Indianapolis, IN 46225	Fax: 317-269-6276
www.ieda.org	

Provides continuity to a statewide community development effort. The organization has two objectives: (1) to utilize the knowledge and resources of the association to make economic development activities in the state more effective, and (2) to cooperate and interact with all state and local organizations engaged in promoting the economic welfare of Indiana.

* Indiana Economic Development Council (IEDC)

One North Capitol, Suite 900	317-234-2371
Indianapolis, IN 46204	Fax: 317-233-0399
www.iedc.org	

Helps to shape long-term state goals, strategies and policies on economic development matters through non-partisan planning, evaluation, policy development and coordination. The role of the IEDC includes providing independent performance reviews and recommendations relating to governmental budgets and the economic development support systems of public and private entities, both state and local.

* Indiana Community Business Credit Corporation (ICBCC)

8440 Woodfield Crossing, Suite 315	
Indianapolis, IN 46240	317-469-9704

Loans for small to medium-sized businesses that exceed banks' customary limits. Loan amounts range from $100,000 to $750,000, and must be at least matched by a participating lender. Minimum project is $200,000.

* Community Development Action Grant (CDAG)

Community Development Division	
Indiana Department of Commerce	
One N. Capitol, Suite 600	317-232-8911
Indianapolis, IN 46204	800-824-2476

Grants to help organizations whose missions include economic development to expand administrative capacity and program development by offsetting miscellaneous expenses. In the case of organizations serving at least two counties, the amount of the grant may not exceed one dollar for every one dollar raised by the organization. The maximum grant award for organizations serving two or more counties may not exceed $75,000.

* Tax-Exempt Bonds

Indiana Development Finance Authority	
One N. Capitol, Suite 900	317-233-4332
Indianapolis, IN 46204	Fax: 317-232-6786

Provide fixed-asset financing at competitive rates. Limits vary according to the type of project. Most manufacturing facilities are limited to $10 million.

* Foreign Trade Zone or Free Trade Zone

International Trade Division	
Indiana Department of Commerce	
One North Capitol, Suite 700	
Indianapolis, IN 46204	317-233-3762

Foreign Trade Zone or Free Trade Zone: An enclosed, secure area that is located outside U.S. Customs territory. A company located within a Foreign Trade Zone does not pay duties or personal property taxes on goods stored within the zone. Foreign and domestic goods may enter a zone to be stored, processed, distributed, manufactured, assembled or exhibited. Benefits to companies located in a Foreign Trade Zone include the following:
- Duty is deferred on imported goods admitted to the zone, thus improving cash flow for the company.
- No U.S. duty is assessed when exporting goods from the zone.
- Processing goods within the zone can eliminate or lower tariffs.
- Duties can be avoided on defective or damaged goods by inspecting and testing imported goods within a zone.

- Savings may be realized in transport insurance.
- Inventory stored in a Foreign Trade Zone is exempt from local property tax.

* Indiana Workforce Development

10 North Senate
Indianapolis, IN 46204   1-888-WorkOne
www.in.gov/dwd

The Department of Workforce Development (DWD) provides employers with a free labor exchange service designed to help build Indiana's workforce by bringing together qualified job seekers and employers seeking qualified workers. Through a statewide network of One-Stop Employment Centers, job seekers and employers have free access to a variety of information to help make the match between employers and job seekers more effective.

* Small Business Administration (SBA)

Robert Gastineau, Deputy Director
Finance Division
429 N. Pennsylvania, Suite 100   317-226-7272
Indianapolis, IN 46204-1873   Fax: 317-226-7259
www.sba.gov/in

The Indiana Small Business Administration Office delivers a variety of programs and services, such as startup and operational assistance through small business training and counseling, financial assistance for startup's, business opportunities and much more.

* Small Business Investment Companies

1st Source Capital Corporation
Eugene L. Cavanaugh, Jr., Vice President
100 North Michigan St.
Mail: P.O. Box 1602, South Bend 46634   219-235-2180
South Bend, IN 46601   Fax: 219-235-2227
Email: cavanaugh@1stsource.com

Cambridge Ventures, LP
Ms. Jean Wojtowicz, President
4181 East 96th Street, Suite 200   317-814-6192
Indianapolis, IN 46240   Fax: 317-844-9815
Email: jwojtowicz@cambridgecapitalmgmt.com

Centerfield Capital Partners, L.P.
D. Scott Lutzke, Contact
3030 Market Tower
10 West Market Street   317-237-2323
Indianapolis, IN 46204   Fax: 317-237-2325
SCOTT@centerfieldcapital.com

Irwin Ventures Incorporated-SBIC
David Meyercord, Contact
500 Washington Street   812-373-1434
Columbus, IN 47201   Fax: 812-376-1709
Email: dave.meyercord@irwinventures.com

White River Venture Partners, LP
Sam Sutphin & Marc DeLong, Managers
3603 East Raymond St.   317-780-7789
Indianapolis, IN 46203-4762   Fax: 317-791-2935
Email: madelong@driversolutions.com

The SBA licenses, regulates, and provides financial assistance to privately owned and operated Small Business Investment Companies. SBICs make venture or risk investments by supplying capital and extending unsecured loans and loans not fully collateralized to small enterprises which meet their investment criteria. Financing is made by direct loans and by equity investments.

* Certified Development Companies

Business Development Corporation
Kate McCahill/Don Inks
1200 County-City Building   574-235-9278
South Bend IN 46601   Fax: 574-235-9021
Area of Operation: St. Joseph County

Community Development Corporation
Matt Blair
840 City-County Building   260-427-1127
Fort Wayne IN 46802   Fax: 260-427-1375
www.fortwayne-ed.org/business_loans.htm
Area of Operation: Allen County

Indiana Statewide Certified Development Corporation
Jean Wojtowicz, President
4181 East 96th Street, Suite 200   317-844-9810
Indianapolis IN 46240   Fax: 317-844-9815
Area of Operation: Statewide

Premier Capital Corporation
David W. Amick, Executive Director
151 N. Delaware, Suite 750   317-974-0504
Indianapolis, IN 46204   Fax: 317-974-0510
www.premiercapitalcorp.com
Area of Operation: Counties of Boone, Hancock, Hendricks, Johnson, Marion, Morgan and Shelby

Northwest Indiana Regional Development Corporation
Dennis M. Henson, President
6100 Southport Road   219-763-6303
Portage IN 46368   Fax: 219-763-2653
www.nwirdc.org
Area of Operation: Jasper, Lake LaPorte, Newton, Porter, Pulaski and Starke Counties

The 504 Certified Development Company (CDC) Program provides growing businesses with long-term, fixed-rate financing for major fixed assets, such as land and buildings. A Certified Development Company is a nonprofit corporation set up to contribute to the economic development of its community or region. CDC's work with the Small Business Administration and private-sector lenders to provide up to 90% financing to small businesses. There are about 270 CDC's nationwide, each covering a specific region.

* Metro Small Business Assistance Corporation

306 Civic Center Complex
1 NW Martin Luther King Blvd.
Evansville, IN 47708   812-426-5857
Service Area: Vanderburgh, Posey, Gibson, and Warrick counties

SBA Loan Guarantees and Direct Loans: Provides technical assistance to implement SBA finance programs.

Working Capital Loan Pool: Provides short-term, working capital financing for small businesses in the city of Evansville and unincorporated areas of Vanderburg county.

* Indiana Small Business Development Center

James Simpson, Comptroller
One North Capital, Suite 900   317-234-2082
Indianapolis, IN 46204   Fax: 317-232-8872
www.isbdc.org

The Indiana Small Business Development Center helps small businesses throughout Indiana grow, expand, innovate and increase success rates.

Consulting: Free one-to-one service that assists new and existing business owners build better businesses.

Workshops: A variety of low-cost programs are available to meet the small business owner's needs.

Access To Information: All of the Centers in Indiana provide libraries with numerous materials on business topics.

* Minority Business Development

Department of Administration
402 West Washington Street, Room W474
Indianapolis, IN 46204   317-232-3061
http://www.in.gov/idoa/minority/index.html

The Department of Administration administers the state of Indiana's Minority Business Enterprise Program. Some of the services provided include: state purchasing opportunities, workshops on state procurement, monitoring and providing networking assistance and matching majority owned businesses with minority owned businesses.

Iowa

* Iowa Department of Economic Development

200 East Grand Ave.   515-242-4700
Des Moines, IA 50309-1827   800-245-IOWA
www.state.ia.us/ided   Fax: 515-242-4809
                                         TTY: 800-735-2942

Workforce Development Fund: Programs under this fund provide training for new and existing employees and include: Jobs Training, Business Network Training, Targeted Industries Training, Innovative Skills Development.

Locating in Iowa: Provides expanding companies with many valuable and unique services, with the end goal of streamlining the site location process. Iowa Department of Economic Development (IDED) confidential services include:
- Working on a confidential basis with companies to determine expansion project needs
- Providing data and information on available buildings, sites and communities
- Coordinating community/site visits
- Packaging appropriate financial assistance and job training programs
- Serving as a liaison with state environmental permitting officials
- IDED Incorporates Information and Technology Into Team Approach

Regulatory Assistance Programs: Provide assistance with environmental permitting, regulations, and compliance with the EPA Clean Air Act.

Community Economic Betterment Account (CEBA): Provides financial assistance to companies that create new employment opportunities and/or retain existing jobs, and make new capital investment in Iowa. The amount of funding is based, in part, on the number of jobs to be created/retained. Funds are provided in the form of loans and forgivable loans. The CEBA program can provide assistance up to $1 million. As an alternative, non-traditional, short-term float loans or interim loans greater than $1 million may be available. The funding level for start-up companies varied depending upon employee wage rates. Assistance through CEBA's "Venture Project" component is provided as an "equity-like" investment, with a maximum award of $250,000. 515-242-4819

Economic Development Set-Aside Program (EDSA): Provides financial assistance to companies that create new employment opportunities and/or retain existing jobs, and make new capital investment in Iowa. The amount of funding is based, in part, on the number of jobs to be created/retained. Funds are provided in the form of loans and forgivable loans. The EDSA program can provide assistance up to $500,000.

Value-Added Products and Processes Financial Assistance Program (VAAPFAP): Seeks to increase the innovative utilization of Iowa's agricultural commodities. It accomplishes this by investing in the development of new agri-products and new processing technologies. The program includes two components:
- Innovative Products and Processes encourages the processing of agricultural commodities into higher-value products not commonly produced in Iowa, or utilizing a process not commonly used in Iowa to produce new and innovative products from agricultural commodities.
- Renewable Fuels and Co-Products encourages the production of renewable fuels, such as soy diesel and ethanol, and co-products for livestock feed.

Any single project may apply for up to $900,000 in assistance. Financial assistance is provided in the form of loans and forgivable loans. Generally, assistance of $100,000 or less is provided as a forgivable loan, while larger awards are usually a combination of loans and forgivable loans, with the forgivable portion decreasing as the award size increases.

Small Business Loan Program and Economic Development Loan Program: Provides financing to new and expanding businesses through the sale of tax-exempt bonds. The maximum loan is $10 million.

USDA Business and Industrial Loan Guarantee Program: Provides guarantees on loans up to $10 million or more made by private lenders for start-up or expansion purposes to for-profit or non-profit businesses or investors of any size.

Iowa Capital Investment Corporation (ICIC): A for-profit venture capital corporation established with funds provided by the state of Iowa and equity investments by Iowa financial institutions, insurance companies and electric utilities. The corporation's primary purpose is to provide an attractive risk-adjusted rate of return on investment to the corporation's shareholders and advance economic development in Iowa. The corporation provides financing for a broad range of business capital needs. Financing may be in the form of equity participation, loans with stock purchase warrants, royalties, etc. and is tailored to the particular business situation. Investments generally range from $50,000 to $1 million, with the average expected to be approximately $250,000.

Rail Economic Development Program: The Iowa Department of Transportation provides funds for construction or rehabilitation of rail spurs to serve new or existing industries. The rail project must be a key to the creation or retention of jobs.

Revitalize Iowa's Sound Economy (RISE): Administered by the Iowa Department of Transportation for expenditures on city, county and state highways to help attract new development or to support growth with existing developments. Projects are evaluated on economic potential and impact. Funding may be used in conjunction with other sources of federal, state, local and private financing for the purpose of improving area highways and specific access to roads.

Public Facilities Set-Aside Program: Administered by the Iowa Department of Economic Development, provides financial assistance to cities and counties to provide infrastructure improvements for businesses which require such improvements in order to create new job opportunities. The form of assistance is limited to grants to cities under 50,000 population and counties for the provision of or improvements to sanitary sewer systems, water systems, streets and roads, storm sewers, rail lines and airports. Assistance is limited to two-thirds of the total cost of the improvements needed. The emphasis of this program is to increase the productive capacity of the state. Priority will be given to projects that will create manufacturing jobs, add value to Iowa resources and/or export out-of-state.

Venture Capital Resource Fund: A for-profit corporation whose mission is to stimulate economic development and provide an attractive rate of return to shareholders by investing in businesses with significant growth potential.

Targeted Small Business Financial Assistance Program (TSBFAP): Designed to assist in the creation and expansion of Iowa small businesses that have an annual gross sales of $3 million and are at least 51% owned, operated and managed by women, minorities or persons with a disability. The business must be certified as a "Targeted Small Business" by the Iowa Department of Inspections and Appeals before applying for or receiving TSB funds. Awards may be obtained in one of the following forms of assistance:
- Low-interest loans - Loans of up to $25,000 may be provided at interest rates of 0-5 percent, to be repaid in monthly installments over a five- to seven-year period. The first installment can be deferred for three months for a start-up business and one month for an existing business.
- Loan guarantees are available up to $40,000. Loan guarantees can cover up to 75% of a loan obtained from a bank or other conventional lender. The interest rate is at the discretion of the lender.
- In limited cases, equity grants - to be used to leverage other financing (SBA or conventional) - are available in amounts of up to $25,000.
- TSB funds may be used to purchase equipment, acquire inventory, provide operating capital or to leverage additional funding.

Self-Employment Loan Program (SELP): This program is designed to assist in the creation and expansion of businesses owned, operated and managed by women, minorities, or persons with a disability. To qualify for a SELP loan, applicants must have an annualized family income that does not exceed current income guidelines for the program. An applicant is automatically eligible for SELP if he or she is receiving Family Investment Plan (FIP) assistance or other general assistance such as disability benefits. The applicant can also qualify for SELP funds if determined eligible under the Job Training Partnership Act, or is certified as having a disability under standards established by the Iowa Department of Education, Division of Vocational Rehabilitation Services. SELP loans of up to $10,000 are available. The interest rate is 5 percent, and the loan is to be repaid in monthly installments over a five-year period. The first installment can be deferred for three months for a start-up business and one month for an existing business.

Entrepreneurs With Disabilities (EWD): Helps qualified individuals with disabilities establish, acquire, maintain or expand a small business by providing technical and financial assistance. To be eligible for the program, applicants must be active clients of the Iowa Department of Education Division of Vocational Rehabilitation Services or the Iowa Department for the Blind. Technical Assistance grants of up to $10,000 may be used to pay for any specific business-related consulting service such as developing a feasibility study or business plan, or accounting and legal services. Financial Assistance grants of up to $10,000 may be used to purchase equipment, supplies, rent or other start-up, expansion or acquisition costs identified in an approved business plan. Total financial assistance provided to an individual may not exceed 50% (maximum of $10,000) of the financial package. EWD financial assistance must be fully matched by funding from other sources.

Assistive Device Tax Credit: Iowa small businesses can reduce their taxes by buying or renting products or equipment, or by making physical changes to the workplace to help employees with disabilities get or keep a job.

Export Trade Assistance Program (ETPA): ETAP provides financial assistance to eligible Iowa businesses wishing to enter new markets by participating in foreign trade shows and trade missions.

State Money and Help For Your Business

Iowa Department of Economic Development Entrepreneurial Service Team: This Team services the needs of high-growth, value-adding entrepreneurs by offering one-on-one management and technical assistance.

* Cooperative Services
USDA-Rural Development
873 Federal Bldg.
210 Walnut St. — 515-284-4663
Des Moines, IA 50309 — Fax: 515-284-4821
www.rurdev.usda.gov/ia

Provides free technical assistance to help rural residents form new cooperative ventures and improve operations of existing cooperatives.

Business & Industrial Guaranteed Loans are used to improve, develop or finance business, industry and employment. Their goal is to improve the economic and environmental climate in rural communities, including pollution abatement and control. This type of assistance is available to businesses located in rural communities with a population of less than 50,000.

Intermediary Relending Program finances business facilities and community development projects in rural communities with population of less than 25,000.

Rural Cooperative Development Grant Program provides grants for cooperative development in rural areas. Grants are to be made for the purpose of establishing and operating centers for rural cooperative development.

Rural Economic Development Loans and Grants make zero interest loans and grants available to rural electric and telephone borrowers to promote rural economic development and job creation projects.

Rural Business Opportunity Grants help provide technical assistance for business development and conduct economic development planning in rural areas. Eligible applicants include public bodies, cooperatives and private non-profit corporations.

Rural Business Enterprise Grants help support the development of small and emerging private businesses located in rural areas. Eligible applicants include public bodies and private non-profit corporations.

Cooperative Development Technical Assistance is available to help rural residents form new cooperative businesses and improve the operation of existing cooperatives.

* Institute of Social and Economic Development
901 23rd Ave. — 319-338-2331
Coralville, IA 52241 — Fax: 319-338-5824
www.ised.org

Focuses on minorities, women, persons with disabilities and low-income individuals. Encourages self-sufficiency through the growth of small business and self-employment opportunities, and provides services for any person who wants to start or expand a business employing up to five employees, including the owner(s).

* Center for Industrial Research and Service
ISU Research Park
2272 Howe Hall, Suite 2620 — 515-294-3420
Ames, IA 50011 — Fax: 515-294-4925
www.ciras.iastate.edu

Assists companies with management, production, marketing, engineering, finance, and technology problems and/or contact with resource people, organizations, and agencies that can help provide solutions, and operates as an industrial arm of University Extension, Iowa State University.

* Iowa Manufacturing Extension Partnership
Advanced Technology Center
2701 E. Convenience Blvd., Suite 13 — 515-289-0600
Ankeny, IA 50021 — Fax: 515-289-0601
www.imep.org

Manufacturing Technology Center: A resource for small and mid-sized manufacturers. Helps identify problems and resources, conducts formal needs assessments, and develops strategic plans. Also assists with modernizing facilities, upgrading processes, and improving work force capabilities through the use of effective training and skill development.

* Strategic Marketing Services
University of Northern Iowa
College of Business Administration — 800-204-1804
The Cirris Building, Suite 5 — 319-273-2886
Cedar Falls, IA 50614 — Fax: 319-273-6830
www.sms.uni.edu

Provides customized market research, analysis, and strategic planning services to existing businesses, primarily manufacturers.

* Link Investments for Tomorrow (LIFT)
Treasurer of State's Office
LIFT Administration
Hoover State Office Building — 515-281-3287
Des Moines, IA 50319 — Fax: 515-281-7562
www.treasurer.state.ia.us/investments

Assists with rural small business transfer, and horticulture and alternative agricultural crops.

* Iowa Finance Authority
General Counsel
Iowa Finance Authority — 800-432-7230
100 E. Grand, Suite 250 — 515-242-4990
Des Moines, IA 50309 — Fax: 515-242-4957
www.ifahome.com

The Economic Development Loan Program: promotes the development and expansion of family farming, soil conservation, housing and business within the State of Iowa. Iowa's Rural Home Building Initiative ("RHBI"): is seeking to increase the construction of affordable single family homes in eligible rural areas of Iowa. The Iowa Finance Authority ("IFA") and USDA Rural Development ("USDA") are soliciting proposals that specifically address innovative methods to develop new single family residential development in eligible rural areas. The RHBI funds available may be used to mitigate the financial risk of construction lending, to provide gap funding to increase affordability and other direct program costs.

* Iowa Department of Natural Resources
Waste Management Assistance Division
502 E Ninth Street
Wallace State Office Building — 515-281-4387
Des Moines, IA 50319-0034 — Fax: 515-281-8895
www.iowadnr.com

Landfill Alternatives Financial Assistance Program provides funds to be used for equipment, construction, education, materials, etc.

* Small Business Administration (SBA)
210 Walnut, Room 749 — 515-284-4422
Des Moines, IA 50309 — Fax: 515-284-4572

215 4th Ave., SE, Suite 200 — 319-362-6405
Cedar Rapids, IA 52401-1806 — Fax: 319-362-7861
www.sba.gov/ia

The Iowa Small Business Administration Office delivers a variety of programs and services, such as startup and operational assistance through small business training and counseling, financial assistance for startup's, business opportunities and much more.

* Small Business Investment Companies
AAVIN Equity Partners I, L.P.
James D. Thorpe, Contact
118 Third Avenue, SE, Suite 630 — 319-247-1072
Cedar Rapids, IA 52401 — Fax: 319-363-9519
Email: jthorp@aavinvc.com

Lewis & Clark Private Equities, L.P.
David R. Schroder, Contact
101 Second Street, SE, Suite 800 — 319-363-8249
Cedar Rapids, IA 52401 — Fax: 319-363-9683
Email: mbenge@investam.com

MorAmerica Capital Corporation
David R. Schroder, President
101 2nd St., SE, #800 — 319-363-8249
Cedar Rapids, IA 52401 — Fax: 319-363-9683
Email: mbenge@investam.com

North Dakota SBIC, L.P.
David R. Schroder, Manager

101 Second Street SE, Suite 800
Cedar Rapids, IA 52401
Email: mbenge@investam.com
701-298-0003
Fax: 701-293-7819

The SBA licenses, regulates, and provides financial assistance to privately owned and operated Small Business Investment Companies. SBICs make venture or risk investments by supplying capital and extending unsecured loans and loans not fully collateralized to small enterprises which meet their investment criteria. Financing is made by direct loans and by equity investments.

* Certified Development Companies

Black Hawk Economic Development, Inc.
Stephen A. Brustkern, Executive Director
304 South Street
Waterloo IA 50704
319-235-2960
Fax: 319-235-9171

Area of Operation: Allamakee, Blackhawk, Bremer, Butler, Buchanan, Chickasaw, Clayton, Grundy, Howard and Winneshiek Counties

Corporation for Economic Development in Des Moine
Mike Ryan, Development Financing Coordinator
400 East First Street
Des Moines, IA 50309
515-283-4017
Fax: 515-237-1667

Area of Operation: Citywide Des Moines

Iowa Business Growth Company
Dan Robeson, Executive Director
7043 Vista Drive
West Des Moines, IA 50266
515-223-4511
Fax: 515-223-5017

E. Iowa Branch: Jerry Trudo, Branch Manager
805 Wright Brothers Blvd. SW
Cedar Rapids, Iowa 52404-9070
319-632-4242
Fax: 319-632-4241

Area of Operation: Statewide

Siouxland Economic Development Corporation
Ken Beekley, Executive Director
428 Insurance Centre
507 7th Street
Sioux City, IA 51101
712-279-6286
Fax: 712-279-6920

Area of Operation: Woodbury, Plymouth, Cherokee, Ida, Monona and Sioux Counties in Iowa; Dakota County in Nebraska; Union and Clay Counties in South Dakota

E.C.I.A. Business Growth, Inc.
Jerry Schroeder, Economic Development Planner
330 Nesler Center, Suite 330
Dubuque IA 52001
563-556-4166
Fax: 563-556-0348

Area of Operation: Cedar, Clinton, Delaware, Dubuque and Jackson Counties as well as the Cities located therein

The 504 Certified Development Company (CDC) Program provides growing businesses with long-term, fixed-rate financing for major fixed assets, such as land and buildings. A Certified Development Company is a nonprofit corporation set up to contribute to the economic development of its community or region. CDC's work with the Small Business Administration and private-sector lenders to provide up to 90% financing to small businesses. There are about 270 CDC's nationwide, each covering a specific region.

* Iowa Capital Investment Corporation (ICIC)

Iowa Department of Economic Development
200 E Grand Avenue
Des Moines, IA 50309
515-242-4817

www.state.ia.us/ided/investiowa

The State Legislature created the ICIC to assemble private venture capital for investment targeted enterprises and communities. The ICIC manages the Fund of Funds, which is organized as a private, for-profit, limited partnership to make investments in private venture capital funds. A venture fund must commit to consider equity investments in businesses in Iowa.

* Institute for Physical Research and Technology

311 TASF
Iowa State University
Ames, IA 50011
515-294-8849
877-251-6520

www.iprt.iastate.edu/assistance

The Institute for Physical Search and Technology helps Iowa companies solve technical problems; create new products and increase productivity and quality. They will also help launch start-up companies.

Kansas

* Kansas Department of Commerce

Kansas Department of Commerce
1000 SW Jackson Street, Suite 100
Topeka, KS 66612-1354
http://kdoch.state.ks.us
785-296-3481
Fax: 785-296-5055
TTY: 785-296-3487

First-Stop Clearinghouse: A one-stop Clearinghouse for general information. It also provides the necessary state applications required by agencies which license, regulate and tax business, and furnishes information about starting or expanding a business.

From the Land of Kansas Trademark Program: Offers marketing opportunities for Kansas produced food, arts, crafts, and plants.

Agricultural Value Added Center: Identifies new technologies and assists companies in commercialization efforts. Both food/feed and industrial related projects are potential candidates for assistance. 785-296-3084

Kansas Match: Promotes economic growth in the state by matching Kansas manufacturers who are currently buying products from outside Kansas with Kansas suppliers of those same products. The benefit to the buyer includes reductions in freight, warehousing, and communication costs. 785-296-3803

Business Retention & Expansion Program: Offered to Kansas communities and counties who wish to sustain existing industry, support its modernization and competitiveness, foster its expansion and provide an environment that encourages new industry creation and recruitment. The Department works with community leaders and volunteers to conduct on-site surveys of local businesses. The information gathered is then analyzed and the results are used to solve immediate short-term problems, as well as to develop long-term local retention and expansion strategies.

Partnership Fund: Provides financial assistance to Kansas cities and counties by making low-interest loans for infrastructure projects needed to encourage and assist in the creation of new jobs either through the relocation of new businesses or the expansion of existing businesses. 785-296-1868

Industrial Training Program (KIT): Provides training assistance primarily to manufacturing, distribution and regional or national service firms in the process of adding five or more new jobs to a new or existing Kansas facility. KIT will pay the negotiated cost of pre-employment, on-the-job and classroom training expenses that include instructor salaries, travel expenses, minor equipment, training aids, supplies and materials, and curriculum planning and development. 785-296-4284

Industrial Retraining Program (KIR): Provides retraining assistance to employees of restructuring industries who are likely to be displaced because of obsolete or inadequate job skills and knowledge. 785-296-8097

Venture Capital & Seed Capital Programs: Instituted to increase the availability of risk capital in Kansas. These programs make use of income tax credits to encourage investment in venture and seed capital pools as a source of early stage financing for small businesses. Businesses demonstrating strong growth potential but lacking the financial strength to obtain conventional financing are the most likely candidates for risk capital funding. The Business Development Division has in operation and continues to develop a network of venture capital resources to assist qualified small businesses in locating potential sources of venture capital financing.

Economic Opportunity Initiatives Fund (KEOIF): A funding mechanism to address the creation/retention of jobs presented by unique opportunities or emergencies. The fund has a higher level of flexibility than do many of the other state financing programs and allows the State to participate as a funding source when other options have been exhausted. 785-296-1868

Existing Industry Expansion Program (KEIEP): Performance based, with a focus on the expansion/ retention of jobs that are associated with the activities of existing firms.

Investments In Major Projects And Comprehensive Training (IMPACT): A funding mechanism designed to respond to the training and capital requirements of major business expansions and locations in the state. SKILL (State of Kansas Investments in Lifelong Learning) funds may be used to pay for expenses related to training a new work force. MPI (Major Project Investment) funds may be used for other expenses related to the project such as the purchase or relocation of equipment, labor recruitment, or building costs. Individual bond size may not exceed 90% of the withholding taxes received from the new jobs over a 10-year period.

Network of Certified Development Companies: Provides financial packaging services to businesses, utilizing state, Small Business Administration, and private financial sources. The state provides supplemental funding to these organizations in recognition of the service they provide.

Private Activity Bonds (PABs): Tax-exempt bonds (IRBs) for facility and equipment financing for qualifying manufacturers and processors. The reduced financing costs generated through these bonds are passed through to the company.

Training Equipment Grants: Provide area technical schools and community colleges an opportunity to acquire instructional equipment to train or retrain Kansas workers.

Kansas Trade Show Assistance Program: Allows a Kansas company to receive a reimbursement of up to 50% of their international trade show expenses to a maximum of $3,500 per show and $7,000 per state fiscal year.

Foreign Trade Zones: Provide a duty-free and quota-free entry point for foreign goods into specific areas under customs' supervision for an unlimited period of time.

Office of Minority & Women Business Development: Promotes and assists in the development of minority-owned and women-owned businesses in Kansas. The program provides assistance in procurement and contracting, financing resources, business planning, and identification of business opportunities. A directory of minority-owned and women-owned businesses in Kansas is published annually. 785-296-3425

Single Source Certification Program: Responsible for certifying minority-and-women-owned businesses as small disadvantaged businesses for non-highway related firms.

Domestic Agricultural Marketing: This program identifies new markets for Kansas products and helps Kansas agricultural producers market their goods.

Export Assistance: The Trade development provides assistance to Kansas companies wishing to begin or expand their international marketing efforts.

Enterprise Zone: Provides potential Kansas sales tax exemption and Kansas income/privilege tax credits to businesses creating net new jobs in Kansas through major capital investment projects.

Micro-Loans Program: Loans are made to county governments to loan to microenterprise businesses with 5 or fewer jobs.

From the Land of Kansas: This trademark program is designed to help small businesses that manufacture products in Kansas.

* Publications

Kansas Department of Commerce
1000 SW Jackson Street, Suite 100   785-296-3481
Topeka, KS 66612-1354   Fax: 785-296-5055
http://kdoch.state.ks.us   TTY: 785-296-3487

The Kansas Department of Commerce & Housing (KDOC&H) distributes a variety of publications to help Kansas residents, businesses and visitors find the information needed about their state. Here are a few:

Data Book: The information found in the *Data Book* gives a good idea of what Kansas has to offer new and expanding businesses. The book is filled with information about the Kansas economy, labor and workforce training. It briefly describes taxes and incentives for new and expanding businesses. It also includes sections on finance, technology and education, markets and transportation, and the environment.

The Kansas Aerospace Directory: A complete resource for aircraft production, parts, equipment, research and development, etc. *Directory* includes a wide range of aviation products and companies.

Kansas Agribusiness Directory: A complete resource for agriculture-related business, the *Kansas Agribusiness Directory* offers assistance in contacting any firm or business as well as finding specialized products or services.

Steps to Success: A Guide to Starting a Business in Kansas: Created to give entrepreneurs and small business owners all the information needed on licenses, forms, rules and regulations required by State agencies. It discusses the aspects of business development including finance, incentives and taxation. Plus, it has referrals to programs such as Small Business Development Centers, development companies, the Kansas Technology Enterprise Corporation, Inc. and the Small Business Administration.

* Rural Development

1303 First America Place, Suite 100   785-271-2700
Topeka, KS 66604   Fax: 785-271-2708
www.rurdev.usda.gov/ks

Business and Industrial Loan Program: Provides loan guarantees to businesses and industries to benefit rural areas. Loans are made in any area outside the boundary of a city of 50,000 or more and its adjacent urbanized areas with population density of no more than 100 persons per square mile. Any legal entity, including individuals, public and private organizations, and federally recognized Indian tribes may borrow under its program. Priority is given to applications for projects in open country, rural communities and towns of 25,000 and smaller. Primary purpose is to create and maintain employment and improve the economic and environmental climate in rural communities. Guarantees of up to 90 percent of the principal and interest.

Intermediary Relending Program Loans: Intermediary Relending Program loans finance business facilities and community development projects in rural areas, including cities with a population of less than 25,000. RBS lends these funds to intermediaries, which, in turn, provide loans to recipients who are developing business facilities or community development projects. Eligible intermediaries include public bodies, nonprofit corporations, Indian tribes, and cooperatives.

Rural Economic Development Loans and Grants: These programs are available to any Rural Utilities Service electric or telecommunications borrower. Zero–interest loans are made primarily to finance start-up ventures and business expansion projects.

Rural Business Enterprise Grants: Rural Business Enterprise Grants help public bodies, nonprofit corporations, and Federally recognized Indian tribal groups finance and facilitate development of small and emerging private business enterprises located in rural areas (this includes all areas other than cities of more than 50,000 people and their immediately adjacent urban or urbanizing areas). Grant funds can pay for the acquisition and development of land and the construction of buildings, plants, equipment, access streets and roads, parking areas, utility and service extensions, refinancing and fees for professional services.

Rural Business Opportunity Grants: Rural Business Opportunity Grant funds provide for technical assistance, training, and planning activities that improve economic conditions in rural areas. Applicants must be located in rural areas (this includes all areas other than cities of more than 50,000 people and their immediately adjacent urban or urbanizing areas). Nonprofit corporations and public bodies are eligible. A maximum of $50,000 per grant is authorized by the legislation. RBS is designing the program to promote sustainable economic development in rural communities with exceptional needs.

* Mid-America Manufacturing Technology Center

10561 Barkley, Suite 602   800-653-4333
Overland Park, KS 66212   Fax: 913-649-4333
www.mamtc.com

The Mid-America Manufacturing Technology Center .(MAMTC) helps small- and medium-sized manufacturers improve their competitiveness by assisting them in modernizing their operations and adopting appropriate technologies, as well as management, marketing and business practices. MAMTC divides its services into three types: 1) one-on-one client consultations, assessments and information searches; 2) programs for groups of manufacturers, such as seminars/workshops, roundtable discussion groups and cooperative networks; and, 3) equipment and software for demonstration, testing, and developing product prototypes. All services are provided in eight core areas: quality, manufacturing processes, business systems, marketing, information systems, human resources, product development and testing, and company assessment.

* Incubator Centers

Alliance for Technology Commercialization
Pittsburg State University
1501 S. Joplin   620-235-4927
Pittsburg, KS 66762   Fax: 620-235-4030
www.atckansas.com

Enterprise Center of Johnson County
8527 Bluejacket   913-438-2282
Lenexa, KS 66214   Fax: 913-888-6928
www.ecjc.com

The ECJC provides services to entrepreneurs in the Kansas City metro area. The Kansas Women's Business Center is located at ECJC.

Lawrence Regional Technology Center
1617 St. Andrews Drive, Suite 210   785-832-2110
Lawrence, KS 66047   Fax: 785-832-8234
www.lrtc.biz

Mid-America Commercialization Corporation
1500 Hayes Drive   785-532-3900

Manhattan, KS 66502   Fax: 785-532-3909
www.ksu.edu/tech.transfer/macc/macc.htm

Quest Business Center for Entrepreneurs
Quest Center
One East Ninth   620-665-8468
Hutchinson, KS 67501   Fax: 620-665-7619
www.hutchquest.com

University of Kansas Medical Center Research Institute
Biotechnology Development Center
3901 Rainbow Blvd.   913-588-1495
Kansas City, KS 66160-7702   Fax: 913-588-5242
www.kcbdc.com

Western Kansas Technology Corporation
1922 Main   620-793-7964
Great Bend, KS 67530   Fax: 620-792-4850

Wichita Technology Center
7829 Rockhill Rd., Suite 307   316-651-5900
Wichita, KS 67206   Fax: 316-684-5640
www.wichitatechnology.com

The Mid-America Manufacturing Technology Center strives to improve the technical capabilities of small manufacturers, ensuring they stay competitive. The incubators are public-private partnerships designed to assist companies and transfer new technology to the marketplace. Each incubator also operates a local seed fund.

* Business Tax Bureau

Kansas Department of Revenue
915 SW Harrison St.
Topeka, KS 66625   785-368-8222
www.ksrevenue.org

The Kansas Department of Revenue provides an economic development outreach program that furnishes information about the tax incentives available to individuals and businesses in Kansas. The department visits with cities, counties, chambers, businesses and other groups to promote the Kansas tax incentives. Their goals are to first make our customers aware of the Kansas tax incentives offered and second to provide their customers with the information necessary to understand and qualify for the tax incentives made available through Kansas law. If you are interested in having a representative from the Kansas Department of Revenue speak to your group about Kansas tax incentives, please contact Tax Incentive Department at 785-296-3070 or by Email: {eco@kdor.state.ks.us}.

* Kansas Technology Enterprise Corporation (KTEC)

214 SW 6th Ave., First Floor   785-296-5272
Topeka, KS 66603-3719   Fax: 785-296-1160
www.ktec.com

Through the following programs, KTEC serves inventors, researchers, corporations, investors and entrepreneurs. In addition, they conduct an annual high tech expo.

Applied Research Matching Grants: KTEC funds 60 percent of the cost of industry R&D projects which lead to job creation in Kansas. Industrially-focused Centers of Excellence are operated at several major universities.

Seed Capital Fund: Provides equity financing for high tech product development. Matching funds are provided for the Small Business Innovation Research Program.

KTEC Centers of Excellence: University based research centers providing product development, seminars, research, consulting, networking and training.

Advanced Manufacturing Institute (AMI): Located on the campus of Kansas State University. Purpose is to improve manufacturing practiced by Kansas companies. These include automated and flexible manufacturing and assembly systems, process planning, processing of engineering materials, special developmental efforts, and technology transfer.

Higuchi Biosciences Center (HBC): Located on the campus of the University of Kansas. Serves as a hub of pharmaceutical research and development. Mission is pre-clinical drug delivery, drug development, drug testing and research.

National Institute for Aviation Research (NIAR): Located at the Wichita State University. Integrates higher education, government and business in cooperative efforts to advance the nation's aviation industry. Conducts research and technology transfer to meet industry challenges.

Kansas Polymer Research Center: Located in Pittsburg State University. Helps companies by providing technical assistance and research facilities for design, testing, development of prototypes, products and processing methods.

Information and Telecommunication Technology Center (ITTC): Located at the University of Kansas, ITTC develops technology and advances knowledge in the areas of information technology, telecommunications, radar systems and remote sensing.

Grant Programs
Small Business Innovation Research (SBIR) Grants: Helps small businesses obtain Federal SBIR awards by providing grants to support proposal preparation. Offers a network for SBIR concept evaluation, identification of appropriate SBIR solicitation topics, federal agency contact, and technical assistance.

* Kansas Development Finance Authority

555 S. Kansas Ave., Suite 202   785-357-4445
Topeka, KS 66603-3761   Fax: 785-357-4478
www.kdfa.org

The Authority is authorized to issue bonds for the purpose of financing capital improvements facilities, industrial enterprises, agricultural business enterprises, educational facilities, health care facilities, and housing developments. Several small projects can be combined into one large bond issue.

* Certified Development Companies

Avenue Area, Inc.
Tom Overby, Executive Director
753 State Avenue, Suite 106   913-371-0065
Kansas City, KS 66101   Fax: 913-321-1019
County served: Wyandotte

Citywide Development Corporation of Kansas City, Kansas
701 North 7th Street, Room 421   913-573-5733
Kansas City, KS 66101   Fax: 913-573-5745
Serves: City of Kansas City

Eastern Kansas Economic Development Group
Wayne Symmonds, Executive Director
702 Commercial, Suite 3A   785-776-0417
Emporia, KS 66801   Fax: 785-776-7204
Counties served: Atchison, Chase, Clay, Coffey, Franklin, Geary, Jackson, Lyon, Marshall, Morris, Nemaha, Osage, Pottawatomie, Riley, Wabaunsee

Four Rivers Development, Inc. (ADC)
Debra J. Peters, Manager
P.O. Box 265   785-738-2185
Beloit, KS 67420   Fax: 785-738-2185
Email: dpeters@nckcn.com
www.ckcn.com/ComEcon/fordi.htm
Counties served: Cloud, Dickinson, Ellsworth, Jewell, Lincoln, Mitchell, Ottawa, Republic, Saline, Washington

Great Plains Development, Inc.
Patty Richardson, Executive Director
100 Military Plaza, Suite 128
P.O. Box 1116   316-227-6406
Dodge City, KS 67801-1116   Fax: 316-225-6051
Counties served: Barber, Barton, Clark, Comanche, Edwards, Finney, Ford, Grant, Gray, Greeley, Hamilton, Haskell, Hodgeman, Kearney, Kiowa, Lane, Meade, Morton, Ness, Pawnee, Pratt, Rush, Scott, Stafford, Seward, Stanton, Stevens, Wichita

Johnson County Certified Development Company
David Long, Executive Director
11111 West 95th Street, Suite 214   913-599-1717
Overland Park, KS 66214   Fax: 913-599-6430
County served: Johnson

McPherson County Small Business Development Association
David A. O'Dell, Executive Director
212 E. Euclid   620-241-3927
McPherson KS 67460   Fax: 620-241-3927
Email: sbda@mpks.net
County served: McPherson

Mid-America, Inc.
Bruce Fairbank, Executive Director
1501 S. Joplin   316-235-4920
Pittsburg, KS 66762   Fax: 316-235-4919
Counties served: Allen, Anderson, Bourbon, Cherokee, Crawford, Labette, Linn, Miami, Montgomery, Neosho, Wilson, Woodson

MoKan Development, Inc.
Director of Economic Development
1302 Faraon   816-233-3144
St. Joseph, MO 64501   Fax: 816-233-8498
Counties served: Atchison, Brown, Doniphan, Jackson, Jefferson, Nemaha

Pioneer Country Development, Inc.
Randy Hrabe, Executive Director
319 North Pomeroy
P.O. Box 248   785-625-6116
Hill City, KS 67642-0248   Fax: 785-628-0533
Counties served: Cheyenne, Decatur, Ellis, Gove, Graham, Logan, Norton, Osborne, Phillips, Rawlins, Rooks, Russell, Sheridan, Sherman, Smith, Thomas, Trego, Wallace

South Central Kansas Economic Development District
Bill Bolin, Executive Director
209 E. William, Suite 300   316-262-7035
Wichita, KS 67202   Fax: 316-262-7062
Counties served: Butler, Chautauqua, Cowley, Elk, Greenwood, Harper, Harvey, Kingman, Marion, McPherson, Rice, Reno, Sedgwick, Sumner

Wakarusa Valley Development, Inc.
Mike O'Donnell, Executive Director
203 Lyon Street
P.O. Box 586   785-865-4425
Lawrence, KS 66044-0367   Fax: 785-865-4400
County served: Douglas
SBA 504 Program: Provides loans using 50 percent conventional bank financing, 40 percent SBA involvement through Certified Development Companies, and 10 percent owner equity. A fixed asset loan in amounts up to $1 million. Loan can be used for land and building, construction, machinery and equipment, and renovation/expansion.

* Small Business Administration (SBA)

271 W. 3rd St. N, Suite 2500   316-269-6616
Wichita, KS 67202-1212   Fax: 316-269-6499
The Kansas Small Business Administration Office delivers a variety of programs and services, such as startup and operational assistance through small business training and counseling, financial assistance for startup's, business opportunities and much more.

* Small Business Investment Companies

Kansas Venture Capital, Inc.
Carol Laddish, Manager
6700 Antioch Plaza, Suite 460   913-262-7117
Overland Park, KS 66204   Fax: 913-262-3509
Email: jdalton@kvci.com

MidStates Capital, L.P.
Timothy J. Keeble, Contact
7300 West 110th Street, 7th Floor   913-962-9007
Overland Park, KS 66210   Fax: 913-962-0699
Email: timkeeble@mail.com
The SBA licenses, regulates, and provides financial assistance to privately owned and operated Small Business Investment Companies. SBICs make venture or risk investments by supplying capital and extending unsecured loans and loans not fully collateralized to small enterprises which meet their investment criteria. Financing is made by direct loans and by equity investments.

Kentucky

* Kentucky Cabinet for Economic Development

2300 Capital Plaza Tower
500 Mero Street   502-564-7670
Frankfort, KY 40601   800-626-2930
www.thinkkentucky.com
Kentucky Cabinet for Economic Development: The Cabinet is the primary state agency responsible for creating new jobs and new investment in the state.

-    Job Recruitment, Placement And Training: Provides a package of time-and cost-saving employee recruiting and placement services to Kentucky employers, at no cost to either employers or employees.
-    Industrial Location Assistance: Provides a comprehensive package of assistance to large manufacturing, services, and administrative facilities, both before and after their location in Kentucky.

Business Information Clearinghouse: 800-626-2250
Provides new and existing businesses a centralized information source on business regulations, licenses, permits, and other business assistance programs.

Kentucky Economic Development Finance Authority (KEDFA): Provides business loans to supplement other financing. KEDFA provides loan funds at below market interest rates. The loans are available for fixed asset financing (land, buildings, and equipment) for business startup, locations, and expansions that create new jobs in Kentucky or have a significant impact on the economic growth of a community. The loans must be used to finance projects in agribusiness, tourism, industrial ventures, or the service industry. KEDFA may participate in the financing of qualified projects with a secured loan for up to $10,000 per new job created, not to exceed 25% of a project's fixed asset cost. The maximum loan amount is $500,000 and the minimum is $25,000. Small businesses with projects of less than $100,000 may receive loans on fixed assets for up to 45% of the project costs if enough jobs are created. Interest rates are fixed for the life of the loan, and are determined by the length of the loan term. 502-564-4554, ext. 4413

Commonwealth Small Business Development Corporation (CSBDC): Works with state and local economic development organizations, banks, and the SBA to achieve community economic development through job creation and retention by providing long-term fixed asset financing to small business concerns. The CSBDC can lend a maximum of 40% of project cost or $750,000 per project (in certain circumstances $1,000,000).

Linked Deposit Program: Provides loans up to $100,000 for small business and agribusiness. Credit decisions are the responsibility of the lender making the loan. The state will purchase certificates of deposit from participating lenders through the State Investment Commission, at the New York Prime interest rate less four percent, but never less than 2%. 502-564-2064

Local Financial Assistance: Several local governments and area development districts offer loans and other financial incentives for economic development projects. The levels and terms of financial assistance provided generally are negotiable, and are based upon the availability of funds, jobs created, economic viability of the project, and other locally determined criteria.

Bluegrass State Skills Corporation (BSSC): An independent dejure corporation within the Cabinet for Economic Development, provides grants for customized skills training of workers for new, expanding and existing industries in Kentucky.

Industrial Revenue Bonds (IRB): Can be used to finance manufacturing projects and their warehousing areas, major transportation and communication facilities, most health care facilities, and mineral extraction and processing projects. 502-564-4554, ext. 4427

Utility Incentive Rates: Electric and gas utility companies regulated by the Kentucky Public Service Commission (excluding municipal systems) can offer economic incentive rates for certain large industrial and commercial customers.

Kentucky Investment Fund (Venture Capital): Encourages venture capital investment by certifying privately operated venture funds, thereby entitling their investors to tax credits equal to 40% of their capital contributions to the fund. 502-564-0531

Kentucky Tourism Development Act: Provides financial incentives to qualifying tourism projects. Tourism projects are defined as a cultural or historical site, recreation or entertainment facility, or area of natural phenomenon or scenic beauty.

Local Government Economic Development Fund: Grants are made to eligible counties for specific project that enable the counties to provide infrastructure to incoming and expanding business and industry.

Job Development Incentive Grant Program: Grants are made to eligible counties from their coal severance accounts for the purpose of encouraging job development. The grant amount cannot exceed $5,000 per job created.

Kentucky Industrial Development Act (KIDA): Investments in new and expanding manufacturing projects may qualify for tax credits. Companies that create at least 15 new full-time jobs and invest at least $100,000 in projects approved under KIDA may receive state income tax credits for up to 100% of annual debt service costs (principal and interest) for up to 10 years on land, buildings, site development, building fixtures and equipment used in a project, or the company may collect a job assessment fee of 3% of the gross wages of each employee whose job is created by the approved project and who is subject to Kentucky income taxes.

Kentucky Rural Economic Development Act (KREDA): Larger tax credits are available for new and expanding manufacturing projects that create at least 15 new full time jobs in counties with unemployment rates higher than the state average in each of the five preceding calendar years and invest at least $100,000.

Kentucky Jobs Development Act (KJDA): Service and technology related companies that invest in new and expanded non-manufacturing, non-retail projects that provide at least 75% of their services to users located outside of Kentucky, and that create new jobs for at least 15 full-time Kentucky residents may qualify for tax credits.

Kentucky Industrial Revitalization Act (KIRA): Investments in the rehabilitation of manufacturing operations that are in imminent danger of permanently closing or that have closed temporarily may qualify for tax credits. Companies that save or create 25 jobs in projects approved under KIRA may receive state income tax credits and job assessment fees for up to 10 years limited to 50% of the costs of the rehabilitation or construction of buildings and the reoutfitting or purchasing of machinery and equipment. 502-564-4554, ext. 4428

Kentuckyenterprise: This program was developed by the Cabinet for Economic Development to assist new businesses through the maze of start-up questions. They publish a "Kentucky Business Guide" to help you through all the requirements of a new business.

Kentucky Economic Opportunity Zone Program: Provides tax credits to companies that establish new or expand existing manufacturing, service, or technology operations in a qualified zone having high unemployment and poverty levels.

Enterprise Zone Program: Encourages new or renewed development to targeted areas of the state by offering special state and local tax incentives to businesses locating in a zone.

Direct Loan Program: Provides financing for manufacturing, warehousing, distribution, non-retail services, agribusiness, and tourism projects to private firms in participation with other lenders.

Craft Loan Program: Provides direct loans to the craft industry to finance inventory, working capital, up to 50% of eligible operating expenses, and renovation or purchase of equipment or other fixed assets.

Bluegrass State Skills Corporation: An independent corporation that brokers skills training for business and industry, from entry-level to advanced training, and from upgrading present employees to retraining experienced workers. Awards grants to new, expanding and existing companies, providing up to 50% reimbursement of eligible costs. Tax credit is available to existing businesses for skills upgrade and occupational upgrade training. The program works in partnership with other employment and job training resources and programs, as well as economic development activities, to package a program customized to meet the specific needs of a company. 502-564-2021

The Small and Minority Business Division: Coordinates small and minority business activities throughout the state.

One-Stop Business Licensing Program: The One-Stop Business Licensing Program was developed to cut through the 'red tape' by simplifying this process. This program allows users to instantly receive a complete listing of all licenses that could be required at the state level. {www.sos.state.ky.us/ONESTOP/PROGRAM/onestop.asp}

Alliance Program: The Commonwealth Alliance Program helps guide entrepreneurs through an organized process of creating and managing strategic, market-driven business relationships with other companies.

Procurement Assistance: If you want to market your products and/or services to federal, state, and local government agencies then the Kentucky Procurement Assistance Program (KPAP) offers services to assist you.

International Trade Division: The International Trade Division within the Kentucky Cabinet for Economic Development assists business owners with international endeavors. Their programs include: export consulting, export marketing, education and training and representatives in Belgium, Japan, Chile and Mexico.

* Rural Development

771 Corporate Dr., Suite 200   859-224-7300
Lexington, KY 40503-4577   Fax: 859-224-7340
www.rurdev.usda.gov/ky

The Office of Kentucky Rural Development's Rural Business-Cooperative Service promotes economic viability of rural communities through partnerships with public and private community based organizations. Their programs provide financial and technical assistance to rural businesses and cooperatives to create and preserve quality jobs in rural areas. Rural Business-Cooperative Service programs include: Business and Industry Guaranteed Loans, Rural Business Opportunity Grants, Rural Business Enterprise Grants, Intermediary Relending Program, Rural Economic Development Loan and Grants, Rural Cooperative Development Grants and Rural Community Value Added Grants. Contact the office or check their web site for additional information.

FmHA Business and Industrial Guarantee Loan Program: Offers loan guarantees of up to 90 percent of principal and interest on conventional loans to businesses and industries in rural areas of Kentucky. The FmHA designates the eligible rural areas and are in areas with populations of less than 50,000. Priority is given where areas are in open country, rural communities, and cities of 25,000 or fewer. Funds can be used to purchase land, buildings, machinery, equipment, furniture, and fixtures; to finance construction, expansion, or modernization of buildings; and to provide start-up and working capital.

* Kentucky Pollution Prevention Center

KPPC
University of Louisville   800-334-8635
420 Academic Building   502-852-0965 (in Louisville)
Louisville, KY 40292   Fax: 502-852-0964
www.kppc.org

KPPC is a waste management resource center that provides information on how to manage, recycle, procedure or exchange waste even the smallest businesses produce, such as drycleaners or auto body shops. The service is free to all Kentucky businesses. They are located at the University of Louisville and provides a toll-free number for your convenience in calling:

* Business Environmental Assistance Program – Air Quality

Center for Business Development
Business Environmental Assistance Program for Air Quality
University of Kentucky
227 Carol M. Gatton College of Business
  and Economics Building   800-562-2327
Lexington, KY 40506-0034   Fax: 859-323-1907
www.kbeap.org

Operated by the Center for Business Development at the University of Kentucky, this non-regulated program offers confidential air quality environmental assistance to businesses while also serving as an advocate for development of environmental regulations which promote economic competitiveness. Services include environmental training seminars, publications to help businesses reduce air emissions through prevention techniques and on-site air quality environmental assessments to individual businesses. The center's reference library and toll-free phone line acts as a clearinghouse for information about techniques, products and equipment that businesses can use to prevent production and release of air pollutants. These services will help businesses comply with federal and state regulations including Title V of the Clean Air Act of 1990.

* Kentucky Tourism Development Cabinet

2200 Capital Plaza Tower
500 Mero Street   502-564-0678
Frankfort, KY 40601   Fax: 502-564-1512
http://tourism.ky.gov

Developers of approved projects will be eligible to recover 25% of their project's cost by having refunded to them the six percent Kentucky sales tax they collect from their visitors. The refund will be paid over a 10-year period. Eligible tourism attractions for Kentucky's incentives are cultural or historic sites, recreation or entertainment facilities, areas of scenic beauty or distinctive natural phenomena, entertainment destination centers, Kentucky crafts and products centers and lodging when built on state or federal parks and recreational land or built with a recreational component that costs more than the lodging facility.

Kentucky Tourism Development Loan Program: The loan program assists smaller tourism facilities obtain financing. The program is targeted to facilities that will attract travelers into the area. Projects approved for funding have included a rock climbing experience, equine shoe facility and a bed & breakfast. Funds are available through this program are for the financing of fixed assets only. The maximum loan amount is $250,000 with an equal amount being provided by another source. The program offers below market interest rates with maximum terms of 15 years.

* Information Technology Resource Center

iTRC-Shelby Campus
9001 Shelbyville Road   502-852-0900
Louisville, KY 40222   Fax: 502-852-4701

iTRC-Downtown
201 East Jefferson St.
Louisville, KY 40202
www.theitrc.com

The iTRC provides incubating facilities for new companies using applications of new technologies. This effort is now being expanded and developed into an international-class offering. The iTRC's incubation program is targeting Information and Telecommunications intensive startup companies or companies less than two years old. They offer an extremely competitive pricing structure for all the facility and infrastructure needs of a new and growing company.

* Small Business Administration (SBA)

Room 188
600 Dr. Martin Luther King, Jr. Place   502-582-5971
Louisville, KY 40202   Fax: 502-582-5009
www.sba.gov/ky

The Kentucky Small Business Administration Office delivers a variety of programs and services, such as startup and operational assistance through small business training and counseling, financial assistance for startup's, business opportunities and much more.

* Small Business Investment Companies

Chrysalis Ventures II, L.P.
Lisa K. Aly, Contact
101 South Fifth Street, Suite 1650   502-583-7644
Louisville, KY 40202   Fax: 502-853-7648
Email: Laly@ChrysalisVentures.com

Equal Opportunity Finance, Inc. (SSBIC)
David L. Davis, President
50E RiverCenter Boulevard
PO Box 391   859-815-3434
Covington, KY 41012   Fax: 859-815-4496
Email: dldavis@ashland.com

Mountain Ventures, Inc.
L. Ray Moncrief, Exec. Vice President
P.O. Box 1738
362 Old Whitley Rd.   606-864-5175
London, KY 40743   Fax: 606-864-5194
Email: BMcDaniel@khic.org

Prosperitas Investment Partners, L.P.
Steven B. Bing, Contact
3600 National City Tower
101 South Fifth Street   502-584-4008
Louisville, KY 40202   Fax: 502-587-1351
Email: sbing@prosperitasfund.com

The SBA licenses, regulates, and provides financial assistance to privately owned and operated Small Business Investment Companies. SBICs make venture or risk investments by supplying capital and extending unsecured loans and loans not fully collateralized to small enterprises which meet their investment criteria. Financing is made by direct loans and by equity investments.

* Certified Development Companies

Commonwealth Small Business Development Corporation
111 St. James Court, Suite 504   502-696-9444
Frankfort KY 40601   Fax: 502-696-9493
Area of Operation: Statewide

Capital Access Corporation - Kentucky
120 Webster Street, Suite 330   502-584-2175
Louisville, KY 40206   Fax: 502-584-2173
Email: billfensterer@yahoo.com

Area of Operation: Jefferson, Oldham, Scott, Hardin, Bullitt, Nelson, Daviess, Estill, Henderson, Meade, Pendleton, Pulaski, Shelby, Spencer and Warren Counties

Community Ventures Corporation
1450 N. Broadway   859-231-0054
Lexington, KY 40505   Fax: 859-231-0261

Area of Operation: Bourbon, Boyle, Clark, Fayette, Jessamine, Kenton, Madison, Taylor, & Woodford Counties

Purchase Area Development District
1002 Medical Drive   502-247-7171
Mayfield KY 42066   Fax: 502-247-9000

Area of Operation: Ballard, Calloway, Carlisle, Fulton, Graves, Hickman, Marshall and McCracken Counties

The 504 Certified Development Company (CDC) Program provides growing businesses with long-term, fixed-rate financing for major fixed assets, such as land and buildings. A Certified Development Company is a nonprofit corporation set up to contribute to the economic development of its community or region. CDC's work with the Small Business Administration and private-sector lenders to provide up to 90% financing to small businesses. There are about 270 CDC's nationwide, each covering a specific region.

* Kentucky Department of Local Government

Division of Community Programs   800-346-5606
1024 Capital Center Dr., Suite 340   502-573-2382
Frankfort, KY 40601   Fax: 502-573-2512
www.dlg.ky.gov

Community Development Block Grant Loan (CDBG): Available to cities and counties for the commercial rehabilitation of existing buildings or structures used for business, commercial, or industrial purposes. The cities and counties loan the grant funds to business to be used for fixed assets and for the creation or retention of jobs. At least 51 percent of the jobs created must be for low-and moderate-income families.

* Community Ventures Corporation

1450 Broadway   800-299-0267
Lexington, KY 40505   859-231-0054
www.cvcky.org   Fax: 859-231-0261

Community Venture Corporation is a community-based, non-profit organization that strives to help improve the quality of life for urban and rural residents throughout central and northern Kentucky. They offer free Business Orientation classes and a free Small Business Resource Guide. In addition they offer a variety of business classes with a sliding fee scale. The Center for Entrepreneurs provides businesses with highly visible rental space, which includes: conference rooms, computer and faxes, workroom, business training, consultants, and free parking starting at $350 per month.

* Kentucky Highlands Investment Corporation (KHIC)

362 Whitley Road
P.O. Box 1738   606-864-5175
London, KY 40743   Fax: 606-864-5194
www.khic.org

A small business investment company licensed by the SBA, provide both short term and long term financing assistance to small businesses in Southeastern Kentucky. Venture capital loans and equity capital investments for higher-risk projects are available for start-ups, expansions, and relocations of manufacturing and services firms. Participation usually ranges from $50,000 to $500,000. Terms and interest rates are negotiated.

* Mountain Association for Community Economic Development

433 Chestnut St., Suite 9   859-986-2373
Berea, KY 40403   Fax: 859-986-1299
www.maced.org

Private Loans: Appalachian Counties: Loans and financial planning assistance are available to qualifying new and expanding manufacturing businesses in the 49 Appalachian counties of Kentucky. Loans range from $10,000 to $150,000. Funds can be used for working capital or to finance fixed assets.

* Office for the New Economy

702 Capital Avenue, #256   502-564-0531
Frankfort, KY 40601   Fax: 502-564-0963
www.one-ky.com

Created by the Kentucky Innovation Act of 2000, the Office of New Economy facilitates a state-wide strategic development plan to spur the growth of the knowledge-based economy in Kentucky. The Office of the

New Economy provides programs for entrepreneurs, science and research, and information technology.

Louisiana

* Louisiana Department of Economic Development

P.O. Box 94185   225-342-3000
Baton Rouge, LA 70804   225-342-5388
www.lded.state.la.us

Quality jobs: Provides an annual refundable credit of up to 6% of payroll for a period of up to 10 years for qualifying companies.

Cost-free training: Louisiana's QuickStart Training Program utilizes the state's vocational-technical institutes to provide cost-free pre-employment training customized to a company's requirements. The Jobs Training Partnership Act Program can help a company find trainees and will also pay a portion of their wages while they are in training.

Workforce development and training: Develops and provides customized pre-employment and workforce upgrade training to existing and prospective Louisiana businesses.

Business Matchmakers: Seeks to pair small and medium-sized suppliers in the state with larger companies which are currently making purchases out of state.

Minority Venture Capital Match Program: Provides for a match investment for qualified minority venture capital funds. The fund must have at least $250,000 of private investment for which LEDC may invest $1.00 for every $2.00 of private capital up to $5 million.

Small Business Loan Program: Provides loan guarantees and participations to banks in order to facilitate capital accessibility for businesses. Guarantees may range up to 75% of the loan amount, not to exceed a maximum of $1.5 million. Loan participations of up to 40% are also available. Applicants must have a business plan and a bank that is willing to fund the loan.

Business Linked Deposit Program: Provides for a 1% to 4% interest rate reduction on a maximum of $200,000 for a maximum of 2 to 5 years on term loans that are funded by banks to Louisiana businesses. Job creation, statistical area employment, and cash flow requirements for underwriting are all criteria, which will effect the percentage and term of the linked deposit.

Micro Loan Program: Provides loan guarantees and participations to banks that fund loans ranging from $5,000 to $50,000 to Louisiana small businesses.

Contract Loan Program: Intended to provide a loan participation and guarantee to a bank for government contract loans. These loans are intended to help businesses finance working capital for contracts with local, state, or federal government agencies. Loans may range from $5000 to $1,000,000 and must be for terms of one year or less.

Exim Bank City/State Program: LEDC has a relationship with the U.S. Export-Import Bank in Washington, DC Under this program, LEDC facilitates export working capital loans for small Louisiana businesses.

Venture Capital Match Program: Provides for a match investment for Louisiana venture capital funds. The fund must have at least $5 million of private investment for which LEDC may provide $5 million.

Venture Capital Co-Investment Program: Provides for a co-investment in a Louisiana business of up to 1/4 of the round of investment, but not more than $500,000, with any qualified venture capital fund with at least $7.5 million in private capital. The venture capital fund may be from outside of Louisiana.

BIDCO Investment Program: Provides for a match or co-investment in certified BIDCOs. BIDCOs are state-chartered, non-depository alternative financing sources for small businesses. BIDCOs frequently provide equity and subordinated debt financing to new and growing companies, as well as to companies requiring turnaround assistance. A BIDCO must have at least $2 million in private capital. LEDC may match the investment $1.00 for $2.00 of private capital up to $2.5 million. Co-investments are considered on a project by project basis and cannot exceed 33% of the total investment.

Specialty BIDCO Investment Program: Provides for a match or co-investment in certified Specialty BIDCOs. Specialty BIDCOs are BIDCOs established with a particular focus on assisting disadvantaged businesses and businesses located in impoverished and economically disadvantaged areas. The BIDCO must have at least $250,000 in private capital. LEDC may

match the investment $1.00 for every $1.00 of private capital up to $2.5 million. Co-investments are considered on a project by project basis and cannot exceed 50% of the total investment.

Small Business Bonding Assistance Program: The primary goal of this program is to aid certified Economically Disadvantaged Businesses (EDBs) in acquiring quality bid, performance, and payment bonds at reasonable rates from surety companies. EDBs receive help reaching required bonding capacity for specific projects. Contractors often do not reach these levels on their own due to balance sheet deficiencies and a lack of adequate managerial and technical skills. After certification by the Division and accreditation by LCAI, contractors are eligible to receive bond guarantee assistance to be used as collateral when seeking bonds. The Division will issue a letter of credit to the surety for an amount up to 25% of the base contract amount or $200,000.

Economic Development Award: Provides financial incentives in the form of linked deposit loans, loan guarantees and grants to industrial or business development projects that promote economic development and that require state assistance for basic infrastructure development.

International Trade: The International Trade Division utilizes trade and catalog shows, identifies trade opportunities, offers counseling, matches exporters with markets and encourages participation in their seminars.

Microenterprise Program: The Microenterprise Program assists low income parents of minor children to start or strengthen a small business. The program provides entrepreneurial and economic literacy training and mentoring; financial counseling; and access to capital through micro loans for the participants. In addition, the program provides ongoing assistance to participants to ensure that microentrepreneurs successfully negotiate the challenges new microenterprise businesses face during the initial phases.

Small Business Development Centers: Louisiana Economic Development provides 12 Small Business Development Centers throughout the state.

Louisiana Seed Capital Program: Provides matching funds to be used to provide seed capital for Louisiana small businesses at the early stages.

* Rural Development Office

USDA, Rural Development
Louisiana State Office
3727 Government Street   318-473-7921
Alexandria, LA 71302   Fax: 318-473-7829
www.rurdev.usda.gov/la

USDA Rural Development provides a full range of rural development credit services in rural Louisiana. Programs in the areas of business and industrial development, community facilities, multi-family and single housing and water and waste disposal are administered through Rural Development state and area offices.

* First Stop Shop

Secretary of State
First Stop Shop Division   225-922-2675
P.O. Box 94125   800-259-0001
Baton Rouge, LA 70804-9125   Fax: 225-922-0439
www.sos.louisiana.gov/comm/fss/fss-index.htm

The First Stop Shop is a "licensing information center" for prospective small business owners. The First Stop Shop gives current and potential business owners a single place to go for licensing information needed to start a business in Louisiana.

* Department of Environmental Quality

Small Business Assistance Program
602 N. Fifth Street   225-219-3296
Baton Rouge, LA 70802   Fax: 225-219-3309
www.deq.state.la.us

The mission of the DEQ's non-regulatory Small Business Assistance Program is to provide technical assistance to small business owners in complying with state and federal environmental regulations. The SBAP is dedicated to: interpreting federal and state environmental regulations and giving guidance on how to comply with them; interpreting the rights and obligations of the small businesses, identifying emission sources and compounds; estimating emissions at each source for inventory questionnaires; assisting in the preparation of environmental permit applications and exemptions; developing pollution programs; and providing guidance with multi-media issues.

* Louisiana Department of Agriculture and Forestry

Office of Marketing
5825 Florida Boulevard, Suite 1158
P.O. Box 3334   225-922-1277
Baton Rouge, LA 70821   Fax: 225-922-1289
www.ldaf.state.la.us

The Office of Marketing provides one-on-one counseling assistance to numerous clients for varied marketing services and economic development needs. The staff is capable of providing a wealth of information about Louisiana aquaculture, agriculture and forestry either directly or through extensive professional networks.

* Incumbent Worker Training

Louisiana Department of Labor
1001 North 23rd Street
P.O. Box 94094
Baton Rouge, LA 70804-9094   225-342-3290
www.ldol.state.la.us

Incumbent Worker Training is designed to benefit business and industry by assisting in the skill development of existing employees, increasing employee productivity and the growth of the company. Both are expected to result in the creation of new jobs, the retention of jobs that otherwise may have been eliminated, and an increase in wages for the trained workers.

* Small Business Administration

One Canal Plaza
365 Canal St., Suite 2250   504-589-6685
New Orleans, LA 70130   Fax: 504-589-2339
www.sba.gov/la

The Louisiana Small Business Administration Office delivers a variety of programs and services, such as startup and operational assistance through small business training and counseling, financial assistance for startup's, business opportunities and much more.

* Small Business Investment Companies

Audubon Capital SBIC, L.P.
Robert Cowin, Contact
1100 Poydras Street, Suite 2000   504-585-7730
New Orleans, LA 70163   Fax: 504-585-7731
Email: rcowin@auduboncapital.com

Bank One Equity Investors, Inc.
Thomas J. Adamek, President
450 Laurel Street, Suite 1450   225-408-3255
Baton Rouge, LA 70801   Fax: 225-408-3090
Email: sgwhittington@stonehengecapital.com

Hibernia Capital Corp.
Thomas Hoyt, President
313 Carondelet Street   504-533-5988
New Orleans, LA 70130   Fax: 504-533-3873
Email: thoyt@hiberniabank.com

Jefferson Capital Partners I, L.P.
William J. Harper, Contact
3501 N. Causeway Blvd., Suite 420   504-828-2088
Metairie, LA 70002   Fax: 504-828-2014
Email: capital@jeffcap.com
Email: wharper@jeffcap.com

The SBA licenses, regulates, and provides financial assistance to privately owned and operated Small Business Investment Companies. SBICs make venture or risk investments by supplying capital and extending unsecured loans and loans not fully collateralized to small enterprises which meet their investment criteria. Financing is made by direct loans and by equity investments.

* Certified Development Companies

Ark-La-Tex Investment & Development Corporation
5210 Hollywood Avenue
Shreveport LA 71109
MAILING ADDRESS:
P.O. Box 37005   318-632-2022
Shreveport LA 71109   Fax: 318-632-2099
Area Of Operation: Parishes of Bienville, Bossier, Caddo, Claiborne, DeSoto, Lincoln, Natchitoches, Red River, Sabine and Webster

JEDCO Development Corporation
3445 North Causeway Boulevard, Suite 300   504-833-1881

Metairie LA 70002   Fax: 504-833-7676
Area Of Operation: Jefferson Parish

Kisatchie-Delta Regional Planning & Development District, Inc.
1611 Arnold Drive, First Floor   318-487-5454
Alexandria, LA 71303   Fax: 318-487-5451
Area Of Operation: Parishes of Avoyelles, Catahoula, Concordia, Grant, La Salle, Rapides, Vernon and Winn

Louisiana Capital Certified Development Company, Inc.
302 La Rue France, Suite 200
Lafayette, LA 70508
MAILING ADDRESS:
302 La Rue France, Suite 200   337-234-2977
Lafayette, LA 70508   Fax: 337-234-5535
Area Of Operation: Parishes of Acadia, Calcasieu, Evangeline, Iberia, Lafayette, St. Landry, St. Martin, St. Mary and Vermilion

New Orleans Regional Business Development Loan Corporation
650 Poydras, Suite 1220   504-524-6172
New Orleans LA 70130   Fax: 504-524-0002
Area Of Operation: Parishes of Assumption, Jefferson, Laforuche, Orleans, Plaquemines, St. Benard, St. Charles, St. James, St. John the Baptist, St. Tammany, Tangipahoa, Terrebonne and Washington

Northeast Louisiana Capital, Inc.
1900 North 18th Street, Suite 304   318-323-0878
Monroe LA 71201   Fax: 318-387-8529
Area Of Operation: Ouachita, Union, Morehouse, Richland, Caldwell, Jackson, Franklin, Tensas, East Carroll, West Carroll and Madison Parishes

The 504 Certified Development Company (CDC) Program provides growing businesses with long-term, fixed-rate financing for major fixed assets, such as land and buildings. A Certified Development Company is a nonprofit corporation set up to contribute to the economic development of its community or region. CDC's work with the Small Business Administration and private-sector lenders to provide up to 90% financing to small businesses. There are about 270 CDC's nationwide, each covering a specific region.

Maine

* Department of Economic and Community Development

Office of Business Development   207-624-9804
59 State House Station   Fax: 207-287-5701
Augusta, ME 04333   TTY: 207-287-2656
www.econdevmaine.com/biz-develop.htm

Business Answers: 800-872-3838
Maine's toll-free business information hotline provides rapid responses to questions about doing business in Maine.

One-Stop Business License Center: This central clearinghouse for state regulatory information helps simplify the process of complying with state business regulations. Callers may request business license and permit applications, as well as information on state regulations.

Business Answers/Small Business Advocate: Serves as a central clearinghouse of information regarding business assistance programs and services available to state businesses. Also helps small businesses resolve problems they may be experiencing with state regulatory agencies.

Maine Products Marketing Program: Provides marketing assistance to producers of Maine-made consumer goods. Members of the program promote their message of Maine quality through the use of product tags and labels, literature and package design, which carry the unified theme, "Maine Made America's Best." The program also publishes the "Maine Made" Buyer's Guide, which is sent to more than 25,000 wholesale buyers. {www.mainemade.com}

* Rural Development Administration (RDA)

967 Illinois Ave.
P.O. Box 405   207-990-9160
Bangor, ME 04402-0405   Fax: 207-990-9165
www.rurdev.usda.gov/me

Maine's Rural Business-Cooperative Services Office offers several programs to assist businesses in Maine.

- *Direct Business and Industry Program*: Loans are made to businesses to benefit rural areas. The primary purpose of this program is to create and maintain employment and improve the economic and environmental climate in rural communities.

- *Guaranteed Business and Industry Programs*: Loans made by conventional lender and guaranteed by the Rural Development Office to improve, develop or finance business, industry and employment.
- *Rural Business Enterprise Grants:* Grants are made to facilitate the development of small emerging businesses in rural areas with populations less than or equal to 25,000.
- *Intermediary Relending Program*: The objective of IRP is to finance business facilities and community development projects in rural areas with populations of less than 25,000. Loans are made to intermediaries to relend the funds ultimately to recipients for business facilities or community development.
- *Cooperative Assistance Program*: The cooperative assistance program provides assistance to help recipients form new cooperatives and improve the operations of existing cooperatives.

* Apprenticeship Program
Kenneth L. Hardt
Maine Apprenticeship Program
Maine Department of Labor
55 State House Station   207-624-6390
Augusta, ME 04333-0055   Fax: 207-624-6499
Email: k.skip.hardt@state.me.us

Maine's Apprenticeship Program provides customized training and instruction so workers can obtain professional credentials. Many of Maine's larger firms have taken advantage of this innovative workforce development program, which will underwrite 50% of apprenticeship-related tuition for new and existing employees.

* School-to-Work Initiatives
Susan Brown
Center for Career Development
Maine Technical College System
SMVTC, Fort Road   207-767-5210, ext. 111
South Portland, ME 04106   Fax: 207-767-2542
Email: susan@ccd.mtcs.tec.me.us
www.mtcs.net

School-to-Work Initiatives: This public-private partnership is designed to provide Maine industry with a competitive workforce. The program employs three strategies to train Maine youth. These include:

- Maine Career Advantage: a nationally recognized two-year combination of business internship and integrated academics, including one free year at the technical college level.
- Registered Pre-Apprenticeship: four years of employer-driven high school academics, coupled with two summers of on-the-job training. This culminates in permanent employment and a Registered Apprenticeship upon high school graduation.
- Tech Prep: sequential, industry-driven academic and technical training beginning in eleventh grade and progressing through completion of Certificate, Associate and/or Bachelor Degrees.

* Maine Quality Centers Program
Maine Quality Centers
Center for Career Development
2 Fort Road   207-767-5210, ext. 4107
South Portland, ME 04106   Fax: 207-629-4048
www.mccs.me.edu/mqc.html

This is an economic development initiative of the Maine Technical College System, which provides new and expanding businesses with a trained and ready workforce. New or expanding firms creating at least eight new full-time jobs with benefits may be eligible to receive state financing for 100% of pre-hire classroom training.

* Governor's Training Initiative
Bureau of Employment Services
Maine Department of Labor   207-624-6390
55 State House Station   888-457-8883
Augusta, ME 04333-0055   Fax: 207-624-6499
Email: caroline.p.morgan@state.me.us
www.mainecareercenter.com

This program reimburses training costs when they are required for business expansion, retention or unique upgrading issues. Businesses that meet eligibility requirements may receive reimbursements for on-the-job training, competitive retooling, specialized recruitment, workplace literacy, high-performance skills or customized technical training.

* Safety Education and Training
Safety Works!
Bureau of Labor Standards
Maine Department of Labor   877-SAFE345
45 State House Station   207-624-6400
Augusta, ME 04333-0045   Fax: 207-624-6449
Email: alan.c.hinsey@state.me.us
www.state.me.us/labor/bls/blsmain.htm

At no cost to a company, Maine's Bureau of Labor Standards provides customized health and safety training, site evaluation and technical support. Priority is given to small and mid-sized employers and large employers with documented health and safety problems

* Maine Revenue Services
24 State House Station
Augusta, ME 04333   207-287-2336
www.state.me.us/revenue

Business Equipment Property Tax Reimbursement Program: Program reimbursed, for up to 12 years, all local property taxes paid on eligible business property.

Employee-Assisted Day Care Credit: Provides an income tax credit of up to $5,000. The credit is limited to the lesser of $5,000, 20% of the cost incurred or $100 for each child of an employee enrolled on a full-time basis or for each full-time equivalent throughout the tax year.

Employer Provided Long-term Care Benefits Credit: Provides an income tax credit equal to the lesser of $5,000, 20% of the cost incurred or $100 per employee covered by a long-term care policy as part of a benefits package.

Research and Development Sales Tax Exemption: Sales of machinery and equipment used by the purchaser directly and exclusively in research and development by any business is eligible for a sales tax exemption.

Fuel and Electricity Sales Tax Exemption: Program exempts any business from sales tax 95% of the sales price of all fuel and electricity purchased for use at the manufacturing facility.

Business Property Tax Reimbursement Program: Maine reimburses what companies pay in local property taxes on facilities built after April 1, 1995. Taxes on this property may be reimbursed by the state for a maximum of 12 years. The definition of qualified business property for this program is broad and specified by law.

Maine Seed Capital Tax Credit Program: FAME authorizes state income tax credits to investors in an amount equal to 30% of the cash equity they provide to eligible Maine businesses.

* Maine International Trade Center
Perry Newman, Trade Director
Maine International Trade Center
511 Congress Street   207-541-7400
Portland, ME 04101   Fax: 207-541-7420
Email: newman@ mitc.com
www.mitc.com

Maine offers businesses and organizations international assistance through the Maine International Trade Center. The Trade Center's mission is to expand Maine's economy through increased international trade in goods and services and related activities such as:

- Trade missions
- Training programs in international trade
- Conferences, such as a major Trade Day event
- Publications, including the Trade Center newsletter
- Special member-only programs and one-on-one counseling and technical service assistance
- Comprehensive international library resources

* Finance Authority of Maine (FAME)
David Markovchick, Director of Business Development
5 Community Dr.   800-228-3734
P.O. Box 949   207-623-3263
Augusta, ME 04332-0949   Fax: 207-623-0095
www.famemaine.com

Commercial Loan Insurance Program: Designed to promote economic development by providing business borrowers access to capital that would otherwise be denied by lender due to unacceptable level of credit risk. Must be exhibit responsible ability to repay loan. Insures up to 90 percent or $7,000,000 of a commercial loan. Loan proceeds may be used for purchase of, and improvements to real estate, and machinery and equipment.

SMART-E Bond Program: Tax-exempt, fixed-asset financing for manufacturing facilities. SMART-E will finance up to 90 percent of a loan by grouping it with other similar loans and selling tax-exempt bonds to finance them. Maximum loan is $7 million. Assets that can be financed with loan proceeds include land and depreciable assets.

Potato Marketing Improvement Fund: Provides direct loans to potato growers and packers to construct modern storages, packing lines, and sprout inhibitor facilities. Long-term, fixed-rate loans at below market interest rates are available to help finance construction or improvements to storage and packing facilities. Participating loans can finance between 45 and 55 percent of the costs of eligible construction and improvements.

Linked Investment Program for Agriculture and Small Business: State funds are invested in financial institutions which then lend out funds at reduced interest rates to Maine farmers and small business people.

Occupational Safety Loan Fund Program: Targeted direct loans to Maine businesses seeking to make workplace safety improvements. A business may borrow up to $50,000 for up to 10 years. Interest rate is 3 percent fixed. Funds can be used to purchase, improve, or erect equipment which reduces workplace hazards or promotes health and safety of employees.

Export Financing Services:
- *Working Capital Insurance* provides additional security to bankers.
- *Export Credit Umbrella Insurance* reduces international credit risks, allows an exporter to offer credit terms to foreign buyers in a competitive market, and offers the opportunity to obtain current cash flow against foreign receivables. Provided by the Export-Import bank of the United States (Eximbank).
- Either the Finance Authority of Maine (FAME) or Eximbank is responsible for up to 100 percent of a loan made by a financial institution to the exporter.

Underground Oil Storage Tank Removal and Replacement Program: Provides 100% loan insurance to lenders, or direct loans to business borrowers, for the removal, replacement and disposal of underground tanks for oil, petroleum products or petroleum by-products. Loans must be used for the removal, replacement and/or disposal of storage tanks for oil, petroleum products or petroleum by-products, or for installation of air quality equipment required by state law.

Economic Recovery Loan Program: Direct lending program designed to assist small businesses in their effort to remain viable during difficult economic times. The program is available to assist both existing firms and new business ventures. Borrower requests should be the minimum amount necessary to complete the project under consideration, not to exceed $200,000.

Overboard Discharge Replacement Program: Provides 100% loan insurance to lenders on loans made for the removal, rehabilitation or replacement of certain wastewater disposal systems which result in discharges into fresh or salt water. Maximum insured loan under this program is $1,000,000. Interest rates and loan terms are negotiated between the borrower and lender. Loan term may not exceed 10 years.

Major Business Expansion Program: Provides taxable bond financing of up to $25,000,000 for major industrial or commercial projects.

Waste Reduction and Recycling Loan Program: The Authority will sometimes request that businesses intending to finance projects designed to reduce and recycle waste submit proposals for loans of up to $100,000.

Revenue Obligation Securities Program: FAME is authorized to issue tax-exempt Industrial Revenue Bonds to finance any project authorized under the U.S. Internal Revenue Code, Section 103, including manufacturing facilities, solid waste projects and loans for non-profit corporations. Proceeds may be used for land, buildings, machinery and equipment, financing and interest charges, engineering, legal services, surveys, cost estimates and studies. Offers low financing rates.

Adaptive Equipment Loan Program: Provides low interest loans to assist disabled persons in becoming more productive member of the community. Businesses may also borrow to make their facilities more accessible to physically challenged individuals. May also be used to enable a business to make physical and structural changes necessary to allow a business to hire disabled workers.

The Agricultural Marketing Loan Program will help natural resource based industries by providing a source of subordinated debt for eligible projects and borrowers. The maximum loan size under this program is $250,000. To be eligible for assistance, projects requesting financing must incorporate new or innovative technology and methodology. For example, it is

anticipated that this new loan program will prove helpful to Maine's fledgling cranberry industry and Maine's aquaculture industry.

Maine Seed Capital Tax Credit Program: In order to encourage equity investments in young, dynamic business ventures the Authority may authorize State income tax credits to investors in an amount equal to 30% of the cash equity they provide to certain Maine businesses.

Nutrient Management Program: Eligible Applicant: Any business or individual identified by the State of Maine Department of Agriculture, Food & Rural Resources ("Agriculture") as required by law to upgrade manure and milk room waste containment and handling facilities. Eligible Uses: Proceeds may be used to finance the construction or improvement of livestock manure and milk room waste containment and handling facilities, the associated costs of design and engineering of these facilities, as well as, related equipment that meets the goals of the State's Nutrient Management Plan.

The Plus 1 Computer Loan Program provides lenders with loan insurance on an expedited basis for small business loans for acquisition and installation of computer equipment and software. Since lenders certify that a loan meets specific credit criteria at the time of application and since FAME does not independently underwrite each loan application, all loans meeting the program's credit criteria are promptly approved (within 48 hours). Loans not meeting the credit criteria for the Business Computer Loan Rapid Response Guarantee may be submitted under FAME's Small Business Loan Insurance Program.

Rapid Response Guarantee Program: The Finance Authority of Maine's Rapid Response Guarantee provides lenders with loan insurance on an expedited basis for small business loans meeting certain minimum credit standards. Since lenders certify that a loan meets specific credit criteria at the time of application and since FAME does not independently underwrite each loan application, all loans meeting the program's credit criteria are promptly approved (within 48 hours). Loans not meeting the credit criteria for the Rapid Response Guarantee may be submitted under FAME's Small Business Loan Insurance Program.

On August 2, 1999, FAME established a Secondary Market for the FAME insured portion of bank loans.

The Small Enterprise Growth Fund was created to provide Maine entrepreneurs with access to "patient" sources of venture capital. Venture capital is typically difficult for Maine small businesses and entrepreneurs to access. This is especially true for smaller projects needing $500,000 or less. Established venture capital firms usually don't invest in increments of less than $500,000.

Waste Oil Furnace Loan Program: an interest rate subsidy to approved lenders who make loans to borrowers to purchase and install an improved waste oil boiler or furnace. Loans may be for up to $5,000 for a term of up to five (5) years. The loan may provide for an interest rate of up to thirteen percent (13%) per annum. The borrower is required to pay an effective interest rate of three percent (3%) per annum on the loan. The Authority will provide a subsidy in an amount which, when invested by the approved lender at an assumed annual return of six percent (6) per annum, will provide the lender with an overall rate of return of thirteen percent (13%).

SMART Bond Program: The Secondary Market Taxable (SMART) Bond Program is similar to the SMART-E Bond Program. It is available (with some exceptions) to those businesses that are not eligible for tax-exempt financing. The process begins when a lending institution provides a business with a loan commitment for acquisition of real estate, equipment or other fixed assets. After reviewing the credit application, FAME may commit to insuring up to 90% of the loan. FAME then helps to place the loan with investors who agree to purchase the insured portion of the loan.

Clean Fuel Vehicle Guarantee: This program provides lenders with loan insurance on loans to businesses for the acquisition or lease of clean fuel vehicles, delivery systems or other clean fuel vehicle components. Funds may be used to cover purchase or lease-related costs.

Dairy Farm Debt Relief Loan Insurance Program: Provides lenders with loan insurance for existing small business loans meeting certain minimum credit standards. The Dairy Farm Debt Relief Program offers up to a 25% leveraged loan insurance. The maximum aggregate insurance is $70,000 per borrower.

Katahdin Loan Insurance Program: Katahdin Loan Insurance Program provides lenders with loan insurance for existing small business loans meeting certain minimum credit standards. The program offers up to a 25% leveraged loan insurance. The maximum aggregate insurance is $50,000 per borrower.

Small Business and Veterans' Small Business Loan Insurance Program: Loan insurance is available for any prudent business activity. This 90% prorata or 25% leveraged insurance program is designed to help businesses gain access to commercial credit financing.

Development Fund: This program is designed to provide subordinated financing to businesses. Funds may be used for any prudent business activity that provides a public benefit, including jobs. 5% fixed interest rates for the life of the loan for 40% of project costs up to a maximum loan amount of $200,000.

Energy Conservation Loan Program: This program provides low-interest loans to improve energy efficiency in Maine workplaces.

Intermediary Relending Program: This program is designed to assist qualifying small businesses by providing gap financing for any prudent business activity.

Linked Investments for Commercial Enterprises: The purpose of this program is to reduce borrower's interest expenses.

Regional Economic Development Revolving Loan Program: The Regional Economic Development Revolving Loan program is designed to make loans through Regional Economic Development Agencies for the purpose of creating or retaining jobs. Qualifying businesses must have sales under $5,000,000 or employ fewer than 50 employees.

Regional Economic Development Revolving Loan Program for Daycare: Loans for up to $100,000 for qualifying daycares for physical improvements.

* Department of Agriculture
Food & Rural Resources
Nutrient Management Program Coordinator
State House Station 28
Augusta, ME 04333　　　　　207-287-3871
www.state.me.us/agriculture

Eligible Applicant: Any business or individual identified by the State of Maine Department of Agriculture, Food & Rural Resources ("Agriculture") as required by law to upgrade manure and milk room waste containment and handling facilities. Eligible Uses: Proceeds may be used to finance the construction or improvement of livestock manure and milk room waste containment and handling facilities, the associated costs of design and engineering of these facilities, as well as, related equipment that meets the goals of the State's Nutrient Management Plan.

* Maine & Company
P.O. Box 7462
120 Exchange Street　　　　　800-871-3485
Portland, ME 04112-7462　　　Fax: 207-775-6716
www.maineco.org

The State offers several performance based incentives to help attract and retain growing companies. In addition to the statewide incentives outlined below, companies coming to Maine can also take advantage of significant local incentives that may include low priced land, low lease rates, tax increment financing, municipal bond financing, and reimbursement for most personal property tax paid on new machinery and equipment.

Workforce Training: Maine has some of the best training programs in the country. The Maine Quality Centers program provides 100% state-financed education and training for new employees, as well as customized recruitment and guaranteed, fast-track training designed to employer specifications. The Governor's Training Initiative (GTI) offers employers partial reimbursement of training costs for new employees or upgrading existing work force skills.

Property Tax Reimbursement: Companies can be reimbursed for taxes on new machinery and equipment. Through the Business Property Tax Reimbursement program, the state may reimburse a company for as many as 12 years. In addition, companies may be eligible for real and property tax reimbursements from communities through tax increment financing.

Maine Income Tax Reimbursements: Companies hiring 5 or more people can receive as much as 75 percent reimbursement on Maine income tax withholdings from new employees. Those employers who provide benefits and pay above average wages are likely to qualify for this program, known as Employment Tax Increment Financing (ETIF).

Tax Increment Financing: Businesses making significant capital investment in a community may be eligible for partial property tax refunds from the municipality.

Sales Tax Exemptions: Maine sales tax exemptions are available for manufacturing, research and development, custom computer programming and biotechnology.

Investment Tax Credit: Employers can save as much as $500,000 per year for seven years by investing $5 million in personal property and creating at least 100 new jobs. Tax credits apply toward Maine income tax.

Small Enterprise Growth Fund: This venture capital fund provides financing for potential high growth companies with fewer than 50 employees or gross sales of less than $5 million within the past 12 months.

* Small Business Administration (SBA)
Edmund S. Muskie Building
68 Sewall St., Room 512　　　207-622-8274
Augusta, ME 04330　　　　　Fax: 207-622-8277
www.sba.gov/me

Trade Missions: The SBA participates by underwriting private firms and assisting them to enter trade missions with other Federal Agencies. SBA promotes and assists in cost share monies to a limited degree. Trade Shows have been sponsored in Europe, Asia, Mid East, Africa and North America.

The Maine Small Business Administration Office delivers a variety of programs and services, such as startup and operational assistance through small business training and counseling, financial assistance for startup's, business opportunities and much more.

* Small Business Investment Companies
North Atlantic Venture Fund II, LP
David M. Coit, Manager
2 City Center, 5th Floor.　　　207-772-1001
Portland, ME 04101　　　　　Fax: 207-772-3257
Email: kniles@northatlanticcapital.com

The SBA licenses, regulates, and provides financial assistance to privately owned and operated Small Business Investment Companies. SBICs make venture or risk investments by supplying capital and extending unsecured loans and loans not fully collateralized to small enterprises which meet their investment criteria. Financing is made by direct loans and by equity investments.

* Certified Development Companies (CDC)
Androscoggin Valley Council of Governments
Robert J. Thompson
125 Manley Road　　　　　207-783-9186
Auburn ME 04210　　　　　Fax: 207-783-5211
Area of Operation: Androscoggin, Franklin and Oxford Counties

Coastal Enterprises, Inc.
Ronald L. Phillips, President
Water Street
P.O. Box 268　　　　　　207-882-7552
Wiscasset ME 04578　　　　Fax: 207-882-7308
Area of Operation: Cumberland, Knox, Lincoln, Sagadahoc and York Counties

Eastern Maine Development Corporation
Victoria Lundgren, Loan Officer
One Cumberland Place, Suite 300
P.O. Box 2579　　　　　　207-942-6389
Bangor ME 04401　　　　　Fax: 207-942-3548
Area of Operation: Hancock, Kennebec, Knox, Penobscot, Piscataquis, Somerset, Waldo and Washington Counties

Certified Development Companies (CDCs) are SBA certified and intended to assist communities, both urban and rural, by stimulating the growth and expansion of small businesses primarily through financial assistance. Financial assistance may be provided through the Development Company loan programs.

* Maine Technology Institute
2E Mechanic Street　　　　　207-582-4790
Gardiner, ME 04345　　　　　Fax: 207-582-4772
www.mainetechnology.org

Marine Infrastructure and Technology Fund: The Marine Infrastructure and Technology Fund provides up to $1,000,000 to private non-profit companies and state agencies that are engaged in marine research.

Marine Biomedical Research Fund: The fund provides grants for capital and expenses for eligible non-profit biomedical research labs in the state of Maine.

Seed Grant Program: 1:1 matching grants of up to $10,000 are available to support very early stages of product development, commercialization or business planning and development.

Development Awards: 1:1 matching awards of up to $500,000 are available to support research and development of new products or services in Maine's targeted technology regions.

Cluster Enhancement Awards: 1:1 matching awards of up to $500,000 per project to help stimulate and support the formation and growth of eligible technology businesses.

Renewable Resource Matching Funds Award Program (RRMF): Investments of up to $50,000 per project to match funding for approved Cluster Enhancement Awards.

Maryland

* Department of Business and Economic Development

217 East Redwood St.
Baltimore, MD 21202
www.mdbusiness.state.md.us

410-767-6300
888-CHOOSE MD
Fax: 410-333-6792
TDD/TTY: 410-333-6926

This office can provide information and expertise in dealing with state, federal, and local agencies. They also have information on financing programs and other services offered by the state government.

Workforce Resources: Maryland offers several training and grants for training programs to meet a variety of workforce needs. The following are two of their many programs:
1. Maryland Job Service: Provides recruitment and screening services based on the specifications of a company at no costs. It maintains a state/ nationwide data bank of job seekers and acts as the state's labor exchange agent to match qualified workers with available employment opportunities.
2. Partnership for Workforce Quality: Targets training grants to manufacturing firms with 500 or fewer employees to upgrade skills for new technologies.

Industrial Training Program: Provides incentive grants for the development and training of new employees in firms locating or expanding their workforce in Maryland. MITP reimburses companies for up to 100% of the direct costs associated with training programs customized to the work process.

Technology Support: Helps companies diversify into new markets. In addition, the office: provides technical assistance to firms seeking to commercialize new technologies; facilitates collaboration between businesses and universities and federal laboratories; and oversees the Strategic Assistance Fund, which provides matching funds to support the cost of private sector consultants to aid in both strategic plan development and new market strategies.

Investment Financing Programs: Provide for direct investment in technology-driven Maryland-based companies through three programs. All three provide a novel alternative to grants, direct loans or credit enhancements available through other State financing programs. All three involve the use of private sector capital, including venture capital, on a co-investment basis, and while having an underlying economic development agenda, are capital gains and return-on-investment driven.

Enterprise Investment Fund: An investment financing tool that enables DBED to make direct equity investments in "second -stage" technology driven companies located in the state. Investments range from $150,000 to $250,000 per entity. Investment decisions are based on the potential for return on investment, as well as the promotion of broad-based economic development and job creation initiatives.

Day Care Special Loan Fund: Direct loans up to $10,000 for minor renovations and upgrades to meet standards.

Maryland Industrial Development Financing Authority (MIDFA): Available to industrial/commercial businesses except certain retail establishments. Normal project range is $35,000 to $5 million. Insured up to lower of 80% of loan or $1 million. The amount of insurance varies with each loan and is determined after discussing the lender's needs. Typically, MIDFA insures from 20% to 50% of the loan.

Seafood & Aquaculture Loan Fund: Available to individuals or businesses involved in seafood processing or aquaculture. Normal Project Range: $20,000 to $800,000. Maximum Program Participation: The lesser of $250,000 or 80% of the total investment needed.

Contract Financing Program: Eligible applicants are businesses owned 70% or more by socially and economically disadvantaged persons. Normal Project Range: Up to $500,000. Maximum Program Participation: Direct up to $500,000. Loan guarantee up to 90% not to exceed a maximum participation of $500,000. Approved Uses of Funds: Working capital required to begin, continue and complete government or public utility contracts. Acquisition of machinery or equipment to perform contracts. Interest Rates: For guaranteed loans, maximum rate is prime plus 2% . For direct loans, maximum is 15% .

Long Term Guaranty Program: Eligible applicants are businesses owned 70% or more by socially and economically disadvantaged persons. Must have 18 successive months of experience in the trade or business for which financing is sought. Normal Project Range: $50,000 to $1 million. Maximum Program Participation: Loan guarantees may not exceed the lesser of 80% of the loan or $600,000.

Surety Bond Program: Eligible applicants are independently owned small businesses generally employing fewer than 500 full-time employees or those with gross annual sales of less than $50 million. Normal Project Range: Guaranty Program - None. Direct Bonding Program - Up to $750,000. Maximum Program Participation: Guaranty Program - Guarantees up to 90% of face value of the bond not to exceed a total exposure of $900,000. Direct Bonding Program - Can directly issue bonds not to exceed $750,000. Approved Uses of Funds: Guaranty Program - Guarantees reimbursement of losses on a bid, payment or performance bond required in connection with projects where the majority of funds are from government or a regulated public utility. Direct Bonding Program - Issues bid, payment or performance bonds on projects where the majority of funds are from government or a regulated public utility.

Equity Participation Investment Program - Technology Component & Business Acquisition Component: Eligible applicants are technology based businesses and business acquisitions which will be owned 70% or more by disabled, socially or economically disadvantaged persons. Normal Project Range: $100,000 to $3 million. Maximum Program Participation: The lesser of $250,000 or 80% of the total investment needed.

Equity Participation Investment Program - Franchise Component: Eligible applicants are franchises that are or will be owned 70% or more by disabled, socially or economically disadvantaged persons. Must have at least 10% of total project cost in owner's equity. Normal Project Range: $50,000 to $1.5 million. Maximum Program Participation: Equity investments or loans up to 45% of initial investment or $100,000, whichever is less.

Challenge Investment Program: Eligible applicants are technology-driven companies, with principal activity located in Maryland; applicants must have complete business plan as a minimum requirement. Size of Investment: $50,000.

Enterprise Investment Program: Eligible applicants are technology-driven companies, with principal activity located in Maryland; applicants must have complete business plan as a minimum requirement. Size of Investment: $150,000 to $500,000.

Foreign Offices & Representatives: Network of foreign offices and representatives provide exporters with in-country resources and expertise around the globe. These foreign offices in China, Japan, the Netherlands and Taiwan -- and representatives in Argentina, Brazil, Chile, Israel and Mexico -- deliver support in the following areas: agent/distributor searches and business appointments; credit reports, competitor analysis and regulatory information, marketing and logistical support at trade shows; market research and analysis.

Day Care Facilities Guarantee Fund: Eligible applicants are individuals or business entities involved in the development or expansion of day care facilities for infants and children, the elderly, and disabled persons of all ages. Normal Project Range: Up to $1 million. Maximum Program Participation: Loan guarantee up to 80%.

Child Care Facilities Direct Loan Fund: Eligible applicants are individuals, business entities involved in the development of day care facilities for children, either center-based or home-based. Normal Project Range: Minimum $15,000. Maximum Program Participation: Maximum of 50% of fixed assets.

Child Care Special Loan Fund: Eligible applicants are individuals, business entities for expanding or improving child care facilities, meeting state and local licensing requirements and improving the quality of care. Normal Project Range: $1,000 to $10,000. Maximum Program Participation: Direct loans up to $10,000.

Governor's Office of Business Advocacy and Small Business Assistance (GOBA): GOBA helps in the development and growth of small businesses in the state. Small and minority businesses are connected to needed resources, provide information, and offered assistance from permits and licensing to the creation of a business plan. 410-767-0545

Business License Information System (BLIS): This online system quickly connects a business to information on permits and licenses that are needed to start, relocate or expand in Maryland. Instant information on business licenses, occupation licenses, permitting information and business start-up information is also available.

Maryland With Pride: Companies whose products are grown, processed, assembled, manufactured or handcrafted in Maryland can benefit from this program. Those businesses can register to use the Maryland With Pride trademark on product packaging, advertising, web sites, stationery, vehicles and buildings. They are also given exclusive marketing opportunities. 410-767-6519

Department of General Services Small Business Preference Program: With this program, small businesses are able to receive part of the State's total purchases of equipment, materials and supplies. Those businesses that are certified with the program may be eligible to receive a 5% award preference on designated solicitations. 410-767-4621

Smart Growth Economic Development Infrastructure Fund (One Maryland): The fund provides a financial resource in cases where the need to develop industrial sites is not fully met by the private sector. Loans are made to counties or municipalities at below market interest rates and are secured by the full faith and credit of the borrowing government. Loans may be used for the acquisition of land, development of industrial parks, improvements to infrastructure of potential industrial sites, installation of utilities, and the rehabilitation of existing buildings for business incubators. The sites must be in a Priority Funding Area.

Sunny Day Fund: Created to allow the State to take advantage of extraordinary economic development opportunities where assistance from other resources are constrained by program design, timing, or available resources. The fund has been an extremely valuable tool in both business retention and recruiting. Maryland has taken advantage of opportunities with rapid and creative proposals that have assisted in the establishment of several high-profile private sector enterprises, including prized technology and research companies. The project must create employment, especially in those areas of high unemployment. The participants must provide a minimum capital investment of at least five times the amount of the Sunny Day assistance.

Maryland Economic Development Assistance Authority and Fund: This incentive program offers five financing means where the assistance goes to the business community and political jurisdictions. The applicants are restricted to businesses located in a specified area and an industry sector. Assistance cannot generally exceed 70% of the total project costs. If the recipient is a Maryland Economic Corporation (MEDCO), they can receive 100% financing. The funding programs are:

- *Significant Strategic Economic Development Opportunities:* This project provides eligible industries with a significant economic development opportunity on a statewide or regional level. Assistance is provided to a business through a loan where the maximum amount cannot exceed the lesser of $10 million or 20% of the current fund balance.
- *Local Economic Development Opportunity:* Designed for businesses that provide valuable economic development opportunities to the jurisdiction in which it is located and is a priority for the governing body in that area. Loans are for up to $5 million; conditional loans and grants may be up to $2 million. The business must be sponsored by the local jurisdiction and must participate by way of guarantee or a direct loan or a grant equal to 10% of the State's assistance.
- *Direct Assistance to Jurisdiction or MEDCO:* Financial assistance to local jurisdictions for local economic development needs.
- *Regional or Local Revolving Loan Fund:* Grants to local jurisdictions to help capitalize local revolving loan funds.
- *Special Purposes Loans:* Specified funding initiatives that are deemed critical to the States' economic health and development. The special purpose initiatives include: Seafood and Aquaculture, Animal Waste, and Day Care Center programs. 407-767-6353

Strategic Assistance Fund: SAF was originally a grant, which offered assistance to businesses with defense conversion and helped dislocated defense entrepreneurs. SAF is now a state funded program offering businesses marketing assistance with new products, product diversification, new markets, or market expansion. Projects may include defense diversification opportunities, diversification of commercial products into related markets, commercialization of new technologies, expansion into international markets and more. Awards range from $5,000 to $25,000 and can be made to individual businesses or groups. 410-767-0095

Maryland Community Colleges' Business Training Network (MCCBTN): Maryland Community College's Business Training Network is a one-stop for businesses interested in workforce training. {www.marylandtraining.com}

The Maryland Industrial Training Program (MITP): The Industrial training Program works with other state and local agencies to assist in the recruitment, assessment and placement of new employees with participating companies.

Maryland Economic Adjustment Fund (MEAF): The Economic Adjustment Fund assists businesses in the State with the modernization of manufacturing operations, the development of commercial applications for technology and exploring and entering new markets.

* Neighborhood Business Development Program (NBDP)

Maryland Department of Housing and Community Development
Neighborhood Business Development Program
100 Community Place   410-514-7288
Crownsville, MD 21032   Fax: 410-685-8270
www.dhcd.state.md.us

Initiative to help stimulate Maryland's established, older communities, NBDP provides flexible, gap financing (up to 50% of total project cost) for many small businesses starting up or expanding in targeted urban, suburban or rural revitalization areas throughout the State. Terms and conditions are established on an individual basis. Financing ranging from $25,000 to $500,000, up to 50% of total project cost, where other funds clearly are unavailable.

* Development Credit Fund, Inc.

2530 N. Charles St.
Suite 200   410-467-7500
Baltimore, MD 21218-4627   Fax: 410-467-7988
www.developmentcredit.com

Development Credit Fund Program: Loan guarantees for businesses owned by socially and economically disadvantaged persons. Must show experience in the trade. Projects range from $5,000 to $575,000. Proceeds may be used for working capital, acquisition of machinery and equipment acquisition, and business acquisitions, business real estate. Interest rates are variable, none more than 2 percent over prime rate.

* Community Financing Group

Department of Business and Economic Development
Redwood Tower
217 East Redwood, 22nd Floor
Baltimore, MD 21202   410-767-6352
www.choosemaryland.org

Community Development Block Grant: Available to cities and counties for the commercial rehabilitation of existing buildings or structures used for business, commercial, or industrial purposes. Grants and loans of between $200,000 and $1 million can be made. Every $15,000 of grant funds invested must create at least one full-time job, and at least 51 percent of the jobs created must be for low- and moderate-income families.

* USDA/Rural Development

4607 South DuPont Highway
P.O. Box 400   302-697-4300
Camden, Delaware 19934   Fax: 302-697-4390
Email: Jack.Walls@de.usda.gov
www.rurdev.usda.gov/md

The Community & Business Programs Division consists of the Rural Utilities Service (RUS) and the Rural Business & Cooperative Service (RBS). RUS programs assist rural America in building infrastructure by providing loans and grants for water and wastewater disposal systems, solid waste disposal systems, storm drainage systems and advanced telecommunications. RBS programs help provide financial as well as technical assistance to businesses, non-profit organizations, educational institutions and cooperatives. The financial assistance is provided in the form of loans, guaranteed loans and grants. It is the intent of the RBS to enhance the quality of life for rural Americans by providing leadership in building competitive businesses and cooperatives.

* Tri-County Council for Western Maryland, Inc.

113 Baltimore St., Suite 302   301-777-2159
Cumberland, MD 21502   Fax: 301-777-2495
www.tccwmd.org

The Tri-County Council Revolving Loan Fund (TCC-RLF) will stimulate and support the development of small to mid-sized businesses in order to diversify the economy and maintain and expand employment opportunities in the Western Maryland-Appalachian area. This will be achieved by providing low cost, flexible financing designed to fill gaps in the local capital market.

* The Dingman Center for Entrepreneurship

Robert H. Smith School of Business	
University of Maryland	
3570 Van Munching Hall	301-405-9545
College Park, MD 20742	Fax: 301-314-7973
Email: dingman@rhsmith.umd.edu	
http://dingman.rhsmith.umd.edu	

The Dingman Center for Entrepreneurship facilitates, supports, and encourages entrepreneurship and new enterprise growth in the mid-Atlantic region through outreach, education and research.

* Technology Advancement Program (TAP)

Engineering Research Center	
University of Maryland	
1105 TAP Building	
387 Technology Drive	301-314-7803
College Park, MD 20742	Fax: 301-226-5378
www.tap.umd.edu	

Incubator facilities offer space and support services for start up and growing companies. By offering companies a supportive environment, the incubator allows a company to reduce start-up obligations while concentrating its limited resources on product development and bringing its product to the marketplace. Incubators are often best suited for businesses engaged in developing technically-oriented products with commercial potential.

* Maryland Department of the Environment

1800 Washington Blvd.	800-633-6101
Baltimore, MD 21230	410-537-3000
www.mde.state.md.us	

The Environmental Permits Service Center, EPSC, which was established in 1994, is a service arm of the Department designed to provide assistance to businesses. The primary responsibility of the EPSC is to track permit applications and streamline the Department's review of permit applications. The EPSC staff work in a multimedia fashion to assist businesses who need environmental permits for a combination of air, water, and waste issues.

The department's Small Business Assistance Program is here to help your small business with environmental permitting and compliance. This free assistance is available to any small business, which means practically any independently owned and operated business with less than 100 employees is eligible. The small business assistance program can help with:
- Understanding environmental requirements
- Getting the proper forms
- Filling out permit applications
- Filling out compliance forms

The Pollution Prevention Program provides information to businesses on how to eliminate potential pollution at the source, which often results in saving businesses money.

* Certified Development Companies

Chesapeake Business Finance Corporation	
John Sower, President	
4606 Wedgewood Boulevard	301-668-1844
Frederick, MD 21603	Fax: 301-668-1845

Area of Operation: Garrett, Allegany, Charles, Talbot, Dorchester, Cecil, St. Mary's, Washington, Montgomery, Wicomico, Prince George, Carroll, Frederick, Baltimore Counties and the City of Baltimore.

Mid-Atlantic Certified Development Company	
Paula Klepper, President	
1410 N. Crain Highway	
Suite 5B	
Glen Burnie, MD 21061	410-863-1600
www.mabfc.com	Fax: 410-863-7446

Area of Operation: Statewide

Prince George's County Financial Services Corporation	
1400 McCormick Drive, Suite 240	301-883-6900
Largo, MD 20774	Fax: 301-883-6160
www.pgfsc.com	

Area of Operation: Prince George's County

The 504 Certified Development Company (CDC) Program provides growing businesses with long-term, fixed-rate financing for major fixed assets, such as land and buildings. A Certified Development Company is a nonprofit corporation set up to contribute to the economic development of its community or region. CDCs work with the SBA and private-sector lenders to provide financing to small businesses.

* Small Business Administration

City Crescent Bldg., 6th Floor	
10 S. Howard St.	410-962-4392
Baltimore, MD 21201	Fax: 410-962-1805
www.sba.gov/md	

The Maryland Small Business Administration Office delivers a variety of programs and services, such as startup and operational assistance through small business training and counseling, financial assistance for startup's, business opportunities and much more.

* Small Business Investment Companies

Allegiance Capital, L.P.	
Gary Dorsch	
2000 West 41st Street	410-338-6314
Baltimore, MD 21211	Fax: 410-662-6816
Email: gdorsch@allcapital.com	

Anthem Capital, LP	
William M. Gust, II, Manager	
16 South Calvert St.	
Suite 800	410-625-1510
Baltimore, MD 21202	Fax: 410-625-1735
Email: espiva@anthemcapital.com	

Legg Mason SBIC Mezzanine Fund, L.P.	
Andrew L. John, Contact	
100 Light Street	410-454-4400
Baltimore, MD 21202	Fax: 410-454-4344
Email: aljohn@leggmason.com	

MMG Ventures, L.P.	
Stanley W. Tucker, Manager	
826 E. Baltimore Street	410-659-7851
Baltimore, MD 21202	Fax: 410-333-2552
Email: cathy.lockhart@mmggroup.com	

Patriot Capital, L.P.	
Chris M. Royston, Contact	
16 West Madison Street	443-573-3010
Baltimore, MD 21201	Fax: 443-573-3020
Email: croyston@patriot-capital.com	

Security Financial and Investment Corp.	
Jim Bonfils, Manager	
7720 Wisconsin Ave.	
Suite 207	301-951-4288
Bethesda, MD 20814	Fax: 301-951-9282
Email: JamesBonfils@aol.com	

Spring Capital Partners, L.P.	
Jay M. Wilson, General Partner	
The Latrobe Building	
2 East Read St.	410-685-8000
Baltimore, MD 21202	Fax: 410-545-0015
Email: mailbox@springcap.com	

Toucan Capital Fund II, L.P.	
Linda Powers	
7600 Wisconsin Avenue, 7th Floor	240-497-4060
Bethesda, MD 20814	Fax: 240-497-4065
Email: info@toucancapital.com	

Walker Investment Fund II SBIC, L.P.	
Gina Dubbe, Contact	
3060 Washington Road, Suite 200	301-854-6850
Glenwood, MD 21738	Fax: 301-854-6235
Email: gina@walkerventures.com	

The SBA licenses, regulates, and provides financial assistance to privately owned and operated Small Business Investment Companies. SBICs make venture or risk investments by supplying capital and extending unsecured loans and loans not fully collateralized to small enterprises which meet their investment criteria. Financing is made by direct loans and by equity investments.

* Governor's Office of Minority Affairs

6 Saint Paul Street, Suite 1502   410-767-8232
Baltimore, MD 21202   Fax: 410-333-7568
www.oma.state.md.us

Massachusetts

* Massachusetts Office of Business Development

10 Park Plaza, 3rd Floor   617-973-8600
Boston, MA 02116   800-5-CAPITAL
www.state.ma.us/mobd   Fax: 617-973-8797

Through five regional offices, they will advise and counsel businesses and individuals in utilizing federal, state, and local finance programs established to help businesses with their capital formation needs.

One-Stop Business Centers: Offers a streamlined approach to economic development assistance. Offices located throughout the state are staffed with professionals who know about Massachusetts' programs and opportunities for businesses throughout the state's diverse regions.

Economic Development Incentive Program (EDIP): To stimulate economic development in distressed areas, attract new businesses, and encourage existing businesses to expand in Massachusetts.

Business Finance Specialists: Assists companies with financing targeted to urban and economically disadvantaged areas through the Community Development Finance Corporation and other public funds.

One-Stop Permitting Program: For all construction-related, state-issued permits. Project Managers act as advocates, assisting with identifying all required permits and moving the application through the entire process.

Starting a Business in Massachusetts: A comprehensive guide for business owners available from MOBD.

The Emerging Technology Fund (ETF): A useful tool for economic growth for technology based companies. Targeting the fields of biotechnology, advanced materials, electronics, medical, telecommunications and environmental technologies, the fund provides companies in these industries with a greater opportunity to obtain debt financing. Loans can be guaranteed for tenant build-out, construction or expansion of facilities and equipment purchased for up to $1.5 million or 50% of the aggregate debt, whichever is less. Loans are also provided for hard asset-owned facilities and equipment, with a maximum amount of $2.5 million or 33 1/3% of the aggregate debt, whichever is less.

State Office of Minority and Women Business Assistance (SOMWBA): Certifies companies as minority or women-owned or controlled, and publishes a directory listing of verified firms. SOMWBA provides management and technical assistance seminars and workshops for minority and women entrepreneurs on a wide variety of business topics.

Minority Business Financing: A MOBD Business Finance Specialist can guide a company to several targeted financing programs including the Community Development Finance Corporation's Urban Initiative Fund, the Economic Development Fund and others.

* Rural Development Administration

USDA Rural Development in Southern New England
451 West Street, Suite 2   413-253-4300
Amherst, MA 01002-2999   Fax: 413-253-4347
www.rurdev.usda.gov/ma

Business Development Programs
This type of assistance is available in rural areas which are outside the boundary of a city or town of 50,000 or more inhabitants and its immediately adjacent urbanized area.

Business and Industry Loans (B&I): Loans are made to improve, develop or finance business, industry and employment and improve the economic and environmental climate in rural communities, including pollution abatement and control. The objective is achieved principally through bolstering a loan made by a private lender with guarantees by the federal government. Direct loans are also available on a limited basis. The funds may be used for real estate purchase or improvement, equipment or capital.

Rural Business Enterprise Grants (RBEG): Grants are made to assist public bodies and non-profit corporations to finance and facilitate development of small and emerging private business enterprises. Small and emerging businesses have 50 or less employees and less than $1.0 million in gross revenues. Grants are primarily to be used by eligible non-profits or public entities to provide technical assistance or establish a revolving loan fund. Revolving loan funds can provide micro-loans to small business which may be for the purchase of land, construction of facilities, and other business purposes.

Intermediary Relending Program Loans (IRP): Loans are made to eligible intermediaries (non-profit or public entities) who in turn provide loans to ultimate recipients for business facilities and community development in a rural area. The interest rate on the loan to the intermediary is one percent with a term of up to 30 years. Eligible applicants must have a record of successfully assisting rural businesses, including experience in making and servicing commercial loans.

* Massachusetts Site Finder Service

Massachusetts Alliance for Economic Development
25 Research Drive   617-247-7800
Westborough, MA 01582   Fax: 617-247-3337
www.massecon.com

Offers confidential, statewide searches for industrial land or buildings to fit defined specifications for expanding businesses. MOBD can also provide up-to-date Community Profiles of communities being considered as a business location. Information provided includes the local tax structure, local permitting requirements, and a demographic profile of area residents.

* Massachusetts Export Center

Massachusetts Export Center
State Transportation Building
10 Park Plaza, Suite 4510   617-973-8664
Boston, MA 02116   Fax: 617-973-8681
www.state.ma.us/export

The Massachusetts Export Center is part of the Massachusetts Small Business Development Center Network (MSBDC). The Export Center operates four offices that are strategically located throughout the state to assist companies locally. The Export Center provides targeted, high-impact services for exporters including: Export Counseling and Technical Assistance, International Market Research and Assessment, International Business Development Assistance, Export Training Programs and Export Publications.

* Massachusetts Department of Food and Agriculture

251 Causeway Street, Suite 500   617-626-1700
Boston, MA 02114   Fax: 617-626-1850
www.state.ma.us/dfa

The Massachusetts Department of Agricultural Resources' mission is to support, promote and enhance the long-term viability of Massachusetts's agriculture. They offer a variety of Technical Assistance and Resource Programs including:

Agriculture Business Training Program: The Agriculture Business Training Program uses several training approaches to help farmers understand their financial situation, plan their operations, track performance and project the effects of anticipated changes. Chief among these is a 10-session, nationally recognized next-level training course for agricultural entrepreneurs entitled "Tilling The Soil of Opportunity".

Agricultural Marketing Grants Program: The Department's Agricultural Marketing Grant Program provides agricultural organizations the opportunity to receive matching grant funds to assist in their promotional efforts. Grants range from $500 to $15,000. All grant recipients are required to acknowledge the Department's support and/or use the "Massachusetts Grown...and Fresher!" or "Mass. Made with Pride" logos in order to receive grant funds. 617-626-1750

Agro-Environmental Technology Grant Program: The Agro Environmental Technology Grant Program is designed to address agriculturally related environmental concerns and agricultural development needs and opportunities. Through an annual request for proposals, the Department will consider projects which must have practical commercial application involving new or alternative technologies, practices or organizational arrangements which will stimulate expanded agricultural development, economic activity and employment growth.

Agricultural Environmental Enhancement Program: The program grants $150,000 a year to farmers to purchase materials to protect water quality from the potential impacts of agricultural practices. Eligible materials include fencing, culverts, seed and gutters. All interested farmers are encouraged to apply for the next round of this new grant program.

Farm Viability Program: This program is designed to improve the economic bottom line and environmental integrity of participating farms through the development and implementation of farm viability plans developed by teams of agricultural, economic and environmental consultants.

Agriculture Preservation Restriction Program (APR): The APR Program is a voluntary program which is intended to offer a non-development alternative to farmers who are faced with a decision regarding the future use of their farms. The program offers to pay farmers the difference between fair market value and the agriculture value of their land in exchange for a permanent deed restriction which precludes any use of the property that will have a negative impact on its agricultural viability.

Massachusetts Aquaculture Grants Program (MAG): The MAG program encourages environmentally responsible aquaculture projects that can demonstrate public and industry benefit through work that will: result in the development and implementation of new technologies, products, processes or services; reduce aquaculture industry operating costs thereby increasing business profitability; increase the productivity of Massachusetts aquatic cultivation endeavors; and preserve existing jobs and/or result in new employment opportunities for the Commonwealth of Massachusetts.

* Commonwealth Corporation

The Schrafft Center
529 Main Street, Suite 110   617-727-8158
Boston, MA 02129   Fax: 617-242-7660
www.commcorp.org

The Commonwealth Corporation provides services that promote workers, businesses, youth, educators and the entire workforce development system. The Commonwealth Corporation sponsors Entrepreneurial Training and Small Business Assistance Programs. The programs include all aspects of starting and operating a business. There are seminars on marketing research, marketing tools, strategic planning, financial management, sales techniques and much more. The Economic Stabilization Trust Program offers direct loans and guarantees for small and medium-sized manufactures on a $7,500 per employee basis, with a minimum of 12 employees. The financing helps these companies in the areas of modernization and competition in the global marketplace. Another service of the Trust is business consultation and financial guidance.

* MassDevelopment

75 Federal Street, 10th Floor
Boston, MA 02110   617-451-2477
www.massdevelopment.com

Mass Development: Their mission is to promote economic development and job creation that is done in partnership with government, communities, and businesses.
- *Real Estate Loans:* Loans up to $3 million can be used for facility acquisition, renovation, construction, or permanent financing.
- *Guarantees:* a portion of private real estate loans are secured thereby providing lenders incentive to extend credit.
- *Equipment loans:* Below-market-rate financing of $50,000 to $500,000 can be used for new equipment.
- *Brownsfield Redevelopment Fund:* Interest-free financing up to $50,000 is available for environmental site assessment.
- *Tech Dollars:* Non-profit organizations with annual revenues of $5 million or less can access 100% financing at below-prime rates for technology equipment purchases and installation.
- *Emerging Technology Fund:* Technology based companies can get loans and guarantees for facilities and specialized equipment.
- *Seafood Loans:* Fixed asset financing can be used to purchase land, building, and equipment for the construction or renovation of seafood-related facilities. Direct loans are also available for facility expansions.
- *Predevelopment Assistance:* Funds are available for early-state economic development projects in communities throughout Massachusetts. Matching fund range between $5,000 and $25,000.
- *Term Working Capital:* Small- and middle-market businesses get help through the replenishing of working capital shortfalls caused by adverse business conditions.
- *Turnaround Management Assistance:* This helps businesses restructure or reposition by funding the services of a turnaround management consultant. A maximum funding of $25,000 is available for the development and implementation of a plan.
- *Tax Exempt Bonds:* Provides very low interest rate financing for capital projects. The four groups eligible for this program are: 501(c)(3) nonprofits for real estate and equipment; exempt facilities for waste recovery and recycling facilities; manufacturers for facilities and equipment; and affordable housing developers for residential housing. All of these businesses must be eligible for tax-exempt financing under the federal tax code.
- *Tax-Exempt Equipment Lease/Purchase Program:* Financing of

$300,000 or more is available for manufacturers, nonprofits, and environmental enterprises for equipment needs.
- *Taxable Bonds:* Businesses have access to capital markets for industrial and commercial real estate projects.
- *Capital Financing 501:* Short-term, tax exempt commercial paper financing which can be borrowed and repaid as needed.

* Certified Development Companies

Bay Colony Development Corporation
David King, Managing Trustee
1601 Trapelo Road, Suite 222   781-891-3594
Waltham MA 02451   Fax: 781-647-4950
Area of Operation: Statewide- except Dukes and Nantucket Counties

Massachusetts Certified Development Corporation
Elizabeth C.Trifone, Vice President
50 Milk Street   617-350-8877
Boston MA 02109   Fax: 617-350-0052
Area of Operation: Statewide

North Central Massachusetts Certified Development Corporation
David McKeehan, President
110 Erdman Way   978-840-4300
Leominster MA 01453   Fax: 978-840-4896
Area of Operation: Cities and towns in the Northern Worcester County and the Western Middlesex County

South Eastern Economic Development Corporation
Maria Gooch, Executive Director
88 Broadway   508-822-1020
Taunton MA 02780   Fax: 508-880-7869
Area of Operation: Counties of Barnstable, Bristol, Dukes, Nantucket and Plymouth

South Shore Economic Development Corporation
Patricia Faiella
36 Miller Stile Road   617-479-1111
Quincy MA 02169   Fax: 617-479-9274
Area of Operation: Plymouth and Norfolk Counties

Worcester Business Development Corporation
William E. Purcell, Vice President
33 Waldo Street   508-753-2924
Worcester MA 01608   Fax: 508-754-8560
Area of Operation: Worcester County

The 504 Certified Development Company (CDC) Program provides growing businesses with long-term, fixed-rate financing for major fixed assets, such as land and buildings. A Certified Development Company is a nonprofit corporation set up to contribute to the economic development of its community or region. CDCs work with the SBA and private-sector lenders to provide financing to small businesses.

* Massachusetts Business Development Corporation

500 Edgewater Drive, Suite 555   781-928-1100
Wakefield, MA 01880   Fax: 781-928-1101
www.mass-business.com

Business Loans: Provides loans to firms which are unable to obtain financing through conventional sources. Loans may be used for purchase or construction of fixed business assets (land, plant, equipment) and for working capital. Can provide up to 100 percent of financing.

* Massachusetts Capital Resource Company

420 Boylston St.   617-536-3900
Boston, MA 02116   Fax: 617-536-7930
www.masscapital.com

Provides unsecured loans in the form of debt and equity financing to small and medium-sized firms that are unable to obtain financing through conventional sources. Maximum loan amount is $5 million.

* Division of Communities Development

Division of Community Services
Department of Housing and Community Development
100 Cambridge St., Suite 300
Boston, MA 02114   617-573-1100
www.state.ma.us/dhcd

Community Development Action Grant: Grants are made to cities and towns for public actions in support of private investments. Projects should create or retain long-term employment and/or housing opportunities and revitalize distressed areas.

Community Development Fund (CDF): CDF is designed to generate and/or retain jobs in small communities. The program provides flexible structured debt financing for businesses which provide, create or retain jobs for low to moderate income residents. CDF can fund up to one third of the total project cost and the loans can be used for purchase of equipment, acquisition of real estate, new construction or rehabilitation, working capital or refinancing.

Massachusetts Downtown Initiative: Seeks to revitalize and strengthen the business and community life or urban centers in cities and towns, while preserving the state's heritage of historic downtown buildings. Funds are offered on a sliding scale for professional staff and technical assistance to non-profit organizations working on downtown revitalization. Staff funding decreases over the life of the three year program, while technical assistance is focused on different issues each year.

Economic Development Industrial Corporations (EDIC): Enables cities and towns to undertake development projects that will generate jobs and stabilize communities. With EDIC, municipalities can designate economic development areas and shape plans for their development. EDICs have the authority to negotiate payments in-lieu of property taxes and may also issue bonds to finance the development of eligible projects, which very often include industrial parks.

* Small Business Administration (SBA)

Boston District Office
10 Causeway St.
2nd Floor, Room 265   617-565-5590
Boston, MA 02222-1093   Fax: 617-565-5598
www.sba.gov/ma

The Massachusetts Small Business Administration Office delivers a variety of programs and services, such as startup and operational assistance through small business training and counseling, financial assistance for startup's, business opportunities and much more.

* Small Business Investment Companies

Ascent Venture Partners II, L.P.
Frank Polestra, General Partner
255 State Street, 5th Floor   617-720-9400
Boston, MA 02109   Fax: 617-720-9401
Email: klittlejohn@ascentvp.com

Axxon Capital, L.P.
Paula E. Groves, Contact
28 State Street, 37th Floor   617-523-7778
Boston, MA 02109   Fax: 617-557-6014
Email: peg@axxoncapital.com

BancBoston Ventures, Inc.
Frederick M. Fritz, President
175 Federal St., 10th Floor   617-434-2442
Boston, MA 02110   Fax: 617-434-1153
Email: john_lamphier@fleet.com

Chestnut Street Partners, Inc.
David D. Croll, President
75 State St., Suite 2500   617-345-7220
Boston, MA 02109   Fax: 617-345-7201
Email: ebroadhurst@mcventurepartners.com

Citizens Ventures, Inc.
Robert Garrow & Gregory Mullligan, Mgrs.
28 State Street, 15th Floor   617-725-5635
Boston, MA 02109   Fax: 617-725-5630
Email: gmccarey@citizenscapital.com

Crescent Private Capital II, L.P.
Nancy S. Amer, Contact
One Copley Place, Suite 602   617-638-0051
Boston, MA 02116   Fax: 617-638-0090
Email: eden@crescentlp.com

Draper Fisher Jurvetson New England Fund I
Scott Johnson, Contact
One Broadway, 14th Floor   617-758-4213
Cambridge, MA 02142   Fax: 617-758-4101
Email: scott@dfjne.com

Gemini Investors III, L.P.
David F. Millet, Contact

20 William Street   781-237-7001
Wellesley, MA 02481   Fax: 781-237-7233
Email: mkeis@gemini-investors.com

Geneva Middle Market Investors, L.P.
James J. Goodman, Manager
20 William Street   781-237-7001
Wellesley, MA 02481   Fax: 781-237-7233
Email: bhardiman@gemini-investors.com

GMN Investors II, L.P.
James J. Goodman, Manager
20 William Street   781-237-7001
Wellesley, MA 02481   Fax: 781-237-7233
Email: bhardiman@gemini-investors.com

Lancet Capital Health Ventures, L.P.
William Golden, Manager
124 Mount Auburn Street
Suite 200N   617-330-9345
Cambridge, MA 02138   Fax: 617-330-9349
Email: golden@lancetcapital.com

Longworth Venture Partners II-A, L.P.
Paul A. Margolis, Contact
1050 Winter Street, Suite 2600   781-663-3600
Waltham, MA 02451   Fax: 781-663-3619
Email: margolis@longworth.com

Marathon Investment Partners, L.P.
Paul Bolger, Managing Director
100 Cummings Center, Suite 326-J   978-720-3520
Beverly, MA 01915   Fax: 978-998-6960
Email: sampson@marathoninvestment.com

New England Partners Capital, L.P.
Robert Hanks, Prin. & Todd Fitzpatrick
One Boston Place, Suite 2100   617-624-8400
Boston, MA 02108   Fax: 617-624-8416
Email: tfitzpatrick@nepartners.com

North Hill Ventures II, L.P.
Brett Rome, Contact
Ten Post Office Square, Suite 1100   617-788-2150
Boston, MA 02109   Fax: 617-788-2152
Email: brett.rome@capitalone.com

RockPort Capital Partners, L.P.
Bettina Metais, Contact
160 Federal Street, 18th Floor   617-912-1420
Boston, MA 02110   Fax: 617-912-1449
Email: bmetais@rockportcap.com

Seacoast Capital Partners, LP
Walt Leonard, Manager
55 Ferncroft Rd.   978-750-1310
Danvers, MA 01923   Fax: 978-750-1301
Email: wleon@seacoastcapital.com

Summer Street Capital Fund I, L.P.
Richard Steele
171 Dwight Rd., Suite 310   413-567-3366
Longmeadow, MA 01106   Fax: 413-567-6556

UST Capital Corp.
Robert E. Garrow, President & Director
28 State Street   617-725-5635
Boston, MA 02108   Fax: 617-725-5630
Email: GMcCarey @citizenscapital.com

Velocity Equity Partners I SBIC, L.P.
David Vogel, Contact
121 High Street   617-338-2545
Boston, MA 02110   Fax: 617-261-3864
Email: dvogel@velocityep.com

Venture Capital Fund of New England IV, L.P
Kevin J. Dougherty, Contact
30 Washington Street   781-431-8400
Wellesley Hills, MA 02481   Fax: 781-237-6578
Email: kdougherty@vcfne.com

Zero Stage Capital V, LP
Paul Kelley, Manager

Kendall Square
101 Main St., 17th Floor
Cambridge, MA 02142 617-876-5355
Email: bjohnson@zerostage.com Fax: 617-876-1248

Zero Stage Capital VI, L.P.
Paul Kelley, Gordon Baty, Stanley Fung
101 Main Street, 17th Floor
Cambridge, MA 02142 617-876-5355
Email: bjohnson@zerostage.com Fax: 617-876-1248

The SBA licenses, regulates, and provides financial assistance to privately owned and operated Small Business Investment Companies. SBICs make venture or risk investments by supplying capital and extending unsecured loans and loans not fully collateralized to small enterprises which meet their investment criteria. Financing is made by direct loans and by equity investments.

* The Massachusetts Workforce Training Fund

Division of Employment and Training
19 Staniford Street 800-252-1591
Boston, MA 02114 Fax: 617-727-8671
www.detma.org

Workforce Training Fund Express Program: This program is for businesses with 50 or fewer employees for 50% of training reimbursement. Total grant request cannot exceed $15,000.

Workforce Training Fund General Program: This program is designed for large and small businesses. Matching training grants are available from $2,000 up to $250,000 for training which will occur over a period not to exceed two years.

* Massachusetts Technology Development Corporation

40 Broad Street, Suite 818 617-723-4920
Boston, MA 02109 Fax: 617-723-5983
www.mtdc.com

Massachusetts Technology Development Corporation is a state-owned venture capital firm that offers assistance to Massachusetts's technology-based manufactures whose principal products or services are innovative enough to be competitive. They have made up to one-half million dollars available to qualifying companies. To receive the fund, the applicant company must show that it cannot secure conventional financing; that funding will produce a significant increase in employment; and that there is a prospect of a high rate of return on investment.

* Massachusetts Trade Office

10 Park Plaza, Suite 3720 617-973-8650
Boston, MA 02116 Fax: 617-227-3488
www.state.ma.us/mobd

This office stimulates export development through an export assistance program and promotes foreign investment and Massachusetts industries. The export assistance programs encompasses the following aspects: product sector marketing, foreign market development, and general export services. Specific services include one-on-one corporate counseling for new-to-export companies, coordination of foreign buying missions to Massachusetts trade, investment, and strategic partnerships, and hosting periodic industry and market seminars on overseas trade opportunities.

* Massachusetts Manufacturing Extension Partnership

100 Grove Street
Worchester, MA 01605 800-MEP-4MFG
www.massmep.org

Small and medium-sized businesses in Massachusetts can get help from over 2,000 manufacturing and business specialists that work through local chapters. They offer assistance in current manufacturing and management technologies such as Lean Manufacturing, plant layout, machinery automation/specification, marketing and business development, and much more. A MEP specialist will visit the business to observe and then sit down with the client and discuss the businesses operations.

* Massachusetts Community Development Finance Corporation (CDFC)

100 City Hall Plaza, Suite 300 617-523-6262
Boston, MA 02108 Fax: 617-523-7676
www.mcdfc.com

One of the goals of the CDFC is to invest in small business, which will result in job growth. They do this through the following programs:

- *Minority & Women Contractor Bond Program:* Technical and financial assistance is available to help contractors to qualify for surety bonds while establishing a relationship with a surety company.
- *Urban Initiative Fund (UIF):* Minority-owned businesses with less than $500,000 in annual sales can get technical assistance and loans to strengthen their business from the fund. It also provides loans and grants for a variety of innovative economic development and human service projects.
- *Massachusetts Enterprise Loan Fund:* This fund provides debt financing to established businesses for expansion. The investment range is from $100,000 to $300,000 with CDFC providing up to one third of the total financing. The funds can be used for equipment, working capital, and expansion or acquisition costs.
- *Real Estate Fund:* This program offers short-to-medium-term flexible financing for CDC development residential, commercial and industrial real estate projects. Up to $250,000 is provided for the financing of recoverable development expenses. The project must offer a clear public benefit such as job creation or revitalization of blighted commercial properties.
- *CDC Working Capital Fund:* This program fills pressing capital gaps for CDC's through flexible financing to cover operating expenses.

Michigan

* Michigan Economic Development Corporation

300 North Washington Square 517-373-9808
Lansing, MI 48913 Fax: 517-335-0198
http://medc.michigan.org

Michigan Business Ombudsman: Serves as a "one-stop" center for business permits. Acts as a mediator in resolving regulatory disputes between business and the various state departments and also provides consultation and referral services.

Economic Development Jobs Training: Provides financial assistance to companies that need to train or retrain workers to meet marketplace needs. Grant average: $2,000 per employee.

Economic Development Corporations: Provides a flexible tool to assist in job creation at the local level by acquiring, developing, and maintaining land, buildings, machinery, furnishings, and equipment necessary to complete a project plan.

Michigan Business Development: Assists existing companies with a wide array of business services which are customized to meet the specific needs of the business.

Michigan Technical Assistance Center Network: Assists companies with government contracting and exporting.

Labor Market Information: Detailed information concerning Michigan's economy and business climate. Information is also available regarding various industrial sectors critical to Michigan.

Employee Ownership Program: Provides information, technical assistance, and financing to enhance the establishment of employee-owned companies and Employee Stock Ownership Plans.

Business and Industrial Development Corporations (BIDCOs): Many sound businesses are unable to obtain growth capital because their finances are considered too risky for conventional bank lending, yet they cannot provide the high rates of return required by venture capitalists. BIDCOs are a new type of private institution designed to fill this growth capital gap. BIDCOs offer an array of financing options that can be structured flexibly to suit the needs of individual companies. In addition, they can provide management assistance to help businesses grow. As a privately owned and operated corporation, each BIDCO establishes its own criteria for the kinds of businesses it will finance and for the types of loans and investments it will make. BIDCOs do not normally finance start ups.

Industrial Development Revenue Bond Program (IDRB): Tax-exempt bonds issued on behalf of the borrower by the Michigan Strategic Fund and purchased by private investors. These loans can be made for manufacturing and not-for-profit corporation projects and solid waste facilities. Bond proceeds can only be used to acquire land, building and equipment. Working capital and inventory are not eligible for this type of financing. These bonds are generally used when financing of $1 million and higher is required.

Export Working Capital Program (EWCP): The EWCP was designed to provide short-term working capital to exporters. It is a combined effort of the SBA and the Export-Import Bank. The two agencies have joined their working capital programs to offer a unified approach to the government's support of export financing.

International Trade Loan (ITL): This program provides short- and long-term financing to small businesses involved in exporting, as well as businesses adversely affected by import competition. The SBA can guarantee up to $1.25 million for a combination of fixed-asset financing and working capital. Loans for facilities or equipment can have maturities of up to 25 years. The working capital portion of a loan has a maximum maturity of three years. Interest rates are negotiated with the lender and can be up to 2.25% over the prime rate.

Minority And Women's Prequalification Loan and the Women's Pre-Qualification Loan Program: Use intermediaries to assist prospective minority and women borrowers in developing viable loan application packages and securing loans. The women's program uses only nonprofit organizations as intermediaries; the minority program uses for-profit intermediaries as well.

Disadvantaged Business Enterprise Certification: Insures that firms owned and controlled by disadvantaged individuals, minorities, and women participate in federal-aid contracts and grant entered into and administered by MDOT.

Community Assistance Team (CAT): The Community Assistance Team provides a variety of economic incentives and programs for Michigan communities.

Consultation Education Training (CET): The Consultation Education & Training Division can help your company's safety performance by developing a safety program to meet your needs.

Export Services: The Michigan Economic Development Corporation has trade specialists to help companies gain or expand access to markets in North America, South America and Asia.

* Michigan Rural Development Office

3001 Coolidge Road, Suite 200   517-324-5190
East Lansing, MI 48823   Fax: 517-324-5225
www.rurdev.usda.gov/mi

Rural Development Business Programs works in partnership with the private sector and the community-based organizations to provide financial assistance and business planning. They fund projects that create or preserve quality jobs and/or promote a clean rural environment. Recipients of these programs may include individuals, corporations, partnerships, cooperatives, public bodies, nonprofit organizations, Indian tribes, and private companies. Business and Industry Loan Guarantees: This program's objective is to create jobs and stimulate rural economics by providing financial backing for rural businesses through a loan guarantee program.

Business and Industry Direct Loans: This program's objective is to create jobs and stimulate rural economics by providing financial backing for rural businesses through a direct loan.

Rural Enterprise Grants: This program finances and facilitates the development of small and emerging private business enterprises through a grant program.

Intermediary Relending Program Loans: This program finances business facilities and community development projects in rural areas through direct loans.

Rural Economic Development Loans and Grants: This program finances economic development and job creation in rural areas for Electric and Telephone Cooperatives.

* Certified Industrial Park Program

Michigan Economic Developers Association
P.O. Box 15096   517-241-0011
Lansing, MI 48901   Fax: 417-241-0089
www.medaweb.org

Industrial park developers and communities have used this identification as a marketing tool to show prospective clients that they are prepared to accept the new client without delay.

* Alternative Investments Division

Michigan Department of Treasury
Alternative Investments Division
P.O. Box 15128
Lansing, MI 48901   517-373-4330
www.michigan.gov/treasury

Invests in businesses with strong management that show a substantially above-average potential for growth, profitability, and equity appreciation. A typical initial investment is $5,000,000 and up.

* Equipment and Real Property Purchases

Michigan Municipal Bond Authority
Treasury Bldg., 3rd Floor
430 West Allegan   517-373-1728
Lansing, MI 48922   Fax: 517-335-2160
www.michigan.gov/treasury

Municipal Bonds provide streamlined tax-exempt, fixed interest rate financing well suited to equipment purchases.

* Freight Economic Development Project Loans/Grants

Michigan Department of Transportation
Bureau of Urban and Public Transportation
Freight Services and Safety Division
425 W. Ottawa
P.O. Box 30050
Lansing, MI 48909   517-325-2580
www.michigan.gov/mdot

Provides financial assistance to non-transportation companies which promote the development or expansion of new business and industries, by financing freight transportation infrastructure improvements needed to operate a new venture.

* Rail Loan Assistance Program

Michigan Department of Transportation
Bureau of Urban and Public Transportation
Freight Services and Safety Division
P.O. Box 30050
Lansing, MI 48909   517-373-1321
www.michigan.gov/mdot

The Michigan Rail Loan Assistance Program helps preserve and improve rail freight infrastructure. Non-interest bearing loans are available to fund eligible rail infrastructure improvement projects with a repayment period of up to ten years.

* Marketing and Communications Division

Michigan Department of Agriculture   571-241-2178
Office of Agriculture Development   800-292-3939
P.O. Box 30017   517-373-1104
Lansing MI 48909   Fax: 517-335-7071
www.michigan.gov/mda

The Marketing Section is the main contact for Michigan food and agricultural companies who seek assistance in international sales. The division works cooperatively to take advantage of the resources and international expertise of the Michigan Jobs Commission (MJC) and the Mid-America International Agri-Trade Council (MIATCO). Michigan exporters have opportunities to attend trade shows and missions, receive sales leads and market statistics, attend export education programs, and apply for federal Market Promotion Program funds via the MDA/MJC liaison. 517-373-1104.

* Michigan Department of Consumer & Industry Services

Corporation and Land Development Bureau
2501 Woodlake Circle
P.O. Box 30004   517-241-6470
Lansing, MI 48909   Fax: 571-241-0538
www.michigan.gov/cis

The Corporation Division promotes economic development and growth by facilitating the formation of business entities in Michigan. The Division provides services that enable corporations, limited liability partnerships to be formed, and for foreign entities to obtain a certificate of authority to transact business in the State, as required by Michigan law. The Division also maintains a record of the documents filed by these business entities, and makes this information available to the public.

* Industrial Assessment Center (IAC)

2350 Hayward Street   734-764-7471
Ann Arbor, MI 48109-2125   Fax: 734-647-0079
http://interpro.engin.umich.edu/mfgeng_prog/IAC

IAC is the Industrial Assessment Center with in the Program in Manufacturing at the University of Michigan (UM). There are thirty such university based centers across the country that are supported by the U.S. Department of Energy (DOE). The University of Michigan center serves manufacturers in Michigan and the upper region of Ohio. Small and medium-size manufacturers of all types of products are welcome to take advantage of the free and confidential services offered by the UM IAC.

* Certified Development Companies

Economic Development Foundation-Certified
1345 Monroe, NW, Suite 132
Grand Rapids, MI 49505   616-458-5416
Area of Operation: Antrim, Barry, Benzie, Charlevoix, Emmet, Grand Traverse, Kalkaska, Kent, Leelanau, Manistee, Mason, Missaukee, Muskegon, Oceana, and Wexford Counties.

Growth Finance Corporation
19498 M-49
PO Box 501
Howard City, MI 49239-0501   231-937-7429
Area of Operation: Allegan, Ionia, Kent, Lake, Mason, Mecosta, Montcalm, Newaygo, Oceana, Osceola, and Wexford Counties.

Lakeshore 504
272 East 8th Street
PO Box 1888
Holland, MI 49422-1888   269-392-2389
Area of Operation: Allegan, Berrien, Cass, Kalamazoo, Muskegon, Oceana, Ottawa, St. Joseph, and Van Buren Counties.

Metropolitan Growth and Development Corporation
600 Randolph Street, 3rd Floor
Detroit, MI 48226   313-224-0820
Area of Operation: Wayne and Macomb Counties.

Michigan Certified Development Corporation
822 Centennial Way, Suite 180
Lansing, MI 48917   517-886-6612
Area of Operation: State of Michigan.

Oakland County Business Finance Corporation
1200 N. Telegraph
Executive Office Building
Pontiac, MI 48341   248-858-0879
Area of Operation: Oakland County.

SEM Resource Capital
17177 N. Laurel Park Drive, Suite 360
Livonia, MI 48152   734-464-4418
Area of Operation: Genesee, Livingston, Macomb, Monroe, Washtenaw, and Wayne Counties.

The 504 Certified Development Company (CDC) Program provides growing businesses with long-term, fixed-rate financing for major fixed assets, such as land and buildings. A Certified Development Company is a nonprofit corporation set up to contribute to the economic development of its community or region. CDCs work with the SBA and private-sector lenders to provide financing to small businesses.

* Small Business Administration (SBA)

Patrick V. MacNamara Bldg.
477 Michigan Ave., Suite 515   313-226-6075
Detroit, MI 48226   Fax: 313-226-4769
www.sba.gov/mi
The Michigan Small Business Administration Office delivers a variety of programs and services, such as startup and operational assistance through small business training and counseling, financial assistance for startup's, business opportunities and much more.

* Small Business Investment Companies

Comerica Ventures, Inc.
Jay K. Oberg, First Vice President
500 Woodward Avenue, 33rd Floor, MC 3379   313-222-7833
Detroit, MI 48226   Fax: 313-222-4013
Email: jay_k_oberg@comerica.com

Dearborn Capital Corp.
Michael J. Kehres, President
c/o Ford Motor Credit Corp.
The American Rd.   313-337-8577
Dearborn, MI 48121   Fax: 313-390-3783
Email: wlang2@ford.com

EDF Ventures, L.P.
Mary Campbell, Contact
425 North Main Street   734-663-3213
Ann Arbor, MI 48104-1147   Fax: 734-663-7358
Email: caskew@edfvc.com

InvestCare Partners, L.P.
Malcolm Moss, Manager
32330 W. 12 Mile Road   248-489-9000
Farmington Hills, MI 48334   Fax: 248-489-8819
Email: lshipley@gmacapital.com

Merchants Capital Partners, L.P.
Pat Beach, Dick Goff, Ross Martin, Mgrs.
24 Frank Lloyd Wright Drive
Lobby L, 4th Floor   734-994-5505
Ann Arbor, MI 48106   Fax: 734-994-1376
Email: jkaplan@captec.com

Motor Enterprises, Inc.
Lindsay Luttenir, Manager
200 Renaissance Center, 10th Floor   316-665-6083
Detroit, MI 48265   Fax: 313-665-6208
Email: lindsey.luttinen@GM.com

North Coast Technology Investor, L.P.
Hugo E. Braun III, Lindsay D. Aspegren
206 S. Fifth Avenue Suite 550   734-662-7667
Ann Arbor, MI 48104-0648   Fax: 734-662-6261
Email: hugo@northcoastvc.com

Pacific Capital, L.P.
900 Victor's Way, Suite 280   734-747-9401
Ann Arbor, MI 48108   Fax: 734-747-9704
Email: cfisher@whitepines.com

Shorebank Capital Corporation
David Shryock, CEO
228 West Washington Street   906-228-6080
Marquette, MI 49855   Fax: 906-228-5572
Email: alan_keaton@sbk.com

TD Lighthouse Capital Fund, L.P.
Joan Neuscheler, Contact
303 Detroit Street, Suite 301   203-629-8700
Ann Arbor, MI 48104   Fax: 203-629-9293
Email: jceliberti@tullisdickerson.com

White Pines
Mr. Ian Bund, President
900 Victor's Way, Suite 280   734-747-9401
Ann Arbor, MI 48108   Fax: 734-747-9704
Email: lmarler@whitepines.com

The SBA licenses, regulates, and provides financial assistance to privately owned and operated Small Business Investment Companies. SBICs make venture or risk investments by supplying capital and extending unsecured loans and loans not fully collateralized to small enterprises which meet their investment criteria. Financing is made by direct loans and by equity investments.

* Department of Environmental Quality

Environmental Science and Services Division
P.O. Box 30457   800-662-9278
Lansing, MI 48909   517-241-8280
www.michigan.gov/deq
Small Business P2 Loan Program: The Small Business P2 Loan Program provides loans of up to $100,000 at an interest rate of 5% to businesses with fewer than 100 employees. The loans must be used to implement pollution prevention projects that either eliminate or reduce waste at the point of generation or result in environmentally sound reuse and recycling.

* Michigan Works!

2500 Kerry Street, Suite 210   517-371-1100
Lansing, MI 48912   Fax: 517-371-1140
www.michiganworks.org
Michigan Works! is the state's workforce development resource agency. Michigan Works! fosters quality employment and training programs serving employers and workers.

* Michigan Manufacturing Technology Center

47911 Halyard   888-414-6682
Plymouth, MI 48170   Fax: 734-451-4201
www.mmtc.org
Michigan Manufacturing Technology Centers offer training and consulting services designed for small to midsize manufacturers in Michigan.

Minnesota

* Minnesota Department of Trade and Economic Development (MTED)

500 Metro Square Blvd.
121 7th Place East
St. Paul, MN 55101-2146
www.dted.state.mn.us

800-657-3858
612-297-1291
Fax: 651-296-1290

Minnesota Small Business Assistance Office: Provides accurate, timely, and comprehensive information and assistance to businesses in all areas of start-up, operation, and expansion. They can also provide referrals to other state agencies.

Business Development and Site Location Services: For businesses interested in expanding or relocating to a Minnesota site, it serves as a bridge between government and the resources that businesses are seeking. Business Development Specialists act as liaisons between businesses and state and local government to access financial and technical resources. The program also serves as an important information source, providing businesses with data on topics ranging from the availability of buildings and property or the labor supply in a particular location, to transportation or tax comparisons. The one-on-one nature of this program provides businesses with assistance throughout every phase of their expansion or location projects.

Computer and Electrical Components Industry Services: Exists to foster the growth of jobs, revenues, and investment in Minnesota's computer and electrical components industries. A specialist provides technical review of projects, coordination of statistical analysis, overview of prospect proposals, participation in development efforts with industry associations and other agencies.

Healthcare and Medical Products Industry Services: Exists to seek business investment and job growth in the healthcare industry while promoting Minnesota companies' capabilities in this industry. A specialist provides information to businesses on financial programs, suppliers, business planning, trade opportunities, venture partners and other needed resources. The specialist also works to attract direct investment in existing Minnesota businesses with problems and opportunities involving sources, product development, marketing, financing, site selection, and by marketing Minnesota actively at industry gatherings.

Printing and Publishing Industry Services: Exists to foster the growth of jobs, revenues, and investment in Minnesota's printing and publishing industry. A specialist provides information on resources, markets, technologies, buildings and sites, transportation, and other issues, both in response to inquiries and by marketing Minnesota actively at industry gatherings.

Wood Products, Plastics, and Composites Industry Services: Exists to foster the growth of jobs and added value in Minnesota's wood processing and related businesses and to attract new industry consistent with environmental protection. A specialist represents the industry and the Department of Trade and Economic Development by reviewing projects, organizing statistical data, participating in development efforts with Department of Natural Resources, University of Minnesota, Minnesota Technology, Inc., National Resources Research Institute and other agencies, and by helping to coordinate demonstration projects like model homes. This position has evolved from a primary focus on wood products, to a wider interest in plastics and composite materials that are more frequently used in conjunction with wood.

A Guide to Starting a Business in Minnesota: Provides a current discussion of many of the major issues faced by persons planning to start a new business in Minnesota, including forms or organizations, business name filing, business licenses and permits, business plans, financing, employers' issues, business taxes and small business resources.

Minnesota Investment Fund: To create new and retain the highest quality jobs possible on a state wide basis with a focus on industrial manufacturing and technology related industries; to increase the local and state tax base and improve the economic vitality for all Minnesota citizens. Grants are awarded to local units of government who make loans to assist new expanding businesses. Maximum available: $500,000. Only one grant per state fiscal year can be awarded to a government unit.

Minnesota Job Skills Partnership Board: Awards grants for cooperative education and training projects between businesses and educational institutions.

Small Business Development Loan Program: Provides loans to industrial, manufacturing or agricultural processing businesses for land acquisition, building construction or renovation, machinery and equipment. Maximum available: $500,000 minimum up to a maximum of $6 million.

Rural Challenge Grant Program: Provides job opportunities for low-income individuals, encourage private investment, and promote economic development in rural areas of the state. The Business and Community Development Division has a partnership with each of six regional organizations to provide low-interest loans to new or expanding businesses in rural Minnesota. Eligible projects: Up to 50% of start-up or expansion costs, including property acquisition, site improvements, new construction, building renovation, purchase of machinery and equipment, and working capital. Maximum available: $100,000. Most loans will be smaller due to the high demand for funds compared with the funds available.

Tourism Loan Program: Exists to provide low-interest financing to existing tourism-related businesses providing overnight lodging. Additionally, the program assists with the development of business plans. Businesses with feasible business plans qualify to receive financing for up to half of all eligible costs. Business owners meet with DTED staff to determine project eligibility and receive counseling. Direct loans, or participation loans in cooperation with financial institutions, can be made for up to 50% of total project cost. The maximum state loan may not exceed 50% of the total project cost, or $65,000, whichever is less. Maximum available Septic System Loans: Participation Loans - State funds are used in conjunction with loaned funds from financial institutions. Loans for septic system replacement or upgrade are eligible for an additional $65,000. Direct Loans - Only septic system projects of under $10,000 may receive a direct loan. The borrower must fund 50% of the project with private financing. The maximum direct loan is $5,000.

Certified Community Development Corporation: Certified CDCs may apply for grant funds for several purposes: 1. specific economic development projects within a designated area, 2 dissemination of information about, or taking application for, programs operated by DTED, or 3 developing the internal organizational capacity to engage in economic development activities.

Capital Access Program: To encourage loans from private lending institutions to businesses, particularly small-and medium sized-businesses, to foster economic development. When loans are enrolled in the program by participating lending institutions, the lender obtains additional financial protection through a special fund created by the lender, borrower and the State. The lender and borrower contribute between 3% and 7% of the loan to the fund. The amount of funds contributed by the borrower/lender must be equal; however, the funds contributed by the bank may be recovered from the borrower as additional fees or through interest rates. If the amount of all enrolled loans is less than $2,000,000, the State contribution will be 150% of the borrower/lender contribution. The borrower/lender contribution can be financed as part of the loan.

Contamination Cleanup/Investigation Grant Program: The Department of Trade and Economic Development can award grants towards contamination investigations and the development of a Response Action Plan (RAP) or for the cleanup of contamination on sites which will be redeveloped. The contamination investigation grants will allow smaller, outstate communities to access sites believed to be contaminated which are typically not addressed due to limited financial resources. The Contamination Cleanup grants address the growing need for uncontaminated, developable land. In both cases, grants are awarded to those sites where there is serious, imminent private or public development potential.

Minnesota Pathways Program: Act as a catalyst between business and education in developing cooperative training projects that provide training, new jobs and career paths for individuals making the transition from public assistance to the workforce. Grants are awarded to educational institutions with businesses as partners. Maximum available: $200,000 of Pathway funds per grant can be awarded for a project.

Underground Petroleum Tank Replacement Program: Exists to provide low interest financing to small gasoline retailers for the replacement of an underground petroleum tank. Business owners submit an application on the approved form along with supporting documentation including third party cost estimates from a certified installer, prior year federal tax return, schedule of existing debt and proof of gasoline volume sold in the last calendar year. Loans can only be made to businesses that demonstrate an ability to pay the loan from business cash flow. The maximum loan in $10,000.

Minnesota Trade Office: Acts as an advocate for Minnesota businesses pursuing international markets and to promote, assist and enhance foreign direct investments that contribute to the growth of Minnesota's economy. Services provided for Minnesota companies include information on trade shows and trade missions; education and training; and financial assistance programs for Minnesota companies.

Services for International Companies: Resources, services and direct counseling for all companies interested in international trade.

Minnesota World Trade Center Corporation: An international business resource for Minnesota and the upper Midwest.

Minnesota Export Finance Authority: Assists with the financing of exports through four focus areas: working capital guarantees for purchase orders, receivable insurance for foreign buyers, ExIm bank, and agency liaison.

Minnesota Job Skills Partnership Program: Acts as a catalyst between business and education in developing cooperative training projects that provide training for new jobs or retraining of existing employees. Grants are awarded to educational institutions with businesses as partners. Preference will be given to non-profit institutions, which serve economically disadvantaged people, minorities, or those who are victims of economic dislocation and to businesses located in rural areas. Maximum available: $400,000 of Partnership funds per grant can be awarded for a project.

Urban Initiative Loan Program: Exists to assist minority owned and operated businesses and others that will create jobs in low-income areas of the Twin Cities. Urban Initiative Board enters into partnerships with local nonprofit organizations, which provide loans and technical assistance to start-up and expanding businesses. Project must demonstrate potential to create jobs for low-income people, must be unable to obtain sufficient capital from traditional private lenders, and must be able to demonstrate the potential to succeed. Eligible projects: Start-up and expansion costs, including normal business expenses such as machinery and equipment, inventory and receivables, working capital, new construction, renovation, and site acquisition. Financing of existing debt is not permitted. Micro-enterprises, including retail businesses, may apply for up to $10,000 in state funds. Maximum available: The maximum total loan available through the Urban Initiative Program is $300,000. The state may contribute 50% of the loan up to $150,000.

* Rural Development State Office

```
410 Farm Credit Service Building
375 Jackson Street                      651-602-7800
St. Paul, MN 55101-1853                 Fax: 651-602-7824
Email: a07dirmn@attmail.com
www.rurdev.usda.gov/mn
```

Their Rural Business Programs offer a variety of options for rural Minnesota.

Business and Industry Guaranteed and Direct Loan Program: This program's goal is to improve, develop, or finance business, industry, and employment and improve the economic and environmental climate in rural communities.

Intermediary Relending Program: The Relding Program is designed to alleviate poverty and increase economic activity and employment in rural communities, through financing targeted primarily toward smaller and emerging business in partnership with other public and private resources.

Rural Business Enterprise Grant Program: The Rural Business Enterprise Grant Program develops small and emerging private business enterprises in rural areas.

Rural Business Opportunity Grant Program: The Rural Business Opportunity Grant Program provides technical assistance to promote sustainable economic development in rural communities.

Rural Cooperative Development Grant Program: This program is designed to facilitate the creation or retention of jobs in rural areas through the development of new rural cooperatives value-added processing, and rural businesses.

Rural Economic Development Loan and Grant Program: The Rural Economic Development Loan and Grant Program promotes rural economic development and job creation.

* Free Workshops - Business Taxes

```
MN Dept. of Revenue
Mail Station 4410                       651-297-4213
St. Paul, MN 55146-4410                 800-888-6231
www.taxes.state.mn.us
```

Practical, real-world business tax information and up-to-the-minute information on state and federal tax laws that apply to your business. 2000 classes are sponsored by the IRS, the Minnesota Department of Revenue, and the Minnesota Department of Economic Security.

* Work Opportunity Tax Credit and the Welfare-To-Work Tax Credit

```
Minnesota Workforce Center
MN Dept. of Economic Security
```

```
5th Floor, 390 N. Robert Street         651-297-2219
St. Paul, MN 55101                      888-234-5521
www.mnwfc.org/wotc/index.htm
```

The Work Opportunity and Welfare-To-Work Tax Credit programs are designed to help individuals from certain target groups secure meaningful employment by providing a federal income tax incentive to employers who hire them. These programs cover only new hires. That is, the person may not have worked for that employer in the past.

* Minnesota Rural Finance Authority

```
Minnesota Department of Agriculture
90 West Plato Boulevard                 800-967-2474
St. Paul, MN 55107                      651-296-4985
www.mda.state.mn.us/agfinance
```

The Seller Assisted Farm Ownership Program is a cooperative financing effort involving a buyer, a seller, a local lender, and the Minnesota Rural Finance Authority (RFA).

The Basic Farm Loan Program was established to help people who want to farm in Minnesota. The program offers affordable financing, a reasonable down payment and built-in safeguards, such as farm management training and financial planning to help minimize the risk all farmers face. This is a partnership approach backed by the State's financial participation. You may finance a purchase or possibly refinance an existing farm debt. Funding an improvement may be possible if done in conjunction with the requested financing package.

The Aggie Bond Loan Program is a federal bonding program administered by the State through its Rural Finance Authority. The program offers affordable financing for a qualified beginning farmer. This is accomplished by securing for the applicant a reduced interest rate on the loan they are submitting for approval under the program.

Livestock Expansion Loan Program: A loan program to assist livestock and dairy producers finance the construction of state-of-the-art facilities is offered through the RFA in the Minnesota Department of Agriculture.

Agricultural Improvement Loan Program: The Rural Finance Authority (RFA) in the Minnesota Department of Agriculture is offering a loan participation program to assist eligible farmers to finance capital improvements to their farming operation. The program may help to improve production, efficiency, and increase farm income. Agricultural improvements means improvements to a farm, including the purchase and construction or installation of improvements to land, buildings and other permanent structures. This includes equipment incorporated in or permanently affixed to the land, buildings, or structures which are useful for and intended to be used for the purpose of farming. For this program, agricultural improvements also includes wind energy conversion facilities with an output capacity of one megawatt or less.

Value-Added Stock Loan Program: Helps farmers finance the purchase of stock in a cooperative proposing to build or purchase and operate a facility located in Minnesota to process or produce marketable products from agriculture crops. Stock in certain cooperatives proposing to own and operate livestock processing facilities or farm-generated wind energy production facilities may also be eligible.

Rural Finance Authority (RFA): A Restructure Program for agricultural debt is available through the Rural Finance Authority (RFA) in the Minnesota Department of Agriculture. The Restructure II loan program is designed to help farmers who remain in good credit standing with their local agricultural lender, but are having trouble with cash flow due to adverse events. Only debt of an agricultural nature is eligible for refinancing.

* Minnesota Office of Environmental Assistance (OEA)

```
520 Lafayette Rd. N, Floor 2            651-296-3417
St. Paul, MN 55155-4100                 800-657-3843
www.moea.state.mn.us                    Fax: 651-215-0246
```

The OEA helps start-up and expanding businesses in Minnesota develop uses for recycled materials by offering technical, business, financial, and marketing assistance.

* MnTAP

```
University of Minnesota Gateway         800-247-0015 (in MN)
200 Oak St, Suite 350                   612-624-1300
Minneapolis MN 55455                    Fax: 612-624-3370
www.mntap.umn.edu
```

The Minnesota Technical Assistance Program (MnTAP) not only helps businesses prevent pollution and better manage waste, we help them save time and money. Located at the University of Minnesota, they provide free technical assistance tailored to individual businesses. MnTAP helps Minnesota companies become more efficient and find alternatives to using hazardous materials. By reducing waste and increasing efficiency, companies save on disposal and raw-material costs and make working conditions healthier and safer for employees.

* Forestry Stewardship Program

Department of Natural Resources
Information Center
500 Lafayette Road — 651-296-6157
St. Paul, MN 55155-4040 — 888-MINNDNR
www.dnr.state.mn.us

The Forest Stewardship Program offers technical assistance and long range planning to landowners. Grants of up to 65% of costs with a maximum of $10,000 per year are available to develop forest plans, tree planting and land stabilization.

* Minnesota Housing Finance Agency

400 Sibley Street, Suite 300 — 651-296-7608
St Paul MN 55101-1998 — 800-657-3769
www.mhfa.state.mn.us

Affordable Rental Investment Fund is a statewide program that will provide zero percent interest first mortgages or deferred loans to help cover the costs of the acquisition and rehabilitation or new permanent construction of low-income rental housing.

HOME Rental Rehabilitation Program provides grants to rehabilitate privately-owned rental property to support affordable, decent, safe and energy efficient housing for lower-income families. This program is administered by local housing agencies throughout most of the state.

Low and Moderate Income Rental Program makes mortgage and rehabilitation funds available for the acquisition and rehabilitation or new construction/conversion of rental apartment buildings housing low- and moderate-income Minnesotans. Funds after an initial selection round are generally available on an open pipeline basis.

Low Income Housing Tax Credit Program provides a federal income tax credit to investors who invest in the construction or substantial rehabilitation of rental housing. Housing must meet income and rent restrictions for at least 15 years. Tax credits are awarded in three allocation rounds each year. Call for the application dates.

Rental Rehabilitation Loan Program provides property improvement loans to residential rental property owners. Financing is available only in certain areas of the state.

* Certified Development Companies

Central Minnesota Development Company
Connie M. Nelson, Executive Director
277 Coon Rapids Boulevard, Suite 212 — 763-784-3337
Coon Rapids, MN 55433 — Fax: 763-784-3338
Area of Operation: Anoka County

Minneapolis Economic Development Company
Michelle Mueller
105 5th Avenue, South, Suite 200 — 612-673-5070
Minneapolis, MN 55401 — Fax: 612-673-5111
www.mcda.org
Area of Operation: Hennepin County

Minnesota Business Finance Corporation
Alexandra Blum, President and CEO
616 Roosevelt Road, Suite 200 — 320-255-1685
St. Cloud MN 56301 — Fax: 320-255-1815
www.mbfc.org
Area of Operation: Statewide

Prairieland Economic Development Corporation
Steve M. Ousek, Director
1 Prairie Drive — 507-836-6656
Slayton MN 56172-1142 — Fax: 507-836-6309
www.prairielandedc.com
Mailing Address:
P.O. Box 265
Slayton MN 56172
Area of Operation: Big Stone, Chippewa, Cottonwood, Jackson, Lac Qui Parle, Lincoln, Lyon, Murray, Nobles, Pipestone, Redwood, Rock, Swift and Yellow Medicine Counties

South Central Business Finance Economic Development Corp.
Jim Snackenberg, Econ. Dev. Planner
209 South Second St., Suite 311 — 507-625-6056
Mankato MN 56002 — Fax: 507-625-6173
Mailing Address:
P.O. Box 666
Mankato MN 56002-0666
Area of Operation: Blue Earth, Brown, Faribault, Le Sueur, Martin, Nicollet, Sibley, Waseca and Watonwan Counties

Saint Paul/Metro East Development Corporation
Kristin Wood, Executive Director
2459 - 15th Street NW, Suite A — 651-631-4900
New Brighton MN 55112 — Fax: 651-631-9498
www.spedco.com
Area of Operation: Counties of Dakota, Ramsey and Washington

Southeastern Minnesota 504 Development, Inc.
Dwayne Lee, Director, Business Development
220 South Broadway, Suite 100 — 507-288-6442
Rochester MN 55904 — Fax: 507-282-8960
Area of Operation: Counties of Dodge, Fillmore, Freeborn, Goodhue, Hosuton, Mower, Olmsted, Rice, Wabasha, Winona and City of Blooming Prairie

Twin Cities-Metro Certified Development Company
Robert Heck, President
4105 Lexington Ave North
Suite 170 Arden Woods — 651-481-8081
Arden Hills MN 55126-6181 — Fax: 651-481-8280
Area of Operation: Counties of Carver, Dakota, Hennepin, Ramsey, Scott and Washington

The 504 Certified Development Company (CDC) Program provides growing businesses with long-term, fixed-rate financing for major fixed assets, such as land and buildings. A Certified Development Company is a nonprofit corporation set up to contribute to the economic development of its community or region. CDCs work with the SBA and private-sector lenders to provide financing to small businesses.

* Minnesota Technology, Inc.

111 Third Ave. South
Suite 400 — 800-325-3073
Minneapolis, MN 55401 — 612-373-2900
www.minnesotatechnology.org — Fax: 612-373-2901

Promotes jobs and economic growth through technology assistance services, and technology information.

* Indian Affairs Council

1819 Bemidji Ave. — 218-755-3825
Bemidji, MN 56601 — Fax: 218-755-3739
and
161 St. Anthony St., Suite 924 — 651-296-0041
St. Paul, MN 55103 — Fax: 651-296-0132
www.indians.state.mn.us

Provides resources for management and technical assistance for businesses owned by Minnesota-based Indians. A special revolving loan fund disburses funds on a case-by-case basis.

* Small Business Administration (SBA)

100 North Sixth St.
Suite 210-C, Butler Square — 612-370-2324
Minneapolis, MN 55403-1563 — Fax: 612-370-2303
www.sba.gov/mn

The Minnesota Small Business Administration Office delivers a variety of programs and services, such as startup and operational assistance through small business training and counseling, financial assistance for startup's, business opportunities and much more.

* Small Business Investment Companies

AAVIN Equity Partners I, L.P.
2500 Rand Tower
Participating Securities and Commitments — 602-375-9966
Minneapolis, MN 55402 — Fax: 319-363-9519

Affinity Ventures III, L.P.
Robin M. Dowdle, Contact

901 Marquette Avenue, Suite 1810 — 612-252-9897
Minneapolis, MN 55402 — Fax: 612-252-9863
Email: rdowdle@affinitycapital.net

Agio Capital Partners I, L.P.
Kenneth F. Gudorf, President & CEO
Interlachen Corporate Center
5050 Lincoln Drive, Suite 420 — 952-938-1628
Edina, MN 55436 — Fax: 952-933-6066
Email: KUMassey@AOL.com

Bayview Capital Partners, L.P.
Cary Musech, Manager
641 East Lake Street, Suite 230 — 952-345-2000
Wayzata, MN 55391 — Fax: 952-345-2001
Email: cmusech@bayviewcap.com

Convergent Capital Partners I, L.P.
John Mason, Keith Bares
5353 Wayzata Boulevard, Suite 205 — 612-595-8022
Minneapolis, MN 55416 — Fax: 612-595-8113
Email: kbares@cvcap.com

Dougherty Opportunity Fund II, L.P.
James A. Bernards, Contact
7200 Metro Boulevard — 952-831-6499
Edina, MN 55439 — Fax: 952-831-1219
Email: jimb@sbbsl.com

Medallion Capital, Inc.
Tom Hunt, President
3000 W. County Rd. 42, Suite 301 — 952-831-2025
Burnsville, MN 55337 — Fax: 952-831-2945
Email: mvannelli@medallioncapital.com

Milestone Growth Fund, Inc.
Esperanza Guerrero-Anderson, President
401 Second Ave. South, Suite 1032 — 612-338-0090
Minneapolis, MN 55402 — Fax: 612-338-1172
Email: mgfinc@uswest.net

Piper Jaffray Healthcare Capital L.P.
Lloyd (Buzz) Benson, Manager
Mailstation: J10122-32
800 Nicollet Mall, Suite 800 — 612-303-5686
Minneapolis, MN 55402-7020 — Fax: 612-303-1350
Email: mharder@pjc.com

Piper Jaffray Healthcare Fund III, L.P.
Lloyd (Buzz) Benson, Ken Higgins
Mailstation: J10122-32
800 Nicollet Mall, Suite 800 — 612-303-5686
Minneapolis, MN 55402-7020 — Fax: 612-303-1350
Email: mharder@pjc.com

Piper Jaffray Technology Capital SBIC, L.P.
Gary Blauer and Buzz Benson, Managers
Mailstation: J10122-32
800 Nicollet Mall, Suite 800 — 612-303-5686
Minneapolis, MN 55402-7020 — Fax: 612-303-1350
Email: mharder@pjc.com

The SBA licenses, regulates, and provides financial assistance to privately owned and operated Small Business Investment Companies. SBICs make venture or risk investments by supplying capital and extending unsecured loans and loans not fully collateralized to small enterprises which meet their investment criteria. Financing is made by direct loans and by equity investments.

* Initiative Funds

Northwest Minnesota Initiative Fund — 218-759-2057
4225 Technology Drive, NW — 800-659-2328
Bemidji, MN 56601 — Fax: 218-759-2328
www.nwmf.org
Area of Operation: Beltrami, Clearwater, Hubbard, Kittson, Lake of the Woods, Mahnomen, Marshall, Norman, Pennington, Polk, Red Lake and Roseau Counties

Northland Foundation
610 Sellwood Building — 800-433-4045
202 West Superior Street — 218-723-4040
Duluth, MN 55802 — Fax: 218-723-4048
www.northlandfdn.org

Area of Operation: Aitkin, Carlton, Cook, Itasca, Koochiching, Lake and St.Louis Counties.

West Central Minnesota Initiative Fund — 800-735-2239
1000 Western Avenue — 218-739-2239
Fergus Falls, MN 56537 — Fax: 218-739-5381
www.wcif.org
Area of Operation: Becker, Clay, Douglas, Grant, Otter Tail, Pope, Stevens, Traverse, and Wilkin Counties.

Southwest Minnesota Foundation
1390 Highway 15 South — 320-587-4848
P.O. Box 428 — 800-594-9480
Hutchinson, MN 55350 — Fax: 320-587-3838
www.swmnfoundation.org
Area of Operation: Big Stone, Chippewa, Cottonwood, Jackson, Kandiyohi, Lac Qui Parle, Lincoln, Lyon, McLeod, Meeker, Murray, Nobles, Pipestone, Redwood, Renville, Rock, Swift, and Yellow Medicine Counties.

Minnesota Initiative Fund — 320-632-8255
405 First Street Southeast — 877-632-9255
Little Falls, MN 56345 — Fax: 320-632-9258
www.ifound.org
Area of Operation: Benton, Cass, Chisago, Crow, Wing, Isanti, Kanabec, Mille, Lacs, Morrison, Pine, Sherburne, Stearns, Todd, Wadena, and Wright Counties.

Southern Minnesota Initiative Foundation
525 Florence Avenue — 800-590-7759
P.O. Box 695 — 507-455-3215
Owatonna, MN 55060-0695 — Fax: 507-455-2098
www.smifoundation.org
Area of Operation: Blue Earth, Brown, Dodge, Faribault, Fillmore, Freeborn, Goodhue, Houston, LeSueur, Martin, Mower, Nicollet, Olmsted, Rice, Sibley, Steele, Wabasha, Waseca, Watonwan, and Winona Counties.

Private, non-profit organizations supplemented with funds from various public and private sources. Funds are distributed in grants and loans. The six initiative funds listed above are separate entities, and each has its own programs, funding levels, and guidelines. Call your regional Initiative Fund.

* Midwest Minnesota Community Development Corp. (MMCDC)

832 Washington Ave
P.O. Box 623 — 218-847-3191
Detroit Lakes, MN 56501-3042 — Fax: 218-847-3192
www.ruralisc.org/mmcdc.htm
Midwest Minnesota Community Development Corp. (MMCDC) receives grants and loans from public and private sources and re-lends these funds to businesses in the form of secured loans. The interest rate charged is normally at or near bank loan rates. The Revolving Loan Fund serves a five county area of Minnesota (Hubbard, Mahnomen, Becker, Clearwater, and Pennington, Polk, and Red Lahr). The Non-Profit National Corporations Loan Program serves rural communities with a population of 20,000 or less.

* Minnesota Rural Partners

P.O. Box 243 — 507-644-8250
Redwood Falls, MN 56283 — Fax: 507-644-8251
www.minnesotaruralpartners.org
Minnesota Rural Partners (MRP) is Minnesota's rural development organization that works to create, promote and sustain programs that will help the rural communities throughout the state.

BizPathways: BizPathways is an online tool that matches entrepreneurs to the resources they need to grow based on location, stage of business development and other criteria.

BizPathways-Finance Avenue: This online tool can connect your business with the resources you may need based on your answers to seven questions.

Mississippi

* Mississippi Development Authority

P.O. Box 849 — 601-359-3499
Jackson, MS 39205-0849 — 800-927-6378
www.mississippi.org — Fax: 601-359-2832
This office can provide information and expertise in dealing with state, federal, and local agencies. They also have information on financing programs and other services offered by the state government.

- *Training*: Customized industrial training programs provided through the State Department of Education. Job Training Partnership Act assistance provided through the Mississippi Department of Economic and Community Development.
- *Site Finding*: The Mississippi Resource Center in Jackson offers an interactive video for site viewing and detailed data on video, computer disk, or hard copy for later study.
- *One-stop environmental permitting*.

Loan Guarantee Program: Provides guarantees to private lenders on loans made to small businesses allowing a small business to obtain a loan that may not otherwise be possible without the guarantee protection. The maximum guarantee is 75% of the total loan or $375,000, whichever is less.

Industrial Development Revenue Bond Program: Reduces the interest costs of financing projects for companies through the issuance of both taxable and tax-exempt bonds. Additionally, ad valorem and sales tax exemptions are granted in conjunction with this type of public financing. There is a $10 million cap.

Small Enterprise Development Program: Provides funds for manufacturing and processing companies to finance fixed assets. Although a company may qualify for more than one loan under this program, the aggregate amount loaned to any company cannot exceed $2 million.

Mississippi Business Investment Act Program: Through the issuance of State General Obligation Bonds, low-interest loans are provided to counties or cities to finance improvements that complement investments by private companies.

Airport Revitalization Revolving Loan Program: Funds from the issuance of state bonds provide loans to airport authorities for the construction and/or improvement of airport facilities. Maximum loan amount is $500,000.

Port Revitalization Revolving Loan Program: Designed to make loans to port authorities for improvement of port facilities. Maximum is $500,000.

Agribusiness Enterprise Loan Program: Designed to encourage the extension of conventional financing by lending institutions by providing interest-free loans to agribusinesses. Maximum loan is 20% of the total project cost or $200,000, whichever is less. Proceeds may be used to finance buildings and equipment and for costs associated with the purchase of land.

Small Business Assistance Program: Established for the purpose of providing funds to establish revolving loan funds to assist in financing small businesses. Maximum is $100,000.

Energy Investment Program: Provides financial assistance to individuals, partnerships or corporations making energy conserving capital improvements or designing and developing energy conservation processes. This program offers low-interest loans of up to $300,000.

Local Industrial Development Revenue Bonds: Local political entities have the authority to issue tax-exempt and taxable industrial development revenue bonds to finance new or expanding industrial enterprises up to 100% of total project costs.

General Obligation Bonds: Local political entities have the authority to issue general obligation bonds for the purpose of acquiring sites and constructing facilities for lease to new or expanding industries.

Minority Business Enterprise Division (MBED): Provides assistance to businesses in those categories. The division acts as principal advocate on behalf of minority- and women-owned business enterprises and promotes legislation that will help them operate more effectively. Developing funding sources, including state funding, bonding resources, federal and local funds, and others is among the major aims of MBED. But identifying funding sources represents only one aspect of MBED's service to Mississippi's women- and minority-owned firms. The division also attempts to put those businesses in touch with potential customers; MBED maintains an outreach program designed to include them in contracting of goods and services and procurement of contracts. A regional and statewide network of workshops, seminars, and trade shows continually provide training to stimulate the role of entrepreneurship in Mississippi's economic development.

Minority Surety Bond Guaranty Program: Program enables minority contractors, not meeting the surety industry's standard underwriting criteria, to obtain bid and performance bonds on contracts with state agencies and political subdivisions. Maximum bond guarantee is 75% of contract bond amount, or $112,500, whichever is less.

Minority Business Enterprise Loan Program: Designed to provide loans to socially and economically disadvantaged minority-or women-owned small businesses. Loan proceeds may be used for all project costs associated with the establishment or expansion of a minority business, including the purchase of fixed assets or inventory or to provide working capital. The minimum loan is $2,000 and the maximum loan is $25,000. MBFC may fund up to 100% of a total project.

Mississippi Tourism Incentive Program: This is an incentive program for qualified developers for the creation or expansion of family-oriented tourism projects. The types of entertainment enterprises that can receive assistance include: a cultural or historical site; a recreation or entertainment facility; campgrounds; indoor or outdoor play or music shows and more.

Rural Economic Development Assistance Program: Companies financing through the Small Enterprise Development or Industrial Revenue Bond Programs may be eligible to participate in this program. Eligible companies receive credits on Mississippi corporate income taxes. These credits may be used to offset up to 80% of the company's state corporate income tax liability.

* Rural Development

State Director, William Simpson
100 West Capitol St.
Suite 831 Federal Building   601-965-4318
Jackson, MS 39269   Fax: 601-965-5384
Email: wsimpson@rdmail.rural.usda.gov
www.rurdev.usda.gov/ms

The primary goals surrounding these programs are to stimulate economic growth, through the use of several programs administered by the Rural Business & Cooperative Service. The objectives focus on the creation of jobs and cooperatives in rural areas across the State of Mississippi.

Business & Industrial Loan Guarantees: This program encourages commercial financing of rural business, through the use of loan guarantees. This enables lenders the flexibility of maintaining the loan with a percentage guarantee, or sale of the loan on the secondary market. These loans are for the purpose of creating jobs, and improving the economic and environmental climate of rural communities.

Intermediary Relending Program (IRP): The IRP program provides a source of funding for community development, establishment of new businesses, expanding existing businesses and creation of jobs. This is primarily accomplished through the use of a revolving loan fund, which is administered by nonprofit corporations, public bodies, Indian tribes, and cooperatives.

Rural Business Enterprise Grants (RBEG): These grants are primarily used to finance or develop small and emerging private business enterprises. These funds are also administered through nonprofit corporations, public bodies, and Indian tribes. The ultimate recipients of these funds must be small and emerging private businesses.

Cooperative Development Grants: The primary purpose of these funds is for improving the economic condition of rural areas by promoting the development (through technological innovation, cooperative development, and adaptation of existing technology) and commercialization of new services and products that can be produced or provided in rural areas. This includes processes that can be utilized in the production of products in rural areas, and new processes that can be utilized in the production of products in rural areas, and new enterprises that can add value to on-farm production through processing or marketing.

Rural Economic Development Loan And Grants: The basic purpose of this assistance is to promote rural economic development or job creation projects. These funds are administered through private phone and electric companies. The ultimate recipients for these funds will be any type of entity, profit or nonprofit, public or private.

Rural Business Opportunity Grants (RBOG): This grant program is used to promote sustainable economic development in rural communities with exceptional needs. Funds may be used to pay for the costs of economic planning for rural communities, technical assistance for rural businesses or training for rural entrepreneurs or economic development officials. Grant limits are $50,000.

* Mississippi Department of Agriculture and Commerce

121 North Jefferson Street   601-359-1100
Jackson, MS 39201   Fax: 601-354-6290
www.mdac.state.ms.us
Mailing Address
P.O. Box 1609
Jackson, MS 39215

The mission of the Mississippi Department of Agriculture and Commerce is to regulate and promote agricultural-related businesses within the state and to promote Mississippi's products throughout both the state and the rest of the world for the benefit of all Mississippi citizens.

* Certified Development Companies

Central Mississippi Development Company, Inc.
Thelman L. Anderson, Executive Director
P.O. Box 4935
1170 Lakeland Drive — 601-981-1625
Jackson, MS 39296-4935 — Fax: 601-981-1515

Three Rivers Local Development Company, Inc.
Vernon R. Kelley, Executive Director
P.O. Drawer B
75 South Main Street — 662-489-2435
Pontotoc, MS 38863 — Fax: 662-489-6815

Southern Development Council, Inc.
Tamara Y. Lee, Executive Director
Leon Darby, Loan Officer — 800-499-3034
8132 Old Federal Road — 334-244-1801
Montgomery, AL 36117 — Fax: 334-244-1421

ALACOM Finance (Alabama Community Development Corporation)
Diane Roehrig, President
117 Southcrest Drive, Suite 100 — 205-870-3360
Homewood, AL 35209 — Fax: 205-942-5984

The 504 Certified Development Company (CDC) Program provides growing businesses with long-term, fixed-rate financing for major fixed assets, such as land and buildings. A Certified Development Company is a nonprofit corporation set up to contribute to the economic development of its community or region. CDCs work with the SBA and private-sector lenders to provide financing to small businesses.

* Small Business Administration (SBA)

Mississippi District Office
AmSouth Bank Plaza
210 E. Capitol Street, Suite 900 — 601-965-4378
Jackson, MS 39201 — Fax: 601-965-5629

Gulfport Branch Office
Bancorp South Plaza
2909 13th Street, Suite 203 — 228-863-4449
Gulfport, MS 39501 — Fax: 228-864-0179
www.sba.gov/ms

The Mississippi Small Business Administration Office delivers a variety of programs and services, such as startup and operational assistance through small business training and counseling, financial assistance for startup's, business opportunities and much more.

* Small Business Investment Companies

CapSource Fund, L.P.
Bobby Weatherly & James Herndon, Mgrs.
795 Woodlands Parkway, Suite 100 — 601-899-8980
Ridgeland, MS 39157 — Fax: 601-952-1334
Email: capsource@capsourcefund.com

Sun-Delta Capital Access Center, Inc.
Howard Boutte, Jr., Vice President
819 Main St. — 662-335-5291
Greenville, MS 38701 — Fax: 662-335-5293
Email: deltafdn@tecinfo.com

The SBA licenses, regulates, and provides financial assistance to privately owned and operated Small Business Investment Companies. SBICs make venture or risk investments by supplying capital and extending unsecured loans and loans not fully collateralized to small enterprises which meet their investment criteria. Financing is made by direct loans and by equity investments.

Missouri

* Department of Economic Development

P.O. Box 1157 — 573-751-4962
Jefferson City, MO 65102-1157 — 800-523-1434
www.ded.state.mo.us — Fax: 573-526-2416

First Stop Shop: Serves to link business owners and state government and provides information on state rules, regulations, licenses, and permits.

Business Assistance Center: — 888-751-2863
Provides information and technical assistance to start-up and existing businesses on available state and federal programs. Offers several useful publications.

University Outreach and Extension: Programs to help citizens apply university research knowledge to solve individual and community problems. Working with business owners and managers on a one-to-one basis, B&I specialists help entrepreneurs identify problem areas and find solutions.

Small Business Incubators: Buildings that have been divided into units of space, which are then leased to new small businesses. In addition to low-cost physical space, incubators can help clients with access to necessary office machines, reception and secretarial services, furniture, conference rooms and technical expertise in business management.

Innovation Centers: Provide a wide range of management and technical assistance to businesses. These centers are familiar with up-to-date business management and technology innovations and help businesses apply these innovations to help increase profits.

Action Fund Program: The program provides a subordinate loan to certain types of for-profit companies that need funds for start-up or expansion and have exhausted other sources. The projected growth of the company, economic impact, the risk of failure, and the quality of management are critical factors for approval. DED must determine that the borrower has exhausted other funding sources and only the least amount needed to complete the project may be provided. In any event, an Action Fund Loan would be limited to the lower of: $750,000 per project; 30% of the total project cost; or $20,000 per new full-time year-round job.

Brownfield Redevelopment Program: The purpose of this program is to provide financial incentives for the redevelopment of commercial/industrial sites owned by a governmental agency that have been abandoned for at least three years due to contamination caused by hazardous substances. The program provides state tax credits for eligible remediation costs. DED may provide a loan or guarantee for other project costs, or a grant for public infrastructure. Also, tax credits may be provided to businesses that create jobs at the facility. The program provides Missouri state income tax credits for up to 100% of remediation costs. Guaranteed loans or direct loans to an owner or operator of the property are limited to $1 million. Grants to public entities are also available up to $100,000 or 50% for feasibility studies or other due diligence costs. Grants can also be issued up to $1 million for the improvement of public infrastructure for the project. The total of grants, loans or guarantees cannot exceed $1 million per project.

CDBG Loan Guarantee Program: The purpose of this program is to provide "gap" financing for new or expanding businesses that cannot access complete funding for a project. "Gap" financing means other sources of financing (including bank loans and owner equity) have been maximized, and a gap exists in the total project cost. The Department of Economic Development (DED) will guarantee 50% to 80% of the principal balance (after liquidation of assets) of a loan made by a financial institution. DED must determine that the borrower has exhausted other funding sources and only the least amount needed to complete the project may be provided. The maximum funding available is based on the lower of: $400,000 per project or $20,000 per new full-time permanent job created or retained. Approval is based on the good character of the owners, sufficient cash flow, adequate management and reasonable collateral.

Certified Capital Companies (CAPCO): Purpose is to induce private investment into new or growing Missouri small businesses, which will result in the creation of new jobs and investment. DED has initiated the formation of private venture capital firms (CAPCOs). These firms have certain requirements to make equity investments in eligible businesses in Missouri. The amount a CAPCO may invest in one Missouri business depends on various factors, however the maximum amount is 15% of the CAPCO's certified capital. Funding decisions are made by each CAPCO based on their evaluation of the return on investment relative to the risk. CAPCO funds may be used for equity investments, unsecured loans or hybrid investments in eligible businesses. Typically, venture capitalists require a projected 25-40% annual ROI, depending on the risk.

Industrial Development Bonds (IDBs): Developed by the US Congress and the Missouri General Assembly to facilitate the financing of business projects. The interest received by the bondholders may be exempt from federal and state income taxes, if the project is eligible.

Urban Enterprise Loan Fund (UEL): A micro lending instrument established by the State of Missouri, Department of Economic Development and administered in Kansas City by the downtown Minority Development Corporation and in St. Louis by the St. Louis Development Corporation. The program is designed to assist Missouri residents with the creation, expansion, and retention of micro-enterprises. Eligible enterprises must be located - or aspire to locate- within the Federally designated Enhanced Enterprise Community and the State Enterprise Zone. One job must be created for every $20,000 in Urban Enterprise Loan proceeds invested. Loans from the State fund range from a minimum of $10,000 up to a maximum of $100,000. The Urban Enterprise Loan Fund also has a matching funds requirement and new job creation criteria.

CDBG Industrial Infrastructure Grant: This program assists local governments in the development of public infrastructure that allows industries to locate new facilities, expand existing facilities or prevent the relocation or closing of a facility. The use of this program is based on the local government exhausting their available resources. DED has targeted a 20% match by the community base upon the availability of unencumbered city or county funds.

Missouri Office Of International Marketing: Services include: International Consulting Service, Competitive Analysis Reports, Trade Show Reports, Trade Exhibitions, Catalog Shows, Missouri International Office Assistance, Foreign Company Background Checks, Rep-Find Service, International Travel Program, Marketing Program, Trade Opportunity Program, Foreign Trade Missions, Strategic Alliance Program, Export Finance Assistance, Made In Missouri Catalogs, Missouri Export Directory, Recognition Program.

Office of Minority Business (OMB): Charged with the responsibility of identifying and developing support systems that assist the minority business community in gaining a foothold in the mainstream of Missouri's economy. This responsibility entails counseling minority small businesses on business start-up, retention, expansion, financing, and procurement; also including but not limited to providing ready access to information regarding current legislation and regulations that affects minority business. The staff of the Office of Minority Business can provide assistance with; administering technical and financial assistance programs; providing new and small businesses with management expertise; business development information; tying minority firms to national and global markets; connecting minority firms to the labor market; accessing research and technology; and other customized assistance.

* Rural Development Administration
601 Business Loop 70 West
Parkade Center, Suite 235   573-876-0976
Columbia, MO 65203   Fax: 573-876-0977
www.rurdev.usda.gov/mo

Business and Industry Loans: Direct loans made by USDA Rural Development and loans made by conventional lenders and guaranteed by USDA Rural Development to help maintain or establish private business and industry enterprises that create employment opportunities. Limited to communities of 50,000 population or less.

Intermediary Relending Program: Loans made to intermediaries at 1% for 30 years. Maximum loan amount $150,000 or 75% of project costs, whichever is less.

Rural Business Enterprise Grants: Grants made to public bodies, not for profits and Indian tribes to support the development of private business enterprise in rural communities of less than 50,000 people.

Rural Business Opportunity Grants: Grants made to public bodies, not for profits, and Indian tribes in rural areas.

Technical Assistance and Training Grants: Grants made to private nonprofit organizations that have been granted tax-exempt status. Grant funds may be used to provide assistance to existing water and water disposal facilities.

Rural Economic Development Grants and Loans: Grants and Loans to rural electric cooperatives and REA telephone borrowers.

* Workforce Development System
Missouri Division of Workforce Development
421 East Durkin Street
P.O. Box 1087   573-751-3999
Jefferson City, MO 65102-1087   Fax: 573-751-4088
www.ded.state.mo.us/employment/workforcedevelopment

Integrates previously fragmented employment and training programs into a comprehensive workforce development system. Services benefit both job seekers and employers through One-Stop Career Centers.

* Missouri First
State Treasurer's Office

P.O. Box 210   573-751-2372
Jefferson City, MO 65102-0210   800-662-8257
www.sto.state.mo.us/link/deposit.htm

The State Treasurer has reserved a portion of available linked deposit funds for small businesses. State funds are deposited with participating lending institutions at up to 3% below the one-year Treasury Bill rate, with the lender passing on this interest savings to the small business borrower. A company must have less than 25 employees, be headquartered in Missouri, and be operating for profit. Small Business MISSOURI FIRST Linked Deposit loans are available for working capital. The maximum loan amount is $100,000.

* Market Development Loans for Recovered Materials
Environmental Improvement and Energy Resources Authority
P.O. Box 744   573-526-5555
Jefferson City, MO 65102   Fax: 573-635-3486
www.dnr.state.mo.us/eiera/eiera.htm

The Environmental Improvement and Energy Resources Authority funds activities that promote the development of markets for recovered materials. Loans of up to $75,000 are available to companies for equipment used in the production or manufacture of products made from recovered materials. After three years, if all contract obligations are met, the loan is forgiven and repayment is not required.

* Financial Aid for Beginning Farmers
Missouri Agricultural and Small Business Development Authority
Beginning Farmer Program
P.O. Box 630   800-735-2966
Jefferson City, MO 65102   573-751-2129
www.mda.state.mo.us

Beginning farmers can receive federally tax-exempt loans from commercial lenders at rates 20 to 30% below conventional rates through this program. A qualified borrower can borrow up to $250,000 to buy agricultural land, farm buildings, farm equipment and breeding livestock in Missouri. The borrower must be a Missouri resident, at least 18 years old and whose chief occupation must be farming or ranching after the loan is closed. The borrower's net worth must not exceed $150,000, and he or she must have adequate working capital and experience in the type of farming operation for which the loan is sought. A beginning farmer is one who has not previously owned more than 15% of the medium-sized farm in their county. Land cannot be purchased from a relative.

* Small Corporation Offering Registration (SCOR)
Securities Division
Secretary of State's Office
600 W. Main St., 2nd Floor
Jefferson City, MO 65101   573-751-4136
www.sos.mo.gov/

Missouri's Small Corporate Offering Registration (SCOR) provides a process for entrepreneurs to register their securities. The SCOR process has been designed by state securities regulators to make it easier and less expensive for small companies to raise needed capital from Missouri residents. All securities registered through this process need to complete form U-7 available from the Secretary of State's Office.

* Working Capital, St. Louis
Working Capital
3830 Washington   314-531-4546
St. Louis, MO 63108   Fax: 314-534-1883
http://stlouis.missouri.org/enterprise/about/worcap.htm

Working Capital is a micro-lending program which identifies small business people in the St. Louis area and makes available to them the commercial credit and business support which enables them to expand their business. Working Capital utilizes a peer-lending technique. At required monthly meetings borrowers receive continuing assistance in the marketing of their goods or services. The maximum first-time loan is $500 payable in four to six months; subsequent loans can have increased amounts (up to $5,000) and longer duration. Working Capital gives priority to individuals already in business to minimize loan risk; will consider applications from start-ups.

* Economic Council of St. Louis County
121 South Meramec St., Suite 900 314-889-7663
St. Louis, MO 63105   Fax: 314-615-7666
http://slcec.com

Services include Business Development Fund (BDF), Metropolitan St. Louis Loan Program, Minority/ Disadvantaged Contractor Loan Guarantee,

Recycling Market Development Loan Program, SBA 504 Loan Program and Minority & Women's Prequalified Loan Program.

* St. Charles County Economic Development Council

St. Charles County Economic Development Council
5988 Midrivers Mall Dr., Suite 100   636-441-6880
St. Charles, MO 63304   Fax: 636-441-6881
www.stcc-edc.com

Program assists eligible companies with fixed asset and working capital needs; acts as the certified development company which packages SBA 504 loans.

* St. Louis Development Corporation

1015 Locust St., #1200
St. Louis, MO 63101   314-622-3400
http://stlouis.missouri.org/sldc

St. Louis City Revolving Loan Fund: Provides direct, low interest, subordinated loans for working capital, machinery and equipment, purchasing land and buildings, renovation and constructing facilities and leasehold improvements. Business must be located in the City of St. Louis and be licensed to do business in the City. Must create one full-time job for every $10,000 of funds. Loans can provide up to 1/3 of the project cost to a maximum loan amount of $150,000.

St. Louis Urban Enterprise Loan, St. Louis Development Corporation: Provides loans to businesses located within the Enterprise Community area or the Enterprise Zone within the City of St. Louis. Eligible borrowers must be for profit businesses with current employment of less than 100. Eligible program activities will include fixed asset or working capital needs. Eligible projects must retain existing or create new jobs (one job created for every $20,000 of funding). The UEL can lend up to 50% of the project costs to a maximum loan amount of $100,000.

LDC Micro Loan Program, St. Louis Development Corporation: Microloans are available to start-up companies or businesses less than one year old located within the City of St. Louis; one job, other than the owner's, must be created. Successful applicants must demonstrate a viable business plans and the inability to secure bank financing. Companies must show the ability to start or grow the business with a maximum loan amount of $25,000. Loans may be used to cover start-up costs, working capital and purchase of machinery and equipment.

* First Step Program, Kansas City

First Step Fund
First Step Program
4747 Troost Avenue   816-235-6116
Kansas City, MO 64110   Fax: 816-235-6162
www.firststepfund.org

The First Step Fund (FSF) offers training in business basics such as record keeping, budgeting and marketing; assistance in completing a feasibility study for a business; opportunity to apply for loans of up to $2,500; and ongoing support group. FSF participants must be residents of Jackson, Clay or Platte counties in Missouri and must meet federal guidelines for low to moderate income. During a 10-week business training program, students work on a feasibility study for the proposed business. Potential borrowers receive continuing education at monthly meetings. Participants review each others' feasibility studies and approve loans. The maximum loan amount for first-time borrowers is $2,500 and $5,000 for second-time borrowers.

* Urban Enterprise Loan Fund

Missouri Department of Economic Development
Office of Business Finance
301 W. High Street
PO Box 118
Jefferson City, MO 65102   573-751-0295
   Fax: 573-526-1567

The Missouri Department of Economic Development administers a micro-lending program, which provides low interest loans to for-profit businesses in the urban areas in St. Louis and Kansas City. Funds may be used to start a new business; purchase business equipment, inventory, working capital, acquisition of business assets or other expansion purposes of the an existing business. It may also be used to provide an equity match for leveraging a commercial loan, secure lines of credit or secure gap financing from a conventional commercial lender. They may not exceed 50% of the entrepreneurs' total financial need. Interested entrepreneurs may contact the local program administer:

St. Louis Minority Business Council
720 Olive Street, Suite 1630

St. Louis, MO 63101   314-241-1143
www.slmbc.org/

Douglass National Bank
1670 East 63rd Street
Kansas City, MO 64110   816-822-8560

* Community Development Corporation of Kansas City

2420 E. Linwood Blvd., Suite 400   816-924-5800
Kansas City, MO 64109   Fax: 816-921-3350
www.cdcofkc.org

Provides microloan business assistance to small businesses located in a five-county area; assists entrepreneurs whose credit needs are $25,000 and under.

* Thomas Hill Enterprise Center

1714 Prospect Dr., Suite A   660-385-6550
Macon, MO 63552   800-470-8625
www.e-center.org

The Thomas Hill Enterprise Center offers a variety of programs and services to help businesses and communities grow. They provide Community Planning, Business Training, and Computer Training.

* Missouri Export Finance Program

P.O. Box 118   573-526-4967
Jefferson City, MO 65102-0118   Fax: 573-526-1567
www.ded.state.mo.us/business/internationalmarketing

Missouri companies that need financial assistance exporting to foreign markets can use programs of the Export and Import Bank of the United States(Ex-Im Bank) and the Small Business Administration (SBA) through a joint project that provides local access for Missouri businesses. There are primarily two programs available, Working Capital Loan Guarantees and Export Credit Insurance. These programs are designed to help small and medium-sized businesses that have exporting potential but need funds or risk insurance to produce and market goods or services for export.

Export Credit Insurance: The state of Missouri offers assistance in obtaining export credit insurance through the Export/Import Bank of the US to take the risk out of selling to customers overseas. The Missouri program, which insures both commercial and political risks, guarantees an exporter that once his goods are shipped, he will be paid. Insured receivables can enhance an exporter's ability to obtain export financing and allow an exporter to offer more attractive credit terms to foreign buyers.

* Workplace Readiness for Women

Trish Rogers
Central Ozarks Private Industry Council
1202 Forum Drive   800-638-1401 ext. 153
Rolla, MO 65401   Fax: 573-364-7030

This particular program provides skills for employment in manufacturing industries for women living in Camden, Laclede, and Pulaski Counties. Training includes classroom instruction, one-on-one instruction and tutoring, computer training and work experience assignments with private employers who agree to provide the necessary supervision and work experience to assist participants with skills development and transition into employment in the manufacturing industry.

* Workforce Preparation for Women

Dr. Nancy Wegge, Consortium Director
Jefferson College   573-431-1951
Hillsboro, MO 63050   Fax: 573-431-9397

This program is currently served in two Missouri locations; Mineral Area College in Park Hills and Jefferson College in Hillsboro. These programs focus on self-esteem, foundation skills and competencies as identified by an assessment process, and a workforce preparation plan developed by each student. Experts from education, business, and industry serve as speakers and consultants for the training sessions. Furthermore, the program matches each student with a mentor.

* Capital for Entrepreneurs

4747 Troost Ave.   816-561-4646
Kansas City, MO 64110   Fax: 816-756-1530

Seed capital fund divided into three separate funds of $1 million each: Fund for Women, Fund for Hispanics, and Fund for African-Americans.

* Missouri Enterprise Business Assistance Center

800 West 14ᵗʰ Street, Suite 111   573-364-8570
Rolla, MO 65401   800-956-2682
www.missourienterprise.org   Fax: 573-364-6323

Missouri Enterprise Business Assistance Center is a nonprofit corporation dedicated to helping Missouri business succeed. Their integrated programs provide the resources you need to build a successful enterprise.

* Certified Development Companies

Clay/Platte County Development Corporation
Gary R. Moore, Executive Director
8320 North Oak Trafficway, Suite 265   816-468-4989
Kansas City, MO 64118   Fax: 816-468-7778
Area of Operation: Clay and Platte County

EDC Loan Corporation
Kathleen Barney, Loan Manager
10 Petticoat Lane, Suite 250   816-221-0636
Kansas City, MO 64106   Fax: 816-221-0189
Area of Operation: Kansas City

Green Hills Rural Development, Inc.
Michael R. Johns
909 Main Street
Trenton, MO 64683   816-359-5086
Area of Operation: Counties of Caldwell, Daviess, Grundy, Harrison, Linn, Livingston, Mercer, Putnam, Sullivan, Chariton and Carroll

Meramec Regional Development Corporation
Mary Elder, Business Development Specialist
#4 Industrial Drive
St. James, MO 65559   573-265-2993
Area of Operation: Phelps, Dent, Crawford, Washington, Gasconade and Maries Counties

Mo-Kan Development, Inc.
Maurice Owen, Director of Ec. Dev.
1302 Faraon Street   816-233-3144
St. Joseph, MO 64501   Fax: 816-233-8498
Area of Operation: Missouri Counties of Andrew, Buchanan,Clinton and Dekalb; Kansas Counties of Atchison, Brown, Doniphan, Jackson, Jefferson, and Nemaha

Business Finance Corporation of St. Louis County
Richard M. Palank, Executive Director
121 South Meramec, Suite 412   314-889-7663
Clayton, MO 63105   Fax: 314-889-7666
Area of Operation: St. Louis County and Jefferson County

Central Ozarks Development, Inc.
James Dickerson, Executive Director
115 West Hwy 54
P.O. Box 786   573-346-5692
Camdenton, MO 65020   Fax: 573-346-2007
Area of Operation: Camden, Laclede, Pulaski, Miller and Morgan Counties

Economic Development Corporation of Jefferson County, MO
Patrick Lamping, Executive Director
5217 Highway B
P.O. Box 623   314-797-5336
Hillsboro, MO 63050   Fax: 314-789-4594
Area of Operation: Jefferson County

Enterprise Development Corporation
Michael Crist, Executive Director
910 East Broadway, Suite A   573-875-8117
Columbia, MO 65201   Fax: 573-443-2319
Area of Operation: Audrain, Boone, Callaway, Cole, Howard, Montgomery and Randolph Counties

Rural Missouri, Inc.
Ken Lueckenotte, Director
1014 Northeast Drive   573-635-0136
Jefferson City, MO 65109   Fax: 573-635-5636
Area of Operation: Statewide

St. Charles County Economic Development Corporation
Gregory Presteman, Executive Director
5988 Mid Rivers Mall Drive   314-441-6880
St. Charles, MO 63304   Fax: 314-441-6881
Area of Operation: Counties of Franklin, Lincoln, St. Charles and Warren

St. Louis Local Development Company (The)
1015 Locust, Suite 1200   314-622-3400
St. Louis, MO 63101   Fax: 314-622-3413
Area of Operation: St. Louis

The 504 Certified Development Company (CDC) Program provides growing businesses with long-term, fixed-rate financing for major fixed assets, such as land and buildings. A Certified Development Company is a nonprofit corporation set up to contribute to the economic development of its community or region. CDCs work with the SBA and private-sector lenders to provide financing to small businesses.

* Environmental Improvement and Energy Resource Authority

Missouri Department of Natural Resources
P.O. Box 744
Jefferson City, MO 65102-0744   573-751-4919
www.dnr.state.mo.us/eiera/eiera.htm

The Authority may issue tax-exempt bonds or notes to companies for projects that would reduce, prevent or control the pollution of air or water, or provide for proper methods of solid waste disposal. The Authority also may issue bonds for the construction or installation of energy producing facilities.

* Environmental Improvement and Energy Resources Authority

Market Development Loans
P.O. Box 744
Jefferson City, MO 65102   573-751-4919
www.dnr.state.mo.us/eiera/eiera.htm

Loans of up to $75,000 are available to companies for equipment purchases which enable the recovering and recycling of materials. After three years, if all the loan criteria are met, the loan is forgiven and repayment is not required.

* State Treasurer's Office

Missouri First Linked Deposit Program
P.O. Box 210   573-751-2372
Jefferson City, MO 65102-0210   800-662-8257
www.sto.state.mo.us

The Small Business Program: A portion of these deposits are reserved for small businesses under 25 jobs with the maximum loan amount of $100,000. The interest rate to the borrower is capped at 75% of an average rate typically imposed on small businesses.

* Missouri Women's Council

421 East Durkin Street
Jefferson City, MO 65101
Mailing Address:
P.O. Box 1684   573-751-0810
Jefferson City, MO 65102   877-426-9284
www.womenscouncil.org   Fax: 573-751-8835

This program is designed to help Missouri's women achieve economic self-sufficiency by supporting education, training, and leadership opportunities. Each year the Missouri Women's Council reviews pilot program proposals across the state and selects projects to fund, which promote training, employment and support Missouri women in the work place.

* Small Business Administration (SBA)

323 West 8th St., Suite 501
Kansas City, MO 64105-1500   816-374-6701

200 N. Broadway, Suite 1500   314-539-6600
St Louis, MO 63102   Fax: 314-539-3785
www.sba.gov/mo

The Missouri Small Business Administration Office delivers a variety of programs and services, such as startup and operational assistance through small business training and counseling, financial assistance for startup's, business opportunities and much more.

* Small Business Investment Companies

American Century Ventures II, L.L.C.
Diane Mulcahy, Contact
4500 Main Street, 9th Floor   816-340-4054
Kansas City, MO 64111   Fax: 816-340-3278
Email: diane_mulcahy@americancentury.com

Bankers Capital Corporation
Raymond E. Glasnapp, President
3100 Gilham Rd.   816-531-1600
Kansas City, MO 64109   Fax: 816-531-1334
Email: cglasnapp@aol.com

BOME Investors II, L.L.C.
Shelley Whittington, Thomas Adamek
8000 Maryland Avenue, Suite 1190   314-721-5707
St. Louis, MO 63105   Fax: 314-721-5135
Email: jmcvey@gatewayventures.com

BOME Investors III, LLC
Shelley G. Whittington, Contact
8000 Maryland Ave., Suite 1190   225-332-7721
Kansas City, MO 64112   Fax: 225-332-7377
Email: sgwhittington@stonehengecapital.com

BOME Investors, Inc.
Gregory R. Johnson & John McCarthy, Mgrs
8000 Maryland Ave., Suite 1190   314-721-5707
St. Louis, MO 63105   Fax: 314-721-5135
Email: gjohnson@gateway ventures.com

CFB Venture Fund I, Inc.
Greg L. Gaeddert
1000 Walnut, 18th Floor   816-234-2357
Kansas City, MO 64106   Fax: 816-234-2952

CFB Venture Fund I, Inc.
James F. O'Donnell, Chairman
11 South Meramec, Suite 1430   314-746-7427
St. Louis, MO 63105   Fax: 314-746-8739
Email: Bill.Witzofsky@capitalforbusiness.com

CFB Venture Fund II, LP
James F. O'Donnell, Chairman
11 South Meramec, Suite 1430   314-746-7427
St. Louis, MO 63105   Fax: 314-746-8739
Email: Bill.Witzofsky@capitalforbusiness.com

Eagle Fund I, L.P.
Scott Fesler
Bush O'Donnell Capital
101 S. Hanley Road, Suite 1250   314-727-4555
St. Louis, MO 63105   Fax: 314-727-8829
Email: sdf@bushodonnell.com

KCEP I, L.P.
William Reisler, Manager
233 West 47th St.   816-960-1771
Kansas City, MO 64112   Fax: 816-960-1777
Email: dhebert@kcep.com

KCEP Ventures II, L.P.
Bill Reisler, Manager
233 West 47th Street   816-960-1771
Kansas City, MO 64112   Fax: 816-960-1777
Email: dhebert@kcep.com

MorAmerica Capital Corporation
Kevin F. Mullane, Vice President
911 Main St., Suite 2424
Commerce Tower Building   816-842-0114
Kansas City, MO 64105   Fax: 816-471-7339

Power Equities, Inc.
800 Market Street, 13th Floor
MO1-800-15-03   314-466-6634
St. Louis, MO 63101   Fax: 314-466-6238

RiverVest Venture Fund I, L.P.
Thomas C. Melzer, Contact
7733 Forsyth Boulevard, Suite 1650   314-726-6700
St. Louis, MO 63105   Fax: 314-726-6715
Email: tmelzer@rivervest.com

UMB Capital Corporation, Inc.
Noel Shull, Manager
1010 Grand Ave.
Mail: P.O. Box 419226   816-860-7914
Kansas City, MO 64141   Fax: 816-860-7143
Email: noel.shull@umb.com

The SBA licenses, regulates, and provides financial assistance to privately owned and operated Small Business Investment Companies. SBICs make venture or risk investments by supplying capital and extending unsecured loans and loans not fully collateralized to small enterprises which meet their investment criteria. Financing is made by direct loans and by equity investments.

Montana

* Department of Commerce

301 S. Park Ave.   406-841-2700
P.O. Box 200501   800-221-8015 (in MT)
Helena, MT 59601-0501   Fax: 406-841-2701
http://commerce.state.mt.us

Economic Development Division: Offers a variety of programs aimed at assisting start-up and existing businesses with the technical and financial assistance necessary for their success. Works closely with other department divisions, state agencies, and federal and private programs, as well as local development groups, chambers and similar organizations.

The Census and Economic Information Center (CEIC): The official source of census data for Montana, the Center maintains a collection of documents and computer-retrievable files that address the economy and population of the state (historical as well as current), including special papers and annual, quarterly and monthly statistical reports from federal agencies and other Montana state agencies.

Montana Health Facility Authority: Issues revenue bonds or notes to finance or refinance projects involving construction, renovation, or equipment purchases for public or private non-profit health care programs. The MHFA lends its bond proceeds to participating health care facilities at costs below those offered by commercial lending institutions, thereby substantially lowering the facilities' borrowing expenses. In some instances, however, the MHFA includes commercial lending institutions in the financing to provide credit enhancement or private placement for the bonds. The MHFA may issue its notes and bonds, which are not general obligations of the state, for a single entity or a pool of health care facilities. Eligible health facilities may include hospitals, clinics, nursing homes, centers for the developmentally disabled or a variety of other health facilities.

Microbusiness Finance: Montana "micro" business companies with fewer than 10 full-time equivalent employees and annual gross revenues under $500,000 can receive loans of up to $35,000 from the program's network of regional revolving loan funds lending directly to businesses. The loan program is designed to fund economically sound business projects that are unable to obtain commercial financing. Companies must provide a detailed written business plan and may be required to participate in business training classes. In addition to financing, borrowers receive technical assistance and consulting to help assure their success.

Research and Development Financing: Montana Science and Technology Alliance provides $13.1 million in matching capital, from the Permanent Coal Tax Trust Fund, for research and development projects at Montana public universities. 406-444-2778

Growth Through Agriculture: Projects must embody innovative agricultural products or processes. Amounts: $50,000 in any one round, $150,000 to any one firm.

Seed Capital Program: provides funding for early-state entrepreneurial companies. The emphasis for funding is on technological companies but other companies can receive financing as well. The program may loan up to $350,000 in a single financing round, and up to a maximum of $750,000 to any one company over time.

Trade Program: Mission is to identify opportunities for worldwide and domestic trade and to provide representation, information and technical assistance. More specifically, the Trade Program provides: trade consultation, Marketing/Country reports, trade leads, trade show assistance, special promotions for Montana made products and services, tourism promotion services in the Far East.

Made in Montana program: Works to elevate the status of Montana-made products in the marketplace and to educate Montanans about the diversity of products manufactured in their state.

NxLevel: This is an on-line program that prepares business owners with basic business training. It also will walk the business owner through each step of preparing a business plan. www.nxlevelmontana.org

Revolving Loan Funds: There are a variety of local and regional revolving loan funds (RFL) in the state, with many of them being co-located. A list of RFL's can be found at http://mtfinanceonline.com/RLFlist.html

Regional Development Office: Montana is divided into five areas with each having a Regional Development Officer (RDO) that serves as a representative for the Department of Commerce. Their primary goal is to provide technical assistance to businesses so they can get funding for start-ups, expansions, and retention projects.
{http://commerce.state.mt.us/BRD/BRD_RD.html}

West Regional Development Office
Eric Hanson
15 Depot Park   406-257-2259
Kalispell, MT 59901   Fax: 406-758-2805
Area of Operation: Lincoln, Flathead, Sanders, Lake, Missoula, Mineral and Ravali Counties.

South Central Regional Development Office
Al Jones
2004 Miles Avenue   406-655-1696
Billings, MT 59102   Fax: 406-655-0899
Area of Operation: Meagher, Park, Carbon, Stillwater, Sweet Grass, Yellowstone, Big Horn, Musselshell, Golden Valley, and Wheatland Counties.

Southwest Regional Development Office
Terry Dimock
301 S Park
Helena, MT 59601
Mailing Address:
P.O. Box 200505   406-841-2737
Helena, MT 59620-0505   Fax: 406-841-2731
Area of Operation: Lewis & Clark, Powell, Granite, Deer Lodge, Jefferson, Broadwater, Silver Bow, Beaverhead, Madison, and Gallatin Counties.

Eastern Montana Regional Development Office
Tod Kasten
P.O. Box 520   405-485-3374
Circle, Mt 59215   Fax: 406-485-3376
Area of Operation: Valley, Daniels, Sheridan, Roosevelt, McCone, Richland, Dawson, Prarie, Wibaux, Fallon, Carter, Powder River, Custer, Treasure, Rosebud, and Garfield counties.

North Central Regional Development Office
Randy Hanson
48 2nd Avenue, Room 211
Havre, MT 59501
Mailing Address:
P.O. Box 311   406-262-9579
Havre, MT 59501-0311   Fax: 406-262-9581
Area of Operation: Glacier, Toole, Liberty, Hill, Blaine, Phillips, Petroleum, Fergus, Judith Basin, Choteau, Cascade, Teton, and Pondera Counties.

* USDA Rural Development State Office

P.O. Box 850   406-585-2580
Bozeman, MT 59771   Fax: 406-585-2565
www.rurdev.usda.gov/mt

B&I Guaranteed Loan Program: The Business and Industry (B&I) Guaranteed Loan program provides up to an 80% guarantee on traditional lender loans to businesses. The primary purpose of the program is to create and maintain employment and improve the economic climate of the rural community by providing the financial backing for new and expanding businesses.

Rural Business Enterprise Grant: The Rural Business Enterprise Grant Program provides grants for development of revolving loan funds and to provide technical assistance to small emerging private businesses.

Cooperative Services: Cooperative Services can help rural residents who are trying to form new cooperative businesses or improve the operations of an existing cooperative by providing technical assistance, conducting cooperative research, and producing information products to promote public understanding of cooperatives.

* Montana Manufacturing Extension Center (MMEC)

MSU Advanced Technology Park
960-A Technology Boulevard
Bozeman, MT 59718
Mailing address:
P.O. Box 174255   406-994-3812
Bozeman, MT 59717-4255   Fax: 406-994-3391
www.mmec.montana.EDU
Improves the competitiveness of Montana manufacturers through direct,

unbiased engineering and managerial assistance in partnership with public and private resources. MMEC field engineers help companies obtain the highest output from their people, equipment, and capital. They make "house calls" and provide free initial consultation. Their assistance includes, but is not limited to: productivity and quality audits, facility layouts, materials handling, ISO 9000 and quality assurance, benchmarking, managing growth, capacity planning, feasibility assessment, equipment justification, process design and improvement, cycle time reduction, production management, cost/benefit analysis, cost reduction, product costing, make/buy analysis, inventory analysis, supplier identification and relations, payroll incentive systems, materials requirements planning (MRP), and more.

* Montana Local Technical Assistance Program LTAP

Montana State University-Bozeman
Civil Engineering Department
416 Cobleigh Hall
P.O. Box 173910   800-541-6671
Bozeman, MT 59717-3910   Fax 406-994-1697
Email: mtltap@coe.montana.edu
www.coe.montana.edu/ltap

Each LTAP Center tailors its resources to meet the particular needs of the clients they serve. Basic responsibilities include: Publish a quarterly newsletter; Serve as a clearinghouse for local transportation agencies to obtain publications, video tape and other technology resource materials; Maintain a comprehensive up-to-date mailing list of local officials having transportation responsibilities; Conduct training for local transportation agencies; Provide information on new and existing technology; Conduct program evaluations to assure the needs of local transportation agencies are being met.

* Montana World Trade Center

Gallagher Business Building, Suite 257
The University of Montana   406-243-6982
Missoula, MT 59812-6798   Fax: 406-243-5259
www.mwtc.org

The Montana World Trade Center is a nonprofit organization whose purpose is to help Montana and regional businesses establish or strengthen their international commercial capabilities. The Center works to develop untapped international trade opportunities for the state and region and help businesses capitalize on opportunities to expand their market share around the world.

* One Stop Licensing Center

Montana Department of Revenue
P.O. Box 8003
Mitchell Building   406-444-6900
Helena, MT. 59604   Fax: 406-444-0750
http://discoveringmontana.com/revenue

Here are a few of the benefits of one-stop licensing: One point of contact for obtaining or renewing a majority of the licenses required to operate the business. One master form to obtain or renew these licenses, eliminating the redundancy of filling out multiple forms. Renewal forms may be completed by telephone. One payment (writing one check) rather than making a separate payment for each license. Credit cards will be accepted. A significant reduction in the labor and paperwork involved in licensing the business.

* Family Business Program

College of Business
Montana State University
P.O. Box 173040   406-994-6796
Bozeman, MT 59717-3040   Fax: 406-994-6206
www.montana.edu/wwwdb/FamilyBusiness/FamilyBusiness.html

The purpose of the Family Business Program is to provide educational opportunities and resources to family-owned businesses; in addition, the program provides educational opportunities and resources to service providers of family businesses.

* Certified Development Companies

Economic Development Corporation of Yellowstone County
Jeff Leuthold
TW I, #109
404 N. 31st   406-245-0415
Billings, MT 59101   Fax: 208-330-4264
Area of Operation: statewide

Montana Community Finance Corporation
Karen Howard, Executive Director
7 West 6th Avenue   406-443-3261

Helena, MT 59624 — Fax: 406-449-5678

The 504 Certified Development Company (CDC) Program provides growing businesses with long-term, fixed-rate financing for major fixed assets, such as land and buildings. A Certified Development Company is a nonprofit corporation set up to contribute to the economic development of its community or region. CDCs work with the SBA and private-sector lenders to provide financing to small businesses.

* Montana Capital Companies

The Glacier Springs Company
P.O. Box 2644 — 406-727-7500
Black Eagle, MT 59403 — Fax: 406-454-1085

Southwest Montana Development Corp.
P.O. Box 507
Butte, MT 59703 — 406-723-4349

Great Falls Capital Corporation
104 2nd Street South, Suite 203
Great Falls, MT 59401 — 406-761-2000

First Montana Capital Corporation
310 West Spruce St. — 406-721-8300
Missoula, MT 59802 — Fax: 403-721-6300

The Montana Capital Companies Act is designed to stimulate economic activity in Montana by providing tax credit incentives to investors in Montana capital companies, who in turn provide debt and equity financing to new or expanding qualified Montana Businesses. The Department of Commerce is responsible for oversight of the tax credits, qualified investments, and general operations of Glacier Venture Fund.

* Department of Agriculture

Agriculture/Livestock Building
P.O. Box 200201 — 406-444-3144
Helena, MT 59620-0201 — Fax: 406-444-5409
http://agr.state.mt.us

Junior Agriculture Loan Program: Direct, lower-interest rate financing to active members of rural youth organizations for junior livestock and other agricultural business loans. May also make direct loans to youths unable to participate as members of such organizations. Projects can involve crop and livestock production, custom farming, marketing and distribution processing. Loans shall not exceed $7,000.

Rural Assistance Loan Program: Provides loans to farmers and ranchers with modes financial investments in agriculture. Available to those who are unable to qualify for financing from commercial lenders. Maximum loan amount is $50,000, not to exceed 80 percent of the loan value. Funds can be used to finance agricultural property such as livestock and farm machinery, improvements such as barns and irrigation systems, annual operating expenses, and agricultural land.

Montana Growth Through Agriculture Act (MGTA): Intent of the MGTA is to create jobs and expand small agricultural business opportunities. The Programs receives a level of coal severance tax revenues for the purpose of funding seed capital loans, market enhancement and research grants, agricultural business incubators and foreign trade office activities.

Seed Capital Loans: Funds are specifically intended for the commercialization and marketing of new and innovative agricultural products or processes. Maximum loan amount in any one round of financing is $50,000.

Beginning Farmer/Rancher Loan Program: The Montana Beginning Farmer/Rancher Loan Program is a tax-exempt bond program designed to assist Beginning Farmers/Raanchers in the State of Montana to acquire agricultural property at lower interest rates.

* Resource Development Bureau

Department of Natural Resources and Conservation
P.O. Box 20161
1625 11th Ave. — 406-444-2074
Helena, MT 59620-1601 — Fax: 406-444-2684
www.dnrc.state.mt.us

Resource Outreach Programs: The state's coal severance tax provides grants, and two bonding authorities fund loans. Loans and grants available for such diverse water development projects as dam and reservoir construction, streambank stabilization and erosion control, development of water conservation measures, and water and sewer projects.

Reclamation and Development Grant Program: Funds projects that protect and restore the environment from damages resulting from mineral

development and projects that meet other crucial state needs. Other projects may qualify if they enhance Montana's economy or develop, promote, protect, or otherwise further Montana's total environment and public interest.

State Revolving Fund Program: A loan program for wastewater systems and is proposed to be used for landfills. This allows communities to obtain loans at 4% to finance these types of infrastructure.

Private Water Development Program: This program is made up of loans and grants. The low-interest loans may be used for the development of water-related projects, efficient use of resources, best management practices for the agricultural community, and water and wastewater projects. The grants are made to help private entities to meet regulatory requirements that pertain to water use in Montana. The grants are for up to $5,000.

Range Improvement Loan Program: Low-interest loans to Montana's farmers and ranchers for rangeland improvements and development.

Renewable Resource Loans to Private Entities: Loans for private water development projects up to $200,000 or 80% of fair market value of the security given for the project.

* Small Business Administration (SBA)

10 West 15th Street, Suite 1100 — 406-441-1081
Helena, MT 59626 — Fax: 406-441-1090
www.sba.gov/mt

The Montana Small Business Administration Office delivers a variety of programs and services, such as startup and operational assistance through small business training and counseling, financial assistance for startup's, business opportunities and much more.

* Montana Department of Revenue

Office of Research and Information
Sam Mitchell Building
125 N. Roberts
P.O Box 5805
Helena, MT 59604-5805 — 406-444-6900
www.state.mt.us/revenue

Montana is one of very few states imposing neither a general sales tax nor a use tax. In addition, Montana also offers specific tax incentives to aid businesses with start-up and expansion. These include such topics as: property tax incentives, general individual income tax and corporation license tax incentives, natural resource-related tax incentives, and other significant tax incentives.

Assistance for Business Clinics: The Department of Revenue, in conjunction with the Internal Revenue Service and various state government agencies, offers workshops statewide designed to assist new business start-ups and small businesses. These informative workshops are offered in a variety of locations each summer and cover many employer-related topics, including tax filing obligations.

* Montana Board of Investments

2401 Colonial Drive, 3rd Floor
Helena, MT 59601
Mailing Address:
P.O. Box 200126 — 406-444-1365
Helena, MT 59620-0126 — Fax: 406-449-6579
www.investmentmt.com

The Montana Board cannot make direct loans to businesses; the staff however is able to work with businesses to develop a loan package tailored to the companies needs. The following programs are accessed through banks and approved lending institutions.

Business Loan Participation Program Funded From the Coal Tax Trust: There is fixed-rate financing up to 25 years in this program. The maximum participation is about $64 million, which 10% of the Trust. Job creation credits can reduce the interest by up to 2.5%.

Linked Deposit Business Loan Program Funded From the Coal Tax Trust: Fixed-rate financing for up to 20 years is available. The Board invests in a one year CD with the lender for the life of the loan. The CD amount is reduced annually in line with the loan principal pay-down. The lender will pledge qualifying investments as collateral with the State Treasurer.

Guaranteed Loan Purchase Program Funded From the Coal Tax Trust: Fixed-rate financing is available for up to 30 years. The Board will purchase 100% of the guarantee portion of the loan. The interest rate is reduced up to 2.5% with job creation credits.

Value-Added Business Loan Funded From the Coal Tax Trust: This offers a maximum 15-year loan with 2 ¼% interest rate for the first five years, 6% for the second five years, and the posted rate for the remaining years. If 10-14 jobs are created/retained, the business qualifies for a loan rate at 4% for five years. If 15 jobs are created/retained, the business qualifies for a loan rate of 2% for 5 years. The loan range is from $250,000 to $6.4 million. The borrow's business must add value material and or products.

* Montana Department of Administration

General Services Division
Room 165 Mitchell Building
125 North Roberts Street
P.O. Box 200135   406-444-2575
Helena, MT 59620-0136   Fax: 406-444-2529
www.discoveringmontana.com/doa/gsd

The department develops and administers a cost-effective, professional procurement program for the State of Montana by ensuring fair competition, maximizing the purchasing value of public funds, and providing leadership and services for innovative, responsive and accountable public procurement. In addition, they offer State Procurement Bureau Training on purchasing, through the Professional Development Center on state procurement issues.

Nebraska

* Department of Economic Development

P.O. Box 94666   402-471-3111
301 Centennial Mall South   800-426-6505 (in NE)
Lincoln, NE 68509   Fax: 402-471-3378
www.neded.org   TDD: 402-471-3441

One-Stop Business Assistance Program: Provides assistance on identifying, marketing and finance information; business information and research, regulations, licenses, fees, and other state requirements for business operation.

Skilled Training Employment Program (STEP): Offers a comprehensive, on-the-job training program for new and expanding businesses.

Government Procurement Assistance: Helps create additional markets.

Match Marketing: Assists with matching Nebraska buyers and suppliers.

Technical Assistance: Increases productivity and competitiveness.

Site Location Assistance: Includes facilitating access to programs.

Industrial Revenue Bonds (IRB): All Nebraska counties and municipalities, as well as the Nebraska Investment Finance Authority, are authorized to issue IRBs to finance land, buildings and equipment for industrial projects. The rate of interest is normally lower than on most loans.

Nebraska Investment Finance Authority: Issues IRBs for land, building and equipment for industrial enterprises, as well as provides financing for housing.

Community Improvement Financing: This is Nebraska's version of Tax Increment Financing, a method of financing public improvements associated with a private development project in a blighted and substandard area by using the projected increase in the property tax revenue which will result from the private development.

Local Option Municipal Economic Development Act: Provides the ability for communities to add a sales or property tax for economic development projects.

Nebraska Energy Fund: Provides low-interest loans for energy efficiency improvements.

Nebraska Redevelopment Act: Authorizes Community Improvement Financing for real estate and equipment in a project that adds at least 500 new jobs and $50 million of new investment.

Office of International Trade and Investment (OITI): Works with existing businesses to expand their international marketing efforts, as well as foster international manufacturing investments in the state.

Toolkit for Start-up and Existing Business: The toolkit site has an enormous amount of information covering business needs. From starting a business to finances, taxes, and business law, owners will be connected to resources they need to accomplish their business goals. http://assist.neded.org

* Rural Development Administration

Federal Building, Room 308
100 Centennial Mall North   402-437-5551
Lincoln, NE 68508   Fax: 402-437-5408
www.rurdev.usda.gov/ne

The mission of the Rural Business Service is to enhance the quality of life for all rural Americans by providing leadership in building competitive businesses that can prosper in both the domestic and global trading marketplace.

Business and Industry Loan Guarantee: This program provides loan guarantees for business and industrial development to create and maintain employment, expand, and to improve economic climate. Projects include: business/industrial acquisition, construction, enlargement, modernization, real estate, buildings, equipment, working capital, and refinancing. Eligible applicants include traditional lenders, individuals, partnerships, non-profits, corporations, Indian tribes, and cooperatives.

Rural Economic Development Loan and Grant Program: This program provides for a wide range of rural economic development and job creation projects that will improve the economic condition of rural areas. Loans and grants are made to the Rural Utilities Service (RUS) electric and telephone borrowers who use the funds to provide financing for business and community development projects. Projects may include: business expansion and start-up, community development, incubator, medical, training and technology projects, and revolving loan funds.

Rural Business Enterprise Grant: This program provides grants that facilitate and finance the development of small and emerging private business enterprises in rural areas through establishing small business revolving loan funds, acquisition of land, buildings, and infrastructure to enhance business development or by providing technical assistance. Eligible applicants include public bodies, non-profits, and Indian tribes.

Rural Business Opportunity Grants: To provide grants for technical assistance for business development and to conduct economic planning in rural areas. Funds may be used to develop project feasibility studies, technical assistance, or for business and economic development, planning and training. Eligible applicants include public bodies, non-profits, federally recognized tribal groups, and cooperatives.

Intermediary Relending Program: To provide intermediary loans to ultimate recipients for community development projects, establishment and expansion of businesses and creation and/or saving of jobs. Eligible applicants include public bodies/agencies (local/state government), non-profits, Indian tribes, and cooperatives.

* Dollar and Energy Saving Loans

Nebraska Energy Office
Box 95085   402-471-2867
Lincoln, NE 68509   Fax: 402-471-3064
www.nol.org/home/NEO/loan/index.html

Energy saving loans are offered statewide by the Nebraska Energy Office and the state's lending institutions. The interest rate is 5% or less, but may be adjusted semi-annually. Adjustments do not affect existing loans. Check with a lender or the Nebraska Energy Office for the current rate.

* Rural Business Development Fund

Robert E. Hobbs, Loan Coordinator
16 West 11th Street
P.O. Box 2288   308-865-5675
Kearney, NE 68848-2288   308-865-5681
www.mnca.net

Small Enterprises Economic Development Project, Rural Economic and Community Development, State of Nebraska. LB144, private grants. Provides microenterprise loans, loan counseling, credit analysis, developing business plan and entrepreneurial training.

* Northeast Nebraska Development District
Business Loan Programs

Northeast Nebraska Economic Development District
111 S. 1st St.
Norfolk, NE 68701   402-379-1150
www.nenedd.org   Fax: 402-379-9207

Exists to promote and assist the growth and development of business and industrial concerns within Northeast Nebraska. Priority will be given to fixed asset financing (land, building, equipment); however, working capital can also be financed. Generally, loans will range from $10,000 to $100,000 (maximum).

* Nebraska Department of Revenue

301 Centennial Mall South
P.O. Box 94818   402-471-5729
Lincoln, NE 58509-4818   800-742-7474
www.revenue.state.ne.us

Employment and Investment Growth Act: With a $3 million investment in qualified property and addition of 30 full-time employees, a business qualifies for: direct refund of all sales and use taxes paid on purchases of qualified property; 5% tax credit on the amount of the total compensation paid to employees; 10% tax credit on total investment in qualified property, 5 and 10% tax credits applied to income tax liability or used to obtain refund of sales and use taxes paid on other purchases.

With a $10 million investment in qualified property and addition of 100 full-time employees, a business qualifies for: all of the above plus up to a 15 year personal property tax exemption on newly acquired: turbine-powered aircraft, mainframe computers and peripheral components, equipment used directly in processing agricultural products. Investment in qualified property resulting in a net gain of $20 million with no increased employment qualifies a business for direct refund of all sales and use taxes paid on purchases of qualified property.

Employment Expansions and Investment Incentive Act: Provides tax credits for any business which increase investment by at least $75,000 and increase net employment by an average of two full-time positions during a taxable year. Credits of $1,500 per net new employee and $1,000 per $75,000 net new investment may be used to reduce a portion of the taxpayer's income tax liability or to obtain a refund of sales and use taxes paid.

Enterprise Zones: Within these areas, tax credits are given for qualifying businesses which increase employment and make investments in the area.

* Nebraska Investment Finance Authority (NIFA)

200 Commerce Court
1230 O St.   800-204-NIFA
Lincoln, NE 68508-1402   402-434-3900
www.nifa.org   Fax: 402-434-3921

Beginning Farmer/Rancher Program: The NIFA Beginning Farmer/Rancher Program enables farmers or ranchers to obtain loans at lower interest rates than those available in the conventional farm credit markets. This is made possible by the issuance of a tax-exempt bond by NIFA to the lender, providing the lender with interest that is exempt from federal and Nebraska state income tax. Therefore, the loan can be priced to provide the lender with a desired effective yield due to the tax savings on the bond.

Community Outreach: NIFA provides community outreach and technical assistance services to housing providers, community organizations, community officials, housing advocates, developers, builders and lenders to initiate, facilitate and expedite the development of affordable housing. The technical assistance provided is to better inform the public of the financial resources available in the State; the various programs NIFA has to offer; and the processes by which housing development occurs.

BINGO Bonds: NIFA's loan guarantee program, Building Infrastructure in Nebraska for Greater Opportunities (BINGO), is designed to stimulate the development of eligible projects in rural and targeted areas by leveraging local resources. When using the BINGO Bond program, the original principal balance of any loan to be guaranteed by NIFA may not exceed $250,000 per phase; $500,000 per project and may only finance costs associated with capital improvement funding. Working capital and operating expenses are not eligible for funding. The loan-to-value ratio should be at least 70 percent and any credit-enhancement must be acceptable to NIFA. Eligible developers include individuals, partnerships, communities and limited liability companies, both non-profit and for-profit, depending on the eligible project, with substantial development experience and/or access to such experience capable of completing the project.

* Commission on Local Government Innovation and Restructuring

521 S. 14th Street, Suite 30   402-471-8697
Lincoln, NE 68508   Fax: 402-471-3079
Email: lwood@mail.state.ne.us
www.state.ne.us/home/clgir

The Goals of the grant program are to stimulate innovation, cooperation, and restructuring of local government in Nebraska; assist in planning innovative, restructuring, or cooperative projects; encourage collaborative or joint use of facilities and capital equipment by local governments; collect evaluations of efforts in government services innovation, restructuring and cooperation; and to identify legislative changes needed to encourage innovation, cooperation and restructuring of local government in Nebraska.

* Nebraska Business Development Center (NBDC)

Nebraska Business Development Center
College of Business Administration
Roskens Hall Room 415
University of Nebraska at Omaha
Omaha, NE 68182-0248   402-554-2521
http://nbdc.unomaha.edu/

NBDC is an educational service designed to help business owners, especially small and medium-sized businesses, compete more evenly with larger firms that have the resources to employ similar consulting services. NBDC works with individuals who wish to start a company, firms that are planning to expand or pursue new business opportunities and firms that are experiencing operations or financial difficulties.

* Nebraska Development Academy

58 Filley Hall
University of Nebraska, Lincoln   800-328-2851
Lincoln, NE 68508-0947   402-472-1724
www.state.ne.us/home/NDN/academy/html

The Nebraska Development Academy committee is the educational arm of the Partnership for Rural Nebraska. The Partnership for Rural Nebraska is a cooperative commitment between the Rural Development Commission, State of Nebraska, University of Nebraska, the United States Department of Agriculture, and the Nebraska Development Network. The Academy provides a systematic way to access education, training and technical assistance in leadership, community, and economic development.

* Nebraska Rural Development Commission

1200 N Street, Suite #610   402-471-6002
Lincoln, NE 68508-2022   877-814-4707
www.rdc.state.ne.us   Fax: 402-471-8690

The Nebraska Cooperative Development Center was created in response to both demand for services and a larger opportunity to create more sustainable rural communities in Nebraska. Cooperative development as a strategy has demonstrated its ability to create economic opportunities that increase the wealth status of its members, improve the economic condition of its area, contribute toward rural community revitalization, and increase the competitiveness of locally owned and operated enterprises. The purpose of the Commission is to foster sustainable community and economic development initiatives. These initiatives should enable Nebraska communities to realize their own goals, thereby contributing to the growth and well-being of the entire state. The Commission is affiliated with National Rural Development Partnership (NRDP). NRDP is a national partnership of states and the national government to support effective development throughout rural America.

Nebraska Rural Partners:
Nebraska Development Network: The Network is a partnership of over 600 public and private organizations committed to supporting community-based development throughout Nebraska.

Nebraska Community Builders: Community Builders is an initiative of the Network and is a process to empower local residents to engage in more effective community building and stimulate regional collaboration through partnerships.

* Nebraska Enterprise Opportunity Network (NEON)

P.O. Box 6605
Lincoln, NE 68506-0605   402-420-9589
Email: neonneb@aol.com
http://neon.neded.org

NEON's mission is to create, expand and support small and micro business opportunities for individuals and communities with limited resources. NEON strives to achieve its mission through networking, training, advocacy, and sharing resources. They are a member-based association of non-profit organizations and public agencies which provide training, technical services, and micro lending assistance (loans up to $25,000) to Nebraska's micro businesses (five or fewer employees).

* Certified Development Company

Nebraska Economic Development Corporation
Alan Eastman
1033 O Street, Suite 548   402-475-2795
Lincoln NE 68508   Fax: 402-475-2849
Area of Operation: statewide

The 504 Certified Development Company (CDC) Program provides growing businesses with long-term, fixed-rate financing for major fixed assets, such as land and buildings. A Certified Development Company is a nonprofit corporation set up to contribute to the economic development of its community or region. CDCs work with the SBA and private-sector lenders to provide financing to small businesses.

* Small Business Administration

11145 Mill Valley Rd.	402-221-4691
Omaha, NE 68154	Fax: 402-221-3680
www.sba.gov/ne	

The Nebraska Small Business Administration Office delivers a variety of programs and services, such as startup and operational assistance through small business training and counseling, financial assistance for startup's, business opportunities and much more.

* Center for Rural Affairs

Rural Enterprise Assistance Project (REAP)	
145 Main St.	
P.O. Box 136	402-687-2100
Lyons, NE 68038	Fax: 402-687-2200
www.cfra.org	

REAP begins with a community commitment to raise seed capital funds to be used for small business loans. Loan sizes range from a few hundred to several thousand dollars. A program is set up to provide training for members, who are generally start-up and home-based businesses, in business planning, management and finance.

* Nebraska Center for Productivity and Entrepreneurship

CBA 209, P.O. Box 880487	402-472-3353
Lincoln, NE 68588-0487	Fax: 402-472-5855
www.cba.unl.edu/outreach/ent	

The Center provides seminars, workshops, and an annual Productivity and Entrepreneurship Conference which are sponsored by the Center to help new businesses, businesses wishing to increase productivity, and people with ideas for new businesses. Persons involved with the Center are also encouraged to participate in the Young Entrepreneurship Program, which provides internships and mentoring for college students wishing to pursue careers in entrepreneurship.

* Nebraska Diplomats, Inc.

P.O. Box 94666	800-426-6505
Lincoln, NE 68509	402-471-3780
http://nediplomats.org/index.html	Fax: 402-471-3778

The Nebraska Diplomats Inc. is a nonprofit corporation with over 475 business executive and community leaders members. They provide a connection for Nebraska leaders without political, organizational or geographical boundaries.

* Agriculture Promotion and Development Division

Department of Agriculture	
P.O. Box 94947	800-422-6692
301 Centennial Mall South	402-471-4876
Lincoln, NE 68509-4847	Fax: 402-471-2759
www.agr.state.ne.us/division/apd/apd.htm	

This division supports and promotes the buying, selling, and development of Nebraska agricultural products by linking buyer to seller. The division works closely with other agencies, commodity groups, and public and private institutions to seek new and expanding markets for Nebraska products. These resources can be accessed through the division□s extensive database.

* Bureau of Business Research

Department of Economics	
University of Nebraska	402-472-2319
Lincoln, NE 68588	Fax: 402-472-3878
www.bbr.unl.edu	

The bureau compiles statistical information on business conditions, produces economic forecasts, and reports economic and demographic information of interest to the business community. The bureau maintains economic and population data files by detailed geographic markets in Nebraska and in the United States.

* Department of Environmental Quality

1200 N St., Suite 400	
Box 98922	402-471-2186
Lincoln, NE 68509	Fax: 402-471-2909
www.deq.state.ne.us	

Funded primarily from a fee on tire sales, the Waste Reduction and Recycle Grant Program allows businesses to seek grants for solid waste management programs and projects. Emphasis is on tire recycling and tire waste reduction, but other projects may be eligible. Grants are awarded twice each year.

* Midland Venture Forum (MVF)

Scott Technology Center	
6825 Pine Street	402-393-0459
Omaha, NE 68106	Fax: 402-955-1790
www.mvforum.com	

This group was put together for the purpose of fostering business development and success of high growth companies; promote economic stability and growth; create jobs and diversify the types of businesses in the midlands. Business owners can get support from resources such as venture capital firms, private investors, educational programs, workshops and more.

* Invest Nebraska Corporation

Invest Nebraska Corporation	
4701 Innovation Drive	402.472.2063
Lincoln, NE 68521	Fax: 402.472.4203
www.investnebraska.com	

Invest Nebraska is a non-profit partnership that helps new and growth-stage companies succeed. They will help businesses find capital, focus on business plans and identify needed resources.

* Nebraska Microenterprise Partnership Fund

P.O. Box 99	
312 Main St., #8	402-846-5757
Walthill, NE 68067	Fax: 402-846-5219
www.nebbiz.org	

Nebraska Microenterprise Partnership Fund (NMPF) raises money from national, state and local levels and then matches those funds with locally based micro-enterprise programs. There are grantees located throughout Nebraska, which offer training and technical assistance in addition to the loans.

Nevada

* State of Nevada Commission on Economic Development

108 E. Proctor St.	775-687-4325
Carson City, NV 89710	800-336-1600
www.expand2nevada.com	Fax: 775-687-4450

555 E. Washington Avenue	
Suite 5400	702-486-2700
Las Vegas, NV 89101	Fax: 702-486-2701

Commission on Economic Development: Publishes a pamphlet, *Business Assistance*. Acts as a clearinghouse for information and technical assistance. Operates several business assistance programs and performs advertising and public relations activities on behalf of Nevada business. Maintains a computerized inventory of available manufacturing and warehousing buildings, land and corporate office space, and customized site selection.

Procurement Outreach Program: Assists businesses in successfully tapping into this lucrative market by: introducing firms to federal agencies that purchase the products and services they sell; providing assistance to ensure that companies are prepared with all of the tools, knowledge and skills necessary to meet the federal government's specifications and standards, and properly complete bids; offering seminars, marketing fairs, mailing lists and direct assistance as well as the Automated Bidline which is a fax-on demand system allowing instant access to the latest bid and requests for proposal information.

Venture Capital: A potential source of venture capital is the State Public Employees Retirement System that disperses funds through several venture capital pools.

Rural Business Loans: Companies in rural Nevada have additional avenues for financial assistance designed to: lend money to small businesses in need of expansion or start-up financing; assist small businesses in obtaining gap financing to complete their business expansion projects; provide financing to small businesses which meet job creation requirements. Assistance is available through the Nevada Revolving Loan Fund, Rural Economic and Community Development Services, and Rural Nevada Development Corporation.

Train Employees Now: Grants to training providers up to 75% of the total eligible costs with a cap of $1,000 per trainee.

Business Assistance Program: Helps businesses understand environmental rules and explain the permitting process as well as identify sources of financing for pollution control equipment and provide access to the latest information regarding environmental issues.

Nevada's International Trade Program: Goal is to assist Nevada businesses to begin, or expand, exporting to international markets. Services include: Trade Missions, Export Seminars, Export Counseling, International Trade Database, Foreign Buyers Delegations, International Trade Directories.

Foreign Trade Zones: Two zones allow international importers duty-free storage and assembly of foreign products.

Export Financing: Assistance is available through private sector financial institution, the International Trade Program and the federal Export/Import Bank.

Made in Nevada Program: Companies that are licensed and headquartered in Nevada and have at least 50% of their product(s) manufactured in the state will benefit from this program. In addition to the network support, those businesses will receive marketing assistance and help to find other beneficial business assistance. 702-486-2710.
{www.expand2nevada.com/MadeinNevada2/index.htm}

* Rural Development State Office

1390 S. Curry Street	702-887-1222
Carson, NV 89703	Fax: 702-885-0841
www.rurdev.usda.gov/nv	

Business And Industry Guarantee And Direct Loans: The guaranteed B&I program provides financial assistance to rural businesses by offering guarantees to lenders as an incentive to extend credit in rural areas. If credit is not available elsewhere, Rural Development may provide direct loans to rural borrowers. Loan funds may be used to support the establishment or expansion of businesses, for working capital, machinery and equipment, buildings and real estate, and certain types of debt refinancing. Businesses involved in forestry, aquaculture, growing of hydroponics and mushrooms and commercial nurseries are eligible for assistance in addition to businesses involved in producing value-added products. The primary purpose is to create and maintain employment and improve the economic climate in rural communities.

Intermediary Relending Program: These loans enable Rural Development to finance business facilities and community development projects in communities of 25,000 or less. This is achieved through loans made by Rural Development to nonprofit intermediaries, which in turn provide loans to businesses in a rural area.

Rural Business Enterprise Grant: Rural Development can make Rural Business Enterprise Grants to tribes, public bodies, and non-profits to assist small and emerging private business enterprises. Funds may be used to conduct feasibility studies, provide technical assistance, or establish a revolving loan fund.

Rural Business Opportunity Grant: Rural Development can make Rural Business Opportunity Grants to tribes, public bodies, and non-profits to promote economic development initiatives in rural communities with exceptional needs. This is accomplished by providing planning, technical assistance, and training.

Rural Economic Development Loans: Rural Development can provide zero interest loans to Rural Utilities Service financed telephone utilities to promote rural economic development and job creation projects.

Rural Economic Development Grants: Rural Development can provide grants from the Rural Business-Cooperative Service to rural communities through Rural Utilities Service borrowers. These grants can be used for the revolving loan fund for community facilities and infrastructure, and for assistance in conjunction with the Rural Economic Development Loans.

Cooperative Services: The Cooperative Services program helps rural residents form new cooperative businesses and improve the operations of existing cooperatives. To accomplish this, Cooperative Services provides technical assistance, conducts cooperative-related research, and produces information products to promote public understanding of cooperatives. They provide a wide range of assistance for people interested in forming cooperatives.

* Community Business Resource Center

116 E. 7th St., Suite 1	775-841-1420
Carson City, NV 89701	800-337-4590
www.cbrc.org	Fax: 775-841-2221

A one-stop center for business information designed to enhance the economic self-sufficiency of low-and moderate-income individuals by developing their entrepreneurial skills. Services available include training, technical assistance and access to credit.

* Nevada State Development Corporation (NSDC)

Nevada Development Corporation	
6572 South McCarran Blvd.	775-826-6172
Reno, NV 89509	800-726-2494
Southern Nevada Development Corporation	
1551 Desert Crossing Rd., Suite 100	702-877-9111
Las Vegas, NV 89114	877-732-7101
www.nsdc-loans.com	

A private development fund designed to finance growth opportunities for small, sound Nevada businesses which do not qualify for conventional financing. The financing provided by NDCC includes but is not limited to the following: working capital loans secured by primary or subordinated assets; loans secured by fixed assets with longer terms than could be provided by conventional lending sources; loans for the acquisition of a business or interest in a business; subordinated loans in cases where available bank financing is sufficient; loans to refinance existing debt in cases where existing terms present a hardship for the business. Most loans will probably be in the $50,000 to $150,000 range.

* Small Business Advocate

Center for Business Advocacy and Services	
2501 East Sahara Ave., Suite 100	702-486-4335
Las Vegas, NV 89104	Fax: 702-486-4340

Assistance in cutting bureaucratic red tape. Information and expertise in dealing with state, federal, and local agencies.

* Certified Development Corporations

Nevada State Development Corporation	
Roberta Bennett, President	775-826-6172
6572 South McCarran Blvd.	800-726-2494
Reno, NV 89509	Fax: 775-826-6398
Area of Operation: Statewide	
New Ventures Capital Development Company	
Earnest Fountain, Vice President	
626 South 9th Street	702-382-9522
Las Vegas NV 89101	Fax: 702-382-0375
Area of Operation: Clark County	
Southern Nevada Certified Development Corporation	
Thomas J. Gutherie, President/CEO	
2770 South Maryland Parkway, Suite 216	
Las Vegas NV 89109	702-732-3998

Area of Operation: Mineral, Esmeralda, Nye, Lincoln, Lyon, Douglas, White Pine and Clark Counties

SBA 504: Provides loans using 50 percent conventional bank financing, 40 percent SBA involvement through Certified Development Companies, and 10 percent owner equity. A fixed-asset loan in amounts up to $750,000. Loan can be used for land and building, construction, machinery and equipment, and renovation/expansion.

* Nevada Housing Division

Department of Business and Industry	
Northern Office	
Evergreen Center	775-687-4258
1802 N. Carson St., Suite 154	800-227-4960
Carson City, NV 89701	Fax: 775-687-4040
Southern Office	
Century Park	
1771 East Flamingo, Suite 206-B	702-486-7220
Las Vegas, NV 89119	Fax: 702-486-7226
http://nvhousing.state.nv.us	

The Housing Division is the designated issuer of tax-exempt mortgage revenue bonds for Nevada. The multifamily bond program provides a financial mechanism for funding affordable housing projects (apartments) via the use of tax-exempt and taxable mortgage revenue bonds.

* NevadaWorks

5905 South Virginia St., Suite 200   775-337-8600
Reno NV, 89502-6024   877-337-8261
www.nevadaworks.com   Fax: 775-337-9589
The Workforce Investment Act provides workforce development services to employers and job seekers through a seamless One-Stop service delivery system. These services are intended to meet both employer demands for a skilled workforce and to increase the employment, retention and earnings of job seekers.

* Nevada Division of Environmental Protection

333 West Nye Lane, Room 104   775-687-4670
Carson City, NV 89706-0851   Fax: 775-687-5856
http://ndep.nv.gov
The Small Business Assistance Program (SBAP) assists with all aspects of compliance, including permitting, reporting, planning, pollution control and prevention technologies. The technical assistance coordinator (TAC) works cooperatively with local governments and other assistance programs to help small businesses comply with environmental regulations. The ombudsman works to inform businesses of the governmental processes, their appeal rights, and promotes small business participation in the development of regulations. The Air Quality Compliance Advisory Panel (CAP) is a panel of professionals who are involved with or own small businesses.

* Industrial Development Revenue Bonds

Nevada Department of Business and Industry
Office of Business Finance and Planning
788 Fairview Lane, Suite 100   775-687-4246
Carson City, NV 89701   Fax: 775-687-4266
http://dbi.state.nv.us/bfp
A special type of loan to qualified manufacturers who are buying land, building new facilities, refurbishing existing buildings and purchasing new equipment.

* Nevada Microenterprise Initiative

Northern Nevada Office
113 W. Plumb Lane   775-324-1812
Reno, NV 89509   Fax: 775-324-1813

Rural Nevada Office
116 E. 7th Street, Suite 1   775-841-1420 x2
Carson City, NV 89701   Fax: 775-841-2221

Southern Nevada Office
1600 E. Desert Inn Road, Suite 210   702-734-3555
Las Vegas, NV 89109   Fax: 702-734-3530
www.nmimicro.org
Nevada MicroEnterprise Initiative is a private non-profit community development financial institution. They provide business tools to assist businesses overcome barriers that they may face in starting or in expanding a business. They offer business training, business loans, and networking.

* Small Business Administration (SBA)

400 South 4th Street, Suite 250   702-388-6611
Las Vegas NV 89101   Fax: 702-388-6469
www.sba.gov/nv
The Nevada Small Business Administration Office delivers a variety of programs and services, such as startup and operational assistance through small business training and counseling, financial assistance for startup's, business opportunities and much more.

* Small Business Investment Companies

Atlanta Investment Company, Inc.
L. Mark Newman, Chairman of the Board
601 Fairview Blvd.
P.O. Box 7718   702-833-1836
Incline Village, NV 89452   Fax: 702-833-1890
Email: mnewman@resortnet.com
The SBA licenses, regulates and provides financial assistance to privately owned and operated Small Business Investment Companies. SBIC's make venture or risk investments by supplying capital and extending unsecured loans and loans not fully collateralized to small enterprises which meet their investment criteria. Financing is made by direct loans and by equity investments.

New Hampshire

* Department of Resources and Economic Development

State of New Hampshire
172 Pembroke Road
P.O. Box 1856   603-271-2411
Concord, NH 03302-1856   Fax: 603-271-2629
www.dred.state.nh.us
Office of Business and Industrial Development: Provides assistance and publications designed to support and promote business and industry in the state. Information in areas such as licensing and permits, financial counseling, marketing, and exporting, labor markets, and more.

Economic Development Data System: A comprehensive database of all the communities and available industrial properties within the state.

Business Visitation Program: Local volunteers visit businesses to gather information about firms' development issues, economic concerns and opinions about their community as a place to do business. Once aware of these issues, local, state and federal programs can be accessed to assist the firms. A referral network coordinates questions, issues and concerns.

Procurement Technical Assistance Program: Provides the necessary tools to be competitive in the federal marketplace through procurement counseling; contract announcements; specifications and standards; and support databases.

Regional and Local Revolving Loan Funds: Many local and regional revolving loan funds exist throughout New Hampshire. These funds have been capitalized from a variety of services, many with federal monies. The administration of these funds is generally handled by a non-profit corporation, while the local funds most often are overseen by governing bodies with the help of a loan committee. The loans may be used in conjunction with other sources to leverage additional monies or independently finance the project.

Finance Clearinghouse: Offers companies assistance in obtaining financing. A complete listing of programs can be obtained through the clearinghouse.

International Trade Resource Center: A one-stop location when businesses, both current and potential exporters, can access the assistance and information necessary to effectively explore, develop and penetrate the foreign marketplace. Offers counseling, education and training seminars, automated trade leads, market research, marketing promotion, library and finance assistance. {www.globalnh.org}

Foreign Trade Zones: Provides economic incentives to companies doing business in foreign countries.

* New Hampshire Industrial Research Center

New Hampshire Industrial Research Center
134 Environmental Technology Building
35 Colovos Road   603-862-0123
Durham, NH 03824   Fax: 603-862-0329
www.nhirc.unh.edu
Assistance in basic and applied research, development and marketing through a matching grants program; hands-on training in Design of Experiment methods; and helping inventors develop patent and commercialize their ideas.

* Workforce Opportunity Council, Inc.

New Hampshire Job Training
64 Old Suncook Rd.   603-228-9500
Concord, NH 03301   Fax: 603-228-8557
www.nhworks.org
Provides job training for citizens while helping businesses gain capable workers.

* New Hampshire Export Finance Program

New Hampshire Office of International Commerce
17 New Hampshire Ave.   603-334-6074
Portsmouth, NH 03801   Fax: 603-334-6110
www.globalnh.org/export
To support export sales in providing working capital for the exporter to produce or buy a product for resale; provide political and/or commercial risk insurance in order to provide open account terms to foreign buyers; provide access to funding to qualified foreign buyers who need medium-term financing in order to purchase capital goods and services from New

Hampshire Exporters. Rates and premiums arranged per sale or as needed. No dollar limit.

* Rural Development

New Hampshire/Vermont Rural Development
Montpelier Office
City Center, 3rd Floor
89 Main Street   802-828-6010
Montpelier, VT 05602   Fax: 802-828-6076
www.rurdev.usda.gov/vt

Cooperative Services Program: The Cooperative Services Program goal is to promote the understanding and use of the cooperative form of business as a viable organizational option for marketing and distributing agricultural products.

Business and Industry Guaranteed Loans: The Business and Industry (B&I) Guaranteed Loan Program helps create jobs and stimulates rural economies by providing financial backing for rural businesses. Loan proceeds may be used for working capital, machinery and equipment, buildings and real estate, and certain types of debt refinancing. The primary purpose is to create and maintain employment and improve the economic climate in rural communities. The maximum aggregate B&I Guaranteed Loan(s) amount that can be offered to any one borrower under this program is $25 million.

Intermediary Relending Program: The purpose of the Intermediary Relending Program (IRP) is to finance business facilities and community development projects in rural areas. Intermediaries re-lend funds to ultimate recipients for business facilities or community development.

Rural Business Enterprise Grants: The Rural Business-Cooperative Service (RBS) makes grants under the Rural Business Enterprise Grants (RBEG) Program to public bodies, private nonprofit corporations, and Federally-recognized Indian Tribal groups to finance and facilitate development of small and emerging private business enterprises located in areas outside the boundary of a city or unincorporated areas of 50,000 or more and its immediately adjacent urbanized or urbanizing area. Grant funds do not go directly to the business.

Rural Economic Development Loans and Grants: Provides zero-interest loans and/or grants to electric and telephone utilities financed by the Rural Utilities Service (RUS), an agency of the United States Department of Agriculture, to promote sustainable rural economic development and job creation projects.

Rural Business Opportunity Grants: The purpose is to promote sustainable economic development in rural communities with exceptional needs. This is accomplished by making grants to pay costs of providing economic planning for rural communities, technical assistance for rural businesses, or training for rural entrepreneurs or economic development officials.

* New Hampshire Housing Finance Authority

32 Constitution Drive
Bedford, NH   800-640-7239 (NH only)
Mailing address: P.O. Box 5087   603-472-8623
Manchester, NH 03108   Fax: (603) 472-8501
www.nhhfa.org

Tax Exempt Bond Financing. Tax exempt private activity bonds can be issued by the Authority to finance multi-family housing. In return for the reduced interest financing, at least thirty percent of the units must be rented to households earning 50% or less of the median area income or fifty percent of the units must be rented to households earning 60% or less of the median area income. The Authority also adds rent restrictions for the compliance period. The restrictions are in effect for the longer of 15 years or the life of the bond. Any for-profit development entity is eligible to participate.

* New Hampshire Community Technical College System

26 College Drive   603-271-2722
Concord, NH 03301-7400   800-247-3420 (in NH)
www.nhctc.edu   Fax: 603-271-2725

The New Hampshire Community Technical College System is a source of highly skilled personnel for business and industry, both through traditional associate degree programs and through customized professional and skills training. Throughout the state, their seven Centers for Training and Business Development (CTBDs) work with businesses to develop and deliver special classes or entire programs on specific topics to maintain and/or upgrade the skills of their employees. They help employers train their employees to maximize new technologies and increase productivity and competitiveness.

* Business Finance Authority (BFA)

14 Dixon Ave., 2nd Floor   603-271-2391
Concord, NH 03301-6313   Fax: 603-271-2396
www.nhbfa.com

Industrial Development Revenue Bond Financing: Tax exempt revenue bond financing through the Business Finance Authority (BFA). Advantages include 100% financing. Lower interest costs to the company and no dilution of equity. Eligible applicants are manufacturing facilities, facilities for the disposal of waste material; small-scale power facilities for producing electric energy; water-powered electric generating facilities; water facilities for the collecting, purifying, storing or distributing of water for use by the general public. Bond proceeds may be used to finance the cost of land, buildings and equipment, as well as bond counsel fees and the development and financing costs of the project.

Guaranteed Loans

The Guarantee of Loans to Small Business Program: Works in conjunction with the U.S. Small Business Administration (SBA). For businesses seeking guarantees on loan amounts that exceed the SBA's capacity. The BFA guarantees amount shall not exceed 90% of the original principal amount of the loan. The BFA guarantee amount and the SBA guarantee amount shall not exceed $1,500,000. The loan amount used to finance working capital shall not exceed $500,000. There is a non-refundable application fee of $250.

The Capital Access Program (CAP): For small businesses experiencing difficulty obtaining lines of credit and funds for start-up or expansion. Encourages banks to make loans to businesses with more than conventional risk by creating an account designed to protect the lender. The account reduces lender risk by decreasing the bank's exposure on the loan. CAP is available to businesses with annual revenues of less than $5,000,000. Total loan amount may not exceed $100,000.

The Guarantee Asset Program (GAP): Designed to provide assistance to capital intensive businesses experiencing difficulty obtaining normal bank financing. BFA will guarantee up to 90% of a loan made by a bank to a qualifying business. The borrower must have at least 25 full time employees. No more than 40% of the gross proceeds of the loan may used to finance working capital. The maturity of a loan shall not exceed 5 years. The terms of the loan will be determined by the participating financial institution.

Assistance to Local Development Organizations Program: To help LDOs create and maintain employment opportunities, the BFA may lend money to LDOs for the purpose of developing and expanding business opportunities in their market area. By providing LDOs with additional resources for financing, the BFA can effectively foster economic growth through existing organizations dedicated to the development of business. Any local development organization dedicated to the promotion and development of business is eligible for this program. The terms of the loan to the business will determined by the participating LDO.

The Working Capital Line of Credit Guarantee (WAG) program allows participating banks or lending institutions to receive a guarantee of up to 75% for a working capital line of credit, not to exceed $2,000,000.

* Small Business Administration (SBA)

District Office
143 N. Main, Suite 202   603-225-1400
Concord, NH 03301   Fax: 603-225-1409
www.sba.gov/nh

The New Hampshire Small Business Administration Office delivers a variety of programs and services, such as startup and operational assistance through small business training and counseling, financial assistance for startup's, business opportunities and much more.

* Small Business Investment Companies

MerchantBanc Venture Partners, L.P.
Jeffrey M. Pollock
Two Wall Street   603-623-5500
Manchester, NH 03101   Fax: 603-623-3972
Email: nlabshier@nhbdc.com.

The SBA licenses, regulates and provides financial assistance to privately owned and operated Small Business Investment Companies. SBIC's make venture or risk investments by supplying capital and extending unsecured loans and loans not fully collateralized to small enterprises which meet their investment criteria. Financing is made by direct loans and by equity investments.

* Certified Development Corporations

Capital Regional Development Council
Niel Cannon, Executive Director

1 South Street
Concord NH 03301

603-228-1872
Fax: 603-226-3588

Mailing Address:
P.O. Box 664
Concord NH 03301

Area of Operation: Belknap, Grafton, Merrimack and Sullivan Counties

Granite State Economic Development Corporation
Alan Abraham, President
1 Cate Street, 5th Floor
Portsmouth NH 03801

603-623-7383
Fax: 603-623-6723

Mailing Address:
P.O. Box 1491
Portsmouth, NH 03801

Area of Operation: Statewide

Northern Community Investment Corporation
Paul Denton, President
20 Main Street
St. Johnsbury VT 05819

802-748-1501
Fax: 802-748-1884

Mailing Address:
P.O. Box 396
St. Johnsbury, VT 05819

Area of Operation: Carroll, Coos, and Grafton Counties

The 504 Certified Development Company (CDC) Program provides growing businesses with long-term, fixed-rate financing for major fixed assets, such as land and buildings. A Certified Development Company is a nonprofit corporation set up to contribute to the economic development of its community or region. CDC's work with the Small Business Administration and private-sector lenders to provide up to 90% financing to small businesses. There are about 270 CDC's nationwide, each covering a specific region.

* Community Development Finance Authority

14 Dixon Avenue, Suite 102
Concord, NH 03301
www.state.nh.us/osp/cdbg

603-271-2170
Fax: 603-271-1728

Community Development Block Grants (CDBG): Grants are awarded to municipalities who in turn loan the funds to help municipalities meet housing and community development needs by alleviating some form of physical or economical distress.

* New Hampshire Port Authority

555 Market St.
Box 369
Portsmouth, NH 03801
www.state.nh.us/nhport

603-436-8500
Fax: 603-436-2780

Foreign Enterprise Zone: Foreign traders can store, mix, blend, repack and assemble various commodities with an exemption from normal custom duties and federal excise taxes. Four areas in New Hampshire have been designated as Foreign Trade Zone 81. They are the Port Authority Terminal, Portsmouth; Portsmouth Industrial Park; Crosby Road Industrial Park, Dover; Manchester Airport (formerly Grenier Air Base, Manchester).

* Industrial Development Manager

Public Service of New Hampshire (PSNH)
1000 Elm St.
P.O. Box 330
Manchester, NH 03105
www.psnh.com

603-669-4000

Development Incentive Rate Contract: PSNH offers an incentive rate to its new or expanding commercial and industrial customers that will provide benefits to all PSNH customers. PSNH negotiates special rate contracts with existing or new customers having incremental load requirements of more than 300 kilowatts.

Small Business Retrofit Program: Through the Small Business Retrofit Program you can get help to improve the efficiency of your businesses electrical appliances. The program can help replace out of date equipment and systems therefore reducing your electric bill.

* NETAAC (New England Trade Adjustment Assistance Center)

600 Suffolk St., 5th Floor North
Lowell, MA 01854
www.netaac.org

978-446-9870
Fax: 978-446-9820

Trade Adjustment Assistance: Manufacturing company must have exper-ienced a decline in production or sales and an actual or threatened decrease in employment, attributable to increased imports of competitive products.

* Manufacturing Management Center

New Hampshire Small Business Development Center
108 McConnell Hall
University of New Hampshire
Durham, NH 03824
www.nhsbdc.org/mmc.htm

603-862-2200
Fax 603-862-4876

The New Hampshire Small Business Development Center is designing a model program and public policy recommendations to help small and medium manufacturers in rural areas of New Hampshire manage growth effectively. In addition, the NH SBDC offers technical, business and financial counseling and training to small manufacturers while enlisting the help of the University's faculty and resources to deliver specialized services on an as-needed basis.

* Merchant Banc

Two Wall Street
Manchester, NH 03101
www.merchantbanc.com

603-623-5500
Fax: 603-623-3972

A non-profit company in the business of funding loans to small businesses that qualify.

* Micro Credit-New Hampshire

New Hampshire Community Loan Fund
7 Wall Street
Concord, NH 03301
www.nhclf.org

800-432-4110
603-224-6669
Fax: 603-225-7425

This program provides assistance to micro business owners that cannot get traditional funding. Loans start at $500 and have a maximum of $10,000.

New Jersey

* New Jersey Economic Development Authority

P.O. Box 990
Trenton, NJ 08625-0990
www.njeda.com

609-292-1800

Division of Economic Development: Develops and administers comprehensive marketing and support programs. Helps access public and private services which address a broad array of issues, ranging from financial, technical and regulatory concerns to employee training and site location.

Office of the Business Advocate and Business Information: Assists businesses that are having difficulty navigating through State regulations. 609-777-0885

Entrepreneurial Training Institute: An eight week program is offered to help new and aspiring entrepreneurs learn the basics of operating a business.

Small Business Contracts: State law requires that at least 15% of the contracts awarded by the State be given to small businesses. In the first half of 1998, these "set-aside contracts" amounted to more than $425 million.

Doing Business in New Jersey Guidebook: Provides information on starting and operating a business in the state. Topics include requirements and advice for starting a new business, information on tax and employee regulations, state and federal financial information, franchising, procurement opportunities, and exporting.

Selective Assistance Vendor Information Database: A computer database designed especially to assist business owners that wish to do business with the State of New Jersey and the private sector. SAVI-II matches buyers and vendors for public and private contracting opportunities.

Maritime Services: New Jersey offers several services to support businesses engaged in this enterprise. These include advice and assistance with permits and economic development issues, facilitation of dredging-related activities, and assistance in reducing or minimizing the creation of sediment.

New Jersey Economic Development Authority's Trade Adjustment Assistance Center: Can provide technical assistance to manufacturers or certify manufacturers for eligibility for federal government assistance.

Real Estate Development Division: Businesses may be able to lease state-of-the-art, affordable laboratory, production, and research facilities in the Technology Centre of New Jersey. New high-technology businesses may be able to utilize inexpensive lab and office space at one of several technology business incubators throughout the state. These incubators typically offer administrative and consulting services to their tenants.

Technology Transfer Program: Businesses may be able to partner with an academic institution, facilitating the transfer of new technology from research to commercial application.

Technology Help Desk Hotline: 800-4321-TEC
Businesses may take advantage of a one-stop Technology Help Desk Hotline, 1-800-4321-TEC. The hotline offers answers to business and technology questions as well as financial advice, referrals to sources of commercialization assistance, help with research and development grant proposals, and advice on using a statewide and national network of business development resource organizations.

The New Jersey Economic Development Authority's Finance Finder: Helps match companies with appropriate finance programs administered by the NJEDA.

Technology Centre of New Jersey: State-of-the-art, affordable laboratory production and research facilities are available for emerging and advanced technology driven companies.

Consulting Assistance for Manufacturers Impacted By Imports: Manufacturers who can demonstrate that their employment and either sales or production have declined due to foreign competition of a like or similar product may be eligible for consulting assistance.

Bond Financing: Bonds are issued to provide long-term loans at attractive, below-market interest rates for real estate acquisitions, equipment, machinery, building construction, and renovations. Minimum loan size is approximately $1 million. Maximum tax-exempt bond amount for manufacturers is $10 million.

Statewide Loan Pool For Business: Loans from $50,000 up to $5 million for fixed assets and up to $1,000,000 for working capital are available to businesses that create or maintain jobs in a financially targeted municipality or represent a targeted industry such as manufacturing, industrial, or agricultural. Assistance usually will not exceed $35,000 per job created or maintained.

Business Employment Incentive Program (BEIP) Grant: Businesses creating at least 25 new jobs in designated urban areas, or 75 jobs elsewhere, may be eligible to receive a BEIP grant. These grants, which may last for up to 10 years, may be for up to 80% of the value of the income taxes withheld annually from the paychecks of new employees.

Loan Guarantees: Guarantees of conventional loans of up to $1 million for working capital and guarantees of conventional loans or bond issues for fixed assets of up to $1.5 million are available to credit worthy businesses that need additional security to obtain financing. Preference is given to businesses that are either job intensive, will create or maintain tax ratables, are located in an economically distressed area, or represent an important economic sector of the state and will contribute to New Jersey's growth and diversity.

Direct Loans: Loans are made for up to $750,000 for fixed assets and up to $500,000 for working capital for up to 10 years to businesses that are unable to get sufficient bank credit on their own or through the Statewide Loan Pool or with and EDA guarantee. Preference is given to job-intensive enterprises located in economically targeted areas or representing a targeted business sector.

New Jersey Seed Capital Program: Loans are made from $25,000 to $500,000 at a market rate of interest for working capital and fixed assets to technology businesses that have risked their own capital to develop new technologies and need additional funds to bring their products to market.

New Jersey Technology Funding Program: EDA participates with commercial banks to make term loans from $100,000 to $5 million for second stage technology enterprises.

Fund For Community Economic Development: Loans and loan guarantees are made to urban-based community organizations that in turn make loans to micro-enterprises and small businesses which may not qualify for traditional bank financing.

Downtown Beautification Program: Loans ranging from $5,000 - $100,000 are available to existing retail and commercial businesses located in the commercial district of a targeted municipality.

Local Development Financing Fund: Loans ranging from $50,000 to $2 million may be made for fixed assets form commercial and industrial projects located in Urban Aid communities.

Hazardous Discharge Site Remediation Loan and Grant Program: Businesses may qualify for loans of up to $1 million for remediation activities due to a closure of operations or transfer of ownership.

Petroleum Underground Storage Tank Remediation Upgrade and Closure Program: Owners/operators may qualify for 100% of the eligible project costs.

Small Business Loans: Loans and loan guarantees administered by the New Jersey Economic Development Authority's Community Development and Small Business Lending Division.

New Jersey Economic Development Authority's Investment Banking Division: Loans may be available for the purchase of manufacturing equipment.

R&D Excellence Grant Program: Businesses may receive financial support for research and development in critical fields, such as healthcare (especially biomaterials, pharmaceuticals, and biotechnologies), software/information, and environmental and civil infrastructure technologies.

Small Business Innovation Research Grants: Applicants for federal grants may receive technical consulting and bridge loans.

Business Relocation Assistance Grant: Provides grants to relocating companies that create a minimum of 75 new full-time jobs in New Jersey.

International Trade Services: Services include financing assistance, strategic advocacy in foreign markets, opportunities to network and receive information and advice regarding international commerce, and assistance in taking advantage of federal international trade programs and Foreign Trade Zones.

Export Financing: Up to a $1 million one-year revolving line of credit will be provided to finance confirmed foreign orders to assist businesses that want to enter the export market or expand export sales but are unable to do so because they cannot get the financing they need on their own.

Foreign Trade Zones: Within these zones, which are outside U.S. Customs territory, businesses may manufacture, assemble, package, process and exhibit merchandise with a substantial duty and cash flow savings.

* New Jersey Department of Commerce and Economic Growth Commission

Division of Development for Small Businesses and
  Women and Minority Businesses
CN 835   609-292-3860
Trenton, NJ 08625   Fax: 609-292-9145
www.state.nj.us/commerce

Services For Businesses Owned By Women And Minorities: Businesses owned by women and minorities play an important role in the New Jersey economy. New Jersey offers a number of services to help these businesses compete and overcome the special challenges they face. These services include financial assistance, advice and instructional materials, training and education, and certification necessary to receive certain contracts.

Set Aside Contracts: State law requires that 7% of the contracts awarded by the State be given to businesses owned by minorities, and 3% to businesses owned by women. In the first half of 1998, these "set-aside contracts" amounted to more than $180 million.

Women and minorities interested in establishing franchise businesses may receive investments from the Small Business Investment Company, which works in conjunction with the New Jersey Economic Development Authority's Commercial Lending Division.

Contractors Assistance Program: Small contracting businesses owned by women or minorities may receive training courses and consultations with experienced executives of large construction companies designed to make it easier to get performance bonds and successfully bid on major construction projects. This service is provided by the New Jersey Economic Development Authority's Community Development and Small Business Lending Division.

New Jersey Development Authority For Small Businesses, Minorities' And Women's Enterprises: This office offers women and minority-owned small businesses financial, marketing, procurement, technical and managerial assistance. Loans of up to $1 million can be made for real estate, fixed asset acquisition, and working capital. Guarantees to banks are also available for fixed asset acquisition and for working capital. To be eligible, a business must be certified as a small, minority-owned or women-owned enterprise. Most of the funds are targeted to enterprises located in Atlantic City or providing goods or services to customers in Atlantic City, including but not limited to the casinos. Limited monies are available for businesses located in other parts of the state.

Regulatory Assistance: Business assistance with obtaining permits and approvals through state regulations.

One-Stop Permit: Assistance in completing the One-Stop form to becoming a business.

Small Business Environmental Ombudsman/Compliance Assistance: This program can help you business deal with specific technical issues, provide free and confidential visits and refer your business to appropriate agencies as necessary.

Business Information Services: One-stop answers and assistance for many new and existing businesses questions. 609-777-0885

License & Certification Hotline: Information that outlines business and occupation requirements. 800-533-0186

Next Step Workshops: Workshops designed to help you do business with the State of New Jersey.

* Rural Development

New Jersey Rural Development Office
5th Floor North, Suite 500
8000 Midlantic Drive   856-787-7000
Mt. Laurel, NJ 08054   Fax: 856-787-7783
www.rurdev.usda.gov/nj

Commercial Lending
Business and Industry Guarantee Loans: The Business and Industry (B&I) Guarantee Loan Program helps create jobs and stimulates rural economies by providing financial backing for rural businesses.

Revolving Loan Funds And Technical Assistance
Intermediary Relending Program Loans: Intermediary Relending Program loans finance business facilities and community development projects in rural areas, including cities with a population of less than 25,000.

Rural Business Enterprise Grants: Rural Business Enterprise Grants help public bodies, nonprofit corporations, and Federally recognized Indian tribal groups finance and facilitate development of small and emerging private business enterprises located in rural areas (this includes all areas other than cities of more than 50,000 people and their immediately adjacent urban or urbanizing areas).

Rural Business Opportunity Grants: Rural Business Opportunity Grant funds provide for technical assistance, training, and planning activities that improve economic conditions in rural areas. Applicants must be located in rural areas (this includes all areas other than cities of more than 50,000 people and their immediately adjacent urban or urbanizing areas).

Rural Economic Development Loans and Grants: This program finances economic development and job creation projects in rural areas based on sound economic plans. Rural Economic Development Loans and Grants are available to any Rural Utilities Service electric or telecommunications borrower to assist in developing rural areas from an economic standpoint, to create new job opportunities, and to help retain existing employment.

* The New Jersey Redevelopment Authority (NJRA)

New Jersey Redevelopment Authority
50 W. State St.
P.O. Box 790
Trenton, NJ 08625   609-292-3739
www.state.nj.us/njra

An independent state financing agency whose mission is to focus on investing in neighborhood-based redevelopment projects. NJRA offers low and no-interest loans, loan guarantees, equity investment and technical assistance to eligible businesses and municipalities.

* Early Stage Enterprises, LP

103 Carnegie Center, Suite 200   609-921-8896
Princeton, NJ 08540   Fax: 609-921-8703
www.esevc.com

Early Stage Enterprises (ESE) Seed Investment Fund: The Commission was a catalyst in the formation of the Early Stage Enterprises (ESE) Seed Investment Fund, which offers equity financing to qualifying start up companies. ESE offers traditional venture capital funding (never requesting more than 50% equity) to companies in the mid-Atlantic region ranging from $500,000 to $1,000,000. ESE is currently funding 12 companies, expecting to increase its portfolio to 25 - 30 companies in the near future.

* The New Jersey Technology Funding Program

Assistant Director of Commercial Lending
Post Office Box 990   609-292-0187
Trenton, NJ 08625-0990   Fax: 609-633-7751
www.njeda.com/high_tech.htm

The New Jersey Technology Funding Program: This is a financing partnership offered by the New Jersey Economic Development Authority (NJEDA) and area banks to fill the financing gaps in the availability of expansion capital for growing second stage technology-based enterprises. The NJEDA can guarantee a portion of the bank's loan. Funds will be lent for working capital and fixed assets such as buildings and equipment.

* Edison Venture Fund

Mr. John H. Martinson, Managing Partner
1009 Lenox Drive, #4   609-896-1900, ext. 18
Lawrenceville, NJ 08648   Fax: 609-896-0066
www.edisonventure.com

The Edison Venture Fund: This fund provides financing and guidance to growing companies in the mid-Atlantic region. The General Partners have backgrounds in venture capital, management buyouts, banking, acquisitions, technology development, business management, investment banking and entrepreneurial enterprise. The fund's capital pool exceeds $215 million in four independent limited partnerships. The Edison Venture Fund seeks promising enterprises with proprietary products, services and market opportunities which will grow rapidly. The initial investment averages $3 million. Providing more than capital, The Edison Venture Fund contributes specialized knowledge, operating skills and an extensive contact network.

* New Jersey Manufacturing Extension Program (NJMEP)

NJIT University Heights
GITC Suite 3200   973-642-7099
Newark, NJ 07102   Fax: 973-596-6056
www.njmep.org

New Jersey Manufacturing Extension Program (NJMEP): is designed to help improve the performance of small and mid-sized manufacturers in New Jersey. It offers various technical and management solutions to competitive problems and represents a valuable resource for the newly growing manufacturing sector in New Jersey.

* New Jersey Business Incubation Network

Mr. Louis Gaburo
Assistant Director of Enterprise Development
105 Lock Street   973-643-4063
Newark, NJ 07103   Fax: 973-643-4502
www.njbin.org

New Jersey Business Incubation Network: Business incubation is a dynamic process of business enterprise development. Incubators nurture young firms, helping them to survive and grow during the startup period when they are most vulnerable. Incubators provide hands-on management assistance, access to financing and orchestrated exposure to critical business or technical support services. They also offer entrepreneurial firms shared office services, access to equipment, flexible leases and expandable space ó all under one roof. An incubation program's main goal is to produce successful graduates ó businesses that are financially viable and freestanding when they leave the incubator usually in two to three years.

* New Jersey Business & Industry Association

102 West State Street
Trenton, NJ 08608-1199   609-393-7707
www.njbia.org

The New Jersey Business & Industry Association is an employer association providing information, services and advocacy for its member companies in order to build a more prosperous New Jersey.

* Certified Development Corporations

New Jersey Business Finance Corp.
Ira Lutsky, President
Bridge Plaza North, Suite 211
P.O. Box 919   201-346-0300
Fort Lee, NJ 07024   Fax: 201-346-1336
Area Of Operation: All New Jersey counties except for Sussex and Warren.

Corporation for Business Assistance in New Jersey
Barbara Bennett
200 South Warren Street
P.O. Box 990   609-292-0184

Trenton NJ 08625   Fax: 609-292-0368
Area Of Operation: Statewide

The 504 Certified Development Company (CDC) Program provides growing businesses with long-term, fixed-rate financing for major fixed assets, such as land and buildings. A Certified Development Company is a nonprofit corporation set up to contribute to the economic development of its community or region. CDCs work with the SBA and private-sector lenders to provide financing to small businesses.

* Small Business Administration (SBA)

Two Gateway Center, 15th Floor   201-645-2434
Newark, NJ 07102   Fax: 201-645-6265
www.sba.gov/nj

The New Jersey Small Business Administration Office delivers a variety of programs and services, such as startup and operational assistance through small business training and counseling, financial assistance for startup's, business opportunities and much more.

* Small Business Investment Companies

Alliance Mezzanine Investors, L.P.
Robert Eberhardt, Douglas Smith
96 Pompton Avenue   973-239-8900
Verona, NJ 07044   Fax: 973-239-8909
Email: bob@mezcap.com

Capital Circulation Corp.
Judy Kao, Manager
2035 Lemoine Ave., 2nd Floor   201-947-8637
Fort Lee, NJ 07024   Fax: 201-585-1965
Email: judykao@bellatlantic.net

DFW Capital Partners, LP
Donald F. DeMuth, Manager
Glenpointe Center East, 5th Floor
300 Frank W. Burr Blvd.   201-836-2233
Teaneck, NJ 07666   Fax: 201-836-5666
Email: DDemuth@DFWCapital.com

Early Stage Enterprises, L.P.
Ronald Hahn and James Miller, Managers
995 Route 518   609-921-8896
Skillman, NJ 08558   Fax: 609-921-8703
Email: tammi@esevc.com

Edison Venture Fund IV SBIC, L.P.
John Martinson, Bruce Luehrs, Contacts
1009 Lenox Drive, #4   609-896-1900
Lawrenceville, NJ 18648   Fax: 609-896-0066
Email: rmartinson@edisonventure.com

Liberty View Equity Partners SBIC, L.P.
Scott Flamm, Richard Meckler Contacts
Waterfront Corporate Center
111 River Street, 10th Floor   201-595-2926
Hoboken, NJ 07030-5776   Fax: 201-216-8605
Email: sflamm@libertyview.com

MidMark Capital II, L.P.
Matthew W. Finlay, Contact
177 Madison Avenue   973-971-9960
Morristown, NJ 07960   Fax: 973-971-9963
Email: mfinlay@midmarkcapital.com

MidMark Capital, L.P.
Denis Newman, Manager
177 Madison Avenue   973-971-9960
Morristown, NJ 07960   Fax: 973-971-9963
Email: jswerner@midmarkcapital.com

Navigator Growth Partners, L.P.
Bernard B. Markey, Contact
P. O. Box 159   908-273-7733
Summit, NJ 07902   Fax: 908-273-5566
Email: bbmarkey@navigatorequity.com

NJTC Venture Fund SBIC, L.P.
4 Becker Farm Road   973-994-0606
Roseland, NJ 07068   Fax: 973-992-6336

NJTC Venture Fund SBIC, L.P.
James T. Gunton, Contact

1001 Briggs Road, Suite 280   856-273-6800
Mt. Laurel, NJ 08054   Fax: 856-273-0990
Email: jim@njtcvc.com

Norwood Venture Corp.
Mark R. Littell, President
65 Norwood Avenue   973-783-1117
Montclair, NJ 07043   Fax: 973-783-1117
Email: nvc@norven.com

Penny Lane Partners, L.P.
William R. Denslow, Jr., Manager
One Palmer Square, Suite 309   609-497-4646
Princeton, NJ 08542   Fax: 609-497-0611
Email: pennylanepartner@msn.com

Sycamore Venture Capital, L.P.
John Whitman
845 Alexander Road   609-759-8888
Princeton, NJ 08543   Fax: 609-759-8900
Email: dlichtenstein@sycamorevc.com

Jeffrey Birnberg, President
Tappan Zee Capital Corporation
Mail: P.O. Box 416
201 Lower Notch Rd.   973-256-8280
Little Falls, NJ 07424   Fax: 973-256-2841
Email: tzcc@aol.com

University Ventures, Inc.
Oscar Figueroa, President
180 University Avenue, 3rd Floor   973-353-5627
Newark, NJ 07102   Fax: 973-353-1175
Email: ofiguero@andromeda.rutgers.edu

Ziegler Healthcare Fund I, L.P.
Douglas Korey, Contact
Executive Center #2, Third Floor
1040 Broad Street   732-578-0533
Shrewsbury, NJ 07702   Fax: 732-578-0501
Email: esmith@zieglerhealthcare.com

Zon Capital Partners, L.P.
William D. Bridgers, Contact
5 Vaughn Drive, Suite 104   609-452-1653
Princeton, NJ 08540   Fax: 609-452-1693
Email: billbridgers@zoncapital.com

The SBA licenses, regulates, and provides financial assistance to privately owned and operated Small Business Investment Companies. SBICs make venture or risk investments by supplying capital and extending unsecured loans and loans not fully collateralized to small enterprises which meet their investment criteria. Financing is made by direct loans and by equity investments.

* New Jersey Commission on Science and Technology

28 West State St.
P.O. Box 832   609-984-1671
Trenton, NJ 08625-0832   Fax: 609-292-5920
www.state.nj.us/scitech

The New Jersey Commission on Science and Technology connects university-based innovation with the most vigorous private sector Research & Development facilities in the world, and facilitates financial and technical assistance to high-technology businesses. Programs include:

Research & Development Excellence Program: The Research & Development Excellence Program (R&D Excellence) is intended to create and/or mature new scientific and technology areas with potential for products, services, or processes important to the State's future economic development. The Commission of Science and Technology supports the R&D Excellence Programs listed below:

Business Assistance Programs: The New Jersey Commission on Science and Technology recognizes the significant contributions that small and medium-sized technology-based companies make to technological and economic development. The Commission, working in conjunction with other state agencies, private organizations, and academic institutions, has developed several pioneering programs to assist New Jersey's technology entrepreneurs.

Funding Opportunities:
Technology Transfer & Commercialization Program (TTCP): This competitive investment program, administered by the Commission, is a

funding source for small, for-profit technology companies, to conduct produce or process development projects with a near-term commercial outcome. Companies eligible for this funding must be New Jersey-based or plan to relocate in New Jersey. The Program offers direct investments of $50,000 to $250,000 to companies, to conduct product or process development projects with near-term commercial outcome.

SBIR Bridge Loan Program: This is a Commission-sponsored business assistance program for New Jersey companies which helps bridge the time and financial gap between the awarding of Phase I and Phase II Federal SBIR grants.

* Casino Reinvestment Development Authority (CRDA)

1014 Atlantic Avenue
P.O. Box 749
Atlantic City, NJ 08401   609-347-0500
www.njcrda.com

Funnels a portion of casino revenues into state development projects, by mandatory investment in CRDA taxable or tax-free bonds (1.25 percent of casino gross receipts). CRDA pays interest at 2/3rds of market rate, freeing funds for development use. The CRDA then makes loans to designated municipalities at below-market rate financing.

* New Jersey Department of Environmental Protection

401 E. State St.
7th Floor, East Wing
P.O. Box 402   602-292-2885
Trenton, NJ 08625-0402   Fax: 609-292-7695
www.state.nj.us/dep

The Department of Environmental Protection strives to build relationships with the business community that promote both environmental and economic health through cooperation and innovation. These innovative efforts include: issuance of the first facility-wide permit int he nation, which replaces more than five dozen individual permits; amnesty and other programs that encourage compliance without the threat of penalties; and introduction of Alternative Dispute Resolution as a means of resolving permit and other disagreements by mediation rather than litigation.

* New Jersey Technology Council Venture Fund

1001 Briggs Road, Suite 280   856-273-6800
Mt. Laurel, NJ 08054   Fax: 856-273-0990

Roseland Office:
4 Becker Farm Road   973-994-0606
Roseland, NJ 07068   Fax: 973-992-6336
www.njtcvc.com

This program provides funding assistance to emerging high-technology companies in New Jersey. This private enterprise works closely with the State of New Jersey, having been selected through a competitive process to manage certain funds on behalf of the New Jersey Economic Development Authority.

New Mexico

* Economic Development Department

Joseph M. Montoya Bldg.
1100 St. Francis Drive   505-827-0382
Santa Fe, NM 87505-4147   800-374-3061
www.edd.state.nm.us   Fax: 505-827-0407

Business Participation Loans: The State Investment Council may invest a portion of the Severance Tax Permanent Fund in real property related business loans. There is a minimum of $500,000 and a maximum of $2 million.

Industrial Development Training Program: Provides funds for classroom or on-the-job training to prepare New Mexico residents for employment. Trainee wages are reimbursed to the company at 50% during hours of training; 65% in rural New Mexico. Instructional costs involving classroom training will be reimbursed to the educational institution at 100% of all costs outlined in the training contract.

Severance Tax Loan Program: New Mexico can purchase up to $20 million of bonds, notes, debentures or other evidence of indebtedness, excluding commercial paper, whose proceeds are used for the establishment or expansion of business outlets or ventures located in state.

International Trade Division: Provides assistance to manufacturing, agricultural and other production concerns in developing their worldwide export capabilities. Services include:
- Export market development counseling
- Foreign trade shows and missions
- Foreign buying and reverse trade missions
- Identifying and disseminating overseas trade leads
- Attracting foreign businesses
- Developing, maintaining and using a database of potential domestic and international customers for New Mexico goods and services.

New Mexico Communities: {www.edd.state.nm.us/COMMUNITIES/}
This web site offers information in three forms:
- Site and Buildings Database: Search for available land and buildings by size or county.
- Community/County Profile: An overview of each incorporated municipality and its available land and buildings. County statistics are also available.
- State Map: A clickable version that shows where each county and community is located in relation to each other and major intersections.

Industrial Revenue Bonds: Municipalities or counties issue IRBs in order to finance privately operated development projects.

Job Training Incentive Program (JTIP): JTIP is designed to provide fast response training to new and expanding businesses in New Mexico. They offer financial assistance to businesses to help with the expenses associated with employee training.

New Mexico 9000 Program: The New Mexico Economic Development Department has teamed up with area large businesses to provide small businesses technical assistance to achieve ISO 9001:2000 compliance certification at affordable costs.

Office of Mexican Affairs and trade Division: This division provides information pertaining to international trade from New Mexico, major exports, and marketing strategies to businesses.

Trade Division Education Programs: The Trade Division Educational Programs include basic export seminars, advanced trade seminars and assisting trade groups with their educational programming.

Export Library: The Trade Division maintains an international trade research library.

Rural Job Tax Credit: Eligible New Mexico employers may earn the rural job tax credit for each qualifying job created after July 1, 2000.

Welfare-to-Work Credit: The state credit piggybacks onto the federal credit and can be applied to New Mexico personal and corporate income tax.

* Rural Development Office

Rural Development Administration
6200 Jefferson St., NE, Room 255
517 Gold Ave. SW   505-761-4950
Albuquerque, NM 87109   Fax: 505-761-4938
www.rurdev.usda.gov/nm

To foster economic development in rural areas, this program offers guarantees to private lenders for projects by healthy, reliable companies that will benefit the community. Loans are for a wide range of rural and industrial purposes, including pollution control and transportation services. Projects should create jobs in areas with populations under 25,000.

The New Mexico Rural Development Office offers a variety of programs including: Business and Industry Direct and Guaranteed Loans, Intermediary Reldending Program, Rural Business Enterprise and Opportunity Grants, and Rural Economic Development Loans and Grants.

* Women's Economic Self-Sufficiency Team

WESST Corp.
414 Silver SW   505-241-4753
Albuquerque, NM 87102   Fax: 505-241-4766
www.wesst.org

Provides consulting, training and support programs as well as financial assistance (loans).

* ACCION

ACCION New Mexico
20 First Plaza NW, Suite 417   505-243-8844
Albuquerque, NM 87102   Fax: 505-243-1551

www.accionnewmexico.org
A private non-profit organization that extend microloans to small business entrepreneurs designed to help home-based and other self-employed people grow to be self sufficient.

* Cibola Foundation Revolving Loan Fund

Cibola Communities
Economic Development Foundation Inc.
P.O. Box 277 505-285-6604
Grants, NM 87020 Fax: 505-285-6746
http://mttaylor.com/cibladev/index.htm
A variety of financial incentives offered to encourage economic development in Cibola County.

* Community Development Loan Fund

NM Community Development Loan Fund
P.O. Box 705 505-243-3196
Albuquerque, NM 87103 Fax: 505-243-8803
www.nmcdlf.org
Provides loans to businesses and organizations that have tangible benefits for low-income people. Typical loans are from $5,000 to $25,000.

* Enchantment Land Certified Development Company

625 Silver SW, Suite 210 505-843-9232
Albuquerque, NM 87102 Fax: 505-764-9153
www.elcdc.com
Enchantment Land Certified Development Company (ELCDC) The ELCDC is an SBA licensed, not-for-profit organization, authorized to administer the SBA 504 loan program. A 504 program provides long-term (20 years), low down payment (10%), fixed rate loans for land, buildings and equipment for expanding small businesses. ELCDC sells a debenture with a 100% SBA guarantee for up to 40% of the project, or $750,000 (in some cases $1 million), and the company provides 10% equity. The remaining 50% is from a first mortgage loan from a private sector lender. Area of Operation: statewide.

* Technology Ventures Corporation

1155 University Blvd. SE 505-246-2882
Albuquerque, NM 87106 Fax: 505-246-2891
www.techventures.org
Technology Ventures Corporation (TVC) TVC was formed by Lockheed Martin to promote the commercialization of technology, particularly in relation to Sandia National Laboratories, TVC serves to link technologies and investment sources with start-up companies and existing business. Also, TVC facilitates technical, business and management assistance for its clients.

* Bureau For Business Research And Services

New Mexico State University
P.O. Box 3001
Las Cruces, NM 88003 505-646-1334
http://bbrs.nmsu.edu
Management training, research services; maintains business and economic data bank.

* NEDA Business Consultants, Inc.

718 Central SW 505-843-7114
Albuquerque, NM 87102 Fax: 505-242-2030
www.nedainc.net
Assists minority entrepreneurs with financing, capital development, marketing, procurement, management, etc.

* Navajo Nation Division Of Economic Development

P. O. Box 663 505-871-6544
Window Rock, AZ 86515 Fax: 505-871-7381
www.navajo.org
Provides counseling, financial planning, and loan packaging for small business development

* New Mexico Department Of Agriculture

Marketing Development Office
New Mexico State University
P. O. Box 30005, MSC 5600

Las Cruces, NM 88003 505-646-4929
http://nmdaweb.nmsu.edu
Technical assistance to agricultural producers and processors with interstate or international exports.

* New Mexico Entrepreneurs Association

New Mexico Entrepreneurs Association
6416 Glen Oak NE 505-293-3811
Albuquerque, NM 87111 Fax: 505-262-0871
www.edd.state.nm.us/cgi-bin/technoview.cgi
Provides forum for entrepreneurs and support groups; promotes local business development.

* New Mexico Farm And Livestock Bureau

421 N. Water St.
P.O. Box 20004
Las Cruces, NM 88004 505-532-4706
www.nmfb.org
Lobbying organization; business services and insurance for members; publishes New Mexico Farm and Ranch Magazine.

* Rio Grande Minority Purchasing Council, Inc.

7216 Washington Street, NE, Suite B
Albuquerque, NM 87109 505-342-9300
www.rgmpc.org
Supports minority businesses and those owned by women through increased corporate and government purchasing.

* Science And Technology Corporation

University of New Mexico
801 University SE, Suite 101 505-272-7900
Albuquerque, NM 87106 Fax: 505-272-7300
http://stc.unm.edu
Provides business assistance to technology-based companies; transfers technology from publicly funded R&D organizations to commercial markets.

* State Investment Council

2025 South Pacheco St.
Suite 100 505-424-2500
Santa Fe, NM 87505 Fax: 505-424-2510
www.state.nm.us/nmsic
The State Investment Council offers a number of programs of interest to developing business in New Mexico.

Venture Capital Investment Program: This program makes investments in qualified New Mexico-based venture capital funds, which are then invested into entrepreneurial businesses. The business must have experienced management; a rapidly growing an d potentially large market; and a competitive advantage where there are barriers to entry for other businesses and significant capital appreciation for investors over a 5 to 7 year period.

The Real Estate Business Loan Participation Program: Allows the Severance Tax Permanent Fund to participate in certain real estate loans up to a total of $2 million. The loan may not exceed 75% of the appraisal and must originate with a New Mexico bank.

The Severance Tax Permanent Fund Policy Governing Purchases of Small Business Administration or Rural Economic and Community Development Service Obligations: Allows the state to use severance tax permanent funds to purchase SBA or RECD loans made to New Mexico businesses.

The New Mexico Venture Capital Fund: Provides capital to venture capital partnerships that already have significant, successful investment experience.

* Department of Finance and Administration

2600 Cerrilos Road 800-432-7108
Santa Fe, NM 87505 505-827-4950
www.nmlocalgov.net Fax: 505-827-4948
This department provides gap financing, often with long term loan amortization, for start-up and expansion projects that address local economic development objectives.

* New Mexico Taxation and Revenue Department

Returns Processing Bureau

P.O. Box 630
Santa Fe, NM 87504-0630
www.state.nm.us/tax

505-827-0700
Fax: 505-827-0331

Investment Tax Credit: Available to manufacturing operations. For each $100,000 of equipment purchased (used directly and exclusively in a manufacturing process and subject to depreciation) by a company that simultaneously hires one employee, that company may receive credit against its gross receipts taxes or withholding tax due. A business must apply for the credit.

* Small Business Administration (SBA)

625 Silver SW
Suite 320
Albuquerque, NM 87102
www.sba.gov/nm

505-346-7909
Fax: 505-346-6711

The New Mexico Small Business Administration Office delivers a variety of programs and services, such as startup and operational assistance through small business training and counseling, financial assistance for startup's, business opportunities and much more.

* Small Business Investment Companies

TD Origen Capital Fund, L.P.
J. Michael Schafer, Manager
150 Washington Avenue Suite 201
Santa Fe, NM 87501
Email: jceliberti@tullisdickerson.com

203-629-8700
Fax: 203-629-9293

The SBA licenses, regulates, and provides financial assistance to privately owned and operated Small Business Investment Companies. SBICs make venture or risk investments by supplying capital and extending unsecured loans and loans not fully collateralized to small enterprises which meet their investment criteria. Financing is made by direct loans and by equity investments.

* Small Business Innovation Research

UNM-Los Alamos Small Business Development Center
P.O. Box 715
Los Alamos, NM 87544
www.nmsbdc.org/losalamos

505-662-0001
Fax: 505-662-0099

Small for-profit United States businesses that are able to answer a specific federal governmental research and development need may compete for up to $850,000 in SBIR contracts. Contracts are awarded in phases. Phase I (up to $100,000) for evaluation and analysis of an idea. Phase II (up to $750,000) for further research and development of idea deemed feasible. And Phase III, which require private or non-SBIR governmental funding for the commercialization of the results of Phase II work.

* New Mexico Industry Corporation

700 4th Street, SW
Albuquerque, NM 87102

505-244-0574
Fax: 505-242 – 8666

Small businesses located in eligible counties can get funding for fixed assets and working capital. The loans generally range from $25,000 to $50,000 with lower than market rates interest. Preference is given to existing businesses that develop, manufacturing, or assemble products using local labor. They must have been turned down by at least two lenders.

* Workforce Training Center

5600 Eagle Rock Avenue NE
Albuquerque, NM 87113
http://planet.tvi.edu/wtc

505-224-5200
Fax: 505-224-5201

The Workforce Training Center provides customized training, skill development and business consulting. They also have two small business development centers in Albuquerque and South Valley to provide counseling, assessment, training and other resources to assist entrepreneurs start and grow their own businesses.

New York

* Empire State Development

30 South Pearl Street
Albany, NY 12245
www.empire.state.ny.us

518-474-7756
800-STATE-NY

633 Third Ave.
New York, NY 10017
www.nylovesbiz.com

212-803-3100

Small Business Division: Offers fast, up-to-date information on the State's economic development programs and can help in making contact with appropriate agencies in such areas as financing, job training, technical assistance, etc. {www.nylovessmallbiz.com}

Technical Advisory Services; Provides free, confidential technical assistance concerning compliance to federal and state air quality requirements for small businesses.

Small Business Stationary Source Technical And Environmental Compliance Assistance Program: Provides technical assistance and advocacy services to eligible businesses in achieving environmental regulatory compliance.

Business Ombudsmen Services: Counseling and problem solving assistance to resolve complaints from small businesses concerning interactions with government authorities available to businesses employing 100 or less that are not dominant in their fields.

Entrepreneurial Assistance Program: Referrals of recipients to ESD funded assistance provides classroom instruction and individual counseling, business plan development for minorities, women, dislocated workers, public assistance recipients, public housing recipients and those seeking to start a new business or who have owned a business for five years or less.

Business Development Office: Industrial and manufacturing companies are targeted for a variety of services.

New York State Contract Reporter: Provides listings of contracts made available for bidding by New York State agencies, public benefit corporations, and its public authorities. {www.nyscr.org}

Procurement Assistance: Provides technical assistance to businesses seeking to compete for contracts valued at $1,000,000 or more from the state.

Workforce Training: Empire State Development offers financial support and technical resources to companies to offset the cost of employee training.

Recycling Assistance: New York State has one of the largest concentrations of recycling companies in the world. Works with companies to demonstrate that, in addition to being an important environmental activity, recycling makes good business sense. To this end, they diagnose the research and development, capital, and marketing needs of recycling companies and tailor-make a package of technical and financial assistance. Identifies new markets and assist companies retooling to reach those markets. Assists companies to implement waste prevention practices.

Technical Assistance: New York State has developed a host of business-friendly products ranging from understanding the federal Clean Air Act and its impact on small business to ownership transition plans that can help a company grow and prosper. A hotline (800-STATE NY) puts business people directly in touch with a business ombudsman. The experts staffing this hotline are ready to answer questions. In addition, they serve as advocates for business.

Advanced Controls for Efficiency Program (ACE): Applied research, product design, demonstration and testing, and product commercialization for individuals or enterprises with an innovative, energy-related product.

Financial Incentives: Companies that plan to locate, expand or modernize their facilities in New York State are eligible for financial assistance. Generally, this assistance supports the acquisition of land and buildings or machinery and equipment. It also can help fund construction or renovation of buildings or the infrastructure and working capital required for the establishment or expansion of an eligible company.

Funds may be available through:
- direct loans to business for a portion of the cost of the project;
- interest rate subsidies to reduce the cost of borrowing from private or public sector financial institutions, in the form of a grant or linked deposit with the lending institution;
- loan guarantees for working capital assistance;
- assistance in the form of a loan and grant combination for a portion of the cost of an infrastructure project.

Economic Development Fund:
1. *Industrial Effectiveness Program*: Direct technical assistance for identifying, developing and implementing improved management and production process and grants to pay the cost of feasibility studies up to $60,000.
2. *Employee Training Assistance*: Offers skills training grant from $15,000 to $25,000.
3. *Commercial Area Development*: Loans, loan guarantees, and grants to improve commercial buildings, commercial strips, downtown areas, and business districts from $75,000 to $100,000.

4. *General Development*: Loans and loan guarantees for manufacturers, non-retail service firms, headquarters facilities of retail firms, retail firms in distressed areas, and businesses developing tourist attractions from $75,000 to $2,000,000.
5. *Capital Access*: For small and medium size businesses including minority and women-owned businesses and day care centers, financing from $100,000 to $300,000.
6. *General Development Financing*: Loans and loan guarantees for manufacturing, non-retail service firms, retail headquarters, retail firms located in distressed areas and businesses which develop recreational, cultural or historical facilities for tourist attractions. Amounts are determined case-by-case.
7. *Competitiveness Improvement Services - Global Export Marketing Service*: Grants up to $5,000 for consulting services to assess organizational and product readiness for exporting. Grants up to $25,000 for an individual business or up to $50,000 for a business or industry group to create market development plans.

Environmental Finance Corporation: Grants for resource recovery facilities, solid waste disposal facilities, hazardous waste treatment facilities, Brownfields redevelopment, water supply and management facilities and sewage treatment works. {www.nysefc.org}

Venture Capital Fund: High Tech entrepreneurs, companies with technologies ready for market, and leading-edge enterprises each have different needs for investment capital. New York State has the seed and growth capital that will enable a high tech business to grow. The Small Business Technology Investment Fund program (SBTIF) is a source of early-stage debt and equity funding for high tech companies. Initial investments range as much as $300,000 and later stage investment up to $500,000. New York State is banking on a strong high tech future.

Transportation Capital Assistance Program: Loans up to $500,000 for small business enterprises and NYS-certified minority and women-owned business enterprises that have transportation-related construction contracts. 518-457-1129

Regional Revolving Loan Trust Fund: Loans and loan guarantees up to $80,000 for businesses employing fewer than 100 people.

Small Business Technology Investment Fund: For small technology based companies, financing from $25,000 to $500,000 for seed or capital.

Job Development Authority: Loans to small and medium sized businesses in manufacturing and services from $50,000 to $1,500,000.

Jobs Now Program: Capital loans and grants to private businesses creating at least 300 new full time jobs not to exceed $10,000 per job.

Linked Deposit Program: Interest rate subsidies to a variety of businesses seeking to improve competitiveness and performance up to $1,000,000.

Empire State Development: International market experts help a company enter and expand in the global economy. Offers a step-by-step analysis of a company's capabilities and matches them with the demands of the international marketplace. If a company has what the global marketplace needs, they will work with that company to find the niche, the spot on the globe where they can sell. Then, they will assist them in determining how to reach those markets. They provide information about tariffs, industry specifications and government regulations. They can put a company in touch with representatives, distributors, agents and strategic allies to sell a product or service abroad. Other services include:
-   Assistance in identifying foreign sales agent or distributor
-   Matching grants of up to $5,000 to assess product sales potential in foreign markets
-   Matching grants of up to $25,000 to assist in creating export market development plans
-   Low cost participation in international trade shows.

Division of Minority and Women's Business Development: Administers, coordinates, and implements a statewide program to assist the development of M/WBE's and facilitate their access to state contracting opportunities. Through the process of certification, the agency is responsible for verifying minority and women-ownership and control of firms participating in the program.

Division of Minority and Women's Business Development Lending Program: Loans up to $7,000 from the Microenterprise Loan Fund and up to $50,000 from the Minority and Women Revolving Loan Trust Fund.

Semiconductor Manufacturing Initiative: To encourage semiconductor manufacturing, New York has facilitated the pre-permitting of industrial sites solely for chip fabrication. {www.semi-ny.com}

Technology Incubators: New York has over 50 incubator facilities.

Environmental Services Unit: Businesses can get assistance in order to understand and comply with environmental regulations.

* Rural Development

441 S. Salina St.
Suite 357, 5th Floor
Syracuse, NY 3202-2245   315-477-6400
www.rurdev.usda.gov/ny   Fax: 315-477-6438

Rural Business-Cooperative Service supports economic and business development in rural communities.

Guaranteed Business and Industry Loans: Rural Development joins together with local banks and other commercial lenders to provide financing for businesses located in rural areas. Lenders are able to offer larger loans and better terms with a guarantee that may cover up to 80% of the lenders exposure on the loan. B&I guarantees are available in all parts of New York except for cities of more than 50,000 population and the urbanized areas surrounding them. Eligible Applicants - Individuals, corporations, partnerships, cooperatives, federally recognized Indian Tribes and other legal entities are eligible borrowers.

Intermediary Relending Program: The Intermediary Relending Program makes funds available to community development organizations that will become intermediaries and relend the funds to rural businesses and community development projects. Eligible Applicants - Organizations eligible to become intermediaries include Not-For-Profit Corporations, Public Agencies, Indian Tribal Groups and Cooperatives.

Rural Business Enterprise Grants: Rural communities can receive assistance in promoting the development of small businesses through the Rural Business Enterprise Grant (RBEG) program. Grants are made to public bodies or not-for-profit organizations. Grantees use the funds to promote the development of small private businesses, which are defined as having 50 or fewer new employees and less than $1 million in projected annual gross revenue. Rural communities include cities with up to 50,000 populations and cannot be within the urbanized area of a larger city.
-   Eligible Applicants - RBEG grants are made to public bodies and private not-for-profit corporations. Public bodies are States, counties, cities, townships, incorporated towns and villages, boroughs, authorities, districts, and federally recognized Indian Tribes.

Rural Cooperative Development Grants: The program provides grants for establishing and operating centers for cooperative development. The primary purpose is to improve economic conditions in rural areas, including cities of up to 50,000 populations. Grant funds can pay up to 75% of the costs for establishing and operating such centers. Grants may be made to public bodies or not-for-profit institution.

Rural Business Opportunity Grants: Rural Business Opportunity Grants (RBOG) are available to promote sustainable economic development in rural communities with exceptional need. Projects funded by the grants will:
-   Promote economic development that is sustainable over the long term without continued need for external support.
-   Improve the quality as well as the quantity of economic development activity.
-   Act as a catalyst by providing critical investments.
-   Serve as examples of "best practices" that merit implementation in rural communities in similar circumstances.
-   Eligible rural areas exclude any area that is within the boundaries of a city with a population in excess of 10,000 inhabitants

Rural Cooperative Stock Purchase: The Rural Cooperative Stock Purchase Program works in conjunction with the Guaranteed Business and Industrial loan program allowing loans to be made to producers of agricultural products seeking to join new cooperatives that produce value-added goods. Family farmers can use the B&I loan program to help pay for stock in a start-up cooperative that will process an agricultural commodity into a value-added product.

Cooperative Agreements: The primary objective of this funding is to encourage research through cooperative agreements on critical issues vital to the development and sustainability of user-owned cooperatives as a means of improving the quality of life in America's rural communities. A cooperative agreement is not a grant. Cooperative agreements are to be awarded on the basis of merit, quality, and relevance to advancing the purpose of federally supported rural development programs that increase economic opportunities in farming and rural communities.

Technical Assistance: Rural Business-Cooperative Service (RBS) is developing plans to provide non-financial business advice and assistance to businesses and cooperative enterprises interested in applying for RBS financial assistance. This assistance will include how to complete application forms, acceptable standards for business plans to be used for RBS financing, methods of feasibility analysis, industry statistics, and financial standards generally required by lenders.

Rural Economic Development Loans and Grants: Loans and grants are available to rural electric cooperative or telephone borrowers to help promote economic and community development projects.

Cooperative Development: The office of Cooperative development offers a wide range of assistance for people interested in forming new cooperatives.

* Agricultural Business Development Assistance

New York State Department of Agriculture and Markets
The Winners Circle   800-554-4501
Albany, NY 12235   518-457-3880
www.agmkt.state.ny.us

Technical assistance to help locate public and private funding for food processors and agricultural producers.

* Apprentice Training Program

Long Island Field Office
303 W. Old Country Road   516-934-8525
Hicksville, NY 11801   Fax: 516-934-8557
Area of Operation: Nassau and Suffolk Counties

New York City Field Office
247 W 54th Street, 5th Floor   212-621-0844
New York, NY 10019   Fax: 212-621-0728
Area of Operation: Bronx, Kings, New York, Queens and Richmond Counties.

Albany Field Office
State Office Building Campus
Building 12, Room 436   518-457-4914
Albany, NY 12240   Fax: 518-457-7154
Area of Operation: Albany, Clinton, Columbia, Essex, Franklin, Fulton, Greene, Hamilton, Montgomery, Rensselaer, Saratoga, Schenectady, Schoharie, Warren and Washington Counties.

Utica Field Office
207 Genesee Street, Room 712   315-793-5339
Utica, NY 13501   Fax: 315-793-2514
Area of Operation: Herkimer, Madison, Oneida, and St.Lawrence Counties.

Binghamton Field Office
Glendale Technology Park
2001 Perimeter Road East, Suite 3   607-741-4577
Endicott, NY 13760   Fax: 607-741-4529
Area of Operation: Broome, Chemung, Chenango, Delaware, Otsego, Schuyler, Steuben, Tompkins, and Tioga Counties.

Syracuse Field Office
450 S. Salina Street, Room 203   315-479-3228
Syracuse, NY 13202   Fax: 315-479-3217
Area of Operation: Cayuga, Cortland, Jefferson, Lewis, Onondaga, and Oswego Counties.

Rochester Field Office
130 W. Main Street, Room 202   585-258-8885
Rochester, NY 14614   Fax: 585-258-8882
Area of Operation: Genesee, Livingston, Monroe, Ontario, Orleans, Seneca, Wayne, Wyoming, and Yates Counties.

Buffalo Field Office
290 Main Street, Room 224   716-851-2726
Buffalo, NY 14202   Fax: 716-851-2797
Area of Operation: Allegany, Cattaraugus, Chautauqua, Erie, and Niagara Counties.

Mid-Hudson Field Office
120 Bloomingdale Road   914-997-9534
White Plains, NY 10605   Fax: 914-997-8463
Area of Operation: Dutchess, Orange, Putnam, Rockland, Sullivan, Ulster, and Westchester Counties.

Provides on-the-job training for more than 250 skilled occupations. Contact the Apprentice Training Office that serves your county. {www.labor.state.ny.us/business_ny/apprenticeship_training/apprenticeship_training.html}

* Rural Employment Program

Room 282, Bldg. 12
State Office Campus
Albany, NY 12240   518-457-6798

Recruits workers for farm, landscaping and food processing industries.

* Division Of Housing And Community Renewal

Hampton Plaza
38-40 State Street
Albany, NY 12207   518-402-3728
and
25 Beaver Street
New York, NY 10004   212-480-6700
www.dhcr.state.ny.us

Low Income Housing Credit Program: The Credit program provides a dollar-for-dollar reduction in federal income tax liability for project owners who develop, rehabilitate and acquire rental housing that serves low-income households. The amount of Credit available to project owners is in direct relation to the number of low-income housing units that they provide.

The Farmworker Housing Program is a low-cost loan program which assists in the improvement of existing housing or construction of new housing for seasonal farmworkers. Under this program loans of up to $100,000 per year are available to agricultural producers who apply to them and demonstrate that these program funds are needed to improve or construct seasonal farmworker housing. DHCR's priority is to provide loan funds for projects which will bring existing seasonal farmworker housing into compliance with applicable building codes

* New York State Office of Science, Technology & Academic Research (NYSTAR)

30 South Pearl Street 11th Floor   518-292-5700
Albany, New York 12207   Fax: 518-292-5780
www.nystar.state.ny.us

NYSTAR makes New York the leader in high-technology academic research and economic development by undertaking a host of new, unprecedented programs and initiatives. These initiatives result in the creation of several world-class, state-of-the-art research centers, the modernization of existing research centers and the rapid transfer of technologies from the research lab to the marketplace. Through programs and other strategic initiatives, NYSTAR strengthens the formation of university-business partnerships to develop and commercialize the most economically promising technologies of tomorrow.

The Technology Transfer Incentive Program is specifically designed to help business make the rapid transfer of new ideas and new technology from the research lab to the marketplace. The Technology Transfer Incentive Program will support a wide array of activities associated with bringing new technologies to the marketplace such as creation of business and marketing plans, obtaining venture capital, filing patent applications and product evaluation and assistance. This program will be structured so that awards may be made several times a year, giving potential applicants greater opportunity to quickly move a product from the research lab to the marketplace.

Science & Technology Law Center Program: As New York's high tech companies bring newly developed technology to market, they need assistance in the business formation and development process. Under NYSTAR's direction, the New York State Science and Technology Law Center will provide low-cost legal consultation and services essential to small and start-up companies as they seek to succeed in a competitive and complex marketplace.

The Centers for Advanced Technology (CAT) Program supports university-industry collaboration in research, education and technology transfer, with a strong focus on helping New York businesses gain a technological edge on their competition. Now this national model for technology transfer will be strengthened to achieve even greater results.

Centers for Advanced Technology:
Center for Advanced Ceramic Technology, Alfred University, Alfred NY 14802, 607-871-2486, {http://cact.alfred.edu}. Research and development of high technology ceramic materials that possess the potential to benefit both the industrial base of New York State and the scientific community.

Center for Ultrafast Photonic Materials & Applications, The City College of CUNY, Dept. of Physics, Room J419, 138th St. & Convent Avenue, New York, NY 10031, 212-650-5531, {http://cunyphotonics.com}. Research and technology development in select areas of photonics that have applications in optical communications, medical diagnostics, laser development, semiconductors, and optical imaging.

Center for Advanced Materials Processing, Clarkson University, Potsdam, Potsdam, NY 13699-5665, 315-268-2336, {www.clarkson.edu/camp/}. Research applied to industrial needs in photocopying and imaging, micro-electronics, pharmaceutical, cosmetic, and environmental control industries, among others.

Center for Advanced Technology in Information Management & Medical Informatics, Columbia University, New York City - Columbia Presbyterian Medical Center, 630 West 168th Street, New York, NY 10032, 212-305-2944, {http://www.cat.columbia.edu}. Specializes in bringing cutting-edge information science to industry for product development and enhancement.

Center for Biotechnology, Cornell University, Ithaca 130 Biotechnology Building, Ithaca, NY 14853-2703, 607-255-4259, {http://www.research. cornell.edu/Biotech/Biotech.html}. Research and development, education and training, and technology transfer that address the economic development needs of New York industry.

Center for Advanced Technology in Digital Multimedia, New York University, New York City, 719 Broadway, 12th Floor, New York, NY 10003, 212-998-3390, {http://www.cat.nyu.edu/}. Fosters industry growth by developing and licensing new technologies and by providing business assistance to new media companies.

Center for Advanced Technology in Telecommunications, Polytechnic University, Brooklyn 5 MetroTech, Brooklyn, NY 11201, 718-260-3050, {http://catt.poly.edu/catthome.html}. Technology transfer, partnering with both providers and users of telecommunications and information systems to help them turn the latest developments in these technologies into competitive and productive resources.

Center for Automation Technologies, Rensselaer Polytechnic Institute, Troy CII Building, Room 8015, Troy, NY 12180, 518-276-8087, {http://cat.rpi. edu/}. CAT engineers are creating automation solutions that will have a powerful, positive impact on the global economy. Cutting edge research applied to the needs of corporate clients and industry in general.

CAT in Electronic Imaging Systems, University of Rochester/Rochester Institute of Technology, Rochester, Taylor Hall, 260 Hutchison Road, Rochester, NY 14627-0194, 585-275-3999, {http://www.ceis.rochester. edu/}. Basic research in the field of electronic imaging, leveraging the results for economic advantage to New York State and the nation.

Center for Advanced Thin Film Technology, State University of New York, 251 Fuller Road, Albany, NY 12203, 518-437-8686, {http://www.albany. edu/cat}. A research, development, education, and economic outreach resource for industries which manufacture, use, or supply micro-electronics, electronics, optoelectronics, bioelectronics, nanotechnology and telecommunications devices and components.

Integrated Electronics Engineering Center, SUNY at Binghamton, Binghamton Thomas J. Watson School of Engineering, Vestal Parkway East, P.O. Box 6000, Binghamton, NY 13902-6000, 607-777-6880, {http://www.ieec.binghamton.edu/ieec/}. Engaged in the process of bringing a semiconductor chip, with its resident circuitry, to a form that can be integrated effectively into a larger microelectronics assembly.

Center for Computer Applications and Software Engineering, Syracuse University, Syracuse 2-212, Center for Science & Technology, Syracuse, NY 13244-4100, 315-443-1060, {http://www.cat.syr.edu/}. Research focused on computer applications and software engineering. Applies traditional university strengths in research and education to economic development.

Center for Biotechnology, State University of New York at Stony Brook, Stony Brook Psychology A, 3rd Floor, Stony Brook, NY 11794-2580, 631-632-8521, {http://www.biotech.sunysb.edu/}. Discovery, development, translation and commercialization of promising biotechnology resulting from academic research centers around the state of New York.

CAT in Sensor Systems, State University of New York at Stony Brook, Stony Brook Light Engineering Building, Room 150, Stony Brook, NY 11794-2350, 631-632-1368, {http://www.sensorcat.sunysb.edu}. Magnetic, optical, X-ray, and infrared sensors; signal processing and image recognition; superconducting electronics for sensor applications; DNA sequencing devices; and MEMS-based sensors and actuators.

* Certified Development Companies

The Bronx Initiative Corporation
Madeline Marquez
98 East 161st Street   718-590-3948
Bronx, NY 10451   Fax: 718-590-5814
Area of Operation: The Bronx

Long Island Development Corporation
Roslyn Goldmacher, Executive Director
255 Executive Drive   516-349-7800
Plainview, NY 11803   Fax: 516-349-7881
Area of Operation: Counties of Nassau and Suffolk

Progress Development Corporation
Cynthia C. Clune, Executive Director
19 East Main Street
P.O. Box 3105   914-858-8358
Port Jervis, NY 12771   Fax: 914-858-8002
Area of Operation: Orange County

Albany Local Development Corporation
George Leveille, Vice President
Eagle Street
City Hall, 4th Floor   518-434-5133
Albany, NY 12207   Fax: 518-434-5098
Area of Operation: City of Albany

Empire State Certified Development Corporation
Robert Lazar, President
41 State Street
P.O. Box 738   518-463-2268
Albany, NY 12207   Fax: 518-463-0240
New York City   212-803-3672
Area of Operation: Statewide; except Nassau, Suffolk and Onondaga Counties

Greater Syracuse Business Development Corporation
Richard Arciero, Executive Director
572 South Salina Street   315-470-1888
Syracuse, NY 13202   Fax: 315-471-8545
Area of Operation: Counties of Onondaga, Cayuga, Cortland and Madison

Mohawk Valley Certified Development Corporation
Michael Reese, Executive VP & CEO
26 West Main Street
P.O. Box 69   315-866-4671
Mohawk, NY 13407   Fax: 315-866-9862
Area of Operation: Oneida, Herkimer, Fulton, Montgomery and Schoharie Counties

Monroe County Industrial Development Corporation
Judy Seil, Assistant Secretary
8100 City Place
50 W. Main Street   716-428-5060
Rochester, NY 14614   Fax: 716-428-2147
Area of Operation: Monroe County

Operation Oswego County, Inc.
L. Michael Treadwell, Area Industrial Dir.
44 West Bridge Street   315-343-1545
Oswego, NY 13126   Fax: 315-343-1546
Area of Operation: Oswego County

Rochester Economic Development Corporation
Fashun Ku, President
30 Church Street, Suite 005A   716-428-6966
Rochester, NY 14614   Fax: 716-428-6042
Area of Operation: City of Rochester

Syracuse Economic Development Corporation
Laurenzo James, Deputy Director
223 City Hall   315-488-8107
Syracuse, NY 13202   Fax: 315-448-8036
Area of Operation: Citywide in Syracuse

* New York State Environment Facilities Corporation (EFC)

625 Broadway   518-402-6924
Albany, NY 12207-2997   800-882-9721
www.nysefc.org   Fax: 518-485-8773

Industrial Finance Program (IFP): The Industrial Finance Program (IFP) provides tax-exempt and taxable conduit financing to private entities in New York State for a variety of environmental purposes. The IFP lends the proceeds of tax-exempt bonds to borrowers seeking financing for capital facilities for the following: solid waste handling, disposal and recycling, including brownfield site remediation; sewage treatment, including limited industrial or other wastewater treatment; drinking water supply and management; limited hazardous waste disposal and remediation; and privatization of New York municipal or state environmental facilities. The use of tax-exempt bonds allows IFP clients to borrow funds at a lower rate of interest than would otherwise be available in the market. For projects or portions of projects that do not qualify for tax-exemption under the federal tax code, the IFP can provide taxable conduit financing. The minimum size of an IFP financing is approximately $1.5 million. However, several projects at one or more sites owned by one or more borrowers may be financed with a single IFP bond issue. IFP financing can be used to privatize certain exempt facilities. For More Information about IFP financing contact: Director of Industrial Finance, 518-457-4100 or 1-800-882-9721 (within NY).

Small Business Assistance Program (SBAP): The SBAP provides small businesses, such as printers, metal and wood furniture manufacturers, autobody shops, drycleaners, and various other manufacturers, with free and confidential technical assistance about air emission requirements. The SBAP suggests measures to help businesses achieve compliance, including permitting assistance, pollution prevention, materials substitution, and process modifications. 800-780-7227.

Financial Assistance to Business Program (FAB): The Financial Assistance to Business (FAB) helps businesses cope with the cost of complying with environmental protection mandates. EFC administers this program with the assistance and approval of local governments. EFC is in the process of awarding some of the $60 million of Bond Act funds available under this program.

Dry Cleaner Program: The New York State Environmental Facilities Corporation ("EFC") proposes to provide funding to the owners of certain eligible dry cleaning facilities to defray costs associated with new environmental protection requirements. Contact Laurie A. Allen, Program Manager, 800-200-2200, Fax: 518-486-9246.

The Industrial Finance Program (IFP) provides tax-exempt and taxable conduit financing to private entities in New York State for a variety of environmental purposes. The IFP lends the proceeds of tax-exempt bonds to borrowers seeking financing for capital facilities for the following: solid waste handling, disposal and recycling, including brownfield site remediation; sewage treatment, including limited industrial or other wastewater treatment; drinking water supply and management; limited hazardous waste disposal and remediation; and privatization of New York municipal or state environmental facilities. Director of Industrial Finance, 518-402-6924 or 800-882-9721.

The Division of Technical Advisory Services (TAS) provides assistance to private- and public-sector clients to help them improve environmental practices and to support management of their environmental projects. Through TAS, EFC offers businesses and government entities a number of pollution prevention, waste reduction and project management services custom-tailored to the needs of the individual client. TAS services are typically provided on a fee-for-service basis, although certain programs are available at no cost to participants. Erick McCandless, Director at 1-800-882-9721.

* New York Business Development Corporation (NYBDC)

New York Business Development Corporation (NYBDC)
50 Beaver Street   800-923-2504
Albany, NY 12207   Fax: 518-463-0240
www.nybdc.com

The New York Business Development Corporations mission is to promote economic activity within New York state by providing innovative loans to small and medium-size businesses; to assist our partner banks in making such loans; and, particularly, to assist minority and women-owned businesses by offering credit opportunities not otherwise available to them.

Agricultural Business Loan Program: This program is committed to financing the growth of agricultural-related business in New York State.

Mezzanine Loan Program: This program aids in financing emerging technology companies and other growth oriented businesses in need of capital.

Capital Access Program: NYBDC administers a pool of funds that are designed to give banks a flexible and non-bureaucratic tool to make business loans that are somewhat riskier than conventional bank loans.

Linked Deposit Program: This program provides businesses with affordable loans based on interest rates subsidized by state deposits.

Micro Loan Program: The Micro Loan Program was designed to provide an alternative to credit scoring for smaller loan requests.

* Small Business Administration (SBA)

Regional Office
26 Federal Plaza, Room 3100   212-264-4354
New York, NY 10278   Fax: 212-264-4963

111 West Huron St., Suite 1311   716-551-4301
Buffalo, NY 14202   Fax: 716-551-4418

401 S. Salina St., 5th Floor   315-471-9393
Syracuse, NY 13202   Fax: 315-471-9288
www.sba.gov/ny

The New York Small Business Administration Office delivers a variety of programs and services, such as startup and operational assistance through small business training and counseling, financial assistance for startup's, business opportunities and much more.

* Small Business Investment Companies

399 Venture Partners
William Comfort, Chairman
399 Park Ave., 14th Floor/Zone 4   212-559-1127
New York, NY 10043   Fax: 212-793-6164
Email: jjarema@cvcltd.com

ACI Capital America Fund, L.P.
Gregory Warner, Thomas Israel
900 Third Avenue, 26th Floor   212-634-3333
New York, NY 10022   Fax: 212-634-3330
Email: jemattutat@ACICapital.com

American Asian Capital Corp.
Howard H. Lin, President
130 Water St., Suite 6-L
New York, NY 10005   212-422-6880
Email: linwillh@cs.com

Argentum Capital Partners, LP
60 Madison Avenue, Suite 701   212-949-6262
New York, NY 10110   Fax: 212-949-8294
Email: sberman@argentumvc.com

Argentum Capital Partners, LP
Daniel Raynor, Chairman
60 Madison Avenue, Suite 701   212-949-8272
New York, NY 10110   Fax: 212-949-8294
Email: sberman@argentumvc.com

Avalon Equity Fund, L.P.
Benjamin E. Brandes, Contact
800 3rd Avenue, 31st Floor   212-421-0600
New York, NY 10022   Fax: 212-421-1742
Email: bbrandes@avalonequity.com

Bank Austria Creditanstalt SBIC, Inc.
245 Park Avenue, 32nd Floor   212-672-5656
New York, NY 10167   Fax: 212-672-5500
Email: jrangeldern@hvbamericas.com

BNP Paribas Principal Incorporated
Steven Alexander, President
787 Seventh Avenue, 32nd Floor   212-841-2000
New York, NY 10019-8018   Fax: 212-841-3558
Email: steve_alexander@paribas.com

BNY Capital Partners, L.P.
Stratton Heath, Paul Echausse
445 Park Avenue   212-821-1909
New York, NY 10022   Fax: 212-832-6949
Email: pechausse@bankofny.com

BOCNY, LLC
152 West 57th Street, 20th Floor   212-944-2542
New York, NY 10019   Fax: 212-656-1344
Email: wskeller@stonehengecapital.com

Brookside Pecks Capital Partners, L.P.
Robert Cresci, Contact
One Rockefeller Plaza, Suite 900   212-332-1346
New York, NY 10020   Fax: 212-332-1334
Email: dbuttolph@brooksideintl.com

Cephas Capital Partners L.P.
Clint Campbell, Jeff Holmes, Mgrs.
16 West Main Street   716-231-1528

Rochester, NY 14614
Email: cephascwc@aol.com
Fax: 716-231-1530

CIBC WG Argosy Merchant Fund 1, L.P.
425 Lexington Avenue, 3rd Floor
New York, NY 10017
Email: steven.a.flyer@us.cibc.com
212-885-4735
Fax: 212-885-4350

CIBC WMV Inc.
Robi Blumenstein, Managing Director
425 Lexington Avenue, 9th Floor
New York, NY 10017
Email: David.Shotland@US.CIBC.com
212-856-3713
Fax: 212-697-1544

Citicorp Venture Capital, Ltd
William Comfort, Chairman of the Board
399 Park Ave.
14th Floor/Zone 4
New York, NY 10043
Email: jjarema@cvcltd.com
212-559-1127
Fax: 212-793-6164

CMNY Capital II, L.P.
Robert G. Davidoff, General Partner
135 East 57th Street, 26th Floor
New York, NY 10022
Email: jtaylor@carlmarks.com
212-909-8428
Fax: 212-980-2630

Coqui Capital Partners, L.P.
Jeffrey S. Davidson, Contact
1775 Broadway, Suite 604
New York, NY 10019
Email: jmcgurk@coquicapital.com
212-247-4590
Fax: 212-247-4801

Critical Capital Growth Fund, L.P.
Steven Sands Mgr; C. Robinson
90 Park Ave., 39th Floor
New York, NY 10016
Email: crobinson@sandsbros.com
212-697-5200
Fax: 212-697-8035

DB Capital Partners SBIC, L.P.
Heide Silverstein, Director
130 Liberty Street, 25th Floor
New York, NY 10006
Email: heide.silverstein@db.com
212-250-8084
Fax: 212-250-7651

Dresdner Kleinwort Benson Private Equity
Richard Wolf, Partner
75 Wall Street, 34th Floor
New York, NY 10005
Email: rwolf@dresdner.com
212-429-3131
Fax: 212-429-3099

East Coast Venture Capital, Inc.
Zindel Zelmanovitch, President
241 Fifth Ave., Suite 302
New York, NY 10016
Email: zindel@eastcoastventure.com
212-686-1515
Fax: 212-686-1131

Easton Hunt Capital Partners, L.P.
John H. Friedman, Contact
641 Lexington Avenue, 21st Floor
New York, NY 10022
Email: schneider@eastoncapital.com
212-702-0950
Fax: 212-702-0952

Elk Associates Funding Corp.
Gary C. Granoff, President
747 Third Ave.
New York, NY 10017
Email: MChance@elkassociates.com
212-421-2111
Fax: 212-759-3338

Emigrant Capital Corporation
Lawrence Adolf and John Hart, Managers
6 East 43rd Street, 8th Floor
New York, NY 10017
Email: adolfl@emigrant.com
212-850-4460
Fax: 212-850-4839

Empire State Capital Corp.
Dr. Joseph Wu, President
170 Broadway, Suite 1200
New York, NY 10038
Email: ESCS131799@aol.com
212-513-1799
Fax: 212-513-1892

Eos Partners SBIC, LP
Steven Friedman, Partner
320 Park Avenue, 22nd Floor
212-832-5800

New York, NY 10022
Email: bbernstein@eospartner.com
Fax: 212-832-5805

Eos Partners SBIC II, L.P.
320 Park Avenue, 22nd Floor
New York, NY 10022
Email: bbernstein@eospartner.com
212-832-5800
Fax: 212-832-5805

Exeter Capital Partners IV, L.P.
Keith Fox, Kurt Bergquist, Jeff Weber
10 East 53rd Street, 32nd Floor
New York, NY 10022
Email: exeter@exeterfunds.com
212-872-1170
Fax: 212-872-1198

Exeter Equity Partners, L.P.
Keith Fox, Timothy Bradley, Jeff Weber
10 East 53rd Street
New York, NY 10022
Email: exeter@exeterfunds.com
212-872-1170
Fax: 212-872-1198

Exeter Venture Lenders, LP
Keith Fox, Manager
10 East 53rd St., 32nd Floor
New York, NY 10022
Email: exeter@exeterfunds.com
212-872-1170
Fax: 212-872-1198

Falcon Private Equity, L.P.
Gregga Baxter, Matthew Snyder, Contacts
335 Madison Avenue, 11th Floor
New York, NY 10017
Email: gregga.baxter@saudibank.com
212-922-2333
Fax: 212-922-2351

First County Capital, Inc.
Orest Glut, Financial Manager
40-48 Main Street, Suite 301
Flushing, NY 11354
Email: FirstCounty@AOL.com
718-461-1778
Fax: 718-461-1835

Flushing Capital Corp.
Frank J. Mitchell, President
39-06 Union St., Room 202
Flushing, NY 11354
Email: Tetsuwa@att.net
718-886-5866
Fax: 178-939-7761

Freshstart Venture Capital Corporation
Alvin Murstein, President
437 Madison Avenue
New York, NY 10022
Email: esanchez@medallionfinancial.com
212-328-2110
Fax: 212-328-2125

Fundex Capital Corp.
Larry Linksman, President
50 Main Street, Suite 1000
White Plains, NY 10606
Email: L.Linksman@fundexcapital.com
212-884-9360
Fax: 212-884-9346

Gefus SBIC, L.P.
William J. Beckett
375 Park Avenue, Suite 2401
New York, NY 10152
Email: wbeckett@gefinorusa.com
212-308-1111
Fax: 212-308-1182

Hanam Capital Corp.
Robert Schairer, President
38 West 32nd St., Suite 1512
New York, NY 10001
Email: hanam@aol.com
212-564-5225
Fax: 212-564-5307

Hudson Venture Partners, L.P.
Lawrence Howard, Marilyn Adler, R. Glaser
660 Madison Avenue, 14th Floor
New York, NY 10021
Email: cfeder@hudsonptr.com
212-644-9797
Fax: 212-644-7430

Ibero American Investors Corp.
Christine Ryan, Loan Officer
Statler Towers Bldg.
107 Delaware Avenue, Suite 64
Buffalo, NY 14202
716-842-9908
Fax: 716-842-9925

Ibero American Investors Corp.
Domingo Garcia, President
104 Scio St.
716-262-3440

Rochester, NY 14604
Email: iberoinv@rochester.rr.com

Fax: 716-262-3441

ING Furman Selz Investments
Brian Friedman, Manager
520 Madison Ave., 8th Floor
New York, NY 10022
Email: mluxenberg@ingprivate.com

212-284-1708
Fax: 212-284-1717

International Paper Cap. Formation, Inc.
Julius A. Weiss, President
Two Manhattanville Rd.
Purchase, NY 10577-2196

914-397-1960
Fax: 914-397-1630

J.P. Morgan Partners (23A SBIC), LLC
Jeffrey Walker, Managing Gen. Partner
1221 Avenue of the Americas, 40th Floor
New York, NY 10036
Email:Mary.Gormley@JPMorganPartners.com

212-899-3500
Fax: 212-622-3799

KBL Healthcare, L.P.
Marlene Krauss, Michael Kaswan
645 Madison Avenue
New York, NY 10022
Email: dcabo@kblhealthcare.com

212-319-5555
Fax: 212-319-5591

LEG Partners Debenture SBIC, L.P.
Lawrence Golub, Manager
555 Madison Avenue, 30th Floor
New York, NY 10022
Email: rzomback@golubassoc.com

212-750-6060
Fax: 212-750-5505

LEG Partners III SBIC, L.P.
Lawrence Golub, Manager
555 Madison Avenue, 30th Floor
New York, NY 10022
Email: rzomback@golubassoc.com

212-750-6060
Fax: 212-750-5505

LEG Partners SBIC, L.P.
Lawrence E. Golub, Manager
555 Madison Avenue, 30th Floor
New York, NY 10022
Email: rzomback@golubassoc.com

212-750-6060
Fax: 212-750-5505

M & T Capital Corporation
Tom Scanlon, President
One Fountain Plaza, 9th Floor
Buffalo, NY 14203
Email: tscanlon@mandtbank.com

716-848-3800
Fax: 716-848-3150

Madison Investment Partners II, L.P.
Susan Goodrich, Contact
52 Vanderbilt Avenue, Suite 1010
New York, NY 10017
Email: smaher@madisonpartners.com

212-949-0400
Fax: 212-949-6049

Medallion Funding Corporation
Alvin Murstein, President
437 Madison Avenue
New York, NY 10022
Email: mrusso@medallionfinancial.com

212-328-2110
Fax: 212-328-2125

Merchants Capital Partners, L.P.
Jake Wessner
1120 Avenue of the Americas, 4th Floor
New York, NY 10036

212-626-6832
Fax: 212-626-6833

Mercury Capitol, L.P.
David W. Elenowitz, Manager
153 East 53rd Street 49th Floor
New York, NY 10022
Email: hal@dlfi.com

212-838-0888
Fax: 212-759-3897

NBT Capital Corporation
Daryl Forsythe & Joe Minor, Managers
19 Eaton Avenue
Norwich, NY 13815
Email: csantullo@ascent.net

607-337-6810
Fax: 607-336-8730

NYBDC Capital Corp.
Chester A. Sadowski, Sr. V. President
633 Third Avenue, 36th Floor
New York, NY 10017

212-803-3672
Fax: 212-803-3675

NYBDC Capital Corporation
Robert W. Lazar, President
41 State St.
P.O. Box 738
Albany, NY 12207
Email: pvannost@nybdc.com

518-463-2268
Fax: 518-463-0240

NYBDC Capital Corp.
Stephen A. Ross, Vice President
16 West Main Street, Suite 236
Rochester, NY 14614

716-232-6250

Needham Capital SBIC, L.P.
John Michaelson, Manager
445 Park Ave.
New York, NY 10022
Email: galban@needhamco.com

212-705-0297
Fax: 212-751-1450

Needham Capital SBIC II, L.P.
George Needham, John Michaelson, Mgrs.
445 Park Avenue
New York, NY 10022
Email: galban@needhamco.com

212-371-8300
Fax: 212-751-1450

Penny Lane Partners, L.P.
William R. Denslow, Manager
108 Forest Avenue
P.O. Box 447
Locust Valley, NY 11560

516-609-8065
Fax: 516-759-4653

Pierre Funding Corp.
Elias Debbas, President
805 Third Ave., 6th Floor
New York, NY 10022
Email: pierrefunding@aol.com

212-888-1515
Fax: 212-688-4252

Psilos Group Partners II SBIC, L.P.
Jeffrey M. Krauss, Contact
625 Avenue of the Americas, 4th Floor
New York, NY 10011
Email: jeffkrauss@psilos.com

212-242-8844
Fax: 212-242-8855

Pyramid Ventures, Inc.
Brian Talbot, Vice President
130 Liberty St., 31st Floor
New York, NY 10006
Email: heide.silverstein@db.com

212-250-9571
Fax: 212-250-7651

Quad Venture Partners SBIC, L.P.
Lincoln E. Frank, Contact
650 Fifth Avenue, 31st Floor
New York, NY 10019
Email: linc@quadventures.com

212-724-2200
Fax: 212-724-4310

Radius Venture Partners II, L.P.
Daniel C. Lubin, Contact
One Rockefeller Plaza, Suite 920
New York, NY 10020
Email: dlubin@radiusventures.com

212-897-7784
Fax: 212-397-2656

Rand Capital SBIC, L.P.
Allen F. Grum, Jr., Contact
2200 Rand Building
Buffalo, NY 14203-
Email: dpenberthy@randcapital.com

716-853-0802
Fax: 716-854-8480

RBC Equity Investments, Inc.
Sindy Jagger, Manager
One Liberty Plaza
New York, NY 10006
Email: sindy.jagger@royalbank.com

212-858-7157
Fax: 212-858-7468

RBS Capital Corporation
Andrew S. Weinberg, Sr. Vice President
101 Park Avenue, 10th Floor
New York, NY 10178
Email: andrew.weinberg@rbos.com

212-401-1330
Fax: 212-401-1390

Regent Capital Partners, L.P.
J. Oliver Maggard, Managing Partner
505 Park Ave., Suite 1700
New York, NY 10022
Email: omaggard@regentcapitalpartners.com

212-735-9900
Fax: 212-735-9908

Rock Maple Ventures, L.P.
David W. Freelove, Contact
5 East 57th Street, 15th Floor   212-308-1935
New York, NY 10022   Fax: 212-308-8641
Email: dfreelove@rockmapleventures.com

SGC Partners II LLC
Christopher M. Neenan, VP & COO
1221 Avenue of the Americas, 8th Floor   212-278-5184
New York, NY 10020   Fax: 212-278-5454
Email: frances.madrid@us.socgen.com

Summer Street Capital Fund I, L.P.
Brian D'Amico
70 West Chippewa St., Suite 500   716-566-2900
Buffalo, NY 14202   Fax: 716-566-2910
Email: bdamico@summerstreetcapital.com

T.S. Capital Corporation
James Trainor, Manager
The Rice Building
216 River Street   518-687-4430
Troy, NY 12180   Fax: 518-687-4435
Email: jtrainor@tscapital.com

The 1818 SBIC Fund, L.P.
Richard J. Ragoza, Contact
59 Wall Street   212-493-7910
New York, NY 10005   Fax: 212-493-7280
Email: rick.ragoza@bbh.com

Toronto Dominion Capital (U.S.A.), Inc.
Brian A. Rich, General Manager
31 West 52nd Street   212-827-7000
New York, NY 10019   Fax: 212-974-8429
Email: gariem@tdusa.com

Triad Capital Corp. of New York
Oscar Figueroa, Manager of Rutgers Inv.
305 Seventh Ave., 20th Floor   212-243-7360
New York, NY 10001   Fax: 212-243-7647
Email: mrobiou@bcf-triad.org

Trusty Capital Inc.
Yungduk Hahn, President
25 West 37th Street, 5th Floor   212-719-3760
New York, NY 10118   Fax: 212-869-8577
Email: ydhahn@earthlink.net

UBS Capital II, LLC
Justin S. Maccarone, President
299 Park Ave.   212-821-6490
New York, NY 10171   Fax: 212-821-6333
Email: marc.unger@ubs.com

Walden Capital Partners, L.P.
John Costantino & Allen Greenberg, Mgrs.
708 Third Avenue, 21st Floor   212-355-0900
New York, NY 10017   Fax: 212-755-8894
Email: ahne@waldencapital.com

Wall Street Technology Partners, L.P.
Richard H. Wolf, Contact
75 Wall Street, 34th Floor   212-429-2817
New York, NY 10005   Fax: 212-429-2261
Email: richard.wolf@dresdnerkc.com

Wasserstein Adelson Ventures, L.P.
Townsend Ziebold, Jr., Manager
1301 Avenue of the Americas, 44th floor   212-702-5688
New York, NY 10019   Fax: 212-969-7879
Email: tz@wasserco.com

Wasserstein SBIC Ventures II, L.P.
Robert Mersten
1301 Avenue of the Americas, 44th Floor   212-969-2698
New York, NY 10019   Fax: 212-702-5635
Email: rm@wasserco.com

Westbury Equity Partners SBIC, L.P.
Richard P. Sicoli, Contact
1400 Old Country Road, Suite 313   516-333-0218
Westbury, NY 11590   Fax: 516-333-2724
Email: rsicoli@westburypartners.com

The Small Business Administration (SBA) licenses, regulates, and provides financial assistance to privately owned and operated Small Business Investment Companies. SBICs make venture or risk investments by supplying capital and extending unsecured loans and loans not fully collateralized to small enterprises which meet their investment criteria. Financing is made by direct loans and by equity investments.

* Housing and Urban Development (HUD) Regional Office

26 Federal Plaza, Suite 3541   212-264-8000
New York, NY 10278-0068   Fax: 212-264-3068
    TDD: 212-264-0927

Community Development Block Grants: Available to cities and counties for the commercial rehabilitation of existing buildings or structures used for business, commercial or industrial purposes. Grants of up to $500,000 can be made. Every $15,000 of grant funds invested must create at least one full-time job, and at least 51 percent of the jobs created must be for low- and moderate-income families.

* Power For Jobs

The New York Power Authority
123 Main Street, 10th Floor   888-562-7697
White Plains, NY 10601   Fax: 914-390-8155
www.nypa.gov/economic.htm

Businesses that remain and expand in the state get low cost electricity. The firm must first retain or create a specified number of jobs.

* New York State Energy Research and Development Authority (NYSERDA)

17 Columbia Circle   866-NYSERDA
Albany, NY 12203-6399   518-862-1090
www.nyserda.org   Fax: 518-862-1091

New York State Energy Research and Development Authority's goal is to help all of New York State solve their energy and environmental problems while developing new, innovative products and services that can be manufactured or commercialized by New York businesses.

Economic Development through Greater Energy Efficiency: Grants and technical support for detailed engineering studies of manufacturing operations up to $50,000. Capital financing for demonstrations of energy efficient process technology up to $250,000.

Energy $mart Loan Fund: Interest rate reductions are provided on loans for energy-efficiency projects and renewable technologies.

Energy Efficiency Services: Technical assistance and financial assistance up to $50,000 per project for the following:
-     Energy Feasibility Studies
-     Energy Operations Management
-     Rate Analysis and Aggregation
-     Combined Heat & Power Renewable Generation Studies

Industrial Waste Minimization Program: Technical assistance and grants up to $50,000 to assist, develop, and demonstrate energy-efficient methods to reduce, reuse or recycle industrial wastes at the point of generation.

* New York State Banking Department

One State Street   800-522-3330
New York, NY 10004-1417   Fax: 212-709-3582
www.banking.state.ny.us/sbusines/sba.htm

The Banking Department has developed a source book of private, public and non-profit small business assistance programs in New York State to be used as a resource tool for financial institutions, as well as a referral source for small business entrepreneurs.

North Carolina

* North Carolina Department of Commerce

301 North Wilmington Street
Raleigh, NC 27601
Mailing Address:
4301 Mail Service Center
Raleigh, NC 27699-4301   919-733-4151
www.commerce.state.nc.us

Retention and Expansion Programs: Professional assistance is provided for all aspects of business including environmental consultation, financing alternative, human resources consulting, marketing information, energy process surveys and other issues that impact business and industry.

Business and Industry ServiCenter: Provides technical and industrial management assistance, conducts applied research, advocates industrial use of technology and modern managerial practices, as well as conducts continuing education programs for business, industry, entrepreneurs, engineers and local governments. 866-259-9846

Biotechnology Center: Carries out a variety of programs and activities strengthening North Carolina's biotechnology community. Call 919-541-9366 or contact their website {www.biotech.org}.

Customized Training Program: State funded customized job training programs for new and expanding industries that create 12 or more new jobs in a community within one year.

SBTDC Special Market Development Assistance:
- *Procurement Technical Assistance Program*: The SBTDC provides comprehensive assistance in selling goods and services to the federal government. Services include help in finding out about contracting opportunities, preparing bid and proposal packages, obtaining 8(a) certification, interpreting regulations, and resolving contract administration problems. An integral part of this program is PRO-BID, a computer-based bid matching service that provides accurate and timely information on procurement opportunities.
- *International Business Development*: North Carolina businesses are increasingly looking at exporting as a vehicle to increase sales and profits. The SBTDC helps successful domestic, new-to-export businesses to identify, target and then penetrate foreign markets. SBTDC counselors provide marketing research information, assist with market planning, and then identify implementation procedures.
- *The Technology Group*: Part of the SBTDC's mission is to help emerging businesses commercialize innovative new technologies, and to facilitate the transfer of technology developed within the small business and university communities. Technology Group services include assistance in maritime technology transfer, identifying markets for scientific discoveries, guiding the development of strategies to protect intellectual property and providing referrals to specialized organizations and resources.
- *Marine Trades Program*: The SBTDC's Marine Trades Program provides business development support to marine industry firms. Specific services include assistance in marketing marine products and services, complying with environmental regulations, and maintaining safe operations. The program also provides marine specific training, education and research.

Industrial Revenue Bonds: Revenue Bonds have a variety of names and purposes but essentially three basic types exist. These bonds whose proper name is Small Issue Industrial Development Bonds are referred to as Industrial Revenue Bond's (IRB's). The state's principal interest in these bonds is assisting new and expanding industry while insuring that North Carolinians get good jobs at good wages. The regulations governing bond issuance are a combination of federal regulations and North Carolina statutes. The amount each state may issue annually is designated by population. There are three types of bond issuances as follows:
- Tax Exempt - Because the income derived by the bondholder is not subject to federal income tax, the maximum bond amount is $10 million in any given jurisdiction. According to federal regulations, the $10 million total includes the bond amount and capital expenditures over a six-year period going both backwards and forwards three years. The maximum any company may have is $40 million nationwide outstanding at any given period.
- Taxable - They are not exempt from federal tax (they are however exempt from North Carolina tax). The essential difference is that the Taxable bond rate is slightly higher to the borrower and not being subject to the federal volume cap, may exceed $10 million in bond amount.
- Pollution Control/Solid Waste Disposal Bond - These bonds are subject to volume cap although there is no restriction on amount, and the interest on these bonds is federally tax exempt.

Industrial Development Fund: Purpose is to provide an incentive for jobs creation in the State's most economically distressed counties, also identified as Tier 1, 2, and 3 areas. Funds for the renovation of manufacturing buildings and the acquisition of infrastructure are made available by the Department of Commerce to eligible counties or their local units of government, which apply for the funds on behalf of their existing or new manufacturing businesses. A commitment to create jobs is executed by the benefiting firm. The amount of funds available to participating firms is determined by multiplying the number of jobs committed to be created times $4,000.00, up to a maximum of $400,000.00 or the cost of the project, whichever is less. Of course, the availability of funds also applies.

Business Energy Improvement: Program provides loans between $100,000 and $500,000 to industrial and commercial businesses located or moving to North Carolina. Loans can be financed for up to seven years at interest rates equal to 50% of the average (high and low) T-bill rate for the past year or five percent, whichever is lower. Current rate is 5%, which is the maximum. Funds are provided from a pool of $2,500,000 designated for energy related capital improvement such as cogeneration, energy saving motors, boiler improvements and low energy use lighting. A participating bank will process loans on a first-come-first-served based upon the date of receipt of a letter of credit.

Partnerships for Regional Economic Development: The counties of North Carolina have been organized into seven regional partnerships for economic development. North Carolina's regional partnerships will enable regions to compete effectively for new investment and to devise effective economic development strategies based on regional opportunities and advantages.

Industrial Access/Road Access Fund: Administered by the Department of Transportation, this program provides funds for the construction of roads to provide access to new or expanded facilities.

The Rail Industrial Access Program: Provides grant funding to aid in financing the cost of constructing or rehabilitating railroad access tracks required by a new or expanded industry which will result in a significant number of new jobs or capital investment.

Export Ready Program: A series of workshops designed to walk a company through every facet of the export process. In cooperation with the North Carolina Community College Small Business Network, the International Trade Division has made this program available in seven regional centers across the state. The Export Outreach Program is a hard-core, intense program where commitment, preparation and action are instilled as the basis for successful exporting. North Carolina is the only state to offer such a program, which increases the quality and competitiveness of North Carolina products.

Trade Events Program: This program consists of Catalog Shows, Trade Fairs and Trade Mission in carefully selected markets worldwide. The Trade Events Calendar is updated periodically to inform North Carolina companies of these opportunities.

International Trade Division: Because North Carolina companies are prepared and committed prior to entering international markets, North Carolina is recognized in the major trading blocs of the world as one of the most aggressive international business development states in the United States. Senior Trade Specialists of the International Trade Division represent the three major trading blocks of the world: Europe/Africa/The Middle East, The Americas, Far East.

* Rural Development

State Director, Rural Development
William A. Tadlock III
4405 Bland Road
Raleigh, NC 27609
Email: william.tadlock@nc.usda.gov
www.rurdev.usda.gov/nc

919-873-2000
Fax: 919-873-2075

Business And Industry Loan Guarantees: The business and industry program provides loan guarantees for expansion and preservation of jobs in rural areas. The guarantees are issued to commercial lenders who make credit available to support business activity in rural areas with populations up to 50,000. Loan funds may be used to purchase land, buildings and equipment; working capital; and refinance debts. The goal of the program is to strengthen the economy of rural communities through the creation of employment opportunities.

Business And Industry Direct Loans: The business and industry program provides for direct loans for expansions and preservation of jobs in rural areas. These loans are made to individuals or corporate businesses to support business activity in rural areas with populations up to 50,000. Loan funds may be used to purchase land, buildings and equipment; working capital; and refinance debts. The goal of the program is to strengthen the economy of rural communities through the creation of employment opportunities.

Intermediary Relending Program: Loans are made to private nonprofit corporations, any state or local government, Indian tribe, or cooperatives who in turn provide credit to finance business facilities and community development projects in rural areas on a revolving loan basis.

Rural Business Opportunity Grants: Rural Business Opportunity Grants provide funding for technical assistance, training, and planning activities that improve economic conditions in rural areas.

Rural Business Enterprise Grants: Rural Business Enterprise Grants finance the development of small and emerging private business enterprises. Public bodies, non-profit corporations and recognized Indian Tribal Groups may be eligible applicants.

Rural Economic Development Loans And Grants: The purpose of the Rural Economic Development Loan and Grant program is to develop projects that will result in a sustainable increase in economic productivity, job creation, and incomes in rural areas. Projects may include business start-ups and expansion, community development incubator projects, medical and training projects, and feasibility studies.

Cooperative Services Technical Assistance: Cooperative Services (CS) assists rural residents in forming new cooperative businesses and improving the operations of existing cooperatives.

Value-Added Program Grants: Grants for independent producers, eligible agriculture producer groups, and farmer or ranch cooperatives. Grants may also be used for feasibility studies to provide capital to establish alliances or business ventures that allow the producers of the value-added agricultural product to better compete in domestic and international markets.

Renewable Energy Grants: This program enables agricultural producers and small businesses to purchase renewable energy systems and make energy improvements to reduce the cost and consumption of the nation's energy needs.

* SBTDC Minority Business Enterprise Development (SBTDC)

Small Business and Technology Development Center
5 West Hargett Street, Suite 600   919-715-7272
Raleigh, NC 27601-1348   800-258-0862 (NC only)
www.sbtdc.org

The Small Business and Technology Development Center is North Carolina's resource for growing companies. Many of the clients counseled are existing businesses. Through their management counseling and educational services, the SBTDC helps owners and managers gain knowledge essential to improving business practices, creating high-value products and services, and enhancing competitiveness. They also provide statewide procurement technical assistance through a partnership with the Defense Logistics Agency. They can help your business export products and services through a partnership with the US Export-Import Bank.

* MCNC

3201 Cornwallis Rd.
P.O. Box 12889   919-248-1800
Research Triangle Park, NC 27709   Fax: 919-248-1455
www.mcnc.org

A private nonprofit corporation that supports advanced education, research and technology programs to enhance North Carolina's technology infrastructure and businesses.

* Sales Tax Exemptions and Discounts

NC Department of Revenue
Box 25000
Raleigh, NC 27640   919-733-3991
www.dor.state.nc.us/

The North Carolina Department of Revenue has information for your business whether you're starting a new business, or have been in business for a while.

* Business License Information

North Carolina Business License Information Office (BLIO)
Department of the Secretary of State
111 Hillsborough St.,   919-807-2166
Raleigh, NC 27603   800-228-8443 (in NC)
www.secretary.state.nc.us/blio

All BLIO services are free of charge and customized to the individual business concept. Services include: one-on-one client consultations either by phone or in person; customized licensing information including employer forms and business structure information; referrals to state occupational licensing boards; referrals to local government licensing and zoning offices; referrals to the appropriate federal government agencies; and assistance in identifying other business resources.

* Aquaculture and Natural Resources

North Carolina Department of Agriculture & Consumer Services
2 West Edenton Street
1001 Mail Service Center   252-633-1477

Raleigh, NC 27699-1001   Fax: 919-716-0090
www.ncagr.com

The North Carolina Department of Agriculture & Consumer Services is the lead agency for the aquaculture industry in North Carolina. The Division of Aquaculture and Natural Resources issues the aquaculture license, is a source of general information on aquaculture, and provides farmers with published information on the economics of aquaculture and with one-one-one business counseling. The Division also participates in the National Association of State Aquaculture Coordinators. The Department also maintains seven veterinary diagnostic labs to help farmers maintain healthy fish, and the Agronomic Division does free soil evaluations to help farmers choose the best site for ponds.

* Department of Environment and Natural Resources

Small Business Assistance Program (SBAP)
1640 Mail Service Center   877-623-6748
Raleigh, NC 27699-1640   Fax: 919-715-7468
www.envhelp.org

The mission of the SBAP is to assist small businesses with air quality and other regulatory requirements, encouraging environmental compliance and stewardship.

Small Business Ombudsman (SBO): The state/territory SBOs serve as the small business community's representative where small businesses are impacted by the CAA. The SBO's key responsibilities may include: Review and provide recommendations to EPA and state/local air pollution control authorities regarding development and implementation of regulations impacting small businesses.

Compliance Advisory Panel (CAP): The CAP is created at the state level and is comprised of at least seven members: 2 members who are not owners of small business stationary sources — selected by the Governor to represent the public. 2 members who are owners of small business stationary sources — selected by the lower house of the state legislature. 2 members who are owners of small business stationary sources — selected by the upper house of the state legislature. 1 member from the state air pollution permit program — selected by the head of that agency. The responsibilities of the CAP are to: Render advisory opinions concerning the effectiveness of the SBTCP, difficulties encountered, and degree and severity of enforcement. Report on the compliance of the SBTCP with the Paperwork Reduction Act, the Regulatory Flexibility Act, and the Equal Access to Justice Act. Submit periodic reports to EPA's SBO. Review information for small business stationary sources to ensure it is understandable to the layperson. Assist in dissemination of information about upcoming air regulations, control requirements, and other matters relevant to small businesses.

Small Business Assistance Program (SBAP): The SBAPs should provide sufficient communications with small businesses through the collection and dissemination of information to the small businesses on matters of: Determining applicable requirements under the Act and permit issuance. The rights of small businesses under the Act. Compliance methods and acceptable control technologies, pollution prevention and accidental release prevention and detection and audit programs.

* North Carolina Department of Transportation

Program Development Branch
Mail Service Center #1534   919-733-2039
Raleigh, NC 27699-1534   Fax: 919-733-3585
www.ncdot.org/planning/development/TIP/TIP/

The TIP Unit develops the Transportation Improvement Program (TIP). The TIP contains funding information and schedules for various transportation divisions including: highways, aviation, enhancements, public transportation, rail, bicycle and pedestrians, and the Governor's Highway Safety Program.

* Carolinas Export Assistance Center

521 E. Morehead Street
Suite 435   704-333-2130
Charlotte, NC 28202   Fax: 704-332-2681

The Center assists clients with information about export finance options. This U.S.E.A.C. consolidates the export promotion and finance services of the U.S. Dept. of Commerce, the U.S. Small Business Administration, and the Small Business and Technology Development Center (SBTDC).

* Crop Production and Marketing Systems

North Carolina Department of Agriculture and Consumer Services
2 West Edenton Street
Raleigh, NC 27601   919-733-7125

www.agr.state.nc.us

Program goals include helping farmers evaluate alternative production practices and markets; helping part-time and limited-resource producers increase the sustainability of their farms; helping agricultural professionals adopt practices to enhance environmental quality and maintain profitability; helping producers understand and successfully comply with regulations; providing citizens with information about biotechnology; and helping farmers, agribusinesses and related organizations understand how to take advantage of local and global market factors.

* Certified Development Companies

Asheville-Buncombe Development Corporation
Robert C. Kendrick
347 Barnardsville Hwy.
Weaverville NC 28787-9696
Mail: P.O. Box 7032   828-645-0439
Asheville, NC 28802-1010   Fax: 828-658-2935
Area of Operation: Buncombe County

Centralina Development Corporation, Inc.
Paul K. Herringshaw, Executive Director
1300 Baxter Street
P.O. Box 35008   704-348-2734
Charlotte, NC 28235   Fax: 704-372-1280
Area of Operation: Cabarrus, Gaston, Iredell, Lincoln, Mecklenburg, Rowan, Stanly & Union Counties

Charlotte Certified Development Corporation
Fred L. Miller, Executive Director
5970 Fairview Rd. Suite 218   704-442-8145
Charlotte, NC 28211   Fax: 704-442-0429
Area of Operation: Mecklenburg County

Neuse River Development Authority, Inc.
Don Stewart, Senior Loan Officer
233 Middle Street
P.O. Box 1717   919-638-6724
New Bern, NC 28563   Fax: 919-638-3187
Area of Operation: Carteret, Craven, Duplin, Greene, Johnston Counties

Northwest Piedmont Development Corporation, Inc.
Charles Malone
Director of Economic Development
400 West Fourth Street, Suite 400   336-761-2111
Winston-Salem, NC 27101-2805   Fax: 336-761-2112
Area of Operation: Davie, Forsyth, Stokes, Surry, Yadkin Counties

Region C Development Corporation, Inc.
Jim Edwards, Executive Director
111 West Court Street
P.O. Box 841   828-287-2281
Rutherfordton, NC 28139-0841   Fax: 828-287-2735
Area of Operation: Cleveland, McDowell, Polk & Rutherford Counties

Region D Development Corp, Inc.
Executive Arts Building
Furman Road
P.O. Box 1820   828-265-5434 x125
Boone, NC 28607   Fax: 828-265-5439
Area of Operation: Alleghany, Ashe, Avery, Mitchell, Watauga Counties

Region E Development Corporation
James E. Chandler, Loan Specialist
736 Fourth Street, SW
Hickory, NC 28602   828-322-9191
                                 Fax: 828-322-5991
Area of Operation: Alexander, Burke, Caldwell & Catawba Counties

Self-Help Ventures Fund
Jim Overton, Commerical Loan Off.
301 W. Main Street
P.O. Box 3619   919-956-4473
Durham, NC 27702   Fax: 919-956-4600
Area of Operation: Statewide

Smokey Mountain Development Corporation
Thomas Fouts, Executive Director
144 Industrial Park Drive   828-452-1967
Waynesville, NC 28786   Fax: 828-452-1352
Area of Operation: Madison, Haywood, Graham, Cherokee, Clay Counties

Wilmington Industrial Development, Inc.
Susie Parker, Office Manager
1739 Hewlett Drive

P.O. Box 1698   910-763-0013
Wilmington, NC 28402   Fax: 910-763-0106
Area of Operation: New Hanover, Brunswick, Pender Counties

The 504 Certified Development Company (CDC) Program provides growing businesses with long-term, fixed-rate financing for major fixed assets, such as land and buildings. A Certified Development Company is a nonprofit corporation set up to contribute to the economic development of its community or region. CDCs work with the SBA and private-sector lenders to provide financing to small businesses.

* North Carolina Technological Development Authority

2 Davis Dr.
P.O. Box 13169   919-990-8558
Research Triangle Park, NC 27709 Fax: 919-558-0156
www.nctda.org

The North Carolina Technological Development Authority, Inc. (TDA) is a public benefit corporation whose mission is to create jobs and wealth throughout North Carolina using business incubation, venture capital, technology transfer and rural initiatives to commercialize promising business opportunities.

Seed and Incubator Capital: Through the Innovation Research Fund, up to $50,000 in seed money is available for development of new products or services. The Authority funds incubator facilities through its Incubator Facilities Program. It also conducts workshops across the state for those small business interested in the IRF and the Small Business Innovation Research program.

* Small Business Administration (SBA)

6302 Fairview Road, Suite 300   704-344-6563
Charlotte, NC 28210   Fax: 704-344-6769
www.sba.gov/nc

The North Carolina Small Business Administration Office delivers a variety of programs and services, such as startup and operational assistance through small business training and counseling, financial assistance for startup's, business opportunities and much more.

* Small Business Investment Companies

BA Capital Company, LP
Walter W. Walker, Jr., Managing Director
100 North Tryon Street, 25th Floor
NCI-007-25-02   704-386-8063
Charlotte, NC 28255   Fax: 704-386-6432
Email: ed.a.balogh@bankofamerica.com

BancAmerica Capital Investors SBIC I, LP
Walter W. Walker, Jr., Managing Director
100 North Tryon Street, 25th Floor
NC-1-007-25-02   704-386-8063
Charlotte, NC 28255   Fax: 704-386-6432
Email: ed.a.balogh@bankofamerica.com

BB&T Capital Partners, LLC
David Townsend & Martin Gilmore, Mgrs.
200 West Second Street, 4th Floor   336-733-2420
Winston-Salem, NC 27101   Fax: 336-733-2419
Email: dgtownsend@bbandt.com

Blue Ridge Investors II, LP
Kevin Jessup, Ronald Stanley, Contacts
300 N. Greene Street, Suite 2100   336-275-7002
Greensboro, NC 27401   Fax: 336-275-9155
Email: kjessup@genevamerchantbank.com

Blue Ridge Investors Ltd. Partnership
Richard MacLean
922 East Boulevard   704-332-3346
Charlotte, NC 28203-5204   Fax: 704-332-4528

CapitalSouth Partners Fund I, L.P.
Joseph B. Alala, III, Contact
1011 East Morehead Street, Suite 150   704-376-5502
Charlotte, NC 28204   Fax: 704-376-5877
Email: edortch@capitalsouthpartners.com

Centura SBIC, Inc.
Robert R. Anders, Jr., President
200 Providence Road, 3rd Floor
P.O. Box 6261   704-686-1451
Charlotte, NC 28207   Fax: 704-686-1761
Email: swestbrook@centura.com

Frontier Fund I, LP
Paul W. Stackhouse, Contact
1900 South Blvd., Suite 300   704-414-2880
Charlotte, NC 28203   Fax: 704-414-2881
Email: lindner@frontierfunds.com

North Carolina Economic Opportunities Fund,
H. Dabney Smith, Contact
316 West Edenton Street, Suite 110   919-256-5007
Raleigh, NC 27603   Fax: 919-256-5015
Email: dsmith@dogwoodequity.com

Oberlin Capital, LP
Robert Shepley, Manager
702 Oberlin Road, Suite 150   919-743-2544
Raleigh, NC 27605   Fax: 919-743-2501
Email: rmountcastle@oberlincapital.com

Venture Capital Solutions, LP
Philip Martin, Contact
112 Cambridge Plaza Drive
P.O. Box 24785   336-768-9343
Winston-Salem, NC 27114   Fax: 336-768-6471
Email: pmartin@vcslp.com

Wachovia Capital Partners, Inc.
Tracey M. Chaffin, Chief Financial Officer
One First Union Center, 12th Floor
301 South College Street   704-374-4791
Charlotte, NC 28288-0732   Fax: 704-374-6711
Email: tracey.chaffin@wachovia.com

Wachovia Private Capital, Inc.
Tracey M. Chaffin, Chief Financial Officer
One First Union Center, 12th Floor
301 South College Street   704-374-4791
Charlotte, NC 28288-0732   Fax: 704-374-6711
Email: michelle.dellinger@capmark.funb.com

The SBA licenses, regulates, and provides financial assistance to privately owned and operated Small Business Investment Companies. SBICs make venture or risk investments by supplying capital and extending unsecured loans and loans not fully collateralized to small enterprises which meet their investment criteria. Financing is made by direct loans and by equity investments.

* North Carolina Biotechnology Center

15 TW Alexander Dr.
P.O. Box 13547   919-541-9366
Research Triangle Park, NC 27709-3547   Fax: 919-990-9544
www.ncbiotech.org

Supports biotechnology research as a means of improving the state's economy. The center does not actually perform research itself, but supports, coordinates, and educates in the field of biotechnology. Grants are available for academic research, large-scale projects at universities and non-profit institutions, economic development, and for groups wishing to organize conferences and workshops. These grants total several million dollars per year.

* Industrial Extension Service (IES)

North Carolina Manufacturing Extension Partnership (NCMEP)
IES Technical Services   800-227-0264
Box 7902   919-515-2358
Raleigh, NC 27695-7902   Fax: 919-515-6159
www.ies.ncsu.edu

Through NCMEP, IES delivers services to North Carolina's manufacturing community, offering engineering assistance, problem solving, technical information, continuing education, and demonstration of new technologies and best practices. Extension specialists are linked through electronic communication, industry advisory councils, networking, and state of the art information resources.

North Dakota

* North Dakota Department of Economic Development and Finance

1600 East Century Ave., Suite 2
P.O. Box 2057   701-328-5300
Bismarck, ND 58502   Fax: 701-328-5320
www.growingnd.com   TTY: 800-366-6888

This office can provide information and expertise in dealing with state, federal, and local agencies. They also have information on financing programs and other services offered by the state government.

North Dakota Manufacturing Technology Partnership (MTP): Approximately 400 targeted manufacturers in the state will be able to receive direct assistance from dedicated manufacturing specialists experienced in manufacturing and will be able to access other appropriate assistance through managed referrals. Manufacturers can expect benefits from improved manufacturing processes; enhanced management skills; better business practices; research and development funding and technical assistance; expanded market opportunities; defense conversion assistance; new product development resources; better trained staff; intercompany working relationships; increased revenue; and increased profit.

The North Dakota Development Fund: Provides gap financing for primary sector businesses expanding or relocating in the state. Primary sector is defined as: "an individual, corporation, partnership or association which, through the employment of knowledge or labor, adds value to a product, process or service that results in the creation of new wealth." Primary sector businesses are typically considered to be manufacturing, food processing, and exported services. Types of investments include equity, debt, and other forms of innovative financing up to a limit of $300,000. One of the criteria for dollars invested is projected job creation within 24 months of funding.

Agricultural Products Utilization Commission: Mission is to create new wealth and jobs through the development of new and expanded uses of North Dakota agricultural products. The commission accomplishes its mission through the administration of a grant program.

Basic and Applied Research Grants: This program centers on research efforts that focus on the uses and processing of agricultural products and by-products. Further, consideration is given to products which develop an expanded use of technology for the processing of these products.

Marketing & Utilization Grants: Funds from this category are used for the development or implementation of a sound marketing plan for the promotion of North Dakota agricultural products or by-products.

Farm Diversification Grants: This category focuses on the diversification of a family farm to non-traditional crops, livestock or non-farm value-added processing of agricultural commodities. Traditional crops and livestock are generally defined as those for which the North Dakota Agricultural Statistics Service maintains records. The proposed project must have the potential to create additional income for the farm unit.

International Trade Program: Mission is to increase the number of jobs in North Dakota by helping companies expand their business into foreign markets. Staff counsels companies on export procedures, international marketing, banking and financing. They also provide referrals to translators, customs brokers, consultants and opportunities for participation in international trade show events. Offers a series of international business workshops, titled "Hands-On Training in International Business," to provide North Dakota businesses with the tools to target global markets and expand export opportunities.

* Rural Development Administration

State Director
Federal Building, Room 208
220 East Rosser
P.O. Box 1737   701-530-2037
Bismarck, ND 58502   701-530-2108
www.rurdev.usda.gov/nd

Business and Industrial Loan Programs: Provides loan guarantees to lenders. Proceeds can be used for working capital, equipment, and real property. Interest rates are negotiated between lender and borrower. Maximum terms: 7 years for working capital, 10 years for equipment, and 25 years for real property. Requires 10 percent equity for existing businesses and 20 percent-25 percent for new businesses. Additional funding allowed from any source. Only rural areas and areas with populations under 25,000 are eligible.

Rural Enterprise Grant Program: Provides grants to public or non-profit agencies to provide loans and/or technical assistance to for-profit enterprises, with the intent of creating jobs for rural residents.

Intermediary Relending Program: Provides loans to rural businesses. The interest rate to the intermediaries is 1%, with repayment terms of up to 30 years. The program is intended to create employment for rural residents.

* Skills and Technology Training Center

    1305 19th Ave. North
    Fargo, ND 58102   701-231-6900
    www.sttc.nodak.edu   Fax: 701-231-6905
Located in Fargo. A partnership between NDSU-Fargo, North Dakota State College of Science, and Wahpeton private sector leaders.

* Job Services North Dakota

    P.O. Box 5507   800-732-9787
    Bismarck, ND 58506-5507   701-328-3096
    www.state.nd.us/jsnd/   Fax: 701-328-1025
Has labor, employment, and other statistical information available.

* One Stop Capital Center

    Bank of North Dakota
    700 E. Main, 2nd Floor
    P.O. Box 5509   701-328-5850
    Bismarck, ND 58506   800-544-4674
    http://webhost.btigate.com/ ~onestop
Located at the Bank of North Dakota, the One Stop Capital Center offers one-stop access to over twenty financing programs. Together, the five partners work with local financial institutions and economic developers to offer integrated financial packages. The One Stop Capital Center has loan officers available from each of the agencies who jointly work to streamline the financing process and provide timely service.

* Center for Technology & Business/ Women & Technology

    P.O. Box 2535   701-223-0707
    Bismarck, ND 58502   Fax: 701-223-2507
    www.techwomen.org
A partnership funded by the Economic Development and Finance Division and the U.S. Small Business Administration brought about this program, which is designed to serve women in business or about to start a business. It also provides technical assistance and training to help women so they may join the technology revolution.

* Center for Innovation

    Bruce Gjovig, Director
    University of North Dakota Rural Technology Center
    4300 Dartmouth Drive
    P.O. Box 8372   701-777-3132
    Grand Forks, ND 58202-8372   Fax: 701-777-2339
    www.innovators.net
The Center for Innovation offers comprehensive, hands-on assistance to technology entrepreneurs, innovators, and manufacturers interested in starting up new ventures, commercializing new products, and licensing new technologies. They can help your business with Marketing Services, Business Plans, Small Business Innovation Research (SBIR) applications, Commercial Evaluations, and Patent & Trademark searches. The Center has helped launch hundreds of new products and companies, including several university-developed spinoffs.

* The Rural Technology Incubator

    Center for Innovation
    4300 Dartmouth Drive
    P.O. Box 8372   701-777-3132
    Grand Forks, ND 58202-8372   Fax: 701-777-2339
    www.innovators.net
The Rural Technology Incubator located in the Center for Innovation is designed to provide a seedbed to help innovators and entrepreneurs grow their businesses. Our highly-diversified staff assists startups by providing them with supportive, creative places in which to work as a team. The Rural Technology Incubator offers university talent, technology, training, and technical assistance to help business startups develop and test-market new products, ideas, technologies, and ventures. They also provide tenants with improved exposure to the entrepreneurial enterprise of the greater Grand Forks community. Tenants enjoy a major cost savings due to below-average market prices, flexible rental space, and reduced overhead through shared infrastructure.

* Pride of Dakota

    North Dakota Department of Agriculture
    Marketing Division   800-242-7535
    600 E Boulevard Ave, Dept 602   701-328-2231
    Bismarck, ND 58505-0020   Fax: 701-328-4567
    Email: ndda@state.nd.us
    www.agdepartment.com/Programs/podhp.html
The program was created to develop, improve and expand domestic and foreign markets for North Dakota products. Pride of Dakota products gain exposure through: sharing booth space at trade shows and fairs; listing in North Dakota Products Guide and brochures ; networking with other North Dakota companies Pride of Dakota Day promotions ; and cooperative advertising and magazine advertisements. Pride of Dakota members have access to a marketing staff who can: assist in gaining consumer exposure for their products ; help make sales and distribution contacts in local, regional, national and international markets; assist in design of company brochures, packaging and labels; and develop marketing strategies and promotional planning. Pride of Dakota members can buy these promotional materials at cost: shelf tags; stickers; advertising slicks; and shelf talkers.

* Certified Development Company

    Dakota Certified Development Company
    Toby Sticka, 504 Prog. Director   701-293-8892
    51 Broadway, Suite 400   800-611-8997
    Fargo ND 58102   Fax: 701-293-7819
The 504 Certified Development Company (CDC) Program provides growing businesses with long-term, fixed-rate financing for major fixed assets, such as land and buildings. A Certified Development Company is a nonprofit corporation set up to contribute to the economic development of its community or region. CDCs work with the SBA and private-sector lenders to provide financing to small businesses.

* Bank of North Dakota

    Bank of North Dakota
    P.O. Box 5509
    700 East Main Ave.   800-472-2166
    Bismarck, ND 58506   Fax: 701-328-5731
PACE (Partnership in Assisting Community Expansion): PACE assists North Dakota communities in expanding their economic base and provide for new job development by reducing the borrower's overall interest rate. The participation by a local lender is a major element, and the borrower must demonstrate that within the first year, there will be a minimum of one job created for every $75,000 of total loan proceeds.

Ag Pace: Provides low-interest financing to on-farm businesses. The program funds are sued to buy down the interest rate on loans which have been approved by a local lender and the Bank of North Dakota. It is available to any business, except traditional agriculture, which is integrated into the farm operation and will be used to supplement farm income.

Oil and Gas Development Loans: Assists North Dakota developers in increasing oil and gas production and job enhancement at existing wells. The Bank's maximum loan participation amount is $100,000.

Small Business Loan Program: Loans of up to $250,000 to any business, through a local lender, for working capital, equipment and real property. Terms are 3-5 years for working capital, 5-7 years for equipment, and 12-15 years for real estate. Equity requirement is 25 percent for new businesses. Local lender is required for 30-40 percent of loan.

Business Development Loans: Available to any business. Local lender is required for up 30 to 40 percent of total loan. BND share is up to $500,000 per project. Fund can be used for working capital, equipment and real property.

Match Program: MATCH is targeted to manufacturing, processing and value-added industries which are financially strong companies and provide interest rates at some of the lowest in the nation.

The SBA Loan Purchase Program is designed to provide low interest rate loans to North Dakota businesses receiving a SBA loan guarantee. This program permits BND to purchase the SBA guaranteed portion of the loan. BND will purchase, at par, the SBA guaranteed portion of any loan. BND's purchase is conditioned upon the borrower receiving the benefit of the lower interest rate. Call 701-328-5670 for further information.

Farm Loan Programs: Agriculture Partnership in Assisting Community Expansion (AG PACE); Beginning Farmer Guaranteed Farm Real Estate Loans; Beginning Farmer Real Estate Loan Program; Value Added Agriculture Equity Program (ENVEST); Established Farmer Real Estate Loan Program; Family Farm Loan Program; Farm Operating Loan Program;

Farm Real Estate Loan Rates; FSA Guaranteed Loan Purchase Program; Irrigation Loan Program; and the ND First Time Farmer Finance Program. Call 701-328-5672.

Developmentally Disabled Facility Loan Fund: This fund assists in the construction facilities to house and train the developmentally disabled, the chronically mentally ill, and the physically disabled persons throughout the State. Loans may be made to nonprofit corporations organized in the locality in which a facility is proposed to be located. The proceeds may be used for the cost of real estate, construction, reconstruction, acquisition, furnishing and equipment and administrative costs related to the establishment of facilities for developmentally disabled, chronically mentally ill, and physically disabled persons. The maximum amount of a loan may not exceed 75% of the project costs.

* Grand Forks Region Economic Development Corporation

600 DeMars Ave., Suite 501	701-746-2720
Grand Forks, ND 58201	Fax: 701-746-2725
www.grandforks.org/localprograms.htm	

Grand Forks Growth Fund: The fund is intended to provide gap and incentive financing for new or expanding businesses which have capacity to create new primary sector jobs and contribute to the local tax base. Funds can be used to provide temporary or permanent financing for capital costs (land, buildings, and infrastructure), equipment, working capital, seed capital, or other miscellaneous feasibility costs. A minimum 10 percent equity contribution is required. For requests in excess of $25,000, the applicant must obtain some levels of bank participation.

* ND Division of Community Services

1600 East Century Avenue, Suite 2	
P.O. Box 2057	701-328-5300
Bismarck, ND 58502-2057	Fax: 701-328-5320
www.state.nd.us/dcs	

Community Development Block Grants: Available to cities and counties for the commercial rehabilitation of existing buildings or structures used for business, commercial, or industrial purposes. Grants of up to $300,000 can be made. Every $15,000 of grant funds invested must create at least one full-time job, and at least 51 percent of the jobs created must be for low- and moderate-income families.

* Agricultural Products Utilization Commission

North Dakota Department of Commerce	
1600 East Century Avenue, Suite 2	
P.O. Box 2057	701-328-5350
Bismarck, ND 58502-2057	Fax: 701-328-5320
www.growingnd.com	

Provides funding and assistance to private industry in the establishment of agricultural processing plants for the manufacturing and marketing of agricultural derived fuels, chemicals and other processed products.

* North Dakota Tax Commissioner

600 E. Boulevard Ave.	701-328-2770
Bismarck, ND 58505-0599	Fax: 701-328-3700
www.state.nd.us/taxdpt	

Special Tax Incentives for Businesses: Incentives include:
- Five year property and corporation income tax exemptions for new business projects
- Wage and salary income tax credits
- Income tax credit for research expenditures and for investment in a North Dakota venture capital corporation
- Deductions for selling or renting a business to a beginning business person or farmland to a beginning farmer

* Fargo-Cass County Economic Development Corporation

51 Broadway, Suite 500	701-237-6132
Fargo, ND 58102	Fax: 701-293-7819
www.fedc.com	

The Fargo-Cass County Economic Development Corporation provides a variety of incentive programs to businesses that locate or expand in Cass County.

* Small Business Administration (SBA)

657 2nd Ave. N., Room 219	701-239-5131
Fargo, ND 58102	Fax: 701-239-5645

www.sba.gov/nd
The North Dakota Small Business Administration Office delivers a variety of programs and services, such as startup and operational assistance through small business training and counseling, financial assistance for startup's, business opportunities and much more.

* Small Business Investment Companies

North Dakota SBIC, L.P.	
51 Broadway, Suite 400	701-298-0003
Fargo, ND 58102	Fax: 701-293-7819

The Small Business Administration (SBA) licenses, regulates, and provides financial assistance to privately owned and operated Small Business Investment Companies. SBICs make venture or risk investments by supplying capital and extending unsecured loans and loans not fully collateralized to small enterprises which meet their investment criteria. Financing is made by direct loans and by equity investments.

* Marketplace of Ideas/ Marketplace for Kids Headquarters

411 Main Street West	701-663-0150
Mandan, ND 58554-3164	888-384-8410
www.marketplaceofideas.com	Fax: 701-663-1032

Marketplace of Ideas holds a yearly conference where entrepreneurs can participate in training and technical assistance. Their web site keeps a directory of ideas and other economic development information.

Ohio

* Ohio Department of Development

77 South High Street	
Columbus, OH 43215-6140	
Mailing Address:	
P.O. Box 1001	614-466-3379
Columbus, OH 43216-1001	800-848-1300
www.odod.state.oh.us	Fax: 614-463-1540

Small Business Innovation Research (SBIR) Technical Assistance Services: Increases the number of research contracts won by Ohio companies from eleven participating federal agencies. Provides small businesses with direct, hands-on assistance in identifying research topics; guides businesses through the proposal writing process from design to review; and offers educational and technical services. Also helps companies prepare proposals for SBIR Phase I awards of up to $100,000 and Phase II awards up to $500,000.

Business Development Assistance: Assists domestic and foreign businesses with up-to-date information on sites, buildings, labor, markets, taxes and financing. Development specialists act as liaison between the companies and state/local agencies. Works to maintain and create Ohio jobs through retention and expansion of established businesses and attraction of new businesses; assists local community development organizations and acts as a liaison for communities when dealing with issues under local control.

Labor Market Information: Measurements of economic conditions. Local and national employment/labor-force data to aid in market research, business development and planning. Attracts new employers by identifying skilled workforce. Supplies free information on the training/education available to help workers meet business needs.

Ohio Data Users Center: Census and statistical data; demographic; economic; specific trade, industry and labor analyses. Develops and disseminates population estimates, projections. Provides tools for better coordinated decision-making in public/private sectors.

Ohio Procurement Technical Assistance: Free in-depth counseling, technical resources and historical contracting data, military specifications, financial guidance and advocacy services for federal procurement opportunities. Increases the federal dollars invested in Ohio; increase job and business market opportunities; increase awareness of procurement programs and opportunities.

One-Stop Business Permit Center: Supplies new entrepreneurs with information about licenses and permits required by the State of Ohio; directs callers to proper area for technical, financial and management resources; acts as advocate for licensing and permit problems. 614-446-4232

Edison Technology Centers: Provides businesses with access to state-of-the-art applied research performed in-house or obtained through linkages with universities, federal laboratories and other institutions; education and training programs; plant site assessments; technical problem solving; conferences, seminars and other networking opportunities.

Edison Technology Incubators: Low-cost space that reduces operating costs during start-up phase for technology-based businesses; access to business, technical, and professional services, including legal, accounting, marketing, and financial counseling. 614-466-3887

Federal Technology Transfer Program: "Gateway" organizations to resources of the federal laboratory system including intellectual property, engineering expertise, facilities, and equipment.

166 Regional Loan Program: Land and building acquisition, expansion or renovation, and equipment purchase; industrial projects preferred. Up to 40% of total eligible fixed cost ($350,000 maximum); rate negotiable for 5-15 years; equity minimum 10%, bank minimum 25%. Ohio prevailing wage rate applies.

Direct Loan (166 Loan): Land and building acquisition, expansion or renovation, and equipment purchase; industrial projects preferred. Up to 30% of total eligible fixed cost ($1 million maximum, $350,000 minimum), two-thirds of prime fixed rate for 10-15 years; equity minimum 10%, bank minimum 25%. In distressed areas of the State, preferential rates and terms are available. However, the Director of Development may authorize a higher loan amount or modified terms that address a unique and demonstrated economic development need. Must show repayment and management capabilities; must create one job for every $15,000 received; Ohio prevailing wage rate applies.

Labor/Management Cooperation Program: Enhances relationship between labor and management through regular meetings, seminars, conferences, and work-site labor/management training programs. Creates a stable and positive work environment by nurturing cooperative labor/management relationships and by dispelling negative labor images. Matching grants support community-based area labor/management committees, regional centers for the advancement of labor-management cooperation, and an employee stock ownership assistance program.

Linked Deposit Program: Fixed assets, working capital and refinanced-debt for small businesses, creating or retaining jobs. A similar Agricultural Linked Deposit Program provides funds for Ohio farmers to help meet planning deadlines. 3% below current lending rate fixed for 2 years (possible 2-year extension); bank may then extend term at current rates. (All other sources of funds allowable.) The Agricultural Linked Deposit Program provides up to $100,000 per farm at reduced rate, approximately 4% below borrower's current rate. Must have Ohio headquarters and no divisions out of state, create one job for every $15,000 to $25,000 received, have 150 or fewer employees, be organized for profit, and have bank loan from eligible state depository. 800-228-1102

Ohio Enterprise Bond Fund: Land and building acquisition, construction, expansion or renovation, and equipment purchase for commercial or industrial projects between $1 million and $10 million in size. Long-term, fixed rate for up to 16 years; interest rate based on Standard & Poor's A-minus rating, for up to 90% of total project amount.

Ohio Coal Development Program: Financial assistance for clean coal research and development projects. Advances promising technology into the commercial market. Installed technologies will result in cleaner air, better use of by-products, greater demand for Ohio coal and the jobs associated with its production and use. Strong potential also exists for the export of the technologies. For research: up to $75,000 or two-thirds of total project costs (TPC). Pilot and demonstration scale projects: up to $5 million or one-half of TPC for a pilot project, or one-third TPC for demonstration project. Funds can be issued in the form of a grant, loan, or loan guarantee.

Defense Adjustment Program: Provides assistance to communities and technology-based companies impacted by economic losses because of company and military base drawdowns, realignments and closures. 614-466-3887

Industrial Training Program: Up to 50% funding for orientation, training, and management program; instructional materials, instructor training.

Economic Development Program: Provides funding for development and revitalization of local communities for fixed assets related to commercial, industrial or infrastructure.

Pioneer Rural Loan Program: Provides direct loans for businesses locating or expanding in Ohio's rural areas. Must demonstrate that they will create new jobs.

International Trade Division: Assists Ohio companies to develop export markets worldwide. Ohio's trade staff in Columbus, Tokyo, Hong Kong, Toronto, Mexico City, Sao Paulo, Brussels, and Tel Aviv provide custom-tailored assistance in international marketing and export finance and lead Ohio companies on trade missions and to the world's leading trade shows.

Services include:
- Export Counseling
- Trade Shows and Trade Missions
- Electronic Trade
- Export Finance
- Export Incentives
- Japan Trade Program

Minority Management and Technical Services: Provides assistance in management analysis, technical assistance, educational services and financial consulting. Supports overall growth and development of minority firms throughout the State. Counseling is provided at no charge.

Minority Contractor and Business Assistance Program: Provides management, technical, financial, and contract procurement assistance; loan, grant, bond packaging services. Networks with all levels of government, private businesses. Aids in economic growth and development of the minority community; increases awareness of local, state, and federal business assistance programs. Counseling is provided at no charge. Fees may be charged for some programs using federal funding. 614-466-5700

Minority Contract Procurement Services: Assists primarily minority firms in procuring public and private sector contracts. Supports efforts of minority firms to obtain contract awards that will aid in sustaining and developing these firms. Counseling is provided at no charge.

Minority Business Bonding Program: Surety bonding assistance for state-certified minority businesses. Maximum bond pre-qualification of up to $1,000,000 per Minority Business. The bond premium for each bond issued will not exceed 2% of the face value of the bond. 614-644-7708

Minority Direct Loan: Purchase or improvement of fixed assets for state-certified minority-owned businesses. Up to 40% of total project cost at 4.5% fixed for up to 15 years (maximum).

Ohio Mini-Loan Program: Fixed assets and equipment for small businesses. Start-up or existing business expansion. Projects of $100,000 or less. Up to 45% guarantee of an eligible bank loan. Interest rate of the State guarantee of the loan is currently 5.5%, and may be fixed for 10 years. Eligibility: Small business entrepreneurs with fewer than 25 employees, targeted 50% allocation to businesses owned by minorities and women.

Women's Business Resource Program: Assistance for start-up, expansion and management of businesses owned by women; assures equal access to state business assistance and lending programs; direction to purchase and procurement opportunities with government agencies. Researches legislation that may impact businesses owned by women. Increases start-ups and successes of women-owned businesses. No charge. 614-466-4945

Office of Energy Efficiency: Training, technical assistance and partnership programs are available to help businesses become more energy efficient thereby reducing costs and to contribute to a cleaner environment.

Office of Investment Training Program: Companies can receive financial assistance and technical resources for customized training for employees of new and expanding businesses. There is a 50% reimbursement for instructional costs, materials and training-related activities. 614-466-4155

Capital Access Program: Small businesses that have less than $10 million in sales and that have trouble securing a loan may be eligible for funding with this program. Financing is available for working capital and construction of fixed assets and refinancing of existing loans. The maximum loan amount is $250,000 for working capital and $500,000 for fixed assets. 614-644-7708

Technology Action Fund: Grants are awarded on a competitive basis in order to support entrepreneurial activity in technology sectors that enhance the economic development in Ohio. 614-466-3887

Microenterprise Business Development Program: Grants given to cities and counties are used to help with the development of local enterprise businesses and also to create and retain long-term jobs. 614-466-2285

Ohio Qualified Small-Issue Bond Program: Low-interest financing for small manufacturing facilities expanding or relocating in Ohio.

Rural Industrial Park Loan: Provides direct loans and loan guarantees to rural, distressed local communities to create industrial parks.

NxLevel: NxLevel is a community-based training program created to help small-to-medium size businesses through classes and materials.

* USDA, Rural Development
Federal Building, Room 507
200 North High Street

Columbus, OH 43215   614-255-2500
www.rurdev.usda.gov/oh

Business & Industry Loan Guarantees (B&I): The B&I program provides loan guarantees for expansion and preservation of jobs in rural areas. The program can provide development credit in rural areas and towns of 50,000 or less. Jobs produced in this manner will help people stay in their own communities and raise their standard of living in the rural environment. The program provides guarantees to commercial lenders who make credit available to establish or maintain businesses. Loan funds may be used to purchase land, buildings and equipment; working capital; and in some cases to refinance debt. Eligible entities include corporations, partnerships, cooperatives, individuals, federally recognized Indian Tribes and other legal entities.

Intermediary Relending Program (IRP): The purpose of the Intermediary Relending Program is to finance business facilities and community development projects in rural areas. This is achieved through low interest loans made by Rural Development to intermediaries. The intermediaries relend the funds to ultimate recipients for business purposes or community development projects. Intermediaries establish revolving loan funds, so that collections from loans to ultimate recipients, in excess of necessary operating expenses and debt payments, will be used for more loans to ultimate recipients. Intermediaries may be private nonprofit corporations, public agencies, Indian groups or cooperatives. Any type legal entity, including individuals and public and private organizations, may be an ultimate recipient.

Rural Business Enterprise Grants (RBEG): These grants provide resources which are utilized to develop small and emerging business enterprises in rural areas or cities up to 50,000 population. Qualifying entities include public bodies and nonprofit corporations. Grants are used by third party lenders to create revolving business loan funds. Funds can also be used to install infrastructure to business locations and house business incubators.

Rural Economic Development Loan and Grant (REDLG): This program is utilized to finance rural economic development and rural job creation projects which are based on sound economic and financial analysis. This is done by making zero-interest loans and/or grants to Rural Utilities Service (RUS) electric and telephone borrowers who use the funds to provide financing for business and community development projects. Eligible project costs include project feasibility studies, start-up costs, purchasing facilities and equipment, business incubator projects and other reasonable expenses for the purpose of fostering rural economic development.

* Certified Development Companies

Cascade Capital Corporation, Inc.
Robert Filipiak, Executive Director
One Cascade Place, 7th Floor   330-379-3160
Akron, OH 44308   Fax: 330-761-0307
Area of Operation: Ashland, Holmes, Portage, Medina, Summit and Wayne Counties

Certified Development Co. of Butler County
Jenea Norris Allen, Executive Director
130 High Street, 6th Floor   513-887-3404
Hamilton, OH 45011   Fax: 513-785-5723
Area of Operation: Butler County

Certified Development Company of Warren County, Inc.
Steve Jacobs, Loan Manager
320 East Silver St   513-695-1223
Lebanon, OH 45036   Fax: 513-695-2933
Area of Operation: Warren County

Citywide Small Business Development Corp.
Janet White, Director, Economic Development Officer
8 North Main Street   937-226-0457
Dayton, OH 45402-1916   Fax: 937-222-7035
Area of Operation: city limits of Dayton

Clark County Development Corp.
Warren Holden, Loan Manager
300 East Auburn Avenue   937-322-8685
Springfield, OH 45505   Fax: 937-322-7874
Area of Operation: Clark County

Community Capital Development Corporation
Brad Shimp, Executive Director
900 Michigan Avenue   614-645-6171
Columbus, OH 43215-1165   Fax: 614-645-8588
Area Of Operation: Counties of Delaware, Fairfield, Fayette, Franklin, Licking, Madison, Muskingum, Perry, Pickaway, Union, Athens, Gallia, Hocking, Lawrence, Meigs, Monroe, Morgan, Noble, Scioto and Washington Counties.

County Corp Development
Marlene J. Flagel, President
40 West Fourth Street, Suite 1600   937-225-6328
Dayton, OH 45402   Fax: 937-225-5089
Area of Operation: Darke, Miami, Montgomery (outside Dayton city limits), Shelby, Greene and Preble Counties.

Greene County Development Corp.
Melissa Frost, SBA 504 Coordinator
61 Greene Street   937-562-5644
Xenia, OH 45385   Fax: 937-562-5645
Area of Operation: Greene County

Growth Capital Corporation
Gerald H. Meyer
200 Tower City Center
50 Public Square   216-621-3300
Cleveland, OH 44113-2291   Fax: 216-621-6013
Area of Operation: Cuyahoga, Lake, Geauga, Lorain, Medina, Portage and Summit Counties

Hamilton County Development Co., Inc.
David K. Main, President
1776 Mentor Avenue   513-631-8292
Cincinnati, OH 45212   Fax: 513-631-4887
Area of Operation: Adams, Brown, Highland, Clermont and Hamilton Counties

Lake County Small Business Assistance Corporation
Catherine Haworth, Assistant Executive Director
7750 Clocktower Drive   440-951-1290
Mentor, OH 44060   Fax: 440-953-4413
Area Of Operation: Lake County

Lucas County Improvement Corporation
Deborah Campbell
One Maritime Plaza, 7th Floor   419-243-8251
Toledo, OH 43604   Fax: 419-243-1835
Area of Operation: Lucas County

Mahoning Valley Economic Development Corporation
Donald L. French, Executive Director
4319 Belmont Avenue   330-759-3668
Youngstown, OH 44505   Fax: 330-759-3686
Area Of Operation: Mahoning, Columbiana and Trumbull Counties

Mentor Economic Assistance Corporation
Elaine Kline, Program Administrator
8500 Civic Center Boulevard   440-255-1100
Mentor, OH 44060   Fax: 440-974-5708
Area of Operation: City of Mentor

Ohio Statewide Development Corp.
Dianne Allen, Executive Director
1335 Dublin Road, Suite 200   614-481-3214
Columbus, OH 43215   Fax: 614-481-3215
Area of Operation: 67 counties through out Ohio

Stark Development Board Finance Corporation
Steve Paquette, President
116 Cleveland Avenue, NW, Suite 600   330-453-5900
Canton, OH 44702-1730   Fax: 330-453-1793
Area Of Operation: Stark, Tuscarawas, Harrison, Carroll, Coshocton and Jefferson Counties

The 504 Certified Development Company (CDC) Program provides growing businesses with long-term, fixed-rate financing for major fixed assets, such as land and buildings. A Certified Development Company is a nonprofit corporation set up to contribute to the economic development of its community or region. CDCs work with the SBA and private-sector lenders to provide financing to small businesses.

* The Clean Air Resource Center (CARC)

Mark R. Shanahan, Executive Director
Clean Air Resource Center   614-224-3383
50 W. Broad Street, Suite 1718   800-225-5051
Columbus, OH 43215   Fax: 614-752-9188
www.ohioairquality.org
CARC seeks to find the most cost-efficient means possible for small businesses to meet these new requirements. They strive to support the critical role played by small business in Ohio's economy and recognize the financial challenges presented by environmental regulations. They are an

independent, non-regulatory (no inspection or enforcement, confidential, one-stop shop for finding solutions to air quality problems. State law requires them to keep all information received from businesses seeking assistance strictly confidential.

* Research and Extension Center

Ohio State University Piketon
Research and Extension Center
1864 Shyville Road   740-289-2071
Piketon, OH 45661   Fax: 740-289-4591
http://southcenters.osu.edu/

The South Center provides research based educational resources including: Entrepreneur Program, Small Business Development Center, Manufacturing SBDC, The Ohio Cooperative Development Center, Business Incubator and Training Center, and The Ohio State Learning Center South.

* Ohio Department of Agriculture

Ohio Rural Development Partnership
Family Farm Loan Guarantee Program   614-466-1490
8995 East Main Street   800-282-1955 (in OH)
Reynoldsburg, OH 43068-3399   Fax: 614-466-4346
www.ohioagriculture.gov

The Ohio Family Farm Loan Guarantee Program provides guarantees to conventional lenders that provide loans to persons engaged in agricultural production, which enhances the economic viability of the state's agricultural areas. Through the Family Farm Loan Guarantee Program, the state provides a partial guarantee to an eligible lender, by placing with the lender up to 40 percent of the lender's loan in an interest bearing account. The lender agrees to pay the state one (1%) percent per annum on the amount of the outstanding guarantee. It also agrees to lend the guaranteed portion of the loan to its borrowers at a reduced interest rate that compensates for the state's reduced interest rate. The maximum interest rate allowed on the guaranteed portion of a loan shall be 5 percent. The remaining unguaranteed portion is loaned at the lender's prevailing interest rate. The two rates are then blended and the new blended rate is passed on to the borrower.

* U.S. Export Assistance Center

600 Superior Ave. East, Suite 700   216-522-4731
Cleveland, OH 44114-2650   Fax: 216-522-2235

The Center assists clients with information about export finance options. This U.S.E.A.C. consolidates the export promotion and finance services of the U.S. Dept. of Commerce, the U.S. Small Business Administration, and the Small Business and Technology Development Center (SBTDC).

* Treasurer of the State

30 East Broad St., 9th Floor   614-466-2160
Columbus, OH 43215   800-228-1102 in OH
www.treasurer.state.oh.us   Fax: 614-644-7313

Small Business Linked Deposit Program: Funds are available for fixed assets, working capital, and refinancing for small businesses, creating or retaining jobs. Rates are 3 percent below current lending rate fixed for two years.

Agricultural Linked Deposit Program: Provides funds for Ohio full-time farmers to help meet planning deadlines. Provides up to $100,000 per farm at reduced rate, approximately 4 percent below borrower's current rate.

Access Ohio Program: Small Ohio businesses organized for profit, which have offices and facilities exclusively in Ohio, employ less than 150 people - a majority of who are Ohio residents and, are borrowing money for the specific purpose of becoming ADA compliant and/or more accessible to persons with disabilities may apply for low interest loans through a State Depository Bank. Approved bank loans are submitted to the Treasury which purchases a reduced interest CD with the lender. (Retrofitting work areas and the purchase of adaptive devices are also eligible.)

* Small Business Administration (SBA)

2 Nationwide Plaza
Suite 1400   614-469-6860
Columbus, OH 43215-2592   Fax: 614-469-2391

1111 Superior Avenue, Suite 630   216-522-4180
Cleveland, OH 44114-2507   Fax: 216-522-2038
www.sba.gov/oh

The Ohio Small Business Administration Office delivers a variety of programs and services, such as startup and operational assistance through small business training and counseling, financial assistance for startup's, business opportunities and much more.

* Ohio Business Connection

eVantage Program
3155 Research Boulevard, Suite 206   937-258-7255 ext. 224
Kettering, OH 45420   Fax: 937-258-9732
www.evantage-ohio.com

eVantage provides small business owners access to eBusiness techniques that can help their business. For a fee, the eVantage program provides 36 instructional hours and 30 individualized assistance.

* Small Business Investment Companies

Banc One Capital Partners, LLC
James Henson
c/o Stonehenge Financial Holdings, Inc.
191 W. Nationwide Blvd., Suite 600   614-246-2440
Columbus, OH 43215   Fax: 614-246-2441
Email jjhenson@stonehengefinancial.com

Clarion Capital Corporation
Tom Niehaus, CFO
Ohio Savings Plaza, Suite 1120
1801 East 9th St.   216-687-1096
Cleveland, OH 44114   Fax: 216-694-3545
Email: karena@clariongrp.com

Enterprise Ohio Investment Company
Janet White, Manager
8 North Main St.   937-226-0457
Dayton, OH 45402   Fax: 937-222-7035
Email: jwhite@citywidedev.com

Key Equity Capital Corp.
David Given, President
127 Public Square, 51st Floor   216-535-4711
Cleveland, OH 44114   Fax: 216-689-3204
Email: 1roof@bluepointcapital.com

Key Mezzanine Capital, LLC
Dennis Wagner
10th Floor, Banc One Building
800 Superior Avenue   216-828-8125
Cleveland, OH 44114   Fax: 216-828-8125
Email: dwagner@mcdinvest.com

National City Capital Corporation
William H. Schecter, President & G.M.
1965 East Sixth St., Suite 1010   216-222-2491
Cleveland, OH 44114   Fax: 216-222-9965
Email: smbreznak@nccapital.com

River Cities Capital Fund II, LP
Edwin Robinson, Contact
221 East Fourth Street, Suite 1900   513-621-9700
Cincinnati, OH 45202   Fax: 513-579-8939
Email: trobinson@rccf.com

River Cities Capital Fund, LP
R. Glen Mayfield, Manager
221 E. Fourth St., Suite 1900   513-621-9700
Cincinnati, OH 45202   Fax: 513-579-8939
Email: trobinson@rccf.com

Walnut Investment Partners, L.P.
Jimmy Gould, Managing Partner
312 Walnut Street, Suite 1151   513-651-3300
Cincinnati, OH 45202   Fax: 513-651-1084
Email Angie.Fischer@TheWalnutGroup.com

The Small Business Administration (SBA) licenses, regulates, and provides financial assistance to privately owned and operated Small Business Investment Companies. SBICs make venture or risk investments by supplying capital and extending unsecured loans and loans not fully collateralized to small enterprises which meet their investment criteria. Financing is made by direct loans and by equity investments.

Oklahoma

* Oklahoma Department of Commerce

900 North Stiles   405-815-6552
P.O. Box 26980   800-879-6552
Oklahoma City, OK 73126-0980   Fax: 405-815-5199

State Money and Help For Your Business

http://busdev3.odoc5.odoc.state.ok.us

Office of Business Recruitment: Provides comprehensive site location assistance to companies considering new investment in Oklahoma.

Business Development Division: Promotes growth by addressing the needs of existing and start-up businesses. Provides information and seminars directly to businesses. Offers business information and a referral network to assist companies through the maze of regulatory requirements and introduces local resource providers.

Site Location Planner: On CD-ROM and the web at {http://busdev3.odoc.state.ok.us}. Provides comprehensive site location data including available buildings, community information, state incentives, and statistical and other information.

Technology Partnerships: Testing of technologies developed by private business may be performed in partnership with research universities. Such institutions may devote resources such as laboratory usage and faculty time to a particular business's need in return for a portion of business's profits.

Training for Industry: Assists qualifying businesses by paying for training for new employees.

Quality Jobs Program: Provides quarterly cash payments of up to 5% of new taxable payroll directly to a qualifying company, for up to ten years.

Small Employer Quality Jobs Program: Provides annual cash payments of 5% of taxable payroll for new employees to a qualifying company, for up to 5 years.

Enterprise Zones: The enterprise district management authorities created in some enterprise districts are empowered to establish venture capital loan programs and to solicit proposals from enterprises seeking to establish or expand facilities in the zones.

International Trade and Investment Division: Provides diverse services including hands on assistance for companies wishing to learn more about exporting to promoting Oklahoma products at trade shows throughout the world. Also works closely with the international business community to develop top of mind awareness of Oklahoma's business climate advantages. Provide confidential, reliable site location assistance, site selection assistance, tax comparisons, and incentive projections.

International Market Insights (IMI): Commercial specialists also regularly report on specific foreign market conditions and upcoming opportunities for U. S. business.

Customized Market Analysis (CMA): Provides detailed information needed to make the most efficient and beneficial export marketing decisions. CMA will give an accurate assessment of how a product or service will sell in a given market.

Trade Opportunities Program (TOP): Up-to-the-minute sales leads from around the world are prescreened and transmitted every work day to commercial specialists in U. S. embassies and consulates abroad.

Agent/Distributor Service (ADS): Customized search needed to successfully launch an export marketing campaign. Provides pertinent information on up to six prequalified potential representatives per market.

Foreign Trade Zones: Businesses engaged in international trade within these zones benefit from special customs procedures.

Export Finance Program: Assistance is available through a relationship with the Export-Import Bank of the United States to facilitate export financing with working capital guarantees, credit insurance and foreign buyer financing.

Women-owned Business Certification Program: Established to facilitate contracting capabilities for women-owned businesses with public and private sector entities.

Minority Business: Provides a forum to network with banking organizations, utility companies, state agencies and other that can be valuable resources for a business. Each month several business owners are selected to give a brief presentation about their business.

Minority Business Development Centers: A vehicle for small minority-owned businesses that are seeking help in start-up information. The centers provide assistance in business plans, procurement assistance and works with the SBA in the certified lenders program and 8(a) certification.

Oklahoma Business Licensing System: Provides one-stop access to state level licensing requirements for businesses. Links are provided to the agency that issues the license and where the needed forms can be downloaded. This site only handles licensing at the state level, however, it will soon cover city, county and federal levels. 800-TRY-OKLA ext 155 (879-6552)

Business Incubator Certification: Business Incubators are facilities that accelerate the development and success of start-up and existing businesses. They provide lease space and a large variety of on-site managerial administrative and financial services. Tenants are exempt from state tax liability on income earned as a result of activities conducted as an occupant for up to 10 years. There are 25 certified business incubators in Oklahoma. 405-815-5143

Business Incentive Analysis: A confidential analysis of all state incentives and abatements can be gathered pertaining to a business project. 405-855-5182

International Seminars and Workshops: Continuing education seminars and workshops provide hands on training to aid businesses prepare for trade shows, break into international marketing and to stay up-to-date on necessary information.

Oklahoma Small Business Regulatory Review Committee: The Committee reviews new government rules that may have an adverse effect on small businesses and suggest alternatives whenever possible.

Export Assistance: An international business specialist will visit your company to consult with you about your export marketing strategy and goals. Your trade advisor will answer your questions, provide you with research regarding your target markets and work with you to assess the viability of your product or service in those markets. There is no fee for this service.

Community and County Profiles: Detailed information on Oklahoma communities and counties.

Census, Economic and Demographic Data Analysis: Commerce provides analysis of census, economic, and demographic data to assist businesses and communities in their growth plans.

Business Retention and Expansion: Assistance for communities to retain existing businesses.

Business Incentives Tax Training: This seminar can help you and your CPA learn about the state's business incentives.

Business Financing: This department can help you find information on capital for your business.

Advocacy in Foreign Markets: A service for Oklahoma firms encountering trade problems, including unfair or illegal trade practices in foreign markets.

Agent and Distributor Search: This agency will help your company search for prospective agents and distributors for your products and will initiate a contact. There is no fee for this service.

County Briefs: This office will give you an overview of Oklahoma's top export markets, including current opportunities, an overview of the market and need-to-know information like regulatory issues, freight, market entry advice and business and cultural tips.

Foreign Market Visit Assistance: Arrangement can be made to meet with prescreened contacts whose market interests and objectives match your own.

International Protocol: This office can help you develop a greater awareness of cultural differences. You can find out about business practices, customs, and manners.

Sister State and Cities Program: Commerce promotes international cooperation, business and understanding through community involvement and relationships in education, business, technology, culture, agricultural and youth and other areas exchanges. The agency will assist communities wanting to establish sister cities overseas.

Trade Mission: Commerce organizes trade missions, often led by state officials, to initiate and nurture relationships with potential international business partners.

Trade Show Assistance: Oklahoma Commerce will help your business exhibit at key international trade shows.

Oklahoma Main Street Program: The Oklahoma Main Street Center provides program training, technical assistance, guidance and resources to people, organizations and communities.

Self-Employment Entrepreneurial Development System (SEEDS): The Self-Employment Entrepreneurial Development System uses states funds to provide training, business plan development and start-up financing of micro-businesses started by low-income and unemployed persons.

* Oklahoma Department of Transportation

200 NE 21st Street
Oklahoma City, OK 73105   800-788-4539
www.okladot.state.ok.us/dbeinfo/indexg.htm

The Department of Transportation has a Disadvantaged Business Enterprise certification program for transportation-related projects and facilities.

* Rural Development Administration

100 USDA Agriculture Building, Suite 108   405-742-1000
Stillwater, OK 74074-2654   Fax: 405-742-1005

Business and Industrial Loan Program: Encourages the retention of jobs in rural areas. RDA will guarantee up to 90 percent of a loan from a commercial institution.

Intermediary Relending Program: This program provides 1% loans to intermediaries to establish revolving loan funds for the purpose of relending to small emerging private businesses.

Rural Business Enterprise Grants: USDA makes Rural Business Enterprise Grants to public bodies, nonprofits and Native American tribes to encourage the development of small and emerging private business enterprises in rural areas.

Rural Business Opportunity Grants: Grants from this program provide technical assistance, training and planning activities that improve economic conditions in rural areas.

Rural Economic Development Loans/Grants: These loans/grants are provided to USDA-financed telephone and electric cooperatives to establish revolving loan funds or single purpose loans for businesses/job creation and community development in rural areas. Recipients receive 10 year, zero percent loans.

Value-Added Agricultural Product Market Development Grants

* Oklahoma Capital Investment Board

301 NW 63rd, Suite 520
Oklahoma City, OK 73116   405-848-9456

Facilitates investment in venture capital companies that focus on investing in quality Oklahoma companies.

* Oklahoma Minority Supplier Development Council (OMSDC)

6701 N. Broadway, Suite 216   405-767-9900
Oklahoma City, OK 73116   Fax: 405-767-9901
www.omsdc.org

The mission of the OMSDC is to assist corporations and public sector agencies in creating a business environment that promotes access and increased opportunities for minority-owned businesses. The Council also helps to promote, educate and develop minority-owned businesses.

* Oklahoma Tax Commission

Business Tax Workshops
2501 North Lincoln Boulevard
Connors Building, Capitol Complex
Oklahoma City, OK 73194   405-521-3160
www.oktax.state.ok.us

The Business Tax Workshops offered by the Oklahoma Tax Commission are designed to meet the needs all business ownership levels from new business owners just starting out to seasoned business owners needing to brush up on the latest tax changes, and everyone in between. For a new business or an individual thinking about setting up a business in Oklahoma, the workshop offers information on formation, business structures, steps for formation types such as incorporation steps, a step-by-step guide to business registration, bookkeeping techniques, and a line-by-line explanation of the primary business tax forms.

* Business Filing Department

2300 N. Lincoln Blvd.
Room 101   405-521-3912
Oklahoma City OK 73105-4897   Fax: 405-521-3771

www.sos.state.ok.us/business/business_filing.htm

The Business Filing Department receives and processes corporation, limited partnership, limited liability company, limited liability partnership, certificate of partnership fictitious name for general partnership and trade name registrations. These include new registrations, amendments, mergers, dissolutions and withdrawals for both domestic and foreign.

Business Records Department: 1-900-555-2424 (A flat fee of $5.00): The Business Records Department provides searches on corporations, limited partnerships, limited liability companies, limited liability partnerships, certificate of partnership fictitious name for general partnerships and trade names. The search includes correct name, status, date of registration, service agent and address, state of domicile, authorized shares and par value, amendments, name changes, mergers, and trade names.

* Oklahoma Agriculture Enhancement and Diversification Program

2800 N. Lincoln Blvd.
Oklahoma City, OK 73105-4298   405-522-5515
www.oda.state.ok.us/gapl.htm

The Oklahoma Agriculture Enhancement and Diversification Program provides funds in the form of loans or grants for the purpose of expanding the state's value added processing sector and to encourage farm diversification. Funds, provided on a cost-share basis, must be used for marketing and utilization, cooperative marketing, farm diversification and basic and applied research. All funding proposals must clearly demonstrate the ability to directly benefit Oklahoma farmers and ranchers.

* Certified Development Companies

Metro Area Development Corporation
Dan Fitzpatrick
4200 North Lindsay
Oklahoma City, OK 73105   405-424-5181
Area of Operation: Canadian, Cleveland, Oklahoma Counties

Rural Enterprises, Inc.
Debbie Partin, Dir. of Fin. Service
422 Cessna
P.O. Box 1335   402-924-5094
Durant, OK 74702   Fax: 405-920-2775
Email: debbiep@ruralenterprises.com
Area of Operation: Atoka, Bryan, Carter, Choctaw, Coal, Creek, Garvin, Haskell, Hughes, Johnston, Latimer, LeFlore, Lincoln, Logan, Love, Marshall, McCurtain, Murray, Okfuskee, Payne, Pittsburg, Pontotoc, Pottawatomie, Pushmataha, Seminole Counties

SWODA Development Corporation
Gary Gorshing, Executive Director
Building 420, Sooner Drive,
Clinton-Sherman Indust. Park
P.O. Box 569
Burns Flat, OK 73624   405-562-4886
Area of Operation: Beckham, Custer, Greer, Harmon, Jackson, Kiowa, Roger Mills, Washita Counties

Small Business Capital Corporation
Tracie Costello, Assistant Director
Bank of America Center
15 W. Sixth St., Suite 1211
Tulsa, OK 74119-5406   918-584-7888
Area of Operation: Creek, Osage, Tulsa, Washington Counties

Tulsa Economic Development Corporation
Frank McCrady, Executive Director
907 S. Detroit Avenue
Suite 1001   918-585-8332
Tulsa, OK 74120   Fax: 918-585-2473
Area of Operation: Citywide Tulsa

Verd-Ark-Ca Development Corporation
L.V. Watkins, Executive Director
600 Emporia, Suite A   918-683-4634
Muskogee, OK 74403   Fax: 918-683-7894
Area of Operation: Adair, Cherokee, Craig, Delaware, Haskell, LeFlore, Mayes, McIntosh, Muskogee, Nowata, Okmulgee, Ottawa, Rogers, Sequoyah, Tulsa, Washington Counties

The 504 Certified Development Company (CDC) Program provides growing businesses with long-term, fixed-rate financing for major fixed assets, such as land and buildings. A Certified Development Company is a nonprofit corporation set up to contribute to the economic development of its community or region. CDCs work with the SBA and private-sector lenders to provide financing to small businesses.

* The Oklahoma Cooperative Extension Service

Rural Development Program
Oklahoma State University-Oklahoma City
139 Agriculture Hall   405-744-5398
Stillwater, OK 74078   Fax: 405-744-5339
http://www1.dasnr.okstate.edu/oces

Cooperative Extension offers educational and technical assistance to aid rural leaders in promoting economic development and providing quality community services. The programs include economic and business development, community services, and local government education.

* Oklahoma Center for the Advancement of Science & Technology

4545 N. Lincoln Blvd., Suite. 116   405-524-1357
Oklahoma City, OK 73105   866-265-2215
Email: info@ocast.state.ok.us   Fax: 405-521-6501
www.ocast.state.ok.us

The Oklahoma Center for the Advancement of Science and Technology is the state's only agency focusing solely on technology - its development, transfer, commercialization and impact on Oklahoma's economy. OCAST continues to pursue its legislative mandate to: Support basic and applied research and development (R&D) Facilitate technology transfer and commercialization (SBIR/STTR) Stimulate seed-capital investment in firms commercializing new technologies Encourage manufacturing competitiveness through modernization. OCAST currently has funding to operate the following programs:
- Oklahoma Health Research (OHR)
- Small Business Research Assistance (SBRA)
- Oklahoma Applied Research Support Program (OARS)
- OARS R&D Faculty and Student Intern Partnerships
- Oklahoma Alliance for Manufacturing Excellence, Inc.
- Oklahoma Technology Commercialization Center
- Oklahoma Inventor's Assistance Program
- Technology Business Finance Program

* Oklahoma Technology Commercialization Center

840 Research Parkway, Suite 250
Oklahoma City, OK 73104   800-337-OTCC
www.otcc.org   Tulsa: 918-582-5592
    Oklahoma City: 405-235-2305

The Tech Center is the Program Manager for OCAST Technology Business Finance Program. This Oklahoma Center for the Advancement of Science & Technology (OCAST)-funded program is designed to provide Oklahoma-based, high-tech, start-up companies with pre-seed financing and early stage risk capital to stimulate additional investments from private sources.

* Oklahoma Industrial Finance Authority (OIFA)

301 NW 3rd, Suite 225
Oklahoma City, OK 73116   405-842-1145

Loans: Available to manufacturers plus recreational, agriculture processing, livestock processing and conditioning, and mine resource processors. Can loan up to 66 2/3% of the cost of land, buildings and fixed equipment on a secured first mortgage and 33 1/3% on a second mortgage. Maximum loan amount is $2 million per project on a first mortgage, $750,000 on a second mortgage.

* Office of the State Treasurer

Link Deposit Loan Programs
2300 N. Lincoln Blvd., Room 217   405-521-3191
Oklahoma City, OK 73105   Fax: 405-521-4994

Oklahoma Small Business Linked Deposit Program: Loans are available of up to $1 million for small businesses and $5 million for industrial parks. Loan must create new jobs or preserve existing ones. Terms not to exceed two years, but may be renewed for 3 additional terms.

Agricultural Linked Deposit Program: Available for farmers who meet certain criteria. The linked deposit commitment cannot exceed 2 years, but may be renewed. The interest rates are fixed and are calculated based on the current T-note auction rate minus 3 percent.

* Small Business Administration (SBA)

District Office
301 NW 6th Street, Suite 116   405-609-8000
Oklahoma City, OK 73102   Fax: 405-609-8990
www.sba.gov/ok

The Oklahoma Small Business Administration Office delivers a variety of programs and services, such as startup and operational assistance through small business training and counseling, financial assistance for startup's, business opportunities and much more.

* Small Business Investment Companies

Chisholm SBIC, L.P.
John B. Frick, Contact
One Leadership Square
211 North Robinson Street, Suite 1910   405-605-1111
Oklahoma City, OK 73102   Fax: 405-605-1115
Email jfrick@chisholmvc.com

Council Oak Investment Corporation
T. Kent Faison, Manager
101 North Broadway
Mail: P.O. Box 26788   405-270-1000
Oklahoma City, OK 73126   Fax: 405-270-1089
Email kfaison@bancfirst.com

First United Venture Capital Corporation
John Massey and Greg Massey, Managers
1400 West Main Street   580-920-4907
Durant, OK 74701   Fax: 580-924-0916
Email bertd@firstunitedbank.com

The SBA licenses, regulates, and provides financial assistance to privately owned and operated Small Business Investment Companies. SBICs make venture or risk investments by supplying capital and extending unsecured loans and loans not fully collateralized to small enterprises which meet their investment criteria. Financing is made by direct loans and by equity investments.

* HUD Regional Office

500 West Main St.   405-553-7509
Oklahoma City, OK 73102-3202   Fax: 405-553-7588
www.hud.gov/local/index.cfm?state=ok

Urban Development Action Grants (UDAG): Awarded to communities which then lend the proceeds at flexible rates to eligible businesses. Projects whose total costs are less than $100,000 are not eligible. UDAG funds should leverage at least three to four times their amount in private sector investment.

* Home Based & Micro Business

Oklahoma State University
104 Human Environmental Sciences, Room 336
Stillwater, OK 74078   405-744-9931
www.fcs.okstate.edu/microbiz

If you are thinking about starting a home based business or micro business, this office can help. They can answer questions from "What kind of business should I start?" to "Do I need a license?"

Oregon

* Oregon Economic Development Department

775 Summer St., NE, Suite 200   503-986-0123
Salem, OR 97301   Fax: 503-581-5115
www.econ.state.or.us/

Economic Development Department: This office can provide information and expertise in dealing with state, federal, and local agencies. They also have information on financing programs and other services offered by the state government.

Oregon Downtown Development Association works to revitalize and maintain the heritage and economic health of Oregon's downtowns and older business districts.

Rural Development Initiatives: A non-profit corporation that builds the capacity of rural communities to make strategic decisions about their futures and to act on those decisions to ensure high quality of life and a vital economy.

Industry Workforce Training: Provides grants to community colleges for the development and implementation of training programs for multiple firms within an industry. Employers must provide matching funds or in-kind services.

Capital Access Program: Offered through the Oregon Economic Development Department, is designed to increase the availability of loans to Oregon small businesses from banks. The program provides loan portfolio insurance so lenders may make loans that carry higher than conventional risks. Borrowers pay a fee of between 3% and 7% of the loan amount, which is matched by the department and contributed to a loan loss reserve account in an enrolled bank. The loans must be within soundness and safety requirements of federal and state banking regulations. A Capital Access Program loan is a private transaction between the borrower and lender. The Oregon Economic Development Department is not a party to loan negotiations or to the loan agreement. The department does not monitor the loan or require reporting from the borrower. Loan may be used for virtually any purpose, except to construct or purchase residential housing, to purchase real property that is not used for business operations of the borrower, or to refinance the principal balance of an existing loan.

Credit Enhancement Fund: Administered by the Oregon Economic Development Department, provides guarantees to enrolled banks to increase capital availability to small Oregon firms, helping them create jobs. The maximum guarantee for a loan is $500,000. The department has authority to guarantee up to $75 million of financial institution loans.

Entrepreneurial Development Loan Funds: Entrepreneurial businesses can receive loans of up to $25,000 through the Oregon Entrepreneurial Development Loan Fund. Additional follow-on loans up to $15,000 are available.

Subordinated and Direct Loans: Subordinated loans usually fill a gap in a financing package, where commercial and private debt financing and equity have been maximized and additional funds are required to complete the financing transaction. Often these loans will "subordinate" or take a lesser security interest in the assets being financed, which will allow the senior lender first priority on project assets in the event of a default. The subordinated loan is often secured with additional assets to help collaterize its position. Direct loans and, in some limited cases, grants are available to finance businesses when the project will further the public objectives of the entity making the loan or grant.

Business Development Fund: Manufacturing, processing and regionally significant tourism projects are eligible for the Oregon Business Development Fund. The fund provides long-term, fixed rate financing for land, buildings, equipment and machinery.

Local Revolving Loan Funds: Many local and regional development groups and local governments throughout Oregon administer revolving loan funds for small business financing. In most cases, funding has been provided by the federal Department of Housing and Urban Development (HUD), the federal Economic Development Administration (EDA), the U.S. Department of Agriculture Rural Economic and Community Development Administration (RECD) or the Oregon Economic Development Department. Loan criteria may reflect some of the objectives of those funding organizations or may have special requirements of those agencies.

Industrial Development Revenue Bonds: The Economic Development Commission may issue industrial development revenue bonds for manufacturing and processing facilities in Oregon. Industrial development bonds can finance fixed assets only, along with some limited transaction costs. If a project qualifies the bonds can be issued on a tax-exempt basis which lowers the overall cost of financing. Revenue bonds are not direct obligations of the State of Oregon. The individual or corporation on whose behalf the bonds are issued is legally obligated to repay them. An eligible company may borrow up to $10 million through the Oregon Industrial Development Revenue Bond Program. Typically, the minimum bond is for $2 million.

Regional Development: Cities, counties and other governmental entities also can obtain loans and grants to help pay for construction projects. The department uses grant and loan funds to support public works, safe drinking water and housing rehabilitation projects. The department also provides funding for community facilities projects to improve or build day care, senior centers, emergency shelters and family counseling facilities, among others.

Business Retention Services: Companies are matched with a consultant based on its specific needs and industry requirements. The maximum benefit for consulting service is $5,000 and the maximum feasibility studies is $30,000. To qualify for a feasibility study, the applicant must contribute 25% of the cost of the study. Consultant fees are treated as an interest-free loan. An application can be downloaded from {www.econ.state.or.us/businessfinance/brs.htm}.

Targeted Workforce Development: Funds are used for a variety of services that can help businesses organize their workforce needs into affordable initiatives that improve worker skills.

Regulatory Assistance: The state's coordinated environmental and regulatory process allows for a streamlined permitting process without an environmental impact statement. Regulatory experts provide one-stop permitting information and assistance.

Project Sitting Assistance: The Department can provide a custom proposal of available sites to traded sector companies. Once a site requirement form is submitted, a list of qualifying sites with specific community information is created. Assistance with scheduling site visits is also available. This service can be accessed online at {www.econ.state.or.us/busform.htm} or call 503-986-0156.

Business Information Center: Business information from six state agencies is available. Referrals for state licensing, regulatory information and other business needs are provided.

Sustainable Business Liaison: Businesses that are looking to learn more about the "triple bottom line" sustainability, will receive information and networking support from this office. 503-986-0158

* Rural Development

Rural Development Services
Business and Cooperative Programs
101 SW Main, Suite 1410
Portland, OR 97204-3222
www.rurdev.usda.gov/or

503-414-3300
Fax: 503-414-3392

Cooperative Development Assistance: The Cooperative Services program helps residents form new cooperative businesses and improve the operations of existing cooperatives. They provide technical assistance, conduct cooperative-related research, and produce information products to promote public understanding of cooperatives.

Direct Business and Industry Loan Program: The Business and Industry Direct Loan Program provides loans to public entities and private parties who cannot obtain credit from other sources.

Guaranteed Business and Industry Loan Program: The Business and Industry Guarantee Loan Program helps create jobs and stimulates rural economies by providing financial backing for rural businesses. This program guarantees up to 80% of a loan made by a commercial lender.

Intermediary Relending Loan Program: Intermediaries may make loans to private individuals, public or private organizations in cities with population of less than 25,000. The loan must be used for the establishment of new business, the expansion of existing businesses, creation of employment opportunities, saving of existing jobs, or community development projects.

Rural Business Enterprise Grants: The Rural Business Enterprise Grants help public bodies, nonprofits and Indian Tribal groups finance and facilitate development of small and emerging private business enterprises located in rural areas.

Rural Economic Development Loans and Grants: This program finances economic development and job creation projects in rural areas based on sound economic plans. The grants are available to any Rural Utility Service to assist in developing rural areas.

Rural Business Opportunity Grants: Rural Opportunity Grants are provided to promote sustainable economic development in rural communities with exceptional needs.

* Oregon Entrepreneurs Forum

222 NW Fifth Ave., Suite 308
Portland, OR 97209
www.oef.org

503-222-2270
Fax: 503-241-0827

Provides assistance to help companies that are in transition by providing mentoring services.

* Oregon Port Revolving Fund Loans

Ports Division
Oregon Economic Development Department
775 Summer Street NE, Suite 200
Salem, OR 97310
www.econ.state.or.us/portrevolve.htm

503-986-0153

Provides long-term loans to ports at below-market interest rates. Individual loans may be made to a maximum of $700,000 per project. The total outstanding loan amount any individual port can have at any one time cannot exceed $2 million. Funding may be used for port development projects (infrastructure) or to assist port-related private business development projects. The 23 legally formed Port Districts are the only entities eligible for Port Revolving Fund loans. The variety of projects eligible is very broad. These include, but are not limited to, water-oriented facilities, industrial parks, airports and eligible commercial or industrial developments. Projects must be located within port district boundaries.

* Small Scale Energy Loan Program

Oregon Office of Energy   800-221-8035 (in OR)
625 Marion Street NE   503-378-4040
Salem, OR 97301   Fax: 503-373-7806
www.energy.state.or.us

The Small Scale Energy Loan Program (SELP), administered by the Oregon Department of Energy, finances energy conservation and renewable energy projects in Oregon, through the issuance of general obligation bonds. Bond proceeds can be loaned to finance eligible equipment costs, construction, certain design and consultation fees, some reserves, construction interest and most loan closing costs. Eligible costs are those incurred after loan approval. Land and working capital are normally not financed. Costs not part of the energy project also are not eligible. All Oregonians, Oregon businesses, nonprofit organizations, municipal corporations and state agencies can apply for loans. Eligible projects are those which conserve conventional energy, such as electricity and natural gas; or projects which produce renewable energy from geothermal or solar sources or from water, wind, biomass and some waste materials.

* International Division of the Oregon Economic Development Department

One World Trade Center
Suite 205, 121 SW Salmon   503-229-6051
Portland, OR 97204   800-448-7512
www.econ.state.or.us/oregontrade

The international arm of state government. It provides "export ready" Oregon companies assistance in export markets, assists the Governor's Office on protocol and other assignments, and works with public and private organizations to promote Oregon in the international business community.

* Southern Oregon Women's Access to Credit

Southern Oregon Women's Access to Credit (SOWAC)
33 N. Central Avenue   866-608-6094 (toll-free)
Suite #209   541-779-3992
Medford, OR 97501   Fax: 541-779 5195
www.sowac.org

Offers a business development program for new and existing business owners in Jackson, Josephine and Klamath counties. Focuses on training, mentoring and financing.

* Oregon Association of Minority Entrepreneurs

4134 N. Vancouver   503-249-7744
Portland, OR 97217   Fax: 503-249-2027
www.oame.org

A non-profit, tax exempt organization formed to promote and develop entrepreneurship and economic development for ethnic minorities in the State of Oregon. OAME works as a partnership between ethnic minorities, entrepreneurs, education, government and established corporate business. OAME provides a core of services to start-up and/or existing minority businesses. These services include:

-    Technical Assistance
-    Access To Capital/Loan Fund
-    Capability And Opportunity Matching (OAME's Marketing/ Clearinghouse)
-    Administrative Services
-    Incubator With & Without Walls Development

* Oregon Department of Environmental Quality

811 SW Sixth Avenue   503-229-5696
Portland, OR 97204   Fax: 503-229-6124
www.deq.state.or.us

Corporate Income Tax Credits; Oregon businesses may be eligible for a number of tax credits allowed under Oregon law. Some of these business-related tax credits include: pollution control tax credit; non-point source pollution control tax credit and clean diesel retrofit tax credits.

* Oregon Department of Revenue

Enterprise Zone Coordinator
955 Center Street NE
Room 256, Revenue Building
Salem, OR 97301   503-945-8318
www.dor.state.or.us

Construction in Progress Exemption: Under Oregon law, new facilities are exempt from property taxes for up to two years while they are under construction and not in use on January 1. The Construction in Progress Exemption also applies to any machinery or equipment installed in the unoccupied facility on January 1. The exemption does not apply to land. The application for this exemption must be filed with the county assessor by April 1 of the taxing year.

* Oregon Advanced Technology Consortium

29353 Town Center Loop East   503-657-6958, ext. 4609
Wilsonville, OR 97070   Fax: 503-682-4494

Technical training, seminars, workshops, one-on-one technical assistance and various course offerings are available through the Oregon Advanced Technology Consortium, which is made up of various community colleges throughout the state. The consortium's primary goal is to help Oregon businesses acquire and implement new technologies and provide workforce training.

* The Performance Center

Performance Center
2459 SE T.V. Highway, PMB #145   503-345-9400
Hillsboro, OR 97123   Fax: 503-345-9409
www.performancecenter.org

To be competitive in the global marketplace, Oregon manufacturers need to meet or exceed applicable international quality standards (ISO 9000). Assistance is available to evaluate whether a product is required to meet these standards. The Performance Center offers a link to a statewide system of total quality training through Oregon's community colleges. The objective is to enable Oregon businesses to acquire the tools to consistently achieve world leadership quality, productivity, service and customer satisfaction.

* ONABEN -- A Native American Business Network

11825 SW Greenburg Road, Suite B-3   800-854-8289
Tigard, OR 97223   503-968-1500
www.onaben.org   Fax: 503-968-1548

ONABEN is a nonprofit public-benefit corporation created by Northwest Indian Tribes to increase the success of private businesses owned by Native Americans. It offers training and support focused on developing entrepreneurship in Native American communities. The network offers courses on starting businesses and small business management. It is a source of micro loans that can be combined with equity to acquire third-party financing. It also provides business owners with technical assistance in completing marketing plans and sponsors various services for Indian businesses.

* Office of Minority, Women, and Emerging Small Business

Department of Consumer & Business Services
350 Winter St. NE, Room 300
Salem, OR 97301-3878   503-947-7922
Mailing Address:
P.O. Box 14480
Salem, OR 97309-0405
Portland Field Office: 503-887-4349
www.cbs.state.or.us/omwesb

The Office of Minority, Women, and Emerging Small Business administers the Disadvantaged Business Enterprise (DBE), Minority Business Enterprise/Women Business Enterprise (MBE/WBE), and Emerging Small Business (ESB) Programs. As the sole certification authority in Oregon for targeted government contracts for disadvantaged, minority-and woman-owned businesses, and emerging small businesses, OMWESB provides "one-stop" certification.

* Certified Development Companies

Business Development Corporation
Wayne Luzier, Executive Director
744 Southeast Rose Street   541-672-6728
Roseburg OR 97470-3941   Fax: 541-672-7011
Email: wluzier@ccdbusiness.com
www.ccdbusiness.com
Area of Operation: State of Oregon, except Wallowa County

CCDBDC North Bend Office:
2455 Maple Leaf, #13B   541-756-4101
North Bend, OR 97459   888-553-1110
Email: thaga@ccdbusiness.com   Fax: 541-756-1167

CCDBDC Portland Office:
6312 SW Capitol Hwy, Suite 441

Portland, OR 97239
Email: ccdbusiness@hevanet.com
503-245-1175

Cascades West Financial Services, Inc.
Mary Merriman-Smith, Director
P.O. Box 686
Albany, OR 97321-0686
Email: msmith@cwcog.cog.or.us
www.cascadeswest.com
541-924-8430
Fax: 541-967-4651
Area of Operation: Benton, Lane, Lincoln, Linn, Marion, Polk, Yamhill
Counties

Evergreen Community Development Association (ECDA)
Jim Bright, Senior Loan Officer
1618 SW First Avenue, Suite 401
Portland, OR 97201
Email: jbright@ecda.com
www.ecda.com
503-222-7496
503-222-7498
Area of Operation: Clackamas, Clatsop, Columbia, Hood River, Multnomah,
Tillamook, Wasco and Washington Counties

Greater Eastern Oregon Development Corporation
Melisa Jo Drugge, Executive Director
2016 Airport Road
P.O. Box 1041
Pendleton OR 97801-1041
Email: mdrugge@OregonVOS.net
541-276-6745
Fax: 541-276-6071
Area of Operation: Gilliam, Grant, Morrow, Umatilla, Wheeler, Union,
Baker and Wallowa Counties

Northwest Business Development Association
Louie Robida, Loan Officer
6312 SW Capitol Hwy, Suite 441
Portland, OR 97239
Email: nwbusiness@hevanet.com
www.nwbusiness.org
503-245-1175
Area of Operation: Clark, Cowlitz, Skamania and Wahkiakum Counties

Northwest Small Business Finance Corporation
Teresa Cowles, President
15455 NW Greenbrier Pkwy., Suite 210
Beaverton OR 97006
Email: teresa@nsbfc.com
www.nsbfc.com
503-629-9662
Fax: 877-296-0703
Area of Operation: Multnomah, Clackamas, Clatsop, Columbia and
Washington Counties

Oregon Certified Business Development Corporation
Jim MacKinnon, Senior Loan Officer
2363 SW Glacier Place
P.O. Box 575
Redmond OR 97756-0575
Email: ;mackinon@coic.org
Email: kmears@coic.org
Email: cfolkens@coic.org
www.coic.org
541-548-8184
Fax: 541-504-3302
Area of Operation: Crook, Deschutes, Harney, Jefferson, Klamath, Lake and
Malheur Counties

The 504 Certified Development Company (CDC) Program provides growing businesses with long-term, fixed-rate financing for major fixed assets, such as land and buildings. A Certified Development Company is a nonprofit corporation set up to contribute to the economic development of its community or region. CDCs work with the SBA and private-sector lenders to provide financing to small businesses

* Business Information Center

Secretary of State Corporation Division
Suite 151
255 Capitol Street NE
Salem, OR 97310-1327
www.filinginoregon.com
503-986-2200
The Business Information Center is a cooperative effort of six state agencies that provides information to the public on state registration and licensing requirements for businesses. The Center handles phone calls and letter inquiries and mails out packets with state business registration information and forms. The packet includes a new publication, the Oregon Business Guide, which provides a consolidated source of information from the participating agencies. The guide also provides a general checklist for starting a business with references to agencies that must be contacted. In addition, the Center's staff provides information on whether a business is required to have a state license, permit or certification and refers the caller to

the appropriate regulatory agencies or boards. The Center also offers referrals to business assistance programs available in Oregon.

* Oregon Housing and Community Services (OHCS)

P.O. Box 14508
Salem, OR 97309-0409
Email: info@hcs.state.or.us
www.hcs.state.or.us
503-986-2000
Fax: 503-986-2020
TTY: 503-986-2100
Tax Exempt Bond Financing: OHCS provides multi-family housing financing, pre-development funds, and other financing options for developing affordable housing to moderate-, low-, and very-low-income Oregonians.

Tax Credits & Grants for Rental Housing Developments: The Housing Resources Section administers OHCS' housing development grant and tax credit programs. Through its activities, the Section provides housing-related technical and financial assistance and carries out the spirit of the OHCS' mission to reach out for opportunities to create partnerships that improve Oregonians' lives and the quality of their communities.

* Oregon Office of Energy

625 Marion St. NE
Salem, OR 97301
www.energy.state.or.us
800-221-8035
503-373-4040
Fax: 503-373-7806
Business Energy Tax Credits: Tax credits for businesses in Oregon that invest in energy conservation, recycling, renewable energy resources and less-polluting transportation fuels. An Oregon business may qualify.

Energy Loan Program: Low-interest, long-term loans for businesses and others that invest in energy conservation, produce energy from renewable resources and use recycled materials to create products.

Building Commissioning: Ensuring that the complex equipment providing lighting, heating, cooling, ventilation and other amenities in buildings works together effectively and efficiently. Studies on commissioning show that the process provides average energy savings of 15 to 30 percent.

* Small Business Administration (SBA)

1515 SW 5th Ave.
Suite 1050
Portland, OR 97201-5494
www.sba.gov/or
503-326-2682
Fax: 503-326-2808
The Oregon Small Business Administration Office delivers a variety of programs and services, such as startup and operational assistance through small business training and counseling, financial assistance for startup's, business opportunities and much more.

* Small Business Investment Companies

Northern Pacific Capital Corporation
Joseph P. Tennant, President
937 SW 14th St., Suite 200
Mail: P.O. Box 1658
Portland, OR 97207
Email: Joetpacmar@aol.com
503-241-1255
Fax: 503-299-6653

Shaw Venture Partners III, LP
Ralph R. Shaw, Manager
400 Southwest Sixth Ave., Suite 1100
Portland, OR 97204
Email: judyb@shawventures.com
503-228-4884
Fax: 503-227-2471

Shaw Venture Partners IV, L.P.
Ralph R. Shaw, Managing General Partner
400 SW Sixth Avenue, Suite 1100
Portland, OR 97204
Email: judyb@shawventures.com
503-275-5710
Fax: 503-275-7565

SmartForest Ventures I, L.P.
Debi Coleman, Contact
209 SW Oak Street, 1st Floor
Portland, OR 97204
Email plans@smartforest.com
503-222-2552
Fax: 503-222-2834

Tamarack Mezzanine Partners, L.P.
Loree Misch, Contact
522 SW Fifth Ave., Suite 915
Portland, OR 97204
Email: john@tamarackcapital.com
503-517-8939
Fax: 503-517-8938

Utah Ventures II L.P.
Alan Dishlip
400 Lincoln Center Tower
10260 SW Greenburg Road   503-293-3588
Portland, OR 97223   Fax: 503-293-3527

The SBA licenses, regulates, and provides financial assistance to privately owned and operated Small Business Investment Companies. SBICs make venture or risk investments by supplying capital and extending unsecured loans and loans not fully collateralized to small enterprises which meet their investment criteria. Financing is made by direct loans and by equity investments.

* Agricultural Development & Marketing Division

Oregon Department of Agriculture
1207 NW Naito Parkway, Suite 104   503-872-6600
Portland, OR 97209-2832   Fax: 503-872-6601
www.oda.state.or.us

The Agricultural Development and Marketing Division offers a variety of programs for the producers of Oregon.

Value-added grants: The bill contains $40 million nationally in grants for value-added projects, up to $500,000 per producer, producer organization, cooperative or business venture to assist in developing a business plan, marketing strategies, and marketing efforts.

Small Business Market Development Workshops: These workshops are presented to entrepreneurs developing new value added products.

* Oregon Contract Assistance Program (GCAP)

1144 Gateway Loop, Suite 203   541-736-1088
Springfield, OR 97477   800-497-7551
www.gcap.org   Fax: 541-736-1090

GCAP provides comprehensive assistance and information to Oregon small businesses desiring to enter the government contracting market.

* Lane Community College

Business Development Center & Contract Training
1445 Willamette Street, Suite 1   541-463-5255
Eugene, OR 97401-4087   Fax: 541-686-0096
www.lanebdc.com

Small Business Management: The program is designed for small business owners who have been in business for at least one year, are willing to try new ideas, and are willing to commit to classes and on-site visits. This is a two year program.

Farm Business Management: The program is designed for full-time or pert-time farm operators and managers. The program combines classroom training with on-site visits to achieve the businesses management goals.

Lane MicroBusiness: This program provides free business assistance and training as well as access to capital to Lane County low-income Micro-enterprise entrepreneurs.

Businesswomen's Mentoring Program: Support for women business owners.

Pennsylvania

* Pennsylvania Department of Community and Economic Development

400 North Street, 4th Floor
Commonwealth Keystone Building
Harrisburg, PA 17120   800-379-7448
www.inventpa.com

or

Governor's Action Team
100 Pine Street, Suite 100   717-787-8199
Harrisburg, PA 17101   Fax: 717-772-5419
www.teampa.com

Entrepreneurial Assistance Office: Established to ensure small business owners receive the support and assistance they require. The Entrepreneurial Assistance Office works to build an environment which encourages the creation, expansion and retention of small, women and minority owned businesses.

PAOpen4Business: The single point of contact and hub of information for small businesses, answering state related and general business questions about licenses and permits. The Center has select state forms and applications available as well as other sources of information and technical assistance. {www.paopen4business.state.pa.us}

Environmental Business Advocate: Assists small businesses in complying with requirements of the Federal Clean Air Act and appropriate state regulations. Housed in the PA Department of Environmental Protection, (DEP), the EBA represents the interests of small businesses in matters affecting them with DCED and the U.S. Environmental Protection Agency.

Industrial Resource Centers: Assists companies in solving problems through the deployment of technologies.

Job Centers: Provide employers with a wide array of employment and training services.

Small Business Incubators: Sites where young businesses can start and grow. Offers businesses the opportunity to rent small units of space at a lower than market rate. Provides tenants with business development services that help to reduce costs and increase profits.

PA Industrial Development Authority: Low-interest financing through Industrial Development Corporations for land and building acquisitions, construction and renovation resulting in the creation or retention of jobs. Amounts: Loans up to $1 million (within Enterprise Zones, $1.5 million) no more than 30 to 40% of the total eligible project costs, advanced technology projects and those in an Act 47 or within an Enterprise Zone qualify for lower interest rates.

Machinery and Equipment Loan Fund: Low-interest loan financing to acquire and install new or used machinery and equipment or to upgrade existing machinery and equipment. Amounts: Loans up to $500,000 or 50% of the total eligible project costs, whichever is less.

Small Business First: Funding for small businesses including: low-interest loan financing to small businesses for land and building acquisition and construction; machinery and equipment purchases and working capital; financing to comply with environmental regulations; for businesses involved in municipal or commercial recycling; and for those impacted by defense conversion. Amounts: $200,000 or 50% of the total eligible project costs, whichever is less. Maximum loan amount is $100,000 for working capital.

PA Infrastructure Investment Authority (PennVEST): Low-interest loans for design, engineering and construction of publicly and privately owned drinking water distribution and treatment facilities, storm water conveyance and wastewater treatment systems. Amounts: Loans up to $11 million per project for one municipality, up to $20 million for more than one municipality, up to $350,000 for design and engineering, up to 100% of the total project costs.

PA Capital Access Program: Through participating banks, loan guarantees are provided to support a wide variety of business purposes. Amounts: Loan guarantees up to $500,000.

PA Economic Development Financing Authority: An issuer of tax-exempt and taxable bonds, both in pooled transactions and stand-alone transactions. Bond funds are loaned to businesses and can be used to finance land, building, equipment, working capital and refinances. Amounts: Loans no less them $400,000 and no more than $10 million for manufacturers, no upper limits for other projects, up to 100% of project costs.

Opportunity Grant Program: Provides grant funds to create or preserve jobs within the Commonwealth. Funds may be used for job training, infrastructure improvements, land and building improvements, machinery and equipment, working capital and environmental assessment and redemption. Amounts: No minimum or maximum grant amount.

Infrastructure Development Program: Grant and low-interest loan financing for public and private infrastructure improvements. Amounts: Loans and grants up to $1.25 million, no more than 20% of the annual appropriation for a single municipality.

Industrial Sites Reuse Program: Grant and low-interest loan financing is provided to perform environmental site assessment and remediation work at former industrial sites. Amounts: Grants and loans up to $200,000 for environmental assessment, grants and loans up to $1 million for remediation.

Rail Freight Assistance: Grants to build or repair rail lines and spurs. Amounts: Grants up to $250,000 for maintenance, up to $100,000 for construction.

Enterprise Zone Program: Grants available for loans to businesses: Planning Grant up to $50,000; Basic Grant up to $50,000; Competitive Grant: up to $250,000.

Seed Venture Program: Provides product development and working capital to early-stage venture companies.

Small Business First Export Loan Program: Provides short-term loans to meet the pre and post-export financing needs of small businesses. Amounts: Pre-Export loans: Up to $350,000 or 50% of total eligible project costs, whichever is less. Post-Export loans: Loans not to exceed 80% of the face amount of the contract.

Underground Storage Upgrade Loan: Loans to assist owners of regulated storage tanks in upgrading their underground storage tank systems to meet federal Environmental Protection Agency upgrade requirements. Amounts: $500,000 or 75% of the total eligible project costs, whichever is less.

Challenge Grant Program: Provides grants ranging from $5,000 to $250,000 for research and development, technology transfer, joint research and development.

PA Minority Business Development Authority: Low-interest loan financing to businesses which are owned and operated by minorities. Amounts: Manufacturing, industrial, high-tech, international trade or franchise companies with loans up to $500,000 (within Enterprise Zones, $750,000) or 75% of total eligible project costs, whichever is less, retail or commercial firms loans of up to $250,000 ($350,000 in Enterprise Zones).

Independence Capital Network Fund: Provides grants to small employers to enable them to make special accommodations for workers with disabilities.

Minority Business Advocate: Encourages the development of minority-owned businesses as part of the overall economic development strategy of the Commonwealth. Serves as an advocate for minority owned business owners in resolving issues with state agencies and interacting with other government agencies.

Women's Business Advocate: Works to assist women businesses in the development of their business, specifically assisting in resolving issues with state agencies, exploring marketing options and identifying financing strategies.

Bureau of Contract Administration and Business Development (Formerly the Minority and Women Business Enterprise Office): Benefits small, minority and women businesses. Provides the necessary resources and direction for business owners to compete for and participate in the state contracting process. Furthermore, it is the statewide agency for certification as a Minority Business Enterprise and Women Business Enterprise.

Office of International Business Development: This office is headquartered in Harrisburg but maintains offices all around the world. They support Pennsylvania firms wishing to do business overseas. 888-PA EXPORT

Guaranteed Free Training Program: Funds for basic skills and information technology training for new employees and new or expanding business is available for businesses in manufacturing, technology-based information technology and those other than point of sale/retail. For basic skills, the maximum funding is up to $450 per trainee and $100,000 per company. The maximum for information technology is up to $700 per trainee and $50,000 per company.

Regional Marketing Initiative Grant: Local tourism promotion agencies and non-profit organizations can get funding to conduct comprehensive destination marketing including research advertising, public relations and other promotional programs that stimulate travel and tourism.

Critical Job Training Grants: Grants to eligible entities for programs that train dislocated workers and other individuals for high-demand jobs or jobs with shortages of skilled workers. A 25% match is required.

Communities of Opportunity: Provides state-funded grants for community revitalization and economic development activities that occur locally.

Community Economic Development Loan Program: Low-interest loans for projects in distressed communities, stimulating self-help initiatives and helping people build assets.

Workforce Leadership Grants: Education programs grants throughout the secondary and post-secondary education system.

Elm Street Program: Grant funds for planning, technical assistance and physical improvements to residential and mixed use areas in proximity to central business districts.

Pollution Prevention Assistance Account (PPAA): Assistance for small businesses that helps implement pollution prevention and energy-efficiency projects, enable these businesses to adopt or install equipment or processes that reduce pollution or energy use.

Customized Job Training (CJT): Grant funds for specialized job training to existing or newly hired employees.

Job Creation Tax Credit Program: The Job Creation Tax Credit Program provides tax credits to eligible businesses that create 25 or more full-time jobs or increase employment by 20% within three years from the start date.

* Bureau of Market Development

Pennsylvania Department of Agriculture
2301 North Cameron Street   717-787-6041
Harrisburg, PA 17110-9408   Fax: 717-783-9115
www.agriculture.state.pa.us

Domestic and International Trade Development Division: The programs provide a platform from which Pennsylvania food, agriculture and wood companies can determine the opportunities available for their products and services beyond the borders of the Commonwealth and present them to the world.

Commodity Promotion Division; Administers programs that provide farmers a means to promote their products or provide funds for production research without the use of public funding; administers a matching grant program that provides public funding for agricultural product promotion by nonprofit agricultural organizations; develops promotional materials and campaigns for Pennsylvania agricultural products.

Division of Aquaculture: The aquaculture program within the is designed to help current and prospective aquaculture farmers to easily access information to help them achieve success. The program provides: Links to information regarding: regulations impacting aquaculture, species production research sales and marketing; Guidance on business development Strategies; Access to local sources for: food fish, ornamental fish, sports fish and bait fish; Marketing initiatives designed to help Pennsylvania fish farmers penetrate new markets and expand current sales. Educational opportunities for aquaculturalists to local venues.

* Tax Credit Program

Manager, Tax Credit Program
Pennsylvania Housing Finance Agency
P.O. Box 8029
Harrisburg, PA 17105-8029
Low Income Housing Tax Credit Program   717-780-3882
www.phfa.org

This program provides owners of and investors in affordable rental housing developments with tax credits that offer a dollar-for-dollar reduction in their tax liability. The credit may be taken for up to ten years. Tax credits are usually sold to investors with the proceeds used to cover project costs.

* Small Business Assistance Program

Department of Environmental Protection
Rachel Carson State Office Building
400 Market Street
Harrisburg, PA 17105   717-787-2814
www.dep.state.pa.us

Act 190 Pollution Prevention (P2)/Energy Efficiency (E2) Grant Program: Grants under the Act 190 P2/E2 Grant Program will be used to fund 80 percent of the total cost of a P2E2 site assessment, up to a maximum of $5,000 for Pennsylvania small businesses with 100 or fewer employees OR up to a maximum of $15,000 for holders of any DEP permit (or holder of an air permit from either the Allegheny County Department of Health or Philadelphia Air Management Services). (6/2/00)

Pennsylvania Environmental Assistance Network (PEAN): PEAN is a partnership of public and private sector service providers offering pollution prevention, energy efficiency, and environmental management systems services.

Small Business Pollution Prevention Assistance Account: The Pollution Prevention Assistance Account is a loan program that helps small Pennsylvania businesses implement pollution prevention and energy-efficiency projects. Go to the Small Business Pollution Prevention Assistance Account web site for more information.

* Keystone Opportunity Zones (KOZ)

Northwest Region:
Northwest Regional Planning & Development Commission
395 Seneca Street   814-677-4800
Oil City, PA 16301   Fax: 814-677-7663

Southwest Region:
Southwestern Pennsylvania Commission
Regional Enterprise Tower

425 Sixth Avenue, Suite 2500 — 412-391-5590, ext. 343
Pittsburgh, PA 15219-1819 — Fax: 412-391-9160

North Central Region:
North Central Pennsylvania Regional Planning and
Development Commission
651 Montmorenci Avenue — 814-773-3162
Ridgway, PA 15853 — Fax: 814-772-7045

Southern Alleghenies Region
Planning & Program Management
Southern Alleghenies Planning & Development Commission
541 58th Street — 814-949-6508
Altoona, PA 16602 — Fax: 814-949-6505

Northern Tier Region:
Northern Tier Regional Planning & Development Commission
507 Main Street — 570-265-9103
Towanda, PA 18848 — Fax: 570-265-7585

Central Region:
Economic Development Programs
SEDA-Council of Governments
201 Furnace Road — 570-524-4491
Lewisburg, PA 17837 — Fax: 570-524-9190

South Central Region:
South Central Assembly for Effective Governance
777 West Harrisburg Pike — 717-948-6324
Middletown, PA 17057 — Fax: 717-948-6306

Lackawanna/Luzerne Region:
Redevelopment Authority of Luzerne County
16 Luzerne Avenue, Suite #210 — 570-655-3329
West Pittston, PA 18643 — Fax: 570-655-3287

Urban Workshop
1020 Mellon Bank Center
8 West Market Street — 570-822-3166
Wilkes-Barre, PA 18711 — Fax: 570-822-3164

Schuykill/Carbon:
Office of Economic Development
401 North Second Street — 570-628-1167
Pottsville, PA 17901 — Fax: 570-628-1210

Lehigh Valley Region:
Lehigh Valley Economic Development Corporation
2158 Avenue C — 610-266-6775
Bethlehem, PA 18017 — Fax: 610-266-7623

Southeastern Region:
Bucks Co. Economic Dev. Corp.
2 East Court Street — 215-348-9031 ext 12
Doylestown, PA 18901 — Fax: 215-348-8829

Philadelphia Region:
Philadelphia Department of Commerce
One Parkway
1515 Arch Street, 12th Floor — 215-683-2015
Philadelphia, PA 19102 — Fax: 215-557-8538
Keystone Opportunity Zones are defined, parcel-specific areas with greatly reduced or no tax burden for property owners, residents and businesses. Keystone Opportunity Zones have been designated by local communities and approved by the state–they are, in fact, a partnership between each community and region among state and local taxing bodies, school districts, economic development agencies and community-based organizations.

* Certified Development Companies

Allentown Economic Development Corporation
Janice Gubich, Director of Finance
718 Hamilton Mall
Portland Place - 7th Floor — 610-435-8890
Allentown, PA 18105 — Fax: 610-435-6166
Area of Operation: Lehigh and Northampton counties

DelVal Business Finance Corporation
Michael Schwartz, President
6100 City Line Avenue
Executive House, Suite P218 — 215-871-3770
Philadelphia, PA 19131 — Fax: 215-871-3776
Area of Operation: Bucks, Chester, Delaware, Lackawanna, Luzerne, Monroe, Montgomery, Northampton, and Philadelphia Counties

PIDC Local Development Corporation
Jim Pawlikowski, Client Relations Officer
2600 Centre Square West
1500 Market Street — 215-496-8106
Philadelphia, PA 19109-2126 — Fax: 215-977-9618
Area of Operation: Philadelphia

SEDA-COG Local Development Corporation
Jerry Bohinski, Chief, Economic Development
R.R. 1 - Box 372, Furnace Road — 570-524-4491
Lewisburg, PA 17837 — Fax: 570-524-9190
Area of Operation: Adams, Bradford, Centre, Clinton, Columbia, Cumberland, Dauphin, Franklin, Juniata, Lancaster, Lebanon, Lycoming, Mifflin, Montour, Northumberland, Perry, Potter, Sullivan, Synder, Tioga, Union, and York Counties

South Eastern Economic Development Company of PA
Jay Lowden, Finance Manager
750 Pottstown Pike — 610-363-6110
Exton, PA 19341 — Fax: 610-363-2160

Certified Development Companies-Pittsburgh
Allegheny-Pittsburgh Business Development Corporation
Dave Thomas, Manager
200 Ross Street — 412-255-6557
Pittsburgh, PA 15219 — Fax: 412-255-6542
Area Of Operation: Allegheny County

Altoona-Blair County Development Corporation
Martin J. Marasco, Executive Director
4500 Sixth Avenue — 814-944-6113
Altoona PA 16602 — Fax: 814-946-0157
Area Of Operation: Counties of Blair, Bedford, Cambria, Clearfield, Franklin, Fulton, Huntingdon, Jefferson and Somerset Counties

Regional Development Funding Corp.
Executive Director
ST425 Sixth Avenue-Suite 1410
Regional Enterprise Tower — 412-471-1030
Pittsburgh PA 15219 — Fax: 412-471-3902
Area Of Operation: Counties of Allegheny, Armstrong, Beaver, Butler, Clarion, Crawford, Erie, Fayette, Forest, Greene, Indiana, Lawrence, Mercer, Venango, Warren, Washington and Westmoreland Counties

3EDA-COG Local Development Corporation
Jerry Bohinski, Chief, Economic Development
Box 372 - RD#1 — 717-524-4491
Lewisburg PA 17837 — Fax: 717-524-9190
Mailing Address:
R.D. #1 Box 372
Lewisburg PA 17837
Area of Operation: Adams, Bradford, Centre, Clinton, Columbia, Cumberland, Dauphin, Franklin, Juniata, Lancaster, Lebanon, Lycoming, Mifflin, Montour, Northumberland, Perry, Potter, Snyder, Sullivan, Tioga, Union And York Counties

Certified Development Companies-Philadelphia
Allentown Economic Development Corporation
Janice Gubich, Director of Finance
718 Hamilton Mall
Portland Place - 7th Floor — 610-435-8890
Allentown, PA 18101 — Fax: 610-435-6166
Mailing Address:
P.O. Box 1400
Allentown, PA 18105
Area of Operation: Lehigh and Northampton Counties

Altoona-Blair County Development Corporation
Martin J. Marasco, President and CEO
4500 Sixth Avenue — 814-944-6113
Altoona, PA 16602 — Fax: 814-946-0157
www.abcdcorp.org
Area of Operation: Bedford, Blair, Cambria, Clearfield, Franklin, Jefferson, Huntingdon and Somerset Counties

DelVal Business Finance Corporation
Michael Schwartz, President
6100 City Line Avenue
Executive House, Suite P218 — 215-871-3770
Philadelphia, PA 19131 — Fax: 215-871-3776
www.delval504.com
Area of Operation: Bucks, Chester, Delaware, Lackawanna, Luzerne, Monroe, Montgomery, Northampton, and Philadelphia Counties

SEDA-COG Local Development Corporation
Jerry Bohinski, Chief, Economic Development
R.R. 1 - Box 372 570-524-4491
Lewisburg, PA 17837 Fax: 570-524-9190
http://finance.seda-cog.org
Area of Operation: Adams, Bradford, Centre, Clinton, Columbia, Cumberland, Dauphin, Franklin, Juniata, Lancaster, Lebanon, Lycoming, Mifflin, Montour, Northumberland, Perry, Potter, Snyder, Sullivan, Tioga, Union, and York

South Eastern Economic Development Company of PA
Jay Lowden, Finance Manager
737 Constitution Drive 610-458-5700
Exton, PA 19341 Fax: 610-458-7770
www.ccdcseed.org
Area of Operation: Berks, Bucks, Chester, Delaware, Lancaster, Lebanon, Montgomery, and Schuykill Counties

The 504 Certified Development Company (CDC) Program provides growing businesses with long-term, fixed-rate financing for major fixed assets, such as land and buildings. A Certified Development Company is a nonprofit corporation set up to contribute to the economic development of its community or region. CDCs work with the SBA and private-sector lenders to provide financing to small businesses.

* Pennsylvania Treasury Department

Linked Deposit Program
129 Finance Building 717-787-2465
Harrisburg, PA 17120-0018 Fax: 717-783-9760
www.treasury.state.pa.us
The Department of Treasury helps small businesses by offering a variety of programs.

State Contract Information: Helps businesses bid for contracts with state agencies by providing information about existing state contracts including: contract descriptions, names of previous bidders, pricing breakdowns and other information that may help an entrepreneur bid for a contract.

Business Referral Service: Helps businesses find resources they need including: publications, web sites, regional lists of professional associations, Small Business Development Centers, consultants, as well as information on how to become a state certified minority or women-owned business.

LowDoc Business Loans: Helps small businesses get fast financing of up to $150,000 through a cooperative effort with the SBA and local banks.

* Revenue Bond and Mortgage Program

Room 466, Forum Building
Harrisburg, PA 17120 717-783-1108
Funds for this program are borrowed through a local Industrial Development Authority, with financing secured from private sector sources. Lenders do not pay taxes on interest earned from the loan and borrowers obtain interest rates lower than conventional ones. Funds may be used for purchase of land, buildings, machinery, or equipment.

* Office of Technology Development

Forum Building, #352 717-787-4147
Harrisburg, PA 17120 Fax: 717-772-5080
Email: tkaufman@doc.state.pa.us
Programs available through the Office of Technology Development include:
- Ben Franklin Centers
- Challenge Grants
- Seed Grants
- R&D Grants
- Environmental Technology R&D Fund
- Technical and Business Assistance

* Ben Franklin Technology Partners

North East Tier BFTP
125 Goodman Dr.
Lehigh University 610-758-5200
Bethlehem, PA 18015 Fax: 610-861-5918

BFTP of Southeastern Pennsylvania
1835 Market St., Suite 1100 215-972-6700
Philadelphia, PA 19103 Fax: 215-972-5588

BFTP of Western Pennsylvania
Innovation Works, Inc.

2000 Technology Dr., Suite 250 412-681-1520
Pittsburgh, PA 15219 Fax: 412-681-2625

BFTP of Central/Northern Pennsylvania
115 Technology Center 814-863-4558
University Park, PA 16802 Fax: 814-865-0960

State Coordinator
200 N. Third St., Suite 400 717-234-1748
Harrisburg, PA 17101 Fax: 717-234-1824
www.benfranklin.org
Seed and Growth Capital: Ben Franklin Technology Partner uses gap financing to help start-up companies by providing a financial bridge between personal assets of entrepreneurs and capital funding from third party investors.

Business and Technical Expertise: Ben Franklin provides ongoing support and mentoring to address business needs.

Resources for Established Manufacturers: Resources to help established manufacturers evaluate processes and operations while implementing solutions.

Ben Franklin Technology Partners: A statewide network that fosters innovation to stimulate Pennsylvania's economic growth.

Technology Company Investment: Flexible financing and investment opportunities are available for technology-oriented businesses.

Technology Development Grants: A grant program to support local initiatives that stimulate the advancement of technology in businesses and communities.

Ben Franklin Venture Investment Forum: This program prepares entrepreneurs to raise equity capital by creating venues in which entrepreneurs and investors can interact.

* Small Business Administration (SBA)

Federal Building - Room 1128
1000 Liberty Avenue 412-395-6560
Pittsburgh, PA 15222 Fax: 412-395-6562

Robert N.C. Nix Federal Building
900 Market Street, 5th Floor 215-580-2SBA
Philadelphia, PA 19107 Fax 215-580-2762
www.sba.gov/pa
The Pennsylvania Small Business Administration Office delivers a variety of programs and services, such as startup and operational assistance through small business training and counseling, financial assistance for startup's, business opportunities and much more.

* Small Business Investment Companies

Anthem Capital, L.P.
Gerald A. Schaafsma, General Partner
919 Conestoga Road
Participating Securities and Commitments 610-526-9982
Rosemont, PA 19010 Fax: 610-526-2234

Argosy Investment Partners, L.P.
Knute Albrecht, Manager
950 West Valley Road, Suite 2902 610-971-9685
Wayne, PA 19087 Fax: 610-964-9524
Email: knute@argosycapital.com

CEO Venture Fund III, L.P.
One North Shore Center, Suite 201
12 Federal Street 414-322-2576
Pittsburgh, PA 15212 Fax: 412-322-3226

CIP Capital L.P.
Winston Churchill, Jr., Manager
435 Devon Park Drive, Bldg 300 610-964-7860
Wayne, PA 19087 Fax: 610-964-8136
Email: jjackson@cipcapital.com

GS Capital, L.P.
435 Devon Park Drive, Suite 612 610-293-9151
Wayne, PA 19087 Fax: 610-293-1979
Email: ahartshorn@safequard.com

Inverness Capital Partners, L.P.
1325 Morris Drive, Suite 207 610-722-0300

Wayne, PA 19087
Email tshang@invernesscap.com
Fax: 610-722-0800

Liberty Ventures I, L.P.
Thomas R. Morse, Manager
One Commerce Square
2005 Market Street, Suite 2040
Philadelphia, PA 19103
Email: mariahahn@usa.net
215-282-4484
Fax: 215-282-4485

Mellon Ventures, L.P.
Lawrence Mock & Ronald Coombs, Managers
One Mellon Bank Center, Suite 5210
Pittsburg, PA 15258
Email: kdollish@mellonventures.com
412-236-3594
Fax: 412-236-3593

Meridian Venture Partners
Robert E. Brown, Jr. General Partner
201 King of Prussia Road
Radnor, PA 19087
Email: rbroderick@meridian-venture.com
610-254-2999
Fax: 610-254-2996

Meridian Venture Partners II, L.P.
Robert E. Brown, Jr., Contact
201 King of Prussia Road, Suite 240
Radnor, PA 19087
Email: rbroderick@meridian-venture.com
610-254-2999
Fax: 610-254-2996

NewSpring Ventures, L.P.
Michael DiPiano, Managing G P
500 North Gulph Road, Suite 500
King of Prussia, PA 19406
Email marc@newspringventures.com
610-567-2387
Fax: 610-567-2388

Select Capital Ventures I, L.P.
Michael E. Salerno, Contact
4718 Old Gettysburg Road, Suite 405 717-972-1304
Mechanicsburg, PA 17055
Email dhellyer@selectcapitalcorp.com
Fax: 717-972-1050

The SBA licenses, regulates, and provides financial assistance to privately owned and operated Small Business Investment Companies. SBICs make venture or risk investments by supplying capital and extending unsecured loans and loans not fully collateralized to small enterprises which meet their investment criteria. Financing is made by direct loans and by equity investments.

* Rural Development

U.S. Department of Agriculture
One Credit Union Place, Suite 330
Harrisburg, PA 17110
www.rurdev.usda.gov/pa
717-237-2299
Fax: 717-237-2191

Rural Business Enterprise Grants: Through the Rural Business Enterprise Grant (RBEG) program Rural Development provides grants to public agencies, private non-profit corporations or Indian groups for financing and facilitating development of small and emerging private business. These grants can be made to public bodies and private non-profit corporations that serve rural areas.

Business and Industry Loan Guarantee Program: The Business and Industry (B&I) Loan Guarantee program is a lender-driven program that provides a loan guarantee to the bank or other approved lender to finance private businesses located in rural areas of 50,000 population or less.

Rural Business Opportunity Grants: The mission of the Rural Business Opportunity Grant is to provide technical assistance for business development and conduct economic development planning in rural areas. The purpose of this program is to promote sustainable economic development in rural communities.

Rural Economic Development Loan and Grant Program: The Rural Economic Development Loan and Grant Program (REDLG) provides zero-interest loans and grants to Rural Utilities Service (RUS) borrowers, who in turn relend the money as a zero interest loan to local entities to promote rural economic development and job creation projects.

Intermediary Relending Program: The Intermediary Relending Program (IRP) provides a loan to private nonprofit organizations, public entities and others (intermediary) to finance business facilities and community development projects in rural areas of 25,000 population or less. The RBS loan is used to establish or fund a revolving loan program to provide financial assistance to ultimate recipients for community development projects, establishment of new businesses or expansion of existing businesses, and saving and/or creation of jobs in rural areas.

Cooperative Services Technical Assistance: Rural Business - Cooperative Service (RBS) assists rural residents in forming new cooperative businesses and improving the operations of existing cooperatives. Assistance to cooperatives located in rural areas is the primary focus.

Rhode Island

* Rhode Island Economic Development Corporation (RIEDC)

One West Exchange St.
Providence, RI 02903
www.riedc.com
401-222-2601
Fax: 401-222-2102

This office can provide information and expertise in dealing with state, federal, and local agencies. They also have information on financing programs and other services offered by the state government.

Industrial Revenue Bonds: Industrial Revenue Bonds may be used to finance qualified commercial and industrial projects. The bonds offer a competitive interest rate and state sales tax exemption on building materials that may be significant for projects involving new construction. Financing is available through the Rhode Island Industrial Facilities Corporation and covers the entire project cost. The project and the credit of the user provides the security for the bonds which may be issued on the financial strength of the user when the user is appropriately rated. The bonds may also be issued with an enhancement letter of credit from a financial institution.

Tax-Exempt "Small Issue Bonds": Under the small-issue bond provisions of the Omnibus Budget Reconciliation Act of 1993, interest on certain bonds with face amounts of less than $10 million is excluded from income if at least 95% of the bonds' proceeds is used to finance manufacturing facilities. Industrial Revenue Bonds are tax-exempt obligations of the issuer, the interest on which is exempt from federal and state income tax. The interest rate on such obligations is normally below that available for conventional mortgages.

Bond and Mortgage Insurance Program: The Program reduces the capital necessary for new manufacturing facilities, renovation of manufacturing facilities, the purchase of new machinery and equipment in financing projects up to $5,000,000.

The Small Business Loan Fund: The SBLF provides eligible Small Business Fixed Asset Loans from $25,000 to a maximum of $250,000 and Working Capital Loans to a maximum of $30,000.

International Trade Partnership: As the official arm of state government, RIEDC is the principal liaison with foreign governments and hosts incoming trade delegations from other countries. As the entity charged with developing the state's economic agenda, RIEDC is the partner responsible for providing business services directly to companies. These services include: development and execution of trade shows and trade missions; customized export management training and general trade assistance to Rhode Island companies.

Every Company Counts Network: This program consists of public and private business development organizations, cities and towns and State agencies dedicated to providing expertise and tools for small businesses.

Job Creation Grant Fund: Matching grants to both in-state companies that are expanding their workforce and to out-of-state companies that are relocating or expanding their operations to Rhode Island.

Excellence Through Training Grant Program: Matching grants of up to $30,000 directly to employers for the upgrading and retraining of existing employees to improve the companies competitiveness.

Export Management Training Grant Program: Match grant of up to $5,000 to businesses to address their international training needs.

Employee Investment Grants Reimbursement of up to 50% of the cost of training to a maximum of $10,000 for upgrading and retraining of existing employees.

Urban Enterprise Equity Fund: A revolving loan fund to assist start-up and existing urban businesses.

Urban Ventures: Urban Ventures is a business incubator located in the City of Providence.

Procurement Technical Assistance Center (PTAC): A network of professionals to help small businesses enter into business with the state and federal government.

* Rural Development

Warwick Service Center
David M Delisle, Rural Development Manager
60 Quaker Lane, Suite 44   401-826-0842
Warwick, RI 02886   Fax: 401-828-6042
www.rurdev.usda.gov/ma

Business and Industry Loans (B&I): Loans are made to improve, develop or finance business, industry and employment and improve the economic and environmental climate in rural communities, including pollution abatement and control. The objective is achieved principally through bolstering a loan made by a private lender with guarantees by the federal government. Direct loans are also available on a limited basis. The funds may be used for real estate purchase or improvement, equipment or capital.

Rural Business Enterprise Grants (RBEG): Grants are made to assist public bodies and non-profit corporations to finance and facilitate development of small and emerging private business enterprises. Small and emerging businesses have 50 or less employees and less than $1.0 million in gross revenues. Grants are primarily to be used by eligible non-profits or public entities to provide technical assistance or establish a revolving loan fund. Revolving loan funds can provide micro-loans to small business which may be for the purchase of land, construction of facilities, and other business purposes.

Intermediary Relending Program Loans (IRP): Loans are made to eligible intermediaries (non-profit or public entities) who in turn provide loans to ultimate recipients for business facilities and community development in a rural area. The interest rate on the loan to the intermediary is one percent with a term of up to 30 years. Eligible applicants must have a record of successfully assisting rural businesses, including experience in making and servicing commercial loans.

* Certified Development Company

Ocean State Business Development Authority
155 South Main Street, Suite 301   401-454-4560
Providence, RI 02903   Fax:401-454-4890
Area Of Operation: Providence, Kent, Washington and Newport Counties

The 504 Certified Development Company (CDC) Program provides growing businesses with long-term, fixed-rate financing for major fixed assets, such as land and buildings. A Certified Development Company is a nonprofit corporation set up to contribute to the economic development of its community or region. CDCs work with the SBA and private-sector lenders to provide financing to small businesses.

* Clean Water Finance Agency

Executive Director: Anthony B. Simeone
235 Promenade Street, Suite 119   401-453-4430
Providence, RI 02908   Fax: 401-453-4094
Email: ricwta@doa.state.ri.us
www.ricwf.state.ri.us

All water pollution abatement projects are financed with loans made through the State Revolving Loan Fund with a subsidized interest rate to save the borrowers 1/3 off the market rate for financing these projects.

* First Stop Business Information Center

100 North Main Street,   401-222-2185
Providence, RI 02903   Fax: 401-222-3890
www.faststart.state.ri.us

The First Stop Business Information Center, within the Secretary of State's Office, is designed to make it easier for businesses to deal with federal, state and local requirements. It gives businesses access to the information they need to be competitive by providing quick, accurate information and performing referral assistance services. The Center helps new businesses cut through the red tape and get off the ground, and gives existing businesses the information they need to grow and expand. Services include customized business checklists, resource manuals, and registration assistance.

* Human Resource Investment Council

1511 Pontiac Avenue, Bldg. 72-2   401-462-8860
Cranston, RI 02910   Fax: 401-462-8865
www.rihric.com

The Rhode Island Human Resource Investment Council (HRIC) was established by state law in 1992. Their primary role is to act as a catalyst, initiating inventive programs, funding innovative solutions and building dynamic networks. The HRIC provides grants directly to businesses to help offset the cost of training their workforce which include: Excellence Through Training Grants, Employee Creation Grants, and Export Assistance Grants.

* The Business Development Company of Rhode Island (BDCRI)

40 Westminster Street, Suite 702   401-351-3036
Providence, RI 02903.   Fax: 401-351-3056
www.bdcri.com

The Business Development Company of Rhode Island (BDCRI) is a for-profit, publicly held corporation whose principal stockholders are the Greater Providence Chamber of Commerce, Greater Providence Chamber Foundation and BDCRI's member banks, which include most Rhode Island banks. Its mission is to provide alternative funding to Rhode Island businesses that require funds and have the ability to repay, but which cannot obtain all necessary funding from traditional sources. BDCRI provides bridge loans, lines of credit and long term loans. BDCRI is an approved Small Business Administration lender for term loans and lender for lines of credit.

* Small Business Administration (SBA)

380 Westminster St.
Room 511   401-528-4561
Providence, RI 02903   Fax: 401-528-4539
www.sba.gov/ri

The Rhode Island Small Business Administration Office delivers a variety of programs and services, such as startup and operational assistance through small business training and counseling, financial assistance for startup's, business opportunities and much more.

* Small Business Investment Companies

Domestic Capital Corporation
Nathaniel B. Baker, President
815 Reservoir Ave.   401-946-3310
Cranston, RI 02910   Fax: 401-943-6708
Email: CHomen@Domestic.com

Fleet Equity Partners VI, L.P.
Robert Van Degna & Habib Y. Gorgi, Mgrs.
50 Kennedy Plaza, 12th Floor
Mail Stop: RI MO F12C   401-278-6770
Providence, RI 02903   Fax: 401-278-6387
Email: SBACONTACT@fleetequity.com

Fleet Venture Resources, Inc.
Robert M. Van Degna, President
50 Kennedy Plaza, 12th Floor
Mail Stop: RI MO F12C   401-278-6770
Providence, RI 02903   Fax: 401-278-6387
Email: SBACONTACT@fleetequity.com

The SBA licenses, regulates, and provides financial assistance to privately owned and operated Small Business Investment Companies. SBICs make venture or risk investments by supplying capital and extending unsecured loans and loans not fully collateralized to small enterprises which meet their investment criteria. Financing is made by direct loans and by equity investments.

* Department of Administration

Rhode Island Division of Taxation
1 Capital Hill   800-481-3700
Providence, RI 02908   401-222-3050
www.tax.state.ri.us

Child Daycare Tax Credits: Credits are available against the business corporation tax and other business taxes at 30 percent of amount of day care purchase and of the cost to establish and/or operate a licensed day care facility. Maximum annual credit is $30,000. Certain restrictions apply.

* RI Department of Environmental Management (RIDEM)

235 Promenade St.   401-222-6800
Providence, RI 02908   Fax: 401-222-3810
www.state.ri.us/dem

Hazardous Waste Reduction, Recycling and Treatment Program: Grants are available to companies in four categories for development of hazardous waste reduction, recycling or treatment facilities. The categories are: feasibility study - 90 percent up to $140,000; project design - 70 percent to 90 percent up to $75,000; construction - 50 percent to 90 percent up to $250,000; evaluation - 90 percent to 100 percent up to $50,000.

Office of Technical Assistance: The Office of Technical Assistance provides small business compliance assistance and pollution prevention technical support to businesses, industry, and governmental agencies to help them prevent and minimize pollution at the source of generation. This outreach function includes: on- site technical assistance; training programs, conferences, and workshops; and both regulatory and economic incentives to prevent pollution and to minimize the generation of pollutant wastes associated with industrial processes. These programs work with businesses to reduce regulatory burdens and to develop cost- effective ways to reduce toxic and hazardous material use and waste in the workplace. DEM staff working with the pollution prevention program do not report regulatory violations nor do they issue enforcement actions with penalties for non-compliance. This separation of DEM's assistance and enforcement functions is designed to make the assistance program more attractive to industry.

* Rhode Island MicroEnterprise Association, Inc.
645 Elmwood Avenue   401-383-7940
Providence, RI 02907   Fax: 401-383-7944
www.rimicroenterprise.org

Rhode Island MicroEnterprise Association: The MicroEnterprise Association partners with community-based organizations to provide free microbusiness training and business technical assistance to persons wishing to start their own business.

* Center For Women & Enterprise
55 Claverick Street, Suite 102   401-277-0800
Providence, RI 02903   Fax: 401-277-1122
www.cweprovidence.org

South Carolina

* South Carolina Department of Commerce
1201 Main Street, Suite 1600   803-737-0400
Columbia, SC 29201   877-751-1262
www.callsouthcarolina.com   Fax: 803-737-0418

This office can provide information and expertise in dealing with state, federal, and local agencies. They also have information on financing programs and other services offered by the state government, including Industrial Revenue Bonds, Jobs-Economic Development Authority (JEDA), Small Business Administration, Economic Development Administration, and Farmers Home Administration.

Enterprise Development, Inc.: Develops strategic initiatives and business resources for new capital investments. Initiatives are in the development of finances, technology and human resources.

Taxable Bond Financing Program: Assists commercial business and real estate development firms with affordable long-term debt financing. Proceeds may be used to fund the acquisition, construction or renovation of buildings and land, the purchase of new or used equipment, and for working capital purposes as well as the refinancing of existing debt.

Venture Capital Funding: Loans to businesses for innovative products or processes.

Trade Development Program: Mission is twofold: to increase awareness among South Carolina companies of world market profitability and the valuable export resources available; and to promote South Carolina companies and products to prospective overseas importers, resulting in an increased international market share and direct sales for South Carolina companies.
-   Hands-on trade services include such matters as answering export-related inquiries and extending referrals to other export assistance providers. In addition, they regularly co-host trade-related conferences and seminars.
-   Promotional activities include assistance to and the recruitment of companies for participation in trade shows and trade missions overseas and the hosting of visiting international trade missions sourcing South Carolina products. These activities are accomplished through staff-organized meetings with South Carolina manufacturers.
-   Technological capabilities allow the trade staff to provide the most efficient service through both targeted events scheduling, and the ability to disseminate the most current international sales leads and trade-related reports to South Carolina firms with the push of a button.
-   Exporters Database & Directory allows the matching of South Carolina firms with overseas requests for products, and serves as a resource for storing useful promotional information on in-state exporters. South Carolina firms may request their addition to this database, which doubles as the trade programs' mailing list, by completing an Export Questionnaire available from their office.

Export Trade and Finance Program: Assistance through financial counseling, facilitating services and lending/guarantee program.

Foreign Trade Zones: Operating with an FTZ offers several cost benefits: possible reduction or elimination of customs duty, deferral of duty payment, efficiency gains of bypassing customs through direct delivery.

Entrepreneurs/Small Business Assistance: Programs and services to help entrepreneurs and small business owners become successful. They provide *Business One Stop*, an online resource for new businesses and the guide *Starting A Business in South Carolina*.

Recycling Market Development: Technical and economic development assistance to the recycling industry.

Small Business Ombudsman: The Ombudsman serves as an initial contact for entrepreneurs who are looking for assistance or support from business experts.

* USDA Rural Development
Charles Sparks, State Director
Strom Thurmond Federal Building
1835 Assembly Street, Room 1007 803-765-5163
Columbia, SC 29201   Fax: 803-765-5633
Email: Bernie.Wright@sc.usda.gov
www.rurdev.usda.gov/sc

Business and Industry (B&I) Guaranteed Loans: The purpose of this program is to improve, develop, or finance business, industry and employment opportunities in rural communities with a population less than 50,000. Up to an 80% guarantee may be provided on quality loans to lenders with terms ranging from 7 to 30 years.

Intermediary Relending Program (IRP) Loans: Loans are made to intermediaries to establish revolving loan funds for relending to ultimate recipients to finance business facilities and community development projects in rural areas where the population is less than 25,000.

Rural Business Enterprise Grants (RBEG): Public bodies and private nonprofit corporations that serve rural areas can apply for RBEG grantfunds to support the development of small and emerging private business enterprises in rural areas where the population is less than 50,000.

Rural Business Opportunity Grants (RBOG): Public bodies and non-profit corporations, Indian tribes and rural cooperatives may apply for the Rural Business Opportunity Grant. The purpose of the RBOG program is to promote sustainable economic development in rural communities with exceptional needs. Rural Economic Development Loans and Grants (REDLG): These loans and grants are made to Rural Utilities Service electric or telephone utility borrowers to assist in financing economic development and job creation projects in rural areas, which may include towns/cities with population under 2,500 and any unincorporated areas not adjacent to urbanized areas with population 50,000 or more.

Rural Economic Development Loans and Grants: These loans and grants are made to Rural Utilities Service electric or telephone utility borrowers to assist in financing economic development and job creation projects in rural areas. Loans at zero-interest are passed through to a third party recipient primarily to finance business start-up ventures and business expansion projects.

Cooperative Programs: This program helps rural residents form new cooperative businesses and improve the operations of existing cooperatives. Cooperative Services provides technical assistance to cooperatives and those thinking of forming them.

* Center for Applied Technology
Office of Technology Transfer
Clemson University
P.O. Box 345701
Clemson, SC 29634   864-656-3466

Provides assistance in the formation and development of technology based companies. The Center also offers access to capital, business development, as well as access to federal laboratory technologies.

* South Carolina Research Authority
1330 Lady Street, Suite 503   800-888-0871
Columbia, SC 29201   803 799 4070
www.scra.org

A public, self-funded, nonprofit organization that works to attract and support technology-based companies in South Carolina by: encouraging collaboration between industry, government, and educational institutions; providing unique site locations in specialized research parks; offering technology management specialization.

* Director Of Market Services

South Carolina Department of Agriculture
P.O. Box 11280
Columbia, SC 29211   803-734-2210
www.scda.state.sc.us   Fax: 803-734-2192

Marketing Services provides quality commodity inspection programs, basic and objective market news services to the livestock, fruit and vegetable industry, and to operate regional farmers markets to assist farmers, growers, shippers, processors, receivers and consumers in the effective and efficient marketing of fruits and vegetables.

* Commercial and Industrial Activities

South Carolina Energy Office   800- 851-8899
1201 Main Street, Suite 1010   803- 737-8030
Columbia, SC, 29201   Fax: 803-737-9846
www.state.sc.us/energy/

By promoting energy efficient technologies, the South Carolina Energy Office hopes to increase energy efficiency and promote economic development in the two sectors. Industrial and commercial customers benefit from savings on energy bills, and producers can expect to see an increase in productivity stemming from improvements in production process monitoring and reductions in machine downtime, in addition to energy savings. All of these factors improve a business's ability to compete in the marketplace, leading to job retention and increasing the viability of SC businesses.

Energy Audits: Free Level II energy audits are available for businesses and industry located in South Carolina. Level II audits involve a walk-through review of the facility and a report on the energy efficient opportunities available there. 803-737-8285

How to Reduce Your Energy Costs: The SCEO distributes this book to encourage energy management in commercial and industrial facilities.

Training and Workshops: The South Carolina Energy Office offers a variety of classes for your business.

ConserFund Loan Program: This program provides low cost financing program for energy efficiency improvements in state agencies, public colleges or universities, school districts, local governments and private non-profit organizations. {www.state.sc.us/energy/Commercial/commercial_index.htm

* Governor's Office of Small & Minority Business Assistance

1205 Pendleton Street, Room 329   803-734-0657
Columbia, SC 29201   Fax: 803-734-2498
www.govoepp.state.sc.us/osmba

The South Carolina Office of Small & Minority Business Assistance provides a Minority Business Directory to help identify small minority businesses that can help support South Carolina's economic development.

* Business Development Corporation

P.O. Box 21823
Enoree Building, Koger Center
111 Executive Center Dr., Suite 225   803-798-4064
Columbia, SC 29221   Fax: 803-798-1224
www.businessdevelopment.org

Business Development Board (BDB): A source of funds for business development and expansion. The BDB operates as a widely-held stock company made up of bank and savings and loan members. The BDB provides loans for companies which cannot obtain them elsewhere. Terms may range to 10 years or longer, and interest rates are usually comparable to the market rate. The BDB also makes loans under SBA guarantees. Funds are available for any sound business purpose, excluding debt financing or speculative purposes.

* Small Business Administration (SBA)

Strom Thurman Federal Building.
1835 Assembly St., Room 358   803-765-5377
Columbia, SC 29201   Fax: 803-765-5962
www.sba.gov/sc

The South Carolina Small Business Administration Office delivers a variety of programs and services, such as startup and operational assistance through small business training and counseling, financial assistance for startup's, business opportunities and much more.

* Small Business Investment Companies

CF Investment Company
William S. Hummers III, Manager
102 South Main Street   864-255-4919
Greenville, SC 29601   Fax: 864-239-6423
Email: mary.gentry@thesouthgroup.com

Charleston Capital Corporation
Thomas Ervin, President
56 Queen St.
P.O. Box 328   803-723-6464
Charleston, SC 29402   Fax: 803-723-1228
Email: yaschik@bellsouth.net

The SBA licenses, regulates, and provides financial assistance to privately owned and operated Small Business Investment Companies. SBICs make venture or risk investments by supplying capital and extending unsecured loans and loans not fully collateralized to small enterprises which meet their investment criteria. Financing is made by direct loans and by equity investments.

* Certified Development Corporations

Catawaba Regional Development Corporation
Mr. Harold S. Shapiro
215 Hampton Street   803-327-9041
Rock Hill SC 29730   Fax: 803-327-1912
Mailing Address:
P.O. Box 450
Rock Hill SC 29731
Area Of Operation: South Carolina counties of Chester, Lancaster, Union and York Counties

Certified Development Corporation of South Carolina
Mr. W.C. Grimes
111 Executive Center Drive
Enoree Building, Suite 225   803-798-4064
Columbia SC 29210   Fax: 803-798-1224
Mailing Address:
P.O. Box 21823
Columbia SC 29201
Area Of Operation: Statewide

Appalachian Development Corporation
David Mueller, Special Projects/Loan Fund Coordinator
30 Century Circle   864-242-9733
Greenville SC 29606   Fax: 864-242-6957
Mailing Address:
P.O. Box 6668
Greenville SC 29606
Area Of Operation: South Carolina Counties of Anderson, Cherokee, Greenville, Oconee, Pickens, and Spartanburg Counties

CSRA Development Companies
Randall E. Griffin - President
3023 Riverwatch Parkway, Suite A   706-210-2010
Augusta, GA 30907   Fax: 706-210-2006
Area Of Operation: South Carolina Counties of Abeville, Aiken, Allendale, Barnwell, Edgefield, McCormick and Saluda Counties

Small Business Assistance Corporation
Tony O'Reilly, Executive Director
111 E. Liberty Street, Suite 100   912-232-4700
Savannah GA 31412   Fax: 912-232-0385
Mailing Address:
P.O. Box 10750
Savannah GA 31412
Area Of Operation: South Carolina Counties of Beaufort, Jasper and Hampton Counties

The 504 Certified Development Company (CDC) Program provides growing businesses with long-term, fixed-rate financing for major fixed assets, such as land or buildings. A Certified Development Company is a nonprofit corporation set up to contribute to the economic development of its community or region. CDC's work with the SBA and private-sector lenders to provide financing to small businesses.

South Dakota

* Governor's Office of Economic Development

711 East Wells Ave.   605-773-5032
Pierre, SD 57501-3369   800-872-6190
www.state.sd.us/goed   Fax: 605-773-3256

This office can provide information and expertise in dealing with state, federal, and local agencies. They also have information on financing programs and other services offered by the state government.

Workforce Development Program: Trains new employees, retrains current employees, and upgrades current employee skills.

Economic Development Finance Authority: Allows enterprises to pool tax-exempt or taxable development bonds for the purpose of constructing any site, structure, facility, service or utility for the storage, distribution or manufacturing of industrial or agricultural or nonagricultural products or the purchase of machinery and equipment used in an industrial process. Generally, the Authority will not consider loan requests for enterprises for amounts less than $300,000 and will not pool projects unless the pool volume is $1 million or more.

Revolving Economic Development and Initiative (REDI) Fund: Objective is to create "primary jobs" in South Dakota. Primary jobs are defined as "jobs that provide goods and services which shall be primarily exported from the state, gain market shares from imports to the state or meet an unmet need in the area resulting in the creation of new wealth in South Dakota. Primary jobs are derived from businesses that bring new income into an area, have a stimulative effect on other businesses or assist a community in diversification and stabilization of its economy." All for-profit businesses or business cooperatives are encouraged to apply, whether they are business start-ups, expansions, or relocations from outside South Dakota. The REDI Fund may provide up to 45% of the total project cost and requires the applicant to secure the matching funds before applying to the Board of Economic Development for the REDI Fund, including a 10% minimum equity contribution.

APEX Fund: The Agriculture Processing and Export Loan (APEX) is designed to assist companies in communities with populations of 25,000 or less or which add value to raw agricultural products through processing. The program may provide up to 75% of the total cost up to $150,000.

* Rural Development Administration

200 4th St., SW, Room 210   605-352-1142
Huron, SD 57350-2477   Fax: 605-352-1146
www.rurdev.usda.gov/sd

Guaranteed Business and Industrial Loans: Loans aimed at creating and maintaining employment and improving the economies of rural areas. Local lenders initiate and service the loans, while the RDA guarantees up to 90 percent of the loan. Potential borrowers who want loans of $500,000 or less should apply to the Small Business Administration. Guarantees are limited to $10 million. Interest rates are determined between the borrower and the lender and can be fixed or variable. Eligible projects and costs are business and industrial acquisitions, construction, conversion, enlargement, repair or modernization; purchase of land, machinery and equipment, furniture and fixtures, and certain housing development sites; processing and marketing facilities, start-up and working capital; pollution control; feasibility studies.

Rural Business Enterprise Grant: These grants are available to finance and facilitate development of small and emerging private business enterprises in rural area of cities up to 50,000 with priority given to towns smaller than 25,000.

Rural Business Opportunity Grants: The purpose of the Rural Business Opportunity Grants Program is to promote sustainable economic development in rural communities with exceptional needs. This is accomplished by making grants to public bodies, nonprofit corporations, Indian Tribes or cooperatives to provide for economic development planning, technical assistance, or training activities that improve economic conditions in rural areas.

Rural Economic Development Grant: The purpose of the Rural Economic Development Grant Program is to make available to rural communities through Rural Utility Service borrowers (1) grants to be used for revolving loan funds for community facilities and infrastructure and (2) grant assistance in conjunction with rural economic development loans.

Rural Economic Development Loan: The purpose of the Rural Economic Development Loan Program is to provide zero-interest loans and grants to borrowers to promote rural economic development and job creation projects.

Intermediary Relending Program: The purpose of the Intermediary Relending Program is to alleviate poverty and increase economic activity and employment in rural communities, especially disadvantaged and remote communities, through financing targeted primarily smaller and emerging businesses. This purpose is achieved through loans made to intermediaries that establish programs for the purpose of providing loans to ultimate recipients for business facilities and community developments in a rural area.

Cooperative Service Program: The mission of the Rural Business-Cooperative Service is to enhance the quality of life for all rural Americans by providing leadership in building competitive businesses and cooperatives. Rural Business Service accomplishes this mission by investing its financial resources and/or technical assistance in businesses, cooperatives, and communities, and by building partnerships that leverage public, private, and cooperative resources to stimulate rural economic activity.

* International Trade Directory

Mr. Joop Bollen
South Dakota International Business Institute – NSU
1200 S. Jay Street   605-626-3149
Aberdeen, SD 57401-7198   Fax: 605-626-3004
Email: bollenj@wolf.northern.edu
www.sd-exports.org

Identifies South Dakota traders (i.e. exporters and importers) of manufactured products, agribusiness products, services and technologies. The directory also offers a list of various private companies and public agencies that are available to serve the special needs of South Dakota exporters and importers. *Exporters Directory* is available in hard copy upon request.

* Department of Agriculture

Foss Building, Top Level
523 East Capitol   800-228-5254
Pierre, SD 57501-3182   605-773-3375
www.state.sd.us/doa/doa.html

The Department of Agriculture is responsible for the promotion and enhancement of South Dakota agriculture. They provide a variety of programs including:

Ag Finance Counseling: Ag counselors provide one-on-one assistance to South Dakota farmers and ranchers in financial management, such as completing loan paperwork, financial planning, or handling financial difficulties.

Business Development: This program assists the state's producers in identifying and developing appropriate opportunities. Assistance can be in the form of technical assistance, business plans, pre-feasibility studies or financial reviews.

Farm Loan Mediation: Mediation brings lenders and borrowers together in a confidential setting to resolve their financial disputes.

Livestock Development and Marketing Program: Offers marketing assistance to South Dakota livestock producers.

Ag Loan Programs: There are a wide variety of loan programs available for producers in the state of South Dakota.

Value-Added and Crop Marketing Program: Assists the state's producers and processors in marketing their products both domestically and internationally.

Feed Finder and Harvest Hotline: The feed finder is a computerized listing designed to match buyers and sellers of all types of feed and open pasture land for livestock. Hotline: 800-228-5254

* Certified Development Companies

First District Development Company
Roger Clark
124 First Avenue, NW
P.O. Box 1207
Watertown, SD 57201   605-886-7225

Area Of Operation: Counties in Eastern South Dakota with the exception of Clay and Union Counties

Black Hills Community Economic Development, Inc.
Jim Doolittle

P.O. Box 218
Sturgis, SD 57785   605-642-7106
Area Of Operation: Counties in Western South Dakota with exception of
Gregory County

South Dakota Development Corporation (The)
Tina Van Camp
711 E. Wells Ave.   605-773-5032
Pierre SD 57501   Fax: 605-773-3256
Area Of Operation: Statewide

Siouxland Economic Development Corporation
Glenda Castleberry
P.O. Box 447
Sioux City, IA 55102   712-279-6286
Area Of Operation: Clay and Union Counties

The 504 Certified Development Company (CDC) Program provides growing
businesses with long-term, fixed-rate financing for major fixed assets, such
as land and buildings. A Certified Development Company is a nonprofit
corporation set up to contribute to the economic development of its
community or region. CDCs work with the SBA and private-sector lenders
to provide financing to small businesses.

* Housing Tax Credit Program

Housing Development Authority
South Dakota Housing Development Authority
P.O. Box 1237   605-773-3181
Pierre, SD 57501-1237   Fax: 605-773-5154
www.sdhda.org

Projects eligible for housing tax credits involve construction and/or
preservation of decent, safe, sanitary and affordable housing in areas of the
greatest housing need. A minimum of either 20 percent of the total units
must be available to tenants whose incomes do not exceed 50 percent of the
area median gross income; or 40 percent of the total units must be available
to tenants whose incomes do not exceed 60 percent of the area median gross
income. Gross rents on the low-income units, including tenant-paid utilities,
cannot exceed 30 percent of the qualifying monthly median income. The
project owner must also enter into an agreement to meet the low income
occupancy requirements for a minimum of 15 years beyond the initial 15
year compliance period.

* State Investment Council

State Treasurer
Capitol Building, Suite 212
500 East Capitol Ave.   605-773-3378
Pierre, SD 57501-5070   Fax: 605-773-3115
www.sdtreasurer.com

Deals solely with venture capital funds that invest in equity or equity-
participating instruments of businesses. The fund can invest only in
businesses which have headquarters and the majority of their employees
located within the state. The Investment Council's participation in a venture
capital fund may not be greater than one-third of the total equity funds
invested in the fund.

* Small Business Administration (SBA)

110 S. Phillips Ave., Suite 200   605-330-4243
Sioux Falls, SD 57104   Fax: 605-330-4215
www.sba.gov/sd

The South Dakota Small Business Administration Office delivers a variety
of programs and services, such as startup and operational assistance through
small business training and counseling, financial assistance for startup's,
business opportunities and much more.

* Small Business Investment Companies

Bluestem Capital Partners II, L.P.
Steve Kirby and Paul Schock, Managers
122 South Phillips Avenue, Suite 300   605-331-0091
Sioux Falls, SD 57104   Fax: 605-334-1218
Email: shorst@bluestemcapital.com

The SBA licenses, regulates, and provides financial assistance to privately
owned and operated Small Business Investment Companies. SBICs make
venture or risk investments by supplying capital and extending unsecured
loans and loans not fully collateralized to small enterprises which meet their
investment criteria. Financing is made by direct loans and by equity
investments.

Tennessee

* Department of Economic and Community Development

Rachel Jackson Building, 8th Floor
312 Eighth Avenue North   615-741-1888
Nashville, TN 37243-0405   Fax: 615-741-7306
www.state.tn.us/ecd

Small Business Incubation Centers: Incubation centers offer a low cost way
for entrepreneurs to start their businesses in an office/light manufacturing
environment. Offering low cost rental rates per square foot, incubators also
offer shared resources such as conference rooms, utility hook ups, office
copiers, some telephone support. The most valuable commodity they offer is
a shared environment in which business owners can discuss common
problems and reach solutions.

Small Business Information Guide: A resource manual that assists start-up
and existing small businesses with issues like state and federal business
taxes, business regulations and government assisted funding programs.

Industrial Training Service: Helps recruit, screen and train new employees,
provide job-specific training and overall workforce development. They
partner with over 40 community colleges, and technical institutes and
technology centers across the state.

*Small And Minority Owned Telecommunications Business Assistance
Program (Loan Guarantee):* Designed to enhance and stimulate the growth,
development and procurement opportunities for small, minority, and women
owned businesses in the telecommunications industry in Tennessee.

Revolving Loan Funds: Available through nine community development
corporations in Tennessee. The revolving loan fund combines funds secured
from the Economic Development Administration and Farmer's Home
Administration with regional funding sources to provide new or expanding
businesses with financing at below market rates.

Tennessee Child Care Facilities Program: Assists child care providers by
enabling them to upgrade facilities, create or expand the number of child
care slots. The Program was established to accomplish two main goals:
assist child care providers in attaining higher standards of safety and
environment; increase the number of child care slots especially in rural and
economically distressed areas. The program also assists companies and
organizations wishing to establish day care centers for employees or groups
of employees. The Program has three components:
- Guarantees to lenders up to $250,000 for new construction
- Direct loans to providers up to $10,000 for upgrade of facilities
- Direct loans to providers up to $25,000 for new or addition of slots
As of spring, 1998, the guarantee portfolio totaled $2.3 million, close to its
cap for prudent risk. Direct loans are subject to funding on an annual basis
from different sources. Maturities as well as interest rates vary based on uses
of the loans.

*Rural Electric Administration (REA), Rural Economic Development
Revolving Loan Program For Rural Electric And Telephone Cooperatives*:
Designed to promote rural economic development and job creation by
providing zero interest loans to REA borrowers. The program will fund up to
$100,000 per project. The maximum term of the loan is ten years at zero
interest rate with a two-year deferred payment. For more information,
contact your local electric utility company.

Small Business Energy Loan Program: Designed to assist in the
identification, installation, and incorporation of approved energy efficiency
measures onto, or into, the existing Tennessee located facilities processes,
and for operations of approved applicants. The Energy Division currently
maintains a loan portfolio of $4,560,000 to 115 borrowers. Approved loan
requests average $39,000.

Rural Business & Cooperative Development Service Loan Guarantees: The
U.S. Department of Agriculture, through the RBCDS (formerly Farmers
Home Administration), guarantees term loans to non-farm businesses in
rural areas; that is, localities with populations below 50,000 not adjacent to a
city where densities exceed 100 persons per square mile. The Tennessee
RBCDS currently maintains a loan portfolio in excess of $40,000,000 (in
addition to their relending program with the Development Districts listed
above) with 40 industrial borrowers. Approved loan requests average just
over $1,000,000.

Small Business Investment Companies: Private investment and loan
companies established to serve the small business market. They are funded
with a combination of private and federal investment. SBICs assist only
businesses below $6,000,000 in net worth and less than $2,000,000 in

annual net income. They may prioritize investments in type (equity or loan); dollar amount, location or industry.

Pollution Prevention Loan Program: Loans for the purchase of equipment and/or construction to complete pollution prevention activities at small and medium sized businesses.

Minority Business Development Center: Provides management, marketing, and technical assistance to increase business opportunities for minority entrepreneurs. Each center provides accounting, administration, business planning, construction, and marketing information to minority firms. The MBDC also identifies minority firms for contract and subcontract opportunities with government agencies and the private sector.

The Valley Coalition for Business Development: This coalition promotes the growth and expansion of minority-owned, women-owned and socially and economically disadvantaged businesses.

Business Incubator Loan Fund: Businesses housed within the TVA Business Incubation Network can apply for money from TVA's Business Incubator Loan Fund. Loans of up to $25,000 are available to help young businesses meet their short-term needs for cash flow and operating capital.

* ACCE$$
Nashville Area Chamber of Commerce
211 Commerce Street, Suite 100
Nashville, TN 37201   615-743-3000
www.nashvillechamber.com

The Nashville Area Chamber of Commerce, U.S. Small Business Administration and area banks started a financing program for small businesses. ACCE$$ serves the small business loan market, booking loans of $5000 and up. The program enables entrepreneurs the opportunity to present their business plans orally to a panel of bank loan officers. Panelists can qualify good credit risks immediately, improving the presenter's chances of obtaining an SBA guarantee. Regardless of the decision, small business owners receive valuable outside appraisal of their business plans.

* Rural Development Authority
Department of Agriculture   615-783-1300
3322 W. End Ave., Suite 300   800-342-3149
Nashville, TN 37203   Fax: 615-783-1301
www.rurdev.usda.gov/tn

Business & Industrial Loan Guarantees: This program guarantees loans, which are designed to promote economic growth. Qualifying businesses are eligible for loan note guarantees that better assist the business in obtaining vital credit through a local lender.

Intermediary Relending Program: This program allows the Rural-Business Service to provide loans to local lending authorities, which in turn provide loans to local businesses.

Rural Business Enterprise Grants: These grants provide resources that are utilized to develop small and emerging business enterprises, such as industrial parks. Qualifying entities include public bodies, nonprofit corporations and federally recognized tribal groups.

Cooperative Development Programs: The Rural-Business Service has the responsibility for providing technical and financial assistance to developing existing cooperatives in rural Tennessee. This assistance is targeted to those cooperatives with an emphasis on value-added agricultural products. The goal is to target the technical and financial resources of USDA to cooperatives involved in the development of new products and markets for farmers.

Rural Economic Development Loans and Grants: This program is utilized to finance rural economic development and rural job creation projects that are based on sound economic and financial analyses. Loans and grants are made to Rural Utilities Service electric and telephone borrowers who use the funds to provide financing for business and community development projects.

* University of Tennessee Center for Industrial Services
193 Polk Avenue, Suite C   888-763-7439
Nashville, TN 37219   615-532-8657
www.cis.utk.edu   Fax: 615-532-4937

Industrial Extension: CIS is a state wide industrial extension program dedicated to helping managers of Tennessee business and manufacturing firms find solutions to technical and managerial problems they face. CIS

provides information and counseling services and strives to link resources of higher education with industrial needs.

* Tennessee Technological University Center for Manufacturing Research and Technology Utilization
Tennessee Tech Manufacturing Center
College of Business Administration
TTU Box 5077   615-372-6634
Cookeville, TN 38505   Fax: 423 372-3362
www.tntech.edu/cmr

The Manufacturing Center was created to help improve the manufacturing productivity of state industry and to enhance instructional quality in manufacturing-related areas. The Center seeks to assist industry not only in research and development, but also in integrating manufacturing processes with a systems approach. At any given time in the Manufacturing Center, over 30 separate, but complimentary projects may be in progress.

* Tennessee Valley Authority Special Opportunity Counties Program
Tennessee Valley Authority
400 W. Summit Hill Dr.
Knoxville, TN 37902-1499   865-632-2101
www.tva.gov/econ

Designed to provide capital to finance projects which support the recruitment of new industry, the expansion of existing industry, the growth of small business, and the creation of new companies in the Tennessee Valley.

The Economic Development Loan Fund (EDLF): $20 million per year revolving loan program targeted on low interest loans to established companies relocating or expanding their operations in the Tennessee Valley. Loans are made for buildings, plant equipment, infrastructure, or property based on the capital investment leveraged, the number of jobs created, power load generated and geographic diversity. TVA Economic Development staff market the program, manage the loan review process, and manage the loan portfolio. Primary Focus: Sustained Growth.

Special Opportunities County Fund: $15 million revolving loan program targeted on low interest loans for companies expanding or relocating in the Tennessee Valley's most economically distressed counties. Loans are made for buildings, plant equipment, infrastructure, or property based on the capital investment leveraged and the number of jobs created. TVA Economic Development staff market the program, manage the loan review process, and manage the loan portfolio. Primary Focus: Sustained Growth.

Minority Business Development Loan Fund.: Revolving loan fund targeted to socially and economically disadvantaged businesses in the Valley.

* Office of Minority Business Enterprise
312 8th Ave. North, 11th Floor
Nashville, TN 37243   615-741-1888
www.state.tn.us/ecd/minority.htm

Facilitates the resources needed in assisting minority businesses in growth and business development by identifying sources of capital; linking successful businesses with minority businesses which need help in areas like training, quality control, supplier development or financial management; providing education and training, specialized technical assistance and identification of procurement opportunities in the public and private sectors; and publishing the *Minority and Women Business Directory* profiling minority businesses and their capabilities for public and private organizations which use their services or products.

* Tennessee Technology Development Corporation
1020 Commerce Park Dr.
Oak Ridge, TN 37830   865-220-8832
www.tennesseetechnology.org

Provides seed capital fund for promising technology companies.

* Occupational Safety And Health Grant
Tennessee Department of Labor
Occupational Safety and Health Grant Program
Gateway Plaza, 2nd Floor   800-249-8510
710 James Robertson Parkway   615-741-2793
Nashville, TN 37243   Fax: 615-253-1623
www.state.tn.us/labor-wfd/tosha.html

The goal of this program is to fund the education and training of employees in safe employment practices and conduct in the employer's own business for the employer's own employees; and promote the development of employer - sponsored health and safety programs in the employer's own business for the employer's own employees. Grants average in the $5000 range with some greater amounts.

* Tennessee Department of Agriculture

Division of Marketing
Ellington Agricultural Center
P.O. Box 40627   615-837-5103
Nashville, TN 37204   Fax: 615-360-0194
www.state.tn.us/agriculture

Offers similar services as the Tennessee Export Office, however specifically catering to the Tennessee farmers and agri-business people in the state. Their services include:
- hosting foreign buyer visits from abroad
- participating in trade shows and sales missions to key agricultural market destinations
- identifying foreign import requirements and assistance in obtaining appropriate documentation
- conducting seminars highlighting agricultural exports
- disseminate trade leads and other trade information

* Purchasing Councils

Tennessee Minority Purchasing Council
Metro Center, Plaza 1 Building
220 Athens Way, Suite 105   615-259-4699
Nashville, TN 37228   Fax: 615-259-9480
www.tmsdc.net

Encourages mutually beneficial economic links between ethnic minority suppliers and major purchasers in the public and private sectors.

* Certified Development Companies

Alacom Finance
Diane Roehrig
4515 Poplar Avenue, #2, Suite 217   901-374-0396
Memphis TN 38119   Fax: 901-347-0397

Area Of Operation: Lake, Obion, Weakley, Henry, Dyer, Gibson, Carroll, Benton, Lauderdale, Crockett, Tipton, Haywood, Madison, Henderson, Decatur, Shelby, Fayette, Hardeman, McNairy, and Chester Counties

Areawide Development Corporation
Don Woods, Loan Officer
5616 Kingston Pike
P.O. Box 19806   865-588-7972
Knoxville TN 37919-2806   Fax: 865-584-5159

Area Of Operation: Scott, Campbell, Claiborne, Anderson, Union, Morgan, Roane, Loudon, Monroe, Blount, Knox, Grainger, Hamblen, Jefferson, Cocke, Carter, Greene, Hancock, Hawkins, Johnson, Sullivan, Unicoi, Washington and Sevier Counties

Mid-Cumberland Area Development Corporation
Tom McAuley, Small Bus. Loan Off.
501 Union Street
Stalman Building, 6th Floor   615-862-8855
Nashville TN 37219-1735   Fax: 615-862-8840

Area Of Operation: Cheatham, Davidson, Dickson, Houston, Humphreys, Montgomery, Robertson, Rutherford, Stewart, Sumner, Trousdale, Williamson and Wilson Counties

South Central Tennessee Business Development Corp.
Doug Williams, Econ. Dev. Director
815 South Main Street
P.O. Box 1346   931-381-2041
Columbia TN 38402   Fax: 931-381-2053

Area Of Operation: Bedford, Coffee, Franklin, Giles, Hickman, Lawrence, Lewis, Lincoln, Marshall, Maury, Moore, Perry and Wayne Counties

Southeast Local Development Corporation
Joe Guthrie, Executive Director
25 Cherokee Boulevard
P.O. Box 4757   423-266-5781
Chattanooga TN 37405   Fax: 423-267-7705

Area Of Operation: Cannon, Clay, Cumberland, DeKalb, Fentress, Jackson, Macon, Overton, Pickett, Putnam, Smith, Van Buren, Warren, White, Grundy, Sequatchie, Bledsoe, Rhea, Meigs, Marion, Hamilton, Bradley, McMinn and Polk Counties

Tennessee Business Development Corporation
Jim Thigpen
P.O. Box 307   731-644-7108
Paris, TN 38242   Fax: 731-644-5984

Area Of Operation: Benton, Bledsoe, Bradley, Campbell, Cannon, Carroll, Carter, Chester, Claiborne, Clay, Crockett, Cumberland, Decatur, Dekalb, Dyer, Fayette, Fentress, Franklin, Gibson, Giles, Grainer, Greene, Grundy, Hancock, Hardeman, Hardin, Henderson, Henry, Hickman, Houston, Jackson, Johnson, Lake, Lauderdale, McNairy, Macon, Marshall, Meigs, Monroe, Moore, Morgan, Obion, Overton, Perry, Pickett, Polk, Putnam, Rhea, Roane, Scott, Sequatchie, Stewart, Sumner, Tipton, Trousdale, Union, Van Buren and Washington Counties

The 504 Certified Development Company (CDC) Program provides growing businesses with long-term, fixed-rate financing for major fixed assets, such as land and buildings. A Certified Development Company is a nonprofit corporation set up to contribute to the economic development of its community or region. CDCs work with the SBA and private-sector lenders to provide financing to small businesses.

* The Southern Appalachian Fund

1020 Commerce Park Drive, Suite 5L   865-220-2020
Oak Ridge, TN 37830   865-220-2030
www.southappfund.com

The Southern Appalachian Fund is a venture capital fund focused on investing in technology-based, early-stage, private companies. The Fund is supported by institutional and private investors and is awaiting approval of its license to become a Small Business Investment Company under the Participating Securities Program. Southern Appalachian Fund can make investments throughout the United States but will focus its investments in Tennessee and the surrounding states.

* Environment and Conservation

21st Floor, L&C Tower
401 Church Street   615-532-0104
Nashville, TN 37243-0454   888-891-8332
www.state.tn.us/environment/dco/p2

Pollution Prevention Programs: Provides multimedia pollution prevention assistance to industry, commercial establishments, schools, institutions, homes, government, etc through the preparation and review of pollution prevention plans, onsite visits, market development, general outreach and training.

* Tennessee Department of Labor and Workforce Development

710 James Robertson Parkway
Andrew Johnson Tower, 8th Floor   615-741-6642
Nashville, TN 37243   Fax: 615-741-5078
www.state.tn.us/labor-wfd

The Work Opportunity Tax Credit and the Welfare-to-Work tax credit programs are intended to further the partnership between the employment and training system and the private sector in dealing with problems of the disadvantaged and the unemployed. These two tax credits are significant complements to the welfare reform effort and can be used as incentives for employers to hire regular as well as long-term welfare recipients. 800-432-5268 (in state only) or fax your request to 615-532-1612.

Employment and Training: We are committed to providing employers access to recruitment and training services for both immediate and long-term needs. We help coordinate services through local partners in the state's local workforce investment areas to help connect employers with the well-trained workforce they need to be productive. 800-255-5872

* International Trade Administration (ITA)

U.S. Dept. of Commerce
Nashville Export Assistance Center
Commerce Center Building
211 Commerce St., 3rd Floor, Suite 100   615-259-6060
Nashville, TN 37201   Fax: 615-259-6064

U.S. Dept. of Commerce
Knoxville Export Assistance Center
601 W. Summit Hill Drive, Suite 300   865-545-4637
Knoxville, TN 37902-2011   Fax: 865-545-4435

U.S. Dept. of Commerce
Memphis Export Assistance Center
Buckman Hall

650 East Parkway South, Suite 348   901-323-1543
Memphis, TN 38103-2190   Fax: 901-320-9128
www.state.tn.us/ecd/rg_ch8.htm

These International Trade Centers operate as a division of the Tennessee Small Business Development Center, the state's primary consulting and technical assistance provider for small- and medium-size businesses. Their export assistance efforts focus on exporting firms that are new to the exporting business. Maintaining offices in Memphis and Knoxville, the ITC can offer one-on-one counseling at any SBDC office across the state. ITC counselors can: Assist in evaluating a company's export potential; Assist in market research; Assist with market entry strategies; Advise on market opportunities; Advise on export practices; and Advise on export procedures. In addition to counseling, ITC sponsors continuing-education seminars and workshops across the state.

* Tennessee Department of State

Business Services Division
William R. Snodgrass Tower, 6th Floor`
312 Eighth Avenue North   615-741-2286
Nashville, TN 37243   Fax 615-741-7310
www.state.tn.us/sos/service.htm

The Division of Business Services can assist with corporate filing transactions, issues certifications, responds to corporate telephone inquiries; UCC filing and search transactions ;issues notary- at-large commissions and registers trademarks.

* Small Business Administration (SBA)

50 Vantage Way
Suite 201   615-736-5881
Nashville, TN 37228-1500   Fax: 615-736-7232
www.sba.gov/tn

The Tennessee Small Business Administration Office delivers a variety of programs and services, such as startup and operational assistance through small business training and counseling, financial assistance for startup's, business opportunities and much more.

* Small Business Investment Companies

Capital Across America, LP
Whitney Johns & Chris Brown, Managers
501 Union Street, Suite 201   615-254-1414
Nashville, TN 37219   Fax: 615-254-1856
Email: CXAChris@aol.com

Commerce Capital, LP
Andrew Higgins, Pres & Rudy Ruark, V.P.
5115 Maryland Way, Suite 304   615-244-1432
Brentwood, TN 37027   Fax: 615-242-1407
Email: billie12@bellsouth.net

Equitas, LP
D. Shannon LeRoy, President of CGP
2000 Glen Echo Rd., Suite 100   615-383-8673
Nashville, TN 37215   Fax: 615-383-8693
Mail To: P.O. Box 158838, Nashville, TN 37215
Email: sleroy@equitaslp.com

Delta Venture Partners I, L.P.
Donald L. Mundie, Contact
c/o Delta Capital Management, LLC
8000 Centerview Parkway, Suite 100   901-755-0949
Cordova, TN 38018   Fax: 901-755-0436
Email yearwood@deltacapital.com

International Paper Cap. Formation, Inc.
Bob J. Higgins, V.P. and Controller
International Place II
6400 Poplar Ave.   901-419-7055
Memphis, TN 38197   Fax: 901-419-7950
Email: Bob.Higgins@ipaper.com

Massey Burch Venture Fund I, L.P.
Don Johnston, President
One Burton Hills Blvd., Suite 350   615-665-3221
Nashville, TN 37215   Fax: 615-665-3240
Email: tcalton@masseyburch.com

Morgan Keegan Mezzanine Fund, L.P.
William J. Nutter, Contact
30 Burton Hills Blvd., Suite 500   615-665-3636

Nashville, TN 37215   Fax: 615-665-3670
Email: bill.nutter@morgankeegan.com

Pacific Capital, L.P.
Jere M. Ervin
Two International Plaza Dr., Suite 200   615-367-0770
Nashville, TN 37217   Fax: 615-367-1771

Petra Mezzanine Fund, L.P.
Michael Blackburn, Joseph O'Brien
172 Second Avenue North, Suite 112   615-313-5999
Nashville, TN 37201   Fax: 615-313-5990
Email: jdo@petracapital.com

Valley Capital Corp.
Lamar J. Partridge, President
Suite 212, Krystal Bldg.
100 W. Martin Luther King Blvd.   423-265-1557
Chattanooga, TN 37402   Fax: 423-265-1588
Email: ValleyCapital@aol.com

West Tennessee Venture Capital Corp.
Frank Banks, President
5 N. Third St.   901-522-9237
Memphis, TN 38103   Fax: 901-527-6901
Email: fjbanks@aol.com

White Pines Limited Partnership I
William D. Orand
Two International Plaza Dr., Suite 200   615-367-0770
Nashville, TN 37217   Fax: 615-367-1771

The SBA licenses, regulates, and provides financial assistance to privately owned and operated Small Business Investment Companies. SBICs make venture or risk investments by supplying capital and extending unsecured loans and loans not fully collateralized to small enterprises which meet their investment criteria. Financing is made by direct loans and by equity investments.

* Tennessee Small Business Development Center (TSBDC)

1415 Murfreesboro Road, Suite 350   615-366-3900
Nashville, TN 37217   877-898-3900
www.tsbdc.org

The TSBDC network is composed of 12 centers and 2 satellite offices throughout the state.

Personalized One-on-One Counseling: A personal consultant is assigned to work with your business for personal attention.

Training: Training on a variety of business subjects are available including: buying and selling abroad, E-commerce, marketing, starting and managing a small business and writing a business plan.

Texas

* Texas Department of Economic Development

P.O. Box 12728   512-936-0100
Austin, TX 78711   800-888-0511
www.tded.state.tx.us   Fax: 512-936-0400

Provides business counseling for both new and established firms. Helps firms locate capital, state procurement opportunities, state certification programs for minority and women-owned businesses, and resources management and technical assistance. An Office of Business Permit Assistance serves as a clearinghouse for permit-related information throughout the state and refers applicants to appropriate agencies for permit and regulatory needs. Publications are available containing information and resources for start-up and existing businesses. Also has a program for corporate expansion and recruitment.

Office of Small Business Assistance: Charged with helping the state's small businesses become more globally competitive. The Office provides information and assistance to establish, operate and expand small and historically underutilized businesses (HUBS). In addition, the Office is charged with being the focal point for comments, suggestions and information regarding HUBS and small businesses to develop and suggest proposals for changes in state and federal policies in response to this information.

Economic Development Clearinghouse: A one-stop center for information about economic development programs and technical assistance offered by state and federal agencies, local governments and other organizations. The clearinghouse's website is {www.edinfo.state.tx.us}.

Office of Defense Affairs: Develops pro-active statewide strategy to prevent future defense closures and realignments and assist defense-dependent communities to prepare for future base realignments or closures.

Linked Deposit Program: Established to encourage lending to historically underutilized businesses, child-care providers, non-profit corporations, and/or small businesses located in distressed communities by providing lenders and borrowers a lower cost of capital. Minimum loan amount is $10,000; maximum loan amount is $250,000, fixed borrower loan rate.

Small Business Industrial Revenue Bond Program: Designed to provide tax-exempt financing to finance land and depreciable property for eligible industrial or manufacturing projects. The Development Corporation Act allows cities, counties, conservation and reclamation districts to form non-profit industrial development corporations or authorities on their behalf. Program objective is to issue taxable and tax-exempt bonds for eligible projects in cities, counties, conservation and reclamation districts. The industrial development corporation acts as a conduit through which all monies are channeled. Generally, all debt services on the bonds are paid by the business under the terms of a lease, sale, or loan agreement. As such, it does not constitute a debt or obligation of the governmental unit, the industrial development corporation, or the State of Texas.

Capital Access Fund: Established to increase the availability of financing for businesses and nonprofit organizations that face barriers in accessing capital. Through the use of the Capital Access Fund, businesses that might otherwise fall outside the guidelines of conventional lending may still have the opportunity to receive financing. The essential element of the program is a reserve account established at the lending institution to act as a credit enhancement, inducing the financial institution to make a loan. Use of proceeds may include working capital or the purchase, construction, or lease of capital assets, including buildings and equipment used by the business. There is no minimum or maximum loan amount, only a maximum amount that the state will provide to the financial institution's reserve fund.

Leverage Fund: An economic development bank offering an added source of financing to communities that have passed the economic development sales tax. This program allows the community to make loans to local businesses for expansion or to recruit new industries.

Office of International Business (OIB) helps Texas companies expand their business worldwide. By providing a forum for international business exchange through international trade missions, trade shows, seminars and in-bound buyers missions, OIB gives Texas companies the opportunity to promote their products and services to international buyers and partners. OIB also helps to connect companies with counseling and training available through the International Small Business Development Centers and works with entities such as the U.S. Department of Commerce, the Japan External Trade Organization, the Texas consular corps and its counterparts in the Mexican border states to ensure that Texas business interests are represented abroad. The State of Texas office in Mexico City is an invaluable resource for facilitating business between Texas and Mexico. Programs include:
- Trade Missions and Trade Shows
- Export Counseling
- Partnerships
- Trade Lead Distribution
- Texas International Center
- Research Publications

State of Texas Mexico Office: Texas businesses and communities receive a variety of services in order to promote Texas tourism and exporting.

Enterprise Zone: This program encourages job creation and capital investment by providing tax incentives to businesses in economically distressed areas.

Defense Zone Program: This program provides tax incentives for businesses in adversely impacted defense-dependent communities.

Business Permit Office: A four-step program to starting a business in Texas.

Texas Marketplace: This is a free online tool that the State of Texas uses to facilitate electronic commerce, including government procurement and private-sector trade opportunities.

* Rural Development Authority
District Office
101 S. Main, Suite 102
Temple, TX 76501   254-742-9700
www.rurdev.usda.gov/tx   Fax: 254-942-9709

Business and Industrial Guaranteed Loans: Commercial loans guaranteed up to 90% for developing improving or financing business, industry and employment in rural areas of less than 50,000.

Business and Industry Direct Loan Program: The Business and Industry Direct Loan Program provides loans to public and entities and who cannot obtain credit from other sources.

Intermediary Relending Program Loans: This program provides assistance to finance business facilities and community development projects in rural areas. These funds are made to intermediaries that ultimately provide loans to recipients for business facilities and community development.

Rural Business Enterprise Grants: This program provides assistance to public and nonprofit corporations to finance and facilitate development of small and emerging private businesses located in rural areas.

Rural Economic Development Loan and Grant Program: Provides uses of loans and grants to promote rural economic development and job creation. These grants can only be made to Rural Utility Service.

Rural Business Opportunity Grants: This program provides grants for technical assistance for business development and economic development planning in rural areas.

* Texas Marketplace
Texas Department of Economic Development
Internet Services Group
P.O. Box 12728
Austin, TX 78711   512-936-0100
www.marketplace.state.tx.us

Offers businesses access to the internet including free web page, daily posting of all major procurement opportunities with the State of Texas, electronic bulletin board for posting information about commodities for sale or to buy, and other resources and government procurement opportunities.

* Business & Industry Data Center (BIDC)
P.O. Box 12728   512-936-2000
Austin, TX 78711   Fax: 512-936-0800
www.bidc.state.tx.us

Provides one-stop access to data, information, and analyses on the Texas economy.

* Texas Agricultural Extension Service
Texas Agricultural Extension Service
112 Jack K. Williams Administration Building   979-845-7808
College Station, TX 77843-7101   Fax: 979-845-9542
http://texasextension.tamu.edu

The Texas Agricultural Extension Service (TAEX) has long been a key element in The Texas A&M University System's effort to reach out to all Texans, from all backgrounds, in all areas of the state. The agency's programs serve all 254 Texas counties providing research-based information and education for agricultural producers, agribusinesses, consumers and families.

* Texas Engineering Extension Service (TEEX)
Texas A&M University
301 Tarrow
College Station, TX 77840   979-458-6800
http://teexweb.tamu.edu

As one of the largest providers of work force training in the nation, the Texas Engineering Extension Service is known for its innovative, customized programs and its hands-on and on-site training. Through a variety of delivery systems, tailored to fit customer needs, TEEX offers technical and vocational work force training, manufacturing and technical assistance and technology transfer services.

* Texas Manufacturing Assistance Center (TMAC)
Technology & Economic Development
Texas A&M University System
College Station, TX 77843-8000   409-862-1670
teex.cy-net.net/TMAC   800-625-4876
www.tmac.org

TMAC's mission is to improve the competitiveness of small Texas manufacturers by helping firms adopt state-of-the-art manufacturing technologies and techniques. TMAC offices are located throughout the region, providing a variety of services to small manufacturers

* Community Reinvestment Fund (CRF)

801 Nicollet Mall   612-338-3050
Suite 1700 West   800-475-3050
Minneapolis, MN 55402   Fax: 612-338-3236
www.crfusa.com/

CRF is a nonprofit organization that provides a secondary market for economic development loans. The fund buys loans from economic development organizations and uses them as collateral to sell bonds to private investors. It tailors each loan purchase to the needs of the client and has auxiliary services like loan servicing portfolio management and training.

* State Grants Team

P.O. Box 12428   512-463-8465
Austin, TX 78711   Fax: 512-936-2681
www.governor.state.tx.us/divisions/stategrants

The Grants Team provides: technical assistance and information about available federal, state and private grants, proposal writing support and review of applications and proposal writing training.

* Texas Business Incubator Association (TBIA)

9600 Long Point Road, Suite 150   713-932-7495, ext. 13
Houston, TX 77055   Fax: 713-932-7498

TBIA's mission is to advance the business incubator industry in Texas; to assist those communities and individuals seeking to open business incubators; to educate managers and operators of business incubators in methods of successfully growing small businesses; to educate those residents in business operations; to influence legislation favorable to small business incubators; and to assist the state of Texas and the United States in economic development and diversification.

* Texas Economic Development Council (TEDC)

1301 Nueces, Suite 101   512-480-8432
Austin, Texas 78701   Fax: 512-472-7907
www.texasedc.org

TEDC provides information, educational and legislative services to its 1,000 members. TEDC's objective is to expand existing industry, recruit new firms to the state and develop strategies that promote a positive business climate in Texas.

* Texas Rural Communities, Inc.

1524 South IH35, Suite 232   512-219-0468
Austin, TX 78704   Fax: 512-219-0416
www.texasrural.org

Texas Rural Communities, Inc. is a nonprofit organization serving rural Texas communities, individuals, groups and support organizations through rural economic development, educational, loan and grant programs.

* Texas Rural Development Council

Cheryl Hinckley, Executive Director
8140 Burnet Road
Suite 218   512-323-6515
Austin, TX 78757-7799   Fax: 512-323-6526
www.trdc.org

The Texas Rural Development Council matches the resources of the federal, state and local governments and the private sector - both profit and non-profit - with locally conceived and driven development strategies.

* Center for Rural Health Initiatives

Office or Rural Community Affairs
1700 N. Congress Suite 220
Austin, TX 78701
Mailing Address:
P.O. Box 12877   512-936-6701
Austin, TX 78711   800-544-2042
www.orca.state.tx.us   512-936-6776

As the Texas State Office of Rural Health, the Center for Rural Health Initiatives administers programs and services designed to ensure health and well-being in rural communities throughout the state. The Center: provides funding opportunities; serves as a rural information clearinghouse; administers scholarship and loan repayment programs for healthcare professionals; provides a comprehensive service for recruitment and retention of healthcare providers by local communities; assists communities with assessments of health care delivery and availability; develops impact statements and policy development in an advocacy role; collaborates and partners with other state agencies and professional organizations and participates in national leadership roles.

* Certified Development Companies

Ark-Tex Regional Development Company, Inc.
James C. Fisher, Jr.
122 Plaza West
Texarkana, TX 75501
Mailing Address:
P. O. Box 5307   903-832-8636
Texarkana, TX 75505-5307   Fax: 903-832-2672
Area Of Operation: Bowie, Cass, Delta, Franklin, Hopkins, Red River, Lamar, Morris and Titus Counties in Texas; also Miller County in Arkansas

Central Texas Certified Development Company
Bruce Gaines, VP of Operations
1103 Airline Drive
P.O. Box 154118   817-799-0259
Waco TX 76715   Fax: 817-799-0294
Area of Operation: Bell, Bosque, Coryell, Falls, Hamilton, Hill, Freestone, Limestone, McLennan, and Milam Counties

Dallas Business Finance Corporation
Charles English, Executive V.P.
1402 Corinth St., Suite 1150   214-428-7332
Dallas TX 75215   Fax: 214-426-6847
Area of Operation: Dallas County

East Texas Regional Development Company, Inc.
Kent Bryson
3800 Stone Road   903-984-8641
Kilgore TX 75662   Fax: 903-983-1440
Area of Operation: Anderson, Camp, Cherokee, Gregg, Harrison, Henderson, Marion, Panola, Rains, Rusk, Smith, Upshur, Van Zandt and Wood

Fort Worth Economic Development Corporation
Larry McNatt, Executive Director
100 East 15th Street, Suite 500
P.O. Box 136   817-336-6420
Fort Worth TX 76102   Fax: 817-335-4513
Area of Operation: Erath, Denton, Ellis, Hood, Kaufman, Palo, Pinto, Dallas, Tarrant, Wise, Parker and Johnson counties; Excluding the City of Dallas

Greater East Texas Certified Development Company
Judy Loden
P.O. Box 1129
Athens, Texas 75751   903-675-7403
Area of Operation: Anderson, Cherokee, Henderson, Kaufman, Shelby, Smith and Van Zandt Counties

North Texas Certified Development Corporation
Webb Cox, President
1101 East Plano Pkwy., Suite A   214-516-0514
Plano TX 75074   Fax: 214-424-7479
Area of Operation: Grayson, Ranes, Fannin, Hunt, Collin, Cooke and Rockwall Counties

Upper Rio Grande Development Company
Justin R. Ormsby, Executive Director
1100 North Stanton, Suite 610   915-533-0998
El Paso TX 79902   Fax: 915-532-9385
Area of Operation: El Paso, Hudspeth, Culberson, Jeff Davis, Presidio and Brewster Counties

Brownsville Local Development Company, Inc.
1150 East Adams, 1st Floor
P.O. Box 911   956-548-6150
Brownsville TX 78520   Fax: 956-548-6144
Area of Operation: Citywide Brownsville

Lower Rio Grande Valley Certified Development Corporation
Kenneth N. Jones, Jr., Executive Director
311 N. 15th Street   956-682-3481
McAllen TX 78501-4705   Fax: 956-631-4670
Area of Operation: Cameron, Hidalgo and Willacy Counties

Bryan-College Station Certified Development Company
Dennis H. Goehring, Representative
2908 Finfeather Road   409-775-3699
Bryan TX 77801   Fax: 409-775-4393
Area of Operation: Brazo County

Houston-Galveston Area Local Development Corporation
Jeff Sjostrom, Sen. Ec. Dev. Spec.
3555 Timmons Lane, Suite 500

P.O. Box 22777
Houston TX 77227
713-627-3200
Fax: 713-621-8129
Area of Operation: Austin, Brazoria, Chambers, Colorado, Fort Bend, Galveston, Harris, Liberty, Matagorda, Montgomery, Walker, Waller and Wharton Counties

Multi-County Small Business Finance Corporation
Amos M. Brown, Executive Director
3100 Timmons Lane, Suite 222
Houston TX 77027
713-840-8804
Area of Operation: Brazoria, Fort Bend, Galveston, Harris, Liberty, Montgomery and Waller Counties

Southeast Texas Economic Development Foundation
Wilson White, Executive Director
450 Bowie
P.O. Box 3150
409-838-6581
Beaumont TX 77704
Fax: 409-833-6718
Area of Operation: Jefferson and Orange Counties

Council Finance, Incorporated
Rick Womble, Ec. Dev. Specialist
909 North Judge Ely Boulevard
P.O. Box 3195
915-672-8544
Abilene TX 79604
Fax: 915-675-5214
Area of Operation: Brown, Callahan, Coleman, Comanche, Eastland, Fisher, Haskell, Jones, Kent, Knox, Mitchell, Nolan, Runnels, Scurry, Shackelford, Stephens, Stonewall, Taylor and Throckmorton Counties

Caprock Business Finance Corporation, Inc.
Tim Pierce, Director of Ec. Dev.
1323 58th Street
P.O. Box 3730
806-762-8721
Lubbock TX 79452-3730
Fax: 806-765-9544
Area of Operation: Baily, Cochran, Crosby, Dickens, Floyd, Garza, Hale, Hockley, King, Lamb, Lubbock, Lynn, Motley, Terry, Gaines, Dawson, Borden, Andrews, Martin, Howard, Winkler, Ector, Midland, Glasscock, Ward, Crane, Upton and Yoakum Counties

Texas Panhandle Regional Development Corporation
Doug Nelson
415 West Eighth Avenue
P.O. Box 9257
806-372-3381
Amarillo TX 79105-9257
Fax: 806-373-3268
Area of Operation: Armstrong, Briscoe, Carson, Castro, Childress,Collingsworth, Deaf Smith, Dallam, Donley, Gray, Hall, Hansford, Hutchinson, Hartley, Hemphill, Lipscomb, Moore, Ochiltree, Randall, Oldham, Parmer, Potter, Roberts, Sherman, Swisher and Wheeler Counties

Capital Certified Development Corporation
Craig Pinkley, Executive Director
Wild Basin One
512-327-9229
110 Wild Basin Road, Suite 270
800-504-2232
Austin, TX 78746
Fax: 512-327-9243
Area Of Operation: Atascosa, Bandera, Bee, Blanco, Burnet, Caldwell, Calhoun, Comal, Dimmit, Edwards, Fayette, Frio, Gillespie, Goliad, Hays, Jackson, Karnes, Kendall, Kinney, La Salle, Lampasas, Lavaca, Lee, Live Oak, Llano, Maverick, McMullen, Real, Refugio, Travis, Uvalde, Val Verde, Victoria and most other counties in Texas

Cen-Tex Certified Development Corporation
Rosa Rios Valdez, Executive Director
2212 South Congress Avenue
P.O. Box 220
Mail Stop L-108
512-912-9884
Austin TX 78703
Fax: 512-912-9869
Area of Operation: Austin, Bastrop, Bandera, Blanco, Brown, Burleson, Caldwell, Colorado, Comal, Concho, Coryell, DeWitt, Edwards, Fayette, Gillespie, Gonzales, Guadalupe, Hamilton, Hays, Kendall, Kerr, Kimble, Lampasas, Lavaca, Lee, Llano, Mason, Matagorda, McCulloch, Medina, Menard, Mills, Real, San Saba, Sutton, Travis, Uvalde, Waller, Washington, Wharton, Williamson, Wilson 43 Central Texas Counties

San Antonio Local Development Corporation
Michael Mendoza, Financial Specialist
215 South San Saba
P.O. Box 830505
210-207-3930
San Antonio TX 78283-0505
Fax: 210-207-3939
Area of Operation: Atascosa, Bandera, Bexar, Comal, Frio, Gillespie, Guadalupe, Karnes, Kendall, Kerr, Medina and Wilson Counties

Texas Certified Development Company, Inc.
Ernest Perales, President

7801 N. IH-35
P.O. Box 6479
800-486-8620
Austin TX 78762
Fax: 512-433-1821
Area of Operation: Aransas, Atascosa, Bandera, Bastrop, Bee, Bell, Bexar, Blanco, Brazoria, Brooks, Burleson, Burnet, Caldwell, Calhoun, Cameron, Comal, Concho, Crockett, Dallas, Denton, DeWitt, Dimmit, Duval, Edwards, Ellis, Fayette, Frio, Ft. Bend, Galveston, Gillespie, Goliad, Gonzales, Grayson, Guadalupe, Hardin, Harris, Hays, Hidalgo, Irion, Jackson, Jefferson, Jim Hogg, Jim Wells, Johnson, Karnes, Kendall, Kenedy, Kerr, Kimble, Kinney, Kleberg, LaSalle, Lampasas, Lavaca, Lee, Liberty, Live Oak, Llano, Mason, Maverick, McCulloch, McLennan, McMullen, Medina, Menard, Montgomery, Nueces, Orange, Parker, Real, Refugio, San Patricio, San Saba, Schleicher, Smith, Starr, Sutton, Tarrant, Tom Green, Travis, Uvalde, Val Verde, Victoria, Walker, Waller, Webb, Wichita, Willacy, Williamson, Wilson, Wise, Zapata, Zavala Counties

The 504 Certified Development Company (CDC) Program provides growing businesses with long-term, fixed-rate financing for major fixed assets, such as land and buildings. A Certified Development Company is a nonprofit corporation set up to contribute to the economic development of its community or region. CDCs work with the SBA and private-sector lenders to provide financing to small businesses.

* Texas Agriculture Finance Authority (TAFA)

Department of Agriculture
P.O. Box 12847
512-463-7476
Austin, TX 78711
Fax: 512-463-1104
www.agr.state.tx.us/eco/finance_ag_development
Linked Deposit Program
512-463-1104
Available for non-traditional alternative crops, processing facilities for agricultural products, and direct marketing initiatives. Funds can be used to purchase or least land, buildings, equipment, seed, fertilizer, etc. Maximum loan is $100,000 for production, $250,000 for processing and marketing.

Texas Agricultural Finance Authority (TAFA
Loans, loan guarantees or revenue bonds available to small and medium size enterprises that contribute to the diversification of Texas agriculture. Funds can be used for fixed assets and working capital.

Young Farmer Loan Guarantee Program: TAFA provides financial assistance through loan guarantees to eligible applicants from 18 to 39 years of age who wish to establish or enhance their farm and/or ranch operation or establish an agricultural-related business. The program provides up to a 90 percent guarantee to a lender for an eligible applicant, not to exceed $250,000.

* Small Business Administration (SBA)

4300 Amon Carter Blvd.
817-684-5500
Dallas/Fort Worth, TX 76155
Fax: 817-684-5516

10737 Gateway West
915-633-7001
El Paso, TX 79935
Fax: 915-633-7005

222 East Van Buren Street, Suite 500
Harlingen, TX 78550
956-427-8533

8701 S. Gessner Dr., Suite 1200
713-773-6500
Houston, TX 77074-1591
Fax: 713-773-6550

1205 Texas Avenue, Room 408
806-472-7462
Lubbock, TX. 79401-2693
Fax: 806-472-4787

17319 San Pedro, Suite 200
210-403-5900
San Antonio, TX 78232-1411
Fax: 210-403-5933

3649 Leopard Street, Suite 411
Corpus Christi, TX 78408
361-879-0017
www.sba.gov/tx
The Texas Small Business Administration Office delivers a variety of programs and services, such as startup and operational assistance through small business training and counseling, financial assistance for startup's, business opportunities and much more.

* Small Business Investment Companies

Alliance Enterprise Corporation
Donald R. Lawhorne, President
2435 North Central Expressway, Suite 200
972-991-1597
Richardson, TX 75080
Fax: 972-991-1647
Email: info@pacesettercapital.com

AMT Capital, Ltd.
Tom H. Delimitros, CGP
5220 Spring Valley Road, Suite 600   214-905-9760
Dallas, TX 75240   Fax: 214-905-9761
Email: TDeliAMT@aol.com

BA Capital Company, L.P.
Doug Williamson, Sr. Vice President
901 Main Street, 22nd Floor   214-508-0900
Dallas, TX 75202   Fax: 214-508-0985

Banc One Capital Partners LLC
Suzanne B. Kriscunas, Managing Director
300 Crescent Court, Suite 1600   214-979-4360
Dallas, TX 75201   Fax: 214-979-4355

Blue Sage Capital, L.P.
Pat M. Baskin, Jr., Contact
114 West 7th Street, Suite 820   512-536-1900
Austin, TX 78701   Fax: 512-236-9215
Email: bo.baskin@lbjhc.com

Capital Southwest Venture Corporation
William R. Thomas, President
12900 Preston Rd., Suite 700   214-233-8242
Dallas, TX 75230   Fax: 214-233-7362
Email: skhodgson@capitalsouthwest.com

Catalyst Fund, Ltd.
Richard L. Herrman, Manager
Two Riverway, Suite 1710   713-623-8133
Houston, TX 77056   Fax: 713-623-0473
Email: gillioz@thecatalystgroup.net

Chen's Financial Group, Inc.
Samuel S. C. Chen, President
10101 SW Freeway, Suite 370   713-772-8868
Houston, TX 77074   Fax: 713-772-2168
Email: chens8868@aol.com

First Capital Group of Texas II, L.P.
Messrs. Blanchard, Greenwood, & Locy
750 East Mulberry, Suite 305   210-736-4233
San Antonio, TX 78212   Fax: 210-736-5449
Email: jpb@texas.net

First Capital Group of Texas II, L.P.
Wm. Ward Greenwood
100 Congress Avenue, Suite 730   512-494-9754
Austin, TX 78701   Fax: 512-494-9756

First Capital Group of Texas III, L.P.
Jeffrey P. Blanchard, Contact
750 E. Mulberry, Suite 305   210-736-4233
San Antonio, TX 78212   Fax: 210-736-5449
Email: jpblanchard@firstcapitalgroup.com

HCT Capital Corp.
Vichy Woodward Young, Jr., President
4916 Camp Bowie Blvd, Suite 200   817-763-8706
Fort Worth, TX 76107   Fax: 817-377-8049
Email: VWYoung@email.msn.com

Independent Bankers Capital Fund, L.P.
Floyd Collins, Barry Conrad, Contacts
1700 Pacific Avenue, Suite 2740   214-765-1350
Dallas, TX 75201   Fax: 214-765-1360
Email: mtaylor@independentbankerscap.com

Jardine Capital Corp.
Lawrence Wong, President
6638 Sharpstown Green Circle, Suite 787   713-271-7077
Houston, TX 77036   Fax: 713-271-7577
Email: jardinecapital@hotmail.com

Main Street Mezzanine Fund, L.P.
Todd A. Reppert, Contact
1300 Post Oak Blvd., Suite 800   713-350-6029
Houston, TX 77056   Fax: 713-350-6042
Email: treppert@mainstreethouston.com

MESBIC Ventures, Inc.
Donald R. Lawhorne, President

2435 North Central Expressway, Suite 200   972-991-1597
Richardson, TX 75080   Fax: 972-991-1647
Email: carolc@mvhc.com

North Texas MESBIC, Inc.
Allan Lee, President
9500 Forest Lane, Suite 430   214-221-3565
Dallas, TX 75243   Fax: 214-221-3566
Email: NTM168@aol.com

PMC Investment Corporation
Andrew S. Rosemore, President
18111 Preston Road, Suite 600   972-349-3200
Dallas, TX 75252   Fax: 972-349-3265
Email: barryb@pmccapital.com

Power Equities, Inc.
Donald Lawhorne and Thomas Gerron
2435 North Central Expressway, Suite 200   972-991-1597
Richardson, TX 75080   Fax: 972-991-4770
Email: info@mvhc.com

Red River Ventures I, L.P.
J. Bruce Duty, Contact
15301 Dallas Parkway, Suite 820   972-687-7770
Addison, TX 75001   Fax: 972-687-7760
Email: bruce@redriverventures.com

Retail & Restaurant Growth Capital, L.P.
Raymond Hemmig, Joseph Harberg, Mgrs.
10000 N. Central Expressway
Suite 1060   214-750-0065
Dallas, TX 75231   Fax: 214-750-0060
Email: jharberg@rrgcsbic.com

SBIC Partners, LP
Gregory Forrest & Jeffrey Brown, Manager
201 Main St., 27th Floor   949-222-1987
Fort Worth, TX 76102   Fax: 949-222-1988
Email: joe@fbbvc.com

Southwest/Catalyst Capital, Ltd.
Ronald Nixon and Rick Herrman, Mgrs.
Two Riverway, Suite 1710   713-623-8133
Houston, TX 77056   Fax: 713-623-0473
Email: gillioz@thecatalystgroup.net

Stratford Capital Partners, LP
Michael D. Brown/John Farmer
300 Crescent Court, Suite 500   214-740-7377
Dallas, TX 75201   Fax: 214-740-7393
Email: shenegar@hmtf.com

Stratford Equity Partners, L.P.
Michael Brown, Manager
200 Crescent Court, Suite 1600   214-740-7377
Dallas, TX 75201   Fax: 214-740-7393
Email: shenegar@hmtf.com

Toronto Dominion Capital (U.S.A.), Inc.
Martha L. Gariepy, VP/Secretary/Treas.
909 Fannin, Suite 1700   713-652-8225
Houston, TX 77010   Fax: 713-652-2647

Trident Growth Fund, L.P.
Larry St. Martin, Contact
700 Gemini, Suite 100   281-488-8484
Houston, TX 77058   Fax: 281-488-8404
Email: larry@tridentgrowthfund.com

Victoria Capital Corp.
Steve Selinske, Acting President
c/o Norwest Bank Texas, N.A.
16416 San Pedro   210-856-8804
San Antonio, TX 78232   Fax: 210-856-8848

Western Financial Capital Corporation
Andrew S. Rosemore, President
18111 Preston Rd., Suite 600   972-349-3200
Dallas, TX 75252   Fax: 972-349-3265
Email: barryb@pmccapital.com

The Small Business Administration (SBA) licenses, regulates, and provides financial assistance to privately owned and operated Small Business Investment Companies. SBICs make venture or risk investments by supplying capital and extending unsecured loans and loans not fully collateralized to small enterprises which meet their investment criteria. Financing is made by direct loans and by equity investments.

Utah

* Business and Economic Development Division

324 South State St., Suite 500   801-538-8700
Salt Lake City, UT 84111   Fax: 801-538-8889
http://dced.utah.gov

Business and Economic Development Division: Provides information on regulations, sources of assistance, and other important information for starting a business.

Short Term Intensive Training (STIT): Programs are customized and designed to meet full-time job openings. Programs are usually less than one year in length and will be designed to meet the specific training needs of a company while matching needs with people seeking employment. Although potential employees must pay tuition to participate, STIT can provide qualified employees from which a company can hire. STIT gives the option of training at 50% - 70% discount of normal training costs. Funding for this program is distributed to State Colleges.

Job Service: A computerized job matching system that quickly screens applicants to ensure that they meet the qualifications set by a company. Over 16,000 active applicants are presently registered with the Salt Lake Office. Job Service personnel can save countless hours by taking all of company applications and then referring only the most qualified applicants.

Centers of Excellence Program: Supports selected research programs at Utah's universities. Programs are selected based on leading edge research activities that have projected commercial value. The primary objective is to encourage the commercialization of leading edge technologies through licensing patented technologies and by creating new companies. The Centers of Excellence Program impacts Utah's economic development by the creation of jobs, the flow of licensing royalties, the expansion of the tax base, and the leveraged use of matching fund dollars to strengthen research and development at Utah's institutions of higher learning.

Utah Directory of Business and Industry: A listing of more than 9,800 individual employers sorted by Standard Industrial Classification (SIC), which is a standard method for classifying what businesses or other organizations do.

Revolving Loan Funds: In an effort to create jobs and improve the business climate of a community, some cities, counties, and Associations of Governments (geographical regions) will lend money to small businesses located in their areas. The amount available to a business goes from a few thousand dollars to over $100,000. Typically, the money is used for plant and equipment, working capital, inventory or accounts receivable financing. Rates are usually less than or equal to conventional lender financing, and the term for repayment may be either short (6 months) or extended (many years). This type of financing is often used in conjunction with other lender financing since most revolving loan programs will accept a second or third position on financed assets.

Industrial Assistance Fund: Can be used for relocation costs. This incentive loan can be repaid as Utah jobs created meet the IAF requirements resulting in higher quality jobs, and as Utah purchases merit enough earned credits to convert the loan to a grant. Three basic programs exist: 1) rural Utah program with funding up to $100,000 for relocation expenses; 2) Corporate Funding which is dependent on the amount of Utah purchases and wages: 3) Targeted Industries which is primarily aimed at information technology, biomedical and aerospace.

Industrial Development Bonds (IDB's): A financing tool used by private sector developers for manufacturing facilities. The federal tax code places a limit of $10.0 million per project on IDB financing.

International Business Development Office: Programs offered include:
- Trade Representatives
- Country Information
- Market Research Reports
- Trade Lead Resource Center
- Foreign Business Directories
- Trade Shows and Exhibits

Offices of Ethnic Affairs: Recognizing that state government should be responsive to all citizens, and wishing to promote cooperation and understanding between government agencies and its ethnic citizens, these offices were created:
- Office Of Asian Affairs
- Office Of Black Affairs
- Office Of Hispanic Affairs
- Office Of Pacific Island Affairs
- Division of Indian Affairs

Minority and Women Owned Business Source Directory: Offered by the Utah PTAC (Procurement Technical Assistance Center). The directory includes approximately 850 companies, and is the most complete such listing available. However, listings are voluntary, having been obtained through surveys, and this is not to be construed as a comprehensive catalog. There are some 4,400 minority-owned employers in the state, and 46,000 that are women-owned.

Utah Technology Alliance: The Utah Technology Alliance acts as a bridge between the high tech business community and Utah State Government. Its goal is to position Utah as the location of choice to grow and nurture high tech companies.

* Custom Fit Training

Utah College of Applied Technology Central Administration
Board of Regents Building, The Gateway
60 South 400 West   801-321-7183
Salt Lake City, UT 84101-1284   Fax: 801-366-8480
www.ucats.org/aboutcustomfit.html

Provides training for new or expanding companies. A Custom Fit representative will discuss with the company the training needs anticipated and then develop a specific customized training plan to meet those needs. The required training can take place at a variety of locations including the business or a local institution. Often training is provided in both locations. The program can provide instructors from the State's learning institutions, private sector, consultants or instructors within the business. The program is designed to be flexible to meet the specific needs of the company.

* Utah Partners in Education

324 South State St., Suite 500   801-538-8628
Salt Lake City, UT 84111   Fax: 801-538-8888
www.utahpartnership.utah.org

Facilitates business/ education/ government partnerships statewide. Purpose is to find ways in which those three entities can work together to meet common needs and thereby strengthen the economy of Utah.

* Utah Ventures

2755 E. Cottonwood Parkway, Suite 520   801-365-0262
Salt Lake City, UT 84121   Fax: 801-365-0233
www.utahventures.com/

Utah Ventures: a privately financed venture fund focusing on investments in the life sciences and information technology in Utah, other Intermountain states and California. Utah Ventures seeks to identify the best opportunities, secure subsequent coinvestments from other venture funds and corporate investors, and works with the entrepreneur to help build the business.

* Utah Microenterprise Loan Fund

3595 S. Main St.
Salt Lake City, UT 84115   801-269-8408
www.umlf.com   Fax: 801-269-1063

Microenterprise Loan Fund (UMLF) is a tax-exempt, nonprofit corporation. It provides a modestly secured form of financing up to $10,000, with terms up to five years, to owners of startup and existing firms who do not have access to traditional funding sources, especially those who are socially or economically disadvantaged. The interest rate is prime plus 3% fixed, and the business must be located in Salt Lake County.

* Utah Technology Finance Corporation (UTFC)

699 East South Temple, Suite 220   801-741-4200
Salt Lake City, UT 84102   Fax: 801-741-4249
www.utfc.org

The Utah Technology Finance Corporation is an independent corporation of the state that makes debt investments in Utah companies. UTFC leverages state and federal funds as a catalyst in capital formation for the creations, growth, and success of Utah Businesses. UTFC offers various types of debt financing through such programs as Early Technology Business Capital, Utah Rural Loan Program, MicroLoan Program, Utah Revolving Loan Fund, Bank Participation Loan Program, and Defense Conversion Loan Program.

* State Tax Commission

210 North 1950 West   800-662-4335

Salt Lake City, UT 84134
801-297-2200
www.incometax.utah.gov
Fax: 801-297-7574

One-Stop Service Center: You can register a business name, file Articles of Incorporation, obtain application for State Sales Tax License and State and Federal Tax Identification Numbers, file a Status Report with the Department of Employment Security, and apply for State Workers' Compensation Insurance. A *Going Into Business Workbook* is also available which includes all the forms and instructions necessary to do any of these activities.

* Mountain West Venture Group (MWVG)

c/o John M. Knab
6952 South High Tech Drive, Suite A
801-984-5103
Midvale, UT 84047-3756
Fax: 801-566-0880
www.mwvgutah100.org

The Mountain West Venture Group is a nonprofit organization that identifies, monitors, and recognizes "deal flow" within the state of Utah. Through the exchange of ideas, services, and acquaintances, the Group seeks to foster the investment of risk funds. Along with a monthly meeting, a monthly newsletter, and the Utah Deal Flow book, the MWVG hosts an annual awards luncheon that identifies and recognizes Utah's 100 fastest growing companies.

* Utah Information Technologies Association (UITA)

2825 E. Cottonwood Parkway, Suite 460
801-568-3500
Salt Lake City, UT 84121
Fax: 801-568-1072
www.uita.org

UITA is an industry association that represents and provides services to Utah's Information Technology (IT) vendors. UITA assists IT vendors with networking, opportunities to learn and market, saving money through group discounts, and other means.

* Utah Small Cities, Inc.

324 South State Street
Suite 500
801-538-8821
Salt Lake City, UT 84111
Fax: 801-538-8889
http://utahreach.usu.edu/rosie/usci

Aids in the recruitment and expansion of businesses in the rural areas of Utah. Responds to requests for information.

* Utah Supplier Development Council

U of U Purchasing Department
151 Annex Building
801-581-8169
Salt Lake City, UT, 84112
Fax: 801-581-8609
www.usdcutah.com

A purchasing council made up of major Utah firms that specifically look for small businesses owned by minorities and women to be suppliers for the Council. The Council also prints a directory of these businesses.

* Business Information Center

310 South Main Street, North Mezzanine
801-746-2269
Salt Lake City, UT 84101
Fax: 801-746-2273
www.utahbic.org

The Business Information Center (BIC) is a library of electronic and hard copy resources available to existing businesses and individuals seeking information on starting a business. The center provides SCORE counseling, training, and access to computers, business software, and video tapes.

* Utah Business Resource Network (UBRN)

SBDC State Director Michael C. Finnerty
1623 South State Street
801-957-3480
Salt Lake City, UT 84115
888-599-UBRN
www.utah.gov/business

The Small Business Development Center is in partnership with the Utah Business Resource Network. The UBRN provides experts in many fields, including finance, marketing, engineering, manufacturing, contracting, and minority owned businesses. The statewide network makes it easy to put together the team, information and resources that will make your business grow.

* Bureau of Economic and Business Research

David Eccles School of Business
University of Utah
1645 E. Campus Center Drive, Room 401
801-581-6333
Salt Lake City, UT 84112-9302
Fax: 801-581-3354

www.business.utah.edu/BEBR

Maintains a comprehensive and timely information base on the Utah and Rocky Mountain regional economies and uses computer models for data analysis. Periodicals include: Utah Economic and Business Review, featuring articles on economic development with monthly selected business statistics; Utah Construction Report reporting statistics on construction permits in Utah; Utah Statistical Abstract

* Business Workshops

Taxpayer Education Coordinator
Internal Revenue Service
50 South 200 East
801-799-6874
Salt Lake City UT 84111
800-829-1040
http://tax.utah.gov/business/resources.html

The Utah State Tax Commission, Internal Revenue Service, State Industrial Commission, Worker's Compensation, and the Utah Department of Employment Security jointly sponsor a one day Employment Tax Workshop to provide information and answer questions about employment and other tax requirements for businesses. The seminars are free and scheduled monthly in Salt Lake City. During the summer months, the workshops are available in Ogden, Provo, and St. George. Other specialized education programs are available for partnerships and corporations through the IRS Small Business Tax Education Program (STEP).

* Small Business Administration (SBA)

Salt Lake District Office
125 South State St., Room 2227
801-524-3209
Salt Lake City, UT 84138-1195
Fax: 801-524-4160
www.sba.gov/ut

The Utah Small Business Administration Office delivers a variety of programs and services, such as startup and operational assistance through small business training and counseling, financial assistance for startup's, business opportunities and much more.

* Small Business Investment Companies

First Security Business Investment Corp.
Greg Vidrine, Manager
405 S. Main St.
801-246-1047
Salt Lake City, UT 84111
Fax: 801-246-1545
Email: gvidrin@fscnet.com

Utah Ventures II L.P.
Alan Dishlip & James Dreyfous, Mgrs.
2755 E. Cottonwood Parkway, Suite 520
801-583-5922
Salt Lake City, UT 84121
Fax: 801-583-4105
Email: jdreyfous@uven.com

UTFC Financing Solutions, LLC
Steve Grizzell, Contact
699 East South Temple, Suite 220
801-741-4215
Salt Lake City, UT 84102
Fax: 801-741-4249
Email: sgrizzell@utfc.org

vSpring SBIC, L.P.
Greg Warnock, Contact
2795 E. Cottonwood Parkway, Suite 360
801-942-8999
Salt Lake City, UT 84121
Fax: 801-942-1636
Email: David@vspring.com

Wasatch Venture Corp.
Todd J. Stevens, Secretary
1 S. Main St., Suite 1400
801-524-8939
Salt Lake City, UT 84133
Fax: 801-524-8941
Email: tstevens@wasatchvc.com

Wasatch Venture Fund II, LLC
Todd Stevens, Manager
1 South Main Street Suite 1400
801-524-8936
Salt Lake City, UT 84133
Fax: 801-524-8941
Email: tstevens@wasatchvc.com

Zions SBIC, L.L.C.
Todd J. Stevens, Contact
One South Main Street, Suite 1660
'801-524-8939
Salt Lake City, UT 84133
Fax: 801-524-8941
Email: tstevens@wasatchvc.com

The SBA licenses, regulates, and provides financial assistance to privately owned and operated Small Business Investment Companies. SBIC's make venture or risk investments by supplying capital and extending unsecured loans and loans not fully collateralized to small enterprises which meet their investment criteria. Financing is made by direct loans and by equity investments.

* Industrial Assistance Fund

324 S. State St., Suite 500   801-538-8698
Salt Lake City, UT 84111   Fax: 801-538-8888
http://dced.utah.gov/iaf/index.html

The Industrial Assistance Fund's mission is to expand the number of high paying jobs and increase in-state purchase of supplies.

* Small Business Assistance Program

Department of Environmental Quality
168 N. 1950 West   800-270-4440
P.O. Box 144810-4810   801-536-4400
Salt Lake City, UT 84116   Fax: 801-536-4401
http://airquality.utah.gov/PERMITS/psba.htm

The Clean Air Act Amendments of 1990 required that all States develop a program to assist small businesses in meeting the requirements of the Act. Since then, these programs have expanded to provide assistance in other environmental areas, including water and waste issues. EPA has established its own Small Business Assistance Program (SBAP) to provide technical assistance to these State small business programs.

* Utah Energy Office

Utah Energy Office
1594 West North Temple, Suite 3610
P.O. Box 146480   801-538-5428
Salt Lake City, UT 84114-6480   800-662-3633

The Utah Energy Office promotes energy efficiency in Utah. They provide businesses with information, research, technical assistance, energy-related policy analysis and access to federal or state programs.

* Venture Capital Programs

Wayne Brown Institute
175 West 200 South, Suite 4002
P.O. Box 2135   801-595-1411
Salt Lake City, UT 84110-2135   Fax: 801-595-1181
www.venturecapital.org

The institute seeks to assist worthy early-state technology based companies raise capital, form partnerships, and strategic alliances for the purpose of creating new wealth, jobs, and tax base.

* Rural Development Office

Wallace F. Bennett federal Building
125 South State Street, Room 4311   801-524-4320
Salt Lake City, UT 84138   Fax: 801-524-4406
www.rurdev.usda.gov/ut

Business & Industry Loan Guaranteed Loan Program: The Guaranteed Business and Industry loan program guarantee loans to quality businesses that support a diversified economic base and provide or save quality jobs in rural areas.

Intermediary Relending Program: Lenders utilize these funds to obtain low interest capital to make loans up to $250,000 to rural businesses.

Rural Economic Development Loan and Grant Program: his program provides loan to utility companies to promote rural economic development and job creation.

Rural Business Enterprise Grant Program: Funds may be used by rural public bodies, private non-profit organizations and federally recognized Native American tribes to provide technical assistance to small and emerging businesses, purchase machinery or equipment, construct business incubators or buildings that will be leased to small and emerging businesses.

Rural Business Opportunity Grant: These grants may be used by rural public bodies, non-profit organizations, cooperatives, and federally recognized Native American tribes to promote economic growth in depressed rural areas.

Value-Added Agricultural Producer Grant Program: These grant funds may be used by eligible producers of agricultural commodities, agricultural producer groups, farmer and rancher cooperatives, and majority-owned producer-based business ventures to plan or implement sales of agricultural products into emerging markets.

Rural Cooperative Development Grants: Rural Cooperative Development Grant funds may be used by selected non-profit corporations or institutions

of higher education to establish and operate centers for rural cooperative development which will facilitate the development of new cooperative, value-added processing and rural businesses that create or retain jobs in rural areas.

Rural Energy Systems & Energy Efficiency Improvements Program: Agricultural producers and small rural businesses with financial need can use these program to obtain matching grant funding up to $500,000 to purchase alternative energy systems or up to $250,000 to make energy efficiency improvements.

* Certified Development Companies

Deseret Certified Development Company
2595 East 3300 South
Salt Lake City, UT 84109   801-474-3232
Email: scott@deseretcdc.com   Fax: 801-493-0111
Area of Operation: Box Elder, Davis, Morgan, and Weber Counties

Northern Utah Capital, Inc.
2404 Washington Boulevard, Suite 1000
Ogden, UT 84401   801-627-1333
Email: rrichards@nucdc.com
Area of Operation: Statewide Utah

Certified Development Companies are private companies licensed by the SBA to provide long-term financing to expanding businesses. The SBA 504 loans provide long-term fixed-asset financing with a maximum SBA share of $750,000 or 40% of the project cost. At least 10% must be provided by the borrowers, and the remaining provided by a bank or other lender.

Vermont

* Vermont Department of Economic Development

National Life Building, Drawer 20   802-828-3080
Montpelier, VT 05620-0501   800-341-2211
www.thinkvermont.com   Fax: 802-828-3258

A one-stop shop ready to help with businesses to support the economic growth of the state through job creation and retention. Areas in which the Department can assist Vermont businesses are entrepreneurs; international trade; financing; government contracts, marketing; permits; site location; and training.

Regional Development Corporations: Twelve RDCs serve every geographic region of the state serving as satellites of the Department of Economic Development, and provide many of the same services. Their primary function is to coordinate job and business development activities within their geographic region.

Business Assistance Network: An accessible series of resources designed to provide timely and pertinent information to businesses interested in participating in new markets for their products or services, increasing competitiveness, or building "teaming arrangements" with other businesses. The information may be accessed through the Internet at {www.state.vt.us}.

Government Marketing Assistance Center: Exists to design, implement, and maintain resources that promote economic expansion by providing assistance to Vermont businesses' which allow them to pursue and compete in the public procurement process and introduce them to new markets for their goods and/or services. The GMAC can provide a business with a customized search to receive Federal bid opportunities, including bids available through Electronic Data Interchange (EDI). A business must be registered to receive Federal Bids opportunities.

Vermont Business Registry: An on-line registry of businesses throughout Vermont involved in manufacturing, manufacturing support, product distribution, services, research and development, and construction. {www.vermontbusinessregistry.com}

Vermont Bid Opportunities: An electronic resource which provides businesses with a current listing of bid opportunities available through Vermont based federal, state and local governments and by the private sector purchasing organizations. {www.vermontbidsystem.com}

Business Calendar of Events: Lists business assistance seminars, training workshops, trade shows, etc., which are sponsored by various organizations.

The Vermonter's Guide to Doing Business: Provides information relating to public and private institutions that can assist local businesses on any aspect of successful business operation.

Department of Employment and Training: Offers a full range of workforce-related services and information through a network of 12 One-Stop Career Resource Centers. Contact {www.det.state.vt.us).

Regional/Local Revolving Loan Funds: Existing through the state, the administration of these funds is generally a non-profit development corporation.

Business and Industrial Loan Guarantees: Designed to serve the credit needs of large rural businesses. Emphasis is placed on loan guarantees between $500,000 and $3 million, but may be issued up to $10 million.

Business and Industry Direct Loans: A limited amount of funding is available for direct business loans in designated areas of economic distress. The program is targeting loans in the $100,000 to $250,000 range.

Intermediary Relending Program: Designed to finance small and emerging business and community development projects in rural areas. Loans are made to qualified intermediaries who in turn relend to small businesses and community development organizations. Business or organizations borrowing from the intermediary must be located in a rural area. The maximum loan to an intermediary is $2 million and the maximum loan that the intermediary can relend for a project is $150,000.

Rural Business Enterprise Grant: Provides grants to public bodies and non-profit corporations for the benefit of small and emerging businesses. Grant funds may be used to establish revolving loan funds, construct facilities, provide planning, or technical assistance.

VEDA Export Financing: In addition to the Export Working Capital Guarantee Program, VEDA offers a number of other loan and insurance programs for Vermont's exporting community. This includes small business credit insurance, and environmental exports program, and export credit insurance short-term multi-buyer policy, and a medium-term single-buyer policy.

Vermont Training Program: The Vermont Training Program promotes industrial expansion and encourages the creation and retention of jobs by providing training for new and existing businesses.

Reach Up Program: This is Vermont's welfare-to-work program which helps welfare recipients access education, vocational training and job placement.

Micro Business Development Program: The Micro Business Development Program promotes self-employment and business opportunities for low income Vermonters. They offer free one-on-one technical assistance, business planning classes, workshops and assistance.

Workplace Literacy and Youth Apprenticeship: Programs provide businesses with the opportunity to update the basic skills of their workforce and to enable vocational/technical students the opportunity to gain work experience.

Women's Small Business Program: Women's Small Business Program through Trinity College offers several services including:
- Getting Serious- A workshop to determine a business idea and whether a business meets personal goals.
- Start-Up: A 15 week intensive course to develop a business plan.
- Working Solutions: Topic specific workshops for micro-business owners.

Vermont Businesses for Social Responsibility: "The Livable Jobs Toolkit" is a hands-on tool for businesses interested in attracting and keeping employees. It features innovative ways to compensate employees and implement workplace practices in businesses.

Direct Loans: VEDA can provide direct loans to eligible facilities for the acquisition of land, buildings and improvements, machinery and equipment.

Financial Access Program: The Vermont Financial Access Program utilizes a "pooled reserve" concept to enhance opportunities for small businesses to access commercial credit.

Small Business Development Corporation: The Vermont Small Business Development Corporation makes loans to low to moderate Vermont business owners.

Industrial Revenue Bonds (IRBs): VEDA issues bonds to businesses eligible for tax-exempt financing. Funds can be used for the acquisition of land, buildings and improvements, or machinery and equipment.

Rural Economic Activity Loans (REAL): REAL provides low interest direct loans for fixed asset financing and for funding inventory and accounts receivable growth through the REAL program. Loan amounts of up to 75% of the fixed projects costs which are under $25,000 and up to 40% of projects which are over $25,000.

Vermont Agricultural Credit Corporation: VEDA provides loans and refinancing for family farms or agricultural facility operators.

Vermont Job Start: Job Start helps develop self-employment opportunities for low and moderate income Vermonters. Loans can be used to start, strengthen or expand small businesses.

* Women's Small Business Program

Trinity College
208 Colchester Ave.
Burlington, VT 05401
www.trinityvt.edu/WSBP.htm   802-846-7339

Offers a continuum of services to women seeking to identify, start, stabilize and expand a small business. Services include: Getting Serious, a workshop to determine a business idea and whether business meets personal goals; Start-Up, a 15 week intensive course to develop a business plan and business management skills; Working Solution, topic specific workshops for micro-business owner; and a graduate association to foster ongoing networking and access to information. They also offer comprehensive skills training and the opportunity to connect with other women entrepreneurs. Grants and scholarships for training are available to income eligible women.

* Vermont Manufacturing Extension Center

VT Technical College
P.O. Box 12   800-MEP-4MFG
Randolph Center, VT 05061-0500   802-728-1432
www.vmec.org   Fax: 802-728-1456

Provides one-on-one support and services through Field Engineers to small and mid-sized manufacturers. Their goal is to assist Vermont manufacturers increase productivity, modernize processes, and improve their competitiveness. Ongoing training opportunities designed specifically for manufacturers are also offered.

* Agricultural Marketing

Department of Agriculture
Development Division
116 State St., Drawer 20   802-828-2416
Montpelier, VT 05620   Fax: 802-828-3831
www.vermontagriculture.com/develop.htm

Provides resource for the promotion of various agricultural projects and works with commodity groups to improve market opportunities. Marketing representatives help with promotion, marketing, packaging, support publications, etc.

* Vermont Economic Development Authority

58 E. State St., Suite 5
Montpelier, VT 05602   802-828-5627
www.vcda.org

Small Business Development Corporation: A non-profit corporation offering loans up to $100,000 to assist growing Vermont small businesses who cannot access conventional sources of credit. Funds may be used to finance the acquisition of fixed assets or for working capital with restrictions.

Job Start Program: Helps develop self-employment opportunities for low and moderate income Vermonters through loans used to start, strengthen or expand small businesses. Funds may be used to purchase equipment, inventory or for working capital.

Financial Access Program: Designed to enhance opportunities for small businesses to access commercial credit utilizing a pooled reserve concept. Loans must be in an amount up to and including $200,000 made to businesses with sales less than $5 million.

Mortgage Insurance Program: Designed to aid businesses by insuring loans made by commercial banks. Proceeds may be used to insure loans made for the acquisition of land, buildings, machinery and equipment or working capital, for use in an eligible facility. Maximum is $2 million per project.

Local Development Corporation Loans: Loans to nonprofit local development corporations are available through VEDA-s Subchapter 3 program. "Spec" buildings and incubators can provided low cost, flexible leased space for businesses which prefer not to own their own facility. Loan proceeds may be used for the purchase of land for industrial parks, industrial park planning and development, and the construction or improvement of speculative buildings or small business incubator facilities.

Industrial Revenue Bonds: Designed to aid businesses through VEDA's issuance of tax-exempt, low interest bonds to provide funds for the acquisition of land, buildings, and/or machinery and equipment for use in a manufacturing facility.

Direct Loan Program: Designed to finance the establishment or expansion of eligible facilities through the acquisition, construction and installation of fixed assets. Provides attractive variable rate loans to business for the purchase of land, the purchase or construction (including renovation) of buildings, and the purchase and installation of machinery and equipment for use in an eligible facility.

* Vermont Sustainable Jobs Fund, Inc.

61 Elm St.   802-828-5320
Montpelier, VT 05602   Fax: 802-223-2336
www.vsif.org

The goal of the fund is to develop and support projects throughout the State leading to the creation or retention of quality jobs, and the protection and enhancement of Vermont's human and natural resources. Grants and technical assistance will be available for collaborative activity including the development of flexible manufacturing networks, business clusters, and networks. A specific area of focus will be adding value to agricultural products that use the natural resource of grass.

* Vermont World Trade Office

National Life Building
6th Floor, Drawer 20   802-828-1175
Montpelier, VT 05620   Fax: 802-828-3258

60 Main Street, Suite 102   802-865-0493
Burlington, VT 05401   877-VTXPORT
www.vermontworldtrade.org

Assists businesses wishing to export their products and services, to expand by developing sales in new markets, and by encouraging suitable foreign companies to establish operations within the state.

* Certified Development Companies

Central Vermont Economic Development Corporation
Richard Angney, Exec. Vice President
1 National Life Drive, 5th Floor
P.O. Box 1439   802-223-4654
Montpelier VT 05601   Fax: 802-223-4655
Area of Operation: Washington and Orange counties

Northern Community Investment Corporation
Paul Denton, President
20 Main Street
P.O. Box 904   802-748-5101
Johnsbury VT 05819   Fax: 802-748-1884
Area of Operation: Caledonia, Essex and Orleans Counties in Vermont; also Coos, Carroll and Grafton Counties in New Hampshire

Vermont 503 Corporation
Jo Bradley, Executive Director
58 East State Street
Montpelier VT 05602   802-828-5627
                  Fax: 802-828-5474
Area of Operation: Statewide

The 504 Certified Development Company (CDC) Program provides growing businesses with long-term, fixed-rate financing for major fixed assets, such as land and buildings. A Certified Development Company is a nonprofit corporation set up to contribute to the economic development of its community or region. CDCs work with the SBA and private-sector lenders to provide financing to small businesses.

* The Women's Agricultural Network

Women's Agricultural Network
617 Comstock Road, Suite 5   802-223-2389
Berlin, VT 05602   Fax: 802-223-6500
www.uvm.edu/~wagn

The Women's Agricultural Network (WAgN) is a collaborative effort of the UVM Extension System, the Women's Small Business Program (WSBP), and the UVM Center for Sustainable Agriculture. Their mission is to assist individuals interested in starting or expanding a farm or agriculture-related business. WAgN provides education, technical assistance, and networking opportunities for each step along the business development continuum. From developing the idea through the planning and implementation phases, the Women's Agricultural Network has a program to meet client's needs.

* Vermont Telecom Advancement Center

163 South Willard Street   802-865-6448
Burlington, VT 05401   Fax: 802-860-2759
www.vtac.org;

VTAC's mission is to introduce users to workable and achievable solutions designed within the field of telecommunications. The goals are to educate small business owners, entrepreneurs, non-profit organizations, and educators concerning the latest available technology, products and services available in Vermont; to place interested users in touch with advanced users, vendors and consultants who can aid in facilitating telecom usage, and to provide a neutral source of information serving state government and legislators.

* The North Atlantic Venture Fund II

The Vermont Venture Capital Fund, L.P.
76 St. Paul Street   802-658-7840
Burlington, VT 05401   Fax: 802-658-5757

The North Atlantic Venture Fund II is managed by North Atlantic Venture Capital Corporation, which, through affiliate funds, has a total of $40 million in venture capital under management. The fund is a private enterprise that seeks to invest from $100,000 to $750,000 in high-quality opportunities that have outgrown seed capital resources and are either not ready for or have exceeded the limits of commercial bank lending resources. Investments are made based on estimated return on investment.

* Vermont Community Loan Fund

P.O. Box 827
15 State St.   802-223-1448
Montpelier, VT 05601   Fax: 802-223-1455
Email: VCLF@VCLF.org.
www.vclf.org

Vermont Community Loan Fund is a statewide nonprofit, private community development financial institution. It strengthens Vermont's communities by promoting equitable access to capital through two loan funds:

Enterprise Fund: The Enterprise fund provides critical funding primarily to businesses, which use Vermont's natural resources and/or are agricultural-based.

Building Community Fund: The Building Community Fund provides funding to create or preserve affordable housing and community-based services, such as child and elder care, women's centers, and elderly housing, and community facilities.

Loans are accompanied by technical assistance designed to help borrowers achieve their goals. Through its services and projects, the VCLF serves low and moderate income Vermonters. VCLF also enables individual investors, contributors, corporations and foundations to use their money for positive social purposes.

Building Bright Futures Fund: The Building Bright Future Fund assists new and existing child care and youth programs to expand quality child care. This grant resource is available to start, relocate, expand or improve the physical facility.

Business Loan Program: Loans of up to $250,000 for entrepreneurs, who increase economic opportunities for low-income or underemployed Vermonters, create or save jobs or add value to Vermont's agricultural or natural resources economy.

Child Care Loan Program: The Child Care Loan Program is available to profit and non-profit childcare providers in Vermont, including home-based facilities. The loans are available to finance major improvements, licensing requirements, renovations and materials or equipment purchases.

* Regional Development Corporations

Addison County Economic Development Corp.
1590 US Route 7S, Suite 3   802-388-7953
Middlebury, VT 05753   Fax: 802-388-0119
www.addisoncountyedc.org

Bennington County Industrial Corp.
P.O. Box 357   802-442-8975

No. Bennington, VT 05257 — Fax: 802-477-1101
www.bcic.org

Brattleboro Development Credit Corp.
76 Cotton Mill Hill — 802-257-7731
Brattleboro, VT 05301 — Fax: 802-257-0294
www.brattleborodevelopment.com

Central Vermont Economic Development Corp.
P.O. Box 1439 — 802-223-4654
Montpelier, VT 05601 — Fax: 802-223-4655
www.central-vt.com/cvedc

Franklin County Industrial Development Corp.
163 N. Main St.
P.O. Box 1099 — 802-524-2194
St. Albans, VT 05478-1099 — Fax: 802-524-6793
www.fcidc.com

Greater Burlington Industrial Corp.
60 Main St., Suite 101
P.O. Box 786 — 802-562-5726
Burlington, VT 05402-0786 — Fax: 802-860-1899
www.vermont.org/gbic

Green Mountain Economic Development Corp.
P.O. Box 246. — 802-295-3710
White River Junction, VT 05001 — Fax: 802-295-3779
www.gmedc.org

Lake Champlain Island Chamber of Commerce
P.O. Box 213 — 802-372-8400
North Hero, VT 05474 — Fax: 802-372-5107
www.champlainislands.com

Lamoille Industrial Development Corp.
P.O. Box 455 — 802-888-5640
Morrisville, VT 05661 — Fax: 802-888-7612
www.lamoilleeconomy.org

Northeastern Vermont Development Association.
P.O. Box 640 — 802-748-5181
St. Johnsbury, VT 05819 — Fax: 802-748-1223
www.nvda.net

Rutland Economic Development Corp.
110 Merchants Row
4th Floor, Suite 3. — 802-773-9147
Rutland, VT 05701-5918 — Fax: 802-773-8009
www.rutlandecomony.com

Springfield Regional Development Corp.
14 Clinton St. — 802-885-3061
Springfield, VT 05156 — Fax: 802-885-3027
www.springfielddevelopment.org

* Northern Community Investment Corporation (NCIC)

P.O. Box 904
347 Portland St. — 802-748-5101
St. Johnsbury, VT 05819 — Fax: 802-748-1884
www.ncic.org

A private, non-profit, community-based corporation that assists development in Vermont and northern New Hampshire. The NCIC provides capital and professional assistance to both small and large businesses and community development projects. Some of its services include: personalized technical assistance, direct financing of $500,000 or more, attracting outside capital to supplement its own resources in order to expand its investments, developing industrial space for new or expanding businesses, and investment in residential and commercial development.

* Small Business Administration (SBA)

87 State St., Room 205 — 802-828-4422
Montpelier, VT 05601 — Fax: 802-828-4485
www.sba.gov/vt

The Vermont Small Business Administration Office delivers a variety of programs and services, such as startup and operational assistance through small business training and counseling, financial assistance for startup's, business opportunities and much more.

* Small Business Investment Companies

Green Mountain Capital, LP
Michael Sweatman, General Manager
25 Cross Rd., Suite 3 — 802-244-8981
Waterbury, VT 05676 — Fax: 802-244-8990
Email: ims@gmtcap.com

North Atlantic Venture Fund II, L.P.
Gregory B. Peters, Vice President
76 St. Paul Street, Suite 600 — 802-658-7820
Burlington, VT 05401 — Fax: 802-658-5757

The SBA licenses, regulates, and provides financial assistance to privately owned and operated Small Business Investment Companies. SBICs make venture or risk investments by supplying capital and extending unsecured loans and loans not fully collateralized to small enterprises which meet their investment criteria. Financing is made by direct loans and by equity investments.

* Northeast Employment and Training Organization (NETO)

P.O. Box 186
17 Center St. — 802-748-8935
St. Johnsbury, VT 05819 — Fax; 802-748-8936
http://vt-neto.org

or

P.O. Box 584
Ridgeview 91 Bldg. — 802-334-7378
Newport, VT 05855 — Fax: 802-334-8148

NETO manages the Entrepreneurial Training Program which provides statewide small business management curses to enterprises of all sizes, including individuals interested in self-employment and microbusinesses. Services are available free to certain income eligible persons as well as on a fee basis.

* Micro Business Development Program (MBDP)

Statewide Facilitator, Bruce Whitney
P.O. Box 437 — 802-387-5029
Putney, VT 05346 — Fax: 802-387-5029
www.vtmicrobusiness.org

Central Vermont Community Action Council, Inc.
195 Route 302 Berlin — 800-639-1053
Barre, VT 05641 — 802-479-1053
Email: cflint@cvcac.org — Fax: 802-479-5353
Area of Operation: Orange, Washington and Lamoille Counties

Champlain Valley Office of Economic Opportunity
431 Pine St. — 800-287-7971
Burlington, VT 05401 — 802-860-1417
Email: mbdp@cvoeo.org — Fax: 802-860-1387
Area of Operation: Addison, Chittenden, Grand Isle and Franklin Counties

Community Action in Southwestern Vermont
60 Center St. — 800-717-2762
Rutland, VT 05701 — 802-775-0878
Email: mrock@broc.org — Fax: 802-775-9949
Area of Operation: Rutland and Bennington Counties

Northeast Kingdom Community Action
108 Cherry Street St. — 800-639-4065
Johnsbury, VT 05819 — 802-748-6048
Email: mbdp@nekca.org — Fax: 802-748-0732
Area of Operation: Caledonia, Orleans and Essex Counties

Southeastern Vermont Community Action
91 Buck Drive — 800-464-9951
Westminster, VT 05158 — 802-722-4575
Email: jjuhasz@sevca.org — Fax: 802-722-4509

MBDP promotes self-employment and business expansion opportunities for low income Vermonters. MBDP offers free one-to-one technical assistance and business development workshops for income eligible persons. Specials work in the regional Community Action Program (CAP) agencies listed above.

* Department of Housing and Community Affairs

Vermont Community Development Program (VCDP)
National Life Bldg., Drawer 20 — 802-828-3211
Montpelier, VT 05620 0501 — 800-622-4553
www.dhca.state.vt.us — Fax: 802-828-2928

VCDP funds can be used for a wide range of economic development activities such as loans to businesses for capital equipment or real property acquisition, or to assist in the construction of infrastructure improvements such as water and sewer lines.

* Department of Public Service

Utility Demand-Side Management Programs
112 State St., Drawer 20   802-828-2811
Montpelier, VT 05620-2601   Fax: 802-828-2342
www.state.vt.us/psd

Individual Vermont utilities have developed energy efficient and/or energy conservation programs providing technical and financial assistance. In some cases, utilities actually invest along with companies, in energy-saving technology.

* Rural Development Service

89 Main St.
City Center, 3rd Floor   802-828-6010
Montpelier, VT 05602   Fax: 802-828-6076
www.rurdev.usda.gov/vt

Business & Industry Guaranteed Loans: The Business and Industry Guaranteed Loan Program helps create jobs and stimulates rural economies by providing financial backing for rural businesses. This program provides guarantees up to 90 percent of a loan made by a commercial lender. Loan proceeds may be used for working capital, machinery and equipment, buildings and real estate, and certain types of debt refinancing.

Cooperative Services Program: Cooperative Services Program is to promote understanding and use of the cooperative form of business as a viable organizational option for marketing and distributing agricultural products.

Intermediary Relending Program: The purpose of the Intermediary Relending Program is to finance business facilities and community development projects in rural areas. This is achieved through loans made by the Rural Business-Cooperative Service to intermediaries. Intermediaries re-lend funds to ultimate recipients for business facilities or community development.

Rural Business-Cooperative Service: The Rural Business-Cooperative Service makes grants under the Rural Business Enterprise Grants Program to public bodies, private nonprofit corporations, and Indian Tribal groups to finance and facilitate development of small and emerging private business enterprises located in areas with population of less than 50,000. The public bodies, private nonprofit corporations and Indian tribes receive the grant to assist a business. Grant funds do not go directly to the business.

Rural Economic Development Loans: This program provides zero-interest loans to electric and telephone utilities to promote sustainable rural economic development and job creation projects.

Rural Economic Development Grants: This program provides grants to electric and telephone utilities to promote sustainable rural economic development and job creation projects through the operation of a revolving loan fund program.

Rural Business Opportunity Grants: The purpose of this program is to provide sustainable economic development in rural communities with exceptional needs. This is accomplished by making grants to pay costs of providing economic planning for rural communities, technical assistance for rural businesses, or training for rural entrepreneurs or economic development officials.

* Participating Micro Lenders

Economic Dev. Council of Northern Vermont, Inc.
155 Lake Street   802-524-4546
Albans, VT 05478   Fax 802-527-1081
Area of Operation: Chittenden, Franklin, Grand Isle, Lamoille, and Washington counties

Northern Community Investments Corporation
20 Main St.
P.O. Box 904   802-748-5101
St. Johnsbury, VT 05819   Fax: 802-748-1884
Area of Operation: Caledonia, Essex, and Orleans Counties

Vermont Development Credit Union
18 Pearl Street   802-865-3404
Burlington, VT 05401   Fax: 802-862-8971
Area of Operation: Addison, Bennington, Orange, Rutland, Windham Counties

The Microloan Program provides small loans ranging from under $500 to $35,000.

Virginia

* Economic Development Partnership

901 East Byrd Street
P.O. Box 798   804-371-8100
Richmond, VA 23218   Fax: 804-371-8112
www.yesvirginia.org

Helps new and expanding businesses by answering questions about licensing, taxes, regulations, assistance programs, etc. The office can also locate sources of information in other state agencies, and it can identify sources of help for business planning, management, exporting, and financing.

Existing Industry Division (EID): Discovers needs and identifies resources that allow existing businesses and industries to take advantage of opportunities and avoid problems. EID professionals generally call on organizations within geographic territories and discuss business conditions. Information collected is processed and analyzed for further action.

Workforce Services Division (WFS): Works with new and existing businesses and industries to recruit and train qualified workers at all skill levels for newly created jobs. The programs addressing these efforts support State and local Economic Development marketing efforts.

Workforce Services: Mission is to train and retrain Virginians for specific employment opportunities. Offers consulting, video production for training purposes, and funding.

Virginia's Business Development Network: Designed to provide management and technical assistance to small and medium-sized companies. Provides one-on-one counseling and group training on a variety of subjects and assists entrepreneurs with pre-business planning.

Financial Services Division (FSD): Identifies potential financial resources to meet the capital needs of Virginia business clients, and administers loan and guarantee programs designed to foster growth and private financing in Virginia business.

Governor's Opportunity Fund: Supports economic development projects that create new jobs and investment in accordance with criteria established by state legislation. Funds can be used for such things as site acquisition and development; transportation access; training; construction or build-out of publicly owned buildings; or grants or loans to Industrial Development Authorities.

Enterprise Zone Job Grants: Businesses creating new-full-time positions are eligible to receive grants of up to $500 per position ($1,000 if a zone resident fills a position). The maximum grant to any one firm is $100,000 a year for the three consecutive years in the grant period.

International Market Planning: Designed to assist companies developing new export markets and increase sales. Offers international marketing research; current market analyses; specific strategies to access selected markets.

New Jobs Program: Funding and assistance are available to qualified companies that make a capital investment of more than $1 million and create a minimum of 25 new jobs.

Small Business New Jobs Program: Funding and assistance are available to qualified companies that have operated in Virginia for at least one year, are for-profit and have fewer that 250 employees. The company must create 5 to 24 jobs within 12 months and make capital investment of at least $100,000.

Retraining Program: Workforce Services will provide consulting services and funds to eligible Virginia businesses to assist in retraining their existing employees.

Virginia Investment Partnership Grant Fund: The Virginia Partnership Grant Fund is a discretionary performance incentive program in which grants are negotiated and made to selected projects that invest in Virginia and promote employment opportunities.

Tobacco Region Opportunity Fund: The Tobacco Opportunity Fund makes grants or loans to localities in Virginia's tobacco producing regions to assist with projects that result in the creation of new jobs.

Loan Guarantee Program: The Loan Guarantee Program is designed to reduce a bank's risk in making loans and increase availability of short-term capital for small businesses.

Small Business Compliance Assistance Fund: The fund is designed to provide Virginia businesses with financing to purchase equipment to comply with federal Clean Air Act, voluntary pollution prevention measures and voluntary agricultural best management practices.

* VWBE Certification Program

Women's Enterprise Program
P.O. Box 446
Richmond, VA 23218
www.dba.state.va.us/mwbusinesses/wob.asp

800-980-VWBE
804-371-8200

Helps Virginia's women-owned and operated companies certify themselves as WBE's to better compete in government and corporate procurement markets. In addition to being listed in the directory, certified companies will be registered in the WBE website, as well as in the Virginia Procurement Pipeline website. Certified WBE's also have the privilege of using the WBE seal on marketing materials and letterhead. They also receive information on other resources available to women-owned businesses regarding government contracting, management issues, and women's ownership.

* Virginia Department of Business Assistance

707 East Main Street, Suite 300
P.O. Box 466
Richmond, VA 23218
www.dba.state.va.us

804-371-8200
Fax: 804-371-2142

A good starting point for new businesses to learn about financial programs, workshops, business planning and more.

* Center for Innovative Technology

2214 Rock Hill Rd, Suite 600
Herndon, VA 20170
www.cit.org

703-689-3000
800-383-2482
Fax: 703-689-3041

Exists to stimulate economic growth by serving technology businesses. Services include: access to 11 technology development centers; assistance with pursuing joint product development with a Virginia university and provide co-funding for projects; entrepreneurship programs designed to help early stage companies bring new products to market; assistance solving manufacturing production problems.

* Virginia Small Business Financing Authority

707 East Main Street, Suite 300
P.O. Box 446
Richmond, VA 23218
www.dba.state.va.us/financing

804-371-8200
Fax: 804-371-8111

Offers financing programs to provide businesses with access to capital needed for growth and expansion. Programs include:

- *Industrial Development Bonds (IDBs) and the Umbrella IDB Program*: VSBFA issues tax-exempt and taxable revenue bonds (IDBs) statewide to provide creditworthy businesses with access to long term, fixed asset financing at favorable interest rates and terms. Tax-exempt IDBs may be used to finance new or expanding manufacturing facilities and exempt projects, such as solid waste disposal facilities. In addition, VSBFA offers an Umbrella IDB Program that provides a cost-effective means for businesses to sell their bonds in the public bond market, particularly for smaller projects with limited access to this market.
- *Virginia Economic Development Revolving Loan Fund*: This fund provides loans of up to $700,000 to bridge the gap between private debt financing and private equity for projects that will result in job creation or retention. Funding is available for fixed asset financing to new and expanding manufacturing companies and other industries that derive 50% or more of their sales outside of Virginia.
- *Virginia Defense Conversion Revolving Loan Fund*: This fund provides loans of up to $700,000 to assist defense dependent companies seeking to expand into commercial markets and diversify their operations. Funding is available for fixed assets and working capital.
- *Loan Guarantee Program*: This program is designed to reduce the risk to banks in making loans thereby increasing the availability of short-term capital for small businesses. Under the program, VSBFA will guarantee up to $250,000 or 50%, whichever is less, of a bank loan. Typical borrowings include revolving lines of credit to finance accounts receivable and inventory, and short-term loans for working capital and fixed asset purchases, such as office or research equipment.

- *Virginia Capital Access Program (VCAP):* VCAP provides a form of loan portfolio insurance for participating banks through special loan loss reserve accounts which are funded by loan enrollment premiums paid by the bank/borrower and matched by the VSBFA. This allows the banks to exceed their normal risk thresholds for commercial loans of all types and, thereby, accommodate a broader array of loan requests from Virginia businesses.
- *Child Day Care Financing Program*: VSBFA provides small direct loans to child day care providers for quality enhancement projects or to meet or maintain child care standards. Eligible loan uses include infant care equipment or equipment needed to care for children with special needs, playground improvements, vans, and upgrades or minor renovations to kitchens, bathrooms, and plumbing and electrical systems.
- *Small Business Environmental Compliance Assistance Fund*: The Small Business Environmental Compliance Assistance Fund is a revolving low-interest loan fund. It is available to small businesses for the purchase and installation of replacement equipment need to comply with the Clean Air Act or to implement voluntary pollution prevention measures.
- *VSBFA DIRECT*: This program is designed to provide access capital to new and existing small businesses and economic development authorities. These loans from the Small Business Finance Authority are to facilitate the financing projects that create economic benefit to Virginia's communities through increased revenues and the creation of new jobs.

* Solar Photovoltaic Manufacturing Grants

Virginia Department of Mines, Minerals, and Energy
202 N. Ninth St.
Ninth Street Office Bldg., 8th Floor
Richmond, VA 23219
www.mme.state.va.us/de/commercialframe.html

804-692-3200
Fax: 804-692-3238

Designed to encourage the product development and manufacture of a high technology, renewable energy source in Virginia. Any manufacturer who sells solar photovoltaic panels, manufactured in Virginia, is entitled to receive an annual grant of up to seventy-five cents per watt of the rated capacity of panel sold.

* Virginia Coalfield Economic Development Authority

The Virginia Southwest Promise
P.O. Box 1060
Lebanon, VA 24266
www.vaswpromise.com

800-735-9999
276-889-0381
Fax: 276-889-1830

Designed to enhance the economic base of specific areas. The Authority provides low interest loans or grants to qualified new or expanding industries through its financing program to be used for real estate purchases, construction or expansion of buildings, and the purchase of machinery and equipment.

* Virginia Capital LP

1801 Libbie Avenue, Suite 201
Richmond, VA 23226
www.vacapital.com

804-648-4802
Fax: 804-648-4809

A private venture capital firm. Investments that are attractive include ownership transactions and profitable, growing companies whose needs exceed senior bank debt capacity. Typical investments range between $500,000 and $1,500,000.

* Virginia Resources Authority

707 East Main Street, Suite 1350
Richmond, VA 23219
www.virginiaresources.org

804-644-3100
Fax: 804-644-3109

VRA's Financing Programs:

Virginia Water Facilities Revolving Fund: VRA acts as the financial administrator and manager for the Virginia Water Facilities Revolving Fund (VWFRF). The VWFRF is co-managed with the Department of Environmental Quality (DEQ), Water Division. Funding for the VWFRF is provided by grants from the Environmental Protection Agency along with a state match of twenty percent.

Virginia Water Supply Revolving Fund: The VWSRF was established as a renewing source of funding for improvements to privately and publicly owned community and nonprofit noncommunity waterworks.

Interim Financing: Is available to borrowers whose loans have been approved by VRA's Board of Directors, and to borrowers that have received a loan commitment from either the wastewater or water supply revolving fund. The interim financing program was created to provide approved borrowers with funds for eligible costs incurred before loans can close, including engineering and construction costs.

* eVa

Department of General Services,
Division of Purchases and Supply (DPS).
P.O. Box 644   804-786-3910
Richmond, VA 23218   Fax: 804-371-7841
www.eva.state.va.us

eVa is a one-stop information source about Virginia state government bidding opportunities. The information summarizes opportunities in general and highway construction, data processing, equipment, printing, supplies, surplus property auctions or sealed bid sales, real property and various services: professional, non-professional, individual and consulting. Each listing includes a contact person for more details.

* Department of Environmental Quality

629 East Main Street   804-698-4394
P.O. Box 10009   800-592-5482
Richmond, VA 23240   Fax: 804-698-4510
www.deq.state.va.us

The Virginia Small Business Assistance Program (VA SBAP) is a "non-regulatory," voluntary program within the Department of Environmental Quality. It offers small businesses free technical assistance on air quality and related environmental requirements. It's mission is to help small businesses comply with the Clean Air Act and Virginia's air regulations.

* Virginia Tourism Corporation

901 East Byrd Street   804-786-2051
Richmond, VA 23219   Fax: 804-786-1919
www.vatc.org

The Corporation develops and implements programs beneficial to Virginia travel-related businesses and consumers that no industry component or organization would be expected to carry out on its own. Through its multifaceted national and international marketing programs, the VTC researches and targets specific, highly profitable audience segments in those geographic markets offering the highest potential of travel to Virginia.

* Virginia Department of Forestry

Fontaine Research Park
900 Natural Resources Drive, Suite 800   804-977-6555
Charlottesville, VA, 22903-0758   Fax: 804-296-2369
www.vdof.org

The Conservation Reserve Enhancement Program (CREP) is a State-federal conservation partnership program targeted to address specific State and nationally significant water quality, soil erosion and wildlife habitat issues related to agricultural use. The program uses financial incentives to encourage farmers and ranchers to voluntarily enroll in contracts of 10 to 15 years in duration to remove lands from agricultural production. This community-based conservation program provides a flexible design of conservation practices and financial incentives to address environmental issues.

* Virginia Department of Housing and Community

Development Planning and Development Office
501 North Second Street
Richmond, VA 23219   804-371-7000
www.dhcd.virginia.gov/

The Department of Housing and Community Development has a variety of programs through their Business Assistance Program. They work with business and communities to help foster economic growth and to help stimulate the creation of new businesses.

Virginia Enterprise Initiative Program: This program supports small business development by assisting entrepreneurs in starting new businesses and helping disadvantaged individuals gain business skills and access to credit.

Virginia Enterprise Zone Program: This program encourages new business activity and expansion by providing state and local tax relief and grants, local regulatory flexibility, and local infrastructure development in selected economically depressed areas.

Virginia Individual Development Account Program: This program is designed to encourage savings in the form of cash matching funds. An eligible participant saves into a designated account at a financial institution for a specific purpose, such as home ownership, education, or business start-up and also receives financial training.

* Certified Development Companies

Crater Development Company
Post Office Box 1808
1964 Wakefield Street   804-861-1666
Petersburg, VA 23805   Fax: 804-732-8972
Area of Operation: Cities of Colonial Heights, Emporia, Hopewell and Petersburg. Counties of Chesterfield, Dinwiddie, Greensville, Prince George, Surry, and Sussex.

James River Dev. Corp.
Capitol Place, Suite 702
1108 East Main Street   804-344-0002
Richmond, VA 23219   Fax: 804-344-0022
Email: fminton@aol.com
Area of Operation: City of Richmond. Counties of Charles City, Goochland, Hanover, Henrico, James City, New Kent, Powhatan, Williamsburg, and York.

Rappahannock Econ. Dev. Corp.
3304 Bourbon Street
P.O. Box 863   540-373-2890
Fredericksburg, VA 22404   Fax: 540-899-4808
Area of Operation: City of Fredericksburg. Counties of Caroline, King George, Stafford, and Spotsylvania.

Tidewater Business Financing Corp.
1226 Suntrust Center
500 E. Main St.   757-623-2691
Norfolk, VA 23510   Fax: 757-623-0660
Area of Operation: Cities of Chesapeake, Hampton, Newport News, Norfolk, Poquoson, Portsmouth, Suffolk, and Virginia Beach.

Virginia Economic Dev. Corp.
101 E. High Street
P.O. Box 1402   434-972-9900
Charlottesville, VA 22902   Fax: 972-9900
Email: towens@rlc.net
Area of Operation: City of Charlottesville.Counties of Albemarle, Fluvanna, Greene, Louisa, and Nelson.

Virginia Asset Financing Corp.
4165 Chain Bridge Road   703-352-0504
Fairfax, VA 22030   Fax: 703-352-9100
Area of Operation: Statewide

The 504 Certified Development Company (CDC) Program provides growing businesses with long-term, fixed-rate financing for major fixed assets, such as land and buildings. A Certified Development Company is a nonprofit corporation set up to contribute to the economic development of its community or region. CDCs work with the SBA and private-sector lenders to provide financing to small businesses.

* Small Business Administration (SBA)

Richmond District Office
400 N. 8th St., Suite 1150   804-771-2400
Richmond, VA 23240   Fax: 804-771-2764
www.sba.gov/va

The Virginia Small Business Administration Office delivers a variety of programs and services, such as startup and operational assistance through small business training and counseling, financial assistance for startup's, business opportunities and much more.

* Small Business Investment Companies

BIA Digital Partners, L.P.
Lloyd R. Sams, Contact
15120 Enterprise Court, Suite 200   703-227-9600
Chantilly, VA 20151   Fax: 703-227-9645
Email: lsams@bia.com

Continental SBIC
Arthur Walters, President
4141 N. Henderson Rd., Suite 8   703-527-5200
Arlington, VA 22203   Fax: 703-527-3700
Email: alwetal@erols.com

Development Capital Ventures, L.P.
Wayne S. Foren, Contact
510 King Street, Suite 311   703-548-3226
Alexandria, VA 22314   Fax: 703-684-8217
Email: dccgrowth@aol.com

East West United Investment Co.
Dung Bui, President
1568 Spring Hill Rd., Suite 100   703-442-0150
McLean, VA 22102   Fax: 703-442-0156
Email: tiffanyd@ewmortgage.com

eCentury Capital Partners, L.P.
Thomas Dann, Contact
8270 Greensboro Drive, Suite 1025   703-442-4480
McLean, VA 22102   Fax: 703-448-1816
Email: tdann@ecenturycapital.com

Esquire Capital Corp.
Frederick Eliassen, Manager
15413 Championship Drive
P.O. Box 909   866-753-9664
Haymarket, VA 20169   Fax: 703-753-9643
Email: esquiremoneta@msn.com

GIV Venture Partners, L.P.
Jeff Tonkel, Contact
8150 Leesburg Pike, Suite 1210   703-442-3300
Vienna, VA 22182   Fax: 703-442-3388
Email: jeff@givinc.com

Virginia Capital SBIC, L.P.
Frederick Russell & Tom Deardorff, Mgrs.
1801 Libbie Avenue, Suite 201   804-648-4802
Richmond, VA 23226   Fax: 804-648-4809
Email: frussell@vacapital.com

Waterside Capital Corporation
Alan Lindauer, President
500 East Main Street, Suite 800   757-626-1111
Norfolk, VA 23510   Fax: 757-626-0114
Email: gmcdonald@watersidecapital.com

The SBA licenses, regulates, and provides financial assistance to privately owned and operated Small Business Investment Companies. SBICs make venture or risk investments by supplying capital and extending unsecured loans and loans not fully collateralized to small enterprises which meet their investment criteria. Financing is made by direct loans and by equity investments.

* Rural Development Administration

1606 Santa Rosa Rd.
Culpeper Building #238   804-287-1550
Richmond, VA 23229-5014   Fax: 8044-287-1718
www.rurdev.usda.gov/va

Business and Industry Loan Guaranteed Loans: The Business and Industry Loan Guarantee Program provides loan guarantees for expansion and preservation of jobs in rural areas in towns of less than 50,000.

Intermediary Re-Lending Program: This program finances business facilities and community development projects in rural areas. This is achieved through loans made by Rural Development to intermediaries. The intermediaries re-lend the funds to ultimate recipients for business facilities or community development. Any type of legal entity, including individuals and public and private organizations may be an ultimate recipient.

Rural Business Enterprise Grants: This program promotes the development and commercialization of new services and products that can be produced in rural areas; new processes that can be produced in rural areas; new processes that can be utilized in the production of products in rural areas; and new enterprises that can add value to on-farm production. Grants may be made to public bodies or nonprofit institutions to pay up to 75% of the costs for establishing and/or operating centers for rural technology and/or cooperative development.

Cooperative Services: The Cooperative Services program helps rural residents form new cooperative businesses and improve the operations of existing cooperatives. To accomplish this, Cooperative Services provides technical assistance, conducts cooperative-related research, and produces information products to promote public understanding of cooperatives.

Rural Cooperative Development Grant Program: Rural Cooperative Development grants are made for establishing and operating centers for cooperative development for the primary purpose of improving the economic condition of rural areas through the development of new cooperatives and improving operations of existing cooperatives.

Rural Business Opportunity Grants: Rural Business Opportunity Grant

funds provide for technical assistance, training, and planning activities that improve economic conditions in rural areas. Applicants must be located in rural. Non-profit corporations and public bodies are eligible. This program is designed to promote sustainable economic development in rural communities with exceptional needs.

Rural Economic Development Loans and Grants: This program finances economic development and job creation projects in rural areas. Loans and Grants are available to any Rural Utilities Service electric or telecommunications borrower to assist in developing rural areas. Loans at zero-interest are made primarily to finance business startup ventures and business expansion projects.

Value-Added Product Market Development Grant: The purpose of the Value-Added Agricultural Product Market Development Grant is to help eligible agricultural producers enter into value-added activities. These grant funds will be used to either develop feasibility studies, business and marketing plans, or other planning activities needed to establish a viable value-added marketing opportunity for an agricultural product.

* Virginia Department of Rail and Public Transportation

1313 E. Main St., Suite 300
P.O. Box 590   804-786-4440
Richmond, VA 23218   Fax: 804-786-7286
www.drpt.state.va.us

The Department of Rail and Public Transportation supports a variety of programs including: Capital Funds, Formula Funds, Rideshare Funds, Technical Assistance Funds, Transportation Efficiency Improvement Funds and more.

* International Trade Division

Director of International Trade
P.O. Box 798
901 East Byrd Street   804-371-0198
Richmond, VA 23218-0798   Fax: 804-371-8860
www.exportvirginia.org

This program provides international business expertise to promote Virginia's products and services in world markets. Services include export counseling, market assistance, educational seminars, international market information and market planning programs.

Washington

* Department of Community, Trade and Economic

Raad Building
128 10th Avenue SW
P.O. Box 42525   360-725-4000
Olympia WA 98504-2525   Fax: 360-586-8440
www.cted.wa.gov

One-Stop Licensing Center: A convenient, one-stop system that takes care of basic registration requirements and offers information about any additional licensing.

Business Retention & Expansion Program: Works with at-risk manufacturing and processing firms to reduce the number of business closures, layoffs and failures that result in significant job loss. State and local staff provide technical and problem solving assistance for these companies.

Downtown Revitalization Service: Encourages partnerships between business and government that revitalize a community's economy, appearance and traditional business image.

Education and Training: Works in partnership with local Economic Development Councils to provide businesses and communities with practical application of economic development techniques.

Child Care Advantages: Provides businesses with financial and technical assistance to develop on-site or near-site child care facilities. Qualified businesses are eligible to receive direct loans, loan guarantees, or grants through the Facilities Fund to start or expand their child care facilities.

Coastal Revolving Loan Fund: This fund lends to public agencies and businesses in Jefferson, Clallam, Grays Harbor, Pacific and Wahkiakum counties. Borrowers must demonstrate job creation and private investment to qualify for loans up to $150,000. The program also provides technical assistance loans up to $50,000 for public agencies and $30,000 for businesses for feasibility studies and planning.

Industrial Revenue Bonds: Up to $10 million may be issued to finance a project. Taxable nonrecourse economic development bonds are also available through the Washington Economic Development Finance Authority.

Forest Projects Revolving Loan Fund: Provides financial assistance to small-and medium-sized forest projects companies. Loans up to $750,000 are available for secondary wood product companies and their suppliers.

Community Development Finance: Program is available to help business and industry secure long-term expansion loans. By combining private financial resources with federal and state lending assistance and local leadership, this program focuses on business expansion through community development activities.

Loan programs are available for real estate, new construction, renovation, major leasehold improvements, machinery, equipment, and working capital. Government financing for a start-up business is possible, but more difficult and requires a larger down payment by the business.

Rural Washington Loan Fund: Gap financing for businesses that will create new jobs or retain existing jobs in non-entitlement areas of the state.

International Trade Division: Works to expand future and existing export markets by distributing trade statistics, a bi-monthly newsletter, industry directories, organizing trade missions, participating in trade shows and managing state office in Europe, Japan, Taiwan, Tokyo, and Vladivostock.

Linked Deposit Loan Program: Allows minority or women-owned businesses with 50 or fewer employees to apply at participating banks for reduced rate loans.

Minority and Women-Owned Business Loan: Loans can be available to assist certified minority and woman-owned businesses that are located in non-metropolitan areas.

* Rural Development Administration

Rural Development
1835 Black Lake Blvd. SW, Suite B   360-704-7740
Olympia, WA 98501-5715   Fax: 360-704-7742
www.rurdev.usda.gov/wa

Business and Industry Loans The purpose of the Business and Industry loan program is to improve develop or finance business, industry and employment and improve the economic and environmental climate in rural communities by guaranteeing quality loans, which will provide lasting community benefits.

Rural Economic Development Loans and Grants: This program provides zero interest loans and grants to Rural Utilities Service borrowers and Rural Electrification Administration to promote rural economic development and job creation projects through direct loans or revolving loan funds.

Rural Business Enterprise Grants: Grants made by USDA Rural Development to public bodies, not for profit entities or Indian tribes to support the development of private business enterprises. Limited to communities of 50,000 population or less.

Rural Business Opportunity Grants: Grants to public bodies, nonprofit corporations, Indian tribes, and cooperatives, which will be used to assist in the economic development of rural areas.

Intermediary Relending Program: Loans made by USDA Rural Development to intermediaries (public bodies, not for profit entities or Indian tribes) at 1% interest-30 years. Intermediaries maximum loan is $250,000 or 75% of project cost, whichever is less. Intermediaries establish revolving loan fund accounts and then relend to individuals or public or private organizations to finance business enterprises or community development. This program is limited to communities of 25,000 population or less.

Rural Cooperative Development Grants: Grants made by USDA Rural Development to nonprofit corporations and institutions of higher education for the purpose of establishing and operating centers for rural cooperative development. Grant will be used to facilitate the creation or retention of jobs in rural areas through the development of new rural cooperatives, value-added processing and rural businesses.

Technical Assistance for Cooperative Development: This program provides Assistance for people interested in forming new cooperatives or existing cooperatives facing specific problems or challenges.

* Business Assistance Center

2001 6th Ave.
Suite 2600   800-237-1233
Seattle, WA 98121   360-956-3135

Education & Training: Efforts are focused on providing practical application of economic development techniques along with providing a forum for practitioners for the interchange of economic development ideas.

The Business Assistance Center Hotline: A statewide, toll-free information and referral service, provides information regarding state business licensing, registration, technical assistance, other state agencies or one-to-one business counseling. To contact a person from the Business Assistance Hotline, call 800-237-1233; 360-586-4840; TDD 360-586-4852.

* Permit Assistance Center

Department of Ecology   800-917-0043
300 Desmond Dr. SE   360-407-7037
Lacey, WA 98503   Fax: 360-407-6904
Mailing Address:
P.O. Box 47600
Olympia, WA 98504
www.ecy.wa.gov

Regional Staff are available to coordinate permit applications for large, complex projects, and to work with applicants, agencies and regulatory authorities to develop a plan for meeting environmental and land-use requirements.

* Export Finance Assistance Center

Export Finance Assistance Center of Washington
2001 Sixth Ave., Suite 650   206-553-5615
Seattle, WA 98121   Fax: 206-553-7253
www.cymma.com/useac.html

Provides information and guidance on the repayment risk of financing aspects of export transactions.

* Office of Minority and Women's Business Enterprises

406 S. Water St.
P.O. Box 41160   360-753-9693
Olympia, WA 98504   Fax: 360-586-7079
www.omwbe.wa.gov

Mission is to enhance the economic vitality of Washington State by creating an environment which mitigates the effects of race and gender discrimination in public contracting and promotes the economic development and growth of minority and women businesses. Certifies Women's business ventures and publishes a directory.

* Minority & Women Business Development

Washington State Office of Minority & Women's Business Enterprises
406 South Water Street   866-208-1064
P.O. Box 41160   360-753-9693
Olympia, WA 98504-1160   Fax: 360-586-7079
www.omwbe.wa.gov

The Office of Minority and Women's Business Enterprises help create and sustain the business environment by promoting public procurement by businesses owned by minorities, women and those who are socially and economically disadvantaged.

* Cascadia Revolving Fund

1901 NW Market Street   206-447-9226
Seattle, WA 98107   Fax: 206-682-4804
www.cascadiafund.org

Private, nonprofit community development loan fund which is lent to small businesses that cannot access traditional sources of credit. Maximum loan is $500,000.

* Washington State Department of Agriculture

Agency Operations/Market Development Division
1111 Washington Street S.E.
P.O. Box 42560   360-902-1800
Olympia, WA 98504-2560   Fax: 360-902-2092
http://agr.wa.gov

Services available include:
Administrative Support Services:
Provides financial services, computer and information technology services,

personnel services, communications, administrative procedures guidance, legal services, and safety and emergency management programs for the department's 25 programs.

Agricultural Fairs: 360-902-1809
Provides financial assistance to agricultural fairs and youth shows.

Commodity Commissions: 360-902-2043
Administers agency responsibilities relative to the state's 26 agricultural commodity commissions.

International Marketing: 360-902-1915
Assists food and agriculture companies to sell their products internationally; helps resolve phytosanitary and other trade barriers; organizes and leads companies on trade missions and to major trade shows; and develops and distributes information to buyers on the state's agricultural suppliers.

Small Farm and Direct Marketing: 360-902-1884
The Small Farm and Direct Marketing Program works with small farms, farmers markets, chefs and non-profit organizations to connect consumers directly to farmers who sell fresh, local products. They partner with public and private organizations to increase the economic viability of small farms and strengthen Washington's local food systems.

"From the Heart of Washington":   360-902-1915
From the Heart of Washington promotes the purchase of local products by Washington consumers, and raises awareness of agriculture's value to the state's economy and its role in sustaining rural communities.

* Certified Development Companies

Evergreen Community Development Association
Philip T. Eng, President
900 Fourth Avenue, Suite 2900   206-622-3731
Seattle, WA 98164   Fax: 206-623-6613
Area of Operation: State of Washington; Oregon Counties of Clackamas, Columbia, Clatsop, Multnomah, Washington, Hood River, Wasco and Tillamook

Northwest Business Development Association
Gary Whelpley, President
9 South Washington St. #215   509-458-8555
Spokane, WA 99201   Fax: 509-458-8553
State of Washington except Pacific County, Idaho Counties of Clearwater, Idaho, Latah, Lewis and Nez Perce

The 504 Certified Development Company (CDC) Program provides growing businesses with long-term, fixed-rate financing for major fixed assets, such as land and buildings. A Certified Development Company is a nonprofit corporation set up to contribute to the economic development of its community or region. CDCs work with the SBA and private-sector lenders to provide financing to small businesses.

* Washington State Energy Office

925 Plum St., SE, Building 4
P.O. Box 43165   360-956-2000
Olympia, WA 98504-3165   Fax: 360-956-2217
www.energy.wsu.edu
Bioenergy Technical Information: Technical assistance is provided to manufacturing and commercial facilities interested in using biomass for energy production. The Office will also help in identifying funding opportunities, local resources, technology, and conduction environmental assessments.

Commercial Education: Provides training for designers and operators of commercial buildings on energy-efficient technologies and practices.

District Heating and Cooling: This program provides assistance to design or implement district heating or cooling systems for commercial, industrial, or public institutions. Assistance is also provided on obtaining project funding from multiple sources.

Electric Ideas Clearinghouse: 800-872-3568
                                                 360-956-2237
                                            Fax: 360-956-2214
Provides a regional resource for professionals involved in commercial building design, construction, operations, and industrial processes. It provides information and technical assistance on products, design, codes, standard, energy programs, training opportunities, job listings, and expert referrals.

* Small Business Administration

Seattle Regional Office
1200 6th Ave., Suite 1700   206-553-7310
Seattle, WA 98101-1128   Fax: 206-553-7099

801 West Riverside Ave., Suite 200   509-353-2800
Spokane WA 99201-0901   Fax: 509-353-2829
www.sba.gov/wa
The Washington Small Business Administration Office delivers a variety of programs and services, such as startup and operational assistance through small business training and counseling, financial assistance for startup's, business opportunities and much more.

* Small Business Investment Companies

Bancshares Capital, L.P.
John E. Thoresen, Contact
22020 17th Avenue S.E., Suite 220   425-424-0058
Bothell, WA 98021-8486   Fax: 425-424-0809
Email: bancshares_lp@msn.com

Integra Ventures III, L.P.
Tim T. Black, Contact
300 E. Pine, 2nd Floor   206-832-1990
Seattle, WA 98122   Fax: 206-832-1991
Email: Black@IntegraVentures.net

Northwest Venture Partners II, L.P.
Thomas Simpson & Jean Balek-Miner, Mgrs.
221 North Wall Street, Suite 628   509-747-0728
Spokane, WA 99201   Fax: 509-747-0758
Email: jbminer@nwva.com

Northwest Venture Partners III, L.P.
Jean Balek-Miner, Contact
221 North Wall Street, Suite 628   509-747-0728
Spokane, WA 99201   Fax: 509-747-0758
Email: jbminer@aol.com
The SBA licenses, regulates, and provides financial assistance to privately owned and operated Small Business Investment Companies. SBICs make venture or risk investments by supplying capital and extending unsecured loans and loans not fully collateralized to small enterprises which meet their investment criteria. Financing is made by direct loans and by equity investments.

West Virginia

* West Virginia Development Office

1900 Kanawha Blvd., East   304-558-2234
Charleston, WV 25305-0311   800-982-3386
www.wvdo.org   Fax: 304-558-0449
This office can provide information and expertise in dealing with state, federal, and local agencies. They also have information on financing programs and other services offered by the state government.

Business Counseling: Confidential free service is available to those exploring the option of starting or purchasing a new business and to current owners of small businesses.

Seminars and workshops: Small group training is provided in areas such as starting a business in West Virginia, the basics of business planning, accounting and record keeping, business management techniques, tax law, personnel management techniques, quality customer service, etc. Most seminars and workshops may be attended for a nominal fee.

Site Selection: Industrial specialists assist out-of-state companies, existing state businesses and site location consultants with the identification of suitable locations for their proposed operations utilizing a computerized inventory.

Small Business Work Force Program: Designed to serve businesses with fewer than 20 employees that are established, viable small businesses with demonstrable growth potential. Training programs will be developed based upon a comprehensive needs analysis and the business plan.

Jobs Investment Trust: A $10 million public venture capital fund that uses debt and equity investments to promote and expand the state's economy.

Governor's Guaranteed Work Force Program: Provides training funds to assist new employees in learning their jobs, as well as to improve and expand the skills of existing employees for companies moving to or expanding in West Virginia.

Office of International Development: Offers export counseling and trade promotion opportunities to West Virginia companies. Maintains overseas offices.

Business and Industry Development Division: The Industrial Development Division of the West Virginia Development Office, in cooperation with the Department of Commerce and SBA, cosponsors workshops in international marketing.

West Virginia Export Council: A non-profit export promotion organization committed to expanding West Virginia exports. The Council assists public sector organizations in planning, promoting, and implementing activities that assist international export efforts.

Minority-owned and Women-owned Business Directory: Each year the West Virginia Small Business Development Center publishes a "Minority-owned and Women-owned Business Directory" This directory is distributed to public and private purchasing agents, Chambers of Commerce, Economic Development Authorities, legislators and many privately owned businesses including contractors and all of the listees. There is no cost for the directory nor is there a charge for being included. The only requirement is that the business be located in West Virginia, be a for profit company and be 51% owned by a minority or woman.

Direct Loan Programs The West Virginia Economic Development Authority provides up to 45% in financing fixed assets by providing low-interest loans to expanding state businesses in West Virginia. Loan proceeds may be used for the acquisition of land, buildings and equipment.

Indirect Loan Programs: The West Virginia Economic Development Authority provides a loan insurance program through participating commercial banks to assist firms that cannot obtain conventional bank financing. This program insures up to 80 percent of a bank loan for a maximum loan term of four years. Loan proceeds may be used for any business purpose except the refinancing of existing debt.

Industrial Revenue Bonds: The Industrial Revenue Bonds program provides for customized financing through federal tax-exempt industrial revenue bonds.

Leveraged Technology Loan Insurance Program: This program expands the loan insurance coverage to 90 percent for those businesses involved in the development, commercialization or use of technology-based products and processes.

West Virginia Infrastructure and Jobs Development Council: The Economic Infrastructure Bond Fund can be used for financial assistance to public utilities, county development authorities and private companies for infrastructure improvements to support economic development projects.

Small Business Development Loans: This program provides capital to entrepreneurs for new or expanded small business with loans from $500 to $10,000. 888-982-7232

Linked Deposit Program: The Linked Deposit program provides low-interest loans to qualified small businesses for amounts up to $150,000 and for terms up to four years.

Competitive Improvement Program: The program targets small (50 or fewer employees) and medium (under 500 employees) sized manufacturers. Grants of up to $1,000 per trainee are available with 50 percent contribution by each employer required.

Workforce Development Initiative Program: The program encourages working partnerships between educational institutions and the business community. To qualify, community and technical colleges must establish their own revolving fund dedicated to work force development initiatives. The program requires a one-to-one match from the private sector.

* Rural Development Administration

75 High Street, Room 320   304-284-4860
Federal Building   800-295-8228
Morgantown, WV 26505   Fax: 304-284-4893
www.rurdev.usda.gov/wv

Guaranteed Business and Industry Loan Program: The Business and Industry program is an incentive program to lenders to make loans to businesses that will result in sustainable jobs in rural areas.

Intermediary Relending Program Loans: The Intermediary Lending Program is a revolving loan program where they lend a non-profit organization or public entity money at 1% for 30 years. The borrower then relends the funds to eligible businesses at a reduced rate.

Rural Business Enterprise Grants: Rural communities can receive assistance in promoting the development of small businesses through the Rural Business Enterprise Grant Program. Grants are made to public bodies or not-for-profit organizations. Grantees use the funds to promote the development of small private businesses, which are defined as having 50 or fewer new employees and less than $1 million in projected annual gross revenue. Rural communities include cities with up to 50,000 population.

Rural Cooperative Development Grants: The program provides grants for establishing and operating centers for cooperative development. The primary purpose is to improve economic conditions in rural areas, including cities of up to 50,000 population. Grant funds can pay up to 75% of the costs for establishing and operating such centers. Grants may be made to public bodies or not-for-profit institutions.

Rural Business Opportunity Grants: Rural Business Opportunity Grants are available to promote sustainable economic development in rural communities with exceptional need.

Cooperative Stock Purchase Program: The Rural Cooperative Stock Purchase Program works in conjunction with the Guaranteed Business and Industrial Loan Program allowing loans to be made to producers of agricultural products seeking to join new cooperatives that produce value-added goods. Family farmers can use the Business and Industry Loan Program to help pay for stock in a start-up cooperative that will process an agricultural commodity into a value-added product.

Cooperative Development: Cooperative Service's professional staff provides technical assistance, research, statistics, education, and information to agricultural cooperatives and to groups planning to form a cooperative type of organization. Rural-Business Service is expanding its technical assistance role to bring the service closer to the users and to make technical assistance available to all types of rural cooperatives, including consumer cooperatives, housing cooperatives, marketing cooperatives and credit unions.

Rural Economic Development Loans and Grants: Loans or grants under the Rural Economic Development Loans and Grants programs are available only to rural electric cooperative or telephone borrowers. The programs are intended to help these utilities promote economic and community development projects within their service areas.

* Robert C. Byrd Institute

Huntington Manufacturing Technology Center
1050 Fourth Avenue   800-469-RCBI
Huntington, WV 25701   304-696-6275
Fax: 304-696-6277

Charleston Manufacturing Technology Center
100 Angus E. Peyton Drive   800-469-RCBI
South Charleston, WV 25303   304-746-8925
Fax: 304-746-8926

Bridgeport Manufacturing Technology Center
2007 Aviation Way
Benedum Airport   800-469-RCBI
Bridgeport, WV 26330   304-842-0777
Fax: 304-842-0436

Rocket Center Manufacturing Technology Center
410 State Route 956   800-469-RCBI
Rocket Center, WV 26726   304-726-9900
Fax: 304-726-7048
www.rcbi.org

A teaching factory to help small and medium-sized manufacturing companies increase their competitiveness through the adoption of world-class manufacturing technologies and modern management techniques.

* West Virginia Development Office

1900 Kanawha Blvd., East   800-982-3386
Charleston, WV 25305   304-558-2234
www.wvdo.org   Fax: 304-558-0449

Direct Loans: The WVDO can provide up to 45% in financing fixed assets by providing low interest, direct loans to expanding state businesses and firms locating in West Virginia. Loan term is generally 15 years for real estate intensive projects and 5 to 10 years for equipment projects.

Indirect Loans: The WVDO provides a loan insurance program and a capital access program through participating commercial banks to assist firms that cannot obtain conventional bank financing. The program insures up to 80% of a bank loan for a maximum loan term of four years.

Industrial Revenue Bonds: This provides for customized financing through the federal tax exempt industrial revenue bonds. $35 million of the state's bond allocation is reserved for small manufacturing projects.

Leveraged Technology Loan Insurance Program: This program expands the loan insurance coverage to 90% for those businesses involved in the development, commercialization, or use of technology- based products and processes.

West Virginia Capital Company Act: WVDO administers a program that provides for debt and equity venture capital investment to small business.

* Center for International Programs

Dr. Will Edwards, Director
Marshall University
One John Marshall Drive
320 Old Main   304-696-6265
Huntington, WV 25755   Fax 304-696-6353
www.marshall.edu/cip

The Center for International Programs' mission is to assist in globalizing the community.

* Center for Economic Options

214 Capitol St., Suite 200   304-345-1298
Charleston, WV 25301   Fax: 304-342-0641
www.centerforeconomicoptions.org

A non-profit statewide, community-based organization which promotes opportunities that develop the economic capacity of West Virginia's rural citizens and communities. Working with members of society who traditionally have been excluded from economic decision-making, the Center advocates equity in the workplace, coordinates alternative approaches for economic development, and works to impact the direction of public policy.

* West Virginia Women's Commission

Building 6, Room 850
1900 Kanawha Boulevard, East   304-558-0070
Charleston, WV 25305   Fax: 304-558-5167
www.wvdhhr.org/women/index.asp

Offers women opportunities to learn to be advocates for themselves and to work with others to address systemic change. Projects include leadership and legislative conference like the Women's Town Meeting and Women's Day at the Legislature among others.

* West Virginia Division of Environmental Protection

Pollution Prevention Services
7012 MacCorkle Avenue, South East   304-926-3647 Ext 351
Charleston, West Virginia 25304   Fax: 304-926-3637
www.dep.state.wv.us

The Pollution Prevention (P2) program was established to promote pollution prevention activities among West Virginia's regulated community. P2 activities include such things as adopting new manufacturing processes or materials substitution, both of which can result in less waste being produced. P2 activities can reduce the burden, and cost, of waste treatment and reduce the impact on the environment.

* Regional Contracting Assistance Center

Charleston Regional Contracting Assistance Center
1116 Smith Street, Suite 202   304-344-2546, ext. 4
Charleston, WV 25301   Fax: 304-344-2574
Area of Operation: Barbour, Braxton, Cabell, Calhoun, Clay, Gilmer, Jackson, Kanawha, Lewis, Mason, Putnam, Roane, Upshur, Wirt Counties

Huntington Regional Contracting Assistance Center
1050 Fourth Avenue   304-696-6275
Huntington, WV 25701   Fax: 304-696-4834
Area of Operation: Statewide

Logan Regional Contracting Assistance Center
Southern WV Community & Technical College
P.O. Box 2900
2900 Dempsey Branch Road   304-792-7098 x100
Mt. Gay, WV 25637   Fax: 304-792-7028
www.rcacwv.com/home.html
Area of Operation: Boone, Lincoln, Logan, McDowell, Mingo, Wayne, Wyoming Counties

Princeton Regional Contracting Assistance Center
130 Scott Street, Suite 3   304-487-3104
Princeton, WV 24740   Fax: 304-487-3125
Area of Operation: Fayette, Greenbrier, Mercer, Monroe, Nicholas, Pocahontas, Randolph, Raleigh, Summers, Webster Counties

Ranson Regional Contracting Assistance Center
401 South Fairfax Blvd.   304-724-7547
Ranson, WV 25438   Fax: 304-728-3068
www.rcacwv.com
Area of Operation: Berkeley, Grant, Hampshire, Hardy, Jefferson, Mineral, Monongalia, Morgan, Pendleton, Preston, Tucker Counties

The Regional Contracting Assistance Center (RCAC) is a private nonprofit corporation founded to create information and assistance programs that help West Virginia businesses understand, adapt to, and excel in the evolving business environment. RCAC is dedicated to providing businesses with the direct marketing and technical assistance needed to more fully participate in markets represented by the Department of Defense, other federal agencies, state and local governments, and private corporations. Their aim is to create and retain jobs in the State of West Virginia. All RCAC services are free. They have offices located in Charleston, Beckley, Ranson, and Huntington, WV.

* Certified Development Companies

Ohio Valley Industrial Business Development Council
Certified Development Corporation
P.O. Box 1029
12th & Chapline Street   304-232-7722
Wheeling, WV 26003   Fax: 304-232-7727
Area of Operation: Brooke, Hancock, Ohio, Marshall and Wetzel Counties

West Virginia Certified Development Corporation
Patrick A. Tony" Benedetto", President
North Gate Business Park
10 Association Drive   304-558-3691
Charleston, WV 25311-1217   Fax: 304-558-0206
Area of Operation: Statewide

The 504 Certified Development Company (CDC) Program provides growing businesses with long-term, fixed-rate financing for major fixed assets, such as land and buildings. A Certified Development Company is a nonprofit corporation set up to contribute to the economic development of its community or region. CDCs work with the SBA and private-sector lenders to provide financing to small businesses.

* The Business Information Center

1000 Technology Drive, Suite 1230   304-368-0023
Fairmont, WV 26554   Fax: 304-367-0867
www.sba.gov/wv/wvbic.html

Business Information Centers, or BICs, are one-stop locations for information, counseling and technical assistance designed to help entrepreneurs start, operate and grow their businesses. This center has reference material on almost all areas of business. There are computers with business plan software to assist you in developing your business guidelines. We also have numerous videos and booklets covering what most any business will need.

* Small Business Administration

West Virginia District Office   304-623-5631
320 West Pike Street, Suite 330   800-767-8052, #8
Clarksburg, WV 26301   Fax: 304-623-4269
www.sba.gov/wv

The West Virginia Small Business Administration Office delivers a variety of programs and services, such as startup and operational assistance through small business training and counseling, financial assistance for startup's, business opportunities and much more.

* Small Business Development Center

State Capitol Complex Building 6, Room 652   304-558-2960
1900 Kanawha Blvd. E   888-982-7232
Charleston, WV 25305   Fax: 304-558-0127
www.sbdcwv.org

The SBDC promotes economic development through a program of practical, interrelated services, providing assistance to existing small businesses and the emerging entrepreneurs. The WVSBDC has 14 sub centers throughout the state serving every county.

* Small Business Investment Companies

Mountaineer Capital, L.P.
Patrick A. Bond, Contact
107 Capitol Street, Suite 300   304-347-7521
Charleston, WV 25301   Fax: 304-347-0072
Email: pabond@mtncap.com

WestVen Limited Partnership
Thomas E. Loehr, President
208 Capital St., Suite 300   304-344-1794
Charleston, WV 25301   Fax: 304-344-1798
Email: tloehr@fourthventure.com

Whitney Capital Corporation
Gale Gray, Manager
707 Virginia Street, East, Suite 1700   304-345-2480
Charleston, WV 25301   Fax: 304-345-7258
Email: ggmcpa@citynet.net

The SBA licenses, regulates, and provides financial assistance to privately owned and operated Small Business Investment Companies. SBICs make venture or risk investments by supplying capital and extending unsecured loans and loans not fully collateralized to small enterprises which meet their investment criteria. Financing is made by direct loans and by equity investments.

Wisconsin

* Department of Commerce (COMMERCE)

201 W. Washington Avenue
Madison, WI 53707   608-266-1018
Business Helpline   800-HELP-BUSiness
Fax Request Hotline   608-264-6154
Export Helpline   800-XPORT-WIsconsin
www.commerce.state.wi.us

The Wisconsin Department of Commerce is the state's primary agency for delivery of integrated services to businesses. Services include business financing, technical and managerial services to a wide range of businesses.

Business Development Resources: The Area Development Manager Program assists business expansions, promotes business retention, and helps local development organizations in their respective territories. Area development managers use their knowledge of federal, state, and regional resources to provide a variety of information to expanding or relocating firms. They also mobilize resources to help struggling businesses.

Brownfields Initiative Technical Assistance Program: Provides information and assistance related to brownfields redevelopment. The program can assist in the identification and resolution of regulatory issues, and electronically link prospective buyers with information on available brownfield sites.

Business Development Assistance Center: Provides assistance to small businesses. The office furnishes information on government regulations, and refers businesses to appropriate resources. Call 800-HELP BUSiness.

Assistance with Environmental Regulations and Permits is available to manufacturers. COMMERCE can also expedite regulatory and permit clearance and resolve delays and communications problems. Businesses storing or handling flammable or combustible liquids can receive compliance assistance.

Wisconsin Health Consultation Program: Provides free assistance to employers who request help to establish and maintain a safe and healthful workplace. Health Consultants will conduct an appraisal of physical work practices and environmental hazards, will perform an ergonomics analysis, review various aspects of the employers present occupational safety and health program, and will present occupational health related training.

Manufacturing Assessment Center: Helps small and medium manufacturers improve quality and productivity through professional assessment of operations, systems, and layouts. The center maintains a list of related seminars available throughout the country, and can arrange plant tours of leading-edge manufacturers in the state.

Plan Review Program provides plan review and consultation for structures, plumbing, elevators, HVAC, lighting, erosion control, and private onsite wastewater treatment systems. The services help designers, installers, and owners protect public safety and promote economic efficiency.

Small Business Clean Air Assistance Program: Designed to help small businesses comply with standards established by the federal Clean Air Act.

Small Business Ombudsman: Provides information on government regulations and financing alternatives to small businesses, particularly entrepreneurs. Through its advocacy function, the office promotes special consideration for small businesses in Wisconsin administrative rules.

WiSCon Safety Consultation Program: Assesses current safety programs and suggests improvements; evaluates physical work practices; identifies available assistance; and provides training and education for managers and employees. The consultants do not issue citations, propose penalties, or report possible safety violations to the Occupational Safety and Health Administration.

Wisconsin TechSearch is the fee-based information outreach program of the Kurt F. Wendt Library. TechSearch offers document delivery and reference services to businesses and industry. On-line literature, patent and trademark searches are available. TechSearch provides access to the information resources of the Wendt Library, which contains outstanding collections in science and engineering, and is a US Patent and Trademark Depository Library and more than 40 libraries and information centers on the UW-Madison campus. For more information and a fee schedule, call 608-262-5913/5917 or Email {wtskfw@ doit.wisc.edu}.

Customized Labor Training Fund: Provides training grants to businesses that are implementing new technology or production processes. The program can provide up to 50% of the cost of customized training that is not available from the Wisconsin Technical College System.

Dairy 2020 Initiative: Awards grants and loans for business and feasibility planning to dairy producers and processors considering a modernization or expansion project.

Employee Ownership Assistance Loan Program: Can help a group of employees purchase a business by providing individual awards up to $25,000 for feasibility studies or professional assistance. The business under consideration must have expressed its intent to downsize or close.

Division of Vocational Rehabilitation Job Creation Program: Designed to increase employment opportunities for DVR clients by providing equipment grants, technical assistance grants, and customized assistance to companies that will hire persons with disabilities as part of a business expansion.

Major Economic Development Program: Offers low-interest loans for business development projects that create a significant economic impact.

Rural Economic Development Program: Makes individual awards up to $30,000 for feasibility studies and other professional assistance to rural businesses with fewer than 25 employees. Businesses and farms that have completed their feasibility evaluations are eligible for individual micro loans up to $25,000 for working capital and the purchase of equipment.

Technology Development Fund: Helps businesses finance Phase I product development research. Firms completing Phase I projects can receive Phase II product-commercialization funding.

Tax Incremental Financing: Helps cities in Wisconsin attract industrial and commercial growth in underdeveloped and blighted areas. A city or village can designate a specific area within its boundaries as a TIF district and develop a plan to improve its property values. Taxes generated by the increased property values pay for land acquisition or needed public works.

BDI Micro Loan Program: Helps entrepreneurs with permanent disabilities and rehabilitation agencies finance business start-ups or expansions.

BDI Self-Employment Program: Helps severely disabled DVR clients start micro-businesses.

Industrial Revenue Bonds (IRBs): A means of financing the construction and equipping of manufacturing plants and a limited number of non-manufacturing facilities. The municipality is not responsible for debt service on IRBs, nor is it liable in the case of default. IRBs are also exempt from federal income tax.

Petroleum Environmental Clean-up Fund: Reimburses property owners for eligible clean-up costs related to discharges for petroleum tank systems.

Recycling Demonstration Grant Program: Helps businesses and local governing units fund waste reduction, reuse, and recycling pilot projects.

Recycling Early Planning Grant Program: Awards funds to new and expanding business plans, marketing assistance, and feasibility studies on the start-up or expansion of a recycling business.

Recycling Loan Program: Awards loans for the purchase of equipment to businesses and nonprofit organizations that make products from recycled waste, or make equipment necessary to manufacture these products.

Recycling Technology Assistance Program: Provides low cost loans to fund research and development of products or processes using recovered or recyclable materials. Eligible activities include product development and testing, process development and assessment, specialized research, and technical assistance.

Wisconsin Fund: Provides grants to help small commercial businesses rehabilitate or replace their privately owned sewage systems.

Wisconsin Housing and Economic Development Authority (WHEDA): Offers a program that buys down commercial interest rates, enabling Wisconsin lenders to offer short-term, below-market-rate loans to small, minority- or women-owned businesses. A loan guarantee program is available for firms ramping-up to meet contract demands; for firms in economically-distressed areas; and for tourism and agribusiness projects. The authority also operates a beginning farmer bond program.

Community-Based Economic Development Program: Awards grants to community-based organizations for development and business assistance projects and to municipalities for economic development planning. The program helps community-based organizations plan, build, and create business and technology-based incubators, and can also capitalize an incubator tenant revolving-loan program.

Early Planning Grant: Helps entrepreneurs and small businesses obtain professional services necessary to evaluate the feasibility of a proposed start-up or expansion.

Economic Diversification Loan Program: Low-interest loan to finance a portion of the costs to establish and expand operations.

Wisconsin Small Business Innovative Research (SBIR) Support Program: Coordinates resources to help businesses pursue federal SBIR grants and contracts. The federal SBIR program provides Phase I awards of up to $100,000 for feasibility studies and Phase II awards of up to $750,000 for project development.

Wisconsin Trade Project Program: Can help small export-ready firms participate in international trade shows. The business covers its own travel and lodging expenses. COMMERCE can then provide up to $5,000 in reimbursements to a business for costs associated with attending a trade show, such as booth rental or product brochure translation.

Trade Shows and Trade Missions: Showcase Wisconsin firms and products to prospective international clients. The Department sponsors a Wisconsin-products booth at approximately 12 international trade fairs per year, and also arranges trade and reverse investment missions abroad, many of them led by the Governor.

Economic Impact Loan Program: This program is designed to help Wisconsin businesses that have been negatively impacted by gaming. Loans are for 75% of the cost of modernizing and/or improvements up to $100,000.

Business Employees' Skills Training (BEST) Program: Helps business in industries facing severe labor shortages upgrade the skills of their workforce with tuition reimbursement grants to help cover the costs associated with training employees.

Financial Consulting and Technical Assistance: The bureau counsels individuals who want to start, buy or expand a business. Economic consultants provide information regarding structuring financial plans, preparing loan applications, strategic planning, and guidance for writing business plans.

Enterprise Development Zone Program (EDZ): EDZ provides site specific tax incentives to new or expanding businesses whose projects will affect distressed areas.

Technology Development Fund: The Technology Development Fund program helps Wisconsin businesses research and develop technological innovations that have the potential to provide significant economic benefit to the state.

Agribusiness Guarantee: Agribusiness Guarantee is administered by Wisconsin Housing and Economic Development Authority (WHEDA). This program provides loan guarantees for projects developing products, markets, method of processing or marketing for a Wisconsin-grown commodity. The maximum guarantee of 80% on loans up to $750,000 can be used for equipment, land, buildings, working capital, inventory and marketing expenses. Contact WHEDA at 1-800-334-6873.

Early Planning Grant Program (EPG): EPG helps individual entrepreneurs and small businesses throughout Wisconsin obtain the professional services necessary to evaluate the feasibility of a proposed start up or expansion.

Entrepreneurial Training Grant Program (ETG): ETG provides grants to help cover a portion of the cost of attending Small Business Development Center's (SBDC) new Entrepreneurial Training Course.

Freight Railroad Infrastructure Improvement Program: The Freight Improvement Program awards loans to businesses or communities wishing to rehabilitate rail lines, advance economic development, connect an industry to the national railroad system, or to make improvements to enhance transportation efficiency, safety, and freight movement. Contact the Department of Transportation, 608-267-9284.

Milk Volume Production Program (MVP): MVP is designed to assist dairy producers that are undertaking capital improvement projects that will result in a significant increase in Wisconsin's milk production.

State of Wisconsin Investment Board (SWIB): The State of Wisconsin Investment Board is a large pension fund designed to explore investments in Wisconsin. The Department of Commerce can help your Wisconsin business seek financing to expand your business.

Going into Business in Wisconsin: An Entrepreneur's Guide: This $5 guide covers many issues involved in the planning and starting new business ventures.

Business Wizard: The Business Wizard uses a series of questions-and-answer pages to provide customized information to help you start and operate a Wisconsin-based business.

Trade Show Grant Program: This program is designed to encourage Wisconsin businesses seek out new international markets. Reimbursement grants of up to $5,000 are available for specific expenses for participating in an approved trade show or matchmaker trade delegation event.

Outreach Consultants: These consultants, located throughout the state, will work one-on-one with businesses to solve export problems. This service is free.

* Rural Development Administration

4949 Kirschling Court   715-345-7615
Stevens Point, WI 54481   Fax: 715-345-7669
www.rurdev.usda.gov/wi

Business and Industry Guaranteed and Loans: Business and Industry Guaranteed Loans are loan guarantees where the cost is a one-time, up-front fee of 2% of the amount guaranteed. Loans are made to businesses, which save or create jobs in rural areas (under 50,000 in population). Borrowers may be an individual, partnership, cooperative, for-profit or non-profit corporation, Indian Tribe, or public body.

Business and Industry Direct Loans: The purpose of the Business and Industry Direct Loan Program is to improve, develop, or finance business, industry, and employment, and improve the economic and environmental climate in rural communities. Loan purposes include purchase and expansion of land, equipment, buildings, and working capital.

Community Facilities Direct Loans and Grants: Community Facilities Direct Loans and Grants provide funding for essential community facilities such as municipal buildings, day care centers, and health and safety facilities. Examples include fire halls, fire trucks, clinics, nursing homes, and hospitals. Community Facility loans and grants may also be used for such things as activity centers for the handicapped, schools, libraries, and other community buildings. Applicant must be unable to borrow money elsewhere at rates and terms to make the project affordable.

Community Facilities Guaranteed Loans: Community Facilities Guaranteed Loans provide funding for essential community facilities such as day care, hospitals, schools, clinics, roads, and fire halls.

Cooperative Development Technical Assistance: Cooperative Development Technical Assistance helps rural residents form new cooperative businesses or to use the cooperative model to address unmet social or economic needs.

Intermediary Relending Program: Intermediary Relending Program money is lent to private non-profit corporations, any state or local government, an Indian Tribe, or a cooperative that in turn is re-lent by the intermediary to the ultimate recipients. The ultimate recipient must be unable to obtain credit elsewhere at reasonable rates and terms.

Rural Business Enterprise Grants: Rural Business Enterprise Grants are for financing and developing small and emerging private businesses with less than $1 million in revenues, and which will have fewer than 50 new employees. There is no maximum dollar limit for any one project. Funds can be used for technical assistance, revolving loan program, incubator/industrial buildings, and industrial park improvements.

Rural Cooperative Development Grants: Rural Cooperative Development Grants are for establishing and operating centers for cooperative development. The grant program will be used to facilitate the creation or retention of jobs in rural areas through the development of new rural cooperatives and operational involvement of existing cooperatives by the centers. Cooperative development activities by the centers include the startup, expansion, or operational improvement of a cooperative.

Rural Business Opportunity Grants: Rural Business Opportunity Grants provide for technical assistance, training, and planning activities that improve economic conditions in rural areas and cities and villages with a population of 10,000 or less.

Rural Economic Development Loans and Grants: Rural Economic Development Loans and Grants help develop projects that will result in a sustainable increase in economic productivity, job creation, and incomes in rural areas. Projects may include business start-ups and expansion, community development, incubator projects, medical and training projects, and feasibility studies. Ineligible purposes are those that directly benefit the borrower, conflicts of interest, and costs incurred prior to the application.

Value-Added Agricultural Product Market Development Grants: Value Added Agricultural Product Market Development Grants help independent producers and producer organizations enter into value-added activities.

* Bureau of Minority Business Development

Department of Commerce
201 W. Washington Ave.
P.O. Box 7970   608-267-9550
Madison, WI 53707   Fax: 308-267-2829
www.commerce.state.wi.us

Certifies companies to be eligible to participate in state's minority business bid preference. Company must be at least 51% owned, controlled, and managed by minority (being a woman is not considered a minority).

Certification to participate in the state's minority business purchasing and contracting program is available to minority vendors. Interested firms may apply through the department. They are then listed in the *Annual Directory of Minority-Owned Firms*.

Marketing Assistance of various kinds is offered to minority-owned firms. Certified minority vendors are listed in the department's database for access by the purchasing community. Minority-owned firms can receive help developing marketing plans. Each year, the department sponsors the Marketplace Trade Fair to encourage business contacts between minority vendors and state and corporate buyers.

Minority Business Development Fund: Offers low-interest loans for start-up, expansion or acquisition projects. To qualify for the fund, a business must be 51-percent controlled, owned, and actively managed by minority-group members, and the project must retain or increase employment.

Minority Business Early Planning Grant Program: Provides seed capital to minority entrepreneurs for feasibility studies, business plans, and marketing plans.

* Solid and Hazardous Waste Education Center

UW- Green Bay Campus
2420 Nicolet Dr., ES317   920-465-2278
Green Bay, WI 54311   Fax: 920-465-2376
www1.uwex.edu/ces/shwec/index.cfm

Provides technical assistance to businesses and communities on emissions reduction, pollution prevention, recycling, and solid waste management. The Center also offers grants that companies can use for hazardous waste reduction audits.

* Wisconsin Housing and Economic Development Authority

Madison Office   608-266-7884
201 W. Washington Ave., Suite 700 800-334-6873
Madison, WI 53703   Fax: 608-267-1099
Mailing Address:
P.O. Box 1728
Madison, WI 53701-1728

Milwaukee Office   414-277-4039
101 W Pleasant Street, Suite 100 800-628-4833
Milwaukee, WI 53212   Fax: 414-277-4704
www.wheda.com

Business Development Bonds: These are essentially industrial revenue bonds issued by the Wisconsin Housing and Economic Development Authority (WHEDA) on behalf of small businesses. Eligible projects qualify for low-cost fixed-rate financing. Businesses need to supply lenders with a letter of credit from WHEDA to guarantee these bonds. Available to manufacturers and first-time farmers with gross sales of $35 million or less. Project funded must create or retain employment. Proceeds can be used for land, building, or equipment purchase or improvement. Other restrictions apply. BDB's are generally range from $500,000 to $1 million with $10 million maximum.

Agribusiness Guarantee; Qualifying businesses are those located in a municipality with a population under 50,000, that purchase a substantial percentage of its raw agricultural commodities from Wisconsin suppliers, and; 1.) Develop a new product, method of processing, market, or improved marketing method for a Wisconsin product, or; 2.) Produce a specialty cheese product that is new to the business, or; 3.) Commercially harvest whitefish in Lake Superior. Maximum guarantee is 80% on loans up to $750,000. Agribusiness can be used for equipment, land, buildings, permanent working capital, inventory and initial product marketing expenses.

Linked Deposit Loan (LiDL) Subsidy: The purpose of this loan is to assist women- and/or minority-owned and controlled businesses in the start-up or expansion of their business by reducing the interest rate on their bank loans.

Neighborhood Business Revitalization Guarantee: This program helps business owners obtain financing to stimulate economic development in urban neighborhoods.

WHEDA Small Business Guarantee (WSBG): The WSBG program can help your business obtain financing to start a business, acquire land or expand a small business.

Credit Relief Outreach Program (CROP): CROP provides guarantees on agriculture production loans to farmers.

Farm Asset Reinvestment Management (FARM): FARM provides loan guarantees for agricultural expansion and modernization.

Beginning Farmer Bond Loan (BFB): BFB gives beginning farmers below-market interest rates on financing to start an operation.

* Certified Development Companies

Great Lakes Asset Corporation
Ms. Cindy Esterling, Loan Officer/Manager
1317 Lombardi Access Rd.   800-281-6444
Green Bay, WI 54304   Fax: 920-499-7331
Email: cdcglac@aol.com
Area of Operation: Brown, Calumet, Kewaunee, Manitowoc, Marinette, Oconto and Shawano Counties

Milwaukee Economic Development Corporation
Ms. Martha Morrison, Asst. Vice President/Secretary
809 North Broadway
P.O. Box 324   414-286-5853
Milwaukee WI 53201-0324   Fax: 414-286-5778
Email: mmorri@mkedcd.org
Area of Operation: Milwaukee, Ozaukee, Washington and Waukesha Counties

Racine County Business Development Corporation
Mr. Gordon M. Kacala, Executive Director
4701 Washington Avenue, Suite 215 414-638-0234
Racine, WI 53406-3938   Fax: 414-638-0250
E-mail: rcedc@execpc.com
Area of Operation: Kenosha and Racine Counties

Western Wisconsin Development Corporation
Mr. William Bay, General Manager

126 Soo Street
Almena, WI 54805   715-357-3334
                                          Fax: 715-357-6233
Area of Operation: Barron, Bayfield, Burnett, Chippewa, Dunn, Polk, Rusk, St. Croix, Sawyer and Washburn Counties

* Entrepreneurial Training Grant (ETG) Program

P.O. Box 7970
Madison, WI 53707   608-263-7680
www.commerce.state.wi.us

Commerce has partnered with the Small Business Development Center (SBDC) to develop a pilot program designed to help individual entrepreneurs and small businesses throughout Wisconsin. Under the Entrepreneurial Training Grant (ETG) program, Commerce can provide applicants with a grant to help cover a portion of the cost of attending SBDC's new Entrepreneurial Training Course.

* Wisconsin Department of Tourism

P.O. Box 8690   608-266-7621
Madison, WI 53708   Fax: 608-261-8213
http://agency.travelwisconsin.com

Tourism Development
Tourism Communication Program:
Responsible for public information, publication production, media assistance, statewide events publicity, and special projects promotions producing the materials and publicity to ensure that Wisconsin tourism is visible to public.

Joint Effort Marketing (JEM) Program: Department may fund up to 75% of advertising expenses of qualifying projects that help promote the state in coordination with the tourism marketing plan.

JEM Newspaper Program: Businesses can take advantage of special low rates and get greater impact by purchasing advertising space in newspapers under the Wisconsin tourism logo.

Tourism Marketing and Customer Service 101: The Department of Tourism provides a series of basic tourism marketing and customer service educational courses. These courses are designed to provide basic information to assist in the marketing and operational aspects of the tourism business.

Tourism Development Specialist Program: Provides information on funding sources and feasibility assessment to individual businesses and developers. Development consultants advise and help promote the industry in their respective territories.

* Export-Import Bank of the United States

Chicago Regional Office & U.S. Export Center
55 W. Monroe Street, Suite 2440   312-353-8081
Chicago, IL 60603   Fax: 312-353-8098
www.exim.gov

Working Capital Guarantee: Loan guarantees to assist small to medium-sized companies having the potential to export but inability to access working capital lines of credit from their banks to finance operations. Funds can be used for inventory, working capital, materials, labor, marketing activities. Other export credit programs available include medium and long term credit, and various types of export/import insurance.

* Small Business Administration (SBA)

310 West Wisconsin Ave., #400
Milwaukee, WI 53203   414-297-3941

740 Regent St., Suite 100
Madison, WI 53715   608-441-5263
www.sba.gov/wi

The Wisconsin Small Business Administration Office delivers a variety of programs and services, such as startup and operational assistance through small business training and counseling, financial assistance for startup's, business opportunities and much more.

* Small Business Investment Companies

Banc One Stonehenge Capital Fund WI, LLC
Mr. Kent Velde, Manager
3424 N. Shepard Avenue   414-906-1702
Milwaukee, WI 53211   Fax: 414-906-1703
Email: kvelde@att.net

Capital Investments, Inc.
Steve Rippl, Exec. Vice-President

1009 West Glenn Oals Lane
Suite 103   414-241-0303
Mequon, WI 53092   Fax: 414-241-8451
Email: dmayer@capitalinvestmentsinc.com

Facilitator Capital Fund, L.P.
Robert Zobel, Gustavus Taylor
5133 West Terrace Drive, Suite 204   608-227-2900
Madison, WI 53718   Fax: 608-227-2901
Email: tracy@facilitatorfunds.com

M & I Ventures, LLC
John T. Byrnes, President
770 North Water St.   414-765-7910
Milwaukee, WI 53202   Fax: 414-765-7850
Email: worthober@masonwells.com

The SBA licenses, regulates, and provides financial assistance to privately owned and operated Small Business Investment Companies. SBICs make venture or risk investments by supplying capital and extending unsecured loans and loans not fully collateralized to small enterprises which meet their investment criteria. Financing is made by direct loans and by equity investments.

* Wisconsin Business Development Finance Corporation

P.O. Box 2717
100 River Place, Suite 1
P.O. Box 2717   608-819-0390
Madison, WI 53701   Fax: 608-819-0393
www.wbd.org

Wisconsin Business Development (WBD): Offers long-term financing at below conventional rates. Fund can be used for land, building, equipment, and certain soft costs such as architect, accounting, legal fees are also eligible. WBD participation may not exceed 40 percent or a maximum of $750,000 of the project cost.

* Venture Capital

Department of Commerce
P.O. Box 7970
Madison, WI 53707   800-HELP-BUS
www.commerce.state.wi.us

Venture capital firms are interested in investing in businesses with especially high growth potential. Venture capital firms expect to recover three to five times their investment in five to seven years. They are typically interested in projects requiring an investment of $300,000 to $2,000,000. For more information on Wisconsin venture capital and procedures for obtaining venture capital write or call the Department of Commerce.

* Wisconsin Women's Business Initiative Corporation

2745 N. Dr. Martin Luther King Jr. Drive   414-263-5450
Milwaukee, WI 53212   Fax: 414-263-5456
www.wwbic.com

The Wisconsin Women's Business Initiative Corporation provides business education, technical assistance and access to capital for entrepreneurs.

Wyoming

* Wyoming Business Council

214 W. 15th St.   307-777-2800
Cheyenne, WY 82002   800-262-3425
www.wyomingbusiness.org   Fax: 307-777-2838

This office can provide information and expertise in dealing with state, federal, and local agencies. They also have information on financing programs and other services offered by the state government.

Science, Technology and Energy Authority: Helps to improve the development of research capability, stimulate basic and applied technological research and facilitate commercialization of new products and processes.

Mid-America Manufacturing Technology Centers: A non-profit organization that assists small and medium-sized manufacturers in becoming more competitive, improve quality, boost sales and locate production resources.

The state offers a wide spectrum of public sector financial and technical assistance programs.

Wyoming Industrial Development Corporation: Matches resources in both private and public sectors that best fit the needs of business.

Workforce Training: Financial support is available for on-the-job training, classroom training, or a combination of both.

Seed Capital Loan Program: The Seed Capital Loan Program makes direct loans to qualifying businesses that can demonstrate the required capital match, collateral and repayment.

Job Training Grants: Job training grants are available to for-profit businesses that have a need for specially trained employees in their workplace.

Economic Development Technical Assistance Grants: Technical assistance grants are available to for-profit businesses wanting to conduct project-planning research.

Challenge Loan Program: The Challenge Loan Program offers matching funds to a local economic development organization for the benefit of a business.

Business Permitting Assistance Office: This office provides one-stop permitting and licensing information for existing Wyoming businesses and businesses relocating in Wyoming.

Grant Station Database: The Business Council provides a database listing over 5,000 funding sources.

GRO-Biz: Gro-Biz is the Wyoming Procurement Technical Assistance center. The center assists small businesses and entrepreneurs throughout the state in selling their products and services to the government.

Industrial Development Revenue Bonds (IRB): Cities and counties can issue Industrial Development Revenue Bonds to provide financing to promote economic growth in Wyoming and to create jobs for in-state residents.

Market Research Center: The Market Research Center provides marketing information that can improve the ability of Wyoming businesses to thrive.

Tradeshow Incentive Program: The Tradeshow Incentive Program encourages Wyoming businesses promote and sell their products to statewide, national and international buyers.

Wyoming Research Products Center: The technology center helps inventors develop their technology innovations into marketable products.

Wyoming Women's Business Center: The Wyoming Women's Business Center offers a variety services to prospective and current women business owners.

* Rural Development Administration

100 East B Street
Federal Building, Room 1005   307-233-6700
Casper, WY 82601   Fax: 307-233-6727
www.rurdev.usda.gov/wy

Business and Industry Direct and Guaranteed Loans: The business and industry program provides direct and guaranteed loans for expansion and preservation of jobs in rural areas. The program can provide development credit in towns of 50,000 or less. Loan funds may be used to purchase land, buildings, and equipment; working capital; and in certain cases to refinance debts. Priorities place special emphasis on saving existing jobs as well as creating employment opportunities.

Intermediary Relending Program: The purpose of the Intermediary Relending Program is to finance business facilities and community development projects not within the outer boundary of any city having a population of 25,000 or more. This is achieved through loans made by Rural Business-Cooperative Service to intermediaries that provide loans to ultimate recipients for business facilities and community development projects in a rural area.

Rural Business Enterprise Grants: This program provides grants to finance and facilitate development of small and emerging private business enterprises in rural areas or cities up to 50,000 population, with priority to applications for projects in open country, rural communities and towns of 25,000 and smaller and economically distressed communities. Rural Business Enterprise Grants include grants made to third party lenders to establish revolving loan programs. Eligibility is limited to public bodies and private nonprofit corporations.

Rural Economic Development Loan and Grant Program: The Rural Economic Development Loan and Grant Program finances rural economic

development and rural job creation projects. Loans and grants are made to Rural Utilities Service electric and telephone borrowers who use the funds to provide financing for business and community development projects.

Rural Cooperative Development Grants: Grants will be made available to non-profit corporations and institutions of higher education for the purpose of establishing and operating centers for rural cooperative development.

Cooperative Services: Rural Business Service provides a wide range of services including assistance for people interested in forming new cooperatives, technical assistance to existing cooperatives facing specific problems or challenges, and research assistance for cooperatives dealing with changing markets and business trends.

* Certified Development Companies

Frontier Certified Development Company
Diane Johnston, Director   800-934-5351
232 East Second Street, Suite 300   307-234-5351
Casper, WY 82601   Fax: 307-234-0501
Area of Operation: Statewide
The 504 Certified Development Company (CDC) Program provides growing businesses with long-term, fixed-rate financing for major fixed assets, such as land and buildings. A Certified Development Company is a nonprofit corporation set up to contribute to the economic development of its community or region. CDCs work with the SBA and private-sector lenders to provide financing to small businesses.

* Department of Environmental Quality

122 West 25th Street,
Herschler Building   307-777-7937
Cheyenne, WY 82002   Fax: 307-777-7682
http://deq.state.wy.us
Small Business Assistance Visits: The Office provides free on-site assistance visits on a rotating basis throughout the state.

* Wyoming Community Development Authority

155 North Beech   307-265-0603
Casper, WY 82601   Fax: 307-266-5414
www.wyomingcda.com
Housing Trust Fund: The WCDA established a Housing Trust Fund for the purpose of financing non-traditional affordable housing other than under its tax-exempt bond program. Loans to projects from the Housing Trust Fund are often combined with other funding sources to accomplish housing goals.

Community Development Block Grant (CDBG) funds: are loaned to applicants for housing-related programs that benefit low-income households. Eligible applicants for these funds are counties and incorporated cities and towns in Wyoming.

Federal Low Income Housing Tax Credits: Housing finance authorities across the county have been designated by federal statute to administer the Federal Low-Income Housing Tax Credit, which was enacted through the Tax Reform Act of 1986. This program provides federal tax credits for developers and contractors as an incentive to develop affordable rental housing projects. An Allocation Plan may be obtained by contacting the WCDA.

* Wyoming Industrial Development Corporation

232 E. Second Street, Suite 300   800-934-5351
Casper, WY 82601   307-234-0501
www.widefrontier.com
Provides non-bank lending through various Small Business Administration programs and other public finance sources for companies with moderately strong credit risks. Funds may be used for acquiring fixed assets, renovation and construction of facilities, financing costs, or working capital. These loans range from $25,000 to $3 million, but most do not exceed $750,000. Some size restrictions and employment requirements apply. Depending on which program is used, the SBA will guarantee between 40 percent-90 percent of a loan. Terms run from between 7 to 10 years, with maturity in 25 years.

SBA 504 Program: Provides loans using 50 percent conventional bank financing, 40 percent SBA involvement through Certified Development Companies, and 10 percent owner equity. A fixed-asset loan in amounts up to $750,000. Loan can be used for land and building, construction, machinery and equipment, and renovation/expansion.

SBA 7(a) Guaranteed and Direct Loan: Guarantees up to 90 percent of a loan made through a private lender, up to 750,000. Can be used for working capital, inventory, machinery and equipment, and land and building.

Available only to those unable to obtain a loan from conventional sources. Direct loans are made up to $150,000.

* Small Business Administration
100 E. B St., Room 4001
Box 2839   307-261-6500

Casper, WY 82602-2839   Fax: 307-261-6535
www.sba.gov/wy

The Wyoming Small Business Administration Office delivers a variety of programs and services, such as startup and operational assistance through small business training and counseling, financial assistance for startup's, business opportunities and much more.

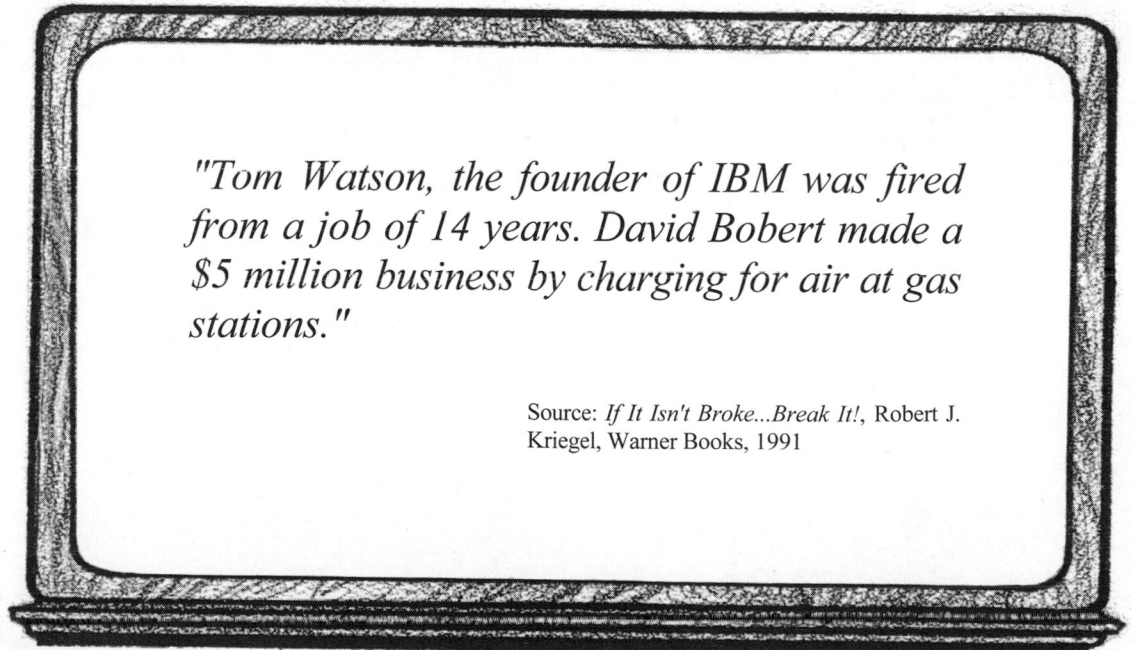

"Tom Watson, the founder of IBM was fired from a job of 14 years. David Bobert made a $5 million business by charging for air at gas stations."

Source: *If It Isn't Broke...Break It!*, Robert J. Kriegel, Warner Books, 1991

Federal Money Programs for Businesses

The following is a description of the federal funds available to small businesses, entrepreneurs, inventors, and researchers. This information is derived from the *Catalog of Federal Domestic Assistance* which is published by the U.S. Government Printing Office in Washington, DC. The number next to the title description is the official reference for this federal program. Contact the office listed below the caption for further details. The following is a description of the terms used for the types of assistance available:

Loans: money lent by a federal agency for a specific period of time and with a reasonable expectation of repayment. Loans may or may not require a payment of interest.

Loan Guarantees: programs in which federal agencies agree to pay back part or all of a loan to a private lender if the borrower defaults.

Grants: money given by federal agencies for a fixed period of time and which does not have to be repaid.

Direct Payments: funds provided by federal agencies to individuals, private firms, and institutions. The use of direct payments may be "specified" to perform a particular service or for "unrestricted" use.

Insurance: coverage under specific programs to assure reimbursement for losses sustained. Insurance may be provided by federal agencies or through insurance companies and may or may not require the payment of premiums.

* Loans to Producers of Cotton, Rice, Soybeans, Canola, Flaxseed, Mustard Seed, Rapeseed, Safflower, Sunflower Seed, Feed Grains, Wheat, Rye, Peanuts, Tobacco, Sugar, and Crambe

(10.051 Commodity Loans and Loan Deficiency Payments)
U.S. Department of Agriculture
Farm Service Agency
Price Support Division
Stop 0512, 1400 Independence Ave., SW
Washington, DC 20250-0512   202-720-7901
www.fsa.usda.gov

This program is designed to improve and stabilize farm income, to create a better balance between supply and demand of the commodities and to assist farmers in the marketing of their crops. Types of assistance: direct payments with unrestricted use; direct loans. Range of money available: $162 to $1,006,400; Average: $22,959.

* Grants to Dairy Farmers Whose Milk is Contaminated Because of Pesticides

(10.053 Dairy Indemnity Program)
U.S. Department of Agriculture
Farm Service Agency
1400 Independence Av., SW
Washington, DC 20250-0512   202-720-7641
www.fsa.usda.gov

This program provides money to dairy farmers and manufacturers of dairy products who are forced to remove their products from commercial markets due to contamination. Fair market value is paid for the milk and dairy products as long as the contamination was not caused by negligence or failure to follow procedures set forth by the Federal government. Possible sources of contamination include pesticides approved for use by the Federal government, chemicals, toxic substances, and nuclear radiation or fallout. Types of assistance: direct payments with unrestricted use. Range of money available: $88 to $95,000; Average: $40,000.

* Grants to Producers of Wheat, Corn, Grain Sorghum, Barley, Oats, Upland Cotton and Rice

(10.055 Production Flexibility Payments for Contract Commodities)
Philip W. Stronce
U.S. Department of Agriculture
Farm Service Agency
Economic and Policy Analysis Staff
Stop 0508, 1400 Independence Ave., SW
Washington, DC 20250-0508   202-720-2711
www.fsa.usda.gov

This program provides financial assistance to farmers in order to ensure a steady supply of food, while maintaining the flexibility necessary to adjust to the condition of the economy while complying with farm conservation and wetland protection requirements. Type of assistance: direct payment with unrestricted use. Range of money available: up to $40,000.

* Money to Run an Agriculture Related Business

(10.406 Farm Operating Loans)
U.S. Department of Agriculture
Farm Service Agency
Director, Loan Making Division
Ag Box 0522
Washington, DC 20250   202-720-1632
www.fsa.usda.gov

Through the extension of credit and supervisory assistance, this program helps the operators of family size farms to make more efficient use of their land, labor, and other resources. It also helps to establish and maintain financially stable farming and ranching operations. Types of assistance: direct loans; guaranteed/insured loans. Range of money available: Direct Loans up to $200,000; average: $47,365. Guaranteed/Insured Loans up to $731,000; average: $157,339.

* Money to Implement Emergency Conservation Programs

(10.054 Emergency Conservation Program)
U.S. Department of Agriculture
Farm Service Agency
Stop 0513, 1400 Independence Ave., SW
Washington, DC 20250-0513   202-720-6221
www.fsa.usda.gov

Any agricultural producer who, as owner, landlord, tenant or sharecropper on a farm or ranch, bears a part of the cost of an approved conservation practice in a disaster area is eligible to apply for cost-share assistance. This program enables farmers to perform emergency conservation measures to control wind erosion on farmlands, to rehabilitate farmlands damaged by wind erosion, floods, hurricanes or other natural disasters and to carry out emergency water conservation or water enhancing measures during periods of severe drought. Type of assistance: direct payments for specified use. Range of money available: $50 to $64,000; average: $2,681.

* Loans to Purchase and Construct On-Farm Storage Facilities

(10.056 Farm Storage Facility Loans)
U.S. Department of Agriculture
Farm Service Agency
Director, Price Support Division
1400 Independence Ave., SW
Washington, DC 20250   202-720-7935
www.fsa.usda.gov/dafp/psd/FSFL.html

The purpose of this program is to support the construction of on-farm grain storage facilities and to help farmers adapt to identity preserved storage and handling requirements for genetically enhanced production. Funding from this program can be used for the purchase and construction of new storage structures, handling equipment, drying equipment, and to finance the remodeling of existing storage structures. Type of assistance: direct loans. Range of money available: $1,000 to $100,000.

* Grants to Livestock Producers

(10.066 Livestock Assistance Program)
U.S. Department of Agriculture
Farm Service Agency
Production, Emergencies and Compliance Division
Emergency Preparedness and Program Branch
Stop 0517, 1400 Independence Ave., SW
Washington, DC 20250-0517   202-720-7641
www.fsa.usda.gov

This program provides grants to eligible livestock producers who suffered grazing losses due to drought, hot weather, disease, insect infestation, fire, hurricane, flood, earthquake, severe storm or other disasters occurring after January 1, 2000. Benefits are provided to producers who suffered 40% or greater grazing loss for three or more months. Eligible livestock producers must be in a county where a severe natural disaster occurred and said county must have been approved as a primary disaster area under a Secretarial or Presidential disaster declaration. Type of assistance: direct payment with unrestricted use. Range of money available: up to $40,000; average: $875.

* Loans to Apple Producers

(10.075 Special Apple Program)
Department of Agriculture
Farm Service Agency
Director, Loan Making Division
Ag Box 0522, 1400 Independence Ave., SW
Washington, DC 20250   202-720-1632
www.fsa.usda.gov

This program is available to producers of apples that are suffering from economic loss due to low prices for apples. Loan funds may be used for payment of costs associated with reorganizing a farm to improve its profitability, payment of annual farm expenses, purchase of farm equipment or fixtures or any other approved purposes related to the production or marketing of apples. Type of assistance: direct loans. Range and average of money available: program is new; this information is not available at this time

* Loans for Seed Producers

(10.076 Emergency Loans for Seed Producers)
Department of Agriculture
Farm Service Agency
Director, Loan Making Division
AgBox 0522, 1400 Independence Ave., SW
Washington, DC 20250   202-720-1632

www.fsa.usda.gov

The aim of this program is to assist seed producers who were adversely impacted by the bankruptcy filing of AgriBiotech. To be eligible, an applicant must have filed a valid proof of claim for seed produced under contract to AgriBiotech in 1999 in the United States or a United States Territory. Type of assistance: direct loans. Range and average of money available: program is new; this information is not available yet.

* Grants to Producers of Cattle, Sheep, Goats, Buffalo, and Catfish

(10.077 Livestock Compensation Program)
U.S. Department of Agriculture
Farm Service Agency
Production Emergency and Compliance Division
Washington, DC 20250   202-720-7641
www.fsa.usda.gov

This program provides financial compensation to livestock producers in counties that received primary disaster designation due to drought in 2001 and 2002. Type of assistance: direct payments with unrestricted use. Range of money available: up to $40,000.

* Grants to Bioenergy Producers

(10.078 Bioenergy Program)
U.S. Department of Agriculture
Farm Service Agency
Kansas City Commodity Office
Contract Reconciliation Division
P.O. Box 419205, Stop 8758
Kansas City, MO 64141-6205   816-926-6525
www.fsa.usda.gov/daco/bio_daco.htm

This program provides financial assistance to producers of Bioenergy. The money is to be used to increase purchases of eligible commodities for the purpose of expanding production of Bioenergy, such as ethanol and biodiesel, and to support new production capacity for Bioenergy. Producers must be able to show an increase in their purchase of eligible commodities and the resulting increase of production as compared to the previous fiscal year. Type of assistance: direct payments for specified use. Range of money available: information not available.

* Money to Farmers, Ranchers, and Aquaculture Businesses

(10.407 Farm Ownership Loans)
U.S. Department of Agriculture
Farm Service Agency
Director, Loan Making Division
AgBox 0522
Washington, DC 20250   202-720-1632
www.fsa.usda.gov

This program assists eligible farmers, ranchers, and aquaculture operators, including farming cooperatives, corporations, partnerships, and joint operations, through the extension of credit and supervisory assistance to become owner-operators of not larger than family farms; make efficient use of the land, labor, and other resources; carry on sound and successful farming operations; and enable farm families to have a reasonable standard of living. Loan funds may be used to enlarge, improve, and buy family farms; provide necessary water and water facilities; provide basic soil treatment and land conservation measures; construct, repair, and improve essential buildings needed in the operation of a family farm; construct or repair farm dwellings; or provide facilities to produce fish under controlled conditions. Types of assistance: direct loans; guaranteed/insured loans. Range of money available for direct loans: up to $200,000; average: $111,762. Range of money available for guaranteed/insured loans: up to $731,000; average: $250,421.

* Loans to Family Farms That Can't Get Credit

(10.437 Interest Assistance Program)
U.S. Department of Agriculture
Farm Service Agency
Director, Loan Making Division
Ag Box 0522
Washington, DC 20250   202-720-1632
www.fsa.usda.gov

This program provides a 4% interest subsidy to farmers and ranchers who do not qualify for standard commercial credit. Operating loans obtained through the Interest Assistance Program can be used to finance livestock or farm equipment; to pay annual operating expenses or family living expenses; or to refinance debts under certain conditions. Type of assistance:

guaranteed/insured loans. Range of money available: $1 to $731,000; average: $158,000.

* Grants to Market Food Related Products Overseas

(10.600 Foreign Market Development Cooperation Program)
U.S. Department of Agriculture
Foreign Agricultural Service
Deputy Administrator
Commodity and Marketing Programs
1400 Independence Ave., SW
Washington, DC 20250   202-720-4761
www.fas.usda.gov/mos/programs/fmd.html

The purpose of this program is to develop, maintain and expand long-term export markets for U.S. agricultural products. This is to be achieved through cost-share assistance and the opportunity to work closely with the Foreign Agricultural Service and its overseas offices. Funding from this program may be used for trade servicing, market research and technical assistance to actual or potential foreign purchasers of U.S. commodities. Type of assistance: direct payments for specified use. Range of money available: $11,000 to $7,000,000; average: $1,243,000.

* Grants to Sell Food Related Products Overseas

(10.601 Market Access Program)
Deputy Administrator
Commodity and Marketing Programs
Foreign Agricultural Service
U.S. Department of Agriculture
1400 Independence Ave., SW
Washington, DC 20250   202-720-4761
www.fas.usda.gov/mos/programs/mapprog.html

This program encourages the creation, maintenance, and expansion of commercial export markets for U.S. agricultural commodities through cost-share assistance to eligible trade organizations that implement programs to develop foreign markets. Program funds may be used for consumer advertising, point of sale demonstrations, public relations, trade servicing activities, participation in trade fairs and exhibits, market research and technical assistance. Type of assistance: direct payments for specified use. Range of money available: $22,000 to $9,611,000; average: $1,375,000.

* Technical Assistance for Farming Cooperatives

(10.350 Technical Assistance to Cooperatives)
Deputy Administrator
Rural Business-Cooperative Service
U.S. Department of Agriculture, Box 3250
Washington, DC 20250-3250   202-720-8460
www.rurdev.usda.gov

This program provides technical assistance, research, and advisory services to farmer cooperatives and to groups of farmers interested in forming cooperatives. It also provides educational programs on the financial, organizational, management, legal, social and economic aspects of farmer cooperatives. Types of assistance: advisory services and counseling; dissemination of technical information.

* Emergency Loans for Farmers, Ranchers and Aquaculture Businesses Hurt by Natural Disasters

(10.404 Emergency Loans)
Department of Agriculture
Farm Service Agency
Director, Loan Making Division
Ag Box 0522
Washington, DC 20250   202-720-1632
www.fsa.usda.gov

The Farm Service Agency provides emergency loans to help farmers, ranchers, and aquaculture businesses recover from production and physical losses due to drought, flooding, other natural disasters, or quarantine. These loan funds may be used to restore or replace essential property; pay all or part of production costs associated with the disaster year; pay essential family living expenses; reorganize the farming operation; or refinance certain debts. Type of assistance: direct loans. Range of money available: $500 to $500,000; average: $58,000.

* Loans and Grants to Build Housing for Farm Laborers

(10.405 Farm Labor Housing Loans and Grants)
Multi-Family Housing Processing Division
Department of Agriculture

1400 Independence Ave., SW
Washington, DC 20250   202-720-1604
www.rurdev.usda.gov

The purpose of this program is to insure decent, safe, and sanitary low-rent housing and related facilities for domestic farm laborers. Funds from this program can be used for construction, repair, or purchase of year-round or seasonal housing; land acquisition and the improvements necessary to build; and developing related support facilities such as central cooking and dining areas, small infirmaries, laundry facilities, day care centers, and other essential equipment and facilities or recreation areas. Types of assistance: project grants; guaranteed/insured loans. Range of money available for grants: $135,000 to $2,300,000; average $1,104,120. Range of money available in loans to individuals: $20,000 to $200,000; average $34,500. Range of money available in loans to organizations: $165,000 to $670,000; average $292,753.

* Money to Local Communities Near National Forests to Help Businesses Grow or Expand

(10.670 National Forest-Dependent Rural Communities)
Deputy Chief
State and Private Forestry
Forest Service
U.S. Department of Agriculture
P.O. Box 96090
Washington, DC 20090-6090   202-205-1657
www.fs.fed.us/links/stateandprivate.shmtl

Through this program, eligible economically disadvantaged rural areas can request assistance in identifying opportunities that will promote economic improvement, diversification, and revitalization of their community. To be eligible, the community must be located in or near a national forest and be economically dependent on forest resources. Assistance is coordinated through a community action plan and team. Programs may include the upgrading of existing businesses, technical assistance, and training and education directed towards meeting the community action plan. Types of assistance: project grants; direct loans; use of property, facilities, and equipment; training. Range of money available: $1,000 to $30,000.

* Loans to Nonprofits to Lend Money to New Businesses

(10.767 Intermediary Relending Program)
Rural Business-Cooperative Service
Room 6867, South Agriculture Building, Stop 3225
Washington, DC 20250-3225   202-690-4100
www.rurdev.usda.gov

This program provides loans to Intermediary Lenders who in turn re-lend the money to finance community development and business facilities in rural areas. Type of assistance: direct loans. Range of money available: $3,000 to $615,000; average $19,684.

* Loans to Businesses in Small Towns

(10.768 Business and Industry Loans)
Administrator
Rural Business-Cooperative Service
U.S. Department of Agriculture   202-690-4730
Washington, DC 20250-3201   Fax: 202-690-4737
www.rurdev.usda.gov

In order to improve the economic and environmental climate, including pollution abatement and control, in rural communities, this program helps public, private, or cooperative organizations (profit and non-profit) obtain quality loans to improve, develop or finance business, industry and employment. These loans may be used in many ways including modernization or developing costs; purchasing and developing land, easements, rights-of-way, buildings, facilities, leases or materials; purchasing equipment, leasehold improvements, machinery and supplies; and pollution control and abatement. Types of assistance available: direct loans; guaranteed/insured loans. Range of money available for direct loans: $35,000 to $10,000,000; average: $559,471. Range of money available for guaranteed/insured loans: $35,000 t0 $25,000,000; average: $1,836,853.

* Grants to Nonprofits to Lend Money to New Businesses

(10.769 Rural Business Enterprise Grants)
Director, Specialty Lenders Division
Rural Business-Cooperative Service
U.S. Department of Agriculture
Washington, DC 20250-3222   202-720-1400
www.rurdev.usda.gov

The goal of this program is to increase employment and the development of small and new private business and industry to improve the economy in rural communities. The grant funds may be used for learning networks or programs that provide educational or job training instruction; to establish revolving loan funds; or refinancing services and fees. Funds may also be used to develop, construct or purchase land, buildings, plants, equipment, access streets and roads, parking areas, utility extensions, or necessary water supply and waste disposal facilities. Television Demonstration Grants (TDG) may be used for television programming to provide information on agriculture and other topics of importance to farmers and rural residents. All uses must assist a small or emerging private business enterprise except for the TDG Program. Type of assistance: project grants. Range of money available: $2,000 to $500,000; average: $83,309.

* Money to Run a Teenage Business

(10.406 Farm Operating Loans)
U.S. Department of Agriculture
Farm Service Agency
Director, Loan Making Division
Ag Box 0522
Washington, DC 20250   202-720-1632
www.fsa.usda.gov

The FSA makes loans to individual rural teens to establish and operate an income-producing business. To be eligible, teens must be associated with a 4-H Club, Future Farmers of America or a similar organization. The business project must be planned and operated under the supervision of the organization advisor, produce enough income to repay the loan, and provide the youth with practical business and educational experience. Loan funds may be used to buy livestock, equipment or supplies; to buy, rent or repair needed tools and equipment; and to pay operating expenses for running the project. Type of assistance: direct loans. Range of money available: up to $5,000.

* Loans to Companies That Provide Electricity to Small Towns

(10.850 Rural Electrification Loans and Loan Guarantees)
Administrator, Rural Utilities Service
U. S. Department of Agriculture
Washington, DC 20250-1500   202-720-9540
www.rurdev.usda.gov

This program provides loans to qualified organizations to supply or improve electric services on a continuing basis in rural areas. Its goal is to assure that people in eligible areas have access to electric services comparable in reliability and quality to the rest of the nation. Types of assistance: direct loans. Range of money available in direct loans: $443,000 to $103,000,000; average: $8,167,383. Range of money available in guaranteed FFB; $698,000 to $269,940,000; average $17,000,000.

* Loans to Companies That Provide Telephone Service to Small Towns

(10.851 Rural Telephone Loans and Loan Guarantees)
Administrator
Rural Utilities Service
U.S. Department of Agriculture
Washington, DC 20250   202-720-9554
www.rurdev.usda.gov

This program provides loans to qualified organizations to finance the improvement, expansion, construction, acquisition and operation of telephone lines, facilities or systems to furnish and improve telecommunications service in rural areas. Its goal is to assure that people in eligible rural areas have access to telecommunications services comparable in quality and reliability to the rest of the nation. Types of assistance: direct loans; guaranteed/insured loans. Range of money available in direct loans: $289,000 to $61,567,000: average: $9,375,000. Range of money available in guaranteed/insured loans: $4,476,000 to $59,389,000; average: $13,333,333.

* Extra Loans to Companies That Provide Telephone Services to Small Towns

(10.852 Rural Telephone Bank Loans)
Assistant Governor
Rural Telephone Bank
U.S. Department of Agriculture
Washington, DC 20250   202-720-9554
www.rurdev.usda.gov

This program provides supplemental financing to qualified organizations to extend and improve telecommunication services in rural areas. Type of assistance: direct loans. Range of money available: $169,050 to $35,918,400; average: $5,468,728.

* Grants and Loans to Telephone Companies That Then Provide Financing to Small Businesses

(10.854 Rural Economic Development Loans and Grants)
Director, Specialty Lenders Division
Rural Business-Cooperative Service
U.S. Department of Agriculture
Washington, DC 20250   202-720-1400
www.rurdev.usda.gov

The goal of this program is to fund rural economic development and job creation projects through electric and telephone utility companies. Program grants and loans may be used for project feasibility studies, start-up costs, incubator projects and other reasonable expenses incurred while promoting rural development. The maximum term for loans is ten years at an interest rate of zero. Type of assistance: direct loans and project grants. Range of money available for loans: $10,000 to $450,000; average: $375,000. Range of money available for grants: $10,000 to $200,000; average: $ 160,000.

* Free Plants for Conservation Studies

(10.905 Plant Materials for Conservation)
Deputy Chief for Science and Technology
Natural Resources Conservation Service
U. S. Department of Agriculture
P.O. Box 2890
Washington, DC 20013   202-720-4630
www.nrcs.usda.gov

This program is limited to conservation co-op properties in conjunction with soil conservation districts. Its goal is to develop technology for land management and restoration with plant materials by promoting the use of new and improved plant materials for soil, water, and related resource conservation and environmental improvement programs. Breeder and foundation quality seed or propagules are provided to commercial seed growers. Type of assistance: provision of specialized services.

* Grants to Communities That Provide Money and Help to Small Business Incubators

(11.300 Grants for Public Works and Economic Development)
David L. McIlwain, Director
Public Works Division
Economic Development Administration
Room H7326, Herbert C. Hoover Building
U.S. Department of Commerce
Washington, DC 20230   202-482-5265
www.doc.gov/eda

The EDA provides funding for special projects to support long-term economic development in areas experiencing substantial economic distress. Eligible projects must fulfill a pressing need in the area; improve the opportunities for the successful establishment or expansion of industrial or commercial businesses, assist in the creation of long term employment or benefit the unemployed/underemployed or low-income residents of the area. Such projects could include water and sewer system improvements, industrial access roads, industrial and business parks, port facilities, railroad sidings, distance learning facilities, skill training facilities, business incubator facilities, eco-industrial facilities and telecommunications infrastructure improvements needed for business retention and expansion. Type of assistance: project grants. Average grant amount: $1,201,991.

* Grants to Communities to Help Small Businesses Start or Expand

(11.302 Economic Development Support for Planning Organizations)
Anthony Meyer
Acting Director, Planning and Development Assistance Division
Economic Development Administration
Room H7317, Herbert C. Hoover Bldg.   202-482-2121
Washington, DC 20230   Fax: 202-482-0466
www.doc.gov/eda

The purpose of this program is to help States, Indian Tribes and/or local governments strengthen their economic development planning, and to formulate and establish comprehensive economic development strategies designed to reduce unemployment and increase income. Grants are used to help defray the cost of economic development and the administrative expenses necessary to carry out the planning. Type of assistance: project grants. Range of money available: $500 to $175,000; average $56,000.

* Grants to Communities That Help Finance New or Old Businesses Due to Military Base Closings

(11.307 Economic Adjustment Assistance)
David F. Witschi, Director
Economic Development Administration

Room H7327, Herbert C. Hoover Building
U.S. Department of Commerce
Washington, DC 20230　　　　　　　　202-482-2659
www.doc.gov/eda

The goal of this program is to assist state and local areas in the development and/or implementation of strategies designed to address structural economic adjustment problems resulting from sudden and severe economic dislocation such as plant closings, military base closures and defense contract cutbacks, and natural disasters, or from long term economic deterioration in the area's economy. Funded activities may include, but are not limited to, the creation or expansion of business development and financing programs such as revolving loan funds, infrastructure improvements, organizational development, and market or industry research and analysis. Type of assistance: project grants. Range of money available: no specific minimum or maximum.

* Grants to Fisherman Hurt by Oil and Gas Drilling on the Outer Continental Shelf

(11.408 Fishermen's Contingency Fund)
Michael Grable
Chief, Financial Services Division
National Marine Fisheries Service
1315 East-West Highway　　　　　　301-713-2396
Silver Spring, MD 20910　　　　　Fax: 301-713-1306
www.noaa.gov

This program compensates U.S. Commercial fishermen for damage/loss of fishing gear and 50% of resulting economic loss due to oil and gas related activities in any area of the Outer Continental Shelf. Type of assistance: direct payments with unrestricted use. Range of money available: $500 50 $54,000; average: $6,000.

* Grants to Develop New Technologies for Your Business

(11.612 Advanced Technology Program)
Barbara Lambis
Advanced Technology Program
National Institute of Standards and Technology
100 Bureau Drive, Stop 4700　　　　301-975-4447
Gaithersburg, MD 20899-4700　　　Fax: 301-869-1150
Email: Barbara.lambis@nist.gov
www.atp.nist.gov/atp
To receive application kits:
ATP customer service staff　　　　　800-ATP-FUND

Working in partnership with industry, the Advanced Technology Program provides funding for development of new, high-risk technologies that offer the potential for significant, broad based economic benefits for the entire country. ATP funding may not be used to fund product development, or existing or planned research programs that would otherwise be conducted in the same time period. Type of assistance: project grants. Range of money available: $434,000 to $31,478,000; average: $3,043,374.

* Grants to Organizations That Help Minorities Start Their Own Businesses

(11.800 Minority Business Development Centers)
Barbara Curry
Business Development Specialist
Room 5071, Minority Business Development Agency
U.S. Department of Commerce
14th and Constitution Ave., NW
Washington, DC 20230　　　　　　　202-482-1940
www.mbda.gov

The Minority Business Development Agency provides funding for Minority Business Development Centers. For a nominal fee, these centers provide a wide range of services from initial consultations, to the identification and resolution of specific business problems. The goal of this program is to provide electronic and one-on-one business development services to minority firms or individuals interested in entering, expanding, or improving their efforts in the marketplace. Type of assistance: project grants. Range of money available: $155,000 to $385,750.

* Grants to Organizations That Help Native Americans Start Their Own Businesses

(11.801 Native American Program)
Barbara Curry
Business Development Specialist
Room 5071, Minority Business Development Agency
U.S. Department of Commerce

14th and Constitution Ave., NW
Washington, DC 20230　　　　　　　202-482-1940
www.mbda.gov

This program provides funding for eight Native American Business Development Centers that provide electronic and one-on-one business development service to Native Americans interested in entering, expanding, or improving their efforts in the marketplace. These centers provide advice and counseling in areas such as preparing financial packages, business counseling, business information and management, accounting guidance, marketing, business/industrial site analysis, production, engineering, construction assistance, procurement, and identification of potential business opportunities. Type of assistance: project grants. Range of money available: $155,000 to $287,500.

* Grants to Help Minority Businesses Enter New Markets

(11.802 Minority Business Development)
Barbara Curry
Room 5071, Minority Business Development Agency
U.S. Department of Commerce
14th and Constitution Ave., NW
Washington, DC 20230　　　　　　　202-482-1940
www.mbda.gov

This Program supports minority business development through indirect business assistance programs that identify and develop private markets and capital sources; expand business information and business services through trade associations; promote and support the utilization of Federal, State and local government resources; and assist minorities in entering new and growing markets. Type of assistance: project grants. Average amount of financial assistance: $300,000.

* Grants to Organizations That Will Help You Sell to the Department of Defense

(12.002 Procurement Technical Assistance for Business Firms)
Defense Logistics Agency
Office of Small and Disadvantaged Business Utilization (DDAS)
8725 John J. Kingman Road, Suite 2533
Fort Belvoir, VA 22060-6221　　　　703-767-1650
www.dla.mil/db

The purpose of the Procurement Technical Assistance Program is to generate employment and to improve the economy of an area by assisting business firms in obtaining and maintaining Federal, State, and local government contracts. Recipients of project funds are to provide marketing and technical assistance to businesses in selling their goods and services to the Department of Defense, other Federal agencies, and local and State governments. Type of assistance: project grants. Range of money available: $30,000 to $300,000; average: $160,185.

* Loans to Start a Business on an Indian Reservation

(15.124 Indian Loans-Economic Development)
Woodrow Sneed
Office of Economic Development
Bureau of Indian Affairs
1849 C Street, NW, MS-4640
Washington, DC 20240　　　　　　　202-208-4796
www.doi.gov/bia/ecodev/loanpgm.html

This program assists Federally Recognized Indian Tribal Governments, Native American Organizations, and individual American Indians in obtaining financing from private sources in order to promote business development on or near Federally Recognized Indian Reservations. Funding may be used to finance commercial, industrial, agricultural, or business activities organized for profit. Types of assistance: guaranteed/insured loans. Range of money available for individuals and tribal enterprises: $2,500 to $500,000; average: $125,000. Range of money available for Federally Recognized Tribal Governments and Native American Organizations: $10,000 to $7,000,000; average: $1,500,000.

* Grants to Small Coal Mine Operators to Clean Up Their Mess

(15.250 Regulation of Surface Coal Mining and Surface Effects of Underground Coal Mining)
Chief, Division of Regulatory Support
Office of Surface Mining Reclamation and Enforcement
U.S. Department of the Interior
1951 Constitution Ave., NW
Washington, DC 20240　　　　　　　202-208-2651

www.osmre.gov

This program provides grants to develop permanent programs that protect society and the environment from the adverse effects of surface coal mining, while maintaining the coal supply necessary to meet the Nation's energy needs. Coal mining operators that have total annual production of less than 300,000 tons at all locations can apply for assistance in meeting certain technical permit application requirements. Types of assistance: project grants; direct payments for specified use. Range of money available: $2,500 to $500,000; average: $125,000.

* Money to Fisherman Who Have Their Boats Seized by a Foreign Government

(19.204 Fisherman's Guaranty Fund)
Mr. Stetson Tinkham
Office of Marine Conservation
Bureau of Oceans and International Environmental and Scientific Affairs
Room 5806
U.S. Department of State   202-647-3941
Washington, DC 20250-7818   Fax: 202-736-7350
www.state.gov

The Fisherman's Guaranty Fund is an insurance program that provides reimbursement for losses incurred as a result of the seizure of U.S. commercial fishing vessels by a foreign country on the basis of rights or claims in territorial waters or on the high seas, which are not recognized by the U.S. Effective November 28, 1990, the United States acknowledges the authority of coastal states to manage highly migratory species, thus reducing the basis for valid claims under the Fishermen's Protective Act. Type of assistance: insurance. Range of money available: up to $500,000.

* Grants to Build or Improve an Airport

(20.106 Airport Improvement Program)
Federal Aviation Administration
Office of Airport Planning and Programming
Airports Financial Assistance Division, APP-500
800 Independence Avenue, SW
Washington, DC 20591   202-267-3831
www.faa.gov

Using grants, advisory services, and counseling, this program's goal is to assist owners or operators of public airports in the development of a nationwide system of airports sufficient to meet needs of civil aeronautics. Grants can be made for integrated airport system planning in a specific area, airport master planning, construction, or rehabilitation of a public-use airport. Eligible work at airports includes airport master plans; airport noise compatibility plans; land acquisition; site preparation; construction, alteration, and rehabilitation of runways, taxiways, aprons, and certain roads within airport boundaries; construction and installation of airfield lighting, navigational aids, and certain offsite work; safety equipment required for certification of the airport facility; required security equipment ; snow-removal equipment; terminal development; aviation-related weather reporting equipment; equipment to measure runway surface friction; burn area training structures and land for that purpose, on or off airport; agency-approved noise compatibility projects; relocation of air traffic control towers and navigational aids ; land, paving, drainage, aircraft deicing equipment and structures for centralized deicing areas; and projects to comply with the Americans with Disabilities Act of 1990, Clean Air Act, and Federal Water Pollution Control. Types of assistance: project grants; advisory services, and counseling. Range of money available: $12,000 to $35,000,000; average: $1,250,000.

* Grants to Bus Companies

(20.509 Formula Grants for Other Than Urbanized Areas)
Federal Transit Administration
Office of Program Management
Office of Capital and Formula Assistance
400 Seventh Street, SW
Washington, DC 20590   202-366-2053
www.fta.dot.gov

In order to improve, introduce or continue public transportation service in rural areas, this program provides technical and financial assistance to rural transportation providers. Funding may be used for operating and administrative expenses, and for the acquisition, construction, and improvement of facilities and equipment. Type of assistance: formula grants.

* Grants to Become a Women-Owned Transportation Related Company

(20.511 Human Resources Program)
Director, Office of Civil Rights

Federal Transit Administration
U.S. Department of Transportation
400 Seventh Street, SW, Room 9102
Washington, DC 20590   202-366-4018
www.fta.dot.gov

This program provides financial assistance to national, regional, and local initiatives that address human resource needs in the area of public transportation. Projects may include employment training programs; outreach programs to increase minority and women's employment in public transportation activities; research on training and public transportation manpower needs; and training and assistance for minority businesses that meet Section 120 program criteria. Types of assistance: project grants (cooperative agreements), dissemination of technical information.

* Money for Airlines to Fly to Small Towns and Make a Profit

(20.901 Payments for Essential Air Services)
Director, Office of Aviation Analysis, X-50
U.S. Department of Transportation
400 Seventh Street, SW
Washington, DC 20590   202-366-1030
www.ost.dot.gov

The purpose of this program is to assure that air transportation services are provided to eligible communities. When necessary, subsidy payments are made to air carriers providing air services to eligible locations in order to ensure the continuation of service. Subsidies are paid to cover the carrier's prospective operating loss plus an element of profit. Type of assistance: direct payment for specified use. Range of money available: $297,636 to $1,871,825 annually per point; average $858,599 annually per point.

* Grants to Women-Owned Businesses to Help Get Contracts from the Department of Transportation

(20.903 Support Mechanisms for Disadvantaged Businesses)
Office of Small and Disadvantaged Business Utilization, S-40
Office of the Secretary
400 Seventh Street, SW   800-532-1169
Washington, DC 20590   202-366-1930
www.dot.gov

This program is designed to help small businesses (minority and non-minority), socially and economically disadvantaged persons, and businesses owned and operated by women increase their participation in Department of Transportation programs and funded projects. Financial assistance may be given to develop support mechanisms, such as liaison and assistance programs, that provide outreach and referrals for technical assistance, information dissemination, and communication networks with government offices. Type of assistance: project grants (cooperative agreements). Average amount of financial assistance: $134,000.

* Loans to Start a Credit Union

Mr. Anthony Lacreta
(44.002 Community Development Revolving Loan Program for Credit Unions)
Community Development Revolving Loan Program for Credit Unions
National Credit Union Administration
1775 Duke Street
Alexandria, VA 22314-3428   703-518-6610
www.ncua.gov

The Community Development Revolving Loan Program for Credit Unions provides funding to support low-income credit unions' efforts to provide a variety of financial and related services designed to meet the needs of their community. Funds from this program may be used to support and stimulate economic development and revitalization efforts in the community; provide member services such as financial counseling; and for programs to increase the membership and capitalization base. Type of assistance: direct loans. Range of money available: $25,000 to $300,000.

* Money if Your Business Was Hurt by a Natural Disaster or Drought

(59.002 Economic Injury Disaster Loans)
Herbert Mitchell
Office of Disaster Assistance
Small Business Administration
409 3rd Street, SW
Washington, DC 20416   202-205-6734
Email: disaster.assistance@sba.gov
www.sba.gov/DISASTER

This program provides assista nce to small businesses, agricultural cooperatives, and nurseries that suffered economic injury as a result of a disaster declared by the President, Small Business Administration, and/or the Secretary of Agriculture. These loans can be used to pay liabilities which the business could have paid if the disaster had not occurred, or as working capital to keep the business in operation until conditions return to normal. Funds are not available for lost income or profits, equipment repair or acquisition. Types of assistance: direct loans; guaranteed/insured loans (including immediate participation loans). Range of money available: up to $1,500,000; average: $76,200.

* Money for Businesses Hurt by Physical Disaster or Drought

(59.008 Physical Disaster Loans)
Herbert Mitchell
Office of Disaster Assistance
Small Business Administration
409 3rd Street, SW
Washington, DC 20416   202-205-6734
Email: disaster.assistance@sba.gov
www.sba.gov/DISASTER

Businesses that have suffered uninsured losses due to a declared physical-type disaster may qualify for loans through this program. Funds may be used to repair or replace damaged or destroyed real property to its pre-disaster condition. Types of assistance: direct loans; guaranteed/insured loans. Range of money available: up to $1,500,000; average: $51,160.

* Money to Start a Venture Capital Company

(59.011 Small Business Investment Companies)
Associate Administrator for Investment
Investment Division
Small Business Administration
409 Third Street, SW
Washington, DC 20416   202-205-6510
www.sba.gov

This program provides funding to establish privately owned and managed investment companies, which are licensed and regulated by the U.S. Small Business Administration. These companies, in turn, provide equity capital, long term loan funds, and advisory services to small businesses. Range of money available: $50,000 to $90,000,000: average: $14,323,000.

* Up to $500,000 to Start Your Own Business

(59.012 Small Business Loans)
Director, Loan Policy and Procedures Branch
Small Business Administration
409 Third Street, SW   202-205-6510
Washington, DC 20416   800-8ASK-SBA
www.sba.gov

The Small Business Loans program provides guaranteed loans to small businesses that are unable to obtain financing elsewhere, but have shown the ability to repay their debts. These loans are made to low-income business owners, businesses located in areas of high unemployment, non-profit sheltered workshops and similar organizations that produce goods or services, small businesses started, acquired or owned by handicapped individuals, and to enable small businesses to manufacture , design, market, install, or services specific energy measures. Loans may be used to construct, expand, or convert facilities, to purchase building equipment or materials, and for working capital. The SBA's 7(a) Lending Authority includes: the Cap Line Program, the Low Documentation Loan Program (Low Doc), Fa$ Trak Program (formerly the Small Loan Express), the Women's Prequalification Program, and the Minority Prequalification Program. Types of assistance: guaranteed/insured loans (including immediate participation loans). Range of money available: up to $500,000; Average: $226,521.

* Help for Contractors and Others to Get Bonded to Obtain Contracts

(59.016 Bond Guarantees for Surety Companies)
Associate Administrator, Robert J. Moffitt
Office of Surety Guarantees
Small Business Administration
409 Third Street, SW
Washington, DC 20416   202-205-6540
www.sba.gov

Under this program, small contractors unable to obtain a bond are guaranteed surety bonds issued by commercial surety companies. Guarantees are for up to ninety percent of the losses incurred and are paid by participating sureties when conditions are met. Types of assistance:

insurance (guaranteed surety bonds). Range of money available: up to $500,000; average: $226,521.

* Money to Local Organizations to Finance Small Businesses

(59.041 Certified Development Company Loans [504 loans])
Office of Financial Assistance
Small Business Administration
409 Third Street, SW
Washington, DC 20416   202-205-6490
www.sba.gov/financing/sbaloan/cdc504.html

The CDC/504 loan program is a long-term financing tool for economic development within a community. The 504 loan program provides growing businesses with long-term fixed rate financing for major fixed assets. A Certified Development Company (CDC) is a non-profit corporation set up to contribute to the economic development of its community. CDC's work with private sector lenders and the SBA to provide financing to small businesses. These loans have either a 10 or 20 year term, and may be used for the acquisition of land and buildings; the construction, expansion, renovation or modernization of buildings; or the acquisition and/or installation of machinery and equipment. Type of assistance: guaranteed/insured loans. Range of money available: up to $1,000,000; average: $350,000.

* Grants to Local Organizations That Help Women Start Their Own Businesses.

(59.043 Women's Business Ownership Assistance)
Sally Murrell
Office of Women's Business Ownership
Small Business Administration
409 Third Street, SW
Washington, DC 20416   202-205-6673
www.sba.gov/womeninbusiness

Private, non profit organizations can receive funding through this program to provide training and counseling to small businesses owned and operated by women in an effort to eliminate discriminatory barriers women may encounter in obtaining credit and promoting their businesses. Type of assistance: project grants (cooperative agreements or contracts). Range of money available: $75,000 to $150,000.

* Grants to Local Organizations That Help Veterans Start Their Own Businesses

(59.044 Veteran's Entrepreneurial Training and Counseling)
Reginald Teamer
Office of Veteran Affairs
Small Business Administration
5th Floor, 409 Third Street, SW
Washington, DC 20416   202-205-6773
www.sba.gov

This program establishes Veteran Business Outreach Centers to provide long term training, counseling, and mentoring to small businesses and potential small businesses owned and operated by eligible U.S. Veterans. Type of assistance: cooperative agreements. Range of money available: $350 to $1,500 per client.

* Money to Local Organizations to Provide Micro-loans

(59.046 Micro-loan Demonstration Program)
Small Business Administration
Office of Financial Assistance
Micro enterprise Development Branch
409 Third Street, SW, Eighth Floor
Washington, DC 20416   202-205-6490
www.sba.gov

The Micro Loan program provides very small loans to start up, newly established or growing small businesses. Its objective is to help business owners, especially women, low-income entrepreneurs, minorities, potential entrepreneurs, and those located in areas with a lack of credit due to economic conditions. To achieve this, the Small Business Administration makes loans and loan guarantees to intermediary lenders, who in turn make short term, fixed interest rate micro loans to start-up, newly established, and growing businesses. These micro-loans can only be used for working capital, supplies, furniture, fixtures, inventory, equipment and/or machinery. The SBA makes grants to participating intermediary lenders to provide marketing, management and technical assistance to micro-loan recipients. The SBA also provides training for the lenders and non-lenders participating in the program, and makes grants to non-profit organizations to provide marketing, technical and managerial assistance to low-income individuals seeking private financing for their businesses. Types of assistance: formula grants; direct loans. Range of money available: up to $35,000; average: $10,500.

* Help for Disabled Veterans to Start New Businesses

(64.116 Vocational Rehabilitation for Disabled Veterans)
Veterans Benefits Administration
Vocational Rehabilitation and Counseling Service (28)
U.S. Department of Veteran Affairs
Washington, DC 20420   202-273-7419
www.va.gov

This Vocational Rehabilitation Program provides services and assistance to help disabled veterans get and keep a suitable job. The program also provides the needed services and assistance to help individuals achieve the necessary skills to maximize independence in daily living. Veterans who meet certain requirements may receive an initial supply of goods and commodities to start a small business. Types of assistance: direct payments with unrestricted use; direct payments for specified use; direct loans; advisory services and counseling. Range of money available: information is not available at this time.

* Help for Retired Military to Start a Business

(64.123 Vocational Training for Certain Veterans Receiving VA Pension)
Veterans Benefits Administration
Vocational Rehabilitation and Counseling Service (28)
U.S. Department of Veterans Affairs
Washington, DC 20420   202-273-7419
www.va.gov

This program provides vocational and counseling to recipients of VA pensions so they may get and keep a suitable job. Veterans who meet certain eligibility requirements may be provided with the goods or commodities to start a small business. Type of assistance: direct payments for specified use; advisory services and counseling. Range of money available: information is not available at this time.

* Money to Invest in Companies Overseas

(70.002 Foreign Investment Financing)
Information Officer
Overseas Private Investment Corporation
1100 New York Ave, NW   202-336-0799
Washington, DC 20527   Fax: 202-336-8700
Email: info@opic.gov
www.opic.gov

The Overseas Private Investment Corporation provides financing for investments in developing countries for projects that contribute to the social and economic development of the host country and at the same time have a positive impact on the U.S. economy. OPIC disqualifies projects that may have a negative effect on the environment, U.S. employment, the host country's development, or would violate internationally recognized worker rights. Direct loans can only be made for private sector projects where there is significant involvement by a U.S. small business. Types of assistance: Guaranteed/insured loans; direct loans. Range of money available: $10,000,000 to $400,000,000; average: $9,000,000.

* Money to Privately Owned Community Drinking Water Utilities for Security Improvements

(66.477 Vulnerability Assessments and Related Security Improvements as Large Privately Owned Drinking Water Utilities)
U.S. Environmental Protection Agency
Private Water Utility Security Grant Program
Room 2104A, EPA East Building
1201 Constitution Avenue, NW   202-564-3750
Washington, DC 20004   800-426-4791
www.epa.gov

Large privately owned community drinking water utilities that serve 100,000 or more people are eligible to apply for this funding. The money may be used to conduct a vulnerability assessment, develop or revise an emergency response operating plan, enhance security plans, or a combination of these efforts. Type of assistance: project grants. Range of money available: up to $115,000.

* Grants for Security Improvements at Drinking Water Utilities

(66.476 Vulnerability Assessments and Related Security Improvements at Large Drinking Water Utilities)
U.S. Environmental Protection Agency

Public Water Utility Security Grant Program
1201 Constitution Ave., NW
Washington, DC 20004   800-426-4791
www.epa.gov

Large publicly owned community drinking water utilities that serve at least 100,000 people are eligible to apply for this funding. Recipients of these grants may use the money to conduct a vulnerability assessment, develop or revise an emergency response operating plan, enhance security measures, or any combination of these efforts. Grant money may not be used for construction or other physical improvements. Type of assistance: project grants. Range of money available: up to $115,000.

* Insurance Against Your Business in Another Country Being Hurt by Foreign Politics

(70.003 Foreign Investment Insurance)
Information Officer
Overseas Private Investment Corporation
1100 New York Avenue, NW   202-336-8799
Washington, DC 20527   Fax: 202-336-8700
Email: info@opic.gov
www.opic.gov

To encourage private U.S. investment in developing countries, OPIC provides insurance to protect against the risks of inconvertibility, expropriation and political violence. Insurance is available for contractors and exporters against arbitrary drawings of letters of credit posted as bid, performance or advance payment guaranties; petroleum exploration, development and production; leasing operations; and debt financials, including securities. Type of assistance: insurance. Range of insurance available: up to $250,000,000.

* Free Patent Licenses to Develop and Market Energy Saving Inventions

(81.003 Granting of Patent Licenses)
Robert J. Marchick
Office of the Assistant General Counsel for Patents
U.S. Department of Energy
Washington, DC 20585   202-586-2802
www.doe.gov

The Department of Energy grants nonexclusive, revocable patent licenses to qualified applicants with plans to develop and/or market one of the more that 1,200 DOE owned U.S. Patents. Type of assistance: dissemination of technical information. Range of money available: not applicable.

* Money to Work on an Energy Related Invention

(81.036 Invention and Innovations)
Lisa Barnett
Office of Industrial Technologies (EE-23)
U.S. Department of Energy
Weatherization and Intergovernmental Programs
1000 Independence Avenue, SW
Washington, DC 20585   202-586-2212
www.eere.energy.gov/inventions

The U.S. Department of Energy's Inventions and Innovation program provides financial and technical support to inventors and businesses to develop energy saving concepts and technologies. Grant recipients are selected through a competitive process. Types of assistance: project grants, advisory services and counseling, and dissemination of technical information. Range of money available for projects in early stage development: up to $40,000. Range of money available for technology near the point of prototype: up to $250,000. Range of money available for technology demonstrations: up to $500,000. Average amount of assistance: $83,000.

* Counseling to Help Women and Minority Owned Businesses Get Department of Energy Contracts

(81.082 Management and Technical Assistance for Minority Business Enterprises)
Sterling Nichols
Office of Economic Impact and Diversity
U.S. Department of Energy
ED-1, Forrestal Building, Room 5B-110
Washington, DC 20585   202-586-8698
www.hr.doe.gov/ed/index.html

This program strives to support increased participation of minority and women owned and operated small businesses; to develop energy related minority small business assistance programs; to encourage public/private partnerships to provide technical assistance to MBE's; to transfer applicable technology from national Federal laboratories to MBE's; and to increase the Department of Energy's high technology research and development contracting activities. Services provided by this program include identification and compilation of DOE procurement opportunities; technical assistance; dissemination of DOE energy technology opportunities; financial proposal and bid assistance; and matching business opportunities in public and private organizations with minority businesses and educational institutions. Type of assistance: advisory services and counseling. Range of money available: not applicable.

* Help for Farmers to Control Plant and Animal Diseases

(97.003 Agricultural Inspections)
Department of Homeland Security
245 Murray Drive, SW
Washington, DC 20528   202-282-8000
www.dhs.gov

This program's objective is to protect U.S. agriculture from harmful plant and animal diseases and pests. It provides for inspections to detect and evaluate infestations and carries out regulatory actions to prevent the interstate spread of diseases and infestations. Type of assistance: project grants (cooperative agreements). Range of money available: not applicable.

* Grants for Commercial Fisheries Failing Due to a Natural Disaster

(11.477 Fisheries Disaster Relief)
Alicia Jarboe
Financial Services Division (F/CS2)
National Marine Fisheries Service
1315 East-West Highway   301-713-2358
Silver Spring, MD 20910   Fax: 301-713-1939
Email: Alicia.jarboe@noaa.gov
www.fakr.noaa.gov/omi/grants/default.htm (Alaska)
http://caldera.sero.nmfs.gov/grants/programs/disaster.htm (Southeast)

This program provides assistance to fishing vessel owners, operators, and crew, and fish processors that are facing failure due to a fishery resource disaster. Disasters may be natural, man-made, or by undetermined causes. Funds may be used to assist affected communities, assess the effect of commercial fishery failures, restore fisheries, or prevent future failures. Type of assistance: project grants (cooperative agreements). Range of money available: $343,500 to $7,000,000: average: $2,781,167.

* Money for Small, Minority, and Women Owned Businesses to Develop an AIDS Prevention Activity

(93.118 Acquired Immunodeficiency Syndrome (AIDS) Activity)
Division Contact:
Ron VanDuyne
Division of HIV/AIDS Prevention
Centers for Disease Control and Prevention
Department of Health and Human Services
1600 Clifton Road, A43
Atlanta, GA 30333   404-639-0930

Grants Management Contact:
Lynn Mercer
Grants Management Branch
Procurement and Grants Office
Centers for Disease Control and Prevention
Department of Health and Human Services
2920 Brandywine Road
Atlanta, GA 30341   770-488-2810
www.cdc.gov

Through this program, small and minority businesses, and businesses owned by women are eligible to apply for funds to develop and implement public information and education programs on HIV prevention and awareness. Type of assistance: project grants. Range of money available: $45,000 to $2,000,000; average: $390,174.

* Grants to Develop Energy Saving Products

(81.086 Conservation Research and Development)
Office of Energy Efficiency and Renewable Energy (EERE)
Mail Stop EE-1
Department of Energy   202-586-9220
Washington, DC 28585   800-DOE-3732
www.eere.energy.gov

This program offers grants to conduct research in the areas of buildings, industry and transportation. Grants are also offered to develop and transfer conservation technology to the non-federal sector. The Department of Energy EERE offices involved in this program are the Office of Building Technology, Office of Freedom CAR and Vehicle Technologies, Office of Industrial Technologies, and the Office of Hydrogen, Fuel Cells and Infrastructure. Type of Assistance: project grants. Range of money available: $50,000 to $500,000.

* Grants to Work on Solar Energy Products

(81.087 Renewable Energy Research and Development)
Office of Energy Efficiency and Renewable Energy (EERE)
Mail Stop EE-1
Department of Energy   202-586-9220
Washington, DC 28585   800-DOE-3732
www.eere.energy.gov

The Department of Energy provides funding to conduct research and development efforts in the following energy technologies: distributed energy and electric reliability, solar, hydrogen, biomass, fuel cells and infrastructure, geothermal, wind and hydropower. Grants are also offered to develop and transfer these renewable energy technologies to the scientific and industrial communities, and state and local governments. Type of assistance: project grants. Range of money available: $10,000 to $100,000.

* Grants to Develop Uses of Fossil Fuels

(81.089 Fossil Energy Research and Development)
Mary J. Roland
Fossil Energy Program, Mail Stop FE-3
19901 Germantown Road
Department of Energy
Germantown, MD 20874   301-903-3514
www.fe.doe.gov

The focus of the Fossil Energy Research and Development program is to promote the development and use of environmentally and economically advanced technologies for supply, conversion, delivery and utilization of fossil fuels. Cooperative agreements will involve industry, DOE laboratories, universities and States. The successes of this program will benefit everyone through lower energy costs, reduced environmental impact, increased technology exports, and reduced dependence on foreign energy sources. Type of assistance: project grants, cooperative agreements. Range of money available: $10,000 to$25,000,000.

* Grants to Businesses That Employ People with Disabilities

(89.234 Projects with Industry)
Lavanna Kia Weems and Lois Vaughan
Rehabilitation Services Administration
U.S. Department of Education
400 Maryland Avenue, SW
OSERS, Room 3332   202-205-8749 (Vaughan)
Washington, DC 20202   202-205-8922 (Weems)
Email: lavanna.weems@ed.gov
Email: lois.vaughan@ed.gov
www.ed.gov/offices/OSERS/RSA/Programs/Discretionary/pwi.html

Projects with Industry grants are awarded to employers, labor unions, profit and non-profit organizations and State vocational rehabilitation agencies. Funds may be used to support projects that create and expand job and career opportunities in the competitive labor market for individuals with disabilities. Type of assistance: project grants, cooperative agreements. Average continuation award: $205,000. Average new award: $230,000.

* Grants to Telecommunications Companies to Provide Services to Schools

(84.203 Star Schools)
Joseph Wilkes
U.S. Department of Education
Office of Innovation and Improvement
Technology in Education Programs
555 New Jersey Ave., NW
Washington, DC 20208-5645   202-219-2186
Email: joseph.wilkes@ed.gov
www.ed.gov/offices/OII

This program provides grants to telecommunications companies to provide facilities and equipment, educational and instructional programming, and necessary technical assistance to elementary and secondary schools. Priority is given to companies that provide services to schools in traditionally underserved areas, individuals excluded from careers in math and science due to discrimination or economic disadvantages, areas with scarce resources, and areas with limited access to courses in math, science, and foreign languages. Type of assistance: project grants. Range of money available: information not available at this time.

* Money to Develop Health and Safety Programs for Construction Workers

(93.955 Health and Safety Programs for Construction Workers)
Grant Management Contact:
Mildred Garner
Grants Management Branch
Procurement and Grants Office
Centers for Disease Control and Prevention
2920 Brandywine Road
Atlanta, GA 30341   770-488-2745

Program Management Contact:
Office of Extramural Programs
National Institute for Occupational Safety and Health
Centers for Disease Control and Prevention
1600 Clifton Road
Mail Stop E-74
Atlanta, GA 30333   404-498-2530
www.cdc.gov

The purpose of this program is to develop health and safety programs for construction workers in order to reduce occupational injuries and illnesses. Funds may be used for salaries of personnel employed specifically for the project, consultant fees, supplies and equipment necessary to conduct the project, essential travel expenses, and other project related expenses. Type of assistance: project grants. Range of money available: up to $5,000,000.

* Grants to Improve Emergency Medical Service in Rural Areas

(93.952 Improving EMS/Trauma Care in Rural Areas)
Richard J. Smith III
Chief, Injury/EMS Branch
Maternal and Child Health Bureau
Health Resources and Services Administration
Public Health Service
Department of Health and Human Services
Parklawn Building, Room 18A-38
5600 Fishers Lane
Rockville, MD 20857   301-443-0324

Grants Management Contact:
Grants Management Branch
Maternal and Child Health Bureau
Health Resources and Services Administration
Public Health Service
Department of Health and Human Services
Parklawn Building, Room 18-12
5600 Fishers Lane
Rockville, MD 20857   301-443-1440
www.mchb.hrsa.gov

This program makes grants for research and demonstration projects designed to improve the quality and availability of emergency medical services in rural areas. Funds may be used to develop and use new, innovative communications technologies; develop model curricula for training emergency medical services personnel; make training, certification, and continuing education more accessible; develop increased access to pre-hospital care and improve the availability of emergency transportation services; and evaluate the effectiveness of current emergency medical services and systems. Type of assistance: project grants. Range of money available: $50,000 to $150,000; average: $100,000.

* Pension Plan Termination Insurance for Small Businesses

(86.001 Pension Plan Termination Insurance)
Pension Benefit Guaranty Corporation
1200 K Street, NW
Washington, DC 20005-4026   202-326-4000
www.pbgc.gov

This program encourages the continuation and maintenance of voluntary private pension plans, provides for timely and uninterrupted payment of pension benefits to participants and beneficiaries in plans covered by the PBGC, and maintains premiums at the lowest possible level. Type of assistance: insurance. Range of monthly benefit available: $10 to $3664.77; average: $383.

* Crop Insurance for Owners or Operators of Farmlands

(10.450 Crop Insurance)
Department of Agriculture
Administrator, Risk management Agency
Ag Box 0801
Washington, DC 2050   202-690-2803
www.fsa.usda.gov

The Federal Crop Insurance Corporation (FCIC) is a government owned corporation created to provide comprehensive crop insurance nation wide. Catastrophic crop insurance protection (CAT) is fully subsidized except for administrative fees paid by the producer. This coverage compensates the producer for yield losses greater than 50% at a price equal to 55% of maximum price. Additional protection is offered at higher levels of coverage and variable levels of premium subsidy. Owners or operators of farmland, who have an insurable interest in a crop in a county where insurance is offered on that crop, are eligible for insurance. Type of assistance: insurance. Range of assistance available: level of assistance varies according to policy, crop, and indemnities paid.

* Crop Loss Assistance for Uninsured Producers of Commercial Crops

(10.451 Noninsured Assistance)
Department of Agriculture
Farm Service Agency
Production, Emergency and Compliance Division
Noninsured Assistance Program Branch
Mail Stop 0517
1400 Independence Avenue, SW
Washington, DC 20250-0526   202-720-5172
www.fsa.gov

This program provides crop loss assistance to producers of commercial crops and other agricultural commodities where crop insurance at the catastrophic risk protection level is not available. Crops that are produced for food or fiber are eligible including: floricultural, ornamental nursery, and Christmas tree crops, turf grass sod, seed crops, aquaculture (including ornamental fish) and industrial crops. To be eligible, producers must be an owner, tenant, sharecropper, or landlord who shares in the risk of producing the crop, must be entitled to share in the crop available for marketing or would have shared had the crop been produced, and whose qualifying gross revenue for the preceding tax year was less than $2 million. Type of assistance: Direct payments with unrestricted use. Range of money available: not applicable.

* Money for Livestock Owners Hurt by a Natural Disaster

(10.452 Disaster Reserve Assistance)
Department of Agriculture
Farm Service Agency
Emergency and Noninsured Assistance Program Division
Mail Stop 0526
1400 Independence Avenue, SW
Washington, C 20250-0526   202-720-3168
www.fsa.usda.gov

This program provides emergency assistance to eligible livestock owners in an area, county or state where an official emergency has been declared due to insect infestation, disease, fire, drought, flood, hailstorm, hurricane, earthquake, hot weather, c old weather, ice, snow, freeze, winter kill, or other natural disaster. Type of assistance: direct payments for specified use. Range of money available: not applicable.

* Health and Safety Education and Training for Mine Operators

(17.602 Mine Health and Safety Education and Training)
Director, Educational Policy and Development
Mine Safety and Health Administration
Department of Labor
4015 Wilson Blvd.   703-235-1515 (Jeffrey Duncan)
Arlington, VA 22203   304-256-3201 (Jack Spadaro)
www.msha.gov

The Mine Safety and Health Administration provides initial and advanced Mine Safety and Health Training for Federal Mine Inspectors, Mine Operators, miners, States, and labor organizations. Assistance is also provided through written and audiovisual training materials dealing with health and mining safety issues. Type of assistance: training. Range of money available: not applicable.

* Money for U.S. Fishermen Whose Vessels are Seized by a Foreign Country

(19.210 Protection of Ships from Foreign Seizure)
Mark A. Clodfelter
Assistant Legal Adviser for International Claims and Investment Disputes
Office of the Legal Advisor
Suite 203, South Building
2430 E Street, NW
Washington, DC 2007-2800   202-776-8360
www.state.gov

U.S. Fishermen whose vessels are seized by a foreign country may be eligible for reimbursement by the State Department. Claims for reimbursement can be filed for fines, license or registration fees, levies, any direct charges paid to a foreign government to secure the prompt release of the vessel and crew, and for fees charged by the government of a foreign country to engage in transit between points in the United States. Seizures made by a country at war with the U.S., or a seizure made in accordance with the provisions of any convention or treaty made with the U.S. and in force at the time of seizure are not eligible for reimbursement. Type of assistance: insurance (reimbursement). Range of money available: dependent on Congressional authorizations.

* Help for Farmers and Ranchers on Indian Lands

(15.034 Agriculture on Indian Lands)
Mark Bradford
Office of Trust Responsibilities
Division of Water and Land Resources
Branch of Agriculture and Range
Bureau of Indian Affairs
1849 C Street, NW
Mail Stop 4513 MIB
Washington, DC 20240   202-208-3598
www.doi.gov/bia/otrhome.htm
www.doi.gov/bureau-indian-affairs.html

This program helps Indian farmers, ranchers and landowners manage and develop their land for farming and grazing. It also provides for noxious weed eradication by means of chemical, mechanical, cultural, and biological control methods. Funds may be used for farmland improvements such as farm drainage, land leveling, crop varieties, cropping patterns, stock water engineering, range inventories, inventories to identify vegetation, range conditions, precipitation zones and current forage utilization; rangeland pest control, livestock control, maintenance of readiness conditions for fire suppression; leasing and permitting support, and performance evaluations. Types of assistance: direct payments for specified use, advisory services and counseling, provision of specialized services. Range of money available for agricultural assistance: $200 to $575,000; average: $50,000. Range of money available for noxious weed eradication: $500 to $300,000; average: $20,000.

* Money to Indian Tribes for Economic Development

(15.032 Indian Economic Development)
Woodrow Sneed
Office of Economic Development
Bureau of Indian Affairs
1849 C Street, NW
Mail Stop 4640
Washington, DC 20240   202-208-4796
www.doi.gov/bia/ecodev/index.htm
www.doi.gov/bureau-indian-affairs.html

Funds from this program can be used to administer revolving loan and guaranty loan programs to promote economic development on tribal lands. Assistance is provided to American Indian owned businesses in obtaining financing from private sectors. Type of assistance: direct payments for specified use. Range of money available: $5,000 to $300,000; average: $215,000.

* Grants to Market Food Related Products to Emerging Markets Overseas

(10.603 Emerging Markets Program)
Director
Marketing Operations Staff
Foreign Agricultural Services
Department of Agriculture
Washington, DC 2020   202-720-4327
www.fas.usda.goc/mos/em-markets/em-markets.html

The Emerging Markets Program's goal is to promote, enhance, or expand the export of U.S. agricultural commodities in low to middle income counties that are likely to emerge as promising export markets in the near future. U.S. agricultural and agribusiness firms, especially those that need assistance in obtaining or maintaining access to overseas markets, may be eligible for cost-share assistance to implement an Emerging Markets Program. Program funds may be used to finance activities such as feasibility studies, market research, sectorial assessments, orientation visits, specialized training, and business workshops. Type of assistance: direct payments for specified use. Range of money available: $5,000 to $500,000.

* Help for Farmers and Ranchers to Conserve Natural Resources

(10.912 Environmental Quality Incentives Program)
Deputy Chief for Natural Resource Conservation Programs
Natural Resources Conservation Service
U.S. Department of Agriculture
P.O. Box 289   202-720-1845
Washington, DC 20013   Fax: 202-72-4265
www.nrcs.usda.gov

This program provides technical, educational and financial assistance to eligible farmers and ranchers to address soil, water and other natural resource concerns on their lands through the implementation of structural, vegetative, and land management practices. Technical assistance is provided for conservation planning measures. Educational and financial assistance is provided for the implementation of structural, vegetative and land management practices. Cost-share payments may be used to implement one or more eligible structural or vegetative practices. Incentive payments can be used to implement one or more land management practices. To be eligible, farmers and ranchers must face serious threats to soil, water and related natural resources or need assistance in complying with Federal and State environmental laws. Type of assistance: direct payments for specified use. Range of money available in cost-share and incentive payments: up to $10,000 per year, $50,000 over the length of the contract; average: $15,000.

* Money for Great Plains Farmers and Ranchers to Conserve Soil and Water

(10.900 Great Plains Conservation)
Deputy Chief
National Resources Conservation Programs
Natural Resources Conservation Services
Department of Agriculture
P.O. Box 2890
Washington, DC 20013   202-720-1873
www.nrcs.usda.gov

In order to conserve and develop the Great Plains water and soil resources, technical and financial assistance is provided to farmers and ranchers to plan and implement conservation practices. Cost-share funds are available for many of the soil and water conservation measures necessary to protect and stabilize a farm or ranch against the effects of climate and erosion in the Great Plains area. Applicants must have control of the land for the period of the contract, between 3 to 10 years. Land must be located in one of the 556 designated counties in Colorado, Kansas, Montana, Nebraska, New Mexico, Oklahoma, South Dakota, Texas or Wyoming. Types of assistance: direct payments for specified use; advisory services and counseling. Range of money available: up to $35,000 per farm operating unit over a contract period of 3 to 10 years.

* Money for Businesses to Reduce High Energy Costs in Rural Communities

(10.859 Assistance to High Energy Cost-Rural Communities)
Administrator
Rural Utilities Service
Department of Agriculture
Washington, DC 20250-1500   202-720-9540
www.rurdev.usda.gov

This program provides assistance to rural communities with extremely high energy costs. Funds must be used to acquire, construct, extend, upgrade, or otherwise improve the energy generation, transmission, or distribution facilities in these communities. Types of assistance: direct loans, project grants. Range of money available: not established yet.

* Grants to Agricultural Producers and Rural Small Businesses to Conserve Energy

(10.775 Renewable Energy Systems and Energy Efficiency Improvements Program)
Rural Business-Cooperative Services
Department of Agriculture
1400 Independence Avenue, SW

Washington, DC 20013   202-720-1400
www.rurdev.usda.gov/rbs

The Rural Business-Cooperative Service provides direct loans, loan guarantees and grants to farmers, ranchers, and rural small businesses for measures to help reduce the cost and consumption of energy. Funds must be used to purchase renewable energy systems or energy efficiency improvements. Types of assistance: direct loans, loan guarantees, and grants. Range of money available: not applicable.

* Money to Enhance Production and Marketing in the Sheep and Goat Industries

(10.774 National Sheep Industry Improvement Center)
National Sheep Industry Improvement Center
U.S. Department of Agriculture
1400 Independence Avenue, SW
Room 2117   202-690-0632
Washington, DC 20250   Fax: 202-236-6576
www.rurdev.usda.gov/coops/cssheep.htm

The National Sheep Industry Improvement Center provides financial assistance to the U.S. Sheep and Goat Industries to strengthen and enhance the production and marketing of sheep, goats, and their products within the United States. Funds may be used for increasing production or improving production efficiency; improving product quality or marketing efficiency; coordinating marketing systems and industry participants; improving communication between the industry, public, and the center; and taking actions that will keep the center viable. Types of assistance: direct loans, guaranteed/insured loans, direct payments for specified use, and project grants. Range of money available: each program or project loan may not exceed $1,000,000.

* Grants for Rural Businesses and Communities

(10.773 Rural Business Opportunity Grants)
Rural Business-Cooperative Service
U.S. Department of Agriculture
Specialty Lenders Division
Mail Stop 3225, Room 6767
1400 Independence Avenue, SW
Washington, DC 20250-1521   202-720-1400
www.rurdev.usda.gov

Grant funds from this program can be used to improve the economic development of rural areas by providing technical assistance for rural businesses, training for rural entrepreneurs and economic development officials, or planning for business and economic development. Type of assistance: project grants. Range of money available: $3,000 to $615,000; average $98,684.

* Money for U.S. Businesses to Train Foreign Interns

(11.114 Special American Business Internship Training Program)
SABIT Program
U.S. Department of Commerce
FCB, Fourth Floor, 4100W
1401 Constitution Avenue, NW
Washington, DC 20230   202-482-2443
www.ita.doc.gov/sabit/sabit.html

The SABIT Program awards funding to qualified U.S. Companies for training scientists and business executives form the New Independent States (NIS) of the former Soviet Union. Recipient firms will be reimbursed up to $13,700 per intern for airline travel, stipends and housing. This program exposes NIS managers and scientists to American methods of management and innovation, and also benefits U.S. businesses who gain business associates and customers in the NIS. Type of assistance: project grants, cooperative agreements. Range of money available: $8,400 to $40,400; average: $18,000.

* Loans to Fishermen and Fisheries

(11.415 Fisheries Finance Program)
Michael Grable
Financial Services Division
National Marine Fisheries Service
Department of Commerce
1315 East-West Highway   301-713-1306
Silver Spring, MD 20910   Fax: 301-713-1306
www.noaa.gov

This program provides loans for certain fisheries costs. Loans are made for up to 80% of the actual cost, for the reconstruction or reconditioning of fishing vessels, and the renovation, repair, or construction of shore side fishery facilities (including aquaculture facilities). Funds from this program may not be used for purposes which could lead to the over capitalization of the fishing industry. Type of assistance: direct loans. Range of money available: $10,000 to $100,000,000; average: $1,000,000.

* Grants to Improve and Extend Public Telecommunications Services in the U.S.

(11.550 Public Telecommunications Facilities-Planning and Construction)
William Cooperman
Director, Public Telecommunications Facilities Program
Office of Telecommunications and Information Application/NTIA
Room 4625
Department of Commerce
1401 Constitution Avenue, NW
Washington, DC 20230   202-482-5802
www.ntia.doc.ov/ptfp

This program's purpose is to assist in the planning, acquisition, installation and modernization of public telecommunication facilities. Grants are given to extend public telecommunications service by the most efficient and economical means; including the use of broadcast and non-broadcast technologies; increasing public telecommunications services and facilities owned and operated by women and minorities; and strengthening the capability of existing public television and radio stations to provide public telecommunications service to the public. Planning grants are awarded for the construction of public telecommunications facilities. Matching grants are given for the equipment needed for the production and distribution of programming, and for the reception of non-commercial educational and cultural radio and television programs. Type of assistance: project grants. Range of money available: $15,073 to $1,800,000; average: $362,575.

* Money to Help Bus Operators Comply With "Transportation for Individuals with Disabilities" Requirements

(20.518 Capital and Training Assistance Program for Over-the Road Bus Accessibility)
Brenda Younger
Program Coordinator
Federal Transit Administration
Office of Program Management
Office of Resource Management and State Programs
400 7th Street, SW
Washington, DC 2059   202-366-2053
www.fta.dot.gov

This program provides funding to private operators of over-the-road buses to assist with the costs and training necessary to comply with the Department of Transportation's "Transportation for Individuals with Disabilities" rule. Capital projects eligible for funding include adding wheelchair lifts and other accessibility equipment to new vehicles, and purchasing lifts to retro-fit existing vehicles. Eligible training costs include sensitivity training, boarding assistance, securement, handling and storage of mobility devices, and training in the proper operation and maintenance of equipment. Type of assistance: project grants. Range of money available: $10,000 to $50,000; average: $20,000.

* Loans to U.S. Shipowners and Shipyards

(20.802 Federal Ship Financing Guarantees)
Associate Administrator for Shipbuilding
Office of Ship Financing
Maritime Administration
Department of Transportation
400 7th Street, SW
Washington, DC 20590   202-366-5744
www.marad.dot.gov

The purpose of this program is to promote the growth and modernization of the U.S. Merchant Marine and U.S. Shipyards. It provides competitive financing, through loan guarantees, to fund the construction, re-construction, or re-conditioning of vessels built in U.S. Shipyards. It also guarantees loans for general shipyard facilities located in the U.S. in order to stimulate commercial ship construction for domestic and export sales, encourage shipyard modernization, and support increased productivity. Loans may be used to finance advanced shipbuilding technology and modern shipbuilding technology of general shipyard facilities located in the U.S. and for vessels which are designed for research or commercial use. Type of assistance: guaranteed/insured loans. Range of money available: past projects have ranged from less than one million to several hundred million dollars.

* Firefighting, Safety and Marine Operations Training for Seafarers

Bruce J. Carlton
Associate Administrator for Policy and International Trade
Maritime Administration
Department of Transportation
400 7th Street, SW
Washington, DC 20590   202-366-5755
www.marad.dot.gov
(20.810 Supplementary Training)

Marad provides supplemental training for seafarers in marine firefighting, safety, marine operations, and defense readiness. Type of assistance: training. Range of money available: fee-paid basis.

* Help for Minority, Women-owned and Disadvantaged Businesses to Get Bonded to Obtain Transportation Related Contracts

(20.904 Bonding Assistance Program)
Bonding Manager
Office of Small and Disadvantaged Business Utilization
S-40, Office of the Secretary
Department of Transportation
400 7th Street, SW   800-532-1169
Washington, DC 20590   202-366-2852
http://osdbuweb.dot.gov

Through this program, small and disadvantaged businesses can get assistance in obtaining bid, performance and payment bonds for transportation related contracts emanating from the DOT. The bonds are issued to support contracts for maintenance, rehabilitation, restructuring, improvement or revitalization of any mode of transportation in the U.S. with any public or commercial provider of transportation or any Federal, State or local transportation agency. Only certified minority, women-owned and disadvantaged businesses are eligible for this assistance. Type of assistance: insurance. Range of money available: average dollar amount of bonds issued is $330,000.

* Short Term Loans for Certified Disadvantaged Business Enterprises, and Minority and Women Owned Businesses

(20.905 Short Term Lending Program)
Office of Small and Disadvantaged Business Utilization
S-40, Office of the Secretary
Department of Transportation
400 7th Street, SW   800-532-1169
Washington, DC 20590   202-366-2852
http://osdbuweb.dot.gov

Short term working capital is provided in the form of a revolving line of credit in support of transportation related contracts through the DOT. Transportation related means a contract for the maintenance, rehabilitation, restructuring, improvement, or revitalization of any mode of transportation in the U.S. with any public or commercial provider of transportation, or any Federal, State, or local transportation agency. Businesses can borrow against the line of credit to meet the short term costs of performing the contract being financed. Loans are repaid as the contracts are completed and paid for. Lines of credit are for one year periods and may be renewed for up to five years. Only certified Disadvantaged Business enterprises, minority owned businesses, or women owned businesses are eligible. Type of assistance: direct loans. Range of money available: up to $750,000.

* Help to Establish and Operate a Credit Union

(44.001 Credit Union Charter, Examination, Supervision, and Insurance)
Chairman
NCUA Board
National Credit Union Administration
1775 Duke Street
Alexandria, VA 22314-328   703-518-6300
www.ncua.gov

NCUA staff will explain Federal Credit Union chartering requirements to any group interested in forming a credit union. They also help with the preparation of the charter application, assist newly chartered credit unions begin operation, and will assist credit unions and their members in consumer matters. Grant of a Federal Charter will provide $100,000 depositor insurance on individual accounts. State chartered credit unions are eligible to apply for depositor insurance in accordance with applicable State laws. Type of assistance: insurance, provision of specialized services, advisory services and counseling. Range of money available: not applicable.

* Money to Improve Services at Art, History, Natural History, Children's, General and Specialized Museums, Aquariums, Zoological Parks, Botanical Gardens, Arboretums, Nature Centers, Science and Technology Centers, and Planetariums

(44.301 Institute of Museum and Library Services, Learning Opportunity Grants)
Christine Henry
Institute of Museum and Library Services
1100 Pennsylvania Avenue, NW
Room 510
Washington, DC 20506   202-606-8687
Email: chenry@imls.gov
www.imls.gov

The Institute of Museum and Library Services supports the efforts of museums to conserve the country's historic, scientific, and cultural heritage by maintaining and expanding the educational roles of museums and libraries, and easing their financial burden as well. Funds from this program may be used for building public access, expanding educational services, reaching families and children, and using technology more effectively in support of these goals. Art, history (including historic buildings and sites), children's, general and specialized museums, aquariums, zoological parks, botanical gardens, arboretums, nature centers, science and technology centers, and planetariums are considered museums and are eligible for assistance through the IMLS. Types of assistance: project grants, direct payments for specified use. Range of money available: $5,000 to $150,000.

* Institutional, Collections Management, Public Dimension and Governance Assessments for Museums, Nature Centers, Science and Technology Centers and Botanical Gardens

(45.302 Museum Assessment Program)
Jeannette Thomas
Institute of Museum and Library Services
1100 Pennsylvania Avenue, NW
Room 510   202-606-8458 (Jeanette Thomas)
Washington, DC 20506   202-606-8339 (Public Affairs)
Email: imlsinfo@imls.gov
www.imls.gov

The Museum Assessment Program (MAP) is funded by the Institute of Museum and Library Services and administered by the American Association of Museums. It is designed to help museums assess their strengths and weaknesses and plan for the future. The program provides non-competitive grants of technical assistance for four types of assessments: Institutional, Collections Management Public Dimension, and Governance. In all Map assessments, members of the museum staff and governing authority complete a self-study and receive a site visit by one or more museum professionals who tour the museum and meet with the staff, governing officials, and volunteers. The surveyors work with MAP staff and the museum to produce a report on the museum's operations, suggesting resources and making recommendations. Museums include art, history (including historic buildings and sites), natural history, children's, general and specialized museums, science and technology centers, planetariums, aquariums, zoological parks, botanical gardens, arboretums, and nature centers. Types of assistance: direct payments for specified use, cooperative agreements
Rage of money available: $1775 to $2970.

* Grants to Museums, Aquariums, Zoological Parks, and Planetariums for Conservation Programs

(45.304 Conservation Assessment Program)
Noelle Giguere
Institute of Museum and Library Services
1100 Pennsylvania Avenue, NW
Room 510   202-606-8550 (Noelle Giguere)
Washington, DC 20506   202-606-8339 (Public Affairs)
Email: imlsinfo@imls.gov
www.imls.gov

The Conservation Assessment Program (CAP) supports a two day site visit by conservation professional to perform the assessment and up to three days to write the report. The general conservation survey or assessment provides an overview of all the museum's collections, as well as its environmental conditions, policies and procedures relating to collections care. The report aids the museum by providing recommendations and priorities for both immediate and long term conservation actions; facilitating the development of long range institutional plans for the care and preservation of the collection; and serving as a fundraising tool for future conservation projects. CAP helps institutions with living animal collections that do not have an assessment of the animal's physical conditions and habitats. Institutions with fully surveyed living animal collections may use the grant to assess the conservation needs of their non-living collections only. Botanical gardens and arboreta may use the grant to asses the conservation needs of both their living and non-living collections. Museums that have received a grant for a general conservation survey through the Conservation Project Support Program are not eligible for the Conservation Assessment Program. Art, history (including historic buildings and sites), natural history, children's, general and specialized museums, science and technology centers, planetariums, aquariums, zoological parks botanical gardens, arboretums and nature centers are eligible for this program. Types of assistance: direct payments for specified use, cooperative agreements. Average grant amount: $6,000.

* Grants to Museums, Botanical Gardens, Arboretums, and Nature Centers for Conservation Projects

(45.303 Conservation Project Support)
Steven Shwartzman
Institute of Museum and Library Services
1100 Pennsylvania Avenue, NW
Room 510   202-606-4641 (Steven Shwartzman)
Washington, DC 20506   202-606-8339 (Public Affairs)
Email: imlsinfo@imls.gov
www.imls.gov

The IMLS Conservation Project Support program awards matching grants to help museums identify conservation priorities and needs, and perform activities to ensure the safekeeping of their collections. The primary goal of each project must be conservation care and not collection management or maintenance. Conservation Project Support also funds exceptional projects with far reaching effects that benefit multiple institutions. Applicants may receive additional funding if their project has a directly related education component. Collections may be in one of four categories: non-living, systemic/natural history, living plants, and living animals. Grants are available for five broad areas of conservation activities: surveys, training, research, treatment, and environmental improvements. Aquariums, zoological parks, botanical gardens, arboretums, nature centers, science and technology centers, planetariums, and art, history (including historic buildings and sites), natural history, children's and specialized museums are eligible for this program. Types of assistance: project grants, direct payments for specified use. Range of money available: up to $50,000; up to $75,000 for exceptional projects; up to $10,000 in additional funds for an education component; average: $35,148.

* Business Development Help for Small Businesses

(59.005 Business Development Assistance to Small Business)
Associate Administrator for Business Initiatives
Small Business Administration
409 3rd Street, SW   800-8ASK-SBA
Washington, DC 20416   202-205-6665
www.sba.gov

This program provides assistance to prospective, as well as present, small business persons to improve the skills necessary to manage and operate a business. The assistance includes workshops for prospective small business owners; management counseling including assistance from the Service Corps of Retired Executives (SCORE) and other volunteer groups; management courses, conferences, and seminars; and educational materials to assist in the management of a small business. Types of assistance: advisory services and counseling, dissemination of technical information, and training. Range of money available: not applicable.

* Help in Obtaining Federal Contracts for Small Businesses

(59.009 Procurement Assistance to Small Businesses)
Associate Administrator for Government Contracting
Small Business Administration
409 3rd Street, SW   202-205-6460
Washington, DC 20416   800-8ASK-SBA
www.sba.gov

This program helps small business obtain a "fair" share of contracts and sub-contracts for Federal government supplies and services, and a "fair" share of property sold by the government. Assistance includes: the application of small business set-asides to increase the Federal procurement and disposal requirements awarded to small business; consultations to optimize small business participation in procurement activities; review and analysis of small firms in order to certify competence as a prime contractor; review of large

prime contractors' sub-contracting plans and programs to insure sub-contracting opportunities for small, disadvantaged, and women owned businesses; consultation and advice for small firms regarding government procurement and property sales matters; assistance in specific contract administration problems; and determination of small business eligibility for SBA's procurement financial programs. Existing and potential small businesses are eligible for assistance through this program. Type of assistance: provision of specialized services. Range of money available: not applicable.

* New Markets Venture Capital for Small Business in Low-Income Geographic Areas

(59.051 New Markets Venture Capital)
Director
New Markets Venture Capital Program
409 3rd Street, NW   202-205-6510
Suite 6300   800-8ASK-SBA
Washington, DC 20416   Fax: 202-205-6013
www.sba.gov/INV/venture.html

The goal of this program is to promote economic development and job opportunities in low-income geographic areas through developmental venture capital investments in smaller businesses located in such areas. The SBA designates New Markets Venture Capital companies which are eligible to receive guaranteed loans and project grants. The guaranteed loan funds are used to make equity capital investments in smaller businesses located in low-income geographic areas. Grant funds are used to provide management and technical assistance to these smaller enterprises in connection with the capital investments. Types of assistance: project grants, guaranteed/insured loans. Range of money available: minimum grant award is $1,500,000.

* Short-Term, Working-Capital Loans for Small Businesses

(59.012 Small Business Loans)
Office of Financial Assistance
CAPLines Program
Small Business Administration
409 Third Street, SW   202-205-6490
Washington, DC 20416   800-UASK-SBA
www.sba.gov/financing/loanprog/caplines.tml

CAPLines is a SBA loan program that helps small businesses meet their short term and cyclical working capital needs. Under the CAPLine program, there are five short term working capital loans: Seasonal line, Contract line, Builders line, Standard asset-based line, and Small asset-based line. The Seasonal line is an advance against anticipated inventory and accounts receivable during peak seasons when businesses experience seasonal sales fluctuations. The loan can be revolving or non-revolving. A Contract line finances the material cost and direct labor associated with performing assignable contracts. It can be revolving or non-revolving. A Builders' line is for small general contractors or builders who are constructing or renovating commercial or residential buildings. The building project serves as collateral, and loans can be revolving or non-revolving. A Standard asset-based line is a revolving line of credit for businesses unable to meet credit requirements for long term credit. It provides financing for cyclical growth and recurring and/or short term needs. A Small asset-based line is a revolving line of credit up to $200,000. It operates like a standard asset-based line except that some of the stricter requirements are waived providing the business demonstrates repayment ability. Type of assistance: direct loans. Range of money available: up o $1,000,000.

* Loans and Technical Assistance for Defense-Dependent Small Businesses Hurt by Defense Reductions

(59.012 Small Business Loans)
Office of Financial Assistance
DELTA Program
Small Business Administration
409 Third Street, SW   202-205-6490
Washington, DC 20416   800-UASK-SBA
www.sba.gov/financing/loanprog/military.html

The Defense Economic Transition Assistance Program (DELTA) provide technical and financial assistance to defense dependent small businesses that have been negatively affected by defense reductions. The goal of the program is to help those businesses diversify into the commercial market while remaining part of the defense industrial base. Loans must be used to retain jobs of defense workers, create new jobs in impacted communities, or to retool and expand in order to remain available to the Department of Defense. Type of assistance: direct loans. Range of money available: up to $1,250,000.

* Loans for Companies Engaged in International Trade

(59.012 Small Business Loans)
Office of Financial Assistance
International Trade Loan Program
Small Business Administration
409 Third Street, SW   202-205-6490
Washington, Dc 20416   800-UASK-SBA
www.sba.gov/financing/loanprog/tradeloans.tml

The International Trade Loan program helps businesses that are preparing to engage in or are already engaged in international trade, or are adversely affected by competition from imports. Applicants must establish that the loan will significantly expand or develop an export market, currently be adversely affected by import competition, upgrade equipment or facilities to improve competitive position, or be able to provide a business plan that reasonably projects sufficient export sales to cover the loan. Loan funds may be used to acquire, construct, renovate, modernize, improve or expand facilities and equipment to be used in the U.S. in order to produce goods or services involved in international trade, and to develop and penetrate foreign markets. International Trade Loan funds cannot be used to repay debt. Type of assistance: guaranteed loans. Range of money available: up to $1,250,000.

* Loans to Businesses to Create Jobs in Communities Impacted by NAFTA

(59.012 Small Business Loans)
Office of Financial Assistance
CAIP Program
Small Business Administration
409 Third Street, SW   202-205-6490
Washington, DC 20416   800-UASK-SBA
www.sba.gov/financing/loanprog/caip.html

The U.S. Community Adjustment and Investment Program (CAIP) was established to aid communities that suffered job losses due to changing trade patterns with Canada and Mexico after the North American Free Trade Agreement (NAFTA). CAIP increases the availability of credit to encourage business development and expansion in impacted areas. Through CAIP, credit is available to businesses in eligible communities to create new, sustainable jobs or to preserve existing jobs. CAIP works with the SBA in both the 7(a) loan program and 504 programs to reduce borrower costs and increase the availability of funds. Eligible businesses must be located in, or relocating to, a specific geographic area designated as eligible for funding under the CAIP by the U.S. Treasury and the NAD Bank. Type of assistance: guaranteed loans. Range of Money Available: up to $750,000.

* Loans to Provide Short-Term Working Capital to Exporters

(59.012 Small Business Loans)
Office of Financial Assistance
Special Purpose Loans
Export Working Capital Program
Small Business Administration
409 Third Street, SW
Washington, DC 20416   202-205-6490
800-UASK-SBA
www.sba.gov/financing/loanprog/ewcp.html

The Export Working Capital Program (EWCP) is designed to provide short term working capital to exporters who have been in business for at least one full year. The EWCP supports export financing to small businesses when other financing is not available on reasonable terms. The program encourages lending by guaranteeing loans up to $1,000,000 or 90% of a loan amount, whichever is less. The EWCP is a combined effort of the SBA and the Export-Import Bank. The SBA handles loan requests of $1,111,111 or less, and the Export-Import Bank processes loans for more than $1,111,111. Loans through the EWCP must be used to finance the working capital needs associated with single or multiple transactions of the exporter. Type of assistance: guaranteed/insured loans. Range of money available: up to $1,250,000.

* Loans to Start or Expand a Small Business

(59.012 Small Business Loans)
Office of Financial Assistance
7(a) Loan Program
Small Business Administration
409 Third Street, SW   202-205-6490
Washington, DC 20416   800-UASK-SBA
www.sba.gov/financing/sbaloa/7a.html

7(a) loans are the most basic and the most used of the SBA's business loan programs. The loans are from commercial lenders, but are guaranteed by the SBA. Small businesses are considered for eligibility based on size, type of business, use of proceeds, and the availability of funds from other sources. 7(a) loan funds may be used to establish a new business, or to assist in the operation, expansion or acquisition of an existing business. Eligible uses include the purchase of land or buildings, new construction as well as expansion or conversion of existing facilities; to acquire equipment, machinery, furniture, fixtures, supplies or materials; long-term working capital including the payment of accounts payable and/or the purchase of inventory; to purchase an existing business; and to refinance existing business debts which are not already structured with reasonable terms and conditions. Type of assistance: guaranteed loans. Range of money available: $2,000,000.

* Loan Prequalification Program for Low-Income Borrowers, Disabled Business Owners, New and Emerging Businesses, Veterans, Exporters, Rural and Specialized Industries

(59.012 Small Business Loans)
Office of Financial Assistance
Prequalification Program
Small Business Administration
409 Third Street, SW   202-205-6490
Washington, DC 20416   800-UASK-SBA
www.sba.gov/financing/sbaloan/prequalification.html

The Prequalification Loan Program uses intermediary organizations to assist prospective borrowers in developing viable loan application packages and securing loans. This program is primarily for rural and specialized industries, veterans, exporters, new and emerging businesses, disabled business owners and low income borrowers. The intermediaries work with applicants to ensure business plans are complete and that the application is eligible and has credit merit. Qualified loan packages are submitted to the SBA for approval. If approval is granted, the SBA will issue a pre-qualification letter on behalf of the applicant that indicates the SBA's willingness to guarantee a loan. The intermediary then helps the borrower to locate an appropriate commercial lender. Type of assistance: guaranteed loans, counseling. Range of money available: up to $250,000.

* Loans to Start or Expand a Business With a One Page Application

(59.012 Small Business Loans)
Office of Financial Assistance
LowDoc Loan Program
Small Business Administration
409 Third Street, SW   202-205-6510
Washington, DC 20416   800-UASK-SBA
www.sba.gov/financing/lendinvest/lowdoc.html

The Low Documentation Loan Program (LowDoc) streamlines the process of making small business loans. Once a small business borrower is approved for credit by a lender, the lender can request a loan guarantee from the SBA. The borrower completes the front of the one page form and the lender completes the back. The lender submits the completed application to the SBA and receives an answer within 36 hours. LowDoc loan funds can be used to start or expand a business. Type of assistance: guaranteed loans. Range of money available: up to $150,000.

* Technical and Financial Assistance to Small Businesses to Develop an Export Market

(59.012 Small Business Loans)
Director
Office of Financial Assistance
Specialty Loan Programs
Small Business Administration
409 Third Street, SW   202-205-6720
Washington, DC 20146   800-UASK-SBA
www.sba.gov/financial/loanprog/exportexpress.html

The SBA Export Express program combines lending assistance and technical assistance to help small businesses that have traditionally has difficulty in obtaining export financing. Export Express helps small businesses that have exporting potential, but need funds to buy or produce goods and/or to provide services for export. Loan funds nay be used to finance export development activities such as: participation in a trade show; general lines of credit for export purposes; translation of product brochures or catalogues for use in overseas markets; service contracts from buyers located outside the U.S.; transaction-specific financing needs associated with completing actual export orders; purchase real estate and/or equipment to be used in the expansion of services and the production of goods; provide loans and other financing to allow small businesses, export trading companies, and export management companies to develop foreign markets; acquire, purchase, renovate, expand, modernize, or improve production facilities or equipment used in the U.S. to produce goods or services for international trade. The Export Express program also offers technical assistance in the form of marketing, management and planning assistance. The Technical assistance is provided by the SBA's U.S. Export Assistance Centers, Small Business Development Centers (SBDC's), and the Service Corps of Retired Executives (SCORE). On approval of an SBA Export Express Loan, a representative from a U.S. Export Assistance Center will contact the borrower to offer appropriate assistance. This assistance may include training offered through the Export Trade Assistance Partnership, SBDC International Trade Center, SCORE, the District Export Council, or the Export Legal Assistance Network. Types of assistance: Guaranteed loans, technical assistance. Range of money available: up to $250,000.

* Help to Start or Expand a Microenterprise

(59.050 Micro-enterprise Development Grants)
Judy Raskind
Office of Financial Assistance
Small Business Administration
409 Third Street, SW   202-205-6497
Washington, DC 20416   800-UASK-SBA
www.sba.gov/INV

The PRIME program was created to help the smallest of small businesses, those with fewer than six employees, at the beginning stage of starting a business when the greatest amount of service and guidance is needed. Under the Program for Investment in Micro-entrepreneurs (PRIME), the SBA provides federal funds to community based organizations that in turn offer training and technical assistance to low-income and very low-income micro-entrepreneurs. Type of assistance: training and technical assistance. Range of money available: not applicable.

* Free Counseling and Mentoring Services for Potential and Existing Small Businesses

(59.026 Service Corps of Retired Executives Association)
W. Kenneth Yancey
National SCORE Association Office
Small Business Administration
409 Third Street, SW   800-634-0245
Washington, DC 20025   202-205-6762
www.score.org
www.sba.gov

SCORE uses the management experience of retired and active business professionals to counsel and train potential and existing small business owners. SCORE members volunteer their counseling and mentoring services to the public free of charge, though small business training workshops are offered for a low fee. Confidential counseling is offered face-to-face or through Email. SCORE is a resource partner with the SBA. Types of assistance: advisory services and counseling, training. Range of money available: not applicable.

* Business Development Help for Asian American, African American, Hispanic American, Native American and Asian Pacific American Businesses

(59.006 8(a) Business Development)
Associate Administrator for 8(a) Business Development
Small Business Administration
409 Third Street, SW   202-205-6421
Washington, DC 20416   800-UASK-SBA
www.sba.gov/8abd

This program offers business development assistance to business owners who are both socially and economically disadvantaged. The assistance provided includes: management and technical assistance, access to capital and other forms of financing, business training and counseling, and access to sole source and limited competition Federal Contract opportunities. Socially and economically disadvantaged individuals and businesses owned and operated by such individuals, economically disadvantaged Indian tribes, Alaskan Native corporations, and Native Hawaiian organizations may be eligible for assistance through this program. Type of assistance: provision of specialized services. Range of money available: not applicable.

* Loans to Small Businesses to Plan, Design or Install a Pollution Control Facility

(59.012 Small Business Loans)
Office of Financial Assistance
Special Purpose Loan Programs
Small Business Administration

409 Third Street, SW   202-205-6490
Washington, DC 20416   800-UASK-SBA
www.sba.gov/financing/lanprog/pollution.html

Pollution Control Loans are SBA 7(a) loans with the special purpose of pollution control. The program provides financing to eligible small businesses for the planning, installation or design of a pollution control facility. This facility must control, abate, reduce or prevent any form of pollution; this also includes recycling. Loan funds can only be used for fixed assets. Type of assistance: direct loans for a specified purpose. Range of money available: up to $2,000,000.

* Loans Guarantees to Foreign Buyers to Purchase Products or Services from U.S. Exporters

(Medium and Long Term Loan Guarantee Program)
Jeffrey Miller
Export Finance Department
Export-Import Bank of the United States
811 Vermont Avenue, NW   202-565-3946
Washington, DC 20571   800-565-3946
www.exim.gov/products/loan_guar.html

Ex-Im Bank assists U.S. Exporters by guaranteeing financing to credit worthy international buyers for purchase of U.S. goods and services, and exports to large scale projects. Financing may also be available for refurbished equipment, software, certain banking and legal fees, and certain local costs and expenses. The benefits of this program include flexible financing options and repayment terms, no limits on transaction size, medium and long term financing, 100% coverage of commercial and political risks, and it enables buyers to obtain loans from lenders. To qualify for Ex-Im support, the product or services must be made up of at least 50% U.S. content, and must be shipped from the U.S. to an international buyer. Military or defense items are not eligible, nor are sales to military buyers. The loans are available for up to 85% of the U.S. export value. The buyer must make a cash payment of at least 15% of the U.S. export value. Type of assistance: loan guarantees. Range of money available: There is no minimum or maximum limit to the size of the export sale that may be financed with Ex-Im Bank's loan guarantee.

* Loans to Exporters to Finance New Project Companies

(Project and Structured Finance)
Barbara O'Boyle
Project and Structured Finance Division
Export-Import Bank of the United States
811 Vermont Avenue, NW   800-565-3976 ext. 3690
Washington, DC 20571   202-565-3377
Email: structuredfinance@exim.gov
www.exim.gov/products/guarantee/proj_finance.html

Ex-Im Bank's Project Finance program is an arrangement in which Ex-Im Bank lends to newly created project companies and looks to the project's future cash flow as the source of repayment of the debt. Eligible project candidates include significant facility or production expansions and Greenfield projects. Ex-Im Bank has no dollar limits on project size, sector, or country. While there is no minimum transaction size, applicants should consider carefully the costs associated with a limited recourse project financing approach. The Ex-Im Bank uses seven major guidelines to determine eligibility of costs related to a project finance transaction. They are foreign content, reach-back, related parties, capital cost, contingencies, local cost and progress payments. This program allows for flexible loan repayment terms to match a project's revenue flow. Project finance transactions can be structured with tailored repayment profiles, more flexible grace periods, and more flexibility on total repayment terms. Through "Structured Finance", Ex-Im Bank considers existing overseas companies as potential borrowers based on their credit worthiness as reflected on heir balance sheet, and other sources of collateral or security enhancements. Type of assistance: direct loans. Range of money available: there is no minimum or maximum dollar amount associated with this program.

* Loan Guarantees to Foreign Purchasers of New and Used U.S. Manufactured Ships

(Transportation Loan Guarantees- Ship Exports)
Robert Morin
Transportation Division
Export-Import Bank of the United States
811 Vermont Avenue, NW   800-565-3976 ext. 3787
Washington, DC 20571   202-565-3550
www.exim.gov/products/transportation/ship.html

The Export-Import Bank of the United States offers a variety of financing options, through its direct loan, loan guarantee, and insurance programs, to assist U.S Manufacturers in the sale of new and used ships. Ships are defined as self-propelled sea going vessels of more than 1000 gross tons. The OECD governs the terms and conditions of Ex-Im Bank's financing support for ship exports. For sales of new ships, Ex-Im Bank can provide financing for the lesser of 85% of the contract price or 100% of the U.S. content. Ex-Im also supports the export of used ships from the United States. A Used Equipment Questionnaire must be completed and an inspection may be required in order to determine the terms of Ex-Im Bank's financing support. Type of assistance: loan guarantees. Range of money available: up to $50,000,000.

* Loan Guarantees to Foreign Purchasers of New and Used U.S. Made Railroad Equipment

(Transportation Loan Guarantees- Railroad Equipment)
Robert Morin
Transportation Division
Export-Import Bank of the United States
811 Vermont Avenue, NW   800-565-3946 ext. 3787
Washington, DC 20571   202-565-3550
www.exim.gov/products/transportation/rail.html

Ex-Im Bank offers financing support to assist U.S. Manufacturers in the sale of new and used, commercial and general railroad equipment to foreign purchasers through its direct loan, insurance and loan guarantee programs. Terms and conditions of the financing support of railroad equipment exports are established by the OECD. Railroad equipment includes locomotives, passenger and freight cars (rolling stock) and infrastructure equipment such as tracks, and switching and signaling equipment. Ex-Im Bank bases its credit decision on the creditworthiness of the borrower, and may require additional security provided by a mortgage on the equipment. For government owned or controlled borrowers a sovereign guarantee may be required. Generally, Ex-Im Bank can support up to 85% of the contract price, but not more than 100% of the U.S. content of the equipment. For new rolling stock equipment, support is usually provided through a medium or long term guarantee program where the Ex-Im Bank guarantees 100% of the principle and interest of a loan extended by a financial institution. Used rolling stock may also be eligible for support provided the equipment meets Ex-Im bank's used equipment criteria. These criteria specify that the equipment must have been manufactured in the U.S., has been used in the U.S. for at least one year, and must be exported from a U.S. port. A Used Equipment Questionnaire must be completed when the application is submitted and will be reviewed by the Ex-Im Bank to determine eligibility. Type of assistance: loan guarantees. Range of money available: up to $50,000,000.

* Loan Guarantees to Foreign Purchasers of New and Used U.S. Manufactured Commercial and General Aviation Aircraft and Helicopters

(Transportation Loan Guarantees- Aircraft Equipment)
Robert Morin
Transportation Division
Export-Import Bank of the United States
811 Vermont Avenue, NW   800-565-3946 ext. 3787
Washington, DC 20571   202-565-3550
www.exim.gov/products/transportation/aircraft.html

Ex-Im Bank offers financing support, through its direct loan, insurance and loan guarantee programs, to foreign purchasers of new and used U.S. Made commercial and general aviation aircraft, including helicopters. The OECD governs the terms and conditions of the Ex-Im Bank's financing support under this program. Credit decisions are based on the credit worthiness of the airline/lessee and the additional security provided by the aircraft. New, large, commercial aircraft (those with passenger seating for 70 or more) are usually financed using an asset-based finance lease structure. New, small aircraft (fewer than 70 seats) are typically financed by other methods. The maximum amount of Ex-m Bank supported financing for a new aircraft is 85% of the U.S contract price net of all manufacturer and supplier memoranda, but not more than 100% of the U.S. content of the aircraft. Spare parts, related ground equipment, training costs, and transaction expenses may be included in sovereign guaranteed large aircraft transactions. Ex-Im Bank considers the financing support of pre-owned or used aircraft on a case by case basis. A Used Equipment Questionnaire must be completed and submitted as part of the application. The amount of financing support granted by the Ex-Im Bank will be based on the net invoice price of the used aircraft, an appropriate advance rate determined by Ex-Im Bank, and an inspection/appraisal performed by an independent third party appraiser. Ex-Im Bank is prohibited from financing the export of military aircraft or the export of civilian aircraft to a foreign military unit. Type of assistance: guaranteed loans. Range of money available: up to $50,000,000.

* Lines of Credit to Support the Export of U.S Goods and Services

(Credit Guarantee Facility Program)
Wayne Gardella
Export-Import Bank of the United States
822 Vermont Avenue, NW   800-565-3976 ext 3787
Washington, DC 20571   202-565-3900
www.exim.gov/products/credt_guar.html

This program facilitates the sale of U.S. goods and services by establishing lines of credit between a U.S. bank and a foreign bank, or occasionally a large foreign buyer. Ex-Im Bank guarantees the repayment of the foreign bank's obligation and the foreign bank then makes credit available to the end user of the U.S. exports and takes the repayment risk of that local company. Standard guarantee coverage is available: 100% of principle and interest up to 85% of the U.S. export value. The buyer must make a 15% cash payment to the exporter. Type of assistance: loan guarantees. Range of money available: $10,000,000.

* Loans for Exporters of Architectural, Industrial Design and Engineering Services

(Engineering Multiplier Program)
Wayne Gardella
Export-Import Bank of the United States
811 Vermont Avenue, NW   800-565-3976 ext. 3787
Washington, DC 20571   202-565-3380
www.exim.gov/ebd-m-03.html

This program finances feasibility studies, pre-construction design, and engineering and architectural services that involve projects that have the potential of generating substantial U.S. export orders. The Engineering Multiplier Program offers fixed rate loans and guarantees to foreign buyers of project related feasibility studies and pre-construction engineering services. In the long term, the program is designed to generate additional overseas sales of U.S. goods and services (the "multiplier effect") since the foreign buyer is more likely to order U.S. equipment and services for a construction project on which U.S. engineers, designers and architects did the feasibility and design work. Type of assistance: loans, loan guarantees. Range of money available: up to $10,000,000.

* Fixed Rate Loans to International Purchasers of U.S. Exports

(Direct Loan Program)
Jeffrey Miller
Export Finance Department
Export-Import Bank of the United States
811 Vermont Avenue, NW   202-565-3946
Washington, DC 20571   800-565-3946
www.exim.gov/products/directloan.html

Ex-Im Bank assists U.S. Exporters by guaranteeing financing to credit worthy international buyers for purchase of U.S. goods and services, and exports to large scale projects. Financing may also be available for refurbished equipment, software, certain banking and legal fees, and certain local costs and expenses. The benefits of this program include flexible financing options and repayment terms, no limits on transaction size, medium and long term financing, 100% coverage of commercial and political risks, and it enables buyers to obtain loans from lenders. To qualify for Ex-Im support, the product or services must be made up of at least 50% U.S. content, and must be shipped from the U.S. to an international buyer. Military or defense items are not eligible, nor are sales to military buyers. The loans are available for up to 85% of the U.S. export value. The buyer must make a cash payment of at least 15% of the U.S. export value. Type of assistance: direct loans. Range of money available: There is no minimum or maximum limit to the size of the export sale that may be financed with direct loan from Ex-Im Bank, though most transactions are over $10,000,000.

* Working Capital Loans for U.S. Exporters

(Working Capital Guarantee Program)
Pamela Bowers
Export-Import Bank of the United States   800-565-3946
811 Vermont Avenue, NW   202-565-3780
Washington, DC 20571   Fax: 202-565-3793
www.exim.gov/products/work_cap.html

Ex-Im Bank's working capital financing allows U.S. exporters to obtain loans to produce or buy goods or services for export. Exporters may use the financing to purchase finished products for export, pay for raw materials, equipment, supplies, labor and overhead to produce goods and/or provide services for export, cover standby letters of credit serving as bid bonds, performance bonds or payment guarantees, or to finance foreign receivables. Eligible exporters must be located in the U.S., have been in business for at least one year, and have a positive net worth. Eligible exports must be shipped from the U.S., services must be performed by U.S. personnel, and products must have at least 50% U.S. content. Military or defense items are not eligible, nor are sales to military buyers. Ex-Im Bank assumes 90% of the bank loan, including principal and interest. For qualified loans to minority, woman-owned, or rural businesses, Ex-Im Bank can increase its coverage to 100%. Type of assistance: loan guarantees. Range of money available: There is no minimum or maximum transaction amount for this program.

* Letter of Credit Insurance for Banks

(Bank Letter of Credit Insurance Policy)
Richard Maxwell
Trade, Finance and Insurance Division
Export-Import Bank of the United States   202-565-3633
811 Vermont Avenue, NW   800-565-3946
Washington, DC 20571   Fax: 202-565-3684
www.exim.gov/products/insurance/loc.html

The Ex-Im Bank's Letter of Credit Insurance Policy reduces a bank's risks on irrevocable letters of credit issued by foreign banks to support U.S. Exports. The policy provides coverage against losses caused by war, revolution, expropriation or confiscation by a governmental authority, cancellation of export or import licenses, foreign exchange inconvertibility, and commercial losses due to insolvency of the foreign issuing bank and failure to pay or reimburse for other reasons. Terms up to 180 days may be extended for consumer goods, spare parts, and raw materials. Agricultural commodities, fertilizer and capital equipment may be insured up to 360 days on a case by case basis. Type of assistance: insurance. Range of coverage available: up to $10,000,000.

* Financing Lease Insurance for Companies that Lease U.S. Goods Overseas

(Financing Lease Policy)
Richard Maxwell
Trade, Finance and Insurance Division
Export-Import Bank of the United States   800-565-3946
811 Vermont Avenue, NW   202-565-3633
Washington, DC 20571   Fax: 202-565-3684
www.exim.gov/products/insurance/leasing,html

The Financing Lease insurance policy is designed to provide protection to leasing companies where the lease contract stipulates there will be little residual value in the leased product and ownership is to be transferred to the lessee at the end of the lease. Ex-Im Bank considers this type of lease structure to be similar to a medium term sale transaction, and requires a 15% advance payment from the lessee to the lessor before delivery of the leased product. Ex-Im Bank will insure the remaining 85% of the lease transaction. Should the lessee default, coverage for the insured percentage of each lease payment is provided to the lessor as it falls due, until the end of the lease term. The Financing Lease policy covers only single transactions. A separate policy is issued for each lease insured by Ex-Im Bank. Type of assistance: insurance. Range of coverage available: up to $10,000,000.

* Stream of Payments Lease Insurance for Overseas Leasing Companies

(Operating Lease Policy-Coverage for Stream of Payments)
Richard Maxwell
Trade, Finance and Insurance Division
Export-Import Bank of the United States   800-565-3946
811 Vermont Avenue, NW   202-565-3633
Washington, DC 20571   Fax: 202-565-3684
www.exim.gov/products/insurance/leasing,html

The Operating Lease Insurance Policy was designed to provide coverage for leases where payments total less than the full value of the lease products, there is no intention on the part of the lessor to transfer title of the leased product to the lessee at the end of the lease period, and the lessor keeps the risk that the leased products will decline in market value at a greater rate than expected. Stream of Payments is one of two types of coverage under the Operating Lease Policy. It provides coverage for the "stream of payments" falling due during a repossession effort period after a default on the part of the lessee. This part of the overall coverage maintains the insured will receive a stream of payments while action is taken to repossess the leased products. The length of repossession efforts period is underwritten on a case by case basis, and usually covers periodic and non-periodic payments which fall due for up to five months. Periodic payments represent the rental portion of the lease, and non-periodic payments include service or maintenance payments. Coverage for the stream of payments is provided at a maximum of 100% for sovereign lessees and 90% for all others. Type of assistance: insurance. Range of coverage available: $10,000,000.

* Insurance for Exporters Against Repossession of Leased Goods Being Prevented By a Foreign Government

(Operating Lease Policy-Government Prevention of Repossession)
Richard Maxwell
Trade, Finance and Insurance Division
Export-Import Bank of the United States   800-565-3946
811 Vermont Avenue, NW   202-565-3633
Washington, DC 20571   Fax: 202-565-3684
www.exim.gov/products/insurance/leasing,html

Coverage against Governmental Prevention of Repossession (GPR) is one of two types of coverage provided by Ex-Im Bank's Operating Lease Policy. This policy is designed to support leasing companies involved in the export of goods by providing coverage in cases where government actions may prevent the repossession, expropriation, or confiscation of leased products, or lead to the cancellation of export licenses. This coverage, usually 100% for all lessee types, comes into effect only after the end of the repossession-efforts period. It is limited to the fair market value of the leased product at the time of the claim. Type of assistance: insurance. Range of coverage available: up to $10,000,000.

* Medium Term Insurance for U.S. Exporters and Banks

(Medium Term Insurance Credit Program)
Richard Maxwell
Trade, Finance and Insurance Division
Export-Import Bank of the United States   800-565-363
811 Vermont Avenue, NW   202-565-3633
Washington, DC 20571   Fax: 202-565-3684
www.exim.gov/products/insurancemedium_term.html

Exporters and Financial Institutions supporting the credit sale of U.S. capital equipment, its installation, and/or spare parts can insure their foreign receivables against losses with Ex-Im Bank's medium term insurance policy. Documentary policies are issued to financial institutions, and non-documentary policies are issued to exporters. These medium term policies cover two types of losses. Commercial losses resulting from non-payment for such reason's as a buyer's insolvency or failure to pay an obligation within six months of the date due, and Political losses from certain specifically defined risks such as war, revolution, cancellation of import or export licenses, and currency inconvertibility. Ex-Im Bank's medium term policies cover credit sales in which payment terms range from 1 to 5 years after the goods arrive at the port of importation. Two types of transaction are covered under these policies: single sales or one time transactions; and repetitive sales in which there is an ongoing relationship between the exporter and a dealer or distributor. All medium term policies require the buyer to pay the insured party a 15% cash payment before delivery of the goods. The remaining financed portion is then insured at 100%. Type of assistance: insurance. Range of coverage available: up to $10,000,000.

* Loans and Insurance for Small Environmental Export Businesses

(Environmental Exports Program)
James A. Mahoney Jr.
Engineering and Environment Division
Export-Import Bank of the United States
811 Vermont Avenue, NW   800-565-3946
Washington, DC 20571   202-565-3946
www.exim.gov/products/special/environment.html

Ex-Im Bank's Environmental Exports Program has several policies to support U.S. Exporters of renewable energy and environmentally beneficial goods and services, and exporters participating in foreign environmental projects. The Short-term Environmental Export Insurance Policy provides short-term, multi-buyer, and single-buyer insurance coverage for small business environmental exporters. The policy enables the exporter to offer credit terms to its foreign customers for up to 180 days. The medium-term export credit insurance policy allows U.S. exporters to offer both technology and financing to their international buyers of capital goods and environmental services. Ex-Im Bank also offers enhanced medium and long tern loans and loan guarantees in support of environmental projects, products and services. Exports qualifying for support under this program include products or services for foreign environmental or renewable energy projects or facilities; the export of products or services specifically used to aid in the prevention, abatement, control or mitigation of air, water and ground pollution or contamination; and the export of products and services which provide protection in the handling of toxic substances and waste. Types of assistance: insurance, loans, and loan guarantees. Range of money available: $10,000,000.

* Short-Term, Single-Buyer, Export Credit Insurance for U.S. Exporters

(Short-Tem, Single-Buyer, Export Credit Insurance)
Richard Maxwell
Trade, Finance and Insurance Division
Export-Import Bank of the United States   800-565-3946
811 Vermont Avenue, NW   202-565-3633
Washington, DC 20571   Fax: 202-565-3684
www.exim.gov/products/insurance/single_buyer.html

Exporters of U.S. goods and services can reduce their risks when selling on credit terms internationally by insuring specific, foreign receivables with Ex-Im Bank's Short-term, Single-Buyer, Export Credit Insurance Policy. This policy insures receivables against non-payment by international buyers, extends competitive credit terms to foreign buyers, and uses insured foreign receivables as additional collateral to get better financing terms with the exporter's lender. This policy covers exports of U.S. goods and services with at least 51% U.S. content, single or multiple shipments to one buyer on credit terms, in an eligible country, and repayment terms of up to 180 days. Confirmed letters of credit, cash-in-advance sales and military or defense related items are not covered. This policy covers losses due to commercial reasons (insolvency, default) and political events (war, revolution, seizure of goods, foreign exchange inconvertibility, and revocation of import/export licenses). Type of assistance: insurance. Range of coverage available: up to $10,000,000.

* Insurance for U.S. Exporters That Sell to Multiple Buyers on Credit Terms

(Multi-Buyer Export Credit Insurance)
Richard Maxwell
Trade, Finance and Insurance Division
Export-Import Bank of the United States   800-565-3946
811 Vermont Avenue, NW   202-565-3633
Washington, DC 20571   Fax: 202-565-3684
www.exim.gov/products/insurance/multi_buyer.html

Exporters of U.S. goods and services can reduce their risk of selling on credit terms by insuring their export accounts receivable with Ex-Im Bank's Short-term, Multi-buyer, Export Credit Insurance. This policy covers exports of U.S. goods and services with at least 51% U.S. content, sold to multiple buyers, on credit terms of up to 180 days. Commercial losses such as bankruptcy and protracted default, and losses due to political events such as war, revolution, seizure of goods, revocation of import license and foreign exchange inconvertibility are covered under this policy. Two coverage options are available: Split coverage (90% for commercial losses, 100% for political losses) and Equalized coverage (95% for both commercial and political losses). For an additional premium, the exporter can choose pre-shipment coverage in cases where goods are special ordered or there is a long manufacturing wait. This policy does not cover confirmed letters of credit, cash-in-advance sales, and military or defense related items. Type of assistance: insurance. Range of coverage available: up to $10,000,000.

* Insurance for New Small Business Exporters

(Small Business Multi-Buyer Export Credit Insurance)
Richard Maxwell
Trade, Finance and Insurance Division
Export-Import Bank of the United States   800-565-3946
811 Vermont Avenue, NW   202-565-3633
Washington, DC 20571   Fax: 202-565-3684
www.exim.gov/products/insurance/small_bus_multi_buyer.html

This policy is a special product for small, financially viable businesses that export occasionally, or are new to exporting. It can help increase international sales by extending competitive credit terms while minimizing risks. To be eligible, the exporter must be a small business as defined by the Small Business Administration, have export credit sales of not more than $5 million, have at least a one year operating history, and a positive net worth. Commercial losses caused by insolvency, bankruptcy and/or default are covered at 95%. Political losses due to war, revolution, cancellation of import/export licenses or currency inconvertibility are covered at 100%. There is no first-loss deductible. Confirmed letters of credit, cash in advance sales and military or defense related items are excluded from coverage. Type of assistance: insurance. Range of coverage available: up to $10,000,000.

* Foreign Currency Guarantees for Banks on Export Credits

(Foreign Currency Guarantee)
Export-Import Bank of the United States
811 Vermont Avenue, NW   800-565-3946
Washington, DC 20571   202-565-3946
www.exim.gov/products/guarantee/foreign_curr.html

The Ex-Im Bank Foreign Currency Guarantee policy (FCG) is designed to help buyers control certain risks associated with export credits by taking the full political and commercial risk of the credit. All lenders are eligible to use the program as long as they enter into a standard Master Guarantee Agreement with Ex-Im Bank. Under the FCG, a commercial bank extends an export credit to a buyer of U.S. goods and/or services, and Ex-Im Bank extends to the commercial bank 100% guarantee of all principal and regular interest. Ex-Im Bank issues guarantees in such currencies as the Australian Dollar, Dutch Guilder, Italian Lira, Austrian Schilling, Euro, Japanese Yen, British Pound, French Franc, Swedish Krona, Canadian Dollar, German Mark, Swiss Franc, CFA Franc, Egyptian Pound, Indian Rupees, Mexican Peso, and South African Rand. Type of assistance: loan guarantees. Range of coverage available: up to $10,000,000.

* Help for U.S. Exporters to do Business in Africa

(Special Initiatives- Africa)
Export-Import Bank of the United States   800-565-3946 ext. 3900
811 Vermont Avenue, NW   202-565-3839 ext. 390
Washington, DC 20571   Fax: 202-565-3839
Email: eximAfrica@exim.gov
www.exim.gov/prodcuts/special/africa/index.html

Ex-Im Bank has several programs to help U.S. exporters compete for business in all regions of Africa, including high-risk and emerging markets. These programs include the working Capital Guarantee Program, Export Credit Insurance, Direct Loans and Guarantees, and the Project Finance Program. These programs offer exporters increased access to working capital, protection against political and commercial risk, and the ability to offer buyers competitive financing. Types of assistance: insurance, loans, loan guarantees. Range: up to $10,000,000.

* Working Capital Loans for Small Business Exporters

(Special Initiatives- Underserved Exporters)
Pamela Bowers
Small and Medium Enterprises Division
Export-Import Bank of the United States
811 Vermont Avenue, NW   800-565-3946
Washington, DC 20571   202-565-3792
www.exim.gov/products/special/underserved.html

Ex-Im Bank offers eligible underserved exporters coverage of 100% of their working capital financing needs with their enhanced working capital guarantee, compared to 90% under their regular working capital guarantee. This program is designed to help small businesses that have not been able to obtain financing for their exports in the traditional market, especially those that are owned by women or minorities, located in an economically depressed or rural area, or specialize in environmentally beneficial goods and services. To be eligible, the borrower must be new to Ex-Im Bank, have total annual sales under $10,000,000, have fewer than 100 employees, and qualify as a small business under Small Business Administration guidelines. Type of assistance: guaranteed loans. Range of money available: up to $2,000,000.

* Insurance for Lenders Who Finance the Export Receivables of Small Business Exporters

(Financial Institution Supplier Credit Multi-Buyer Insurance Policy)
Richard Maxwell
Trade, Finance and Insurance Division
Export-Import Bank of the United States   800-565-3946
811 Vermont Avenue, NW   202-565-3633
Washington, DC 20571   Fax: 202-565-3684
www.exim.gov/products/insurance/supplier.html

The Financial Institution Supplier Credit Multi-Buyer Insurance Policy protects lenders who finance the export receivables of small businesses on a non-recourse basis. It is available in documentary and non-documentary formats. Eligible financial institutions must have a minimum of 3 years financing or purchasing export or domestic receivables; a minimum short term debt rating of Standard & Poors "A" or better, or Moody's "P-2" or better; and a written business plan to finance or purchase export receivables including identifying sufficient credit management and staffing resources to process large transaction volumes. Type of assistance: insurance. Range of coverage available: up to $10,000,000.

* Insurance for Lenders Who Make Reimbursement and Short Term Direct Buyer Credit Loans to Foreign Buyers

(Financial Institution Buyer Credit Export Insurance)
Richard Maxwell

Trade, Finance and Insurance Division
Export-Import Bank of the United States 800-565-3946
811 Vermont Avenue, NW 202-565-3633
Washington, DC 20571 Fax: 202-565-3684
www.exim.gov/proucts/insurance/buyercredit.html

Financial Institutions can lower their risks on a short term direct buyer credit loan or reimbursement loan made to a foreign buyer for the financing of U.S. exports through an Ex-Im Bank Financial Institution Buyer Credit Insurance Policy (FBIC) also call a Bank Buyer Credit Policy. The policy provides coverage against political risks such as war, revolution, expropriation or confiscation by a government authority, cancellation of import or export licenses after shipment, and foreign exchange inconvertibility, and commercial losses due to protracted default, insolvency of the buyer or failure to reimburse for other reasons. Devaluation is not considered a political risk. The policy is issue in two formats: a documentary policy for buyer credits and certain supplier credits when the supplier is a small business; and a non-documentary policy for supplier credits when the supplier is not a small business or otherwise does not meet the criteria. Type of assistance: insurance. Range of coverage available: up to $10,000,000.

* Grants to Museums for Projects that Sustain Our Cultural Heritage and Support Life Long Learning in the Community

(Museums for America)
Christine Henry
Senior Program Officer
Office of Museum Services, Room 609
Institute of Museum and Library Services
1100 Pennsylvania Avenue, NW 202-606-8687
Washington, DC 20506 Fax: 202-606-0010
Email: chenry@imls.gov
www.imls.gov/grants/museum/mus_mfa.htm

Museums for America Grants support projects and activities that strengthen museums as active resources and centers of community engagement. These grants may be used to fund ongoing museum activities; purchase equipment or services; research and scholarships; upgrading and integration of new technology; improve institutional infrastructure; or to plan new programs or activities. Grants are available to all types and sizes of museums. Funding falls into one of three categories: $5,000 to $24,999; $25,000 to $74,999; and $75,000 to $150,000. A 1:1 funding match is required in each category. All applications must show evidence of strategic planning and the relationship between the museum's plan and the funding applied for. Projects should be investments for the future, not one-time activities with no long term impact. Type of assistance: grants. Range of money available: $5,000 to $150,000.

* Grants to Non-Profit Museums for Innovations in Public Services and Meeting Community Needs

(45.312 National Leadership Grants for Museums)
Dan Lukash
Senior Program Officer
Office of Museum Services, Room 609
Institute of Museum and Library Services
1100 Pennsylvania Avenue, NW 202-606-4644
Washington, DC 20506 Fax: 202-606-0010
Email: dlukash@imls.gov
www.imls.gov/grants/museum/mus_nlgm.asp

National Leadership Grants support innovation in providing public service and meeting community needs through the creative use of new technologies; model projects to be replicated though out the field; increased public access to museum collections; and collaborative projects to extend the impact of funding. Funding falls into one of three grant categories. Museum Online Grants address the technological needs and issues of museums. They are designed to make technology resources available to all types of museums. Projects should address the challenges and potential application of new technology and/or demonstrate the educational impact of connecting museums and communities through technology. Museums in the Community Grants support museum and community partnerships that enhance the quality of community life. Projects should focus on developing long term relationships between museums and community organizations with an emphasis on how the project meets documented community needs. Professional Practise Grants support projects that improve the professional practises in the museum field. This includes projects that use research to improve museum operations, projects to collect, assess or develop information and research that will serve the field, and projects that create opportunities to improve professional practises through training or the development of new materials. Museums of all disciplines are eligible including youth, children's, art, natural history, history, anthropology, science, technology and nature centers, zoos, arboreta, aquariums, botanical

gardens, planetariums, historic houses and sites, general, specialized, museum agencies and museum consortia. Federal and For-Profit museums are not eligible. Type of assistance: grants. Range of money available: $15,000 to $500,000.

* Grants to Improve Native American Libraries

(45311 Native American Library Services)
Alison Freese
Senior Program Specialist
Office of Library Services, Room 802
Institute of Museum and Library Services
1100 Pennsylvania Avenue, NW 202-606-5408
Washington, DC 20506 Fax: 202-606-1077
Email: afreese@imls.gov
www.imls.gov/grants/library/lib_nat.asp

This program offers three types of grants to support libraries for Native Americans. Basic Grants are non-competitive and are distributed in equal amounts among eligible applicants. They are used to support core library operations and ensure a minimum level of public library service. Professional Assistance Grants are also non-competitive and can be used to support professional assessments of library operations. Consultants provide advice on a full range of library services including staffing, financial management, types and levels of services, and collections development and management. Enhancement Grants are competitive grants that fund projects to enhance existing library services, or implement new library services. Type of assistance: grants. Range of money available: up to $150,000.

* Grants to Libraries that Serve Native Hawaiians

Alison Freese
Senior Program Specialist
Office of Library Services, Room 802
Institute of Museum and Library Services
1100 Pennsylvania Avenue, NW 202-606-5408
Washington, DC 20506 Fax: 202-606-1077
Email: afreese@imls.gov
www.imls.gov/grants/library/lib_nhls.asp

Grants from the Native Hawaiian Library Services Program can be used to support improvements in library services to Native Hawaiians. Funds may be used to establish or enhance electronic links between libraries; link libraries electronically with social, educational or information services; help libraries access information through electronic networks; encourage libraries in different areas, and different types of libraries to establish consortia and share resources; pay costs for libraries to acquire or share computer systems and telecommunications technologies; and target library and information services to persons having difficulty using a library and to underserved urban and rural communities. Type of assistance: grants. Range of money available: up to $150,000.

* Help for Manufacturers and Producers Hurt by Increased Imports

(Trade Adjustment Assistance Program)
David A. Sampson
Economic Development Administration
Department of Commerce
1401 Constitution Avenue, NW
Washington, DC 20230 202-482-5081
www.eda.gov/InvestmentsGrants/Investments.xml

The EDA provides assistance to manufacturers and producers injured by increased imports. A network of 12 Trade Adjustment Assistance Centers (TAAC) help affected firms complete and submit an eligibility petition to the EDA. Once approved, the TAAC helps the firm to prepare an adjustment proposal that includes an objective analysis of the firm's weaknesses, strengths, and opportunities. After the EDA approves the adjustment plan, the firm can receive cost share assistance from the TAAC. Types of assistance provided through this program include; market research; development of new marketing materials such as e-commerce; completion of a quality assurance program; and identification of technology, software and computer systems to meet the specific needs of the firm. Types of assistance: technical assistance; cost-share assistance. Range of money available: up to $75,000.

* Help for Marine Suppliers and Owners and Operators of U.S. Shipbuilding and Repair Facilities to Improve Their Competitiveness in International Markets

(National Maritime Resource and Education Center)
Joseph Byrne

Director, Office of Shipbuilding and Marine Technology
Maritime Administration
U.S. Department of Transportation
400 7th Street, SW
Washington, DC 20590
www.marad.dot.gov/NMREC/index.html
800-99-MARAD
202-366-1931
Fax: 202-366-7197

The Maritime Administration (MARAD) established the National Maritime Resource and Education Center to assist marine suppliers, and the owner/operators of U.S. shipbuilding and repair facilities in improving their international competitiveness. Some of the services provided by NMREC include conferences and workshops; information on the Title XI Federal Ship Financing Program; energy technologies information; Standards Organizations and Information; MARAD Guideline Specifications for Merchant Ship construction; Maritime Industry Standards Library; the ISO 9000 family of standards for quality management and assessment handbook and training courses; and environmental information. Type of assistance: technical assistance and training. Range of money available: not applicable.

* Help for Owners and Operators of U.S. Flag Ships to Construct, Reconstruct or Acquire New Vessels

(Capital Construction Fund, CCF)
Office of Ship Financing
Maritime Administration
U.S. Department of Transportation
400 7th Street, SW, Room 8122
Washington, DC 20950
www.marad.dot.gov/TitleXI/ccf.html
202-366-5744
800-99-MARAD

The CCF Program was established to help owners and operators of U.S. Flag vessels accumulate the capital necessary to modernize and expand the U.S. Merchant Marine. The program promotes the construction, reconstruction or acquisition of vessels by deferring Federal Income Taxes on money or property placed into a Capital Construction Fund. CCF vessels must be built in the U.S., and be documented under U.S. laws for operation in the Nation's foreign, Great Lakes, or noncontiguous domestic trade or its fisheries. The CCF program can lower the effective cost to a company of replacing or adding new vessels, and hasten the time frame for accumulating the necessary capital. CCF funds may also be used to pay existing indebtedness on vessels if it is a part of an overall building program. Type of assistance: financial assistance through tax deferrals. Range of money available: not applicable.

* Help for Owners of U.S. Flag Ships to Buy, Build or Purchase Vessels

(Construction Reserve Fund, CRF)
Director, Office of Ship Financing
Maritime Administration
U.S. Department of Transportation
400 7th Street, SW, Room 8122
Washington, DC 20590
www.mrad.dot.gov/TitleXI/crf.html
800-99-MARAD
202-366-5744

The CRF is a financial assistance program that provides tax deferral benefits to owners of U.S. Flag Ships. Eligible owners can defer the gain from the sale or loss of a vessel as long as the proceeds are used to expand or modernize the U.S. Merchant fleet. The main goal of the Construction Reserve Fund is to promote the construction, re-construction, or acquisition of merchant vessels which are necessary to the development of U.S. commerce and national defense. Type of assistance: financial assistance through tax deferrals. Range of money available: not applicable.

* Help for Exporters of U.S. Dairy Products

(Dairy Export Incentive Program, DEIP)
Operations Division, Export Credits
Foreign Agricultural Service, USDA
Mail Stop 1035
1400 Independence Avenue, SW
Washington, DC 20250-1035
www.fas.usda.gov/excredits/deip.html
202-720-3224
202-720-6211
Fax: 202-720-0938

The Dairy Export Incentive Program helps exporters of U.S. dairy products meet world prices for certain dairy products and destinations. Through this program, the USDA pays cash bonuses to exporters, allowing them to sell certain U.S. dairy products at prices lower that their acquisition costs. The goal of this program is to develop export markets for dairy products where U.S. products are not competitive due to the presence of subsidized products from other countries. Eligible products include milk powder, butter fat and various cheeses. Type of assistance: cash bonuses. Range of money available: bonus values vary with each agreement.

* Cash Bonuses to Exporters of U.S. Agricultural Products

(Export Enhancement Program, EEP)
Operations Division, Export Credits
Foreign Agricultural Service, USDA
Mail Stop 1035
1400 Independence Avenue, SW
Washington, DC 20250-1035
www.fas.usda.gov/excredits/eep.html
202-720-3224
202-720-6211
Fax: 202-720-0938

The main objectives of the program are to expand U.S. agricultural exports and to challenge unfair trade practices. The EEP helps products produced by U.S. farmers meet competition from subsidized products from other countries, and especially the European Union. To achieve these objectives, the USDA pays cash bonuses to exporters, allowing them to sell U.S. agricultural products in targeted countries at prices below their cost of acquiring them. Type of assistance: financial assistance in the form of cash bonuses. Range of money available: bonus values vary with each agreement.

* Loan Guarantees for Exporters of U.S. Agricultural Products

(Export Credit Guarantee Program, GSM-102, GSM-103)
Program Planning, Development, and Evaluation Division
Export Credits
Foreign Agricultural Service, USDA
1400 Independence Avenue, SW
Washington, DC 20250-1034
www.fas.usda.gov/excredits/exp-cred-guar.html
202-720-4221
Fax: 202-690-0251

The USDA's Export Credit Guarantee Programs help ensure that credit is available to finance commercial exports of U.S. agricultural products, while at the same time providing competitive credit terms to buyers. Credit guarantees support exports to buyers, mainly in developing countries, where credit is needed to increase or maintain U.S. sales, but may not be available without such guarantees. The Export Credit Guarantee Program (GSM-102) covers credit terms p to 3 years, and the Intermediate Export Credit Guarantee Program (GSM-103) covers credit terms up to 10 years. Both programs are administered by the Foreign Agricultural Service on behalf of the Commodity Credit Corporation (CCC), which issues the credit guarantees. The CC guarantees payments due from approved foreign banks to exporters of banks in the U.S. The CCC only provides the guarantees; financing must be obtained through normal commercial sources. Usually, 98% of principal and a portion of the interest are covered by a guarantee. Type of assistance: loan guarantees. Range of money available: not applicable.

* Short Term Credit Guarantees for Exporters of U.S. Agricultural Products to Offer to their Foreign Buyers

(Supplier Credit Guarantee Program, SCGP)
Program Planning, Development, and Evaluation Division
Export Credits
Foreign Agricultural Service, USDA
1400 Independence Avenue, SW
Washington, DC 20250-1034
www.fas.usda.gov/excredits/scgp.html
202-720-4221
Fax: 202-690-0251

This program reduces the financial risk to exporters by guaranteeing a large portion of the payments due from importer s, where financing has been arranged for a 180 day period. The direct credit extended by the exporter to the importer must be for the purchase of U.S. agricultural products and secured by a promissory note signed by the importer. The USDA's Foreign Agricultural Service administers this program on behalf of the Commodity Credit Corporation (CCC). The CCC issues credit guarantees only, the exporter or the exporter's bank provides the financing. SCGP guarantees 65% of the value of the exports. Type of assistance: credit guarantees. Range of money available: not applicable.

* Money for Farmers to Incorporate Conservation into their Farming Operations

(Agricultural Management Assistance)
David B. Mason
National AMA Program Manager
Natural Resources Conservation Service, USDA
1400 Independence Avenue, SW
Room 5242-S
Washington, DC 20250
Email: dave.mason@usda.gov
www.nrcs.usda.gov/programs/ama
202-720-1873

Agricultural Management Assistance (AMA) provides cost share assistance to agricultural producers to voluntarily incorporate conservation efforts, such as water management, water quality and erosion control, into their farming operations. AMA provides the personnel and resources needed to conduct conservation planning, conservation practice surveys, layout design, installation and certification, quality assurance and assessment of the program. Cost-share payments are 75% of the cost of eligible installed conservation practices. Producers may construct or improve water management structures or irrigation systems, plant trees to provide windbreaks or to improve water quality, practice resource conservation, control soil erosion, practice product diversification, integrate pest management or transition to organic farming. Types of assistance: cost-share financial assistance; technical assistance. Range of money available: up to $50,000 for any fiscal year, no more than $150,000 over the course of the contract.

* Money for Farmers and Ranchers to Conserve Soil and Water

(Soil and Water Conservation Assistance, SWCA)
Walley Turner
National Program Manager
Natural Resources Conservation Service, USDA
1400 Independence Avenue, SW
Washington, DC 20250   202-720-1875
Email: walley.turner@usda.gov
www.nrcs.usda.gov/programs/swca

The SWCA program helps farmers and ranchers address threats to water, soil and other related natural resources, including grazing land, wetlands and wildlife habitat, by providing cost share and incentive payments. SWCA also helps landowners comply with Federal and state environmental laws, and make cost effective changes to nutrient management, irrigation, grazing management and cropping systems. NRCS will work with the landowner to develop a conservation plan which will become the basis of the SWCA contract. Contracts are for 5 to 10 years and the landowners must agree to maintain cost shared practices for the length of the contract. Eligible land includes cropland, hay land, pasture, rangeland, land used for subsistence purposes and land that produces crops or livestock where there is a serious threat to soil, water or related natural resources. Cost share payments are 75% of the cost of an eligible conservation practice. Type of assistance: cost share financial assistance. Range of money available: up to $50,000.

* Grants to Convert Military Airfields for Civilian Use

(Military Airport Program)
Oliver Murdock
Office of Airport Planning and Programming
Federal Aviation Administration
Military Airport Branch (APP-420)
800 Independence Avenue, SW
Washington, DC 20591   202-267-8244
www.faa.gov/planning/MAP

The Military Airport Program (MAP) provides financial assistance to civilian sponsors who are converting or have already converted a military airfield for civilian or joint military/civilian use. Eligible projects include utility work, building or rehabilitating surface parking lots, access roads, hangars, fuel farms, passenger terminal facilities, and projects to construct, improve or repair building facilities with up to 50,000 square feet of floor space. Type of assistance: grants. Range of money available: up to $7,000,000.

* Grants to Business Partnerships to Provide Technical Skills Training to American Workers

(H-1B Technical Skills Training Grant)
Mindy Feldbaum
Program Officer
U.S. Department of Labor
Employment and Training Administration
Room 4659
200 Constitution Avenue, NW   202-693-3382
Washington, DC 20210   Fax: 202-693-2982
Email: Feldbaum.Mindy@dol.gov
www.doleta.gov/h-1b/h-1b_index.cfm

The goal of the H-1B Technical Skills Training Grant Program is to raise the technical skill levels of American workers so firms can lessen their dependence on highly skilled foreign workers. Grants are awarded to local Workforce Investment Boards and business partnerships made up of at least two businesses or a businesses related non-profit organization. The grants are to be used for training workers in high technology, information technology and biotechnology skill areas, including software and communications services, telecommunications, systems installation and

integration, computers and communication hardware, advanced manufacturing, health care technology, biomedical research and manufacturing, and innovation services. Type of assistance: matching grants. Range of money available: $10,000 to $3,000,000.

* Loans and Technical Assistance for Small Businesses in New Market Areas

(Community Express Loans)
Office of Financial Assistance
Special Purpose Loan Programs
Small Business Administration
409 Third Street, SW   800-UASK-SBA
Washington, DC 20416   202-205-6490
www.sba.gov/financing/lendinvest/comexpress.html

Community Express is a SBA loan program with the National Community Reinvestment Coalition (NCRC). It is offered in pre-designated geographic areas that primarily serve low and moderate incomes and New Market small businesses. The program also includes hands-on technical and management assistance. Loan funds may be used for start-up, working capital, expansion, real estate acquisitions or equipment purchases. Types of assistance: loans and technical assistance. Range of money available: up to $250,000.

* Loans to Locate a Business at an Army Industrial Facility

(Armament Retooling and Manufacturing Support (ARMS) Loan guarantee Program)
Ms. Donnetta Rigney
United States Department of Agriculture
Rural Business Cooperative Service
Business Programs
Room 5045-S, Mail Stop 3201
1400 Independence Avenue, SW
Washington, DC 20250-3201   202-720-9812
Email: donnetta.rigney@usa.gov
www.rurdev.usda.gov/rbs/bp-arms.htm

This program is a cooperative effort between the U.S. Department of Agriculture and the U.S. Army. The ARMS Asset Management program offers mature infrastructure and services to businesses looking for manufacturing, warehouse, office and other industrial park resources. The ARMS Loan Guarantee Program provides tenants with money for working capital, equipment acquisition, building modification and other business resources to locate at an eligible Army Industrial facility. Type of assistance: guaranteed loans. Range of money available: up to $10,000,000.

* Loans to Beginners to Make a Down Payment on a Ranch or Farm

(Down Payment Farm Ownership Loan Program)
Carolyn Cooksie
Farm Loan Programs
Farm Service Agency
U.S. Department of Agriculture
1400 Independence Avenue, SW
Washington, DC 20250   202-720-4671
www.fsa.usda.gov/pas/services.htm

The Farm Service Agency helps beginning farmers and ranchers purchase a farm or ranch. with its Down Payment Farm Ownership Loan Program. A beginning farmer or rancher is a person who has not operated a farm or ranch for more than ten years and substantially participates in the operation. Applicants must make a cash down payment of at least 10% of the purchase price. FSA can provide up to 40% of the appraised value or purchase price whichever is less. The purchase price/appraised value can not be greater than $250,000. FSA also acquires property from retiring farmers and ranchers and offers it to beginning ranchers and farmers first. Type of assistance: direct and guaranteed loans. Range of money available: up to $100,000.

* Loans to Beginning Farmers and Ranchers to Purchase or Operate a Farm or Ranch

(Loans for Beginning Farmers and Ranchers)
Carolyn Cooksie
Farm Loan Programs
Farm Service Agency
U.S. Department of Agriculture
1400 Independence Avenue, SW
Washington, DC 20250   202-720-4671
www.fsa.usda.gov/daf/deafult.htm

The Farm Service Agency has several loan programs to help beginning farmers and ranchers who are unable to get financing from commercial credit sources. Included are direct and guaranteed loans for farm ownership (FO) and farm operation (OL). A beginning farmer or rancher is a person who has not operated a farm or ranch for more than 10 years, participates significantly in the operation, and owns a farm less than 30% of the average size farm in the county. Type of assistance: direct and guaranteed loans. Range of money available: for direct FO or OL loans- up to $200,000; for guaranteed FO or OL loans- up to $782,000.

* Loans for Socially Disadvantaged Persons to Buy and Operate Family Size Farms and Ranches

(Loans for Socially Disadvantaged Persons)
Carolyn Cooksie
Farm Loan Programs
Farm Service Agency
U.S. Department of Agriculture
1400 Independence Avenue, SW
Washington, DC 20250   202-720-4671
www.fsa.usda.gov/daf/deafult.htm

The Farm Service Agency makes and guarantees loans to qualified socially disadvantaged applicants to purchase and operate family size farms and ranches. For this program's purposes, socially disadvantaged persons include women, Pacific Islanders, African Americans, Asian Americans, Alaskan Natives, Hispanics, and American Indians. Direct loans are made by FSA and may be farm operating (OL) or farm ownership (FO) loans. Guaranteed loans are made by commercial lenders and guaranteed by FSA. They also can be used for farm ownership or operating purposes. Farm Ownership loans can be used to purchase easements or rights of way necessary to the farm's operation, erect or improve buildings, promote soil and water conservation and development, pay closing costs, and to purchase or enlarge a farm or ranch. Direct farm operating loans can only be used to purchase a farm or ranch, guaranteed loan funds may also be used to refinance debt. Farm Operating Loans (OL) may be used for hail and other crop insurance, hired labor, medical care, food, clothing, livestock, poultry, chemicals, farm equipment, fuel, fertilizer, seed and feed. Funds may also be used to refinance debt, to install or improve water systems for home use, irrigation or other improvements. Type of assistance: direct and guaranteed loans. Range of money available: for direct FO or OL loans- up to $200,000; for guaranteed FO or OL loans- up to $782,000.

* Loan Guarantees for Farmers and Ranchers

(FSA Guaranteed Loans)
Carolyn Cooksie
Farm Loan Programs
Farm Service Agency
U.S. Department of Agriculture
1400 Independence Avenue, SW
Washington, DC 20250   202-720-4671
www.fsa.usda.gov/daf/guaranteed.htm

This program provides lenders with a FSA guarantee for up 95% of the loss of principal and interest on a loan. Farmers and ranchers apply to an agricultural lender which then arranges for the guarantee. FSA guaranteed loans are for both farm ownership and operating purposes. Guaranteed Farm Ownership Loans (FO) may be used to purchase farmland, refinance debt, construct or repair buildings and other fixtures, or to develop farmland to promote soil and water conservation Guaranteed Operating Loans (OL) may be used for operating expenses, livestock, farm chemicals, fuel, feed, seed, farm equipment, and insurance. Under certain conditions, they can also be used to pay for minor improvements to buildings, family living expenses, costs associated with land and water development, and to refinance debt. Type of assistance: loan guarantees. Range of money available: up to $782,000.

* Money for Agricultural Land Owners to Establish Long-Term Resource Conserving Covers on Eligible Farmland

(Conservation Reserve Program)
Robert Stephenson
Conservation and Environmental Programs Division
Farm Service Agency
U.S. Department of Agriculture
1400 Independence Avenue, SW
Washington, DC 20250   202-720-6221
www.fa.usda.gov/dafp/cepd/crp.htm

The Conservation Reserve Program (CRP) is a voluntary program for agricultural producers to help them protect environmentally sensitive land. Producers taking part in CRP plant long term, resource conserving, ground covers to improve the quality of water, control soil erosion, and enhance wildlife habitats. In return, FSA provides participants with rental payments and cost share assistance. CRP contracts are for ten to fifteen years. To be eligible for the CRP program, land must be cropland or pasture land, have a weighted average erosion index of 8 or higher, be expiring CRP acreage, or be located in a state/national CRP conservation priority area. FSA provides participants in the CRP program with annual rental payments, maintenance incentive payments and cost share assistance. Rental rates are based on the relative productivity of the soils within each county and the average dry-land cash rent or cash rent equivalent. In addition CRP may include an additional amount, not more than $5.00 per acre per year, to perform maintenance obligations. Cost share assistance is up to 50% of the participant's cost to establish an approved cover on eligible cropland. FSA may offer additional financial incentives of up to 20% of the annual payment for certain continuous sign up practices. Type of assistance: cost sharing, rent, incentive payments. Range of money available: not applicable.

* Grants for Small Businesses to Research and Develop High-Tech Innovations

(Small Business Innovation Research Program)
Robert Connolly
SBIR/STTR Program
Office of Technology
U.S. Small Business Administration
409 Third Street, SW
Mail Code: 6540   202-205-6450
Washington, DC 20416   Fax: 202-205-6390
Email: robert.connolly@sba.gov
www.sba.gov/sbir

The Small Business Innovation Research Program encourages small businesses to conduct research and development on high-tech innovation. Many small businesses lack the resources to conduct serious research and development efforts. The SBIR is able to help by reserving a portion of their Federal research and development funds just for small businesses enabling them to compete on the same level as larger firms. SBIR funds the start up and development stages of the technology, product or service and encourages its commercialization. Small businesses must be American owned and independently operated, for-profit, have less than 500 employees, and the principal researcher must be employed by the business to be eligible for this program. The Departments of Agriculture, Commerce, Defense, Education, Energy, Health and Human Services and Transportation, Environmental Protection Agency, National Aeronautics and Space Foundation and the National Science Foundation participate in the SBIR Program. They designate the Research and Development topics and accept the proposals. Awards are based on small business qualification, degree of innovation, technical merit, and future market potential. Small businesses that receive awards or grants then enter into a three phase program. The start-up phase is Phase I. Awards, up to $100,000, are given for six months to explore the technical merit or feasibility of an idea or technology. Phase II consists of up to $750,000 for as long as 2 years to expand Phase I results. Research and development is completed and the developer evaluates commercial potential. Only Phase I award winners are eligible for Phase II. Phase III is where the innovation moves from the lab into the marketplace. There are no SBIR funds to support this phase. The small business must acquire funding from the private sector or other non-SBIR federal agencies. Type of assistance: grants. Range of money available: Phase I- up to $100,000; Phase II- up to $750,000.

Program Contacts

Department of Agriculture
Charles Cleland PhD.
Director, SBIR Program
Cooperative State Research, Education & Extension Service
U.S. Department of Agriculture
Stop 2243, Waterfront Centre, Suite 2312
1400 Independence Avenue, SW   202-401-6852
Washington, DC 20250-2243   Fax: 202-401-6070
Email: CCLeland@reeusda.gov
www.reeusda.gov/sbir

Department of Commerce
Joseph Bishop, Ph.D.
Director, Office of Research and Technology Applications
U.S. Department of Commerce/NOAA
1335 East-West Highway, Room 106   301-713-3565
Silver Spring, MD 20910   Fax: 301-713-4100
Email: Joseph.Bishop@NOAA.GOV
www.ofa.noaa.gov/~amd/sbir/sbir.html

Department of Defense
Jeff Bond
Acting SBIR/STTR Program Coordinator
OSD/SADBU

U.S. Department of Defense
1777 North Kent Street, Suite 9100
Arlington, VA 22209 — 703-588-8616
Email: Jeff.Bond@osd.mil — Fax: 703-588-7561
www.defenselink.mil

Department of Education
Joseph G. Teresa, Ph.D.
U.S. Department of Education
Institute of Education Sciences
Room 620
555 New Jersey Avenue, SW — 202-219-2046
Washington, DC 20208 — Fax: 202-501-3005
Email: Joe.teresa@ed.gov
www.ed.gov/programs/sbir/index.html

Department of Energy
Arlene M. DeBlanc, J.D.
SBIR/STTR Program
Office of Science
U.S. Department of Energy
100 Independence Avenue, SW
SC-32, Germantown Building — 301-903-3199
Washington, DC 20585-1290 — Fax: 301-903-5488
Email: Arlene.deblanc@science.doe.gov
www.scicnce.doc.gov/sbir

Department of Health and Human Services
Debbie Ridgely
Director
OSBDU, Office of the Secretary
U.S. Department of Health and Human Services
200 Independence Avenue, Room 360G — 202-690-7235
Washington, DC 20201 — Fax: 202-260-4872
Email: Debbie.ridgely@hhs.gov
www.hhs.gov/osdbu

Department of Transportation
Joseph D. Henebury
SBIR Program Director
U.S. Department of Transportation
Volpe Center
55 Broadway, Kendall Square — 617-494-2712
Cambridge, MA 02142-1093 — Fax: 617-494-2370
Email: Henebury@volpe.dot.gov
www.volpe.dot.gov/sbir

Environmental Protection Agency
James Gallup, Ph.D.
Office of Research and Development
U.S. Environmental Protection Agency
ORD/NCER (8722R)
1200 Pennsylvania Avenue, NW — 202-564-6823
Washington, DC 20460 — Fax: 202-565-2447
Email: Gallup.James@epa.gov
http://es.epa.gov/ncer/sbir

NASA
Robert L. Norwood, Ph.D.
Director, Commercial Development and Technology Transfer
National Aeronautics and Space Administration-HQ
300 E Street, SW
Code XC — 202-358-2320
Washington, DC 20546-0001 — Fax: 202-358-3878
http://sbir.gsfc.nasa.gov/SBIR/SBIR.html

National Science Foundation
Kesh S. Narayanan
Director
Industrial Innovation Programs
U.S. National Science Foundation
SBIR Program
4201 Wilson Boulevard, Room 550 — 703-292-7076
Arlington, VA 22230 — Fax: 703-292-9057
Email: knarayan@nsf.gov
www.eng.nsf.gov/sbirspecs

* Grants for Small Business and Non-profit Research Partners to Research and Develop High-Tech Innovations
(Small Business Technology Transfer Program)
Robert Connolly

SBIR/STTR Program
Office of Technology
U.S. Small Business Administration
409 Third Street, SW
Mail Code: 6540 — 202-205-6450
Washington, DC 20416 — Fax: 202-205-6390
Email: robert.connolly@sba.gov
www.sba.gov/sbir

The Small Business Technology Transfer Program (STTR) is a competitive program that sets aside a certain percentage of federal research and development funds for awards to small business and non-profit research institution partnerships. To be eligible, small businesses must be American owned and independently operated, for profit, and have fewer than 500 employees. The principal researcher does not need to be employed by small business. The non-profit research center must be located in the U.S, and be either a non-profit college or university, a domestic non-profit research organization, or a federally funded research and development center (FFRDC). The Department of Defense, Department of Energy, Department of Health and Human Services, the National Aeronautics and Space Administration, and the National Science Foundation all participate in the STTR Program. These departments and agencies designate research and development topics and accept proposals for the program. STTR awards are based on the qualifications of the small business/non-profit research institution, degree of innovation, and future market potential. Small businesses that receive awards or grants enter into a three phase program. Phase I is the start up phase. It consists of awards up to $100,000 for one year to fund the exploration of the technical, scientific and commercial feasibility of an idea or technology. Phase I consists of awards up to $500,000 for two years to expand on Phase I results. Research and development work is performed and commercial potential considered, Phase I must be completed in order to be considered for Phase II. During Phase III, the innovation moves from the laboratory into the marketplace. This phase is not supported by STTR funds. The small business must acquire funding from the private sector or other non-STTR federal agencies. Type of assistance: grants. Range of money available: Phase I -up to $100,000; Phase II- up to $500,000.

Program Contacts:

National Science Foundation
Kesh S. Narayanan
Director
STTR Program
National Science Foundation
4201 Wilson Boulevard, Room 550 — 703-292-7076
Arlington, VA 22230 — Fax: 703-292-9057
Email: knarayan@nsf.gov
www.nsf.gov

National Aeronautics and Space Administration
Robert L. Norwood, Ph.D.
Director, STTR Program
National Aeronautics and Space Administration-HQ
300 E Street, SW
Code-XC — 202-358-232
Washington, DC 20546-0001 — Fax: 202-358-3878
www.nasa.gov

Department of Health and Human Services
Debbie Ridgely
Director, STTR Program
OSBDU, Office of the Secretary
U.S. Department of Health and Human Services
200 Independence Avenue, Room 360G — 202-690-7235
Washington, DC 20201 — Fax: 202-260-4872
Email: Debbie.ridgely@hhs.gov
www.hhs.gov/osdbu

Department of Energy
Arlene M. DeBlanc, J.D.
STTR Program
Office of Science
U.S. Department of Energy
1000 Independence Avenue, SW
SC-32, Germantown Building — 301-903-3199
Washington, DC 20585-1290 — Fax: 301-903-5488
Email: Arlene.deblanc@science.doe.gov
www.science.doe.gov/sbir

Department of Defense
Jeff Bond
Acting STTR Program Coordinator
OSD/SADBU
U.S. Department of Defense

1777 North Kent Street, Suite 9100
Arlington, VA 22209
Email: jeff.bond@osd.mil
www.defenselink.mil

703-588-8616
Fax: 703-588-7561

* Venture Capital to Start a Water Related Business in an Emerging Market County

(Aqua International Partners Fund)
John Sylvia
Chief Operating Officer
Texas Pacific Group
345 California Street, Suite 3300
San Francisco, CA 94104
Email: jlyvia@texpac.com
www.opic.gov/investmentfunds

415-743-1570
Fax: 415-743-1504

This fund supports equity investments in operating and special purpose companies involved in the treatment, bulk supply and distribution of water in emerging market countries. The Aqua International Partners Fund is a privately owned, privately managed investment fund supported by the Overseas Private Investment Corporation. It is designed to promote and facilitate U.S. investment in emerging markets by working with private capital to make direct equity and equity related investments. This investment fund is designed to complement OPIC's insurance and loan products. Each investment fund must meet OPIC policy requirements, including impact on the U.S. economy and employment. Type of assistance: venture capital. Range of money available: $5,000,000 to $40,000,000.

* Venture Capital to Start Infrastructure Projects in the Baltic Region

(AIG Brunswick Millennium Fund)
Peter Yu
American International Group
175 Water Street, 24th Floor
New York, NY 10038
www.opic.gov/investmentfunds

212-458-2156
Fax: 212-458-2153

This fund provides equity investments in the Baltic, Russia, and NIS for large infrastructure projects including transportation, power, natural resource development and related industries. The AIG Brunswick Millennium Fund is a privately owned, privately managed investment fund supported by the Overseas Private Investment Corporation. It is designed to promote and facilitate U.S. investment in emerging markets by working with private capital to make direct equity and equity related investments. This investment fund is designed to complement OPIC's insurance and loan products. Each investment fund must meet OPIC policy requirements, including impact on the U.S. economy and employment. Type of assistance: venture capital. Range of money available: $5,000,000 to $30,000,000.

* Venture Capital to Start a Business in Russia

(Russia Partners Fund, A)
Drew Guff
Managing Director
Siguler, Guff & Company
630 Fifth Avenue, 16th Floor
New York, NY 10111
www.opic.gov/investmentfunds

212-332-5108
Fax: 212-332-5120

This program supports equity investments in Russia in natural resource related companies, telecommunications, light manufacturing, and consumer services and products. This fund may also invest in other OPIC covered NIS states. The Russia Partners Fund, A is a privately owned, privately managed investment fund supported by the Overseas Private Investment Corporation. It is designed to promote and facilitate U.S. investment in emerging markets by working with private capital to make direct equity and equity related investments. This investment fund is designed to complement OPIC insurance and loan products. Each investment fund must meet OPIC policy requirements, including impact on the U.S. economy and employment. Type of assistance: venture capital. Range of money available: $4,500,000 to $15,000,000.

* Venture Capital to Start a Business in the Ukraine, Russia and Other East European Countries

(New Century Capital Partners LP Fund)
George Rohr
Chief Executive Officer
NCH Advisors
712 Fifth Avenue, 46th Floor
New York, NY 10019-4018

212-641-3229
Fax: 212-641-3201

www.opic.gov/investmentfunds
This fund provides equity investment in consumer products, financial and service industries, and diversified manufacturing in the following target areas: Latvia, Ukraine, Lithuania, Russia, Estonia, Kazakhstan, Moldova, Armenia, Bulgaria, Romania, Belarus, and Georgia. The direct equity investments of this OPIC supported fund complement OPIC's insurance and loan products. By supplementing the capital of privately owned, privately managed investment funds, OPIC can help profit oriented enterprises in emerging market areas gain access to venture capital, management guidance and financial expertise. Type of assistance: venture capital. Range of money available: $7,000,000 to $20,000,000.

* Venture Capital to Start a Telecommunications Business in South East Asia

(Asia Development Partners LP Fund)
Daniel Mintz
Managing Director
Olympus Capital Holdings, Asia
153 East 53rd Street, 43rd Floor
New York, NY 10022
Email: dmintz@zbi.com
www.opic.gov/investmentfunds

212-292-6531
Fax: 212-292-6570

This program funds equity investment in consumer products, financial services and telecommunication in the emerging market areas of Bangladesh, India, Vietnam, Thailand, Indonesia, Korea, Sri Lanka, Laos and the Philippines. The direct equity investments of this OPIC supported fund complement OPIC's insurance and loan products. By supplementing the capital of privately owned, privately managed investment funds, OPIC can help profit oriented businesses in emerging market areas gain access to venture capital, management guidance, and financial expertise. Type of assistance: venture capital. Range of money available: $450,000 to $18,000,000.

* Venture Capital to Start a Business in South America

(South American Private Equity Growth Fund)
Varel D. Freeman
Vice President and Managing Director
Baring Latin American Partners, LLC
230 Park Avenue
New York, NY 10169
www.opic.gov/investmentfunds

212-309-1795
Fax: 212-309-1794

This program supports equity investments in South America, with emphasis on Argentina, Brazil, Chile and Peru, for diversified manufacturing, service and financial services. The direct equity investments of this OPIC supported fund complement OPIC's insurance and loan products. By supplementing the capital of privately owned and managed investment funds, OPIC can help profit oriented enterprises in emerging market areas gain access to venture capital, management guidance and financial expertise. Type of assistance: venture capital. Range of money available: $1,000,000 to $18,000,000.

* Venture Capital to Start a Business in Southern Africa

(New Africa Opportunity Fund)
Thomas C. Barry
Chief Executive Officer
Zephyr Management, LP
320 Park Avenue
New York, NY 10022-6815
Email: info@opic.gov
www.opic.gov/investmentfunds

212-508-9410
Fax: 212-508-9494

This fund provides equity investment in South Africa and regional SADC countries for financial and service industries and diversified manufacturing. The direct equity investments of this OPIC supported fund complement OPIC's insurance and loan products. By supplementing the capital of privately owned and managed investment funds, OPIC can help profit oriented businesses in emerging market areas gain access to venture capital, management guidance, and financial expertise. Type of assistance: venture capital. Range of money available: $3,600,000 to $14,000,000.

* Venture Capital to Start a Manufacturing or Computer Business in India

(India Private Equity Fund)
Michele J. Buchignani
Managing Director
CIBC Oppenheimer & Company
Oppenheimer Tower

World Financial Center
New York, NY 10281
212-667-8190
Fax: 212-667-4468
Email: Michele.buchignani@us.cibc.com
www.opic.gov/investmentfunds

This fund supports equity investment in India for basic manufacturing, consumer goods, computer, banking and related industries. The direct equity investments of this OPIC supported fund complement OPIC's insurance and loan products. By supplementing the capital of privately owned and managed investment funds, OPIC can help profit oriented enterprises in emerging market areas gain access to venture capital, management guidance and financial expertise. Type of assistance: venture capital. Range of money available: $4,200,000 to $16,800,000.

* Venture Capital to Start a Business in Latin America

(Newbridge Andean Partners LP Fund)
Bernard Aronson
ACON Investments, LLC
1133 Connecticut Avenue, NW, Suite 700
Washington, DC 20036
202-861-6060 ext. 103
202-861-6061
Email: infp@opic.gov
www.opic.gov/investmentfunds

This program funds equity investments in Belize, Bolivia, Brazil, Columbia, Ecuador, Peru, Argentina, Venezuela, El Salvador, Costa Rica, Honduras, Guatemala, Uruguay, Panama, Paraguay, Nicaragua and Chile for diversified manufacturing, financial and service industries. The direct equity investments of this OPIC supported fund complement OPIC's insurance and loan products. By supplementing the capital of privately owned, privately managed investment funds, OPIC can help profit oriented businesses in emerging market areas gain access to venture capital, management guidance and financial expertise. Type of assistance: venture capital. Range of money available: $4,800,000 to $16,000,000.

* Venture Capital to Start an Environment Related Business in an Emerging Market

(Global Environment Emerging Markets Fund I)
H. Jeff Leonard
President
GEF Management
1225 Eye Street, NW, Suite 900
Washington, DC 20005
202-789-4500
Fax: 202-789-4508
Email: info@opic.gov
www.opic.gov/investmentfunds

This fund provides equity investments in all OPIC eligible countries for environment oriented sectors relating to the development, financing, operating or supplying of infrastructure relating to clean water and energy. The direct equity investments of this OPIC supported fund complement OPIC's insurance and loan products. By supplementing the capital of privately owned, privately managed investment funds, OPIC can help profit oriented enterprises in emerging market areas gain access to venture capital, management guidance and financial expertise. Type of assistance: venture capital. Range of money available: $2,000,000 to $6,000,000.

* Venture Capital to Start a Business in Southeast Europe

(Soros Investment Capital Ltd)
David Matheson
Manager
Soros Private Funds Management, LLC
888 Seventh Avenue
New York, NY 10106
212-333-9727
Fax: 212-397-0139
Email: info@opic.gov
www.opic.gov/investmentfunds

This program provides equity investments in Albania, Bosnia, Bulgaria, Croatia, Herzegovina, FYR Macedonia, Montenegro, Romania, Slovenia, Turkey, and should they become eligible, Serbia and Kosovo. The direct equity investments of this OPIC supported fund complement OPIC's insurance and loan products. By supplementing the capital of privately owned, privately managed investment funds, OPIC can help profit oriented businesses in emerging market areas gain access to venture capital, management guidance and financial expertise. Type of assistance: venture capital. Range of money available: $4,000,000 to $15,000,000.

* Venture Capital to Start an Agriculture Business in the Baltic Region

Agribusiness Partners International)
Robert Peyton
President
Agribusiness Management Company
c/o America First Companies
11004 Farnam Street
Omaha, NE 68102
402-930-3060
Fax: 402-930-3007
Email: bpeyton@am1st.com
www.opic.gov/investmentfunds

This program provides equity investments in the NIS/Baltic region for agriculture, food firms, infrastructure projects, privatizations, and food storage and distribution facilities. The direct equity investments of this OPIC supported fund complements OPIC's insurance and loan products. By supplementing the capital of privately owned, privately managed investment funds, OPIC can help profit oriented enterprises in emerging market areas gain access to venture capital, management guidance and financial expertise. Type of assistance: venture capital. Range of money available: $2,945,000 to $14,915,000.

* Venture Capital to Start an Environment Related Business in an Emerging Market

(Global Environment Emerging Markets Fund II)
H. Jeff Leonard
President
GEF Management
1225 Eye Street, NW, Suite 900
Washington, DC 20005
202-789-4500
Fax: 202-789-4508
Email: info@opic.gov
www.opic.gov/investmentfunds

This fund provides equity investments in all OPIC eligible countries for environment oriented sectors relating to the development, financing, operating or supplying of infrastructure relating to clean water and energy. The direct equity investments of this OPIC supported fund complement OPIC's insurance and loan products. By supplementing the capital of privately owned, privately managed investment funds, OPIC can help profit oriented enterprises in emerging market areas gain access to venture capital, management guidance and financial expertise. Type of assistance: venture capital. Range of money available: $3,600,000 to $14,400,000.

* Venture Capital to Start a Business in a Sub-Sahara Country

(Modern Africa Growth and Investment Fund)
Steve Cashin
Managing Director
Modern Africa Fund Managers
1100 Connecticut Avenue, NW, Suite 500
Washington, DC 20036
202-887-1772
Fax: 202-887-1788
Email: info@opic.gov
www.opic.gov/investmenfunds

This fund supports equity investments in all sub-Saharan countries, except South Africa, with a focus on telecommunications, natural resources and manufacturing. The direct equity investments of this OPIC supported fund complement OPIC's insurance and loan products. By supplementing the capital of privately owned, privately managed investment funds, OPIC can help profit oriented businesses in emerging market areas gain access to venture capital, management guidance and financial expertise. Type of assistance: venture capital. Range of money available: $3,000,000 to $11,000,000.

* Venture Capital to Start a Business in Central Europe

(Bancroft Eastern Europe Fund)
Fred Martin
President
Bancroft UK, LTD
7/11 Kensington
High Street
London W8 5NP
44-20-7368-334
Fax: 44-20-738-3348
Email: martin@bancroftgroup.com
www.opic.gov/investmentfunds

This fund supports equity investments in basic manufacturing, distribution networks, consumer goods and related services networks. Eligible countries include Central Europe/Baltic Republics, Albania, Bulgaria, Croatia, the Czech Republic, Estonia, Hungary, Latvia, Lithuania, Poland, Romania, Slovakia and Slovenia. The direct equity investments of this OPIC supported fund complement OPIC's insurance and loan products. By supplementing the capital of privately owned, privately managed investment funds, OPIC can help profit oriented enterprises in emerging market areas gain access to venture capital, management guidance and financial expertise. Type of assistance: venture capital. Range of money available: $2,850,000 to $9,500,000.

* Venture Capital to Start a Telecommunications Business in Armenia, Georgia or Azerbaijan

(Caucasus Fund)
Irakli Rukhadze
CEO
Caucasus Advisors
Suite 901, 31 Milk Street   617-646-4512
Boston, MA 02109   Fax: 617-646-4512
Email: info@opic.gov
www.opic.gov/investmentfunds

This fund provides equity investments for telecommunications projects in Georgia, Armenia and Azerbaijan. The direct equity investments of this OPIC supported fund complement OPIC's loan and insurance products. By supplementing the capital of privately owned, privately managed investment funds, OPIC can help profit oriented enterprises in emerging markets gain access to venture capital, management guidance and financial expertise. Type of assistance: venture capital. Range of money available: $2,850,000 to $9,200,000.

* Venture Capital to Start a Business in Southeast Asia

(Asia Pacific Growth Fund)
Ta-Lin Hsu
Chairman
Hambrecht & Quist Asia Pacific
156 University Avenue   650-838-8098
Palo Alto, CA 94104   Fax: 650-838-0801
Email: info@opic.gov
www.pic.gov/investmentfunds

This program supports equity investments in financial, construction, high tech, light manufacturing and telecom services in Indonesia, Singapore, Taiwan, Malaysia, Thailand and the Philippines. The Asia Pacific Growth Fund is a privately owned, privately managed investment fund supported by the Overseas Private Investment Corporation. It is designed to promote and facilitate U.S. investment in emerging markets by working with private capital to make direct equity and equity related investments. This investment fund is also designed to complement OPIC's insurance and loan products. Each investment must meet OPIC policy requirements, including impact on the U.S. economy and employment. Type of assistance: venture capital. Range of money available: @2,250,000 to $7,500,000.

* Venture Capital to Start a Business in West Bank/Gaza and Jordan

(West Bank/Gaza & Jordan Fund)
Scott Stupay
International Capital Advisors
6862 Elm Street, Suite 720   703-847-0870
McLean, VA 22101   Fax: 703-847-3068
E-ail: info@opic.gv
www.opic.gov/investmentfunds

This program provides equity investments in West Bank/Gaza and Jordan for basic services and manufacturing companies. The West Bank/Gaza & Jordan Fund is a privately owned, privately managed investment fund supported by the Overseas Private Investment Corporation. It promotes and facilitates U.S. investment in emerging markets by working with private capital to make direct equity and equity related investments. This fund is designed to complement OPIC's insurance and loan products. Each investment must meet OPIC policy requirements, including impact on the U.S. economy and employment. Type of assistance: venture capital. Range of money available: $1,200,000 to $6,500,000.

* Venture Capital to Start a Business in Central and Eastern Europe

(Emerging Europe Fund)
Jamie Halper
Managing Director
TDA Capital Partners, Inc
15 Valley Drive   203-625-4525
Greenwich, CT 06831   Fax: 203-625-4525
Email: jhalper@templeton.com
www.opic.gov/investmentfunds

This program supports equity investments in Central and Eastern Europe for sustainable development industries. Eligible countries include Poland, Czech Republic, Slovakia, Romania, Bulgaria, Hungary and Slovenia. Investments are capped at 40% of commitments in any single country. The direct equity investments of this OPIC supported fund complement OPIC's insurance and loan products. By supplementing the capital of privately owned, privately managed investment funds, OPIC can help profit oriented enterprises in

emerging market areas gain access to venture capital, management guidance and financial expertise. Type of assistance: venture capital. Range of money available: $1,800,000 to $6,000,000.

* Venture Capital For Starting a Business in India

(Draper International India Fund)
Robin Richard Donohoe
Draper International
50 California Street, Suite 2925   415-616-4056
San Francisco, CA 94111   Fax: 415-616-4060
Email: rarichards@draperintl.com
www.opic.gov/investmentfunds

This program supports equity investments in India for information technology, telecommunications and consumer goods. Draper International India Fund is a privately owned, privately managed investment fund supported by the Overseas Private Investment Corporation. It promotes and facilitates U.S. investment in emerging markets by working with private capital to make direct equity and equity related investments. This fund is designed to complement OPIC's insurance and loan products. Each investment must meet OPIC policy requirements, including impacts on the U.S. economy ad employment. Type of assistance: venture capital. Range of money available: $1,650,000 to $5,500,000.

* Venture Capital for Starting a Business in Poland

(Poland Partners LP Fund)
Landon Butler
President
Landon Butler & Company
700 Thirteenth Street, NW, Suite 1150   202-737-7360
Washington, DC 20005   Fax: 202-737-7604
Email: info@opic.gov
www.opic.gov/investmentfunds

This program provides equity investments in Poland for consumer goods, manufacturing, distribution networks, merchandising, and related service networks. The Poland Partners LP Fund is a privately owned, privately managed investment fund supported by the Overseas Private Investment Corporation. OPIC promotes and facilitates U.S. investment in emerging markets by working with private capital to make direct equity and equity related investments. This fund is designed to complement OPIC's insurance and loan products. Each investment must meet OPIC policy requirements, including impact on the U.S. economy and employment. Type of assistance: venture capital. Range of money available: $1,500,000 to $5,000,000.

* Venture Capital for Starting a Business in Oman, Jordan and West Bank/Gaza

(Inter-Arab Investment Fund)
Dr. Fuad S. Abu Zayyad
Chairman
Inter-Arab Management, Inc
2468 Embarcadero Way   650-917-0390
Palo Alto, CA 94303   Fax: 650-856-9864
Email: info@opic.gov
www.opic.gov/investmentfunds

This program supports equity investments in Oman, Jordan and West Bank/Gaza for basic industries that create intra/inter-regional synergies. The direct equity investments of this OPIC supported fund complement OPIC's insurance and loan products. By supplementing the capital of privately owned and managed investment funds, OPIC can help profit oriented enterprises in emerging market areas gain access to venture capital, management guidance and financial expertise. Type of assistance: venture capital. Range of money available: $1,000,000 to $4,500,000.

* Venture Capital to Start a Business in Israel

(Israel Growth Fund)
Allan Barkat
General Manager
Apax-Leumi Partners, Inc
Herzliya Business Park
2 Maskit Street, 6th Floor
P.O. Box 2034   972-3-696-5992
Herliza, Israel 46120   Fax: 972-9-958-8366
Email: allan@apax.co.il
www.opic.gov/investmentfunds

This program supports equity investment in Israel for technology, telecommunications, consumer retail and consumer products. The Israel Growth Fund is a privately owned, privately managed investment fund supported by the Overseas Private Investment Corporation. OPIC promotes and facilitates U.S. investment in emerging markets by working with private capital to make direct equity and equity related investments. This fund is designed to complement OPIC's insurance and loan products. Each investment must meet OPIC policy requirements, including impact on the U.S. economy and employment. Type of assistance: venture capital. Range of money available: $1,000,000 to $4,000,000.

* Venture Capital for Starting a Mining or Manufacturing Business in Sub-Sahara Africa

(Africa Growth Fund)
Joe Jandreau
Managing Director
Equator Overseas Services, LTD
45 Glastonbury Boulevard
Glastonbury, CT 06033
Email: info@opic.gov
www.opic.gov/investmentfunds

860-633-9999
Fax: 860-633-6799

This program provides equity investments in Sub-Sahara Africa for mining, manufacturing and financial services. The Africa Growth Fund is a privately owned, privately managed investment fund supported by the Overseas Private Investment Corporation. OPIC promotes and facilitates U.S. investment in emerging markets by working with private capital to make direct equity and equity related investments. This fund is designed to complement OPIC's insurance and loan products. Each investment must meet OPIC policy requirements, including impact on the U.S. economy and employment. Type of assistance: venture capital. Range of money available: $750,000 to $3,000,000.

* Venture Capital to Start a Small Business Overseas

(Allied Small Business Fund)
Cabell Williams
Allied Capital Corporation
1919 Pennsylvania Avenue, NW
Washington, DC 20006-3434
Email: info@opic.gov
www.opic.gov/investmentfunds

202-973-6319
Fax: 202-659-2053

This program supports equity investments for basic manufacturing and service industries sponsored by qualifying U.S. small businesses in any OPIC eligible country. The Allied Small Business Fund is a privately owned, privately managed investment fund supported by the Overseas Private Investment Corporation. OPIC promotes and facilitates U.S. investment in emerging markets by working with private capital to make direct equity and equity related investments. This fund is designed to complement OPIC's insurance and loan products. Each investment must meet OPIC policy requirements, including impact on the U.S. economy and employment. Type of assistance: venture capital. Range of money available: $^00,000 to $2,000,000.

* Loans for Small Businesses to Invest Overseas

(Corporate Finance Loans)
Robert Drumheller
Vice-President, Finance Department
Overseas Private Investment Corporation
1100 New York Avenue, NW
Washington, DC 20527
Email: info@opic.gov
www.opic.gov/Finance

202-336-8400
Fax: 202-408-9866

This program is designed to promote U.S. investment in emerging market economies by providing medium term loans to OPIC eligible U.S. small or medium sized businesses or the overseas subsidiary of such a business. The loans may be used to fund an overseas investment, including fixed assets, permanent working capital, and expansion of facilities. This type of loan is intended to provide long term support for credit worthy U.S. small businesses that desire to make overseas investments when the overseas project is not intended to be the sole source of repayment. Borrowers should own at least 25% of the investment overseas. Type of assistance: loans. Range of money available: $100,000 to $2,000,000.

* Loans to Start a Franchise Business Overseas

(Franchise Loans)
Robert Drumheller
Vice-President, Finance Department
Overseas Private Investment Corporation
1100 New York Avenue, NW
Washington, DC 20527
Email: info@opic.gov
www.opic.gov/Finance

202-336-8400
Fax: 202-408-9866

This program s designed to promote U.S. investment in emerging market economies by providing franchise loans to U.S. small businesses that have a 25% ownership in the franchisee or significant involvement of the small business U.S. franchiser in the project.

The franchise projects must be financially sound, foster private initiative and competition in the host country, and promise significant benefits to the social and economic development of the host country. Type of assistance: loans. Range of money available: $100,000 to $4,000,000.

* Hybrid Loans for Businesses to Invest Overseas

(Hybrid Loans)
Robert Drumheller
Vice-President, Finance Department
Overseas Private Investment Corporation
1100 New York Avenue, NW
Washington, DC 20527
Email: info@opic.gov
www.opic.gov/Finance

202-336-8400
Fax: 202-408-9866

This program is designed to promote U.S. investment in emerging market economies by providing hybrid loans to qualified businesses. Hybrid loans combine features of the Corporate Finance Loan and the Project Finance Loan. Hybrid loans use the cash flow and collateral from the domestic parent company and the project company to create an acceptable loan structure. These loans may be used when the domestic partner has already pledged assets to its existing bank. OPIC may be able to see sufficient value in the cash flow and collateral overseas to consider the loan, whereas a local bank may not. OPIC can lend up to 50% of the cost of the start up operation, or up to 75% of the costs for the expansion of a successful existing business. Loan funds may be used for feasibility studies, organizational expenses, land, construction, machinery, equipment, training, market development, interest payments during construction, and start up expenses including initial losses and adequate working capital. Type of assistance: loans. Range of money available: $100,000 to $200,000,000.

* Medium Term Loans for Businesses to Invest Overseas

(Project Finance Loan)
Robert Drumheller
Vice-President, Finance Department
Overseas Private Investment Corporation
1100 New York Avenue, NW
Washington, DC 20527
Email: info@opic.gov
www.opic.gov/Finance

202-336-8400
Fax: 202-408-9866

This program is designed to promote U.S. investment in emerging market economies by providing medium term loans and guarantees. OPIC provides financing for overseas investments that are completely owned by U.S. companies, or joint ventures where the U.S. sponsoring firm is a participant. The U.S. investor must have at least 25% equity in the project. Projects must be financially and commercially sound and must be able to repay the loan from the project cash flow. Projects that are owned or controlled by governments, or have a negative impact on U.S. employment, the U.S. economy, or the host country are not eligible. OPIC can lend up to 50% of the cost of the start up operation, or up to 75% of the costs for the expansion of a successful existing business. Loan funds may be used for feasibility studies, organizational expenses, land, construction, machinery, equipment, training, market development, interest payments during construction, and start up expenses including initial losses and adequate working capital. Type of assistance: loans and guarantees. Range of money available: loans-$100,000 to $1,000,000; guarantees up to $250,000,000.

* Insurance Coverage for Overseas Contractors and Exporters

(Contractors and Exporters Insurance Coverage)
Michael T. Lempres
Vice President
Insurance Department
1100 New York Avenue, NW
Washington, DC 20527
Email: info@opic.gov
www.opic.gov/Insurance

202-336-8400
Fax: 202-408-9866

This program offers coverage to companies and investors that are acting as contractors pursuant to international construction, sales, or services contracts. It also covers companies that export heavy machinery, turbines, computers, medical equipment, and other goods. This program protects against the wrongful calling of bid, performance, advance payment guaranties, custom bonds and other guaranties. Coverage is provided against the loss of physical assets and bank accounts due to confiscation or political violence, inconvertibility of proceeds from the sale of equipment used at a site, and losses due to certain breaches by foreign buyers of contractual disputes resolution procedures. Type of assistance: insurance. Range of coverage available: up to$250,000,000.

* Insurance Protection for Overseas Financial Transactions

(Capital Markets Insurance Program)
Michael T. Lempres
Vice President
Insurance Department
1100 New York Avenue, NW
Washington, DC 20527
Email: info@opic.gov
www.opic.gov/Insurance

202-336-8400
Fax: 202-408-9866

This program insures capital market transactions including new bond financing of existing ventures, Rule 144A bond issuances, and Private Placements. This coverage protects U.S. based bond holders who provide 50% of the funding for at least 40 days, and companies in developing countries and emerging markets with strong underlying credit that can pierce the sovereign ceiling and move from sub investment to investment rating by insuring their foreign currency denomination bonds against inconvertibility. Type of assistance: insurance. Range of coverage available: up to $250,000,000.

* Insurance Coverage for Financial Institutions Who Make Loans in Emerging Market Economies

(Financial Institution Insurance Program)
Michael T. Lempres
Vice President
Insurance Department
1100 New York Avenue, NW
Washington, DC 20527
Email: info@opic.gov
www.opic.gov/Insurance

202-336-8400
Fax: 202-408-9866

This program protects financial institutions engaged in activities that result in financial exposure in developing countries or emerging markets. Coverage may be tailored to reflect the specific nature of the project. Activities insured by this program include loans made or arranged by banks, Capital Market transactions, cross-border leases, debt for equity investments, commodity price or interest rate swaps, and gold loans. Type of assistance: insurance. Range of coverage available: up to $250,000,000.

* Insurance Protection for Overseas Leasing Arrangements

(Leasing Coverage Insurance Program)
Michael T. Lempres
Vice President
Insurance Department
1100 New York Avenue, NW
Washington, DC 20527
Email: info@opic.gov
www.opic.gov/Insurance

202-336-8400
Fax: 202-408-9866

This program provides protection for capital leases, operating leases and coverage against unlawful host government actions that prevent a lessor from enforcing its right to repossess, re-export and de-register leased equipment. Capital leases, where ownership of the asset is expected to be transferred to the lessee at the end of the lease, are protected against default on lease payments due to inconvertibility, expropriation, and/or political violence. Operating leases, where the lessor expects to recover the leased asset at the end of the lease, are insured for the value of the asset including

installation, transportation costs, and for inconvertibility resulting in default on lease payments. Type of assistance: insurance. Range of coverage available: up to $250,000,000.

* Insurance Coverage for Overseas Mineral Exploration

(Natural Resources Insurance, other than oil or gas)
Michael T. Lempres
Vice President
Insurance Department
1100 New York Avenue, NW
Washington, DC 20527
Email: info@opic.gov
www.opic.gov/Insurance

202-336-8400
Fax: 202-408-9866

Natural Resources Insurance protects investors from risks involved in large scale natural resource projects. Coverage is provided to protect against traditional political risks, and may also insure against unlawful withdrawal or breach by the host government involving mineral exploitation rights and other types of risk. Type of assistance: insurance. Range of coverage available: up to $250,000,000.

* Insurance Coverage for Overseas Gas and Oil Projects

(Oil and Gas Insurance Program)
Michael T. Lempres
Vice President
Insurance Department
1100 New York Avenue, NW
Washington, DC 20527
Email: info@opic.gov
www.opic.gov/Insurance

202-336-8400
Fax: 202-408-9866

The Oil and Gas Insurance Program offers coverage to any large or small U.S. investor involved in oil and gas exploration and/or production. This program provides enhanced and special protection with expropriation coverage designed especially for oil and gas projects. Expropriation includes losses caused by material change in project agreements unilaterally imposed by the host government. Coverage is also available for confiscation of tangible assets and bank accounts, and interference with operations as a result of political violence that cases the cessation of operations for 6 or more months. Type of assistance: insurance. Range of coverage available: up to $250,000,000.

* Insurance Coverage for Technical Assistance Companies Doing Business Overseas

(Technical Assistance Insurance Program)
Michael T. Lempres
Vice President
Insurance Department
1100 New York Avenue, NW
Washington, DC 20527
Email: info@opic.gov
www.opic.gov/Insurance

202-336-8400
Fax: 202-408-9866

This policy provides insurance coverage for U.S. investors who provide only technology or services, or provide technology or services as part of the financing plan for a project in which it has other equity and/or debt investment. This program protects investments in the form of technology and "know-how", or services, pursuant to technical assistance agreements between the U.S and foreign companies. Coverage is provided for 90% of payment accrued but unpaid as a result of inconvertibility, expropriation or political violence. Type of assistance: insurance. Range of coverage available: up to $250,000,000.

Government Contracts:
How to Sell Your Goods and Services
To The World's Largest Buyer

If you produce a product or service, you've probably always wondered how you could offer what you produce to the biggest client in the world — the Federal government. Have you thought of the government as being a "closed shop" and too difficult to penetrate? Well, I'm happy to say that you're entirely wrong on that score. The Federal government spends over $200 billion each year on products ranging from toilet paper to paper clips and writes millions of dollars in contracts for services like advertising, consulting, and printing. Most Americans believe that a majority of those federal purchasing contracts have been eliminated over the last few years, but that's simply not true — they've just been replaced with new contracts that are looking for the same kinds of goods and services. Last year the government took action (either initiating or modifying) on over 500,000 different contracts. They buy these goods and services from someone, so why shouldn't that someone be you? To be successful doing business with the government, you need to learn to speak "governmenteze" to get your company into the purchasing loop, and I can show you how to accomplish that in just a few easy steps.

Step 1

Each department within the Federal government has a procurement office that buys whatever the department requires. Most of these offices have put together their own Doing Business With the Department of _____ publication, which usually explains procurement policies, procedures, and programs. This booklet also contains a list of procurement offices, contact people, subcontracting opportunities, and a solicitation mailing list. Within each department there is also an Office of Small and Disadvantaged Business Utilization, whose sole purpose is to push the interests of the small business, and to make sure these companies get their fair share of government contracts. Another good resource is the listing in this book for Federal Procurement Technical Assistance Offices in your state.

Step 2

Once you have familiarized yourself with the process, you need to find out who is buying what from whom and for how much. There are three ways to get this important information.

A. Federal Business Opportunities (FedBizOpps)
FedBizOpps lists products and services (costing more than $25,000) needed by Government buyers directly on the Internet. Businesses wanting to sell to the Federal Government can search, monitor and retrieve opportunities solicited by the entire Federal contracting community. Department, then office within that agency, and then each specific office location lists opportunities. For instance, the General Services Administration has recently posted 4,125 solicitations for each of their offices throughout the states. Within that, the Public Building Services has posted 167 business possibilities. Synopses and solicitations are listed by posted date, class code, award and set aside. They can also be searched by the same criteria as well as zip code, agency, and office.

Sellers can sign up for the Vendor Notification Service. This sends emails containing announcements, presolicitations and their modification, notices of solicitation and amendment releases, and general procurement announcements. Notices can be received based on solicitation number, specific organizations, and product service classification, or all procurement notices. Other items of interest to sellers are the FBO Datafeed, which lists daily postings in html format daily, and Interested Vendors Module that promotes teaming opportunities for businesses wanting to sell to the government.

The General Services Administration Federal Supply Service publishes the FBO Vendors Guide that explains the system in detail. To begin viewing the vast amounts of potential opportunities, go to {www.fedbizopps.gov}. For information, call 877-472-3779; {fbo.support@gsa.gov}.

B. Federal Procurement Data System (FPDC)

This Center distributes consolidated information about federal purchases, including research and development. FPDC can tell you how much the Federal government spent last quarter on products and services, which agencies made those purchases, and what contractors did business with the government. FPDC summarizes this information through two types of reports: The FPDC standard report and the FPDC special report. The standard report compilation containing statistical procurement information in "snapshot" form for over 60 federal agencies, as well as several charts, graphs, and tables which compare procurement activities by state, major product and service codes, method of procurement, and contractors can be printed out, in whole or in part, at the website below. The report also includes quarterly and year-to-year breakdowns of amounts and percentages spent on small, women owned, and minority businesses. Special reports are prepared upon request for a fee, based on computer and labor costs. They are tailored to the specific categories, which can be cross-tabulated in numerous ways. A special report can help you analyze government procurement and data trends, identify competitors, and locate federal markets for individual products or services. Your Congressman may have access to the Federal Procurement Database from his/her office in Washington, which you may be able to use for free. For more information, contact: General Services Administration, Government Wide Information Systems Division, Federal Procurement Data System, 7th and D St., SW, Room 5652, Washington, DC 20407; 202-401-1529; {www.fpdc.gov/}.

C. Other Contracts

For contracts under $25,000, you must be placed on a department's list for solicitation bids on those contracts. The mailing list forms are available through the Procurement Office, the Office of Small and Disadvantaged Business Utilization, or your local Small Business Association office. Last year 18.7 billion dollars was spent on these "small" purchases, so these contracts should not be overlooked. Smaller contracts, completed over the course of a fiscal year, can mean lots of revenue for your business bottom line.

Step 3: Subcontracting Opportunities

All of the federal procurement offices or Offices of Small and Disadvantaged Business Utilization (SDBU) can provide you with information regarding subcontracting. Many of the departments' prime contracts require that the prime contractor maximize small business subcontracting opportunities. Many prime contractors produce special publications which can be helpful to those interested in subcontracting. The SDBU Office can provide you with more information on the subcontracting process, along with a directory of prime contractors. Another good source for subcontract assistance is your local Small Business Administration (SBA) office, 1-800-827-5722. SBA develops subcontracting opportunities for small business by maintaining close contact with large business prime contractors and by referring qualified small firms to them. The SBA has developed agreements and close working relationships with hundreds of prime contractors who cooperate by offering small firms the opportunity to compete for their subcontracts. In addition, to complete SBA's compliance responsibilities, commercial market representatives monitor prime contractors in order to assess their compliance with laws governing subcontracting opportunities for small businesses. Check the website at {www.sba.gov}. For a list of major federal OSDBU offices, check the listing in this book entitled "Offices of Small and Disadvantaged Business Utilization."

Step 4: Small Business Administration's 8(a) Program

Are you a socially or economically disadvantaged person who has a business? This group includes, but is not limited to, Black Americans, Hispanic Americans, Native Americans, Asian Pacific Americans, and Subcontinent Asian Americans. Socially and economically disadvantaged individuals represent a significant percentage of U.S. citizens, yet account for a disproportionately small percentage of total U.S. business revenues. The 8(a) program assists firms in participating in the business sector and to become independently competitive in the marketplace. SBA may provide participating firms with procurement, marketing, financial, management, or other technical assistance. A Business Opportunity Specialist will be assigned to each firm that participates, and is responsible for providing the firm with access to assistance that can help the firm fulfill its business goals. SBA undertakes an extensive effort to provide government contracting opportunities to participating businesses. To apply for the 8(a) program, you must attend an interview session with an official in the SBA field office in your area. For more information, contact your local Small Business Administration Office, or call 1-800-827-5722 or {www.sba.gov/8abd} for the SBA office nearest you.

Step 5: Bond

A Surety bond is often a prerequisite for government and private sector contracts. This is particularly true when the contract involves construction. In order for the company to qualify for an SBA Guarantee Bond, they must make the bonding company aware of their capabilities based on past contract performance and meeting of financial obligations. SBA can assist firms in obtaining surety bonding for contracts that do not exceed $6,000,000. SBA is authorized, when appropriate circumstances occur, to guarantee as much as 90 percent of losses suffered by a surety resulting from a breach of terms of a bond. Check their website at {www.sba.gov/osg}.

Step 6: Publications

The Government Printing Office has several publications for sale which explain the world of government contracts. For ordering information, contact: Superintendent of Documents, Government Printing Office, Washington, DC 20402; 202-512-1800; {www.gpo.gov}.

* *Guidebook for Performance-Based Services Acquisition in the Department of Defense.* This publication highlights the key elements of performance-based services acquisition and encourages innovative business practices within the Department of Defense acquisition process. S/N 008-020-01501-6 $7.00
* *Code of Federal Regulations, Title 41, Public Contracts and Property Management.* Chapter 1-100. S/N 869-044-00162-4 $22.00
* *Best Practices: How to Avoid Surprises in the World's Most Complicated Technical Process, The Transition From Development to Production.* This is a guide for defense contractors that shows common mistakes that were made at all stages of the procurement process, form proposal submission to research, test and development. S/N 008-050-00234-4 $33.50
* *Federal Acquisition Regulation (FAR Subscription)* Access to all critical information you need to profitably contract with the Federal Government. Subscribe to the FAR and get all the information you need to fully understand the solicitation bids that interest you. S/N 922-006-00000-8 $220.00 On CD-ROM S/N 721-034-00000-3 $70.00

* *Defense Acquisition Deskbook CD-ROM* This easy-to-use reference system is an encyclopedia of information invaluable to anyone who wants to do business with Department of Defense (DoD) or other Government agencies. Provided on CD-ROM, it contains a comprehensive library of all the policies and regulations. S/N 708-097-00000-4 $37.00

Step 7: What is GSA?

General Services Administration (GSA) is the Government's business agent. On an annual budget of 16 billion dollars, it directs and coordinates nearly $8 billion a year worth of purchases, sales, and services. Its source of supply is private enterprise, and its clients include all branches of the Federal government. GSA plans and manages leasing, purchase, or construction of office buildings, laboratories, and warehouses; buys and delivers nearly $10 billion worth of goods and services; negotiates the prices and terms for an additional $2.3 billion worth of direct business between federal groups and private industry; sets and interprets the rules for federal travel and negotiates reduced fares and lodging rates for federal travelers; and manages a 185,000 vehicle fleet with a cumulative yearly mileage of over 1 billion. For a copy of *Doing Business With GSA* go to {www.gsa.gov/smallbusiness} and click on "Publications" or call Office of Small Business Utilization headquarters at 202-501-1021 or your regional Small Business Utilization Center. For information on GSA's architect and engineer services, such as who is eligible for GSA professional services contracts, how to find out about potential GSA projects, what types of contracts are available, and where and how to apply, contact: Public Buildings Service, GSA, 1800 F Street, NW, Washington, DC 20405; 202-501-1100.

Step 8: Bid and Contract Protests

The General Accounting Office (GAO) resolves disputes between agencies and bidders of government contracts, including grantee award actions. The free publication, *Bid Protests at GAO; A Descriptive Guide*, contains information on GAO's procedures for determining legal questions arising from the awarding of government contracts. Contact General Accounting Office, 441 G Street, NW, Room LM, Washington, DC 20548; 202-512-6000. For Contract Appeals, the GSA Board of Contract Appeals works to resolve disputes arising out of contracts with GSA, the Departments of Treasury, Education, Commerce, and other independent government agencies. The Board also hears and decides bid protests arising out of government-wide automated data processing (ADP) procurements. A contractor may elect to use either the GSA Board or the General Accounting Office for resolution of an ADP bid protest. Contractors may elect to have their appeals processed under the Board's accelerated procedures if the claim is $50,000 or less, or under the small claims procedure if the claim is $10,000 or less. Contractors may also request that a hearing be held at a location convenient to them. With the exception of small claims decisions, contractors can appeal adverse Board decisions to the U.S. Court of Appeals for the Federal Circuit. For more information, contact: Board of Contract Appeals, General Services Administration, 1800 F Street, NW, Washington, DC 20405; 202-501-0116; {www.gsbca.gsa.gov}. There are other Contract Appeals Boards for other departments. One of the last paragraphs in your government contract should specify which Board you are to go to if a problem with your particular contract should arise.

Free Local Help:
The Best Place To Start To Sell To The Government

Within each state there are offices that can help you get started in the federal procurement process. As stated previously, your local Small Business Administration (SBA) office is a good resource. In addition to their other services, the SBA can provide you with a list of Federal Procurement Offices based in your state, so you can visit them in person to gather valuable information. Another place to turn is your local Small Business Development Center (look under Economic Development in your phone book). These offices are funded jointly by federal and state governments, and are usually associated with the state university system in your area. They are aware of the federal procurement process, and can help you draw up a sensible business plan that will be successful.

Some states have established programs to assist businesses in the federal procurement process for all departments in the government. These programs are designed to help businesses learn about the bidding process, the resources available, and provide information on how the procurement system operates. They can match the product or service you are selling with the appropriate agency, and then help you market your product. Several programs have online bid matching services, whereby if a solicitation appears on FedBizOpps that matches what your company markets, then the program will automatically contact you to start the bid process. The program office can then request the appropriate documents, and assist you in achieving your goal. These Procurement Technical Assistance Centers (PTAC) are partially funded by the Department of Defense to assist businesses with Defense Procurement. For a current listing of PTACs contact:

Defense Logistics Agency
Office of Small and Disadvantaged Utilization
Bldg. 4, Cameron Station, Room 4B110
Alexandria, VA 22304-6100   703-767-1661
{www.dla.mil/db}, then go to the small business site

Let Your Congressman Help You

Are you trying to market a new product to a department of the Federal government? Need to know where to try to sell your wares? Is there some problem with your bid? Your Congressman can be of assistance. Because they want business in their state to boom, most Congressmen will make an effort to assist companies in obtaining federal contracts. Frequently they will write a letter to accompany your bid, or if you are trying to market a new product, they will write a letter to the procurement office requesting that they review your product. Your Congressman can also be your personal troubleshooter. If there is some problem with your bid, your Congressman can assist you in determining and resolving the problem, and can provide you with information on the status of your bid. Look in the blue pages of your phone book for your Senators' or Representatives' phone numbers, or call them in Washington at 202-224-3121.

Small Business Set-Asides

The Small Business Administration (SBA) encourages government purchasing agencies to set aside suitable government purchases for exclusive small business competition. A purchase which is restricted to small business bidders is identified by a set aside clause in the invitation for bids or request for proposals. There is no overall listing of procurements which are, or have been, set aside for small business. A small business learns which purchases are reserved for small business by getting listed on bidders' lists. It also can help keep itself informed of set aside opportunities by referring to the FedBizOpps. Your local SBA office can provide you with more information on set asides, and so can the Procurement Assistance Offices listed at the end of this section. To locate your nearest SBA office, call 1-800-827-5722 or {www.sba.gov}.

Veterans Assistance

Each Small Business Administration District Office has a Veterans Affairs Officer which can assist veteran-owned businesses in obtaining government contracts. Although there is no such thing as veterans set aside contracts, the Veterans Administration does make an effort to fill its contracts using veteran-owned businesses whenever possible. Contact your local SBA office for more information, or check the following websites: {www.sba.gov/VETS}; {www.va.gov}.

Woman-Owned Business Assistance

There are over 3.7 million women-owned businesses in the United States, and the number is growing each year. Current government policy requires federal contracting officers to increase their purchases from women-owned businesses. Although the women-owned firms will receive more opportunities to bid, they still must be the lowest responsive and responsible bidder to win the contract. To assist these businesses, each SBA district office has a Women's Business Ownership Representative, who can provide you with information regarding government programs. Most of the offices hold a *Selling to the Federal Government* seminar, which is designed to educate the business owner on the ins and outs of government procurement. There is also a helpful publication, *Women Business Owners: Selling to the Federal Government*, which provides information on procurement opportunities available. Contact your local SBA office or your Procurement Technical Assistance Center (listed below) for more information; or check the website at {http://onlinewbc.gov}.

Minority and Labor Surplus Area Assistance

Are you a socially or economically disadvantaged person who has a business? This group includes, but is not limited to, Black Americans, Hispanic Americans, Native Americans, Asian Pacific Americans, and Subcontinent Asian Americans. Socially and economically disadvantaged individuals represent a significant percentage of U.S. citizens yet account for a disproportionately small percentage of total U.S. business revenues. The 8(a) program assists firms to participate in the business sector and to become independently competitive in the marketplace. SBA may provide participating firms with procurement, marketing, financial, management, or other technical assistance. A Business Opportunity Specialist will be assigned to each firm that participates, and is responsible for providing that company with access to assistance that can help it fulfill its business goals. Check the website at {www.sba.gov/8adb}

Some areas of the country have been determined to be labor surplus areas, which means there is a high rate of unemployment. Your local SBA office can tell you if you live in such an area, as some contracts are set asides for labor surplus areas. For more information, contact your local Small Business Administration office (call 1-800-827-5722 for the SBA office nearest you; or online at {www.sba.gov}), or call the Procurement Technical Assistance Center in your state (listed below).

Federal Procurement Technical Assistance Centers

Alabama

Charles Hopson
Alabama Small Business Development
Consortium
2800 Milan Ct., Suite 124
Birmingham, AL 35211
205-934-6750
Fax: 205-934-7645
Email: charlesh@uab.edu
www.asbdc.org/procurement

Alaska

Mike Taylor
University of Alaska Anchorage
Small Business Development Center
430 W. 7th Ave., Suite 110
Anchorage, AK 99501-3550
907-274-7232
800-478-7232
Fax: 907-274-9524
Email: angmt1@uaa.alaska.edu
www.ptacalaska.org

Procurement Technical Assistance Center of
Alaska
613 Cushman Street, Suite 209
Fairbanks, AK 99701
907-456-7232
800-478-1701
Fax: 907-456-7233
www.ptacalaska.org

Arizona

Elaine Young
The National Center for AIED
National Center Headquarters
953 E. Juanita Ave.
Mesa, AZ 85204
480-545-1298, ext. 223
Fax: 480-545-4208
Email: Ncaiedely@aol.com
www.ncaied.org/mpsp

APTAN, Inc
459 North Gilbert Road
Suite A215
Gilbert, AZ 85234
480-632-1800
Fax: 480-632-1931
Email: aptan@primenet.com
www.aptan.com

Cyndi Bosworth
Maricopa County PTAC
201 N. Central Avenue, 27th Floor
Phoenix, AZ 85073
602-495-6467
Fax: 602-495-8913
Email: cbosworth@phoenixchamber.com

Arkansas

Sue Coates
University of Arkansas
Cooperative Extension Service
103 East Page St.
Malvern, AR 72104
501-337-5355
Fax: 501-337-5045
Email: apac@uaex.edu
www.arcommunities.org/APAC/default.asp

California

Bob Truex
Riverside Community College District
Procurement Assistance Center
13745 Riverside Drive
Riverside, CA 92518
909-571-6442
Fax: 909-653-1051

Email: Bob.Truex@rcc.edu
www.rcchelpsbusiness.com

Jane E. McGinnis
Action Business Center
California Central Valley PTAC
2000 "M" St.
Merced, CA 95340
209-385-7686
Fax: 209-383-4959
Email: ptac1@pacbell.net
www.abc.merced.ca.us/ptac.html

Ken Hollis
Imperial County Community and Economic
Development
836 Main Street
El Centro, CA 92243
760-337-7814
800-317-8432
Fax: 760-337-8907
www.icced.com

J. Gunnar Schalin
Southwestern Community College
Contracting Opportunities Center
3443 Camino Del Rio South, Suite 116
San Diego, CA 92108-3913
619-285-7020, ext. 3005
Fax: 619-285-7030
Email: sdcoc@pacbell.net
www.ptac-sandiego.org

Debbie Johnson
Los Angeles County Office of Small Business
and Procurement Technical Assistance
4800 Cesar E. Chavez Avenue
Los Angeles, CA 90022
323-260-2311
800-555-3815
Fax: 323-881-1871
Email: dcabrier@lacdc.org
www.laosb.org

Jack Tooney
Federal Technology Center PTAC
4700 Roseville Road, Suite 105
Sacramento, CA 95660
916-334-9388
866-FTC-PTAC
Fax: 916-334-9078
Email: jack@TheFTC.org
www.theftc.org/ptac

Colorado

Denver Small Business Development
Procurement Center
1445 Market Street
Denver, CO 80202
303-620-8076
Fax: 303-534-3200
Email: Denver.sbdc@den-chamber.org
www.denverchamber.org/chamber/programs/s
bdc/index.htm

Connecticut

Arlene M. Vogel
Southeastern Connecticut Enterprise Region
(seCTer)
190 Governor Winthrop Blvd., Suite 300
New London, CT 06320
860-437-4659, ext. 208
1-888-6-SECTER
Fax: 860-437-4662
Email: ptap@secter.org
www.secter.org/

Delaware

Juanita Beauford

Delaware Government Marketing Assistance
Program
Small Business Development Center
1318 North Market Street
Wilmington, DE 19801
302-571-1555
Fax: 302-571-5222
www.delawarecontracts.com

District of Columbia

No PTAC awarded

Florida

Laura Subel
University of West Florida
Florida PTA Program
401 East Chase St., Suite 100
Pensacola, FL 32502
850-473-7806
Fax: 850-473-7813
Email: lsubel@uwf.edu
www.fptac.com
Serving: Pensacola, Panama City and
Tallahassee areas.

Regina Bell
University of West Florida Purchasing
Department
Minority Enterprise Procurement Program
11000 University Parkway
Pensacola, FL 32514
850-474-2632
Email: rbell@uwf.edu
www.fptac.org

Paul Briere
University of West Florida
34 Miracle Strip Parkway, S.E. (US 98)
Ft. Walton Beach, FL 32548
850-243-3514
Email: pbriere@uwf.edu
www.fptac.org
Serving Ft. Walton Beach and Crestview areas

Bob Raiser
Chamber of Commerce Small Business Center
5000-3 Norwood Avenue
Jacksonville, FL 32208
904-924-1100 ext 231
Email: bob.riser@myjaxhamber.com
www.fptac.org
Serving the Jacksonville area

Glenda Rife
University of North Florida
110 E. Silver Springs Boulevard
Ocala, FL 34470-6613
352-622-8763 (Mondays and Fridays)
352-334-7230 (Tuesdays)
Email: ger-sbdc@atlantic.net
www.fptac.org
Serving Ocala and Gainesville areas

Charlene Bostic
University of South Florida
1101 Channelside Drive, Suite 210
Tampa, FL 33602
813-905-8526
800-733-7232
Email: cbostic@coba.usf.edu
www.fptac.org
Serving Tampa, Bartow, Orlando, Ocala and
Melbourne areas

Carol Bowers
University of South Florida
The Pinellas Park Technical Services Building
6051 78th Avenue
Pinellas Park, FL 33780

727-541-0805 ext 2108
Email: cbowers@coba.usf.edu
www.fptac.org
Serving St. Petersburg, Sarasota and Pasco
counties

Carole Hart
Florida Atlantic University
777 Glades Road T-9
Boca Raton, FL 333431
561-291-1145
Email: chart@fau.edu
www.fptac.org
Serving the Boca Raton area

Jackie Rule
Florida Atlantic University
8500 SW 8th Street, Suite 224
Miami, FL 33144-4002
561-297-1145
Email: jrule1@fau.edu
www.fptac.org
Serving the Miami area

Dan Telep
Florida Gulf Coast University
12751 Westlinks Drive, Building 3, Unit 7
Ft. Myers, FL 33913-8615
239-225-4218
Email: dtelep@fgcu.edu
www.fptac.org
Serving Lee, Collier, Charlotte, Glades and
Hendry counties

Georgia

Georgia Institute of Technology
Georgia Tech Procurement Assistance Center
760 Spring Street, Suite 330
Atlanta, GA 30332-0640
478-953-3155
888-272-2104
Fax: 478-953-3169
Email: gtpac@edi.gatech.edu
www.edi.gatech.edu

Alan Barfoot
Georgia Institute of Technology
Georgia Tech Procurement Assistance Center
Dublin Regional Office
1200-A Hillcrest Parkway
Dublin, GA 31201
478-275-6543
Fax: 478-275-6544
Email: centralregion@edi.gatech.edu
www.edi.gatech.edu

Jill Winkelman
Georgia Institute of Technology
Georgia Tech Procurement Assistance Center
Savannah Regional Office
210 Technology Circle
Savannah, GA 31407
912-963-2509
Fax: 912-963-2522
Email: coastalregion@edi.gatech.edu
www.edi.gatech.edu

Todd Hurd
Georgia Institute of Technology
Georgia Tech Procurement Assistance Center
Augusta Regional Office
1054 Claussen Road, Suite 301
Augusta, GA 30907
706-737-1414
Fax: 706-737-1420
Email: eastregion@edi.gatech.edu
www.edi.gatech.edu

Karen Fite
Georgia Institute of Technology
Georgia Tech Procurement Assistance Center
Athens Regional Office
1180 E. Broad Street
Chicopee Complex

Athens, GA 30602-5413
706-542-8900
Fax: 706-542-8899
Email: northeastregion@edi.gatech.edu
www.edi.gatech.edu

Jerry Zolkowski
Georgia Institute of Technology
Georgia Tech Procurement Assistance Center
Dalton Regional Office
213 N. College Drive
Dalton, GA 30720
706-272-2702
Fax: 706-272-2701
Email: northwestregion@edi.gatech.edu
www.edi.gatech.edu

Art Ford
Georgia Institute of Technology
Georgia Tech Procurement Assistance Center
Albany Regional Office
125 Pine Avenue
Suite 220
P.O. Box 587
Albany, GA 31702-0587
229-430-4188
Fax: 229-430-4200
Email: southregion@edi.gatech.edu
www.edi.gatech.edu

Jennifer Trapp
Georgia Institute of Technology
Georgia Tech Procurement Assistance Center
Newman Regional Office
31-B Postal Parkway
Newman. GA 30263
770-254-7381
Fax: 770-254-7449
Email: westregion@edi.gatech.edu
www.edi.gatech.edu

Tyler McGhee
United Indian Development Association
Consulting Group, Inc.
86 South Cobb Drive, MZ 0510
Marietta, GA 30063-0510
770-494-0431
Fax: 770-494-1236
Email: uida@uida.org
www.uida.org/ptac.html

Hawaii

No PTAC awarded

Idaho

Larry Demirelli
Idaho Department of Commerce
State of Idaho
700 West State St.
Boise, ID 83720-0093
208-334-2470
Fax: 208-334-2631
Email: ibn@idoc.state.id.us
www.idahoworks.com

Illinois

Pedro Pereira
Latin American Chamber of Commerce
The Chicago Pac
3512 W. Fullerton
Chicago, IL 60647
773-252-5211
Fax: 773-252-7065
Email: cmontoya@lacc1.com
www.lacc1.com

Lois Van Meter
State of Illinois
Dept. of Commerce and Community Affairs
620 E. Adams St., Third Floor
Springfield, IL 62701
217-557-1823
Fax: 217-785-6328

Email: ivanmete@commerce. state.il.us
www.commerce.state.il.us

Al Meroz
Moraine Valley Community College
10900 S. 88th Avenue
Palos Hills, IL 60465-0937
708-974-5452
Fax: 708-974-0078
Email: meroz@morainevalley.edu
www.morainevalley.edu/ptac/default.htm

Rita Hatcher
College of DuPage PTAC
425 Fawell Boulevard
Glen Ellyn, IL 60137-6599
630-942-2184
Fax: 630-942-3789
Email: hatcher@cdnet.cod.edu
www.cod.edu/BPI/ptac.htm

Susan Gorman
Illinois Central College PTAC
124 S.W. Adams Street
Suite 300
Peoria, IL 61602-1388
309-495-5970
Fax: 309-676-7534
Email: sgorman@icc.edu
www.icc.edu/ptac

Marc N. Violante
College of Lake County PTAC
19351 West Washington Street
Grayslake, IL 60030-1198
847-543-2025
Fax: 847-223-9371
Email: clcptac@clc.cc.il.us
www.clcillinois.edu/ddd/dept/pta.asp

Teresa Ebeler
East St. Louis PTAC
Southern Illinois University
601 J.R. Thompson Drive, Room 2090
East St. Louis, IL 62001
618-482-8330
Email: tmeehan@siue.edu
www.siue.edu/ESL/small_business/small_busi
ness.htm

Rich Fyke
John A. Logan College PTAC
700 Logan College Road
Carterville, IL 62918
618-985-2828
800-851-4720
Fax: 618-985-2867
Email: rich.fyke@jal.cc.il.us
www.jal.cc.il.us/bus_ind/ptac.html

William Hett-Dobricky
NORBIC PTAC Center
5353 West Armstrong Avenue
Chicago, IL 60646
773-594-9562
Fax: 773-594-9416
Email: whdobricky@norbic.org
www.norbic.org/procurement_assistance.htm

John DiGiacoma
Rock Valley College PTAC
3301 North Mulford Road, Room 262
Rockford, IL 61114-5640
Phone: 815-921-2086
Fax: 815-921-3059
Email: jdigiacomo@rvc.cc.il.us
www.rvc.cc.il.us/business/procure

David Talbot
South Suburban College
15800 South State Srteet
South Holland, IL 60473-1270
708-596-2000 Ext. 2431
Fax: 708-225-5834

Email: dtalbot@southsuburbancollege.edu
www.ssc.cc.il.us/bci/ptac.html

Kristin Johnson
Women's Business Development Center
PTAC
8 South Michigan Avenue, Suite 400
Chicago, IL 60603-3302
312-853-3477 Ext. 18
Fax: 312-853-0145
Email: kjohnson@wbdc.org
www.wbdc.org

Carol Cusumano, Freida Schreck
Central Illinois Regional PTAC
P.O. Box 203
Riverton, IL 62561
217-789-1017
Fax: 217-522-3512
Email: PRAXIS535@aol.com

Indiana
Kathy DeGuilio-Fox
Partners in Contracting Corporation
PTA Center
6100 Southport Rd.
Portage, IN 46368
219-762-8644
Fax: 219-763-1513
Email: picc@piccorp.org
www.piccorp.org

Iowa
Bruce Coney
Iowa State University
Iowa Procurement Center
2272 Howe Hall
Ames, IA 50011-2270
515-294-4473
800-458-4465
Fax: 515-294-4483
Email: bruce.coney@ciras.iastate.edu
www.ciras.iastate.edu/ipoc

Kansas
Terri Bennett
Heartland Procurement Technical Assistance
Center
Missouri Southern State College
3950 E. Newman Rd.
Joplin, MO 64801-1595
417-625-9538
Fax: 417-625-9782
Email: heartlandptac@mail.mssc.edu
www.mssc.edu/heartlandptac

Jesse James III
Heartland Procurement Technical Assistance
Centers
Entrepreneurial Growth Resource Center
Bloch School of Business University of
Missouri - Kansas City
4747 Troost Building, 203
Kansas City, MO 64110
816-235-2891
Fax: 816-235-2947
Email: jamesje@umkc.edu

Kentucky
Tim Back
Kentucky Cabinet For Economic Development
Department of Community Development
500 Mero St.
2200 Capital Plaza Tower
Frankfort, KY 40601
800-838-3266
502-564-4252
Fax: 502-564-5932
Email: tback@mail.state.ky.us
www.thinkkentucky.com/kyedc/proassist.asp

Louisiana
Sherrie Mullins

Louisiana Productivity Center
University of Southwest Louisiana
P.O. Box 44172
241 E. Lewis St.
Lafayette, LA 70504-4172
337-482-6767
Fax: 337-482-5837
Email: sbm3321@louisiana.edu
www.louisiana.edu

Kelly Ford
Northwest Louisiana Government
Procurement Center
Shreveport COC
400 Edwards St.
P.O. Box 20074
Shreveport, LA 71120-0074
318-677-2500
Fax: 318-677-2541
Email: kellyford@shreveportchamber.org
www.lagpc.org

Maine
Rick Alexander
Eastern Maine Development Corp.
Market Development Center
One Cumberland Pl., Suite 300
P.O. Box 2579
Bangor, ME 04402-2579
207-942-6389
800-339-6389
Fax: 207-942-3548
Email: ralexander@emdc.org
www.mdcme.org

Rick Alexander
Market Development Center
95 Park Street
Suite 411
Lewistown, ME 04240
207-777-5067
Email: ralexander@emdc.org
www.mdcme.org

Rick Alexander
Market Development Center
P.O. Box 1517
Portland, ME 04101
207-780-8894
Email: egray@clinic.net
www.mdcme.org

Maryland
Greg Prouty
Maryland PTAC
Small Business Development Center
7100 Baltimore Avenue, Suite 303
College Park, MD 20740
301-403-2739
866-228-0432
Fax: 301-403-8303
Email: gprouty@mdptap.edu
www.mdptap.umd.edu

Massachusetts
Peter J. Cokotis
University of Massachusetts at Amherst
Office of Grants and Contracts
121 Presidents Drive
Room 227 S.O.M.
Amherst, MA 01033-9310
413-737-6712
Email: pcokotis@som.umass.edu
http://msbdc.som.umass.edu/ptac

Michigan
Sandy Gelman
Schoolcraft College Business Development
Center
18600 Haggerty Rd.
Livonia, MI 48152-2696
734-462-4438
Fax: 734-462-4439

Email: sgelman@schoolcraft.cc.mi.us
www.schoolcraft.cc.mi.us/bdc/default.htm

Mike Black
Southwest Michigan Technical Assistance
Center
Western Michigan University
4717 Campus Drive, Box 100
Kalamazoo, MI 49008
269-372-3941
Fax: 269-353-5569
Email: Michael.black@wmich.edu
www.michigantac.org

Paula Boase
Downriver Community Conference
Economic Development
15100 Northline Road
Southgate, MI 48195
734-362-3477
Fax: 734-281-6661
Email: paulab@dccwf.org
www.dccwf.org

James Millhench
Warren, Center Line
Sterling Heights Chamber of Commerce
30500 Van Dyke Ave., Suite 118
Warren, MI 48093
586-751-3939
Fax: 586-751-3995
Email: jmillhench@wcschamber.com
www.michigantac.org

Pamela Vanderlaan
West Central Michigan Works!
PTA Center
110 Elm St.
Big Rapids, MI 49307
231-796-4891, ext. 16
Fax: 231-796-8316
Email: ptac@michworkswc.org
www.michworks.swc.org

James F. Haslinger
Northwestern Michigan Council of
Governments
PTA Center
1209 South Garfield Ave.
Traverse City, MI 49685-0506
231-929-5036
Fax: 231-929-5042
Email: jhasling@nwm.cog.mi.us
www.nwm.org/business/procure/

Pennie Southwell
Technical Assistance Center of South Central
Michigan
The Enterprise Group of Jackson, Inc.
One Jackson Square
Jackson, MI 49201
517-788-4680
Fax: 517-782-0061
Email: pennie@enterprisegroup.org
www.enterprisegroup.org

Pemale Vanderlaan
Michigan Works! West Central
900 Third Street, Suite 113
Muskegon, MI 49440
231-722-7700
800-528-8776
Fax: 231-722-6182
Email: psvander@wmis.net
www.michworks.swc.org

Dustin Frigy
Flint-Genesee Economic Growth Alliance
519 South Saginaw Street, Suite 210
Flint, MI 48502
810-238-8845
Fax: 810-238-7866
Email: dfrigy@flint.org
www.michigantac.org

Sally Beck
Economic Development Alliance of St. Clair
County
735 Erie Street, Suite 250
Port Huron, MI 48060
810-982-9511
Fax: 810-982-9531
Email: sbeck@edaofstclaircounty.com
www.edaofstclaircounty.com

Delena Spates-Allen
Saginaw Future, Inc.
301 East Genesee, Suite 300
Saginaw, MI 48607
989-754-8222
Fax: 989-754-1715
Email: dsallen@saginawfuture.com

Jody Wilson
Michigan Works!
3270 Wilson St.
Marlette, MI 48453
989-635-3561
Fax: 989-635-2230
Email: wilsonjo@thumbworks.org

Denise Hoffmeyer
NE Michigan Consortium
P.O. Box 711
Onaway, MI 49765
989-733-8548
Fax: 989-733-8069
Email: denise@miworks-nemc.gen.mi.us

John Chichester
Wayne State University
Room 240 Rands
Detroit, MI 48202
313-577-2241
Fax: 313-577-4354
Email: ac1538@wayne.edu

Denise Hoffmeyer
Northeast Michigan Consortium
20709 State Street
P.O. Box 711
Onaway, MI 49765
517-733-8548
800-371-2533
Fax: 517-733-8069
Email: General@miworks-nemc.gen.mi.us
www.miworks-nemc.gen.mi.us/index.html

Minnesota

George Johnson
Minnesota Project Innovation, Inc.
Procurement Technical Assistance Center
100 Mill Place
111 Third Ave. South
Minneapolis, MN 55401-2551
612-338-3280
Fax: 612-349-2603
Email: gjohnson@mpi.org
www.mpi.org/ptac/index.htm

Tom Allen
Minnesota Project Innovation, Inc.
2720 River Woods Lane
Burnsville, MN 55337
952-707-6301
Email: tcallen@mpi.org
www.mpi.org

Rodney McGee
Minnesota Project Innovation, Inc.
1821 University Avenue, Suite S-340
St. Paul, MN 55104
651-644-3786
Fax: 651-603-6764
Email: rmcgee@mpi.org
www.mpi.org

Sherri Komrosky
Minnesota Project Innovation, Inc.

Moorhead State University
Box 303
MSU 615 - 11th Street
Moorhead, MN 56563-0001
218-299-5801
Fax: 218-236-2280
Email: skom@linkup.net
www.mpi.org

Christina Nebel
Minnesota Project Innovation, Inc.
616 Roosevelt Rd
St. Cloud, MN 56301
320-202-6496
Fax: 320-654-5412
Email: cnebel@mpi.org
www.mpi.org

Charles Wallschlaeger
Minnesota Project Innovation, Inc.
560 Dunnell Dr
Merrill Building Suite 214
Owatonna, MN 55060
507-446-2310
Fax: 507-446-2311
Email: cwallsch@mpi.org
www.mpi.org

Mississippi

Richard L. Speights
Mississippi Contract Procurement Center, Inc.
1636 Poppsferry Rd., Suite 229
Biloxi, MS 39532
228-396-1288
Fax: 228-396-2520
Email: mprogoff@aol.com
www.mscpc.com

Bill Estes
Central Mississippi Contract Procurement
Center
Jackson Enterprise Center
931 Highway 80, West #32
Jackson, MS 39204
601-352-0804
Fax: 601-948-3250
Email: cmpc@mscpc.com
www.mscpc.com
Serving Adams, Claiborne, Copiah, Franklin,
Hinds, Jefferson, Jefferson Davis, Lawrence,
Lincoln, Madison, Rankin, Simpson, Warren
counties

Beth Woodyard
Delta Mississippi Contract Procurement
Center
P.O. Box 1179
Greenville, MS 38702
662-334-2656
Fax: 662-334-2709
Email: dcpc@mscpc.com
www.mscpc.com
Serving Bolivar, Carroll, Coahoma, DeSoto,
Grenada, Holmes, Humphreys, Issequena,
LeFlore, Panola, Quitman, Sharkey,
Sunflower, Tallahatchie, Tate, Tunica,
Washington, Yalobusha, Yazoo counties

Bill Burge
Northeast Mississippi Contract Procurement
Center
P.O. Box 1328
Columbus, MS 39703-1328
662-329-1077
Fax: 662-327-6600
Email: nmcpc@mscpc.com
www.mscpc.com
Serving Alcorn, Attala, Benton, Calhoun,
Chickasaw, Choctaw, Clay, Itawamba,
Lafayette, Lee, Lowndes, Marshall, Monroe,
Montgomery, Noxubee, Oktibbeha, Pontotoc,
Prentiss, Tippah, Tishomingo, Union,
Webster, Winston counties

Bill Mabry
East Central Mississippi Contract Procurement
Center
Meridian Community College
910 Highway 19 N
Meridaian, MS 39307
601-482-7658
Fax: 601-482-5803
Email: eccpc@mscpc.com
www.mscpc.com
Serving Clarke, Covington, Jasper, Jones,
Kemper, Lauderdale, Leake, Neshoba,
Newton, Scott, Smith, Wayne counties

Richard L. Speights
South Mississippi Contract Procurement
1636 Popps Ferry Road, Suite 229
Biloxi, MS 39532
228-396-1288
Fax: 228-396-2520
Email: smcpc@mscpc.com
www.mscpc.com
Serving Amite, Forrest, George, Greene,
Hancock, Harrison, Jackson, Lamar, Marion,
Pearl River, Perry, Pike, Stone, Walthall,
Wilkinson counties

Missouri

Mark Hudson
Missouri Procurement Technical Assistance
Center
University of Missouri-Columbia
300 University Place
Columbia, MO 65211
573-882-3597
Fax: 573-884-4297
Email: hudsonm@missouri.edu
www.smallbusinesslearning.net/ptac/index.asp

Lauren Tucker
Missouri Procurement Technical Assistance
Center-St. Louis
100 North Tucker, Suite 530
St. Louis, MO 63101
314-621-7280
Fax: 314-621-9871
Email: tuckerlh@missouri.edu
www.smallbusinesslearning.net/ptac/index.asp

Donna Leonard
Missouri Procurement Technical Assistance
Center
University of Missouri-Kansas City
4747 Troost Building, Room 227
Kansas City, MO 64110
816-235-2891
Fax: 816-235-2947
Email: leonardd@umkc.edu
www.bloch.umkc.edu/egrc/MissouriPTAC/

Terri Bennett
Missouri Southern State College
3950 E. Newman Rd.
Joplin, MO 64801-1595
417-625-9538
Fax: 417-625-9782
Email: heartlandptac@mail.mssc.edu
www.mssc.edu/heartlandptac

Montana

Maureen Jewell
Big Sky Economic Development Authority
222 North 32nd Street
Billings, MT 59101-1931
406-256-6871
Fax: 406-256-6877
Email: jewell@bigskyeda.org
www.bigskyeda.org/PTAC

Karl J. Dehn
Montana PTAC
710 First Avenue North
P.O. Box 2568
Greta Falls, MT 59403-2568

406-454-1934
Fax: 406-454-2995
Email: karl@gfdevelopment.org
www.gfdevelopment.org/govtcont.htm

Nebraska

Michael Hall
Economic Business Development Center
PTA Omaha Business Technology Center
2505 North 24th Street, Suite 103
Omaha, NE 68182-0072
402-595-3511
Fax: 402-595-3832
Email: mikehallneptac@netscape.net

Joe Breault
Nebraska Business Development Center
Lincoln Chamber Building
1135 M Street, Suite 200
City Campus Mailboc 0224
Lincoln, NE 68588-0224
402-472-1177
Fax: 402-472-3363
Email: JBreaultNEPTAC@netscape.net
http://nbdc.unomaha.edu/consulting/growth/pt
ac.cfm

Mike Hall
Nebraska Business Development Center
Peter Kiewit Conference Center
1313 Farnum, Suite 230
Omaha, NE 68182
402-595-3511
Fax: 402-595-2385
Email: MikeHallNEPTAC@netscape.net
http://nbdc.unomaha.edu/consulting/growth/pt
ac.cfm

Nevada

Rick Horn
555 East Washington, Suite 5400
Las Vegas, NV 89101
702-486-2716
800-336-1600
Fax: 702-486-2701
Email: lvpop8@bizopp.state.nv.us
www.nvoutreachcenter.com

Kathy Dow
Procurement Outreach Program
108 E. Proctor
Carson City, NV 89701
775-687-1913
Fax: 775-687-4450
Email: kdow@bizopp.state.nv.us
www.nvoutreachcenter.com

New Hampshire

Joseph Flynn
State of New Hampshire
Office of Business and Industrial Development
P.O. Box 1856
172 Pembroke Rd.
Concord, NH 03302-1856
603-271-2591
Fax: 603-271-6784
Email: j-flynn@dred.state.nh.us
www.nheconomy.com/nheconomy/ptac/main/i
ndex.php

New Jersey

Shashee Joshi
Union County Economic Development Corp.
PTA Program
1085 Morris Ave.
Suite 531
Lib Hall Center
Union, NJ 07083
908-527-1166
Fax: 908-527-1207
Email: sjoshi@ucedc.com
www.ucedc.com/services/contracts.shtml

Dolcey Chaplin
Foundation at New Jersey Institute of
Technology (NJIT)
240 Martin Luther King Blvd.
Newark, NJ 07102
973-596-3105
Fax: 973-596-5806
Email: chaplin@admin.njit.edu
www.nyit.edu/old/DPTAC

Madeline Britman
New Jersey Small Business Development
Centers
Procurement Program
43 Bleeker Street
Newark, NJ 07102
973-353-5960
Fax: 973-353-1930
Email: britman@njsbdc.com
www.njsbdc.com/procurment

Jan D. Mirijanian
New Jersey Institute of Technology
Atlantic Community College
1535 Bacharach Boulevard, Room 211
Atlantic City, NJ 08401
609-343-4845
Fax: 609-343-4823
www.njit.edu/old/DPTAC/

New Jersey Institute of Technology
Camden Office
One Federal Street
Camden, NJ 08103
856-614-5486
Fax: 856-614-5498
www.njit.edu/old/DPTAC/

New Jersey Institute of Technology
Trenton Office
Mary G. Roebling Building
20 W. State Street
Trenton, NJ 08650
609-292-3861
www.njit.edu/old/DPTAC/

New Jersey Institute of Technology
Mt. Holly Office
60 High Street
Mt. Holly, NJ 08060
609-267-5618
www.njit.edu/old/DPTAC/

New Mexico

Michael Vinyard
State of New Mexico General Services
Department
Procurement Assistance Program
P.O. Drawer 26110
Santa Fe, NM 87502
505-827-0425
Fax: 505-827-0499
Email: mvinyard@state.nm.us
www.state.nm.us/spd/pap/index.html

New York

Dina Terry
South Bronx Overall Economic Development
Corporation
55 Bergen Avenue
Bronx, NY 10455
718-292-3113
Fax: 718-292-3115
Email: dterry@sobro.org
www.sobro.org

Joseph J. Williams
Cattaraugus County
Department of Economic Development
Plan and Tour
303 Court St.
Little Valley, NY 14755
716-938-9111, ext. 2331
Fax: 716-938-9431

Email: josewi@lv.co.cattaraugus.ny.us
www.co.cattaraugus.ny.us/economic-
development/gma/index.asp?did=6

Solomon Soskin
Long Island Development Corporation
PTA Program
45 Seamon Ave.
Bethage, NY 11714
516-433-5000
Fax: 516-433-5406
Email: gov-contracts@lidc.org
www.lidc.org/assist.htm

Gordon Richards
New York City Dept. of Business Services
Procurement Outreach Program
110 William St., 2nd Floor
New York, NY 10038
212-513-6472
Fax: 212-618-8899
Email: grichard@sbs.nyc.gov
www.nyc.gov/html/sbs/html/pop.html

Rockland Economic Development Corporation
Procurement
One Blue Hill Plaza, Suite 1110
Pearl River, NY 10965-1575
845-735-7040
Fax: 845-735-5736
Email: ptac@redc.org
www.redc.org/business/sell_to_gov/index_sell
_to_gov.html

Benjamin Hunt
Laguardia Community College
Urban Center for Economic Development
31-10 Thomson Ave., Room E-405
Long Island City, NY 11101
718-482-5315
Fax: 718-482-5176
Email: bhunt@lagcc.cuny.edu
www.lagcc.cuny.edu/ace/luced

Paulette Birch
Rochester Business Alliance
150 State Street
Rochester, NY 14614
585-327-5907
Email: pauletteb@RBAlliance.com
www.RochesterPTAC.com

North Carolina

Tom Elam
Small Business and Technology Development
Center
5 West Hargett Street, Suite 600
Raleigh, NC 27601-1348
919-715-7272
800-258-0862 (NC only)
Email: info@sbtdc.org
www.sbtdc.org/services/gov_procurement.asp

North Dakota

No PTAC awarded

Ohio

Bob Fenn
NE Ohio PTAC
Lake Erie College
391-W. Washington St.
Painesville, OH 44077
440-357-2294
Fax: 440-357-2296
Email: neoptac@lcedc.org
www.lcedc.org/neoptac.htm

Kelly Lawhorn
Lawrence Economic Development
Corporation
Procure Outreach Center
216 Collins Ave.
P.O. Box 488

South Point, OH 45680-0488
740-377-4550
800-408-1334
Fax: 740-377-2091
Email: klawhorn@zoominternet.net
www.lawrencecountyohio.org/5.htm

Eric Van Otteren
Ohio Department of Development
Procurement Technical Assistance Centers of
Ohio
77 South High Street, 28th Floor
P.O. Box 1001
Columbus, OH 43216-1001
614-466-5700
800-848-1300
Fax: 614-466-4172
Email: evanotteren@odod.state.oh.us
www.odod.state.oh.us/dmba/ptac.htm

Stephen J. Danyi
Mahoning Valley Economic Development
Corporation
4319 Belmont Ave.
Youngstown, OH 44505-1005
330-759-3668
Fax: 330-759-3686
Email: steve@mvedc.com
www.mvedc.com/development.htm

Keith Tarbett
Kent PTAC Satellite
Kent Regional Business Alliance
Kent State University
College of Business Room 300B
Kent, OH 44242
330-672-9448
Fax: 330-672-9338
Email: ktarbett@bsa3.kent.edu
http://business.kent.edu/KRBA/PTAC.asp

Sharon Williams
Appalachian PTAC
20 Circle Drive, The Ridge Ohio University
143 Technology and Enterprise Building
Athens, OH 45701
740-597-1868
Fax: 740-597-1399
Email: sharonw@voinovichcenter.edu
www.ohiou.edu/ptac/

Richard Archer
Bowling Green/Toledo PTAC
Bowling Green State University
140B Jerome Library
Bowling Green, OH 43403
419-372-9257
Fax: 419-372-7996
Email: rarcher@bgnet.bgsu.edu
www.bgsu.edu/colleges/library/ptac

Jeanatta Brown
Cincinnati PTAC TechSolve
1111 Edison Drive
Cincinnati, OH 45216
513-948-2083
Fax: 513-948-2083
Email: brown@techsolve.org
www.techsolve.org

Deborah Wallace-Flagg
Dayton PTAC
3155 Research Boulevard, Suite 106
Dayton, OH 45420
937-259-1321
Fax: 937-259-1303
Email:
dwallace@emtec.org;dwallaceflagg@who.rr.c
om
www.dayptac.org

Oklahoma
Scott Dean
Oklahoma Department of Vocational and

Technical Education
Oklahoma Bid Assistance Network
1500 W. Seventh Ave.
Stillwater, OK 74074-4364
405-743-5592
Fax: 405-743-6821
Email: sdean@careertec.org
www.okcareertech.org/business/oban/oban.ht
m

Roy Robert Gann, Jr.
Tribal Government Institute
421 E. Comanche, Suite B
Norman, OK 73071
405-329-5542
Fax: 405-329-5543
Email: tgi40019@worldnet.att.net

Terry Henneke
Autry Technology Center
1201 West Willow
Enid, OK 73703-2598
580-242-2750
Fax: 580-233-8262
Email: thenneke@autrytech.com
www.autrytech.com

David Hoffmeier
Gordon Cooper Technology Center
One John C. Bruton Blvd
Shawnee, OK 74804
405-273-7493 Ext 314
Fax: 405-273-6354
Email: davidh@gctech.org
www.gctech.org

Clayton Evans
High Plains Technology Center
3921 34th Street
Woodward, OK 73801-7000
580-571-6155
Fax: 580-571-6186
Email: cevans@hptc.net
www.hptc.net

John Hasler
Indian Capital Technology Centers
2403 N. 41st Street East
Muskogee, OK 74403-1799
918-687-6383 Ext. 253
Fax: 918-687-6624
Email: john@azalea.net
www.icavts.tec.ok.us/

Wendell Marley
Kiamichi Technology Centers
301 Kiamichi Dr
McAlester, OK 74501
918-426-1560
Fax: 918-426-1626
Email: wmarley@kavts.tec.ok.us
www.kiamichi-
mcalester.tec.ok.us/new_page_8.htm

Mitchell Slemp
Mid-America Technology Centers
POB H
Wayne, OK 73095-0210
405-449-3391
Fax: 405-449-3421
Email: mslemp@matech.org
www.matech.org/adult.htm

Bill Crain
Mid-Del Technology Centers
1621 Maple Drive
Midwest City, OK 73110-4825
405-739-1712
Fax: 405-739-1751
Email: wacrain@hotmail.com
www.mid-del.tec.ok.us/

Teresa Smith
Pioneer Technology Center

2101 N. Ash
Ponca City, OK 74601-1110
580-718-4261
Fax: 580-765-5101
Email: teresas@pioneertech.org
www.pioneertech.org

Dana Harwell
Red River Technology Centers
P.O. Box 1807
Duncan, OK 73534-1807
580-255-2903 Ext. 270
Fax: 580-255-0491
Email: dharwell@redriver.tec.ok.us
www.redriver.tec.ok.us

Dale Latham
Southwest Technology Center
711 W. Tamarack
Altus, OK 73522-8086
580-477-2250
Fax: 580-477-0138
Email: dlatham@swtc.org
www.swtc.org/BID.HTM

Judy Robbins
Francis Tuttle Technology Center
3500 NW 150th Street
Oklahoma City, OK 73134
405-717-4750
Fax: 405-752-0307
Email: bis@francistuttle.com
www.francistuttle.com/bis/training/gc/default.
asp

Pat Young
Tri County Technology Center
6101 SE Nowata Road
Bartlesville, OK 74006-6010
918-331-3311
Fax: 918-335-2197
Email: pyoung@tctc.org
www.tctc.org

Lynda Speller
MetroTech Economic Development Center
1700 Springlake Drive
Oklahoma City, OK 73111
405-605-4792
Email: lynda.speller@metrotech.org
www.metrotech.org

Oregon
Jan Hurt
The Organization for Economic Initiatives
Government Contract Assistance Program
1144 Gateway Loop, Suite 203
Springfield, OR 97477
541-736-1088
800-497-7551
Fax: 541-736-1090
Email: info@gcap.org
www.gcap.org

Pennsylvania
Daniel Shade
Southern Alleghenies Planning and
Development Commission
541 58th Street
Altoona, PA 16602
814-949-6528
Fax: 814-949-6505
Email: shade@sapdc.org
www.sapdc.org

Ron Moreau
Indiana University of Pennsylvania
650 South 13th Street
Robert Shaw Building, Room 10
Indiana, PA 15705-1087
724-357-7824
Fax: 724-357-3082
Email: rfmoreai@iup.edu
www.eberly.iup.edu/gcap

Deborah S. Wojcik
Mon-Valley Renaissance
CA University of Pennsylvania
250 University Ave.
California, PA 15419
724-938-5881
Fax: 724-938-4575
Email: wojcik@cup.edu
www.cup.edu

Dianne McCartney
NW Pennsylvania Regional Planning and
Development Commission
395 Seneca Street
Oil City, PA 16301
814-677-4800
Fax: 814-677-7663
Email: diannem@newcommission.org
www.nwcommission.org

Pete Chirillo
Johnstown Area Regional Industries
Defense PAC
111 Market St.
Johnstown, PA 15901
814-535-8675
Fax: 814-535-8677
www.jari.com

Chris Wilusz
Seda Council of Governments
201 Furnace Road
Lewisburg, PA 17837
570-524-4491
Fax: 570-524-9190
Email: cwilusz@seda-cog.org
www.seda-cog.org/seda_cog/site/default.asp

Clyde Stoltzfus
University of Pennsylvania-Wharton
SE-PA PTAP
3733 Spruce St.
Vance Hall, 4th Floor
Philadelphia, PA 19104-6374
215-898-1282
Fax: 215-573-2135
Email: clycles@wharton.upenn.edu
www.pasbdc.org/consulting

David Kern
Economic Development Council of Northeast
Pennsylvania
Local Development District
1151 Oak St.
Pittston, PA 18640
570-655-5581
Fax: 570-654-5137
Email: dkk@nepa-alliance.org
www.nepa-alliance.org/ptac.htm

Puerto Rico
Carmen Y. Rosario
Commonwealth of Puerto Rico
Economic Development Administration
P.O. Box 362350
San Juan, PR 00936-2350
787-753-6861
Fax: 787-751-6239
Email: prptac@hotmail.com

Rhode Island
Dorothy Reynolds
Rhode Island Development Corporation
Business Expansion Division
One W. Exchange St.
Providence, RI 02903
401-222-2601
Fax: 401-222-2102
Email: dreynolds@riedc.com
www.riedc.com/growth/procure/procurementfr
ame.html

South Carolina
University of South Carolina
Frank L. Roddey SBDC of South Carolina
1200 Woodruff Rd., Suite C-38
Greenville, SC 29607
864-297-1016
Fax: 864-329-0453
http://business.clemson.edu/sbdc/page7.htm

South Dakota
Kareen H. Dougherty
The University of South Dakota
414 Clark Street
Vermillion, SD 57069-2390
605-677-5287
Fax: 605-677-5238
Email: kdougher@usd.edu

Tennessee
Jim Slizewski
Center for Industrial Services
University of Tennessee
193C Polk Avenue
Nashville, TN 37210
615-532-8657
888-763-7439
Fax: 615-532-4937
Email: cjs@tennessee.edu
www.cis.utk.edu/PTAC

Texas
Edmond Esparza
Panhandle Regional Planning Commission
Economic Development Unit
P.O. Box 9257
Amarillo, TX 79105-9257
806-372-3381
Fax: 806-373-3268
Email: eesparza@prpc.cog.tx.us
www.prpc.cog.tx.us/programs/econ/econ_cont
ract.htm

Jim Hicks
University of Texas at Arlington
Automation and Robotics Research Institute
Cross Timbers Procurement Center
Box 19125
Arlington, TX 76019
817-272-5978
Fax: 817-272-5952
Email: jhicks@arri.uta.edu
http://arri.uta.edu/crosstimbers

Rosalie Manzano
University of Texas at Brownsville/ITSC
Center for Business and Economic
Development
1600 E. Elizabeth St.
Brownsville, TX 78520
956-548-8713
Fax: 956-548-8717
Email: vptac@utb1.utb.edu
www.utb.edu

Carey Joan White
University of Houston, TIPS
2302 Fannin, Suite 200
Houston, TX 77002
713-752-8444
Fax: 713-756-1515
Email: cwhite@uh.edu
http://SmBizSolutions.uh.edu

Otilo Castellano
Texas Technical University
VP for Research and Tech Transfer
2579 S. Loop 289, Suite 210
Lubbock, TX 79423
806-745-3973
Fax: 806-745-6207
Email: o.castellano@nwtsbdc.org
www.nwtsbdc.org/pac/pac.htm

Thomas E. Brewer, Jr.
Angelina College
Procurement Assistance Center
P.O. Box 1768
Lufkin, TX 75902-1768
936-639-1301
888-326-5223
Fax: 936-639-4299
Email: acpac@texucom.net
www.angelina.cc.tx.us/comserv/cs%20procur.
htm

Albert Vela
San Antonio Procurement Outreach Program
Economic Development Department
P.O. Box 839966
215 S. San Saba
San Antonio, TX 78283
210-207-3900
Fax: 210-207-3909
Email: albertv@sanantonio.gov
www.sanantonio.gov/edd/small_bus/contractin
g/ptac.asp

Don Bostic
El Paso Community College
Office of Workforce Development and
Lifelong Learning
P.O. Box 20500
El Paso, TX 79998
915-831-7722
Fax: 915-831-4420
Email: donb@epcc.edu
www.epcc.edu/admin/wfd/contract_opportunit
y_ctr.htm

Sean Smith
Del Mar College
Division of Business
101 Bladwin and Ayers
Corpus Christi, TX 78401
361-698-1023
Fax: 361-698-1024
Email: spsmith@delmar.edu
www.delmar.edu/sbdc/ptac.html

Utah
Ron Spindler
Utah Department of Community and
Economic Development
Utah Procurement Technical Assistance
Center (UPTAC)
324 South State St., Suite 500
Salt Lake City, UT 84111
801-538-8680
Fax: 801-538-8611
Email: uptac@utah.gov
http://dced.utah.gov/procure

Vermont
Greg Lawson
State of Vermont
Department of Economic Development
109 State St.
Montpelier, VT 05609
802-828-5237
Fax: 802-828-3258
Email: greg@thinkvermont.com
www.vermontbidsystem.com/

Virginia
James Regan
George Mason University
Mason Enterprise Center
4031 University Dr., Suite 200
Fairfax, VA 22030
703-277-7757
Fax: 703-352-8195
Email: ptap@gmu.edu
www.gmu.edu/gmu/PTAP

John Fedkenheuer
Crater Planning District Commission

Crater Procurement Assistance Center
1964 Wakefield St.
P.O. Box 1808
Petersburg, VA 23805
804-861-1666
Fax: 804-732-8972
Email: jfedkenheuer@cpd.state.va.us
www.craterpdc.state.va.us/PAC/pacmain.htm

Glenda D. Calver
Southwestern Virginia Community College
Economic Development Division
P.O. Box SVCC
Richlands, VA 24641
276-964-7334
Fax: 276-964-7575
Email: glenda.calver@sw.vccs.edu
www.sw.vccs.edu/ptac2

Linda Hutson Green
Virginia Center for Innovative Technology
530 Main Street, Suite 204
Danville, VA 24541
434-791-5376
Fax: 434-791-5378
Email: lgreen@cit.org
www.cit.org/ptac-04.asp

Washington

John Tamble
Economic Development Council of
Snohomish County
728 134th St., SW, Bldg. A, Suite 219
Everett, WA 98204
425-743-4567
Fax: 425-745-5563
Email: ptac@snoedc.org
www.snoedc.org/securing_government_contra
cts.jsp

Diane McLeod
Economic Development Association of Skagit
County
204 W. Montgomery
P.O. Box 40
Mount Vernon, WA 98273
360-336-6114
Fax: 360-336-6116
Email: diane@skagit.org
www.skagit.org/subcategorypages/procuremen
t.htm

Angela Brooks
Bellingham Whatcom Economic Development
Council
105 E. Holly Street
P.O. Box 2803
Bellingham, WA 98227
360-676-4255
Fax: 360-647-9413
Email: angela@bwedc.org
www.bwedc.org/ptac.html

Deb Wallace
Columbia River Economic Development
Council
1101 Broadway, Suite 120
Vancouver, WA 98660
360-567-1061
Fax: 360-694-9927
Email: dwallace@credc.org
www.credc.org/ptac.htm

Teresa Lemmons Tom Westerlund
Metropolitan Development Council
Economic Development Services
15 N Broadway, #B
Tacoma, WA 98403
253-591-7026
Fax: 253-572-5583
Email: ceo@mdc-tacoma.org
www.snoedc.org/securing_government_contra
cts.jsp

Johann Curtiss
WSU Tri-City Business LINKS
2710 University Drive
Richland, WA 99352
509-372-7142
Fax: 509-372-7512
Email: buslinks@tricity.wsu.edu
www2.tricity.wsu.edu/links/ptac.htm

West Virginia

Bridgette Venanzi
Regional Contracting Assistance Center, Inc.
1116 Smith St., Suite 202
Charleston, WV 25301
304-344-2546
Fax: 304-344-2574
Email: bvenanzi@rcacwv.com
www.rcacwv.com

Belinda Sheridan
Mid-Ohio Valley Regional Council
PTA Center
P.O. Box 5528
Parkersburg, WV 26105
304-428-6889
Fax: 304-428-6891
Email: ptac@access.mountain.net
www.wvptac.org

West Virginia Procurement Technical Center
#2 Rosemar Circle, Suite B
Parkersburg, WV 26101
304-428-6889
Fax: 304-428-6891
Email: Belinda@cssiwv.con
www.wvptac.org

Wisconsin

Denise Kornetzke
Madison Area Technical College
Business PAC
3591 Andersen St., Suite 100
Madison, WI 53704
608-243-4490
Fax: 608-243-4486
Email: bpac@matcmadison.edu
http://matcmadison.edu/bpac/home.htm

Ania Vilumsons
Wisconsin Procurement Institute, Inc.
756 N. Milwaukee St.
Milwaukee, WI 53202
414-270-3600
Fax: 414-270-3610
Email: info@wispro.com
www.wispro.com

Wyoming

Rudy Nesvik
University of Wyoming
Government Resources and Opportunities for
Business (GRO-BIZ)
1400 E. College Dr.
Cheyenne, WY 82007
307-637-5029
Fax: 307-632-6061
Email: nesvik@wyoming.com
www.gro-biz.com

How To Become a Consultant With The Government

If you are between jobs or just thinking about quitting the one you have and want something to tide you over until you get your next one, you should seriously think about freelancing for the Federal government.

The Interior Department hires ecologists and geologists. The Justice Department hires business consultants. The Department of Energy hires conservation consultants. Here's a sample listing of the kinds of projects freelance consultants do for the Federal government:

Types of Government Freelancing

Landscaping
Carpentry Work
Painting and Paper Hanging
Security Guards
Computer Services
Data Processing
Detective Services
Electrical Work
Plumbing
Accounting Services
Chaplain Services (Priest)
Management Consulting
Engineering Services
Information Retrieval
  Services
Real Estate Agents
Secretarial Services
Court Reporting
Legal Services
Business Consulting
Photography
Insurance Agents
Computer Programming
Research
Drafting
Interior Decorating
Library Services
Word Processing

Translation Services
Courier and Messenger Services
Cleaning Services
Food Service
Auditing Services
Advertising Services
Nursing Services
Housekeeping Services
Administrative Support
  Services
Education and Training
Medical Services
Social Services
Special Study and Analysis
Wildlife Management
Salvage Services
Travel Agent
Personnel Testing Services
Photography
Animal Care
Mathematics and Computer
  Science
Environmental Research
Historians
Recreation Research
Economic Studies
More, More, More...

Practically every major government agency hires freelance consultants to work on both small and large projects — which might be exactly what you need until you land a full time job down the road.

The feds hire all kinds of professionals to perform consulting work, from accountants and business specialists, to computer experts, social scientists, and security and surveillance consultants. The offices listed below, called Offices of Small and Disadvantaged Business Utilization, specialize in helping individuals and small businesses get involved in contracting with their agency.

Subcontracting

Not only do the feds themselves hire consultants, so do the large prime contractors who sell their products and services to the government. By law, any large company that receives contracts worth $500,000 or more from the Federal government must make an effort to subcontract some of that work to small businesses. So, for example, if a company gets a large computer consulting contract with the Defense Department, they have to make an effort to hire some freelance computer consultants to work on that contract. And that could be you.

How to Find Subcontracting Work

All of the federal procurement offices or Offices of Small and Disadvantaged Business Utilization (SADBU) (see list below) can provide you with information regarding subcontracting. Many of the departments' prime contracts require that the prime contractor maximize small business subcontracting opportunities. The SADBU offices can show you the way to get this work.

Each of the large federal agencies listed below, except the Department of Education, maintain directories of large contractors who are looking to do work with the feds in your area of expertise. And since the companies listed in these directories, for the most part, have just landed big government contracts, they might very well be looking to take on more full-time employees to help fulfill those contracts. A great lead on new job openings that probably won't be listed in the Sunday newspaper!

Offices of Small and Disadvantaged Business Utilization

Note: Offices designated as Offices of Small and Disadvantaged Business Utilization (OSDBUs) provide procurement assistance to small, minority, 8(a) and women-owned businesses. Their primary function is to ensure that small and disadvantaged businesses receive their fair share of U.S. Government contracts. "OSDBUs" are the contacts for their respective agencies and are excellent sources of information.

Agency for International Development
Ronald Reagan Building
1300 Pennsylvania Ave., NW
Washington, DC 20523-7800
202-712-1500
Fax: 202-216-3056
www.usaid.gov/procurement_bus_opp/osdbu/

Air Force Department
The Pentagon
SASSB 1060 Air Force
Washington, DC 20330-1060
703-696-1103
Fax: 703-696-1170
www.selltoairforce.org/sell2airforce/toc.htm

Army Corps of Engineers
441 G Street, NW
Washington, DC 20314-1000
202-761-0725
Fax: 202-761-4609
www.usace.army.mil/business.html

Army Department
106 Army Pentagon
Washington, DC 20310-0106
703-697-2868
Fax: 703-693-3898
www.sellingtoarmy.info

Corporation for National and Community Service
1201 New York Ave., NW
Washington, DC 20525
202-606-5000

Fax: 202-565-2777
www.nationalservice.org

Defense Contract Management Agency
6350 Walker Lane
Alexandria, VA 22310
703-428-0786
Fax: 703-428-3578
www.dcma.mil/DCMAHQ/dcma_sb/index.htm

Defense Information Systems Agency
701 S. Courthouse Road
D04 Room 1108B
Arlington, VA 22204-2199
703-607-6436
Fax: 703-607-4173
www.disa.mil/main/sadbu.html

Defense Logistics Agency
8725 John J. Kingman Road
DB Room 1127
Ft. Belvoir, VA 22060-6221
703-767-1662
Fax: 703-767-1670
www.dla.mil.db

Department of Agriculture
14th and Independence, SW
Room 1566, South Bldg.
Washington, DC 20250-9400
202-720-7117
Fax: 202-720-3001
www.usda.gov/osdbu

Department of Commerce
14th and Constitution Ave, NW
Room 6411
Washington, DC 20230
202-482-1472
Fax: 202-482-0501
www.osec.doc.gov/osdbu

Department of Defense
1177 North Kent Street, Suite 9100
Washington, DC 22209
703-588-8620
Fax: 703-588-7561
www.acq.osd.mil/sadbu

Department of Education
400 Maryland Ave., SW
Room 3120-ROB-3
Washington, DC 20202
202-708-9820
Fax: 202-401-6477
www.ed.gov/fund/contracts/about/booklet1.html

Department of Energy
1000 Independence Ave., SW
Room 5B148
Washington, DC 20585
202-586-7377
Fax: 202-586-5488
http://smallbusiness.doe.gov

Department of Health and Human Services
200 Independence Ave., SW, Room 517D
Washington, DC 20201
202-690-7300

Fax: 202-260-4872
www.hhs.gov/osdbu

Department of Homeland Security
Attn: OSDBU Room 3514
Washington, DC 20528
202-205-0050
www.dhs.gov

Department of Housing and Urban Development
451 7th St., SW, Room 3130
Washington, DC 20410
202-708-1428
Fax: 202-708-7642
www.hud.gov/offices/osdbu/index.cfm

Department of the Interior
1331 Pennsylvania Ave., NW
National Place Building, Room 1010
Washington, DC 20240
202-208-3493
Fax: 202-219-2131
www.doi.gov/osdbu

Department of Justice
Director, OSDBU
U.S. Department of Justice
Washington, DC 20530
202-616-0521
800-345-3712
Fax: 202-616-1717
www.usdoj.gov/jmd/osdbu/index.html

Department of Labor
200 Constitution Ave., NW, Room C-2318
Washington, DC 20210
202-693-6460
Fax: 202-693-6485
www.dol.gov/osbp/programs/osdbu.htm

Department of State
SA-6, Room L500
Washington, DC 20522-0602
703-875-6822
Fax: 703-875-6825
www.state.gov/m/a/sdbu

Department of Transportation
400 7th St., SW, Room 9414
Washington, DC 20590
202-366-1930
800-532-1169
Fax: 202-366-7538
http://osdbuweb.dot.gov

Department of the Treasury
1500 Pennsylvania Ave., NW
Room 1310 G, 400 West
Washington, DC 20220
202-622-0530
Fax: 202-622-4963
www.ustreas.gov/sba

Department of Veterans Affairs
810 Vermont Ave., NW
Washington, DC 20420
202-565-8124
800-949-8387
Fax: 202-565-8156
www.va.gov/osdbu

Environmental Protection Agency
1200 Pennsylvania Ave., NW
Mail Code 1230-A
Washington, DC 20460
202-564-4142

Fax: 202-401-1080
www.epa.gov/osdbu

Export-Import Bank of the U.S.
811 Vermont Ave., NW, Room 1023
Washington, DC 20571
202-565-3338
Fax: 202-565-3528
www.exim.gov/

Federal Communications Commission
Office of Communications Business
Opportunities
445 12th Street SW
Washington, DC 20554
202-418-0990
Fax: 202-418-0235
www.fcc.gov/ocbo

Federal Emergency Management Agency
Financial and Acquisition Management
500 C St., SW
Washington, DC 20472
202-646-3743
Fax: 202-646-3846
www.fema.gov/ofm

Federal Trade Commission
600 Pennsylvania Ave., NW, Room 600
Washington, DC 20580
202-326-2258
Fax: 202-326-3529
www.ftc.gov/ftc/oed/fmo/procure/procure.htm

General Services Administration
Office of Enterprise Development
1800 F Street, NW
Washington, DC 20405
202-501-1021
Fax: 202-208-5938
www.gsa.gov/

National Aeronautics and Space Administration
Headquarters, Code K
300 E St., SW
Washington, DC 20546
202-358-2088
Fax: 202-358-3261
www.hq.nasa.gov/office/codek

National Institute of Health
6100 Executive Blvd., Room 6D05
Bethesda, MD 20892-7540
301-496-9639
Fax: 301-480-2506
http://sbo.od.nih.gov/sbomain.htm

National Science Foundation
4201 Wilson Blvd., Room 5505
Arlington, VA 22230
703-292-7082
Fax: 703-292-9057
www.nsf.gov/bfa/dacs/contracts/start.htm

Navy Department
720 Kennon Street SE, Room 207
Washington Navy Yard, DC 20374-5015
202-685-6485
Fax: 202-685-6865
www.hq.navy.mil/sadbu

Nuclear Regulatory Commission
Small Business Program
Washington, DC 20555
301-415-7380

Fax: 301-415-5953
www.nrc.gov/who-we-are/small-business.html

Executive Office of the President
725 17th St., NW, Room 5001
Washington, DC 20503
202-395-7669
Fax: 202-395-3982

Office of Personnel Management
Contracting Division
1900 E St., NW
Washington, DC 20415
202-606-2180
Fax: 202-606-1464
www.opm.gov/procure/index.htm

Small Business Administration
Office of Government Contracting
409 Third St., SW, 8th Floor
Washington, DC 20416
202-619-1850
Fax: 202-693-7004
www.sba.gov/sdb

Smithsonian Institution
Small and Disadvantaged Business Utilization
Program
905 L'Enfant Plaza, SW
Washington, DC 20560-0921
202-287-3588
Fax: 202-287-3492
www.si.edu/oeema

Social Security Administration
Office of Acquisition and Grants
1710 Gwynn Oak Avenue
Baltimore, MD 21207-5279
410-965-9498 Office of Contracts and Grants
Fax: 410-965-9560
410-965-9478 Office of Information
Technology Acquisition
Fax: 410-966-9310
www.socialsecurity.gov/oag/acq/oagacq_small
business.htm

Tennessee Valley Authority
P.O. Box 292409
Nashville, TN 37229-2409
615-232-6169
www.tva.gov

Transportation Security Administration
7th and D Streets, SW
Room 3124-A
Washington, DC 20590
202-385-1842
www.tsa.dot.gov/public/display?theme=3

U.S. Postal Service
475 L'Enfant Plaza, SW, Room 3821
Washington, DC 20260-5616
202-268-6578
Fax: 202-268-6573
www.usps.gov/purchasing

U.S. Agency for International Development
Ronald Reagan Building
1300 Pennsylvania Avenue, NW
Room 7.8 E
Washington, DC 20523-7800
202-712-1500
Fax: 202-216-3056
www.usaid.gov/procurment_bus_opp/osdbu

Veteran Affairs

OSDBU Office
810 Vermont Avenue, NW
202-565-8124
800-949-8387
Fax: 202-565-8156
www.va.gov/OSDBU

Office of Federal Procurement Policy

725 17th St., NW, Room 9013

Washington, DC 20503
202-395-6811
Fax: 202-395-5105
www.whitehouse.gov/omb/procurement/index
.html

Railroad Retirement Board

844 N. Rush St.
Chicago, IL 60611
312-751-4987
Fax: 312-751-4923
www.rrb.gov

Minority Business Development Agency

Department of Commerce
Herbert C. Hoover Bldg.
14th & Constitution Ave., NW
Room 5093
Washington, DC 20230
202-482-1712
Fax: 202-482-5117
www.mbda.gov

State Procurement Assistance

Have you ever wondered where the government buys all of the products that it works with each day? You might be surprised to learn that they buy from small businesses just like yours that produce products such as:

- work clothing
- office supplies
- cleaning equipment
- miscellaneous vehicles
- medical supplies and equipment

Imagine what your bottom line could look like each year if you won just ONE lucrative government contract that would provide your business with a secure income! It might even buy you the freedom to pursue other clients that you wouldn't have the time or money to go after otherwise. If your business performs well and completes a government contract satisfactorily, chances are you'll have a shot at more and maybe even bigger contracts.

The offices listed below are starting places for finding out who in the state government will purchase your products or services.

State Procurement Offices

Alabama
Finance Department
Purchasing Division
100 N. Union, Suite 192
Montgomery, AL 36104
334-242-7250
Fax: 334-242-4419
www.purchasing.state.al.us

Alaska
State of Alaska
Department of Administration
Division of General Services
P.O. Box 110210
Juneau, AK 99811-0210
907-465-2250
Fax: 907-465-2189
www.state.ak.us/local/akpages/ADMIN/dgs/purchasing/home.htm

Arizona
State Procurement Office
100 North 15th Ave., Suite 104
Phoenix, AZ 85007
602-542-5511
Fax: 602-542-5508
http://sporas.ad.state.az.us

Arkansas
Office of State Procurement
P.O. Box 2940
Little Rock, AR 72203
501-324-9316
Fax: 501-324-9311
www.accessarkansas.org/dfa/purchasing/index.html

California
Procurement Division
Department of General Services
707 Third Street, 2nd Floor

West Sacramento, CA 95605
916-375-4400
800-559-5529
Fax: 916-375-4613
www.pd.dgs.ca.gov/default.htm

Colorado
State Purchasing Office
225 E. 16th Ave., Suite 802
Denver, CO 80203
303 866-6100
Fax: 303-894-7445
www.gssa.state.co.us

Connecticut
State of Connecticut
Department of Administrative Services
Bureau of Procurement/Purchasing
165 Capitol Ave., Room G-8a
Hartford, CT 06106
860-713-5086
Fax: 860-622-2915
www.das.state.ct.us/busopp.asp

Delaware
Division of Support Services
820 Silver Lake Blvd., Suite 100
Delaware City, DE 19904
302-739-5371
Fax: 302-739-3779
www.state.de.us/purchase

District of Columbia
Office of Contracts and Procurement
441 4th St. NW, Suite 700 South
Washington, DC 20001
202-727-0252
Fax: 202-724-5673
http://ocp.dc.gov/main.shtm

Florida
Department of Management Services
State Purchasing Office
4050 Esplanade Way
Tallahassee, FL 32301
850-488-8440
www.myflorida.com/myflorida/business/purchasing.html

Georgia
Administrative Services Department
State Purchasing Office
200 Piedmont Ave., Room 1308 West Tower
Atlanta, GA 30334-9010
404-656-3240
Fax: 404-657-8444
www.doas.state.ga.us

Hawaii
State Procurement Office
Dept. of Accounting and General Services
1151 Punch Bowl St.
Honolulu, HI 96813
808-586-0554
Fax: 808-586-0570
www.spo.hawaii.gov

Idaho
Division of Purchasing and Bids
Administration Department
5569 Kendall St.
Boise, ID 83720
208-327-7465
Fax: 208-327-7320
www2.state.id.us/adm/purchasing

Illinois
Department of Central Management Services
Procurement Services Division
401 South Spring

801 Stratton Bldg.
Springfield, IL 62706
217-782-2301
Fax: 217-782-5187
www.state.il.us/cms/purchase/default.htm

Indiana
Department of Administration
Procurement Division
402 W. Washington St., Room W-468
Indianapolis, IN 46204
317-232-3053
Fax: 317-232-7312
www.state.in.us/idoa/proc

Iowa
State of Iowa
Department of General Services
Operations/Purchasing Division
Hoover State Office Building
Des Moines, IA 50319
515-281-6355
Fax: 515-242-5974
www.state.ia.us/government/dgs/purchase/bus
iness.htm

Kansas
Division of Purchasing
900 Jackson, Room 102N
Landon State Office Bldg.
Topeka, KS 66612
785-296-2376
Fax: 785-296-7240
http://da.state.ks.us/purch

Kentucky
Purchases, Department of Finance
Room 367, Capital Annex Building
Frankfort, KY 40601
502-564-4510
877-973-HELP
Fax: 502-564-7209
www.thinkkentucky.com/kyedc/proassist.asp

Louisiana
State Purchasing Office
Division of Administration
1201 N. 3rd Street, Suite 2-160
P.O. Box 94095
Baton Rouge, LA 70804-9095
225-342-8010
Fax: 225-342-8688
www.doa.state.la.us/osp/osp.htm

Maine
Division of Purchases
Burton Cross Building, 4th Floor
9 State House Station
Augusta, ME 04333
207-624-7340
Fax: 207-287-6578
www.state.me.us/purchase

Maryland
Office of Procurement and Contracting
301 W. Preston St.
Mezzanine, Room M3
Baltimore, MD 21201
410-767-4628
Fax: 410-333-5482
www.dgs.state.md.us

Massachusetts
Purchasing Agent Division
One Ashburton Place
Room 1017
Boston, MA 02108
617-720-3197
Fax: 617-727-4527
www.comm-pass.com

Michigan
Office of Purchasing
Mason Bldg., 2nd Floor
P.O. Box 30026
Lansing, MI 48909
or 530 W. Ellegan, 48933
517-335-0230
Fax: 517-335-0046
www.michigan.gov/doingbusiness

Minnesota
State of Minnesota
Materials Management Division
112 Administration Bldg.
50 Sherburne Ave.
St. Paul, MN 55155
651-296-2600
Fax: 651-297-3996
www.mmd.admin.state.mn.us

Mississippi
Office of Purchasing and Travel
1401 Woolfolk Building, Suite A
501 North West St.
Jackson, MS 39201
601-359-3409
Fax: 601-359-3910
www.mmrs.state.ms.ujs/Purchasing/ms_pur.ht
m

Missouri
State of Missouri
Division of Purchasing and Materials
Management
P.O. Box 809
301 W. High St., Room 630
Jefferson City, MO 65102
573-751-2387
Fax: 573-751-2387
www.oa.state.mo.us/purch/purch.htm

Montana
Department of Administration
State Procurement Bureau
165 Mitchell Bldg.
125 North Roberts St.
Helena, MT 59620-0135
406-444-2575
Fax: 406-444-2529
www.discoveringmontana.com/doa/gsd/css/de
fault.asp

Nebraska
State Purchasing Bureau
DAS Material Division
301 Centennial Mall S., Mall Level
P.O. Box 94847
Lincoln, NE 68509
402-471-2401
Fax: 402-471-2089
www.das.state.ne.us/material/purchasing/purc
hasing.html

Nevada
Nevada State Purchasing Division
755 N. Roop Street
Metcalf Building, Room 211
Carson City, NV 89701
775-684-0170
Fax: 775-684-0188
http://purchasing.state.nv.us/

New Hampshire
State Purchasing Department
25 Capitol St.
State House Annex, Room 102
Concord, NH 03301
603-271-2201
Fax: 603-271-2700
http://admin.state.nh.us/purchasing/index.html

New Jersey
Division of Purchase and Property
P.O. Box 230
Trenton, NJ 08625
609-292-4700
Fax: 609-292-0490
www.state.nj.us/treasury/purchase

New Mexico
State Purchasing Division
1100 St. Frances Dr.
Joseph Montoya Bldg., Room 2016
Santa Fe, NM 87505
505-827-0472
Fax: 505-827-2484
www.state.nm.us/spd

New York
Procurement Services Group
Corning Tower, Room 3711
Empire State Plaza
Albany, NY 12242
518-474-6717
Fax: 518-474-2437
www.ogs.state.ny.us/purchase/default.asp

North Carolina
Department of Administration
Division of Purchase and Contract
116 W. Jones St.
Raleigh, NC 27603-8002
919-733-3581
Fax: 919-733-4782
www.doa.state.nc.us/PandC

North Dakota
Central Services Division
State Procurement Office
14th Floor, Capital Tower
600 E Blvd., Dept. 012
Bismarck, ND 58505-0310
701-328-2683
Fax: 701-328-1615
www.state.nd.us/csd.spo

Ohio
State Procurement
Rhodes Tower
30 Broad St., 40th Floor
Columbus, OH 43215-3414
614-466-8218
Fax: 614-466-7525
http://procure.ohio.gov/proc/index.asp

Oklahoma
Office of Public Affairs
Central Purchasing Division
Suite 116, Rogers Bldg.
2401 N. Lincoln
P.O. Box 528803
Oklahoma City, OK 73152
405-522-0955
Fax: 405-521-4475
www.dcs.state.ok.us/okdcs.nsf/htmlmedia/cent
ral_purchasing.html

Oregon
General Services
State Procurement Office
1225 Ferry St., SE
Salem, OR 97310
503-378-4642
Fax: 503-373-1626
http://das.state.or.us/purchasing

Pennsylvania
Bureau of Purchases
414 N. Office Bldg.
Harrisburg, PA 17125
717-787-5733

Fax: 717-783-6241
www.dgs.state.pa.us

Rhode Island

Department of Administration
Purchases Office
One Capital Hill
Providence, RI 02908-5855
401-222-2317
Fax: 401-222-6387
www.purchasing.ri.gov

South Carolina

Materials Management Office
General Service Budget and Control Board
1201 Main St., Suite 600
Columbia, SC 29201
803-737-0600
Fax: 803-737-0639
www.state.sc.us/mmo/

South Dakota

Offices of Purchasing and Printing
523 E. Capitol Ave.
Pierre, SD 57501
605-773-3405
Fax: 605-773-4840
www.state.sd.us/boa/opm

Tennessee

Department of General Services
Division of Purchasing
Third Floor, Tennessee Towers
312 8th Ave. North
Nashville, TN 37243-0557
615-741-1035
Fax: 615-741-0684
www.state.tn.us/generalserv/purchasing

Texas

Texas Building and Procurement Commission
P.O. Box 13047
Austin, TX 78711
512-463-3420
Fax: 512-463-8872
www.tbpc.state.tx.us/stpurch

Utah

Division of Purchasing and General Services
Department of Administrative Services
3150 State Office Bldg.
Capitol Hill
Salt Lake City, UT 84114
801-538-3026
Fax: 801-538-3882
www.purchasing.state.ut.us

Vermont

Purchasing and Contract Administration
1078 US Route 2-Middlesex
Drawer 33
Montpelier, VT 05633-7601
802-828-2211
Fax: 802-828-2222
www.bgs.state.vt.us/pca

Virginia

Department of General Services
Division of Purchasing and Supply
P.O. Box 1199
805 E. Broad St.
Richmond, VA 23218
804-786-3842
Fax: 804-371-8936
http://dps.dps.virginia.gov/dps

Washington

Office of State Procurement
Department of General Services
210 11th Ave. SW, Room 201
P.O. Box 41017
Olympia, WA 98501
360-902-7400
Fax: 360-586-2426
www.ga.wa.gov/purchase

West Virginia

Department of Administration
Purchasing Division
2019 Washington St. East
P.O. Box 50130
Charleston, WV 25305-0130
304-558-2538, ext. 213
Fax: 304-558-6026
www.state.wv.us/admin/purchase

Wisconsin

Division of State Agency Services
Bureau of Procurement
101 E. Wilson, 6th Floor
P.O. Box 7867
Madison, WI 53707-7867
608-266-7897
Fax: 608-267-0600
http://vendornet.state.wi.us/vendornet/default.asp

Wyoming

Department of Administration
General Services Division
801 West 20th Street
Cheyenne, WY 82002
307-777-7253
Fax: 307-777-5852
http://ai.state.wy.us/generalservices/procurement.asp

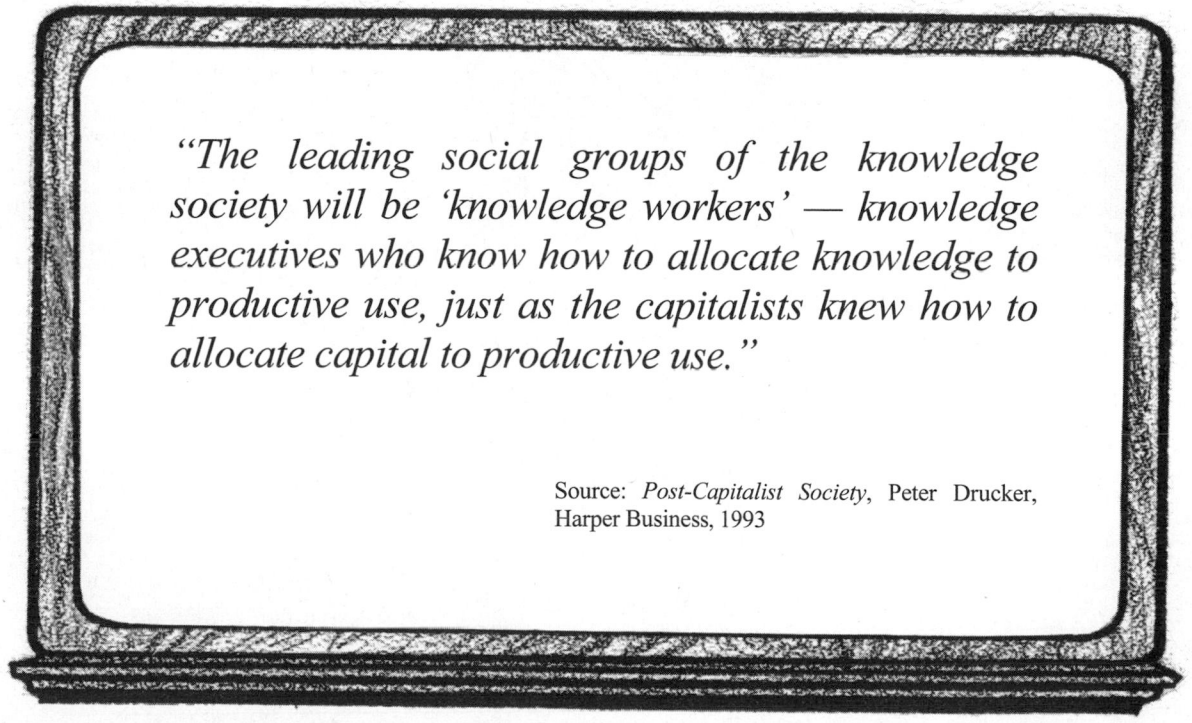

"The leading social groups of the knowledge society will be 'knowledge workers' — knowledge executives who know how to allocate knowledge to productive use, just as the capitalists knew how to allocate capital to productive use."

Source: *Post-Capitalist Society*, Peter Drucker, Harper Business, 1993

Venture Capital:
Finding A Rich Angel

With federal and state money getting harder to come by, and banks experiencing serious problems of their own that restrict their willingness to loan money, anyone interested in starting his own business or expanding an existing one may do well to look into venture capital. Venture capitalists are willing to invest in a new or growing business venture for a percentage of the equity. Below is a listing of some of the associations, government agencies, and businesses that have information available on venture capital.

In addition, there are Venture Capital Clubs throughout the country where entrepreneurs have a chance to present their ideas to potential investors and learn about the process of finding funds for ventures that might be long on innovative ideas for a business, but short on proven track records.

Associations

The National Association of Seed and Venture Funds
301 NW 63rd Street, Suite 500   405-843-6550
Oklahoma City, OK 73116   Fax: 405-842-3299
www.nasvf.org
The National Association of Seed and Venture Funds is an organization of venture capitalists who invest in businesses. The Association helps these organizations network with each other to learn how to better serve their clients. They also offer seminars, conferences, and training programs to better serve their members.

The National Venture Capital Association (NVCA)
1655 N. Fort Meyer Dr., Suite 850   703-524-2549
Arlington, VA 22209   Fax: 703-524-3940
www.nvca.org
The association works to improve the government's knowledge and understanding of the venture capital process. Staff members can answer questions about federal legislation and regulations, and provide statistical information on venture capital. NVCA members include venture capital organizations, financiers, and individuals interested in investing in new companies.

The association publishes a membership directory that includes a listing of their members with addresses, phone numbers, tax numbers and contacts. There are currently about 289 members. The directory is available for $99.

The Western Association of Venture Capitalists
3000 San Hill Rd.
Bldg. 1, Suite 190
Menlo Park, CA 94025   650-854-1322
www.wavc.net
Publishes a directory of its 140 members. The cost is $100.

National Association of Investment Companies
1300 Pennsylvania Ave., NW, Suite 700   202-289-4336
Washington, DC 20004   Fax: 202-289-4329
www.naicvc.com

It is composed of specialized Small Business Investment Companies (SSBICs). The SSBIC Directory lists about 120 companies across the country including names, addresses, and telephone numbers. It also describes each company's investment preferences and policies. The 23-page publication costs $25.98.

It also publishes *Perspective*, a monthly newsletter geared toward specialized small business investment companies. This newsletter includes articles about legislation and regulations affecting SSBICs. (Note: This association was formerly called the American Association of Minority Enterprise Small Business Investment Companies (AAMESBIC)).

Technology Capital Network at MIT
222 Third St., Suite 0350   617-253-2337
Cambridge, MA 02142   Fax: 617-258-7395
www.tcnmit.org
This nonprofit corporation tries to match entrepreneurs in need of capital with venture capital sources. Investors and entrepreneurs register with the network for up to 12 months for $300.

Venture Capital Clubs

There are more than 150 Venture Capital Clubs worldwide where inventors can present their ideas to potential investors. At a typical monthly meeting, several entrepreneurs may give short presentations of their ideas. It is a great way for entrepreneurs and potential investors to talk informally.

The International Venture Capital Institute (IVCI)
P.O. Box 1333
Stamford, CT 06904   203-323-3143
The IVCI publishes an annual directory of domestic and international venture groups (venture capital clubs). The cost of the *1995 IVCI Directory of Domestic and International Venture Groups*, which includes contact information for all of the clubs, is $19.95.

Below is a partial listing of clubs in the United States.

Venture Capital Clubs

Alabama
Birmingham Venture Club
Chamber of Commerce
505 20th St., N
Birmingham, AL 35203
205-241-8113
www.birminghamchamber.com

Mobile Venture Club
c/o Mobile Area Chamber of Commerce
451 Government St.
Mobile, AL 36652
251-433-6951
Fax: 251-431-8646

www.mobcham.org
Attn: Walter Underwood

Arkansas
Venture Capital Investors
400 W. Capital, Suite 1845
Little Rock, AR 72201
501-372-5900
Fax: 501-372-8181

California
Tech Coast Venture Network
195 S. C St., Suite 250
Tustin, CA 92780

714-505-6493
Fax: 714-669-9341
www.tcvn.org
Attn: Alonzo

Orange Coast Venture Group
P.O. Box 2011
Laguna Hills, CA 92654
949-859-3646
Fax: 949-859-1707
www.ocvg.net

San Diego Venture Group
P.O. Box 9357
San Diego, CA 92169

414

619-308-9423
Fax: 619-308-9433
www.sdvgroup.org

Colorado

Rockies Venture Club, Inc.
1805 S. Bellaire St., Suite 480
Denver, CO 80222
303-831-4174
Fax: 303-758-3885
www.rockiesventureclub.org

Connecticut

Connecticut Venture Group
1895B Post Rd.
Fairfield, CT 06430
203-256-5955
Fax: 203-256-9949
www.ct-venture.org

District of Columbia

Baltimore-Washington Venture Group
Michael Dingman Center for Entrepreneurship
College Park, MD 20742-7215
301-405-2144
Fax: 301-314-9152
www.rhsmith.umd.edu/dingman

Florida

Gold Coast Venture Capital Club
22783 S. State Rd. 7, #56
Boca Raton, FL 33428
561-488-4505
Fax: 561-451-4746
www.beaconmgmt.com/gcvcc

Hawaii

Hawaii Venture Group
University of Hawaii, OTTED
2800 Woodlawn Dr., Suite 280
Honolulu, HI 96822
805-533-1400
Fax: 808-524-2775
www.hawaiiventuregroup.com

Idaho

Rocky Mountain Venture Group
2300 N. Yellowstone, Suite E
Idaho Falls, ID 83402
208-526-9557
Fax: 208-526-0953
Attn: Dennis Cheney

Treasure Valley Venture Capital Forum
Idaho Small Business Development Center
Boise State University College of Business
1910 University Dr.
Boise, ID 83725
208-426-1640
Fax: 208-426-3877
www.idahosbdc.org

Iowa

Iowa City Development
ICAD Group
P.O. Box 2567
Iowa City, IA 52244
319-354-3939
Fax: 319-338-9958
Attn: Marty Kelley

Illinois

Madison Dearborn Partners
3 First National Plaza, Suite 3800
Chicago, IL 60602
312-895-1000
Fax: 312-895-1001
www.mdcp.com

Kentucky

Mountain Ventures Inc.

P.O. Box 1738
London, KY 40743
606-864-5175
Fax: 606-864-5194
www.khic.org

Maryland

Mid Atlantic Venture Association (MAVA)
2345 York Rd.
Timonium, MD 21093
410-560-5855
Fax: 410-561-2238
www.mava.org

Massachusetts

Venture Capital Fund of New England
160 Federal St., 23rd Floor
Boston, MA 02110
617-439-4646
Fax: 617-439-4652

Michigan

New Enterprise Forum
Ann Arbor Chamber of Commerce
425 S. Main St.
Ann Arbor, MI 48104
734-214-0104
www.nef.bizserve.com
Attn: Barb Sprague

Minnesota

St. Paul Venture Capital
10400 Viking Drive, Suite 550
Bloomington, MN 55444
952-995-7474
Fax: 952-995-7475
www.st.paulvc.com

Missouri

Missouri Innovation Center
5650 A S. Sinclair Rd.
Columbia, MO 65203
573-884-0492

Nebraska

Grand Island Industrial Foundation
309 W. 2nd St.
P.O. Box 1486
Grand Island, NE 68802-1486
308-382-9210
Fax: 308-382-1154
www.gichamber.com
Attn: Andrew G. Baird, II CED

New Jersey

Venture Association of New Jersey, Inc.
177 Madison Ave
CN 1982
Morristown, NJ 07962
973-267-4200
www.vanj.com
Attn: Amy or Jay Trien

New York

Long Island Venture Group
Scott Skodnek Business Development Center
Room 243-F, East Wing
145 Hofstra University
Hampstead, NY 11549
516-463-6326
Fax: 516-463-3907
www.livg.com

New York Venture Group
605 Madison Ave., Suite 300
New York, NY 10022-1901
212-832-7300
Fax: 212-832-7338
www.nybusiness.com
Attn: Burt Alimansky

Westchester Venture Capital Network
c/o Chamber of Commerce
235 Mamaroneck Ave.
White Plains, NY 10605
914-948-2110
Fax: 914-948-0122
www.westchesterny.org

Rochester Venture Capital Group
100 Corporate Woods, Suite 300
Rochester, NY 14623
www.rcvg.org

Ohio

Greater Columbus Chamber of Commerce
Columbus Investment Interest Group
37 N. High St.
Columbus, OH 43215
614-225-6938
Fax: 614-469-8250
www.columbus.org
Attn: Diane Essex

Ohio Venture Association, Inc.
1120 Chester Ave.
Cleveland, OH 44114
216-566-8884
Fax: 216-696-2582
Attn: Joan McCarthy
www.ohioventure.org

Oregon

Oregon Entrepreneur Forum
222 NW Fifth Ave., #308
Portland, OR 97209
503-222-2270
Fax: 503-241-0827
www.oef.org

Portland Venture Group
P.O. Box 2341
Lake Oswego, OR 97035
503-697-5907
Fax: 503-697-5907
Attn: Glen Smith

Pennsylvania

Enterprise Venture Capital Corporation of
Pennsylvania
111 Market St.
Johnstown, PA 15901
814-535-7597
Fax: 814-535-8677
www.jari.com

South Dakota

Dakota Ventures Inc.
P.O. Box 8194
Rapid City, SD 57709
605-348-8441
Fax: 605-348-8452
Attn: Don Frankenfeld

Texas

Capital Southwest Venture Corporation
12900 Preston Rd., Suite 700
Dallas, TX 75230
972-233-8242
Fax: 972-233-7362
www.capitalsouthwest.com

Utah

Utah Ventures
2755 E. Cottonwood Pkwy., Suite 520
Salt Lake City, UT 84121
801-365-0262
Fax: 801-365-0233
www.utahventures.com

Vermont

Vermont Venture Network
P.O. Box 5839

Burlington, VT 05402
802-658-7830
Fax: 802-658-0978
www.b2law.net/vvn.html

Virginia
Richmond Venture Capital Club
c/o 4900 Augusta Ave., Suite 103
Richmond, VA 23230
804-897-7411
www.ventureclub.com

Washington
Northwest Venture Group
P.O. Box 21693
Seattle, WA 98111-3693
425-746-1973

West Virginia
Enterprise Venture Capital Company
P.O. Box 460
Summerville, WV 26651

304-872-3000
Fax: 304-872-3040
Attn: William Bright

Wisconsin
Wisconsin Innovation Network
P.O. Box 510103
Milwaukee, WI 53203
414-224-7070

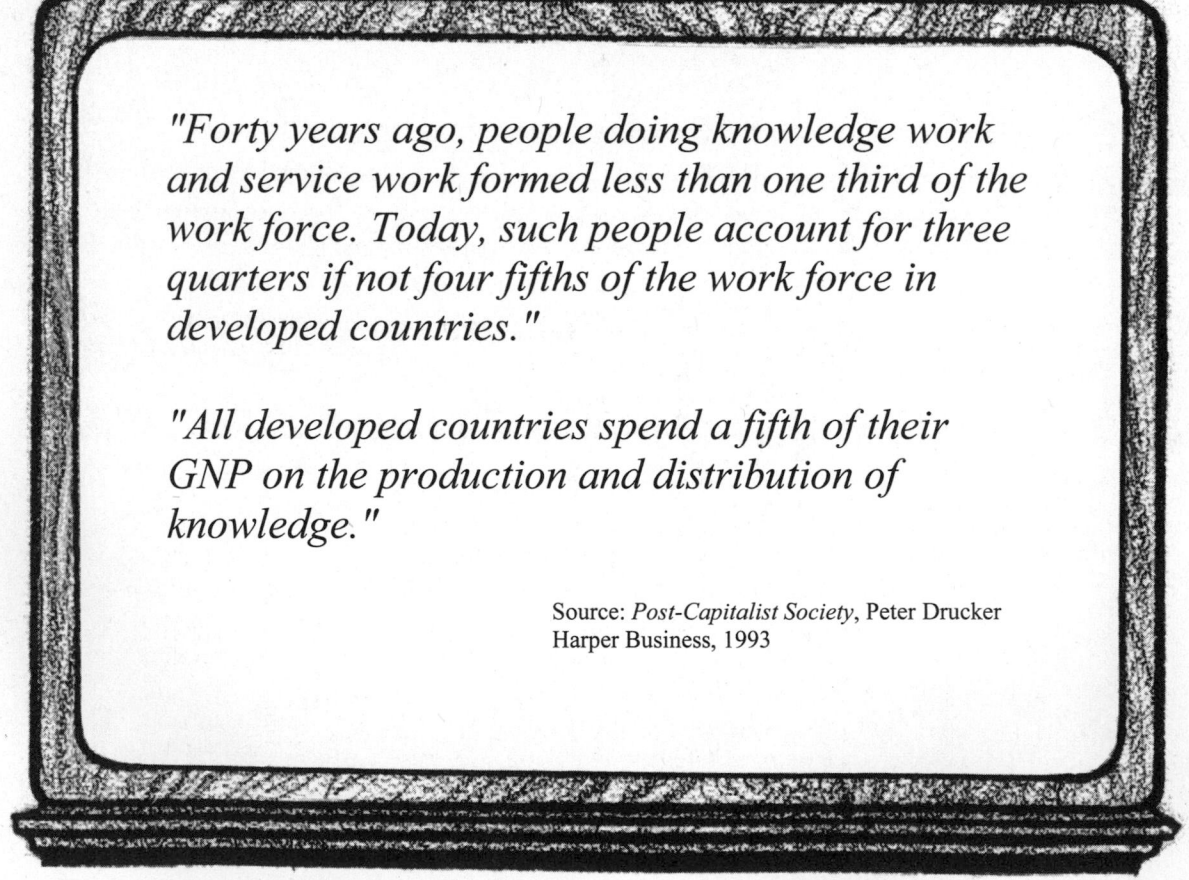

"Forty years ago, people doing knowledge work and service work formed less than one third of the work force. Today, such people account for three quarters if not four fifths of the work force in developed countries."

"All developed countries spend a fifth of their GNP on the production and distribution of knowledge."

Source: *Post-Capitalist Society*, Peter Drucker
Harper Business, 1993

Uncle Sam's Venture Capital

What Do Federal Express, Apple Computer, Staples and A Porno Shop on 42nd Street All Have In Common? They All Used Government Venture Money To Get Started

A few years ago I read that the government provided money to a porno shop in New York City through a program call Small Business Investment Companies (SBIC). Since 1960 these organizations have provided venture capital to over 75,000 businesses, so it's easy to see that one of those businesses might be a porno shop. Porno is a legitimate businesses in many areas of the country.

SBICs are licensed by the U.S. Small Business Administration but are privately owned and operate on a for profit basis. Their license allows companies to pool their money with borrowed money from the government in order to provide financing to small businesses in the form of equity securities or long-term debt. These government subsidized investment companies have helped Compaq, Apple, Federal Express and Staples make it to the big time. They have also helped smaller companies achieve success. They've financed Spencer and Vickie Jacobs' hot tub business in Columbus, Ohio, as well as taxi drivers in New York City who needed money to pay for the medallions which allows them to operate their own cabs.

Uncle Sam's Venture Capital Boom

In 1994, new government regulations were imposed that make it easier to become an SBIC. The budget for this program was also greatly expanded. As a result of this change, there will now be over $6 billion worth of financing available to entrepreneurs over the next several years. Now, that's not small change, even to a hotshot entrepreneur. With these new regulations and budget in place, the government expects that there will soon be 200 additional SBICs waiting to serve American entrepreneurs.

Who Gets The Money?

Basically you have to be a small business to apply for this money, and the government's definition includes companies that have less than $18 million in net worth and less than $6 million in profits. Wow, that's some small business! They seem particularly interested in businesses that offer a new product or service that has a strong growth potential. There is special consideration given to minorities and Vietnam Veterans applying for this money.

You do have to be armed with a business plan which should include the following:
1) Identify Your Company
2) Identify Your Product Or Service
3) Describe Your Product Facilities And Property
4) Detail Your Marketing Plan
5) Describe Your Competition
6) Describe Your Management Team
7) Provide A Financial Statement

Where to Apply

You can apply to more than one SBIC at the same time. Each acts as an independent company and they can provide money to both local or out-of-state businesses. At the end of this section is a listing of SBA licensed Small Business Investment Companies. However, this list is growing every day so it would be wise to contact the following office to obtain a current list: Associate Administrator for Investment, U.S. Small Business Administration, Washington, DC 20416; 202-205-6510; {www.sba.gov/inv}.

States Have Venture Money, Too

It's not enough to only look at federal venture capital programs, because some state governments also have venture capital programs. More and more states continue to start new programs every month. Some states, like Maryland, see the value in the new rule changes for becoming an SBIC, and are beginning to apply to become a licensed participant of the Small Business Administration's program. Here is what is available from state governments at the time this book went to press. Be sure to check with your state to see what's new:

1) Arkansas - Seed Capital Investment Program
2) Connecticut - Risk Capital
    - Product Design Financing
    - Seed Venture Fund
3) Illinois - Technology Investment Program
    - Illinois Venture Capital Fund
4) Iowa - Venture Capital Resources Fund
5) Kansas - Venture Capital and Seed Capital
    - Seed Capital Fund
    - Ad Astra Fund
    - Ad Astra Fund II
6) Louisiana - Venture Capital Incentive Program
7) Massachusetts - Venture Capital Program
8) Michigan - Enterprise Development Fund
    - Onset Seed Fund
    - Diamond Venture Associates
    - Semery Seed Capital Fund
    - Michigan Venture Capital Fund
9) Montana - Venture, Equity & Risk Capital
10) New Mexico - Venture Capital Investment Program
11) New York - Corporation for Innovation Development
12) North Carolina - North Carolina First Flight Inc.
13) North Carolina - Seed and Incubator Capital
14) Pennsylvania - Seed Venture Capital
15) South Carolina - Venture Capital Funding Program
16) Tennessee - Venture Capital

Contact your state office of economic development in your state capital for further information on venture capital available in your state (also see the chapter entitled "State Money and Help For Your Business").

Small Business Investment Companies

Alabama

FJC Growth Capital Corporation
William B. Noojin, Manager
165 West Park Loop
P.O. Box 1290
Huntsville, AL 35807
256-922-2918
Fax: 256-922-2909
http://www.fjcgrowth.com/index.html

Harbinger Mezzanine Partners, L.P.
John Harrison, Contact
One Riverchase Parkway South
Birmingham, AL 35244
615-301-6400
Fax: 615-301-6401
Email: nhartin@harbert.net

Hickory Venture Capital Corp.
J. Thomas Noojin, President
301 Washington St., Suite 100
Huntsville, AL 35801
256-539-1931
Fax: 256-539-5130
www.hvcc.com

TD Javelin Capital Fund II, L.P.
Lyle Hohnke, Manager
2850 Cahaba Road, Suite 240
Birmingham, AL 35223
203-629-8700
Fax: 203-629-9293
www.tullisdickerson.com

Arkansas

Diamond State Ventures, L.P.
Joe T. Hays, Contact
200 South Commerce Street, Suite 400
Little Rock, AR 72201-1728
501-374-9247
Fax: 501-374-9425
www.arcapital.com

Small Business Investment Capital, Inc.
Jerry W. Davis, President
12103 Interstate 30
P.O. Box 3627
Little Rock, AR 72203
501-455-6599
Fax: 501-455-6556
Email: jmills@afslr.com

Grayhawk Venture Fund I, L.P.
Sherman Chu, Contact
5050 North 40th Street, Suite 310
Phoenix, AZ 85018
602-956-8700
Fax: 602-956-8080
www.gvp.us

Magnet Capital, L.P.
Gregory Mischel/Michael Shields, Contact
3550 North Central Ave., Suite 1400
Phoenix, AZ 85012
602-222-4801
Fax: 602-222-4807
www.magnetcapital.com

California

AltoTech II, L.P.
Walter Lee, Contact
707 Menlo Avenue, Suite 120
Menlo Park, CA 94025
650-330-0881
Fax: 650-330-0885
www.altotechventures.com

American River Ventures, L.P.
Corley Phillips, Contact

2270 Douglas Blvd., Suite 212
Roseville, CA 95661
916-780-2828
Fax: 916-780-5443
www.arventures.com

Aspen Ventures III, L.P.
Alex Cilento, Thaddeus Whalen, Contacts
1000 Fremont Avenue, Suite 200
Los Altos, CA 94024
650-917-5670
Fax: 650-917-5677
www.AspenVentures.com

AVI Capital, L.P.
P. Wolken, B. Weinman & B. Grossi, Mgrs.
One First Street, Suite 12
Los Altos, CA 94022
650-949-9862
Fax: 650-949-8510
www.avicapital.com

Bank of America Ventures
Hayley Hoad, Manager, Administration
950 Tower Lane, Suite 700
Foster City, CA 94404
650-378-6000
Fax: 650-378-6040
www.bankofamerica.com

Bay Partners L.S. Fund, L.P.
John Freidenrich, Marcella Yano
10600 N. De Anza Blvd., Suite 100
Cupertino, CA 95014
408-725-2444
Fax: 408-446-4502
www.baypartners.com

Bentley Capital (SSBIC)
John Hung, President
592 Vallejo Street, Suite #2
San Francisco, CA 94133
415-362-2868
Fax: 415-398-8209
Email: bc8081@aol.com

Canaan SBIC, L.P.
Eric Young, Manager
2884 Sand Hill Road
Menlo Park, CA 94025
650-854-8092
Fax: 650-854-8127
www.canaan.com

Celerity Partners SBIC, L.P.
Clifford A. Lyon, Contact
11111 Santa Monica Blvd., Suite 1127
Los Angeles, CA 90025
310-268-1710
Fax: 310-268-1712
www.celeritypartners.com

Charterway Investment Corporation (SSBIC)
Edmund C. Lau, Chairman
9660 Flair Dr., Suite 328
El Monte, CA 91731
626-279-1189
Fax: 626-279-9062
Email: toysanaba@aol.com

Cardinal Venture Capital, SBIC, L.P.
Christopher J. Hadsell, Contact
1010 El Camino Real, Suite 250
Menlo Park, CA 94025
650-614-4860
Fax: 650-614-4865
www.cardinalvc.com

Draper Associates, a California LP
Timothy C. Draper, President

400 Seaport Court, Suite 250
Redwood City, CA 94063
650-599-9000
Fax: 650-599-9726
www.dfj.com

Draper-Richards L.P.
William Draper III, President
50 California Street, Suite 2925
San Francisco, CA 94111
415-616-4050
Fax: 415-616-4060
www.draperintl.com

East Gate Private Equity Fund III, L.P.
Ken Choi, Contact
514 High Street, Suite #5
Palo Alto, CA 94301
650-325-5077
Fax: 650-325-5072
www.eg-group.com

Far East Capital Corp.
Eduardo Ho, Manager
350 S. Grand Ave., Suite 4100
Los Angeles, CA 90071
213-687-1200
Fax: 213-687-8511
www.fareastnationalbank.com

Fulcrum Venture Capital Corporation (SSBIC)
Brian Argrett, President
300 Corporate Pointe, Suite 380
Culver City, CA 90230
310-645-1271
Fax: 310-645-1272
www.fulcrumventures.com

Geraro Klauer Mattison (GKM) SBIC, L.P.
Jonathan R. Bloch, Contact
11150 Santa Monica Blvd., Suite 800
Los Angeles, CA 90025
310-268-2600
Fax: 310-268-0870
www.gkm.com

Hall, Morris & Drufva II, L.P.
Ronald J. Hall, Managing Director
26161 La Paz Road, Suite E
Mission Viejo, CA 92691
714-707-5096
Fax: 714-707-5121

Hamilton Apex Technology Ventures, L.P.
Richard Crosby, Contact
12526 High Bluff Drive, Suite 260
San Diego, CA 92130
858-314-2350
Fax: 858-314-2355
www.hamiltonventures.com

Housatonic Equity Investors SBIC, L.P.
Barry Reynolds, Will Thorndike
44 Montgomery Street, Suite 4010
San Francisco, CA 94104
415-955-9020
Fax: 415-955-9053
www.housatonicpartners.com

Huntington Capital, L.P.
Morgan Miller and Barry Wilson, Contacts
11988 El Camino Real, Suite 160
San Diego, CA 92130
858-259-7654
Fax: 858-259-0074
www.huntingtoncapital.com

Inglewood Ventures, L.P.
Dr. M. Blake Ingle, Daniel Wood
12526 High Bluff Drive, Suite 300

San Diego, CA 92130
858-792-3579
Fax: 858-792-3417
www.inglewoodventures.com

J.P. Morgan Partners (SBIC), LLC
101 California Street, 27th Floor
San Francisco, CA 94111
415-393-1283
Fax: 415-393-1205
www.jpmorgan.com

Kline Hawkes California SBIC, L.P.
Frank R. Kline, Manager
11726 San Vicente Blvd., Suite 300
Los Angeles, CA 90049
310-442-4700
Fax: 310-442-4707
www.klinehawkes.com

LaiLai Capital Corp. (SSBIC)
Danny Ku, President
18249-2 Valley Boulevard
City of Industry, CA 91744
626-333-5420
Fax: 626-934-9699
Email: lailaicapital@aol.com

Magna Pacific Investments (SSBIC)
Howard Wong
330 North Brand Boulevard, Suite 670
Glendale, CA 91203
818-547-0809
Fax: 818-547-9303
Email: Magnapacific@cs.com

Marwit Capital Company, L.P.
Matthew Witte, President
180 Newport Center Drive, Suite 200
Newport Beach, CA 92660
949-640-6234
Fax: 949-720-8077
www.marwit.com

Milepost Ventures, L.P.
Christine Cordaro, Contact
One Embarcadero Center, Suite 3250
San Francisco, CA 94104
415-391-8950
Fax: 415-391-8937
www.milepostventures.com

Montreux Equity Partners II SBIC, L.P.
Daniel K. Turner III, Contact
2500 Sand Hill Road, Suite 215
Menlo Park, CA 94025-7073
650-234-1200
Fax: 650-234-1250
www.montreuxequity.com

New Vista Capital Fund, L.P.
Roger Barry & Frank Greene, Managers
540 Cowper Street, Suite 200
Palo Alto, CA 94301
650-566-2200
Fax: 650-329-6889
www.nvcap.com

Novus Ventures II, L.P.
Daniel D. Tompkins, Managing GP
20111 Stevens Creek Blvd.
Suite 130
Cupertino, CA 95014
408-252-3900
Fax: 408-252-1713
www.novusventures.com

Opportunity Capital Corporation (SSBIC)
J. Peter Thompson, President
2201 Walnut Avenue, Suite 210
Fremont, CA 94538
510-795-7000
Fax: 510-494-5439
www.ocpcapital.com

Outlook Ventures III, L.P.
Carl Nichols, Contact
135 Main Street, Suite 1350
San Francisco, CA 94105
415-547-0000
Fax: 415-547-0010
www.iminds.com

Pacific Mezzanine Fund, L.P.
Nathan W. Bell, General Partner
2200 Powell St., Suite 1250
Emeryville, CA 94608
510-595-9800
Fax: 510-595-9801
www.pacmezz.com

Peninsula Equity Partners SBIC, L.P.
Gregory C. Ennis, Contact
3000 Sand Hill Road
Building 3, Suite 125
Menlo Park, CA 94025
650-854-0314
Fax: 650-854-0670
www.peninsulaequity.com

Pinecreek Capital Partners, L.P.
Randall F. Zurbach, President
24 Corporate Plaza, Suite 180
Newport Beach, CA 92660
949-720-4620
Fax: 949-720-4629
www.pinecreekcap.com

Positive Enterprises, Inc. (SSBIC)
Kwok Szeto, President
1489 Webster Street, Suite 228
San Francisco, CA 94115
415-885-6600
Fax: 415-928-6363
www.pei-sba.com

Red Rock Ventures II, L.P.
Robert Todd, Jr., Curtis K. Meyers
180 Lytton Avenue
Palo Alto, CA 94301
650-325-3111
Fax: 650-853-7044
www.redrockventures.com

Rocket Ventures II SBIC, L.P.
David Adams
3000 Sand Hill Road, Building 1, Suite 170
Menlo Park, CA 94025
650-561-9100
Fax: 650-561-9183
www.rocketventures.com

Seacoast Capital Partners, L.P.
Jeff Holland
425 Market Street, Suite 2200
San Francisco, CA 94105
415-956-1400
Fax: 415-956-1459
www.seacoastcapital.com

Selby Venture Partners II, L.P.
Robert Marshall, Contact
3500 Alameda De Las Pulgas, 2nd Floor
Menlo Park, CA 94025
650-854-7399
Fax: 650-854-7039
www.selbyventures.com

Shepherd Ventures II, L.P.
George C. Kenney, Contact
12250 El Camino Real, Suite 116
San Diego, CA 92130
858-509-4744
Fax: 858-509-3662
www.shepherdventures.com

Smart Technology Ventures III SBIC, L.P.
Joseph Marks, Contact
1801 Century Park West, 5th Floor

Los Angeles, CA 90067
310-203-3800
Fax: 310-203-3801
www.smarttechnologyventures.com

Sorrento Growth Partners I, L.P.
Robert Jaffe, Manager
4370 La Jolla Village Drive, Suite 1040
San Diego, CA 92122
858-452-3100
Fax: 858-452-7607
www.sorrentoventures.com

St. Cloud Capital Partners, L.P.
Terrence Ng, Contact
10866 Wilshire Blvd., Suite 1450
Los Angeles, CA 90024
310-475-2700
Fax: 310-475-0550
www.stcloudcapital.com

Stone Canyon Venture Partners, L.P.
Kenneth R. Kilroy, Contact
2121 Avenue of the Stars
Suite 2800
Los Angeles, CA 90067
310-551-2210
Fax: 310-551-0591
www.stonecanyonvp.com

Tangent Growth Fund, L.P.
Alexander H. Schilling, Manager
180 Geary St., Suite 500
San Francisco, CA 94108
415-392-9228
Fax: 415-392-1928
www.tangentfund.com

TeleSoft Partners IA L.P.
Arjun Gupta, Manager
1450 Fashion Island Boulevard, Suite 610
San Mateo, CA 94404
650-358-2500
Fax: 650-358-2501
www.telesoftvc.com

UnionBanCal Venture Corporation
Robert S. Clarke, President
445 South Figueroa Street, Suite 2100
Los Angeles, CA 90071
213-236-6566
Fax: 213-236-7619
www.uboc.com

Utah Ventures II L.P.
Allan Wolfe
720 31st Street
Manhattan Beach, CA 90266
310-546-2777
Fax: 310-546-6757
www.utahventures.com

Walden-SBIC, L.P.
Arthur S. Berliner, Manager
750 Battery Street, 7th Floor
San Francisco, CA 94111
415-391-7225
Fax: 415-391-7262
www.waldenvc.com

Wells Fargo SBIC, Inc.
Steven W. Burge, Managing Director
333 South Grand Avenue, Suite 1150
Los Angeles, CA 90071
213-253-3671
Fax: 213-621-2623
www.wellsfargo.com

Wells Fargo SBIC, Inc.
Richard R. Green, Managing Director
One Montgomery Street
West Tower #2530
San Francisco, CA 94104
415-222-1800

Fax: 415-765-1569
www.wellsfargo.com

Western General Capital Corporation (SSBIC)
Alan Thian, President
13701 Riverside Drive, Suite 610
Sherman Oaks, CA 91423
818-907-8272
Fax: 818-905-9220

Woodside Fund III SBIC, L.P.
Vincent Occhipinti & Frank Mendicino
350 Marine Parkway, Suite 300
Redwood Shores, CA 94065
650-610-8050
Fax: 650610-8051
www.woodsidefund.com

Colorado

CapEx L.P.
Jeffrey Ross, Manager
518 Seventeenth Street, 17th Floor
Denver, CO 80202
303-869-4700
Fax: 303-869-4602
www.capexsbic.com

Cornerstone Ventures, L.P.
John R. Ord, Contact
11001 West 120th Avenue, Suite 310
Broomfield, CO 80021
303-410-2500
Fax: 303-466-9316
www.cornerstoneventures.com

Hanifen Imhoff Mezzanine Fund, L.P.
Edward C. Brown, Manager
1125 17th Street, Suite 2260
Denver, CO 80202
303-297-1701
Fax: 303-297-1702
www.rockycapital.com

NewWest Mezzanine Fund, L.P.
David Henry, Managing General Partner
1700 Lincoln Street, Suite 2000
Denver, CO 80203
303-764-9677
Fax: 303-832-6154
www.mezzcap.com

Rocky Mountain Mezzanine Fund II, L.P.
Edward Brown & Paul Lyons, Mgrs.
1125 17th Street, Suite 2260
Denver, CO 80202
303-297-1701
Fax: 303-297-1702
www.rockycapital.com

The Roser Partnership III, SBIC, L.P.
James Roser and Christopher Roser, Mgrs.
1105 Spruce Street
Boulder, CO 80302
303-443-6436
Fax: 303-443-1885
www.roserventures.com

Vista Ventures Advantage, L.P.
Catharine M. Merigold, Contact
103 West Mountain Avenue
Fort Collins, CO 80524
970-482-3037
Fax: 970-482-3840
www.vistavc.com

Wolf Venture Fund III, L.P.
David Wolf, Contacts
1600 Stout Street, Suite 1510
Denver, CO 80202
303-321-4800
Fax: 303-321-4848
www.wolfventures.com

Connecticut

AB SBIC, Inc.
Adam J. Bozzuto, President
275 Schoolhouse Road
Cheshire, CT 06410
203-272-3511
Fax: 203-250-2954
www.bozzutos.com

Bon Secours Community Investment Fund, L.P.
Jennifer Plourde, CFO
c/o Smith Whiley & Company
242 Trumbull Street, 8th Floor
Hartford, CT 06103
860-548-2513
Fax: 860-548-2518
www.smithwhiley.com

Brookside Pecks Capital Partners, L.P.
80 Field Point Road, Third Floor
Greenwich, CT 06830
203-618-0202
Fax: 203-618-0984

Canaan SBIC, L.P.
Gregory Kopchinsky, Manager
105 Rowayton Avenue
Rowayton, CT 06853
203-855-0400
Fax: 203-854-9117
www.canaan.com

Cygnet Capital Partners L.P. SBIC
Owen S. Crihfield, Contact
281 Tresser Boulevard, 4th Floor
Stamford, CT 06901
203-602-0011
Fax: 203-602-2206
www.hrco.com

FieldPoint Partners SBIC, L.P.
Nestor J.Olivier
80 Field Point Road
Greenwich, CT 06830
203-869-5444
Fax: 203-869-6345
www.dublindpartners.com

First New England Capital 2, L.P.
Richard Klaffky, Manager
100 Pearl Street
Hartford, CT 06103
860-293-3333
Fax: 860-293-3338
www.firstnewenglandcapital.com

GreenLeaf Capital, L.P.
Jon Atkeson, Attorney
177 Broad Street
Stamford, CT 06901
203-973-1400
Fax: 203-973-1422
www.whitney.com

Imprimis SB, LP
Charles Davidson, Joseph Jacobs, Mgrs.
411 West Putnam Avenue
Greenwich, CT 06830
203-862-7000
Fax: 203-862-7374
www.wexford.com

Ironbridge Mezzanine Fund, L.P.
Marc Reich, President, Contact
200 Fisher Drive
c/o Ironwood Capital Advisors LLC
Avon, CT 06001
860-409-2100
Fax: 860-409-2120
www.ironwoodcap.com

Murketing 1 to 1 Ventures, L.P.
Bruce Blasnik, Contact

One Landmark Square
Stamford, CT 06901
203-325-4000
Fax: 203-325-8900
www.1to1ventures.com

Main Street Resources MSR I SBIC, L.P.
Daniel A. Levinson
8 Wright Street
Westport, CT 06880
203-227-5320
Fax: 203-227-5312
www.mainstreet-resources.com

RFE Capital Partners, L.P.
Robert M. Williams, Managing Partner
36 Grove Street
New Canaan, CT 06840
203-966-2800
Fax: 203-966-3109
www.rfeip.com

Saugatuck Capital Company, L.P. IV, SBIC
Frank Hawley, Thomas Berardino
One Canterbury Green
Stamford, CT 06901
203-348-6669
Fax: 203-324-6995
www.saugatuckcapital.com

TD Javelin Capital Fund II, L.P.
Two Greenwich Plaza, 4th Floor
Greenwich, CT 06830
203-629-8700

Valentis SB, L.P.
Paul M. Jacobi
411 West Putnam Avenue
Greenwich, CT 06830
203-862-7300
Fax: 203-862-7374
www.wexford.com

Delaware

Blue Rock Capital, L.P.
Virginia Bonker & Paul Collison, Mgrs.
5700 Kennett Pike, 2nd floor
Wilmington, DE 19807-1312
302-426-0981
Fax: 302-426-0982
www.bluerockcapital.com

Inflection Point Ventures II, L.P.
Jeffrey A. Davison, Contact
Delaware Technology Park
15 Innovation Way, Suite 280
Newark, DE 19711
302-452-1120
Fax: 302-452-1122
www.inflectpoint.com

District of Columbia

Allied Investment Corporation
Kelly Anderson, Controller
1919 Pennsylvania Avenue, NW
Washington, DC 20006-3434
202-331-1112
Fax: 202-659-2053
www.alliedcapital.com

Broadcast Capital, Inc. (SSBIC)
John E. Oxendine, President
1001 Connecticut Avenue, Suite 705
Washington, DC 20036
202-496-9250
Fax: 202-496-9259
Email: broadcap@aol.com

Core Capital Partners, L.P.
William Dunbar, Jonathan Silver, Contact
901 15th Street, Suite 950
Washington, DC 20005
202-589-0090

Fax: 202-589-0091
www.core-capital.com

Florida

Stonehenge Capital BOCF, LLC
Steven F. Lux, Stephen A. Bennett
777 S. Harbour Island Blvd. Suite 375
Tampa, FL 33602
813-223-9335
Fax: 813-221-6453
www.stonehengecapital.com

Crossbow Venture Partners LP
Stephen J. Warner, Contact
One North Clematis Street, Suite 510
West Palm Beach, FL 33401-5523
561-838-9005
Fax: 561-838-4105
www.cb-ventures.com

Market Capital Corp.
Eugene C. Langford, President
1715 W. Cleveland Street
P.O. Box 3277
Tampa, FL 33606
813-251-5533
Fax: 813-251-1900
www.langfordhill.com

Power Equities, Inc.
Maureen Beavers
50 N. Laura Street, 9th Floor
FL9-001-09-03
Jacksonville, FL 32202
904-791-7601
Fax: 904-791-7516

Georgia

Cordova Enhanced Fund, L.P.
Paul DiBella & Ralph Wright, Managers
2500 North Winds Parkway, Suite 475
Alpharetta, GA 30004
678-942-0300
Fax: 678-942-0301
www.cordovaventures.com

EGL/NatWest Equity Partners USA, L.P.
Salvatore Massaro, Manager
3495 Piedmont Road
Building Ten, Suite 412
Atlanta, GA 30305
404-949-8303
Fax: 404-949-8311
www.eglholdings.com

First Growth Capital, Inc.
Vijay K. Patel, President
P.O. Box 815
I-75 & GA 42, Best Western Plaza
Forsyth, GA 31029
478-994-9260
Fax: 478-994-1280
Email: vidya.patel@anjgroup.biz

Global Capital Funding Group, L.P.
Brad A. Thompson, Contact
106 Colony Park Drive, Suite 900
Cumming, GA 30040
678-947-0028
Fax: 678-947-6499
Email: bthompson@gcaltd.com

Wachovia Capital Associates, Inc.
Matt Sullivan, Managing Director
1170 Peachtree Street, Suite 1610
Atlanta, GA 30309
404-253-6388
Fax: 404-253-6377
www.peachtreeequity.com

Hawaii

HMS Hawaii
Richard Grey, Contact

Davies Pacific Center
841 Bishop Street, Suite 860
Honolulu, HI 96813
650-906-0488
Fax: 650-856-9864
www.hmsgroup.com

Pacific Century SBIC, Inc.
Darlene Blakeney, Manager
130 Merchant St., 12th Floor
Honolulu, HI 96813
Mailing address:
P.O. Box 2900
Honolulu HI 96846-6000
808-537-8088
Fax: 808-521-7602
www.boh.com

Pacific Venture Capital, Ltd.
Frank Tokioka
222 South Vineyard Street, PH.1
Honolulu, HI 96813
808-521-6502
Fax: 808-521-6541
Email: dperk@lava.net

Illinois

ABN AMRO Capital (USA) Inc.
Paul Widuch, Chairman
135 South LaSalle Street
Chicago, IL 60674
312-904-6445
Fax: 312-904-6376
www.abnamro.com

Alpha Capital III SBIC, L.P.
Andrew H. Kalnow, Contact
122 South Michigan Avenue, Suite 1700
Chicago, IL 60603
312-322-9800
Fax: 312-322-9808
Email: AmyColeman@earthlink.net

Banc One Equity Capital SBIC Fund II, L.L.C
Susan Klaus, Contact
55 West Monroe Street, 16th Floor
Chicago, IL 60670
312-732-9825
Fax: 312-732-7495
www.bankone.com

BancAmerica Capital Investors SBIC II, L.P.
Dennis McCrary, Robert Perille
231 South LaSalle Street, 7th Floor
Chicago, IL 60697
312-828-1781
Fax: 312-828-6298
www.BankofAmerica.com

BMO Nesbitt Burns Equity Investments, Inc.
William C. Morro, President
111 West Monroe Street, 20th Floor
Chicago, IL 60603
312-461-3855
Fax: 312-765-8000
www.bmonb.com

Cardinal Growth, L.P.
Joseph M. McInerney, Contact
311 South Wacker Drive
Suite 5500
Chicago, IL 60606
312-913-1000
Fax: 312-913-1001
www.cardinalgrowth.com

Channel Medical Partners, L.P.
Gregory Shearer, Contact
5750 Old Orchard Road, Suite 310
Skokie, IL 60077
847-779-1550
Fax: 847-779-1535
www.chanmed.com

Chicago Venture Partners, L.P.
John Fife, Manager
303 East Wacker Drive, Suite 311
Chicago, IL 60601
312-297-7000
Fax: 312-819-9701
www.chicagoventure.com

CIVC Partners Fund, LLC
Christopher Perry, Marcus Wedner
231 South LaSalle Street, Seventy Floor
Chicago, IL 60697
312-828-6570
Fax: 312-987-0763
Email: christopher.perry@bankofamerica.com

Continental Illinois Venture Corp.
Christopher J. Perry, President
209 South LaSalle Street
Mailing address:
231 South LaSalle Street
Chicago, IL 60697
312-828-8023
Fax: 312-987-0887
Email: christopher.perry@bankofamerica.com

DNJ Leasing II, L.P.
Jeffery S. Pfeffer, Contact
150 N. Wacker Drive
Suite 3025
Chicago, IL 60606
312-629-2877
Fax: 312-629-2874
www.dnjcapital.com

First Chicago Equity Corporation
David J. Vitale, President
Three First National Plaza, Suite 1330
Chicago, IL 60670
312-895-1000
Fax: 312-895-1001
Email: susan.e.klaus@em.fcnbd.com

High Street Capital III SBIC, L.P.
Joseph R. Katcha, Contact
11 South LaSalle Street, 5th Floor
Chicago, IL 60603
312-423-2650
Fax: 312-423-2655
www.Highsrt.com

Mercantile Capital Partners I, L.P.
Steven Edelson, Contact
1372 Shermer Road
Northbrook, IL 60062
847-509-3711
Fax: 847-509-3715
www.MercantilePartners.com

Midwest Mezzanine Fund II, L.P.
David Gezon & Allan Kayler, Mgrs.
135 South LaSalle Street, 20th Floor
Chicago, IL 60603
312-992-4587
Fax: 312-995-4595
www.midwestmezzanine.com

Open Prairie Ventures I, L.P.
Dennis D. Spice, Contact
115 North Neil Street, Suite 209
Champaign, IL 61820
217-351-7000
Fax: 217-351-7051
www.openprairie.com

Peterson Finance and Investment Company
(SSBIC)
James S. Rhee, President
3300 West Peterson Avenue, Suite A
Chicago, IL 60659
773-539-0502
Fax: 773-583-6714
Email: jsrhee@aol.com

Prairie Capital II, L.P.
C. Bryan Daniels, Contact
300 South Wacker Drive, Suite 2400
Chicago, IL 60606
312-360-1133
Fax: 312-360-1193
www.prairie-capital.com

Prism Opportunity Fund SBIC, L.P.
Robert A. Finkel, Contact
444 N. Michigan Avenue, Suite 1910
Chicago, IL 60611
312-464-7900
Fax: 312-464-7915
www.prismfund.com

Shorebank Capital Corporation (SSBIC)
David Shryock, CEO
7936 S. Cottage Grove Ave.
Chicago, IL 60619
773-371-7030
Fax: 773-371-7035
www.sbk.com

SvoCo, L.P.
John Svoboda, Michelle Collins, Contacts
1 North Franklin Street, Suite 1500
Chicago, IL 60606
312-267-8750
Fax: 312-267-6025
www.svoco.com

USHCC Private Equity, L.P.
Victor L. Maruri, Contact
311 South Wacker Drive
Chicago, IL 60606
312-697-4600
Fax: 312-697-0115
www.dufflic.com

Indiana

1st Source Capital Corporation
Eugene L. Cavenaugh, Jr., Vice President
100 North Michigan Street
South Bend, IN 46601
574-235-2250
Fax: 574-235-2227
www.1stsource.com

Cambridge Ventures, LP
Ms. Jean Wojtowicz, President
4181 East 96th Street, Suite 200
Indianapolis, IN 46240
317-814-6192
Fax: 317-844-9815
Email:
jwojtowicz@cambridgecapitalmgmt.com

Centerfield Capital Partners, L.P.
D. Scott Lutzke, Contact
3030 Market Tower
10 West Market Street
Indianapolis, IN 46204
317-237-2323
Fax: 317-237-2325
www.centerfieldcapital.com

Irwin Ventures SBIC LLC
David Meyercord, Contact
500 Washington Street
Columbus, IN 47201
812-373-1434
Fax: 812-376-1709
www.irwinventures.com

White River Venture Partners, LP
Sam Sutphin & Marc DeLong, Managers
3603 East Raymond St.
Indianapolis, IN 46203-4762
317-780-7789
Fax: 317-791-2935
Email: madelong@driversolutions.com

Iowa

AAVIN Equity Partners I, L.P.
James D. Thorpe, Contact
118 Third Avenue, S.E., Suite 630
Cedar Rapids, IA 52401
319-247-1072
Fax: 319-363-9519
www.aavinvc.com

Berthel SBIC, LLC
Henry Royer & Larry Duncan, Contacts
701 Tama Street, Building B
P.O. Box 609
Marion, IA 52302
319-447-5700
Fax: 319-447-4250
www.berthel.com

MorAmerica Capital Corporation
David R. Schroder, President
101 2nd Street, SE, Suite 800
Cedar Rapids, IA 52401
319-363-8249
Fax: 319-363-9683
Email: mbenge@investam.com

Kansas

Kansas Venture Capital, Inc.
John Delton, Manager
6700 Antioch Plaza, Suite 460
Overland Park, KS 66204
913-262-7117
Fax: 913-262-3509
www.kvci.com

MidStates Capital, L.P.
Timothy J. Keeble, Contact
7300 West 110th Street, 7th Floor
Overland Park, KS 66210
913-962-9007
Fax: 913-962-0699
Email: timkeeble@mail.com

Kentucky

Chrysalis Ventures II, L.P.
Lisa K. Aly, Contact
101 South Fifth Street, Suite 1650
Louisville, KY 40202
502-583-7644
Fax: 502-853-7648
www.ChrysalisVentures.com

Equal Opportunity Finance, Inc. (SSBIC)
David L. Davis, President
50 E RiverCenter Boulevard
PO Box 391
Covington, KY 41012
859-815-3434
Fax: 859-815-4496
www.ashland.com

Mountain Ventures, Inc.
L. Ray Moncrief, President
P.O. Box 1738
362 Old Whitley Road
London, KY 40743
606-864-5175
Fax: 606-864-5194
www.khic.org

Prosperitas Investment Partners, L.P.
Steven B. Bing, Contact
3600 National City Tower
101 South Fifth Street
Louisville, KY 40202
502-584-4008
Fax: 502-587-1351
www.prosperitasfund.com

Louisiana

Audubon Capital SBIC, L.P.
Robert Cowin, Contact
1100 Poydras Street, Suite 2000

New Orleans, LA 70163
504-585-7730
Fax: 504-585-7731
www.auduboncapital.com

Bank One Equity Investors-BIDCO, Inc.
Thomas J. Adamek, President
c/o Stonehenge Capital Corporation
450 Laurel Street, Suite 1450
Baton Rouge, LA 70801
225-408-3000
Fax: 225-408-3090
www.stonehengecapital.com

Hibernia Capital Corp.
Thomas Hoyt, President
313 Carondelet Street
New Orleans, LA 70130
504-533-5988
Fax: 504-533-3873
www.hiberniabank.com

Jefferson Capital Partners I, L.P.
William J. Harper, Contact
3501 N. Causeway Blvd., Suite 420
Metairie, LA 70002
504-828-2088
Fax: 504-828-2014
www.jeffcap.com

Maine

North Atlantic Venture Fund II, L.P.
David M. Coit, Manager
Two City Center, 5th Floor
Portland, ME 04101
207-772-4470
Fax: 207-772-3257
www.northatlanticcapital.com

Maryland

Allegiance Capital, L.P.
Gary Dorsch
2000 West 41st Street
Baltimore, MD 21211
410-338-6314
Fax: 410-662-6816
www.allcapital.com

Anthem Capital II, L.P.
C. Edward Spiva, Contact
16 South Calvert Street, Suite 800
Baltimore, MD 21202
410-625-1510
Fax: 410-625-1735
www.anthemcapital.com

Meridian Management Group Ventures, L.P.
(SSBIC)
Stanley W. Tucker, Manager
826 E. Baltimore Street
Baltimore, MD 21202
410-333-2548
Fax: 410-333-2552
www.mmggroup.com

Patriot Capital, L.P.
Chris M. Royston, Contact
16 West Madison Street
Baltimore, MD 21201
410-576-2975
Fax: 410-752-2978
www.bengurbryan.com

Security Financial and Investment Corp.
Jim Bonfils, Manager
7720 Wisconsin Avenue, Suite 207
Bethesda, MD 20814
301-951-4288
Fax: 301-951-9282
Email: JamesBonfils@aol.com

Spring Capital Partners, L.P.
Jay M. Wilson, General Partner
The Latrobe Building, 5th Floor

2 East Read Street
Baltimore, MD 21202
410-685-8000
Fax: 410-545-0015
www.springcap.com

Toucan Capital Fund II, L.P.
Linda Powers
7600 Wisconsin Avenue, 7th Floor
Bethesda, MD 20814
240-497-4060
Fax: 240-497-4065
www.toucancapital.com

Walker Investment Fund II SBIC, L.P.
Gina Dubbe, Contact
3060 Washington Road, Suite 200
Glenwood, MD 21738
301-854-6850
Fax: 301-854-6235
www.walkerventures.com

Massachusetts

Ascent Venture Partners II, L.P.
Frank Polestra, General Partner
255 State Street, 5th Floor
Boston, MA 02109
617-720-9400
Fax: 617-720-9401
www.ascentvp.com

Axxon Capital, L.P.
Paula E. Groves, Contact
28 State Street, 37th Floor
Boston, MA 02109
617-772-0980
Fax: 617-557-6014
www.axxoncapital.com

BancBoston Ventures, Incorporated
Frederick M. Fritz, President
175 Federal Street, 10th Floor
Boston, MA 02110
617-434-2442
Fax: 617-434-1153
www.fleet.com

Chestnut Venture Partners, L.P.
David D. Croll, President
75 State Street, Suite 2500
Boston, MA 02109
617-345-7220
Fax: 617-345-7201
www.mcventurepartners.com

Citizens Ventures, Inc.
Robert Garrow & Gregory Mulligan, Mgrs.
28 State Street, 15th Floor
Boston, MA 02109
617-725-5633
Fax: 617-725-5630
www.citizenscapital.com

Crescent Private Capital II, L.P.
Nancy S. Amer, Contact
One Copley Place, Suite 602
Boston, MA 02116
617-638-0050
Fax: 617-638-0090
www.cresentlp.com

Gemini Investors III, L.P.
David F. Millet, Contact
20 William Street
Wellesley, MA 02481
781-237-7001
Fax: 781-237-7233
www.gemini-investors.com

Lancet Capital Health Ventures, L.P.
William Golden, Manager
124 Mount Auburn Street, Suite 200N
Cambridge, MA 02138
617-330-9345

Fax: 617-330-9349
www.lancetcapital.com

Longworth Venture Partners II-A, L.P.
Paul A. Margolis, Contact
1050 Winter Street, Suite 2600
Waltham, MA 02451
781-663-3600
Fax: 781-663-3619
www.longworth.com

Marathon Investment Partners, L.P.
Paul Bolger, Managing Director
100 Cummings Center, Suite 326-J
Beverly, MA 01915
978-720-3520
Fax: 978-998-6960
www.marathoninvestment.com

New England Partners Capital, L.P.
Robert Hanks, Prin. & Todd Fitzpatrick
One Boston Place, Suite 2100
Boston, MA 02108
617-624-8400
Fax: 617-624-8416
www.nepartners.com

North Hill Ventures II, L.P.
Brett Rome, Contact
Ten Post Office Square
Suite 1100
Boston, MA 02109
617-788-2150
Fax: 617-788-2152
Email: brett.rome@capitalone.com

RockPort Capital Partners, L.P.
Bettina Metais, Contact
160 Federal Street, 18th Floor
Boston, MA 02110
617-912-1420
Fax: 617-912-1449
www.rockportcap.com

Seacoast Capital Partners II, L.P.
Walt Leonard, Contact
55 Ferncroft Road
Danvers, MA 01923
978-750-1300
Fax: 978-750-1301
www.seacoastcapital.com

Summer Street Capital Fund I, L.P.
Richard Steele
171 Dwight Rd., Suite 310
Longmeadow, MA 01106
413-567-3366
Fax: 413-567-6556
www.summerstreetcapital.com

UST Capital Corp.
Robert E. Garrow, President & Director
28 State Street
Boston, MA 02109
617-725-5635
Fax: 617-725-5630
www.citizenscapital.com

Velocity Equity Partners I SBIC, L.P.
David Vogel, Contact
121 High Street, Suite 400
Boston, MA 02110
617-338-2545
Fax: 617-261-3864
www.velocityep.com

Venture Capital Fund of New England IV, L.P
Kevin J. Dougherty, Contact
30 Washington Street
Wellesley Hills, MA 02481
781-431-8400
Fax: 781-237-6578
www.vcfne.com

Zero Stage Capital SBIC VII, L.P.
Paul M. Kelly, Contact
101 Main Street, 17th Floor
Cambridge, MA 02142
617-876-5355
Fax: 617-876-1248
www.zerostage.com

Michigan

Comerica Ventures, Inc.
Jay K. Oberg, First Vice President
500 Woodward Avenue, 33rd Floor, MC 3379
Detroit, MI 48226
313-222-7833
Fax: 313-222-4013
www.comerica.com

Dearborn Capital Corp. (SSBIC)
William D. Lang, President
c/o Ford Motor Credit Corporation
The American Road
Dearborn, MI 48121
313-337-8577
Fax: 313-390-3783
www.ford.com

EDF Ventures, L.P.
Mary Campbell, Contact
425 North Main Street
Ann Arbor, MI 48104-1147
734-663-3213
Fax: 734-663-7358
www.edfvc.com

InvestCare Partners, L.P.
Malcolm Moss, Manager
32330 W. 12 Mile Road
Farmington Hills, MI 48334
248-489-9000
Fax: 248-489-8819
www.gmacapital.com

Merchants Capital Partners, L.P.
G. Cohen, P. Beach, R. Martin, Mgrs.
24 Frank Lloyd Wright Drive
Lobby L, 4th Floor
Ann Arbor, MI 48106
734-994-5505
Fax: 734-994-1376
www.merchantscapitalpartners.com

Motor Enterprises, Inc. (SSBIC)
Lindsey Luttinen, VP and Treasurer
200 Renaissance Center, 10th Floor
PO Box 200, Mail Code: 482-B10-C76
Detroit, MI 48265-2000
316-665-6083
Fax: 313-665-6208
Email: lindsey.luttinen@GM.com

North Coast Technology Investor, L.P.
Hugo E. Braun III, Lindsay D. Aspegren
206 S. Fifth Avenue Suite 550
Ann Arbor, MI 48104-0648
734-662-7667
Fax: 734-662-6261
www.northcoastvc.com

Pacific Capital, L.P.
Dan Boyle
900 Victor's Way, Suite 280
Ann Arbor, MI 48108
734-747-9401
Fax: 734-747-9704
www.whitepines.com

TD Lighthouse Capital Fund, L.P.
Joan Neuscheler, Contact
303 Detroit Street, Suite 301
Ann Arbor, MI 48104
734-623-6300
Fax: 734-623-2956
www.tullisdickerson.com

White Pines Limited Partnership I
Mr. Ian Bund, President
900 Victor's Way, Suite 280
Ann Arbor, MI 48108
734-47-9401
Fax: 34-47-9704
www.whitepines.com

Minnesota

AAVIN Equity Partners I, L.P.
Daryl Erdman
2500 Rand Tower
Participating Securities and Commitments
Minneapolis, MN 55402
612-375-9966
Fax: 319-363-9519
www.aavininc.com

Affinity Ventures III, L.P.
Robin M. Dowdle, Contact
901 Marquette Avenue, Suite 1810
Minneapolis, MN 55402
612-252-9897
Fax: 612-252-9863
www.affinitycapital.net

Agio Capital Partners I, L.P.
Kenneth F. Gudorf, President & CEO
Interlachen Corporate Center
5050 Lincoln Drive, Suite 420
Edina, MN 55436
952-938-1628
Fax: 952-933-6066
www.agio-capital.com

Bayview Capital Partners, L.P.
Cary Musech, Manager
641 East Lake Street, Suite 230
Wayzata, MN 55391
952-345-2000
Fax: 952-345-2001
www.bayviewcap.com

Convergent Capital Partners I, L.P.
John Mason, Keith Bares
5353 Wayzata Boulevard, Suite 205
Minneapolis, MN 55416
952-595-8102
Fax: 952-595-8113
www.cvcap.com

Dougherty Opportunity Fund II, L.P.
James A. Bernards, Contact
7200 Metro Boulevard
Edina, MN 55439
952-831-6499
Fax: 952-831-1219
www.sbbsl.com

Medallion Capital, Inc.
Tom Hunt, President
3000 W. County Road 42, Suite 301
Burnsville, MN 55337-4827
952-831-2025
Fax: 952-831-2945
Email: mvannelli@medallioncapital.com

Milestone Growth Fund, Inc. (SSBIC)
Esperanza Guerrero-Anderson, President
401 Second Avenue South, Suite 1032
Minneapolis, MN 55401
612-338-0090
Fax: 612-338-1172
www.milestonegrowth.com

Norwest Equity Partners VII-SBIC, L.P.
John Whaley, Contact
3600 IDS Center
80 S. 8th St.
Minneapolis, MN 55402
612-215-1600
Fax: 612-215-1601
www.nep.com

Piper Jaffray Healthcare Capital L.P.
Lloyd (Buzz) Benson, Manager
800 Nicollet Mall, Suite 800
Minneapolis, MN 55402-7020
612-303-5664
Fax: 612-303-1350
www.piperventures.com

Wells Fargo SBIC, Inc.
John Whaley
3600 IDS Center
80S 8th St.
Minneapolis, MN 55402
612-215-1600
Fax: 612-215-1601
www.nep.com

Mississippi

CapSource 2000 Fund, L.P.
James R. Herndon, Contact
795 Woodlands Parkway, Suite 100
Ridgeland, MS 39157
601-899-8980
Fax: 601-952-1334
www.capsources.com

Sun-Delta Capital Access Center, Inc.
(SSBIC)
Harry Bowie, President
819 Main Street
Greenville, MS 38701
662-335-5291
Fax: 662-335-5295
Email: deltafdn@tecinfo.com

Missouri

American Century Ventures II, L.L.C.
Diane Mulcahy, Contact
4500 Main Street, 9th Floor
Kansas City, MO 64111
816-340-4054
Fax: 816-340-3278
www.americancentury.com

Bankers Capital Corp.
Raymond E. Glasnapp, President
3100 Gillham Road
Kansas City, MO 64109
816-531-1600
Fax: 816-531-1334
Email: cglasnapp@aol.com

BOME Investors II, L.L.C.
Shelley Whittington, Thomas Adamek
c/o Gateway Capco II, LLC
8000 Maryland Avenue, Suite 1190
St. Louis, MO 63105
314-721-5707
Fax: 314-721-5135
www.gatewayventures.com

CFB Venture Fund I, Inc.
James F. O'Donnell, Chairman
11 South Meramec, Suite 1430
St. Louis, MO 63105
314-746-7427
Fax: 314-746-8739
www.capitalforbusiness.com

Eagle Fund I, L.P.
Scott Fesler
Bush O'Donnell Capital
101 S. Hanley Road, Suite 1250
St. Louis, MO 63105
314-727-4555
Fax: 314-727-8829
Email: sdf@bushodonnell.com

Kansas City Equity Partners Ventures II, L.P.
William Reisler, Manager
233 West 47th Street
Kansas City, MO 64112
816-960-1771

Fax: 816-960-1777
www.kcep.com

MorAmerica Capital Corporation
Kevin F. Mullane, Vice President
911 Main Street, Suite 2424
Commerce Tower Building
Kansas City, MO 64105
816-842-0114
Fax: 816-471-7339

Power Equities, Inc.
Craig Fowler
800 Market Street, 13th Floor
MO1-800-15-03
St. Louis, MO 63101
314-466-6634
Fax: 314-466-6238

RiverVest Venture Fund I, L.P.
Thomas C. Melzer, Contact
7733 Forsyth Boulevard, Suite 1650
St. Louis, MO 63105
314-726-6700
Fax: 314-727-6715
www.rivervest.com

UMB Capital Corporation, Inc.
Noel Shull, Manager
1010 Grand Boulevard
Mailing address:
P.O. Box 419226
Kansas City, MO 64141
816-860-7914
Fax: 816-860-7143
www.umb.com

Nevada

Atalanta Investment Company, Inc.
L. Mark Newman, Chairman of the Board
601 Fairview Blvd.
P.O. Box 7718
Incline Village, NV 89452
775-833-1836
Fax: 775-833-1890
Email: mark@marknewman.net

New Hampshire

MerchantBanc Venture Partners, L.P.
Jeffrey M. Pollock
Two Wall Street
Manchester, NH 03101
603-623-5500
Fax: 603-623-3972
www.merchantbanc.com

New Jersey

Alliance Mezzanine Investors, L.P.
Robert Eberhardt, Douglas Smith
96 Pompton Road
Verona, NJ 07044
973-239-8900
Fax: 973-239-8909
www.mezcap.com

Blue Rock Capital, L.P.
Virginia G. Bonker
230 Lackawanna Drive
Andover, NJ 07821
973-426-1767
Fax: 973-426-0224
www.bluerockcapital.com

Capital Circulation Corporation (SSBIC)
Judy Kao, Manager
2035 Lemoine Avenue, Second Floor
Fort Lee, NJ 07024
201-947-8637
Fax: 201-585-1965
Email: judykao@bellatlantic.net

DFW Capital Partners, L.P.
Donald F. DeMuth, Manager

Glenpointe Center East, 5th Floor
300 Frank W. Burr Blvd.
Teaneck, NJ 07666
201-836-6000
Fax: 201-836-5666
www.DFWCapital.com

Early Stage Enterprises, L.P.
Ronald Hahn and James Millar, Managers
995 Route 518
Skillman, NJ 08558
609-921-8896
Fax: 609-921-8703
www.esevc.com

Edison Fund V, L.P.
Ross Martinson, Contact
1009 Lenox Drive, #4
Lawrenceville, NJ 08648
609-896-1900
Fax: 609-896-0066
www.edisonventure.com

Liberty View Equity Partners SBIC, L.P.
Scott Flamm, Richard Meckler Contacts
Waterfront Corporate Center
111 River Street, 10th Floor
Hoboken, NJ 07030-5776
201-595-2926
Fax: 201-216-8605
Email: dmancilla@cprus.com

MidMark Capital II, L.P.
Matthew W. Finlay, Contact
177 Madison Avenue
Morristown, NJ 07960
973-971-9960
Fax: 973-971-9963
www.midmarkcapital.com

Navigator Growth Partners, L.P.
Bernard Markey
47 Summit Avenue
Summit, NJ 07901
908-273-7733
Fax: 908-273-5566
www.navigatorequity.com

Norwood Venture Corp.
Mark R. Littell, President
65 Norwood Avenue
Montclair, NJ 07043
973-783-1117
www.norven.com

Penny Lane Partners, L.P.
William R. Denslow, Jr., Manager
One Palmer Square
Suite 309
Princeton, NJ 08542
609-497-4646
Fax: 609-497-0611
Email: pennylanepartner@msn.com

Sycamore Venture Capital, L.P.
John Whitman
845 Alexander Road
Princeton, NJ 08540
609-759-8888
Fax: 609-759-8900
www.sycamorevc.com

Tappan Zee Capital Corporation
Jeffrey Birnberg, President
201 Lower Notch Road
Mailing address:
    P.O. Box 416
    Little Falls, NJ 07424
973-256-8280
Fax: 973-256-2841
Email: tzcc@aol.com

University Ventures, Inc. (SSBIC)
Oscar Figueroa, President

180 University Avenue, 3rd Floor
Newark, NJ 07102
973-0353-5627
Fax: 973-353-1175
Email: ofiguero@andromeda.rutgers.edu

Ziegler Healthcare Fund I, L.P.
Douglas Korey, Contact
Executive Center #2, Third Floor
1040 Broad Street
Shrewsbury, NJ 07702
732-578-0533
Fax: 732-578-0501
www.zieglerhealthcare.com

Zon Capital Partners, L.P.
William D. Bridgers, Contact
5 Vaughn Drive, Suite 104
Princeton, NJ 08540
609-452-1653
Fax: 609-452-1693
www.zoncapital.com

New Mexico

Tullis-Dickerson Origen Capital Fund, L.P.
Tom Dickerson
150 Washington Avenue, Suite 201
Santa Fe, NM 87501
505-982-7007
Fax: 505-982-7008
www.tullisdickerson.com

New York

399 Venture Partners
William Comfort, Chairman
399 Park Avenue, 14th Floor/Zone 4
New York, NY 10043
212-559-1127
Fax: 212-793-6164
Email: jjarema@cvcltd.com

ACI Capital America Fund, L.P.
Gregory H. Warner, Thomas Israel
900 Third Avenue, 26th Floor
New York, NY 10022-4728
212-634-3333
Fax: 212-634-3330
www.acicapital.com

American Asian Capital Corporation (SSBIC)
Howard H. Lin, President
130 Water Street, Suite 6-L
New York, NY 10005
212-422-6880
Fax: 212-422-6880
Email: linwillh@cs.com

Argentum Capital Partners II, L.P.
Daniel Raynor, Chairman
60 Madison Avenue, Suite 701
New York, NY 10110
212-949-6262
Fax: 212-949-8294
www.argentumgroup.com

Avalon Equity Fund, L.P.
Benjamin E. Brandes, Contact
800 3rd Avenue, 31st Floor
New York, NY 10022
212-421-0600
Fax: 212-421-1742
www.avalonequity.com

Bank Austria Creditanstalt SBIC, Inc.
Christopher Wrenn, President
245 Park Avenue, 32nd Floor
New York, NY 10167
212-672-5656
Fax: 212-672-5500
Email: jvangeldern@hvbamericas.com

BNP Paribas Principal Incorporated
Steven Alexander, President
787 Seventh Avenue, 32nd Floor

New York, NY 10019-8018
212-841-3070
Fax: 212-841-3251
www.bnpparibas.com

Bank of New York Capital Partners, L.P.
Stratton Heath, Paul Echausse
445 Park Avenue
New York, NY 10022
212-821-1909
Fax: 212-832-6949
www.bankofny.com

BOCNY, LLC
W. Stephen Keller
c/o Stonehenge Capital Corporation
152 West 57th Street, 20th Floor
New York, NY 10019
212-944-2542
Fax: 212-656-1344
www.stonehengecapital.com

Brookside Pecks Capital Partners, L.P.
Robert Cresci, Contact
One Rockefeller Plaza, Suite 900
New York, NY 10020
212-332-1346
Fax: 212-332-1334
Email: rcresci@pecks.com

Cephas Capital Partners L.P.
Clint Campbell, Jeff Holmes, Mgrs.
16 West Main Street
Rochester, NY 14614
716-231-1528
Fax: 716-231-1530
Email: cephascwc@aol.com

Champlain Capital Partners, L.P.
Dennis M. Leary, Contact
45 Rockefeller Plaza, Suite 2000
New York, NY 10020
212-332-7164
Fax: 212-332-3401
Email: dennis.leary@champlaingroup.com

CIBC WG Argosy Merchant Fund 1, L.P.
Steven A. Flyer, Executive Director
425 Lexington Avenue, 3rd Floor
New York, NY 10017
212-885-4735
Fax: 212-885-4350
Email: steven.a.flyer@us.cibc.com

Citicorp Venture Capital, Ltd.
William Comfort, Chairman of the Board
399 Park Avenue, 14th Floor/Zone 4
New York, NY 10043
212-559-1127
Fax: 212-793-6164
Email: jjarema@cvcltd.com

Carl Marks NY Capital II, L.P.
Robert G. Davidoff, General Partner
135 East 57th Street, 26th Floor
New York, NY 10022
212-909-8400
Fax: 212-980-2630
www.carlmarks.com

Coqui Capital Partners, L.P.
Jeffrey S. Davidson, Contact
1775 Broadway, Suite 604
New York, NY 10019
212-247-4590
Fax: 212-247-4801
www.coquicapital.com

Critical Capital Growth Fund, L.P.
Steven Sands Mgr; C. Robinson
90 Park Ave., 39th Floor
New York, NY 10016
212-697-5200

Fax: 212-697-8035
www.sandsbros.com

Deutsche Bank Capital Partners SBIC, L.P.
Heide Silverstein, Director
130 Liberty Street, 25th Floor
New York, NY 10006
212-250-8084
Fax: 212-250-7651
www.db.com

Dresdner Kleinwort Capital, LLC
Richard Wolf, Partner
75 Wall Street, 34th Floor
New York, NY 10005
212-429-3131
Fax: 212-429-3099
www.drkw.com

East Coast Venture Capital, Inc. (SSBIC)
Zindel Zelmanovitch, President
241 Fifth Avenue
Suite 302
New York, NY 10016
212-686-1515
Fax: 212-686-1131
Email: fstart@aol.com

Easton Hunt Capital Partners, L.P.
John H. Friedman, Contact
641 Lexington Avenue, 21st Floor
New York, NY 10022
212-702-0950
Fax: 212-702-0952
www.eastoncapital.com

Elk Associates Funding Corporation
Gary C. Granoff, President
747 Third Avenue
New York, NY 10017
212-355-2449
Fax: 212-759-3338
www.elkassociates.com

Emigrant Capital Corporation
Lawrence Adolf and John Hart, Managers
6 East 43rd Street, 8th Floor
New York, NY 10017
212-850-4460
Fax: 212-850-4839
www.emigrant.com

Empire State Capital Corporation (SSBIC)
Dr. Joseph Wu, President
170 Broadway, Suite 1200
New York, NY 10038
212-513-1799
Fax: 212-513-1892
Email: ESC5131799@aol.com

Eos Partners SBIC II, L.P.
Steven Friedman & Brian Young, Manager
320 Park Avenue, 22nd Floor
New York, NY 10022
212-832-5800
Fax: 212-832-5815
www.eospartners.com

Esquire Capital Corp. (SSBIC)
Frederick Eliassen, Manager
69 Veterans Memorial Highway
Commack, NY 11725
631-462-6944
Fax: 631-864-8152
Email: esquiremoneta@msn.com

Exeter Capital Partners IV, L.P.
Keith Fox, Kurt Bergquist, Jeff Weber
10 East 53rd Street, 32nd Floor
New York, NY 10022
212-872-1172
Fax: 212-872-1198
www.exeterfunds.com

Falcon Private Equity, L.P.
Gregga Baxter, Matthew Snyder, Contacts
335 Madison Avenue - 11th Floor
New York, NY 10017
212-922-2333
Fax: 212-922-2351
Email: gregga.baxter@saudibank.com

First County Capital Inc. (SSBIC)
Orest Glut, Financial Manager
40-48 Main Street, Suite 301
Flushing, NY 11354
718-461-1778
Fax: 718-461-1835
Email: FirstCounty@AOL.com

Flushing Capital Corporation (SSBIC)
Frank J. Mitchell, President
39-06 Union Street, Room 202
Flushing, NY 11354
718-886-5866
Fax: 718-939-7761
Email: flushing.capital@verizon.net

Freshstart Venture Capital Corporation
Alvin Murstein, President
437 Madison Avenue
New York, NY 10022
212-328-2110
Fax: 212-328-2125
www.medallionfinancial.com

Fundex Capital Corp.
Larry Linksman, President
387 Park Avenue South, 9th Floor
New York, NY 10016
212-759-2690
Fax: 212-319-1976
www.fundexcapital.com

Gefus SBIC, L.P.
William J. Beckett
375 Park Avenue, Suite 2401
New York, NY 10152
212-308-1111
Fax: 212-308-1182
Email: wbeckett@gefinorusa.com

Hanam Capital Corp.
Robert Schairer, President
38 West 32nd Street, Suite 1512
New York, NY 10001
212-564-5225
Fax: 212-564-5307
Email: hanam@aol.com

Hudson Venture Partners II, L.P.
Dr. Lawrence A. Howard, Contact
660 Madison Avenue, 14th Floor
New York, NY 10021
212-644-9797
Fax: 212-644-7430
www.hudsonptr.com

Ibero American Investors Corp. (SSBIC)
Domingo Garcia, President
104 Scio Street
Rochester, NY 14604
716-262-3440
Fax: 716-262-3441
www.iberoinvestors.com

Ibero American Investors Corp. (SSBIC)
Christine Ryan, Loan Officer
Statler Towers Bldg.
107 Delaware Avenue, Suite 64
Buffalo, NY 14202
716-842-9908
Fax: 716-842-9925

ING Furman Selz Investments
Brian Friedman, Manager
520 Madison Avenue, 8th Floor
New York, NY 10022

212-284-1708
Fax: 212-284-1717
Email: mluxenberg@ingprivate.com

International Paper Cap. Formation, Inc.
(SSBIC)
Julius A. Weiss, President
Two Manhattanville Road
Purchase, NY 10577-2196
914-397-1960
Fax: 914-397-1630

J.P. Morgan Partners (23A SBIC), LLC
Jeffrey Walker, Managing Gen. Partner
1221 Avenue of the Americas, 40th Floor
New York, NY 10036
212-899-3500
Fax: 212-622-3799
www.JPMorganPartners.com

KBL Healthcare, L.P.
Marlene Krauss, Michael Kaswan
645 Madison Avenue
New York, NY 10022
212-319-5555
Fax: 212-319-5591
www.kblhealthcare.com

LEG Partners Debenture SBIC, L.P.
Lawrence Golub, Manager
555 Madison Avenue, 30th Floor
New York, NY 10022
212-750-6060
Fax: 212-750-5505
www.golubassoc.com

M & T Capital Corp.
Tom Scanlon, President
One Fountain Plaza, 9th Floor
Buffalo, NY 14203
716-848-3800
Fax: 716-848-3150
www.mandtbank.com

Madison Investment Partners II, L.P.
Susan Goodrich, Contact
52 Vanderbilt Avenue, Suite 1010
New York, NY 10017
212-949-0400
Fax: 212-949-6049
www.madisonpartners.com

Medallion Funding Corporation
Alvin Murstein, President
437 Madison Avenue
New York, NY 10022
212-328-2110
Fax: 212-328-2121
www.medallionfinancial.com

Merchants Capital Partners, L.P.
Jake Wessner
1120 Avenue of the Americas - 4th Floor
New York, NY 10036
212-626-6832
Fax: 212-626-6833

Mercury Capital, L.P.
David W. Elenowitz, Manager
153 East 53rd Street, 49th Floor
New York, NY 10022
212-838-0888
Fax: 212-759-3897
Email: hal@dlfi.com

NBT Capital Corporation
Daryl Forsythe & Joe Minor, Managers
19 Eaton Avenue
Norwich, NY 13815
607-337-6810
Fax: 607-336-8730
www.nbtbank.com

Needham Capital SBIC II, L.P.
George Needham, John Michaelson, Mgrs.
445 Park Avenue
New York, NY 10022
212-371-8300
Fax: 212-751-1450
www.needhamco.com

New York Business Development Corp.
Capital Corp.
Stephen A. Ross, Vice President
16 West Main Street
Suite 236
Rochester, NY 14614
716-232-6250
www.nybdc.com

New York Business Development Corp.
Capital Corp.
Robert W. Lazar, President
41 State Street
P.O. Box 738
Albany, NY 12207
518-463-2268
Fax: 518-463-0240
www.nybdc.com

New York Business Development Corp.
Capital Corp.
Chester A. Sadowski, Sr. V. President
633 Third Avenue, 36th Floor
New York, NY 10017
212-803-3672
Fax: 212-803-3675
www.nybdc.com

Penny Lane Partners, L.P.
William R. Denslow, Manager
108 Forest Avenue
P.O. Box 447
Locust Valley, NY 11560
516-609-8065
Fax: 516-759-4653

Pierre Funding Corp.
Elias Debbas, President
805 Third Avenue, 6th Floor
New York, NY 10022
212-888-1515
Fax: 212-688-4252
Email: PierreFunding@AOL.COM

Psilos Group Partners II SBIC, L.P.
Jeffrey M. Krauss, Contact
625 Avenue of the Americas, 4th Floor
New York, NY 10011
212-242-8844
Fax: 212-242-8855
www.psilos.com

Pyramid Ventures, Inc.
Brian Talbot, Vice President
130 Liberty Street, 31st Floor
New York, NY 10006
212-250-9571
Fax: 212-250-7651
Email: heide.silverstein@db.com

Quad Venture Partners SBIC, L.P.
Lincoln E. Frank, Contact
650 Fifth Avenue, 31st Floor
New York, NY 10019
212-724-2200
Fax: 212-724-4310
www.quadventures.com

Radius Venture Partners II, L.P.
Daniel C. Lubin, Contact
One Rockefeller Plaza
Suite 920
New York, NY 10020
212-897-7778
Fax: 212-397-2656
www.radiusventures.com

Rand Capital SBIC, L.P.
Allen F. Grum, Jr., Contact
2200 Rand Building
Buffalo, NY 14203
716-853-0802
Fax: 716-854-8480
www.randcapital.com

RBC Equity Investments, Inc.
Sindy Jagger, Manager
One Liberty Plaza
New York, NY 10006
212-858-7157
Fax: 212-858-7468
www.rbcap.com

RBS Capital Corporation
Andrew S. Weinberg, Sr. Vice President
101 Park Avenue, 10th Floor
New York, NY 10178
212-401-1330
Fax: 212-401-1390
Email: andrew.weinberg@rbos.com

Regent Capital Partners, L.P.
J. Oliver Maggard, Managing Partner
505 Park Avenue, Suite 1700
New York, NY 10022
212-735-9900
Fax: 212-735-9908
Email: oliverm@cpequity.com

Rock Maple Ventures, L.P.
David W. Freelove, Contact
5 East 57th Street, 15th Floor
New York, NY 10022
212-308-1935
Fax: 212-308-8641
www.rockmapleventures.com

SGC Partners II LLC
Christopher M. Neenan, VP & COO
1221 Avenue of the Americas, 8th Floor
New York, NY 10020
212-278-5184
Fax: 212-278-5454
Email: frances.madrid@us.socgen.com

Sixty Wall Street SBIC Fund, L.P.
John A. Mayer, Jr., Managing Director
1221 Avenue of the Americas, 40th Floor
New York, NY 10036
212-648-7778
Fax: 212-648-5032
www.JPMorganPartners.com

Summer Street Capital Fund I, L.P.
Brian D'Amico
70 West Chippewa St., Suite 500
Buffalo, NY 14202-
716-566-2900
Fax: 716-566-2910
www.summerstreetcapital.com

T.S. Capital Corporation
James Trainor, Manager
The Rice Building
216 River Street
Troy, NY 12180
518-687-4430
Fax: 518-687-4435
www.troysavingsbank.com

The 1818 SBIC Fund, L.P.
Richard J. Ragoza, Contact
59 Wall Street
New York, NY 10005
212-493-7910
Fax: 212-493-7280
www.bbh.com

Toronto Dominion Capital (U.S.A.), Inc.
Mr. Marc H. Michel, President
31 West 52nd Street

New York, NY 10019
212-827-7000
Fax: 212-974-8429
www.tdcapital.com

Triad Capital Corp. of New York (SSBIC)
Oscar Figueroa, Manager of Rutgers Inv.
305 Seventh Avenue, 20th Floor
New York, NY 10001
212-243-7360
Fax: 212-243-7647
Email: mrobiou@bcf-triad.org

Trusty Capital Inc. (SSBIC)
Yungduk Hahn, President
25 West 37th Street, 5th Floor
New York, NY 10118
212-719-3760
Fax: 212-869-8577
Email: ydhahn@earthlink.net

UBS Capital II LLC
Justin S. Maccarone, President
299 Park Avenue
New York, NY 10171
212-821-6490
Fax: 212-821-6333
www.ubs.com

Walden Capital Partners, L.P.
John Costantino & Allen Greenberg, Mgrs.
708 Third Avenue, 21st Floor
New York, NY 10017
212-355-0090
Fax: 212-755-8894
www.waldencapital.com

Wall Street Technology Partners, L.P.
Richard H. Wolf, Contact
75 Wall Street, 34th Floor
New York, NY 10005
212-429-2817
Fax: 212-429-2261
Email: richard.wolf@dresdnerkc.com

Wasserstein Adelson Ventures, L.P.
Townsend Ziebold, Jr., Manager
1301 Avenue of the Americas, 44th floor
New York, NY 10019
212-702-5600
Fax: 212-702-5635
www.wasserco.com

Westbury Equity Partners SBIC, L.P.
Richard P. Sicoli, Contact
1400 Old Country Road
Suite 313
Westbury, NY 11590
516-333-0218
Fax: 516-333-2724
www.westburypartners.com

Winfield Capital Corp.
R. Scott Perlin, CFO
237 Mamaroneck Avenue
White Plains, NY 10605
914-949-2600
Fax: 914-949-7195
www.winfieldcapital.com

North Carolina

BA Capital Company, L.P.
J. Travis Hain, Managing Member
100 North Tryon Street, 25th Floor
NCI-007-25-02
Charlotte, NC 28255
704-386-8063
Fax: 704-386-6432
www.bankofamerica.com

BB&T Capital Partners, LLC
David Townsend & Martin Gilmore, Mgrs.
200 West Second Street, 4th Floor
Winston-Salem, NC 27101

336-733-2420
Fax: 336-733-2419
www.bbandt.com

Blue Ridge Investors II, L.P.
Kevin Jessup, Ronald Stanley, Contacts
300 N. Greene Street, Suite 2100
Greensboro, NC 27401
336-275-7002
Fax: 336-275-9155
www.genevamerchantbank.com

Blue Ridge Investors Ltd. Partnership
Richard MacLean
922 East Boulevard
Charlotte, NC 28203-5204
704-332-3346
Fax: 704-332-4528

CapitalSouth Partners Fund I, L.P.
Joseph B. Alala, III, Contact
1228 East Morehead Street, Suite 102
Charlotte, NC 28204
704-376-5502
Fax: 704-376-5877
www.capitalsouthpartners.com

Centura SBIC, Inc.
Robert R. Anders, Jr., President
200 Providence Road, 3rd Floor
P.O. Box 6261
Charlotte, NC 28207
704-686-1451
Fax: 704-686-1761
www.centura.com

Frontier Fund I, L.P.
Paul W. Stackhouse, Contact
1900 South Boulevard, Suite 300
Charlotte, NC 28203
704-414-2880
Fax: 704-414-2881
www.frontierfunds.com

North Carolina Economic Opportunities Fund
H. Dabney Smith, Contact
316 West Edenton Street, Suite 110
Raleigh, NC 27603
919-256-5000
Fax: 919-256-5015
www.dogwoodequity.com

Oberlin Capital, L.P.
Robert Shepley, Manager
702 Oberlin Road, Suite 150
Raleigh, NC 27605
919-743-2544
Fax: 919-743-2501
www.oberlincapital.com

Venture Capital Solutions, L.P.
Philip Martin, Contact
112 Cambridge Plaza Drive
Mailing address:
P.O. Box 24785
Winston-Salem, NC 27114
336-768-9343
Fax: 336-768-6471
www.vcslp.com

Wachovia Capital Partners, Inc.
Tracey M. Chaffin, Chief Financial Officer
One First Union Center, 12th Floor
301 South College Street
Charlotte, NC 28288-0732
704-374-4791
Fax: 704-374-6711
www.wachovia.com

North Dakota

North Dakota SBIC, L.P.
John G. Cosgriff, Manager
51 Broadway, Suite 400
Fargo, ND 58102

701-298-0003
Fax: 701-293-7819

Ohio

Banc One Capital Partners, LLC
James Henson
c/o Stonehenge Financial Holdings, Inc.
191 W. Nationwide Blvd., Suite 600
Columbus, OH 43215
614-246-2500
Fax: 614-246-2441
www.stonehengefinancial.com

Clarion Capital Corp.
Tom Niehaus, CFO
Ohio Savings Plaza
1801 East 9th Street, Suite 1120
Cleveland, OH 44114
216-687-1096
Fax: 216-694-3545
www.clariongrp.com

Enterprise Ohio Investment Company
(SSBIC)
Janet White, Manager
8 North Main Street
Dayton, OH 45402
937-226-0457
Fax: 937-222-7035
www.citywidedev.com

Financial Opportunities, Inc.
300 Executive Parkway West
Hudson, OH 44236
330-342-6664
Fax: 330-342-6752
Email: gbudoi@dairymart.com

Key Equity Capital Corporation
David Given, President
127 Public Square, 51st Floor
Cleveland, OH 44114
216-535-4711
Fax: 216-689-3204
www.bluepointcapital.com

Key Mezzanine Capital, LLC
Dennis Wagner
800 Superior Avenue, 10th Floor
Cleveland, OH 44114
216-828-8125
Fax: 216-263-3577
www.mcdinvest.com

National City Equity Partners, Inc.
William H. Schecter, President & G.M.
1965 East Sixth Street, Suite 1010
Cleveland, OH 44114
216-575-2491
Fax: 216-575-9965
www.nccapital.com

River Cities Capital Fund II, L.P.
Edwin Robinson, Contact
221 East Fourth Street, Suite 1900
Cincinnati, OH 45202
513-621-9700
Fax: 513-579-8939
www.rccf.com

Walnut Investment Partners, L.P.
Jimmy Gould, Managing Partner
312 Walnut Street, Suite 1151
Cincinnati, OH 45202
513-651-3300
Fax: 513-929-4441
www.TheWalnutGroup.com

Oklahoma

Chisholm SBIC, L.P.
John B. Frick, Contact
One Leadership Square
211 North Robinson Street, Suite 1910
Oklahoma City, OK 73102

405-605-1111
Fax: 405-605-1115
www.chisholmvc.com

Council Oak Investment Corporation
T. Kent Faison, Manager
101 North Broadway
Mailing address:
P.O. Box 26788
Oklahoma City, OK 73126
405-270-1000
Fax: 405-270-1089
Email: kfaison@bancfirst.com

First United Venture Capital Corporation
John Massey and Greg Massey, Managers
1400 West Main Street
Durant, OK 74701
580-924-2256
Fax: 580-924-2430
www.firstunitedbank.com

Oregon

Northern Pacific Capital Corporation
Joseph P. Tennant, President
937 S.W. 14th Street, Suite 200
Mailing address:
P.O. Box 1658
Portland, OR 97207
503-241-1255
Fax: 503-299-6653
Email: Joetpacmar@aol.com

Shaw Venture Partners III, L.P.
Ralph R. Shaw, Manager
400 Southwest Sixth Avenue, Suite 1100
Portland, OR 97204
503-228-4884
Fax: 503-227-2471
Email: judyb@shawventures.com

SmartForest Ventures I, L.P.
Debi Coleman, Contact
209 SW Oak Street, 1st Floor
Portland, OR 97204
503-222-2552
Fax: 503-222-2834
www.smartforest.com

Tamarack Mezzanine Partners, L.P.
John Woolley, Contact
522 SW Fifth Ave., Suite 915
Portland, OR 97204
503-517-8939
Fax: 503-517-8938
www.tamarackcapital.com

Utah Ventures II L.P.
Alan Dishlip
400 Lincoln Center Tower
10260 SW Greenburg Road
Portland, OR 97223
503-293-3588
Fax: 503-293-3527

Pennsylvania

Anthem Capital, L.P.
Gerald A. Schaafsma, General Partner
919 Conestoga Road
Building 1, Suite 301
Rosemont, PA 19010
610-526-9982
Fax: 610-526-2234
www.anthemcapital.com

Argosy Investment Partners II, L.P.
Knute C. Albrecht
950 West Valley Road
Suite 2902
Wayne, PA 19087
610-971-9685
Fax: 610-964-9524
www.argosycapital.com

I Wanna Start My Own Business

CIP Capital L.P.
Winston Churchill, Jr., Manager
435 Devon Park Drive, Bldg 300
Wayne, PA 19087
610-964-7860
Fax: 610-964-8136
Email: ecarey@safeguard.com

GS Capital, L.P.
Kenneth Sweet, Richard Gessner
435 Devon Park Drive
Suite 612
Wayne, PA 19087
610-293-9151
Fax: 610-293-1979
Email: ahartshorn@safeguard.com

Liberty Ventures I, L.P.
Thomas R. Morse, Manager
One Commerce Square
2005 Market Street, Suite 2040
Philadelphia, PA 19103
215-282-4484
Fax: 215-282-4485
www.libertyvp.com

Mellon Ventures, L.P.
Lawrence Mock & Ronald Coombs, Managers
One Mellon Center, Room 151-5210
Pittsburgh, PA 15258
412-236-3594
Fax: 412-236-3593
www.mellonventures.com

Meridian Venture Partners
Robert E. Brown, Jr. General Partner
201 King of Prussia Road, Suite 240
Radnor, PA 19087
610-254-2999
Fax: 610-254-2996
www.meridian-venture.com

NewSpring Ventures, L.P.
Michael DiPiano, Managing G P
500 North Gulph Road, Suite 500
King of Prussia, PA 19406
610-567-2380
Fax: 610-567-2388
www.newspringventures.com

Select Capital Ventures I, L.P.
Michael E. Salerno, Contact
4718 Old Gettysburg Road, Suite 405
Mechanicsburg, PA 17055
717-972-1304
Fax: 717-972-1050
www.selectcapitalcorp.com

Puerto Rico

North America Investment Corporation
(SSBIC)
Marcelino Pastrana Torres, President
Mercantil Plaza Bldg., Suite 813
Mailing address:
P.O. Box 1831
Hato Rey Sta., PR 00919
787-754-6178
Fax: 787-754-6181
Email: namerica@prtc.net

Puerto Rico Entrepreneurs Fund, L.P.
Abdon G. Ruiz, Contact
Union Plaza, Suite 1500
416 Ponce de Leon Avenue
San Juan, PR 00918
787-620-0062
Fax: 787-620-0131
Email: info@miraderocapital@.com

Rhode Island

Domestic Capital Corp.
Nathaniel B. Baker, President
815 Reservoir Avenue
Cranston, RI 02910

401-946-3310
Fax: 401-943-6708
www.Domestic.com

Fleet Equity Partners VI, L.P.
Brian T. Moynihan, Manager
50 Kennedy Plaza, 12th Floor
Mail Stop: RI MO F12C
Providence, RI 02903
401-278-6770
Fax: 401-278-6387

South Carolina

CF Investment Company
William S. Hummers III, Manager
102 South Main Street
Greenville, SC 29601
864-255-4919
Fax: 864-239-6423
Email: mary.gentry@thesouthgroup.com

Charleston Capital Corporation
Thomas Ervin, President and Secretary
56 Queen Street
P.O. Box 328
Charleston, SC 29402
843-723-6464
Fax: 843-723-1228
Email: yaschik@bellsouth.net

South Dakota

Bluestem Capital Partners II, L.P.
Steve Kirby and Paul Schock, Managers
122 South Phillips Avenue, Suite 300
Sioux Falls, SD 57104
605-331-0091
Fax: 605-334-1218
www.bluestemcapital.com

Tennessee

Capital Across America, L.P.
Whitney Johns & Chris Brown, Managers
501 Union Street, Suite 201
Nashville, TN 37219
615-254-1414
Fax: 615-254-1856
www.capitalacrossamerica.org

Commerce Capital, L.P.
Andrew Higgins, Pres & Rudy Ruark, V.P.
5115 Maryland Way, Suite 304
Brentwood, TN 37027
615-244-1432
Fax: 615-242-1407
www.commercecap.com

Delta Venture Partners I, L.P.
Donald L. Mundie, Contact
c/o Delta Capital Management, LLC
8000 Centerview Parkway, Suite 100
Cordova, TN 38018
901-755-0949
Fax: 901-755-0436
www.deltacapital.com

International Paper Cap. Formation, Inc.
(SSBIC)
Bob J. Higgins, V.P. and Controller
International Place II
6400 Poplar Avenue
Memphis, TN 38197
901-763-6282
Fax: 901-763-6076
Email: Bob.Higgins@ipaper.com

Massey Burch Venture Fund I, L.P.
Don Johnston, President
One Burton Hills Boulevard, Suite 350
Nashville, TN 37215
615-665-3221
Fax: 615-665-3240
www.masseyburch.com

Morgan Keegan Mezzanine Fund, L.P.
William J. Nutter, Contact
30 Burton Hills Blvd., Suite 500
Nashville, TN 37215
615-665-3636
Fax: 615-665-3670
www.morgankeegan.com

Pacific Capital, L.P.
Jere M. Ervin
Two International Plaza Drive, Suite 200
Nashville, TN 37217
615-367-0770
Fax: 615-367-1771

Petra Mezzanine Fund, L.P.
Michael Blackburn, Joseph O'Brien
172 Second Avenue North, Suite 112
Nashville, TN 37201
615-313-5999
Fax: 615-313-5990
www.petracapital.com

Valley Capital Corp. (SSBIC)
Lamar J. Partridge, President
Suite 212, Krystal Building
100 W. Martin Luther King Blvd.
Chattanooga, TN 37402
423-265-1557
Fax: 423-265-1588
Email: ValleyCapital@aol.com

West Tennessee Venture Capital Corporation
(SSBIC)
Frank Banks, President
5 North Third Street
Memphis, TN 38103
901-522-9237
Fax: 901-527-6091
Email: fjbanks@aol.com

White Pines Limited Partnership I
William D. Orand
Two International Plaza Drive, Suite 200
Nashville, TN 37217
615-367-0770
Fax: 615-367-1771

Texas

Alliance Enterprise Corporation
Donald R. Lawhorne, President
2435 North Central Expressway, Suite 200
Richardson, TX 75080
972-991-1597
Fax: 972-991-4770
www.pacesettercapital.com

AMT Capital, Ltd.
Tom H. Delimitros, CGP
5220 Spring Valley Road, Suite 600
Dallas, TX 75254
214-905-9760
Fax: 214-905-9761
www.amtcapital.com

BA Capital Company, L.P.
Doug Williamson, Sr. Vice President
901 Main Street, 22nd Floor
Dallas, TX 75202
214-508-0900
Fax: 214-508-0985

Capital Southwest Venture Corp.
William R. Thomas, President
12900 Preston Road, Suite 700
Dallas, TX 75230
972-233-8242
Fax: 972-233-7362
www.capitalsouthwest.com

The Catalyst Fund, Ltd.
Richard L. Herrman, Manager
Two Riverway, Suite 1710
Houston, TX 77056

713-623-8133
Fax: 713-623-0473
www.thecatalystgroup.net

Chen's Financial Group, Inc. (SSBIC)
Samuel S. C. Chen, President
8303 Southwest Freeway, Suite 750
Houston, TX 77074
713-772-8868
Fax: 713-772-2168
Email: chens8868@aol.com

First Capital Group of Texas II, L.P.
Messrs. Blanchard, Greenwood, & Locy
750 East Mulberry, Suite 305
San Antonio, TX 78212
210-736-4233
Fax: 210-736-5449
www.firstcapitalgroup.com

First Capital Group of Texas II, L.P.
Wm. Ward Greenwood
1601 Rio Grande, Suite 345
Austin, TX 78701
512-494-9754
Fax: 512-494-9756
www.firstcapitalgroup.com

HCT Capital Corp.
Vichy Woodward Young, Jr., President
4916 Camp Bowie Boulevard, Suite 200
Fort Worth, TX 76107
817-763-8706
Fax: 817-377-8049
Email: VWYoung@email.msn.com

Independent Bankers Capital Fund, L.P.
Floyd Collins, Barry Conrad, Contacts
1700 Pacific Avenue, Suite 2740
Dallas, TX 75201
214-765-1350
Fax: 214-765-1360
www.independentbankerscap.com

Jardine Capital Corp.
Lawrence Wong, President
6638 Sharpstown Green Circle
Houston, TX 77036
713-271-7077
Fax: 713-271-7577
www.jardinecapital.com

Main Street Mezzanine Fund, L.P.
Todd A. Reppert, Contact
1300 Post Oak Blvd., Suite 800
Houston, TX 77056
713-350-6029
Fax: 713-350-6042
www.mainstreethouston.com

MESBIC Ventures, Inc.
Donald R. Lawhorne, President
2435 North Central Expressway, Suite 200
Richardson, TX 75080
972-991-1597
Fax: 972-991-4770
www.paccsettcrcapital.com

North Texas MESBIC, Inc. (SSBIC)
Allan Lee, President
9500 Forest Lane, Suite 430
Dallas, TX 75243
214-221-3565
Fax: 214-221-3566
Email: NTM168@aol.com

PMC Investment Corporation (SSBIC)
Andrew S. Rosemore, President
18111 Preston Road, Suite 600
Dallas, TX 75252
972-349-3200
Fax: 972-349-3265
www.pmccapital.com

Power Equities, Inc.
Donald Lawhorne and Thomas Gerron
2435 North Central Expressway
Suite 200
Richardson, TX 75080
972-991-1597
Fax: 972-991-4770
Email: info@mvhc.com

Red River Ventures I, L.P.
J. Bruce Duty, Contact
15301 Dallas Parkway, Suite 820
Addison, TX 75001
972-687-7770
Fax: 972-687-7760
www.redriverventures.com

Retail & Restaurant Growth Capital, L.P.
Raymond Hemmig, Joseph Harberg, Mgrs.
10000 N. Central Expressway, Suite 1060
Dallas, TX 75231
214-750-0065
Fax: 214-750-0060
www.rrgcsbic.com

SBIC Partners II, L.P.
Nicholas Binkley & Gregory Forrest, Mgrs
201 Main Street, 27th Floor
Fort Worth, TX 76102
949-222-1987
Fax: 949-222-1988
Email: joe@fbbvc.com

Southwest/Catalyst Capital, Ltd.
Ronald Nixon and Richard Herrman, Mgrs.
Two Riverway, Suite 1710
Houston, TX 77056
713-623-8133
Fax: 713-623-0473
www.thecatalystgroup.net

Stratford Capital Partners, L.P.
Michael D. Brown/John Farmer
300 Crescent Court, Suite 500
Dallas, TX 75201
214-740-7377
Fax: 214-740-7393
Email: shenegar@hmtf.com

Stratford Equity Partners, L.P.
Michael Brown, Manager
200 Crescent Court, Suite 1600
Dallas, TX 75201
214-740-7377
Fax: 214-740-7393
Email: shenegar@hmtf.com

Toronto Dominion Capital (U.S.A.), Inc.
Martha L. Gariepy, VP/Secretary/Treas.
909 Fannin, Suite 1700
Houston, TX 77010
713-653-8225
Fax: 713-652-2647

Trident Growth Fund, L.P.
Larry St. Martin, Contact
700 Gemini, Suite 100
Houston, TX 77058
281-488-8484
Fax: 281-488-5353
www.tridentgrowthfund.com

Victoria Capital Corp.
Steve Selinske, Acting President
c/o Norwest Bank Texas, N.A.
16416 San Pedro
San Antonio, TX 78232
210-856-8804
Fax: 210-856-8848

Western Financial Capital Corporation
Andrew S. Rosemore, President
18111 Preston Road, Suite 600
Dallas, TX 75252

972-349-3200
Fax: 972-349-3265
www.pmccapital.com

Utah

First Security Business Investment Corp.
Greg Vidrine, Manager
405 S. Main St
Salt Lake City, UT 84111
801-246-1047
Fax: 801-246-1545
Email: gvidrin@fscnet.com

Utah Ventures II L.P.
Alan Dishlip & James Dreyfous, Mgrs.
2755 E. Cottonwood Parkway, Suite 520
Salt Lake City, UT 84121
801-365-0262
Fax: 801-365-0233
www.uven.com

UTFC Financing Solutions, LLC
Steve Grizzell, Contact
699 East South Temple, Suite 220
Salt Lake City, UT 84102
801-741-4200
Fax: 801-741-4249
www.utfc.org

vSpring SBIC, L.P.
Greg Warnock, Contact
2795 E. Cottonwood Parkway
Suite 460
Salt Lake City, UT 84121
801-942-8999
Fax: 801-942-1636
www.vspring.com

Wasatch Venture Corporation
Todd J. Stevens, Secretary
1 South Main Street, Suite 1400
Salt Lake City, UT 84133
801-524-8939
Fax: 801-524-8941
www.wasatchvc.com

Virginia

BIA Digital Partners, L.P.
Lloyd R. Sams, Contact
15120 Enterprise Court, Suite 200
Chantilly, VA 20151
703-818-2425
Fax: 703-803-3299
www.bia.com

Continental SBIC
Arthur Walters, President
4141 N. Henderson Road, Suite 8
Arlington, VA 22203
703-527-5200
Fax: 703-527-3700
Email: alwetal@erols.com

Development Capital Ventures, L.P.
Wayne S. Foren, Contact
510 King Street, Suite 311
Alexandria, VA 22314
703-548-3226
Fax: 703-684-8217
www.dccgrowth.com

East West United Investment Company
(SSBIC)
Dung Bui, President
1568 Spring Hill Road
Suite 100
McLean, VA 22102
703-442-0150
Fax: 703-442-0156
Email: tiffanyd@ewmortgage.com

eCentury Capital Partners, L.P.
Thomas Dann, Contact
8270 Greensboro Drive, Suite 1025

McLean, VA 22102
703-442-4480
Fax: 703-448-1816
www.ecenturycapital.com

GIV Venture Partners, L.P.
Jeff Tonkel, Contact
8150 Leesburg Pike, Suite 1210
Vienna, VA 22182
703-442-3300
Fax: 703-442-3388
www.givinc.com

Virginia Capital SBIC, L.P.
Frederick Russell & Tom Deardorff, Mgrs.
1801 Libbie Avenue, Suite 201
Richmond, VA 23226
804-648-4802
Fax: 804-648-4809
www.vacapital.com

Waterside Capital Corporation
Alan Lindauer, President
500 East Main Street, Suite 800
Norfolk, VA 23510
757-626-1111
Fax: 757-626-0114
www.watersidecapital.com

Vermont
Green Mountain Capital, L.P.
Michael Sweatman, General Manager
25 Cross Road, Suite 3
Waterbury, VT 05676
802-244-8981
Fax: 802-244-8990
www.gmtcap.com

North Atlantic Venture Fund II, L.P.
Gregory B. Peters, Vice President
76 St. Paul Street, Suite 600
Burlington, VT 05401
802-658-7820
Fax: 802-658-5757

Washington
Bancshares Capital, L.P.
John E. Thoresen, Contact
22020 17th Avenue S.E.
Suite 220
Bothell, WA 98021-8486
425-424-0058
Fax: 425-424-0809
Email: bancshares_lp@msn.com

Integra Ventures III, L.P.
Tim T. Black, Contact
300 E. Pine, 2nd Floor
Seattle, WA 98122
206-832-1990
Fax: 206-832-1991
www.IntegraVentures.net

Northwest Venture Partners II, L.P.
Thomas Simpson & Jean Balek-Miner, Mgrs.
221 North Wall Street, Suite 628
Spokane, WA 99201
509-747-0728
Fax: 509-747-0758
www.nwva.com

West Virginia
Mountaineer Capital, L.P.
Patrick A. Bond, Contact
107 Capitol Street
Suite 300
Charleston, WV 25301
304-347-7525
Fax: 304-347-0072
www.mtncap.com

WestVen Limited Partnership
Thomas E. Loehr, President
208 Capitol Street, Suite 300
Charleston, WV 25301
304-344-1794
Fax: 304-344-1998
www.fourthventure.com

Whitney Capital Corporation
Gale Gray, Manager
707 Virginia Street East, Suite 1700
Charleston, WV 25301
304-345-2480
Fax: 304-345-7258
Email: glg.ggm@wvdsl.net

Wisconsin
Banc One Stonehenge Capital Fund WI, LLC
Mr. Kent Velde, Manager
3424 N. Shepard Avenue
Milwaukee, WI 53211
414-906-1702
Fax: 414-906-1703
Email: kvelde@att.net

Capital Investments, Inc.
Steve Rippl, Exec. Vice-President
1009 W Glen Oaks Lane, Suite 103
Mequon, WI 53092
262-241-0303
Fax: 262-241-8451
www.capitalinvestmentsinc.com

Facilitator Capital Fund, L.P.
Robert Zobel, Gustavus Taylor
5133 West Terrace Drive, Suite 204
Madison, WI 53718
608-227-2900
Fax: 608-227-2901
www.facilitatorfunds.com

M & I Ventures, L.L.C.
John T. Byrnes, President
770 North Water Street
Milwaukee, WI 53202
414-765-7910
Fax: 414-765-7850
www.masonwells.com

Money to Start a Business if You Are a Minority

If you want to start or expand a business and you belong to a minority group, the Department of Commerce has something special just for you. The Minority Business Development Agency funds Business Development Centers nationwide to assist with the start-up, expansion, and acquisition of competitive minority owned firms offering quality goods and services. These centers provide business assistance for bonding, bidding, estimating, financing, procurement, international trade, franchising, acquisitions, mergers, and joint ventures to increase opportunities in domestic and international markets for minority entrepreneurs. Individuals eligible for the centers' business assistance are Hispanics, Asians, Native and African-Americans, Aleuts, Eskimos, and Hasidic Jews.

These centers are operated by private firms, nonprofit organizations, state and local government agencies, Native American tribes, and educational institutions. The centers provide accounting, administration, business planning, construction, and marketing information. They also identify minority owned firms for contract and subcontract opportunities with federal, state, and local government agencies, and the private sector. The centers identify both private and public sector sources of financing for minority owned firms and assist with the preparation of financial documents and plans for submission to lenders.

The following lists contain the local Business Development Centers to contact. If you need more information, you may contact the national headquarters at Minority Business Development Agency, U.S. Department of Commerce, Room 5099, Washington, DC 20230; 202-482-3007.

Minority Business Development Centers

Alabama
Birmingham MBDC
1718 Fifth Ave., North
Birmingham, AL 35203
205-251-2040

Mobile MBDC
801 Executive Park Dr., Suite 102
Mobile, AL 36606
205-471-5165

Alaska
Alaska MBDC
1577 C St. Plaza, Suite 304
Anchorage, AK 99501
907-274-5400

Arizona
Arizona NABDC
953 E. Juanita Ave.
Mesa, AZ 85204
602-831-7524

Phoenix MBDC
702 Osborne St., Suite 150
Phoenix, AZ 85014
602-225-0740

Tucson MBDC
1200 N. El Dorado Square, Suite D-440
Tucson, AZ 85715
602-721-1187

American Indian Consultants, Inc.
2070 E. Southern Ave.
Tempe, AZ 85282
602-945-2635

California
Bakersfield MBDC
1706 Chester Ave., Suite 407
Bakersfield, CA 93301
805-633-2787

California NABDC
9650 Flair Dr., Suite 303
El Monte, CA 91731-3008
818-442-3701

Fresno MBDC
2300 Tulare St., Suite 210
Fresno, CA 93721
209-266-2766

Oxnard MBDC
741 S. A St., Suite A
Oxnard, CA 93030
805-385-6277

Riverside MBDC
Vanir Tower
290 N. D St.
Suite 303
San Bernadino, CA 92401
909-381-4008

Sacramento MBDC
1779 Tribute Rd., Suite J
Sacramento, CA 95815
916-649-2551

Salinas MBDC
14 Maple St., Suite D
Salinas, CA 93901
408-422-8825

San Diego MBDC
7777 Alvarado Rd., Suite 310
La Mesa, CA 91941
619-668-6232

San Francisco MBDC
221 Main St., Suite 1350
San Francisco, CA 94105
415-243-8430

Oakland MBDC
1212 Broadway, Suite 900
Oakland, CA 94612
510-271-0180

San Jose MBDC
150 Almaden Blvd.
Suite 600
San Jose, CA 95113
408-275-9456

Santa Barbara MBDC
331 N. Milpas St., Suite G
Santa Barbara, CA 93103
805-965-2611

Colorado
Denver MBDC
930 W. 7th Ave.
Denver, CO 80204
303-623-5660

District of Columbia
Washington MBDC
1133 15th St. NW, Suite 1120
Washington, DC 20005
202-785-2886

Florida

Miami/Ft.Lauderdale MBDC
1200 NW 78th Ave., Suite 301
Miami, FL 33126
305-591-7355

Orlando MBDC
132 E. Colonial Dr., Suite 211
Orlando, FL 32801
407-422-6234

West Palm Beach MBDC
2001 Broadway, Suite 301
Riviera Beach, FL 33404
407-863-0895

Georgia

Atlanta MBDC
75 Piedmont Ave., NE, Suite 256
Atlanta, GA 30303
404-586-0973

Augusta MBDC
1394 Laney-Walker Blvd.
Augusta, GA 30901-2796
706-722-0994

Columbus MBDC
233 12th St., Suite 621
Columbus, GA 31920
706-324-4253

Hawaii

Honolulu MBDC
1132 Bishop St., Suite 1000
Honolulu, HI 96813-3652
808-531-6232

Indiana

Gary MBDC
567 Broadway
P.O. Box 9007
Gary, IN 46402
219-883-5802

Indianapolis MBDC
4755 Kingsway Dr., Suite 103
Indianapolis, IN 46205
317-257-0327

Kentucky

Louisville MBDC
609 W. Main St., 3rd Floor
Louisville, KY 40202
502-589-6232

Louisiana

Baton Rouge MBDC
2036 Wooddale Blvd., Suite D
Baton Rouge, LA 70806
504-924-0186

New Orleans MBDC
10001 Lake Forest Blvd., Suite 408
New Orleans, LA 70127
504-241-8664

Maryland

Baltimore MBDC
301 N. Charles St., Suite 902
Baltimore, MD 21201
410-752-7400

Michigan

Detroit MBDC
645 Griswold St., Suite 2156
Detroit, MI 48226
313-963-6232

Minnesota

Minneapolis MBDC
2021 E. Hennepin Ave., Suite LL 35
Minneapolis, MN 55413
612-331-5576

Missouri

Kansas City MBDC
1101 Walnut St., Suite 1900
Kansas City, MO 64106-2143
816-471-1520

St.Louis MBDC
231 S. Bemiston St., Suite 750
St. Louis, MO 63105
314-721-7766

New Jersey

Middlesex/Somerset/Hunterdon MBDC
390 George St., Suite 401
New Brunswick, NJ 08901
908-249-5511

New Mexico

Albuquerque MBDC
718 Central Ave. SW
Albuquerque, NM 87102
505-843-7114

Statewide New Mexico MBDC
718 Central SW
Albuquerque, NM 87102
505-843-7114

New York

Brooklyn MBDC
300 Flatbush Ave., Suite 423
Brooklyn, NY 11217
718-522-5880

Buffalo MBDC
570 E. Delavan Ave.
Buffalo, NY 14211
716-895-2218

Manhattan MBDC
51 Madison Ave., Suite 2212
New York, NY 10010
212-779-4364

Nassau/Suffolk MBDC
150 Broad Hollow Rd., Suite 304
Melville, NY 11747
516-549-5454

Queens MBDC
125-10 Queens Blvd.
Suite 2705
Kew Gardens, NY 11415
718-793-3900

Rochester MBDC
350 North St.
Rochester, NY 14605
716-232-6120

Williamsburg/Brooklyn MBDC
12 Heyward St.
Brooklyn, NY 11211
718-522-5620

North Carolina

Charlotte MBDC
700 E. Stonewall St., Suite 360
Charlotte, NC 28202
704-334-7522

Cherokee NABDC
Alquoni Bldg.
Acquoni Rd.
P.O. Box 1200
Cherokee, NC 28719
704-497-9335

Cherokee NABDC
70 Woodfin Place, Suite 305

Asheville, NC 28801
704-252-2516

Fayetteville MBDC
114 1/2 Anderson St.
Fayetteville, NC 28302
910-483-7513

Raleigh/Durham MBDC
817 New Bern Ave., Suite 8
Raleigh, NC 27601
919-833-6122

North Dakota

North Dakota NABDC
3315 University Dr.
Bismarck, ND 58504-7596
701-255-6849

Ohio

Cincinnati MBDC
1821 Summit Rd., Suite 111
Cincinnati, OH 45237-2810
512-679-6000

Cleveland MBDC
601 Lakeside, Suite 335
Cleveland, OH 44114
216-664-4155

Dayton MBDC
Society Bank Building
32 N. Main St., Suite 903
Dayton, OH 45402
513-2228-0290

Oklahoma

Oklahoma City MBDC
3017 N. MLK Ave.
Oklahoma City, OK 73111
405-424-0082

Tulsa MBDC
240 East Apache St.
Tulsa, OK 74106-3799
918-592-1995

Oregon

Portland MBDC
8959 SW Barbur Blvd., Suite 102
Portland, OR 97219
503-245-9253

Pennsylvania

Philadelphia MBDC
125 N. 8th St., 4th Floor
Philadelphia, PA 19106
215-569-3500

Pittsburgh MBDC
Nine Parkway Center
Suite 250
Pittsburgh, PA 15220
412-921-1155

Puerto Rico

Mayaguez MBDC
70 West Mendez Vigo
P.O. Box 3136 Marina Station
Mayaguez, PR 00681
809-833-7783

Ponce MBDC
Edificio El Pardo
19 Salud St.
Ponce, PR 00731
809-840-8100

San Juan MBDC
122 Eleanor Roosevelt Ave.
Hato Rey, PR 00919
809-753-8484

South Carolina

Charleston MBDC
4 Carriage Ln., Suite 201
Charleston, SC 29407
803-556-3040

Columbia MBDC
2111 Ball St.
Columbia, SC 29201
803-779-5905

Tennessee

Memphis MBDC
5 N. 3rd St., Suite 301
Memphis, TN 38103
901-527-2298

Nashville MBDC
14 Academy Place, Suite 2
Nashville, TN 37210-2026
615-255-0432

Texas

Austin MBDC
1524 S. International Hwy. 35, Suite 218
Austin, TX 78704
512-447-0800

Beaumont MBDC
330 Liberty, 2nd Floor
Beaumont, TX 77701
409-835-0440

Brownsville MBDC
2100 Boca Chica Blvd., Suite 301
Brownsville, TX 78521-2265
512-546-3400

Corpus Christi MBDC
3649 Leopard St., Suite 514
Corpus Christi, TX 78404
512-887-7961

Dallas/Ft. Worth MBDC
501 Wynnewood Village Shopping Ctr.
Suite 202
Dallas, TX 75224-1899
214-943-4095

El Paso MBDC
6068 Gateway E., Suite 200
El Paso, TX 79905
915-774-0626

Houston MBDC
1200 Smith St., Suite 2870
Houston, TX 77002
713-650-3831

McAllen MBDC
1701 W. Bus. Hwy. 83
Suite 306
McAllen, TX 78501
210-664-0073

San Antonio MBDC
1222 N. Main St., Suite 750
San Antonio, TX 78212
210-558-2480

Utah

Salt Lake City MBDC
350 East 500 S., Suite 101
Salt Lake City, UT 84111
801-328-8181

Virginia

Hampton Roads MBDC
129 W. Virginia Beach
Suite 105
Hampton, VA 23510
804-626-1635

Richmond MBDC
3805 Cutshaw Ave., Suite 402
Richmond, VA 23230
804-353-6227

Virgin Islands

Virgin Islands MBDC
31 Dronningens Gade
Drake's Passage, 2nd Floor
St. Thomas, VI 00802
809-777-4103

Washington

Northwest NABDC
100 W. Harrison
South Tower, Suite 530
Seattle, WA 98119
206-285-2190

Seattle MBDC
155 NE 100th Ave., Suite 401
Seattle, WA 98105
206-525-5617

Wisconsin

Milwaukee MBDC
1442 N. Farwell Ave., Suite 500
Milwaukee, WI 53202
414-289-3422

Native American Business Development Centers (NABDCs)

Arizona

The National Center for American Indian
Enterprise Development
953 East Juanita Ave.
Mesa, AZ 85204
602-831-7524
Fax: 602-491-1332

Native American Business Consultant
American Indian Consultants, Inc.
2070 East Southern Ave.
Tempe, AZ 85282
602-966-2061
Fax: 602-491-5035

California

The National Center for American Indian
Enterprise Development
9650 Flair Dr., Suite 303
El Monte, CA 91731-3008

818-442-3701
Fax: 818-442-7115

Minnesota

Minnesota Chippewa Tribe
P.O. Box 217
Cass Lake, MN 56633
218-335-8583
Fax: 218-335-6562

North Carolina

Eastern Band of Cherokee Indians
Acquoni Rd.
P.O. Box 1200
Cherokee, NC 28719
704-497-9335
Fax: 704-497-9009

North/South Dakota

United Tribes Technical College

3315 University Dr.
Bismarck, ND 58504
701-255-6849
Fax: 701-255-1844

Oklahoma

T3RC Associates, Inc.
5727 South Garnett, Suite C
Tulsa, OK 74146
918-250-5950
Fax: 918-250-9784

Washington

National Center for American Indian
Enterprise Development
100 West Harrison
South Tower, Suite 530
Seattle, WA 98119
206-285-2190

Matthew Lesko, Information USA, Inc., 12081 Nebel Street, Rockville, MD 20852 • 1-800-955-7693 • www.lesko.com

I Wanna Start a Business And I Have No Money

Matthew Lesko, Information USA, Inc., 12081 Nebel Street, Rockville, MD 20852 • 1-800-955-7693 • www.lesko.com

Unconventional Loan Programs

The following is a description of loan programs available to low and moderate income individuals, minorities, Native Americans, Hispanics, refugees, unemployed individuals, welfare recipients, youths, and low and moderate income individuals who don't qualify for credit through conventional methods.

Most of these programs allow individuals (depending on the situation) to roll closing costs and fees into the amount of the loan. So you actually go to the closing with NO money in your pocket.

The aim of these programs is to stimulate economic growth through small businesses or microenterprises. Helping individuals become self-sufficient is the main focus, and also to challenge conventional methods of providing credit. All of the programs hope to demonstrate that persons with limited incomes are responsible, will repay, and can become successful if given access to knowledge and resources.

Some programs are designed just for youths, (15-21 years old), to develop their own businesses, avoid drugs and crime, sharpen academic skills and form positive attitudes about themselves and their communities. This is accomplished by utilizing the leadership, communication, management and business skills they may have acquired through affiliation with the illegal drug trade and other street activities. Loan amounts can range from $50 to $2,000 with terms from six months to two years.

The following is a small sample of many success stories that we found:

Susanna Rodriquez started making ceramic figurines for children's parties. Susanna is a former teacher's assistant who presently works in the kitchen of her small apartment. Her creations fill every free corner. She was constantly looking for ways to expand her business. One day she was in a store where the owner sold similar products. As they were comparing notes, the owner mentioned ACCION New York. After four loans as a result of working with that organization, Susanna's monthly revenue from her ceramics business has increased from $350 a month to $800 a month. In time, she hopes to open her own store. She feels that if it were not for ACCION, she would not be at the advanced stage of business that she is enjoying now.

Jeff Hess of Virginia had fished and hunted with his father since the age of five. He earned his associates degree in business and was working in an assembly plant for a moderate hourly wage, but wanted more. At the age of 24 he didn't see opportunity coming to call on him because he had no money and no credit. He and his wife, Cherylanna enrolled in the BusinessStart class at People, Inc. With this training, assistance in small business planning and a small loan, Jeff and Cherylanna were able to buy a bait shop in Honaker and turn it into Bucks and Bass, a full service hunting and fishing store. Located in prime hunting and fishing country, Bucks and Bass has nearly doubled its sales in its first year alone. Both Jeff and Cherylanna have left their jobs and run Bucks and Bass full time.

Loan Programs

National Programs

* The Abilities Fund

    332 S. Linn St., Suite 15   866-720-3863
    Iowa City, IA 52240   319-338-2521
    http://www.abilitiesfund.org   Fax: 319-338-2528

The Abilities Fund is a national organization committed to advancing the entrepreneurial opportunities for Americans with disabilities. Their MicroLoans range from $300 to $25,000 to qualified entrepreneurs. Equity Grants of up to $10,000 are available to entrepreneurs with disabilities in geographic areas where they do not have an established equity grant-making relationship with a microenterprise organization. Qualified businesses for all of these programs must be at least 51% owned by an individual with a disability.

* Association for Enterprise Opportunity

    1601 North Kent Street, Suite 1101   703-841-7760
    Arlington, VA 22209   Fax: 703-841-7748
    http://www.microenterpriseworks.org/

The Association for Enterprise Opportunity is committed to microenterprise development. It primarily assists organizations to promote opportunities for people with limited access to economic resources. They do have a wide variety of resources and a list of organizations in your area.

* FIELD (Microenterprise Fund for Innovative, Effectiveness, Learning and Dissemination)

    The Aspen Institute
    One Dupont Circle, NW, Suite 700   202-736-1071
    Washington, DC 20036   Fax: 202-467-0790
    http://fieldus.org/home/index.html

FIELD's mission is to identify, develop and disseminate the best practices throughout the United States about microenterprise programs as an anti-poverty intervention. They offer publications, access to information as well as a directory of microenterprise organizations.

Alabama

* Community Development Metro Loan Fund

    Community Service Program of West Alabama
    601 17th Street   205-752-5429
    Tuscaloosa, AL 35401   Fax 205-758-7229
    http://www.cspwal.com/comdev-new-1.htm

Loans are made to open or expand small businesses owned by minorities, women and low-income individuals. Loan Amounts range from $1,000 to $25,000 for up to 5 years with a 10% interest rate. Loans are made only to businesses located within the City of Tuscaloosa.

* Alabama Microenterprise Network

    110 12th St., North   205-250-6380
    Birmingham, AL 35203   Fax: 205-250-6384

Help is available in a variety of ways for entrepreneurs who wish to start or expand their business.

* Birmingham Business Resource Center

    110 12th St., North   205-250-6380
    Birmingham, AL 35203   Fax: 205-250-6384
    www.bbrc.biz

The Birmingham Business Resource Center offers a variety of loan programs to help new or expanding businesses in the area. In addition they offer seminars, entrepreneurial training, support groups, one on one counseling and a learning center.

* Central Alabama Women's Business Center

    110 12th St., North   205-250-6380
    Birmingham, AL 35203   Fax: 205-250-6384
    www.cawbc.org

The Central Alabama Women's Business Center offers educational scholarships and loans through the Schlarb Foundation for Women

Entrepreneurs. They also offer classes, resources, newsletters and more to help women businesses in the area.

* Human Resource Development Corp.

    100 Wallace Dr.
    P.O. Box 311407   334-347-0881 ext. 22
    Enterprise, AL 36331   Fax: 334-393-0048

Help is available in a variety of ways for entrepreneurs who wish to start or expand their business.

* Huntsville Revitalization

    700 Adventist Blvd.   256-726-7139
    Huntsville, AL 35896   Fax: 256-726-8329

Huntsville Revitalization is working towards helping to revitalize the downtown area by offering a variety of programs and incentives.

* Tuskegee/Macon County Community Development Corp.

    P.O. Box 831134
    Tuskegee, AL 36083   334-724-9662

The Tuskegee/Macon County Community Development Corp. offers a variety of incentives to help improve the economic and employment opportunities in the region.

Alaska

* Southeast Alaska Revolving Loan Fund

    Juneau Economic Development Council
    612 W. Willoughby Ave., Suite A   907-463-3662
    Juneau, AK 99801-1732   Fax: 907-463-3929
    www.jedc.org

If you have a project that will create or retain jobs in Southeast Alaska, the Revolving Loan Fund might be the lender you've been looking for. Its purpose is to bridge the financial gap between what banks will finance and what the business community needs. Their goal is to provide financing for viable projects that will create and retain quality jobs and help to diversify local economies in Southeast Alaska. Loan amounts range from $35,000 - $350,000.

* Microloan Fund

    Kenai Peninsula Economic Development District
    14896 Kenai Spur Hwy., Suite 103A   907-283-3335
    Kenai, AK 99611   Fax: 907-283-3913
    www.kpedd.org

This fund is designed for the home-based entrepreneur who is primarily producing an Alaskan craft or artwork or is involved in a trade within the Kenai Peninsula. Applicants have to live in a rural area or, if in a city, a city of less than 5,000 in population. Applicants have to be financially challenged. Traditional financing sources have either denied or are under serving the applicant. Loan amounts range from $250-$1,000.

* Revolving Loan Fund

    Kenai Peninsula Economic Development District
    14896 Kenai Spur Hwy., Suite 103A   907-283-3335
    Kenai, AK 99611   Fax: 907-283-3913
    www.kpedd.org

The Kenai Peninsula Economic Development District's Revolving Loan Fund provides alternative financing options to small businesses. Financing is available to support the startup and expansion of businesses within the borough; which create long-term employment and diversify. Loan amounts range from $5,000-$50,000. Projects that are financed with Revolving Loan Fund proceeds must be located within the Kenai Peninsula Borough and stay within the Borough until paid off.

* KAWERAK CED

    P.O. Box 948   907-443-9231
    Nome, AK 99762   Fax: 907-443-4452
    www.kawerak.org

KAWERAK provides technical assistance to Bering Strait communities in small business start-up and expansion, and economic development planning. CED's mission is to promote economic growth thru increased employment and income in the Bering Strait Region; and to create an economic climate that promotes businesses development.

Arizona

* MicroBusiness Advancement Center
P.O. Box 42108   520-620-1241
Tucson, AZ 85733   Fax: 520-622-2235
www.mac-sa.org
Offers a variety of loan programs, one on one counseling, business classes and more to help new and expanding businesses succeed.

* PPEP Microbusiness and Housing Development Corp.
901 E. 46th St.   520-806-9513
Tucson, AZ 85713   Fax: 520-806-9515
www.azsmallbusinessloans.com
The PPEP Microbusiness and Housing Development Corp. provides business and housing loans designed to help with community development. Loans offered include a Microenterprise loan of up to $25,000, A Bridge Loan of up to $75,000, and a Small Business Loan of up to $250,000. They also provide business assistance in the form of business planning, bookkeeping referrals, grant writing, technical assistance, training, and more.

* Self Employment Loan Fund, Inc.
1601 N. 7th St., Suite 340   602-340-8834
Phoenix, AZ 85006   Fax: 602-340-8953
www.selfloanfund.org
The Self Employment Loan Fund offers a variety of services to help new or expanding entrepreneurs. A 10 week course on how to run a business, which covers topics such as writing a business plan, bookkeeping, marketing and more. Technical assistance includes networking, counseling, and business assistance. Two loan programs are offered. Peer Lending can be for up to $5,000 and can be sued for equipment, materials, and more. You receive continual peer support and encouragement for your business. The Individual Lending Program loans funds for up to $15,000 and you must have been in business for at least one year.

* Gila River Entrepreneurship Program
P.O. Box 97   520-562-6138
Sacation, AZ 85247   Fax: 520-562-6125
http://www.gilariverdevelopment.com/entrepreneurship.htm
The Gila River Entrepreneurship Program is designed to assist those in the Gila River Indian Community to start and run businesses to help improve the local economy. A variety of microloans, loan guarantees, and other loan programs are available. In addition, business counseling covers topics such as financing, marketing, accounting, and business planning. Classes are offered on how to run a business, as well as computer classes on different computer programs. Workshops, seminars, and artisan's cooperative are also available to entrepreneurs.

Arkansas

* Good Faith Fund
2304 W. 29th Ave.   870-535-6233
Pine Bluff, AK 71603   Fax: 870535-7883
www.goodfaithfund.org
Help is available in a variety of ways for entrepreneurs who wish to start or expand their business.

* Beacons and Bridges Business Development Center
231 S. Fisher St.   870-931-1707
Jonesboro, AR 72401   Fax: 870-910-3516
Help is available in a variety of ways for entrepreneurs who wish to start or expand their business.

* Central Arkansas Development Council
722 Gaunt St.
P.O. Box 580
    501-315-1121

Benton, AR 72018   Fax: 501-778-9120
www.cadconline.net
The Central Arkansas Development council makes small loans available to those wishing to start or expand a business. In addition would be entrepreneurs can take education and training classes to learn how to best run a successful business.

California

* California Association for Microenterprise Opportunity (CAMEO)
655 13th Street   510-238-8260
Oakland, CA 94612   Fax: 510-238-8361
http://www.microbiz.org/members.htm
CAMEO is a statewide membership organization designed to build the capacity of microbusiness organizations. CAMEO provides referrals to microbusiness owners seeking assistance. Use the site above or call to find a member service provider or for entrepreneur information in your area.

* Micro Loan
ACCESS San Diego
2612 Daniel Ave   858-560-0871
San Diego, CA 92111   Fax: 858-560-8135
www.access2jobs.org
ACCESS has created a micro loan program with funding from the San Diego Foundation. This micro loan program provides small loans to local entrepreneurs to help them "jump start" their small businesses.

* Home Based and Small Business Loans
ACCION San Diego
World Trade Center San Diego
1250 6th Avenue, Suite 500   619-685-1380
San Diego, CA 92101   Fax: 619-685-1470
http://www.accionsandiego.org/
As a community lender, this program provides low- to moderate-income small business owners loans ranging from $300-$25,000. The program is particularly geared to those businesses which are home-based, whose efforts not only support their families but, create jobs and contribute to the revitalization of their neighborhoods. First loans are usually termed between 9 and 24 months, which can enable an entrepreneur to grow their business and succeed. Serving San Diego County.

* Micro Loan Program
California Coastal Rural Development Corporation
Cal Coastal Micro Loan Program
221 Main Street   831-424-1099
Salinas, CA 93901   Fax: 831-424-1094
www.calcoastal.org/indexnew.html
Cal Coastal is a California chartered Financial Development Corporation which provides loan capital and other financial services to businesses and farms located on the Central Coast. They serve the counties of Monterey, Santa Cruz, San Benito, Santa Clara, San Luis Obispo, Santa Barbara and Ventura.

* Micro Loans
California Capital Small Business Development Corporation
926 J Street, Suite 1500   916-442-1729
Sacramento, CA 95814   Fax: 916-442-7852
cwilliams@capital.com
Serving ethnic minorities, immigrants, and women to provide counseling and individual development accounts in the Sacramento area.

* Industrial Development Bonds
City of Los Angeles Community Development Department
215 West 6th Street, 10th Floor   213-473-0311
Los Angeles, CA 90014   Fax: 213-485-8151
www.cityofla.org/cdd
City of Los Angeles Industrial and Commercial Division offers loans for projects in low to moderate-income communities in the LA and area. Loan amounts range from $500,000 to $10 million.

* Micro Enterprise Loan Program
City of Long Beach California Business Development Center
200 Pine Avenue, Suite 400   562-570-3800

Long Beach, CA 90802
www.ci.long-beach.ca.us/bdc/index.htm
Fax: 562-570-3897

The City of Long Beach Micro Enterprise Loan program provides up to $25,000 to start-up and existing businesses. The purpose for these programs is to make capital available to underserved and disadvantaged businesses, specifically those unable to obtain financing from conventional sources. Businesses must be located within the City of Long Beach.

* Community Development Financial Institute

Clearinghouse CDFI
23861 El Toro Rd, #401
Lake Forest, CA 92630
http://clearinghousecdfi.com
949-859-3600
Fax: 949-859-8534

The Clearinghouse CDFI, Community Development Financial Institution, is a corporation that is addressing unmet credit needs in Southern California. The CDFI provides direct loans for small business.

* Capital Partners, SEED Loan Program, Small Expansion Loan Program

Community Financial Resource Center
4060 So. Figueroa St.
Los Angeles, CA 90037
www.cfrc.net
323-233-1900
Fax: 323-235-1686

Community Financial Resource Center offers a variety of financial loan options for the LA area. The Capital Partners Program provides self-employed business owners and entrepreneurs access to working capital. Loans range from $500-$5,000. Start-ups as well as existing businesses are eligible. The SEED Loan program provides low cost commercial loans for businesses in operation for one year or more. SEED loans range from $5,000 to $30,000. The Small Expansion Loan Program is for businesses ready to expand. Loans range from $30,000 to $250,000.

* Micro-Enterprise Loan Fund

East Bay Asian Local Development Corporation
310 8th Street, Suite 200
Oakland, CA 94607
http://www.ebaldc.com/
510-287-5353
Fax: 510 763-4143

The East Bay Asian Local Development Corporation is a community economic development organization dedicated to the betterment of the East Bay community, particularly the low-income and Asian and Pacific Islander population. East Bay Asian Local Development Corporation provides business planning and marketing assistance to small businesses located in its commercial properties. A revolving micro-loan fund is available to commercial tenants and others seeking small business loans.

* Emergency Interest Free Loans

Jewish Free Loan Association
6505 Wilshire Boulevard, Suite 715
Los Angeles, CA 90048
www.jfla.org
323-761-8830
Fax: 323-761-8841

The Jewish Free Loan Association of Los Angeles offers interest-free loans on a non-sectarian basis to individuals, families and businesses whose needs are urgent and who may not qualify through normal financial resources. They serve the residents of Los Angeles and surrounding communities. A satellite office operates in West Hills, providing service to residents of the San Fernando and Conejo Valleys.

* Community Development Loan

Lenders for Community Development
111 West St. John Street, 10th Floor
San Jose, CA 95113
www.L4CD.org
408-297-0204
Fax: 408-297-4599

Lenders for Community Development (LCD), is a non-profit, community development financial institution whose mission is to increase the flow of capital into low-income communities throughout the Silicon Valley. LCD provides small business loans of between $5,000 and $50,000.

* Financial Assistance

Madera County Economic Development Commission
413 W. Yosemite Ave., Suite 103
Madera, CA 93637
www.maderaindustry.org
559-675-7768
800-357-5231
Fax: 559-675-3252

The Madera County Economic Development Commission provides a full range of financing and consulting services for businesses in the Madera area. This assistance could include: financial assistance through grants, loan packaging assistance, and bond funding.

* Revolving Loan Fund

Micro-Entrepreneurs Support Association
MESA Governing Council
C/O Merced County CAA
P.O. Box 2085
Merced, CA 95344-0085
www.mercedcaa.org
209-723-4565
Fax: 209-725-8574

Merced County members of the Micro-Entrepreneurs Support Association are eligible for loans for start-up or expansion of their business. Loan preference is given to micro-enterprise loans that create or retain local jobs, are to State certified women and minority owned businesses, to previous borrowers with an excellent payment record, and to finance projects that improve business by upgrading micro-enterprise employee(s) skills and wages. Loans will be for as little as $500 but no more than $10,000.

* Start-up Loans

Micro enterprise Assistance Program
2118 K Street
Sacramento, CA 95816
www.mapsac.org
916-492-2591
Fax: 916-492-2603

Microenterprise Assistance Program (MAP) empowers underserved individuals in the Sacramento area to become self-employed by providing financial assistance. MAP manages a loan pool and works with other financial agencies in Sacramento to secure funding for clients' start-up businesses.

* Loan Fund

Northern California Community Loan Fund
870 Market Street, Suite 677
San Francisco, CA 94102
www.ncclf.org
415-392-8215
Fax: 415-392-8216

The Northern California Community Loan Fund (NCCLF) was founded to help revitalize the economy of low-income communities by providing nonprofit loans to create healthier communities. NCCLF estimates that more than 61% of the clients served by NCCLF borrowers are ethnic minority and more than 40% are women. NCCLF's geographic focus is Northern California with a majority of the current portfolio focused in the San Francisco Bay Area. Loans range from $10,000 to $450,000.

* Financial Resource Center

Renaissance Entrepreneurship Center
275 5th Street
San Francisco, CA 94102
www.rencenter.org
415-541-8580
Fax: 415-541-8589

The Financing Resource Center assists San Francisco Bay Area new and established small business owners in understanding their company's financial position and growth options. A major component of the FRC is helping small business owners access needed capital to start or grow their businesses. The FRC helps entrepreneurs to package and secure loans. Loans range in size from $1,500 to $250,000.

* Micro Enterprise Loan Program

Riverside County Community Investment Corporation
4250 Brockton Avenue, Suite 100
Riverside, CA 92501
www.cicontheweb.com
909-786-1370
Fax: 909-786-0050

Community Investment Corporation extends credit to start-ups and established businesses as part of their Micro Enterprise Loan Program in the low-income areas throughout the Inland Empire. Maximum loan amounts are $25,000

* North Coast Microloan Program

SAFE-BIDCO
1211 N. Dutton Ave, Suite D
Santa Rosa, CA 95401-4638
www.safe-bidco.com
707-577-8621
Fax: 707-577-7348

SAFE-BIDCO is a catalyst for economic development of the North Coast Region, serving as a non-traditional financing source. This program is open to small businesses that are looking for financing to start-up or expand operations. Loan amounts range from $1,000-$25,000.

* Revolving Loan

Silicon Valley Economic Development Corporation
City of San Jose Revolving Loan Fund
1155 N. First Street, Suite 107
San Jose, CA 95112
www.sved.org/dsp_main.htm
408-298-8455
Fax: 408-971-0680

The Revolving Loan Fund was established to advance the economic development of San Jose by creating jobs in the community. Businesses must be in San Jose and be able to create jobs in order to obtain the loan. Loans range from $5,000 to $40,000 with no loan fees and competitive fixed rates.

* Lenders for Community Development

Start Up EPA
1395 Bay Road
East Palo Alto, CA 94303
For East Palo Alto/ East Menlo Park   650-321-2548
For Santa Clara or San Mateo counties   408-297-4554
www.startupepa.org

Start Up is a private, nonprofit organization whose mission is to promote economic development in and around East Palo Alto, California by providing training, capital, and other assistance to help establish and support locally-owned and operated small businesses. Lenders for Community Development provide fixed-rate term loans to small businesses ranging from $5,000 to $50,000. The program is targeted to women and minority-owned businesses, low-income-owned businesses, and businesses located in low-income communities.

* Business Development Loan Program

Superior California Economic Development District
737 Auditorium Dr.   530-225-2760
Redding, CA 96001   Fax: 530-225-2769
www.scedd.org

Superior California Economic Development District (SCEDD) is a four county economic development district with its main office in Redding. SCEDD offers communities and businesses in Modoc, Shasta, Siskiyou and Trinity counties loans for start-up and established businesses. Loan amounts range from $5,000 to $250,000.

* Community Capital

TELACU
5400 E. Olympic Blvd., Suite 300   323-721-1665
Los Angeles, CA 90022   Fax: 323-724-3372
www.telacu.com

TELACU Community Capital works closely with the Los Angeles Community Development Bank, serving as one of the Bank's micro-loan intermediaries. TELACU makes micro-loans on behalf of the Bank ranging from $3,000 to $25,000. The micro-loan program assists clients in gaining entry to the mainstream of the business world.

* Microenterprise Resource for Medocino County

West Company: Ukiah Office
367 N State St., Suite 201   707-468-3553
Ukiah, CA 95482   Fax: 707-468-3555
info@westcompany.org

West Company: Coast Office
306 E. Redwood Ave., Suite 2   707-964-7571
Fort Bragg, CA 95437   Fax: 707-64-7576
www.westcompany.org

If you live in Mendocino County and are interested in starting or growing a micro business the West Company may be able to help you. Recognizing that access to capital has been the most restrictive barrier to low-income people who seek self-employment, West Company makes small loans from the West Company Loan Fund to people enrolled in their program. West Company particularly strives to empower low-income persons, women and minorities by helping them to build financial stability, self-confidence, and social and personal responsibility. Opportunity Loans provide short-term access to capital to individuals needing immediate financial assistance for a discrete business use. Loan amounts range from $100 to $250. Graduate Loans are also available in the $5,001 to $10,000 range for clients who have successfully paid back a West Company loan and are in an expansion stage.

* Loan Fund

Women's Economic Ventures
Small Business Fund of Santa Barbara
1136 E. Montecito Street   805-965-6073
Santa Barbara, CA 93103   Fax: 805-962-9622
http://www.wevonline.org/

The goal of the Loan Fund is to diversify and expand the local economy and create new jobs by providing start-up and expansion capital to small businesses that do not qualify for conventional bank financing. SBLF loans are targeted to low and moderate-income men and women, minorities and others who have been traditionally underserved by lenders. Applicants must have resided within Santa Barbara for at least one year. Loans range from $1,000 to $25,000.

* Loans for Women

Women's Initiative for Self-Employment
1390 Market Street, Suite113   415-247-9473
San Francisco, CA 94102   Fax: 415-247-9471
www.womensinitiative.org

Women's Business Center
1611 Telegraph Avenue, Suite 702   415-247-9473
Oakland, CA 94612   Fax: 510-451-3428
www.womensinitiative.org/Revolving_Loan_fund.htm

Women's Initiative for Self Employment is a private, non-profit agency providing comprehensive business training, on-going technical assistance and financing to San Francisco Bay Area low-income women. Women's Initiatives lends money to women who have graduated from their "Managing Your Small Business," are starting or growing their businesses, and who show the cash-flow capacity to pay back the loan. Loans are made to businesses located in Alameda, Contra Costa, Marin, San Francisco and San Mateo Counties. The loan limit is $10,000.

* Revolving Loan

Yuba-Sutter Enterprise Zone   530-741-6463
1364 Sky Harbor Drive   530-742-6280
Marysville, CA 95901   Fax: 530-742-7835
www.yubacounty.org
www.yubasutterez.com

Yuba County, Sutter County, Yuba City, and Marysville have established revolving loan fund programs to assist businesses and industries in satisfying capital needs. These loans are often used as "gap" financing to complete a financing package. The maximum loan amount available is $150,000.

* Micro Loans

Yuba-Sutter Enterprise Zone   530-741-6463
1364 Sky Harbor Drive   530-742-6280
Marysville, CA 95901   Fax: 530-742-7835
www.yubacounty.org
www.yubasutterez.com

If you are just getting started in business and are from the Yuba County, Sutter County, Yuba City, and Marysville area this type of fund may be for you. The loan amount begins at $150 to a maximum of $25,000. Designed for the individual just starting out. Applicants must complete the 12-hour Micro enterprise Training Program.

* Anew America Community Corp.

2974 Adeline St.   510-540-7785
Berkeley, CA 94703   Fax: 510-540-7786
www.anewamerica.org

Anew American provides training and coaching to people wishing to start of expand a business. They help with marketing and planning, and provide access to capital by linking entrepreneurs with funding sources.

* Economic and Employment Development Center

2200 W. Valley Blvd., Suite A   626-281-3792
Alhambra, CA 91803   Fax: 626-281-8064

Help is available in a variety of ways for entrepreneurs who wish to start or expand their business.

* Santa Cruz Credit Union

Community Ventures
P.O. Box 1877   831-425-7708
Santa Cruz, CA 95061   Fax: 831-425-4824
www.scruzccu.org

Provides a variety of loans to entrepreneurs.

* Vermont Slauson Economic Development Corp.

5918 S. Vermont Ave.   323-753-2335
Los Angeles, CA 90044   Fax: 323-753-6710
www.vsedc.org

Vermont Slauson provides a variety of programs and services to help improve the economic environment of the community.

* Arcata Economic Development Corporation

100 EricsonCr., Suite 100 707-822-4616
Arcata, CA 95521 Fax: 707-822-8982

The Arcata Economic Development Corporation offers a variety of loan and business service assistance to those interested in starting or expanding a business.

* CHARO Community Development Corp.

4301 East Valley Blvd. 323-269-0751
Los Angeles, CA 90032 Fax: 323-343-9485
www.charocorp.com

CHARO provides a business incubator, business training, technical assistance, and loan information to the Latino community in the area.

* Jacobs Center for Non-profit Innovation

P.O. Box 740650 619-527-6161
San Diego, CA 92174 Fax: 619-527-6162
www.jacobscenter.org

The Jacobs Center for Non-profit Innovation uses a variety of financial strategies, such as equity investments, loans, loan guarantees, and more to help the people of the Diamond Neighborhoods. They work together with the residents to help make the community stronger and more vital.

* Tulare County Redevelopment Agency

5961 S. Mooney Blvd. 559-733-6291
Visalia, CA 93277 Fax: 559-730-2591
www.co.tulare.ca.us

The Tulare County Redevelopment Agency woks to help improve the economy of the area. They offer incentives to businesses and have an entrepreneur training program to help new businesses.

* Valley Economic Development Center

5121 Van Nuys Blvd., 3rd Floor 818-907-9977
Van Nuys, CA 91403 Fax: 818-907-9720
www.vedc.org

The Valley Economic Development Center offers training, consulting, technical assistance and financing to small and medium-sized businesses. They offer several different types of loan and loan guarantee programs, as well as an extensive entrepreneurial training program.

Colorado

* Colorado Alliance for Microenterprise Initiatives

3003 Arapahoe St., Suite 110 303-996-0045
Denver, CO 80205 Fax: 303-996-4939
www.coloradoalliance.org

Colorado Alliance for Microenterprise Initiatives (CAMI) is a coalition of microenterprise development organizations dedicated to providing entrepreneurs in under-served communities the opportunity and resources to become self-sufficient through private enterprise. Check with them frequently because members are added regularly.

* Initiative Loans for Small Businesses

Business Capital of Colorado, Inc.
1410 Grant St., Suite B-203 303-832-8647
Denver, CO 80203 Fax: 303-832-8649
www.bcc-colorado.com

Business Capital of Colorado, Inc. (BCC) provides loans to eligible small businesses located in Denver Metro and Boulder, Colorado. Business Capital of Colorado, Inc. serves small businesses that cannot qualify for conventional bank financing due to lack of collateral, personal credit issues, or length of time in business. Loans range from $100 up to $50,000.

* Business Loans

Colorado Lending Source 877-852-6799
730 17th Street, #1A 303-657-0010
Denver, CO 80202-3580 Fax: 303-657-0140
http://coloradolendingsource.org

Colorado Lending Source is a private, non-profit community based organization dedicated to assisting diverse small businesses within the Denver community. Loans from $10,000 are available.

* MicrocreditWorks! And BusinessWorks!

MicroBusiness Development Corporation
3003 Arapahoe St., Suite 112A 303-308-8121
Denver, CO 80205 Fax: 303-308-8120
www.microbusiness.org

Microbusiness Development Corporation is a Colorado organization that provides many services for area business owners. The Direct Lending Peer Loan Program called MicrocreditWorks! Makes small loans without credit checks or collateral for business start-up and expansion. They also provide Small Business Loans for access capital. Loans range from $500 to $30,000.

* San Juan 2000 Development Association

P.O. Box 722
1315 Snowden 970-387-5101
Silverton, CO 81433 Fax: 970-387-5104
www.sanjuan2000.org

San Juan 2000 Development Association tries to improve the community and the economy of the Silverton area by providing loans and technical assistance to new or expanding businesses. Loans can range for $500-$5,000 to help businesses grow and prosper. Technical assistance can be had in the form of bookkeeping help, marketing and planning.

* Youth Works

MicroBusiness Development Corporation
3003 Arapahoe St., Suite 112A 303-308-8121
Denver, CO 80205 Fax: 303-308-8120
www.microbusiness.org

YouthWorks helps the youth of Denver enter into the business world. Youth Works Management helps coach and support youth run businesses. They also manage the youth loan process and create opportunities for the young adults to start businesses. YouthWorks Enterprise is an entrepreneurial training program, where youth learn what it takes to run a successful business.

* Christian Community Services

Entrepreneur Loan Center
P.O. Box 984
309 San Juan Ave. 719-589-5192
Alamosa, CO 81101 Fax: 719-589-4330

Small loan is available to residents in the area for new or expanding businesses.

Connecticut

* Loaves and Fishes Ministries

360 Farmington Ave. 860-524-1730
Hartford, CT 06105 Fax: 860-249-2871

Loaves and Fishes Ministries offers a Business Initiative$ Program for low to moderated income entrepreneurs. There is a 14-week business training course and access to capital for new businesses.

Delaware

* Microloan and Business Growth Fund

First State Community Loan Fund 800-652-4779
100 West 10th Street, Suite 1005 302-652-6774
Wilmington, DE 19801 Fax: 302-656-1272
www.firststateloan.com

The First State Community Loan Fund (FSCLF) is a not-for-profit Community Development Financial Institution (CDFI) that supports small businesses and micro-enterprises particularly for the underserved populations. They have created a micro enterprise program to lend $300 to $15,000 to small businesses to be repaid with interest over a 4-month to 3-year period. For larger amounts they have a Business Growth Fund where business owners can borrow $15,001 to $50,000 to be repaid with interest over a 1-5 year period.

Florida

* Florida Community Loan Fund

3107 Edgewater Drive, Suite 2 407-246-0846
Orlando, FL 32804 888-578-2030
www.fclf.org Fax: 407-246-0856

The Florida Community Loan Fund provides capital to qualifying organizations with insufficient access to capital, from conventional lending sources. In addition, the fund has bridge loans for job training programs in Florida. At least one job must be created or retained for each $10,000 borrowed. Projects must be located in a low-income area and must employ low-income people

* Business Loan Fund of the Palm Beaches Inc.

1016 N. Dixie Hwy.   561-838-9027
West Palm Beach, FL 33401   Fax: 561-838-9029
www.businessloanfund.org

The Business Loan Fund offers several different types of funds for new or expanding businesses in the area Microloans range from $500-$7,500. Generally these loans are used to buy a new piece of equipment. Small Business Loans range from $5,000- $50,000. Typically the loans are used for new equipment, inventory or expansion. The Rural Development Intermediary Re-lending Program offers loans to those in rural areas in Palm Beach County. Loans range from $25,000- $150,000. The business Loan Fund also offers classes to train entrepreneurs in bookkeeping, marketing, planning, and more.

* Florida WWINS,Inc.

Doris Reeves-Lipscomb
3318 San Pedro St.
Clearwater, FL 33759   727-723-7714

Florida WWINS Inc. helps women entrepreneurs in a variety of areas.

* Minority/Women Business Enterprise Alliance, Inc.

625 East Colonial Drive   407-428-5860
Orlando, FL 32803   Fax: 407-428-5869
www.allianceflorida.com

The Minority/Women Business Enterprise Alliance, Inc., provides assistance to small and medium sized business in the Orlando and Orange County area, focusing on the needs of minority and women businesses. The Alliance offers a variety of loan programs. Most are available to those located in Brevard, Hillsborough, Lake, Marion, Orange, Osceola, Polk, Seminole, Sumter and Volusia counties. The Alliance Micro Loan provides loans from $1,000-$35,000 for inventory, supplies, and equipment. The Contracts/Accounts Receivable Program loans up to $10,000 based on accounts receivable financing. The Walt Disney Micro Loan program loans up to $50,000 for start-up, expansion, inventory and more for women and minority businesses. SOHO (Small Office Home Office) Community Express Loan Program offers loan of $5,000, $10,000 and $15,000 for start up, inventory, business purchase, equipment, and more. The Alliance Community Express Loan Program is a loan program of up to $5,000 for start-up, expansion, equipment, and more. Most of these loan programs come with technical assistance.

Georgia

* ACCION USA

100 Peachtree Street, Suite 700   404-521-0594
Atlanta, GA 30303   Fax: 404-521-0597
http://www.accionatlanta.org/

ACCION USA's lending methodology is character-based. Unlike traditional lenders, they don't make loans based on credit history or collateral alone. Instead, they focus on a potential borrower's initiative and desire to succeed, knowledge of his or her business and market, as well as on references from customers and neighbors. Loans range from $500 to $50,000 with terms of 3 to 36 months. They offer loans designed to match the credit needs of each business, the borrower's character and the business/family income and expenses. ACCION USA serves the following counties in Georgia: Clayton, Cobb, DeKalb, Douglass, Fulton, Gwinnett, Henry, the northern portion of Fayette county and the southern portion of Cherokee county and the Atlanta metro area.

* Mountain Partnership Loan Fund

Appalachia Community Enterprises, Inc.
1727 Turner's Corner Road   706-348-6609
Cleveland, GA 30528   877-434-6609 toll free
www.acenorthgorgia.org   Fax: 706-219-4976

The Mountain Partnership Loan Fund is a loan source for residents of Fannin, Lumpkin, White, Franklin, Hart, Stephens, Rabun, Towns, Union, Habersham, Banks, and Elbert counties who want to start or grow a small

enterprise and are not able to secure traditional financing. Loans are provided to businesses for working capital as well as business asset purchases. Maximum loan amounts are $5,000.

* Loan Fund

Business NOW
Goodwill Industries of North Georgia, Inc.
2201 Glenwood Ave., SE   404-486-8400
Atlanta, GA 30316   Fax: 404-486-8500
www.biznow.org

BusinessNOW assists women of low and moderate income who want to achieve economic self-sufficiency through self-employment. They assist women living in the Crim, Douglass and Harper Clusters of The Atlanta Project and metropolitan Atlanta who want to start and grow their own businesses. Loans range from $50 to $5,000 to qualified participants.

* Micro Loan Funds

Cobb Microenterprise Center
Kennesaw State University
Small Business Development. Center
1000 Chastain Rd - BB423   770-499-3228
Kennesaw, GA 30144   Fax: 770-423-6564
www.cobbmicro.org

The services provided by the Cobb Microenterprise Center are for low-to-moderate-income individuals who have an "entrepreneurial spirit" and need development and capital to start or grow a business. If you are on welfare, unemployed, underemployed, disable, elderly, and you have a good business idea, you can participate in this opportunity. During a 12-week training program participants will have access to credit through microloan funds, revolving loan funds, financial institutions and asset building accounts with the microenterprise Individual Development Accounts (IDA).

* East Athens Development Corporation

410 McKinley Drive   706-208-0048
Athens, GA 30601   Fax: 706-208-0015
www.eadcinc.com

The East Athens Development Corporation, Inc. (EADC) is a nonprofit community based development organization. They provide loans to micro enterprise businesses in Athens that do not yet qualify for conventional loans. The program targets businesses owned by low to moderate income, minority, and women entrepreneurs and businesses located in underserved areas. To be eligible, businesses must be located in Athens and must be for-profit. Priority will be given to low-to-moderate income, minority, and women business owners and businesses creating jobs for low-to-moderate income individuals. Loan maximums are $3,500 for terms of up to 3 years.

* Atlanta Micro Fund

AHAND
P.O. Box 11387   404-586-0808
Atlanta, GA 30310   Fax: 404-586-0805
http://ahand.org

Atlanta Micro Fund offers first-time loans for up to $1,500 for low-income people interested in starting a business. Once that loan is repaid, the business can request a larger loan.

* Refugee Women's Network

4151 Memorial Dr.
Suite 103-F
Decatur, GA 30032   404-299-0180
www.riwn.org

The Refugee Women's Network helps women start and expand their own businesses by assisting them with their microenterprise and microloans.

Hawaii

* Hawaii Community Loan Fund

677 Ala Moana Blvd., Suite 702   808-523-0075
Honolulu, HI 96813   Fax: 808-534-1199
www.hclf.org

The Hawaii Community Loan Fund (HCLF) is a certified Community Development Financial Institution that provides capital to businesses, nonprofit organizations and projects that create jobs, build wealth, and improve the quality of life for disadvantaged communities and people. HCLF's provides loans to individuals and organizations whose work and success benefits low-income individuals and communities across the state of

Hawaii. Maximum loans are $25,000 that can be used for start-up or growth of microbusinesses generally defined as businesses with five or fewer employees.

* Micro Lending

Maui Economic Opportunity, Business Development Corporation
99 Mahalani Street   808-249-2990
Wailuku, HI 96793   Fax: 808-249-2991
www.meoinc.org

Maui Economic Opportunity, Business Development Corporation is a private, nonprofit Community Action Agency that helps low-income entrepreneurs start and expand their businesses. They provide funding for low-income entrepreneurs who do not have access to traditional lending. They serve the residents of Maui and Kauai counties.

Illinois

* ACCION Chicago

3245 W. 26th Street   773-376-9004
Chicago, IL 60623   Fax: 773-376-9048
http://www.accionchicago.org/

ACCION Chicago's lending methodology is character-based. Unlike traditional lenders, they don't make loans based on revenue, collateral or credit alone. Instead, they focus on a client's commitment to their business, as well as references from customers and suppliers. ACCION Chicago offers a variety of loan products for the small business owner including individual and group loans, start-up loans and lines of credit. Loans range from $500 to $35,000. If you live in the greater Chicago area, can't qualify for conventional bank loans or have a poor credit history, ACCION may be able to help.

* LCP and IDFA Micro Loans

Lake County Partners
28055 Ashley Circle, Suite 212   847-247-0137
Libertyville, IL 60048   Fax: 847-247-0423
www.lakecountypartners.com

Have you always wanted to start a business or expand your existing one, but have been unable to access capital? You may be eligible to acquire a small business loan through the Lake County Integrated Financing Program for Small Business Micro Loan Program. They help people start or expand a small business within Lake County, Illinois. Lake Count Partners Micro Loan program loans range from $500 to $50,000 with terms of 3 to 5 years. The Illinois Development Finance Authority Micro Loan assists start-up and existing small business with access to capital of up to $25,000 and terms of up to 3 years.

* Community Development Publications

Woodstock Institute
407 S. Dearborn, Suite 550   312-427-8070
Chicago, IL 60605   Fax: 312-427-4007
www.woodstockinst.org

The Woodstock Institute offers a variety of business related publications including descriptions of community development banks, community development loan funds, community development credit unions, and microenterprise funds.

* Jewish Vocational Service - Chicago

Duman Microenterprise Center & Loan Fund
One South Franklin Street   312-357-4548
Chicago, IL 60606   Fax: 312-553-5544
www.jvschicago.org

The Duman Microenterprise Center and Loan Fund helps those wishing to start or expand a small business. You can apply for zero or low interest loans up to $15,000, business assistance, seminars, mentoring, network opportunities, and more.

* Tri-County Opportunities Council

405 Emmons Avenue
Rock Falls, IL 61071   800-323-5434
www.tcochelps.com/

The Tri-County Opportunities Council offers assistance to small businesses to help increase employment opportunities. The loan program is coordinated with banks and other financial organizations. Training is also provided to those wishing to start or expand their business.

Indiana

* Community Action Program, Inc. of Western Indiana

418 Washington St.
P.O. Box 188   765-793-4881
Covington, IH 47932   Fax: 765-793-4884
www.capwi.org

The Community Action Program of Western Indiana offers a revolving loan of $10,000 (or possibly more) for people wishing to start or expand a business. Funds can be used for working capital, inventory, or even fixed assets. Funds cannot be used for construction or the purchase of real estate.

* Neighborhood Self-Employment Initiative

Concord Community Development Corporation
324 W. Morris   317-917-3266
Indianapolis, IN 46225   Fax: 317-917-1447
http://concordindy.org

Neighborhood Self-Employment Initiative (NSI) is a program targeting low to moderate income people wishing to start or expand their business in urban Indianapolis. The NSI offers business assistance, which includes training, mentoring, financing, and more. They offer a 20 hour business course for those wishing to start a business.

Louisiana

* Acadiana Regional Development District

601 Loire Ave., Suite C
P.O. Box 90070   337-886-7782
Lafayette, LA 70507   Fax: 337-886-7081
www.ardd.org

Acadiana Regional Development District provides small business loans through the Revolving Loan Fund Program for businesses based in Acadia, Evangeline, Iberia, Lafayette, St. Landry, St. Martin, St. Mary and Vermilion Parishes. Financing is provided on a mid-level scale, ranging from $10,000 up to $150,000.

* Louisiana Department of Economic Development

Mailing address:
P.O. Box 94185
Baton Rouge, LA 70804
Physical address:
Capital Annex
1051 N. 3rd Street   225-342-3000
Baton Rouge, LA 70802   Fax: 225-342-5389
www.lded.state.la.us

The Louisiana Economic Development Corporation (LEDC) administers several loan programs for small Louisiana businesses. The Micro Loan Program provides loan guarantees and participations to banks that fund loans ranging from $5,000 to $50,000 to Louisiana small businesses.

* Micro Loans for Women

Microenterprise Development Alliance of Louisiana
1200 S. Acadian Thruway, Suite 204   225-387-1166
Baton Rouge, LA 70806   Fax: 225-343-6935
www.microenterprisela.org

The MicroEnterprise Development of Alliance Louisiana (MEDAL) is a statewide not for profit alliance committed to helping entrepreneurs through the establishment of microenterprises, particularly by women and youth. MEDAL will provide loans as well as other financial services to women microentrepreneurs.

Maine

* Penquis C.A.P., Inc.

262 Harlow Street   207-973-3612
Bangor, ME 04401   Fax: 207-973-3699
www.penquiscap.org

Penquis Community Action Program primarily serves low- and moderate-income individuals in Penobscot and Piscataquis Counties. Their Economic Development Department provides assistance to individuals interested in starting or expanding a microenterprise, a business with five or fewer employees. Small Business Loans are available to low-income residents who want to start or expand a business and who are unable to receive financing from traditional sources, such as a bank or other lending institutions.

* Women, Work, and Community

Administrative Office
46 University Drive
Augusta, ME 04330-9410   800-442-2092
http://www.womenworkandcommunity.org/

Women, Work, and Community was begun to help women re-enter the job market, but has since expanded to include a variety of programs to improve the lives of women in Maine. They offer assistance in business planning development, access to financing, and other programs to help women-owned businesses succeed. Services include workshops, training courses, and a mentoring. Self-employment Assistance for TANF is a program to help those on welfare start a business and run it successfully.

Maryland

* Garrett County Community Action MicroWorks

104 E. Center Street   301-334-9431
Oakland, MD 21550   Fax: 301-34-8555
www.garrettcac.org

Garrett County Community Action Corporation is a not for profit corporation committed to improving the quality of life for persons with needs by helping them become more self sufficient. The Microenterprise Loan offers a variety of options for the small business owners of Garrett County, Maryland. Loan amounts range from $500 to $15,000.

* Maryland Capital Enterprises, Inc.

P.O. Box 1844   866-MARY-CAP
Salisbury, MD 21802   410-546-1900
www.marylandcapital.org   Fax: 410-546-9718

Maryland Capital Enterprises work to build economically distressed communities by supporting micro businesses. They offer many small community-based businesses the resources they need to grow. The loan program is solely based on the individual. Loan amounts range from $2,000 to $15,000.

Massachusetts

* ACCION USA

56 Roland Street   617-625-7080
Suite 300, South Lobby   Toll-free: 866-245-0783
Boston, MA 02129   Fax: 617-625-7020
www.accionusa.org/boston/

ACCION USA's lending methodology is character-based. Unlike traditional lenders, they don't make loans based on credit history or collateral alone. Instead, they focus on a potential borrower's initiative and desire to succeed, knowledge of his or her business and market, as well as on references from customers and neighbors. Loans range from $500 to $50,000 with terms of 3 to 36 months. If you are an entrepreneur who lives in the greater Boston area, can't qualify for conventional bank loans or have a poor credit history, ACCION may be able to help.

ACCION USA
450 Essex Street, 2nd Floor   978-725-5934
Lawrence, MA 01840   Fax: 978-794-7600
www.accionusa.org/lawrence/
Serving greater Lawrence area.

ACCION USA
One Federal Street
Building 101   413-734-6679
Springfield, MA 01105   Fax: 413-755-6101
www.accionusa.org/springfield/
Serving greater Springfield area.

ACCION USA
11 Pleasant Street, Suite 300   508-799-0029
Worcester, MA 01609   Fax: 508-799-7771
www.accionusa.org/worcester/
Serving greater Worcester area.

* Day Care Business Loans

Acre Family Day Care Corporation
14 Kirk Street   978-937-5899
Lowell, MA 01852   Fax: 978-937-5148
www.acrefamily.org

The Acre Family Day Care not for profit organization that helps low-income women in Greater Lowell become financially independent by providing child care training and assistance in setting up licensed child care businesses in their own homes. Acre can offer business loans for start-up or expansion of family day cares.

Michigan

* Renaissance MicroLoan Development Fund

Cornerstone Alliance
P.O. Box 428
38 W. Wall Street   269-925-6100
Benton Harbor, MI 49023   Fax: 616-925-4471
www.cstonealliance.org

The Renaissance Development Fund was created by the Cornerstone Alliance to promote economic development in the most distressed region of the Twin Cities area of Benton Harbor and St. Joseph, Michigan. The fund provides credit to small businesses in the service area that do not have access to traditional financing. They offer a Neighborhood Venture Loan for entrepreneurs who are facing start-up costs. Loans range from $500 to $3,000 with terms of 6 months to two years. The Commercial Micro Loan program is for small businesses that have been in business for at least 6 months. Loan amounts range from $500 to $25,000 with terms from 6 months to 5 years. The Renaissance Development Fund also offers larger loan for more established businesses.

* Detroit Entrepreneurship Institute, Inc.

455 W. Fort St., 4th Floor   313-961-8426
Detroit, MI 48226   Fax: 313-961-8831
www.deibus.org

The Detroit Entrepreneurship Institute (DEI) provides entrepreneurship training to those interested in starting or expanding a business. The DEI provides an incredible number of programs and services, almost all of which are free. Business consultants and assigned to help you with your business. A computer center is available and has accountants on duty to help with bookkeeping. For those who complete the training program, DEI has several loan funds to help with business needs. A library and graphic design services as also available. The Self-Employment Initiative offers workshops, training, consultations, business cards, and more. The Enterprise Development Initiative offers consultations, training, design services, and a loan fund. The Young CEO & Investor Program teaches children ages 14-17 how to operate a business.

* Kent Area MicroBusiness Loan Services

Masonic Temple Building
233 E. Fulton, Suite 101   616-771-6880
Grand Rapids, MI 49503   Fax: 616-771-8021
www.kamls.org

KAMLS offers loans and assistance to new or expanding companies in the Grand Rapids or Kent County Area. Microloans are available for up to $3,000. Money can be used for working capital, inventory, furniture, or equipment. You may not purchase real estate or pay off debt. In addition, KAMLS offers support to help your business succeed.

Minnesota

* Neighborhood and Small Business Loans

Neighborhood Development Center, Inc
651-½ University Avenue   651-291-2480
St. Paul, MN 55104   Fax: 651-291-2597
www.windndc.org

The Neighborhood Development Center, Inc (NDC) is a community-based non-profit organization that works with entrepreneurs in the inner city of Minneapolis and St. Paul develop successful businesses and stronger neighborhoods. NDC provides access to credit for start-up businesses and other entrepreneurs who do not qualify for traditional financing. The Neighborhood Entrepreneurs Fund is available to graduates of NDC's training programs. Loan amounts range from $500 to $10,000. NDC's Small Business Loan Fund makes loans available up to $30,000 to established small businesses in the St. Paul inner city neighborhoods.

* Child Care Business Loan

Tri-County Community Action Program, Inc.
501 LeMieur St.
P.O. Box 368   320-632-3691
Little Falls, MN 56345   Fax: 320-632-3695
www.tccaction.com

The Tri-County Community Action Program is a not for profit corporation committed to creating opportunities for self-sufficiency for citizens in Crow Wing, Morrison and Todd Counties. The Child Care Business Loan Program is exclusively for Family Day Care Providers. Loans can be used to start or expand a business. In addition, loan recipients are eligible for business skills training. Loan amounts range from $300 to $3,000.

* MEDA

250 Second Ave., South, Suite 106   612-332-MEDA
Minneapolis, MN 55401   Fax: 612-317-1002
www.meda.net

MEDA provides assistance to new and expanding businesses owned by ethnic minorities. MEDA offers a loan program to help those who typically are denied financing through traditional lenders. Loans can be for up to $300,000 and are for working capital, equipment, capital expenditures, and more.

* Arrowhead Community Economic Assistance Corporation

8880 Main Street Bank Building, POB 406   218-735-8201
Mountain Iron, Minnesota 55768   Fax: 218-735-8202
Email: aceac@rangenet.com

Arrowhead Community Economic Assistance Corporation (ACEAC) is a community-based non-profit providing primary service to Cook, Lake and St. Louis counties, excluding the City of Duluth. ACEAC also provides service to Aitkin, Carlton, Itasca, and Koochiching counties in cooperation with individual communities, other agencies and organizations. Services include community development and business planning, technical assistance, business loans and other types of financial assistance that will benefit low- and moderate-income persons. This includes providing technical assistance coupled with small business loans, a micro-business loan and TA project and a peer group-lending project. Loans can range up to $50,000. Money can be used for assets, equipment, and capital expenditures. New or expanding businesses are eligible, as well as home based businesses

* North Star Community Development Corporation

301 West 1st Street, Suite 604   218-727-6690
Duluth, MN 55802   Fax: 218-723-7120
www.nstarcdc.org

North Star Community Development Corp. helps local businesses by providing financing, training, seminars, workshops, and other forms of assistance to help them succeed. Many of those served are low-income individuals wishing to start or expand a business. Business located in Duluth are eligible for assistance. Loans are available up to $20,000 and businesses must be located in Duluth. Businesses must also agree to hire low to moderate income people to fill new jobs created at their business.

* Initiative Foundation

405 First Street Southeast   320-632-9255
Little Falls, MN 56345   Fax: 320-632-9258
Email: info@ifound.org
http://www.ifound.org/

The Initiative Foundation helps promote economic development throughout the state. They offer four different types of loan funds to help improve the job environment and increase wages by providing assistance to businesses. The Microenterprise Loan Guarantee Program offers loans up to $50,000 for women, minorities, and young adults who generally lack the needed capital. Seed Capital Fund has money for up to $50,000 for new businesses. The Direct Business Loan Program offers up to $250,000 for new or expanding companies that will increase the number of jobs available. The Technology Capital Fund has $500,000 to support new technology ventures.

* Southeastern MN Development Corporation

P.O. Box 684   507-864-7557
Rushford, MN 55971   Fax: 507-864-2091
Email: mthein@acegroup.cc
www.semdc.com/

The Southeastern Minnesota Microenterprise Fund makes available up to $35,000 to new or expanding businesses in the area. Money can be used for capital expenditures, inventory, equipment, real estate, and renovation. Business must exist in any of eight communities in the Southeastern part of the state.

Mississippi

* Micro Loan

Minority Business Enterprise Division
Mississippi Development Authority
501 North West Street
P. O. Box 849   601-359-3448
Jackson, MS 39205   Fax: 601-359-5290
www.mississippi.org

The Mississippi Development Authority administers the state Minority

Business Loan Program as a source of financing for small businesses. A minority business is an economically disadvantaged small business with at least on minority or female owner. Loan amounts range from $2,000 to $15,000 with terms up to 5 years.

* Micro Loan

Quitman County Development Organization, Inc.
201 Humphrey Street
PO Box 386   662-326-4000
Marks, MS 38646   Fax: 662-326-3904
www.qcdo.org

The Quitman County Development Organization (QCDO) Micro-Enterprise Loan and Business Development Program is dedicated to assisting women, minority and small businesses in Quitman County and surrounding areas. The Micro Loan Program provides loans for all types of businesses start-ups and expansions. Loan are reviewed and determined on a per loan basis, with loan amounts typically ranging from $500 to $25,000.

* Minority Capital Fund of Mississippi

2530 Bailey Ave.   601-713-3322
P.O. Box 11305   877-713-3322
Jackson, MS 39283   Fax: 601-713-3610
www.mincap.org

The Minority Capital Fund of Mississippi provides financing and other types of assistance to minority and women owned businesses located in Mississippi. This is designed to help with the disparity between the minority owned and majority owned businesses. The goal of all is to help improve the economic and employment opportunities in the area. Loans are available up to $150,000, and money can be used for equipment, working capital, inventory, and other capital expenditures. In addition, the Fund provides technical assistance with marketing, accounting, business planning, and more.

Missouri

* Micro Loans

Growth Opportunity Connection
4747 Troost Avenue   816-235-6146
Kansas City, MO 64110   Fax: 816-235-6177
Email: acorbet@goconnection.org
www.goconnection.org

The Growth Opportunity Connection is a non-profit organization, specializing in assisting small businesses prepare and obtain financing. The Micro Loan Program provides funds for micro-entrepreneurs who do not qualify for conventional lending. They help both start-up and expanding businesses. Loan amounts are up to $35,000 with terms of up to 5 years.

* International Institute

3654 S. Grand Blvd.   314-773-9090
St. Louis, MO 63118   Fax: 314-773-6047
http://www.intlinst.org/

The Micro Enterprise Development Program is designed to assist refugees in the St. Louis area. The program offers business planning, training, marketing, technical, and other types of assistance to those not yet citizens. The services are offered free of charge.

Montana

* Small Business Loans

Montana Department of Commerce
301 S Park Ave
Helena, MT 59601
Mailing address:
P.O. Box 200501   406-841-2751
Helena, MT 59620-0501   Fax: 406-841-2701
www.commerce.state.mt.us

The Montana Department of Business Resources provides small businesses with 10 or fewer employees and gross revenue of less than $500,000 the opportunity to apply for a revolving loan of up to $35,000. They have a close relationship with resource providers to help low-to-moderate income people interested in self-employment

* District 7 Human Resources Development Council

7 North 31st St.   406-247-4732
Billings, MT 59101   Fax: 406-248-2943

www.hrdc7.org

The Human Resources Development Council offers a revolving loan program to business wishing to start or expand. The loans are for up to $35,000 and can be used for working capital, inventory, and more.

Nebraska

* Micro Loan Fund

Lincoln Action Program
210 "O" Street
Lincoln, NE 68508
www.lincoln-action.org

402-471-4515
Fax: 402-471-4844

The Microenterprise Program is designed to help low-to-moderate incomes establish their own small businesses. Access to small loans through peer lending are available. Loan Funds are provided by the Nebraska Microenterpriese Development Partnership Fund and Union Bank and Trust Company.

* Micro Business Directory

Nebraska Department of Economic Development
Nebraska Micro Business Resource Directory
P.O. Box 6605
Lincoln, NE 68506-0605
http://neon.neded.org/mbrd/index.html

402-420-9589

The Nebraska Micro Business Resource Directory provides a wide variety of loan options available to micro businesses in Nebraska.

* Small Business Loans

Community Development Resources
1135 M Street
3rd Floor, Suite 116
Lincoln, NE 68508-3169
http://www.self-lincoln.org/about.html

402-436-2386
Fax: 402-436-2360

SELF provides business loans for small and home-based businesses in the City of Lincoln, Nebraska. Loan amounts range from $250-$25,000.

New Hampshire

* Microbusiness Loans

MicroCredit-NH
7 Wall Street
Concord, NH 03301
http://www.microcreditnh.org/

603-224-2069
Fax 603-225-7425

MicroCredit-NH provides small loans to microbusinesses in New Hampshire. Loan amounts range from $500 to $5,000.

New Jersey

* Small Business Loans

New Jersey Economic Development Authority
PO Box 990
Trenton, NJ 08625-0990
http://www.njeda.com/

609-292-1800

The New Jersey Economic Development Authority offers direct loans for small businesses, minority-owned and women-owned businesses. Generally loans are available to enterprises located in Atlantic City although monies are available for other areas.

* Microbusiness Loans

Prudential Young Entrepreneur Program
NJIT-Enterprise Development Center
105 Lock Street
Newark, NJ 07103
www.njit-edc.org/PYEP.htm

973-643-4063

The program assists entrepreneurs between 18-30 years of age starting businesses. Microloans are available to qualified young adults establishing businesses in targeted urban areas.

* Micro Loan Fund

Tri-County Community Action Agency
River's Edge Community Campus
110 Cohansey Street
Bridgetown, NJ 08302

856-451-6330
Fax: 856-455-7288

http://www.tricountycaa.org/

Tri-County Community Loan Fund provides loans to small businesses in Cumberland, Gloucester and Salem counties. Loans amounts range from $5,000 to $30,000.

* Bergen County Economic Development Corporation

One Bergen County Plaza, Suite 440
Hackensack, NJ 07601
www.bergen4business.com

201-336-7500
Fax: 201-336-7513

The Bergen County Economic Development Corporation (BCEDC) wants to help businesses succeed in the area. They have partnered with many different agencies to offer assistance and training to business owners. The Bergen County Small Business Loan Program provides loans for people to open new or expand their businesses.

* Elizabeth Development Company

288 North Broad St., 3rd Floor
P.O. Box 512
Elizabeth, NJ 07207
http://www.edcnj.org/

908-289-0262
Fax: 908-558-1142

The Elizabeth Development Company offers a variety of programs to help new or expanding business in the city of Elizabeth. Business financing, site location, and an Urban Enterprise Program are just some of the ways businesses can start and grow in the area.

* Hudson County Economic Development Corporation

601 Pavonia Ave., Suite 302
Jersey City, NJ 07306
http://www.hudsonedc.org/

201-222-1900
Fax: 201-222-6350

The Hudson County Economic Development Corporation helps businesses in a variety of ways including loan programs. The Business Loan Program offers funds up to $100,000 that can be used for capital, inventory, equipment, real estate purchase, and more. The MicroLoan Program offers funds up to $25,000 to business in East Newark, Guttenberg, Harrison, Hoboken, Kearney, Secaucus, Weehawken, and West New York. The HCEDC also has a bonding program.

New Mexico

* ACCION Loan

ACCION New Mexico
20 First Plaza NW, Suite 417
Albuquerque, NM 87102
http://www.accionnewmexico.org/

505-243-8844
800-508-7624
Fax: 505-243-1551

ACCION is a community-based organization that provides loans to entrepreneurs in targeted counties of New Mexico. Loan amounts range from $200 to $20,000.

* Loan Fund

New Mexico Community Development Loan Fund
Mailing Address:
PO Box 705
Albuquerque, NM 87103
Street Address:
700 Fourth Street, SW
Albuquerque, NM 87102
http://www.nmcdlf.org/

505-243-3196
Fax: 505-243-8803

The New Mexico Community Development Loan Fund provides loans for small businesses in New Mexico. Particular emphasis is placed on helping low-income people; minority and women based businesses that are unable to obtain traditional financing.

New York

* ACCION New York

235 Havemeyer St.
Brooklyn, NY 11211
http://www.accionnewyork.org/

718-599-5170
Fax: 718-387-9686

ACCION New York provides loans for businesses to expand or start a new business. ACCION serves all 5 boroughs of New York City. Loan amounts range from $500 to $25,000.

* Start-up Loan

Appleseed Trust
220 Herald Place, 2nd Floor   315-424-9485
Syracuse, NY 13202   Fax: 315-424-7056
http://www.appleseedtrust.org/

Appleseed Trust is a not for profit organization that is committed to assisting low- to moderate-income residents of Syracuse to start or expand their own business. Entrepreneurs with an idea for a product or service can pay a small monthly fee to participate in an eight-week training program. The process includes applying for an initial loan.

* Community Loan Fund

Capital District Community Loan Fund
255 Orange Street
Albany, NY 12210   518-436-8586
http://www.cdclf.org/1024.html

The Community Loan Fund provides loans to small businesses and micro businesses in the New York State Capital region. Loans of up to $10,000 are available for business start-ups and up to $25,000 for business expansions.

* Loan Fund

Chautauqua Microenterprise Loan Fund
Chautauqua Opportunities for Development
402 Main Street   716-366-2334
Dunkirk, NY 14048   Fax 716-366-7407
http://www.codi-wny.com

The Chautauqua Microenterprise Loan Fund provides loans to small businesses with fewer than 5 employees in Chautauqua County. Loans must have a positive impact on low-income to moderate-income individuals. Loan amounts range from $1,000 to $15,000.

* Micro-Loans

Homesteaders Federal Credit Union
2052 Adam Clayton Powell Jr. Blvd   212-222-0328
New York, NY 10027   Fax: 212-222-1035
http://www.homesteadersfcu.org/

The Homesteaders Federal Credit Union is a not-for-profit financial institution that provides affordable financing for people in the Harlem and New York City areas. Loans of up to $25,000 are available.

* Peer Micro Lending

Project Enterprise
144 West 125th St., 4th Floor   212-678-6734
New York, NY 10027   Fax: 212-678-6737
http://www.projectenterprise.org/

Project Enterprise lending practices provides business credit to New York's low-income individuals. It is a comprehensive program delivering microcredit, business training and networking opportunities to entrepreneurs in New York City's economically disadvantages communities. Members interested in credit may access loans starting at a maximum of $1,500. After each successful loan repayment, the member may increase their available credit in steps up to a maximum of $12,000.

* Loans

Rural Opportunities, Inc
400 East Avenue   716-340-3387
Rochester, NY 14607-1910   Fax: 716-340-3326
www.ruralinc.org

Rural Opportunities, Inc is a not-for-profit community development organization providing services to low to moderate-income people and economically depressed communities throughout New York and Ohio. The aim is to promote self-sufficiency and economic independence through the creation and expansion of microenterprises. Loan amounts of up to $50,000.

* Trickle Up

104 W. 27th Street, 12th Floor   212-255-9980
New York, NY 10001   Fax: 212-255-9974
www.trickleup.org

Over 75% of the recipients of this program either have no credit and cannot even apply for a microloan. Entrepreneurs are given $700 in grant money, not loans for start-up capital. Grants are awarded in two installments with requirements, which are required of the recipient. Most of the businesses are home based with grants being used to buy supplies such as flour for baking or yarn for sewing products to sell.

* Loans for Women

Women's Venture Fund, Inc
240 West 35 Street, Suite 201   212-563-0499
New York, NY 10001   Fax: 212-868-9116
www.womensventurefund.org

The Women's Venture Fund relies on character-based lending principles in approving loans to low-income women who lack business experience. Women applicants must establish their skills of business concepts submit a business plan and possess a willingness to comply with program requirements. The Assessment Committee identifies businesses that can implement growth plans with loans up to $15,000.

* Washington Heights and Inwood Development Corporation

57 Wadsworth Ave.   212-795-1600
New York, NY 10033   Fax: 212-781-4051
www.members.aol.com/whidc

The Washington Heights and Inwood Development Corporation offers a variety of programs to help new and expanding businesses in the area. The Business Operating Success System offers a micro loan program, as well as a business assistance center. They also offer a mentoring program and a street vendor program.

* ACCORD Corp.

84 Schuyler Street   585-268-7605
Belmont, NY 14813   Fax: 585-268-7241
www.accordcorp.org/

The Allegany County Community Opportunities and Rural Development offers entrepreneurial assistance through 120 hours of classroom instruction and mentoring. Topics covered include business planning, bookkeeping, marketing, finances, and more. They also offer a Micro Enterprise Revolving Loan Fund of up to $3,500.

North Carolina

* Loans for Crafts People

HandMade in America
P.O. Box 2089   828-252-0121
Asheville, NC 28802   Fax: 828-252-0388
www.handmadeinamerica.org

HandMade in America works closely with financial institutions in Western North Carolina that understand craft businesses and offer alternative lending programs. Contact their office for additional information on loan options.

* Individual Development Account

Mountain Microenterprise Fund
29 ½ Page Avenue   828-253-2834
Asheville, NC 28801   Fax: 828-389-3089
www.mtnmicro.org

Mountain Microenterprise Fund (MMF) provides entrepreneurs with the option to set up an Individual Development Account. The fund matches your $1,000 for capitalizing your business with matches as large as $2,000, which means you triple your savings. Members of MMF also receive assistance in obtaining loans.

* Group and Individual-Based Lending

North Carolina Microenterprise Loan Program
4021 Carya Drive   919-250-4314
Raleigh, NC 27610   Fax 919-250-4325
ckperry@ncruralcenter.org
http://www.ncruralcenter.org/grants/micro.htm

The North Carolina Microenterprise Program provides rural people with small business loans to help them become self-sufficient through business ownership. The program helps low-income and rural area individuals who have sound business ideas but do not qualify for traditional financing. Loan amounts are up to $25,000.

Ohio

* ASSETS Toledo

333 14th St.   419-381-2721
Toledo, OH 43624   Fax: 419-720-0079
http://www.assetstoledo.com/

ASSETS Toledo assists individuals in Lancaster County who strive for self-employment but have limited resources. They provide capital through their Loan Fund to graduates of their business course.

* Food and Technology Loans

ACEnet –Appalachian Center for Economic Networks
94 Columbus Road   740-592-3854
Athens, OH 45701   Fax: 740-593-5451
www.acenetworks.org

The fund works with the food and technology sectors, including start-ups that have the potential to create wealth for low-income entrepreneurs. The fund provides capital for any business activities not served by conventional financial institutions. Loans are awarded packaged with technical assistance provided by ACEnet's staff to increase the likelihood of business success.

* Revolving Loan Funds

Community Action Committee of Pike County
MicroEnterprise/Business Development Department
941 Market Street
P.O. Box 799   740-289-2371
Piketon, OH 45661   Fax: 740-289-4291
www.pikecac.org

The Community Action Committee of Pike County administers three revolving loan funds available to those clients who successfully complete the Business Training program. The fund offers financial assistance to potential entrepreneurs who are not able to get loans through traditional lenders. Rates and terms are based upon each business's ability to repay. Loans range from $200 to $100,000, which cannot exceed 8 years.

* Greater Cincinnati Microenterprise Initiative

1501 Madison Rd., 1st Floor Rear   513-569-4816
Cincinnati, OH 45206   513-569-4816
www.gcmi.org   Fax: 513-569-0075

Greater Cincinnati Microenterprise Initiative (GCMI) provides access to microloans to individual business owners who are low to moderate income. Loans may be used to start or expand a small business. Microloan amounts range from $500 to $10,000 with a repayment period of 36 months.

Oklahoma

* Micro-Enterprise Development Program

Cherokee Nation
P. O. Box 948   918-456-0671
Tahlequah, OK 74465   800-256-0671 in Oklahoma only
http://www.cherokee.org

Loans are available to Native American entrepreneurs residing and operating their business in rural area of the Cherokee Nation. Loans of up to $25,000 with a maximum term of 7 years.

Oregon

* Micro Loans

Mercy Enterprise
936 SE Ankeny, Suite 1
Portland, OR 97214   503-236-1580
http://www.mercyenterprise.org/

Mercy is a nonprofit organization, which provides financing to entrepreneurs in the Portland area who may not have perfect credit but have the "entrepreneurial spirit". Loans from $500 to $25,000 with terms up to 36 months and competitive rates.

* Childcare Neighborhood Network Loan Fund

ROSE Community Development
5215 SE Duke Street
Portland, OR 97206-6839   503-788-0826 ext. 109
http://www.rosecdc.org/childcare.htm

Through community based micro enterprise development, ROSE Community Development Corporation helps to increase the character of childcare and secure providers' businesses. These loans are established in order to help the childcare providers who have difficulty getting conventional loans. Loan amounts range from $500 to $5,000 for child care business expenses such as equipment, education, and minor facility renovations.

* Shorebank Enterprise Pacific

429 Spruce Street
P. O. Box 56   541-572-5172
Myrtle Point, OR 97458   Fax: 541-572-5261
http://www.sbpac.com/index.cfm

Shorebank Enterprise is a nonprofit rural economic development corporation assisting entrepreneurs build business and market ventures, which improve the social and environmental conditions of rural communities. Loan amounts range from $3,000 to $350,000 for new business start-up or new equipment for existing businesses.

Pennsylvania

* Community Capital Works

Philadelphia Development Partnership
1334 Walnut Street, 7th Floor   215-545-3100
Philadelphia, PA 19107   Fax: 215-546-8055
http://www.pdp-inc.org/

Community Capital Works' mission is to increase self-employment, employment and income-generating opportunities through microenterprise activities with a focus on entrepreneurs from socially and economically distressed communities in the City of Philadelphia and the City of Chester. Loan amounts range from $500 to $5,000.

* Prudential Young Entrepreneur Program (PYEP)

The Enterprise Center
4548 Market Street
Philadelphia, PA 19139   215-895-4000
www.theenterprisecenter.com/forentre/start_business/pyep.asp

The Prudential Young Entrepreneur Program (PYEP) is an innovative microenterprise initiative funded by The Prudential Foundation to help provide young adults with the skills and resources they need to make their entrepreneurial dreams a reality. The PYEP is an extensive, multi-year business development and job creation program for young adults between the ages of 18-30. It combines business training, technical assistance and microloans to qualified young adults establishing businesses in targeted urban areas.

* Revolving Loan Fund

Rural Enterprise Development Corp.
10 East Main Street
P.O. Box 276   570-784-7003
Bloomsburg, PA 17815-0276   Fax: 570-784-7030
http://www.redc-leap.org/

The Local Enterprise Assistance Program through the Rural Enterprise Development Corporation loans funds for new business startups as well as business expansions. Loan amounts range from $500 to $25,000.

Rhode Island

* ACCION USA

775 Mineral Spring Avenue   401-722-5558
Pawtucket, RI 02860   Fax: 401-722-0629
http://www.accionusa.org/rhodeisland/
Serving all of Rhode Island

South Dakota

* Loan Fund

Four Bands Community Fund, Inc.
Cheyenne River Lakota Nation
101 South Main Street
P.O. Box 932   605-964-3687
Eagle Butte, SD 57625   Fax: 605-964-3689
http://www.fourbands.org/loan_fund.htm

Four Bands Community Fund, Inc., is a non-profit corporation, which assists entrepreneurs of the Cheyenne River Indian Reservation by providing access to capital, encouraging economic development and enhancing the quality of life for all communities and residents of the reservation. They offer a MicroLoan that of $100 to $1,000 and Small Business Loans of $1,000 to $25,000.

Tennessee

* Central Appalachian Microenterprise Program (CAMP)

East Tennessee Community Partnership Center
300 East Main Street, Suite 301   423-232-5730
Johnson City, TN 37601   Fax: 423-232-5760
http://www.etsu.edu/keystone/microenterprise.html
Microenterprise loan funds are structured to make loans to individuals much like traditional bank lending model.

Texas

* ACCION Texas

2014 S. Hackberry   888-215-2373
San Antonio, TX 78210   Fax: 210-533-2940
http://www.acciontexas.org/   210-226-3664 (San Antonio inquiries)
Serving San Antonio, Austin, Brownsville, Dallas, El Paso, Fort Worth, Harlingen, Houston and McAllen

* Loan Program

Alliance for Multicultural Community Services
6440 Hillcroft, Suite 411   713-776-4700
Houston, TX 77081   Fax: 713-776-4730
http://www.allianceontheweb.org
The Alliance's mission is to assist refugees, immigrants, and other low-income residents of Harris County. They offer an Individual Development Account, which provides matching funds for entrepreneurs in addition to small business workshops. Through their newly established Multicultural Community Development Corporation (MCDC), they have added a microenterprise loan program.

* PLAN Fund

2008 Didsbury Rd., Apt. B   214-942-6698
Dallas, TX 75224   Fax: 214-942-5430
www.planfund.org
The PLAN Fund (Peer Lending Action Network) is a micro-lending program for low-income people, especially women, who would like to start a new business. Anyone interested in a loan will be part of a group of people similarly driven to become entrepreneurs. The group works together reviewing business plans and training. You are accountable to the group. There are three different loan types: General loans of up to $1,500; Short Term Loans payable over ten weeks; and Technology Loans for computer equipment. For more information contact PLAN.

Utah

* Micro-Loan, Childcare and "Under 3-Step" Loan Programs

Utah Microenterprise Loan Fund
3595 South Main St   801-269-8408
Salt Lake City, UT 84115   Fax 801-269-1063
http://www.umlf.com/
The Utah Microenterprise Loan Fund is a private, non-profit, multi-bank community development financial institution, whose mission is to provide financing to entrepreneurs in start-up and existing firms that do not have access to traditional funding sources; especially those who are socially and economically disadvantaged. UML offers three loan products for businesses. Their Traditional Micro-Loan is available for start-up and existing businesses in Boxelder, Davis, Morgan, Salt Lake, Summit, Tooele, Utah or Weber counties. Loan amounts of up to $10,000 for 5 years at a fixed 5% interest rate. Childcare Provider Loan's are available for working capital and construction of day care facilities in Salt Lake County. "Under 3 Step Loan" program is designed businesses needing even smaller loans between $0-$3,000. The "stepped" program means that borrowers receive a small first loan (0-$500) for short terms with follow-up loans offered in progressively larger amounts. Businesses must be located in Salt Lake County.

Vermont

* Vermont Job Start

58 E. State Street, Suite 5   802-828-5466
Montpelier, VT 05602   Fax: 802-828-5474
http://www.vermontjobstart.org

Vermont Job Start's mission is to help develop self-employment opportunities for low to moderate-income entrepreneurs of Vermont. Loan amounts up to $20,000 are available with terms of up to 5 years at a fixed 8% interest rate.

* Community Economic Development Program

Central Vermont Community Action
195 US Rt. 302   800-639-1053
Barre, VT 05641   802-479-1053
The Community Economic Development Program provides financing, support, and assistance to low income individuals who would like to start or expand a business. The community Capital of Central Vermont offers up to $50,000 loans and other assistance to help small businesses.

Virginia

* Micro-Loan Program

Community Business Partnership
6911 Richmond Hwy., Suite 290   703-768-1440
Alexandria, VA 22306   Fax: 703-768-0547
http://www.cbponline.org
Community Business Partnership was formed in response to an identified need for small business financing services, particularly to low-moderate income and disadvantaged individuals, including minorities, women and the disabled. Loans are available from $3,500 to $25,000 to benefit low-moderate-income individuals in Fairfax County. Loan recipients do not have to be low-moderate income to qualify, however all loans must in some way benefit low-moderate income individuals

* New Enterprise Fund

Community Housing Partners Corporation
930 Cambria Street, NE   540-382-2002
Christiansburg, VA 24073   Fax: 540-382-1935
http://www.communityhousingpartners.org/
The New Enterprise Fund provides entrepreneurs with microloans from $1,000 to $25,000 with terms of one to four years at 8% interest rate. Individual Development Accounts are available with a matching 3:1 program for income qualifying individuals. They serve low to moderate-income individuals. Women, minorities and youth are encouraged to apply. Businesses must be located in the counties of Floyd, Giles, Montgomery, Pulaski, and the City of Radford.

* Micro Loans

New Visions, New Ventures, Inc.
801 East Main Street, Suite 1100   804-643-1081
Richmond, VA 23219   Fax: 804-643-1085
http://nvnv.org/index.html
New Visions, New Ventures supports women in difficult life situations, striving to become independent by providing microenterprise development. They provide clients access to capital through Individual Development Accounts that match savings accounts. New Visions, New Ventures works closely with community micro lenders to provide loans to clients.

* Valley Microenterprise Alliance

1251 Virginia Avenue
Harrisonburg, VA 22802   540-433-5624
http://www.vmalliance.org/
Valley Microenterprise Alliance offers microloans to encourage underemployed and low to moderate-income individuals to start or expand a microenterprise in the Shenandoah Valley Region. Valley Microenterprise Alliance offers character-based microloans for small business purposes to graduates of the Blueprint for Business Success training class

* Middle Peninsula Business Development Partnership

125 Bowden St.
P.O. Box 286   804-758-4917
Saluda, VA 23149   Fax: 804-758-3221
www.mppdc.com
The Business Development Partnership helps small businesses start or expand in the Middle peninsula of Virginia. They offer up to $25,000 loans to help your business. In order to be eligible for the loan, you must complete an 8 course business training program and have five or fewer employees.

Washington

* Microloan Program

Center for Economic Opportunity
202 North Tacoma Avenue   253-591-7026
Tacoma, WA 98402   Fax: 253-593-2744
http://www.mdc-tacoma.org/page26.html
The Center for Economic Development provides low-income adults in Tacoma Pierce County access to loans in support of their microenterprise development.

* Shorebank Enterprise Pacific

203 Howerton Way SE
P.O. Box 826   360-642-4265
Ilwaco, WA 98624   Fax: 360-642-4078
http://www.sbpac.com/index.cfm
Shorebank Enterprise is a nonprofit rural economic development corporation assisting entrepreneurs build business and market ventures, which improve the social and environmental conditions of rural communities. Loan amounts range from $3,000 to $350,000 for new business start-up or new equipment for existing businesses.

* Microenterprise Loan

Spokane Neighborhood Action Program
212 South Wall Street   509-456-7174
Spokane, WA 99201   Fax: 509-456-7170
http://www.snapwa.org/microent.html
The Microenterprise Development Program is designed to assist low to moderate-income individuals and families to realistically enter into business, expand an existing small or home-based business. They offer a term loan from $500 to $10,000 in conjunction with technical support.

West Virginia

* Micro Loans Fund

Unlimited Future, Inc.
1650 Eighth Avenue
Huntington, WV 25703   304-697-3007
http://www.unlimitedfuture.org
Unlimited Future, Inc. offers access to micro loans for graduates of their Business Basic Training Course.

Free Business Assistance Programs

A helping hand is just a phone call away for individuals who want to enter into a small business or microenterprise. If you fall into any of the following categories: low to moderate income, Native American, minorities, women, welfare recipients, or have little or no money, you may be eligible for a wide range of assistance. These programs are aimed to assist individuals toward self-sufficiency.

Imagine getting training, counseling, peer support and exchange, and mentoring for free to help you get the knowledge you need to start your own business. Learn how to prepare a business plan and get guidance from the best instructors in the country. One such program is NOVA, located in Arkansas. Their program has four major components: Group Training; Individual Sessions; Business Start-Up; and Networking and Mentoring.

Imagine youths able to receive effective business course training. One such program is Kidpreneur Enterprises, located in Michigan. This program is available to all youths who express an interest in owning and operating their own small business. Kidpreneur is designed to provide and instill concepts and experiences in the minds of youths.

Doors can open for entrepreneurs, like Adina Rosenthal, owner of Threadbearer, a fabric and accessory shop located on Capitol Hill. At a very young age, Adina knew she wanted to work with fabrics. At age 17, she lost the use of her right arm when she was hit by a logging truck. After receiving her degree from the Fashion Institute of Design and Merchandising she attempted to get work at various design companies only to be passed over time and time again. A friend suggested she join the Black Dollar Days' program for entrepreneurs. After completing their entrepreneurial program, Adina opened Threadbearer. She accredits her success to the assistance she received, and is still receiving, from the Black Dollar Days Task Force.

Daryl Anderson an experienced roofer, lacked the necessary skills to run a business of his own. In 1994, Daryl began his involvement with the Cottage Industry Programs offered by the Portsmouth Community Development Group (PCDG) in Montana. After a year of technical assistance, the use of an office, and hours of encouragement, Daryl and his wife Karen were able to open Quality Roofing and Siding. Daryl admits he never would have made it without PCDG's commitment to business counseling and training.

The aim of these programs is to develop a participant's confidence and skills in understanding business enterprise and to further the development of viable business ideas.

Technical Assistance Programs

National Programs

* The Abilities Fund

332 S. Linn St., Suite 15
Iowa City, IA 52240
http://www.abilitiesfund.org

866-726-3863
319-338-2521
Fax: 319-338-2528

The Abilities Fund is a national organization committed to advancing the entrepreneurial opportunities for Americans with disabilities. They provide a unique combination of financial products, training, technical assistance services, and advisory supports to individuals with disabilities.

* Association for Enterprise Opportunity

1601 North Kent Street, Suite 1101
Arlington, VA 22209
http://www.microenterpriseworks.org/

703-841-7760
Fax: 703-841-7748

The Association for Enterprise Opportunity is committed to microenterprise development. It primarily assists organizations to promote opportunities for people with limited access to economic resources. They do have a wide variety of resources and a list of organizations in your area.

* FIELD (Microenterprise Fund for Innovative, Effectiveness, Learning and Dissemination)

The Aspen Institute
One Dupont Circle, NW, Suite 700
Washington, DC 20036
http://fieldus.org/home/index.html

202-736-1071
Fax: 202-467-0790

FIELD's mission is to identify, develop and disseminate the best practices throughout the United States about microenterprise programs as an anti-poverty intervention. They offer publications, access to information as well as a directory of microenterprise

* Hobbies into Cash

http://www.make-stuff.com/home_business/index.html
Make-Stuff.com is an on-line resource for crafters, hobbyist and

Matthew Lesko, Information USA, Inc., 12081 Nebel Street, Rockville, MD 20852 • 1-800-955-7693 • www.lesko.com

entrepreneurs. They provide information in turning your craft or hobby into a marketable business.

* Free On-Line Training

My Own Business Inc.
13181 Crosswoods Parkway North, Suite 190   562-463-1800
City of Industry, CA 91746   Fax: 562-463-1802
http://www.myownbusiness.org/

My Own Business Inc. is a non-profit organization dedicated to educating entrepreneurs by giving them access to vital information about business. They provide a free 12-session business course intended for both start-up and established businesses.

* ONABEN

11825 SW Greenburg Road, Suite B-3   800-854-8289
Tigard, OR 97223   503-968-1500
http://www.onaben.org/   Fax: 503-968-1548

ONABEN is a non-profit organization created by Northwest Indian Tribes to increase the success of private businesses owned by Native Americans regardless of tribe. They offer free workshops on a variety of topics including: Website Planning and Development and Website Building Computer-Based Workshop. Their business classes: Financial Literacy and Starting a Successful Business are available for a fee. ONABEN is available to Native Americans living in Oregon, Washington, Idaho, or Northern California.

Alabama

* Birmingham Business Resource Center

110 12th St., North   205-250-6380
Birmingham, AL 35203   Fax: 205-250-6384
www.bbrc.biz

The Birmingham Business Resource Center offers a variety of loan programs to help new or expanding businesses in the area. In addition they offer seminars, entrepreneurial training, support groups, one on one counseling and a learning center.

* Central Alabama Women's Business Center

110 12th St., North   205-250-6380
Birmingham, AL 35203   Fax: 205-250-6384
www.cawbc.org

The Central Alabama Women's Business Center offers educational scholarships and loans through the Schlarb Foundation for Women Entrepreneurs. They also offer classes, resources, newsletters and more to help women businesses in the area.

Alaska

* Business Innovation Center

Kenai Peninsula Economic Development District
14896 Kenai Spur Hwy., Suite 103A   907-283-3335
Kenai, AK 99611   Fax: 907-283-3913
www.kpedd.org

The mission of the Kenai Peninsula Economic Development Center is to serve the Kenai Peninsula Borough residents by enhancing their quality of life through responsible and sustainable regional economic and workforce development. The Business Innovation Center (BIC) is a small business incubator designed to provide assistance for new and expanding businesses in the Kenai Peninsula Borough.

Arizona

* Self Employment Loan Fund, Inc.

1601 N. 7th St., Suite 340   602-340-8834
Phoenix, AZ 85006   Fax: 602-340-8953
www.selfloanfund.org

This program provides a variety of services to help those in the area who wish to start or expand a business.

Arkansas

* Business Assistance

Alt.Consulting
Delta Region Office:
6210 Dollarway Road, Suite 5-1   870-267-1725

Pine Bluff, AR 71602   Fax: 870-267-1726
www.altconsulting.org/

Alt.Consulting is a non-profit, economic development organization that operates like a management-consulting firm but is driven by a passion for economic justice. They provide on-site business assistance for the clients they serve.

* MicroEnterprise Development and Training

Central Arkansas Development Council
P.O. Box 580   501-315-1121
Benton, AR 72018   Fax: 501-778-9120
http://www.cadconline.net/

This initiative helps make credit accessible to the low-income through a combination of education, training, mentoring, and resource development. Economic Literacy classes gives persons in all areas the tools needed to get out of debt and to build sound financial futures. Pre-Business Classes helps individuals develop plans to become entrepreneurs in their communities. Serving Calhoun, Clark, Columbia, Dallas, Hot Spring, Lonoke, Montgomery, Ouachita, Pike, Pulaski, Saline, Union counties.

California

* California Association for Microenterprise Opportunity (CAMEO)

655 13th Street   510-238-8260
Oakland, CA 94612   Fax: 510-238-8361
http://www.microbiz.org/members.htm

CAMEO is a statewide membership organization designed to build the capacity of microbusiness organizations. CAMEO provides referrals to microbusiness owners seeking assistance. Use the site above or call to find a member service provider or for entrepreneur information in your area.

* Micro Business Training

ACCESS San Diego
2612 Daniel Ave   858-560-0871
San Diego, CA 92111   Fax: 858-560-8135
www.access2jobs.org

ACCESS offers microenterprise training and development to prepare low-income individuals especially those in low-income communities impacted by immigrants. Clients are taught how to start and operate a small business in fields where they have expertise including handcrafts or cultural or ethnic services

* One-On-One Training

ACCION San Diego
World Trade Center San Diego
1250 6th Avenue, Suite 500   619- 685-1380
San Diego, CA 92101   Fax: 619-685-1470
http://www.accionsandiego.org/

ACCION helps clients build favorable credit histories and improve their business skills with one-on-one training in bookkeeping, preparation of financial statements and credit repair. They support the leadership and entrepreneurial spirit of their clients energy in San Diego's low-income neighborhoods.

* Micro Loans

California Capital Small Business Development Corporation
926 J Street, Suite 1500   916-442-1729
Sacramento, CA 95814   Fax: 916-442-7852
cwilliams@capital.com

Serving ethnic minorities, immigrants, and women to provide microloans in the Sacramento area.

* Business Development Center

Central California Small Business Development Center
Fresno Office
3419 W. Shaw, Suite 102   559-275-1223
Fresno, CA 93711   800-974-0664

Visalia Office
720 West Mineral King
P.O. Box 787
Visalia, CA 93279   559-625-3051
www.ccsbdc.org

The mission of the Central California Small Business Development Center

(CCSBDC) is to enhance economic growth by making the Central Valley's small businesses more competitive through entrepreneurial assistance. The CCSBDC provides one-on-one counseling, business training and a variety of workshops.

* Child Care Home Business

Chicano Federation of San Diego County, Inc
Southeastern Regional Resource Center.
610 22nd Street
San Diego, CA 92102-2909   619-236-1228, Ext. 315
www.chicanofederation.org

The Southeastern Regional Resource Center builds child care capacity in unserved and underserved communities in San Diego, Orange and Imperial Counties through training and technical assistance for small private child care centers, community based organizations, ethnic organizations and family child care providers to increase and enhance quality child care centers. Provides family child care home (FCCH) training, accelerated child development training, subsidized child care for infants and toddlers (birth to 36 months), center-based child care and development for pre-school children (3 to 5 years old), financial reimbursements for meals provided to children in licensed child care homes.

* Technical Assistance

Community Financial Resource Center
4060 So. Figueroa St.   323-233-1900
Los Angeles, CA 90037   Fax: 323-235-1686
www.cfrc.net

The Center offers technical assistance in English and Spanish to help entrepreneurs in the LA area prepare loan packages and develop business plans.

* Business Training for Women

Creating Economic Opportunities for Women (CEO)
971 Regal Road
Berkeley, CA 94708   510-526-3258
www.ceowomen.org

CEO Women is an organization dedicated to helping immigrant women create economic opportunities for themselves and their families. They offer micro-enterprise business training, technical assistance, and asset education to women who are planning to start or expand their own business. CEO Women concentrates its efforts on assisting low to moderate-income women within the San Francisco Bay Area but also assists the broader population of women in need of micro-enterprise support services. All CEO Women programs are offered on a sliding scale basis.

* East Bay Small Business Development Center

519 17th Street, Suite 210   510-893-4114
Oakland, CA 94612-1528   Fax: 510-893-5532
www.ebsbdc.org

The East Bay Small Business Development Center (EBSBDC) provides training, one-on-one counseling and workshops throughout Alameda County. All of the programs are designed to assist business owners in developing the critical tools needed for long-term success. Consulting services and most training events are available at no cost.

* Small Business Development Center

Eastern Los Angeles County Small Business Development Center
363 S. Park Ave., Suite 101   909-629-2247
Pomona, CA 91766   Fax 909-629-8310
Email: sbdcpom@ibm.net
www.companyhelp.org

The Eastern Los Angeles County Small Business Development Center provides management and business technical assistance at no cost to small businesses and entrepreneurs in Eastern Los Angeles County.

* Business Assistance

El Pájaro Community Development Corporation
23 East Beach Street, #209   831-722-1224
Watsonville, CA 95076   Fax: 831-722-3128
www.elpajarocdc.org

El Pájaro Community Development Corporation has more than twenty years of experience in the provision of bilingual/bicultural small business assistance and job creation for primarily minority and low-income entrepreneurs. Serving the El Pájaro community.

* Business Programs

Fresno West For Economic Development
Fresno Street, Suite 212   559-485-1273
Fresno, CA 93706   Fax: 559-485-1276
www.fwced.org

The Fresno West Coalition for Economic Development's (FWCED) overall mission and goal is to improve the physical and socio-economic condition of the Southwest Fresno area and its residents. They develop programs for small businesses located in or desiring to locate within the Fresno area.

* Training and Technical Assistance

Jefferson Economic Development Institute
711 Pine Street
P.O. Box 1586   530-926-6670
Mt. Shasta, CA 96067   Fax: 530-926-6676
www.e-jedi.org

The Jefferson Economic Development Institute (JEDI), is located in Mt. Shasta, California, and serves all of Siskiyou County. They offer free and low-cost services to Siskiyou County residents who would like to receive help to grow or start a business along with individualized technical assistance.

* BusinesStarts Program

Job Starts, Inc.
3010 West 48th Street
Los Angeles, CA 90043
www.jobstarts.org

BusinesStarts Program targets the poorest of the economically active persons in south Los Angeles communities to assist emerging entrepreneurs start or improve a business enterprise in order to help families improve their economic well being. The Program consists of Business Design and Management Training Workshops, Volunteer Mentors, Technical Assistance, and Access to Credit Classes.

* Legal Assistance

Legal Aid Foundation of Los Angeles
8601 South Broadway   231-640-3968
Los Angeles, CA 90003   Fax: 231-640-3988
www.lafla.org

Legal Aid Foundation of Los Angeles provides legal help for low-income people; they promote access to justice, strengthen communities, combat discrimination, and provide community education.

* Los Angeles Business Assistance Program

City of Los Angeles Community Development Department
216 West 6th Street, 10th Floor   231-473-0311
Los Angeles, CA 90014   Fax: 231-485-8151
www.cityofla.org/cdd

Los Angeles Business Assistance Program (LABAP) provides technical assistance, support and growth for area entrepreneurs and microenterprises in the LA area. Training is provided for microenterprises and start-ups using high quality, reasonably priced technical services.

* Training and Technical Assistance

Madera County Economic Development Commission
413 W. Yosemite Ave., Suite 103   559-675-7768
Madera, CA 93637   800-357-5231
www.maderaindustry.org   Fax: 559-675-3252

The Madera County Economic Development Commission (MCEDC) provides counseling and guidance for small businesses and assists in their development and expansion in the Madera area. Resources include the business and marketing plans, finance analysis, access to capital and technical assistance.

* Business and Technical Assistance

Micro-enterprise Assistance Program
2118 K Street   916-492-2591
Sacramento, CA 95816   Fax: 916-492-2603
www.map-srm.org

Micro-enterprise Assistance Program (MAP) empowers underserved individuals in the Sacramento area to become self-employed by providing business and technical assistance. MAP has developed and continues to refine a program of training and assistance specifically tailored to meet the needs of our clients.

Free Business Assistance Programs

* Technical Assistance

Mission Economic Development Association
3505 20th Street
San Francisco, CA 94110
415-282-3334
Fax: 415-282-3320
www.medasf.org

The Mission Economic Development Association is a community-based corporation located in the Mission District of San Francisco. MEDA targets minority and women-owned businesses and provides them with technical assistance and business training.

* Micro Business Incubation

Technical Assistance
The New America Foundation
2974 Adeline St.
Berkeley, CA 94703
510-540-7785
Fax: 510-540-7786
www.anewamerica.org

The New America Foundation offers a 3-year holistic program of asset building for families and communities. The current programs serve Latino and Indo-Chinese communities in the San Francisco Bay Area through micro business incubation, networking and technical assistance.

* Business Assistance

North Coast Small Business Development Center (NCSBDC)
520 E Street
Eureka, CA 95501
707-443-5057
Fax: 707-445-9652
www.northcoastsbdc.org

North Coast Small Business Development Center provides business assistance, education and resources not available in isolated rural communities to small business owners. They serve new and established businesses in the Del Norte and Humboldt Counties. Free services include general information, referrals and consulting assistance. Low cost services include troubleshooting, problem solving and technical support.

* Business Resource Center

North San Diego County
1823 Mission Avenue
Oceanside, CA 92054
760-795-8740
Fax: 760-795-8728
www.sandiegosmallbiz.com

The Small Business Development and Resource Center serves North San Diego County providing business assistance. They offer one-on-one business consulting, workshops, training, referral resources and a business resource center.

* Business Assistance

PACE Business Development Center
1541 Wilshire Boulevard, Suite 310
Los Angeles, CA 90017
213-353-9400
213-353-4665
www.pacela.org

The Pacific Asian Consortium in Employment (PACE) was founded in 1975 to address the employment and job training needs of the Asian Pacific Islander communities. There are a variety of business assistance programs for entrepreneurs in the LA area.

* Outreach

Planada Community Development Center
9167 East Stanford Avenue
P.O. Box 1045
Planada, CA 95365
209-382-2321
Fax: 209-82-2316
www.planadacdc.org/abcd.htm

Planda CDC goals are to provide low-income entrepreneurs, especially women, minorities and immigrants with support through increased outreach.

* One-On-One Counseling

Redwood Empire Small Business Development Center
606 Healdsburg Avenue
Santa Rosa, CA 95401
707-524-1770
Fax: 707-524-1772
www.santarosa.edu/sbdc

The Redwood Empire Small Business Development Center, hosted by Santa Rosa Junior College, is a valuable resource for the small business communities in Marin, Sonoma, and Mendocino Counties of California. The program assists small businesses by providing one-on-one, no cost, business consulting, low-cost workshops and technical assistance.

* Business Training

Renaissance Entrepreneurship Center

275 5th Street
San Francisco, CA 94102
415-541-8580
Fax: 415-541-8589
www.rencenter.org

Training classes and workshops provide hands-on practical experiences that teach you what you need to know to start and grow your own business. The business incubator provides office space, consultation and support services for growing businesses. There is also a Women's Business Center offering programs to help women succeed in business.

* Investment Corporation

Riverside County Community Investment Corporation
4250 Brockton Avenue, Suite 100
Riverside, CA 92501
909-786-1370
Fax: 909-786-0050
www.cicontheweb.com

Community Investment Corporation provides mentoring and coaching to help entrepreneurs in low-income areas throughout the Inland Empire overcome obstacles of business ownership.

* Business Training and Childcare Provider Services

Silicon Valley Economic Development Corporation
1155 N. First Street, Suite 107
San Jose, CA 95112
408-298-8455
Fax: 408-971-0680
www.sved.org/dsp_main.htm

Silicon Valley Economic Development Corporation provides opportunities for low-income persons, and other disadvantaged individuals in Santa Clara County to become entrepreneurs. Services are offered through a variety of programs, including: Entrepreneur training, business assistance center, childcare provider services and classes for developmentally disabled entrepreneurs.

* One-On-One Counseling

Business Resource Center
Small Business Development and International Trade Center
Southwestern College (SBDITC)
900 Otay Lakes Road, Building 1600
Chula Vista, CA 91910
619-482-6393
Fax: 619-482-6387
www.sbditc.org

The Small Business Development and International Trade Center provides, free of charge, many resources to assist potential and existing entrepreneurs in the San Diego and Imperial counties. Their small business services include: one-on-one counseling, seminars, classes, import/export assistance, and a business resource center.

* Capital Access Initiative

Start Up EPA
1395 Bay Road
East Palo Alto, CA 94303
650-321-2193 ext. 15
Fax: 650-321-1025
www.startupepa.org

Start Up is a private, nonprofit organization whose mission is to promote economic development in and around East Palo Alto, California by providing training, capital, and other assistance to help establish and support locally-owned and operated small businesses. Start Up's Capital Access (CAP) initiative aims to help clients' access a broad array of financing resources and technical assistance needed to launch and sustain viable enterprises.

* MicroEnterprise Development Program

Superior California Economic Development District
737 Auditorium Dr.
Redding, CA 96001
530-225-2760
Fax: 530-225-2769
www.scedd.org

Superior California Economic Development District (SCEDD) is a four county economic development district with its main office in Redding. SCEDD offers communities and businesses in Modoc, Shasta, Siskiyou and Trinity counties economic, technical and business assistance.

* Technical Assistance

Vermont Slausen Economic Development Corporation
VSEDC Headquarters
5918 S. Vermont Avenue
Los Angeles, CA 90044
323-753-2335
Fax: 323-753-6710
http://vsedc.org/

VSEDC Business Enterprise Center
6109 S. Western Avenue
Los Angeles, CA 90047
323-789-4515

http://vsedc.org/   Fax: 323-789-4524

The VSEDC facilitates community development of the Vermont Slauson area by providing programs structured to revitalize the community. VSEDC has developed and implemented a comprehensive approach to community economic development that includes business development, technical assistance and training,

* Microenterprise Resource for Medocino County

West Company: Ukiah Office
367 N State St., Suite 201   707-468-3553
Ukiah, CA 95482   Fax: 707-468-3555

West Company: Coast Office
306 E. Redwood Ave., Suite 2   707-964-7571
Fort Bragg, CA 95437   Fax: 707-964-7576
www.westcompany.org

If you live in Mendocino County and are interested in starting or growing a microbusiness the West Company may be able to help you. West Company delivers Technical Assistance to business owners through consultations. Technical Assistance is conducted on a one-on-one basis with clients.

* Business Cooperative

Women's Action to Gain Economic Security (WAGES)
1214 Webster St. Suite B
P.O. Box 71885   510-272-0564
Oakland, CA 94612   Fax: 510-272-0384
www.wagescooperatives.org

WAGES is designed to help women move out of poverty through cooperative ownership. They use the cooperative model to allow women to pool their skills and work together to succeed. A cooperative is a business owned and controlled by those who work in it. WAGES is currently helping Latina women establish environmentally sound housecleaning cooperatives in the greater San Francisco Bay Area.

* Business Training for Women (And Men Too)

Women's Economic Ventures
1136 E. Montecito Street   805-965-6073
Santa Barbara, CA 93103   Fax: 805-962-9622
www.wevonline.org

Women's Economic Ventures (WEV) is a local, non-profit organization dedicated to helping women become economically self-sufficient through entrepreneurship development. Although they primarily target women, business counseling and loans are available to men, especially minority and low-income men who have not had access to traditional job opportunities, training and business capital. Training opportunities include: self-employment training, mentoring programs, business consulting and business owner roundtables.

* Business Classes

Women's Enterprise Development Corp.
235 East Broadway, Suite 506   562-983-3747
Long Beach, CA 90802   Fax: 562-983-3750
www.wedc.org

Women's Enterprise Development Corporation (WEDC) is a private, non-profit, community supported organization providing a broad range of training and support programs to help entrepreneurs from all cultures and economic levels successfully start, manage, expand and diversify their businesses. Classes are available in "Starting Your Own Business", "Starting you Own Home Based Childcare Business", "Managing Your Business", and "Manage Your Business for Growth". Course fees vary and scholarships are available.

* Microenterprise Training Program

Yuba-Sutter Enterprise Zone
1364 Sky Harbor Drive   530-741-6463
Marysville, CA 95901   530-742-6280
www.yubacounty.org   Fax: 530-742-7835
www.yubasutterez.com

The training program is a 14-week training session that includes a comprehensive reference book, hands-on assistance and instruction from real practitioners. This program includes the areas of Yuba County, Sutter County, Yuba City, and Marysville.

* Asian Pacific Islander Small Business Program

231 E. 3rd St.   213-473-1605
Los Angeles, CA 90013   Fax: 213-473-1601
www.apisbp.org

This program provides a variety of services to help those in the area who wish to start or expand a business.

* Center for Community Futures

6621 Elverton Dr.   510-339-3801
Oakland, CA 94611   Fax: 510-339-3803
www.cencomfut.com

The Center for Community Futures provides information on how to start and run a business.

* Economic and Employment Development Center

2200 W. Valley Blvd., Suite A   626-281-3792
Alhambra, CA 91803   Fax: 626-281-8064

This program provides a variety of services to help those in the area who wish to start or expand a business.

* Mayfair Improvement Initiative

2342 Alum Rock Ave.   408-251-6900
San Jose, CA 95116   Fax: 408-251-6987
www.mayfairneighborhood.org

This program provides a variety of services to help those in the area who wish to start or expand a business.

* Arcata Economic Development Corporation

100 Ericson Cr., Suite 100   707-822-4616
Arcata, CA 95521   Fax: 707-822-8982

The Arcata Economic Development Corporation offers a variety of loan and business service assistance to those interested in starting or expanding a business.

* Bay Area Entrepreneur Association

1714 Franklin St., #100-134   510-663-0656
Oakland, CA 94612   Fax: 510-663-0657

This association provides a variety of programs and services to those wishing to start or expand a business.

* CHARO Community Development Corp.

4301 East Valley Blvd.   323-269-0751
Los Angeles, CA 90032   Fax: 323-343-9485
www.charocorp.com

CHARO provides a business incubator, business training, technical assistance, and loan information to the Latino community in the area.

* Southeast Asian Community Center

875 O'Farrell St.   415-885-2743
San Francisco, CA 94019   Fax: 415-8853253

The Community center works with the Southeast Asian population to help them pursue their goals.

* Tulare County Redevelopment Agency

5961 S. Mooney Blvd.   559-733-6291
Visalia, CA 93277   Fax: 559-730-2591
www.co.tulare.ca.us

The Tulare County Redevelopment Agency woks to help improve the economy of the area. They offer incentives to businesses and have an entrepreneur training program to help new businesses.

* Valley Economic Development Center

5121 Van Nuys Blvd., 3rd Floor   818-907-9977
Van Nuys, CA 91403   Fax: 818-907-9720
www.vedc.org

The Valley Economic Development Center offers training, consulting, technical assistance and financing to small and medium-sized businesses. They offer several different types of loan and loan guarantee programs, as well as an extensive entrepreneurial training program.

Colorado

* Colorado Alliance for Microenterprise Initiatives

3003 Arapahoe St., #35   303-996-0045
Denver, CO 80205   Fax: 303-996-4939

www.coloradoalliance.org

Colorado Alliance for Microenterprise Initiatives (CAMI) is a coalition of microenterprise development organizations dedicated to providing entrepreneurs in under-served communities the opportunity and resources to become self-sufficient through private enterprise. Check with them frequently because members are added regularly.

* One-Stop Center

Colorado Business Assistance Center
2413 Washington St.   303-592-5920 (Denver Metro)
Denver, CO 80205   800-333-7798 (Nationwide)
www.state.co.us/oed/sbdc/bac.html

The Colorado Business Assistance Center is a one-stop center for new and existing business owners in Colorado.

* Training for Women

Colorado Women's Business Office
1625 Broadway, Suite 1700   303-892-3840
Denver, CO 80202   Fax: 303-892-3848
www.state.co.us/oed/wbo

The Colorado Women's Business Office offers a variety of services for the women business owners of Colorado. They have training and counseling for start-ups and expansions along with internet resources.

* Business Incubator

Denver Enterprise Center
3003 Arapahoe St.   303-296-9400
Denver, CO 80205   Fax: 303-296-5542
www.thedec.org

The Denver Enterprise Center is a small business incubator. The incubator provides new and existing companies affordable light manufacturing and office space. Business can also share office and administrative services that include: copier, fax, business library, consulting services technical assistance and the newly added commercial kitchen.

* Business Center

Denver Minority Business Development Center
1011 West 45th Ave.   303-455-3099
Denver, CO 80211   Fax: 303-455-3076
www.denvermbdc.com

The Denver Minority Business Development Center (DMBDC) provides consulting services in the areas of business plan development, financial planning and loan packaging.

* Entrepreneurial Training for Latinas

Mi Casa Resource Center for Women, Inc.
360 Acoma   303-573-1302
Denver, CO 80223   Fax: 303-595-0422
Http://miscasadenver.org

Mi Casa strives to advance self-sufficiency for primarily low-income Latinas and youth. Mi Casa Resource Center offers a free 3-hour business workshop to help you decide if becoming a business owner is for you. The center also offers classes for entrepreneurs to learn more about their business. Classes offered include: Secrets to Becoming a Successful Small Business Owner, Legal and Tax Matters, Marketing and many more. They also have a computer lab for clients to work on technical aspects of their business.

* Technical Assistance

MicroBusiness Development Corporation
3003 Arapahoe St., Suite 112A 303-308-8121
Denver, CO 80205   Fax: 303-308-8120
www.microbusiness.org

MicroBusiness Development Corporation offers PACEWorks!, a technical assistance program for entrepreneurs. They offer workshops on a variety of topics, usually at no or low cost to the client. In addition, they offer fee based one-to-one services and a mentoring program. They offer loans from $500-$50,000 and business training and development.

* Counseling and Technical Assistance

SCORE Denver
721 19th Street, 4th Floor
Denver, CO 80202   303-844-3985
www.scoredenver.org

Counselors to America's Small Business (SCORE) is a non-profit organization that provides entrepreneur education to form, grow and succeed

in small business. They conduct free counseling and low-cost workshops in addition to a business information center and speakers bureau.

* San Juan 2000 Development Association

P.O. Box 722
1315 Snowden   970-387-5101
Silverton, CO 81433   Fax: 970-387-5104
www.sanjuan2000.org

San Juan 2000 Development Association tries to improve the community and the economy of the Silverton area by providing loans and technical assistance to new or expanding businesses. Loans can range for $500-$5,000 to help businesses grow and prosper. Technical assistance can be had in the form of bookkeeping help, marketing and planning.

Connecticut

* Aid to Artisans, Inc.

331 Wethersfield Avenue   860-947-3344
Hartford, CT 06114   Fax: 860-947-3350
http://www.aidtoartisans.org/

The mission of Aid to Artisans, Inc. is to create employment opportunities for disadvantaged artisans worldwide. They provide assistance with business training, product development, marketing and small grants. Their plans are to develop relationships between American and foreign artisans worldwide.

* The Entrepreneurial Center at Hartford College for Women

50 Elizabeth Street   860-768-5681
Hartford, CT 06105   Fax: 860-768-5622
http://uhaweb.hartford.edu/entrectr

The mission of The Entrepreneurial Center is to help women and men achieve financial independence through self-employment. Entrepreneurs of all income levels are encouraged to participate. They provide a self-assessment workshop for Connecticut entrepreneurs to discover what's involved in starting a Connecticut small business. They provide a 16-week program "Comprehensive Small Business Training. In addition they provide one-on-one counseling, business workshops and special events for women from start-up to established business owner. Services are available on a sliding scale to eligible individuals.

Florida

* Business Development Center and Disadvantaged Business Enterprise Assistance

City of Petersburg Economic Development
P.O. Box 2842   800-874-9026
St. Petersburg. FL 33731   727-893-7146
www.stpete.org/bdc.htm   Fax: 727-551-3360

The Business Development Center (BDC) is a one-stop center that helps current and future small business owners research ideas and receive technical assistance and training in business development. It provides a comprehensive array of financial and technical information, training, services, and follow up. Technical and financial assistance, workshops, seminars and training programs are available through the Business Development Center for Disadvantaged Business Enterprises.

* Florida Community Loan Fund

3107 Edgewater Drive, Suite 2 407-246-0846
Orlando, FL 32804   888-578-2030
www.fclf.org   Fax: 407-246-0856

The Florida Community Loan Fund provides technical assistance to qualifying organizations with insufficient access to capital from conventional lending sources. They provide assistance with: design development, budgeting, finances, management and needs assessment. The services may also include the assignment of a Technical Assistant Consultant to work with your organization.

* Center for Urban Redevelopment and Empowerment

111 E. Las Olas Blvd., Suite 604 954-762-5270
Fort Lauderdale, FL 33301   Fax: 954-762-5278
www.cure.fau.edu/Programs/microbusiness.htm

FAU-CURE provides entrepreneurial training twice a year in the form of a

15-week microbusiness training course. Topics covered include bookkeeping, marketing, taxes, planning, financing, and more. Courses are offered in English, Spanish and Haitian Creole.

* Miami Urban Ministries

2850 SW 27th Ave.   305-442-8306
Miami, FL 33133   Fax: 305-442-9726
www.mum-umc.org

ASSETS Miami is an entrepreneur training program offered through the Miami Urban Ministries. This is an eleven week training program for those who want to start or expand a business. The program includes classroom work, coaching, computer lab, and assistance in securing loans.

Georgia

* Technical Support for Atlanta Union Mission Alumni

Atlanta Mission Entrepreneur Network (AMEN)
P.O. Box 76956   707-952-0862
Atlanta, GA 30358   Fax: 707-984-8627
www.ameninc.org

AMEN is designed with the purpose to help overcome the resource barriers faced by men and women who have completed the Atlanta Union Mission program and who exhibit strong interest in starting their own businesses. Additionally, AMEN will provide the tools and the support necessary to help these startup businesses to be successful.

* Technical Assistance

Appalachia Community Enterprises, Inc.
1727 Turner's Corner Road   706-348-6609
Cleveland, GA 30528   877-434-6609 toll free
www.acenorthgorgia.org   Fax: 706-219-4976

The Appalachia Community Loan Fund provides ongoing support, technical assistance and business education to loan recipients by the loan fund through partner organizations.

* Athens-Clarke Microenterprise Program for Women

UGA-School of Environmental Design
609 Caldwell Hall
Athens, GA 30602   706-542-0936
http://www.sed.uga.edu/pso/athensmicro/default.htm

The Athens-Clarke Microenterprise Program for Women is a public service program of the University of Georgia School of Environmental Design. The program's mission is to assist women with minimum income levels achieve economic self-sufficiency through microenterprise development. They provide a 12-week program of intensive business and personal effectiveness training for women who have viable business ideas or who are engaged in some business activity. The program is open to women residents in Athens-Clarke County whose income does not exceed $47,950. If your income exceeds the limit, please contact the director to discuss your options.

* Micro Business Center

BusinessNOW- Neighborhood Organization for Women
Goodwill Industries of North Georgia, Inc.
2201 Glenwood Ave., SE   404-486-8400
Atlanta, GA 30316   Fax: 404-486-8500
www.biznow.org

Entrepreneurs living in the Atlanta Metropolitan Area have a Micro Business Center to help them bridge the gap between a great idea and a successful business. The Center provides many resources to assist the small business owner with business strategies, from designing business cards to technical assistance to legal advice the center is a one-stop-center. The Micro-Business Center offers: computers with internet access, business resources, fax and phone services, copiers, meeting facilities and training workshops. Daily admission for the Center is $3.00.

* Center for Black Women's Wellness, Inc.

477 Windsor Street, SW, Suite 309   404-688-9202
Atlanta, GA 30039   Fax: 404-880-9435
www.cbww.org

The Center for Black Women's Wellness, Inc. (CBWW) is a non-profit community-based, family-service center. CBWW assists low-to-moderate income women who are starting micro businesses by providing personal and business development training, counseling, business-to-business networking

sessions, and access to financial resources They offer 19 workshop sessions that include: How to Conduct Market Research; Marketing and Advertising Strategies; Pricing Your Product/Service; Legal Structure; Record Keeping; and more.

* Business Training Program

Cobb Microenterprise Center
Kennesaw State University--Small Business Development Center
1000 Chastain Rd - BB423   770-499-3228
Kennesaw, GA 30144   Fax: 770-423-6564
www.cobbmicro.com

The services provided by the Cobb Microenterprise Center are for low-to-moderate-income individuals who have an "entrepreneurial spirit" and need development and capital to start or grow a business. If you are on welfare, unemployed, underemployed, disable, elderly, and you have a good business idea, you can participate in this opportunity. Cobb Microenterprise offers a 12-week training program in business development, technical assistance, access to its business incubator and many other services.

* Technical Assistance

East Athens Development Corporation
410 McKinley Drive   706-208-0048
Athens, GA 30601   Fax: 706-208-0015
www.eadcinc.com

The East Athens Development Corporation, Inc.(EADC) is a nonprofit community based development organization. EADC manages and collaborates with other agencies to provide technical assistance and training to businesses in the East Athens Community. Some services include: business plan development, cooperative marketing and advertising, micro loans, micro enterprise development, business incubator and adult and youth entrepreneurial training.

* Partnership for Community Action

3597 Covington Hwy.   404-929-2415
Decatur, GA 30088   Fax: 404-508-9330
www.pcaction.org

The Microenterprise Initiative is a 12-week curriculum which helps those wanting to develop a business plan and are in need of financing. Many of those who attend are refugees.

Hawaii

* Hawaii Community Loan Fund

677 Ala Moana Blvd., Suite 702   808-523-0075
Honolulu, HI 96813   Fax: 808-534-1199
www.hclf.org

The Hawaii Community Loan Fund (HCLF) is a certified Community Development Financial Institution that provides technical assistance to their clients. The objective of technical assistance is to build healthy businesses that result in better internal management and to increase employment within local neighborhoods. Programs include: organizational assessment, management training, one-to-one counseling and loan packaging.

* Business Training

Maui Economic Opportunity
Business Development Corporation
99 Mahalani Street   808-249-2990
Wailuku, HI 96793   Fax: 808-249-2991
www.meoinc.org

Maui Economic Opportunity, Business Development Corporation is a private, nonprofit Community Action Agency that helps low-income entrepreneurs start and expand their businesses. They provide a FastTrac New Venture, an 11-week course that teaches entrepreneurs the tools needed to write a feasibility study for any business they may be thinking of starting.

Illinois

* Small Business Development Center

Jane Adams Hull House Association
Uptown Center Development
4520 N. Beacon   773-561-3500
Chicago, IL 60640-5519   Fax: 773-561-3507
www.hullhouse.org/sbdu.asp

The Jane Adams Hull House Small Business Development Center operates on the north and south sides of Chicago to help revitalize local neighborhoods.

They work with new and expanding businesses to find the resources to operate a successful business venture. A variety of small business programs to available for entrepreneurs, including: individual counseling, small business workshop series, small business training programs and networking opportunities.

* Financial and Technical Assistance

Lake County Partners
28055 Ashley Circle, Suite 212   847-247-0137
Libertyville, IL 60048   Fax: 847-247-0423
www.lakecountypartners.com

The Financial and Technical Services Committees help all businesses in Lake County have access to loans and capital for starting and growing their business. They can help your business thrive.

* Project Now

418 19th St.   309-793-6391
Rock Island, IL 61201   Fax: 309-793-6352
www.projectnow.org

Project Now offers and eight week Self-Employment Training Program. The program provides information on how to write a business plan, bookkeeping, marketing, sales, and more. A Revolving Loan Fund can provide you with a $15,000 loan for each job created. This service targets the unemployed or low-income persons.

Indiana

* Community Action of Southern Indiana

1613 E. 8th Street   812-288-6451 ext. 123
Jeffersonville, IN 47130   Fax: 812-284-8314
www.casijeff.net/

The Community Action of Southern Indiana offers assistance to small businesses in planning, marketing, training, and more. The Micro Enterprise Business Development Program targets small businesses with less than five people.

Kansas

* The First Step Fund

4747 Troost Ave.
Kansas City, MO 64110   816-235-6116
www.firststepfund.org

The First Step Fund's mission is to serve low- to moderate-income individuals; there are income requirements for all class participants. First Step Fund offers two types of business training classes: general business and child care entrepreneurship. The general business class they offer is a 36-hour course to help entrepreneurs with their businesses, called First Step FastTrac. The Family Child Care Entrepreneur Course is an interactive 54-hour course. In addition to training, First Step students receive assistance with personal challenges and referrals. Child Care reimbursement and transportation assistance is also available.

Kentucky

* Business Training and Business Center

Community Ventures Corporation
1450 North Broadway   859-231-0054
Lexington, KY 40505   800-299-0267
www.cvcky.org   Fax: 859-231-0261

The Community Ventures Corporation (CVC) is a community-based, non-profit organization that exists to improve the quality of life for urban and rural residents throughout central and northern Kentucky. CVC's mission is to provide individuals and families with the skills, income, and assets; they need to achieve financial independence. They offer a variety of classes including: computer courses, business planning, and a free business orientation. The Business Center offers entrepreneurs: copiers, faxes, computer access, conference rooms, work rooms and office space with lease rates starting at $350 per month.

* Center for Microenterprise Development

Jewish Family and Vocational Services
3587 Dutchmans Lane   502-452-6341
Louisville, KY 40205   Fax: 502-452-6718
www.jfvs.com

The Jewish Family and Vocational Services help immigrants start their own small businesses by providing economic training, business planning and technical assistance.

* Mountain Association for Community Economic Development

433 Chestnut St.   859-986-2373
Berea, KY 40403   Fax: 859-986-1299
www.maced.org

The Mountain Association for Community Economic Development provides an accessible clearinghouse of information, access to training, and opportunities to learn from other entrepreneurs. Their program called Business First Stop provides these resources for communities in Kentucky and Central Appalachia.

Louisiana

* Entrepreneurial Training

Acadiana Regional Development District
601 Loire Ave., Suite C
P.O. Box 90070   337-886-7782
Lafayette, LA 70507   Fax: 337-886-7081
www.ardd.org

The Acadiana Regional Development District Small Business Entrepreneurial Training Program (SBET) is available to assist individuals interested in starting their own small business. SBET is designed to assist those with little or no experience in running a business. The program focuses on three training models in the areas of business plan preparation, loan packaging, and finding financial resources. The District serves the eight parishes of Region Four: Acadia, Evangeline, Iberia, Lafayette, St. Landry, St. Martin, St. Mary and Vermilion.

* Louisiana Department of Economic Development

Mailing address:
P.O. Box 94185
Baton Rouge, LA 70804
Physical address:
Capital Annex
1051 N. 3rd Street   225-342-3000
Baton Rouge, LA 70802   Fax: 225-342-5389
www.lded.state.la.us

The Louisiana Economic Development Department provides a variety of programs for beginning and existing small businesses. The Microenterprise Program assists low- income parents of minor children to start or strengthen a small business. The program provides entrepreneurial and economic literacy training and mentoring; financial counseling; and access to capital through micro loans for the participants. The Small and Emerging Business Development Program (SEBD) offers workshops to small business owners with assistance in marketing, technical training, and management. These programs are offered through statewide Small Business Development Centers (SBDC).

* Microenterprise Development Alliance of Louisiana

1200 S. Acadian Thruway, Suite 204   225-387-1166
Baton Rouge, LA 70806   Fax: 225-343-6935
www.microenterprisela.org

The MicroEnterprise Development of Alliance Louisiana (MEDAL) is a statewide not for profit alliance committed to helping entrepreneurs through the establishment of microenterprises, particularly by women and youth. MEDAL provides technical assistance in the areas of marketing, recruiting, program design, evaluation design, technology, sector service and start-up.

Maine

* Penquis C.A.P., Inc.

262 Harlow Street   207-973-3612
Bangor, ME 04401   Fax: 207-973-3699
www.penquiscap.org

Penquis Community Action Program primarily serves low- and moderate-income individuals in Penobscot and Piscataquis Counties. Their Economic Development Department provides assistance to individuals interested in starting or expanding a microenterprise, a business with five or fewer employees. One-On-One Technical Assistance for Entrepreneurs offers assistance to low-income individuals starting or expanding a business. After completing a business plan class, participants meet with a business coach to determine their needs and goals. Areas of assistance may include: business plan completion, marketing, technical assistance, and general supporting services.

Maryland

* Garrett County Community Action MicroWorks

104 E. Center Street   301-334-9431
Oakland, MD 21550   Fax: 301-334-8555
www.garrettcac.org

Garrett County Community Action Corporation is a not for profit corporation committed to improving the quality of life for persons with needs by helping them become more self sufficient. They provide training and technical assistance to small business owners in Garrett County, Maryland that have microloans with the Action Corporation and those not seeking loans. Their program includes: training, seminars, product design, tax issues, marketing, financial counseling, a lending library and many other services.

* Maryland Capital Enterprises, Inc.

P.O. Box 1844   866-MARY-CAP
Salisbury, MD 21802   410-546-1900
www.marylandcapital.org   Fax: 410-546-9718

Maryland Capital Enterprises work to build economically distressed communities by supporting micro businesses. They offer many small community based businesses the resources they need to grow. The Enterprise also offers business skills workshops, business networks, and business support groups.

* Entrepreneurial Training and Merchant Development Initiative

Microenterprise Development Center, Inc.
2401 Liberty Heights Ave., Suite 310   410-669-5782
Baltimore, MD 21215   Fax: 410-669-8348
http://microdc.homestead.com

Microenterprise Development Center, Inc. is a not for profit corporation dedicated to promoting self-sufficiency of distressed communities through entrepreneurial training activities. The Center offers an Entrepreneurial Training class with over 64 hours of classroom instruction. The students will visit successful businesses, receive technical assistance and prepare a business plan. They also offer a 12-week Merchant Development Initiative for retail clients to educate themselves in customer service, marketing, sales and other retail issues.

* Technical Training

Women Entrepreneurs of Baltimore, Inc.
1118 Light St., Suite 202   410-727-4921
Baltimore, MD 21230   Fax: 410-727-4989
www.webinc.org

Women Entrepreneurs of Baltimore, Inc (WEB) is a nonprofit organization that provides entrepreneurial training, technical assistance and follow-up services for microbusiness start-ups in the Baltimore metro area. WEB screens potential entrepreneurs with a viable business idea to participate in their Business Skills Training Course, a 12-week class. Graduates of the training class are eligible to receive free technical assistance, resources and support for the 12 months following graduation. WEB has a large variety of programs to offer including but not limited to: internet training, mentoring, networking, financial strategies, and business consultation.

Massachusetts

* Day Care Training

Acre Family Day Care Corporation
14 Kirk Street   978-937-5899
Lowell, MA 01852   Fax: 978-937-5148
www.acrefamily.org

The Acre Family Day Care not for profit organization that helps low-income women in Greater Lowell become financially independent by providing child care training and assistance in setting up licensed child care businesses in their own homes. Family Day Care Businesses in Lowell can benefit from continued support of day care training and business support.

* Business Training

Center for Women and Enterprise
1135 Tremont Street, Suite 480   617-536-0700 x248
Boston, MA 02120   Fax: 617-536-7373
www.cweboston.org

The Center for Women and Enterprise (CWE) is a nonprofit organization dedicated to the mission of empowering women in the Boston and Worcester areas, to become economically self-sufficient through entrepreneurship. Training programs are offered in Business Planning, Business Basics: Starting a Retail Business Community Entrepreneur Programs and many more. All fees are on a sliding scale.

* Business and Technical Training, Incubator

Commonwealth Corporation
529 Main Street, Suite 110   617-727-8158
Boston, MA 02129   800-439-0183
www.commcorp.org   Fax: 617-242-7660

The Commonwealth Corporation administers a variety of training for the entrepreneurs of Massachusetts. For the beginning small business owner, they offer a 10-week Entrepreneurial Training Program and a 20-week Starting Your Own Business class. In addition, they offer classes in marketing, business plan writing, preparing financial documents and even a business incubator.

* Berkshire Enterprises

One Fenn St., Suite 301   413-448-2755
Pittsfield, MA 01201   Fax: 413-448-2749
www.berkshireenterprises.com

Berkshire Enterprises offer a variety of classes to help people wishing to start or expand their business. They have a Daytime Dislocated Worker Program designed to teach the skills necessary to run a successful business. Marketing, financing, business planning and more are covered in the course. Berkshire Enterprises offers a fee based evening program as well.

* Lowell Business Assistance Center

169 Merrimack St.
Lowell, MA 01852   978-441-1889
www.comteam.org

For businesses located in Lowell, the Lowell Business Assistance Center is a wonderful resource. They offer workshops, seminars, and more to help with starting or expanding a business. They also provide support and other resources to help your business succeed.

* This Neighborhood Means Business!

Dorchester Center for Adult Education
269 East Cottage St.
Dorchester, MA 02125   617-474-1170
www.fdnh.org/Programs/adults.htm

This Neighborhood Means Business! is a program designed to help improve the community by offering assistance to businesses to help them succeed. Workshops are offered that cover topics necessary to operating a business. such as marketing, bookkeeping, and more. Additional workshops cover important computer programs with a business focus.

* M.A.D.E. for Business

Commonwealth Corp.
529 Main St., Suite 110
Boston, MA 02129   617-727-8158
www.weiu.org

M.A.D.E. for Business (Manufacturers, Artisans, Designers, Entrepreneurs) is a micro enterprise program begun by the Women's Union. The focus was on helping women artisans start their own business. participants in the program can attend workshops on business planning, financing, selling, and more. Services also include lectures, referrals, and business counseling.

* Women's Business Opportunity Program

The Elizabeth Stone House
P.O. Box 59
Jamaica Plain, MA 02130   617-522-3659
www.elizabethstonehouse.org

The Elizabeth Stone House is a program run for women and provides services necessary for women to take control of their lives. Transitional housing, mental health services and more are provided. In addition, they run a Community Education for Economic Development Program to help improve the communities in the area. Women can take classes in personal finances, and participate in the Women's Business Opportunity program where they learn how to create and run a business.

Michigan

* Technical Assistance

Cornerstone Alliance
P.O. Box 428
38 W. Wall Street
Benton Harbor, MI 49023
www.cstonealliance.org

269-925-6100
Fax: 616-925-4471

Cornerstone Alliance is committed to economic growth and civic development in the cities of Benton Harbor and St. Joseph, the charter townships of Benton, St. Joseph, Lincoln and Royalton. The technical assistance program provides business and financial technical assistance to low-income entrepreneurs. Programs include: entrepreneurial support, pre-loan and loan packaging classes.

* Small Business and Entrepreneurial Training

Grand Rapids Opportunities for Women
25 Sheldon Blvd., SE, Suite 210
Grand Rapids, MI 49503
www.growbusiness.org

616-458-3404
Fax: 616-458-6557

(GROW) is a not for profit economic development organization which provides women, many who face economic barriers, with the skills to be achieve economic independence. GROW focuses on small businesses with training and counseling plus several support services to start or expand a business. The "Minding Your Own Business" class is offered on a sliding fee scaled based on income and up to two hours of counseling if free. Seminars vary in cost but no one is turned away solely on their ability to pay.

Minnesota

* Neighborhood Development Center, Inc

651 ½ University Avenue
St. Paul, MN 55104
www.windndc.org

651-291-2480
Fax: 651-291-2597

The Neighborhood Development Center, Inc (NDC) is a community-based non-profit organization that works with entrepreneurs in the inner city of Minneapolis and St. Paul develop successful businesses and stronger neighborhoods. NDC provides training programs to applicants living in some of the lowest income neighborhoods in the Twin Cities. Neighborhood Entrepreneur Training, Ethnic Entrepreneur Training, and RECIPE for Business Success are the three training programs currently available. After initial training, technical assistance is available for business owners in marketing, management, legal issues, and accounting.

* Self Employment Program

Tri-County Community Action Program, Inc.
501 LeMieur St.
P.O. Box 368
Little Falls, MN 56345
www.tccaction.com

320-632-3691
Fax: 320-632-3695

The Tri-County Community Action Program is a not for profit corporation committed to creating opportunities for self-sufficiency for citizens in Crow Wing, Morrison and Todd Counties. The Self-Employment Program provides training to citizens to help them start their own business. Eligibility is based on income.

Mississippi

* Technical Assistance

Minority Business Enterprise Division
Mississippi Development Authority
501 North West Street
P. O. Box 849
Jackson, MS 39205
minority@mississippi.org

601-359-3448
Fax: 601-359-5290

The Minority Business Enterprise Division provides business and educational assistance to minority and women-owned businesses to promote entrepreneurship in Mississippi. Assistance includes: business start-up and expansion training, counseling, referrals and outreach. The Minority Business Enterprise Division also has several publications that may be of assistance to businesses.

* Technical Assistance

Quitman County Development Organization, Inc.
201 Humphrey Street

P.O. Box 386
Marks, MS 38646
www.qcdo.org

662-326-4000
Fax: 662-326-3904

The Quitman County Development Organization (QCDO) provides technical assistance through the Micro-Enterprise Loan Program to promote and grow successful businesses before and after loans are made. They offer business development workshops, seminars for women and cooperative groups.

Missouri

* Technical Assistance

Economic Opportunity Corporation Community Action Agency
817 Monterey St.
P.O. Box 3068
St. Joseph, MO 64503
www.eoccaa.org

816-223-8281
Fax: 816-233-8262

The EOC Community Action Agency serves the needs of low-income families in Andrew, Buchanan, Clinton and DeKalb Counties in Northwest Missouri. They have created a micro-enterprise program that includes the First Step FastTrac training program with follow-up technical assistance for two years. Participants must meet income guidelines, live in the ABCD area and be ready to start or expand a business. Tuition waivers and scholarships are available to persons of low-to-moderate income.

* General Business and Child Care Training

First Step Fund
4747 Troost Avenue
Kansas City, MO 64110
www.firststepfund.org

816-235-6116
Fax: 816-35-6177

The First Step Fund is a nonprofit agency providing business training and support to low-to-moderate-income entrepreneurs in the metro Kansas City area. The agency uses the First Step FastTrac curriculum to offer general business and childcare training classes. The business training class is a 36-hour course covering marketing, budgeting, finances and other concepts for $20. The Family Child Care Entrepreneur course trains individuals on childhood development and business skills. This 54-hour course costs $25.

* Community Development Corporation of Kansas City

2420 E. Linwood Blvd., Suite 400
Kansas City, MO 64109
www.cdcofkc.org

816-924-5800
Fax: 816-921-3350

The Community Development Corp. Small Business Technical Assistance Program provides help to those wishing to start or expand a business in the Kansas City area. The program offers assistance in business planning, financing, bookkeeping, marketing, and more. All of this is free of charge.

Montana

* Microbusiness Technical Assistance

Montana Department of Commerce
301 S Park Ave
Helena, MT 59601
Mailing address:
P.O. Box 200501
Helena, MT 59620-0501
www.state.mt.us

406-721-3663
Fax: 406-841-2701

The Montana MicroBusiness Technical Assistance Program focuses on providing technical assistance to low and moderate-income individuals to assist them in obtaining financing of up to $35,000 to start or expand a small business. The focus of the Montana program is to provide business management training through a combination of traditional classroom and Internet training. The NxLevel Online Training Program is offered at various locations throughout the state to offer in-depth training for entrepreneurs.

Nebraska

* Microbusiness Training

Lincoln Action Program
210 "O" Street
Lincoln, NE 68508
www.lincoln-action.org

402-471-4515
Fax: 402-471-4844

The Microenterprise Program is an economic development program designed to help low-to-moderate incomes entrepreneurs establish their own small businesses. The program provides self-assessment, business training and technical support. They also have a Computer Microenterprise Development (CDM) to help very low-income people start a business from their home by providing services using computers. After training, the graduates work from home on their very own home-based computer business.

* Microbusiness Technical Assistance
Nebraska Department of Economic Development
Nebraska Micro Business Resource Directory
P.O. Box 6605
Lincoln, NE 68506-0605   402-420-9589
http://neon.neded.org/mbrd/index.html
The Nebraska Micro Business Resource Directory provides a wide variety of technical assistance options available to microbusinesses in Nebraska.

* Technical Training
Nebraska EDGE Program
University of Nebraska   402-472-4138
58 Filey Hall   800-328-2851
Lincoln, NE 68583-0947   Fax: 402-472-0688
The Nebraska EDGE (Enhancing, Developing and Growing Entrepreneurs) is an organization for rural entrepreneurial training programs hosted by local communities and organizations. They offer a variety of classes and training programs, including some online.

* Technical Assistance
Community Development Resources
1135 M Street
3rd Floor, Suite 116   402-436-2386
Lincoln, NE 68508-3169   Fax: 402-436-2360
http://www.self-lincoln.org/about.html
SELF offers one-on-one technical assistance in many areas of business including: financing, planning, marketing and advertising. The services are free.

New Jersey

* New Jersey Economic Development Authority
P.O. Box 990
Trenton, NJ 08625-0990   609-292-0187
http://www.njeda.com/finance_mstr.htm
The New Jersey Economic Development Authority offers an eight-week program for small businesses, minority-owned and women-owned businesses. The program helps entrepreneurs learn the basics of operating a business. Sessions are held bi-annually throughout the state.

* Business Training for Young People
Prudential Young Entrepreneur Program
NJIT-Enterprise Development Center
105 Lock Street
Newark, NJ 07103   973-643-4063
www.njit-edc.org/PYEP.htm
Interested entrepreneurs 18-30 years old may enroll for a 9-week course that provides them with the fundamentals needed to run a small business. Examples of the topics covered include: marketing, sales, financial statements, and how to write a business plan. Students are encouraged to write a business plan, and set it into motion.

* Tri-County Community Action Agency
River's Edge Community Campus
110 Cohansey Street   856-451-6330
Bridgetown, NJ 08302   Fax: 856-455-7288
http://www.tricountycaa.org/
Tri-County Community Loan Fund provides a six-week Entrepreneurial Training Program to small businesses in Cumberland, Gloucester and Salem counties. The class provides training in 16 areas including: marketing, credit, financing and other areas of business.

* Middlesex County Economic Opportunities Commission
1215 Livingston Ave.   732-846-6600
North Brunswick, NJ 08902   Fax: 732-846-3728
www.mceoc.org
The Middlesex County Economic Opportunities Commission helps

microenterprises in a variety of ways. They have a 12 hour business course for those interested in starting or expanding their businesses. They also operate a print shop offering lower prices to help new businesses

New Mexico

* Free Technical Training
New Mexico Community Development Loan Fund
Mailing Address:
P.O. Box 705
Albuquerque, NM 87103
Street Address:
700 Fourth Street, SW   505-243-3196
Albuquerque, NM 87102   Fax: 505-243-8803
http://www.nmcdlf.org/
The New Mexico Community Development Loan Fund provides free personalized pre-loan and post-loan technical training.

New York

* Business Training
Appleseed Trust
220 Herald Place, 2nd Floor
Syracuse, NY 13202   315-424-9485
http://www.appleseedtrust.org/
Appleseed Trust is a not for profit organization that is committed to assisting low- to moderate-income residents of Syracuse to start or expand their own business. Entrepreneurs with an idea for a product or service can pay a small monthly fee to participate in an eight-week training program. The process includes applying for an initial loan.

* Technical Assistance
Capital District Community Loan Fund
255 Orange Street
Albany, NY 12210   518-436-8586
http://www.cdclf.org/1024.html
The Community Loan Fund provides technical assistance to its small businesses and micro businesses clients in the New York State Capital region.

* Loan Fund Technical Assistance
Chautauqua Microenterprise Loan Fund
Chautauqua Opportunities for Development
402 Main Street   716-366-2334
Dunkirk, NY 14048   Fax 716-366-7407
http://www.codi-wny.com
The Chautauqua Microenterprise Loan Fund provides technical assistance to loan applicants and recipients of small businesses with fewer than 5 employees in Chautauqua County.

* Technical Assistance
Homesteaders Federal Credit Union
2052 Adam Clayton Powell Jr. Blvd   212-222-0328
New York, NY 10027   Fax: 212-222-1035
http://www.homesteadersfcu.org/
The Homesteaders Federal Credit Union is a not-for-profit financial institution that provides affordable financing and technical assistance for people in the Harlem and New York City areas. Members may receive technical assistance for their small business.

* Ongoing Training and Technical Assistance
Project Enterprise
144 West 125th St., 4th Floor   212-678-6734
New York, NY 10027   Fax: 212-678-6737
http://www.projectenterprise.org/
Project Enterprise lending practices provides business credit to New York's low-income individuals. It is a comprehensive program delivering microcredit, business training and networking opportunities to entrepreneurs in New York City's economically disadvantages communities. All clients receive ongoing, personalized business training and technical assistance.

* Technical Assistance and Training
Rural Opportunities, Inc
400 East Avenue   716-340-3387
Rochester, NY 14607-1910   Fax: 716-340-3326

www.ruralinc.org

Rural Opportunities, Inc is a not-for-profit community development organization providing services to low to moderate-income people and economically depressed communities throughout New York and Ohio. The aim is to promote self-sufficiency and economic independence through the creation and expansion of microenterprises. Technical assistance is available for small business entrepreneurs.

* Family Day Care Training
Women's Housing and Economic Development Corporation
50 E. 168th, Suite 702   718-839-1100
Bronx, NY 10452   Fax: 718-839-1170
www.whedco.org

The Women's Housing and Economic Development Corporation (WHEDCO) offers microenterprise support for individuals to be their own boss by opening or expanding a Family Day Care Program from their home. They offer a bilingual training program, which exceeds state requirements. Members receive continuing education, access to a resource library, loan application assistance and other programs to help them become successful business owners.

* Training Services
Women's Venture Fund, Inc
240 West 35 Street, Suite 201   212-563-0499
New York, NY 10001   Fax: 212-868-9116
www.womensventurefund.org

The Women's Venture Fund provides entrepreneurs with a comprehensive offering of business classes necessary to build the essential building blocks for an aspiring business owner, as well as the established business owner. All classes are open to the public and there is a nominal fee for classes. Contact them for a current listing of classes, workshops and seminars.

* Micro Technical Training Programs
Worker Ownership Resource Center
104 Scio Street   585-338-7822
Rochester, NY 14604   Fax: 585-338-1232
www.atworc.net

Worker Ownership Resource Center, Inc (WORC) is a non-profit organization that helps refugees and economically disadvantaged people in the Southern Tier of New York State start their own microbusinesses. WORC has developed training and technical assistance programs that provide a comprehensive package of classes for the disadvantaged entrepreneur. The package includes assessment, workshops, one-on-one technical assistance, business planning and other support services.

North Carolina

* Construction, Child Care and General Business Assistance
Good Work, Inc.
115 Market Street, Suite 470   919-682-8473
Durham, NC 27701   Fax: 919-687-7033
www.goodwork.org

Good Works is a non-profit organization, which provides entrepreneurs with business and technical assistance. Entrepreneurs in the Chapel Hill, Durham and Raleigh area may learn more about becoming a member of this organization by attending a free information session. Nearly all of the members are businesses owned by women, minorities, and/or low-income individuals. Good Work offers three types of classes for entrepreneurs starting or expanding a small business: Building Your Business, Building Your Child Care Business, and Managing Your Construction Trade Business.

* Craft Business Assistance
HandMade in America
P.O. Box 2089   828-252-0121
Asheville, NC 28802   Fax: 828-252-0388
www.handmadeinamerica.org

HandMade in America works with organizations in Western North Carolina to provide learning opportunities about business issues for craftspeople. Topics include business planning, marketing, sales techniques, and others.

* Training Programs
Mountain Microenterprise Fund
29 ½ Page Avenue   828-253-2834
Asheville, NC 28801   Fax: 828-389-3089

www.mtnmicro.org

Mountain Microenterprise Fund offers programs in everything you need to know to start a new business: marketing, cash flow, budgeting, and sales forecasting. They also offer a 21-hour course for businesses ready to expand.

* Technical Training
North Carolina Rural Economic Development Center
4021 Carya Drive   919-250-4314
Raleigh, NC 27610   Fax 919-250-4325
http://www.ncruralcenter.org/grants/micro.htm

The North Carolina Microenterprise Program provides North Carolina rural residence with small business loans to help them become self-sufficient through business ownership. They provide their clients with technical assistance in conjunction with their loan program.

* Entrepreneurship Education Training
REAL Enterprises
115 Market Street, Suite 320   919-688-7325
Durham, NC 27701   Fax: 919-682-7621
www.realenterprises.org

REAL Enterprises (Rural Entrepreneurship through Action Learning) makes entrepreneurial training accessible to rural communities through hands-on education. Programs for youth and adult are available.

Ohio

* ASSETS Toledo
333 14th St.   419-381-2721
Toledo, OH 43624   Fax: 419-720-0079
http://www.assetstoledo.com/

ASSETS Toledo assists individuals in Lancaster County who strive for self-employment but have limited resources. They provide hands-on training, peer mentoring and a support network.

* Food Venture Assistance
ACEnet –Appalachian Center for Economic Networks
94 Columbus Road   740-592-3854
Athens, OH 45701   Fax: 740-593-5451
www.acenetworks.org

Food Ventures assists small specialty food businesses in southeastern Ohio. They provide information to businesses including a Community Kitchen incubator. The aim is to transform relationships within communities to allow people with low-incomes to successfully enter the economic mainstream.

* Technical Assistance
Community Action Committee of Pike County
MicroEnterprise/Business Development Department
941 Market Street
P.O. Box 799   740-289-2371
Piketon, OH 45661   Fax: 740-289-4291
www.pikecac.org

Community Action Committee of Pike County offers technical assistance in developing business plans and marketing strategies, as well as advertisements and basic business counseling. In addition they offer one-on-one assistance to small business owners in Pike, Ross, Jackson and Scioto Counties.

* Technical Assistance
EnterpriseWorks
88 East Broad Street, Suite 1770   614-228-1043
Columbus, OH 43215   Fax: 614-621-9222
www.enterpriseworksinc.org

EnterpriseWorks is designed to identify entrepreneurship as an employment option, to improve the success rate of business start-ups and to generate new jobs. They provide Ohioans two types of classes and technical assistance: self-assessment and Business Plan Development. Programs are offered throughout the state.

* Greater Cincinnati Microenterprise Initiative
1501 Madison Rd.
PNC Building, 1st Floor Rear   513-569-4816
Cincinnati, OH 45206   Fax: 513-569-0075
www.gcmi.org

The Greater Cincinnati Microenterprise Initiative provides Business Coaches who guide their clients through the steps to start and operate their own small business. The Coach will customize a training program to meet your specific needs. Training is provided through a variety of settings including classroom training, small business workshops, one-to-one coaching and technical assistance. If you already have a business they will work with you to achieve your expansion plans.

Oklahoma

* Technical Assistance
Cherokee Nation
P. O. Box 948   918-456-0671
Tahlequah, OK 74465   800-256-0671 in Oklahoma only
http://www.cherokee.org
Technical assistance is available to help Native American entrepreneurs living and running their business in the Cherokee Nation with writing a business plan.

Oregon

* Mercy Enterprise
936 SE Ankeny, Suite 1
Portland, OR 97214   503-236-1580
http://www.mercyenterprise.org/
Mercy offers a 7 week Business Basics class for its clients which address a variety of topics including: market research, taxes, writing a business plan and many others. Mercy Enterprise also offers a yearly training called Business Seminars Series on a variety of business topics.

* Neighborhood Pride Team
9117 SE Foster Rd.   503-774-4880
Portland, OR 97266   Fax: 503-774-4832
http://www.neighborhoodpride.org/
The Neighborhood Pride Team offers a variety of technical and business classes to entrepreneurs to realize their dreams by making concrete business plans.

* Food Innovation Center
Oregon State University
1207 NW Naito Parkway
Portland, OR 97209   503-872-6680
http://fic.oregonstate.edu/
The Food Innovation Center offers one-stop access to important services for food entrepreneurs. They have a staff of technologists, engineers, economists, and business professional which have a breath of real-world experience and depth of technical understanding.

* Child Care Neighbor Network
ROSE Community Development
5215 SE Duke Street
Portland, OR 97206-6839   503-788-0826 ext. 109
http://www.rosecdc.org/childcare.htm
The Child Care Neighbor Network brings together home-based family child care providers in order to improve quality of care. Technical assistance is also available to help providers run their home-based business.

* Shorebank Enterprise Pacific
429 Spruce Street
P O Box 56   541-572-5172
Myrtle Point, OR 97458   Fax: 541-572-5261
http://www.sbpac.com/index.cfm
Shorebank Enterprise is a nonprofit rural economic development corporation assisting entrepreneurs build business and market ventures, which improve the social and environmental conditions of rural communities. Development services are specifically designed for small rural businesses. Their staff's services include financial planning, business strategy, deal structuring, business plan preparation assistance, and management assistance.

Pennsylvania

* ASSETS Lancaster
1821 Oregon Pike, Ste. 201   717-560-6546
Lancaster, PA 17601-6466   Fax: 717-560-6549
http://www.geocities.com/AssetsL/

ASSETS Lancaster is dedicated to serving the low to moderate-income entrepreneurs of Lancaster County. They offer a Business Design and Management Course in English and in Spanish. In addition, they provide technical assistance and mentors for their clients.

* ASSETS Montco Inc (A Service for Self-Employment Training Support)
3 East Marshall Street   610-275-3520
Norristown, PA 19401   Fax: 610-272-7802
http://www.assetsmontco.org/index.html
ASSETS offers business training and peer lending groups to entrepreneurs. Volunteers teach a 13-week training course that teaches the basics of setting up and running a small business. Participants are later matched with volunteer mentors who encourage and counsel participants as they develop or grow their business. During monthly contacts over a six-month period, mentors help participants learn the practical realities of the business world and ways to solve problems.

* Market Access for Neighborhood Enterprises (MANE)
Philadelphia Development Partnership
1334 Walnut Street, 7th Floor   215-545-3100
Philadelphia, PA 19107   Fax: 215-546-8055
http://www.pdp-inc.org/
MANE is a marketing and growth management service for small neighborhood businesses. Their mission is to promote neighborhood economic development to help business succeed and grow.

* Prudential Young Entrepreneur Program (PYEP)
The Enterprise Center
4548 Market Street
Philadelphia, PA 19139   215-895-4000
www.theenterprisecenter.com/forentre/start_business/pyep.asp
Interested entrepreneurs enroll for a 9-week course that provides them with the fundamentals needed to run a small business. Examples of the topics covered include: marketing, sales, financial statements, and how to write a business plan. Students are encouraged to write a business plan, and set it into motion.

* Local Enterprise Assistance Program (LEAP)
Rural Enterprise Development Corp.
10 East Main Street
P.O. Box 276   570-784-7003
Bloomsburg, PA 17815-0276   Fax: 570-784-7030
http://www.redc-leap.org/
The Rural Enterprise Assistance Program provides introductory and intermediate level business training classes - specifically designed for LEAP participants. These non-credit classes usually include 48 hours of instruction. Principles of marketing, management, finance, accounting, taxes, insurance, and business law are topics, which are covered. Technical assistance and peer networking are also provided through LEAP.

* Trehab Center Inc.
P.O. Box 366
10 Public Avenue   570-278-5227
Montrose, PA 18801   Fax: 570-278-1889
http://www.trehab.org/
The ASSETS-TREHAB Program is a training, mentoring and technical support program for entrepreneurs, with emphasis on serving low- to-middle income participants. They provide a six-week, three-hour long Business Design and Management course twice a year. Serving Susquehanna, Bradford, Sullivan, Tioga and Wyoming counties.

Rhode Island

* Rhode Island MicroEnterprise Association
8 Abbott Park Place   401-598-2256
Providence, RI 02903   Fax: 401-598-2257
http://www.rimicroenterprise.org/
The Rhode Island MicroEnterprise Association provides free microbusiness training and business technical assistance to persons wishing to start their own small business. Their services are available to microbusinesses and home-based businesses in Rhode Island. They offer a four-week Microbusiness Training Program; all worksheets, planning guides, and other written materials are provided free of charge.

South Dakota

* Four Bands Community Fund, Inc.

Cheyenne River Lakota Nation
101 South Main Street
P.O. Box 932   605-964-3687
Eagle Butte, SD 57625   Fax: 605-964-3689
http://www.fourbands.org/loan_fund.htm

Four Bands Community Fund, Inc., is a non-profit corporation which assists entrepreneurs of the Cheyenne River Indian Reservation by providing training and business incubation encouraging economic development and enhancing the quality of life for all communities and residents of the reservation. They offer the CREATE Program (Cheyenne River Entrepreneurial Assistance, Training & Education), a 10-week class which meets two times a week for two hours.

Tennessee

* Central Appalachian Microenterprise Program (CAMP)

East Tennessee Community Partnership Center
300 East Main Street, Suite 301   423-232-5730
Johnson City, TN 37601   Fax: 423-232-5760
http://www.etsu.edu/keystone/microenterprise.html

Technical assistance and individual counseling are available to entrepreneurs.

* Community Kitchen

Jubilee Project, Inc.
123 N. Jockey St.
P.O. Box 657   423-733-4195
Sneedville, TN 37869   Fax: 423-733-1624
http://jubileeproject.holston.org

Clinch-Powell Community Kitchens can help you turn a good idea or a great recipe into a successful food product business. Entrepreneurs renting the kitchens have access to a variety of assistance at no additional cost, which include food safety and equipment training, recipe development, product testing and business assistance. Consulting and technical assistance are also available on a fee-for-service basis for businesses not renting space in the kitchen.

* Alt.consulting

P.O. Box 40210   901-312-9797
Memphis, TN 38104   Fax: 901-312-9798
www.altconsulting.org

alt.consulting is a non-profit that will help all businesses grow and develop. They offer a wide variety of services at a below market rate.

Texas

* MicroEnterprise Assistance

Alliance for Multicultural Community Services
6440 Hillcroft, Suite 411   713-776-4700
Houston, TX 77081   Fax: 713-776-4730
http://www.allianceontheweb.org/

The Alliance's mission is to assist refugees, immigrants, and other low-income residents of Harris County. They offer an Individual Development Account that provides matching funds for entrepreneurs in addition to small business workshops. Through their newly established Multicultural Community Development Corporation (MCDC), they have added microenterprise training.

* Urban Business Initiative

2223 North Main Street, Suite 203   713-222-8085
Houston, TX 77009   Fax: 713-222-8097
http://www.urbanbusiness.org

The Urban Business Initiative believes a good foundation is needed for any business to succeed. That foundation is a well-written business plan. Their volunteers provide assistance in the development of this key business component. They assist the client with the consulting, research, and analysis needed to compile the plan.

Utah

* Technical Assistance

Utah Microenterprise Loan Fund
3595 South Main St   801-269-8408
Salt Lake City, UT 84115   Fax: 801-269-1063
http://www.umlf.com/

The Utah Microenterprise Loan Fund is a private, non-profit, multi-bank community development financial institution, whose mission is to provide management support to entrepreneurs in start-up and existing firms that do not have access to traditional funding sources; especially those who are socially and economically disadvantaged. They offer free Business Counseling and low-cost training, workshops and seminars

Vermont

* BROC Community Action in Southwestern Vermont

60 Center Street   802-775-0878
Rutland, VT 05701   800-717-BROC (2762)
http://www.broc.org/

BROC's Micro Business Development Program provides technical assistance and training for low to moderate income residents of Vermont interested in starting or expanding a small business. Programs offered include a comprehensive training course, computer class, virtual incubator program as well as a child care business initiative program. All classes are free for income eligible entrepreneurs. BROC also offers an Individual Development Account savings plan. Program participant's savings are matched while saving for their business.

* Micro Business Development Program

P.O. Box 437
Putney, VT 05346   802-387-5029
http://www.vtmicrobusiness.org/

The Micro Business Development Program provides counseling and education to low to moderate income Vermont entrepreneurs striving to start or expand small businesses. Micro Business Development Program services include: one-on-one counseling, classroom training, seminars, loan packaging, and market research.

* Women's Agricultural Network

590 Main Street, UVM
Burlington, VT 05405   802-656-3276
http://www.uvm.edu/~wagn/

Women's Agricultural Network (WAgN) offers several educational and assistance opportunities that help individuals develop and/or further expand an ag-based enterprise. They offer workshops in all aspects of business development, from starting to expanding projects. There is a cost for the workshops however; grants are available for eligible participants.

Virginia

* Business Development Assistance Group

George Mason University Enterprise Center
3401 N. Fairfax Drive, #225   703-993-8127
Arlington, VA 22201   Fax: 703-993-8130
http://www.bdag.org/index.html

Business Development Assistance Group's mission is to help small and minority-owned businesses become more viable in American economic life through educational programs, workshops and training seminars. Most of the services to individuals are provided free of charge if they meet certain income levels.

* Community Business Partnership

6911 Richmond Hwy., Suite 290   703-768-1440
Alexandria, VA 22306   Fax: 703-768-0547
http://www.cbponline.org

Community Business Partnership was formed in response to an identified need for small business technical assistance, particularly to low-moderate income and disadvantaged individuals, including minorities, women and the disabled. A variety of workshops are available for entrepreneurs in Fairfax County.

* New Enterprise Fund

Community Housing Partners Corporation
930 Cambria Street, NE   540-382-2002
Christiansburg, VA 24073   Fax: 540-382-1935
http://www.communityhousingpartners.org/enterprise/me.html
The New Enterprise Fund requires training for applicants. Scholarships are available to attend training to qualified entrepreneurs. After small business training, counseling services or a loan has been funded, on-going technical assistance is provided to those entrepreneurs participating in the Micro-Enterprise Program.

* New Visions, New Ventures, Inc.

801 East Main Street, Suite 1100   804-643-1081
Richmond, VA 23219   Fax: 804-643-1085
http://nvnv.org/index.html
New Visions, New Ventures supports women in difficult life situations, striving to become independent by providing microenterprise development. They provide entrepreneurial training, technical assistance, peer networking and a technology resource center.

* Valley Microenterprise Alliance

1251 Virginia Avenue
Harrisonburg, VA 22802   540-433-5624
http://www.vmalliance.org/
Valley Microenterprise Alliance offers training and business assistance to encourage underemployed and low to moderate-income individuals to start or expand a microenterprise in the Shenandoah Valley Region. Valley Microenterprise Alliance offers a wide variety of classes, workshops and counseling for every aspect of entrepreneurial process.

Washington

* Technical Assistance

Center for Economic Opportunity
202 North Tacoma Avenue   253-591-7026
Tacoma, WA 98402   Fax: 253-593-2744
http://www.mdc-tacoma.org/page26.html
The Center for Economic Development provides low-income adults in Tacoma Pierce County with technical assistance in support of their microenterprise development.

* Shorebank Enterprise Pacific

203 Howerton Way SE
P.O. Box 826   360-642-4265
Ilwaco, WA 98624   Fax: 360-642-4078
http://www.sbpac.com/index.cfm
Shorebank Enterprise is a nonprofit rural economic development corporation assisting entrepreneurs build business and market ventures, which improve the social and environmental conditions of rural communities. Development services are specifically designed for small rural businesses. Their staff's services include financial planning, business strategy, deal structuring, business plan preparation assistance, and management assistance.

* Microenterprise Assistance

Spokane Neighborhood Action Program
212 South Wall Street   509-456-7174
Spokane, WA 99201   Fax: 509-456-7170
http://www.snapwa.org/microent.html
The Microenterprise Development Program is designed to assist low to moderate-income individuals and families to realistically and successfully enter into business, or expand an existing very small or home-based business. They offer a variety of assistance from Business Training to counseling.

West Virginia

* Appalachian by Design

208 South Court Street
Lewisburg, WV 24901   304-647-3455 ext. 14
http://www.abdinc.org
Appalachian by Design provides a training program which teaches Appalachian women the technical and business aspect of hand loomed knitwear.

* Business Development Center

Unlimited Future, Inc.
1650 Eighth Avenue
Huntington, WV 25703   304-697-3007
http://www.unlimitedfuture.org/
Unlimited Future, Inc. provides small business and entrepreneurial classes and training. Classes are free of charge to eligible clients. They also provide one-on-one counseling free of charge.

I Wanna Be a
Real Estate Entrepreneur

Federal Money for Housing and Real Estate

The following is a description of the federal funds available to renters, homeowners, developers, and real estate investors for housing assistance in urban and rural areas. This information is derived from the *Catalog of Federal Domestic Assistance* which is published by the U.S. Government Printing Office in Washington, D.C. The number next to the title description is the official reference for this federal program. Contact the office listed below the caption for further details. The following is a description of some of the terms used for the types of assistance available:

Loans: money lent by a federal agency for a specific period of time and with a reasonable expectation of repayment. Loans may or may not require a payment of interest.

Loan Guarantees: programs in which federal agencies agree to pay back part or all of a loan to a private lender if the borrower defaults.

Grants: money given by federal agencies for a fixed period of time and which does not have to be repaid.

Direct Payments: funds provided by federal agencies to individuals, private firms, and institutions. The use of direct payments may be "specified" to perform a particular service or for "unrestricted" use.

Insurance: coverage under specific programs to assure reimbursement for losses sustained. Insurance may be provided by federal agencies or through insurance companies and may or may not require the payment of premiums.

* Money for Conserving the Water and Soil During an Emergency

(10.054 Emergency Conservation Program (ECP))
U.S. Department of Agriculture
Farm Service Agency, Stop 0513
1400 Independence Avenue, SW
Washington, DC 20250 202-720-6221
www.fsa.usda.gov
Objectives: To enable farmers to perform emergency conservation measures to control wind erosion on farmlands, or to rehabilitate farmlands damaged by wind erosion, floods, hurricanes, or other natural disasters and to carry out emergency water conservation or water enhancing measures during periods of severe drought. Types of assistance: direct payments for specified use. Estimate of annual funds available: (Direct payments) $147,093-033.

* Money to Improve Your Water and Soil

(10.069 Conservation Reserve Program (CRP))
U.S. Department of Agriculture
Farm Service Agency, Stop 0513
Washington, DC 20250-0513 202-720-6221
www.fsa.usda.gov
Objectives: To protect the Nation's long-term capability to produce food and fiber; to reduce soil erosion; to reduce sedimentation; to improve water quality; to create a better habitat for fish and wildlife; to curb production of some surplus commodities; and to provide some needed income support for farmers. Types of assistance: direct payments for specified use. Estimate of annual funds available: $1,787-722,000.

* Money to Change Your Country Property Into a Wetlands

(10.070 Colorado River Basin Salinity Control Program (CRBSCP))
National Resources
Conservation Service
U.S. Department of Agriculture
P.O. Box 2890
Washington, DC 20013 202-720-1873
www.nrcs.usda.gov
Objectives: To provide financial and technical assistance to: (1) Identify salt source areas; (2) develop project plans to carry out conservation practices to reduce salt loads; (3) install conservation practices to reduce salinity levels; (4) carry out research, education, and demonstration activities; (5) carry out monitoring and evaluation activities; and (6) to decrease salt concentration and salt loading which causes increased salinity levels within the Colorado River and to enhance the supply and quality of water available for use in the United States and the Republic of Mexico. Types of assistance: direct payments for specified use. Estimate of annual funds available: (Direct payments) $649,873.

* Loans to Help Your Country Property Recover From an Emergency

(10.404 Emergency Loans)
Loan Making Division
U.S. Department of Agriculture
Farm Service Agency
AG Box 0522
Washington, DC 20250 202-720-1632
www.fsa.usda.gov
Objectives: To assist established (owner or tenant) family farmers, ranchers and aquaculture operators with loans to cover losses resulting from major and/or natural disasters, which can be used for annual farm operating expenses, and for other essential needs necessary to return disaster victims' farming operations to financially sound bases in order that they will be able to return to private sources of credit as soon as possible. Types of assistance: direct loans. Estimate of annual funds available: $40,571,000.

* Money to Build Houses for Your Employees

(10.405 Farm Labor Housing Loans and Grants (Labor Housing))
Multifamily Housing Processing Division
Rural Housing Service
U.S. Department of Agriculture
Washington, DC 20250 202-720-1604

www.rurdev.usda.gov

Objectives: To provide decent, safe, and sanitary low rent housing and related facilities for domestic farm laborers. Types of assistance: project grants; guaranteed/insured loans. Estimate of annual funds available: (Loans) $28,522,532. (Grants) $15,000,000.

* Money to Buy, Fix Up or Build Houses in Small Towns

(10.410 Very Low to Moderate Income Housing Loans (Section 502 Rural Housing Loans))
Director
Single Family Housing
Direct Loan Division
U.S. Department of Agriculture
Washington, DC 20250   202-720-1474
Or
Direct Single Family Housing Guaranteed Loan Division
Rural Housing Service
U.S. Department of Agriculture
Washington, DC 20250   202-720-1452
www.rurdev.usda.gov

Objectives: To assist lower income rural families through direct loans to buy, build, rehabilitate, or improve decent, safe, and sanitary dwellings and related facilities for use by the applicant as a permanent residence. Subsidized funds are available only on direct loans for low and very low income applicants. Nonsubsidized Funds (loan making) are available for very low and low income applicants who are otherwise eligible for assistance, but based on the amount of the loan requested, the interest credit assistance formula results in no interest credit. Nonsubsidized funds (loan servicing) are available to very low, low and moderate income applicants/ borrowers who do not qualify for interest credit assistance for: (1) Subsequent loans for repair and rehabilitation; and (2) subsequent loan part only (repair or rehabilitation or the payment of equity) in connection with transfers by assumption or credit sales. Loan guarantees are also available to assist moderate income rural families in home acquisition. Types of assistance: direct loans; guaranteed/insured loans. Estimate of annual funds available: (Direct Loans) $1,076,998,750 (for subsidized low or moderate income loans for servicing and repairs). (Guaranteed loans) $3,136,429,000.

* Money to Help Low Income Rural Families Get Housing

(10.441 Technical and Supervisory Assistance Grant)
Rural Housing Service (RHS)
USDA
14th Street and Independence Ave., SW
Washington, DC 20250   202-720-1474
www.rurdev.usda.gov

Objectives: To assist low-income rural families in obtaining adequate housing to meet their families needs and/or to provide the necessary guidance to promote their continued occupancy of already adequate housing. These objectives will be accomplished through the establishment or support of housing delivery and counseling projects run by eligible applicants. This program is intended to make use of any available housing program that provides the low-income rural resident access to adequate rental properties or homeownership. Types of assistance: project grants. Estimate of annual funds available: $1,687,543.

* Money for Nonprofits to Build Rental Houses in Small Towns

(10.415 Rural Rental Housing Loans)
Multi-Family Housing Processing Division
Rural Housing Service
U.S. Department of Agriculture
Washington, DC 20250   202-720-1604
www.rurdev.usda.gov

Objectives: To provide economically designed and constructed rental and cooperative housing and related facilities suited for independent living for rural residents. Types of assistance: direct loans. Estimate of annual funds available: (Direct Loans) $49,000,000.

* Loans and Grants to Fix Up Your House in the Country ($5,000 Grants)

(10.417 Very Low Income Housing Repair Loans and Grants) (Section 504 Rural Housing Loans and Grants)
Single-Family Housing Processing Division
Rural Housing Service
U.S. Department of Agriculture
Washington, DC 20250   202-720-1474

www.rurdev.usda.gov

Objectives: To give very low income rural homeowners an opportunity to make essential repairs to their homes to make them safe and to remove health hazards to the family or the community. Types of assistance: direct loans; project grants. Estimate of annual funds available: (Loans) $32,396,000. (Grants) $30,000,000.

* Money for Needy Families to Keep Their Homes

(10.420 Rural Self-Help Housing Technical Assistance) (Section 523 Technical Assistance)
Director, Single-Family Housing Processing Division
Rural Housing Service (RHS)
U.S. Department of Agriculture
Washington, DC 20250   202-720-1474
www.rurdev.usda.gov

Objectives: To provide financial support for programs of technical and supervisory assistance that will aid needy and very low and low-income individuals and their families in carrying out mutual self-help housing efforts in rural areas. Types of assistance: project grants. Estimate of annual fund available: (Grants and Contracts) $34,000,000

* Help for Low-Income Families to Reduce Their Rent

(10.427 Rural Rental Assistance Payments) (Rental Assistance)
Director, Multi-Family Housing Portfolio Management Division
Rural Housing Service
U.S. Department of Agriculture
Washington, DC 20250   202-720-1600
www.rurdev.usda.gov

Objectives: To reduce the tenant contribution paid by low-income families occupying eligible Rural Rental Housing (RRH), Rural Cooperative Housing (RCH), and Farm Labor Housing (LH) projects financed by the Rural Housing Service (RHS) through its sections 515, 514 and 516 loans and grants. Types of assistance: direct payment for specified use. Estimate of annual funds available: $679,000,000

* Application Assistance for Low-Income Rural Residents

(10.442 Housing Application Packaging Grants) (Section 509 Grants)
Director, Single Family Housing Processing Division
Rural Housing Service
Department of Agriculture
Washington, DC 20250   202-720-1474
www.rurdev.usda.gov

Objectives: To package single family housing applications for very low and low-income rural residents into colonials and designated counties who wish to buy, build, or repair houses for their own use and to package applications for organization wishing to develop rental units for lower income families. Types of assistance: project grants. Estimate of annual funds available: (Grants) $755,821

* Money for Emergency Assistance for Natural Disasters

(10.444 Direct Housing-Natural Disaster Loans and Grants) (Section 504, Rural Housing Loans and Grants)
Director, Single Family Housing Processing Division
Rural Housing Service
Department of Agriculture
Washington, DC 20250   202-720-1474
www.rurdev.usda.gov

Objectives: To assist qualified recipients to meet emergency assistance needs resulting from natural disaster. Funds are only available to the extent that funds are not provided by the Federal Emergency Management Agency (FEMA) for the purpose of administering these funds, natural disaster will only include those counties identified by a Presidential declaration. Types of assistance: project grants, direct loans. Estimate of annual funds available: (Loans) $1,056,000 (Grants) $4,143,000, Funds under this program are based on supplemental funding provided by Congress in response to a natural disaster.

* Money to Improve Housing After a Natura Disaster

(10.445 Direct Housing-Natural Disaster) (Section 502 Very Low and Low Income Loans)
Director
Single Family Housing Processing Division
Rural Housing Service

Department of Agriculture
Washington, DC 20250
www.rurdev.usda.gov
202-720-1474

Objectives: To assist qualified lower income rural families to meet emergency, assistance needs resulting from natural disaster to buy, build, rehabilitate, or improve dwelling in rural areas. Funds are only available to the extent that funds are not provided by the Federal Emergency Management Agency (FEMA) for the purpose of administering these funds, natural disaster will only include those counties identified by a Presidential declaration. Types of assistance: direct loans. Estimate of annual funds available: (Loans) $10,495,428. Funds under this program are based on supplemental funding provided by Congress in response to a natural disaster.

* Money to Conserve Soil and Water in Small Towns

(10.900 Great Plains Conservation)
Deputy Chief
National Resources Conservation Program
National Resources Conservation Service
U.S. Department of Agriculture
P.O. Box 2890
Washington, DC 20013
www.nrcs.usda.gov
202-720-1873

Objectives: To conserve and develop the Great Plains soil and water resources by providing technical and financial assistance to farmers, ranchers, and others in planning and implementing conservation practices. Types of assistance: direct payments for specified use; advisory services and counseling. Estimate of annual funds available: (Grants) $400,144. (Salaries and expenses) $0.

* Money to Fix Up an Abandoned Coal Mine

(10.910 Rural Abandoned Mine Program (RAMP))
Deputy Chief for Programs
Natural Resources Conservation Service
U.S. Department of Agriculture
P.O. Box 2890
Washington, DC 20013
www.nrcs.usda.gov
202-720-1873

Objectives: To protect people and the environment from the adverse effects of past coal mining practices, and to promote the development of soil and water resources of unreclaimed mined lands. Types of assistance: direct payments for specified use; advisory services and counseling. Estimate of annual funds available: (Grants) $164,470. (Salaries and expenses) $10,538.

* Money for Farmers and Ranchers to Improve Water and Soil

(10.912 Environmental Quality Incentives Program EQIP)
Deputy Chief for Natural Resources
Conservation Programs
Natural Resources Conservation Service
U.S. Department of Agriculture
P.O. Box 2890
Washington, DC 20013
www.nrcs.usda.gov
202-720-1845
Fax: 202-720-4265

Objectives: Technical, education and finance assistance to eligible farmers and ranchers to address soil, water and related natural resource concerns on their lands in an environmentally beneficial and cost-effective manner. This program provides assistance to farmers and rancher in complying with Federal, State and tribal environmental laws and encourage environmental enhancement. The purpose of this program is achieved through the implementation of structural, vegetative, and land management practices eligible land. This program is funded through the Commodity Credit Corporation (CCC). NRCS provides overall program management and implementation leadership for conservation planning and implementation. The Farm Service Agency provides leadership for administrative processes and procedures for the program. Types of assistance: direct payment and specified use. Estimate of annual funds available: (Grants) $162,000,000 (Salaries and Expenses) $38,000,000 (Education Assistance) not to exceed 1% of grants estimate.

* Loans to Fix Up Houses That Are More Than One Year Old

(14.108 Rehabilitation Mortgage Insurance (203(k)))
Contact your State Homeownership Center or local HUD office
www.hud.gov/progdesc/snglindx.html
Objectives: To help families repair or improve, purchase and improve, or refinance and improve existing residential structures more than one year old.

Types of assistance: guaranteed/insured loans. Estimate of annual funds available: (Loans insured) $1,395,000,000.

* Loans to Buy Trailers

(14.110 Manufactured Home Loan Insurance-Financing Purchase of Manufactured Homes as Principal Residences of Borrowers (Title I))
Chief
Home Mortgage Insurance Division
451 7th Street, SW, Room 9272
U.S. Department of Housing and Urban Development
Washington, DC 20410
www.hud.gov/progdesc/manuf14.cfm
202-708-2121

Objectives: To make possible reasonable financing of manufactured home purchases. Types of assistance: guaranteed/insured loans. Estimate of annual funds available: (Loans insured) $70,000,000.

* Loans to Co-op Investors

(14.112 Mortgage Insurance for Construction or Substantial Rehabilitation of Condominium Projects (234(d) Condominiums))
Chief
Home Mortgage Insurance Division
Room 9272
U.S. Department of Housing and Urban Development
Washington, DC 20410
www.hud.gov/progdesc/condo14.cfm
202-708-1212

Objectives: To enable sponsors to develop condominium projects in which individual units will be sold to home buyers. Types of assistance: guaranteed/insured loans. Estimate of annual funds available: (Mortgages insured) $0.

* Loans to Homeowners Anywhere With 1 to 4 Family Units

(14.117 Mortgage Insurance-Homes (203(b)))
Contact your State Homeownership Center or local HUD office.
Objectives: To help people undertake home ownership. Types of assistance: guaranteed/insured loans. Estimate of annual funds available: (Mortgages insured) $121,673,546,000.

* Loans to Buy Single Family Homes for Disaster Victims

(14.119 Mortgage Insurance-Homes for Disaster Victims (203(h)))
Contact your State Homeownership Center or local HUD office.
Objectives: To help victims of a major disaster undertake homeownership on a sound basis. Types of assistance: guaranteed/insured loans. Estimate of annual funds available: (Mortgages insured) reported under Program No. 14.117.

* Money for Homes in Outlying Areas

(14.121 Mortgage Insurance-Homes in Outlying Areas (203(i)))
Contact your State Homeownership Center or local HUD office.
www.hud.gov
Objectives: To help people purchase homes in outlying areas. Types of assistance: guaranteed/insured loans. Estimate of annual funds available: (Mortgages insured) reported under program No. 14.117.

* Money for Homes in Urban Renewal Areas

(14.122 Mortgage Insurance-Homes in Urban Renewal Areas (220 Homes))
Contact your State Homeownership Center or local HUD office.
www.hud.gov
Objectives: To help families purchase or rehabilitate homes in urban renewal areas. Types of assistance: guaranteed/insured loans. Estimate of annual funds available: (Mortgages insured) Reported under Program 14.113.

* Money for Homes in Older Areas of Town

(14.123 Mortgage Insurance-Housing in Older, Declining Areas (223(e)))
Contact your State Homeownership Center or local HUD office
www.hud.gov
Objectives: To assist in the purchase or rehabilitation of housing in older, declining urban areas. Types of assistance: guaranteed/insured loans. Estimate of annual funds available: (Mortgages insured) Reported under Program 14.113.

* Money to Buy a Co-op Apartment

(14.126 Mortgage Insurance-Cooperative Projects (213 Cooperatives))
Office of Multifamily Housing Development
U.S. Department of Housing and Urban Development
451 7th Street, SW
Washington, DC 20410   202-708-1142
www.hud.gov/offices/hsg/hsgmulti.cfm

Objectives: To make it possible for nonprofit cooperative ownership housing corporations or trusts to develop or sponsor the development of housing projects to be operated as cooperatives and to allow investors to provide good quality multifamily housing to be sold to such nonprofit corporations or trusts upon completion of construction or rehabilitation. Types of assistance: guaranteed/insured loans. Estimate of annual funds available: (Mortgages insured) Reported under Program 14.117.

* Money to Buy a Trailer-Home Park

(14.127 Mortgage Insurance-Manufactured Home Parks (207(m) Manufactured Home Parks))
Office of Multifamily Development
U.S. Department of Housing and Urban Development
451 7th Street, SW
Washington, DC 20410   207-708-1142
www.hud.gov/offices/hsg/hsgmulti.cfm

Objectives: To make possible the financing of construction or rehabilitation of manufactured home parks. Types of assistance: guaranteed/insured loans. Estimate of annual funds available: (Mortgages insured) Reported under Program No. 14.135.

* Money to Buy a Hospital

(14.128 Mortgage Insurance-Hospitals (242 Hospitals))
Office of Insured Health Care Facilities
U.S. Department of Housing and Urban Development
Washington, DC 02410   202-708-0599
or
Division of Facilities Loans
U.S. Department of Health and Human Services
Rockville, MD 20857   301-443-5317
www.hud.gov/officeshsg/hosp/hsghospi.cfm

Objectives: To facilitate the affordable financing of hospitals for the care and treatment of persons who are acutely ill or who otherwise require medical care and related services of the kind customarily furnished only or most effectively by hospitals. Types of assistance: guaranteed/insured loans. Estimate of annual funds available: (Mortgages insured) $500,000,000.

* Money to Buy a Nursing Home

(14.129 Mortgage Insurance-Nursing Homes, Intermediate Care Facilities and Board and Care Homes (232 Nursing Homes))
Office of Multifamily Development
U.S. Department of Housing and Urban Development
451 7th Street, SW
Washington, DC 20412   202-708-1142
www.hud.gov/offices/hsg/hsgmulti.cfm

Objectives: To make possible financing for construction or rehabilitation of nursing homes, intermediate care facilities and board and care homes, to allow purchase or refinancing with or without repairs of projects currently insured by HUD, but not requiring substantial rehabilitation, and to provide loan insurance to install fire safety equipment. Types of assistance: guaranteed/insured loans. Estimate of annual funds available: (Guaranteed/Insured Loans) $1,300,000,000.

* Money to Buy Your Co-op

(14.132 Mortgage Insurance-Purchase of Sales-Type Cooperative Housing Units (213 Sales))
Contact your State Homeownership Center or local HUD office.

Objectives: To make available, good quality, new housing for purchase by individual members of a housing cooperative. Types of assistance: guaranteed/insured loans. Estimate of annual funds available: (Mortgages insured) Reported under program 14.135.

* Money to Buy a Condominium

(14.133 Mortgage Insurance-Purchase of Units in Condominiums (234(c)))
Contact your State Homeownership Center or local HUD office.
www.hud.gov/progdesc/234c--df.cfm

Objectives: To enable families to purchase units in condominium projects. Types of assistance: guaranteed/insured loans. Estimate of annual funds available: (Mortgages insured) $8,482,000,000.

* Housing Money for Middle Income Families

(14.134 Mortgage Insurance-Rental Housing) (207)
Office of Multifamily Development
Department of Housing and Urban Development
451 7th Street, SW
Washington, DC 20410
202-708-1142
www.hud.gov/offices/hsg/mfh/progdesc/progdesc.cfm

Objectives: To provide good quality housing for middle income families. Types of assistance: mortgages insured. Estimate of annual funds available: Reported under Program 14.135.

* Money to Invest in Apartment Buildings for Middle Class Families

(14.135 Mortgage Insurance-Rental and Cooperative Housing for Moderate Income Families and Elderly, Market Interest Rate (221(d)(3) and (4) Multifamily - Market Rate Housing))
Office of Multifamily Development
U.S. Department of Housing and Urban Development
Washington, DC 20410   202-708-1142
www.hud.gov/offices/hsg/hsgmulti.cfm

Objectives: To provide good quality rental or cooperative housing for moderate income families and the elderly and handicapped. Single Room Occupancy (SRO) may also be insured under this section (see 14.184). Types of assistance: guaranteed/insured loans. Estimate of annual funds available: (Mortgages insured excluding coinsurance) $4,050,000,000.

* Money to Invest in Rental Housing for the Elderly

(14.138 Mortgage Insurance-Rental Housing for the Elderly (231))
Office of Multifamily Development
U.S. Department of Housing and Urban Development
451 7th Street, SW
Washington, DC 20410   202-708-1142

Objectives: To provide good quality rental housing for the elderly. Types of assistance: guaranteed/insured loans. Estimate of annual funds available: (Mortgages insured) Reported under program 14.135.

* Money to Invest in Rental Housing in Urban Renewal Areas

(14.139 Mortgage Insurance-Rental Housing in Urban Renewal Areas (220 Multifamily))
Office of Multifamily Development
U.S. Department of Housing and Urban Development
451 7th Street, SW
Washington, DC 20410   202-708-1142
www.hud.gov/offices/hsg/hsgmulti.cfm

Objectives: To provide good quality rental housing in urban renewal areas, code enforcement areas, and other areas designated for overall revitalization. Types of assistance: guaranteed/insured loans. Estimate of annual funds available: (Mortgages insured) Reported under Program 14.135.

* Money to Fix Up Your Home

(14.142 Property Improvement Loan Insurance for Improving All Existing Structures and Building of New Nonresidential Structures (Title I))
Contact your State Homeownership Center or local HUD office
800-767-7468
www.hud.gov/progdesc/title-i.cfm

Objectives: To facilitate the financing of improvements to homes and other existing structures and the building of new nonresidential structures. Types of assistance: guaranteed/insured loans. Estimate of annual funds available: $117,750,000.

* Money to Fix Up Multifamily Projects

(14.151 Supplemental Loan Insurance-Multifamily Rental Housing (241(a)))
Policies and Procedures Division
Office of Multifamily Development
U.S. Department of Housing and Urban Development
451 7th Street, SW
Washington, DC 20411   202-708-1142
www.hud.gov/offices/hsg/hsgmulti.cfm

Objectives: To finance repairs, additions and improvements to multifamily projects, group practice facilities, hospitals, or nursing homes already insured by HUD or held by HUD. Major movable equipment for insured nursing homes, group practice facilities or hospitals may be covered by a mortgage under this program. Types of assistance: guaranteed/insured loans. Estimate of annual funds available: (Loans insured) $50,000,000.

* Money to Investors to Purchase or Refinance Multifamily Housing

(14.155 Mortgage Insurance for the Purchase or Refinancing of Existing Multifamily Housing Projects (Section 223(f) Insured Under Section 207))
Office of Multifamily Development
U.S. Department of Housing and Urban Development
451 7th Street, SW
Washington, DC 20410 202-708-1142
www.hud.gov/offices/hsg/hsgmulti.cfm
Objectives: To provide mortgage insurance to lenders for the purchase or refinancing of existing multifamily housing projects, whether conventionally financed or subject to federally insured mortgages at the time of application for mortgage insurance. Types of assistance: guaranteed/insured loans. Estimate of annual funds available: (Mortgages Insured) $960,000,000.

* Money to Build Housing for the Elderly That Also Provides Support Services

(14.157 Supportive Housing for the Elderly (202))
Office of Housing Assistance and Grants Administration
U.S. Department of Housing and Urban Development
Washington, DC 20410 202-708-2866
www.hud.gov/cfda/2001/14157.cfm
Objectives: To expand the supply of housing with supportive services for the elderly. Types of assistance: direct payment for specified use. Estimate of annual funds available: $1,024,151,000.

* Money to Buy a House With Graduated Mortgage Payments

(14.159 Section 245 Graduated Payment Mortgage Program)
Contact your State Homeownership Center or local HUD office.
www.hud.gov/progdesc/245--dft.cfm
Objectives: To facilitate early home ownership for households that expect their incomes to rise. Program allows homeowners to make smaller monthly payments initially and to increase their size gradually over time. Types of assistance: guaranteed/insured loans. Estimate of annual funds available: Reported under Program 14.117.

* Money to Buy a Trailer and Trailer Lot

(14.162 Mortgage Insurance-Combination and Manufactured Home Lot Loans (Title I))
Chief, Mortgage Insurance Division
U.S. Department of Housing and Urban Development
451 7th Street, SW, Room 9272
Washington, DC 20410 202-708-2121
www.hud.gov/progdesc/manuf14.cfm
Objectives: To make possible reasonable financing for the purchase of a manufactured home and a lot on which to place the home. Types of assistance: guaranteed/insured loans. Estimate of annual funds available: (Mortgages insured) Reported under program No. 14.110.

* Money to Finance Coop Buildings

(14.163 Mortgage Insurance-Single Family Cooperative Housing (203(n)))
Contact your State Homeownership Center or local HUD office.
www.hud.gov/progdesc/203n--df.cfm
Objectives: To provide insured financing for the purchase of the Corporate Certificate and Occupancy Certificate for a unit in a cooperative housing project. Ownership of the corporate certificate carries the right to occupy the unit located within the cooperative project. Types of assistance: guaranteed/insured loans. Estimate of annual funds available: (Mortgages Insured) Reported under program No. 14.117.

* Money to Developers in Financial Trouble

(14.164 Operating Assistance for Troubled Multifamily Housing Projects (Flexible Subsidy Fund) (Troubled Projects))
Office of Housing Assistance and Grants Administration
U.S. Department of Housing and Urban Development
Washington, DC 20420 202-708-2866
www.hud.gov/offices/hsg/mfh/progdesc/progdesc.cfm
Objectives: To provide loans to restore or maintain the physical and financial soundness, to assist in the management and to maintain the low to moderate income character of certain projects assisted or approved for assistance under the National Housing Act or under the Housing and Urban Development Act of 1965. Types of assistance: direct payments for specified use. Estimate of annual funds available: (Obligations) $1,503,000.

* Money to Buy Houses in Areas Hurt by Defense Cuts

(14.165 Mortgage Insurance-Homes-Military Impacted Areas (238(c)))
Contact your State Homeownership Center or local HUD office.
www.hud.gov/funds/singlefamily.cfm
Objectives: To help families undertake home ownership in military impacted areas. Types of assistance: guaranteed/insured loans. Estimate of annual funds available: (Mortgages Insured) Reported under Program 14.133.

* Loans to Developers in Trouble During Their First Two Years of Operation

(14.167 Mortgage Insurance-Two Year Operating Loss Loans, Section 223(d) (Two Year Operating Loss Loans))
Office of Multifamily Development
U.S. Department of Housing and Urban Development
451 7th Street, SW
Washington, DC 20410 202-708-21142
www.hud.gov/offices/hsg/hsgmulti.cfm
Objectives: To insure a separate loan covering operating losses incurred during the first two years following the date of completion of a multifamily project with a HUD-insured first mortgage. Types of assistance: guaranteed/insured loans. Estimate of annual funds available: (Loans insured) $8,500,000.

* Money to Buy a Home Using Increased Equity Payments

(14.172 Mortgage Insurance-Growing Equity Mortgages (GEMs))
Contact your State Homeownership Center or local HUD office.
www.hud.gov/progdesc/245a--df.cfm
Objectives: To provide a rapid principal reduction and shorter mortgage term by increasing payments over a 10-year period, thereby expanding housing opportunities to the homebuying public. Types of assistance: guaranteed/insured loans. Estimate of annual funds available: (Mortgages insured) Reported under program 14.117.

* Money to Buy a Home Using an Adjustable Rate Mortgage

(14.175 Adjustable Rate Mortgages (ARMS))
Contact your State Homeownership Center or local HUD office.
www.hud.gov/origdesc.251--df.cfm
Objectives: To provide mortgage insurance for an adjustable rate mortgage which offers lenders more assurance of long term profitability than a fixed rate mortgage, while offering consumer protection features. Types of assistance: guaranteed/insured loans. Estimate of annual funds available: (Mortgages Insured) Reported under 14.117.

* Money to Invest in Houses for Those With Disabilities

(14.181 Supportive Housing for Persons with Disabilities (811))
Office of Housing Assistance and Grants Administration
U.S. Department of Housing and Urban Development
Washington, DC 20410 202-708-2866
Objectives: To provide for supportive housing and related facilities for persons with disabilities. Types of assistance: direct payments for specified use. Estimate of annual funds available: Reported under program 14.157

* Money to Help Elderly Homeowners Convert Their Equity into a Monthly Income

(14.183 Home Equity Conversion Mortgages (255))
Director
Insured Family Development Division
Office of Single Family Housing
U.S. Department of Housing and Urban Development
Washington, DC 20410 202-708-2121
www.hud.gov/progdesc/hecm--df.cfm
Objectives: To enable elderly homeowners to convert equity in their homes to monthly streams of income or, except for Texas, lines of credit. Types of assistance: guaranteed/insured loans. Estimate of annual funds available: (Mortgages insured): Reported under program 14.133.

* Money to Help Rid Low-Income Housing of Drug Related Crime

(14.193 Federally Assisted Low-Income Housing Drug Elimination)
Office of Housing Assistance and Grants Administration
Department of Housing and Urban Development
451 7th Street, SW, Room 6142
Washington, DC 20410   202-708-2866

Objectives: The purposes of the Assisted Housing Drug Elimination program are to reduce/eliminate drug-related crime and related problems in and around the premises of federally assisted low income housing; encourage owners of such housing to develop a plan for addressing the problem of drug-related crime in and around the premises of federally assisted low income housing proposed for funding under this part; and make available Federal grants to help the owners of federally assisted low-income housing to carry out their plans. Types of assistance: project grants. Estimate of annual funds available: (Grants) $19,477,678

* Money for Supportive Housing for the Homeless

(14.235 Supportive Housing Program) (Transitional Housing; Permanent Housing for Homeless Persons with Disabilities; Innovative Supportive Housing; Supportive Services for Homeless Persons not in Conjunction with Supportive Housing; and Safe Havens)
Director
Office of Special Needs Assistance Programs
Community Planning and Development
U.S. Department of Housing and Urban Development
451 7th Street, SW
Washington, DC 20410   202-708-4300
www.hud.gov/homeless/fedprog.cfm

Objective: The Supportive Housing Program is designed to promote the development of supportive housing and supportive services to assist homeless persons in the transition from homelessness and to enable them to live as independently as possible. Program funds may be used to provide:(I) transitional housing within a 24 month period as well as up to six months of follow-up services to former residents to assist their adjustment to independent living, (ii) permanent housing provided in conjunction with appropriate supportive services designed to maximize the ability of person with disabilities to live as independently as possible; (iii) supportive housing that is, or is part of, a particularly innovative project for, or alternate method of, meeting the immediate and long-term needs of homeless individuals and families; (iv) supportive services for homeless individuals not provided in conjunction with supportive housing, and (v) safe havens for homeless individuals with serious mental illness currently residing on the streets who may not yet be ready for supportive services. Types of assistance: project grants, direct payment for specified use. Estimate of annual funds available: (Grants) $799,000,000.

* Money to Rid Low-Income Housing of Crime

(14.312 New Approach Anti-Drug Grants)
Program Analysts
Office of Housing Assistance and Grants Administration
U.S. Department of Housing and Urban Development
451 7th Street, SW, Room 6146
Washington, DC 20410   202-708-2866, ext. 5787
www.hud.gov

Objectives: to use a comprehensive, coordinated neighborhood/community based approach to eliminate drug-related and other crime problems on the premises and in the vicinity of low-income housing, which may be privately or publicly owned and is financially supported or assisted by public or nonprofit private entities. To emphasize and facilitate the partnership of owners/operators of eligible housing with Federal and local law enforcement as well as other units of general local government and other stake holders to address crime in an assisted project or in an entire neighborhood which may have more than one assisted housing project. Types of assistance: project grants. Estimate of annual funds available: (Grants) $28,883,796

* Rent Supplements to Building Owners With Tenants That Have Low Incomes

(14.856 Lower Income Housing Assistance Program-Section 8 Moderate Rehabilitation (Section 8 Housing Assistance Payments Program for Very Low Income Families-Moderate Rehabilitation))
Office of the Deputy Assistant Secretary for Public Assisted Housing Development
Real Estate and Housing Performance Division
U.S. Department of Housing and Urban Development
Washington, DC 20410   202-708-0477
www.hud.gov/progdesc/pihindx.cfm

Objectives: To aid very low income families and homeless individuals in obtaining decent, safe and sanitary rental housing. Types of assistance: direct payments for specified use. Estimate of annual funds available: (Outlays) not separately identifiable.

* Money to Have Your State Buy Your Old Farm and Turn It into a Park

(15.916 Outdoor Recreation-Acquisition, Development and Planning (Land and Water Conservation Fund Grants))
Chief
Recreation Programs
National Park Service (2225)
U.S. Department of the Interior
1849 C Street, NW, Room 3622
Washington, DC 20240   202-565-1200
www.nps.gov/lwcf

Objectives: To provide financial assistance to the States and their political subdivisions for the preparation of Statewide Comprehensive Outdoor Recreation Plans (SCORPs) and acquisition and development of outdoor recreation areas and facilities for the general public, to meet current and future needs. Types of assistance: project grants. Estimate of annual funds available: (Grants) $146,000,000.

* Grants to Build Houses on Indian Reservations

(15.141 Indian Housing Assistance)
Division of Human Services
Office of Tribal Services
Bureau of Indian Affairs
MS 4660 MIB
1849 C Street, NW
Washington, DC 20240   202-208-3667

Objectives: To use the Indian Housing Improvement Program (HIP) and Bureau of Indian Affairs resources to substantially eliminate substandard Indian housing. This effort is combined with the Indian Health Service (Department of Health and Human Services). Types of assistance: project grants (contracts); dissemination of technical information. Estimate of annual funds available: (Total amount of award: Self-determination contracts and direct grants) $16,781,640.

* Appalachian Local Development District Assistance

(23.009 Appalachian Local Development District Assistance LDD)
Inquiries and proposals for projects should be submitted first to:
Appalachian State Office designated by the Governor
Other inquiries:
Executive Director
Appalachian Regional Commission
1666 Connecticut Avenue, NW
Washington, DC 20235   202-884-7700
www.arc.gov

Objectives: To provide planning and development resources in multi county areas; to help develop the technical competence essential to land development assistance; and to meet the objectives stated under the program entitled Appalachian Regional Development (23.001). Types of assistance: project grants. Estimate of annual funds available: (Grants) $5,900,000.

* Physical Disaster Loans

(59.008 Physical Disaster Loans) (7 (b) Loans (DL))
Office of Disaster Assistance
Small Business Administration
409 3rd Street, SW
Washington, DC 20416   202-205-6734
www.sba.gov/disaster

Objectives: To provide loans to the victims of declared physical type disasters for uninsured losses. Types of assistance: direct loans. Estimate of annual funds available: (Loans) $814,000,000 (Obligations include funds for 59.002 and 59.008).

* Homeless Providers Grant

(64.024 VA Homeless Providers Grant and Per Diem Program)
Program Manager
VA Homeless Providers Grant and Per Diem Program
Mental Health Strategic Healthcare Group (116E)
Department of Veteran Affairs
810 Vermont Avenue, NW   202-273-8966
Washington, DC 20420   Toll free 877-322-0334
www.va.gov

Objectives: To assist public and nonprofit private entities in establishing new programs and service centers to furnish supportive services and supportive housing for homeless veterans through grants that may be used to acquire, renovate, or alter facilities, and to provide per diem payments, or in-kind assistance in lieu of per diem payments, to eligible entities which established programs after November 10, 1992 that provide supportive services and supportive housing for the homeless veterans. Types of assistance: project grants. Estimate of annual fund available: $31,653,000.

* Paraplegic Housing

(64.106 Specially Adapted Housing for Disabled Veteran) (Paraplegic Housing)
Department of Veteran Affairs
Washington, DC 20420   202-273-7355
www.va.gov
Objectives: To help certain severely disabled veteran acquire a home which is suitable adapted to meet the special needs of their disability. Types of assistance: direct payment for specified use. Estimate of annual funds available: (Direct Payments) $22,805,000

* Money for Veterans Who Want to Buy a House

(64.114 Veterans Housing-Guaranteed and Insured Loans (VA Home Loans))
U.S. Department of Veterans Affairs
Washington, DC 20420   202-273-7390
www.va.gov
Objectives: To assist veterans, certain service personnel, and certain unremarried surviving spouses of veterans, in obtaining credit for the purchase, construction or improvement of homes on more liberal terms than are generally available to non-veterans. Types of assistance: guaranteed/insured loans. Estimate of annual funds available: (Closed Loans Guaranteed) $29,535,181,000.

* Loans for Disabled Veterans to Buy a House

(64.118 Veterans Housing-Direct Loans for Disabled Veterans)
U.S. Department of Veterans Affairs
Washington, DC 20420   202-273-7390
www.va.gov
Objectives: To provide certain severely disabled veterans with direct housing credit in connection with grants for specially adaptive housing with special features or movable facilities made necessary by the nature of their disabilities. Types of assistance: direct loans. Estimate of annual funds available: (Loans) $33,000.

* Money for Veterans to Buy Mobile Homes

(64.119 Veterans Housing-Manufactured Home Loans)
U.S. Department of Veterans Affairs
Washington, DC 20420   202-273-7390
www.va.gov
Objectives: To assist veterans, servicepersons, and certain unremarried surviving spouses of veterans in obtaining credit for the purchase of a manufactured home on more liberal terms than are available to non-veterans. Types of assistance: guaranteed/insured loans. Estimate of annual funds available: (Guaranteed Loans) $0.

* Loans for Native American Veterans to Buy or Build a Home

(64.126 Native American Veteran Direct Loan Program (VA Native American Home Loan Program))
U.S. Department of Veterans Affairs
Washington, DC 20420
202-273-7377
www.va.gov
Objectives: To provide direct loans to certain Native American veterans for the purchase or construction of homes on trust lands. Types of assistance: direct loans. Estimate of annual funds available: (Loans): $3,225,000.

* Grants for Storm Windows or to Weatherize Your Home

(81.042 Weatherization Assistance for Low Income Persons)
Director
Office of Building and Technology Assistance
Mail Stop EE-42
Office of Energy Efficiency and Renewable Energy
U.S. Department of Energy
Forrestal Building
Washington, DC 20585   202-586-4074
www.eren.doe.gov/buildings/weatherization_assistance

Objectives: To insulate the dwellings of low income persons, particularly the elderly and handicapped low income, in order to conserve needed energy and to aid those persons least able to afford higher utility costs. Types of assistance: formula grants. Estimate of annual funds available: $154,000,000.

* Government Subsidized Flood Insurance to Homeowners

(83.100 Flood Insurance)
Edward L. Connor
Federal Insurance Administration
Federal Emergency Management Agency
Washington, DC 20472   202-646-3429
www.fema.gov
Objectives: To enable persons to purchase insurance against losses from physical damage to or loss of buildings and or contents therein caused by floods, mudflow, or flood-related erosion in the United States and to promote wise flood plain management practices in the Nation's flood-prone and mudflow-prone areas. Types of assistance: insurance. Estimate of annual funds available: $1,539,166,000.

* Individual and Family Grants

(83.543 Individual and Family Grants)
Director
Readiness Recovery Division
Response and Recovery Directorate
Federal Emergency Management Agency
Washington, DC 20472   202-646-3685
www.fema.gov
Objectives: To produce funds for the necessary expenses and serious needs of disaster victims which cannot be met through other forms of disaster assistance or through other means such as insurance. Types of assistance: project grants. Estimate of annual fund available: (Grants) Not separately identifiable.

* Disaster Housing Program

(83.545 Disaster Housing Program)
Director
Recovery Division, Readiness, Response and Recovery Directorate
Federal Emergency Management Agency
Washington, DC 20472   202-646-3685
www.fema.gov
Objectives: To provide assistance to households affected by a disaster to assist with their disaster created housing needs. Types of assistance: direct payment for specified use; provision of specialized services. Estimate of annual funds available: (Housing Assistance) Not separately identifiable.

* Grants for Renovation or Construction of Non-Acute Health Care Facilities

(93.887 Health Care and Other Facilities (Renovation or Construction Projects)
Program:
Director
Division of Facilities Compliance and Recovery
Office of Special Programs
Health Resources and Services Administration
Department of Health and Human Services
Parklawn Building
5600 Fishers Lane, Room 10C-16
Rockville, MD 2085   301-443-5656
Grants:
Grants Management Specialist
Grants Management Branch
Office of Program Support
HIV/AIDS Bureau
Health Resources and Services Administration
5600 Fishers Lane, Room 7-89
Rockville, MD 2085   301-443-5906
www.hrsa.gov/osp
Objectives: To renovate, expand, repair, equip, or modernize non-acute health care facilities. Types of assistance: project grants. Estimate of annual funds available: (Grants) $0

* Money For Nonprofits to Provide Rural Housing Site Loans

(10.411 Rural Housing Site Loans and Self-Help Housing Land Development Loans (Section 523 and 524 Site Loans))
Director

Single-Family Housing Processing Division
Rural Housing Service
U.S. Department of Agriculture
Washington, DC 20250   202-720-1474
www.rurdev.usda.gov

Objectives: To assist public or private nonprofit organizations interested in providing sites for housing, to acquire and develop land in rural areas to be subdivided as adequate building sites and sold on a cost development basis to families eligible for low and very low income loans, cooperatives, and broadly based nonprofit rural rental housing applicants. Types of assistance: direct loans. Estimate of annual funds available: (Loans) $5,009,000.

* Money to Fix Up Your Home in the Country

(10.433 Rural Housing Preservation Grants)
Multiple Family Housing Processing Division
Rural Housing Service
U.S. Department of Agriculture
Washington, DC 20250   202-720-1660
www.rurdev.usda.gov

Objectives: To assist very low and low income rural residents individual homeowners, rental property owners (single/multi-unit) or by providing the consumer cooperative housing projects (co-ops) the necessary assistance to repair or rehabilitate their dwellings. These objectives will be accomplished through the establishment of repair/rehabilitation, projects run by eligible applicants. This program is intended to make use of and leverage any other available housing programs which provide resources to very low and low income rural residents to bring their dwellings up to development standards. Types of assistance: project grants. Estimate of annual funds available: (Grants) $8,000,000.

* Money for Homes for Low Income Indian Families

(14.850 Public and Indian Housing)
Assistant Secretary for Public and Indian Housing
U.S. Department of Housing and Urban Development
Washington, DC 20410   202-708-0950
www.hud.gov/progdesc/pihindx.html

Objectives: To provide and operate cost-effective, decent, safe and affordable dwellings for lower income families through an authorized local Public Housing Agency (PHA) or Indian Housing Authority (IHA). Types of assistance: direct payments for specified use. Estimate of annual funds available: $3,530,000,000.

* Money to Provide Affordable Rental Housing for Low-Income Families

(14.239 HOME Investment Partnerships Program)
Mary Kolesar, Director
Office of Affordable Housing Programs
Community Planning and Development
U.S. Department of Housing and Urban Development
451 7th St., SW, Room 7164
Washington, DC 20410   202-708-2470
www.hud.gov/offices/cpd

Objectives: (1) To expand the supply of decent and affordable housing, particularly rental housing, for low and very low income Americans; (2) To strengthen the abilities of State and local governments to design and implement strategies for achieving adequate supplies of decent, affordable housing; (3) To provide both financial and technical assistance to participating jurisdictions, including the development of model programs for developing affordable low income housing and; (4) To extend and strengthen partnerships among all levels of government and the private sector, including for-profit and nonprofit organizations, in the production and operation of affordable housing. Types of assistance: formula grants. Estimate of annual funds available: (Grants) $2,084,100,000.

* Money to Invest in Rental Housing for Lower Income Families

(14.856 Lower Income Housing Assistance Program-Section 8 Moderate Rehabilitation)
Office of the Deputy Assistant Secretary for Public Assisted Housing Delivery
Real Estate and Housing Performance Division
U.S. Department of Housing and Urban Development
Washington, DC 20410   202-708-0477
www.hud.gov/progdesc/pihindx.html

Objectives: To aid very low income families in obtaining decent, safe and sanitary rental housing. Types of assistance: direct payments for specified use. Estimate of annual funds available: (Outlays) not separately identifiable.

* Loans to Investors, Builders, Developers of Affordable Housing

(14.189 Qualified Participating Entities QPE Risk Sharing Pilot Program)
Office of Multifamily Development
U.S. Department of Housing and Urban Development
451 7th Street, SW
Washington, DC 20410   202-708-1142
www.hud.gov/offices/hsg/hsgmulti.cfm

Objectives: Under this program HUD will provide reinsurance on multifamily housing projects whose loans are originated, underwritten, serviced, and disposed of by qualified participating entities (QPEs) and/or its approved lenders. The program is a pilot designed to assess the feasibility of risk-sharing partnerships between HUD and QPEs, including Government Sponsored Enterprises, State and local housing finance agencies, financial institutions and the Federal Housing Finance Board, in providing affordable housing for the nation. Types of assistance: guaranteed/insured loans. Estimate of annual funds available: (Loans insured) $105,000,000.

* Money for Developers, Investors, and Builders of Low Income Housing

(14.188 HFA Risk Sharing Pilot Program)
Office of Multifamily Development
U.S. Department of Housing and Urban Development
451 7th Street, SW
Washington, DC 20412   202-708-1142
www.hud.gov/offices/hsg/hsgmulti.cfm

Objectives: Under this program, HUD will provide credit enhancement for mortgages for multifamily housing projects whose loans are underwritten, processed, serviced, and disposed of by HFAs, HUD, and the Housing Finance Agencies share in the risk of the mortgage. Types of assistance: guaranteed/insured loans. Estimate of annual funds available: (Loans Insured) $650,000,000

State Money for Housing and Real Estate

State Initiatives

While affordable housing has long held an important place on the Federal government's policy agenda, budget cutbacks in recent years have forced the government to turn over many housing responsibilities to the states. Housing finance agencies (HFAs) have been created by states to issue tax-exempt bonds to finance mortgages for lower income first-time home buyers and to build multifamily housing.

States are involved in a host of initiatives throughout the broad spectrum of housing finance and development. Interim construction financing programs which can reduce the basic costs of lower income housing projects have been initiated in a number of states, together with innovative home ownership programs and programs directed toward rehabilitation and improved energy conservation.

States are also venturing into areas which have not received as much public sector attention until recently. By encouraging non-traditional types of housing, such as accessory units, shelters, and single room occupancy housing, states are addressing important elements of the housing market.

In Colorado, the state Housing and Finance Authority (CHFA) has issued more than $2.6 billions of bonds and notes since its establishment in 1973, providing housing for more than 47,000 families and individuals of low and moderate income; 27,200 first-time home buyers and over 20,500 rental housing units. In recent years the state has broadened CHFA's authority to allow it to develop finance programs to assist the growth of small business, help exports with insurance on goods sold overseas, and similar projects.

Colorado has done more than simply help its citizens find housing: the programs have resulted in construction employment of more than 20,000 jobs, with wages estimated at almost $20 million in new local real estate taxes and an indirect gain of $1.6 billion for the state.

Wisconsin, Maine and New York each have between 18 and 20 programs including special ones for women and minorities, for disabled persons, and for environmental hazard removal.

Maryland operates 26 programs, including those to help people with closing costs and settlement expenses. It also has special funds available for the elderly and is developing an emergency mortgage fund to help people who have fallen behind in their payments. Nonprofit developers can also tap the state for money to build low cost rental units.

Among Michigan's 29 programs and Minnesota's 25 are several for neighborhood revitalization. Minnesota also offers programs targeting the needs of urban Indians and migrant farm workers. Alaska, Oregon and Vermont offer financing for tenant acquisition of mobile home parks.

Funds are also available for persons who take steps to make their homes more energy efficient, for homeowners and landlords who remove lead paint from dwelling units, for houses without plumbing or those with plumbing that is dysfunctional, for handicapped persons, and to help landlords defray the costs of bringing low income housing into compliance with state and local housing codes. There are also funds for nonprofit organizations to acquire or renovate existing houses and apartments for use as group homes for special needs such as the mentally retarded.

In many states, elderly homeowners can look to the HFA to obtain financing and/or support services they need to remain in their homes and avoid institutionalization. Some of the states have more than one agency dedicated to housing and we have attempted to list them all here. Also, many cities and counties have quasi-federal/quasi-local "housing authorities" with additional programs. Check your local government listings for these.

The following is a complete listing of state housing programs.

Housing Offices

Alabama

Alabama Housing Finance Authority
2000 Interstate Park Dr., Suite 408
Montgomery, AL 36109
Mailing Address:
P.O. Box 230909   334-244-9200
Montgomery, AL 36123-0909   800-325-2432
www.ahfa.com
Email: webmaster@ahfa.com

1. Mortgage Revenue Bond Program: low rate loans for income eligible first-time homebuyers. Contact the Alabama Housing Finance Authority for application information.
2. Step Up Program: designed specifically for moderate-income home buyers: those whose incomes can sustain a market-rate mortgage but whose savings fall short of the amount needed for entry costs like a down payment, closing costs and prepaid items. The application can be found in the Appendix Manual, Appendix 45, page 104 at the web site, {www.ahfa.com/StepUpmanuals.htm}.
3. Habitat For Humanity Loan Purchase Program: loan purchasing program in which AHFA purchases loans from Alabama's 32 Habitat affiliates. The affiliate uses the up-front money to build more housing for low-income families.
4. Building Blocks To Homeownership: free seminar that educates Alabama's potential or current homebuyer in money management, credit, financing and home maintenance.
5. Low Income Housing Tax Credit Program: federal tax credits for owners of low-income rental housing. The program increases the supply of affordable housing for economically disadvantaged families. {www.ahfa.com/LIHTCprgm.htm}.
6. HOME Program: provides additional opportunities for the production of affordable housing for low-income families. For an application, fill out the request form on the back of the HOME brochure booklet; {www.ahfa.com/HOMEprgm.htm}.
7. Multifamily Mortgage Revenue Bonds: Lower than market interest rates for developers of multifamily housing that reserve some of their units for very-low income renters. Contact the Alabama Housing Finance Authority for application information.
8. Alabama Multifamily Loan Consortium: long-term financing for affordable multifamily housing development and rehabilitation. To view the Charter Members of the Consortium go to {www.ahfa.com/AMLCmembers.htm}.

Alaska

Alaska Housing Finance Corporation
4300 Boniface Parkway
Anchorage, AK 99504
Mailing Address:
P.O. Box 101020
4300 Boniface Parkway   907-338-6100
Anchorage, AK 99510-1020   800-478-2432
www.ahfc.state.ak.us

1. Mobile Home Program: low down payment for affordable homes. To view a list of approved lenders, go to {www.ahfc.state.ak.us/Department_Files/Mortgage/approved-lenders.htm}.
2. Veteran Mortgage Program: low interest loans to qualified veterans. To view a list of approved lenders, go to {www.ahfc.state.ak.us/Department_Files/Mortgage/approved-lenders.htm}.
3. Refinance Program: reduce monthly payments on existing loans. To view a list of approved lenders, go to {www.ahfc.state.ak.us/Department_Files/Mortgage/approved-lenders.htm}.
4. Non-Conforming Program: financing for homes which cannot be financed through traditional financing. To view a list of approved lenders, go to {www.ahfc.state.ak.us/Department_Files/Mortgage/approved-lenders.htm}.
5. Senior Housing Plan: potential borrowers may apply for financing to purchase, construct, rehabilitate or improve various kinds of housing that would meet the needs of persons 60 or older. To obtain an application, call 800-478-AHFC, 907-330-8436, or email {jmccall@ahfc.state.ak.us}.
6. Energy Efficient Interest Rate Reduction Program: participants of an AHFC loan may qualify for an interest-rate reduction depending on the energy efficiency of their home. To view a list of approved lenders, go to {www.ahfc.state.ak.us/Department_Files/Mortgage/approved-lenders.htm}.
7. Low-Income Weatherization Program: eligible low-income Alaskans can lower the cost of heating their homes by providing energy-efficient improvements. To view a list of service providers, go to {www.ahfc.state.ak.us/Department_Files/RIC/Energy/weatherization-providers.htm}.
8. Affordable Housing Enhanced Loan Program: down payment assistance to moderate-income borrowers. To view a list of approved lenders, go to {www.ahfc.state.ak.us/Department_Files/Mortgage/approved-lenders.htm}.
9. Assistance Provider interest Rate Reduction: subsidized interest rates for housing with a live-in care provider for physically or mentally disabled occupants. For a loan application, call 800-478-AHFC, 907-338-6100, or email {ehaveloc@ahfc.state.ak.us}.
10. Association Loan Program: funds to Homeowners' Associations for improvements to common-area that if not corrected could threaten the health and safety of the residents. For loan information, call 800-478-AHFC, 907-338-6100, or email {ehaveloc@ahfc.state.ak.us}.
11. Conventional Loan Program(Taxable Loan Program): loans for borrowers that do not meet the criteria of other special AHFC programs for eligible property. To view a list of approved lenders, go to {www.ahfc.state.ak.us/Department_Files/Mortgage/approved-lenders.htm}.
12. First Time Homebuyer Program: (Tax-Exempt Loan Program) loan program for income eligible first-time homebuyers. To view a list of approved lenders, go to {www.ahfc.state.ak.us/Department_Files/Mortgage/approved-lenders.htm}.
13. Interest Rate Reduction for Low Income Buyer: interest rate subsidy for low-income borrower. To view a list of approved lenders, go to {www.ahfc.state.ak.us/Department_Files/Mortgage/approved-lenders.htm}.
14. Rural Owner-Occupied Loan Program: low interest financing for the construction or rehabilitation of a primary residence to qualified borrowers that live in "small communities" in rural Alaska. To view a list of approved lenders, go to {www.ahfc.state.ak.us/Department_Files/Mortgage/approved-lenders.htm}.
15. Second Mortgage program: funds to qualified borrowers for home improvements or for the purchase of a home subject to an exiting first mortgage. To view a list of approved lenders, go to {www.ahfc.state.ak.us/Department_Files/Mortgage/approved-lenders.htm}.
16. Second Mortgage for Health and Safety Repair: funding for health and safety repairs to a financed property of AHFC. To view a list of approved lenders, go to {www.ahfc.state.ak.us/Department_Files/Mortgage/approved-lenders.htm}.
17. Small Building Material Loan Program: financing for qualified borrowers to purchase materials to rehabilitate primary residences in areas that are defined as "small communities". Contact the Alaska Housing Finance Corporation for application information.
18. Streamline Refinance Program: applicants can get financing secured by property that is currently financed by AHFC without income, credit, or appraisal qualifications. To view a list of approved lenders, go to {www.ahfc.state.ak.us/Department_Files/Mortgage/approved-lenders.htm}.
19. Rural Enhanced Loan Program (RELP): offers an interest rate reduction, reduced mortgage requirements, and one step construction loans to low-moderate income borrowers in remote communities. To view a list of approved lenders, go to {www.ahfc.state.ak.us/Department_Files/Mortgage/approved-lenders.htm}.
20. Multifamily, Congregate and Special Needs Housing Loan: assists qualified nonprofit housing providers and for-profit companies in financing multifamily complexes for low- and moderate-income housing. Contact the Alaska Finance Corporation for information.

21. GOAL Program: provides grants, federal tax credits, and zero interest loans to for profit and non-profit developers who build affordable rental housing for low-to-moderate income families and seniors. This program is funded through three programs: For applications to this program, go to {www.ahfc.state.ak.us/Download/download-main-page.htm}.

22. HOME Investment Partnership Program (HOME): funding for the development of affordable housing for low-to-moderate income families.

23. Low-Income Housing Tax Credits (LIHTC): tax credits to owners of rental property where a number of units are set aside for low- to moderate-income families.

24. Senior Citizens Housing Development Fund (SCHDF): grants to non-profit agencies.

25. Senior Housing Loan Program: potential borrowers may apply for financing to purchase, construct, rehabilitate or improve various kinds of housing that would meet the needs of persons 60 or older. To obtain an application, call 800-478-AHFC, 907-330-8436, or email {jmccall@ahfc.state.ak.us}.

26. Assistance Provider Interest Rate Reduction: subsidized interest rates for housing with a live-in care provider for physically or mentally disabled occupants. For a loan application, call 800-478-AHFC, 907-338-6100, or email {ehaveloc@ahfc.state.ak.us}.

27. Multifamily Federally Insured Loan Program: up to 85% of financing for the acquisition, rehabilitation, or refinance of existing multifamily properties. To view a list of approved lenders, go to {www.ahfc.state. ak.us/Department_Files/Mortgage/approved-lenders.htm}.

28. Loans to Sponsors: funding to sponsors of affordable housing for low to moderate income people or those living in remote, underdeveloped, or blighted areas of the state. For a loan application, call 800-478-AHFC, 907-338-6100, or email {ehaveloc@ahfc.state.ak.us}.

29. Multi Family Loan Purchase Program: loans for the acquisition, rehabilitation, and refinance of multifamily properties with at least 5 units. For an application, go to {www.ahfc.state.ak.us/Department_Files/mortgage/Loan-Programs/multi-family-loan-purchase-program.htm}.

30. Taxable First Time Home Buyer Program: reduced interest rate to eligible borrowers, without income limits. To view a list of approved lenders, go to (www.ahfc.state.ak.us/Department_Files/Mortgage/approved-lenders.htm).

31. Rural Teacher Housing Loan Program: conventional loans to purchase or renovate housing occupied by educators in rural "small communities" of Alaska.

32. State Veterans Interest Rate Preference: a one percent rate reduction on the first $50,000 to low-to-moderate income qualified veterans.

33. Public Housing Rental Program: safe, decent, and affordable rental housing to low-income Alaskans. To view a list of available rental housing locations, go to {www.ahfc.state.ak.us/Department_Files/Public_Housing/public-housing-program.htm}.

Arizona

Arizona Department of Commerce
Office of Housing Development
1700 W. Washington St., Suite 210
Phoenix, AZ 85007
www.housingaz.com   602-771-1000
Email: webmaster@azcommerce.com

1. Low Interest Mortgages: affordable mortgages for first-time homebuyers that can include down payment assistance. Contact the Governor's Office of Housing Development for a list of participating lenders.

2. Down Payment Assistance: down payment and closing cost assistance offered in the area in which you live. The Homebuyer Counseling Agencies list is at {www.housingaz.com/homeownershipassistance/default.asp}.

3. Rural Home Purchase Program: assistance to qualified low-income family or individuals purchasing a home. Contact the Governor's Office of Housing Development for information on this program.

4. Weatherization Assistance Program: helps low-income families and individuals reduce their home energy costs. A list of agencies to apply to is located at {www.commerce.state.az.us/Etips/Weatherization.htm}.

5. HOME Program: provides help for low-income families with various housing needs from rehabilitation to rental assistance. Applications related to this program are available at {www.commerce.state.az.us/housing.ahtf1.shtml}.

6. Special Needs Housing Program: grants to provide planning, technical assistance, and services to groups that serve low-income special needs groups. Contact the Governor's Office of Housing Development for application information.

7. State Housing Trust Fund: funding for the development of affordable housing for low-income families in Arizona. Applications related to this program are available at {www.commerce.state.az.us/housing/ahtf1.shtml}.

8. Low Income Housing Tax Credits: federal income tax credits for owners of low income housing units. The application is available at {www.housingaz.com/library/default.asp}.

9. Tenant Based Rental Assistance Program: rental assistance to income eligible households. The application can be downloaded from {www.housingaz.com/library/default.asp}.

10. Project Based Rental Assistance: project based rent subsidies to income eligible households. Contact the Governor's Office of Housing Development for application information.

11. Publicly Assisted Affordable Rental Properties: affordable rental property available to income eligible households. Contact the Governor's Office of Housing Development for application information.

12. Low Income Housing Tax Credits: federal income tax credits for owners of low income housing units. The application is available at {www.housingaz.com/library/default.asp}.

Arkansas

Arkansas Development Finance Authority
423 Main Street, Suite 500
Little Rock, AR 72201   501-682-5900
www.accessarkansas.org/adfa
Email: mdodson@adfa.state.ar.us

1. Home To Own (Mortgage Revenue Bond Program): low interest rate loans to low and moderate income first time homebuyers. For a list of participating lenders, go to {www.acessarkansas.org/adfa/programs/H2OProgramGuide.htm}.

2. Down Payment Assistance Program: closing cost assistance for low to moderate-income first time homebuyers. The Homebuyer Counseling Agencies list can be viewed at {www.accessarkansas.org/adfa/programs/dpap.html}.

3. Low Income Housing Tax Credit Program: federal tax credits for owners of low-income rental housing. The application can be found at {www.accessarkansas.org/adfa/programs/lihtcp.html}.

4. HOME Program: funds are used for a variety of activities to develop and support affordable housing for low-income households. Eligible activities include: Tenant Based Rental Assistance, Rental Rehabilitation, new construction, and assistance to homeowners and homebuyers. Download an application at {www.accessarkansas.org/adfa/home_program_2000.htm}.

5. Tax Exempt Multi Family Housing Bonds: below market rate loans for developers that agree to set affordable rental rates for low to moderate-income families. Contact the Arkansas Development Finance Authority for application information.

California

California Housing Finance Agency
1121 L Street
Sacramento, CA 95814   916-322-3991
www.calhfa.ca.gov
Email: homeownership@calhfa.ca.gov
Visit {www.hcd.ca.gov/clearinghouse/} to find information on over 200 housing programs, government, private leaders and foundation grants. Each program listing identifies the goals, eligible activities and type of funding, as well as such critical and timely information as application deadlines and current funding availability

1. 100% Loan Program (CHAP): provides low interest financing along with CalHFA down payment assistance to qualified first-time homebuyers.

2. The Affordable Housing Partnership Program (AHPP): assists first-time homebuyers with closing cost and/or down payment. The Approved Subordinate Localities and Programs list can be viewed at {www.calhfa.ca.gov/homeownership/downpayment/ahpp-approved.pdf}.

3. Extra Credit Teacher Program: provides qualified teachers and principals down payment assistance to first-time homebuyers. The documents needed for this program are at {www.calhfa.ca.gov/homeownership/requirements/lender/index.htm}.

4. Oakland Teacher Program: provides affordable loans and down payment assistance to qualified teachers and principals on the purchase of their first home. For a list of approved lenders to apply to, go to {www.calhfa.ca.gov/quick/forms/homeownership/oakland_teacher_program/lenders.pdf}.

5. High Cost Area Home Purchase Assistance Pilot Program (HiCAP): designed to assist first-time homebuyers in the highest housing cost areas of the state. Eligible counties are: San Francisco, San Mateo, Santa Clara, Alameda, Contra Costa, and Sonoma. An application can be obtained from an approved lender, see the list at {www.calhfa.ca.gov/homeownership/requirements/lender/index.htm}.

6. Builder Lock (BLOCK) Program: Builders/Developers may purchase forward commitments for permanent mortgage financing for CalHFA-eligible borrowers tied to their construction/marketing program at single-family new-home developments anywhere in the state. On any day, builders/developers may lock-in, through an approved CalHFA

Lender, an interest rate for a pool of funds for terms of 6, 9, or 12 months (nonprofits up to 18 months) into the future for commitment fees of 0.5%, 1.5%, and 2% respectively. Contact the California Housing Finance Agency for application information.

7. Loan to Lender Financing: available to eligible sponsors to help reduce the cost of construction financing for affordable housing projects by providing low cost funds to eligible construction lenders. Contact the California Housing Finance Agency for application information. {www.calhfa.ca.gov/special/help/index.htm}.

8. Mulitfamily Housing Program: loans for new construction, rehabilitation preservation of permanent and transitional rental housing for lower income households. The application can be downloaded at {www.calhfa.ca.gov/rental/financing/mf_loanapp.doc}.

9. Energy Efficient Mortgages: loans to finance energy-efficient improvements to new and existing homes.

10. California Housing Loan Insurance Fund: helps homeowners with the restrictions of conventional mortgage insurance by encouraging lenders to serve borrowers with limited funds for a down payment or closing costs.

11. Self-Help Builder Assistance Program: permanent low interest loans for single family homes built by owner-builders through self-help construction. This gives families with limited down payments the opportunity to use their "sweat equity" to obtain homeownership. To view a list of nonprofit builders who have participated go to {www.calhfa.ca.gov/homeownership/programs/sffdpap/builders.PDF}.

California Department of Housing and Community Development
1800 Third Street
P.O. Box 952050
Sacramento, CA 94252   916-445-4782
www.hcd.ca.gov

1. California Self-Help Housing Program: assists low- and moderate-income families to build and rehabilitate their homes with their own labor. The application can be downloaded at the following website, {www.hcd.ca.gov/ca/cshhp}.

2. HOME Program: assists communities and community housing development organization (CHDOs) in activities that create or retain affordable housing. The application can be found at {www.hcd.ca.gov/ca/home/nofa2001}.

3. Emergency Housing Assistance Program: grants to provide emergency shelters, transitional housing and services for the homeless. The forms for this program can be downloaded from the following website, {www.hcd.ca.gov/ca/ehap/ehapforms.html}.

4. California Indian Assistance Program: assists tribal organizations to obtain and administer housing, infrastructure. Call 916-445-4727 to check if funding is available and information on the application procedure.

5. Mobile Home Park Resident Ownership Program: loan to mobile home park resident organizations, nonprofit housing sponsors, or local public agencies that are purchasing the park. Go to {www.hcd.ca.gov/ca/mprop} for the necessary forms.

6. Federal Emergency Shelter Grant Program: grants to fund emergency shelters, services and transitional housing for the homeless. Applications and Request for Proposal (RFP) forms are available at {www.hcd.ca.gov/ca/fesg}.

7. Child Care Facilities Finance Program: loan guarantees and direct loans for the development and or expansion of child care facilities, child development facilities and family child care homes. Call 916-323-2180 for information on funding availability and the application process.

8. Families Moving to Work Program: loans to Cal WORKS welfare reform program recipients for limited-term housing assistance, childcare, employment assistance and other services. The forms can be found at {www.hcd.ca.gov/ca/fmtw}.

9. Housing Assistance Program: rent assistance for extremely low and very-low income households in rural counties without housing authorities. For information on the application process, call 916-324-7696.

10. Office of Migrant Services: loans and grants to provide safe, decent and affordable seasonal rental housing and support services for migrant farm worker families during peak harvest season. Call 916-324-0695 for funding availability and application information.

Colorado

Colorado Housing and Finance Authority
1981 Blake Street   303-297-2432
Denver, CO 80202-1272   800-877-2432
www.colohfa.org

1. HomeStart Program (tax-exempt bond program): first-mortgage financing program for eligible Colorado home buyers that offers a competitive interest rate loan and optional cash assistance to help pay down payment and closing expenses. For a list of participating lenders to apply with, go to {www.colohfa.org/hf_homestart_info.shtml}.

2. HomeStart Plus (taxable bond program): provides competitive interest rates and includes cash assistance. Eligibility Income limits are higher than the CHFA HomeStart program but are still below market. For a list of participating lenders to apply with, go to {www.colohfa.org/hf_homestart_info.shtml}.

3. Home Access and Home Access Plus Program: CHFA can possibly make it easier for those with disabilities to purchase their first home with a low interest rate loan. CHFA also offers a second mortgage program for down payment and closing costs. Call 800-877-2432 ext. 376 or 303-297-7376 for application assistance.

4. Mortgage Credit Certificate Program: reduction of federal income tax for homebuyers to pay their monthly mortgage. Call 303-297-7376 for application information.

5. Down Payment Assistance: low interest second mortgage loan to help eligible homebuyers with down payment and closing costs; only available to those who get CHFA Forward Commitment Loans. Call 303-572-9445 for application information.

6. Tax Exempt Private Activity Bonds: provides tax-exempt financing for construction loans and/or permanent mortgage loans. Call Colorado Housing and Finance Authority for a developer pack; 303-297-7351 or 800-877-2432.

7. Risk Sharing Program: provides long term, fully amortizing loans for new construction or acquisition with rehabilitation of rental housing for families or elderly. Contact the Colorado Housing and Finance Authority for application information.

8. Taxable Loans: combined with the Low Income Housing Tax Credit for new construction, acquisition, or rehabilitation of rental property to house families or the elderly. For an application, go to {www.colohfa.org/rf_forprof.shtml}.

9. Low Income Housing Tax Credit: federal tax credits for owners of low-income rental housing. For a application, you can email the tax credit staff; {Paulah@colohfa.org} or go to {www.colohfa.org/tc_lihtc.shtml}.

10. Small Affordable Rental Transaction (SMART): provides long term financing for small rental housing projects; also minimizes the paperwork, document costs and the time it takes to close the loan. The application is available at {www.colohfa.org/rf_forprof.shtml}.

Connecticut

Connecticut Housing Finance Authority
999 West Street
Rocky Hill, CT 06067-4005   860-721-9501
www.chfa.org/
Email: info@chfa.org

1. Home of Your Own Program (HOYO): offers 30-year fixed rate mortgages to first time homebuyers with disabilities. Contact the Connecticut Housing Finance Authority for application information.

2. Urban Rehabilitation Home Ownership (UR Home) Program: a 2-year pilot program with hopes of revitalizing 16 targeted urban communities in Connecticut. This program offers a low interest rate, 30-year CHFA mortgage loan with low-cost down payment assistance. For a list of participating lenders to apply with, go to {www.chfa.org/FirstHome/UR%20Home.asp}.

3. Military Homeownership Program: a special, low-interest rate mortgage for full-time enlisted military personnel. If you are serving in the military full-time, whether it be U.S. Army, Navy, Air force, Marine Corps, Coast Guard, or National Guard, you may be eligible. Call 860-571-3502 for application information.

4. Teachers Mortgage Assistance Program: low interest rate mortgage available to Connecticut certified public school teachers. Call 860-571-3502 for application information.

5. Home Buyer Mortgages: below market interest rates for first time low or moderate income homebuyers that purchase moderate priced homes. Call 860-571-3502 for application information.

6. Rehabilitation Mortgage Loan Program: loans to income eligible home buyers that purchase a home that needs to be repaired, refinancing of a home in need of repair for income eligible homeowners. Call 860-571-3502 for application information.

7. Homeownership Program: mortgages for public housing tenants and certain public assisted housing residents that meet income requirements; a home buyer education seminar must be attended. Call 860-571-3502 for application information.

8. Police Homeownership Program: low interest rate mortgages to police officers that purchase a home in certain communities; must not have owned a home within the past 3 years unless they purchase in targeted areas. Call 860-571-3502 for application information.

9. Down Payment Assistance Program: down payment assistance to eligible homebuyers; closing costs assistance to low income buyers in the Homeownership Program. To download an application, go to {www.chfa.org/mainpages/dap_forms.htm}.

10. Apartment Conversion for the Elderly: funding for elderly homeowners so they can renovate or add an addition on their home to create an accessory apartment to provide rental income. Call 860-571-3502 for application information.

11. Reverse Annuity Mortgage Program: elderly low-income homeowners can use the equity in their home as tax-free income which can be repaid after their death or when they no longer occupy the home. Call 860-571-3502 for application information.

12. Common Interest Community Common Element Repair Program: financing for repairs to common elements of condominiums and housing cooperatives where other financing is not available. Call 860-571-4216 for application information.

13. Employer Assisted Housing Tax Credit Program: state tax credits to employers that create loan funds for low and moderate income employees so they can purchase or rent a home. For information on the application, go to {www.chfa.org/TaxCredits/application.pdf}.

14. Community Development and Preservation Loan Fund: financing for developers to acquire, rehabilitate, and/or construct one to four family housing for income eligible buyers. Call 860-571-4374 for application information.

15. Multifamily Rental Housing Program: construction and permanent first mortgages to developers that build or rehabilitate affordable housing where some units are set aside for low income residents. Call 860-571-4216 for application information.

16. Mobile Manufactured Home Parks Pilot Program: financing for resident associations and certain non-profits to purchase mobile home park land to convert it to condominiums or cooperative ownership. Call 860-571-4216 for application information.

17. Low Income Housing Tax Credit: federal tax credits for developers of rental housing for low income tenants. Call 860-571-4216 for application information.

18. Housing Tax Credit Contribution Program: tax credits to non-profits that develop, sponsor or mange housing for very low, low, and moderate income individuals or families. Call 860-571-4216 for application information.

Delaware

Delaware State Housing Authority
18 The Green
Dover, DE 19901   302-739-4263
www2.state.de.us/dsha

1. Home Fix-Up Program: offered in Northeast Wilmington, this program provides housing rehabilitation loans to low- and moderate-income home owners and to landlords renting to low-income persons, to bring properties up to State Housing Code standards or to add handicapped-accessible modifications. Call the Delaware State Housing Authority for application information.

2. Housing Rehabilitation Loan Program: loans to low-to moderate-income homeowners or landlords who rent to low-income tenants of $35,000 for ten years at 3% for repairs or handicapped accessibility modifications. Call the Delaware State Housing Authority for application information.

3. Single-Family Mortgage Revenue Bond Program: low interest loans to first time homebuyers with low and moderate income. For a list of participating lenders to apply with, go to {www2.state.de.us/dsha/sfmrb_frame.htm}.

4. Second Mortgage Assistance Program: down payment and closing costs assistance to persons who have not owned a home in the past year. For a list of participating lenders to apply with, go to {www2.state.de.us/dsha/smal_frame.htm}.

5. Delaware Housing Partnership Program: second mortgages for settlement assistance to low to moderate-income families purchasing homes in targeted new construction subdivisions. For a list of participating lenders to apply with, go to {www2.state.de.us/dsha/home_buy_frame.htm}.

6. Acquisition/Rehabilitation Loan Program: loans for low- and moderate-income first time buyers to purchase homes that are in need of repair and then get a 3% interest loan to make the repairs all with one application. Call the Delaware State Housing Authority for application information.

7. Multifamily Mortgage Revenue Bond Program: tax-exempt mortgage revenue bonds, for the acquisition, new construction or rehabilitation of an apartment, which will be rented to low-income individuals and families. Call the Delaware State Housing Authority for application information.

8. Home Fix-Up Program: offered in Northeast Wilmington, this program provides housing rehabilitation loans to low- and moderate-income homeowners and also to landlords renting to low-income persons, to bring properties up to State Housing Code standards or to add handicapped-accessible modifications. Call the Delaware State Housing Authority for application information.

9. Housing Development Funds: loans to developers of housing for low- and moderate-income persons and families. Call the Delaware State Housing Authority for application information.

10. Community Development Block Grant: funding to maintain or improve housing, in Kent and Sussex counties, of low/moderate income households. Call the Delaware State Housing Authority for application information.

11. Emergency Shelter Grant Program: federal funds for local communities in Kent and Sussex counties, to rehabilitate, expand and operate emergency shelters. Call the Delaware State Housing Authority for application information.

12. HOME Program: designed to expand affordable housing through tenant and homebuyer assistance, rehabilitation, and new construction. Call the Delaware State Housing Authority for application information.

13. Neighborhood Revitalization Fund: low-interest loans to help entire communities restore their homes to State Housing Code standards. To download the application, go to {www2.state.de.us/dsha/nrf frame. htm}.

14. Low Income Housing Tax Credit: federal income tax credit to owners and investors of affordable rental housing that rent to low-income tenants. For an application, go to {www2.state.de.us/dsha/2002_QAP. htm}.

15. Housing Capacity Building Program: a range of assistance to providers of affordable housing to increase their capacity to build and maintain the housing. For an application, go to {www2.state.de. us/dsha/hcbp_frame.htm}.

16. Public Housing (PH): offers low-income persons in Kent and Sussex Counties who are in need of assistance to afford month-to-month rent payments. Call the Delaware State Housing Authority for application information.

17. Section 8 Vouchers (SEC8V): assistance for low-income households to meet costs of rental housing for DSHA-approved private rental residency. Call the Delaware State Housing Authority for application information.

18. Moving to Work Demonstration Program (MTW): Applicants on the two programs (MTW and SEC8V) are placed on a combined waiting list for assistance. They are given the first available subsidy location, whether it is at a public housing site, a DSHA-owned apartment complex, or it is in the form of a Section 8 Voucher for use in the private market. Most residents, with the exception of the elderly and disabled, are eligible to receive subsidy under these programs for a maximum of 5 years (with some one-year extensions) while they take part in a mandatory self-sufficiency program. Call the Delaware State Housing Authority for application information.

19. Resident Services (RS): this self-sufficiency program provides its residents with social workers, counseling and programs to assist them with becoming independent of government housing assistance. Call the Delaware State Housing Authority for application information.

20. Section 8 New Construction (SEC 8 NC): affordable housing to very low-income people at 30 different sites in the state where participants pay about 30% of their income for rent. Call the Delaware State Housing Authority for application information.

District of Columbia

DC Department of Housing and Community Development
801 North Capitol Street, NE, Suite 8000
Washington, DC 20002   202-442-7200
http://dhcd.dc.gov

For application information on the following programs, please contact the Department of Housing and Community Development.

1. Home Purchase Assistance Program: low or no interest loans for low and moderate-income homebuyers.

2. First Right Purchase Assistance Program: low cost loans for low and moderate income individuals and tenant groups to exercise their right to purchase their rental housing that is being offered for sale.

3. Homestead Housing Preservation Program: repossessed properties are sold to eligible District residents at low cost and with deferred payment loans.

4. Handicapped Access Improvements Program: grants to remove barriers and improve accessibility; for homeowners or landlords on behalf of handicapped tenants.

5. D.C. Employer Assisted Housing Program: grants and deferred loans to first-time homebuyers that are employees of the District of Columbia government.

6. D.C. Metropolitan Police Housing Assistance Program: assistance to members of the Metropolitan Police Department for down payment and closing costs.

7. Senior Citizen Home Repair and Improvement Program: loans to senior citizens so that they can make emergency repairs to their home that would otherwise threaten their health and safety.

8. Distressed Properties Improvement Program: tax incentives to encourage the repair of occupied or vacant rental housing and retain low-income residents.

9. Housing Finance for the Elderly, Dependent and Disabled: loans for the development of housing for special needs households.

10. Low Income Housing Tax Credit Program: tax credits for owners of low and moderate income rental housing.

11. Single-Family Housing Rehabilitation Program: low cost financing for the rehabilitation of one to four unit low-income housing in designated areas.

12. Handicapped Access Improvements Program: grants to remove barriers and improve accessibility; for homeowners or landlords on behalf of handicapped tenants.
13. Homeownership Developer Incentive Fund: grant to development entities to lower the development costs so that they are affordable to low and moderate-income residents.
14. Apartment Improvement Program: technical assistance to rental housing owners to make comprehensive property improvement plans that involve a cooperative effort between owners, renters and financial institutions.
15. Construction Assistance Program: assistance to nonprofit land trusts to develop acquired land and buildings to create low- and moderate-income housing.
16. Community Land Acquisition Program: assistance to nonprofits to acquire land and buildings to create low and moderate income housing.
17. Housing Production Trust Fund Program: financial assistance to developers for the planning and production of low- to moderate-income housing and related facilities; there are a wide rang of housing initiates concerning housing production and preservation.

Florida

Florida Housing Finance Corporation
227 North Bronough St., Suite 5000
Tallahassee, FL 32301-1329
www.floridahousing.org

850-488-4197
Fax: 850-488-9809

1. First-Time Homebuyer Mortgage Revenue Bond Program: below market rate financing for first-time homebuyers with low/moderate income. Contact the Florida Housing Finance Corporation for application information.
2. Home Ownership Assistance Program: 0% interest, non-amortized 2nd mortgage loans to low-income families; 3% interest rate loan for nonprofit to develop or substantially rehabilitate affordable housing. Contact the Florida Housing Finance Corporation for application information.
3. State Housing Initiative Program (SHIP): funds for the development and maintenance of affordable housing through public/private partnerships. Contact the Florida Housing Finance Corporation for application information.
4. State Apartment Incentive Loan Program (SAIL): low rate financing for developers who build or rehabilitate rental housing that is affordable to very low-income people. For an application, go to {www.floridahousing.org/sail/sail.html}.
5. HOME Program: provides states their opportunity to administer federally funded homeownership housing program. To download an application, go to {www.floridahousing.org/home-own/home.html}.
6. HOME Rental Program: mortgage loans to construct, rehabilitate, or acquire and rehabilitate affordable housing for low-income households. To obtain an application, go to {www.floridahousing.org/dpts/notice_universalapp.html}.
7. Housing Credit Program: federal tax reduction to acquire and rehabilitate or construct rental housing units for low- and very low-income renters. For an application, go to {www.floridahousing.org/combined-cycle/hc/housing_credits.html}.
8. Florida Affordable Housing Guarantee Program: issues guarantees on obligation of the financing of affordable housing in order to encourage lending activities. To download an application, go to {www.foridahousing.org/guarantee.html}.
9. Predevelopment Loan Program: financial assistance to non-profits with limited or no experience that develop affordable housing for very low- or low-income households. Download the Application Package Request Form at {www.floridahousing.org/plp.html}.
10. Multifamily Revenue Bonds: below market rate loans to developers who set aside 20% of the units to low-income or 40% of units to very low-income persons. For an application, go to {www.floridahousing.org/mrb.html}.
11. Home Ownership Assistance Program: 0% interest, non-amortized 2nd mortgage loans to low-income families; 3% interest rate loan for nonprofit to develop or substantially rehabilitate affordable housing.

Georgia

Georgia Department of Community Affairs
60 Executive Parkway South NE
Atlanta, GA 30329
www.dca.state.ga.us/

404-679-4940

1. Own Home Down payment Program: loan to cover most of the down payment, closing costs and prepaid expenses to first time homebuyers. For a list of participating lenders to apply to, go to {www.dca.state.ga.us/housing/SFH/index.html}.
2. Home Buyer Program: low interest rate mortgages to qualified first-time homebuyers. For a list of participating lenders to apply to, go to {www.dca.state.ga.us/housing/SFH/index.html}.
3. The Redevelopment Fund Program: provides flexible financial assistance to local governments to assist them in implementing challenging economic and community development projects that cannot be undertaken with existing public sector grant and loan programs. For an application, go to {www.dca.state.ga.us/economic/RedevFund.html}.
4. The CDBG Loan Guarantee Program (Section 108 Program): program is a method of assisting non-entitlement local governments with certain unique and large-scale economic development projects that cannot proceed without the loan guarantee. A pre-application manual can be downloaded from {www.dca.state.ga.us/economic/108manual.html}.
5. Bond Allocation Program: long-term low-interest financing to businesses and individuals for the construction or improvements of manufacturing facilities, single and multi-family housing projects exempt financing is available both at the state and local level. For an application, go to {www.dca.state.ga.us/economic/bond.html}.
6. The Community HOME Investment Program (CHIP): used for the production, acquisition, or rehabilitation of decent, safe, and sanitary housing units which will be occupied by income eligible homebuyers, homeowners, or tenants. For an application, use the "Small Cities" Program application at the website, {www.dca.state.ga.us/grants/grantprogram.html}.
7. Affordable Rental Housing Development Financing: DCA's rental housing finance programs work with for-profit, nonprofit and government partners to build or rehabilitate rental housing in Georgia. Download the application from the website, {www.dca.state.ga.us/housing/rentalfin.html}.
8. Appalachian Regional Commission: grants for site development and technical assistance for low- and moderate-income housing projects. For an application, go to {www.dca.state.ga.us/economic/arc.html}.
9. Emergency Shelter Grant Program: grants to shelter facilities for their operation and for the essential services for the homeless they service. To download an application, go to {www.dca.state.ga.us/housing/hopwamemo.html}.
10. Housing Opportunities for Persons with AIDS Program: direct subsidies of Federal funds to nonprofit groups that operate housing and provide supportive services to people with AIDS and related diseases. To download an application, go to {www.dca.state.ga.us/housing/hopwamemo.html}.
11. Community Development Block Grant Program: grant program including those for housing improvement projects, and economic development projects. For an application, go to {www.dca.state.ga.us/grants/grantprogram.html}.
12. Local Development Fund: matching grants to fund community improvement projects. {www.dca.state.ga.us/grants/developfund.html}.
13. Downtown Development Revolving Loan Fund: loans to eligible applicants to carry out downtown development projects. To download the application, go to {www.dca.state.ga.us/economic/ddrlf2.html}.
14. Housing Opportunities for Persons with AIDS Program: direct subsidies of Federal funds to nonprofit groups that operate housing and provide supportive services to people with AIDS and related diseases. To download an application, go to {www.dca.state.ga.us/housing/hopwamemo.html}.

Hawaii

Housing and Community Development Corporation of Hawaii
677 Queen Street, Suite 300
Honolulu, HI 96813
www.hcdch.state.hi.us
Email: hcdch@hcdch.state.hi.us

808-587-0597

1. Lease to Fee Conversion: provides a method for lessee homeowners to acquire the fee simple title to their house lots. Contact the Housing and Community Development Corporation of Hawaii for application information.
2. Hula Mae Single Family Program: low interest loans to first-time homebuyers. For a list of participating lenders, go to {www.hcdch.state.hi.us/hulamae.htm}.
3. Mortgage Credit Certificate Program: direct federal tax credit to potential homebuyers so that they have more available income to qualify for a loan and to help make payments. For a list of participating lenders, go to {www.hcdch.state.hi.us/mortgagecredit.html}.
4. Housing Alteration Revolving Loan Fund Program: low interest loans to persons with physical disabilities to adapt their home or rental unit. For application information, call 808-587-0567.
5. Down Payment Loan Program: down payment loans for borrowers that meet certain criteria. For a list of participating lenders, go to {www.hcdch.state.hi.us/downpay_loan.html}.
6. Interim Financing: a developer may receive interim construction financing from the Corporation at a reduced interest rate. Contact the Housing and Community Development Corporation of Hawaii for application information.
7. Rental Housing Trust Fund: provides "Equity Gap" low-interest loans or grants to qualified owners and developers constructing affordable

housing units. Contact the Housing and Community Development Corporation of Hawaii for application information.

8. Rental Assistance Program: provides qualified owners monthly subsidies to assist eligible tenants who live in rental housing developments to make their rental payments. Also provides for interim construction financing for rental projects. Contact the Housing and Community Development Corporation of Hawaii for application information.

9. Low Income Housing Tax credit: tax credit for developers that construct or rehabilitate affordable rental housing. Contact the Housing and Community Development Corporation of Hawaii for an application.

10. Seed Money Loan: loans or grants to help with the costs to initiate a low- to moderate-income housing project. Contact the Housing and Community Development Corporation of Hawaii for application information.

11. Rental Assistance Program: provides qualified owners monthly subsidies to assist eligible tenants who live in rental housing developments to make their rental payments. Also provides for interim construction financing for rental projects. Contact the Housing and Community Development Corporation of Hawaii for application information.

12. Homeless Program: shelter and social services for homeless families and individuals. Contact the Housing and Community Development Corporation of Hawaii for application information.

13. State Rent Supplement Program: rent subsidies to tenants in approved projects. Contact the Housing and Community Development Corporation of Hawaii for an application.

14. Section 8 Housing Voucher Program: rental housing subsidies. Contact the Housing and Community Development Corporation of Hawaii for application information.

15. Housing Alteration Revolving Loan Fund Program: low interest loans to persons with physical disabilities to adapt their home or rental unit. Contact the Housing and Community Development Corporation of Hawaii for application information.

16. Lease Rent Renegotiation Program: arbitration of a lease renegotiation for one and two family residences leased by cooperative housing corporations. Contact the Housing and Community Development Corporation of Hawaii for application information.

Idaho

Idaho Housing and Finance Association
565 West Myrtle
P.O. Box 7899
Boise, ID 83707-1899   208-331-4882
www.ihfa.org

1. First-Time Home Buyer Program: low interest rate loans for first-time low- to moderate-income homebuyers. Contact the Idaho Housing and Finance Association for application information.

2. Finally Home Program: after completing the education, program participants may be eligible for financial assistance to purchase a home. Contact the Idaho Housing and Finance Association for information.

3. IHFA Housing Bonds: low-interest mortgage loans to first-time homebuyers, developers and nonprofit sponsors of affordable multifamily developments, for both families and seniors. Contact the Idaho Housing and Finance Association for application information.

4. 501(c)(3) Nonprofit Facilities Bonds: provides loans for nonprofit facilities to be owned by qualified nonprofit organizations. Contact the Idaho Housing and Finance Association for application information.

5. HOME Program: funds used for the construction and rehabilitation of affordable rental housing for low-income families across the state. The application can be obtained from {www.ihfa.org/mulitfamily_taxcredit.html}.

6. Emergency Shelter Grant Program: grants to improve the quality of emergency homeless shelters. For an application go to {www.ihfa.org/grants_homeless.html}.

7. Homeless Program Assistance: provides technical assistance to participants in homeless care programs. For an application go to {www.ihfa.org/grants_homeless.html}.

8. Section 8 Rental Assistance Program: assistance for low-income households to meet costs of rental housing. Contact the Idaho Housing and Finance Association for application information.

9. Family Self-Sufficiency Program: recipients receive assistance to eventually free themselves of federal and state welfare assistance. Contact the Idaho Housing and Finance Association for application information.

10. Public Housing in Idaho: IHFA operated public housing in target areas where lower income renters pay 30% of their income towards rent. Contact the Idaho Housing and Finance Association for application information.

11. Housing Opportunities for Persons Living with HIV/AIDS: 45 units with rental assistance to people who have a family member with HIV/AIDS. To download the application, go to {www.ihfa.org/rental_housingopps.html}.

12. Supportive Housing Program: supportive housing services to help the homeless with the transition to independent living; long-term assisted housing for persons with disabilities; supportive services for hard-to-reach homeless person with severe mental illness. Contact the Idaho Housing and Finance Association for application information.

13. Shelter Plus Care Program: rental and supportive services for seriously mentally ill homeless people. Contact the Idaho Housing and Finance Association for application information.

Illinois

Illinois Housing Development Authority
401 North Michigan Ave., Suite 900   312-836-5200
Chicago, IL 60611   800-942-8439
www.ihda.org

1. First-Time Home Buyer Program: low interest mortgages for first-time income eligible homebuyers. For a list of participating lenders, go to {www.ihda.org/sf_search_form.htm}.

2. Mortgage Credit Certificate Program: federal tax credit to first-time income eligible homebuyers. For a list of participating lenders, go to {www.ihda.org/sf_search_form.htm}.

3. Affordable Housing Trust Fund: grants and loans to profit and nonprofit developers of low-income housing projects. For an application, go {www.ihda.org/cd2.htm}.

4. HOME Program: this program is designed to expand the availability of affordable housing for low and very low income persons. The application can be found at the following website; {www.ihda.org/home6.htm}.

5. Low Income Housing Tax Credit: tax credit to investors for new construction and rehabilitation of rental housing for low-income families. For an application, go to {www.ihda.org/lihtc2.htm}.

6. Multifamily Program: low interest loan to build or rehabilitate low-income housing. The application can be downloaded at the following website, {www.ihda.org/mf2.htm}.

Indiana

Indiana Housing Finance Authority
115 West Washington Street   317-232-7777
Suite 1350, South Tower   800-872-0371
Indianapolis, IN 46204   Fax: 317-232-7778
www.in.gov/ihfa

1. First Time Home Program: loans to first-time homebuyers below the market rate. For a list of participating lenders, go to {www.in.gov/ihfa/county/county.htm}.

2. Mortgage Credit Certificate Program: tax credit to low and moderate income families to purchase a single-family residence. For a list of participating lenders, go to {www.in.gov/ihfa/county/county.htm}.

3. First Home 100 Program: works with the First Home and Rural Development Direct Loan Programs for further financial assistance to eligible homebuyers. For a list of Rural Development Offices, go to {www.rurdev.usda.gov/in/}.

4. First Home/One Down Program: 0% interest forgivable loan to assist qualified first-time home buyers with a down payment. For a list of participating lenders, go to {www.in.gov/ihfa/county/county.htm}.

5. First Home/Plus Program: a 5% - 10% down payment assistance loan 0% in conjunction with a First Home Loan. For a list of participating lenders, go to {www.in.gov/ihfa/county/county.htm}.

6. The Housing Opportunities for People with AIDS (HOPWA) Program: provides housing assistance and related services for about 500 low-income persons with HIV/AIDS and their families.

7. Rental Housing Tax Credits: federal tax credit to owners of low-income rental housing. For information on how to request an application, go to {www.in.gov/ihfa/rental/tax/allo/programs/programs.htm}

8. HOME Program: funds used for a number of different purposes to create affordable housing. For an application, go to {www.in.gov/ihfa/comdev/allo/apps/subrecipients/subrec.htm}.

9. Community Development Block Grant: funding to create affordable housing for low and very low income families. Contact the Indiana Housing Finance Authority for information.

10. Build-A-Home: grants to non-profit developers for construction or rehabilitation of single-family homes. Contact the Indiana Housing Finance Authority for information.

11. The Low-Income Housing Trust Fund: uses various State funding sources to provide additional financing options and may be used by not-for-profit housing developers to obtain financing for various kinds of housing development. Contact the Indiana Housing Finance Authority for application information.

12. Market-to-Market: subsidies to bring rent down to market level. Contact the Indiana Housing Finance Authority for application information.

13. First Home Community: enables teacher, fire fighters, law enforcement, state and municipal workers purchase a home with as

little as 1% of the purchase price or $500, whichever is less, of their own funds.

14. First Home Opportunity: enables qualified buyers the ability to purchase a home with as little as 1% of the purchase price or $500, whichever is less, of their own funds.

Iowa

Iowa Finance Authority
100 East Grand, Suite 250   `515-242-4990
Des Moines, IA 50309   800-432-7230
www.ifahome.com   Fax: 515-242-4957
Email: webmaster@ifahome.com

1. First-Time Home Buyer Mortgage Loan Program: low interest rate mortgage loans for first-time homebuyers. For a list of participating lenders, go to {www.ifahome.com/docs/sf_lenders.pdf}.
2. First Home Plus Program: designed to help first-time homebuyers or individuals who have not owned a home in the last three years pay for closing costs, down payment and required repairs. For a list of participating lenders, go to {www.ifahome.com/docs/sf_lenders.pdf}.
3. Multifamily Preservation Loan Program: loans available to help preserve the existing supply of affordable rental units at risk of being lost – either from physical deterioration or the need for financial restructuring, loans are made available to eligible nonprofit and for-profit sponsors. For information on the application, contact the Iowa Finance Authority.
4. Transitional Housing: grants for existing non-profit providers of transitional housing to increase the number of transitional housing units they provide OR for domestic violence shelters/homeless shelters and other non-profits who wish to develop transitional housing units. To download an application, go to {www.ifahome.com/partner_2002_Strategic_Initiative.htm}.
5. Transitional Housing Technical Assistance: provide technical assistance for a variety of purposes. To download an application, go to {www.ifahome.com/partner_2002_Strategic_Initiative.htm}.
6. Capacity Building: grants for non-profit organizations producing affordable multi-family and/or single family housing units in Iowa. For an application, go to {www.ifahome.com/partner_2002_Strategic_Initiative.htm}.
7. LHAP (housing production): loans, grants or combination of loans and grants to focus on the creation of additional units that serve single-family and multi-family rental housing needs. The housing must be affordable to low and moderate income individuals and families. For an application, go to {www.ifahome.com/partner_2002_Strategic_Initiative.htm}.
8. Main Street Revitalization Loan Program: partnership between Main Street Iowa, the Iowa Finance Authority and the Federal Home Loan Bank of Des Moines created a program to make available funds for lending to Main Street communities in Iowa. The pre-application form can be downloaded from {www.ifahome.com/docs/mainstreet-preapp.doc}
9. Housing Assistance Funds Program: a flexible program of financial assistance dedicated to a variety of housing projects, programs and activities which contribute to the goal of providing decent, safe and affordable housing for limited income persons. Contact the Iowa Finance Authority for application information.

Kansas

Kansas Housing Resources Corp.
1000 SW Jackson Street, Suite 100   785-296-3481
Topeka, KS 66612-1354   800-752-4422
www.kshousingcorp.org   Fax: 785-296-5055
Email: nphillips@kansascommerce.com

1. Kansas Accessibility Program: assists individuals with disabilities needing funds to make modifications of their primary residence allowing them to better fulfill their abilities to use their home. The KAMP Service Providers list can be viewed at {http://kdoch.state.ks.us/ProgramApp/program_docs_display.jsp?PROG_RECNO=995637399238}.
2. First Time Homebuyers Down Payment Assistance Program: loan for qualified homebuyers for down payment, closing costs, and legal fees associated with the purchase of a home. Forms for the program are available at the website, {http://kdoch.state.ks.us/ProgramApp/program_docs_display.jsp?PROG_RECNO=995462043556}.
3. Homeowner Rehabilitation of Existing Property Program: funds to help homeowners to repair and rehabilitate their property, priority is given to elderly homeowners and families with school-age children. Forms for this program are available at the website, {http://kdoch.state.ks.us/ProgramApp/program_docs_display.jsp?PROG_RECNO=995466474226}.
4. Weatherization Assistance Program: a multi-funded program used to increase energy efficiency in low-income homes. A list of State provides and income limits is available at {http://kdoch.state.ks.us/ProgramApp/program_docs_display.jsp?PROG_RECNO=995659080528}.

5. State Housing Trust Fund: assists homeownership, rental housing, and housing with supportive services developments. The application can be found at {http://kdoch.state.ks.us/ProgramApp/program_docs_display.jsp?PROG_RECNO=996502435748}.
6. Private Activity Bond Allocation: provide lower interest and longer term financing which reduces financing costs for multifamily housing. For an application, go to {http://kdoch.state.ks.us/ProgramApp/program_docs_display.jsp?PROG_RECNO=996505406828}.
7. Low Income Housing Tax Credit: tax credits for developers who rent to low-income families. For an application, go to {http://kdoch.state.ks.us/ProgramApp/program_docs_display.jsp?PROG_RECNO=996507865348}.
8. Emergency Shelter Grant Program: grants to local government agencies to provide emergency shelters for the homeless. To download the application, go to {http://kdoch.state.ks.us/ProgramApp/program_docs_display.jsp?PROG_RECNO=995487751206}.
9. Interim Development Loan: financial assistance to aid difficult-to-develop rental housing projects. The application can be downloaded from the following website; {http://kdoch.state.ks.us/ProgramApp/program_docs_display.jsp?PROG_RECNO=995639301908}.
10. Community Services Block Grant: funding for community action agencies to combat the causes and condition of poverty in the community.
11. Tenant Based Rental Assistance Program: grants to the owners of a rental unit to help renters with monthly rent payments. The application is available from the following website; {http://kdoch.state.ks.us/ProgramApp/program_docs_display.jsp?PROG_RECNO=995483275116}.
12. Rural Housing Incentive District: encourages local governments to develop housing in rural cities and counties. To download the application, go to {http://kdoch.state.ks.us/ProgramApp/program_docs_display.jsp?PROG_RECNO=1002566038629}.
13. Community Housing Development Organization: helps communities, through non-profit housing developers address housing issues. To download the application, go to {http://kdoch.state.ks.us/ProgramApp/program_docs_display.jsp?PROG_RECNO=995308226134}.

Kentucky

Kentucky Housing Corporation
1231 Louisville Road   502-564-7630
Frankfort, KY 40601   800-633-8896
www.kyhousing.org   TTY: 800-648-6056
Email: webmaster@kyhousing.org

1. Home Ownership Program: low interest loans to homebuyers who currently do not own property and meet income requirements. Contact the Kentucky Housing Corporation for application information.
2. Homeownership Trust Fund: low fixed interest rate for very low-income families with special needs. Contact the Kentucky Housing Corporation for application information.
3. Yes You Can…Own a Home Program: free homeownership education program. For the Qualified Counselor list, go to {www.kyhousing.org/programs/yesyoucan}.
4. Homeownership Counseling Program: homeownership counseling services to eligible potential homebuyers. Contact the Kentucky Housing Corporation for application information.
5. Repair Affair: assistance to homeowners that do not qualify for other existing programs to complete needed home repairs. Contact the Kentucky Housing Corporation for application information.
6. Kentucky Appalachian Housing Program: site development grants and loans for housing development in 49 eastern KY counties. Contact the Kentucky Housing Corporation for application information.
7. New Construction/Substantial Rehabilitation Program: funds to create or substantially rehabilitate housing to make it affordable for very low-income residents. For a list of complexes to apply directly to, go to {www.kyhousing.org/programs/newconstruction}.
8. Risk Sharing Program: low interest, permanent rate financing to developers of new construction or substantial rehabilitation of apartment units. For an application, go to {www.kyhousing.org/programs/risksharing}.
9. Assisted Living Program: low interest rate financing to developers of housing/service units for the elderly. To download an application, go to {www.kyhousing.org/programs/assistedliving}.
10. Small Multi Family Affordable Loan Program: loans to be used for construction and/or permanent financing of rental housing development not exceeding 11 units for lower-income people. The application can be downloaded at the following website; {www.kyhousing.org/programs/smal}.
11. HOME Program: program to fund affordable housing production and rehabilitation. For an application, go to {www.kyhousing.org/programs/home}.
12. Nonprofit Housing Production and Repair Program: very low-interest loans for the production and repair of lower income housing. To download an application, go to {www.kyhousing.org/programs/nonprofithousing}.

13. Housing Development Fund: flexible loan terms and low-interest rates to build affordable housing. Contact the Kentucky Housing Corporation for application information.
14. Affordable Housing Trust Fund: funds to acquire, rehabilitate, and/or build housing for very low-income residents. To download an application, go to {www.kyhousing.org/programs/affordablehtf}.
15. Housing Opportunities for Person with AIDS: funds to meet the housing needs of people with AIDS or related diseases. Download the application at {www.kyhousing.org/programs/hopwa}.
16. Renaissance Kentucky: assists communities to revitalize their downtown. Call the Kentucky Housing Corporation for application information.
17. Housing Credit Program: offer eligible property owners a ten-year tax credit for each unit set aside for low-income families. Download the application at {www.kyhousing.org/programs/taxcredits}.
18. Rental Housing Deposits Program: assistance with utility and security deposits for low-income households. Contact the Kentucky Housing Corporation for application information.
19. Housing Choice Voucher Program: recipients can locate and rent a dwelling that meets the guideline on their own, provides rental assistance. For a list of housing contacts that will provide and application, go to {www.kyhousing.org/programs/housingvoucher}.
20. Family Self-Sufficiency Program: rental assistance and supportive services for very low-income people that are willing to commit to a goal of being free of government assistance. Contact the Kentucky Housing Corporation for application information.
21. Mark-to-Market: assistance to owners of properties with expiring Section 8 contracts to achieve market-rate rents and affordable rental units. Contact the Kentucky Housing Corporation for application information.
22. Continuum of Care Program: variety of programs that offer transitional housing, rental assistance, supportive services, and permanent housing for disabled homeless persons and operating funds for emergency shelters. Download the application at {www.kyhousing.org/programs/continuum}.
23. New Construction/Substantial Rehabilitation Program: offers rental units throughout the state. For a list of rental complexes, go to {www.kyhousing.org/programs/newconstruction/}.

Louisiana

Louisiana Housing Finance Agency   225-763-8700
2415 Quail Drive   888-454-2001
Baton Rouge, LA 70808   Fax: 225-763-8710
www.lhfa.state.la.us

1. Low Income Housing Tax Credit: federal tax credits to developer/owners of rental units for low-income families. The application can be downloaded from {www.lhfa.state.la.us/programs/rental/htc-dwnlds.html}.
2. HOME Programs
   ▪ Community Housing Development Organizations (CHDOs): Section 231 of the Cranston-Gonzalez National Affordable Housing Act requires that 15% of HOME allocations are to be set-aside for CHDOs. The purpose of the set aside is to be used by CHDOs in housing activities to develop, sponsor or own. Contact the Louisiana Housing Finance Agency for information.
   ▪ Substandard Housing Assistance for Rural Economies (SHARE): funds used for the purpose of rehabilitating owner occupied dwellings. Contact the Louisiana Housing Finance Agency for information.
   ▪ HOME/Mortgage Revenue Bond Program (MRB): offers a lower interest rate to assists those homebuyers whose annual income does not exceed 80 percent of median income (adjusted for family size) in the parish in which the property being purchased is located. The list of participating lenders can be found at . The application can be downloaded from {http://204.196.244.8/programs/homeownership/firsthome.html}.
   ▪ HOME Rental Program (5 or more units): provided to non-profits and for profits to develop new construction or rehabilitate existing housing. The application can be downloaded from {www.lhfa.state.la.us/programs/rental/home-dwnlds.html}.
3. First-Time Homebuyer Program: low interest rate loans for first time low-to-moderate income homebuyers. For additional information, go to {www.lhfa.state.la.us/programs/programs.html}.
4. Teachers' Homebuyers Program: designed to help state classroom teachers buy single-family homes. Additional 4% grant to homebuyers to cover closing costs with no repayment. For additional information, go to {www.lhfa.state.la.us/programs/homeownership/teacher/teacherhome.html}.
5. Low Income Home Energy Assistance Program: assists low-income households meet their energy costs. For additional assistance, go to {www.lhfa.state.la.us/programs/energy/liheap.html}.
6. TANF Energy Assistance Program: energy assistance voucher program to prevent the loss of utility services for families participating in Family Independence Temporary Assistance Program (FITAP) and Kinship Subsidy Program (KSCP). For additional information, go to {www.lhfa.state.la.us/programs/energy/tanf.html}.
7. Weatherization Assistance Program: funds are distributed to nonprofit community agencies to assist low-income households through energy efficiency. For additional information, go to {www.lhfa.state.la.us/programs/energy/wap.html}.

Maine

Maine State Housing Authority
353 Water Street   207-626-4600
Augusta, ME 04330-4633   Fax: 207-626-4678
www.mainehousing.org   TTY: 800-452-4603

1. hoMEworks program: a network of homebuyer education that give potential homebuyers an opportunity to sort through the complex process of buying a home, including building good credit, shopping for a home, qualifying for a loan, and life as a homeowner. *Check the statewide schedule for available classes on the hoMEworks web site at:* {www.mainehomeworks.org}.
2. Mortgage Insurance Program for Tribal Land: insures mortgage loans for individuals purchasing or refinancing homes on Passamaquoddy and Penobscot Tribal land where restrictions on ownership prevent lenders from ever taking possession of the property. For a list of participating lenders, go to {www.mainehousing.org/1stbuyer.html}.
3. Home Rehabilitation Program (Pilot): provides loans to income eligible households to perform necessary repairs. Currently offered in four counties (Cumberland, Knox, Hancock and Washington Counties). For a list of contacts that you may apply to, go to {www.mainehousing.org/homerepair.html}.
4. Low Income Assistance Plan (LIAP): bill payment assistance program to eligible low and very low-income households who receive residential electric service. For a list of CAP agencies that will have an application, go to {www.mainehousing.org/liap.html#CAP%20Agencies}.
5. Homeownership Program; low down payment and low rate financing for first-time income eligible homebuyers. For a list of participating lenders, go to {www.mainehousing.org/1stbuyer.html}.
6. Purchase Plus Improvement: home improvement loans for borrowers to make immediate repairs. For a list of participating lenders, go to {www.mainehousing.org/1stbuyer.html}.
7. Low Income Energy Assistance Program: offers assistance to fuel vendors to provide heatng for low-income homeowners and renters. For a list of CAP agencies, go to {www.mainhousing.org/liheap.html#CAP%20Agencies}.
8. Closing Cost Assistance: a loan of 2% of the mortgage to eligible applicants to cover closing costs. For a list of participating lenders, go to {www.mainehousing.org/1stbuyer.html}.
9. Down Home Loan: allows a minimum cash contribution of $750 or $1,000 in out-of-pocket expenses for income eligible borrowers. For a list of participating lenders, go to {www.mainehousing.org/1stbuyer.html}.
10. New Neighbors Program: special financing to buy a home in inner city, low-income neighborhoods in specified areas. For a list of participating lenders, go to {www.mainehousing.org/1stbuyer.html}.
11. Great Rate Program: low interest rate for low-income applicants; a homebuyer education course must first be completed. For a list of participating lenders, go to {www.mainehousing.org/1stbuyer.html}.
12. Lead Hazard Control Program: grants and loans to low-income homeowners and renters with a child under 6 in the household to get rid of lead-based paint problems. For a list of CAP agencies to apply to, go to {www.mainehousing.org/leadpaint.html}.
13. Residential Energy Assistance Challenge Program (REACH): program to help low-income households reduce their energy costs. For a list of CAP agencies to apply to, go to {www.mainhousing.org/reach.html#CAP%20Agencies}.
14. Weatherization/Central Heating Improvement Program: delivers weatherization and central heating repair/replacement to low-income homeowners and renters. For a list of CAP agencies to apply to, got to {www.mainehousing.org/weather.html#CAP%20Agencies}.
15. Pre-development Loan Program: provides interest-free capital to cover mortgageable pre-development costs to nonprofit borrowers developing affordable housing projects. To download an application, go to {www.mainehousing.org/download/download.html#PDL}.
16. Subsequent Loan Program: provides funds to existing MSHA mortgagors to make capital improvements, including converting electrically heated projects to another energy source; to make major repairs or to create new affordable units within an existing project. Contact the Maine State Housing Authority for application information.
17. Preservation Financing Program: a program to preserve the future affordability of MSHA-financed Section 8 projects. Download an application from the following website, {www.mainehousing.org/download/download.html#Pres}.

18. Project-Based Rental Assistance: offered to housing developers, owners, and managers to maintain financial and physical viability of subsidized housing in order to continue providing affordable housing to very low and low income elderly, disabled and families. Contact the Maine State Housing Authority for application information.

19. Transitional Housing Request for Proposals Program: MSHA solicits proposals for the development of new transitional housing for youth, families and victims of domestic violence who are homeless. These funds may be used for acquisition, acquisition and rehabilitation, and new construction. The application can be downloaded from {www.mainehousing.org/TransHousRFP.html}.

20. Rental Loan Program: below market rate loan for new or rehabilitated rental housing affordable to low- and very-low income households. Download an application at {www.mainehousing.org/download/download.html#RLP}.

21. Housing Program: funding to operate or improve shelters. For a list of CAP Agencies to apply to, go to {www.mainehousing.org/hhp.html#CAPAgencies}.

22. Low Income Energy Assistance Program: offers assistance to fuel vendors to provide heating for low-income homeowners and renters. For a list of CAP Agencies to apply to, go to {www.mainehousing.org/hhp.html#CAPAgencies}.

23. New Lease Program: reduced interest rate loans for the acquisition and rehabilitation of housing for low- and very low-income renters. To download an application, go to {www.mainehousing.org/download/download.html#NL}.

24. Supportive Housing Program: reduced interest rate mortgage financing and subsidy funding for nonprofits to create housing for persons who need supportive housing and services. For an application, go to {www.mainehousing.org/shp.html}.

25. Low Income Assistance Plan (LIAP): bill payment assistance program to eligible low and very low-income households who receive residential electric service. For a list of CAP agencies to apply to, go to {www.mainehousing.org/liap.html#CAP%20Agencies}.

26. Preservation Financing Program: a program to preserve the future affordability of MSHA-financed Section 8 projects. Download an application from the following website, {www.mainehousing.org/download/download.html#Pres}.

27. Project-Based Rental Assistance: offered to housing developers, owners, and managers to maintain financial and physical viability of subsidized housing in order to continue providing affordable housing to very low and low income elderly, disabled and families. Contact the Maine State Housing Authority for application information.

28. The Continuum of Care Homeless Assistance Program: funds to assist homeless persons move to self-sufficiency and permanent housing. For an application, go to {www.mainehousing.org/download/download.html#CofC}.

29. Shelter Plus Care Program: provides housing and supportive services on a long-term basis for homeless people with disabilities, (primarily those with serious mental illness, chronic problems with alcohol or drugs, or acquired immunodeficiency (AIDS) or related diseases). The program provides rental vouchers that are matched with supportive services. Contact the Maine State Housing Authority for application information.

30. Section 8 Moderate Rehabilitation for Single Room Occupancy (SRO) Dwellings for Homeless Individuals: SRO housing contains units for occupancy for one person. The SRO program provides rental assistance on behalf of homeless individuals in connection with the moderate rehabilitation of SRO dwellings. Contact the Maine State Housing Authority for application information.

31. Low Income Energy Assistance Program: offers assistance to fuel vendors to provide heating for low-income homeowners and renters. For a list of CAP agencies to apply to, go to {www.mainehousing.org/liheap.html#CAP%20Agencies}.

32. Lead Hazard Control Program: grants and loans to low-income homeowners and renters with a child under 6 in the household to get rid of lead-based paint problems. For a list of CAP agencies to apply to, go to {www.mainehousing.org/leadpaint.html}.

33. Residential Energy Assistance Challenge Program (REACH): program to help low-income households reduce their energy costs. For a list of CAP agencies to apply to, go to {www.mainhousing.org/reach.html#CAP%20Agencies}.

34. Weatherization/Central Heating Improvement Program: delivers weatherization and central heating repair/replacement to low-income homeowners and renters. For a list of CAP agencies to apply to, go to {www.mainhousing.org/weather.html#CAP%20Agencies}.

35. Tenant Assistance Program: federal rent subsidies to very low-income elderly, disabled, or families. Contact the Maine State Housing Authority for application information.

Maryland

Department of Housing and Community Development
100 Community Place
Crownsville, MD 21032-2023

410-514-7000
800-756-0119

www.dhcd.state.md.us; Email: customerservice@dhcd.state.md.us

1. The Homeownership for Individuals with Disabilities Program: provides low-interest mortgage loans to eligible disabled homebuyers. Contact the Center for Community Development at 800-638-7781 to be referred to a housing counselor.

2. The HotSpot Homeownership Initiative: an initiative to promote homeownership in HotSpot neighborhoods. A HotSpot neighborhood is an at-risks high-crime neighborhood that has been targeted to receive additional federal and State funding for crime control and prevention efforts. Contact the Maryland Department of Housing and Community Development for application information.

3. Mortgage Program: below market interest rate mortgage financing for low- and moderate-income first time homebuyers. For a list of lenders to apply to, go to {www.dhcd.state.md.us/mmp.cfm}.

4. Housing Rehabilitation Program-Single Family: loans to limited income homeowners and owners of small nonresidential properties to preserve and improve the property. For a list of local housing offices to apply to, go to {www.dhcd.state.md.us/mhrp-sf/index.cfm#local}.

5. Downpayment and Settlement Expense Loan Program: borrowers through the *Mortgage Program* can get a 0% loan to help cover settlement expenses. Contact the Maryland Department of Housing and Community Development for application information.

6. Live Near Your Work Program: employees that purchase a home near their work in targeted areas receive a grant for costs associated with the purchase of a home. For an application, go to {www.dhcd.state.md.us/lnyw/index.cfm}.

7. Lead Hazard Reduction Grant and Loan Program: funds to homeowners and landlords to reduce or eliminate lead-based paint hazard.

8. Weatherization Assistance Program: low interest rate loans assist eligible low-income households to install energy conservation materials. For a list of local government or non-profit organizations to apply to, go to {www.dhcd.state.md.us/weather/index.cfm}.

9. Special Targeted Applicant Rehabilitated Program (STAR): funds to help single-family homeowners to bring their property up to code. Contact the Maryland Department of Housing and Community Development for application information.

10. Community Housing Support Program (CHSP): for eligible non-profit organizations to renovate and resell properties to owner/occupants. Thus, reducing vacancies and encourages the health and vitality of those neighborhoods. For a list of available properties, go to {www.dhcd.state.md.us/chsp/index.cfm}.

11. Rental Housing Funds: provides loans to nonprofit and profit developers for new construction and rehabilitation projects for the development of affordable multi-family housing in priority funding areas. To download an application, go to {www.dhcd.state.md.us/rhfunds/index.cfm}.

12. The Self-Help Homeownership Technical Assistance Program: provides funds to non-profit organizations and local governments that operate self-help housing programs. To download an application, go to {www.dhcd.state.md.us/shhtag/index.cfm}.

13. Maryland Affordable Housing Trust (MAHT); a variety of opportunities that promote affordable housing for very low-income households earning less than 50% of area or Statewide median income. To download an application, go to {www.dhcd.state.md.us/maht/index.cfm}.

14. Operation Assistance Grant Program: - consists of two types of grants -- production and capacity building. To download the applications, go to {www.dhcd.state.md.us/oagp/index.cfm}.
   - Production Grants: for nonprofit organizations who are engaged in the production and/or rehabilitation of affordable housing.
   - Capacity Building Grants: for inexperienced nonprofit organizations or existing nonprofit organizations that are undertaking new types of affordable housing activities, for the development of affordable housing.

15. Group Home Financing Program: low interest, no interest deferred payment loans to nonprofit organizations to purchase and modify housing for use as group homes and shelters. For information on the application process, call the Maryland Department of Housing and Community Development.

16. Multifamily Bond Program: below-market financing for low-income multifamily rental housing development. For information on the application process, call the Maryland Department of Housing and Community Development.

17. Accessory, Shared and Sheltered Housing Program: low rate loans to finance additions and improvement to create accessory, shared or sheltered housing for low-income households. For information on the application process, call the Maryland Department of Housing and Community Development.

18. Low Income Housing Tax Credit Program: federal tax credit to owners of low-income rental housing. To download an application, go to {www.dhcd.state.md.us/lihtc/index.cfm}.

19. Shelter and Transitional Housing Facilities Program: provides grants to improve or create transitional housing and emergency shelters. For

information on the application process, call the Maryland Department of Housing and Community Development.

20. Lead Hazard Reduction Grant and Loan Program: funds to homeowners and landlords to reduce or eliminate lead-based paint hazard. For a listing of local housing offices to apply to, go to {www.dhcd.state.md.us/lead/index.cfm#local}.

21. HOME Program: funds for the construction, acquisition and rehabilitation of rental housing, owner occupied housing, and special needs housing. To download an application, go to {www.dhcd.state.md.us/home/index.cfm}.

22. Office and Commercial Space Conversion Initiative: financing to convert older offices and commercial space downtown into new affordable rental housing. To download an application, go to {www.dhcd.state.md.us/ocsci/index.cfm}.

23. RAP to Work Program: subsidies to very low income individuals with emergency needs or that are homeless who are making the transition from welfare to work. To download the RAP Handbook, go to {www.dhcd.state.md.us/rap/index.cfm}.

24. Rental Allowance Program: subsidies to very low-income individuals with emergency needs or that are homeless. To download the RAP Handbook, go to {www.dhcd.state.md.us/rap/index.cfm}.

25. Section 8 Existing Certificate/Voucher Program: rent subsidies for low-income households. For application information, contact the Maryland Department of Housing and Community Development.

26. Lead Hazard Reduction Grant and Loan Program: funds to homeowners and landlords to reduce or eliminate lead-based paint hazard. For a listing of local housing offices to apply to, go to {www.dhcd.state.md.us/lead/index.cfm#local}.

Massachusetts

MassHousing
One Beacon Street
Boston, MA 02108
www.mhfa.com
Email: information@masshousing.com

617-854-1000
Fax: 617-854-1029
TDD: 617-854-1025

1. Group Home Financing Program: low interest, no interest deferred payment loans to nonprofit organizations to purchase and modify housing for use as group homes and shelters. Contact the Massachusetts Housing Finance Agency for information.

2. Municipal Mortgage Program: financing available to police, firefighters, school teachers and other municipal employees that requires no down payment. For a list of participating banks, go to {http://mhfadata.com/municipal_results.asp}.

3. Home Improvement Loan Program: loans of up to $25,000 to eligible homeowners to make needed permanent general improvements to their homes. For a list of lenders to apply to, go to {www.mhfa.com/sf/sf_products.htm#1stTIMEHOMEBUYERS}.

4. General Lending: special loans for income eligible first time homebuyers. Contact the Massachusetts Housing Finance Agency for information.

5. Mortgage Insurance Fund: provides private mortgage insurance on mortgage loan down payments below 20%. Contact the Massachusetts Housing Finance Agency for information.

6. Get the Lead Out Program: provides low cost financing to owners of 1 to 4 family homes to remove lead paint. For a listing of local rehabilitation agencies, go to {www.mhfa.com/sf/sf_lra.htm}.

7. FreshRate Program: loan of 4% of the loan amount for down payment and closing cost assistance to qualified buyers. For a list of lenders to apply to, go to www.mhfa.com/sf/sf_products.htm#FRESHRATE}.

8. Septic Repair Loan Program: financial assistance for income eligible homeowners to repair a failed septic system. For a list of lenders to apply to, go to {www.mhfa.com/sf/sf_septic_lenders.htm}.

9. Elder 80/20: Supportive Housing for Seniors Program: for the development of housing that will serve elders who wish to live in independent rental apartments with on-site access to supportive services as needed. At least 20% of the units must be reserved for low-income occupancy. Contact the Massachusetts Housing Finance Agency for application information.

10. Elder Choice Program: fills the gap between independent living and a nursing home by providing a home-like setting coupled with on-site services that support the needs of frail elderly persons. To download the forms for this program, go to {www.mhfa.com/dev/dp_elderch guide.htm}.

11. Construction Loan Program: loans available to builders who agree to price 25% of their units at or below MHFA's acquisition cost limits. Thus, creating homeownership opportunities for low- and moderate-income persons and assist small-scale home builders who may not be able to access conventional sources of construction financing. Contact the Massachusetts Housing Finance Agency for application information.

12. Low Income Housing Tax Credit Program: federal tax credits for owners of low-income rental housing. Contact the Massachusetts Housing Finance Agency for application information.

13. Get the Lead Out Program: provides low cost financing to owners of 1 to 4 family homes to remove lead paint. For a listing of local rehabilitation agencies, go to {www.mhfa.com/sf/sf_lra.htm}.

14. The Massachusetts Affordable Housing Trust Fund: designed to provide resources to create or preserve affordable housing throughout the state for low-income households. To download an application, go to {www.mhfa.com/dev/da_1stpmnpg.htm}.

15. Expanding Rental Affordability Program (ERA): assistance for rental housing where at least 20% of the units are set aside for low-income renters. For information, contact the Massachusetts Housing Finance Agency.

16. Demonstration Disposition Program: funding to renovate development in specified areas. To download an application, go to {www.mhfa.com/dev/rfp_homepage.htm}.

17. Options for Independence Program: financing to community based residences for previously mentally institutionalized persons, homeless mentally ill, and other special needs persons. For information, contact the Massachusetts Housing Finance Agency.

18. Bridge Loan Financing: for developers of low-income rental housing in conjunction with construction/permanent financing. For information, contact the Massachusetts Housing Finance Agency.

19. 504/ADA Technical Assistance: technical assistance for housing providers, residents, applicants, and service providers. For information, contact the Massachusetts Housing Finance Agency.

20. Project TAP (Tenant Assistance Program): training for project residents and management for drug and alcohol-related problems. For information, contact the Massachusetts Housing Finance Agency.

21. Get the Lead Out Program: provides low cost financing to owners of 1 to 4 family homes to remove lead paint. For a listing of local rehabilitation agencies, go to {www.mhfa.com/sf/sf_lra.htm}.

22. Expanding Rental Affordability Program: assistance for rental housing where at least 20% of the units are set aside for low-income renters. For information, contact the Massachusetts Housing Finance Agency.

23. 504/ADA Technical Assistance: technical assistance for housing providers, residents, applicants, and service providers. For information, contact the Massachusetts Housing Finance Agency.

24. Youth Resident Activities Program: programs and activities for youths that reside in MHFA properties in specified areas. For information, contact the Massachusetts Housing Finance Agency.

25. MassAdvantage: below-market-rate mortgages or home improvement loans available to low-to-moderate income first-time homebuyers. For additional information, go to {www.mhfa.com}.

26. MassAdvantage100: 100% financing available to low-to-moderate first-time homebuyers. For additional information, go to {www.mhfa.com}.

27. Purchase and Rehabilitation Program: program covering purchase price plus necessary rehabilitation costs for first-time homebuyers. For additional information, go to {www.mhfa.com}.

28. RHS Loan Guarantee Loan: mortgage program for low-to-moderate income borrowers in identified rural areas. For additional information, go to {www.mhfa.com}.

29. Take the "T" Home Mortgage Program: provides 100% financing to qualified regular public transportation ("T") riders buying a home in close proximity to public transportation. For additional information, go to {www.mhfa.com}.

Massachusetts Department of Housing and Community Development
One Congress Street, 10th Floor
Boston, MA 02114
www.state.ma.us/dhcd
Email: dhcdweb@hotmail.com

617-727-7765

The following websites provide location listings:

- Local Housing Authorities:
{www.state.ma.us/dhcd/publications/HOW_TO2K.HTM#LHAs}
- Department of Transitional Assistance (DTA):
{www.state.ma.us/dhcd/publications/HOW_TO2K.HTM#DTAs}
- Neighborhood Housing Services Offices:
{http://www.state.ma.us/dhcd/publications/HOW_TO2K.HTM#NHS}
- Community Development Corporations:
{www.state.ma.us/dhcd/publications/HOW_TO2K.HTM#CDCs}
- Community Action Agencies:
{www.state.ma.us/dhcd/publications/HOW_TO2K.HTM#CAAs}
- Area Agencies on Aging:
{www.state.ma.us/dhcd/publications/HOW_TO2K.HTM#AaonA}
- Independent Living Centers:
{www.state.ma.us/dhcd/publications/HOW_TO2K.HTM#ILC}
- Shelter Referral / Placement Services:
{www.state.ma.us/dhcd/publications/HOW_TO2K.HTM#SR/PS}
- Temporary Shelters:
{www.state.ma.us/dhcd/publications/HOW_TO2K.HTM#TSs}

Other available resources:
For The Elderly:
   Statewide Elder Hotline: 1-800-882-2003
   Massachusetts Executive Office of Elder Affairs: 617-727-7550

For The Disabled
Independent Living Information Center 1-800-462-5015

For Special Needs Housing:
Massachusetts Department of Mental Health: 617-626-8000
Massachusetts Department of Mental Retardation: 617-727-5608, {www.dmr.state.ma.us/}

1. The State Soft-Second Mortgage Program: a state funded program that will helps first time homebuyers purchase a home. For more information, contact the Massachusetts Housing Partnership at 617-338-7868 or visit their website at {www.mhpfund.com}.
2. Homebuyer Counseling: educates first-time home buyers of the home buying process.
   - Contact the *Massachusetts Homeownership collaborative* for information on homebuyer counseling agencies across the state. Call 1-800-HOME-111 or visit the web site at {www.baystatehomebuyer.com}.
   - The *City of Boston* operates the Boston Home Center. Call 617-635-4663 or visit the web site at {www.ci.boston.ma.us/dnd}.
   - The *Massachusetts Housing Finance Agency* has a list of homebuyer counseling agencies. Call 614-854-1000 or visit the web site at {www.mhfa.com}.
3. Home Rehabilitation Loans: loans made available to moderate and low income homeowners.
4. Low Income Home Energy Assistance Program (LIHEAP): helps low-income households to pay winter heating bills. Contact the Massachusetts Department o f Housing and Community Development for an application.
5. Weatherization Assistance Program: funds for full-scale energy conservation services in low-income households. Contact the Massachusetts Department o f Housing and Community Development for information.
6. Heating Emergency Assistance Retrofit Task Weatherization Assistance Program (HEARTWAP): provides heating system repair and replacement services to low-income households. Contact the Massachusetts Department o f Housing and Community Development for information.
7. Low Income Sewer and Water Assistance Program: financial assistance to homeowners that have excessive water and sewer bills. Contact the Massachusetts Department o f Housing and Community Development for information.
8. Homeownership Opportunity Program (HOP): reduced rate first mortgage loans to buyers of HOP units. Call 617-727-7824 for application information.
9. Community Development Block Grant Program: variety of programs that fund housing and/or public facilities and infrastructure programs. Contact the Massachusetts Department of Housing and Community Development for application information.
10. Community Enterprise Economic Development Program: assistance for residents and their local community development corporation to revitalize their neighborhoods. Contact the Massachusetts Department of Housing and Community Development for application information.
11. HOME Program: funds available for rental housing production and rehabilitation, first time homebuyer assistance, rehabilitation assistance for homeowners, and tenant based rental assistance. Contact the Massachusetts Department of Housing and Community Development for application information.
12. Housing Innovations Fund: Deferred payment loans to non-profit developers who reserve at least 50% of the housing units to low-income families. Contact the Massachusetts Department of Housing and Community Development for application information.
13. Housing Stabilization Fund Program: funding for three specific programs. Contact the Massachusetts Department of Housing and Community Development for application information.
    - Neighborhood Restoration Initiative (NRI): funds used for neighborhood revitalization to support affordable rental housing and affordable homeownership.
    - The Rehabilitation Initiative (RI): funds to support the acquisition, rehabilitation, and reuse of distressed, reused, or abandoned properties as affordable housing.
    - Soft Second Loan Program: creates homeownership opportunities by subsidizing mortgages, or providing closing cost assistance and down payments.
14. Local Initiative Program: technical assistance to communities and developers that are working together to create housing that sets aside 25% of its units for low and moderate income households.
15. Neighborhood Housing Services Program: support for agency or individual housing rehabilitation projects. Contact the Massachusetts Department of Housing and Community Development for application information.
16. Contact the Massachusetts Department of Housing and Community Development for application information on these programs.

- Rental Voucher Program (MRVP): subsidies for very low-income families.
- Section 8 Certificate/Voucher Program: rent subsidies for very low-income families, the elderly and the disabled.
- Section 8 Designated Housing Program: tenant based subsidies for non-elderly disabled individuals who are on waiting lists at MHFA developments.
- Section 8 Family Self-Sufficiency Program: assists eligible families to achieve economic independence.
- Section 8 Family Unification Program: eligible families are issued a Section 8 voucher. The family is then given up to 180 days to locate their own rental housing.
- Section 8 Housing Choice Voucher Program: eligible families are issued a Section 8 voucher. The family is then given up to 180 days to locate their own rental housing.
- Section 8 Housing Options Program: Section 8 vouchers for eligible low-income disabled individuals that are living in transitional housing.
- Section 8 Mainstream Housing Program: available to eligible families where the head of household is disabled.
- Section 8 Moderate Rehab Single Room Occupancy Program: available to very low-income homeless individuals that may or may not have a need for supportive services.
- Section 8 Raising Next Generation Program: targeted for low-income families living independently in the community but need special support services for both the elderly and young children.
- Section 8 Tenant Based Rental Assistance for Persons Living with HIV / AIDS: section 8 vouchers, and supportive services for those eligible very low-income persons living with HIV / AIDS.
- Section 8 Veterans Administration Supported Housing Program: provides section 8 rental vouchers along with ongoing case management and clinical services administered by the Veterans Administration Supportive Housing (VASH) to homeless disabled veterans.
- Alternative Housing Voucher Program (AHVP): provides rental assistance to people with disabilities under age 60 who either live in, or are eligible to live in elderly/disabled state-assisted public housing.
- Low Income Home Energy Assistance Program (LIHEAP): helps low-income households to pay winter heating bills.
- Weatherization Assistance Program: funds for full scale energy conservation services in low-income households.
- Heating Emergency Assistance Retrofit Task Weatherization Assistance Program (HEARTWAP): provides heating system repair and replacement services to low-income households.
- Homeless Intervention and Housing Services Program: supportive services that help people in a housing crisis situation, find housing.
- McKinney Emergency Shelter Grant Program: provides emergency shelter and homelessness prevention to low-income families and individuals.
- McKinney Local Housing Authority Transitional Housing Program: transitional housing and individual service plans that include job training, education, counseling, employment assistance, daycare, and life skills enhancements.
- McKinney Shelter Plus Care Program: provides rental assistance and support services for homeless families or individuals with disabilities - primarily those with mental illness, chronic substance abuse, and / or HIV/AIDS.
- Scattered Site Transitional Apartment Program (SSTAP): transitional housing provided to individuals, and their families, who are victims of domestic violence, and are homeless as a result of domestic violence.

Michigan

Michigan State Housing Development Authority
735 East Michigan Avenue   517-373-8370
P.O. Box 30044   Fax: 517-335-4797
Lansing, MI 48912   TTY: 800-382-4568
www.mshda.org

1. Property Improvement Loan: home improvement loans for owner and non-owner occupied homes over 20 years old at a low interest rate. Contact the Michigan State Housing Development Authority for application information.
2. Homeownership Counseling Network: free counseling for potential MSHDA borrowers. To use the counselor locator, go to the following web site: {www.michigan.gov/mshda/1,1607,7-141-5485_5498---/00.htm}.
3. Mortgage Credit Certificate: federal income tax credits that give homebuyers more income to qualify for a mortgage. To view the list of participating lenders, go to {www.michigan.gov/mshda/1,1607,7-141-5485_5494-24810—00.html}.
4. Single Family Mortgage Program: low interest loans for the purchase single family homes and condominiums. For a list of participating lenders to apply with, go to {www.michigan.gov/mshda/1,1607,7-141-5485_5486---00.html}.

5. Housing Resource Fund: funds for nonprofit and local government to create affordable housing projects. Contact the Michigan State Housing Development Authority for application information.

6. Community Development Block Grant: grants to small communities and counties so that lower income homeowners can upgrade their homes and carry out other housing activities. Contact the Michigan State Housing Development Authority for application information.

7. Habitat for Humanity Housing Grant Fund: grants to Habitat for Humanity to build or rehabilitate homes. Contact the Michigan State Housing Development Authority for information on this program.

8. Contractor's Assistance Program: provides working capital loans to small contractors who have been selected to work on rental housing projects. Contact the Michigan State Housing Development Authority for application information.

9. Low Income Housing Tax Credit Program: federal tax credit for owner/developers of low-income rental housing. Contact the Michigan State Housing Development Authority for application information.

10. More Independence Through HOME: funds used to finance nonprofit projects that provide rental units for disabled people. Contact the Michigan State Housing Development Authority for application information.

11. Section 8 Existing Rental Allowance Program: rent subsidies for very low-income persons who find their own housing in private homes and apartment buildings. Contact the Michigan State Housing Development Authority for application information.

12. Tax Exempt Apartment for Michigan (TEAM): program for rental units where 20% of the units are for low income people and another 20% for very low income people. Contact the Michigan State Housing Development Authority for application information.

13. Family Self Sufficiency Program (FSS): help for families in assisted housing that contract to be off of government support. Contact the Michigan State Housing Development Authority for application information.

14. Taxable Bond Program: loans for rental housing where most tenants will have very low incomes. Contact the Michigan State Housing Development Authority for application information.

15. Acquisition Rehabilitation Mortgages: available to qualified homebuyers with repair costs or improvements of at least $5,000. Contact the Michigan State Housing Authority for application information.

Minnesota

Minnesota Housing Finance Agency
400 Sibley Street, Suite 300
St. Paul, MN 55101-1998
www.mhfa.state.mn.us
Email: mhfa@state.mn.us

612-296-7608
800-657-3769
TDD: 651-297-2361

1. Minnesota Mortgage Program (MMP): below market rate loans for low/moderate income first-time homebuyers. For a list of lenders, go to {www.mhfa.state.mn.us/homes/MMP.htm}.

2. Minnesota City Participation Program (MCPP): low interest mortgage loans for low to moderate income first-time homebuyers. For a list of communities and lenders, go to {www.mhfa.state.mn.us/homes/MCPP.htm}.

3. Urban Indian Housing Program: loans at below market interest rates for low to moderate income Indian families buying their first home in an urban area. Contact the Minnesota Housing Finance Agency for application information.

4. Home Equity Conversion Counseling (HECC): a Home Equity Conversion or Reverse Mortgage is designed to assist primarily senior homeowners (as defined by the participating lender), to be able to spend the equity in their home while still continuing to live there. In order to receive this type of mortgage, homeowners are required to receive counseling specifically designed to educate the homeowner on the options available under a reverse mortgage. Contact the Minnesota Housing Finance Agency for program information.

5. Home Ownership Assistance Fund (HAF): down payment and monthly payment assistance to low to moderate income MHFA mortgage recipients. Contact the Minnesota Housing Finance Agency for application information.

6. Entry Cost Homeownership Opportunity (ECHO): provides down payment and closing cost assistance to those purchasing a home through a community lending program. Contact the Minnesota Housing Finance Agency for application information.

7. Fix Up Fund Loans: loans offering below market interest rates to fix up your home. Contact the Minnesota Housing Finance Agency for application information.

8. Rehabilitation Loan Program: loans to low to moderate-income homeowners for home improvements directly affecting the safety, habitability, energy efficiency and accessibility of their home. Contact the Minnesota Housing Finance Agency for application information.

9. Community Fix-Up Fund: home improvement loans offered to low to moderate income homeowners who occupy the property to be improved, in participating communities. Eligible homeowners must also meet any additional targeting criteria established by the community. Contact the Minnesota Housing Finance Agency for application information.

10. Foreclosure Prevention Assistance Program: provides case management services and, if applicable, mortgage payment, or other financial assistance to homeowners facing foreclosure, due to a temporary financial crisis. For a list of FPAP Administrators, go to {www.mhfa.state.mn.us/homes/homes_foreclosure.htm}.

11. Urban Indian Housing Program: loans at below market interest rates for low to moderate income Indian families buying their first home in an urban area, low interest rate loans for rental housing development for Indian families that have a low income. Contact the Minnesota Housing Finance Agency for application information.

12. Preservation Affordable Rental Investment Fund: a statewide program that will provide zero to one percent interest-deferred loans to help cover the costs of preserving permanent affordable rental housing with long term project-based federal subsidies that are in jeopardy of being lost. To download an application, go to {www.mhfa.state.mn.us/multifamily/multifamily_preserving.htm}.

13. Economic Development and Housing Challenge Program: supports economic development activities by providing loans and grants for construction, acquisition, rehabilitation, construction financing, permanent financing, interest rate reduction, refinancing, and gap financing of both single and multi-family homes. Contact the Minnesota Housing Finance Agency for application information.

14. Housing Trust Fund (HTF): zero interest deferred loans for acquisition, contraction or rehabilitation of a development of low-income rental and co-op housing. To download an application, go to {www.mhfa.state.mh.us/multifamily/RAFS.htm}.

15. Low to Moderate Income Rental Program: funds for the refinance or rehabilitation OR acquisition/rehabilitation or new construction of existing properties for low income people; funds for the acquisition and rehabilitation or new construction/conversion of rental housing for low and moderate income people. To download an application, go to {www.mhfa.state.mn.us/managers/LMIRP%20Program%20Guide.pdf}.

16. Rental Rehabilitation Loan Program: low interest loans to rental property owners to rehabilitate the property. For an application, go to {www.mhfa.state.mn.us/multifamily/RRLP.htm}.

17. HOME Rental Rehabilitation Program: grants to rental property owners to rehabilitate property so that it is safe and affordable for low-income people. To download an application, go to {www.mhfa.state.mn.us/multifamily/HomeRRG.htm}.

18. Family Homeless and Prevention Assistance Program: grants to support or establish support systems relating to homelessness, funds can be used in an existing home, shelter, or with the transition to permanent affordable housing. To download an application, go to {www.mhfa.state.mn.us/multifamily/FHPAP.htm}.

19. Rental Assistance for Family Stabilization: rental assistance to families on public service enrolled in self-sufficiency programs that reside in specified counties. To download an application, go to {www.mhfa.state.mn.us/multifamily/RAFS.htm}.

20. Bridges: housing subsidy for low-income households that have at least one adult member with a serious and persistent mental illness. To download an application, go to {www.mhfa.state.mn.us/multifamily/bridges.htm}.

21. Section 8 New Construction: subsidized housing to assist low and moderate income families in need of housing. Contact the Minnesota Housing Finance Agency for application information.

22. Section 8 Existing Housing (Certificate Voucher Program): administered by local, county, or regional housing and redevelopment authorities (HRA) to help pay the rent on housing the applicant can find in the private market. For a list of local HRAs, go to {www.mhfa.state.mn.us/renters/section8.htm}.

23. Housing Opportunities for Persons with AIDS: grants for housing assistance and services to people with AIDS and/or related diseases and their families. Contact the Minnesota Housing Finance Agency for application information.

24. 4dPrperty Tax Classification: property tax reduction for owners of residential rental property that pledge to comply with 4d requirements for 5 years. To download an application, go to {www.mhfa.state.mn.us/managers/property_4d.htm}.

25. Accessibility Home Fund: provides loans to borrowers with a disabled family member to buy, remodel or refinance a home.

Mississippi

Mississippi Home Corporation
840 River Place, Suite 605
P.O. Box 23369
Jackson, MS 39225-3369
www.mshomecorp.com
Email: emailus@mshc.com

601-718-4642
Fax: 601-718-4643

1. Down Payment Assistance Program: for lower income buyers who can afford mortgage payments but not a down payment. Contact the Mississippi Home Corporation for application information.
2. Mortgage Revenue Bond Program: interest rate at or below market rate and 3% down payment assistance. For a list of participating lenders to apply to, go to {www.mshomecorp.com/news_pub.html}.
3. Mortgage Credit Certificate Program: reduction of the amount of Federal Income Tax paid by income eligible borrowers. For a list of participating lenders to apply to, go to {www.mshomecorp.com/news_pub.html}.
4. HomeRun: loan for down payment and closing costs to low to moderate income for first time homebuyers. For a list of participating lenders to apply to, go to {www.mshomecorp.com/news_pub.html}.
5. Housing Assistance for Teachers Program: down payment and closing cost assistance to licensed teachers that teach in a specified area. For a list of participating lenders to apply to, go to {www.mshomecorp.com/news_pub.html}.
6. Mississippi Affordable Housing Development Fund: loans to owners for construction, mortgage, predevelopment costs and rehabilitation of hosing for moderate income households. To download an application, go to {www.mshomecorp.com/mahdf.html}.
7. Housing Tax Credit Program: tax credits for owners of low-income rental housing. For an application, go to {www.mshomecorp.com/htc%20program.htm}.
8. Mississippi Affordable Housing Development Fund: loans to owners for construction, mortgage, predevelopment costs and rehabilitation of hosing for moderate income households. To download an application, go to {www.mshomecorp.com/mahdf.html}.
9. Get on the Track Mortgage: provides prospective homebuyers with impaired credit a predetermined lease period to establish their credit reputation. For additional information, contact the Mississippi Home Corporation.
10. Mississippi Home of Your Own Project (HOYO): assistance for persons with disabilities to locate financial counseling which may allow them to purchase a home. For additional information, contact the Mississippi Home Corporation.

Missouri

Missouri Housing Development Commission
3435 Broadway   816-759-6600
Kansas City, MO 64111-2415   TDD: 816-758-6839
www.mhdc.com
Email: info@mhdc.com

1. Mortgage Revenue Bond Program: mortgage financing at interest rates below conventional market rates. For a list of participating lenders, go to {www.mhdc.com/lenders_list1.htm}.
2. MHDC Rental Housing Production Program: funding to developers who acquire, rehabilitate, and/or construct rental housing for low- and moderate-income families. For an application, go to {www.mhdc.com/rental_production/forms/default.htm}.
3. HOME Rental Housing Program: provides financing for the acquisition and rehabilitation of housing for low- to very low-income families. For an application, go to {www.mhdc.com/rental_production/forms/default.htm}.
4. MISSOUI Housing Trust Fund: funds for eligible activities to meet the housing needs of very low income families; activities include rental housing production, housing and related services for the homeless, and rental subsidies. Contact the Missouri Housing Development Commission for an application package.
5. Affordable Housing Assistance Program (AHAP): tax credit for firms that donate cash, services, or property to a non-profit community organization that develops affordable housing. To download an application, go to {www.mhdc.com/rental_production/ahap/ahapapplication.doc}.
6. More Help Program "Home Repair": assistance for low-to-moderate income families to make improvements and repairs to their homes. To download an application, go to {www.mhdc.com/rental_production/pdf/home%20repair%20app%20packet.pdf}.
7. Cash Assistance Payment: 4% cash assistance to eligible homebuyers of their loan amount that does not have to be repaid. The payment may be applied to down payment, closing costs, prepaid taxes or other loan expenses. For additional information, go to {www.mhdc.com/homebuyer_programs/MRB_guidelines.htm}.

Montana

Montana Board of Housing
Department of Commerce
301 S. Park Ave.
Helena, MT 59601
Mailing Address:
P.O. Box 200501   406-841-2700
Helena, MT 59620-0501   Fax: 406-841-2701
http://commerce.state.mt.us/Housing/hous_prog_bhb.html

1. Reverse Annuity Mortgage Loan: home equity loans for lower income senior 68+ homeowners. Contact the Board of Housing for application information.
2. Single Family Bond Program: assists low and moderate income people in the purchase of a first home; in targeted areas it does not need to be a first time purchase. Contact a participating lender in your area for application information.
3. Disabled Accessible Affordable Homeownership Program: assists people with disabilities to acquire affordable architecturally accessible homes enabling them to live independently. Contact the Board of Housing for application information.
4. Recycled Single Family Mortgage Program: below market rate funds are often coupled with federal grants or local funds to make purchasing a home more affordable for lower income families and individuals. Contact the Board of Housing for application information.
5. HOME Program: funds to government and community housing organizations to create affordable housing and provide financial and technical assistance for low-income persons. To download an application, go to {http://commerce.state.mt.us/HOUSING/Hous_Prog_HOME.html}.
6. Risk Sharing Program: permanent mortgage financing for affordable rental housing to low income people. Contact the Board of Housing for application information.
7. Section 8 Housing Program: subsidies for rent and utilities to very low-income families. Contact the Board of Housing for application information.
8. Low Income Housing Tax Credit Program: federal tax credits for owners of low-income housing Contact the Board of Housing for application information.
9. Risk Sharing Program: permanent mortgage financing for affordable rental housing to low-income people. Contact the Board of Housing for application information.

Nebraska

Nebraska Investment Finance Authority
200 Commerce Court
1230 "O" Street   402-434-3900
Lincoln, NE 68508-1402   800-204-6432
www.nifa.org/
Email: webmaster@nifa.org

A special telephone operator has a Telephone Device for the Deaf (TDD) and acts as an intermediary between the hearing impaired caller and the NIFA personnel. Call 1-800-833-7352 and ask the operator to call 402-434-3900.

1. Agricultural Finance Programs: low interest rate loans to farmers and ranchers. Contact a local financial institution or a NIFA office for an application.
2. Single Family Home Ownership Program: loans for first time homebuyers that are income eligible. For a list of participating lenders, go to {www.nifa.org/programs/sfamily/sfamily.html#le}.
3. Affordable Housing Trust Fund: funds to help low and moderate income households obtain affordable housing. Contact the Nebraska Investment Finance Authority for application information.
4. Technical Assistance Review Process (TARP): provides technical assistance on financial resources, application, housing projects and more. Contact the Nebraska Investment Finance Authority for application information.
5. Low Income Housing Tax Credit Program: Federal tax credits for owners of low income housing. To download an application, go to {www.nifa.org/programs/lihtc/lihtc.html#download}.
6. Super-Targeted Mortgage Program: low interest loans for low-to-moderate income potential homeowners to purchase a home. Homebuyer education is required. For additional information, contact the Nebraska Investment Finance Authority.
7. Community Empowerment Resource Funds (CERF): funds for the development of affordable housing development projects for low-to-moderate income individuals. Certain restrictions may apply. For additional information, contact the Nebraska Investment Finance Authority.
8. Credits to Own (CROWN): provides qualified low-income individuals the resources to plan and save to but a home. The 15-year rental period in affordable housing allows time for the tenant to participate in homebuyer education, build equity and correct credit problems. For additional information, contact the Nebraska Investment Finance Authority.

Nevada

Nevada Housing Division
1802 North Carson St., Suite 154   775-687-4258
Carson City, NV 89701   800-227-4960
http://nvhousing.state.nv.us   Fax: 775-687-4040
Email: nhd@govmail.state.nv.us

1. Single Family Mortgage Program: loans to moderate-income families with no previous home ownership interest in the past 3 years. For a

list of participating lenders, go to {www.nvhousing.state.nv.us/single_family/participatinglenders.htm}.

2. Low Income Housing Trust Fund: funds available to homeowners for down payment assistance or rehabilitation of owner-occupied housing. Funds can also be used by developers to develop and support affordable rental housing through Acquisition, New Construction, Reconstruction, Moderate or Substantial Rehabilitation, Site Improvements, Conversion, Demolition and certain finance costs. Trust Funds may also be used for technical assistance. The application for developers can be found at {www.nvhousing.state.nv.us/low_income/developer%20information.htm}.

3. Low Income Weatherization Program: assist eligible low-income households with their utility bills by providing for various energy conservation measures. Contact the Nevada Housing Division for application information.

4. Emergency Shelter Grant Program: provides funding to help improve existing shelters, make available additional emergency shelters, as well as provide social and supportive services to homeless individuals. The forms for this program can be found at {www.nvhousing.state.nv.us/emer_shelter/Forms.htm}.

5. Low Income Housing Tax Credit Program: tax credits to developers of low and very low income housing. To download an application, go to {www.nvhousing.state.nv.us/tax_credit/tax%20credit%20index.htm}.

6. Multi-Family Project Bond Financing Program: funding to developers of affordable housing projects. For an applications, go to {http://nvhousing.state.nv.us/bond_program/mfindex.htm}.

7. Low Income Housing Trust Fund: funds available to homeowners for down payment assistance or rehabilitation of owner-occupied housing. Funds can also be used by developers to develop and support affordable rental housing through Acquisition, New Construction, Reconstruction, Moderate or Substantial Rehabilitation, Site Improvements, Conversion, Demolition and certain finance costs. Trust Funds may also be used for technical assistance. The application for developers can be found at {www.nvhousing.state.nv.us/low_income/developer%20information.htm}.

8. HOME Program: federally funded programs to expand the number of rental housing and improve ownership opportunities for low income people. To download an application, go to {www.nvhousing.state.nv.us/fed_home/HOMEindex.htm}.

9. Down Payment and Closing Cost Loan Program: provides second mortgage loans to qualified buyers for down payment and closing cost assistance. For a list of participating lenders, go to {www.nvhousing.state.nv.us/single_family/participatinglenders.htm}.

10. Energy Efficient Mortgages (EEMs): loans to promote borrowers to purchase energy efficient homes or homes that can be made energy efficient through improvements. For additional information, go to {www.nvhousing.state.nv.us/single_family/energy%20efficient%20mortgages.htm}.

New Hampshire

New Hampshire Financing Authority
P.O. Box 5087
Manchester, NH 03108   603-472-8623
Fax: 603-472-8501   800-640-7239
www.nhhfa.org   TDD: 603-472-2089

1. Single-Family Mortgage Program: low interest mortgage funds to qualifying individuals and households. For a list of participating lenders, go to {www.nhhfa.org/incpurln_lenders.htm}.

2. Cash Assistance Option: provides cash assistance grant to help defray down payment, closing, and prepaid escrow expenses. Contact the New Hampshire Financing Authority for application information.

3. First Time Homebuyers Seminar: free seminars on the process of buying a home. To view the seminar schedule, go to {www.nhhfa.org/homeown.htm#1sttime}.

4. HELP (Housing Expense Loan Program): closing cost funds to income eligible homebuyers. For a list of participating lenders, go to {www.nhhfa.org/incpurln_lenders.htm}.

5. Philip S. Rader Divorced Borrower Initiative: qualifying borrowers with minor children can refinance and retain their principal residence in connection with a divorce. Contact the New Hampshire Financing Authority for information.

6. Voucher Assisted Mortgage Option: uses Housing Choice (Section 8 Vouchers) as a portion of the monthly mortgage payment provides very-low income families the opportunity to purchase a home. For a list of participating lenders, go to {www.nhhfa.org/vamolenders.htm}.

7. Emergency Home Repair Loan (EHRL): affordable loans to borrows with existing mortgages through the Single-Family Mortgage program to cover costs of repairs when an emergency occurs in their home that is not covered by insurance and that affects the livability of the home. Contact the New Hampshire Financing Authority for application information

8. Purchase/Rehab Program: loans to eligible new homebuyers to make improvements to a home in need of repair. For a list of participating lenders, go to {www.nhhfa.org/incpurln_lenders.htm}.

9. Home of Your Own Program (HOYO): homeownership opportunities for developmentally disabled people that are income eligible. Contact the New Hampshire Financing Authority for application information.

10. HomeAccess Program: helps low and moderate-income borrowers acquire a home and/or make it accessible for a permanently disabled household member. For a list of participating lenders, go to {www.nhhfa.org/incpurln_lenders.htm}.

11. Low Income Housing Tax Credit Program: tax credits for owners of low income rental housing. To download an application, go to {www.nhhfa.org/mffinancingapp.htm}.

12. HOME Rental Housing Production Program: provides funds to support the development of rental housing opportunities for low- and very-low income households. To download an application, go to {www.nhhfa.org/mffinancingapp.htm}.

13. Special Needs Housing: permanent financing for the development of rental housing for low and very low income special needs people that also provide social services. An application can be downloaded from {www.nhhfa.org/multifam.htm#specneeds}.

14. Affordable Housing Fund: funds to support rental housing, group homes and manufactured housing co-ops for low income people. An application can be downloaded from {www.nhhfa.org/multifam.htm}.

15. Housing Finance Fund: funds for short-term construction and bridge financing for new or rehabilitated rental housing. An application can be downloaded from {www.nhhfa.org/multifam.htm}.

16. Tax Exempt Bond Financing: for multifamily housing that rents to moderate, low and very low income people. An application can be downloaded from {www.nhhfa.org/multifam.htm}.

17. Multi-Family Housing Production Initiative and the Senior Housing Production Initiative: in an effort to meet the demands for new affordable housing units, funding is available for the construction, or the adaptive reuse of non-residential structures An application can be downloaded from {www.nhhfa.org/multifam.htm}.

18. Section 8 Existing Housing Program: Rental assistance for low income households. For an application, go to {www.nhhfa.org/tenant.htmS8}.

19. Housing to Work Rental Assistance Program: rental assistance to families that either are eligible or are currently receiving TANF (Temporary Assistance to Needy Families) funds and sign an employment agreement. Request an application at {www.nhhfa.org/tenant.htm#htw}.

20. Family Self-Sufficiency Program: families receiving Section 8 rental assistance that participate in a program to become economically self-sufficient. An application can be downloaded from {www.nhhfa.org/tenant.htm#FSS}.

21. Section 8 New Construction/Substantial Rehabilitation (Project-Based Rental Assistance): rental assistance to eligible persons that live in housing complexes financed by NHFA's tax exempt bonds or other public, private sources. Contact the New Hampshire Financing Authority for application information.

22. Supportive Services Program: technical assistance and training to managers of senior housing complexes so that they can provide quality supportive services for senior. The Service Directory can be viewed at {www.nhhfa.org/ssdirectory_temp.htm}.

23. Emergency Housing Program: short term rental assistance to eligible households when municipalities cannot help them. Contact the New Hampshire Financing Authority for application information.

24. Manufactured Housing Program: financing to low-to-moderate-income borrowers to purchase new manufactured home located in a NHHFA approved Housing Community. For a list of participating lenders, go to {www.nhhfa.org/incpurln_lenders.htm}.

New Jersey

New Jersey Housing and Mortgage Finance Agency
637 S. Clinton Avenue
P.O. Box 18550   609-278-7400
Trenton, NJ 08650-2085   800-NJ-HOUSE
www.state.nj.us/dca/hmfa/
Email: webmaster@jnhmfa.state.nj.us

1. Home Buyer Mortgage Program: low interest loans to urban area, income eligible, first-time buyers with a 3% down payment. For a list of lenders, go to {www.state.nj.us/dca/hmfa/singfam/lenderlist07201.htm}.

2. Home Ownership for Performing Employees (HOPE): employer guaranteed below market, fixed rate loans to eligible employees. Contact the New Jersey Housing and Mortgage Finance Agency for application information.

3. Home Plus Program: low rate financing for income-eligible first time homebuyers in urban areas that need immediate home improvements. For a list of approved lenders, go to {www.state.nj.us/dca/hmfa/singfam/homeplus.htm}.

4. One Hundred Percent Mortgage Program: no down payment, no mortgage insurance, mortgage loans for qualified first time and urban area buyers at pre-approved single family housing developments. For a list of approved lenders, go to {www.state.nj.us/dca/hmfa/sinfgam/ndpfact.htm}.

5. Police and Firemen's Retirement System Mortgage Program: loans for active members of the New Jersey Police and Fireman's Retirement System with at least 1 year of active duty for purchase or refinancing of a home. For a list of approved lenders, go to {www.state.nj.us/dca/hmfa/singfam/pfrsfact.htm}.

6. Potable Water Loan Program: loans available to owners of single family residences to pay for an alternative water supply or adequate treatment of drinking water that comes from a private well that violates the State's Primary Drinking Water standards or the standards for sodium, chloride, lead, mercury, iron or manganese. Contact the New Jersey Housing and Mortgage Finance Agency for application information.

7. Purchase/Rehabilitation Mortgage Program: below market rate financing to qualified first time buyers and urban target area buyers that purchase and rehabilitate a home or rehabilitate a presently owned home. For a list of approved lenders, go to {www.state.nj.us/dca/hmfa/singfam/buy&fix.htm}.

8. Reverse Mortgage Program: allows seniors to access the equity in their home without a monthly repayment schedule. Counseling is required. To view the list of lenders, go to {www.state.nj.us/dca/hmfa/singfam/lenderlist070201.htm}.

9. Upstairs-Downtown Mortgages: below market rate funds to acquire and rehabilitate, or refinance and rehabilitate residential structures with a storefront commercial component. To view the list of lenders, go to {www.state.nj.us/dca/hmfa/singfam/lenderlist070201.htm}.

10. Urban Home Ownership Recovery Program: construction financing for developers of urban for sale housing. For information on the application process, contact the New Jersey Housing and Mortgage Finance Agency.

New Mexico

New Mexico Mortgage Finance Authority
344 4th Street, SW   505-843-6880
Albuquerque, NM 87102   800-444-6880
www.nmmfa.org   TTY: 800-659-8331

1. Help Program: loans to first-time, income eligible homebuyers who participate in the Mortgage Saver Home Program for down payment and closing costs. To view the list of lenders, go to {www.nmmfa.org/consumer/lender.asp}.

2. Helping Hand Program: down payment and closing cost assistance to low income families where a member has a disability. Contact the New Mexico Mortgage Finance Authority for application information.

3. Mortgage Saver Program: loans to first time homebuyers at two interest rates; one below market value and one about even with conventional market rate. To view the list of lenders, go to {www.nmmfa.org/consumer/lender.asp}.

4. Mortgage Saver Plus: buyers that choose the higher rate in the *Mortgage Saver Program*, get credit towards closing costs up to 3.5% of the principal. To view the list of lenders, go to {www.nmmfa.org/consumer/lender.asp}.

5. Payment Saver Program: first time, income eligible, buyers get a below market interest rate and a 2nd zero percent interest loan to pay for up-front costs. To view the list of lenders, go to {www.nmmfa.org/asp/consumer/lenders.asp}.

6. "Take 5" Program: down payment assistance to low-income first-time homebuyers. To download the forms for this program go to {www.nmmfa.org/forms/formsLentake5.htm}.

7. Weatherization Assistance Program: assistance to low-income homeowners to improve the energy efficiency of their homes. The forms for this program can be downloaded at {www.nmmfa.org/consumer/conswap.htm}.

8. Low Income Energy Assistance Program: assistance for low-income households to pay their energy bills. Call 800-285-4465 for information on this program.

9. Housing Opportunities for Persons with AIDS: provides housing and supportive services to persons with AIDS/HIV; funding to enhance and expand housing opportunities for people with AID/HIV. The application can be downloaded at {www.nmmfa.org/AllPrograms;Hopwa/HOPWA_ProgSheets.htm}.

10. Building Trust: assistance for Native Americans interested in buying, building or repairing a home on trust land. For additional information, go to {www.nmmfa.org/consumer/consBuildingTrust.asp}.

11. Section 8 Assisted Housing Program: permanent financing for 5 multi-family housing projects in specified areas. Call the New Mexico Mortgage Finance Authority for application information.

12. 501(c) (3) Bond Program: funds for the acquisition, new construction, rehabilitation, or refinance of residential rental projects of nonprofit corporations. Call the New Mexico Mortgage Finance Authority for application information.

13. Build It: guaranties of conventional interim loans to nonprofit organizations, tribal, or public agencies to develop affordable housing. Call the New Mexico Mortgage Finance Authority for application information.

14. Primero Investment Fund: seed money to nonprofit, tribal, and public agencies to develop multifamily rental or special needs housing projects. Call the New Mexico Mortgage Finance Authority for application information.

15. Rental HOME: gap financing for projects that create low income housing and special needs projects. The application for this program can be downloaded at {www.nmmfa.org/multifamily/rentalhome program.htm}.

16. Emergency Shelter Grants Program: assistance to improve the quality of emergency shelters, help with operational costs, and of providing essential services to the homeless. Contact the New Mexico Mortgage Finance Authority for application information.

17. State Homeless Assistance Program: assistance to shelters that provide emergency shelter or short-term services to homeless people and their families. The application can be downloaded at {www.nmmfa.org/consumer/conshomelessassit.htm}.

18. Housing Opportunities for Persons with AIDS: provides housing and supportive services to persons with AIDS/HIV; funding to enhance and expand housing opportunities for people with AID/HIV. The application can be downloaded at {www.nmmfa.org/forms/documents/frmcommHOPWA_Application.pdf}.

19. State Homeless Assistance Program: assistance to shelters that provide emergency shelter or short-term services to homeless people and their families. The application can be downloaded at {www.nmmfa.org/consumer/conshomelessassit.htm}.

20. Housing Tax Credits: federal tax credits for owners of low-income rental housing. The application can be downloaded from {www.nmmfa.org/multifamily/HTC/HTC_Allocations.htm}.

21. Emergency Shelter Grants Program: assistance to improve the quality of emergency shelters; help with operational costs, and of providing essential services to the homeless. Contact the New Mexico Mortgage Finance Authority for application information.

22. Low Income Energy Assistance Program: assistance for low-income households to pay their energy bills. Call 800-285-4465 for information on this program.

23. Shelter Plus Care Program (S+C): funding to service providers to help disabled homeless persons through supportive services. Contact the New Mexico Mortgage Finance Authority for application information.

24. Supportive Housing: funding for transitional housing with supportive services enabling the homeless to live more independently. Contact the New Mexico Mortgage Finance Authority for application information.

25. Tenant Based Rental Assistance Program: one time cash assistance for security deposits, utility deposits, and/or first month's rent, and up to 6 months of rent subsidy to low income tenants in order to obtain permanent or transitional housing.

26. Special Needs Rental Program: below market rate loans to develop affordable rental housing projects with a maximum of 20 units where half are set aside for special needs people.

New York

New York State Division of Housing and Community Renewal
Hampton Plaza
38-40 State Street
Albany, NY 12207   518-473-2517
www.dhcr.state.ny.us

1. Weatherization Assistance Program: services to low-income households include life-saving health and safety tests and fuel consumption analysis to identify the potential to save energy.

2. Residential Emergency Services to Offer Repairs to the Elderly Program (RESTORE): funds to make emergency repairs in order to eliminate hazardous conditions in elderly owned homes when the homeowner cannot afford to make the repairs.

3. Rural Preservation Program: funds to local not-for-profit organizations engaging in a variety of activities for the benefit of low and moderate income persons in rural areas.

4. Neighborhood Preservation Program: funding to defray administrative costs of nonprofit agencies performing neighborhood preservation activities.

5. HOME Program: provides funds for a variety of housing needs for low-income families.

6. Disaster Recovery Initiative Grant: grants to help cities, counties, and States recover from declared disasters, especially in low income areas.

7. Farmworker Housing Program: low-cost loans for the improvement of existing housing or construction of new housing for seasonal farmworkers

8. Homes for Working Families Initiative: substantial rehabilitation or new construction of affordable rental housing.

9. Senior Housing Initiative: funding for projects that substantially rehabilitate or construct rental housing for seniors.

10. Housing Development Fund: loans to nonprofits for development of low-income housing projects
11. Low-Income Housing Credit Program: reduction in federal income tax liability for project owners that develop, rehabilitate, and acquire rental housing for low-income families.
12. Residential Emergency Services to Offer Repairs to the Elderly Program (RESTORE): funds to make emergency repairs in order to eliminate hazardous conditions in elderly owned homes when the homeowner cannot afford to make the repairs.
13. Low Income Housing Trust Fund: funds to nonprofit sponsors to rehabilitate existing properties into affordable low income housing.
14. Rural Rental Assistance Program: rent subsidies for multifamily project development of rental housing for elderly, and family, low-income tenants.
15. Mitchell-Lama Housing Program: low-interest mortgage loans to build affordable housing for middle-income people.
16. Rural Rental Assistance Program: rent subsidies for multifamily project development of rental housing for elderly, and family, low-income tenants.
17. Section 8 Statewide Program: rent subsidies for low income households.

New York Housing Finance Agency
641 Lexington Avenue
New York, NY 10022 212-688-4000
www.nyhomes.org/

1. 80/20 Program: loans for projects that will rent 80% of the units to individuals or families at market-rate rents, while the other 20% must be rented to low income households. Contact the New York Housing Finance Agency for application information.
2. The All Affordable Program: for production of new construction or rehabilitation of multi-family rental housing that all the units are affordable to low-income families. Contact the New York Housing Finance Agency for application information.
3. The Senior Housing Financing Program: financing for new construction or acquisition/rehabilitation of senior housing; Assisted Living, Rental or State Licensed housing. Contact the New York Housing Finance Agency for application information.
4. 501(c) (3) Bond Program: funds to nonprofit organizations for new construction, or rehabilitation of existing multi-family rental housing projects, or residential rental projects of nonprofit organizations. Contact the New York Housing Finance Agency for application information.
5. Manufactured Homes Cooperative Fund Program: technical and financial assistance to encourage and facilitate cooperative ownership of mobile home parks. Contact the New York Housing Finance Agency for application information.
6. Low Income Housing Tax Credit Program: federal tax credits for owners of low-income housing. Contact the New York Housing Finance Agency for application information.
7. Empire Housing Fund Program: low interest or no-interest loans made to developers to subsidize costs for the construction or rehabilitation or low-income housing. Contact the New York Housing Finance Agency for application information.

North Carolina

North Carolina Housing Finance Agency
3508 Bush Street 919-877-5700
Raleigh, NC 27609 7509 800-393-0988
www.nchfa.com
Email: webmaster@nchfa.com

1. Low Interest Home Loans: below market, fixed rate loans for first-time homebuyers with low/moderate income. For a list of participating lending institutions, go to {www.nchfa.com/lib/html/ Homeownership%20Programs/For20Individuals/mortgage%20partici pating_lenders.htm}.
2. Mortgage Credit Certificate: federal tax-credit for first-time income eligible homebuyers. {www.nchfa.com/lib/html/Homeownership%20 Programs/For%20Individuals/mortgage%20participating_lenders.htm}.
3. Urgent Repair Program: grants to fix housing conditions that pose a threat to health and safety in low-income homes. The application can be downloaded from {www.nchfa.com/lib/html/Urgent%20Repair% 20&%20Rehab/URP2003_application_guidelines.doc}.
4. Mortgage Revenue Bond (MRB) Program: reduced rate loans to low and moderate-income first-time homebuyers. Contact the North Carolina Housing Finance Agency for application information.
5. Self-Help Housing Program: funding for nonprofit organizations building 1-5 homes a year. Homebuyer sweat equity and volunteer labor must be used to reduce the construction costs by at least 30% from the cost of conventional construction. The application can be downloaded at {www.nchfa.com/lib/html/Homeownership%20 Programs/For%20Govts%20&%20Nonprofits/Self-Help%20Housing%20Program.htm}.

6. Supportive Housing Development Program: loans for the production of transitional and permanent housing and for the rehabilitation of emergency housing for people with special needs. An application can be downloaded at {www.nchfa.com/lib/html/Special%20Needs%20 Housing/Supportive%20Housing%20Page.htm}.
7. Multifamily Rental Development Program: federal and state tax credits for developers of low-income housing and below market rate loans to develop the housing. The application can be downloaded at {www.nchfa.com/lib/html/rental/Rental%20Development%20Home %20Page.htm}.
8. Low Income Housing Tax Credit Program: federal tax credit for owners of low-income housing. The application can be downloaded at {www.nchfa.com/lib/html/rental/Tax%20Credit/Application%20Form s%20Page.htm}.
9. Affordable Homeownership Program: loans for the purchase of newly constructed, rehabilitated, or existing homes for income-eligible homebuyers. Contact the North Carolina Housing Finance Agency for information.
10. Rental Production Program: financing for the construction f rental housing for low income households. The application can be downloaded at {www.nchfa.com/lib/html/rental/Tax%20Credit/ Application%20Forms%20Page.htm}.
11. Low Income Housing Tax Credit Program: federal tax credit for owners of low income housing. The application can be downloaded at {www.nchfa.com/lib/html/rental/Tax%20Credit/Application%20Form s%20Page.htm}.

North Dakota

North Dakota Housing Finance Agency
1500 E. Capital Ave. 701-328-8080
P.O. Box 1535 800-292-8621
Bismarck, ND 58502-1535 Fax: 701-328-8090
www.ndhfa.org TTY: 800-366-6888

1. HomeSmart Homebuyer Education Incentive Program: after completion of the course to help first-time homebuyers prepare for home ownership, borrowers may receive a $100 grant to be used towards closing costs. A listing of the homebuyer education providers is available at {www.ndhfa.org/HMFP/HMFP.Asp?FileName= Programs/homesmart.htm}.
2. Home Mortgage Finance Program: low interest rate mortgages for first-time income eligible homebuyers. Contact the North Dakota Housing Finance Agency for application information.
3. Rural Real Estate Mortgage Program: creates a secondary market for residential real estate mortgages for purchases of a single-family, owner occupied, non-farm, principal residence. Contact the North Dakota Housing Finance Agency for application information.
4. Start Program: a low interest second mortgage for first-time homebuyers for down payment assistance. Contact the North Dakota Housing Finance Agency for application information.
5. Down Payment and Closing Cost Assistance Program: zero percent interest loans to participants of a single-family mortgage loan from NDHFA for down payment and closing costs.
6. HomeWork: down payment and closing cost assistance to employees of those employers have partnered with the North Dakota Housing Finance Agency (NDHFA). Contact the North Dakota Housing Finance Agency for application information.
7. Major Home Improvement Program: low interest rate loans to income eligible borrowers to buy and rehabilitate single-family homes or to rehabilitate their existing homes. Contact the North Dakota Housing Finance Agency for application information.
8. Homeownership Acquisition and Rehabilitation Program: low-income households receive home owner education, assistance in finding an affordable home, rehabilitation funds to make the property safe and sanitary and if necessary, help in acquiring the home. For a list of Community Action Agencies to contact, go to {www.ndcaa.org/index.htm}.
9. HomeKey Program: one-percent interest rate reduction for the first three years of a Home Mortgage Finance Program loan. Borrowers must meet income-eligible guidelines.
10. Rental Rehab Assistance Program: funds for property improvement to rental units that address the needs of physically disabled people. The application can be downloaded at {www.ndhfa.org/Grants/Grants. asp?cFileName=./Rental/RRAP.htm}.
11. Helping Housing Across North Dakota (Helping Hand): funds to Habitat for Humanities Affiliates, Native American Reservations, and North Dakota Community Action Agencies to support new or existing single family or multi-family housing rehabilitation programs for low-income housing. The application can be downloaded from {www.ndhfa.org/Grants/Grants.asp?cFileName=helping_hand.htm}.
12. Moderate Rehabilitation Program: provides low-income households the ability to acquire affordable, safe and descent housing through the use of rent subsidies available to qualified individuals in specified locations. Contact the North Dakota Housing Finance Agency for application information.

13. Low Income Housing Tax Credit Program: federal tax credits for owners of low-income rental housing. The application can be downloaded from {www.ndhfa.org/Rental/Rental.asp?cFileName=LIHTC.htm.&Detail=59}.

14. Rental Rehab Assistance Program: funds for property improvement to rental units that address the needs of physically disabled people. The application can be downloaded at {www.ndhfa.org/Grants/Grants.asp?cFileName=../Rental/RRAP.htm}.

Ohio

Ohio Housing Finance Agency
57 E. Main St.   614-466-7970
Columbus, OH 43215-5135   Fax: 614-644-5393
www.odod.state.oh.us/ohfa   TDD: 614-466-1940

1. First-Time Homebuyer Program: below market financing for first-time, low- to moderate-income homebuyers. A listing of participating lenders to apply to is available at {www.odod.state.oh.us/ohfa/Owner/1stBUYER/Default.htm}.

2. Housing Credit Program: federal tax credits for owners of low-income rental housing. The application can be downloaded at {www.odod.state.oh.us/ohfa/RENTAL/LIHTC/default.htm}.

3. Affordable Housing Loan Program: loans to developers of low- to moderate-income residents. The application can be downloaded at {www.odod.state.oh.us/ohfa/RENTAL/AHL/downld2.htm}.

4. Housing Development Assistance Program: financing available for eligible housing projects to expand housing for very low-income individuals and households. The application can be downloaded at {www.odod.state.oh.us/ohfa/RENTAL/HDAP/downld4.htm}.

5. Multifamily Bond Program: financial assistance with the acquisition, construction, and substantial rehabilitation of multifamily dwelling units and single-family housing. The application can be downloaded at {www.odod.state.oh.us/ohfa/RENTAL/MRDBP/downld3.htm}.

6. Loan Guaranteed Program: the OHFA may guarantee the repayment of all or part of a loan for costs of development housing for low- and moderate-income families and the elderly. The application is located in Appendix B of the Affordable Housing Loan application. To download that form, go to {www.odod.state.oh.us/ohfa/RENTAL/LOANGUAR/default.htm}.

7. CHDO Competitive Operating Grant Program: funding to develop self-sufficient organizations with the capacity to create affordable housing. For additional information, go to {www.odod.state.oh.us/ohfa/RENTAL/CHDO/default.htm}.

8. Housing Credit Program: federal tax credits for owners of low-income rental housing. The application can be downloaded at {www.odod.state.oh.us/ohfa/RENTAL/LIHTC/default.htm}.

9. Section 8 Rental Assistance Program: rent subsidies on behalf of low-income people and families including the elderly and handicapped. Contact the Ohio Housing Finance Agency for application information.

Oklahoma

Oklahoma Housing Finance Agency
100 N. 63rd Street, Suite 200   405-848-1144
P.O. Box 26720   800-256-1489
Oklahoma City, OK 73126-0720   TDD: 405-848-7471
www.ohfa.org

1. Mortgage Revenue Bond Program: low rate loans to first-time home buyers. For a list of participating lenders, go to {www.ohfa.org/hdt/bond1/lendermap.html}.

2. 1st Four: statewide down payment and closing cost assistance for first-time homebuyers and non-first time homebuyers in Targeted areas. For additional information, go to {www.ohfa.org/HDT/Bond1/Types/1stfour.html}.

3. Market Best: statewide low interest rate assistance for first-time homebuyers and non-first time homebuyers in Targets areas. For additional information, go to {www.ohfa.org/HDT/Bond1/Types/Market.html}.

4. Future Foundation: statewide low interest rate assistance for first-time homebuyers and non-first time homebuyers in Targets areas that want to build a new home. For additional information, go to {www.ohfa.org/HDT/Bond1/Types/Future.html}.

5. HOME Plus: low interest rate loans for homebuyers with limited or fixed income. Loans not available in Norman, Lawton, Tulsa or Oklahoma City. For additional information, go to {www.ohfa.org/HDT/Bond1/Types/HOMEPlus.html}.

6. Housing Tax Credit Program: tax credits for new construction and rehabilitation of existing rental properties. The application can be downloaded from {www.ohfa.org/hdt/tcredits1/ohfalihp.html}.

7. HOME Program: funding for programs that increase the supply of housing and single family new construction. The application can be downloaded from {www.ohfa.org/hdt/home1/homepage.html}

8. Section 8 Rental Assistance Program: rent subsidies for low-income households who locate their own housing. The application can be downloaded at {www.ohfa.org/rental/preapp/works.html}.

9. Transitional Housing Pilot Program: pays maintenance and utility bills at transitional homes. Contact the Oklahoma Housing Finance Agency for application information.

10. Housing Opportunities for People with AIDS (HOPWA): provides assistance that can help a family find a place to rent, provide utility or rental assistance, or provide housing counseling to people with AIDS that are homeless or at risk of becoming homeless. Contact the Oklahoma Housing Finance Agency for application information.

11. Moderate Rehabilitation "Mod Rehab": section project based rental assistance. For additional information, go to {www.ohfa.org/Rental/Modrehab/contact.htm}.

12. Family Self-Sufficiency Program: helps families work towards economic independence. The application can be downloaded from {www.ohfa.org/rental/fss/ohfafsspsk.html}.

Oregon

Oregon Housing Agency
P.O. Box 14508   503-986-2000
Salem, OR 97309-0409   Fax: 503-986-2020
www.hcs.state.or.us/   TTY: 503-986-2100

1. Residential Energy Assistance Challenge Program (REACH): provides low-income households assistance with utility payments, energy education, weatherization assistance, and family services related to budget management. A list of participating lenders can be viewed at {www.hcs.state.or.us/community_resources/energy_wx/reach-agencies.htm}.

2. Low-Income Energy Assistance Program: helps low-income households pay heating bills. A listing of local Community Action Agencies can be viewed at {www.hcs.state.or.us/community_resources/energy_wx/lieap.html}.

3. Low-Income Weatherization Assistance Program: free weatherization and energy conservation services to income eligible households. A listing of local Community Action Agencies can be viewed at {www.hcs.state.or.us/community_resources/energy-wx/liwap.html}.

4. Energy Rated Home of Oregon (ERHO): provides Oregon home-builders and home-buyers with Home Energy Ratings which can be used to qualify for certain mortgages and programs. Contact the Oregon Housing Agency for application information.

5. Homebuyer Training: classes offered to help the first-time homebuyer understand the home buying process. Contact the Oregon Housing Agency for program information.

6. Downpayment and Closing Cost Assistance Program: assistance to low-income, first-time homebuyers with down payment and closing costs. A list of participating lenders can be viewed at {www.hcs.state.or.us/housing/homebuying/downpayment.htm}.

7. Residential Loan Program: below market interest rate loans to low and moderate-income homebuyers. Contact the Oregon Housing Agency for application information.

8. Manufactured Dwelling Park Ombudsman Program: assists park owners and residents to resolve conflicts and provides technical assistance. Contact the Oregon Housing Agency for application information.

9. Multi-Family Housing Finance Program: financing for multi-unit rental housing for moderate, low, and very low-income families. Contact the Oregon Housing Agency for application information.

10. Elderly and Disabled Loan Program: offers below market rate permanent mortgages to profit and non-profit developers for the development of newly constructed properties or the acquisition / rehabilitation of existing properties for elderly and/or disabled residents. The application can be downloaded at {www.hcs.state.or.us/housing/multi_family_finance/elderly_disabled.html}.

11. Loan Guarantee Program: provides partial loan repayment guarantees to assist the financing of new housing construction or the acquisition and/or rehabilitation of existing housing for low- and very low-income families. A list of Regional Advisors to the Director can be viewed at {www.hcs.state.or.us/rads/rads.html}.

12. Oregon Rural Rehabilitation Loan Program: funding specifically for the construction or rehabilitation of farm worker housing. A list of Regional Advisors to the Director can be viewed at {www.hcs.state.or.us/rads/rads.html}.

13. Seed Money Advance Loan: loans to help cover predevelopment costs for the production of housing for low-income individuals and families. A list of Regional Advisors to the Director can be viewed at {www.hcs.state.or.us/rads/rads.html}.

14. Risk Sharing Program: below market financing for the development of affordable housing for low- and very low-income individuals or families. The application can be downloaded from {www.hcs.state.or.us/housing/multi_family_finance/risk_sharing.html}.

15. HELP Program: assistance for the development of housing for very-low income families. The Consolidated Funding Cycle form can be downloaded from {www.hcs.state.or.us/housing/help}.

16. HOME Investment Partnership: provides funding for the development of affordable housing for low and very low-income families and

individuals. The Consolidated Funding Cycle form can be downloaded from {www.hcs.state.or.us/housing/home}.

17. Housing Development Grant Program: funding for the acquisition, construction, and/or rehabilitation of housing for low and very low-income families. The Consolidated Funding Cycle form can be downloaded from {www.hcs.state.or.us/housing/hsgdevgrant}.

18. Low Income Housing Tax Credit: federal income tax credit to developers who construct, rehabilitate, or acquire qualified low-income rental housing. The application can be downloaded at {www.hcs.state.or.us/housing/lihtc}.

19. Oregon Affordable Housing Tax Credits: tax credits for housing projects or community rehabilitation projects for low-income people, savings must be passed on to the tenants by reduced rents. The application can be downloaded at {www.hcs.state.or.us/housing/oahtc}.

20. Residential Energy Assistance Challenge Program (REACH): provides low-income households assistance with utility payments, energy education, weatherization assistance, and family services related to budget management. A list of participating lenders can be viewed at {www.hcs.state.or.us/community_resources/energy_wx/reach-agencies.htm}.

21. Low-Income Energy Assistance Program: helps low-income households pay heating bills. A listing of local Community Action Agencies can be viewed at {www.hcs.state.or.us/community_resources/energy_wx/lieap.html}.

22. Low-Income Weatherization Assistance Program: free weatherization and energy conservation services to income eligible households. A listing of local Community Action Agencies can be viewed at {www.hcs.state.or.us/community_resources/energy_wx/liwap.html}.

23. Emergency Housing Account: assistance to homeless people or those at risk of becoming homeless to pay for emergency shelter, services and housing assistance. A list of participating agencies is available at {www.hcs.state.or.us/community_resources/housing_shelter/index.html}.

24. Emergency Shelter Grant: money to increase the number of beds in emergency shelters. A list of participating agencies is available at {www.hcs.state.or.us/community_resources/housing_shelter/index.html}.

25. HOME Tenant Based Assistance (TBA): rental assistance to very low-income tenants for housing costs and security deposits. A list of service agencies can be viewed at {www.hcs.state.or.us/community_resources/housing_shelter/hometba.html}.

26. Housing Stabilization Program: assistance to households with children that are at risk of becoming homeless or are homeless. Contact the Oregon Housing Agency for application information.

27. Low Income Rental Housing Fund: rental assistance to very low-income families. A list of local service providers is available at {www.hcs.state.or.us/community_resources/housing_shelter/lirhf.html}.

28. State Homeless Assistance Program: funding to emergency shelters and services directly related to them. Contact the Oregon Housing Authority for application information.

29. Low Income Housing Tax Credit: federal income tax credit to developers who construct, rehabilitate, or acquire qualified low-income rental housing. The application can be downloaded from {www.hcs.state.or.us/housing/lihtc}.

30. Manufactured Dwelling Park Ombudsman Program: assists park owners and residents to resolve conflicts and provides technical assistance. Contact the Oregon Housing Agency for application information.

Pennsylvania

Pennsylvania Housing Finance Agency
2101 North Front Street
P.O. Box 8029
Harrisburg, PA 17105-8029
www.phfa.org

717-780-3800
TDD: 717-780-1869

1. Future Home Buyer Program: teaches high school student the importance of budgeting, the use of credit and the ramifications of credit abuse and some of the everyday legal issues they may face in the near future. Contact the Pennsylvania Housing and Finance Agency for information on this program.

2. Homeowners Emergency Assistance Program; loans to keep delinquent homeowners from losing their homes to foreclosure. A list of counseling agencies is available at {www.phfa.org/programs/hemap/index.htm}.

3. PennVest Individual On-Lot Sewage System Loans: very low interest rate loan up to $25,000 for homeowners to repair or upgrade malfunctioning on-lot sewer systems in rural areas. The Participating Lending Institutions list can be viewed at {www.phfa.org/programs/singlefamily/pennvest.htm}.

4. Access Down Payment and Closing Cost Assistance Loan Program: loans for down payment and closing cost assistance for those persons with disabilities or who have a family member(s) living in the

household with disabilities who are purchasing a home. Contact the Pennsylvania Housing and Finance Agency for application information.

5. Access Home Modification Program: no-interest accessibility improvement loans ranging from $1,000 to $10,000 in conjunction with PHFA first mortgage financing. Contact the Pennsylvania Housing and Finance Agency for application information.

6. Closing Cost Assistance Program: pays up to $2,000 toward closing costs for homes that are bought by participants in the Lower Income Home Ownership Program, qualified participants must have dependent children or be disabled. Contact the Pennsylvania Housing and Finance Agency for application information.

7. FHA 203(k) Program: loans to acquire property in need of repair and to finance the improvements. Contact the Pennsylvania Housing and Finance Agency for application information.

8. Homestead Second Mortgage Program: non-interest loans from $1,000 to $10,000 to income eligible families with at least one child or a member with a disability, for down payment and closing costs. Contact the Pennsylvania Housing and Finance Agency for application information.

9. Joint Financing Program: below-market interest rate loans to first-time buyers in specified areas of the Commonwealth. Contact the Pennsylvania Housing and Finance Agency for application information.

10. Low Income Homeownership Program: provides mortgage loans to low income first time homebuyers that have children or a member with a disability and meet income and home purchase price guidelines. Contact the Pennsylvania Housing and Finance Agency for application information.

11. PHFA/Fannie Mae Disability Access Modification Loan Program: provides mortgage assistance to those with disabilities or who have a family member(s) with a disability to retrofit the home to meet accessibility needs of the household member with the disability. To view a list of lenders, go to {www.phfa.org/programs/singlefamily/lenders/index.htm}.

12. Purchasing-Improvement Program: allows up to $15,000 in improvements in conjunction with an Agency first mortgage loan. Contact the Pennsylvania Housing and Finance Agency for application information.

13. Statewide Homeownership Program: low interest financing for first-time qualified home buyers or buyers of property in targeted areas. To view a list of lenders, go to {www.phfa.org/programs/singlefamily/lenders/index.htm}.

14. Construction Loan Program: construction loans to sponsors of low-income rental housing who have permanent take-out financing from other lenders. To view a list of lenders, go to {www.phfa.org/programs/singlefamily/lenders/index.htm}.

15. Low Income Housing Tax Credit Program: tax credits to owners and investors of affordable rental housing. To download an application, go to {www.phfa.org/programs/multifamily/taxcredit.htm}.

16. PennHOMES Program: provides interim and permanent mortgage financing to developers of low income rental housing. An application can be downloaded at {www.phfa.org/mfapg/index.htm}.

17. Taxable and Tax Exempt Bond Financing: below market loans for the development of or rehabilitation of affordable rental units. To view a list of lenders, go to {www.phfa.org/programs/singlefamily/lenders/index.htm}.

18. Low Income Housing Tax Credit Program: tax credits to owners and investors of affordable rental housing. To download an application, go to {www.phfa.org/programs/multifamily/taxcredit.htm}.

19. Supportive Services Program: provides on-site supportive housing services for residents of PHFA-financed rental developments. Contact the Pennsylvania Housing and Finance Agency for application information.

Rhode Island

Rhode Island Housing and Mortgage Finance Corporation
44 Washington Street
Providence, RI 02903-1721
www.rihousing.com/

401-751-5566
TDD: 401-427-9799

Contact the Rhode Island Housing and Mortgage Finance Corporation for application information for the following programs.

1. First HOMES: low interest rates with low down payment requirements for first time home buyers, assistance with down payment costs for lower income first time homebuyers.

2. Jump Start Program: low interest rate loans with up to $5,000 in down payment and closing cost assistance.

3. Opening Doors Program: first mortgages from other banks with down payment and closing cost assistance from RIHMFC for minority purchases; employment and credit history requirements are relaxed.

4. Purchase Plus Program: loans for income-eligible, first time homebuyers to purchase a home and make up to $10,000 worth of repairs or improvements.

5. Buy It/Fix It Program: low-interest mortgage with construction financing to first time income eligible purchasers; current income eligible homeowners can refinance their mortgage providing they make at least $5,000 worth of need repairs.

6. Zero Down Program: low-interest loans with federal loan guarantees that allow you to borrow up to 100% of the purchase price for down payment assistance to first-time, income-eligible buyers.

7. Equity Rebate: a grant to income eligible homebuyers that equals 2% of the purchase price of the home you buy or $1,000, whichever is less, to be used to pay closing costs.

8. Silent Second Mortgage: a deferred payment second mortgage that must be repaid when you sell your home.

9. Closing Costs Assistance Loan: income eligible homebuyers can borrow up to 5% of the purchase price, or $5,000, whichever is less, to pay closing costs.

10. Home Repair: fixed rate loans to make needed repairs to owner occupied homes and on one to four unit dwellings that meet income requirements.

11. Lead Hazard Reduction: loans to income eligible homeowners and landlords who rent to income eligible tenants to make eligible repairs so their homes/units are lead safe.

12. EquiSense Program: low interest rate, second mortgage based on home equity that has no points or application, title, credit report or appraisal fees.

13. Reverse Mortgages Program: elderly income eligible home owners can use their home equity to provide them with tax-free income; no monthly payments and no repayment as long as they own the home.

14. Access Independence Program: low-interest loans and grants for qualified low- and moderate-income owner-occupied single family homes so they can remodel for persons with functional disabilities.

15. HOME: grants and low interest loans to encourage the construction or rehabilitation of affordable housing.

16. Low Income Housing Tax Credit Program: tax credits for owners of rental housing for low income households.

17. Predevelopment Loan: qualified nonprofit developers can get short-term loans to cover pre-closing costs incurred in determining development feasibility.

18. Preservation Loan Program: below market rate loans to preserve affordability of existing subsidized rental housing.

19. Rental Housing Production Program: a combination of financing programs to construct or rehabilitate affordable housing where portions of the units are rented to low income people.

20. Targeted Loans Program: loans for the construction or rehabilitation of affordable apartments; generally available only with first mortgage financing.

21. Technical Assistance Program: technical help and short-term loans to individuals, municipalities, and nonprofit groups to help preserve affordable housing.

22. Thresholds Program: grants for the development of housing that introduces persons with long-term mental illness into the community.

23. Home Repair: fixed rate loans to make needed repairs to owner occupied homes and on one to four unit dwellings that meet income requirements.

24. Lead Hazard Reduction: loans to income eligible homeowners and landlords who rent to income eligible tenants to make eligible repairs so their homes/units are lead safe.

25. Low Income Housing Tax Credit Program: tax credits for owners of rental housing for low income households.

26. Next Step Program: loans to nonprofit social service agencies for the development of transitional apartments for people in crisis.

27. Family Self Sufficiency Program: education and training available to Section 8 certificate and voucher holders to help them move from welfare into a job that will give them financial independence.

28. Foundation for Senior Health Program: funding for homemaker services to frail elderly and disabled residents of specified Section 8 apartments.

29. Youth RAP: funding for tutoring, employment and self-esteem building activities for disadvantaged children living in RIHMFC financed apartments.

South Carolina

South Carolina State Housing Finance and Development Authority
919 Bluff Road
Columbia, SC 29201   803-734-2000
www.sha.state.sc.us
Email: webmaster@sha.state.sc.us

1. Homeownership Mortgage Purchase Program: below market rate financing for income eligible homebuyers funded through the sale of bonds. A list of participating lenders is available at {www.sha.state.sc.us/Programs/HomeOwnership/lenders/lenders.html}.

2. Mortgage Assistance Loan Program: loans for down payment and for up-front closing costs not in excess of $2,000 for qualified home buyers that participate in one of the Homeownership Programs. The list of participating lenders is located at {www.sha.state.sc.us/Programs/HomeOwnership/Lenders/lenders.html}.

3. MultiFamily Tax-Exempt Bond Financing Program: permanent financing for property being developed for low- to moderate-income multifamily rental projects. The application can be downloaded at {www.sha.state.sc.us/Programs/Rental/Multifamily/multifamily.html}.

4. Low Income Housing Tax Credit Program: tax credits for developers of low-income rental housing. An application can be downloaded at {www.sha.state.sc.us/Programs/Rental/Tax_Credit/tax_credit.html}.

5. HOME Program: affords state and local government the flexibility to fund a wide range of low income housing activities. An application can be downloaded from {www.sha.state.sc.us/Programs/Other/HomeInvest/homeinvest.html}.

6. Section 8 Certificates and Vouchers: rental subsidies for low-income households. The application is available at {www.sha.state.sc.us/Programs/Rental/Section-8/section-8.html}.

South Dakota

South Dakota Housing Development Authority
221 South Central Ave.   605-773-3181
Pierre, SD 57501-1237   Fax: 605-773-5154
www.sdhda.org   TTY: 605-773-6107

1. First-Time Homebuyer Program: below market rates to income qualified first-time homebuyers. For a list of participating lenders, go to {www.sdhds.org/hofthb.htm}.

2. Mortgage Assistance Program: provides down payment and closing costs assistance up to $2,000.to qualified first-time homebuyers. For a list of participating lenders, go to {www.sdhds.org/homap.htm}.

3. Employer Mortgage Assistance Program (EMAP): provides down payment and closing cost assistance to income eligible employees with a participating employer. For a list of current participating employers, go to {www.sdhda.org/hoemap.htm}. For a list of participating lenders, go to {www.sdhds.org/hofthb.htm}.

4. Cooperative Home Improvement Program: low interest loans for up to seven years for the improvement, repair, or addition to the borrower's home. For a list of participating banks, go to {www.sdhda.org/hochip.htm}.

5. Housing Tax Credit: tax credits for the construction and rehabilitation of rental housing for low-income households. The application can be downloaded from {www.sdhda.org/planapp.htm#htc}.

6. HOME Program: designed to expand the supply of affordable housing for very low- and low-income families. The application is available at {www.sdhda.org/planapp.htm#home}.

7. Multifamily Bond Financing Program: mortgage loans to finance the construction of multifamily housing. The application can be downloaded from {www.sdhda.org/planapp.htm#bond}.

8. Emergency Shelter Grant Program: financing of shelters for homeless people. The application can be downloaded from {www.sdhda.org/planapp.htm#esg}.

9. Rural Site Development Program: funding for the development of new affordable housing in rural areas. Contact the South Dakota Housing Development Authority for a pre-application meeting.

10. The Governor's House: provides reasonably sized, affordable, energy efficient homes to income eligible families. Contact the South Dakota Housing Development Authority for information on this program.

11. Services to the Aging Residents Program: owners of SDHDA financed housing developments targeted for the elderly can provide supportive services to their residents. Housekeeping, transportation, meals, service coordination, and other services are available. Contact the South Dakota Housing Development Authority for information.

Tennessee

Tennessee Housing Development Agency
404 James Robertson Parkway, Suite 1114
Nashville, TN 37243-0900   615-741-2400
www.state.tn.us/thda

1. Great Rate Mortgage Program: loans for low- and moderate-income first-time homebuyers for homes that meet certain requirements. Contact the Tennessee Housing Development Authority for application information.

2. Great Start Mortgage Program: loans for low and moderate-income first-time homebuyers at a slightly higher interest rate, but offers down payment and closing cost assistance. Contact the Tennessee Housing Development Authority for application information.

3. New Start 0% Mortgage Loan Program: loans for nonprofit organizations for the construction of new single-family homes for very low-income families. An application can be downloaded from {www.state.tn.us/thda/Programs/Mortgage/0startmemo.htm}.

4. HOME Programs: federal funding to create affordable housing programs for income eligible people. An application can be downloaded from {www.state.tn.us/thda/Programs/grants00/grants.htm}.

5. Low Income Housing Tax Credit: tax credits for 10 years to owners of low-income housing. An application can be downloaded from {www.state.tn.us/thda/Programs/lihtc/lihtccvr.html}.

6. Tax Exempt Multi Family Bond Authority: loans for development of multifamily housing that sets aside units for certain income households. An application can be downloaded from {www.state.tn.us/thda/Programs/temfba/mfcvr.html}.

7. Family Self-Sufficiency Program: provides access to the supportive services families need to become free of public assistance within five years. Contact the Tennessee Housing Development Authority for application information.

8. Housing Choice Voucher Program: subsidy funds to low-income households that find their own dwelling. An application can be downloaded from {www.state.tn.us/thda/Programs/section8/sec8cvr.html}.

Texas

Texas Department of Housing and Community Affairs
507 Sabine Street
Austin, TX 78701
Mailing Address:
P.O. Box 13941
Austin, TX 78711-3941   512-475-3800
www.tdhca.state.tx.us
Email: info@tdhca.state.tx.us

1. Comprehensive Energy Assistance Program (CEAP): case management, education, and financial assistance to very low- and extremely low-income families to help reduce utility bills to comfortable level. Services include utility payment assistance, energy education and budget counseling. A list of service providers is available at {www.tdhca.state.tx.us/ea.htm#consumer CEAP}.

2. Emergency Nutrition/Emergency Relief Program (ENERP): provides Texans with emergency and energy related assistance to low-income households. Services include utility assistance, housing, cloths, food, medical assistance and transportation. Contact the Texas Department of Housing and Community Affairs for application information.

3. Weatherization Assistance Program: provides energy related improvements to homes, and also provides education about energy conservation. Priority is given to those families with children, the elderly and/or disabled, and those households with the highest energy costs, and the lowest income. The Service Provider list is at {www.tdhca.state.tx.us/ea.htm#consumersWAP}.

4. Down Payment Assistance Program: assists low and very low-income families with an interest fee loan to be used for a down payment and certain closing costs on a home purchased through the First Time Homebuyer Program. Contact the Texas Department of Housing and Community Affairs for application information.

5. First time Homebuyer Program: low interest revenue bonds channeled through certain Texas lenders to eligible families purchasing their first home. For a list of participating lenders, go to {www.tdhca.state.tx.us/hf_sfbp.htm}.

6. HOME Program: To download the application for this program, go to {www.tdhca.state.tx.us/HOMEApps2002.htm}.
   - Owner Occupied Housing Assistance Program: funds to rehabilitate single family, owner occupied, homes where the owner meets income requirements.
   - Homebuyer Assistance Program: loans up to $10,000 to income eligible borrowers for down payment, closing costs and gap financing.

7. Housing Trust Fund Program: funds to nonprofit, local government, public housing authorities, community housing developments and income eligible families to acquire, rehabilitate, or construct affordable housing for low and very low income people. The application can be downloaded at {www.tdhca.state.tx.us/htf.htm}.

8. "Bootstrap" Homebuilder Loan Program: loans to low-income families who agree to help build their house. An application is available at {www.tdhca.state.tx.us/bootstrap.htm}.

9. Contract for Deed Consumer Education Program: class to teach consumers about contract for deed sales. Contact the Texas Department of Housing and Community Affairs for information on this program.

10. Contract for Deed Conversion Initiative: available to residents who are currently purchasing residential property within 150 miles of the Texas-Mexico border and reside in a colonia identified by the Texas Water Development Board or meet the Department's definition of a colonia. Residents interested in converting their contract for deed into a traditional note and deed of trust may apply. Contact the Texas Department of Housing and Community Affairs for information on this program.

11. Mortgage Revenue Bond Program: finances below market loans to nonprofit and for profit developers of apartment projects that agree to set aside units for rental to low income families and special needs people. The application can be downloaded from {www.tdhca.state.tx.us/hf_mfbp.htm}.

12. HOME Program:
   - Rental Housing Development Program: funds to build, acquire, and/or rehabilitate rental property for mixed income, mixed use, single room occupancy, or transitional housing. The application is available at {www.tdhca.state.tx.us/HOMEApps2002.htm}.

13. Housing Trust Fund Program: funds to nonprofit, local government, public housing authorities, community housing developments and income eligible families to acquire, rehabilitate, or construct affordable housing for low and very low income people. The application can be downloaded from {www.tdhca.state.tx.us/htf.htm}.

14. Low Income Housing Tax Credit Program: tax credit to developers of low-income rental housing used to offset a portion of their federal tax liability in exchange for the production of affordable rental housing. The application can be downloaded from {www.tdhca.state.tx.us/lihtc.htm}.

15. Emergency Nutrition/Emergency Relief Program (ENERP): provides Texans with emergency and energy related assistance to low-income households. Services include; utility assistance, housing, clothes, food, medical assistance and transportation. Contact the Texas Department of Housing and Community Affairs for application information.

16. Emergency Shelter Grants Program: provides grants to entities that provide shelter and related services for the homeless. Also provides grants to assist those at risk of becoming homeless. An application can be downloaded from {www.tdhca.state.tx.us/pubs.htmHCS}.

17. HOME Program:
   - Tenant Based Rental Assistance Program: rent subsidies and security deposit payments to tenants that participate in a self-sufficiency program. The application is available at {www.tdhca.state.tx.us/HOMEApps2002.htm}.

18. Section 8 Housing Assistance Program: rental assistance via subsidies for low income households, elderly, disabled and handicapped people. Contact the Texas Department of Housing and Community Affairs for application information.

Utah

Utah Housing Corporation
554 South, 300 East   801-521-6950
Salt Lake City, UT 84111   800-284-6950 (UT only)
800-344-0452 (outside UT)   Fax: 801-359-1701
www.utahhousingcorp.org
Email: info@utahhousingcorp.org

1. First Home Program: below market rate mortgage loans to qualifying first time home buyers; purchases made in targeted areas do not need to meet the first time homebuyer requirements. The list of participating mortgage lenders is located at {www.utahhousingcorp.org/homebuyer_firsthome.html}.

2. Low Income Housing Tax Credit Program: tax credits for developers/owners of rental housing for income eligible people. The application can be downloaded at {www.utahhouingcorp.org/multifamily_lowincome.html}.

3. Tax Exempt Bond Financing: financing for the development of multifamily housing for low to moderate income persons. The application is available at {www.utahhousingcorp.org/multifamily_taxexempt.html}.

4. Low Income Housing Tax Credit Program: tax credits for developers/owners of rental housing for income eligible people. The application can be downloaded at {www.utahhouingcorp.org/multifamily_lowincome.html}.

5. Low Income Housing tax Credit Program: tax credits for developers/owners of rental housing for income eligible people. The application can be downloaded at {www.utahhouingcorp.org/multifamily_lowincome.html}.

Vermont

Vermont Housing Finance Agency
One Burlington Square
P.O. Box 408   802-864-5743
Burlington, VT 05402-0408   Fax: 802-864-5746
www.vhfa.org
Email: home@vhfa.org

1. Mortgages for Vermonters (MOVE): offers several interest rate and point options with flexible down payment requirements. A list of participating lenders is at {www.vhfa.org/partners/index.htm}.

2. Cash Assistance Rate Option: provides up to 3% of the loan amount to be used towards down payment and closing costs associated with a VHFA loan. Contact the Vermont Housing Finance Authority for application information.

3. Homeownership Opportunities Using Shared Equity: loans with stepped interest rates to nonprofit housing organizations that work together to reduce the purchase price and related costs; they agree to keep the property affordable to future home buyers by sharing any profit when it is sold. A list of participating lenders is at {www.vhfa.org/partners/index.htm}.

4. Limited Refinance: provides qualified homeowners the opportunity to replace high interest rate mobile home loan and all other property types can replace shared appreciation financing. Borrowers can also finance the cost of property improvements, and all associated closing costs. A list of participating lenders is at {www.vhfa.org/partners/index.htm}.

5. Construction and Permanent Loan Financing Program: financing for the development and preservation of affordable rental housing where at least 51% of the units are rented to low and moderate income people. The application can be downloaded at {www.vhfa.org/development/loan-programs.htm#cplfp}.

6. Nonprofit Housing Predevelopment and Bridge Loan Program: low cost financing to eligible nonprofit housing developers for projects such as transitional housing, nursing homes, co-op housing, single family homes and more. Call the Vermont Housing Finance Agency for and application.

7. Low Income Housing Tax Credit Program: tax credits for developers/owners of rental housing for low-income households. The application is available at {www.vhfa.org/development/lihtc.htm}.

Vermont State Housing Authority
One Prospect Street   802-828-3295
Montpelier, VT 05602   Fax: 802-828-3248
www.vsha.org

1. Section 8 HomeOwnership Program: allows some people to convert Section 8 Rental vouchers into HomeOwnership vouchers. This can provide those eligible, assistance meeting monthly costs associated with owning a home. The Questionnaire and Mutual Release can be downloaded from {www.vsha.org/homeown.htm}.

2. Development Program: assistance for the development and preservation of affordable multi-unit complexes and mobile home parks. Contact the Vermont State Housing Authority for application information.

3. New Construction/Substantial Rehabilitation Program: creates new and rehabilitated housing in communities without safe and sanitary housing for low-income families and the elderly. Contact the Vermont State Housing Authority for application information.

4. Section 8 Rental assistance Program: rental assistance to eligible persons who choose their own housing. An application can be downloaded at {www.vsha.org/ra.htm}.

5. Shelter Plus Care Program: rental assistance to disabled homeless people. Contact the Vermont State Housing Authority for application information.

6. Project Based Certificates and Moderate Rehabilitation Program: a rent subsidy that is attached to the unit and not the tenant. The application can be downloaded from {www.vsha.org/ra.htm}.

7. Family Unification Program: promotes family unification by providing rental assistance to families for whom the lack of adequate housing is a primary factor in the separation, or threat of imminent separation, of children from their families. The Department of Social and Rehabilitative Services refer eligible households to VSHA. Contact the Vermont State Housing Authority for application information.

8. Mainstream Housing: rental assistance for disabled families. Contact the Vermont State Housing Authority for application information.

Virginia

Virginia Housing Development Authority
601 South Belvidere Street   804-782-1986
Richmond, VA 23220   800-968-7837
www.vhda.com

1. Home Ownership Education: helps prepare first-time homebuyers with the purchase of their first home. A list of class schedules is located at {www.vhda.com/sf/singlefam.asp}.

2. Fresh Start Loan Program: offers low rate interest loans to qualified first-time homebuyers that have had difficulty purchasing a home due to past credit issues. The list of housing counseling agencies is at {www.vhda.com/sf/freshstart.asp}.

3. FHA Plus Loan Program: assists qualified borrowers who need down payment assistance. Contact a local VHDA originating lender (www.vhda.com/sf/singlefam.asp) for information.

4. Flexible Alternative Program: optioning for a slightly higher interest rate, allows up to 100% loan-to-value financing without mortgage insurance to eligible buyers. The application can be downloaded at {www.vhda.com/sf/SF_Flex_Apply_right.asp}.

5. Flexible Alternative Step Rate Program: couples the flexible features of the *Flexible Alternative Program* with the lower interest rate loan of the Step Rate program; lower interest rate for the first two years of the loan. Contact the Virginia Housing Development Authority for application information.

6. Flexible Alternative Home Enhancer Program: offers qualified borrowers the same features as the *Flexible Alternative Program*. But also offers financing for modest home improvements. Contact the Virginia Housing Development Authority for application information.

7. Flexible Alternative Home Access Program: a variation of the *Flexible Alternative Program* offering up to 100% of the sale price, but also offers an additional 10% more to be used for home modifications for accessibility. Contact the Virginia Housing Development Authority for application information.

8. Fixed Rate Loan: lower interest fixed rate loans for eligible homebuyers. Contact the Virginia Housing Development Authority for application information.

9. Step Rate Loan Program: lower interest rate for the first two years of the loan creating lower mortgage payments for those years. Contact the Virginia Housing Development Authority for application information.

10. Home Improvement Loan: loan for home improvement with a lower interest rate, low closing costs, and no points for low and moderate income homeowners. Contact the Virginia Housing Development Authority for application information.

11. Low Income Housing Tax Credit Program: federal tax credits for owners of low-income rental housing. The application can be downloaded at {www.vhda.com/multifam/taxcredframes.htm}.

12. Virginia Housing Fund: low interest rate funds for multi-family projects available to for-profits and non-profits for minority, and rural area developers. The application can be downloaded from {www.vhda.com/multifam/mfvhf.htm}.

13. Bond-Funded program: funding for multi-family projects that rent to low and very low-income tenants. An application is available at {www.vhda.com/multifam/mfbond.htm}.

14. Low Income Housing Tax Credit Program: federal tax credits for owners of low-income rental housing. The application can be downloaded at www.vhda.com/multifam/taxcredframes.htm.

15. State Credit Rent Reduction Program: tax credit to property owners who fill vacant units and/or reduce rent amounts for elderly, disabled, and homeless persons. Contact the Virginia Housing Development Authority for application information.

Washington

Washington State Housing Finance Commission
1000 Second Avenue, Suite 2700   206-464-7139
Seattle, WA 98104-1046   800-767-4663
www.wshfc.org

1. Home Choice Program: down payment assistance and lower interest rates for low and moderate income people with a disability, or that have a family member with a disability that are first time buyers or are buying in a targeted area; must complete an education counseling course. For the Service Provider list, go to {www.wshfc.org/buyers/homechoice.htm}.

2. House Key Program: below market rate loans for income eligible first time home buyers and buyers of residences in target areas. The list of participating lenders is at {www.wshfc.org/buyers/key.htm}.

3. House Key Plus Program: loans to income eligible buyers to help pay down payment and closing costs in conjunction with the *House Key Program*. The list of participating lenders is at {www.wshfc.org/buyers/keyplus.htm}.

4. House Key Teacher Program: offers lower down payment requirements to eligible full-time employed teacher, administrator, principal, vice-principal, librarian, or health care professional (such as nurse or counselor) who is a first-time homebuyer or buying in a targeted area. For a list of House Key Loan originaters, go to {www.wshfc.org/buyers/key.htm#lenders}.

5. House Key Extra: mortgage loan for income eligible first time home buyers with a disability, or a family member with a disability in a rural area and the home is within the specified price range. Contact the Washington State Housing Finance Commission for application information.

6. House Key Rural (Pilot Program): down payment and closing cost assistance available to first time homebuyers buying in a rural area. If buying in a rural targeted area, you do not need to be a first time homebuyer. The list of participating lenders is at {www.wshfc.org/buyers/krural.htm}.

7. Open Door Second Mortgage Loan Program: down payment and closing cost assistance to eligible first time homebuyers in the city of Tacoma. The list of participating lenders is at {www.wshfc.org/buyers/open.htm}.

8. Low Income Housing Tax Credit Program: federal tax credits to developers/owners of low-income rental housing. The application can be downloaded at {www.wshfc.org/tax-credits/index.htm}.

9. For Profit Multifamily Developer Program: financing for developers of rental projects or new construction, acquisition and/or rehabilitation, and predevelopment costs. The application can be downloaded from {www.wshfc.org/bonds/fp-bond.htm}.

10. Bonds for Nonprofit Capital Projects: funding to nonprofits for a range of real estate and capital equipment projects. {www.wshfc.org/bonds/np-capital.htm}.

11. Bonds for Nonprofit Housing: funding to nonprofits for housing projects such as transitional housing, group homes, independent living

apartments and more. The application is available at {www.wshfc.org/bonds/np-housing.htm}.

12. Low Income Housing Tax Credit Program: federal tax credits to developers/owners of low-income rental housing. The application can be downloaded at {www.wshfc.org/tax-credits/index.htm}.

West Virginia

West Virginia Housing Development Fund
814 Virginia Street, East   304-345-6475
Charleston, WV 25301   800-933-9843
www.wvhdf.com
Email: wvhdf@wvhdf.com

1. Teacher and Education Employee Loan Assistance Program: designed for employees of the West Virginia school system who have sufficient income to support a monthly payment, but have limited funds to cover down payment and closing cost expenses. Contact a local banking or financial institution for application information.
2. Single Family Bond Program: low interest rate financing for low- and moderate-income families to buy a home in a specified price range. For a list of participating lenders, go to {www.wvhdf.com/home_ownership/limitsandlenders/index.cfm}.
3. Secondary Market Program: below market rate loans or refinancing for eligible homebuyers. For a list of participating lenders, go to {www.wvhdf.com/home_ownership/limitsandlenders/index.cfm}.
4. Closing Cost Assistance Program: assistance with closing costs for participants of the *Single Family Bond Program*. For a list of participating lenders, go to {www.wvhdf.com/home_ownership/limitsandlenders/index.cfm}.
5. Closing cost and Down Payment Assistance Loan: loan to be used towards down payment and closing costs available to income eligible participants in the *Secondary Market Program*. For a list of participating lenders, go to {www.wvhdf.com/home_ownership/limitsandlenders/index.cfm}.
6. HOME Program: a mortgage program providing funding for low-income families. The application is available when funding is available. It can be downloaded at {www.wvhdf.com/home_ownership/home/index.cfm}.
7. Housing Emergency Loan Program (HELP): funding for structural or construction problems that threaten the health and safety of low-income homeowners. For a list of participating lenders, go to {www.wvhdf.com/home_ownership/limitsandlenders/index.cfm}.
8. Mini-Mod Rehabilitation Program (MMRP): offers landlords affordable financing for upgrading rental units for low-income households. The Area Manager list is available at {www.wvhdf.com/area_managers/index.cfm}.
9. Constructing Affordable Sensible Homes (CASH) Program: provides a guaranteed sales program for single-family homebuilders. This program is only offered in counties affected by the 2001 flood. Contact the West Virginia Housing Development Fund for application information.
10. Construction Loan Incentive Program (CLIP): construction loans for low- and moderate-income multifamily or elderly housing in designated rural areas. Contact the West Virginia Housing Development Fund for application information.
11. Low Income Housing Tax Credit Program: federal tax credits for developers/owners of low-income multifamily housing. Contact the West Virginia Housing Development Fund for application information.
12. Low Income Housing Tax Credit Program: federal tax credits for developers/owners of low-income multifamily housing. Contact the West Virginia Housing Development Fund for application information.

Wisconsin

Wisconsin Housing and Economic Development Authority
201 West Washington, Suite 700   608-266-7884
P.O. Box 1728   800-334-6873
Madison, WI 53701-1728   Fax: 608-267-1099

www.wheda.com
Email: info@wheda.com

1. HOME Loan: mortgage loans with low interest rates for low- and moderate-income people for first time home buyers. The list of lenders is at {www.wheda.com/programs/singlefamily/sfbuyers/lenderlist/lenderlist.stm}.
2. CROP Program: loan guarantees for agricultural production loans. The list of lenders is at {www.wheda.com/programs/agricultural/lenderlist/lenderlist.stm}.
3. FARM Program: guarantees for agricultural expansion and modernization loans. The list of lenders is at {www.wheda.com/programs/agricultural/lenderlist/lenderlist.stm}.
4. Beginning Farmer Bond Program: low interest rate funding for the first time purchase of a farm, including land, equipment, livestock, or buildings. The list of lenders is at {www.wheda.com/programs/agricultural/lenderlist/lenderlist.stm}.
5. Home Improvement Loans: home improvement loans of up to $17,500 to low-to-moderate-income Wisconsin homeowners. For additional information, go to {www.wheda.com/programs/single family/sfbuyers/hilp.stm}.
6. Tax-Exempt Bond Financing: below-market-rate loans for development of multifamily rental housing. Loans can be used for new construction, acquisition and rehabilitation of one-to-three story apartment buildings. For additional information, go to {www.wheda.com/programs/multifamily/bmrfinan.stm}.
7. Affordable Housing Tax Credit: federal tax incentive to encourage the creation of affordable rental housing. For additional information, go to {www.wheda.com/programs/multifamily/ahtc/taxcred.stm}.
8. Section 8 Preservation Options: offer mortgage-restructuring options that provide incentive for owners to maintain affordable Section 8 housing for low-income tenants. Contact the Wisconsin Housing and Economic Development Authority for application information.

Wyoming

Wyoming Community Development Authority
155 North Beech   307-265-0603
Casper, WY 82602   Fax: 307-266-5414
www.wyomingcda.com
Email: curry@wyoming.cda.com

1. Qualified Rehabilitation Loan: low interest rate loans for rehabilitation projects from extensive major structural repair to major disrepairs. Contact the Wyoming Community Development Authority for application information.
2. Mortgage Revenue Bond (MRB): low interest rate mortgages for first-time Wyoming homebuyers with low and moderate incomes. For additional information, go to {www.wyomingcda.com/firsthome.html}.
3. HOME Investment Partnership Program: funds for the development of affordable housing for low and very low income households. The application can be downloaded at {www.wyomingcda.com/hs-prog1.htm}.
4. Low Income Housing Tax Credit Program: tax credits for owners of rental housing affordable to low income households. The application can be downloaded at {www.wyomingcda.com/hs-prog2.htm}.
5. Housing Trust Fund: financing of non-traditional affordable housing. Contact the Wyoming Community Development Authority for application information.
6. Community Development Block Grant (CDBG): loans for housing-related programs that benefit low-income households of Wyoming. For additional information, go to {www.wyomingcda.com/hs-prog3.html}.
7. Low Rent Public Housing: rental program of single family detached units for very-low income large families. Contact the Wyoming Community Development Authority for application information.

Section 8 Rental Assistance Program: certificates and vouchers to assist low income rental households. Contact the Wyoming Community Development Authority for application information.

Free Grants, Low Interest Loans, and Tax Credits to Renovate Historic Homes and Buildings

Renovating an old house can be very time consuming and expensive. If only there were a way to get someone else to pay for all that time consuming work... well, there is, if you know where to look. About 20 states offer some kind of grant or loan program for individual homeowners who are renovating historic homes. Here are a few examples:

- Iowa offers matching grants for renovation projects
- Kansas offers up to $75,000 in matching grants for renovation
- South Carolina offers up to $25,000 in matching grants.
- Maryland offers low interest loans for historic renovation
- Tennessee offers 50/50 matching grants for renovation

To qualify for these grant and loan programs, you first need to have your house qualify for the National Register of Historic Places. This isn't as difficult as it might seem. Your house doesn't have to have national significance, such as at one time being George Washington's weekend retreat. It can have local historic or architectural significance to qualify for the National Register. It could be an early example of 18th century Greek Revival style — or have been owned at one time by a locally significant family. You'd be surprised how many older houses have some sort of local significance, and that might be just enough to qualify for these programs. Contact your State Office of Historic Preservation listed below for more information about how to get your property qualified for historic status.

Federal Tax Credits

If you happen to live in one of the 30 states that don't offer renovation grants to individual homeowners, you still may be able to qualify for some types of financial benefits. Under the Federal Tax Credit Program, individuals who have rehabilitated an income producing building used for commercial or industrial purposes can receive a 20% tax credit on expenses incurred during that renovation. To be eligible for funding, buildings must be listed on the National Register of Historic Places or be eligible for membership into that organization.

What this means is that if you renovate your house and use part of it to run your own business, like a gift shop, you may be able to receive a federal tax deduction of 20% of the renovation costs. If you spent $50,000 on renovations, that comes out to a $10,000 tax deduction on next year's taxes. Not bad. Not only would you get the benefit of writing off 20% of your renovation expenses, but you'll also be able to write off part of your mortgage as a business expense.

Nonprofits Get The Breaks

Starting up a nonprofit, or looking to relocate an existing one? Think of moving into an historic building in need of renovation. Most states offer nonprofits matching grant money and low interest loans to buy and renovate historic buildings. Yes, that's right — some states actually offer nonprofits money to buy historic buildings.

Matthew Lesko, Information USA, Inc., 12081 Nebel Street, Rockville, MD 20852 • 1-800-955-7693 • www.lesko.com

Check In Often

The availability of money for historic renovation changes from year to year, depending on the state in which you live. Just because your state isn't awarding grants or loans this year, they may change within the next year or two, so continue to check the resources. Don't forget that some states, like South Dakota and Iowa, allow renovating homeowners of historic places up to 8 years of not having to pay property taxes — in the long run that could be even better for you than getting grant money.

Alabama

Alta Cassady
State Historic Preservation Officer
Alabama Historical Commission
468 South Perry   334-242-3184
Montgomery, AL 36104   Fax: 334-240-3477
www.preserveala.org
Email: acassady@mail.preserveala.org

There are no state grant funds available to individual homeowners. However, owners of commercial property listed in the National Register of Historic Places are eligible for a 50% reduction in property taxes. Nonprofits, local government, and universities are eligible to apply for the Alabama Cultural Resources Preservation Trust Fund, a 50/50 matching grant program. Eligible funding categories include survey and registration, education and public awareness, planning for historic rehabilitation, and planning archaeological project and eligible projects are those encourage good community preservation. The agency also administers the Federal Rehabilitation Tax Credit Program. Individuals who have rehabilitated an income producing building used for commercial or industrial purposes can receive a 20% tax credit on eligible expenses incurred during renovation. To be eligible for funding, buildings must be listed on the National Register of Historic Places or be eligible for membership.

Alaska

Judith Bittner
State Historic Preservation Officer
Alaska Department of Natural Resources
Office of History and Archeology
550 West 7th Avenue, Suite 1310907-269-8721
Anchorage, AK 99501-3565   Fax: 907-269-8908
www.dnr.state.ak.us/parks/oha_web
Email: oha@alaska.net

There are no funding programs available to individual property owners. Communities can become eligible for matching grant funds for historic preservation activities through Alaska's Historic Preservation Program. In order to qualify, the community must first become a Certified Local Government. As such, they can share in the 10% of federal funds that are passed on to the State Historic Preservation Office. The Federal Tax Rehabilitation Tax Credit is also available, it offers a 20% tax credit on money spent on an eligible rehabilitation of an income producing building that will be used for commercial or industrial purposes. Buildings must be listed on the National Register of Historic Places or be eligible for membership to qualify.

Arizona

Joe Roth
State Historic Preservation Officer
Arizona State Parks
1300 West Washington   602-542-4009
Phoenix, AZ 85007   Fax: 602-542-4180
www.pr.state.az.us
Email: jroth@pr.state.az.us

Although $1.7 million is available in historical renovation grants, funds are not directly awarded to individual property owners. Homeowners must have the support of a sponsoring agency to apply for funding. This may include a certified local government, nonprofit organization, Indian tribe, or a national register listed district or educational institution. Matching funds of 40% are usually required. The office also administers the Federal Investment Tax Credit Program. Through this program, individuals receive a 20% tax credit on expenses they incurred while rehabilitating an income producing building that will be used for commercial or industrial purposes. There is also a State property tax reduction program for non-income producing properties and a State property tax incentive program for commercial or industrial properties. Buildings must be listed on the National Register of Historic Places or be eligible for membership to qualify.

Arkansas

Cathie Matthews
State Historic Preservation Officer
Suite 1500 Tower Buildings

323 Center Street   501-324-9880
Little Rock, AR 72201   Fax: 501-324-9184
www.arkansaspreservation.org
Email: info@arkansaspreservation.org

Owners of historic homes can apply for a 50/50 matching grant from the Historic Preservation Restoration Program. The property must be listed on the Arkansas Register of Historic Places and if the grant will make it eligible for the National Register of Historic Places, the owner must follow through with the listing. The Federal Rehabilitation Tax Credit Program offers a 20% tax credit to individuals who have spent money rehabilitating an income producing building to be used for commercial, industrial, or residential rental purposes. Federal tax deductions can be gained through the donation of a conservation easement of a historic structure. Buildings must be listed on the National Register of Historic Places to qualify for either of these benefits. The Arkansas city governments that participate in the Certified Local Government (CLG) program are eligible for federal pass-through grants. These funds can be used for local historic preservation projects which include the rehabilitation of local historic structures. Individuals that are currently renovating or considering a renovation can receive technical assistance. The agency will provide on-site visits, consultations, and explanations. While cemeteries are not generally included in the National Register of Historic Places, they can be eligible under some circumstances. The Cemetery Preservation Program will consider assistance to those cemeteries where there are a significant amount of older markers and where the graves contain people of historic importance, or if there is a distinctive design feature.

California

Dr. Knox Mellon
Acting State Historic Preservation Officer
Office of Historic Preservation
Department of Parks and Recreation
P.O. Box 942896   916-653-6624
Sacramento, CA 94296-0001   Fax: 916-653-9824
http://ohp.parks.ca.gov
Email: calshpo@ohp.parks.ca.gov

There are occasionally state grants available to nonprofit organizations, local governments, and educational organizations. Various cities in California are Certified Local Governments. As such, they are eligible for 10% of the federal funds given to this agency. That money is used for historic preservation actives in each of their communities. The Mills Act provides property tax relief for owners of historic buildings. If the owner pledges to rehabilitate and maintain the historical and architectural character of their building, for a 10 year period they may receive a property tax savings of around 50%. This is not a state program, it is adopted by city and county governments. Another program the agency administers the Federal Historic Preservation Tax Incentive program. Individuals who have rehabilitated an income producing building used for commercial or industrial purposes can receive a 20% tax credit on expenses incurred during renovation. To be eligible for funding, buildings must be listed on the National Register of Historic Places or be eligible for membership.

Colorado

Georgianna Contiguglia
State Historic Preservation Officer
Colorado Historical Society
1300 Broadway   303-866-3395
Denver, CO 80203   Fax: 303-866-2711
www.coloradohistory-oahp.org

The State Historical Fund awards grants to public and non-profit entities. Individuals can obtain funding if they find a public or non-profit organization to apply for and administer funds on their behalf. Eligible categories include acquisition and development, education, and survey and planning projects. Funding is divided into four types: 1) General Grant: Competitive grants from $10,000 or less to multi-year grants; 2) Preservation Initiative Grants: No dollar amount specified; 3) Historic Structure Assessment Grants: Non-competitive grants of $10,000 or less whose purpose is to prepare a historic building for assessment; 4) Emergency Grants: Non competitive grants that generally do not exceed $10,000 for historic properties in danger of being destroyed or seriously damaged. The agency also administers the Colorado Historic Preservation

Income Tax Credit. Approved preservation/ rehabilitation projects that cost more than $5,000 and are completed within a 24 month period can receive a 20% credit on state income taxes. Properties must be over 50 years old and listed on the State Register of Historic Places or be landmarked by a Certified Local Government. Another tax savings can be attained through the donation of a preservation easement to this agency. The property must be listed on the National or State Registers of Historic Places to be eligible. There is also the Federal Rehabilitation Tax Credit Program. This is a 20% tax credit on the expenses incurred during the renovation of an income producing building that is used for commercial or industrial purposes. The building must be listed on the National Register of Historic Places or be eligible for a membership.

Connecticut

John W. Shannahan
State Historic Preservation Officer
Connecticut Historical Commission
59 South Prospect Street   860-566-3005
Hartford, CT 06106   Fax: 860-566-5078
www.chc.state.ct.us
Email: cthist@neca.com

There are no state grants or loans for homeowner's renovation projects at this time. There is a state tax incentive program, but it is only available to corporations that purchase homes in certain census tracts. There is however, the Federal Rehabilitation Tax Credit Program. This is a 20% tax credit on the expenses incurred during the renovation of an income producing building that is used for commercial or industrial purposes. The building must be listed on the National Register of Historic Places or be eligible for a membership. Another program available is the federally funded program called the Certified Local Government Program. The CLG's receive 10% of the funds passed on to the Historical Commission to be used for local restoration projects.

Delaware

Daniel R. Griffith
State Historic Preservation Officer
Division of Historical and Cultural Affairs
Hall of Records
P.O. Box 1401
406 Otis Drive   302-739-5313
Dover, DE 19901   Fax: 302-739-6711
www.state.de.us/shpo/index.htm
Email: dgriffith@state.de.us

There are no funding programs available to individuals. The office does administer the Federal Rehabilitation Tax Credit Program. Through this program individuals receive a 20% tax credit on expenses they incurred while rehabilitating a commercial or industrial building. Buildings must be listed on the National Register of Historic Places or be eligible for membership to qualify. The Certified Local Government Program is a federally funded program. The CLG's receive 10% of the funds passed on to the Department of Consumer and Regulatory Affairs to be used for local restoration projects.

District of Columbia

David Maloney, Deputy SHPO
Historic Preservation Division
801 N. Capitol St., NE, 3rd Floor   202-442-8818
Washington, DC 20002   Fax: 202-535-2497
www.planning.dc.gov/main.shtm

At this time there are no funds available from the District of Columbia for individuals to complete restoration projects. However, the agency does administer the Federal Rehabilitation Tax Credit Program. Individuals who have rehabilitated an income producing building used for commercial or industrial purposes can receive a 20% tax credit on expenses incurred during renovation. To be eligible for funding, buildings must be listed on the national Register of Historic Places or be eligible for membership. A federally funded program is the Certified Local Government Program. The CLG's receive 10% of the funds passed on to the Department of Consumer and Regulatory Affairs to be used for local restoration projects.

Florida

Dr. Janet Snyder Matthews
State Historic Preservation Officer
Division of Historical Resources
Department of State
R.A. Gary Building, Room 305
500 S. Bronaugh Street   850-245-6300
Tallahassee, FL 32399-0250   Fax: 850-488-3353
http://dhr.dos.state.fl.us/

State agencies, units of local government, and nonprofit organizations are eligible to submit applications and compete for funding. Funding categories include acquisition and development, survey and planning and community education. In general, grants will provide 50/50 matching assistance. The

agency also administers the Federal Rehabilitation Tax Credit Program. Individuals who have rehabilitated an income producing building used for commercial or industrial purposes can receive a 20% tax credit on expenses incurred during renovation. To be eligible for funding, buildings must be listed on the National Register of Historic Places or be eligible for membership. Another federal program is the Certified Local Government Program. With this, the CLG's receive 10% of the funds passed on to the Division of Historical Resources to be used for local restoration projects.

Georgia

Ray Luce
State Historic Preservation Officer
156 Trinity Avenue, SW, Suite 101   404-656-2840
Atlanta, GA 30303-3600   Fax: 404-651-8739
www.dnr.state.ga.us/dnr/histpres

There are no state grant programs available to home owners. However, this office does administer two federal and one state tax incentive programs. The Federal Rehabilitation Tax Credit Program allows for a 20% tax credit on expenses incurred while rehabilitating an income producing building used for commercial or industrial purposes. The Historic Preservation State Tax Incentive Program offers an 8 year freeze on property tax assessments when a substantial rehabilitation has been done an individual or business property. There is also a Charitable Contribution Deduction that gives a one time tax deduction to the owner of a historic property that donates a conservation easement. For all of these programs the building must be listed in the National Register of Historic Places or be eligible for membership, have approval for the project to qualify. There are also cities that are Certified Local Governments in Georgia. Those cities are eligible for a portion of the federal funding to be used for their communities' historic preservation projects and technical assistance.

Hawaii

Don Hibbard
Department of Land and Natural Resources
State Historic Preservation Division
Kakuhihewa Building
601 Kamokila Boulevard, Suite 555
P.O. Box 621   808-692-8015
Honolulu, HI 96809   Fax: 808-692-8020
www.hawaii.gov/dlnr/hpgreeting.htm
Email: dlnr@exec.state.hi.us

A state grant program provides funding, if funds are available, to local and county governments, nonprofit organizations and responsible corporations and individuals. These are 50/50 matching grants, although there are rarely funds for historic property renovation. The agency also administers the Federal Rehabilitation Tax Credit Program Individuals who have rehabilitated an income producing building used for commercial or industrial purposes can receive a 20% tax credit on expenses incurred during renovation. To be eligible for funding, building must be listed on the National Register of Historic Places or be eligible for membership. There is also a property tax exemption available to individuals who won homes listed on the Historic Register. Local county tax offices can provide information and materials. A local government that is deemed a Certified Local Government becomes eligible for federal funding to fund historic renovation projects and technical assistance.

Idaho

Steve Guerber
State Historic Preservation Officer
Idaho State Historical Society
1109 Main Street, Suite 250   208-334-2682/3847
Boise, ID 83702-5640   Fax: 208-334-2774
www.idahohistory

There are no funding programs available to individuals in Idaho. However, this office does administer the Federal Tax Credit Program. Through this program individuals receive a 20% tax credit on expenses they incurred while rehabilitating a building used for commercial or industrial purposes. Buildings must be listed on the National Register of Historic Places or be eligible for membership to qualify. They also have the Certified Local Government Program in which CLG's receive 10% of the federal funds passed on to the Historical Society in the form of matching grants. The funds are used for local preservation projects in the CLG's community.

Illinois

William Wheeler, SHPO
State Historic Preservation Agency   217-785-4512
1 Old State Capitol Plaza   TDD: 217-524-7128
Springfield, IL 62701-1512   Fax: 217-524-7525
www.state.il.us/HPA
Email: historicpreservation@yahoo.com

Homeowners must have a sponsoring agency to apply for state grant funding. Sponsoring agencies include nonprofit organizations or Certified Local Governments. The agency administers the Federal Tax Credit

Program. Individuals who have rehabilitated a building used for commercial or industrial purposes can receive a 20% tax credit on approved expenses that were incurred. Another tax incentive program for owner-occupied residences is the State Property Tax Assessment Freeze. When at least 25% of the fair market value of the property is spent on a rehabilitation project, the owner can receive a freeze of the assessed valuation of the property at the pre-rehabilitation level for 8 years. After that time, the assessed value will increase in quarter increments for 4 years. Buildings must be listed on the National Register of Historic Places or be eligible for membership to qualify. They also have the Certified Local Government program. With this, a CLG will receive 10% of the federal funds given to the Historic Preservation Agency to be used for historic preservation of their community.

Indiana

Larry D. Macklin, Director, DNR
Division of Historic Preservation & Archaeology
402 Washington Street, Room W274
Indiana Government Center South   317-232-1646
Indianapolis, IN 46204   Fax: 317-232-0693
www.in.gov/dnr/historic
Email: dhpa@dnr.state.in.us

Grants are available to public agencies, nonprofit organizations with a ceiling up to $30,000. These are 50/50 matching grants. The agency also administers the Federal Rehabilitation Tax Credit Program. Individuals who have rehabilitated an income producing building used for commercial or industrial purposes can receive a 20% tax credit on approved expenses incurred during renovation. To be eligible for funding, the building must be listed on the National Register of Historic Places or be eligible for membership. With the Certified Local Government Program, local communities that have preservation zoning ordinances receive 10% of the federal funds passed on to the Historic Preservation Office. With these matching grants, the CLG's fund local preservation activities in their community.

Iowa

Anita Walker
State Historic Preservation Officer
State Historical Society of Iowa
Capitol Complex
600 E. Locust Street   515-281-5111
Des Moines, IA 50319   Fax: 515-242-6498
www.iowahistory.org/preservation/
Email: anita.walker@dca.state.ia.us

The Historic Resource Development Program offers matching grants for work on historic properties, museums and their collections, and documentary collections. The program is open to individuals, nonprofit organizations, Certified Local Governments, businesses, state agencies, school districts and Native American tribes. There is another matching grant available to nonprofits, government bodies and Indian Tribes. For both the buildings must be listed on the National Register of Historic Places or be reviewed by the State Preservation Office to determine eligibility. Local government agencies that become Certified Local Governments receive federal matching grants to fund local preservation planning activities in their communities. This agency also offers a state tax incentive for substantial rehabilitation. This is a combination of a 4 year exemption from any increase of property valuation because of the project and 4 years of decreasing exemptions. Buildings must be evaluated as eligible for membership on the National Register of Historic Places. There is a Federal Rehabilitation Tax Credit Program for rehabilitated income producing buildings used for industrial or commercial purposes. They will receive a 20% tax credit for approved renovations to the buildings. The property must be listed on the National Register of Historic Places or be eligible for membership to participate in the program.

Kansas

Mary R. Allman
State Historic Preservation Officer
Kansas State Historical Society
6425 SW Sixth Avenue   785-272-8681
Topeka, KS 66615-1099   TTY: 785-272-8683
www.kshs.org/resource/histpres.htm   Fax: 785-272-8682
Email: rpowers@kshs.org

Nonprofit organizations, city or county governments, or individuals may apply for the Heritage Trust Fund Program, an annual grant with a funding ceiling of $75,000. This is a matching grant with 80% provided in grant money and a 20% cash match required on the part of the recipient. The deadline for applications is in February. Eligible properties must be listed on national or state registers of historic places. The agency also administers the Federal Rehabilitation Tax Credit Program. Individuals who have rehabilitated an income producing building used for commercial or industrial purposes can receive a 20% tax credit on approved expenses incurred during renovation. To be eligible for funding, the building must be listed on the National Register of Historic Places or be eligible for membership. With the

Certified Local Government Program, local communities that have preservation zoning ordinances receive 10% of the federal funds passed on to the Historic Preservation Office. With these matching grants, the CLG's fund local preservation activities in their community.

Kentucky

David Morgan, Director, SHPO
Kentucky Heritage Council
300 Washington Street   502-564-7005
Frankfort, KY 40601   Fax: 502-564-5820
www.state.ky.us/agencies/khc/khchome.htm
Email: dmorgan@mail.state.ky.us

The State Restoration Grant Program that is available to all owners of historic properties, including individuals. However, nonprofit organizations and government agencies that restore structures for public use generally take precedence. It is a 50/50 matching grant. They have an African American Heritage Grant Program that has funding for projects relating to African American sites. The grants are sometimes used for building restoration, otherwise, it is for research and exhibits. The agency also administers the Federal Tax Credit Program from which individuals may benefit. Individuals who have rehabilitated an income producing building used for commercial or industrial purposes can receive a 20% tax credit on approved expenses incurred during renovation. To be eligible for the credit, buildings must be listed on the National Register of Historic Places or be eligible for membership. With the Certified Local Government Program, local communities that have preservation zoning ordinances receive 10% of the federal funds passed on to the Historic Preservation Office. With these matching grants, the CLG's fund local preservation activities in their community.

Louisiana

Laurel Wyckoff
State Historic Preservation Officer
Department of Culture, Recreation & Tourism
Division of Historic Preservation
P.O. Box 44247   225-342-8200
Baton Rouge, LA 70804-4247   Fax: 225-342-8173
www.crt.state.la.us/crt/ocd/hp/ocdhp.htm

At present, state funding is not available to individual property owners. They may however, apply to a Certified Local Government for renovation funding. The CLG's receive a portion of the federal funds given to the Division of Historic Preservation to be used for renovation programs in their communities. These are generally matching grants. The agency does administer the Federal Preservation Tax Credit Program. Individuals who have rehabilitated an income producing building used for commercial or industrial purposes can receive a 20% tax credit on approved expenses incurred during renovation. They also have the Restoration Tax Abatement Program available for business and owner occupied properties that are going to improve, renovate, or create an addition on their buildings. The program creates a freeze on the assessed value and property taxes at the re-improvement level for 5 years. That can be renewed for an additional 5 years in many parishes. This state program can be used in addition to the Federal Tax Credit Program. To be eligible for funding, the building must be listed on the National Register of Historic Places or be eligible for membership.

Maine

Earle G. Shettleworth, Jr.
State Historic Preservation Officer
Maine Historic Preservation Commission
55 Capitol Street
State House Station 65   207-287-2132
Augusta, ME 04333-0065   Fax: 207-287-2335
www.state.me.us/mhpc
Email: earle.shettleworth@state.me.us

At present, federal and state funding is not available to individual property owners, nonprofit organizations or local county governments. The agency does administer the Federal Historic Preservation Tax Credit Program. Individuals who have rehabilitated an income producing building used for commercial or industrial purposes can receive a 20% tax credit on approved expenses incurred during renovation. To be eligible for funding, the building must be a certified historic structure. With the Certified Local Government Program, local communities that have preservation zoning ordinances receive 10% of the federal funds passed on to the Historic Preservation Office. With these matching grants, the CLG's fund local preservation activities in their community.

Maryland

Rodney Little
State Historic Preservation Officer
Maryland Historical Trust
100 Community Place, 3rd Floor   410-514-7600
Crownsville, MD 21032-2023   Fax: 410-514-7678
www.marylandhistoricaltrust.net

Email: mdshpo@ari.net

There is a loan and a grant program available to individuals for projects to acquire, rehabilitate or restore eligible properties. The Historic Preservation Grant Fund has awards of $40,000 per year, per project. In order to participate in this program, the owner must give a perpetual historic preservation easement to the Trust before receiving any funds. The Historic Preservation Loan Fund is a low interest loan. They are available on a first come, first serve basis. A perpetual historic preservation easement must be conveyed for this program also. The agency also administers the Federal Rehabilitation Tax Credit Program. Individuals who have rehabilitated an income producing building used for commercial or industrial purposes can receive a 20% tax credit on approved expenses incurred during renovation. To be eligible for funding, the building must be listed on the National Register of Historic Places or be eligible for membership. The state tax incentive program is the Heritage Preservation Tax Credit Program. The owner of a certified heritage structure can receive a tax credit equal to 25% of the qualified capital costs of the rehabilitation project. It also includes a mortgage credit certificate option. With this, a property owner can choose to transfer the credit to his/her mortgage lender for a reduction in the principal amount or interest rate of the loan. There is also a Certified Local Government Program where those local governments receive a portion of the federal funds given to the Historical Division for historic preservation programs.

Massachusetts

Cara Metz
State Historic Preservation Officer
Massachusetts Historical Commission
220 Morrissey Boulevard
Boston, MA 02125-3314
www.state.ma.us/sec/mhc
Email: cara.metz@sec.state.ma.us

617-727-8470
TDD: 800-392-6090
Fax: 617-727-5128

At present, state grants are not available to individual property owners. The Massachusetts Preservation Projects Fund will provide approximately $9 million in matching grants over the next 3 years available to municipalities and non-profits.. Money will be used to support the preservation and maintenance of properties and sites listed in the State Register of Historic Places. Eligible categories will include pre-deveopment, development and acquisition projects. Request for pre-development costs range from $5,000 to $30,000; requests for development or acquisition projects can range from $7,500 to $100,000. Local governments that become Certified Local Governments will receive 10 % of the federal funds given to the Historical Commission for renovation projects in their communities. Individual property owners may benefit from the Federal Rehabilitation Tax Credit Program. Individuals who have rehabilitated an income producing building used for commercial or industrial purposes can receive a 20% tax credit on approved expenses incurred during renovation. To be eligible for funding, the building must be listed on the National Register of Historic Places or be eligible for membership.

Michigan

Brian Conway
State Historic Preservation Office
Michigan Historical Center
Box 30740
Department of History, Arts and Libraries
702 W. Kalamazoo St.
Lansing, MI 48909
www.sos.state.mi.us/history/preserve/preserve.html
Email: preservation@sos.state.mi.us

517-373-1630
Fax: 517-373-1630

State grants are not available to individual property owners. The agency does, however, administer the Federal Rehabilitation Tax Credit Program. Individuals who have rehabilitated an income producing building used for commercial or industrial purposes can receive a 20% tax credit on expenses incurred during renovation. There is also the Michigan Historic Preservation Tax Incentive. This is an income tax credit of up to 25% for owners of a historical home that are going to start a rehabilitation project. To be eligible for funding, buildings must be listed on the National Register of Historic Places or be eligible for membership. There is a federal funding program for Certified Local Governments. They receive 10% of the State Historical Center's federal appropriation in the form of matching grants. These funds are used for local preservation projects in the CLG's community.

Minnesota

Nina Archabal
State Historic Preservation Officer
Minnesota Historical Society
345 West Kellogg Boulevard
St. Paul, MN 55102-1906
www.mnhs.org

651-296-6126
Fax: 651-296-1004

There is no state funding program available to individual property owners. The agency does, however, offer technical advice concerning restoration projects. They do administer a Federal Rehabilitation Tax Credit Program to

individuals that have rehabilitated an income producing building. The credit is for 20% of eligible expenses incurred during renovation and the building must be used for commercial or industrial purposes. In order to be eligible, the building must be listed on the National Register of Historic Places, or be eligible for membership. They also have the Certified Local Government Program. With this program, cities, townships, and counties with qualified local historic preservation ordinances receive federally funded matching grants to be used for local preservation projects.

Mississippi

Elbert Hilliard
State Historic Preservation Officer
Mississippi Department of Archives and History
618 East Pearl Street
Jackson, MD 39201
Mailing Address:
P.O. Box 571
Jackson, MS 39205-0571
www.mdah.state.ms.us/hpres/hprestxt.html
Email: msshpo@mdah.state.ms.us

601-359-6940
Fax: 601-359-6975

They do have a pending program called the Mississippi Landmark Program. If a property is designated as a Landmark it can be eligible for funding, however, it is not clear if individual property owners will be able to benefit from the grants. They do have the Certified Local Government Program. With this program, cities, townships, and counties with qualified local historic preservation ordinances receive federally funded matching grants to be used for local preservation projects. They also administer a Federal Rehabilitation Tax Credit Program to individuals that have rehabilitated an income producing building. The credit is for 20% of eligible expenses incurred during renovation and the building must be used for commercial or industrial purposes. In order to be eligible, the building must be listed on the National Register of Historic Places, or be eligible for membership.

Missouri

Stephen Mahfood
State Historic Preservation Officer
State Department of Natural Resources
Division of State Parks
205 Jefferson
P.O. Box 176
Jefferson City, MO 65102
www.dnr.state.mo.us/shpo/homepage.htm

573-751-4422
Fax: 573-751-7627

The Historic Preservation Fund Grant is a federal 60/40 matching grant that is open to individuals, state agencies, municipal governments, incorporated organizations, non-profits and educational institutions. The eligible activities for funding are survey, National Register, predevelopment, development and planning. These activities must be directly related to the protection of historical or architectural resources, among other things. The recipient of the grant must fund the entire project and then receive a reimbursement up to the total amount of the grant. The agency also administers the Federal Tax Credit Program. It offers a 20% tax credit on money spent on approved rehabilitation of an income producing building that will be used for commercial or industrial purposes. There is a state investment tax credit for 25% of qualified rehabilitation efforts. Homeowners as well as developers of income producing buildings can qualify for this credit and it can be used in combination with the federal credit for owners of eligible buildings. The Certified Local Government is a federal program administered through local communities. The CLG's receive 10% of the federal funds passed on to the Historical Division to be used for local renovation projects.

Montana

Mark Baumler, Program Manager
State Historic Preservation Office
1410 8th Avenue
P.O. Box 201202
Helena, MT 59620-1202
www.his.state.mt.us/
Email: mbaumler@state.mt.us

406-444-7717
Fax: 406-444-6575

There is not any funding available for individual homeowners. The Certified Local Government Program is a federal program administered through local communities. The CLG's receive 10% of the federal funds passed on to the Historical Division to be used for local renovation projects. The agency also administers the Federal Tax Credit Program. It offers a 20% tax credit on money spent on approved rehabilitation of an income producing building that will be used for commercial or industrial purposes. There is a state investment tax credit for 25% of qualified rehabilitation efforts. Homeowners as well as developers of income producing buildings can qualify for this credit and it can be used in combination with the federal credit for owners of eligible buildings.

Nebraska

Lawrence Sommer
State Historic Preservation Officer

Nebraska State Historical Society
P.O. Box 82554
1500 R Street
Lincoln, NE 68501   402-471-4745
www.nebraskahistory.org   Fax: 402-471-3316
Email: hpnshs@nebraskahistory.org/histpres.index.htm

There are no state grant programs that provide funds for historic preservation to homeowners. Individual property owners may apply for the Federal Tax Credit Program if they have rehabilitated an income producing property used for commercial or industrial purposes. They would receive a 20% tax credit on expenses they incurred during the project. To be eligible, the building must be either listed on the National Register of Historic Places, or be eligible for membership. With the Certified Local Government Program, local communities that have preservation zoning ordinances receive 10% of the federal funds passed on to the Historic Preservation Office. With these matching grants, the CLG's fund local preservation activities in their community.

Nevada

Ronald James
State Historic Preservation Officer
Historic Preservation Office
100 N. Stewart Street   775-684-3448
Carson City, NV 89710-4285   Fax: 775-684-3442
http://dmla.clan.lib.nv.us/docs/shpo

Presently, there are no state grant programs for individuals. They do have a program to rehabilitate buildings that are used for cultural purposes. However, they do have the Certified Local Government Program. With this program, cities, townships, and counties with qualified local historic preservation ordinances receive federally funded matching grants to be used for local preservation projects. Individuals may be able to become sponsored through the CLG Program for their restoration project. Individual property owners may also apply for the Federal Rehabilitation Tax Credit Program. Rehabilitation of an income producing building that is used for commercial or industrial purposes can receive a 20% tax credit on expenses incurred during renovation. To be eligible for funding, buildings must be listed on the National Register of Historic Places or be eligible for membership.

New Hampshire

James McConaha
State Historic Preservation Officer
State Historic Preservation Office
Division of Historical Resources and
State Historic Preservation Office
19 Pillsbury Street   603-271-3483/3558
P.O. Box 2043   TDD: 800-735-2964
Concord, NH 03301-2043   Fax: 603-271-3433
http://webster.state.nh.us/nhdhr
Email: preservation@mndhr.state.nh.us

Presently, there are no state grants available for individuals or nonprofit organizations. However, they do have the Certified Local Government Program. With this program, cities, townships, and counties with qualified local historic preservation ordinances receive federally funded matching grants to be used for local preservation projects. There is also the Federal Rehabilitation Tax Credit Program that may benefit individual property owners. They can receive a 20% tax credit on eligible expenses incurred during a renovation of an income producing building used for commercial or industrial purposes. To be qualify, the building must be listed on the National Register of Historic Places or be eligible for membership.

New Jersey

Robert C. Shinn
State Historic Preservation Officer
New Jersey Historic Trust
P.O. Box 404   609-292-2023
Trenton, NJ 08625-0404   Fax: 609-984-0578
www.state.nj.us/dep/hpo

The state has both grant and loan programs for nonprofits, government agencies, and educational institutions, however, none for individual homeowners. There are two programs that individuals can use as tax benefits. With the New Jersey Legacies Program, the charitable donation of a historic property allows for reduced estate tax as well as other tax benefits. The Preservation Easement Program gives legal protection to a historic property by the donation of an easement. It also has property and federal tax benefits. The property must be listed on the National Register of Historic Places. There is also the Federal Rehabilitation Tax Credit Program that may benefit individual property owners. They can receive a 20% tax credit on eligible expenses incurred during a renovation of an income producing building used for commercial or industrial purposes. To be qualify, the building must be listed on the National Register of Historic Places or be eligible for membership. With the Certified Local Government Program, local communities that have preservation zoning ordinances receive 10% of the federal funds passed on to the Historic Preservation Office. With these matching grants, the CLG's fund local preservation activities in their community.

New Mexico

Elmo Baca
State Historic Preservation Officer
Historic Preservation Division
Office of Cultural Affairs
Room 320, LaVilla Rivera
228 East Palace Avenue   505-827-6320
Santa Fe, NM 87501   Fax: 505-827-6338
www.museums.state.nm.us/hpd

While there are no state grants currently available, funds from the federal Historic Preservation Fund are being administered by this division through categorical projects. There are ten small grants of up to $2,000 for the promotion of preservation activities available to individuals, local governments, historic and archaeological and preservation groups. The New Mexico Historic Preservation Loan Fund offers rehabilitation incentives to owners of registered cultural properties. This revolving loan fund combines monies of the state and participating local lenders. To obtain funding, projects must be on the State and/or National Register of Historic Places and reviewed for compliance with the Secretary of the Interior's Standards for Rehabilitation and with the Historic Preservation Division Staff. Borrowers are subject to the lending criteria applied by the participating bank. The maximum principal for a loan is $200,000 with a low interest rate and a term of 5 years. Individual property owners can also apply for the Federal Tax Credit Program. Through this program building owners receive a 20% tax credit on allowed expenses they incurred while rehabilitating a building used for commercial or industrial purposes. Buildings must be listed on the National Register of Historic Places or be eligible for membership to qualify. There is a state tax credit program that is available to homeowners and business owners for expenses incurred during a restoration/rehabilitation project. Those projects that have been approved by the Cultural Properties Review Committee are eligible for a 50% credit for expenditures up to a maximum credit of $25,000. Certified Local Governments get a portion of the federal funding received by the Historic Preservation Division in the form of matching grants. The grants fund local preservation actives in the CLG's community.

New York

Ruth Pierpont
Deputy State Historic Preservation Officer
Field Services Bureau
New York State Parks, Recreation and Historic Preservation
New York State Parks
Albany, NY 12238
Physical Address:
20th Floor, Agency Building #1
Empire State Plaza   518-474-0456
Albany, NY 12238   TTY: 518-486-1899
Email: ruth.pierpont@oprhp.state.ny.us
http://nyparks.state.ny.us/

There are no state funds available to individual property owners. Funding to nonprofit organizations and local municipal governments made available by the Environmental Protection Act of 1993 and provides up to 50% matching grants fo4r acquisition and restoration. Also, the Historic Barn Tax Credit has established a state income tax credit which provides a reduction in state income tax to barn owners based on the rehabilitation of the barn. This office administers the Federal Rehabilitation Tax Credit Program. Through this program individuals receive a 20% tax credit on allowable expenses they incurred while rehabilitating a building used for commercial or industrial purposes. Buildings must be listed on the National Register of Historic Places or be eligible for membership to qualify. New York also has two tax abatement programs that allow local municipalities to establish property tax abatement programs for locally designated landmarks. These will allow for the increase in assessed value of a rehabilitated historic building or barn to be phased-in over time. With the Certified Local Government Program, local communities that have preservation zoning ordinances receive 10% of the federal funds passed on to the Historic Preservation Office. With these matching grants, the CLG's fund local preservation activities in their community.

North Carolina

David Brook
Deputy State Historic Preservation Officer
State Historic Preservation Office
Department of Culture Resources
Division of Archives and History
4617 Mail Service Center   919-733-4763
Raleigh, NC 27699-4617   Fax: 919-733-8653
www.hpo.dcr.state.nc.us
Email: dbrook@ncsl.dcr.state.nc.us

North Carolina has no state funding program for individual property owners.

The Division of Archives and History provides grants to nonprofit organizations and local county governments for historical preservation activities. Individual property owners can, however, benefit from the Federal Tax Credit Program. Through this program individuals receive a 20% tax credit on expenses they incurred while rehabilitating a building used for commercial or industrial purposes. Buildings must be listed on the National Register of Historic Places or be eligible for membership to qualify. Private residences that are going to take on a substantial rehabilitation of their historic home may take advantage of a 30% state tax credit. The project must be certified and the home must be listed on that National Register or be located within a National Register district. The Certified Local Government Program funds local community preservation activities in communities that have preservation zoning ordinances.

North Dakota

Merlan Paaverud, Jr.
State Historic Preservation Officer
State Historical Society of North Dakota
Archeology & Historic Preservation Division
Heritage Center
612 East Boulevard 701-328-2666
Bismarck, ND 58505-0830 Fax: 701-328-3710
www.state.nd.us/hist
Email: mpaaverud@state.nd.us

The Restoration Grant Program is available to individuals, but it is offered sporadically. The matching grant comes from federal sources and can be used for approved rehabilitation projects of homes listed on the National Register of Historic Places. The agency also administers the Federal Preservation Tax Credit Program. Individuals who have rehabilitated an income producing building used for commercial or industrial purposes can receive a 20% tax credit on eligible expenses incurred during renovation. To be eligible, the building must be either listed on the National Register of Historic Places, or be eligible for membership. With the Certified Local Government Program, local communities that have preservation zoning ordinances receive 10% of the federal funds passed on to the Historic Preservation Office. With these matching grants, the CLG's fund local preservation activities in their community.

Ohio

Amos J. Loveday
State Historic Preservation Officer
Ohio Historical Society
Historic Preservation Office
567 East Hudson Street 614-298-2000
Columbus, OH 43211-1030 Fax: 614-298-2037
www.ohiohistory.org/resource/histpres
Email: ajloveday@aol.com

There is no state funding available to individual property owners. However, they do have the Certified Local Government Program. With this program, cities, townships, and counties with qualified local historic preservation ordinances receive federally funded matching grants to be used for local preservation projects. Individual property owners may benefit from the Federal Tax Credit Program. Individuals who have rehabilitated an income producing building used for commercial or industrial purposes can receive a 20% tax credit on expenses incurred during renovation. To be eligible for funding, buildings must either be listed on the National Register of Historic Places or be eligible for membership. Federal Rehabilitation Tax Credit Program.

Oklahoma

Bob Blackburn
State Historic Preservation Officer
State Historic Preservation Office
2704 Villa Prom
Shepherd Mall 405-521-6249
Oklahoma City, OK 73107 Fax: 405-947-2918
www.ok-history.mus.ok.us

There is no state or federal funding available to individual property owners at the present time. The agency does, however, administer the Federal Tax Credit Program. Individuals who have rehabilitated an income producing building used for commercial or industrial purposes can receive a 20% tax credit on eligible expenses incurred during renovation. They also have a state tax credit that can be used on top of the federal credit for historic hotels and historic economic development areas. To be eligible for funding for both credits, the buildings must be listed on the National Register of Historic Places, or be eligible for membership. They have another federal program called the Certified Local Government Program. With this program, cities, townships, and counties with qualified local historic preservation ordinances receive federally funded matching grants to be used for local preservation projects.

Oregon

Michael Carrier
State Historic Preservation Officer
State Parks and Recreation Department
State Historic Preservation Office
1115 Commercial St., NE, Suite 2 503-378-6305
Salem, OR 97301-1012 Fax: 503-378-8936
www.prd.state.or.us/about_shpo.html
Email: shpo.info@state.or.us

They offer competitive grants programs for assistance to National Register properties when they have funding available. Currently, there is no funding but they hope to have it available next year. However, they do have the Certified Local Government Program. With this program, cities, townships, and counties with qualified local historic preservation ordinances receive federally funded matching grants to be used for local preservation projects. Individual property owners may also benefit from the Special Assessment for Historic Properties Program which provides a fifteen year tax abatement on increases in land and improvement. Properties must be listed on the National Register of Historic Places and be approved by a State Historic Preservation committee. This office also administers the Federal Rehabilitation Tax Credit Program. Income producing buildings that are used for commercial or industrial purposes can receive a 20% tax credit for eligible expenses incurred during a renovation. To be eligible, the building must be listed on the National Register of Historic Places, or be eligible for membership.

Pennsylvania

Brent Glass
State Historic Preservation Officer
Bureau for Historic Preservation
400 North Street 717-783-8946
Harrisburg, PA 17108-0093 Fax: 717-772-0920
www.phmc.state.pa.us

There are no state funds available to residential homeowners at the present time. Nonprofit organizations and public agencies may apply for the Keystone Historic Preservation Grant to renovate/restore historic properties that are open to the public. This is a 50/50 matching grant program. The agency also administers the Federal Tax Credit Program. There is also the Certified Local Government Program. With this program, cities, townships, and counties with qualified local historic preservation ordinances receive federally funded matching grants to be used for local preservation projects. Individuals who have rehabilitated an income producing building used for commercial or industrial purposes can receive a 20% tax credit on approved expenses incurred during renovation. To be eligible for funding, buildings must be listed on the National Register of Historic Places or be eligible for its membership.

Rhode Island

Frederick C. Williamson
State Historic Preservation Officer
Historical Preservation Commission
Old State House
150 Benefit Street 401-222-2678
Providence, RI 02903 Fax: 401-222-2968
www.rihphc.state.ri.us

While there are no state grant programs, they do have a low interest loan program that individual homeowners can apply to for restoration projects. The Historical Preservation Loan Fund has an interest rate of 2% less than prime. The maximum loan is for $200,000 with a term of 5 years. The agency also administers the Federal Rehabilitation Tax Credit Program. Individuals who have rehabilitated an income producing building used for commercial or industrial purposes can receive a 20% tax credit on expenses incurred during renovation. To be eligible for funding, buildings must be listed on the national Register of Historic Places or be eligible for membership. The state's Historic Preservation Residential Tax Credit Program provides a 10% income tax credit for eligible rehabilitation and maintenance costs for homeowners. With the Certified Local Government Program, local communities that have preservation zoning ordinances receive 10% of the federal funds passed on to the Historic Preservation Office. With these matching grants, the CLG's fund local preservation activities in their community.

South Carolina

Roger E. Stroup
State Historic Preservation Officer
Historic Preservation Office
8301 Parklane Rd. 803-896-6100
Columbia, SC 29223-4905 Fax: 803-896-6168
www.state.sc.us/scdah

This office administers both federal and state grant programs to support preservation efforts of individuals, organizations, institutions and local governments. Owners of South Carolina properties that are listed in the National Register of Historic Places or determined eligible for membership may apply for State Development Grants and Federal Survey & Planning Grants. Funds from State Development grants assist preservation work on historic structures.. Awards generally range from $5,000 to $20,000. The Federal Survey & Planning Grant assists historic preservation projects in a variety of categories. The work must be done by professionals and must comply with the agencies' guidelines and standards. Both of these are reimbursable 50/50 matching grants. They do also have the Certified Local Government Program. With this program, cities, townships, and counties with qualified local historic preservation ordinances receive federally funded matching grants to be used for local preservation projects. There are two tax incentive programs available. The Special Property Tax Assessments for Rehabilitated Historic Buildings encourages the revitalization of neighborhoods and downtown commercial districts. Municipal and county governments can freeze tax assessments when a property owner finishes a substantial rehabilitation of a historic building and low and moderate income rental properties. The freeze is in effect for up to 2 years if the rehabilitation is completed within those years. For the following 8 years, it will be taxed at the greater of 40% of the post-rehabilitation assessment, or 100% of the pre-rehabilitation assessment.

South Dakota

Jay D. Vogt
State Historic Preservation Officer
State Historical Society Historic Preservation Center
900 Governor's Drive   605-773-3458
Pierre, SD 57501-2217   Fax: 605-773-6041
www.state.sd.us/state/executive/deca/cultural/histpres.htm
Email: jay.vogt@state.sd.us

There are no state grants available to individual property owners at the present time. However, individuals, public agencies and nonprofits are eligible to apply for the Deadwood Fund which makes loans and grants available to purchase, restore, or develop historic property for residential, commercial, or public purposes. The agency also administers the Federal Rehabilitation Tax Credit Program. Individuals who have rehabilitated an income producing building used for commercial or industrial purposes can receive a 20% tax credit on expenses incurred during renovation. There is an additional 10% credit for the renovation of buildings that were constructed before 1936. To be eligible for funding, buildings must be listed on the national Register of Historic Places or be eligible for membership. The South Dakota Legislature has also approved and eight year moratorium on property tax assessment for improvements on historical buildings. Buildings must be on the National Register of Historic Places to qualify. There is also the Certified Local Government Program. With this program, cities, townships, and counties with qualified local historic preservation ordinances receive federally funded matching grants to be used for local preservation projects.

Tennessee

Herbert L. Harper
Deputy State Historic Preservation Officer
Tennessee Historical Commission
Clover Bottom Mansion
2941 Lebanon Road   615-532-1550
Nashville, TN 37243-0422   Fax: 615-532-1549
www.state.tn.us/environment/hist/index.html

The Federal Preservation Grant is open to individuals, local governmental bodies, private organizations or educational institutions. While historic survey projects will be emphasized, funding is also available for other projects that are needed to undertake a restoration. The agency also administers the Federal Renovation Tax Credit Program. Individuals who have rehabilitated an income producing building used for commercial or industrial purposes can receive a 20% tax credit on expenses incurred during renovation. To be eligible for funding, buildings must be listed on the National Register of Historic Places or be eligible for its membership. There is also the Certified Local Government Program. With this program, cities, townships, and counties with qualified local historic preservation ordinances receive federally funded matching grants to be used for local preservation projects.

Texas

Lawrence Oaks
State Historic Preservation Officer
Texas Historical Commission
P.O. Box 12276   512-463-6100
Austin, TX 78711-2276   Fax: 512-463-8222
www.thc.state.tx.us
Email: l.oakes@thc.state.tx.us

The Texas Preservation Trust Fund Grant Program provides funding to public or private entities in the form of two for one matching grants. Although individuals may apply, the large majority of grants are awarded to nonprofit organizations and municipal governments. There is also the Certified Local Government Program. With this program, cities, townships, and counties with qualified local historic preservation ordinances receive

federally funded matching grants to be used for local preservation projects. This agency administers the Federal Renovation Tax Credit Program. Individuals who have rehabilitated an income producing building used for commercial or industrial purposes can receive a 20% tax credit on expenses incurred during renovation. To be eligible for funding, buildings must be listed on the national Register of Historic Places or be eligible for its membership.

Utah

Max Evans
State Historic Preservation Officer
Utah State Historical Society
Office of Preservation   801-533-3500
300 South Rio Grande   TDD: 801-533-3502
Salt Lake City, UT 84101-1143   Fax: 801-533-3503
http://history.utah.org
Email: ushs@history.state.ut.us

At present, there are no state or federal funds directly available to individual property owners. However, individuals may be able to apply for funding through Utah's Certified Local Government Program. Homeowners qualify if they have support of a sponsoring agency. Matching funds are usually required. The agency also administers the State and Federal Tax Credit Programs. Through these programs individuals can receive a 20% tax credit on expenses they incurred while rehabilitating a building that will be used for residences (state tax credit only), commercial or industrial purposes. Buildings must be either listed on the National Register of Historic Places, or be eligible for membership to qualify.

Vermont

Emily Wadhams
State Historic Preservation Officer
Vermont Division for Historic Preservation
National Life Building, Drawer 20
Montpelier, VT 05620-0501   802-828-3211
www.historicvermont.org

Vermont has no state funding for privately owned properties other than a state grant program that provides funding for the renovation of old barns. There is a 50/50 matching grant program available to nonprofit organizations and municipalities. The agency also administers the Federal Tax Credit Program. Individuals who have rehabilitated an income producing building used for commercial or industrial purposes can receive a 20% tax credit on expenses incurred during renovation. To be eligible for funding, buildings must be listed on the National Register of Historic Places or be eligible for its membership. There is also the Certified Local Government Program. With this program, cities, townships, and counties with qualified local historic preservation ordinances receive federally funded matching grants to be used for local preservation projects.

Virginia

Kathleen Kilpatrick
State Historic Preservation Officer
Department of Historic Resources
Commonwealth of Virginia
2801 Kensington Avenue   804-367-2323
Richmond, VA 23221   Fax: 804-367-2391
www.dhr.state.va.us
Email: kkilpatrick@dhr.state.va.us

The state grant program is available for local governments, nonprofit historical associations, and museum organizations. However, individuals with state tax liability may benefit from the State Rehabilitation Tax Credit Program which provides a 25% credit for eligible rehabilitation expenses. The agency also administers the Federal Tax Credit Program. Individuals who have rehabilitated an income producing building used for commercial or industrial purposes can receive a 20% tax credit on expenses incurred during renovation. To be eligible for funding, buildings must be listed on the National Register of Historic Places or be eligible for its membership. There is also the Certified Local Government Program. With this program, cities, townships, and counties with qualified local historic preservation ordinances receive federally funded matching grants to be used for local preservation projects.

Washington

Allyson Brooks
State Historic Preservation Officer
Office of Archeology and Historic Preservation
1063 S. Capitol Way, Suite 106
P.O. Box 48343   360-586-3065
Olympia, WA 98504-8343   Fax: 360-586-3067
www.ocd.wa.gov/info/lgd/oahp

At present, state grant funding is not available to individual property owners, nonprofit organizations or local county governments, although, there is the Certified Local Government Program. With this program, cities, townships, and counties with qualified local historic preservation ordinances receive federally funded matching grants to be used for local preservation projects. This agency administers the Federal Rehabilitation Tax Credit Program. Individuals who have rehabilitated an income producing building used for commercial or industrial purposes can receive a 20% tax credit on expenses incurred during renovation. To be eligible for funding, buildings must be either listed on the National Register of Historic Places, or be eligible for membership.

West Virginia

Susan Pierce
Deputy State Historic Preservation Officer
West Virginia Division of Culture and History — 304-558-0220
1900 Kanawha Boulevard, East — TDD: 304-558-3562
Charleston, WV 25305-0300 — Fax: 301-558-2779
www.wvculture.org/shpo/index.html

State Development Grants are available to individuals who wish to renovate a historical home. Grants range from $1,000 to $20,000 depending upon the scope of the project. There is also the Certified Local Government Program. With this program, cities, townships, and counties with qualified local historic preservation ordinances receive federally funded matching grants to be used for local preservation projects. The Federal Rehabilitation Tax Credit Program is administered by this agency. Individuals who have rehabilitated an income producing building used for commercial or industrial purposes can receive a 20% tax credit on expenses incurred during renovation. In addition, there is a state tax credit program for both residential and commercial property owners that undergo a rehabilitation project. To be eligible for funding, buildings must be either listed on the National Register of Historic Places, or be eligible for membership.

Wisconsin

George Vogt
State Historic Preservation Officer
Historic Preservation Division

State Historical Society
816 State St. — 608-264-6500
Madison, WI 53706-1842 — Fax: 608-264-6504
www.shsw.wisc.edu/about/index.html

There are no state or federal grants available to individual homeowners. Individuals can, however, apply for tax assistance under the Federal Tax Credit Program. Individuals who have rehabilitated an income producing building used for commercial or industrial purposes can receive a 20% tax credit on expenses incurred during renovation. To be eligible for funding, buildings must be either listed on the National Register of Historic Places, or be eligible for membership. There is also the Certified Local Government Program. With this program, cities, townships, and counties with qualified local historic preservation ordinances receive federally funded matching grants to be used for local preservation projects.

Wyoming

Richard Currit
State Historic Preservation Officer
2301 Central Avenue, 3rd Floor — 307-777-7013
Cheyenne, WY 82002 — Fax: 307-777-3543
http://wyoshpo.state.wy.us

There are currently no state or federal grant programs available to individuals. Individuals can, however, apply for tax assistance under the Federal Tax Credit Program. Those who have rehabilitated an income producing building used for commercial or industrial purposes can receive a 20% tax credit on expenses incurred during renovation. To be eligible for funding, buildings must be either listed on the National Register of Historic Places, or be eligible for membership. There is also the Certified Local Government Program. With this program, cities, townships, and counties with qualified local historic preservation ordinances receive federally funded matching grants to be used for local preservation projects.

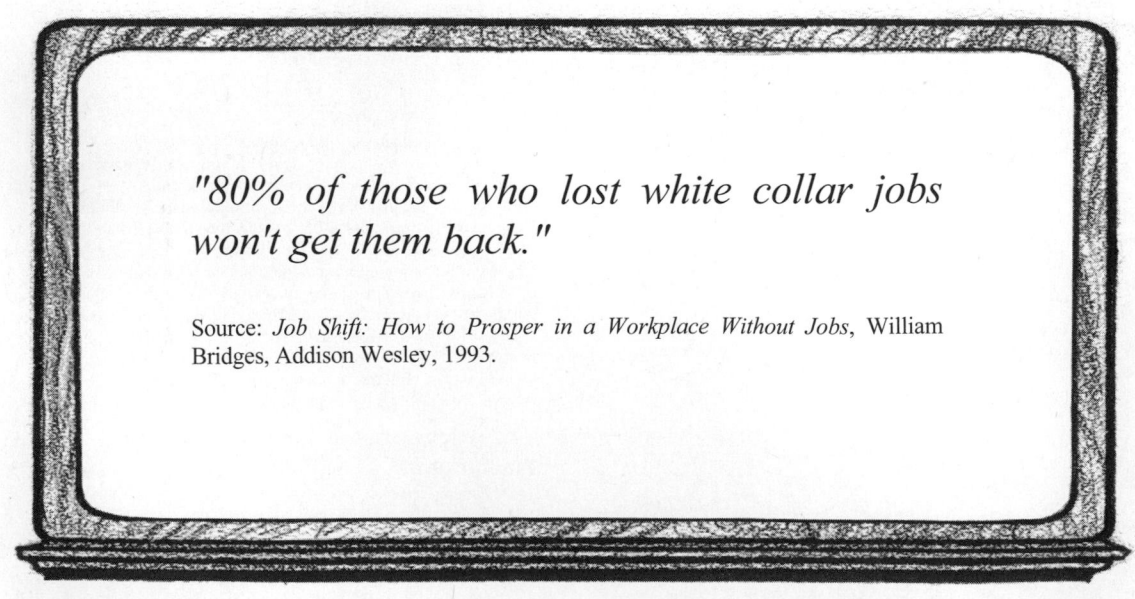

"80% of those who lost white collar jobs won't get them back."

Source: *Job Shift: How to Prosper in a Workplace Without Jobs*, William Bridges, Addison Wesley, 1993.

I Wanna Be an Inventor

Matthew Lesko, Information USA, Inc., 12081 Nebel Street, Rockville, MD 20852 • 1-800-955-7693 • www.lesko.com

Help For Inventors:
Patents, Trademarks, and Copyrights

Most inventors realize that it's vitally important to protect their idea by copyrighting it and obtaining the necessary patents and copyrights, but did you know that it's also important to look around for loans and other grants to support your business while working on your invention? If you want an idea to become an actual product, you have to invest an awful lot of your time into its research, and not just on a part time basis. Loans and grants programs for inventors help you do just that. For example, Hawaii offers low cost loans to inventors, as do other states around the country. First, let's talk about getting the necessary information concerning trademark and patent procedures.

Patent and Trademark Office

United States patent and trademark laws are administered by the Patent and Trademark Office (PTO). States also have trade secret statutes, which generally state that if you guard your trade secret with a reasonable amount of care, you will protect your rights associated with that secret. The PTO examines patent and trademark applications, grants protection for qualified inventions, and registers trademarks. It also collects, assembles, and disseminates the technological information patent grants. The PTO maintains a collection of almost 6 million United States patents issued to date, several million foreign patents, and more than 2.2 million trademarks, together with supporting documentation. Here's how to find out what you need to do to patent your idea.

What a Great Idea

To help you get started with patenting your invention, the Patent and Trademark Offices will send you a free booklet upon request called *General Information Concerning Patents*. There are three legal elements involved in the process of invention: the conception of the idea, diligence in working it out, and reducing it to practice - i.e., getting a finished product that actually works. If you have a great idea you think might work, but you need time to develop it further before it is ready to be patented, what should you do? For answers to general questions on patent examining policies and procedures, contact the Patent Assistance Center at 800-PTO-9199 or 703-308-HELP; TTY: 703-305-7785; Email: {usptoinfo@uspto.gov}. They will not answer legal questions or opinions. Applications, forms, and part or all of pamphlets are at their website; {www.uspto.gov}. You can order them online from {http://bookstore.gpo.gov}. To order them through the mail write to:

Superintendent of Documents
U.S. Government Printing Office
P.O. Box 371954
Pittsburgh, PA 15250-7954
www.access.gpo.gov/su_docs

202-512-1800
Fax: 202-512-2250

What is a Patent

A patent is a grant of a property right to the inventor for an invention. It lasts for 20 years from the date that the application is filed. United States patent grants are effective within the US, its territories and its possessions. By the language of the grant it is "the right to exclude others from making, using, offering for sale, or selling" the invention in the US or "importing" the invention into the US. It is not the right of the inventor to do so himself that is granted. It is personal property and can be sold or mortgaged, bequeathed or transferred and that person then has the same rights as the original grantee.

What Can Be Patented

A patent can be received for an invention or discovery of any new and useful process, machine, manufacture, or composition of matter, or any new and useful improvement to the original. A design patent is the invention of any new and non-obvious ornamental design for an article of manufacture. Its appearance is protected, not its structural or functional features. A plant patent is the invention or discovery and asexually reproduction of any distinct and new variety of plant. This includes cultivated sports, mutants, hybrids, and newly found seedlings, other than a tuber-propagated plant or a plant found in an uncultivated state. Physical phenomena, abstract ideas, and laws of nature can not be patented. There must be a complete description and not just an idea or suggestion of a subject. It must also do what it claims to do; it must work.

If an invention has been described in a publication anywhere in the world, or has been used publicly, or put up for sale, a patent must be applied for before one year passes, or the right to a patent is lost.

Who May Apply

There are only a few situations where a person other than the inventor may apply for a patent application.
- a representative if the inventor has died
- a guardian if the inventor is insane
- a joint inventor or a person that has ownership interest if the inventor refuses to apply or can not be found

If two or more persons are the inventors, they may file jointly. However, someone who contributed only financially, is not a joint inventor and cannot be included on the application.

Non-Provisional Application

The application must include:
1) a written document consisting of the specifications of the invention, and an oath or declaration
2) a drawing where it is necessary
3) the filing fee.

It must be in English, legible and written on only one side of white paper with a typewriter or its equivalent. The applicant will be notified if all the requirements are not met. The date that the completed application is filed will then become the filing date. Specifications must include a written description of the invention and the method and process of how it was made and is to be used. It must be in clear, concise, and exact terms to allow any skilled person related to the area of the invention to make and use the same discovery. The oath or declaration is a statement made by the inventor that he/she is the original and first inventor of the subject matter, as well as various other statements, made in front of a notary. The filing fee, excluding design and plant inventions, is a basic fee and additional fees. The basic fee covers 20 claims, including not more than 3 in independent form. There is an additional fee for each claim over 20, whether independent or dependent. The filing fees are cut in half for applicants that file a verified statement claiming small entity status; independent inventor, small business or non-profit. The drawing must show every feature of the invention specified in the claim. Generally, photographs are not accepted. Applications have legal requirements and must be followed precisely.

Provisional Application

These applications create an early effective filing date and the term "Patent Pending" can be applied to the invention. There must be a written description of the invention, any necessary drawings and the name of the inventor(s). Claims and oath or declarations are not required. Also needed, is a cover sheet that states it is a provisional application and a filing fee. The filing date is the date that the PTO receives the application. This type of application can not be filed for design inventions. A non-provisional application must be filed within 12 months or else it will be discarded.

Protect Your Idea for $10

You can file a Disclosure Document with the Patent and Trademark Office, and they will keep it in confidence as evidence of the date of conception of the invention or idea.

Disclosure Document
Commissioner for Patents
Box DD
Washington, DC 20231
Disclosure Office   800-786-9199
www.uspto.gov/web/offices/pac/disdo.html   703-308-HELP

Send an 8 1/2 x 11" drawing, a copy, signed disclosure, SASE, and a check or money order for $10 to file. Upon request, the above office will also send you a free brochure on Disclosure Documents.

This is the best way to keep the idea you are working on completely secret and yet document the date you conceived the idea. You can file the Disclosure Document at any time after the idea is conceived, but the value of it will depend on how much information you put into it - so put as much detail into this statement as you can.

The Purpose of Documenting The Date of Conception

If someone else should try to patent your idea, filing a Disclosure Document shows that you thought of it first, although filing this statement does not legally protect your invention. Documentation of the conception date gives you time to patent your invention, and is invaluable if you need to prove when you thought of your idea if a dispute should arise. (Note that filing a Disclosure Document gives you limited defensive legal protection only if you follow it up with a patent in two years. Unlike a patent, it cannot be used offensively, to stop someone else from patenting the same idea.) When you go to file for a patent, if you and a competitor get into a dispute as to who was the first to invent it, the Patent and Trademark Office (PTO) will hold an Interference Proceeding. If you thought of the idea first, your Disclosure Document will go a long way towards establishing that you were the first inventor and should therefore receive the patent for it.

Examining the Application

They look to see that the application follows the legal requirements and also that the invention is new, useful and non-obvious and meets all requirements. It is not unusual for some, or all, of the claims to be rejected on the first examination few are accepted as filed The applicant will be notified in writing of any errors found. Then the inventor must request reconsideration, specifically pointing out and addressing any errors found and any amend any claims that to be revised. The second examination will generally be made final. Patents are granted in about every 2 out of 3 applications that are filed.

Patent Electronic Business Center

This is the center where you can do business electronically with the USPTO. In order to check the status of your patent application and also find general patent information, you can access the Patent Application Information Retrieval (PAIR). You will also be able to search for specific patents or applications by their number. The Electronic Filing System (EFS) accepts electronically filed applications, but you must have a digital certification and meet other requirements first. This program is only open to select number of people at this time because it is in the beginning stages of operation. Contact the office to see if you may participate!

Research Resources That Can Help You Turn Your Idea Into Reality

While diligently working out the details of your invention you can use the extensive resources of over 190,000 scientific and technical journals, articles, and books at the Scientific and Technical Information Center in Arlington, VA.

Facilitating public access to the more than 25 million cross-referenced United States patents is the job of PTO's Technology Assessment and Forecast Program (TAF); 703-306-2600. It has a master database which covers all United States patents, and searches are available free. A TAF search will not result in an in-depth patent search. (More on that, and how to find classifications in the *Conducting Your Own Patent Search* section below.) TAF extracts information from its database and makes it available in a variety of formats, including publications, custom patent reports, and statistical reports. The purpose of most of the reports generated by a TAF search is to reveal statistical information.

Copies of the specifications and drawings of all patents are available from PTO. Design patents and trademark copies are $3 each. Plant patents in color are $15 each. To make a request, you must have the patent number. For copies, contact:

Office of Public Records (OPR)   800-972-6382
Crystal Gateway 4, Suite 300   703-308-9726
Arlington, VA 22202   Fax: 703-305-8759
Email: {dsd@uspto.gov}

Assistant Secretary and Commissioner
P.O. Box 9
ATTN: PTCS
Washington, DC 20231
Public Information Line   703-305-8716

Conducting Your Own Patent Search

Before investing too much time and money on patenting your idea, you will want to see if anyone has already patented it. You may conduct the search yourself on the PTO website at {http://www.uspto.gov} or hire someone to do it for you. If you wish to hire a professional to do your patent search, consult the local yellow pages or again, search the PTO website for a roster of patent attorneys. Even if your search is not as in-depth as that of a patent attorney or a patent agent, you may still find the information that you need. You may also conduct your patent search at the Patent and Trademark Office Search Room.

Patent and Trademark Office (PTO)
Patent and Trademark Search Room
Crystal Plaza 3, 1A01
2021 Jefferson Davis Highway
Arlington, VA 22202   703-305-4463

For information about the Patent and Trademark Depository Library, contact the office listed below.

Patent and Trademark Depository Library (PTDL)
U.S. Patent and Trademark Office
Crystal Park 3, Suite 481   703-308-5558
Washington, DC 20231   Fax: 703-306-2654

You may also conduct your patent search at any of the 83 Patent Depository Libraries (PDLs) throughout the country as listed below.

Patent and Trademark Depository Libraries
Alabama
Ralph Brown Draughon Library, Auburn University, 231 Mell Street, Auburn, AL 36849-5606; 334-844-1737; {www.lib.auburn.edu/scitech/resguide/patents/ptd/html}.

Birmingham Public Library, 2100 Park Place, Birmingham, AL 35203; 205-226-3620; {www.bplonline.org/GovDocs/patents.html}.

Alaska
Z.J. Loussac Municipal Library, 3600 Denali Street, Anchorage, AK 99503-6093; 907-343-2975; {www.muni.org/library1/index.cfm }.

Arkansas
Arkansas State Library, One Capitol Mall, Little Rock, AR 72201; 501-682-2053; Fax: 501-682-1529; {www.asl.lib.ar.us/patents/index.html}.

California
Los Angeles Public Library, 630 West Fifth Street, Los Angeles, CA 90071; 213-228-7220; Fax: 213-228-7209; {www.lapl.org/central/science.html}.

California State Library, Library & Courts Building I, 914 Capitol Mall, Sacramento, CA 95814; 916-654-0069; {www.library.ca.gov/index.html}.

San Diego Public Library, 820 E Street, San Diego, CA 92101-6478; 619-236-5813; {www.sandiego.gov/public-library/index.shtml}.

San Francisco Public Library, 100 Larking Street, San Francisco, CA 94102; 415-557-4500; {http://sfpl.lib.ca.us}.

Sunnyvale Center for Innovation, Invention & Ideas, 665 West Olive Avenue, Sunnyvale, CA 94086; 408-730-7300; Fax: 408-735-8762; {www.sci3.com}.

Colorado
Denver Public Library, 10 West 14th Avenue Parkway, Denver, CO 80204; 720-865-1111; {www.denver.lib.co.us/index.html}

Connecticut
Hartford Public Library, 500 Main Street, Hartford, CT 06103; 860-695-6300; {www.hartfordpl.lib.ct.us}.

Delaware
University of Delaware Library, 181 South College Avenue, Newark, DE 19717-5267; 302-831-2965; {www.lib.udel.edu}.

District of Columbia
Founders Library, Howard University, 500 Howard Place, NW, Washington, DC 20059; 202-806-7234; {www.founders.howard.edu}.

Florida
Broward County Main Library, 100 South Andrews Avenue, Fort Lauderdale, FL 33301; 954-357-7444; {www.co.broward.fl.us/lil12515.htm}.

Dade Public Library, 101 West Flagler Street, Miami, FL 33130; 305-375-2665; {www.mdpls.org}.

University of Central Florida Libraries, 4000 Central Florida Blvd., Orlando, FL 32816; 407-823-2562; {http://library.ucf.edu/GovDocs/PAT_TRAD.htm}.

Tampa Campus Library, 4202 East Fowler Avenue, Tampa, FL 33620-5400; 813-974-2729; {www.lib.usf.edu/virtual/govdocs}.

Georgia
Library and Information Center, Georgia Institute of Technology, 2nd Floor-East Building, Atlanta, GA 30332; 404-894-4508; {http://gtel.gatech.edu/patents}.

Hawaii
Hawaii State Library, 478 South King Street, 2nd Floor, Honolulu, HI 96813-2994; 808-586-3477; {www.state.hi.us/libraries/feddocs}

Idaho
University of Idaho Library, Rayburn St., Moscow, ID 83844-2350; 208-885-6235; {www.lib.uidaho.edu/internet/links/intellectual_property}

Illinois
Chicago Public Library, 400 South State St., 4th Floor, Chicago, IL 60605; 312-747-4450; {www.chipublib.org/008subject/009scitech/patents.html}

Illinois State Library, 300 South 2nd Street, Springfield, IL 62701-1796; 217-782-5659; {www.cyberdriveillinois.com/library/isl/isl.html}

Indiana
Indianapolis-Marion County Public Library, 40 E. St. Clair St., Indianapolis, IN 46204; 317-269-1741; {www.imcpl.lib.in.us/bst_patents.htm}.

Siegesmund Engineering Library, Purdue University, 1530 Stewart Center, Potter Room 160, W. Lafayette, IN 47907; 765-494-2869; {www.lib.purdue.edu/engr/patent.html}.

Iowa
State Library of Iowa, 1112 East Grand Avenue, Des Moines, IA 50319; 515-281-6541; {www.silo.lib.ia.us}.

Kansas
Ablah Library, Wichita State University, 1845 Fairmont, Wichita, KS 67260-0068; 316-978-3622; 800-572-8368; {http://library.wichita.edu/govdoc/patents.html}.

Kentucky
Louisville Free Public Library, 301 York Street, Louisville, KY 40203; 502-574-1611; {http://lfpl.org/govdoc.htm}.

Louisiana
Troy H. Middleton Library, Louisiana State University, Baton Rouge, LA 70803; 225-388-5652; {www.lib.lsu.edu/index.html}.

Maine
University of Maine, 5729 Raymond H. Fogler Library, Orono, ME 04469-5729; 207-581-1678; {http://library.umaine.edu/patents/default.htm}.

Maryland
Engineering and Physical Sciences Library, University of Maryland, College Park, MD 20742-7011; 301-405-9152; {www.lib.umd.edu/ENGIN/working/patents.html}.

Massachusetts
Physical Sciences and Engineering Library, Lederle Graduate Research Center, Room 273, University of Massachusetts, Amherst, Amherst, MA 01003-4630; 413-545-1370; {www.library.umass.edu/subject/science/scieng8.htm}.

Boston Public Library, 700 Boylston St., Copley Sq., Boston, MA 02116; 617-536-5400, ext. 2226; {www.bpl.org/research/govdocs/patent_trademark.htm}.

Michigan
Media Union Library, University of Michigan, 2281 Bonisteel Boulevard, Ann Arbor, MI 48109-2094; 734-647-5735; {www.lib.umich.edu/ummu/pattm.html}.

Abigail S. Timme Library, Ferris State University, Big Rapids, MI 49307-2747; 231-591-3500; {www.ferris.edu/library/patent/homepage.html}.

Great Lakes Patent and Trademark Center, Detroit Public Library, 5201 Woodward Avenue, Detroit, MI 48202; 313-833-3379, 800-547-0619; {www.detroit.lib.mi.us/glptc}.

Minnesota
Minneapolis Public Library, 250 Marquette Ave., Minneapolis, MN 55401-1992; 612-630-6000; {www.mplib.org}.

Mississippi
Mississippi Library Commission, 1221 Ellis Ave., Jackson, MS 39289-0700; 601-961-4120, 877-KWIK-REF; {www.mlc.lib.ms.us/reference_and_information_services/patent_&_trademark/index.htm}.

Missouri
Linda Hall Library, Science, Engineering, & Technology, 5109 Cherry Street, Kansas City, MO 64110-2498; 816-363-4600, 800-662-1545; {www.lindahall.org}.

St. Louis Public Library, 1301 Olive Street, St. Louis, MO 63103; 314-241-2288, ext. 390; {www.slpl.lib.mo.us/library.htm}.

Montana
Montana Tech Library, 1300 West Park Street, Butte, MT 59701; 406-496-4281; {www.mtech.edu/library/ patents.htm}.

Nebraska
Engineering Library, Nebraska Hall, 2nd Floor West, City Campus 0516, Lincoln, NE 68588-0410; 402-472-3411; {www.unl.edu/libr/libs/engr/engr.html}.

Nevada
Clark County Library, 1401 East Flamingo Road, Las Vegas, NV 89119; 702-507-3400; {www.lvccld.org/special_collections/patents/index.htm}.

Getchell Library, University of Nevada, 2nd Floor, Reno, NV 89557; 775-784-6500 ext. 309; {www.library.unr.edu/depts/bgic}.

New Hampshire
New Hampshire State Library, 20 Park Street, Concord, NH 03301; 603-271-2143; {www.state.nh.us/nhsl/patents/index.html}.

New Jersey
Newark Public Library, 3rd Floor, Main Library, 5 Washington St., Newark, NJ 07101; 973-733-7779; {www.npl.org/Pages/Collections/bst.html}.

Library of Science and Medicine, Rutgers University, 165 Bevier Road, Busch Campus, Piscataway, NJ 08854-8009; 732-445-3854; {www.libraries.rutgers.edu/rul/libs/lsm_lib/lsm_lib.shtml}.

New Mexico
Centennial Science and Engineering Library, The University of New Mexico, Albuquerque, NM 87131; 505-277-5327; {http://zoobert@unm.edu/newcse/}

New York
New York State Library, Cultural Education Center, Empire State Plaza, Albany, NY 12230; 518-474-5355; {www.nysl.nysed.gov/patents.htm}.

Buffalo and Erie County Library, 1 Lafayette Square, Buffalo, NY 14203-1887; 716-858-8900; {www.buffalolib.org/home}.

Science Industry and Business Library, New York Public Library, 188 Madison Avenue, New York, NY 10016; 212-592-7000; {www.nypl.org/research/sibl/pattrade/pattrade.htm}.

Central Library of Rochester & Monroe County, 115 South Ave., Rochester, NY 14604-1896; 585-428-8110; {www.rochester.lib.ny.us/central}.

Science & Engineering Library, SUNY at Stony Brook, Stony Brook, NY 11794; 631-632-7148; {www.sunysb.edu/sciencelibs/patents.htm}.

North Carolina
D.H. Hill Library, North Carolina State University, 2205 Hillsborough Street, Raleigh, NC 27695-7111; 919-515-2935; {www.lib.ncsu.edu/risd/govdocs}.

North Dakota
Chester Fritz Library, University of North Dakota, University Station, Grand Forks, ND 58202; 701-777-4888; {www.und.nodak.edu/dept/library/resources/patents/ptdlp.new.jsp}.

Ohio
Akron-Summit County Public Library, 55 South Main Street, Akron, OH 44326; 330-643-9000; {http://ascpl.lib.oh.us/pat-tm.html}.

Public Library of Cincinnati and Hamilton County, 800 Vine Street, 2nd Floor, North Building, Cincinnati, OH 45202-2071; 513-369-6971; {www.cincinnatilibrary.org/info/main/pd}.

Cleveland Public Library, 325 Superior Avenue, NE, Cleveland, OH 44114-1271; 216-623-2800; {www.cpl.org/}.

Paul Laurence Dunbar Library, Wright State University, Dayton, OH 45435; 937-775-2925; {www.libraries.wright.edu/libnet/subj/gov/ptdl/}

Science and Engineering Library, Ohio State University, 175 West 18th Avenue, Columbus, OH 43210-1150; 614-292-3022; {www.lib.ohio-state.edu/OSU_profile/phyweb}.

Toledo-Lucas County Public Library, 325 N. Michigan Street, Toledo, OH 43624; 419-259-5209; {www.toledolibrary.org/discover/maintwo.htm}.

Oklahoma
Oklahoma State University, 206 CITD, Stillwater, OK 74078-8085; 405-744-7086; {www.library.okstate.edu/patents/index.htm}.

Oregon
Paul L. Boley Law Library, Northwestern School of Law Lewis and Clark College, 10015 SW Terwilliger Boulevard, Portland, OR 97219; 503-768-6786; {www.lclark.edu/~lawlib/ptointro.html}.

Pennsylvania
The Free Library of Philadelphia, 1901 Vine Street, Philadelphia, PA 19103; 215-686-5331; {www.library.phila.gov/}.

Carnegie Library of Pittsburgh, Science and Technology Department, 4400 Forbes Avenue, 3rd Floor, Pittsburgh, PA 15213; 412-622-3138; {www.clpgh.org/clp/Scitech/PTDL/}.

Schreyer Business Library, 301 Paterno Library, 3rd Floor, University Park, PA 16802; 814-865-6369; {www.libraries.psu.edu/crsweb/business/patents}.

Puerto Rico
General Library, University of Puerto Rico at Mayaguez, Mayaguez, PR 00681; 787-832-4040, ext. 2022; {www.uprm.edu/library/patents}.

General Library, Bayamon Campus, #170 Road 174 Minillas Industrial Park, Bayamon, PR 00959; 787-786-5225; {www.uprb.upr.edu}.

Rhode Island
Providence Public Library, 225 Washington Street, Providence, RI 02903-3283; 401-455-8027; {www.provlib.org}.

South Carolina
R.M. Cooper Library, Clemson University, Clemson, SC 29634-3001; 864-656-3024; {www.lib.clemson.edu/govdocs/patents/newpat.htm}.

South Dakota
Devereaux Library, 501 East Saint Joseph Street, 2nd Floor, Rapid City, SD 57701; 605-394-1275; {www.sdsmt.edu/services/library/library.html}.

Tennessee
Stevenson Science & Engineering Library, 3200 Stevenson Center, Nashville, TN 37240; 615-322-2717; {www.library.vanderbilt.edu/science/patents..html}.

Texas
McKinney Engineering Library, University of Texas at Austin, ECJ 1.300, Austin, TX 78713; 512-495-4500; {www.lib.utexas.edu/engin/patent/uspat.html}.

Evans Library, Texas A&M University, College Station, TX 77843; 409-845-5745; {http:// library.tamu.edu/govdocs/intprop.html}.

Dallas Public Library, 1515 Young Street, 6th Floor, Dallas, TX 75201; 214-670-1468; {http://dallaslibrary.org/central.htm}.

Fondren Library, MS225 Rice University, Houston, TX 77251-1892; 713-348-5483; {www.rice.edu/Fondren/PTDL}.

Texas Tech University Libraries, 18th and Boston, Lubbock, TX 79409-0002; 806-742-2282; {www.lib.ttu.edu/govdocs/index.htm}

San Antonio Public Library, 600 Soledad, 2nd Floor, San Antonio, TX 78205; 210-207-2500; {www.sanantonio.gov/library/central/govdocs.asp}.

Utah
Marriott Library, University of Utah, 295 South 1500 E, Salt Lake City, UT 84112; 801-581-8394; {www.lib.utah.edu/govdocs}.

Vermont
Bailey/Howe Library, University of Vermont, Burlington, VT 05405; 802-656-2542; {http://library.uvm.edu/reference/government/patent.html}.

Virginia
James Branch Cabell Library, Virginia Commonwealth University, 901 Park Avenue, 1st Floor, Richmond, VA 23284-2033; 804-828-1104; {www.library.vcu.edu/jbc/govdocs/govhome.html}.

Washington
Engineering Library, University of Washington, Box 352170, Seattle, WA 98195; 206-543-0740; {www.lib.washington.edu/Engineering/ptdl}.

West Virginia
Evansdale Library, West Virginia University, P.O. Box 6105, Morgantown, WV 26506; 304-293-4696; {www.libraries.wvu.edu/patents/index.htm}.

Wisconsin
Wendt Library, University of Wisconsin, 215 North Randall Ave., Madison, WI 53706; 608-262-6845; {www.wisc.edu/wendt/patent/patent.html}.

Milwaukee Public Library, 814 West Wisconsin Avenue, Milwaukee, WI 53233; 414-286-3051; {www.mpl.org/}.

Wyoming
Wyoming State Library, 2301 Capitol Ave., Cheyenne, WY 82002; 307-777-7281; {www-wsl.state.wy.us/sis/ptdl/index.html}.

The Patent and Trademark Library Program distributes the information to the 83 PDLs. The information is kept on CD-Rom discs, which are constantly updated, and you can use them to do a patent search. CD-Rom discs have been combined to incorporate CASSIS (Classification and Search Support Information System). CD-Rom discs do not give you online access to the PTO database. Online access is available through APS (Automated Patent Systems), and is presently available to public users of the PTO Search Room and to the 83 Patent Libraries. Each PDL with the online APS has its own rules regarding its use. To use the online APS at the PTO Search Room, it is recommended that you take a class at the Search Room. West, East, and X-Search classes are offered once per month for a cost of $25. Off Schedule 3-hour personal training sessions are available for a fee of $120. Online access costs $40 per connect hour, and the charge for paper used for printouts is an additional $.25 per sheet. Public user Ids are required to access all Public Search Facilities. They are available at the Search Room Reception Desk with a valid government issued photo ID.

If you do not live near a PDL, several CD-Rom discs are available through subscription. You may purchase the Classification disc, which dates back to 1790, for $300; the Bibliography disc, which dates back to 1969, for $300; and the ASIST disc, which contains a roster of patent attorneys, assignees, and other information for $200. You can also conduct your patent search and get a copy of it through commercial database services such as:

MeadData Central, Nexis, Lexis: 1-800-422-1337; Fax: 1-800-421-5585; {www.lexisnexis.com/patentservices}. Printouts are billed per page plus shipping. Copies are available via email, mail, fax, or on a CD-Rom. If you intend on doing many searches over time, Nexis Lexis will customize a package for you as a subscriber for approximately $250 per month.

Derwent, 1725 Duke St., Suite 250, Alexandria, VA 22314; 1-800-337-9368, Fax: 1-800-457-0850; {www.derwent.com}. Patent searches are free, but the printouts range from $3.95 to $29.50 per page plus shipping.

If you are going to do your own patent search at your local Patent Depository Library, begin with the Manual and Index to U.S. Patent Classifications to identify the subject area where the patent is placed. Then use the CD-Rom discs to locate the patent. CD-Rom discs enable you to do a complete search of all registered patents but do not enable you to view the full patent, with all its specific details. Lastly, view the patent, which will be kept on microfilm, cartridge, or paper. What information there is to view varies by library, depending on what they have been able to purchase. If the library you are using does not have the patent you want, you may be able to obtain it through inter-library loan.

Copies of patents can be ordered from the PTO at 703-308-9726; 800-972-6382; Fax: 703-305-8759, for $3 per copy.

To obtain a certified copy of a patent, call 703-308-9726 (Patent Search Library at the PTO). The fee is $25 and you must have the patent number. For a certified copy of an abstract of titles, the fee is $25. For a certified copy of patent assignments, with a record of ownership from the beginning until present, call 703-308-9726. The cost is $25, and to request specific assignments you must have the reel and frame number.

Now You Have Got Your Patent

Once a Notice of Allowance stating that your application for patents approved, you have 3 months to pay another filing fee. If not, the application will be deemed abandoned. There are also maintenance fees due at 31/2, 71/2, and 111/2 years after the original grant. After it has expired, anyone may make, use, offer for sale, or sell or import the invention without the patentee's approval. A patent is personal property.

Tips

- Most importantly, do not reveal the details of your invention to anyone! If you need to do so, establish a confidential relationship with them by law or regulation, or a written agreement. Your plans and information you have gathered can be trade secrets and you must protect them.

- Record your discovery in detail as soon as possible and keep a record as you go. Have it witnessed by two reliable persons with a confidentiality agreement.

- Developing a new product is time consuming and expensive. Determine how much of your time, money, and effort you can invest. Know your personal limitations and when to get professional help.

- Twenty percent of patents issued each year are to private inventors. They must be effective business people to also research business concepts.

- Read articles by successful inventors for tips on what it took for them to market their product. Talk to potential customers to see what they would look for in the type of product that you are discovering.

- Remember, if a product similar to yours exists, you can still patent an improvement that is significant.

- Lastly, many times it is not the first try at inventing a product that is successful, it gets better as you go.

What Are Trademarks and Servicemarks?

A trademark is a word, name, symbol or device used in trade with goods to indicate the source of the goods and to set them apart from the goods of others. A servicemark is used to distinguish the source of a service instead of a product. Trademark or mark is generally the term used to refer to both trademarks and servicemarks. They are to keep others from using a confusingly similar mark, but not to keep others from making or selling the same goods or services under a clearly different mark. The Trademark Assistance Center will provide general information about the registration process and will respond to questions concerning the status of a specific trademark application and registration. They are available Monday through Friday from 8:30am to 5pm at 703-308-9000; {www.uspto.gov/main/trademarks.htm}.

Trademarks

Registering a trademark for your product or service is the way to protect the recognition quality of the name you are building. The PTO keeps records on more than 2.2 million trademarks and records. Over 500,000 active trademarks are kept on the floor of the library, while "dead" trademarks are kept on microfilm. Books contain every registered trademark ever issued, starting in 1870. You can visit the Patent and Trademark Office to research a trademark using the US Trademark Search Database at www.uspto.gov/tmdb/index.html. However, it will be replaced by the US Trademark Electronic Search System (TESS) soon. For now, both systems will be running. You can access TESS at http://tess.uspto.gov. You can then conduct your search manually for no charge or use their Trademark Search System (T-Search) for $40 per hour, plus $.25 cents per page.

Assistant Commissioner of Trademarks
Trademark Search Library
2900 Crystal Dr.
Second Floor, Room 2B30
Arlington, VA 22202   703-308-9800/9805

If you can't do it yourself, you can hire someone to do the search for you. For an agent to do this, consult the local yellow pages under "Trademark Agents/Consultants" or "Trademark Attorneys". You can also locate an agent by calling your local bar association for a referral.

To conduct your own search at a Patent Depository Library, use the CD-Rom disc on trademarks. It is available for purchase. The CD-Rom discs deliver patent and trademark information including full-text facsimile images and searchable text records. Images can be found in the *Official Gazette*, which contains most current and pending trademarks. The price for an annual subscription to the *Official Gazette* for trademarks is $980. It is issued every Tuesday and can be ordered from the U.S. Government Printing Office. You can also purchase an image file which contains pending and registered trademarks and corresponding serial or registration numbers through Thomson and Thomson by calling 1-800-692-8833. The information contained in it dates back to April 1, 1987 and is updated by approximately 500 images weekly. However, the PDL you use is likely to have an image of the trademark on microfilm or cartridge, and also have copies of the *Official Gazette*. If not, and you have the registration number, you may obtain a copy of the trademark you want for $3 from the PTO. Contact:

Assistant Commissioner of Trademarks
2900 Crystal Dr.
Second Floor, Room 2B30
Arlington, VA 22202   703-308-9800

There are also several commercial services you can use to conduct trademark searches.

Trademark Scan produced by Thomson and Thomson. It can be purchased by calling 1-800-692-8833 (ask for online services), or accessed directly via Saegis. Trademark Scan is updated three times per week, and includes state and federal trademarks, foreign and domestic. To access Trademark Scan you must already have Dialog or Saegis. Many online options are free. The Internet address is {www.thomson-thomson.com}.

Derwent, 1-800-337-9368, is a commercial service that will conduct patent searches only. The cost ranges from $100 and up with a turnaround time of 2-5 days. The Internet address is {www.derwent.com}.

Online services and database discs for both patents and trademarks are constantly being expanded. For information on an extensive range of existing and projected products, call the PTO Office of Electronic Information at 703-306-2600 and ask for the U.S. Department of Commerce, PTO Office of Information Systems' *Electronic Products Brochure*. For example, there is a Weekly Text File, containing text data of pending and registered trademarks. Information can be called up by using almost any term. It can be purchased from AvantIQ and Thomson & Thomson. You can reach AvantIQ at 1-800-320-6366, 973-594-0076, or online at {http://www.avantiq.lu/}. You can reach Thomson & Thomson at 1-800-692-8833 or online at {www.thomson-thomson.com}.

How to Register a Trademark

The right of a trademark comes from either the actual use of the mark, or by filing the correct application. There are two types of rights in a mark, the right to register it and the right to use the mark. The right to register is given to the first party that uses a mark in commerce, or who files an application at the PTO. The right to use a mark can be a complicated matter. For example, in the case where two people who do not know each other, start to use the same or similar marks without a registration. A court will have to decide who has the right to use the mark. Trademark rights last indefinitely if the owner continues its use. The registration last 10 years with 10 year renewal periods. You can order a free copy of Basic Facts about Trademarks from the U.S. Government Printing Office, or by calling the Trademark Search Library at 703-308-9000.

Types of Applications

The "use" application is for an applicant that already has been using their mark in commerce. The "intent-to-use" application is for those who have a bona fide intention of using the mark in commerce. These offer protection only in the US and it territories. Applications must be filed in the name of the owner of the mark.

For automated information about the status of a trademark application and registration, call 703-305-8747.

The Trademark Electronic Center

The Trademark Electronic Application System (TEAS) has step-by-step instructions for filling out forms and also contains information about the USPTO's procedures and practices. It also allows you to fill out the trademark forms, check them to be sure they are complete, and using e-TEAS, submit it on-line. You must be able to attach either a black-and-white GIF or JPG file to apply for a stylized or design mark. If a sample of actual use in commerce is needed, a scanned image or digital photo in GIF or JPG format must be attached. The final requirement is payment with a credit card or from an account already set up with the PTO. One mark can be filed with each application for a fee of $325, except for Class 9 and Class 25, where there is a $650 fee. E-TEAS will not accept applications from 11pm Saturday to 6am Sunday. Also, if you prefer to send the forms by mail, you can use PrinTEAS to print out your completed forms. You can send check, money order, or make arrangements for payment through a USPTO account. This system can be accessed 24 hours a day, 7 days a week.

You can check the status of marks using TARR-Trademark Applications and Registrations Retrieval at {http://tarr.uspto.gov}.

Symbols

Anyone who claims rights in a mark can use the symbols, TM (trademark) or SM (servicemark) to show that right. However, the registration symbol, an r in a circle ®, can not be used until the mark is registered.

The Right Way to Get a Copyright

Copyrights are filed on intellectual property. A copyright protects your right to control the sale, use of distribution, and royalties from a creation in thought, music, films, art, or books. It is an automatic form of protection for authors of published and unpublished "original works of authorship." The concrete form of expression as opposed to the subject matter is what is protected. Since a copyright is automatic when a work is created, registration is not required for protection. However, there are advantages to registration. If it is registered within 5 years of publication of the work, it establishes prima facie evidence of its validity and can be helpful in case of a court action. Generally the work is protected for the author's life plus 70 years after death.

For more information, contact:

Library of Congress
Copyright Office
101 Independence Avenue SE
Washington, DC 20559-6000   TTY: 202-707-6737
Public Information Office   202-707-3000
Email: copyinfo@loc.gov
www.loc.gov
www.loc.gov/copyright
www.copyright.gov

If you know which copyright application you require, you can call the Forms Hotline, open 7 days per week, 24 hours per day at 202-707-9100. The fee is $30 for each registration. Information on all of the different types of copyrights and their applications can be found at their web site.

The Library of Congress provides information on copyright registration procedures and copyright card catalogs that cover several million works that have been registered since 1870. The Copyright Office will research federal copyrights only for varying fees. Requests must be made in writing and you must specify exactly what information you require. If a work does not show any elements of copyright notice, you can search the Copyright Office's catalogs and records. The records from January 1, 1978, to the present can be searched on the Internet through the Library of Congress Information System (LOCIS). That web site address is {www.loc.gov/copyright/rb.html}.

Contact the Copyright Office, Reference and Bibliography, Library of Congress, 101 Independence Ave., SE, Washington, DC 20559; 202-707-6850, Public Information 202-707-3000.

What is Not Protected by Copyright

Works that have not been notated, recorded, or written can not be protected by copyright. Here are some others:

- titles, short phrases, and slogans; familiar symbols or designs; variations of ornamentation, lettering or coloring, listings of ingredients or contents
- concepts, methods, systems, principles, or devices, as opposed to description, explanation, and illustration
- works that are entirely made of information that is common property and do not contain any original authorship

Invention Scams: How They Work

Fake product development companies prey on amateur inventors who may not be as savvy about protecting their idea or invention as experienced inventors might be. Most of the bogus/fake companies use escalating fees.

The following is a description of how most of them operate:

- The inventor is invited to call or write for free information.

- The inventor is then offered a free evaluation of his idea.

- Next comes the sales call. The inventor is told he has a very good potential idea and that the company is willing to share the cost of marketing, etc. Actual fact, there is no sharing with these companies. Most times the inventor has to come up with the money (usually several hundred dollars or more) for a patent search and a market analysis. Neither of these are worth anything.

- Then the inventor receives a professional/ impressive looking portfolio which contains no real information at all. All the paper crammed into this portfolio looks topnotch, but it's all computer generated garbage.

- Upon receiving this portfolio, the inventor is lured into signing a contract that commits him to giving the company thousands of dollars to promote/license the product. The company sends some promotional letters to fulfill their obligation, but large manufacturers simply toss them into the trash.

After all this, the inventor has spent thousands of dollars, wasted a lot of time, and gotten nowhere with his product.

How To Avoid Losing a Fortune

According to the experts, the inventor should:

- Beware of the come-ons offered by these unethical companies. Avoid using the invention brokers who advertise on TV late in the evening; in public magazines; those who offer 800 numbers; and those on public transit display signs.

- When upfront money is required, look out. There are very few legitimate consultants who insist on a retainer or hourly fee.

- Don't allow the enthusiasm of your idea to take over your inherent common sense. Talk to your patent attorney and see if he knows anything about this company. Plus, check with inventors associations in the state, and see what they have to say about this particular company.

- Demand to know what percentage of ideas the company accepts. Legitimate brokers might accept 2 ideas out of every 100. The fake companies tend to accept about 99 out of 100.

- Find out their actual success rate. Any corporation/ company that will not give you their success rate (not licensing agreements) is a company to stay away from.

- Get an objective evaluation of your invention from reputable professionals. This will save you plenty of money on a bad idea.

A number of highly recommended programs are listed in the next section.

Free Help for Inventors

If you have a great idea and want to turn it into reality, don't rush out and spend what could be thousands of dollars for a private invention company and a patent attorney. You can get a lot of this help for free or at a fraction of the cost. There is a lot of help out there; university-sponsored programs, not-for-profit groups, state affiliated programs, profit-making companies, etc. Depending on the assistance and the organization, some services are free, others have reasonable fees.

Many of the inventors' organizations hold regular meetings where speakers share their expertise on topics such as licensing, financing and marketing. These groups are a good place for inventors to meet other inventors, patent attorneys, manufacturers, and others with whom they can talk and from whom they can get help.

If the listings in the state-by-state section of this chapter do not prove to be useful, you can contact one of the following organizations for help.

1. Small Business Development Center
    Washington State University
    Parkplace Building
    1200 6th Ave., Suite 1700 — 206-553-7328
    Seattle, WA 98101 — Fax: 206-553-7044
    www.wsbdc.org
    This service will evaluate your idea for a fee. They also provide counseling services and can assist you with your patent search.

2. Wisconsin Innovation Service Center/Technology
    Small Business Development Center
    Melissa Rick, Director
    University of Wisconsin - Whitewater
    402 McCutchan Hall — 262-472-1365
    Whitewater, WI 53190 — Fax: 262-472-1600
    www.sbdc.uww.edu
    The only service that is guaranteed is the evaluation. However, efforts are made to match inventors with exceptional high evaluation scores with manufacturers seeking new product ideas. (Do not offer direct invention development or marketing services). WISC charges a $495 flat fee for an evaluation. The goal is to keep research as affordable as possible to the average independent inventor. Most evaluations are completed within 30 - 45 days. Those inventions from specialized fields may require more time. WISC also provides preliminary patent searches via on-line databases to client.

3. Drake University
    Small Business Development Center
    Ms. Sherry Shafer, Director
    Drake Business Center — 515-271-2655
    2507 University — 1-800-532-1216
    Des Moines, IA 50311-4505 — Fax: 515-271-1899
    www.iabusnet.org
    INVENTURE is a program of the Drake University Business Development and Research Institute designed to encourage the development of valid ideas through the various steps to becoming marketable items. INVENTURE has no paid staff. The entire panel is made up of volunteers. The administration of the program is handled by existing staff from the Small Business Development Center and the College of Business and Public Administration. They will review items from **any person** regardless of their place of residence. They will review a product idea and check it for market feasibility. INVENTURE may link individuals with business and/or financial partners.

    INVENTURE screens every product submitted, but will not consider toy/game or food items. Products are evaluated on 33 different criteria, (factors related to legality, safety, business risk, and demand analysis, to market acceptance/ competition). It normally takes up to 6 weeks to receive results of the evaluation. Evaluators are experienced in manufacturing, marketing, accounting, production, finance and investments.

    INVENTURE acts in a responsible manner to maintain confidence of an idea, but cannot guarantee confidentiality.

For assistance with business plans, financial projections, and marketing help, you're encouraged to contact your Small Business Development Center (SBDC).

4. U.S. Department of Energy
    Mail Stop EE-24
    1000 Independence Ave., SW — 202-586-1478
    Washington, DC 20585-0121 — Fax: 202-586-7114
    www.oit.doe.gov/inventions/
    Financial assistance is available at 2 levels: up to $40,000 and up to $200,000 by the Inventions and Innovations program as stated by the Office of Industrial Technologies (OIT) Department of Energy (DOE) for ideas that significantly impact energy savings and future commercial market potential. Successful applicants will find technical guidance and commercialization support in addition to financial assistance.

    DOE has given financial support to more than 500 inventions with nearly 25% of these reaching the marketplace bringing in nearly $710 million in cumulative sales.

5. **U.S. Environmental Protection Agency**
    Center for Environmental Research Information
    Cincinnati, OH 45268 — 513-569-7578
    www.epa.gov
    Directory Description: Environmental Protection Agency, Office of Research and Development, 1200 Pennsylvania Ave., NW, Mail Code 8101R, Washington, DC 20460; 202-564-6620, Fax: 202-565-2910.
    The Office of Research and Development conducts an Agency wide integrated program of research and development relevant to pollution sources and control, transport and fate processes, health/ecological effects, measurement/monitoring, and risk assessment. The office provides technical reviews, expert consultations, technical assistance, and advice to environmental decision-makers in federal, state, local, and foreign governments.

    Center for Environmental Research Information
    26 W. ML King Drive, Cincinnati, OH 45268; 513-569-7578; Fax: 513-569-7585.
    A focal point for the exchange of scientific/ technical information both within the federal government and to the public.

    Office of Research and Development
    Is responsible for working with laboratories, program offices, regions to produce information products that summarize research, technical, regulatory enforcement information that will assist non-technical audiences in understanding environmental issues. Contact Office of Research and Development, U.S. Environmental Protection Agency, 1200 Pennsylvania Ave., NW, Washington, DC 20460; 202-564-6620; Fax: 202-565-2910.

    Office of Exploratory Research
    1200 Pennsylvania Ave., NW, Washington, DC 20460; 202-564-6825.
    The Office of Exploratory Research (OER) plans, administers, manages, and evaluates the Environmental Protection Agency's (EPA) extramural grant

research. It supports research in developing a better understanding of the environment and its problems. Main goals are: to support the academic community in environmental research; maintain scientific/technical personnel in environmental science/ technology; to support research for the identification/solution of emerging environmental problems.

Goals are accomplished through four core programs:

1.   **The Research Grants Program:**
Supports research initiated by individual investigators in areas of interest to the agency.

2.   **The Environmental Research Centers Program:**
Has two components: The Academic Research Center Program (ARC) and the Hazardous Substance Research Centers Program (HSRC).

3.   **The Small Business Innovation Research (SBIR) Program:**
Program supports small businesses for the development of ideas relevant to EPA's mission. Focuses on projects in pollution control development. Also receives 1.5% of the Agency's resources devoted to extramural Superfund research.

4.   **The Visiting Scientists Program:**
Components are an Environmental Science and Engineering Fellows Program and a Resident Research Associateship Program. The Fellows Program supports ten mid-career post-doctoral scientists and engineers at EPA headquarters & regional offices. The Research Associateship Program attracts national and international scientists and engineers at EPA research laboratories for up to 3 years to collaborate with Agency researchers on important environmental issues.

Other programs available are:
A Minority Fellowship Program
A Minority Summer Intern Program
The Agency's Senior Environmental Employment Program (SEE)
The Federal Workforce Training Program
An Experimental Program to Stimulate Competitive Research (EPSCoR).

To learn more, contact Grants Administration, U.S. Environmental Protection Agency, 1200 Pennsylvania Ave., NW, Washington, DC 20460; 202-260-2090. The best way, though, is to search for the word "grant" at the EPA's website, {www.epa.gov}.

State Sources for Inventors

Below is a listing of a variety of inventors groups, listed state by state. Some organizations listed under the state where they are located are regional or national in scope. In states where there is no specific program for inventors, the Small Business Development Centers (under the U.S. Small Business Administration) can often be of help. They are usually found at the colleges and universities. The Small Business Development Center office is located at 409 Third St., SW, Suite 4600, Washington, DC 20416; 202-205-6766; 800-UASK-SBA; {www.sba.gov}.

Alabama

Office for the Advancement of Developing Industries
University of Alabama - Birmingham
2800 Milan Ct.   205-934-6560
Birmingham, AL 35211   205-934-6563
http://main.uab.edu/oadi/show.asp?durkj=29458

Inventors can receive help on the commercialization and patent processes and critical reviews of inventions in this office. Assessments can be made on an invention's potential marketability and assistance is available for patent searches. There is a charge for services.

Small Business Development Center
University of Alabama at Birmingham
901 S. 15th St.   205-934-6760
Birmingham, AL 35294   Fax: 205-934-0538
www.business.uab.edu/SBDC/Index.htm

The center offers counseling for a wide range of business issues and problems.

U.S. Small Business Administration
Business Development
801 Tom Martin Drive   205-290-7101
Birmingham, AL 35211   Fax: 205-290-7443
www.sba.gov

This office offers counseling for a wide range of business issues and problems.

Invent Alabama
Bruce Koppenhoefer
137 Mission Circle   205-663-9982
Montevallo, AL 35115   Fax: 205-250-8013
Email: brucek@quixnet.net

Alaska

UA Small Business Development Center of Alaska
430 W. 7th Ave., Suite 110   907-274-7232
Anchorage, AK 99501   Fax: 907-274-9524
www.aksbdc.org

The SBDC provides general assistance, including free counseling to inventors on commercialization and patent processes, and arranging meetings between inventors, investors, manufacturers, and others who can be of help.

Alaska Inventors and Entrepreneurs Association
P.O. Box 241801
Anchorage, AK 99524   907-563-4337 (phone and fax)
www.artic.net/~inventor
Email: inventors@artic.net

They provide access to the tools and resources needed in order to empower inventors to bring their product to market. The InventorNet Resource Directory lists professional service providers, agents, designers, and much more. There are also monthly meetings, magazine subscription discounts, free access to the Internet and other benefits. There is a membership fee.

Inventors Institute of Alaska
Al Jorgensen
PO Box 876154
Wasilla, AK 99687   907-376-5114

Arizona

Arizona SBDC Network
2411 West 14th Street   480-731-8720
Tempe, AZ 85281   Fax: 480-731-8729

www.dist.maricopa.edu/sbdc

The center offers counseling for a wide range of business issues and problems.

Inventors Association of Arizona   520-721-9966
3104 E. Camelback #344   888-299-6787
Phoenix, AZ 85016   Fax: 602-912-9455
www.azinventors.org/
Email: linda@kangaring.com

Their goal is to guide the creativity of the members through experience, support and confidentiality so that they will be able to market their new invention or idea. Some of the areas they offer assistance in are, patent, trademark, and copyrights, manufacture, finance, and obtaining a product license. Benefits include discounts for legal services, Trade Magazine subscriptions, and consulting, as well as comprehensive information concerning the steps from concept to market. There is a membership fee.

Arkansas

Small Business Development Center
University of Arkansas at Little Rock   800-862-2040 (AR only)
100 S. Main, Suite 401   501-324-9043
Little Rock, AR 72201   Fax: 501-324-9049
http://asbdc.ualr.edu

The center offers counseling for a wide range of business issues and problems.

Inventors Congress Inc.
Garland Bull
Rt 2, Box 1630
Dandanell, AR 72834   501-229-4515

California

Small Business Development Center
1410 Ethan Way   916-563-3210
Sacramento, CA 95825   Fax: 916-563-2366
www.sbdc.net
Email: info@sbdc.net

The center offers counseling for a wide range of business issues and problems.

Inventors' Alliance
P.O. Box 390219   650-964-1576
Mountain View, CA 94039-390219   Fax: 650-964-1576
www.inventorsalliance.org
Email: president@inventorsalliance.org

They have monthly meeting with guest speakers on topics such as marketing and product development. These meetings are designed to increase the inventors knowledge and create contacts for a successful production of a product.

Inventors Forum
80 Huntington St. #9   714-540-2491
Huntington Beach, CA 92648   Fax: 714-668-0583
www.inventorsforum.org
Email: infor@inventorsforum.org

This nonprofit group teaches inventors about the invention process. Some of the products and services they provide are, the Invention Showcase, a listing of service providers for a number of different services, and an inventors message base with a range of topics.

Redwood Empire Small Business
Development Center   888-346-SBDC
606 Healdsburg Avenue   707-524-1770

Santa Rosa, CA 95401
www.santarosa.edu/sbdc/
Email: sbdc@santarosa.edu

Fax: 707-524-1772

They have a Patent Information Network where inventor clients perform initial patent searches to help in forming an assessment of an idea or design. They also offer one-on-one professional business consulting. There is no charge for these services.

Central Valley Inventor's Assn.
John Christensen
P.O. Box 1551
Manteca, CA 95336
Email: cdesigns@softcom.net

209-239-8090

Inventors Forum of San Diego
Greg Lauren
11292 Poblado Road
San Diego, CA 92127
Email: Enovex@aol.com

858-451-1028
Fax: 858-451-6154

Bruce Sawyer Center
Steve Schneider
4261 Brookshire Circle
Santa Rosa, CA 95405
Email: sbdc1@ap.net

707-524-1773

American Inventor Network
Jeff McGrew
1320 High School Rd.
Sebastopol, CA 95472

707-823-3865
Fax: 707-823-0913

Inventors Alliance of Northern California
Jim DeLang
6514 Elmira Drive
Redding, CA 96001
Email: sagn@charter.net
www.inventorsnorcal.org

530-241-5222

Established in 1999, the IANC assists inventors in the patent process, and the development and marketing of ideas and products.

Idea to Market Network
Sidnee Cox
P.O. Box 12248
Santa Rosa, CA 95406
www.ideatomarket.org
Email: sidnee@ap.net

1-800-ITM-3210

Idea to Market is a network of inventors who guide fellow members through the inventive process.

Colorado

Affiliated Inventors Foundation, Inc.
1405 Porter St., #107
Colorado Springs, CO 80909
To order free Info Kit
www.affiliatedinventors.com
Email: info@affiliatedinventors.com

719-380-1234
Fax: 800-380-3862
800-525-5885

This foundation counsels inventors on commercialization and patent processes, and provides detailed information on the steps needed to reach commercialization. Preliminary appraisals, evaluations and other services are available for a fee.

Small Business Development Center
Office of Economic Development
1625 Broadway, Suite 1710
Denver, CO 80202
www.state.co.us/oed/sbdc

303-892-3864
Fax: 303-892-3848

The center offers counseling for a wide range of business issues and problems.

Rocky Mountain Inventors & Entrepreneurs
Congress (RMIC)
P.O. Box 36233
Denver, CO 80236-0233
www.RMinventor.org
Email: info@RMinventor.org

303-670-3760
Fax: 720-962-5026

Their mission is to help people with new ideas to fulfill their greatest potential. Their members include new and established inventors, prototypers, manufactures, marketers, patent attorneys and others connected to the invention process. Besides dinner and round table meetings, they have networking sessions, monthly educational meetings and an annual conference. They offer information on the invention process, the tools needed and advice on what to do with the invention. Three is a dinner meeting fee.

Connecticut

Small Business Development Center
University of Connecticut
2100 Hillside Road, Unit 1094
Storrs, CT 06269-1094
www.sbdc.uconn.edu
Email: CSBDCinformation@sba.uconn.edu

860-486-4135
Fax: 860-486-1576

The center offers counseling for a wide range of business issues and problems.

Inventors Association of Connecticut
9-B Greenhouse Road
Bridgeport, CT 06606-2130
www.inventus.org
Email: IACTWinventus.org

203-866-0720
Fax: 781-846-6448

This is a nonprofit group who has members that include inventors, designers, engineers, attorneys, and business people. They look to nurture, stimulate creativity and advance the image of independent inventors by education, promotion and sharing of member resources. They have monthly meeting with pre-meeting session, and a newsletter to accomplish this goal. There is a monthly fee.

Inventors Assn. of Connecticut
Pal Asija
7 Woonsocket Ave.
Shelton, CT 06484
Email: pal@ourpal.com

203-924-9538

Delaware

Small Business Development Center
University of Delaware
One Innovation Way, Suite 301
Newark, DE 19711
www.delawaresbdc.org

302-831-1555
Fax: 302-831-1423

The office offers management counseling and seminars on various topics, and can counsel inventors on areas such as the commercialization and patenting processes. Services are by appointment only.

Delaware Economic Development
99 Kings Highway
Dover, DE 19901
www.state.de.us/dedo/departments/finance/sbir.htm

302-739-4271
Fax: 302-739-2028

Assistance is available to any applicant located in Delaware or relocating to Delaware, who has been granted a phase I SBIR award and has submitted a Phase II SBIR application.

Early Stage East
3 Mill Road, Suite 201A
Wilmington, DE 19806
Email: info@earlystageeast.org

302-777-2460

District of Columbia

U.S. Department of Commerce
U.S. Patent and Trademark Office
Crystal Plaza 3, Room 2C02
Washington, DC 20231
www.uspto.gov
Email: usptoinfo@uspto.gov

800-PTO-9199
703-308-4357

District of Columbia Small Business Development Center
Howard University
2600 6th St., NW, Suite 128
Washington, DC 20059
www.bschool.howard.edu/sbdc/index.htm
Email: husbdc@cldc.howard.edu

202-806-1550
Fax: 202-806-1777

The center offers counseling for a wide range of business issues and problems.

U.S. Small Business Administration
1110 Vermont Ave., NW, 9th Floor
Washington, DC 20005
www.sba.gov

202-606-4000
Fax: 202-606-4225

This office provides general assistance and information on funding.

Inventors Network of the Capital Area
Ray Gilbert
6501 Inwood Drive
Springfield, VA 22150
Email: Raybik@aol.com
http://inca.hispeed.com

703-971-7443
Fax: 703-971-9216

This is a non-profit educational organization offering monthly meetings, guest speakers, and networking with fellow inventors.

Florida

Small Business Development Center
University of North Florida   904-620-2476
12000 Alumni Drive   800-450-4624 (in FL)
Jacksonville, FL 32224   Fax: 904-620-2567
www.sbdc.unf.edu
Email: smallbiz@unf.edu
The center offers counseling for a wide range of business issues and problems.

Small Business Development Center
University of West Florida
1170 Martin L. King, Jr. Blvd.   850-863-6543
Fort Walton Beach, FL 32547   Fax: 850-863-6543
www.sbdc.uwf.edu
The center offers counseling for a wide range of business issues and problems.

Florida SBDC Network
19 W. Garden St., Suite 302   850-595-5480
Pensacola, FL 32501   Fax: 850-595-5487
www.floridasbdc.com
The network provides general assistance; conducts market/ technical assessments; offers legal advice on patents and licensing; provides funding information; and assists in building a prototype. Inventors get to showcase their inventions and meet with other inventors and investors.

University of Central Florida
Small Business Development Center
12565 Research Parkway, Suite 300   407-823-5554
Orlando, FL 32826-2909   Fax: 407-384-2868
www.bus.ucf.edu/sbdc
The center provides general assistance, funding information and conducts market assessments. Inventors meet other inventors.

Edison Inventors Association
P.O. Box 07398   941-275-4332
Ft. Meyers, FL 33919   Fax: 941-267-9746
www.edisoninventors.org
Email: drghn@aol.com
They are a non-profit group whose goal is to aid creativity and assistance inventors and entrepreneurs to be successful. They have monthly meetings.

Inventors Society of South Florida
P.O. Box 4306
Boynton Beach, FL 33424   954-486-2426
Email: abbysideas@aol.com
They consider themselves a non-profit educational society. The guest speakers include patent agents, attorneys, government sources, engineers, technicians and more. You will be able to ask questions of the guest and also network with other inventors at monthly meetings.

Tampa Bay Inventors' Council
5901 Third Street South
St. Petersburg, FL 33705   727-866-0669 (phone/fax)
http://patent-faq.com/tbichome.htm
Email: KIEWIT@patent-faq.com
This non-profit organization educates its members and others about invention product development and marketing. The meetings are a public forum for people who have information for inventors and for inventors that have questions. Members also get a monthly newsletter, a current member directory and reference materials. There is a membership fee.

Space Coast Inventors Guild
1221 Pine Tree Drive
Indian Harbour Beach, FL 32937   321-773-4031 (phone/fax)
They accept the challenge to help people in the development of an idea so they can present for a patent. The monthly meetings are open to the public and there is no charge to attend.

Inventors Council of Central Florida
David Flinchbaugh
4855 Big Oaks Ln.
Orlando, FL 32806-7826   407-859-4855

Georgia

Small Business Development Center
University of Georgia
Chicopee Complex
1180 East Broad Street   706-542-7436
Athens, GA 30602   Fax: 706-542-6803
www.sbdc.uga.edu
The center offers counseling for a wide range of business issues and problems.

Inventor Associates of Georgia
P.O. Box 888163
Dunwoody, GA 30356   478-474-6948
www.geocities.com/iaggroup/   Fax: 478-474-2602
Email: miquelon80@aol.com
A group of experts and novices that assist independent inventors with the process of developing their ideas so that they can be marketed. Partly, this is accomplished by Q&A with members and impartial evaluations of inventions. There are monthly meetings with roundtable discussions afterwards. There is a membership fee.

Inventor Assoc. of Georgia, Inc.
Scott Parker
PO Box 888163
Dunwoody, GA 30356   770-908-7386 (phone/fax)
Email: tropez99@yahoo.com
www.geocities.com/iaggroup
IAG, Inc. assists independent inventors in getting their product to market.

Hawaii

Small Business Development Center
University of Hawaii at Hilo
308 Kamehameha Avenue, Suite 201   808-974-7515
Hilo, HI 96720   Fax: 808-974-7683
http://hawaii-sbdc.org
The center offers counseling for a wide range of business issues and problems.

Idaho

Idaho Research Foundation, Inc.
University of Idaho
Morrill Hall 103
P.O. Box 443003   208-885-4550
Moscow, ID 83844   Fax: 208-885-0105
www.irf.uro.uidaho.edu
Email: irf@uidaho.edu
This foundation counsels inventors on commercialization and patent processes, and provides critical reviews on inventions. Computerized data searching and marketing service is available. It takes a percentage of intellectual property royalties.

Small Business Development Center
Boise State University   800-225-3815 (in ID)
1910 University Drive   208-426-1640
Boise, ID 83725   Fax: 208-426-3877
www.idahosbdc.org
Email: info@idahosbdc.org
The center offers counseling for a wide range of business issues and problems.

Idaho Small Business Development Center
College of Southern Idaho
P.O. Box 1238
315 Falls Ave.   208-733-9554
Twin Falls, ID 83303-1238   Fax: 208-733-9316
www.csi.edu/support/isbdc/sbdc.html
Email: srust@csi.edu
The center conducts market assessments and provides funding information.

Idaho Small Business Development Center
Lewis-Clark State College
500 8th Ave.   208-792-2465
Lewiston, ID 83501   Fax: 208-792-2878
www.lcsc.edu/isbdc
Email: SLWagner@lcsc.edu
The center provides general assistance and funding information. They also conduct market assessments.

Idaho State University
Small Business Development Center
2300 N. Yellowstone   208-523-1087
Idaho Falls, ID 83401   Fax: 208-528-7127
Email: woodrhon@isu.edu
The center provides general assistance and funding information, and conducts technical assessments. Inventors meet with other inventors and investors.

Illinois

Small Business Development Center
Department of Commerce and Community Affairs

620 East Adams St., 3rd Floor   217-782-7500
Springfield, IL 62701   Fax: 217-785-6328
www.commerce.state.il.us
The center offers counseling for a wide range of business issues and problems, including commercialization and patent processes.

Small Business Development Center
Evanston Business Investment Corp.
1840 Oak Avenue   847-866-1817
Evanston, IL 60201-3670   Fax: 847-866-1808
The center provides general assistance and funding information.

Western Illinois University
Technical Center and Small Business Development Center
Seal Hall 214   309-298-2211
Macomb, IL 61455-1390   Fax: 309-298-2520
The center provides general assistance; conducts market/technical assessments; provides investment and funding information; and aids in building a prototype. Inventors meet with other inventors and investors, and get the chance to showcase their inventions.

Illinois Innovators and Inventor's Club
P.O. Box 623
Edwardsville, IL 62025   618-656-7445
Email: invent@charter-IL.com
They are a non-profit group created to exchange useful information and ideas. Membership fees cover monthly meetings, newsletters, and events.

Inventors' Council
431 South Dearborn, Suite 705   312-939-3329
Chicago, IL 60605   Fax: 312-922-7706
www.donmoyer.com
Email: patent@donmoyer.com
There is a multitude of information and links to information at this web site. Patent searching tools, how to get a free patent application if you are eligible, technology information, science facts, where to look for money, and so much more is available. Mostly, their workshops are in virtual reality on the web, but they still hold some of them in person, and they are free! They list tips from them, such as The Fool Rule, The secrets Rule and other basics. Mr. Moyer cannot answer questions over the phone, but he will do so through Email.

Indiana

Small Business Development Center   Toll-free: 888-ISBD-244
One North Capitol, Suite 900   317-234-2082
Indianapolis, IN 46204   Fax: 317-232-8872
www.isbdcorp.org
The center offers counseling for a wide range of business issues and problems.

Indiana Inventors Association
5514 South Adams   765-674-2845
Marion, IN 46953   Fax: 765-733-0579
Email: arhumbert@bpsinet.com
This is an informal non-profit group. Their members include inventors, engineers, educators and more. They are concerned with the innovation process and look to answer questions and solve problems at the monthly meetings. There is no fee.

Iowa

Small Business Development Center
Iowa State University
2501 N. Loop Drive   800-373-7232
Bldg. 1, Suite 1615   515-296-7828
Ames, IA 50010-8283   Fax: 515-296-6714
www.iabusnet.org
The center offers counseling for a wide range of business issues and problems.

Drake Small Business Development Center and
Inventure Program
2507 University Avenue   515-271-2655
Des Moines, IA 50311   Fax: 515-271-1899
The Inventure Program is a program within the Small Business Development Center. In the program, they will evaluate a product so that the inventor can decide if it is feasible to go to market. There is a fee of $125 and it is open to all people in the nation. The Small Business Development Center offers counseling on commercialization and other business aspects. There is no charge for this and it is only open to residents of Iowa.

Kansas

Small Business Development Center
Wichita State University
Campus Box 148
1845 Fairmont   316-978-3193
Wichita, KS 67260-0148   Fax: 316-978-3647
http://webs.wichita.edu/depttools/user_home/?view=ksbdc
Email: wsusbdc@wichita.edu
The center offers counseling for a wide range of business issues and problems.

Inventors' Association of South Central Kansas
2302 Amarado
Wichita, KS 67205   316-721-1866
www.networksplus.net/aledarich
Email: aledarich@networksplus.net
They have monthly meetings with a guest speaker who takes questions after finishing the speech. Reports of important information concerning the group, discussions and workshops are included. Guests and members must sign a non-disclosure agreement to protect the ideas that are discussed. There is a membership fee.

Kansas Association of Inventors
Clayton Williamson
272 W. 6th St.
Hoisington, KS 67544   316-653-2165
Email: clayton@hoisington.com

Kentucky

Small Business Development Center
University of Louisville
Burhans Hall, Room 122
Shelby Campus   502-852-7854
Louisville, KY 40292   Fax: 502-852-8573
www.ksbdc.org
This center counsels inventors on commercialization and patent processes and provides critical reviews of inventions. It provides assistance in technically refining inventions. There are no fees.

Small Business Development Center
Kentucky Small Business Development Center
Center for Business Development
College of Business and Economics Building
225 Business and Economics Building
University of Kentucky   859-257-7668
Lexington, KY 40506-0034   Fax: 859-323-1907
www.ksbdc.org
The center offers counseling for a wide range of business issues and problems.

Kentucky Transportation Center
176 Oliver H. Raymond Bldg.   859-257-4513
Lexington, KY 40506-0281   Fax: 859-257-1815
www.engr.uky.edu/ktc
The center works closely with various federal, state and local agencies, as well as the private sector to conduct research supported by a wide variety of sources.

Central Kentucky Inventors & Entrepreneurs
117 Carolyn Drive   606-885-9593
Nicholosville, KY 40356   Fax: 606-887-9850
Email: nashky@IBM.net
This is a nonprofit group that helps each other with patents, analysis, and a business plan so that their products can be marketed. Membership fees cover monthly meetings and a newsletter.

Central Kentucky Inventors Council, Inc.
Donald L. West, President
3060 Pine Ridge Road
Winchester, KY 40391   859-842-4110
Email: dlwest3@yahoo.com

Louisiana

Small Business Development Center
Northeast Louisiana University
College of Business Administration
700 University Avenue, Room 2-57   318-342-1224
Monroe, LA 71209   Fax: 318-342-1209
The center offers counseling for a wide range of business issues and problems.

Louisiana Department of Economic Development
P.O. Box 94185
101 France St.
Baton Rouge, LA 70804-9185   225-342-3000
www.lded.state.la.us
The department provides general assistance.

Maine

Department of Industrial Cooperation
5717 Corbet Hall, Room 480   207-581-2200
Orono, ME 04469-5711   Fax: 207-581-1479
www.umaine.edu/dic

On March 15, 1984, the Inventors Forum of Maine, Inc. (IFM), was formed and became a nonprofit corporation in the state of Maine. It was organized to stimulate inventiveness and entrepreneurship, and to help innovators and entrepreneurs develop and promote their ideas. It allows inventors and entrepreneurs to join together, share ideas and hopefully improve the chance for success. It gives encouragement, professional expertise, evaluation assistance, confidentiality and moral support of the University of Maine's Network and the University of Southern Maine's Small Business Development Center.

The Inventors Forum of Maine generally meets on the first Tuesday evening of each month at the University of Southern Maine, Campus Center, Room A, B & C on Bedford Street in Portland. Membership is open to all. For information regarding the Inventors Forum of Maine, contact Jake Ward, 207-581-1488.

Portland Inventors' Forum
5717 Corbett Hall, Room 480
University of Maine   207-581-1488
Orono, ME 04469-5717   Fax: 207-581-1479
www.umaine.edu/DIC/Invent/IFM.htm
Email: jsward@maine.edu

This group of inventors and business people offer encouragement, professional expertise, confidentiality and evaluation assistance to its members. At the monthly meeting they have Show & Tell, speakers and open discussions. There is no membership fee.

Maryland

Inventions and Innovations
Department of Energy
Forrestal Building
1000 Independence Ave., SW
Washington, DC 20585-0121   202-586-2079
www.oit.doe.gov/inventions

The office evaluates all promising non-nuclear energy-related inventions, particularly those submitted by independent inventors and small companies for the purpose of obtaining direct grants for their development from the U.S. Department of Energy.

Small Business Development Center
MMG, Inc.
826 E. Baltimore Street   410-333-2548
Baltimore, MD 21202   Fax: 410-333-2552
www.mmggroup.com

The center offers counseling for a wide range of business issues and problems.

Massachusetts

Massachusetts Small Business Development Center
Salem State College
121 Loring Avenue, Suite 310
Salem, MA 01970   978-542-6343
www.salemsbdc.org

The center offers counseling for a wide range of business issues and problems.

Small Business Development Center
227 Isenberg School of Management
121 Presidents Drive
University of Massachusetts   413-545-6301
Amherst, MA 01003-9310   Fax: 413-545-1273
http://msbdc.som.umass.edu

The center provides general assistance and funding information.

Smaller Business Association of New England
204 2nd Ave.   781-890-9070
Waltham, MA 02451   Fax: 781-890-4567
www.sbane.org

The association provides general assistance and funding information.

Inventors Association of New England (IANE)
P.O. Box 335   978-433-2397
Lexington, MA 02420-0004   Fax: 978-433-3516
www.inventne.org
Email: crholt@aol.com

At the monthly meetings, they discuss things such as patent protection, licensing, manufacturing and avoiding scams. They also have guest speakers and free workshops. Their inventor shows and exhibits showcase member's inventions. Membership dues cover meetings, a monthly newsletter, and discounts to trade shows, and some publications.

Inventors Resource Network
P.O. Box 137
Shutesbury, MA 01072-0137   413-259-2006
http://pages.prodigy.net/pwassoc/irn.html
Email: info@irnetwork.org

The center of this group of inventors and business people have either created successful businesses with their invention, or they have been licensed. They focus on getting the product to market. Monthly meeting alternate between public and private. They involve networking, announcements, assistance and a guest speaker.

Worcester Area Innovators
132 Sterling Street   508-835-6435
West Boylston, MA 01583   Fax: 805-799-2796
Email: lore1930@aol.com

This group has monthly meetings with informal networking and guest speakers. There are no summer meetings. They put out a monthly newsletter and there is a minimal membership fee.

Cape Cod Inventors Association
Ernest Bauer
Briar Main
P.O. Box 143
Wellfleet, MA 02667   508-349-1628

Greater Boston Inventors Association
Inventors Association of New England
Chris Holt
P.O. Box 577   978-433-2397
Pepperal, MA 01463   Fax: 978-433-3516
Email: crholt@aol.com
www.inventne.org

Expert speakers and members join together to provide guidance to inventors in the areas of patents, marketing, and product development.

Michigan

Small Business Development Center
Grand Valley State University
Seidman School of Business
510 W. Fulton Street   616-336-7480
Grand Rapids, MI 49504   Fax: 616-336-7485
www.mi-sbdc.org

The center offers counseling for a wide range of business issues and problems.

Inventors Club of America
524 Curtis Road
East Lansing, MI 48823   517-332-3561

They meet monthly where a roll call is kept. They have an open quorum and look to help each other with past experiences.

Inventor's Council of Mid-Michigan (ICMM)
519 South Saginaw Street, Suite 200   810-232-7909
Flint, MI 48502   Fax: 810-233-7437
www.flintchamber.org
Email: bross@flint.org

The goal is to help members with patents, trademarks, and copyrights and to get their inventions to market without a large cost. The monthly dues cover meetings and a 2 year subscription to Inventors Digest.

Inventors Association of Metropolitan Detroit
Frank Wales
749 Clairepointe Circle
St. Clair, MI 48081
Email: unclefj@yahoo.com

Minnesota

Minnesota Project Innovation, Inc.
100 Mill Place
111 Third Ave. S.   612-338-3280
Minneapolis, MN 55401   Fax: 612-349-2603

www.mpi.org
This project is affiliated with the Minnesota Dept. of Energy and Economic Development, U.S. Small Business Administration, and private companies. It provides referrals to inventors for sources of technical assistance in refining inventions.

Minnesota Inventors Congress (MIC)
P.O. Box 71   507-637-2344
Redwood Falls, MN 56283   Fax: 507-637-8399
www.invent1.org   800-INVENT1
Email: mic@invent1.org

The Minnesota Inventors Congress (MIC) is a nonprofit organization established in 1958 to promote creativity, innovation, entrepreneurship by assisting the inventor and entrepreneur with education, promotion and referral. It's a professional organization composed of private individuals and corporations, who are creating and developing useful technologies. MIC is for inventors at every development stage - the novice and experienced; male or female; young and old; and supporters of invention and innovation. Workshops are also available. These are for individuals with ideas or inventions not yet successfully on the market; for companies, entrepreneurs looking for such inventions or new products.

"World's Oldest Annual Invention Convention," promotes the spirit of invention and innovation. Each year a 3-day convention presents more than 200 inventions and attracts some 10,000 visitors from around the world. The MIC provides a meeting place for:

1. Inventors to showcase their new products, connecting with manufacturers/investors, product test market, educational seminars, publicity, inventors network, and $1,500 in cash awards.

2. Manufacturers, marketers, investors and licenses seeking new products.

3. Inventors, viewers and exhibitors, seeking free counsel and literature on the invention development process.

4. Public to view the latest inventions, by adults and students, purchase MarketPlace products and meet global inventors.

University of Minnesota, Duluth
Center for Economic Development
Duluth Technology Village   Toll free: 888-387-4594
11 East Superior Street, Suite 210.   218-726-7298
Duluth, MN 55802   Fax: 218-726-6338
www.umdced.com

The center offers counseling for a wide range of business issues and problems.

Society of Minnesota Inventors
10355 Riverdale Drive, Suite 500-236   763-753-2766
Cedar Rapids, MN 55448   Fax: 763-753-6817
www.inventorsnetwork.org
Email: paulparis@uswest.net

With two meetings a month, this group aims to educate inventors. They have inventor question and answer, discussion sessions, and conduct general business. There is a small monthly fee.

Inventors' Network (Mpls./St.Paul)
Bill Baker
23 Empire Dr., Suite 105
St. Paul, MN 55103

Mississippi

Mississippi State University
Small Business Development Center
P.O. Box 5288   662-325-8684
Mississippi State, MS 39762   Fax: 662-325-4016
www.cbi.msstate.edu/cobi/sbdc/sbdc.html

The center provides general assistance; conducts market assessments; and provides funding information.

Small Business Development Center
Meridian Community College   800-MCC-THE1
910 Highway 19 North   601-482-7445
Meridian, MS 39307   Fax: 601-482-5803
www.mcc.cc.ms.us/webbcenter/sbdchome.htm

The center provides general assistance and funding information; conducts market/technical assessments; and offers legal advice on patents and licensing. Inventors meet with other inventors and investors.

Society of Mississippi Inventors
B19 Jeannette Phillips Dr.
P.O. Box 1848
                                   800-725-7232 (MS)

University of Mississippi   601-232-5001
University, MS 38677-1848   Fax: 601-232-5650
www.olemiss.edu/depts/msbdc/invent.html
Email: msbdc@olemiss.edu

This Small Business Development Center specializes in assisting inventors. They help inventors to get started with an idea, give them sources for evaluation, patents, trademarks, finance, and specialized assistance. There are also seminars and workshops.

Mississippi SBDC Inventor Assistance
Bob Lantrip   662-915-5001
B 19 Jeanette Phillips Dr.   800-725-7232 (in MS only)
Fax: 662-915-5650
Email: blantrip@olemiss.edu
http://www.olemiss.edu/depts/mssbdc/invent.html

This organization provides a wide range of services to assist Mississippi residents through the invention process.

Missouri

Missouri Innovation Center
5650 S. Sinclair Rd.   573-446-3100
Columbia, MO 65203   Fax: 573-443-3748
www.marketmaker.org/aboutus.htm
Email: info@marketmaker.org

This group provides communications among inventors, manufacturers, patent attorneys and venture capitalists, and provides general consultations. It is sponsored by the state, city of Columbia, and the University of Missouri. There are fees for some services.

Inventors Association of St. Louis
P.O. Box 410111
St. Louis, MO 63141   314-432-1291
www.uspto.gov/web/offices/com/comm06feb2002.html
Email: dayjobiasl@webtunet

The group holds monthly meetings, provides communications among inventors, manufacturers, patent attorneys, and venture capitalists. It publishes a newsletter. There are annual dues.

Small Business Development Center
University of Missouri - Columbia
1205 University Ave.
Suite 1800 University Pl.   573-882-7096
Columbia, MO 65211   Fax: 573-882-9931
Email: sbdc-c@ext.missouri.edu
www.mo-sbdc.org

The center offers counseling for a wide range of business issues and problems.

Women's Inventor Project
Betty Rozier
7400 Foxmount
Hazlewood, MO 63042

Mid-America Inventors Association
Carl Minzes
8911 East 29th St.   816-254-9542
Kansas City, MO 64129-1502   Fax: 816-221-3995

Montana

Small Business Development Center
Montana Department of Commerce
301 South Park
P.O. Box 200505   406-841-2746
Helena, MT 59620   Fax: 406-841-2728
www.commerce.state.mt.us
Email: adesch@state.mt.us

The center offers counseling for a wide range of business issues and problems.

Montana Inventors Association
5350 Love Lane   406-586-1541
Bozeman, MT 59715   Fax: 406-585-9028

They have a yearly 2-day meeting for inventors. The guest speaker is a known inventor or a patent officer. They will answer questions and have discussions and some of the inventors talk about the process they used to market their product. They also have a member directory.

Blue Sky Inventors
Warren George
1200 Blair Lane, Apt. #1
Billings, MT 59102   406-259-9110

Nebraska

University of Nebraska – Lincoln
Engineering Extension
W 191 Nebraska Hall   402-472-5600
Lincoln, NE 68588-0525   Fax: 402-472-0015
www.engext.unl.edu/engext.html

Upon request, the University will send a packet of information so that the individual may go to the location and conduct their own Patent and Trademark search.

Nebraska Business Development Center
University of Nebraska at Omaha
Roskens Hall
CBA, Room 415   402-554-2521
Omaha, NE 68182-02458   Fax: 402-554-3473

The center offers counseling for a wide range of business issues and problems.

Lincoln Inventors Association
Roger Reyda
92 Ideal Way
Brainard, NE 68626   402-545-2179 (phone/fax)

Nevada

Nevada Small Business Center
University of Nevada - Reno
College of Business Administration, Room 411
Reno, NV 89557-0100   775-784-1717
www.nsbdc.org   Fax: 775-784-4337
Email: nsbdc@unr.nevada.edu

The center provides general assistance and funding information. Inventors meet with other inventors and get to showcase their inventions.

Nevada Small Business Center
3720 Howard Hughes Pkwy., Suite 130   702-734-7575
Las Vegas, NV 89109   Fax: 702-734-7633
www.nsbdc.org
Email: nsbdc@univ.edu

The center provides general assistance and funding information. Inventors meet with other inventors.

Inventors Society of Southern Nevada
3627 Huerta Drive
Las Vegas, NV 89121   702-435-7741
Email: InventSSN@aol.com

Here inventors will learn the process from A to Z. The group will answer questions and send its members in the correct direction to accomplish their goals. They host different speakers from the field at monthly meetings which are open to the public. All ideas are kept confidential. There are yearly dues that cover all of this plus a newsletter.

Nevada Inventors Association
P.O. Box 11008   702-677-0123
Reno, NV 89510-1108   Fax: 702-677-1322
www.nevadainventors.org
Email: inventors@nevadainventors.org

They offer education, assistance, and networking to their members. Anywhere from one to nine guests will show up at the monthly meetings. They also put together a monthly newsletter.

New Hampshire

Small Business Development Center
University of New Hampshire
108 McConnell Hall   603-862-2200
Durham, NH 03824   Fax: 603-862-4876
www.nhsbdc.org
Email: mary.collins@unh.edu

The center offers counseling for a wide range of business issues and problems.

Small Business Development Center
670 N. Commercial Street
Fourth Floor, Suite 1   603-624-2000
Manchester, NH 03101   Fax: 603-647-4410
www.nhsbdc.org
Email: rte@cisunix.unh.edu

The Small Business Development Center provides general assistance and funding information, and offers legal advice on patents and licensing. Inventors meet with other inventors.

New Hampshire Inventors Association
P.O. Box 2772
Concord, NH 03302   603-526-6939
www.patentcafe.com/inventor_orgs/nhia.html
Email: dunmark@tdk.net

It is their mission to encourage and assist inventors in evaluating, patenting and commercializing their products. They teach them about the patent process and supply them with information and resources. There are speakers at the monthly meetings, workshops, and seminars. Inventors will be able to learn from others through networking. The membership fee covers all of this and a newsletter.

New Jersey

Small Business Development Center
Rutgers University
43 Bleeker St.   973-353-5950
Newark, NJ 07102-1897   Fax: 973-353-1030
http://njsbdc.com/home

The Small Business Development Center offers counseling for a wide range of business issues and problems.

Jersey Shore Inventors Club
416 Park Place Avenue   732-776-8467
Bradley Beach, NJ 07720   Fax: 732-776-5418
Email: 2edeilmcclain@msn.com

They have monthly meetings where inventors can learn from each other.

National Society of Inventors
94 North Rockledge Dr.   973-994-9282
Livingston, NJ 07039-1121   Fax: 973-535-0777

This group is "Inventor Friendly". They are inventors helping each other in the New Jersey area. They offer meetings that either have speakers or round table discussions that are open to the public. There is a minimal membership fee.

Kean Univ. SBDC
Mira Kostak
215 North Ave., Room 242   908-527-2946
Union NJ 07083   Fax: 908-527-2960
Email: mkostak@cougar.kean.edu

New Jersey Entrepreneurs Forum
Jeff Millinetti
325 Kimball Ave   908-789-3424
Westfield, NJ 07090   Fax: 908-789-9761

New Mexico

New Mexico Invention Club
P.O. Box 30062
Albuquerque, NM 87190   505-266-3541 (phone/fax)

The contact is Dr. Albert Goodman, president of the club. The club meets on a monthly basis for speakers and presentations by different inventors. Members include patent attorneys, investors, and manufacturers.

Small Business Development Center
Santa Fe Community College   800-281-7232
6401 Richards Ave.   505-428-1362
Santa Fe, NM 87505   Fax: 505-428-1469
www.nmsbdc.org
Email: info@nmsbdc.org

The center offers counseling for a wide range of business issues and problems.

New York

Small Business Development Center
University of Albany
One Pinnacle Place, Suite 218   518-443-9567
Albany, NY 12203-3439   Fax: 518-443-9572
www.nyssbdc.org
Email: albsbdc@nycap.rr.com

The center offers counseling for a wide range of business issues and problems.

New York State Energy Research and Development Authority
17 Columbia Circle   Toll free: 866-NYSERDA
Albany, NY 12203-6399   518-862-1090
www.nyserda.org   Fax: 518-862-1091

The office provides general assistance and investment and funding information. It assists in building a prototype.

SUNY Institute of Technology
Small Business Development Center
P.O. Box 3050 315-792-7547
Utica, NY 13504 Fax: 315-792-7554
www.sbdc.sunyit.edu
Email: sbdc@sunyit.edu

The center provides general assistance and funding information; conducts market/technical assessments; offers legal advice on patents and licensing, and assists in building a prototype. Inventors meet with other inventors.

Small Business Technology Investment Fund
New York State Science and Technology Foundation
30 South Pearl St. 800-782-8369
Albany, NY 12245 518-473-9741
www.empire.state.ny.us/
Email: sbtif@empire.state.ny.us

The program provides financing assistance for technology-based start-up companies with initial investment as much as $300,000.

Inventors Alliance of America-Rochester Chapter
97 Pinebrook Drive 716-225-3750
Rochester, NY 14616 Fax: 716-225-2712
Email: InventNY@aol.com

This non-profit group helps inventors by educating them to develop their business and offer support and recognition. The members and guest speakers offer useful information and contacts at the monthly meetings.

New York Society of Professional Inventors
Box 216 516-798-1490
Farmingdale, NY 11735-9996 Fax: 516-799-1362
Email: dan.weiss.pe@juno.com

They are a networking group that meets once a month. Speakers that are experts on different areas of inventing attend. There is a membership fee.

Long Island Forum for Technology, Inc.
Phil Orlando 631-755-3321
Farmingdale, NY 11735 Fax: 631-755-9264
Email: porlando@lift.org

Inventors Society of Western New York
Bob Murray
52 Manor Hill Drive.
Fairport, NY 14450 585-223-1225
Email: inventnewyork@aol.com

Innovators Resource Network of Central NY
Mark Pierson
65 Hospital Hill Road
Binghamton, NY 13901 607-648-4626
Email: mvpierson@aol.com

North Carolina

Small Business Development Center
University of North Carolina
333 Fayetteville Street Mall, #1150 919-715-7272
Raleigh, NC 27601 Fax: 919-715-7777

The center offers counseling for a wide range of business issues and problems.

North Dakota

Center for Innovation
University of North Dakota
4300 Dartmouth Drive
P.O. Box 8372 701-777-3132
Grand Forks, ND 58202-8372 Fax: 701-777-2339
www.innovators.net

This center conducts occasional seminars and workshops with speakers; counsels on the commercialization and patenting process; provides communications among inventors, manufacturers, and patent attorneys. There are fees for services, but the first consultation is free.

Small Business Development Center
118 Gamble Hall
University of North Dakota
Box 7308 701-777-3700
Grand Forks, ND 58202-7308 Fax: 701-777-3225
www.und.nodak.edu/dept/

The center offers counseling for a wide range of business issues and problems.

North Dakota Inventors Congress
Michael S. Neustel

2534 South University Drive, Suite 4 800-281-7009
Fargo, ND 58103 Fax: 701-237-0544
Email: neustel@patent-ideas.com
www.ndinventors.com

The NDIC provides inventors and entrepreneurs with all the information needed to see an idea through to fruition.

Ohio

Inventors Council of Dayton
Mr. George Pierce, President
P.O. Box 611 937-224-8513
Dayton, OH 45409 Fax: 413-691-1630
www.xec.com/invent/index.html
email: geopierce@earthlink.net

This association meets on a regular basis and provides communication among inventors, manufacturers, patent attorneys, etc., and often publishes newsletters.

Docie Marketing
73 Maplewood Drive 740-594-5200
Athens, OH 45701 Fax: 740-594-4004
http://docie.com
Email: idea@docie.com

Docie Marketing provides assistance to inventors worldwide, including free educational material, free referrals to legitimate invention service providers, commission-based brokerage, and fee-based services for inventors.

Small Business Development Center
Department of Development
77 S. High Street 800-848-1300
P.O. Box 1001 614-466-2480
Columbus, OH 43216-1001 Fax: 614-466-5167
www.connectohio.com
Email: connect@odod.state.oh.us

The center offers counseling for a wide range of business issues and problems.

Inventors Connection of Greater Cleveland, Inc.
P.O. Box 360804 216-226-9681
Strongsville, OH 44136 Fax: 440-543-0354
http://members.aol.com/icgc/index.htm
Email: icgc@usa.com

This is a non-profit organization of inventors helping inventors that help to make ideas into marketable products. They provide information on patent developments, educate them on things pertaining to the inventing process, and identify needs for those inventions that have a possible market. Monthly meetings cover many topics, but stress the introduction of ideas into the marketplace.

Inventors Council of Canton
303 55th Street, NW
North Canton, OH 44720 330-499-1262
Email: fleisherb@aol.com

The Council provides an opportunity for inventors to meet and share ideas. They hold monthly meetings to further this goal.

Inventors Network
1275 Kinnear Road
Columbus, OH 43212 614-470-0144
Email: 13832667@msn.com

This is a nonprofit group with members in varying occupations. Entrepreneurs and inventors are educated on the invention process and production. They meet monthly to network and question various guest speakers. They cover topics like manufacturing, prototyping, and marketing. They also have a yearly seminar.

Inventor's Council of Cincinnati
Andrea Brady, President
121 Bradford Drive 513-831-0664
Milford, OH 45150 Fax: 513-831-6328
Email: InventorsCouncil@fuse.net

Youngstown-Warren Inv. Assn.
Robert J. Herberger
500 City Center One
PO Box 500
Youngstown, OH 44501-0500 330-744-4481
Email: rjh@mm-lawyers.com

Oklahoma

Small Business Development Center
Southeastern Oklahoma State University

517 University
P.O. Box 2584
Durant, OK 74701
405-924-0277
Fax: 405-924-7071

The center offers counseling for a wide range of business issues and problems.

Inventors Assistance Program
877-577-7632 (in OK)
395 Cordell South
405-744-8727
Stillwater, OK 74078-8015
Fax: 405-744-8516
http://techweb.ceat.okstate.edu/ias

This is a service to help inventors navigate the process from idea to marketplace using information, education and referrals. The service itself is free.

Oklahoma Inventors Congress
3212 NW 35th Street
405-947-5782
Oklahoma City, OK 73112
Fax: 405-947-6950
Email: wbaker@tanet.net

They are a self-help group that shares knowledge and experience with each other in order to help in the invention process. They hold monthly meetings.

Oregon

Eastern Oregon University
Small Business Development Center
One University Blvd.
541-962-3391
La Grande, OR 97850
Fax: 541-962-3668
Email: lagrande@bizcenter.org

Oregon Institute of Technology
Small Business Development Center
3201 Campus Dr.
Boivin Hall, Room 119
541-885-1760
Klamath Falls, OR 97601-8801
Fax: 541-885-1761
www.oit.edu/sbdc/5
Email: sbdc@oit.edu

Southern Oregon University
Small Business Development Center
332 W. 6th St.
541-772-3478
Medford, OR 97501
Fax: 541-734-4813
www.sou.edu/business/sbdc.htm

Small Business Development Centers (SBDCs) at three state colleges and the community colleges can counsel inventors and direct them where to go for patent process, etc.

Oregon Small Business Development Center
44 W. Broadway, Suite 501
541-726-2250
Eugene, OR 97401-3021
Fax: 541-345-6006
www.bizcenter.org

The center provides general assistance and funding information.

Small Business Development Center
2025 Lloyd Center mall
503-978-5080
Portland, OR 97232
Fax: 503-288-1366
www.sbdc.citysearch.com
Email: yjohnson@pcc.edu

The center provides general assistance and funding information.

Oregon State Library
State Library Building
250 Winter St., NE
503-378-4277
Salem, OR 97310-3950
Fax: 503-588-7119
www.osl.state.or.us

Organization's name and address may be given to individual inventors for referrals.

Southern Oregon Inventors Council
332 West 6th Street
541-772-3478
Medford, OR 97501
Fax: 541-734-4813
Email: sbdc@s.oregonstate

This is a group that supports each other through the sharing of ideas. They learn the process of going about developing an invention and answer each others' questions at monthly meetings. They also have guest speakers who cover topics such as, marketing, on-line marketing, and manufacturing. The meetings are open to the public. There is a small membership fee.

South Coast Inventors Group
Lori Capps
c/o Southwestern Business Development Center
2110 Newmark
541-888-7100
Coos Bay, OR 97420
Fax: 541-888-7113
lcapps@southwestern.cc.or.us

Pennsylvania

Small Business Development Center
Bucknell University
Toll free: 866-375-6010
125 Dana Engineering Bldg.
570-524-1249
Lewisburg, PA 17837
Fax: 570-524-1768
www.departments.bucknell.edu/sbdc/
Email: sbdc@bucknell.edu

The center offers counseling for a wide range of business issues and problems.

Pennsylvania Small Business Development Center
Vance Hall
3733 Spruce Street
215-898-4861
Philadelphia, PA 19104
Fax: 215-898-1063
www.pasbdc.org

The center provides general assistance and funding information. It also conducts market and technical assessments. It also oversees all centers in Pennsylvania.

American Society of Inventors
(ATTN: Henry H. Skillman)
P.O. Box 58426
Philadelphia, PA 19102-5426
215-546-6601
www.asoi.org
Email: hskillman@ddhs.com

This group offers members legal, technical, and business information. Some of the services that they have are, the Information Index, the Inventors Notebook, and the Invention Conception, all provided to help the member become creative and successful. They have bi-monthly meetings and newsletters. At the Board Meeting, 2 members will be allowed to have their inventions evaluated.

Pennsylvania Inventors Association
2317 East 43rd
Erie, PA 16510
814-825-5820
www.pa-invent.org
Email: dhbutler@velocity.net

"What we are able to conceive, we are meant to create", is the motto of this group. They bring together people with ideas, link inventors to industry, and get support for inventors. Meetings are open to local inventors and others interested in promoting creativity.

Central Pennsylvania Inventors Assn.
Scott Pickford
9 First Avenue
Wormleysburg, (Harrisburg) PA 17043
717-763-5742
Email: S1Pickford@aol.com

Puerto Rico

Puerto Rico Inventors Association
Bill Diaz
PO Box 1081
Saint Just, PR 00978
787-760-5074
Email: acuhost@novacomm-inc.com

Rhode Island

Service Corps of Retired Executives (SCORE)
c/o U.S. Small Business Administration
380 Westinghouse, Room #511
Providence, RI 02903
401-528-4571
www.swns.net/score/main1.html

Volunteers in the SCORE office are experts in many areas of business management and can offer advice to inventors in areas including marketing and the commercialization process.

Small Business Development Center
30 Exchange Terrace
Providence, RI 02903
401-831-1330

The center offers counseling for a wide range of business issues and problems.

Small Business Development Center
Bryant College
1150 Douglas Pike
401-232-6111
Smithfield, RI 02917-1284
Fax: 401-232-6933
www.risbdc.org

The center provides general assistance and conducts market and technical assessments.

The Center for Design & Business
Cheryl A. Daria, Director

20 Washington Place 401-454-6108
Providence, RI 02903 Fax: 401-454-6559
Email: cfaria@risd.edu

South Carolina

Small Business Development Center
South Carolina State University
School of Business
300 College Ave.
Campus Box 7176 803-536-8445
Orangeburg, SC 29117 Fax: 803-536-8066
The center offers counseling for a wide range of business issues and problems.

South Carolina Small Business Development Center
University of South Carolina
1710 College Street
College of Business Administration 803-777-4907
Columbia, SC 29208 Fax: 803-777-4403
The center provides general assistance and funding information.

Inventors & Entrepreneurs Association of South Carolina
Charles Sprouce
P.O. Box 4123
Greenville, SC 29608 864-244-1045

Carolina Inventors Council
Johnny Sheppard
2960 Dacusville Highway
Easley, SC 29640 864-859-0066
Email: john17@home.com

South Dakota

Small Business Development Center
University of South Dakota
School of Business
414 East Clark St. 605-677-5287
Vermillion, SD 57069-2390 Fax: 605-677-5427
www.usd.edu/brbinfo
Email: brbinfo@usd.edu
The center offers counseling for a wide range of business issues and problems.

South Dakota Inventors Congress
Kent Rufer
P.O. Box 2220
SDSU-EERC 605-688-4184
Brookings, SD 57007 Fax: 605-688-5880
Email: kent_rufer@sdstate.edu

Tennessee

Jackson State Community College
Small Business Development Center
2046 North Parkway Street 901-424-5389
Jackson, TN 38301 Fax: 901-425-2641
The center offers counseling for a wide range of business issues and problems.

Tennessee Inventors Association
P.O. Box 11225
Knoxville, TN 37939-1225 865-981-2927
www.uscni.com/tia
Email: bealaj@aol.com
Their main goal is the advancement of technology through Tennessee by providing guidance, information, and encouragement. They have a TIA Inventor's Guide that has topics such as the Inventors Log, how to market your product yourself, prototypes, and licensing. Their members include inventors, small business developers, research scientist and more to network with. There is a lot more information available with this group.

Inventors' Association of Middle Tennessee and South Kentucky
Marshal Frazer
3908 Trimble Rd.
Nashville, TN 37215 615-269-4346

Texas

North Texas-Dallas Small Business Development Center
Dallas Community College District
1402 Corinth Street 214-860-5900

Dallas, TX 75215 Fax: 214-565-5815
www.billpriestinstitute.org/dallas_sbdc.htm
The center offers counseling for a wide range of business issues and problems.

Texas Tech University
Small Business Development Center
2579 S. Loop 289, St. 114 806-745-1637
Lubbock, TX 79423 Fax: 806-745-6717
www.lubbock-sbdc.org
The center provides general assistance and funding information.

Amarillo Inventors Association
7000 West 45th Street, Suite 2 806-352-6085
Amarillo, TX 79109 Fax: 806-352-6264
Email: kiefer7000@aol.com
They have monthly meetings in order to inform inventors of steps that they can take to enhance their invention.

Houston Inventors Association
2916 West T.C. Jester Blvd., Suite 105 713-686-7676
Houston, TX 77018 Fax: 281-326-1795
www.inventors.org
Email: kenroddy@nol.net
Speakers at monthly meeting discuss their success stories, technical areas, and share tips on making money from inventions. There are also monthly workshops on patent fundamentals, injection moldings and more. They will put together members having a problem with members who can help them.

Technology Advocates of San Antonio
Inventors & Entrepreneurs SIG
9406 Hays Point
San Antonio, Texas 78250
Richard Rodriguez - Co-Chair 210-680-5754
Email: richard@kenrod.biz Fax: 210-680-5755
Edward Hopkins - Co-Chair
Email: hopkinsedward@msn.com 210-452-7405
www.tasa.org

Texas Inventors Association
Barbara Pitts
P.O. Box 251248
Plano, TX 75025 972-312-0090
Email: barb@asktheinventors.com
www.asktheinventors.com
Successful inventors providing experienced advice for new inventors.

Utah

Utah Small Business Development Center
1623 S. State St. 801-957-3840
Salt Lake City, UT 84115 Fax: 801-957-3489
www.slcc.edu/schools/cce/atc/cad/sbac.html
Email: finnermi@slcc.edu
The center provides general assistance and funding information, and conducts market research and strategy.

Vermont

Economic and Development Office
State of Vermont
National Library Bldg.
6th Floor North 802-828-3211
Montpelier, VT 05620-0501 Fax: 802-828-3258
www.state.vt.us/dca
Inventors will be given references to businesses that can assist with the commercialization and marketing process.

Small Business Development Center
P.O. Box 188 Toll free: 800-464-7232 (in VT)
Randolph Center, VT 05061 802-728-9101
www.vtsbdc.org Fax: 802-728-3026
The center offers counseling for a wide range of business issues and problems.

Inventors Network of Vermont
Dave Dionne
4 Park Street 802-885-5100
Springfield, VT 05156 802-885-8178
Email: comtu@turbont.net

Invent Vermont
Norman Elkind
PO Box 82
Woodbury, VT 05681 802-472-8741
Email: Netkind@att.net

Virginia

Virginia Small Business Development Center
707 E. Main St., Suite 300
P.O. Box 446   804-371-8111
Richmond, VA 23218-0446   804-371-8200
www.dba.state.va.us
The center offers counseling for a wide range of business issues and problems.

Small Business Development Center
2000 Holiday Drive, Suite 200   434-295-8198
Charlottesville, VA 22901   Fax: 434-817-0664
http://monticello.avenue.org/Market/SBDC
Email: sbdc@cstone.net
The center provides general assistance, conducts market studies, and refers inventors to companies that conduct market and technical assessments.

Blue Ridge Inventor's Club
P.O. Box 6701   804-973-3708
Charlottesville, VA 22906-6701   Fax: 804-973-2648
www.inventorclub.org
Email: mac@luckycat.com
The purpose of this club is to help people protect their innovations, provide information on patents, trademarks, and copyrights, and inform them how the US Patent and Trademark Office operates.

Inventors Network of the Capital Area
Ray Gilbert
6501 Inwood Drive   703-971-7443
Springfield, VA 22150   Fax: 703-971-9216
Email: Raybik@aol.com
http://inca.hispeed.com
This is a non-profit educational organization offering monthly meetings, guest speakers, and networking with fellow inventors.

Washington

Innovation Assessment Center
180 Nickerson St., Suite 207   206-464-5450
Seattle, WA 98109   Fax: 206-464-6357
www.wsbdc.org/services/innovation_assessment.htm
Part of the Small Business Development Center, this center performs commercial evaluations of inventions, counseling and provides assistance with patentability searches. There are fees for services.

Small Business Development Center
Washington State University
Spokane, WA 99201   509-358-7765
www.wsbdc.org
Email: sbdc@wsu.edu
The center offers counseling for a wide range of business issues and problems.

Small Business Development Center
Western Washington University
Bellingham Towers
119 N. Commercial St., Suite 195   360-733-4014
Bellingham, WA 98225   Fax: 360-733-5092
www.cbe.wwu.edu/sbdc
The center provides general assistance, and investment and funding information.

Inventors Network
P.O. Box 5575
Vancouver, WA 98668   503-239-8299
This is a nonprofit inventor's self-help club whose goal it is to make an invention a reality. They will not do it for you, but rather help you to do it yourself. There is an annual membership fee.

Whidbey Island Inventor Network
Matthew Swett
P.O. Box 1026
Langley, WA 98260   360-678-0269
Email: wiin@whidbey.com
http://www2.whidbey.net/wiin
WIIN is designed as a forum for independent inventors to network with one another.

West Virginia

Small Business Development Center
West Virginia University
912 Main St.   304-465-1434

Oak Hill, WV 25901   Fax: 304-465-8680
The center offers counseling for a wide range of business issues and problems.

West Virginia Small Business Development Office
2000 7th Ave.   304-696-6246
Huntington, WV 25703-1527   Fax: 304-696-4835
www.marshall.edu/ibd/sbdc.htmlx
The center provides information on investment and funding.

West Virginia Inventors Council, Inc.
Katherine Morgan
The Discovery Lab
Eng. Research Building
West Virginia University
P.O. Box 6070
Morgantown, WV 26506   304-293-3612, ext. 3730

Wisconsin

Wisconsin Innovation Service Center
402 McCutchan Hall
UW-Whitewater   262-472-1365
Whitewater, WI 53190   Fax: 262-472-1600
http://academics.uww.edu/BUSINESS/innovate/innovate.htm
Email: innovate@uwwvax.uww.edu
Provides early stage market research for inventors. There is a flat fee of $495 for services.

Small Business Development Center
University of Wisconsin
975 University Ave., Room 3260   608-263-7680
Madison, WI 53706   Fax: 608-263-0818
www.wisconsinsbdc.org
Email: sbdc@uwex.edu
The center offers counseling for a wide range of business issues and problems.

Wisconsin Department of Commerce
201 W. Washington Ave.
P.O. Box 7970   608-266-1018
Madison, WI 53707   Fax: 608-267-8969
www.commerce.state.wi.us
The office provides information on investment and funding.

Central Wisconsin Inventors Association
P.O. Box 915
Manawa, WI 54949   920-596-3092
Email: dr.heat@mailexcite.com

Inventors Network of Wisconsin
1066 St. Paul Street
Green Bay, WI 54304   920-429-0331
http://inventor.tsnnet.com
Email: inventorgb@msn.com
This group holds monthly meetings to advance the knowledge of its members. They do this through speakers, networking, and other resources.

Wyoming

Small Business Development Center   800-348-5207
300 South Wolcott, Suite 300   307-234-6683
Casper, WY 82601   Fax: 307-577-7014
http://uwadmnweb.uwyo.edu/sbdc
Dr. Leonard Holler, who works in the office, is able to help inventors on a wide range of issues including patenting, commercialization and intellectual property rights. There are fees for services.

National Organizations

United Inventors Association of the USA
Carol Oldenburg
P.O. Box 23447   585-359-9310
Rochester, NY 14692   Fax: 585-359-1132
Email: UIAUSA@aol.com
http://www.uiausa.com
The MISSION of the UIA is to provide leadership, support and services to inventor support groups and independent inventors.

National Congress of Inventor Organizations
Stephen Gnass
P.O. Box 93669   213-878-6952
Los Angeles, CA 90093-6690   Fax: 213-962-8588

Email: ncio@inventionconvention.com
http://inventionconvention.com/ncio/index.html

International Organizations

International Federation of Inventors' Associations (IFIA)
http://www.invention-ifia.ch
A nongovernmental organization created by inventor associations in 1968. Its membership represents some 100 countries.

Canada

Canadian Innovative Centre   800-265-4559
490 Dutton Drive, Unit 1A   519-885-5870
Waterloo, Ontario Canada N2L 6H7   Fax: 519-5885-5729
www.innovationcentre.ca
Email: info@innovationcentre.ca
Provides inventors with market research, idea testing, and helps guide inventors up to the patent stage.

Inventors Alliance of Canada
Mark Ellwood
350 Sunnyside Ave.
Toronto, Ontario M6R 2R6   416-410-7792
Email: ellwood@netcom.ca
http://www.inventorsalliance.com
The Inventor's Alliance is a non-profit group designed to help inventors develop their business through education, recognition, friendship, and support.

British Columbia Inventors' Society
Richard Parson
P.O. Box 78055

Vancouver, BC Canada V5N 5W1
Joann Robertson   604-707 0250
Email: admin@bcinventor.com
www.bcinventor.com

Durham East Independent Inventors Group
George Cheung
1945 Denmar Rd., Ste.#56
Pickering, Ontario
Canada L1V 3E2   905-686-7172
Email: gc7591@hotmail.com

Inter Atlantic Inventors Club
Tomas Romero
28021 Tacoma PO   902-435-5218
Dartmouth NS Canada B2W 6E2   Fax: 902-434-4221

Saskatchewan Research Council
Marie Savostianik
15 Innovation Blvd.
Saskatoon - Saskatc Canada S7N 2X8   306-933-5400

Waterloo - Wellington Inventors Club
Harry VanDyke
65 Woodland Drive
Cambridge, ONT Canada N1R 2X7   519-653-8848
Email: svandyk@bserv.com

Women's Inventor's Project - Toronto Canada
107 Holm Crescent   905-731-0328
Thornhill, Ontario L3T 5J4   Fax: 905-731-9691
Canada
http://www.interlog.com/~womenip

Government Buys Bright Ideas From Inventors: Small Business Innovative Research Programs (SBIR)

The Small Business Innovative Research Program (SBIR) stimulates technological innovation, encourages small science and technology based firms to participate in government funded research, and provides incentives for converting research results into commercial applications. The program is designed to stimulate technological innovation in this country by providing qualified U.S. small business concerns with competitive opportunities to propose innovative concepts to meet the research and development needs of the Federal government. Eleven federal agencies with research and development budgets greater than $100 million are required by law to participate: The Departments of Defense, Health and Human Services, Energy, Agriculture, Commerce, Transportation, and Education; the National Aeronautics and Space Administration; the National Science Foundation; the Nuclear Regulatory Commission; and the Environmental Protection Agency.

Businesses of 500 or fewer employees that are organized for profit are eligible to compete for SBIR funding. Nonprofit organizations and foreign owned firms are not eligible to receive awards, and the research must be carried out in the U.S. All areas of research and development solicit for proposals, and the 2001 budget for SBIR is $1.158 billion. There are three phases of the program: Phase I determines whether the research idea, often on high risk advanced concepts, is technically feasible; whether the firm can do high quality research; and whether sufficient progress has been made to justify a larger Phase II effort. This phase is usually funded for 6 months with awards up to $100,000. Phase II is the principal research effort, and is usually limited to a maximum of $750,000 for up to two years. The third phase, which is to pursue potential commercial applications of the research funded under the first two phases, is supported solely by nonfederal funding, usually from third party, venture capital, or large industrial firms. SBIR is one of the most competitive research and development programs in the government today. About one proposal out of ten received is funded in Phase I. Generally, about half of these receive support in Phase II. Solicitations for proposals are released once a year (in a few cases twice a year). To assist the small business community in its SBIR efforts, the U.S. Small Business Administration publishes the Pre-Solicitation Announcement (PSA) in December, March, June, and September of each year. Every issue of the PSA contains pertinent information on the SBIR Program along with details on SBIR solicitations that are about to be released. This publication eliminates the need for small business concerns to track the activities of all of the federal agencies participating in the SBIR Program. In recognition of the difficulties encountered by many small firms in their efforts to locate sources of funding essential to finalization of their innovative products, SBA has developed the Commercialization Matching System. This system contains information on all SBIR awardees, as well as financing sources that have indicated an interest in investing in SBIR innovations. Firms interested in obtaining more information on the SBIR Program or receiving the PSA, should contact the Office of Technology, Small Business Administration, 409 3rd St., SW, MC/6470, Washington, DC 20416, 202-205-6450.

SBIR representatives listed below can answer questions and send you materials about their agency's SBIR plans and funding:

Department of Agriculture
Dr. Charles Cleland, Directory SBIR Program, U.S. Department of Agriculture, Stop 2243, Waterfront Centre, Suite 2312, 1400 Independence Avenue, SW, Washington, DC 20250-2243; 202-401-6852, Fax: 202-401-6070; Email: Ccleland@reeusda.gov

Department of Commerce
Dr. Joseph Bishop, Department of Commerce, 1335 East-West Highway, Room 106, Silver Springs, MD 20910, 301-713-3565, Fax: 301-713-4100, Email: Joseph.Bishop@NOAA.GOV

Department of Defense
Ivory Fisher, SBIR/STTR Program Manager, Office Under Secretary of Defense, U.S. Department of Defense, 1777, North Kent Street, Rosslyn Plaza North, Suite 9100, Arlington, VA 22209, 800-382-4634, 703-588-8616, Fax: 703-588-7561, Email: fisherij@acq.osd.mil

Department of Education
Lee Eiden, SBIR Program Coordinator, Department of Education, Room 508 D-Capitol Place, 555 New Jersey Avenue, NW Washington DC 20208, 202-219-2004, Fax: 202-219-1407, Email: Lee_Eiden@ed.gov

Department of Energy
Dr. Robert E. Berger, SBIR/STTR Program Manager, US Department of Energy, SC-32 19901 Germantown Road, Germantown, MD 20874-1290, 301-903-2900, Fax: 301-903-5488, Email: Robert.Berger@science.doe.gov

Department of Health and Human Services
Debbie Ridgely, Director OSDBU, Office of the Secretary, U.S. Department of Health and Human Services, 200 Independence Ave., Washington, DC 20201; 202-690-7235, Fax: 202-260-4872; Email: debbie.ridgely@hhs.gov.

Department of Transportation
Joseph D. Henebury, SBIR Program Director, DTS-22, US Department of Transportation, Volpe Center, 55 Broadway, Kendall Square, Cambridge, MA 02142-1093, 617-494-2712, Fax: 617-494-2370, Email: Henebury@volpe.dot.gov

Environmental Protection Agency
James Gallup, Office of Research and Development, US Environmental Protection Agency, ORD/NCER (8722R), 1200 Pennsylvania Ave., NW, Washington DC 20460, 202-564-6823, Fax: 202-565-2447, Email: Gallup.James@epa.gov

National Aeronautics and Space Administration
Dr. Robert L. Norwood, SBIR Program, National Aeronautics Space Administration-HQ, 300 E. St, SW, Code XC, Washington, DC 20546-0001; 202-358-2320, Fax: 202-358-3878

Small Business Administration
Maurice Swinton, US Small Business Administration, 409 3rd Street, SW, Mail Code:6540, Washington, DC 20416, 202-205-6450, Fax: 202-205-6390, Email: maurice.swinton@sba.gov

I Wanna Start
My Own Nonprofit

I Wanna Start My Own Nonprofit

You say you're committed to a particular social issue, and would like to set up a nonprofit to further your cause? But you're afraid that the paperwork involved makes it much too complicated and time consuming? Contrary to popular belief, you don't have to hire a lawyer and have thousands of dollars in the bank to consider starting your own nonprofit. With as little as $35 and 30 minutes of paperwork that you can complete sitting at your kitchen table, you can be well on your way to raising funds and raising the consciousness of the country.

Try The Easy, Cheap Way - First!

Dan Meeks of Columbus, Ohio had a dream of starting his own nonprofit that could be staffed by Vietnam veterans who would help local kids tackle various personal and community-related problems. He called a lawyer to investigate the costs associated with becoming a nonprofit. He was astounded to hear that it would cost $800, and that it would take several months to complete the lengthy process. Since theirs was a new and fledgling organization, Dan and the other interested participants didn't have that kind of money. Through a friend, Dan heard of a special IRS office that does nothing but assist people in starting nonprofits. They sent Dan the necessary forms and instructions which were easily completed in a few hours, after clarifying a few points over the telephone with the IRS office. A letter soon followed notifying Dan that his organization had qualified as a nonprofit, and the entire process cost him less than $20.00! Within a few months, Dan had raised $5,000 through a fundraiser and donated the money to several other nonprofit organizations, including the local Ronald McDonald House. Success stories like Dan's don't necessarily take lots of time and effort — just the right information.

Tamara Gates is another individual determined to make a difference. She wanted to start a chapter of V-COPS (Veteran-Civilian Observation Patrol) in Cleveland, to tackle the dual problem of a high crime rate coupled with a high number of homeless veterans residing on the city's streets. The V-COPS program offers shelter for homeless veterans in exchange for their services patrolling the streets at night, acting as the eyes and ears of the police. Ms. Gates contacted the special IRS office to find out how to apply for nonprofit status, and was sent the appropriate forms. It took her a little over a week to complete the forms, and several months later she received her confirmation as a nonprofit. Because of the budget for her organization, Ms. Gates was required to pay a fee of several hundred dollars, but it was still much less than the $50,000 that a consultant estimated that she would be required to pay. Thanks to her commitment to forge ahead and get the right information, Ms. Gates can point to the very tangible shelter services that her V-COPS program offers to Cleveland's homeless veterans, in exchange for the valuable services that they provide to the local community.

If you are thinking about establishing a nonprofit, check out this FREE source of valuable information before you decide that the obstacles are too great. Just like Dan and Tamara, you may find yourself pleasantly surprised and able to achieve your goal, without handing over a ton of your hard earned money to someone just to figure it out for you!

How To Become A Nonprofit

* Filing With The IRS

Internal Revenue Service Forms Line   800-829-3676
www.irs.ustreas.gov/forms_pubs/forms.html

or

Your Local IRS Office
Listed in the government section of your telephone book

To help you determine if your organization may qualify for tax exempt status or to find out what you will need to do to qualify, request Publication 557, *Tax-Exempt Status For Your Organization*. This publication takes you step-by-step through the filing process, and contains instructions and checklists to help you provide all of the necessary information required to process your application correctly the first time around.

Most organizations seeking tax exempt status from the Federal government must use either: Form 1023, *Application for Recognition of Exemption Under Section 501(c)(3) of the Internal Revenue Code*, or Form 1024, *Application for Recognition of Exemption Under Section 501(a) or for Determination Under Section 120*. The forms will ask you to provide:

- a description of the purposes and the activities of your organization,
- financial information, and if you have not yet begun operation, a proposed budget, along with a statement of assets and liabilities (if you have any),
- information on how you intend to finance your activities, through fundraisers, grants, etc.

Examples of who qualifies under each of the laws and samples of forms are provided in these publications. If the necessary forms have been properly completed and all goes well, a ruling or determination letter should be on its way to you in no time.

* Getting Help From The IRS

Internal Revenue Service Info-Line   800-829-1040

or

Your local IRS Office
Listed in the government section of your telephone book

or

Exempt Organizations Division
Internal Revenue Service
U.S. Department of the Treasury
1111 Constitution Ave., NW, Room 6411
Washington, DC 20224   202-622-8100
www.irs.gov/exempt/

The first two offices listed above can provide you with the answers to any questions that might arise in filling out the necessary forms. If the first person that you speak with in that office cannot answer your question completely, they can put you in touch with a specialist who will discuss your question in detail. The Exempt Organization Technical Division is not set up to handle every question that might arise in completing forms, but it can serve as a good backup when all else fails. This is the office that will actually process your application.

* Filing With The State Government

See page 545 for a state by state listing

You will also be required to file as a nonprofit organization with your state government. This is normally done at the same time that you file with the IRS. Although it is the IRS who gives you the authority to raise money as a tax-exempt organization, your state government will also want to know about the proposed activities of your organization. Relevant information that they will be interested in includes:

- the name and address of registrant,
- the purpose of the nonprofit,
- any articles of incorporation,
- and the names and addresses of any Board of Directors.

The charge for filing this information with the state is minimal, usually from $30.00 to $50.00. Contact the appropriate state listed on page 545 to obtain the necessary forms.

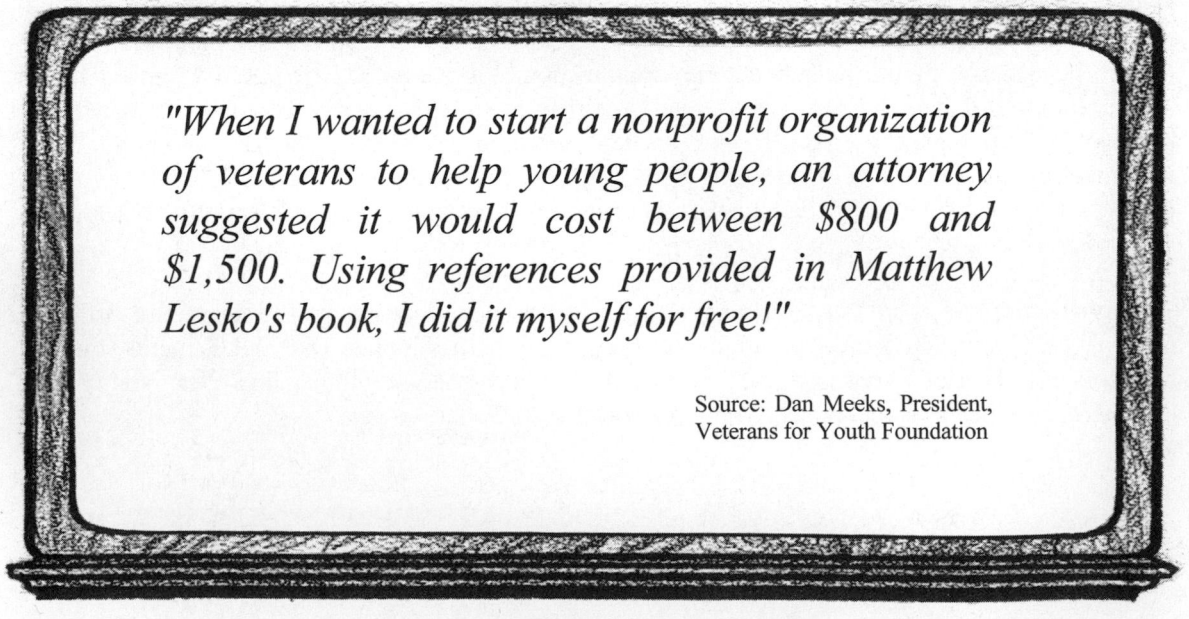

"When I wanted to start a nonprofit organization of veterans to help young people, an attorney suggested it would cost between $800 and $1,500. Using references provided in Matthew Lesko's book, I did it myself for free!"

Source: Dan Meeks, President,
Veterans for Youth Foundation

How To Raise Money For Your Nonprofit

* Grants and Foundation Support Resource List

Your Local Representative's or Senator's Office

or

Your Representative or Senator
U.S. Capitol
Washington, DC 20515   202-224-3121
http://rothman.house.gov/grantinfo.htm

A free report called *Grants And Foundation Support* (IP50G), describes sources of funding (both government and private), as well as information regarding grant proposal development. It is available from your congressman's office.

***

* Catalogue Of Federal Grant Programs

Federal Domestic Assistance Catalogue Staff
General Services Administration
300 7th St., SW
Reporters Building, Room 101   202-708-5126
Washington, DC 20407   800-669-8331
www.cfda.gov/default.htm

Everything you will need to get you started in searching for grants is found in this concise government publication. The *Catalog of Federal Domestic Assistance* is available in most libraries and describes Federal government programs providing funds or other non-financial assistance to organizations. Included in the publication are various programs' eligibility requirements, application procedures, information contacts, and more. This manual of more than 1,000 pages provides the most comprehensive information on federal funds currently available. This database can be accessed at the website listed above. You will be able to search there for programs for which you are eligible. The Catalog may be purchased in three different formats: hard copy for $60/year; CD-ROM, single copy for $45 or an annual subscription for $75; or diskettes for $85 (issued semi-annually).

* The Center For Foundation Support

The Foundation Center
79 Fifth Ave/16th St.
New York, NY 10003-3076   800-424-9836
http://fdncenter.org

The Foundation Center is a nonprofit organization which gathers and disseminates factual information on foundations. The Center's libraries contain copies of foundations' tax returns, collections of books, documents, and reports about the foundation field, and related material. They also publish funding directories specific to certain fields, and offer programs to assist individuals in information searches. You may also request a list of cooperating libraries in each state where Center publications containing foundation information may be consulted. The Center has the following regional offices:

The Foundation Center
1627 K St., NW, 3rd Floor   202-331-1400
Washington, DC 20006-1708   Fax: 202-331-1739

The Foundation Center
312 Sutter St., #606   415-397-0902
San Francisco, CA 94108   Fax: 415-397-7670

The Foundation Center
1422 Euclid Ave., Suite 1600   216-861-1934
Cleveland, OH 44115   Fax: 216-861-1936

The Foundation Center
50 Hurt Plaza, Suite 150   404-880-0094
Atlanta, GA 30303   Fax: 404-880-0087

The Foundation Center
79 Fifth Ave.   212-620-4230
New York, NY 10003   Fax: 212-691-1828

* How Someone Can Give You Money And Make It Tax Deductible

Internal Revenue Service Forms Line   800-829-3676
www.irs.ustreas.gov/forms_pubs/pubs.html

or

Your Local IRS Office
Listed in the government section of your telephone book

Obtain a free copy of Publication 526 entitled *Charitable Contributions*. It will explain the kinds of charitable contributions that are tax deductible and the type of organizations that can qualify for this deduction.

Information About Existing Nonprofits

* The One Book of Nonprofits

Exempt Organizations Division
Internal Revenue Service
U.S. Department of the Treasury
1111 Constitution Ave., NW
Room 6411
Washington, DC 20224   202-622-8100

To find out about other nonprofits that have filed with the Internal Revenue Service, subscribe to the *Cumulative List of Organizations* (Publication #78), which includes a complete listing of names and addresses of exempt organizations. You can search the publication online, or download your own copy from this website: www.irs.gov/faqs/

* Mailing Lists Of Nonprofits

Internal Revenue Service
P.O. Box 2608   202-874-0700
Washington, DC 20013-2608   Fax: 202-874-0964
www.irs.ustreas.gov/

A database of over 1,000 tax-exempt organizations is maintained by the Internal Revenue Service from which you can access a wealth of priceless information. You may access this database through the website given above. In order to understand the codes in these files, you will also have to download the Instructions Booklet, which is available on the same link. This information is also available on CD-ROM and includes more financial information per organization that the Internet data. Ask for Statistics of Income (SOI) samples of Forms 990 and 990-EZ. Years 1993-1996 are available. Years 1993 and 1994 are available for $100 and years 1995 and 1996 are $300. From the website listed above, choose Charities & Non-Profits. From the menu on the left, choose Charitable Orgs. Choose More from the Topics menu on the left, then choose Publication 78, *Search for Tax Exempt Organizations*.

Freebies and Cheapies For Nonprofits

* Americorp And You

Corporation for National and Community Service
1201 New York Ave., NW
Washington, DC 20525   202-606-5090
www.americorps.org

Does your nonprofit work to eliminate poverty or poverty-related problems? Americorp provides full-time, full-year volunteers to local organizations, with participants working to improve the community's ability to solve its own problems. Americorp has assisted in setting up drug abuse action centers, literacy programs, food distribution efforts, and shelters for runaway youth and the homeless. The benefits for the Americorp Volunteer include college loan deferment or cancellation, a modest subsistence allowance, an education award of $4,725, health insurance, training, and travel. Contact the office listed above to learn how your organization can apply for Americorp volunteers.

* Local Community Service

Corporation for National and Community Service
Learn and Serve Program
1201 New York Ave., NW
Washington, DC 20525   202-606-5090
www.learnandserve.org

If your nonprofit needs help addressing the needs of the poor, you can get some energetic help from high school and college students who take part in Service-Learning projects. Student Volunteers have assisted in a variety of programs including Headstart, drug abuse prevention, runaway youth, and elderly assistance. The volunteers receive no stipend, but projects utilizing the services of these students are awarded grants for staff salaries, project support expenses, and much more. For information on how your organization can take advantage of this wonderful volunteer program, contact Corporation for National and Community Service.

* Tons Of Free Books

Surplus Books Section
Anglo-American Acquisitions Division
Library of Congress
101 Independence Ave., SE   202-707-9514
Washington, DC 20540   Fax: 202-707-0380
Email: otsa@loc.gov
www.loc.gov/acq/surplus.html

Need to raise a little cash? Why not appeal to the intellectual side of most folks and hold a book sale? Thousands of surplus books from the Copyright Division and private gifts in a variety of subject areas are available to nonprofit organizations from the Library of Congress. All you need is a letter from your nonprofit which includes the names of the person or persons coming to select books and your organization's name. The only cost to you will be shipping and handling charges for the publications that your representatives select. Your organization may also be eligible to have the shipping and handling charges due on these books paid for by your Congressman's office through the use of franks (the means by which a Congressional office pays postage expenses).

* Cheap Postage

U.S. Postal Service
Consumer Information and Product Support
475 L'Enfant Plaza West, SW
Room 5092
Washington, DC 20260
www.usps.gov

Bulk mailings are easier with Uncle Sam picking up part of the tab. Your organization can send its mail for almost half of the regular rate just by filing an application for nonprofit status. Contact your local post office for information on application procedures and request publications entitled *Nonprofit Standard Mail Eligibility* (Publication 417) which incldes cooperative mailing information.

* Conserve And Improve Your Part Of The World

Natural Resource Conservation Service
U.S. Department of Agriculture
Room 6121-S
P.O. Box 2890
Washington, DC 20013
www.nrcs.usda.gov/NRCstate.html

Why not raise money for a new park or save a crumbling edifice in your area? Resource Conservation and Development (RC&D) Councils may be able to help you do this, as each council identifies priorities and sets goals to achieve them. The Resource Conservation and Development Councils may be able to provide some funding and necessary technical assistance. For more information on RC&D and the location of a council near you, contact your local Soil Conservation Representative listed in the blue pages of your phone book under U.S. Government Agriculture.

* Strike Up The Band

Blue Angel Public Affairs Office
Navy Flight Demonstration Squadron
390 San Carlos Road, Suite A   850-452-4784
Pensacola, FL 32508-5508   Fax: 850-452-2681
www.blueangels.navy.mil

RE: Golden Knights
Department of the Army
Office of the Chief of Public Affairs
Attn: SAPA POPD
1500 Army Pentagon   703-695-5732
Washington DC 20310-1500   Fax: 703-695-6159
www.usarec.army.mil/hq/GoldenKnights/index.htm

USAFADS Thunderbirds
4445 Tyndall Avenue   702-652-4018
Nellis AFB, NV 89191   Fax: 702-652-6367
www.airforce.com/thunderbirds/index.htm

Your parade can get a little noisier and a lot more colorful with a band and color guard supplied by local Defense Department installations. Most installations have community relations officers who handle requests from nonprofit organizations for these and other little-known services, so contact them for information on availability and restrictions. If you would like an aerial flyover from the Blue Angels or the Thunderbirds, or a parachute show from the Golden Knights, you must put your request in writing. There are obviously some costs involved in providing some of these highly specialized services, but some are actually free.

* Free Food For Nonprofits And The Homeless

Food Distribution Division
Food and Nutrition Service
U.S. Department of Agriculture
3101 Park Center Dr., Room 510   703-305-2882
Alexandria, VA 22302   Fax: 703-305-2420
Email: fdd-pst@fns.usda.gov
www.fns.usda.gov/fdd/default.htm

Does your nonprofit offer meals or bulk foods to those in need? Through the Food Distribution Program, the U.S. Department of Agriculture (USDA) distributes foods to state agencies for use by eligible local agencies. The foods go to schools and institutions participating in child and elderly nutrition programs, to needy families on Indian reservations, and to food banks, soup kitchens, hospitals, and prisons. The foods are also used to assist victims of natural disasters and in situations of distress. A directory of State Distributing Agency contacts is available at the website.

* A Home For The Homeless

U.S. Department of Health and Human Services
Division of Property Management
Program Support Center
Room 5B-41, Parklawn Building
5600 Fishers Lane
Rockville, MD 20857   800-927-7588
www.hud.gov/offices/cpd/homeless/programs/ts/index.cfm

If you are part of a nonprofit organization ministering to the homeless, the government is now taking applications for eligible groups to receive excess or unused federal buildings or land for homeless people. Homeless organizations pay operating and repair costs on the surplus properties that are leased rent-free and in "as is" condition. The program is administered by a combination of the Department of Housing and Urban Development (HUD), which screens applications, the General Services Administration (GSA), which makes the properties available, and the Department of Health and Human Services (HHS), which reviews applications. In accordance with Title V of the McKinney Homeless Assistance Act, HUD publishes a list of properties available in the Federal Register. Additional information regarding the properties (as well as the Title V process) can be obtained by calling 800-927-7588, a toll-free number established by HUD. After a property is published, homeless providers must submit expressions of interest by providing a written notice to the Division of Health Facilities Planning at HHS within 60 days of publication. You will then receive an application packet containing complete instructions on how to apply for the property. You can also request the following helpful publications:

- *How To Acquire Federal Surplus Real Property for Public Health Purposes*
- *Obtaining Federal Property for the Homeless*
- *Questions and Answers About Federal Property Programs*
- *HHS/HUD/GSA joint regulation covering specific information on Title V process*

* Government Property And Land If You Use It For Education Or Training

Federal Real Property Assistance Program
Office of the Administrator for Management Services
U.S. Department of Education
600 Independence Ave.., SW.
Washington, DC 20202   202-401-0500
http://aspe.hhs.gov/cfda/p84145.htm}

No need to put a bond issue on the ballot. The Federal government is giving away surplus buildings and properties for educational use, including higher education, elementary and secondary education, libraries, educational television and radio, and more. The buildings are free, but recipients must cover all expenses for improvement, renovation, repair, maintenance, and operation of the program and facilities. Some of the properties range from improved or unimproved land in rural and urban settings (such as former Nike missile sites), to complete military bases (such as former Air Force stations). For information on properties available, contact the Federal Real Property Assistance Program.

* Money For Nonprofit Radio and TV Stations

Office of Telecommunications and Information Applications
National Telecommunications and Information Administration
Room 4096
U.S. Department of Commerce
1401 Constitution Ave., NW   202-482-5802
Washington, DC 20230   Fax: 202-501-5136
www.ntia.doc.gov/otiahome/otiahome.html

If you always wanted to operate or appear on public or noncommercial television or radio, the Federal government can help you get started or improve your existing facilities. There are grants for planning and construction of facilities, and matching grants for equipment necessary for production. For information on application procedures, contact the office listed above.

* Donations Or Loan Of Military Equipment For Museums And Towns

Office of Public Affairs
Defense Reutilization and Marketing Service (DRMS)   616-961-7015
74 N. Washington   888-352-9333
Battle Creek, MI 49017   Fax: 616-961-7410
Email: custservice@dlis.dla.mil
www.drms.dla.mil

Veterans' groups and museums should take note: the Federal government donates or lends obsolete combat materials to veterans' organizations, libraries, museums, and municipalities. Items include books, manuscripts, works of art, drawings, plans, models, and other specified items to be used only for historical, ceremonial or display purposes. It's no joke ☐ you can even get a Navy vessel! Contact your nearest military installation for general information on this program, or write to the office listed above.

* Tools For Schools

Attn: Sue Ellen Walbridge
Office of Science
Used Energy Related Equipment
U.S. Department of Energy
1000 Independence Ave., SW
Washington, DC 20585   202-586-7231
http://erle.osti.gov/erle/

Is the equipment in your college's laboratories broken, outdated, or just worn out? The U.S. Department of Energy (DOE) will send your school energy-related lab equipment that they no longer need for no charge, other than shipping and handling. The equipment list and application are available at their website.

* Change An Outdated Military Base Into A New Public Park

National Park Service
Rivers, Trails and Conservation Service
U.S. Department of the Interior
1849 C St., NW
Washington, DC 20240   202-565-1200

States or local governments can apply to receive surplus property (even closed military bases) from the Federal government to be used for public parks and recreation and historic monument purposes. Properties must be converted to nature study areas, play areas, state and regional parks, arts and crafts centers, or senior citizen areas. For information regarding properties available and the necessary application procedures, contact the office listed above.

* Help The Needy Buy A Home

Frances Bush
Office of Affordable Housing
451 7th St., SW, Room 7218
Washington, DC 20410   202-708-3226
To request Fact Sheet: Hope for
Homeownership of Single Family Homes   800-998-9999
www.hud.gov/progdesc/hope3fin.cfm

Help those in your community become homeowners through the HOPE 3 Program. The U.S. Department of Housing and Urban Development (HUD) administers the HOPE 3 Program which provides federal grant funds to eligible organizations that, in turn, select eligible families to purchase single-family properties at affordable prices. All single-family properties used in the program were previously owned by federal, state, or local governments. The funds can be used for financial assistance in mortgage financing, reductions in the sale price of homes, counseling in personal financial management, home maintenance training, or job training. For information on how your nonprofit organization can compete for HOPE 3 funds, contact the number listed above.

* $50,000 For Local Community Groups To Fight Area Polluters

Office of Solid Waste (5305W)
U.S. Environmental Protection Agency
1200 Pennsylvania Ave., NW   703-412-9810
Washington, DC 20460   800-424-9346
www.epa.gov/epaoswer/hotline

The Superfund Technical Assistance Grants (TAG) provide $50,000 for community groups to hire technical advisors to assist them in interpreting technical information about potential hazards and the selection and design of appropriate remedies to clean up sites under the Superfund program. The program is designed to benefit homeowners, land/property owners, as well as other individuals living near a site or otherwise affected by a site. You can be referred to your regional TAG officer who will explain the application procedure by contacting RCRA/Superfund Hotline, U.S. Environmental Protection Agency, 401 M St., SW, Washington, DC 20460. (800-424-9346)

* Free Art Films And Videos From The National Gallery Of Art

Department of Education Resources
Extension Programs Section
National Gallery of Art   202-842-6263
Washington, DC 20565   Fax: 202-842-6937
www.nga.gov/resources/derdesc.htm

Impress your women's group or art organization by borrowing free slide programs, videocassettes, and films from the National Gallery of Art. The available materials might cover specific artists, time periods for a particular art form, or present an overview of the Gallery's extensive collection. To receive a complete catalogue and ordering information, contact the Extension Programs Office.

* Government Real Estate To Nonprofits

Office of Property Disposal
Federal Property Resources Service
General Services Administration
1800 F St., NW   202-501-0084
Washington, DC 20405   Fax: 202-208-1714
http://propertydisposal.gsa.gov/property

The government has surplus property that they want to lease, sell, exchange, or donate. These properties can be used for public parks or other recreational uses, public health or educational purposes, public airports, wildlife conservation areas, correctional facilities, replacement housing, and for historic monument purposes. State and local government agencies are eligible to apply for any of the above reasons, and tax-supported and nonprofit medical and educational institutions can apply for property to be used for health, educational, and homeless uses. For more information regarding the application process, as well as appropriate use and restrictions of the properties, contact the office listed above.

* Government Goods To Nonprofits

GSA
Property Management Division
1941 Jefferson Davis Highway, Room 804
Arlington, VA 22202   703-305-5809
www.gsa.gov/Portal/
See page 547 for state by state listing.

Need some desks, chairs, or even hospital beds for your nonprofit? Here's how you can. Nonprofits (which include medical institutions, clinics, schools, museums, libraries and others), can receive free furniture, clothing, and equipment from Uncle Sam through their state surplus property agency which receives items for distribution from the Federal government. To find out about the office nearest you, use the website listed above, or contact your state agency listed on page 547.

* Access $200 Million Products

Gifts In Kind International
333 North Fairfax St.   703-836-2121
Alexandria, VA 22314   Fax: 703-549-1481
www.giftsinkind.org

Nonprofits now have a way to tap into the resources and donations from companies across the country. Through Gifts In Kind America, nonprofits can register for The Agency Partnership program. This program entitles you to receive monthly catalogues of donated goods including computers, office equipment, software, children's items, personal care items, building materials, and clothing. Each year over 600 million dollars worth of products become available. Your nonprofit can then apply to receive these goods. Gifts In Kind America also has a Transportation and Logistics Center to help reduce the costs of shipping and handling. There is a minimal registration fee based upon the revenue of the nonprofit (under $1 million costs $125; over $1 million costs $250). Some states require State Charitable Solicitation Registration. Contact Gifts in Kind America to learn if your state requires certification and where you need to apply.

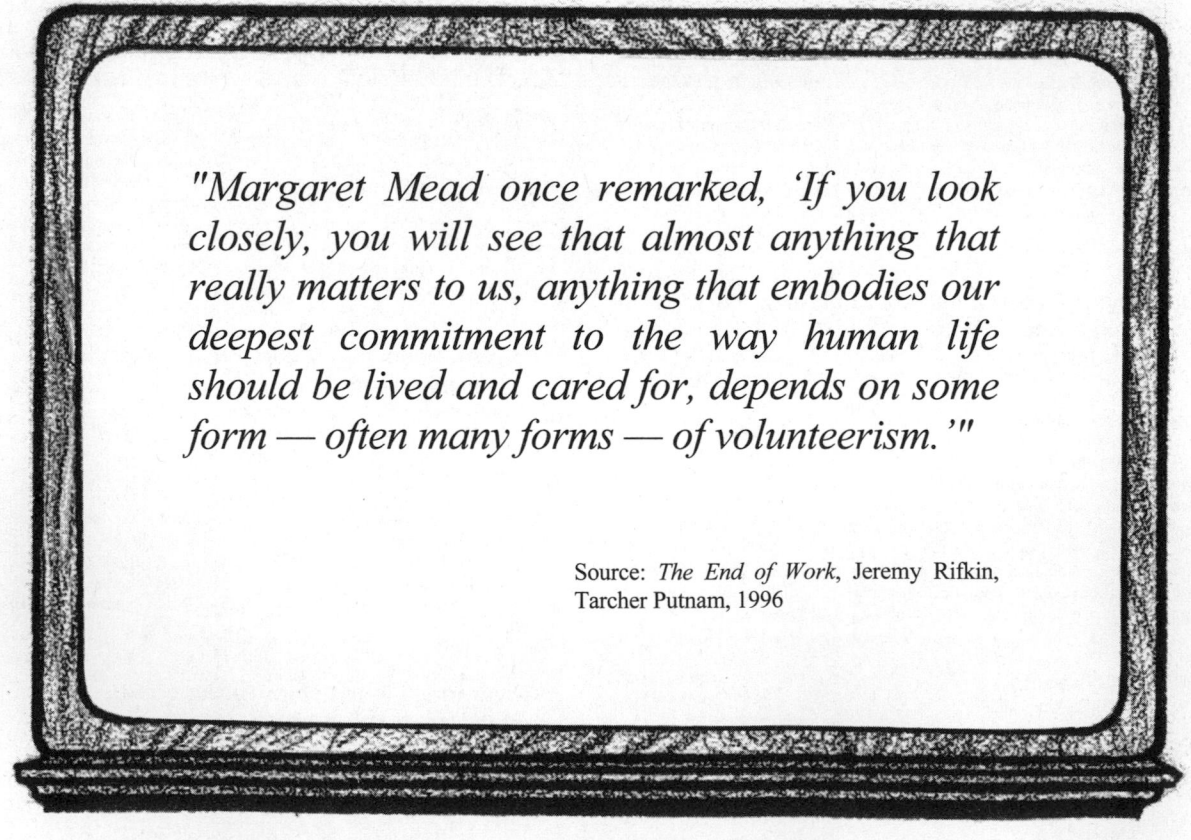

"Margaret Mead once remarked, 'If you look closely, you will see that almost anything that really matters to us, anything that embodies our deepest commitment to the way human life should be lived and cared for, depends on some form — often many forms — of volunteerism.'"

Source: *The End of Work*, Jeremy Rifkin, Tarcher Putnam, 1996

State Government Corporation Offices

Alabama
Corporation Section
Secretary of State
11 S. Union St., Suite 207
P.O. Box 5616
Montgomery, AL 36103-5616
334-242-5324
www.sos.state.al.us/business/corporations.cfm

Alaska
Banking, Securities and Corporation Division
P.O. Box 110808
Juneau, AK 99811-0808
907-465-2521
Fax: 907-465-3257
www.dced.state.ak.us/bsc/corps.htm

Arizona
Corporation Commission
1300 W. Washington St.
Phoenix, AZ 85007
602-542-3026
800-345-5819
www.cc.state.az.us/

Arkansas
Corporations Division
Suite 310, Services Building
501 Woodlane
Little Rock, AR 72201-1023
501-682-3409
888-233-0325
www.sosweb.state.ar.us/business.html

California
Corporations Unit
Main Office
1500 11th Street
Sacramento, CA 95814
916-657-5448
www.ss.ca.gov/business/corp/corporate.htm

Colorado
Corporations Office
State Department
1560 Broadway, Suite 200
Denver, CO 80202
303-894-2251
www.state.co.us/gov_dir/sos/divinfo.
html#Commercial

Connecticut
Commercial Recording Division
Secretary of State
30 Trinity St.
Hartford, CT 06106
860-509-6001
Fax: 860-509-6068
www.sots.state.ct.us/CommercialRecording/
CRDIndex.html

Delaware
State Department
Division of Corporations
P.O. Box 898
Dover, DE 19903
302-739-3073
Fax: 302-739-3812
www.state.de.us/corp/

Federal Express
Division of Corporations
401 Federal Street, Suite 4
Dover, DE 19901

District of Columbia
Dept. of Consumer and Regulatory Affairs
Corporations Division
941 N. Capitol Street NE
Washington, DC 20002-4259
202-442-4430
http://dcra.dc.gov/

Florida
Division of Corporations
P.O. Box 6327
Tallahassee, FL 32314
850-488-9000
www.dos.state.fl.us/doc/

Georgia
Corporations Division
2 Martin Luther King Jr. Dr.
315 West Tower
Atlanta, GA 30334
404-656-2817
Fax: 404-657-2248
www.sos.state.ga.us/corporations/default.htm

Hawaii
Dept. of Commerce and Consumer Affairs
Business Registration Division
P.O. Box 40
1010 Richards Street, 2nd Floor
Honolulu, HI 96813
808-586-2744
www.state.hi.us/dcca/breg-seu

Idaho
Secretary of State
Attn. Commercial Division
P.O. Box 83720
Boise, ID 83720-0080
208-334-2301
Fax: 208-334-2847
www.idsos.state.id.us/corp/corindex.htm

Illinois
Department of Business Services
5015 2nd St., Suite 328
Springfield, IL 62756
217-782-2201
800-252-8980
www.sos.state.il.us/departments/business_
services/business.html

Indiana
Business Services Division
302 W. Washington, Room E018
Indianapolis, IN 46204
317-232-6576
www.in.gov/sos/business/corporations.html

Iowa
Business Services Division
Secretary of State
1st Floor, Lucas Building
Des Moines, IA 50319
515-281-5204
www.sos.state.ia.us/Business

Kansas
Business Development
Business Assistance
1000 SW Jackson St., Suite 100
Topeka, KS 66612
785-296-5298
http://kdoch.state.ks.us

Kentucky
Kentucky Secretary of State
Business Services
700 Capitol Avenue, Suite 152
State Capitol
P.O. Box 718
Frankfort, KY 40601
502-564-2848
Fax: 502-564-4075
www.kysos.com/BUSSER/
CORPORATIONS/corporations.asp

Louisiana
Secretary of State
Commercial Division
P.O. Box 94125
Baton Rouge, LA 70804-9125
225-925-4704
www.sec.state.la.us/comm/comm_index.htm

Maine
Corporations, Elections and Commissions
101 State House Station
Augusta, ME 04333-0101
207-624-7736
Fax: 207-287-5428
www.state.me.us/sos/cec/cec.htm

Maryland
Department of Assessments and Taxation
Charter Division
301 W. Preston Street, Room 809
Baltimore, MD 21201
410-767-1340
888-246-5941
www.dat.state.md.us/sdatweb/charter.html

Massachusetts
Corporations Division
Secretary of the Commonwealth
1 Ashburton Place, 17th Floor
Boston, MA 02108
617-727-9640
www.state.ma.us/sec/cor/coridx.htm

Michigan
Bureau of Commercial Services
Corporation Division
6546 Mercantile Way
P.O. Box 30054
Lansing, MI 48909
517-241-6470
www.commerce.state.mi.us/bcs/
corp/home.htm

Minnesota
Secretary of State
Business Services Division
180 State Office Building
St. Paul, MN 55155
651-296-2803
877-551-6SOS (6767)
www.state.mn.us/ebranch/sos/business/
index.html

Mississippi
Business Services Division
Corporations Unit
Secretary of State
P.O. Box 136
Jackson, MS 39205-0136
601-359-1633
800-256-3494
Fax: 601-359-1607
www.sos.state.ms.us/busserv/corp/
corporations.html

Missouri

Corporation Division
Secretary of State
P.O. Box 778
Jefferson City, MO 65102
573-751-4153
http://mosl.sos.state.mo.us/bus-ser/soscor.html

Montana

Business Services Bureau
Secretary of State
Room 260, Capitol
P.O. Box 202801
Helena, MT 59620-2801
406-444-3665
Fax: 406-444-3976
http://sos.state.mt.us/crs/BSB/Contents.asp

Nebraska

Corporation Division
Secretary of State
Room 1305, State Capitol
P.O. Box 94608
Lincoln, NE 68509-4608
402-471-4079
Fax: 402-471-3666
www.nol.org/home/SOS/htm/services.htm

Nevada

Commercial Recordings Division
Secretary of State, Annex Office
202 N. Carson Street
Carson City, NV 89701-4271
775-684-5708
http://sos.state.nv.us/comm_rec/index.htm

New Hampshire

Corporations Division
Secretary of State
State House, Room 204
25 Capitol St.
Concord, NH 03301
603-271-3244
www.state.nh.us/sos/corporate/index.htm

New Jersey

Division of Revenue
NJ Business Gateway
P.O. Box 628
Trenton, NJ 08646
609-292-9292
www.state.nj.us/njbgs/

New Mexico

Corporation Bureau
P.O. Drawer 1269
Santa Fe, NM 87504-1269
505-827-4508
800-947-4722
www.nmprc.state.nm.us/corporation.htm

New York

Division of Corporations, State Records and
UCC
State Department
41 State Street
Albany, NY 12231-0001
518-473-2492
Fax: 518-474-1418
www.dos.state.ny.us/corp/corpwww.html

North Carolina

North Carolina Secretary of State
Corporations Division
P.O. Box 29622
Raleigh, NC 27626-2225

919-807-2225
www.secretary.state.nc.us/Corporations

North Dakota

Secretary of State
Business Information/Registration Division
600 E. Boulevard Ave., Dept. 108
Bismarck, ND 58505-0500
701-328-4284
800-352-0867, ext. 4284
Fax: 701-328-2992
www.state.nd.us/sec/Business/
businessinforegmnu.htm

Ohio

Business Services Division
30 E. Broad Street, Lower Level
Columbus, OH 43215
614-466-3910
877-SOS-FILE (767-3453)
Fax: 614-466-3899
www.state.oh.us/sos/
business_services_information.htm

Oklahoma

Business Filing Department
2300 N. Lincoln Blvd., Room 101
Oklahoma City, OK 73105-4897
405-522-4560
www.sos.state.ok.us/business/
business%20information.htm

Oregon

Corporation Division
Public Service Building
255 Capitol Street NE, Suite 151
Salem, OR 97310-1327
503-986-2200
www.sos.state.or.us/corporation/corphp.htm

Pennsylvania

Department of State
Corporation Bureau
P.O. Box 8722
Harrisburg, PA 17105-8722
717-787-1057
www.dos.state.pa.us/corp/corp.htm

Rhode Island

Corporations Division
100 N. Main Street, 1st Floor
Providence, RI 02903-1335
401-222-3040
Fax: 401-222-1309
www.corps.state.ri.us

South Carolina

Corporations Division
Secretary of State
P.O. Box 11350
Columbia, SC 29211
803-734-2158
www.scsos.com/corporations.htm

South Dakota

Corporations Division
Secretary of State
Capitol Building
500 E. Capitol Ave., Suite 204
Pierre, SD 57501-5070
605-773-4845
www.state.sd.us/sos/Corpadmn.htm

Tennessee

Division of Business Services
Secretary of State
312 Eight Ave., N

6th Floor, William R. Snodgrass Tower
Nashville, TN 37243
615-741-2286
www.state.tn.us/sos/service.htm

Texas

Secretary of State
Corporations Section
P.O. Box 13697
Austin, TX 78711-3697
512-463-5555
Fax: 512-463-5709
www.sos.state.tx.us/corp/index.shtml

Utah

Department of Commerce
Division of Corporations and Commercial
Code
160 E. 300 S.
Salt Lake City, UT 84111
801-530-4849
877-526-3994
www.commerce.utah.gov/cor/index.html

Vermont

Corporations Division
Secretary of State
81 River St., Drawer 09
Montpelier, VT 05609
802-828-2386
Fax: 802-828-2853
www.sec.state.vt.us/corps/corpindex.htm

Virginia

Virginia State Corporation Commission
P.O. Box 1197
Richmond, VA 23218
804-371-9967
800-552-7945
www.state.va.us/scc

Washington

Corporations Division
Secretary of State
Dolliver Bldg., 801 Capitol Way South
P.O. Box 40234
Olympia, WA 98504-0234
360-753-7115
www.secstate.wa.gov/corporations

West Virginia

Business Organizations Division
Secretary of State
Building 1, Suite 157K
1900 Kanawha Blvd. E.
Charleston, WV 25305-0770
304-558-8000
Fax: 304-558-0900
www.wvsos.com/business/main.htm

Wisconsin

Department of Financial Institutions
Division of Corporate and Consumer Services
Corporation Section, 3rd Floor
P.O. Box 7846
Madison, WI 53707
608-261-7577
Fax: 608-267-6813
www.wdfi.org/corporations

Wyoming

Corporations Division
Secretary of State
State Capitol
Cheyenne, WY 82009
307-777-7311
http://soswy.state.wy.us/corporat/corporat.htm

State Agencies For Surplus Property

Alabama
Mr. Shane T. Bailey, Director
Surplus Property Division
P.O. Box 210487
Montgomery, AL 36121-0487
334-277-5866
Fax: 334-223-7320
www.adeca.state.al.us/adeca/pages/
ages_stm/surplus%20Property.stm

Alaska
Department of Administration
General Services Property
Property Management Office
2400 Viking Drive
Anchorage, AK 99501
907-279-0596
Fax: 907-278-0352
www.state.ak.us/local/akpages/ADMIN/
dgs/property/home.htm

American Samoa
American Samoa State Agency for Surplus
Property
c/o Office of Procurement
American Samoa Government
Pago, Pago AS 96799
684-699-1170
Fax: 684-699-2387
www.samoanet.com/asg/asgoop97.html

Arizona
Surplus Property Management Office
1700 W. Washington, Room 2244
Phoenix, AZ 85007
602-542-5675
Fax: 602-542-2010
www.msd.ad.state.az.us

Arkansas
Arkansas State Agency for Surplus Property
8700 Remount Road
North Little Rock, AR 72118
501-835-3111
Fax: 501-834-5240
www.work_ed.state.ar.us

California
Department of General Services
Procurement Division
1700 National Dr.
Sacramento, CA 95834-1938
916-928-4630
Fax: 916-928-0304
www.pd.dgs.ca.gov/default.
asp?mp=/materials/surplus.asp

Colorado
Colorado Surplus Property Agency
4200 Garfield Street
Denver, CO 80216-6517
303-370-2165
Fax: 303-320-1050
www.cijvp.com/

Connecticut
State and Federal Property Distribution
165 Capitol Avenue, 5th Floor
Hartford, CT 06106
860-713-5159
Fax: 860-713-7476

Delaware
Delaware Surplus Services

Division of Support Services
P.O Box 299
Delaware City, DE 19706
302-836-7640
Fax: 302-836-7298
www.state.de.us/purchase/html/
delaware_surplus_services.htm

District of Columbia
District of Columbia
Office of Contracting and Procurement
441 4th St., NW, Suite 800 South
Washington, DC 20002
202-576-6472
Fax: 202-576-7111
www.ocp.dcgov.org/main.shtm

Florida
Florida Department of Management Services
Bureau of Federal Property Assistance
813-A Lake Bradford Road
Tallahassee, FL 32304
850-488-3524
Fax: 850-487-3222
www.state.fl.us/fcn/centers/purchase/
fedsurp/sppage.html

Georgia
Georgia State Agency for Surplus Property
1050 Murphy Avenue
Building 12
Atlanta, GA 30310
404-756-4800
Fax: 404-756-4845
http://gasurplus.doas.state.ga.us/apps/
gss/surplus.nsf

Guam
Government of Guam
Department of Administration
P.O. Box 884
Agana, GU 96932
671-472-1725, ext. 47
Fax: 671-472-4217

Hawaii
Surplus Property Branch
729 Kakoi Street
Honolulu, HI 96819
808-831-6757
Fax: 808-831-6786

Idaho
Bureau of Federal Surplus Property
6941 South Supply Way
P.O. Box 83720
Boise, ID 83720-0086
208-334-3477
Fax: 208-334-5320
www2.state.id.us/adm/purchasing/
surplus/index.htm

Illinois
Illinois State Agency for Surplus Property
3550 Great Northern Avenue
Springfield, IL 62707
217-785-6903
Fax: 217-785-6905
www.state.il.us/cms/property/federal/
default.htm

Indiana
State of Indiana
Department of Administration

State and Federal Surplus Property
5700 W. Raymond St.
Indianapolis, IN 46241
317-260-4201
Fax: 317-260-4201
www.ai.org/idoa/surplus/index.html

Iowa
Iowa Federal Surplus Property
Department of General Services
6291 Chaffee Rd.
Des Moines, IA 50315
515-953-5747
Fax: 515-953-5767
www.state.ia.us/government/dgs/
Business/federalsurplus.htm

Kansas
Kansas Federal Surplus Property
3400 SE 10th Street
Topeka, KS 66607-2513
785-296-2351
Fax: 785-296-4060

Kentucky
Surplus Property Division
514 Barrett Avenue
Frankfort, KY 40601
502-564-4836
Fax: 502-564-2215
www.state.ky.us/agencies/adm/
mars/auction.htm

Louisiana
Louisiana Federal Property
1635 Foss Drive
Baton Rouge, LA 70802
225-342-7860
Fax: 225-342-7863

Maine
Surplus Property Program
85 Leighton Rd.
Augusta, ME 04333
207-287-5753
Fax: 207-287-7861
www.state.me.us/purchase/surplus/surplus.htm

Maryland
Federal Surplus Property
Maryland Department of General Services
8037 Brock Bridge Road
P.O. Box 1039
Jessup, MD 20794
410-799-0770
Fax: 410-799-2725
www.dgs.state.md.us/surplus

Massachusetts
State Agency for Surplus Property
Division of Capital Asset Management
One Ashburton Place, Room 1017
Boston, MA 02108-1552
508-792-7453
Fax: 508-368-1511
www.magnet.state.ma.us/cam/dcposp.htm

Michigan
Michigan State Agency for Surplus Property
3369 N. Martin Luther King Blvd.
P.O. Box 30026
Lansing, MI 48906
517-335-9105
Fax: 517-335-9559
www.state.mi.us/dmh/mgmt/
services/oss/mibid

Minnesota

Minnesota Surplus Services
Department of Administration
5420 Highway 8, Arden Hills
New Brighton, MN 55112
651-296-0726
Fax: 651-297-3996
www.mmd.admin.state.mn.us/mn03000.htm

Mississippi

Mississippi Office of Surplus Property
P.O. Box 5778
Jackson, MS 39288-5778
601-939-2050
866-281-6589
Fax: 601-939-4505
www.dfa.state.ms.us/surplusx.html

Missouri

Missouri State Agency for Surplus Property
117 N. Riverside Drive
Jefferson City, MO 65101
573-751-3415
Fax: 573-751-1264
www.oa.state.mo.us/purch/surplus.html

Montana

Property Supply Bureau
930 E. Lyndale Avenue
P.O. Box 200137
Helena, MT 59620-0137
406-495-6000
800-896-4481
Fax: 406-449-4952
www.mt.gov/doa/ppd/surplus.htm

Nebraska

Federal Surplus Property
2700 West Van Dorn
P.O. Box 94661
Lincoln, NE 68509-4661
402-471-2677
Fax: 402-471-2769
www.corrections.state.ne.us/surplus

Nevada

Personal Property management Program
2250 Barnett Way
Reno, NV 89512-3807
775-688-1161
Fax: 775-688-1503
http://purchasing.state.nv.us/property/prop.htm

New Hampshire

Department of Administrative Services
Bureau of Purchase and Property
State House Annex, Room 102
25 Capitol St.
Concord, NH 03301
603-271-2201
Fax: 603-271-2700
www.state.nh.us/das/purchasing/index.html

New Jersey

New Jersey State Agency for Surplus Property
152 U.S. Highway 206 South, Bldg. 15F
Somerville, NJ 08876
908-685-9562
Fax: 908-685-9578
www.state.nj.us/lps/njsp/ems/comb.html

New Mexico

New Mexico Federal Property Assistance
Program
1990 Siringo Road
Santa Fe, NM 87505-4757
505-827-4603
Fax: 505-827-4610
www.state.nm.us/spd/surprop/

New York

Bureau of Federal Property Assistance
1220 Washington Avenue
Building # 18
State Office Building Campus
Albany, NY 12226-1855
518-457-3264
Fax: 518-457-5436
www.ogs.state.ny.us/fedsurplus/default.asp

North Carolina

North Carolina Federal Property Agency
1950 Garner Road
1311 Mail Service Center
Raleigh, NC 27699-1311
919-733-3885
Fax: 919-733-3883
www.doa.state.nc.us/doa/fsp/fsp.htm

North Dakota

North Dakota State Agency
Igoe Industrial Park, Bldg. 12
P.O. Box 7293
Bismarck, ND 58507-7293
701-328-9665
Fax: 701-328-9669
www.state.nd.us/csd/surplus/

Northern Mariana Islands

Agency for Surplus Property
P.O. Box 11355
Saipan, MP 96950
670-664-1500
Fax: 670-664-1515

Ohio

Federal Surplus Property Program
4200 Surface Road
Columbus, OH 43228-1395
614-466-4485
Fax: 614-466-1584
www.state.oh.us/das/gsd/surplus/
fedSURP.html

Oklahoma

Oklahoma Property Distribution Division
3100 North Creston
Oklahoma City, OK 73111
405-425-2700
800-789-6776
Fax: 405-425-2713
www.dcs.state.ok.us/okdcs.nsf/htmlmedia/
property_distribution.html

Oregon

Department of Administrative Services
1655 Salem Industrial Drive, NE
Salem, OR 97303
503-378-4714
Fax: 503-378-8558
http://tpps.das.state.or.us/surplus/

Pennsylvania

Pennsylvania State Agency for Surplus
Property
2221 Forster Street, Room 6-50
P.O. Box 1365
Harrisburg, PA 17105-1365
717-787-9724, Extension 3205
Fax: 717-772-2491
www.dgs.state.pa.us/ssurplus/about.htm

Puerto Rico

State Agency for Federal Property Asst.
P.O. Box 7428
San Juan, PR 00916
787-759-7676, ext. 2321
Fax: 787-759-7385

Rhode Island

Rhode Island State Agency for Federal
Surplus Property
701 Power Road
Cranston, RI 02920
401-464-3452
Fax: 401-946-9518

South Carolina

Disposable Property Office
1441 Boston Avenue
West Columbia, SC 29170-2194
803-896-6880
Fax: 803-896-6899
www.ogs.state.sc.us/disposable/OGS-
disposable-index.html

South Dakota

South Dakota Federal Property Agency
Bureau of Administration
20 Colorado Avenue, SW
Huron, SD 57350-1898
605-353-7150
Fax: 605-353-7164
www.state.sd.us/boa/fsp.htm

Tennessee

Tennessee Department of General Services
Property Utilization Division
6500 Centennial Boulevard
Nashville, TN 37243-0543
615-350-3373
Fax: 615-350-3379
www.state.tn.us/generalserv/ba04s/

Texas

General Services Commission
Federal and State Surplus Property
1711 San Jacinto
P.O. Box 13047
Austin, TX 78711-3047
512-463-3438
888-472-0500
Fax: 512-463-3573
Email: dan.bremer@gsc.state.tx.us
www.gsc.state.tx.us/surplus/index.html

Utah

State Agency for Surplus Property
447 West 13800 South
Draper, UT 84020
801-619-7219
Fax: 801-619-7229
http://fleet.state.ut.us/

Vermont

Surplus Property Section
Rural Route 2, Box 520
124 Gallison Hill Rd.
Montpelier, VT 05602
802-828-3394
Fax: 802-828-3396
www.bgs.state.vt.us/GSC/surplus/

Virginia

Acting Surplus Property Administrator
Virginia Federal Property Agency
1910 Darbytown Road
Richmond, VA 23231
804-236-3664
Fax: 804-236-3663
http://159.169.222.200/dps

Virgin Islands

State Agency for Surplus Property
Sub Base Bldg. No.1
St. Thomas, VI 00802
809-774-0828
Fax: 809-777-8362

Washington

Washington State Agency for Surplus
Property
P.O. Box 41000
Olympiz, WA 98504-1000
253-333-4905
Fax: 253-333-4908
www.ga.wa.gov/surplus/surplus.htm

West Virginia
West Virginia State Agency for Surplus
Property
2700 Charles Avenue
Dunbar, WV 25064
304-766-2626
800-576-7587
Fax: 304-766-2631
www.state.wv.us/admin/purchase/surplus

Wisconsin
Wisconsin Division of Federal Property
One Foundation Circle
Waunakee, WI 53597-8914
608-849-2449
Fax: 608-849-2468
http://wtcsf.tec.wi.us/federal/

Wyoming
Wyoming Surplus Property
Department of Administration and Information
2045 Westland Road
Cheyenne, WY 82002-0060
307-777-7901
Fax: 307-634-5710
http://ai.state.wy.us/generalservices/index.asp

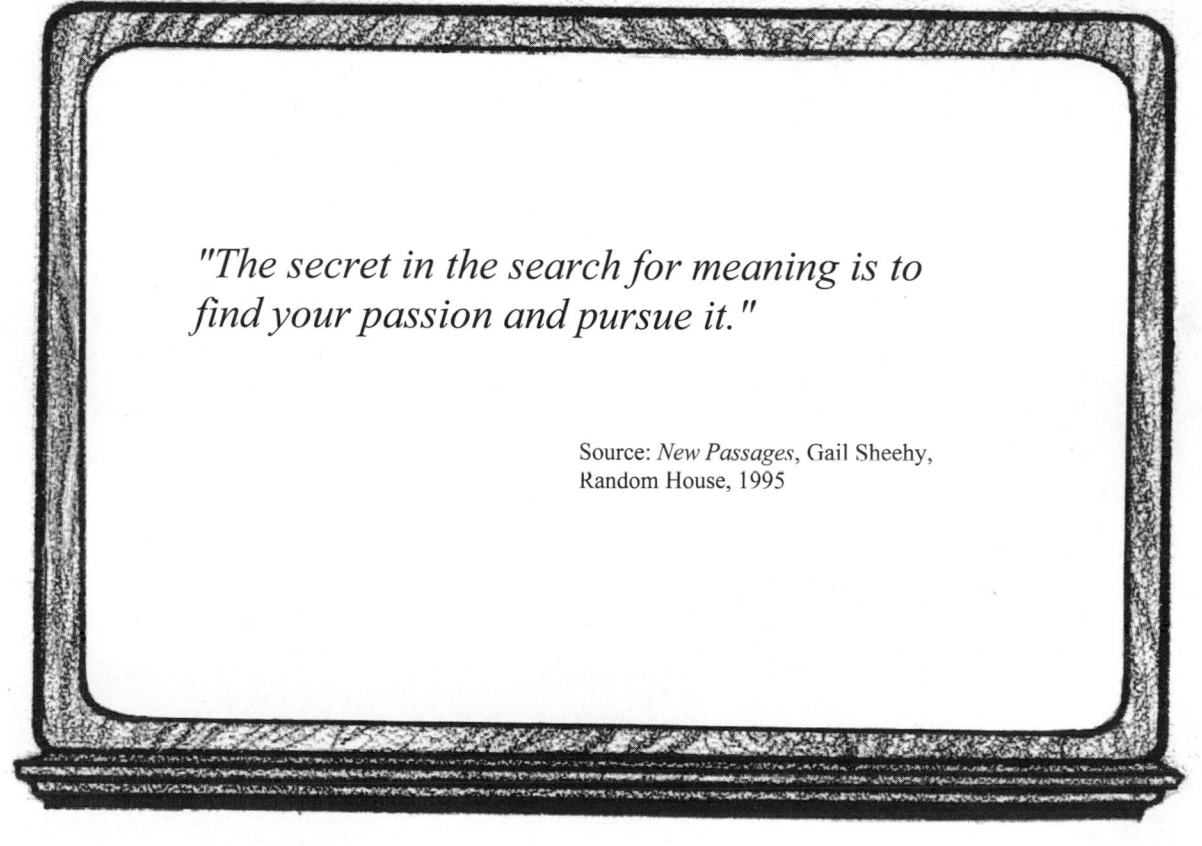

"The secret in the search for meaning is to find your passion and pursue it."

Source: *New Passages*, Gail Sheehy,
Random House, 1995

Matthew Lesko, Information USA, Inc., 12081 Nebel Street, Rockville, MD 20852 • 1-800-955-7693 • www.lesko.com

I Wanna Be a Volunteer

I Wanna Be a Volunteer

Volunteers are the backbone of almost every community service or public organization: Meals would not be delivered to seniors; children would not have scout masters; our parks would not be maintained. Volunteerism is also a great way to get the experience you may need to get a job. You can even try out a profession before you spend four years in college pursuing that career. You can meet people whose life experiences are different from yours and from whom you may learn a new way to look at an old problem. Being a volunteer also gets your foot in the door with potential new employers. They can see how you could fit into their organization and learn your work habits, skills, and abilities (at no real risk to them) before they might employ you on a full time basis. The Federal government has also provided an added onus for those who join the AmeriCorp program. Every volunteer earns $4,250 which is targeted for college or job training tuition. While you are an AmeriCorp volunteer, you also receive child care funds and health care coverage. Now, who says it doesn't pay to be a volunteer?

Below are some programs sponsored by the Federal government, but let these be a starting point for you. Your church, school, library, and other service organizations can provide you with other examples and opportunities to dedicate your free time towards helping to improve your own little corner of the world.

* America Reads
Corporation for National Service
1201 New York Ave., NW   202-606-5000
Washington, DC 20525   800-USA-LEARN
www.ed.gov/inits/americareads

America Reads is looking for programs and individuals who want to help kids learn to read. They have a resource kit available online.

* AmeriCorps*VISTA
Corporation for National Service
AmeriCorp Programs
1201 New York Ave., NW   202-606-5000
Washington, DC 20525   800-942-2677
www.americorps.org/vista

For more than 30 years, AmeriCorps*VISTA members have been serving disadvantaged communities. The program increases the capability of people to improve their lives. Members of AmeriCorps*VISTA work and live in the communities they serve, creating programs that can continue after they complete their service. Members must be at least 18 years old, and there is no upper age limit.

* Community Based Programs
Corporation for National Service
Learn and Serve Programs
1201 New York Ave., NW
Washington, DC 20525   202-606-5000, ext. 117
www.learnandserve.org

In Learn and Serve's Community Based Programs, state offices and nonprofit organizations implement, expand, and replicate service learning programs in local communities. Participants are between the ages of 5 and 17 and include students and youth who are not in school.

* Fish and Wildlife Service
U.S. Fish and Wildlife Service
4401 N. Fairfax Dr., Room 670
Arlington, VA 22203   703-358-1730
http://volunteers.fws.gov

Would you like to spend some time banding birds at a national wildlife refuge, feeding fish at a national fish hatchery, or doing research in a laboratory? Then consider volunteering with the U.S. Fish and Wildlife Service. There are no age requirements; however, anyone under 18 must have written parental approval. Young people under 16 years of age are encouraged to volunteer as part of a supervised group, such as a Boy Scout troop, Girl Scout troop, or 4H Club. Contact one of the U.S. Fish and Wildlife regional offices for possible volunteer programs in your area. Applications are also available online from the website above.

* Forest Service Volunteers
Public Affairs Office
Forest Service
U.S. Department of Agriculture
P.O. Box 96090   202-205-1760
Washington, DC 20090-6090   Fax: 202-205-0885
www.fs.fed.us/people/programs/volunteer.htm

The Forest Service has a volunteer program for almost everyone--retirees, professionals, housewives, students, teenagers, and youngsters. Typical jobs include working with specialists in resource protection and management, cooperative forestry, or research. You may also work at a Visitor Information Center by conducting interpretive natural history walks.

* Foster Grandparents Program
Corporation for National Service
National Senior Service Corps
1201 New York Ave., NW   202-606-5000
Washington, DC 20525   800-424-8867
www.seniorcorps.org/joining/fgp/index.html

Since 1965, the Foster Grandparents Program has provided valuable aid to children and youth with exceptional needs. Foster Grandparents serve 20 hours a week in schools, hospitals, drug treatment centers, correctional institutions, and Head Start and day care centers — helping children who have been abused or neglected, mentoring troubled teenagers and young mothers, and caring for premature infants and children with physical disabilities.

* Health Research Volunteers
National Institutes of Health
Warren Grant Magnuson Clinical Center   800-411-1222
Bethesda, MD 20892   Fax: 301-480-9793
www.nimh.nih.gov/studies/index.cfm

Many of the research programs at National Institutes of Health require normal volunteers who can provide clinicians with indices of normal body functions. There is a small compensation for their participation.

* Higher Education
Corporation for National Service
Learn and Serve Programs
1201 New York Ave., NW

Washington, DC 20525 202-606-5000, ext. 117
www.learnandserve.org

Learn and Serve America: Higher Education helps create and strengthen community service and service learning initiatives at colleges and universities, which involve a wide array of students and organizations working together to address community needs. Grants also support technical assistance for expanding the field of service learning.

* National Archives and Genealogy

Volunteer and Visitor Services
The National Archives and Records
 Administration 202-501-5205
Washington, DC 20408 Fax: 202-502-5248
www.nara.gov/professional/volunteer/naravol.html

Volunteers are needed to lead tours, welcome visitors at the information desk, assist staff with information and administrative services, and to become genealogical staff aides to assist new genealogical researchers. Positions are available in the Washington, DC area, regional facilities, and Presidential libraries.

* National Civilian Community Corp.

Corporation for National Service
AmeriCorp Programs
1201 New York Ave., NW
Washington, DC 20525 800-942-2677
www.americorps.org/nccc/index.html

A full time residential service program, AmeriCorps*NCCC (the National Civilian Community Corps) combines the best practices of civilian service with the best aspects of military service, including leadership and team building. Men and women, ages 18-24, serve full time and are based at one of the five AmeriCorps*NCCC campuses — in Perry Point, MD; Charleston, SC; Denver, CO, San Diego, CA, and Washington, DC.

* National Park Service

National Park Service
1849 C St., NW
Washington, DC 20240 202-208-6843
www.nps.gov/volunteer

The National Park Service provides many opportunities for volunteers to help at their many parks and historic sites. A volunteer application along with a listing of opportunities is available at their website. Contact the National Park nearest you for more information.

* Retired Business Executives

Service Corps of Retired Executives (SCORE)
National SCORE Office
U.S. Small Business Administration
409 Third St., SW, 6th Floor
Washington, DC 20024 800-634-0245
www.score.org

Retired business executives volunteer their time and services to help small business solve their operating and management problems. Assigned SCORE counselors visit the owners in their places of business to analyze the problems and offer guidance. In addition to learning more about the SCORE program by calling the toll-free SBA Answer Desk, also refer to your local telephone directory to contact the community-based SCORE center.

* Peace Corps Volunteers

Office of Private Sector Relations
Peace Corps
1111 20th St., NW
Washington, DC 20526 800-424-8580
www.peacecorps.gov

Here is your chance to travel to a distant land to offer a much needed helping hand. The Peace Corps' purpose is to promote world peace and friendship. Volunteers serve for two years, living among the people with whom they work. Volunteers are expected to become a part of the community. Projects are designed to match the skills of the volunteers to help solve specific development problems.

* Retired and Senior Volunteer Program

Corporation for National Service
National Senior Service Corps
1201 New York Ave., NW 202-606-5000

Washington, DC 20525 800-424-8867
www.seniorcorps.org/joining/rsvp/index.html

One of the largest volunteer efforts in the nation, the Retired and Senior Volunteer Program (RSVP) matches local problems with older Americans who are willing to help. RSVP members choose how and where they want to serve — and determine how many hours a week they can serve. They organize neighborhood watch programs, tutor teenagers, renovate homes, teach English to immigrants, program computers, help people recover from natural disasters — whatever their skills and interest lead them to do.

* School Based Programs

Corporation for National Service
Learn and Serve America Programs
1201 New York Ave., NW
Washington, DC 20525 202-606-5000, ext. 117
www.learnandserve.org

In Learn and Serve's School Based Programs, schools plan, implement, and expand service activities for elementary and secondary students. Schools also use Learn and Serve grants for adult volunteer programs and teacher training.

* Senior Companion Program

Corporation for National Service
National Senior Service Corps
1201 New York Ave., NW 202-606-5000
Washington, DC 20525 800-424-8867
www.seniorcorps.org/joining/scp/index.html

Providing assistance and friendship to seniors who have difficulties with daily living tasks, members of the Senior Companion Program help other seniors retain their dignity and independence. In their 20 hours of service each week, Senior Companions help clients with chores such as paying bills, buying groceries, and finding transportation to medical appointments. Senior Companions receive training in topics such as Alzheimer's Disease, stroke, diabetes, and mental health — and alert doctors and family members of potential health problems.

* Smithsonian Curatorial-Aides

Visitor Information and Associates'
 Reception Center
Smithsonian Institution
SI Building, Room 153
Washington, DC 20560 202-357-2700
www.si.edu/resource/faq/volunteer

Volunteers can participate in an independent program in which their educational and professional backgrounds are matched with curatorial or research requests from within the Smithsonian Institution. Go to their website to find a program that interests you.

* Smithsonian Museums Tour Guides

Visitor Information and Associates'
 Reception Center
Smithsonian Institution
SI Building, Room 153
Washington, DC 20560 202-357-2700

Volunteers are needed and welcomed at the Smithsonian Institution to serves as information volunteers or tour guides at many of the museums and Smithsonian programs and activities.

* Speakers for Community Groups

See all other Chapters.

Every federal department and many government agencies have a speakers bureau to inform interested organizations and citizen groups about many of the major community concerns. Many resources are available on medical issues such as health fairs and cholesterol screening. Public education, space programs, housing programs, weapons systems are some of the other areas where federal experts might be available to come to speak.

* Veterans Voluntary Service

Chief of Voluntary Services
810 Vermont Ave., NW
Washington, DC 20420 202-273-8952
www.va.gov/volunteer

Refer to your local telephone directory for the nearest VA hospital or medical center. Many opportunities exist for volunteers to help veterans.

I Wanna Be Trained

Free On-The-Job Training
Apprenticeship Skills Programs

Program: Apprenticeship Training — 17.201

Description: Getting a good job does not always mean that you must attend college or trade school, but no one will readily admit that. There are apprenticeship programs all over the country that will provide free on-the-job training — and you'll learn while you earn. Take that, frat rats.

Why would a company offer to train you for free? Simple — they get a skilled worker that they've trained themselves. And if they hire you after you complete your apprenticeship, they'll know exactly what they're getting.

Apprentices learn each skill of a job by carrying it out step by step under the close supervision of a skilled craftworker. An apprenticeship involves planned, day-by-day supervised training on the job, combined with technical instruction. Training may also include taking courses outside of working hours in such subjects as math, blueprint reading, applied English, and other technical courses.

Length of training varies depending on the job and is determined by standards adopted by a particular industry. For example, to learn welding may take you four years, while learning to paint houses may take only one or two years. The minimum term of apprenticeship is one year.

Who Is Eligible: An apprentice usually has a high school diploma or GED, and is at least 16 years or older, with manual dexterity and other characteristics directly related to the apprenticeable job to be learned. For the most part, there is no maximum age limit, although some construction area and industrial shop trades do have specific age limits.

Also, there are no income requirements: you can be rich, middle class, or poor, as long as you're willing to put in the time and work for the current apprenticeship rate. Remember, apprenticeships are not just for men: women comprise 7% of apprentices in the country, depending on the state, and the number is growing.

Wages Or Costs: You don't have to pay anything for the training. You may, however, be required to buy your own tools. Because an apprentice is technically a company employee, you will be paid an hourly wage by the company determined by how long you're in the program — therefore, the more you learn, the more you'll earn.

Wages begin at about half of what fully trained craftworkers make, and pay usually advances at six month intervals until you complete training. Then you too will be paid the full craftworker wage.

In Alabama, for example, apprentices can make up to $9 per hour to start (depending on the trade), and up to $18 per hour within a year or two. In North Carolina, the average starting pay for an apprentice is about $5 per hour, and the starting salary for a graduate apprentice can be as high as $20 per hour. Now, try to find those kind of pay increases anywhere else.

Types Of Jobs: Apprenticeable occupations can be found in such industries as construction, service, metal working, public administration, and the medical and health care fields. There are approximately 800 apprenticeable occupations currently recognized by the U.S. Department of Labor and the State Apprenticeship Agencies.

Programs may be sponsored by an employer, a group of employers, or a union. Often employers and unions form joint apprenticeship committees that determine industry needs for particular skills, the kind of training required, and then set the standards for acceptance into the programs.

Money Available: The Apprenticeship Training program receives $17,531,000 in annual funds from the Federal government.

National Office:

Office of Apprenticeship, Training, Employer and Labor Service
Bureau of Apprenticeship and Training
U.S. Department of Labor
200 Constitution Ave., NW
Washington, DC 20210
202-693-3812
www.doleta.gov/atels_bat/

Local Offices:

For more information, contact your state Bureau of Apprenticeship and training listed at the end of this section.

The following is a listing of some of the more popular occupations which use the apprenticeship program.

Apprenticeable Occupations
(Number refers to the required number of years of apprenticeship)

Occupation	Yrs
Accordion maker	4
Acoustical carpenter	4
Actor (amusement and recreation)	2
Air and hydronic balance technician	3
Air-conditioning mechanic (automotive services)	1
Air-conditioning installer, window	3
Aircraft mechanic, armament	4
Aircraft mechanic, electrical	4
Aircraft mechanic, plumb and hydraulics	4
Aircraft-armament mechanic (government services)	4
Aircraft-photograph-equipment mechanic	4
Airframe and power plant mechanic	4
Airplane coverer (aircraft)	4
Airplane inspector	3
Alarm operator (government services)	1
Alteration tailor	2
Ambulance attendant (EMT)	1
Animal trainer (amusement and recreation)	2
Architectural coatings finisher	3
Arson and bomb investigator	2
Artificial-glass-eye maker	5
Artificial-plastic-eye maker	5
Asphalt-paving machine operator	3
Assembler-installer, general	2
Assembler, aircraft, power	2
Assembler, aircraft, structures	4
Assembler, electromechanical	4
Assembler, metal building	2
Assembly technician	2
Assistant press operator	2
Audio operator	2
Audio-video repairer	2
Auger press operator, manual control	2
Automobile cooling system diagnostic technician	2
Automobile-maintenance-equipment servicer	4
Automobile-radiator mechanic	2
Automated equipment engineer-technician	4

Occupation	Yrs
Automatic-equipment technician (telephone and telegraph)	4
Automobile mechanic	4
Automobile tester (automotive services)	4
Automobile upholsterer	3
Automobile-body repairer	4
Automobile-repair-service estimator	4
Automotive-generator-and-starter repairer	2
Aviation safety equipment technician	4
Aviation support equipment repairer	4
Avionics technician	4
Baker (bakery products)	3
Baker (hotel and restaurant)	3
Baker, pizza (hotel and restaurant)	1
Bakery-machine mechanic	3
Bank-note designer	5
Barber	2
Bartender	1
Batch-and-furnace operator	4
Battery repairer	2
Beekeeper (agriculture and agricultural service)	4
Ben-day artist	6
Bench hand (jewelry)	2
Bindery worker	4
Bindery-machine setter	4
Biomedical equipment technician	4
Blacksmith	4
Blocker-and-cutter, contact lens	1
Boatbuilder, wood	4
Boiler operator (any industry)	4
Boilerhouse mechanic	3
Boilermaker fitter	4
Boilermaker I	4
Boilermaker II mechanic	3
Book binder	5
Bootmaker, hand	1
Bracelet and brooch maker	4
Brake repairer (automotive services)	2
Bricklayer (brick and tile)	4
Bricklayer, firebrick and refractory tile	4

Occupation	Yrs
Bricklayer (construction)	3
Brilliandeer-lopper (jewelry)	3
Butcher, all-round	3
Butcher, meat (hotel and restaurant)	3
Buttermaker (dairy products)	2
Cabinetmaker	4
Cable installer-repairer	3
Cable splicer	4
Cable television installer	1
Cable tester (telephone and telegraph)	4
Calibration laboratory technician	4
Camera operator	3
Camera repairer	2
Canal-equipment mechanic	2
Candy maker	3
Canvas worker	3
Car repairer (railroad locomotive and car building)	4
Carburetor mechanic (automotive services)	4
Card cutter, jacquard	4
Card grinder (asbestos products)	4
Carpenter	4
Carpenter, interior systems	4
Carpenter, maintenance	4
Carpenter, mold	6
Carpenter, piledriver	4
Carpenter, rough	4
Carpenter, ship (ship and boat building and repairing)	4
Carpet cutter (retail trade)	1
Carpet layer	3
Cartoonist, motion picture	3
Carver, hand	4
Cash-register servicer	3
Casing-in-line setter (printing and publishing	4
Casket assembler	6
Caster (jewelry)	2
Caster (nonferrous metal alloys and primary products)	2
Cell maker (chemicals)	1

Apprenticeship Training Program

Cement mason	2
Central-office installer (telephone and telegraph)	4
Central-office repairer	4
Chaser (jewelry; silverware)	4
Cheesemaker	2
Chemical operator III	3
Chemical-engineering technician	4
Chemical-laboratory technician	4
Chief of party (professional and kindred)	4
Chief operator (chemicals)	3
Child care development specialist	2
Chimney repairer	1
Clarifying-plant-operator (textiles)	1
Cloth designer	4
Coin-machine-service repairer	3
Colorist, photography	2
Commercial designer	4
Complaint inspector (light, heat, and power)	4
Composing-room machinist	6
Compositor	4
Computer operator	3
Computer programmer	2
Computer-peripheral-equipment-operator	1
Construction craft laborer	2
Construction-equipment-mechanic	4
Contour wire specialist, denture	4
Control equipment elec-tech	5
Conveyor-maintenance mechanic	2
Conveyor-system operator	4
Cook (any industry)	2
Cook (hotel and restaurant)	3
Cook, pastry (hotel and restaurant)	3
Cooling tower technician	2
Coppersmith (ship and boat building and repairing)	4
Coremaker	4
Cork insulator, refrigeration plant	4
Correction officer	1
Corrosion-control fitter	4
Cosmetologist	2
Counselor	2
Cupola tender	3
Custom tailor (garment)	4
Customer service representative	3
Cutter, machine I	3
Cylinder grinder (printing and publishing)	5
Cylinder-press operator	4
Dairy equipment repairer	3
Dairy technologist	4
Decorator (any industry)	4
Decorator (glass manufacturing)	4
Dental assistant	1
Dental ceramist	2
Dental-equipment installer and servicer	3
Dental-laboratory technician	3
Design and patternmaker (boot and shoe)	2
Design drafter, electromechanisms	4
Detailer	4
Diamond selector (jewelry)	4
Dictating-transcribing-machine servicer	3
Die designer	4
Die finisher	4
Die maker (jewelry)	4
Die maker (paper goods)	4
Die maker, bench, stamping	4
Die maker, stamping	3
Die maker, trim	4
Die maker, wire drawing	3
Die polisher (nonferrous metal alloys and primary products)	1
Die setter (forging)	2
Die sinker	4
Diesel mechanic	4
Diesel-engine tester	4
Director, funeral	2
Director, television	2
Dispatcher, service	2
Display designer (professional and kindred)	4
Displayer, merchandise	1

Door-closer mechanic	3
Dot etcher	5
Drafter, automotive design	4
Drafter, automotive design layout	4
Drafter, architectural	4
Drafter, cartographic	4
Drafter, civil	4
Drafter, commercial	4
Drafter, detail	4
Drafter, electrical	4
Drafter, electronic	4
Drafter, heating and ventilating	4
Drafter, landscape	4
Drafter, marine	4
Drafter, mechanical	4
Drafter, plumbing	4
Drafter, structural	3
Drafter, tool design	4
Dragline operator	1
Dredge operator (construction, mining)	1
Dressmaker	4
Drilling-machine operator	3
Dry cleaner	3
Dry-wall applicator	2
Electric-distribution checker	2
Electric-meter installer I	4
Electric-meter repairer	4
Electric-meter tester	4
Electric-motor assembler and tester	4
Electric-motor repairer	4
Electric-motor-and-generator assembler	2
Electric-sign assembler	4
Electric-tool repairer	4
Electric-track-switch maintainer	4
Electrical technician	4
Electrical-appliance repairer	3
Electrical-appliance servicer	3
Electrical-instrument repairer	3
Electrician	4
Electrician (ship and boat building and repairing)	4
Electrician (water transportation)	4
Electrician, aircraft	4
Electrician, automotive	2
Electrician, locomotive	4
Electrician, maintenance	4
Electrician, powerhouse	4
Electrician, radio	4
Electrician, substation	3
Electromechanical technician	3
Electromedical-equipment repairer	2
Electronic prepress system operator	5
Electronic-organ technician	2
Electronic-production-line-maintenance mechanic	1
Electronic-sales-and-service technician	4
Electronics mechanic	4
Electronics technician	4
Electronics tester	3
Electronics utility worker	4
Electrotyper	5
Elevating-grader operator	2
Elevator constructor	4
Elevator repairer	4
Embalmer (personal service)	2
Embosser	2
Embossing-press operator	4
Emergency medical technician	3
Engine model maker	4
Engine repairer, service	4
Engine turner (jewelry)	2
Engine-lathe set-up operator	2
Engine-lathe set-up operator, tool	2
Engineering assistant, mechanical equipment	4
Engraver glass	2
Engraver I	5
Engraver, block (printing and publishing)	4
Engraver, hand, hard metal	4
Engraver, hand, soft metal	4
Engraver, machine	4
Engraver, pantograph I	4

Engraver, picture (printing and publishing)	10
Engraving press operator	3
Envelope-folding-machine adjuster	3
Environmental analyst	3
Equipment installer (telephone and telegraph)	4
Estimator and drafter	4
Etcher, hand (print and publishing)	5
Etcher, photoengraving	4
Experimental mechanic (motor and bicycles)	4
Experimental assembler	2
Exterminator, termite	2
Extruder operator plastics	1
Fabricator-assembler, metal products	4
Facilities locator	2
Farm-equipment, mechanic I	3
Farm-equipment mechanic II	4
Farmer, general (agriculture and agricultural service)	4
Farmworker, general I	1
Fastener technologist	3
Field engineer (radio and television broadcasting)	4
Field service engineer	2
Film developer	3
Film laboratory technician	3
Film laboratory technician I	3
Film or videotape editor	4
Finisher, denture	1
Fire apparatus engineer	3
Fire captain	3
Fire engineer	1
Fire fighter	3
Fire fighter, crash, fire	1
Fire inspector	4
Fire medic	3
Fire-control mechanic	2
Firer, kiln (pottery and porcelain)	3
Fish and game warden (government services)	2
Fitter (machine shop)	2
Fitter I (any industry)	3
Fixture maker (lighting fixtures)	2
Floor layer	3
Floral designer	1
Floor-covering layer (railroad locomotive and car building)	3
Folding-machine operator	2
Forge-shop-machine repairer	3
Forging-press operator I	1
Form builder (construction)	2
Former, hand (any industry)	2
Forming-machine operator	4
Foundry metallurgist	4
Four-slide-machine setter	2
Fourdrinier-machine tender	3
Freezer operator (dairy products)	1
Fretted-instrument repairer	3
Front-end mechanic	4
Fuel injection servicer	4
Fuel-system-maintenance-worker	2
Fur cutter (fur goods)	2
Fur designer (fur goods)	4
Fur finisher (fur goods)	2
Furnace installer	3
Furnace installer and repairer	4
Furnace operator	4
Furniture designer	4
Furniture finisher	3
Furniture upholsterer	4
Furrier (fur goods)	4
Gang sawyer, stone	2
Gas appliance servicer	3
Gas utility worker	3
Gas-engine repairer	4
Gas-main fitter	4
Gas-meter mechanic I	3
Gas-regulator repairer	3
Gauger (petroleum products)	2
Gear hobber set-up operator	4

Gear-cutting mach set-up operator	3	Landscape technician	2	Miller, wet process	3
Gear-cutting mach set-up operator, tool	3	Last-model maker	4	Milling-machine set-up operator	2
Gem cutter (jewelry)	3	Lather	3	Millwright	4
Geodetic computer	2	Laundry-machine mechanic	3	Mine-car repairer	2
Glass bender (signs)	4	Lay-out technician	4	Miner I (mining and quarry)	1
Glass blower	3	Lay-out worker (any industry)	4	Mock-up builder (aircraft)	4
Glass blower, laboratory apparatus	4	Lead burner	4	Model and mold maker (brick and tile)	2
Glass installer (automotive services)	2	Leather stamper	1	Model and mold maker, plaster	4
Glass-blowing-lathe operator	4	Legal secretary	1	Model builder (furniture)	2
Glazier	3	Letterer (professional and kindred)	2	Model maker (clocks, watches, and	
Glazier, stained glass	4	Licensed practical nurse	1	allied products)	4
Grader (woodworking)	4	Light technician	4	Model maker (aircraft manufacturing)	4
Graphic designer	1	Line erector	3	Model maker II	4
Greenskeeper II	2	Line installer-repairer	4	Model maker pottery	4
Grinder I (clocks, watches, and		Line maintainer	4	Model maker (automobile manufacturing)	4
allied products)	4	Line repairer	3	Model maker, firearms	4
Grinder operator, tool, precision	4	Liner (pottery and porcelain)	3	Model maker, wood	4
Grinder set-up operator, jig	4	Linotype operator (printing and		Mold maker (pottery and porcelain)	3
Grinder set-up operator, universal	4	publishing)	5	Mold maker II (jewelry)	2
Gunsmith	4	Lithograph-press operator tin	4	Mold maker (jewelry)	4
		Lithographic platemaker	4	Mold maker, die-casting and	
Harness maker	3	Locksmith	4	plastic molding	4
Harpsichord maker	2	Locomotive engineer	4	Mold setter	1
Hat-block maker (woodwork)	3	Loft worker (ship and boat		Molder	4
Hazardous-waste material technician	2	building and repairing)	4	Molder, pattern (foundry)	2
Head sawyer	3	Logger, all-round	2	Monotype-keyboard operator	3
Health care sanitary technician	1	Logging-equipment mechanic	4	Monument setter (construction)	4
Heat treater I	4	Logistics engineer	4	Mosaic worker	3
Heat-transfer technician	4	Loom fixer	3	Motor-grader operator	3
Heating/air-conditioning installer				Motorboat mechanic	3
and servicer	3	Machine assembler	2	Motorcycle repairer	3
Heavy forger	4	Machine builder	2	Multi-operation-forming-machine setter	4
Horse trainer	1	Machine erector	4	Multi-operation-machine operator	3
Horseshoer	2	Machine fixer (carpet and rug)	4	Multi-story window/build	3
Horticulturist	3	Machine fixer (textile)	3		
Housekeeper	1	Machine operator I	1	Neon-sign servicer	5
Hydraulic-press servicer (ammunition)	2	Machine repairer, maintenance	4	Nondestructive tester	1
Hydraulics repairer	4	Machine set-up operator, paper	4	Numerical-control-machine operator	4
Hydroelectric-machinery mechanic	3	Machine set-up operator	2	Nurse assistant	1
Hydroelectric-station operator	3	Machine setter	3		
Hydrometer calibrator	2	Machine setter	4	Office-machine servicer	3
		Machine setter (clocks, watches,		Offset-press operator I	4
Illustrator (professional and kindred)	4	and allied products)	4	Oil-burner-servicer and installer	2
Industrial designer	4	Machine setter (woodwork)	4	Oil-field equipment mechanic	2
Industrial engineering technician	4	Machine try-out setter	4	Operating engineer	3
Injection-molding-machine operator	1	Machinist	4	Operational test mechanic	3
Inspector, building	3	Machinist, automotive	4	Optical-instrument assembler	2
Inspector, electromechanical	4	Machinist, experimental	4	Optician	5
Inspector, metal-fabricating	4	Machinist, linotype	4	Optician (optical goods)	4
Inspector, outside production	4	Machinist, marine engine	4	Optician-dispensing	2
Inspector, precision	2	Machinist, motion-pic equipment I	2	Optomechanical technician	4
Inspector, quality assurance	3	Machinist, outside (ship and boat		Ordinance artificer (government services)	3
Inspector, motor vehicles	2	building and repairing)	4	Ornamental-iron worker	3
Inspector, set-up and lay-out	4	Machinist, wood	4	Ornamental-metal worker	4
Instrument repairer (any industry)	4	Mailer	4	Orthopedic-boot-and-shoe designer	
Instrument technician (light, heat,		Maintenance mechanic (any industry)	4	and maker	5
and power)	4	Maintenance mechanic (grain and		Orthotics technician	1
Instrument maker	4	feed milling)	2	Orthotist	5
Instrument maker and repairer	5	Maintenance mechanic (petroleum		Orthodontic technician	2
Instrument mechanic (any industry)	4	products; construction)	4	Outboard-motor mechanic	2
Instrumentation technician	4	Maintenance repairer, industrial	4	Overhauler (textile)	2
Instrument mechanic, weapons system	4	Maintenance machinist	4		
Insulation worker	4	Maintenance mechanic, (compressed		Painter	3
Interior designer	2	and liquified gases)	4	Painter (professional and kindred)	1
Investigator, private	1	Maintenance mechanic, telephone	3	Painter, hand (any industry)	3
		Maintenance repairer, building	2	Painter, shipyard (ship and boat	
Jacquard-loom weaver	4	Manager, food service	3	building and repairing)	3
Jacquard-plate maker	1	Manager, retail store	3	Painter, sign	4
Jeweler	2	Marble finisher	2	Painter, transportation equipment	3
Jig builder wood box	2	Marble setter	3	Pantograph-machine set-up operator	2
Job printer	4	Marine-service technician	3	Paperhanger	2
Joiner (ship and boat building		Material coordinator (clerical)	2	Paralegal	3
and repairing)	4	Materials engineer	5	Paramedic	2
		Meat cutter	3	Paste-up artist	3
Kiln operator (woodworking)	3	Mechanical-engineering technician	3	Patternmaker (textiles)	3
Knitter mechanic	4	Mechanic, endless track vehicle	4	Patternmaker (metal prod)	4
Knitting-machine fixer	4	Mechanic, industrial truck	4	Patternmaker (stonework)	4
		Mechanical-unit repairer	4	Patternmaker, all-around	5
Laboratory assistant	3	Medical secretary	1	Patternmaker, metal	5
Laboratory assistant metallurgical	2	Medical-laboratory technician	2	Patternmaker, metal, bench	5
Laboratory technician	1	Metal fabricator	4	Patternmaker, plaster	3
Laboratory tester	2	Meteorological equipment repairer	4	Patternmaker, plastics	3
Landscape gardener	4	Meteorologist	3	Patternmaker, wood	5
Landscape management technician	1	Meter repairer (any industry)	3	Pewter caster	3

Apprenticeship Training Program

Pewter fabricator	4	Quality-control inspector	2	Sound technician	3
Pewter finisher	2	Quality-control technician	2	Spinner, hand	3
Pewterer	2			Spring coiling machine setter	4
Pharmacist assistant	1	Radiation monitor	4	Spring maker	4
Photo-equipment technician	3	Radio mechanic (any industry)	3	Spring manufacturing set-up technician	4
Photocomposing-perforator-machine		Radio repairer (any industry)	4	Spring repairer, hand	4
operator	2	Radio station operator	4	Stage technician	3
Photoengraver	5	Radiographer	4	Stained glass artist	4
Photoengraving finisher	5	Recording engineer	2	Station installer and repairer	4
Photoengraving printer	5	Recovery operator (paper)	1	Stationary engineer	4
Photoengraving proofer	5	Refinery operator	3	Steam service inspector	4
Photogrammetric technician	3	Refrigeration mechanic (any industry)	3	Steel-die printer	4
Photographer retoucher	3	Refrigeration unit repairer	3	Stencil cutter	2
Photographer, lithographic	5	Reinforcing metal worker	3	Stereotyper	6
Photographer, photoengraving	6	Relay technician	2	Stoker erector-and-service	4
Photographer, still	3	Relay tester	4	Stone carver	3
Photographic-equipment-maintenance		Repairer I (chemical)	4	Stone polisher	3
technician	3	Repairer, handtools	3	Stone setter (jewelry)	4
Photographic-plate maker	4	Repairer, heavy	2	Stone-lathe operator	3
Piano technician	4	Repairer, welding equipment	2	Stonecutter, hand	3
Piano tuner	3	Repairer, welding system and equipment	3	Stonemason	3
Pilot, ship	1.5	Reproduction technician	1	Street-light servicer	4
Pinsetter adjuster, automatic	3	Research mechanic (aircraft)	4	Stripper (printing and publishing)	5
Pinsetter mechanic, automatic	2	Residential carpenter	2	Stripper, lithographic II	4
Pipe coverer and insulator (ship and		Retoucher, photoengraving	5	Structural-steel worker	3
boat building)	4	Rigger	3	Substation operator	4
Pipe fitter (construction)	4	Rigger (ship and boat building		Supercargo (water transportation)	2
Pipe organ builder	3	and repairing)	2	Surface-plate finisher	2
Pipe fitter (ship and boat building		Rocket-engine-component mechanic	4	Surveyor assistant, instru.	2
and repairing)	4	Rocket-motor mechanic	4	Swimming-pool servicer	2
Pipe-organ tuner and repairer	4	Roll threader operator	1	Switchboard operator (light, heat,	
Plant operator	3	Roller engraver, hand	2	and power)	3
Plant operator, furnace process	4	Roofer	3		
Plaster-pattern caster	5	Rotogravure-press operator	4	Tank setter (petroleum products)	2
Plasterer	2	Rubber tester (rubber goods)	4	Tape-and-die maker technician	4
Plastic process technician	4	Rubber-stamp maker	4	Tape-recorder repairer	4
Plastic tool maker	4	Rubberizing mechanic	4	Taper	2
Plastic-fixture builder	4	Rug cleaner, hand	1	Taxidermist (professional and kindred)	3
Plastics fabricator	2			Teacher aide I	2
Plate finisher (printing and publishing)	6	Saddle maker (leather)	2	Technician, submarine cable equipment	2
Platen-press operator	4	Safe and vault service mechanic	4	Telecommunications technician	4
Plater	3	Salesperson, parts	2	Telecommunicator	4
Plumber	4	Sample maker, appliances	4	Telegraphic-typewriter operator	3
Pneumatic-tool repairer	4	Sample stitcher (garment)	4	Television and radio repairer	4
Pneumatic-tube repairer	2	Sandblaster, stone	3	Template maker	4
Podiatric assistant	2	Saw filer (any industry)	4	Template maker, extrusion die	4
Police officer I	2	Saw maker (cutlery and tools)	3	Terrazzo finisher	2
Pony edger (sawmill)	2	Scale mechanic	4	Terrazzo worker	3
Post-office clerk	2	Scanner operator	2	Test equipment mechanic	5
Pottery-machine operator	3	Screen printer	2	Test technician (professional and kindred)	5
Power-plant operator	4	Screw-machine operator, multiple spindle	4	Test-engine operator	2
Power-saw mechanic	3	Screw-machine operator, single spindle	3	Tester	3
Power-transformer repairer	4	Screw-machine set-up operator	4	Testing and regulating technician	4
Powerhouse mechanic	4	Screw-machine set-up operator,		Thermometer tester	1
Precision assembler	3	single spindle	3	Tile finisher	2
Precision assembler, bench	2	Script supervisor (motion pictures)	1	Tile setter	3
Precision-lens grinder	4	Service mechanic (automobile		Tool builder	4
Press operator, heavy duty	4	manufacturing)	2	Tool design checker	4
Printer, plastic	4	Service planner	4	Tool designer	4
Printer-slotter operator	4	Sewing-machine repairer	3	Tool grinder I	3
Process/shipping technician	4	Sheet metal worker	4	Tool maker	4
Program assistant	3	Ship propeller finisher	3	Tool maker, bench	4
Programmer, engineering and scientific	4	Shipfitter (ship and boat building		Tool-and-die maker	4
Project printer (photofinishing)	4	and repairing)	4	Tool-grinder operator	4
Proof-press operator	5	Shipwright (ship and boat building		Tool-machine set-up operator	3
Proofsheet corrector (printing and		and repairing)	4	Tool programmer, numerical	3
publishing)	4	Shoemaker, custom	3	Tractor mechanic	4
Prop maker (amusement and recreation)	4	Shop optician, surface room	4	Transformer repairer	4
Propulsion-motor-and-generator repairer	4	Shop optician, benchroom	4	Transmission mechanic	2
Prospecting driller (petroleum products)	2	Shop tailor (garment)	4	Transportation clerk	1.5
Prosthetics technician	4	Siderographer (printing and publishing)		Treatment-plant mechanic	3
Prosthetist (personal protective		Sign erector I	4	Tree surgeon (agriculture and	
and medical devices)	5	Sign writer, hand	1	agricultural service)	3
Protective-signal installer	4	Signal maintainer (railroad		Tree trimmer	2
Protective-signal repairer	3	locomotive and car building)	4	Trouble locator, test desk	2
Prototype model maker	4	Silk-screen cutter	3	Trouble shooter II	3
Private-branch-exchange installer		Silversmith II	3	Truck driver, heavy	1
(telephone and telegraph)	4	Sketch maker I (printing and publishing)	5	Truck-body builder	4
Private-branch-exchange repairer	4	Sketch maker II	4	Truck-crane operator	3
Pump erector (construction)	2	Small-engine mechanic	2	Tuck pointer, cleaner caulker	3
Pump servicer	3	Soft-tile setter (construction)	3	Tumor registrar	2
Pumper-gauger	3	Soil-conservation technician	3	Tune-up mechanic	2
Purchasing agent	4	Solderer (jewelry)	3	Turbine operator	4
Purification operator II	4	Sound mixer	4	Turret-lathe set-up operator	4

Upholsterer	2	Water treatment-plant operator		Wildland fire fighter specialist	1
Upholsterer, inside	3	(waterworks)	3	Wind tunnel mechanic	4
		Weather observer	2	Wind-instrument repairer	4
Violin maker, hand	4	Web-press operator	4	Wine maker (vinous liquor)	2
		Welder, arc	4	Wire sawyer (stonework)	2
Wallpaper printer I	4	Welder, combination	3	Wire weaver, cloth	4
Wardrobe supervisor	2	Welder-fitter	4	Wirer (office machine)	2
Waste-treatment operator	2	Welding technician	4	Wood-turning-lathe operator	1
Wastewater-treatment-plant operator	2	Welding-machine operator, arc	3		
Watch repairer	4	Well-drill operator (construction)	4	X-ray equipment tester	2

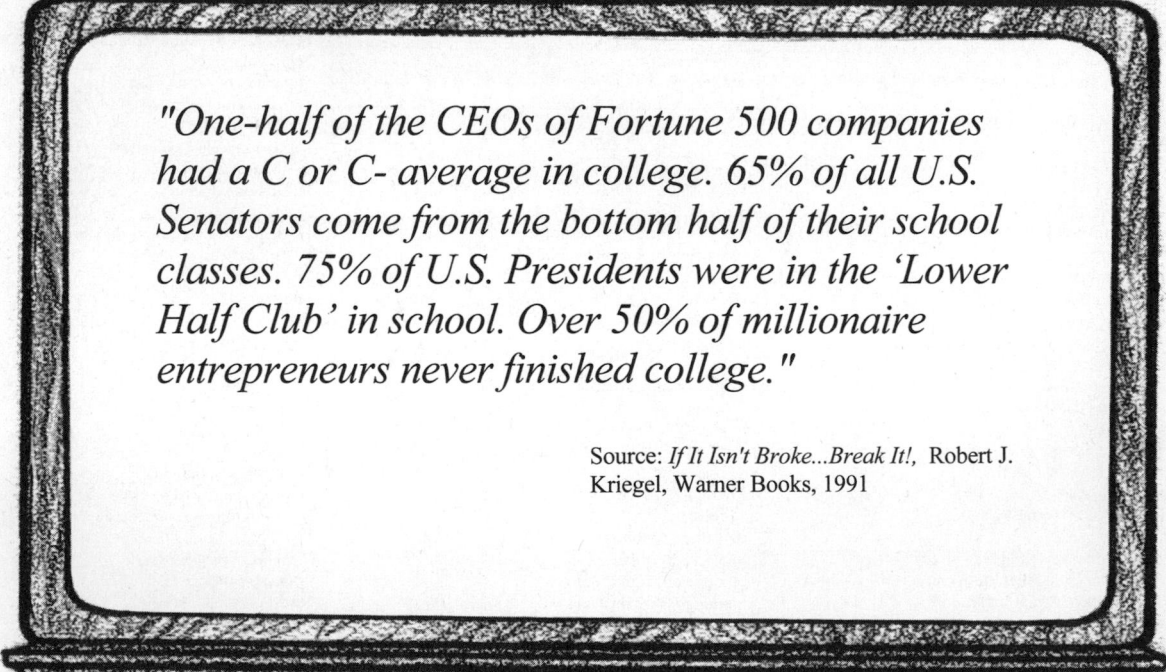

"One-half of the CEOs of Fortune 500 companies had a C or C- average in college. 65% of all U.S. Senators come from the bottom half of their school classes. 75% of U.S. Presidents were in the 'Lower Half Club' in school. Over 50% of millionaire entrepreneurs never finished college."

Source: *If It Isn't Broke...Break It!,* Robert J. Kriegel, Warner Books, 1991

Matthew Lesko, Information USA, Inc., 12081 Nebel Street, Rockville, MD 20852 • 1-800-955-7693 • www.lesko.com

State Bureaus of Apprenticeship and Training

The following is a state by state listing of offices to contact for information on apprenticeship programs in your area.

Alabama
Bureau of Apprenticeship and Training
U.S. Department of Labor
950 22nd Street N
Medical Forum Building
Room 648
Birmingham, AL 35203
205-731-1308

Alabama Department of Industrial Relations
649 Monroe Street
Montgomery, AL 36131
334-242-8990
www.dir.state.al.us/index.html

Alaska
Bureau of Apprenticeship and Training
U.S. Department of Labor
605 West 4th Avenue
Anchorage, AK 99501
907-271-5035

Department of Labor and Workforce
Development
P.O. Box 21149
Juneau, AK 99802
907-465-2700
www.ajcn.state.ak.us/apprentice

Arizona
Bureau of Apprenticeship and Training
U.S. Department of Labor
3221 North 16th Street
Suite 105
Phoenix, AZ 85106
602-640-2964

Department of Commerce
Workforce Development
3800 North Central Avenue
Suite 1500
Phoenix, AZ 85102
602-280-8133
www.commerce.state.az.us/wfd/cover.html

Arkansas
Bureau of Apprenticeship and Training
U.S. Department of Labor
Federal Building, Room 3507
700 West Capitol Street
Little Rock, AR 72201
501-324-5415

Employment Security Department
#2 Capitol Mall
P.O. Box 2981
Little Rock, AR 72203
501-682-2121
www.state.ar.us/esd

California
Bureau of Apprenticeship and Training
U.S. Department of Labor
1301 Clay Street
Oakland, CA 94612
510-637-2951

California Employment Development
Department
800 Capitol Mall, MIC 83
Sacramento, CA 95814
916-653-0707
wwwedd.cahwnet.gov/emptran.htm

Colorado
Bureau of Apprenticeship and Training
U.S. Department of Labor
721 19th Street, Room 469
Denver, CO 80202
303-844-4794

Colorado Department of Labor & Employment
1515 Arapahoe, Tower 2, Suite 400
Denver, CO 80202
303-318-8000
www.coworkforce.com

Connecticut
Bureau of Apprenticeship and Training
U.S. Department of Labor
Federal Building
135 High Street, Room 367
Hartford, CT 06103
203-240-4311

Employment and Training
Connecticut Labor Department
200 Folly Brook Boulevard
Wethersfield, CT 06109
860-263-6085
www.ctdol.state.ct.us/progsupt/appren/
appren.htm

Business Services Unit
2 Lafayette Square
Bridgeport, CT 06604
203-330-4830
www.ctdol.state.ct.us/bridgept/bridgefacts.htm

Business Services Unit
152 West Street
Danbury, CT 06813
203-731-2929
www.ctdol.state.ct.us/danbury/danbfacts.htm

Business Services Unit
95 Westcott Road
Danielson, CT 06239
860-779-5850
www.ctdol.state.ct.us/danielsn/dnlsnfacts.htm

Business Services Unit
37 Marne Street
Hamden, CT 06514
203-789-7683
www.ctdol.state.ct.us/hamden/hamdfacts.htm

Business Services Unit
3580 Main Street
Hartford, CT 06120
860-566-5727
www.ctdol.state.ct.us/hartford/htfdfacts.htm

Business Services Unit
290 Pratt Street
Meriden, CT 06450
203-238-6148
www.ctdol.state.ct.us/meriden/merifacts.htm

Business Services Unit
260 Lafayette Street
New Britain, CT 06053
860-827-4460
www.ctdol.state.ct.us/newbritn/nbritfacts.htm

Business Services Unit
Shaw's Cove Six
New London, CT 06320

860-447-6208
www.ctdol.state.ct.us/newlondn/newlfacts.htm

Business Services Unit
249 Thomaston Avenue
Waterbury, CT 06702
203-596-4130
www.ctdol.state.ct.us/waterbry/wtbyfacts.htm

Delaware
Bureau of Apprenticeship and Training
U.S. Department of Labor
Lock Box 36
Federal Building
844 King Street
Wilmington, DE 19801
302-573-6113
(Temporarily Closed)

Apprenticeship and Training
Division of Employment and Training
State Department of Labor
4425 North Market Street
Wilmington, DE 19802
302-368-6909
www.delawareworks.com/services.htm

District of Columbia
Apprenticeship Information and Training
Office
Department of Employment Services
609 H Street, NE
Washington, DC 20002
202-698-5099
http://does.dc.gov/services/appren.shtm

Florida
Bureau of Apprenticeship and Training
U.S. Department of Labor
City Centre Building, Suite 4140
227 North Bronough Street
Tallahassee, FL 32301
850-942-8336

Florida Division of Workforce Development
325 West Gaines Street
Turlington Building, Room 714
Tallahassee, FL 32399
850-922-5021
www.firn.edu/doe/bin00057/index.html

Service Area I & II: Pensacola, Tallahassee,
and Jacksonville
215 Market Street, Suite 300
Jacksonville, FL 32202-2885
904-359-6080 ext. 102

Service Area III: Orlando
2133 All Children Way
Orlando, FL 32818-5272
407-521-2510

Service Area IV: Melbourne
Cocoa/Melbourne, FL
Beeper: 321-883-0002 (Rob Grisar)

Service Area V & VI: West Palm Beach,
Hollywood
2550 West Oakland Park Boulevard
Fort Lauderdale, FL 33311
954-677-5816

Service Area VII: Miami
2550 West Oakland Park Boulevard

Fort Lauderdale, FL 33311
954-677-5816

Service Area III: Sarasota
Beeper: 941-988-0002 (Donna Beasley)

Service Area X: Tampa, St. Petersburg
Tampa Employment Center
9215 North Florida Avenue, Suite 106
Tampa, FL 33612
813-930-7588

Service Area XI: Pinellas Park
Clearwater, FL
Beeper: 727-559-3012 (Cindy Durant)

Georgia
Bureau of Apprenticeship and Training
U.S. Department of Labor
61 Forsyth Street, SW
Room 6T80
Atlanta, GA 30303
404-562-2323

Georgia Department of Labor
148 International Boulevard, NE
Atlanta, GA 30303
404-656-3017
www.dol.state.ga.us

Hawaii
Bureau of Apprenticeship and Training
U.S. Department of Labor
300 Ala Moana Boulevard
Honolulu, HI 96850
808-541-2519

Department of Labor and Industrial Relations
Apprenticeship Division
830 Punchbowl Street
Honolulu, HI 96813
808-586-8877
www.dlir.state.hi.us

Idaho
Bureau of Apprenticeship and Training
U.S. Department of Labor
1150 North Curtis Road
Suite 204
Boise, ID 83706-1234
208-321-2973

Idaho Department of Labor
Workforce Development Division
317 West Main Street
Boise, ID 83735-0600
208-334-6252
www.idahoworks.org

Illinois
Bureau of Apprenticeship and Training
U.S. Department of Labor
230 South Dearborn Street
Room 656
Chicago, IL 60604
312-353-4690

Department of Employment Security
Apprenticeship Information Center
6 South, 401 South State Street
Chicago, IL 60605
312-793-5700
www.ides.state.il.us/individual/special/
apprentc.htm

Chicago
2550 West Addison Street, 773-296-6021
244 West Lawrence Avenue, 773-334-6646
4931 West Diversey Avenue, 773-889-6820
5101 South Cicero Avenue, 773-838-3100
3500 West Grand Avenue, 773-227-7117
1657 Sout Blue Island Avenue, 312-243-5100
1515 East 71st Street, 773-947-2500

8750 South Stony Island Avenue, 773-221-
3737
837 West 119th Street, 773-821-4100
715 East 47th Street, 773-538-9811
Richard J. Daley College, 7500 South Pulaski
Road, Building 100, 773-838-6415
Wright College-South, 3400 North Austin
Avenue, Room 352, 773-736-5627

Arlington Heights
723 West Algonquin Road, 847-981-7400

Bolingbrook
321 Quadrangle Drive, 630-759-0647

Burbank
5608 West 75th Place, 708-458-0500

Chicago Heights
1010 Dixie Highway, 708-709-3000

Cicero
2138 South 61st Court, 708-222-3100

Elgin
30 DuPage Court, 847-888-7900

Evanston
1527 Maple Avenue, 847-864-3530

Grayslake
800 Lancer Lane (on the College of Lake
County), 847-543-7400

Harvey
14829 Dixie Highway, 708-596-2325

Joliet
1115 Plainfield Road, 815-727-4444

Kankakee
255 North Schuyler, 815-932-0035

Lombard
837 South Westmore-Myers Road, 630-495-
4345

Maywood
35 South 19th Avenue, 708-338-6900

North Aurora
2 Smoke Tree Plaza, 630-844-6640

Woodstock
500 Russel Court, 815-338-7940

Indiana
Bureau of Apprenticeship and Training
U.S. Department of Labor
Federal Building and U.S. Courthouse
46 East Ohio Street, Room 414
Indianapolis, IN 46204
317-226-7592

Indiana Department of Labor
Workforce Development Division
10 North Senate
Indianapolis, IN 46204
888-WORKONE
www.ai.org/dwd

Iowa
Bureau of Apprenticeship and Training
U.S. Department of Labor
210 Walnut Street, Room 715
Des Moines, IA 50309
515-284-4690

Iowa Workforce Development
1000 East Grand Avenue
Des Moines, IA 50319-0209
515-281-5387
www.iowaworkforce.org

Kansas
Bureau of Apprenticeship and Training
U.S. Department of Labor
444 SE Quincy Street, Room 247
Topeka, KS 66683
785-295-2624

Employment and Training Division
Department of Human Resources
401 SW Topeka Boulevard
Topeka, KS 66603-3182
785-296-4299
http://entkdhr.ink.org/Apprenticeship.htm

Kentucky
Bureau of Apprenticeship and Training
U.S. Department of Labor
Federal Building, Room 168
600 Martin Luther King Place
Louisville, KY 40202
502-582-5223

Kentucky Department of Employment
Services
275 East Main Street
Frankfort, KY 40621
502-564-5331
www.desky.org

Louisiana
Bureau of Apprenticeship and Training
U.S. Department of Labor
Afton Village Condo
3535 Sherwood Forest Boulevard
Baton Rouge, LA 70816
504-389-0263
(Temporarily Closed)

Apprenticeship Program
Louisiana Department of Labor
1001 North 23rd Street
Baton Rouge, LA 70804-9094
225-342-7820
www.ldol.state.la.us/websponsorsearch.asp

Maine
Bureau of Apprenticeship and Training
U.S. Department of Labor
Federal Building
68 Sewall Street, Room 401
Augusta, ME 04330
207-622-8235

Department of Labor
Bureau of Employment Services
54 State House Station
Augusta, ME 04333-0054
207-287-3516
888-457-8883
www.mainecareercenter.com/MAPlink.html

Maryland
Bureau of Apprenticeship and Training
U.S. Department of Labor
Federal Building, Room 430B
31 Hopkins Plaza
Baltimore, MD 21201
410-962-2676

Division of Labor and Industry
Apprenticeship & Training Program
1100 North Eutaw Street, Room 606
Baltimore, MD 21201
410-767-2229
www.dllr.state.md.us/labor/appr.html

Massachusetts
Bureau of Apprenticeship and Training
U.S. Department of Labor
JFK Federal Building, Room E-370
Boston, MA 02203
617-565-2288

Massachusetts Division of Employment
Training
Charles F. Hurley Building
19 Staniford Street
Boston, MA 02114
617-626-5400
www.detma.org

Michigan
Bureau of Apprenticeship and Training
U.S. Department of Labor
801 South Waverly, Room 304
Lansing, MI 48917
517-377-1746

Michigan Department of Civil Service
Lansing, MI 48933
517-373-3030
www.state.mi.us/mdcs/index.htm

Minnesota
Bureau of Apprenticeship and Training
U.S. Department of Labor
316 North Robert Street, Room 144
St. Paul, MN 55101
651-290-3951

Apprenticeship Unit
Minnesota Department of Labor and Industry
443 Lafayette Road North
St. Paul, MN 55155-4303
651-296-2371
www.doli.state.mn.us/appr.html

Mississippi
Bureau of Apprenticeship and Training
U.S. Department of Labor
Federal Building, Suite 410
100 West Capital Street
Jackson, MS 39269
601-965-4346

Mississippi Employment Security
Commission
15201 Capitol Street
Jackson, MS 39203
601-354-8711
www.mesc.state.ms.us/index.html

Missouri
Bureau of Apprenticeship and Training
U.S. Department of Labor
1222 Spruce, Room 9.102E
Robert A. Young Federal Building
St. Louis, MO 63103
314-539-2522

Missouri Department of Labor and Industrial
Relations
3315 West Truman Boulevard, Room 213
P.O. Box 504
Jefferson City, MO 65102-0504
573-751-4091
www.dolir.state.mo.us

Montana
Bureau of Apprenticeship and Training
U.S. Department of Labor
Federal Office Building
301 South Park Avenue
Room 396, Drawer 10055
Helena, MT 59626-0055
406-441-1076

Job Service Division
Department of Labor and Industry
P.O. Box 1728
Helena, MT 59624-1728
406-444-3478
http://jsd.dli.state.mt.us

Nebraska
Bureau of Apprenticeship and Training
U.S. Department of Labor

106 South 15th Street, Room 801
Omaha, NE 68102
402-221-3281

Nebraska Workforce Development
550 South 16th Street
P.O. Box 94600
Lincoln, NE 68509-4600
402-471-9000
www.dol.state.ne.us

Nevada
Bureau of Apprenticeship and Training
U.S. Department of Labor
301 Stewart Avenue, Room 311
Las Vegas, NV 89101
702-388-6396

State Apprenticeship Council
555 East Washington Avenue, Suite 4100
Las Vegas, NV 89101
702-486-2738
www.labor.state.nv.us/atr/atr.htm

New Hampshire
Bureau of Apprenticeship and Training
U.S. Department of Labor
143 North Main Street, Suite 205
Concord, NH 03301
603-225-1444

Apprenticeship Director
New Hampshire Labor Department
State Office Park South
95 Pleasant Street
Concord, NH 03301
603-271-6850
www.state.nh.us/dol/dol-st/rap/index.html

New Jersey
Bureau of Apprenticeship and Training
U.S. Department of Labor
Woodbridge Corporate Plaza
Building E-Room 300
485 Route 1, South
Iselin, NJ 08830
908-750-9191

State of New Jersey Department of Education
Division of Academic and Career Standards
P.O. Box 500
Trenton, NH 08625-0500
609-633-0665
http://wnjpin.state.nj.us/OneStopCareerCenter/
STW/apprentice1.html

County Apprentice Coordinators
Atlantic County
Atlantic County Vocational School, 5080
Atlantic Avenue, Mays Landing, NJ 08330;
609-625-2249 ext. 1209; www.acvts.org

Bergen County
Bergen County Vocational School, East 285
Pascack Road, Paramus, NJ 07652; 201-986-
0008 ext. 8402; www.bergen.org

Burlington County
Burlington Count Vocational School, 10
Hawkins Road, Medford, NJ 08055; 609-654-
0220 ext. 406; www.bcit.tec.nj.us

Camden County
Camden Count Vocational School, 343,
Berlin-Cross Keys Road, Sicklerville, NJ
08081; 609-767-7000 ext. 5299;
www.cyberenet.net/~camnet/ccts

Cape May County
Cape May Vocational School, 148 Crest
Haven Road, Cape May Court House, NJ
08210; 609-465-2161 ext. 616;
www.capemaytech.com

Cumberland County
Cumberland County Vocational School, 601
Bridgetown, NJ 08302; 856-451-9000 ext.
258; www.cumberland.tec.nj.us

Essex County
Essex County Vocational School, 50 South
Clinton Street, 5th Floor, East Orange, NJ
07018; 973-395-8554; www.essextech.org

Glouchester County
Glouchester County Vocational School; 1360
Tanyard Road, P.O. Box 800, Sewell, NJ
08080; 609-468-1445 ext. 2720; www.gcit.org

Hudson County
Hudson County Vocational School, 8511
Tonnelle Avenue, North Bergen, NJ 07047;
201-854-2398; www.hcst.tec.nj.us

Hunterdon County
Hunterdon County Vocational School, North
Hunterdon Campus, 14445 Route 31,
Annandale, NJ 08801; 908-735-6774 ext. 11;
www.co.hunterdon.nj.us/polytech

Mercer County
Mercer County Vocational School, Adult
Evening Schools, 1085 Old Trenton Road,
Trenton, NJ 08690; 609-586-5146;
www.mctec.net

Middlesex County
Middlesex County Vocational School, Box
1070, 112 Rues Lane, East Brunswick, NJ
08816; 732-257-3300 ext. 1921; www.mc-
votech.org

Monmouth County
Monmouth County Vocational School, West
end Avenue, Long Branch, NJ 07740; 732-
229-3019; www.mcv.mcvsd.k12.nj.us

Morris County
Morris County Vocational School, 400 East
Main Street, Denville, NJ 07834; 973-627-
4600 ext. 233; www.mcvts.org

Ocean County
Ocean County Vocational School 1299 Old
Freehold & Bey Lea Road, Toms River, NJ
08753; 732-473-3159/3133; www.ocvts.org

Passaic County
Passaic County Vocational School, 45
Reinhardt Road, Wayne, NJ 07470; 973-389-
4101; www.pcti.tec.nj.us

Salem County
Salem County Vocational School; P.O. Box
350, RD #2, Woodstown, NJ 08098; 856-769-
0102 ext. 349; www.scvts.org

Somerset County
Somerset County Vocational School, P.O. Box
6350, Vogt Drive, Bridgewater, NJ 08807;
908-526-8900 ext. 7265/7234; www.scti.org

Sussex County
Sussex County Vocational School, 105 North
Church Road, Sparta, NJ 07871; 973-383-
6700 ext. 285; www.sussex.tec.nj.us

Union County
Union County Vocational School, 1776
Raritan Road, Scotch Plains, NJ 07076; 908-
889-8288 ext. 309; www.ucvts.tec.nj.us

Warren County
Warren County Vocational School, 1500
Route 57, Washington, NJ 07882; 908-835-
2841; www.warrennet.org

Department of Labor, Employment and
Training Programs
P.O. Box 933
Trenton, NJ 08625-0933
609-984-3534
www.wnjpin.net/employer.html

New Mexico
Bureau of Apprenticeship and Training
U.S. Department of Labor
505 Marquette, Room 830
Albuquerque, NM 87102
505-766-2398

New Mexico Department of Labor
Labor and Industrial Division
Apprenticeship Council
501 Mountain Road
Albuquerque, NM 87102
505-841-8990
www.dol.state.nm.us/WIA_PartnerA3.html

New York
Bureau of Apprenticeship and Training
U.S. Department of Labor
Leo O'Brien Federal Building, Room 809
North Pearl and Clinton Avenue
Albany, NY 12207
518-431-4008

New York Department of Labor
State Office Building Campus, Room 500
Albany, NY 12240-0003
518-457-9000
www.labor.state.ny.us/working_ny/
apprenticeship_training/
apprenticeship_training.html

Albany
Building 12, State Office Campus, Room 440,
Albany, NY 12240; 518-457-1996

Binghamton
Glendale Technology Park, 2001 Perimeter
Road East, Suite 3, Endicott, NY 13760; 607-
741-4577

Buffalo
290 Main Street, Buffalo, NY 14202; 716-
851-2726

Long Island
303 Old Country Road, Hicksville, NY 11801;
516-934-8526

New York City
247 West 54th Street, 5th Floor, New York,
NY 10019; 212-621-0844

Rochester
130 West Nain Street, Room 202, Rochester,
NY 14614; 716-258-8885

Syracuse
450 South Salina Street, Room 203, Syracuse,
NY 13202; 315-479-3228

Utica
207 Genessee Street, Room 603, Utica, NY
13501; 315-793-2296

White Plains
120 Bloomingdale Road, White Plaza, NY
10605; 914-997-9534

North Carolina
Bureau of Apprenticeship and Training
U.S. Department of Labor
Somerset Park
4407 Bland Road, Suite 205
Raleigh, NC 27609
919-790-2801

North Carolina Department of Labor
Apprenticeship and Training Bureau
4 West Edenton Street
Raleigh, NC 27601
919-733-7533
www.dol.state.nc.us

North Dakota
Bureau of Apprenticeship and Training
U.S. Department of Labor
304 East Broadway, Room 332
Bismarck, ND 58501
701-250-4700

Job Service North Dakota
P.O. Box 5507
Bismarck, ND 58506
701-328-2868
800-732-9787
www.state.nd.us/jsnd

Ohio
Bureau of Apprenticeship and Training
U.S. Department of Labor
200 North High Street
Room 605
Columbus, OH 43215
614-469-7375

Ohio State Apprenticeship Council
145 South Front Street
P.O. Box 1618
Columbus, OH 43216
614-644-2242
www.state.oh.us/odjfs/apprenticeship/
index.stm

Oklahoma
Bureau of Apprenticeship and Training
U.S. Department of Labor
1500 South Midwest Boulevard
Suite 202
Midwest City, OK 73110
405-732-4338

Oklahoma Employment Security Commission
P.O. Box 52003
Oklahoma City, OK 73152
405-557-0200
www.oesc.state.ok.us

Oregon
Bureau of Apprenticeship and Training
U.S. Department of Labor
256 Warner-Milne Road, Room 3
Oregon City, OR 97045
503-557-8257

Apprenticeship and Training Division
Bureau of Labor and Industries
State Office Building, Suite 1105
800 NE Oregon
Portland, OR 97232
503-731-4200 ext. 3
www.boli.state.or.us/apprenticeship/
index.html

Portland
800 NE Oregon #32, Portland, OR 97232;
503-731-4200 ext. 3

Salem
3865 Wolverine NE, E-1, Salem, OR 97305;
503-378-3287

Eugene
1400 Executive Parkway, Suite 200, Eugene,
OR 97401; 541-686-7623

Medford
700 East Main, Room 105, Medford, OR
97504; 541-776-6270

Bend
2480 NE Twin Knolls Drive, Bend, OR
97701; 541-322-2428

Pennsylvania
Bureau of Apprenticeship and Training
U.S. Department of Labor
Federal Building
228 Walnut Street, Room 356
Harrisburg, PA 17108
717-221-3496

Apprenticeship and Training
Labor and Industry Building
7th and Forster Street, Room 1700
Harrisburg, PA 17120
717-787-5279
www.dli.state.pa.us/landi/site/default.asp

Rhode Island
Bureau of Apprenticeship and Training
U.S. Department of Labor
Federal Building
100 Hartford Avenue
Providence, RI 02909
401-528-5198

Department of Labor & Training
Division of Professional Regulation
P.O. Box 20247
Cranston, RI 02920
401-462-8536
www.det.state.ri.us/appren/appren.htm

South Carolina
Bureau of Apprenticeship and Training
U.S. Department of Labor
Thurmond Federal Building
1835 Assembly Street, Room 838
Columbia, SC 29201
803-765-5547

Employment Security Commission
1500 Gadsden Street
P.O. Box 995
Columbia, SC 29202
803-737-2400
www.sces.org/ms_index.htm

South Dakota
Bureau of Apprenticeship and Training
U.S. Department of Labor
Room 205, 320 East Capitol
Pierre, SD 57501
605-224-6693

Department of Labor
700 Governors Drive
Pierre, SD 57501-2291
605-773-3101
www.state.sd.us/dol/dol.htm

Tennessee
Bureau of Apprenticeship and Training
U.S. Department of Labor
Airport Executive Plaza
1321 Murfreesboro Road, Suite 541
Nashville, TN 37210
615-781-5318

Department of Labor & Workforce
Development
710 James Robertson Parkway
Andrew Johnson Tower, 4th Floor
Nashville, TN 37243
651-253-1324
www.state.tn.us/labor-wfd

Texas
Bureau of Apprenticeship and Training
U.S. Department of Labor
VA Building, Room 2105

2320 LaBranch Street
Houston, TX 77004
713-718-3696

Texas Workforce Commission
101 East 15th Street
Austin, TX 78778
512-463-9767
www.twc.state.tx.us/svcs/apprentice.html

Apprenticeship & Training Representatives
Dallas, North Central & Northeast Texas: 214-767-9263/9264

San Antonio, Austin & Rio Grande Valley: 210-308-4592/4594

El Paso, West Texas: 505-248-5038

Panhandle: 405-732-4338

Houston & College Station: 713-983-7916

Port Arthur & Southeast Texas: 409-727-1780

Utah
Bureau of Apprenticeship and Training
U.S. Department of Labor
1600 West 220 South, Suite 101
Salt Lake City, UT 84119
801-975-3650

Cash Career Apprenticeship
Grand County School District
264 South 400 East
Moab, UT 84532
435-259-5317
www.grand.k12.ut.us/cash/home.htm
(web site temporarily offline)

Vermont
Bureau of Apprenticeship and Training
U.S. Department of Labor
Federal Building
11 Elmwood Avenue, Room 109
Burlington, VT 05401
802-951-6278

Department of Labor and Industry
Apprenticeship Division
National Life Building
Drawer 20
Montpelier, VT 05620-3401
802-828-2157
www.det.state.vt.us/miscfile/apprent.htm

Barre: 802-476-2600
Bennington: 802-442-6376
Brattleboro: 802-254-4555
Brulington: 802-863-7698
Middlebury: 802-388-4921
Morrisville: 802-888-4545
Newport: 802-334-6545
Rutland: 802-786-5837
St. Albans: 802-524-6585
St. Johnsbury: 802-748-3177
Springfield: 802-885-2167
White River Junction: 802-295-8805

Virginia
Bureau of Apprenticeship and Training
U.S. Department of Labor
400 North 8th Street
Federal Building, Suite 404
Richmond, VA 23219
804-771-2488

Virginia Occupational Information
Coordinating Committee
P.O. Box 1358
Richmond, VA 23211
804-786-5881

Division of Apprenticeship Training
Virginia Department of Labor and Industry
Powers-Taylor Building
13 South 13th Street
Richmond, VA 23219
804-786-2381
www.doli.state.va.us

Apprenticeship Representatives
Central Virginia Regional Office
1500 East Main Street, Suite 222
Richmond, VA 23219
804-786-3075 or 804-371-0296

Northern Virginia Regional Office
10515 Battleview Parkway
Manassas, VA 20109
703-392-0900 ext. 102/103

Tidewater Regional Office
Interstate Corporate Center
Building 6
Norfolk, VA 23502
757-455-0891 ext. 126/145

Valley Regional Office
201 Lee Highway
Verona, VA 24482
540-248-9280

Southwest Virginia Regional Office
Brammer Village
3013 Peters Creek Road
Roanoke, VA 24019
540-562-3580 ext. 120

Abingdon Field Office
Brooksfield Square
966 West Main Street, Suite 4
Abingdon, VA 24210
540-676-5465

Lynchburg Field Office
3704 Old Forest Road, Suite B
Lynchburg, VA 24501
804-385-0806

Washington
Bureau of Apprenticeship and Training
U.S. Department of Labor
1400 Talbot Road South
Renton, WA 98055
425-277-5214

Department of Labor and Industry
7273 Linderson Way, SW
Tumwater, WA 98501
P.O. Box 44851
Olympia, WA 98504-4851
360-902-5320
www.lni.wa.gov/scs/apprenticeship/default.htm

Apprenticeship Program Coordinators
Olympia
State Department of Labor and Industries
P.O. Box 44530, MS: 4530
Olympia, WA 98504-4530
360-902-5320

Mt. Vernon
525 College Way, Suite H
Mount Vernon, WA 98273
360-416-3026

Seattle
P.O. Box 69050
Seattle, WA 98168-1050

Tukwila
12806 Gateway Drive
Tukwila, WA 98168-3346
206-248-8250

Tacoma
950 Broadway, Suite 200
Tacoma, WA 98402-4453
253-596-3930

Longview
900 Ocean Beach Highway
Longview, WA 98632
360-757-6927

Olympia
P.O. Box 44181
Olympia, WA 98504-4181
360-902-6781

Moses Lake
3001 Broadway
Moses Lake, WA 98837
509-764-6906

Spokane
901 North Monroe, Suite 100
Spokane, WA 99201-218
509-324-2590

West Virginia
Bureau of Apprenticeship and Training
U.S. Department of Labor
One Bridge Place, 2nd Floor
No. 10 Hale Street
Charleston, WV 25301
304-347-5794

Bureau of Employment Programs
112 California Avenue
Charleston, WV 25305
304-558-2630
www.state.wv.us/bep

Wisconsin
Bureau of Apprenticeship and Training
U.S. Department of Labor
740 Regent Street, Suite 104
Madison, WI 53715-1233
608-441-5377

Bureau of Apprenticeship Standards
201 East Washington Avenue, Room 229
P.O. Box 7972
Madison, WI 53707
608-266-3332
www.dwd.state.wi.us/dweappr

Field Representatives District Assignments
Area 2-Eau Claire Assignments
c/o Chippewa Valley Technical College
620 West Clairmont, Room 7A
Eau Claire, WI 54701
715-833-6444

Area 3- LaCrosse Area Assignments
402 North Eighth Street
LaCrosse, WI 54601
608-785-9176

Area 4-Wausau Area Assignments
c/0 North Central Technical College
1000 Campus Drive
Wausau, WI 54401
715-675-3331 ext. 4238

Area 5- Madison Area Assignments
co MATC
2125 Commercial Avenue
Madison, WI 53704
608-246-3887

Area 6- Madison & Rock County Assignments
MATC-Apprenticeship Center
2125 Commercial Avenue
Madison, WI 53704
608-246-7900

Area 7- Green Bay Assignments
c/o Northeast Wisconsin Technical College
2740 West Mason Street
P.O. Box 19042
Green Bay, WI 54307-9042
920-492-5618

Area 8- Appleton Area Assignments
1825 North Bluemound Drive
P.O. Box 2277
Appleton, WI 54913
920-832-5303

Area 9- Fond du Lac Area Assignments
N5887 County Road West
Fond du Lac, WI 54935
920-929-3184

Areas 11 & 13- Milwaukee Kenosha & Racine
Area Assignments
c/o State Office Building
819 North 6th Street, Room 516
Milwaukee, WI 53203
414-227-4398

Area 12-Milwaukee & Waukesha Area
Assignments
Workforce Development Center
892 Main Street, Suite J
Pewaukee, WI 53702
414-695-7778

U.S. Department of Labor
Bureau of Apprenticeship and Training
Federal Center

740 Regent Street, Suite 104
Madison, WI 53715
608-264-5377

Wyoming
Bureau of Apprenticeship and Training
U.S. Department of Labor
American National Bank Building
1912 Capitol Avenue, Room 508
Cheyenne, WY 82001
307-772-2448

Department of Employment
Office of Workforce Development
3120 Old Faithful Road, Suite 300
Cheyenne, WY 82002
307-777-3465
http://wydoe.state.wy.us/doe.asp?ID=445

Free Training or $6,000 For College
If You're Laid Off Or Can't Get A Job

Program: Employment and Training Assistance — Dislocated Workers 17.246

Description: If you've found yourself on the losing end of a plant closing or mass layoff, apply for money and re-training under the Economic Dislocation and Worker Adjustment Assistance Act (EDWAA). The program is administered by each state, and because of that, the program differs from state to state. Some even offer help to out-of-work cowboys and displaced housewives. The program's goal is to help workers find unsubsidized jobs through re-training and other employment services. Some states will even lend you money to help you pay bills until you're back at work in a new job.

What You Can Get: Workers can receive classroom, occupational and on-the-job training in skills currently in demand — such as entry level positions in health care or training to work with computers. Basic and remedial training, as well as entrepreneurial training is also available. So if you need to brush up on your math or want to start a business, this could be the place to start. Programs also include literacy classes and courses in English as a second language.

The programs also provide testing and counseling, development of personal service plans (including child care and transportation allowances), and help with relocation expenses once you have a solid job offer out of state. It is also possible to receive some pre-layoff assistance, but remember, services vary by state.

Workers in the program who have exhausted state unemployment benefits can apply for "needs related" allowances, up to the amount they formerly received from that state, while they complete their training.

Many states let you chart your own career course. If you know what you want to do, say to open a pet store, you can apply to the state for the appropriate training.

Who Is Eligible: While the program is intended to help workers affected by plant closings and layoffs on a grand scale, others are not necessarily excluded. Most benefits are also available to long-term unemployed workers with limited prospects of ever finding another job in that field. For example, farmers and ranchers who have fallen on hard times, and other self-employed people who have lost their income due to general economic conditions, including displaced "homemakers" are eligible.

Money Available: The Federal government gives each state an annual allotment, depending on how many unemployed workers live there. It spends over a billion dollars each year to help workers get back on track. In 1994 alone, half a million workers received help through this program.

National Office:
Office of Worker Retraining and Readjustment Programs
U.S. Department of Labor
Room N-5426, 200 Constitution Ave., NW
Washington, D.C. 20210
202-219-5577
www.doleta.gov/layoff/

State Offices:

Because each state administers and manages its own program, it would be wise to start there to find out specific program details.

Dislocated Worker Unit Contacts

Alabama
Alabama Department of Economic and Community Affairs
Workforce Development Division
401 Adams Avenue
P.O. Box 5690
Montgomery, AL 36103
334-242-5525
www.adeca.state.al.us/ADECA/Pages/Pages_stm/ADECAdefault.stm

Alaska
Department of Labor and Workforce Development
P.O. Box 21149
Juneau, AK 99802
907-465-2700
www.labor.state.ak.us

Arizona
Department of Economic Security
Workforce Development Division
Job Training Partnership Program
1789 West Jefferson, Site Code 920Z
Phoenix, AZ 85007
602-542-2478
www.de.state.az.us/links/esa/index.html

Arkansas
Arkansas Employment Security Department
125 West 4th Street
P.O. Box 2981
Little Rock, AR 72203
501-682-1818
www.state.ar.us/esd/gdwtf.htm

California
Workforce Investment Division, MIC 691
Employment Development Department
P.O. Box 826880
Sacramento, CA 94280
916-653-4803
www.edd.ca.gov/wiaind.htm

Colorado
Colorado Department of Labor and Employment
Dislocated Worker Unit
1515 Arapahoe
Tower 2, Suite 400
Denver, CO 80202
303-318-8840
www.coworkforce.com/emp/layoffassistance.asp

Connecticut
State Department of Labor
Rapid Response Unit
200 Folly Brook Boulevard
Wethersfield, CT 06109
860-263-6589
www.ctdol.state.ct.us/progsupt/jobsrvce/rrfaq.htm

Delaware
Delaware Department of Labor
Division of Employment and Training
4425 North Market Street
P.O. Box 9828
Wilmington, DE 19809
302-761-8102
www.delawareworks.com

District of Columbia
Dislocated Worker Unit
Department of Employment Services
500 C Street, NW
Washington, DC 20001
202-727-4099
http://does.ci.washington.dc.us/main.shtm

Florida
Agency for Workforce Innovation/REACT
325 John Knox Road
Building L, Suite 101
Tallahassee, FL 32303
850-921-3325
www2.myflorida.com/awi/react

Georgia
Employment and Training
Department of Labor
148 International Boulevard, Suite 440
Atlanta, GA 30303
404-656-6336
www.dol.state.ga.us/eshtml/warn.html

Hawaii
Office of Employment and Training Administration
Department of Labor and Industrial Relations
830 Punchbowl Street, Room 329
Honolulu, HI 96813
808-586-8814
www.dlir.state.hi.us

Idaho
Workforce Systems Bureau
Department of Labor
317 West Main Street
Boise, ID 83735
208-334-6298
www.labor.state.id.us/wia1/wiaservices.htm

Illinois
Job Training Division
Department of Employment Security
325 West Adams, 3rd Floor
Springfield, IL 62704
217-785-6006
www.ides.state.il.us

Indiana
Workforce Development
Worker Transition Unit
10 North Senate Street
Indianapolis, IN 46204
317-232-2371
www.in.gov/dwd

Iowa
Workforce Development
1000 East Grand Avenue
Des Moines, IA 50319
515-281-9027
www.iowaworkforce.org

Kansas
Department of Human Resources
Division of Employment and Training
401 SW Topeka Boulevard
Topeka, KS 66603
785-296-5115
http://entkdhr.ink.org

Kentucky
Office of Training and Re-employment
Division of Field Services
209 St. Claire Street, 4th Floor
Frankfort, KY 40601
502-564-5360
http://otr.state.ky.us

Louisiana
Louisiana Department of Labor
Dislocated Worker Unit
1001 North 23rd Street
P.O. Box 94094
Baton Rouge, LA 70809
225-342-7633
www.ldol.state.la.us

Maine
Workforce Development
Maine Department of Labor
Bureau of Employment Services
State House Station 55
Augusta, ME 04333
207-624-6399
www.mainecareercenter.com

Maryland
Office of Employment Training
Department of Labor, Licensing and Regulations
1100 North Eutaw Street, Room 601
Baltimore, MD 21201
410-767-2832
www.careernet.statemd.us

Massachusetts
Commonwealth Corporation
Schrafft Center
529 Main Street, Suite 400
Boston, MA 02129
617-727-8158 ext. 1346
www.commcorp.org/BES/WRC/default.htm

Michigan
Michigan Jobs Commission
Workforce Transition Unit
201 North Washington Square
Victor Office Center, 7th Floor
Lansing, MI 48913
517-373-6234
www.mdcd.org/Core/dislocated.htm

Minnesota
Minnesota Department of Trade and Economic Development
500 Metro Square Building
121 East 7th Place
St. Paul, MN 55101
612-296-7918
www.dted.state.mn.us/06x01f.asp

Mississippi
Employment Training Division
Mississippi Development Authority
P.O. Box 849
Jackson, MS 39205
601-329-9266
www.dced.state.ms.us/main/job/job_main.htm

Missouri
Division of Workforce Development
Department of Economic Development

P.O. Box 1087
Jefferson City, MO 65102
573-751-7896
800-877-8698
www.ecodev.state.mo.us/wfd/jobseek/
dislocated.htm

Montana

State Job Training Bureau
Montana Department of Labor and Industry
P.O. Box 1728
Helena, MT 59624
406-444-1827
http://dli.state.mt.us

Nebraska

Nebraska Department of Labor
Workforce Development
Office of Workforce Services
550 South 16th Street
Lincoln, NE 68509
402-471-9878
www.dol.state.ne.us/nwd/
center.cfm?PRICAT=1&SUBCAT=1F

Nevada

State Job Training Office
505 East King, Room 501
Carson City, NV 89710
775-684-4210
http://detr.state.nv.us

New Hampshire

New Hampshire Job Training Coordinating
Council
64 Old Suncook Road
Concord, NH 03301
603-228-9500
www.nhworks.org

New Jersey

Rapid Response Team
Labor Management Committee
New Jersey Department of Labor
John Fitch Plaza, CN 058
Trenton, NH 08625
800-343-3919
www.state.nj.us/labor

New Mexico

New Mexico Department of Labor
Job Training Division
1596 Pacheco Street, Suite 201
Santa Fe, NM 87502
505-827-6895
www3.state.nm.us/dol/dol_dirr.html

New York

New York State Department of Labor
State Office Campus Building, #12
Albany, NY 12240
518-457-3101
www.labor.ny.us

North Carolina

Division of Employment and Training
North Carolina Department of Commerce
4316 Mail Service Center
Raleigh, NC 27699-4316
919-662-6333
www.det.commerce.state.nc.us/wrkfrcedev/
programs/adults.asp

North Dakota

Job Training Division
Job Service North Dakota
1000 East Divide Avenue
P.O. Box 5507
Bismarck, ND 58506
701-328-3066
www.state.nd.us/jsnd/docs/workforce/
jsnd5001.pdf

Ohio

Department of Jobs and Family Services
30 East Broad Street, 32nd Floor
Columbus, OH 43266-0433
614-995-7474
www.state.oh.us/odjfs

Oklahoma

Oklahoma Employment Security Commission
Employment and Training Division
Will Rogers Building, Room 408
2401 North Lincoln Boulevard
Oklahoma City, OK 73152
405-557-5344
www.oesc.state.ok.us/Emp-
Trng/programs.html

Oregon

Department of Community Colleges and
Workforce Development
255 Capitol Street, NE, 3rd Floor
Salem, OR 97310
503-378-8648 ext. 226
www.odccwd.state.or.us

Pennsylvania

Dislocated Worker Unit
Bureau of Workforce Investment
12th Floor Labor and Industry building
7th and Forster Street
Harrisburg, PA 17120
717-772-0781
www.dli.state.pa.us

Rhode Island

Department of Employment and Training
Center General Complex
1511 Pontiac Avenue
Building 73
Cranston, RI 02920
401-462-8803
www.dlti.state.ri.us

South Carolina

Employment Security Commission
1550 Gadsden Street
Columbia, SC 29202
803-737-2601
www.sces.org/ms_index.html

South Dakota

South Dakota Department of Labor
Workforce Investment
Kneip Building
700 Governors Drive
Pierre, SD 57501
605-773-5017
www.state.sd.us/dol/WIA/index.html

Tennessee

Tennessee Department of Labor and
Workforce Development

Division of Employment and Workforce
Development
Gateway Plaza
500 James Robertson Parkway, 12th Floor
Nashville, TN 37245
615-741-1031
www.state.tn.us/labor-wfd/empwfd.html

Texas

Work Force Development Division
101 East 15th Street, Room 202T
Austin, TX 78778-0001
512-936-0425
888-562-7489
www.twc.state.tx.us/svcs/jtpa/dislocat.html

Utah

Department of Workforce Services
324 South State Street, Suite 500
P.O. Box 45249
Salt Lake City, UT 84145-0249
801-526-4312
www.dws.state.ut.us

Vermont

Department of Employment and Training
5 Green Mountain Drive
P.O. Box 488
Montpelier, VT 05601
802-828-4177
www.det.state.vt.us

Virginia

Employment Security Supervisor
Virginia Employment Commission
703 East Main, Room 308
Richmond, VA 23219
804-786-3037
www.vec.state.va.us

Washington

Employment Security Department
P.O. Box 9046
Olympia, WA 98507
360-438-3275
www.wa.gov/esd

West Virginia

Governor's Workforce Investment Office
Dislocated Worker Service Unit
112 California Avenue, Room 208
Charleston, WV 25305
304-558-5927
www.wvgwio.org

Wisconsin

Department of Workforce Development
Division of Workforce Excellence
201 East Washington Avenue
Madison, WI 53707
608-266-0745
www.dwd.state.wi.us/dwepfe/programs.htm

Wyoming

Employment Resources Division
Department of Employment
100 West Midwest
P.O. Box 2760
Casper, WY 82602
307-235-3200
http://wydoe.state.wy.us

Free Training For Those Who Lose Their Jobs Because of Increased Trade With Mexico or Canada

Program: NAFTA Transitional Adjustment Assistance Program

Description: NAFTA is not a dirty word, but a lot of U.S. workers swear it is a plan to put them out of work and ship their jobs where labor costs are cheaper — Canada, but more significantly, to Mexico and other Latin American countries. In a dog-eat-dog global economy there are no real borders — read the label on the shirt you're wearing or check the "made in" stamps on every toy you buy your kids for Christmas.

Who Is Eligible: If you were laid off or lost your job because of the North American Free Trade Agreement (NAFTA), the government wants to help you find a new one, and probably one that pays you more than your last job. The NAFTA Transitional Adjustment Assistance Program is like a job skills and retraining SWAT team geared to provide rapid and early response to the threat of unemployment. It is an opportunity to engage in long term job retraining while receiving income assistance from Uncle Sam.

The program includes:
- on-site services to let workers know if they are eligible
- assessment of individual skills and abilities
- financial and personal counseling to prepare for job transition
- career counseling
- job placement assistance
- child care
- transportation
- occupation skills training
- basic and remedial education
- entrepreneurial training
- English as a second language
- income support for up to 52 weeks after worker has exhausted unemployment compensation while the worker is enrolled in training
- job search allowances to pay expenses for workers who search for work beyond their normal commuting area
- relocation allowances

National Office:
Division of Trade Adjustment Assistance
Employment and Training Administration
U.S. Department of Labor
Room C-5311, 200 Constitution Ave., NW
Washington, DC 20210
202-693-3560
http://wdsc.doleta.gov/trade_act

Local Offices: For more information contact your local employment service office or your state Dislocated Worker Unit contact (see page 570).

Matthew Lesko, Information USA, Inc., 12081 Nebel Street, Rockville, MD 20852 • 1-800-955-7693 • www.lesko.com

Free Training If You Lose Your Job
From Increased Imports From Other Countries

Program: Trade Adjustment Assistance — Workers - 17.245

Description: Ever notice how so many products have gotten less expensive over the last ten years? Shirts that once cost $30 are now sold for $15. Televisions and VCRs — not to mention computers — have never been cheaper. Visit any shopping mall, and you'll see bargains galore! So what's the deal? Simple, almost everything we now buy in the U.S. is being made overseas. But the downside to bargain hunting is that each of these products has cost Americans jobs. "Made in Japan" was a joke in the 1950s — it meant really cheapo products — but now it's a sign of quality. And U.S. workers have suffered in the long run because of these dramatic changes.

Ever the diplomat, Uncle Sam doesn't get angry, he gets even. And the government is willing to train anyone displaced by foreign imports to learn new job skills.

If you lost your job because of imports, you can get $800 in travel expenses to look for a new job, and 90% of your moving costs will be paid if you get a solid offer. Or stay at home and let the government pay you to learn a new marketable job skill. Computer programming, anyone?

Since 1974, the Employment and Training Administration at the Department of Labor has given away several billion dollars helping workers who have lost jobs because of imports. This year alone, the Trade Adjustment Assistance (TAA) program will spend $96.6 million to help workers learn more marketable job skills and to move to greener employment pastures. An additional $183 million will be spent on weekly allowances to help program participants pay their bills if they have exhausted state unemployment benefits.

What You Can Get: If you qualify, there are a number of career counseling and retraining opportunities, all free. Again, the program will pay some workers to learn new skills, then help pay travel expenses while they search for a new job. Opportunities include remedial education, vocational and technical retraining, as well as on-the-job training. If you qualify for a Trade Readjustment Allowance (TRA), you can receive a weekly allowance equal to state unemployment benefits, for up to two years.

The program will reimburse you up to $800 for travel expenses if there is a lack of good jobs in your area and you have to look elsewhere. If you find a job and need to relocate, the program will pay 90 percent of your moving costs and a lump sum payment of three times your former average weekly paycheck (up to $800) to help you get settled in.

Who Is Eligible: Any worker, no matter what their prior income level, can apply for assistance. Go to your local State Employment Security Agency, to the unemployment insurance office, and fill out an "application for determination" to learn whether you qualify under the program. They will investigate your case and determine to what degree imports caused your layoff. If your hours were cut back by at least 80 percent, or you have lost at least 80 percent of your prior income, you may qualify.

To qualify for an allowance while you participate in the program, you must have worked at least 26 weeks — and earned more than $30 a week — for one year prior to losing a job due to imports. You also must have exhausted all other unemployment benefits; you must meet the same weekly job search requirements as you did when receiving state unemployment benefits, including actively looking for work and accepting any offers. In addition, you must be enrolled in, or have completed, an approved job training program, but sometimes states waive this last requirement.

To be eligible for a relocation allowance, you have to find a job with the possibility of it being long term employment or an offer somewhere in the U.S. You cannot receive moving expenses if you have received a relocation allowance in the past, and you must be entirely unemployed or have had your hours cut back substantially in anticipation of a total layoff.

You must file for relocation funds within 425 days after you receive TAA certification or 182 days after completing a TAA retraining program. To file for a Trade Readjustment Allowance, you must wait 60 days after certification. But even if your application is rejected, you can qualify for reemployment help, retraining, relocation expenses and other job search allowances.

In general, the readjustment allowance is the same as your state unemployment benefits. Remember, all unemployment benefits must be exhausted in order to qualify. The amount will be reduced by any other earnings or income. The allowance continues for two years, starting your first week off the job, once you are certified. You can receive an additional 26 weeks of TRA if you apply for retraining within 210 days of a layoff and need the additional benefits to complete the program. Maximum benefits are capped at 52 times your weekly allowance, unless an extension is approved.

So what happens if you find a job during the 104-week allowance period but imports cost you that job too? As long as you are still within the certification period, the 104-week allowance period is recalculated, starting the first week of your second layoff.

Money Available: In fiscal year 1996, the program will spend $183 million in TRA payments and another $96.6 million to retrain workers and help them search for new jobs, and to relocate, if necessary.

National Office:
> Division of Trade Adjustment Assistance
> Employment and Training Administration
> U.S. Department of Labor
> 200 Constitution Ave., NW, Room C-5311
> Washington, D.C. 20210
> 202-693-3560
> http://wdsc.doleta.gov/trade_act/wdp.asp

Regional Offices:
There also are program representatives at each of DOL's regional offices:

Boston - 617-565-2217
New York - 212-337-2159
Philadelphia - 215-596-83366
Atlanta - 404-347-2122
Chicago - 312-353-0313
Dallas - 214-767-8263
Kansas City, Mo. - 816-426-3796
Denver - 303-391-5740
San Francisco - 415-975-4610
Seattle - 206-553-7700

Local Offices:
The best source of further information on how the TAA program works is the local office of your State Employment Security Agency.

State Employment Security Agencies

Alabama
Alabama Department Industrial Relations
649 Monroe Street, Room 2813
P.O. Box 5690
Montgomery, AL 36130
334-242-8635
www.dir.state.al.us/es

Alaska
Employment Security Division
Department of Labor
P.O. Box 25509
Juneau, AK 99802
907-465-5954
www.labor.state.ak.us/handbook/aes2.htm

Arizona
Department of Economic Security
P.O. Box 6666
Phoenix, AZ 85005
602-495-1861
www.de.state.az.us/links/esa/service.html

Arkansas
Arkansas Employment Security Department
125 West 4th Street
P.O. Box 2981
Little Rock, AR 72203
501-682-2121
www.state.ar.us/esd/gdwtf.htm

California
Employment Development Department
P.O. Box 826880
Attn: MIC40
Sacramento, CA 94280
916-654-8555
www.edd.ca.gov/

Colorado
Colorado Department of Labor and
Employment
NAFTA/TAA Unit
1515 Arapahoe
Tower 2, Suite 400
Denver, CO 80202
303-318-8814
www.coworkforce.com/EMP/
trade_adjustment_assistance_prog.asp

Connecticut
State Department of Labor
200 Folly Brook Boulevard
Wethersfield, CT 06109
860-263-6070
www.ctdol.state.ct.us/progsupt/jobsrvce/
naftataa.htm

Delaware
Delaware Department of Labor
Division of Employment and Training
4425 North Market Street
P.O. Box 9828
Wilmington, DE 19809
302-761-8110
www.delawareworks.com

District of Columbia
Department of Employment Services
609 H Street, NE
Washington, DC 20002
202-727-7000
http://does.ci.washington.dc.us/main.shtm

Florida
Department of Labor and Employment
Security
325 John Knox Road
Building L
Tallahassee, FL 32303
850-921-3268
www2.myflorida.com/awi/nafta/faq.htm

Georgia
Department of Labor
148 International Boulevard, Suite 440
Atlanta, GA 30303
404-656-6336
www.dol.state.ga.us/eshtml/warn.htm#
tradeadjustments

Hawaii
Department of Labor and Industrial Relations
830 Punchbowl Street, Room 329
Honolulu, HI 96813
808-586-8820
www.dlir.state.hi.us

Idaho
TAA Coordinator
Department of Labor
317 West Main Street
Boise, ID 83735
208-334-6328
www.labor.state.id.us

Illinois
Department of Employment Security
401 South State Street, 7th Floor
Chicago, IL 60605
312-793-6805
www.ides.state.il.us/program/employer.htm#
trade

Indiana
Workforce Development
10 North Senate Street
Indianapolis, IN 46204
317-232-7186
www.in.gov/dwd/policy/taa/formfact/
TAAFacts.PDF

Iowa
Workforce Development
1000 East Grand Avenue
Des Moines, IA 50319
515-281-9008
www.iowaworkforce.org

Kansas
Department of Human Resources
401 SW Topeka Boulevard
Topeka, KS 66603
786-296-7290
http://entkdhr.ink.org/Naftaa.htm

Kentucky
Department for Employment Service
275 East Main Street
2nd Floor, CHR Building
Frankfort, KY 40621
502-564-2420
www.desky.org/jobservices/othserv/
othserv.htm

Louisiana
Louisiana Department of Labor
3rd Floor Annex
P.O. Box 94094

Baton Rouge, LA 70804-9094
225-342-8753
www.ldol.state.la.us/laworksweb/text/
trade.htm

Maine
Maine Department of Labor
Bureau of Employment Security
State House Station 55
Augusta, ME 04333
207-624-6390
www.mainecareercenter.com

Maryland
Department of Labor, Licensing and
Regulations
1100 North Eutaw Street, Room 310
Baltimore, MD 21201
410-767-2833
www.careernet.state.md.us

Massachusetts
Trade Programs
Commonwealth Corporation
Schrafft Center
529 Main Street, Suite 110
Boston, MA 02129
617-727-8158
www.commcorp.org/BES/Trade/default.htm

Michigan
Employment Service Development and
Services Division
Michigan Department of Career Development
201 North Washington Square
Victor Office Center, 7th Floor
Lansing, MI 48913
517-373-5308
www.mdcd.org/Core/dislocated.htm

Minnesota
Reemployment Programs
Minnesota Dept. of Employment Security
390 North Robert Street
St. Paul, MN 55101
612-296-5657
www.mnsworkforcecenter.org/taa/tra.htm

Mississippi
Mississippi Employment Security
Commission
P.O. Box 1699
Jackson, MS 39215
601-961-7544
www.mesc.state.ms.us

Missouri
Division of Employment Security
P.O. Box 59
421 East Dunklin Street
Jefferson City, MO 65104
573-751-9832
www.dolir.state.mo.us/es/d4c21.htm

Montana
TAA Program
Montana Department of Labor and Industry
P.O. Box 1728
Helena, MT 59624
406-444-3351
http://dli.state.mt.us

Nebraska
Nebraska Department of Labor
Workforce Development

550 South 16th Street
P.O. Box 94600
Lincoln, NE 68509
402-471-9878
www.dol.state.ne.us/nwd/center.cfm?
PRICAT=1&SUBCAT=1F&ACTION=nafta

Nevada

Department of Employment Training and
Rehabilitation
500 East Third Street
Carson City, NV 89713
775-684-0325
http://detr.state.nv.us/es/es_index.htm

New Hampshire

New Hampshire Department of Employment
Security
32 South Main Street
P.O. Box 9505
Concord, NH 03108
603-656-6608
www.nhworks.state.nh.us/esb/eb/taa.htm

New Jersey

New Jersey Department of Labor
John Fitch Plaza
Labor and Industry Building
P.O. Box 058
Trenton, NH 08625
609-292-5156
www.state.nj.us/labor/uiex/uiinfo/otherui.htm

New Mexico

New Mexico Department of Labor
Employment Security Department
P.O. Box 1928
Albuquerque, NM 87103
505-841-8452
www3.state.nm.us/dol/dol_trad.htm

New York

New York State Department of Labor
State Office Campus Building, #12, Room 425
Albany, NY 12240
518-457-7595
www.labor.ny.us

North Carolina

Employment Security Commission
Workforce Development
P.O. Box 26990
Raleigh, NC 27611
919-733-6745
www.exc.state.nc.us/personal/training.asp

North Dakota

Job Service North Dakota
1000 East Divide Avenue
P.O. Box 5507
Bismarck, ND 58506
701-328-3066
www.state.nd.us/jsnd/jobinsurance.htm?
bookmark=taatra

Ohio

Department of Jobs and Family Services
Trade Adjustment Assistance Program
30 East Broad Street, 32nd Floor
Columbus, OH 43266-0433
614-644-2706
www.state.oh.us/odjfs

Oklahoma

Oklahoma Employment Security Commission
2401 North Lincoln Boulevard
Oklahoma City, OK 73152
405-557-7274
www.oesc.state.ok.us/ES/default.htm

Oregon

Employment Department
875 Union Street, NE
Salem, OR 97311
503-947-1665
www.emp.state.or.us

Pennsylvania

Office of Employment Security
Department of Labor and Industry
P.O. Box 1899
Harrisburg, PA 17105
717-783-3284
www.dli.state.pa.us/landi/cwp/view.asp?
a=152&q=53924

Rhode Island

Department of Employment and Training
Center General Complex
1511 Pontiac Avenue, Building 73
Cranston, RI 02920
401-462-8800
www.dlti.state.ri.us

South Carolina

Employment Security Commission
1550 Gadsden Street
P.O. Box 1406
Columbia, SC 29202
803-737-3096
www.sces.org/employerws/rapidresponse/
index.htm

South Dakota

South Dakota Department of Labor
Kneip Building
700 Governors Drive
Pierre, SD 57501
605-773-5017
www.state.sd.us/dol/dolui/benefits/
BE_facts.htm#TRADE

Tennessee

Tennessee Department of Labor and
Workforce Development
Division of Employment and Workforce
Development
710 James Robertson Parkway, 12th Floor
Nashville, TN 37243

615-741-3780
www.state.tn.us/labor-wfd/TAA.HTML

Texas

Workforce Commission
101 East 15th Street, Room 506T
Austin, TX 78778
512-463-2227
www.twc.state.tx.us/svcs/taa/taahp.html

Utah

Department of Workforce Services
P.O. Box 45249
Salt Lake City, UT 84145
801-526-4311
ui.dws.state.ut.us/jobseeker/tradehuide.asp#
TradeAdjustmentAssistance (TAA)

Vermont

Department of Employment and Training
5 Green Mountain Drive
P.O. Box 488
Montpelier, VT 05601
802-828-4177
www.det.state.vt.us

Virginia

Virginia Employment Commission
703 East Main, Room 308
Richmond, VA 23219
804-786-8825
www.vec.state.va.us/seeker/seeker.htm

Washington

Employment Security Department
P.O. Box 9046
Olympia, WA 98507
360-438-4611
www.wa.gov/esd/work/programs.htm

West Virginia

Bureau of Employment Programs
Division of Employment Services
112 California Avenue
Charleston, WV 25305
304-558-2850
www.www.state.wv.us/bep

Wisconsin

Department of Workforce Development
Division of Workforce Excellence
201 East Washington Avenue
P.O. Box 7946
Madison, WI 53707
608-266-0745
www.dwd.state.wi.us/dwepfe/programs.htm

Wyoming

Department of Employment
P.O. Box 2760
Casper, WY 82602
307-235-3284
http://wydoe.state.wy.us/doe.asp?ID=354

Free Training for Teens and Low-Income Unemployed Adults

Program: Workforce Investment Act

Description: Under the Workforce Investment Act (WIA), your state receives millions of dollars each year to train teenagers, unskilled adults, the elderly, and others who have special needs to overcome in order to find and keep good jobs.

Free services can include an assessment of an unemployed individual's needs and abilities and a strategy of services such as classroom training, on-the-job training, job search assistance, work experience, counseling, basic skills training, and support services, such as transportation and child care.

What You Can Get: For young people, WIA offers jobs and training during the summer that could include basic and remedial education, work-experience programs, and support services such as transportation. WIA also provides year-round training and employment programs for youth, both in and out of school. Program services may include limited internships, school-to-work transition services, and alternative high school services.

Who Is Eligible: Those eligible to take advantage of WIA services include economically disadvantaged adults and youth (ages 14-21), dislocated workers, and others who face significant employment barriers.

Money Available: The goal of WIA is to move jobless individuals into permanent self-sustaining employment. The federal budget for this program is $1,054,813,000. For more information, contact one of the WIA sites listed below, or contact the Office of Career Transition Assistance, U.S. Department of Labor, 200 Constitution Ave., NW, Room S4231, Washington, DC 20210; 202-693-3045; {http://usworkforce.org}.

Workforce Investment Act

Alabama

Alabama Workforce Investment Area (counties) Autauga, Baldwin, Barbour, Bibb, Blount, Bullock, Butler, Calhoun, Chambers, Cherokee, Chilton, Choctaw, Clarke, Clay, Cleburne, Coffee, Colbert, Conecuh, Coosa, Covington, Crenshaw, Cullman, Dale, Dallas, De Kalb, Elmore, Escambia, Etowah, Fayette, Frankline, Geneva, Greene, Hale, Henry, Houston, Jackson, Lumar, Lauderdale, Lawrence, Lee, Lime-stone, Lowndes, Macon, Madison, Marengo, Marion, Marshall, Monroe, Montgomery, Morgan, Perry, Pickens, Pike, Randolph, Russell, St. Clair, Shelby, Sumter, Talladega, Tallapoosa, Tuscaloosa, Walker, Washington, Wilcox, Winston
Mr. Steve Walkley
Alabama Department of Economic and Community Affairs
401 Adams Ave.
P.O. Box 5690
Montgomery, AL 36103-5690
334-242-5300
Fax: 334-242-5855
Email: steve@adeca.state.al.us

Birmingham/ Jefferson County Workforce Investment Area
Mr. Robert E. Lunsford
Birmingham/ Jefferson County Workforce Inveestment Area
805 N. 22nd Street
Birmingham, AL 35203
205-325-5671
Fax: 205-325-5095
Email: lunsfordb@jcc.co.jefferson.al.us

Mobile Works
Mr. Sidney Raine
Mobile Works, Inc.
P.O. Box 889
Mobile, AL 36601
251-432-0909
Fax: 251-432-1004
Email: sraine@mobile0works.org

Alaska

Governor and State WIA Liaison
Mr. Ronald Hull
Division of Community and Regional Affairs
Employment Security

P.O. Box 25509
Juneau, AK 99802-5509
907-465-5937
Fax: 907-465-4537
Email: ron_hull@labor.state.ak.us

Municipality of Anchorage/ Mat-Su
Ms. Ruth DeCamp
Career Development and Training
Anchorage/Mat-Su Consortium
P.O. Box 196650
235 E. 8th Ave.
Municipality of Anchorage
Anchorage, AK 99519-6650
907-343-6560
Fax: 907-258-6584
Email: decampra@ce.anchorage.ak.us

Statewide
(counties) Bristol Bay, Fairbanks-North Star, Greater Juneau, Greater Sitka, Haines, Kenai Penninsula, Ketchikan Gateway, Kodiak Island, Matanuska Susitna, North Slope
Mr. Sean O'Brien
Department of Labor and Workforce Development

P.O. Box 25509
Juneau, AK 99802-5509
907-465-4892
Fax: 907-465-3212
Email: sean_o'brien@labor.state.ak.us

Arizona

Governor's Liaison and State Director
Mr. Stan Flowers
Department of Economic Security
1789 W. Jefferson St.
P.O. Box 6123
Site Code 920Z
Phoenix, AZ 85007
602-542-1784
Fax: 602-542-2491
Email: sflowers@de.state.az.us

Apache County
Ms. Cheri Castillo
Apache County Workforce Development
P.O. Box 606
Springerville, AZ 85938
520-333-4454
Fax: 520-333-2903

Cochise County
Ms. Vada Phelps
Cochise County Workforce Office
650 E. Wilcox Dr.
Sierra Vista, AZ 85635-2534
520-417-9913
Fax: 520-417-9910
Email: vphelps@cpic_cas.org

Coconino County
Ms. Carol Curtis
Coconino County Workforce Center
110 E. Cherry Ave.
Flagstaff, AZ 86001
520-522-7900
Fax: 520-522-7919
Email: ccurtis@co.coconino.az.us

Gila/Pinal Consortium
Ms. Deanna Jonovich
Gila County Community Services Division
P.O. Box 1254
Globe, AZ 85501
520-425-3281
Fax: 520-425-7521
Email: djonovich@mail.co.gila.az.us

Graham County
Mr. Neil Karnes
Graham County WIA Office
826 W. Main St.
Safford, AZ 85546
520-428-7386
Fax: 520-428-3944
Email: nkarnes@graham_cnty.org

Greenlee County
Ms. Evangelina Esquivel
Greenlee Career Center
Highway 191
Wards Canyon Highway
Clifton, AZ 85533
520-865-4151
Fax: 520-865-3566
Email: vesquivel@aepnet.com

Maricopa County
Mr. Darcy Bucholz
Maricopa Employment and Training Office
2801 W. Durango

Phoenix, AZ 85009
602-506-5911
Fax: 602-506-8789
Email: dubcholz@mail.maricopa.gov

Mohave-Lapaz Consortium
Ms. Susie Parel-Duranceau
Mohave Workforce Development Division
P.O. Box 7000
Kingman, AZ 86401
520-753-0723
Fax: 520-753-0776
Email: susie.parel-duranceau@co.mohave.az.us

Navajo County
Ms. Gail Sadler
Navajo County Workforce Investment Board
155 West Center Street
Snowflake, AZ 85937
520-537-3668
Fax: 520-537-5376
Email: sadler_gail@hotmail.com

Navajo Nation
(parts of counties) San Juan, San Miguel
(reservations) Canoncito, Alamo, Ramah
Ms. Rosalyn Curtis
Navajo Department of Employment and Training
P.O. Box 1889
Window Rock, AZ 86515
520-871-7707
Fax: 520-871-7116

Nineteen Tribal Nations WIA
Ms. Nadine Talayumptewa
Workforce Job Training Administration
1789 West Jefferson
Site Code 920Z
Phoenix, AZ 85007
602-542-3957
Fax: 602-542-2491
Email: ntalayumptewa@de.state.az.us

Phoenix (city)
Mr. Jim Moore
City of Phoenix Employment and Training Division
200 W. Washington, 19th Floor
Phoenix, AZ 85003-1611
602-534-0539
Fax: 602-534-3915
Email: jmoore@ci.phoenix.az.us

Pima County
Mr. Hank Atha
Regional Employment Center
32 N. Stone, 16th Floor
Tucson, AZ 85701
520-740-5205
Fax: 520-798-3203
Email: hatha@csd.co.pima.az.us

Santa Cruz County
Mr. Carlos Rivera
Santa Cruz County Board of Supervisors
2150 North Congress Drive, Room 119
Nogales, AZ 85621
520-761-7800

Yavapai County
Ms. Teri Drew
NACOG-Economic/Workforce Development
P.O. Box 2451
221 N. Marina, Suite 201
Prescott, AZ 86302

520-778-1422
Fax: 520-778-1756
Email: tdrew@cabelone.net

Yuma County
Mr. John Morales
Yuma Private Industry Council
3834 W. 16th St.
Yuma, AZ 85364
520-329-0990
Fax: 520-783-0886
Email: jmorales@ypic.com

Arkansas

State Liaison
Ms. Jane English
Arkansas Workforce Investment Board
320 Executive Court, Suite 302
Little Rock, AR 72205
501-371-1020
Fax: 501-371-1030
Email: jane.english@mail.state.ar.us

Central
(counties) Faulkner, Lonoke, Monroe, Prairie,
Pulaski, Saline
Mr. John Guthrie
Central Arkansas PDD, Inc.
1109 S. 16th St.
P.O. Box 2067
Ft. Smith, AR 72902
501-785-2651
Fax: 501-785-1964
Email: jguthrie@wapdd.org

Eastern
(counties) Crittenden, Cross, Lee, Phillips, St.
Francis
Ms. Sharon Williams
Workforce, Inc.
310 Mid-Continent Bldg., Suite 600
P.O. Box 1388
West Memphis, AR 72303
870-735-6730
Fax: 870-732-4995
Email: sharon@thewib.org

Little Rock (city)
Ms. Dorothy Nayles
Community Programs
500 W. Markham St., Room 220W
Little Rock, AR 72201
501-399-3424
Fax: 501-399-3425
Email: dnayles@littlerock.state.ar.us

North Central
(counties) Cleburne, Fulton, Independence,
Izard, Jackson, Sharp, Stone Van Buren,
White Woodruff
Mr. Van Thomas
White River PDD, Inc.
1652 White Dr.
P.O. Box 2396
Batesville, AR 72501
870-793-5233
Fax: 870-793-4035
Email: thomas@wrpdd.org

Northeast
(counties) Clay, Craighead, Greene,
Lawrence, Mississippi, Poinsett, Randolph
Mr. Sammy McGuire
Employment and Training Services, Inc.
2805 Forrest Home Rd.

Jonesboro, AR 72401
870-932-1564
Fax: 870-932-5310
Email: etsine@cox-internet.com

Northwest
(counties) Baxter, Benton, Boone, Carroll,
Madison, Marion, Newton, Searcy,
Washington
Mr. Mike Norton
Northwest Arkansas EDD
818 Hwy 62-65, 412 North
P.O. Box 190
Harrison, AR 72602-0190
870-741-5404
Fax: 870-741-1905
Email: jmnorton@alltel.net

Southeast
(counties) Arkansas, Ashley, Bradley, Chicot,
Cleveland, Desha, Drew, Grant, Jefferson,
Lincoln
Mr. Glenn Bell
Southeast Arkansas EDD, Inc.
721 Walnut
P.O. Box 6806
Pine Bluff, AR 71601
870-536-1971
Fax: 870-536-7718
Email: glenbell@earthlink.net

Southwest
(counties) Calhoun, Columbia, Dallas,
Hempstead, Howard, Lafeyette, Little River,
Miller, Nevada, Ouachita, Sevier, Union
Mr. John Guthrie
Southwest Arkansas PDD, Inc.
P.O. Box 2067
1109 S. 16th St.
Ft. Smith, AR 72902
501-785-2652
Fax: 501-785-1964
Emaiil: jguthrie@wapdd.org
Magnolia, AR 71753

West Central
(counties) Clark, Conway, Garland, Hot
Spring, Johnson, Montgomery, Perry, Pike,
Pope, Yell
Ms. Pat Heusel
West Central PDD, Inc.
1820 Higdon Ferry Rd., Suite D
P.O. Box 21100
Hot Springs, AR 71903
501-525-7577
Fax: 501-575-7677
Email: pheusel@hsnp.com

Western
(counties) Crawford, Franklin, Logan, Polk,
Scott, Sebastian
Mr. John Guthrie
Southwest Arkansas PDD, Inc.
P.O. Box 2067
1109 South 16th Street
Ft. Smith, AR 72902
501-785-2651
Fax: 501-785-1964
Email: jguthrie@wapdd.org

California
Governor's Liaison
Mr. Michael Bernick
Employment Development Department
800 Capitol Mall, MIC 81

P.O. Box 826880
Sacramento, CA 94280-0001
916-654-8210
Fax: 916-657-5294
Email: mbernick@edd.ca.gov

State Workforce Development
Mr. Bill Burke
Employment Development Department
Workforce Investment Division
MIC 69
P.O. Box 826880
Sacramento, CA 94280-0001
916-654-7111
Fax: 916-654-8039
Email: bburke@edd.ca.gov

Alameda County
(counties) Alameda; (cities) Alameda, Albany,
Brekeley, Dublin, Emeryville, Fremont,
Hayward, Livermore, Newark, Piedmont,
Pleasanton, San Leandro, Union City
Ms. Dorothy Chen
Alameda County WIB
24100 Amador St., 6th Floor
Hayward, CA 94544
510-670-5700
Fax: 510-670-5706
Email: dchen@alcopic.com

Anaheim (city)
Mr. Ruben Acaves
City of Anaheim
50 S. Anaheim Blvd., #200
Anaheim, CA 92805
714-765-4342
Fax: 714-765-4363
Email: raceves@anaheim.net

Carson/ Lomita/ Torrance Consortium
Ms. Patricia Unangst
Carson/Lomita/Torrance
1 Civic Plaza, Suite 500
Torrance, CA 90745
310-518-8130
Fax: 310-518-8214
Email: unangst.patrick@mail.ci.torrance.ca.us

Contra Costa County
Mr. Ronald Wetter
Contra Costa County WIB
2425 Bisso Lane, Suite 100
Concord, CA 94520
925-646-5239
Fax: 925-646-5517
Email: rwetter@ehsd.co.contra-costa.ca.us

Foothill Consortium
(cities) Arcadia, Duarte, Monrovia, Pasadena
Sierra Madre, South Pasadena
Mr. Phillip L. Dunn
Foothill WIB
1207 E. Green St.
Pasadena, CA 91106
626-584-8381
Fax: 626-584-8375
Email: npdunn@ci.pasadena.ca.us

Fresno Consortium
City and County of Fresno
Ms. Cindy Merzon
Fresno Area WIG
2035 Tulare St., Suite 203
Fresno, CA 93721
559-266-3742
Fax: 559-233-9633
Email: cmerzon@jobsfresno.com

Golden Sierra Consortium
(counties) Alpine, El Dorado, Nevada, Placer,
Sierra
Ms. Kim Hemmer
Golden Sierra Job Training
Dewitt Center
11549 F Ave.
Auburn, CA 95603
530-823-4631
Fax: 530-885-5579
Email: khemmer@psyber.com

Humboldt County
Mr. Farrel Starr
Humboldt Co. Employment Training Dept.
930 Sixth St.
Eureka, CA 95501
707-441-4631
Fax: 707-445-6228
Email: fgstarr@northcoast.com

Imperial County
Ms. Helen Lopez
Imperial County Office of Employment and
Training
760 Main St.
El Centro, CA 92243
760-353-5050
Fax: 760-353-6594
Email: helen.lopez@hotmail.com

Kern/ Inyo/ Mono Consortium
Mr. John Nilon
Kern/Inyo/Mono Consortium
2001 28th St.
Bakersfield, CA 93301
661-336-6849
Fax: 661-336-6855
Email: nilonj@co.kern.ca.us

Kings County
Mr. John Lehn
Job Training Office
124 N. Irwin St.
Hanford, CA 93230
559-585-3532
Fax: 559-589-7395
Email: jslehn@yahoo.com

Long Beach (city)
Mr. Ray Warden
City of Long Beach
Business Development Center
200 Pine Ave., Suite 400
Long Beach, CA 90802
562-570-3800
Fax: 562-570-3897
Email: raworde@ci.long-beach.ca.us

Los Angeles (city)
Ms. Ann Giagni
Workforce Development Division
Community Development Department
215 W. Sixth St., 10th Floor
Los Angeles, CA 90014
213-485-5019
Fax: 213-473-3749
Email: agiagni@cbd.lacity.org

Los Angeles County
Mr. Kenneth Kessler
Workforce Program
Los Angeles County Department of
Community and Senior Services
3175 W. Sixth St., Room 302
Los Angeles, CA 90020

213-738-2620
Fax: 213-385-3893
Email: kkesler@co.la.ca.us

Madera County
Mr. Herman Perez
Employment and Training Office
Madera County Department of Education
209 E. 7th St.
Madera, CA 93638
559-662-4600
Fax: 559-673-1794
Email: hperez@maderacoe.k12.ca.us

Marin County
Ms. Mary Donovan
Marin County Office of Workforce
Investment Board
2980-A Kerner Blvd.
San Rafael, CA 94901
415-499-7845
Fax: 415-499-7847
Email: mdonovan@marin.org

Mendocino
Mr. Charles R. Hall
County of Mendocino
631 S. Orchard Ave.
Ukiah, CA 95453
707-463-6390
Fax: 707-463-6392
Email: colstonm@medss.org

Merced County
Merced Training Department
1880 W. Wardrobe Ave.
Merced, CA 95340
209-385-7324
Fax: 209-725-3592

Monterey County
Mr. Joseph Werner
Office for Employment Training Monterey
County
730 LaGuardia St.
Salinas, CA 93902
831-759-6644
Fax: 831-755-3246
Email: wernerj@redshift.com

Mother Lode Consortium
(counties) Amador, Calaveras, Mariposa,
Tuolumne
Ms. Candace Katosic
Mother Lode Job WIA
19900 Cedar Rd. North
Sonora, CA 95370
209-533-3396
Fax: 209-533-1079
Email: candace@mljt.org

Napa County
Ms. Donna DeWeerd
WIB
1700 Second St., #378
Napa, CA 94559
707-259-8680
Fax: 707-259-8681
Email: ddeweerd@co.napa.ca.us

Nortec Consortium
(counties) Butte, Del Norte, Lassen, Modoc,
Plumas, Shasta, Siskiyou, Tehama, Trinity
Mr. Charles Brown
NORTEC Governing Board
7420 Skyway
Paradise, CA 95969

530-872-9600
Fax: 530-872-5647
Email: cbrown@ncen.org

North Central Counties Consortium
(counties) Colusa, Glenn, Lake, Sutter, Yuba
Mr. Charles A. Peterson
North Central Counties Consortium
1215 Plumas St., Suite 1800
Yuba City CA 95991
530-822-7145
Fax: 530-822-7150
Email: cpeterson@ncen.org

Nova Job Training Consortium
(cities) Cupertino, Los Altos, Mountain View,
Palo Alto, Santa Clara, Sunnyvale
Mr. Michael J. Curran
NOVA Consortoi,
Department of Employment Development
505 W. Olive, Suite 550
Sunnyvale, CA 94086
408-730-7248
Fax: 408-730-7643
Email: mccuran@novapic.org

Oakland (city)
Mr. Al Auletta
City of Oakland Community and Economic
Development Department
250 Frank Ogawa Plaza, Suite 3315
Oakland, CA 94612-3025
510-238-3752
Fax: 510-238-2230

Orange County
Mr. Andrew Munoz
Orange County WIB
1300 S. Grand, Bldg. B, 36th Floor
Santa Ana, CA 92705
714-567-7370
Fax: 714-834-7132
Email: amunoz@csa.co.orange.ca.us

Richmond (city)
Mr. Upesi Mtambuzi
Employment and Training Program
City of Richmond
330 25th St.
Richmond, CA 94804
510-307-8153
Fax: 510-307-8072
Email: umtambuzi@richmondworks.org

Riverside County
Mr. Jerry Craig
County of Riverside Economic Development
Agency
1151 Spruce St.
Riverside, CA 92607
909-955-3100
Fax: 909-955-3131
Email: eda2.jcraig@co.riverside.ca.us

Sacramento Consortium
(county and city) Sacramento
Ms. Kathy Kossick
Sacramento Employment and Training
Agency
1217 Del Paso Blvd.
Sacramento, CA 95815
916-263-3800
Fax: 916-263-3825
Email: kathy@delpaso.seta.net

San Benito County
Ms. Kathy Flores
San Benito County Department of Community

Services/ Workforce Development
1131 San Felipe Rd.
P.O. Box 2107
Hollister, CA 95023
831-637-9293
Fax: 831-637-0996
Email: kflores@hollinet.com

San Bernardino (city)
Mr. Ernest Dowdy
San Bernardino Employment and Training
Agency
599 N. Arrowhead Ave.
San Bernardino, CA 92401-1201
909-888-7881
Fax: 909-889-7833
Email: ebdowdy@sbeta.com

San Bernardino County
Ms. Janice Eisenbelsz
County of San Bernardino
Jobs and Employment Services Department
851 S. Mt. Vernon Ave., Suite 22
Colton, CA 92324
909-433-3330
Fax: 909-433-3333

San Diego Consortium and Private Industry
Council
(city and county) San Diego
Mr. Lawrence G. Fitch
San Diego Workforce Partnership, Inc.
1551 Fourth Ave., Suite 600
San Diego, CA 92101
619-238-1445
Fax: 619-238-6063
Email: lgfitch@workforce.org

San Francisco City and County
(city and county, a single political
jurisdiction)
Ms. Pamela S. Calloway
PIC of San Francisco, Inc.
1650 Mission St., Suite 300
San Francisco, CA 94103-2490
415-923-4003
Fax: 415-923-6966
Email: rrholland@picsf.org

San Joaquin County
Mr. John M. Sollis
Employment and Economic Development
Department
County of San Joaquin
850 N. Hunter St.
Stockton, CA 95202
209-468-3500
Fax: 209-462-9063
Email: jsolis@sjcworknet.org

San Luis Obispo County
Mr. Lee Ferrero
San Luis Obispo County Private Industry, Inc.
4111 Broad St., Suite A
San Luis Obispo, CA 93401
805-788-2600
Fax: 805-541-4117
Email: lferrero@co.sio.ca.us

San Mateo County
Mr. Robert Schwab
San Mateo County WIB
262 Harbor Blvd., Bldg. A
Belmont, CA 94002
650-802-5171
Fax: 650-802-5173
Email: rschwab@co.sanmateo.ca.us

Santa Ana (city)
Ms. Patricia Nunn
Santa Ana Work Center
20 Civic Center Plaza (M-25)
Santa Ana, CA 92701
714-647-6991
Fax: 714-647-6949
Email: pnunn@ci.santa-ana.ca.us

Santa Barbara County
Mr. Bob Shapiro
Department of Social Services
234 Camino del Remedio
Santa Barbara, CA 93110
805-681-4650
Fax: 805-681-4403
Email: shapiro@co.santa-barbara.ca.us

Santa Cruz County
Ms. Kathy Zwart
Career Works Division
Santa Cruz County
1040 Emeline Ave.
Santa Cruz, CA 95060
831-454-4080
Fax: 831-454-4651
Email: hra716@hra.co.santa-cruz.ca.us

Silicon Valley
(county) San Jose
Mr. Blake Konzcal
Silicon Valley Workforce Investment Board
60 South Market Street, Suite 470
San Jose, CA 95113
408-277-5880
Fax: 408-277-3615
Email: blake.konczal@ci.sj.ca.us

Solano County
Mr. Robert Bloom
Solano County WIB
320 Campus Lane
Suisun, CA 94585
707-864-3370
Fax: 707-864-3386
Email: rbloom@solanowib.org

Sonoma County
Mr. Jerald C. Dunn
Sonoma County WIB
2227 Capricorn Way, Suite 207E
Santa Rosa, CA 95407
707-565-8501
Fax: 707-565-8515
Email: jdunn@sonoma-county.org

South Bay Consortium
(cities) El Segundo, Gardena, Hawthorne,
Hermosa Beach, Inglewood, Lawndale,
Manhattan Beach, Redondo Beach
Ms. Jan Vogel
South Bay WIB
11539 Hawthorne Blvd., Suite 500
Hawthorne, CA 90250
310-970-7700
Fax: 310-970-7711
Emil: jvogel@sbwib.org

Southeast Los Angeles County Consortium
(Selaco)
(cities) Bellflower, Downey, Hawaiian
Gardens, Lakewood, Norwalk
Mr. Bill R. Plaster
SELACO
10900 E. 183rd St., Suite 350
Cerritos, CA 90703
562-402-9336

Fax: 562-860-4701
Email: billp@selaco.com

Stanislaus County
Mr. Terry Plett
Stanislaus County Department of Employment
and Training
251 E. Hackett Rd., C-2
Modesto, CA 95358-0031
209-558-2100
Fax: 209-558-2164
Email: plettT@mail.co.stanislaus.ca.us

Tulare County
Mr. Joseph Daniel
Tulare County WIB
4025 W. Noble Ave., Suite A
P.O. Box 3146
Visalia, CA 93278-3146
559-713-5200
Fax: 559-713-5263
Email: main.jdaniel@tcpic.org

Ventura County
Mr. Bruce Stenslie
Workforce Investment Office of Ventura
County
505 Poli Street
Ventura, CA 93001
805-652-7621
Fax: 805-648-9533
Email: bruce.stenslie@mail.co.ventura.ca.us

Verdugo Consortium
(cities) Burbank, Glendale, La Canada,
Flintridge
Ms. Madalyn Blake
Community Development and Housing
Verdugo WIB
141 N. Glendale Ave., Room 202
Glendale, CA 91206-1996
818-548-2053
Fax: 818-548-3724
Email: mblake@ci.glendale.ca.us

Yolo County
Mr. Dana Johnson
Dept. of Employment and Social Services
120 W. Main St.
Woodland, CA 95695
916-661-2772
Fax: 530-666-8193

Colorado
State Workforce Development Liaison
Ms. Vickie L. Armstrong
Colorado Department of labor and
Employment
1515 Arapahoe Street
Denver, CO 80202-2117
303-620-4701
Fax: 303-620-4714
Email: vickie.armstrong@state.co.us

Adams County
Ms. Judy Richendifer
Adams County One Stop Career Center
7190 Colorado Blvd., 5th Floor
Commerce City, CO 80022
303-227-2026
Fax: 303-227-2050
Email: jrichendifer@co.adams.co.us

Arapahoe and Douglas Counties
Ms. Pat Buys
Arapahoe/Douglas Works!

1210 S. Havana, Unit E-3
Aurora, CO 80012
303-752-5820
Fax: 303-752-5850
Email: pbuys@adworks.org

Big Ten Counties Northeast CO
(counties) Cheyenne, Elbert, Kit Carson,
Lincoln, Logan, Morgan, Phillips, Sedgwick,
Washington, Yuma
Ms. Elizabeth Romick
Eastern Colorado Workforce Center
411 Main Street
Fort Morgan, CO 80701
970-867-9401
Fax: 970-867-0226
Email: TaylorRomick@worldnet.att.net

Boulder County
Mr. Tom Miller
Workforce Boulder County
2905 Center Green Court, Suite C
Boulder, CO 80301
303-441-3985
Fax: 303-939-0054
Email: tom.miller@wfoc.org

Denver
Mr. Shepard Nevel
Mayor's Office of Workforce Development
1391 N. Speer Blvd., Suite 710
Denver, CO 80204
303-376-6722
Fax: 303-376-6721
Email: nevels@ci.denver.co.us

Eastern Region
(counties) Cheyenne, Elbert, Kit Carson,
Lincoln, Logan, Morgan, Phillips, Sedgwick,
Washington, Yuma
Ms. Jane Paterson
Colorado Department of Labor and
Employment
1515 Arapahoe, Tower 2, Suite 400
Denver, CO 80202
303-620-4718
Fax: 303-620-4717
Email: jane.patterson@state.co.us

Larimer County
Ms. Joni Friedman
Larimer County Workforce Center
3842 S. Mason St.
Fort Collins, CO 80525
303-223-2470
Fax: 303-223-7456
Email: friedmjb@co.larimer.co.us

Mesa County
Ms. Sue Tuffin
Mesa County Workforce Center
2897 North Avenue
Grand Junction, CO 81501
970-248-0871
Fax: 970-257-2219
Email: tufsa@mesaworkforce.org

Northwest Region
(counties) Grand, Jackson, Moffat, Rio
Blanco, Toutt
Ms. Rosemary Pettus
Colorado Department of Labor and
Employment
602 Galena
Frisco, CO 80443
970-668-5360

Fax: 970-668-3216
Email: rpettus@cwfc.net

Pikes Peak Region
(counties) El Paso, Teller
Ms. Peggy Herbertson
Pikes Peak Workforce Center
2306 East Pikes Peak Avenue
Colorado Springs, CO 809109
719-667-3792
Fax: 719-667-3752
Email: herbertson.-@ppwfc.org

Pueblo Region
Mr. John Martinez
Pueblo Work Link
201 Lamkin
Pueblo, CO 81003
719-253-7821
Fax: 719-253-7946
Email: martinez@co.pueblo.co.us

Rural Resort Region
(counties) Eagle, Garfield, Lake Pitkin, Summit
Ms. Rosemary Pettus
Colorado Department of Labor and Employment
602 Galena
Frisco, CO 80443
970-668-5360
Fax: 970-668-3216
Email: rpettus@cwfc.net

South Central Region
(counties) Alamosa, Conejos, Costilla, Huerfano, Las Animas, Mineral, Saguache, Rio Grande
Mr. Scot Simons
South Central Region
639 East 18th Avenue
Denver, CO 80203
303-830-3099
Fax: 303-894-9313
Email: scot.simons@moet.org

Southeast Region
(counties) Baca, Bent, Crowles, Kiowa, Otero, Prowers
Ms. Jane Paterson
Colorado Department of Labor and Employment
1515 Arapahoe
Tower 2, Suite 400
Denver, CO 80202
303-620-4718
Fax: 303-620-4714
Email: jane.paterson@state.co.us

Southwest Region
(counties) Archuleta, Dolores, La Plata, Montezuma, San Juan
Ms. Maxine Maestas
217 West Main Street
Cortez, CO 81321
970-565-3759
Fax: 970-565-0916
Email: mmaestas@cwf.net

Tri-County Workforce Center
(counties) Clear Creek, Gilpin, Jefferson
Ms. Sherri Almond
Tri-County Workfroce Center
730 Simms Street, Suite 300
Golden, CO 80401
303-271-4747

Fax: 303-271-4708
Email: salmond@co.jefferson.co.us

Upper Arkansas Region
(counties) Chaffee, Custer, Fremont Park
Ms. Rosemary Pettus
Colorado Department of Labor and Employment
602 Galena
Frisco, CO 80443
970-668-5360
Fax: 970-668-3216
Email: rpettus@cwfc.net

Weld County
Ms. Linda Perez
Employment Services of Weld County
1517 N. 17th Ave.
Greeley, CO 80632
970-353-3800
Fax: 970-356-3975
Email: lperez@co.weld.co.us

Western Region
(counties) Delta, Gunnison, Hinsdale, Montrose, Ouray, San Miguel
Ms. Annie Lupp
Western Colorado Workforce Center
Workforce Development
525 Main Street
Montrose, CO 81401
970-249-7783
Fax: 970-249-0445
Email: annie@ocinet.net

Connecticut
State Workforce Development Liaison
Mr. Shaun B. Cashman
Department of Labor
200 Folly Brook Boulevard
Wethersfield, CT 06109
860-263-6505
Fax: 860-263-6529

Ansonia/ Bridgeport/ Norwalk/ Stamford
(towns) Ansonia, Bridgeport, Darien, Derby, Easton, Fairfield, Greenwich, Milford, Monroe, New Canaan, Norwalk, Oxford, Seymour, Shelton, Stamford, Stratford, Trumbull, Weston, Westport, Wilton
Mr. Joseph m. Carbone
The WorkPlace, Inc.
350 Fairchild
Bridgeport, CT 06604
203-576-7030
Fax: 203-335-9703
Email: carbone@workplace.org

Danbury/ Torrington
(towns) Barkhamsted, Bethel, Bridgewater, Brookfield, Canaan, Colebroook, Cornwall, Danbury, Goshen, Hartland, Harwinton, Kent, Litchfield, Morris, New Fairfield, New Hartford, New Milford, Newton, Norfolk, North Canaan, Redding, Ridgefield, Roxbury, Salisbury, Sharon, Sherman, Torrington, Warren, Washington, Winchester
Mr. Owen Quinn
Danbury/ Torrington Workforce Investment Board
Fuessenich Park Fieldhouse, Coe Place
Torrington, CT 06790
860-489-3556
Fax: 860-482-8391

Danielson/ Windham
(towns) Ashford, Brooklyn, Canterbury, Chaplin, Columbia, Coventry, Eastford, Hampton, Killingly, Lebanon, Mansfield, Plainfield, Pomfret, Putnam, Scotland, Sterling, Thompson, Union, Windham, Woodstoc, Willington
Ms. Virginia Sampietro
Workforce One
128 Chaplain Street
P.O. Box 305
Chaplain, CT 06235-0305
860-455-8009
Fax: 860-455-8025
Email: virginia.sampietro@po.state.ct.us

Hartford
(towns) Andover, Avon, Bloomfield, Bolton, Canton, East Granby, East Hartford, East Windsor, Ellington, Enfield, Farmington, Glastonbury, Granby, Hartford, Hebron, Manchester, Marlborough, Newington, Rocky Hill, Simsbury, Somers, South Windsor, Stafford, Suffield, Tolland, Vernon, West Hartford, Wethersfield, Windsor, Windsor Locks
Mr. Thomas Phillips
Capital Region Workforce Development Board
99 Pratt Street
Hartford, CT 06103
862-522-1111
Fax: 862-722-2486
Email: thomas.phillips@po.state.ct.us

Mid-Connecticut
(municipalities) Berlin, Bristol, Burlington, Chester, Cromwell, Deep River, Durham, East Haddam, East Hampton, Essex, Haddam, Killingworth, Meriden, Middlefield, New Britain, Old Saybrook, Plainville, Plymouth, Portland, Southington, Westbrook
Mr. George Brusznicki
Workforce Partners, Inc.
136 Main Street
New Britian, CT 06051
860-223-4421
Fax: 860-832-9103

New Haven
(towns) Bethany, Branford, Clinton, East Haven, Guilford, Hamden, Madison, New Haven, North Branford, North Haven, Orange, Wallingford, West Haven, Woodbridge
Mr. William Villano
Regional Workforce Development Board
560 Ella T. Grasso Blvd.
New Haven, CT 06519
203-624-1493
Fax: 203-562-1106
Email: wvillano@rwdb.org

New London/ Norwich
(towns) Bozrah, Colchester, East Lyme, Franklin, Griswold Groton, Ledyard, Lisbon, Lyme Montville, New London, North Stongton, Norwich, Old Lyme, Preston, Salem, Sprague, Stonington Voluntown, Waterford
Mr. John Beauregard
Workforce Investment Board of Southeastern Connecticut
113 Salem Turnpike
North Building, Suite 200
Norwich, CT 06360
860-859-5740
Fax: 860-859-5741
Email: sectpic@snet.net

Waterbury
(towns) Beacon Falls, Bethlehem, Cheshire,
Middlebury, Naugatuck, Prospect, Southbury,
Thomaston, Waterbury, Watertown, Wolcott,
Woodbury
Ms. Catherine Awward
Workforce Connection
249 Thomaston Ave.
Waterbury, CT 06702
203-574-6971
Fax: 203-573-8951

Delaware

State Workforce Development Liaison
Ms. Anne Farley
Department of Labor
Division of Employment and Training
Fox Valley-14425 North Market Street
Wilmington, DE 19802
302-761-8129
Fax: 302-761-6617
Email: afarley@state.de.us

Single State Workforce Area
Ms. Patricia Cannon
Delaware WIB
Community Services Bldg.
100 10th St., Suite 707
Wilmington, DE 19801
302-577-6202
Fax: 302-577-6247
Email: pcannon@state.de.us

District of Columbia

Single State Workforce Area
Mr. Gregory Irish
District of Columbia Department of
Employment Services
500 C St., NW, Suite 600
Washington, DC 20001
202-724-7100
Fax: 202-724-7112
Email: girish@does.dcgov.org

Florida

Governor's Liaison
Ms. Mary B. Hoooks
Dept. of Labor and Employment Security
2012 Capital Circle, Southeast
Suite 303, Hartman Bldg.
Tallahassee, FL 32399-2152
850-922-7021
Fax: 850-488-8930
Email: mary_b_hooks@fdles.state.fl.us

State Workforce Development
Mr. Larry McIntyre
Dept. of Labor, Employment and Training
1320 Executive Center Dr., #200
Tallahassee, FL 32399 0667
850-488-9250
Fax: 850-488-0249
Email: larry_mcintyre@jb.fdles.state.fl.us

Alachura/Bradford Counties-Region 9
Ms. Rachel Bishop-Cook
BCN Association, Inc.
408 University Avenue, Suite 604
Gainesville, FL 32601
352-334-4088
Fax: 352-377-5242
Email: rachel@bcnassociates.com

Big Bend-Region 5
(counties) Gadsden, Leon, Wakulla
Dr. J. Wyatt Pope

Big Bend Jobs and Education Council, Inc.
565 East Tennessee Street
Tallahassee, FL 32308
850-414-6085
Fax: 850-410-2595
Email: wyatt.pope@bigbend-workforce.org

Brevard County-Region 13
Ms. Linda South
Brevard Workforce Development Board
597 Haverty Court, Suite 40
Rockledge, FL 32955
321-504-2060
Fax: 321-504-2065
Email: lsouth@job-link.net

Broward County
Mr. Mason Jackson
Workforce One
3800 Inverarry Blvd., Suite 400
Lauderhill, FL 33319
954-535-2345
Fax: 954-535-2346
Email: masonjacks@broward-workforce.org

Central Florida-Region 12
(counties) Lake, Orange, Osceola, Seminole,
Sumter
Mr. Gray Earl
Workforce Central Florida
1801 Lee Road, Suite 270
Winter Park, FL 32789-2165
407-741-4365
Fax: 407-741-4376
Email: gearl@msn.com

Chipola-Region 3
(counties) Calhoun, Holmes, Jackson, Liberty,
Washington
Ms. Freida Sheffield
Chipola Regional Workforce Planning Board,
Inc.
P.O. Box 947
Chipley, FL 32428
850-638-6081
Fax: 850-638-3093
Email: freidas@jep3.state.fl.us

Citrus/Levy/Marion-Region 10
Mr. Thomas "Rusty" Skinner
CLMWorks
Workforce Development Board
2300 SE 17th Street, Suite 1000
Ocala, FL 34471
352-732-1355
Fax: 352-732-1718
Email: tskinner@clmworkforce.com

Dade & Monroe Counties-Region 23
Ms. Harriet Spivak
Job and Education Partnership Region Board
for Dada & Monroe Counties
3403 NW 82nd Avenue, Suite 300
Miami, FL 33122-1029
305-594-1029
Fax: 305-594-7615
Email: harriet@jeb-tec.org

Escarosa-Region 1
(counties) Escambia, Santa Rosa
Ms. Susan Simpler
Escarosa Regional Workforce Development
Board, Inc.
9111 Sturdevant Drive
Pensacola, FL 32514
850-473-0939

Fax: 850-473-0935
Email: escarosa@bellsouth.net

First Coast-Region 8
(counties) Clay, Duval, Nassau, Putnam, St.
Johns
Mr. Lynn Grafet
First Coast Workforce Development Board,
Inc.
2141 Loch Rane Boulevard, Suite 107
Orange Park, FL 32073-4239
904-213-3050
Fax: 904-272-8927
Email: worksource@worksource.fl.com

Flagler/ Volusia Counties; WDB11
Mr. Laurence Tomasetti
Workforce Development Board of Flager &
Volusia Counties
1901 Mason Ave., Suite 110
Daytona Beach, FL 32117
386-274-3850
Fax: 385-274-3864
Email: larryt@web-fvc.org

Florida-Crown-Region 7
(counties) Baker, Columbia, Dixie, Gilchrist,
Union
Mr. James E. Carr
Florida Crown Workforce Development Board
1430 South 1st Street, Suite 2
Lake City, FL 32025-5750
386-752-5713
Fax: 386-752-6461
Email: jecarr@flcrown.org

Gulf Coast-Region 4
(counties) Bay, Franklin, Gulf
Ms. Kimberly L. Shoemaker
Gulf Coast Workforce Board
Gulf Coast Community College
5230 West US Highway 98
Panama, FL 32401-1058
850-913-3285
Fax: 850-913-3264
Email: kshoemaker@mail.gc.cc.fl.us

Heartland; Region 19
(counties) De Soto, Hardee, Highlands
Mr. James L. Gose
Heartland WIB
600 W. College Dr.
Avon Park, FL 33825
863-453-6661
Fax: 863-784-7209
Email: gosej@sfcc.cc.fl.us

Hillsborough County; WDB15
Mr. Max Selko
Hillsborough County Workforce Board
9250 Bay Plaza Blvd., Suite 320
Tampa, FL 33619
813-744-5547
Fax: 813-744-5764
Email: selkom@workforcetampa.com

North Florida-Region 6
(counties) Hamilton, Jefferson, Lafayette,
Madison, Suwannee, Taylor
Mr. William M. Deming
North Florida Workforce Development
Board/WAGES Coalition
400 West Base Street, 2nd Floor
P.O. Box 267
Madison, FL 32341
850-973-2672

Fax: 850-973-6497
Email: deminggm@nfwdb.org

Okaloosa/ Walton Counties; Region 2
Ms. Mary Lou Reed
Workforce Development Board of Okaloosa
& Walton
109 Eighth Ave.
Shalimar, FL 32579
850-651-2315
Fax: 850-651-3165
Email: mireed@seii.net

Palm Beach County; WDB 21
Mr. Ken Montgomery
Palm Beach County Workforce Development
Board, Inc./WAGES Coalition
2051 Martin Luther King Jr. Boulevard #302
Rivera Beach, FL 33404
561-841-0207
Fax: 567-841-0280
Email: kmontgomery@pbcwdb.com

Pasco/Hernando Counties; Region 16
Mr. Lee Elizey
Pasco-Hernando Jobs & Education
Partnership Regional Board
P.O. Box 15790
Brooksville, FL 34609
352-797-5781
Fax: 352-797-5785
Email: lee@paso-hernando.com

Pinellas County; Region 14
Ms. Bonnie Moore
Worknet Pinellas
4525 140th Ave., North, Suite 906
Clearwater, FL 33760
727-524-4334
Fax: 727-524-4350
Email: bamoore@co.pinellas.fl.us

Polk County; Region 17
Ms. Nancy Thompson
Polk County Workforce Development Board,
Inc.
205 East Main Street, Suite 107
Bartow, FL 33830
863-519-0100
Fax: 803-534-8501
Email: nancy_thompson@polkworks.org

Southwest Florida; Region 24
(counties) Dade, Monroe
Mr. Joseph Paterno
Southwest Florida Workforce Development
Board
24311 Walden Center Drive #200
Bonita Springs, FL 34134
941-992-8000
Fax: 941-948-3359
Email: paterno_joe@hotmail.com

Suncoast; WDB18
(counties) Manatee, Sarasota
Ms. Mary Helen Kruss
Suncoast Workforce Development Board
1750 17th Street, Building J-2
Sarasota, FL 34234
941-361-6090
Fax: 941-361-6141
Email: mhdress@swdb.org

Treasure Coast; WDB 20
(counties) Indian River, Martin, St. Lucie,
Okeechobee
Ms. Nan Rose Griggs

Workforce Development Board of the
Treasure Coast
9350 South Federal Highway
Port. St. Lucie, FL 34952
561-335-3030
Fax: 561-335-0677
Email: ngriggs@tcjobs.org

Georgia
State Workforce Development Liaison
Ms. Andrea Harper
Georgia Department of Labor
Job Training Division
148 International Boulevard, Suite 650
Atlanta, GA 30303
424-656-7392
Fax: 404-651-9377
Email: aharper@dol.state.ga.us

Atlanta (City)
Ms. Patricia Atkins
Atlanta Workforce Development Agency
818 Pollard Boulevard, SW
Atlanta, GA 30315
404-658-9675
Fax: 404-658-7091
Email: psermon@ci.atlanta.ga.us

Atlanta Regional
(counties) Cherokee, Clayton, Douglas,
Fayette, Gwinnett, Henry, Rockdale
Ms. Mary Margaret Garrett
Atlanta Regional Commission
40 Courtland Street, NE
Atlanta, GA 30303-2538
404-463-3327
Fax: 404-463-3105
Email: mmgarrett@atlantaregional.com

Coastal
(counties) Bryan, Bulloch, Camden, Chatham,
Effingham, Glynn, Liberty, Long, McIntosh
Ms. Donna Happach
Mayor's Office
P.O. Box 1027
Savannah, GA 31402
912-651-4280
Fax: 912-651-4287
Email: dhappach@hotmail.com

Cobb County
Mr. John Helton
Cobb County Resource Center
590 Commerce Park Dr., Suite 175
Marietta, GA 30060
770-528-4300
Fax: 770-528-4302
Email: jhelton@cobbworks.org

Dekalb County
Mr. Pete Burke
Dekalb Workforce Development Dept.
320 Church St.
Decatur, GA 30030
404-687-3430
Fax: 404-687-3443
Email: pfburke@co.dekalb.ga.us

East Central Georgia
(counties) Columbia, Glascock, Hancock,
Jefferson, Jenkins, Lincoln, McDuffie,
Screven, Taliaferro, Warren, Washington,
Wilkes
Ms. Mary Braxton
East Central Georgia Consortium
P.O. Box 179

Thompson, GA 30824
706-595-8941
Fax: 706-597-9713
Email: mbraxton@thomson.net

Fulton County
Ms. Valerie Wilson
Fulton County Human Services
132 Mitchell St., SW
Atlanta, GA 30303
404-730-7944
Fax: 404-730-6889
Email: rwilson@co.fulton.ga.us

Georgia Mountains
(counties) Banks, Dawson, Forsyth, Franklin,
Habersham, Hall, Hart, Lumpkin, Rabun,
Stephens, Towns, Union, White
Ms. Kimberly Wilson
Georgia Mountains Workforce Investment
Board
2481 Hilton Drive, Suite 8
Gainesville, GA 30501
770-538-2727
Fax: 770-538-2730
Email: Kimberlee.Wilson@dol.state.ga.us

Heart of Georgia
(counties) Appling, Bleckley, Candler, Dodge,
Emanuel, Evans, Jeff Davis, Johnson,
Laurens, Montgomery, Tattnall, Telfair,
Toombs, Treultlen, Wayne, Wheeler, Wilcox
Ms. Reba VanMeter
Job Training Unlimited
7 South Duval Street
Claxton, GA 30417
912-739-7158
Fax: 912-739-7126
Email: jobtraining@g-net.net

Lower Chattahoochee
(counties) Chattahoochee, Clay, Harris,
Muscogee, Quitman, Randolph, Stewart,
Talbot
Mr. Howard T. Pendleton
Job Training Division
City of Columbus
P.O. Box 1340
Columbus, GA 31902-1340
706-653-4529
Fax: 706-653-4533
Email: hpendleton@columbusga.org

Macon-Bibb
Mr. Al Chandler
Macon-Bibb Workforce Development Agency
682 Cherry Street, Suite 600
Decatur, GA 31202
478-751-7333
Fax: 478-751-7335
Email: Al.Chandler@macon.ga.us

Middle Georgia
(counties) Baldwin, Crawford, Houston,
Jones, Monroe, Peach, Pulaski, Putnam,
Twiggs, Wilkinson
Mr. Don McRae
Middle Georgia Consortium
124 Osigian Boulevard, Suite A
Warner Robbins, GA 31088
478-953-4771
Fax: 478-953-2509
Email: dmcrae@compunet1.net

Northeast Georgia
(counties) Barrow, Clarke, Elbert, Greene,

Jackson, Jasper, Madison, Morgan, Newton, Oconee, Oglethorpe, Walton
Ms. Carol Rayburn
NE Georgia RDC
305 Research Dr.
Athens, GA 30610
706-369-5703
Fax: 706-369-5792
Email: crayburn@negrdc.org

Northwest Georgia
(counties) Bartow, Catoosa, Chatooga, Dade,
Fannin, Floyd, Gilmer, Gordon, Haralson,
Murray, Paulding, Pickens, Polky, Walker,
Whitfield
Mr. Gwen Dellinger
Coosa Valley Regional Development Center
P.O. Box 1793
Rome, GA 30162
706-295-6485
Fax: 706-802-5567
Email: gwend@jtpa.cvrdc.org

Richmond/Burke Counties
Ms. Aray Darden
Richmond/Burke Job Training Authority
209 7th Street
P.O. Box 1446
Augusta, GA 30913
706-722-3001
Fax: 706-721-7395

South Georgia
(counties) Ben Hill, Berrien, Brooks, Cook,
Echols, Irwin, Lanier, Lowndes, Tift, Turner
Ms. Haley Rosenburg
South Georgia WIB
327 W. Savannah Ave.
Valdosta, GA 31601
229-333-5277
Fax: 229-333-5312
Email: haley@sgrdc.com

Southeast Georgia
(counties) Atkinson, Bacon, Brantley,
Charlton, Clinch, Coffee, Pierce, Ware
Ms. Wanda Taft
Southeast Georgia RDC
3395 Harris Rd.
Waycross, GA 31601
229-285-6097
Fax: 229-285-6126

Southwest Georgia
(counties) Baker, Calhoun, Colquitt, Decatur,
Dougherty, Early, Grady, Lee, Miller,
Mitchell, Seminole, Terrell, Thomas, Worth
Ms. June Richey
Southwest Georgia Workforce Investment Board
P.O. Box 647
Camilla, GA 31730
229-522-3594
Fax: 229-522-3597
Email: June.Richey@dol.state.ga.us

West Central Georgia
(counties) Butts, Carroll, Coweta, Heard,
Lamar, Meriwether, Pike, Spaulding, Troup,
Upson
Ms. Diane Davis
West Central Georgia Workforce Investment Board
1435 North Expressway, Suite 304
Griffin, GA 30223
770-229-3220

Fax: 770-229-3200
Email: ddavis5756@aol.com

Guam
Territory
Ms. Sheila S. Torres
Agency for Human Resources Development
Government of Guam
125 Tun Jesus Crisostomo Street
Suite 306, Sunny Plaza
Tamuning, Guam 96911
671-647-7161
Fax: 671-647-7162
Email: sstorres@mail.gov.gu

Hawaii
State Workforce Development Liaison
Ms. Elaine Young
Department of Labor and Industrial Relations
830 Punchbowl St., Room 329
Honolulu, HI 96813
808-586-8813
Fax: 808-586-8822
Email: wdd@dlir.state.hi.us

County and City of Hawaii
Mr. Edwin Taira
Office of Housing and Community Development
50 Wailuka Drive
Hilo, HI 96720
808-961-8379
Fax: 808-961-8685
Email: ohcd@interpac.net

County of Kauai
Ms. Virginia Kapali
Office of Economic Development
4444 Rice Street, Suite 200
Lihue, HI 96766-9591
808-241-6390
Fax: 808-241-6399

County of Maui
Ms. Rosalyn Baker
Office of Economic Development
200 South High Street, 6th Floor
Wailuka, HI 96793
808-270-7710
Fax: 808-270-7995
Email: rosalyn.baker@co.mdui.hi.us

Honolulu
(city and county)
Mr. Mike Amii
Department of Community Services
715 S. King St., 5th Floor
Honolulu, HI 96813
808-527-5311
Fax: 808-527-5498
Email: mamii@co.honolulu.hi.us

Idaho
Governor's Liaison
Ms. Roger B. Madsen
Idaho Department of Labor
317 W. Main St.
Boise, ID 83735
208-334-6110
Fax: 208-334-6430
Rmadsen@labor.state.id.us

WIA State Contact
Ms. Cheryl Brush
Workforce Systems Bureau
Department of Labor

317 W. Main St.
Boise, ID 83735
208-334-6303
Fax: 208-332-7417
Email: cbrush@labor.state.id.us

East Central Idaho
(counties) Bonneville, Butte, Clark, Custer,
Fremont, Jefferson, Lemhi, Madison, Teton
Mr. Terry Butikofer
310 North 2nd, East, Suite 115
Rexburg, ID 83440-1604
208-356-4524
Fax: 208-356-4544
Email: terry.ecipda@nstep.net

North Central
(counties) Nez Perce, Idaho, Latah, Lewis
Ms. Rachel Stocking
1626 6th Ave., North
Lewiston, ID 83501
208-746-0015
Fax: 208-743-0576

North Idaho
(counties) Benewah, Boundary, Booner,
Kootenat, Shoshone
Mr. Jim Flowers
North Idaho WIA
11100 N. Airport Dr.
Hayden, ID 83835
208-772-0588
Fax: 208-772-6196
Email: jflowers@pacni.org

South Central Idaho
(counties) Cassia, Blaine, Camas, Goodling,
Jerome, Lincoln, Minidoka, Twin Falls
Ms. Candy McElfresh
P.O. Box 5079
Twin Falls, ID 83303-5079
208-732-5727
Fax: 208-732-5454
Email: candy@rivda.org

Southeast Idaho
(counties) Bannock, Bear Lake, Bingham,
Caribou, Frankling, Oneida, Power
Mr. Bob Perky
P.O. Box 6079
Pacatello, ID 83205-6079
208-233-4032
Fax: 208-233-4841
Email: bobp@sicog.org

Southwest Idaho
Ada, Adams, Boise, Canyon, Elmore, Gem,
Owyhee, Payette, Valley, Washington
Mr. Bob Barber
Southwest WIA
10624 W. Executive Dr.
Boise, ID 83713
208-322-7033
Fax: 208-321-8008
Email: bbarber@ida-ore.com

Illinois
State Workforce Development Liaison
Mr. Herbert D. Dennis
Department of Employment Security
Job Training Division
325 West Adams, 3rd Floor
Springfield, IL 62704
217-785-6006
Fax: 217-558-2444
Email: hdennis@ides.state.il.us

Boone/ Winnebago Counties; # 3
Ms. Carol Houghtby
Rock River Training Corporation
3134 11th Street
Rockford, IL 61109-2275
815-395-6600
Fax: 815-229-2796
Email: sda3@xta.com

Bureau/ Lasalle/ Lee/ Putnam #12
Mr. Dale Broadway
Business Employment Skills Team, Inc.
LaSalle County Courthouse, Suite 406
Ottawa, IL 61350
815-434-8676
Fax: 815-434-3381
Email: bestinc12@aol.com

Champaign Consortium; # 17
(counties) Champaign, Ford, Iriquois, Piatt
Mr. Al Anderson
Champaign Consortium
1008 W. University Ave.
Urbana, IL 61801-2441
217-278-5700
Fax: 217-384-3875
Email: chamcons@aol.com

Chicago
Ms. Jackie Edens
Mayor's Office of Workforce Development
1615 West Chicago Avenue, 5th Floor
Chicago, IL 60622
312-746-7777
Fax: 312-744-9001
Email: jedens@ci.chi.il.us

City of Peoria; #15
(counties) Marshall, Peoria, Stark, Woodford
Mr. Bashir Ali
Workforce Development Department
City of Peoria
211 Fulton St., 3rd Floor
Peoria, IL 61602-1309
309-495-8900
Fax: 309-495-8999
Email: bali@workforcenetwork.com

Cook County Balance of #7
Mr. Rudolph Sanchez
Cook County President's Office of
Employment & Training
69 West Washington Street, #2860
Chicago, IL 60602-3007
312-603-0200
Fax: 312-603-9994

Dupage County #6
Ms. Sue Clark
Dupage County Workforce Development
Job Training Division
837 South Westmore/Meyers Road
Lombard, IL 60148
630-495-4345
Fax: 630-495-4374
Email: sclark@ietc-dupageco.com

Grundy/ Kankakee/ Livingston #11
Ms. Margaret Cooper
Kankakee Community College
Employment and Training
P.O. Box 888
817 River Rd.
Kankakee, IL 60901
815-933-0372

Fax: 815-933-0370
Email: mcooper1@keynet.net

Kane/ Dekalb/ Kendall Counties
Ms. Sheila McCraven
Kane County Department of Employment and
Education
719 S. Batavia Ave.
Geneva, IL 60134
630-208-1402
Fax: 630-208-1055

Lake County; # 1
Ms. Chris Stevens
Workforce Development Board
18 N. County St., Room 901
Waukegan, IL 60085
847-377-2224
Fax: 847-360-6732
Email: pic@co.lake.il.us

Land of Lincoln Consortium; # 20
(counties) Cass, Christian, Logan, Menard,
Sangamon
Mr. Andre Mostert
Sangamon County Land of Lincoln
Consortium
P.O. Box 19493
Springfield, IL 62794-9493
217-524-5996
Fax: 217-524-6096
Email: lrtc@fgi.net

Local Workforce Area #24
(counties) Clinton, Monroe, Randolph, St.
Clair, Washington
Mr. Steven Schneider
Employment and Training
St. Clair County Intergovernmental Grants
Department
19 Public Square, Suite 200
Belleville, IL 62220
618-277-6790
Fax: 618-236-1190
Email: schneider@igd.org

Macon/ Dewitt Counties; #19
Ms. Elsie Sorenson
Macon Dewitt Job Training
1075 West Pershing Road, Suite B
Decatur, IL 62526
217-872-5870
Fax: 217-872-2275
Email: sdal9@aol.com

Madison/ Bond Counties; #22
Mr. David Stoecklin
Madison County Employment and Training
Department
130 Hillsboro Ave., Suite 200
P.O. Box 670
Edwardsville, IL 62025
618-692-7040
Fax: 618-656-6945
Email: mcetd@plantnet.com

Man-Tra-Con Corporation #25
(counties) Franklin, Jackson, Jefferson, Perry,
Williamson
Mr. Greg Clark
Management, Training & Consulting
Corporation
1301 Enterprise Way, Suite 60
P.O. Box 1727
Marion, IL 62896

618-998-0970
Fax: 618-998-1291
Email: gregclark@mantracon.org

McHenry County; #2
Mr. Carl Martens
McHenry County Job Training
500 Russel Court
Woodstock, IL 60098
815-338-7100
Fax: 815-338-7125
Email: russ500@mc.net

Northern Cook County; #8
(Cook County Townships) Barrington, Elk
Grove, Evanston, Hanover, Maine, Niles, New
Trier, Northfield, Palatine, Schaumberg,
Wheeling
Ms. Mary Pepperl
The Workforce Board of Northern Cook
County
2604 E. Dempster St., Suite 502
Park Ridge, IL 60068
847-699-9195
Fax: 847-699-9155

Rock Island County Consortium #13
(counties) Henry, Mercer, Rock Island
Mr. Charles O. Stewart
Rock Island Tri-County Consortium
1504 Third Ave.
Rock Island, IL 61201
309-793-5200
Fax: 309-793-5204
Email: ritccdir@aol.com

Vermillion County #18
Ms. Renee Beasley-Poke
Vermillion County Job Training Partnership
Illinois Employment/ Training Center
407 N. Franklin St., Suite B
Danville, IL 61832
217-442-0296
Fax: 217-442-0305
Email: vcjtp@soltec.net

West Central Illinois Valley; SDA 21
(counties) Calhoun, Green, Jersey, Macoupin,
Montgomery, Morgan, Scott, Shelby
Ms. Amy Arnett
W. Central Workforce Development Council
116 S. Plum St.
P.O. Box 260
Carlinville, IL 62626
217-854-9642
Fax: 217-854-8082
Email: jobcntr@accunet.net

Western Illinois #14
(counties) Adams, Brown, Hancock,
Henderson, Knox, McDonough, Pike,
Schuyler, Warren
Ms. Blanche Shoup
Workforce Investment Office
40 N. Prairie St., Suite B
P.O. Box 231
Galesburg, IL 61402-0231
309-344-1575
Fax: 309-344-2446
Email: sda14wil@gallatinriver.net

WIA #23
(counties) Clark, Clay, Coles, Crawford,
Cumberland, Douglas, Edgar, Effingham,
Fayette, Jasper, Lawrence, Marion, Moultrie,
Richland

Mr. Brian Noe
CEFS Economic Opportunity Corporation
1805 South Banker Street
P.O. Box 928
Effingham, IL 62401-0928
217-342-2193
Fax: 217-342-4109
Email: noeone@advant.com

Workforce Area #4
(counties) Carroll, Jo Davies, Ogle,
Stephenson, Whiteside
Ms. Nancy Sweitzer
NW Illinois Workforce Partnership
24711 Emerson Rd.
Sterling, IL 61081
815-625-3623
Fax: 815-625-3664
Email: nwilwia4@essex1.com

Workforce Development Area #16
(counties) Fulton, Mason, Mclean, Tazewell
Mr. Norman Hill
United Workforce Development Board
200 S. 2nd St., Suite 10
Pekin, IL 61555
309-353-4475
Fax: 309-353-1632
Email: uwdb@gallatinriver.net

Workforce Development Area #26
(counties) Alexander, Edwards, Fallatin,
Hamilton, Hardin, Johnson, Massac, Pope,
Pulaski, Saline, Union, Wabash, Wayne,
White
Mr. James Murphy
Southern 14 Workforce Investment Board
210 Airport Road
P.O. Box 186
Cormi, IL 62821-0186
618-382-5024
Fax: 618-382-7038
Email: pic26@midwest.net

Will County; #10
Ms. Sharon May
Workforce Development Council of Will
County
1115 Plainfield Rd.
Joliet, IL 60435
815-727-4444
Fax: 815-727-6008

Indiana

Governors Liaison and State Workforce
Development Liaison
Dr. Craig E. Hartzer
Indiana Department Workforce Development
10 N. Senate Ave.
Indianapolis, IN 46204-2277
317-232-7670
Fax: 317-233-4793
Email: chartzer@dwd.state.in.us

Circle Seven Training Council
(counties) Boone, Hamilton, Hancock,
Hendricks, Johnson, Morgan, Shelby
Mr. Lance Ratliff
Interlocal Association
836 S. State St.
P.O. Box 69
Greenwood, IN 46140-0069
317-467-0248
Fax: 317-467-6340
Email: lanceratliff@netscape.net

East Central
(counties) Blackford, Delaware, Henry, Jay,
Randolph
Ms. Barbara Street
East Central Opportunities, Inc.
201 E. Charles St.
P.O. Box 1081
Muncie, IN 47308-1081
765-741-5863
Fax: 765-741-5869
Email: bstreet@ecoinc.org

Kankakee Valley SDA
(counties) Jasper, Laporte, Newton, Porter,
Pulaski, Starke
Ms. Linda Woloshansky
Workforce Innovations, Inc.
2800 Boilermaker Ct., Suite E
Valparaiso, IN 46383
219-462-2940
Fax: 219-465-6860
Email: lwolo@crown.net

Madison/ Grant Counties
Mr. Marc Scharnowske
JobSource
222 E. 10th St., Suite C
P.O. Box 149
Anderson, IN 46015-0149
765-642-4981
Fax: 765-641-6548
Email: shark1@netusa1.net

Marion County
Ms. Kelley D. Gulley
Private Industry Council
17 W. Market St., Suite 500
Indianapolis, IN 46204
317-684-2222
Fax: 317-639-0103
Email: kgulley@ipic.org

North Central Indiana
(counties) Cass, Fulton, Howard, Miami,
Tipton, Wabash
Ms. Vicki Byrd
Workforce Development Strategies, Inc.
1810 W. Hoosier Blvd.
P.O. Box 47
Peru, IN 46970-0047
765-689-9950
Fax: 765-689-9971
Email: vbyrd@lquest.net

Northeast Indiana
(counties) Adams, Allen, Dekalb, Hunting,
Noble, Steuben, Wells, Whitley, LaGrange
Ms. Patty Weddle
Northeast Indiana WIB
201 E. Rudisill Blvd., Suite 206
Fort Wayne, IN 46806
219-745-2000
Fax: 219-745-0114
Email: ppw10623@aol.com

Northern Indiana Partnership
(counties) Elkhart, Kosciusko, Marshall, St.
Joseph
Mr. Juan Manigault
Northern Indiana Workforce Investment
Board of Northern Indiana
401 East Colfax Avenue
South Bend, IN 46617
219-239-2380
Fax: 219-239-2386
Email: jam@niwib.com

Northwest Indiana
(county) Lake
Mr. James H. McShane III
Integrated Services Delivery Board
840 Broadway, 3rd Floor
Gary, IN 46402-2412
219-882-0033
Fax: 219-882-9253
Email: lcisdb@netnitco.net

Shawnee Trace
(counties) Daviess, Dubois, Gibson, Greene,
Knox, Lawrence, Martin, Pike, Sullivan
mr. Charles L. Roche
Employment and Training Center
Vincennes University
P.O. Box 887
525 N. 4th St.
Vincennes, IN 47591-0887
812-888-5306
Fax: 812-888-5455
Email: cruche@indian.vinu.edu

South Central Indiana
(counties) Bartholomew, Brown, Jackson,
Jennings, Monroe, Owen
Mr. Charles Roche
Vincennes University
Employment and Training Center
525 North 4th Street
P.O. Box 887
Vincennes, IN 47591-0887
812-888-5306
Fax: 812-888-5455
Email: croche@indian.vinu.edu

Southeastern Indiana
(counties) Dearborn, Decatur, Fayette,
Franklin, Jefferson, Ohio, Ripley Rush,
Switzerland, Union, Wayne
Mr. Don Richardson
River Valley Resources, Inc.
Training Center
319 E. Main St.
Madison, IN 47250
812-265-2652
Fax: 812-265-2664
Email: rvradmin@seidata.com

Southern Seven
(counties) Clark, Crawford, Floyd, Harrison,
Orange, Scott, Washington
Mr. Don Richardson
River Valley Resources
319 East Main Street
Madison, IN 47250
812-265-2652
Fax: 812-226-5266
Email: rvradmin@seidata.com

Southwest Indiana SDA
(counties) Perry, Posey, Spencer,
Vanderburgh, Warrick
Mr. Jerry Yazbick
Southwest Indiana WIB
701 N. Weinbach Ave., Suite 810
Evansville, IN 47711-6608
812-475-1147
Fax: 812-475-1149
Email: jerryy@sigecom.net

Tecumseh Area Partnership
(counties) Benton, Carroll, Clinton, Fountain,
Montgomery, Tippecanoe, Warren, White
Mr. Roger Feldhaus
Tecumseh Area Partnership

2301 Concord Rd.
P.O. Box 4729
Lafayette, IN 47903
765-474-5411
Fax: 765-474-7036
Email: rfeldhaus@tap.lafayette.in.us

Western Indiana
(counties) Clay, Parke, Putnam, Vermillion,
Vigo
Ms. Lisa Lee
Western Indiana Employment and Training
630 Wabash Ave., Suite 205
Terre Haute, IN 47807
812-238-5616
Fax: 812-238-2466
Email: wiwibdir@aol.com

Iowa

Governor's Liaison and State WIA Liaison
Mr. Richard Running
Iowa Workforce Development Department
1000 E. Grand Ave.
Des Moines, IA 50309
515-281-2365
Fax: 515-281-4698
Email: Richard.Running@iwd.state.ia.us

Upper Explorerland; Region 1
(counties) Allamakee, Chicksaw, Clayton,
Delaware, Dubuque, Fayette, Howard,
Winneshiek
Ms. Fern Rissman
Upper Explorerland Regional Planning
Commission
134 W. Greene St.
P.O. Box 219
Postville, IA 52162
563-864-7554
Fax: 563-864-7445
Email: fern.rissman@iwd.state.ia.us

Coordinating Services Provider; Region 2
(counties) Cerro, Gordon, Floyd, Franklin,
Hancock, Mitchell, Winnebago, Worth
Ms. Nancy Blair
Iowa Workforce Development
600 South Pierce, Suite Two
Mason City, IA 50401-4836
515-422-1521
Fax: 515-422-1506
Email: nancy.blair@iwd.state.ia.us

Western Iowa Tech Community College,
Region 12
(counties) Cherokee, Ida, Monona, Plymouth,
Woodbury
Mr. Chris Jensen
Western Iowa Technical Community College
4647 Stone Ave.
P.O. Box 5199
Sioux City, IA 51102-5199
712-274-6401
Fax: 712-274-6407
Email: chris.jensen@iwd.state.ia.us

Iowa Central Community College, Region 5
(counties) Buena Vista, Calhoun, Hamilton,
Humbolt, Pocahontas, Webster, Wright
Mr. Terry Augustus
Iowa Central Community College
2700 First Ave., South
Fort Dodge, IA 50501
515-576-3131
Fax: 515-955-1420
Email: terry.augustus@iwd.state.ia.us

Iowa Valley Community College, Region 6
(counties) Hardin, Marshall, Poweshiek,
Tama
Ms. Sue Greenwood
Iowa Valley Employment and Training
3405 S. Center St.
P.O. Box 497
Marshalltown, IA 50158-1116
641-754-1400
Fax: 641-754-1443
Email: sue.greenwood@iwd.state.is.us

Hawkeye Community College, Region 7
Mr. Dave Mazur
Hawkeye Community College
3420 University Ave.
Waterloo, IA 50701
800-299-3430
Fax: 319-291-2723
Email: dave.mazur@iwd.state.ia.us

Eastern Iowa Community College-Region 9
(counties) Clinton, Jackson, Muscatine, Scott
Ms. Cathy Wiebel
Eastern Iowa Community College District
304 West 2nd Street
Davenport, IA 52801-1212
563-336-3467
Fax: 563-336-3494
Email; cathy.wiebel@iwd.state.ia.us

Central iowa E&T Consortium, Region 11
(counties) Boone, Dallas, Jasper, Madison,
Marion, Polk, Story, Warren
Ms. Ramona Cunningham
Central Iowa Employment and Training
Consortium
215 Watson Powell Jr. Way, Suite 100
Des Moines, IA 50309-1728
515-281-9728
Fax: 515-281-9727
Email: ramona.cunningham@iwd.state.ia.us

Region XIICOG; Region 8
(counties) Audubon, Carroll, Crawford,
Greene, Guthrie, Sac
Ms. Karen Burchfield
Region 12 Council of Governments
P.O. Box 768
Carroll, IA 51401-0768
712-792-2685
Fax: 712-792-6605
Email: karen.burchfield@iwd.state.ia.us

Southwestern Community College, Region 13
(counties) Cass, Fremont, Harrison, Mills,
Page, Pottawattamie, Shelby
Mr. Gary Johnson
Iowa Western Community College
300 W. Broadway, Suite 13
Council Bluffs, IA 51503
712-242-2112
Fax: 712-242-2115
Email: gary.johnson@iwd.state.ia.us

WIA Matura Action, Region 14
(counties) Adair, Adams, Clarke, Decatur,
Montgomery, Ringgold, Taylor, Union
Mr. Jerry Smith
WIA Matura Action Corporation
215 N. Elm
Creston, IA 50801
515-782-2119
Fax: 515-782-5101
Email: jerry.smith@iwd.state.ia.us

Indian Hills Community College, Region 15
(counties) Appanoose, Davis, Jefferson,
Keokuk, Lucas, Mahaska, Monroe, Van
Buren, Wapello, Wayne
Ms. Marilyn Runnells
Indian Hills Community College
651 Indian Hills Dr., Suite 1
Ottumwa, IA 52501
641-682-8577
Fax: 641-682-0102
Email: marilyn.runnels@iwd.state.ia.us

Job Training Partnership Activities
(counties) Benton, Cedar, Iowa, Johnson,
Jones, Linn, Washington
Mr. Bob Ballantyne
Kirkwood College
1030 5th Avenue, SE
P.O. Box 5454
Cedar Rapids, IA 52403-5454
319-398-5105
Fax: 319-398-5252
Email robert.ballantyne@iwd.state.ia.us

Northwest Iowa Planning Regions 3&4
(counties) Clay, Dickinson, Emmet, Palo Alto,
Kossuth (counties region 4) Lyon, Oscelon,
Sioux, O'Brien
Ms. Anne Scott
Northwest Planning and Development
Commission
217 West 5th Street
P.O. Box 1493
Spencer, IA 51301
712-262-7662
Fax: 712-262-7665
Email anne.scott@iwd.state.ia.us

Southeast Community College; Region 16
(counties) Des Moines, Henry, Lee, Louisa
Ms. Linda Gidley
Southeastern Community College
Iowa Workforce Development
1000 North Roosevelt
P.O. Box 609
Burlington, IA 52601-1671
319-753-1671
Fax: 319-753-5881
Email linda.gidley@iwd.state.ia.us

Upper Exploreland; Region 1
(counties) Allamakee, Chickasaw, Clayton,
Delaware, Dubuque, Fayette, Howard,
Winneshiek
Mr. David Leary
Iowa Workforce Development Center
P.O. Box 757
Dubuque, IA 52004-0757
563-556-5800
Fax: 563-556-0154
Email Dave.Leary@iwd.state.ia.us

Workforce Development; Region 10
(counties) Benton, Iowa, Linn, Johnson,
Jones, Cedar, Washington
Mr. Steve Rackis
Iowa Workforce Development
800 Seventh Street, SE
P.O. Box 729
Cedar Rapids, IA 52406-0729
319-365-9474
Fax: 319-365-9270
Email steve.rackis@iwd.state.ia.us

Kansas

State Workforce Development Liaison
Mr. Richard E. Beyer
Kansas Department of Human Resources
Employment and Training Division
401 SW Topeka Blvd.
Topeka, KS 66603
785-296-7474
Fax: 785-368-6294
Email: rbeyer@hr.state.ks.us

WIA Administrative Entity #3
(counties) Johnson, Leavensworth,
Wyandotte; (city) Kansas City, Overland Park
Mr. Al Rolls
Department of Human Resources
552 State Ave.
Kansas City, KS 66101
913-281-3000
Fax: 913-281-0069
Email: alrolls@hr.state.ks.us

WIA Administrative Entity #1
(counties) Barber, Barton, Chase, Cheyenne,
Clark, Cloud, Comanche, Decatur, Dickinson,
Edwards, Ellis, Ellsworth, Finney, Gord,
Graham, Grant, Gray, Greeley, Hamilton,
Harvey, Haskell, Hodgeman, Jewel, Kearny,
Kiowa, Lane, Lincoln, Logan, Mcpherson,
Marion, Meade, Mitchell, Morris, Morton,
Ness, Norton, Osborne, Ottawa, Pawnee,
Phillips, Pratt, Rawlins, Republic, Rice,
Rooks, Rush, Russell, Saline, Scott, Seward,
Sheridan, Sherman, Smith, Staford, Stanton,
Stevens, Thomas, Trego, Wallace, Wichita;
(cities) Colby, Dodge City, Garden City,
Great Bend, Hays, Hutchinson, Liberal,
Norton, Salina
Mr. Glenn Fondoble
WESTCO Management, Inc.
1401-B Main St.
Hays, KS 67601
785-623-4485
Fax: 785-623-4508
Email: glenn@gowestco.net

WIA Administrative Area #2
(counties) Atchison, Brown, Clay, Doniphan,
Douglas, Franklin, Geary, Jackson, Jefferson,
Marshall, Nemaha, Osage, Pottawatomie,
Riley, Shawnee, Webaunsee, Washington;
(cities) Atchison, Lawrence, Manhattan,
Topeka
Ms. Kris Kitchen
Heartland Works, Inc.
1035 SW Topeka Blvd.
Topeka, KS 66612
785-234-0500
Fax: 785-234-0552
Email: krisk@heartlandworks.org

WIA Administrative Entity #4
(counties) Butler, Cowley, Harper, Kingman,
Sedgwick, Sumner; (cities) Arkansas City, El
Dorado, Wichita
Ms. Sarah Gilbert
Department of Human Services
444 E. Williams St.
Wichita, KS 67202
316-337-9444
Fax: 316-337-9452
Email: Gilbert_S@ci.wichita.ks.us

WIA Administrative Entity #5
(counties) Allen, Anderson, Bourbon,
Chautauqua, Cherokee, Coffey, Crawford,
Elk, Greenwood, Labette, Linn, Lyon, Miami,
Montgomery, Neosho, Wilson, Woodson;
(cities) Chanute, Emporia, Independence,
Pittsburg
Mr. Jim Stowell
Kansas Department of Human Resources
320 N. Locust St.
Pittsburg, KS 66762
620-232-2620
Fax: 620-232-1222
Email: jastowell@hr.state.ks.us

Kentucky

State Workforce Investment Act
Ms. Clyda Henderson
Office of Training and Reemployment
209 St. Clair St., 4th Floor
Frankfort, KY 40601
502-564-5360
Fax: 502-564-8974
Email: clydal.henderson@mail.state.ky.us

Barren River
(counties) Allen, Barren, Butler, Edmonson,
Hart, Logan, Metcalfe, Monroe, Simpson,
Warren
Mr. George Leamon
Barren River Training & Unemployment
P.O. Box 90005
Bowling Green, KY 42102-9005
270-781-2381
Fax: 270-842-0768
Email: george.leamon@bradd.org

Bluegrass
(counties) Anderson, Bourbon, Boyle, Clark,
Estill, Fayette, Franklin, Garrard, Harrison,
Jessamine, Lincoln, Madison, Mercer,
Nicholas, Powell, Scott, Woodford
Ms. Susan Craft
Bluegrass WIB
699 Perimeter Dr.
Lexington, KY 40517
606-269-8021
Fax: 606-269-7917
Email: scraft@bgadd.org

Cumberlands
(counties) Adair, Casey, Clinton, Cumberland,
Green, Laurel, Mccreary, Pulaski, Rockcastle,
Russell, Taylor, Wayne, Whitley
Mr. Darryl McGaha
Cumberland Training & Employment
P.O. Box 1570
Russell Springs, KY 42642
270-866-4200
Fax: 270-866-2044
Email: lcadd@aol.com

Eastern Kentucky CEP
(counties) Bell, Breathitt, Carter, Clay, Elliott,
Floyd, Harlan, Jackson, Johnson, Knott,
Knox, Lawrence, Lee, Leslie, Letcher,
Magoffin, Martin, Menifee, Morgan, Owsley,
Perry, Pike, Wolfe
Ms. Mable Duke
Eastern Kentucky Concentrated Employment
Program
941 N. Main St.
Hazard, KY 41701
606-436-5751
Fax: 606-436-5755
Email: ekcep@mis.net

Green River
(counties) Daviess, Hancock, Henderson,
McLean, Ohio, Union, Webster
Ms. Sonya Fife

Green River Training & Employment
3860 US Highway 60 West
Owensboro, KY 42301
270-926-4433
Fax: 270-684-0714
Email: sonyahoward@gradd.com

Lincoln Trail
(counties) Breckinridge, Grayson, Hardin,
Larue, Marion, Meade, Nelson, Washington
Ms. Sherry Johnson
Lincoln Trail Training & Employment
P.O. Box 604
Elizabethtown, KY 42702-0604
270-769-2393
Fax: 270-769-2993
Email: sherry@ltadd.org

Louisville/ Jefferson Counties
(county) Jefferson; (city) Louisville
Mr. Robert Huffman
Louisville/ Jefferson County WIB
410 W. Chestnut St., Suite 200
Louisville, KY 40202
502-574-2500
Fax: 502-574-4288
Email: rhuffman@louky.org

North Central Kentucky Council
(counties) Bullitt, Henry, Oldham, Shelby,
Spencer, Trimble
Mr. Robert Huffman
North Central Kentucky Workforce Council
410 W. Chestnut St., Suite 200
Louisville, KY 40202
502-574-2500
Fax: 502-574-4288
Email: rhuffman@louky.org

Northern Kentucky
(counties) Boone, Campbell, Carroll,
Gallatin, Grant, Kenton, Owen, Pendleton
Mr. Barbara Stewart
Employment and Traiing Division of Northern
Kentucky Area Development District
P.O. Box 668
Florence, KY 41022
859-283-1885
Fax: 859-283-8178
Email: barbara.stewart@mail.state.ky.us

Purchase/ Pennyrile
(counties) Ballard, Caldwell, Calloway,
Carlisle, Christian, Crittenden, Fulton,
Graves, Hickman, Hopkins, Livingston, Lyon,
McCracken, Marshall, Muhlenberg, Todd,
Trigg
Ms. Sheila Clark
Training & Employment
300 Hammond Dr.
Hopkinsville, KY 42240
270-886-9484
Fax: 270-886-3211
Email: sheila.clark@mail.state.ky.us

Tenco
(counties) Bath, Boyd, Bracken, Fleming,
Greenup, Lewis, Mason, Montgomery,
Robertson, Rowan
Ms. Marlene Duffy
Tenco WIB
P.O. Box 460
Maysville, KY 41056
606-564-6894
Fax: 606-564-0955
Email: marlene.duffy@mail.state.ky.us

Louisiana

State Workforce Development Liaison
Ms. Susan Boutte
Louisiana Department of Labor
Office of Workforce Development
1001 N. 23rd St.
P.O. Box 94094
Baton Rouge, LA 70804-9094
225-342-7692
Fax: 225-342-7960
Email: sboutte@ldol.state.la.us

Calcasieu Consortium; SDA 51
(parishes) Calcasieu, Cameron, Jefferson
Davis
Ms. Jean Augustine
Calcasieu Workforce Center
1015 Pithon St.
Lake Charles, LA 70602
337-437-3380
Fax: 337-437-3475
Email: jaugustine@structureX.net

East Baton Rouge Parish
Mr. Sidney Longwell
East Baton Rouge WIB
4523 Plank Rd.
Baton Rouge, LA 70805
225-358-4606
Fax: 225-357-9675

Fifth Planning District Consortium
(parishes) Allen, Beauregard, Vernon
Mr. Charles J. Maxie
Fifth Planning District Consortium
P.O. Box 779
408 W. Fertitta Blvd.
Leesville, LA 71496-0779
337-238-2950
Fax: 337-238-0066
Email: vpwiacc@worldnetla.net

First Planning District; WIA 10
(parishes) Plaquemines, St. Bernard, St.
Tammany
Mr. Al Waller
First Planning District Consortium
8201 W. Judge Perez Dr., Room 212
Chalmette, LA 70043
504-278-4263
Fax: 504-278-4266
Email: fpd@st_bernard.la.us

Jefferson Parish
Ms. Arleeta Terrell
Jefferson Parish Department of Employment
and Training
1221 Elmwood Park Blvd.
Jefferson, LA 70123
504-736-6471
Fax: 504-736-6765
Email: aterrell@jeffparish.net

Lafayette Parish
Mr. Glenn Dugas
Lafayette Consolidated Government
P.O. Box 4017-C
Lafayette, LA 70502
337-291-7152
Fax: 337-291-7113
Email: glennd@cox-internet.com

Lafourche Parish Consortium
(parishes) Assumption, Lafourche,
Terrebonne
Mr. Frank Lewis
LAT board

911 Bond Street
P.O. Box 4115
Houma, LA 70361
985-580-7249
Fax: 985-580-7248
Email: frank@internet8.com

Orleans Parish
Ms. Thelma French
1300 Perdido Street, Suite 2E10
New Orleans, LA 70112
504-565-6414
Fax: 504-565-6976
Email: THELMAF@new-orleans.la.us

Ouachita Parish
Ms. Doretha Bennett
Ouachita Parish Police Jury
Workforce Investment Board
P.O. Box 3007
1333 State Farm Drive
Monroe, LA 71210-3007
318-657-7025
Fax: 318-398-7427
Email: dbennett@oppj.org

Rapides Parish
Ms. Jan Haworth
Office of Economic Workforce Development
5608 Coliseum Blvd.
P.O. Box 7556
Alexandria, LA 71306
318-448-1591
Fax: 318-442-7834
Email: jhaworth@cenlaworks.org

Franklin Parish Consortium
(parishes) Caldwell, East Carroll, Franklin,
Jackson, Madison, Richland, Tensas
Mr. C.W. Frazier, Jr.
WIB
P.O. Box 14667
1504 Stubbs Ave.
Monroe, LA 71207-4269
318-387-7962
Fax: 318-361-0279
Email: frazier@bayou.com

Second Planning District
(parishes) Ascension, East Feliciana,
Iberville, Livingston, Pointe Coupee, St.
Helena, Tangipahoa, Washington, West Baton
Rouge, West Felciana
Ms. Gloria Abels
Tangipahoa Parish School System
Workforce Center
1745 SW Railroad Ave., Suite 201
Hammond, LA 70403
985-345-4461
Fax: 985-542-8535
Email: gabels@jtap-ham.org

Seventh Planning District
(parishes) Bienville, Bossier, Balance of
Caddo, Claiborne, Desoto, Lincoln,
Natchitoches, Red River, Sabine, Webster
Mr. Harold LaBorde, Jr.
Coordinating and Developing Corporation
5210 Hollywood Ave.
P.O. Box 37005
Shreveport, LA 71133-7005
318-632-2022
Fax: 318-632-2099
Email: cdsport@shreve.net

Shreveport
(city)
Mr. Herman Vital
Department of Community Services
Community Development Department
1234 Texas Ave.
P.O. Box 31109
Shreveport, LA 71130
318-673-7500
Fax: 318-673-7512
Email: hvital@ci.shreveport.la.us

Sixth Planning District Consortium
(parishes) Avoyelles, Catahoula, Concordia,
Grant, Lasalle, Winn
Ms. Azelea Pullin
Lasalle Community Action Association
Courthouse Building, Room 23
P.O. Box 1230
Jena, LA 71342
318-992-8271
Fax: 318-992-8750
Email: azpullin@centurytel.net

River Parish Consortium
(parishes) St. Charles, St. James, St. John the
Baptist
Ms. Sharon G. Simpkins
Employment and Training Office
River Parishes Consortium
P.O. Box 1010
Hahnville, LA 70057
985-783-5034
Fax: 985-785-8372
Email: sgs_wia@mail.com

Union Parish Consortium; SDA 82
(parishes) Morehouse, Union, West Carroll
Mr. David Creed
North Delta Regional Planning and
Development, Inc.
2115 Justice Street
Monroe, LA 71201
318-387-2572
Fax: 318-387-9054
Email: dcreed@bayou.com

Workforce Investment Board #40
(parishes) Acadia, Evangeline, Iberia, St.
Landry, St. Martin, St. Mary, Vermilion
Mr. Chris Dunbar
Private Industry Council
284 West Bloch Street
Opelousas, LA 70570
337-942-5678
Fax: 337-942-9654
Email: jtpa40@aol.com

Maine

Governor's Liaison
Ms. Valerie Landry
Department of labor
20 Union St.
54 State House Station
Augusta, ME 04333-0054
207-287-3788
Fax: 207-287-5292
valerie.r.landry@state.me.us

State Workforce Development
Mr. Tim McLellan
Bureau of Employment Services
Department of Labor
55 State House Station
Augusta, ME 04333-0055
207-624-6390

Workforce Investment Act

Fax: 207-624-6499
tim.mclellan@state.me.us

Local Area 1
(counties) Aroostook, Washington,
Mr. Douglas F. Bealieu
Aroostook/Washington Local Workforce
Investment Board
144 Sweden Street, Suite 205
Caribou, ME 04736
207-493-3496
Fax: 207-493-3498
Email: doug@aroostook.me.us

Local Area 2
(counties) Hancock, Pemobscto, Piscataquis
Mr. Barry Martin
Tri-County Workforce Investment Board,
EMDC
P.O. Box 2579
Bangor, ME 04402-2579
207-942-6389
Fax: 207-942-3548
Email: bmartin@emdc.org

Local Area 3
(counties) Androscoggin, Franklin, Kennebec,
Oxford, Somersset
Mr. Bryant E. Hoffman
Central/Western Maine Workforce Investment
Board
5 Mollison Way
Lewiston, ME 04240-5805
207-753-9000
Fax: 207-783-5301
Email: bryant.hoffman@state.me.us

Local Area 4
(counties) Cumberland, Knox, Lincoln,
Sagadahoc, Waldo, York
Mr. Mike Bourrat
Coastal Communities Workforce Board
1 Main Street, Suite 206
Topsham, ME 04086
207-725-5472
Fax: 207-725-5472
Email: director@coastalcounties.org

Marshall Islands

Marshall Islands
Republic of the Marshall Islands
Workforce Investment Board
P.O. Box 136
Majuro, MH 96960
692-625-6594
Fax: 692-625-6595
Email: rmjtpa@ntamar.com

Maryland

Governor's Liaison
Ms. Ellen Miller
Division of Employment/Training
Department of Labor Licensing and
Regulations
1100 N. Eutaw St., Room 600
Baltimore, MD 21201
410-767-2400
Fax: 410-767-2986
Email: ellen@dllr.state.md.us

State Workforce Development
Mr. Gary Moore
Department of Labor Licensing and
Regulations
Employment and Training Office
1100 N. Eutaw St., Room 310

Baltimore, MD 21201
410-767-2800
Fax: 410-767-2842
Email: gmoore@careernet.state.md.us

Anne Arundel County
Ms. Dorothy McGuinness
Business and Workforce Development Center
of Anne Arundel County
877 Baltimore/ Annapolis Blvd., Suite 305
Severna Park, MD 21146
410-315-9680
Fax: 410-315-8664
Email: dmcguiness@bwdc.org

Baltimore
(city)
Ms. Karen Sitnick
Office of Employment Development
417 E. Fayette St., Suite 468
Baltimore, MD 21202
410-396-1910
Fax: 410-752-6625
Email: ksirnick@oedworks.com

Baltimore County
Ms. Terri Boblooch
Baltimore County Office of Employment and
Training
1 Investment Place, Suite 409
Towson, MD 21204-3911
410-887-4400
Fax: 410-887-5673
Email: tboblooch@co.ba.md.us

Frederick County
Ms. Bonnie Gann
Frederick County Job Training Agency
520 N. Market St.
Frederick, MD 21701
301-694-1174
Fax: 301-696-2906
Email: bgann@fredco-md.net

Lower Shore
(counties) Somerset, Wicomico, Worcester
Mr. B.J. Corbin
Lower Shore PIC
P.O. Box 99
Snow Hill, MD 21863-0099
410-632-3300
Fax: 410-632-1466
Email: bjcorbin@lowershore.org

Mid-Maryland
(counties) Carroll, Howard
Ms. Dorothy Lehman
Howard County Employment and Training
Center
10650 Hickory Ridge Rd.
Columbia, MD 21044-5613
410-313-4600
Fax: 410-313-7383
Email: dlehman@flash.net

Montgomery County
Mr. Ed Trumbull
Montgomery County Workforce Development
Corporation
451 Hungerford Dr., Suite 515
Rockville, MD 20850
301-738-0015
Fax: 301-738-8792
Email: etrumbull@mcwdc.com

Prince George's County
Mr. Joseph Puhalla
Prince George's County Workforce
Corporation
1802 Brightseat Rd.
Landover, MD 20785
301-583-2063
Fax: 301-386-5533
Email: jpuhalla@pgworkforce.org

Southern Maryland
(counties) Calvert, Charles, St. Mary's
Ms. Ellen Flowers-Field
Southern Maryland Works, Inc.
2670 Crain Highway, Suite 207
Waldorf, MD 20601
301-885-0020
Fax: 301-885-0018
Email: effields@somdworks.org

Susquehanna Region
Mr. Bruce England
Susquehanna Workforce Network, Inc.
410 Girard St.
Havre De Grace, MD 21078
410-939-4240
410-939-5171
Email: bengland@swnetwork.org

Upper Shore
(counties) Caroline, Dorchester, Kent, Queen
Anne's, Talbot
Mr. Daniel McDermott
Upper Shore WIB
P.O. Box 8
Chesapeake College
Wye Mills, MD 21679
410-822-1716
Fax: 410-827-5874
Email: dmcdermott@chesapeake.org

Western Maryland
(counties) Allegany, Garrett, Washington
Mr. Peter Thomas
Western Maryland Consortium
The Training Place
P.O. Box 980
33 W. Washington St.
Hagerstown, MD 21741
301-791-3076
Fax: 301-790-3502
Email: peterthomas@mindspring.com

Massachusetts

Governor's Liaison
Mr. John A. King
Department of Employment and Training
C.F. Hurley Bldg., 3rd Floor
19 Staniford St.
Boston, MA 02114
617-626-6600
Fax: 617-727-0315
Email: jking@detma.org

State Workforce Development Liaison
Mr. Jonathan Raymond
Commonwealth Corporation
529 Main Street
The Schrafft Center, Suite 110
Boston, MA 02129
617-727-8158
Fax: 617-242-7660
Email: jraymond@commcorp.org

Berkshire County
(municipalities) Adams, Alford, Becket,

Cheshire, Clarksburg, Dalton, Egremont, Florida, Hancock, Gr. Barrington, Hinsdale, Lee, Lenox, Lanesborough, Monterey, Mt. Washington, New Ashford, New Marlborough, N. Adams, Otis, Peru, Pittsfield, Richmond, Sandisfield, Savoy, Sheffeild, Stockbridge, Tyringham, Washington, West Stockbridge, Williamstown, Windsor
Mr. Michael Herrick
Berkshire Employment and Training Program
184 North St.
Pittsfield, MA 01201-5111
413-499-2220
Fax: 413-499-0503

Boston
Ms. Conny Doty
Office of Jobs and Community Service
43 Hawkins St.
Boston, MA 02114
617-918-5200
Fax: 617-918-5299

Bristol
(municipalities) Attleboro, Berkley, Dighton, Fall River, Mansfield, N. Attleborough, Norton, Raynham, Rehoboth, Seekonk, Somerset, Swansea, Taunton, Westport
Mr. James Calkins
Bristol County Training Consortium
One Government Center, 5th Floor
Fall River, MA 02722
508-675-1161
Fax: 508-675-1166

Brockton
(municipalities) Abington, Avon, Bridgewater, Brockton, Easton, East Bridgewater, Hanson, Stoughton, Whitman, West Bridgewater
Mr. Kevin O'Rourke
Brockton Area PIC
One Center St., 2nd Floor
Brockton, MA 02301
508-584-1887
Fax: 508-587-1944

Cape Cod/ Martha's Vineyard/ Nantucket
(municipalities) Barnstable, Bourne, Brewster, Chatham, Chilmark, Dennis, Eastham, Edgartown, Falmouth, Gay Head, Gosnold, Harwich, Mashpee, Nantucket, Oak Bluffs, Orleans, Provincetown, Sandwich, Tisbury, Truro, Wellfleet, West Tisbury, Yarmouth
Ms. Kristina E. Dower
JTEC/ Job Training and Employment Corp.
297 North St.
Building 3
Hyannis, MA 02601
508-790-0400
Fax: 508-790-0969
Email: jtecked@aol.com

Franklin and Hampshire
(municipalities) Amherst, Ashfield, Athol, Belchertown, Bernardston, Buckland, Charlemont, Chesterfield, Colrain, Conway, Cummington, Deerfield, Easthampton, Erving, Gill, Goshen, Granby, Greenfield, Hadley, Hatfield, Hawley, Heath, Huntington, Leyden, Leverett, Middlefield, Monroe, Montague, New Salem, Northfield, Northampton, Orange, Pelham, Petersham, Phillipston, Plainfield, Royalston, Rowe, Shelburne, Shutesbury, Southampton, South Hadley, Sunderland, Ware, Warwich, Wendell, Westhampton, Whately, Williamsburg, Worthington

Mr. Michael Truckey
Franklin/ Hampshire Employment and Training Consortium
One Arch Place
Greenfield, MA 01301
413-774-3182
Fax: 413-784-1765
Email: mtruckey@detma.org

Hampden County
(municipalities) Agawam, Blandford, Brimfield, Chester, Cricopee, E. Longmeadow, Granville, Hampden, Holland, Holyoke, Longmeadow, Ludlow, Montgomery, Monson, Palmer, Russell, Southwick, Springfield, Rolland, Wales, Westfield, Wilbraham, West Springfield
Mr. James W. Asselin
Hampden County Employment and Training Consortium
1176 Main St.
Springfield, MA 01103
413-781-6900
Fax: 413-736-0650

Lower Merrimack Valley
(county) Northern Essex; (municipalities) Amesbury, Andover, Boxford, Georgetown, Groveland, Haverhill, Lawrnece, Methuem, Merrimac, Newbury, Newburyport, N. Andover, Rowely, Salisbury, West Newbury
Mr. Shaw Rosen
Lower Merrimack Valley WIB
11 Lawrence St., 6th Floor
Lawrence, MA 01840
978-682-7099
Fax: 978-794-1901
Email: lmvwib@detma.org

Metro South/ West
(municipalities) Acton, Ashland, Bedford, Bellingham, Boxborough, Brookline, Carlisle, Canton, Concord, Dedham, Dover, Framingham, Franklin, Foxborough, Holliston, Hopkinton, Hudson, Lexington, Lincoln, Littleton, Marlborough, Maynard, Medfield, Medway, Millis, Natich, Needham, Newton, Norfolk, Norwood, Plainville, Sharon, Sherborn, Southborough, Stow, Sudbury, Walpole, Waltham, Wayland, Wellesley, Weston, Westwood, Wrentham
Ms. Anne M. Whooley
Metro South/ West Employment and Training Administration
P.O. Box 740
275 Prospect St.
Norwood, MA 02062
781-769-4120
Fax: 781-769-5226

New Bedford
(municipalities) Acushnet, Dartmouth, Fairhaven, Freetow, Lakeville, Marion, Mattapoisett, New Bedford, Rochester, Wareham
Mr. Jessie Ealy
New Directions
181 Hillman St.
New Bedford, MA 02740
508-979-1616
Fax: 508-979-1656

Northern Middlesex/Southern Essex
(municipalities-Northern Middlesex) Billerica, Chelmsford, Dracut, Dunstable, Lowell, Tewksbury, Tyngsborough, Westford

(municipalities Southern Essex) Beverly, Danvers, Essex, Glouchester, Hamilton, Ipswich, Lynn, Lymfield, Manchester, Marblehead, Middleton, Nahant, Peabody, Rockport, Salem Saugus, Swampscott, Topsfield, Wenham
Mr. Henry Przydzial
Lowell Office of Employment and Training
107 Merrimack St.
Lowell, MA 01852
978-459-2336
Fax: 978-459-2111

Northern Worcester
(municipalities) Ashburnham, Ashby, Ayer, Barre, Berlin, Bolton, Clinton, Fitchburg, Gardner, Groton, Harvard, Hubbardston, Lancaster, Leominster, Luneburg, Pepperell, Princeton, Shirley, Sterling, Templeton, Townsend, Westminster, Winchendon
Ms. Rosemary Chandler
North Central Massachusetts Regional Employment Board, Inc.
80 Erdman Way, Suite 201
Leominster, MA 01453
978-534-1481
Fax: 978-534-1375
Email: ncentral@ma.ultranet.com

South Coastal
(municipalities) Braintree, Carver, Cohassett, Duxbury, Halifax, Hanover, Hingham, Holbrook, Hull, Kingston, Marshfield, Middleborough, Milton, Norwell, Pembroke, Plymouth, Plympton, Randolph, Rockland, Scituate, Quincy, Weymouth
Mr. Paul L. Berrini
South Coastal Career Development Administration
1431 Hancock St., 3rd Floor
Quincy, MA 02169
617-745-4000
Fax: 617-328-0215

Southern Worcester
(municipalities) Auburn, Blackstone, Boylston, Brookfield, Charlton, Douglas, Dudley, E. Brookfield, Grafton, Hardwick, Holden, Hopedale, Leicester, Mendon, Milbury, Milford, Millville, New Braintree, N. Bridge, Northborough, North Brookfield, Oakham, Oxford, Paxton, Rutland Shrewsbury, Southbridge, Spencer, Sturbridge, Upton, Uxbridge, Warren, Webster, Westborough, West Boylston, W. Brookfield, Worcester
Mr. Donald Anderson
Workforce Central
44 Front St., 7th Floor
Worcester, MA 01608
508-799-8000
Fax: 508-799-8012

Michigan

State Workforce Liaison
Dr. Barbara Bolin
Michigan Department of Career Development
201 N. Washington Square
Lansing, MI 48913
517-241-4000

Capital Area Michigan Works
(counties) Clinton, Eaton, Ingham (cities) Lansing, East Lansing
Mr. Douglas E. Stites
Capital Area Michigan Works
2110 South Cedar Street

Lansing, MI 48910
517-492-5599
Fax: 517-492-5598
Email: dstites@camw.net

MI Works! Agency Q
Ms. Cathy Simons
Ottawa County Department of Employment
and Training
12251 James St.
Holland, MI 49424
616-393-5600
Fax: 616-393-5612
Email: grillo@novagate.net

MI Works! Agency R
(counties) Arenac, Clare, Gladwin, Iosco,
Ogemaw, Roscommon
Mr. Mark L. Berdan
Region 7B Employment and Training
Consortium
402 N. First St.
P.O. Box 408
Harrison, MI 48625
989-539-2173
Fax: 989-539-6053
Email: reg7b@michworks4u.org

MI Works! Agency S
(counties) Bay, Midlands, Saginaw
Mr. Dennis Brieske
Saginaw/ Midland/ Bay Michigan Works!
1600 N. Michigan, Room 400
Saginaw, MI 48602
989-754-1144
Fax: 989-754-1439
Email: smb@michiganworks.com

MI Works! Agency B
(counties) Berrien, Cass, Van Buren
Mr. Charles McCallum
Office of Michigan Works! Berrien-Cass-Van
Buren
185 E. Main St.
Benton Harbor, MI 49022
616-927-1064
Fax: 616-927-1399
Email: omw@omw.org

MI Works! Agency I
(counties) Alger, Delta, Dickinson, Marquette,
Menominee, and Schoolcraft
Mr. Orrin Baily
Michigan Works! The Job Force/
Six County Employment Alliance
2831 N. Lincoln Rd.
Escanaba, MI 49829
906-789-0558
Fax: 906-789-9952
Email: orrin@jobforce.org

MI Works! Agency E
(city) Detroit
Mr. Willie Walker
City of Detroit Employment and Training
Department
707 W. Milwaukee St., 5th Floor
Detroit, MI 48202
313-876-0674
Fax: 313-876-0686
Email: detroitmwa@emptrain.ci.detroit.mi.us

MI Works! Agency F
(counties) Chippewa, Luce, Mackinac
Ms. Gwen Worley
E.U.P. Employment and Training Consortium

1122 E. Easterday Ave.
Sault Saint Marie, MI 49783
906-635-1752
Fax: 906-635-0115
Email: miworks@northernway.net

MI Works! Career Alliance
(counties) Genesee, Shiawasee
Ms. Pamela Y. Loving
MI Works! Career Alliance, Inc.
711 N. Saginaw St., Suite 300
Flint, MI 48503
810-233-5974
Fax: 810-233-8652
Email: admin@careeralliance.org

Central Area Michigan Works Consortium
(counties) Gratiot, Ionia, Isabella, Montcalm
Mr. Ralph Loeschner
Central Area MI Works Consortium
904 Oak Dr. - Turk Lake
P.O. Box 368
Greenville, MI 48838
231-754-9315
Fax: 231-754-9310
Email: ralphl@serv.net

MI Works! Agency A
(county) Allegan, Kent; (city) Grand Rapids
Ms. Beverly Drake
Area Community Services
Employment and Training Council
144 E. Fulton St.
Grand Rapids, MI 49503
616-336-4100
Fax: 616-336-4118
Email: acset@nwd.org

MI Works! Agency X
(counties) Lake, Mason, Mecosta, Newaygo,
Osceola
Mr. Paul Griffith
West Central MI Works!
110 Elm St.
Big Rapids, MI 49307
231-796-4891
Fax: 231-796-8316
Email: westcent@wmis.net

MI Works! Agency L
(counties) Macomb, St. Clair
Mr. John Bierbusse
Macomb/ St. Clair Workforce Development
Board, Inc.
21885 Dunham Rd., Suite 11
Verkuilen Bldg.
Clinton Twp., MI 48036-1030
810-469-5220
Fax: 810-469-7488
Email: linda!macomb-stclairworks.org

MI Works! Agency M
(counties) Muskego, Oceana
Mr. Paul Roy
Dept. of Employment and Training
Muskegon County
1611 Oak Ave.
Muskegon, MI 49442-2405
231-724-6381
Fax: 231-724-6687
Email: temp082@gte.net

MI Works! Agency N
(counties) Alcona, Alpena, Cheboygan,
Crawford, Montmorency, Oscoda, Otsego,
Presque Isle

Mr. Kurt Ries
Northeast Michigan Consortium
P.O. Box 711
20709 State St.
Onaway, MI 49765
989-733-8548
Fax: 989-733-8069
Email: kurt@miworks-nemc.gen.mi.us

MI Works! Agency O
(counties) Antrim, Benzie, Charlevoix, Emmet,
Grand Traverse, Kalkaska, Leelanau,
Manistee, Missaukee, Wexford
Mr. Alton Shipstead, Jr.
Northwest Michigan Council of Governments
2194 Dendrinos Dr.
P.O. Box 506
Traverse City, MI 49685-0506
231-929-5000
Fax: 231-929-5012
Email: nwmwa@nwm.cog.mi.us

MI Works! Agency P
(county) Oakland
(excluding Pontiac Consortium)
Mr. John Almstadt
Oakland County
Department of Public Services
1200 N. Telegraph Rd.
Pontiac, MI 48341-0437
248-452-2256
Fax: 248-542-2260
Email: laked@co.oakland.mi.us

MI Works! Agency V
(counties) Huron, Lapeer, Sanilac, Tuscola
Mr. Marvin Pichla
Thumb Area Employment and Training
Consortium MI Works!
3270 Wilson St.
Marlette, MI 48453
989-635-3561
Fax: 989-635-2230
Email: centraladm@thumbworks.org

MI Works! Agency W
(county) Washtenaw
Ms. Trenda Rusher
Washtenaw County Workforce Development
Board
555 Towner St.
P.O. Box 915
Ypsilanti, MI 48197-0915
734-484-6650
Fax: 734-484-7271
Email: rushert@co.washtenaw.mi.us

MI Works! Agency Y
Western Upper Peninsula
(counties) Baraga, Gogebic, Houghton, Iron,
Keweenaw, Ontonogan
Mr. James Saari
Western Upper Peninsula MI Works!
100 W. Cloverland Dr.
Ironwood, MI 49938
906-932-4059
Fax: 906-932-3992
Email: mwa@portup.com

MI Works! Agency K
(county) Livington
Mr. William S. Sleight
Livingston County Job Training Services
828 E. Grand River Ave.
Howell, MI 48843
517-546-7450

Fax: 517-546-2353
Email: sleightw@htonline.com

Michigan Works! Agency C
(counties) Barry, Branch, Calhoun
Dr. Roger T. LaBonte
Michigan Works! Agency C
Calhoun Intermediate School District
17111 G Drive North
Marshall, MI 49068
616-789-2409
Fax: 616-781-8792
Email: bujdosj@calhoun-isd.k12.mi.us

Michigan Works! Agency G
(counties) Kalamazoo, St. Joseph
Mr. Robert A. Straits
Kalamazoo-St. Joseph Michigan Works!
536 West Lovell Street
Kalamazoo, MI 49007-4614
616-349-1533
Fax: 616-349-5505
Email: straits@we.upjohninst.org

Michigan Works! Agency T
(counties) Hillsdale, Jackson, Lenawee
Mr. Scott A. Menzel
South Central Michigan Works!
2075 West Bacon Road
Hillsdale, MI 49242
517-437-0990
Fax: 517-439-4388
Email: menzel@scnc.hcisd.k12.mi.us

Michigan Works! Agency U
(counties) Monroe, Wayne
Southeast Michigan Community Alliance
(SEMCA)
Michigan Works!
8750 South Telegraph Road, Suite 400
Taylor, MI 48180
313-295-1200
Fax: 313-295-7742
Email: semca@semca.org

Micronesia
Mr. Lanny L Kabua
Republic of the Marshall Islands
Workforce Investment Board
P.O. Box 136
Majuro, Marshall Islands 96960
692-625-6594
Fax: 692-625-6595
Email: rmjtpa@ntamar.com

Minnesota
State Workforce Development Liaison
Earl Wilson
Minnesota Department of Economic Security
390 N. Robert St.
St. Paul, MN 55101
651-296-1821
Fax: 651-296-0994
Email: earl.wilson@state.mn.us

Anoka County
Mr. Jerry Vitzthum
Anoka County /MN Workforce Center
1201 89th Ave., NE, Suite 235
Blaine, MN 55434
763-783-4800
Fax: 763-783-4844
Email: jdvitzth@co.anoka.mn.us

Central Minnesota #5
(counties) Chisago, Isanti, Kanabec,
Kandiyohi, McLeod, Meeker, Millie Lacs,
Pine, Renville, Sherburne, Wright
Ms. Barb Chaffee
Central Minnesota Jobs and Training Services
106 Pine Street
Monticello, MN 53362
763-271-3711
Fax: 763-271-3701
Email: bchaffee@ngwmail.des.state.mn.us

Dakota County
Ms. Helen Dahlberg
Dakota County workforce Services
60 East Marie Avenue, Suite 220
West St. Paul, MN 55118
651-450-2633
Fax: 651-450-2656
Email: helen.dahlberg@co.dakota.mn.us

Duluth
(city)
Ms. Sharon Finch
Workforce Development
332 City Hall
411 W. First St.
Duluth, MN 55802
218-723-3419
Fax: 218-723-3636

Minneapolis
Mr. F.A. Wells
Minneapolis Employment and Training
Program
250 S. 4th St., Room 510
Minneapolis, MN 55415-1372
612-673-5700
Fax: 612-673-2108
Email: chip.wells@ci.minneapolis.mn.us

Northeast Minnesota
(counties) Aitkin, Carlton, Cook, Itasca,
Koochiching, Lake, St. Louis
Mr. Dennis Wain
Northeast Minnesota Office of Job Training
820 N. 9th, Suite 240
P.O. Box 1028
Virginia, MN 55792
218-748-2200
Fax: 218-748-2240
Email: dwain@ngwmail.des.state.mn.us

Northwest Minnesota; SDA 1
(counties) Kittson, Marshall, Norman,
Pennington, Polk, Red Lake, Roseau
Mr. Rodger L. Coauette
Northwest Private Industry Council, Inc.
Workforce Council
1730 University Avenue
Crookston, MN 56716-1912
218-281-6020
Fax: 218-281-6025
Email: roger.coauette@state.mn.us

Ramsey County
Ms. Patricia Brady
Workforce Solution Department
2098 11th Avenue East
North St. Paul, MN 55109
651-779-5651
Fax: 651-779-5240
Email: patricia.brady@co.ramsey.mn.us

Rural Minnesota CEP
(counties) Becker, Beltrami, Cass, Clay,
Clearwater, Crow Wing, Douglas, Grant,
Hubbard, Lake of the Woods, Mahnomen,

Morrison, Otter Tail, Pope, Stevens, Todd,
Traverse, Wadena, Wilkin
Mr. Larry Buboltz
Rural Minnesota CEP, Inc.
P.O. Box 1108
Detroit Lakes, MN 56502
218-846-7400
Fax: 218-846-7404
Email: lbuboltz@wfc.des.state.mn.us

South Central
(counties) Blue Earth, Brown, Faribault, Le
Sueur, Martin, Nicollet, Sibley, Waseca,
Watonwan
Ms. Sandra Oppegard
South Central Workforce Council
P.O. Box 3327
410 Jackson St.
Mankato, MN 56002-3327
507-549-3452
Fax: 507-345-2414
Email: sandy@mnic.net

Southeastern Minnesota
(counties) Dodge, Fillmore, Freeborn,
Goodhue, Houston, Mower, Olmsted, Rice,
Steele, Wabasha
Mr. Randy Johnson
Minnesota Workforce Development, Inc.
300 11th Ave., SW, Suite 110
Rochester, MN 55901
507-292-5153
Fax: 507-292-5173
Email: rjohnson@semnpic.org

Southwest Minnesota
(counties) Big Stone, Chippewa, Cottonwood,
Jackson, Lac Qui Parle, Lincoln, Lyon,
Murray, Nobles, Pipestone, Redwood, Rock,
Swift, Yellow Medicine
Ms. Juanita Lauritsen
Southwest Minnesota PIC
607 W. Main St.
Marshall, MN 56258-3021
507-537-6987
Fax: 507-537-6997
Email: jlauritsen@ngwmail.des.state.nmate.
mn.us

Stearns, Benton
Ms. Kathy Zavala
Stearns-Benton Employment and Training
Council
3333 W. Division St., Suite 210
St. Cloud MN 56301-3783
320-202-2100
Fax: 320-650-1717
Email: kzavala@sbetc.des.state.mn.us

Washington County
Mr. Robert L. Crawford
Washington County Workforce Center
14949 62nd St., North
Stillwater, MN 55082
651-430-6850
Fax: 651-430-6864

Hennepin/Scott/Carver Workforce Area
(counties) Carver, Hennepin (excluding City
of Minneapolis), Scott
Mr. William Brumfield
Hennepin County Training and Employment
Assistance Department
300 S. 6th St.
Minneapolis, MN 55487-0012
612-348-8953

Fax: 612-348-3932
Email: bill.brumfield@co.hennepin.mn.us

Winona County
Mr. Michael Haney
Winona County Workforce Council
1250 Homer Road, Suite 200
Winona, MN 55987-4842
507-453-2920
Fax: 507-453-2960
Email: mhaney@ngwmail.des.state.mn.us

Mississippi
State Workforce Liaison
Mr. James R. Lott
MDA-Employment Training Division
P.O. Box 24568
Jackson, MS 39225-4568
601-359-9250
Fax: 601-359-9252
Email: jlott@mississippi.org

Delta Area #1
(counties) Bolivar, Carroll, Coahoma,
Holmes, Humphreys, Issaquena, Leflore,
Panola, Quitman, Sharkey, Sunflower,
Tallahatchie, Tunica, Washington
Mr. William B. Haney
South Delta Planning and Development
District
P.O. Box 1776
Greenville, MS 38702-1776
662-378-3831
Fax: 662-378-3834
Email: sdpddwia@tecinfo.com

Hinds County Area #4
Dr. Eugene Mc Lemore
Hinds County
420 East Woodrow Wilson Drive
Jackson, MS 39216
601-368-2928
Fax: 601-368-2915
Email: lthomas@co.hinds.ms.us

Mississippi Partnership Area #2
(counties) Alcorn, Attlla, Benton, Calhoun,
Choctaw, Clay, DeSoto, Grenada, Itawamba,
Lafayette, Lee, Lowndes, Marshall, Monroe
Mr. Vernon R. Kelley III
Three Rivers Planning and Development
District
P.O. Box 690
Pontotoc, MS 38863
662-489-2415
Fax: 662-489-6815
Email: threerivers@trpdd.com

Southern Mississippi Area #3
(counties) Adams, Amite, Claiborne, Copiah,
Franklin, Jefferson, Lawrence, Lincoln,
Madison, Pike, Rankin, Simpson, Warren,
Wilkinson, Yazoo
Mr. F. Clarke Holmes
Central Mississippi Planning and
Development District
P.O. Box 4935
Jackson, MS 39296
601-981-1511
Fax: 601-981-1515
Email: gyates@cmpdd.org

Twin Districts Area #5
(counties) Clarke, Covington, Forrest,
Greene, Jasper, Jefferson, Davis, Jones,
Kemper, Lamar, Lauderdale, Leake, Marion,

Neshoba, Newton, Pearl, River, Perry, Scott,
Smith, Wayne
Mr. Gary Lukens
Southern Mississippi Planning and
Development District
700 Hardy Street
Hattiesburg, MS 39401
601-545-2137
Fax: 601-545-2164
Email: glukens@hotmail.com

Gulf Coast #6
(counties) Hancock, Harrison, George,
Jackson and Stone
Ms. Mary Lee McNeil
Gulf Coast Business Services Corporation
330 Courthouse Rd.
Gulfport, MS 39507-1807
228-897-1881
Fax: 228-897-3687
Email: mlmcneil@prodigy.net

Missouri
Missouri Workforce Division
Mr. Tom Jones
Workforce Development
421 East Dunklin
P.O. Box 1087
Jefferson City, MO 65102-1087
573-751-3349
Fax: 573-751-8162
Email: thones@works.state.mo.us

Northwest Region
(counties) Andrew, Atchison, Buchanan,
Caldwell, Clinton, Daviess, Dekalb, Gentry,
Grundy, Harrison, Holt, Linn, Livingston,
Mercer, Nodaway, Putnam, Sullivan, Worth
Mr. Beck Steele
North Central Missouri College
912 Main St.
Trenton, MO 64683
660-359-3622
Fax: 660-359-3082
Email: bsteele@mail.ncmc.cc.mo.us

Northeast Region
(counties) Adair, Clark, Knox, Lewis, Lincoln,
Macon, Marion, Monroe, Montgomery, Pike,
Ralls, Randolph, Schuyler, Scotland, Shelby,
Warren
Ms. Sharon Hayes
NEMBO WIB, Inc.
111 W. Monroe
Paris, MO 65275
660-327-5125
Fax: 660-327-5128
Email: shays@mcmsys.com

EastJjackson County Region
(counties) Cass, Clay, Platte, Ray, Jackson
Mr. Clyde McQueen
Full Employment Council
1740 Paseo, Suite D
Kansas City, MO 64108
816-254-3297
Fax: 816-471-0132
Email: cmcqueen@works.state.mo.us

West Central Region
(counties) Bates, Benton, Carroll, Chariton,
Cedar, Henry, Hickory, Johnson, Lafayette,
Pettis, St. Clair, Saline, Vernon
Mr. Harlan McGinnis
Western Missouri Workforce Development
Board.
P.O. Box 701

2905 W. Broadway
Sedalia, MO 65302-0701
660-827-3722
Fax: 660-826-3789
Email: wdb@iland.net

Southwest Region
(counties) Barry, Barton, Dade, Jasper,
Lawrence, McDonald, Newton
Mr. Harry Rogers
211 S. Main St., Suite 210
Joplin, MO 64801
417-782-3517
Fax: 417-782-2043
Email: hrogers@talleytech.com

Ozark Region
(counties) Christian, Dallas, Greene, Polk,
Stone, Taney, Webster
Ms. Kathy Clancy
Job Council of the Ozarks
1514 S. Glenstone
Springfield, MO 65804-1436
417-891-1690
Fax: 417-887-1892
Email: kclancy@works.state.mo.us

Central Region
(counties) Audrain, Boone, Camden, Cole,
Cooper, Crawford, Dent, Gasconade,
Laclede, Maries, Miller, Moniteau, Morgan,
Osage, Phelps, Pulaski, Washington
Ms. Janet Vaughn
Central Ozarks Workforce Investment Board
1202 Forum Dr.
Rolla, MO 65401
573-364-7030
Fax: 573-364-1865
Email: jvaughn@copic.ext.missouri.edu

South Central Region
(counties) Butler, Carter, Douglas, Howell,
Oregon, Ozark, Reynolds, Ripley, Shannon,
Texas, Wayne, Wright
Ms. Tana Holder
Ozark Action, Inc.
710 E. Main St.
West Plains, MO 65775
417-256-6147
Fax: 417-256-7318
Email: tholder@www.oaiwp.org

Southeast Region
(counties) Bollinger, Cape Girardeau,
Dunkin, Iron, Madison, Mississippi, New
Madrld, Pemiscot, Perry, St. Francois, Ste.
Genevieve, Scott, Stoddard
Mr. Ron Swift
Southeast Missouri WIB
760 S. Kingshighway St., Suite F
Cape Girardeau, MO 63703
573-334-0990
Fax: 573-334-0335
Email: ron@job4you.org

Jefferson Franklin Consortium Region
(counties) Franklin, Jefferson
Ms. Shirley Wilson
Jefferson/ Franklin Counties, Inc.
Office of Job Training
P.O. Box 350
Hillsboro, MO 63050
636-467-2307
Fax: 636-467-5254
Email: sdwilson@east.wfd.state.mo.us

Kansas City Region
(city) Kansas City
Ms. Billie Carson
Full Employment Council
1740 Paseo
Kansas City, MO 64108
816-471-2330
Fax: 816-471-0132

St. Charles County Region
(county) St. Charles
Mr. Marvin Freeman
St. Charles County Government
Work Connection Center
2020 Parkway Drive
St. Peters, MO 63376
636-441-2422
Fax: 636-441-7045
Email: mfreem02@mail.win.org

St. Louis City Region
(city) St. Louis
Ms. Sherry Vogel
St. Louis Agency on Training and
Employment
1017 Olive Street, Suite 13
St. Louis, MO 63101-2019
314-589-8000
Fax: 314-589-6410
Email: svogel@works.state.mo.us

St. Louis County Region
(county) St. Louis
Mr. Don Holt
Workforce Development Board of St. Louis
City
26B North Oaks Plaza
St. Louis, MO 63121
314-679-3300
Fax: 314-671-3301
Email: donald_holt@stlouisco.com

Montana
State WIA
Ms. Ingrid Childress
Department of Labor and Industry
P.O. Box 1728
Helena, MT 59624
406-444-2416
Fax: 406-444-3037
Email: ichildress@state.mt.us

Concentrated Employment Program
Concentrated Employment Program (CED)
SDA: Beaverhead, Broadwater, Deer, Lodge,
Granite, Jefferson, Lewis & Clark, Madison,
Meagher, Powell, & Silver Bow Counties.
Balance of State (BOS) SDA: remaining 46
counties in Montana
Ms. Sue Mohr
Montana Job Training Partnership, Inc.
302 North Last Chance Gulch, Suite 409
Helena, MT 59601
406-444-1331
Fax: 406-444-1316
Email: smohr@mjtp.org

Nebraska
Governor's Liaison
Mr. Fernando Lecuona III
Department of Labor
P.O. Box 94600
550 S. 16th St.
Lincoln, NE 68509-4600
Fax: 402-471-9792
Fax: 402-471-2318
Email: flecuona@dol.state.ne.us

State Workforce Development
Ms. Joan Modrell
Nebraska Department of Labor
Office of Workforce Services
550 South 16th Street
P.O. Box 94600
Lincoln, NE 68509-4600
402-471-9948
Fax: 402-471-8239
Email: jmodrell@dol.state.ne.us

Greater Lincoln
(counties) Lancaster, Saunders (city) Lincoln
Mr. Dan Cain
Urban Development Department
1010 "N" Street, #174
Lincoln, NE 68508
402-441-7121
Fax: 402-441-6038
Email: dcain@ci.lincoln.ne.us

Greater Nebraska
(counties) Adams, Antelope, Arthur, Banner,
Blaine, Boone, Box, Boyd, Brown, Buffalo,
Burt, Butler, Butte, Cass, Cedar, Chase,
Cherry, Cheyenne, Clay, Colfac, Cuming,
Custer, Dakota, Dawes, Dawson, Deuel,
Dixon, Dodge, Dundy, Fillmore, Franklin,
Frontier, Furnas, Gage, Garden Garfield,
Gosper, Grant, Greeley, Hall, Hamilton,
Harlan, Hayes, Hitchcock, Holt, Hooker,
Howard, Jefferson, Johnson, Kearney, Keith,
Keya Paha, Kimball, Knox, Lincoln, Logan,
Loup, Madison, Mcpherson, Merrick, Morrill,
Nance, Nemaha Muckolls, Otoe, Pawnee,
Perkins, Phelps, Pierce, Platte, Polk, Red
Willow, Richardson, Rock, Saline, Saunders,
Scotts Bluff, Seward, Sheridan, Sherman,
Sioux, Stanton, Thayer, Thomas, Thurston,
Valley, Wayne, Webster, Wheller, York
Ms. Cathy Plager
Greater Nebraska Job Training Program
550 S. 16th St.
P.O. Box 94600
Lincoln, NE 68509
402-471-9928
Fax: 402-471-3050
Email: cplager@dol.state.ne.us

Greater Omaha
(counties) Douglas, Sarpy, Washington; (city)
Omaha
Mr. David Catalan
Greater Omaha Workforce Development
2421 N. 24th St.
Omaha, NE 68110
402-444-3449
Fax: 402-444-3755
Email: dcatalan@ci.omaha.ne.us

Nevada
Governor's Administrative Entity
Ms. Myla C. Florence
Nevada Department of Employment, Training
& Rehabilitation
500 East Third Street, Room 200
Carson City, NV 89713
775-684-3911
Fax: 775-684-3908

Northern Nevada
(counties) Churchill, Douglas, Elko, Eureka,
Humboldt, Lander, Lyon, Mineral, Pershing,
Storey, Washoe, White Pine; (city) Carson
City
Mr. Thomas C. Fitzgerald
Nevada Works of Northern Nevada

600 Mill Street
Reno, NV 89502
775-337-8600
Fax: 775-337-9589

Southern Nevada
(counties) Clark, Esmeralda, Lincoln, Nye
Mr. Richard Blue, Jr.
Nevada Business Services
P.O. Box 4428
Las Vegas, NV 89127
702-638-8750
Fax: 702-638-8774
Email: rblue@snwib.org

New Hampshire
State Workforce Development Liaison
(counties) Balknap, Carroll, Cheshire, Coos,
Grafton, Hillsborough, Merrimack,
Rockingham, Strafford, Sullivan
Ms. Kelly Clark
New Hampshire Workforce Opportunity
Council, Inc.
64 Old Suncook Rd.
Concord, NH 03301
603-229-3303
Fax: 603-228-8557
Email: kclark@nhworkforce.org

New Jersey
Governor's Liaison
Mr. Mark B. Boyd
NJ Department of Labor
John Fitch Plaza
P.O. Box 110
Trenton, NJ 08625-0110
609-292-2975
Fax: 609-633-9271
Email: cmycoff@dol.state.nj.us

State Workforce Liaison
Ms. Janice Pointer
Division of Employment and Training
P.O. Box 055
Trenton, NJ 08625
609-292-5834
Fax: 609-633-2556
Email: jpointer@dol.state.nj.us

Atlantic/Cape May
Mr. Stephen J. Brunner
Atlantic/Cape May WIB
Private Industry Council
1333 Atlantic Avenue, Floor 6
Atlantic City, NJ 08401
609-343-2345
Fax: 609-343-2189
Email: brunner_steve@aclink.org

Bergen County
Mr. Paul Calocino
Bergen County WIB
25 East Salem St., Room 602
Urban Plaza Bldg.
Hackensack, NJ 07601
201-752-4003
Fax: 201-752-4180
Email: pcalocino@co.bergen.nj.us

Burlington County
Ms. Kelly A. West
Burlington County Department of Economic
Development
124 High St.
P.O. Box 6000
Mount Holly, NJ 08060

609-265-5055
Fax: 609-265-5006
Email: kwest@mail.burlco.lib.nj.us

Camden County
Mr. Thomas S. Billet
Camden County WIB
Job Training Resource Center
800 Kings Highway, North, Suite 305
Cherry Hill, NJ 08034
856-414-0044
Fax: 856-414-9050
Email: ccwib@rcn.com

Cumberland/ Salem Consortium
Mr. Charles A. Thomas
Cumberland/ Salem Consortium
P.O. Box 1398
220 N. Laurel St.
Bridgeton, NJ 08302
856-451-8920
Fax: 856-451-2514
Email: cthomas@ccoel.org

Essex County
Ms. Geri Durso
Essex County Workforce Investment Board
50 South Clinton Street, East
Orange, NJ 07018
973-395-8681
Fax: 973-395-8667
Email: gdurso@bellatlantic.net

Gloucester County
Ms. Tamara Primas Thomas
Gloucester County WIB
Route 45 and Budd Blvd.
P.O. Box 337
Woodbury, NJ 08096
609-384-6970
Fax: 609-384-0207
Email: tthomas@co.gloucester.nj.us

Greater Raritan
Ms. Maria Guerriero
Greater Raritan WIB
P.O. Box 330
Room L 208
Somerville, NJ 08876
908-526-1200
Fax: 908-725-2831
Email: mguerrie@raritanval.edu

Hudson County
Mr. Anthony J. Corsi
Hudson County WIB
Career Development Center
4800 Broadway, Room 208
Union City, NH 07087
201-271-4555
Fax: 201-271-4557
Email: tcorsi@hest.tec.nj.us

Jersey City
Mr. Benjamin Lopez
Jersey City Office of Employment and
Training
121-125 Newark Ave., 3rd Floor
Jersey City, NJ 07302
201-413-7580
Fax: 201-860-0007

Mercer County
Ms. Cathy Tramontana
Mercer WIB
P.O. Box 8068
640 S. Broad St., Suite 408

Trenton, NJ 08650
609-989-6827
Fax: 609-989-6882
Email: ctramontana@mercercounty.org

Middlesex County
Ms. Patricia Roman
Middlesex County WIB
506 Jersey Ave.
New Brunswick, NJ 08901-2053
732-745-3920
Fax: 732-745-4050
Email: proman@dol.state.nj.us

Monmouth County
Mr. William J. Wood
Monmouth County WIB
170 Monmouth St.
Red Bank, NJ 07701
732-747-2282
Fax: 732-741-6553
Email: wjwood@dol.state.nj.us

Morris/ Sussex/ Warren
Mr. Jack Patten
Morris, Sussex, Warren WIB
P.O. Box 900
Morristown, NJ 07963-0900
973-829-8662
Fax: 973-829-8500
Email: jpattern123@aol.com

Newark
(city)
Mr. Daniel Akwei
Newark WIB
Mayor's Office of Employment and Training
24-38 Lock Street
Newark, NH 07103
973-733-4820
Fax: 973-424-4229
Email: akwei@ci.newark.nj

Ocean County
Ms. Faith C. Liguori
Ocean County WIB
1027 Hooper Avenue
Building Two, Third Floor
Toms River, NH 08754
732-506-5312
Fax; 732-341-4539
Email: fliguori@co.ocean.nj.us

Passaic County
Mr. Gary Altman
Passaic County WIB
388 Lakeview Ave.
Clifton, NJ 07011
973-340-3400
Fax: 973-340-7214
Email: gary@wibpc.org

Union County
Mr. Carol Ford
Union County WIB
Administration Bldg., 4th Floor
Elizabeth, NJ 07207
908-558-2562
Fax: 908-558-2562
Email: cford@unioncounty.org

New Mexico
Governor's Liaison
Mr. Clinton D. Harden, Jr.
New Mexico Department of Labor
401 Broadway, NE

Albuquerque, NM 87103
505-841-8409
Fax: 505-841-8491
Email: charden@state.nm.us

Administrative Entity
Mr. Alan Richardson
New Mexico Department of Labor
Job Training Division
P.O. Box 4128
Santa Fe, NM 87502
Fax: 505-827-6823
Fax: 505-827-6812
Email: arichardson@state.nm.us

New Mexico Central Area
(counties) Sandoval, Bernalillo, Valencia,
Torrance
Ms. Becky Darrow
New Mexico Central Job Training Program
One Civic Plaza, NW Albuquerque, NM
87102
505-768-4650
Fax: 505-768-4329
Email: bdarrow@mercury.bernco.gov

New Mexico Eastern Area
(counties) Union, Harding, Quay, Guadalupe,
De Baca, Roosevelt, Lincoln, Chaves, Otero,
Eddy, Lea
Ms. Rachel Sayer
New Mexico Eastern Job Training Program
P.O. Box 4128
Santa Fe, NM 87502
505-827-6823
Fax: 505-827-6812

New Mexico Northern Area
(counties) San Juan (excluding Navajo
Nation) McKinley (excluding Navajo Nation),
Cibola, Rio Arriba, Taos, Santa Fe, Calfax,
Mora, San Miguel
Mr. Jerry Lgaussoin
New Mexico Northern Job Training Program
Private Industry Council
P.O. Box 4218
Santa Fe, NM 505-827-6812
Fax: 505-827-6812

New Mexico Southwestern Area
(counties) Catron, Socorro, Grant, Sierra,
Hidalgo, Luna, Dona Ana
Tenchie Overcash
New Mexico Department of Labor
P.O. Box 1928
Albuquerque, NM 87103
505-841-8406
Fax: 505-841-8409
Email: clehman@state.nm.us

New York
Governor's Liaison
Ms. Linda Angello
New York State Department of Labor
State Office Campus
Building 12, Room 500
Albany, NY 12240
518-457-2741
Fax: 518-457-6908

State Workforce Development
Ms. Margaret Moree
NY Department of Labor
State Office Campus Building
Building #12
Albany, NY 12240
518-457-0380

Fax: 518-457-9526
Email: usgmmm@labor.state.ny.us

Albany/ Rensselaer/ Schenectady
Mayranne Gronau
Department of Employment and Training
1600 7th Ave.
Troy, NY 12180
518-270-2860
Fax: 518-270-2865'Email: crrc5@albany.net

Broome/ Tioga
(counties) Broome, Tioga
Mr. Patrick Doyle
Broome-Tioga Workforce Development
System
P.O. Box 1766
Binghamton, NY 13902
607-778-2109
Fax: 607-778-2044
Email: pdoyle@co.broome.ny.us

Cayuga/ Cortland; SDA 22
Ms. Judy K. Davison
Department of Employment and Training
Grant Administration
60 Central Ave.
Cortland, NY 13045
607-753-5201
Fax: 607-753-5199
Email: jdavison@cortland-co.org

Cattaraugus/Allegany
Ms. Joan Sinclair
Cattarugus-Allegany Workforce Investment
Board, Inc.
One Blue Bird Square
Olean, NY 14760
716-806-0660
Fax: 716-806-0062
Email: catt_allegany@yahoo.com

Chautaulua County
Dr. Susan McNamara
Workforce Development
10785 Bennett Road
Dunkirk, NY 14048
716-366-7281
Fax: 716-366-6819
Email: wibboard@netsync.net

Chemung/Schuyler/Steuben
Mr. Matt Schick
Workforce Development One-Stop
20 Denison Parkway West
Corning, NY 14830-2607
607-937-8337
Fax 607-937-5420
Email: csswfd@stny.rr.com

Chenango/Delaware/Otsego
Mr. Kevin Price
Chenango Workforce Investment Board
19 Eaton Avenue
Morwich, NY 13815-1495
607-334-1405
Fax: 607-336-2638
Email: wibexec@norwich.net

Clinton/ Essex/ Franklin/ Hamilton; SDA 16
Mr. James E. Calnon
North County WIB
185 Margaret St.
Plattsburgh, NY 12901-1837
518-561-4295

Fax: 518-561-0229
Email: jcalnon@ncworkforce.com

Columbia/ Greene Counties
Ms. Mary Alane Wiltse
Columbia Greene Community College
Office of Employment and Training
4400 Route 23
Hudson, NY 12534
518-828-4181
Fax: 518-828-8543
Email: wiltse@sunycgcc.edu

Dutchess
Ms. Connie Fowle
Dutchess Works
3 Neptune Rd.
Poughkeepsie, NY 12601
845-463-0947
Fax: 845-463-0247
Email: dcwib@aol.com

Erie County/City of Buffalo
Mr. James Finamore
Buffalo and Erie County Workforce
Investment Board, Inc.
275 Oak Street
Buffalo, NY 14203
716-504-1480
Fax: 716-504-1483
Email: finamore@becwib.org

Fulton/ Montgomery/ Schoharie; SDA 14
Ms. Gail Breen
Fulton/ Montgomery/ Schoharie Counties
199 S. Main St.
Gloversville, NY 12078
518-725-6473
Fax: 518-773-8202
Email: gbreen315@hotmail.com

Gennessee/ Livingston/ Orleans/ Wyoming
Ms. Mary Lou Pullinzi
Gennessee County Career Center
587 E. Main St., Suite 100
Batavia, NY 14020
716-344-2042
Fax: 716-344-3266
Email: mlpullin@co.genessee.ny.us

Hempstead/ Long Beach Consortium
Mr. Clinton Boone
Town of Hempstead
Department of Occupational Resources
50 Clinton St., 4th Floor
Hempstead, NY 11550
516-485-5000
Fax: 516-538-5260
Email: ekenny@universalresources.nassau.ny

Jefferson/ Lewis Counties
Mr. Martin A. DelSignore
County of Jefferson Employment and Training
Administration
1222 Coffen St.
Watertown, NY 13601-1822
315-782-9252
Fax: 315-785-2073
Email: odelm@mailrelay.sunyjefferson.edu

Monroe County/Rochester
(county) Monroe (city) Rochester
Mr. Matthew C. Hurlbutt
Rochester Resource Alliance, Inc.
34th Paul Street
Rochester, NY 14604

716-258-3534
Fax: 716-232-6033
Email: mhurlbutt@RNYworks.com

New York City/Adult
Mr. Amy Peterson
Human Resources Administration
180 Water Street, 25th Floor
New York, NY 10038
212-331-6183
Fax: 212-331-6154

New York City/Youth and Dislocated Worker
Ms. Dorothy Lehman
Workforce Investment Board
180 Water Street, #1402
New York, NY 10038
212-331-4843
Fax: 212-331-3457
Email: lehmando@hra.nyc.gov

Niagara County
Mr. Paul J. Parise
Niagara County Employment & Training
Trott ACCESS Center
1001 Eleventh Street, 2nd Floor
Niagara Falls, NY 14301-1201
716-278-8140
Fax: 716-278-8149
Email: paul.parise@niagaracounty.com

Oneida/Herkimer/Madison
Mr. John E. Holt
Oneida county Workforce Development
The Paul Building
209 Elizabeth Street, 2nd Floor
Utica, NY 13501
315-793-6037
Fax: 315-798-5409
Email: jholt@co.oneida.ny.us

Onondaga
Ms. Sylvia Connolly
City/County Job Training Agency
677 S. Salina St., Suite 200
Syracuse, NY 13202
315-473-8250
Fax: 315-472-9492
Email: sconnolly@cnyworks.com

Ontario, Wayne, Seneca, Yates
Ms. Karen Springmeier
Finger Lakes Workforce Investment Board
Employment and Training Services Facility
3010 County Complex Drive
Canadaigua, NY 14424
716-396-4028
Fax: 716-396-4281
Email: Karen.Springmeier@co.ontario.ny.us

Orange County; SDA 9
Mr. Charles Bruno
Orange County WIB
30 Matthews St., Suite 106
Goshen, NY 10924
845-291-2450
Fax: 845-291-2503
Email: eta@co.orange.ny.us

Oswego County
Ms. Kathleen Casella
Oswego County Employment and Training
100 Spring Street
P.O. Box 1320
Mexico, NY 13114
315-963-5294

Fax: 315-963-5263
Email: kathyc@co.oswego.ny.us

Oyster Bay/North Hempstead/Glen Grove
(towns) Oyster Bay, North Hempstead; (city)
Glen Cove
Mr. Eugene Faber
Employment and Training Division
Town of Oyster Bay
977 Hicksville Rd.
Massapequa, NY 11758
516-797-4575
Fax: 516-797-4589

Rockland County
Ms. Pamela Weisberg
Tomorrow's Workplace
One Perlman Drive
Spring Valley, NY 10977
845-356-5100
Fax: 845-356-5949
Email: pam@tomorrowsworkplace.com

Saratoga/ Warren/ Washington
Mr. Anthony Scavone
Saratoga County Employment and Training
152 W. High St.
Ballston Spa, NY 12020
518-884-4170
Fax: 518-884-4262
Email: saremtra@govt.co.saratoga.ny.us

St. Lawrence County
Mr. Edmund Russell, Jr.
Office of Economic Development
48 Court St.
Canton, NY 13617
315-379-2283
Fax: 315-379-2394
Email: erussell@co.st-lawrence.ny.us

Suffolk County
Mr. John O'Donnell
Suffolk County Department of Labor
Building 17, North County Complex
Veteran's Memorial Highway
Hauppague, NY 11788
631-853-6500
Fax: 631-853-6614
Email: jack.o'donnell@co.suffolk.my.us

Sullivan County
Ms. Laura Quigley
Sullivan County Center for Workforce
Development
County Government Center
100 North St.
Monticello, NY 12701
845-794-3000
Fax: 845-794-0762
Email: LAQ@health.co.sullivan.ny.us

Tompkins
Ms. Debra L. Giordano
Tompkins County Workforce Development
Center
Administrative Office Center Ithaca
Suite 258, Box 154
171 East State Street
Ithaca, NY 14850
607-273-1913
Fax: 607-272-2835
Email: dgiordano@tompkins-co.org

Ulster County
Mr. Dominick Stregola
Ulster County Workforce Investment Board

Office of Employment and Training
651 Development Court
Kingston, NY 12401-1955
845-340-3170
Fax: 845-340-3165
Email: dsfr@co.ulster.ny.us

Yonkers City
Ms. Tracey Mitchell
Yonkers Employment Center
20 S. Broadway, Suite 1209
Yonkers, NY 10701
914-964-0105
Fax: 914-964-0322
Email: tracey@ypic.net

North Carolina

Governor's Liaison
Mr. Michael Aheron
North Carolina Commission on Workforce
Development
4327 Mail Service Center
Raleigh, NC 27699-4327
919-715-3300
Fax: 919-715-3974
Email: maheron@nccommerce.com

Cape Fear Local Area
(counties) Brunswick, Columbus, New
Hanover, Pender
Ms. Margie Parker
Cape Fear Job Training Consortium
1480 Harbour Dr.
Wilmington, NC 28401
910-395-4553
Fax: 910-395-2684
Email: mparker@capefaercog.org

Capital Area
(counties) Wake, Johnston
Ms. Brenda Savage
Capital Area Workforce Development
Consortium
P.O. Box 550
Raleigh, NC 27602
919-856-6040
Fax: 919-856-6038
Email: bsavage@co.wake.nc.us

Central Piedmont
(county) Durham
Mr. Ted Abernathy
Central Piedmont
101 City Hall Plaza
Durham, NC 27702
919-560-4965
Fax: 919-560-4986
Email: tabernathy@ci.durham.nc.us

Centralina
(counties) Anson, Cabarrus, Iredell, Lincoln,
Rowan, Stanly, Union
Mr. David Hollars
Centralina Workforce Development Board,
Inc.
P.O. Box 35008
Charlotte, NC 28235
704-348-2717
Fax: 704-347-4710
Email: dhollars@centralina.org

Charlotte/Mecklenburg
Ms. Deborah Mikysa
Charlotte/Mecklenburg Consortium
Workforce Development Board
700 Parkwood Ave.
Charlotte, NC 28205

704-336-3952
Fax: 704-336-7259
Email: dlmikysa@ci.charlotte.nc.us

Cumberland County
Mr. Patrick Hurley
Cumberland County Workforce Development
Center
410 Ray Ave.
P.O. Drawer 1829
Fayetteville, NC 28302-1829
910-323-3421
Fax: 910-323-5755
Email: hurley.patrick@esc.state.nc.us

Davidson County
Ms. Pat Everhart
Davidson County Job Training and
Employment Center
P.O. Box 1067
Lexington, NC 27293-1067
336-242-2065
Fax: 336-248-5410
Email: peverhart@co.davidson.nc.us

Eastern Carolina
(counties) Carteret, Craven, Duplin, Greene,
Jones, Lenoir, Onslow, Pamlico, Wayne
Ms. Tammy Childers
Eastern Carolina Workforce Consortium
233 Middle Street, Suite 109
P.O. Box 87
New Bern, NC 28563
252-636-6901
Fax: 252-638-3569
Email: childers@ecwdb.org

Greensboro/ High Point/ Guilford
(county) Guilford
Ms. Lillian Plummer
Greensboro/High Point/Guilford Consortium
303 N. Raleigh St.
Greensboro, NC 27401
910-373-5922
Fax: 910-373-5840
Email: lillian.plummer@ci.greensboro.nc.us

Kerr-Tar
(counties) Franklin, Granville, Person,
Warren, Vance, Caswell
Ms. Jane Ball-Groom
Kerr-Tar Interlocal Cooperative Consortium
for Job Training
P.O. Box 709
Henderson, NC 27536
252-436-2040
Fax: 252-436-2055
Email: jballgroom@kerrtarcog.org

Lumber River
(counties) Bladen, Hoke, Robeson, Scotland
Mr. Jim Perry
Lumber River Council of Governments
Consortium
4721 Fayetteville Rd.
Lumberton, NC 28358
910-618-5533
Fax: 910-618-5516
Email: jpb@mail.lrcog.dst.nc.us

Mid-Carolina
Ms. Mary Ann Dolister
Mid-Carolina Council of Governments
P.O. Drawer 1510
Fayetteville, NC 28302
910-323-4191

Fax: 910-323-9330
Email: madolister@fayetteville.net

Mountain Area
(counties) Buncombe, Henderson, Madison,
Transylvania
Ms. Helen R. Beck
Mountain Area
P.O. Box 729
Asheville, NC 28802-0729
828-250-4760
Fax: 828-255-5833
Email: helen.beck@ncmail.net

Northeastern Consortium
(counties) Camden, Chowan, Currituck, Dare,
Gatus, Hyde, Pasquotank, Perquimans,
Tyrrell, Washington
Ms. Cathy Long
Northeastern Workforce Investment
Consortium
P.O. Box 757
2522 South Croatan Highway
Nags Head, NC 27959
252-480-3500
Fax: 252-480-0121
Email: cathy.long@ncmail.net

Northwest Piedmont
(counties) Davie, Rockingham, Stokes, Surry,
Yadkin
Ms. Theresa Reynolds
Northwest Piedmont Job Training Consortium
400 West Fourth Street, Suite 400
Winston-Salem, NC 27101
336-761-2111
Fax: 336-761-2112
Email: treynolds@nwpcog.dst.nc.us

Regional Partnership
(counties) Alamance, Orange, Randolph
Ms. Janice Scarborough
Regional Partnership Local Area
 P.O. Box 1883
Asheboro, NC 27204-1883
336-629-5141
Fax: 336-629-1290
Email: janices@regionalcs.org

Region C
(counties) Cleveland, McDowell, Polk,
Rutherford
Mr. Bill Robertson
Region C Job Training Consortium
P.O. Box 841
Rutherford, NC 28139
828-287-0262
Fax: 828-287-2735
Email: brobertson@regionc.org

Region D
(counties) Alleghany, Ashe, Avery, Mitchell,
Watauga, Wilkes, Yancey
Ms. Carole Coates
Region D Council of Governments
P.O. Box 1820
Boone, NC 28607
828-265-5434
Fax: 828-265-5439
Email: ccoates@regiond.org

Region L
(counties) Edgecombe, Halifax, Nash,
Northampton, Wilson
Ms. Pamela Whitaker
Region L Job Training Consortium

P.O. Drawer 2748
Rocky Mount, NC 27802
252-446-0411
Fax: 252-446-5651
Email: pwhitacker#vcpcog.org

Region Q
(counties) Beaufort, Bertie, Hertford, Martin,
Pitt
Mr. Walter Dorsey
Region Q Workforce Investment Consortium
P.O. Drawer 1787
Washington, NC 27889
252-940-1600
Fax: 252-940-1601
Email: wdorsey@mideastcom.org

Southwestern NC
(counties) Cherokee, Clay, Graham,
Haywood, Jackson, Macon, Swain
Ms. Susan Fouts
Southwestern North Carolina
P.O. Drawer 850
Bryson City, NC 28713
828-488-9211
Fax: 828-488-3950
Email: susan@regiona.org

Western Piedmont
(counties) Alexander, Burke, Caldwell,
Catawba
Ms. Sheila Dotson
Western Piedmont Workforce Development
Consortium\736 4th Street, SW
P.O. Box 9026
Hickory, NC 28603
828-322-9191
Fax: 828-322-5991
Email: sdotson@wdcog.dst.nc.us

Winston-Salem/ Forsyth County
(county) Forsyth; (city) Winston-Salem
Dr. Otis B. Robinson
City of Winston-Salem/Forsyth County
Consortium
P.O. Box 2511
Winston-Salem, NC 27102
336-727-2866
Fax: 336-748-3303
Email: otisr@ci.winston-salem.nc.us

North Dakota
Governor's Liaison; Single Statewide
Ms. Maren Daley
Job Service North Dakota
P.O. Box 5507
Bismarck, NC 58506-5507
701-328-2836
Fax: 701-328-1612
Email: mdaley@state.nd.us

Ohio
State Workforce Development
Mr. John Weber
Ohio Department of Jobs and Families
145 S. Front St.
Columbus, OH 43216
614-644-8836
Fax: 614-728-5938
Email: weberj@odjfs.state.oh.us

WIA Area 1- Summit County
(county) Summit (city) Akron
Dr. Daisy Alford-Smith
Workforce Development Agency
Summit Department of Human Services

47 North Main Street, Building 1
Akron, OH 44308-1991
330-643-7200
Fax: 330-643-7351
Email: smithct19@odhs.state.oh.us

WIA Area 2- Cuyahoga County
(county) Cuyahoga (not including city of
Cleveland)
Mr. Jerry Slabe
Cuyahoga Workforce Development
1275 Ontario Street, 1st Floor
Cleveland, OH 44113
216-443-3224
Fax: 216-443-5950

WIA Area 3- Cleveland (City)
(city) Cleveland
Mr. Jeffery K. Patterson
Cleveland Workforce Development
Human Resources Division
601 Lakeside Avenue, Room 121
Cleveland, OH 44114-1015
216-664-3531
Fax: 216-664-3489
Email: jpatterson@4cleveland.com

WIA Area 4- Lorain County
Mr. William D. Ogle
Lorain Employment and Training
Administration
42495 North Ridge Road
Elyria, OH 44035-1055
440-322-5262
Fax: 440-322-1663
Email: wdouglas@lceta.org

WIA Area 5- Lake County
Ms. Donna Mona
Workforce Development Agency
125 East Erie Street
Painesville, OH 44077
440-350-2767
Fax: 440-639-2796
Email: donna2767@yahoo.com

WIA Area 6- Stark/Tuscarawas Counties
(counties) Stark, Tuscarawas (city) Canton
Ms. Sharon Perry
The employment Source
Regional COG 822 30th Street NW
Canton, OH 44709
330-433-9675
Fax: 330-491-2600
Email: sparry@workforceinitiative.com

WIA Area 7
(counties) Adams, Allen, Ashland, Ashtabula,
Athens, Auglaize, Belmount, Brown, Carroll,
Champaign, Clark, Clinton, Columbiana,
Coshocton, Crawford, Darke, Defiance,
Delaware, Erie, Fairfield, Fayette, Franklin,
Fulton, Gallia, Geauga, Greene, Guernsey,
Hamilton, Hancock, Harrison, Henry,
Highland, Hocking, Holmes, Huron, Jackson,
Jefferson, Knox, Lawrence, Licking, Logan,
Lucas, Madison, Mahaning, Marion, Medina,
Meigs, Mercer, Miami, Monroe, Montgomery,
Morgan, Morrow, Muskingum, Noble, Ottawa,
Paulding, Perry, Pickway, Pike, Portage,
Preble, Putnam, Richland, Ross, Sandusky,
Scioto, Seneca, Shelby, Trumbull, Union, Van
Wert, Vinton, Warren Washington, Wayne,
Williams, Wood, Wyandotte, (city) Cincinnati
Mr. John Weber
Ohio Department of Jobs & Family Services

145 South Front Street
Columbus, OH 43216-1618
614-644-8836
Fax: 614-728-5938
Email: weberj@odjfs.state.oh.us

Oklahoma

State Workforce Development Liaison
Mr. Glen Robards, Jr.
Employment Security Commission
2401 N. Lincoln Blvd.
Oklahoma City, OK 73152
405-557-5329
Fax: 405-557-7256
Email: glen.robards@oesc.state.ok.us

State Workforce Director
Mr. Eddie Foreman
2401 North Lincoln Boulevard
Oklahoma City, OK 73152
405-557-7294
Fax: 405-557-1478
Email: eddie.foreman@oesc.state.ok.us

Central Oklahoma
(counties) Canadian Logan (city) Oklahoma City
Mr. Bill Bryant
ACOG
21 East Main Street, #100
Oklahoma City, OK 73104
405-234-2200
Fax: 405-234-2217
Email: bbryant@acogok.org

Cleveland County
Ms. Joan Barker
Cleveland Workforce Development Board
P.O. Box 5345
Norman, OH 73070
405-701-2000
Fax: 405-701-2042
Email: joan.barker@oesc.state.ok.us

East Central Oklahoma
(counties) Hughes, Lincoln, Okfuskee, Pawnee, Payne, Pottawatomie, Seminole
Mr. Art Johnson
East Central Workforce Development, Inc.
P.O. Box 484
Chandler, OK 74834-0484
405-258-1470
Fax: 405-258-5285
Email: artj@brightok.net

North Central Oklahoma
(counties) Alfalfa, Blaine, Garfield, Grant, Kay, Kingfisher, Major, Noble
Mr. Larry Tip
NODA 2901 North Van Buren
Enid, OK 73703-2505
580-237-4810
Fax: 580-237-8230
Email: larry@nodadistrict.com

Eastern
(counties) Adair, Cherokee Mcintosh, Muskogee, Okmulgee, Sequoyah, Wagoner
Mr. Luther Sowder
Eastern Workforce Development Board
P.O. Box 2698
Muskogee, OK 74402-2698
918-682-5000
Fax: 918-682-3258
Email: lsowder@azalea.net

Northeast
(counties) Craig, Delaware, Mayes, Nowata, Ottawa, Rogers, Washington
Mr. Jim Craun
Job Training Northeast
104 Hester Place
Clelsea, OK 74016
918-789-2574
Fax: 918-789-2400
Email: newoeta@swbell.net

Northwest
(counties) Beaver, Cimarron, Dewey, Ellis, Harper, Texas, Woods, Woodward
Mr. Mike Bostic
Oklahoma Economic Development Authority
P.O. Box 668
Beaver, OK 73932
580-625-4531
Fax: 580-625-3420
Email: oedaxdir@ptsi.net

Balance of Oklahoma County
Ms. Norma Noble
Oklahoma County Workforce Development Board / Private Industry COuncil
7401 NE 23rd St.
Oklahoma City, OK 73141
405-713-1890
Fax: 405-713-1898
Email: norma.noble@oesc.state.ok.us

South Central
(counties) Caddo, Comanche, Cotton, Grady, Jefferson, Mcclain, Stephens, Tillman
Mr. Ray Friel
ASCOG
P.O. Box 1647
Duncan, OK 73534
580-252-0595
Fax: 580-252-6170
Email: frie_ra@ascog.org

Southeast
(counties) Choctaw, Haskell, Latimer, Leflore, Mccurtain, Pittsburg, Pushmataha
Ms. Susan Wall
KEDDO
P.O. Box 638
Wilburton, OK 74578
918-465-2367
Fax: 918-465-3873
Email: suwall@eosc.cc.ok.us

Southern
(counties) Atoka, Bryan, Carter, Coal, Garvin, Johnston, Love, Marshall, Murry, Pontotoc
Mr. Bill Haddock
Big 5 Community Services
P.O. Box 1577
Durant, OK 74702
405-924-5331
Fax: 405-920-2004
Email: bigfive@fullnet.net

Southwest
(counties) Beckham, Custer, Greer, Harmon, Jackson, Kiowa, Roger Mills, Washita
Mr. Pat Cochtan
SWODA
P.O. Box 569
Burns Flat, OK 73624
580-562-4553
Fax: 580-562-4274
Email: pat.cochran@swoda.org

Tulsa City and County
(counties) Creek, Osage, Pawnee, Tulsa (city)
Tulsa
Mr. Steve Gilbert
Tulsa Workforce Investment Board, Inc.
6111 East Skelly Drive, Suite 100
Tulsa, OK 74135-6101
918-828-5321
Fax: 918-828-5329
Email: admin@workforcetulsa.com

Oregon

Governor's Office
Ms. Cam Preus-Braly
Community Colleges and Workforce Development
255 Capitol Street, NE
Salem, OR 97310
503-378-8648
Fax: 503-378-3365
Email: cam.preus-braly@state.or.us

Clackamas County
Ms. Maureen Thompson
Employment Training and Business Services
P.O. Box 215
Marylhurst, OR 97036
503-534-5460
Fax: 503-635-8946
Email: mautha@co.clakamus.or.us

Jackson/ Josephine
Mr. Bruce McGregor
The Job Council
673 Market St.
Medford, OR 97504
541-776-5100
Fax: 541-776-0458
Email: brucem@jobcouncil.org

Benton/Linn/Lincoln
Mr. Tom Clancy
Burns Community Services Consortium
545 SW 2nd Street, Suite A
Corvallis, OR 97333
541-752-1010
Fax: 541-752-2348
Email: tcburns@csc.gen.or.us

Lane County
Mr. Chuck Forster
Lane Workforce Partnership
300 County Club Road, Suite 120
Eugene, OK 97401
541-682-7227
Fax: 541-686-3570
Email: chuck.forster@co.lane.or.us

Marion/Pok/Yamhill
Mr. Ron Bassett-Smith
Mid-Willamette Workforce Network
Chemeketa Community College
P.O. Box 14007, Building 48, Suite 102
Salem, OR 97309
503-399-6924
Fax: 503-589-7772
Email: rons@chemeketa.edu

Multnomah/Washington/Tillamook
Mr. John Ball
Workforcesystems, Inc.
711 SW Adler, Suite 200
Portland, Or 97205-3504
503-478-7300
Fux: 503-241-4622
Email: jball@worksystems.org

The Oregon Consortium
(counties) Baker, Clatsop, Coos, Crook, Columbia, Curry, Deschutes, Douglas, Grant, Gilliam, Harney, Jefferson, Klamath, Hood River, Lake, Morrow, Sherman, Malheur, Umatilla, Union, Wallowa, Wasco, Wheeler
Mr. Bill Demestihas
The Oregon Consortium and Workforce Alliance
260 SW Ferry St., Suite 102
Albany, OR 97321
503-928-0241
800-888-7611
Fax: 503-928-3096
Email: bill@tocowa.org

Pennsylvania

State Workforce Development Liaison
Mr. Tim Bittle
Bureau of Workforce Investment
PA Department of Labor and Industry
7th and Forster Streets, Room 1719B
Harrisburg, PA 17120
717-772-4966
Fax: 717-783-7115
Email: tbittle@dli.state.pa.us

Tri-County
(counties) Armstrong/ Butler/ Indiana
Mr. Fred Fornataro
Tri-County WIB
121 Sunnyview Circle, Suite 121
Butler, PA 16001-3596
724-282-4700
Fax: 724-282-4896
Email: tcpic@nauticom.net

Southern Alleghenies
(counties) Bedford, Blair, Cambria, Fulton, Huntington, Somerset
Ms. Pebble Bulvin-Albertelli
Southern Alleghenies Planning Development Commission
541 58th St.
Altoona, PA 16602-1158
814-949-6540
Fax: 814-949-6505
Email: albertelli@sapdc.org

Northern Tier
(counties) Bradford/ Sullivan/ Susquehanna/ Tioga/ Wyoming
Mr. Nicholas Schultz
Northern Tier Reg. Planning and Development Commission
312 Main St.
Towanda, PA 18848
570-265-9103
Fax: 570-265-7585
Email: schultz@northerntier.org

Bucks County
Mr. John Walsh, Jr.
Bucks County Office of Employment and Training
4259 Swamp Rd., Suite 303
Doylestown, PA 18901
215-340-2020
Fax: 215-340-2030
Email: jvwalsh@voicenet.com

North Central PA
(counties) Cameron, Clearfield, Elk, Jefferson, Mckean, Potter
Mr. Mike Lawrence
North Central Pennsylvania Regional Planning and Development Commission

P.O. Box 488
651 Montmorenci Ave.
Ridgway, PA 15853
814-773-3162
Fax: 814-772-7045
Email: mike@newib.org

Pocono Counties
(counties) Carbon/ Monroe/ Pike/ Wayne
Mr. Keith Ramsey
Pocono Counties SDA
76 Susquehanna St.
Jim Thorpe, PA 18229
570-325-2462
Fax: 717-325-8547
Email: kramsay@ptd.net

Chester County
Mr. Thomas McIntyre
Chester County Office of Employment and Training
601 Westown Rd., Suite 365
P.O. Box 2747
West Chester, PA 19380-0990
610-344-6900
Fax: 610-344-6925
Email: tmcintyre@chesco.org

Northwest PA
(counties) Clation, Crawford, Erie, Forest, Venango, Warren
Mr. Robert J. Cooke
NW Pennsylvania Training Partnership Consortium, Inc.
Highway 322 East
P.O. Box 1
Franklin, PA 16323
814-437-3000
Fax: 814-437-9516
Email: fin@nwpatrng.org

Southcentral Eight County Region
(counties) Adams, Cumberland, Dauphin, Franklin, Juniata, Lebanon, Perry, York
Mr. James MacDonald
Southcentral Employment Corporation
100 N. Cameron St., First Floor
Harrisburg, PA 17101-2424
717-236-7931
Fax: 717-236-4426
Email: dnornhold@pasec.org

Delaware County
Mr. Francis Carey
Delaware County Office of Employment and Training
9 S. 69th St., 3rd Floor
Upper Darby, PA 19082
610-713-2200
Fax: 610-713-2224
Email: careyf@dcoet.org

Southwest Corner
(counties) Beaver, Greene, Washington
Ms. Linda Bell
Washington/ Greene Job Training Agency
100 W. Beau St., Room 302
Washington, PA 15301
724-228-6870
Fax: 724-228-6939
Email: lbell08@cobweb.net

Berks County
Mr. Edward J. McCann
Berks County Career Link
501 Crescent Avenue

Reading, PA 19605-3050
610-988-1363
Fax: 610-988-1301
Email: emccann@bccl.org

Fayette/Westmoreland
Mr. William Thompson
Westmoreland County Community College
400 Armbrust Road
Youngwood, PA 15697
724-755-2145
Fax: 724-755-0914
Email: wthompson@westfaywib.org

Lancaster County
Mr. Rod Kopp
Lancaster Employment and Training Agency
1016 North Charlotte Street
P.O. Box 83480
Lancaster, PA 17603
717-291-1231
Fax: 717-295-9846
Email: koppr@co.lancaster.pa.us

Mid-State
(counties) Centre, Clinton, Columbia, Lycoming, Mifflin, Montoor, Northumberland, Snyder, Union
Mr. William C. Brock
Central PA Workforce Development Corporation
3 Kelly Square
Route 15 North
Lewisburg, PA 17837
570-568-0800
Fax: 570-568-0814
Email: wbrock@mail.csrlink.net

Lackawanna County
Mr. Fred Lettieri
Scranton-Lackawanna Human Development Agency
200 Adams Ave., 2nd Floor
Scranton, PA 18503
570-963-6836
Fax: 570-963-1317
Email: slhda@aol.com

West Central PA
(counties)Lawrence, Mercer
Mr. Gregg K. Dogan
West Central Job Partnership
44 S. Beaver St.
New Castle, PA 16101
724-658-2501
Fax: 724-658-4252
Email: gdogan@wcjp.org

Lehigh Valley
(counties) Lehigh, Northhampton
Mr. Edward Murray
PIC of Lehigh Valley, Inc.
1601 Union Blvd.
P.O. Box 20490
Lehigh Valley, PA 18002-0490
610-439-1123
Fax: 610-437-1715
Email: emurray@ptdprolog.net

Luzerne and Schuylkill Counties
Mr. Frank Sauchak
Luzerne County Human Resources Development Department
32 E. Union St., 2nd Floor
Wilkes-Barre, PA 18701-2793
570-822-1101

Fax: 570-824-4514
Email: fsauchak@yahoo.com

Montgomery County
Mr. Gerald Birkelbach
Montgomery County Training and
Employment Program
P.O. Box 311
Norristown, PA 19401
610-278-5950
Fax: 610-278-5949
Email: gbirkelb@montcopa.org

Philadelphia
(city) Philadelphia
Mr. Ernest E. Jones
Philadelphia PIC, Inc.
1617 JFK Blvd., 13th Floor
Philadelphia, PA 19103
215-963-2100
Fax: 215-557-2821
Email: ejones@pwdc.org

Three River WIB
(city) Pittsburgh (county) Allegheny
Mr. Ron Painter
Three Rivers WIB
Room 433 City/ County Bldg.
Pittsburgh, PA 15219
412-255-2696
Fax: 412-255-8909
Email: r.painter@trwib.org

Puerto Rico

Governor's Liaison and Balance of State
Mr. Juan Martinez, CPA
Right to Employment Administration
P.O. Box 364452
San Juan, PR 00936
787-754-0690
Fax: 787-758-0690

Caguas/ Guayama Consortium
Mr. Joaquin Santiago
Box 8518
Caguas, PR 00726
787-744-5333
Fax: 787-744-5334
Email: concg@coqui.net

Carolin-Trujillo Alto
(pueblos) Carolina, Trujillo, Alto
Mr. Rey Marrero
Carolina-Trujillo Alto
P.O. Box 899
Pueblo Station
Carolina, PR 00985
787-776-7745
Fax: 787-701-1375
Email: caralto@prtc.net

Guaynabo/Toa Baja
(pueblos) Catano, Guaynabo, Toa Alto, Toa Baja
Mr. Edward Gonzalez
Guaynabo-Toa Baja
Call Box 11864
Caparra Height Station
San Juan, PR 00922
787-782-9898
Fax: 787-749-0405

La Montana
(pueblos) Aguas, Buenas, Cidra, Corozal, Orocovis, Villaba
Mr. Robert Ramos

Cidra/Villalba
RR-1 Box 2004
Calle Jose de Diego
Cidra, PR 00739-9601
787-739-1370
Fax: 787-739-6903

Manati/Dorado
(pueblos) Barceloneta, Ciales, Dorado, Florida, Manati, Morovis, Vega Alta, Vega Baja
Mr. Edward Nunez Mendez
North Central
P.O. Box 3160
Manati, PR 00674-3160
787-884-6900
Fax: 787-884-7010

Mayaguez/Las Marias
(pueblos) Las Marias, Mayaguez
Ms. Elen Martinez
Mayaguez-Las Marias
P.O. Box 447
Mayaguez, PR 00681-0447
787-805-7730
Fax: 787-831-5195
Email: emez@coqui.net

North Central (Arecibo)
(pueblos) Arecibo, Adjuantas, Camuy, Hatillo, Jayuya, Lares, Quebradilla, Utuado
Mr. Jose R. Acevedo Santiago
North Central
P.O. Box 9933
Cotto Station
Arecibo, PR 00613-9933
787-879-4872
Fax: 787-878-6255

Northeast (Rio Grande)
(pueblos) Canovanas, Ceiba, Culebra, Fajardo, Loiza, Luquillo, Naguabo, Rio Grande, Vieques
Mr. Carlos J. Mendez Nunez
Northeast
P.O. Box 1750
Rio Grande, PR 00745
787-888-3030
Fax: 787-888-3031
Email: cnorespe@coqui.net

Northwest (Aguadilla)
(pueblos) Aguada, Aguadilla, Anasco, Isabela, Moca, Rincon, San Sebastian
Mr. Aurelio Gonzalez
Northwest
P.O. Box 992
Aguadilla, PR 00605-0992
787-882-2500
Fax: 787-882-1555

San Juan
Mr. Felipe Candelaria Acosta
Program Adiestramiento y Empleo
Edificio Trade Center
Fernandez Juncos 163
Pta. Tierra
San Juan, PR 00901
787-289-0460
Fax: 787-289-0481
Email: adiestyempleomsj@prtc.net

South Central (Salinas)
(pueblos) Barranquitas, Coamo, Juana, Diaz, Naranjito, Salinas, Santa Isabel
Mr. Dimas Torres Sanchez

South Central
P.O. Box 193
Salinas, PR 00751
787-824-1060
Fax: 787-824-3054
Email: Csentra@siful.org

Southeast (San Lorenzo)
(pueblos) Humacao, Juncas, Las Piedras, Maunabo, Pitillas, San Lorenzo, Yubucoa
Mr. Luis E. Gonzale
Southeast
Apartado 731
San Lorenzo, PR 00771
787-716-0730
Fax: 787-716-0515
Email: csurest@coqui.net

Southwest (San German)
(pueblos) Cabo, Rojo, Guanica, Guyanilla, Hormiguero, Lajas, Maricao, Penuelas, Sabana, Grande, San German, Yauco
Mr. Rafael Montalvo Vasquez
Southwest
P.O. Box 85
San German, PR 00683
787-892-1000
Fax: 7887-892-0810

Bayamon/ Comerio
Mr. Jose Rivera
Bayamon/Comerio Consortium
P.O. Box 1588
Bayamon, PR 00960
787-785-4202
Fax: 787-780-1777

Municipality of Ponce
Mr. Ramon Anglada
Municipality of Ponce
P.O. Box 1709
Ponce, PR 00733
787-840-2900
Fax: 787-844-8569

Republic of Palau

Republic of Palau
Ms. Josephine Ulengchong
Palau Combined Private industry Council/
SJTCC
P.O. Box 1000
Koror, Republic of Palau 96940
9-1-0288-011-680-488-2513
Fax: 9-1-0288-011-680-488-1725

Rhode Island

Governor's State Workforce
Mr. Lee Arnold
Department of Labor and Training
1511 Pontiac Avenue
Cranston, RI 02920
401-462-8870
Fax: 401-462-8872
Email: larnold@dlt.state.ri.us

Greater Rhode Island
Mr. Michael Koback
Workforce Partnership of Greater Rhode Island
877 Broadway
East Providence, RI 02917
401-222-2090
Fax: 401-222-1476
Email: Mkoback@dlt.state.ri.us

Providence/ Cranston Job Training Partnership
Mr. Robert Ricci

Workforce Development Office
180 Westminster St.
Providence, RI 02903-1918
401-861-0800
Fax: 401-861-9650

South Carolina

State Workforce Development Liaison
Mr. Sam Jordan
Employment and Training
South Carolina Employment Security
Commission
P.O. Box 1406
Columbia, SC 29202
803-737-2611
Fax; 803-737-2119
Email: sjordan@sces.org

Cherokee/Spartanburg/Union
Ms. Ann Fesperman
Upstate Workforce Investment Board
P.O. Box 5666
Spartanburg, SC 29304
864-596-2028
Fax: 864-596-2199
Email: fesperma@bellsouth.net

Lowcountry
(counties) Beaufort, Colleton, Hampton,
Jasper
Ms. Sandy Watkins
Lowcountry COG
P.O. Box 98
Yemassee, SC 29945
843-726-5536
Fax: 843-726-5165
Email: lwaia@hargray.com

Pendelton District
(counties) Anderson, Oconee, Pickens
Ms. Julia McLellan
Pendelton District Workforce Investment
Board
P.O. Box 587
Pendelton, SC 29670
864-646-8361
Fax: 864-646-2814
Email: jmclellan@tricounty.tec.sc.us

Trident
(counties) Berkeley, Charleston, Dorchester
Ms. Evelyn Delaine-Hart
Trident Workforce Development Board
4045 Bridge View Drive, Suite 226B
North Charleston, SC 29405
843-202-6960
Fax: 843-202-6961
Email: edelainehart@charlestoncoutny.org

Waccamaw
(counties) Georgetown, Harry, Williamsburg
Ms. Shirley Graham
Waccamaw Regional Planning Council
1230 Highmarket Street
Georgetown, SC 29440
843-546-4231
Fax: 843-520-0642
Email: sgraham29@yahoo.com

Upper Savannah
(counties) Abbeville, Edgefield, Greenwood,
Laurens, McCormick, Newberry, Saluda
Ms. Sandra M. Johnson
Upper Savannah COG
P.O. Box 1366
Greenwood, SC 29648

800-922-7729
Fax: 803-941-8090
Email: sjohnson@uppersavannah.com

Midlands
(counties) Fairfield, Lexington, Richland
Ms. Bonnie Austin
South Carolina Employment Security
Commission
Midlands Workforce Development Board
P.O. Box 995
Columbia, SC 29202
803-737-0107
Fax: 803-737-2132
Email: baustin@sces.org

Greenville County
Ms. Vivian Anthony
Greenville County Workforce Development
Board
301 University Ridge, Suite 500
Greenville, SC 29601
864-467-7220
Fax: 864-467-7051

PeeDee
(counties) Chesterfield, Darlington, Dillon,
Florence, Marion, Marlboro
Ms. Vicky Tyner
Pee Dee COG
P.O. Box 5719
Florence, SC 29502
800-884-3741
Fax: 803-669-0511
Email: vtyner@usns.net

Lower Savannah
(counties) Aiken, Allendale, Bamberg,
Barnwell, Calhoun, Orangeburg
Mr. Ollie Saulsby
Lower Savannah COG
P.O. Box 850
Aiken, SC 29802
803-649-7981
Fax: 803-649-2248
Email: osaulsby@lscog.org

Catawba
(counties) Chester, Lancaster, York
Mr. Robert A. Barber
Catawba Regional Planning Council
100 Dave Lyle Blvd., Suite 300
P.O. Box 450
Rock Hill, SC 29731
803-327-9041
Fax: 803-327-1912
Email: wia1@catawbacog.org

Santee Lynches
(counties) Clarendon, Kershaw, Lee, Sumter
Mr. Jim Darby
Santee Lynches COG
P.O. Box 1837
Sumter, SC 29151
803-775-7381
Fax: 803-773-9903
Email: slsda@slcog.org

South Dakota

Governor's Liaison Single State SDA
Mr. Lloyd Schipper
Department of Labor
700 Governor's Dr.
Pierre, SD 57501
605-773-3101

Fax: 605-773-4211
Email: lloyd.schipper@state.sd.us

Tennessee

Governor's Liaison
Mr. Michael E. Magill
Department of Labor and Workforce
Development
710 James Robertson Pkwy.
Nashville, TN 37243-0655
615-253-1324
Fax: 615-253-1329
Email: mmagill@mail.state.tn.us

State Workforce Development
Ms. Maria Persulas Draper
Tennessee Department of Labor and
Workforce Development
710 James Robertson Pkwy., 4th Floor
Nashville, TN 37243-0658
615-741-1031
Fax: 615-741-3003
Email: mdraper2@mail.state.tn.us

LWIA 01
(counties) Carter, Johnson, Sulivan, Unicoi,
Washington
Mr. J.B. Shepherd
Alliance for Business and Training, Inc.
386 Highway 91
P.O. Box 249
Elizabethton, TN 37644-0249
423-547-7500
Fax: 423-547-7522

Fayette and Shelby Counties; LWIA 14
Dr.. Elma Mardis
City of Memphis PIC
100 N. Main Bldg., Suite 2810
Memphis, TN 38103-5010
901-576-6536
Fax: 901-576-6297

Knox County LWIA 03
Mr. Vaughn Smith
Knoxvile/ Knox County WIB
P.O. Box 51650
2247 Western Ave.
Knoxville, Tn 37950-1650
865-544-5200
Fax: 865-544-5269
Email: vsmith@knxcac.org

LWIA 04
(counties) Anderson, Blount, Campbell,
Cumberland, Loudon, Moroe, Morgan,
Roane, Scott
Mr. Bobby Renfro
ETHRA Workforce Development
 1743 Harriman Highway
Harriman, TN 37748
865-590-1502
Fax: 865-590-1081
Email: Renfro@lwia4.org

LWIA 05
(counties) Bradley, McMinn, Meigs, Monroe,
Polk
Workforce Development Center
P.O. Box 3570
3750 Adkison Dr.
Cleveland, TN 37320-3570
423-478-6240
Fax: 423-478-6256
Email: jcate@clscc.cc.tn.us

LWIA 06
(counties) Bledsoe, Grundy, Hamilton, Marion, Rhea, Sequatchie
Mr. Wanza Lee
SE Tennessee WIB
535 Chestnut St., Suite 300
Chattanooga, TN 37402
423-757-5013
Fax: 423-757-5491

LWIA 07
(counties) Cannon, Clay, DeKalb, Fentress, Jackson, Macon, Overton, Pickett, Putnam, Smith, Van Buren, Warren, White
Mr. Pat Callahan
Upper Cumberland Human Resource Agency
3111 Enterprise Drive
Cookeville, TN 38506
931-528-1127
Fax: 931-526-8305
Email: jtpa@multipro.com

LWIA 08
(counties) Cheatham, Dickson, Houston, Humphreys, Montgomery, Robertson, Stewart, Sumner, Trousdale, Williamson, Wilson
Mr. Ross Jackson
North Tennessee WIB
P.O. Box 1125
110 Main St.
Clarksville, TN 37041
931-551-9110
Fax: 931-551-9026
Email: rjackson@workforceessentials.com

Davidson County: Lwia 09
Ms. Christine Bradley
Nashville Career Advancement Center
621 Mainstream Dr., Suite 210
Nashville, TN 37228-1210
615-862-8890
Fax: 615-862-8910
Email: jobs@nashville.org

LWIA 10
(counties) Bedford, Coffee, Franklin, Lincoln, Moore, Rutherford
Mr. Gary D. Morgan
Motlow State Community College
Job Training
412 Wilson Ave.
Tullahoma, TN 37388
931-455-9596
Fax: 931-455-9580
Email: gdmorgan@charter.net

LWIA 11
(counties) Benton, Carroll, Chester, Crockett, Decatur, Gibson, Hardeman, Hardin, Haywood, Henderson, Henry, McNairy, Madison, Weakley
Mr. Lafayette McKinnie
1314 Highway 45 North, Suite D
Henderson, TN 38340
731-989-0533
Fax: 731-983-3149
Email: lmckinnie@onemain.com

LWIA 11
(counties) Giles, Hickman, Lawrence, Lewis, Marshall, Maury, Perry, Wayne
Ms. Jan O. McKeal
8 Courthouse Square, 2nd Floor
Columbia, TN 38401
931-381-0068
Fax: 931-381-7643
Email: mckeel@coscc.cc.tn.us

LWIA 13
(counties) Dyer, Lake, Lauderdale, Obion, Tipton
Mr. Henry Lewis
Dyersburg State Community College
620B-1 Mall Boulevard
Dyersburg, TN 38024-1640
731-286-3585
Fax: 731-286-3584
Email: lewis@wfdlan.dscc.cc.tn.us

Texas
State Workforce Development Liaison
Ms. Barbara Cigainero
Texas Workforce Commission
101 East 15th Street, Room 504BT
Austin, TX 78778
512-463-2654
Fax: 512-463-2799
Email: Barbara.Cigainero@twc.state.tx.us

Alamo
(counties) Atascosa, Bandera, Bexar, Comal, Frio, Gillespie, Guadalupe, Karnes, Kendall, Kerr, Medina, Wilson
Mr. Dennis Blythe
Alamo Workforce Development, Inc.
115 E. Travis St., Suite 220
San Antonio, TX 78205
210-272-3250
Fax: 210-272-3290
Email: dennis.blythe@twc.state.tx.us

Alamo
Mr. Alan D. Miller
115 East Travis, Suite 220
San Antonio, TX 78205-1603
210-272-3250
Fax: 210-272-3290
Email: alan.miller@twc.state.tx.us

Brazos Valley
(counties) Brazos, Burleson, Grimes, Leon, Madison, Robertson, Washington
Mr. Tom Wilkinson
Brazos Valley Workforce Development Board
P.O. Drawer 4128
Bryan, TX 77805
979-775-4244
Fax: 979-775-3466
Email: twilkinson@bvcog.org

Cameron County
Ms. Stella Garcie
Cameron Works,Inc.
245 E. Levee
Brownsville, TX 78520
956-548-6719
Fax: 956-548-6704
Email: sgarcia@camwksinc.org

Capital Area
(county) Travis
Ms. Shirley Clowers
Capital Area Workforce Development Board
5930 Middle Fiskville Road, 5th Floor
Austin, TX 78752
512-223-7970
Fax: 512-454-6935
Email: shirley.clowers@twc.state.tx.us

Central Texas
(counties) Bell, Coryell, Hamilton, Lampasas, Milam, Mills, San Saba
Ms. Susan Kamas
Central Texas WIB
P.O. Box 450
Belton, TX 76513
254-939-3771
Fax: 254-939-3207
Email: susank@workforcelink.com

Coastal Bend
(counties) Aransas, Bee, Brooks, Duval, Jim Wells, Kenedy, Kleberg, Live Oak, McMullen, Nueces, Refugio, San Patrick
Mr. Alan Meriwether
Coastal Bend Workforce Development Board
4444 Corona, Suite 215
Corpus Christi, TX 78411
361-225-1098
Fax: 361-814-3450
Email: allen.meriwether@twc.state.tx.us

Concho Valley
(counties) Coke, Concho, Crockett, Irion, Kimble, Mcculloch, Mason, Menard, Reagan, Schleicher, Sterling, Sutton, Tom Green
Mr. Johnny Griffin
Concho Valley WDB
P.O. Box 2779
San Angelo, TX 79602-2779
915-655-2005
Fax: 915-482-8900
Email: johnny.griffin@twc.state.tx.ux

Dallas City & County
Ms. Laurie Bouillion Larrea
WorkSource for Dallas County
1201 Main Street, Suite 2700
Dallas, TX 75202
214-290-1000
Fax: 214-745-1110

Deep East Texas
(counties) Angelina, Houston, Jasper, Nacogdoches, Newton, Polk, Sabine, San Augustine, San Jacinto, Shelby, Trinity, Tyler
Ms. Charlene Meadows
Deep East Texas Workforce Development Board
1318 South John Redditt, Suite C
Lufkin, TX 75904
800-649-5241
Fax: 936-633-7491
Email: charlene.meadows@twc.state.tx.us

East Texas
(counties) Anderson, Camp, Cherokee, Gregg, Harrison, Henderson, Marion, Panola, Rains, Rusk, Smith, Upshur, Wood, Van Zandt
Mr. Wendell Holcombe
East Texas COG
Occupational Training Programs
3800 Stone Rd.
Kilgore, TX 75662-9604
903-984-8641
Fax: 903-983-1440
Email: wendell.holcombe@twc.state.tx.us

Golden Crescent
(counties) Calhoun, Dewitt, Goliad, Gonzales, Jackson, Lavaca, Victoria
Ms. Laura G. Sanders
Golden Crescent WDB
P.O. Box 77902
Victoria TX 77902
361-576-5872
Fax: 361-573-0225
Email: laura.sanders@twc.state.tx.us

Gulf Coast
(counties) Austin, Brazoria, Chambers,
Colorado, Fort Bend, Galveston, Liberty,
Matagorda, Montgomery, Walker, Waller,
Wharton; (city) Houston
Mr. Rodney Bradshaw
Houston-Galveston Area Council
3555 Timmons Lane, Suite 500
P.O. Box 22777
Houston, TX 77227-2777
713-627-3200
Fax: 713-993-4578
Email: rbradshaw@hgac.cog.tx.us

Heart of Texas
(counties) Bosque, Falls, Freestone, Hill,
Limestone, McLennan
Ms. Gaylen Lange
Heart of Texas Council of Governments
300 Franklin Ave.
Waco, TX 76701-2244
254-756-7822
Fax: 254-756-4065
Email: gaylen.lange@hot.cog.tx.us

Lower Rio Grande Valley
(counties) Hildago, Willacy
Mr. Carlos Herrera
Lower Rio Grande Valley Workforce
Development Board
3406 West Alberta
Edinburg, TX 78539
956-928-5000
Fax: 956-664-8987
Email: carlos.herrera@twc.state.tx.us

Middle Rio Grande
(counties) Dimmit, Edwards, Kinney, Lasalle,
Maverick, Real, Uvalde, Val Verde, Zavalla
Mr. Ricky McNiel
Middle Rio Grande Workforce Development
Board
P.O. Box 760
Uvalde, TX 78801
830-591-0141
Fax: 830-591-0004
Email: ricky.mcniel@twc.state.tx.us

North Central Texas
(counties) Collin, Denton, Ellis, Erath, Hood,
Hunt, Johnson, Kaufman, Nevarro, Palo
Pinto, Parker, Rockwell, Somervell, Wise
Ms. Linda K. Davis
North Central Texas Workforce Development
Board
c/o North Central Council of Governments
P.O. Box 5888
Arlington, TX 76005-5888
817-695-9176
Fax: 817-640-6480
Email: ldavis@dfwinfo.com

North Texas
(counties) Archer, Baylor, Clay, Cottle,
Foard, Hardeman, Jack, Montague, Wichita,
Wilbarger, Young
Mr. Mona Statser
North Texas Workforce Development Board
P.O. Box 4671
Wichita Falls, TX 76308-4671
940-767-1432
Fax: 940-322-2683
Email: mona.statser@twc.state.tx.us

Northeast Texas
(counties) Bowie, Cass, Delta, Franklin,
Hopkins, Lamar, Morris, Red River, Titus

Ms. Jeanie Callicott
Northeast Texas Workforce Development
Board
1902 West Ferguson
Mt. Pleasant, TX 75545
903-794-9490
Fax: 903-794-4884
Email: jeanie.callicott@twc.state.tx.us

Panhandle
(counties) Armstrong, Briscoe, Carson,
Castro, Childress, Collingsworth, Dallam,
Deaf Smith, Donley, Gray, Hall, Hansford,
Hartley, Hemphill, Hutchinson, Lipscomb,
Moore, Ochiltree, Oldham, Parmer, Potter,
Randall, Roberts, Sherman, Swisher, Wheeler
Mr. Tom Dressler
Panhandle Regional Planning Commission
415 West 8th St.
P.O. Box 9257
Amarillo, TX 79105-9257
806-372-3381
Fax: 806-373-3268
Email: tdressler@prpc.cog.tx.us

Permian Basin
(counties) Andrews, Borden, Crane, Dawson,
Ector, Gaines, Glasscock, Howard, Loving,
Martin, Midland, Pecos, Reeves, Terrell,
Upton, Ward, Winkler
Mr. Willie Taylor
Permian Basin WDB
P.O. Box 61947
Midland, TX 79711-1947
915-563-5239
Fax: 915-563-8785
Email: willie.taylor@twc.state.tx.us

Rural Capital
(counties) Bastrop, Blanco, Burnet, Caldwell,
Fayett, Hays, lee, Llano, Williamson
Mr. James Satterwhite
Rural Capital Area WDB
P.O. Box 5279
Round Rock, TX 78683-5279
512-244-7966
Fax: 512-244-9023
Email: james.satterwhite@twc.state.tx.us

South Plains
(counties) Bailey, Cochran, Crosby, Dickens,
Floyd Hale, Garzea, Hockley, King, Lamb,
Lubbock, Lynn, Motley, Terry, Yoakum
Ms. Mary Ann Rojas
South Plaines Workforce Development Board
1301 Broadway, Suite 201
Lubbock, TX 79401
806-744-1987
Fax: 806-744-5378
Email: maryann.rojas@twc.state.tx.us

South Texas
(counties) Jim Hogg, Starr, Webb, Zapata
Mr. Eduardo Guerra
South Texas WDB
P.O. Box 1757
Laredo, TX 78044-1757
956-722-3973
Fax: 956-725-2341
Email: eguerra@netscorp.net

Southeast Texas
(counties) Hardin, Jefferson, Orange
Ms. Linda Brown-Turk
Southeast Texas Workforce Development
Board

P.O. Drawer 1387
Nederland, TX 77627-1387
409-727-2384
Fax: 409-727-6431
Email: linda.turk@twc.state.tx.us

Tarrant County
Ms. Judy McDonald
Tarrant County Workforce Development
Board
2601 Scott Ave., Suite 400
Fort Worth, TX 76103
817-531-6760
Fax: 817-531-6754
Email: judy.mcdonald@twc.state.tx.us

Texoma
(counties) Cooke, Fannin, Grayson
Texoma WDB
305 W. Woodard, Suite 217
Denison, TX 75020-8399
903-465-7408
Fax: 903-465-1745
Email: janie.bates@twc.state.tx.us

Upper Rio Grande
(counties) Brewster, Culberson, El Paso,
Hudspeth, Jef Davis, Presidio
Mr. Martin Aguirre
Upper Rio Grande Workforce Development
Board
221 North Kansas, Suite 1000
El Paso, TX 79901-1441
915-772-2002
Fax: 915-351-2790
Email: martin.aguirre@urgwdb.org

West Central Texas
(counties) Brown, Callahan, Coleman,
Comanche, Eastland, Fisher, Haskell, Jones,
Kent, Knox, Mitchell, Nolan, Runnels, Scurry,
Shackelford, Stephens, Stonewall, Taylor,
Throckmorton
Ms. Mary Ross
West Central Texas WDB
400 Oak Street
Abilene, TX 79602
915-795-4200
Fax: 915-795-4382
Email: mross@camalott.com

Utah
State Workforce Development
Mr. Robert Gross
Utah Department of Workforce Services
140 East 300 South
P.O. Box 143001
Salt Lake City, UT 84111-3001
801-526-9210
Fax: 801-526-9211
Email: wsadmpo.rgross@state.ut.us

Central Region
Mr. Brad Maughan
Utah Department of Workforce Services
Central Region
1385 South State Street
Salt Lake City, UT 84115
801-468-0280
Fax: 801-468-0211
Email: bmaug@ws.state.ut.us

Eastern Region
Ms. Judy Chambley
Utah Department of Workforce Services
Eastern Region
1680 West Highway 40, Suite 203B

Vernal, UT 84078
435-789-7597
Fax: 435-789-7525
Email: JCHAMBL@ws.state.ut.us

Mountainland Region
Ms. Melissa K. Finch
Utah Department of Workforce Services
Montainland Region
150 East Center, Suite 3200
Provo, UT 84006
801-374-7876
Fax: 801-374-7717
Email: prmain.mfinch@state.ut.us

North Region
Mr. Harold B. Hess
Utah Department of Workforce Services
Northern Region
2540 Washington Boulevard, 7th Floor
Ogden, UT 84401
801-626-3444
Fax: 801-626-5720
Email: hhess@ws.state.ut.us

Western Region
Ms. Jan Thompson
Utah Department of Workforce Services
Western Region
168 North 100 East
St. George, UT 84770
435-674-3815
Fax: 435-674-4310
Email: jthomps@ws.state.ut.us

Vermont

State Workforce Development Liaison
Mr. Steven Gold
Vermont Department of Employment and
Training
P.O. Box 488
Five Green Mountain Dr.
Montpelier, VT 05601
802-828-4000
Fax: 802-828-4181
Email: sgold@pop.det.state.vt.us

Single State Workforce Area
Mr. Bill Cormany
Vermont Department of Employment and
Training
5 Green Mountain Drive
P.O. Box 488
Montpelier, VT 05601-0488
802-828-4301
Fax: 802-828-4355
Email: bcormany@det.state.vt.us

Virgin Islands

WIA Director
Ms. Loretta Petersen
Virgin Island Department of Labor
2203 Church Street
Christiansted, St. Croix, VI 00820-4612
340-773-1994
Fax: 340-773-0094

Virginia

State Workforce Development
Dr. Thomas J. Touberman
Virginia Employment Commission
703 East Main Street
Richmond, VA 23219
804-786-3001
Fax: 804-225-3923
Email: vec@vaworkforce.com

Arlington/Alexandria #6
(county) Arlington (city) Alexandria
Ms. Carla Leap
Arlington Employment Center
3033 Wilson Boulevard, Suite 400 B
Arlington, VA 22201
703-228-1400
Fax: 703-228-1044
Email: cleap@co.arlington.va.us

Bay Consortium
*(counties) Accomack, Caroline, Essex, King
and Queen, King George, King William,
Lancaster, Mathews, Middlesex,
Northampton, Northumberland, Richmond,
Spotsylvania, Stafford, Westmoreland; (city)
Fredericksburg*
Mr. Michael Jenkins
Bay Consortium
P.O. Box 1117
Warsaw, VA 22572
804-333-4048
Fax: 804-333-6378
Email: mjenkins@crosslink.net

Capital Area WIB
*(counties) Charles City, Chesterfield,
Goochland, Hanover, Henrico, New Kent,
Powhatan*
Ms. Rosalyn Key
Capital Area WIB
5410 Williamsburg Rd.
Sandston, VA 23150-1222
804-226-1941
Fax: 804-236-0503
Email: key@co.henrico.va.us
Fax: 703-981-2773

Crater Area
Ms. Helen Leonard
114 North Union Street
Petersburg, VA 23803
804-732-7053
Fax: 804-732-6668
Email: crater@techcomm.net

Greater Peninsula
*(counties) Gloucester, James City, York;
(cities) Hampton, Newport News, Poquoson,
Williamsburg*
Mr. William Mann
Greater Peninsula PIC
P.O. Box 7489
Hampton, VA 23666
804-838-5206
Fax: 804-838-4809
Email: wmann@ci.netport-news.va.us

Hampton Roads
*(counties) Isle of Wright, Southampton (cities)
Chesapeake, Franklin, Norfolk, Portsmouth,
Suffolk, Virginia Beach*
Mr. Roy Budd
Opportunity Inc. of Hampton Roads
420 Bank Street
Norfolk, VA 23510
757-664-2523
Fax: 757-622-5563
Email: rbudd@hrccva.com

New River/ Mount Rogers
*(counties) Bland, Carroll, Floyd, Giles,
Grayson, Montgomery, Pulaski, Smyth,
Washington, Wythe; (cities) Bristol, Galax,
Radford*
Mr. Ronnie E. Martin
New River/Mount Rogers PIC
6580 Valley Center Drive

Box 23
Radford, VA 24141
540-633-6764
Fax: 540-633-2502
Email: rmartin@nrvdc.org

Northern Virginia
*(counties) Fairfax, Loudoun, Prince William;
(cities) Fairfax, Falls Church, Manassas,
Manassas Park*
Mr. Juani Diaz
Fairfax County Department of Family
Services
12011 Government Center Pkwy., Suite 500
Fairfax, VA 22035-1102
703-324-7749
Fax: 703-222-7332
Email: jdiazr@co.fairfax.va.us

Workforce Today
*(counties) Albemarle, Culpeper, Fauquier,
Fluvanna, Greene, Louisa, Madison, Nelson,
Orange, Rappahannock; (city) Charlottesville*
Ms. Nancy O'Brien
Workforce Today
P.O. Box 1505
Charlottesville, VA 22902
434-979-7310
Fax: 434-979-1597
Email: nobrien.tjpd@state.va.us

Northern Shenandoah Valley
*(counties) Frederick, Clarke, Shenandoah,
Warren (city) Winchester*
Mr. Thomas Carter
Northern Shenandoah Valley
P.O. Box 825
Winchester, VA 22604
540-678-1909
Fax: 540-678-1939
Email: thomascarter@springgap.com

Richmond City
Mr. Surnease Drew
201 West Broad Street
Richmond, VA 23220
804-780-4146
Fax: 804-780-4177

Southwestern Virginia
*(counties) Buchanan, Dickenson, Lee, Russell,
Scott, Tazewell, Wise; (city) Norton*
Mr. Ron Ratliff
Southwestern Virginia Workforce Investment
Board
P.O. Box 2439
Lebanon, VA 24266
276-883-4034
Fax: 276-883-4036
Email: director@wiaone.com

Shenandoah Valley
*(counties) Augusta, Bath, Highland, Page,
Rockbridge, Rockingham,(cities) Buena Vista,
Harrisonburg, Lexington, Staunton,
Waynesboro*
Mr. Bob Satterwhite
Shenandoah Valley WIB
P.O. Box 869
Harrisonburg, VA 22803
540-442-7134
Fax: 540-434-0803
Email: spic@cfw.com

South Central; SDA 9
*(counties) Amelia, Brunswick, Buckingham,
Charlotte, Cumberland, Dinwiddie,
Greensvile, Halifax, Lunenburg,
Mecklenburg, Nottoway, Prince Edward,*

Prince George, Surry, Sussex; (cities)
Colonial Heights, Emporia, Hopewell,
Petersburg, South Boston, Farmville
Ms. Betty Lou Weaver
South Central Private Industry Council
Drawer S
Farmville, VA 23901-0290
434-392-2300
Fax: 434-392-3808
Email: south@farmvilleez.net

West Piedmont
Ms. Becky Aydlett
West Piedmont Workforce Investment Area
P.O. Box 1112
Martinsville, VA 24112
276-656-5338
Fax: 276-656-1386
Email: baydlett@ci.martinsville.va.us

Western Virginia
(counties) Alleghany, Botetourt, Craig,
Franklin, Roanoke (cities) Clifton, Forge,
Covington, Roanoke, Salem
Ms. Jeannine Blackburn
Fifth District Employment and Training
Consortium
108 North Jefferson Street, Suite 312
Roanoke, VA 24016
540-767-6145
Email: staff@fdetc.org

Washington
State Workforce Development Liaison
Mr. Garry Gallwas
Employment Security Department
P.O. Box 9046
Olympia, WA 98507-9046
360-438-3132
Fax: 360-438-3174
Email: ggalwas@esd.wa.gov

Benton/Franklin
Ms. Michelle M. Mann
Benton/Franklin Workforce Development
Council
815 North Kellogg Street, Suite C
Kennewick, WA 99336
509-734-5980
Fax: 509-734-5999
Email: mmann@bf-wdc.org

Eastern Washington Workforce #10
(counties) Asotin, Columbia, Ferry, Garfield,
Lincoln, Pend Oreille, Stevens, Walla Walls,
Whitman
Mr. Tom O'Brien
Eastern Washington Partnership Workforce
Development Council
320 North Main
Colville, WA 99114
509-684-8421
Fax: 509-684-4740
Email: tobrien@ruralresources.org

Northwest Washington # 3
(counties) Island, San Juan, Skagit, Whatcom
Ms. Gay Dubigk
Northwest Washington Workforce
Development Council
P.O. Box 2009
Bellingham, WA 98227
360-671-1660
Fax: 360-671-4948
Email: gdubigk@nwpic.bellingham.wa.us

Olympic Consortium
(counties) Clallam, Kitsap, Jefferson
Mr. Bert Furuta
Kitsap Personnel and Human Resources
614 Division St., MS 23
Port Orchard, WA 98366
360-377-7185
Fax: 360-377-7187

Snohomish County
Ms. June Sekera
Workforce Development Council of
Snohomish County
917 134th St., SW, B-3
Everett, WA 98204
425-921-3491
Fax: 425-921-3484
Email: jsekera@snocowdc.org

Southwest Washington
(counties) Clark, Cowlitz, Skamania,
Wahkiakum
Ms. Beth Taylor
Southwest Washington Workforce
Development Council
111 West 39th Street
Vancouver, WA 98660-1955
360-699-3071
Fax; 360-696-8999
Email: beth@wdcsw.org

Spokane City and County
Mr. Larry Lengyel
Spokane Workforce Development Council
West 808 Spokane Falls Blvd.
Room 606
Spokane, WA 99201
509-625-6210
Fax: 509-625-6929
Email: llengyel@wdcspokane.com

The Pacific Mountain Consortium
(counties) Grays Harbor, Lewis, Mason,
Pacific, Thurston
Mr. Michael Kennedy
Thurston County Workforce Development
Council
719 Slater Kinney Rd. SE, Suite 200
360-754-4113
Fax: 360-754-4119
Email: kennedm@co.thurston.wa.us

The Pentad
(counties) Adams, Chelan, Douglas, Grant,
Okanoghan
Mr. Dave Petersen
North Central Washington/Columbia Basin
Workforce Development Council
P.O. Box 2360
234 N. Mission Ave.
Wenatchee, WA 98807
509-663-3091
Fax: 509-663-5649
Email: dave@picw.com

The Seattle/ King County
(county) King; (city) Seattle
Ms. Kris Stadelman
The Seattle/ King County Workforce
Development Council
2003 Western Ave.
Seattle, WA 98121
206-448-0474
Fax: 206-448-0484

The Tacoma/ Pierce Consortium
(county) Pierce; (city) Tacoma
Mr. Colin Conant
Tacoma/ Pierce County Employment and
Training Consortium
3650 S. Cedar St.
Tacoma, WA 98409
253-591-5450
Fax: 253-594-7932
Email: cconant@pic.tacoma.wa.us

Tri-Valley Consortium
(counties) Kittitas, Klickitat, Yakima
Mr. Patrick Baldoz
Tri-County Workforce Development Council
120 South 3rd Street, Suite 200-A
Yakima, WA 98901-2868
509-574-1950
Fax: 509-574-1951
Email: PatrickB@co.yakima.wa.us

West Virginia
State Workforce Development Liaison
(counties) Barbour, Berkeley, Boone, Braxton,
Brooke, Cabell, Calhoun, Clay, Doddridge,
Fayette, Gilmer, Grant, Greenbrier,
Hampshire, Hancock, Hardy, Harrison,
Jackson, Jefferson, Lewis, Lincoln, Logan,
Mcdowell, Marion, Marshall, Mason, Mercer,
Mineral, Mingo, Monongalia, Monroe,
Morgan, Nicholas, Ohio, Pendleton,
Pleasants, Pocahontas, Preston, Putnam,
Raleigh, Randolph, Ritchie, Roane, Summers,
Taylor, Tucker, Tyler, Upshur, Wayne,
Webster, Wetzel, Wirt, Wood, Wyoming
Mr. Robert J. Smith
Bureau of Employment Programs
112 California Ave.
Charleston, WV 25305-0112
304-558-2630
Fax: 304-558-1136

Region 1
(counties) Fayette, Greenbrier, McDowell,
Mercer, Monroe, Nicholas, Pocahontas,
Raleigh, Summers, Webster, Wyoming
Mr. Bill Loope
Region 1 Workforce Investment Board
210 Gray Flats Road
Beckley, WV 25801
304-253-3611
Fax; 304-253-0176
Email: wloope@wvdsl.net

Region 2
(counties) Boone, Cabell, Lincoln, Logan,
Mongo, Putnam, Wayne
Mr. Gary Pommerenck
South Western West Virginia Region 2
Workforce Investment Board
720 Fourth Avenue
Huntington, WV 25701
304-523-4800
Fax: 304-523-3739
Email: wib2ed@ezwv.com

Region 3
Mr. Curtis Hardman
Kanawah County WIB
P.O. Box 3726
Charleston, WV 25337
304-344-5760
Fax: 304-344-5762
Email: Chardman@citynet.net

Region 4
(counties) Calhoun, Clay, Jackson, Mason, Pleasant, Ritchie, Roane, Wirt, Wood
Ms. Joyce Okes
Mid-Ohio Valley Regional Workforce
Investment Board
P.O. Box 247
531 Market Street
Parkersburg, WV 26101
304-424-7271
Fax: 304-424-6196
Email: Joyce.Okes@mourc.org

Region 5
(counties) Brooke, Hancock, Marshall, Ohio, Tyler, Wetzel
Ms. Rosemary Guida
Northern Panhandle Workforce Investment
Board
109 Mount Wood Road
Wheeling, WV 26003-2632
304-231-1170
Fax: 304-231-1172
Email: npwib@yahoo.com

Region 6
(counties) Barbour, Braxton, Doddridge, Gilmer, Harrison, Lewis, Marion, Monongailia, Preston, Randolph, Taylor, Tucker, Upshur
Mr. Jeff Smith
Fairmont WORK4WV Center
P.O. Box 1468
Fairmont, WV 26554
304-363-5550
Fax; 304-368-9532
Email: st1400@stmail.wvnet.edu

Region 7
(counties) Berkeley, Grant, Hampshire, Hardy, Jefferson, Mineral, Morgan, Pendelton
Mr. Don Thorne
Region 8 Planning and Development Council
Grant County Industrial Park
P.O. Box 849
Petersburg, WV 26847
304-257-2448
Fax: 304-257-2292
Email: dont7@hotmail.com

Wisconsin
State Workforce Development Liaison
Mr. Ronald Hunt
Department of Workforce Development
201 East Washington Avenue, Room 231X
Madison, WI 53702
608-266-2687
Fax: 608-267-2392
Email: huntro@dwd.state.wi.us

Bay Area: WDA #5
(counties) Brown, Door, Florence, Kewaunee, Manitowoc, Marienette, Menominee, Oconto, Shawano, Sheboygan
Mr. James Golembeski
Bay Area PIC
3019 Holmgren Way, Suite 201
Green Bay, WI 54304
920-339-4202

Fax: 920-339-4201
Email: golemjim@new.rr.com

Fox Valley: WDA #4
(counties) Calumet, Fond du Lac, Green lake, Outagamie, Waupaca, Waushara, Winnebago
Ms. Cheryl Welch
Fox Valley Workforce Development Board, Inc.
996 South Green Bay Road
Neenah, WI 54956
920-720-5600
Fax: 920-720-5606
Email: cwelch@athenet.net

Milwaukee County; WDA #2
Mr. Gerald Randall
Workforce Development Board of Milwaukee
County
101 W. Pleasant St., Suite 201
Milwaukee, WI 53212
414-225-2360
Fax: 414-225-2375
Email: grandall@milwjobs.com

North Central Wisconsin: WDA #6
(counties) Adams, Forest, Langlade, Lincoln, Marathon, Oneida, Portage, Vilas, Wood
Mr. Dough Wellumson
North Central Wisconsin Workforce
Development Board, Inc.
2800 9th Street South
Wisconsin Rapids, WI 54494
715-422-4700
Fax: 715-422-4715
Email: dwellums@wctc.net

Northwest Wisconsin; WDA #7
(counties) Ashland, Bayfield, Burnett, Douglas, Iron, Price, Rusk, Sawyer, Taylor, Washburn
Mr. Fred Schnook
Northwest Wisconsin CEP, Inc.
100 W. Main St.
P.O. Box 616
Ashland, WI 54806
715-682-9141
Fax: 715-682-9181
Email: fschnook@nwcep.org

South Central Wisconsin: WDA#10
(counties) Columbia, Dane, Dodge, Jefferson, Marquette, Sauk
Mr. Dale Hopkins
Workforce Development Board of South
Central Wisconsin, Inc.
1819 Abery Avenue, Room 16
Madison, WI 53704-4201
608-249-9001
Fax: 608-249-9356
Email: dhopkins@execpc.com

Southeastern Wisconsin; WDA #1
(counties) Kenosha, Racine, Walworth
Ms. Cheryl Zimmerman
Southeastern WI Workforce Development
Board
Racine County Workforce Development
Center
1717 Taylor Ave.
Racine, WI 53404-2497

262-638-6622
Fax: 262-638-6970
Email: czimm@racineco.com

Southwestern Wisconsin; WDA #11
(counties) Grant, Green, Iowa, Lafayette, Richland, Rock
Ms. Roberta Early
Southwestern Wisconsin WDB, Inc.
319 Elaines Court
Dodgeville, WI 53533
608-935-3116
Fax: 608-935-5072
Email: r.early@jobcenter.org

West Central Wisconson; WDA #8
(counties) Barron, Chippewa, Clark, Dunn, Eau, Claire, Pepin, Pierce, Polk, St. Croix
Mr. Richard Best
West Central Wisconsin WDB
401 Technology Dr. E, Suite 100
Menomonie, WI 54751
715-232-1412
Fax: 715-232-2240
Email: bestd@workforceresource.org

Western Wisconsin; WDA #9
(counties) Buffalo, Crawford, Jackson, Juneau, Lacrosse, Monroe, Trempealeau, Vernon
Mr. Jerry Hanoski
Western Wisconsin PIC & WDB
402 N. 8th St., Third Floor
P.O. Box 2908
La Crosse, WI 54602-2908
608-789-5620
Fax: 608-785-9939
Email: hanoskij@western.tec.wi.us

WOW; WDA #3
(counties) Waukesha, Ozaukee, Washington
Mr. Francisco Sanchez
WOW WDB, Inc.
892 Main St., Suite A
Pewaukee, WI 53072
262-695-7880
Fax: 262-695-7890
Email: fsanchez@waukesha.tec.wi.us

Wyoming
Workforce Development Liaison
Ms. Beth Nelson
Employment Resources Division
Department of Employment
122 W. 25th St.
Casper, WY 82002
307-235-3254
Fax: 307-235-3278
Email: bnelso@state.wy.us

Single State Workforce Area
Wyoming Department of Employment
Employment Resources Division
100 W. Midwest
P.O. Box 2760
Casper, WY 82602
307-235-3242
Fax: 307-235-3293
Email: ccorli@state.wy.us

Free Job Training and Education
For Kids and High School Dropouts

Program: Job Corps

Description: Just because you dropped out of high school or barely made it through doesn't mean you'll have to survive on a bare-bones income digging ditches, flipping burgers or pumping gas for the rest of your life. Uncle Sam never even went to school. But he pays almost $800 million each year on the Job Corps program to help people like you learn skills that can later translate into better paying jobs and a rosy future.

What You Can Get: The Job Corps is a free job training and basic education program for high school dropouts and disadvantaged youth. Once accepted, students usually live at one of 108 program centers across the country. They live in dorms — just like college — and have their room, meals, and medical expenses paid for. It's a great deal! While there, participants become full time students and get the basic education they missed, along with job training in an area of their choice.

Each year over 40,000 kids participate in the Job Corps. About 66.5% of the students leaving the Job Corps find meaningful jobs, while another 16.4% go on to further their education or get additional training. Others join the military services. Job placement and other support services are provided to all students leaving the program.

Students in the program receive the following free services:

- basic education
- General Educational Development (GED)
- occupational exploration programs
- vocational skills training
- social skills training
- work experience programs
- counseling
- leadership training
- residential living programs, including meals, lodging, and clothing
- health care
- substance abuse programs
- incentive-based allowances

Currently, Job Corps conducts training and education at three types of facilities:

Civilian Conservation Centers
There are 30 residential centers located in national parks, forests, and wildlife refuges, and on other public lands owned and operated by the U.S. Departments of the Agriculture and Interior for the U.S. Department of Labor.

Contract Centers
There are 81 residential and nonresidential centers operated by major corporations and nonprofit organizations under contractual agreements with the U.S. Department of Labor, selected through open competition.

Matthew Lesko, Information USA, Inc., 12081 Nebel Street, Rockville, MD 20852 • 1-800-955-7693 • www.lesko.com

Extension Programs

These programs offer advanced training and education at Job Corps centers, special training sites, and other locations such as community colleges under contract with unions and public and private institutions. Examples are advanced food service training operated by the National Maritime Union (NMU), advanced clerical training programs operated by the Transportation-Communication International Union, and Advanced Career Training programs operated by various community colleges in conjunction with nearby Job Corps centers.

Who Is Eligible: Job Corps enrolls young people who are between 16 and 24 years of age. In addition, applicants must:

-   Be economically disadvantaged
-   Be a high school dropout, or if graduated, in need of additional education or training to get a meaningful job
-   Be a U.S. citizen, national, legal resident, permanent resident alien, or lawfully admitted alien
-   Not be on probation or parole, unless court does not require personal supervision
-   Be living in an environment that is so disruptive that the prospects of participating in a non-residential program are impaired
-   Have signed consent from a parent or guardian, if under 18
-   Be free of serious medical or behavioral problems
-   Have the motivation and capability to succeed in Job Corps

The typical Job Corps student is an 18-year-old high school dropout who reads at the 7th grade level, comes from an economically disadvantaged family, belongs to a minority group, and has never held a full time job.

Depending on the trade they want to learn, students can enroll in any Job Corps Center with openings in their state and within their Job Corps region, of which there are ten throughout the country.

If the skill you would like to learn is not available in your region, you will need to petition with your region to transfer elsewhere.

Wages Or Costs: Job Corps students don't pay anything. Tuition, room, and meals are all free of charge. The government picks up the entire bill, which runs over $22,000 per year per student — that's comparable to what you might spend for a year at Harvard or Yale.

Students are also given a cash clothing allowance every six months for up to two years. And to cover personal expenses, they also receive a $40 per month living allowance to start, which can increase to as much as $100 per month if they stay in the program the entire two years. At some centers, free child care is provided for Job Corps student/parents.

Types of Jobs

Landscape Technician	Medical Assistant	Surgical Technician
Groundskeeper	Medical Laboratory Assistant	Ward Clerk
Horticultural Worker I	Medical Records Clerk	Accounting Clerk
Ornamental Horticulture	Medical Secretary	Bookkeeper
Dental Technician	Nurses Aide	Clerical, Occupations
Dispensing Optician	Nurse, Licensed Practical	Computer Operator
EKG Technician	Nurse, General Duty	Computer Programmer
Environmental Control	Program Aide	Computer Service Technician
Health Occupations	Radiological Technician	Computer Specialist
Home Health Aide	Respiratory Therapist	Computer Systems Configuration Technology

Data Entry
Legal Secretary
Microcomputer Graphics and Desktop
Publishing
Secretary
Stenographer
Teller
Terminal Operator
Ticket Agent
Train Clerk
Word Processing, Advanced
Construction
Bricklayer
Building and Apartment Maintenance
Cable TV Installer
Carpenter
Cement Mason
Construction Equipment Worker
Construction Estimator
Electrician
Electrician, Appliance
Floor Layer
Glazier
Janitor I
Painter
Painter, Auto
Pipefitter, Marine

Plasterer
Plumber
Solar Installer
Tilesetter
Barber
Cosmetologist
Nursery School Attendant
Teacher Aide
Drafter
Electronics Technician
Electrician, Tester
Interior Design
Surveyor Assistant
Auto Parts Clerk
Cashier Checker
Hotel Clerk
Sales Clerk Retail Trades
Salesperson, General
Stock Control Clerk
AC Refrigerator Mechanic
Auto Body Repair
Auto Diagnostic Technician
Auto Repair Technician
Construction Equipment Mechanic
Diesel Mechanic
Electronic Assembler

Front End Mechanic
Heavy Equipment Mechanic
Small Engine Mechanic
Station Installer
Commercial Artist
Furniture Upholsterer
Visual Arts
Lithographic Printer
Machinist
Painter, Sign
Offset Duplication Machine Operator
Peripheral Equipment Operator
Welder
Correctional Officer
Security Guard
Forester Aide
Ranger Training
Pointing, Corking and Cleaning
Deckhand
Heavy Equipment Operator
Industrial Truck Operator
Material Handler
Operating Engineer
Seamanship
Truck Driver, Light
Food Service
Meat Cutter

National Office

Office of Job Corps
U.S. Department of Labor
200 Constitution Ave., NW, Room N4510
Washington, DC 20210
202-219-8550
800-733-JOBS
www.jobcorps.org

Local Offices:

For more information, contact your Job Corps office listed below. This section provides a list of vocational courses offered at 109 Job Corps centers located in 43 States, the District of Columbia, and Puerto Rico. Each entry includes the following:

- Name of center
- Job Corps region
- Address
- Phone/Fax numbers
- Special features of program
- Job training

Job Corps Offices

Alabama

Gadsden Job Corps Center
Region 3
P.O. Box 286
600 Valley Street
Gadsden, AL 35902
256-547-6222
Fax: 256-547-9040
Email: gadsd@jcdc.jobcorps.org
Job Training: Facilities Maintenance, Health Occupations, Business Clerical, Culinary Arts, Electrician, Cement Mason, Carpenter

Montgomery Job Corps Center
Region 3
1145 Air Base Blvd.
Montgomery, AL 36108
334-262-8883
Fax: 334-265-2339
Email: mont@jcdc.jobcorps.org
Job Training: Building and Apartment Maintenance, Business Clerical, Electrician, Health Occupation, Painter, Carpentry, Heat and Air Conditioning, Legal Secretary, Medical Assistant

Alaska

Alaska Job Corps Center
Region 6
750 Cope Industrial Way
Palmer. AK 99645
907-746-8800
Fax: 907-746-8810
Email: alaska@jcdc.jobcorps.org
Job Training: Carpentry, Building and Apartment Maintenance, Painter, Clerical, Culinary Arts, Electrician, Welder, Brick Layer

Arizona

Phoenix Job Corps
Region 6
518 South Third Street
Phoenix, AZ 85004
602-254-5921
Fax: 602-340-1965
Email: phone@jcdc.jobcorps.org
Job Training: Off-center Programs, Business Clerical, Networking Systems, Health Occupations, Electronics Assembly, Building and Apt Maintenance, Bricklayer, Carpenter, Plasterer, Painter

Fred G Acosta Job Corps Center
Region 6
901 South Campbell Avenue
Tucson, AZ 85719-6596
520-792-3015
Fax: 520-628-1552
Email: accost@jcdc.jobcorps.org
Job Training: Business Clerical, Sale Cl Ret Tr., Auto Repair, Health Occupations, Home Health Aide, Building and Apartment Maintenance, Plumber, Electrician, Data Entry, Accounting, Nurse Assistant

Arkansas

Cass Job Corps Center
Region 4
21424 N. Hwy 23
Ozark, AR 72949
501-667-3989
Fax: 501-667-3689
Email: cass@jcdc.jobcorps.org
Job Training: Culinary Arts, Welder, Building and Apartment Maintenance, Cement Mason, Painter, Bricklayer, Carpenter, Operating Engineer

Little Rock Job Corps Center
Region 4
2020 Vance Street
Little Rock, AR 72206
501-376-4600
Fax: 501-376-6152
Email: little@jcdc.jobcorps.org
Job Training: Business Clerical, Culinary Arts, Act, Plumber, Building and Apartment Maintenance, Nurses Aide

Ouachita Job Corps Center
Region 4
570 Job Corps Road
Royal, AR 71968
501-767-2707
Fax: 501-767-2768
Email: ouach@jcdc.jobcorps,org
Job Training: Welder, Painter, Plasterer, Bricklayer, Carpenter, Cement Mason, Building and Apartment Maintenance

California

Inland Empire Job Corps Center
Region 6
P.O. Box 9550
3173 Kerry Street
San Bernardino, CA 92427
909-887-6305
Fax: 909-887-8635
Email: inlan@jcdc.jobcorps.org
Job Training: Business Clerical, Facilities Maintenance, Tilesetter, Landscape Tech Act., Culinary Arts, Electronics Assembly, Surveyor Assist I, Welder, Off-Center Programs

Long Beach Job Corps
Region 6
1903 Santa Fe Ave
Long Beach, CA 90810-4050
562-983-1777
Fax: 562-983-0053
Email: longb@jcdc.jobcorps.org
Job Training: Telecommunication, Automotive, Health Occupations, Building and Apartment Maintenance, Landscaping, Hotel/Hospitality, Business Clerical, Culinary Arts, Glazier, Painting

Los Angeles Job Corp Center
Region 6
1031 Hill Street
Los Angeles, CA 90015
213-748-0135
Fax: 213-741-5359
Email: losan@jcdc.jobcorps.org
Job Training: Lic Practical Nurse, Business Clerical, Culinary Arts, Lithographic Printing, Electronics Tech, Computer Support Spec., Radiology Cl. Tech., Accounting, Data Entry, Heat and AC., Medical Assistant, Building and Apartment Maintenance, Administrative Clerical, Welding, Auto Repair Tech., Machinist, Health Occupations, Auto Body Repair, Child Care Worker, Drafter, Electrician

Sacramento Job Corp Center
Region 6
3100 Meadowview Road
Sacramento, CA 95832-1498
916-394-0770
Fax: 916-394-0751
Email: sacra@jcdc.jobcorps.org
Job Training: Off-Center Programs, Business Clerical, Facilities Maintenance, Carpenter, Heavy Equipment Operator, Heavy Equipment Mechanic, Retail Sales, Culinary Arts, Data Entry, Health Occupations, Cement Mason, Plasterer, Security and Investigations, Landscape Tech.

San Diego Job Corps Center
Region 6
1325 Iris Avenue, Building 60
Imperial Beach, CA 91932
619-429-8500
Fax: 619-429-4909
Email: sandi@jcdc.jobcorps.org
Job Training: Business Clerical, Bookkeeper, Sales Cl Ret Tr., Culinary Arts, Nurse Aide, Landscape Tech., Auto Repair Tech., Child Care Worker, Facility Maintenance, Computer Repair, Act, Solar Installer, Tilesetter, Bricklayer, Carpenter, Cement Mason, Plasterer, Painter, Welder, Security Guard, Hotel/Motel Clerk

San Jose Job Corps Center
Region 6
3485 East Hills Drive
San Jose, CA 95127-2970
408-254-5627
Fax: 408-254-5663
Email: sanjo@jcdc.jobcorps.org
Job Training: Building and Apartment Maintenance, Culinary Arts, Electronics Tech., Drafter Assistant, Office Skills, Advanced Clerical, Auto Repair Tech., Offset Duplicating Machine Operator, Welder, Cabinetmaker, Computer Apps., Electronic Repair, Truck Mechanics, Machinist, Landscape Maintenance, Air Conditioning and Refrigeration, Bookkeeping/Accounting, Auto Body Repair, Dental Assistant, Carpenter, Electrical Maintenance, Word Processing, Computer Maintenance, Data Entry, Cement Mason, Medical Office

Treasure Island Job Corps Center
Region 6
655 H Avenue, Building 42
Treasure Island, CA 94130-5027

415-277-2400
Fax: 415-277-2438
Email: tisla@jcdc.jobcorps.org
Job Training: Advanced Culinary Arts, Plumbing, Cement Mason, Painting, Database Administrator, Basic Culinary Arts, Carpentry, Electrical Word Processing, Accounting

Colorado

Collbran Job Corps Center
Region 4
57608 Highway 330
Route 1 Box 12
Collbran, CO 81624-9702
970-487-3576
Fax: 970-487-3823
Email: collb@jcdc.jobcorps.org
Job Training: Cement Mason, Carpenter, Culinary Arts, Business Tech 101, Welder, Painter, Building and Apartment Maintenance

Connecticut

Connecticut Job Corps Center
Region 1
455 Wintergreen Avenue
New Haven, CT 06515
203-397-3775
Fax: 203-392-0299
Email: conne@jcdc.jobcorps.org
Job Training: Business Clerical, Hotel/Motel Clerk, Culinary Arts, Health Occupations, Plasterer, Bldg. and Apt. Maintenance, Carpenter, Electronics Assem., Painter

Delaware

Region 2
This state does not have a Job Corps Center. Contact the regional Office for more information.

District of Columbia

Potomac Job Corps Center
Region 2
No.1 D.C. Village Lane SW
Washington, DC 20032
202-574-5000
Fax: 202-574-9451
Email: potom@jcdc.jobcorps.org
Job Training: Business Clerical, Data Entry, Bookkeeper, Nurses Aide, Security Guard, Landscape Tech, Electrician, Train Clerk, Plumber, Bricklayer, Carpenter, Cement Mason, Plasterer, Painter

Florida

Gainesville Job Corps Center
Region 3
5301 NE 40th Terrace
Gainesville, FL 32609-1670
352-377-2555
Fax: 352-374-8257
Email: gaine@jcdc.jobcorps.org
Job Training: Business and Computer Services, Business Retail, Culinary Arts, Health Occupations, Pre-Law Enforcement, Auto Repair Tech., Plasterer, Tile Setter, Carpenter, Painter, Auto Body Repair, Building and Apartment Maintenance

Homestead Job Corps Center
Region 3
12350 Southwest 285 Street
Homestead, FL 33033
305-257-3916
Fax: 305-257-3920

Email: homes@jcdc.jobcorps.org
Job Training: Collision Repair Tech, Business Clerical, Health Occupation, Medical Records Tech., Bricklayer, Carpenter, Culinary Arts, Auto Repair, Computer Repair Tech, Medical Assistant, Heat and Air Conditioning Tech, Facilities Maintenance, Glazing

Jacksonville Job Corps Center
Region 3
205 West Third Street
Jacksonville, FL 32206
904-353-5904
Fax: 904-359-4747
Email: jacks@jcdc.jobcorps.org
Job Training: Business Clerical, Secretary, Culinary Arts, Auto Body Repair, Bricklayer, Electrician, Carpenter, Plumber

Miami Job Corps Center
Region 3
3050 NW 183rd Street
Carol City, FL 33056
305-626-7800
Fax: 305-626-7857
Email: miami@jcdc.jobcorps.org
Job Training: Business Clerical, Child Development, Food Service, Landscape Tech, Carpentry, Facilities Maintenance, Health Occupations, Hotel Clerk, Accounting Clerk, Painter

Georgia

Atlanta Job Corps Center
Region 3
239 West Lake Avenue NW
Atlanta, GA 30314
404-794-9512
Fax: 404-794-8426
Email: atlan@jcdc.jobcorps.org
Job Training: Business Clerical, Culinary Arts, Nurses Aides, Off-Center Programs, Data Entry, Building and Apartment Maintenance, Act

Brunswick Job Corps Center
Region 3
4401 Glynco Parkway
Brunswick, GA 31525
912-264-8843
Fax: 912-267-7192
Email: bruns@jcdc.jobcorps.org
Job Training: Business Clerical, Culinary Arts, Welder, Auto Body Repair, Home Health Aide, Landscape Tech., Tile Setter, Electrician, Painter, Carpenter, Plumber, Building and Apartment Maintenance

Turner Job Corps Center
Region 3
2000 Schilling Avenue
Albany, GA 31705
912-883-8500
Fax: 912-434-0383
Email: turne@jcdc.jobcorps.org
Job Training: Business Clerical, Sales Clerk Retail, Culinary Arts, Health Occupations, Medical Assistant, Security Guard, Offset Dup Machine Operator, Welder, Heavy Equipment Operator, Plasterer, Cement Mason, Building and Apartment Maintenance, Bricklayer, Carpenter, Electrician, Painter, Landscape Tech, Heavy Construction Mechanic

Hawaii

Hawaii Job Corps Center
Region 6
41-467 Hihimanu Street
Honolulu, HI 96795
808-259-6010
Fax: 808-259-7907
Email: hawai@jcdc.jobcorps.org
Job Training: Business Clerical, Off-Center Programs, Culinary Arts, Retail Sales, Auto Repair Tech, Building and Apartment Maintenance, Desktop Publishing, Word Processing, Horticulture

Idaho

Centennial Job Corps Center
Region 6
3201 Ridgecrest Dr.
Nampa, ID 83687
208-442-4500
Fax: 208-442-4506
Email: cente@jcdc.jobcorps.org
Job Training: Culinary Arts, Health Occupations, Carpentry, Building and Apartment Maintenance, Painting, Accounting Clerk, Business Clerical, Computer Services, Electrician, Plasterer, Welder

Illinois

Chicago Job Corps Center
Region 5
3348 South Kedzie Avenue
Chicago, IL 60623
773-847-9820
Fax: 773-847-9823
Email: chic@jcdc.jobcorps.org
Job Training: No information available

Golconda Job Corps Center
Region 5
Route 1, Box 104A
Golconda, IL 62938
618-285-6601
Fax: 618-285-3121
Email: golco@jcdc.jobcorps.org
Job Training: Building and Apartment Maintenance, Culinary Arts, Welder, Business Clerical, Urban Forestry, Electrician, Bricklayer, Carpenter, Painter

Joliet Job Corps Center
Region 5
Joliet, IL 60433
815-727-7677
Fax: 815-723-7052
Email: jolie@jcdc.jobcorps.org
Job Training: Building and Apartment Maintenance, Culinary Arts, Business Clerical, Health Occupations, Tile Setter, Painter, Auto Repair Tech, Act

Indiana

Atterbury Job Corps Center
Region 5
P.O. Box 187
1025A Hospital Road
Edinburg, IN 46124
812-526-5581
Fax: 812-526-9551
Email: atter@jcdc.jobcorps.org
Job Training: Business Clerical, Culinary Arts, Health Occupation, Tech, Building and Apartment Maintenance, Welder, Cement Mason, Legal Secretary, Landscape Tech, Heavy Equipment Mechanic, Carpenter, Bricklayer, Painter, Glazier, Retail Sales, Heavy Equipment Operator, Sign Painter, Computer Operator, Computer Repair, Electrician

IndyPendence Job Corps Center
Region 5
17 West Market Street, Suite 400
Indianapolis, IN 46204
317-684-2555
Fax: 317-684-7640
Email: indyp@jcdc.jobcorps.org
Job Training: Business Clerical, Retail Sales, Hotel Clerk, Off-Center Training

Iowa

Denison Job Corps Center
Region 5
P.O. Box 610
10 Opportunity Drive
Denison, IA 51442
712-263-4192
Fax: 712-263-6910
Email: denis@jcdc.jobcorps.org
Job Training: Business Clerical, Security Guard, Culinary Arts, Nurses Aide, Home Health Aide, LPN, Bricklayer, Carpenter, Painter, Welder, Building and Apartment Maintenance, Automotive

Kansas

Flint Hills Job Corps Center
Region 5
4620 Eureka Drive
Manhatten, KS 66503-8488
785-821-7000
Fax: 785-537-9517
Email: flint@jcdc.jobcorps.org
Job Training: Business Office Tech, Culinary Arts, Health Occupations, Cement Mason, Carpenter, Facility Maintenance, Tech.

Kentucky

Carl D. Perkins Job Corps Center
Region 2
363 Meadows Branch
Prestonsburg, KY 41653-1501
606-886-1037
Fax: 606-886-6048
Email: perki@jcdc.jobcorps.org
Job Training: Culinary Arts, Electrician, Carpenter, Act, Health Occupations, Retail Sales, Building and Apartment Maintenance, Bricklayer, Business Clerical, Mayo Vo-Tech School

Earle C. Clements Job Corps Center
Region 2
2302 US Highway 60 E
Morganfield, KY 42437
270-389-2419
Fax: 270-389-1134
Email: earle@jcdc.jobcorps.org
Job Training: Auto Body Repair, Bricklayer, Bldg. and Apt Maintenance, Carpenter, Medical Secretary, Plumber, Electrician, Culinary Arts, Medical Records, Health Occupations, Adv Auto Tech, Security Officer, Tile Setter, Auto Repair Tech, Retail Sales, Painter, Business Clerical, Cement Mason, Heat and Air Conditioning, Welder, Material Handler

Frenchburg Job Corps Center
Region 2
HCR-68- Box 2170
Highway 77
Mariba, KY 40322
606-768-2111
Fax: 606-768-3080
Email: frenc@jcdc.jobcorp.org
Job Training: Business Clerical, Culinary Arts, Auto Repair tech, Painter, Bricklayer, Carpenter, Cement Mason, Bldg and Apt Maintenance

Great Onyx Job Corps Center
Region 2
3115 Ollie Ridge Road
Mammoth Cave, KY 42259-9801
270-286-4515
Fax: 270-286-8824
Email: great@jcdc.jobcorps.org
Job Training: Business Clerical, Landscape Tech, Hotel/Motel Clerk, Welder, Bldg. and Apt Maintenance, Bricklayer, Carpenter, Painter

Muhlenberg Job Corps Center
Region 2
3875 State Rte., Hwy 181 North
Greenville, KY 42345
270-338-5460
Fax: 270-338-3615
Email: muhle@jcdc.jobcorps.org
Job Training: Culinary Arts, Bricklayer, Bldg. and Apt Maintenance, Business Clerical, Heavy Equipment Operator, Heavy Equipment Construction Mechanic, Auto Repair Tech

Pine Knot Job Corps Center
Region 2
US Hwy 27
Pine Knot, KY 42635
606-354-2176
Fax: 606-354-2170
Email: pknot@jcdc.jobcorps.org
Job Training: Culinary Arts, Bricklayer, Welder, Bldg. and Apt
Maintenance, Carpenter, Urban Forestry, Dispensing Optician, Auto Repair
Tech

Whitney Young Job Corps Center
Region 2
P.O. Box 307
8460 Shelbyville Road
Simpsonville, KY 40067
502-722-8862
Fax: 502-722-8719
Email: whitn@jcdc.jobcorps.org
Job Training: Secretary, Culinary Arts, Home Health Aide, Welder, Cement
Mason, Bricklayer, Carpenter, Bldg. and Apt Maintenance, Painting,
Accounting Clerk

Louisiana

New Orleans Job Corps Center
Region 4
3801 Hollygrove Street
New Orleans, LA 70118
504-486-0641
Fax: 504-486-0823
Email: newor@jcdc.jobcorps.org
Job Training: Cement Mason, Carpenter, Culinary Arts, Business Tech 101,
Welder, Painter, Building and Apartment Maintenance

Shreveport Job Corps Center
Region 4
2815 Lillian Street
Shreveport, LA 71109
318-227-9331
Fax: 318-222-0768
Email: shrev@jcdc.jobcorps.org
Job Training: Business Clerical, Carpentry, Culinary Arts, Nurses Aide,
Security Guard, Off-Center Programs, Cement Mason, Painter, Welder,
Building and Apartment Maintenance

Maine

Penobscot Job Corps Center
Region 1
1375 Union Street
Bangor, ME 04401
207-990-3000
Fax: 207-942-9828
Email: penob@jcdc.jobcorps.org
Job Training: Secretary, Business Clerical, Bookkeeper, Culinary Arts,
Carpenter, Multi-Media and Computer Graphics Designer, User Training &
Software Support Specialist, Bldg. and Apt Maintenance, welder, Nurses
Aide, Home Health Aide, web Page Designer

Loring Job Corps Center
Region 1
RR#1 Box 1727
Limestone, ME 04750
207-328-4212
Fax: 207-328-4219
Email: lorin@jcdc.jobcorps.org
Job Training: Business Clerical, Computer Repair Tech, Culinary Arts,
Gas/Diesel Mechanic, Painter, Business Accounting, Outdoor Rec-Act.,
Electrician, Cement Mason, Carpenter, Auto Body Repair, Outdoor Rec,
Nurses Aide

Maryland

Woodland Job Corps Center
Region 2
3300 Fort Mead Road
Laurel, MD 20724

301-725-7900
Fax: 301-497-8978
Email: woodl@jcdc.jobcorps.org
Job Training: Business Clerical, Data Entry, Bookkeeper, Culinary Arts,
Nurses Aide, Cement Mason, Bldg. and Apt Maintenance, Carpenter,
Painter, Plasterer

Woodstock Job Corps Center
Region 2
P.O. Box 300
10900 Old Court Road
Woodstock, MD 21133-0395
410-461-1100
Fax: 410-461-5794
Email: woods@jcdc.jobcorps.org
Job Training: Business Clerical, Bookkeeper, Culinary Arts, Nurses Aide,
Welder, Carpenter, Sales Clerk Retail, Bricklayer, Painter, Electrician,
Landscape Tech, Bldg. and Apt Maintenance

Massachusetts

Sargent Shriver Job Corps Center
(Formerly known as Fort Devons Job Corps Center)
Region 1
192 MacArthur Avenue
Devens, MA 01432
978-784-2610
Fax: 978-784-2721
Email: deven@jcdc.jobcorps.org
Job Training: Business Clerical, Computer Tech, Transportation
Communications Union, Sun Microsystems, Certified Nursing Assistant
(CAN), Food Services/Culinary Arts, Automotive, Cement Masonry (NTC),
Carpentry (NTC), Painting (NTC)

Grafton Job Corps Center
Region 1
P.O. Box 575
100 Pine Street
North Grafton, MA 01536
508-839-6904
Fax: 508-839-9781
Email: graft@jcdc.jobcorps.org
Job Training: Business Clerical, Culinary Arts, Nurses Aide, Facility Maint
I and II, Painter, Cement Mason, Electrician

Westover Job Corps Center
Region 1
103 Johnson Road
Chicopee, MA 01022
413-593-5731
Fax: 413-593-5170
Email: westo@jcdc.jobcorps.org
Job Training: Business Clerical, Hotel/Motel Clerk, Culinary Arts, Auto
Repair Tech, welder, Plumber, Glazier, Sign Painter, Accounting,
Electrician, Bricklayer, Carpenter, Painter, Landscape Tech, Retail Sales,
Telecommunications

Michigan

Detroit Job Corps Center
Region 5
10410 East Jefferson Avenue
Detroit, MI 48214
313-821-7000
Fax: 313-821-0004
Email: detro@jcdc.jobcorps.org
Job Training: Business Clerical, Health Occupation, Welder, Building and
Apartment Maintenance, Computer Operator

Grand Rapids Job Corps Center
Region 5
110 Hall Street SE
Grand Rapids, MI 49507
616-243-6877
Fax: 616-243-1701
Email: grand@jcdc.jobcorps.org

Job Training: Business Clerical, Culinary Arts, Health Occupation, Painter, Dispensing Optician, Building and Apartment Maintenance, Carpenter

Flint-Genesee Job Corps Center
Region 5
2400 North Saginaw Street
Flint, MI 48505
810-232-9102
Fax: 810-232-6835
Email: genes@jcdc.jobcorps.org
Job Training: Business Clerical, Accounting Clerk, Computer Support Specialist, Health Occupation, Dispensing Optician, Carpenter, Painter, Act.

Minnesota

Hubert Humphrey Job Corps Center
Region 5
1480 North Snelling Avenue
ST Paul, MN 55108
651-642-1133
Fax: 651-642-0123
Email: huber@jcdc.jobcorps.org
Job Training: Business Clerical, Culinary Arts, Health Occupation, Data Entry, Act., Customer Service, Train Clerk, Building and Apartment Maintenance, Painting and Wallpapering

Mississippi

Batesville Job Corps Center
Region 3
821 Highway 51 South
Batesville, MS 38606
662-563-4656
Fax: 662-563-0569
Email: bates@jcdc.jobcorps.org
Job Training: Business Clerical, Retail Sales, Culinary Arts, Health Occupations, Painter, Act, Auto Repair Tech, Welder, Carpenter, Lithograph Printer, Bricklayer

Gulfport Job Corps Center
Region 3
3300 20th Street
Gulfport, MS 39501
228-864-9691
Fax: 228-865-0154
Email: gulfp@jcdc.jobcorps.org
Job Training: Fiber Optics, Secretary, Data Entry, Home Health Aide, Welder, Act, Building and Apartment Maintenance, Plumber, Bricklayer, Carpenter, Electrician, Air Cond/Heating

Mississippi Job Corps Center
Region 3
P.O. Box 817
400 Harmony Road
Crystal Springs, MS 39059
601-892-3348
Fax: 601-892-3719
Email: missi@jcdc.jobcorps.org
Job Training: Bricklayer, Plumber, Building and Apartment Maintenance, Carpenter, Business Clerical, Act, Electrician, Welder, Culinary Arts, Sales Clerk Retail, Health occupations, Landscape Tech

Missouri

Excelsior Spring Job Corps Center
Region 5
701 St. Louis Avenue
Excelsior Springs, MO 64024
816-630-5501
Fax: 816-637-1806
Email: excel@jcdc.jobcorps.org
Job Training: Culinary Arts, Business Clerical, Health Occupation, Data Entry, Act., Customer Service, Train Clerk, Building and Apartment Maintenance, Painting and Wallpapering

Mingo Job Corps Center
Region 5
4253 State Highway T
Puxico, MO 63960-9585
573-222-3537
Fax: 573-222-2681
Email: mingo@jcdc.jobcorps.org
Job Training: Culinary Arts, Business Clerical, Nurses Aide, Auto Repair Tech., Bricklayer, Carpenter, Operating Engineer, Building and Apartment Maintenance

St. Louis Job Corps Center
Region 5
4333 Goodfellow Blvd.
St. Louis, MO 63120
314-679-6200
Fax: 314-383-5717
Email: stlou@jcdc.jobcorps.org
Job Training: Culinary Arts, Business Clerical, Data Entry, Nurses Aide, Security Guard, Welder, Act., Building and Apartment Maintenance, Carpenter, Cement Mason, Plasterer, Train Clerk, Painter, Bricklayer, Dispensing Optician

Montana

Anaconda Job Corps Center
Region 4
1407 Foster Creek Road
Anaconda, MT 59711
406-563-3476
Fax: 406-563-8243
Email: anaco@jcdc.jobcorps.org
Job Training: Welder, Business Clerical, Painter, Carpenter, Operating Engineer, Construction Equipment Mechanic, Bricklayer, Culinary Arts

Kicking Horse Job Corps Center
Region 4
2000 Mollman Pass Trail
Ronan, MT 59864
406-644-2217
Fax: 406-644-2343
Email: kicki@jcdc.jobcorps.org
Job Training: Business Clerical, Forester Aide, Diesel Mechanic, Medical Assistant, Dental Assistant, Building and Apartment Maintenance, Carpenter, Heavy Equipment Operator, Food Service Occupation

Trapper Creek Job Corps Center
Region 4
5139 West Fork Road
Darby, MT 59829-5139
406-821-3286
Fax: 406-821-3290
Email: trapp@jcdc.jobcorps.org
Job Training: Welder, Business Clerical, Culinary Arts, Painter, Carpenter, Electrician, Stock Clerk, Cement Mason, Building and Apartment Maintenance, Natural Resources

Nebraska

Pine Ridge Job Corps Center
Region 5
15710 Hwy. 385
Chadron, NE 69337
308-432-3316
Fax: 308-432-4145
Email: pridg@jcdc.jobcorps.org
Job Training: Union Construction Trades- Carpentry, Bricklaying, Painting, Plastering, Cement Masonry. Non Union Trades- Business Clerical, Health Occupation, Warehouse, Welding, Facility Maintenance

Nevada

Sierra Nevada Job Corps Center
Region 6
5005 East Echo Avenue
Reno, NV 89506

775-972-5627
Fax: 775-972-7480
Email: sierr@jcdc.jobcorps.org
Job Training: Medical Assistant, Health Occupations, Business Clerical, Culinary Arts, Security Guard, Carpenter, Cement Mason, Auto Repair Tech, Facility Maintenance, Plumber, Plasterer, Painter, Welder

New Hampshire
Region 1
This state does not have a Job Corps Center. Contact the Regional Office for more information

New Jersey
Edison Job Corps Center
Region 1
500 Plainfield Avenue
Edison, NJ 08817-2587
732-985-4800
Fax: 732-985-8551
Email: ediso@jcdc.jobcorps.org
Job Training: Carpenter, Bricklayer, Tile Setter, Auto Repair Tech, Painter, Office Tech, Health Occupations, LPN, College, Electrician, Security Guard, Facilities Maintenance, Plumber, Accounting, Culinary Arts, Transmission Repair, Microsoft/A plus Certification

New Mexico
Albuquerque Job Corps Center
Region 4
1500 Indian School Road
Albuquerque, NM 87104
505-346-2562
Fax: 505-346-2769
Email: albuq@jcdc.jobcorps.org
Job Training: Welder, Business Clerical, Data Entry, Nurses Aide, Medical Assistant, Painter, Carpenter, Electrician, Cement Mason, Building and Apartment Maintenance, Plumber, Plasterer

Roswell Job Corps Center
Region 4
P.O. Box 5970
57 G Street
Roswell, NM 88203
505-347-5414
Fax: 505-347-2243
Email: roswe@jcdc.jobcorps.org
Job Training: Welder, Business Clerical, Painter, Carpenter, Electrician, Stock Clerk, Cement Mason, Building and Apartment Maintenance, Natural Resources

New York
Cassadaga Job Corps Center
Region 1
8115 Glasgow Road
Cassadaga, NY 14718-9619
716-595-8760
Fax: 716-595-3963
Email: cassa@jcdc.jobcorps.org
Job Training: Advanced Business Clerical, Business Clerical, Culinary Arts, Painter, Off-Center Programs, Nurses Aide, Bldg. and Apt Maintenance, Plumber, Carpenter, Act

Delaware Valley Job Corps Center
Region 1
P.O. Box 846
9368 State Rt. 97
Callicoon, NY 12723-0846
845-887-5400
Fax: 845-887-4762
Email: delaw@jcdc.jobcorps.org
Job Training: Business Clerical, Health Occupations, Culinary Arts, Bldg. and Apt Maintenance, Painter, Retail Sales, Electrician, Auto Body Repair, Computer Repair Tech, Auto Repair Tech, Hotel/Motel Clerk, Security Guard

Glenmont Job Corps Center
Region 1
P.O. Box 993
822 River Road
Glenmont, NY
12077-0993
518-767-9371
Fax: 518-767-2106
Email: glenm@jcdc.jobcorps.org
Job Training: EKG Tech, Medical Assistant, Data Entry, Cosmetology, Bldg. and Apt Maintenance, Culinary Arts, Auto Body Repair, Auto Body Tech, Nurses Aide, Business Clerical, Act

Iroquois Job Corps Center
Region 1
11780 Tibbets Road
Medina, NY 14103
716-798-7000
Fax: 716-798-7046
Email: iroqu@jcdc.jobcorps.org
Job Training: Business Clerical, Bricklayer, Plasterer, Health Occupations Carpenter, Painter

Oneonta Job Corps Center
Region 1
Box 51 A, R.D. #4
21 Homer Folks Avenue
Oneonta, NY 13820
607-433-2111
Fax: 607-433-1629
Email: oneon@jcdc.JobCorps.org
Job Training: Business Clerical, Culinary Arts, Nurses Aides, Electrician, Welder, Act, Child care Worker, Tile Setter, Auto Repair Tech, Auto Body Repair, Cement Mason

South Bronx Job Corps Center
Region 1
1771 Andrews Avenue
Bronx, NY 10453-6803
718-731-7700
Fax: 718-731-3543
Email: south@jcdc.jobcorps.org
Job Training: Business Clerical, Bookkeeper, Ward Clerk, Culinary Arts, Nurses Aides, Bldg. and Apt Maintenance, Plumber, Carpenter, Retail Sales, Data Entry, Health Occupations, Cement Mason, Plasterer, Security and Investigations, Landscape Tech

Brooklyn Job Corps Center
585 DeKalb Avenue
Brooklyn, NY 11205
718-623-4000
Fax: 718-623-9626

North Carolina
Kittrell Job Corps Center
Region 3
P.O. Box 278
1096 US Hwy #1 South
Kittrell, NC 27544
252-438-6161
Fax: 252-492-9630
Email: kittr@jcdc.jobcorps.org
Job Training: Business Clerical, Sales Clerk Retail, Culinary Arts, Nurses Aide, Building and Apartment Maintenance, Bricklayer, Carpenter, Painter

Lyndon Johnson Job Corps Center
Region 3
3170 Wayah Road
Franklin, NC 28734
828-524-4446
Fax: 828-369-7338
Email: lbj@jcdc.jobcorps.org

Job training: Culinary Arts, Carpenter, Welder, Business Clerical, Bricklayer, painter, Building and Apartment Maintenance, Cement Mason,

Oconaluftee Job Corps Center
Region 3
502 Oconaluftee Job Corps Road
Cherokee, NC 28719
828-497-5411
Fax: 828-497-4417
Email: ocona@jcdc.jobcorps.org
Job Training: Business Clerical, Plasterer, Cement Mason, Carpenter, Painter, Health Occupation, Building and Apartment Maintenance

Schenck Job Corps Center
Region 3
98 Schenck Drive
P.O. Box 98
Pisgah Forest, NC 28768
828-862-6100
Fax: 828-877-3028
Email: schen@jcdc.jobcorps.org
Job Training: Culinary Arts, Auto Repair Tech, Welder, Painter, Health Occupations, Adv. Pre-Forestry, Building and Apartment Maintenance, Bricklayer, Carpenter, Landscape Tech, High School Program

North Dakota

Quentin Burdick JCC Job Corps Center
Region 4
1500 University Avenue West
Minot, ND 58703
701-857-9600
Fax: 701-838-9979
Email: quent@jcdc.jobcorps.org
Job Training: Auto Repair Tech, Auto Parts Clerk, Culinary Arts, Business Clerical, Facilities Maintenance, Welding, Retail Sales, Data Entry, Health Occupations, Carpenter, Medical Records Clerk

Ohio

Cincinnati Job Corps Center
Region 5
1409 Western Avenue
Cincinnati, OH 45214
513-651-2000
Fax: 513-651-2004
Email: cinci@jcdc.jobcorps.org
Job Training: Food Service, Business Clerical, Welder, Oct, Act, Carpenter, Auto Repair Tech, Facilities Maintenance

Cleveland Job Corps Center
Region 5
10660 Carnegie Avenue
Cleveland, OH 44106
216-795-8700
Fax: 216-721-9518
Email: cleve@jcdc.jobcorps.org
Job Training: Business Clerical, Dispensing Optician, Health Occupation, Act., Building and Apartment Maintenance, Painter, Floor Covering

Dayton Job Corps Center
Region 5
3849 Germantown Pike
Dayton, OH 45418
937-268-6571
Fax: 937-267-3822
Email: dayto@jcdc.jobcorps.org
Job Training: Business Clerical, Hotel/Motel Clerk, Culinary Arts, Building and Apartment Maintenance, Carpenter, Electronics, Assembler, Painter

Oklahoma

Guthrie Job Corps Center
Region 4
3106 West University
Guthrie, OK 73044

405-282-9930
Fax: 405-282-9501
Email: guthr@jcdc.jobcorps.org
Job Training: Welder, Building and Apartment Maintenance, Medical Office Specialist, Business Office Tech, Culinary Arts, Offset Dup Mac op, Act, Computer Operator, Security Guard, Health Occupation

Talking Leaves Job Corps Center
Region 4
P.O. Box 1066
5700 Bald Hill Road
Tahlequah, OK 74465
918-456-9959
Fax: 918-456-1270
Email: talki@jcdc.jobcorps.org
Job Training: Business Clerical, Electrical Wiring, Diesel Mechanic, Advanced Clerical, Culinary Arts, Building and Apartment Maintenance, Health Occupation

Treasure Lake Job Corps Center
Region 4
Route 1, Box 30
Indiahoma, OK 73552
580-246-3203
Fax: 580-246-8222
Email: tlake@jcdc.jobcorps.org
Job Training: Culinary Arts, Health Occupations, Cement Mason, Electrician, Painter, Plumbing, Plasterer

Tulsa Job Corps Center
Region 4
1133 North Lewis Avenue
Tulsa, OK 74110
918-585-9111
Fax: 918-592-2430
Email: Tulsa@jcdc.jobcorps.org
Job Training: Business Clerical, Nurses Aide, Barber, Electronics Assem, Cosmetology, Culinary Arts, Painter, Building and Apartment Maintenance, Carpenter, Security Guard

Oregon

Angell Job Corps Center
Region 6
335 N.E. Blodgett Road
Yachats, OR 97498
541-547-3137
541-547-4236
Email: angel@jcdc.jobcorps.org
Job Training: Business Clerical, Culinary Arts, Painter, Forester Aide, Auto Repair Tech, Welder, Bricklayer, Carpenter

Pivot Job Corps Center
Region 6
2508 NE Everett
Portland, OR 97232
503-916-6170
Fax: 503-916-2710
Email: pivot@jcdc.jobcorps.org
Job Training: Business Clerical

Springdale Job Corps Center
Region 6
31224 East Historic
Columbia River Highway
Troutdale, OR 97060
503-695-2245
Fax: 503-695-2254
Email: sprin@jcdc.jobcorps.org
Job Training: Business Clerical, Culinary Arts, Building and Apartment Maintenance, Auto Body Paint and Repair, Nurse Aide, Marketing

Timber Lake Job Corps Center
Region 6
59868 East Highway 224
Estacada, OR 97023

503-834-2291
Fax: 503-824-2333
Email: timbe@jcdc.jobcorps.org
Job Training: Culinary Arts, Forester Aide, Welder, Painter, Building and Apartment Maintenance, Carpenter, Plasterer

Tongue Point Job Corps Center
Region 6
37573 Old Highway 30
Astoria, OR 97103-7000
503-325-2131
Fax: 503-325-5375
Email: tongu@jcdc.jobcorps.org
Job Training: Facilities Maintenance, Landscape Tech, Culinary Arts, Medical Assist, Welder, Painter, Plasterer, Cement Mason, Carpenter, Business Clerical, Accounting Clerk, Dental Assistant, Nurse Aide, Lithograph Printer, Electrician, Seamanship, Glazier

Wolf Creek Job Corps Center
Region 6
2010 Opportunity Lane
Glide, OR 97443
541-496-3507
Fax: 541-496-8515
Email: wolfc@jcdc.jobcorps.org
Job Training: Culinary Arts, Forester Aide, Carpenter, Painter, Business Clerical, Welder, Plasterer, Cement Mason

Pennsylvania

Keystone Job Corps Center
Region 2
P.O. Box 37
Foothills Drive
Drums, PA 18222
570-788-1164
Fax: 570-788-1119
Email: keyst@jcdc.jobcorps.org
Job Training: Business Clerical, Culinary Arts, Medical Assistant, Floor Layer, Plasterer, Cement Mason, Bricklayer, Painter, Carpenter, Electrician, Nurses Aide, Security Guard, Material Handler, Plumber, Facilities Maintenance, Fencing, Hotel/Motel

Philadelphia Job Corps Center
Region 2
4601 Market Street
Philadelphia, PA 19139
215-471-9693
Fax: 215-747-8552
Email: phila@jcdc.jobcorps.org
Job Training: Business Clerical, Culinary Arts, Act/Oct, Hotel Clerk, Facilities Maintenance, Nurses Aide, Carpenter

Pittsburgh Job Corp Center
Region 2
7175 Highland Drive
Pittsburgh, PA 15206
412-441-8700
Fax: 412-441-1586
Email: pitts@jcdc.jobcorps.org
Job Training: Accounting Specialist, Admin. Office Prof., Court Reporter, Hotel/Restaurant Mgt., Health Info Tech, Business Mgt, Retail Merchandising, Medical Lab Asst., Medical Asst., Respiratory Therapy, Paralegal, Computer Operator, Social Work Tech, Mechanic, Drafting/Design, Child Development/Care, Human Services Infant, Youth and Adult Care, Transportation/Whse, Facilities Maintenance, Collision Repair, Nurses Aide, Business Office Tech, Culinary Arts, Diesel Mechanic, Heavy Equipment Operator, Physical Therapist, Dietetic Tech, Phlebotomist, Radiation Therapy Tech, Pharmacy Tech, Corrections Admin., Civil Engineer Tech, Arch Drafting /Design, Legal Office Prof, Early Childhood Ed, MH/MR Specialist

Red Rock Job Corps Center
Region 2
P.O. Box 218
Route 487 North

Lopez, PA 18628
570-477-2221
Fax: 570-477-3046
Email: redro@jcdc.jobcorps.org
Job Training: Business Clerical, Bookkeeper, Nurses Aide, Landscape Tech, Auto Repair Tech, Cosmetologist, Sales Clerk Retail, Bldg and Apt Maintenance, Painter, Electrician, Plumber, Bricklayer, Carpenter

Puerto Rico

Arecibo Job Corps Center
Region 1
P.O. Box 544
Garrochales, PR 00652-0544
877-881-2300
Fax: 877-881-0971
Email: areci@jcdc.jobcorps.org
Job Training: Nurse License Prac., Business Clerical, Electrician, Auto Body Repair, Bldg. and Apt Maintenance, Home Health Aide

Barranquitas Job Corps Center
Region 1
Bo. Quebradillas Carr.
152 K.M. 3.0
P.O. Box 68
Barranquitas, PR 00794
787-857-5200
Fax: 787-857-2262
Email: barra@jcdc.jobcorps.org
Job Training: Nurse License Pract., Business Clerical, Tapiceria, Ayudante de Electricdad, Albanileria, Mantenimiento de Edificios

Ramey Job Corps Center
Region 1
P.O. Box 250463
Aquadilla, PR 00604-0463
787-890-2030
Fax: 787-890-4749
Email: ramey@jcdc.jobcorps.org
Job Training: Business Clerical, Culinary Arts, Nurse License Pract, Cement Mason, Home Health Aide, Electrician, Front End Mechanic, Carpenter, Plumber

Rhode Island
Region 1
This state does not have a Job Corps Center. Contact the Regional Job Corps Office for more information.

South Carolina

Bamberg Job Corps Center
Region 3
P.O. Box 967
Bamberg, SC 29003
803-245-6302
Fax: 803-245-5915
Email: bambe@jcdc.jobcorps.org
Job Training: Business Clerical, Culinary Arts, Nurses Aide, Auto Body Repair, Welder, Cement Mason, Carpenter, Plumber, Building and Apartment Maintenance

South Dakota

Boxelder Job Corps Center
Region 4
P.O. Box 110
Nemo, SD 57759
605-348-3636
Fax: 605-578-1157
Email: boxel@jcdc.jobcorps.org
Job Training: Business Clerical, Health Occupation, Welder, Culinary Arts, Painter, Building and Apartment Maintenance, Carpenter, Bricklayer

Tennessee

Jacobs Creek Job Corps Center
Region 3
984 Denton Valley Road
Bristol, TN 37620-1430
423-878-4021
Fax: 423-878-7034
Email: jacob@jcdc.jobcorps.org
Job Training: Culinary Arts, Construction Equipment Mechanic, Welder, Painter, Security Guard, Bricklayer, Carpenter, Operating Engineer, Cement Mason, Optician Technician

Memphis Job Corps Center
Region 3
1555 McAlister Drive
Memphis, TN 38116
901-396-2800
Fax: 901-396-8712
Email: memph@jcdc.jobcorps.org
Job Training: Accounting Clerk, Computer SVC Tech, Material Handler, Medical Lab Tech, Carpenter, Electronic Tech. Medical Assistant, Medical Office Support

Texas

David L. Carrasco Job Corps Center
Region 4
11155 Gateway West
El Paso, TX 79935
915-594-0022
Fax: 915-591-0166
Email: david@jcdc.jobcorps.org
Job Training: Business Clerical, Rehabilitation Tech, Culinary Arts, Health Occupations, Act, Facilities Maintenance, Welder, Electronics Tester, Auto Repair Tech, Cosmetology

Gary Job Corps Center
Region 4
P.O. Box 967
2800 Airport Highway 21
San Marcos, TX 78667-0967
512-396-6652
Fax: 512-396-6666
Email: garycd@jcdc.jobcorps.org
Job Training: Business Clerical, Dental Assistant, Retail Sales, Building and Apartment Maintenance, Culinary Arts, Meat Cutting, Auto Repair Tech, Plumber, Health Occupations, Electrician, Material Handler, Lithograph Printer, Welder, Machinist, Carpenter, Accounting Clerk, Bricklayer

Laredo Job Corps Center
Region 4
P.O. Box 1819
1701 Island Street
Laredo, TX 78044-1819
956-727-5147
Fax: 956-727-1937
Email: lared@jcdc.jobcorps.org
Job Training: Business Clerical, Bookkeeping, Culinary Arts, Welder, Act, Carpenter, Electrician

North Texas Job Corps Center
Region 4
P.O. Box 8003
1701 North Church Street
McKinney, TX 75069
972-542-2623
Fax: 972-542-8870
Email: ntexa@jcdc.jobcorps.org
Job Training: Business Clerical, Culinary Arts, Act/Oct, Hotel Clerk, Facilities Maintenance, Nurses Aide, Carpenter

Utah

Clearfield Job Corps Center
Region 4
P.O. Box 160070

20 West 1700 South
Clearfield, UT 84016-0070
801-774-4000
Fax: 801-774-4135
Email: clear@jcdc.jobcorps.org
Job Training: Business Clerical, Welder, Facilities Maintenance, Offset Dup Mac Op., Auto Body Repair, Culinary Arts, Off-Center Programs, Plastering, Retail Sales, Tile Setter, Sign Painting, Plumbing, Carpentry, Computer Repair Tech, Electrician, Floor Covering, Health Occupations, Machinist, Landscape Tech., Desktop Publisher, Painter, Security Officer, Auto Repair tech., Diesel Mechanic, Auto Parts Clerk

Weber Basin Job Corps Center
Region 4
7400 South Cornia Drive
Ogden, UT 84405-9605
801-479-9806
Fax: 801-476-5985
Email: weber@jcdc.jobcorps.org
Job Training: Business Clerical, Welder, Health Occupations, Culinary Arts, Bricklayer, Carpenter, Building and Apartment Maintenance, Painter

Vermont

Northlands Job Corps Center
Region 1
100-A Macdonough Drive
Vergennes, VT 05491
802-877-0298
Fax: 802-877-2699
Email: north@jcdc.jobcorps.org
Job Training: Business Clerical, Bookkeeper, Culinary Arts, Nurses Aide, Bldg and Apt Maintenance, Welder, Auto Body Repair, Auto Repair Tech

Virginia

Blue Ridge Job Corps Center
Region 2
P.O. Box 425
245W Main Street
Marion, VA 24354
540-783-7221
Fax: 540-783-1751
Email: bluer@jcdc.jobcorps.org
Job Training: Accounting Clerk, Nurses Aide, Sales Clerk Retail, Business Clerical, Culinary Arts, Welder, Machinist, Diesel Mechanic, Bldg. and Apt Maintenance, Act

Flatwoods Job Corps Center
Region 2
2803 Dungannon Road
Coeburn, VA 24230
540-395-3384
Fax: 540-395-2043
Email: flatw@jcdc.jobcorps.org
Job Training: Welder, Painter, Plasterer, Cement Mason, Electrician, Plumber, Bricklayer, Carpenter

Old Dominion Job Corps Center
Region 2
1073 Father Judge Road
Monroe, VA 24574
434-929-4081
Fax: 434-929-0812
Email: olddo@jcdc.jobcorps.org
Job Training: Business Clerical, Medical Clerical, Marketing, Culinary Arts, Nurses Aide, Auto Repair Tech, Electrician, Landscape Tech, Facilities Maintenance, Plumber, Bricklayer, Carpenter, Painter

Washington

Cascades Job Corps Center
Region 6
P.O. Box 819
7782 Northern State Road
Sedro Woolley, WA 98284

360-854-3400
Fax: 360-854-3419
Email: casca@jcdc.jobcorps.org
Job Training: Dental Assistant, Business Clerical, Culinary Arts, Facilities Maintenance, Painter, Act,
Nursing Assistant, Carpenter, Cement Mason, Plasterer, Electrician, Medical Office Specialist

Columbia Basin Job Corps Center
Region 6
6739 24th Street
Building 2402
Moses Lake, WA 98837-2402
509-762-5581
509-762-9540
Email: colum@jcdc.jobcorps.org
Job Training: Dental Assistant, Building and Apartment Maintenance, Culinary Arts, Painter, Welder, Act, Nurses Aide, Business Clerical, Carpenter, Cement Mason, Plasterer

Curlew Job Corps Center
Region 6
3 Campus Street
Curlew, WA 99118
509-779-4611
Fax: 509-779-7680
Email: curle@jcdc.jobcorps.org
Job Training: Business Clerical, Culinary Arts, Forester Aide, Painter, Building and Apartment Maintenance, Bricklayer, Carpenter, Welder, Construction Worker

Fort Simcoe Job Corps Center
Region 6
40 Abella Lane
White Swan, WA 98952
509-874-2244
Fax: 509-874-2342
Email: forts@jcdc.jobcorps.org
Job Training: Business Clerical, Culinary Arts, Auto Repair Tech, Truck Driver Light, Auto Body Repair, Painter Plasterer, Heavy Equipment Operator, Heavy Equipment Mechanic, Bricklayer, Carpenter

West Virginia
Charleston Job Corps Center
Region 2
1000 Kennawa Drive
Charleston, WV 25311
304-925-3200
Fax: 304-925-7127
Email: charl@jcdc.jobcorps.org
Job Training: Word Processing, Secretary, Receptionist, Culinary Arts, Home Health Aide, Drafter, Cosmetology, Electronic Tech, Nurses Aide, Hotel Clerk, Painting, Auto Body Repair, Child Care Worker, Computer Repair Tech, Welder, Bldg. and Apt Maintenance, Carpenter, Medical Assistant

Harpers Ferry Job Corps Center
Region 2
P.O. Box 237
237 Job Corps Road
Harpers Ferry, WV 25425
304-728-5708
Fax: 304-728-8200
Email: harpe@jcdc.jobcorps.org
Job Training: Painter, Bricklayer, Cement Mason, Bldg. and Apt Maintenance, Business Clerical, Carpenter, Health Occupations

Wisconsin
Blackwell Job Corps Center
Region 5
4155 Count Highway H
Laona, WI 54541
715-674-2311
Fax: 715-674-4305
Email: black@jcdc.jobcorps.org

Job Training: Culinary Arts, Electrician, Painter, Carpenter, Building and Apartment Maintenance, Welder, Bricklayer, Business Clerical

Wyoming
Region 4
This State does not have a Job Corps Center. Contact the Regional Office listed for more information.

Regional Offices
Region 1 (Boston/New York)
Marcus F. Gray
US Department of Labor, ETA
Offices of Youth Services and Job Corps
Room E-350
John F. Kennedy Federal Building
Boston, MA 02203
617-565-2166
Fax: 617-565-2170

Joseph A. Semansky
US Department of Labor, ETA
Office of Youth Services and Job Corps
201 Varick Street, Room 897
New York, NY 10014
212-337-2282
Fax: 212-337-2305

Region 2 (Philadelphia)
Lynn Intrepidi
US Department of Labor, ETA
Office of Youth Services and Job Corps
The Curtis Center, Suite 815
170 South Independence Mall
West Philadelphia, PA 19106
215-861-5500
Fax: 215-861-5520

Region 3 (Atlanta)
Don Scott
US Department of Labor, ETA
Office of Youth Services and Job Corps
Room 6T95, 61 Forsyth Street
Atlanta, GA 30303
404-562-2372
Fax: 404-562-2396

Region 4 (Dallas/Denver)
Jose DeOlivares
US Department of Labor, ETA
Office of Youth Services and Job Corps
Room 403, 525 Griffin Street
Dallas, TX 75202
214-767-2567
Fax: 214-767-2148

Greg Evans
US Department of Labor, ETA
Office of Youth Services and Job Corps
Federal Office Building
1999 Broadway, Suite 1720
Denver, CO 80202
303-844-1630
Fax: 303-844-1638

Region 5 (Chicago/Kansas City)
Stephen H. Garlington
US Department of Labor, ETA
Office of Youth Services and Job Corps
Federal Building, Room 676
230 South Dearborn Street
Chicago, IL 60604
312-353-1311
Fax: 312-353-3026

Tom Deuschle
US Department of Labor, ETA
Office of Youth Services and Job Corps
1100 Main Street, Suite 1000
Kansas City, MO 64105
816-426-3661
Fax: 816-426-5307

Region 6 (San Francisco/ Seattle)

Jacqueline Roberts
US Department of Labor, ETA
Office of Youth Services and Job Corps
71 Stevenson Street, Suite 1015

San Francisco, CA 94105
415-975-4680
Fax: 415-975-4715

Ernest Priestly
US Department of Labor, ETA
Office of Youth Services and Job Corps
1111 Third Avenue, Suite 960
Seattle, WA 98101
206-553-7938
Fax: 206-553-4009
800-733-5627

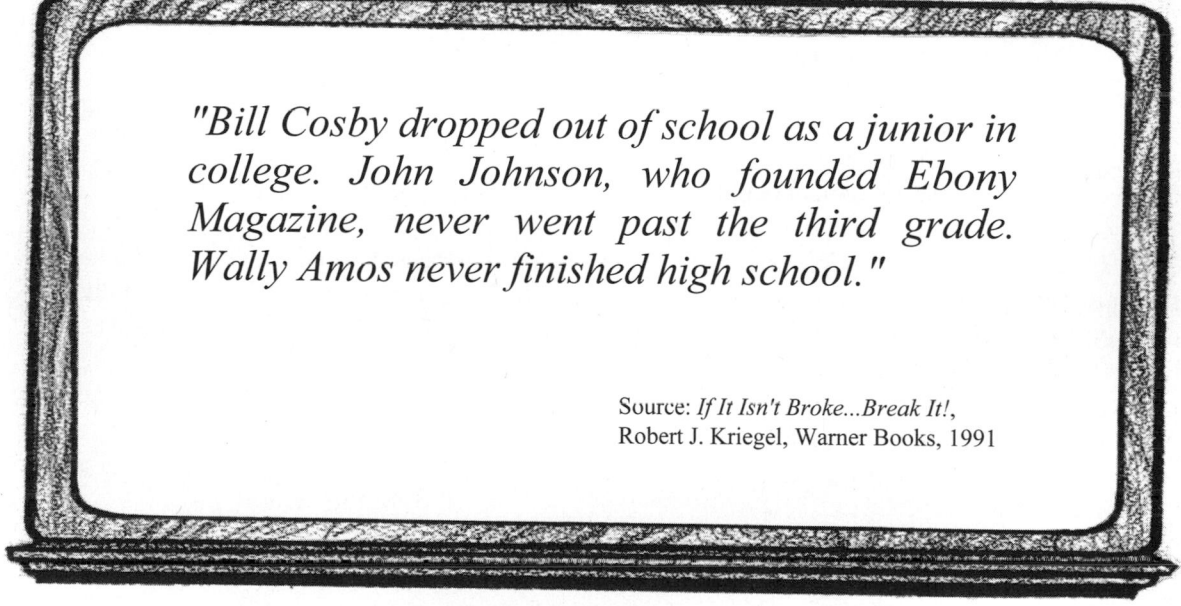

"Bill Cosby dropped out of school as a junior in college. John Johnson, who founded Ebony Magazine, never went past the third grade. Wally Amos never finished high school."

Source: *If It Isn't Broke...Break It!*,
Robert J. Kriegel, Warner Books, 1991

Free Training For Workers Who Are Laid Off Because Their Factories Complied With Air Pollution Laws

Program: Clean Air Employment Transition Assistance Program

Description: First, federal air pollution laws currently on the books are certainly better than none at all. Look at Mexico City, where they are laying the groundwork for respiratory fatalities due to industrial smoke — laying them in the ground, in fact. Second, even though the government may have shut down your factory here in the U.S. — because of pollution or environmental problems, Uncle Sam will help you get back on your feet with free training programs and unemployment services.

What You Can Get: Under the Clean Air Employment Transition Assistance Program, workers who have lost jobs due to a company complying with air pollution laws can receive the following free services:
- classroom studies
- job skills
- on-the-job training
- remedial education
- entrepreneurial training
- English as a second language
- job search and placement
- child care
- transportation allowances
- relocation assistance
- additional unemployment benefits so you can complete your retraining or education

Who Is Eligible: Those eligible for this program include dislocated workers who are unlikely to return to their previous industries or occupations, and who have been terminated or laid off due to a decision to reduce employment as a result of a company's compliance with the requirements of the Clean Air Act.

Money Available: The current budget for this program is $50,000,000 per year.

National Office:
Office of Worker Retraining and Adjustment Programs
Employment and Training Administration
U.S. Department of Labor
Room N5426, 200 Constitution Ave., NW
Washington, DC 20210
202-219-5577

Or, contact the Dislocated Worker Unit contact for your state (see page 570).

Matthew Lesko, Information USA, Inc., 12081 Nebel Street, Rockville, MD 20852 • 1-800-955-7693 • www.lesko.com

Free Training If You Are Laid Off
Due To Defense Cutbacks

Program: Defense Conversion Adjustment (DCA) Program

Description: Thousands of communities around the country have felt the fallout of the end of the Cold War. And the fallout has been economic, not nuclear. Base closings mean no jobs - pure and simple. Fortunately, the Defense Conversion Adjustment (DCA) Program provides retraining and other assistance for workers hurt by defense cutbacks.

What You Can Get: The DCA Program offers retraining and readjustment services, tailored to meet each individual participant. Long term training, including educational and occupational, is encouraged to enable the dislocated worker to become competitive in the future workforce. Some of the services available include:
-   classroom and occupational skills
-   on-the-job training
-   basic and remedial education
-   entrepreneurial training
-   English as a second language
-   job development
-   job search and placement
-   child care
-   transportation allowances
-   relocation assistance
-   needs-related payments for those who have exhausted their unemployment benefits

Who Is Eligible: Those eligible include workers who lose their jobs because of plant closings or mass layoffs due to reduced U.S. defense expenditures or closed military facilities.

National Office:
Office of Worker Retraining and Adjustment Programs
Employment and Training Administration
U.S. Department of Labor
Room N5426, 200 Constitution Ave., NW
Washington, DC 20210
202-219-5577

Local Offices:
For more information contact your local employment service office, or the Dislocated Worker Unit contact for your state (see page 570).

Free Training If You Were Laid Off
By A Defense Contractor

Program: Defense Diversification Program (DDP)

Description: If you have been laid off or fired because the company you worked for was on the wrong end of cutbacks at the U.S. Department of Defense, you may qualify to be retrained for another job. The Defense Diversification Program (DDP) provides retraining and readjustment assistance to workers and military personnel dislocated by defense cutbacks and base closings, as well as career planning support and assistance.

What You Can Get: The DDP offers a variety of retraining and readjustment services tailored to meet each participants' needs. The program offers long term training (both education and occupational) that will help you to be more competitive in the workforce of the future. Services include:
- classroom, job skills, and on-the-job training
- remedial education
- entrepreneurial training
- job development
- job search and placement
- child care and transportation allowance and relocation assistance
- needs-related payments for those who have exhausted their unemployment insurance

Additional support includes assistance in converting facilities to prevent closure or mass layoff and retraining workers to new technologies.

Who Is Eligible: Those eligible for the program include civilian employees of the Department of Defense, Department of Energy, and defense contractors who have been terminated or laid off, or have a notice of termination or layoff.

National Office:
Office of Worker Retraining and Adjustment Programs
Employment and Training Administration
U.S. Department of Labor
Room N5426, 200 Constitution Ave., NW
Washington, DC 20210
202-219-5577

Local Offices:
For more information contact your local employment services office, or the Dislocated Worker Unit contact for your state (see page 570).

How To Make A High School Diploma
Worth More Than The Paper It's Written On

Program: School-To-Work

Description: Each year millions of young people across the country are faced with making the difficult transition from being in school for 12 straight years, to being out in the real world and making it on their own. How do you go about translating a high school education into a good paying job that allows young people to take responsibility for their lives? For too many students, this just doesn't happen. And this is where the government thinks it can help.

What You Can Get: The School-To-Work approach to learning is based on the fact that individuals learn best by doing and by relating what they learn in school to their experiences as workers. The approach has come to be accepted as a better way to educate all young people. Instead of traditional general track and vocational education programs that were based on the theory that students who didn't go to college needed to be taught a skill they could use to make a living for the rest of their lives, the school-to-careers approach is based on the concept that education for all should be made more relevant and useful to multiple future career and lifelong learning. School-To-Work sets up partnerships between schools, employers, educators, students, and others to help students make the connection between what they learn in school and what will be required of them out in the working world. Developed with the input of business, education, labor, and community-based organizations that have a strong interest in how American students prepare for careers, the effort to create a national school-to-work system contains three fundamental elements:

- School-based learning: school-to-work programs restructure the educational experience so that students learn how academic subjects relate to the world of work. Teachers work together with employers to develop broad-based curricula that help students understand the skills needed in the workplace. Students actively develop projects and work in teams, much like the modern workplace.

- Work-based learning: employers provide learning experiences for students that develop broad, transferable skills. Work-based learning provides students with opportunities to study complex subject matter as well as vital workplace skills in a hands-on, "real life" environment.

- Connecting activities: connecting schools and workplaces does not happen naturally. It requires a range of activities to integrate the worlds of school and work to ensure that the student is not the slender thread that connects the two. Connecting activities provide program coordination and administration, integrate the worlds of school and work through school and business staff exchanges, and provide student support, such as career counseling and college placements.

Who is Eligible: The program is open to any young person, including high school students, out-of-school youth, and at-risk youth.

Money Available: This program is no longer funded by the Federal government. Many states have chosen to continue the program on their own. Contact your state contact or your state Department of Education to learn more.

National Office:
National School-To-Work Learning and Information Center
400 Virginia Ave., SW, Room 210
Washington, DC 20024
800-251-7236
Website: http://www.stw.ed.gov.

Local Offices:
The School-To-Work program may look different from state to state, but each local system provides relevant education, marketable skills, and valued credentials to all of its learners. A list is provided which includes state contacts, as well as local partnership information.

School-To-Work State Contacts

Alabama
Dr. Kenneth H. Hollingsworth
Alabama School-to-Career Office
401 Adams Avenue
P.O. Box 5690
Montgomery, AL 36103-5690
334-242-5436
Fax: 334-353-4239
http://www.adeca.state.al.us/School-to-Career/
Email: kenh@adeca.state.al.us

Alaska
Eva Mullen
Alaska Department of Labor & Workforce Development
3301 Eagle Street, Suite 106
Anchorage, AK 99503-4418
907-269-4658
Fax: 907-269-4661
http://www.akbec.com/
Email: eva_mullen@labor.state.ak.us

Arizona
Paula Burnam
Arizona Dept. of Commerce, STW Division
3800 North Central Avenue, Suite 1500
Phoenix, AZ 85012
602-280-8134
Fax: 602-280-1358
http://www.state.azcommerce.com
Email: paulab@azcommerce.com

Arkansas
Dr. Tanny Harper
Arkansas Career Opportunities Initiative
3 Capitol Mall
Little Rock, AR 72201
501-682-1535
Fax: 501-682-1805
http://www.work-ed.state.ar.us/
Email: tanny.harper@mail.state.ar.us

California
Patrick Ainsworth
High School Leadership Division
660 J Street, Suite 300
Sacramento, CA 95814
916-327-5055/445-2652
Fax: 916-327-5868
http://www.cde.ca.gov
Email: painswor@cde.ca.gov

Samuel Rodriguez
Employment Development Department
800 Capital Mall, MIC 83
Sacramento, CA 95814
916-651-6051
Fax: 916-657-5294
http://www.stc.ca.gov/
Email: srodrigu@edd.ca.gov

Connecticut
George A. Coleman
Connecticut State Department of Education
25 Industrial Park Rd
Middletown, CT 06457-1543
860-807-2005
Fax: 860-635-7125
http://www.state.ct.us/sde/
Email: george.coleman@po.state.ct.us

Delaware
Regina Greenwald
Delaware Department of Education
P.O. Box 1402
Dover, DE 19903
302-739-3743
Fax: 302-739-1318
http://www.doe.state.de.us/etc
Email: rgreenwald@state.de.us

District of Columbia
Janice Cannon
Career and Technical Education
825 N. Capitol, NE, Room 8112
Washington, DC 20002-4232
202-442-5650
Fax: 202-442-5081
http://www.dcschooltocareers.com
Email: janice.cannon@k12.dc.us

Georgia
Sue Chandler
Georgia School-to-Work
3103 Clairmont Road, NE, Suite B
Atlanta, GA 30329
404-327-6953
Fax: 404-679-1661
http://www.dtae.org/gastw
Email: schandler@dtae.org

Patt Stonehouse
Georgia Department of Technical and Adult Education
Office of Technical Education
1800 Century Place, Suite 400
Atlanta, GA 30345-4304
404-679-1658
Fax: 404-982-3485

http://www.dtae.org/gastw
Email: pstonehouse@dtae.org

Hawaii
Aileen Ah Yat
Hawaii School-to-Work
Kalani High School
4680 Kalanianaole Hwy., Room A-12
Honolulu, HI 96821
808-377-2436
Fax: 808-377-2499
http://www.hcc.hawaii.edu/stw/frames/index.htm
Email: aileen_ah_yat@notes.k12.hi.us

Katherine Kawaguchi
OCISS
1390 Miller St., Room 316
Honolulu, HI 96813
808-586-3446
Fax: 808-586-3645
http://www.doe.k12.hi.us
Email: kathy_kawaguchi@notes.k12.hi.us

Idaho
Burton Waite
Idaho School-to-Work
650 W. State Street
P.O. Box 83720
Boise, ID 83720-0095
208-332-3216
Fax: 208-334-2365
http://www.pte.state.id.us
Email: bwaite@pte.state.id.us

Illinois
Sandy Dunkel
Illinois State Board of Education
100 North First Street
Springfield, IL 62777-0001
217-782-4620
Fax: 217-782-0710
http://www.isbe.net/etc/
Email: sdunkel@isbe.net

Indiana
Peggy O'Malley
Department of Workforce Development
10 N. Senate Avenue, SE
Room 302, IN Government Center South
Indianapolis, IN 46204-2277
317-232-1832
Fax: 317-233-1670
http://www.dwd.state.in.us
Email: pomalley@dwd.state.in.us

Iowa

Laurie Phelan
Iowa Department of Education
Grimes State Office Building, 3rd Floor
Des Moines, IA 50319
515-242-5611
Fax: 515-242-5618
Email: laurie.phelan@ed.state.ia.us

Kansas

Shelly McDonald
Kansas School to Career
Kansas Dept. of Commerce & Housing
1000 SW Jackson, Suite 100
Topeka, KS 66612-1354
785-296-0908
Fax: 785-296-3490
http://www.kdoch.state.ks.us
Email: smcdonald@kansascommerce.com

Kentucky

Dianne H. Smithers
Kentucky Office of School-to-Work
229 West Main Street, Suite 304
Frankfort, KY 40601
502-564-5901
Fax: 502-564-5904
http://www.state.ky.us/agencies2/stw/
Email: dianneh.smithers@mail.state.ky.us

Louisiana

Chris Weaver
Louisiana Workforce Commission
224 FL Blvd, Suite 301
Baton Rouge, LA 70802-9004
225-342-2094
Fax: 225-342-1494
http://www.laworkforce.net/STW
Email: cweaver@idsmail.com

Maine

Yvonne Davis
Department of Education
Workforce Education
23 State House Station
Augusta, ME 04333-0023
207-624-6730
Fax: 207-624-6731
Email: yvonne.davis@state.me.us

Maryland

Katharine M. Oliver
Division of Career Technology and Adult
Learning
Department of Education
200 West Baltimore Street
Baltimore, MD 21201-2595
410-767-0158
Fax: 410-333-8666
http://www.msde.state.md.us
Email: koliver@msde.state.md.us
Email: jseay@msde.state.md.us

Massachusetts

Mary Ellen McDonagh
MA Office for School-to-Work Transition
Massachusetts Department of Education
350 Main Street
Malden, MA 02148-5023
781-338-3932
Fax: 781-338-3350
http://www.doe.mass.edu/stc/
Email: mmcdonagh@doe.mass.edu

Michigan

Patty Cantu
Michigan Department of Career Development
Office of Career and Technical Preparation
P.O. Box 30712
Lansing, MI 48909
517-373-3373
Fax: 517-373-8776
http://www.michigan.gov/mded
Email: cantup@michigan.gov

Minnesota

Dan Smith
Division of Life Work Development
1500 Highway 36 West
Roseville, MN 55113-4266
651-582-8330
Fax: 651-582-8492
http://children.state.mn.us
Email: dan.smith@state.mn.us

Mississippi

Nancy Chaney
Mississippi Department of Education
P.O. Box 771
Jackson, MS 39205-0771
601-359-1737
Fax: 601-576-4300
http://www.fastforwardms.com/
Email: nchaney@mde.k12.ms.us

Missouri

Doug Sutton
Missouri Department of Elementary &
Secondary Education
205 Jefferson Street
Jefferson Building 5th Floor
Jefferson City, MO 65102
573-751-4192
Fax: 573-526-4261
http://www.dese.state.mo.us/divvoced/
commcareered/misscommcareers/menu.html
Email: dsutton1@mail.dese.state.mo.us

Montana

Cathy Yetter
Montana University System
PO Box 203101
2500 Broadway
Helena, MT 59620-3101
406-444-0313
Fax: 406-444-1469
http://www.montanaschooltowork.com/
Email: cyetter@oche.montana.edu

Nebraska

Deb Fritch
Nebraska Economic Development
301 Centennial Mall South
P.O. Box 94666
Lincoln, NE 68509-4666
402-471-6284
Fax: 402-471-3365
http://stc.neded.org/
Email: dfritch@neded.org

Nevada

John Griffin
Nevada Department of Education
700 E Fifth Street
Carson City, NV 89701-5096
775-687-9152
Fax: 775-687-9114
Email: griffinprism@aol.com

New Hampshire

Kim Runion
Department of Education
101 Pleasant Street
Concord, NH 03301
603-271-7977
Fax: 603-271-4079
http://www.ed.state.nh.us/SchoolToWork/
Sch-T-Wk.htm
Email: Krunion@ed.state.nh.us

New Jersey

Thomas Henry
New Jersey Department of Education
P.O. Box 500
Trenton, NJ 08625-0500
609-633-0665
Fax: 609-984-5347
http://www.state.nj.us/njded/voc/
Email: tom.henry@doe.state.nj.us

New Mexico

Vonell Huitt
Office of the Governor State Capitol
State Capitol Building, Suite 400
Santa Fe, NM 87503
505-827-3078
Fax: 505-827-3026
http://www.edd.state.nm.us/STW
Email: huittv@gov.state.nm.us

New York

Jean Stevens
NY State Education Department
89 Washington Avenue
Room 319EB
Albany, NY 12234
518-474-8892
Fax: 518-474-0319
http://www.emsc.nysed.gov/workforce
Email: jstevens@mail.nysed.gov

North Carolina

Beth Lucas
Workforce Outreach
4327 Mail Service Center
Raleigh, NC 27699-4331
919-715-3300
Fax: 919-715-3974
http://www.jobready.state.nc.us/
Email: blucas@nccommerce.com

North Dakota

Wayne Kutzer
State Division of Vocational Education
State Capitol, 15th Floor
600 E. Boulevard Ave., Dept. 270
Bismarck, ND 58505-0610
701-328-2254
Fax: 701-328-1255
Email: wkutzer@state.nd.us

Ohio

Kristen Howard
Office of Career-Technical and Adult
Education
25 South Front Street, 605
Columbus, OH 43215-4183
614-466-3904
Fax: 614-728-6176
http://www.stwclearinghouse.org
Email: Kristen.howard@ode.state.oh.us

Oklahoma
Robin Schott
Career Tech
1500 West Seventh Avenue
Stillwater, OK 74074-4364
405-743-5554
Fax: 405-743-5142
http://www.okcareertech.org/STW
Email: rscho@okcareertech.org

Oregon
Mr. Salam Noor
Oregon Department of Education
255 Capitol Street, N.E.
Salem, OR 97310
503-378-3600 x 2230
Fax: 503-378-5156
http://www.ode.state.or.us
Email: salam.noor@state.or.us

Pennsylvania
Jim Potts
Pennsylvania Department of Education
333 Market Street, 5th Floor
Harrisburg, PA 17126-0333
717-787-8022
Fax: 717-783-6672
http://www.pastw.psu.edu
Email: japotts@state.pa.us

Puerto Rico
Miriam R. Hernandez
Puerto Rico School-to-Work Office
Plaza Alverio Building, Floor 2
566 Cabo Alverio, Urb. La. Merced
Hato Rey, PR 00918
787-282-8392
Fax: 787-281-5619
Email: miroman@interempleo.org

Rhode Island
Linda Soderberg
Rhode Island School-to-Careers Office
1511 Pontiac Avenue
Building #72, 3rd Floor
Cranston, RI 02920
401-462-8880/94
Fax: 401-462-8865

http://www.RISTC.org
Email: lsoderberg@dlt.state.ri.us

South Carolina
Dr. James R. Couch
South Carolina Department of Education
1429 Senate Street
Room 912A, Rutledge Bldg
Columbia, SC 29201
803-734-8410
Fax: 803-734-5686
http://www.myschools.com
Email: jcouch@sde.state.sc.us

South Dakota
Deb Halling
Department of Labor
700 Governors Drive
Pierre, SD 57501
605-773-5017
Fax: 605-773-6184
http://www.state.sd.us/dol/jtpa/stw.htm
Email: deb.halling@state.sd.us

Tennessee
Betsy Houston
Department of Education
Andrew Johnson Tower
710 James Robertson Parkway, 4th Floor
Nashville, TN 37243-0379
615-532-2718
Fax: 615-532-4792
http://www.state.tn.us/education/eehpage.htm
Email: brhouston@mail.state.tn.us

Texas
James P. Cooper
Texas School-to-Work
101 East 15th Street, Room 104-T
Austin, TX 78778-0001
512-936-3314
Fax: 512-463-6689
Email: jim.cooper@school.
careers.twc.state.tx.us

Utah
Marvin Johnson
Utah State Office of Education

250 East 500 South
P.O. Box 144200
Salt Lake City, UT 84111-4200
801-538-7843
Fax: 801-538-7868
http://www.usoe.k12.ut.us/stc/stc.htm
Email: mjohnson@usoe.k12.ut.us

Virginia
Lynne Talley
Virginia Business Education Partnership
701 East Franklin Street, Suite 811
Richmond, VA 23219
804-692-0244 x 16
Fax: 804-371-8654
http://www.vbep.state.va.us
Email: ltalley@vbep.state.va.us

Washington
Jill teVelde
Office of Superintendent of Public Instruction
Old Capitol Building
600 Washington Street, SE
P.O. Box 47200
Olympia, WA 98504-7200
360-725-6248
Fax: 360-586-9321
http://www.k12.wa.us/STW/
Email: jtevelde@ospi.wednet.edu

Wisconsin
Aleta Murray
Governor's Work-Based Learning Board
131 W. Wilson Street, Suite 1001
P.O. Box 7891
Madison, WI 53707-7891
608-261-4588
Fax: 608-261-4862
http://www.dwd.state.wi.us/gwblb/stw.htm
Email: murraal@dwd.state.wi.us

Wyoming
Lori Morrow
Office of Workforce Development
3120 Old Faithful Road, Suite 300
Cheyenne, WY 82002
307-777-7654
Fax: 307-777-6966
Email: lmorro@state.wy.us

Free Job Training for Dead Beat Dads

Program: Child Support Enforcement Research — 93.564

Description: No one likes a dead beat dad, but Uncle Sam understands that many fathers fall behind in child support not because they're evil, wicked, mean or nasty. Some just don't have a job and have never been trained to make them qualified for many jobs. The Parents Fair Share Program helps these parents get the training they need to get a paycheck that will help them set things straight with their children. According to the latest data, almost two-thirds of custodial mothers receive no child support from the fathers of their children.

What You Can Get: Fair Share provides fathers with training on how to:
- get ready for a job
- search for a job
- build job skill levels

Since it is important to get participants earning paychecks fast, sites are encouraged to offer on-the-job training, paid work experience, and other activities that mix skills training or education with part time employment. The program also forms and directs support groups to help participants learn about their rights and obligations to their children, and to help them to become better parents. Mediation programs help parents discuss disagreements regarding visitation, household expenditures, child care and other issues that arise between divorced parents.

Who Is Eligible: Any non-custodial parent whose children are on welfare is eligible for job training. Many participants are court ordered to participate, but others are accepted, provided there is space.

National Office:
Mark Gucello
Office of Planning, Research and Evaluation
Administration for Children and Families
U.S. Department of Health and Human Services
901 D St., SW
Washington, DC 20447
202-401-4538

Local Offices:
Currently the program is only being offered in seven states. For more information, contact one of the sites listed below.

California
Los Angeles County Fair Share
Bureau of Family Support Operations
5770 South Eastern Ave.
Commerce, CA 90024
213-889-2877

Florida
Duvall County Parents' Fair Share
Employment and Training Security
Department of Labor
215 Market St.
Jacksonville, FL 32202
904-359-6080

Massachusetts
Massachusetts JOBS Parents' Fair Share
Project
Springfield Employment Resource Center, Inc.
140 Wilbraham Ave.
Springfield, MA 01109
413-737-9544

Michigan
Kent County Parents' Fair Share Project
Kent County Friend of the Court
50 Monroe Ave., NW
Grand Rapids, MI 49503
616-336-2800

New Jersey
Operation Fatherhood
Union Industrial Home for Children
864 Bellevue Ave.
Trenton, NJ 08618
609-695-1492

Ohio
Options for Parental Training and Support
Montgomery County Department of Human Services
14 W. Fourth St.
Dayton, OH 45402
513-225-4077

Tennessee
Fair Share
Youth Service, USA, Inc.
67 Madison Ave., Suite 804
Memphis, TN 38103
901-527-6255

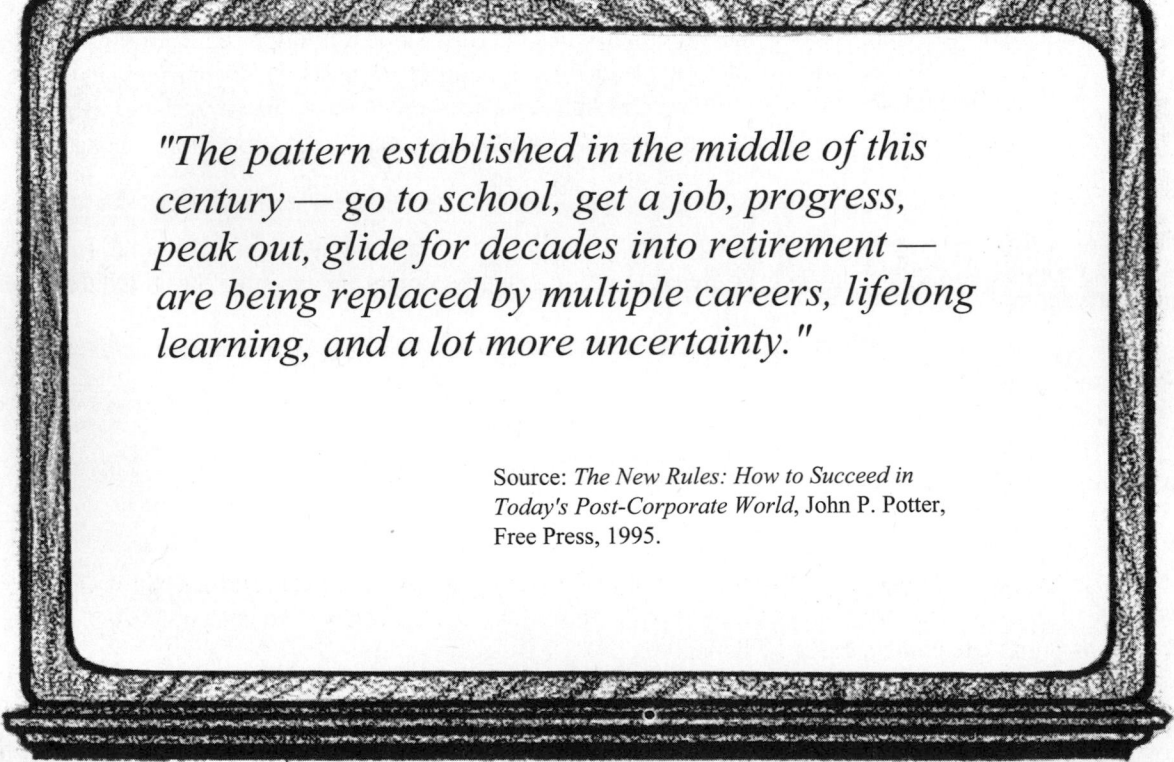

"The pattern established in the middle of this century — go to school, get a job, progress, peak out, glide for decades into retirement — are being replaced by multiple careers, lifelong learning, and a lot more uncertainty."

Source: *The New Rules: How to Succeed in Today's Post-Corporate World*, John P. Potter, Free Press, 1995.

Free Job Training and More For Foster Care Teens

Program: Independent Living - 93.674

Description: All kinds of free help is out there for teenagers in foster care — and young adults who have been raised in foster homes — to get the job skills they need to make a good life on their own. The Independent Living program provides help for foster care youth between the ages of 16 and 21, help in getting a GED or a driving permit, even assistance in filling out college applications. Those who live out in the country can even get free transportation to job training programs that can assure them of a good paying career track. The goal of the program is to ease the transition from foster care to independent living.

What You Can Get: Job training is only part of the program. Kids are also given lessons on handling day to day problems, such as:

- budgeting money
- opening checking accounts
- looking for an apartment
- parenting skills
- finding health care
- training in social skills
- independent or group counseling

Independent Living programs will point you to the free programs you'll need to get ahead in the world, including:

- GED preparation
- job placement
- on-the-job training
- job interviewing skills
- career planning

Who Is Eligible: If you are in foster care or have recently left a foster home, and are between the ages of 16 and 21, this program could be a gold mine for you. To apply, contact your foster care worker or your state contact from the list below.

Money Available: The Independent Living program receives $70,000,000 each year from the government.

National Office:
Michael Ambrose, Director
Division of Child Welfare
Children's Bureau
Administration for Children and Families
P.O. Box 1182
Washington, DC 20013
202-205-8740

Independent Living State Coordinators

Alabama
Linda Stephens
Alabama Department of Human Resources
Family Services Partnership - ILP
50 Ripley Street
Montgomery, AL 36130
334-353-7984
Fax: 334-353-1491
Email: lstephens@dhr.state.al.us

Alaska
Matthew Turner
Alaska Division of Family and Youth Services
P.O. Box 110630
Juneau, AK 99811-0630
907-465-3209
Fax: 907-465-3397
Email: Matthew_Turner@health.state.ak.us

Arizona
Beverlee B. Kroll
Arizona Department of Economic Security
P.O. Box 6123
Phoenix, AZ 85005
602-542-5120
Fax: 602-542-3330
Email: beverlee.kroll@childs.de.state.az.us

Arkansas
Jim Dennis
Arkansas Division of Children and Family
Services
P.O. Box 1437, Slot 818
Little Rock, AR 72203-1437
501-682-8453
Fax: 501-682-8991
Email: james.dennis@mail.state.ar.us

Calfornia
Sonya St. Mary
California Department of Social Services
744 P Street, M.S. 19-70
Sacramento, CA 95814
916-323-6214
Fax: 916-445-9874
Email: Sonya.St.Mary@dss.ca.gov

Colorado
Valerie D. Jenkins
Independent Living Coordinator
Child Welfare Alive/e Program
Colorado Department of Human Services
1575 Sherman Street, 2nd Floor
Denver, CO 80203
303-866-4539
Email: valerie.jenkins@state.co.us

Meg Williams
Colorado Department of Human Services
1575 Sherman Street, Ground Floor
Denver, CO 80203-1714
303-866-4706
Fax: 303-866-5563
Email: meg.williams@state.co.us

Connecticut
Bill Pinto
Connecticut Department of Children and
Families
505 Hudson Street
Hartford, CT 06106

860-550-6471
Fax: 860-566-8022
or 860-566-3453
Email: william.pinto@po.state.ct.us

Delaware
Truman Bolden
Independent Living Program Manager
Division of Family Services
1825 Faulkland Road
Wilmington, DE 19805
302-633-2638
Fax: 302-633-2652
Email: tbolden@state.de.us

District of Columbia
Cecille Hollingsworth
ILP Coordinator
D.C. Child & Family Services Agency
400 6th Street Southwest
Washington, DC 20024
202-727-7500
Fax: 202-546-1798

Florida
JoAnne Richmond
State IL Coordinator
Florida Department of Children and Families
1317 Winewood Blvd., Bldg. 7
Tallahassee, FL 32399-0700
850-921-4118
Fax: 850-448-0751
Email: joanne_richmond@dcf.state.fl.us

Georgia
Walter C. Pitman
Georgia Division of Family and Children
Services
Independent Living Program
P.O. Box 3249
Albany, GA 31706
912-430-3385
Fax: 912-430-4355
Email: wapitman@dhr.state.ga.us

Milicent Houston
Georgia Division of Family and Children
Services
Independent Living Program
2 Peachtree Street, 18th Floor
Atlanta, GA 30303
404-657-3482
Email: mjhouston@dhr.state.ga.us

Hawaii
Lee Dean
Hawaii Department of Human Services
Social Services Division
810 Richards St., Suite 400
Honolulu, HI 96813
808-586-5704
Fax: 808-586-4806
Email: ldean@dhs.state.hi.us

Idaho
Steve Green
Idaho Department of Health and Welfare
P.O. Box 83720
Boise, ID 83720-0036

208-334-5700
Fax: 208-334-6664
Email: greens@idhw.state.id.us

Illinois
Nyle Robinson
Illinois Dept. of Children and Family Services
1921 S. Indiana
Chicago, IL 60616
312-808-5241
Fax: 312-808-5784
Email: NRobinso@idcfs.state.il.us

Indiana
Audrea T. Mitchell
Indiana Family and Social Services
Administration/
Division of Family and Children
402 W. Washington St., Room W364
Indianapolis, IN 46204
317-232-4439
Fax: 317-232-4436
Email: amitchell@fssa.state.in.us

Iowa
Holli Noble
Transition Planning Program
Manager, Iowa Dept. of Human Services
Hoover State Office Building
Des Moines, IA 50319-0114
515-281-6786
Fax: 515-281-4597
Email: hnoble@dhs.state.ia.us

Kansas
Angie Casey
Kansas Children and Family Services
Commission
Docking State Office Bldg., 5th Floor South
915 SW Harrison
Topeka, KS 66606-1570
785-368-8172
Fax: 785-368-8159
Email: AGC@srskansas.org

Kentucky
Mike Yocum
Kentucky Department for Community Based
Services
Division of Protection and Permanency
275 E. Main Street
Mail Stop 3C-E
Frankfort, KY 40621
502-564-2147
Fax: 502-564-5995
Email: mike.yocum@mail.state.ky.us

Louisiana
Ernie Chapman
Louisiana Office of Community Services
Division of Social Services
P.O. Box 3318
Baton Rouge, LA 70821-3318
225-342-2279
Fax: 225-342-9087
Email: rdernie@ocs.dss.state.la.us

Betty Becker
Louisiana Office of Community Services
Division of Social Services

P.O. Box 57149
New Orleans, LA 70157-7149
504-568-8003
Fax: 504-599-0936
Email: 71bettyb@ocs.dss.state.la.us

Maine

Hugh E. Sipowicz
IL Coordinator
Bureau of Children & Family
Maine Department of Human Services
SHS #11 - 221 State Street
Augusta, ME 04333
207-287-6259
Fax: 207-287-5282
Email: hugh.e.sipowicz@state.me.us

Maryland

Gale Fulton
State Independent Living Coordinator
Maryland Department of Human Services
311 West Saratoga Street
5th Floor, Room 571
Baltimore, MD 21201
410-767-7634
Fax: 410-333-0127
Email: gfulton@dhr.state.md.us

Massachusetts

Maureen Fallon Messeder
Associate Director
Adolescent Services
Massachusetts Department of Social Services
24 Farnsworth Street
Boston, MA 02210
617-748-2311
Fax: 617-748-2311
Email: maureen.fallon@state.ma.us

Michigan

Knud Hansen
Michigan Department of Social Services
235 S. Grand, Suite 510
Lansing, MI 48909
517-335-3983
Fax: 517-241-7047
Email: hansenk@state.mi.us

Minnesota

Claire Hill
Minnesota Department of Human Services
Family and Children's Services
444 Lafayette Road
St. Paul, MN 55155-3832
651-296-4471
Fax: 651-297-1949
Email: claire.d.hill@state.mn.us

Missouri

Lee Temmen
Program Development Specialist
Missouri Division of Family Services
615 Howerton Court
Jefferson City, MO 65103
573-751-2427
Fax: 573-526-3971
Email: Ltemmen@mail.state.mo.us

Mississippi

Pearl Holloway
IL Coordinator Administrator
Mississippi Department of Human Resources
750 N. State St.
Jackson, MS 39205
601-359-4982

Fax: 601-359-2525
Email: gyoung@mdhs.state.ms.us

Montana

Betsy Stimatz
Montana Department of Public Health and
Human Services
P.O. Box 8005
1400 Broadway
Helena, MT 59604
406-444-1675
Fax: 406-444-2547
Email: bstimatz@state.mt.us

Nebraska

Debbie Dominick (Interim)
Nebraska Department of Health and Human
Services
Division of Protection and Safety
P.O. Box 95044
Lincoln, NE 68509
402-471-6786
Fax: 402-471-9034
Email: debbie.dominick@hhss.state.ne.us

Nevada

Kathleen Shane
ILP Coordinator/Specialist
Division of Children and Family Services
711 East Fifth Street
Carson City, NV 89701-5092
775-684-4450
Fax: 775-684-4457
Email: kshane@govmail.state.nv.us

New Hampshire

Dorothy Doucette Melzard
Program Specialist
Department of Health and Human Services
129 Pleasant Street
Concord, NH 03301-3857
603-271-4706
Fax: 603-271-4729
Email: dmelzard@dhhs.state.nh.us

New Jersey

Nancy Caplan
New Jersey Division of Youth and Family
Services
Placement Services
50 East State Street, CN 717
Trenton, NJ 08625-0717
609-292-0887
Fax: 609-984-8199
Email: ncaplan@dhs.state.nj.us

New Mexico

Eric Gallegos Interim-Program Manager
New Mexico Children, Youth and Families
Department
760 Motel Blvd., Suite A
Las Cruces, NM 88005
505-524-6400, ext. 105
Fax: 505-524-6415
Email: edgallegos@cyfd.state.nm.us

New York

Nancy Martinez
NYS Office of Children and Family Services
Capital View Office Park
Room 313 South
52 Washington Street
Rensselaer, NY 12144
518-474-9586
Fax: 518-402-6826

Email: 0fb030@dfa.state.ny.us
(All Zeroes in address)

North Carolina

Joan S. McAllister
Independent Living Coordinator
North Carolina Division of Social Services
MSC 2408
325 N. Salisbury Street
Raleigh, NC 27699-2408
919-733-4622
Fax: 919-715-6714
Email: joan.mcallister@ncmail.net

North Dakota

Don Snyder
North Dakota Department of Human Services
Children and Family Services Division
600 E. Boulevard Avenue
3rd Floor - Judicial Wing
Bismarck, ND 58505
701-328-4934
Fax: 701-328-3538
Email: sosnyd@state.nd.us

Ohio

Heidi Stone
Ohio Department of Human Services
255 East Main St., 3rd Floor
Columbus, OH 43081
614-752-6269
Fax: 614-466-0164
Email: stoneh@odhs.state.oh.us

Ron Pollard
Ohio Department of Human Services
65 E. State St., 5th Floor
Columbus, OH 43215
614-752-6208
Fax: 614-466-0164

Oklahoma

Claudia Hunter
Oklahoma Department of Human Services
P.O. Box 25352
Oklahoma City, OK 73125
405-521-4364
Fax: 405-521-4373
Email: claudia.hunter@okdhs.org

Oregon

Rosemary Iavenditti
ILP Coordinator
SCF-Independent Living Program, E76
500 Summer Street NE
Salem, OR 97301-1069
503-945-5688;
Email: Rosemary.Iavenditti@state.or.us

Pennsylvania

David Derbes
Department of Public Welfare
Office of Children, Youth and Families
P.O. Box 2675
Harrisburg, PA 17105-2675
717-705-2911
Fax: 717-703-0364
Email: dderbes@state.pa.us

Puerto Rico

Maria Carillo de Sevilla
Department of the Family
Families with Children Program
P.O. Box 15091
San Juan, PR 00902

787-724-7532
Fax: 787-725-5443

Rhode Island.
John P. O'Riley
Rhode Island DCYF
610 Mt. Pleasant Avenue
Providence, RI 02908
401-222-5235
Fax: 401-222-6960
Email: orileyj@dcyf.state.ri.us

South Carolina
Petri Carrington-Jones
South Carolina Department of Social Services
P.O. Box 1520
1535 Confederate Avenue
Columbia, SC 29202-1520
803-898-7159
Fax: 803-898-7792
Email: pcarrington-jones@dss.state.sc.us

Don Adams
South Carolina Department of Social Services
P.O. Box 1520
Columbia, SC 29202
903-898-7567
Fax: 803-898-7792

South Dakota
Joyce Panzer
South Dakota Department of Social Services
700 Governors Drive
Pierre, SD 57501-2291
605-773-3227
Fax: 605-773-6834
Email: joyce.panzer@state.sd.us

Tennessee
Gayle York Crawford
Tennessee Department of Children's Services
8th Floor, Cordell Hull Bldg.
436 6th Avenue North
Nashville, TN 37243
615-532-5644
Fax: 615-532-6495
Email: gcyork@mail.state.tn.us

Texas
Janet L. Luft
Texas Department of Protective and Regulatory Services
P.O. Box 149030
M.C. E-557
Austin, TX 78714-9030
512-438-5442
Fax: 512-438-3782
Email: luftj@tdprs.state.tx.us

Utah
Duane Betournay
Utah Department of Human Services
Division of Children and Family Services
120 N. 200 West
Salt Lake City, UT 84103
801-538-4341
Fax: 801-538-3993
Email: hsadmin1.dbetourn@email.state.ut.us

Dana Lawrence
Vermont Department of Social Services
103 South Main
Osgood Bldg.
Waterbury, VT 05676
802-241-2153
Fax: 802-241-2980
Email: lawrence@srs.state.vt.us

Virginia
Yvonne Vaughan
Independent Living Program Coordinator
Virginia Department of Social Services
730 E. Broad Street, 2nd Floor
Richmond, VA 23219
804-692-1293
Fax: 804-692-1284
Email: yhv2@email1.dss.state.va.us

Washington
Erica Shrack
Washington Children's Administration
115 Washington Street
P.O. Box 45710
Olympia, WA 98504-5710
360-902-8262
Fax: 360-902-7903
Email: shca300@dshs.wa.gov

West Virginia
Shirlee Lively
West Virginia Office of Social Services
350 Capitol Street, Room 691
Charleston, WV 25301-3704
304-558-7980
Fax: 304-558-4563
Email: slively@wvdhhr.org

Christine Craig
West Virginia Department of Health and Human Resources
Building 6, Room 850
1900 Washington St. East
Charleston, WV 25305
304-558-7980 or 2968
Fax:304-558-8800
Email: ccraig@wvdhhr.org

Wisconsin
Ruth Murphy
Wisconsin Dept. of Health and Family Services
P.O. Box 8916
Madison, WI 53708
608-266-5330
Fax: 608-264-6750
Email: murphr@dhfs.state.wi.us

Paula L. Brown
Independent Living and Kinship Coordinator
DHFS/DCFS/BPP
One West Wilson, Rm. 527
P.O. Box 8916
Madison, WI 53708-8916
608-267-7287
Fax: 608-264-6750
Email: brownpl@dhfs.state.wi.us

Wyoming
Jim Palmer
Wyoming Division of Social Services
Hathaway Building, 3rd Floor
Cheyenne, WY 82002-0490
307-777-6203
Fax: 307-777-3693
Email: jpalme2@state.wy.us

Federal Contacts
Pamela Johnson
National Program Officer for Independent Living
ACF/DHHS
Children's Bureau
330 C Street, SW, Room 2058
Washington DC 20447
202-205-8086
Fax: 202-205-8221
Email: pjohnson@acf.dhhs.gov

Carlotta Garcia
Intergovernmental Personnel Act Appointee
ACF/DHHS
Children's Bureau
330 C Street, SW, Room 2411
Washington DC 20447
202-205-8175
Fax: 202-205-8221
Email: cgarcia@acf.dhhs.gov

Mary E. Furnas
Children's Bureau
Casey Family Programs Fellow
Chafee Foster Care Independence Program
330 C Street, SW - Room 2412
Washington DC 20447
202-260-0334
Fax: 202-205-8221
Email: mfurnas@acf.dhhs.gov

Triple Your Salary With Job Training
for Migrant and Farmworkers

Program: Migrant and Seasonal Farmworkers — 17.247

Description: Migrant workers and seasonal laborers are some of the hardest working people in America. Yet when the crops are all picked or the economy sags, they are some of the first to be out of a job. And most of these people live just at the poverty level to begin with. Fortunately, the government has a special job training program to help them find less backbreaking work, jobs that last past the harvest — and can mean an actual shot at the American Dream.

The Department of Labor's Employment and Training Administration pays public agencies and nonprofit groups almost $80 million a year to provide free job training, job search, and support services for migrant workers living at or below the poverty line. The program is offered in every state except Alaska, Rhode Island, and the District of Columbia.

What You Can Get: Participants can receive a weekly allowance at the current minimum wage and learn new work skills in classroom and on-the-job training programs, work experience in new employment areas, job development and placement services, relocation and education assistance — and even some health care. In some states where the poverty level is relatively high, a family with two children could take advantage of the program even if they earned $20,000 or more the year before and only worked six months.

Who Is Eligible: Any seasonal worker and their dependents are eligible if they worked for any consecutive 12-month period in the two years prior to applying to the program. Applicants must have earned at least half of their income — or worked at least 50 percent of their time — in seasonal farmwork in the 12 months before they apply for aid. Families must be receiving some type of public assistance, and their annual income must be at either the poverty level or at 70 percent of the state's lower-living-standard income level.

Money Available: Uncle Sam provides these funds based on grant applications from public and nonprofit groups. In 1995, $79 million was spent and more than one-third of participants received some job retraining. Of those who finish the program, almost 65 percent found new work in higher paying jobs.

National Office:
> U.S. Department of Labor
> National Office
> Office of Special Targeted Programs
> Division of Migrant and Seasonal Farmworker Programs
> Room N-4641, 200 Constitution Ave., N.W.
> Washington, DC 20210
> 202-219-5501
> Fax: 202-219-5500

Local Offices: Program benefits are delivered through grants to various retraining and outreach facilities in each state. (See listing below.)

Migrant and Seasonal Farmworker Programs

Alabama

Mickey Hutto
Executive Director
Alabama Department of Economic and
Community Affairs
401 Adams Ave.
P.O. Box 5690
Montgomery, AL 36103-5690
334-242-5886
Fax: 334-242-5855

E.C.Rentz, II
State Coordinator
Alabama Opportunity Program
Suite D, 224 Church St
P.O. Box 18724
Huntsville, AL 35801
205-536-8218
Fax: 205-533-2039

Arizona

John Arnold
Chief Executive Officer
Portable Practical Educational Preparation, Inc
806 East 46th St.
Tucson, AZ 85713
520-622-3553
Fax: 520-622-1480

Elise Arnold
Executive Director
Portable Practical Educational Preparation, Inc
806 East 46th St.
Tucson, AZ 85713
602-792-5708
Fax: 602-622-1480

Arkansas

Clevon Young
Executive Director
Arkansas Human Development Corporation
Suite 800, 300 South Spring St.
300 Spring Building
Little Rock, AR 72201-2424
501-374-1103
Fax: 501-374-1413

California

John Nilon
Executive Director
Employers Training Resources
County of Kern
2001 28th St.
Bakersfield, CA 93301
805-336-6843 Ext 6994
Fax: 805-336-6858

Hermelinda Sapien
Executive Director
Center for Employment Training
701 Vine St.
San Jose, CA 95110
408-287-7924
Fax: 408-294-7849

James Gordon
Chief Executive Officer
Proteus, Inc
1830 North Dinuba Blvd
P.O. Box 727
Visalia, CA 93279
209-733-5423

Fax: 209-738-1137
www.proteusinc.org

Ernie Flores
Executive Director
Central Valley Opportunity Center, Inc.
1748 Miles Court
P.O. Box 2307
Merced, CA 95348
209-383-2415
Fax: 209-383-2859
www.elite.net/~cvocplan/

George Ortiz
Corporate President
California Human Development Corporation
(CHDC)
3315 Airway Dr.
Santa Rosa, CA 95403
707-523-1155
Fax: 707-523-3776
www.chdcorp.org

Colorado

Charles P. Tafoya
Executive Director
Rocky Mountain Ser/Jobs Progress, Inc.
3555 Pecos St.
P.O. Box 11148
Denver, CO 80211
303-480-9394
Fax: 303-480-9214

Connecticut

Eugene Caro
State Director
New England Farm Workers' Council, Inc.
191 Franklin Ave.
Hartford, CT 06114
860-296-3518
Fax: 860-296-3713

Delaware

Karen Webster
State Director
Telamon Corporation
504 North Dupont Highway
Dover, DE 19901
302-734-1903
Fax: 302-734-0382

Florida

Carlod Saavedra, Director
Adult Migrant and Seasonal Farmworker
Program
Suite 200, 3802 Corporex Park Dr.
Corporex Plaza Two
Tampa, FL 33619
813-744-6303
Fax: 813-744-6296

Frank T Brogan
Florida Department of Education
Division of Applied Technology and Adult
Education
Adult Migrant Program and Services Section
The Capital
Plaza Level
Tallahassee, FL 32399
904-487-1785
Fax: 904-488-1492

Georgia

Herb Williams
State Director
Telamon Corporation
Suite 140, Building "D"
2720 Sheraton Dr
Macon, GA 31204-1167
912-750-7134
Fax: 912-750-7375
www.telamon.org

Hawaii

Gladys C Baisa
Executive Director
Maui Economic Opportunity, Inc
189 Kaahumanu
P.O. Box 2122
Kahului, HI 96733
808-871-9591
Fax: 808-871-2426

Idaho

Andres R Rodriguez
Employment Training Director
Idaho Migrant Council, Inc
104 North Kimball
P.O. Box 490
Caldwell, ID 83696-0490
208-454-1652
Fax: 208-459-0448

Humberto Fuentes
Educational Director
317 Happy Day Blvd.
Suite 400
Caldwell, ID 83605
208-454-1652
Fax: 208-459-0448

Illinois

Eloy Salazar
Executive Director
Illinois Migrant Council
16th Floor
28 East Jackson Blvd.
Chicago, IL 60604
312-663-1522 Ext 215
Fax: 312-663-1994

Indiana

L. Diane Swift
State Director
Transition Resource Corporation
5809 North Post Rd.
Indianapolis, IN 46216
317-547-1924
Fax: 317-547-6594

Iowa

Terry Mack
Executive Director
Proteus, Inc.
P.O. Box 10385
Des Moines, IA 50306
515-244-5694
Fax: 515-244-4166
www.netins.net/showcase/proteus/

Kansas

Richard E. Lopez
Executive Director
SER Corporation of Kansas

709 East 21st
Wichita, KS 67214
316-264-5372
Fax: 316-264-0194

Kentucky

Ronald J. Ramsey
Executive Director
Kentucky Farmworker Programs, Inc.
Suite 210, 1844 Lyda St
P.O. Box 51146
Bowling Green, KY 42102-4446
502-782-2330
Fax: 502-781-9820

Louisiana

Kevin Boyd, State Director
Motivation Education and Training, Inc.
1055 Laurel St.
Baton Rouge, LA 70802
504-343-0301
Fax: 504-343-7977

Maine

Jon Farley
Senior Vice President
Training and Development Corporation
18 School St.
Bucksport, ME 04416-1669
207-469-6385
Fax: 207-469-6348

Jack. A Frost
402 Project Manager
Training and Development Center
14 High St.
P.O. Box 476
Ellsworth, ME 04605-0476
207-667-7543
Fax: 207-667-3780

Maryland

Karen Webster
State Director
Telamon Corporation
237 Florida Ave.
Salisbury, MD 21801
410-546-4604
Fax: 410-546-0566

Massachusetts

Heriberto Flores
Executive Director
New England Farm Workers' Council, Inc.
1628-1640 Main St.
Springfield, MA 01103
413-781-2145
Fax: 713-781-5928

Michigan

Sam R. Garcia
State Director
Telamon Corporation
6250 West Michigan Ave., Suite C
Lansing MI 48917
517-323-7002
Fax: 517-323-9840

Minnesota

Lee Starken·
State Director
Motivation Education and Training, Inc.
1900 Highway 294, NE
Suite 2040
Wilmar, MN 56201-9423

320-231-5174
Fax: 320-231-6054

Mississippi

Joseph W Wheatley
Executive Director
Mississippi Delta Council For Farm Workers
Opportunities, Inc.
1005 State St.
Clarksdale, MS 38614
662-627-1121
Fax: 662-624-5087

Missouri

Ken Lueckenotte
Executive Director
Rural Missouri, Inc.
1014 Northeast Dr.
Jefferson City, MO 65109
314-635-0136
Fax: 314-635-5636
www.rmiinc.org

Montana

Sharon Liederman
Executive Director
Rural Employment Opportunities, Inc.
318 N. Last Chance Gulch, Suite 2A
P.O. Box 831
Helena, MT 59624-0831
406-442-7850
Fax: 406-442-7855
www.mt.net/~reo

Nebraska

Ella Ochoa
Executive Director
NAF Multicultural Human Development
Corporation
416 East 4th St.
P.O. Box 1459
North Platte, NE 69103-1459
308-534-2630
Fax: 308-534-9541

Nevada

Marcel Fernando Schaerer
Division Director
Center For Employment Training
520 Evans Ave.
Reno, NV 89512-3301
702-348-8668
Fax: 702-348-2034

New Hampshire

Ed Clark
Area Director
Farmworkers' Council, Inc.
370 Union St.
Manchester, NH 03103-5301
603-622-8199
Fax: 603-622-8230

New Jersey

John Schmidt Jr.
Executive Director
Rural Opportunities, Inc.
510-12 E. Landis Ave.
Vineland, NJ 08360
609-696-1000
Fax: 609-696-4892

New Mexico

Ernest E. Ortega
Executive Director

Home Education Livelihood Programs, Inc.
5101 Copper, N.E.
Albuquerque, NM 87108
505-265-3717
Fax: 505-265-5412

New York

Stuart J. Mitchell
Chief Executive Officer
Rural Opportunities, Inc.
400 East Ave.
Rochester, NY 14607
716-546-7180
Fax: 716-340-3337

Velma Smith
Executive Director
Rural Opportunities, Inc.
400 East Ave.
Rochester, NY 14607
716-546-7180
Fax: 716-340-3337

North Carolina

Richard A Joanis
Telamon Corporation
3937 Western Blvd.
P.O. Box 33315
Raleigh, NC 27636-3315
919-851-7611 Ext. 201
Fax: 919-851-1139

Thom Myers
State Director
Telamon Corporation
Suite 200
4917 Waters Edge Dr.
Raleigh, NC 27606
919-851-6141
Fax: 919-851-2605

North Dakota

Todd Wensloff
State Coordinator
Motivation Education Training
1326 25th St., SW
Fargo, ND 58106-9262
701-241-8442
Fax: 701-241-7016

Ohio

Michal Urrutia
State Director
Rural Opportunities, Inc.
2-453 Co. Road V
Liberty Center, OH 43532
419-875-6654
Fax: 419-875-4010

Oklahoma

Jose Angel Gomez
Executive Director
ORO Development Corporation
308 SW 25th St
Oklahoma City, OK 73109
405-840-7077
Fax: 405-848-7871

Oregon

Ronald J Hauge
Executive Director
Oregon Human Development Corporation
Suite 110, 9620 S.W. Barbur Blvd.
Portland, OR 97219

503-245-2600
Fax: 503-245-9602
www.ohdc.org

Pennsylvania

B. Kay Laracuente
Executive Director
Rural Opportunities, Inc.
1300 Market St., Suite 202
Lemoyne, PA 17043
717-731-8120
Fax: 717-731-8196

Puerto Rico

Cesar J. Almodovor-Marchany
Secretary
Commonwealth of Puerto Rico
Department of Labor and Human Resources
21st Floor
505 Munoz Rivera Ave.
Hato Rey, PR 00918
FTS 8-472-6620
Phone: 787-754-5247
Fax: 809-754-9244

Radames La Menza
Director
Commonwealth of Puerto Rico
Department of Labor and Human Resources
19th Floor, 505 Munoz Rivera Ave.
Hato Rey, PR 00918
FTS 8-754-5246
Phone: 787-754-5247
Fax: 809-754-9244

South Carolina

Barbara B Coleman
State Director
Telamon Corporation
P.O. Box 12217 (Capitol Station)
Columbia, SC 29211-2217
803-256-7411
Fax: 803-256-8528

South Dakota

William Podhradsky
Division Director
Black Hill Special Services Cooperative
221 South Central Ave.
Pierre, SD 57501
605-224-5336
Fax: 605-224-8320

Randy Morris
Executive Director
P.O. Box 218
Surgis, SD 57785
605-347-4467
Fax: 605-347-5223

Tennessee

Thomas Barnes
Executive Director
Tennessee Opportunity Program, Inc.
1370 Hazelwood Dr., Suite 207
P.O. Box 925
Smyrna, TN 37167
615-459-3600
Fax: 615-459-9326

Texas

Frank Acosta
Executive Director
Motivation Education and Training, Inc.
307 North College
P.O. Box 1749
Cleveland, TX 77328-1749
713-592-6483
Fax: 713-592-1690

Utah

Eulogio Alejandre
Director Operations
Futures Through Training, Inc.
533 26th St., Suite 204
P.O. Box 1309
Ogden, UT 84402
801-394-9774
Fax: 801-394-9841

Vermont

Hal Cohen
Executive Director
Central Vermont Community Action Council, Inc.
195 US Route 302 Berlin
Barre, VT 05641
802-479-1053
Fax: 802-479-5353

Virginia

Sharon L. Saldarridga
State Director
Telamon Corporation
4915 Radford Ave., Suite 202A

Richmond, VA 23230
804-355-4676
Fax: 804-355-6407

Washington

Gilberto Alaniz
402 Program Director
Yakima Valley OIC
815 Fruitvale Blvd.
Yakima, WA 98902
5090-248-6751
Fax: 509-575-0482
www.yvoic.org

West Virginia

Jim Dlhosh
State Director
Telamon Corporation
100 Williamsport Ave.
Martinsburg, WV 25401
304-263-0916
Fax: 304-263-4809

Wisconsin

Lupe Martinez
Executive Director
United Migrant Opportunity Services
929 West Mitchell St.
P.O. Box 04129
Milwaukee, WI 53204
414-671-5700
Fax: 414-671-4833

Wyoming

Edwin M. Stolns
Executive Director
Northwestern Community Action Programs of Wyoming, Inc.
1922 ½ Robertson Ave.
P.O. Box 158
Worland, WY 82401
307-347-6185
Fax: 307-347-4008

National

Lynda D. Mull
Executive Director
Association of Farmworker Opportunity Programs
1611 North Kent St., Suite 910
Arlington, VA 22209
703-528-4141
Fax: 703-528-4145

Free Job Training, GED Courses, and Guaranteed Jobs For High School Kids and Poverty Zone Drop Outs

Program: Youth Opportunity Program (YOP)

Description: Growing up in poverty today isn't what it was earlier this century. In years past, a life of poverty was much harder. There was no government assistance, no food stamps, no volunteer organizations willing to spend time helping anyone out. But many people who grew up in the rough-and-tumble, hand-to-mouth reality of the Great Depression — not to mention immigrants who arrived here with nothing more than a dream and a coat on their back — made good. Some even went on to become millionaires, professors, doctors, lawyers and political leaders. This is what America was all about. Guess what? It still is.

Youth Opportunity Program is a new community based program that gives money directly to areas where problems for kids are greatest — high poverty zones. And not just in inner cities. There are more kids living in poverty in rural parts of our country than in our cities. They've never seen crack dealers, and never heard the pop-pop-pop of gunfire in the night, but they are poor, and their chances of rising from poverty are slim. Fortunately, there is help available for them.

What You Can Get: The purpose of Youth Opportunity Program is to serve kids who just aren't getting what they need from traditional job training and placement programs. Here are some of the special kinds of help they give kids who participate:

- employment and training
- help staying in school
- ways to curb teen pregnancy
- assistance in dealing with drug and gang involvement
- participation in sports and recreation
- family support
- child development and health

Who Is Eligible: Kids and young adults between 14-21 years of age who reside in rural, Native American and urban communities are eligible to take part in the program. These communities even include migrant or seasonal farmworker communities, native Alaskan villages, or Indian reservations.

Youth Opportunity Program serves these kids, both in and out of school. For those still in school, the program offers:

- school to work help
- broad-based education improvement
- training and employment opportunities
- work-based learning
- school-based learning
- student-employer matching

For kids and young adults who are out of school, Youth Opportunity Program offers centers for continuing education and training. These centers offer:

- remedial education
- GED preparation
- occupational training
- English as a Second Language classes
- job search assistance
- support services
- recreation and sports programs

Money Available: Some of the Youth Opportunity Program projects will actually pay employers to hire participants in the program — up to 50% of the kids' wages on the job.

National Office:
Office of Policy and Research
Employment and Training Administration
U.S. Department of Labor
200 Constitution Ave., NW
Washington, DC 20210
202-219-5677
www.doleta.gov/youth_services/yog.asp

Local Offices: For more information on this program, contact the site nearest you from the list below.

Youth Opportunity Grants

Alabama
United Way-Birmingham Works for Youth
Jefferson County Office of Community Development
P.O. Box 320189
Birmingham, AL 35232
205-929-6668
Fax: 205-323-2872
Carmen Haley-Smith

Alaska
Youth Opportunity Grant
670 West Fireweed Lane
Anchorage, AK 99503
907-265-5900
Fax: 907-265-5996
M.J. Longley

Arkansas
Phoenix Youth And Family Services
Southeast Arkansas Economic Development District
PO Box 654
Crossett, AR 71635
870-364-1676
Fax: 870-364-1779
Toyce Newton

Arizona
Pima County Youth Opportunity
340 N. Commerce Loop, Suite 100
Tucson, AZ 85745
520-798-0534
Fax: 520- 884-5076
Arnold Palacios

Window Rock Youth Opportunity Grant
P.O. Box 3150
Window Rock, AZ 86515
928-872-6373/6372
Fax: 928-871-7116
John Hunt

California
L.A. Youth Opportunity Movement
2130 East First St., Suite 7
Los Angles, CA 90014
323-526-5817
Robert Sainz

San Diego Workforce Partnership
1551 Fourth Avenue, Suite 600
San Diego, CA 92101
619-238-1445
Fax: 619-235-8105
Margie Rosas

YO! San Francisco
Private Industry Council of San Francisco
YO! SF Headquarters
1650 Mission St., #300
San Francisco, CA 94103
415-431-8700
Fax: 415-431-8702
Glenda Gutierrez,

Steps of Success (SOS)
Imperial County Office of Employment Training
c/o SOS, 302 Main St
Brawley, CA 92227
760-344-9759

Fax: 760-344-9760
Marilyn Boyle

California Indian Manpower Consortium, Inc.
738 N. Market St.
Sacramento, CA. 95834
916-920-0285
Fax: 916-641-6338
Naomi Wilson

Colorado
Mayors Office of Workforce Development: Generation Y2K Project
City and County of Denver
1391 N. Speer Blvd.
Denver, CO 80206
720-865-5664
Fax: 303-276-6721
Rosanne Martillaro

Towaoc, Colorado
Youth Opportunity Grant Program
P.O.Box 514
Towaoc, CO 81334
970-564-5422
Fax: 970-564-5528
Tina Galyon

Connecticut
YO! Hartford Progress Collaborative
Capital Region Workforce Development Board
427 Franklin Avenue
Hartford, CT 00114
860-296-5068, ext. 110
Fax: 860-296-3477
Bob Rath

District of Columbia

Youth Opportunity Initiative
DC Department of Employment Services
77 P Street, N.E.
Washington, DC 20006
202-698-4204
Fax: 202-724-7347
Noel Meekins

Florida

Tampa Youth Opportunity
Tampa Metropolitan Area YMCA
110 E. Oak Avenue
Tampa, FL 33602
813-223-4202
Fax: 813-229-5949
Mark Dufva

Georgia

Georgia Department Of Labor
Albany/Dougherty Community Partnership for
Education
901 N. Jackson
P.O. Box 1726
Albany, GA 31702-1726
912-888-0999
Fax: 912-888-2664
Jo Granberry

Hawaii

County of Maui
Moloka'i Community Service Council
(MCSC)
P.O. Box 1046
125 Kamehameha V, Highway
Kaunakakai, HI 96748
808-553-3654
Fax: 808-553-3659
B.J. Dudoit

Kentucky

Project Empower YO!
Louisville and Jefferson County Workforce
Investment Board
410 E. Chestnut St., Suite 200
Louisville, KY 40202
502-574-2500
Fax: 502-574-4600
Irebe Britt

Louisiana

Northeast Louisiana Delta
Workforce Investment Board SDA-83, Inc.
P.O. Box 14269
1504 Stubbs Ave.
Monroe, LA 71207
318-387-7962
Fax: 318-361-0279
Keith Guice

Maryland

Youth Opportunity Movement
Office of Employment Development
417 East Fayette Street, Suite 468
Baltimore, MD
410-396-6722
Fax: 410-545-3702
Ernest Dorsey

Massachusetts

Brockton Rise Youth Opportunity Center
Brockton Area Private Industry Council
4 Main Street
Brockton, MA 02301
508-584-1888, ext. 21

Fax: 508-587-1994
Lisa Johnson

Youth Opportunity Boston
Boston Office of Jobs and Community
Services/EDIC
43 Hawkins Street
Boston, MA 02114
617-541-635-0874
Fax: 617-918-5299
Michael Mitchell

Michigan

YO! Detroit
City of Detroit YO! Detroit
5555 Conner Avenue,
Detroit, MI 48213
313-579-4900, ext. 2037;
Fax: 313-579-4903
Donald Hurt

Ottawa and Chippewa Indians
Grand Traverse Band of Ottawa and
Chippewa Indians
2605 N.W. Bayshore Dr.
Suttons Bay, MI 49682
231-271-7267
Fax: 231-271-7646

Mississippi

Ms. Jean Denson, Bureau Director
Employment and Training Division
Department of Economic and Community
Development
301 W. Pearl St.
Jackson, MS 39203
601-949-2234

Missouri

YO! Program
Full Employment Council (FEC)
1740 Paseo
Kansas City, MO 64108
816-471-2330, X285
Fax: 816-471-3828
Richard Salazar

New York

Buffalo and Erie County Workforce
Development Consortium
Buffalo and Erie County
Workforce Development Consortium
77 Goodell Street
Buffalo, NY 14203
716-856-JOBS
Fax: 716-856-5680
Felicia Beard

North Carolina

Lumber River YO!
Lumber River Council of Governments
4721 Fayetteville Rd.
Lumberton, NC 28358
910-618-5533
Fax: 910-618-5716
Blondell McIntyre

Ohio

YO! Cleveland
City of Cleveland, YO Cleveland
540 E. 105th St. 4th Floor
Cleveland, OH 44108
216-249-2020
Fax: 216-249-2119
Reuben Sheperd

Oregon

Portland YO!
Worksystems, Inc.
Youth Opportunity Center
3034 NE MLK Blvd
Portland, OR 97212
503-528-7510
Fax: 503-528-7575
Antoinette Edwards

Pennsylvania

Youth Opportunity Initiative
Workforce Investment Board of Philadelphia
734 Schuykill Avenue, Room 681
Philadelphia, PA 19146
215-875-3829
Fax: 215-875-5470
Angie Pabon

South Dakota

Sioux Tribe Pine Ridge, South Dakota
Oglala Sioux Tribe
P.O Box H
Pine Ridge, SD 5770
605-867-2200
Fax: 605-867-1579
Leticia Decory

Tennessee

YO! Memphis
Greater Memphis Area Workforce
Development Agency
2140 South Third Street
Memphis, TN 38109
901-947-5353
Fax: 901-547-5341
Dr. Marie Milam

Texas

Houston YO!
Houston Galveston Area Council
HoustonWorks
600 Jefferson Ave., Suite 900
Houston, TX 77002
713-654-1919
Fax: 713-793-0751
Johnny Bright

YO! Youth Opportunity Program
Alamo Workforce Development, Inc.
115 E. Travis Street, Suite 220
San Antonio, TX 78205
210-272-3260
Fax: 210-272-3283
Alan Miller

Washington

Seattle YO!
Seattle King County Workforce Development
Council
2003 Western Avenue, Suite 250
Seattle, WA 98121
206-448-0474
Fax: 206-448-0484
Dan Fey, Robert Roach

Wisconsin

Reach-Milwaukee
Private Industry Council of Milwaukee
County Reach Program
101 W. Pleasant St., Suite 201
Milwaukee, WI 53212
414-270-1701
Fax: 414-225-1071
Lois O'Keefe

Free Jobs And Training For Dropouts
Interested In Careers In The Construction Industry

Program: Youthbuild — 14.243

Description: Bottom line: most construction jobs pay really well. If you like the work, training in the construction industry can fatten the paycheck even further. If you get the itch, you might even want to become an engineer — or better yet — become someone who gets to use the wrecking ball to tear down old houses and buildings. What a job! But how do you get started?

What You Can Get: Young men and women can get experience in the construction trades while helping to build housing for the homeless under the Youthbuild program. It's a win-win deal for everyone involved. High school dropouts and other disadvantaged young adults can get a boost in life by enrolling in Youthbuild. Participants get hands-on training in the rehabilitation and construction of housing, as well as valuable off-site education. Youthbuild teaches participants how to tear down or rehabilitate old houses and how to build new houses from the ground up. Other benefits include:

- living allowances
- job development activities
- job placement services
- job seeking skills
- on-the-job training
- driver's education courses

Who Is Eligible: Low income kids between the ages of 16 and 24 are eligible to participate.

Money Available: The federal budget for the program is currently $50 million.

National Office:
Office of Economic Development
Community Planning and Development
U.S. Department of Housing and Urban Development
451 7th Street, SW
Washington, DC 20410
202-708-2290/1112
www.hud.gov/

Local Offices: For more information on the program, contact the site nearest you from the list below.

Youthbuild Grants

Alabama
Birmingham Health Care for Homeless
Jonathon Dunning
712 25th Street North
Birmingham, AL 35203
205-439-7201
Twenty participants will learn on-site construction skills by working to rehabilitate a vacant four unit building.

Mobile Housing Board
Steven Gregory
151 S. Claiborne Street
Mobile, AL 36602
334-434-2201
Twenty participants will learn on-site construction skills by working to construct eight affordable housing units.

Matthew Lesko, Information USA, Inc., 12081 Nebel Street, Rockville, MD 20852 • 1-800-955-7693 • www.lesko.com

Alaska

Southeast Alaska Guidance Association
Joe Parrish
P.O. Box 33037
Juneau, AK 99803
907-789-6403
Fourteen participants will be learning on-site construction skills by working on the construction of residences affordable to low and very low income households.

Arizona

City of Phoenix Human Services Department
Deborah Larkins
200 West Washington
Phoenix, AZ 85003-1611
602-262-4032
Thirty-six participants will learn on-site construction skills by working on the construction of three homes.

Town of Guadalupe
9050 S. Avenida Del Yaqui
Guadalupe, AZ 85283
602-730-3080

Arkansas

Mid-South Community College
Charles Tillman
2000 West Broadway
West Memphis, AR 72301
870-733-6755

California

Century Freeway Affirmative Action Committee, Inc.
Andrew Delgado
110 South Labrea Ave., Suite 430
Inglewood, CA 90301
310-419-8003
Twenty-five participants will be learning on-site construction skills by rehabilitating 12 units of low income housing. Half of the units will be owner-occupied, and half will be residential rental units.

Youth Employment Partnership, Inc.
Michelle Clark-Clough
1411 Fruitvale Ave., Third Floor
Oakland, CA 94601
510-533-3447
Forty participants will be learning on-site construction skills by working to rehabilitate twelve 3-bedroom rental units.

San Diego County SER/Jobs For Progress Inc.
George Lopez
3355 Mission Ave., Suite 223
Oceanside, CA 92054
619-754-6500

City of Vacaville
Cyndi Johnston
40 Eldridge Ave., Suites 1-5
Vacaville, CA 95688
707-449-5675

Asian Neighborhood Design
Joyce Pisnanont
1182 Market Street, Suite300
San Francisco, CA 94102
415-593-0423
Twenty-five selected participants will learn on-site construction skills by working on one apartment units.

Black Contractors Association
Abdur-Rahim Hameed
6125 Imperial Avenue

San Diego, CA 92114
619-263-9791
Twenty-eight participants will learn on-site construction skills by working to construct two single story three-bedroom homes for homeownership.

Century Center for Economic Opportunity
Andrew Delgado
17216 S. Figueroa Street
Gardena, CA 90248
310-225-3070
Forty-three participants will learn on-site construction skills by working to construct eight affordable single-family units.

Pacific Asian Consortium in Employment (PACE)
Kerry Doi
1541 Wilshire Boulevard, Suite 210
Los Angeles, CA 90017
213-353-3982
Twenty-five participants will learn on-site construction skills by working to construct two single residences.

Watsonville Redevelopment Agency
Richard S. Koch
P.O. Box 50000
Watsonville, CA 95077
831-728-6162
Sixteen participants will learn on-site construction skills by working to construct four new townhouse-style homes for Watsonville Redevelopment Agency's Low and Moderate Income Housing Fund.

Youth Employment Systems
James P. Smith
1772 East Century Boulevard
Los Angeles, CA 90002
213-473-3713
Thirty participants will learn on-site construction skills by working to construct 36 town homes.

Connecticut

City of New Britain
Department of Municipal Development
Kenneth A Malinowski
27 West Main Street
New Britain, CT 06051
860-826-3330
Fifty participants will learn on-site construction skills by working in conjunction with the City of New Britain, and HUD-Multi-Family Division. The project calls for demolishing an entire block and the construction of five single-family homes along with a recreational facility.

Co-opportunity, Inc
State of Connecticut
Department of Economic and Community Development
505 Hudson Street
Hartford, CT 06106-7107
860-270-8000
Forty to forty-eight participants will learn on-site construction skills by building five new homes.

District of Columbia

Sasha Bruce Youthwork
Deborah Shore
741 Eighth St., SE
Washington, DC 20003
202-675-9340

ARCH Training Center
Clement E. Idun
2427 Martin Luther King, Jr. Ave, SE
Washington, DC 20020
202-783-0958
Fifty-five participants will be learning on-site construction skills by working to rehabilitate three residential houses. Activities will include lead paint abatement, construction of wheelchair access ramps, and gut rehab.

Latin American Youth Center
Lori Kaplan
3045 15th St., NW
Washington, DC 20009
202-462-5696
Fifty participants will be learning on-site construction skills by working to construct two single residences.

Florida

Centro Campesino-Farmworker Center, inc.
Steven Mainster
P.O. Box 3483
Florida City, FL 33034
305-245-7738
Thirty participants will be learning on-site construction skills by working to build four single-family homeownership units.

City of Jacksonville
John Griffith
421 West Church St.
Suite 201-216
Jacksonville, FL 32202
904-630-3640
Twenty-four participants will be learning on-site construction skills by working to rehabilitate ten units.

DISC Village
Jan Hendricks
3333 West Pensacola St
Tallahassee, FL 32304
850-575-4388
Twenty participants will learn on-site construction skills by working to construct two new housing units.

Gainesville Housing Authority
Sally Lawrence
1900 SE 4th Street
Gainesville, FL 32602
352-371-3180
Fifteen participants will learn on-site construction skills by working to construct two new housing units.

Georgia

MONTEZUMA
Flint Area Consolidated Housing Authority
137 Richardson Street
Montezuma, GA 31063
478-472-8209

Illinois

Chicago Housing Authority
Kathryn Greenberg
626 West Jackson Blvd.
Chicago, IL 60661
312-791-8500, ext. 4741
Twenty-five participants will learn on-site construction skills by working to rehabilitate three single-family homes.

Chicago Housing Authority Youthbuild
Kathryn Greenberg
626 West Jackson Blvd.
Chicago, IL 60661
312-791-8500, ext. 4741
Twenty-five participants will learn on-site construction skills by working to construct five units of single-family housing.

Comprehensive Community Solutions, Inc
Kerry Knodle
310 S. Avon Street
Rockford, IL 61102
815-963-6263
Twenty-eight participants will learn on-site construction skills by working to construct three new single-family residences.

Emerson Park Development Corporation
Vickie Kimmel Forby
1405 State Street
East Saint Louis, IL
618-874-1671
Forty participants will learn on-site construction skills by working to rehabilitate two homes and construct two new homes.

Genesis Housing Development Corporation
Donnie Brown
607 East Oakwood Boulevard
Chicago, IL 60653
773-285-1685
Twenty-one participants will learn on-site construction skills by working to rehab Taherah Towers, a 16 unit residential facility for the homeless.

Indiana

Tree of Life Community Development Corporation
Bettye J. Brooks
561 Broadway Street
Gary, IN 46402
219-886-7475
Fifty participants will learn on-site construction skills by working to rehabilitate a three-story building for use as transitional housing for low-income homeless persons.

Iowa

City of Des Moines, Iowa
602 East First Street
Des Moines, Iowa 50309-1881
515-283-4568

Kansas

United Way of Wyandotte County, Inc.
434 Minnesota Avenue
P.O. Box 17-1042
Kansas City, KS 66117
913-371-3674
Fax: 913-371-2718

Kentucky

Community Action Council for Lexington-Fayette, Bourbon, Harrison, and Nicholas Counties, Inc
Mark Hundley
P.O. Box 11610
Lexington, KY 40576
859-244-2211
Forty participants will learn on-site construction skills by working to construct two residences for homeownership.

YouthBuild Louisville
P.O. Box 638
Louisville, KY 40202
502-213-4257

Louisiana

Louisiana Technical College
Patrick T. Murphy
Old Highway 65 South
Tallulah, LA 71284
318-574-4820
Fifty participants will learn on-site construction skills by working to construct two single residences in Tallulah and Lake Providence.

Mirabeau Family Learning Center
Christine Sartoris
4908 Haik Dr.
New Orleans, LA 70122
504-282-5559
Thirty participants will learn on-site construction skills by working to rehabilitate eight housing units. These units will be used for rental housing.

Rapides Parish Police Jury
Terry G. Bounds
P.O. Box 7556
Rapides Parish
Alexandria, LA 71306
318-448-1591
Thirty participants will learn on-site construction skills by working to construct two single residences.

Renaissance Development Corporation
Michael Vales
1623 Main Street
Baton Rouge, LA 70802
504-669-0566
Thirty participants will learn on-site construction skills by working to construct two single residences.

Maine

Portland West Neighborhood Planning Council
Thomas Pearson
155 Brackett St.
Portland, ME 04102
207-775-0105
Sixty-two participants will be learning on-site construction skills by working to rehabilitate six residences. When completed, one low income family will purchase each building.

Maryland

Community Building in Partnership
Tamara Jones-Short
1137 North Gilmore St.
Baltimore, MD 21217
410-523-4472
Thirty-five participants will be learning on-site construction skills by working on the rehabilitation of four residences for homeownership.

Massachusetts

YouthBuild Boston
Jackie Gelb
173A Norfolk Ave.
Boston, MA 02119
617-445-8887
Forty-nine participants will be learning on-site construction skills by working on the gut rehabilitation of four units of housing in two abandoned buildings in the inner city. Two low-income families will purchase the properties, and the new owner of the four unit building will rent the other three units to low income families.

Just A Start Corporation
Gordon Gottsche
432 Columbia St., Unit 12
Cambridge, MA 02141
617 494 0444
Thirty-two participants will be learning on-site construction skills by working to rehabilitate six housing units for homeownership and rental in three low income neighborhoods.

The Lawrence Youth Commission
Patricia Karl
11 Lawrence St., Room 615
Lawrence, MA 01840
Eighteen participants will be learning on-site construction skills by working to construct four units of new housing. The homes will be sold to low income new owners.

Michigan

Shiawassee Employment and Training
Margaret McAvoy
201 North Shiawassee St.
Corunna, MI 48817
517-743-5691

Young Detroit Builders
Ruby Kennedy
3535 Cass Ave.
Detroit, MI 48201
313-831-2385
Twenty-eight participants will be learning on-site construction skills by rehabilitating 12 housing units. The homes will be sold to low income families.

YouthBuild Detroit
Beverly Manick
Young Detroit Builders
3546 Trumbull
Detroit, MI 48208
313-831-1318
Fax: 313-831-0537

Minnesota

Bi-County Community Action Programs, Inc.
Mahlon Swentkofske
P.O. Box 579
Bemidji, MN 56601
218-751-4631
Forty participants will be learning on-site construction skills by working to rehabilitate six units of transitional housing for the homeless and one unit of homeownership housing.

Summit Academy
Louis King
935 Olson Memorial Highway
Minneapolis, MN 55405
612-377-0150
Fifty-six participants will learn on-site construction skills by assisting in the rehab of twenty-five homes being provided by the city for lead safe rehabilitation.

Mississippi

Coahoma Community College
Dr. Hazeltine Woods-Fouche
Coahoma Community College
3240 Friars Point Road
Clarksdale, MS 38614
662-627-5446
Thirty participants will learn on-site construction skills by working with the College's ongoing project to rehab between 5 and 15 homes and work with Habitat for Humanity on new construction of homes for low-income residents.

West Jackson Community Development Corporation
Howard Boutte', Jr.
1060 John R Lynch Street
Jackson, MS 39203
601-352-6993
Selected participants will learn on-site construction skills by working to construct and rehabilitate 7 residential units.

Missouri

Youth Education in Health in Soulard
Joyce Sonn
1921 South 9th St.
St. Louis, MO 63104
314-436-1400
Fifty-six participants will be learning on-site construction skills by working to construct five units for low income housing.

The Housing Authority of St. Louis County
Neil Molloy
8865 Natural Bridge
St. Louis, MO 63121
314-428-3200
Twenty-eight participants will be learning on-site construction skills by working to construct two rental single family homes.

Housing Authority of St. Louis County
Julie Tibbs
8865 Natural Bridge Road
St. Louis, MO 63121
314-428-3200
Thirty participants will learn on-site construction skills by working to construct two new residential houses for homeownership.

Nebraska

High Plains Community Development Corporation Inc.
Marguerite Miller
130 E. 2nd Street
Chadron, NE
308-432-4346
Fifteen participants will learn on-site construction skills by working to construct two single residences.

Lincoln Action Program
210 "O" Street
Lincoln, NE 68508
402-471-4515, ext. 108
Beatty Brasch

New Hampshire

Odyessey House, Inc
Joseph Diament
34 Winnacunnet Rd.
Hampton, NH
603-929-3038, ext. 341
Fourteen participants will learn on-site construction skills by working to rehabilitate two housing units. These units will be used for rental housing.

New Jersey

New Jersey Community Development Corporation
13 ½ Van Houten Street
Suite 200
Paterson, NJ 07505
973-225-0555

New Mexico

Taos County Government
Samuel Montoya
P.O. Box 1914
Taos, NM 87571
505-751-1542

Youthbuild New Mexico Coalition, Inc
Mary Sagbakken
115 Second Street, SW
Albuquerque, NM 87102
505-765-5517
Twenty-four participants will learn on-site construction skills by working to construct two single residences.

New York

Banana Kelly Community Improvement Association
Yolanda Rivera
863 Prospect Ave.
Bronx, NY 10459
718-328-1064

Episcopal Social Services
Stephen Chinlund
18 West 18th St.
New York, NY 10011
212-675-1000
Twenty participants will be learning on-site construction skills by working to rehabilitate a four unit vacant building. After renovation, it will be sold to owner occupants.

The YMCA of Greater New York
Michael Kllidas
333 Seventh Ave.
15th Floor
New York, NY 10001
212-630-9680
Eighty participants will be learning on-site construction skills by rehabilitating 105 housing units for homeless individuals.

Youth Action Programs and Homes, Inc.
Sierra Stoneman-Bell
1325 Fifth Ave.
New York, NY 10029
212-860-8170
Fifty-five participants will be learning on-site construction skills by working to rehabilitate two contiguous, vacant, city-owned buildings. A total of 20 permanent rental units will be created for homeless families.

Episcopal Social Services
Yaniyah Pearson
305 Seventh Avenue, 4th Floor
New York, NY 10001
718-221-1414
Twenty-seven participants will learn on-site construction skills by working to rehab ten vacant units in three multi-family dwellings located in Brownsville.

Utica Community Action, Inc
John Furman
253 Genesee Street
Utica, NY 13501
315-797-7364
Twenty participants will learn on-site construction skills by working to construct eight townhomes for single-family residences.

West Seneca Youth Program
2001 Union Road
West Seneca,
New York, NY 14224
716-674-5600, ext. 325

North Carolina

Housing Authority of High Point
Wayne Woodell
P.O. Box 1779
500 East Russell Avenue
High Point, NC 27261
336-878-2310
Twenty participants will learn on-site construction skills by working to construct four single family detached housing units for homeownership.

Housing Authority of Wilmington
Bob Dennis
508 Front Street
Wilmington, NC 28401
910-341-7700
Thirty participants will learn on-site construction skills by working to assist in the major conversion of a 250 unit complex and converting it into 190 rental units and homeownership for low income residents.

River City Community Development Corporation
Lenora Jarvis-Mackey
501 E. Main Street
Elizabeth City, NC 27909
252-331-2925
Thirty participants will learn on-site construction skills by working to construct two single residences.

UDI Community Development Corporation
Edward Stewart
631 United Drive
Durham, NC 27702
919-544-4597
Forty-five participants will learn on-site construction skills by working to construct two single residences.

Ohio

Buckeye Community Hope Foundation
Gilbert Barno
261 W. Johnstown Road
Gahanna, OH 43203
614-337-9718, ext. 106
Twenty-eight participants will learn on-site construction skills by working to rehabilitate four residences for homeownership.

Improved Solutions for Urban Systems, Inc
Ann Higdon
140 North Keowee Street
Dayton, OH 937-223-2322
Forty participants will learn on-site construction skills by working to construct three single residences that will be used for homeownership.

Quest Recovery Systems, Inc
Caroloyn Hess
1341 Market Avenue, N.
Canton, OH 44714
330-454-4246
Twenty participants will learn on-site construction skills by working to construct two new single residences.

Sojourners Care Network
Richard Games
P.O. Box 312
McArthue, OH 45651
740-596-1117
Twenty-eight participants will learn on-site construction skills by working to construct four homes for homeownership.

Oklahoma

City of Oklahoma City
Mayor Ronald Norik
420 East Main St.
Suite 920
Oklahoma City, OK 73102
405-297-2424
Twenty-four participants will be learning on-site construction skills by working to rehabilitate four vacant single family houses. When completed, the homes will be made available for purchase by low-moderate income families or individuals.

Oregon

Community Services Consortium
Mark Bemetz
545 S.W. 2nd St., Suite A
Corvallis, OR 97333
541-752-1010
Twenty-two participants will learn on-site construction skills by working to construct two single residences.

City of Portland's Bureau of Housing and Community Development
Jill Walters
City of Portland
421 SW 6th Avenue, Suite 1100-A
Portland, OR 97004
503-286-9350
Fifty participants will learn on-site construction skills by working to construct three single residences.

Pennsylvania

Philadelphia Youth for Change
Ms. Taylor Frome
619 Catherine St.
Philadelphia, PA 19147
215-627-8671
Seventy-five participants will be learning on-site construction skills by working to rehabilitate 12 single family homes for subsidized homeownership.

Resources for Human Development
Robert Fishman
4333 Kelly Dr.
Philadelphia, PA 19129
215-951-0300
Twenty-one participants will be learning on-site construction skills by working to convert a school building into 36 townhouses for residential rental and also by working to rehabilitate a home for homeownership.

Crispus Attucks Community Development Corp.
Cynthia Dotson
605 South Duke St.
York, PA 17403
717-843-3610
Participants will be learning on-site construction skills by working to rehabilitate eight efficiency rental apartments in a vacant building.

Alliance for Building Communities
Ed Pawlowski
830 Hamilton Street
Allentown, PA 18101
610-439-7007
Twenty participants will learn on-site construction skills by working to renovate homes for qualifying low-income families.

Rhode Island

Providence Plan
Chinyelu Martin
56 Pine Street
Providence, RI 02903
401-273-7528
Sixty participants will learn on-site construction skills by working to construct two single residences.

South Carolina

Telamon Corporation
Richard Joanis
P.O. Box 12217
Columbia, SC 29211
919-851-7611

Benedict-Allen CDC, Inc
Larry K. Salley
1600 Harden Street
Columbia, SC 29204
803-253-5121
Twenty participants will learn on-site construction skills by working to construct three new single family homes to be sold to low-income residents.

Low Country Community dba Palmetto Community
Helen Whitcher
3346-C Rivers Ave
North Charleston, SC 29405
843-974-6400
Thirty participants will learn on-site construction skills by working to construct a Historical Freedom Cottage for homeownership.

South Sumter Resources Center
Lana A. Odom
13 East Canal Street
Sumter, SC 29150
803-436-2276
Twenty participants will learn on-site construction skills by working to construct one new home and assist Habitat for Humanity in rehabbing homes of elderly and handicapped homebound residents.

Tennessee

Shelby County Government
Maggie Conway
1075 Mullins Station Road
Memphis, TN 38143
901-387-5700
Sixteen participants will learn on-site construction skills by working to rehabilitate three homes.

Texas

Dallas Youth Services Corp.
Patrick McNeil
501 North Stemmons
Dallas, TX 75207
214-939-3972

The Houston Community College System
Charles Green
P.O. Box 7849
Houston, TX 77270
713-718-5209
Forty participants will be learning on-site construction skills by helping to construct two single homes and rehabilitate two homes.

South Plains Community Action Association, Inc.
W.D. Powell
411 Austin St., L
Loveland, TX
806-894-1621

American Institute for Learning
Richard H. Halpin
216 E. 4th Street
Austin, TX 78701
512-472-3395
Fifty-six participants will learn on-site construction skills by working to construct eight new homes.

Community Development Corporation
Don Currie
1150 E. Adams, 2nd Floor
Brownsville, TX 78520
404-810-0090
Forty participants will learn on-site construction skills by working to construct ten new homes.

George Gervin Youth Center
Barbara Hawkins
6903 Sunbelt Drive South
San Antonio, TX 78218
210-804-1786
Thirty-five participants will learn on-site construction skills by working to construct four rental units.

Gulf Coast Trades Center
Thomas Buzbee
P.O. Box 515
New Waverly, TX 77358
936-344-6677
Forty-five participants will learn on-site construction skills by working to construct five housing units.

Vermont

Youth Building for the Future, Inc
J. Tim Parsons
14 S. Williams Street
Burlington, VT 05401
802-658-3397
Thirty participants will learn on-site construction skills by working to construct three units in the 25 unit historic Bus Barns housing complex single-family homes.

YouthBuild Burlington
14 South Williams Street
Burlington, VT 05401
802-847-2222
Fax: 802-847-2111

Virginia

Norfolk State University
Thomas Dawes
700 Park Avenue
Norfolk, VA

757-832-2396
Sixty participants will learn on-site construction skills by working to construct two single-family homes in the new Brambleton Community for public housing residents.

Total Action Against Poverty (TAP)
145 Campbell Avenue SW
P.O. Box 2868
Roanoke, VA 24001-2868
540.345.6781
Fax: 540.345.4461

Petersburg Urban Ministries, Inc
Dwalz Ferrell
P.O. Box 708
Petersburg, VA 23804
804-862-1104
Fourteen participants will learn on-site construction skills by working to rehabilitate two residences for homeownership.

Washington

King County Department of Community and Human Services
George Dignan
King County, City of Seattle
821 Second Ave., Suite 500
Seattle, WA 98104
206-296-5220
One-hundred participants will learn on-site construction skills by working to construct four single-family homes.

West Virginia

The Randolph County Housing Authority
Bruce Betler
P.O. Box 1579
Elkins, WV 26241
304-636-6495
Twenty participants will be learning on-site construction skills by working to construct two single family dwellings.

Human Resource Development and Employment Inc.
Homer Kincaid
1644 Mileground
Morgantown, WV 26505
304-296-8223
Twenty-four participants will be learning on-site construction skills by working to construct a single-family home and two apartment units to provide affordable housing.

Multi-County Community Action Against Poverty, Inc
Paul R Skaff
1007 Bigley Ave
Charleston, WV
304-342-1300
Thirty participants will learn on-site construction skills by working to rehabilitate 15 housing units and construct three new units.

Southern Appalachian Labor School Coalfield Housing
John P David
PO Box 127
Kincaid, WV 25119
304-442-3157
Twenty-eight participants will learn on-site construction skills by working to rehab coal camp houses for single-family occupancy.

Wisconsin

The Housing Authority of the City of Milwaukee
Ricardo Diaz
809 North Broadway, Third Floor
Milwaukee, WI 53202
414-286-5670
Twenty-seven participants will be learning on-site construction skills by rehabilitating three houses. The completed homes will be sold to low income families.

Operation Fresh Start, Inc
Connie Ferris Bailey
1925 Winnebago Street
Madison, WI 53704
608-224-4721
Thirty participants will learn on-site construction skills by working to
construct two single-family homes.

"The percent of the U.S. working population working in Fortune 500 firms rose from 14.6% in 1954 to 19.4% in 1974. Since then, the movement has been away from these large industrial companies. In 1992, only 10.9% of the working population were in Fortune 500 firms."

Source: *The New Rules: How to Succeed in Today's Post-Corporate World*, John P. Potter, Free Press, 1995

Go To One-Stop Career Centers
For Free Money And Help

Over 1,000 centers around the country offer free telephones, fax machines, photocopiers, computers, Internet access, help with day care, job search, resume preparation, free education and training money and more. It's a place that job seekers should start with to begin the process of finding out how you can get help to improve your career.

Each community has tailored their own system to meet the needs of its citizens. In Nevada, you will find the Career Information System whose resources include Discover Your Career Options and how to establish long-term career goals. The employment services staff at the Ohio Job Net will match you to the job that fits your skills. Idaho's Job Search Workshops teach techniques on how to target employers, interview, and get a job by employment experts.

The number of centers is growing every day. To find a center near you contact your local employment office; look in the Appendix for your state Department of Labor; or online at {www.ttrc.doleta.gov/onestop/pdf/1stop.pdf}.

Alabama
Alabama Career Center System
Alabama Department of Industrial Relations
649 Monroe Street
Montgomery, AL 36131
334-242-8003
Fax: 334-242-8012
www.dir.state.al.us
Email: webmaster@dir.statel.al.us

Alaska
Alaska Job Center Network
Department of Labor and Workforce
Development
P.O. Box 25509
Juneau, AK 99802-509
907-465-2712
Fax: 907-465-4537
www.jobs.state.ak.us

Arizona
One-Stop Career Center Project
Arizona Department of Economic Security
P.O. Box 21149
Phoenix, AZ 85005
602-542-1250
Fax: 602-542-2273
www.de.state.az.us/oscc
Email: onestop@de.state.az.us

Arkansas
Arkansas Career Development Network
Employment Security Department
P.O. Box 2981
Little Rock, AR 72203
501-682-7719
Fax: 501-682-7797
www.state.ar.us/esd/

California
California Workforce Investment Division
Employment Development Department
P.O. Box 826880
Sacramento, CA 94280-0001

916-653-6347
Fax: 916-657-0055
www.sjtcc.cahwnet.gov/SJTCCWEB
ONE-STOP/
Email: onestop@edd.ca.gov

Colorado
Colorado Department of Labor and
Employment
1515 Arapahoe, Tower 2, Suite 400
Denver, CO 80202
303-318-8000
www.coworkforce.com/EMP/

Connecticut
Connecticut Works
Connecticut Labor Department
200 Folly Brook Blvd
Wethersfield, CT 06109
860-263-6785
www.ctdol.state.ct.us/index.htm

Delaware
Delaware Works
DOL/Division of Employment and Training
4425 N. Market Street
Wilmington, DE 19809-0828
302-761-8102
Fax: 302-761-6617
www.vcnet.net
Email: dlabor@state.de.us

District of Columbia
DOES One-Stop Career Center
Department of Employment Services
500 C Street, NW, Suite 600
Washington, DC 20001
202-698-4817
TDD: 202-724-7000
Fax: 202-724-1357
http://does.ci.washington.dc.us

Florida
Workforce Florida

Agency for Workforce Innovation
Office of Workforce Services
320 Executive Center Drive, Suite 300
Tallahassee, FL 32399-0667
850-921-1119
Fax: 850-921-1101
www.floridajobs.com

Georgia
Georgia One-Stop Career Network
Georgia Department of Labor
Sussex Place, Suite 400
148 International Blvd., NE
Atlanta, GA 30303-1751
404-656-7392
www.g1careernet.com

Hawaii
Workforce Development
Department of Labor and Industrial Relations
830 Punchbowl Street, Room 329
Honolulu, HI 96819
808-586-8820
Fax: 808-586-8822
http://dlir.state.hi.us/wdd
Email: wdd@dlir.state.hi.us

Idaho
Idaho Works
Idaho Department of Labor
317 Main Street
Boise, ID 83735-0600
208-334-6303
Fax: 208-334-6430
www.idahoworks.state.id.us

Illinois
Illinois Employment and Training Center
Network
Department of Employment Security
400 West Monroe Street
Springfield, IL 62704
217- 785-5069
Fax: 312-793-9306
www.ides.state.il.us/ietc/map.htm

Matthew Lesko, Information USA, Inc., 12081 Nebel Street, Rockville, MD 20852 • 1-800-955-7693 • www.lesko.com

Indiana

Indiana Workforce Development
Department of Workforce Developoment
10 N. Senate Avenue
Indianapolis, IN 46204-2277
1-888-WorkOne
317-232-4259
Fax: 317-233-4793
www.dwd.state.in.us
Email: workone@dwd.state.in.us

Iowa

Iowa Department of Workforce Development
1000 East Grand Avenue
Des Moines, IA 50319-0209
515-281-5387
800-JOB-IOWA
www.state.ia.us/government/wd/
Email: IWD.CustomerService@iwd.state.ia.us

Kansas

Kansas Job Link
Department of Human Resources
Division of Employment and Training
401 SW Topeka Blvd.
Topeka, KS 66603-3182
866-444-LINK
785-296-0295
Fax: 785-296-5112
www.kansas.joblink.com.prod

Kentucky

Kentucky Cabinet for Workforce
Development
Department of Employment Services
275 East Main Street
Frankfort, KY 40601
502-564-5114
http://kycwd.org/one_stop.htm

Louisiana

Louisiana Works
Department of Labor
1001 N. 23rd Street
P.O. Box 94094
Baton Rouge, LA 70804-9094
225-342-3111
Fax: 225-342-7664
www.ldol.state.la.us
Email: os@ldol.state.la.us

Maine

Maine Career Centers
Maine Department of Labor
20 Union Street
P.O. Box 309
Augusta ME 04330
888-457-8883
207-287-3788
Fax: 207-287-5292
www.mainecareercenter.com

Maryland

CareerNet
Maryland Department of Labor, Licensing and
Regulation
Office of Employment Services
1100 Eutaw Street, Room 208
Baltimore, MD 21201
One-Stop Lead
410-767-2173
www.careernet.state.md.us

Massachusetts

One-Stop Career Center Network
Department of Labor and Workforce
Development
1 Ashburton Place Room 1402
Boston, MA 02108
617-727-6573
Fax: 617-727-1090
www.detma.org/offices/careercenters.htm

Michigan

Michigan Works
The Association of Michigan Works Agencies
2500 Kerry Street
Lansing, MI 48912
517-371-1100
Fax: 517-371-1140
www.michiganworks.org
Email: info@michiganworks.org

Minnesota

Minnesota WorkForce Center
Department of Economic Security
390 North Robert Street
St. Paul, MN 55101
888-GET-JOBS
Fax: 651-296-0994
TTY: 651-282-5909
www.mnworkforcecenter.org

Mississippi

Job Centers
Mississippi Employment Security
Commission
P.O. Box 1699
Jackson, MS 39215-1699
601-961-7593
Fax: 601-961-7540
www.wininmississippi.org

Missouri

Missouri Wins
Division of Workforce Development
421 Dunklin Street
Jefferson City, MO 65102-1928
573-751-3999
www.ecodev.state.mo.us/wfd/wfds/
frontpagewfds.htm
Email: wfd.state.mo.us

Montana

Job Service Division
Montana Department of Labor and Industry
P.O. Box 1728
Helena, MT 59624
406-444-2607
Fax: 406-444-3037
www.mtjoblinc.com

Nebraska

Nebraska Workforce Development Centers
Department of Labor
P.O. Box 94600
550 South 16th Street
Lincoln, NE 68509-4600
402-471-9928
Fax: 402-471-2318
www.dol.state.ne.us

Nevada

Job Link
Nevada Department of Employment, Training
and Rehabilitation
Employment Security Division
500 East Third Street
Carson City, NV 89713
1-877-US-JOBS

702-687-4440
Fax: 702-687-3903
http://detr.state.nv.us/
Email: detrinfo@nvdetr.org

New Hampshire

New Hampshire Works
Department of Employment Security
32 South Main Street
Concord, NH 03301-3860
603-224-3311
800-852-3400
www.nhworks.state.nh.us
Email: webmaster@nhes.state.nh.us

New Jersey

Workforce New Jersey
New Jersey Department of Labor
John Fitch Plaza, CN 055
Trenton, NJ 08625
609-292-6236
Fax: 609-777-0483
www.wnjjpin.state.nj.us

New Mexico

New Mexico Works
Department of Labor
401 Broadway, NE
Albuquerque, NM 87102
505-841-2000
www.dol.state.nm.us/dol_dirr.html
Email: dolinfo@state.nm.us

New York

Workforce Development System
New York State Department of Labor
State Campus Building 12
Albany, NY 12240
518-457-0380
Fax: 518-457-9526
www.wdsny.org
Email: onestop@labor.state.ny.us

North Carolina

Joblink Career Centers
North Carolina Department of Commerce
301 N. Wilmington Street
Raleigh, NC 27601
919-733-4151
www.joblink.state.nc.us

North Dakota

Job Service North Dakota
P.O. Box 5507
Bismarck, ND 58506-5507
800-732-9787
701-328-2868
TTY: 800-366-6888
Fax: 701-328-4193
www.state.nd.us/jsnd
Email: jsndweb@state.nd.us

Ohio

One-Stop System
Ohio Department of Job and Family Services
145 Front Street
Columbus, OH 43215
Fax: 614-728-5938
Email: www.state.oh.us/odjfs/onestop

Oklahoma

Workforce Oklahoma
Employment Security Commission
P.O. Box 53003

Oklahoma City, OK 73152
405-557-0200
Fax: 405-557-7256
www.oesc.state.ok.us

Oregon
Oregon Employment Department
Public Service Building
255 Capitol Street NE
Salem, OR 97310
503-378-8648
www.emp.state.or.us
Email: job_search@emp.state.or.us

Pennsylvania
Pennsylvania Works
Department of Labor and Industry
1720 Labor and Industry Building
Seventh and Forster Streets
Harrisburg, PA 17120
717-783-7184
Fax: 717-772-1461
http://pacareerlink.state.pa.us

Rhode Island
NetWorki
Department of Employment and Training
101 Friendship St.
Providence, RI 02903
888-616-JOBS
401-222-1133
Fax: 401-222-1136
www.networkri.org
Email: brutherford@networkri.org

South Carolina
South Carolina Workforce System
Employment Security Commission
1550 Gadsden Street
P.O. Box 995
Columbia, SC 29202
803-737-9935
Fax: 803-737-0202
www.sces.org/1stop/1stopmain.asp
Email: jobs@sces.org

South Dakota
One-Stop Career Center System
South Dakota Department of Labor
Kneip Building

700 Governors Drive
Pierre, SD 57501-2291
605-773-3101
Fax: 605-773-4211
www.state.sd.us/dol/sdjob/js-home.htm
Email: info@dol-pr.state.sd.us

Tennessee
Tennessee Career Center System
Office of Workforce Development
Davy Crockett Tower, 12th Floor
500 James Robertson Parkway
Nashville, TN 37243
615-741-7973
800-576-3467
Fax: 615-741-1500
www.state.tn.us/labor-wfd/cchome:htm
Email: lkelley@mail.state.tn.us

Texas
Texas Workforce Commission
101 E. 15th Street
Austin, TX 78201
800-735-2988
512-463-6438
TDD: 800-735-2989
Fax: 512-463-8547
www.twc.state.tx.us

Utah
Career Centers
Department of Workforce Services
P.O. Box 45249
Salt Lake City, UT 84145-0249
801-526-WORK
Fax: 801-536-9211
www.dwsa.state.ut.us/default.ht
Email: www@dwsa.state.ut.us

Vermont
Vermont Job Bank
Department of Employment & Training
5 Green Mountain Drive
P.O. Box 488
Montpelier, VT 05601-0488
802-828-4000
Fax: 802-828-4022
www.det.state.vt.us
Email: dcopeland@det.state.vt.us

Virginia
Career Connect
Workforce Development System
P.O. Box 1358
Richmond, VA 23218-1358
804-786-8531
www.careerconnect.state.va.us

Washington
Work Source Washington
Washington State Employment Security
Department
605 Woodland Square Loop
P.O. Box 9046 MS/600
Olympia, WA 98507-9046
360-438-4128
Fax: 360-438-3284
www.to2worksource.com
Email: iws@esd.wa.gov

West Virginia
Job Service
West Virginia Bureau of Employment
Programs
112 California Avenue - 5204
Charleston, WV 25305-0112
304-558-3461
www.state.wv.us/bep/jobs/default.HTM
Email: haydep@wvnvm.wvnet.edu

Wisconsin
Wisconsin Employment Connection
Department of Workforce Development
P.O. Box 7972
201 E. Washington Ave., Rm. A200(C)
Madison, WI 53707-7972
608-266-2687
888-258-9966
Fax: 608-261-6376
www.dwd.state.wi.us/dwepfe

Wyoming
Wyoming Job Network
Department of Employment
Employment Resources Division
P.O. Box 2760
100 West Midwest
Casper, WY 82602-2760
307-235-3254
Fax: 307-235-3278
http://wydoe.state.wy.us/erd

State Employment Agencies

You don't have to look to Washington to get help finding a new job, because the answer is probably in your own back yard — or at least down the street. Every state offers programs to get people the training and job counseling they need to earn a steady paycheck, and overlooking these programs can really minimize your chances for advancement. Utilize your state program and soon you'll be laughing — all the way to the bank.

What's next is a state-by-state listing of State Employment Agencies for you to contact to find out about specific programs in your state. Each entry will give you the following information:

- state employment agency address and phone number
- local employment office in state capital
- whether career counseling is available
- what vocational testing is offered
- what special services and publications are available

Examples of special training and job services offered by individual states include:

- free job retraining if you're injured on the job (WA)
- translation assistance for Hispanic workers (NY)
- tuition waivers for courses at community colleges (RI)
- special training for welfare mothers (CT)
- free child care and transportation during job search (HI)
- job networking for laid off professionals (KY)
- job training and help for laid off timber workers (OR, WA)
- list of federal contractors with hiring preferences (VA)

Alabama
Department of Industrial Relations
State Employment Service
649 Monroe Street
Montgomery, AL 3613
334-242-8004
Monegomery local office: 334-286-3700
www.dir.state.al.us/es

Alaska
Employment Security Division
Alaska Department of Labor and Workforce
Development
P.O. Box 25509
Juneau, AK 99802-5509
Juneau local office: 907-465-2711
www.labor.state.ak.us/esd/home.htm

Arizona
Department of Economic Security
DES Public Information Office
1789 W. Jefferson, 2nd Floor
Phoenix, AZ 85007
602-542-4791
www.de.state.az.us/links/esa/index.html

Arkansas
Arkansas Employment Security Department
#1 Pershing Circle
North Little Rock, AR 72114
501-682-2121
www.state.ar.us/esd/index.html

California
Employment Development Department
800 Capitol Mall, Room 5000
Sacramento, CA 95814
Mailing Address:
   P.O. Box 826880
   Sacramento, CA 94280-0001
916-653-0707
www.edd.ca.gov

Colorado
Colorado Department of Labor and
Employment
Division of Employment and Training
1515 Arapahoe, Tower 2, Suite 400
Denver, CO 80202
303-318-8800
www.coworkforce.com

Connecticut
Connecticut Department of Labor
200 Folly Brook Boulevard
Wethersfield, CT 06109
860-263-6000
www.ctdol.state.ct.us

Delaware
Department of Labor
Employment and Training Division
P.O. Box 9499
Newark, DE 19714-9499
302-761-8129
www.delaware.gov/agencies/DeptLabor/Empl
oyment_Services

District of Columbia
Department of Employer Services
609 H. Street, NE
Washington, DC 20002
202-727-7000
http://does.ci.washington.dc.us/main.shtm

Florida
Department of Labor and Employment
Security
3023 Capital Circle, SE
Suite 303, Hartman Bldg.
Tallahassee, FL 32399-2152
850-922-7021
www2.myflorida.com/les

Georgia
Employment Services Division
Department of Labor
148 Andrew Young International
Atlanta, GA 30303

404-656-6380
www.dol.state.ga.us

Hawaii
hawaii State Employment Service
830 Punchbowl St., #112
Honolulu, HI 96813
808-586-8700
www.dlir.state.hi.us

Idaho
Access Idaho
999 Main St, W
Boise, ID 83702
208-332-3570
Boise local office: 208-334-6211
www.labor.state.id.us

Illinois
Department of Employment Security
401 South State Street
Chicago, IL 60605
312-793-5700
www.ides.state.il.us

Indiana
Department of Workforce Development
10 North Senate
Indianapolis, IN 46204
1-888-WorkOne
317-232-7670
Local Indianapolis office: 317-684-2400
www.state.in.us/dwd

Iowa
Job Service Program Bureau
Department of Employment Services
1000 East Grand Avenue
Des Moines, IA 50319
515-281-5387
800-JOB-IOWA
Des Moines local office: 512-281-9619
www.state.ia.us/government/des/index

Kansas
Division of Employment and Training
Department of Human Resources
401 Topeka Ave.
Topeka, KS 66603
785-296-7874
www.kansasjobs.org

Kentucky
Department for Employment Services
275 East Main Street, 2nd Floor
Frankfort, KY 40621
502-564-5331
Frankfort local office: 502-564-7046
www.desky.org

Louisiana
Office of Employment Security
Louisiana Department of Labor
P.O. Box 94094
Baton Rouge, LA 70804-9094
225-342-3111
www.ldol.state.la.us

Maine
Department of Labor
Bureau of Employment Services
20 Union Street
P.O. Box 259

Augusta, ME 04332-0259
202-287-3516
Augusta local office: 207-624-5120
www.state.me.us/labor

Maryland
job Service
Department of Employment and Economic
Development
1100 North Eutaw Street, Room 208
Baltimore, MD 21201
410-767-2000
www.dllr.state.md.us

Massachusetts
Division of Employment and Training
19 Staniford Street
Boston, MA 02114
617-626-5400
Boston local office: 617-626-6000
www.detma.org

Michigan
Michigan Department of Career Development
201 N. Washington Square
Victor Office Center, 7th Floor
Lansing, MI 48913
517-241-0592
866-MY GOALS
www.michigan.gov/mdcd

Minnesota
Minnesota Department of Economic Security
390 Roberts Street, 5th Floor
St. Paul, MN 55101
651-297-2177
888-GET-JOBS
St. Paul local office: 651-642-0363
www.mnwfc.org

Mississippi
Mississippi Employment Security
Commission
1520 West Capitol St.
P.O. Box 1699
Jackson, MD 39203
601-354-8711
www.mesc.state.ms.us

Missouri
Employment Service
Division of Employment Security (DOLIR)
PO Box 59
Jefferson City, MO 65104
Gracia Yancey Backer, Director
573-751-8086
www.dolir.state.mo.us/es

Montana
Job Service/Employment and Training
Division
P.O. Box 1728
Helena, MT 59624
406-444-2840
http://dli.state.mt.us

Nebraska
Job Training program
Department of labor
P.O. Box 94600
Lincoln, NE 68509
402-471-2600
www.dol.state.ne.us

Nevada
Nevada Department of Employment, Training
and Rehabilitation

Employment Security Division
500 East Third Street
Carson City, NV 89713
775-684-3849
http://detr.state.nv.us

New Hampshire
Employment Service Bureau
Department of Employment Security
32 South Main Street
Concord, NH 03301
603-224-3311
www.nhes.state.nh.us

New Jersey
Employment Services
New Jersey Department of Labor
P.O. Box 055
Trenton, NJ 08625
609-292-5005
www.state.nj.us/labor/index.html

New Mexico
New Mexico Department of Labor
401 Broadway NE
Albuquerque, NM 87102
505-841-8409
www.dol.state.nm.us

New York
New York State Department of Labor
State Office Building Campus, Room 500
Albany, NY 12240
518-457-9000
www.labor.state.ny.us

North Carolina
Employment Security Commission
700 Wade Ave.
P.O. Box 25903
Raleigh, NC 27611
919-733-4329
www.ncesc.com

North Dakota
Employment and Training Division
Job Service
PO Box 5507
Bismarck, ND 58506
701-328-2868
www.state.nd.us/jsnd

Ohio
Ohio Department of Job and Family Services
145 South Front St., 6th Floor
Columbus, OH 43215
614-752-3091
www.state.oh.us/odjfs

Oklahoma
Oklahoma Employment Service
Employment Security Commission
Will Rogers Memorial Office Bldg.
P.O. Box 52003
Oklahoma City, OK 73152
405-557-0200
www.oesc.state.ok.us

Oregon
Oregon Employment Department
875 Union St., NE
Salem, OR 97311
503 947-1387
www.emp.state.or.us

Pennsylvania

Pennsylvania Department of Labor and
Industry
Seventh and Forster Sts., Room 1700
Harrisburg, PA 17120
717-787-5279
www.dli.state.pa.us

Rhode Island

Department of Labor and Training
101 Friendship St.
Providence, RI 02903
401-222-3682
www.det.state.ri.us

South Carolina

S.C. Employment Security Commission
P.O. Box 995
Columbia, SC 29202
803-737-9935
www.sces.org

South Dakota

South Dakota Department of Labor
700 Governors Drive
Pierre, SD 57501
605-773-3101
TTY: 605-773-3101
www.state.sd.us/dol/dol.asp

Tennessee

Department of Labor and Workforce
710 James Robertson Parkway
Andrew Jackson Tower, 4th Floor

Nashville, Tennessee 37243
615-253-1324
800-255-5872
www.state.tn.us/labor-wfd/esdiv.html

Texas

Texas Emploument Commission
101 E. 15th Street
Austin, TX 78778
512-463-2236
www.twc.state.tx.us

Utah

Utah Department of Workforce Services
P.O. Box 45249
Salt Lake City, UT, 84115-0249
801-526-WORK
http://jobs.utah.gov

Vermont

Employment Service Administration
Department of Employment and Training
P.O. Box 488
5 Green Mountain Drive
Montpelier, VT 05601
802-828-4000
www.det.state.vt.us

Virginia

Virginia Employment Commission
703 East Main Street
Richmond, VA 23219
804-786-1485
www.vec.state.va.us/index.cfm

Washington

Washington Employment Security Department
TRB2 Unit
PO Box 9046
Olympia, WA 98507-9046
360-438-4611
www.wa.gov/esd/

West Virginia

West Virginia Bureau of Employment
Programs
112 California Ave.
Charleston, WV 25305-0112
304-558-2630
www.state.wv.us/bep

Wisconsin

Department of DILHR
Job Service, 2nd Floor
201 East Washington Ave., (GEF-1)
Madison, WI 53702
Mailing Address:
  P.O. Box 7946
  Madison, WI 53707-7946
608-266-3131
www.dwd.state.wi.us

Wyoming

Wyoming Department of Employment
122 West 25th Street
Cheyenne, WY 82002
307-777-7672
http://wydoe.state.wy.us

State Funded Job Training Assistance

A priority in all states is job training and education because a well trained, employed work force is a prime asset. Programs that assist businesses with the costs involved in training or upgrading job skills of new or existing workers are available in all states except New Hampshire, Montana, and Wyoming. These states choose to use only the federal programs available for this purpose. All states have a wide variety of federally funded programs and services for job seekers and employers. State money is used in many of these programs, also. For instance, in Oregon the JOBS Program, which provides welfare recipients with a variety of education, training, and job placement services is comprised of 35% federal funds and 65% state funds. State funded programs tend to target small individual groups, so each state must consider its own unique economic, social, demographic and political issues when deciding on the state budget. The advantage of a state funding its own program is that the state can decide (with federal approval) what restrictions are required to be eligible for some programs. As an example, the state of Washington has no income restrictions for the Displaced Homemaker program, allowing individuals to receive assistance before they reach poverty level.

There are programs like New York's Green Thumb Program for seniors and Youth Conservation Corps programs in Iowa, Michigan, Wisconsin and Ohio which not only help the people who are involved in these programs but the state benefits as well. While these individuals are learning job skills, earning an income, and improving their self esteem, the state benefits from the results of their labor by improving the appearances of state highways, parks, and other recreational areas. Other programs that have had positive results at a minimal cost are: Arkansas's Educators-in-Industry program which provides educators the opportunity to learn about employers needs, and allows employers to express their views on the types of employees needed in the workforce; the Kansas Parole Job Fair which had a total cost of approximately $200 in 1996, and provided information regarding the job skills of offenders to the attention of local employers who were often unaware of the skills learned, developed and practiced by inmates; Maine's Professionals in Transition program, an organized support group for professionals to meet and make positive changes in their careers; and Hawaii's Career Kokua, a computerized library of occupational and educational information.

The following chapter will give you an idea of what types of programs each state offers. Some of them, although operated with state funds, are administered through federal agencies.

Alabama

* Alabama Industrial Development Training

Alabama Industrial Development Training (AIDT)
One Technology Court   334-242-4158
Montgomery, AL 36116-3200   Fax: 334-242-0299
www.aidt.edu/index.html   TDD: 334-280-4475

Alabama Industrial Development Training (AIDT) is a state-funded education institution established to develop and coordinate training programs for companies that are creating jobs in Alabama. They recruit and assist companies in selecting Alabama residents for enrollment in training programs. Training programs average 60 to 80 hours in length. Trainees usually attend a three to four hour training session on two nights a week for about ten weeks. Training sessions may be conducted at the company receiving the training, in AIDT mobile training units, in classrooms and labs at one of AIDT's three training centers in Huntsville, Montgomery and Mobile, or at a local community college.

* Veterans Benefits

Department of Veterans Affairs
P.O. Box 1509   334-242-5077
Montgomery, AL 36102-1509   Fax: 334-242-5102
www.va.state.al.us

Preference in State Classified Employment: All persons who have been honorably discharged from the US Armed Forces at any time shall have five points added to any earned ratings in examination for entrance to the state classified service. Those honorably discharged and entitled to pension, compensation, or disability allowance under existing laws shall have 10 points added to any earned ratings. Wives and widows of certain disabled or deceased veterans may have the 10 point preference extended to them and added to any earned ratings.

Educational Benefits: This program is administered by the Alabama Department of Veterans Affairs and veterans must meet certain qualifications to establish eligibility for his/her dependents. Programs offered include the American Legion and Auxiliary Scholarship Program and the Disabled American Veterans Scholarship Program G.I. Dependents' Scholarship Program. Complete details can be obtained by contacting the office listed above.

Alaska

* State Training and Employment Program (STEP)

State Training and Employment Program Manager
Department of Labor and Workforce Development
Employment Security Division
3301 Eagle Street, Suite 106   907-269-4660
Anchorage, AK 99503   Fax: 907-269-4611
www.ajcn.state.ak.us/jt/step.html

The State Training and Employment Program (STEP) attempts to prevent future claims against unemployment benefits by: attracting new business due to an available skilled labor force and lower employer unemployment insurance costs; training or retraining workers for new or emerging industries and technologies; and promoting local hire. STEP is funded by 1/10% of employee contributions to the Unemployment Insurance (UI) Trust Fund. These contributions are deposited in a special account within the state general fund. Persons are eligible who are unemployed and receiving unemployment insurance benefits, or who have exhausted their UI benefits; are employed but likely to lose their job within 6 months due to the job's elimination; or due to obsolescence of their job skills; or have worked in a job covered by unemployment insurance during the last 3 years but are ineligible for benefits because the job was seasonal, temporary, part-time, or wage contributions were insufficient, or due to underemployment. These programs are typically conducted in classrooms or other institutional settings; foster economic development in high growth industry; and are tailored to meet specific needs of a particular employer or group of employers. The employer must commit to hiring those who successfully complete training.

Arizona

* Apprenticeship Program

Department of Commerce
Apprenticeship & Job Training Program
1700 West Washington, Suite 600
Phoenix, AZ 85007   602-771-1181
www.commerce.state.az.us/jobtraining/default.html

Apprenticeship is a combination of on-the-job and related classroom instruction in which workers learn the practical and theoretical aspects of a highly skilled occupation. Programs are operated voluntarily by employers, employer associations or management and labor groups. Related classroom instruction is given in the sponsor's training facility or a local technical school or community college. Apprentices earn wages while they learn on the job, starting from about half the journeymen's rate up to 95% of full pay near the end of their apprenticeship. Training periods range from 1 to 6 years. Most trades require 3 to 4 years. The State Apprenticeship Council sponsors and funds the program.

* Veterans Benefits

Department of Veterans Services
Veterans Service Division
3225 North Central Ave., Suite 420   602-255-4183
Phoenix, AZ 85012-2409   Fax: 602-255-1244
www.azvcts.com

Tuition and Fees-Deferred Payment: A veteran or eligible dependent who has applied for education benefits under the GI Bill at state-supported community colleges. Colleges and universities may defer payment of tuition, fees and required books for a period of 120 days with no interest charges. If, at the end of such period, the person has not received from the US Department of Veterans Affairs the initial benefit monies for tuition and fees, an extension may be granted until such time benefits are received.

Employment Preferences: An honorably discharged veteran shall be eligible for employment preference, rights, and privileges under any merit system in the state or any political subdivisions thereof, regardless of age, if otherwise qualified.

* Job Training Grant Program

Arizona Department of Commerce
1700 West Washington, Suite 220
Phoenix, AZ 85007   602-771-1181
www.commerce.state.az.us/Workforce/default.asp

This state funded program provides business with grants for short-term customized, job and business specific training for new employees. The Department administers the program but works with training providers such as community colleges, private post-secondary institutions, and trade schools. Businesses must maintain or exceed current level of training expenditures and attempt to leverage other training resources. Eligible costs include: recruitment, screening, intake, assessment, interviewing, training design, materials design and accession, trainer costs, equipment, management and administration of training project and travel (not to exceed 10% of project). Ineligible costs are trainee wages and fringe benefits, and basic skills training. Selection is based on: number of new jobs created, location of business, average wages for new employees, total cost of training, training cost per employee, amount of business matching funds, use of local labor force, use of target groups, employee benefit package, financial well-being of business, and community support for the project. Start-up financing for new business ventures is not available. Eligible companies must have a profitable operating history of at least 2 years.

Arkansas

* Arkansas Industry Training Program

Department of Economic Development
Arkansas Industry Training Program   501-682-7675
One Capitol Mall   800-ARKANSAS
Little Rock, AR 72201   Fax: 501-682-7394
www.1800arkansas.com/business/Incentives/Customized_Training.htm

The primary function of the Arkansas Industry Training Program (AITP) is to offer pre-employment training, free of charge, to companies and to underemployed and unemployed persons in Arkansas. Trainees are not paid while in training. On-the-job training is offered if the equipment is too large, unique, or proprietary to set up in a training area. Training takes place in the community in which the company locates. Classes may be held in an educational institution, at the company site, in a donated community site, or a leased AITP facility. Classes are normally conducted at night, 3 to 4 hours a night, 3 to 4 nights a week, for 3 to 15 weeks. AITP provides training for possible jobs; it does not subsidize companies or trainees. All AITP funds are expended for direct training costs. Trainees voluntarily enroll in the classes so they are not obligated to accept employment, nor are they assured of employment and may accept or reject any job offered.

* Existing Workforce Training Program

Department of Economic Development   501-682-7675
One State Capitol Mall   800-ARKANSAS
Little Rock, AR 72201   Fax: 501-682-7394
www.1800arkansas.com/business/Incentives/Customized_Training.htm

The focus of this program is skills upgrade training, specific to a company's current workforce at any level. Skills upgrade training is defined as instruction conducted in a classroom environment at a worksite, an education institution, or a neutral location, that provides an existing, full-time employee with the new skills necessary to enhance productivity, improve performance, and/or retain employment. Skills upgrade training programs provide skills development to help a company and its employees adapt to new or altered technologies, management/supervisory systems, continuous quality improvement initiatives, or production methods or the new skills needed by the company to remain competitive, productive, and economically viable. To be considered for financial assistance, a manufacturing industry must: submit an application prior to the beginning of training; provide assurance that the participants involved in the proposed training program possess the prerequisite literacy skills; and clearly tie the proposed training to specific business goals and performance objectives. The Existing Workforce Training Program will pay a portion of the costs for the approved training program; grants will range from 20-70% of allowable training costs, depending upon a series of scoring criteria; and the maximum funding for any one company site cannot exceed $50,000 per year.

* Youth Apprenticeship/Work Based Learning Consortia Project

Ron Schertzer, Program Manager
Arkansas Department of Workforce Education
Three Capitol Mall   501-682-1360
Little Rock, AR 72201-1083   Fax: 501-682-1355

The primary objective of the program is to link resources of business and industry, education and the community to bridge the gap between the classroom and the workplace. It gives high school students an opportunity to develop career skills, evaluate their own potential for success, establish personal goals, earn paid apprenticeships, obtain college-level experience and gain personal contact within a specific occupation. All consortia are funded with state funds and other individually acquired sources.

* Dependents Educational Benefits
Arkansas Department of Veterans Affairs
P.O. Box 1280501-370-3820
North Little Rock, AR 72115   Fax: 501-370-3829
www.nasdva.com/arkansas

This program of the Department of Veterans' Affairs provides for free tuition at state-supported institutions of higher learning and vocational-technical schools for dependents of vets or Arkansas citizens that were prisoners of war or missing in action or killed in action, after January 1, 1960. Contact the office above for the specifics of the program.

* Elderly Employment Services
Division of Aging and Adult Services
Department of Human Services
P.O. Box 1437, Slot S-530
Little Rock, AR 72203   501-682-2441
www.state.ar.us/dhs/aging/index.html

Individuals over the age of 55 with limited incomes can get training, employment placement, counseling, and other employment services with this program. Financial eligibility requirements vary.

California

* Apprentice Program
Apprenticeship Program
Department of Industrial Relations
455 Golden Gate Avenue
San Francisco, CA 94102   415-703-5070
www.dir.ca.gov/apprenticeship.html

Apprenticeship is a combination of on-the-job and related classroom instruction in which workers learn the practical and theoretical aspects of a highly skilled occupation. Programs are operated voluntarily by employers, employer associations or management and labor groups. Related classroom instruction is given in the sponsor's training facility or a local technical school or community college. Apprentices earn wages while they learn on the job, starting from about half the journeymen's rate up to 95% of full pay near the end of their apprenticeship. Training periods range from 1-6 years. Most trades require 3-4 years. The State Apprenticeship Council sponsors and funds the program.

* Employment Training Panel
Employment Training Panel (ETP)
1100 J St., 4th Floor
Sacramento, CA   916-327-5640
          Fax: 916-327-5260

The Employment Training Panel (ETP) program is designed to assist business in acquiring and retraining highly skilled workers and staff needed to increase competitiveness and productivity. A performance-based contract is developed and a cost reimbursement per trainee is negotiated. Trainees must remain on the payroll 90 days after training in order for employer to earn cost reimbursement. The average cost reimbursement ranges between $1,000-$2,500 per trainee that successfully completes the program. Trainees eligible include someone who is unemployed and receiving unemployment insurance benefits or has exhausted his benefits within the past 2 years; an employee covered by the Unemployment Insurance System and is in danger of being laid off; and an employee in a firm that is becoming a high performance or diversified workforce. Priorities of the program are: growth of the California economy by stimulating exports and the production of goods and services that are imported from outside the state; new employees for firms locating or expanding in the state; development of a high performance workplace for the future; training displaced workers; joint developments with business management and worker representatives; and retention and expansion of manufacturing workforce.

* Technology-to-Teaching Program
Employment Development Division
800 Capitol Mall, MIC 83
Sacramento, CA 95814   916-654-8210
www.edd.ca.gov/wiarep/wiattp.htm

This program was created to meet the demand for new teachers, particularly in the Math and Science fields. Laid-off technology workers can receive training to become Math and Science teachers in K-12 public schools. Each local area created its own requirements due to the specific needs, however, the minimum requirements for the trainee are: the trainee must be a laid-off worker, preferably from the technology industry; must have a 4-year degree, preferably in Math or Science; and must qualify to receive services under the Workforce Investment Act.

* Veterans Dependents Educational Assistance
Division of Veterans Services
1227 O Street, Suite 101
Sacramento, CA 95814   916-503-8397
www.cdva.ca.gov/service/feewaiver.asp

The dependent child, spouse or unmarried surviving spouses of a service connected disabled or deceased veteran may be eligible for tuition and fee waiver benefits at any campus of the California State University system, University of California or a California Community College. The student must meet the residency requirement of the school that will be attended.

Colorado

* Colorado FIRST & Existing Industries Job Training Program
Business Development and Finance   303-892-3840
1625 Broadway, Suite 1710   Fax: 303-892-3848
Denver, CO 80202   TDD: 303-659-2656

Colorado FIRST Customized Training Program provides quality training for companies that are relocating, expanding, or facing new competition. The program will assist employers in training new or current workers in permanent, non-seasonal jobs and provide short-term, job specific training designed to fit the company's needs. Program requirements include: jobs must pay above minimum wage levels and be accompanied by a health care coverage plan; companies must participate in the training costs, directly and indirectly; and Colorado FIRST funds do not pay wages of trainees. Financial assistance for direct training costs include: instructor wages, travel, and per diem allowances; development of curriculum and instructional materials; cost of essential training supplies, equipment and space; and training at employer's location or local community college or vocational school. The Existing Industry portion helps those companies that are adopting new technologies or that are determined to become more competitive.

* State Veterans Benefits
Colorado Department of Human Services
Division of Veterans Affairs
789 Sherman, Suite 460   303-894-7474
Denver, CO 80203   Fax: 303-894-7442

Some of the benefits Colorado provides for veterans include:

Educational Benefits: Reduced or Free Tuition at certain designated state institutions of post-secondary education for members of the Colorado National Guard (must serve 2 years for each year of education granted).

Educational Opportunities for Children: Free Tuition in certain state-supported schools for children of POW or MIA who were Colorado residents when they entered the Armed Forces, or for children of Colorado national guardsmen who died or were permanently disabled. Limited to dependents who do not qualify for federal educational benefits.

Employment Preference, Privileges: Disabled veterans shall have 10 points added to their grade and non-disabled veterans or widows of veterans whose death was due to military service shall be credited with an additional 5 points on civil service examinations.

Connecticut

* Apprenticeship
Connecticut Department of Labor
Office of Apprenticeship Training
200 Folly Brook Boulevard   860-263-6085
Wethersfield, CT 06109-1114   Fax: 860-263-6323
www.ctdol.state.ct.us/progsupt/appren/appren.htm

This program provides trade-related classroom instruction to apprentices registered with the State Department of Labor. Thirty six hours of classroom instruction per apprentice course are set up in 13 locations, based on the number of registered apprentices and the types of apprentice trades. No state or federal money is used. State-registered apprentices must pay $100 tuition fee per course and half will be reimbursed by the employer.

* Community Services

Programs and Treatment Division
Connecticut Department of Corrections
24 Wolcott Hill Road   860-692-7494
Wethersfield, CT 06109   Fax: 860-692-7495
www.doc.state.ct.us/org/DivProg.htm

This program provides services in a residential or non-residential setting for inmates returning to the community including: pre-release planning, counseling, job development and placement counseling, substance abuse counseling, follow-up and other necessary services. The program, Correctional Enterprise of Connecticut, gives offenders an opportunity for real-life work experience while producing and marketing items for state and non-profit institutions. Also, Unified School District #1 provides instruction on topics such as special education, technical, trade, vocation, and post-secondary opportunities.

* Customized Job Training (CJT)

Program Manager
Connecticut Department of Labor
200 Folly Brook Blvd.
Wethersfield, CT 06109   860-263-6024
www.ctdol.state.ct.us/progsupt/bussrvce/cjt.htm

The goal of the Connecticut Workplace-Based Customized Job Training Center (CJT) Program is to help businesses grow and prosper in Connecticut by becoming highly productive and globally competitive and to build a stable, highly skilled workforce. The program is designed to stimulate the creation and retention of jobs in the state by providing financial assistance for training which the company could not have provided through its own resources. Non-financial assistance in the form of assessment of training needs and brokering of services is also given to businesses. Programs and contracts are developed on a discretionary basis to address specific training needs. Most programs have no client eligibility standards. Others may target dislocated workers or other populations.

* Displaced Homemaker Program

Program Manager
Connecticut Department of Labor
200 Folly Brook Blvd.
Wethersfield, CT 06109   203-566-2450
www.ctdol.state.ct.us/progsupt/jobsrvce/discjt.htm

This program coordinates a statewide network of job training and support services for the displaced homemaker population. A broad program of support services and occupational training provided through four multi-purpose service centers and their satellites in different parts of the state. Participants must be someone who has worked in the home providing unpaid household services for family members; has been dependent on the income of another family member but is no longer supported by that income or is receiving public assistance; and has had or would have difficulty in securing employment sufficient to provide for economic independence. Activities include referral, counseling, assessment of skills, job training for various occupations, job placement, and supportive services, such as child care and transportation assistance.

* Institute of Technology & Business Development

Dr. Edward Rybczyk
Central Connecticut State University
185 Main St.
New Britain, CT 06051   203-827-7966
www.ccsu.edu/ITBD

IIET is an outreach function of the School of Technology (SOT) at Central Connecticut State University (CCSU) and offers non-credit courses and services to industry. The SOT has had a proven record of success by providing its services to over 1200 companies in Connecticut. IIET was selected to assist in delivering applications oriented problem solving services to organizations for them to stay competitive. Programs may be designed for individual organizations and employers for individuals. IIET has four Centers designed to provide services; the Manufacturing Applications Center, and the Procurement Technical Assistance Center receive both federal and state money. The remaining two centers are self-sufficient; the Technical Training Center focuses on training companies on advanced manufacturing technologies and concepts ranging from quality

assurance to engineering design and analysis. The Conference Center hosts conferences, seminars, meeting and training sessions.

* Job Development Unit

Job Development and Placement Specialist
Commission on the Deaf and Hearing Impaired
1245 Farmington Ave.   TTY/Voice: 800-708-6796
West Hartford, CT 06107   TTY/Voice: 860-566-7414
www.state.ct.us/cdhi/job_dev.htm

This program provides job counseling, locations and/or develops job opportunities for deaf and hard of hearing persons, assists employers as well as deaf and hard of hearing persons with on-site training and in resolving on-the-job problems, arranges for sign language interpreting services in vocational situations. Any Connecticut resident of working age exhibiting a hearing loss (including deafness) is considered eligible to pursue vocational services through the Job Unit.

* Opportunities Industrialization Centers

Executive Director
Opportunities Industrialization Centers
180 Clinton Street
New Britain, CT 06053   860-224-7151

State funding is offered to Opportunities industrialization Centers (OIC) in order to provide basic education, skill training, plus job counseling toward employment to unemployed and/or underemployed young adults. OIC's services are only available to low-income and welfare recipients.

* Services for the Blind

Board of Education and Services for the Blind
Industries Division
184 Windsor Avenue, Suite B
Windsor, CT 06095   860-602-4000

Basic rehabilitation services for persons age 17-21 may include: low vision aids, diagnostic evaluation, counseling and guidance, physical restoration, vocational training, rehabilitation technology evaluation, adaptive equipment and services to assure a client is satisfactorily placed. Additional services provided to individuals who are blind may include: rehabilitation teaching evaluation and training, such as activities of daily living, Braille and/or technology orientation and mobility, may include evaluation and training in cane travel techniques as well as orientation to home and work environments. Staff can provide in-service training to employers and community agencies who request it.

* Workers Rehabilitation

Director
Division of Workers' Rehabilitation
Connecticut Workers' Compensation Commission
21 Oak St.
Hartford, CT 06106   203-493-1500
http://wcc.state.ct.us/wcc/rehabemployee.htm

The Workers Compensation Commission provides Vocational Rehabilitation services to individuals injured under the Connecticut Workers' Compensation Act. Funding is provided from part of the Workers' Compensation Commission Budget which is an assessment against the insurance industry. To be eligible for the services of this program, an individual must have an accepted workers' compensation case and the injury must prevent return to former, or most recent, work and pose permanent restrictions. Workers' Rehab provides aptitude testing, evaluation, job development, job-seeking skills, counseling, formal training, job placement, and on the job training.

* Employment and Training Consulting Services

Department of Labor
Business Services Unit
200 Folly Brook Boulevard   860-263-6575
Wethersfield, CT 06109-1114   Fax: 860-236-6529
www.ctdol.state.ct.us/progsupt/bussrvce/etcon.htm

The Department of Labor offers workplace consultation services to help businesses to become high-performance work organizations. The staff of the Business Services Unit will develop a plan of action which outlines the following: Employment and training services/resources needed; Identification o service deliver(s); Development of project time frame for follow-up/case management. The services and resources are provided through the Department of Labor, Department of Economic & Community Development, CONN/STEP, colleges, and others in partnership with the Department.

Delaware

* Apprenticeship Program

Department of Labor
Council on Apprenticeship and Training
Lock Box 36 Federal Building
Wilmington, DE 19801   302-761-8121

Apprenticeship is a combination of on-the-job and related classroom instruction in which workers learn the practical and theoretical aspects of a highly skilled occupation. Programs are operated voluntarily by employers, employer associations or management and labor groups. Related classroom instruction is given in the sponsor's training facility or a local technical school or community college. Apprentices earn wages while they learn on the job, starting from about half the journeymen's rate up to 95% of full pay near the end of their apprenticeship. Training periods range from 1-6 years. Most trades require 3-4 years. The State Apprenticeship Council sponsors and funds the program.

* Department of Corrections Education and Training

Bureau of Prisons
Department of Corrections
Administration Building
245 McKee Road
Dover, DE 19904   302-739-5601 ext. 221
www.state.de.us/correct/Data/BOP.htm

One of the biggest concerns officials for the Department of corrections have, as it relates to its clients, is education and absence of essential job skills. The agency offers a variety of vital programs to equip clients with some of the basic skills needed to obtain employment upon release. The Volunteers of America provide a Literacy Program which provides reading skills to anyone from non-readers to 4th grade level and Literacy Training which trains residents to tutor other residents.

* Economic Development Job Training

Department of Economic Development
Workforce Development Division
99 Kings Highway   302-739-4271
Dover, DE 19901   Fax: 302-739-2028
www.state.de.us/dedo

This office has a variety of employment and training services for new and expanding businesses. The Customized Training Grants Program offers customized training based on the specific needs of the business. Training can be on-site or off-site, entry level, transferable skills, job retention/retraining, provide increases in individual productivity, and other necessary training. There are also special training programs. The Workplace Basic Skills Training program allows existing companies to upgrade employees' basic reading, math, communication, and computer skills. The Pre-employment Training program offers custom pre-employment training in order to provide job applicants with the job skills required for a business' entry-level positions. The Information Technology Training Grant funds IT training for small and medium sized businesses.

* Educational Benefits for Children of Vets

Delaware Commission on Veterans Affairs
Robbins Building302-739-2792
800 Silver Lake Boulevard, Suite 100   800-344-9900 (DE)
Dover, DE 19904   Fax: 302-739-2794
www.state.de.us/veteran/vetben.htm

Children of veterans that are deceased, held prisoner of war, or missing in action are eligible for educational benefits. The child should be between the ages of 16 and 24 and be a resident of the State for at least 3 years prior to the application for benefits. The benefit may include funds for room, board, tuition, and required institutional fees for the academic year. Benefits are limited to four years of education.

Florida

* Department of Labor

State Apprenticeship Council
325 West Gaines Street, Suite 714   850-922-5021
Tallahassee, FL 32399   Fax: 850-487-1735
www.firn.edu/doe/apprenticeship/index.html

Apprenticeship is a combination of on-the-job and related classroom instruction in which workers learn the practical and theoretical aspects of a highly skilled occupation. Programs are operated voluntarily by employers, employer associations or management and labor groups. Related classroom instruction is given in the sponsor's training facility or a local technical school or community college. Apprentices earn wages while they learn on the job, starting from about half the journeymen's rate up to 95% of full pay near the end of their apprenticeship. Training periods range from 1-6 years. Most trades require 3-4 years. The State Apprenticeship Council sponsors and funds the program.

* Quick Response Training Program

Workforce Florida, Inc.
Quick Response Training
1974 Commonwealth Lane   850-921-1119
Tallahassee, FL 32303   Fax: 850-921-1101
www.workforceflorida.com

The Quick Response Training Program is a customer-driven training program designed as an inducement to secure new businesses to Florida as well as provide existing businesses the necessary training programs for expansion. Through this program, Florida is able to effectively retain, expand and attract employers offering high-quality jobs. Eligible projects are new or expanding/existing businesses that produce exportable goods or services, create new jobs and employ workers who require customized entry-level skills training. Training Requirements include: 1)Training services can be provided through community colleges, school districts, area vocational-technical centers, state universities, and when approved, at licensed and certified post-secondary private institutions. Training is limited to 18 months or less. 2) Training can be conducted at the business's own facility, at the training provider's facility, or at a combination of sites. 3) Program instructors can be either full or part time educators or professional trainers from the business. 4) The selection of trainees is the responsibility of the business, although assistance is available. The business is also responsible for establishing criteria to select trainees.

* Veterans Preference in Employment

Mary Grizzle Building, Suite 332-A
11351 Ulmerton Road
Largo, FL 33778-1630   727-518-3202 ext. 548
www.floridavets.org/benefits/veteranspref.htm

Florida laws relating too veterans are intended to provide selected veterans with an advantage in employment as a recognition of their sacrifices in the service of the nation, and also as compensation for deferring their civilian careers. There are 4 Veterans' Preference categories: 1) Persons with a service connected disability which is compensable under public laws, 2) the spouse of any person who has a total and permanent service disability and who, because of this disability cannot qualify for employment; 3) any veteran of any war who served one day on active duty during a wartime period; 4) the unmarried widow or widower of a veteran who died as a result of a service connected disability. Specific questions regarding preference eligibility, including required documentation, should be referred to the office listed above.

* Veterans Scholarship Programs

Bureau Chief
State Approving Agency
9500 Bay Pines Boulevard
Bay Pines, FL 33744   727-319-7423
www.floridavets.org/benefits/edu.html

The State of Florida provides scholarships for dependent children of deceased or disabled veterans or children of servicemen classified as prisoners of war or missing in action. Applicants must be between the ages of 16 and 22. The value of each award will be the amount of tuition and fees charged for 2 semesters or the equivalent by the institution the applicant is attending. The payment is made directly to the institution, no disbursement is made to the student. For more information or an application, contact the Public Information Division.

* Displaced Homemaker Program

Agency for Workforce Innovation
107 East Madison Street
Caldwell Building
Tallahassee, FL 32399   850-245-7476

www.floridajobs.org

The Displaced Homemaker Program allows the participants to achieve independence and economic security through job retraining, employment assistance, educational services and other services. To participate, the individual must be at least 35 years old; worked in the home providing unpaid household services for family members; are not adequately employed; will likely have a difficult time gaining adequate employment; and have been dependent on the income of another family member but is no longer supported by them.

* Migrant and Seasonal Farmworker Adult Education

Division of Workforce Development
Florida Department of Education
8402 Laurel Fair Circle, Suite 212   813-744-6306
Tampa, FL 33610   Fax: 813-744-6296
www.firn.edu/doe/bin00051/migrant_farmprog.htm

Services included in this program are provided to migrant and seasonal farm workers in order for them to become economically self-sufficient by obtaining employment outside of agriculture or upgrading their skills and stabilizing their employment in agriculture. Educational and skill training is provided by local school districts, community colleges and private for-profit and non-profit agencies. Participants may receive a $2/hour of instruction allowance and needs-based payments for transportation and child care. Emergency services such as food medical care, clothing, rent, transportation and more.

Georgia

* HOPE Grants

Student Finance Commission
2082 East Exchange Place   770-724-9000
Tucker, GA 30084-5305   800-546-HOPE

The Helping Outstanding Pupils Educationally (HOPE) program provides scholarships and grants to students attending public and approved private institutions. The intent of this award is to encourage advance training and education. This HOPE award may be applied toward tuition, books, and other education-related expenses. Funding is received from the Georgia Lottery for Education.

* Quick Start

Georgia Department of Technical and Adult Education
1800 Century Place, Suite 300   404-679-1700
Atlanta, GA 30345   Fax: 404-679-1710

Quick Start provides high-quality training services at no cost to new or expanding businesses in Georgia. Some of the elements of Quick Start training include: training needs analysis, examines the needs and develops recommendations for training that will be required; a detailed training plan gives a description of the training services and training schedule that will be custom-designed to meet a company's needs; high-quality training using advanced instructional technologies; and an expert in manufacturing and business technologies, instructional designers, computer experts, video production technicians and other professionals, Every company works with a Certified Economic Developer Trainer (CEDT). The CEDT is located at one of the Georgia's Department of Technical and Adult Education's 34 technical institutes, 18 satellite campuses or one of the four colleges affiliated with Quick Start.

* New Connections to Work

State Coordinator
Special Workforce Services Unit
1800 Century Place, Suite 400
Atlanta, GA 30345   404-679-4953
www.dtae.org/teched/CTS/newconn.html

Single parents, displaced homemakers, single pregnant women and TANF recipients are eligible to participate in the comprehensive training and employment program. It operates out of the state's 34 technical colleges and 3 colleges with technical divisions in partnership with the Department of Human Resources, Department of Labor, and other state agencies. The types of services offered are skills training, job readiness/job search activities, career guidance, assessment training, and life management/employability workshops.

Hawaii

* Apprenticeship Program

Department of Labor and Industrial Relations
Workforce Development Division
Apprenticeship Program
830 Punchbowl Street, Room 329   808-586-8877
Honolulu, HI 96813   Fax: 808-586-8876
http://dlir.state.hi.us

Apprenticeship is a combination of on-the-job and related classroom instruction in which workers learn the practical and theoretical aspects of a highly skilled occupation. Programs are operated voluntarily by employers, employer associations or management and labor groups. Related classroom instruction is given in the sponsor's training facility or a local technical school or community college. Apprentices earn wages while they learn on the job, starting from about half the journeymen's rate up to 95% of full pay near the end of their apprenticeship. Training periods range from 1-6 years. Most trades require 3-4 years. The State Apprenticeship Council sponsors and funds the program.

* Career Kokua

Research and Statistics Office
Career Kokua Program
Department of Labor and Industrial Relations
830 Punchbowl St., Room 322   808-587-5515
Honolulu, HI 96813   Fax: 808-586-9099

Career Kokua, the Hawaii Career Information Delivery System, is a computerized library of occupational and educational information. This information is accurate, up-to-date, and easily retrievable. Its information covers career exploration, occupations, how to prepare for specific jobs, wages, schools, programs of study, job search aides, military careers, community resources, and financial aid. The general public can use Career Kokua computers at Employment offices. Career Kokua computers are located at all secondary schools, community colleges, University of Hawaii's Manoa campus, some community agencies, the Employment Resource Centers and at some military bases. The user agencies receive handbooks and training so their counselors can assist students, clients, and interested persons. Funds for this service are provided by the state and by user fees.

* Employment and Training Fund Program

Department of Labor and Industrial Relations
830 Punchbowl St., Room 322   808-586-8838
Honolulu, HI 96813   Fax: 808-586-8822
www.dlir.state.hi.us/wdd/etf%20Home.htm

The Employment and Training Fund (EFT) Program makes available to employers and individuals timely and innovative programs in business-specific training, upgrade training, new occupational skills training, management skills training and similar activities. EFT may be used to fund: the operation of the state employment service for which no federal funds have been allocated; business-specific training programs to create a more diversified job base and to carry out the purposes of the new industry training program; industry or employer-specific training programs where there are critical skill shortages in high growth occupational or industry areas; training and retraining programs to assist workers who have become recently unemployed or are likely to be unemployed; programs to assist residents who do not qualify for federal or state job training programs to overcome employment barriers; and training programs to provide job-specific skills for individuals in need of such assistance to improve career employment prospects.

* Employment Training and Job Placement Services for Low-Income Persons

Office of Community Services
Department of Labor and Industrial Relations
830 Punchbowl St., Room 420   808-586-8675
Honolulu, HI 96813   Fax: 808-586-8685

Gaps in services or special needs to assist low-income persons and low-income persons with disabilities in becoming employed are addressed by Chapter 42D Contracts with Private Sector Service Agencies. The services assist low-income persons and low-income persons with disabilities with employment through pre-employment training, occupational skills training including on-the-job training, and job development and placement.

* Offender/Ex-Offender Program

Offender/Ex-Offender Project
Alu Like Inc.
567 South King Street, Suite 105
Honolulu, HI 96813   808-535-6790
www.alulike.org

The Project will complete an in-depth assessment on the capabilities, needs, and vocational potential of the ex-offenders seeking services from the project. A determination on the course of training, work, and services most appropriate to address each individual's employment goals and needs will be jointly agreed to by the ex-offender and the project's Employment Specialist. The service plan will identify employment goals and projected timetable of services. The Project will assist with referrals to Job Training Partnership Act (JTPA) programs to provide classroom training in basic education and/or vocational skills, worksite experience, on-the-job and other training designed to enhance the employment potential of participants. On-the-job training sites will be developed by the project prior to referral to a JTPA program. Referrals to JTPA programs will be initiated due to the project not having training monies for participants. Due to recent budget cuts, this program is currently available only on the island of Oahu.

* Psychosocial Rehabilitation Program

Adult Mental Health Division
Department of Health
1250 Punchbowl Street
Honolulu, HI 96813   808-586-4686
www.state.hi.us/doh/index.html

Through the Department of Health's nine Community Mental Health Centers' Psychosocial Rehabilitation program, the following vocational rehabilitation services are provided to persons with severe disabling mental illness: 1) Functional assessment/evaluation to determine the individual's capabilities and level of functioning. 2) Work-activity programs to assist individuals in their development of desired work habits and attitudes. 3) Psycho-educational classes to assist the individual with the understanding of their illness, medication, symptoms, and stress. 4) Social skills training for the development of interpersonal, communication, problem-solving, and independent living skills. 5) Vocational counseling services to individuals referred and participating in the Psychosocial Rehabilitation Services during the time that they are with the programs. 6) Support services for individuals who are employed and/or interested in employment.

Idaho

* Workforce Training Network

Division of Professional-Technical Education
650 West State St.
P.O. Box 83720
Boise, ID 83720-0095   208-334-3216   Fax: 208-334-2365
www.pte.state.id.us/wtn/wtn.htm

Short-term training programs for adults are supported primarily by employer contributions, user fees, and business and industry donations. The goal is to deliver customized training for employer needs that actively contributes to Idaho's continued economic, rural and community development. The Idaho technical college system helped more than 37,500 Idaho employees upgrade their skills or learn brand new ones in fiscal year 1995 and provided customized training to numerous Idaho businesses.

* Workforce Development Training Fund

Idaho Department of Labor
317 West Main Street
Boise, ID 83735
www.labor.state.id.us

The Workforce Development Training Fund was created to fund a trained workforce for Idaho employers. This Fund provides training and retraining opportunities that would not otherwise exist for Idaho's workforce. It is dedicated to provide training for: skills necessary for specific economic opportunities and industrial expansion initiatives; and upgrading skills of currently employed workers at risk of being permanently laid off. It is funded by a small portion of the state's share of the unemployment tax.

* Older Worker Program

Idaho Commission on Aging
3380 Americana Terrace, Suite 120   208-334-3833
Boise, ID 83706   877-471-2777

www.idahoaging.com

These programs are concerned with low-income unemployed senior citizens. They give those persons, 55 and older, basic skills and occupational training which allows them to gain economic independence as well as self-sufficiency. The programs are administered by a partnership between the Idaho Commission on Aging and the Department of Labor.

* Centers for New Direction

Idaho Division of Professional-Technical Education
650 West State Street
Len B. Jordan Building, Room 324   208-334-3216
Boise, ID 83720   Fax: 208-334-2365
www.pte.state.id.us/specproj/efnd.htm

The Centers have worked with single parents and displaced homemakers to help meet their employment needs. Recently, they have extended their services to other adults in transition that are in need of assistance. The Centers are located on the campuses of the state's six technical colleges. The services provided include pre-employment and pre-training, preparation, career and educational counseling, and assessment and testing. These services are designed to get the participants ready for employment opportunities.

Illinois

* Displaced Homemakers

Melissa Lake
Illinois Department of Labor
Displaced Homemakers Program   312-793-7111
160 North LaSalle   Fax: 312-793-5257
Chicago, IL 60601   TDD: 312-782-2000
www.state.il.us/agency/idol

A displaced homemaker is a person who 1) has worked in the home for a substantial number of years providing unpaid services for family members; 2) is not gainfully employed; 3) has difficulty in securing employment; and 4) was dependent on the income of another family member but is no longer supported by such income, or was dependent on federal assistance and is no longer eligible for such assistance. Agencies eligible to apply for program funds are those which can demonstrate that they are currently providing some type of services to the population. Allowable activities for individuals include assessment; career guidance and testing; self-confidence building; assertiveness training, job readiness workshops, job development and placement; work experience; supportive services, and referrals.

* Earnfare

Department of Human Services
1200 South Grand Avenue E   217-557-1601
Springfield, IL 62762   Fax/TTY: 217-557-2134

Participants engage in assigned employment activities equal to the amount of the Food Stamp benefits divided by the federal minimum wage. Subsequently, minimum wage assistance is earned for each additional hour of performance in Earnfare activity up to a maximum of $294 per month. Participants continue working at the initial Earnfare provider worksite for six months out of any twelve consecutive month period or until reassigned or reassessed. Participants must accept bona fide offers of employment and apply for jobs for which the provider makes a referral. Transportation expenses are provided for job interviews arranged by Earnfare employers. A clothing allowance is available which allows an individual to receive up to $100 in a 12-month period for clothing needed to go to the Earnfare assignment.

* Educational Opportunities for Children of Disabled or Deceased War Veterans

Vickey Campbell
Illinois Department of Veterans Affairs
833 South Spring   217-782-3418
P.O. Box 19432   Fax: 217-524-0344
Springfield, IL 62794-9432   TDD: 217-524-4645
www.state.il.us/agency/dva/benefits.htm

With certain restrictions, this state funded program offers payments of $250 for matriculation and tuition fees, board, room rent, books and supplies at elementary school, high school, and other institutions in Illinois for youth between the ages of 10-18 years. Requirements are extensive; details are available from the office listed above.

* Employer Training Assistance Program

Dennis Sienko
Prairie State 2000 Authority
James R. Thompson Center
Suite 4-800, 100 West Randolph St.   312-814-2700
Chicago, IL 60601   Fax: 312-814-2703
www.state.il.us/ps2000/index.htm   TDD: 312-814-3842

Prairie State 2000 is an Illinois State Agency that invests in currently employed worker training tied to technological or productivity quality changes in the workplace. The focus is on assisting job retention through skills upgrading. Funds are awarded under two programs: the Employer Training Assistance Program (ETAP) and the Individual Training Assistance Program (ITAP). Prairie State receives referrals from local and state economic development groups, trade associations, community colleges and directly from employers. Grants and loans are awarded to businesses on the basis of financial need and type of retraining planned. Allowable activities include trainer costs, materials, and supplies.

* Individual Training Assistance Program

Dennis Sienko
Prairie State 2000 Authority
James R. Thompson Center
Suite 4-800
100 West Randolph St.   312-814-2700
Chicago, IL 60601   Fax: 312-814-2703
www.state.il.us/ps2000/index.htm   TDD: 312-814-3842

Prairie State 2000 is an Illinois State Agency that invests in currently employed worker retraining tied to technological or productivity/quality changes in the workplace. The focus is upon assisting job retention through skills upgrading. Experienced Illinois employed workers are candidates for retraining vouchers. Unemployed workers may be eligible, assuming all other training resources have been exhausted.

* Industrial Training Program

Office of Industrial Training
620 East Adams   217-785-6284
Springfield, IL 62701   Fax: 217-558-6971
www.illinoisbiz/bus/employ_ind_training.html   TDD: 217-785-6055
or

Office of Industrial Training
James R. Thompson Center
100 West Randolph St., Suite 3-400   312-814-5963
Chicago, IL 60601   Fax: 312-814-8420

The purpose of this program is to increase economic development activities to small and medium-sized businesses and to increase the cost efficiency of state-delivered economic development programs and services. Any multi-company project sponsored by manufacturing associations, community colleges, strategic manufacturing partnerships, and grant recipients or administrative entities under the Job Training Partnership Act is eligible to apply for funding. Individual companies may apply for funding if they are retraining their workforce or training new employees in conjunction with an expansion or new location.

* MIA/POW Scholarships

Vickey Campbell
Illinois Department of Veterans Affairs
833 South Spring
P.O. Box 19432   217-782-3564
Springfield, IL 62794-9432   Fax: 217-524-0344
TDD: 217-524-46455
www.state.il.us/agency/dva/benefits.htm

The Missing-in-Action/Prisoner of War scholarship includes full payment of tuition and certain fees to any state supported Illinois institution of higher learning consisting of the equivalent of four calendar years of full-time enrollment including summer terms for any spouse, natural child or step-child of an eligible veteran. Application is made through the state controlled university or college that the applicant wished to attend or through any local Department of Veterans Affairs service office. The child must begin using the scholarship prior to his or her 26th birthday.

* Senior Employment Specialist Program

Illinois Department on Aging
Senior Employment Specialist
State of Illinois Center
Suite 10-350   312-814-2630

100 West Randolph St.   Fax: 312-814-2916
Chicago, IL 60601-3220   TDD: 800-2552-8966
www.state.il.us/aging

The Illinois Department on Aging (IDOA) is mandated by the Illinois Act on Aging to coordinate training and employment-related activities for the state's older individuals. IDOA funds the Area Agencies on Aging to hire Senior Employment Specialists, whose main responsibilities are to establish an effective system of coordination and delivery of training and employment services for older individuals by tapping the resources and coordinating with Illinois' 26 Job Training Partnership Act private industry councils, Employment Service Office, private and public sector employers, universities and colleges, the Older Americans act Title V Senior Community Service Employment Program and other training and employment-related services. The purpose of the program is to provide older individuals the maximum opportunity for training and employment programs and services.

* State Literacy Grant Program

Illinois Secretary of State Literacy Office
300 South Second Street   217-785-6921
Springfield, IL 62701   Fax: 217-785-6927
TDD: 217-524-0040

The Literacy Office administers two grant programs to improve the basic skills of adults. The community literacy program currently uses volunteers to upgrade the basic skills of adults functioning below the ninth grade level. The workplace literacy grant provides dollars to businesses which match the public money to provide job-specific basic skills at the worksite.

* Illinois Veteran Grant Program (IVG)

Department of Veteran Affairs
833 South Spring Street
P.O. Box 19432   217-782-6641
Springfield, IL 62794-9432   Fax: 217-524-0344
www.state.il.us/agency/dva/benefits.htm

Illinois Student Assistance Commission
1755 Lake Cook Road   847-948-8550
Deerfield, IL 60016   800-899-ISAC
www.isac1.org

The IVG program will pay for tuition and certain fees for undergraduate or graduate study at an Illinois public school of higher learning for eligible veteran. Grant assistance covers up to a maximum of 120 eligibility units. Information and applications for this program are available at either of the addresses above.

* Food Stamp Employment and Training Job Placement

Department of Human Services
Office of Employment and Training
100 South Grand Avenue E   800-843-6154
Springfield, IL 62762   TTY: 800-447-6404
www.dhs.state.il.us/ts/et/fsetjp.asp

This program offers assistance to TANF clients that have reached their 60 month lifetime limit and are not eligible for additional TANF cash benefits. Participants will receive intensive case management education, job skills training, pre-employment services and unsubsidized job placement with retention services. This program will allow these clients to improve their work skills and find employment, which will ultimately lead to self-sufficiency.

* Job Training Economic Development Program

Illinois Department of Commerce and Economic Opportunity
620 East Adams Street
Springfield, IL 62701   217-782-7500
www.illinoisbiz.biz/bus/employ_job_training.html

The program was created with the goal of fostering local economic development by linking the needs of the low wage/low skilled employed workers and disadvantaged individuals with the workforce needs of local industry. Community-based providers create partnerships with economic development organizations in order to identify local industries having difficulty in recruiting skilled entry-level employees. The partnership then provides training to fill those industries needs.

* Apprenticeship Program

Illinois Department of Economic Security
401 South State Street, 6 South

Chicago, IL 60605   312-793-5700
www.ides.state.il.us/individual/special/apprentc.htm

Apprenticeship is a combination of on-the-job and related classroom instruction in which workers learn the practical and theoretical aspects of a highly skilled occupation. Employers, employer associations or management and labor groups operate programs voluntarily. Related classroom instruction is given in the sponsor's training facility or a local technical school or community college. Apprentices earn wages while they learn on the job, starting from about half the journeymen's rate up to 95% of full pay near the end of their apprenticeship. Training periods range from 1-6 years. Most trades require 3-4 years. The State Apprenticeship Council sponsors and funds the program.

Indiana

* Gain Education & Training (GET)

Indiana Department of Workforce Development
Indiana Government Center South
10 North Senate Avenue
Indianapolis, IN 46204   888-WORKONE
www.in.gov/dwd/employer/advanceindiana/program/index.html

GET is a training program that looks to increase the skill level of incumbent workers. The training activity must result in a college degree, General Equivalency Diploma, apprenticeship status, Certificate of Technical Achievement, or other recognizable certification for the worker.

* Workforce Investment Now (WIN)

Indiana Department of Workforce Development
Indiana Government Center South
10 North Senate Avenue   317-233-5724
Indianapolis, IN 46204   888-WORKONE
www.in.gov/dwd/employer/advanceindiana/program/index.html

This program is for those workers that face a substantial risk of workforce reduction due to advanced technology, declining productivity, loss of product lines, cutbacks, and other factors. Indiana provides training of the employees' transferable skills, those skills that enhance their general knowledge, employability and flexibility in the workplace.

* Workforce Literacy

Department of Workforce Development
Office of Workforce Literacy
10 North Senate Avenue
Indianapolis, IN 46204   317-232-4785
www.in.gov/dwd/education/workforce_lit2.html

The Workforce Literacy Division has a goal to build up the skills of the state's workforce through on-site customized, specific job-related training.

* TECH Fund

Business Development Division
Indiana Department of Commerce
One North Capitol, Suite 700
Indianapolis, IN 46204   317-232-1888
www.in.gov/doc/skills2016/tech

The Technology Enhancement Certification for Hoosiers Fund is a pilot program that was developed to quickly increase the number of certified information technology workers. Workers will earn professional-level certifications with the training.

* Skills Enhancement Fund (SEF)

Business Development Division
Indiana Department of Commerce
One North Capitol, Suite 700
Indianapolis, IN 46204   317-232-1888
www.in.gov/doc/skills2016/skills

Funds are available to new and expanding businesses that are committed to training their workforce. Training activities include basic skills, transferable skills, company-specific skills, and quality-assurance skills.

* New Directions Program

Single Parent Specialist
Henry Reis Educational center
1900 Stringtown Road
Evansville, IN 47711   812-435-8275

www.evsc.k12.in.us/cirriculum/adulted/newdir/index.html

Displaced homemakers and single parents can gain marketable job skills through participation in this program. An individual Employment/Training Plan and Career Assessment will be completed for each participant. After the vocational training and employment plans are completed, they will receive assistance with employment placement. Support services in such areas as transportation, childcare and books are available.

Iowa

* Iowa Jobs Training Program

Iowa Department of Economic Development
Division of Work Force Development
200 East Grand Avenue   515-242-4867
Des Moines, IA 50309   Fax: 515-242-4749
www.iowasmart.com/services/workforce/njtp.html

The program provides for job training services to current employees of eligible businesses located in Iowa. Job training is defined as any training that is needed to enhance the performance of a business' employees. Business sites are allowed a maximum award of $25,000 per project. Those projects that cost more than $5,000 require a 25% cash match from the business. The program is administered by the Iowa Department of Economic Development and training services are provided by the state's 15 Community Colleges.

* Iowa Industrial New Jobs Training Program

Iowa Department of Economic Development
200 East Grand Avenue   515-242-4867
Des Moines, IA 50309   Fax: 515-242-4749
www.iowasmart.com/services/workforce/iinjtp.html

Funding for this program comes from the sale of bonds by the Community Colleges that provide the training. Training is available to businesses that are creating new positions in their company. The employees that are to receive the training must occupy job positions that did not exist 6 months prior to the training project date. The businesses get back up to 50% of the annual gross payroll costs for the on-the-job training for up to one year after the new job was filled.

* Apprenticeship Program

Iowa Department of Economic Development
200 East Grand Avenue   515-242-4867
Des Moines, IA 50309   Fax: 515-242-4749
www.iowasmart.com/services/workforce/appren.html

The Iowa program has been established to fund high-technology apprenticeship programs. Apprenticeship is a combination of on-the-job and related classroom instruction in which workers learn the practical and theoretical aspects of a highly skilled occupation. Employers, employer associations or management and labor groups operate programs voluntarily. Related classroom instruction is given in the sponsor's training facility or a local technical school or community college. Apprentices earn wages while they learn on the job, starting from about half the journeymen's rate up to 95% of full pay near the end of their apprenticeship. Training periods range from 1-6 years. Most trades require 3-4 years. The State Apprenticeship Council sponsors and funds the program.

* CareerLink

Iowa Department of Economic Development
200 East Grand Avenue   515-242-4783
Des Moines, IA 50309   Fax: 515-242-4749
www.community.state.ia.us/workforce/career.html

CareerLink is an industry driven training program designed to invest in projects that provide assistance to the underemployed and working poor. The goal is to help them to obtain the training and skills necessary to move into available higher skill, higher wage jobs.

Kansas

* Apprenticeship Program

Kansas Department of Human Resources
Kansas Apprenticeship Council
401 Topeka Boulevard   785-296-4161
Topeka, KS 66603-3182   Fax: 785-291-3512
http://entkdh.state.ks.us/Apprenticeship.htm

Apprenticeship is a combination of on-the-job and related classroom instruction in which workers learn the practical and theoretical aspects of a highly skilled occupation. Programs are operated voluntarily by employers, employer associations or management and labor groups. Related classroom instruction is given in the sponsor's training facility or a local technical school or community college. Apprentices earn wages while they learn on the job, starting from about half the journeymen's rate up to 95% of full pay near the end of their apprenticeship. Training periods range from 1-6 years. Most trades require 3-4 years. The State Apprenticeship Council sponsors and funds the program.

* Kansas Industrial Retraining (KIR) Program

Kansas Department of Commerce & Housing
Business Development Division
1000 S.W. Jackson Street, Suite 100   785-296-8097
Topeka, KS 66612-1354   Fax: 785-296-3490
                                    TDD: 785-296-3487

This program is a job retention tool which assists employees of restructuring industries who are likely to be displaced because of obsolete or inadequate job skills and knowledge. Eligible industries include basic enterprises that are restructuring their operations through incorporation of existing technology, development and incorporation of existing diversification of production, or the development and implementation of new production activities. At least one existing employee must be trained to qualify for assistance.

* State of Kansas Investments in Lifelong Learning (SKILL)

Kansas Department of Commerce & Housing
Business Development Division
1000 S.W. Jackson Street, Suite 100
Topeka, DS 66612-1354   785-296-3339
http://kdoch.state.ks.us

The SKILL program may be utilized by individual business or consortiums of companies adding new jobs. Like the KIT program, SKILL is intended to help companies offset the costs of training employees for new jobs. SKILL's funding capacity, however, is substantially larger because the number and average wages of the new employees determine the project funding limit. Training projects costs are financed through tax exempt, public purpose bonds issued on an as needed basis by the Kansas Development Finance Authority. The maximum amount of assistance for which a company qualifies is directly tied to the number of new jobs created and the taxable wages of those jobs over 10 years. If a company is unable to create jobs in sufficient numbers to generate withholding tax revenue according to its annual projections, the business may be required to repay a portion of the training funds on a shared basis with the state. If a company leaves the state before the bonds are retired, the full cost must be repaid, less any withholding tax contributions collected prior to the company's departure.

* Kansas Industrial Training Program (KIT)

Workforce Training Specialist
Business Development
1000 S.W. Jackson, Suite 100   785-296-4284
Topeka, KS 66612-1354   Fax: 785-296-3490

KIT is a flexible workforce training program for new and expanding companies that are creating at least one new job, excluding the jobs of recalled workers, replacement workers, or jobs that formerly existed. Training includes both pre-employment and on-the-job training. Pre-employment training may be used so that the potential employee and the company have the chance to evaluate each other before committing to employment. The likely employee is given the knowledge and specific skills needed for the job. With on-the-job training, trainees may get instruction on the company's own production equipment or on similar machinery in a classroom.

Kentucky

* Apprenticeship Program

Kentucky Labor Cabinet
Employment Standards, Apprenticeship & Training
1047 US Highway 127 South, Suite 4
Frankfort, KY 40601   502-564-3070
http://labor.ky.gov/esat/apprent.htm

Apprenticeship is a combination of on-the-job and related classroom instruction in which workers learn the practical and theoretical aspects of a highly skilled occupation. Programs are operated voluntarily by employers, employer associations or management and labor groups. Related classroom instruction is given in the sponsor's training facility or a local technical school or community college. Apprentices earn wages while they learn on the job, starting from about half the journeymen's rate up to 95% of full pay near the end of their apprenticeship. Training periods range from 1-6 years. Most trades require 3-4 years. The State Apprenticeship Council sponsors and funds the program.

* Bluegrass State Skills Corporation (BSSC)

Cabinet for Economic Development
Capitol Plaza Tower
500 Mero St.   502-564-7670
Frankfort, KY 40601   Fax: 502-564-3256

BSSC provides grants for the customized skills training of workers for new, expanding, and existing industries in Kentucky. Grants are awarded for portions of an employer's eligible costs of training Kentucky residents in job skills ranging from entry level to advanced, including retraining and skills upgrading of existing employees. BSSC works with other employment, job training resources, and financial incentive agencies to design a training program customized to meet the specific needs of a company. Approved training can be provided by an educational institution, private training specialists, or by the company's own trainers. Funds can be used for curriculum design and customization, instructor salaries and instructional materials. BSSC also can help to cover a portion of the travel costs for the employees of new and expanding Kentucky industries that must be sent outside of Kentucky or the USA for training as company instructors. The instructor must return to the company and train other employees on similar equipment, processes, and procedures. BSSC can reimburse the company partially for the instructor/trainer's out-of-state travel, food, and lodging expenses.

* Kentucky TECH System

Cabinet for Workforce Development
Department for Technical Education
500 Mero St.
Capitol Plaza Tower   502-564-4286
Frankfort, KY 40601   Fax: 502-564-4800
http://kytech.ky.gov/ProgramOffering.htm

The Department for Technical Education manages state-supported technical education programs and facilities, including the Kentucky TECH system. Kentucky TECH offers technical training in more than 50 job areas at 25 post-secondary and 54 secondary facilities across the state, retraining for employed adults who need new or upgraded skills, and vocational assessment. Customized employee training and assessment programs are provided to businesses and industries at technical schools, in mobile facilities or at work sites. The Kentucky TECH System guarantees employers that graduate state-operated vocational-technical schools have demonstrated competence in the skills listed on the approved task lists which represent industry-validated specification for each occupational program. Should a former student be considered by the employer as performing below a satisfactory level on any skill on the approved task lists, the Kentucky TECH System agrees to provide specific retraining at no charge for instructional costs to the employee or employer. This guarantee extends for two years from the date of graduation.

* SKILL

Kentucky Department for Adult Education & Literacy
Workplace Training
500 Mero Street
Capital Plaza Tower, 3rd Floor   502-564-5114
Frankfort, KY 40601   800-928-7323
http://adulted.state.ky.us/Workplace%20Skill%20Branch.htm

State of Kentucky's Investment in Lifelong Learning (SKILL) is a program that provides basic workplace essential skills training which upgrades employee skills. These skills improve performance, productivity, and profitability at the worksite. Eligible training activities include; Contexted Workplace Essential Skills training to employees on company time; Pre-technical training in conjunction with advanced classes; Contexted pre-employment training with a goal to hire at least 50% of the trainees; Traditional, on-site, Adult Basic Education; and Work-based skills training. The program is funded through the Council on Postsecondary Education Adult Education Fund.

Louisiana

* Apprenticeship Program

Department of Labor
Apprenticeship Division
1001 North 23rd Street
P.O. Box 94094
Baton Rouge, LA 70804-9094   225-342-3111

Apprenticeship is a combination of on-the-job and related classroom instruction in which workers learn the practical and theoretical aspects of a highly skilled occupation. Programs are operated voluntarily by employers, employer associations or management and labor groups. Related classroom instruction is given in the sponsor's training facility or a local technical school or community college. Apprentices earn wages while they learn on the job, starting from about half the journeymen's rate up to 95% of full pay near the end of their apprenticeship. Training periods range from 1-6 years. Most trades require 3-4 years. The State Apprenticeship Council sponsors and funds the program.

* Customized Workforce Training

Louisiana Department of Economic Development
P.O. Box 94185   225-342-5375
Baton Rouge, LA 70804-9185   Fax: 225-342-5349
www.lded.state.la.us/businessresources/workforcetraining.asp

Businesses that existing or expanding and companies locating inside of the state can receive customized training assistance through the Department. The goal is to increase productivity and competition while promoting employment stability. A minimum of 10 new jobs must be created unless the training is for upgrading skills. Upgrade training must be provided to a minimum of 10 full-time permanent employees. Both pre-employment and on-the-job training are eligible.

* Veterans State Aid Program

Department of Veterans Affairs
P.O. Box 94095
Capitol Station   225-922-0500
Baton Rouge, LA 70804-9095   Fax: 225-922-0511
www.ldva.org/benefits.html

This program provides financial assistance to the children and surviving spouses of certain veterans that died in service or of a service connected disability during wartime. The same benefits are allowed for children of living veterans that are 90% or above disabled. These dependents may attend any state supported college, university, or trade vocational technical school and are exempt from paying tuition or school imposed fees. Student imposed fees are not included. Students are eligible for four years of schooling, which is to be completed in not more than 5 years. If funds are available, a small cash allowance will be paid.

Maine

* Apprenticeship Program

Department of Labor
State Apprenticeship Council
Federal Building
68 Sewall St., Room 401
Augusta, ME 04330   207-622-8235

Apprenticeship is a combination of on-the-job and related classroom instruction in which workers learn the practical and theoretical aspects of a highly skilled occupation. Programs are operated voluntarily by employers, employer associations or management and labor groups. Related classroom instruction is given in the sponsor's training facility or a local technical school or community college. Apprentices earn wages while they learn on the job, starting from about half the journeymen's rate up to 95% of full pay near the end of their apprenticeship. Training periods range from 1-6 years. Most trades require 3-4 years. The State Apprenticeship Council sponsors and funds the program.

* Business Visitation Program

Department of Labor
Bureau of Employment Services
55 State House Station   207-624-6390
Augusta, ME 04333-0055   Fax: 207-624-6499
www.mainecareercenter.com/BVPlink.html   TDD: 207-794-1110

80% of all new jobs come from existing businesses. This is why the Business Visitation Program (BVP) assists local companies and communities to identify and resolve business problems. The program enlists local volunteers and the Chamber of Commerce to gather information about development problems, and economic and community concerns. It then links businesses with a variety of financial, technological, business planning, marketing and job training concerns. The goal of the BVP program is to stimulate local economic growth and prevent dislocation.

* Maine's Veterans Services

Maine Veterans Services Bureau
117 State House Station   207-626-4464
Augusta, ME 04333   Fax: 207-626-4471

Veterans Dependents Educational Benefits Program: Free tuition (waiver) will be granted to eligible dependents who attend a State of Maine Supported Institution of higher learning. Eligible dependents are granted benefits for a maximum of 8 semesters which must be completed within 6 consecutive academic years from the date of first entrance. Call this office for eligibility requirements.

* Maine Pre-Apprenticeship Program (Pre-MAP)

Bureau of Employment Services   888-457-8883
55 State House Station   207-624-6390
Augusta, ME 04333-0055   Fax: 207-624-6499
www.mainecareercenter.com/PreMap.html

Students enter the program in their junior year of high school and work part-time with an employer through their junior and senior years. The program length is usually between 2000 to 8000 hours, and takes anywhere from 2-5 years to complete depending on the occupation and the employer. Upon graduating from the program, they will receive a Certificate of Completion from the State Apprenticeship and Training Council. At that point, the graduate can choose to enter the Maine Apprenticeship Program and if so, their time in the Pre-MAP program will count towards their training.

* Governor's Training Initiative (GTI)

Bureau of Employment Services   888-457-8883
55 State House Station   207-624-6390
Augusta, ME 04333-0055   Fax: 207-624-6499
www.mainecareercenter.comGTIlink.html

GTI provides training funds for employers who are hiring new employees and/or retraining or upgrading their existing workforce. Eligible services include recruitment, assessment, job task analysis, workplace literacy, high performance skills, technical training, higher education, on-the-job training, workplace safety and competitive retooling.

* On-The-Job Training Program (OJT)

Bureau of Employment Services   888-457-8883
55 State House Station   207-624-6390
Augusta, ME 04333-0055   Fax: 207-624-6499
www.mainecareercenter.comOJTlink.html

This is an employer-based training program where the trainee learns occupational skills on-the-job under the skilled supervision of an employer. Trainees are recruited through the Maine Career Centers where a training program is negotiated and a contracted is completed before the trainees first day of work.

* Women, Work & Community Program

Stoddard House
University of Maine at Augusta
46 University Drive   207-621-3440
Augusta, ME 04330   800-442-2092
www.womenworkandcommunity.org/index.shtml

Women are provided with assistance after divorce, or the death or disability of a spouse of family member. Services that are available include career exploration and training in job-seeking skills, counseling, and education and training connections. The goal is to provide them support, guidance, and the tools needed to take the next steps to a successful future. Advocacy and assistance are provided in the areas of workforce development, microenterprise development, asset development, and leadership development.

* Maine Quality Centers

Maine Quality Centers
Center for Career Development   207-767-5210 ext. 107
2 Fort Road   800-491-3121

South Portland, ME 04106   Fax: 207-767-2542
www.mtcs.net

Businesses, or a consortium of businesses, that have the identical training needs for at least 8 new employees will benefit from the Centers work. State-financed education and training in support of job creation, as well as customized recruitment and guaranteed fast-track training are available. Services are provided at on of the state's seven technical colleges and can be for either pre-hire or post-hire.

Maryland

* Apprenticeship Program
Department of Labor and Industry
State Apprenticeship and Training
1100 North Eutaw Street, Room 606   410-767-2229
Baltimore, MD 21201   Fax: 410-767-2220
www.dllr.state.md.us/labor/appr.html

Apprenticeship is a combination of on-the-job and related classroom instruction in which workers learn the practical and theoretical aspects of a highly skilled occupation. Programs are operated voluntarily by employers, employer associations or management and labor groups. Related classroom instruction is given in the sponsor's training facility or a local technical school or community college. Apprentices earn wages while they learn on the job, starting from about half the journeymen's rate up to 95% of full pay near the end of their apprenticeship. Training periods range from 1-6 years. Most trades require 3-4 years. The State Apprenticeship Council sponsors and funds the program.

* DIsplaced Homemaker Program
Maryland Department of Human Resources   410-767-6681
311 West Saratoga St.   Fax: 410-333-0079
Baltimore, MD 21201-3521   TDD: 410-767-7025
www.dhr.state.md.us/oci/dishome.htm

The Displaced Homemaker Program provides services to women who have been homemakers for most of their adult lives and have lost their primary source of income because of separation, divorce or death of a spouse. These programs help the homemaker cope with the immediate crisis, increase her self-confidence and develop the skills needed to support herself and her family. Displaced Homemaker Programs offer: Individual and career counseling, career development workshops, assistance in obtaining education and training, support groups, job referral and placement. To be eligible homemakers must be over 30, depended for support on the income of a family member and lost that income because of separation, divorce, death, disability of a spouse, or who have been dependent of government assistance as the parent of a dependent child and are no longer eligible for that assistance.

* Partnership for Workforce Quality
Department of Business and Economic Development
Division of Regional Development
Office of Regional Response
217 East Redwood St.   888-CHOOSEMD
Baltimore, MD 21202   410-767-0095

The Partnership for Workforce Quality (PWQ) provides matching grants to reimburse Maryland business (targeting manufacturers with 500 or fewer employees) for direct costs related to training activities for upgrading the skills of the business's current employees. The objectives of the program are to improve the competitiveness and productivity of the workforce and business community; to upgrade employees skills for new technologies or production process; and to assist Maryland businesses in promoting employment stability. For qualifying companies that make a commitment to the training goals, PWQ will reimburse up to 50% of the direct cost of training. The PWQ program is a catalyst to assist businesses in establishing a formalized training program. Program staff assist business with related activities which include the following: provides connections to other state services; guides businesses to resources available for productivity and training needs assessments; and advises business of the appropriate training curriculum in accordance with program guidelines and recommends resources for curriculum development.

* Maryland Industrial Training Program (MITP)
DBED
Division of Regional Development
217 East Redwood Street
Baltimore, MD 21202   888-ChooseMD

www.choosemaryland.org/business/workforce/training.asp

The Department of Business and Economic Development in a partnership with other state agencies, works to recruit, assess and place new employees with participating companies. This customized training program works through local business expansion teams to assure that trained workers are available to new or expanding businesses. Companies that participate in MITP are also eligible for state and local assistance with site selection, financing, technology needs and other business concerns they might face.

Massachusetts

* Apprenticeship Program
Department of Labor and Workforce Development
Division of Apprentice Training
399 Washington Street, 4th Floor
Boston, MA 02108-5223   617-727-3486
www.state.ma/dat

Apprenticeship is a combination of on-the-job and related classroom instruction in which workers learn the practical and theoretical aspects of a highly skilled occupation. Programs are operated voluntarily by employers, employer associations or management and labor groups. Related classroom instruction is given in the sponsor's training facility or a local technical school or community college. Apprentices earn wages while they learn on the job, starting from about half the journeymen's rate up to 95% of full pay near the end of their apprenticeship. Training periods range from 1-6 years. Most trades require 3-4 years. The State Apprenticeship Council sponsors and funds the program.

* Commonwealth Corporation
Commonwealth Corporation   617-727-8158
529 Main Street, Suite 110   800-439-0183
Boston, MA 02129   Fax: 617-242-7668
www.commcorp.org

The Commonwealth Corporation, a quasi-public agency, administers four categories of training programs for businesses, each of which targets a specific population and works closely with private industry to develop and provide the training needed for a changing employment market.

* Tuition Waiver for Veterans
Department of Veterans Services
239 Causeway Street, Suite 100   617-727-3578
Boston, MA 02114   Fax: 617-727-5903
www.state.ma.us/veterans

Veterans of Massachusetts can be eligible for any state-supported course in an undergraduate degree program or certified program offered by a public college or university. To be eligible, a veteran must also be a legal resident of Massachusetts for one year and he/she must not be in default of any federal student loans. Veterans will be eligible on a space-available basis for a waiver of full or partial tuition based on proper documentation of the eligibility of the veteran. There is also the Public Service Scholarship Program which awards scholarships to children of veterans who were killed in action or are missing in action. Contact the Veterans Services Department for complete details.

* Veterans Employment Preference
Department of Veterans Services
239 Causeway Street, Suite 100   617-727-3578
Boston, MA 02114   Fax: 617-727-5903
www.state.ma.us/veterans

Veterans are given preference in the eligibility lists of civil service positions. Civil service uses a system of absolute veteran's preference in which someone qualifying as a veteran who receives 70 points or above on an Open Competitive Exam (including police and firefighter) is immediately placed at the head of the eligibility list. On Promotional Exams all types of veterans have two points added to their scores but are not placed at the head of the list. For Labor Service, there is no exam required and veterans, whether disabled or not, are placed at the top of the eligibility list.

* Pre-Apprenticeship Program
Department of Labor and Workforce Development
Division of Apprentice Training
399 Washington Street, 4th Floor

Boston, MA 02108-5223   617-727-3486
www.state.ma/dat

Students enter the program in their junior year of high school and work part-time with an employer through their junior and senior years. The program length is usually between 2000 to 8000 hours, and takes anywhere from 2-5 years to complete depending on the occupation and the employer. Upon graduating from the program, they will receive a Certificate of Completion from the State Apprenticeship and Training Council. At that point, the graduate can choose to enter the Apprenticeship Program, and if so, their time in the Pre-Apprenticeship program will count towards their training.

* Workforce Training Fund

Massachusetts Division of Employment and Training
Charles F. Hurley Building
19 Staniford Street
Boston, MA 02114   617-626-6560
www.detma.org/workforcehome.htm

In order to improve employee skills and to maintain the economic strength of the state's businesses, the Workforce Training Fund was created. The fund places the following types of training as a priority: 1) Projects that will result in job retention, job growth or increased wages; 2) Projects where training would make a difference in the company's productivity, competitiveness, and ability to do business in the state; 3) Projects where the applicant has made a commitment to provide significant private investment in training for the duration of the grant and after the grant has expired. The fund's major focus is in on small to mid-sized businesses that would not be able to make this type of training investment without assistance. The type of training that is done and what is taught, is up to the business. Training can last up to 2 years.

Michigan

* Economic Development Job Training Program

Michigan Economic Development Corporation
300 North Washington Square
Lansing, MI 48913   517-373-9807
http://medc.michigan.org/miadvantage/laborforce

The Economic Development Jog Training (EDJT) Program helps Michigan businesses create new jobs or retain existing jobs which are at risk by improving the skills and competitiveness of Michigan's workforce. Any Michigan business which agrees to create jobs or retain jobs at risk of being lost in manufacturing, research and development, warehousing and distribution, a world headquarters, or a business which exports goods and services outside Michigan is eligible to receive education and training services funded by this program. Funded applications must show a specific employer need for the worker training, a written commitment from the employer to hire or retain the workers after completion of training, and training for full-time jobs of sufficient skill, wage, and benefit level to warrant training costs. Employers must provide a 25% match for training existing workers. Grants are awarded on a competitive application process and grant applications will be continuously accepted throughout the year until funding is exhausted.

* Manpower Information and Services for Troubled Youth (MISTY)

Michigan Family Independence Agency
MISTY Program Manager
P.O. Box 30037   517-373-2035
Lansing, MI 48909   Fax: 517-335-6101
www.michigan.gov/fia

MISTY is a statewide comprehensive employment, vocational, and job training program which provides funding for services to eligible youths involved with the Family Independence Agency. MISTY eligible youths must be in a community placement and must be engaged in employment-related endeavors. Eligible for funding are activities related to: employment testing; academic needs evaluation; job placement and follow-up services; assistance while in training; cost or fees for training; subsidized employment; and work related clothing and tools. State wards age 15 to 20 years of age are eligible, with priority consideration for youths over age 16, who lack marketable skills and experience difficulty in finding employment.

* Michigan Civilian Conservation Corps

Michigan Department of Natural Resources
Michigan Civilian Conservation Corps (MCCC)
Parks and Recreation Division

P.O. Box 30257   517-373-9900
Lansing, MI 48909   Fax: 517-373-4625
www.michigan.gov/dnr

Activities are funded that improve Michigan's natural resources and help participants obtain work records, skills, and work experience to increase their likelihood of obtaining permanent employment. Services provided include basic education; GED preparation; work experience; job skills training, subsidized food, shelter and clothing; public information activities; life skills and placement assessment. Corps members are paid at least the minimum wage for employment activities.

* Michigan Occupation Information System (MOIS)

MOIS Office (Career Exploration)
Ingham Intermediate School District
611 Hagadorn Rd.   517-676-1051 ext. 338
Mason, MI 48854   Fax: 517-676-3399
www.michigan.gov/careers

MOIS is the primary source of career information customized to the state of Michigan. It is a major career exploration tool for both young people and adult workers. The system is used at over 1,400 sites around Michigan. The computer system searches through thousands of pages of information and allows users to explore over 2,000 job titles arranged in over 400 occupational clusters. The major file in the MOIS system is the occupational file covering the nature of the occupation, working conditions, worker requirements, earnings and advancement, employment and outlook, education and training, and sources of additional information. MOIS supports self-awareness and world-of-work awareness through 16 different search strategies covering work and personal characteristics such as aptitudes, interests, education, training, physical demands and job content. Many schools, libraries, and public agencies make it available for use by the public. The MOIS system is supported totally by user fees.

* BeeFreeway

BeeFreeway
Suite G, 3101 Technology Parkway
Lansing, MI 48910   877-844-8385
www.beefreeway.com

Business e-education Freeway (BeeFreeway) was created to help small businesses effectively and efficiently train their employees. The BeeFreeway web site has over 1,300 self-paced employee training modules, which have been pre-paid by the Michigan Department of Career Development. The modules range in subject matter from management techniques to office skills to advanced technical skills. Michigan businesses with 25 or fewer full-time employees are eligible to participate.

* Career Training for the Disabled

Michigan Career & Technical Institute (MCTI)
11611 West Pine Lake Road
Plainwell, MI 49080   877-901-7360
www.michigan.gov/mdcd

MCTI conducts vocational and technical training programs and provides supportive services that are needed in order to prepare Michigan citizens with disabilities for competitive employment. All of the programs are market driven by the needs of the state's businesses and citizens. Career training programs are in the areas of Automotive Technology, Cabinetmaking, Computer Programming, Retail Marketing, Custodial, Drafting, and more. Eligible adults with a physical, mental, or emotional disability can get tuition and room in the dormitory at not charge.

* STRA-School to Registered Apprenticeship

Michigan Department of Career Development
201 North Washington Square
Victor Office Center, 7th Floor
Lansing, MI 48913   888-253-6855
www.stra.org

Students enter the program in their junior year of high school and work part-time with an employer through their junior and senior years. The program length is usually between 2000 to 8000 hours, and takes anywhere from 2-5 years to complete depending on the occupation and the employer. Upon graduating from the program, they will receive a Certificate of Completion from the State Apprenticeship and Training Council. At that point, the graduate can choose to enter the Apprenticeship Program and if so, their time in the STRA program will count towards their training.

Minnesota

* Apprenticeship Program

Department of Labor & Industry
Apprenticeship Unit   651-284-5090
443 Lafayette Road North   800-DIAL-DLI
St. Paul, MN 55155   Fax: 651-284-5736
www.doli.state.mn.us/appr.html

Apprenticeship is a combination of on-the-job and related classroom instruction in which workers learn the practical and theoretical aspects of a highly skilled occupation. Programs are operated voluntarily by employers, employer associations or management and labor groups. Related classroom instruction is given in the sponsor's training facility or a local technical school or community college. Apprentices earn wages while they learn on the job, starting from about half the journeymen's rate up to 95% of full pay near the end of their apprenticeship. Training periods range from 1-6 years. Most trades require 3-4 years. The State Apprenticeship Council sponsors and funds the program.

* Displaced Homemaker Program

Minnesota Department of Economic Security
Minnesota Displaced Homemaker Program
390 North Robert St., Room 125
St. Paul, MN 55101   651-296-6060
www.mnwfc.org/programs/disphome.htm

Twelve Displaced Homemaker programs are delivered through five nonprofit corporations, five community action agencies, and two community colleges. The programs provide the transitional services and vocational preparation needed to allow displaced homemakers to learn to make choices concerning training or employment. A displaced homemaker is defined as a person who worked in the home for a minimum of two years caring for home and family, but due to separation, divorce, death or disability of spouse, or other loss of financial support, must support self and family. Eligibility is based on income guidelines; enrollment is limited to one year. Services are free to those eligible. Workshops, groups for support and networking, self esteem building, one-to-one personal or vocational counseling, job seeking methods, and resume development are among the resources used to help participants build confidence, identify skills, and seek training or employment.

* Extended Employment Program

David Sheerwood-Gabrielson
Extended Employment Program
Minnesota Department of Economic Security
Rehabilitation Services Branch   651-296-9150
390 North Robert St.   800-657-3973
St. Paul, MN 55101   TDD: 651-296-3900
www.mnwfc.org/programs/extempl.htm

This program provides on-going employment support services to individuals in a variety of work settings including community rehabilitation program in-house sites, community-based group sites, and community-based individual sites. Individuals work in a variety of occupations including manufacturing, food service, office occupations, hospitality occupations, janitorial, and other service industries. The focus has been to increase the number and types of employment choices available to people with the most severe disabilities, paying particular attention to supporting integrated employment in the communities in which the individuals live.

* Minnesota Job Skills Partnership

Minnesota Department of Trade and
  Economic Development
500 Metro Square   800-657-3858
121 7th Place East   651-296-0388
St. Paul, MN 55101-2146   Fax: 651-296-5287
www.dted.state.mn.us   TDD: 612-282-6142

The Partnership was created to act as a catalyst between business and education in developing cooperative training projects that provide training for new jobs or retrain existing employees. Grants are awarded to public and/or private educational institutions with new or expanding businesses as partners. All projects must have at least one educational institution and one business working together. Funds may be used for educational infrastructure improvements necessary to support businesses located or intending to locate in Minnesota. Up to $400,000 of Partnership funds per grant can be awarded for a project, and a cash or in-kind contribution from the contribution business must match Partnership funds. A project may be funded for up to three years.

* Youth Program

Kay Tracy or Peggie Jackson
Youth Program
Minnesota Department of Economic Security
390 North Robert St.   651-296-6064
St. Paul, MN 55101   Fax: 651-456-8519
www.mnwfc.org/programs/youthpgm.htm

A young person may receive a combination of the following services based on an assessment of individual need: academic enrichment and basic skills training, private sector limited internships, work experience, personal counseling, vocational counseling, life training, mentoring, peer support groups, and tutoring services. The education component of the program focuses on applied basic skills with a problem solving emphasis.

* Youthbuild Program

Minnesota Department of Economic Security
390 North Robert Street
St. Paul, MN 55101   651-296-6064
www.mnwfc.org/programs/youthbui.htm

At-risk youths between the ages of 16 and 24 can get assistance in making a successful transition to the workforce. Services that will help to attain that goal are construction skills training, work experience, job readiness training, leadership development and basic academic skills. There are currently 12 organizations in the state that provide training.

* Opportunities Industrialization Centers (OIC)-Employment Program

Minnesota State Council of OIC
390 North Robert Street   651-296-6174
St. Paul, MN 55101   TTY: 651-296-3900
www.mnwf.org/programs/pooind.htm

This program provides community-based specialized employment and training services. The participants are unemployed, underemployed and otherwise economically disadvantaged persons; minorities, welfare recipients, at-risk youth, refugees and ex-offenders. Services of OIC include outreach/recruitment, counseling, pre-vocational training, skills training and job development and placement. The program is funded through state, city and county, corporate contributions, and earned income and private contributions.

* Minnesota Pathways Program

Minnesota Department of Trade and Economic Development
500 Metro Square
121 7th Place East   651-297-3314
St. Paul, MN 55101-2146   800-657-3858
www.dted.state.mn.us

The program was created to act as a catalyst between business and education in developing co-operative training projects that provide training, new jobs and career paths for person that are at or below 200% of federal poverty guidelines or are making the transition from public assistance to work. Grants are awarded to educational institutions with businesses as partners. Up to $400,000 of Pathways funds per grant can be used for a project and it can last for up to three years.

Mississippi

* Education Opportunities

Mississippi Office of Student Financial Aid
Student Financial Aid
3825 Ridgewood Rd.   601-432-6997
Jackson, MS 39211-6453   In MS: 800-327-2980

The Mississippi Office of Student Financial Aid offers unique programs which are not offered through the financial aid offices on the campuses of institutions of higher learning but are administered in conjunction with the financial aid offices of the individual campuses. Some of the programs available include: Mississippi Psychology Apprenticeship Program, Health Care Professions Loan/Scholarship Program, Nursing Education Loan/Scholarship, Nursing Teacher Stipend Program, Mississippi Law Enforcement Officers and Firemen Scholarship Program, and Mississippi Public Management Graduate internship Program. A catalog listing all programs, eligibility requirements and who to contact is available from the office listed above.

* Industrial Training Program

Adult Vocational & Technical Education
Mississippi State Department of Education
P.O. Box 771   601-359-3989
Jackson, MS 39205   Fax: 601-359-6619

The state-funded industrial training program's purpose is to assist new and existing industries in meeting their training requirements. Customized training is provided to applicants before they are hired. This training is to prepare trainees for immediate placement in new jobs. Post-employment training is customized to include on-the-job programs that are conducted after the employees have been hired. This training provides job specific training. Retraining and upgrade training is customized retraining developed for existing company employees to meet changing skill requirements caused by new technology. Upgrade training consist of courses designed to assist industry employees in advancing from one job level to another. The training program is delivered through the 15 community or junior colleges, each of which has an industrial coordinator.

Missouri

* Educare

Department of Social Services
Division of Family Services
P.O. Box 1527
Jefferson City, MO 65103-1527   573-751-3221
www.dss.mo.gov/pr_family.htm

Educare is part of the governor's approach to welfare reform. To enable families to move from welfare to work, Missouri's program invests in both generations. By developing, strengthening and improving a child's learning and nurturing environment, their chances for success in adulthood can be vastly improved. While their parents are in job training, pre-school children can be receiving assistance that will increase their chances for success.

* Missouri Customized Training Program

Department of Economic Development
Division of Workforce Development
Missouri Customized Training Program   800-877-8698
P.O. Box 1087   573-526-8254
Jefferson City, MO 65102-1087   Fax: 573-522-9496
www.ded.state.mo.us/business/expandrelocate/customizedtraining.shtml

The purpose of this program is to increase and improve the state's work force by: helping new or expanding businesses recruit and train new workers for newly created jobs; and, helping retrain existing workers as a result of sizable new capital investment, introduction of new products or services, or to upgrade quality and/or increase productivity. Employees are custom trained to meet specific needs of employers in one or all three of the following methods: Skill Training is in a classroom setting at the employer's place of business or at one of more than 80 educational facilities throughout Missouri; On-the-Job Training at the worksite provides hands-on experience on the employer's own equipment, employers will be reimbursed 50% of an eligible trainee's wages.

* Missouri Community College New Jobs Training Program

Department of Economic Development
Division of Workforce Development   573-526-8254
P.O. Box 1087   800-877-8698
Jefferson City, MO 65102-1087   Fax: 573-522-9496
TDD: 800-347-8699
www.ded.state.mo.us/business/expandrelocate/commcollege.shtml

This program provides education and training to workers employed in newly created jobs in Missouri. Whether the new jobs are a result of a new industry or an existing industry that is expanding, this program can offer the resources necessary to train workers in new jobs at a reduced cost. Missouri is one of the few states that provides this program to companies. Training assistance can include skill assessment, orientation, pre-employment training, training facilities and equipment, instructor, curriculum development, travel and a variety of other training related services. Through On-the-Job Training, the employer can be reimbursed up to 50% of wages paid to workers in the new jobs. Eligible participants include all businesses with a sound credit rating currently located in or locating to Missouri, engaged in interstate or intrastate commerce for the purpose of manufacturing, processing, or assembling products. Companies that conduct research and development or provide services in interstate commerce are also eligible. Retail businesses, health and professional services do not qualify for the program. The program is offered at community colleges located in 12 districts in Missouri.

* Skills Training Development Program

Department of Economic Development
Division of Workforce Development
421 East Dunklin   573-526-8254
P.O. Box 1087   800-877-8698
Jefferson City, MO 65102   Fax: 573-522-9496
www.ded.state.mo.us/business/expandrelocate/skillsdevelopment.shtml

Businesses that are located in distressed areas of the state can be reimbursed for the training to upgrade the occupational skills of their employees. They can receive a tax credit for 50% of the actual training costs. Only classroom training is eligible and the employer has complete discretion in choice of the training provider. The credit has a maximum of $1,500 per year and may be claimed for 2 years, with a possible credit of $3,000 per trainee.

* Veterans Tuition Waiver

Missouri Veterans Commission
1719 Southridge Dr.
P.O. Drawer 147   573-751-3779
Jefferson City, MO 65102-0147   Fax: 573-751-6836
www.mvc.state.mo.us

The state of Missouri offers tuition-free scholarships for certain surviving family members of veterans who died as a possible result of exposure to Agent Orange or similar toxic chemicals during the Vietnam War.

Montana

* Apprenticeship Program

Department of Labor and Industry
Workforce Services Division
P.O. Box 1728
Helena, MT 59624-1728   Fax: 406-444-3037
http://jsd.dli.state.mt.us/lsc/apprenticeship.htm

Apprenticeship is a combination of on-the-job and related classroom instruction in which workers learn the practical and theoretical aspects of a highly skilled occupation. Programs are operated voluntarily by employers, employer associations or management and labor groups. Related classroom instruction is given in the sponsor's training facility or a local technical school or community college. Apprentices earn wages while they learn on the job, starting from about half the journeymen's rate up to 95% of full pay near the end of their apprenticeship. Training periods range from 1-6 years. Most trades require 3-4 years. The State Apprenticeship Council sponsors and funds the program.

* Displaced Homemaker Program

Workforce Services Division
Department of Labor and Industry
P.O. Box 1728   406-444-4571
Helena, MT 59624-1728   Fax: 406-444-3037
TDD: 406-444-0532

The Department of Labor and Industry administers the State Displaced Homemaker Program, which is funded through state dollars. This program provides training, counseling and services to help displaced homemakers achieve independence and economic security. Although there is no income requirement for this program, individuals must be 18 years of age or older; have worked as an adult without remuneration to care for the home and family and for that reason has diminished marketable skills; has been dependent on public assistance or on an income of a relative but is no longer supported by that income; will become ineligible for public services; is unemployed or underemployed; or is a criminal offender.

* Dislocated Worker Program for State Employees

Department of Labor and Industry   406-444-1827
P.O. Box 1728   Fax: 406-444-3037
Helena, MT 59624-1728   TDD: 406-444-0532

Dislocated employees whose employment loss means they are unlikely to return to their previous occupation are eligible for assistance. The program emphasizes a comprehensive, timely array of retraining and re-employment services, tailored to workers' individual needs, including long term job preparation.

Nebraska

* Nebraska's Customized Job Training

Job Training Coordinator
Department of Economic Development
301 Centennial Mall South, 4th Floor   800-426-6505
P.O. Box 94666   402-471-3780
Lincoln, NE 68509-4666   Fax: 402-471-3365
http://assist.neded.org/jobtrcust.html

The purpose of customized job training is to provide state training assistance on projects which offer an opportunity for economic development in Nebraska. Use of the funds is limited to eligible companies and eligible training projects. In general, the types of companies qualifying are those engaged in activities which sell goods or services primarily to a non-Nebraska market: manufacturing, processing, warehousing, and headquarters facilities are some samples. Eligible training projects in these industries will include new investment in Nebraska which expand full-time employment or assist in upgrading job skills of existing employees in order to retain the jobs in the state.

* Tuition Waiver

Department of Veterans Affairs
301 Centennial Mall South, 6th Floor
P.O. Box 95083
Lincoln, NE 68509-5083
www.vets.state.ne.us   402-471-2458

Tuition may be waived by the University of Nebraska, state colleges, and technical community colleges on behalf of any child, spouse, widower, or widow, resident of the State of Nebraska, whose parent was a member of the Armed Forces of the U.S., and who died or was totally disabled due to a service-connected disability, classified as Missing in Action or a Prisoner of War, and meet other eligibility requirements.

* Short Term Job Customized Job Training Through the Community College System

Job Training Coordinator
Department of Economic Development
301 Centennial Mall South, 4th Floor
P.O. Box 94666
Lincoln, NE 68509-4666   402-471-3780
http://assist.neded.org/jobtrshort.html

The funds may be used to upgrade skills training or training for new jobs created by business expansion. The length of the program may vary, but generally the training will be completed in 80 hours or less. A preference will be given to a company that targets a specified continuous process improvement system: Quality Assurance, School-To-Career, Applied Academics, Robotics, and other types of training. A priority will also be given to training programs that serve multiple companies or businesses within a local community. The company must provide a match of 50%.

Nevada

* Apprenticeship Program

Office of Nevada Labor Commission
555 East Washington Avenue, Suite 4100   702-486-2738
Las Vegas, NV 89101   Fax: 702-486-2660
www.laborcommissioner.com/atr/atr.htm

Apprenticeship is a combination of on-the-job and related classroom instruction in which workers learn the practical and theoretical aspects of a highly skilled occupation. Programs are operated voluntarily by employers, employer associations or management and labor groups. Related classroom instruction is given in the sponsor's training facility or a local technical school or community college. Apprentices earn wages while they learn on the job, starting from about half the journeymen's rate up to 95% of full pay near the end of their apprenticeship. Training periods range from 1-6 years. Most trades require 3-4 years. The State Apprenticeship Council sponsors and funds the program.

* Career Enhancement Program

Employment Security Division
Employment, Training and Rehabilitation Department
500 East Third St.   702-687-4635
Carson City, NV 89713   Fax: 702-687-8351

http://detr.state.nv.us/es/es_cep.htm

The Career Enhancement Program (CEP) serves Nevada employers by building a stronger, more skilled and reliable work force by placing program-qualified claimants of Unemployment insurance (UI) into training and re-training situations increasing their employability and decreasing the probability of future unemployment. CEP offers classroom, vocational and on-the-job training to help unemployed claimants gain necessary skills to find and keep jobs. The program offers employers the opportunity to enhance their work force with qualified, competent employees trained to the employer's unique needs. And, CEP offers unemployed Nevadans enhanced employment futures.

* Train Employees Now (TEN)

Commission for Economic Development   775-687-4325
108 East Proctor Street   800-336-1600
Carson City, NV 89701   Fax: 775-687-4450
www.expand2nevada.com/newsite/workforce/ten.html

The Nevada Train Employees Now (TEN) provides short-term, intensive job training to assist new and expanding firms to reach productivity quickly. A customized program is designed covering recruitment, hiring and job training. Each project is tailored to fit the firm's needs. Major elements include the development of a job applicant list, preparation of the training program and materials, and classroom training. A firm participating in the program is required to contribute, either in-kind or cash, an amount equal to 25% of the state portion of the project budget. The program is available for training in jobs with wages exceeding the average statewide annual hourly wage. The program may be used prior to plant opening and up to 90 days following. Depending on the extent of training required, a maximum of $1,000 per trainee is available for classroom training.

New Hampshire

* Apprenticeship Program

Department of Labor
State Apprenticeship Council
143 North Main St., Room 205
Concord, NH 03301   603-225-1444
www.labor.state.nh.us/apprenticeship.asp

Apprenticeship is a combination of on-the-job and related classroom instruction in which workers learn the practical and theoretical aspects of a highly skilled occupation. Programs are operated voluntarily by employers, employer associations or management and labor groups. Related classroom instruction is given in the sponsor's training facility or a local technical school or community college. Apprentices earn wages while they learn on the job, starting from about half the journeymen's rate up to 95% of full pay near the end of their apprenticeship. Training periods range from 1-6 years. Most trades require 3-4 years. The State Apprenticeship Council sponsors and funds the program.

* Job Training Program for Economic Growth

Job Training Program for Economic Growth
NH Community Technical College System
26 College Drive
Concord, NH 03301   800-247-3420
www.nhctcs.tec.nh.us

The funds from this program provide state-subsidized training services through the Centers for Training & Business Development. Eligible training includes: basic skills, technical skills, management and supervision, and other skills that will help the business grow and remain competitive. A 50% match is required from the company. These funds must supplement and not replace existing company funds for training.

* Children of Veterans Education Benefits

State Veterans Council   800-622-9230
275 Chestnut Street, Room 321   603-624-9230
Manchester, NH 03103-2411   Fax: 603-624-9236
www.state.nh.us/nhveterans/bene.html

The child of a reported/listed missing veteran that was missing after February 28, 1961, is eligible for education benefits. The child is entitled to free tuition at a vocational-technical college. The children of certain deceased veterans who died from a service-connected disability are entitled to free tuition in a state college-grade institution. If the children are in need of financial assistance, they will be furnished with board, room, rent, books and supplies up to $1,000 per year for not more that 4 years.

New Jersey

* Customized Training Program

New Jersey Department of Labor
Office of Customized Training
P.O. Box 933
Trenton, NJ 08625-0933
www.nj.gov/labor/bsr/custrain.html

609-292-2239
Fax: 609-777-1768

Customized training is provided to prevent job loss caused by obsolete skills, technological change or national or global competition; or for employees at a facility being relocated into New Jersey. To be eligible employers, labor organization or community-based organization must be seeking to create, upgrade or retain jobs in a labor demand occupation for their workers. Each employer that receives customized training services must contribute a minimum of 40% of the total cost of the customized training service. A minimum of 3% of the total funds is dedicated to occupational safety and health training and is linked to skills training and workplace needs.

* Construction Trades Training Program for Women and Minorities

New Jersey Department of Labor
P.O. Box 933
Trenton, NJ 08625-0933
www.nj.gov/labor/bsr/bsprog.html

609-292-6852
609-633-3645

There are two objectives with this program: 1) Increase opportunities for women and minorities to acquire skills and construction employment, and to benefit from school construction projects in their community; and 2) assist contractors and trade unions in recruiting and training women and minorities to fill their workforce needs. The trainers operate under a consortium in the Abbott district. Training consists of assessment; orientation and pre-training preparation; and literacy training. These services will provide the necessary training so the participant can move on to school-based training or a registered apprenticeship program.

* Apprenticeship Program

New Jersey Department of Labor
P.O. Box 933
Trenton, NJ 08625-0933
www.nj.gov/labor/bsr/bsprog.html

609-633-8596

Apprenticeship is a combination of on-the-job and related classroom instruction in which workers learn the practical and theoretical aspects of a highly skilled occupation. Employers, employer associations or management and labor groups operate programs voluntarily. Related classroom instruction is given in the sponsor's training facility or a local technical school or community college. Apprentices earn wages while they learn on the job, starting from about half the journeymen's rate up to 95% of full pay near the end of their apprenticeship. Training periods range from 1-6 years. Most trades require 3-4 years. The State Apprenticeship Council sponsors and funds the program.

* War Orphans Tuition Assistance

Military & Veterans Affairs
P.O. Box 340
Trenton, NH 08625
www.state.nj.us/military

609-530-6927
Fax: 609-530-8193

Children of personnel who died while in the military or due to service-connected disabilities, or who are officially listed as missing in action may claim $500 per year for four years of college or equivalent training. To qualify, the child must be a resident of New Jersey for at least one year immediately preceding the filing of the application and be between the ages of 16 and 21 at the time of application. The veteran must have been a state resident.

* POW-MIA Tuition Benefit Program

Military & Veterans Affairs
P.O. Box 340
Trenton, NH 08625
www.state.nj.us/military

609-530-6927
Fax: 609-530-8193

Free undergraduate college tuition is available to any child born or adopted before or during the period of time his or her parent was officially declared a prisoner of war (POW) or person missing in action (MIA) after Jan. 1, 1960. The POW-MIA must have been a New Jersey resident at the time he or she entered the service or whose official residence is in N.J. The child must attend either a public or private institution in N.J.

* Veterans Tuition Credit Program

Military & Veterans Affairs
P.O. Box 340
Trenton, NH 08625
www.state.nj.us/military

609-530-6927
Fax: 609-530-8193

Veterans attending any approved educational institution may apply for the Veterans Tuition Credit Program. Under the program, partial reimbursement is provided to the institution to offset the cost of the veteran's tuition. Maximum reimbursement is $400 per year for full-time students, $200 for part-time students. To qualify, the veteran must have been on active duty between Dec. 31, 1960, and May 7, 1975, and have been a legal resident of N.J. at the time of entrance into or discharge from the service, or two years immediately prior to application.

* Literacy Training

Department of Labor
Customized Training Office, 7th Floor
P.O. Box 933
Trenton, NJ 08625
www.state.nj.us/labor/bsr/custrain.html

609-292-6852

This program provides funds for a business to upgrade the basic skills and enhance the knowledge and work-related abilities of their employees. Some examples of literacy skills are; communication skills, work readiness skills, and basic computer literacy.

New Mexico

* Apprenticeship Program

New Mexico Department of Labor
1596 Pacheco Street
Aspen Building
Santa Fe, NM 87501
www.dol.state.nm.us

505-841-8990

Apprenticeship is a combination of on-the-job and related classroom instruction in which workers learn the practical and theoretical aspects of a highly skilled occupation. Programs are operated voluntarily by employers, employer associations, or management and labor groups. Related classroom instruction is given in the sponsor's training facility or a local technical school or community college. Apprentices earn wages while they learn on the job, starting from about half the journeymen's rate up to 95% of full pay near the end of their apprenticeship. Training periods range from 1-6 years. Most trades require 3-4 years. The State Apprenticeship Council sponsors and funds the program.

* Industry Development Training Program

New Mexico Economic Development Department
Joseph M. Montoya Building
1100 St. Francis
Santa Fe, NM 87505
www.edd.state.nm.us/SERVICES/TRAINING/index.html

505-827-0323
800-374-3061
Fax: 505-827-6696

The Industrial Development Training Program is designed to provide quick-response manpower training to new or expanding businesses in New Mexico. Under the program financial assistance is available to assist new or expanding business with the cost associated in training employees. The amount of funding allocated is determined by the number of trainees (minimum of 3 individuals) and the amount of training needed. Training can be customized to meet the companies' needs and may be classroom, on-the-job, or a combination of both. Training assistance of up to 1,040 hours per trainee is available under the program. However, a wage scale is used to determine number of training hours required. Costs are reimbursed to the employer at the rate of one-half of the hourly wage rate paid to the trainee. Trainees must be guaranteed full-time employment upon successful completion of the training program.

* Senior Employment Program

New Mexico State Agency on Aging
228 East Palace Ave.
Santa Fe, NM 87501
www.nmaging.state.nm.us

505-827-7640
In NM: 800-432-2080
Fax: 505-827-7649

The New Mexico State Agency on Aging operates a state funded Senior Employment Program serving older workers 55 years of age and older whose income is at or below 125% of poverty level. The program funds 125 positions in which approximately 250 older workers are employed and trained throughout an average year.

* Vietnam Veteran Scholarship

Veterans Service Commission
P.O. Box 2324   505-827-6300
Santa Fe, NM 87504   Fax: 505-827-6372
www.state.nm.us/veterans

Veterans who entered the service from New Mexico and received the Vietnam Service Medal may receive a scholarship to a state sponsored college or university. The fund pays for tuition, required fees and books. The maximum amount of funding is $1,520 for tuition and $500 for books each year.

* Children of Deceased Veterans Scholarship

Veterans Service Commission
P.O. Box 2324   505-827-6300
Santa Fe, NM 87504   Fax: 505-827-6372
www.state.nm.us/veterans

Children of veterans that were killed in action or as a result of that action may receive a scholarship to a state supported school. The veteran must have been a resident of New Mexico at the time of entering the service at a time of armed conflict. The fund will pay for all marticular fees, board and room, and books and supplies. The child must be between the ages of 16 and 26 and will be chosen by the Veterans Service Commission based on need and merit. This program also extends to the children of State Police Officers and National Guard members killed on active duty.

New York

* Adolescent Vocational Exploration (AVE)

Workforce Development & Training
Youth Programs
New York State Department of Labor
State Campus, Building 12   518-457-0380
Albany, NY 12240   Fax: 518-457-9526
www.labor.state.ny.us/working_ny/workforce_development/wiayouth.htm

Thirteen AVE projects provide services to economically disadvantaged 14-17 year olds who are at risk of dropping out of school and failing to develop the skills needed for employment. Services provided include academic and skills assessment, career and vocational exploration, tutoring and/or basic skills remediation, counseling and career and life skills instruction. This is a one year program. Like the Progressive Adolescent Vocational Exploration (PAVE) program, students completing programs that meet established criteria may be eligible to receive one academic credit which may be used toward the completion of high school requirements. The New York State Department of Labor contracts with the State Education Department to provide training and technical assistance to service providers, and to assist in establishing academic credit guidelines.

* Adult Literacy Education Aid Grants

Scott Jill
Workforce Preparation and Continuing Education
Department of Education
Education Building Annex
Hawk and Elk Sts.   518-479-8940
Albany, NY 12234   Fax: 518-474-0319

This program provides funds for literacy and basic skill instruction, GED preparation, English as a Second Language (ESL) and life skills programs operated by post-secondary institutions, community based organizations, volunteer literacy agencies, and libraries.

* AIDS Institute Educational Services

Richard Cotronio
Department of Health
AIDS Institute
Educational Services
Empire State Plaza
Corning Tower, Room 270   518-474-3045
Albany, NY 12237   Fax: 518-474-5450
www.health.state.ny.us/nysdoh/aids/traiing.htm

This program provides job training and technical assistance to health and human service providers. Activities provided include: Overview of HIV Infection and AIDS, HIV Test Counselor Training, Semi-annual HIV/AIDS Physicians' Training and Infection Control Training for health care providers. Other contracts provide a variety of HIV/AIDS educational activities. Some training is done by the AIDS Institute staff. Appropriation amounts include funds to support the HIV/AIDS Physicians Training and Infection Control Training.

* Another Chance Initiative for Education, Vocation, or Employment (ACHIEVE)

Joseph Baez
Workforce Development
Department of Labor
State Campus, Building 12   518-457-0380
Albany, NY 12240   Fax: 518-457-9526

ACHIEVE focuses on increasing employment readiness and the basic skills of school drop-outs through on-the-job training, work experience, job search assistance, counseling, wage subsidy, stipends, literacy and/or basic or remedial education, life skills instruction, day care, and transportation. The focus group for this program is 18-19 year olds, but ages range from 16-21 years of age.

* Apprenticeship Program

Department of Labor
State Apprenticeship Program
Leo O□Brien Federal Building, Room 809
North Pearl & Clinton Ave.
Albany, NY 12207   518-431-4008

Apprenticeship is a combination of on-the-job and related classroom instruction in which workers learn the practical and theoretical aspects of a highly skilled occupation. Programs are operated voluntarily by employers, employer associations or management and labor groups. Related classroom instruction is given in the sponsor's training facility or a local technical school or community college. Apprentices earn wages while they learn on the job, starting from about half the journeymen's rate up to 95% of full pay near the end of their apprenticeship. Training periods range from 1-6 years. Most trades require 3-4 years. The State Apprenticeship Council sponsors and funds the program.

* Career Exploration Internship Program

Tony Schilling
Department of Education
Room 320EB   518-474-4486
Albany, NY 12234   Fax: 518-474-4909

Services provided include structured on-site career exploration, mentoring, and related instruction for youth enrolled in secondary schools, and also for secondary school dropouts. It is a program of structured, supervised, non-paid intensive career exploration for students ages 14 and above.

* Chamber of Commerce On-The-Job Training Program

Workforce Development & Training Division
Department of Labor
State Campus, Building 12, Room 450   518-457-0380
Albany, NY 12240   Fax: 518-457-9526

The On-The-Job Training (OJT) Program provides financial incentives to employers by helping them offset the high cost of training new workers. A company can receive a reimbursement of up to 50% of an employees' wages while the employee acquires the skills necessary to perform the job. The length of training is determined by the individuals background and the complexity of the job. In addition to this wage subsidy, other benefits may be provided to reduce an employer's training cost. Some of these include: cost of related classroom instruction; reasonable cost of tools, materials and equipment; 75% reimbursement if a new job is created or an Unemployment Insurance recipient is hired under the program; and although the OJT Program is designed primarily for new workers, some Chambers can provide reimbursement to companies who are upgrading the skills of their current workforce.

* Children of Veterans Awards

Executive Department
Division of Veterans Affairs
5 Empire State Plaza, Suite 2836   518-474-7606
Albany, NY 12223-1551   Fax: 518-473-0379
www.veterans.state.ny.us

The award provides student financial aid to children of veterans who served in the United States Armed Forces during specified periods of war or national emergency and, as a result of service, died, suffered a 40% or more disability, were a prisoner of war or are Missing in Action. The student must enroll full time in an approved post-secondary educational program in New York State, be a New York State resident, meet U.S. citizenship requirements, and be in good academic standing. Contact this office for additional information on specific requirements.

* Displaced Homemaker Program

Karen Coleman
Department of Labor
State Campus, Building 12   518-457-6998
Albany, NY 12240   Fax: 518-457-6908

This program assists displaced homemakers in becoming economically independent by providing the counseling, on-the-job training or internships, job search assistance, skills upgrading, skills retraining, pre-vocational skills training, literacy instruction, basic or remedial education, employability skills instruction, life skills instruction, and day care and transportation assistance. Services available may vary from center to center. There are 24 programs statewide, operated by 19 contractors.

* Dislocated Worker Assistance Center

Dislocated Worker Assistance Center (DWAC)
State Office Building
207 Genesse St., Suite 201   315-793-2229
Utica, NY 13501   Fax: 315-793-2509

DWAC is a program jointly administered by the New York State AFL-CIO and New York State Department of Labor, designed to help individuals who have permanently lost their jobs. The Center provides a full array of services to dislocated workers and their families, including peer counseling, assessment, job training, education and worker literacy programs, job development, program eligibility certification, and referral for all training programs and benefits available to dislocated workers. In addition to dislocated workers, the Center offers services to Displaced Homemakers-- those who have been in the role of a homemaker and are now reentering the labor market due to a change in income resulting from death, divorce, separation, or permanent dislocation or disability of a spouse. This center serves individuals from a three county area consisting of Oneida, Herkimer, and Madison counties.

* Firm/Industry Specific Training

Empire State Development Corporation
633 3rd Ave.
New York, NY 10017   212-803-3100
www.iloveny.com

Firm/Industry Specific Training is one form of assistance available through the Regional Economic Development Partnership Program. Services available include entry level skills training, literacy and English as a second language instruction, and basic or remedial education.

* Green Thumb Program

Green Thumb Environmental
74 Main St.
P.O. Box 214
Stamford, NY 12167   607-652-2015

Enacted by the State Legislature in 1974, the Green Thumb Program provides meaningful and fulfilling work for senior citizens through various service activities designed to enhance the state's natural beauty and to play a vital role in maintaining the natural and man-made resources in New York State. To be eligible individuals must be at least 55 years old and fall within the income guidelines provided within state law. A certificate from a physician stating that one is healthy enough to work is required. Green Thumb will provide $30 toward the cost of a physical. The program is operated to ensure that employees earnings remain below the threshold that would impact social security benefits. This arrangement provides senior citizens with an opportunity to remain active, supplement their income, and provide a valuable service to the state without incurring a financial penalty. Work is part time, averaging three days a week for 7 hours per day. Payment for Green Thumb work is equal but not limited to the prevailing New York State minimum wage.

* Health Care Worker Training Program

Anne Bryant
Workforce Development & Training Division
Department of Labor
State Office Campus, Building 12

Albany, NY 12240   518-457-0380
www.labor.state.ny.us

This program was designed to facilitate career advancement for employed health care workers by providing cross training and retraining opportunities to workers being affected by changes in the industry. The training program design may include, but is not limited to, one or more of the following: an on-the-job training program and/or site education program for credentials or a licensed health care professional; training in multiple skills to upgrade or retrain current employees by adding additional competencies and skills; retraining opportunities for workers that will prepare them to meet changes in patient care needs and/or work in alternative patient care settings. Funding for projects is awarded on a yearly basis through a Request for Proposal process. Eligible applicants include health care worker unions, joint labor management committees, health care providers (hospitals, long term care facilities) or consortia of health care providers. The program requires a 100% match from other funding sources for all funds requested.

* Job Training for Individuals with Disabilities

Office of Mental Retardation and Developmental Disabilities
44 Holland Ave.   518-474-6601
Albany, NY 12229   Fax: 518-473-1271
www.omr.state.ny.us

Services provided include sheltered workshops which provide developmentally disabled individuals a range of vocational services and employment in a protected environment; supported employment including job-site training both in job skills and interpersonal skills; the Employment Training Program for youth and adults providing basic life skills and on-the-job training for developmentally disabled; and the Youth Opportunity Program which provides employment and training to economically and educationally disadvantaged youth.

* Jobs For Youth

Joseph Baez
Workforce Development
Department of Labor
State Campus, Building 12   518-457-0380
Albany, NY 12240   Fax: 518-457-9526
www.labor.state.ny.us

The Jobs for Youth (JFY) Apprenticeship Program serves in-school and out-of-school Job Opportunity and Basic Skills (JOBS) eligible youth, 17-21 years of age. This two-year program offers an integrated program of study that includes academic curriculum, work-related instruction, and supervised, structured on-the-job training. Following this program, youth will be placed into entry level or full-time registered apprenticeships, exclusively or in combination with post-secondary studies.

* Liberty Partnerships

Department of Education
Office of K-16 Infinitives and Access Program
Pre-Collegiate Preparation Program Unit
Room 965 EBA   518-473-6810
Albany, NY 12234   Fax: 518-474-7468
www.highered.nysed.gov/kiap/PCPPU/lpp/home1.htm

The Program awards grants to post-secondary institutions for the purpose of providing supportive services to students in public and non-public schools who are identified as having a high risk of dropping out of school. Awards are made on a competitive basis to degree-granting institutions, individually or in consortia, in cooperation with school districts and no-for-profit community-based organizations. The purpose of the program is to provide those students with a broad range of services designed to increase their motivation and ability to complete secondary education and seek entry into post-secondary education or the work force.

* Progressive Adolescent Vocational Exploration (PAVE)

New York State Department of Labor
Workforce Development and Training
State Campus, Building 12   518-473-6810
Albany, NY 12240   Fax: 518-457-9526
www.labor.state.ny.us/working_ny/workforce_development/pave.htm

PAVE is a two-year program which replaced the Structured Education Support Program. It is a career exploration and educational support program which focuses on serving economically disadvantaged youth who are at risk of dropping out of school or graduating without marketable skills. Supportive services include classroom instruction, remedial support, counseling, employment assistance, and personal development activities.

During the second year of the PAVE program, students will have the opportunity to participate in internships, apprenticeship programs, entrepreneurial programs and activities, and other individual work exploration activities. Students completing programs that meet established criteria may be eligible to receive one academic credit which may be used toward the completion of high school requirements. The New York State Department of Labor contracts with the State Education Department to provide training and technical assistance to service providers, and to assist in establishing academic credit guidelines. There are 21 PAVE projects throughout New York State.

* Osborne Association

> Osborne Association
> Division of Probation and Correctional Alternative
> 80 Wolf Road
> Albany, NY 12205   518-457-5800
> www.dpca.state.ny.us/nysdpca

Osborne Association provides vocational assessment, pre-employment training, and job placement services to work release participants at New York City Work Release Facilities. Vocational assessment services are provided to referred inmates to examine their capabilities, needs, and vocational potential and to develop a service strategy and employment goal. Clients are evaluated by taking into account his or her family situation, work history, education, occupational skills, interests, aptitudes, attitude towards work, motivation, behavior patterns affecting employment, potential financial resources and supportive service needs, and personal employment information as it relates to the local labor market.

* Teacher Opportunity Corps

> Bureau of Professional Career
> Opportunity Program
> Room 976, EBA
> Albany, NY 12234   518-486-6042
> www.highered.nysed.gov/pcop/toc.htm

The goals of the Teacher Opportunity Corps (TOC) program are to enhance the preparation of teachers and prospective teachers in addressing the learning needs of students at risk of truancy, academic failure or dropping out of school, and to increase participation in teaching careers by individuals who are from economically disadvantaged backgrounds or from minority groups historically underrepresented in teaching. Participants in the 17 current TOC projects are provided with specialized curricula addressing the needs of at-risk students; internships; clinical experiences; mentoring during the first year of teaching; counseling and other supportive services; and financial assistance.

* Teacher Resource and Computer Training Center

> New York State Department of Education
> Regional School & Community Service
> Room 475, EBA   518-473-1234
> Albany, NY 12234   Fax: 518-474-1403
> www.emsc.nysed.gov/rscs

These centers provide skills upgrading and life skills instruction; professional support and staff development primarily for teachers, other school professionals, and parents. Services are provided by teachers, administrators, consultants, and university faculty. There are 117 centers statewide. Approximately 290,000 teachers, other school professionals, and parents are served annually.

* Vera Institute of Justice

> Division of Probation and Correctional Alternative
> 80 Wolf Road
> Albany, NY 12205   518-457-5800
> www.dpca.state.ny.us/nysdpca

Vera is a non-residential work incentive, skills training program comprised of a Vocational Development Program (VDP) and Neighborhood Work Projects (NWP) located in New York city which encompasses releasees from the five boroughs of the metropolitan area. The program is designed to enhance the employability and future employment opportunities by enrolling releasees and providing work experience in structured settings. Counseling services are also available. This is a not-for-profit organization which specializes in inmate follow-up job placement services where releasees can return to work with NWP and work with their VDP job developers to find further employment.

* Skills Exchange

> Donald Menze
> The City University of New York
> Workforce Development Center
> New York, NY 10021   212-220-8350
> www.bmcc.cuny.edu/skills

This is a comprehensive array of workforce related initiatives for employed adults addressing the following goals: promoting and supporting small business; retraining and skill upgrading; meeting the shortages of qualified teachers, preparing undergraduates for skill shortage occupations; job creation and economic development; and labor market research, planning, and program coordination.

* Workplace Literacy Program

> Adult and Family Education Team
> Office of Workforce Preparation and Continuing Education
> Department of Education Building, Room 317
> Albany, NY 12234   518-474-5808

The Workplace Literacy Program is designed to build the capacity of labor organizations, expand literacy opportunities for union members and other workers, as well as to encourage the establishment of job-related literacy and basic skills education. To be eligible to participate in a Workplace Literacy Program in New York State, a person must be an employee of a public or private employer or a member of a union and have a demonstrated need for job-related literacy and/or basic skills education.

* Vietnam and Persian Gulf Veterans Tuition Award

> New York State Division of Veterans Affairs
> #5 Empire State Plaza, Suite 2836   888-VETS-NYS
> Albany, NY 12223-1551   518-474-7606
> www.veterans.state.ny.us

Those that served in Southeast Asia and the Persian Gulf can receive a maximum of $1,000 per semester for full-time study or $500 a semester for part-time study at any institution of higher learning in New York. Study in an approved vocational training program will also receive funding.

North Carolina

* Apprenticeship Program

> Department of Labor
> State Apprenticeship Program
> Somerset Part, Suite 205
> 4407 Bland Rd.
> Raleigh, NC 27609   919-790-2801
> www.nclabor.com/appren/appindex.htm
> www.ncccs.cc.nc.us/Business_and_Industry/index.html

Apprenticeship is a combination of on-the-job and related classroom instruction in which workers learn the practical and theoretical aspects of a highly skilled occupation. Programs are operated voluntarily by employers, employer associations or management and labor groups. Related classroom instruction is given in the sponsor's training facility or a local technical school or community college. Apprentices earn wages while they learn on the job, starting from about half the journeymen's rate up to 95% of full pay near the end of their apprenticeship. Training periods range from 1-6 years. Most trades require 3-4 years. The State Apprenticeship Council sponsors and funds the program.

* Focused Industrial Training

> Glynda Lawrence, Associate Director
> Business and Industry Services
> N.C. Department of Community Colleges
> 200 West Jones St.   919-733-7051
> Raleigh, NC 27603-1337   Fax: 919-733-0680
> www.ncccs.cc.nc.us/Business_and_Industry/index.html

Focused Industrial Training (FIT) is a special training program for North Carolina's traditional industries. Serving primarily manufacturing clients, FIT uses individualized needs assessments and consultations to design and implement targeted, customized training for organizations who need to upgrade workers' skills because of technological or process advances. FIT is designed to serve the special needs of existing industry. This program keeps North Carolina's economy strong and healthy. Qualified instructors conduct classes at the company site, or in one of the 58 community colleges throughout the state.

* New and Expanding Industry Training

Joe Sturdivant, Director
Business and Industry Services
N.C. Community College system
200 West Jones St.   919-733-7051
Raleigh, NC 27603-1337   Fax: 919-733-0680
www.ncccs.cc.nc.us/Business_and_Industry/index.html

Companies that create at least 12 new production jobs are eligible for training programs which are administered at one of the 58 community colleges throughout the state. Industrial training specialists visit an existing operation to study the job skills, work schedules, production processes and any other pertinent variables and then prepare a proposal regarding the nature of the jobs and the skills they require. Companies may use their own instructors or the local college may assign faculty members or recruit special instructors. Employees can be trained before they're hired, after they're hired, or programs can be designed to include both options. The State of North Carolina finances this program completely, including all classroom materials such as texts, workbooks, and some computer-based packages.

* Employment and Training Grant Program

Public Affairs
Department of Commerce
301 North Wilmington St.   919-733-7651
Raleigh, NC 27626-0571   Fax: 919-733-8356

The purpose of the grant program is to make grants available to local agencies operating on behalf of the Private Industry Councils serving Job Training Partnership Act service delivery areas for the purpose of upgrading the foundation of basic skills of the adult population and existing workforce in North Carolina.

* Training Initiatives

New & Expanding Industry Training
N.C. Department of Community Colleges
200 West Jones Stree   t919-733-7051
Raleigh, NC 27603-1337   Fax: 919-733-0680
www.ncccs.cc.nc.us/Business_and_Industry/index.html

The Department of Labor develops and operates model, pilot, and demonstration programs which can be replicated for system wide or statewide applications. These programs are able to field test new tools or processes which can more efficiently serve targeted populations. They operate programs which address target populations or address skill or labor shortages in either an industry or business sector or specific geographic area.

North Dakota

* New Jobs Training Program

Workforce Programs
Job Service ND
P.O. Box 5507   701-328-3358
Bismarck, ND 58506   Fax: 701-328-4894
www.state.nd.us/jsnd/workforce.htm

The New Jobs Training Program is administered by the Job Service of North Dakota in cooperation with education and training providers: to assist in designing training for a company's specific needs; business loans for training for a company's specific needs; business loans for training are obtained from the North Dakota Department of Economic Development & Finance and repaid through state income tax withholding credits. Instead of the state income tax on the wages paid to new employees going to the state general fund, that income tax revenue is used to pay off the loan. Once the loan is repaid, state income taxes on wages revert to the state's general fund. Qualifying criteria includes: businesses location in the state must create a minimum of five new jobs, expanding businesses must increase employment by at least one employee; business must not be closing or reducing its operations in one area of the state and relocating the same operation to another part of the state; every employee participating in the new jobs training program must be paid at least $7.50 an hour plus benefits within the first 12 months; and business must have an economically and socially desirable purpose.

* Workforce 2000

Job Training Division
Job Service of North Dakota
P.O. Box 5507   701-328-3358
Bismarck, ND 58502   Fax: 701-328-4894

www.state.nd.us/jsnd/workfoce.htm

Job Service North Dakota, the State Board for Vocational & Technical Education, and the Department of Economic Development & Finance collaborated to form Workforce 2000. This is a unique job training resource that goes beyond the Federal government's federally funded programs which are limited in helping expanding or modernizing business. Workforce 2000 provides state funds for supporting business start-ups, expansion, and retention by making available customized retraining and upgrade training for any worker. Workforce 2000 will help businesses undergoing major technological changes, where training is critical to remain competitive.

* Veterans Educational Benefits

Department of Veterans Affairs
1411 32nd Street S   701-239-7165
P. O. Box 9003   866-634-8387
Fargo, ND 58106-9003   701-239-7166
www.state.nd.us/veterans

Any dependent of a veteran who was killed in action or died from wounds or other service-connected causes, was totally disabled as a result of service-connected causes, died from service-connected disabilities, was a prisoner of war, or was declared missing in action, upon being duly accepted for enrollment into any North Dakota state-supported institution of higher education or state-supported technical or vocational school, must be allowed to obtain a bachelor's degree or certificate of completion, as long as the dependent is eligible, free of any tuition and fee charges. The bachelor's degree or certificate of completion must be earned within a thirty-six month or an eight-semester period or its equivalent. Costs for aviation flight charges or other such expenses are not included with the benefits.

* National Guard Tuition Waiver

Department of Veterans Affairs
1411 32nd Street S   701-239-7165
P. O. Box 9003   866-634-8387
Fargo, ND 58106-9003   701-239-7166
www.state.nd.us/veterans

Any qualifying member of the National Guard who enrolls in any state-controlled school, shall, receive a waiver of the tuition charged by the school. The tuition waiver is valid only so long as the member of the National Guard maintains satisfactory performance with the guard, meets the qualification requirements, and pursues a course of study in a manner that satisfies the normal requirements of the school.

Ohio

* Adult Vocational Education Full Service Centers

Ohio Department of Education
Office of Career Technical & Adult Education
65 South Front St., Room 907   614-466-3430
Columbus, OH 43215   Fax: 614-644-5702

There are 40 adult workforce full service centers located across the state of Ohio. Center programs and services include job assessment, employee testing and assessment, technical skill training, customized training for specific business and industry needs, seminar development, career counseling, and job placement. For businesses and other organizations, the Centers serve as an out-of-house training and development solution. They are also a human resources tool for classifying job skills and evaluating related individual abilities. In addition, the Centers offer support programs which help students access needed resources such as child care and financial aid.

* Apprenticeship Program

Department of Labor
State Apprenticeship Council
145 South Front Street
P.O. Box 1618   614-644-2242
Columbus, OH 43215   Fax: 614-644-24710
www.state.oh.us/odjfs/apprenticeship

Apprenticeship is a combination of on-the-job and related classroom instruction in which workers learn the practical and theoretical aspects of a highly skilled occupation. Programs are operated voluntarily by employers, employer associations, or management and labor groups. Related classroom instruction is given in the sponsor's training facility or a local technical school or community college. Apprentices earn wages while they learn on the job, starting from about half the journeymen's rate up to 95% of full pay near the end of their apprenticeship. Training periods range from 1-6 years.

Most trades require 3-4 years. The State Apprenticeship Council sponsors and funds the program.

* Ohio Career Information System

OCIS Supervisor
Department of Education
25 South Front Street
Mail Stop 609   614-644-6771
Columbus, OH 43215-4183   Fax: 614-466-7097
www.ocis.org

The Ohio Career Information System (OCIS) is a computer-based information system which provides users with educational and occupational information. Approximately 1,700 user sites exist throughout the state, Users include youth and adults affiliated with public, primary and secondary schools; two and four-year colleges; correctional facilities; the Ohio Industrial Commission; the Ohio Rehabilitation Services Commission; and other public, non-profit, and private job training institutions. A combination of state funds and user fees support the program. The target population starts with the 7th grade, continues through 12th grade, and also is used by adults.

* Ohio Investment in Training Program

Ohio Department of Development
Office of Investment in Training
77 South High St.   614-466-4155
P.O. Box 1001   800-848-1300
Columbus, OH 43266-0101   Fax: 614-644-1789
www.odod.state.oh.us/OITP.htm

The Ohio Investment in Training Program (OITP) is designed to provide financial assistance and resources for customized training involving employees of new and expanding Ohio manufacturing businesses and will consider other industries creating a large number of new jobs. The program links Ohio's public educational system (vocational, technical, and universities) to the needs of industry by acting as a brokering source of specialized training services. Financial assistance may be provided for business and industry where there is manufacture and/or assembly of goods or information production, for verifiable retention of jobs, expansion of industry through capital investments, or for new industry. Funding is conducted through the regional OITP Office on reimbursement basis, for a portion of training expenses incurred, including (but not limited to): instructor costs, materials, special needs, such as assessment, curriculum development and software rentals. Companies that are requesting up to $10,000 in training funds may apply for the OITP Mini-Grant. Regardless of the size of the company, the training proposals are evaluated on the same criteria as the standards competitive proposals (number of new or retained jobs, number trained, etc) and are subject to the same guidelines as the standard grants.

* Ohio Tech Prep

Vocational and Adult Education Division
Employment Education Section
Department of Education
25 South Front Street   614-466-5910
Columbus, OH 43215   Fax: 614-466-5702

This program prepares youths and adults to make informed career choices; to achieve personal and family goals; and to successfully enter, compete, and advance in a changing work world. All of Ohio's 11th and 12th grade secondary students have access to comprehensive vocational education programs through 94 Vocational Education Planning Districts (VEPD). Approved educational agencies within the VEPD's determine the programs to be implemented based on analysis of state and local labor markets. Students are offered a variety of programs targeting those occupations projected to have the largest annual growth in Ohio through the year 2000.

* Ohio Displaced Homemaker Network

Vocational & Adult Education
Department of Education
Room 915, 25 South Front Street
Columbus, OH 43215   614-466-3892

The Displaced Homemaker Program allows the participants to achieve independence and economic security through job retraining, employment assistance, educational services and other services. To participate, the individual must have worked in the home providing unpaid household services for family members; are not adequately employed; will likely have a difficult time gaining adequate employment; and have been dependent on the income of another family member but is no longer supported by them.

Oklahoma

* Training for Industry Program

Economic Development Liaison
Oklahoma Department of Career & Technology Education
900 North Stiles
P.O. Box 26980   405-815-5110
Oklahoma City, OK 73126-0980   Fax: 405-743-6821
www.sde.state.ok.us/default.html

Training for new and expanding industry is provided through the Training for Industry Program (TIP). It is delivered through a statewide network of 54 technology centers and 39 colleges and universities equipped at a cost of more than $50 million. TIP provides customized training that meets companies specific needs. Employees are trained in the process and on the equipment used by the company. Programs range from basic skills, through Total Quality Management and ISO 9000, to the latest in organizational design and management training. TIP will assist with the recruitment and assessment of a customized employee training program at no cost. Representatives from the company and Vo-Tech meet to assess the competencies needed in each job category and to design the training program. A statement of understanding that outlines responsibilities, areas and length of training, number of employees to be trained, and any special requirements will be developed. There are no applications to complete or reviews by committees.

* Customized Business & Industry Training

Oklahoma Department of Career & Technology Education
1500 West 7th Avenue   405-377-2000
Stillwater, OK 74074   Fax: 405-743-5541

Oklahoma's technology centers have been providing customized upgrade training to local businesses for years. Many types of companies are served, including retail, manufacturers, and warehouse and distribution. Services and training include technical skills, team skills, quality/TQM/ISO processes, skills safety training, computer training and any other skill needed by the company.

* Existing Industry Training

Oklahoma Department of Career & Technology Education
1500 West 7th Avenue   405-377-2000
Stillwater, OK 74074   Fax: 405-743-5541

This program's mission is to assist Oklahoma businesses to ensure their existing employee's skills are up-to-date on the latest technologies and processes. It mainly serves business types such as manufacturers, distribution centers, and business service centers, which bring new money into the state. Customized training and services are provided at very little cost or not cost at all. It' services can be used with the installation of new equipment, technology process, computerized manufacturing applications and/or training for new product lines.

* Vocational Services

Development Disabilities Services Division
Oklahoma Department of Health
P.O. Box 25352
Oklahoma City, OK 73125   405-521-3646
www.okdhs.org/ddsd

Employment services are available to disabled persons. The services include prevocational training, job placement and on-the-job training and supervision. Both sheltered and community employment services are available. Center-based training is provided in a controlled environment with a large group of other disabled trainees. Community Integrated Employment is provided through other entities such as trade school, Vo-Techs and others.

Oregon

* Apprenticeship Program

Director of Apprentice and Training Division
Bureau of Labor and Industries
800 N.E. Oregon St., #32   503-731-4200, ext. 3
Portland, OR 97232   Fax: 503-731-4103

This state funded program registers apprentices and employers who serve as training agents. Apprenticeship is a combination of on-the-job training and related classroom instruction in which workers learn the practical and theoretical aspects of a high skilled occupation. Apprenticeship programs

I Wanna Be Trained

are operated voluntarily by employers, employer associations, or management and labor groups. Apprentices earn wages while they learn on the job, starting from about half the journeymen's rate up to 95% of full pay near the end of their apprenticeship. There are currently more than 7,000 registered apprentices with over 4,500 employers registered as training agents in Oregon.

* Career Information System

Cheryl Buhl, Director
Career Information System   800-459-1266
1244 University of Oregon   541-346-3872
Eugene, OR 97403-1244   Fax: 541-346-2346
http://oregoncis.uoregon.edu

The mission of the Career Information System (CARES) is to collect current labor market and educational data and develop it into useful career information; provide a practical means of access to career information by individuals who need it; and to promote the integration of career information into schools and social agencies. Using this system you can obtain information on such topics as: occupational descriptions and preparations; industry descriptions and employment; programs of study and training, including short-term training programs, descriptions, and schools in Oregon; job search and employers; entrepreneurship; and military occupations and worklife. Currently CARES has 545 user sites located across the state.

* Educational Aids for Veterans

Public Information
Department of Veterans Affairs   800-633-6826
Oregon Veterans' Building   503-373-2085
700 Summer St., N.E., Suite 150   Fax: 503-373-2362
Salem, OR 97310-1201   TDD: 503-373-2217

Oregon Educational Aid benefits, up to $200 each semester, are available to certain veterans who take approved college courses. These courses must be taken in an accredited Oregon school, except when the course of study is not available in Oregon. Benefits are paid for classroom instruction needed as part of an apprenticeship program or other on-the-job training programs. Benefits are also paid for home study courses and for vocational flight training. This program is available for Veterans who served during the Korean War and post-Korean vets who received a campaign or expeditionary medal ribbon.

* Employer-at-Injury Program

Reemployment Assistance Unit
Workers' Compensation Division
Department of Consumer and Business Services   800-445-3948
350 Winter N.E., Room 240   Salem: 503-947-7816
Salem, OR 97301   Medford: 541-947-7581
www.clos.state.or.us/external/wed/rds/rau/returntowork.html

The Employer-at-Injury Program helps reduce employer claim costs and helps workers remain productive while recovering from on-the-job injuries. The program offers reimbursements to eligible Oregon employers who return their injured workers to light duty work while their claims are open. Reimbursements can include up to three months 50% wage subsidy; $2,500 for worksite modification; $750 for tuition, books and fees necessary to update the worker's existing skills or to meet the requirements of the job; $1,000 for tools and equipment required for the job; and $400 for required clothing. This program is funded by worker and employer cents-per-hour assessments and contributions to the Worker Benefit Fund.

* JOBS Plus

Oregon Employment Department
875 Union Street, NE   800-237-3710
Salem, OR 97311   503-947-1847
http://findit.emp.state.or.us/emprsvcs/jobsplus.cfm

JOBS Plus is an added component of the existing federal JOBS Program in six Oregon counties. Use of $2.7 million in lottery funding was approved to cover start-up costs of the three-year demonstration project. JOBS Plus participants are placed in limited duration, on the job training in private businesses, where they earn at least the minimum wage. Participants are paid by employers, who are then reimbursed by the state for minimum wages and payroll taxes. The employer assigns a workplace mentor to help participants learn job skills and good work habits. Participants do not lose any benefits and in most cases brings an increase. Each participant has an Individual Education Account established, into which the employer contributes $1 for each hour worked. These funds will be available to the participant for further education after the worker finds unsubsidized employment.

* Preferred Worker Program

Reemployment Assistance Unit
Workers' Compensation Division
Department of Consumer and Business Services   800-445-3948
350 Winter N.E., Room 240   Salem: 503-945-7575
Salem, OR 97301   Medford: 541-776-6032

The Preferred Worker Program provides incentives to Oregon employers who hire or reemploy workers with a permanent disability who can't return to regular work because of an Oregon on-the-job injury. The incentives include six months at 50% wage subsidy; up to $25,000 for worksite modification; exemption from paying workers compensation premiums for the Preferred Worker for up to three years; full claim cost payment for the life of the claim if the Preferred Worker has a new accepted, compensable on-the-job injury during the premium exemption period; and payment for certain items needed to obtain or maintain employment, such as tools, clothing, or tuition, books and fees for a class or course of instruction to update existing skills or to meet the requirements of an obtained job. This program is funded by worker and employer cents-per-hour assessments and contributions to the Worker Benefit Fund.

* Workforce Development Programs

Oregon Economic Community Development   503-986-0206
Workforce Development Section   In OR: 800-223-3306
775 Summer St., N.E.   Fax: 503-581-5115
Salem, OR 97310   TDD: 503-986-0123
www.econ.state.or.us/Blworkassis.htm

The Department directly operates three industry workforce development programs: Targeted Training, Industry Workforce & Training and Oregon Workforce System. The Targeted Training program works with business, develops the need for and negotiates to award grants to community colleges and others for training programs customized to the needs of the specific new, or expanding businesses. Industry Workforce Training Program is guided by the needs of business and industry. Grants are awarded to educational institutions, unions, and trade associations in order to help businesses build training programs that are normally provided by public higher education institutions. Oregon's Workforce System is a partnership between industry, stat agencies, educational institutions and service providers. A variety of workforce services are available to job seekers and employers at one place. All three programs are funded through the Oregon State Lottery.

Pennsylvania

* Apprenticeship Program

Department of Labor
State Apprenticeship Council
Federal Building
228 Walnut St., Room 773
Harrisburg, PA 17108   717-782-3496

Apprenticeship is a combination of on-the-job and related classroom instruction in which workers learn the practical and theoretical aspects of a highly skilled occupation. Programs are operated voluntarily by employers, employer associations, or management and labor groups. Related classroom instruction is given in the sponsor's training facility or a local technical school or community college. Apprentices earn wages while they learn on the job, starting from about half the journeymen's rate up to 95% of full pay near the end of their apprenticeship. Training periods range from 1-6 years. Most trades require 3-4 years. The State Apprenticeship Council sponsors and funds the program.

* Customized Job Training Program

Pennsylvania Department of Commerce and Economic Development
400 North Street, 4th Floor
Commonwealth Keystone Building   717-720-7060
Harrisburg, PA 17120-0225   Fax: 717-720-7069
www.inventpa.com

The objectives of the Customized Job Training (CJT) Program are to improve skill levels of employees and their ability to obtain higher quality jobs through training; creation of new jobs or retention of jobs that would otherwise be lost; inclusion in the work force of significant number of dislocated workers, displaced homemakers and public assistance recipients; and the improvement of the ratio of net new hires to upgraded jobs funded by the CJT Program. CJT enables businesses to improve efficiency, lower costs or otherwise better compete in the global marketplace through the expansion of existing businesses; new business start-ups or relocation of firms from out of state; and increased levels of capital investment which will require training. Costs covered under this program include the trainer's salary, materials, administration costs, and some curriculum development.

* Education Programs

Office of Postsecondary and Higher Education
Department of Education
333 Market St.   717-787-4313
Harrisburg, PA 17126-0333   Fax: 717-783-5420

The Department of Education administers a wide range of programs designed to serve various target groups. Most funds are directed to local education agencies including school districts, area vocational-technical schools, and community colleges, for the support of secondary and post-secondary education. Programs include Secondary Vocational Education which subsidizes school districts and area vocational technical schools for the higher costs of secondary vocational education and to improve vocational educational programs; Adult Affidavits subsidizes school districts and area vocational technical schools for providing vocational extension and pre-employment training for out-of-school youths and adults; Health Occupations/Schools of Practical Nursing subsidizes secondary education agencies for providing health occupational/licensed practical nursing programs for out-of-school youths and adults; and community college Variable Stipend supports the higher costs of occupational-technical training programs in community colleges, and to encourage community colleges to develop curricula designed to further industrial development, reduce unemployment and improve employability skills.

* The New Directions Program

Special Programs Unit
Department of Labor and Industry   717-787-3266
Harrisburg, PA 17121   Fax: 717-787-5785

The New Directions Program focuses on the extensive use of education, skill training, employment services and supportive services such as child care, transportation, extended medical coverage, etc., to increase the potential for clients to secure and maintain long-term employment that will enable them to be self-supporting. The program builds on the strengths of previous employment and training activities while redirecting resources and efforts to provide a wider range of services to all welfare clients who can most benefit from these services. New Directions is driven fundamentally by client needs. Because the aspiration and needs of individual welfare clients vary depending upon their educational background, prior work history and family circumstances, a wide range of employment and training services are needed to help these welfare clients achieve self-sufficiency.

* Pennsylvania Literacy Corps

PA Literacy Corps
Institute for the Study of Adult Literacy
105 Rackley Building
University Park, PA 16802   814-863-3777
www.ed.psu.edu/paliteracycorps

The purpose of the Pennsylvania Literacy Corps is to increase training of citizens in need of literacy instruction by preparing college students to serve as tutors through a credit-bearing college course. Since the beginning of the program in fiscal year 1989 1990, 2,000 tutors have provided services to approximately 5,500 individuals.

* Single Point of Contact (SPOC) Program

Special Programs Unit
Department of Labor and Industry   717-787-6915
Harrisburg, PA 17121   Fax: 717-787-5785

The SPOC Program was specifically designed to provide intensive educational, employment services, and skill training to clients of welfare and eligible General Assistance (GA) clients. The resources from three state departments (Labor and Industry, Public Welfare and Education) were combined and utilized to provide services to New Directions clients who could benefit from enhanced educational, training, and employment services. The full implementation of the Family Support Act has provided additional resources to the Commonwealth to expand services to AFDC, AFDC/U and GA clients (in all 67 counties of Pennsylvania) who require educational, training and employment services in order to reduce their dependency on welfare.

* Vocational Rehabilitation On-The-Job Training

Office of Vocational Rehabilitation   717-787-5244
909 Green Street   TTY: 717-783-8917
Harrisburg, PA 17102   Fax: 717-783-5221

www.dli.state.pa.us

The office can reimburse employers for a percentage of the weekly wage of a trainer for a specified amount of time. This is dependent on the job and the time it takes to train the employee. Job Coaching is also available for disabled individuals requiring intensive on-site job training. The Office can hire a Job Coach who will work along side of the employer until the training is completed. The Coach will provide follow up support to both the employee and the employer.

* Guaranteed Free Training Program (GFT)

WEDnetPA
Dixon University Center
2986 North 2nd Street   717-720-7060
Harrisburg, PA 17110   Fax: 717-720-7069
www.inventpa.com

This program is a supplement to the CJT program. GFT provides assistance to companies in the following areas: Basic Skill Training- up to $450 per employee; and Information Technology Training- up to $700 per employee for new or existing employees that are IT professionals, front-line employees or supervisors of manufacturing companies; and Internet-Based Training- for basic skills and information technology, HIPPA, healthcare certifications, OSHA and technician training. Training is provided through WEDnetPA, and educational alliance.

* Critical Job Training Grant

Pennsylvania Department of Commerce and Economic Development
400 North Street, 4th Floor
Commonwealth Keystone Building   717-720-7060
Harrisburg, PA 17120-0225   Fax: 717-720-7069
www.inventpa.com

This grant funds job training for dislocated workers and other individuals for high-demand jobs or jobs with a shortage of skilled workers. The funds may be used for instructional costs, supplies, consumable materials, and contracted services. A 25% match is required.

Rhode Island

* Apprenticeship Program

Rhode Island Department of Labor & Training
Division of Professional Regulation
P.O. Box 20247
Cranston, RI 02920   401-462-8536
www.dlt.ri.gov/profregs/appren/appren.htm

Apprenticeship is a combination of on-the-job and related classroom instruction in which workers learn the practical and theoretical aspects of a highly skilled occupation. Programs are operated voluntarily by employers, employer associations or management and labor groups. Related classroom instruction is given in the sponsor's training facility or a local technical school or community college. Apprentices earn wages while they learn on the job, starting from about half the journeymen's rate up to 95% of full pay near the end of their apprenticeship. Training periods range from 1-6 years. Most trades require 3-4 years. The State Apprenticeship Council sponsors and funds the program.

* Job Training Assistance for Business

Rhode Island Human Resources investment Council (HRIC)
1511 Pontiac Avenue, Building 72-2   401-462-8860
Cranston, RI 02910   Fax: 401-462-8865
www.rihric.com

The HRIC provides assistance to businesses to provide job training skills to their employees. The HRIC is a significant component of the state's employment and training coordination efforts by responding to the workforce and economic development challenges which are not addressed by federally funded programs. Key HRIC initiatives include: Excellence Through Training Grants, Job Creation Grants, Employee Investment Grants, the Export Management Training Grant, Regional Employment and Training Boards, grants to the Rhode Island Economic Development Corporation to finance training for new jobs resulting from economic expansion, funding support for Rhode Island Manufacturing Extension Service, support for the Rhode Island Export Assistance Center, support of Rhode Island Area Coalition for Excellence, funding for Rhode Islands School-to-Work Program, support of Rhode Island Skills Commission activities, funding for Jobs for Rhode Island Grads Program, funding for HRIC/United Way "Making it Work" Project, and creation of a statewide customer-friendly "One-Stop" system.

South Carolina

* Continuing Education Programs

Economic Development Division
State Board for Technical and Comprehensive Training
111 Executive Center Dr.   803-896-5280
Columbia, SC 29210   Fax: 803-896-5281

Continuing education programs can be structured as certificate programs or as customized programs designated to improve specific workplace skills. Courses are often customized to meet the employer's specific training objectives. State technical colleges have worked directly with employers to train workers using proprietary processes producing proprietary products. South Carolina's technical colleges provide instructors and develop course materials and education programs are offered at Technical College campuses, employer's facilities, and mobile training facilities.

* Center for Accelerated Technology Training

Economic Development Division
State Board for Technical and Comprehensive Training
111 Executive Center Drive   803-896-5334
Columbia, SC 29210   Fax: 803-896-5281
www.sctechsystem.com/catt.htm

This program has been designed to provide tailor-made training to new and expanding industries in South Carolina. The system was founded on the idea that the state would be better served by training its citizens and employ them inside of South Carolina with jobs created by the state. Its main purpose is still to offer trained employees to a company when it first begins operations. An example of some of the programs used in training are ISO 9000, Total Quality Management Team Building, Supervisory Development Training, and Statistical Process Control.

South Dakota

* Customized Industrial Training

Governor's Office of Economic Development
711 East Wells Ave.   800-872-6190
Pierre, SD 57501-3369   605-773-5032
TDD: 605-773-3256

The Governor's Office of Economic Development coordinates all employee training programs for the Department of Labor and the four Technical Institutes located in the state. The Customized Industrial Training program allows training to be customized to meet the needs of any new or expanding South Dakota employer. Training is normally done in a classroom setting with a qualified instructor coordinated through one of the eight Technical Institutes. Companies help design curriculum content and participant screening requirements, and commit to hire trained participants. Funding is available to train eligible participants for entry level employment. The payment made to the employer is considered compensation for extraordinary training costs. Employers who commit to a post training wage or $8 per hour are eligible for this program.

* Technical Institutes Training

Economic Development Division
State Board for Technical and Comprehensive Training
111 Executive Center Dr.   803-737-9321
Columbia, SC 29210   Fax: 803-737-9371
www.sdgreatprofits.com/labor/training.htm

South Carolina's technical education (TECH) system is regarded as one of the nation's best. TECH's 15 resource centers offer specialized training programs for manufacturers and non-manufacturing businesses. The resource centers constantly update offerings in keeping with the business climate. The TECH system also offers mobile training units, making equipment and instructors available throughout the state.

* Veterans Education Benefits

SD Division of Veterans Affairs
500 East Capitol
Pierre, SD 57501   605-773-3269
www.state.sd.us/military/VetAffairs/benefits.html

Eligible veterans can receive tuition for undergraduate courses at a state university. They are eligible for one month of free tuition for each month of qualifying service with a minimum of one year and a maximum of four.

* Free Tuition for Children of Deceased Veterans

SD Division of Veterans Affairs
500 East Capitol
Pierre, SD 57501   605-773-3269
www.state.sd.us/military/VetAffairs/benefits.html

Children under the age of 25, whose parent was killed in action or died of other causes while on active duty, are eligible for free tuition at a state supported school. The veteran must have been a bona-fide resident of the state for at least 6 months prior to entering the service.

* Free Tuition for Dependents of POW's and MIA's

SD Division of Veterans Affairs
500 East Capitol
Pierre, SD 57501   605-773-3269
www.state.sd.us/military/VetAffairs/benefits.html

Children and spouses of prisoners of war, or of persons listed as missing in action, are entitled to attend a state supported school without the payment of tuition or mandatory fees provided they are not eligible for equal or greater federal benefits.

Tennessee

* Industrial Training Service

Tennessee Department of Economic and Community Development
Industrial Training Service   615-741-1746
10th Floor, William R. Snodgrass TN Tower   In TN: 800-342-8470
312 8th Avenue North   Outside TN: 800-251-8594
Nashville, TN 37243   Fax: 615-741-0607
www.state.tn.us/ecd/its.htm

The Industrial Training Service (ITS) offers customized training as an incentive for creating new jobs. The Service is offered to manufacturing and service sector businesses. Using ITS a business can open its doors quickly and expand as new production technologies are developed. The major ITS benefits include: Preemployment Training has special programs designed to focus on developing basic skills in new employees; On-the Job Training focuses on the development of specific skills and knowledge vital to production; System Support Training may include courses on new methods for increased mechanization, personnel interaction, quality and materials handling; Supervisory and Leadership Skills is designed to develop those skills essential for general supervision as well as the basics of leadership behavior; Training for Unique Equipment and Processes, in some cases, training programs are developed for companies involved in new equipment or processes within the new plant or expansion; and Training Materials developed for new employees and instructors participating in ITS programs.

* TN Job Skills

Tennessee Department of Economic and Community Development
Industrial Training Service
10th Floor William R. Snodgrass TN Tower
312 8th Avenue North   615-741-1746
Nashville, TN 37243   Fax: 615-741-0607
www.state.tn.us/ecd/tnjobskill.htm

Through training, the program will give priority to the creation and retention of high-wage jobs. Focus is on the industries and employers that promote high-skill, high-wage jobs for emerging, demand, and high technology manufacturing occupations. Employers must certify that a job or job opening exists at the end of training and that the training participants will fill it. An Industrial Training Service staff member will monitor the training.

Texas

* Skills Development Fund

Texas Workforce Commission
101 East 15th St., Room 104-T   512-463-8844
Austin, TX 78778   Fax: 512-475-2321

The Skills Development fund (SDF) is intended to aid public community and technical colleges in meeting industry and workforce training needs. SDF will award grants to businesses and labor unions for training programs designed for their specific needs and carried out through contracts with public community and technical colleges throughout the state. In regions without a community or technical college, businesses may request a non-local college to provide training. SDF grants are designed to cover the costs of program design, actual instruction, texts, and reusable equipment. Businesses or labor unions that need equipment specialized to their operations will be expected to supply it. SDF has two distinct goals: the creation of new jobs, whether through business start-ups or the expansion or relocation of existing businesses in Texas; and the creation of a highly trained and competitive Texas workforce.

* Apprenticeship Program

Texas Workforce Commission
101 East 15th Street, Room 420-T
Austin, TX 75778   512-463-9767
www.twc.state.tx.us

Apprenticeship is a combination of on-the-job and related classroom instruction in which workers learn the practical and theoretical aspects of a highly skilled occupation. Employers, employer associations or management and labor groups operate programs voluntarily. Related classroom instruction is given in the sponsor's training facility or a local technical school or community college. Apprentices earn wages while they learn on the job, starting from about half the journeymen's rate up to 95% of full pay near the end of their apprenticeship. Training periods range from 1-6 years. Most trades require 3-4 years. The State Apprenticeship Council sponsors and funds the program.

* Self-Sufficiency Fund

Texas Workforce Commission
101 East 15th Street, Room 420-T
Austin, TX 75778   512-463-9767
www.twc.state.tx.us/svcs/funds/ssfintro.html

This is a customized job-training program that was designed to help TANF and/or Food Stamp recipients get training, receive jobs, and become independent of government financial assistance. Since the training prepares the participants for jobs with specific employers, both the employer and participant must participate in the application process.

Utah

* Career Apprenticeship Starts Here (C.A.S.H.) Program

Utah State Office of Education
250 East 500 South   801-538-7639
Salt Lake City, UT 84111   Fax: 801-538-7521
www.grandk12.ut.us/cash/home.htm

The C.A.S.H. Program is a state-of-the-art program developed to provide high school students with a carefully supervised combination of the on-the-job training and classroom instruction they will need to prepare them to achieve their career goals. Any student at least 16 years of age who wishes to begin a career in an apprenticeable occupation may participate in the program. The advantages for employers who participate in the program includes: identifies training which is nationally recognized by the industry; provide systematic and structured form of training; attracts applicants who possess a firm background in reading, writing, and mathematics; promotes long-term employee commitment; and reduces training cost. This is a voluntary program involving no cost to the employer or the apprentice.

* General Assistance Self Sufficiency Program

Department of Workforce Services
140 East 300 South, 4th Floor 801-536-7400
Salt Lake City, UT 84111 Fax: 801-536-7420
http://jobs.utah.gov

This program either provides money to correct a client's medical problem so that the client can return to work or provides direction in pursuing another line of work that does not conflict with the medical condition. These clients are paid a monthly grant in line with TANF grant levels. Additional services are assessment and development of a self-sufficiency plan, assignment to one or more self-sufficiency activities, follow up and referral to allied agencies. Contract services are provided such as self esteem groups, legal services for Social Security Insurance appeals, and Job Service Workshops. Clients served are individuals and couples without children and those over 60 years of age who are medically unable to work at least 30 days or who are marginally employable. Clients normally posses a statement of disability that is provided by a psychologist, the Office of Rehabilitation, or a doctor or other who determines disability.

* Short Term Intensive Training

Department of Community and Economic Development
Division of Business and Economic Development
324 South State, Fifth Floor 801-538-8700
Salt Lake City, UT 84114 Fax: 801-538-8888

The Short Term Intensive Training (STIT) programs are customized and designed to meet full-time job openings. Programs are usually less than one year in length and will be designed to meet the specific training needs of a company while matching needs with people seeking employment. Although potential employees must pay tuition to participate, STIT can provide qualified employees from which a company can hire. STIT gives the option of training at 50-70% discount of normal training cost. Funding for this program is distributed to State Colleges.

* Single Head of Household Program

Department of Community & Economic Development
Office of Job Training for Economic Development
324 South State St., Fifth Floor
Salt Lake City, UT 84114-7162 801-538-8750

The Single Head of Household Program is designed to break the cycle of welfare dependency by moving economically disadvantaged single parents into permanent, self sustaining employment through a variety of education, job training, and support services. The programs goals are: placement in a job with a beginning wage which exceeds $6 per hour with health benefits; placements are made in areas with opportunities for advancement; and the long term impact of the program is measured by decreased welfare payments made by the state and an increase in taxes paid.

* Utah Custom Fit Training

Department of Economic Development
Utah State Office of Education
250 East 500 South   801-538-7867
Salt Lake City, UT 84111 Fax: 801-538-7521
http://dced.utah.gov/iaf/customfit.html TDD: 801-538-7876

Custom Fit Training is a tool for bringing business and education together by assisting businesses with their training needs. New and expanding businesses can participate as well as businesses in need of revitalization. Activities include instruction, curriculum development, assessment, and on-the-job training. Eligible applicants are for-profit enterprises or services. State priorities are technical training needs for business to encourage economic growth in the state and to involve education institutions assisting these businesses/industries. The following guidelines apply: training is short-term; company must be new, expanding, or in need of revitalization; trainees must be full time; company must meet regional minimum wage standards; and all funding is subject to legislative appropriation and State Board of Education approval. The range and average of financial assistance is a maximum of $500 per trainee, with an average of $250 per trainee. Actual levels of funding are determined by regional coordinators based on need and availability of funds.

* Vocational Rehabilitation

Utah State Office of Rehabilitation
250 East 500 South   800-473-7530
Salt Lake City, UT 84111 Fax: 801-538-7522
www.usor.utah.gov Voice/TDD: 801-538-7530

Persons whose disability prevents them from getting or keeping suitable employment may apply for vocational rehabilitation services. After eligibility is determined, assessment information is used to develop an Individualized Written Rehabilitation Program plan that is designed to assist the individual in preparing for and obtaining employment. Throughout the planning process, emphasis is placed on informed client choice of a vocational goal, services, and providers of services. When the client is ready for a job, placement service assistance is provided according to need identified in the individual plan. After the client begins working, the counselor provides follow-up to make sure the client is satisfied and the job is appropriate.

Vermont

* Apprenticeship Program

Department of Employment and Training
5 Green Mountain Drive
P.O. Box 488
Montpelier, VT 05601   802-828-5082
www.det.state.vt.us/jt/apprent.cfm

Apprenticeship is a combination of on-the-job and related classroom instruction in which workers learn the practical and theoretical aspects of a highly skilled occupation. Programs are operated voluntarily by employers, employer associations, or management and labor groups. Related classroom instruction is given in the sponsor's training facility or a local technical school or community college. Apprentices earn wages while they learn on the job, starting from about half the journeymen's rate up to 95% of full pay near the end of their apprenticeship. Training periods range from 1-6 years. Most trades require 3-4 years. The State Apprenticeship Council sponsors and funds the program.

* Vermont Training Program

Vermont Training Program Director
National Life Building, Drawer 26   802-828-5235
Montpelier, VT 05620   Fax: 802-828-3258
www.thinkvermont.com/workforce/vt_train.cfm

The Vermont Training Program promotes industrial expansion and encourages the creation of jobs in manufacturing by providing training for new and existing businesses. Individually designed programs may include on-the-job, classroom, skill upgrade, or other specialized training which are mutually agreed upon between the state and the employer. The program helps companies with new labor force for start-up or expansion, attracts new companies to the state, assists existing companies to remain competitive in production technology and product lines, helps currently employed individuals raise their skill levels and obtain better jobs within their company and improves the skills of a regional labor pool in anticipation of the needs for existing or incoming industries. Requirements for companies requesting assistance include agreeing to pay wages equal to at least twice minimum wage at the completion of training and providing a minimum of 50% of the overall training costs.

* Veterans Preference in State Employment

Vermont Department of Employment and Training
5 Green Mountain Drive
P.O. Box 488
Montpelier, VT 05601   603-431-0762/7115
www.det.state.vt.us/~vets/stavetpf.htm

In certification for appointment, in appointment, in employing, in retention of employment position, whether in classified or unclassified civil service, whether for temporary or for extended time, wherever state funds furnish the payroll, preference is given to veterans, their wives or widows. Contact this office for complete information on this program and for more information on eligibility requirements.

* Vermont Offender Work Programs

Vermont Department of Corrections
103 South Main Street   802-241-1103
Waterbury, VT 05671-1101   Fax: 802-241-2565
www.vtowp.com

In coordination with the community, these programs provide work and training opportunities to offenders allowing them to make reparations and return value to communities and victims while learning work habits and skills.

* Rural and Farm Family Vocation Rehabilitation Program

UVM Extension System
P.O. Box 53010   802-656-5433
Burlington, VT 05405-3010   Fax: 802-656-5423
www.dad.state.vt.us/dvr/rffp/rff.htm

This program works with members of rural and farm families with disabilities to place them into jobs consistent with their abilities and interests, or helps them to stay in their current job. Evaluation, counseling and assistance in job placement are available to eligible persons. Assistance is in the areas of vocational training and placement, machinery/equipment adaptations, education and training, work site/home site modification, and more.

Virginia

* Apprenticeship Program

Bureau of Apprenticeship & Training
Federal Building
400 North 8th Street, Suite 404   804-771-2488
Richmond, VA 23240   Fax: 804-771-8679

www.doli.state.va.us/whatwedo/apprenticeship/apprenticeship_p1.html
Apprenticeship is a combination of on-the-job and related classroom instruction in which workers learn the practical and theoretical aspects of a highly skilled occupation. Programs are operated voluntarily by employers, employer associations, or management and labor groups. Related classroom instruction is given in the sponsor's training facility or a local technical school or community college. Apprentices earn wages while they learn on the job, starting from about half the journeymen's rate up to 95% of full pay near the end of their apprenticeship. Training periods range from 1-6 years. Most trades require 3-4 years. The State Apprenticeship Council sponsors and funds the program.

* Transportation Trainee and Intern Programs

Internship Coordinator
VDOT Learning Center
VA Department of Transportation
1404 East Broad Street
Richmond, VA 23219-1939
http://virginiadot.org/careers/default.asp

The Virginia Department of Transportation (VDOT), sponsors two entry-level programs: the Engineer Trainee Program and the Administrative Intern Program. The objective of the Engineer Trainee Program is to orient the entry level engineer to the major functions of the Department; provide a system of diverse, structured training assignments to assist the trainee in gaining practical experience and developing their abilities more rapidly than would otherwise be possible; and produce knowledgeable and skilled transportation engineers who are prepared to advance into increasingly responsible engineering, supervisory, and administrative positions within VDOT. The Administrative Trainee Program's objective is to provide job incumbents who have undergraduate or graduate degrees and little or no work experience with two years of structured practical work experience related to their academic field, within the agency's administrative divisions.

* Virginia VIEW Program

Virginia Tech
205 West Roanoke St.   In VA:800-542-5780
Blacksburg, VA 24061-0527   540-231-7571
www.vaview.vt.edu

The Commonwealth of Virginia funds Virginia VIEW as its Career Information Delivery Service. Virginia VIEW is a state project operated through Virginia Tech. The project provides information on specific occupations and other relevant labor force information that is updated annually. Occupation Search generates a list of occupations matching users personal preferences in including preferences in the area of work, interests, and education. College Search matches users preferences with Virginia community colleges and 2 & 4 year public and private institutions. This information is available in an interactive computer program, in tabloid form and on microfiche. Each fall, 25 workshops are conducted across the state to distribute the updated products and train clients in their use. Users are typically counselors at schools, colleges, in private practice and rehabilitative services, or employment services professions. Virginia VIEW also operates a toll free Career information Hotline (800-542-5870) that people may call with career questions.

* Workforce Services

Department of Business Services
707 East Main Street, Suite 300
P.O. Box 446   804-371-8200
Richmond, VA 23218   Fax: 804-371-8137

Since 1965, Workforce Services has been a unique program which offers consulting services and training assistance for new and expanding industries. The programs offered are; New Jobs, Small Business New Jobs, and Retraining, each comes with its own requirements. Workforce Services will assist in coordinating the client's specific training needs with any one or more of Virginia's institutions of education including: vocational education, community college, and the four-year institutions. The following activities are legitimate uses for the program funds: consulting services, training analysis, recruitment/pre-employment assessment, video production services, train-the-trainer, instructors, productivity/continuous improvement programs, and training. Funding for each program will be based on estimated tax benefits generated within a one-year period for each new job created and filled and the cost estimate developed during the program's design. Companies will be reimbursed three months after the new employee's hire date.

Washington

* Apprenticeship Program

Department of Labor & Industry
Specialty Compliance Services Division
P.O. Box 4440
Olympia, WA 98504   360-902-5320
www.lni.wa.gov/scs/apprenticeship

Apprenticeship is a combination of on-the-job and related classroom instruction in which workers learn the practical and theoretical aspects of a highly skilled occupation. Programs are operated voluntarily by employers, employer associations or management and labor groups. Related classroom instruction is given in the sponsor's training facility or a local technical school or community college. Apprentices earn wages while they learn on the job, starting from about half the journeymen's rate up to 95% of full pay near the end of their apprenticeship. Training periods range from 1-6 years. Most trades require 3-4 years. The State Apprenticeship Council sponsors and funds the program.

* Career Services Program

Department of Personnel
P.O. Box 47500   360-664-1990
Olympia, WA 98504   Fax: 360-586-4694
http://hr.dop.wa.gov/RIF

State employees impacted by reduction-in-force (RIF) have a wide range of resources and services available to them through Career Services. Workshops have been developed to help employees with the various aspects of their job search. New workshops are added as the need arises for additional topics to be covered. Other services available include: one-on-one guidance from professional employment specialists on all aspects of conducting a job search; the RIF Transition Pool offers employees impacted by RIF an alternative opportunity for finding reemployment within state service; and the Office of Personnel will place the names of eligible employees on agency and service-wide reduction-in-force registers for referral to appropriate vacancies. Resources available include personal computers and printers, career and job search handbooks, copiers, telephones and fax machines.

* Claimant Placement Program

Dwight Wood
Employment Security Department
212 Maple Park
Olympia, WA 98504   360-438-4124

Participants are provided assistance in developing plans for successfully seeking employment. Services include workshops teaching job search skills, assistance in contacting employers, and other employment seeking skills. The program protects the solvency of the Washington State Unemployment Insurance Trust Fund by reducing the average length of a claimant's period of unemployment. The Claimant Placement Program is delivered through a network of 20 Job Service Centers throughout the state. The program services are available for long term unemployed and older workers.

* Corrections Clearinghouse

Doug Jacques
Employment Security Department
P.O. Box 9046, MS 6000
Olympia, WA 98507-9046   360-438-4124
www.wa.gov/esd/work/programs.htm

The Corrections Clearinghouse (CCH) provides offenders with employment and training enhancement services. It provides institutional and community linkages, liaison, and advocacy for the offender who is about to be released or has recently been released from a correctional institution. The Offender Employment Program allows individuals to gain knowledge and skills necessary to find and retain employment and training opportunities. Additional functions of CCH include career awareness, pre-release employment preparation, youth employment preparation and youth transition services.

* Displaced Homemaker Program

Displaced Homemaker Program
Higher Education Coordination Board
917 Lakeridge Way   360-753-7823
P.O. Box 43430   Fax: 360-753-7808
Olympia, WA 98504-3430   TDD: 360-753-7809
www.hecb.wa.gov

A displaced homemaker is an individual who: has worked in the home for ten or more years providing unsalaried household services for family members on a full-time basis; is not gainfully employed; needs assistance in securing employment; and has been dependent on the income of another family member but is no longer supported by that income, or has been dependent on federal assistance but is no longer eligible for that assistance, or is supported as the parent of minor children by public assistance or spouse support but whose children are within two years of reaching 18 years of age. An important objective of the Displaced Homemaker Program is to provide necessary training opportunities, counseling, and services to increase the employability of displaced homemakers. The program established guidelines under which the higher Education Coordinating Board shall contract to establish Multipurpose Service Centers and programs to provide a wide range of educational retraining services, including job readiness, job search and/or job training and job placement for eligible participants.

* Industry-Specific Training at Community and Technical Colleges

Dan McConnon or Roy Schmidt
State Board for Community and Technical Colleges
P.O. Box 42495   360-753-2000
Olympia, WA 98504-2495   Fax: 360-753-6440

Each of the 32 community and technical colleges across the state offers workforce skills training and management classes and seminars for business. Customized training can range from basic skills for the workplace, new employee training, upgrade training, and management training. Community and technical colleges can assess the training needs of business or set of businesses and fashion customized training programs for the membership. Both small and large businesses can be served. Fees depend upon the type of training to be offered and the number of people to be trained. In addition to customized training that is open to any worker, colleges offer the state funded training programs for dislocated workers. An association might consider this option if member businesses wish to hire and train dislocated workers.

* Job Skills Program (JSP)

State Board for Community and Technical College
WA State Business Development
210 11th Avenue SW, Suite 101
Olympia, WA 98504-2500   360-725-5050
www.oted.wa.gov/cd/busdev/jobskills.asp

This statewide program funds industry-education partnerships from which customized training materials are developed and short-term, job-specific training is delivered. JSP supports up to one-half the total cost of training with the participating companies providing a dollar-for-dollar cash or in-kind match. JSP supports entry-level training for prospective employees before a new plant opens or when a company expands; retraining of a company's current employees when the training is required to prevent the dislocation of those employees; and upgrade skills training of current employees when new vacancies will be created as a result of their promotion into new positions. Awards are granted four times each year, however, accommodation can be made to award funds at other times of the year if the company or companies have an urgent need for training.

* Pre-Apprenticeship Training

Department of Labor & Industry
Specialty Compliance Services Division
P.O. Box 4440
Olympia, WA 98504   360-902-5320
www.lni.wa.gov/scs/apprenticeship/preappen.htm

Washington offers a variety of pre-apprenticeship programs throughout the state. Programs are geared towards low-income men and women, and high school students. They range in services but all of them provide on-the-job and classroom training in order for the participants to move up to the Apprenticeship program. The web site listed above provides a listing of all of the available programs.

West Virginia

* Governor's Guaranteed Work Force Programs

West Virginia Development Office
1900 Kanawha Blvd., East
Capitol Complex   877-967-5498
Building 6, Room 553   304-558-7024
Charleston, WV 255308-0311   Fax: 304-967-7029

The Governor's Guaranteed Work Force Program (GGWFP) is West

Virginia's customized job training program for both new and existing businesses. The GGWFP can provide up to $1,000 per employee to new companies which create at least 10 new jobs within a 12-month period. The program can also provide up to $1,000 per employee to existing companies which are either expanding or in need of training to retrain employees. The program works with outside training resources to provide a wide range of services. Through its partnerships with agencies such as the Department of Education and the Bureau of Employment Programs, the GGWFP office serves as a one-stop center for businesses requiring work force development.

* Competitive Improvement Program

West Virginia Development Office   304-558-7024
1900 Kanawha Boulevard, East   877-967-5498
Charleston, WV 255308-0311   Fax: 304-967-7029
www.wvdo.org/workforce/index.html

This program is for small (50 or fewer employees) and medium (less than 500 employees) sized manufacturers. A maximum grant of $1,000 per trainee is available for training programs to upgrade the skill of employees. A 50% cash contribution is required from the employer and they must document an in-kind contribution toward the project.

* Small Business Workforce Program

West Virginia Development Office   304-558-7024
1900 Kanawha Boulevard, East   877-967-5498
Charleston, WV 255308-0311   Fax: 304-967-7029
www.wvdo.org/workforce/index.html

For-profit small businesses are eligible for reimbursement for the cost of pre-approved technology and technology training. The grants have a maximum amount of funding for $5,000 and are designed to enhance competitiveness and expand markets. The maximum grant for a technology business is $10,000.

Wisconsin

* Adult Literacy Incentive Grant Program

Technical College System Board
P.O. Box 7874   608-266-0025
Madison, WI 53707-7874   Fax: 608-266-1690
www.board.tec.wi.us/grants

Funds are awarded on a competitive basis to Wisconsin Technical College districts that implement educational programs designed to improve basic educational skills of educationally disadvantaged adults. The program provides basic education courses, such as adult high school classes and English as a Second Language classes. Eligible participants are adults who are functioning below the 12th grade level, with priority given to the unemployed, minorities, and persons with disabilities.

* Apprenticeship Program

Bureau of Apprenticeship Standard
201 East Washington Avenue, Room 229
P.O. Box 7972   608-266-3332
Madison, WI 53707   Fax: 608-266-0766
www.dwd.state.wi.us/dws/appr/default.htm

Apprenticeship is a combination of on-the-job and related classroom instruction in which workers learn the practical and theoretical aspects of a highly skilled occupation. Programs are operated voluntarily by employers, employer associations, or management and labor groups. Related classroom instruction is given in the sponsor's training facility or a local technical school or community college. Apprentices earn wages while they learn on the job, starting from about half the journeymen's rate up to 95% of full pay near the end of their apprenticeship. Training periods range from 1-6 years. Most trades require 3-4 years. The State Apprenticeship Council sponsors and funds the program.

* Aviation Careers Education (ACE) Program

Bureau of Aeronautics
Department of Transportation
4802 Sheboygan Avenue
Madison, WI 53702   608-266-8166
www.dot/wisconsin.gov/travel/air/ace.htm

The objectives of this program include: making learning more interesting and meaningful so students stay in school; offering clubs that enhance students experiences through contact with individuals at the airport and through extracurricular activities; and providing part time jobs in the field

of aviation that will educate students, provide participants with work experience, and fulfill airline employment objectives. Although three Milwaukee public schools currently provide services through the program, only the high school students actually participate in the employment and job training aspects of the program by enrolling in work experience placements through 12 aviation-related businesses and government agencies. Placements typically provided participants with work experience in maintenance, customer service, parking and aircraft fueling, baggage handling, and clerical and food service work. A coordinator from Milwaukee Public Schools provides oversight of the day-to-day activities of students participating in the work experience program.

* Basic Skills Incentive Grant Program

Technical College System Board
P.O. Box 7874   608-266-1207
Madison, WI 53707-7874   Fax: 608-266-1690
www.board.tec.wi.us/grants

The Board awards state funds designated for the Basic Skills Incentive Grant Program to provide additional support to Wisconsin Technical College districts that have implemented programs to improve the reading and employability skills of educationally disadvantaged adults. Specifically, the Basic Skills Incentive Grant Program provides instruction in writing, mathematics, and critical thinking and problem solving. Eligible participants are adults who are functioning below the 12th grade level, with priority given to the unemployed, minorities, and persons with disabilities.

* Customized Labor Training Program

Department of Commerce
201 West Washington Avenue
P.O. Box 7970   800-HELP-BUS
Madison, WI 53702-7970   608-266-1018
www.commerce.state.wi.us

The Customized Labor Training Program (CLT), encourages businesses, primarily manufacturing, to invest in the retooling and upgrading of equipment, productivity and the labor forces by providing up to 50% of the costs of a workforce training program. Eligible training includes: job training that focuses on new technology, industrial skills or manufacturing processes that are new to the company; job training that is not currently available from other resources and would not take place without state funds; and job training for new or retained positions that will be guaranteed by the company. Quality improvement training my be reimbursed after participation in a manufacturing assessment program. Eligible costs and match include: wages of production-related staff, not including benefits or premiums; training materials; trainer costs, except certain costs for publicly supported schools; and training travel costs. Any business making a firm commitment to locate in Wisconsin or expanding within Wisconsin that is upgrading a product, process, or service that requires worker training in new technology and industrial skills is eligible for the program.

* Displaced Homemakers' Program

Technical College System Board
P.O. Box 7874   608-266-1207
Madison, WI 53707-7874   Fax: 608-266-1690
www.board.tec.wi.us/grants

This program provides job development and support services to displaced homemakers throughout the state. Its goal is to help displaced homemakers successfully locate and obtain employment and is designed to reduce barriers to employment by offering participants the opportunity to gain marketable skills and eventually secure a job. The Board awards funds designated for the Displaced Haymakers' Program to Wisconsin Technical College districts and community organizations that implement programs to help displaced homemaker successfully find employment. The services available to qualified participants include career counseling, employability assessment, post-placement follow-up, classroom training, and dependent care. The program receives additional funding from the Department of Health and Social Services, which administers a block grant to fund services for displaced homemakers. The program is open to individuals who have worked in the home for a substantial number of years providing unpaid household services for family members, are not gainfully employed, are experiencing difficulty obtaining a job, and have been dependent on the income of another family member or on public assistance but are no longer supported by such income.

* New and Expanding Occupations Incentive Grant Program

Technical College System Board
P.O. Box 7674   608-266-1207

Madison, WI 53707-7874   Fax: 608-266-1690

The Board awards designated state funds on a competitive basis to the Wisconsin Technical College districts that implement programs to improve the employability skills of adults. Grants for New and Expanding Occupations are used to develop and maintain programs, provide instruction in the use of new technology, foster the provision of apprenticeship programs, and upgrade the instruction of journey workers. Program funding primarily supports curriculum development and instructors. The program is available to individuals in the general public who qualify to enroll in postsecondary education programs, with priority given to educationally disadvantaged, unemployed, minorities, and persons with disabilities.

* Veterans Education Benefits

Department of Veterans Affairs
Tuition and Fee Reimbursement Grant Programs
P.O. Box 7843
30 West Mifflin St.   800-947-8387
Madison, WI 53707-7843   608-266-1311
http://dva.state.wi.us/BENEFITS.ASP

Veterans, and unremarried spouses and dependents of deceased veterans, who have served on active duty under honorable conditions for other than training purposes in the United States Armed Forces for at least 90 days during a wartime period or conflict are eligible for the following educational benefits: Personal Loan Program for education, Part-Time Study Grant Program, Part Time Study Grant, and the Tuition and Fee Reimbursement Grant Program. Contact the office listed above for complete information on programs and other eligibility requirements.

* Workplace Education Incentive Grant Program

Technical College System Board
P.O. Box 7874   608-266-1207
Madison, WI 553707-7874   Fax: 608-266-1690

This state grant program funds adult education programs that provide courses below the post-secondary level, and is designed to improve the occupational skill level of educationally disadvantaged working adults. Courses provided through this program include adult basic education and English as a Second Language, provided by Wisconsin technical colleges in the workplace. This program is available to adults who are functioning below the 12th grade level in Wisconsin businesses, with priority given to small businesses.

* Business Employees Skills Training (BEST) Programs

Department of Commerce
201 West Washington Avenue
P.O. Box 7970   800-HELP-BUS
Madison, WI 53702-7970   608-266-1018
www.commerce.state.wi.us

The State Legislature established this program to help small businesses in industries that are facing severe labor shortages upgrade the skill of their workforce. Applicants will receive a tuition reimbursement grant, which will cover a portion of the training costs. A match of 25% is required from the company. Eligible companies are those with 25 or fewer full time employees.

* Youth Apprenticeship

Bureau of Apprenticeship Standard
201 East Washington Avenue, Room 229
P.O. Box 7972   608-266-3332
Madison, WI 53707   Fax: 608-266-0766
www.dwd.state.wi.us/dws/appr/default.htm

Students enter the program in their junior year of high school and work part-time with an employer through their junior and senior years. The program length is usually between 2000 to 8000 hours, and takes anywhere from 2-5 years to complete depending on the occupation and the employer. Upon graduating from the program, they will receive a Certificate of Completion from the Bureau of Apprenticeship Standard. At that point, the graduate can choose to enter the Apprenticeship Program and if so, their time in the Youth Apprenticeship program will count towards their training.

Wyoming

* Light-Duty Work Program

The Division of Workers' Safety and Compensation has a light-duty work provision which allows injured workers to go back to work for their previous employer in a light-duty capacity if they meet the medical requirements as set forth by law. This encourages injured workers to go to work rather than
continuing to receive benefits through the program. Injured workers can actually earn more money than they would on the Workers' Compensation program by going back to light-duty work.

* Vocational Rehabilitation Benefit

Department of Employment
Division of Workers' Safety and Compensation
1510 East Pershing Boulevard   307-777-7441
Cheyenne, WY 82002   Fax: 307-777-6552
http://wydoe.state.wy.us

The Wyoming Division of Workers' Safety and Compensation has a provision that allows injured workers that qualify the option of receiving a disability award or opting for enrollment in a vocational rehabilitation program. This vocational rehabilitation program is designed to get injured workers back to work by retraining and job placement. An individually written rehabilitation program outlines the specific steps necessary for the injured worker to achieve a vocational goal.

* Apprenticeship Program

Apprenticeship & Training Bureau
1912 Capitol Avenue
Cheyenne, WY 82001   307-772-2448
http://dwsweb.state.wy.us/jobs/apprenticeship

Apprenticeship is a combination of on-the-job and related classroom instruction in which workers learn the practical and theoretical aspects of a highly skilled occupation. Employers, employer associations or management and labor groups operate programs voluntarily. Related classroom instruction is given in the sponsor's training facility or a local technical school or community college. Apprentices earn wages while they learn on the job, starting from about half the journeymen's rate up to 95% of full pay near the end of their apprenticeship. Training periods range from 1-6 years. Most trades require 3-4 years. The State Apprenticeship Council sponsors and funds the program.

* Workforce Development Training Fund

Department of Workforce Services
Program Manager
P.O. Box 2760   307-235-3294
Casper, WY 82602-2760   Fax: 307-235-3293
http://dwsweb.state.wy.us/employes/trainingfund.asp

Revenues generated from the interest of the State Unemployment Insurance Trust Fund supplies the funds for this program. It is used for the training of newly hired or current employees from businesses that have expanded or relocated. Training must be necessary due to changes in the skill required to continue the operation of the business. A job must exist at the end of training and the trainee must fill it. Only expenses directly related to the training; instructor fees, materials, travel expenses, workshop fees, will be reimbursed.

I Wanna Get Experience to Get a Better Job

Federal Government Jobs, Internships, and Student Educational Employment Programs

Have you ever dreamed of:

- Making $2,000 a month during the summer learning how Congress really works?
- Spending the summer earning $550 a week tracking endangered species for the Department of the Interior?
- Taking a semester off to help the Environmental Protection Agency crack down on illegal polluters?
- Going to school and getting a part time job making $10 an hour helping NASA prepare for the next manned space flight?

No one but the Federal government can provide students with full and part time jobs helping the victims of floods, hurricanes or earthquakes; helping in the fight against homelessness; understanding the inner workings of volcanoes; or learning about the reshaping of the USSR.

The U.S. government is the world's **LARGEST** single employer with over 3 million people on its payroll. Students should not miss out on the opportunity available for full time or part time employment, as well as cooperative education programs. Remember only about 13% of those U.S. government employees actually work in Washington, DC. So if you want to find opportunities in your own community, you can still take advantage of these wonderful programs.

Utilizing one of these student programs is also one of the surest ways of landing a full time job with the government after graduation. Many agencies view these programs as a "win/win" situation for everyone. An agency acquires an employee that is enthusiastic and hardworking, while the student acquires good experience and the opportunity for possible employment after graduation.

Increase your chances of success by matching up your area of interest with the mission of an agency you are interested in. For example, business majors may find a better match at the U.S. Department of Commerce than at the U.S. Fish And Wildlife Service. On the other hand, if you're a business major with an interest in nature, you may find work in the accounting department at the Fish and Wildlife Service. You can get information about an agency's mission by requesting a copy of their annual report (which will be sent to you free), or by taking a look at the *U.S. Government Manual* available in most libraries. It is printed by the U.S. Government Printing Office, and is a powerhouse of important information in your search for the best programs and the best employment opportunities.

* Student Educational Employment Program

U.S. Office of Personnel Management
Washington Area Service Center
1900 E St. NW
Washington, DC 20415-0001   202-606-1800
USA Jobs (recording)   703-724-1850
www.opm.gov/employ/students/index.htm   202-606-2700

The Federal government is the largest employer of students in the United States. By working for the government, students gain valuable work experience while still in school and get paid for it. The U.S. Office of Personnel Management has consolidated the previous programs (e.g., Cooperative Education, Stay-in-School, Federal Junior Fellowship, and Summer Aid Programs) into the new Student Educational Employment Program. The new program combines key features of the old program along with added flexibilities to provide a more effective and streamlined program. The Federal government has always looked to educational institutions to find people who have the skills needed to meet its future employment needs. Students who are U.S. citizens or national residents of American Samoa or Swains Island, non-citizens may be eligible for employment if permitted by a federal agency's appropriation act or are eligible to work under U.S. immigration laws. Students must be enrolled or accepted for enrollment as a degree-seeking student (diploma, certificate, etc.), and taking at least a half-time academic or vocational and technical course load in an accredited high school, technical or vocational school, two year or four year college or university, graduate or professional school. The schedule is flexible and would depend on the needs of the agency you are interested in. Positions are paid and salary is based on education, work experience, and assignment. Thousands of students at different academic levels have participated in this program. Most federal agencies throughout the United States use this program as well as developing additional student, intern or fellowship programs to meet their specific business needs. Every agency of the government requires that you submit a resume and/or an Optional Form 612 which you can get from the Office of Personnel Management or the agency of interest. To apply, contact your school guidance office, career planning and placement office, or federal agency employment office where you are interested in working. To get more information about the program, you may also contact the Office of Personnel Management at the office listed above or call the Career America Connection.

* Internships and Volunteers

(Volunteer Service Program)

The Volunteer Service Program gives students the opportunity to gain career-related work experience while attending school. The program allows one to develop personal and professional skills and enhance their knowledge of public service. The Volunteer Service Program has also been equated to the Internship Program, and in some instances is referred to as the Volunteer Internship Program. In a few agencies there might be the possibility of payment to the student, but this is very limited. There are opportunities in many different government agencies throughout the United States. Students will be doing a variety of functions ranging from policy to research oriented tasks and projects. The assignments are always very rewarding. Students must be enrolled on at least a part-time basis in an accredited high school or trade school, a technical or vocational institution, a college or university, or any other accredited educational institution. Volunteers usually work three to four months on a part-time basis. Volunteers are not permitted to be compensated. There are thousands of students throughout the different agencies who have participated. Students work all over the United States in various agencies. Every agency of the government requires that you submit a resume or OPT. 612 (optional form). This form can be obtained from the office you wish to work for, the Office of Personnel Management listed below, or from the Personnel Office of a government office anywhere in the United States. Most agencies will request letters of recommendation and a copy of your school or college transcript. For official internships, you must also contact your school's career counseling center internship office, as well

as the agency of interest. Although most agencies do offer this program, budget constraints may force some offices not to participate each and every year. The list of agency contacts at the end of this section identifies the contact person at the time of publication. If the agency listed does not contain a contact person for the Student Educational Employment Program, you can write or call one of the other contacts listed to see if a program will soon begin at that agency.

* Presidential Management Intern Program (PMI)

Presidential Management Intern Program
U.S. Office of Personnel Management
1900 E Street, NW, Room 1425
Washington, DC 20415   202-606-1040
USA Jobs (recording)   703-724-1850
www.pmi.opm.gov/index.htm
Email: pmi@opm.gov

The Presidential Management Intern Program (PMI) is an entry level career development and training program designed to attract to the federal service outstanding men and women who are interested in a career in public service. Applicants must be nominated by their graduate school dean, director, or chairperson. Individuals must have management and leadership potential. There is a very rigorous and competitive screening process. Once chosen, the two-year program will have PMIs rotate to federal agencies where they will participate in training conferences, seminars, and Congressional briefings. Recent PMIs have worked on issues related to government reinvention, health care, criminal justice, and the environment. There are opportunities throughout the United States. To obtain an application, you may call or write the Office of Personnel Management or the Career Connection. Graduate degree recipients will have been nominated by their graduate school dean, director, or chairperson. PMIs work full time for two years. Starting salary is a GS-9 ($30,658) plus benefits, with salaries 8% higher in San Francisco, New York City, and Los Angeles. Applicants must first obtain an application and be nominated. Be sure to complete and submit all of the required information to the appropriate address. The number of positions varies based on need, but in the past there have been as many as 750 appointments annually. PMIs work all over the United States in various agencies, departments, and bureaus. Applicants can obtain an application and nomination information from the above address.

* Special U.S. Congress Internship Programs

Honorable _____
United States House of Representatives
Washington, DC 20510   202-224-3121

Honorable _____
United States Senate
Washington, DC 20510   202-224-3121

The following programs are special internships offered by the U.S. Congress. For more information on applying for these programs, or for a free copy of *Internships and Fellowships* (#IP 631), you can contact the office of your Representative or either of your Senators at the addresses listed above.

Congressional Internships

Congressional Internships are available through members of Congress and private organizations and are highly competitive. Members of the House of Representatives, Senators, Congressional committees, and other congressional groups may appoint a person to the regular staff and designate that person as an intern or volunteer.

Congressional Senior Citizen Internship Program

This program brings senior citizens to Washington, DC for one week in May where they will attend seminars and briefings on the workings of the Federal government. Particular interest is paid to informing participants how the Federal government serves seniors.

Legislative Branch

* Architect of the Capitol
Jeannie Smith
Human Resource Division
U.S. Capitol Building   202-225-1231
Washington, DC 20515   Fax: 202-225-7315
Program Available: Student Educational Employment Program.

* U.S. Botanic Garden
Jeannie Smith
Human Resource Division
U.S. Capitol Building   202-225-1231
Washington, DC 20515   Fax: 202-225-7315
Program Available: Student Educational Employment Program.

* Congressional Budget Office
Ford House Office Building, 4th Floor   202-226-2628
Washington, DC 20515-6925   Fax: 202-225-7539
www.cbo.gov/Intern.cfm
Programs Available: Internship Program.

* Congressional Research Service
Library of Congress
LM-208   202-707-8803
Washington, DC 20515   Fax: 202-707-7615
Email: employment@crs.loc.gov
Programs Available: Internship Program; Presidential Management Intern Program

* General Accounting Office
Student Employment Program Coordinator
Office of Recruitment
441 G St. NW, Room 1050   202-512-3429
Washington, DC 20548   Fax: 202-512-2539
Programs Available: Student Educational Employment Program; Internship Program.

* Library of Congress
Leon Turner, Cooperative Education Program Manager
Library of Congress/Librarian's Office
101 Independence Ave., SE   202-707-2087
Washington, DC 20540-2530   Fax: 202-252-2045
Email: letu@loc.gov
Programs Available: Student Educational Employment Program; Volunteer Service Program; Presidential Management Intern Program.

Judicial Branch

* Administrative Office of the U.S. Courts
Tony Robinson
Student Employment Program Coordinator
Administrative Office of the U.S. Courts
Thurgood Marshall Federal Judicial Building
One Columbus Circle, NE
Washington, DC 20544   202-273-2777
Program Available: Volunteer Service Program.

* Federal Judicial Center
Elaine Lewis Clark
Summer Program Coordinator
Personnel Office
Federal Judicial Center
Thurgood Marshall Federal Judicial Building
One Columbus Circle, NE   202-273-2777
Washington, DC 20002-8003   Fax: 202-273-2782
Program Available: Student Educational Employment Program.

Jeanette Sisson
Student Employment Program Coordinator
Personnel Office
Federal Judicial Center
Thurgood Marshall Federal Judicial Building

One Columbus Circle, NE   202-273-4165
Washington, DC 20002-8003   Fax: 202-273-2782
Program Available: Internship Program.

Executive Branch

* The White House
Michael Sanders, Intern Coordinator
Old Executive Office Building
17th and Pennsylvania Ave., NW   202-456-2742
Washington, DC 20500   Fax: 202-456-5123
www.whitehouse.gov/government/wh-intern.html
Program Available: Internship Program.

* Department of Agriculture
Marilyn Jenkins
Student Employment Program Coordinator
U.S. Department of Agriculture
14th and Independence Ave., SW
Administrative Building, Room 316-W   202-720-7168
Washington, DC 20250-9600   Fax: 202-720-7850
Email: marilyn.jenkins@usda.gov
www.usda.gov/da/employ/intern.htm
Programs Available: Student Educational Employment Program; Volunteer Service Program.; Presidential Management Intern Program

* Department of Agriculture-Economic Research Service
Kate Muir
Economic Research Service
1800 M Street, NW N4122   202-694-5014
Washington, DC 20036-5828   Fax: 202-694-5747
Email: kmuir@ers.usda.gov
Program Available: Presidential Management Intern Program

* Department of Agriculture-Farm and Foreign Agricultural Services
Dawn Ferguson
PMI Program Coordinator
Mail Stop 0593
1400 Independence Avenue, SW   202-418-9008
Washington, DC 20250-9600   Fax: 202-418-9127
Email: dawn.ferguson@usda.gov
Program available: Presidential Management Intern Program

* Department of Agriculture-Food and Nutrition Service
Mike Vost
Food and Nutrition Service
3101 Park Center Drive, Room 620   703-305-2372
Alexandria, VA 22032-1594   Fax: 703-305-2299
Email: mike.vost@fns.usda.gov
Program available: Presidential Management Intern Program

* Department of Agriculture-Food Safety and Inspection Service
Tonya M. Johnson
Human Resources Development
Room 3141 South Building
1400 Independence Avenue, SW   202-690-1787
Washington, DC 20250   Fax: 202-720-5124
Email: tonya.johnson7@fsis.usda.gov
Program available: Presidential Management Intern Program

* Department of Agriculture- Forest Service
Vernetta Fields
PMI Program Coordinator
U.S. Forest Service
1621 North Kent Street
Room 900 RPE   703-605-0821
Arlington, VA 22209   Fax: 703-605-0825
Email: vfields@fs.fed.us
Program available: Presidential Management Intern Program

* Department of Agriculture-Natural Resources Conservation Service

Kathy Huey
Natural Resource Conservation Services
1400 Independence Avenue, SW
Mail Stop 1600-2890   202-720-2631
Washington, DC 20250   Fax: 202-720-0717
Email: Kathy.huey@usda.gov
Program available: Presidential Management Intern Program

* Department of Agriculture-OCIO/Resource Management Staff

Lisa Acure
PMI Program Coordinator
1400 Independence Avenue, SW
Room 0177, S Building   202-720-4109
Washington, DC 20250   Fax: 202-690-0647
Email: lisa.acure@usda.gov
Program available: Presidential Management Intern Program

* Department of Agriculture-Office of the Chief Economist

Donna Carter
PMI Program Coordinator
1400 Independence Avenue, SW   202-720-5806
Washington, DC 20250-3810   Fax: 202-690-1067
Email: donna.carter@usda.gov
Program Available: Presidential Management Intern Program

* Department of Agriculture-Office of Human Resources Management

Renee Jones
Office of Human Resources Management
14th and Constitution Avenue, NW
Room 5005   202-482-8078
Washington, DC 20230   Fax: 202-501-2641
Email: rjones@doc.gov
Program available: Presidential Management Intern Program

* Department of Agriculture-Office of the Inspector General

Joanne Poag
Office of the Inspector General
Room 46 E
1400 Independence Avenue, SW   202-720-0966
Washington, DC 20250-2306   Fax: 202-720-4321
Email: japoag@oig.usda.goc
Program available: Presidential Management Intern Program

* Department of Agriculture-Rural Development

Junius Scott
Rural Development
MS 0730
1400 Independence Avenue, SW   202-692-0199
Washington, DC 20250-0730   Fax: 202-692-0295
Email: JScott@rurdev.usda.gov
Program available: Presidential Management Intern Program

* Department of Commerce - Main Office

Colette Davis
Student Employment Program Coordinator
U.S. Department of Commerce
Human Resources Department
1401 Constitution Ave.   202-482-6402
Washington, DC 20230   Fax: 202-482-2898
Email: cdavis@doc.gov
Programs Available: Student Educational Employment Program; Volunteer Service Program; Presidential Management Intern Program.

* Department of Commerce - Bureau of The Census

Bureau of the Census
College Relations Office
4700 Silver Hill Road

Department of Commerce   301-457-4748
Washington, DC 20233   Fax: 301-457-4575
Email: recruiter@census.gov
www.census.gov/hrd
Program Available: Student Educational Employment Program.

* Department of Commerce-Census Bureau

Donna Yee
Bureau of Census
Human Resource Development
4700 Silver Hill Road
Room 3039-3   301-763-3274
Washington, DC 20233   Fax: 301-457-4005
Email: donna.yee@census.gov
Program Available: Presidential Management Intern Program

* Department of Commerce-International Trade Administration

Tina James
International Trade Administration-HCHB
1401 Constitution Avenue, NW
Room 7417   202-482-0653
Washington, DC 20230   Fax: 202-482-1903
Email: tina_james@ita.doc.gov
Program Available: Presidential Management Intern Program

* Department Of Commerce - National Institute of Standards and Technology

Student Employment Program Coordinator
National Institute of Standards and Technology (NIST)
100 Bureau Drive, Stop 3550   301-975-3039
Gaithersburg, MD 20899   Fax: 301-948-6107
Program Available: Student Educational Employment Program; National Institute of Standards and Technology (NIST)

* Department of Commerce - National Oceanic and Atmospheric Administration (NOAA)

Theodoris Corbett
Student Employment Coordinator
National Oceanic and Atmospheric Administration
Department of Commerce
1315 East West Hwy., Room 12612   301-713-0539
Silver Spring, MD 20910   Fax: 301-713-2083
Email: theodoris.l.corbett@noaa.gov
Program Available: Student Educational Employment Program; Presidential Management Intern Program.

* Department of Commerce - National Technical Information Service (NTIS)

National Technical Information Service
Personnel Department
5285 Port Royal Rd.
Springfield, VA 22161   703-605-6000
Program Available: Student Educational Employment Program.

* Department of Commerce-Office of the General Counsel

Katy Kalb
Office of the General Counsel
1401 Constitution Avenue, NW
Room 5875   202-482-3611
Washington, DC 20230   Fax: 202-501-4695
Email: kkalb@doc.gov
Program Available: Presidential Management Intern Program

* Department of Commerce - Office of the Inspector General

Mary Good
Special Employment Program Coordinator
Office of the Inspector General
1401 Constitution Ave., Room 7713   202-482-5727
Washington, DC 20230   Fax: 202-482-3006
Email: mgood@oig.doc.gov

Program Available: Student Educational Employment Program; Presidential Management Intern Program.

* Department of Commerce - Patent and Trademark Office

Shirley Robinson, Student Employment Coordinator
Patent and Trademark Office
P.O. Box 171   703-305-1709
Washington, DC 202302   Fax: 703-305-9864
Email: shirley.robinson@uspto.gov
Programs Available: Student Educational Employment Program; Volunteer Service Program; Presidential Management Intern Program.

* Department Of Defense

Jeanne Raymos
Student Employment Program Coordinator
4000 Defense, The Pentagon, Room 30267   703-693-5404
Washington, DC 20301   Fax: 703-697-4850
Program Available: Student Educational Employment Program; Presidential Management Intern Program.

* Department of Defense - Defense Contract Management Agency

Marianne Bailey
Defense Contract Management Agency
Personnel Department
6350 Walker Lane, Suite 300   703-428-0804
Alexandria, VA 22304   Fax: 703-428-1931
Email: marianne.bailey@dcma.mil
Program Available: Student Educational Employment Program; Presidential Management Intern Program.

* Department of Defense - Defense Information Systems Agency

Defense Information Systems Agency
Civilian Personnel Division
701 South Court House Rd.   703-607-4432
Arlington, VA 22204-2199   Fax: 703-607-4530
Program Available: Student Educational Employment Program; Presidential Management Intern Program.

* Department of Defense-Defense Threat Reduction Agency

Ree Nee Carrington
Defense Threat Reduction Agency
8725 John J. Kingman Road, MS6201   703-767-5768
Fort Belvoir, VA 22060-6201   Fax: 703-767-5750
Email: reenee.carrington@dtra.mil
Program available: Presidential Management Intern Program

* Department of Defense-Defense Security Service

Joanne Moffett
Defense Security Service
881 Elkridge Landing Road   410-865-2662
Linthicum, MD 21090   Fax: 410-865-2669
Email: Joanne.moffett@mail.dss.mil
Program available: Presidential Management Intern Program

* Department of Defense-Missile Defense Agency

Janice Siemsen
Office of the Secretary-Missile Defense Agency
7100 Defense Pentagon
Washington, DC 20301   703-697-6538
Email: Janice.siemsen@mda.osd.mil
Program available: Presidential Management Intern Program

* Department of Defense-Office of Economic Adjustment

Martha Sands
Office of the Secretary of Defense
400 Army Navy Drive, Suite 200   703-604-6131
Arlington, VA 20301-4704   Fax: 703-604-5843

Email: Martha.sands@osd.mil
Program available: Presidential Management Intern Program

* Department of Defense-Office of the Secretary of Defense

Eugene Bruseau
5111 Leesburg Pike, Suite 810   703-681-8705
Falls Church, VA 22041   Fax: 703-681-7706
Email: Eugene.bruseau@tma.osd.mil
Program available: Presidential Management Intern Program

* Department of Defense-Office of the Secretary of Defense

Melinda Gillis
Office of the Secretary of Defense
5001 Eisenhower Avenue, H2N58   703-617-7941
Alexandria, VA 22333-0001   Fax: 703-617-7287
Email: gillim@psd.whs.mil
Program available: Presidential Management Intern Program

* Department of the Air Force

Barbara Hayman
ZHWAF/DPPH
Room 4E235, The Pentagon
1040 Air Force   703-695-7383
Washington, DC 20330-1040   Fax: 703-692-9939
Program Available: Student Educational Employment Program; Presidential Management Intern Program.

* Department of the Army

Edward David
OASA (M&RA), SFCP-COA
200 Stovall St.   703-325-1553
Alexandria, VA 22332-0320   Fax: 703-325-1493
Email: edward.david@asamra.hoffman.army.mil
Programs Available: Student Educational Employment Program; Volunteer Service Program; Presidential Management Intern Program.

* Department of the Navy

David Nettleton
ODASN(OCHR)13
U.S. Department of the Navy
3801 Nebraska Ave., NW   703-764-0841
Washington, DC 20393-5441   Fax: 202-764-0588
Email: dave.nettleton@navy.mil
Programs Available: Student Educational Employment Program; Volunteer Service Program; Presidential Management Intern Program.
Program Available: Presidential Management Intern Program

* Department of Education

Joyce Boykin
Student Employment Program Coordinator
Department of Education
400 Maryland Ave., SW, Room 2C134   202-401-3603
Washington, DC 20202   Fax: 202-401-0520
Email: joyce.boykin@ed.gov
Program Available: Student Educational Employment Program; Presidential Management Intern Program.

* Department of Energy

Rhonda Kennedy
Student Employment Program Coordinator
U.S. Department of Energy
Office of Personnel
Room 4H080, RS NA 352
1000 Independence Ave., SW   202-586-3544
Washington, DC 20585   Fax: 202-586-8101
Email: rhonda.kennedy@hq.doe.gov
Program Available: Student Educational Employment Program; Presidential Management Intern Program.

* Department of Health and Human Services

Dave Dunlap

Department of Health and Human Services
Intern Program Manager
Humphrey Building, Room 536E
200 Independence Ave., SW   202-690-7833
Washington, DC 20201   Fax: 202-690-7925
Email: ddunlap@os.dhhs.gov
www.hhs.gov/ohr
Programs Available: Student Educational Employment Program; Volunteer Service Program; Presidential Management Intern Program.

* Department of Health and Human Services-
Administration for Children & Families
Lee Kernan-Ivery
Administration for Children & Families
OA/OMS-6th Floor East
370 L'Enfant Promenade, SW   202-401-5602
Washington, DC 20447   Fax: 202-401-5450
Email: lkernan@acf.dhhs.gov
Program available: Presidential Management Intern Program

* Department of Health and Human Services-
Administration on Aging
Donna Blake
Administration on Aging
U.S. Department of Health and Human Services
300 Independence Avenue, SW
Room 4651
Washington, DC 20202   770-488-1725
Program available: Student Educational Employment Program, Presidential Management Intern Program

* Department of Health and Human Services-
Administration on Aging, Program Support Center
Edith McIlwain
Office of the Secretary
8455 Colesville Road
Suite 700, SSC   301-504-6175
Silver Spring, MD 20910   Fax: 301-504-3663
Email: emcilwain@psc.gov
Program available: Presidential Management Intern Program

* Department of Health and Human Services-
Agency for Healthcare Research and Quality
Patti Brown
Agency for Healthcare Research and Quality
Wilco Building, Suite 309
6000 Executive Boulevard   301-594-2408
Rockville, MD 20852   Fax: 301-443-8602
Email: pbrown@ahcpr.gov
Program available: Presidential Management Intern Program

* Department of Health & Human Services - Center
For Disease Control (CDC)
Daryl Bible
Centers for Disease Control and Prevention
Mailstop K-04
1600 Clifton Road, NE   770-488-1725
Atlanta, GA 30333   Fax: 770-488-1948
Email: dcb4@cdc.gov
Program Available: Volunteer Service Program; Student Educational Employment Program; Presidential Management Intern Program.

* Department of Health and Human Services-Food
and Drug Administration
Roger Laird
Food and Drug Administration
Room 7-B-24, Parklawn Building
Mail Stop HFA-410
5600 Fishers Lane   301-827-4136
Rockville, MD 20857   Fax: 301-827-6457
Program available: Presidential Management Intern Program

* Department of Health and Human Services-
Health Care Financing Administration
Vera Dorsey
Health Care Financing Administration
C2-15-26 Center Building
7500 Security Boulevard   410-786-5568
Baltimore, MD 21244   Fax: 410-786-4341
Email: vdorsey@cms.hhs.gov
Program Available: Presidential Management Intern Program

* Department of Health and Human Services-
Health Resources and Services Administration
Tony DeJesus
Health Resources and Services Administration
Chief Training & Development Branch
5600 Fisher Lane, Room 13A-38   301-443-4054
Rockville, MD 20857   Fax: 301-480-5695
Email: tdejesus@hrsa.gov
Program Available: Presidential Management Intern Program

* Department of Health & Human Services -
National Institutes of Health
Carol Storm
Student Employment Program Coordinators
National Institutes of Health (NIH)
6120 Rockville Pike, Suite 100   301-402-3383
Bethesda, MD 20892   Fax: 301-496-0986
Email: cs23j@nih.gov
Programs Available: Student Educational Employment Program; Volunteer Service Program; Management Interns; Presidential Management Intern Program

* Department of Health & Human Services -
Substance Abuse and Mental Health Services Administration (SAMHSA)
Sherry Preusch
Substance Abuse and Mental Health Services and Administration
OHR/SAMHSA, Room 14C-24
5600 Fishers Lane   301-443-5030
Rockville, MD 20857   Fax: 301-443-5866
Email: spreusch@samhsa.gov
Programs Available: Student Educational Employment Program; Volunteer Service Program; Presidential Management Intern Program.

* Department of Homeland Security-Bureau of
Customs & Border Protection
Audrey Blackwell
1300 Pennsylvania Avenue, NW
HRM Suite 2.5B   202-927-3671
Washington, DC 20229   Fax: 202-927-5447
Email: Audrey.blackwell@dhs.gov
Program available: Presidential Management Intern Program

* Department of Homeland Security-Bureau of
Citizenship & Immigration Service
Julia Peeler
Bureau of Citizenship & Immigration Service
800 K Street, NW
Techworld, Room 5000   202-616-2447
Washington, DC 20536   Fax: 202-305-4886
Email: Julia.e.peeler@usdoj.gov
Program available: Presidential Management Intern Program

* Department of Homeland Security-
Transportation Security Administration
Phyllis Throckmorton
Transportation Security Administration
601 South 12th Street   571-227-2884
Arlington, VA 22202   Fax: 571-227-2554
Email: Phyllis.throckmorton@dhs.gov
Program available: Presidential Management Intern Program

* Department of Housing and Urban Development
Charlene Paige
Student Employment Program Coordinator
U.S. Department of Housing and Urban Development
Room 2180
451 Seventh St., SW
Washington, DC 20410   202-708-0614
Email: charlene_paige@hud.gov
Programs Available: Student Educational Employment Program; Volunteer Service Program; Presidential Management Intern Program.

* Department of the Interior
Claudia Gleicher
Special Employment Programs Coordinator
1849 C St., NW
Mail Stop 1800G   202-343-2542
Washington, DC 20240   Fax: 202-343-2544
Programs Available: Student Educational Employment Program; Volunteer Service Program; Presidential Management Intern Program.

* Department of the Interior - Office of the Secretary
Deborah Perry
Special Employment Program Coordinators
Office of the Secretary
MS 2400
381 Elden Street   703-787-1404
Herndon, VA 20170-4817   Fax: 703-787-1046
Email: deborah.perry@mms.gov
Program Available: Student Educational Employment Program.

* Department of the Interior - U.S. Geological Survey
Sarah Griffin
Special Employment Program Coordinator
U.S. Geological Survey
12201 Sunrise Valley Dr.
Mail Stop 601   703-648-7395
Reston, VA 20192   Fax: 703-648-7451
Email: sgriffin@usgs.gov
Program Available: Student Educational Employment Program; Presidential Management Intern Program.

* Department of the Interior - Bureau of Land Management
Norma Frazier
Special Employment Program Coordinator
1849 C Street, NW   202-452-5105
Washington, DC 20249-0036   Fax: 202-653-9120
Email: normafrazier@doi.blm.gov
Programs Available: Student Educational Employment Program; Volunteer Service Program; Presidential Management Intern Program.

* Department of the Interior - Office of Surface Mining, Reclamation, and Enforcement
Brenda Garrett Freeman
Special Employment Program Coordinator
Office of Surface Mining, Reclamation, and Enforcement
1951 Constitution Ave., NW
Room 332-SIB   202-208-2771
Washington, DC 20240   Fax: 202-219-3107
Email: bgarrett@osmre.gov
Program Available: Student Educational Employment Program; Presidential Management Intern Program.

* Department of the Interior - U.S. Fish and Wildlife Service
Carmen Andujar
Special Employment Program Coordinator
U.S. Fish and Wildlife Service
4501 N. Fairfax Dr., Room 2032-D   202-208-4562
Arlington, VA 22203   Fax: 202-358-2115
Email: carmen_andujar@fws.gov
Programs Available: Student Educational Employment Program; Volunteer Service Program; Presidential Management Intern Program.

* Department of the Interior - National Park Service
Ella Drummond
Special Employment Program Coordinators
National Park Service
1201 I Street, NW, Room 2653   202-354-1996
Washington, DC 20240   Fax: 202-371-1762
Email: ella_drummond@nps.gov
Programs Available: Student Educational Employment Program; Volunteer Service Program; Presidential Management Intern Program.

* Department of the Interior - Minerals Management Service
Rosa Thomas
Special Employment Program Coordinator
Minerals Management Service
381 Elden St.   703-787-1314
Herndon, VA 20170-4817   Fax: 703-787-1601
Email: rosa_thomas@nms.gov
Programs Available: Student Educational Employment Program; Volunteer Service Program; Presidential Management Intern Program.

* Department of the Interior - Bureau of Reclamation
Special Employment Program Coordinator
Bureau of Reclamation
Federal Center
PO Box 25007, Attn. D4000   303-236-5610
Denver, CO 80225   Fax: 303-236-0544
Program Available: Student Educational Employment Program.

* Department of Justice
Lashon Adams
Student Employment Program Coordinator
Department of Justice, Policy Group
1331 Pennsylvania Ave., Suite 1110   202-305-0120
Washington, DC 20530   Fax: 202-514-6827
Email: lashon.a.adams@usdoj.gov
Programs Available: Presidential Management Intern Program.

Angeline Thomas
Student Employment Program Coordinator
Department of Justice
1331 Pennsylvania Ave., Suite 1110   202-616-3249
Washington, DC 20530   Fax: 202-514-3076
Email: thomasa@ojp.usdoj.gov
Program Available: Worker-Trainee Program; SCEP; STEP; Student Volunteer Service.

* Department of Justice-Antitrust Division
Terricita Scott
Antitrust Division
950 Pennsylvania Avenue, NW   202-514-5372
Washington, DC 20530   Fax: 202-514-0580
Email: terricita.ls.scott@usdoj.gov
Program available: Student Educational Employment Program; Volunteer Service Program

* Department of Justice-Bureau of Alcohol, Tobacco, Firearms & Explosives
Kimberly Porter
Bureau of Alcohol, Tobacco, Firearms & Explosives
650 Massachusetts Avenue, NW
Room 4100   202-927-6374
Washington, DC 20226   Fax: 202-927-3464
Email: Kimberly.Porter@atf.gov
Programs available: Volunteer Service Program; Student Educational Employment Program

* Department of Justice - Bureau of Prisons
Mary Doyle
Bureau of Prisons
Student Employment Program Coordinator
320 First St., NW   202-307-3177
Washington, DC 20534   Fax: 202-514-8198
Email: medoyle@bop.gov

Programs Available: Student Educational Employment Program; Volunteer Service Program (Internship).

* Department of Justice-Civil Rights Division

Harry Vickers
Civil Rights Division
950 Pennsylvania Avenue, NW   202-514-3934
Washington, DC 20530   Fax: 202-514-6603
Email: harry.vickers2@usdoj.gov
Programs available: Student Educational Employment Program; Volunteer Service Program

* Department of Justice-Civil Division

Towanna Williams
Laura Gann
Civil Division-Personnel Management Branch
Ben Franklin Station NW   202-307-0261
Washington, DC 20044-4660   Fax: 202-514-7968
Email: laura.gann@usdoj.gov
Email: towanna.williams@usdoj.gov
Programs available: Presidential Management Intern Program; Student Educational Employment Program; Volunteer Service Program

* Department of Justice-Criminal Division

Kia Johnson
Department of Justice, Criminal Division
950 Pennsylvania Avenue   202-305-3960
Washington, DC 20530-0001   Fax: 202-514-1792
Email: kia.johnson@usdoj.gov
Programs available: Student Educational Employment Program; Volunteer Service Program

Gail Hunter
Criminal Division-Personnel Programs Staff
1400 New York Avenue, Room 5000   202-514-9887
Washington, Dc 20530   Fax: 202-353-0775
Email: gail.hunter@usdoj.gov
Program available: Presidential Management Intern Program

* Department of Justice - Drug Enforcement Administration

Doris Turner
Office of Personnel
2401 Jefferson Davis Hwy.   202-307-4094
Alexandria, VA 22301   Fax: 202-307-4173
Program Available: Student Educational Employment Program; Volunteer Service Program

Janice Johnson
Office of Personnel
2401 Jefferson Davis Hwy.   202-307-4058
Alexandria, VA 22301   Fax: 202-307-4173
Program Available: Presidential Management Intern Program.

* Department of Justice-Environment and Natural Resource Division

Ann Dublin
Environment and Natural Resource Division
601 D Street, NW   202-616-2678
Washington, DC 20004   Fax: 202-616-3362
Email: ann.dublin@usdoj.gov
Programs available: Student Educational Employment Program; Volunteer Service Program

Betsy Preston
Environment and Natural Resources Division
601 D Street, NW   202-616-2636
Washington, DC 20004   Fax: 202-616-3362
Email: betsy.preston@usdoj.gov
Program available: Presidential Management Intern Program

* Department of Justice-Executive Office for Immigration Review

Judy Berryhill
Executive Office for Immigration Review
5107 Leesburg Pike, Suite 2300   703-305-0370

Falls Church, VA 22041   Fax: 703-305-1456
Email: judith.berryhill@usdoj.gov
Program available: Summer Law Intern Program

Dorothy Ambrose
Executive Office for Immigration Review
5107 Leesburg Pike, Suite 2300
Falls Church, VA 22041   703-305-5827
Email: Dorothy.ambrose@usdoj.gov
Program available: Presidential Management Intern Program

* Department of Justice-Executive Office for U.S. Trustees

Valerie Rice
Student Employment Coordinator
20 Massachusetts Avenue, N.W.   202-616-1013
Washington, DC 20530   Fax: 202-616-1192
Email: vrice@usdoj.ghov
Program available: Student Educational Employment Program

* Department of Justice-Justice Management Division

Brenda Hurst
Justice Management Division
1331 Pennsylvania Avenue, NW, Room 1400   202-307-1800
Washington, DC 20530   Fax: 202-307-1853
Email: brenda.hurst2@usdoj.gov
Program available: Presidential Management Intern Program

* Department of Justice - Federal Bureau of Investigation

Ava Deberry
Federal Bureau of Investigation
935 Pennsylvania Ave., NW, Room PA1301-200   202-278-2440
Washington, DC 20535   Fax: 202-278-2428
Email: personnel.recruiting@fbi.gov
Program Available: Volunteer Service Program (Internship); Presidential Management Intern Program.

* Department of Justice-Office of Attorney Recruitment and Management

Kathleen C. Smith
Office of Attorney Recruitment & Management
Suite 5200
20 Massachusetts Avenue, NW   202-514-8905
Washington, Dc 20530-0001   Fax: 202-514-0713
Email: Kathleen.c.smith@usdoj.gov
Programs available: Summer Law Intern Program; Legal Intern Program

* Department of Justice-Office of the Inspector General

Helen D. Keiler
Office of the Inspector General
950 Pennsylvania Avenue, Suite 4322   202-616-4501
Washington, DC 20536-0001   Fax: 202-616-4532
Email: Helen.keiler2@usdoj.gov
Programs available: Student Educational Employment Program; Summer Law Intern Program

* Department of Justice-Tax Division

Mary Michael
Student Employment Coordinator
USDOJ/Tax Division Human Resources Office
P.O. Box 813
Ben Franklin Station   202-616-2774
Washington, DC 20044   Fax: 202-616-1973
Email: mary.o.michael@usdoj.gov
Programs available: Summer Law Intern Program; Legal Intern Program

* Department of Justice - United States Attorney's Office

Marie Blackmon
Student Program Coordinator

Department of Justice
Bicentennial Building
600 E St., NW, Room 8200 — 202-616-6900
Washington, DC 20530-0001 — Fax: 202-616-6648
Email: marie.blackmon@usdoj.gov
Program Available: Student Educational Employment Program; Presidential Management Intern Program.

* Department of Justice - United States Marshals Service

Debbie Harlow
Student Program Coordinator
U.S. Marshals Service
Human Resources Division, Suite 890 — 202-307-5258
Washington, DC 20530-1000 — Fax: 202-307-9455
Email: debbie.harlow@usdoj.gov
Program Available: Student Educational Employment Program; Presidential Management Intern Program.

* Department of Labor

Melissa Naudin
Intern Coordinator
U.S. Department of Labor
200 Constitution Ave., NW, Room N5460 — 202-219-0118
Washington, DC 20210 — Fax: 202-219-8127
Program Available: Student Educational Employment Program.

Karen Terrell
Career Map. Human Resource Center
200 Constitution Avenue, NW, Room N-5464 — 202-693-7654
Washington, DC 20210 — Fax: 202-693-7681
Email: Terrell-karen@dol.gov
Program available: Presidential Management Intern Program

* Department of Labor - Bureau of Labor Statistics

Dorothy Wigglesworth
Division of Human Resources
Bureau of Labor Statistics
U.S. Department of Labor
2 Massachusetts Ave., NE, Suite 4280 — 202-606-6600
Washington, DC 20212-0001 — Fax: 202-606-6610
Program Available: Student Educational Employment Program.

* Department of Labor - Employment Standards Administration

Student Employment Program Coordinator
Employment Standards Administration
U.S. Department of Justice
200 Constitution Ave., NW, Room S3316 — 202-219-7545
Washington, DC 20210 — Fax: 202-273-3590
Programs Available: Student Educational Employment Program; Volunteer Service Program.

* Department of Labor - Office of the Solicitor

Student Employment Program Coordinator
Office of the Solicitor
U.S. Department of Justice
200 Constitution Ave., NW, Room N2431 — 202-219-5276
Washington, DC 20210 — Fax: 202-219-9255
Program Available: Student Educational Employment Program.

* Department of Labor - Occupational Safety and Health Administration

Student Employment Coordinator
Occupational Safety and Health Administration
200 Constitution Ave., NW, Room N3308
Washington, DC 20210 — 202-693-1800
Programs Available: Student Educational Employment Program; Volunteer Service Program.

* Department of Labor - Employment and Training Administration

Office of Human Resources
Student Employment Program Coordinator

Employment Training Administration
200 Constitution Ave., NW — 877-US-2JOBS
Room S5214 — 202-219-5754
Washington, DC 20210 — Fax: 202-219-8732
Program Available: Student Educational Employment Program.

* Department of Labor - Office of the Inspector General

Student Employment Program Coordinator
Office of the Inspector General
200 Constitution Ave., NW, Room S-5028 — 202-693-5122
Washington, DC 20210 — Fax: 202-693-5121
Programs Available: Student Educational Employment Program; Volunteer Service Program.

* Department of Labor - Mine Safety and Health Administration

Joe Stormer
Student Employment Program Coordinator
Ballston Towers #3
4015 Wilson Blvd., Room 500 — 202-693-9855
Arlington, VA 22203 — Fax: 202-693-9856
Program Available: Student Educational Employment Program.

* Department of State

Danita Hickson
Student Employment Program Coordinator
U.S. Department of State
Bureau of Resource Management
2401 E Street, NW, Room H518 — 202-261-8909
Washington, DC 20522 — Fax: 202-261-8842
Email: hicksonDX@state.gov
Programs Available: Student Educational Employment Program; Volunteer Service Program; Presidential Management Intern Program.

* Department of Transportation

Student Employment Program Coordinator
Ric Brady
Office of the Secretary (OST)
400 Seventh St., SW, Room 7411, M-15 — 202-366-9435
Washington, DC 20590 — Fax: 202-366-6806
Email: ric.brady@ost.dot.gov
Programs Available: Student Educational Employment Program; Volunteer Service Program; Presidential Management Intern Program.

* Department of Transportation - United States Coast Guard (USCG)

Marty Siegel
Student Employment Coordinator
Office of Civilian Personnel
U.S. Coast Guard
2100 Second St., SW — 202-267-1711
Washington, DC 20293 — Fax: 202-267-4580
Email: msiegel@comdt.uscg.mil
Program Available: Volunteer Service Program; Presidential Management Intern Program.

* Department of Transportation - Federal Aviation Administration (FAA)

Human Resources Management Division
Student Employment Coordinator
Federal Aviation Administration
800 Independence Ave., SW — 202-267-8007
Washington, DC 20591 — Fax: 202-267-8330
Programs Available: Student Educational Employment Program; Volunteer Service Program.

* Department of Transportation - Federal Highway Administration (FHWA)

Edith Romero-Bruner
Student Employment Coordinator
Federal Highway Administration
400 Seventh St., SW, Room 4323 — 202-366-1161
Washington, DC 20590 — Fax: 202-366-7523

Email: edith.romero-bruner@fhwa.dot.gov
Program Available: Student Educational Employment Program; Presidential Management Intern Program.

* Department of Transportation-Federal Motor Carrier Safety Administration

Lee Leatrice
Federal Motor Carrier Safety Administration
400 7th Street, SW
Room 8213   202-366-0860
Washington, DC 20590   Fax: 202-366-3502
Email: leatrice.lee@fmcsa.dot.gov
Program available: Presidential Management Intern Program

* Department of Transportation - Federal Railroad Administration (FRA)

Renee Clark
Student Employment Coordinator
Federal Railroad Administration
Radio, Mail Drop 30
1120 Vermont Avenue, NW   202-366-0592
Washington, DC 20590   Fax: 202-366-7439
Email: renee.clark@fra.dot.gov
Program Available: Volunteer Service Program; Presidential Management Intern Program.

* Department of Transportation - National Highway Traffic Safety Administration (NHTSA)

Student Employment Coordinator
National Highway Traffic Safety Administration (NHTSA)
400 Seventh St., SW   202-366-2606
Washington, DC 20590   Fax: 202-366-7402
Program Available: Student Educational Employment Program; Summer Medical Student Internship.

* Department of Transportation - Federal Transit Administration (FTA)

Pamela Payton
Student Employment Coordinator
Federal Transit Administration
400 Seventh St., SW
Room 9113   202-366-2228
Washington, DC 20590   Fax: 202-366-7890
Email: pamela.bell-payton@fta.dot.gov
Program Available: Student Educational Employment Program; Presidential Management Intern Program.

* Department of Transportation - Maritime Administration (MARAD)

Ray Pagliarni
Student Program Coordinator
Maritime Administration
400 Seventh St., SW
Room 8101   202-366-4141
Washington, DC 20590   Fax: 202-366-3791
Program Available: Student Educational Employment Program.

* Department of Transportation - Research and Special Programs Administration (RSPA)

Shenita Wells
Student Program Coordinator
Research and Special Programs Administration
400 Seventh St., SW, Room 7108   202-366-4432
Washington, DC 20590   Fax: 202-366-0502
Email: shenita.wells@rspa.dot.gov
Program Available: Student Educational Employment Program; Presidential Management Intern Program.

* Department of Transportation - Office of the Inspector General (OIG)

Vivian Jarcho
Student Program Coordinator
Office of the Inspector General

400 Seventh St., SW, Room 7422   202-366-1490
Washington, DC 20590   Fax: 202-366-2003
Email: vivian.jarcho@oig.dot.gov
Program Available: Student Educational Employment Program; Presidential Management Intern Program.

* Department of the Treasury

Student Employment Coordinator
Treasury Annex
1500 Pennsylvania, NW   202-622-1400
Washington, DC 20220   Fax: 202-633-2405
Program Available: Student Educational Employment Program.

* Department of Treasury- Bureau of Alcohol, Tobacco and Firearms

Personnel Division
Bureau of Alcohol, Tobacco and Firearms
650 Massachusetts Avenue, NW, Room 4100
Washington, DC 20226   202-927-8610
Programs available: Student Temporary Employment Program; Student Volunteer Program

Eldora Womack
Bureau of Alcohol, Tobacco and Firearms
650 Massachusetts Avenue, NW, Room 4170   202-927-7993
Washington, DC 20226   Fax: 202-927-3464
Email: eewomack@atfhq.atf.treas.gov
Program available: Presidential Management Intern Program

* Department of the Treasury - Bureau of Engraving and Printing

Student Program Coordinator
Bureau of Engraving and Printing
Fourteenth and C St., SW   202-874-3568
Washington, DC 20228   Fax: 202-874-3182
Program Available: Student Temporary Employment Program.

* Department of Treasury-Community Development Financial Institution

Lori Stormer
Community Development Financial Institution
601 13th Street, NW
Suite 200 S   202-622-8209
Washington, DC 20005   Fax: 202-622-7754
Email: stormerl@cdfi.treas.gov
Program available: Presidential Management Intern Program

* Department of the Treasury - Federal Law Enforcement Training Center

Mona Dubose
College Intern Program Coordinator
Federal Law Enforcement Training Center
Building 94   912-267-2849
Glynco, Georgia 31524   Fax: 912-267-2701
www.fletc.gov/intern.htm
Program Available: Volunteer Service Program (Internship).

* Department of the Treasury - Financial Management Service

Human Resources Division
Attn: SEEP Coordinator
Financial Management Service
Department of the Treasury
3700 East-West Highway, Room 170A   202-874-8090
Hyattsville, MD 20782   Fax: 202-874-6684
Email: job.opportunities@fms.treas.gov
www.fms.treas.gov/hrd/students.html
Program Available: Student Educational Employment Program; Volunteer Service Program.

* Department of the Treasury - Internal Revenue Service

Susie Williams

Student Employment Program Coordinator
Internal Revenue Service
Room C-2-466
500 Ellin Road   202-283-1774
Lanham, MD 20706   Fax: 202-283-7295
Email: susie.williams@irs.gov
Programs Available: Student Educational Employment Program; Volunteer Service Program; Presidential Management Intern Program.

* Department of Treasury-Office of the Inspector General
Student Employment Program Coordinator
Office of the Inspector General
740 15th Street, NW, Suite 510   202-927-5414
Washington, DC 20220   Fax: 202-927-4827
Program available: Presidential Management Intern Program

* Department of Treasury-Trade and Tax Bureau
Trade and Tax Bureau
Student Employment Program Coordinator
650 Massachusetts Avenue, NW
Washington, Dc 20226   202-927-9380
www.ttb.gov/jobs/studentprog/htm
Program available: Student Temporary Employment Program; Student Volunteer Program

* Department of the Treasury - United States Customs Service
Roland Mozie
Personnel Division
U.S. Customs Service
Department of the Treasury
2070 Chainbridge Road, Suite 200
Vienna, VA 22182   202-634-5005
Email: mozier@fincer.treas.gov
Program Available: Student Educational Employment Program; Presidential Management Intern Program.

* Department of Treasury-United States Mint
Beverly Spears
United States Mint
Office of Human Resources
801 9th Street, NW, 7th Floor   202-354-7226
Washington, DC 20220   Fax: 202-756-6170
Email: bspears@usmint.treas.gov
Program available: Presidential Management Intern Program; Student Career Experience Program; Student Temporary Employment Program

* Department of the Treasury - United States Secret Service
Secret Service Personnel Division
Student Program Coordinator
United States Secret Service   888-813-8777
1800 C St., NW   202-406-5800
Washington, DC 20223   Fax: 202-406-5613
Program Available: Student Educational Employment Program.

* Department of Veterans Affairs
Max Collier
Student Employment Program Coordinator
Department of Veterans Affairs
Office of Human Resources Development
810 Vermont Ave., NW, Room 227   202-273-9758
Washington, DC 20420   Fax: 202-273-5797
Email: max.collier@mail.va.gov
Programs Available: Student Educational Employment Program; Volunteer Service Program; Presidential Management Intern Program.

Independent Establishments and Government Corporations

* Broadcasting Board of Governors
Janice Albritton

Office of Human Resources
300 Independence Avenue, SW
Room 1543   202-619-2124
Washington, DC 20237   Fax: 202-205-8427
Email: jalbritt@ibb.gov
www.voa.gov/interns
Program available: Presidential Management Intern Program

* Central Intelligence Agency
CIA Employment Center
Office of Personnel Management   800-368-3886
P.O. Box 12727   703-482-1100
Arlington, VA 22209-8727   Fax: 703-482-7814
Program Available: Specialized programs are available.

* Commission on Civil Rights
Human Resources Division
U.S. Commission on Civil Rights
624 Ninth St., NW   202-376-8364
Washington, DC 20425   Fax: 202-376-7577
Email: vacancies@usccr.gov
www.usccr.gov/jobs/jobs.htm
Programs Available: Student Educational Employment Program; Volunteer Service Program.

* Commodity Futures Trading Commission
Office of Human Resources
Student Employment Program Coordinator
Commodity Futures Trading Commission
1155 21st St., NW, Suite 7200   202-418-5003
Washington, DC 20581   Fax: 202-418-5530
Programs Available: Student Educational Employment Program; Volunteer Service Program.

* Consumer Product Safety Commission
Student Employment Program Coordinator
Consumer Product Safety Commission
4330 East West Highway
East West Towers   301-504-7925
Bethesda, MD 20814   Fax: 301-504-0025
Email: recruitapps@cpsc.gov
Programs Available: Student Career Experience Program; Volunteer Service Program; Student Temporary Employment Program.

* Corporation for National Service
Internship Coordinator
Corporation for National Service
1201 New York Ave., NW   202-606-5000
Washington, DC 20525   Fax: 202-565-2794
www.cns.gov/jobs/internships/index.html
Programs Available: Student Educational Employment Program; Volunteer Service Program.

* Environmental Protection Agency
Jamie Langlie
Office of Human Resources
Environmental Protection Agency
1200 Pennsylvania Ave., NW   202-564-7576
Washington, DC 20460   Fax: 202-564-7771
Email: langlie.jamie@epa.gov
www.epa.gov/epahome/intern.htm
Programs Available: Student Educational Employment Program; Volunteer Service Program (Internship); Presidential Management Intern Program.

* Equal Employment Opportunity Commission
Virginia Gilmore
Student Employment Program Coordinator
Equal Employment Opportunity Commission
First Floor Training Center
1801 L St., NW   202-663-4146
Washington, DC 20507   Fax: 202-663-7139
Email: vgilmor@eeoc.gov
Programs Available: Student Educational Employment Program; Volunteer Service Program; Presidential Management Intern Program.

* Export Import Bank of the United States

Ana Guzman-Evans
Student Employment Program Coordinator
Export Import Bank of the United States
811 Vermont Ave., NW   202-565-3407
Washington, DC 20571   Fax: 202-565-3627
Email: ana.guzman-evans@exim.gov
Program Available: Student Educational Employment Program; Presidential Management Intern Program.

Nancy Layhill, Student Employment Program Coordinator
Export Import Bank of the United States
811 Vermont Ave., NW   202-565-3300
Washington, DC 20571   Fax: 202-565-3627
Program Available: Volunteer Service Program.

* Farm Credit Administration

David Mclerran
Student Employment Program Coordinator
Farm Credit Administration
1501 Farm Credit Dr.   703-883-4132
McLean, VA 22102-5090   Fax: 703-893-2608
Email: mclerrand@fca.gov
Program Available: Student Educational Employment Program; Presidential Management Intern Program.

* Federal Communications Commission

Doreen Fisher
Human Resources
Federal Communications Commission
445 12th Street, SW, Room 1A064   202-418-0028
Washington, DC 20024   Fax: 202-418-2643
Email: doreen.fisher@fcc.gov
Program Available: Volunteer Service Program; Presidential Management Intern Program.

* Federal Deposit Insurance Corporation

Student Employment Program Coordinator
Federal Deposit Insurance Corporation
550 17th St. NW, Room PA1730-6014   202-942-3347
Washington, DC 20429   Fax: 202-942-3309
Program Available: Student Educational Employment Program; Presidential Management Intern Program.

* Federal Emergency Management Agency

Sheryl Withers
Office of Human Resources
Federal Emergency Management Agency
500 C St., SW, Room 816   202-646-4081
Washington, DC 20427   Fax: 202-646-2913
Email: sheryl.withers@dhs.gov
Programs Available: Student Educational Employment Program; Volunteer Service Program; Presidential Management Intern Program.

* Federal Housing Enterprise Oversight

Anna Reiss-Keeve
Office of Federal Housing
1700 G Street, NW   202-414-3743
Washington, DC 20552   Fax: 202-414-8938
Email: areiss-keeve@ofheo.gov
Program available: Presidential Management Intern Program

* Federal Labor Relations Authority

Student Employment Program Coordinator
Federal Labor Relations Authority
607 14th St., NW, Suite 430   202-482-6660
Washington, DC 20424   Fax: 202-482-6659
Program Available: Volunteer Service Program.

* Federal Maritime Commission

Hatsie Charbonneau
Student Employment Program Coordinator
Federal Maritime Commission
800 North Capitol St., NW, Room 924   202-523-5773
Washington, DC 20573-0001   Fax: 202-523-7842

Email: hatsiec@fmc.gov
Program Available: Student Educational Employment Program; Presidential Management Intern Program.

* Federal Reserve System

Student Employment Coordinator
Federal Reserve System
20th and Constitution Ave., NW   202-452-3850
Washington, DC 20551   Fax: 202-452-3863
Program Available: Various programs available.

Lori Carrington
Student Employment Coordinator
Federal Reserve System
Mail Stop 65
20th and Constitution Ave., NW   202-452-3851
Washington, DC 20551   Fax: 202-452-3863
Program Available: Volunteer Service Program (Internship).

* Federal Retirement Thrift Investment Board

Personnel Division
Federal Retirement Thrift Investment Board
1250 H St., NW   202-942-1682
Washington, DC 20005-3952   Fax: 202-942-1674
Program Available: Student Educational Employment Program.

* Federal Trade Commission

Human Resources Management Office
600 Pennsylvania Ave., NW, Room 723   202-326-2021
Washington, DC 20580   Fax: 202-326-2534
Programs Available: Student Educational Employment Program; Volunteer Service Program; Summer Legal Intern Program.

* General Accounting Office

Madeline Daniels
Office of Recruitment
441 G Street, NW, Room 1165   202-512-3429
Washington, DC 20548   Fax: 202-512-2539
Email: danielsm@gao.gov
Program available: Presidential Management Intern Program

* General Services Administration

Cass Willett
Student Employment Program Coordinator
General Services Administration
18th and F St., NW, Room 1107   202-501-1223
Washington, DC 20405   Fax: 202-208-1875
Email: cassie.willett@gsa.gov
Program Available: Student Educational Employment Program; Presidential Management Intern Program.

* Institute of Museum and Library Services

Teresa Lahaie
Institute of Museum and Library Services
1100 Pennsylvania Avenue, NW, Suite 223   202-606-8637
Washington, DC 20506   Fax: 202-606-0395
Email: tlahaie@imls.gov
Program available: Presidential Management Intern Program

* Inter-American Foundation

Ronald Arms
Personnel/Student Volunteer Service Program
901 North Stuart Street, 10th Floor   703-306-4304
Arlington, VA 22203-000   Fax: 703-306-4365
Email: rarms@iaf.gov
www.iaf.gov/about_iaf/iaf_jobs_en.asp?job_id=3D123
Programs available: Volunteer Service Program; Presidential Management Intern Program

* Joint Financial Management Improvement Program

Doris Chew
Joint Financial Management Improvement Program
1990 K Street, NW, Suite 430   202-219-0526

Washington, DC 20006-000
Email: doris.chew@gsa.gov
Fax: 202-219-0549
Program available: Presidential Management Intern Program

* Library of Congress
Analisa Archer
Congression Research Service
101 Independence Avenue, SE
202-707-1423
Washington, DC 20540-7490
Fax: 202-707-2615
Email: aarcher@crs.loc.gov
Program available: Presidential Management Intern Program

* Merit Systems Protection Board
Human Resources Division
Student Employment Program Coordinator
Merit Systems Protection Board
1615 M Street, NW
202-653-6772
Washington, DC 20419
Fax: 202-653-7130
Programs Available: Student Educational Employment Program; Volunteer Service Program.

* National Aeronautics and Space Administration (NASA)
Rhonda Horton-Taylor
Student Employment Program Coordinator
NASA Headquarters
300 E Street, SW
202-358-0444
Washington, DC 20546
Fax: 202-358-3493
Email: rhonda.l.taylor@hq.nasa.gov
Programs Available: Student Educational Employment Program; Volunteer Service Program; Presidential Management Intern Program.

Stacey Medina
Johnson Space Center
2101 NASA Road, 1
281-244-1069
Houston, TX 77058
Fax: 281-483-3789
Email: Stacey.r.medina@nasa.gov
Program available: Presidential Management Intern Program

Lori Moore
Goddard Space Flight Center
Code 114
301-286-5087
Greenbelt, MD 20771
Fax: 301-286-1679
Email: lori.a.moore@nasa.gov
Program available: Presidential Management Intern Program

* National Archives and Records Administration
Deborah Hilton
Personnel Division
National Archives and Records Administration
9770 Page Avenue, Room 4210
St. Louis, MO 63132-5100
Email: deborah.hilton@stlouis.nara.gov
Programs Available: Student Educational Employment Program; Volunteer Service Program; Presidential Management Intern Program.

* National Capital Planning Commission
Student Employment Program Coordinator
401 9th Street, NW
Suite 500, North Lobby
202-482-7200
Washington, DC 20576
Fax: 202-482-7272
Program Available: Student Educational Employment Program.

* National Labor Relations Board
Personnel Branch
Room 6000
1099 14th Street, NW
202-273-3988
Washington, DC 20570
Fax: 202-273-2921
Program available: Presidential Management Intern Program

* National Science Foundation
Division of Human Resources
Student Employment Program Coordinator
National Science Foundation
4201 Wilson Blvd., Suite 315
703-292-4373

Arlington, VA 22230
Fax: 703-292-9279
Programs Available: Student Educational Employment Program; Volunteer Service Program; Presidential Management Intern Program.

* National Transportation Safety Board
Shawne Boddie
Student Employment Program Coordinator
Human Resources Division
National Transportation Safety Board
490 L'Enfant Plaza, SW
202-314-6238
Washington, DC 20594
Fax: 202-382-1948
Email: boddies@ntsb.gov
Programs Available: Student Educational Employment Program; Volunteer Service Program.

* Nuclear Regulatory Commission
Student Employment Program Coordinator
Nuclear Regulatory Commission
301-415-1534
Washington, DC 20555
Fax: 301-415-3818
Programs Available: Student Career Experience Program; Summer Employment Program.

* Office of National Drug Control Policy
Briggitte Lafontant
Office of National Drug Control Policy
750 18th Street, NW, Room 544
202-395-6695
Washington, DC 20503
Fax: 202-395-6724
Email: briggette_r._lafontant@ondcp.eop.gov
Program available: Presidential Management Intern Program

* Office of Management and Budget
Sharon Warner
New Executive Office Building
725 17th Street, NW, Room 9026
202-395-4665
Washington, DC 20503
Fax: 202-395-3504
Email: swarner@mb.eop.gov
Program available: Presidential Management Intern Program

* Office Of Personnel Management
Latonya Brown
Student Employment Program Coordinator
Human Capital Management Services Group
1900 E St. NW, Room 1469
202-606-1759
Washington, DC 20415
Fax: 202-606-1732
Email: llbrown@opm.gov
Programs Available: Student Educational Employment Program; Volunteer Service Program; Presidential Management Intern Program.

* Office of Special Counsel
Student Temporary Employment Coordinator
Office of Special Counsel
Suite 218, 1730 M St., NW
202-653-9485
Washington, DC 20036-4505
Fax: 202-653-8939
Programs Available: Student Temporary Employment Program.

* Peace Corps
Student Employment Program Coordinator
Peace Corps Headquarters
1990 L St., NW
Washington, DC 20001
202-692-1200
Programs Available: Student Educational Employment Program; Volunteer Service Program (Internship).

* Pension Benefit Guarantee Corporation
Student Employment Program Coordinator
Pension Benefit Guarantee Corporation
1200 K St., NW, Suite 120
202-326-4110
Washington, DC 20005
Fax: 202-326-4114
Program Available: Student Educational Employment Program.

* Securities and Exchange Commission
Theresa Ellison
450 5th Street, NW

Washington, DC 20549   202-942-4062
Fax: 202-628-1453   Email: ellisont@sec.gov
Program available: Presidential Management Intern Program

* Small Business Administration

Jose Mendez
Student Employment Program Coordinator
Small Business Administration
409 3rd St., SW, Suite 4200   202-205-6178
Washington, DC 20416   Fax: 202-481-2707
Email: jose.mendez@sba.gov
Programs Available: Student Educational Employment Program; Volunteer Service Program; Presidential Management Intern Program.

* Social Security Administration

Joyce Brooks Brown
6401 Security Blvd
East High Rise Building, Suite 100   410-965-2962
Baltimore, MD 21235-6401   Fax: 410-966-4046
Email: joyce.brown@ssa.gov
Program available: Presidential Management Intern Program

Susan Dwyer
6401 Security Boulevard
Suite 100, East High Rise Building   410-965-0583
Baltimore, MD 21235   Fax: 410-966-4046
Email: susan.dwyer@ssa.gov
Program available: Presidential Management Intern Program

* Tennessee Valley Authority

Jim Dodson
TVA Intern/Co-op Program
1101 Market Street, EB8B   423-751-0011
Chattanooga, TN 37402-2801   Fax: 865-632-4452
Program Available: Student Educational Employment Program.

* Trade and Development Agency

Carolyn Hum, Administrative Officer
Trade and Development Agency
1000 Wilson Blvd., Suite 1600   703-875-4357
Arlington,, VA 22209-3901   Fax: 703-875-4009
Program Available: Volunteer Service Program (Internship).

Caroline Hum
Trade and Development Agency
1621 North Kent Street, Suite 200
Arlington, VA 22209   703-875-4296
Email: chum@tda.gov
Program available: Presidential Management Intern Program

* United States Information Agency

United States Information Agency

M/HRCO-Volunteer Internships
301 4th St., SW, Room 518   202-619-4656
Washington, DC 20547   Fax: 202-205-0496
Program Available: Volunteer Service Program (Internship).

* United States International Development

Mary Satterwhite
Student Employment Coordinator
U.S. International Development Cooperation Agency
1300 Pennsylvania Ave., NW
Ronald Reagan Building, Room 2-8-141   703-712-5045
Washington, DC 20523-2700   Fax: 202-216-3248
Email: msatterwhite@usaid.gov
Programs Available: Student Educational Employment Program; Volunteer Service Program; Presidential Management Intern Program.

* United States International Trade Commission

Susan Austin
Student Employment Coordinator
United States International Trade Commission
Office of Human Resources
500 E St., SW, Room 314   202-205-2660
Washington, DC 20436   Fax: 202-205-2659
Email: saustin@usitc.gov
Programs Available: Summer Employment Program; Volunteer Service Program; Presidential Management Intern Program.

"Quasi-Official" Agencies

* Smithsonian Institution

Student Internship Coordinator
750 9th Street, NW, Suite 9300
MRC 902
P.O. Box 37012
Smithsonian Institution   202-275-0655
Washington, DC 20013-7012   Fax: 202-275-0489
Programs Available: Various programs are available.

Office of Fellowships and Grants
750 9th Street, NW, Suite 9300
MRC 902
P.O. Box 37012
Smithsonian Institution   202-275-0655
Washington, DC 20013-7012   Fax: 202-275-0489
Email: siofg@si.edu
Book Available: A book is available that has internship and fellowship possibilities.

* United States Institute of Peace

United States Institute of Peace
1200 17th Street, NW   202-457-1700
Washington, DC 20036   Fax: 202-429-6063
Program Available: Volunteer Service Program (Internship).

State Government Internships For Students

Much like Federal government programs, almost every state offers many opportunities for students to earn money and college credits while they learn about their own unique state government. Unlike some other programs, eligibility for these state programs does not depend upon financial need.

Did you know that:

- States like Arizona offer a Governor's Internship program that hires several interns each year to work on issues such as education, women's issues, and public administration?

- If you are a college student in the state of Hawaii, you can earn a decent hourly wage as an intern assisting a state agency that is working on issues of special interest to you?

- If you are a student and resident of Maine, you can earn a cash stipend **and** academic credit to work in a state agency of your choice?

Whether you are looking for part time or full time employment, during the school year or just for the summer, the agencies we have listed will give you the information you need to find the job that suits you best.

Many state agencies offer exciting internships, work/study programs, or other special positions designed exclusively for students. Unfortunately, most states lack a central clearinghouse to easily keep track of the numerous positions, let alone the specific qualifications and application procedures for each position. We have provided an up-to-date listing of offices in each state that can assist you in your search for the program that fits your interests, needs, and schedule.

While it is possible to "earn while you learn" in almost every state in this country, you have to know **where to look**, and that's where this book can help you.

Alabama

* Capital Intern Program
Robert L. McCurley Director
Alabama Law Institute
P.O. Box 861425
Tuscaloosa, AL 35486-0013
205-348-7411
Fax: 205-348-8411
www.ali.state.al.us

The Alabama Law Institute has announced a new program known as the Capital Intern Program. It was established to train student interns in state government by allowing them to observe and participate in the process of the legislative and executive branches of government.

- One intern will be assigned to work with the Governor and will attend functions with him, as well as participate in the day to day functions of the office.
- There will also be an intern assigned to work with the Lieutenant Governor doing similar work.
- The House of Representatives will also have an intern that will learn every aspect of the Legislature.

Applicants must be residents of Alabama and be at least a junior at a college or university. Preference is given to students with a keen interest in government. Students work full time for the legislative session. Interns are paid $3,300 for their participation. Send application to the office listed. There are three positions available for the legislative session.

* State Agency Program
State Personnel
64 North Union Street

Folsom Administrative Building
Montgomery, AL 36130
334-242-3389
Fax: 334-242-1110

In the state of Alabama, there is a Student Aid Program for students of Alabama schools. The program is similar to an internship, but students must contact the agencies they are interested in to find out if the program is available at that agency. If one needs assistance in locating a number, state personnel will help.

Alaska

* Alaska State Internship
Students need to contact the agency of interest directly, but assistance is available through the following:
Division of Personnel
Department of Administration
333 Willoughy Avenue, 10th Floor
Juneau, AK 99811-0201
907-465-4430
Fax: 907-465-2576

The Alaska State Internship Program provides an opportunity for a student to have planned, productive experience directly related to their field of interest. Interns work throughout the state, including opportunities in the Office of the Governor. The tasks that the student will perform will be based on the student's level of education. At the high school level, student interns will do basic tasks. College interns will be involved in the professional knowledge and skills of an area. Graduate interns solve problems and actively manage a department with some assistance. High school, undergraduate, and graduate students that are residents of Alaska may apply. Full time and part time are options for employment, depending on agency requirements. Funding is limited and wages may vary from agency to agency. Send resume and cover letter to the office listed. The number of positions varies based on need.

Arizona

* Governor's Internship Program

Melodee Jackson
Director of Constituent Services
Office of the Governor
1700 West Washington   602-542-1318
Phoenix, AZ 85007   Fax: 602-542-1381

The Governor's Internship Program has several positions available, each with a different emphasis. Students are placed in positions based on interests and expertise and all interns must possess good writing skills.

- Interns will be doing research, responding to mail, working on projects, and gaining important hands-on experience.
  Areas to be focused on are:
  - Communications
  - Education
  - Women's Issues
  - Public Administration and much more.

Undergraduate or graduate students who are residents of Arizona may apply. Interns will work a minimum of 20 hours per week. Unpaid academic credit is available. Send resume and cover letter to the office listed. The number of positions varies based on need.

* State Agency Programs

Arizona Department of Administration
100 N. 15th Avenue   602-542-5216
Phoenix, AZ 85007   Fax: 602-542-2588
Job Hotline   602-542-4966

State internships are handled by each agency. If a student is interested in a particular department, they would need to contact that agency directly. The State Personnel Office will assist in directing their call to the appropriate agency or the Job Hotline will give them additional information on available internships.

Arkansas

* Governor's Internship Program

Internship Program
Office of the Governor
State Capitol Building Room 250   501-682-3695
Little Rock, AK 72201   Fax: 501-682-3597
www.state.ar.us/governor/programs/programs.html
Brooke Crane, Office Administrator

The Governor's Internship Program gives students insight into working within the executive branch of government. Interns will be assigned projects based on their respective areas of interest, and will also spend time with the Governor attending meetings and receptions. Other exciting opportunities include but are not limited to the following:

- working in the Press Office, interns will be able to participate in research, press clipping, and monitoring news stories from around the state;
- learning about and participating in the discussion of health care issues by working in the Health and Human Services Department;
- finding out what happens at the local and county level by working in the area of city, county, and local affairs.

Undergraduate and graduate students who are residents of Arkansas may apply. Hours are flexible allowing students to work full time or part time for a semester. These are unpaid positions, but the program will work with the student's university or college to provide academic credit. Four to six positions are available per semester. Send application with resume, two letters of recommendation, and a brief essay to the office listed.

* State Agency Programs

State Information
One Capitol Mall
Little Rock, AK 72203   501-682-3000

The State of Arkansas does not have one central contact for internships as each agency is responsible for their own programs. To get information you must contact those agencies directly that are of interest to you. The contact number is the best source for additional information.

California

* Governor's Internship Programs

Intern Coordinator
Office of the Governor
State Capitol Building   916-445-2841
Sacramento, CA 95814   Fax: 916-445-4633

The Office of the Governor offers a broad range of opportunities for interns providing important work experience in various departments. Students are placed in specific departments based on their particular area of study or interest. Here are just a few of the many different opportunities available:

- The Public Affairs Office oversees all of the Governor's verbal and written communication. Speech writers research and write speeches, public service announcements, talking points, and radio addresses for the Governor.
- The legal unit serves as the in-house counsel for the Governor and his staff. The unit reviews requests for clemency, handles extraditions, reviews lifer parole decisions, and monitors significant litigation against the state.
- The communications and press relations unit is responsible for overseeing communication between the Governor's Office and the press. This unit writes and releases statements to the press, schedules media interviews, and press conferences.

Undergraduate and graduate students may apply. Interns must work a minimum of 20 hours per week for a 10 to 12-week period. These positions are unpaid. 25 to 40 positions are available per semester. Send application, resume, brief writing sample, and school transcript to the office listed.

* State Agency Programs

State Personnel Board
801 Capitol Mall
P.O. Box 944201   916-653-1705
Sacramento, CA 94244-2010   Fax: 916-653-4096

In the State of California available internships are handled by individual agencies. Call the agencies that you are interested in directly for information on internships that they offer, or call the State Information or Personnel number to get a phone number for a particular agency.

Colorado

* Governor's Internship Program

Camile Loui
Internship Coordinator
Office of the Governor
127 State Capitol   303-866-2855
Denver, CO 80203   Fax: 303-866-4824

The Governor's Office of Policy and Initiative has several internships available to qualified students. The office is responsible for developing and implementing the Governor's policy agenda. Interns will assist in the preparation of briefings for the Governor in advance of events, researching and compiling his speeches, drafting letters, and conducting background research on a variety of issues.

Some of the possible policy areas for interns include:
- Education
- Advocacy and Outreach
- Environmental Protection and Preservation
- Legislation
- Criminal Justice/Legal Issues

Rising juniors, seniors, graduate students, or recent graduates (within the past year) may apply. Preference is given to applicants attending or graduates from a Colorado college or graduates from a Colorado high school. Applicants must have strong written communication skills. The internship must be no shorter than 3 months nor longer than 12 months. Hours are flexible and can be worked on a part time or full time basis. Unpaid academic credit is available. The number of positions varies based on need. Send resume, writing sample, and cover letter to the office listed.

* State Agency Programs

Division of Human Resources
Colorado Department of Personnel and Administration
1313 Sherman Street, Room 122   303-866-2323
Denver, CO 80203   Fax: 303-866-2021

State internships are handled by each agency. Call the individual agency to find out if internships are available in a student's area of interest. The personnel department will assist in locating the needed phone numbers of agencies.

Connecticut

* Governor's Internship Program

Internship Coordinator
Office of the Governor
State Capitol
210 Capitol Avenue   860-566-4840
Hartford, CT 06106   Fax: 860-524-7395

The Governor's Internship Program gives students the opportunity to work in various units while learning about the Executive Branch of the state government.

- Interns are assigned to positions based on interest and need. In the press unit, interns will work on press releases, as well as assemble press clippings and other projects.
- Legal Counsel will assign interns research work regarding various legal issues.

Undergraduate or graduate students may apply. Hours are flexible, but 3 days 20 hours per week for one semester is preferred. Unpaid academic credit is available. Two to four positions are available per semester. Send resume and cover letter to the office listed.

* Connecticut General Assembly Internships

Program Directors
Legislative Office Building, Room 5150
Hartford, CT 06106-1591   860-240-0520
www.cga.state.ct.us/isc

The Connecticut General Assembly has a Legislative Internship Program available which allows students to acquire hands-on experience in the area of legislation. Interns perform functions such as bill analysis and tracking, in-depth research, drafting of news releases and speeches, liaison work, and more. Applicants must be undergraduate students who are attending two or four-year institutions of higher education in Connecticut and state residents attending out-of-state colleges. Students may work on a full or part time basis. A stipend based on number of miles traveled to the Capitol is paid to defray travel expenses. Academic credit is available. Approximately 90 interns are selected to serve the legislative session. Submit application to the office listed.

Delaware

* Governor's Internship Program

Intern Coordinator
Office of the Governor
Tatnall Building
William Penn Street   302-577-3210
Dover, DE 19901   Fax: 302-577-3118

The Governor's Internship Program gives students opportunities in many different areas. Students are assigned to positions based on interest and expertise.

- Interns who work in the Press Office will be able to participate in projects, do research, and, assemble press articles.
- In Constituent Relations, interns will be involved in correspondence from the Governor's Office and assist with problems that are of concern to citizens.
- The Policy Office deals with issues such as health care. Interns will work with this office doing research.

Juniors, seniors, or graduate students from a college or university may apply. Interns work a minimum of 15 hours and on a full time basis in the summer. Some positions are paid $7.50 per hour and some are unpaid. The summer program is unpaid. Two positions are available per semester. Send resume, cover letter, and writing sample to the office listed.

* State Agency Programs

State Personnel
Employment Services
Townsend Building
401 Federal Street, Suite 5   302-739-4195
Dover, DE 19903   Fax: 302-739-3000

As there is no centralized office to answer questions about agencies, it is necessary for the student to call the agency that they are interested in directly. The number of a particular agency may be obtained from the State Personnel office.

District of Columbia

* Mayor's Office Internships

Office of Policy and Performance Management
441 4th Street, NW
Suite 310 South   202-442-9644
Washington, DC 20001   Fax: 202-727-5486

The District of Columbia offers internships in the Mayor's Office. Interns will perform a variety of different functions in various departments. One such department is in the Office of Employment and Evaluation. Undergraduate and graduate students may apply. Interns work a minimum of 8 hours. Unpaid academic credit is available. The number of positions varies based on need. Send cover letter and resume to the office listed.

Florida

* Governor's Internship Program

Patrick McQuillan
Executive Office of the Governor
The Capitol, Room PL-05
Tallahassee, FL 32399-0001   850-488-9041
www.myflorida.commyflorida/government/bushteam/internships.html

The Governor's Internship Program allows students to work in areas based on their particular experience and interest. Students usually call the area or unit they are interested in directly. However, the personnel office will be able to direct calls and answer questions about this program.

- Interns have the opportunity to work in Planning and Budgeting doing research and special projects.
- The Press Office gives interns a chance to go to press conferences and participate in the communication process between the Governor and the public, along with other activities.
- Communications is another area where interns will be assigned, learning various aspects of the Governor's office.

Undergraduate and graduate students who have an interest in public service may apply. The schedule is flexible, on a full or part time basis, with a minimum of 20 hours. The positions are unpaid currently, but a paid program is anticipated in the future. Six to seven positions are available per year. Send application and cover letter to the office listed.

* State Agency Programs

State of Florida
Department of Management Services
4050 Esplanade Way, Suite 250
Tallahassee, FL 32301   850-488-1234

Internships in Florida are handled by each agency directly. The Department of Management Services does have a listing of Personnel Office phone numbers which will help in locating the agencies.

Georgia

* Governor's Intern Program

Governor's Intern Program
Office of the Governor
245 State Capitol   404-656-3804
Atlanta, GA 30334   Fax: 404-651-5110
www.ganet.org/governor/intern

The Governor's Intern Program offers valuable field experience for one academic term in a governmental or nonprofit agency. Interns will learn about the executive branch of government in the Governor's Office, as well as in other areas. Interns will work in various units based on their particular area of interest, maturity, expertise, and availability. Here is a listing of just a few of the units that utilize interns:

- Press Office
- Georgia Chamber of Commerce
- Georgia Council on Child Abuse
- Georgia Bureau of Investigation
- Legislation

Work may consist of research, special projects, daily functions of the office, and correspondence. Applicants must be college students with a GPA of at least a 2.5 who are juniors, seniors, masters level, or first or second-year law students. Students must also be enrolled in a Georgia college or university, or be a resident of Georgia. The schedule is 20-40 hours for a 10-week or 13-week period. Interns are paid a stipend from $1070 to $2782 depending on the hours and length of the internship. Law students are paid $3000. Academic credit is also available. 260 positions are available per year. Send application to the office listed.

Hawaii

* State Executive Intern Program

Office of the Governor
State Capitol 808-586-0034
Honolulu, HI 96813 Fax: 808-586-0006

The State Executive Intern Program is administered by the Office of the Governor. The program gives students the opportunity to observe firsthand the process of executive decision making. Assignments are made by the Governor's Office to departments within the Executive Branch. A few of the many possible departments are: Office of Children and Youth, Economic Development, and the Department of Human Resources. Applicants must be full time students who are juniors or seniors of the UH Manoa and are in good academic standing. Schedule is flexible on a full or part time basis for one term. Interns are unpaid, but academic credit is available. The number of positions varies based on need. Submit resume and cover letter to the office listed.

* State Agency Programs

Jim Dote
Student Intern Program
Department of Personnel Services
235 S. Beretania St. 808-587-1161
Honolulu, HI 96813-2437 Fax: 808-587-1003

The Student Intern Program was established to provide college students in Hawaii with the opportunity to gain practical experience in their chosen fields, while assisting state government agencies with productive work. It is also an opportunity to encourage students to consider a career in state government. Interns are placed with agencies based on their expertise and area of interest. Possible departments include: Agriculture, Transportation, Human Services, and many others. Upper-level undergraduate and graduate students may apply. The college or university you are attending must be participating in the Student Intern Program. The schedule is full time during breaks and part time with a minimum of 10 hours during the school year. The intern must commit to two semesters. Interns are paid hourly. The number of positions varies based on need. Students must be referred by their University's Cooperative Education staff and sign an agreement.

Idaho

* Governor's Internship Programs

Sara Nye, Intern Coordinator
Office of the Governor
State Capitol Building 208-334-2100
Boise, ID 83720 Fax: 208-334-3454

There are two different internship programs offered through the Governor's Office in Idaho. There is a winter program and a summer program which offer different opportunities:

- The winter program allows interns to work in the Legislative Office. The office tracks and records legislation in progress and will give interns the opportunity for hands-on experience.
- The summer program offers a variety of different possibilities. Interns will be doing research, working on long-term projects, or answering inquiries.

Applicants must be undergraduate or graduate students of an Idaho school. It is also beneficial to be familiar with the state. Interns are required to work full time for one semester for both programs. The summer session is 12 weeks and the winter session is 10 to 12 weeks. Interns are paid a stipend of $100 per week. The winter program utilizes five interns, and the summer program requires three interns. Send application and cover letter to the office listed. Be sure to work with your college or university career center in preparing your application.

* State Agency Programs

Division of Human Resources
700 West State Street 208-334-2263
Boise, ID 83720 Fax: 208-334-3182

Internships in Idaho are handled individually by each agency. Students should contact agencies that they are interested in directly. The Personnel Commission does have a listing of Personnel Office phone numbers which will help in locating the agencies.

Illinois

* Office of the Governor Programs

Program Coordinator
Name of Program
107 William G. Stratton Building
Springfield, IL 62706 217-782-5213

The State of Illinois Office of the Governor has several different fellowship and internship opportunities. The programs consist of positions in the Governor's Office and state agencies. The four different programs are:

- James Dunn Jr. Memorial Fellowship Program
- Vito Marzullo Internship Program
- Michael Curry Summer Internship Program
- Rod R. Blagojevich Governmental Internship

Qualifications and job responsibilities vary based on the department to which an intern is assigned. Students who work in the Governor's Office may be working in one of the following areas:

- In the Press Office, interns will be assisting in answering phones, typing, filing, and writing press releases.
- The Legal Office will give students the opportunity to conduct research, draft correspondence, place calls, and handle scheduling.
- The Legislative Office responds to all issues dealing with legislation, including the monitoring of legislative committees.
- Interns who work in the Department of Agriculture serve as public relations assistants drafting news releases, newsletter articles, and public service announcements.

James Dunn Jr. Fellowship Program

Applicants must have a bachelor's degree and have demonstrated a commitment to excellence through academic honors, leadership ability, and involvement in community/public service. The schedule is full time, with 3 1/2 month intervals through different offices. The program is one year in length. The intern is paid $27,900 annually, with full benefits. Send application, three letters of recommendation, and a current copy of transcript to the office listed.

Vito Marzullo Program

Applicants must be college graduates who are Illinois residents. Interns work full time for one year in the Governor's Office. The intern is paid $27,900 annually and receives state benefits. Send application, three letters of recommendation, and a current copy of transcript to the office listed.

Michael Curry Summer Internship Program

Applicants must be Illinois residents who are college juniors, seniors, or graduate students. Interns work full time for the summer. The intern is paid a stipend of $1,200 per month. Send application and transcript to the office listed.

Indiana

* Fellowship Program

The Governor's Fellowship Program
Governor's Office
Statehouse Room 206
Indianapolis, IN 46204 317-233-1053

The Fellowship Program provides a unique 12-month training experience in state government. The Governor's Fellows are assigned on a rotating basis to different state agencies where they observe and train. Here are a few of the many different agencies:

- Governor's Office
- Department of Family and Social Services
- Civil Rights Commission

All participants complete the Fellowship having gained an unforgettable learning experience while contributing to state government. Applicants must be college graduates who have just received their bachelor's degree and those seniors who will be getting their degrees. Preference is given to Indiana residents. Applicants must have an academic record of B or better and exhibit strong leadership qualities. The schedule is full time for one year. Fellows will receive a salary of approximately $22,000 per year, plus full benefits. Ten positions are available per year. Send application, references, transcripts, and an essay to the office listed.

* Indiana State Government

Kristin Witherbee
The Governor's Public Service Internship Program

c/o State Personnel Department
Indiana Government Center-South
402 West Washington Street
Room W161
Indianapolis, IN 46204-2261   317-233-3777

There are two different internship opportunities with the State of Indiana. Each program has different qualifications and offers different learning experiences. The Governor's Public Service Internship Program is a summer program that is offered to students who have just graduated from an accredited college or university. Interns get first-hand experience working in various agencies. Applicants must be students who have just graduated from an accredited college or university. The schedule is full time for the summer. The intern is paid $798 on a bi-weekly basis. 100 positions are available. Send application to the office listed.

Iowa

* Governor's Internship Program

Office of the Governor
State Capitol
Des Moines, IA 50139   515-281-5211
                              Fax: 515-281-6611

The Governor's Internship Program gives students an opportunity to work in the Governor's Office. Experiences will vary based on the department to which students are assigned. Some of the possibilities include:

- Interns may be assigned to work in Office Administration where duties include daily activities conducted in the Governor's Office.
- In the Press Office interns do research and monitor news stories about the state.
- There are also opportunities for interns to travel with the Governor and to assist with various events.

Undergraduate or graduate students may apply. Most students are from Iowa schools. Interns are required to work 2 or 3 days and at least 20 hours per week for one semester. Interns are unpaid, but academic credit is available. 30 to 40 interns are assigned per year. Send application and resume to the office listed.

* State Agency Programs

Department of Administrative Services
Human Resources Enterprise
Internship Program Coordinator
400 East 14th Street
Des Moines, IA 50319-0150   515-281-3087
                                   Fax: 515-242-6450

Internships in Iowa are handled by each agency. Students should contact an agency directly for further information regarding internships. The Personnel Department will assist in locating phone numbers of various agencies.

Kansas

* Governor's Internship Program

Director of Constituent Services
Office of the Governor   800-748-4405
State House   785 296-3232
Topeka, KS 66612   Fax: 785-368-8788

The Governor's Intern Program gives students the opportunity to work in various offices based on availability and interest.

- In the Office of Constituents Services, students will assist in writing responses to letters of concern, as well as responding to telephone inquiries.
- The Policy Department allows students to become involved in doing research and working on projects.
- Interns who work in the Legislative Office will be involved with tracking legislation and working closely with the legislative staff.

Students from any college or university may apply. Students may work on a full or part time basis. This is very flexible, based on the intern's school schedule. Interns who work full time for two semesters receive a stipend of $500. All other internships are unpaid. Four positions are available per year. Send cover letter and resume to the office listed.

* State Agency Programs

Personnel Services
Civil Service and Employment
Landon State Office
900 SW Jackson   785-296-4278
Topeka, KS 66612   Fax: 785-296-6793

To find out which agencies offer internships, the student must contact the agency directly. Applicants should be aware of the fact that most positions are unpaid. The Personnel Services department can also furnish an applicant with the phone number of a particular agency.

Kentucky

* Governor's Internship Program

Constituent Services
Office of the Governor
State Capitol Building
700 Capitol Avenue, Suite 100   502-564-2611
Frankfort, KY 40601   Fax: 502-564-2517

The Governor's Office offers an internship program that is flexible and allows students to work in various areas based on need and interest. Students from any college or university may apply. Students may work on a full time or part time basis. The schedule is very flexible. Positions are unpaid, but academic credit is available. The number of positions varies based on need. Send resume and cover letter to the office listed above.

* State Agency Programs

Department of Personnel
200 Fair Oaks Lane, Suite 517   502-564-6920
Frankfort, KY 40601   Fax: 502-564-3588

State internships are handled by each agency. To obtain information about a particular internship, you must contact the agency directly. The Department of Personnel or state information will be happy to furnish applicants with the phone numbers of agencies.

Louisiana

* Governor's Internship Program

Connie Nelson
Executive Assistant to Chief of Staff
Office of the Governor
P.O. Box 94004   225-342-7015
Baton Rouge, LA 70804   Fax: 225-342-7099

The Louisiana Internship Program is available for students enrolled in a master's program at a university. Interns will have the opportunity to work in various departments, depending on their expertise. Listed below are a few of the departments where students could be assigned:

- Press Office
- Public Administration
- Legal Office

Special projects, research, and correspondence are just some of the experiences interns will gain. Applicants must be master's degree students. The schedule is 20 hours minimum. Interns are unpaid. The number of positions is discretionary. Send resume and cover letter to the office listed.

* State Agency Programs

Department of Civil Service
P.O. Box 94111
Capitol Station   225-342-8536
Baton Rouge, LA 70804-9111   Fax: 225-342-2386

The State of Louisiana offers no formalized internship program. Each agency makes its own decision on whether or not to have interns, so students should contact agencies directly to find out about these limited opportunities. Interns are usually paid through their college or university when positions are available. State Information or the Department of Civil Service will provide the phone numbers of various agencies.

Maine

* Governor's Internship Program

Office of the Governor
State House Station 1
Augusta, ME 04333-0001   207-287-3531
                                Fax: 207-287-1034

The Governor's Office offers an internship program that is flexible and allows students to work in various areas based on need and interest. Students from any college or university may apply. Students may work on a full time or part time basis. The schedule is very flexible. Positions are unpaid but academic credit is available. The number of positions varies based on need. Send resume and cover letter to the office listed above.

* Maine State Government

Margaret Chase Smith Center for Public Policy
University of Maine
5715 Coburn Hall   207-581-1648
Orono, ME 04469-5715   Fax: 207-581-1266

The Maine State Government Summer Internship Program combines both work experience and education in allowing students the opportunity to contribute and participate in Maine state government. Interns are assigned to various agencies gaining valuable hands-on experience. Here is a listing of a few of the possible areas where interns might be placed:

- Department of Environmental Protection
- Department of Labor
- Department of Economic and Community Development

Students must be residents of Maine and have completed two years of college. Applicants cannot have participated in the program previously. The schedule is full time for the summer. Interns are paid $300 per week and academic credit is also available. The number of positions varies based on need and funding. Send application to the office listed.

Maryland

* Governor's Internship Program

Office of the Governor
State House
100 State Circle   410-974-3591
Annapolis, MD 21401   Fax: 410-974-3275

The intern will be integrated into and become a part of the regular staff assigned to the Governor's Office. It is important that interns be very flexible and respond quickly to any requests by the Governor, staff, constituents, and elected officials.

- Research is an integral part of the intern's duties. This includes personal contact with Cabinet Secretaries, their deputies and staff, as well as working in the Legislative Reference Library and similar other duties.
- Interns are also placed in Scheduling and Public Affairs and are expected to participate in the details of arranging a social or political event.
- There are also opportunities for interns to act as forward liaisons for the Governor.

Students who are rising juniors or seniors, or graduate students who have a 3.0 average may apply. Interns must work at least three full days or a minimum of 20 hours at specific days and times for one semester. Unpaid academic credit is available. 3 to 15 positions are available per semester. Send application, resume, unofficial academic transcript, a short essay, and three references to the office listed.

* Maryland State Government

Christine Krajewski
Attn: Governor's Summer Internship Program
The Shriver Center at UMBC
1000 Hilltop Circle
Baltimore, MD 21250   410-455-2493

The Governor's Summer Internship Program gives students the opportunity to get valuable first-hand experience working in a top level state government office. Interns are matched with a mentor who will supervise and support them throughout their work experience. Duties will include attending meetings, drafting correspondence, tracking legislation, assisting constituents, and researching policy options. Applicants must be rising juniors and seniors attending a college or university in Maryland, or Maryland residents who attend an out-of-state college or university. The schedule is full time for the summer. Both unpaid and paid internships are available along with academic credit. 20 positions are available. Interested candidates should contact the President's Office of their college or university for more information on the nomination and application process.

Massachusetts

* Governor's Internship Program

Theresa Dolan
Director, Office Administration
Office of the Governor
Room 360, State House   617-725-4040
Boston, MA 02133   Fax: 617-727-8685

The Executive Office of the Governor offers a number of opportunities to qualified students. Some programs have a work/study component, while the other positions are on a volunteer basis. Here are some of the exciting possibilities for students:

- External Relations gives interns the opportunity to work in the Correspondence Office or Constituent Services responding to telephone requests, complaints, or opinion calls. Interns may draft and proofread responses sent to the Governor.
- The Chief Secretary handles personnel matters, government issues, and a wide variety of projects that involve team work.
- There is a great opportunity for hands-on experience in the Executive Office of Public Safety if you are an intern interested in law enforcement and public safety.

Undergraduate or graduate students may apply. For the spring and fall/winter programs, a minimum of ten hours per week for the entire academic year is required. For the summer program, internships are full time. The summer program has five positions that are paid at a $200/week stipend. The balance of the positions are work/study or volunteer. The fall/winter and spring programs are unpaid. In the summer, 35 positions are available; in the fall/winter, 60 positions are available, and in the spring, 60 positions are available. Applicants must send a resume, cover letter, a two-to-three page writing sample, and up to three letters of recommendation to the office listed.

* Massachusetts Senate Internship

Ms. Anne Reilly Ziaja, Director
Senate Legislative Education Office
State House
Boston, MA 02133-1053   617-722-1380
Call ahead for fax.

The Massachusetts Senate Internship Program gives students the opportunity to get hands-on experience learning about various offices and functions. Undergraduate or graduate students may apply. Interns work at least six weeks, 12 to 15 hours per week. Unpaid academic credit is available. The number of positions varies based on need. Applicants should submit application, resume, transcript, and sample of writing to the office listed.

Michigan

* The Governor's Management Intern Program

Office of the Governor
Operations Division
Attn: Internship Program Director
P.O. Box 30013   517-373-3400
Lansing, Michigan 48909   Fax: 517-335-0118

The Governor's Management Intern Program was established to develop Michigan's managers of tomorrow. The program familiarizes interns with a wide range of public management issues and provides career development. Interns will work in various departments gaining first-hand experience. Any candidate who is about to receive a graduate degree from a Michigan college or university or any Michigan resident who has received a graduate degree from another state is eligible to apply. The schedule is full time. Interns are paid based on department and individual expertise. The number of positions varies based on need. Submit application, transcripts, nomination from graduate school, and two letters of recommendation to the office listed.

* Michigan State Government

Bureau of Human Resources Services
Michigan Department of Civil Service
Capitol Commons Center
400 S. Pine Street   800-788-1766
P.O. Box 30002   517-373-3030
Lansing, Michigan 48909   Fax: 517-373-7690

The State of Michigan Student Programs provides students with the opportunity to obtain work experience in the state government while pursuing a degree. Interns will work with an agency that is related to their educational goals and objectives. Interns will be working with engineers, social workers, conservation officers, and many others. Any student attending a higher education institution on a full time basis is eligible to apply. Interns usually work part time. There are four levels of pay for interns, with the average being $8.72 per hour. 800 positions are available per year. Contact the Student Programs Coordinator and fill out an application.

Minnesota

* Governor's Internship Program

Director of Operations
Office of the Governor   800-657-3717

130 State Capitol
St. Paul, MN 55155

651-296-3391
Fax: 651-296-2089

The Governor's Internship Program is a flexible program, giving students the opportunity to learn about various departments. Below are just a few of the options available:

- Interns in the Press Office have the opportunity to assist with the writing of press releases and general office work.
- The Legislative Affairs Office tracks and records legislation in progress and deals with a variety of issues of importance to the state.
- In Constituent Services interns will respond to telephone requests, complaints, opinion calls, and comments. It is important for students to have patience, diplomacy, and excellent communication skills in this office.

Undergraduate and graduate students from any university or college may apply. The schedule is 20 hours minimum per week for one semester. Interns are unpaid, but academic credit is available. 1 to 5 positions are available per semester. Send resume and cover letter to the office listed.

* State Agency Programs

Department of Employee Relations
200 Centennial Office Building
658 Cedar Street
St. Paul, MN 55155

651-297-1184

The Minnesota Internship Program has been decentralized so each agency does its own recruitment and selection of interns. Interns usually work four weeks to one year on a full or part time basis. If an intern is to be paid, the rate will be no less than minimum wage. If one needs assistance in getting a phone number for an agency, you may contact the number listed.

Mississippi

* Governor's Office Internship Program

Felicia Gavin
Internship Program
Office of the Governor
P.O. Box 139
Jackson, MS 39205-0139

601-359-3150
800-405-0733

The Office of the Governor has an internship program that allows students to learn about the executive branch and gain experience before entering the work force on a full time basis. Listed below are just a few of the intern possibilities:

- Interns have the opportunity to assist with managing TEAMISSISSIPPI (Governor's Office Public Relations) -legislative agenda.
- A new information management system is currently being developed by interns and staff.
- Interns can assist with constituent relations by serving as a liaison between citizens of Mississippi and various state agencies.

Seniors and graduate students of any college or university may apply. The schedule is very flexible and can be full time or part time. Unpaid academic credit is available. Seven positions are available per semester. Send resume and cover letter to the office listed.

* State Agency Programs

Dr. Ed Clynch
Public Management Intern Program Coordinator
Mississippi State University
P.O. Box P.C.
121 Bowen Hall
Mississippi State, MS 39762

662-325-7852
In Mississippi 800-327-2980

Mississippi has a Management Graduate Internship Program that allows students pursuing graduate degrees in specific areas to gain practical experience working for a state government agency. A few of the many possible agencies to which interns are assigned include: the State Board of Health, Highway Patrol, and the Forestry Commission. Applicants must be students who are U.S. citizens or possess a green card and are enrolled at Jackson State University, Mississippi State University, University of Mississippi, or the University of Southern Mississippi. Students must also be pursuing graduate degrees in Public Administration, Public Policy and Administration or Criminal Justice Administration and have completed at least one semester, maintaining a B average or better. The schedule is full time for one semester. Interns receive a stipend of $1,000 per month, plus one percent fringe benefits. 10 positions are available per year. Contact your Public Administration Coordinator or Criminal Justice Coordinator to find out how to be nominated.

Missouri

* Governor's Internship Program

Governor's Office
Office of the Governor
State Capitol
P.O. Box 720
Jefferson City, MO 65102-0387

573-751-3222
Fax: 573-751-1495

The Governor's Office offers an internship program that is flexible and allows students to work in various areas based on need and interest. Students from any college or university may apply. Students may work on a full time or part time basis. The schedule is very flexible. Positions are unpaid, but academic credit is available. The number of positions varies based on need. Send resume and cover letter to the office listed above.

* State Agency Programs

Division of Personnel
P.O. Box 388
Jefferson City, MO 65102

573-751-4162
Fax: 573-751-8641

State internships are handled by each agency. Contact the agency directly that you are interested in for further information. The Department of Personnel will assist in directing your call or you may call state information for the phone numbers of various agencies.

Montana

* Governor's Internship Program

Rosie Robinson
Press Secretary
Governor's Office
Office of the Governor
State Capitol
Helena, MT 59620

406-444-3111
Fax: 406-444-5529

The Governor's Internship program offers very interesting and challenging opportunities. Interns are given the opportunity to work in many different areas including the Office of Economic Development and the Office of Communications. Duties include doing advance work for the governor and drafting communications. Students with strong writing and communication skills who are juniors or seniors at any college or university may apply. Students may work on a full time or part time basis. The schedule is very flexible. Positions are unpaid, but academic credit is available. The number of positions varies based on need. Send resume, cover letter, and writing samples to the office listed above.

* Montana State Government

Montana Personnel Division
125 N. Roberts, Room 130
Mitchell Building
Helena, MT 59620

406-444-3871
Fax: 406-444-0703

The State of Montana does not have a internship program that is associated with the Job Services Division. If you are attending school in Montana, it would be best to contact your career office to find out what state jobs might be available to students.

Nebraska

* Governor's Internship Program

Director of Public Affairs
Office of the Governor
State Capitol
P.O. Box 94848
Lincoln, NE 68509-4848

402-471-2244
Fax: 402-471-6031

The Governor's Office Internship Program gives insight into working in the executive branch of government. Interns are assigned based on their particular area of interest. Below are just a few of the possible departments in which interns may work:

- The Public Affairs office has the responsibility of ensuring that all communication from the Governor's office is accurate. Interns will be actively involved with assisting in research projects conducted in this office.
- Interns who work in Constituent Services will also conduct research and assist with correspondence.
- The Boards and Commission Department is another area where interns will gain valuable hands-on experience.

Undergraduate and graduate students may apply. Flexible hours can be arranged on a full time or part time basis. Interns are unpaid, but academic credit is available. Five positions are available per semester. Send resume and cover letter to the office listed.

* State Agency Programs
Recruitment Coordinator
Department of Administrative Services
Personnel Division
301 Centennial Mall South   402-471-2075
Lincoln, NE 68509-4905   Fax: 402-471-3754

Internships in the state of Nebraska are currently not centralized, so students should contact the agency of interest directly. Limited information on various agencies is available through personnel.

Nevada

* Governor's Internship Program
Office of the Governor
State Capitol Building   775-684-5670
Carson City, NV 89701   Fax: 775-684-5683

The Governor's Internship Program is very limited at this time, and in the past, most positions have been on a volunteer basis. The program is also very informal. To get additional information about possible opportunities, you may contact the Office of the Governor.

* State Agency Programs
Peggy Martin
Personnel Analyst
Department of Personnel
209 E Musser Street
Carson City, NV 89701   775-684-0140

The State of Nevada has a Public Service Intern Program that gives students the opportunity to receive training and complete a variety of exciting assignments. Interns are placed based on their particular interest and emphasis in school. To get additional information about the intern program, contact the office listed.

New Hampshire

* Governor's Internship Program
Office of the Governor
25 Capitol Street   603-271-2121
Concord, NH 03301   Fax: 603-271-2130

Internships in the Governor's Office are very rewarding and interesting, allowing students to get hands-on experience in state government. Interns will be given significant responsibilities that could include:

- Tracking of Legislation
- Research
- Constituent Services

Positions are very competitive and limited. Applicants must be enrolled in a New Hampshire institution of learning. Interns must work a minimum of 20 hours per week for one semester. Interns are unpaid. One or two positions are available per semester. Applicants must be sponsored by a faculty member and must submit a letter through their college or university.

* State Agency Programs
Division of Personnel
25 Capitol Street   603-271-3262
Concord, NH 03301   Fax: 603-271-1422

State internships are handled by each agency. For additional information, contact the agency that you are interested in directly. The Division of Personnel will assist in directing your call or you may call state information for the phone numbers of various agencies.

New Jersey

* Governor's Internship Program
Office of the Governor
125 West State Street
State House
Trenton, NJ 08625   609-292-6000
    Fax: 609-292-5212

The Governor's Office offers an internship program that is flexible and allows students to work in various areas based on need and interest. Students from any college or university may apply. Students may work on a full time or part time basis. The schedule is very flexible. Positions are unpaid, but academic credit is available. The number of positions varies based on need. Send resume and cover letter to the office listed above.

New Mexico

* New Mexico Fellows Program
Rita Nunez
Deputy for Administration
Office of the Governor
State Capitol, Suite 400
Santa Fe, NM 87501   505-476-2200

The Office of the Governor has a Fellows Program which gives students the opportunity to experience work in the field of public service. Fellows are placed in different government agencies as well as in the Governor's Office. Students at any New Mexico public university who have at least a 3.0 average may apply. The schedule is eight weeks on a full time basis. Interns are paid $3,000, less expenses, for the eight-week period. 10 to 12 positions are available. Send resume and cover letter to the office listed.

* New Mexico State Government
State Personnel Office
2600 Cerrillos Road   505-476-7777
Santa Fe, NM 87505-0127   Fax: 505-476-7798

The State Government Intern Program allows students to gain experience while attending school. Students are placed in different agencies and work on projects required within the area. In order to be considered, an applicant must meet all of the minimum requirements. Possible departments include but are not limited to the following:

- Department of Agriculture
- Department of Health and Human Services
- Department of Transportation

Students need to contact agencies directly. Personnel will provide some assistance with the phone numbers of various agencies.

New York

* Governor's Internship Program
Ms. Terri Brennan
Special Office Assistant
Executive Chamber
State Capitol   518-474-8390
Albany, NY 12224   Fax: 518-474-0495

The Governor's Intern Program gives students an excellent opportunity to learn about the Governor's Office and its many different departments. Some of the possibilities are listed below:

- Interns are assigned to work in the Office of Research where they will do research on different topics that are of concern to the state.
- In the Legal Department interns will learn about litigation involving the state, as well as requests for clemency or reviews of parole decisions.
- The Environmental Department deals with environmental issues and concerns of the state and its constituents.

Undergraduate or graduate students of a college or university may apply. The schedule is 10 to 25 hours for one semester. Interns are unpaid, but academic credit is available. 13 positions are available per semester. Send resume and cover letter to the office listed.

* New York State Government
Department of Civil Service
Staffing Service Section 5
Building 1
Albany, NY 12239   518-457-2487

There are two different internship programs available in the State of New York. The Department of Civil Service has some limited information available regarding summer internships. If you are interested in more specific information, an applicant should call the agency directly to get details such as salary/stipend, schedule, and other requirements.

The Public Management Internship Program has brought exceptional women and men into exciting careers in New York State government. Interns are placed in positions that coincide with training and expertise. Detailed information and qualifications are available by contacting the office listed.

North Carolina

* North Carolina State Government

Jan Wichman
Internship Program Coordinator
Youth Advocacy and Involvement Office
217 West Jones Street, Suite 218
Elks Building   919-733-9296
Raleigh, NC 27603-1334   Fax: 919-733-1461

The North Carolina State Government Summer Internship Program gives students the opportunity to learn about state government. Interns are placed in various departments based on interest, expertise, and availability. There are also opportunities in the Governor's Office. A few of the many possible departments that interns may work in are:

- Department of Environment, Health and Natural Resources
- Department of Labor
- Department of Administration

Interns will work on special projects, conduct research, and in some areas, develop programs. Rising juniors, seniors, graduate students, and second-year law students may apply. The schedule is full time for the summer. Interns are paid approximately $200 per week. 100 positions are available. Send application, cover letter, and transcript to the office listed.

North Dakota

* Governor's Internship Program

Office Manager
Office of the Governor
State Capitol   701-328-2200
Bismarck, ND 58505   Fax: 701-328-2205

The North Dakota Governor's Internship Program is very flexible in order to accommodate students and their schedules. Interns will work in various departments, based on their expertise and criteria. The departments that usually have a need for interns are:

- Press Office
- Legal Department
- Legislative Affairs

Assignments will include research, special projects, correspondence, and many other responsibilities. Undergraduate and graduate students may apply. The schedule is flexible, depending on the student's schedule. A student may also work as an intern for more than one semester. Interns are unpaid, but academic credit is available. The program strives to accommodate as many students as possible. Send resume and cover letter to the office listed.

* State Agency Programs

William Gumeringer
Internship Coordinator
Human Resource Management Services
600 East Boulevard, 14th Floor   701-328-3345
Bismarck, ND 58505-0120   Fax: 701-328-1475

There are very limited opportunities available through the state. Applicants should contact the agencies of interest directly or seek further information from their college or university. The Department of Personnel will assist you with phone numbers of various agencies.

Ohio

* Governor's Internship Program

Office of the Governor
State House   614-644-0860
Columbus, OH 43215   Fax: 614-466-9354

The Governor's Internship Program gives students the opportunity to learn about the executive branch of government. Interns have the opportunity to work in a variety of areas. A few of the possibilities are listed below:

- In the area of Communications, interns could work in Public Affairs or Media. Responsibilities include fielding calls and assisting with press releases.
- Interns in the Legislative Office will track legislation and compile information for the Governor.

- Constituent Services can give interns the opportunity to work in the Executive Office, Human Services, or Multi-Cultural Affairs.

High school, undergraduate, or graduate students who are residents of Ohio may apply. The schedule is full time or part time, with flexible schedules available. Interns are unpaid, but academic credit is available. The number of positions varies based on need. Send resume and cover letter to the office listed.

* State Agency Programs

State Information
30 East Broad Street
Columbus, OH 43085   614-466-2000

Internships in the State of Ohio are handled by each agency, so students should contact them directly. State information will give you the phone numbers of various agencies.

Oklahoma

* Governor's Office Internship Program

Director of Public Affairs
Office of the Governor
212 State Capitol   405-521-2342
Oklahoma City, OK 73105   Fax: 405-521-3353

The Governor's Internship Program gives students the opportunity to work in all major divisions. The program is informal, but still allows students a good learning experience. A few of the possible areas where an intern might work are listed below:

- In Legislative Affairs, interns will track and review legislation.
- Interns who have knowledge of computers will be given the opportunity to assist in entering data from the Governor's Office on to a new computer system.
- In Constituent Services, interns will respond to inquiries by writing letters, and answering other correspondence.

Undergraduate or graduate students who have been recommended by their university or college may apply. Interns must work a minimum of 12 hours per week per semester. Interns may work more than one semester. Most positions are unpaid, but occasionally there are paid opportunities. 2 or 3 positions are available per semester. Send resume and cover letter to the office listed.

* State Agency Programs

Oklahoma Office of Personnel Management
Jim Thorpe Building   405-521-2177
Oklahoma City, OK 73105   Fax: 405-524-6942

There is no centralized internship program in Oklahoma. Students need to contact agencies directly to find out what is available. Information through personnel is very limited, but they can provide the phone numbers of various agencies.

Oregon

* Governor's Intern Program

Gin Ann Denison
Governor's Advocate for Human Resources
Governor's Advocacy Office   503-945-6904
500 Summer Street NE   800-442-5238
Salem, OR 97310-1012   Fax: 503-378-6532

The Governor's Intern Program has interns working in the Department of Human Resources Governor's Advocacy Office. The office provides information and referral services to citizens of the state of Oregon. Frustrated citizens and others requiring more assistance will turn to the Advocacy Office.

- Interns will be responsible for interviewing citizens and responding to inquiries by referring them to the appropriate state agency.
- If a referral is not appropriate, the intern will handle the investigation and write a follow-up letter to the citizen.
- Interns will also be expected to provide information over the phone, work on special projects, and enter data into the computer.

Undergraduate or graduate students may apply. Interns must work 20 hours minimum, full time in the summer, with the intern usually working two terms. Interns are unpaid, but academic credit is available. Six positions are available per semester. Send resume and cover letter to the office listed.

* State Agency Programs

Department of Education
255 Capitol St., NE
503-378-3569
Salem, OR 97310
Fax: 503-373-5156

Internships are not centralized. Applicants should contact an agency directly for further information. The Department of Higher Education will attempt to assist you in whatever way they can.

Pennsylvania

* Pennsylvania State Government

Bureau of State Employment
511 Finance Building, Room 110
Harrisburg, PA 17120
717-787-5703
Call for fax
TTY: 717-787-0570

There are two different Internship Programs available in Pennsylvania: the Management Intern Program and the Capital Semester Internship Program. Both programs offer different types of learning experiences and have different requirements. The Management Internship Program is a one-year training experience designed to accelerate the intern's understanding of state government. Interns will get on-the-job training in budgetary operations, employee relations, financial management, management information systems, policy, and program management. The Capital Semester Internship Program offers students the opportunity to earn money and credit while getting practical experience in their area of interest. Job responsibilities will vary, based upon assigned projects.

Management Intern Program

Applicants must be residents of Pennsylvania, and be candidates for master's degrees or have had an advanced degree conferred within 12 months of the starting date. Pennsylvania residents who attend a college or university in Pennsylvania are given preference. The schedule is full time for 18 months. Interns are paid approximately $27,000 per year, plus benefits. The number of positions varies based on need. Applicants must fill out a Management Intern Program application and supplement application and return those materials to a college liaison, where applicants must then be recommended.

Capital Semester Internship Program

Junior, senior, or graduate students who are residents of Pennsylvania attending a four-year college or university and have a 3.0 GPA may apply. Students work full time for 16 weeks, either in the spring or fall. Interns are paid $10.31 per hour. The number of positions varies based on need. Send application, resume, transcript, and one letter of recommendation to the office listed.

Rhode Island

* Rhode Island State Government

Rhode Island State Government
Internship Administrators
Room 8AA, State Capitol
401-222-6782
Providence, RI 02903
Fax: 401-222-4447

The Rhode Island State Government Intern Programs offer opportunities for experience and research in the governmental process. There are several programs available, all with different requirements. Students work in various offices, depending on their interest and expertise. One of the areas available is the Office of the Governor where interns are assigned to work in departments based on their particular expertise. Undergraduate, graduate, and law students who are residents of Rhode Island and have a GPA of 2.5 may apply. The schedule can be full time or part time, depending on program requirements. Minimum requirement is 8 to 10 hours per week for part time employment. Summer programs require 35 hours per week. Interns are paid in both programs, as well as receive academic credit. The number of positions varies based on need. Send resume, cover letter and letter of recommendation to the office listed.

South Carolina

* Governor's Internship Program

Office of the Governor
P.O. Box 12267
804-734-2100
Columbia, SC 29211
Fax: 804-734-5167

The South Carolina Intern Program gives students the opportunity to learn about the Governor's Office and its responsibilities. To get additional information, students should contact the Office of the Governor directly.

* South Carolina State Government

Internship opportunities are very limited throughout the state. Students attending the University of South Carolina have the best chance of obtaining a position. Contact the university for further information.

South Dakota

* South Dakota Government

Executive Intern Coordinator
PMB 0141-1
Bureau of Personnel
500 East Capitol
605-773-3148
Pierre, SD 57501-5070
Fax: 605-773-4344
www.state.sd.us/bop/jobs/Intern/home.htm

The State of South Dakota Executive Intern Program provides administrative internships to college students to expand their knowledge and understanding of the governmental process. Students will work in various agencies based on expertise, interest, and availability. A few of the many possible agencies where interns might work are listed below:

- Department of Social Services, where interns will work on developing informational materials and a training strategy.
- Department of Labor, where there are many opportunities for Job Service Representative Interns to be assigned duties related to seasonal programs such as: Rent a Kid and the Summer Youth Program.
- Department of Transportation, where there is a position for an engineering student. The intern will be expected to assist in all engineering functions of various projects.

Students may apply for more then one internship, but they must submit separate applications and resumes for each position. Any junior, senior, or graduate student in good academic standing at a college or university is eligible. Preference is given to those students who are residents of South Dakota or attending an institution of higher learning in South Dakota. Most positions are full time. Interns are paid from $5 to $8.86 per hour. Summer 65 internships are available, Fall 6 to 10 internships are available, and Spring 6 to 10 internships are available. Send application and resume to the office listed.

Tennessee

* Governor's Internship Program

Governor's Internship Program
State Capitol
615-532-4582
Nashville, TN 37243-0001
Fax: 615-532-9712

The Governor's Office offers an internship program that allows interns to meet interesting people, learn new skills, work in a variety of policy areas, and produce products that will be useful to the Governor's staff.

- Each intern will be required to do at least one major project, preferably in an area of interest to the intern and of value to the office.
- Interns will also be expected to participate in routine office work, including correspondence and materials summaries.
- Independence is also very important and interns are encouraged to work independently.

Undergraduate and graduate students may apply. The majority of positions are full time. Positions are unpaid, but academic credit is available. The number of positions varies based on need. Send cover letter and resume to the office listed.

* State Agency Programs

Department of Personnel
James K. Polk Building
505 Dedrick Street
615-741-4841
Nashville, TN 37243-0635
Fax: 615-741-6985

In the State of Tennessee internships are handled by each agency. Students should contact agencies directly for further information. State information or personnel will provide applicants with the phone numbers for various agencies.

Texas

* Governor's Office Internship Program

Director of Human Resources
Office of the Governor
P.O. Box 12428
512-463-5873
Austin, TX 78711-2428
Fax: 512-463-8464

The Governor's Office Internship Program allows students the opportunity to work in various departments based on expertise, interest, and availability. A few of the possible areas and departments are listed below:

- Interns who are assigned to the Policy Department will conduct research and work on various projects.
- In the Constituent Services area, interns draft correspondence, handle casework, and answer telephone inquiries.
- During the Legislative session, interns will file bills, track legislation, and conduct research as needed.

Undergraduate and graduate students may apply. The schedule is flexible, but there is a 20-hour minimum per week for one semester. Interns are unpaid, but academic credit is available. The number of positions varies based on need. Send resume and cover letter to the office listed.

Utah

* Governor's Internship Program

Heather Henderson
Office Manager
Office of the Governor
210 State Capitol
Salt Lake City, UT 84114-0601   801-538-1000
Fax: 801-538-1528

The Governor's Office offers an Internship Program that gives students the opportunity to work in areas based on their expertise and interest. All interns must have good written skills. Some of the possibilities are listed below:

- Constituent Services
- Education
- Legal Counsel

Interns will be given guidance and direction by staff, but will be expected to do research, attend meetings, draft reports, work on projects, and write correspondence. Undergraduate and graduate students may apply. Interns must work a minimum of 20 hours for one semester. Interns are unpaid, but academic credit is available. Two to three positions are available per semester. Send resume, cover letter, and writing sample to the office listed.

* State Agency Programs

Department of Human Resources
2120 State Office Building   801-538-3025
Salt Lake City, UT 84114-1531   Fax: 801-538-3081

Students should contact an agency directly for further information. The Department of Human Resources or state information will give phone numbers of various agencies to applicants.

Vermont

* Governor's Internship Program

Ray Walker
Special Assistant for Boards and Commission
Office of the Governor
109 State Street   802-828-3333
Montpelier, VT 05609-0101   Fax: 802-828-3339

The Internship Program in the Governor's Office is very flexible. Interns are assigned to work in areas based on interest and expertise. There are many different possible areas including those mentioned below:

- Legal Department
- Administration
- Public Affairs

The responsibilities will vary based on individual assignments, but all interns may be doing research, special projects, office work, and correspondence. High school, undergraduate, graduate, and law students may apply. The schedule is Full time or part time, depending on a student's schedule. Interns are unpaid, but academic credit is available. The number of positions varies based on need. Send resume and cover letter to the office listed.

* State Agency Programs

Department of Personnel
110 State Street
Drawer 20   802-828-3483
Montpelier, VT 05620-3001   Fax: 802-828-3409

Students should contact agencies directly for further information. State information or the Personnel office will provide the phone numbers of various agencies.

Virginia

* Governor's Fellows Summer Program

Mark Smith
Assistant Secretary of Education
Governor's Fellow Program
State Capitol
P.O. Box 1475   804-786-2211
Richmond, VA 23218   Fax: 804-371-6351

The Governor's Fellows Summer Program offers first-hand experience in the process of state government. The program is designed to bring fresh ideas into the government and give students the chance to see what it is like to work for the state. Interns work at the highest level and are given projects and assignments based on expertise and need. Below are a few of the possible departments or offices where fellows might work:

- Policy
- Constituent Affairs
- Press Office

Applicants must be graduating seniors or enrolled as degree candidates in a graduate or professional school. Students must also be attending a Virginia college or university or be a Virginia resident. The schedule is full time for the summer. Fellows are unpaid. 20 to 25 positions are available per year. Send cover letter, resume, official transcript, and two or three letters of recommendation to the office listed.

Washington

* Governor's Internship Program

Heather Rehaume, Program Coordinator
The Governor's Internship Program
Division of Vocational Rehabilitation
612 Woodland Square Loop SE, Building C
Lacey, WA 98504   360-438-8046

The Governor's Internship Program consists of two different opportunities. Both programs give students the opportunity to get hands-on experience with state government. Below are the two possible programs that students can participate in:

Undergraduate Internship Program

The Undergraduate Internship Program gives students the opportunity to work in specially created jobs in state agencies. Interns will manage projects, people, fiscal resources, and public policy. A few of the possible departments that interns may be assigned to are:

- In the Department of Transportation, interns work on planning, traffic sign designing, and computer projects.
- The Department of Social and Health Services gives interns the opportunity to work on computer projects related to the department, as well as working as an information consultant.
- The Liquor Control Board has interns doing research projects.

Applicants must have completed at least one term of full time study, but have not yet graduated. The schedule is full time for three to six months. Interns are paid $1,873 to $2,148 per month, depending on qualifications and type of internship. 50 positions are available per year. Send cover letter, resume, transcript, and references to the office listed.

Executive Fellowship Program

The Executive Fellowship Program offers Fellows the opportunity to work in a managerial capacity with state government. In the past, Fellows have worked as analysts, program managers, and project managers. Agencies and departments include: Department of Economic Development, Department of Health and Labor and Industries. Applicants must be enrolled but not yet graduated from an accredited graduate program. The schedule is full time for two years in a managerial training position. Fellows are paid $2,246 to $3,3134 per month, depending on qualifications and the type of fellowship one does. 25 positions are available per year. Send cover letter, resume, transcript, and references to the office listed.

West Virginia

* Governor's Summer Intern Program

Frank Chambers
Governor's Summer Intern Program
1900 Kanawha Blvd., East
Building 6, Room 420
Charleston, WV 25305   304-558-3950, ext. 260

In West Virginia, the Governor's Summer Intern Program gives students the opportunity to learn about state government by being assigned to different agencies. Interns must have leadership abilities and a strong interest in community service. Economic Development, Health and Human Services, and the Department of Tourism and Parks are just a few of the many agencies participating. Applicants must be undergraduate or graduate students attending a university or college in West Virginia, or a resident of West Virginia attending a college in or out of West Virginia. The schedule is full time for the summer. Interns are paid $5.15 per hour. 100 positions or more are available per year. Send resume and cover letter to the office listed.

Wisconsin

* Governor's Internship Program

Office Manager
Office of The Governor
115 East State Capitol
P.O. Box 7863   608-266-1212
Madison, WI 53707   Fax: 608-267-8983

The Governor's Office offers a great learning experience for eager students of government. There are a limited number of positions available on a semester basis. Interns will work with various teams throughout the Governor's different offices. There are many possibilities, some of which are listed below:

-   Internship participants who work with the Constituent Relations Team will be drafting correspondence in response to different inquiries.
-   When the Legislature is in session, interns may be asked to observe Legislative floor action and attend committee hearings and press conferences.
-   The Legal and Appointments Team are responsible for research and special projects and interns assist them in these tasks.

Advanced standing undergraduate, graduate, or law students are eligible. Students usually attend schools in Wisconsin. Hours are flexible and students can work part time or full time for one semester. Interns are unpaid, but academic credit is available. 3 to 15 positions are available per semester. Applicants must send resume, cover letter, and writing samples to the office listed. There is also the requirement of a personal interview once all information has been reviewed.

* Wisconsin State Government

Georgia Euler
Intern Coordinator
Human Resources Specialist
Dept. of Natural Resources
101 S. Webster Street
P.O. Box 7921   608-266-9462
Madison, WI 53707-7921   Fax: 608-267-1000

Wisconsin Department of Natural Resources Intern Program provides an opportunity for students to earn credit while getting valuable experience in their chosen field. Positions available include fisheries, wildlife, computer science, law enforcement, and many other areas. The experience is invaluable for the student and the agency. Junior, senior, or graduate students usually from local colleges and universities are eligible. Most positions are 8 to 12-week summer jobs, however full and part time internships are available during a regular semester. Interns are paid directly through their college. Academic credit is also available. 150 positions are available per year. Send application to the office listed.

Wyoming

* Governor's Internship Program

Intern Program Supervisor
Office of the Governor
State Capitol
220 West 24th Street   307-777-7434
Cheyenne, WY 82002   Fax: 307-632-3909

The Governor's program is very flexible and has no restrictions other than that interns should be eager to learn. Every effort is made to match the student's interests and abilities with work possibilities. Some of those areas open to interns are listed below:

-   The Intergovernmental Affairs Office gives students the opportunity to attend meetings and do correspondence and casework, gaining a basic understanding of the overlapping roles of government agencies.
-   In the Press Office, interns will work on various projects that include attending press conferences, issuing press releases, and covering events the Governor is scheduled to attend.
-   Boards and Commissions keeps a historical logbook that needs to be updated with current information by an intern on a regular basis.

Any undergraduate or graduate student can apply. Preference is given to students from the University of Wyoming. Flexible hours can be arranged for the intern, on a full or part time basis for one semester. Interns are unpaid, but academic credit is available. In the past, the program has always been able to accommodate all interested students. Send resume and cover letter to the office listed.

* State Agency Programs

Department of Administration and Information
Human Resources Division
2001 Capitol Ave.
Emerson Building   307-777-7188
Cheyenne, WY 82002   Fax: 307-777-6562

Students should contact agencies directly for further information. Preference is always given to students attending the University of Wyoming. Internships are usually paid and salary is based on the position and year of school of the intern. The Personnel office will assist in locating telephone numbers of various agencies.

Smithsonian Institution
Internships and Fellowships

If you have always dreamed of working in a museum, or would like to actually touch a work of art, maybe an internship or fellowship with one of the Smithsonian Museums might be just what you need to fulfill your dream. There are interns and fellows working and studying at all of the various Smithsonian Institution museums and offices. These are not limited in any way to art majors. The fields of interest are wide and varied, and include anthropology, science and technology, linguistics, biology, geological science, astrophysics, conservation, music, and more. Many of the internships do not provide a stipend, but the experience you receive is invaluable. When stipends are offered, they generally are in the range of $300 per week. Internships are for high school, undergraduate, and graduate students to provide them with the experience of working at the Smithsonian, and helping the museum with their shows, exhibits, and other services. Fellowships are usually for predoctoral and post doctoral candidates who would like to use the facilities and services of the Smithsonian to further their research or work.

Internships

* Center For Museum Studies
Internship Coordinator
Smithsonian Center For Education and Museum Studies
Arts and Industries Building
Room 2235, MRC 427
Smithsonian Institution
Washington, DC 20560-0427   202-357-3102

The Center for Museum Studies coordinates a central internship referral service for museum professionals, undergraduate (completed sophomore year), and graduate students, and individuals interested in a museum career.

Interns are placed in Smithsonian departments and offices in projects emphasizing museum methods and current practices in the field: for example, curatorial practices, educational programming, collections management, museum registration, public relations, and exhibit design and production).

This office publishes a directory of internship projects at the Smithsonian Institution. To order a copy of *Internship Opportunities at the Smithsonian Institution*, send $5.00 (payable to the Smithsonian Institution) to: Center for Museum Studies, Arts and Industries Building, Room 2235, MRC 427, Smithsonian Institution, Washington, DC 20560; 202-357-3102.

Applicants seeking an internship in museum practices and/or wish to be considered for internship appointments at two or more Smithsonian bureaus are encouraged to apply through the Center for Museum Studies. Submission deadlines are February 15, June 15, and October 15.

* Office of Imaging, Printing and Photographic Services (OIPPS)
Intern Coordinator
American History Building
Smithsonian Institution, Room CB-054
Washington, DC 20560-0649   202-786-2707

Internships are available to undergraduate and graduate students throughout the year in museum photography collection management, custom black and white and color darkroom procedures and electronic imaging. Applicants should have some knowledge of photography and wish to pursue photography as a career goal.
Term: 6 to 8 weeks
Applications: Considered year-round; best time summer and fall
Stipend: No

* Office of Product Development and Licensing
Intern Coordinator
Office of Product Development and Licensing
Smithsonian Institution
600 Maryland Ave. SW, Suite 260
Washington, DC 20024   202-287-3620

The Office of Product Development and Licensing develops museum-related products and product lines primarily through licensed manufacturers. Depending on background and experience, interns may expect to work as an assistant in specific product categories or work independently on projects under the supervision of an office member. Retail knowledge or experience is a plus as well as an arts background, but knowledge of specific museums or academic disciplines is not required.
Term: To be arranged between student and supervisor
Applications: Considered year-round
Stipend: No

* Anacostia Museum and Center for African American History and Culture
Intern Coordinator
Anacostia Museum
Smithsonian Institution
1901 Fort Place, SE, MRC 520
Washington, DC 20020   202-287-3369

The Anacostia Museum is a national resource devoted to the identification, documentation, protection, and interpretation of the African American experience and the people of African descent and heritage living in the Americas. Internships offer opportunities to undergraduate and graduate students with an interest in African American history and culture, and are available in the Registrar's office and the following departments: research, exhibits design and production, education, public programs and public affairs.
Applications: Will be considered and accepted based on staff availability and museum schedules.
Stipend: No

* Archives of American Art
Intern Coordinator
Archives of American Art
750 9th Street, NW, Suite 220
Smithsonian Institution
Washington, DC 20560-0937   202-275-1682

The Archives of American Art collects the personal papers of American artists, art dealers, critics, and others concerned with American art. Internships are available to undergraduate seniors and graduate students who have a background in American art history or American studies and are looking for the opportunity to conduct research in primary sources and prepare written descriptions for publication in archival guides and finding aids.
Term: Variable, twelve weeks or more.
Applications: Considered year-round.
Stipend: No

* Cooper-Hewitt National Design Museum — New York
Intern Coordinator
Cooper-Hewitt National Design Museum
Smithsonian Institution

2 East 90th St.
New York, NY 10128 (212) 849-8400

During the academic year, internships are available to undergraduate and graduate students. Participants become fully acquainted with a specific department of the museum and also gain a general overview of museum operations. Must be in an academic program or have just graduated.
Term: Minimum of 1 month
Applications: Resumes are accepted and reviewed at any time
Stipend: No

Summer internships are offered on a competitive basis to those who have completed at least 2 years of College. Interns become acquainted with the programs, policies, and procedures of the Museum in such operations as research in the field of design and decorative arts, exhibition development, library services, and museum education. Individuals without previous museum experience are encouraged to apply.
Term: 10 weeks, June-August
Applications: Submission deadline February 1
Stipend: Yes

* Asian Art

Intern Coordinator
P.O. Box 37012
Arthur M. Sackler Gallery
MRC 707
Smithsonian Institution
Washington, DC 20560 202-357-4880, ext. 246
www.asia.si.edu

The Freer Gallery houses one of the most distinguished collections of Asian art in the world, as well as one of the largest collections of James Whistler's works. The Gallery supports advanced research and distributes the results through exhibitions and publications. A limited number of internships for high school, undergraduate, and graduate students are available for special projects and for general departmental work in the following departments: administration, conservation, curatorial, design, education, fabrication, library, photography, publications, public affairs, and registration.
Applications: Considered year-round
Stipend: No

* Zoos, Biology and Writing

ZooGoer Internship
FONZ Communications Office
c/o National Zoological Park
Washington, DC 20008 202-673-4711

Internships are available for students and recent graduates who have a strong background in writing, editing, and biology or a related field. Interns work in Friends of the National Zoo's Communications Office, which publishes ZooGoer magazine and other zoo-related publications.
Term: Minimum of 10 weeks
Applications: Considered year-round
Stipend: Yes

* Art History

Intern Coordinator
Department of Education
Hirshhorn Museum, MRC 350, Room 409
Smithsonian Institution
Washington, DC 20560-0350 202-357-3235

Summer internships are offered for college juniors and seniors who have completed at least 12 semester hours in art history. This is a competitive program through which interns are placed in one of several departments in the museum.
Term: 10 weeks
Applications: Submission deadline March 1
Stipend: Varies

Graduate student internships are available for students in accredited art history graduate programs and are offered during an academic semester. If college tuition is paid for the internship, the museum requests a tuition-sharing arrangement with the university.
Term: 1-2 semesters
Applications: Deadlines: March 1, June 1, and November 1
Stipend: No

* Horticulture

Intern Program
Horticulture Services Division
Arts and Industries Building, Room 2282

Smithsonian Institution
Washington, DC 20560 202-357-1926

Applicant is required to have a B.A. or B.S. degree, or be enrolled in an accredited college or university in horticulture or one of its related fields. Assignments vary from one specific project to a full range of activities in all branches of this Division.
Term: 10-16 weeks
Applications: 3 months prior to proposed start date
Stipend: Yes (limited)

* International Museum Program

Intern Coordinator
International Center
Quad 3123
Smithsonian Institution 202-357-2519
Washington, DC 20560-0705 Fax: 202-786-2557

The International Center explores, monitors, coordinates, and enhances Smithsonian international activities through its component parts. Internships are available to undergraduate and graduate students. Assignments may include work on a database; help in the preparation of reports and newsletters and with conferences or symposia; and coordination activities involving staffs of the Smithsonian and other government agencies; foreign scholars, and other international organizations.
Terms: Minimum of 2 months
Applications: Considered year-round
Stipend: No

* Aviation, Space Science, Photography, Journalism, Education

Student Services Coordinator
Educational Services Department
National Air and Space Museum, Room P700
Smithsonian Institution 202-357-4223
Washington, DC 20560-0305 TTY: 202-357-1505
www.nasm.si.edu

Internships are offered during the summer semester to undergraduates and graduate students studying science, museology, history, aviation, space science, photography, journalism, education, aircraft restoration and preservation, earth and planetary studies, archives, public affairs, development, exhibits, and library disciplines.
Term: 10 weeks
Applications: January - February 15
Stipend: Yes

* African Arts

Intern Coordinator
National Museum of African Art
950 Independence Ave., SW
Smithsonian Institution 202-357-4600, ext. 225
Washington, DC 20560-0708 TTY: 202-357-4814

Fall, spring, and summer internships are offered to students enrolled in undergraduate and graduate programs and to individuals interested in exploring museum professions. Internship opportunities are available in the following departments: administration, photographic archives, public affairs, exhibition and design, curatorial, conservation, registration, and education. Candidates must have a background in art history, anthropology, museum studies, or a related discipline. Specific training in African art or other aspects of African culture is desirable.
Term: 10 weeks, 20 hours per week
Applications: Deadlines June 15, October 15, February 15
Stipend: No

* American Art

Intern Program Officer
Office of Intern Programs
Smithsonian American Art Museum
Washington, DC 20560-0210 202-275-1554

Advanced Level Scholarships: A graduate degree in art history, American studies, or studio art with museum practice is offered by various universities in cooperation with the National Museum of American Art. To participate in this program, students must have completed 12 or more graduate hours of art history; however, this program may be pursued for self-enrichment without academic credit. In addition, exceptional undergraduates (seniors) may be recommended by their university for this program.
Term: Fall and Spring semester 20 hours weekly, or one semester 40 hours weekly.
Applications: Deadline March 1.
Stipend: One stipend is awarded annually to an exceptional graduate student with financial need.

Summer Internships: Internships are designed for both undergraduates in their senior year and graduate students with strong backgrounds in art history, American studies, or studio art, and who have had little or no previous museum experience. The Museum matches well-qualified applicants' objectives with the activities of the professional staff.

Term: 8 weeks starting in early June

Applications: Deadline March 1

Stipend: Availability varies yearly

* American History

Intern Coordinator
Office of Internships and Fellowships
National Museum of American History
MRC 605, Room 1040
Smithsonian Institution
Washington, DC 20560   202-357-1606

Internships focus on research, museum practicees and professional skills. All internships are designed around a specific project of mutual interest to the intern and the museum supervisor.

Term: Minimum 2 months

Applications: Considered year-round

Stipend: No

Internships are also offered in the following areas: exhibit design and fabrication; museum registration; design and production of educational materials and publications; and administration and production of museum programs and performances, including programs in Hispanic and African American cultures.

Term: Minimum 2 months

Applications: Considered year-round

Stipend: No

* Natural History

Intern Coordinator
Education Office
National Museum of Natural History
Smithsonian Institution   202-357-4548
Washington, DC 20560   Fax: 202-786-2563

Internships are available at various levels in the natural science disciplines that are currently being pursued by the museum.

Term: To be arranged between student and supervisor

Applications: Considered year-round

Stipend: No, academic credit can sometimes be obtained

* National Portrait Gallery

Intern Coordinator
Office of Education
P.O. Box 37012
National Portrait Gallery
Victor Building
Suite 8300, MRC 973
Smithsonian Institution
Washington, DC 20013-70120   202-275-1811

The availability of internships depends on departmental projects and staff needs, as well as the background, skills, and interest of the applicant.

Term: 3 month minimum at 20 hrs per week

Applications: Considered year-round

Stipend: No

* Exhibit Design, Script Writing and Editing

Internship Coordinator
Office of Exhibits Central
1111 N. Capitol, NE, MRC 808
Smithsonian Institution
Washington, DC 20560-0808   202-357-3183

The Office Exhibits Central supports museums and bureaus throughout the Smithsonian in the areas of exhibition design, script writing and editing, and all phases of exhibit production.

Design and Editing Internships: Limited internships are offered to candidates based on the availability of a suitable project. In the design area, interns should know how to do presentation sketches and prepare scale drawings. The editing area requires strong language skills. Interns will work under the guidance of a senior exhibit designer or editor on current exhibit projects.

Fabrication Unit Internship: Interns will be exposed to the four sections under the Fabrication Unit: cabinet shop, sheet plastics shop, paint shop, and specimen handling and crafting shop. Interns should have some basic carpentry skills and be able to lift and move heavy loads on occasion.

Applications: Considered year-round

* Minority Museologists

Office of Fellowships and Grants
P.O. Box 37012
Victor Building
Suite 9300, MRC 902
Smithsonian Institution
Washington, DC 20013-7012   202-275-0655
Email: siofg@si.edu

Minority Internships: are available to minority undergraduates and graduate students to provide an opportunity to participate in ongoing research or museum-related activities around the Smithsonian.

Term: 10 weeks

Applications: Deadline February 15th

Stipend: Yes

Native American Program: Internships are designed to encourage North American Indians to pursue research projects related to Native American history and cultures. These internships promote the use of the Smithsonian Native American collections and provide and opportunity for interns to work in collaboration with research staff.

Term: 9 to 12 weeks

Applications: Deadlines March 1, July 1, and November 1

Stipend: Yes

* Center for Folklife and Cultural Heritage

Intern Coordinator
Center for Folklife and Cultural Heritage
750 9th Street, NW, Suite 4100
Smithsonian Institution
Washington, DC 20560-0953   202-275-1180

Internships are offered year-round in the fields of folklore, cultural anthropology, and ethnomusicology of the U.S. and other countries. Intern projects often center around research for the Festival of American Folklife, the Smithsonian/Folkways Collection, or the Folklife Archive.

Term: 4 weeks to 1 year, full- or part-time

Applications: Considered year-round; deadline for summer internships is March 15th

Stipend: No

* Smithsonian Associates Program

Internship Program
The Smithsonian Associates
1100 Jefferson Dr., SW, Room 3077
Smithsonian Institution
Washington, DC 20560-0701   202-786-3234

The Smithsonian Associates Program is the continuing education, cultural, membership, and outreach arm of the Smithsonian Institution for members in the Washington, D.C., metro area. Internships are arranged in the following areas: Campus-on-the-Mall (adult courses); Lectures, Films, Seminars; Discovery Theater; African American Studies Center; Performing Arts; Studio Arts; Tours; Young Associates and Family Activities; and Public Affairs Office.

Term: Varies

Applications: Considered year-round

Stipend: No

* Asian and Near Eastern Art

Intern Coordinator
Arthur M. Sackler Gallery
P.O. Box 37012
Quad, MRC 707
Smithsonian Institution
Washington, DC 20560   202-357-4880, ext. 246
www.asia.si.edu

The Sackler Gallery contains pre-eminent collections of Near Eastern and Asian Art. Internships are available to high school, undergraduate, and graduate students for special projects and general departmental work in the following departments: administration, conservation, curatorial, design, education, fabrication, library, photography, publication, public affairs, and registration. Curatorial interns must have a working knowledge of pertinent Asian and Near Eastern languages.

Term: Varies

Applications: Considered year-round

Stipend: No

* Smithsonian Environmental Research Center

Intern Coordinator
Smithsonian Environmental Research Center
P.O. Box 28
Edgewater, MD 21037-0028   443-482-2217

This competitive program for undergraduate and graduate students offers a unique opportunity to gain exposure to and experience in environmental research.
Term: 10-16 weeks
Applications: November 15, February 1
Stipend: Yes

* Archival Research

Intern Coordinator
Smithsonian Institution Archives
Arts and Industries Building
Room 2135, MRC 414   202-786-2747
Washington, DC 20560-0414   Fax: 202-357-2395

The Archives program offers internships to graduate students interested in gaining hands-on experience in the application of archival techniques and procedures. Work is chiefly in the arrangement and description of institutional records, collections of personal papers, oral history collections, and photograph collections.
Term: 10 weeks
Applications: Considered year-round
Stipend: Yes (Might go unfunded due to a lack of funding).

* Library and Information Science

Intern Coordinator
Smithsonian Institution Libraries
National Museum of Natural History
Room 26A, MRC 154   202-357-1851
Washington, DC 20560-0154   TTY: 202-357-2328

Internship opportunities are available to undergraduate students who are interested in exploring a career in library and information sciences, graduate students, and library professionals. Assignments may include a discrete project or a structured practical experience and are available in SIL's four divisions: Research Services, Systems and Technical Services, Collections Management, and Planning and Administration.
Term: Varies, minimum of one month
Applications: Considered year-round
Stipend: No

* Exhibition Design and Management

Intern Coordinator
SITES
1100 Jefferson Dr., SW, Room 3146
Smithsonian Institution
Washington, DC 20560   202-357-3168

Internships are available throughout the year, with preference given to students on the graduate level. A variety of academic backgrounds is encouraged. Interns may apply or choose to work in the areas of programming, registration, public relations, and publications for the development and organization of traveling exhibitions.
Term: Not specified
Applications: Considered year-round
Stipend: No

* Tropical Research

Educational Coordinator
Smithsonian Tropical Research Institute
Unit 0948 APO AA 34002-0948   Fax: 507-212-8148

Smithsonian Tropical Research Institute (STRI) is the U.S. leading basic tropical biology research center, located in the Republic of Panama. Undergraduate or recent graduate students from Panama or other developing countries may apply to serve as field assistants to staff scientists, visiting researchers, and fellows in a wide range of tropical research projects.
Term: 3 months
Applications: Varying deadlines
Stipend: Yes (limited)

* Architectural History and Historic Preservation

Intern Coordinator
Arts and Industries Building, Room 2263
P.O. Box 37012
Smithsonian Institution
Washington, DC 20560-0417

Architectural History and Historic Preservation, Office of the Physical Plant, offers internships to both undergraduate and graduate students in the study of the history and preservation of the Smithsonian Buildings. Some previous course work or experience in art history, architectural history or historic preservation is required.
Term: 8 weeks
Applications: Deadlines: April 1, July1, and January 1
Stipend: no

* National Museum of the American Indian

Internship Coordinator
Smithsonian Institution
National Museum of the American Indian
Cultural Resources Center
4220 Silver Hill Road   301-238-6624
Suitland, MD 20746-2863   207-746-2863
Email: interns@nmai.si.edu
www.si.edu/nmai

This program provides learning opportunities in the area of museum practice through work/research experiences. Past projects include: developing and evaluating visitor guides, cataloging photos, monitoring collections, installing exhibits, exhibit research, developing databases and press kits.
Term: 10 weeks, 20-40 hours per week
Applications: reviewed in October, November, February and July
Stipend: varies

* Research Training Program

Program Director
Research Training Program
National Museum of Natural History
10th and Constitution Avenue, N.W.   202-357-4548
Washington, DC 20560-0166   Fax: 202-786-2563
www.nmnh.si.edu/rtp

Students participating in the Research Training Program develop and test a scientific hypothesis and communicate the results in the form of written manuscripts and oral presentations, Research topics are limited to collection based investigation in Anthropology, Botany, Entomology, Invertebrate Zoology, Mineral Sciences, Paleobiology, and Vertebrate Zoology. The research project is supplemented by lectures, discussions, demonstrations, field trips and tours.
Term: 10 weeks
Applications: Deadline February 1
Stipend: yes

* National Postal Museum

Intern Coordinator
National Postal Museum
Education Department
Smithsonian Institution   202-357-2991
Washington, D.C. 20560   Fax: 202-633-9393

The National Postal Museum showcases one of the largest and most comprehensive collections of stamps and philatelic materials in the world. The museum houses six major galleries that highlight a range of topics, from the earliest history of the mail and its rapid growth as a modern enterprise, to the art of letter writing and the beauty and lore of stamps. Internships are available to undergraduate and some high school students. Areas of study include American studies, Postal History, Transportation history, Philately, Education, Exhibits, Collections Management, and Public Affairs.
Term: determined for each position
Applications: accepted year round
Stipend: no

* Office of Information Technology (OIT)

Intern Coordinator
Smithsonian Institution
Office of Information Technology
900 Jefferson Avenue, SW   202-357-4220
Washington, DC 20560   Fax: 202-633-9466

The OIT provides the Smithsonian's central computing and telecommunications services. Applicants should have a strong interest and knowledge of computers. Internships are available in the Information Technology Services Division, the Infrastructure Technologies Division, and the System Engineering Division.
Applications; accepted year round
Stipend: no

* Office of Policy and Analysis (OP&A)

Intern Coordinator
Office of Policy and Analysis

Smithsonian Institution
Washington, DC 20560-0405   202-786-2232

OP&A internships are open to undergraduate and graduate students. These internships provide experience in conducting quantitative and qualitative policy related studies of major Smithsonian programmatic and administrative activities. A background in social science and some course work in qualitative or qualitative research methods are helpful.
Term: minimum of 2 months
Applications: considered year round
Stipend: no (financial assistance is available on a limited basis)

* Art Conservation

Senior Conservator
Department of Conservation
Smithsonian American Art Museum
Room 233, MRC
Smithsonian Institution
Washington, DC 20560-0211   202-357-2685

Students enrolled in graduate art conservation programs may apply for internships at the National Museum of American Art. Intern projects in the past have dealt with painting, paper, and objects conservation.
Term: 1 academic year
Deadline: March 1st
Stipend: Yes (Available through candidates school only)

* Smithsonian Affiliations Intern Partnership (SAIP)

SAIP Program
Smithsonian Affiliations Office
Arts and Industries Building, Suite 1360
900 Jefferson Drive, S.W.
Washington, D.C. 20560-0455   202-633-9157

Interns participating in SAIP internships spend 10 weeks at the Smithsonian Institution working full-time on projects developed to assist with Smithsonian Affiliate projects. Following their time at the Smithsonian, interns work at their Affiliate organization applying the information and knowledge gained from the Smithsonian experience.
Candidates for the Smithsonian Affiliations Intern Partnership Program MUST go through Smithsonian Affiliate Organizations for initial selection. To find an affiliate organization in your area, please see the list of Smithsonian Affiliate Organizations at: {http://affiliations.si.edu}.
Term: 10 weeks
Stipend: Yes. $4000 (Smithsonian and Affiliate museum jointly fund)

* Administrative or Accounting/Financial Internship in Grant/Contract Administration

Intern Coordinator
Office of Sponsored Projects
Smithsonian Institution
P.O. Box 37012   202-275-0677
Washington, DC 20013-7012   Fax: 202-275-0497

The Office of Sponsored Projects (OSP) provides assistance to Smithsonian staff that is seeking or has obtained external funding for sponsored project(s). A "sponsored project" is a research, education, exhibit, training or other activity that receives partial or full funding through the mechanism of a federal or non-federal grant or contract. OSP assists with the acquisition and usage of grants and contract funding for Smithsonian research, education and training. Interns should have a background in accounting, finance, management, public administration, information systems or liberal arts.
Term: minimum 2 months, 10-15 hours per week
Applications: accepted anytime
Stipend: No

Fellowships

* Smithsonian Center for Materials Research and Education (SCMRE)

Internship Secretary
Museum Support Center
4210 Silver Hill Road   301-238-3700
Suitland, MD 20746-2863   Fax: 301-238-3709

Fellowships in Archaeological Conservation: Postgraduate fellowships and graduate internships provide training in archaeological conservation, both in the field and in the Objects Conservation laboratory at CAL.
Term: 1 year
Applications: Deadline February 1

Stipend: Yes
Contact: Carol A. Grissom, 301-238-3700, ext. 153/154

Fellowships in Conservation of Archival Materials: Postgraduate fellowships and third-year internships provide specialized training in preventive care and conservation of archival materials.
Term: 1 year
Applications: Deadline February 1
Stipend: Yes
Contact: Harriet Beaubien, 301-238-3700, ext. 154; Fax: 301-238-3709

Pre-Program and Summer Internships in Conservation and Conservation Science/Technology: Students will work with specialists in conservation, archaeology, art history, chemistry, and materials science.
Term: Pre-program internships range from 8 months to 1 year; Summer internships extend from 8 to 10 weeks.
Applications: Deadline February 1
Stipend: Yes
Contact: Internship Secretary, 301-238-3700, ext. 102

* Freer Gallery of Art

Director
Freer Gallery of Art
P.O. Box 37012
Smithsonian Institution, MRC 707
Washington, DC 20560   202-357-4880, ext. 246
www.asia.si.edu

Harold P. Stern Memorial Fund: Grants support projects that will increase the understanding and appreciation of Japanese art using Freer Collections. Application is by invitation only and is based upon outstanding scholarly achievements in the field of Japanese art.

* National Air and Space Museum

Fellowship Coordinator
National Air and Space Museum
P.O. Box 37012
Smithsonian Institution
Washington, DC 20013-7012   202-357-2515

Guggenheim Fellowship: This 1-year fellowship is designed for pre- or post doctoral research. Scholars interested in research broadly related to the history of aerospace science and technology are encouraged to apply.
Applications: Deadline January 15
Stipend: Yes

Verville Fellowship: This one year competitive fellowship is intended for analysis of major trends, developments, and accomplishments in aviation or space studies. It is open to all interested candidates who can provide a critical, analytical approach and possess good writing skills.
Applications: Deadline January 15
Stipend: Yes

* Office of Fellowships and Grants

Victor Building
750 9th Street, NW, Suite 9300
MRC 902
P.O. Box 37012
Smithsonian Institution   202-275-0655
Washington, DC 20013-7012   Fax: 202-275-0489
Email: siofg@si.edu
www.si.edu/research+study

Predoctoral, Postdoctoral, and Senior Postdoctoral Fellowships: Offerings in most disciplines studied at the Smithsonian.
Term: 3 to 12 months
Applications: Deadline January 15
Stipend: Yes

Graduate Student Fellowships: Offerings in most disciplines studies at the Smithsonian.
Term: 10 weeks
Applications: Deadline January 15
Stipend: Yes

Native American Program: Community Scholar appointments are designed to encourage North American Indians to pursue research related to Native American history and culture. These fellowships promote the use of the Smithsonian Native American collections and resources and provide an opportunity for fellows to work with Smithsonian research staff.
Term: Up to 6 weeks
Applications: Reviewed in January, April, July, and October
Stipend: Yes

* Center for Museum Studies

Center for Museum Studies
Arts and Industries Building
Suite 2235, MRC 427
Smithsonian Institution
Washington, DC 20560-0427   202-357-3175

Fellowships are awarded to professionals in museums and allied fields to study policies, practices, and techniques in museums and education.
Term: 2 to 6 months
Applications: April 1
Stipend: Yes

* James Renwick Fellowship Program in American Crafts Since 1930

Renwick Gallery
Smithsonian American Art Museum
P.O. Box 37012
Smithsonian Institution
Washington, DC 20013-7012   202-357-2531

The Smithsonian Institution, with funding from the James Renwick Alliance, provides senior and graduate fellowships for research in American crafts since 1930.
Term: Up to 1 year
Applications: Deadline January 15
Stipend: Yes

* Smithsonian Astrophysical Observatory

SAO Summer Internship Program Director

Harvard-Smithsonian Center for Astrophysics
60 Garden St., MS 83
Cambridge, MA 02138   (617) 496-7586

The Smithsonian Astrophysical Observatory offers a summer internship program to undergraduate students interested in pursuing careers in the physical sciences. Potential areas of study may include observational and theoretical cosmology, extragalactic and galactic astronomy, interstellar medium and star formation, laboratory astrophysics, supernovae and supernova remnants and planetary science. Applicants should be enrolled in an academic program leading to a bachelor's degree.
Term: 10 weeks
Applications: Deadline April 15
Stipend: Yes

* Smithsonian Tropical Research Institute

Educational Coordinator
Smithsonian Tropical Research Institute   507-212-8031
Unit 0948 APO AA 34002-0948   Fax: 507-212-8148
Email: fellows@tivoli.si.edu
www.stri.org

Smithsonian Tropical Research Institute (STRI) is the United States' leading basic tropical biology research center, located in the Republic of Panama. STRI short-term fellowships are awarded 4 times a year to graduate students and advanced undergraduates who wish to conduct a self-contained project at STRI facilities.
Term: Approximately 3 months
Applications: Deadlines Feb. 15, May 15, Aug. 15, Nov. 15
Stipend: Yes

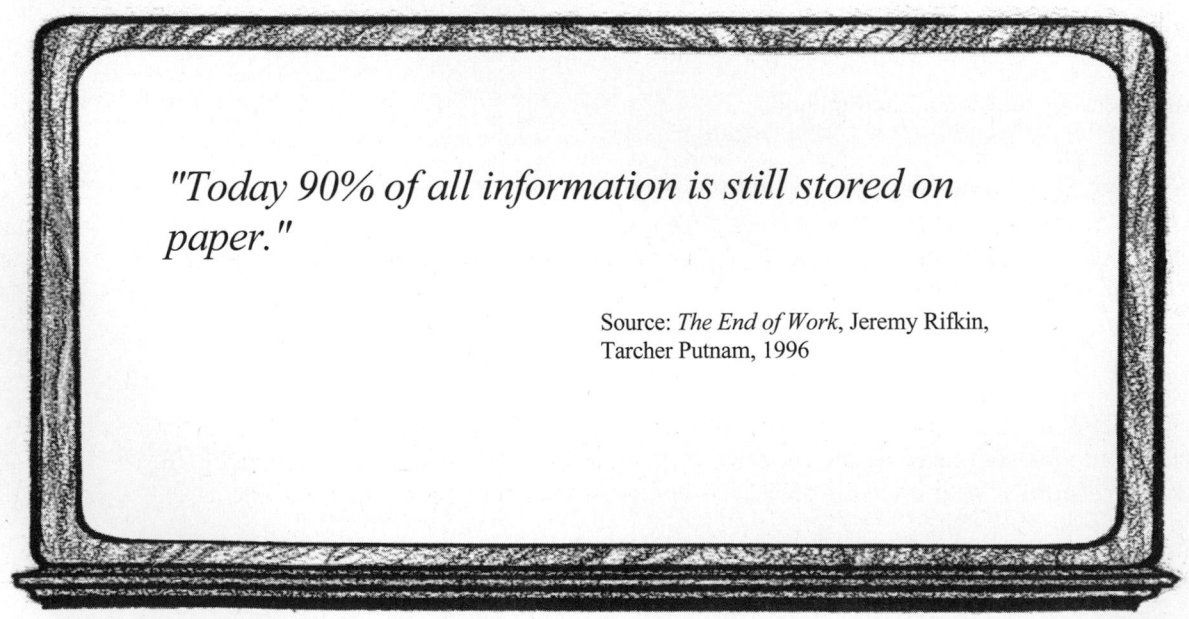

"Today 90% of all information is still stored on paper."

Source: *The End of Work*, Jeremy Rifkin, Tarcher Putnam, 1996

U.S. Department of State Internships

Anyone who's interested in getting some valuable work experience in fields ranging from accounting and African studies to print making and political science should consider doing an internship with the U.S. Department of State. The State Department administers U.S. foreign policy and maintains diplomatic relations throughout the world, with 250 Embassies and Consulates abroad, in over 150 countries. In fact, some interns may qualify to be posted to one of these far off, exotic places.

Each year the State Department sponsors various internships in which highly qualified college juniors, seniors, and graduate students have the opportunity to get first-hand knowledge of American foreign affairs. These internships are open only to currently enrolled students who are taking at least one-half of a full time course load, but the types of students they are open to are widely varied, including students studying the following disciplines:

Accounting	Information Management
African Studies	International Relations
Architecture	Journalism
Art History	Latin American Studies
Business	Law
Communications	Linguistics
Computer Science	Mathematics
Criminal Justice	Natural Sciences
Economics	Personnel Management
Engineering	Political Science
Finance	Print Making
Government	Public Administration
History	Public Relations
	Social Work

The State Department hires two types of interns: paid and unpaid. Most internships are in Washington, D.C., but some openings occur each year for interns to serve abroad. Depending on what the Department needs at the time, interns are assigned junior-level professional duties, which may include research, report writing, correspondence, computer science, analysis of issues, and more. Women and minorities are particularly encouraged to apply for these internships.

Unpaid Internships

These interns usually serve for one semester or quarter during the academic year, or approximately 10 weeks during the summer, and are expected to work a 40 hour week. The Government will not defray any expenses associated with unpaid internships; however, many colleges give academic credit for completing an internship.

Paid Internships

Paid internships are limited and available during the summer only. Interns serve for a minimum of ten weeks.

Candidates selected for the program will be appointed at the GS-4 through GS-7 grade levels, depending on their specific qualifications. The salary range is from $20,000 - $29,000 annually. Paid interns also receive paid leave and retirement credit. Competition for paid internships is intense; only 10% of the internships offered by the Department are paid.

How To Apply

All applicants must submit:

- Computer scannable application form DS-1950

- Statement of Interest that should include your objective and motivation in seeking an internship and how your academic courses and other experiences relate to the Bureau or office to which you are applying

- College transcripts

- Employment Data Form

For more complete application procedures and copies of any of the necessary forms, write:

Intern Coordinator
U.S. Department of State
2401 E Street, NW, 5th Floor
Washington, DC 20522-0151
703-875-4847
703-875-7200 (recorded message)

Deadlines

Applications must be postmarked by the following dates:

Summer Internships -- November 1
Fall Internships -- March 1
Spring Internships -- July 1

What follows is a listing of the different Bureaus and Offices in the State Department that run internship programs. Find the one you're most interested in and apply specifically to that Bureau — or Bureaus — when filling out your application.

* Art Bank Program

The Art Bank program acquires, exhibits, and maintains a collection of 1,400 limited edition prints and original works on paper by American artists.

This program selects fourth-year undergraduate students majoring in art history or art studio and prefers graduate students in art history or print-making.

Unpaid internships are available in Washington, D.C., throughout the year.

* Art in Embassies Program

The Art in Embassies Program administers loans and donations of American works of art and places them at overseas posts, residences of ambassadors, and UN representatives.

Selection of applicants is based on their demonstrated appreciation of art, cultural diversity, and international diplomacy and/or experience or education in visual art/art history.

Unpaid internships are available in Washington, D.C.

* Bureau for Nonproliferation

The Bureau for Nonproliferation is responsible for developing and implementing all policies to curb the proliferation of nuclear, chemical and biological weapons and missiles and other delivery systems, and promoting peaceful uses of nuclear energy and enhanced nuclear safety practices worldwide.

Unpaid internships are available in Washington, D.C. year-round.

* Bureau of Administration

The Bureau of Administration provides domestic and worldwide support services for the State Department to effectively plan and conduct foreign policy. It also constructs and maintains offices and residences overseas and offices in the Washington, D.C., metro area. Further, the Bureau provides safety, occupational health, language services, and a wide range of administrative services.

Interns are selected from applicants majoring in architecture, engineering, business, economics, computer science, accounting, and political science.

Paid and unpaid internships are available in Washington, D.C., throughout the year.

* Bureau of African Affairs

The Bureau African Affairs conducts foreign relations with the countries of sub-Saharan Africa, and directs U.S. Government activities within those countries.

Unpaid internships are available for both graduate and undergraduate students in the Washington, D.C., area throughout the year. Interns posted abroad are provided housing and transportation to and from the post. Internships abroad are available only during the summer

U.S. Department of State Internships

* Bureau of Arms Control

The Bureau of Arms Control strengthens national security by expediting effective arms control and disarmament policies and is responsible within State for arms control verification and monitoring.

Unpaid internships are available in Washington, D.C. throughout the year.

* Bureau of Consular Affairs

The Bureau of Consular Affairs directs consular services relating to the protection, assistance, and documentation of American citizens abroad. They also conduct all passport activities, including documentation and control of travel of U.S. citizens and nationals.

Paid and unpaid internships are available in Washington, D.C. throughout the year.

* Bureau of Democracy, Human Rights, and Labor

The Bureau of Democracy, Human Rights, and Labor applies human rights to the conduct of foreign policy and aid by working closely with international and nongovernmental human rights organizations. It also reviews political asylum requests. Interns work on special projects and normal operations.

Unpaid internships are available in Washington, D.C., year-round.

* Bureau of Diplomatic Security

The Bureau of Diplomatic Security investigates passport and visa fraud; conducts personnel security investigations; and provides general security services to the State Department, including anti-terrorism initiatives.

Applicants pursuing degrees in criminal justice, history, government, or other related fields are preferred. Engineering internships are also offered.

Unpaid internships are available in Washington, D.C., and occasionally at selected field offices in the U.S. such as Dallas, New York, San Francisco, and Los Angeles throughout the year.

* Bureau of East Asian and Pacific Affairs

The Bureau of East Asian and Pacific Affairs conducts foreign relations with countries in the East Asian and Pacific region. Selections of interns will be made from among applicants pursuing degrees in East Asian studies, political science, international relations, economics, business, and related subjects.

Unpaid internships are available in Washington, D.C., and abroad at most U.S. embassies and consulates only during the summer.

* Bureau of Economic and Business Affairs

The Bureau of Economic and Business Affairs develops and implements U.S. international economic policy that protects U.S. economic, political, and security interests.

Unpaid internships are available in Washington, D.C., year-round.

* Bureau of Educational and Cultural Affairs

The Bureau fosters mutual understanding between the people of the U.S. and other countries. Academic and professional exchange programs identify future leaders and build a foundation of trust with current and potential leaders throughout the world.

Unpaid internships are available in Washington, D.C. throughout the year.

* Bureau of European Affairs

The Bureau of European Affairs conducts U.S. foreign relations with countries in Europe.

Internships are offered to those pursuing degrees in political science and/or regional languages of the area. Interns will be involved in research, analysis, and reporting on a wide range of topics relevant to the regions.

Unpaid internships are available in Washington, D.C., and abroad at certain U.S. embassies and consulates year-round.

* Bureau of Human Resources

This Bureau runs the recruitment and examination for the Foreign Service, including administration of the Foreign Service written examination and oral assessments.

Unpaid internships are available in Washington, D.C., year-round.

* Bureau of Information Resource Management

The Bureau is responsible for the State Department's voice communications, telecommunications, transmission networks, automated data processing, personal computers, electronic media products, mass data storage, and more.

Unpaid internships are available in Washington, D.C., year-round.

* Bureau of Intelligence and Research

The Bureau of Intelligence and Research directs the Department's program of policy-oriented analysis and research, and acts as a liaison with the intelligence community. Intern applicants for this bureau are requested to include in their application packets a 3-10 page research paper related to international affairs/political science.

Unpaid internships are offered in Washington, D.C., year-round.

* Bureau of International Narcotics and Law Enforcement Affairs

This Bureau plans, implements, and oversees international narcotics and control activities; negotiates cooperative agreements with foreign governments; and works closely with other government agencies on domestic drug issues.

Intern projects include: monitoring narcotics control programs in South America, the Caribbean, Central America, Mexico, Asia, or Africa; reporting on narcotics activities; and researching narcotics trafficking policies. Proficiency in Spanish is desirable.

Unpaid internships are offered in Washington, D.C., during the summer only.

* Bureau of International Organization Affairs

This Bureau provides guidance for U.S. participation in international organizations and conferences.

Unpaid internships are offered throughout the year in Washington, D.C., and overseas in Vienna and Geneva.

* Bureau of Legislative Affairs

This Bureau supervises and coordinates all legislative and liaison activities between the Department and Congress and the Office of Management and Budget.

Unpaid internships are available in Washington, D.C., year-round.

* Bureau of Near Eastern Affairs

This Bureau conducts U.S. foreign relations with countries reaching from Morocco to Nepal.

Selections will be made from applicants pursuing degrees in political science, international relations, economics, business, and/or languages of the region.

Unpaid internships are available in Washington, D.C., throughout the year and abroad at U.S. Embassies and Consulates in the region only during the summer. Overseas posts provide housing at no cost to the interns.

* Bureau of Oceans and International Environmental and Scientific Affairs

This Bureau focuses on developing policy in the areas of environmental protection, global climate change, nuclear energy, oceans and fisheries, and population affairs.

Unpaid internships are available in Washington, D.C., year-round.

* Bureau of Politico-Military Affairs

The Bureau advises in the development of policies relating to the national security of the U.S. and in policies arising from the U.S. military activities affecting foreign relations.

Unpaid internships are available in Washington, DC.

* Bureau of Populations, Refugees and Migration

This Bureau runs the programs involving issues of refugee camps in the U.S., including selecting and processing those refugees seeking to be admitted to the U.S. It also develops and implements U.S. policies on international population, refugee and migration matters.

Unpaid internships are available in Washington, D.C., throughout the year.

* Bureau of Public Affairs

This Bureau executes all public information policies and programs. Selections are generally made from among those students majoring in public communications and relations, journalism, history, political science, international relations, and public diplomacy.

Unpaid internships are available in Washington, D.C., year-round.

* Bureau of Resource Management

The Bureau of Resource Management manages the financial affairs of the Department, including worldwide financial reporting and accounting programs. Intern selections will be made from those pursuing degrees in accounting, information systems, economics, public administration, mathematics, and computer science.

Paid and unpaid internships are available in Washington, D.C., year-round.

* Bureau of South Asian Affairs

The Bureau conducts U.S. foreign relations with the South Asian countries of India, Nepal, Sri Lanka, Bhutan, the Maldives, Pakistan, Afghanistan, and Bangladesh, and directs, coordinates, and supervises activities within those countries.

Unpaid internships are available in Washington, DC, and abroad at certain Embassies and Consulates during the summer only. Overseas posts provide housing at no cost to the interns.

* Bureau of Verification and Compliance

The Bureau of Verification and Compliance leads the verification and compliance effort for existing arms control and nonproliferation agreements.

Unpaid internships are available in Washington, D.C. year-round.

* Bureau of Western Hemisphere Affairs

The Bureau of Western Hemisphere Affairs conducts foreign relations with Mexico, Central and South America, and the Caribbean. Intern selections will be made from among applicants pursuing degrees in political science, foreign affairs, Latin American studies, economics, public administration, and related fields.

Unpaid internships are available in Washington, D.C. and abroad at certain U.S. embassies year-round.

* Family Liaison Office

The Family Liaison Office responds to the needs of Foreign Service families in the areas of employment and education through the development of programs. It also helps families experiencing crises, whether personal or other disasters. Interns will work on special projects in one or more of the above areas.

Unpaid internships are available in Washington, D.C., throughout the summer.

* Foreign Service Grievance Board

The major function of the Foreign Service Grievance Board is to provide a forum for the fair review and adjudication of grievance appeals.

Unpaid internships are available in Washington, D.C. throughout the year.

* Foreign Service Institute

The Foreign Service Institute trains State Department employees involved in foreign affairs, including instruction in over 50 languages. It also helps personnel and families going overseas. Intern selection will be made from those pursuing degrees in political science, economics, international relations, foreign affairs, language, linguistics, computers, and management.

Unpaid internships are available in Washington, D.C., year-round.

* Interior Planning, Design and Furnishing Division

This Division plans, provides and maintains the functional interior elements for overseas Department of State residences, and identifies and maintains antiques, works of art, and other cultural objects in properties abroad.

Paid and unpaid internships are available in Washington, D.C. throughout the year.

* Office of Equal Employment Opportunity and Civil Rights

This Office manages all Department of State programs and activities which promote equal employment opportunity and affirmative action for employees and applicants for employment. It directs the complaints processing program which addresses complaints of discrimination based on race, color, religion, sex, national origin, age, or disabling condition. It also advises the Secretary of State and senior Department management on affirmative action and diversity issues and develops and implements policies and procedures to eliminate barriers to equal employment opportunity.

Unpaid internships are available to undergraduate, graduate, and law students with an interests in equal employment opportunity and civil rights issues. Internships are available in Washington DC throughout the year.

* Office of Foreign Missions

The Office of Foreign Missions helps operate U.S. foreign missions and international organizations.

Paid internships are available in Washington, D.C., New York, Chicago, San Francisco, Los Angeles, and Miami throughout the year.

* Office of Inspector General

The Office of Inspector General conducts independent audits, investigations, inspections, and security oversight reviews in the Department.

Paid and unpaid internships are available in Washington, D.C., throughout the year. Internships are also available to second-year law students.

* Office of International Information

This office is the principal international communications service for the foreign affairs community. It writes and edits material to explain U.S. Foreign Policy to overseas audiences.

Unpaid internships are available in Washington, D.C., year-round.

* Office of the Chief of Protocol

This Office provides the President and the Secretary of State with advice on fulfilling the government's obligations relating to national and international protocol.

Paid and unpaid internships are available in Washington, D.C. throughout the year.

* Office of the Coordinator for Counter-terrorism

This Office coordinates the U.S. overseas counter-terrorism policy and response to international terrorist incidents that take place outside of U.S. territory.

Paid and unpaid internships are available year-round in Washington, D.C.

* Office of the Legal Advisor

This Office provides legal advice on all domestic and international legal problems arising in the course of the Department's activities.

Paid internships are offered those who are at least second-year law students. Unpaid work-study internships are available for fall and spring semester for second-year students and in the fall for third year students.

Applicants for this office must submit their application package directly to:
Personnel Officer
Office of Legal Advisor
L/EX, Room 5519

U.S. Department of State
Washington, DC 20520-6310
Fax: 202-736-7508

* Office of the Science and Technology Advisor to the Secretary

This office's initiative is to strengthen the science and technology literacy and capacity of the Department as a whole by increasing the number of scientists in the Department and by increasing training and exposure of diplomatic and civil service personnel to science and technology issues.

STAS can accommodate up to two interns during any internship period, but will also assist in identifying regional and functional bureaus, as well as embassies abroad, that may require science and technology interns.

* Office of the Secretary of Policy Planning Staff

This Staff coordinates different policy decisions between Bureaus and recommends alternatives on prospective policy issues when necessary.

Unpaid internships area available in Washington, D.C., year-round.

* Office of the Under Secretary for Arms Control and International Security Affairs

The Under Secretary provides policy direction for non-proliferation, including missile and nuclear, as well as chemical, biological, and conventional weapons; arms control, including negotiation, ratification, and implementation of agreements on strategic, non-conventional, and conventional forces; regional security and defense relations, which involves policy regarding U.S. security commitments worldwide as well as use of U.S. military forces in unilateral or international peacemaking and peacekeeping roles; and export control policy that deals with U.S. government control of exports that might contribute to proliferation of otherwise harm U.S. interests, while at the same time allowing legitimate exports that help U.S. business.

Unpaid internships are available in Washington, DC year-round.

* Office of the Undersecretary for Global Affairs

The Under Secretary coordinates U.S. foreign relations on a variety of global issues, including democracy and human rights, population and the environment, narcotics control, migration, and refugees, and oversees activities for four Bureaus: Democracy, Human Rights and Labor; International Narcotics and Crime; Oceans and International Environmental and Scientific Affairs; and Population, Refugees, and Migration.

Selections will be made from applicants with demonstrable knowledge of, and interest in, one or more global issues. Unpaid internships are available in Washington, DC.

* Program Execution Office

The Program Execution Office manages a $400 million Facility Management Program which includes over 2,000 properties worldwide. The Program acquires real property through lease and purchase, designs, constructs, and maintains offices abroad, and supports rehabilitation and repair of said properties.

Paid and unpaid internships are available year-round in Washington, D.C.

* United States Diplomacy Center

The Diplomacy Center will enable interns to participate in the creation of a new facility. When completed, the museum and center for U.S. diplomacy will feature the history of U.S. diplomacy, the practice and purpose of U.S. diplomacy, and the challenges of U.S. diplomacy past and present.

Unpaid internships are available throughout the year in Washington, D.C.

* United States Mission to the Organization of American States

The United States Mission to the Organization of American States is the main multilateral forum for dealing with political issues in the Western Hemisphere.

Unpaid internships are available in political affairs, economic and social affairs, and resource management in Washington, D.C. throughout the year.

* United States Mission to the United Nations

The United States Mission to the United Nations was established to assist the President and the Department of State in conducting U.S. policy at the United Nations. It carries out our nation's participation in the world body, and recommends what course of action the U.S. should pursue in the world organization.

Internships may be in: political affairs, economic and social affairs, UN resource management, military staff committee, research and reference, legal section, host country affairs, press and public affairs, and regional security office.

Unpaid internships are available in New York City throughout the year.

Millions in Fellowships and Training Opportunities for Students Interested in a Career in Health Care

The National Institutes of Health (NIH) offer students from high school and above who are interested in pursuing a career in health care all kinds of research training and career development programs. One of the best things about these programs is that they actually pay students during their training period.

Here's just a sample of the money offered by NIH:

For High School Students
- $13,000 per year to work full-time while they study
- $1,600 per month over the summer to study neurosciences
- $1,600 per month to study cancer
- $1,400 per month over the summer to study biomedicine

For High School Teachers
- $5,750 for the summer to study physiology

For College Students
- $1,000 to attend a conference on physiology research
- $1,600 per month to study cancer
- $2,800 per month over the summer to do biomedical research
- $1,400 per month to study the neurosciences
- $700 per month to study heart disease

For Graduate Students
- $8,000 per year to study cancer
- $2,400 per summer for research
- $60,000 over six years to earn a PhD/MD degree

For Postdoctoral Students
- $42,000 per year to study your specialty
- $30,000 to study biomedicine in Finland for a year
- $45000 to study your specialty overseas
- $2,500 plus travel, housing, and allowances to study for two months in Japan

These programs aren't just for students who are able to get to the Washington, D.C. area. NIH has made it possible for students all over the U.S. to participate by having two kinds of programs:

Extramural: these programs are located throughout the country at different research institutions, colleges, and universities

Intramural: these programs are located at NIH in the Washington, D.C., area

The assistance and training programs covered are designed to attract students into research careers from all levels of school, including:

Matthew Lesko, Information USA, Inc., 12081 Nebel Street, Rockville, MD 20852 • 1-800-955-7693 • www.lesko.com

- high school
- college
- graduate schools
- medical school
- dental school
- health-professional schools
- postdoctoral trainees
- independent researchers

There are hundreds of fellowships and internships available from NIH. To find out more about them you can request the publication, "Research, Training and Career Development Programs" from the ASK NIH hotline at Ask NIH, Extramural Outreach and Information Resources Office, Division of Research Grants, National Institutes of Health, 6701 Rockledge Dr., Room 1040 MSC 7710, Bethesda, MD 20892-7710; 301-435-0714. This publication is also available online. To access this information, start at the NIH homepage at http://www.nih.gov/ Next click on Grants and Contracts, then click on Grants page, then Funding Opportunities, then Research Training. You can then select the appropriate level of schooling to discover the fellowships and internships available. Both the book and the online service include: information about eligibility, other programs that may be of interest, the expected funding rates during the current fiscal year, and how to apply. Remember that these programs are not conducted exclusively in Washington, DC, but throughout the world.

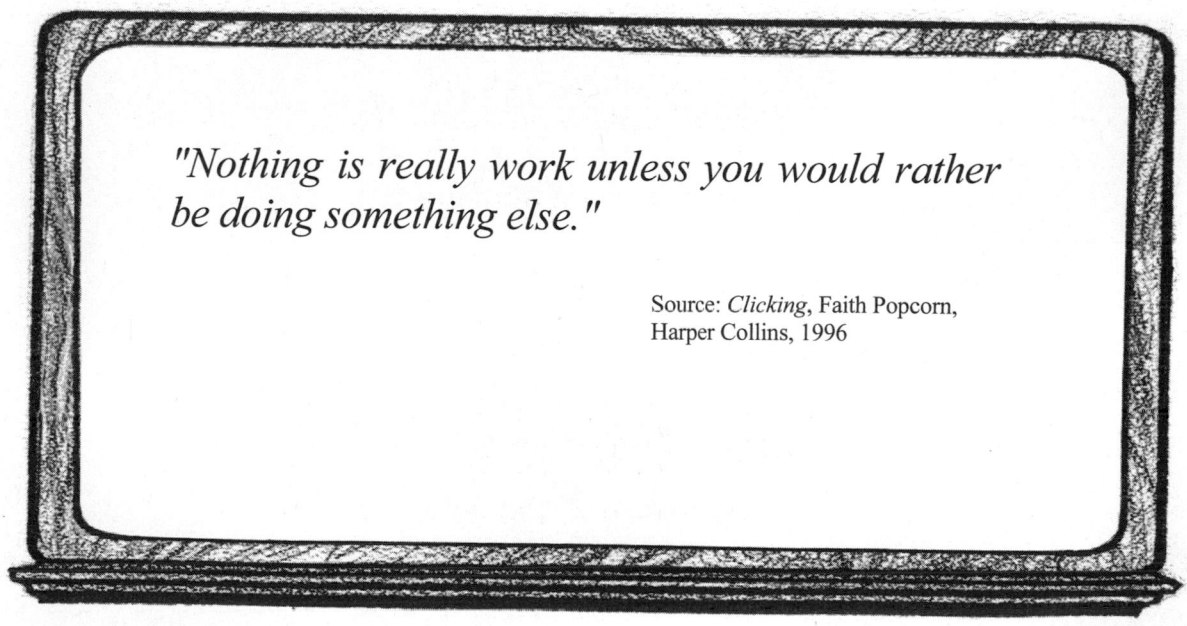

"Nothing is really work unless you would rather be doing something else."

Source: *Clicking*, Faith Popcorn,
Harper Collins, 1996

Matthew Lesko, Information USA, Inc., 12081 Nebel Street, Rockville, MD 20852 • 1-800-955-7693 • www.lesko.com

I Wanna Government Job

Matthew Lesko, Information USA, Inc., 12081 Nebel Street, Rockville, MD 20852 • 1-800-955-7693 • www.lesko.com

Looking For a Job With the Federal Government

You may hear about the downsizing of the government in the news every day, but did you know that the Federal government hires 432,000 new employees every year? In fact, counting the Postal Service, the federal branch of the government has approximately 2,868,588 loyal workers. The benefits are great, and the average full time salary (excluding postal workers) is $42,610. Not a bad day at the office. These jobs are not just located in Washington, DC, but throughout the U.S. and the world. This could be great way to see the country or live overseas while supporting yourself with a stable government job. Jobs in every profession are represented in the Federal government. There is even a listing later in the chapter of jobs by occupation available and the kind of college majors that may fit the bill. Roughly a third of all government employees have college degrees.

The government has made your task of finding employment a little easier. They have done away with the cumbersome Form SF-171. Now you can send your resume directly to many agencies. You can perform your personal job search by using your telephone, your personal computer, or by visiting a touch screen computer kiosk located in various locations nationwide. In addition, there are several automated systems available on the Federal Employment Information Superhighway which are noted below.

The Office of Personnel Management's (OPM) USA JOBS website at {www.usajobs.opm.gov} is the official jobsite of the Federal Government. It provides current worldwide federal job opportunities, salaries, employee benefits information, special recruitment messages, and much more. You can also record your request to have application packages, forms, and other related information sent to you by calling 703-724-1850. This service is available 24 hours a day, 7 days a week.

Keep in mind that your state government also hires workers. We have included addresses and email addresses (where available) to help you on your search.

U.S. Office of Personnel Management
Federal Employment Information Centers

Alabama
520 Wynn Dr., NW
Huntsville, AL 35818-3426
205-837-0894

Alaska
222 West 7th Ave., #22 Room 156
Anchorage, AK 99513-7522
907-271-5821
Outside Alaska: 912-757-3000

Arizona
(see New Mexico)

Arkansas
(see San Antonio, Texas)

California
9650 Flair Dr., Suite 100A
El Monte, CA 91731
818-575-6510

1029 J St., Room 202
Sacramento, CA 95814
416-744-5627

Federal Building, Room 4260
880 Front St.
San Diego, CA 92101
818-575-6510

120 Howard St., Suite B
P.O. Box 7405
San Francisco, CA 94120
415-744-5627

Colorado
12345 W. Alameda Parkway
P.O. Box 25167
Lakewood, CO 80225
303-969-7050

Connecticut
(see Boston, Massachusetts)

Delaware
(see Philadelphia, Pennsylvania)

District of Columbia
Theodore Roosevelt Federal Building
1900 E St., NW
Room 1416
Washington, DC 20415
202-606-2700

Florida
(see Georgia)

Georgia
Richard B. Russell Building
Room 940A
75 Spring St., SW
Atlanta, GA 30303
404-331-4315

Hawaii
Federal Building, Room 5316
300 Alamoana Blvd.
Honolulu, HI 96850
808-541-2791
Outside Hawaii: 912-757-3000

Idaho
(see Seattle, Washington)

Illinois
230 South Dearborn St., Room 2916
Chicago, IL 60804
312-353-6192
(for Madison and St. Clair counties, see St. Louis, MO)

Indiana
(for Clark, Dearborn and Floyd counties, see Ohio; all other counties, see Michigan)

Iowa
(for Scott County, see Illinois; all other counties, see Kansas City, Missouri)

Kentucky
(for Henderson County, see Michigan; for all other counties, see Ohio)

Louisiana
(see San Antonio, Texas)

Maine
(see Boston, Massachusetts)

Maryland
(see Philadelphia, Pennsylvania)

Massachusetts
10 Causeway St.
Boston, MA 02222
617-565-5900

Michigan
477 Michigan Ave.
Room 565
Detroit, MI 48226
313-226-6950

Minnesota
Bishop Henry Whipple Federal Building
1 Federal Dr., Room 501
Fort Snelling, MN 55111
612-725-3430

Mississippi
(see Alabama)

Missouri
Federal Building
Room 134
601 E. 12th St.
Kansas City, MO 64106
816-426-5702

400 Old Post Office Building
815 Olive St.
St. Louis, MO 63101
314-539-2285

Montana
(see Colorado)

Nebraska
(see Kansas City, Missouri)

Nevada
(for Clark, Lincoln, and Nye counties, see Los Angeles, California; all other counties see Sacramento, California)

New Hampshire
(see Boston, Massachusetts)

New Jersey
(see New York City, New York or Philadelphia, Pennsylvania)

New Mexico
505 Marquette Ave.
Suite 910
Albuquerque, NM 87102
505-766-5583

New York
Jacob K. Javits Building
30th Floor, Rooom 3036
26 Federal Plaza
New York City, NY 10278
212-264-0422.0423

James M. Hanley Federal Building
P.O. Box 7267
100 South Clinton St.
Syracuse, NY 13261
315-448-0480

North Carolina
4407 Bland Rd.
Suite 202
Raleigh, NC 27609
919-790-2822

North Dakota
(see Minnesota)

Ohio
Federal Building, Room 506
200 W. 2nd St.
Dayton, OH 45402
513-225-2720

Oklahoma
(see San Antonio, Texas)

Oregon
Federal Building, Room 376
1220 SW Third Ave.
Portland, OR 97204
503-326-3141

Pennsylvania
Federal Building, Room 168
P.O. Box 761
Harrisburg, PA 17108
717-782-4494

William J. Green, Jr. Federal Building
600 Arch St.
Philadelphia, PA 19106
215-597-7440

Federal Building
1000 Liberty Ave., Room 119
Pittsburgh, PA 15222
(see Philadelphia for telephone)

Puerto Rico
U.S. Federal Building, Room 328
150 Carlos Chardon Ave.
San Juan, PR 00918
809-766-5242

Rhode Island
(see Boston, Massachusetts)

South Carolina
(see Raleigh, North Carolina)

South Dakota
(see Minnesota)

Tennessee
(see Alabama)

Texas
(Corpus Christi: see San Antonio)
512-884-8113

Dallas
(see San Antonio)

Harlingen
(see San Antonio)
512-412-0722

Houston
(see San Antonio)
713-759-0455

8610 Broadway, Room 305
San Antonio, TX 78217
210-805-2402

Utah
(see Colorado)

Vermont
(see Boston, Massachusetts)

Virgin Islands
(see Puerto Rico)
809-774-8790

Virginia
For Mail Only:
Federal Building
Room 500
200 Granby St.
Norfolk, VA 23510
804-441-3355

For Walk-in Only:
Virginia Employment Commission
5145 E. Virginia Beach Blvd.
Norfolk, VA 23510

Washington
Federal Building
Room 110
915 Second Ave.
Seattle, WA 98174
206-220-6400

Washington, DC
(see District of Columbia)

West Virginia
(see Ohio)
513-225-2866

Wisconsin
(for Dane, Grant, Green, Iowa, Lafayette,
Jefferson, Walworth, Milwaukee, Racine,
Waukkesha, Rock and Kenosha, see Illinois
listing, 312-353-6189; for all other counties
see Minnesota, 612-725-3430)

Wyoming
(see Colorado)

"A study of lottery winners, comparing them with people not involved in lotteries, shows that the winners are not happier than the others now, nor do they expect to be in the future. In fact, the winners rated seven ordinary activities as less enjoyable now, such as talking with a friend, eating breakfast, getting a compliment reading a magazine, or buying clothes."

Source: *Ambition: How We Manage Success and Failure Throughout Our Lives*, Gilbert Brim, Basic Books, 1992

Government Job Information

Every department and bureau within the Federal government has their own personnel office that can tell you about specific employment opportunities. These job openings are also posted on the Career America Connection and the Internet. What follows is a complete listing of employment offices, as well as online information. If one department interests you more than another, you may contact them directly. A job could be waiting for you.

AMTRAK National Railroad Passenger Corporation
Office of Human Resources
900 Second St., NW
Washington, DC 20001
202-906-3287
877-268-7251 Job Line
202-906-3349 Fax
703-724-1850 USA JOBS
www.amtrak.com/about/careers.html

Central Intelligence Agency
Employment Center
P.O. Box 12727
Arlington, VA 22209-8727
703-482-1100
703-482-7814 Fax
703-724-1850 USA JOBS
www.cia.gov/employment/index.html

Commission on Civil Rights
Human Resources Division
624 Ninth St., NW
Washington, DC 20425
202-376-8364
202-376-7577 Fax
703-724-1850 USA JOBS
Email: vacancies@usccr.gov
www.usccr.gov/jobs/jobs.htm

Commodity Futures Trading Commission
Office of Human Resources
1155 21st St., NW
Washington, DC 20581
202-418-5003
202-418-5009 Job Line
202-418-5530 Fax
703-724-1850 USA JOBS
Email: employment@cftc.gov
www.cftc.gov/cftc/cftcjobs.htm

Consumer Product Safety Commission
Office of Human Resources
4330 East West Highway, Room 523
Bethesda, MD 20814-4408
310-504-7925
301-504-0432 Fax
703-724-1850 USA JOBS
Email: recruitapps@cpsc.gov
www.cpsc.gov/about/hr.html

Corporation for National Service
Human Resources
1201 New York Ave.
Washington, DC 20525
202-606-5000
800-942-2677 Job Line
202-565-2782 Fax
703-724-1850 USA JOBS

Email: jobs@cns.gov
www.nationalservice.org/jobs/index.html

U.S. Department of Agriculture (USDA)
Office of Human Resources Management
1400 Independence Ave., SW
Washington, DC 20250
202-720-3585
202-750-9148 Fax
703-724-1850 USA JOBS
www.usda.gov/da/employ.html

Agricultural Research Service (ARS)
U.S. Department of Agriculture
Employment Information Service
Recruitment Office
5601 Sunnyside Ave., Mail Stop 5144
Beltsville, MD 20705-5141
301-504-1709
301-504-1740 Fax
703-724-1850 USA JOBS
Email: lcollier@ars.usda.gov
www.ars.usda.gov/careers

Food, Nutrition and Consumer Service (FNCS)
U.S. Department of Agriculture
Mission Area Personnel Offices
3101 Park Center, Room 314
Alexandria, VA 22303
703-305-2326
703-305-1474 Job Line
703-305-2299 Fax
703-724-1850 USA JOBS

U.S. Department of Commerce
Office of Human Resources Management
1401 Constitution Ave., NW, Room 5001
Washington, DC 20230
202-482-4807
202-482-5138 Job Line
202-482-0249 Fax
202-482-1533 Flash Fax: 24 Hour Personnel Hotline
703-724-1850 USA JOBS
Email: dlewis@doc.gov
www.johrm.doc.gov

Bureau of the Census
U.S. Department of Commerce
Human Resources Division
4700 Silver Hill Road
Washington, DC 20233-0001
301-763-4748
301-457-4499 Job Line and Personnel
301-457-4714 Fax
703-724-1850 USA JOBS
Email: recruiter@census.gov
www.census.gov/hrd/www/index.html

Economic Development Administration
U.S. Department of Commerce
Office of Personnel
14th St. and Constitution, NW
Washington, DC 20230

202-482-5112
202-482-5138 Job Line
202-482-1533 Flash Fax: 24 Hour Personnel Hotline
703-724-1850 USA JOBS
http://12.39.209.165/xp/EDAPublic/Home/EDAHomePage.xml

International Trade Administration
U.S. Department of Commerce
Human Resources
Washington, DC 20230
202-482-3301
202-482-5138 Job Line
202-482-5133 Flash Fax: 24 Hour Personnel Hotline
703-724-1850 USA JOBS
Email: Melanie_Hazlett@ita.doc.gov
www.ita.doc.gov/jobs

National Oceanic and Atmospheric Administration (NOAA)
U.S. Department of Commerce
Human Resources Central Division
1305 East West Highway
Silver Spring, MD 20910
301-713-0534
301-713-0677 Job Line
301-713-2083 Fax
703-724-1850 USA JOBS
www.noaa.gov/jobs.html

National Institute of Standards and Technology
U.S. Department of Commerce
Office of Human Resources Management
100 Bureau Drive, Bldg. 101
Gaithersburg, MD 20899
301-975-6478
301-926-4851 Personnel/Job Line
703-724-1850 USA JOBS
www.nist.gov/public_affairs/employment.htm

Technology Administration
U.S. Department of Commerce
1401 Constitution Ave., NW
Washington, DC 20230
301-926-4851 Personnel/Job Line
703-724-1850 USA JOBS
Email: info@ta.doc.gov

National Technical Information Service
5285 Port Royal Rd.
Springfield, VA 22161
301-926-4851 Personnel/Job Line
703-724-1850 USA JOBS
www.ntis.gov

Patent and Trademark Office
U.S. Department of Commerce
Office of Human Resources
2011 Crystal Dr.
Arlington, VA 22202
703-305-8231
703-305-9864 Fax
703-724-1850 USA JOBS
Email: usptoinfo@uspto.gov
www.uspto.gov/web/offices/ac/ahrpa/ohr

Western Regional Center
NOAA Human Resources Division
U.S. Department of Commerce
7600 Sands Point Way NE
Seattle, WA 98101
206-526-6294 Job Line
703-724-1850 USA JOBS
www.wrh.noss.gov

U.S. Department of Defense
The Pentagon
Washington, DC 20350
703-617-7174
703-724-1850 USA JOBS
www.defenselink.mil

Defense Threat Reduction Agency
U.S. Department of Defense
6801 Telegraph Rd.

Alexandria, VA 22310
703-767-0311
703-617-0765 Fax
703-724-1850 USA JOBS
Email: RM@dtra.mil
www.dtra.mil/jb/jb_index.html

U.S. Department of the Air Force
Recruitment Service Center
550 C Street West, Suite 57
Randolph AFB, TX 78150
210-527-2377
800-699-4473 job Line
Email: recruitment.center@randolph.af.mil
http://ss2.afpc.randolph.af.mil/resweb

U.S. Department of the Army
Civilian Personnel
The Pentagon
Washington, DC 20310
703-695-3881
http://cpol.army.mil

U.S. Department of the Navy
Civilian Personnel
The Pentagon
Washington, DC 20350-1000
703-697-7391
www.dohhr.navy.mil/default.asp

National Security Agency
Civilian Employment Office
Attention M3212
9800 Savage Road
Fort Meade, MD 20755
301-688-6311
www.nsa.gov/programs/employ/index.html

U.S. Marine Corps
Headquarters
Civilian Human Resources Office
3280 Russell Road
Quantico, VA 22134-5103
703-784-9375
703-784-9815 Fax
703-724-1850 USA JOBS
https://Inweb1.manpower.usmc.mil/CCLD/index.htm

U.S. Department of Education
Office of Human Resources Services
400 Maryland Ave., SW
Washington, DC 20202
202-401-3618
202-401-0520 Fax
703-724-1850 USA JOBS
www.ed.gov/offices/OM/edjobs.html

Gallaudet University
Personnel Office
800 Florida Ave., NE
Washington, DC 20002
202-651-5352
202-651-5358 Job Line
202-651-5344 Fax
www.gallaudet.edu/po/personnel.html

Howard University
U.S. Department of Employment
400 Bryant St., NW
Washington, DC 20059
202-806-7714
202-806-7711 Job Line
202-806-5304 TTY
www.hr.howard.edu/employment

U.S. Department of Energy
Office of Human Resources Management
1000 Independence Ave., SW
Washington, DC 20585
202-586-4171
703-724-1850 USA JOBS
www.ma.mbe.doe.gov/pers/

U.S. Department of Energy
National Nuclear Security Administration
P.O. Box 5400
Albuquerque, NM 87185-5400
505-845-5651
703-724-1850 USA JOBS
www.doeal.gov/hrd/jobinfo/menu.htm

Federal Energy Regulatory Commission (FERC)
Human Resources Department
888 First St., NE
Washington, DC 20426
202-502-8990
202-502-6157 TTY
703-724-1850 USA JOBS
Email: work@ferc.gov
www.ferc.gov/about/employment.asp

U.S. Department of Health and Human Services

Division of Personnel Operations
Mary Switzer Bldg., Room 1100
330 C Street, SW
Washington, DC 20201
202-619-1869
202-619-0488 Fax
703-724-1850 USA JOBS
www.hhs.gov/jobs/index.html

U.S. Department of Health and Human Services
Centers for Medicare and Medicaid Services
U.S. Department of Health and Human Services
C2-09-27 Central Building
7500 Security Blvd.
Baltimore, MD 21224-1850
410-786-5489
410-786-9580 Fax
703-724-1850 USA JOBS
http://cms.hhs.gov/careers

Centers for Disease Control (CDC)
U.S. Department of Health and Human Services
Human Resource Management Office
4770 Buford Highway, MS K16
Atlanta, GA 30341-3724
770-488-1735
770-488-1945 Fax
770-488-1821 TDD
888-CDC-HIRE Job Line
703-724-1850 USA JOBS
www.cdc.gov/train.html

Food and Drug Administration
U.S. Department of Health and Human Services
Office of Human Resources Management
5600 Fishers Lane
Rockville, MD 20857
301-827-4120
301-443-6684 Fax
301-443-1969 Job Line
703-724-1850 USA JOBS
www.fda.gov/jobs/default.htm

Indian Health Service
U.S. Department of Health and Human Services
Office of Personnel
Room 4B-44, Parklawn Building
5600 Fishers Lane
Rockville, MD 20857
301-443-6520
301-594-3146 Fax
703-724-1850 USA JOBS
www.his.gov/JobsCareerDevelop/Jobs_index.asp

National Institutes of Health
U.S. Department of Health and Human Services
Division of Human Resources
Building 1, Room B1-60
9000 Rockville Pike
Bethesda, MD 20892
301-496-3592
301-402-0345 Fax
301-496-2403 Job Line
703-724-1850 USA JOBS

Email: careers@box-c.nih.gov
www.jobs.nih.gov

Substance Abuse and Mental Health Services Administration
U.S. Department of Health and Human Services
Personnel Management
5600 Fishers Lane
Rockville, Md 20857
301-443-5407
301-443-2282 Job Line
703-724-1850 USA JOBS
Email: info@samhsa.gov
www.samhsa.gov/jobs/jobs.html

Health Resources and Service Administration
U.S. Department of Health and Human Services
Office of Human Resources and Development
5600 Fishers Lane, Room 14A46
Rockville, MD 20857
301-443-5460
301-443-2682 Fax
301-443-3143 TDD
301-443-1230 Job Line
703-724-1850 USA JOBS
www.hrsa.gov/jobs/jobs.htm

U.S. Department of Homeland Security

Human Resources Office
Washington, DC 20528
703-724-1850 USA JOBS
www.dhs.gov/dhspublic/display?theme=40

Animal and Plant Health Inspection Service
U.S. Department of Homeland Security
Office of Human Resources
4700 River Road
Riverdale, MD
301-734-8428
301-734-4984 Fax
703-724-1850 USA JOBS
www.aphis.usda.gov/mb/mrphr

Bureau of Citizenship and Immigration Services
Office of Personnel
425 I St., NW
Room 2038
Washington, DC 20536
202-514-4316
202-514-4301 Job Line
703-724-1850 USA JOBS
www.immigration.gov

Customs and Border Protection
U.S. Department of Homeland Security
Office of Human Resources Management
1300 Pennsylvania Avenue, NW
Washington, DC 20229
202-354-1000
202-927-3955 Recruitment Hotline
703-724-1850 USA JOBS
www.customs.gov/xp/cgov/careers

Federal Emergency Management Agency (FEMA)
U.S. Department of Homeland Security
Office of Human Resources
500 C St. SW
Washington, DC 20472
202-646-4040
202-646-3244 Job Line
202-646-4349 Fax
703-724-1850 USA JOBS
www.fema.gov/career/index.jsp

Federal Law Enforcement Center
Human Resources Division
Glynco, GA 31524
912-267-2287 Job Line
912-267-2289
912-280-5101 Fax
703-724-1850 USA JOBS
Email: jobinfo@fletc.treas.gov
www.fletc.gov/recruit1.htm

Transportation Security Administration
U.S. Department of Homeland Security
Department of Human Resources
400 Seventh Street, SW
Washington, DC 20590
800-887-1895 Job Line
800-887-5506 TDD
703-724-1850 USA JOBS
www.tsa.gov/public/display?theme=2

U.S. Department of Housing and Urban Development (HUD)

Office of Human Resources
451 Seventh St., SW
Washington, DC 20410
202-708-2000
703-724-1850 USA JOBS
www.hud.gov/jobs/index.cfm

U.S. Department of the Interior

Office of Human Resources and Workforce Diversity
1849 C St., NW
Washington, DC 20240
202-208-6943
800-336-4562 Job Line
202-219-2184 Fax
703-724-1850 USA JOBS
Email: ppm@ios.doi.gov
www.doi.gov/hrm/doijobs.html

Bureau of Indian Affairs
U.S. Department of Interior
Office of Personnel
1951 Constitution Ave., NW
Washington, DC 20245
202-208-7581
703-724-1850 USA JOBS
www.doi.gov/bureau_indian_affairs.html

Bureau of Land Management
U.S. Department of the Interior
National Human Resources Management Center
Denver Federal Center
Building 50
P.O. Box 25047
Denver, CO 80225-0047
303-236-6503
303-236-6685 Fax
703-724-1850 USA JOBS
www.blm.gov

Bureau of Reclamation
U.S. Department of the Interior
Office of Human Resources
Denver Federal Center
Building 67
Attn: D-4320
Denver, CO 80225
303-445-2684
800-336-4562 Job Line
703-724-1850 USA JOBS
www.usbr.gov/pmts/hr

Minerals Management Service
U.S. Department of the Interior
Office of Personnel
1849 C Street, NW
Washington, DC 20240
202-208-3512
703-724-1850 USA JOBS
www.mms.gov/occ/jobopp.html

Fish and Wildlife Service
U.S. Department of the Interior
Division of Human Resources
4401 N. Fairfax Dr., Room 110
Mail Stop 2000
Arlington, VA 22203
703-358-1743
703-724-1850 USA JOBS
http://hr.fws.gov

Geological Survey Headquarters
U.S. Department of the Interior
12201 Sunrise Valley
Reston, VA 20192
703-648-7442
703-724-1850 USA JOBS
www.usgs.gov/ohr

National Park Service
U.S. Department of the Interior
1849 C St., NW
Washington, DC 20240
202-354-1996
703-724-1850 USA JOBS
Email: NPSjobfairs@nps.gov
www.nps.gov/personnel

U.S. Department of Justice

Office of Attorney Recruitment and Management
20 Massachusetts Ave., NW, Suite 5200
Washington, DC 20530-0001
202-514-3397
202-514-3396 Job Line
202-616-2113 TDD
703-724-1850 USA JOBS
Email: ASKDOJ@usdoj.gov
www.usdoj.gov/oarm

Bureau of Alcohol, Tobacco, Firearms and Explosives
U.S. Department of Justice
Personnel Division
650 Massachusetts Ave., NW, Room 4100
Washington, DC 20226
202-927-8610
202-927-8649 Fax
703-724-1850 USA JOBS
www.atf.gov/jobs/index.htm

Bureau of Prisons
U.S. Department of Justice
Human Resource Management Division
320 First St., NW
Washington, DC 20534
202-307-2886
800-347-7744 Job Line
703-724-1850 USA JOBS
Email: BOP-HRM/Recruitment@bop.gov
www.bop.gov

Drug Enforcement Administration (DEA)
U.S. Department of Justice
Office of Personnel
2401 Jefferson Davis Highway
Alexandria, VA 22301
202-307-4177
800-DEA-4288 Job Line
703-724-1850 USA JOBS
www.usdoj.gov/dea/resources/job_applicants.htm

Federal Bureau of Investigation (FBI)
U.S. Department of Justice
Office of Personnel
935 Pennsylvania Ave., NW
Washington, DC 20535-0001
202-324-3674 Job Line
703-724-1850 USA JOBS
http://fbijobs.com

United States Marshal Service
U.S. Department of Justice
Human Resources Division
950 Pennsylvania Ave. NW
Washington, DC 20001
202-307-9625
202-307-9600 Personnel/Job Line
703-724-1850 USA JOBS
Email: usmarshals@usdoj.gov
www.usdoj.gov/marshals

U.S. Department of Labor

Office of Human Resources
200 Constitution Ave., NW, Room C5516

Washington, DC 20210
202-693-7690
202-693-3046 Job Line
703-724-1850 USA JOBS
www.dol.gov/oasam/dol/jobs.htm

U.S. Department of State

(Employment in the Foreign Service)
HR/DE
2201 C Street, NW
Washington, DC 20520
202-261-8133
202-261-8888 Job Line
703-724-1850 USA JOBS
www.state.gov/employment

U.S. Department of State
(Civil Service Positions)
HR/CSP
2201 C Street, NW
Washington, DC 20520
202-663-2128
202-647-7284 Job Line
703-724-1850 USA JOBS
www.state.gov/employment

U.S. Department of Transportation (DOT)

Departmental Office of Human Resource Management
400 Seventh St., SW, Room 7411
Washington, DC 20590
202-366-4088
202-366-6806 Fax
703-724-1850 USA JOBS
Email: hr@ost.dot.gov
http://dothr.ost.dot.gov/index.html

Federal Aviation Administration (FAA)
U.S. Department of Transportation (DOT)
Human Resources Department
800 Independence Ave., SW
Washington, DC 20591
202-267-8008
202-267-8007 Job Line
800-525-2878 DOT Job Line/Fax on Demand
202-267-8330 Fax
703-724-1850 USA JOBS
http://jobs.faa.gov

Federal Highway Administration (FHWA)
U.S. Department of Transportation (DOT)
Office of Human Resources
HAHR-22, Room 4334
400 Seventh St., SW
Washington, DC 20590
202-366-0541
800-525-2878 DOT Job Line/Fax on Demand
202-366-3749 Fax
703-724-1850 USA JOBS
Email: vacancy.system@fhwa.dot.gov
www.fhwa.dot.gov/vacancy/index.htm

Federal Railroad Administration (FRA)
U.S. Department of Transportation (DOT)
Office of Human Resources
1120 Vermont Ave., NW
Washington, DC 20590
202-493-6112
202-493-6169 Fax
202-366-0584 Job Line
800-525-2878 DOT Connection
703-724-1850 USA JOBS
www.fra.dot.gov/hr/index.htm

Federal Transit Administration (FTA)
U.S. Department of Transportation (DOT)
Office of Human Resources
400 Seventh St., SW
Washington, DC 20590
202-366-2513
202-366-2450 Job Line
800-525-2878 DOT Job Line/Fax on Demand
202-366-7890 Fax
703-724-1850 USA JOBS

Email: ftajobs@fta.dot.gov
www.fta.dot.gov/library/admin/jobs/ftajobs.html

Maritime Administration (MARAD)
U.S. Department of Transportation (DOT)
Office of Human Resources
400 Seventh St., SW
Washington, DC 20590
202-366-4141
202-366-9391 Job Line
800-525-2878 DOT Job Line/Fax on Demand
202-366-3791 Fax
703-724-1850 USA JOBS
www.marad.dot.gov/acareerafloat/index.htm

National Highway Traffic Safety Administration (NHTSA)
U.S. Department of Transportation (DOT)
Office of Human Resources
400 Seventh St., SW
Washington, DC 20590
202-366-1784
202-366-9391 Job Line
800-525-2878 DOT Job Line/Fax on Demand
202-366-7402 Fax
703-724-1850 USA JOBS
www.nhtsa.dot.gov

United States Coast Guard (USCG)
U.S. Department of Transportation (DOT)
Office of Personnel
2100 Second St., SW
Washington, DC 20593-0001
202-267-4756
202-267-1803 Fax
202-366-9397 Job Line
800-525-2878 DOT Job Line/Fax on Demand
703-724-1850 USA JOBS
www.gocoastguard.com

U.S. Department of the Treasury

Office of Human Resources
1500 Pennsylvania Ave., NW
Washington, DC 20220
202-622-2000
202-622-1029 Job Line
202-622-6415 Fax
703-724-1850 USA JOBS
Email: dashr@do.treas.gov
www.ustreas.gov/offices/management/hr

Internal Revenue Service
Office of Personnel
1111 Constitution Ave., NW
Washington, DC 20224
202-622-5000
703-724-1850 USA JOBS
www.jobs.irs.gov

United States Custom Service
U.S. Department of the Treasury
Office of Human Resources Management
1300 Pennsylvania Ave., NW
Washington, DC 20229
202-634-2534
800-944-7725 Job Line
202-634-5613 Fax
703-724-1850 USA JOBS
www.customs.ustreas.gov/xp/cgov/careers

United States Secret Service
Personnel Division
950 H Street, NW
Washington, DC 20223
202-406-5800
202-406-5613 Fax
703-724-1850 USA JOBS
www.ustreas.gov/usss/opportunities.shtml

U.S. Department of Veterans Affairs

Office of Human Resources
810 Vermont Ave., NW
Washington, DC 20420

202-273-4950
202-273-6798 Fax
703-724-1850 USA JOBS
www.va.gov/jobs

Environmental Protection Agency

Office of Human Resources
1200 Pennsylvania Ave., NW
Washington, DC 20460
202-272-0167
703-724-1850 USA JOBS
Email: EZHire@EPA.gov
www.epa.gov/epahome/jobs.htm

Equal Employment Opportunity Commission

Human Resource Management Services
1801 L St., NW
Washington, DC 20507
202-663-4601
202-663-4324 Fax
703-724-1850 USA JOBS
Email: jobs@ecoc.gov
www.ecoc.gov/soars/index.html

Executive Office of the President

Personnel Division
Office of Administration
Washington, DC 20500
202-395-5892 Job Line
703-724-1850 USA JOBS
www.whitehouse.gov/oa

Export-Import Bank

Office of Human Resources
811 Vermont Ave., NW
Washington, DC 20571
202-565-3946
202-565-3946 Job Line
202-565-3627 Fax
703-724-1850 USA JOBS
Email: jobapps@exim.gov
www.exim.gov/about/jobs/jobs.html

Farm Credit Administration

Office of Human Resources
1501 Farm Credit Dr.
McLean, VA 22102-5090
703-883-4135
703-883-4139 Job Line
703-724-1850 USA JOBS
Email: info-line@fca.gov
www.fca.gov/careersatfca.htm

Federal Communications Commission

Human Resources Management
445 12th Street, NW
Washington, DC 20554
202-418-0130
202-418-0101 Job Line
202-418-2830 Fax on Demand
703-724-1850 USA JOBS
Email: fccinfo@fcc.gov
www.fcc.gov/jobs

Federal Deposit Insurance Corporation

Office of Human Resources
1730 Pennsylvania Ave., NW
Washington, DC 20006
202-942-3311
202-942-3540 Job Line
202-942-3532 Fax
703-724-1850 USA JOBS
Email: careers@fdic.gov
www.fdic.gov/about/jobs/index.html

Federal Election Commission

Office of Personnel
999 E St. NW
Washington, DC 20463
202-694-1100
800-424-9530
202-219-3336 TTY
703-724-1850 USA JOBS
Email: fecjobs@fec.gov
www.fec.gov/jobs.htm

Federal Housing Finance Board

Human Resources Division
1777 F St. NW
Washington, DC 20006-5210
202-408-2500
202-408-2808 Job Line
703-724-1850 USA JOBS
Email: jobs@fhfb.gov
www.fhfb.gov/CareerOps/Jobs.htm

Federal Labor Relations Authority

Human Resources Division
607 14th St. NW, Suite 430
Washington, DC 20424
202-482-6660
877-303-8945
202-482-6659 Fax
202-482-6537 Job Line
703-724-1850 USA JOBS
www.flra.gov/29-jobs.html

Federal Maritime Commission

Office of Human Resources
800 North Capitol St., NW
Washington, DC 20573-0001
202-523-5773 Job Line/Personnel
202-523-7842 Fax
703-724-1850 USA JOBS
Email: hatsiec@fmc.gov
www.fmc.gov/jobs/jobs/htm

Federal Reserve System

Division of Human Resource Management
20th and C St. NW
Washington, DC 20551
202-452-3880
800-448-4894 Job Line
202-452-3863 Fax
202-872-4984 TDD
703-724-1850 USA JOBS
www.federalreserve.gov/careers/default.cfm

Federal Retirement Thrift Investment Board

Office of Personnel
1250 H St., NW
Washington, DC 20005
202-942-1682
202-942-1674 Fax
202-942-1687 Job Line
703-724-1850 USA JOBS
www.frtib.gov/personnel/index.html

Federal Trade Commission

Human Resources Management Office
600 Pennsylvania Ave., NW
Washington, DC 20580
202-326-2021
202-326-2020 Job Line
202-326-2543 Fax
703-724-1850 USA JOBS
Email: HRMOEmployment@ftc.gov
www.ftc.gov

General Accounting Office
Human Capital Office
441 G St., NW
Washington, DC 20548
202-512-3299
202-512-6092 Job Line
703-724-1850 USA JOBS
Email: recruit@gao.gov
www.gao.gov

General Services Administration
Office of Human Resources
1800 F St., NW
Washington, DC 20405
202-501-0370
202-501-0141 Fax
703-724-1850 USA JOBS
Email: GSAjobs@gsa.gov
www.gsa.gov

Library of Congress
Human Resources Employment Office
101 Independence Ave., SE
Washington, DC 20540
202-707-4315 Personnel/Job Line
703-724-1850 USA JOBS
www.loc.gov/hr/employment

Merit Systems Protection Board
Human Resources Division
1615 M Street, NW
Washington, DC 20419
202-653-6772, ext. 1207
202-254-8013 Job Line
202-653-7130 Fax
703-724-1850 USA JOBS
Email: mspb@mspb.gov
www.mspb.gov/business/humanresource.html

National Aeronautics and Space Administration (NASA)
Office of Human Resources
Washington, DC 20546
202-358-1560
301-286-5326 Job Line
202-358-3047 Fax
703-724-1850 USA JOBS
www.nasajobs.nasa.gov

National Archives and Records Administration
Office of Human Resources
8601 Adelphi Rd., Room 1200
College Park, MD 20740-6001
301-713-6760
800-827-4898 Job Line
301-713-7272 Fax
703-724-1850 USA JOBS
www.archives.gov/careers/index.html

National Credit Union Administration
Office of Human Resources
1775 Duke St.
Alexandria, VA 22314-3428
703-518-6510
703-518-6539 Fax
703-724-1850 USA JOBS
Email: ohrmail@ncua.gov
www.ncua.gov/news/vacancies/vacancies.html

National Endowment for the Arts
Office of Human Resources
1100 Pennsylvania Ave., NW
Washington, DC 20506
202-682-5405
202-682-5666 Fax
703-724-1850 USA JOBS
Email: jobapplications@arts.endow.gov
www.arts.gov/learn/Jobs/JobsMenu.html

National Endowment for the Humanities
Office of Human Resources
1100 Pennsylvania Ave., NW
Washington, DC 20506
202-606-8415
202-606-8281 Job Line
703-724-1850 USA JOBS
Email: humanresources@neh.gov
www.neh.fed.us/whoweare/jobs.html

National Gallery of Art
Office of Personnel
2000B South Club Drive
Landover, MD 20785
202-842-6282
202-842-6298 Job Line
202-789-3011 Fax
703-724-1850 USA JOBS
Email: staffing@nga.gov
www.nga.gov/resources/employ.htm

National Labor Relations Board
Human Resources Branch
1099 14th St., NW
Washington, DC 20570
202-273-3980
202-273-2921 Fax
703-724-1850 USA JOBS
www.nlrb.gov/jobs/jobs.html

National Mediation Board
Office of Human Resources
1301 K St., NW, Suite 250 East
Washington, DC 20005-7011
202-692-5000
703-724-1850 USA JOBS
www.nmb.gov/index.html

National Science Foundation
Division of Human Resource Management
4201 Wilson Blvd., Suite 315N
Arlington, VA 22230
703-292-8180
703-306-0080 Job Line
703-292-9184 Fax
703-724-1850 USA JOBS
www.nsf.gov/oirm/hrm/jobs/start.htm

National Transportation Safety Board
Human Resources Division
490 L'Enfant Plaza, SW
Washington, DC 20594
202-314-6232
800-573-0937 Job Line
202-314-6260 Fax
703-724-1850 USA JOBS
www.ntsb.gov/vacancies/listing.htm

Nuclear Regulatory Commission
Office of Human Resources
Washington, DC 20555
301-415-1534/7400
301-415-3818 Fax
703-724-1850 USA JOBS
www.nrc.gov/who-we-are/employment.html

Office of Personnel Management
1900 E St., NW
Washington, DC 20415-0001

202-606-2400
202-606-2329 Fax
703-724-1850 USA JOBS
www.opm.gov

Peace Corps
Office of Human Resource Management
1111 20th Street, NW, Room 2300
Washington, DC 20526
800-424-8580 Recruiting/Job Line
202-692-1200 Fax
703-724-1850 USA JOBS
www.peacecorps.gov/employment/index.cfm

Securities and Exchange Commission
Office of Administrative and Personnel Management
450 Fifth St., NW
Washington, DC 20549
202-942-4000
202-942-4150 Job Line
202-942-9630 Fax
703-724-1850 USA JOBS
Email: recruit@sec.gov
www.sec.gov/jobs.shtml

Small Business Administration
Office of Human Resources
409 Third St., SW, Suite 4200
Washington, DC 20416
202-205-6190
202-205-6172 Fax
703-724-1850 USA JOBS
Email: OHR@sba.gov
www.sba.gov/aboutsba/indexjobs.html

Smithsonian Institution
Office of Human Resources
750 9th Street, NW, Suite 6100
Washington, DC 20560
202-275-1102
202-387-3102 Job Line
202-275-1110 TDD
703-724-1850 USA JOBS
www.si.edu.ohr

Social Security Administration
Office of Personnel
6401 Security Blvd.
Baltimore, MD 21235

410-965-4506
703-724-1850 USA JOBS
www.ssa.gov/careers/index.htm

Trade and Development Agency
1000 Wilson Boulevard, Suite 1600
Arlington, VA 22209
703-875-4357
703-875-4009 Fax
703-724-1850 USA JOBS
Email: info@tda.gov
www.tda.gov/abouttda/jobs.html

United States Agency for International Development
Recruitment Unit
M/HR/POD/SP, 2.08, RRB
Washington, DC 20523-2808
202-712-0665
202-619-0909 Job Line
202-216-3418 Fax
www.usaid.gov/careers

United States International Trade Commission
Office of Human Resources
500 E St., SW
Washington, DC 20436
202-205-2651
202-205-2008 Fax
703-724-1850 USA JOBS
Email: jdouglas@usitc.gov
www.usitc.gov/jobs.htm

U.S. Postal Service
Office of Personnel
475 L'Enfant Plaza, SW
Washington, DC 20260-0010
202-268-3646
800-JOB-USPS Job Line
703-724-1850 USA JOBS
www.usps.com/employment

Voice of America
Office of Personnel
330 Independence Ave., SW
Washington, DC 20237
202-619-0909 Job Line
703-724-1850 USA JOBS
www.voa.gov/vacancies/personnel.html

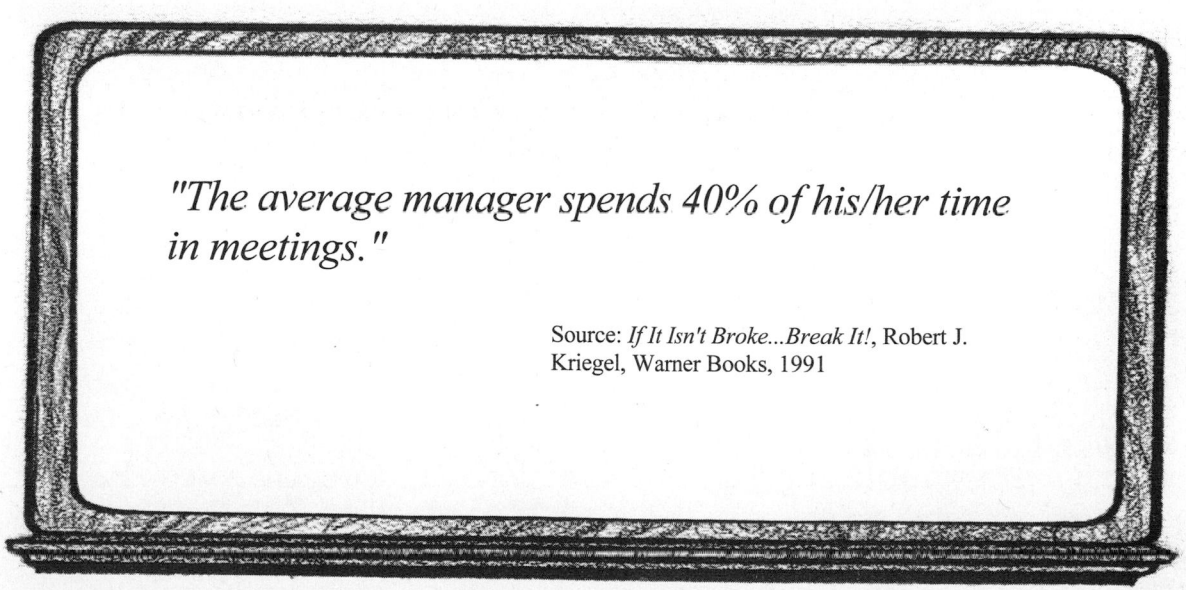

"The average manager spends 40% of his/her time in meetings."

Source: *If It Isn't Broke...Break It!*, Robert J. Kriegel, Warner Books, 1991

Federal Jobs by College Major

To help you choose the right career field, we have prepared the following table that groups federal jobs that are often filled by college graduates with appropriate academic majors. As you study the table, please keep these facts in mind: 1) The jobs listed under each major are usually **examples**, not an all-inclusive list. 2) Many jobs **do not require** a college degree; job-related experience is just as good. And 3), you can qualify for a large number of administrative jobs with a degree in **any academic major**. To illustrate this third point, we are leading off the table with a list of some of the most popular jobs for which **any major** is qualified.

Any Major
Environmental Protection
Civil Rights Analyst
Personnel Occupations
Administrative Officer
Management Analyst
Logistics Management
Paralegal Specialist
Contact Representative
Claims Examining
Public Affairs
Writing and Editing
Internal Revenue Officer
Contract Administration
General Investigator
Air Traffic Controller
Supply Management

Accounting
Accountants
Auditors
Contract Specialists
Financial Managers
Financial Administrators
Financial Institution Examiners
Intelligence Specialists
Internal Revenue Agents
GAO Evaluators

Agriculture
Soil Conservationists
Agricultural Commodity Graders
Agricultural Engineers
Agricultural Management Specialists
Agricultural Program Specialists
Agricultural Market Reporters
Agricultural Marketing Specialists
Foreign Agriculture Affairs Specialists
Soil Scientists

Agronomy
Agronomists
Agricultural Management Specialists
Soil Conservationists
Soil Scientists

Anthropology
Anthropologists
Museum Curators
Museum Specialists
Program Analysts
Management Analysts

Archaeology
Archaeologists
Museum Curators
Museum Specialists

Architecture
Architects

Construction Analysts
Construction Control Inspectors
Landscape Architects
Naval Architects
Program Analysts

Arts, Fine and Applied
Arts Specialists
Audio-Visual Production Specialists
Recreation and Creative Arts Therapists
Exhibits Specialists
General Arts and Information Specialists
Illustrators
Photographers
Visual Information Specialists

Astronomy
Astronomers and Space Scientists
Geodesists

Aviation
Air Safety Investigators
Air Traffic Controllers
Aircraft Operators
Aviation Safety Inspectors
Air Navigators
Aircrew Technicians

Biology
General Biological Scientists
Entomologists
Fishery Biologists
Microbiologists
Range Conservationists
Wildlife Biologists
Zoologists
GAO Evaluator

Botany
Agronomists
Botanists
Forestry Technicians
Geneticists
Horticulturists
Plant Pathologists
Plant Physiologists
Plant Protection and Quarantine Specialists
Range Conservationists

Business
Budget Analysts
Business and Industry Specialists
Commissary Store Managers
Import Specialists
Internal Revenue Officers
Miscellaneous Administrative and Programs Specialists
Quality Assurance Specialists
Trade Specialists

Contract Specialists
GAO Evaluators

Cartography
Cartographers
Cartographic Technicians
Geodetic Technicians

Chemistry
Chemical Engineers
Chemists
Consumer Safety Officers
Environmental Engineers
Food Technologists
Health Physicists
Intelligence Specialists
Toxicologists
GAO Evaluators

Communications
Telecommunications Managers
Communications Specialists
Public Affairs Specialists
Technical Writers and Editors
Writers and Editors

Computer Science
Computer Science Specialists
Computer Specialists
Program Managers
Management Analysts
Computer Programmers

Corrections
Correctional Institution Administrators
Correctional Officers
Program Analysts

Counseling
Chaplains
Education and Vocational Training Specialists
Personnel Specialists
Psychologists
Psychology Aids and Technicians
Social Service Aids and Assistants
Social Service Representatives
Vocational Rehab Specialists
Equal Opportunity Compliance Specialists
Educational Services Specialists

Criminal Justice/Law Enforcement
Border Patrol Agents
Criminal Investigators
Game Law Enforcement Agents
Internal Revenue Officers
Police Officers
United States Marshals
GAO Evaluators

Dietetics and Nutrition
Dietitians
Food Technologists
Nutritionists

Economics
Actuaries
Budget Analysts
Contract Specialists
Economists
Financial Analysts
Financial Institution Examiners
Loan Specialists
Trade Specialists
Transportation Industrial Analysts
GAO Evaluators

Education
Education and Training Specialists
Education and Vocational Training Specialists
Vocational Rehabilitation Specialists
Educational Program Specialists
Employee Development Specialists
Public Health Educators
Training Instructors
Instructional Systems Specialists
Educational Services Specialists

Electronics Technology
Communications Specialists
Electronics Technicians
Patent Examiners
Electronics Mechanics

Employee/Labor Relations
Contractor Industrial Relations Specialists
Employee Relations Specialists
Hearing and Appeals Specialists
Labor Management Relations Examiners
Labor Relations Specialists
Mediators
Salary and Wage Administrators
Workers Compensation Claims Examiners

Engineering (Any Specialty)
General Engineers
Civil Engineers
Mechanical Engineers
Electrical Engineers
Electronics Engineers
Aerospace Engineers
Industrial Engineers
Nuclear Engineers
Computer Engineers
Biomedical Engineers
(11 other Engineering fields)

English and Literature
Editorial Assistants
Printing Specialists
Public Affairs Specialists
Technical Writers and Editors
Writers and Editors
Miscellaneous Administrative and Programs Specialists
Program Analysts
Program Managers
Management Analysts

Environmental Studies
Ecologists
Environmental Health Technicians
Environmental Protection Assistants
Environmental Protection Specialists
General Fish and Wildlife Administrators
Fish and Wildlife Refuge Management
Miscellaneous Administrative and Programs Specialists
Toxicologists
GAO Evaluators

Epidemiology
Environmental Health Technicians
General Health Scientists
Industrial Hygienists
Microbiologists

Finance
Appraisers and Assessors
Budget Analysts
Financial Administrators
Financial Analysts
Financial Institution Examiners
Securities Compliance Examiners
Tax Examiners
Trade Specialists

Fish, Game, and Wildlife Management
General Fish and Wildlife Administrators
Fish and Wildlife Refuge Management
Fishery Biologists
Game Law Enforcement Agents
Soil Conservationists
Wildlife Biologists
Wildlife Rescue Managers
General Biological Scientists

Food Technology and Safety
Consumer Safety Inspectors
Consumer Safety Officers
Dietitians and Nutritionists
Food Assistance Program Specialists
Food Technologists
Toxicologists

Foreign Language
Air Safety Investigators
Border Patrol Agents
Customs Inspectors
Language Specialists
Equal Employment Opportunity Specialists
Foreign Affairs Specialists
Foreign Agricultural Affairs Specialists
Intelligence Specialists

Forestry
Foresters
Soil Conservationists
Management Analysts
Program Analysts
General Fish and Wildlife Administrators
Fish and Wildlife Refuge Management

Geography
Cartographers
Geographers

Geology
Geodesists
Geologists
Hydrologists
Oceanographers
General Physical Scientists

Geophysics
Geophysicists
General Physical Scientists

Health
Environmental Health Technicians
General Health Scientists
Health Physicists
Health System Administrators
Health System Specialists
Industrial Hygienists
Public Health Programs Specialists
Safety and Occupational Health Management Specialists

History
Archives Technicians

Archivists
Exhibits Specialists
Historians
Intelligence Specialists
Museum Curators
Miscellaneous Administrative and Programs Specialists
Management Analysts
Program Analysts

Home Economics
Consumer Safety Officers
Food Technologists

Horticulture
Agricultural Management Specialists
General Biological Scientists
Horticulturists
Plant Protection and Quarantine Specialists
Plant Physiologists

Hospital Administration
Administrative Officers
Health System Administrators
Health System Specialists
Hospital Housekeepers
General Health Scientists
Public Health Programs Specialists
Miscellaneous Administrative and Programs Specialists

Human Resource Management
Apprenticeship and Training Representatives
Employee Development Specialists
Equal Employment Opportunity Specialists
Military Personnel Management Specialists
Personnel Management Specialists
Personnel Staffing Specialists
Position Classification Specialists

Hydrology
Environmental Engineers
Environmental Protection Specialists
Hydrologists
General Fish and Wildlife Administrators
Fish and Wildlife Refuge Management
Program Analysts

Industrial Management
Business and Industrial Specialists
Equipment Specialists
Industrial Hygienists
Industrial Property Managers
Industrial Specialists
Management Analysts
Production Controllers
Program Analysts
Property Disposal Specialists
Quality Assurance Specialists

Insurance
Crop Insurance Administrators
Social Insurance Administration
Social Insurance Claims Examiners
Unemployment Insurance Specialists
Miscellaneous Administrative and Programs Specialists
Program Analysts

International Relations
Foreign Affairs Specialists
Foreign Agricultural Affairs Specialists
Intelligence Specialists
Language Specialists
Public Affairs Specialists
Trade Specialists
International Relations Workers

Journalism
Agricultural Market Reporters
Printing Specialists
Public Affairs Specialists

Writers and Editors
Technical Writers and Editors
Program Analysts

Law
Administrative Law Judges
Attorneys
Hearing and Appeals Specialists
Legal Instruments Examiners
Paralegal Specialists
Patent Attorneys
Tax Law Specialists
GAO Evaluators

Law Enforcement
Alcohol, Tobacco, and Firearms Inspectors
Border Patrol Agents
Criminal Investigators
Customs Inspectors
Game Law Enforcement Agents
Immigration Inspectors
Inspec., Invest. and Compliance Specialists
Police Officers
United States Marshals

Liberal Arts/ Humanities
Contact Representatives
Customs Inspectors
Equal Opportunity Compliance Specialists
Management Analysts
Personnel Management Specialists
Program Analysts
Social Insurance Claims Examiners
Veterans Claims Examiners
Education Services Specialists

Library Science
Librarians
Library Technicians
Medical Record Librarians
Technical Information Services

Management Information Systems
Computer Science Specialists
Computer Specialists
Financial Managers
Logistics Management Specialists
Management Analysts
Miscellaneous Administrative and Programs
Specialists
Operations Research Analysts
Program Analysts
Program Managers

Management, Facilities
Commissary Store Managers
Correctional Institution Administrators
Distribution Facility and Storage Managers
Equipment Specialists
Facility Managers
General Facilities and Equipment Manager
Housing Managers
Industrial Property Managers
Production Controllers

Management
Administrative Officers
Logistics Management Specialists
management Analysts
Manpower Development Specialists
Miscellaneous Administrative and Program
Specialists
Program Analysts
Support Services Administrators

Marketing
Agriculture Marketing Specialists
Bond Sales Promotion Representatives
Contract Specialists
Inventory Management Specialists
Packaging Specialists

Property Disposal Specialists
Supply Specialists
Trade Specialists
Business and Industry Specialists

Mathematics
Actuaries
Cartographers
Computer Science Specialists
Mathematical Statisticians
Mathematicians
Operations Research Analysts
Statisticians

Medical Support
Diagnostic Radiological Technicians
Medical Instrument Technicians
Medical Record Technicians
Medical Technicians
Nuclear Medicine Technicians
Pathology Technicians
Therapeutic Radiological Technicians

Meteorology
Meteorologists
General Physical Scientists

Natural Resource Management
Fish and Wildlife Administrators
General Biological Scientists
Program Analysts
Wildlife Biologists
Wildlife Refuge Management

Nursing
Nurses
Physician's Assistants

Park and Recreation Management
Foresters
Outdoor Recreation Planners
Park Rangers
Recreation Specialists
Recreation and Creative Arts Therapists
Management Analysts

Pharmacy
Consumer Safety Inspectors
Consumer Safety Officers
Pharmacists
Pharmacologists

Physical Education
Corrective Therapists
Outdoor Recreation Planners
Recreation and Creative Arts Therapists
Recreation Specialists
Recreation Aids and Assistants
Sports Specialists
Program Analysts

Physical Science
General Physical Scientists
Metallurgists
Physicists

Physics
Astronomers and Space Scientists
Geodesists
Geophysicists
Health Physicists
Hydrologists
Oceanographers
Patent Examiners
Physicists
General Physical Scientists

Community or City Planning
Community Planners
Realtors

Political Science/Government
Archivists
Budget Analysts
Historians
Foreign Affairs Specialists
Miscellaneous Administrative and Programs
Specialists
Program Analysts
Public Affairs Specialists
Social Scientists
GAO Evaluators

Psychology
Recreation and Creative Arts Therapists
Employee Development Specialists
Personnel Management Specialists
Psychologists
Personnel Staffing Specialists
Position Class. Specialists
Educational Services Specialists
GAO Evaluators

Public Health
Environmental Health Technicians
Food Assistance Program Specialists
Food Inspectors
Health System Administrators
Health System Specialists
industrial Hygienists
Public Health Programs Specialists
Public Health Educators
Social Insurance Administrators
Veterans Claims Examiners

Public Administration
Budget Analysts
Employee Development Specialists
Employee Relations Specialists
Housing Managers
Management Analysts
Manpower Development Specialists
Miscellaneous Administrative and Programs
Specialists
Program Analysts
Public Utilities Specialists
GAO Evaluators

Public Relations
Contact Representatives
Foreign Affairs Specialists
Foreign Agriculture Affairs Specialists
Public Affairs Specialists

Purchasing
Commissary Store Managers
Contract Specialists
Purchasing Specialists
Business and Industry Specialists

Real Estate
Building Managers
Housing Managers
Realtors
Business and Industry Specialists
Contract Specialists

Rehabilitation Therapy
Corrective Therapists
Manual Arts Therapists
Occupational Therapists
Physical Therapists
Prosthetic Representatives
Rehabilitation Therapy Assistants

Social Work
Food Assistance Program Specialists
Psychology Aids and Technicians

Social Science Aids and Technicians
Social Scientists
Social Service Aids and Assistants
Social Service Representatives
Social Workers
Recreation Specialists

Sociology

Social Science Aids and Technicians
Social Scientists
Social Service Aids and Assistants
Social Service Representatives
Program Analysts
Sociologists
GAO Evaluators

Statistics

Actuaries
Computer Science Specialists
Mathematical Statisticians

Operations Research Analysts
Program Analysts
Statisticians
Transportation Industry Analysts

Surveying

Geodesists
Land Surveyors

Systems Analysis

Computer Science Specialists
Computer Specialists
Miscellaneous Administrative and Programs
Specialists
Management Analysts
Program Analysts

Theology

Chaplains

Social Workers
Program Analysts

Transportation

Cargo Schedulers
Highway Safety Specialists
Marine Cargo Specialists
Traffic Management Specialists
Transportation Industry Analysts
Transportation Loss/Damage Claims
Examiners
Transportation Operators
Transportation Specialists
Travel Assistants

Zoology

Animal Scientists
Zoologists
Physiologists

Federal Occupational Groups

The U.S. Office of Personnel Management (OPM) has established occupational groups and series that are used to classify the work of positions. This classification is made in terms of the kind or subject matter of the work, the level of difficulty and responsibility, and the qualification requirements of the work. The classification is made to ensure similar treatment for positions within a class in personnel and pay administration.

Occupational groups have been established for both white and blue collar positions. The following is a list of occupational groups (bold type) and the specific series in each group. Use series "9999" for summer jobs.

White Collar (general schedule)

GS-0000	**Miscellaneous Occupations**
GS-0006	Correctional Institution Administration
GS-0007	Correctional Officer
GS-0011	Bond Sales Promotion
GS-0018	Safety and Occupational Health Management
GS-0019	Safety Technician
GS-0020	Community Planning
GS-0021	Community Planning Technician
GS-0023	Outdoor Recreation Planning
GS-0025	Park Ranger
GS-0028	Environmental Protection Specialist
GS-0029	Environmental Protection Assistant
GS-0030	Sports Specialist
GS-0050	Funeral Directing
GS-0060	Chaplain
GS-0062	Clothing Design
GS-0072	Fingerprint Identification
GS-0080	Security Administration
GS-0081	Fire Protection and Prevention
GS-0082	United States Marshal
GS-0083	Police
GS-0084	Nuclear Materials Courier
GS-0085	Security Guard
GS-0086	Security Clerical and Assistance
GS-0090	Guide
GS-0095	Foreign Law Specialist
GS-0099	General Student Trainee
GS-0100	**Social Science, Psychology, And Welfare**
GS-0101	Social Science
GS-0102	Social Science Aid and Technician
GS-0105	Social Insurance Administration
GS-0106	Unemployment Insurance
GS-0110	Economist
GS-0119	Economics Assistant
GS-0120	Food Assistance Program Specialist
GS-0130	Foreign Affairs
GS-0131	International Relations
GS-0132	Intelligence
GS-0134	Intelligence Aid and Clerk
GS-0135	Foreign Agricultural Affairs
GS-0136	International Cooperation
GS-0140	Manpower Research and Analysis
GS-0142	Manpower Development
GS-0150	Geography
GS-0160	Civil Rights Analysis
GS-0170	History
GS-0180	Psychology
GS-0181	Psychology Aid and Technician
GS-0184	Sociology
GS-0185	Social Work
GS-0186	Social Services Aid and Assistant
GS-0187	Social Services
GS-0188	Recreation Specialist
GS-0189	Recreation Aid and Assistant
GS-0190	General Anthropology
GS-0193	Archeology
GS-0199	Social Science Student Trainee

GS-0200	**Personnel Management and Industrial Relations**
GS-0201	Personnel Management
GS-0203	Personnel Clerical and Assistance
GS-0204	Military Personnel Clerical & Technician
GS-0205	Military Personnel Management
GS-0212	Personnel Staffing
GS-0221	Position Classification
GS-0222	Occupational Analysis
GS-0223	Salary and Wage Administration
GS-0230	Employee Relations
GS-0233	Labor Relations
GS-0235	Employee Development
GS-0241	Mediation
GS-0243	Apprenticeship and Training
GS-0244	Labor Management Relations Examining
GS-0246	Contractor Industrial Relations
GS-0249	Wage and Hour Compliance
GS-0260	Equal Employment Opportunity
GS-0270	Federal Retirement Benefits
GS-0299	Personnel Management Student Trainee
GS-0300	**General Administration, Clerical, Office Services**
GS-0301	Miscellaneous Admin. and Program
GS-0302	Messenger
GS-0304	Miscellaneous Clerk and Assistant
GS-0304	Information Receptionist
GS-0305	Mail and File
GS-0309	Correspondence Clerk
GS-0312	Clerk-Stenographer and Reporter
GS-0313	Work Unit Supervising
GS-0318	Secretary
GS-0319	Closed Microphone Reporting
GS-0322	Clerk-Typist
GS-0326	Office Automation Clerical
GS-0332	Computer Operation
GS-0334	Computer Specialist
GS-0335	Computer Clerk and Assistant
GS-0340	Program Management
GS-0341	Administrative Officer
GS-0342	Support Services Administration
GS-0343	Management and Program Analysis
GS-0344	Management Clerical and Assistance
GS-0346	Logistics Management
GS-0350	Equipment Operator
GS-0351	Printing Clerical
GS-0356	Data Transcriber
GS-0357	Coding
GS-0359	Electric Accounting Machine Operation
GS-0360	Equal Opportunity Compliance
GS-0361	Equal Opportunity Assistance
GS-0362	Elec. Accounting Machine Project Plan.
GS-0382	Telephone Operating
GS-0385	Teletypist
GS-0388	Cryptographic Equipment Operation
GS-0389	Radio Operating
GS-0390	Communications Relay Operation
GS-0391	Telecommunications
GS-0392	General Communications
GS-0394	Communications Clerical
GS-0399	Administration and Office Support Student Trainee

GS-0400	**Biological Sciences**
GS-0401	General Biological Science
GS-0403	Microbiology
GS-0404	Biological Technician
GS-0405	Agricultural Extension
GS-0408	Ecology
GS-0410	Zoology
GS-0413	Physiology
GS-0414	Entomology
GS-0415	Toxicology
GS-0421	Plant Protection Technician
GS-0430	Botany
GS-0434	Plant Pathology
GS-0435	Plant Physiology
GS-0436	Plant Protection and Quarantine
GS-0437	Horticulture
GS-0440	Genetics
GS-0454	Range Conservation
GS-0455	Range Technician
GS-0457	Soil Conservation
GS-0458	Soil Conservation Technician
GS-0459	Irrigation System Operation
GS-0460	Forestry
GS-0462	Forestry Technician
GS-0470	Soil Science
GS-0471	Agronomy
GS-0475	Agricultural Management
GS-0480	General Fish & Wildlife Administration
GS-0482	Fishery Biology
GS-0485	Wildlife Refuge Management
GS-0486	Wildlife Biology
GS-0487	Animal Science
GS-0493	Home Economics
GS-0499	Biological Science Student Trainee
GS-0500	**Accounting and Budget**
GS-0501	Financial Administration and Program
GS-0503	Financial Clerical and Assistance
GS-0505	Financial Management
GS-0510	Accounting
GS-0511	Auditing
GS-0512	Internal Revenue Agent
GS-0525	Accounting Technician
GS-0526	Tax Technician
GS-0530	Cash Processing
GS-0540	Voucher Examining
GS-0544	Civilian Pay
GS-0545	Military Pay
GS-0560	Budget Analysis
GS-0561	Budget Clerical and Assistance
GS-0570	Financial Institution Examining
GS-0592	Tax Examining
GS-0593	Insurance Accounts
GS-0599	Financial Management Student Trainee
GS-0600	**Medical, Hospital, Dental, and Public Health**
GS-0601	General Health Science
GS-0602	Medical Officer
GS-0603	Physician's Assistant
GS-0610	Nurse
GS-0620	Practical Nurse
GS-0621	Nursing Assistant
GS-0622	Medical Supply Aide and Technician
GS-0625	Autopsy Assistant
GS-0630	Dietitian and Nutritionist
GS-0631	Occupational Therapist
GS-0633	Physical Therapist
GS-0635	Corrective Therapist
GS-0636	Rehabilitation Therapy Assistant
GS-0637	Manual Arts Therapist
GS-0638	Recreation/Creative Arts Therapist
GS-0639	Educational Therapist
GS-0640	Health Aid and Technician
GS-0642	Nuclear Medicine Technician
GS-0644	Medical Technologist
GS-0645	Medical Technician
GS-0646	Pathology Technician
GS-0647	Diagnostic Radiologic Technologist
GS-0648	Therapeutic Radiologic Technologist
GS-0649	Medical Instrument Technician
GS-0650	Medical Technical Assistant
GS-0651	Respiratory Therapist
GS-0660	Pharmacist
GS-0661	Pharmacy Technician
GS-0662	Optometrist

GS-0664	Restoration Technician
GS-0665	Speech Pathology and Audiology
GS-0667	Orthotist and Prosthetist
GS-0668	Podiatrist
GS-0669	Medical Record Administration
GS-0670	Health System Administration
GS-0671	Health System Specialist
GS-0672	Prosthetic Representative
GS-0673	Hospital Housekeeping Management
GS-0675	Medical Record Technician
GS-0679	Medical Clerk
GS-0680	Dental Officer
GS-0681	Dental Assistant
GS-0682	Dental Hygiene
GS-0683	Dental Laboratory Aid and Technician
GS-0685	Public Health Program Specialist
GS-0688	Sanitarian
GS-0690	Industrial Hygiene
GS-0696	Consumer Safety
GS-0698	Environmental Health Technician
GS-0699	Medical and Health Student Trainee
GS-0700	**Veterinary Medical Science**
GS-0701	Veterinary Medical Science
GS-0704	Animal Health Technician
GS-0799	Veterinary Student Trainee
GS-0800	**Engineering and Architecture**
GS-0801	General Engineering
GS-0802	Engineering Technician
GS-0803	Safety Technician
GS-0804	Fire Protection Engineering
GS-0806	Materials Engineering
GS-0807	Landscape Architecture
GS-0808	Architecture
GS-0809	Construction Control
GS-0810	Civil Engineering
GS-0817	Surveying Technician
GS-0818	Engineering Drafting
GS-0819	Environmental Engineering
GS-0828	Construction Analyst
GS-0830	Mechanical Engineering
GS-0840	Nuclear Engineering
GS-0850	Electrical Engineering
GS-0854	Computer Engineering
GS-0855	Electronics Engineering
GS-0856	Electronics Technician
GS-0858	Biomedical Engineering
GS-0861	Aerospace Engineering
GS-0871	Naval Architecture
GS-0873	Ship Surveying
GS-0880	Mining Engineering
GS-0881	Petroleum Engineering
GS-0901	**General Legal and Kindred Administration Series**
GS-0904	Law Clerk
GS-0905	General Attorney
GS-0920	Estate Tax Examining
GS-0930	Hearings and Appeals
GS-0945	Clerk of Court
GS-0950	Paralegal Specialist
GS-0958	Pension Law Specialist
GS-0962	Contact Representative
GS-0963	Legal Instruments Examining
GS-0965	Land Law Examining
GS-0967	Passport and Visa Examining
GS-0986	Legal Clerk and Technician
GS-0987	Tax Law Specialist
GS-0991	Workers' Comp. Claims Examining
GS-0993	Claims Examining Railroad Retirement
GS-0996	Veterans Claims Examining
GS-0998	Claims Assistance and Examining
GS-0999	Legal Occupations Student Trainee
GS-1000	**Information and Arts Group**
GS-1001	General Arts and Information
GS-1008	Interior Design
GS-1010	Exhibits Specialist
GS-1015	Museum Curator
GS-1016	Museum Specialist and Technician
GS-1020	Illustrating
GS-1021	Office Drafting
GS-1035	Public Affairs
GS-1040	Language Specialist

GS-1046	Language Clerical		GS-1420	Archivist
GS-1051	Music Specialist		GS-1421	Archives Technician
GS-1054	Theater Specialist		GS-1499	Library and Archives Student Trainee
GS-1056	Art Specialist			
GS-1060	Photography		**GS-1500**	**Mathematics and Statistics Group**
GS-1071	Audio-Visual Production		GS-1510	Actuary
GS-1082	Writing and Editing		GS-1515	Operations Research
GS-1083	Technical Writing and Editing		GS-1520	Mathematics
GS-1084	Visual Information		GS-1521	Mathematics Technician
GS-1087	Editorial Assistance		GS-1529	Mathematical Statistician
GS-1099	Information and Arts Student Trainee		GS-1530	Statistician
			GS-1531	Statistical Assistant
GS-1100	**Business and Industry Group**		GS-1540	Cryptography
GS-1101	General Business and Industry		GS-1541	Cryptoanalysis
GS-1102	Contracting		GS-1550	Computer Science
GS-1103	Industrial Property Management		GS-1599	Math and Statistics Student Trainee
GS-1104	Property Disposal			
GS-1105	Purchasing		**GS-1600**	**Equipment, Facilities, and Services Group**
GS-1106	Procurement Clerical and Technician		GS-1601	General Facilities and Equipment
GS-1107	Property Disposal Clerical and Technician		GS-1630	Cemetery Administration
GS-1130	Public Utilities Specialist		GS-1640	Facility Management
GS-1140	Trade Specialist		GS-1654	Printing Management
GS-1144	Commissary Store Management		GS-1658	Laundry and Dry Cleaning Plant Mgt.
GS-1145	Agricultural Program Specialist		GS-1667	Steward
GS-1146	Agricultural Marketing		GS-1670	Equipment Specialist
GS-1147	Agricultural Market Reporting		GS-1699	Equipment and Facilities Management Student Trainee
GS-1150	Industrial Specialist			
GS-1152	Production Control		**GS-1700**	**Education Group**
GS-1160	Financial Analysis		GS-1701	General Education and Training
GS-1161	Crop Insurance Administration		GS-1702	Education and Training Technician
GS-1162	Crop Insurance Underwriting		GS-1710	Educational and Vocational Training
GS-1163	Insurance Examining		GS-1712	Training Instruction
GS-1165	Loan Specialist		GS-1715	Vocational Rehabilitation
GS-1169	Internal Revenue Officer		GS-1720	Education Program
GS-1170	Realty		GS-1725	Public Health Educator
GS-1171	Appraising		GS-1730	Education Research
GS-1173	Housing Management		GS-1740	Education Services
GS-1176	Building Management		GS-1750	Instructional Systems
GS-1199	Business and Industry Student Trainee		GS-1799	Education Student Trainee
GS-1200	**Copyright, Patent, and Trademark Group**		**GS-1800**	**Investigation Group**
GS-1202	Patent Technician		GS-1801	Gen'l. Inspection, Inv., & Compliance
GS-1210	Copyright		GS-1802	Compliance Inspection and Support
GS-1211	Copyright Technician		GS-1810	General Investigating
GS-1220	Patent Administration		GS-1811	Criminal Investigating
GS-1221	Patent Advisor		GS-1812	Game Law Enforcement
GS-1222	Patent Attorney		GS-1815	Air Safety Investigating
GS-1223	Patent Classifying		GS-1816	Immigration Inspection
GS-1224	Patent Examining		GS-1822	Mine Safety and Health
GS-1226	Design Patent Examining		GS-1825	Aviation Safety
GS-1299	Copyright and Patent Student Trainee		GS-1831	Securities Compliance Examining
			GS-1850	Agricultural Commodity Warehouse Examining
GS-1300	**Physical Sciences Group**		GS-1854	Alcohol, Tobacco & Firearms Inspection
GS-1301	General Physical Science		GS-1862	Consumer Safety Inspection
GS-1306	Health Physics		GS-1863	Food Inspection
GS-1310	Physics		GS-1864	Public Health Quarantine Inspection
GS-1311	Physical Science Technician		GS-1884	Customs Patrol Officer
GS-1313	Geophysics		GS-1889	Import Specialist
GS-1315	Hydrology		GS-1890	Customs Inspection
GS-1316	Hydrologic Technician		GS-1894	Customs Entry and Liquidating
GS-1320	Chemistry		GS-1896	Border Patrol Agent
GS-1321	Metallurgy		GS-1897	Customs Aid
GS-1330	Astronomy and Space Science		GS-1899	Investigation Student Trainee
GS-1340	Meteorology			
GS-1341	Meteorological Technician		**GS-1900**	**Quality Assurance, Inspection, and Grading Group**
GS-1350	Geology		GS-1910	Quality Assurance
GS-1360	Oceanography		GS-1980	Agricultural Commodity Grading
GS-1361	Navigational Information		GS-1981	Agricultural Commodity Aid
GS-1370	Cartography		GS-1999	Quality Inspection Student Trainee
GS-1371	Cartographic Technician			
GS-1372	Geodesy		**GS-2000**	**Supply Group**
GS-1373	Land Surveying		GS-2001	General Supply
GS-1374	Geodetic Technician		GS-2003	Supply Program Management
GS-1380	Forest Products Technology		GS-2005	Supply Clerical and Technician
GS-1382	Food Technology		GS-2010	Inventory Management
GS-1384	Textile Technology		GS-2030	Distribution Facilities and Storage Mgt.
GS-1386	Photographic Technology		GS-2032	Packaging
GS-1397	Document Analysis		GS-2050	Supply Cataloging
GS-1399	Physical Science Student Trainee		GS-2091	Sales Store Clerical
			GS-2099	Supply Student Trainee
GS-1400	**Library and Archives Group**			
GS-1410	Librarian		**GS-2100**	**Transportation Group**
GS-1411	Library Technician		GS-2101	Transportation Specialist
GS-1412	Technical Information Services		GS-2102	Transportation Clerk and Assistant

GS-2110	Transportation Industry Analysis
GS-2121	Railroad Safety
GS-2123	Motor Carrier Safety
GS-2125	Highway Safety
GS-2130	Traffic Management
GS-2131	Freight Rate
GS-2135	Tran. Loss & Damage Claims Examining
GS-2144	Cargo Scheduling
GS-2150	Transportation Operations
GS-2151	Dispatching
GS-2152	Air Traffic Control
GS-2154	Air Traffic Assistance
GS-2161	Marine Cargo
GS-2181	Aircraft Operation
GS-2183	Air Navigation
GS-2185	Aircrew Technician
GS-2199	Transportation Student Trainee

Blue Collar * (Wage Grade)

WG-2500	**Wire Communications Equip. and Maintenance**
WG-2502	Telecommunications Mechanic
WG-2504	Wire Communications Cable Splicing
WG-2508	Comm. Line Installing and Repairing
WG-2600	**Electronic Equipment Installation and Maintenance**
WG-2602	Electronic Measurement Equipment Mechanic
WG-2604	Electronics Mechanic
WG-2606	Electronic Industrial Controls Mechanic
WG-2608	Electronic Digital Computer Mechanic
WG-2610	Electronic Integrated Sys. Mechanic
WG-2800	**Electrical Installation and Maintenance**
WG-2805	Electrician
WG-2810	Electrician (High Voltage)
WG-2854	Electrical Equipment Repairing
WG-2892	Aircraft Electrician
WG-3100	**Fabric and Leather Work**
WG-3103	Shoe Repairing
WG-3105	Fabric Working
WG-3106	Upholstering
WG-3111	Sewing Machine Operating
WG-3119	Broom and Brush Making
WG-3300	**Instrument Work**
WG-3306	Optical Instrument Repairing
WG-3314	Instrument Making
WG-3359	Instrument Mechanic
WG-3400	**Machine Tool Work**
WG-3414	Machining
WG-3416	Toolmaking
WG-3417	Tool Grinding
WG-3428	Die Sinking
WG-3500	**General Services and Support Work**
WG-3502	Laboring
WG-3511	Laboratory Working
WG-3513	Coin/Currency Checking
WG-3515	Laboratory Support Working
WG-3543	Stevedoring
WG-3546	Railroad Repairing
WG-3566	Custodial Working
WG-3600	**Structural and Finishing Work**
WG-3602	Cement Finishing
WG-3603	Masonry
WG-3604	Tile Setting
WG-3605	Plastering
WG-3606	Roofing
WG-3609	Floor Covering Installing
WG-3610	Insulating
WG-3611	Glazing
WG-3653	Asphalt Working
WG-3700	**Metal Processing**
WG-3702	Flame/Arc Cutting
WG-3703	Welding
WG-3705	Nondestructive Testing
WG-3707	Metalizing
WG-3711	Electroplating
WG-3712	Heat Treating
WG-3716	Leadburning
WG-3725	Battery Repairing
WG-3727	Buffing and Polishing
WG-3735	Metal Phototransferring
WG-3736	Circuit Board Making
WG-3741	Furnace Operating
WG-3769	Shot Peening Machine Operating
WG-3800	**Metal Work**
WG-3802	Metal Forging
WG-3806	Sheet Metal Mechanic
WG-3807	Structural/Ornamental Iron Working
WG-3808	Boilermaking
WG-3809	Mobile Equipment Metal Mechanic
WG-3816	Engraving
WG-3819	Airframe Jig Fitting
WG-3820	Shipfitting
WG-3833	Transfer Engraving
WG-3858	Metal Tank and Radiator Repairing
WG-3869	Metal Forming Machine Operating
WG-3872	Metal Tube Making, Installing, and Repairing
WG-3900	**Motion Picture, Radio, Television, and Sound Equipment Operating**
WG-3910	Motion Picture Projection
WG-3940	Broadcasting Equipment Operating
WG-4000	**Lens and Crystal Work**
WG-4005	Optical Element Working
WG-4010	Prescription Eyeglass Making
WG-4100	**Painting and Paper**
WG-4102	Painting
WG-4103	Paperhanging
WG-4104	Sign Painting
WG-4200	**Plumbing and Pipefitting**
WG-4204	Pipefitting
WG-4206	Plumbing
WG-4255	Fuel Distribution Systems Mechanic
WG-4300	**Pliable Materials Work**
WG-4351	Plastic Molding Equipment Operating
WG-4352	Plastic Fabricating
WG-4360	Rubber Products Molding
WG-4361	Rubber Equipment Repairing
WG-4370	Glassblowing
WG-4373	Molding
WG-4400	**Printing**
WG-4402	Bindery Working
WG-4403	Hand Composing
WG-4405	Film Assembly-Stripping
WG-4406	Letterpress Operating
WG-4413	Negative Engraving
WG-4414	Offset Photography
WG-4416	Platemaking
WG-4417	Offset Press Operating
WG-4419	Silk Screen Making and Printing
WG-4425	Photoengraving
WG-4440	Stereotype Platemaking
WG-4441	Bookbinding
WG-4445	Bank Note Designing
WG-4446	Bank Note Engraving
WG-4447	Sculptural Engraving
WG-4448	Siderographic Transferring
WG-4449	Electrolytic Intaglio Platemaking
WG-4450	Intaglio Die and Plate Finishing
WG-4454	Intaglio Press Operating
WG-4600	**Wood Work**
WG-4602	Blocking and Bracing
WG-4604	Wood Working
WG-4605	Wood Crafting
WG-4607	Carpentry
WG-4616	Patternmaking
WG-4639	Timber Working
WG-4654	Form Block Making
WG-4700	**General Maintenance and Operations Work**
WG-4714	Model Making
WG-4715	Exhibits Making/Modeling
WG-4716	Railroad Car Repairing
WG-4717	Boat Building and Repairing
WG-4737	General Equipment Mechanic
WG-4741	General Equipment Operating

WG-4742	Utility Systems Repairing-Operating		**WG-5700**	**Transportation/Mobile Equipment Operation**
WG-4745	Research Laboratory Mechanic		WG-5703	Motor Vehicle Operating
WG-4749	Maintenance Mechanic		WG-5704	Fork Lift Operating
WG-4754	Cemetery Caretaking		WG-5705	Tractor Operating
			WG-5706	Road Sweeper Operating
WG-4800	**General Equipment Maintenance**		WG-5716	Engineering Equipment Operating
WG-4804	Locksmithing		WG-5725	Crane Operating
WG-4805	Medical Equipment Repairing		WG-5729	Drill Rig Operating
WG-4806	Office Appliance Repairing		WG-5736	Braking-Switching and Conducting
WG-4807	Chemical Equipment Repairing		WG-5737	Locomotive Engineering
WG-4808	Custodial Equipment Servicing		WG-5738	Railroad Maintenance Vehicle Operating
WG-4816	Protective and Safety Equipment Fabricating and Repairing		WG-5767	Airfield Clearing Equipment Operating
WG-4818	Aircraft Survival and Flight Equipment Repairing		WG-5782	Ship Operating
WG-4819	Bowling Equipment Repairing		WG-5784	Riverboat Operating
WG-4820	Vending Machine Repairing		WG-5786	Small Craft Operating
WG-4840	Tool and Equipment Repairing		WG-5788	Deckhand
WG-4845	Orthopedic Appliance Repairing			
WG-4848	Mechanical Parts Repairing		**WG-5800**	**Transportation/Mobile Equipment Maintenance**
WG-4850	Bearing Reconditioning		WG-5803	Heavy Mobile Equipment Mechanic
WG-4855	Domestic Appliance Repairing		WG-5806	Mobile Equipment Servicing
			WG-5823	Automotive Mechanic
WG-5000	**Plant and Animal Work**		WG-5876	Electromotive Equipment Mechanic
WG-5002	Farming			
WG-5003	Gardening		**WG-6500**	**Ammunition, Explosives, and Toxic Materials Work**
WG-5026	Pest Controlling		WG-6502	Explosives Operating
WG-5031	Insects Production Working		WG-6505	Munitions Destroying
WG-5034	Dairy Farming		WG-6511	Missile/Toxic Materials Handling
WG-5035	Livestock Ranching/Wrangling		WG-6517	Explosives Test Operating
WG-5042	Tree Trimming and Removing			
WG-5048	Animal Caretaking		**WG-6600**	**Armament Work**
			WG-6605	Artillery Repairing
WG-5200	**Miscellaneous Occupations**		WG-6606	Artillery Testing
WG-5205	Gas and Radiation Detecting		WG-6610	Small Arms Repairing
WG-5210	Rigging		WG-6641	Ordnance Equipment Mechanic
WG-5220	Shipwright		WG-6652	Aircraft Ordnance Systems Mechanic
WG-5221	Lofting		WG-6656	Special Weapons Systems Mechanic
WG-5235	Test Range Tracking			
			WG-6900	**Warehousing & Stock Handling**
WG-5300	**Industrial Equipment Maintenance**		WG-6903	Coal Handling
WG-5306	Air Conditioning Equipment Mechanic		WG-6904	Tools and Parts Handling
WG-5309	Heating & Boiler Plant Equip. Mechanic		WG-6907	Materials Handler
WG-5310	Kitchen/Bakery Equipment Repairing		WG-6910	Materials Expediting
WG-5313	Elevator Mechanic		WG-6912	Materials Examining and Identifying
WG-5317	Laundry & Dry Cleaning Equip. Repairing		WG-6913	Hazardous Waste Disposing
WG-5318	Lock and Dam Repairing		WG-6914	Store Working
WG-5323	Oiling and Greasing		WG-6941	Bulk Money Handling
WG-5330	Printing Equipment Repairing		WG-6968	Aircraft Freight Loading
WG-5334	Marine Machinery Mechanic			
WG-5335	Wind Tunnel Mechanic		**WG-7000**	**Packing and Processing**
WG-5341	Industrial Furnace Building and Repairing		WG-7002	Packing
WG-5350	Production Machinery Mechanic		WG-7006	Preservation Servicing
WG-5352	Industrial Equipment Mechanic		WG-7009	Equipment Cleaning
WG-5364	Door Systems Mechanic		WG-7010	Parachute Packing
WG-5365	Physiological Trainer Mechanic			
WG-5378	Powered Support Systems Mechanic		**WG-7300**	**Laundry, Dry Cleaning, and Pressing**
WG-5384	Gasdynamic Facility Installing and Repairing		WG-7304	Laundry Working
			WG-7305	Laundry Machine Operating
WG-5400	**Industrial Equipment Operating**		WG-7306	Pressing
WG-5402	Boiler Plant Operating			
WG-5403	Incinerator Operating		**WG-7400**	**Food Preparation and Serving**
WG-5406	Utility Systems Operating		WG-7402	Baking
WG-5407	Electric Power Controlling		WG-7404	Cooking
WG-5408	Wastewater Treatment Plant Operating		WG-7405	Bartending
WG-5409	Water Treatment Plant Operating		WG-7407	Meatcutting
WG-5413	Fuel Distribution System Operating		WG-7408	Food Service Working
WG-5415	Air Conditioning Equipment Operating		WG-7420	Waiter
WG-5419	Stationary-Engine Operating			
WG-5423	Sandblasting		**WG-7600**	**Personal Services**
WG-5424	Weighing Machine Operating		WG-7603	Barbering
WG-5426	Lock and Dam Operating		WG-7641	Beautician
WG-5427	Chemical Plant Operating			
WG-5433	Gas Generating Plant Operating		**WG-8200**	**Fluid Systems Maintenance**
WG-5435	Carton/Bag Making Machine Operating		WG-8255	Pneudraulic Systems Mechanic
WG-5438	Elevator Operating		WG-8268	Aircraft Pneudraulic Systems Mechanic
WG-5439	Testing Equipment Operating			
WG-5440	Packaging Machine Operating		**WG-8600**	**Engine Overhaul**
WG-5446	Textile Equipment Operating		WG-8602	Aircraft Engine Mechanic
WG-5455	Paper Pulping Machine Operating		WG-8610	Small Engine Mechanic
WG-5478	Portable Equipment Operating		WG-8675	Liquid Fuel Rocket Engine Mechanic
WG-5479	Dredging Equipment Operating			
WG-5484	Counting Machine Operating		**WG-8800**	**Aircraft Overhaul**
WG-5485	Aircraft Weight and Balance Operating		WG-8810	Aircraft Propeller Mechanic
			WG-8840	Aircraft Mechanical Parts Repairing
			WG-8852	Aircraft Mechanic

WG-8862	Aircraft Attending		
WG-8882	Airframe Test Operating		
WG-9000	**Film Processing**		
WG-9003	Film Assembling and Repairing		
WG-9004	Motion Picture Developing/Printing Machine Operating		

* =

Those occupational groups not listed have yet to be established. The data for Blue Collar occupational groups originated from the *Handbook of Occupational Groups and Families*, Release Date August 2001, from OPM's Classification Programs Division.

Selected Federal White Collar Pay Schedules
Effective January 1996

General Schedule (2.54%)

	Step 1	Step 2	Step 3	Step 4	Step 5	Step 6	Step 7	Step 8	Step 9	Step 10
GS1	$15,214	$15,722	$16,228	$16,731	$17,238	$17,536	$18,034	$18,538	$18,559	$19,031
GS2	17,106	17,512	18,079	18,559	18,767	19,319	19,871	20,423	20,975	21,527
GS3	18,664	19,286	19,908	20,530	21,152	21,774	22,396	23,018	23,640	24,262
GS4	20,952	21,650	22,348	23,046	23,744	24,442	25,140	25,838	26,536	27,234
GS5	23,442	24,223	25,004	25,785	26,566	27,347	28,128	28,909	29,690	30,471
GS6	26,130	27,001	27,872	28,743	29,614	30,485	31,356	32,227	33,098	33,969
GS7	29,037	30,005	30,973	31,941	32,909	33,877	34,845	35,813	36,781	37,749
GS8	32,158	33,230	34,302	35,374	36,446	37,518	38,590	39,662	40,734	41,806
GS9	35,519	36,703	37,887	39,071	40,255	41,439	42,623	43,807	44,991	46,175
GS10	39,115	40,419	41,723	43,027	44,331	45,635	43,939	48,234	49,547	50,851
GS11	42,976	44,409	45,842	47,275	48,708	50,141	51,574	53,007	54,440	55,873
GS12	51,508	53,225	54,942	56,659	58,376	60,093	61,810	63,527	65,244	66,961
GS13	61,251	63,293	65,335	67,377	69,419	71,461	73,503	75,545	77,587	79,629
GS14	72,381	74,794	77,207	79,620	82,033	84,446	86,859	89,272	91,685	94,098
GS15	85,140	87,978	90,816	93,654	96,432	99,330	102,168	105,006	107,844	110,682

State Government Jobs

Basic Information

Applying for state government jobs takes time and a lot of follow-up. Below are a few pointers to keep in mind when applying:

- The majority of states require applications which must be filled out properly and in detail. Never assume that the personnel reviewing applications know what you do based on the position title. Even if you are attaching a resume, always complete the application.

- Detailed information will make a difference in your ranking and could make a difference in whether or not you are granted an interview.

- Make sure that applications are sent before the deadline on the announcement.

- If a job has specific qualifications and you have them, be sure to emphasize those qualifications.

- Always send the application to the appropriate agency or department.

- If you send a resume, most states will simply send it back to you along with an application that must be completed.

- Grade levels are used for salary determination which takes education, position, and experience into consideration.

- All states give veterans and those with disabilities preference.

- State employees who have been laid off are hired back before new people are hired.

- If testing is required for the position, be sure to follow up and take the appropriate examination.

Alabama
State Personnel Department
300 State Administration Bldg.
64 North Union St.
Montgomery, AL 36130
334-242-3389
www.personnel.state.al.us

Alaska
Alaska Division of Personnel
Department of Administration
333 Willoughy Avenue, 10th Floor
Juneau, AK 99811-0201
907-465-4430
Job Bank: 907-465-8910
http://dop2.state.ok.us/index.cfm

Arizona
Arizona Human Resources Division
Department of Administration
100 North 15th Avenue
1st Floor, Suite 103
Phoenix, AZ 85007
602-542-3644
Job Bank: 602-542-4966
http://www.hr.state.az.us

Arkansas
Office of Personnel Management
Department of Finance and Administration
1509 W. 7th St., Room 201
Little Rock, AR 72201
501-682-1823
Job Bank: 501-682-5627
http://www.state.ar.us/dfa/opm

California
California State Personnel Board
P.O. Box 944201
Sacramento, CA 94244-2010
916-653-1705
Los Angeles: 213-620-6450
San Diego: 619-237-6163
San Francisco: 415-557-7871
Sacramento: 916-445-0538
www.spb.ca.gov/indexrd.cfm

Colorado
Colorado Department of Personnel and Administration
1600 Broadway, #1030

Denver, CO 80202
303-866-6559
http://www.colorado.gov/dpa

Connecticut
Department of Administrative Services
165 Capitol Ave.
Hartford, CT 06106
860-713-5205
http://www.das.state.ct.us/default.asp

Delaware
Delaware State Personnel Office
Townsend Building
401 Federal Street, Suite 5
Dover, DE 19901
302-739-4195
http://www.delawarepersonnel.com

District of Columbia
Office of Personnel
441 4th St. NW, Suite 300S
Washington, DC 20001
202-442-9700
http://dsop.dc.gov/main.shtm

Matthew Lesko, Information USA, Inc., 12081 Nebel Street, Rockville, MD 20852 • 1-800-955-7693 • www.lesko.com

Florida

Human Resource Management
Room 1902
The Capitol
Tallahassee, FL 32301
850-922-5449
Fax: 850-922-5542
http://jobsdirect.state.fl.us

Georgia

Georgia Merit System
#2 MLK Jr., Drive, SE
Suite 504 West
Atlanta, GA 30334-5100
404-656-2705
Fax: 404-656-5979
http://www.gms.state.ga.us

Hawaii

Hawaii Department of Human Resource
Development
235 South Beretania St., 11th Floor
Honolulu, HA 96813-2437
808-587-0977
Job Link: 808-587-0977
TDD: 808-587-1148
www.ehawaiigov.org/dhrd/statejobs/html

Idaho

Division of Human Resources
700 W. State St.
P.O. Box 83720
Boise, ID 83720-0066
208-334-2263
800-554-JOBS
Job Bank: 208-334-2568
Fax: 208-334-3182
http://www.dhr.state.id.us

Illinois

Bureau of Personnel
Department of Central Management Services
William G. Stratton Office Bldg.
401 S. Spring St., Room 500
Springfield, IL 62706
217-782-7100
TDD: 217-785-3979
http://www.state.il.us/cms/persnl/default.htm

Indiana

Indiana Department of Personnel
402 West Washington St., Room W161
Indiana Government Center South
Indianapolis, IN 46204-2261
317-232-0200
Fax: 317-233-0236
http://www.in.gov/jobs

Iowa

Iowa Department of Personnel
Grimes State Office Building
East 14th and Grand
Des Moines, IA 50319-0150
515-281-3087
Fax: 515-242-6450
http://www.state.ia.us/government/idop

Kansas

Kansas Division of Personnel Services
Department of Administration
Room 951, South Landon Bldg.
900 Jackson
Topeka, KS 66612-1251
785-296-4278
TDD: 785-296-8404
Fax: 785-296-6793
http://da.state.ks.us/ps

Kentucky

Kentucky Personnel Cabinet
200 Fair Oaks Lane, Suite 517
Frankfort, KY 40601
502-564-6920

Fax: 502-564-3588
http://personnel.ky.gov/index.html

Louisiana

Louisiana Department of State Civil Service
P.O. Box 94111
Capitol Station
Baton Rouge, LA 70804-9111
225-342-8536
Fax: 225-342-2386
http://www.dscs.state.la.us

Maine

Bureau of Human Resources
4 Statehouse
Augusta, ME 04333-0004
207-624-7761
Fax: 207-287-4414
TTY: 207-287-4537
http://www.state.me.us/bhr/index.html

Maryland

Maryland Department of Budget and
Management
45 Calvert Street
Annapolis, MD 21401
800-705-3493
www.dbm.maryland.gov

Massachusetts

Human Resources Division
1 Ashburton Place
Boston, MA 02108
617-727-3777
Fax: 617-727-3970
http://www.state.ma.us/hrd/hrd.htm

Michigan

Michigan Department of Civil Service
400 South Pine
P.O. Box 30002
Lansing, MI 48909
800-788-1766
517-373-3030
Fax: 517-373-7690
www.michigan.gov/mdcs

Minnesota

Minnesota Department of Employee Relations
200 Centennial Office Building
658 Cedar St.
St. Paul, MN 55155
612-279-1184
Job Info Hotline: 651-296-2616
http://www.doer.state.mn.us

Mississippi

Mississippi State Personnel Board
301 North Lamar St.
Suite 100
Jackson, MS 39201
601-359-2339
Fax: 601-359-2380
http://www.spb.state.ms.us

Missouri

Missouri Division of Personnel
P.O. Box 388
Truman Office Building, Room 430
Jefferson City, MO 65102
573-751-4162
TDD: 573-526-4488
Fax: 573-751-8641
http://www.oa.state.mo.us/pers

Montana

Montana Personnel Division
Mitchell Building, Room 130
125 N. Roberts
Helena, MT 59620-0127
406-444-3871

Fax: 406-444-0703
http://discoveringmontana.com/doa/spd/css

Nebraska

DAS Personnel Division
301 Centennial Mall South
P.O. Box 94905
Lincoln, NE 68509
402-471-2075
Job Bank: 402-471-2200
Fax: 407-471-3754
http://www.das.state.ne.us/personnel

Nevada

Nevada Department of Personnel
209 East Musser St., Room 101
Carson City, NV 89710-4204
775-684-0150
TDD: 800-326-6868
http://dop.nv.gov

New Hampshire

New Hampshire Division of Personnel
25 Capitol St., Room 1
Concord, NH 03301
603-271-3262
TDD: 800-735-2964
Fax: 603-271-1422
http://www.state.nh.us/hr/employment.html

New Jersey

New Jersey Department of Personnel
44 South Clinton Ave.
P.O. Box 310
Trenton, NJ 08625
609-292-4144
http://www.state.nj.us/personnel

New Mexico

New Mexico State Personnel Office
P.O. Box 26127
2600 Cerrillos Road
Santa Fe, NM 87502-0127
505-476-7777
TDD: 505-476-7798
http://www.state.nm.us/spd/

New York

New York State Personnel Board
Department of Civil Services
State Campus
Building #1
Albany, NY 12239
518-457-2487
http://www.cs.state.ny.us

North Carolina

North Carolina Office of State Personnel
116 West Jones St.
1331 Mail Service Center
Raleigh, NC 27699-1331
919-733-6316
http://www.osp.state.nc.us/ExternalHome

North Dakota

North Dakota Central Personnel Division
State Capitol
600 East Boulevard Avenue
Bismarck, ND 58505-6120
701-328-3290
Fax: 701-328-1475
http://www.state.nd.us/cpers

Ohio

Ohio Division of Personnel
Division of Human Resources
30 East Broad St., 28th Floor
Columbus, OH 43215
614-466-8044
Job Bank: 614-466-4026
http://www.state.oh.us/das/dhr

Oklahoma

Office of Personnel Management
Jim Thorpe Building
2101 N. Lincoln Blvd.
Oklahoma City, OK 73105
405-521-2177
Fax: 405-524-6942
www.opm.state.ok.us

Oregon

Human Resource Services Division
155 Cottage St., NE, U 30
Salem, OR 97310-3967
503-378-8344
Fax: 503-373-7684
http://www.hr.das.state.or.us

Pennsylvania

Bureau of State Employment
Office of Administration
110 Finance Building
Harrisburg, PA 17120
717-787-5703
TTY: 717-787-0570
http://www.hrm.state.pa.us/oahrm/site/default/asp

Rhode Island

Department of Labor and Training
Center General Complex
1511 Pontiac Avenue
Cranston, RI 02920
401-462-8000
www.dlt.state.ri.us

South Carolina

South Carolina Human Resources
Management Division
2221 Divine St., Suite 100
Columbia, SC 29250
803-734-9080
Fax: 803-734-9098
http://www.state.sc.us/ohr

South Dakota

South Dakota Office of Executive
Management

Bureau of Personnel
500 East Capitol Ave.
Pierre, SD 57501-5070
605-773-3148
Fax: 605-773-4344
http://www.state.sd.us/bop/bop.htm

Tennessee

Tennessee Department of Personnel
James K. Polk Building
505 Deadrick St.
Nashville, TN 37243-0001
615-741-2598
Fax: 615-741-0728
http://www.state.tn.us/personnel

Texas

State of Texas Human Resources
101 East 15th St.
Austin, TX 78778
512-463-2294
http://www.hr.state.tx.us

Utah

Utah Department of Human Resources
Management
2120 State Office Building
Salt Lake City, UT 84114-1531
801-538-3025
Job Bank: 801-538-3118
Fax: 801-538-3081
http://www.dhrm.state.ut.us

Vermont

Vermont Department of Personnel
110 State St., Drawer 20
Montpelier, VT 05602-3001
802-828-3491
Job Bank: 802-828-3483
Fax: 802-828-3409
http://www.vermontpersonnel.org

Virginia

Virginia Department of Personnel and
Training
James Monroe Building, 12th Floor

101 North 14th St.
Richmond, VA 23219
804-225-2131
Fax: 804-371-7401
http:www.dpt.state.va.us

Washington

Washington Department of Personnel
521 Capitol Way South
P.O. Box 47500
Olympia, WA 98504-7500
360-664-1960
TDD: 360-664-6211
http://hr.dop.wa.gov

West Virginia

West Virginia Division of Personnel
Capitol Complex Building, #6
Room 420
1900 Kanawha Blvd. East
Charleston, WV 25305-0139
304-558-3950
TDD: 304-558-1237
http://www.state.wv.us/admin/personnel/default.htm

Wisconsin

Wisconsin Department of Employment
Relations
345 W. Washington Avenue
P.O. Box 7855
Madison, WI 53707-7855
608-266-9820
Job Bank: 608-266-1731
Fax: 608-267-1000
http://der.state.wi.us/home

Wyoming

Wyoming Human Resources Division
Department of Administration and Information
2001 Capitol Ave., Emerson Building
Cheyenne, WY 82002-0060
307-777-7188
Fax: 307-777-6562
http://personnel.state.wy.us

"Winston Churchill is among the great cases of later life success (in his late sixties and early seventies), but one of his contemporaries said this about his early years ... 'capable, industrious, and supremely courageous, but not a pathfinder or great leader of men.'"

Source: *Ambition: How We Manage Success and Failure Throughout Our Lives*, Gilbert Brim, Basic Books, 1992

I Wanna Get Money
And I'm Out of Work

Matthew Lesko, Information USA, Inc., 12081 Nebel Street, Rockville, MD 20852 • 1-800-955-7693 • www.lesko.com

I Wanna Get Money and I'm Out of Work

If you have been laid off or downsized from your job through no fault of your own, then help is out there for you. Unemployment compensation is the government's first line of defense against the ripple effects of unemployment. By cash payments made directly to laid off workers, the program ensures that at least a significant proportion of the necessities of life, such as food, shelter, and clothing, can be met while a search for work takes place. This program is unique in that it is almost totally funded by employer taxes — only three states collect taxes from employees.

Originally, most states paid benefits for a maximum duration of 13 to 16 weeks; most now pay a maximum of 26 weeks, and a few extend them somewhat further. In periods of very high unemployment, individual states may extend the benefits up to 13 additional weeks. Almost all wage and salary workers are now covered by this system.

There are no federal standards for benefits, in terms of qualifying requirements, benefit amounts, or duration of the regular benefits. Which means that every state operates this program somewhat differently. All states do require that a person must have worked a certain amount of time or earned a specified amount of wages to qualify for the program. This is to ensure that the unemployment benefits go to workers who are genuinely attached to the work force. You also must be able and available to work. You would be disqualified for benefits if you voluntarily left a job without good cause, were fired for misconduct, or you refused to take a suitable job.

Your weekly benefit amount depends upon your past wages within certain minimum and maximum limits. The period of past wages used and the formulas for computing benefits from these past wages vary greatly among the states. The number of dependents you have also affects your benefit amount.

If you want to move to another state and still collect unemployment benefits, you can. What happens is that the state you move to will file an Interstate Claim. Your benefits and the length of benefits are determined by the rules set in the state in which you earned your previous wages. In other words, you can't move from Colorado to Connecticut just to get a higher unemployment benefit. You will just get what you would have gotten while living in Colorado, and that's it.

You are allowed to receive benefits if you are participating in a job retraining program. In fact, many of the programs such as the Trade Adjustment Assistance program, will continue to provide you benefits once your unemployment runs out if you still haven't found a job or are participating in a retraining program.

Disaster Unemployment Assistance is provided to any individual who is unemployed as a result of a major natural disaster. In general, people living or working in areas affected by a disaster are eligible for assistance if they are not eligible for unemployment benefits or other wage replacement payments.

As stated earlier, the weekly unemployment benefit amounts varies greatly. In Hawaii, you can earn as little as $5 per week to a high of $347. The length you can receive benefits also varies from a low of four weeks to a high of 26 weeks in Oregon. What follows is a listing of state contacts for unemployment benefits. These offices can tell you the rules for receiving the benefits, as well as the formula used to calculate the amount you would receive. Also included is the general range of weekly payments and the duration of the payments. Remember, certain things such as the number of dependents can affect the amount you receive, and states can extend the duration under certain conditions. Obviously your first point of contact should be your local unemployment office which can be found by looking in the blue pages of your phone book. If you need more information, you may also contact the main office at Unemployment Insurance Service, Employment and Training Administration, 200 Constitution Ave., NW, Washington, DC 20210; 202-219-5200.

Unemployment Insurance Contacts

Alabama
Unemployment Compensation Division
Department of Industrial Relations
649 Monroe St., Room 629
Montgomery, AL 36131
334-242-8025
www.dir.state.al.us/uc.htm
Weekly benefit range: $45-190
Duration of benefits: 15-26 weeks

Alaska
Unemployment Insurance Program Manager
Employment Security Division
P.O. Box 25509
Juneau, AK 99802
907-465-2712
www.labor.state.ak.us
Weekly benefit range: $44-248
Duration of benefits: 16-26 weeks

Arizona
ESA Administrator
P.O. Box 6123-910A
Phoenix, AZ 85007
602-255-3722
Weekly benefit range: $40-185
Duration of benefits: 12-26 weeks

Arkansas
Unemployment Insurance Director
Arkansas Employment Security Department
P.O. Box 2981
Little Rock, AR 72203
501-682-3200
Weekly benefit range: $47-264
Duration of benefits: 9-26 weeks

California
Unemployment Insurance
Employment Development Department
P.O. Box 826880-MIC 86
Sacramento, CA 94280
916-654-9047
wwwedd.cahwnet.gov/uiind.htm
Weekly benefit range: $40-230
Duration of benefits: 12-26 weeks

Colorado
Office of Unemployment Insurance
1515 Arapahoe St.- Tower 2, Suite 400
Denver, CO 80202
303-620-4712
http://unempben.cdle.state.co.us
Weekly benefit range: $25 -272
Duration of benefits: 13-26 weeks

Connecticut
State Labor Department
200 Folley Brook Blvd.
Wethersfield, CT 06109
203-566-4280
www.ctdol.state.ct.us/progsupt/
unemplt/unemploy.htm
Weekly benefit range: $15-362
Duration of benefits: 26 weeks

Delaware
Division of Unemployment Insurance
P.O. Box 9950
Wilmington, DE 19809

302-761-8350
Weekly benefit range: $20-300
Duration of benefits: 24-26 weeks

District of Columbia
Office of Unemployment Compensation
Department of Employment Services
500 C St., NW, Room 515
Washington, Dc 20001
202-724-7274
Weekly benefit range: $50-359
Duration of benefits: 20-26 weeks

Florida
Division of Unemployment Compensation
201 Caldwell Building
Tallahassee, FL 32399
904-921-3889
Weekly benefit range: $10-250
Duration of benefits: 10-26 weeks

Georgia
Assistance Commissioner
Unemployment Insurance
Georgia Department of Labor
148 International Blvd.,NE
Suite 718
Atlanta, GA 30303
404-656-3050
Weekly benefit range: $37-205
Duration of benefits: 9-26 weeks

Hawaii
Administrator
Unemployment Insurance Division
Department of Labor and Industrial Relations
830 Punchbowl St., Room 325
Honolulu, HI 96813
808-586-9069
www.aloha.net/~edpso/uitext.html
Weekly benefit range: $5-347
Duration of benefits: 26 weeks

Idaho
Administrator
Unemployment Insurance Division
Department of Employment
317 Main St.
Boise, ID 83735
208-334-6280
www.doe.state.id.us/id-ui.htm#menu
Weekly benefit range: $44-248
Duration of benefits: 10-26 weeks

Illinois
Unemployment Insurance Manager
Illinois Department of Employment Security
401 S. State St., Room 622
Chicago, IL 60605
312-793-1837
http://il.jobsearch.org/html/worker.htm
Weekly benefit range: $51-269
Duration of benefits: 26 weeks

Indiana
Department of Workforce Development
Indiana Government Center South
10 N. Senate Ave., Room 302
Indianapolis, IN 46204

317-233-5724
Weekly benefit range: $87-217
Duration of benefits: 8-26 weeks

Iowa
Bureau Chief of Job Insurance
Department of Employment Services
1000 E. Grand Ave.
Des Moines, IA 50319
515-281-5387
www.state.ia.us/government/wd/ui/index.html
Weekly benefit range: $33-274
Duration of benefits: 11-26 weeks

Kansas
Director
Division of Employment Security
Department of Human Resources
401 Topeka Ave.
Topeka, KS 66603
785-296-5486
www.hr.state.ks.us/ui/html/enui.htm
Weekly benefit range: $65-260
Duration of benefits: 10-26 weeks

Kentucky
Director
Division for Unemployment Insurance
Department of Employment Services
275 E. Main St., 2nd Floor
Frankfort, KY 40621
502-564-2900
www.des.state.ky.us/agencies/wforce/des/
ui/ui.htm
Weekly benefit range: $32-180
Duration of benefits: 15-26 weeks

Louisiana
Director, Unemployment Insurance
Louisiana Department of Labor
P.O. Box 94094
Baton Rouge, LA 70804
504-342-3017
www.ldol.state.la.us/faqfoldr/faqui.html
Weekly benefit range: $10-181
Duration of benefits: 26 weeks

Maine
Director
Unemployment Compensation Division
Maine Department of Labor
P.O. Box 309
Augusta, ME 04332
207-287-3176
www.state.me.us/labor/ucd/homepag1.htm
Weekly benefit range: $35-303
Duration of benefits: 21-26 weeks

Maryland
Executive Director
Office of Unemployment Insurance
Department of Labor, Licensing, and
Regulation
1100 N. Eutaw St., Room 501
Baltimore, MD 21201
410-767-2464
www.dllr.state.md.us/employment/
unemployment.html
Weekly benefit range: $25-250
Duration of benefits: 26 weeks

Massachusetts

Unemployment Insurance Director
Department of Employment and Training
19 Staniford St., 2nd Floor
Boston, MA 02114
617-727-6560
www.detma.org/claimant.htm
Weekly benefit range: $14-402
Duration of benefits: 10-30 weeks

Michigan

Michigan Employment Security Commission
7310 Woodward Ave., Room 510
Detroit, MI 48202
313-876-5000
800-638-3995
www.cis.state.mi.us/ua/homepage.htm
Weekly benefit range: $42-300
Duration of benefits: 15-26 weeks

Minnesota

Assistant Commissioner
Minnesota Department of Economic Security
Job Services and Reemployment Insurance
390 N. Robert St.
St. Paul, MN 55101
651-296-3611
888-438-5627
www.des.state.mn.us/manuals/220.htm
Weekly benefit range: $38-386
Duration of benefits: 10-26 weeks

Mississippi

Director, Unemployment Insurance Division
Employment Security Commission
P.O. Box 1699
Jackson, MS 39215
601-961-7700
www.mesc.state.ms.us
Weekly benefit range: $30-180
Duration of benefits: 13-26 weeks

Missouri

Director, Unemployment Insurance
Division of Employment Security
P.O Box 59
Jefferson City, MO 65104
573-751-3670
www.dolir.state.mo.us/es/doli.-46_htm
Weekly benefit range: $45-175
Duration of benefits: 11-26 weeks

Montana

Administrator
Unemployment Insurance Division
P.O. Box 1728
Helena, MT 59624
406-444-3783
http://jsd.dli.mt.gov/ui/ui.htm
Weekly benefit range: $57-228
Duration of benefits: 8-26 weeks

Nebraska

Unemployment Insurance Director
Nebraska Department of Labor
P.O. Box 94600
550 S. 16th St.
Lincoln, NE 68509
402-471-9979
www.dol.state.ne.us/uihome.htm
Weekly benefit range: $20-184
Duration of benefits: 20-26 weeks

Nevada

Unemployment Insurance
Employment Security Department
500 E. Third St.
Carson City, NV 89713
702-687-4510
www.state.nv.us/detr/ui.html
Weekly benefit range: $16-258
Duration of benefits: 12-26 weeks

New Hampshire

Unemployment Compensation Bureau
Department of Employment Security
32 South Main St.
Concord, NH 03301
603-228-4031
www.nhworks.state.nh.us
Weekly benefit range: $32-216
Duration of benefits: 26 weeks

New Jersey

Director, Division of Unemployment and
Disability Insurance
New Jersey Department of Labor
CN 058
Trenton, NJ 08625
609-292-2460
www.wnjpin.state.nj.us
Weekly benefit range: $60-390
Duration of benefits: 15-26 weeks

New Mexico

Chief, Unemployment Insurance Bureau
New Mexico Department of Labor
401 Broadway Blvd., NE
P.O. Box 1928
Albuquerque, NM 87103
505-841-8431
www.state.nm.us/dol/dol_form.html
Weekly benefit range: $42-212
Duration of benefits: 19-26 weeks

New York

Director, Unemployment Insurance Division
New York State Department of Labor
State Campus, Building 12
Albany, NY 12240
518-457-2878
www.labor.state.ny.us/html/wimdinpg.htm
Weekly benefit range: $40-300
Duration of benefits: 26 weeks

North Carolina

Unemployment Insurance Division
Employment Security Commission of North
Carolina
P.O. Box 25903
Raleigh, NC 27611
919-733-3121
www.esc.state.nc.us/html/wi_division.html
Weekly benefit range: $15-322
Duration of benefits: 13-26 weeks

North Dakota

Director, Job Insurance Division
Job Service North Dakota
P.O. Box 5507
Bismarck, ND 58506
701-328-5000
www.state.nd.us/jsnd/uins.html
Weekly benefit range: $43-243
Duration of benefits: 12-26 weeks

Ohio

Director, Unemployment Insurance
Ohio Bureau of Employment Services
145 S. Front St.
Columbus, OH 43215
614-466-9755
www.state.oh.us/obes/shared.htm
Weekly benefit range: $66-339
Duration of benefits: 20-26 weeks

Oklahoma

Unemployment Insurance Director
Employment Security Commission
2401 North Lincoln
203 Will Rogers Memorial Office Building
Oklahoma City, OK 73152
405-557-7190
www.desc.state.ok.us/iu/default.htm

Weekly benefit range: $16-262
Duration of benefits: 20-26 weeks

Oregon

Programs and Methods
Employment Department
875 Union St., NE
Salem, OR 97311
503-947-1470
www.emp.state.or.us/benefits/uiinfo.htm
Weekly benefit range: $70-301
Duration of benefits: 4-26 weeks

Pennsylvania

Bureau of U.C. Benefits and Allowances
Department of Labor and Industry
Room 615 Labor and Industry Building
Seventh and Forster Sts.
Harrisburg, PA 17121
717-787-3547
www.li.state.pa.us/ben.html
Weekly benefit range: $33-375
Duration of benefits: 16-26 weeks

Puerto Rico

Director, Unemployment Insurance Division
Bureau of Employment Security
505 Munoz Rivera Ave., FL 12
Hato Rey, PR 00918
809-754-5352
Weekly benefit range: $7-133
Duration of benefits: 26 weeks

Rhode Island

Assistant Director
Unemployment Insurance
Department of Employment and Training
101 Friendship St.
Providence, RI 02903
401-222-3652
www.det.state.ri.us/webdev/ui/html
Weekly benefit range: $41-404
Duration of benefits: 15-26 weeks

South Carolina

Deputy Executive Director
Unemployment Compensation
Employment Security Commission
P.O. Box 995
Columbia, SC 29202
803-737-2787
www.sces.org
Weekly benefit range: $20-238
Duration of benefits: 15-26 weeks

South Dakota

Director, Unemployment Insurance Division
Department of Labor
P.O. Box 4730
Aberdeen, SD 57402
605-626-2312
www.state.sd.us/dol/ui/ui-home.htm
Weekly benefit range: $28-194
Duration of benefits: 15-26 weeks

Tennessee

Deputy Commissioner
Tennessee Department of Employment
Security
500 James Robertson Pkwy., 12th Floor
Nashville, TN 37245
615-741-2131
www.state.tn.us/empsec/ui/ui.htm
Weekly benefit range: $30-200
Duration of benefits: 12-26 weeks

Texas

Director, Unemployment Insurance
Texas Workforce Commission
15th and Congress, Room 668
Austin, TX 78778
512-463-0735

www.twc.state.tx.us/ui/bnfts/benehp.html
Weekly benefit range: $47-287
Duration of benefits: 9-26 weeks

Utah

Director, Unemployment Insurance
Workforce Services
140 East 300 South
P.O. Box 11249
Salt Lake City, UT 84147
801-536-7423
http://dwsa.state.ut.us/default.htm
Weekly benefit range: $20-284
Duration of benefits: 10-26 weeks

Vermont

Unemployment Insurance
Department of Employment and Training
5 Green Mountain Dr.
P.O. Box 488
Montpelier, VT 05602
802-828-4100
www.det.state.vt.us/~detui/ui-dir.htm
Weekly benefit range: $25-275
Duration of benefits: 26 weeks

Virginia

Field Operations
Virginia Employment Commission
703 E. Main St.
Richmond, VA 23219
804-786-3004
www.vec.state.va.us
Weekly benefit range: $55-228
Duration of benefits: 12-26 weeks

Washington

Assistant Commissioner
Employment Security Department
P.O. Box 9046
Olympia, WA 98507
360-902-9303
www.wa.gov/esd/ui.htm
Weekly benefit range: $82-384
Duration of benefits: 10-30 weeks

West Virginia

Director
Unemployment Compensation Division
Bureau of Employment Programs
112 California Ave.
Charleston, WV 25305

304-558-2624
www.state.wv.us/bep/uc/default.htm
Weekly benefit range: $24-290
Duration of benefits: 26 weeks

Wisconsin

Administrator
Division of Unemployment Insurance
201 East Washington Ave., Room 371
P.O. Box 7905
Madison, WI 53707
608-266-7074
www.dwd.state.wi.us/ui/
Weekly benefit range: $52-274
Duration of benefits: 12-26 weeks

Wyoming

Administrator
Division of Unemployment Insurance
Department of Employment
P.O. Box 2760
Casper, WY 82602
307-235-3254
http://wydoe.state.wy.us/erd/ui/
Weekly benefit range: $18-250
Duration of benefits: 12-26 weeks

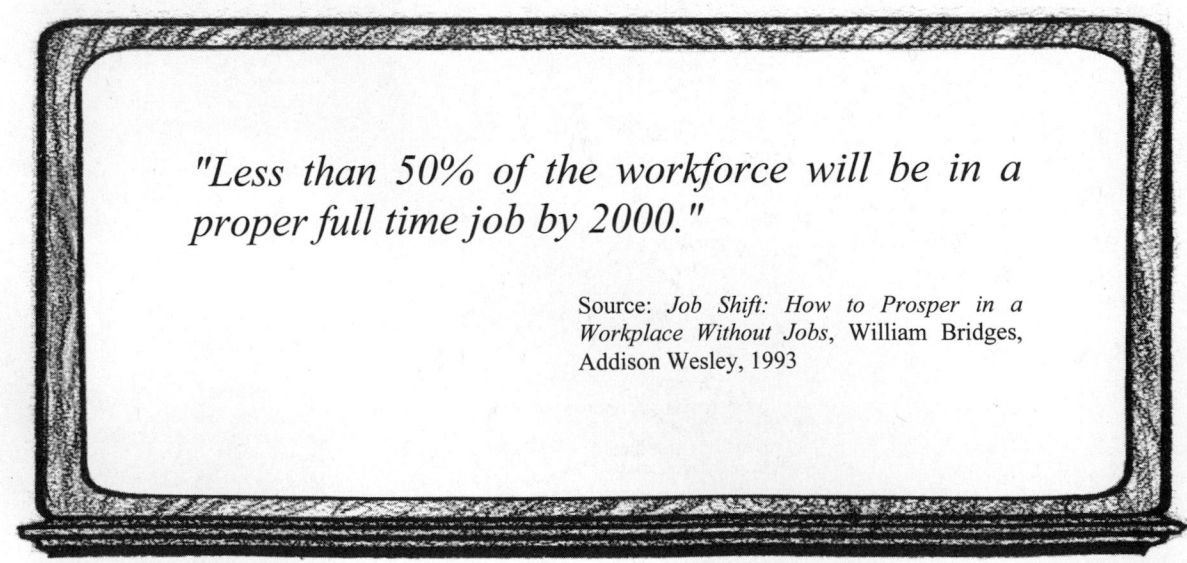

"Less than 50% of the workforce will be in a proper full time job by 2000."

Source: *Job Shift: How to Prosper in a Workplace Without Jobs*, William Bridges, Addison Wesley, 1993

I Wanna Get My GED
Or More Adult Education

I Wanna Get My GED

People drop out of or fail to complete high school for many different reasons. But one thing is clear; getting your high school diploma or GED is the key to advancement. You can join the privileged ranks of people like Bill Cosby, Mary Lou Retton, and 10 million other people famous and not so famous who have obtained their GED.

What is a GED and how do you get one? GED stands for General Educational Development. When you take a GED test, it tests your knowledge and ability in five different areas: writing skills, social studies, science, interpreting literature and the arts, and mathematics. This is a way for you to earn your GED diploma, which you can then use to apply for jobs, enter training programs, or even attend college!

GED tests are given at sites all across the United States. There are several ways to learn where the nearest GED test site is located. You can contact your local Board of Education, your State Department of Adult Education, or the GED Information Hotline at 800-62-MY-GED. This hotline is operated by the American Council on Education (P.O. Box 81826, Lincoln, NE 68501) which administers the GED tests.

You can take the GED without studying if you feel prepared. However, many people who have been out of school for awhile may need a little time to study. There are different ways to do this. Your local library or bookstore offer a variety of GED study books, many of which come with practice tests. The GED hotline listed above can also provide you with information on how to purchase a practice test. Many local school boards, community organizations, and community colleges offer adult education courses. Your local public television station may also run programs to help you study for the test.

Another wonderful resource is the National Literacy Hotline at 800-228-8813 (Contact Center, P.O. Box 81826, Lincoln, NE 68501). This hotline maintains a database of resources and organizations that focus on literacy and can connect you to literacy resources and contacts in your area.

Other Resources

Clearinghouse on Adult Education and Literacy
400 Maryland Ave., SW
Washington, DC 20202   202-205-9996
This clearinghouse can direct you to state contacts for assistance and has publications which review different types of training and education programs.

ERIC Clearinghouse on Adult, Career and Vocational Education
Ohio State University
Center on Education and Training for Employment
1900 Kenny Rd.   614-292-4353
Columbus, OH 43210   800-848-4815
This clearinghouse has literature and relevant materials covering the topics of adult and continuing education, ranging from basic literacy training through professional skill upgrading. They can conduct a database search for materials on a specific subject of interest and has a publications list of resource summaries.

State Directors of Adult Education

Most of us learned the basics — reading, writing, and math — in school. But there are millions of Americans who never learned how to read, much less mastered any of the other fundamental skills necessary to survive in the world today. Without the ability to read, one can't check the want ads, fill out a job application, or attempt to take a job placement test. The road to literacy is never easy, but it's even more difficult as you get older. It takes a great deal of time and effort to achieve your goal of literacy, but reading is the only way to get ahead.

There are many ways to learn what you missed in high school. Nonprofits across this country have been established to deal with illiteracy. They have programs throughout the United States where volunteers work one on one with participants to improve their reading and math skills. The National Literacy Hotline at 800-228-8813 is designed to put callers in touch with literacy programs close by. You may also contact some of the nonprofits listed below to help a loved one learn to read and enjoy a more satisfying life.

Literacy Volunteers of America, 635 James Street, Syracuse, NY 13203; 315-472-0001; {www.literacyvolunteers.org}.

Reading is Fundamental, Smithsonian Institution, 1825 Connecticut Ave., NW, Suite 400, Washington, DC 20009; 202-673-1616; {www.rif.org}.

National Institute for Literacy, 1400 I Street, NW, Suite 730, Washington, DC 20006; 202-233-2025; {www.nifl.gov}.

Barbara Bush Foundation for Family Literacy, 1112 16th Street, NW, Suite 340, Washington, DC 20036; 202-955-6183; {www.barbarabush foundation.com}.

The Federal government supports programs as well. The local board of education may provide classes, as may the nearest community college. The following is a list of state Adult Education Directors. Contact the Director for your state if you are having trouble locating the services you need, or you may contact the headquarters at Clearinghouse on Adult Education and Literacy, Division of Adult Education and Literacy, U.S. Department of Education, 400 Maryland Ave., SW, Washington, DC 20202; 202-205-8270.

Alabama
Nancy Beggs
State Administrator
GED Testing Program
Adult Basic Education Section
Division of Federal Administrative Services
Department of Education
Gordon Persons Building, Room 5343
50 North Ripley St.
Montgomery, AL 36130
334-242-8181
Fax: 334-242-2236
www.alsde.edu

Alaska
Christopher Snyder
State Supervisor, Adult Basic Education
Department of Labor and Workforce
P.O. Box 25509
Juneau, AK 99802-5509
907-465-8714
Fax: 907-465-4537
www.labor.state.ak.us

American Samoa
Ms. Fa'au'uga Achica
Dean of Continuing and Adult Education
American Samoa Community College
Board of Higher Education
Mapusaga Campus
Pago Pago, AS 96799
011-684-699-9155
Fax: 011-684-699-2062
www.amsamoacc.as

Arizona
Karen Liersch
State Administrator
Adult Education Services
Department of Education
1535 West Jefferson
Phoenix, AZ 85007
602-258-4986
Fax: 602-258-2410
www.ade.state.az.us/Adult-Ed/

Arkansas
Mr. Garland Hankins
Deputy Director
Adult Education Section
Department of Education
Luther S. Hardin Building, #506
Third Capitol Mall
Little Rock, AR 72201-1083
501-682-1970/1978
Fax: 501-682-1706
www.work-ed.state.ar.us/adult.html

California
Mary Tobias Weaver
State Director
Adult Education
Department of Education
660 J Street, Suite 400
Sacramento, CA 95814
916-322-2175
Fax: 916-327-7089
www.cde.ca.gov/adulteducation/

Colorado
Pamela Smith
State Director, ABE

Matthew Lesko, Information USA, Inc., 12081 Nebel Street, Rockville, MD 20852 • 1-800-955-7693 • www.lesko.com

State Directors of Adult Education

Division of Adult Education
201 E. Colfax Ave.
Denver, CO 80203
303-866-6640
Fax: 303-866-6947
www.cde.state.co.us/index.adult.htm

Connecticut
Ms. Roberta Pawloski
Director, Division of Vocational Technical
and Adult Education
Department of Education
25 Industrial Park Rd.
Middletown, CT 06457
860-807-2100
Fax: 860-807-2127
www.state.ct.us/sde/deps/adult/index.htm

Delaware
Dr. Fran Tracy-Mumford
State Supervisor
Adult and Community Education
Department of Public Instruction
P.O. Box 1402
J.G. Townsend Building
Dover, DE 19903
302-739-3743
Fax: 302-739-1318
www.state.de.us

District of Columbia
K. Brisbane
Assistant Superintendent
Adult Education Office
University of the District of Columbia
4200 Connecticut Ave., NW
Washington, DC 20008
202-724-7181
Fax: 202-724-7188

Federated States of Micronesia
Dr. Catalino L. Cantero
Secretary, Department of Education
P.O. Box P.S. 87
Palikir, Pohnpei, FM 96941
011-691-320-2609
Fax: 11-691-320-5500

Florida
Adult and Vocational Education (Florida)
State Department of Education
Division of Workforce Development
644 FEC Building
Tallahassee, FL 32399-0400
850-487-6191
Fax: 850-487-4911
www.firn.edu/doe/workforce/adult_ed.htm

Georgia
Dr. Jean DeVard-Kemp
Assistant Commissioner for Adult Literacy
Department of Technical and A.E.
1800 Century Place
Atlanta, GA 30345-4304
404-679-1635
Fax: 404-679-1630
www.dtae.org

Guam
Phyllis Apiag
Occupational Education Services, Academic
Education Services and Student Services
Guam Community College
P.O. Box 23069
Main Postal Facility
Guam, 96921
011-671-735-5517
Fax: 011-671-734-1003
www.guamcc.net

Hawaii
Community Education Section
Department of Education
634 Pensacola Street, Room 222
Honolulu, HI 96814
808-594-0170
Fax: 808-594-0181
http://doe.k12.hi.us/communityschools.htm

Idaho
Dr. Shirley Spencer
Director, A.E.
Department of Education
Len B. Jordon Office Building
650 W. State St.
P.O. Box 83720
Boise, ID 83720
208-332-6931
Fax: 208-334-4664
www.sde.state.id.us

Illinois
John Klit
Director, A.E.
Business Community and Family Partnerships
State Board of Education
100 N. First St., MC C418
Springfield, IL 62777
217-782-3370
Fax: 217-782-9224
www.isbe.net/partnerships/default.htm

Indiana
L. Warner
Director, Division of Adult Education
Department of Education
Room 229, State House
Indianapolis, IN 46204
317-232-0522
Fax: 317-233-0859
http://doe.state.in.us/adulted/welcome.html

Iowa
John Hartwig
Chief, Adult Education
Department of Education
Grimes State Office Building
Des Moines, IA 50319-0146
515-281-3636
Fax: 515-281-6544
www.state.ua.us/educate

Kansas
Adult Education (Kansas)
Kansas Board of Regents
700 SW Harrison, Suite 1410
Topeka, KS 66603
785-296-7159
Fax: 785-296-0983
www.ksbe.state.ks.us/welcome.html

Kentucky
Cheryl King
Office Head
Adult Education Services
Department for Adult and Technical Education
Capital Plaza Tower, 3rd Floor
500 Mero St.
Frankfort, KY 40601
502-564-5114
Fax: 502-564-5436
http://adulted.state.ky.us

Louisiana
Mr. Glenn Gossett, Director
Bureau of Adult and Community Education
Department of Education
P.O. Box 94064
Baton Rouge, LA 70804-9064
225-342-3336
Fax: 225-219-4439
www.doe.state.la.us

Maine
Dr. Paul (Randy) Walker, Director
Adult and Community Education
Department of Education
State House Station 23
Augusta, ME 04333
207-624-6730
Fax: 207-624-6731
www.state.me.us

Maryland
P. Bennett, Director
Adult Education and Literacy Services Branch
Division of Career Technology and Adult
Learning, 3rd Floor
Maryland State Department of Education
200 West Baltimore St.
Baltimore, MD 21201
410-767-0168
Fax: 410-333-2099
www.research.umbc.edu/~ira/

Massachusetts
Mr. Robert Bickerton, Director
Adult and Community Service
Department of Education
350 Main St., 4th Floor
Malden, MA 02148
781-338-3850
Fax: 781-338-3394
www.doe.mass.edu/acis/

Michigan
Adult Education Unit (Michigan)
State Department of Career Development
Victor Office Center
201 North Washington Square, First Floor
Lansing, MI 48913
517-241-4000
Fax: 517-373-0314
www.mdcd.org/Core/2frame2.html

Minnesota
Christine Jax
Adult Basic Education (Minnesota)
Department of Children, Families & Learning
1500 Highway 36 West
Roseville, MN 55113
651-582-8442
Fax: 651-582-8496
http://children.state.mn.us/

Mississippi
Ms. Eloise Johnson
Director of Literacy
State Board for Community and Junior
Colleges
Education and Research Center
3825 Ridgewood Rd.
Jackson, MS 39211
601-432-6481
Fax: 601-432-6365
www.sbcjc.cc.ms.us

Missouri
Steve Coffman
Director, Adult Education
Department of Elementary and Secondary
Education
P.O. Box 480
Jefferson City, MO 65102
573-751-1249
Fax: 573-526-5710
www.dese.state.mo.us/divvoced/aed/
index.html

Montana
David Strong
Director, Adult Education
State Office of Public Instruction
P.O. Box 2022501
1300 11th Avenue

Helena, MT 59620
406-444-4443
Fax; 406-444-1373
www.metnet.state.mt.us

Nebraska

Vicki Bauer
Director, Adult and Community Education
Department of Education
301 Centennial Mall South
P.O. Box 94987
Lincoln, NE 68509
402-471-4807
Fax: 402-471-8127
www.nde.state.ne.us

Nevada

Laura Hale
Adult Education Office (Nevada)
Nevada Department of Education
Workforce Education Team
700 East Fifth Street
Carson City, NV 89701
775-687-9104
Fax: 775-687-9114
www.nde.state.nv.us

New Hampshire

Mr. Art Ellison
Supervisor, ABE
Department of Education
101 Pleasant St.
Concord, NH 03301
603-271-6698
Fax: 603-271-1953
www.ed.state.nh.us

New Jersey

Diane Bates
Adult Education Office (New Jersey)
Department of Education
Office of School-to-Career
River View Executive Plaza Building 100
Route 29, P.O. Box 500
Trenton, NJ 08625-0500
609-984-2420
Fax: 609-984-0573
www.doe.state.nj.us

New Mexico

Ms. Muriel Lawler
State Director, ABE
Department of Education
Education Building
300 Don Gaspar
Santa Fe, NM 87501
505-827-6672
Fax: 505-827-4041
www.nmabe.org/ABE.htm

New York

Jean Stevens
Director, Division of Continuing Education
State Education Department
Room 319, Education Building
Albany, NY 12234
518-474-8892
Fax: 518-474-0319
www.emsc.nysed.gov/workforce/home.html

North Carolina

Randy Whitfield
Basic Skills Program (North Carolina)
North Carolina Community College System
Caswell Building
5024 Mail Service Center
Raleigh, NC 27699-5024
919-733-7051
Fax: 919-733-0680
www.ncccs.cc.nc.us

North Dakota

Mr. G. David Massey
Director, Adult Education
Department of Public Instruction
600 Boulevard Ave. East
Department 201
Bismarck, ND 58505-0440
701-328-2393
Fax: 701-328-4770
www.dpi.state.nd.us/adulted/index.shtm

Northern Mariana Islands

Jack Sablan, Jr.
Director, Adult Education
Northern Marianas College
Commonwealth of the Northern Mariana Islands
P.O. Box 501250
Saipan, MP 96950
011-670-234-3690
Fax: 011-670-234-4940
www.nmcnet.edu

Ohio

James Bowling
Adult Basic and Literacy Education (Ohio)
Ohio Department of Education
Mail Stop 406
25 South Front Street
Columbus, OH 43215-4183
614-466-5015
Fax: 614-752-1640
www.ode.state.oh.us/ctae/adult/ABLE/

Oklahoma

Linda Young
Director, Lifelong Learning
Department of Education
Oliver Hodge Memorial Education Building
2500 N. Lincoln Blvd., Room 180
Oklahoma City, OK 73105-4599
405-521-3321
Fax: 405-522-5394
http://sde.state.ok.us/pro/abe.html

Oregon

Sharon Walker
Assistant Commissioner, Office of Community College Services
255 Capitol St., NE
Salem, OR 97310
503-378-8648
Fax: 503-378-8434
www.odccwd.state.or.us

Pennsylvania

Ms. Cheryl Keenan
Director, Bureau of Adult, Basic and Literacy Education
Department of Education
333 Market St., 12th Floor
Harrisburg, PA 17126-0333
717-772-3737
Fax: 717-783-0583
www.able.state.pa.us/able/site/default.asp

Puerto Rico

Puerto Rico Literacy and Adult Education Resource Center
P.O. Box 190759
San Juan, PR 00919
787-281-0271
Fax: 787-282-6312
Email: oliver_f@de.prstar.net

Republic of Palau

Office of Adult Education (Palau)
Ministry of Education
Bureau of Curriculum and Instruction
P.O. Box 1346
Koror, PW 96940
680-488-1003

Fax: 680-488-2830
Email: emesiocm@palaunet.com

Republic of the Marshall Islands

Ms. Biram Stege
State Director
Republic of the Marshall Islands
College of the Marshall Islands
Majuro, Marshall Islands 96960
011-692-625-3394
Fax: 011-692-625-7203
http://literacynet.org/marshall

Rhode Island

Robert Mason
Rhode Island Department of Elementary and Secondary Education
Shepard Building
255 Westminster Street
Providence, RI 02903-3414
401-222-4600, Ext.
Fax: 401-222-2537
www.ridoe.net/adulted_ged/Default.htm

South Carolina

Mr. Sam Drew
State Director
Office of Community Education
South Carolina Department of Education
1429 Senate St.
902 Rutledge Office Building
Columbia, SC 29201
803-734-8071
Fax: 803-734-2780
www.myschools.com/offices.ace

South Dakota

Marcia Hess
Adult Education and Literacy Office
Department of Labor
700 Governors Dr.
Pierre, SD 57501-2291
605-773-5821
Fax: 605-773-6184
www.state.ad.us/dol/abe/index.html

Tennessee

Mr. Phil White
Office of Adult Education (Tennessee)
Department of Labor and Workforce Development
Davy Crockett Tower, 11th Floor
500 James Robertson Parkway
Nashville, TN 37245
615-741-7054
Fax: 615-532-4899
Email: pwhite@mail.state.tn.us

Texas

Dr. Sheila Rosenberg
Program Director
Adult Education
Division of A.E./Employment Training, Funding and Compliance
Texas Education Agency
1701 North Congress Ave.
Austin, TX 78701
512-463-9294
Fax: 512-475-3661
www.tea.state.tx.us/adult

Utah

Mr. David Steele
Adult Education Services
Office of Education
250 East 500 South St.
Salt Lake City, UT 84111
801-538-7824
Fax: 801-538-7882
www.usoe.k12.ut.us/adulted/home.htm

Vermont
Ms. Sandra Robinson
Chief, Adult Education Unit
Department of Education
State Office Building
120 State Street
Montpelier, VT 05620-2501
802-828-3134
Fax: 802-828-3146
www.state.vt.us/educ/cwd/index.htm

Virginia
Dr Yvonne V Thayer
Office of Adult Education and Literacy
(Virginia)
State Department of Education
P.O. Box 2120
Richmond, VA 23218-2120
804-225-2293
Fax: 804-225-3352
www.pen.k12.va.us/

Virgin Islands
Anna C. Lewis
Office of Vocational, Technical, and Adult
Education (Virgin Islands)

Department of Education
44-46 Kongens Gade
St. Thomas, VI 00801
340-776-3484
Fax: 340-776-3488

Washington
Israel David Mendoza
Director
Office of Adult Literacy
State Board for Community and Technical
Colleges
P.O. Box 42495
Olympia, WA 98504-2495
360-753-3662
Fax: 360-664-8808
www.sbctc.ctc.edu

West Virginia
Ms. Kathi Polis
Assistant Director, A.E.
Department of Education
Building 6, Room 230
Capitol Complex
1900 Kanawha Blvd., East
Charleston, WV 25305

304-558-6318
Fax: 304-558-3946
http://wvabe.state.k12.wv.us

Wisconsin
Mr. Dwight A. York
State Director, Vocational, Technical and
Adult Education
Board of Vocational, Technical and Adult
State and Adult Education
310 Price Place
P.O. Box 7874
Madison, WI 53707
608-266-1207
Fax: 608-266-1690
www.board.tec.wi.us

Wyoming
Bruce Snyder
Adult Basic Education Office (Wyoming)
Wyoming Community College Commission
2020 Carey Avenue, Eighth Floor
Cheyenne, WY 82002
307-777-3545
Fax: 307-777-6567
www.commission.wcc.cdu

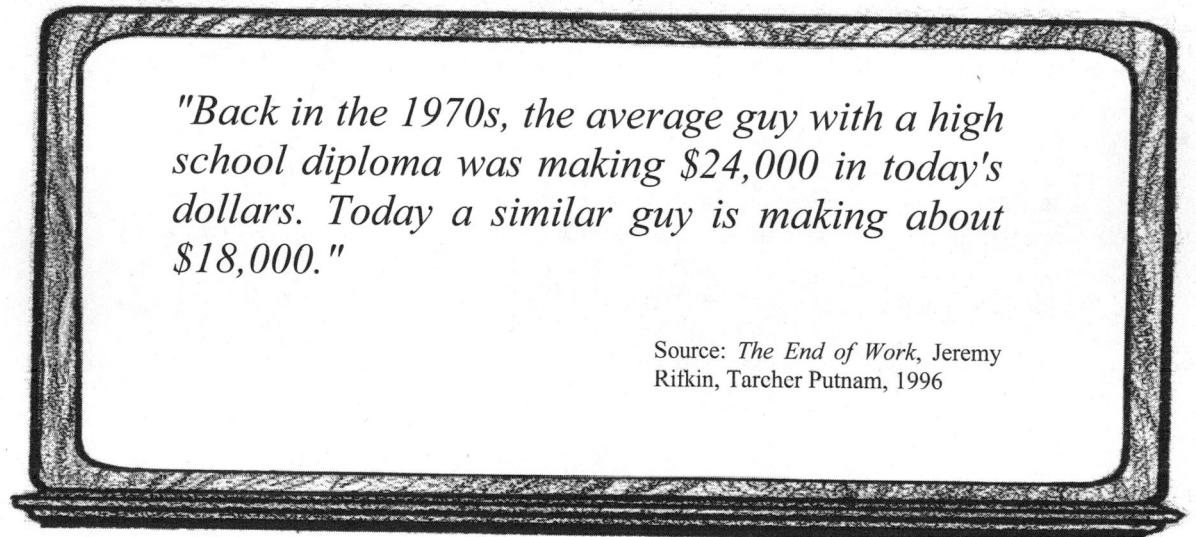

"Back in the 1970s, the average guy with a high school diploma was making $24,000 in today's dollars. Today a similar guy is making about $18,000."

Source: *The End of Work*, Jeremy
Rifkin, Tarcher Putnam, 1996

Free Help For Migrant Workers
Who Want To Get Their GEDs

Program: Migrant Education — High School Equivalency Program - 84.141

Description: Migrant farmworkers who missed out completing high school because of the demands of seasonal work schedules now qualify for a little known program called the Migrant Education High School Equivalency Program. Over 25 different nonprofit groups across the country receive money under this program to offer free help to migrant workers who want to earn their GEDs, enabling them to get better jobs and perhaps go on to college.

What You Can Get: This program provides:
- transportation to and from classes
- weekly stipend
- GED preparation and classroom instruction
- housing for those in the residential programs
- tutorial assistance
- academic and vocational counseling
- career advisement
- assistance in applying to universities, colleges, junior colleges, vocational institutions, military services

Many programs will pay expenses to get students to their sites. Some of the programs are residential programs, where you can live while you are studying to complete your GED. They even give you meals there. Other programs offer satellite sites, which may be within driving range. Your commuting costs can be covered. Remember, these programs are free, so take advantage of them and get your GED.

Who Is Eligible: To be eligible you must be a migrant or seasonally employed worker or their children who, within the last 24 months, has worked a minimum of 75 days in farmwork.

Money Available: The annual budget for this program is $3,000,000.

National Office:
Office of Migrant Education
U.S. Department of Education
400 Maryland Ave., SW
Washington, DC 20202
202-260-1164
www.ed.gov/offices/OESE/MEP/index.html

Local Offices:
For more information, contact the site nearest you from the list below. Each listing gives you the person to contact, address, phone number, recruitment area, and special services that the program offers.

High School Equivalency Program Sites

Alabama
see Florida

Arizona
see Texas

California
Dr. Joyce Bishop
California State University - Sacramento
CSUS High School Equivalency Program
6000 J St.
Sacramento, CA 95819
916-278-3708
Recruitment Area: California Central Valley Area
Program Services: 2 sites in Sacramento area; GED instruction in 3 hour blocks-morning, afternoon, and evening; Counseling and other support services; Social and cultural activities; Referral services and job placement; Summer Transition Enrichment Program (STEP) for students interested in enrolling in college; Vocational instruction/career education to help place students in employment.

Colorado
Leonard Baca
University of Colorado-Boulder
(BUENO Center for Multicultural Education)
Campus Box 249
Boulder, CO 80309-0249
303-492-5416
Recruitment Area: Colorado-Statewide
Program Services: GED course of study; Tutoring; Personal counseling; Cultural and social enrichment activities; Student stipends; Post HEP job or college placement; Some computer skills; Vocational orientation and skills training; College prep GED alternative; Career counseling; Career development plan.

Delaware
see Maryland

Florida
Ann Cranston-Gingras
University of South Florida/Tampa
College of Education/Special Education Department
4202 Fowler Ave., Edu 162
Tampa, FL 33620-5650
813-974-5806
www.coedu.usf.edu/cme/
Recruitment Area: Florida, Alabama, Georgia, Mississippi, South Carolina, Louisiana and Kentucky
Program Services: Individualized academic skills program; Special academic assistance; Vocational training; Job placement; Advanced educational placement; Community living/awareness skills; Mentor system; Social and cultural development activities; To provide academic instruction to enhance career/academic opportunities, academic/career guidance and counseling; Assist students in identifying and applying for positions in vocational training, employment, and armed forces.

Georgia
see Florida

Idaho
Scott Willison
Boise State University
College of Education
1910 University Drive
Boise, ID 83725
208-426-3292
Recruitment Area: Southern Idaho, Northern Utah, Northern California, Northern Nevada, and Eastern Oregon
Program Services: Academic services (GED and government classes, computer assisted instruction and resume preparation, video cassette instruction, individualized and small group tutorial assistance)
Placement (aid students enrolling in post-secondary institutions, assist in securing financial aid and veteran's benefits, train in job interviewing techniques, positive language skills, vocational fields, etc.).

Kentucky
see Florida

Louisiana
see Florida

Maryland
George Ullah
Center for Human Services
7200 Wisconsin Ave., Suite 600
Bethesda, MD 20814
301-941-8451
Recruitment Area: Adams County, PA; Somerset County, MD; Kent and Sussex, DE; Gloucester County, NJ
Program Services: Instructional Courses-mathematics, science, social studies, reading, ESL, and writing.
Transition Skills-financial management, health, alcohol and drug prevention, use of community services.

Mississippi
Bobbie Harris
Mississippi Valley State University
Office of Continuing Education
P.O. Box 7229
Itta Bena, MS 38941
601-254-3468
Recruitment Area: State of Mississippi with emphasis in the Delta region
Program Services: Reading laboratory to determine reading level and individualized student plan; Computer assisted instruction; College preparatory classes; Student newsletter; Diagnostic monitoring of student's progress; Opportunity for personal growth and self-expression; Individualized and group counseling in academic, career, personal area, student development, communication, problem-solving and assertiveness; Daily tutorial services from University students; Job placement/training and apprenticeship program; Cultural and recreational activities.
Student Council: Learn parliamentary procedures and organize social activities.

Montana
see Washington

Nevada
see Idaho

New Jersey
See Maryland

New Mexico
Annette Garcia
Northern New Mexico Community College
Planning & Development
General Delivery
El Rito, NM 87530
505-581-4116
Recruitment Area: Recruitment activities will be conducted throughout North Central New Mexico, particularly the Espanola, El Rito and Taos areas
Program Services: Individualized academic instruction; Tutorial assistance
Career Counseling: Employability development plan, job finding and job holding skills, placement assistance, career advisement.
Personal development and support services: Counseling, cultural enrichment, medical services.
Financial aid: stipend, meal assistance, travel allocation, room and board for commuter students.

New York
HEO
Robert Apicella
SUNY at Oneonta
Bugbee Hall, Room 300
Oneonta, NY 13820
607-436-2767
www.oneonta.edu/external/hep
Recruitment Area: Eastern Stream
Program Services: GED course of study and tutoring; Vocational or college orientation; Counseling services for career exploration and personal development; Social/cultural enrichment activities; Student stipends; Room and board for residents; Post HEP job placement; Independent study/mentor component.

North Carolina
see Tennessee

Oregon
Emilio Hernandez
University of Oregon
College of Education
1685 East 17th Ave.
Eugene, OR 97403
503-346-0882
Recruitment Area: Oregon, Northern California, Southwestern Idaho, and Southern Washington
Program Services: Majority of students live on campus and participate in campus activities.
GED classes five days a week for six hours a day in science, social studies, math, literature, and grammar. Classes offered in Spanish for students with limited English. Counseling and placement services.

Pennsylvania
See Maryland

Puerto Rico
Orlando Colon
Pontifical Catholic University of Puerto Rico
Postal Sub Station #6
Ponce, Puerto Rico 00732
809-843-3265
Recruitment Area: Puerto Rico
Program Services: GED course of study and tutoring; Counseling services for career exploration and personal development; Vocational orientation; computer awareness; Cultural and recreational activities; Room and board; Post HEP job or college placement.

Sylvia Robles
Inter American University
San German Campus
Box 5100
San German, Puerto Rico 00735
787-892-6380
Recruitment Area: Southwestern and North Central Puerto Rico
Program Services: Academic services; Counseling and Guidance; Tutorial services; Financial Aid Guidance
Extracurricular activities: recreation, athletics, and social activities, Post-HEP job of college placement.

South Carolina
See Florida and Tennessee

Tennessee
Loida C. Velazquez
University of Tennessee
College of Education
600 Henley, Suite 312
Knoxville, TN 37996-0140
865-974-7929
Recruitment Area: Southeastern U.S.--Alabama, Florida, California, Kentucky, South Carolina
Program Services: 4 sites in North Carolina, South Carolina, Georgia and Tennessee; GED computer-based and videotape instruction; Academic instructional support; Counseling and career exploration; Social and cultural activities; Referral services; Job placement; Post-HEP.

Texas
Norma Chacon
University of Texas at El Paso
500 W. University Ave.
El Paso, TX 79968-0587
915-747-7652
Recruitment Area: Upper Rio Grande Valley--Texas, New Mexico, Arizona
Program Services: The El Paso HEP provides a quality program of academic and supporting services and financial assistance to 110 migrant/seasonal farmworker youth per year. The project has strong networking and interagency activity.

University of Texas-Pan American
1201 West University Dr.
Edinburg, TX 78539-2999
956-381-2521
Recruitment Area: Rio Grande Valley--Hidalgo, Willacy, Starr, and Cameron Counties
Program Services: The project operates an evening satellite program in cooperation with the Edcouch elsa I.S.D. to provide services to (1) students who work during the day and are unable to attend the daytime on-campus program; (2) teenage mothers unable to attend the on-campus program due to the lack of available child care services; and (3) students who do not have access to public transportation services. The on-campus program provides instruction in mathematics, science, literature, grammar, social studies, and essay writing. In addition, the program provides counseling and placement services, a life skills development class, computer assisted instruction, health services, housing, a stipend, and noon meal service for all students.

Dorcas Garcia
Southwest Texas State University
601 University Dr.
Education Building, Room 1002
San Marcos, TX 78666
512-245-8049
Recruitment Area: State of Texas
Program Services: SWT/HEP offers an on-campus program for both residential and commuter students and, subject to available funds, a satellite program at multiple adult education center sites throughout the service delivery area. All students, whether completing the program on-campus or through a satellite center, are able to participate in on-campus orientation and exit sessions.

Efrain Sanchez
SER-Jobs for Progress of Southwest Texas
P.O. Box 440149
Laredo, TX 78044
956-724-1844
Recruitment Area: Dimmit, Maverick, Starr, Val Verde, Webb, and Zavala Counties, Texas
Program Services: Provide HEP related services in six south and southwest Texas counties with the State's highest migrant and seasonal farmworker population. SER's HEP program is a decentralized commuter program which has classrooms in six South Texas sites. These sites are not "satellite programs" of a main campus, but each is a fully equipped and staffed classroom with a variety of services. Operates in cooperation with Laredo Junior College in Laredo; Laredo State University (a Texas A&M University campus); Southwest Texas Junior College in Uvalde, Eagle Pass and Del Rio; and Texas State Technical College in McAllen and Harlingen.

Kobla Osayande
University of Houston
4800 Calhoun, Suite 425FH
Houston, TX 77204-5874
713-743-4985
Recruitment Area: Houston, Harris, Texas, Hidalgo, Webb, Uvaldo, Dallas, Van Verde Counties
Program Services: The University Houston-HEP is well known in the community as a provider of tailored academic and counseling services to migrant seasonal farmworker youth. The project has as one of its goals to provide instruction in the use of computers. Interagency coordination and cooperation is particularly strong. Subject to available funds, HEP program has proposed to establish a satellite program at a Dallas Independent School district facility for prospective participants who reside in the Dallas area.

Mary Gonzales
Texas A&M University
Campus Box 1B1
Kingsville, TX 78363
361-593-2708
Recruitment Area: Texas--Regions I, II, and XX
Program Services: Academic instruction will be provided through one campus residential site and two satellite centers (Carrizo Springs and Harlingen). Student programs are entirely individualized, allowing each to receive instruction and services relative to specific need.

Utah
see Idaho

Washington
Dr. James Shoemaker
Washington State University/College of Education
23 Cleveland Hall
Pullman, WA 99164-5652
509-335-2454
Recruitment Area: Washington, Montana, Northern Idaho and parts of Oregon and California
Program Services: All students are residential and participate in a variety of on-campus activities; GED classes five days a week from 8:00 AM to 4:00 PM in literature and arts, writing skills, math, science, and social studies; Provide personal, vocational, and career counseling; Classes taught in English, Spanish, or bilingually, depending on students' abilities

Wisconsin

Marla Possell
Milwaukee Area Technical College
700 West State St., Room M246
Milwaukee, WI 53233
414-297-6752, ext 6752
Recruitment Area: Primarily the greater Milwaukee metropolitan area,
Midwest and selected areas of south and Southeast

Program Services: Bilingual, GED instruction; Basic skills, ESL and remedial training; Occupation skills training option; Career exploration and counseling; Job placement; Support services; Tutorial services; computer-assisted instruction; Two outreach sites.

"According to a study of 'Adult Literacy in America,' sponsored by the Department of Education, upwards of 90 million Americans are so poorly educated that they cannot even 'write a brief letter explaining an error on a credit card, figure out a Saturday departure on a bus schedule, or use a calculator to determine the difference between a sale price and a regular price.'"

Source: *The End of Work*, Jeremy Rifkin, Tarcher Putnam, 1996

Free Tutoring and Financial Counseling For Migrant Workers Who Want to Go to College

Program: Migrant Education — College Assistance Migrant Program - 84.149

Description: Migrant workers who are attending college for the first time experience a number of difficulties that are unique to them. To help these workers make a smooth transition into the academic environment of college, the Federal government has awarded a number of colleges money to set up College Assistance Migrant Programs (CAMP) to address the special needs of migrant students.

What You Can Get: The CAMP program provides intensive services during students' first year in college and is available to assist them throughout their stay at the university. CAMP provides:
- campus tours
- application assistance
- university orientation
- housing orientation
- academic advising
- tutoring
- personal counseling
- educationcultural field trips
- leadership development
- extracurricular activities
- financial aid
- health services

Who Is Eligible: Those eligible for the program are any migrant or seasonally employed agricultural worker or their children who within the last 24 months has worked a minimum of 75 days in farmwork.

Money Available: The annual budget for the program is $2,224,000.

National Office:
Mary Suazo
Office of Migrant Education
U.S. Department of Education
400 Maryland Ave., SW
Washington, DC 20202
202-260-1164
www.ed.gov/offices/OESE/MEP/index.html

Local Offices:
For more information, contact the site nearest you from the list below.

California
Marcos Sanchez
California State University-Sacramento
6000 J St.
Sacramento, CA 95819
916-278-7241
Recruitment Area: Northern California (75%), 25% other California regions
Program Services: Outreach, orientation, counseling, tutoring, cultural enrichment, health, housing, student financial assistance counseling, leadership, basic computer training

Raul Moreno
California State University-Fresno
5150 N. Maple
Fresno, CA 93726
559-278-1787
Recruitment Area: Central Valley and San Joaquin Valley
Program Services: Orientation, summer bridge, counseling, career assessment, remediation in academic skills, small group seminars, health, dental, social, cultural, tutoring, financial counseling, leadership training, peer advising.

Matthew Lesko, Information USA, Inc., 12081 Nebel Street, Rockville, MD 20852 • 1-800-955-7693 • www.lesko.com

Jorge Moreno
California Department of Education
721 Capitol Mall, 2nd Floor
Sacramento, CA 95814
916-657-3681
Fax: 916-657-3353
CAMP helps students from migrant and seasonal farmworker backgrounds succeed in college. It offers a pre-college transition and first year support system to assist students in developing the skills needed to stay in school and successfully graduate from college.

Eastern States
see Pennsylvania

Florida
see Texas

Georgia
Rocio Cardenas
Abraham Baldwin Agricultural College
ABAV 12
2802 Moore Highway
Tifton, GA 31794-2601
912-391-6934

Idaho
Scott Willison
Boise State University
Department of Teacher Education
1910 University Drive
Boise, ID 83725
208-426-3292
Recruitment Area: Southern Idaho, Eastern Washington, Eastern Oregon, Northern California, Northern Nevada, and Northern Utah
Program Services: Academic assistance including advising, counseling, tutoring and supervised study, to enable students to successfully complete first year of college; Assistance with financial aid requirements and student stipends; Job placement; Support services including career mentoring, Freshman orientation, health services, and follow-up support.

Michigan
Luis Garcia
Michigan State University
MSU CAMP
528 Wonders Hall
East Lansing, MI 48825
517-432-9900
Michigan State University's College Assistance Migrant Program was initiated in 2000 and is a unique program designed to service incoming migrant and seasonal farmworker students at Michigan State University.

Nevada
see Idaho

Oregon
Linda Herrera

Chemeketa Community College
4000 lancaster Drive, NE
Salem, OR 97309
503-589-7764

Pennsylvania
Melissa Rodriguez
Pennsylvania State University
208 Boucke Bldg.
University Park, PA 16802
814-863-9799
Recruitment Area: Eastern Stream
Program Services: Financial assistance; Counseling
Academic — assessment and academic placement; Skills building in reading, math, science, computer literacy
Personal — peer assistance; Career and guidance; English proficiency for students who do not speak English as their first language; Study skills; Tutorial assistance; Cultural enrichment; Health services

Texas
Ester Yacono
St. Edward's University
3001 South Congress Ave.
Austin, TX 78704-6489
512-488-8626
Recruitment Area: Texas, Florida
Program Services: Instruction — writing, reading, mathematics, listening skills, and English
Counseling — career, goals clarification, interview techniques, and financial aid

Felipe Salinas
University of Texas-Pan American
1201 W. University Dr.
Edinburg, TX 78539
956-318-5333

Utah
see Idaho

Washington
Norberto Espindola
Heritage College
3240 Fort Road
Toppenish, WA 98948
509-865-8505

Wisconsin
Arturo Martinez
Milwaukee Are Technical College CAMP
700 W. State St.
Milwaukee, WI 53233
414-297-8368
The MATC College Assistance Migrant Program (CAMP) is one of several programs nationwide funded by the U.S. Department of Education to assist migrant or seasonal farmworkers or their dependent children during their freshman year of college.

Free Tutors and Other Services
To Help Low-Income School Dropouts Reach College

Program: Talent Search — 84.044

Description: Talent Search is a special program that provides funding to help youth from disadvantaged backgrounds re-enter the educational system, complete high school and go on to the college of their choice.

What You Can Get: Program services include academic, financial and personal counseling on re-entering the school system; career exploration and aptitude testing; tutorial services; information on post-secondary education; exposure to life on college campuses; help in completing college admission and financial aid applications; assistance in preparing for college entrance exams; mentoring programs; special activities for sixth, seventh and eighth grade students; and workshops for the parents of participants.

Who is Eligible: Talent Search programs are sponsored by colleges, public or private agencies or organizations, and, in some cases, secondary schools. Candidates for participation must be between the ages of 11 and 27 years and have completed at least the 5th grade. Two-thirds of participants in any program must be potential first-generation college students from low-income homes.

Money Available: Talent Search awards grants to schools and other agencies to provide services for participants. While students do not receive any direct funds, they can receive help in locating and applying for financial aid. In 2001, $106 million was awarded and over a quarter of a million students were helped. The minimum institutional grant award is $295,000.

National Office:

> Council for Opportunity in Education
> 1025 Vermont Ave., NW, Suite 900
> Washington, DC 20005
> 202-347-7430
> Fax: 202-347-0786
> www.trioprograms.org

Local Offices:

You will find a listing below of participating schools, offices, and organizations. You may also contact the national office for more information.

Alabama

Rhonda Dees
Alabama Southern Community College
P.O. Box 2000
Monroeville, AL 36461
334-575-3156
Fax: 334-575-5356

Karyn Scissum-Guan
Alabama State University
915 South Jackson St.
Montgomery, AL 36101
334-229-4475
Fax: 334-229-4941

Suzanne Combs
Beville State Community College
Box 800
Sumiton, AL 35148

205-648-3271, ext. 5200
Fax: 205-648-2288

Jeanette Baxley
Chauncey Sparks State Technical College
P.O. Drawer 2530
Eufalula, AL 36072-2530
334-687-3543
Fax: 334-687-0255
Email: jbaxley@sstc.cc.al.us

Ward Webster
Faulkner University
2130 Chapel Hill Road, SW
Decatur, AL 35603
334-272-5820
Fax: 334-386-7271
Email: wweb8@aol.com

Cherlyn C. Stowe
Gadsden State Community College
P.O. Box 227
Gadsden, AL 35902-0227
256-549-8374
Fax: 256-549-8404

Bruce Gearhart
John Patterson State Technical College
3920 Troy Highway
Montgomery, AL 36116
334-288-1080, ext. 208
Fax: 334-284-9357

Jean Hardwick
Northwest Alabama Community College
2080 College Rd.
Phil Campell, AL 35581
205-331-6230
Fax: 205-331-6272

Matthew Lesko, Information USA, Inc., 12081 Nebel Street, Rockville, MD 20852 • 1-800-955-7693 • www.lesko.com

Lanetta Phillips
Northwest Shoals Community College
P.O. Box 2545
Colbert County
Muscle Shoals, AL 35662
256-331+5348
Fax: 256-331-5222
Email: lanetta.phillips@nwscc.cc.al.us

Bessie German
Shelton State Community College
9500 Old Greensboro Rd.
Tuscaloosa, AL 35405
205-759-3741, ext. 2242
Fax: 205-759-2495

Beverly Ross
Trenholm State Technical College
1225 Air Base Blvd.
Montgomery, AL 36108
334-832-9000
Fax: 334-832-9777

Manuel W. Jones
1006 Old Administration Bldg.
Tuskegee University
Tuskegee, AL 36088
334-727-8207
Fax: 334-724-4402

Harriet Burroughs
University of South Alabama
5700 University Commons
Mobile, AL 36688
334-380-2620
Fax: 334-380-2651

Betty Bentley
Wallace Community College/Selma
Route 6, Box 62
Dothan, AL 36303
334-875-2634
Fax: 334-874-7116

Suzanne Harbin
Wallace State Community College
P.O. Box 2000
Hanceville, AL 35077-2000
205-352-8208
Fax: 256-352-8188

John White
Alabama Southern Community College
P.O. Box 489
Thomasville, AL 36784
334-636-9642
Fax: 334-636-1380

Tom Michael
Auburn University at Montgomery
7300 University Drive
Montgomery, AL 36117
334-244-3213
Fax: 334-244-3967

Andrea Agnew
Bishop State Community College
414 Stanton Street
Mobile, AL 36617
334-473-8692 ext. 36
Fax: 334-479-6669
Email: aagnew@bscc.cc.al.us

Charlotte Kirkland
Southeast Alabama Education Outreach
Center
P.O. Box 884
412 South Oates Street
Dothan, Al 36302
334-673-9996
Fax: 334-673-9475
Email: Ckirkums@aol.com

Alaska

No talent search programs listed.

Arkansas

Laura Yarbrough
Mississippi County Community College
P.O. Box 1109
Blyhteville, AR 72315-1109
870-762-1020, ext. 1161
Fax: 870-763-1654

Pam Richiert
North Arkansas College
1515 Pioneer Drive
Harrison, AR 72601-5599
870-391-3135
Fax: 870-391-3190

Lewis Sheppard
Quachita Baptist University
Box 3779
Arkadelphia, AR 71998
870-245-5158
Fax: 870-245-5165
Email: shepardl@alpha.obu.edu

Betty K. Clerc
Rich Mountain Community College
1100 College Dr.
Mena, AR 71953
501-394-7622, ext. 1642
Fax: 501-394-2825

Shauna Sterling
University of Arkansas/Fayetteville
715 Hotz Hall
Fayetteville, AR 72701
501-575-3553
Fax: 501-575-4279

Vance Simelton
University of Arkansas/Little Rock
2801 South University Ave.
Little Rock, AR 72204
501-907-2470
Fax: 501-907-2480

Arizona

Elsie Watchman-Brown
Northern Arizona University
P.O. Box 6035
Flagstaff, AZ 86011-6035
520-523-9152
Fax: 520-523-9466
Email: elsie.watchman-brown@nau.edu

Adam Ysaguirre
Pima County Community College District
5901 South Calle Santa Cruz
Tucson, AZ 85706-6070
520-206-4056
Fax: 520-206-5046
Email: aysaguirre@pimcc.pima.edu

Lonnie Dufort-Densberger
Yavapai College
1100 East Sheldon St.
Prescot, AZ 86301
520-776-2048
Fax: 520-776-2009
Email: lonnie_densberger@yavapai.cc.az.us

Linda Heard
Garland County Community College
101College Drive
Hot Springs, AR 71913-9174
501-760-4229
Fax: 501-760-4127
Email: Lheard@admin.gccc.cc.ar.us

California

Rebeka Palomino
CS/Los Angeles

University Auxiliary Services
5151 State University Dr.
Los Angeles, CA 90032
323-343-3190
Fax: 323-343-6426

Donald Towns
CSU/Bakersfield
9001 Stockdale Highway
Bakersfield, CA 93311-1099
805-664-3124
Fax: 804-664-3194
Email: dtowns@csub.edu

Allen Bee
CSU/Chico
102A Sutter Hall
Chico, CA 95929-0612
503-898-4429
Fax: 503-898-5528
Email: abee@oavax.csuchico.edu

Alejandro Juarez
CSU/Fresno
2450 San Ramon #3, Room 3R71
Fresno, CA 93740
559-278-2276
Fax: 559-278-4715

Loretta Enriquez-Najera
CSU/Long Beach
1250 Bellflower Blvd.
Long Beach, CA 90840
562-985-5387
Fax: 562-985-7646

Richard W. Hicks
Humboldt State University Foundation
One Harpst Street
Arcata, CA 95201
707-826-4791
Fax: 707-826-5212

Dolores Diaz
Imperial Valley College
P.O. Box 158
Imperial, CA 92251
760-352-8320
Fax: 760-355-2663

Emalyn Lapus
Japanese Community College Youth
1596 Post St.
San Francisco, CA 94109
415-921-5537
Fax: 415-563-7109
Email: elapus@aol.com

Renee Hernandez
NAPA Valley College
2277 NAPA-Vallejo Highway
Napa, CA 94558
707-253-3009
Fax: 707-259-8030
Email: rhernand@campus.nvc.cc.ca.us

Marco Cruz
National Hispanic University
14271 Story Rd.
San Jose, CA 95107
408-254-6900
Fax: 408-254-1369

W. Charlene Folsom
Pact, Inc.
635 Divisadero St.
San Francisco, CA 94117
415-922-2550
Fax: 415-922-6306
Email: cfolsom@pactinc.org

Victor Edinburg
Provisional Educational Service Inc.
Box 7100

San Bernardino, CA 92411
909-887-7002
Fax: 909-887-8942
Email: palcenter@ece.org

Dr. Cynthia D. Park
San Diego State
5250 Campanile Dr.
San Diego, CA 92182
619-594-2349
Fax: 619-594-7821
Email: cpark@mail.sdsu.edu

Jose L. Hernandez
Sonoma State University
1801 East Cotati Ave.
Rohnert Park, CA 94928
707-664-2428
Fax: 707-664-2505

Lianna Boren
University of California/Davis
207 3rd St., Suite 120
Davis, CA 95616
530-757-3321
Fax: 530-757-3133

Jeffrey L. Clayton
University of Southern California/LA
3714 South Figuerosa St.
Los Angeles, CA 90007
213-743-6395
Fax: 213-746-8142

Myrna R. Joseph
Volunteers of America
3761 Stocker St., Suite 202
Los Angeles, CA 90008
213-381-1353
Fax: 213-381-1162

Victor P. Shupp
Wahupa Educational Services
3251 Fourth Ave.
San Diego, CA 92103
619-297-4471
Fax: 619-297-2351
Email: wahupa@aol.com

Regina Jennings
Yosemite Community College District
435 College Ave.
Modesto, CA 95354
209-575-6508
Fax: 209-575-6843
Email: jenningsr@yosemite.cc.ca.us

Jose Martinez-Saldana
California State University- Monterey Bay
100 Campus Center 86B
Seaside, CA 93955
831-582-3657
Fax: 831-582-3663
Email: josemartinez-saldana@monterey.edu

Jacqueline Jones-Castellano
Diablo Valley College
321 Golf Club Road
FO Annex
Pleasant Hill, Ca 94523
925-685-1230 ext. 677
Fax: 925-685-1551

Romeo Garcia
Mills College
5000 MacArthur Blvd.
Oakland, CA 94613-1399
510-430-2177
Fax: 510-430-3314

Janie Marcus
Santa Ana College
17th at Bristol St.
Santa Ana, CA 92706

714-564-6182
Fax: 714-5422-0896

Norris Sanders
University of California-Berkeley
Educational Guidance Center
2150 Kittredge Street, #1060,
2nd Floor
Berkeley, CA 94720-1060
510-643-3223
Fax: 510-643-3216

Dolores Valdes
University of California-San Diego
9500 Gilman Drive, 0305-B
La Jolla, CA 92093-0305
858-822-3051
Fax: 858-534-8996

Colorado
Ana Armijo
Adam State College
ASC Campus Box 25
Alamosa County
Alamosa, CO 81101
719-589-7895
Fax: 719-589-7522

Oscar Felix
Colorado State University
304 Student Services Bldg.
Fort Collins, CO 80523
970-491-6473
Fax: 970-491-1077

Yvette Hunt
Community College of Denver
1205 5th St., Suite 325
Denver, CO 80217-3363
303-629-9226
Fax: 303-620-4805

Mary Ann Griffin
Fort Lewis College
1000 Rim Dr.
Durango, CO 81301
970-247-7472
Fax: 970-247-7689
Email: griffin_m@fortleewis.edu

Charlott Himenez
Greeley Dream Team, Inc.
811 15th St.
Greeley, CO 80631
970-351-6410
Fax: 970-353-8042

Geraldine L. Garcia Swift
Trinidad State Junior College
Campus Box 168
Los Animas, CO 81082
719-846-5562
Fax: 719-846-5613
Email: jerrye.gracia_swift@tsjc.ccoes.edu

Connecticut
Georgia F. Day
Fairfield University
Dolan 150
Fairfield, CT 06430-7524
203-254-4064
Fax: 203-254-4296

Marjorie A. Bernard
141 Linden Ave.
University of Bridgeport
Bridgeport, CT 06601
203-576-4287
Fax: 203-576-4276
Email: m.bernard@snet.net

Donna Miller-Benjamin
University of Connecticut
150 Fornier St.

New Haven, CT 06511
203-946-6040
Fax: 203-946-6056

Delaware
Ginny Verosko
Delaware Technical Community College
Southern Campus
P.O. Box 660, Route 18
Georgetown, DE 19947
302-855-1600
Fax: 302-856-5635

Kathleen Perkins
Delaware Technical Community
College/Wilmington
333 Shipley St.
Wilmington, DE 19801
302-888-5290
Fax: 302-577-6432

District of Columbia
Linda Ayala
Lulac National Educational Service Center
2000 L St., NW, Suite 610
Washington, DC 20036
202-835-9646
Fax: 202-835-9685

Saundra Carter
University of the District of Columbia
4200 Connecticut Ave., NW
Washington, DC 20008
202-274-5032
Fax: 202-274-7412

Jane Collins
Consortium of Universities of Washington, Dc
901 G Street, NW
313 MLK Library
Washington, DC 20001
202-393-1100
Fax: 202-727-1129
Email: jcollins@collegeinfo.org

Florida
Raul Martinez, Executive Director
Aspira of Florida, Inc.
1300 Memorial Hwy.
Miami, FL 33161
305-576-1512
Fax: 305-576-0810

Femande Lecuova
Bethune-Cookman College
141 S. MLK Jr. Blvd.
Daytona Beach, FL 32114
904-255-1401, ext. 398
Fax: 904-255-2323

Carolyn Hiers
Florida A&M University
103 Unit A, Gore Education Center
Tallahassee, FL 32307
850-599-3055
Fax: 850-599-3967

Dorie Stein
Sante Fe Community College
401 NW 6th St.
Gainsville, FL 32601
392-395-5960
Fax: 352-395-5774

Ann Smith
Pensacola Junior College
1000 College Blvd., Bldg. 6
Pensacola, FL 32504
850-484-2533
Fax: 850-484-1650
Email: asmith@pjc.cc.fl.us

Udeth Lugo
Rollins College
1000 Holt Ave., #2758
Winter Park, FL 32789
407-646-1558
Fax: 407-646-2318
Email: udeth@rollins.edu

Miquel Gonzalez
Lake-Sumter Community College
Talent Search
9501 U.S. Hwy 441 South
Leesburg, FL 34788-8751
352-323-3606
Fax: 352-323-3553

Charles Richardson
Polk Community College
999 Avenue H, N.E.
Winter Haven, FL 33881-4299
863-297-1097
Fax: 863-297-1053

Georgia
Vermell Jenkins McIntyre
Alpha Phi Alpha Fraternity Inc.
566 Monroe St., Box 6071
Macon, GA 32108
912-746-4518
Fax: 912-746-2912

Vivian Ralston-Erkins
Andrew College
Box 306
Cuthbert, GA 31740
912-732-2146
Fax: 912-732-2176

Phyllis Wyatt-Woodruff
Clark Atlanta University, Box 84
James Brawley Dr., Fair St. SW
Atlanta, GA 30314
404-880-8263
Fax: 404-880-8222

Carolyn Crume
Concerted Services, Inc.
111 Medical Arts Dr., Box 1550
Reidsville, GA 30453
912-557-6687
Fax: 912-557-3004

Shirley McCellan
Fort Valley State College
1005 State College Dr.
Fort Valley, GA 31030
912-825-6932
Fax: 912-825-6394

Randy Gunter
Georgia Southern University
Landrum Box 8071-01
1026 Williams Center
Bulloch County
Statesboro, GA 30460
912-681-5458
Fax: 912-681-0863

Rubye Byrd
Morehouse College
830 Westview Dr., SW
P.O. Box 134
Atlanta, GA 30314
404-215-2671
Fax: 404-788-2215
Email: rbyrd@morehouse.edu

Brenda McBride
Morris Brown College
643 Martin Luther King Junior Dr., NW
Atlanta, GA 30314
404-739-1410
Fax: 404-739-1415

Doretha S. Tyson
Savannah State College
240 Whiting Dr.
P.O. Box 20265
Savannah, GA 31404
912-356-2799
Fax: 912-356-2490

Betty Garner
University of Georgia
480 N. Thomas St.
Athens, GA 30602
706-369-5660
Fax: 706-369-5925

Mitchel Haralson, Jr.
Georgia State University
420 One Park Place
Atlanta, GA 30303-3083
404-651-2822
Fax: 404-463-9714
Email: coemhhx@panther.gsu.edu

Melanie Martin
Thomas University
1501 Millpond Road
Thomasville, GA 31792-7499
921-226-1621 x231
Fax: 912-226-1653
Email: mmartin@thomasu.edu

Guam
Norma Guarnes
University of Guam
UOG Station
Mangilo, GU 96923
671-734-9143
Fax: 671-734-7514

Hawaii
Jan Lindsey
Kamehamha Schools
1887 Makuakane St.
Honolulu, HI 96817
808-842-8302
Fax: 808-848-0080

Melven Yoshimoto
University of Hawaii at Manoa
2600 Campus Rd.
Honolulu, HI 96822
808-956-8111

Idaho
Sue Huizinga
Boise State University
1910 University Dr.
Boise, ID 83725
208-385-3572
Fax: 208-385-4334
Email: shuizin@boisestate.edu

James Yizar, Jr.
Idaho State University
Campus Box 8345
Pocatello, ID 83209
208-236-3242
Fax: 208-236-4864

Connie Fleener
University of Idaho/Moscow
Education Building
Moscow, ID 83843
208-885-6475
Fax: 208-885-7607

Illinois
Silas Purnell
ADA McKinley Community Services, Inc.
725 South Well, Suite 1A
Chicago, IL 60607
312-225-3477
Fax: 312-225-6461

Ernesto Rodriguez
Aspira Inc. Of Illinois
2435 N. Western Ave.
Chicago, IL 60647
773-252-0970, ext. 27
Fax: 773-252-0994
Email: titorodriguez@netscape.net

David Henry
Community and Economic Development
Association/Cook County
515 St. Charles Rd.
P.O. Box 950
Maywood, IL 60153
708-450-1445
Fax: 708-450-0589

Joe Young
College of Lake County
19351 West Washington St.
Grayslake, IL 60030
708-223-6601
Fax: 708-223-1017

Edwin Flannigan
East Central Illinios
56 North Vermilion
Danville, IL 61832
217-442-2791
Fax: 217-442-4952
Email: eflann1ets@aol.com

Bernard Clay
Introspect Youths Services, Inc.
430 North Cicero Ave.
Chicago, IL 60644-2002
773-287-2290
Fax: 773-287-4444

Sandra Walters
John Wood Community College
150 South 48th St.
Quincy, IL 62301
217-222-3451
Fax: 217-222-9459

Jewell Dennis
Joilet Junior College
1215 Houbolt Rd., H-1001
Joilet, IL 60431
815-729-9020
Fax: 815-744-5507

George C. Terry
Lewis and Clark Community College
5800 Godfrey Rd.
Godfrey, IL 62035
618-466-3411, ext. 6000
Fax: 618-466-9271
Email: gterry@lc.cc.il.us

Deon Brown
Northeastern Illinois University
770 N. Halsted St.
Chicago, IL 60622
312-733-7330, ext. 450
Fax: 312-733-8188
Email: d-brown2@neiu.edu

Songie Milhouse
South Suburban College
15800 South State St.
South Holland, IL 60473
708-596-2000, ext. 2694
Fax: 708-210-5712
Email: smilhouse@ssc.cc.il.us

John Long
University of Illinois/Chicago
1200 W. Harrison St.
M/C 343, Suite 2720
Chicago, IL 60607
312-996-5046

Fax: 312-996-9298
Email: jlong@uic.edu

Rodney Ranes
Illinois Eastern Community College
305 North West Street
Olney, IL 62450
618-395-7777 ext 2282
Fax: 618-392-3293
Email: ranesr@iecc.cc.il.us

Christine Stutz
Kankakee Community College
P.O. Box 888, River Road
Kankakee, IL 60901
815-935-9613
Fax: 815-933-0217
Email: cshultz@kee.ccil.us

Ivonne Sambolin
Kennedy-King College
3901 South State
Chicago, IL 60609
773-451-2020
Fax: 773-451-2014

Karen Sue Smith
Parkland College
2400 West Bradley R237
Champaign, IL 61821
217-373-3820
Fax: 217-353-2333
Email: kssmith@parkland.cc.il.us

Angelia Millender
Robert Morris College
401 South State Street
Chicago, IL 60605
312-935-6870
Fax: 312-935-6861

Kimberly R. Washington-Pearse
Roosevelt University
430 South Michigan Avenue
HCC Room 310B
Chicago, IL 60605
312-341-3875
Fax: 312-341-3735
Email: kwashing@acfsysv.roosevelt.edu

Charles Hayes
Southern Illinois University- Edwardsville
411 East Broadway
East Street Louis, IL 62201
618-482-6960
Fax: 618-482-6990
Email: chhayes@siue.ed

Indiana

Roxanne Mills
Oakland City University
143 Lucretia St.
Oakland, IN 47660
812-749-4781
Fax: 812-749-1419
Email: rmills@oak.edu

Deborah Birch
Purdue University
North Central
1401 South US Highway
Westville, IN 46391
219-785-5432
Fax: 219-785-5355
Email: dbirch@purduenc.edu

Warren Outlan
University of Notre Dame
P.O. Box 1139
Notre Dame, IN 46556
219-631-5670
Fax: 219-631-5854

LeAnn Luce
Vincennes University
1002 North First St.
Vincennes, IN 47591
812-888-4298
Fax: 812-888-5958

Willa Kline
Educational Opportunity Center
2513 South Calhoun Street
Fort Wayne, IN 46807
219-745-4781
Fax: 219-744-1363

Verenda Hooks
Ivy Technical State College-Northwest
1440 East 35th Avenue
Gary, IN 46409-1499
219-981-4420
Fax: 219-981-4405

Melvyn Harding
Purdue University-Calumet
2233 171st Street
Hammond, IN 46323
219-989-2084
Fax: 219-989-2929
Email: harding@calumet.purdue.edu

Iowa

Maria Anderson
Briar Cliff College
3303 Rebecca St.
P.O. Box 2100
Sioux City, IA 51104-2100
712-279-5321
Fax: 712-279-5410
Email: anderson@briar-cliff.edu

Nancy Wright, President
Central College
812 University
Pella, IA 50219
515-628-5294
Fax: 515-628-5912
Email: wright@central.edu

Susie Catanzareti
Graceland University
One University Place
Lamoni, IA 50140
515-784-5210
Fax: 515-784-5411
Email: catanzar@graceland.edu

Julie Carlson
Iowa Lakes Community College
3200 College Dr.
Emmitsburg, IA 50536
712-856-5302
Fax: 515-652-5344
Email: jcarlson@ilcc.cc.ia.us

Jane Agyeman
Iowa State University
N002 Lagomarcino Hall
Ames, IA 50011
515-294-5546
Fax: 515-294-1219
Email: jagyeman@iastate.edu

Bonnie Gioiella
Iowa Western Community College
2700 College Rd., Box 4C
Council Bluffs, IA 51503
712-325-3282
Fax: 712-325-3424
Email: bgioiello@iwcc.cc.ia.us

Tony Stevens
University Northern Iowa/Waterloo
715-East 4th St.

Waterloo, IA 50703
319-234-6819
Fax: 319-232-5039

Ann Craft
Luther College
700 College Drive
Decorah, IA 51301
319-387-1297
319-387-2213

Tawnya Beermann
Western Iowa Technical Community College
4647 Stone Avenue
P.O. Box 5199
Sioux City, IA 51102-0265
712-274-8733 x1491
Fax: 712-274-6412
Email: beermat@witcc.ia.us

Kansas

Beverly G. Temaat
Dodge City Community College
2501 North 14th Ave.
Dodge City, KS 67801
316-227-9303
Fax: 316-227-9356

Trudi Benjamin
Emporia State University
1200 Commercial, Box 4016
Emporia, KS 66801
316-341-5097
Fax: 316-341-5073

Maritza Williams
The University of Kansas
7 Strong Hall
Lawrence, KS 60045
785-864-7270
Fax: 785-864-5188

Barbara Preston
Wichita State University
1845 N. Fairmont
Wichita, KS 67208
316-689-3137
Fax: 316-689-3528

Sue Saia
Cowley College
125 South Second Street
Arkansas City, KS 67005
316-441-5289
Fax: 316-441-5350

Lea Ann Curtis
Garden City Community College
801 Campus Drive
Garden City, KS 67846
316-276-9513
Fax: 316-276-9630
Email: lcurtis@gccc.cc.ks.us

Kentucky

Darla Phillips
Berea College
P.O. Box 2212
Berea, KY 40404
859-985-3271
Fax: 859-985-3241

Beth Sullivan
Eastern Kentucky University
Begley Building, Room 605
Richmond, KY 40475
606-622-5425
Fax: 606-622-1020

Claudette Nelson
Kentuciana Metroversity
546 S. 1st St.

Louisville, KY 40202
502-584-0475
Fax: 502-584-9781
Email: keop@worldnet.att.net

Donald Long
Lexington Community College
Cooper Dr.
247 Oswald Bldg.
Lexington, KY 40506
606-257-3419
Fax: 606-323-3653
Email: schaoo@ukcc.edu

Anna Leisure
Madisonville Community College
2000 College Dr.
Madisonville, KY 42431
270-821-2250
Fax: 270-825-8553

Michael Pennington
Morehead State University
112 Waterfield Hall
Morehead, KY 40351
606-783-5488
Fax: 606-783-5033

Odessa Torian
Murray State University
Trio Bldg.
P.O. Box 9
Murray, KY 42071
270-762-3165
Fax: 270-762-3096

Michael Berry
Northern Kentucky University
1401 Dixie Hwy.
208 Hankins Hall
Covington, KY 41011
606-392-2410
Fax: 606-392-2418

Greg Marable
Hopkinsville Community College
P.O. Box 2100
North Dr.
Hopkinsville, KY 42241-2100
270-886-3921
Fax: 270-886-8066

Teresa Y. Ward
Western Kentucky University
124 Jones-Jaggers Hall
Bowling Green, KY 42101
270-745-3757
Fax: 270-745-6850

Louisiana

Juanita S. Boniface
Dillard University
2601 Gentilly Blvd.
New Orleans, LA 70122
504-286-4781
Fax: 504-286-4781

Robert P. McFarland
New Orleans Education
Talent Search
4215 South Claiborne Ave.
New Orleans, LA 70125
504-821-8844
Fax: 504-821-2334

James Cozine
University of Louisiana-Monroe
112 Stubbs Hall
Monroe, LA 71209
318-342-1000
Fax: 318-342-1088

Dayne Sherman
Southeastern Louisiana University/Hammond

SLU 10568
Hammond, LA 70402
504-549-5559
Fax: 504-549-3477

Avon R. Honey
Southern University A&M
P.O. Box 9694
Baton Rouge, LA 70813
225-771-5100
Fax: 225-771-2414

Janice H. Winder
Southern University/New Orleans
6400 Press Dr.
Trio Programs
New Orleans, LA 70126
504-286-5209
Fax: 504-284-5448

Gwendolyn Lewis
Southern University-Shreveport/Bossier
610 Texas St.
210 Metro Center
Shreveport, LA 71107
318-674-3462
Fax: 318-676-6511

Brenda Brown
University of New Orleans
BA 159 Lakefront Campus
New Orleans, LA 70148
504-280-6979
Fax: 504-280-5564

Robert L. Carmouche
University of Louisiana/Lafayette
P.O. Box 43452
Lafayette, LA 70504
337-482-6831
Fax: 337-482-6833

Maine

David Megquier
University of Maine/Orono
5713 Chadbourne Hall, Room 300
Orono, ME 04469
207-581-2533
Fax: 207-581-2532

Maryland

Willie Reeves
Anne Arundel Community College
101 College Parkway
Arnold, MD 21012
410-541-2813
Fax: 410-541-2368

Jean Richie
Baltimore City Community College
2901 Liberty Heights Ave., Room 235
Baltimore, MD 21215
410-462-8405
Fax: 410-462-7677

William Sigmon
W. Baltimore County Community College
800 South Rolling Rd.
Catonsville, MD 21228
410-455-4486
Fax: 410-455-4254

Edith Patterson
Charles Community College
P.O. Box 910
Mitchell Rd.
LaPlata, MD 20646
301-934-2251
Fax: 301-934-7678

Shirley Morman
University of Maryland
3103 Turner Hall
College Park, MD 20742

301-314-7763
Fax: 301-314-9201

Massachusetts

Diane Dickerson
Educational Resources Institution
100 Boylston St.
Boston, MA 02111
617-542-3500
Fax: 617-574-5048

Isa Perez
Hispanic Office of Planning
165 Brookside Ave.
Jamaica Plains, MA 02130
617-522-1212
Fax: 524-8888

Evette Layne
Massachusetts Institute of Technology
77 Massachusetts Ave.
Room N52-130
Cambrige, MA 02139
617-253-5124
Fax: 617-258-5616

Mary Ann Miller, President
Middlesex Community College
35 Kearney Square
Lowell, MA 01853
978-656-3385
Fax: 978-656-3389

Virginia DiMola
Mount Wachusett Community College
444 Green St.
Gardner, MA 01440
978-632-6600, ext. 280
Fax: 978-630-1543

Gloria deGuevara
University of Massachusetts/Amherst
208 Whitmore Building
Amherst, MA 01003
413-545-0428
Fax: 413-545-1992

William Pollard
University of Massachusetts/Boston
100 Morrisey Blvd.
Suffolk County, MA 02125
617-287-7390
Fax: 617-287-5844

Pamela K. Bosivert
Worcester Consort for Higher Education
37 Fruit St.
Worcester, MA 01609
508-754-6829
Fax: 508-797-0069

Michigan

Robert Newton
Alpena Community College
666 Johnson St.
Alpena, MI 49707
517-356-9021
Fax: 517-356-0980

June Fletcher
Grand Valley State University
10 Zumberge Library
Allendale, MI 49401
616-336-7110
Fax: 616-336-7115

Florence Harris
Michigan State University
209 Bessey Hall
East Lansing, MI 48823
517-353-5210
Fax: 517-432-2962

Barbara Zupin
Northwestern Michigan College

1701 East Front St.
Traverse City, MI 49684
231-922-1363
Fax: 231-922-8523

Hazel Crosbie
Southwestern Michigan College
58900 Cherry Grove Rd.
Dowgaic, MI 49047
616-782-1367
Fax: 616-782-8414

Charles M. Green
Wayne State University
Helen North 1 East
Wayne County
Detroit, MI 48202
313-993-7510
Fax: 313-993-7510

John Bur
Finlandia University
601 Quincy Street
Hancock, MI 49930
906-487-7390
Fax: 906-487-8509

Minnesota

Nessa Kleinglass
Century Community and Technical College
3300 Century Ave. North
White Bear Lake, MN 55110
651-779-3980
Fax: 651-779-5807

Charles Cantale
Mankato State University
MSU Box 114 EXCEL
Mankato, MN 56002
507-389-1111
Fax: 507-389-6372

Katherine Davis
Minneapolis Community College
1501 Hennepin Ave.
Minneapolis, MN 55403
612-341-7682
Fax: 612-341-7214

Helen Gerhardson
Minnesota Chippewa Tribe
P.O. Box 217
Education Division
Cass Lake, MN 56633
218-759-8496
Fax: 218-759-8498

Cary Waterman
Normandale Community College
9700 France Ave., South
Bloomington, MN 55431
612-832-6728
Fax: 612-832-6571

Janis Johnson
St. Olaf College
2510 Saint Olaf Ave.
Northfield, MN 55057
507-646-3780
Fax: 507-646-3552

Sue Hollis
College Of St. Scholastica
1200 Kenwood Avenue
Duluth, MN 55811-4199
218-723-5910
Fax: 218-723-6472

Mississippi

Irma McKinney
Mississippi Valley State University
14000 Highway 82 West
Box 1053

Itta Bena, MS 38941
662-254-3471
Fax: 662-254-7552

Henry L. Berry
North Mississippi Center for Higher Education
P.O. Box 704
West Point, MS 39773
601-494-0660
Fax: 601-494-0550

Aneitha Keith
Rust College
150 East Rust Ave.
Holly Springs, MS 38635
662-252-4661
Fax: 662-252-6107

Valvia Wilson
Tougaloo College
P.O. Box 216
Tougaloo, MS 39174
601-977-7844
Fax: 601-977-7930
Email: valvia.wilson@tougaloo.edu

Tiffany Anderson
Hinds Community College-Utica
P.O. Box 1245
Utica, MS 39175-9599
601-885-7123
Fax: 601-885-6026

Terri R. Sharpe
Newton Municipal School District
P.O. Box 150
123 Scanlan Street
Newton, MS 39345
601-683-2451
Fax: 601-683-7131
Email: tsharp@nmsd.k12.us

Missouri

Linda Todoroff
Harris-Stowe State College
3026 Laclede Ave.
St. Louis, MO 63103
314-340-5740
Fax: 314-340-3550

Robert Jenkins
Higher Education Center of St. Louis
8420 Delmar Blvd.
Suite 504
St. Louis, MO 63108
314-535-4600
Fax: 314-991-2874

Kathern Harris
Three Rivers Community College
2080 Three Rivers Blvd.
Popular Bluff, MO 63901
573-840-9554
Fax: 573-840-9553

Montana

Loren "Bum" Stiffarm
Fort Belknap Education Department
RR 1, Box 66
Harlem, MT 59526
406-353-2205
Fax: 406-353-4574

Rene Dubay
Montana Board of Regents
2500 Broadway
Helena, MT 59620
406-444-0335
Fax: 406-444-6565

Nebraska

Harold Harris
Creighton University

2500 California Plaza
Omaha, NE 68178
402-280-2115
Fax: 402-280-5579
Email: hharris@creighton.edu

Jimmi Smith
University of Nebraska/Lincoln
220 Administration Building
Lincoln, NE 68588
402-472-2027
Fax: 402-472-9338
Email: jsmith3@unl.edu

Nevada

William E. Sullivan
University Nevada/Las Vegas
Box 452006
4505 Maryland Ave.
Las Vegas, NV 89154
702-895-4777
Fax: 702-895-4786
Email: docbill@ccmail.nevada.edu

New Hampshire

Marsha Johns
University of New Hampshire
Robinson House
Rosemary Lane
Durham, NH 03824
603-862-1562
Fax: 603-862-3270

New Jersey

Miguel Melendez
Aspria, Inc. of New Jersey
600 Penn Street
Camden, NJ 08102
856-964-9115
Fax: 856-964-2339

W. Barry McLaughlin
Cumberland County College
P.O. Box 517
Vineland, NJ 08362
856-691-8600, ext. 252
Fax: 856-690-0059

Betty Foster
Essex County College
303 University Ave.
Room 3310
Newark, NJ 07102
201-973-3196
Fax: 210-973-3044

Donald Davis
Mercer County Community College
P.O. Box B
N. Broad and Academy
Trenton, NJ 08690
609-486-4800
Fax: 690-394-8167

Henry McCloud
New Jersey Institute of Technology
323 ML King Jr. Blvd.
Newark, NJ 07102
973-596-5841
Fax: 973-642-4857
Email: mccloud@admin.njit.edu

Lillian Perez
Seton Hall University
400 South Orange Ave.
South Orange, NJ 07079
973-761-9230
Fax: 973-761-9788
Email: perexlil@lanmail.shu.edu

James Johnson
College Preparatory Incentive Program, Inc.
83 Wayne Street

Jersey City, NJ 07303
201-309-0500
Fax: 201-309-0473

New Mexico
Mary Watson
Eastern New Mexico University/Protales
186 SAS Bldg., Station 34
Portales, NM 88130
505-562-2447
Fax: 505-562-2530

Joyce Cross
Eastern New Mexico University/Rosewell
Box 6000
Rosewell, NM 88202
505-624-7201
Fax: 505-624-7216

Cheryl A. Connell
Eight Northern Indian Pueblos
P.O. Box 3270
Santa Fe, NM 87501
505-455-3185
Fax: 505-455-3055

John Olgiun
Southwestern Indian Ploytech Institute
9169 Coors Rd., NW
P.O. Box 10146
Albuquerque, NM 87184
505-897-5383
Fax: 505-897-5113

VeraJean Gilleland
New Mexico Junior College
5317 Lovington Highway
Hobbs, NM 88240-9121
505-392-5791
Fax: 505-392-3668
Email: vgilleland@nmjc.cc.nm.us

New York
Isabel Pradas
Aspira of New York, Inc.
470 Seventh Ave., 3rd Floor
New York, NY 10018
212-564-6880, ext. 114
Fax: 212-564-7152
Email: jpradas@ny.aspira.org

Crystal Floyd
Boys Harbor, Inc.
1 East 104th St.
New York, NY 10029
212-427-2244
Fax: 212-427-6667

Lily Adams-Dudley
Canisius College
2001 Main St.
Buffalo, NY 14028
716-888-3280
Fax: 716-888-3218

Olger C. Twyner III
Columbia University
306 Alfred Lerner Hall MC 2604
2920 Broadway
New York, NY 10027
212-854-3897
Fax: 212-854-7457
Email: ddc@columbia.edu

Stacy Brown
CUNY
Brooklyn College
2900 Bedford Ave., Room 2438-N
Brooklyn, NY 11210
718-951-5593
Fax: 718-951-5680

Josefina Couture
CUNY

John Jay College
555 W. 57th St., Suite 600
New York, NY 10019
212-237-8275
Fax: 212-237-8742

Wsarren Heusner
CUNY
Medgar Evers College
1150 Carroll St., Room CP400
Brooklyn, NY 11225
718-270-6495
Fax: 718-270-6496

June Bernardin
CUNY
York College
94-43 160th St., Room CL-104
Jamaica, NY 11451
718-262-3860
Fax: 718-262-3812

Paula Martin, Board Chairman
East Harlem College and Career Program
1 East 104th St.
New York, NY 10029
212-348-9200
Fax: 212-831-8202
Email: paulaj24@aol.com

Elliot Palais
Fordham University
201 Faculty Memorial Hall
Bronx, NY 10458
718-817-5985
Fax: 718-817-2513
Email: palais@fordham.edu

Gloria Garretson
SUNY College of Brockport
315 New Campus Dr.
Cooper Hall C-7
Brockport, NY 14420
716-395-5891
Fax: 716-395-2745

Ken Gillman
SUNY Research Foundation/New Platz
110 Humanity
New Platz, NY 12561
914-257-3592
Fax: 914-257-3555

Jo Malin
SUNY Research Foundation/Binghamton
44 Hawley St., 16th Floor
Binghamton, NY 13901
607-721-8281
Fax: 607-721-8680

Sheila Marshal
SUNY Research Foundation
Pottsdam College
119 Sisson Hall
Pottsdam, NY 13676
315-267-2614
Fax: 315-267-2342

Joseph Collins
University Settlement Society
184 Eldridge St.
New York, NY 10002
212-674-9120
Fax: 212-475-3278

Shirley H. Smith
Settlement College Readiness Program
1761 Third Avenue
New York, NY 10029
212-828-6136
Fax: 212-828-6140

Moises Jimenez
St. John's University

8000 Utopia Pkwy
104 Saint Albert Hall
Jamaica, NY 11439
718-990-2381
Fax: 718-990-2383

Yolanda Belle
Buffalo State College
College Learning Lab E-103
1300 Elmwood Avenue
Buffalo, NY 14222
716-878-4099 x20
Fax: 716-878-4015
Email: belleyn@buffalostate.edu

North Carolina
Deborah Kingsberry
Central Piedmont Community College
P.O. Box 35009
Charlotte, NC 28235
704-342-6961
Fax: 704-330-6610

Cheryl J. Lewis
Elizabeth City State
1704 Weeksville Rd.
Elizabeth City, NC 27909
252-335-3494
Fax: 252-335-3758

Joyce Watson, Director
Lees-Mcrae College
P.O. Box 3750
Banner Elk, NC 28604
828-898-5241
Fax: 828-898-8814
Fax: watson@bobcat.lmc.edu

Rick Wilson
Lumbee Regional Development Association
Robertson County
Pembroke, NC 28372
919-733-5998

Mickey Locklear
North Carolina Community of Indians
1317 Mail Service Center
Raleigh, NC 27699
919-733-5998
Fax: 919-733-1207
Email: mickey.locklear@ncmail.net

Marsha Boyd Pharr
North Carolina State University
Box 7319 NCSU
Raleigh, NC 27695-7319
919-515-6447
Fax: 919-515-4581

Sylvia Walker
Southeastern Community College
P.O. Box 151
Whiteville, NC 28472
910-642-7141
Fax: 910-642-5658

Donald Armstrong
St. Augistine's College
721 Penn Ave.
P.O. Box 2042
Rocky Mount, NC 27801
252-446-1921
Fax: 252-446-1435

Todd Murdock
Western Carolina University
G50 Stillwell Building
Cullowhee, NC 28723
828-227-7137
Fax: 828-227-7344
Email: tmurdock@wcu.edu

Maureen Schwind
Western Piedmont Community College

1001 Burkemont Ave.
Morganton, NC 28655
828-439-2316
Fax: 828-438-6065

Dorothy Holmes
Fayetteville State University
1200 Murchison Road
Fayetteville, NC 28301
910-486-1172
Fax: 910-437-2565

Marjorie Kornegay
James Sprunt Community College
P.O. Box 398
Kenansville, NC 28349
910-296-2508
Fax: 910-296-1222

North Dakota

Imogene Belgarde
Little Hoop Community College
P.O. Box 269
Fort Totten, ND 58335
701-766-1318
Fax: 701-766-4022

Neil Reuter
University of North Dakota
P.O. Box 9027
Grand Forks, ND 58202
701-777-3427
Fax: 701-777-3627

Tim Mueller
University Of Mary
7500 University Drive
Bismarck, ND 58504
701-255-7500
Fax: 701-255-7687

Ohio

Bonita Bembry
Bowling Green State University
37 College Park Office Building
Bowling Green, OH 43403
419-392-2381
Fax: 419-372-0399

Daniel Schneider
University of Cincinnati-Clermont College
551 Cinncinnati-Batavia Pike
Cincinnati, OH 45244
513-558-7437
Fax: 513-528-1308
dan.schneider@uc.edu

Jacqueline Dupree
Cuyahoga Community College
2900 Community College Ave.
Cleveland, OH 44115
216-987-4921
Fax: 216-987-3210

Stephan Gregory
Shawnee State University
940 Second St.
Portsmouth, OH 45662
740-355-2444
Fax: 740-355-2687

A. Bradley McClain
University of Akron
115 Gallucci Hall
Akron, OH 44325
330-972-5771
Fax: 330-972-5886

DeeAnn Peterson
Washington State Community College
710 Colegate Dr.
Marietta, OH 45750
740-374-8716
Fax: 740-373-7496

Cheri Westmorland
Cincinnati Youth Collaborative
411 Oak Street
Cincinnati, OH 45219
513-487-1560
Fax: 513-487-6594

Carrie Reeves
Case Western Reserve
425 Parder Hall
10900 Euclid Avenue
Cleveland, OH 44106-7045
216-368-3750
Fax: 216-368-1267

Emily Evans Ford
Cleveland Scholarship Programs
850 Euclid Avenue, Suite 1000
Cincinnati, OH 44114
216-241-5587
Fax: 216-241-6184
Email: eford@cspohio.org

Goldean Gibbs
Ohio Dominican College
12 Sanbury Road
Columbus, OH 43219-2099
614-251-4442
Fax: 614-252-0776

Sandra A. Tucker
Ohio Education Commission
333 West First Street, Suite 170
Dayton, OH 45402
937-223-5074
Fax: 937-223-8388

Oklahoma

Wathene Young
American Indian Resource Center
328 East Downing
Tahlequah, OK 74464
918-456-5581
Fax: 918-458-5415

Cheryl Dorris
Cameron University
2800 West Gore Blvd.
Lawton, OK 73505
580-581-5581
Fax: 580-581-5514
Email: cheryld@cameron.edu

Deborah Herr
Carl Albert State College
1507 South McKenna
Poteau, OK 74953
918-647-1377
Fax: 918-647-1207

Debi Boettcher
East Central University
1000 East 14th St.
Ada, OK 74820
580-332-8000
Fax: 580-436-0334

Gregory McCarroll
Langston University
P.O. Box 838
Langston, OK 73050
405-466-3441
Fax: 405-466-3271

Brock Rutledge
Rogers State College
1701 W. Will Rogers Blvd.
Claremore, OK 74017
918-343-7777
Fax: 918-343-7891

Merry Sunday
Rose State College
6420 SE 15th St.

Midwest City, OK 73110
405-733-7429
Fax: 405-733-7923

Mary Ann hill
Seminole Junior College
P.O. Box 351
Seminole, OK 74868
405-382-9950
Fax: 405-382-2998

Al White
Southeastern Oklahoma State University
SOSU Box 4112
Durant, OK 74701
580-745-2440
Fax: 580-745-7453

Oregon

Ed Bohart
Clatsop Community College
1653 Jerome Ave.
Astoria, OR 97103
503-325-0910
Fax: 503-325-5738

Phillip Dirks
Portland State University
Box 751
Portland, OR 97207
503-725-4458
Fax: 503-725-8514
Email: dirksr@pdx.edu

Connie Nelson
Southwestern Oregon Community College
1988 Newmark Ave.
Coos Bay, OR 97420
541-888-7366
Fax: 541-888-7247

Michael Evans
Chemeketa Community College
4000 Lancaster Drive NE
P.O. Box 14007
Salem, OR 97301
503-399-2391
Fax: 503-399-2580
Email: evans@chemeketa.edu.

Pennsylvania

Evelyn Briganty
Aspira Inc. of Pennsylvania
4322 N. 5th St.
Philadelphia, PA 19133
215-455-1300
Fax: 215-455-6310

Rhonda McMillen-Toth
Clarion University of Pennsylvania
840 Wood St.
Clarion, PA 16214
814-226-2071
Fax: 814-226-1804

Jean Moore
Deleware Valley College
700 East Butler Ave.
Doylestown, PA 18901
215-489-2904
Fax: 215-230-2964

Donna Cargle
Educational Opportunity Center
Rear 845 Wyoming Ave.
Wilkes-Barre, PA 18704
610-432-4839
Fax: 610-432-5467

Nicole Miller
Greater Erie Community Action Committee
18 West Ninth St.
Erie, PA 16501
814-459-4581

Fax: 814-456-0161
Email: nmlgeca@erie.net

Edward McAfee
Northwest Tri-County IU#5
1600 Peninsula Dr., Suite C
Erie, PA 16508
814-866-0870
Fax: 814-836-8690

Teresa Tassotti
Pennsylvania State University
Spruce Cottage
University Park, PA 16802
814-863-8195
Fax: 814-863-8617
Email: dea5@email.psu.edu

Sandra Sorrels
Reading Area Community College
10 South 2nd St.
P.O. Box 1706
Reading, PA 19603
610-372-4721
Fax: 610-607-6266

Gerald Sheridan
Seton Hill College
Greensburg, PA 15601
724-837-6199
Fax: 724-837-0703
Email: sheridan@setonhill.edu

Daniel Wafford
Philadelphia Education Fund
Suite 7007, Ben Franklin Parkway
Philadelphia, PA 19103
215-665-1400 x3341
Fax: 215-864-2494
Email: dwafford@philaedfund.org

Annette Hampton
University of Pennsylvania
3820 Locust Walk, Suite 209
Philadelphia, PA 19104-6225
215-764-2086
Fax: 215-764-2084
Email: hampton@pobox.upenn.edu

Puerto Rico

William Gomez Cedeno
Aspira, Inc. of Puerto Rico
P.O. Box 29132
65 Infantry Station
Rio Piedras, PR 00928
787-768-1985, ext. 228
Fax: 787-257-2725

Maria Yolanda Perez
International American University PR/San
German
Box 5100 C-40
U.I. Station
San German, PR 00753
787-264-0424
Fax: 787-892-5400

Felix A. Roman
University of Puerto Rio/Rio Peidras
Box 23323, UPR Station
Rio Piedras, PR 00931
787-764-8063
Fax: 787-754-4394

Nora Cabrera Cruz
University of Puerto Rico/Utuado
Call Box 2500
Utuado, PR 00641
787-894-2828
Fax: 787-894-2891

Alba Lebron de Ayala
Universidad Del Turabo
Box 3030 University Station

Gurabo, PR 00778
787-746-3999
Fax: 787-746-3999

Myriam Ruiz-Reyes
Universidad Metropolitana
Central #53, Urb. Bahia
Catano, PR 00619
787-269-1713
Fax: 787-269-1730

Josefina Sanchez
University of Puerto Rico-Humacao
Chancellor's Office
CUH Station
100 Carr 908
Humacao, PR 00791
787-850-9376
Fax: 787-852-4638

Rhode Island

Philomena Fayanjuola
Community College of Rhode Island
One Hilton St.
Providence, RI 02905
401-333-7150

South Carolina

Gayle Robertson
Florence-Darlington Technical College
P.O. Box 100548
Florence, SC 29501
803-661-8154
Fax: 803-661-8041

Wanda Hendricks-Bellany
Horry-Georgetown Technical College
2050 Highway 501 East
Conway, SC 29526
803-347-3186, ext. 270
Fax: 803-347-4207

Michael Kelly
Midlands Technical College
P.O. Box 2408
Columbia, SC 29202
803-822-3623
Fax: 803-822-3619
Email: kellym@mtc.mid.tec.sc.us

Patty Hix
Piedmont Technical College
P.O. Box 1467
Greenwood County
Greenwood, SC 29648
864-941-8606
Fax: 864-941-8555

Beverly Starks
Technical College of the Lowcountry
100 South Ribaut Rd.
Box 1288
Beaufort, SC 29901
843-525-8324
Fax: 843-525-8346

Brenda Taylor
Tri-County Technical College
P.O. Box 857
Pendleton, SC 29670
864-646-8361
Fax: 864-646-8256

Arnold Prioleau
Trident Technical College
P.O. Box 118067, CD-B
Charleston, SC 29423
843-899-8022
Fax: 843-899-8081

Karen Burks
University of South Carolina/Columbia
Booker T. Washington Auditorium
Columbia, SC 29208

803-777-5127
Fax: 803-777-7380

Joseph Adams
Williamsburg Technical College
601 Martin Luther King Blvd.
Kingstree, SC 29556
843-354-2021
Fax: 843-354-4197

Anita Davis-DeFoe
York Technical College
452 South Anderson Rd.
Rock Hill, SC 29730
803-981-7217
Fax: 803-981-7332

South Dakota

Charles Swick
University of South Dakota
414 East Clark St.
Vermillion, SD 57069
605-677-5308
Fax: 605-577-5756

Tennessee

Kay Goode
Clinch-Powell Educational Co-op
P.O. Box 279
Tazewell, TN 37879
423-626-1566
Fax: 423-626-8246

Linda Crutchfield
Douglas-Cherokee Economic Authority, Inc.
P.O. Box 1218
Morristown, TN 37814
423-587-4500
Fax: 423-587-4509

William Jackson
Girls Incorporated of Memphis
60 N. 3rd St.
Memphis, TN 38103
901-523-0217, ext. 1203
Fax: 901-523-0456

Gayle C. Brown
Hiwassee College
225 Hiwassee College Dr., Box 633
Madisonville, TN 37354
423-442-2001
Fax: 423-420-1909

Clara D. Hewitt
Lane College
545 Lane Ave.
Jackson, TN 38301
901-426-7500
Fax: 901-426-7527

Victoria Hayes
Tennessee State University
3500 John Merritt Blvd.
P.O. Box 9540
Nashville, TN 37209
615-963-7442
Fax: 615-963-7443

Jeanne Stokes
Tusculum College/Greeneville
Box 5053
Greeneville, TN 37743
423-636-7325
Fax: 423-638-7166

Barbara Lonas
University of Tennessee/Knoxville
1914 Andy Holt Ave.
25 HPER Bldg.
Knoxville, TN 37996
865-974-4466
Fax: 865-974-3961

Ronnie Gross
East Tennessee State University
1227 Volunteer Parkway
Bristol, TN 37620
423-844-6304
Fax: 423-844-6303
Email: grossrd@etsu.edu

Texas

Velma Elizalde
Coastal Bend College
3800 Charco Rd.
Beeville, TX 78102
361-358-2838
Fax: 361-354-2704

Elizabeth Retamozo
Boys and Girls Club/Greater Ft. Worth
3218 Belknap St.
Fort Worth, TX 76111
817-831-2911
Fax: 817-759-1209

Willie Thomas
Communities In Schools
1616 E. Commerce Bldg. #1
San Antonio, TX 78205
210-520-8440
Fax: 210-520-1104

Eddie Anaya
Learn, Inc.
P.O. Box 953358
2161 50th St., #107
Lubbock, TX 79412
806-763-4256
Fax: 806-763-0791

Kimberly Kozel
Paris Junior College
2400 Clarksville St.
Paris, TX 75460
903-782-0228
Fax: 903-782-2232
Email: kkozel@paris.cc.tx.us

Oscar Hernandez, Chairman of the Board
Project: Stay, Inc.
700 South Zarzamora, Suite 103
San Antonio, TX 78207
210-433-9307
Fax: 210-435-0711

Juan Vasquez
Southwest Texas State University
2406 Rosewood St.
Austin, TX 78702
512-476-2450
Fax: 512-476-2452

Cheryl McWilliams
Southwest Texas State University
601 University Ave.
ASB North #308
San Marcos, TX 78666
512-245-8135
Fax: 512-245-8589

Jackie Gildon
Texarkana College
2500 North Robison Rd.
Texarkana, TX 75501
903-838-4541, ext. 258
Fax: 903-832-5030

Virginia Day
Texas Southern University
3100 Clegurne Ave.
Houston, TX 77004
713-313-7275
Fax: 713-313-7842

Jennifer Hightower
University of Houston/Downtown

One Main St., South, Room 936
Houston, TX 77002
713-221-8992
Fax: 713-226-5257

Kathy Taylor
University of North Texas
P.O. Box 310888
Denton, TX 76203
940-565-2125
Fax: 940-565-2089
Email: taylor@coefs.coe.unf.edu

Pamela Flores
University of Texas at Brownsville
1614 Irdgely Road
Brownsville, TX 78520
956-544-3806
Fax: 956-983-7003

Sonia del Angel
University of Texas/Pan American
1201 West University Dr.
Edinburg, TX 78539
956-381-3651
Fax: 956-316-7015

Lyndon McClure
Dallas Community College District
701 Elm Street, Suite 300
Dallas, TX 75202-3299
214-860-2456
Fax: 214-860-2107

Carol Hicks
University of Texas–El Paso
500 W. University Ave. at
Hawthorne
El Paso, TX 79968
915-747-6611
Fax: 915-747-8879
Email: chicks@utep.edu

Rita E. Cortez
University of Texas–San Antonio
6900 North Loop
1604 W.M.S. Building
Room 3.02.49
San Antonio, TX 78249-0645
210-691-5852
Fax: 210-691-5848

Utah

Keele Johnson
College of Eastern Utah
San Juan Campus
639 West 100 South
Blanding, UT 84511
435-678-2201, ext. 162
Fax: 435-678-2220

Ross Taylor
Dixie College
225 South 700 East
Brown Building #207
St. George, UT 84770
801-652-7656
Fax: 801-674-4469

Kenneth Jackson
Snow College
150 College Ave.
Ephraim, UT 84627
435-283-4021
Fax: 435-283-6284

Leanne Maxwell
Southern Utah University
351 West Center
Cedar City, UT 84720
435-586-7771
Fax: 435-865-8235

Maraia Weingarten
Utah Valley State College
800 West 1200 South
Orem, UT 84058
801-222-8076
Fax: 801-222-8812

Virginia

Anita Clayton
Dabney S. Lancaster Community College
P.O. Box 1000
Clifton Forge, VA 24422
540-862-4246
Fax: 540-862-2398

Bertha Medford
Hampton University
P.O. Box 6183
Hampton, VA 23668
804-727-5607
Fax: 804-727-5084

Wendell Howlett
J. Sargent Reynolds Community College
P.O. Box 85622
Richmond, VA 23285
804-786-5987
Fax: 804-786-0974

Regina Massey
Mountain Empire Community College
P.O. Drawer 700
Big Stone Gap, VA 24219
540-523-2400
Fax: 540-523-8297

Jay McCallum
Southwest Virginia Community College
Buchanan Hall
P.O. Box SVCC
Richmond, VA 24641
540-964-7249
Fax: 540-964-7579

Jackie Craft
Virginia Highland Community College
P.O. Box 828
Abingdon, VA 24210
540-628-6094
Fax: 540-676-5487

Tom Wilson
Virginia Polytech Institute
State University
Hillcrest Hall-Lower Level
Blacksburg, VA 24061
540-231-6911
Fax: 540-231-4522
Email: tgwilson@vt.edu

Zelda Tucker-Dugger
Virginia State University
P.O. Box 9001
Petersburg, VA 23806
804-524-5811
Fax: 804-524-5142

Pamela Webb
Wytheville Community College
1000 East Main St.
Wytheville, VA 24382
540-223-4793
Fax: 540-223-4778

Vermont

Linda Shiller
Vermont Student Assistance Corporation
P.O. Box 2000
Champlin Mill, 4th Floor
Winooski, VT 05404
802-655-9602

Matthew Lesko, Information USA, Inc., 12081 Nebel Street, Rockville, MD 20852 • 1-800-955-7693 • www.lesko.com

Fax: 802-654-3765
Email: shiller@vsac.org

Washington

Lucretia Folks
Centralia College
600 West Locust
Centralia, WA 98531
360-736-9391, ext. 360
Fax: 360-330-7503
Email: lfolks@centralia.ctc.edu

Julian Argel
University of Washington
1107 NE 45th St., Suite 428
Box 354809
Seattle, WA 98105
206-616-1948
Fax: 206-616-3089

Beth D. Boyd
Northwest Indian College
2522 Kwina Road
Bellingham, WA 98226-9217
360-676-2772 x257
Fax: 360-752-1627

Karleen Wolfe
South Seattle Community College
6000 16th Avenue SW
Seattle, WA 98106-1499
206-768-6476
Fax: 206-768-6692

West Virginia

Claudia Wilkerson-Black
Greater Appalachian Outreach, Inc.
102 Park St.
Bluefield, WV 24701
304-324-8700
Fax: 304-324-8724

Donna Burgraff
Southern West Virginia Community College
1601 Armory Dr.
P.O. Box 2900
Williamson, WV 25661
304-235-6046
Fax: 304-235-6042

Fredda Chappel
University System of West Virginia
1018 Kanawha Blvd. East, Suite 700
Charleston, WV 25301
304-558-4620
Fax: 304-347-1347

Wisconsin

Kathleen Hirsch
University of Wisconsin/Stout
428 Bowman Hall
Menomonie, WI 54751
715-232-3383
Fax: 715-232-1366

Jane Stahmer
Forward Service Corporation
21A South Brown St.
P.O. Box 597
Rhinelander, WI 54501
715-362-7811
Fax: 715-362-5621

Jim Campbell
Milwaukee Area Technical College
700 W. State St.
Milwaukee, WI 53233
414-297-7991
Fax: 414-297-7401

Dennis Baskin
University of Wisconsin/Whitewater
800 West Main St.

Whitewater, WI 53190
262-472-6207
Fax: 262-472-2794

Deloise Shaw
University of Wisconsin/Milwaukee
P.O. Box 413
Milwaukee, WI 53201
414-229-3813
Fax: 414-229-5699

Paul T. Spraggins
Wisconsin Department of Public Instruction
101 West Pleasant Street
Suite 204
Milwaukee, WI 53212
414 227-4466
Fax: 414 227-4462

Wyoming

Carol Eckhardt
University of Wyoming/Laramie
Box 3808, University Station
Laramie, WY 82071
307-766-6189
Fax: 307-766-4010

Pacific Islands

Heinrich Palik
College of Micronesia-FSM
P.O. Box 159
Kolonia, FM 96941
691-320-3795
Fax: 691-320-2479

Vince Riley
Northern Marianas College
Box 1250
Saipan, MP 96950
670-234-9571
Fax: 670-234-0054

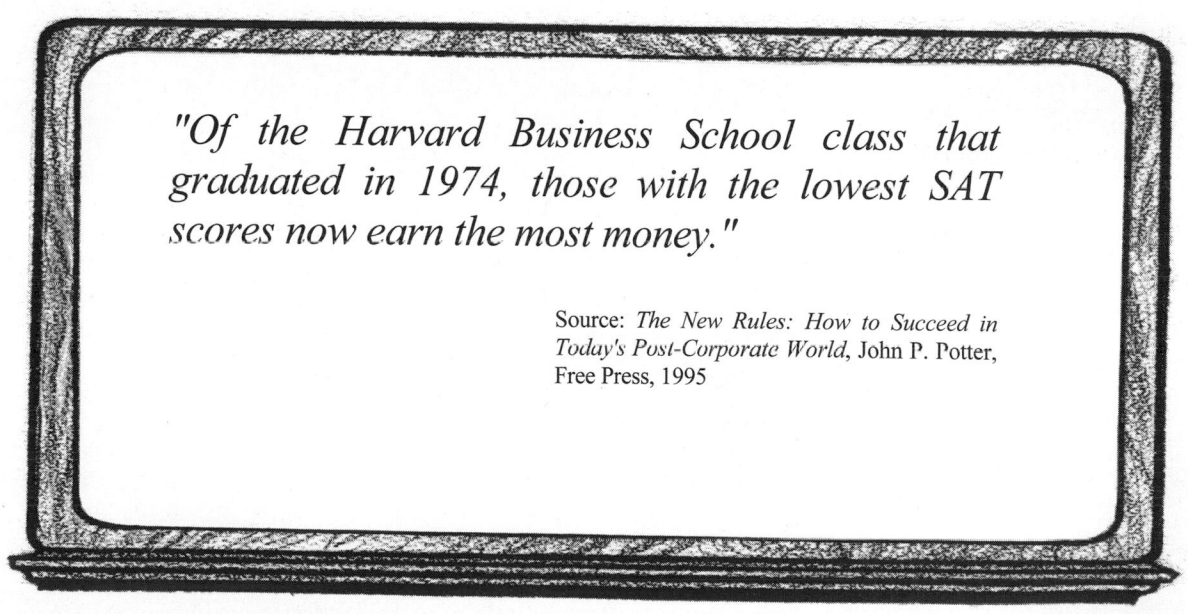

"Of the Harvard Business School class that graduated in 1974, those with the lowest SAT scores now earn the most money."

Source: *The New Rules: How to Succeed in Today's Post-Corporate World*, John P. Potter, Free Press, 1995

Free Help in Getting a College Degree
If You Are a Low Income High School Student

Program: Upward Bound — 84.047

Description: Upward Bound helps disadvantaged high school students prepare for college entrance by helping them improve pre-college performance, locating financial aid and other services, including preparation for entrance exams. It also provides these services for students from families where neither parent holds a college degree and for first-generation military veterans.

What You Can Get: Program services include instruction in reading, writing and study skills; academic, financial and personal counseling; exposure to academic and cultural events; tutorial services; information on postsecondary education opportunities; assistance in completing college entrance and financial aid applications; and help preparing for college entrance exams.

Who Is Eligible: Students must have completed the 8th grade and be between the ages of 13 and 19 (except veterans) and demonstrate a need for support. Students must apply before entering 12th grade, however exceptions are made. Students must be from low income families or be potential first-generation college students. Like Talent Search, the program requires that two-thirds of program participants be both from low-income households and be potential first-generation college students. Candidates are chosen on recommendations from local educators, clergy, or social workers.

Money Available: No direct financial help is made available through the program for students, however counselors will help participants locate and apply for aid from other sources. In 2001, $251 million was awarded, and almost 57,000 students received help.

National Office:
Council for Opportunity in Education
1025 Vermont Ave., NW, Suite 900
Washington, DC 20005
202-347-7430
Fax: 202-347-0786
www.trioprograms.org

Local Offices

Alabama
John C. Calhoun State Community College
Vinetta Wesley
P.O. Box 2216
Decatur, AL 35602
255-306-2765
Fax: 256-350-2656

Wallace Community College-Sparks Campus
Upward Bound
Linda Strickland
P.O. Drawer 2530
Eufaula, AL 36072-2530
334-687-3543
Fax: 334-687-0255
Email: upward@sstc.cc.al.us

Spring Hill College
Upward Bound
Chuck Mason
4000 Dauphin St.
Mobile, AL 36608

334-380-3464
Fax: 334-380-4399

Gadsden State Community College
Upward Bound
Patricia Rutledge
P.O. Box 227
Gadsden, AL 35902-0227
256-549-8396
Fax: 256-549-8404
Prutledge@gadsdenst.cc.al.us

Troy State University
Upward Bound
Mary Griffin
104 Pace Hall
Troy, AL 36082
334-670-3669
Fax: 334-670-3810

Gadsden State Community College
Veterans Upward Bound

Valerie Richardson
P.O. Box 227
Gadsden, AL 35902-0227
256-549-8396
Fax: 256-549-8404

Miles College
Upward Bound
Shirley Ellis
5500 Myron Massey Blvd.
Fairfield, Al 35064
205-929-1527
Fax: 205-929-1453

Lawson State Community College
Upward Bound Program
Mattie Crawford
3060 Wilson Rd., SW
Birmingham, AL 35221
205-929-6339
Fax: 205-929-6313
Email: mcrawford@cougar.ls.cc.al.us

Matthew Lesko, Information USA, Inc., 12081 Nebel Street, Rockville, MD 20852 • 1-800-955-7693 • www.lesko.com

The University of West Alabama
Upward Bound
Carole W. Smith
Station #37
Livingston, AL 35470
205-652-3756
Fax: 205-652-3708

Lurleen B Wallace State Junior College
Upward Bound Program
Bridges Anderson
P.O. Box 1418
Andalusia, AL 36420-1418
334-222-6591, ext. 2247
Fax: 334-222-6567
Email: banderson@hotmail.com

Bevill State Community College-Walker
Campus
Upward Bound
Carolyn Johnson
Box 800
Sumiton, AL 35148
205-648-3271
Fax: 205-648-2288

Stillman College
Upward Bound Program
Math/Science
Vernon Freeman
P.O. Drawer 1430
Tuscaloosa, AL 35403
205-349-4240
Fax: 205-758-3162

Bishop State Community College
Upward Bound
Ervin Thornton
351 North Broad St.
Mobile, AL 36603-5898
334-690-6805
Fax: 334-438-3249

Tuskegee University
Upward Bound
Edna Woodson
Russell Nursery Room 1
Tuskegee, AL 36088
334-727-8209
Fax: 334-724-4402

North Alabama Center for Educational
Excellence
Math/Science
Harold G. Dickerson
1515 Sparkman Dr., Suite B
Huntsville, AL 35816
256-722-9632
Fax: 256-722-9795

Northwest-Shoals Community College
Upward Bound
Charlene Freeman
2080 College Road
Phil Campbell, AL 35581
256-331-6277
Fax: 256-331-6272

Auburn University at Montgomery
Upward Bound
Carolyn Armstrong
Center for Special Services
7300 University Dr.
Montgomery, AL 36117-3596
334-244-3946
Fax: 334-244-3967
Email: carmstro@aum.edu

Talladega College
Upward Bound
Terry Mosley
627 W. Battle St.
Talladega, AL 35160
256-362-0206
Fax: 256-362-2268

Jefferson Davis Community College
Upward Bound
Beth Billy
P.O. Box 958
Brewton, AL 36427
334-809-1500
Fax: 334-809-0178

Central Alabama Community College
Upward Bound
Joyce Giddens
P.O. Box 389
Childersburg, AL 35044
256-378-5576, ext. 6413
Fax: 256-378-5281

University of Montevallo
Upward Bound Station 6268
Cheri Flow
Montevallo, AL 35115
205-665-6268
Fax: 205-665-6255
Email: flowc@um.montevallo.edu

Alabama A&M University
Upward Bound
P.O. Box 347
Normal, AL 35762
205-851-5660
Fax: 205-851-5663

Alabama Southern Community College
Upward Bound
P.O. Box 489
Thomsville, AL 36784
334-636-9642
Fax: 334-636-1380

Alabama Southern Community College
Upward Bound
P.O. Box 130
Gilbertown, AL 36908
334-575-3156
Fax: 334-575-5356

Alabama Southern Community College
Upward Bound
P.O. Box 2000
Monroeville, AL 36461
334-575-3156
Fax: 334-575-5356

Faulkner State Community College
Upward Bound
Lena Dexter
1900 Highway 31 South
Bay Minette, AL 36507
334-580-2170
Fax: 334-580-2182

Alabama State University
Upward Bound
Valerie Pittman
915 S. Jackson St., Box 271
Montgomery, AL 36116
334-229-4475
Fax: 334-229-4941
Email: valpittman@aol.com

Concordia College
Concordia College Center
Math and Science
Gracie Hollins
P.O. Box 1329
Selma, AL 36701
334-874-7143
Fax: 334-874-5735

Bevill State Community College-Fayette
Max Weaver
2631 Temple Avenue North
Brewer Campus
Fayette, Al 35555

205-932-3221
Fax: 205-932-3294

Bevill State Community College- Hamilton
Sara Franks
P.O. Drawer 9
Hamilton, AL 35570
205-921-3177, ext. 5318
Fax: 205-921-9620
Email: sgfranks@bevillst.cc.al.us

Concordia College
Ronnie Harrison
1804 Green Street
Selma, Al 36701
334-874-5727
Fax: 334-872-5755

Harry M. Ayers State Technical College
Lynn Newell
1801 Coleman Road
Anniston, AL 36201
256-835-5447
Fax: 256-832-1224
Email: lnewell@ayers.cc.al.us

Jefferson State Community College
Yvette Busby
2601 Carson Road
Birmingham, AL 35215
205-856-6064
Fax: 205-856-8572
Email: ybusby@jscc.cc.al.us

Lawson State Community College
Upward Bound Math/Science
Michelle Stevenson
3060 Wilson Road, Southwest
Birmingham, AL 35221
205-929-2515, ext. 241
Fax: 205-929-6316

University of South Alabama
Bernita M. Pulmas
307 University Boulevard
Mobile, AL 36688
334-460-7212
Fax: 334-460-6157

Wallace Community College-Aviation
Campus at Ozark
Helen F. Nichols
P.O. Box 1209
Ozark, AL 36361-1209
334-774-5113
Fax: 334-774-6399
Email: mabbott@mail.wallace.edu

Alaska

University of Alaska Fairbanks
Upward Bound Program
Andrew Angaiak
P.O. Box 756320
Fairbanks, AK 99775-6320
907-474-5685
Fax: 907-474-6001
Email: fnapa@uaf.edu

University of Alaska- Fairbanks
Upward Bound Math/Science
Don Lakken
P.O. Box 7556320
Fairbanks, AK 99775-6320
907-474-5938
Fax: 907-474-7900
Email: ffdal@aurora.alaska.edu

University of Alaska- Anchorage
Eric Peterson
2221 East Northern Lights, Suite 106
Anchorage, AK 99508
907-258-0487
Fax: 907-258-4589

Arizona

Arizona State University/Tempe
Upward Bound
Irvin Coin
P.O. Box 870817
Tempe, AZ 85287-0812
480-965-6483

Arizona State University
Veterans Upward Bound
William Weir
1000 E. Apache Blvd.
Tempe, AZ 85281
408-894-8451
Fax: 408-894-9538

Northern Arizona University
Upward Bound
Eliot Schipper
P.O. Box 6035
Flagstaff, AZ 86011-6035
520-523-6988
Fax: 520-523-9466

Pima County Community College District
Upward Bound
Angie Listo
8181 East Irvington Rd.
Tucson, AZ 85709
520-206-7601
Fax: 520-206-7851
Email: alisto@pimacc.pima.edu

Northern Arizona University
Math and Science
Box 6035
Flagstaff, AZ 86011-6035
602-523-1308
Fax: 602-523-9466
Email: terry.hubbard@nau.edu

Embry-Riddle Aeronautical University
Upward Bound Math/Science
Matthew Benney
3200 Willow Creek Rd.
Prescott, AZ 86301
520-708-3874
Fax: 520-708-6678
Email: benney@pr.erau.edu

Arizona Western College
Terry Shove
9500 South Avenue 8E
Yuma, AZ 85365
520-317-6035
Fax: 520-344-7755
Email: slshove@awc.cc.az.us

Dine College
Laura Smith
P.O. Box 218
Tsaile, AZ 86556
520-724-6691
Fax: 520-724-3327
Email: akuslik@crystal.ncc.cc.nm.us

Maricopa County Community College District
Debbie Stanfield
2411 West 14th Street
Tempe, AZ 85281
602-392-5170
Fax: 602-392-5329

Yavapai College
Veterans Upward Bound
Jake Lindsay
1100 East Sheldon Street
Box 6043
Prescott, AZ 86301
520-776-2309
Fax: 520-771-9097
Email: jake_lindsay@yavapai.cc.az.us

Arkansas

University of Arkansas
Veterans Upward Bound
Gerald Hudder
725 Hotz Hall
Fayetteville, AR 72701
501-575-2821
Fax: 501-575-5748
Email: ghudder@comp.uark.edu

University of Arkansas
Upward Bound
Shauna Sterling
715 Hotz Hall
Fayetteville, AR 72701
501-575-3553
Fax: 501-575-4279
Email: ssterli@comp.uark.edu

Lyon College
Upward Bound
Marilynn Chlebak
P.O. Box 2317
Batesville, AR 72503-2317
870-698-4263
Fax: 870-698-4622

University of Arkansas at Pine Bluff
Upward Bound
Verna Cottonham
P.O. Box 4914
1200 N. University Dr.
Pine Bluff, AR 71611
870-543-8256
Fax: 870-543-8261

Arkansas State University/Beebe Branch
Upward Bound
C/o Constance Nowell
P.O. Drawer H
Beebe, AR 72012
501-882-8363
Fax: 501-882-8370

Arkansas State University
Upward Bound
Paula Bradberry
P.O. Box 1390
State University, AR 72467
870-972-2080
Fax: 870-972-2520
Email: pbradberry.pawnee.astate.edu

Southern Arkansas University
Upward Bound
Jerry Thomas
100 East University
P.O. Box 9283
Magnolia, AR 71753
501-235-4160
Fax: 501-235-4995

Ouachita Baptist University
Upward Bound
Math/Science
Lewis Shepherd
410 Ouachita St.
OBU Box 3779
Arkadelphia, AR 71998-0001
870-245-5158
Fax: 870-245-5165
Email: shepherdl@alpha.obu.edu

Rich Mountain Community College
Upward Bound
Betty Clere
1100 College Dr.
Mena, AR 71953
501-394-7622, ext. 1642
Fax: 501-394-2828
Email: bclere@rmcc.cc.ar.us

Philander Smith College
Upward Bound
Gloria Billingsley
812 W. 13th St.

Little Rock, AR 72202
501-370-5210
Fax: 501-370-5396
Email: gabill2628@aol.com

Phillips County Community College
Upward Bound
Betty Darnell
P.O. Box 785
Helena, AR 72342
870-338-6474
Fax: 870-338-7542

Cossatot Technical College
Kay Stroud
P.O. Box 960183
Highway 399
De Queen, AR 71832-0960
870-584-4471
Fax: 870-642-8766

Harding University
Jennifer Smith
HU Box 2275
Searcy, AR 72149-0001
501-279-4170
Fax: 501-279-4169
Email: jsmith@harding.edu

Lyon College
Upward Bound Math/Science
Paul Reynolds
P.O. Box 2317
Batesville, AR 72503
870-698-1783
Fax: 870-698-4622
Email: mosley@shire.ac.arknet.edu

University Of Arkansas Community College
at Hope
Terry Kirchhoff
P.O. Box 140
Hope, AR 71802
870-777-5722
Fax: 870-777-5957

University of Arkansas-Monticello
LaQuieta Grayson
P.O. Box 3629 UAM
Monticello, AR 71656
870-460-1010
Fax: 870-460-1810

California

Humboldt State University
Veterans Upward Bound
Cai Williams
158 University Annex
Arcata, CA 95521-2400
707-826-4971
Fax: 707-826-5237
Email: cwl@axe.humboldt.edu

San Jose State University
Upward Bound
Priscilla Peebles
233 Wahlquist Library
San Jose, CA 95190
408-924-2567
Fax: 408-924-2526
Email: priscill@eopnet.sjsu.edu

Occidental College
Upward Bound
Susan Madrid-Simon
1600 Campus Rd.
Los Angeles, CA 90041
323-259-2691
Fax: 323-341-4981
Email: madridsi@oxy.edu

Humboldt State University
Upward Bound
Jennifer Dyke

203 NHE
Arcata, CA 95521
707-826-3553
Fax: 707-826-4499
Email: jd7000@axe.humboldt.edu

University of California, Riverside
Upward Bound
Gustavo Ocquero
205 W. Big Springs Rd.
Riverside, CA 92507
909-787-4685
Fax: 909-787-4762
Email: ocquera@ucr.edu

University of Southern California
Upward Bound Math/Science
Jeffrey Clayton
3708 S. Figueroa St.
Los Angeles, CA 90007
213-743-6395
Fax: 213-743-8142

Compton Community College
Upward Bound
Oscar Caliman
1111 East Artesia Blvd.
Compton, CA 90221
310-900-1600
Fax: 310-900-1699

College of the Siskiyous
Upward Bound
Kim DeCosta
800 College Ave.
Weed, CA 96094
530-938-5278
Fax: 530-938-5383

California State University-San Bernadino
Upward Bound
Denise Benton
5500 University Parkway, UII 346
San Bernadino, CA 92407-2397
909-880-5914
Fax: 909-880-7000
Email: dbenton@wiley.csusbedu

California State University-Fresno
Upward Bound
Perry Angle
5240 N. Jackson Ave.
Mail Stop #35
Fresno, CA 93740-8023
559-278-2693
Fax: 559-278-4306
Email: perry_angle@csufresno.edu

California State University/Chico
Upward Bound
David Ferguson
Warner St.
102 Siskiyou Hall
Chico, CA 95929
916-898-5181
Fax: 916-898-4837
Email: dferguson@oavax.csuchico.edu

California State University/Fullerton
Upward Bound Program
Janet Lang
800 N. State College Blvd.
215University Hall
Fullerton, CA 92634
714-278-2011
Fax: 714-278-2364

Reedley College
Upward Bound Program
Diana Banuelos
995 North Reed
Reedley, CA 93654
209-638-3641, ext. 247
Fax: 209-638-5040
Email: banuelos_d@scccd.cc.ca.us

California Lutheran University
Upward Bound
Oscar Cobain
60 West Olsen Rd., #3800
Thousand Oaks, CA 91360-2787
805-493-3350
Fax: 805-493-3048
Email: cobain@clunet.edu

West Hills Community College
Upward Bound Program
300 Cherry Lane
Coalinga, CA 93210
559-935-0801
Fax: 559-935-5655
Email: costamd@whccd.cc.ca.us

College of the Desert
Upward Bound Program
Adrian Gonzales
43500 Monterey Ave.
Palm Desert, CA 92260
760-773-2541
Fax: 760-766-7247

University of San Francisco
Upward Bound
Janice Dirden-Cook
2130 Fulton St.
LM/UND #29
San Francisco, CA 94117-1080
415-422-2491
Fax: 415-244-2496
Email: cookj@usfca.edu

East Los Angeles Community College
Upward Bound
Michael Lopez
1301 Avenida Cesar Chavez
Monterey Park, CA 91754-6099
323-265-8981
Fax: 323-265-8655
Email: lopezmc@laccd.cc.ca.us

Napa Valley College
Upward Bound Program
Ana Martinez
2277 Napa Vallejo Highway
Napa, CA 94558-6236
707-253-3077
Fax: 707-259-8030

Long Beach City College
Upward Bound
Jesus Solano
1301 S. Pacific Coast Highway
Long Beach, CA 90808
562-938-3179
Fax: 562-938-3912

California State University/Long Beach
Upward Bound Program
Willie Elston
6300 State University Drive, Suite 332
Long Beach, CA 90815-1203
310-985-4291
Fax: 310-985-7646

California State University
Upward Bound Program
Wayne Kitchen
25800 Carlos Bee Blvd.
Hayward, CA 94542
510-885-2960
Fax: 510-885-4687

Los Angeles City College
Upward Bound Program
Fred Fate
855 N. Vermont Ave.
Los Angeles, CA 90029
323-953-4500

Fax: 323-953-4500
Email: ffate@aol.com

Sonoma State University
Upward Bound Program
Howard Willis
1801 East Cotati Ave.
Rohnert Park, CA 94928-3609
707-664-2428
Fax: 707-664-2505
Email: howard.willis@sonoma.edu

Cal State L.A. University
Upward Bound Math/Science
Maria Godoy
5151 State University Dr.
E + TA 130
Los Angeles, CA 90032
323-343-3238
Fax: 323-343-3234
Email: mgodoy@calstate_la.edu

Imperial Valley College
Upward Bound Program
Rosalie Lopez
P.O. Box 158
380 East Aten Rd.
Imperial, CA 92251-0158
760-352-8320
Fax: 760-355-2663
Email: roslop@imperial.cc.ca.us

The National Hispanic University
Upward Bound
Marco Cruz
14271 Story Rd.
San Jose, CA 95127-3823
408-254-6900
Fax: 408-254-1369

California State University/San Marcos
Upward Bound Program
Carolina Cardenas
Craven Hall, Room 4109
San Marcos, CA 92096-0001
760-750-4872
Fax: 760-750-3089
Email: cardenas@mailhost1

Regents of the University of California
Upward Bound Math/Science
Keith Hori
2150 Kitteredge St., 2nd Floor #1060
Berkeley, CA 94720-1060
510-642-3719
Fax: 510-643-8421
Email: keith_hori@maillink.berkeley.edu

College of the Redwoods
Upward Bound
Jay McCauliff
7351 Tomokins Hill Rd.
Eureka, CA 95501
707-445-6968
Fax: 707-445-6990
Email: upward@humboldt1.com

Telacu Education Foundation
Telacu Veterans Upward Bound Project
Frank Alderete
5400 E. Olympic Blvd.
Suite 100
Los Angeles, CA 90022
323-838-8955
Fax: 323-838-8960

Japanese Community Youth Council/AACE
Upward Bound
Ron Muriera
1596 Post St.
San Francisco, CA 94109-6511
415-202-7900
Fax: 415-563-7109
Email: rpmuriera@aol.com

Pasadena City College
Upward Bound Program
Scott Thayer
1570 East Colorado Blvd.
Pasadena, CA 91106-2003
626-585-7696
Fax: 626-585-7909
Email: swthayer@paccd.cc.ca.us

Fresno City College
Upward Bound Program
Edward Wright
1101 E. University Ave.
Fresno, CA 93741
559-442-8297
Fax: 559-265-5739
Email: wright_e@sccod.cc.ca.us

Rio Hondo Community College District
Upward Bound
Sylvia Diaz
3600 Workman Mill Rd.
Whittier, CA 90601-1699
310-908-3467
Fax: 310-695-8098

California Polytechnic State University
Upward Bound Program
Samuel Cortez
Student Academic Services
San Luis Obispo, CA 93407
805-756-2301
Fax: 805-756-5122
Email: scortez@calpoly.edu

Volunteers of America
Upward Bound
Myrna Joseph
3761 Stocker St., Suite 202
Los Angeles, CA 90008
213-381-1353
Fax: 213-383-1162

Holy Names College
Upward Bound
Barbara Essig
3500 Mountain Blvd.
Oakland, CA 94619-9989
510-436-1504
Fax: 510-879-1876

Wahupa
Upward Bound
Victor Shupp
3251 Fourth Ave.
San Diego, CA 92103
619-297-4471
Fax: 619-297-2351
Email: wahupa@aol.com

University of California
Joanne Madison
Room 110, Building 434
Santa Barbara, CA 93106-7170
805-893-3515
Fax: 805-933-3656
Email: saa3madi@ucsbvm.ucsb.educ

California State University/Dominguez Hills
Upward Bound Program
Melonka Renaldo-McCray
1000 East Victoria St.
SC 11325
Carson, CA 90747
310-243-2817
Fax: 310-217-6987
Email: mmcray@lausd.k-12.us

Cal Poly Pomona Foundation, Inc.
Upward Bound Program Math/Science
Frank Torres
3801 West Temple Ave. 15-13
Pomona, CA 91768-4038
909-869-3231

Fax: 909-869-5154
Email: fjtorres@csupomona.edu

University of California/Davis
Upward Bound
Ping Chan
One Shields Ave.
Davis, CA 95616-8772
916-757-1101
Fax: 916-752-9326
Email: szpingie@ucdavis.edu

Harvey Mudd College
Upward Bound
James Sullivan
301 East 12th St.
Claremont, CA 91711-5990
909-621-8123
Fax: 909-621-8465

University of California/San Diego
Upward Bound Math/Science
Eustacio Beenitez
9500 Gilman Dr.
Dept. 0305-B
La Jolla, CA 92093-0305
858-534-8273
Fax: 858-534-8996
Email: dvaldes@ucsd.edu

Stanford University
Upward Bound Program
Nancy Vandenberg
558 Salvatierra Walkway
Haas Center for Public Service
Stanford, CA 94305-8620
650-725-1663
Fax: 650-725-7339

Yosemite Community College District
Upward Bound
Roberto Mendez
435 College Ave.
Modesto, CA 95354
209-575-6715
Fax: 209-575-6630

San Diego State University Foundation
Upward Bound - Math and Science
Cynthia Park
5250 Campanile Dr.
San Diego, CA 92182
619-594-2349
Fax: 619-594-7821
Email: cpark@mail.sdsu.edu

Harvey Mudd College
Math and Science
Daniel Marquez
301 East 12th St.
Claremont, CA 91711-5990
909-621-8665
Fax: 909-621-8360
Email: dmarquez@thuband.ac.hmc.edu

Monterey Peninsula College
Math and Science
Mary Ann Hamann
980 Fremont St.
Monterey, CA 93940-4799
831-646-4246
Fax: 831-392-1001

California Lutheran University
Upward Bound Math/Science
Joy Brittain
60 West Olsen Road
Thousand Oaks, CA 91360-2787
805-493-3292
Fax: 805-493-3048

California State University-Bakersfield
Donald Towns
9001 Stockdale Highway

Bakersfield, CA 93311-1099
805-664-3124
Fax: 804-664-3194
Email: dtowns@csub.edu

California State University-Fullerton
Upward Bound Math/Science
Patricia Bejarano-Vera
800 North State College Boulevard
215 University Hall
Fullerton, CA 92634
714-278-7327
Fax: 714-278-2364

California State University-Monterey Bay
Jose Martinez-Saldana
100 Campus Center 86B
Seaside, CA 93955
831-582-3657
Fax: 831-582-3663
Email: josemartinez-saldana@monterey.edu

Compton Community College
Upward Bound Math/Science
Ronald Chatman
1111 East Artesia Boulevard
Compton, CA 90221
310-900-1600
Fax: 310-900-1697

Los Angeles Harbor College
Rochelle Hudson
1111 Figueroa Place
Wilmington, CA 90744
310-522-8353
Fax: 310-522-8473

Los Angeles Mission College
John Klitsner
13356 Eldridge Avenue
Sylmar, CA 91342
818-364-7886
Fax: 818-364-7826
Email: klitsnjn@laccd.cc.ca.us

Los Angeles Southwest College
Penelope Jarecke
1600 West Imperial Highway
Los Angeles, CA 90047
323-241-5399
Fax: 323-241-5476
Email: pjarecke@cnt.net

Palomar College
Marsha Gable
1951 East Valley Parkway
Escondido, CA 92027
760-744-1150, ext. 8127
Fax: 760-738-4530

Pasadena City College
Upward Bound Math/Science
Jeff Holmes
1570 East Colorado Boulevard
Pasadena, CA 91106-2003
626-585-7696
Fax: 626-585-7909

Provisional Accelerated Learning Center
Victor Edinburgh
2450 Blake Street
P.O. Box 7100
San Bernardino, CA 92411
909-887-7002
Fax: 909-887-8942
Email: palcenter@eee.org

Riverside Community College
Jose Chavez
4800 Magnolia Avenue
Riverside, CA 92506-1299
909-372-7082
Fax: 909-372-7060

Santa Ana College
David Guzman
1530 W. 17th. Street
Santa Ana, CA 92706
714-564-6287

University Of California-Irvine
Juan Lara
437 Administration Building
Irvine, CA 92697-2510
949-824-6362
Fax: 949-824-1371
Email: jflara@uci.edu

University Of California-Riverside
Upward Bound Math/Science
Javier Hernandez
Office of Res. Affairs
Riverside, CA 92521-0217
909-787-4695
Fax: 909-787-4762

University Of California-Santa Cruz
Upward Bound Math/Science
Tamala Brown
3004 Mission Street
220 Ed. Partnership Center
Santa Cruz, CA 95060
831-460-3009
Fax: 831-460-3002
Email: tammib@cats.ucsc.edu

University Of San Diego
Jocbethem M. Tahapary
5998 Alcala Pike
San Diego, CA 92110
619-295-3530
Fax: 619-295-3539
Email: jtahapal@san.rr.com

Yuba College
Yvette Santana
2088 North Beale Road
Marysville, CA 95901-7605
530-749-3857
Fax: 530-634-7703

Colorado

Metropolitan State College of Denver
Veterans Upward Bound
Glenn Morris
Campus Box 89
P.O. Box 173362
Denver, CO 80217-3362
303-556-3947
Fax: 303-556-6245
Email: morris@mscd.edu

Trinidad State Junior College
Upward Bound
Allen Bachoroski
600 Prospect
Trinidad, CO 81082
719-846-5657
Fax: 719-846-5667
Email: allen.bachoroski@tsjc.ccoes.edu

Pueblo Community College
Upward Bound
Patricia Maes-Garcia
900 West Orman Ave.
Pueblo, CO 81004-1499
719-549-3463
Fax: 719-846-7566
Email: pat.maes-garcia@pcc.colorado.edu

Adams State College
Upward Bound
Mike Garcia
Box 18 Richardson Hall
Alamosa, CO 81102
719-587-7865
Fax: 719-587-7522
Email: mgarcia@ascadms.edu

University of Southern Colorado
Upward Bound
Mike Medina
2200 Bonforte Blvd.
Pueblo, CO 81001-4901
303-549-2750
Fax: 303-549-2942
Email: medina@meteor.uscoloedu.

Colorado State University
Upward Bound
Oscar Felix
304 Student Services Bldg.
Fort Collins, CO 80523
970-491-6473
Fax: 970-491-1077

Metropolitan State College of Denver
High School Upward Bound
Charles Maldonado
Campus Box 66
P.O. Box 173362
Denver, CO 80217-3362
303-556-2812
Fax: 303-556-4035

Trinidad State Junior College
Math and Science
Judy MacLaren
600 Prospect
Trinidad, CO 81082
719-846-5554
Fax: 719-846-5667
Email: judy.maclaren@tsjc.ccoes.edu

University of Northern Colorado
Math and Science
John C. Moore
Department of Biological Sciences
Greeley, CO 80639
970-351-2751
Fax: 970-351-1571

Colorado Mountain College
Collen Moran
3000 County Road
114 Spring Valley Campus
Glenwood Springs, CO 81602
970-947-8278
Fax: 970-947-8017
Email: cmoran@cloradomtn.edu

Fort Lewis College
Glenna Witt Sexton
Office of Student Affairs
1000 Rim Drive
Durango, CO 81301
970-247-7331
Fax: 970-247-7680

University Of Colorado at Denver
Kathy Jackson
P.O. Box 173364
Campus Box 145
Denver, CO 80217-3364
303-556-2802
Fax: 303-556-2280

University Of Colorado-Boulder
Upward Bound Math/Science
Lindy B. Waters
Campus Box 107
202 Willard Hall
Boulder, CO 80309
303-492-6134
Fax: 303-492-3035
Email: lindy.waters@colorado.edu

Connecticut

Central Connecticut State University
Upward Bound
Petra Clark-Dufner
1615 Stanley St.
Copernicus Hall

New Britain, CT 06050
860-832-1904
Fax: 860-832-0191
Email: clarkduferp@ccsu.edu

Fairfield University
Upward Bound
Georgia Day
N. Benson Rd.
Dolan 150
Fairfield, CT 06430-7524
203-254-4064
Fax: 203-254-4296
Email: gfday@fairl.fairfield.edu

Wesleyan University
Upward Bound
Donna Thompson
41 Lawn Ave.
Middletown, CT 06457
860-685-3186
Fax: 860-685-3115
Email: dmthompson@wesleyand.edu

Sacred Heart University
Upward Bound Program
Caryl Rice-Ehalt
5151 Park Ave.
Fairfield, CT 06432-1000
203-371-7864
Fax: 203-371-7759
Email: ehalt@shu.sacredheart.edu

University of Connecticut
Susana Ulloa-Beal
341 Mansfield Road, U-170
Storrs, CT 06269-1170
860-486-4040
Fax: 860-486-4024
Email: capadm16@uconnvm.uconn.edu

Western Connecticut State University
Ismael Diaz
181 White Street
Danbury, CT 06810
203-837-8547
Fax: 203-837-8539

Delaware

Delaware Technical and Community College
Upward Bound
Margaret Hurley
P.O. Box 660
Georgetown, DE 19947
302-856-5400
Fax: 302-856-5635
Email: mhurley@outland.dtcc.edu

Kenneth Geckle, President
Upward Bound Program
1832 N. DuPont Parkway
Dover, DE 19901
302-739-6183
Fax: 302-739-6169

Delaware Technical and Community College
Upward Bound
Eugene Barnes
333 Shipley St.
Wilmington, DE 19801
302-573-5438
Fax: 302-657-5187

Delaware State University
Veterans Upward Bound
Mariko Taylor
1200 N. DuPont Highway
Dover, DE 19901-2277
302-857-6130
Fax: 302-857-6131
Email: mtaylor@dsc.edu

University of Delaware
Upward Bound

Barbara Y. Thomas
5 West Main St.
Academic Services Center
Newark, DE 19716-1101
302-831-6373
Fax: 302-831-4128
Email: by.thomas@mvs.udel.edu

Delaware Technical & Community College
Upward Bound Math/Science
Rosetta Henderson
333 Shipley Street
Wilmington, DE 19801
302-573-5438
Fax: 302-657-5187

Upward Bound Math/Science
Brenda F. Stover
P.O. Box 660, Route 18
Georgetown, DE 19947
302-856-5400, ext. 9890
Fax: 302-856-5635
Email: bstover@outland.dtcc.edu

University of Delaware
Upward Bound Math/Science
Lysbet Murray
5 West Main Street
Newark, DE 19716
302-831-8923
Fax: 302-831-4128
Email: lysbet@udel.edu

District of Columbia

Trinity College
Upward Bound
Altrue Johnson
125 Michigan Ave., N.E.
Washington, DC 20017
202-884-9148
Fax: 202-884-9145
Email: johnson@trinitydc.edu

Howard University
Upward Bound Math/Science
Joseph Bell
2395 Sixth St., N.W.
Washington, DC 20059
202-806-5132
Fax: 202-806-5148
Email: jbell@howard.edu

University of the District of Columbia
Upward Bound
Saundra Carter
4200 Connecticut Ave., N.W., MB 3805
Washington, DC 20008
202-274-5032
Fax: 202-274-7412

Academic Improvement, Inc.
Veterans Upward Bound
Roosevelt Marshall
1425 4th Street, SW #501A
Washington, DC 20024
202-554-8074
Fax: 202-554-8074

The College Board
Constance Clark
1233 20th Street, NW, Suite 600
Washington, DC 20036-2304
202-822-5900
Fax: 202-274-7412

George Washington University
Claudia Nichols
2300 Eye Street, NW
237A Ross Hall
Washington, DC 20037
202-994-4269
Fax: 202-994-7651
Email: mcdcpn@gwumc.edu

Lulac National Education Service Centers, Inc.
Zaida Vasquez
1133 20th Street, NW, Suite 750
Washington, DC 20036
202-835-9646
Fax: 202-835-9685

National Council Of La Raza
Lupi Quinteros
Latin American Youth Center
1419 Columbia Road NW
Washington, DC 20009
202-785-1670
Fax: 202-776-1792
Email: lupi@mail.layc-dc.org

Florida

Florida State University
Upward Bound
Charles Forster
5200A University Center
Tallahassee, FL 32306-2470
904-644-5478
Fax: 904-644-5435

University of South Florida
Upward Bound
Robert Davis
4202 E. Fowler Ave.
FAO 100U
Tampa, FL 33620-7750
813-974-2802
Fax: 813-974-3684

Rollins College
Upward Bound
Udeth Lugo
1000 Holt Ave. @2758
Winter Park, FL 32789-4496
407-646-1558
Fax: 407-646-2318
Email: udeth@rollins.edu

Embry-Riddle Aeronautical University
Upward Bound
Regan Morris
600 S. Clyde Morris Blvd.
Daytona Beach, FL 32114
904-226-6728
Fax: 904-226-6728

Indian River Community College
Upward Bound
Reginald Floyd
3209 Virginia Ave.
Fort Pierce, FL 34981
561-462-4528
Fax: 561-462-4796
Email: rfloyd@ircc.cc.fl.us

Miami-Dade Community College
Veterans Upward Bound
Bernice Belcher
11011 S.W. 104th St.
Miami, FL 33176
305-237-0940
Fax: 305-347-0868
Email: bbelcher@mdcc.edu

University of Miami/Coral Gables
Upward Bound
Marie Grimes-Davis
5600 Merrick Dr.
Coral Gables, FL 33124-5590
305-284-3015
Fax: 305-284-4268

Florida International University
Upward Bound
Sofia Santiesteban
GC-225 University Park Campus
Miami, FL 33199
305-348-1742

Fax: 305-348-1743
Email: santiest@servac.fiu.edu

Santa Fe Community College
Upward Bound
Lou Ann Cooper
3000 N.W. 83 St., P-148
Gainesville, FL 32606-6200
352-395-7357
Fax: 352-395-4440
Email: lou.ann.cooper@santafe.cc.fl.us

University of Florida
Upward Bound
Gwenuel W. Mingo
P.O. Box 118115
Gainesville, FL 32611-8130
352-392-2281
Fax: 352-392-2286
Email: mingo@oasis.ufl.edu

Florida A&M University
Upward Bound
Van WIlliams
Trio Programs
103 GEC-A
Tallahassee, FL 32307-5800
850-599-3055
Fax: 850-599-3967

Jacksonville University
Upward Bound Program
Glori White Peters
2800 University Blvd., N.
Jacksonville, FL 32211-3394
904-745-7150
Fax: 904-745-7159

Edison Community College
Michelle B. Releford
8099 College Parkway, S.W.
Fort Myers, FL 33919
941-489-9028
Fax: 941-489-9291

Edward Waters College
Emma Okari-Brooks
Box 70753
Jacksonville, FL 32202
904-366-2537
Fax: 904-366-2855

Florida A&M University
Upward Bound Math/Science
Errol Wilson
MLK Jr. Boulevard South
400 Lee Hall
Tallahassee, FL 32307
850-561-2109
Fax: 850-599-3967

Florida Community College-Jacksonville
Nini Smiley
4501 Capper Road
Jacksonville, FL 32218
904-766-4446
Fax: 904-766-4449
Email: nsmiley@fccj.org

Florida National College
Angela Rodriguez
4206 West 12th Avenue
Hialeah, FL 33012
305-821-3333
Fax: 305-362-0595

Miami Museum Of Science, Inc.
Upward Bound Math/Science
Jennifer Schooley
3280 South Miami Avenue
Miami, FL 33129
305-646-4254
Fax: 305-646-4300
Email: jennifer@miamisci.org

North Dade Concerted Services, Inc.
Bernice Belchar
1830 NW 188th. Terrace
Opa Locka, FL 33056
954-986-6971
Fax: 954-986-6972

Okaloosa-Walton Community College
Veterans Upward Bound
Ned Couey
100 College Boulevard
Niceville, FL 32578
850-729-5366
Fax: 850-729-5278
Email: coueyn@owcc.net

Palm Beach Community College- Central
Richard Marshall
4200 Congress Avenue
Lake Worth, FL 33461
561-357-1361
Fax: 561-434-5056

Polk Community College
Catherlyn F. Lewis-Brim
999 Avenue H, N.E.
Winter Haven, FL 33838
863-297-1010, ext. 5250
Fax: 863-297-1053
Email: clewis-brim@mail.polk.cc.fl.us

Valencia Community College
Upward Bound
Fred Robinson, Jr.
190 South Orange Avenue
Orlando, FL 32801-3204
407-299-5000, ext. 2625
Fax: 407-382-2061

Upward Bound
Joyce Romano
P.O. Box 3028
Orlando, FL 32802
407-299-5000, ext. 2625
Fax: 407-382-2061
Email: jromano@gwmail.valencia.cc.fl.us

Federated States of Micronesia

College Of Micronesia-FSM
Upward Bound
Penny Weilbacher
P.O. Box 159
Kolonia, FM 96941
691-320-3795
Fax: 691-320-3799

Upward Bound
Morgan Jonas
P.O. Box 37
Kosrae, FM 96944
691-370-2135
Fax: 691-370-2335

Upward Bound
Deliver Salle
P.O. Box 879
Weno Chuuk, FM 96942
691-330-3288
Fax: 691-330-3627
Email: dsalle@mail.fm

Upward Bound
Director
P.O. Box 614
Pohnpei, FM 96941
691-320-3795
Fax: 691-320-3799

Georgia

Georgia Southern University
Upward Bound
Randy Gunter

1026 Williams Center
Landrum Box 8071
Statesboro, GA 30460-8071
912-681-5458
Fax: 912-681-0863

Clark Atlanta University
Upward Bound
Maxine Hutchinson
Box 55
240 J.P. Brawley Dr. at Fair St., S.W.
Atlanta, GA 30314
404-880-8263
Fax: 404-880-6278

Thomas University
Upward Bound
Faye Johnson
1501 Millpond Rd.
Thomasville, GA 31792-7499
912-226-1621
Fax: 912-226-1653
Email: fjohnson@thomasu.edu

Paine College
Upward Bound
Earnestine Bell
1235 Fifteenth St.
Augusta, GA 30901-2799
706-821-8200
Fax: 706-724-6646

Abraham Baldwin Agricultural College
Upward Bound
Kenneth Newkirk
Bpx #1, 2802 Moore Hwy.
Tifton, GA 31794-2601
912-386-7269
Fax: 912-386-7006

Fort Valley State College
Upward Bound Program
Arenetta Hall
1005 State College Dr.
P.O. Box 4620
Fort Valley, GA 31030-3298
912-825-6965
Fax: 912-825-6131

Georgia State University
Upward Bound
Shirley Arnold
420 One Park Place South 240
Atlanta, GA 30303
404-651-2818
Fax: 404-463-9712

University of Georgia
Upward Bound
Melvin Rambeau
Division of Academic Assistance
480 North Thomas St.
Athens, GA 30602-5550
706-369-5660
Fax: 706-369-5925

Morehouse College
Upward Bound
Rubye Byrd
830 Westview Dr., SW
P.O. Box 134
Atlanta, GA 30314
404-215-2671
Fax: 404-788-2215
Email: rbyrd@morehouse.edu

Savannah State University
Upward Bound Project
Erma Jean Mobley
P.O. Box 20488
706 Tatum Street
Savannah, GA 31404
912-356-2196
Fax: 912-353-3050

Andrew College
Upward Bound Program
James Leroy Lewis
413 College St.
Cuthbert, GA 31740
912-732-2932
Fax: 912-732-2176

The University of Georgia
Upward Bound Program
Harriet Church
315 Milledge Hall
Athens, GA 30602-5554
706-542-4128
Fax: 706-542-0476
Email: hchurch@uga.cc.uga.edu

Georgia Southwestern State University
Upward Bound
Gene Thomas
800 Wheatley St.
Americus, GA 31709-4693
912-931-2294
Fax: 912-931-2832

Morris Brown College
Upward Bound
Charlie Mae Wilson
643 Martin Luther King Jr. Dr., NW
Atlanta, GA 30314
404-739-1410
Fax: 404-739-1415

Corporation of Mercer University
Upward Bound
Samuel Hart
1400 Coleman Ave.
Macon, GA 31207-0001
912-301-2686
Fax: 912-301-5306
Email: hart_sf@mercer.edu

Atlanta Metropolitan College
Upward Bound
Willetta Phipps
1630 Metropolitan Pkwy., S.W.
Atlanta, GA 30310
404-756-4060
Fax: 404-756-4460

Morris Brown College
Math and Science
Joyce Lewis
643 Martin Luther King Jr. Dr., NW
Atlanta, GA 30314
404-739-1410
Fax: 404-739-1415

Clark Atlanta University
Math and Science
Maxine Hutchinson
240 James P. Brawley Dr. at Fair St., SW
Box 55
Atlanta, GA 30314
404-880-8263
Fax: 404-880-6278

Veterans Opportunity And Resource Center
Incorporated
Veterans Upward Bound
Arthur Barham
P.O. Box 92425
Atlanta, GA 30314
404-755-7675
Fax: 404-775-5228
Email: vorci@bellsouth.net

Guam

University of Guam
Upward Bound Program
Yoichi K. Rengiil
UOG Station
Mangilao, GU 96923
671-735-2249

Fax: 671-734-7514
Email: yrengiil@uog9.uog.edu

Hawaii

University of Hawaii at Hilo
Upward Bound Program Math/Science
Cornellia L. Anguay
200 West Kawili St.
Hilo, HI 96720-4091
808-974-7372, ext. 7337
Fax: 808-974-7615
Email: anguay@hawaii.edu

Windward Community College
Math and Science
Sandra Matsui
2530 Dole St.
Sakamaki Hall D-200
Honolulu, HI 96822
808-235-7466
Fax: 808-247-5362
Email: s_matsui@wcc.hawaii.edu

Leeward Community College
Upward Bound
David Kong
96-045 Ala Ike
Pearl City, HI 96782
808-455-0249
Fax: 808-455-0471
Email: davidfk@nueworld.com

Upward Bound Math/Science
Michael Moser
96-045 Ala Ike
Pearl City, HI 96782
808-455-0249
Fax: 808-455-0471
Email: tmoser@hawaii.edu

Idaho

Boise State University
Upward Bound
Sue Huizinga
1910 University Dr.
Boise, ID 83725
208-385-3572
Fax: 208-385-4334
Email: shuizin@boisestate.edu

University of Idaho
Upward Bound
Tona TreeTop
College of Education
P.O. Box 443092
Moscow, ID 83844-3092
208-885-2992
Fax: 208-885-9143
Email: ttreetop@uidaho.edu

Idaho State University/Pocatello
Upward Bound
James Vizar
Trio Student Services
P.O. Box 8345
Pocatello, ID 83209-8345
208-236-3242
Fax: 208-236-4864
Email: yizajame@fs.isu.edu

University of Idaho
Math and Science
Isabel Bond
College of Education, Room 107
Moscow, ID 83844
208-885-6205
Fax: 208-885-2825
Email: ibond@uidaho.edu

Illinois

Illinois Eastern Community College
Upward Bound
LeAnn Hartleroad

305 North West St.
Olney, IL 62450
618-395-7777, ext. 2273
Fax: 618-392-3293
Email: hartleroadl@iecc.cc.il.us

Chicago State University
Upward Bound
Carol Carson-Warner
95th Street at King Drive
Library, Room 132
9501 South King Dr.
Chicago, IL 60628-1598
773-995-2566
Fax: 773-995-2591
Email: drcarsonwarnerol@aol.com

University of Chicago
Project Upward Bound
Larry Hawkins
5845 S. Ellis/Gates Blake 113
Chicago, IL 60637
773-702-8288
Fax: 773-702-0189
Email: lhawkins@midway.uchicago.edu

Ada S. McKinley Community Services, Inc.
Upward Bound
Bonnie Spears
10001 S. Woodlawn
Chicago, IL 60628
773-995-5572
Fax: 773-660-4798

Community Services West, Inc.
Upward Bound
Antoinette Kelley
1231 South Pulaski Rd.
Chicago, IL 60623
312-762-2272
Fax: 312-762-2065

Roosevelt University
Upward Bound
Michael Ford
430 South Michigan Ave.
Chicago, IL 60605
312-341-2035
Fax: 312-341-3885
Email: mford@roosevelt.edu

Kankakee Community College
Upward Bound
Richard Braun
River Rd., Box 888
Kankakee, IL 60901-0888
815-933-0281
Fax: 815-933-0217

Northern Illinois University
Upward Bound
Felicia Bohanon
309 Williston Hall East
Dekalb, IL 60115-2854
815-753-1867
Fax: 815-753-6276
Email: fbohanon@niu.edu

Southern Illinois University at Edwardsville
Upward Bound
Charles Hayes
East St. Louis Center
411 East Broadway
East St Louis, IL 62201
618-482-6960
Fax: 618-482-6990
Email: chhayes@siue.ed

Columbia College/Chicago
Upward Bound
Craig Kirsch
600 South Michigan Ave.
Chicago, IL 60605-1996
312-344-7161

Fax: 312-344-7161
Email: ckirsch@popmail.colum.edu

Richard J. Daley College
Upward Bound
Gina Blake
7500 South Pulaski Rd.
Chicago, IL 60652
773-838-7783
Fax: 773-838-7524

Triton College
Upward Bound
Bertha Zagore
2000 North 5th Ave.
River Grove, IL 60171
708-456-0300
Fax: 708-583-3121

Highland Community College
Upward Bound
Jim Bangasser
2998 West Pearl City Rd.
Freeport, IL 61032-9341
815-235-6121
Fax: 815-235-6130
Email: jbangasser@admin.highland.cc.il.us

Lewis and Clark Community College
Upward Bound
5800 Godfrey Rd.
Godfrey, IL 62035-2466
618-466-3411
Fax: 618-466-9271

University of Illinois-Chicago
Upward Bound
John W. Long
1200 W. Harrison St.
M/C 343 Suite 2720
Chicago, IL 60607
312-996-5046
Fax: 312-996-9298
Email: jlong@uic.edu

Northeastern Illinois University
Upward Bound
Deon Brown
770 N. Halsted St.
Chicago, IL 60622
312-733-7330, ext. 450
Fax: 312-733-8188
Email: d-brown2@neiu.edu

Roosevelt University
Veterans Upward Bound
Christopher Chalko
430 South Michigan Ave.
HCC Room 321
Chicago, IL 60605
312-341-6382
Fax: 312-341-6382

Southern Illinois University at Carbondale
Upward Bound
Kevern Donnell Wilson
C310 Woody Hall
Carbondale, IL 62901-4706
618-453-3354
Fax: 618-453-8038

Illinois Central College
Upward Bound
Phyllis Young
One College Dr.
East Peoria, IL 61635
309-694-5300
Fax: 309-694-5450

University of Illinois at Urbana-Champaign
Upward Bound
Sandra Kate-Wright
610 E. John St.
130 Student Services

Champaign, IL 61821
217-333-1889
Fax: 217-244-0349
Email: skatowright@turner.odos.uiuc.edu

Robert Morris College
Upward Bound
J.G. Martinez
401 S. State St.
Chicago, IL 60605
312-935-6869
Fax: 312-935-6861

Southern Illinois University at Edwardsville
Math and Science
Charles Hayes
East St Louis Center
411 East Broadway
East St Louis, IL 62201
618-482-6960
Fax: 618-482-6990
Email: chhayes@siue.ed

Carl Sandburg College
Jill Johnson
2232 South Lake Storey Road
Galesburg, IL 61402
309-341-5320
Fax: 309-341-3291
Email: jjohnson@csc.cc.ul.us

East-West University
Upward Bound Math/Science
Farid Muhammad
816 South Michigan Avenue
Chicago, IL 60605
312-939-0111
Fax: 312-939-0083

Elgin Community College
Upward Bound Math/Science
Bruce Austin
1700 Spartan Drive, Ict 109
Elgin, IL 60123-7193
708-888-7366
Fax: 708-888-7995

Governors State University
Sharon Spence
One University Parkway
University Park, IL 60446
708-534-4045
Fax: 708-235-2127

Rend Lake College
Joe West
468 North Ken Gray Parkway
Ina, IL 62846
618-437-5321
Fax: 618-437-5677
Email: west@rlc.cc.il.us

Rock Valley College
Adam Smith
3301 North Mulford Road
Rockford, IL 61114-5699
815-654-4460
Fax: 815-654-4339

The Family Centered Educational Agency
Jonathan McKenzie
650 East Phoenix Center Drive
Harvey, IL 60426
708-210-1771
Fax: 708-210-1785
Email: jmcken8927@aol.com

Indiana

Indiana University Purdue University
Indianapolis
Upward Bound
Ron Trabue
815 W. Michigan
Indianapolis, IN 46202-5171

317-278-1927
Fax: 317-274-7589

Indiana State University-Terre Haute
Upward Bound Program
Lynn White
200 North Seventh St.
Terre Haute, IN 47809
812-237-3067
Fax: 812-237-8461

Vincennes University
Upward Bound
Dawn Mann
1002 North 1st St.
CSC-YB29
Vincennes, IN 47591-4201
812-888-5373
Fax: 812-888-5958
Email: dmann@indiana.vinu.edu

University of Notre Dame
Upward Bound
Dorine Blake-Smith
University of Notre Dame
120 Brownson
Notre Dame, IN 46556
219-631-5669
Fax: 219-631-3127

Indiana Welseyan University
Upward Bound
Herb Hughes
4201 South Washington St.
Marion, IN 46953-4999
765-677-2935
Fax: 765-677-2938
Email: hhughs@indwes.edu

Oakland City University
Upward Bound
Patricia Swails
143 North Lucretia
Oakland City, IN 47660
812-749-4781
Fax: 812-749-1275
Email: swailsp@evansville.net

Vincennes University
Veterans Upward Bound
Kim Kaiser
1002 North 1st St.
Vincennes, IN 47591-5201
317-927-5373
Fax: 812-888-5958

Indiana University-Bloomington
Marshal Chaifetz
203 Ashton Aley East
Bloomington, IN 47402
812-856-5203
Fax: 812-855-2045
Email: mchaifet@indiana.edu

Purdue University-Calumet
Cheryl L. Berry
2233 171st Street
Hammond, IN 46323-2094
219-989-2392
Fax: 219-989-2036
Email: jarevalo@calumet.purdue.edu

Iowa

Briar Cliff College
Upward Bound
Cheryl Perez
3303 Rebecca St.
Box 2100
Sioux City, IA 51104-2100
712-279-5599
Fax: 712-279-5499

Coe College
Upward Bound

Barbara Gibbs
1220 First Ave., N.E.
Cedar Rapids, IA 51404
319-399-8536
Fax: 319-399-8667
Email: bgibbs@coe.edu

Central College
Upward Bound/Trio Programs
Louise Esveld
812 University
Pella, IA 50219-1999
515-628-5246
Fax: 515-628-5338

Luther College
Upward Bound
Phyllis Gray
700 College Dr.
Decorah, IA 51301
319-387-1136
Fax: 319-387-2213
Email: grayphy1@martin.edu

Iowa Lakes Community College
Upward Bound
Julie Carlson
3200 College Dr.
Estherville, IA 50536
712-852-5302
Fax: 515-652-5344
Email: jcarlson@ilcc.cc.ia.us

Des Moines Area Community College
Upward Bound
Benita Slater
1100 7th St.
Des Moines, IA 50314
515-248-7225
Fax: 515-248-7253

Graceland University
Jeannie McKinney
One University Place
Lamoni, IA 50140
515-784-5297
Fax: 515-784-5449

Iowa State University
Jane Agyeman
N002 Lagomarcino Hall
Ames, IA 50011-3187
515-294-5546
Fax: 515-294-1219
Email: jagyeman@iastate.edu

Simpson College
Lisa Negus
701 North C Street
Indianola, IA 50125
515-961-1961
Fax: 515-961-1674
Email: negus@simpson.edu

Southeastern Community College
Kathy Meyers
1015 South Gear Avenue
Box 180
West Burlington, IA 52655
319-752-2731
Fax: 319-752-4957
Email: kmeyers@sccc.cc.ia.us

St. Ambrose University
Janice Anderson
518 West Locust Street
Davenport, IA 52803
319-333-6486
Fax: 319-333-6486
Email: jandern@saunix.sau.edu

University Of Iowa
Jeanne Meyer
1105 Quadrangle

Iowa City, IA 52242-1123
319-335-6708
Fax: 319-335-9975

University Of Northern Iowa
Upward Bound
Wilfred M. Johnson
214 Student Service Center
Cedar Falls, IA 56014
319-234-6819
Fax: 319-232-5039
Email: wilfred.johnson@uni.edu

Upward Bound Math/Science
Michele Mullings-Shand
214 Student Services Center
Cedar Falls, IA 50614-0388
319-234-6819
Fax: 319-232-5039

Kansas

University of Kansas
Veterans Upward Bound
Ngondi Kamatuks
301 Pearson Hall
Lawrence, KS 66045-2330
785-272-5828
Fax: 785-272-4408
Email: kamatuka@falcon.cc.ukans.edu

Kansas State University/Manhattan
Upward Bound Program
Reginland McGowan
201 Holton Hall
Manhattan, KS 66506
913-532-6497
Fax: 913-532-6457

Dodge City Community College
Upward Bound
V. James Sherer
2501 North 14th Ave.
Dodge City, KS 67801-2399
316-227-9395
Fax: 316-227-9356
Email: jsherer@dccc.cc.ks.us

Emporia State University
Upward Bound
Trudi Benjamin
1200 Commercial
Box 4016, PA 206
Emporia, KS 66801
316-341-5097
Fax: 316-341-5073

Wichita State University
Upward Bound Wichita Prep
Deltha Colvin
1845 Fairmount, Box 94
Wichita, KS 67260-0094
316-978-3314
Fax: 316-978-3650
Email: colvin@twsuvm.uc.twsu.edu

Independence Community College
Upward Bound
Janece English
College Ave. and Brookside Dr.
P.O. Box 708
Independence, KS 67301-0708
316-331-4100
Fax: 316-331-0946

Barton County Community College
Jackie Elliott
245 Northeast 30th Road
Great Bend, KS 67530
316-792-9324
Fax: 316-786-1160

Cowley College
Pamela Doyle
125 South Second Street

P.O. Box 1147
Arkansas City, KS 67005
316-441-5358
Fax: 316-441-5377
Email: doyle@cowley.cc.ks.us

Haskell Indian Nations University
William Reese
155 Indian Avenue
Lawrence, KS 66046
785-749-8405
Fax: 785-832-6618
Email: breese@ross1.dd.haskell.edu

Kansas State University
Upward Bound Math/Science
Lynne Davy
201 Holton Hall
Manhattan, KS 66506
913-532-6374
Fax: 913-532-6457

Neosho County Community College
James O. Hill
800 West 14th Street
Chanute, KS 66720-2639
316-431-2820, ext. 211
Fax: 316-431-4336
Email: jhill@neosho.cc.ks.us

Kentucky

Northern Kentucky University
Upward Bound
Eric Brose
Nunn Dr.
Highland Heights, KY 41099-5975
606-442-3521
Fax: 606-442-3524
Email: brosee@nku.edu

Murray State University
Upward Bound
Myra Yates
P.O. Box 9
Murray, KY 42071-0009
502-762-4492
Fax: 502-762-3251

Kentucky State University
Upward Bound
Deborah Downs
P.O. Box 193
East Main St.
Frankfort, KY 40601
502-227-6536
Fax: 502-227-5914

Eastern Kentucky University
Upward Bound
Milly Burkhart
500 Begley Building
Richmond, KY 40475-3105
606-622-1080
Fax: 606-622-1020

Union College
Upward Bound
William Butler
310 College St.
Barbonville, KY 40906
606-546-4151
Fax: 606-546-2754
Email: wbutler@unionky.edu

Hopkinsville Community College
Upward Bound
Joey Nunn
P.O. Box 2100
734 North Dr.
Hopkinsville, KY 42241-2100
270-886-3921, ext. 6219
Fax: 270-288-2009

University of Louisville
Upward Bound

Mary Thorpe
Strickler Hall, Room 127
Louisville, KY 40292
502-852-6719
Fax: 502-852-8133

Berea College
Upward Bound
Mary McLaughlin
P.O. Box 2295
Berea, KY 40404
606-986-9341
Fax: 606-986-0323
Email: mary_mclaughlin@berea.edu

University of Kentucky
Southeast Community College
Upward Bound Program
Carolyn Sundy
120 Newman Hall
700 College Road
Cumberland, KY 40823
606-589-2145
Fax: 606-589-5423

Madisonville Community College
Upward Bound
William Hailey
2000 College Dr.
Madisonville, KY 42431
502-821-2250
Fax: 502-821-7328

Western Kentucky University
Veterans Upward Bound
Randy Wilson
Western Kentucky University
114 Jones Jaggers Hall
One Big Red Way
Bowling Green, KY 42101-3576
270-745-5008
Fax: 270-745-3487

Lexington Community College
Upward Bound
Tania Crawford
Cooper Dr.
246 Oswald Bldg.
Lexington, KY 40517
606-257-4071
Fax: 606-257-4339
Email: tlcraw1@ukcc.uky.edu

Pikeville College
Upward Bound
Russel McIntosh
CPO Box 26
Pikeville College
Pikeville, KY 41501
606-432-9314
Fax: 606-432-9375

Morehead State University
Upward Bound
Jennifer Cady
UPO 783, 205 Allie Young Hall
Morehead, KY 40351
606-783-2611
Fax: 606-783-5083
Email: j.cady@morehead-st.edu

Hazard Community College
Upward Bound
Venetia Strunk
1 Community College Dr.
Hazard, KY 41701
606-436-5721, ext. 554
Fax: 606-439-1600
Email: venita.strunk@kctcs.edu

Western Kentucky University
Upward Bound
Linda Gaines
College of Ed. and Behavioral Science

Matthew Lesko, Information USA, Inc., 12081 Nebel Street, Rockville, MD 20852 • 1-800-955-7693 • www.lesko.com

121 Jones Jaggers/
1 Big Red Way
Bowling Green, KY 42101
270-745-4873
Fax: 270-745-6850
Email: linda.gaines@wku.edu

Murray State University
Upward Bound Math/Science
Doris Clark-Parham
303 Ordway Hall
Murray, KY 42071
270-762-5429
Fax: 270-762-4351

Louisiana

Southeastern Louisiana University
Upward Bound Math/Science
Kay Gersch
SLU Box 10568
Hammond, LA 70402
504-549-5319
Fax: 504-549-3477
Email: kgersch@selu.edu

McNeese State University
Upward Bound
Stella Miller
P.O. Box 92687
Lake Charles, LA 70609-2687
337-475-5445
Fax: 337-475-5449

Nicholls State University
Upward Bound
Beatrice Wallace
University Station
P.O. Box 2088
Thibodaux, LA 70310
504-448-4083
Fax: 504-448-4373

Delgado Community College
Veterans Upward Bound
Building 2, 615 City Park Ave.
New Orleans, LA 70119-4399
504-483-4114
Fax: 504-483-4386

University of New Orleans
Upward Bound
Brenda Brown
Business Building, Room 159
Lakefront Campus
New Orleans, LA 70148-1510
504-280-6979
Fax: 504-286-5564
Email: bmbjd@uno.edu

Southeastern Louisiana University
Veterans Upward Bound
Kim Barker
SLU-10571
Hammond, LA 70402-0548
504-549-2955
Fax: 504-549-3389
Email: kbarker@selu.edu

Louisiana State University at Eunice
Upward Bound Program
Marvette Thomas
P.O. Box 1129 LSUE
2048 Johnson Highway
Eunice, LA 70535-1129
337-550-1206
Fax: 337-550-1268
Email: mthomas@llsue.edu

Grambling State University
Upward Bound
Shirley Jackson
P.O. Drawer 8
Grambling, LA 71245-0000

318-274-2661
Fax: 318-274-3800

University of Louisiana-Lafayette
Veterans Upward Bound
Robert Carmouche
P.O. Box 43452
106 Declouet Hall
Lafayette, LA 70504-3452
337-482-6831
Fax: 337-482-6833
Email: rlc1713@usl.edu

Southern University at New Orleans
Suno Upward Bound Program
Andrell Washington-Edwards
6400 Press Dr.
New Orleans, LA 70126
504-286-5280
Fax: 504-286-5448

Loyola University Administration Office
Upward Bound
Mattie Stone-Williams
6363 St. Charles Ave.
P.O. Box 154
New Orleans, LA 70118
504-865-3223
Fax: 504-865-3280

University of Louisiana-Lafayette
Upward Bound Program
Robert Carmouche
P.O. Box 43452
106 Declouet Hall
Lafayette, LA 70504-3452
337-482-6831
Fax: 337-482-6833
Email: rlc1713@usl.edu

Southeastern Louisiana University
Upward Bound - Livingston/St. Helena
Kimberly Caruso
SLU Box 10568
Hammond, LA 70402
504-549-3864
Fax: 504-549-3477

Xavier University of Louisiana
Upward Bound
Marie DeLarge
7325 Palmetto St.
P.O. Box 41B
New Orleans, LA 70125
504-483-7664
Fax: 504-485-7946
Email: mdelarge@zula.edu

Southeastern Louisiana University-
Tangipahoa
Sandra Williams
SLU Box 10568
Hammond, LA 70402
504-549-3395
Fax: 504-549-3477
Email: slwilliams@selu.edu

Dillard University
Dione Sibley
2601 Gentilly Boulevard
New Orleans, LA 70122
504-286-4662
Fax: 504-286-4883

Southern University
A&M-Baton Rouge
Upward Bound
Lois St.Amant
12596 Southern Branch Office
Baton Rouge, LA 70813
225-771-3880
Fax: 225-771-4612

Upward Bound Math/Science
Charles Bryant
P.O. Box 9426
Baton Rouge, LA 70813-9426
225-771-3880
Fax: 225-771-4612

Tulane University
Tanis Dasher
210 Gibson
6823 St Charles Avenue
New Orleans, LA 70118
504-862-3322
Fax: 504-862-8705

Maine

University of Maine
Linda Ives
Upward Bound/Room 226
5713 Chadbourne Hall
Orono, ME 04469-5713
207-581-2523
Fax: 207-581-2532
Email: Linda.Ives@umit.maine.edu

University of Maine/Presque Isle
Upward Bound Program
Kristi Pierce
181 Main St., Box 517
Presque Isle, ME 04769
207-768-9456
Fax: 207-768-9464
Email: pierce@polaris.umpi.maine.edu

University of Maine at Farmington
Upward Bound
Lynn Ploof-Davis
224 Maine St.
Farmington, ME 04935
207-778-7297
Fax: 207-778-7298

Bowdoin College
Upward Bound
Bridget Mullen
3400 College Station
Brunswick, ME 04011
207-725-3559
Fax: 207-725-3078
Email: bmullen@bowdoin.edu

University of Southern Maine
Upward Bound
David Agan
111 Woodward Hall
37 College Ave.
Gorham, ME 04038
207-780-4141
Fax: 207-228-8259
Email: agan@usm.maine.edu

Maryland

Morgan State University
Upward Bound Program
Michael Bryant
1700 E. Coldspring Lane
Baltimore, MD 21251
410-885-3448
Fax: 410-319-3936
Email: michaelabryant@hotmail.com

Gilman School
Upward Bound
William A. Greene
5407 Roland Ave.
Baltimore, MD 21210-1991
410-323-3800
Fax: 410-323-3449

Community College of Baltimore County
Upward Bound
Diane Drake
800 South Rolling Rd.
Catonsville, MD 21228

410-455-4198
Fax: 410-719-6506

Baltimore City Community College
Upward Bound
Gregory Hunter
2901 Liberty Heights Ave., Room 239
Baltimore, MD 21215-7893
410-462-8560
Fax: 410-462-7677

University of Maryland Eastern Shore
Upward Bound
Fedder Williams
Princess Anne, MD 21853
410-651-6458
Fax: 410-651-6363

University of Maryland-College Park
Upward Bound and UB Math/Science
Georgette Hardy Dejesus
West Education Annex
Building #66, Room 1107
College Park, MD 20742-8515
301-405-6776
Fax: 301-314-9155
Email: gh39@umail.umd.edu

Frostburg State University
Upward Bound
Timothy Malloy
102 Pullen Hall
Frostburg, MD 21532-1099
301-687-4994
Fax: 301-687-4207
Email: tmalloy@frostburg.edu

University of Maryland Baltimore County
Upward Bound
Lynda Robertson
1000 Hilltop Circle
Math/Psychology Building, Room 007
Baltimore, MD 21228
410-455-2700
Fax: 410-455-1062

Coppin State College
Meredith Davis
2500 West North Avenue
Baltimore, MD 21216
410-383-5800
Fax: 410-383-2246
Email: mdavis@wye.coppin.edu

Frostburg State University
Upward Bound Math/Science
Johnston Hegeman
20 Braddock Street
Frostburg, MD 21532
301-687-4994
Fax: 301-687-4207

University Of Maryland-Baltimore County
Upward Bound Math/Science
Donald G. Hoes
Office of the President
1000 Hilltop Circle
Baltimore, MD 21250
410-455-3124
Fax: 410-455-1183

Massachusetts
University of Massachusetts Boston
Veterans Upward Bound
Charles Diggs
Chancellor's Office
Quinn Admin. Bldg.
Boston, MA 02125-3393
617-287-5870
Fax: 617-265-7173

University of Massachusetts Boston
Upward Bound
Shelley Joyner
Chancellor's Office

Quinn Admin. Bldg.
Boston, MA 02125-3393
617-287-5845
Fax: 617-287-5844

Northfield Mount Hermon School
Upward Bound
Gisele Litalien
28 Mount Hermon Rd.
Northfield, MA 01360
413-498-3416
Fax: 413-498-3415

North Shore Community College
Upward Bound Program
Christopher Anderson
1 Ferncroft Rd.
Box 3340
Danvers, MA 01923-3340
781-593-2161
Fax: 781-477-2110
Email: canderson@nscc.edu

Holyoke Community College
Upward Bound
Sonia Pope
303 Homestead Ave.
Holyoke, MA 01040-1048
413-552-2157
Fax: 413-534-8975

Bristol Community College
Upward Bound Program
Sarah Morrell
64 Durfee St.
Fall River, MA 02720
508-678-2811
Fax: 508-674-4483
Email: smorrell@bristol.mass.edu

Massachusetts Institute of Technology
Upward Bound Program
Evette Layne
77 Massachusetts Ave.
Room N52-130
Cambridge, MA 02139-4307
617-253-5124
Fax: 617-258-5616
Email: emlayne@mit.edu

Fitchburg State College
Upward Bound
Carol mcFarland
Academic Affairs
160 Pearl St.
Fitchburg, MA 01420-2697
978-665-3368
Fax: 978-653-3693

Choice Thru Education Inc.
Upward Bound
Susan Clark
140 Pearl St.
P.O. Box 505599
Chelsea, MA 02150-5599
617-884-4706
Fax: 617-884-1601

Salem State College, Learning Center
Upward Bound
Wendy Porter
352 Lafayette St.
Salem, MA 01970
978-542-6215
Fax: 978-542-6214

University of Massachusetts Dartmouth
Upward Bound Program
Bruce Rose
285 Old Westport Rd.
North Dartmouth, MA 02747
508-999-8712
Fax: 508-999-9257
Email: brose@umassd.edu

Boston University
Michael Dennehy
Collaborative Office
605 Commonwealth Avenue
Boston, MA 02215
617-353-3551
Fax: 617-353-3924
Email: mdennehy@bu.edu

Middlesex Community College
Mary Anne Miller
35 Kearney Square
Lowell, MA 01853
978-656-3385
Fax: 978-656-3389
Email: millerm@middlesex.cc.ma.us

Roxbury Community College
Mark A. Barfield
1234 Columbus Avenue
527 Academic Building
Boston, MA 02123
617-427-0060
Fax: 617-541-5312
Email: mabtrenton@hotmail.com

Simmons College
Upward Bound Math/Science
Lisa Smith
300 The Fenway
Boston, MA 02115
617-521-2620
Fax: 617-521-2622

University Of Massachusetts-Boston
Upward Bound Math/Science
Marcella Maldinado
Harbor Campus
Boston, MA 02125-3393
617-287-5840
Fax: 617-287-5844

Youth Opportunities Upheld, Inc.
Bill Raynor
81 Plantation Street
Worcester, MA 01604
Phone: 508-849-5600, ext. 232
Fax: 508-849-5617

Michigan
Lake Michigan College
Upward Bound
Selene Anderson-Thompson
2755 E. Napier Ave.
Benton Harbor, MI 49022-1899
616-927-7061
Fax: 616-927-8188
Email: anderson@raptor.imc.cc.mi.us

Mott Community College
Upward Bound
Delores Deen
1401 E. Court St.
Flint, MI 48503-2089
810-762-0450
Fax: 810-232-9520

Wayne-Westland Community School District
Upward Bound
Ann Green
3001 Fourth St.
Wayne, MI 48184
313-595-2012
Fax: 313-595-2207

Oakland University
Upward Bound Project
Geraldine Thomas
264 S. Foundation Hall
Rochester, MI 48309-4401
810-370-3218
Fax: 810-370-3218
Email: geri@oakland.edu

Grand Valley State University
Upward Bound
Arnie Smith-Alexander
One Campus Drive
230 STU
Allendale, MI 49401-9403
616-895-3441
Fax: 616-895-3440
Email: smithala@gvsu.edu

WMU
Upward Bound
Maleeka Love
A 314 Ellsworth
Kalamazoo, MI 49008
616-387-3324
Fax: 616-387-3390

Alpena Community College
Upward Bound
Donna Gilmet
666 Johnson St.
Alpena, MI 49707
517-356-9021
Fax: 517-356-3058

Wayne State University
Upward Bound
William Tandy
5425 Woodward Ave., Suite 200
Detroit, MI 48202
313-577-1943
Fax: 313-577-1944
Email: wtandy@wayne.edu

Northwestern Michigan College
Upward Bound
Barbara Zupin
1701 E. Front St.
Traverse City, MI 49684
231-922-1363
Fax: 231-922-8523
Email: bzupin@mcssagc.nmc.cdu

Siena Heights College Upward Bound
Upward Bound
Anita Galnares
1247 E. Siena Heights
Adrian, MI 49221
517-263-0731
Fax: 517-264-7704

Lake Superior State University
Upward Bound
Heidi Witacki
650 W. Easterday Ave.
Sault Ste Marie, MI 49783-1699
906-635-2590
Fax: 906-635-6668
Email: hwitucki@gw.lssu.edu

Hope College
Upward Bound
Elizabeth Colburn
P.O. Box 9000
Graves Hall
263 College Ave.
Holland, MI 49422-9000
616-395-7745
Fax: 616-395-7922
Email: colburn@hope.edu

Wayne State University
Veterans Upward Bound
Paul Rease
3127 E. Canfield
Detroit, MI 48207
313-571-9500
Fax: 313-571-9727
Email: prease@.cc.wayne.edu

Northern Michigan University
Upward Bound
Sharon Jensen
1401 Presque Isle Ave.

Marquette, MI 49855-5398
906-227-2252
Fax: 906-227-2259

Cranbrook
Upward Bound
520 Lone Pine Rd.
Box 801
Bloomfield Hills, MI 48303-0801
810-645-3676
Fax: 810-645-3081

Grand Rapids Community College
Upward Bound
Michael Hopson
143 Bostwick, N.E.
Grand Rapids, MI 49503
616-234-4150
Fax: 616-234-3628

Eastern Michigan University
Upward Bound
Amy Prevo-Johnson
84 Goddard Hall
Ypsilanti, MI 48197
734-487-0488
Fax: 734-487-5088

Kellogg Community College
Upward Bound
Diane Storey
450 North Ave.
Battle Creek, MI 49017-3397
616-965-9550
Fax: 616-965-9558
Email: lmarshal@remc12.k12.mi.us

Cranbrook Educational Community
Math Science
William Washington
520 Lone Pine Rd.
P.O. Box 801
Bloomfield Hills, MI 48303-0801
810-645-3676
Fax: 810-645-3081

Northern Michigan University
Upward Bound Center for Science and Math
Stacy Schwenke
1401 Presque Isle
Marquette, MI 49855-5394
906-227-2115
Fax: 906-227-2013

Grand Valley State University
Math and Science
Arnie Smith-Alexander
1 Campus Dr.
230 Student Services Bldg.
Allendale, MI 49401
616-895-3441
Fax: 616-895-3440
Email: smithala@gvsu.edu

Central Michigan University
Montisa Counts
319 Warriner Hall
Mount Pleasant, MI 48859
313-873-3019
Fax: 517-774-1832
Email: count1ma@cmich.edu

Finlandia University
Cindy Karvonen
601 Quincy Street
Hancock, MI 49930
906-487-7259
Fax: 906-487-8509

Michigan State University
Glenda Hammond
192 East Bessey Hall
East Lansing, MI 48824-1033
517-353-6701
Fax: 517-432-1030

Southwestern Michigan College
Lauren Longwell
58900 Cherry Grove Road
Dowagiac, MI 49047
616-782-5113
Fax: 616-782-8414

Western Michigan University
Upward Bound Math/Science
Lynn Riptoe
A-314 Ellsworth Hall
Kalamazoo, MI 49008
616-387-1000
Fax: 616-387-3390

Minnesota

Rochester Community and Technical College
Upward Bound Program
Molly Rohe
851 30th Ave. S.E.
Box #19
Rochester, MN 55904-4999
507-280-2931
Fax: 507-285-7496
Email: molly.rohe@roch.edu

University of Minnesota
Upward Bound
Aloida Zaragoza
2 Appleby Hall
128 Pleasant St., S.E.
Minneapolis, MN 55455
612-625-0772
Fax: 612-625-0704
Email: zaragoo3@maroon.tc.umn.edu

Normandale Community College
Upward Bound
Cary Waterman
9700 France Ave., S.
Bloomington, MN 55431-4399
612-832-6728
Fax: 612-832-6571
Email: c.waterman@nr.cc.mn.us

Bemidji State University
Upward Bound
Barry yocum
1500 Birchmont Dr., N.E.
Bemidji, MN 56601-2699
218-755-2092
Fax: 218-755-4208
Email: byocom@vax1.bemidji.msu.edu

University of Minnesota Duluths
Upward Bound
John Beaulieu
112 Cina Hall
10 University Dr., UMD
Duluth, MN 55812-2496
218-725-7064
Fax: 218-726-6105
Email: jbeaulie@d.umn.edu

Minnesota State University-Mankato
Upward Bound
Charles Cantale
P.O. Box 114 EXCEL
Mankato, MN 56002-8400
507-389-1111
Fax: 507-389-6372
Email: chuck_cantale@msl.mankato.msus.edu

Minneapolis Community & Technical College
Veterans Upward Bound
Jim Kilps
1501 Hennepin Ave.
Minneapolis, MN 55403
612-341-7076
Fax: 612-341-2797

Northern Minnesota-Itasca Campus
Upward Bound
1855 East Highway 169

Grand Rapids, MN 55744
218-327-4460
Fax: 218-327-4297
Email: dfreeman@it.cc.mn.us

St. Olaf College
Upward Bound Program
Heather Campbell
1520 St. Olaf Ave.
Northfield, MN 55057-1098
507-646-3708
Fax: 507-646-3552
Email: campbelh@stolaf.edu

College of St. Scholastica
Upward Bound
Jill Emery
1200 Kenwood Ave.
Duluth, MN 55811-4199
218-723-6463
Fax: 218-723-6482
Email: jemery@css.edu

Minneapolis Community & Technical College
High School Upward Bound
Shirley Sanders
1501 Hennepin Ave.
Minneapolis, MN 55403
612-341-7023
Fax: 612-373-2797

Century Community and Technical College
Upward Bound
Suzanne Nordsving
3401 Century Ave. N
White Bear Lake, MN 55110-5697
651-779-3287
Fax: 651-779-5807
Email: s.nordsving@cctc.cc.mn.us

The College of St. Scholastica
Math and Science
Christine Penney
1200 Kenwood Ave.
Duluth, MN 55811
218-723-6467
Fax: 218-723-6472
Email: asigford@stfl.css.edu

Century Community and Technical College
Math and Science
Michael Smith
3401 Century Ave. N
White Bear Lake, MN 55110-5697
651-779-3445
Fax: 651-779-3949
Email: m.smith@cctc.cc.mn.us

Anoka Ramsey Community College
Cindy Nutter
TRIO Programs
Minneapolis, MN 55433
612-422-3454
Fax: 612-422-3341

College Of St. Benedict
Dora Schumacher
37 College Avenue South
Saint Joseph, MN 56374
320-363-5268
Fax: 320-363-5269

Lake Superior College
R. Jeannette Turchi
2101 Trinity Road
Duluth, MN 55811
218-733-5931
Fax: 218-733-5945
Email: j.turchi@lsc.cc.mn.us

Mississippi
Coahoma Community College
Upward Bound
Charles Barnes
3240 Friars Point Rd.

Clarksdale, MS 38614
662-627-5446, ext. 130
Fax: 662-621-9451

Hinds Community College - Utica
Upward Bound Program
Daisy Lacour
P.O. Box 1063
Utica, MS 39175
601-885-6062
Fax: 601-885-6026

Mississippi Band of Choctaw Indians
Upward Bound
Hilda Nickey
Route 7
P.O. Box 6008
Choctaw Branch
Philadelphia, MS 39350
601-656-2712
Fax: 601-656-4099

Alcorn State University
Upward Bound
Donnell Bell
1000 ASU Dr. #240
Lorman, MS 39096
601-877-6224
Fax: 601-877-6229

Rust College
Upward Bound
John Peaches
150 Rust Ave.
Holly Springs, MS 38635
662-252-4661
Fax: 662-252-6107

Mississippi Valley State University
Upward Bound
Christine Williams
P.O. Box 1053
14000 Highway 82 W.
Itta Bena, MS 38941-1400
662-254-3472
Fax: 662-254-7552

Jackson State University
Upward Bound
Alvin Clark
P.O. Box 17899
Jackson, MS 39217
601-968-2465
Fax: 601-968-2419

Copiah-Lincoln Community College
Upward Bound
Brenda Brown
P.O. Box 649
Wesson, MS 39191-0649
601-643-8704
Fax: 601-643-8277
Email: brenda.brown@colin.cc.ms.us

Mary Holmes College
Upward Bound
Dorothy Edwards
P.O. Drawer 1257
West Point, MS 39773
601-494-6820
Fax: 601-494-6625

Tougaloo College
Upward Bound and U.B. Math/Science
Valvia Wilson
P.O. Box 216
Tougaloo, MS 39174
601-977-7844
Fax: 601-977-7930
Email: valvia.wilson@tougaloo.edu

Missouri
Truman State University
Upward Bound
Lana Brown
220 Kirk Building

Kirksville, MO 63501-4221
660-785-4244
Fax: 660-785-4245

Mineral Area College
Upward Bound
Jerry Sullivan
Highway 67 and 32
P.O. Box 1000
Park Hills, MO 63601-1000
573-518-3766
Fax: 573-518-2144
Email: jsulliva@mail.mac.cc.mo.us

Saint Louis University
Upward Bound
Charles Dyson
221 N. Grand Blvd.
St. Louis, MO 63103
314-977-2938
Fax: 314-977-3315

University of Missouri Kansas City
Upward Bound
Linda Carter
5100 Rockhill Rd.
101F SASS Building
Kansas City, MO 64110-2499
816-235-1115
Fax: 816-235-5156
Email: ljcarter@cctr.umkc.edu

Avila College
Upward Bound
Brian Moore
1901 Wornall Rd.
Kansas City, MO 64145-1698
816-942-8400
Fax: 816-942-3362
Email: mooreb@mail.avila.edu

Northwest Missouri State University
Upward Bound
Basil Lister, Jr.
Admin. Bldg. #352
800 University Dr.
Maryville, MO 64468
660-562-1630
Fax: 660-562-1900

Harris-Stowe State College
Upward Bound
Carolyn Sweets
3026 Laclede Ave.
St. Louis, MO 63103
314-340-3568
Fax: 314-340-3322

Southeast Missouri State University
Upward Bound
Debra Mitchell-Braxton
One University Plaza
Cape Girardeau, MO 63701-4799
573-651-5186
Fax: 573-986-6042

St. Louis University
Math and Science
Don Black
221 North Grand Blvd.
St. Louis, MO 63103
314-977-2930
Fax: 314-977-3315

Northwest Missouri State University
Math and Science
James Clark
Admin. Bldg. 357
800 University Dr.
Maryville, MO 64468-6001
660-562-1630
Fax: 660-562-1900
Email: jclark@acad.nwmissouri.edu

Crowder College
Upward Bound and Math and Science
Pam Hudson
601 Laclede Ave.
Neosho, MO 64850-9165
417-451-3226
Fax: 417-451-2132
Email: phudson@mail.crowder.cc.mo.us

Missouri Southern State College
Susan Craig
3950 East Newman Road
Joplin, MO 64801
417-625-9830
Fax: 417-625-9831
Email: craig-s@mssc.edu

North Central Missouri College
Kendra Wolgast
1301 Main Street
Trenton, MO 64683
660-359-3948
Fax: 660-359-3202

St. Louis Community College
Carolyn Jackson
5600 Oakland Avenue, G-311
St. Louis, MO 63110
314-951-9481
Fax: 314-644-9951
Email: cjackson@fpmail.stlcc.cc.mo.us

Montana
Salish Kootenai College
Upward Bound
Heather Light
P.O. Box 117
Pablo, MT 59855
406-675-4800
Fax: 406-675-4801

University of Montana
Upward Bound
Jon Stannard
002 Brantly Hall
Missoula, MT 59812
406-243-2219
Fax: 406-243-5296

Flathead Valley Community College
Upward Bound
Lynn Vollmer
777 Grandview Dr.
Kalispell, MT 59901
406-756-3880
Fax: 406-756-3854

Hope Speakthunder
Fort Belknap Education Dept.
RR 1, Box 66
Harlem, MT 59526
406-353-2205
Fax: 406-353-4571

Montana Tech of the University of Montana
Upward Bound
Amy Verlanic
1300 West Park St.
Butte, MT 59701-8997
406-496-4690
Fax: 406-496-4696

Montana State University Billings
Upward Bound
Daniel Benge
Cisel Hall
Billings, MT 59101-0298
406-657-2180
Fax: 406-657-2388

Montana State University-Northern
Veterans Upward Bound
Luke Petriceione
1500 N. 30th St.

Billings, MT 59101-9849
406-657-2075
Fax: 406-657-4077
Email: lukevets@hotmail.com

Western Montana College Of Um
Upward Bound Math/Science
Brian Pilcher
Campus Box 114
710 South Atlantic
Dillon, MT 59725
406-683-7537
Fax: 406-683-7809
Email: b_pilcher@wmc.edu

Nebraska
Creighton University
Upward Bound
Jennifer Lynch
Markoe Hall
2500 California Plaza
Omaha, NE 68178-0024
402-280-2958
Fax: 402-280-5579
Email: jlynch@creighton.edu

Western Nebraska Community College
Upward Bound and Veterans Upward Bound
Cecilia Merrigan
1601 E. 27th St.
Scottsbluff, NE 69361
308-635-6123
Fax: 308-635-6055
Email: merrigan@wncc.net

Creighton University
Math and Science
Jocelyn Perkins
Markoe Hall
2500 California Plaza
Omaha, NE 68178
402-280-2938
Fax: 402-280-5579

Applied Information Management Institute
Upward Bound Math/Science
Kandace Bragg
118 South 19th Street
Omaha, NE 68102-1313
402-345-5025
Fax: 402-345-5028

Metropolitan Community College
John Jeanette
P.O. Box 3777
Omaha, NE 68103-0777
402-457-2468
Fax: 402-457-2559

University Of Nebraska-Lincoln
Upward Bound Math/Science
Jimmi Smith
220 Canfield Administration Building
Lincoln, NE 68588
402-472-2027
Fax: 402-472-9338
Email: jsmith3@unl.edu

Upward Bound
Joan Mendoza-Gorham
201 Administration Building
Lincoln, NE 68588-0419
402-472-8883
Fax: 402-472-9338

Nevada
University of Nevada, Reno
Upward Bound
Leonard Woods
203 Edmund J. Cain Hall
Mail Stop 062
Reno, NV 89557-0077
702-784-4978

Fax: 702-784-6254
Email: woodsl@scs.unr.edu

Truckee Meadows Community College
Veterans Upward Bound
Robert Hernandez
7000 Dandini Blvd.
Reno, NV 89512
775-829-9007
Fax: 775-829-9048

University Of Nevada-Las Vegas
Upward Bound Math/Science
William W. Sullivan
4505 Maryland Parkway
Box 452006
Las Vegas, NV 89154
702-895-4777
Fax: 702-895-4786
Email: docbill@ccmail.nevada.edu

New Hampshire
Keene State College
Upward Bound
Alan Glotzer
229 Main St.
Box 1801
Keene, NH 03435-1801
603-358-2356
Fax: 603-358-2257
Email: aglotzer@keene.edu

University of New Hampshire
Upward Bound Program
Daniel Gordon
Robinson House
Rosemary Lane
Durham, NH 03824
603-862-1563
Fax: 603-862-3270
Email: dpg@hopper.unh.edu

New Jersey
New Jersey Institute of Technology
Upward Bound
Henry McCloud
University Hall
323 MLK Jr. Blvd.
Newark, NJ 07102
973-596-5841
Fax: 973-642-4857
Email: mccloud@admin.njit.edu

Seton Hall University
Upward Bound
Erwin Ponder
400 S. Orange Ave.
South Orange, NJ 07079-2681
973-761-9419
Fax: 973-275-2197

Bloomfield College
Upward Bound
467 Franklin St.
Bloomfield, NJ 07003
201-748-7615
Fax: 201-743-3998

Mercer County Community College
Upward Bound
Donald Davis
P.O. Box B
N. Broad and Academy Sts.
Trenton, NJ 08690
609-586-4800
Fax: 609-394-8167

Stevens Institute of Technology
Upward Bound
Anthony C. Culpepper, Jr.
Castle Point on the Hudson
Wesley J. Howe Center, 5th Floor
Hoboken, NJ 07030

201-216-5387
Fax: 201-216-8341

Camden County College
Upward Bound
Gilbert Shaw
P.O. Box 200
College Dr.
Blackwood, NJ 08012
856-227-7200
Fax: 856-374-4923
Email: gshaw@camdencc.edu

Essex County College
Upward Bound
Betty Foster
303 University Ave., Room 3310
Newark, NJ 07102-1798
201-973-3196
Fax: 201-973-3044
Email: foster@essex.edu

Essex County College
Veterans Upward Bound
Betty Foster
303 University Ave., Room 3310
Newark, NJ 07102-1798
201-973-3196
Fax: 201-973-3044
Email: foster@essex.edu

Rutgers the State University
Upward Bound
Janice Robinson
58 Bevier Rd.
Piscataway, NJ 08854
973-353-5416
Fax: 973-353-3519

Ramapo College of New Jersey
Math and Science
Carol Frishberg
505 Ramapo Valley Rd.
Mahwah, NJ 07430-1680
201-529-7031
Fax: 201-529-7508
Email: cfrishbe@ramapo.edu

New Jersey Institute of Technology
Math and Science
Henry McCloud
University Hall
323 ML King Jr., Blvd.
Newark, NJ 07102
201-596-5841
Fax: 201-642-4857
Email: mccloud@admin.njit.edu

Montclair State University
Donna Lorenzo
Normal Avenue & Valley Road
Upper Montclair, NJ 07043
973-655-4128
Fax: 973-655-5150
Email: lorenzod@mail.montclair.edu

New Jersey City University
Louise Diaz
2039 Kennedy Blvd.
Jersey City, NJ 07305
201-200-2347
Fax: 201-200-2348
Email: ldiaz@njcu.edu

New Mexico

New Mexico State University
Upward Bound
Laura Nystal
P.O. Box 30001
Dept. 5278
Las Cruces, NM 88003-0001
505-646-5732
Fax: 505-646-8082
Email: lnystul@nmsu.edu

New Mexico Eastern Univ/Portales
Upward Bound
Doris Ananya
Station #34, ENMU
SAS Building
Portales, NM 88130
505-562-2452
Fax: 505-562-2220
Email: anaya@enmu.edu

New Mexico Highlands University
Upward Bound
Alfredo Gallegos
National Ave.
P.O. Box 9000
Las Vegas, NM 87701
505-454-3468
Fax: 505-454-3179

University of New Mexico
Upward Bound
Juan Candelaria
2021 Mesa Vista Hall
Albuquerque, NM 87131-2101
505-277-3506
Fax: 505-277-8650

Southwestern Indian Polytechnic Institute
Upward Bound
Cathy Abeita
9169 Coors Rd., NW
P.O. Box 10146
Albuquerque, NM 87184
505-897-5387
Fax: 505-346-7713

Eastern New Mexico University-Roswell
Andrew Gamboa
P.O. Box 6000
Roswell, NM 88202-6000
505-624-1786
Fax: 505-624-7216

New Mexico Junior College
Emily Navarrete
5317 North Lovington Highway
Hobbs, NM 88240-9121
505-392-6515
Fax: 505-392-3668
Email: enavarrete@nmjc.cc.nm.us

New York

Houghton College
Upward Bound
Rebecca Ashe
Houghton, NY 14744
716-567-9200
Fax: 716-567-9572

Le Moyne College
Upward Bound
Johnnie Hill-Marsh
1419 Salt Springs Road
Romero Hall
Syracuse, NY 13214-1399
315-445-4532
Fax: 315-445-4534
Email: hillmajm@maple.lemoyne.edu

Research Foundation of Suny College at
Brockport
Upward Bound
Isabella Mark
13 S. Main St.
Holley, NY 14470
716-638-5274
Fax: 716-638-5275
Email: imark@frontiernet.net

Suny Research Foundation/Plattsburgh
Upward Bound Suny Plattsburgh
101 Broad St.
Plattsburgh, NY 12901

518-564-2030
Fax: 518-564-2157
Email: leavite@spla.cc.plattsburgh.edu

New York University
Upward Bound
Patricia Ryan
32 Washington Pl., 7 Floor
New York, NY 10003
212-998-5115
Fax: 212-995-4199

Boys Harbor Inc.
Upward Bound
Crystal Floyd
One E. 104 St.
New York, NY 10029
212-427-2244
Fax: 212-427-6667

Fordham University
Upward Bound
Elliot Palais
Faculty Memorial Hall 201
Bronx, NY 10458
718-817-5985
Fax: 718-817-2313
Email: palais@fordham.edu

St. Lawrence University
Upward Bound Program
Bruce Kelly
Hepburn Hall, RM 16
Canton, NY 13617
315-229-5749
Fax: 315-229-5819

Suny/Queens College
Upward Bound
Paula Anderson
65-30 Kissena Blvd.
Flushing, NY 11367-1597
718-520-7606
Fax: 718-997-5895

Bronx Community College
Upward Bound
Michelle Danvers
6AH, 517 Faust
W. 181st. St., University Ave.
Bronx, NY 10453
718-220-6026
Fax: 718-220-6028

Columbia University
Upward Bound
Olger C. Twyner III
306 Alfred Lerner Hall
2920 Broadway
Mail Code 2604
New York, NY 10027
212-854-3897
Fax: 212-854-7457
Email: ddc.columbia.kmns

Suny/Search Foundation
Upward Bound
UB Commons
520 Lee Entrance, Suite 211
Amherst, NY 14228-2567
716-829-3474
Fax: 716-829-3655

Laguardia Community College
Upward Bound
Robert Levine
31-10 Thomson Ave.
Room M 418-B
L.I.C., NY 11101
718-482-5413
Fax: 718-482-5443

Hofstra University
Upward Bound Math/Science

James Johnson
217 Mason Hall
Hempstead, NY 11549
516-463-5840
Fax: 516-463-6503

Cuny Research Foundation/
John Jay College
Upward Bound
Karen Texeira
555 W. 57th St.
New York, NY 10019-1029
212-237-8280
Fax: 212-237-8906

Marist College
Upward Bound
Joseph Parker
290 North Rd.
Poughkeepsie, NY 12601-1387
914-575-3000
Fax: 914-471-6213

Suny/Binghampton University
Upward Bound
Daniel McCormack
P.O. Box 6000
Binghampton, NY 13902-6000
607-777-2024
Fax: 607-777-2671
Email: dmccorma@bingsuns.cc.
binghamton.edu

Pace University
Upward Bound
Margaret Boyle
101 Murray St.
New York, NY 10007
212-346-1107
Fax: 212-346-1078

Suny Research Foundation/College at Buffalo
Upward Bound
Melody Carter-Neal
1300 Elmwood Ave., CCL E-103
Buffalo, NY 14222
716-878-3446, ext. 13
Fax: 716-878-4015

Adirondack Community College
Jamin Totino
640 Bay Road
Queensbury, NY 12804
518-743-2300, ext. 410
Fax: 518-743-2317
Email: totinoj@acc.sunyacc.edu

Boys Harbor, Inc.
Upward Bound Math/Science
Robert J. North
One East 104th Street
New York, NY 10029
212-427-2244
Fax: 212-427-2334

CUNY-Borough Of Manhattan Community College
Romilio Castillo
199 Chambers Street
New York, NY 10007
212-346-8011
Fax: 212-346-8086

CUNY-City College Of New York
Heather Gresham
Convent Ave. at 138th Street
New York, NY 10031
212-650-6219
Fax: 212-650-5197
Email: hgresham39@hotmail.com

CUNY-New York City Technical College
Upward Bound Math/Science
Carolyn Musser

300 Jay Street
Brooklyn, NY 11201
718-260-5173
Fax: 718-260-5446

Genesee Community College
Ruth Andes
One College Rd
Batavia, NY 14020
716-345-6811
Fax: 716-343-4541

Mercy College
Patricia Giorgi
555 Broadway
Dobbs Ferry, NY 10522
914-674-7510
Fax: 914-674-7221

Monroe Community College
Carmelita Brown-Wallace
1000 East Henrietta Road
Rochester, NY 14623
716-262-1610
Fax: 716-262-1615

SUNY–Buffalo
Upward Bound
Upward Bound Math/Science
Dwane Hodges
2 Diefendorf Annex
Buffalo, NY 14214
716-829-3474
Fax: 716-829-3655
Email: dthodges@acsu.buffalo.edu

Buffalo State College
Upward Bound Math/Science
Michele Parente
1300 Elmwood Avenue
ESSE - Science Building 130
Buffalo, NY 14222
716-878-4732
Fax: 716-878-4039
Email: parentwm@buffalostate.edu

SUNY–Purchase
Peter Corfield
735 Anderson Hill Road
Purchase, NY 10577
914-251-6675
Fax: 914-251-6635
Email: pwrc@purvid.purchse.edu

North Carolina
Winston-Salem State University
Upward Bound
Addie Hymes
P.O. Box 13093
601 Martin Luther King Dr.
Winston-Salem, NC 27110
910-750-2670
Fax: 910-750-2663

St. Augustine College
Upward Bound Program
Donald Armstrong
721 Penn Avenue
P.O. Box 2042
Raleigh, NC 27611
252-446-1921
Fax: 252-446-1435

Chowan College
Chowan College Upward Bound
Frank Stevenson
200 Jones Dr.
Murfeesboro, NC 27855
919-398-6364
Fax: 919-398-1301

Mars Hill College
Upward Bound
Steve Rudolph

P.O. Box 1839
Mars Hill, NC 28754
828-689-1381
Fax: 828-689-1290

Elizabeth City State University
Upward Bound
Maxine Baskerville
1704 Weeksville Rd.
Campus Box 785
Elizabeth City, NC 27909
252-335-3369
Fax: 252-335-3793

Southeastern Community College
Upward Bound
Queen Lewis-Odom
P.O. Box 151
Whiteville, NC 28472
919-642-7141
Fax: 919-642-5658
Email: qlewisodom@mail.southeast.cc.nc.us

North Carolina State University
Upward Bound
Marsha Boyd Pharr
Box 7319 NCSU
Raleigh, NC 27693-7319
919-515-6447
Fax: 919-515-4581

Wilson Technical Community College
Upward Bound
William James
902 Herring Ave.
P.O. Box 4305
Wilson, NC 27893
252-291-1195
Fax: 252-243-7148

N.C. A&T State University
Upward Bound
Beverly J. Wallace
P.O. Box A-22
1020 E. Windover
Greensboro, NC 27411
336-334-7659
Fax: 336-334-7286
Email: beverly2@ncat.edu

Bladen County Schools
Upward Bound
Jackie Williams
P.O. Box 37
Highway 701 S
Elizabethtown, NC 28337
910-862-4136
Fax: 910-862-4277
Email: jpwilliams@bladen.k12.nc.us

University of North Carolina at Pembroke
Upward Bound
Larry McCallum
P.O. Box 1510
Pembroke, NC 28372-1510
910-521-6276
Fax: 910-521-6496
Email: mccallum@nat.uncp.edu

Johnson C. Smith University
Upward Bound
Magdalyn Lowe
100 Beatties Ford Rd.
P.O. Box 4
Charlotte, NC 28216
704-378-1102
Fax: 704-378-3503
Email: mlowe@jcsu.edu

University of North Carolina at Chapel Hill
Upward Bound
Joyce Daye Clayton
225 Hill Building
Chapel Hill, NC 27599-3310

919-962-1281
Fax: 919-962-4381
Email: jdclayto@email.unc.edu

Fayettesville State University
Upward Bound
Benita Scriven-Tillman
1200 Murchison Rd.
Fayetteville, NC 28301
910-486-1126
Fax: 910-437-2565
Email: btillman@uncfsu.edu

North Carolina State University
Upward Bound
Box 7317
Raleigh, NC 27695-7317
919-515-3632
Fax: 919-515-7065
Email: cynthia_harris@ncsu.edu

Appalachian State University
Upward Bound
Susan McCracken
Room 200 D.D. Dougherty Hall
Box 32087
Boone, NC 28607
828-262-2291
Fax: 828-262-3877
Email: mccrackensd@appstate.edu

Western Carolina University
Math and Science
Daniel Perlmutter
Room 71 McKee Bldg.
Cullowhee, NC 28723
828-227-3875
Fax: 828-227-7022
Email: dperlmutr@wcu.edu

Central Piedmont Community College
Deborah Kingsberry
P.O. Box 35009
7th Street Building
Charlotte, NC 28235
704-342-6961
Fax: 704-330-6610

Halifax: County Schools
Juanita B. Tate
1132 Bacon Road
Littleton, NC 27850
252-586-6645
Fax: 252-586-7827

James Sprunt Community College
Debra Morrisey
P.O. Box 398
Kenansville, NC 28349
910-296-2446
Fax: 910-296-1222

Johnson C. Smith University
Upward Bound Math/Science
Sunday Coward
P.O. Box 4
100 Beaties Ford Road
Charlotte, NC 28216
704-378-1005
Fax: 704-378-1294

Southwestern Community College -Sylva
Tracy Chapple
447 College Drive
Sylva, NC 28779
828-586-4091, ext. 333
Fax: 828-586-3129

North Dakota

University of North Dakota/Grand Forks
Upward Bound
Neil Reuter
P.O. Box 9027
Grand Forks, ND 58202-9027

701-777-3427
Fax: 701-777-3627
Email: nereuter@prarie.nodak.edu

North Dakota State University
Bruce Steele
University Station
P.O. Box 5625
Fargo, ND 58105-5625
701-231-8543
Fax: 701-231-9669

Ohio

Ohio Wesleyan University
Upward Bound
Deborah Lipscomb
219 Phillips Hall
Delaware, OH 43015
740-368-3218
Fax: 740-368-3220
Email: dblipsco@cc.owu.edu

University of Cincinnati
Upward Bound
Philip Cathey
Office of Sponsored Programs
P.O. Box 210118
Cincinnati, OH 45221-0118
513-556-1625
Fax: 513-556-3007
Email: phil.cathey@u.c.edu

The University of Akron
Upward Bound
Bradley McClain
115 Gallucci Hall
Akron, OH 44325-2102
330-972-5771
Fax: 330-972-5886
Email: mcclain@univcoll.uakron

Oberlin College
Upward Bound
Clifton McNish
155 N. Professor St.
Griswold 133
Oberlin, OH 44074
216-775-8759
Fax: 216-775-8886

Bowling Green State University
Upward Bound
Bonita Bembry
37 College Park Office Bldg.
Bowling Green, OH 43403
419-372-2381
Fax: 419-372-0399
Email: bonitag@lognet.bgsu.edu

Ohio State University Ag-Tech
Upward Bound
Gail Miller
1328 Dover Rd.
Wooster, OH 44691
800-647-8283
Fax: 216-262-7634

The Ohio State University Research
Foundation
Upward Bound
Roland Bittles
025 Mount Hall
1050 Carmack Rd.
Columbus, OH 43210-1002
614-292-3724
Fax: 614-292-4603
Email: bugno.2@osu.edu

University of Cincinnati
Veterans Upward Bound
Rosana Nelson
Student Affairs/
Office of Spon. Programs
P.O. Box 210119

Cincinnati, OH 45221-0119
513-556-8387
Fax: 513-556-2089
Email: rosana.nelson@uc.edu

Kent State University
Upward Bound
Geraldine Chabez
225 Michael Schwartz Center
Kent, OH 44242-0001
330-672-2920
Fax: 330-672-2073
Email: gchavez@kentvm.kent.edu

Cuyahoga Community College
Upward Bound
Shirrell Greene
2900 Community College Ave.
Hum 301
Cleveland, OH 44115-3196
216-987-4958
Fax: 216-987-4941

Shawnee State University
Upward Bound
Barbara Bradbury
940 Second St.
Portsmouth, OH 45662
740-355-2439
Fax: 740-355-2416
Email: bbradbury@shawnee.edu

Case Western Reserve University
Upward Bound
Carrie Reeves
10900 Euclid Ave.
Cleveland, OH 44106-7045
216-368-3750
Fax: 216-368-1267
Email: car6@po.cwru.edu

Cuyahoga Community College
Veterans Upward Bound
Eric Weimer
3740 Carnegie Ave.
Cleveland, OH 44115-2716
216-987-4196
Fax: 216-987-4941

University of Cincinnati/Clermont College
Upward Bound
Daniel Schneider
551 Cincinnati-Batavia Pike
Cincinnati, OH 45244
513-558-7437
Fax: 513-558-1308

Central State University
Upward Bound
Michele Franklin
P.O. Box 501
Wilberforce, OH 45384
937-376-6164
Fax: 937-376-6661

Ohio University, Athens
Upward Bound
Michele Smith
College of Education
124F McCracken Hall
Athens, OH 45701-2979
614-593-4417
Fax: 614-593-0714
Email: smithm@ouvaxa.cats.ohiou.edu

Baldwin Wallace College
Upward Bound
Barbara Berry
275 Eastland Rd.
Berea, OH 44017-2005
440-826-2208
Fax: 440-828-3494
Email: bberry@baldwinw.edu

Wittenberg University
Upward Bound
Eddie Chambers
P.O. Box 720
Springfield, OH 45501-0720
937-327-7535
Fax: 937-327-6340
Email: echam@wittenberg.edu

Sinclair Community College
Upward Bound
Brenda Payne
444 W. Third St.
Dayton, OH 45402-1460
937-512-2331
Fax: 937-512-2382
Email: bpayne@sinclair.edu

Ohio Dominican College
Upward Bound
Michael Boyd
12 Sunbury Rd.
Columbus, OH 43219-2099
614-251-4774
Fax: 614-251-0776

University of Toledo
Upward Bound
David Young
2801 W. Bancroft St.
4007 Gillman Hall
Toledo, OH 43606-3390
419-530-2786
Fax: 419-530-6123
Email: dyoung@utnet.utoledo.edu

The University of Akron
Math and Science
A. Bradley McClain
115 Gallucci Hall
Akron, OH 44325-2102
330-972-5771
Fax: 330-972-8099

Cleveland State University
Louis Brownlowe
1935 Euclid Avenue, Room 408
Cleveland, OH 44115
216-687-2594
Fax: 216-687-5510

College Of Mount Saint Joseph
Barbara Crosset-Hoffmeier
5701 Delhi Road
Cincinnati, OH 45233
513-244-5400
Fax: 513-244-4222

Columbus State Community College
R. Renee Davis-Hampton
550 East Spring Street
P.O. Box 1609
Columbus, OH 43216-1609
614-287-2426
Fax: 614-621-6506

Lourdes College
Kimberly Grieve
6832 Convent Blvd.
Sylvania, OH 43560-2898
419-885-3211
Fax: 419-882-3987
Email: kgrieve@lourdes.edu

Washington State Community College
Gary Williams
710 Colegate Drive
Marrieta, OH 45750
740-374-8716
Fax: 740-373-7496

Youngstown State University
Jennifer E. Roller
One University Plaza
Youngstown, OH 44555
330-742-1939
Fax: 330-742-3228

Oklahoma

Redlands Community College
Upward Bound
Deborah White
1300 S. Country Club Rd.
El Reno, OK 73036-5300
405-262-2552
Fax: 405-422-1200

Southwestern Oklahoma State University
Upward Bound
Lou Ann Largent
100 Campus Dr.
Weatherford, OK 73096
580-774-7029
Fax: 580-774-7049

East Central University
Veterans Upward Bound
Mary Huckleberry
ECU Box S-36
Ada, OK 74820
580-310-5541
Fax: 580-436-4563
Email: mhuckleb@mailclerk.ecok.edu

Choctaw Nation of Oklahoma
Upward Bound
Tim Amas
Drawer 1210
Durant, OK 74702-1210
580-924-8280
Fax: 580-924-8292

Bacone College
Upward Bound
Laura Holloway
2299 Old Bacone Rd.
Muskogee, OK 74403-1597
918-683-4581, ext. 255
Fax: 918-687-5913
Email: holloway@mail.bacone.edu

Seminole State College
Upward Bound
Clifton Conatser
P.O. Box 351
Seminole, OK 74868-0351
405-382-9950
Fax: 405-382-2998

Seminole State College
Veterans Upward Bound
Darren Wise
P.O. Box 351
Seminole, OK 74868-0351
405-382-0059
Fax: 405-382-0167

Rogers State College
Upward Bound
Brock Rutledge
Will Rogers and College Hill
1701 W. Will Rogers Blvd.
Claremore, OK 74017
918-343-7777
Fax: 918-343-7891
Email: bmrutled@rsu.edu

Oklahoma State University
Upward Bound
Bennie Boykin
900 N. Portland Ave.
Oklahoma City, OK 73107-6195
405-945-3243

Fax: 405-945-8628
Email: bennie#u#b@mailgate.osuokc.okstate

East Central University
Upward Bound
Janet Borders
ECU Box P-4
Ada, OK 74820
580-332-8000
Fax: 580-332-1708

Langston University
Upward Bound
Glenda Nash
P.O. Box 838
Warner, OK 73050
405-466-3433
Fax: 405-466-2966
Email: gbnash@lunet.edu

Cameron University
Upward Bound Program
Cheryl Dorris
2800 W. Gore Blvd.
Lawton, OK 73505-6377
580-581-5581
Fax: 580-581-5514
Email: cheryld@cameron.edu

Southeastern Oklahoma State University
Upward Bound
Larry Dresser
SOSU Box 4114
Durant, OK 74701-0609
580-924-0121
Fax: 580-920-7481

Chickasaw Foundation
Upward Bound
Michael Cox
P.O. Box 1726
Ada, OK 74820-1726
580-371-9903
Fax: 580-371-9584

Oklahoma City Community College
Upward Bound
Margo Delaune
7777 S. May Ave.
Oklahoma City, OK 73159
405-682-1611, ext. 7625
Fax: 405-682-7529

Carl Albert State College
Upward Bound
David Robinson
1507 S. McKenna
Poteau, OK 74953
918-647-1386
Fax: 918-647-1286

East Central University Bound Math/Science
Math and Science
Rhonda Pettit
200 Stadium Dr.
Ada, OK 74820
580-332-8000
Fax: 580-332-3546

Carl Albert State College
Math and Science
Beverly Afzali
1507 South McKenna
Poteau, OK 74953-5208
918-647-1369
Fax: 918-647-8660

Southeastern Oklahoma State University
Math and Science
Michele Clayton
SOSU Box 4222
Durant, OK 74701-0609
580-924-0121
Fax: 580-920-7404

Choctaw Nation of Oklahoma
Upward Bound Math and Science Program
Robert Ray
HCR 74, Box 102-5
Durant, OK 74547
918-297-2518
Fax: 918-297-2364

Rogers State College
Math and Science
Brock Rutledge
Will Rogers College Hill
1701 W. Will Rogers Blvd.
Claremore, OK 74017
918-343-7777
Fax: 918-343-7891
Email: bmrutled@rsu.edu

Connors State College
Upward Bound
Gretchen Morgan
P.O. Box 1000
Warner, OK 74469
918-463-2931
Fax: 918-463-2233

Veterans Upward Bound
James Wydeman Sanders
1000 College Road
Route 1, Box 1000
Warner, OK 74469
918-463-2931
Fax: 918-463-2233

Northeastern Oklahoma A&M College
Julie Rice
200 I Street Northeast
Miami, OK 74354
918-540-6208
Fax: 918-540-6137

Oklahoma State University-Stillwater
Pam Bowers
201 Whitehurst
Stillwater, OK 74078
405-744-7440
Fax: 405-744-6438

University Of Central Oklahoma
Barry Lofton
100 North University Drive
Box 95
Edmond, OK 73034
405-974-2526
Fax: 405-974-3881

Western Oklahoma State College
Randy Cumby
2801 North Main Street
Altus, OK 73521-1397
580-477-7711
Fax: 580-477-7716

Oregon
Pacific University
Upward Bound
Roberta Nickels
2043 College Way
Forest Grove, OR 97116-1797
503-357-8169
Fax: 503-359-2242
Email: nicke1sb8d8c1ficu-edu

Clatsop Community College
Upward Bound
Ed Bohart
1653 Jerome
Astoria, OR 97103
503-325-0910
Fax: 503-325-5738
Email: ebohart@clatsop.cc.or.us

Umpqua Community College
Upward Bound
Margaret Ellis

1140 College Rd.
P.O. Box 967
Roseburg, OR 97470-0226
541-440-4600
Fax: 541-440-4612
Email: ellism@umpqua.cc.or.us

Portland State University
Upward Bound at Portland State University
Phillip Dirks
219 Shattuck Hall
P.O. Box 751
Portland, OR 97207-0751
503-725-4458
Fax: 503-725-8514

Linfield College
Upward Bound
Madeline Jepson
900 South Baker
McMinnville, OR 97128-6894
503-434-2277
Fax: 503-434-2215
Email: mjepson@linfield.edu

Chemeketa Community College
Roberto Casarez
4000 Lancaster Drive NE
P.O. Box 14007
Salem, OR 97309-7020
503-589-7661
Fax: 503-589-2580
Email: cab@chemeketa.edu

Western Oregon University
Charleen Barrett-Lee
345 North Monmouth Avenue
Monmouth, OR 97361
503-838-8719
Fax: 503-838-8723

Pennsylvania
Saint Francis College
Upward Bound Program
Anne Heinzeroth
P.O. Box 600
Loretto, PA 15940-0600
814-472-3023
Fax: 814-472-3863
Email: aheinzeroth@sspca.edu

Wilkes University
Upward Bound
Paul McHenry
129 S. Franklin St.
P.O. Box 111
Sturdevant Hall
Wilkes-Barre, PA 18766
570-408-3232
Fax: 570-408-1003

Clarion University of Pennsylvania
Upward Bound
John Kula
B-20 Campbell Hall
840 Wood St.
Clarion, PA 16214-1232
814-226-2342
Fax: 814-226-2368
Email: jkula@vaxa.clarion.edu

University of Pittsburgh
Upward Bound
Renee Frazier
SA 18 Forbes Quadrangle
Pittsburgh, PA 15260
412-624-7070
Fax: 412-624-7070

California University of PA
Upward Bound
Gary Seelye
250 University Ave.
Noss Building
California, PA 15419-1394

724-938-4230
Fax: 724-935-5981

Millersville University
Upward Bound
Doris Cross
Acad Aff/Sch of Ed
Somerset House
Millersville, PA 17551-0302
717-872-3256
Fax: 717-872-3253
Email: dcross@mu3.millersv.edu

Chatham College
Upward Bound
Josephine Barnett
Woodland Rd.
Pittsburgh, PA 15232
412-365-1263
Fax: 412-365-1844
Email: jbarnett@chatham.edu

Swarthmore College
Upward Bound
Mike Robinson
500 College Ave.
Swarthmore, PA 19081-1397
610-328-8345
Fax: 610-328-8673

Harcum College
Upward Bound
Judith Greene
750 Montgomery Ave.
Bryn Mawr, PA 19010-3476
610-526-6151
Fax: 610-526-6170

East Stroudsburg University of PA
Upward Bound
Wilfredo Lopez
200 Prospect St.
East Stroudsburg, PA 18301-2999
570-422-3477
Fax: 570-422-3432

University of PA
Veterans Upward Bound
Annette Hampton
3933 Walnut St.
Philadelphia, PA 19104-3246
215-898-6892
Fax: 215-764-2082

The Pennsylvania State University
Upward Bound
Maureen Mulderig
204 Calder Way, Room 201
University Park, PA 16801
814-865-2320
Fax: 814-865-2320
Email: mem5@oas.psu.edu

Bloomsburg University of PA
Upward Bound
Maureen Mulligan
400 E. Second St.
Wilson House
Bloomsburg, PA 17815-1301
717-389-4280
Fax: 717-389-4201
Email: mulligan@planetx.bloomu.edu

Temple University
Upward Bound
Namorah Byrd
1700 N. Broad St.
206 Vivacqua Hall
Philadelphia, PA 19122
215-204-3251
Fax: 215-204-5415

Lincoln University
Upward Bound
Herschel Baily

B-3 University Hall
Lincoln University, PA 19352-0999
610-932-8300, ext. 3551
Fax: 610-932-3489
Email: bailey@lu.lincoln.edu

University of Pennsylvania
Upward Bound
Angela McIver
3933 Walnut St.
Philadelphia, PA 19104-6184
215-898-3185
Fax: 215-898-3684

Temple University
Math/Science
Fred Vincent
202 Vivacqua Hall
1700 N. Broad St.
Philadelphia, PA 19122
215-204-3112
Fax: 215-204-8412

Pennsylvania State Univ/Univ Park
Math and Science
Ron Williams
401 Boucke Building
University Park, PA 16802
814-863-4291
Fax: 814-863-8617
Email: dqw8@oas.psu.edu

Community College Of Philadelphia
Lovell Pugh-Bassett
1700 Spring Garden Street
W1-1C
Philadelphia, PA 19130
215-751-8042
Fax: 215-972-6299

Greater Erie Community Action Committee
Nicole Miller
18 West Ninth Street
Erie, PA 16501
814-459-4581
Fax: 814-456-0161
Email: nmlgeca@erie.net

Gwynedd-Mercy College
Carole Doring
Campbell Hall
P.O. Box 901
Gwynedd Valley, PA 19437-0901
215-646-7300, ext. 123
Fax: 215-641-5573

Kutztown University Of Pennsylvania
Ulysses J. Connor Jr.
153 Beckey Education Center
Kutztown, PA 19530
610-683-4219
Fax: 610-683-1357
Email: connor@kutztown.edu

Lock Haven University Of Pennsylvania
Nicole Chartas
North Fairview Street
Lock Haven, PA 17745
570-893-6292
Fax: 717-893-2432
Email: nchartas@eagle.lhup.edu

Puerto Rico

Cayey University College
Upward Bound
Gladys Ramos
Ave. Barcelo Office 203
Computer Building
Cayey, PR 00634
787-738-2161
Fax: 787-738-8039

University of the Sacred Heart
Upward Bound
Maria Rullan

Loiza Station
P.O. Box 12383
San Turce, PR 00914
787-728-1515
Fax: 787-728-1692

Carmen Marrero
Upward Bound Program
Colegio Universitario Del Este
P.O. Box 2010
Carolina, PR 00984-2010
787-758-2535
Fax: 787-758-7171

Aspira Inc. De Puerto Rico
Upward Bound
Jose Vargas
Box 29132
65th Infantry Station
San Juan, PR 00929-132
787-768-1985
Fax: 787-257-2725

Pontifical Catholic University of Puerto Rico
Upward Bound
Louisa Pillot-Torres
2250 Ave Las Americas, Suite 577
Ponce, PR 00731-6382
787-841-2000, ext. 476
Fax: 787-841-2000, ext. 1795

Inter American University/Rico San German
Upward Bound
Maria Perez
Box 5100 C-40
U.I. Station
San German, PR 00753
787-264-0424
Fax: 787-892-5400

University of Puerto Rico
Upward Bound
Jose Antonio Cruz Rios
P.O. Box 4800
Carolina, PR 00984-4800
787-257-0000
Fax: 787-257-2000

Caribbean University
Upward Bound Project
Herman Perez
P.O. Box 493
Bayamon, PR 00960-6093
787-780-0070
Fax: 787-785-0101

Aspira Inc. De Puerto Rico
Veterans Upward Bound
Francisco Feliciano
Box 21509
UPR Station
San Juan, PR 00931
787-768-1985, ext. 232
Fax: 787-257-2725
Email: ffelicia@rrpac.upr.clu.edu

Inter American University/Barranquitas
Campus
Upward Bound
Marcelina Torres
Box 517
Barranquitas, PR 00794
787-857-3590
Fax: 787-857-3590

Inter American University/San German
Campus
Math and Science
Maria Perez
Box 5100 C-40
U.I. Station
San German, PR 00753
787-264-2320
Fax: 787-892-5400

Inter-American University Of Puerto Rico-
Bayamon
Upward Bound Math/Science
Migdala Mangual
RD 830, #500
Minillas Industrial Park
Bayamon, PR 00957
787-279-2220
Fax: 787-279-2205

Inter American University Of Puerto Rico-
Ponce
Upward Bound Math/Science
Dolores Pinero-Caparros
P.O. Box 363255
San Juan, PR 00936
787-758-0899
Fax: 787-250-7984
Email: dpiero@inter.edu

Universidad Central De Bayamon
Alma Martinez Martinez
P.O. Box 1725
Bayamon, PR 00621
787-786-3030
Fax: 787-740-2200
Email: amartinez@ubc.edu.pr

University Of Puerto Rico-Humacao
Myrian Cintron
Chancellor's Office
CUH Station, 100 Carr 908
Humacao, PR 00791
787-850-9376
Fax: 787-852-4638

Rhode Island

Rhode Island College
Upward Bound
Mariam Boyajian
600 Mount Pleasant Ave.
Providence, RI 02908-1991
401-456-8081
Fax: 401-456-4725
Email: mboyajian@grog.ric.edu

South Carolina

Claflin College
Upward Bound Program
Gwendolyn Phillips
P.O. Box 10
Orangeburg, SC 29115
803-535-5283
Fax: 803-531-2860

Florence-Darlington Technical College
Upward Bound
Shirley March
P.O. Box 100548
Florence, SC 29501-0548
803-661-8072
Fax: 803-661-8041
Email: march@flo.tec.sc.us

Trident Technical College
Upward Bound
Dann Hazel
P.O. Box 118067 SS-B
Charleston, SC 29423
843-899-8005
Fax: 843-899-8100

Morris College
Upward Bound
King Singleton
100 W. College St.
Sumter, SC 29150-3599
803-775-9371
Fax: 803-773-3687

Williamsburg Technical College
Upward Bound
Millicent Jackson
601 Martin Luther King Jr. Ave.

Kingstree, SC 29556-4197
843-354-2021
Fax: 843-354-7269
Email: jacksonm@wil.tec.sc.us

Peidmont Technical College
Upward Bound
E. Jim Oree
P.O. Box 1467
Greenwood, SC 29648-1467
803-941-8607
Fax: 803-941-8555

Technical College of the Low Country
Upward Bound
Frances McCollough
P.O. Box 1288
921 Ribaut Rd.
Beaufort, SC 29901-1288
843-525-8228
Fax: 843-525-8330

University of South Carolina/Spartanburg
Upward Bound
Carolyn Frye
800 University Way
Columbia, SC 29303
803-599-2644
Fax: 803-599-2375

Tri-County Technical College
Upward Bound
David Pressley
Student Services Division
P.O. Box 587
Pendleton, SC 29670
864-646-8361, ext. 2443
Fax: 864-646-8256
Email: dpressley@tricty.tricounty.tec.sc.us

Voorhees College
Upward Bound
Lillian Mullino
1400 Voorhees Rd. - Box 22
Denmark, SC 29042-1400
803-793-3351
Fax: 803-793-4584

Midlands Technical College
Upward Bound
David Long
P.O. Box 2408
Columbia, SC 29202
803-822-3384
Fax: 803-822-3619
Email: longd@mtc.mid.tec.sc.us

University of South Carolina, Trio Programs
Upward Bound Program
Attie Baker
Booker T Washington Aud. Bldg.
1400 Wheat St.
Columbia, SC 29208
803-777-5122
Fax: 803-777-7380

The College of Charleston
Upward Bound Program
Joyce Coakley
66 George St.
Charleston, SC 29424-0001
843-953-5469
Fax: 843-953-4902

Benedict College
Upward Bound Project
Sue Hawks-Foster
1600 Harden
MSP2
Columbia, SC 29204
803-253-5342
Fax: 803-755-4469
Email: fosters@benedict.edu

Trident Technical College
Upward Bound Math and Science Center
P.O. Box 118067, SS-B
Charleston, SC 29423-8067
843-899-8005
Fax: 843-899-8100

Claflin College
Math and Science
Gwendolyn Phillips
P.O. Box 10
Orangeburg, SC 29115
803-535-5283
Fax: 803-531-2860

Greenville Technical College
Lottie B. Gibson
P.O. Box 5616
South Pleasantburg Drive
Greenville, SC 29606-5616
864-250-8380
Fax: 864-250-8193

University Of South Carolina-Lancaster
Thelathia Bailey
207 Medford Library
Lancaster, SC 29728
803-285-7471
Fax: 803-289-7106

University Of South Carolina-Salkehatchie
Andy Thomas
P.O. Box 617
Allendale, SC 29810
803-584-3446
Fax: 803-584-5038
Email: athomas@gwm.sc.edu

South Dakota

Black Hills State University
Upward Bound
Carol Gritts
1200 University
USB 9516
Spearfish, SD 57799-9516
605-642-6120
Fax: 605-642-6214
Email: cgritts@mystic.bhsu.edu

The University of South Dakota
Upward Bound
Charles Swick
414 East Clark St.
Vermillion, SD 57069-2390
605-677-5308
Fax: 605-677-5756

Northern State University
Virginia Laredo Elkhader
1200 South Jay Street
Aberdeen, SD 57401
605-626-2633
Fax: 605-626-3317

Tennessee

Douglas-Cherokee Economic Authority, Inc.
Appalachian Upward Bound
Linda Crutchfield
P.O. Box 1218
Morristown, TN 37816-1218
423-587-4500
Fax: 423-587-4509

The University of Tennessee/Knoxville
Upward Bound Program
Connie Hollingsworth
1914 Andy Holt Ave.
Knoxville, TN 37996-2745
865-974-4466
Fax: 865-974-3961

Lemoyne-Owen College
Upward Bound
Mae Harris

807 Walker Ave.
Memphis, TN 38126-0645
901-942-7365
Fax: 901-942-7810

Lane College
Upward Bound Program
Clara Hewitt
545 Lane Ave.
Jackson, TN 38301-4598
901-426-7500
Fax: 901-426-7527

Tennessee State University
Upward Bound
Rosa Hudson
3500 John A. Merritt Blvd.
P.O. Box 9540
Nashville, TN 37209-1561
615-963-7442
Fax: 615-963-7443

East Tennessee State University
Veterans Upward Bound
Ronnie Gross
1227 Volunteer Parkway
Bristol, TN 37620
423-844-6304
Fax: 423-844-6303

Austin Peay State University
Veterans Upward Bound
Arthur Neal
P.O. Box 4455
Clarksville, TN 37044
931-221-6235
Fax: 931-503-1526
Email: neala@apsu02.apsu.edu

Hiwassee College
Upward Bound
James Cheek
HC Box 606
225 Hiwassee College Dr.
Madisonville, TN 37354
423-420-1233
Fax: 423-420-1909
Email: cheekjam@hiwassee.edu

Austin Peay State University
Upward Bound
Barbara Wilbur
P.O. Box 4427
Clarksville, TN 37044-4427
931-221-6200
Fax: 931-221-7987
Email: wilburb@apsu02.apsu.edu

Lincoln Memorial University
Upward Bound
David Wilhoit
P.O. Box 885
Campus Center
Harrogate, TN 37752
423-869-6320
Fax: 423-869-6426
Email: dwilhoit@inetlrou.Imunet.edu

Tusculum College
Upward Bound
Jeanne Stokes
P.O. Box 5083
Greeneville, TN 37743-9997
615-636-7325
Fax: 615-638-7166

East Tennessee State University
Upward Bound/Trio Programs
Ronnie Gross
1227 Volunteer Pkwy
Bristol, TN 37620
423-844-6304
Fax: 423-844-6303
Email: grossrd@etsu.edu

University of Tennessee/Knoxville
Math and Science Upward Bound Program
Nancy Headlee
1914 Andy Holt Ave.
25 HPER Bldg.
Knoxville, TN 37996-2745
865-974-4466
Fax: 865-974-3961

Dyersburg State Community College
Robert Jones
1510 Lake Road
Dyersburg, TN 38024
901-285-1305
Fax: 901-285-1305
Email: b.jones@dscclan.dscc.cc.tn.us

Southwest Tennessee Community College
Cynthia Lanier
P.O. Box 40568
737 Union Avenue
Memphis, TN 38174-0568
901-333-5117
Fax: 901-333-5534

University Of Tennessee-Chattanoga
Booker T. Scruggs, II
212 Race Hall
615 McCallie Avenue
Chattanooga, TN 37403
423-755-4691
Fax: 423-785-2111
Email: scruggs@utc.edu

Upward Bound Math/Science
Sandra Abbate
615 McCallie Avenue
Chattanooga, TN 37403-2598
423-785-2248
Fax: 423-785-2249
Email: sabbate@utc.edu

University Of Tennessee-Knoxville
Veterans Upward Bound
Joel Coates
1914 Andy Holt Avenue
25 HPER Building
Knoxville, TN 37996-2745
865-974-4466
Fax: 865-974-3961

Texas

Laredo Community College
Upward Bound Program
Gerardo Martinez
P.O. Box 738
West End Washington St.
Laredo, TX 78041
956-721-5238
Fax: 956-721-5438
Email: gmartinez@laredo.cc.tx.us

Tarleton State University
Upward Bound
Jane McClain
Box T-0710
Tarleton Station
Stephenville, TX 76402
254-968-9294
Fax: 254-958-9295

University of Texas at Brownsville
Upward Bound
Hilda Silva
80 Fort Brown
Upward Bound University Program
Brownsville, TX 78520
956-544-8212
Fax: 956-544-8825
Email: hsilva@utb1utb.edu

Southwest Texas State University
Upward Bound
Cheryl McWilliams

ASB North #308
601 University Dr.
San Marcos, TX 78666
512-245-8135
Fax: 512-245-8589
Email: cm16@swt.edu

West Texas A&M University
Upward Bound
Martin Lopez
WTAMU Box 60094
Canyon, TX 79016-0001
806-656-2351
Fax: 806-656-2925

El Paso Community College
Upward Bound
Carlos Caballero
919 Hunter Dr.
El Paso, TX 79998
915-594-2641
Fax: 915-594-2155

Midwestern State University
Upward Bound
Lisa Estrada-Hamby
3410 Taft Blvd. #42
Wichita Falls, TX 76308-2095
940-397-4080
Fax: 940-397-4695

Abilene Christian University
Upward Bound
Bernadette Boglin
ACU Box 29206
Avilene, TX 79699-9206
915-674-2448
Fax: 915-674-2847
Email: bernadette.boglin@upward.acu.edu

Upward Bound Program
Lyndon McClure
Dallas Cmty. College Dist.
701 Elm St., Suite 300
Dallas, TX 75202-3299
214-860-2456
Fax: 214-860-2107

Southwestern Christian College
Upward Bound
Albert Rice
P.O. Box 10
Terrell, TX 75160
972-524-4052
Fax: 972-563-7133

Richland College
Upward Bound Program
12800 Abrams Rd.
Dallas, TX 75243-2199
972-238-3739
Fax: 972-238-3741

University of Texas at El Paso
Upward Bound
Sandra Braham
202 Graham Hall
El Paso, TX 79968
915-747-5149
Fax: 915-747-8879
Email: sbrahman@tep.edu

University of North Texas
Upward Bound
Diane Newman
P.O. Box 310888
Denton, TX 76203-0888
940-565-2090
Fax: 940-565-2089

The University of Texas at San Antonio
Upward Bound Program Science/Math
Rita Cortez
6900 N. Loop

1604 WMS Bldg.
San Antonio, TX 78249-0645
210-691-5852
Fax: 210-691-5848

Communities in Schools
Upward Bound
Willie Thomas
1616 E. Commerce Bldg. #1
San Antonio, TX 78205
210-520-8440
Fax: 210-520-1104

Houston Community College System
Upward Bound
Maria Cisneros
1420 Alabama
Houston, TX 77003
713-630-7210
Fax: 713-630-7212

Texas Christian University
Upward Bound
J. Steven Hodnett
Box 297760
Fort Worth, TX 76129-2977
817-921-7946
Fax: 817-921-7467
Email: shodnett@gamma.is.tcu.edu

Texas A&M University/Kingsville
Upward Bound Regular
Consuelo Martinez
Campus Box 201
Kingsville, TX 78363
361-593-2708
Fax: 361-593-2494

Texas Tech University
Eric Strong
Office of Research Services
Box 4490
Lubbock, TX 79409-1035
806-742-3616
Fax: 806-742-0983

University of Houston/Downtown
Upward Bound
Dawana Lewis
One Main St., Suite 946-S
Houston, TX 77002
713-221-8575
Fax: 713-221-8064
Email: lewis@dt.uh.edu

St. Mary's University
Upward Bound
Jacqueline Dansby
One Camino Santa Maria St.
San Antonio, TX 78228-8589
210-436-3206
Fax: 210-436-3500

Wiley College
Upward Bound
Theresa Adams
711 Wiley Ave.
Marshall, TX 75670
903-927-3247
Fax: 903-938-8554

Texas Southern University
Upward Bound
William Nealy
3100 Cleburne Ave.
Houston, TX 77004
713-313-7233
Fax: 713-313-1876

Houston-Tillotson College
Upward Bound
Mark Terry
900 Chicon St.
Austin, TX 78702-2795

512-505-3000
Fax: 512-505-3190

McLennan Community College
Upward Bound Program
Brenda Wilkinson
1400 College Dr.
Waco, TX 76708
817-750-3538
Fax: 817-756-0934

The University of Texas at Arlington
Upward Bound
Lisa Thompson
Division of Student Affairs
P.O. Box 19356
Arlington, TX 76019-0356
817-272-2610
Fax: 817-272-2616
Email: lthompson@uta.edu

University of Texas/Pan American
Upward Bound Program
Dora Martinez
1201 W. University Dr.
ESRH RM #202
Edinburg, TX 78539
956-381-2596
Fax: 956-316-7108

Paris Junior College
Upward Bound
Carole Pickering
2400 Clarksville St.
Paris, TX 75460
903-782-9280
Fax: 903-782-9370
Email: cpickering@paris.cc.tx.us

Coastal Bend College
Upward Bound Program
Velma Elizalde
3800 Charco Rd.
Beeville, TX 78102
361-358-2838
Fax: 361-354-2704

Odessa College
Upward Bound Program
Max Mufti
201 W. University
Odessa, TX 79764
915-335-6312
Fax: 915-335-6319
Email: mmufti@odessa.edu

Trinity University/Education Department
Upward Bound
Joyce McQueen
715 Stadium Dr.
San Antonio, TX 78212-7200
210-999-7591
Fax: 210-999-7592
Email: jmcqueen@trinity.edu

Wiley College
Math and Science
Leonard Wilmer
711 Wiley Ave.
Marshall, TX 75670
903-927-3301
Fax: 903-934-8100

Texas Southern University
Math and Science
William Nealy
3100 Cleburne St.
Houston, TX 77004
713-313-7233
Fax: 713-313-1876

The University of Texas at Arlington
Math and Science
Lisa Thompson

Division of Student Affairs
P.O. Box 19356
Arlington, TX 76019-0356
817-272-2636
Fax: 817-272-2616
Email: lthompson@uta.edu

Cedar Valley College
Mwauna D. Maxwell
3030 North Dallas Avenue
Lancaster, TX 75134-3799
972-860-8064
Fax: 972-860-8014
Email: mdm3320@dcccd.edu

Eastfield College
Romolio Castillo
3737 Motley Drive
Mesquite, TX 75150-2099
972-860-7277
Fax: 972-860-7291

Education Plus, Inc.
Sylvia Longoria
5415 Keystone Drive
San Antonio, TX 78229
210-523-0031
Fax: 210-681-0538

Houston Community College-Southeast
Paulette Wellington
6815 Rustic
P.O. Box 7849
Houston, TX 77087
713-718-7004
Fax: 713-718-7062

Jarvis Christian College
Mary McKinney
P.O. Box 1470
Hawkins, TX 75765
903-769-2174
Fax: 903-769-5005

Midland College
Judy Merritt
3600 North Garfield
Midland, TX 79705
915-685-6457
Fax: 915-685-4761

North Harris Montgomery Community
College District
Suzanne Acevedo
250 N. Sam Houston Pkwy, East
Houston, TX 77060
281-618-5434
Fax: 281-618-5402

North Lake College
Guy Melton
5001 North MacArthur Blvd.
Irving, TX 75038-3804
972-273-3325
Fax: 972-273-3388

Northeast Texas Community College
Melody Henry
P.O. Box 1307
Mount Pleasant, TX 75456
903-572-1911
Fax: 903-572-6712

Palo Alto College
Judy Camargo
1400 West Villaret Blvd.
San Antonio, TX 78224
210-921-5281
Fax: 210-921-5357
Email: jcamargo@accd.edu

Paul Quinn College
Grace Gonzales
3837 Simpson Stuart Road

Dallas, TX 75241
214-302-3518
Fax: 214-302-3603
Email: ggonzales@pqc.edu

San Jacinto College-North
J.D. Mota
5800 Uvalde Rd
Houston, TX 77049-4513
281-458-4050
Fax: 281-459-7605

South Texas Community College
Patrick Murray
P.O. Box 9701
Mcallen, TX 78504
956-928-3491
Fax: 956-928-3582

Southern Methodist University
Thomas A. Edwards
P.O. Box 750455
Dallas, TX 75275-0455
214-768-2364
Fax: 214-768-1001
Email: t.edwards@mail.smu.edu

Southwestern University
Samuel Wheeler
1001 East University Avenue
Georgetown, TX 78626
512-863-1177
Fax: 512-863-1170

Sul Ross State University
Eleazar R. Cano
Box C-31
Alpine, TX 79832
915-837-8753
Fax: 915-837-8754
Email: ecano@sulross.edu

Texas A&M University-Commerce
Ronnie Brooks
E.T. Station
P.O. Box 3011
Commerce, TX 75429
903-886-5836
Fax: 903-468-3220
Email: ronnie_brooks@tamu-
commerce.edu

Texas A&M University-Corpus Christi
Veronica Guerra
6300 Ocean Dr
Corpus Christi, TX 78412-5503
512-994-6092
Fax: 512-994-5943
Email: vguerra@faclon.tamucc.edu

Texas A&M University-Kingsville
Upward Bound Math/Science
Consuelo Martinez
Office of Sponsor Research
Campus Box 201
Kingsville, TX 78363
361-595-2708
Fax: 361-593-2494

The Boys & Girls Clubs Of Greater Ft. Worth
Elizabeth Retamozo
3218 East Belknap Street
Ft. Worth, TX 76111
817-831-2911
Fax: 817-759-1209

University Of North Texas
Upward Bound Math/Science
Doug Elrod
P.O. Box 310888
Denton, TX 76203
940-565-4184
Fax: 940-565-2089
Email: delrod@coefs.coe.unt.edu

University Of Texas–Brownsville
Upward Bound
Alberto Carlos Villarreal
80 Fort Brown
Brownsville, TX 78520
956-544-3846
Fax: 956-983-7003
Email: avillarreal@utb1.utb.edu

Upward Bound Math/Science
Margie Mancillas
20 Fort Brown
Brownsville, TX 78520
956-548-6502
Fax: 956-544-8823

University Of Texas–San Antonio
Rene Cantu
1222 North Maine, Suite 650-B
San Antonio, TX 78212-5713
210-558-2315
Fax: 210-558-2318
Email: rcantu@ltcpost1.utsa.edu

Weatherford College
Danny Boitnott
225 College Park Drive
Weatherford, TX 76086
817-594-4083
Fax: 817-594-6381
Email: dboitnott@wc.edu

Utah

University of Utah
Upward Bound
Kathryn Felker
1901 E. South Campus Dr.
Annex 2075
Salt Lake City, UT 84112
801-581-7188
Fax: 801-581-4325
Email: kfelker@ssb1.utah.edu

Snow College Upward Bound
Kenneth Jackson
150 College Ave.
Ephraim, UT 84627
435-283-4021
Fax: 435-283-6284
Email: kenj@storm.snow.edu

College of Eastern Utah
Upward Bound
Dennis Gutke
639 W. 100 S.
Blanding, UT 84511
435-678-2201, ext. 162
Fax: 435-678-2220
Email: dgutke@sanjuan.ceu.edu

Weber State University
Upward Bound
David Trujillo
3201 University Circle
Ogden, UT 84408-3201
801-626-6798
Fax: 801-626-7930
Email: dtrujillo@weber.edu

Weber State University
Veterans Upward Bound
James Kopecky
1308 University Circle
Ogden, UT 84408-1308
801-626-7173
Fax: 801-626-6826

Southern Utah University
Upward Bound Program
Leanne Maxwell
351 W. Center St.
Cedar City, UT 84720
435-586-7771

Fax: 435-865-8235
Email: maxwell_l@edu-suu-gc.gc.suu.edu

Dixie State College of Utah
Upward Bound
Nelda Kissinger
225 S. 700 East
St. George, UT 84770-3876
435-656-7659
Fax: 435-656-4006

Utah Valley State College
Upward Bound
Maria Weingarten
800 W. 1200 South #150
Orem, UT 84058-5999
801-222-8076
Fax: 801-222-8812
Email: weingama@uvsc.edu

Vermont

Johnson State College
Upward Bound
Tony Blueter
Box 1875
Johnson, VT 05656
802-635-7051
Fax: 802-635-9745

Southern Vermont College
Upward Bound
Robin Forsyth
Monument Rd.
Bennington, VT 05201
802-447-5213
Fax: 802-447-5529

Lyndon State College
Robert McCabe
Vail Hill
Lyndonville, VT 05851
802-626-9371
Fax: 802-626-9770

University Of Vermont
Nancy Boldt
D100 Living & Learning Center
Burlington, VT 05465
802-656-4185
Fax: 802-656-7957
Email: nbolt@zoo.uvm.edu

Vermont Technical College
Upward Bound Math/Science
John Anderson
Main Street
P.O.Box 500
Randolph Center, VT 05061
802-728-1583
Fax: 802-728-1390

Virginia

Saint Paul's College
Upward Bound Program
Josephine Reid
1115 College Dr.
Lawrenceville, VA 23868
804-848-3347
Fax: 804-848-0303

Virginia State University
Upward Bound Program
Mary Wilson
P.O. Box 9014
Petersburg, VA 23806
804-524-5811
Fax: 804-524-5142

Hampton University
Upward Bound Program
Carolyn Hutcheson
P.O. Box 6167
Hampton, VA 23668
804-727-5307
Fax: 804-727-5084

Old Dominion University
Upward Bound
Ollie Tolliver
Division of Student Services
Academic Skills Center, Room 111
Norfolk, VA 23529-0069
757-683-4315
Fax: 757-683-3201
Email: otollive.odu.edu

Wytheville Community College
Upward Bound
Maynard Joyce
1000 Main St.
Wytheville, VA 24382
540-223-4750, ext. 411
Fax: 540-223-4778
Email: wcbyrnd@vocscent.bitnet

Virginia Union University
Upward Bound
Louis Hearn
1500 N. Lombardy St.
Richmond, VA 23228
804-257-5883
Fax: 804-257-5832

University of Virginia/Charlottesville
Upward Bound
Leah Puryear
231 Minor Hall
Charlottesville, VA 22903
804-982-5576
Fax: 804-982-4554

Norfolk State University
Veterans Upward Bound
Lucy Haawkins
700 Park Ave.
Norfolk, VA 23504
757-823-2471
Fax: 757-823-8803

Roanoke College
Upward Bound Program
Theresa Jackson
221 College Lane
Salem, VA 24153-3794
540-375-2245
Fax: 540-375-2213
Email: jackson@acc.roanoke.edu

Norfolk State University
Upward Bound Program
Tanya Perry
700 Park Ave.
Norfolk, VA 23504
757-823-2346
Fax: 757-823-2343

Virginia Polytechnic Institute and State
University
Upward Bound
Tom Wilson
Hillcrest Hall - Lower Level
Blacksburg, VA 24061-0146
540-231-6911
Fax: 540-231-4522
Email: tgwilson@vt.edu

Tidewater Community College
Upward Bound
Johanna Coleman-Yates
1428 Cedar Rd.
Chesapeake, VA 23320
757-822-5240
Fax: 757-822-5221
Email: tccolej@tc.cc.va.us

Danville Community College
Mark T. Gibson
1008 South Main Street
Danville, VA 24541

804-797-8582
Fax: 804-797-8541

Rappahannock Community College
Robert Griffen
52 Campus Drive
Warsaw, VA 22572
804-333-6750
Fax: 804-333-3082

Southwest Virginia Community College
Upward Bound
Upward Bound Math/Science
Karen Hudson
Buchanan Hall, Box SVCC
Richlands, VA 24641-1510
703-964-2555, ext. 315
Fax: 703-964-7579

University Of Virginia's College At Wise
Teresa Adkins
One College Avenue
Wise, VA 24293
540-328-0175
Fax: 540-376-1098
Email: tah7a@mail.wise.virginia.edu

Virginia Highlands Community College
Mimi Hull
P.O. Box 828
Abingdon, VA 24212-0828
540-676-5484
Fax: 540-676-5591

Virgin Islands
University of the Virgin Islands
Upward Bound Program
Rosalia Rhymer-Rohan
#2 Brewers Bay, Charlotte Amalie
St. Thomas, VI 00802-9990
340-693-1133
Fax: 340-693-1131
Email: rrohan@gecko.uvi.edu

Washington
Columbia Basin College
Upward Bound
Susan Vega
2600 N. 20th Ave.
Pasco, WA 99301
509-547-0511
Fax: 509-546-0401

South Seattle Community College
Upward Bound
Brian Sturdivant
6000-16th Ave., SW
Seattle, WA 98106-1499
206-768-6676
Fax: 206-764-6692
Email: ahayden@sccd.ctc.edu

The Evergreen State Colleges
Upward Bound
Deborah Walker
2700 Evergreen Parkway, NW
Library Building, Room 2211
Olympia, WA 98505
360-866-6000, ext. 6028
Fax: 360-866-6794
Email: walkerd@elwha.evergreen.edu

North Seattle Community College
Upward Bound
Ben Wright
9600 College Way, North
Seattle, WA 98103
206-527-7762
Fax: 206-527-3692
Email: bwright@sccd.ctc.edu

Metropolitan Development Council
Upward Bound
Michaael Paulson

12108 S. Pacific
Tacoma, WA 98447
206-725-3921
Fax: 206-725-6779

University of Washington
Upward Bound
Karen Morell
PC-45
Seattle, WA 98195-5845
206-543-9288
Fax: 206-685-2457
Email: kmorell@u.washington.edu

City of Seattle
Upward Bound
Mary Ellen Vinson
618 Second Ave., 5th Floor
Seattle, WA 98104-2222
206-386-1189
Fax: 206-386-1138
Email: maryellen.vinson@ci.seattle.wa.us

Big Bend Community College
Upward Bound
Patrick Palmerton
7662 Chanute, Bldg. #1400
Moses Lake, WA 98837-3299
509-762-5351
Fax: 509-762-6329

Yakima Valley Community College
Upward Bound Program
Marc Coomer
P.O. Box 22520
Yakima, WA 98907
509-574-6886
Fax: 509-574-6885
Email: mcoomer@yvcc.cc.wa.us

West Virginia
Concord College
Upward Bound
Pamela McPeak
Campus Box 41
P.O. Box 1000
Athens, WV 24712-1000
304-384-6036
Fax: 304-384-9044

Davis and Elkins College
Upward Bound
Carol Suder-Howes
100 Campus Dr.
Elkins, WV 26241
304-637-1989
Fax: 304-637-1428
Email: cshowes@dne.edu

Davis and Elkins College
Veterans Upward Bound
Michael Fisher
100 Campus Dr.
Elkins, WV 26241
304-637-1257
Fax: 304-637-1428
Email: mfisher@dne.edu

Potomac State College of West Virginia University
Upward Bound
Todd Stoops
101 Fort Ave.
Keyser, WV 26726
304-788-6963
Fax: 304-788-6848
Email: tstoops@wvu.edu

Salem-Teikyo University
Upward Bound Program
Rob Freedlander
223 W. Main St.
Salem, WV 26426
304-782-5520

Fax: 304-782-5592
Email: freedlander@salem.wvnet,.edu

Marshall University Multicultural Affairs
Upward Bound
Jacquelyn Hersman
126 Prichard Hall
Huntington, WV 25755
304-696-6846
Fax: 304-696-6565
Email: hersman@marshall.edu

Bluefield State College
Veterans Upward Bound
Ron Holt
219 Rock St.
Bluefield, WV 24701
304-327-4030
Fax: 304-327-4427

West Virginia State College
Upward Bound
Barbara Cary
P.O. Box 100
Campus Box 172
Institute, WV 25112-1000
304-766-3058
Fax: 304-766-5122

West Virginia Institute of Technology
Upward Bound
Beverly Wattie
Box 52
Learning Center
Montgomery, WV 25136
304-442-3196
Fax: 304-442-1033

Concord College
Upward Bound Math/Science
Darrell Taylor
Campus Box 41
P.O. Box 1000
Athens, WV 24712
304-384-6074
Fax: 304-384-6037
Email: tayloub@concord.edu

West Virginia University
Anita Mayer
POB 2612UASC
Morgantown, WV 26506
304-293-3998
Fax: 304-293-7435

Wisconsin
Beloit College
Upward Bound
Robert Obrohta
700 College St.
Beloit, WI 53511-5595
608-363-2725
Fax: 608-363-2718
Email: obrohtar@beloit.edu

University of Wisconsin/Green Bay
Upward Bound
Cassandra Nicholson
2420 Nicolet Dr.
SS 1929
Green Bay, WI 54311-7001
920-465-2671
Fax: 920-465-2954

Northland College
Upward Bound
Joseph Maday
1411 Ellis Ave.
Ashland, WI 54806
715-682-4531
Fax: 715-682-1693
Email: jmaday@wheeler.northland.edu

University of Wisconsin Centers
Upward Bound
Nancy Harrison
UWC-Manitowoc County
705 Viebahn St.
Manitowoc, WI 54220-6699
920-683-4705
Fax: 920-683-4776
Email: nharriso@uwcmail.uwc.edu

Marquette University
Upward Bound
Kevin Ingram
1217 W. Wisconsin Ave., Room 409
Milwaukee, WI 53233
414-288-7368
Fax: 414-288-1769
Email: kevin.ingram@marquette.edu

University of Wisconsin/La Crosse
Upward Bound
Sara Bentley
Wilder Hall
La Crosse, WI 54601
608-785-8539
Fax: 608-785-8757
Email: bcntley@mail.uwlax.edu

Milwaukee School of Engineering
Upward Bound
Donald Ashby
1025 North Broadway
Milwaukee, WI 53201
414-277-7261
Fax: 414-277-7498

University of Wisconsin/Eau Claire
Upward Bound
Kimamo Wahome
281 Fine Arts
105 Garfield Ave.
Eau Claire, WI 54701
715-836-4088
Fax: 715-836-5983
Email: wahomek@uwec.edu

St. Norbert College
Upward Bound
Bridgit Couture
100 Grant St., Pac 108
De Pere, WI 54115
920-403-1349

Fax: 920-403-1325
Email: coutba@sncac.edu

College Of Menominee Nation
Veterans Upward Bound
Alan Caldwell
P.O. Box 1179
Keshena, WI 54135
715-799-5602
Fax: 715-799-1326
Email: acaldwell@menominee.com

Marquette University
Upward Bound Math/Science
Kevin Ingram
1217 West Wisconsin Avenue, Room 409
Milwaukee, WI 53233
414-288-7368
Fax: 414-288-1769
Email: kevin.ingram@marquette.edu

Northcentral Technical College
Dot Kalmon
1000 W. Campus Drive
Wausau, WI 54401
715-675-3331, ext. 4566
Fax: 715-675-9776
Email: kalmon@northcentral.tec.wi.us

University Of Wisconsin–Green Bay
Upward Bound Math/Science
Michael Casbourne
2420 Nicolet Drive
Green Bay, WI 54311-7001
920-465-2671
Fax: 920-465-2954

University Of Wisconsin–Milwaukee
Veterans Upward Bound
Ketmani Kouanchao
324 Johnston Hall
P.O. Box 413
Milwaukee, WI 53201
414-229-6799
Fax: 414-229-2859
Email. ketmani@uwm.edu

Upward Bound Math/Science
David Camacho
324 Johnston Hall
P.O. Box 413
Milwaukee, WI 53201

414-229-5399
Fax: 414-229-2859

University Of Wisconsin–River Falls
Linda L. Bentz
410 South 3rd Street
127 WEB
River Falls, WI 54022
715-425-3774
Fax: 715-425-0622
Email: linda.bentz@uwrf.edu

University Of Wisconsin–Stevens Point
Henry Wojnicki
202 Student Services Center
Stevens Point, WI 54481-3897
715-346-3337
Fax: 715-346-3957

University Of Wisconsin–Superior
Vince Repesh
Belknap & Catlin
P.O. Box 2000
Superior, WI 54880
715-394-8219
Fax: 715-394-8107
Email: vrepesh@uwsuper.edu

University Of Wisconsin–Whitewater
Elizabeth Ogunsola
800 West Main Street
321 McCutchen Hall
Whitewater, WI 53190
262-472-1119
Fax: 262-472-2794
Email: ogunsola@uwwvax.uww.edu

Wyoming
University of Wyoming/Laramie
Upward Bound Math/Science
Manuel Gallegas
P.O. Box 3808
Laramie, WY 82071-3808
307-766-4121
Fax: 307-766-4010
Email: mangal@uwyo.edu

Central Wyoming College
Roena Stone
2600 Peck Avenue
Riverton, WY 82501
307-855-2186
Fax: 307-855-2065

Free Training for Parents
To Make Them Better at Doing Homework

Program: Even Start — 84.213

Description: We all want to be better parents, and the U.S. Department of Education wants that, too. It gives money to hundreds of programs across the country that show parents how to become more involved in their children's education. The idea here is that the more involved parents become, the better education their kids will get — more reading at home, more attention to homework assignments, etc. The program is called Even Start, and it focuses on parents of children up through seven years old.

What You Can Get: Even Start is a family literacy program that integrates early childhood education and adult literacy training. It provides adult basic education, including helping parents learn to read or teach English as a second language. It also integrates parenting education with early childhood education. The goal is for parents to become full partners in their child's education and help kids reach their full potential.

Who Is Eligible: The programs are run year round and are open to families eligible for adult basic education, which includes English as a second language and those who have limited reading and writing skills. Child care is provided when parents are taking separate classes. Even Start programs are located in Chapter 1 school districts, which are areas that have predominately low income residents.

Money Available: Even Start has a budget of $102,024,000.

National Office:
Even Start
U.S. Department of Education
600 Independence Ave., SW, Room 4400
Washington, DC 20202-6132
202-260-0958

Local Offices:
Below is a listing of the 50 or so state coordinators for Even Start programs across the country. By contacting the coordinator in your state, you'll be given the name of the Even Start programs serving your local area.

Alabama
Saundra Gwinn
State Department of Education
50 North Ripley St.
Montgomery, AL 36130-3901
334-242-8167

Alaska
Kathi Wineman
Education Program Specialist
State Department of Education
801 W. 10th St., Suite 200
Juneau, AK 99801-1894
907-465-8706

Arizona
June Torrance
Director, Chapter 1 ESEA
State Department of Education
1535 West Jefferson
Phoenix, AZ 85007
602-542-5235

Arkansas
Shirley Thomas
Coordinator, Chapter 1, ESEA
State Department of Education
Arch Ford Education Building
Little Rock, AR 72201
501-682-4847

California
Sallie L. Wilson
State Department of Education
721 Capitol Mall, 2nd Floor
P.O. Box 944272
Sacramento, CA 95814
916-654-6369

Colorado
Paul Johnson
Even Start Coordinator
State Department of Education
201 East Colfax Ave.
Denver, CO 80203
303-866-6860

Connecticut
Judy Carson
State Department of Education
25 Industrial Park Rd.
Middletown, CT 06457
203-638-4222

Delaware
Frances Tracy-Mumford
State Supervisor
State Department of Public Instruction
P.O. Box 1402
Dover, DE 19903
302-739-4681

District of Columbia
Maurice Sykes
SEA/LEA Operations and Special Programs
Logan Administrative Bldg.
215 G St., NE
Washington, DC 20002
202-724-4099

Florida
Patty Ball-Thomas
State Department of Education
325 West Gains, Suite 754
Tallahassee, FL 32399-0400
904-922-0034

Georgia
Mary Murphy
State Department of Education
1962 Twin Towers East
Atlanta, GA 30334-5040
404-656-0476

Hawaii
Elaine Takenaka
Special Programs Management Section
3430 Leahi Ave.
Honolulu, HI 96817
808-735-9024

Idaho
Zan Payne
State Department of Education
Len B. Jordan Office Building
P.O. Box 83720
Boise, ID 83720-0027
208-334-2196

Illinois
Kay Henderson
Manager
Early Childhood Education
State Board of Education
100 North First St. (E-228)
Springfield, IL 62777
217-524-4835

Indiana
Donna Marks
Room 229 State House
State Department of Education
Indianapolis, IN 46204
317-232-0540

Iowa
Susan Andersen
Early Childhood Consultant
State Department of Education
Grimes State Office Building
Des Moines, IA 50319-0146
515-281-4747

Kansas
Norma Cregan
State Department of Education
120 East 10th St.
Topeka, KS 66612
913-296-4906

Kentucky
Annette Bridges
Division of Primary Education
500 Mero St.
Capital Plaza Tower
Frankfort, KY 40601
502-564-3064

Louisiana
Debi Faucette
Program Manager
ESEA, Chapter 1
654 Main St., 3rd Floor
State Department of Education
Baton Rouge, LA 70801
504-342-3336

Maine
Jackie Thoroughman
Division of Compensatory Education
State Department of Education
State House Station #23
Augusta, ME 04333-0019
207-287-5854

Maryland
Ronald E. Friend, Chief
Compensatory Education Branch
State Department of Education
200 West Baltimore St.
Baltimore, MD 21201
410-767-0286

Massachusetts
Arlene Dale
Director, Early Learning
Massachusetts State Department of Education
350 Main St.
Malden, MA 02148
617-388-3300 ext. 378

Michigan
Mike McGraw
Compensatory Education Programs
State Department of Education
P.O. Box 30008
608 West Allegan St.
Lansing, MI 48909
517-335-4859

Minnesota
Bonnie Griffiths
State Department of Education
873 Capitol Square Building
550 Cedar St.
St. Paul, MN 55101
612-296-2181

Mississippi
Rita Lane
Division of Compensatory Education
State Department of Education
P.O. Box 771
Jackson, MS 39205
601-359-3499

Missouri
Delores Beck
Supervisor of Special Federal Programs
P.O. Box 480
Jefferson City, MO 65102-0480
314-751-9437

Montana
Joan Morris
ESEA Chapter 1/Even Start Specialist
Office of Public Instruction
State Capitol
P.O. Box 202501
Helena, MT 59620-2501
406-444-3083

Nebraska
Harriet Egertson
Administrator, Office of Child Development
State Department of Education
301 Centennial Mall South
Box 94987
Lincoln, NE 68509-4987
402-471-3184

Nevada
Roy Casey
Federal Programs Consultant
State Department of Education
700 E. 5th St.
Carson City, NV 89710
702-687-3187

New Hampshire
Jane Weissman
Chapter 1 Consultant
State Department of Education
101 Pleasant St.
Concord, NH 03301
603-271-3776

New Jersey
Mary Guess Flamer
State Department of Education
CN 500
Trenton, NJ 08625-0500
609-633-6892

New Mexico
Ann Trujillo
State Department of Education
300 Don Gaspar
Santa Fe, NM 87501
505-827-6692

New York
Barbara Shay
Adult and Family Education
State Department of Education
307 EB
Albany, NY 12234
518-474-5808

North Carolina
Susan Reilly
Early Childhood Team
State Department of Public Instruction
301 North Wilmington St.
Raleigh, NC 27601
919-715-1845

North Dakota
Leila Norris
Adult Education
State Department of Public Instruction
State Capitol Building, 9th Fl.
Bismarck, ND 58505
701-328-4646

Ohio
Connie Ackerman
Educational Consultant
State Department of Education
933 High St.
Worthington, OH 43085
614-466-4161

Oklahoma
Lawana Kunze
Administrator, Even Start
State Department of Education
2500 North Lincoln Blvd.
Oklahoma City, OK 73105
405-521-2846

Oregon
Anita McClanahan
Early Childhood Education
State Department of Education
255 Capitol St. NE
Salem, OR 97310-0203
503-378-5585, ext. 665

Pennsylvania

Donald Paquette
Division of Early Childhood and Family
Education
333 Market St., 5th Fl.
Harrisburg, PA 17126-0333
717-772-2813

Puerto Rico

Eileen Loiz-Reyes
Chapter 1 & 2 State Coordinator
Department of Education
P.O. Box 190759
San Juan, PR 00919-0759
809-759-8910

Rhode Island

Charlotte Diffendale
Literacy Division
22 Hayes St.
Providence, RI 02908
401-277-2705, ext. 2138

South Carolina

Peggy May
Literacy Resource Center
State Department of Education
Rutledge Office Bldg.
1722 Main St., Suite 104
Columbia, SC 29201
803-929-2573

South Dakota

Betsy Pollock
Department of Education
Richard F. Kneip Bldg.

700 Governors Dr.
Pierre, SD 57501-2291
605-773-4640

Tennessee

Jeannie Bellephant
Tennessee Department of Education
Office of Special Programs
5th Floor, Gateway Plaza
Nashville, TN 37243-0375
615-741-7054

Texas

Ramona Jo DeValcourt
Adult and Community Education
Texas Education Agency
1701 North Congress Ave.
Austin, TX 78701
512-463-9294

Utah

Marilyn Treshow
Department of Education
250 East 500 South St.
Salt Lake City, UT 84111
801-538-7565

Vermont

Jennifer Howard
State Department of Education
120 State St.
Montpelier, VT 05620
802-828-2753

Virginia

Cheryl Strobel

State Department of Education
101 N. 14th St.
James Monroe Bldg., 20th Fl.
Richmond, VA 23219
804-371-7578

Washington

Mary Carr
Supervisor of Early Childhood
Education/Child Care/Even Start
P.O. Box 47200
Olympia, WA 98504
360-586-2263

West Virginia

Sharon Flack
State Department of Education
Building No. 6, Rm. 330
1900 Canola Blvd. E.
Charleston, WV 25305
304-558-7805

Wisconsin

Darcy Wirebaugh
125 S. Webster St.
P.O. Box 7841
Madison, WI 53707
608-267-9146

Wyoming

Roger Hammer
Coordinator, Chapter 1
State Department of Education
Hathaway Bldg., 2nd Fl.
2300 Capital Ave.
Cheyenne, WY 82002-0050
307-777-7633

"If we have anything to worry about legitimately, it is less the opportunities than our capacity to equip people to take advantage of these opportunities."

Source: *The New Rules: How to Succeed in Today's Post-Corporate World*, John P. Potter, Free Press, 1995

I Wanna Fix Up
My Neighborhood

Matthew Lesko, Information USA, Inc., 12081 Nebel Street, Rockville, MD 20852 • 1-800-955-7693 • www.lesko.com

Federal Empowerment Zones Offer Jobs, Job Training and Small Business Help

Each year, the Federal government awards billions of dollars in grant money and low interest loans to communities and nonprofit groups that want to rebuild their neighborhoods. And what makes it even better, if your community falls within a federally designated Empowerment Zone (EZ), your community will actually receive a special preference when you apply for any grant money.

What exactly is an Empowerment or Enterprise Zone? They are specific geographic areas that typically have high unemployment, low incomes, and show a great need for financial and technical help in tackling chronic economic problems. In the case of Empowerment Zones, the Federal government has designated over 100 such areas that require large amounts of money to get things moving in a positive direction.

Entrepreneurs Can Use Empowerment/Enterprise Zones

If you want to start a business, look at starting one in these zones. Just by committing a business to one of these zones, you can get special breaks from the Federal government such as:

- $3,000 tax credit for hiring or training Empowerment Zone employees
- $20,000 additional write offs for tangible property expenses
- low rate tax exempt bond financing

Job Seekers Can Take Advantage of Empowerment/Enterprise Zones

If a business is going to get $3,000 in tax breaks just to train you, job seekers should look at businesses in these zones for ready and available employment. If you don't have the skills employers want to hire you, you can show them where they can get money to train you for free.

There are also a number of employment training programs that will give special consideration if the job seeker lives in one of these zones. The programs that fit this category and are described in detail in this chapter include:

- Money to Provide Poor Kids with Special Job Training
- Money to Train Poor Adults for New Jobs
- Money for Summer Jobs for Poor Kids
- Money to Train Poor Kids in New Job Skills
- Money to Set Up Job Information Centers
- Money to Train High School Dropouts

Fix Up Your Neighborhood

In addition to helping yourself and your business, you can also help your neighborhood. Remember, that's the main reason for the programs. Be sure that your elected officials and local organizations know how to take full advantage of these programs. You might even be able to educate a politician about money he didn't even know existed!

Once an area has been designated by the Federal government as an Empowerment Zone, it becomes eligible to receive special preferences when applying for federal money to help rebuild the area. The federal funding programs outlined in this section provide communities with money to achieve hundreds of different goals, including:

- job training
- summer jobs for kids
- making schools safer
- child care for the poor
- rebuilding public utilities
- drug reduction programs
- environmental cleanup
- low income housing loans
- lead poisoning reduction
- community bank investment
- getting rid of noisy airplanes
- keeping kids out of gangs
- building a local health information database
- helping the homeless

List of Empowerment/Enterprise Zones

Empowerment Zones

Urban Empowerment Zones
Atlanta, GA
Baltimore, MD
Chicago, IL
Detroit, MI
New York, NY
Philadelphia, PA
Camden, NJ

Urban Supplemental Zones
Los Angeles, CA
Cleveland, OH

Rural Empowerment Zones
Kentucky Highlands (Clinton, Jackson, Wayne Counties, KY)
Mid-Delta Mississippi (Bolivar, Holmes, Humphreys, Leflore Counties, MS)
Rio Grande Valley Texas (Cameron, Hidalgo, Starr, Willacy Counties, TX)

Urban Enhanced Enterprise Communities
Boston, MA
Houston, TX
Kansas City, KS - Kansas City, MO
Oakland, CA

Urban and Rural Enterprise Communities

Alabama
Rural: Chambers County, Greene and Sumter Counties
Urban: Birmingham

Arizona
Rural: Arizona Border Region (Cochise, Santa Cruz, and Yuma Counties)
Urban: Phoenix

Arkansas
Rural: Mississippi County, Eastern Arkansas (Cross, Lee, Monrow, and St. Francis County)
Urban: Pulaski County

California
Rural: Imperial County, City of Watsonville (Santa Cruz County)
Urban: Los Angeles (South Central/Huntington Park), San Diego, San Francisco (Hunters Point)

Colorado
Urban: Denver

Connecticut
Urban: Bridgeport

Delaware
Urban: Wilmington

District of Columbia
Urban: Washington

Florida
Rural: Jackson County
Urban: Dade County/Miami, Tampa

Georgia
Rural: Crisp and Dooly Counties, Central Savannah River Area (Burke, Hancock, Jefferson, McDuffie, Taliaferro, and Warren Counties)
Urban: Albany

Illinois
Urban: East St. Louis, Springfield

Indiana
Urban: Indianapolis

Iowa
Urban: Des Moines

Kentucky
Rural: McCreary County
Urban: Louisville

Louisiana
Rural: Northeast Louisiana Delta (Madison County), Macon Ridge (Catahoula, Concordia, Franklin, Morehouse, and Tensas County)
Urban: Ouachita Parish

Massachusetts
Urban: Lowell, Springfield

Michigan
Rural: Lake County
Urban: Flint, Muskegon

Minnesota
Urban: Minneapolis, St. Paul

Mississippi
Rural: North Delta (Panola, Quitman, and Tallahatchie Counties)
Urban: Jackson

Missouri
Rural: City of East Prairie (Mississippi County)
Urban: St. Louis

Nebraska
Urban: Omaha

Nevada
Urban: Clark County/Las Vegas

New Hampshire
Urban: Manchester

New Jersey
Urban: Neward

New Mexico
Rural: Mora, Taos, and Rio Ariba Counties
Urban: Albuquerque

New York
Urban: Albany, Buffalo, Newburgh-Kingston, Rochester

North Carolina
Rural: Halifax, Edgecombe, and Wilson Counties
Urban: Charlotte

Ohio
Rural: Greater Portsmouth (Scioto County)
Urban: Akron

Oklahoma
Rural: Southeast Oklahoma (Choctaw and McCurtain Counties)
Urban: Oklahoma City

Oregon
Rural: Josephine County
Urban: Portland

Pennsylvania
Rural: City of Lock Haven (Clinton County)
Urban: Harrisburg

Rhode Island
Urban: Providence

South Carolina
Rural: Williamsburg County and Lake City (Florence and Williamsburg Counties)
Urban: Charleston

South Dakota
Rural: Beadle and Spink Counties

Tennessee
Rural: Fayette and Haywood Counties, Scott County
Urban: Memphis Nashville

Texas
Urban: Dallas, El Paso, San Antonio, Waco

Utah
Urban: Ogden

Vermont
Urban: Burlington

Virginia
Rural: Accomack and Northampton Counties
Urban: Norfolk

Washington
Rural: Lower Yakima County
Urban: Seattle, Tacoma

West Virginia
Central Appalachia (Braxton, Clay, Fayette, Nicholas, and Roane Counties)
Urban: Huntington

Wisconsin
Urban: Milwaukee

Who To Contact For Further Information

Community Connections
P.O. Box 7189
Gaithersburg, MD 20898-7189
800-998-9999

Empowerment/Enterprise Zone Programs

For each program, you'll find the following information:

- Program title: this is the official title of the grant program used by officials in Washington, D.C.
- Contact person: this is the person designated by a particular agency to handle questions about a specific program.
- Telephone number: use this number to get more information on how to apply for these money programs.
- Program description: offers a brief explanation of what the money is used for.
- Type of preference: describes what kind of special consideration Empowerment Zone communities receive when applying for programs.
- Program amount: gives amount federal government has to spend each year on a program.

Individual states have their own Enterprise Zone programs, and among all 50 states, there are over 1,000 areas that have been targeted to receive special financial awards to help in their redevelopment efforts. Following this section of the federal redevelopment programs for Empowerment Zones, you will find a state-by-state listing of programs designed to help communities redevelop. But first, see what's available from the Federal government:

* General Development Grants
(Community Development Block Grant Program)
HUD Building
Block Grant Assistance, CPD
U.S. Department of Housing and Urban Development
451 7th St., SW, Room 7282
Washington, DC 20410   202-708-1577
or
Zita Blankenship, rural areas
HUD Building
Block Grant Assistance, CPD
U.S. Department of Housing and Urban Development
451 7th St., SW, Room 7184
Washington, DC 20410   202-708-1322

Annual formula grants to entitled metropolitan cities and urban counties and to states for distribution to nonentitled communities. The program allows these entities to carry out a wide range of community development activities directed toward neighborhood revitalization, economic development, and improved community facilities and services.
Type of Preference: States may give priority for Empowerment Zone/Enterprise Community small cities. Entitlement communities may also target funds received to designated areas.
Program Amount: $4.6 billion.

* Money for Drug and Violence Prevention Programs in Schools
(Safe and Drug-Free Schools and Communities)
Bill Modzeleski
U.S. Department of Education
4000 Portals Building
600 Independence Ave., SW
Washington, DC 20202-6123   202-260-3954

The current Drug Free Schools and Communities Program is the Federal government's major effort in the area of drug and violence and education and prevention. The program targets resources where they are most needed. States will receive 50 percent of their funds based on the Title I formula; the other 50 percent will be based on their school age population and states will determine criteria for selecting high need local educational agencies (LEAs) and target funds to these districts. States and local communities continue to have the primary role in developing and implementing drug and violence prevention and education programming. The Department of Education will provide national leadership in the areas of drug and violence prevention through information, technical assistance evaluation efforts, and direct loans.

In addition, the Safe and Drug Free Schools Communities Act authorizes state grants for Drug and Violence Prevention Programs which provide funding to state and local educational agencies as well as governors. The new program authorizes a broader range of prevention activities. Newly authorized activities include mentoring, comprehensive health education, community service and character education, acquisition of metal detectors, and hiring of security personnel. States and local educational agencies will still be required to assess needs and measure program outcomes and use this information to formulate policies and program initiatives. A new national evaluation system will be established to assess the impact of the program.
Type of Preference: none
Program Amount: Estimated to be $565 million for the entire program.

* Money for Urban Colleges to Help in Redevelopment
(Urban Community Service Program)
Sarah Babson
Center for International Education
U.S. Department of Education
600 Independence Ave., SW
Washington, DC 20202-5247   202-260-3472

The Urban Community Service Program provides grants to urban institutions of higher education (IHEs) to assist projects designed to encourage the use of urban IHEs as sources of skills, talents, and knowledge that can serve the urban areas in which they are located. Grants are made for planning activities, applied research, training, resource exchanges or technology transfers, delivery of services, and activities to design and implement programs to assist urban communities to meet and address their pressing and most severe problems. In awarding the grants, priority is given to applications proposing joint projects with existing local, state and federal programs.
Type of Preference: Priority to Empowerment Zones/Enterprise Communities.
Program Amount: $1.5 million.

* Money to Lend to Others
(Community Development Financial Institutions)
Mark Bender
HUD Building
U.S. Department of Housing and Urban Development
451 7th St., SW, Room 7136
Washington, DC 20410   202-622-0201

Proposed legislation would provide funding for Community Development Banks and other community development financial institutions to provide money for development in financially underserved areas.

Type of Preference: Language in legislative proposal would give priority to CDBs serving Empowerment Zones/Enterprise Communities.
Program Amount: $382 million proposed over 4 years.

* Money to Develop New Housing and Businesses

(John Heinz Neighborhood Development Program)
Stella Hall
American Communities
P.O. Box 7189   202-708-2186
Gaithersburg, MD 20898-7189   800-998-9999

Under this program, U.S. Department of Housing and Urban Development funds community based organizations to increase their capacity to carry out housing and community development activities and to achieve long term financial support for these activities. The activities must benefit low and moderate income persons within the neighborhood. Eligible activities are those which will:
- create permanent jobs in the neighborhood;
- establish or expand businesses within the neighborhood, such as a business incubator program;
- develop new housing;
- rehabilitate existing housing;
- manage housing stock within the neighborhood;
- deliver essential services with lasting benefit to neighborhoods;
- plan or finance voluntary neighborhood improvement efforts.

Type of Preference: Competitive preference for Empowerment Zones/ Enterprise Communities.
Program Amount: $5 million.

* Help in Planning Health Care Services

(Rural Health Technical Assistance)
Jerry Coopey
Office of Rural Health
5600 Fishers Lane, Room 9-05
Rockville, MD 20857   301-443-0835

Support to empower designated rural Empowerment Zones/Enterprise Communities through leadership training, strategic planning, and health systems development.
Type of Preference: Preference for rural Empowerment Zone/Enterprise Community designees.
Program Amount: Technical Assistance.

* Money to Help Create New Jobs

(Urban and Rural Community Economic Development Priority Area)
Joseph Carroll
Administration for Children and Families
Office of Community Services
370 L'Enfant Promenade, SW
Washington, DC 20447   202-401-9346

Grants to private locally initiated nonprofit community development corporations to support business development activities which create employment opportunities for low income people. Funds are used by grantees to develop job creation projects through business, physical or commercial development. More generally, they are used to improve the quality of the economic and social environment of low income residents including displaced workers, at-risk teenagers, public housing residents, and homeless individuals.
Type of Preference: Weighted consideration for serving Empowerment Zones/Enterprise Communities and Empowerment Zone/Enterprise Community eligible areas.
Program Amount: $21.834 million.

* Money for Drug Abuse Prevention Programs

(Substance Abuse Prevention Demonstrations)
Kent Auguston
Center for Substance Abuse Prevention
5600 Fishers Lane
Rockwall Building 2, Room 9D10
Rockville, MD 20857   301-443-0365

Grants to states, local governments, and nonprofit and for-profit entities for substance abuse prevention demonstration projects. Grants will support development and assessment of innovative models for addressing high risk youth and community-wide approaches to substance abuse preventions, including community partnerships in managed care settings, and linkages with primary care programs and programs such as HEAD Start.
Type of Preference: Weighted consideration for serving Empowerment Zones/Enterprise Communities and Empowerment Zone/Enterprise Community eligible areas.
Program Amount: $42.0 million.

* Money to Help Improve Your School

(Community Schools Program)
Terry Lewis

Family and Youth Services
U.S. Department of Health and Human Services
300 C St., SW
Washington, DC 20201   202-205-8102

Funds consortia of community-based organizations, schools, and others to develop neighborhood strategies to curb violence and promote positive academic and social achievement. Grants will be awarded in every state.
Type of Preference: Weighted consideration for serving Empowerment Zones/Enterprise Communities and Empowerment Zone/Enterprise Community eligible areas.
Program Amount: $25.9 million.

* Money for Food Programs

(Community Food and Nutrition Program)
Joseph Carroll
Administration for Children and Families
Office of Community Services
370 L'Enfant Promenade, SW
Washington, DC 20447   202-401-9346

Grants to states, public agencies, and private nonprofit organizations to coordinate existing food assistance resources, assist in identifying sponsors of child nutrition programs and to develop innovative approaches for meeting the nutrition needs of low income people. Health prevention is an important element of this program.
Type of Preference: Weighted consideration for serving Empowerment Zones/Enterprise Communities and Empowerment Zone/Enterprise Community eligible areas.
Program Amount: $4 million.

Early Childhood
Development Programs

* Money for Child Care Programs for Parents in Public Housing

(Early Child Care Program)
Maggie Taylor
U.S. Department of Housing and Urban Development
Room 7262, 451 7th St., SW
Washington, DC 20410   202-708-4300

Child care program for parents of children living in or near public housing, including parents who are homeless or are at risk of being homeless. Funds for a section of this program are administered through a joint memorandum of understanding between U.S. Department of Housing and Urban Development and U.S. Department of Health and Human Services. A portion of the U.S. Department of Housing and Urban Development-administered funds are targeted toward homeless families.
Type of Preference: Preference for Empowerment Zones/Enterprise Communities.
Program Amount: Funded at $15 million; set aside of $9 million for "homeless" child care.

* Money for Early Childhood Education Programs

(Early Childhood Education)
Ray Miner
U.S. Department of Education
Room 4627, 600 Independence Ave., SW
Washington, DC 20202-6123   202-205-9805

The purpose of the Early Childhood Education program is to improve special education and early intervention services for infants, toddlers, and children with special needs from birth through eight years of age. This group includes infants and toddlers birth through age 2 with developmental delays or conditions that are likely to cause developmental delays, and those at risk of substantial developmental delays if they do not receive early intervention services. Children ages 3 through 8 are also included if they need special education because of a disability. The Early Childhood Education program supports research, development, outreach, technical assistance, and training activities that together constitute a systematic approach for improving services for young children with disabilities. Grants, contracts, and cooperative agreements are authorized to public agencies and private nonprofit and, in some cases, profit organizations.
Type of Preference: Competitive preference for Empowerment Zones/ Enterprise Communities.
Program Amount: $2 million.

* Money for Lead Poisoning Prevention Programs

(Childhood Lead Poisoning Prevention Projects -
State and Community-Based)
David L. Forney
Lead Poisoning Prevention Branch
Centers for Disease Control

4770 Buford Hwy, NE
Mail Stop F-42
Atlanta, GA 30341   404-488-7330

Grants to state governments and local governments serving areas with more than 500,000 people for developing, improving, and expanding their capacity to address the problem of childhood lead poisoning in high-risk populations. Grantees undertake various activities, including lead poisoning screening; medical management to ensure that children exposed to lead receive proper treatment and follow-up services; environmental investigation; program evaluations; and other related activities.

Type of Preference: Weighted consideration for serving Empowerment Zones/Enterprise Communities and Empowerment Zone/Enterprise Community eligible areas.

Program Amount: $7.5 million.

* Learn and Serve (K-12)

(Learn and Serve - K-12)
Hugh Bailey
The Corporation for National and Community Service
1201 New York Ave., NW
Washington, DC 20525

The major purpose of Learn and Serve is to fund school and community based service-lending programs for school age youth via State Education Agencies (SEAs), local school districts, Indian tribes, U.S. Territories, grant making entities, and State Commissions. These programs engage youth in service to their communities to enrich academic learning, promote personal growth, and help youth develop skills needed for productive citizenship.

Type of Preference: Not applicable.

Program Amount: $37.5 million.

Economic Development/ Job Creation Programs

* Money for General Housing and Business Development

(Section 108 Loan Guarantee)
Paul Webster
U.S. Department of Housing and Urban Development
Financial Management Division
451 7th St., SW, Room 7180
Washington, DC 20410   202-708-1871

Under this program, U.S. Department of Housing and Urban Development guarantees notes issued by units of general local government. Section 108 funds may be used to finance a wide array of economic revitalization and development activities that include housing and rehabilitation of privately owned buildings for residential purposes; expansion of for-profit businesses including equipment and physical plant; financing and rehabilitation of low income and public housing; acquisition, construction, or rehabilitation of neighborhood and community facilities; site improvement on community owned land which could be leased to a developer to carry out a commercial or industrial development project; site development including structural removal and land clearing; purchase of land or buildings for any authorized economic development use; and infrastructure development which can include street reconstruction and/or sewer system repairs.

Type of Preference: Set aside of $500 million in loan guarantees for Empowerment Zones/Enterprise Communities.

Program Amount: $2.054 billion in loan guarantee authority.

* Money to Supplement General Development Grant Programs

(Section 108 Economic Revitalization Grants)
Paul Webster
U.S. Department of Housing and Urban Development
Section 108 Loan Guarantee
451 7th St., SW, Room 7180
Washington, DC 20410   202-708-1871

The program provides grants to be used in tandem with Section 108 guaranteed loans for economic revitalization projects located in Empowerment Zones/Enterprise Communities. These grants will enhance the viability of such projects (through interest rate subsidies, debt service/operating reserves, etc.) and increase the likelihood that the Section 108 loans can be repaid from project revenue.

Type of Preference: Set aside of up to $300 million in grants for Empowerment Zones.

Program Amount: $300 million.

* Money and Help for General Community Development Projects

(Community Development Block Grant (CDBG) Program)
U.S. Department of Housing and Urban Development

Block Grant Assistance, CPD
451 7th St., SW, Room 7282
Washington, DC 20410   202-708-1577

or

Zita Blankenship, rural areas
U.S. Department of Housing and Urban Development
Block Grant Assistance, CPD
451 7th St., SW, Room 7282
Washington, DC 20410   202-708-1322

Also see the description of CDBG under "Community Building." CDBG funds may be used to provide direct assistance and technical assistance to for-profit businesses (including microenterprises) and to public and private organizations to facilitate economic development by owners of microenterprises and persons developing microenterprises by providing credit, technical assistance and general support such as peer support programs and counseling. CDBG funds may also be used for business incubators and public infrastructure serving businesses. Special consideration in meeting the programs's targeting requirements for low-and moderate-income benefit will be given to employees who reside in, or businesses that are located in, census tracts that meet the Federal Empowerment Zone/Enterprise Community criteria.

Type of Preference: States may give priority for Empowerment Zone/Enterprise Community small cities. Entitlement communities may also target funds received to designated areas.

Program Amount: $4.6 billion.

* Money and Help for Small Business Owners

(One Stop Capital Shop)
Karen Hontz
Small Business Administration
409 3rd St., SW
Suite 7125
Washington, DC 20416   202-205-6573

Deliver financial, business and technical assistance to small, minority and women-owned businesses through the following components:

- Small Business Lending Companies
- Micro-Enterprise Lenders
- Regular/Specialized Small Business Investment Companies
- Certified Development Companies
- Business Information Centers
- Service Corps of Retired Executives (SCORE)
- Small Business Development Centers

Additional assistance will be provided on federal contracting, surety bonds and SBIR. Also, technical assistance will be provided to minority firms through Small Business Administration's (7)(j) grant programs and to women-owned firms through Small Business Administration's women's demonstration projects.

Type of Preference: Located in Empowerment Zones or Enterprise Communities.

Program Amount: $3.2 billion over 5 years.

* Money for General Small Business Development

(Development Grants (RBEG))
Bonnie S. Justice
U.S. Department of Agriculture
Rural Business and Cooperative Development Service
14th and Independence Ave.
Washington, DC 20250   202-720-1490

The Rural Development Administration assists public bodies and nonprofit corporations to finance and facilitate development of small and emerging private business enterprises located in areas outside the boundary of a city of 50,000 or more and its immediately adjacent urbanized area.

Type of Preference: Set aside for Empowerment Zones/Enterprise Communities.

Program Amount: $9.5 million set aside.

* Money to Help Refinance Community Development Projects

(Intermediary Relending Program)
Pandor H. Hadjy
U.S. Department of Agriculture
Rural Business and Cooperative Development Service
14th and Independence Ave., SW
Washington, DC 20250-3200   202-690-4106

The Rural Development Administration finances business facilities and community development projects not within the outer boundary of any city having a population of 25,000 or more. This is achieved through loans made by the Rural Development Administration to intermediaries that provide loans to ultimate recipients for business facilities and community development projects in a rural area.

Type of Preference: Set aside for Empowerment Zones/Enterprise Communities.

Program Amount: $10 million set aside.

* Money to Improve Roads, Water Projects, Sewers

(Economic Development Administration Public Works Program)
David McIllwain
U.S. Department of Commerce
Economic Development Administration
14th and Constitution Ave., NW
Room 7326
Washington, DC 20230   202-482-5265

Grants are provided to units of government, and public or private nonprofit organizations to help distressed communities attract new industry, encourage business expansion, diversify their economies, and generate long-term, private sector jobs. Among the types of projects funded are water and sewer facilities primarily serving industry and commerce; access roads to industrial sites or parks; port improvements; and business incubator buildings. Proposed project must be located within an Economic Development Administration-designated Redevelopment Area or directly benefit an RA, and must be consistent with an approved Overall Economic Development Program.

Type of Preference: Points added to Empowerment Zones/Enterprise Communities.

Program Amount: $195 million.

* Money to Create Redevelopment Plans

(Title IX Economic Adjustment)
David Witschi
Director of Economic Adjustment Division
Economic Development Administration
U.S. Department of Commerce
14th and Constitution Ave., NW
Washington, DC 20230   202-482-2659

Grants to units of government, and public or private nonprofit organizations to develop and implement local economic adjustment strategies designed to address a serious contraction of their economic base which may have occurred suddenly or over time. The impact on jobs and income must be severe, and actually, or potentially, long term. The economic contraction may be the consequence of increasing global competition, technological innovation, changing consumption patterns, federal actions, such as elimination of trade restrictions and cutbacks in defense spending and natural disasters. Economic Development Administration may provide communities with virtually any of the tools that may be needed, singularly or in combination, to design and/or implement economic adjustment strategies appropriate to the particular circumstances. This flexibility may be used to promote and support the use of innovative approaches to addressing different types of economic adjustment problems. Such tools include construction of public facilities, technical/management assistance, and business development assistance including Revolving Loan Funds.

Type of Preference: Targeted to communities including Empowerment Zone/Enterprise Community eligible communities which meet the dislocation criteria.

Program Amount: $45 million.

* Money To Plan and Implement Economic Development

(Planning Programs for States and Urban Areas)
Luis Bueso
Director of Planning Division
HCHB, Room 7319
Economic Development Administration
U.S. Department of Commerce
14th and Constitution Ave., NW
Washington, DC 20230   202-482-2873

Grants to help economically distressed states, cities, and urban counties undertake significant new economic development planning, policy-making, and implementation efforts. The grants finance the administrative expenses to support significant economic development planning and implementation activities, such as economic analysis, definition of project goals, determination of project opportunities, and formulation and implementation of a development program.

Type of Preference: Points added to Empowerment Zones/Enterprise Communities.

Program Amount: $4.87 million.

* Money to Help Organize Development and Solve Problems

(Local Technical Assistance Program)
Dick Hage
Acting Director of Technical Assistance and Research
HCHB, Room 7315
Economic Development Administration
U.S. Department of Commerce
14th and Constitution Ave., NW
Washington, DC 20230   202-482-4085

Grants designed to assist in solving specific economic development problems, respond to developmental opportunities, and build and expand local organizational capacity in distressed areas.

Type of Preference: Points added to Empowerment Zones/Enterprise Communities.

Program Amount: $1.5 million.

* Money to Guarantee Private Development Loans

(Business and Industry)
Pandor H. Hadjy
U.S. Department of Agriculture
Rural Business and Cooperative Development Service
14th and Independence Ave., SW
Washington, DC 20250-3200   202-690-4106

The Rural Development Administration improves, develops or finances business, industry, and employment and improves the economic and environmental climate in rural communities, including pollution abatement and control. This purpose is achieved through bolstering the existing private credit structure through guarantee of quality loans that will provide lasting community benefits. It is not intended that the guarantee authority will be used for marginal or substandard loans or to "bail out" lenders having such loans. This type of assistance is available only to businesses located outside the boundary of a city with a population of 50,000 or more and its immediately adjacent urbanized area.

Type of Preference: Set aside for Empowerment Zones/Enterprise Communities.

Program Amount: $11 million.

* Money to Develop Technology Outreach Programs

(Manufacturing Extension Partnership (MEP))
Kevin Carr
National Institute of Standards and Technology
Building 301, Room C121
Gaithersburg, MD 20899   301-975-4676

The Manufacturing Extension Partnership (MEP) provides matching grants (50% declining to 33% over 6 years) to nonprofit organizations, states, local governments, universities and community colleges to establish manufacturing technology and outreach centers. Centers provide assistance to small- and medium-sized manufacturing firms in adopting advanced manufacturing methods and technologies. Additionally, MEP provides one-time planning grants to states to develop and/or coordinate state-wide technology infrastructure which provides service to such industries. The ultimate mission of the MEP is to improve U.S. manufacturing competitiveness by providing small businesses access to a national network of technical, business and training resources necessary to become world-class.

Type of Preference: None

Program Amount: $80.1 million.

* Money to Improve Your Community

Richard Saul
Office of Community Services
370 L'Enfant Promenade, SW, Fifth Floor
Washington, DC 20447   202-401-9341

Grants to Community Action Agencies for developing and implementing innovative approaches to address the critical needs of the poor common to a number of communities. Grantees, in partnership with other public and private organizations, develop an array of innovative programs, including homelessness, microenterprise/self-employment, minority youth life skills, case management, teenage pregnancy, and comprehensive integrated services.

Type of Preference: Weighted consideration for service Empowerment Zones/Enterprise Communities and Empowerment Zone/Enterprise Community eligible areas.

Program Amount: $7.977 million.

* Money for You to Open Your Business

(Job Opportunities for Low-Income Individuals)
Nolan Lewis
Office of Community Services
370 L'Enfant Promenade, SW, Fifth Floor
Washington, DC 20447   202-401-5282

Grants to nonprofit organizations (including community development corporations) to demonstrate and evaluate ways to create new employment and business opportunities for AFDC recipients and other low-income individuals. Grantees must develop programs that create new jobs through self-employment/microenterprise, expansion of existing businesses, and/or development of business ventures.

Type of Preference: Weighted consideration for service Empowerment Zones/Enterprise Communities and Empowerment Zone/Enterprise Community eligible areas.

Program Amount: $5.5 million.

Education and Job Linkages

* Money for Training Programs for Students Not Going to College
(School to Work Opportunities)
J.D. Hoye (U.S. Department of Education)
School to Work Program
400 Virginia Ave., SW, Room 210
Washington, DC 20024   202-401-6209
It will assist students in making the transition from school to a good first job in a high skill, high wage career track. Each school-to-work program must include work-based learning activities, school-based learning activities and connecting activities. Communities, through collaboration of secondary and post secondary educators, employers, labor, parents and other key parties, will be responsible for giving youth access to skills and employment opportunities that will launch them on paths leading to high skills, high wage careers.
Type of Preference: Competitive grant programs.
Program Amount: $100 million ($50m U.S. Department of Labor; $50m U.S. Department of Education).

* Money for Training Programs in Poor Urban Areas
(School-to-Work Urban/ Rural Opportunities Grants)
Karen Clark (U.S. Department of Education)
School to Work Program
400 Virginia Ave., SW, Room 210
Washington, DC 20024   202-219-6214
School-to-work Urban/ Rural Opportunities Grants will be awarded on a competitive basis to demonstration projects providing school-to-work opportunities programs aimed at youth residing in high-poverty areas in urban and rural communities.
Type of Preference: Limited to high poverty areas. Coordination between the Empowerment Zone or Enterprise Community activities and the School-to-Work High Poverty grants is encouraged.
Program Amount: $25 million.

* Money to Help Start School To Work Programs
(Federal School-To-Work Implementation Grants to Local Partnership Grants)
Marian Banfield (U.S. Department of Education)
School to Work Program
400 Virginia Ave., SW, Room 210
Washington, DC 20024   202-401-6222
or
Janet Moore (U.S. Department of Labor)
School to Work Program
400 Virginia Ave., SW, Room 210
Washington, DC 20024   202-401-3822
Federal School-to-Work Implementation Grants to Local Partnerships will be competitively awarded to communities that are prepared to undertake a school-to-work program. This program is designed to provide support and funds to communities that have built a sound planning and development base for School-to-Work Opportunities programs and that are ready to begin implementing a local School-to-Work Opportunities program. Local grants are to involve local partners directly and accelerate actual operation of programs nationwide by enrolling significant numbers of school-to-work participants.
Type of Preference: Coordination between the Empowerment Zone or Enterprise Community activities and the Federal School-to-Work Implementation grants is encouraged.
Program Amount: $10-12 million.

Education and Training Programs

* Money for Low-Income Education Programs
(Title I of the Improving America's Schools Act)
Mary Jean LeTendre
U.S. Department of Education
600 Independence Ave., SW
Room 4400 Portals
Washington, DC 20202-6132   202-260-0826
Chapter 1 of the Elementary and Secondary Education Act provides extra instruction to help low-achieving students in low-income areas reach high academic standards. Chapter 1 funds, which are distributed to local educational agencies on a formula basis, can be used for a variety of purposes including coordination of services, mentoring and tutoring programs, and after-school and summer educational activities. Empowerment Zones and Enterprise Communities are encouraged to incorporate these pre-existing Chapter 1 resources in their strategic plans. In addition, pending legislation would create a new authority under this program to carry out demonstration projects that show the most promise of enabling children served under the program to meet challenging state standards. Among the projects that could be funded would be those that demonstrate promising strategies of integration of education services with each other and with health, family and other social services, particularly in Empowerment Zones and Enterprise Communities. State and local educational agencies, other public agencies, nonprofit agencies and consortia of those bodies would be eligible for discretionary grants.
Type of Preference: Pending
Program Amount: $7.2 billion for entire Chapter 1 program.

* Money for Gifted and Talented Student Programs
(Jacob K. Javits Gifted and Talented Students Education Program)
Caroline Warren, OERI
U.S. Department of Education
555 New Jersey Ave., NW
Washington, DC 20202   202-219-2206
Under pending legislation, this program would demonstrate that programs and strategies for gifted and talented students can be used to help all students in a school to achieve their potential and to meet challenging state performance standards. The program would target discretionary grants to schoolwide efforts to provide challenging curricula and enriching instruction (often offered in gifted and talented programs) to all students. At least half of the awards will be given to high poverty schools.
Type of Preference: Competitive preference to Empowerment Zones/Enterprise Communities.
Program Amount: Estimated to be $3 million.

* Access To Training and Education Programs
(Family Investment Centers (FIC))
Marcia Martin
U.S. Department of Housing and Urban Development
Office of Community Relations and Involvement
Room 4112
451 7th St., SW
Washington, DC 20410   202-708-4214
Under FIC, families living in Public and Indian Housing will be provided better access to training and educational opportunities.
Type of Preference: Competitive preference for Empowerment Zones/Enterprise Communities.

* Money to Set Up Literacy Programs at Work
(National Workplace Literacy Program)
Dr. Carol Towey
U.S. Department of Education
Division of Adult Education and Literacy
600 Independence Ave., SW
Washington, DC 20202-7240   202-205-9872
The National Workplace Literacy Program provides assistance for demonstration projects that teach literacy skills needed in the workplace through exemplary education partnerships between (1) business, industry, or labor organizations, and (2) state educational agencies, local educational agencies, institutions of higher education or schools (including area vocational schools, employment and training agencies, or community-based organizations). This program must give priority to applications from partnerships that include small businesses.
Type of Preference: Competitive preference to Empowerment Zones/Enterprise Communities.
Program Amount: No new funding.

* Money to Develop New Programs for the Disabled
(Rehabilitation Act Special Demonstration Projects)
Pamela Martin
Rehabilitation Services Administration
U.S. Department of Education
Washington, DC 20202-2531   202-205-8494
The Special Demonstration projects are designed to establish programs for providing rehabilitation services to expand and improve rehabilitation services to individuals with disabilities. Emphasis is given to providing services to those who are unserved or underserved, and those who are blind or deaf who can benefit from comprehensive services. In addition, projects to increase client choice and other activities are authorized.
Type of Preference: Competitive preference for Empowerment Zones/Enterprise Communities.
Program Amount: $2 million.

* Money for Programs That Create Jobs for the Disabled
(Rehabilitation Act Projects with Industry Program)
Fred Ibister
Rehabilitation Services Administration
U.S. Department of Education
Washington, DC 20202-2531   202-205-9297

The Projects with Industries Program initiates programs to create and expand job and career opportunities for individuals with disabilities in the competitive labor market. Services generally include intake, evaluation, pre-vocational training, job development and placement. Services to employers may include job-site and equipment modification, application of rehabilitation technology, and employee recruitment. Each grantee must develop a Business Advisory Council with representation from private industry, organized labor and individuals with disabilities and their representatives.
Type of Preference: Competitive preference for Empowerment Zones/Enterprise Communities.
Program Amount: $1.7 million.

* Money to Create Public Charter Schools

(Charter Schools)
John Fiegle
U.S. Department of Education
1250 Maryland Ave., SW
Room 4000 Portals Building
Washington, DC 20024   202-260-2671
Pending legislation would create a new authority to fund the planning and start up of public charter schools in states that have passed legislation approving charter school experiments. In these states, most regulatory requirements have been removed, leaving schools free to sharpen their focus, mission and identity. Charter schools are operated by key stakeholders such as teachers and parents. Under the proposal, state educational agencies or local educational agencies would be able to apply for a single grant of up to three years, in partnership with the teachers, parents, or others developing the public charter school. An application could cover any combination of one or more schools.
Type of Preference: Competitive preference
Program Amount: Estimated to be $6 million.

* Learn and Serve America: Higher Education

(Learn and Serve America: Higher Education)
Hugh Bailey
The Corporation for National and Community Service
1201 New York Ave., NW
Washington, DC 20525
This program engages diversity of communities, students, and institutions in service-learning efforts that meet critical needs while enhancing education for citizenship. Higher Education programs address community needs in four key areas: education, public safety, human needs, and environment.
Type of Preference: None
Program Amount: $12.5 million.

* Money for Bilingual Education Programs

(Bilingual Education)
Terry Sullivan
Office of Bilingual Education and Minority Language Affairs
Room 5619 MES, 600 Independence Ave., SW
Washington, DC 20202   202-205-9752
Title VII of the Elementary and Secondary Education Act, also known as the Bilingual Education Act, authorizes three grant competitions to fund discrete programs tailored to the needs of the various client school districts.
Enhancement Grants - Local educational agencies can apply for a grant of two years in order to develop new programs, to enhance existing programs, or to meet the short-term needs of districts that currently have no bilingual programs.
Type of Preference: Competitive
Program Amount: $22.4 million.
System-Wide Grants - These grants are for district-wide programs for applicants with significant concentrations of language minority students. These five-year grants are likely to serve all eligible students in a district.
Type of Preference: Competitive
Program Amount: $17.4 million.
Comprehensive Grants - These grants provide assistance to all eligible students within a single school or small group of schools. Such a grant might be appropriate in districts having concentrations of language minority students in a number of selected schools within a district.
Type of Preference: Competitive
Program Amount: $74.1 million.

* Money to Train Kids in the Construction Industry

(Youthbuild)
Ronald J. Herbert
Office of Community Planning and Development
U.S. Department of Housing and Urban Development
451 7th St., SW, Room 7134
Washington, DC 20410   202-708-2035
The Youthbuild program consists of two parts: planning and implementation grants. The purpose of the program is to expand the supply of permanent affordable housing for homeless and low- and very low-income persons and to provide economically disadvantaged young adults with opportunities to obtain an education, employment skills and meaningful on-site work experiences as a service to their communities.
Type of Preference: Preference points to Empowerment Zones.
Program Amount: $74.1 million.

Employment Programs

* Money to Provide Poor Kids With Special Job Training

(Youth Fair Chance)
Beverly M. Bachemin
U.S. Department of Labor
Room N5637
200 Constitution Ave., NW
Washington, DC 20210   202-219-7674
This program is designed to provide comprehensive employment and training services to youth (14-21 years) and young adults (22-30 years) in high poverty areas of urban and rural communities. The program concentrates resources in small geographic areas to provide an integrated array of services and thereby increases the chances that high-risk youth will find jobs, develop careers and lead productive lives.
Type of Preference: Targeted to high-crime, high-poverty urban and rural areas. Additional points given to applications from Empowerment Zones and Enterprise Communities.
Program Amount: $25 million.

* Money to Train Poor Adults for New Jobs

(Job Training Partnership Act (JTPA) Title II-A,
Adult Training Program)
Dolores Battle
U.S. Department of Labor
Room N4459
200 Constitution Ave., NW
Washington, DC 20210   202-219-6236
This job training program is designed to increase the employability of poor adults. When they are job ready, the program helps them find and keep employment. Funds are provided to states and local areas based on unemployment and poverty levels. A wide range of employment and training services are eligible activities, including: a required skills and services assessment and development of an employment plan, vocational counseling, literacy and basic skills training, occupations skills training (either in classrooms or on the job), job search assistance, job placement and support services.
Type of Preference: Formula to states and localities. (States and localities may provide preference for assistance to Empowerment Zones/Enterprise Communities.)
Program Amount: $1,054.8 billion.

* Money for Summer Jobs for Poor Kids

(Job Training Partnership Act (JTPA) Title II-B,
Summer Youth Employment Program)
Donald Kulick
U.S. Department of Labor
Room N4463, 200 Constitution Ave., NW
Washington, DC 20210   202-219-6236
This program provides grants to states and local areas for summer youth employment programs. Funds are provided to states and local areas based on unemployment and poverty levels. Eligible activities include a wide range of activities that are available during the summer vacation months that enhance basic skills, encourage school completion, provide exposure to the world of work and enhance citizenship skills. These activities include assessment, vocational counseling, basic and remedial education, job skills training (either in classrooms or on-the-job), work experience and limited supportive services.
Type of Preference: Formula to states and localities. (States and localities may provide preference for assistance to Empowerment Zones/Enterprise Communities.)
Program Amount: $867 million.

* Money to Train Poor Kids Job Skills

(Job Training Partnership Act (JTPA), Title II-C,
Youth Training Program)
Josephine Nieves
U.S. Department of Labor
Room N4459, 200 Constitution Ave., NW
Washington, DC 20210   202-219-6236
This program provides grants to states and local areas for job training programs for economically disadvantaged youth. Funds are provided to states and local areas based on unemployment and poverty levels. Eligible activities include: a required skills and services assessment and development of an employment plan, vocational counseling, literacy and basic skills training, occupational skills training (either in classrooms or on-the-job), job search

assistance, job placement, and support services. The program requires that youth be provided with pre-employment and work maturity skills training and work experience combined with skills training.

Type of Preference: Formula to states and localities. (States and localities may provide preference for assistance to Empowerment Zones/Enterprise Communities.)

Program Amount: $598.7 million.

* Money to Set Up Job Information Centers

(One-Stop Career Centers)
Grace Kilbane
U.S. Department of Labor
Room N4470
200 Constitution Ave., NW
Washington, DC 20210   202-219-5257

This is a system of career centers to provide any job seeker, student, or employer with streamlined access to a comprehensive menu of state of the art, user friendly, employment, education and training information and services. These centers will enable workers, students, and employers to access a wide range of high quality information about jobs and careers, labor markets, skill standards, education and training programs, and financing options.

Type of Preference: Special consideration given to proposals for locating centers in Empowerment Zones/Enterprise Communities.

Program Amount: $120 million.

* Money to Train High School Dropouts

(Job Corps, Job Training Partnership Act (JTPA) Title IV)
Peter Rell
U.S. Department of Labor
Room N4510
200 Constitution Ave., NW
Washington, DC 20210   202-219-8550

This is a highly intensive, primarily residential training program for severely disadvantaged youth ages 16 through 21. It is designed to make these youth more responsible citizens, prepared to obtain and hold productive jobs or enroll in vocational and technical schools, junior colleges or other institutions for further education or training. Job Corps is a federally administered program through a network of 108 Job Corps centers (including 2 new centers) located in 44 states, Puerto Rico, and the District of Columbia.

Type of Preference: Targeted to most economically disadvantaged youth. New Job Corps sites will be selected competitively. Additional points will be awarded for sites located in Empowerment Zones and Enterprise Communities.

Program Amount: $1.1 billion.

Environmental Protection Programs

* Money to Develop Recreation Areas and Parks

(Urban Park and Recreation Recovery Program)
Chris Ashley
National Park Service
Recreation Grants Division
800 N. Capitol St., NW, Suite 400
Washington, DC 20020   202-343-3700

Under this program, federal grants are provided to local governments for the rehabilitation of recreation areas and facilities, demonstration of innovative approaches to improve park system management and recreation opportunities, and development of improved recreation planning. Eligible activities include resource and needs assessments, coordination, citizen involvement and planning, and program development activities to encourage public definition of goals.

Recovery Action Program grants have a 50 percent local match requirement to local governments for the development of local park and recreation system recovery plans. They assist local efforts to develop priorities and strategies for overall recreation recovery. State, local and private funds may be used as the nonfederal share of project costs. U.S. Department of Housing and Urban Development CDBG funds are the type of federal funds used for local match. All properties assisted through this program must be open to the public.

Rehabilitation grants are matching capital grants (70% federal and 30% local) to local governments for purpose of rebuilding, remodeling, or expanding existing facilities.

Innovative grants are matching (70% federal and 30% local) to local governments to cover costs of personnel, facilities, equipment, supplies or services designed to demonstrate innovative and cost effective ways to enhance park and recreation opportunities at the neighborhood level. Innovative grant funds may be used to address common problems related to facility operations and the delivery of recreation services.

Type of Preference: Priority to applicants located in Empowerment Zones and Enterprise Communities.

Program Amount: $7.5 million.

* Money to Study Clean Up of Contaminated Land Sites

(Brownfields Economic Redevelopment Initiative)
Superfund
Environmental Protection Agency
401 M St., SW
Washington, DC 20460   800-424-9346

Funding to examine ways to convert contaminated sites to clean, productive uses.

Program Amount: $200,000.

* Money to Show Industries How To Prevent Pollution

(Eco-Industrial Parks and Environmental Technology Initiatives)
EPA's ETI Information Line
Environmental Protection Agency
401 M St., SW, Mail Code 2111
Washington, DC 20460   202-260-2686

Funding to demonstrate how industrial parks can prevent pollution, minimize waste generation, and maximize energy and water efficiency.

Program Amount: $5 million.

* Money to Help Businesses Prevent Pollution

(Pollution Prevention Grants Program)
Lena Hann
Environmental Protection Agency
401 M St., SW
Washington, DC 20460   202-260-2237

This program helps to promote the use of source reduction techniques by businesses. Includes funding for experts to provide on-site technical advice and to assist in the development of source reduction plans, targeting assistance to businesses that lack information, and provide training in source reduction techniques.

Type of Preference: Program favors candidates pursuing multi-media source reduction.

Program Amount: $6 million.

* Money to Study How Pollution Affects Minorities and the Poor

(Environmental Justice Grants Program)
Dr. Clarice Gaylord and Daniel Gogal
Office of Environmental Justice
Environmental Protection Agency
Room 2710, Mail Code 3103
Washington, DC 20460   800-962-6215

Grants to examine the impacts of environmental problems on minority and economically disadvantaged communities.

Program Amount: $3 million.

* General Help With Environmental Problems

(Technical Assistance in Understanding Environmental Problems, Regulations and Permits; Training Environmental Management)
Harriet Tregonning
Environmental Protection Agency
401 M St., SW
Washington, DC 20460   202-260-2778

U.S. Environmental Protection Agency Headquarters and regional office contacts are being provided to applicants and designees who wish to address the environmental protection, health and safety aspects of their Empowerment Zone or Enterprise Community strategic plan. These contacts can provide information on the grants, technical assistance and training opportunities that are available.

Program Amount: variable

Equal Opportunity Programs

* Money to Help Fight Housing Discrimination

(Fair Housing Initiatives Program (FHIP))
Maxine Cunningham
HUD Building
U.S. Department of Housing and Urban Development
451 7th St., SW, Room 5234
Washington, DC 20410   202-708-0800

A competitive funding program that funds public and private nonprofit organizations, state and local government agencies and other public and private groups formulating or carrying out programs to prevent or eliminate discriminatory housing practices.

Type of Preference: Competitive preference for areas unserved or underserved by fair housing enforcement organizations.

Program Amount: $17 million.

* Money to Study Gender Discrimination in Education

(Women's Educational Equity)
Carolyn Andrews
U.S. Department of Education
Women's Educational Equity
600 Independence Ave., SW
Portals Room 4500
Washington, DC 20202-6140   202-260-2670

This program promotes educational equity for girls and women, including those who suffer multiple discrimination based on gender and race, ethnicity, national origin, disability or age. It supports the development of model curricula and teacher training programs designed to help women and girls become active participants in academic fields and careers in which they have been historically under represented. The program supports demonstration and local implementation projects to prevent sexual harassment, increase opportunities for women and girls in nontraditional fields through leadership training and school-to-work transition programs, and help pregnant and parenting teens remain in school, graduate, and prepare their children for preschool. Discretionary grants would be available to public agencies, private nonprofit agencies, organizations and institutions.

Type of Preference: competitive preference for Empowerment Zones/Enterprise Communities.

Program Amount: $3.1 million.

Family Support Programs

* Money to Train Parents of Disabled Parents

(Training Personnel for the Education of Individuals with Disabilities ⬚ Parent Training and Information Center Program [Individuals With Disabilities Education Act, Part D, Section 631(c)])
Jack Tringo
Office of Special Education Programs
U.S. Department of Education
600 Independence Ave., SW
MES Room 3517
Washington, DC 20202   202-205-9032

The purpose of the Parent Training program is to provide training and information centers for parents of children with disabilities and persons who work with parents to enable them to participate more effectively with professionals in meeting the educational and early intervention needs of children with disabilities.

Awards are made to private, nonprofit organizations that have governing boards or committees that have a majority of members who are parents of children with disabilities and that include professionals in the fields of special education and early intervention.

Type of Preference: Competitive preference for Empowerment Zones/Enterprise Communities.

Program Amount: $2.7 million.

* Money to Train Parents How to Be Better Parents

(Even Start)
Donna Campbell
Compensatory Education Programs
U.S. Department of Education
600 Independence Ave., SW
Room 4400 Portals Building
Washington, DC 20202-6132   202-260-0996

Even Start is a family focused program providing participating families with an integrated program of early childhood education, adult literacy and basic skills instruction, and parenting education. All projects have some home-based instruction and provide for the joint participation of parents and children. The program is administered by states. Legislation requires collaboration between schools and communities in the application and implementation process and gives priority to projects serving families in eligible Title I schoolwide attendance areas.

Type of Preference: Legislation requires states to give preference to Empowerment Zones/Enterprise Communities.

Program Amount: $102 million.

* Money for Family Violence Prevention

(Family Violence Prevention and Services Discretionary Funds Program)
William Riley
Administration for Children and Families
U.S. Department of Health and Human Services
901 D St., SW
Fifth Floor West Wing
Washington, DC 20447   202-401-5529

Grants to state and local agencies, and Native American Tribes and Tribal organizations who are, or have been recipients of Family Violence Prevention

and Services Act grants; state and local private nonprofit agencies experienced in the field of family violence prevention; and public and private nonprofit educational institutions, community organizations and community-based coalitions, and other entities that have designed and implemented family violence prevention information activities or community awareness strategies.

Type of Preference: Weighted consideration for Empowerment Zones/Enterprise Communities and Empowerment Zone/Enterprise Community eligible areas.

Program Amount: $500,000.

* Money for Family Support Centers

(Family Support Center Demonstration Program)
Sheldon Shalit
Office of Community Services
U.S. Department of Health and Human Services
370 L'Enfant Promenade, SW, Fifth Floor
Washington, DC 20447   202-401-4807

The Family Support Center Demonstration Program provides grants to support the design, development and operation of Family Support Centers to prevent family homelessness. Family Support Centers provide comprehensive and intensive support services that enhance the physical, social and educational development of low and very low income individuals and families who were previously homeless and currently residing in government subsidized housing or at risk of becoming homeless.

Type of Preference: Weighted consideration for service Empowerment Zones/Enterprise Communities and Empowerment Zone/Enterprise Community eligible areas.

Program Amount: $7.4 million.

* Money to Address the Critical Needs of the Poor

(Demonstration Partnership Program)
Richard Saul
Office of Community Services
U.S. Department of Health and Human Services
370 L'Enfant Promenade, SW, Fifth Floor
Washington, DC 20447   202-401-9341

Grants are provided to Community Action Agencies for developing and implementing innovative approaches to address critical needs of the poor common to a number of communities. Grantees, in partnership with other public and private organizations, develop an array of innovative programs including homelessness, micro enterprise/self-employment, minority youth life skills, case management, teenage pregnancy, and comprehensive integrated services.

Type of Preference: Weighted consideration for service Empowerment Zones/Enterprise Communities and Empowerment Zone/Enterprise Community eligible areas.

Program Amount: $7.977 million.

Homelessness Programs

* Money to Address General Needs of the Homeless

(U.S. Department of Housing and Urban Development's Homeless Programs)
Jacquie Lawing
Division of Housing and Urban Development
Office of Community Planning and Development
Deputy Assistant Secretary for Economic Development
451 7th St., SW, Suite 7204
Washington, DC 20410   202-708-0270

U.S. Department of Housing and Urban Development administers each of the homeless assistance programs listed below. However, the Department is working to restructure the delivery of homeless assistance to foster better coordination of homeless assistance within communities, improve the ability of communities to assess and meet the individual needs of homeless persons, and increase the placement of homeless individuals and families into permanent housing. The goal is to replace the currently fragmented approach with a "continuum of care" system. This will be reflected in the competition structure for these programs.

* Money to Develop Transitional Housing for the Homeless

(Supportive Housing Program (SHP))
Jean Whaley
HUD Building
U.S. Department of Housing and Urban Development
451 7th St., SW, Room 7254
Washington, DC 20410   202-708-4300

The program promotes the development of supportive housing and supportive

services, including innovative approaches to assist homeless persons in the transition from homelessness and to enable them to live as independently as possible. Funds can be used to provide: transitional housing; permanent housing provided in conjunction with supportive services; innovative supportive housing projects; supportive services; and facilities in which supportive services are provided.
Type of Preference: Competitive preference points to Empowerment Zones/Enterprise Communities.
Program Amount: $600 million.

* Money to Build Emergency Shelters and Services for the Homeless

(Emergency Shelter Grants Programs (ESG))
Mark Johnston
HUD Building
U.S. Department of Housing and Urban Development
451 7th St., SW, Room 7262
Washington, DC 20410   202-708-1226, ext. 4487

Provides grants to states, metropolitan cities, urban counties, and territories according to the formula used for Community Development Block Grants (CDBG). Eligible activities include renovation, major rehabilitation, or conversion of buildings for use as emergency shelters for the homeless. With certain limitations, grantees may also spend funds on essential services for the homeless, and homeless prevention efforts. In addition, grantees may spend funds on shelter operating costs such as maintenance, insurance, utilities, rent and furnishings. To receive a grant each grantee must have an approved Comprehensive Housing Affordability Strategy (CHAS).
Type of Preference: Funds are distributed by formula (localities can target to Empowerment Zones/Enterprise Communities.)
Program Amount: $156.8 million.

* Money for Rental Assistance Programs for the Homeless

(Shelter Plus Care (S+C))
David Pollock
HUD Building
U.S. Department of Housing and Urban Development
451 7th St., SW, Room 7266
Washington, DC 20410   202-708-1234, ext. 4494

Provides grants for rental assistance through four component programs:
Tenant-based Rental Assistance - Participants reside in housing of their choice;
Sponsor-based Rental Assistance - Provides grants to provide rental assistance through contracts with sponsor organizations;
Project Based Rental Assistance - grants to provide rental assistance through contracts between the grant recipient and owners of existing structures.
Single Room Occupancy for Homeless Individuals - provides grants for rental assistance in connection with the moderate rehabilitation of single room occupancy housing units.
Type of Preference: Competitive preference for Empowerment Zones/Enterprise Communities.
Program Amount: $150 million.

* Money to Create Single Room Occupancy for the Homeless

(Single Room Occupancy (SRO) Dwellings for Homeless Individuals)
David Pollock
HUD Building
U.S. Department of Housing and Urban Development
451 7th St., SW, Room 7262
Washington, DC 20410   202-708-1234, ext. 4494

The purpose of the Section 8 Moderate Rehabilitation Program for Single Room Occupancy Dwellings for Homeless Individuals is to provide rental assistance on behalf of homeless individuals in connection with the moderate rehabilitation of SRO dwellings. Resources to fund the cost of rehabilitating the dwellings must be from other sources. However, the rental assistance covers operating expenses of the SRO housing, including debt service for rehabilitation financing, provided the monthly rental assistance per unit does not exceed the moderate rehabilitation fair market rent for an SRO unit, as established by U.S. Department of Housing and Urban Development.
Type of Preference: Competitive preference for Empowerment Zones/Enterprise Communities.
Program Amount: $150 million.

* Free Unused Federal Properties for the Homeless

(Title V - Surplus Federal Property for Use to Assist the Homeless)
Mark Johnston
HUD Building
U.S. Department of Housing and Urban Development
451 7th St., SW, Room 7262
Washington, DC 20410   202-708-1226, ext. 4487

This program allows suitable federal properties that are categorized as unutilized, under utilized, excess, or surplus to be made available to states, units of local government and nonprofit organizations for use to assist the homeless. Properties can be used to provide shelter, services storage, or other uses of benefit to the homeless. The program provides no funding and properties are made available on an "as is" basis. Properties are leased without charge, although the homeless organization must pay for operating and repair costs. Depending on the availability of the property, and other factors, leases may also be from one-to twenty years. Surplus properties may also be deeded to the organization.
Type of Preference: Applies to any surplus federal property in an Empowerment Zone/Enterprise Community eligible area.

* Money to Support the Family

(Family Support Center Demonstration Program)
Elise Morgan
Administration for Children and Families
U.S. Department of Housing and Urban Development
370 L'Enfant Plaza Promenade, SW
Sixth Floor Aerospace Building
Washington, DC 20447   202-401-4621

Grants to a variety of public and private community based organizations to support the design, development, and operation of Family Support Centers to prevent family homelessness. Family Support Centers provide comprehensive and intensive supportive services that enhance the physical, social, and educational development of low and very low-income individuals and families, who were previously homeless, currently residing in government subsidized housing or at risk of becoming homeless.
Type of Preference: Weighted consideration for Empowerment Zones/Enterprise Communities and Empowerment Zone/Enterprise Community eligible areas.
Program Amount: $7.4 million.

Housing Programs

* Money to Help Make Housing More Affordable to Low Incomes

(Home Investment Partnerships (HOME))
Mimi Kolesar
HUD Building
U.S. Department of Housing and Urban Development
451 7th St., SW, Room 7162
Washington, DC 20410   202-708-2470

Grants to states and units of general local government to implement local housing strategies designed to increase homeownership and affordable housing opportunities for low- and very-low-income persons. Eligible uses of funds include tenant-based assistance, housing rehabilitation, assistance to first-time homebuyers, and new construction, under certain circumstances. Under the HOME program, U.S. Department of Housing and Urban Development is developing and testing model housing programs, in conjunction with the private sector and participating jurisdictions.
Type of Preference: Funds are distributed by formula to states and units of general local government.
Program Amount: $1.4 billion.

* Money to Help Low Income Families Pay Their Rent

(Rental Assistance Certificates)
John H. Greer
Deputy Assistant Secretary for
 Multi-Family Housing Programs
U.S. Department of Housing and Urban Development
451 7th St., SW, Room 6106
Washington, DC 20410   202-708-2495

Project-Based Rental Assistance Certificates. A project-based certificate program encourages owners to construct or rehabilitate rental housing for very low income families at rents within the U.S. Department of Housing and Urban Development-established fair market rents for the area. Assistance is tied to specific units under an assistance contract with the owner for specified term.
Type of Preference: Up to $500 million* set aside to designated Empowerment Zones/Enterprise Communities.
Program Amount: Up to $500 million proposed for project-based certificates in designated Empowerment Zones/Enterprise Communities.

* Money to Insure Multifamily Housing Projects Mortgages

(Multifamily Insurance Processing)
John H. Greer
Deputy Assistant Secretary for

Multi-Family Housing Programs
U.S. Department of Housing and Urban Development
451 7th St., SW, Room 6106
Washington, DC 20410   202-708-2495
FHA would direct all field offices to give priority to processing any application for multifamily mortgage insurance for a project located in an Empowerment Zone.
Type of Preference: Priority processing in Empowerment Zones only.

* Money for Social Service Directors for Elderly Housing Projects

(Service Coordinator Program)
John H. Greer
Deputy Assistant Secretary for Multi-Family Housing Programs
U.S. Department of Housing and Urban Development
451 7th St., SW, Room 6106
Washington, DC 20410   202-708-2495
This program makes funds available to Section 8 elderly project owners to employ an on-site social service coordinator and, in some cases, aides. U.S. Department of Housing and Urban Development will award additional points to applications for projects within Empowerment Zones.
Type of Preference: Points in Empowerment Zones only.
Program Amount: $9 million.

* Money to Counsel Homeowners on Money Matters

(SF Housing Counseling Grants)
Joan Morgan
U.S. Department of Housing and Urban Development
451 7th St., SW, Room 9282
Washington, DC 20410   202-708-0614
Grants to public or nonprofit entities to serve as U.S. Department of Housing and Urban Development-approved housing counseling agencies providing counseling to homebuyers, homeowners, and tenants under U.S. Department of Housing and Urban Development programs and for homeowners with conventional mortgages or mortgages insured or guaranteed by other governmental agencies.
Type of Preference: Points in Empowerment Zones only.
Program Amount: $12 million.

* Money to Spread the Word About FHA Mortgage Insurance

(SF Program Outreach)
Emelda Johnson
Deputy Assistant Secretary for Single Family Housing
U.S. Department of Housing and Urban Development
451 7th St., SW, Room 9282   202-708-3175
Washington, DC 20410   800-CALL-FHA
U.S. Department of Housing and Urban Development outreach effort to commercial lenders to encourage their use of FHA single family mortgage insurance programs for home purchase and home improvement loans in Empowerment Zone/Enterprise Communities. U.S. Department of Housing and Urban Development offices would also make special efforts to market the U.S. Department of Housing and Urban Development-owned single family inventory to nonprofits, local governments, and other low-income housing providers.
Type of Preference: Available in all Empowerment Zone/Enterprise Communities as appropriate.
Program Amount: No funds required.

* Money to Improve U.S. Department of Housing and Urban Development Owned or Insured Properties

(Flexible Subsidy Program)
John H. Greer
Deputy Assistant Secretary for Multi-Family Housing Programs
U.S. Department of Housing and Urban Development
451 7th St., SW, Room 6106
Washington, DC 20410   202-708-2495
This program makes operating assistance and capital improvement loans to owners of certain subsidized projects where U.S. Department of Housing and Urban Development holds the note or insures the loan.
Type of Preference: Points in Empowerment Zones only.
Program Amount: $116.4 million.

* Money to Insure Mortgages on Multifamily Housing Projects

(Multifamily Housing)
David Villano
Farmers Home Administration (FMHA)
Multi-Family Housing Division

Room 5337 South Building
14th and Independence Ave., SW
Washington, DC 20250   202-720-1608
Under this program, Farmers Home Administration provides insured loans to construct new facilities or to purchase/rehabilitate existing facilities to provide modernized rental or cooperative housing for persons with very-low, low and moderate incomes, for those age 62 and older, and for handicapped persons in communities of not more than 10,000 and 20,000 population if the community is not within an MSA. The loans are repayable in not more than 50 years. Provisions are made for interest reductions so that low-income tenants may pay a rent within their means. Rent paid by low-income tenants also can be supplemented through a rental assistance program administered by the Farmers Home Administration.
Type of Preference: Set aside for Empowerment Zones/Enterprise Communities.
Program Amount: $152 million.

* Money to Fix Up Your House

(Rural Community Housing Development)
Joseph Carroll
Office of Community Services
U.S. Department of Housing and Urban Development
370 L'Enfant Promenade, SW
Washington, DC 20447   202-401-9346
Grants to states, public agencies, and private nonprofit organizations to help low-income homeowners improve their housing through self-help rehabilitation.
Type of Preference: Weighted consideration for serving Empowerment Zones/Enterprise Communities and Empowerment Zone/Enterprise Community eligible areas.
Program Amount: $3 million.

Infrastructure Improvement Programs

* Money to Develop Sewers and Sanitation Services

(Water and Waste Loans)
Laurence G. Bowman
AG Box 1548
U.S. Department of Agriculture
Rural Development Administration
Water and Waste Disposal Division
14th and Independence Ave., SW
Washington, DC 20250   202-720-9589
The Rural Development Administration Water and Waste Disposal Loan funds are used to develop water and waste disposal (including solid waste disposal and storm drainage systems in rural areas and towns with a population not in excess of 10,000. The funds are available to public entities such as municipalities, counties, special purpose districts, Indian tribes, and corporations not operated for profit. The Rural Development Administration also guarantees water and waste disposal loans made by banks and other eligible lenders.
Type of Preference: Set aside for Empowerment Zones/Enterprise Communities.
Program Amount: $1.5 million set aside.

* Money to Reduce Cost of Water and Waste Disposal

(Water and Waste Grants)
Laurence G. Bowman
AG Box 1548
U.S. Department of Agriculture
Rural Development Administration
Water and Waste Disposal Division
14th and Independence Ave., SW
Washington, DC 20250   202-720-9589
The Rural Development Administration Water and Waste Disposal Grant funds are used to reduce water and waste disposal costs to a reasonable level for rural users. Grants may be made up to 75 percent of eligible project costs in some cases. Eligible applicants are the same types that are eligible for loans.
Type of Preference: Set aside for Empowerment Zones/Enterprise Communities.
Program Amount: $19 million set aside.

* Money for Airport Planning and Development

(Airport Improvement Program)
James Borsori
Airport Financial Support Division

U.S. Department of Transportation
400 7th St., SW
Washington, DC 20590   202-267-8822

The Airport Improvement Program provides grants to states, units of local government, airport authorities, Indian Tribes and some private owners for airport planning and development.

Type of Preference: Discretionary funding prioritized according to specific statutory set-asides and priorities.

Program Amount: $1.45 million.

* Money for Bridges

(Bridge Replacement and Rehabilitation Program)
Charles Chambers
Office of Engineering Bridge Division
U.S. Department of Transportation
400 7th St., SW
Washington, DC 20590   202-366-4617

The Bridge Replacement and Rehabilitation Program provides for the construction, reconstruction, rehabilitation, resurfacing, restoration, and operational improvements for bridges (including bridges on public roads of all functional classifications). Up to 40% of these funds may be transferred to its NHS or STP Programs.

Type of Preference: Funds are distributed by formula to the states.

Program Amount: $2.55 billion.

* Money for Roadways

(National Highway System (NHS) (23 U.S.C. Section 104(b) (1)))
Tom Weeks
U.S. Department of Transportation
400 7th St., SW
Washington, DC 20590   202-366-5002

The National Highway System provides funds for the construction, reconstruction, rehabilitation, resurfacing, restoration, and operational improvements for roadways designated on the National Highway System. Up to 50% of a state's NHS apportionment may be transferred to its STP Program. Transit projects may be eligible for non-transferred NHS funds under certain conditions.

Type of Preference: Funds are distributed by formula to the states.

Program Amount: $3.331 billion.

* Money for Rural Areas to Develop Essential Utilities

(Community Facility)
John R. Bowles
South Agricultural Building
U.S. Department of Agriculture
Rural Development Administration
Room 6312, 14th and Independence Ave., SW
Washington, DC 20250   202-720-1496

The Rural Development Administration provides funds to construct, enlarge, extend, or otherwise improve community facilities providing essential services in rural areas and towns with a population of 20,000 or less. The funds are available to public entities such as municipalities, counties, special-purpose districts, Indian tribes, and corporations not operated for profit. The Rural Development Administration also guarantees community facility loans made by banks or other eligible lenders.

Type of Preference: Set aside for Empowerment Zones/Enterprise Communities.

Program Amount: $6.1 million set aside.

* Money to Develop the Information Superhighway

(National Information Infrastructure Grants)
Larry Parks
U.S. Department of Commerce
14th and Constitution Ave., NW
Room 5415
Washington, DC 20230   202-482-6050

50% matching grants to state and local governments, nonprofit educational entities, health-care providers, libraries and community information providers for planning and demonstration projects of information networks that will permit interconnection and inter-operability among and between user communities and national "backbone" networks. The purpose of the program is to facilitate the development of the national telecommunications and information infrastructure by promoting the widespread availability of advanced telecommunications technologies especially to: enhance the delivery of social services, traditionally provided by the Government, such as education and health care; and support the formation of a nationwide, multimedia, high-speed interactive infrastructure of varied information technologies.

Type of Preference: Priority for Empowerment Zone/Enterprise Community eligible areas.

Program Amount: $26 million.

* Money to Develop Community Transportation Projects

(Section 26 Planning and Research Funds)
Lynn Sahaj
Office of Budget and Policy
U.S. Department of Transportation
400 7th St., SW, Room 9310
Washington, DC 20590   202-366-2053

Provides funds for research planning, training, and design of local transportation facilities and projects, including such activities in Empowerment Zones/Enterprise Communities.

Type of Preference: Additional consideration for Empowerment Zone/Enterprise Community status.

Program Amount: $92 million.

* Money for Bus and Railroad Stations

(Section (3) Capital Program)
Lynn Sahaj
Office of Budget and Policy
U.S. Department of Transportation
400 7th St., SW, Room 9310
Washington, DC 20590   202-366-2053

Provides federal discretionary funds for the construction and rehabilitation of transit bus and rail facilities, station improvements, the purchase and lease of vehicles, and supportive design elements such as walkways, transit malls, and open space in local areas, including Empowerment Zone/Enterprise Community areas.

Type of Preference: Additional consideration for Empowerment Zone/Enterprise Community status.

Program Amount: $1.724 billion.

* Money for Local Transit Services

(Urbanized Area Formula Program (as amended))
Lynn Sahaj
Office of Budget and Policy
U.S. Department of Transportation
400 7th St., SW, Room 9310
Washington, DC 20590   202-366-2053

Provides formula-based operating and capital assistance for local transit services, including services in Empowerment Zone/Enterprise Community areas.

Type of Preference: Expedited administrative processing for Empowerment Zone/Enterprise Community status.

Program Amount: $2.299 billion.

* Money for Transportation Services in Rural Areas

(Nonurbanized Area)
Lynn Sahaj
Office of Budget and Policy
U.S. Department of Transportation
400 7th St., SW, Room 9310
Washington, DC 20590   202-366-2053

Provides capital and operating assistance for transportation programs in rural areas and urban areas smaller than 50,000 population, including Empowerment Zone/Enterprise Community areas.

Type of Preference: Administrative preference for Empowerment Zone/Enterprise Community status.

Program Amount: $132.9 million.

* Money to Coordinate Transportation Plans

(Transportation Planning/Community Participation Training)
Lynn Sahaj
Office of Budget and Policy
U.S. Department of Transportation
400 7th St., SW, Room 9310
Washington, DC 20590   202-366-2053

Technical assistance to communities to work with regional and state planning organizations on transportation plans (necessary to ensure Empowerment Zone/Enterprise Community projects are in the state's pipeline for federal funding).

Type of Preference: Targeted to Empowerment Zones/Enterprise Communities.

* Money to Reduce Air Pollution Caused by Traffic

Surface Transportation Program (STP) Congestion Mitigation and Air Quality Improvement (CMAQ))
Lynn Sahaj
Office of Budget and Policy
U.S. Department of Transportation
400 7th St., SW, Room 9310
Washington, DC 20590   202-366-2053

These funds support projects that reduce vehicle emissions in Clean Air non-attainment areas. Eligible activities might include the transit and transit-related portions of pedestrian-oriented and mixed use development projects

and other transportation projects that reduce automobile emissions.
Type of Preference: Expedited administrative processing consideration for
Empowerment Zone/Enterprise Community status.
Program Amount: $1.028 billion.

Public Safety Programs

* Money To Stop Drug Crime in Public Housing

(Public Housing Drug Elimination Program)
Sonja Burgess
U.S. Department of Housing and Urban Development
451 7th St., SW, Room 4102
Washington, DC 20410   202-619-8201
Grants to eligible Public and Indian Housing Authorities (HAs) to eliminate
drug-related crime in and around the premises of public and Indian housing
developments. HAs are encouraged to develop a plan to sustain drug
elimination activities over a period of years. Eligible activities include
employment of security personnel, HA police, and investigators,
implementation of physical improvements to enhance security, development
of voluntary tenant patrols, and drug prevention, intervention and treatment
programs to reduce the use of drugs.
Type of Preference: none
Program Amount: $251.75 million total funding.

* Money to Develop Community Policing Programs

(Community Policing)
Joe Brann
Discretionary Grant Programs Division
U.S. Department of Justice
633 Indiana Ave., NW, Room 602
Washington, DC 20531   202-514-2058
Grantees will demonstrate a comprehensive model of community policing,
which will result in a department-wide change in philosophy and mode of
providing law enforcement services to the community. Training and technical
assistance will be provided to the demonstration programs and other
interested jurisdictions.
Type of Preference: Priority consideration to Empowerment Zones/Enterprise
Communities.

* Money to Help Kids Stay Out of Gangs

(Youth and Gangs)
Thomas Albrecht
Bureau of Justice Assistance
U.S. Department of Justice
633 Indiana Ave., NW, Room 1042
Washington, DC 20531   202-514-5948
Grants to develop prevention and intervention strategies to assist youth in
avoiding pressures to use drugs and/or become involved in criminal activities
or gangs will be continued. New programs will assist criminal justice agencies
in providing effective services to children and their families, and train teenage
students to manage anger and resolve conflict without violence.
Type of Preference: Targeted technical assistance to Empowerment
Zones/Enterprise Communities.

* Money for Jails, Boot Camps, and Correctional Programs

(Demonstration Programs)
Thomas Albrecht
Bureau of Justice Assistance
U.S. Department of Justice
633 Indiana Ave., NW, Room 1042
Washington, DC 20531   202-514-5943
Grants for the development and implementation of correctional options that
include community-based incarceration, weekend incarceration, correctional
boot camps, transitional programs, aftercare services, drug courts, day
reporting, structured fines, etc.
Type of Preference: Targeted technical assistance to Empowerment
Zones/Enterprise Communities.
Program Amount: $12 million.

* Free Help to Develop Alternatives to Jail

(Technical Assistance)
Thomas Albrecht
Bureau of Justice Assistance
U.S. Department of Justice
633 Indiana Ave., NW, Room 1042
Washington, DC 20531   202-514-5943
Technical assistance and support to public agencies to help them plan,
develop, implement, improve or expand alternatives to traditional modes of
incarceration.
Type of Preference: Targeted technical assistance to Empowerment

Zones/Enterprise Communities.
Program Amount: see above.

* Money and Help to Develop Boot Camp Jail Programs

(Boot Camp Prisons)
Thomas Albrecht
Bureau of Justice Assistance
U.S. Department of Justice
633 Indiana Ave., NW
Room 1042
Washington, DC 20531   202-514-5948
Grants to implement boot camp programs.
Type of Preference: Targeted technical assistance to Empowerment
Zones/Enterprise Communities.
Program Amount: see above.

* Money to Reduce and Prevent Crime

(Byrne Discretionary Grant Program)
Dick Ward
U.S. Department of Justice
633 Indiana Ave., NW
Washington, DC 20531   202-514-5943
The Bureau of Justice Assistance (BJA) assists states and local jurisdictions in
making communities safe through the Edward Byrne Memorial State and
Local Law Enforcement Assistance Discretionary Grant Program.
Discretionary grant funds are used for demonstration programs, training,
technical assistance, and national scope programs to reduce and prevent crime
and violence and for criminal justice system improvement at the state and
local levels.
Type of Preference: Priority consideration is given to Empowerment
Zones/Enterprise Communities.
Program Amount: $50 million.

Juvenile Justice and Delinquency Prevention

* Money for Youth/Adult Mentoring Programs

(Mentoring (U.S. Department of Justice))
Cora Roy
U.S. Department of Justice
633 Indiana Ave., NW
Washington, DC 20531   202-616-3659
This new program authorizes the Administrator to award three-year grants to
local education agencies for mentoring program designed to link at-risk youth
with responsible adults to provide guidance, promote personal and social
responsibility, increase educational participation, discourage use of illegal
drugs, violence, weapon use, and other criminal activity, discourage gang
involvement, and encourage participation in community service and activities.
Type of Preference: Funding priority is to be given to high crime areas with a
high percentage of Elementary and Secondary Education Act fund eligible
youth and high dropout rates.
Program Amount: $4 million.

* Money to Reduce Crime and Revitalize Communities

(Weed and Seed)
Steve Rickman
U.S. Department of Justice
633 Indiana Ave., NW
Washington, DC 20531   202-616-1152
Grants to develop comprehensive, multi-agency approaches to combating
violent crime, drug use, and gang activity, and to coordinate efforts to
revitalize distressed neighborhoods. Grants will also be available for Safe
Haven programs that provide an integrated array of social services and
activities for youth and their families in a safe setting. Thirty-six communities
received funding.
Type of Preference: Special consideration for Empowerment
Zones/Enterprise Communities.
Program Amount: $28.5 million ($225,000 for new sites).

* Money to Help Retrain Juvenile Delinquents

(Prevention)
Donna Bowres
U.S. Department of Justice
633 Indiana Ave., NW
Washington, DC 20531   202-616-9618
This program supports Title V of the JJDP Act, which authorizes the
Administrator to make grants, through state advisory groups, to units of local
government for a broad range of delinquency prevention programs and

activities to benefit youth who have had contact with or are likely to have contact with the juvenile justice system. Services to children, youth and families include recreation, tutoring and remedial education, work skills, health and mental health, alcohol and substance abuse prevention, leadership development and accountability. Eligible units must be in compliance with OJJDP's Formulate Grants Program, submit a three-year plan to the state and to the Administrator, appoint a local policy board empowered to administer the local program, plan for coordination of services, and provide a 50% cash or in-kind match.

Type of Preference: Priority in awards is given to applicants that coordinate and collaborate in the provision of services, involve the private nonprofit and business sectors and develop or enhance a statewide subsidy program to local governments that are dedicated to early intervention and delinquency prevention.

Program Amount: $20 million.

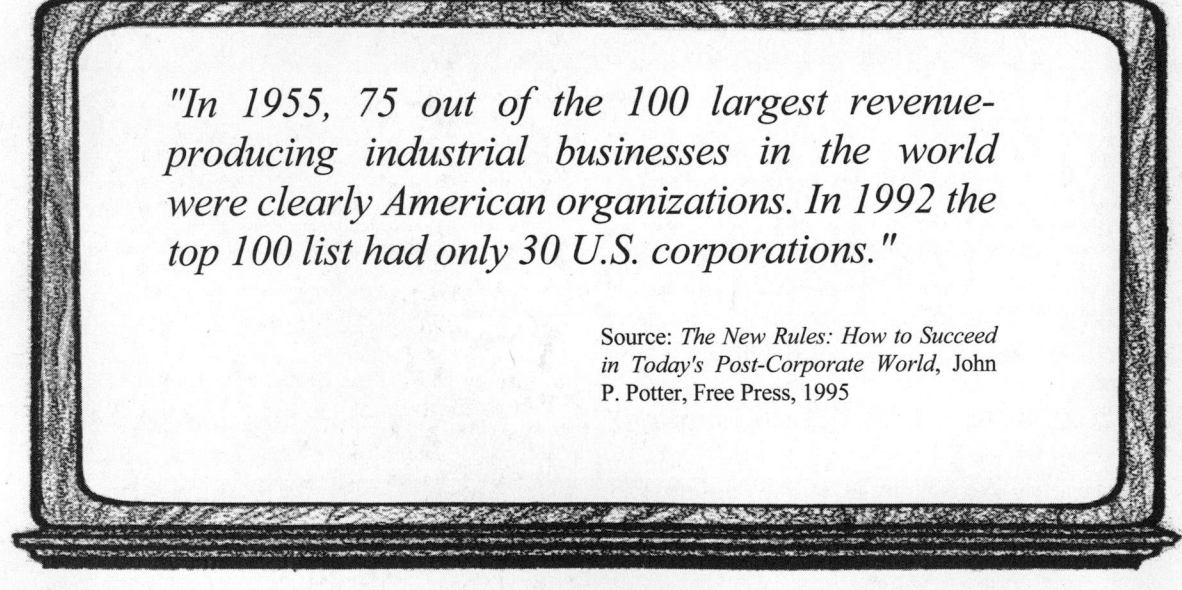

"In 1955, 75 out of the 100 largest revenue-producing industrial businesses in the world were clearly American organizations. In 1992 the top 100 list had only 30 U.S. corporations."

Source: *The New Rules: How to Succeed in Today's Post-Corporate World*, John P. Potter, Free Press, 1995

State Enterprise Zones Offer Jobs and Small Business Help

Like the Federal Empowerment Zone programs, each state has its own benefit programs for designated areas in need of economic rebuilding. As designated Enterprise Zones, thousands of economically depressed communities all across the country have been earmarked to receive billions of dollars in economic stimulation packages.

Entrepreneurs Can Use Empowerment/Enterprise Zones

If you want to start a business, look at starting it in one in these zones. By simply locating a business in one of these zones, you can receive all kinds of benefits. For example:

- California will pay up to 50% of a new employee's wages in the form of a tax credit.

- In Kansas, if your small town retail store creates two new jobs, you won't have to pay sales tax to the state.

- New Jersey businesses receive a $1,500 tax credit for hiring an employee who lives in the enterprise zone where the business operates.

- New York offers businesses lower utility rates in enterprise zones.

- Texas offers special tax reductions for franchises in enterprise zones.

- Arizona offers women business owners an 80 percent reduction on property taxes.

- Florida offers a $50,000 corporate income tax credit.

By using these generous tax credits, states hope to lure businesses into these economically depressed Enterprise Zones and bring jobs to the area. These efforts to stimulate economic growth in depressed areas will ultimately prove beneficial for hundreds of thousands of citizens.

Job Seekers Can Take Advantage of Empowerment/Enterprise Zones

If you're out of work, try to locate businesses that you'd like to work for in a state-designated Enterprise Zone. Let the business know that they'll receive a big tax break if they hire you. For example:

- Alabama will give an employer $2500 of tax credit for every new employee (they get $2500 for hiring you).

- California will give half the cost of an employee's salary in tax credits (they can hire you at $50,000, but it only costs them $25,000).

- Colorado gives employers $200 toward health insurance for an employee.

- Connecticut gives $500 grants for every job created.

- Indiana gives $7,500 of tax credit per employee (they can pay you $25,000, but it really only costs them $17,500).

- Louisiana gives $5000 if a business hires an ex-aerospace employee.

How to Find Your State Empowerment/Enterprise Zones

If you are not sure where the enterprise zones are located in your state, contact the office listed in the state-by-state listing below.

State by State Listing of Programs

Below you will find a state-by-state listing of Enterprise Zone Programs. The following states have programs in place: Alabama, Arizona, Arkansas, California, Colorado, Connecticut, Delaware, Florida, Hawaii, Illinois, Indiana, Kansas, Kentucky, Louisiana, Maryland, Michigan, Minnesota, Missouri, Nebraska, New Jersey, New York, Ohio, Oklahoma, Oregon, Pennsylvania, Rhode Island, South Carolina, Tennessee, Texas, Utah, Virginia, West Virginia, and Wisconsin.

For each state entry, you will find the number of zones in the state, the incentives available to businesses in those zones, eligibility requirements, and a contact for more information. The state contact is usually located in the Department of Commerce of the Department of Economic Development for the state, and can provide you with a listing of credits, incentives, and zones for the state.

Alabama

Number of Zones: 27

Zone and Tax Incentives:
- An employer's maximum tax credit for operating in the zone can't exceed $2,500 per new permanent employee hired
- Income tax credit for hiring 30% of new employees who were formerly unemployed, of 80% during the first year, 60% in the second, 40% in the third year and 20% in the fourth and fifth year
- Tax credit for new investment of 10% of the first $10,000 invested, 5% on the next $90,000 invested and 2% on the remaining
- $1,000 tax credit for training each new employee
- Sales and use tax refund for building materials, machinery and equipment
- Certain income and corporate franchise tax exemptions for a five year period

Eligibility Criteria:
Must be located in or locating within the boundaries on an enterprise zone
- Must generally fall into Standard Industrial Classification (SIC) codes 20-42, 44-49 or consist of major warehousing, distribution center, regional or corporate headquarters of companies in the referenced SIC codes
- Must expand its labor force, make new capital investment or prevent loss of employment
- May not have closed or reduced employment elsewhere in Alabama in order to expand into the enterprise zone
- Must obtain an endorsement resolution approved by the appropriate local governing authority prior to participation in the program

For additional benefits, a business must meet the criteria outlined above and:
- Businesses must certify that at least 35% of their new qualified employees are residents of the zone
- Must give preference and priority to Alabama manufacturers, suppliers, contractors and labor, except when not reasonably possible

To apply, contact:
Bill Babington
Enterprise Zone Program Coordinator
401 Adams Ave.
P.O. Box 5690
Montgomery, AL 36103-5690
334-242-0492

Alaska

The state does not have an authorized enterprise zone program.

Arizona

Number of Zones: 22

Zone and Tax Incentives:
Businesses must certify that at least 35% of their new qualified employees are residents of the zone.
- One fourth of the taxable wages paid to each qualified employee, not to exceed $500 in the first year
- One third of the taxable wages paid to each previously qualified employee, not to exceed $1,000 in the second year of continuous employment
- One-half the taxable wages paid to each previously qualified employee, not to exceed $1,500, in the third year of continuous employment
- Qualified "new employee" considered economically disadvantaged for purposes of the Job Training Partnership Act
- Small minority or women-owned manufacturing businesses are eligible for an assessment ratio of 5% on all personal and real property in the zone for 5 years

Eligibility Criteria:
- Must be at least one-quarter square mile
- Must have a population of at least 1,000 persons

- Must have one of the following two:
  - Unemployment rate of 150% of the statewide rate for the preceding two years, or
  - Poverty rate of 150% of the statewide rate

To apply, contact:
Patty Duff
Enterprise Zone Program Administrator
Arizona Department of Commerce
3800 N. Central Ave., Suite 1650
Phoenix, AZ 85012-1908
602-280-1340
Email: Pattyd@azcommerce.com

Arkansas

Number of Zones: Legislation in July, 1996 established the entire state as one enterprise zone, referred to as Advantage Arkansas.

Zone and Tax Incentives:
- Sales and use tax refund for building materials, machinery and equipment
- $3,000 employer tax credit per net new employee, if at least 35% of the employees live in the same or adjacent county and receive some form of public assistance or have been considered hard to employ, or lacking in basic skills

Eligibility Criteria:
- Manufacturers with Standard Industrial Classification codes (SIC) 20 to 39 adding at least one new employee
- Warehouse operations (no retail sales) and 25 or more new employees
- Computer firms defined as SIC 7375 (Information Retrieval Services) and 7376 (Computer Facilities Management Services) adding at least one new employee
- Office sector business or control center with no retail sales and 100 or more new employees
- Corporate headquarter with no retail sales and 25 or more new employees
- Trucking sector business defined as SIC 4231 with no retail sales and 25 or more new employees
- To be eligible to apply for tax benefits, a company or business must have an expansion (or new plant) project which will result in a new increase in employment

Application Process:
To apply, the company must fill out an application form and project plan with the local governing body of municipality or county in whose jurisdiction the facility is located. If the local governing body approves, they must pass a resolution endorsing the project. The application form, project plan and the resolution must be forwarded to the Arkansas Industrial Development Commission.

To apply, contact:
Gregory Dale
Enterprise Zone Program Coordinator
Arkansas Department of Economic Development
One State Capitol Mall
Little Rock, AR 72201
501-682-7310

California

Number of Zones: 39 enterprise zones. Trade or business must be conducted within the zone.

Zone and Tax Incentives:
- Sales and Use Tax Credits: 100% for the purchase of qualifying machinery and parts. Limits: Individuals--$1 million; Corporations--$20 million
- Hiring Tax Credit: Up to 50% (declines by 10% each year) of wages paid to each qualified employee
- Business Expense Deduction: Tangible personal property may be deducted as a business expense in the first year it is place in service. Limit: $10,000.
- Interest Expense Deduction: Deduction from income is allowed on the amount of "net interest" earned on loans made to a trade or business in an enterprise zone.
- Net Operating Loss Carryover: Net operating losses of individuals or corporations doing business in an enterprise zone may be carried over to future years to reduce the amount of taxable enterprise zone income for those years.

- Local enterprise zone incentives include the expeditious processing of plans and permits.
- Reduced utility rates
- Low-interest revolving loans
- Expeditious processing of plans and permits

Eligibility Requirements:
Qualified businesses must:
- Employ at least 50% of its program area employees who are residents of high density unemployment areas; or
- Employ at least 30% of its program area employees who are residents of high density unemployment areas, and contributes to an approved community service program; or
- Have at least 30% of its owners who are residents of high density unemployment areas

To apply, contact:
Keith Coppage
Enterprise Zone Program Manager
Department of Commerce
801 K St., Suite 1700
Sacramento, CA 95814
916-324-8211
www.commerce.ca.gov

Colorado

Number of Zones: 18

Zone and Tax Incentives:
- Three Percent Investment Tax Credit. Businesses making investments in equipment used exclusively in an enterprize zone may claim a credit against their Colorado income taxes equal to 3% of the amount of the investment, subject to limitations.
- $500 Job Tax Credit. Businesses hiring new employees in connection with a "new business facility" located in an enterprise zone may claim a tax credit against state income taxes of $500 for each new employee, subject to limitations.
- Double Job Tax Credit for Agricultural Processing. An additional credit of $500 per new business facility employee may be claimed by businesses which add value to agricultural commodities through manufacturing or processing.
- $200 Job Tax Credit for Employer Health Insurance. A taxpayer with a qualifying new business facility is allowed a two-year $200 tax credit for each new facility employee who is insured under a qualifying employer-sponsored health insurance program.
- R&D Tax Credit. Taxpayers who make private expenditures on research and experimental activities (as defined by federal tax law) conducted in an enterprise zone qualify for an income tax credit of 3 percent, subject to limitations.
- Credit to Rehabilitate Vacant Buildings. Owners or tenants of commercial buildings in an enterprise zone which are at least 20 years old and which have been vacant for at least two years may claim a credit of 25% of the cost of rehabilitating each building. The credit is limited to $50,000.
- Credit for Contribution to Zones. There is a 25% credit, up to $100,000 for private contributions to local administrators for enterprise zone development projects and for promoting child care in zones.
- Exemption from state sales and use tax for manufacturing, mining, and aircraft equipment. Purchases of manufacturing machinery, machine tools, and parts are exempt form the 3% sales and use tax statewide.
- Local Government Tax Incentives. Any city or county within an enterprise zone is authorized to negotiate with individual taxpayers who have qualifying new business facilities: (a) an incentive payment equal to not more than the amount of the increase in property tax liability over pre-enterprise zone levels; and (b) a refund of local sales taxes on purchases of equipment, machinery, machine tools, or supplies used in the taxpayer's business in the enterprise zone.

Eligibility Criteria:
- Unemployment rate at least 25% above the state 12-month average
- Population growth rate less than 25% of the state average rate for the most recent 5-year period for which data are available; or
- Per capita income less than 75% of the state average
- Total zone population may not exceed 50,000

To apply, contact:
Evan Metcalf
Colorado Department of Local Affairs
1625 Broadway, Room 1700
Denver, CO 80202
303-892-3840

Connecticut

Number of Zones: 17

Zone and Tax Incentives:
- Five-year, 80% abatement of local property taxes on real estate improvements and personal property acquisitions
- Ten-year, 50% credit on corporate business taxes, and a $1,500 grant ($75,000 maximum) for each new job (minimum of three) created within a 24-month period for qualifying manufacturing firms, if at least 30% of all new hires are from urban enterprise zones or form the community's disadvantaged population
- Certain service companies may be eligible for a $500 grant per job created
- Low-cost loans and free technical assistance
- Job training and job placement assistance
- Exemptions from state real estate conveyance taxes, and sales taxes on machinery replacement parts
- A minimum 7-year graduated tax deferral on increased assessments for improvements to property

Eligibility Criteria:
- 25% or more of the population below poverty level
- 25% or more of the population dependent on welfare
- An unemployment rate twice that of the state average

To apply, contact:
Anne Karas
Department of Economic and Community Development
Infrastructure and Real Estate Division
505 Hudson St.
Hartford, CT 06106
860-270-8143

Delaware

Number of Zones: 30 targeted low income census tracts plus additional public and non-profit economic development areas in the City of Wilmington, plus New Castle, Kent and Sussex counties.

Zone and Tax Incentives:
- Delaware exporters who qualify as an Export Trading Company can receive exemption from Delaware income and mercantile taxes
- Corporate income tax credits and gross receipts tax reductions are available to: manufacturers, wholesalers, laboratories or similar facilities used for scientific, agricultural or industrial research, development or testing; computer processors, engineering firms, consumer credit reporting services or any combination of these activities, the administration and management support required for any of these activities who invest a minimum of $200,000 in a new or expanded facility and hires a minimum of five new employees
- The program provides credits of $450 for each new qualified employee and $450 for each $100,000 investment. During the 10-year life of the credits, credits can't exceed 50% of the company's pre-credit tax liability in any one year. Unused credits may be carried forward for ten years.
- Firms which qualify for targeted industry credits and locate in one of the targeted areas, qualify for corporate income tax credits of $650 for each new employee and $650 for each new $100,000 investment. (Blue Collar Jobs Act)
- Qualifying firms are not subject to gross receipts taxes for the first five years and will then have these gross receipts taxes reduced on a declining scale for a period of ten years
- Selected commercial and retail businesses which locate in one of the 30 targeted census tracts and meet the minimum investment and employment criteria, qualify for corporate income tax credits of $450 per new qualified employee and $450 for each $100,000 investment. These businesses also qualify for the ten-year reduction in gross receipts taxes.

Eligibility Criteria:
"Targeted Areas" for targeted industries are:
- Any real property located within the state or any political subdivision, or instrumentality thereof.
- Any real property located within the state and owned by an IRS section 501(c)(3) organization which is organized and operated solely for the purpose of fostering economic development within the state
- Any Foreign Trade Zone located within the state
- 30 specifically identified targeted Census tracts

"Targeted Areas" for commercial and retail businesses are:
- Thirty specifically identified low-income census tracts

Highlights:
Green Industries Initiative: Tax credits through "Blue Collar Jobs Act" to promote reduction of wastes - recycling. Greatest success coming from the development of industrial parks.

To apply, contact:
Donna A. Murray
Senior Business Development Specialist
820 N. French St.
Wilmington, DE 19801
302-577-8472

District of Columbia

The District of Columbia does not have an authorized enterprise zone program.

Florida

Number of Projected Zones: 34

Zone and Tax Incentives:
- Enterprise Zone Jobs Tax Credit (Corporate Income Tax)
- Enterprise Zone Jobs Tax Credit (Sales and Use Tax)
- Enterprise Zone Property Tax Credit
- Sales tax refund for building materials used in rehabilitation of real property
- Sales tax refund for business machinery and equipment
- Sales tax exemption for electrical energy
- Community Contribution Tax Credit Program

In addition to these state incentives, local governments may offer additional incentives. For additional information, please call the contact person in the enterprise zone in which you are interested.

Area Eligibility Criteria:
- Housing conditions
- Per capita income
- Percent of elderly and youth residents
- Unemployment
- Per capita local taxes
- Percent of vacant commercial space
- Crime rate
- Increase in property values

To apply, contact:
Burt Von Hoff
Office of Tourism, Trade and Economic Development
2001 The Capitol
Tallahassee FL 32399-0001
850-487-2568

Georgia

The state does not have an authorized enterprise zone program.

Hawaii

Number of Zones: 17

Zone and Tax Incentives

State Incentives:
- Seven-year exemption from general excise taxes on the gross proceeds from all business within the zone
- 80% income tax abatement the first year, decreasing 10% each year over the next six years
- Income tax credit equal to 80% of the unemployment insurance premium paid during the first year declining 10% each year for the next six years

County Incentives:
May include, but are not limited to the following:
- Property tax abatement or freeze, or tax increment financing
- "Fast track" or priority permit processing
- Zoning or building permit waivers or variances

- Priority consideration for Community Development Nebel Block Grant or other federal programs
- 3 year exemption from any increase in property tax resulting from new construction

Eligibility Criteria:

A nominated area must consist of contiguous U.S. census tracts based on the 1980 U.S. Census and meet one of the following two requirements:

- At least 25% of the population must have incomes below 80% of the median income of the county or
- An unemployment rate 1.5 times the state average

Eligibility Criteria:

In order to be eligible to participate in the program, a business located in an enterprise zone must be engaged in manufacturing, wholesaling, or the repair and/or maintenance of tangible property and must also derive at least 50% of its annual gross receipts from eligible transactions conducted within the zone. Eligible businesses must satisfy low income hiring or employment requirements.

New Business:

Businesses that startup in or move to an EZ (Enterprise Zone) must increase their average annual number of full-time employees by at least 10% in the first year. The average annual number of full-time employees in the years 2 to 7 can fluctuate, but cannot be less than the average number of employees required in the first year. (Note: New businesses will be considered "new" throughout their seven years of eligibility.)

Existing Businesses:

Businesses already in an EZ must increase their average annual number of full-time employees by at least 10% in the first year. The average annual number of full-time employees must also increase by at least 10% annually in years 2 to 7.

To apply, contact:

Tom Brandt
Enterprise Zone Coordinator
Business Services Division
Dept. of Business, Economic Development and Tourism
#1 Capital District Bldg.
250 S. Hotel St.
Honolulu, HI 96813
808-586-2593
Fax: 808-586-2589

Mailing address:

P.O. Box 2359
Honolulu, HI 96804

Idaho

The state does not have an authorized enterprise zone program.

Illinois

Number of Zones: 93

Zone and Tax Incentives:

- Sales Tax Exemption: A state sales tax exemption is permitted on building materials used in an enterprise zone. The materials must be purchased from a place of business which is located in the municipality or county which has established the enterprise zone.
- Enterprise Zone Machinery and Equipment/Pollution Control Facilities Sales Tax Exemption; A state sales tax exemption is available on purchases of specified building materials that will be used or consumed in the manufacturing or assembly process or in the operation of a pollution control facility within an enterprise zone. Businesses must make a $5 million investment which causes the creation of 200 full-time equivalent jobs or an investment of $40 million for the retention of 2,000 full-time jobs.
- Enterprise Zone Utility Tax Exemption: State utility tax exemption on gas, electricity and the Illinois Commerce Commission's administrative charge. Businesses must make a $5 million investment which causes the creation of 200 full-time jobs or an investment of $20 million for the retention of 1,000 full-time jobs.
- Enterprise Zone Investment Tax Credit: State investment tax credit of .5% is allowed a taxpayer who invests in qualified property in a zone.
- Jobs Tax Credit: A taxpayer conducting a trade or business in an

Enterprise Zone may receive a $500 tax credit per eligible employee hired to work in a zone during the taxable year, if the taxpayer hires 5 or more eligible employees.

- Dividend Income Deduction: Individuals, corporations, trusts, and estates are not taxed on dividend income from corporations doing substantially of their business in a zone.
- Interest Deduction: Financial institutions are not taxed on the interest received on loans for development within an enterprise zone.
- Contribution Deduction: Businesses may deduct, from taxable income, double the value of a cash or in-kind contribution to an approved project on a designated zone organization.

Local Incentives:

- Abatement of property taxes on new improvements
- Homesteading and shopsteading programs
- Waiver of business licensing and permit fees
- Special local financing programs and other resources

To apply contact:

Thomas R. Henderson
Dept. of Commerce and Community Affairs
Enterprise Zone Program
620 East Adams, 3rd Floor
Springfield, IL 62701
217-785-6145

Indiana

Number of Zones: 23

Zone and Tax Incentives:

- Gross Income Tax Exemption: All enterprise zone income exceeding the income earned in the enterprise zone prior to its designation is exempt from the state gross income tax
- Employment Expense Credit: Employer income tax for 10% of resident employee wages up to $1,500 per employee
- Inventory Tax Credit: A taxpayer will receive a credit against the personal property tax liability equal to the personal property tax on all inventory located in the zone
- Equity Investment Credit: Individual investors receive up to a 30% income tax credit for the purchase of equity in start-up or expanding enterprise zone firms
- Loan Interest Credit: A tax credit of 5% of interest earned on loans to enterprise zone businesses or on loans for improvements to real property, including residential property
- Employee Tax Deduction: A tax deduction equal to one-half of adjusted gross income up to $7,500 for employees who live and work in the zone
- Neighborhood Assistance Program: Priority will be given to the enterprise zone program for state Neighborhood Assistance Program tax credits

Eligibility Criteria:

- 25% of resident households are below the poverty level established by the U.S. Census; or average rate of unemployment for the most recent 18 month period at least 150 percent of the statewide rate for the same period
- An area greater than .75 square miles, but less than 3 square miles with a continuous boundary
- Property suitable for a mix of development - commercial, industrial, residential
- The designation of an Urban Enterprise Association meeting requirements of the Act
- General distress of area
- A statement by the applicant indicating its willingness to provide specified economic development incentives

To apply, contact:

Urban Enterprise Zone Program Director
Department of Commerce
One North Capitol, Suite 700
Indianapolis, IN 46204
317-232-8911

Iowa

The state does not have an authorized enterprise zone program.

Kansas

Number of Zones: 78

Method of Designation
- The minimum will be a county and several counties may join into a region. Each city over 2,000 in population must agree to participate in the program

Zone and Tax Incentives:
- Sales tax exemption for manufacturing, if two or more net new jobs are created
- Sales tax exemption for all other non-retail business if five or more net new jobs are created
- Sales tax exemption for retail in cities under 2,500 if two or more net new jobs are created
- Investment tax credit of $1,000/$100,000 for non-retail businesses, with same criteria noted above
- Job creation tax credit of $1,500 for non-manufacturing and if five or more net new jobs are created
- $2,500 per employee in a non-metropolitan region, same conditions

In all areas of the state:
- Sales tax exemption for specific qualified business facilities if two or more new jobs are created
- Investment tax credit for specific business facilities of $1,000/$100,000
- Job creation tax credit of $1,500 per new job created for specific qualified business facilities

To apply contact:
Dave Ross
Business Finance Specialist
Kansas Department of Commerce and Housing
700 Southwest Harrison St., Suite 1300
Topeka, KS 66603-3712
785-296-5298

Kentucky

Number of Zones: 10

Zone and Tax Incentives:
- Building materials used in remodeling, rehabilitation, or new construction within the zone area, and new and used equipment and machinery purchased by a qualified business for use in the zone are exempt from sales and use taxes.
- Commercial vehicles purchased and used for a qualified business solely for business purposes shall be exempt from motor vehicle usage taxes.
- Vehicles purchased and used by a qualified business solely for business purposes are exempt from motor vehicle usage taxes, limited to the first $20,000 of the retail price of the vehicle
- A qualified business is allowed a credit against the tax levied equal to 10% of wages paid to each employee who has been unemployed for at least 90 days or who has received public assistance benefits, based on need and intended to alleviate poverty, for at least 90 days prior to employment with the qualified business, up to $1,500 per employee. Any unused credit may be carried forward for up to five years
- A local government has the option to levy an ad valorem tax rate on qualified property within a zone of one-tenth of one cent upon each $100 of value

Eligibility Criteria:
- A continuous boundary
- An average rate of unemployment at least 1.5 times the national average for the past 18 months
- 70% of its residents with incomes below 80% of the locality's median income, or
- Experienced a population decline of 15% or more between 1970 and 1980

Rural as well as urban areas are eligible.

Business Eligibility:
To qualify for zone incentives, businesses must meet requirements related to location of work, resident employees, unemployment and welfare.

To apply, contact:
Business Information Clearinghouse
Division of Business and Entrepreneurship Development
Department of Community Development
Cabinet for Economic Development
Capital Plaza Tower, 22nd Floor
Frankfort, KY 40601
502-564-4252, ext. 4317
1-800-626-2250 (in Kentucky)

Louisiana

Number of Zones: 1,670

Zone and Tax Incentives:
- Qualified businesses receive $2,500 tax credit per new employee if they hire a minimum of five new employees in the first 5 years of the project
- Qualified businesses receive a $5,000 credit for an aerospace or aviation employee, or AFDC recipient
- Business identified under standard industrial classification code may qualify for $5000 tax credit for each certified new employee

Area Eligibility Criteria:
- Urban and rural parishes are eligible
- Considerations are given for:
    - unemployment and youth unemployment
    - per capita income
    - migration
    - residents receiving public assistance

Local government must agree to:
- apply to the U.S. Department of Commerce to have the enterprise zone declared to be a free trade zone
- devise and implement a program to improve police protection within the zone
- assist the State Department of Economic Development (DED) in certifying employers to be eligible for the zone benefits
- authorize the DED to supersede certain specified local regulations and ordinances which may serve to discourage economic development within the zone
- assist the DED in evaluating progress made in any enterprise zone within its jurisdiction

To apply, contact:
Ed Baker or Marylyn Friedkin
Louisiana Department of Economic Development
Business Incentive Division
P.O. Box 94185
Baton Rouge, LA 70804-9185
225-342-9228
225-342-5402

Maine

Program authorization expired June, 1992. No reauthorization has been issued.

Maryland

Number of Zones: 29. Zone designation is for ten year periods.

Zone and Tax Incentives:
- Local real property tax credit for new investment for 10 years
- Income tax credit for each new full-time job created of 500; for disadvantaged workers the credit is $3,000 ($1,500 the first year, $1,000 the second year, $500 the third year). Reimbursement for on the job training--OJT (20-50%).
- Larger loans for qualified businesses form Maryland's existing loan programs
- Amount of the credit is 80% of the taxes due on any expansion, renovation or capital improvement in the property over the first 5 years, for the next 5 years the credit decreases 10% annually

Eligibility Criteria:
Must meet one of the following requirements:
- Unemployment rate of 150% of the u.S. or the Maryland unemployment rate, whichever is higher, for the preceding eighteen months
- Poverty rate, as measured by the U.S. Census, of 125% of the national average
- 70% of the residents with incomes less than 80% of the median family income in the city or county
- Population decline or loss

Background:
No more than six zones may be designated in any 12 month period. No more than one zone may be designated within any county during a calendar year.

To apply, contact:
Jerry Wade
Enterprise Zone Program Administrator
Department of Employment and Economic Development
217 East Redwood St.
Baltimore, MD 21202
410-767-6438
Fax: 410-333-8309

Massachusetts

The state does not have an authorized enterprise zone program.

Michigan

Number of Zones: The state's Renaissance Zones programs works by granting virtually tax-free status to any business or resident presently in a zone or moving into a zone. The zones are designed to provide selected communities with the most powerful market-based incentive, virtually no state or local taxes, to spur new jobs and investment.

To apply, contact:
John Czarnecki or Karla Campbell
Michigan Economic Development Corporation
201 N. Washington Square
Victor Office Center
Lansing, MI 48913
517-373-9148

Minnesota

Number of Zones: 6 border city zones

Zone and Tax Incentives:
- $1,500 income tax credit per existing employed worker in the zone
- State paid property tax credit for a portion of property taxes paid by existing or new commercial or industrial facilities located in the zone

Eligibility Criteria:
- A city with a contiguous border with a city in another state or with a contiguous border with a city in Minnesota which has a contiguous border with a city in another state
- Qualifying local contributions
- Determined to be economically or fiscally distressed

To apply, contact:
Meredith Udoibok
Department of Trade and Economic Development
500 Metro Square
121 7th Place East
St. Paul, MN 55101
651-297-4132

Mississippi

The state does not have an authorized enterprise zone program.

Missouri

Number of Zones: 61

Zone and Tax Incentives:
- Up to $400 in training credits other than JTPA or state training program
- Refund of unused tax credits earned by new facilities at a rate of 50% or up to $50,000 for the first year, and 25% or up to $25,000 for the second year
- State income tax exemption of 50% for 10 years to be earned by a zone business if 30% if the firm's employee's are zone residents or have exhausted their unemployment compensation benefits
- Tax credits if 30% of new employees are zone residents or are considered "difficult to employ", available for 10% of the first $10,000 in investment, 5% of the next $90,000 and 2% of excess over $100,000

- New Jobs Credit: Up to $400 in tax credits for each new job
- Improved Real Property Tax Abatement (local incentive):
  - For improvements; 50-100% for 10-25 years

Eligibility Criteria:
The following minimum job and investment qualification requirements must be maintained as an annual average in offer to receive tax credits each tax year of the 10-year period.
- New Facility: Two new jobs and $100,000 new investment credit
- Expanding Facility: Two new jobs and $100,000 new investment credit or if less, 25% more than the previous investment at the old facility
- Replacement of old facility with new facility: two new jobs and business facility credit of $1,000,000

To apply, contact:
Mike Heimericks
Coordinator, Enterprise Zone Program
Tax Benefits Programs
Missouri Department of Economic Development
P.O. Box 118
Jefferson City, MO 65102
573-751-9051

Montana

The state does not have an authorized enterprise zone program.

Nebraska

Number of enterprise zones: Five enterprise zones are established

Zone and Tax Incentives:
Qualified businesses can receive tax credits up to $75,000;
- $4,500 for each new employee and $3,000 per $75,000 of investment provided at least 50% of the new employees are zone residents
- $4,500 for each new employee who is a zone resident, $1,500 for non-zone residents, and $1,000 per $75,000 of investments; or
- the normal provisions for tax credits provided by the Employment Expansion and Investment Incentive Act
  -- $1,500 per employee and $1,000 per $75,000 of investment

Eligibility Criteria:
Local Government Eligibility Criteria:
Any city, village, tribal government area, or county may apply for designation of an area within the city village, tribal government area, or county as an enterprise zone.
- Must encompass an area which is at least one but no more than sixteen square miles of one or more discrete areas
- If it is composed of more than one discrete area, each separate area must meet eligibility criteria
- Must have a combined total population of not less than 250 persons

Community Eligibility Criteria:
Communities must meet statutory thresholds of economic distress and areas must meet two of the following three criteria:
- An unemployment rate at least 200% above the state's average unemployment rate, as determined by the 1990 Census
- The average poverty rate exceeds 20% in the census tracts or block groups within the area for metropolitan or primary class cities; or, the average poverty rate exceeds 20% for the area as determined by the 1990 Census
- Documentation of population loss in the area has decreased by at least 10% between decennial censuses

Application Process:
The enterprise zone application must include:
- Geographic description of the proposed target area
- Adoption of a Resolution of Intent to establish a zone
- Conducting a Public Hearing on the question of establishing a local enterprise zone
- A vote of approval by the local governing body
- Appointment of an Enterprise Zone Association Board
- Preparation of an economic redevelopment plan and redevelopment strategies
- Documentation of commitments by local governments of general revenue and other resources to encourage community economic development
- Preparation of a formal application
- Approval of application by the enterprise zone board
- Submission of an enterprise zone application to the Nebraska Department of Economic Development for Review

Qualified zone business activities include:
- The assembly, fabrication, manufacture or procession of tangible personal property
- Farming, ranching or the feeding or raising of livestock
- The performance of data processing, telecommunications, or insurance services
- The performance of financial services
- The administrative headquarters for any business may qualify for enterprise zone tax incentives, even if the activities of the business are excluded because of its retail sales

To apply, contact:
Ron Troutman
Nebraska Dept. of Revenue
301 Centennial Mall South
P.O. Box 94818
Lincoln, NE 68509-4818
402-471-5880
Fax: 402-471-5608

Nevada

The state does not have an authorized enterprise zone program.

New Hampshire

(Labor Surplus Areas). The state does not have an authorized enterprise zone program.

New Jersey

Number of Zones: 20

Zone and Tax Incentives:
- A one-time tax credit of $1,500 for the full-time hiring of residents of a city where a zone is located who have been unemployed or dependent upon public assistance for at least 90 days, or
- Credit of $500 for hiring certain full-time employees
- If an eligible firm does not qualify for employee tax, it may receive an incentive tax credit of eight percent of investment in the zone by an approved "in lieu" agreement
- Sales tax exemptions for materials and for tangible personal property
- Possible state regulatory relief by zone request
- Priority for financial assistance from New Jersey Local Development Financing Fund (LDFF) and Job Training Program

Eligibility Criteria:
- Businesses must be certified as a qualified business within a designated zone by the Urban Enterprise Zone Authority
- A business must either be located in the zone when it becomes effective, or meet certain employment tests if the business is started or moves into the zone after the zone is effective
- An area is defined by a continuous border
- Must have one of the following
    - have an unemployment rate 50% above the national average
    - Income of 25% of the populations is below the poverty level
    - 20% of the residents depend on public assistance

To apply, businesses must make an application to the local municipal zone coordinator on an Authority application form. The local coordinator verifies that the business is within the zone and forwards the application to the Authority for review and approval. For information, contact:
Kelly A. Woods
NJ Urban Enterprise Zone Program
New Jersey Dept. of Commerce and Economic Development
20 W. State St., CN-829
Trenton, NJ 08625-0829
609-292-1912

New Mexico

Number of Zones: 2

Zone and Tax Incentives:
- Fast tracking of infrastructure projects (based on the community's and county's ICIP)
- Tax credits to property owner for rehab-qualified business facilities
- Special set aside and preferences from the state Housing Department
- Tax increment method of financing a locally controlled enterprise zone

fund
- Local property tax abatement for 10 years on qualified property
- Special CDBG funds for infrastructure grants and low-interest economic development loans
- Special technical assistance for all development issues
- The federal Empowerment Zone/Enterprise Community program with over $7 billion in resources
- The coordinated federal and state Technology Transfer initiative
- NAFTA and the growing trade corridors
- HUD's Colonias program with over $200 million targeted at the border states.

To apply contact:
Karen Wentworth
State Enterprise Zone Program Officer
NM Economic Development Dept.
1100 St. Francis Dr.
Santa Fe, NM 87503
505-827-0300

New York

Number of Zones: 52. Upon passage of the 2000-2001 state budget, the Zones Program is now called Empire Zones. The Empire Zones are virtually tax-free zones designed to attract new businesses to New York, as well as encourage the growth of existing businesses.

Zone and Tax Incentives:
- A 100% exemption from increases in assessment based on improvements for up to 7 years.
- A 50% refundable wage tax credit for up to 5 years for hiring full time employees in newly created jobs
- Increased investment tax credit at 8-10% for new investments in the zone
- Capital corporation investment tax credit equal to 25% of the stock of the corporations
- State sales tax exemption on building materials used in construction or rehabilitation of commercial or industrial real property
- Local real property tax abatements at the local level
- Special reduction on utility rates
- Priority for programs and services available through other state agencies

Eligibility Criteria:
Size of Zones:
- Up to 2 square miles within a town with a population of less than 25,000

Eligible Census Tracts:
- Poverty rate of at least 20%
- Unemployment rate of at least 25% above the state unemployment rate
- Zone population of at least 2,000

Counties which do not contain an eligible census tract may apply based on the following criteria:
- Poverty rate of at least 13%
- Unemployment rate of at least 25% above the state unemployment rate
- Zone population of at least 2,000
- Of the total land, 25% must be vacant, abandoned, or otherwise available for industrial or commercial development

Application Process:
A city, town, village or county may apply to have an area designated as a zone. However, in New York City, an individual borough may not apply on its own; only the New York City government may apply for a zone within New York City. Each application must include:
- A map of the proposed zone showing existing streets, highways, etc.
- A statement from the local private industry council governing board of the service delivery area established under the Job Training Partnership Act describing the resources and assistance to be provided to the proposed zone by that program
- Evidence that the views of the residents of the proposed zone and the state and local elected officials and private organizations representing those residents have been considered in the preparation of the application
- A development plan for the proposed zone

To apply, contact:
Fred DiMaggio
Director, Empire Zones Program
30 S. Pearl St.
Albany, NY 12245
518-292-5240

North Carolina

The state does not have an authorized enterprise zone program.

North Dakota

The state does not have an authorized enterprise zone program.

Ohio

Number of Zones: 330

Method of Designation:
Distress-based: A distress-based (full authority) zone may be created if the local authority petitions with certification documents that specific distress levels exist within the designated zone. The six distress criteria are:
- 125% of the state average unemployment during the most recent 12 months.
- at least 10% population loss between 1970-1990.
- prevalence (minimum of 5%) of vacant or demolished commercial or industrial facilities.
- specific vacant industrial facilities.
- income weighted tax capacity of the school district is below 70% of the state average.
- 51% of the population is below 80% of the area's median income

Non Distress-Based: Non Distress-Based zones are not required to document distress. Under this limited zone authority, communities may not consider projects involving intra-state relocations unless a waiver is obtained.

Zone and Tax Incentives:
- Exemption of real and/or personal property assessed values of up to 75% for up to 10 years or an average of 60% over the term of the agreement on new investments in buildings, machinery/equipment and inventory and improvements to existing land and buildings for a specific project. These statutory limits can reach 100% with school board approval.

For information about Ohio's Enterprise Zone Program contact:
> Ohio Department of Development
> Economic Development Division
> Office of Tax Exemption Incentives
> 77 S. High St., 28th Floor
> Columbus, OH 43266
> 614-466-2480

Oklahoma

Number of Zones: Over 200 areas, including counties, communities, and census tracts.

Zone and Tax Incentives: (limited to manufacturing firms)
- Double the regular state investment new job tax credits available elsewhere in the state.
- Low interest loans by Enterprise Zone districts.

Eligibility Criteria:
An area must be economically distressed, as determined by the Oklahoma Department of Commerce.

To apply, contact:
> Jeff Wallace
> Director of Programs
> Oklahoma Department of Commerce
> Box 26980
> Oklahoma City, OK 73126-0980
> 405-815-6552

Oregon

Number of Zones: 48

Zone and Tax Incentives:
- Property tax exemption of 100% for three years to eligible business firms making an investment in qualified property. Qualified property includes new construction and machinery and equipment not already on the county tax rolls for the following kinds of investments:

- New building or structure with a cost of a $25,000 or more.
- Addition to or modification of an existing building or structure with a cost of $25,000 or more (only the increase in value is eligible).
- Site preparation that was necessary for and undertaken within six months before qualifying new construction (only the increase in value is eligible).
- Machinery and equipment that was newly purchased, leased or transferred from outside the country.

Eligibility Criteria:
To qualify, a pre-certification form must be filed by an eligible business with the local enterprise zone manager before the firm makes an investment and before it hires new employees.
- Firms must receive at least 75% of their annual gross receipts by providing goods, products, or services to other businesses through activities such as manufacturing, assembly, fabrication, processing, shipping or storage.
- The firm must invest in qualified property which may be owned or leased by the firm.
- New business firms must hire at least one employee after pre-certification and must increase employment by at least 110% over the firm's employment at recertification.
- Contiguous area no larger than 12 square miles, excluding navigable waters
- Urban businesses (contiguous urbanized portion) must meet one of the following three criteria:
  - Per capita income less than 80% of the state or MSA (Metropolitan Statistical Average) in which the zone is located:
  - Incidence of poverty at least twice as great as the state or MSA average; or
  - Unemployment rate at least twice the state or MSA rate
- Non-urban businesses must be entirely within the economically lagging area as certified by the Governor.

Application Process:
Upon completion of the investment and after the employees have been hired, the pre-certified business firm files its "Oregon Enterprise Zone Property Tax Exemption Application" form with the county assessor between July 1 and August 31. A late application may be filed with the count assessor between Sept. 1 and Sept. 15 with a late filing fee. Approval of an application is based on the provisions of the Oregon Enterprise Zone Act and Oregon Department of Revenue administrative rules.

To apply, contact:
> Oregon Economic and Community Development Department
> 775 Summer St., NE, Suite 200
> Salem, OR 97301-1280
> 1-800-233-3306 TTY and Toll-Free (in Oregon)
> 503-945-8318

Pennsylvania

Number of Zones: The state is divided into 6 regions.

Zone and Tax Incentives:
- Assistance in preparing and revising business plans to ensure that commercial loan applications are given appropriate consideration.
- Low-interest gap loans to reduce bank risk exposure and secure ban approval of commercial loan applications.
- Export market development
- Federal procurement bid assistance
- New product market assessment
- Customized job training
- A 20% tax credit on state Corporate Net Income Tax for the value of investments to rehabilitate or improve buildings or land which are located within boundaries of designated enterprise zones.

Eligibility Requirements:
Financially disadvantaged areas are eligible based upon information compiled by the Department of Community and Economic Development.

Application Process:
An eligible municipality can apply directly to the Department for planning funding or through a redevelopment authority. The application must be accompanied by a copy of a resolution by the local governing body authorizing submittal of the application directly to the Department or on behalf of the local governing body by the county redevelopment authority.

To apply, contact:
> David S. Messner
> Coordinator, Enterprise Zone Program

Strategic Planning and Operations Office
Department of Community and Economic Development
551 Forum Bldg., Room 318
Harrisburg, PA 17120
717-787-7400

Rhode Island

Number of Zones: 11

Zone and Tax Incentives:
- Priority use of job training community development funds.
- Resident business owner tax deduction -- $50,000 per year from net worth of income during first three years, $25,000 per year during 4th and 5th years.
- Donation tax credit -- A taxpayer is eligible for a credit of 20% for any cash donation against the state tax imposed for donations to public supported improvement projects in the zone.
- Payroll tax credit -- maximum of $10,000 credit per employee during the first five years of zone operation.
- Tax benefits for business -- A qualified business must have a minimum of 25% Enterprise Workers to receive credits. The credit is 50% of wages and salaries paid to qualified enterprise zone workers in excess of the wages and salaries paid to employees in the prior year.
- Interest Income Credit -- a maximum $10,000 tax credit on interest earned on loans to qualified businesses.
- Enterprise Worker Tax Exemption -- enterprise workers receiving more than 90% of gross income from a qualified business in the zone may deduct from state gross income either $5,000 or the amount earned per year for a period of two taxable years (or whichever is less).

Eligibility Criteria:
- Businesses must complete an application and submit it to their local zone point of contact
- Poverty within the zone
- A locally developed course of action
- Businesses must add new employees to their company and are also encouraged to hire unemployed, underemployed and disadvantaged individuals
- The zone can't consist of more than five contiguous census tracts or portions, thereof

To apply, contact:
Victor Barrows
Urban Development Manager
Economic Development Corporation
Division of Planning
One West Exchange St.
Providence, RI 02903
401-222-2601

South Carolina

Number of Zones: Entire state is considered an enterprise zone.

Job Tax Credits: For firms engaged in manufacturing, processing, warehousing, wholesaling, research and development and service related industries there is a credit against corporate income tax of:
- $4,500 per job in less developed counties;
- $2,500 per job in moderately developed counties
- $1,500 per job in developed counties and
- $3,500 per job in underdeveloped counties

The four classifications have a 10 job minimum to qualify.

Business enterprises locating in a business or industrial park jointly established and developed by two or more counties:
- may qualify for the dollar credit of the participating county which has the greatest dollar credit, regardless the participating county in which the business is located
- are permitted additional job tax credits, for each new full-time job created, of $500 annually for five years, beginning with year two through six after the creation of the job

Expansions which occur within the five-year certification period are also eligible to receive job tax credits. Credits may be applied against corporate income taxes.
- The number of jobs must meet the minimum criteria of 10
- Credits are $300, $600, or $1,000, depending upon the county of location
- Credits are for a five year period for each full-time job created

Multi-County Industrial Park Incentives:
- Special income tax credit
- Businesses are entitled to the greater jobs tax credit allowed for the most disadvantaged county within the multi-county compact at the least job creation threshold; and, the dollar amount of the credit is increased by $500 per year for each employee during the five year tax credit window

Eligibility Criteria:
- The Tax Commission classifies each county as "less developed," "moderately developed," "developed," or "underdeveloped" and may offer tax incentives to qualified businesses throughout the county according to designation
- Classification is determined annually by the county's relative ranking in the state for levels of average unemployment and average per capital income

To apply, contact:
South Carolina Department of Commerce
P.O. Box 927
Columbia, SC 29202
800-868-7232 or 803-734-9818

South Dakota

The state does not have an authorized enterprise zone program.

Tennessee

Number of Zones: 2. One zone designated in Memphis and one in Nashville.

Zone and Tax Incentives:
- Job creation payments of up to $1,000 per net new employee. Businesses must not make retail sales and employ at least 25 persons within the zone
- Reimbursement of sale and use taxes (local and state) for building materials bought by qualified businesses with the zone
- Reimbursement of 1.3% of the purchase price of industrial machinery for use within the zone
- Reimbursement of 20% (up to $100,000) of the qualified business' contribution to a public school within an enterprise zone
- Exemption from business tax imposed by state and local government on the privilege of selling goods or services
- All income from interest earned on loans to qualified businesses for improvements, operations, or real property is exempt from state income tax
- Funds for state educational assistance grants and guaranteed student loans ar set aside for zone residents

Eligibility Criteria:
- Eligibility for the designation is based on poverty, unemployment and general distress
- Businesses must meet new hire requirements
  - 30% of new hires must be residents of zone and/or be economically disadvantaged individuals
  - Must meet new hire requirements through increase in employment
  - Businesses with multiple locations can use only the employee population working in the zone to meet certification requirements

To apply, contact:
Don Waller
Director, Local Planning
Department of Economic and Community Development
William R. Snodgrass Tennessee Tower, 10th Floor
312 Eighth Ave. North
Nashville, TN 37243-0405
615-741-2211

Texas

Number of Zones: 182

Zone and Tax Incentives:
- Refund of up to $1.25 million in state sales or use tax paid or taxes paid for building materials and machinery and equipment for use in the enterprise zone by a state-designated enterprise project at the rate of no more than $250,000 per year. The project is allowed up to a $2,000

refund for each of 110% of the new or retained permanent jobs for a 5-year designation period for up to 625 jobs.

- Franchise tax reductions for state-designated enterprise projects to be based on 50% reduction of increased apportioned taxable capital or 5% apportioned earned surplus income as calculated on each franchise tax report during the 5-year designation period.
- One-time state sales tax refund of up to $5,000 paid for machinery and equipment. The refund is based upon $500 for each job retained.
- One-time franchise tax refund of up to $5,000 based upon $500 for each new job created by a qualified business in a state-designated enterprise zone when at least 20 new jobs have been created.
- Five percent reduction n electric utility rates
- Priority and preference for all economic development programs of the Texas Department of Commerce and potential priority or preference for other programs administered by the state.

Eligibility Criteria:
- Must have a continuous boundary that encompasses at least one square mile but no more than 20 square miles, excluding waterways and transportation arteries.
- Must have an unemployment rate of at least 1.5 times the national, state or local average for the preceding 12 months or has experienced at least a 9% population loss during the most recent six-year period, or has experienced a population loss of at least 3% for the most recent three-year period.
- Must meet one of seven criteria based on income levels, structural conditions, tax arrearages, loss of jobs or business, declaration as a state or federal disaster area.
- Businesses must be located in or committed to located in a state designated enterprise zone. The business must also commit to hire at least 25% of its new employees from residents of the enterprise zone or to hire economically disadvantaged persons as defined by state law.

Highlights:
More than 35,000 jobs have been committed to be created since 1987. Over 210 Enterprise Zone Projects have been approved to date, stimulating investment of more than $5 billion into Texas communities.

To apply, contact:
Craig Pinkley
Texas Department of Economic Development
Texas Enterprise Zone Office
P.O. Box 12728
Austin, TX 78711-2728
512-936-0269

Utah

Number of Zones: 10. Zones are designated on a county basis.

Zone and Tax Incentives:
- 10% of the first $100,000
- 5% of the next $250,000

- Job Tax Credit Consisting of:
  - $750 per job for manufacturing businesses
  - $1,250 per job if the business is in one of the three targeted groups designated by the county

Eligibility Criteria:
County must meet two of the following criteria:
- Unemployment of 150% of the state average
- Net out migration during the past three years
- Poverty rate of 120% of the state average

An Enterprise Zone plan indicating the local contributions must be submitted. In addition, the county must also complete an economic development plan.

To apply, contact:
John Wilkinson
Enterprise Zone Coordinator
Division of Business and Economic Development
324 South State, Suite 50
Salt Lake City, UT 84111
801-538-8782

Vermont

Program authorization expired December, 1992. No reauthorization has been issued.

Virginia

Number of Zones: 52

Zone and Tax Incentives:
Businesses that qualify for state incentives are provided:
- A general tax credit against state business income, franchise or license tax
- State business income tax credit, decreasing from 80% in the first year to credit 60% for the second through tenth year
- A Sales Tax Exemption (in the form of a refund) for purchases of any qualified business for up to five years
- Refundable Real Property Improvement Tax Credit: A credit of 30% not to exceed $125,000 over a 5 year period is available for rehabilitation projects that cost at least $50,000
- In addition to the state incentives, each designated locality offers its own package of incentives including local tax rebates, business loans, job training, public improvements, fast track permitting and development fee waivers.

Eligibility Criteria:
- A business is required to incur at least 50% of its adjusted gross expenses for a taxable year as a result of business activity within the zone.
- A new business must hire a work force in which 40% or more of those employed have incomes below 80% of the median income of the locality prior to employment.
- An existing business must increase its full-time work force by 10% or more over the average of the base taxable year with at least 40% of the increase meeting the same employee income criteria.

Zone Designation Criteria:
- At least 25% of the population has an income level below 80% of the median income for the jurisdiction, or
- The unemployment rate is at least 50% above the state average, or
- Demonstrate a floor area vacancy rate of industrial and/or commercial properties of 25% or more

To apply, contact:
Nicole Thompson
Enterprise Zone Program Manager
Department of Housing and Community Development
501 N. 2nd St.
Richmond, VA 23219-1321
804-371-7030

Washington

The state does not have an authorized enterprise zone program.

West Virginia

The state does not have an authorized enterprise zone program.

Wisconsin

Legislation was enacted in 1988. Program was expanded in 1993. Legislation authorizes the designation of up to 14 zones. Designation period is seven years. Up to three one-year extensions may be authorized.

Number of Zones: 12

Zone and Tax Incentives:
State tax credits of $21 million are available with 10% held in a reserve fund. The remaining credits are allocated to each zone based on population within the zone with minimums established depending on the size of community. Businesses must be certified by the state before they can incur eligible expenses or claim tax credits. The development zone tax credits include:
- Non-refundable sales tax credit for the amount of sales tax paid on building materials and equipment used in a trade or business.
- A non-refundable 2.5% location credit for the costs of acquiring, constructing, rehabilitating, remodeling, or repairing real property that is used in a trade or business.
- A non-refundable jobs credit for hiring certain target groups equal to 20% of the first $13,000 in qualified wages for the first and second years of employment.
- A non-refundable 2.5 percent investment credit on depreciable tangible personal property used in a trade or business.

- A non-refundable 5% additional research credit on increased expenditures.
- Non-refundable resident credit for employees who are residents of the zone of 10% of the first 2 years wages up to $6,000; a maximum of $600 per employee.
- Non-refundable dependent care credit up to $1,200 per child, per year for the first 2 years of employment.

Eligibility Criteria

Cities, towns, villages, Indian reservations, and, in some cases, counties may apply to designate areas within their jurisdictions as development zones. In order to be considered, the area must meet at least two of the following six criteria:

- The unemployment rate is at least 150% of the state average over the last 18 months
- At least 40% of those residing in the area are members of households that have household income levels at or below 80% of the statewide median household income
- The area is Urban Development Action Grant program eligible
- The property value of the last assessment is lower than the assessment two years earlier
- The percentage of households receiving Aid for Families with Dependent Children (AFDC) in the area is at least 150% of the percentage of households receiving AFDC in the state
- At least 5% of the work force of the locality submitting the application was permanently laid off within the last 18 months

Areas must also meet the following criteria:

- Continuous border following natural or man-made boundaries
- Contiguous blocks, census tracts, or similar units
- If located within an MSA (Metropolitan Statistical Area), the zone must:
  - Contain less than 5% of the valuation of the property of the city, village, or town

- If located, within an MSA, the zone must:
  - Contain less than 5% of the valuation of the property of the city, village, or town
  - If located in a city or the first class, the population of the area is not less than 4,000 nor greater than 5% of the city's population
- If located in a village, town, or city other than a first class city, the population cannot be less than 4,000
- If not part of a MSA, the population must be at least 1,000 but not more than 5,000
- If located within the boundaries of an Indian reservation, the population must be 5,000 or less

Designation is competitive and based on:
- The degree of distress
- Economic development strategy
- Expansion of employment opportunities for the target population
- Coordination of employment and training programs
- Organizational capacity
- Other impacts

Highlights:

Through July 1996, the Wisconsin Department of Development has certified 261 businesses. It also created a Development Opportunity Zone in 1994 that generates projects specifically geared to particular company expansions. One was created in West Alice, WI with an allocation of $3 million in tax credits.

To apply, contact:
  Bill Wheeler
  P.O. Box 7970
  Madison, WI 53707
  608-267-2045

Wyoming

The state does not have an authorized enterprise zone program.

Money For Communities and Nonprofits

The federal money programs outlined here are designed to help communities solve many of today's difficult problems. Economic development opportunities such as job training funds are identified. Community improvement programs for emergency shelters, rural housing, senior centers, and mass transit services are described as well as airport modernization loans and grants. You will discover various services such as school lunch and nutrition programs, runaway halfway houses and health clinics. This information is derived from the *Catalog of Federal Domestic Assistance* which is published by the U.S. Government Printing Office in Washington, DC. The number next to the title description is the reference number listed in this *Catalog*. Contact the office listed below the title for more details.

* Rural Self-Help Housing Technical Assistance (Section 523 Technical Assistance) 10.420

Administrator
Rural Housing and Community Development Service
U.S. Department of Agriculture
Washington, DC 20250   202-720-1474
To provide financial support for the promotion of a program of technical and supervisory assistance that will aid needy very low and low-income individuals and their families in carrying out mutual self-help housing efforts in rural areas. Types of assistance: grants. Estimate of annual funds available: $40,000,000.

* Housing Application Packaging Grants 10.442

Director
Single Family Housing Processing Division
Rural Housing and Community Development
U.S. Department of Agriculture
Washington, DC 20250   202-720-1474
To package single family housing applications for very low- and low-income rural residents in communities and designated counties who wish to buy, build, or repair houses for their own use and to package applications for organizations wishing to develop rental units for lower income families. Types of assistance: grants. Estimate of annual funds available: $495,000.

* Cooperative Extension Service 10.500

Cooperative State Research Education and Extension Service
U.S. Department of Agriculture
Washington, DC 20250   202-720-2810
To help people and communities identify and solve their farm, home, and community problems through the practical application of research findings of the U.S. Department of Agriculture (USDA) and the Land-Grant Colleges and Universities. Types of assistance: grants. Estimate of annual funds available: $406,554,060.

* Food Distribution 10.550

Food Distribution Division
Food and Consumer Service
U.S. Department of Agriculture
Alexandria, VA 22302   703-305-2680
To improve the diets of school and preschool children; the elderly; needy persons in charitable institutions; other individuals in need of food assistance; and to increase the market for domestically produced foods acquired under surplus removal or price support operations. Types of assistance: sale, exchange, or donation. Estimate of annual funds available: $119,252,280.

* Child Nutrition: State Administrative Expenses 10.560

Director, Child Nutrition Division
Food and Consumer Service
U.S. Department of Agriculture
Alexandria, VA 22302   703-305-2590
To provide each state agency with funds for its administrative expenses in supervising and giving technical assistance to local schools, school districts and institutions in their conduct of child nutrition programs. Types of assistance: grants. Estimate of annual funds available: $127,321,000.

* Nutrition Education and Training Program (NET Program) 10.564

Nutrition and Technical Services Division
Food and Consumer Service
U.S. Department of Agriculture
Alexandria, VA 22302   703-305-2554
To help subsidize state and local programs that encourage the dissemination of nutrition information to children participating, or eligible to participate in the school lunch and related child nutrition programs. Types of assistance: grants. Estimate of annual funds available: $2,000,000.

* Temporary Emergency Food Assistance (Administrative Costs) 10.568

Food Distribution Division, FNS
U.S. Department of Agriculture (USDA)
Room 502, Park Office Center
3101 Park Center Drive
Alexandria, VA 22302   703-305-2680
To make funds available to states for storage and distribution costs incurred by nonprofit eligible recipient agencies in providing food assistance to needy persons. Types of assistance: grants. Estimate of annual funds available: $45,000,000.

* Temporary Emergency Food Assistance (Food Commodities) 10.569

Food Distribution Division, FNS
U.S. Department of Agriculture (USDA)
Room 502, Park Office Center
3101 Park Center Drive
Alexandria, VA 22302   703-305-2680
To make food commodities available to states for distribution to the needy. Types of assistance: grants. Estimate of annual funds available: $100,000,000.

* Cooperative Forestry Assistance 10.664

Deputy Chief
State and Private Forestry
Forest Service
U.S. Department of Agriculture
P.O. Box 96090
Washington, DC 20090-6090   202-205-1657
With respect to nonfederal forest and other rural lands to assist in the advancement of forest resources management; the encouragement of the production of timber; the control of insects and diseases affecting trees and forests. Types of assistance: grants. Estimate of annual funds available: $144,320,000.

* Schools and Roads - Grants to States (25 Percent Payments to States) 10.665

Al Smith
Director of Procurement and Property
Forest Service, Room 706 RPE
U.S. Department of Agriculture (USDA)
P.O. Box 96090

Washington, DC 20090-6090   703-235-8007

To share receipts from the National Forests with the states in which the National Forests are situated. To be used for the benefit of the public schools and public roads of the county or counties in which the National Forest is situated. Types of assistance: grants. Estimate of annual funds available: $217,337,000.

* Schools and Roads - Grants to Counties (Payments to Counties) 10.666

Al Smith
Director of Procurement and Property
Forest Service, Room 701 RPE
U.S. Department of Agriculture (USDA)
P.O. Box 96090
Washington, DC 20090-6090   703-235-8007

To share receipts from National Grasslands and Land Utilization Projects with the counties in which the National Grasslands and Land Utilization Projects are situated. To be used for school or road purposes or both. Types of assistance: grants. Estimate of annual funds available: $6,038,000.

* Empowerment Zones Program 10.772

U.S. Department of Agriculture
Rural Business and Cooperative Development Servicing
EZ/EC Team
300 7th St., SW, Room 701
Washington, DC 20024   202-619-7981

Provides for the establishment of empowerment zones and enterprise communities in rural areas to stimulate the creation of new jobs, particularly for the disadvantaged and long-term unemployed, and to promote revitalization of economically distressed areas. Types of assistance: grants. Estimate of annual funds available: $280,000,000.

* Livestock, Meat and Poultry Market Supervision 10.800

Administrator for Packers and Stockyards Administration
Room 3039, South Building
U.S. Department of Agriculture
Washington, DC 20250   202-720-7051

To protect producers and consumers against unfair business practices in the marketing of livestock, meat and poultry; and members of the livestock marketing and meat and poultry industries against unfair, deceptive, discriminatory, and monopolistic practices of competitors. Types of assistance: grants. Estimate of annual funds available: $19,348,000.

* Rural Electrification Loans and Loan Guarantees 10.850

Administrator
Rural Utilities Service
U.S. Department of Agriculture
Washington, DC 20250   202-720-9540

To assure that people in eligible rural areas have access to electric services comparable in reliability and quality to the rest of the Nation. Types of assistance: direct loans. Estimate of annual funds available: $350,000,000.

* Rural Telephone Loans and Loans Guarantees 10.851

Assistant Administrator
Rural Utilities Service
U.S. Department of Agriculture
Washington, DC 20250   202-720-9554

To assure that people in eligible rural areas have access to telecommunications services comparable in reliability and quality to the rest of the Nation. Types of assistance: direct loans. Estimate of annual funds available: $120,000,000.

* Rural Telephone Bank Loans 10.852

Assistant Governor
Rural Telephone Bank
U.S. Department of Agriculture
Washington, DC 20250   202-720-9554

To provide supplemental financing to extend and improve telecommunications services in rural areas. Types of assistance: direct loans. Estimate of annual funds available: $175,000,000.

* Rural Economic Development Loans and Grants 10.854

Administrator
Rural Business and Cooperative Development Service
U.S. Department of Agriculture
Washington, DC 20250   202-720-1400

To promote rural economic development and job creation projects, including funding for project feasibility studies, startup costs, incubator projects, and other reasonable expenses for the purpose of fostering rural development. Types of assistance: direct loans. Estimate of annual funds available: Loans $15,000,000; Grants $4,000,000.

* Distance Learning and Medical Link Grants 10.855

Assistant Administrator
Telecommunications, Rural Utilities Service
Room 4056, South Building
U.S. Department of Agriculture
14th and Independence Ave., SW
Washington, DC 20250   202-720-9554

To encourage and improve the use of telecommunications, computer networks, and related advanced technologies to provide educational and medical benefits to people living in rural areas. Types of assistance: grants. Estimate of annual funds available; $20,000,000.

* Watershed Protection and Flood Prevention (Small Watershed Program; PL-566 Program) 10.904

Deputy Chief for Programs
Natural Resources Conservation Service
U.S. Department of Agriculture
P.O. Box 2890
Washington, DC 20013   202-720-4527

To provide technical and financial assistance in planning and carrying out works of improvement to protect, develop, and utilize the land and water resources in small watersheds. Types of assistance: grants. Estimate of annual funds available: $31,989,000.

* Economic Development - Grants for Public Works and Development Facilities 11.300

David L. McIlwain, Director, Public Works Division
Economic Development Administration
Room H7326, Herbert Hoover Bldg.
U.S. Department of Commerce
Washington, DC 20230   202-482-5265

To promote long-term economic development and assist in the construction of public works and development facilities needed to initiate and encourage the creation or retention of permanent jobs in the private sector in areas experiencing severe economic distress. Types of assistance: grants. Estimate of annual funds available: $251,200,000.

* Economic Development-Support for Planning Organizations (Development District Program; Redevelopment Area Program; and Indian Program) 11.302

Luis F. Bueso
Director Planning Division
Economic Development Administration
Room H2319, Herbert Hoover Bldg.
Washington, DC 20230   202-377-2873

To assist in providing administrative aid to multi-county district and redevelopment area (primarily Indian reservations and lands) economic development planning and implementation capability and thereby promote effective utilization of resources in the creation of full-time permanent jobs for the unemployed and the underemployed in high distress areas. Types of assistance: grants. Estimate of annual funds available: $20,000,000.

* Economic Development-Technical Assistance 11.303

Richard E. Hage, Technical Assistance Programs
Economic Development Administration
Room H7319, Herbert Hoover Bldg.
U.S. Department of Commerce
Washington, DC 20230   202-482-2127

To promote economic development and alleviate under-employment and unemployment in distressed areas, EDA operates a technical assistance program. Types of assistance: grants. Estimate of annual funds available: $10,300,000.

* Special Economic Development and Adjustment Assistance Program-Sudden and Severe Economic Dislocation and Long-term Economic Deterioration (SSED and LTED) 11.307

David Witschi, Director
Economic Adjustment Division
Economic Development Administration
Room H7327, Herbert Hoover Bldg.
U.S. Department of Commerce
Washington, DC 20230   202-482-2659

To assist state and local areas develop and/or implement strategies designed to address adjustment problems resulting from sudden and severe economic dislocation such as plant closings (SSED), or from long-term economic deterioration in the area's economy (LTED). Types of assistance: grants. Estimate of annual funds available: $ 199,950,000.

* Research and Evaluation Program 11.312

Richard Hage
Room H-7315, EDA
U.S. Department of Commerce
Washington, DC 20230   202-482-4085

To assist in the determination of causes of unemployment, underemployment, underdevelopment, and chronic depression in various areas and regions of the Nation. Types of assistance: grants. Estimate of annual funds available: $500,000.

* Anadromous and Great Lakes Fisheries Conservation 11.405

Director
Office of Fisheries Conservation and Management
National Marine Fisheries Service
1315 East-West Hwy.
Silver Spring, MD 29010   202-713-2334

To cooperate with the states and other nonfederal interests in the conservation, development, and enhancement of the nation's anadromous fish and the fish in the Great Lakes and Lake Champlain that ascent streams to spawn, and for the control of sea lamprey. Types of assistance: grants. Estimate of annual funds available: $1,992,000.

* Interjurisdictional Fisheries Act of 1986 11.407

Director
Office of Fisheries Conservation and Management
National Marine Fisheries Service
1315 East-West Hwy.
Silver Spring, MD 20910   301-713-2334

To assist states in managing interjurisdictional fisheries resources. Types of assistance: grants. Estimate of annual funds available: $3,283,000.

* Coastal Zone Management Program Administration Grants 11.419

Chief, Coastal Programs Division
Office of Ocean Coastal Resource Management
National Ocean Service
National Oceanic and Atmospheric Administration (NOAA)
U.S. Department of Commerce
1305 East West Highway
Silver Spring, MD 20910   301-713-3102

To assist states in implementing and administering Coastal Zone Management programs that have been approved by the Secretary of Commerce. Types of assistance: grants. Estimate of annual funds available: $151,000,000.

* Coastal Zone Management Estuarine Research Reserves 11.420

Chief, Marine and Estuarine Management Div.
Office of Ocean and Coastal Resource Management
National Ocean Service
National Oceanic and Atmospheric Administration (NOAA)
U.S. Department of Commerce
1305 East West Highway
Silver Spring, MD 20910   301-713-3125

To assist states in the acquisition, research, development and operation of national estuarine research reserves for the purpose of creating natural field laboratories to gather data and make studies of the natural and human processes occurring within the estuaries of the coastal zone. Types of assistance: grants. Estimate of annual funds available: $18,000,000.

* Fisheries Development and Utilization Research and Development Grants and Cooperative Agreements Program 11.427

Office of Trade and Industry Services
National Marine Fisheries Service
National Oceanic and Atmospheric Administration (NOAA)
U.S. Department of Commerce
1315 East West Hwy.
Silver Spring, MD 20910   301-713-2358

To foster the development and strengthening of the fishing industry of the United States and increase the supply of wholesome, nutritious fish and fish products available to consumers. Types of assistance: grants. Estimate of annual funds available: $1,000,000.

* Regional Centers for the Transfer of Manufacturing Technology 11.611

Mr. Kevin Carr
Director, NIST MTC Program
Room C121, Metrology Bldg.
National Institute of Standards and Technology (NIST)
Gaithersburg, MD 20899   301-975-5020

To establish regional centers, the functions of which are to accelerate the transfer of advanced manufacturing technology from the National Institute of Standards and Technology (NIST) automated manufacturing research facility and similar research and development laboratories to small and medium sized U.S. based manufacturing firms. Types of assistance: grants. Estimate of annual funds available: $87,182,000.

* Minority Business Resource Development 11.802

Assistant Director
Office of Program Development
Minority Business Development Agency
U.S. Department of Commerce (MB and IA/C of C)
14th and Constitution Ave, NW, Room 5096
Washington, DC 20230   202-482-5770

To provide financial assistance for Minority Business and Industry Association/ Minority Chambers of Commerce (MB and IA/C of C) which act as advocates for their members and the minority community. Types of assistance: grants. Estimate of annual funds available: $1,000,000.

* Military Construction, National Guard 12.400

Director of Engineering
NGB-AEN, ARNG Readiness Center
111 S. George Mason Dr.
Arlington, VA 22204   703-607-7900

To provide a combat-ready reserve force and facilities for training and administering the Army and Air Force National Guard units in the 50 states, District of Columbia, Commonwealth of Puerto Rico, Virgin Islands, and Guam. Types of assistance: grants. Estimate of annual funds available: $66,363,000.

* Community Economic Adjustment Planning Assistance 12.607

Director
Office of Economic Adjustment, OASD (ES)
400 Army Navy Dr., Suite 200
Arlington, VA 22202   703-604-6020

To assist local governments or states, on behalf of local government to undertake community economic adjustment planning activities to respond to military base closures and realignments. Types of assistance: grants. Estimate of annual funds available: $40,000,000.

* Joint Studies Land Use 12.610

Director
Office of Economic Adjustment, OASD
400 Army Navy Dr., Suite 200
Arlington, VA 22202   703-604-6020

To enable the Army, Navy, Air Force, and Marine Corps to participate in development and implementation of Joint Military/ Community Comprehensive Land Use Plans. Types of assistance: grants. Estimate of annual funds available: $300,000.

* Community Base Reuse Plans 12.612

Director
Office of Economic Adjustment, OASD (ES)
400 Army Navy Dr., Suite 200
Arlington, VA 22202   703-604-6020

To assist local governments or states, on behalf of local governments, to conduct community base reuse plans at closing or realigning military installations. Types of assistance: grants. Estimate of annual funds available: $500,000.

* Mortgage Insurance-Hospitals (242 Hospitals) 14.128

Insurance Division
Office of Insured Multifamily Housing Development
U.S. Department of Housing and Urban Development
Washington, DC 20410   202-708-0599

To make possible the financing of hospitals. Types of assistance: loan guarantee. Estimate of annual funds available: $1,030,000,000.

* Mortgage Insurance-Nursing Homes, Intermediate Care Facilities and Board and Care Homes (232 Nursing Homes) 14.129

Insurance Division
Office of Insured Multifamily Housing Development
U.S. Department of Housing and Urban Development
Washington, DC 20412   202-708-2556

Types of assistance: loan guarantee. Estimate of annual funds available: $5,449,000,000.

* Community Development Block Grants/ Entitlement Grants 14.218

Entitlement Cities Division
Office of Block Grant Assistance
Community Planning and Development
451 7th St., SW
Washington, DC 20410   202-708-1577

To develop viable urban communities, by providing decent housing and a suitable living environment. Types of assistance: grants. Estimate of annual funds available: $3,140,410,000.

* Community Development Block Grants/Small

Cities Program (Small Cities) 14.219
State and Small Cities Division
Office of Block Grant Assistance Community Planning
 and Development
U.S. Department of Housing and Urban Development (HUD)
451 7th St., SW
Washington, DC 20410   202-708-1322

The primary objective of this program is the development of viable urban communities by providing decent housing, a suitable living environment, and expanding economic opportunities. Types of assistance: grants. Estimate of annual funds available: $5,238,000.

* Community Development Block Grants/ Secretary's Discretionary Fund/Insular Area 14.225

Office of Program Policy Development
Community Planning and Development
U.S. Department of Housing and Urban Development (HUD)
451 7th St., SW
Washington, DC 20410   202-708-1322

To provide community development assistance to American Samoa, Guam, the Northern Mariana Islands, Palau and the Virgin Islands. Types of assistance: grants. Estimate of annual funds available: $7,000,000.

* Community Development Block Grants/State's Program 14.228

State and Small Cities Division

Office of Block Grant Assistance
Community Planning and Development
U.S. Department of Housing and Urban Development (HUD)
451 7th St., SW
Washington, DC 20410   202-708-1322

The primary objective of this program is the development of viable urban communities by providing decent housing, a suitable living environment and expanding economic opportunities principally for persons of low and moderate income. Types of assistance: grants. Estimate of annual funds available: $1,340,651,000.

* Emergency Shelter Grants Program (ESGP) 14.231

Barbara Richards
Division of Special Needs Assistance
U.S. Department of Housing and Urban Development (HUD)
451 7th St., SW, Room 7262
Washington, DC 20410   202-708-4300

The program is designed to help improve the quality of existing emergency shelters for the homeless, to help make available additional emergency shelters, and to help pay the costs of operating emergency shelters. Types of assistance: grants. Estimate of annual funds available: $150,000,000.

* Empowerment Zones Program 14.244

Office of Community Planning and Development
U.S. Department of Housing and Urban Development   800-998-9999

To provide for the establishment of Empowerment Zones and Enterprise Communities in urban areas, to stimulate the creation of new jobs, particularly for the disadvantaged and long-term unemployed, and to promote revitalization of economically distressed areas. Types of assistance: grants. Estimate of annual funds available: $150,000,000.

* Fair Housing Assistance Program-State and Local (FHAP) 14.401

Assistant Secretary for Fair Housing
 and Equal Opportunity
U.S. Department of Housing and Urban Development (HUD)
451 7th St., SW
Washington, DC 20410   202-708-0455

To provide to those agencies to whom the U.S. Department of Housing and Urban Development (HUD) must refer Title VIII complaints both the incentives and resources required to develop an effective work force to handle complaints and provide technical assistance and training. Types of assistance: grants. Estimate of annual funds available: $21,000,000.

* Employment Opportunities for Lower Income Persons and Businesses 14.412

Maxine Cunningham
Office of Fair Housing and Equal Opportunity
U.S. Department of Housing and Urban Development
451 7th St., SW
Washington, DC 20410   202-708-3633

To promote affirmative action by Public Housing Agencies (PHAs) and to expand the Department's Title VI Compliance Program beyond the HUD-initiated compliance review process. Types of assistance: advisory services and counseling. Estimate of annual funds available: not known.

* Community Outreach Partnership Center Program 14.511

HUD USER
P.O. Box 6091
Rockville, MD 20849   800-245-2691

This program is a five-year demonstration program to determine the feasibility of facilitating partnerships among institutions of higher education and communities to solve urban problems through research, outreach and exchange of information. Types of assistance: grants. Estimate of annual funds available: $15,000,000.

* Community Development Work-Study Program 14.512

HUD USER
P.O. Box 6091
Rockville, MD 20849   800-245-2691

To make grants to institutions of higher education for the purpose of providing assistance to economically disadvantaged and minority students who participate in community development work-study programs are enrolled in full-time graduate or undergraduate programs in community and economic development and community planning. Types of assistance: grants. Estimate of annual funds available: $3,000,000.

* Edward Byrne Memorial State and Local Law Enforcement Assistance Discretionary Grants Program 16.580

Office of Justice Programs
Bureau of Justice Assistance
U.S. Department of Justice
633 Indiana Ave., NW
Washington, DC 20531   202-514-5947

To enhance the capacity of each state to define the drug problem and to focus on program development on areas of greatest need. Types of assistance: grant. Estimate of annual funds available: $57,546,000.

* Crime Victim Assistance/Discretionary Grants 16.582

Marti Speights, Division Director
Office for Victims of Crime
Office of Justice Programs
U.S. Department of Justice
633 Indiana Ave., NW
Washington, DC 20531   202-616-3582

One percent of the Crime Victims Fund is statutorily reserved by the Office for Victims of Crime for grants to provide training and technical assistance services to eligible crime victims assistance programs and for financial support of services to victims of federal crime by eligible crime victims assistance programs. Types of assistance: grants, direct payments. Estimate of annual funds available: $7,793,222.

* Children's Justice Act Discretionary Grants for Native American Indian Tribes (Children's Justice Act for Native American Indian Tribes) 16.583

Marti Speights, Division Director
Office for Victims of Crime
Office of Justice Programs
U.S. Department of Justice
633 Indiana Ave., NW
Washington, DC 20531   202-616-3578

Fifteen percent of the funds from the Crime Victims Services that are transferred to the U.S. Department of Health and Human Services as part of the Children's Justice Act are to be statutorily reserved by the Office for Victims of Crime to make grants for the purpose of assisting native American Indian tribes in developing, establishing and operating programs. Types of assistance: grants, direct payments. Estimate of annual funds available: $1,500,000.

* Corrections-Training and Staff Development 16.601

National Institute of Corrections
320 First St., NW, Room 5007
Washington, DC 20534   202-307-3156

To devise and conduct in various geographical locations, seminars, workshops and training programs for law enforcement officers, judges and judicial personnel, probation and parole personnel, correctional personnel, welfare workers and other personnel, including lay ex-offenders and paraprofessionals, connected with the treatment and rehabilitation of criminal and juvenile offenders. Types of assistance: grants. Estimate of annual funds available: $3,063,000.

* Corrections-Technical Assistance/ Clearinghouse 16.603

Technical Assistance Coordinator
National Institute of Corrections
320 First St., NW, Room 5007
Washington, DC 20534   202-307-3106

To encourage and assist federal, state, and local government programs and services, and programs and services of other public and private agencies, institutions, in their efforts to develop and implement improved corrections programs. Types of assistance: grants. Estimate of annual funds available: $6,125,000.

* Employment Service 17.207

John Robinson, Director
United States Employment Service
Employment and Training Administration
U.S. Department of Labor
Washington, DC 20210   202-219-5257

To place persons in employment by providing a variety of placement-related services without charge to job seekers and to employers seeking qualified individuals to fill job openings. Types of assistance: grants. Estimate of annual funds available: $761,735,000.

* Dislocated Workers: Employment and Training Assistance 17.246

Employment and Training Administration
U.S. Department of Labor
200 Constitution Ave., NW
Room N5426
Washington, DC 20210   202-219-5577

To assist dislocated workers obtain unsubsidized employment through training and related employment services using a decentralized system of state programs. Types of assistance: grants. Estimate of annual funds available: $1,770,510,000.

* Migrant and Seasonal Farmworkers (Migrant and Other Seasonally Employed Farmworker Programs) 17.247

Office of Special Targeted Programs
Division of Seasonal Farmworker Programs
Employment and Training Administration
U.S. Department of Labor
Room N4641
200 Constitution Ave., NW
Washington, DC   202-219-5500

To provide job training, job search assistance, and other supportive services for those individuals who suffer chronic seasonal unemployment and underemployment in the agricultural industry. Types of assistance: grants. Estimate of annual funds available: $74,445,000.

* Employment Services and Job Training-Pilot and Demonstration Programs 17.249

Administrator
Office of Policy and Research
Employment and Training Administration
U.S. Department of Labor
200 Constitution Ave., NW
Washington, DC   202-219-5677

To provide, foster, and promote job training and other services which are most appropriately administered at the national level and which are operated in more than one state to groups with particular disadvantage in the labor market. Types of assistance: grants. Estimate of annual funds available: $35,000,000.

* Job Training Partnership Act (JTPA) 17.250

Donald Kulick
Employment and Training Administration
U.S. Department of Labor
200 Constitution Ave., NW
Washington, DC 20210   202-219-6236

To provide job training and related assistance to economically disadvantaged individuals and others who face significant employment barriers. Types of assistance: grants. Estimate of annual funds available: unknown.

* Native American Employment and Training Programs 17.251

Division of Indian and Native American Programs
Employment and Training Administration
U.S. Department of Labor
200 Constitution Ave., NW
Room N4641
Washington, DC   202-219-8502

To afford job training to Native Americans facing serious barriers to employment, who are in special need of such training to obtain productive employment. Types of assistance: grants. Estimate of annual funds available: $55,000,000.

* Mine Health and Safety Grants 17.600

Assistant Secretary of Labor for Mine Safety and Health
Mine Safety and Health Administration
U.S. Dept. of Labor
4015 Wilson Blvd.
Arlington, VA 22203   703-235-8264

To assist states in developing and enforcing effective mine health and safety laws and regulations. Types of assistance: grants. Estimate of annual funds available: $7,639,000.

* Disabled Veterans Outreach Program 17.801

Veterans Employment and Training Service
Office of the Assistant Secretary for Veterans
Employment and Training
U.S. Department of Labor
200 Constitution Ave., NW, Room S-1316
Washington, DC 20210   202-219-9105

To provide funds to states to provide job and job training opportunities for disabled and other veterans through contacts with employers. Types of assistance: grants. Estimate of annual funds available: $80,215,000.

* Local Veterans Employment Representative Program (LVER Program) 17.804

Veterans Employment and Training Service
Office of the Asst. Secretary for Veterans
Employment and Training
U.S. Dept. of Labor, Room S1316
200 Constitution Ave., NW
Washington, DC 20210   202-219-9105

To provide funds to State Employment Service/Job Service Agencies to ensure that there is local supervision of compliance with federal regulations, performance standards, and grant agreement provisions in carrying out requirements of 38 USC 2004 in providing veterans with maximum employment and training opportunities. Types of assistance: grants. Estimate of annual funds available: $77,253,000.

* Boating Safety Financial Assistance 20.005

Commandant
U.S. Coast Guard
Washington, DC 20593-0001   202-267-0857

To encourage greater state participation and uniformity in boating safety, particularly to permit the states to assume the greater share of boating safety education , assistance, and enforcement activities. Types of assistance: grants. Estimate of annual funds available: $57,000,000.

* Airport Improvement Program (AIP) 20.106

Federal Aviation Administration (FAA)
Office of Airport Planning and Programming
Grants-in-Aid Division, APP-500
800 Independence Ave., SW
Washington, DC 20591   202-267-3831

To assist sponsors, owners, or operators of public-use airports in the development of a nationwide system of airports adequate to meet the needs of civil aeronautics. Types of assistance: grants. Estimate of annual funds available: $1,800,000,000.

* Highway Planning and Construction (Federal-Aid Highway Program) 20.205

William Weseman, Director
Office of Engineering
Federal Highway Agency (FHA)
400 7th St., SW
Washington, DC 20590   202-366-4853

To assist state highway agencies (SHA) in the development of an integrated, interconnected network of highways by constructing and rehabilitating the interstate highway system and building or improving primary, secondary and urban systems roads, and streets. Types of assistance: grants. Estimate of annual funds available: $30,321,332,000.

* Motor Carrier Safety Assistance Program (MCSAP) 20.218

Associate Administrator for Motor Carriers
Federal Highway Agency (FHA)
Washington, DC 20590   202-366-2519

To reduce the number and severity of accidents and hazardous materials incidents involving commercial motor vehicles by substantially increasing the level of enforcement activity and the likelihood that safety defects, driver deficiencies, and unsafe carrier practices will be detected and corrected. Types of assistance: grants. Estimate of annual funds available: $185,000,000.

* Federal Transit Capital Improvement Grants (Capital Grants) 20.500

Federal Transit Administration
U.S. Department of Transportation
400 7th St., SW
Washington, DC 20590   202-366-1660

To assist in financing the acquisition, construction, reconstruction and improvement of facilities and equipment for use, by operation, lease, or otherwise in mass transportation service in urban areas. Types of assistance: grants. Estimate of annual funds available: $3,113,000,000.

* Federal Transit-Metropolitan Planning Grants (Metropolitan Planning) 20.505

Director, Office of Planning Assistance
Office of Grants Management
Federal Transit Administration
U.S. Department of Transportation (DOT)
400 7th St., SW
Washington, DC 20590   202-366-6385

To assist in planning, engineering and designing of urban mass transportation projects, and other technical studies in a program for a united or officially coordinated urban transportation system. Types of assistance: grants. Estimate of annual funds available: $52,113,600.

* Federal Transit Formula Grants (Urbanized Area Formula Program) 20.507

Director, Office of Planning Assistance
Office of Grants Management
Federal Transit Administration
U.S. Department of Transportation (DOT)
400 7th St., SW
Washington, DC 20590   202-366-1662

To assist in financing the acquisition, construction, cost effective leasing, planning and improvement of facilities and equipment for use by operation or lease or otherwise in mass transportation service. Types of assistance: grants. Estimate of annual funds available: $3,049,966,000.

* Formula Grants for Other Than Urbanized Areas (Section 18) (Nonurbanized Area Formula Program) 20.509

Federal Transit Administration
Office of Grants Management
Office of Capital and Formula Assistance
400 7th St., SW
Washington, DC 20590   202-366-6385

To improve, initiate, or continue public transportation services in nonurbanized areas by providing financial assistance for the acquisition, construction and improvement of facilities and equipment and the payment of operating expenses by operating contract, lease or otherwise. Types of assistance: grants. Estimate of annual funds available: $226,628,000.

* Federal Transit Technical Assistance (Research, Development and Demonstration Project) 20.512

Associate Administrator for Technical Assistance and Safety (TTS-1)
Federal Transit Administration
U.S. Department of Transportation (DOT)
400 7th St., SW, Room 6431
Washington, DC 20590   202-366-4052

To improve mass transportation service, to contribute toward meeting total urban transportation needs at a minimum cost, and to assist in the reduction of urban transportation needs by improving the ability of transit industry operating officials to plan, manage, and operate their systems more effectively and safely. Types of assistance: grants. Estimate of annual funds available: unknown.

* Capital Assistance Program for Elderly Persons and Persons with Disabilities (Section (b)(2)) 20.513

Federal Transit Administration
Office of Grants Management

Office of Capital and Formula Assistance
400 7th St., SW
Washington, DC 20590   202-366-2053
To provide financial assistance in meeting the transportation needs of elderly and handicapped persons where public transportation services are unavailable. Types of assistance: grants. Estimate of annual funds available: $78,851,000.

* State and Community Highway Safety 20.600

Adele Derby
Coordinator of Regional Operations
National Highway Traffic Safety Administration
Washington, DC 20590   202-366-6902
To provide a coordinated national highway safety program to reduce traffic accidents, deaths, injuries, and property damage. Types of assistance: grants. Estimate of annual funds available: $155,000,000.

* Pipeline Safety 20.700

Tom Fortner
Research and Special Programs Administration
U.S. Department of Transportation
400 7th St., SW
Washington, DC 20590   202-366-4564
To develop and maintain state natural gas, liquified natural gas, and hazardous liquid pipeline safety programs. Types of assistance: grants. Estimate of annual funds available: $17,519,000.

* Tax Counseling for the Elderly 21.006

Tax Counseling for the Elderly
Taxpayer Service Division
Internal Revenue Services
1111 Constitution Ave., NW
Washington, DC 20224   202-622-7664
To authorize the Internal Revenue Service to enter into agreement with private or public nonprofit agencies or organizations to establish a network of trained volunteers to provide free income tax information and return preparation assistance to elderly taxpayers. Types of assistance: direct payment. Estimate of annual funds available: $3,950,000.

* Appalachian Supplements to Federal Grant-In-Aid Community Development 23.002

Executive Director
Appalachian Regional Commission
1666 Connecticut Avenue, NW
Washington DC 20235   202-884-7700
To meet the basic needs of local areas and assist in improving creation of jobs and private sector involvement and investment by funding development facilities such as water and sewage systems, sewage treatment plants, industrial sites and providing basic water and sewer facilities. Types of assistance: grants. Estimate of annual funds available: $61,000,000.

* Appalachian Development Highway System (Appalachian Corridor) 23.003

Executive Director
Appalachian Regional Commission
1666 Connecticut Ave., NW
Washington, DC 20235   202-884-7700
To provide a highway system which, in conjunction with other federally aided highways, will open areas with development potential within the Appalachian region where commerce and communication have been inhibited by lack of adequate access. Types of assistance: grants. Estimate of annual funds available: $105,000,000.

* Appalachian Local Access Roads 23.008

Executive Director
Appalachian Regional Commission
1666 Connecticut Ave., NW
Washington, DC 20235   202-884-7700
To provide access to industrial, commercial, educational, recreational, residential and related transportation facilities which directly or indirectly relate to the improvement of the areas determined by the states to have significant development potential. Types of assistance: grant. Estimate of annual funds available: $2,000,000.

* Appalachian Local Development District Assistance (LDD) 23.009

Executive Director
Appalachian Regional Commission
1666 Connecticut Ave., NW
Washington, DC 20235   202-884-7700
To provide planning and development resources in multicounty areas; to help develop the technical competence essential to sound development assistance. Types of assistance: grant. Estimate of annual funds available: $5,400,000.

* Appalachian State Research, Technical Assistance, and Demonstration Projects (State Research) 23.011

Executive Director
Appalachian Regional Commission
1666 Connecticut Ave., NW
Washington, DC 20235   202-884-7700
To expand the knowledge of the region to the fullest extent possible by means of state-sponsored research studies, technical assistance and demonstration projects in order to assist the Commission in accomplishing the objectives of the Act. Types of assistance: grant. Estimate of annual funds available: $900,000.

* Presidential Management Intern Program 27.013

Office of Marketing and Information
Workforce Training Service
Office of Personnel Management
1400 Wilson Blvd.
Arlington, VA 22209   703-312-7282
To attract to the federal service graduate students of exceptional potential who are receiving advanced degrees in a variety of academic disciplines and who have a clear interest in and commitment to a career in the analysis and management of public programs and policies. Types of assistance: federal employment. Estimate of annual funds available: unknown.

* Employment Discrimination-State and Local Fair Employment Agency Contracts 30.002

Lawrence Koziarz
State and Local Programs Division
Office of Program Operations
Equal Employment Opportunity Commission (EEOC)
1801 L St., NW, Room 8030
Washington, DC 20507   202-663-4856
To assist EEOC in the enforcement of Title VII of the Civil Rights Act of 1964, as amended and of the age discrimination in employment act of 1967 by investigating and resolving charges of employment discrimination based on race, color, religion, sex, national origin, etc. Types of assistance: direct payment. Estimate of annual funds available: $29,000,000.

* Employment Discrimination Project Contracts - Indian Tribes 30.009

Lawrence Koziarz
State and Local Programs Division
Office of Program Operations
Equal Employment Opportunity Commission (EEOC)
1801 L St., NW, Room 8030
Washington, DC 20507   202-663-4856
To insure the protection of employment rights of Indians working on reservation. Types of assistance: direct payments for specified use. Estimate of annual funds available: included in program 30.002.

* Labor-Management Cooperation 34.002

Division of Labor Management Grant Programs
Federal Mediation and Conciliation Service
2100 K St., NW
Washington, DC 20247   202-606-8181
Types of assistance: grants. Estimate of annual funds available: $1,500,000.

* Community Development Revolving Loan Program for Credit Unions (CDCU) 44.002

Mr. Floyd Lancaster
Community Development Revolving Loan
 Program for Credit Unions
National Credit Union Administration

1775 Duke St.
Alexandria, VA 22314   703-518-6610

To support community based credit unions in their efforts to stimulate economic development activities which result in increased income, ownership and employment opportunities for low-income residents and to provide basic financial and related services to residents of their communities. Types of assistance: direct loans. Estimate of annual funds available: $1,000,000.

* Management and Technical Assistance for Socially and Economically Disadvantaged Businesses: 7(j) Development Assistance Program 59.007

Associate Administrator for Minority Small Business
409 3rd St., SW
Washington, DC 20416   202-205-6410

To provide management and technical assistance through qualified individuals, public or private organizations to existing or potential businesses which are economically and socially disadvantaged or which are located in areas of high concentration of unemployment. Types of assistance: grants. Estimate of annual funds available: $5,000,000.

* Physical Disaster Loans (7(b) Loans (DL)) 59.008

Office of Disaster Assistance
Small Business Administration (SBA)
409 3rd St., SW
Washington, DC 20416   202-205-6734

To provide loans to the victims of designated physical-type disasters for uninsured loans. Types of assistance: loans, loan guarantee. Estimate of annual funds available: $934,000,000.

* Small Business Development Center (SBDC) 59.037

Small Business Administration
Office of Small Business Development Center
409 3rd St., SW, 4th Floor
Washington, DC 20416   202-205-6776

To provide management counseling, training and technical assistance to the small business community through Small Business Development Centers (SBDCs). Types of assistance: grants. Estimate of annual funds available: $62,000,000.

* Veterans State Domiciliary Care 64.014

Assistant Chief Medical Director
  for Geriatrics and Extended Care
U.S. Department of Veterans Affairs
Washington, DC 20420   202-535,7538

To provide financial assistance to states furnishing domiciliary care to eligible veterans in State Veterans Homes which meet the standards prescribed by the Secretary of Veterans Affairs. Types of assistance: grants. Estimate of annual funds available: $30,573,000.

* Veterans State Nursing Home Care 64.015

Assistant Chief Medical Director
  for Geriatrics and Extended Care
U.S. Department of Veterans Affairs
Washington, DC 20420   202-535,7538

To provide financial assistance to states furnishing nursing home care to eligible veterans in State Veterans Homes which meet the standards prescribed by the Secretary of Veterans Affairs. Types of assistance: grants. Estimate of annual funds available: $285,050,000.

* Veterans State Hospital Care 64.016

Assistant Chief Medical Director
  for Geriatrics and Extended Care
U.S. Department of Veterans Affairs
Washington, DC 20420   202-535,7538

To provide financial assistance to states furnishing hospital care to eligible veterans in State Veterans Homes which meet the standards prescribed by the Secretary of Veterans Affairs. Types of assistance: grants. Estimate of annual funds available: $4,514,000.

* State Cemetery Grants 64.203

Director, State Cemetery Grant Program
National Cemetery System
U.S. Department of Veterans Affairs

810 Vermont Ave., NW
Washington, DC 20420   202-273-5350

To assist states in the establishment, expansion and improvement of veterans cemeteries. Types of assistance: grants. Estimate of annual funds available: $25,000,000.

* Air Pollution Control Program Support 66.001

Steve Hitte
Air Quality Management Division
Office of Air and Radiation
Environmental Protection Agency (EPA)
Research Triangle Park, NC 27711   919-541-0876

To assist state, municipal, intermunicipal, and interstate agencies in planning developing, establishing, improving and maintaining adequate programs for prevention and control of air quality standards. Types of assistance: grants. Estimate of annual funds available: $167,323,000.

* Water Pollution Control-State and Interstate Program Support (106 Grants) 66.419

Carol Crow, Director
Analysis and Evaluation Division
Office of Water Regulations and Standards
Office of Water
Environmental Protection Agency (EPA)
Washington, DC 20460   202-260-6742

To assist states, territorial Indian Tribes and interstate agencies in establishing and maintaining adequate measures for prevention and control of surface and ground water pollution. Types of assistance: grants. Estimate of annual funds available: $160,529,300.

* State Public Water System Supervision 66.432

Craig Damron
Office of Drinking Water
Office of Water
Environmental Protection Agency (EPA)
Washington, DC 20460   202-260,5556

To foster development and maintenance of state programs which implement the Safe Drinking Water Act. Types of assistance: Grant. Estimate of annual funds available: $93,305,500.

* State Underground Water Source Protection 66.433

Francoise Brasier, Chief
Underground Injection Control Branch
Office of Drinking Water
Office of Water
Environmental Protection Agency (EPA)
401 M St., SW
Washington, DC 20460   202-260-7077

To foster development and implementation of underground injection control (UIC) programs under the Safe Drinking Water Act. Types of assistance: grants. Estimate of annual funds available: $10,975,000.

* Water Quality Management Planning (205(j)(2)) 66.454

Don Kunkoski, Director
Assessment and Watershed Protection Division
Office of Water
Environmental Protection Agency (EPA)
401 M St., SW, 4503F
Washington, DC 20460   202-260-7103

To assist states (including territories and the District), public comprehensive planning organizations, and interstate organizations in carrying out water quality management planning. Types of assistance: grants. Estimate of annual funds available: $9,455,900.

* National Estuary Program 66.456

Marilyn Mlay, Chief
Oceans and Coastal Protection Division
Office of Wetlands, Oceans, and Watersheds Protection
Environmental Protection Agency (EPA)
Washington, DC 20460   202-260-1952

To authorize the Agency to convene Management Conferences with participants from states, legislatures, etc., to develop programs to protect and restore coastal resources in estuaries of national significance. Types of assistance: grants. Estimate of annual funds available: $11,900,000.

* Capitalization Grants for State Revolving Funds (State Revolving Fund) 66.458
Don Niehus
Delegation Management Branch
Municipal Construction Division
Office of Municipal Control
Environmental Protection Agency (EPA)
Washington, DC 20460   202-260-7366
To create State Revolving Funds through a program of capitalization grants to states which will provide a feasible transition to state and local financing of municipal wastewater treatment facilities. Types of assistance: grants. Estimate of annual funds available: $800,000,000.

* Environmental Protection Consolidated Grants - Program Support (Consolidated Program Support Grants) 66.600
Richard Mitchell
Grants Administration Division
PM 3903, Environmental Protection Agency
Washington, DC 20460   202-260-6077
The consolidated program support grant is an alternative assistance delivery mechanism which allows a state or local agency responsible for continuing pollution control programs to develop an integrated approach to pollution control. Types of assistance: grants. Estimate of annual funds available: $5,000,000.

* Consolidated Pesticide Enforcement Cooperative Agreements 66.700
John Neylan, Director
Office of Compliance Monitoring
Office of Pesticides and Toxic Substances, 2222A
Environmental Protection Agency (EPA)
Washington, DC 20460   202-564-2385
To assist states in developing and maintaining comprehensive pesticide enforcement programs. Types of assistance: grants. Estimate of annual funds available: $19,911,600.

* Toxic Substances Compliance Monitoring Cooperative Agreements 66.701
John Neylan, Director
Office of Compliance Monitoring
Office of Pesticides and Toxic Substances, 2222A
Environmental Protection Agency (EPA)
Washington, DC 20460   202-564-2385
To assist states in developing and maintaining comprehensive Toxic Substance enforcement programs. Types of assistance: grants. Estimate of annual funds available: $7,364,200.

* Hazardous Waste Management State Program Support 66.801
Grants Administration Division, PM-216F
Environmental Protection Agency (EPA)
Washington, DC 20460   703-308-8757
To assist state governments in the development and implementation of an authorized hazardous waste management program for the purpose of controlling the generation, transportation, treatment, storage and disposal of hazardous waste. Types of assistance: grants. Estimate of annual funds available: $106,598,000.

* Superfund State Site-Specific Cooperative Agreements (Superfund) 66.802
Carolyn Offutt, Chief
State Involvement Section
Office of Emergency and Remedial Response
Environmental Protection Agency (EPA)
Washington, DC 20460   703-603-8797
To determine level of hazard at sites listed in the CERCLA Information System. Types of assistance: grants. Estimate of annual funds available: $110,000,000.

* State Land Tribal Underground Storage Tanks Program (UST Program) 66.804
Dana Tulis, Director
Implementation Division
Underground Storage Tank Program (OSWER)
Environmental Protection Agency (EPA)
401 M St., SW
Washington, DC 20460   703-308-8891
To assist states in development and implementation of their own underground storage tank programs to operate in lieu of the federal program. Types of assistance: grants. Estimate of annual funds available: $11,944,700.

* Leaking Underground Storage Tank Trust Fund Program 66.805
Dana Tulis, Director
Implementation Division
Office of the Underground Storage Tanks
Environmental Protection Agency (EPA)
Waterside Mall
401 M St., SW
Washington, DC 20460   703-308-8891
To support the development of state corrective action and enforcement programs that address releases from underground storage tanks containing petroleum. Types of assistance: grants. Estimate of annual funds available: $58,050,000.

* Superfund Technical Assistance Grants for Citizen Groups at Priority Sites 66.806
Nicole Lacoste
Office of Emergency and Remedial Response
Environmental Protection Agency (EPA)
401 M St., SW
Washington, DC 20460   703-603-8842
To provide resources for community groups to hire technical advisors who can assist them in interpreting technical information concerning the assessment of potential hazards and the selection and design of appropriate remedies. Types of assistance: grants. Estimate of annual funds available: $2,000,000.

* Reimbursement for Firefighting on Federal Property 83.007
Clyde A. Bragdon, Jr., Administrator,
U.S. Fire Administration
16825 S. Seton Ave.
Emmitsburg,, MD 21727   301-447-1080
To provide that each fire service organization which engages in firefighting operations on federal property may be reimbursed for their direct expenses and direct losses incurred in firefighting Types of assistance: direct payment. Estimate of annual funds available: $500,000.

* Emergency Food and Shelter National Board Program (Emergency Food and Shelter) 83.523
Fran McCarthy
Preparedness, Training, and Exercises Directorate
Federal Emergency Management Agency (FEMA)
Washington, DC 20472   202-646-3652
To supplement and expand on-going efforts to provide shelter, food and supportive services for needy families and individuals. Types of assistance: grants. Estimate of annual funds available: $140,000,000.

* Federal Perkins Loan Cancellations 84.037
Susan Morgan
Policy Development Division
Student Financial Assistance Programs
Office of Assistant Secretary for Postsecondary Education
1600 Independence Ave., SW
Washington, DC 20202   202-708-8242
To reimburse institutions for their share of loans canceled for National Defense Student Loan recipients who become teachers or who perform active military service in the U.S. Armed Forces. Types of assistance: direct payment. Estimate of annual funds available: $60,000,000.

* Impact Aid
Charles Hansen
Impact Aid Program
Office of Elementary and Secondary Education
U.S. Department of Education
1250 Maryland Ave., SW
Washington, DC 20202   202-260-3907

To provide financial assistance to local educational agencies when enrollments or availability of revenue are adversely affected by federal activities. Types of assistance: formula grants. Estimate of annual funds available: $760,000,000.

* Indian Education-Grants to Local Educational Agencies 84.060
Office of Indian Educations
U.S. Department of Education
600 Independence Ave., SW
Washington, DC 20202   202-260-1441
To develop and carry out elementary and secondary school programs designed to meet the special educational and culturally related academic needs of Indian children. Types of assistance: grants. Estimate of annual funds available: $92,765,000.

* Rehabilitation Services-Vocational Rehabilitation Grants to States 84.126
Office of Program Operations
Rehabilitation Services Administration
U.S. Department of Education
Washington, DC 20202   202-205-9406
To provide vocational rehabilitation services to persons with mental and/or physical handicaps. Types of assistance: grants. Estimate of annual funds available: $2,375,792,000.

* Rehabilitation Services-Service Projects 84.128
Rehabilitation Services Administration
Office of Asst. Secretary for Special Education and Rehabilitative Services
U.S. Department of Education
Washington, DC 20202   202-205-9297
To provide funds to state vocational rehabilitation agencies and public nonprofit organizations for projects and demonstration which hold promise of expanding and otherwise improving services for groups of mentally and physically handicapped individuals over and above those provided by the Basic Support Program. Types of assistance: grants. Estimate of annual funds available: $2,850,000.

* Migrant Education - Coordination Program 84.144
Office of Migrant Education
Office of Elementary and Secondary Education
U.S. Department of Education
600 Independence Ave., SW, Room 4104
Washington, DC 20202   202-260-1164
To carry out activities to improve the interstate and intrastate coordination of migrant education between state and local education agencies. Types of assistance: grants. Estimate of annual funds available: $10,000,000.

* Rehabilitation Services-Client Assistance For Handicapped Individuals (CAP) 84.161
U.S. Department of Education
Associate Commissioner for Program Operations
Office of Special Education and Rehabilitative Services
Washington, DC 20202   202-205-9406
To provide assistance in informing and advising clients and client applicants of available benefits under the Rehabilitation Act. Types of assistance: grants. Estimate of annual funds available: $11,147,000.

* Magnet Schools Assistance 84.165
Equity and Educational Excellence Division
600 Independence Ave., SW
Washington, DC 20202   202-260-2476
To provide grants to eligible local educational agencies for use in magnet schools that are part of approved desegregation plans. Types of assistance: grants. Estimate of annual funds available: $110,000,000.

* Handicapped-Preschool Grants 84.173
Division of Educational Services
Office of the Asst. Secretary for Special Education and Rehabilitative Services
U.S. Department of Education
600 Independence Ave., SW

Washington, DC 20202   202-205-9097
To provide grants to states to assist them in providing a free appropriate public education to preschool age handicapped children. Types of assistance: grants. Estimate of annual funds available: $390,000,000.

* Education for Homeless Children and Youth 84.196
Compensatory Education Programs
Office of Elementary and Secondary Education
U.S. Department of Education
600 Independence Ave., SW
Washington, DC 20202   202-260-2777
To establish or designate an office in each state educational agency and Outlying Area for the coordination of education for homeless children and youth. Types of assistance: grants. Estimate of annual funds available: $31,700,000.

* Native Hawaiian Family Based Education Centers 84.209
Beth Baggett
School Improvement Programs
U.S. Department of Education
600 Independence Ave., SW
Washington, DC 20202   202-260-2502
To develop and operate a minimum of eleven family based education centers throughout the Hawaiian Islands. Types of assistance: direct payment. Estimate of annual funds available: $8,900,000.

* Capital Expenses 84.216
Mary Jean LeTendre
Compensatory Education Programs
U.S. Department of Education
600 Independence Ave., SW
Washington, DC 20202   202-260-0826
To provide payments to local educational agencies for increases in capital expenses paid from Chapter 1 funds for the purpose of regaining levels of instructional services to eligible private school children. Types of assistance: grants. Estimate of annual funds available: $-0-.

* Native Hawaiian Special Education 84.221
Lynda Glidewell   202-205-9099
To operate projects addressing the special education needs of Native Hawaiian Students. Types of assistance: grants. Estimate of annual funds available: $2,190,000.

* Mental Health Planning and Demonstration Projects 93.125
Community Support Programs Section
Division of Demonstration Programs
National Institute of Mental Health (NIMH)
Parklawn Bldg., Room 11C-22
5600 Fishers Lane
Rockville, MD 20857   301-443-3653
To promote the development of community support systems for the long-term mentally ill, including inappropriately institutionalized individuals, mentally disturbed children and youth, and homeless individuals in communities. Types of assistance: grants. Estimate of annual funds available: $-0-.

* Emergency Medical Services for Children (EMS for Children) 93.127
Maternal and Child Health Bureau
Health Resources and Services Admin.
Room 18A-39, 5600 Fishers Lane
Rockville, MD 20857   301-443-4026
To support demonstration projects for the expansion and improvement of emergency medical services for children who need treatment for trauma or critical care. Types of assistance: grants. Estimate of annual funds available: $15,000,000.

* Technical and Non-Financial Assistance to Health Centers and National Health Service Corps (NHSC) Delivery Sites 93.129
Director

Division of Community and Migrant Health
Bureau of Primary Health Care
Health Resources and Services Admin.
4350 East West Hwy., 7th Floor
Bethesda, MD 20814   301-594-4310

To provide assistance to community health centers (CHCs) in the following areas: the initiation of new shared services activities involving specific CHCs within a state or region; and the enhancement of the clinical capability of centers within a state or region including assistance in retention and recruitment of providers. Types of assistance: grants. Estimate of annual funds available: $15,500,000.

* Primary Care Services-Resource Coordination and Development-Primary Care Offices (Primary Care Offices) 93.130

Director
Div. of Community and Migrant Health
Bureau of Primary Health Care
Health Resources and Services Admin.
Room 7A-55
4350 East West Hwy., 7th Floor
Bethesda, MD 20894   301-594-4310

To coordinate local, state, and federal resources contributing to primary care service delivery in the state to meet the needs of medically under-served populations through community and migrant health centers, and the retention, recruitment and oversight of the National Health Service Corps and other health professions. Types of assistance: grants. Estimate of annual funds available: $12,200,000.

* Minority Community Health Coalition Demonstration 93.137

Ms. Sonia Hunt Gray
Office of Minority Health
Rockwall II Bldg., Suite 1000
5515 Security Lane
Rockville, MD 20852   301-594-0769

To demonstrate that coalitions of local community agencies can be formed to effectively impact on the disease risk factors and related health problems of minority groups, through unique and innovative methods of modifying behavioral and environmental factors involved. Types of assistance: grants. Estimate of annual funds available: $5,084,000.

* AIDS Education and Training Centers 93.145

Director
Division of Medicine
Bureau of Health Professions
Health Resources and Services Admin.
Room 9A27, 5600 Fishers Lane
Rockville, MD 20857   301-443-6190

To provide education and training to primary care providers and others on the treatment and prevention of acquired immune deficiency syndrome (AIDS) in collaboration with health professions schools, local hospitals and health departments. Types of assistance: grants. Estimate of annual funds available: $28,000,000.

* Health Center Grants for Homeless Populations (Health Care for the Homeless) 93.151

Harold Dame, Director
Health Care Services for the Homeless Program
Health Resources and Services Admin.
4350 East West Hwy., 11th Floor
Bethesda, MD 20814   301-594-4260

To provide health care services to homeless persons. Types of assistance: grants. Estimate of annual funds available: $92,325,000.

* Rural Health Research Centers 93.155

Office of Rural Health Policy
Health Resources and Services Admin.
Parklawn Bldg., Room 14-22
5600 Fishers Lane
Rockville, MD 20857   301-443-0835

To support the development of rural health research centers to provide an information base and policy analysis capacity on the full range of rural health issues. Types of assistance: grants. Estimate of annual funds available: $3,000,000.

* Health Program for Toxic Substances and Disease Registry 93.161

Dr. Barry Johnson, Assoc. Administrator
Centers for Disease Control
Public Health Service (PHS)
1600 Clifton Rd., NE
Mail Stop E28
Atlanta, GA 30333   404-639-0700

To work closely with state, local, and other federal agencies to reduce or eliminate illness, disability and death resulting from exposure to the public and workers to toxic substances at spill and waste disposal sites. Types of assistance: grants. Estimate of annual funds available: $9,155,000.

* Childhood Lead Poisoning Prevention Projects 93.197

Mr. David Forney
Lead Poisoning Prevention Branch
Division of Environmental Hazards and Health Effects
National Center for Environmental health
Centers for Disease Control and Prevention
MSF-42, Public Health Service
4770 Buford Highway
Atlanta, GA 30341   404-488-7330

To assure that children in communities with demonstrated high risk for lead poisoning are screened; to identify infants and young children with elevated lead levels; to identify possible sources of lead exposure; and to provide information on childhood lead poisoning. Types of assistance: grants. Estimate of annual funds available: $26,700,000.

* Family Planning-Services 93.217

Deputy Asst. Secretary for Population Affairs
U.S. Department of Health and Human Services
West Tower, Suite 200, East West Hwy.
5600 Fishers Lane
Rockville, MD 20857   301-594-4000

To provide educational, counseling, comprehensive medical and social services necessary to enable individuals to freely determine the number and spacing of their children, and by doing so helping to reduce maternal and infant mortality and promote the health of mothers and children. Types of assistance: grants. Estimate of annual funds available: $210,000,000.

* Community Health Centers 93.224

Director
Division of Community and Migrant Health
Health Resources and Services Admin.
4350 East West Hwy., 7th Floor
Bethesda, MD 20814   301-594-4300

To support the development and operation of community health centers which provide primary health services, supplemental health services and environmental health services to medically under-served populations. Types of assistance: grants. Estimate of annual funds available: $866,884,000.

* Indian Health Service-Health Management Development Program (Indian Health) 93.228

Division of Community Services
Indian Health Service
Public Health Service (PHS), Room 6A-05
5600 Fishers Lane
Rockville, MD 20857   301-443-6840

To improve the quality of the health of American Indians and Native Alaskans by providing a full range of curative, preventative and rehabilitative health services. Types of assistance: grants. Estimate of annual funds available: $6,500,000.

* Health Centers Grants for Migrant and Seasonal Farmworkers 93.246

Director
Migrant Health Branch
Health Resources and Services Administration
4350 East West Hwy., 7th Floor
Bethesda, MD 20814   301-594-4303

To support the development and operation of migrant health centers and projects which provide primary health care services, supplemental health services and environmental health services which are accessible to migrant and seasonal agricultural farm workers and their families. Types of assistance: grants. Estimate of annual funds available: $91,376,000.

* Family Planning-Personnel Training 93.260

Office of the Assistant Secretary for Health
U.S. Department of Health and Human Services
West Tower, Suite 200
East West Hwy.
Rockville, MD 20857   301-594-4008
To provide job specific training for personnel to improve the delivery of
family planning services. Types of assistance: grants. Estimate of annual
funds available: $5,000,000.

* Immunization Grants (Section 317, Public Health Service Act; Immunization Program) 93.268

Kathy Cahill
Centers for Disease Control
Public Health Service (PHS)
U.S. Department of Health and Human Services
1600 Clifton Rd., NE
Atlanta, GA 30333   404-639-8208
To assist states and communities in establishing and maintaining preventive
health service programs to immunize individuals against vaccine-preventable
diseases. Types of assistance: grants. Estimate of annual funds available:
$289,000,000.

* Centers for Disease Control and Prevention - Investigations and Technical Assistance 93.283

Dr. David Satcher, Acting Director
Centers for Disease Control
Public Health Service (PHS)
U.S. Department of Health and Human Services
1600 Clifton Rd., NE
Atlanta, GA 30333   404-639-3291
To assist state and local health authorities and other health related
organizations in controlling communicable disease, chronic diseases, and
other preventable health conditions. Types of assistance: grants. Estimate of
annual funds available: $276,446,384.

* Family Preservation and Support Services 93.556

Commissioner
Administration on Children, Youth and Families
P.O. Box 1182
Washington, DC 20013   202-205-8618
To fund community-based family support services that promote the
well-being of children and families by enhancing family functioning and child
development. Types of assistance: grants. Estimate of annual funds available:
$230,000,000.

* Refugee Land Entrant Assistance-Voluntary Agency Programs 93.567

Barbara Chesnik
Office of Refugee Resettlement
Administration for Children and Families
U.S. Department of Health and Human Services
6th Floor, 370 L'Enfant Promenade SW
Washington, DC 20447   202-401-4558
To assist refugees in becoming self-supporting and independent members of
American society, by providing grant funds to private nonprofit organizations
to support case management, transitional assistance, and social services for
new arrivals. Types of assistance: grants. Estimate of annual funds available:
$54,000,000.

* Refugee and Entrant Assistance Discretionary Grants 93.576

Allan Gall
Office of Refugee Resettlement
Administration for Children and Families
U.S. Department of Health and Human Services
370 L'Enfant Promenade, SW, 6th Floor
Washington, DC 20447   202-401-9251
To decrease the numbers of refugees on public assistance, to promote refugee
community and family stability, to enhance services to refugees and to
encourage placement of families in good locations. Types of assistance:
grants. Estimate of the annual funds available: $76,241,000.

* Native American Programs Grants 93.612

Administration for Native Americans
U.S. Department of Health and Human Services
Room 348-F, 200 Independence Ave., SW
Washington, DC 20201   202-690-5780
To provide financial assistance to public and private nonprofit organizations
including Indian Tribes, urban Indian centers, Native Alaskan villages, Native
Hawaiian organizations, rural off-reservation groups, and Native American
Pacific Island groups for the development and implementation of social and
economic development strategies that promote self-sufficiency. Types of
assistance: grants. Estimate of annual funds available: $ 1,000,000.

* Developmental Disabilities Basic Support and Advocacy Grants 93.630

Director
Program Operations Division
U.S. Department of Health and Human Services
Washington, DC 20201   202-690-5962
To assist states in the development of a comprehensive system and a
coordinated array of services in order to support the developmentally disabled
to achieve their maximum potential and ensure the protection of their legal
and human rights. Types of assistance: grants. Estimate of annual funds
available: $93,860,000.

* Developmental Disabilities Projects of National Significance 93.631

Program Development Division
Administration on Developmental Disabilities
U.S. Department of Health and Human Services
Washington, DC 20201   202-690-6961
To provide grants and contracts for projects of national significance to
increase and support the independence, productivity, and integration into the
community of persons with developmental disabilities. Types of assistance:
grants. Estimate of annual funds available: $10,244,000.

* Children's Justice Grants to States 93.643

James Auchter
National Center on Child Abuse and Neglect
Administration for Children, Youth and Families
P.O. Box 1182
Washington, DC 20013   202-205-8807
To encourage states to enact child protective reforms which are designed to
improve the handling of child abuse cases and the investigation and
prosecution of cases of child abuse. Types of assistance: grants. Estimate of
annual funds available: $8,500,000.

* Child Welfare Services - State Grants 93.645

Daniel Lewis, Associate Commissioner
Children's Bureau
Administration for Children, Youth and Families
P.O. Box 1182
Washington, DC 20013   202-205-8618
To establish, extend, and strengthen child welfare services provided by state
and local public welfare agencies to enable children to remain in their own
homes. Types of assistance: grants. Estimate of annual funds available:
$291,986,000.

* Social Services Research and Demonstration 93.647

Richard Greenberg, Director
Division of Research and Evaluation
U.S. Department of Health and Human Services
370 L'Enfant Promenade SW, 7th Floor
Washington, DC 20447   202-401-6971
To promote effective social services for dependent and vulnerable populations
such as the poor, the aged, children and youth, Native Americans, and the
handicapped. Types of assistance: grants. Estimate of annual funds available:
$6,500,000.

* Foster Care - Title IV-E 93.658

Associate Commissioner
Children's Bureau
P.O. Box 1182
Washington, DC 20013   202-205-8618
To provide Federal Financial Participation (FFP) in assistance on behalf of

eligible children needing care away from their families (in foster care) who are in the placement and care of the state agency administering the program. Types of assistance: grant. Estimate of annual funds available: $5,063,500,000.

* Adoption Assistance 93.659

Associate Commissioner
Children's Bureau
P.O. Box 1182
Washington, DC 20013   202-205-8618
To provide Federal Financial Participation (FFP) to states which meet certain eligibility tests, in the adoption subsidy costs for the adoption of children with special needs. Types of assistance: grants. Estimate of annual funds available: $1,197,600,000.

* Social Services Block Grant 93.667

Director, Office of Policy, Planning and Legislation
Office of Community Services
370 L'Enfant Promenade, SW
Washington, DC 20447   202-401-2333
To enable each state to furnish social services best suited to the needs of the individuals residing in the state. Types of assistance: grant. Estimate of annual funds available: $1,775,000,000.

* Child Abuse and Neglect State Grants 93.669

Donna Litton
National Center on Child Abuse and Neglect
Children's Bureau
P.O. Box 1182
Washington, DC 20013   202-205-8640
To assist states in improving and increasing activities for the prevention and treatment of child abuse, and to develop, strengthen, and carry out the program objectives through State grants. Types of assistance: grants. Estimate of annual funds available: $21,026,000.

* Family Violence Prevention and Services/Grants for Battered Women's Shelters-Grants to States and Indian Tribes 93.671

Office of Policy, Planning and Legislation
Office of Community Services
370 L'Enfant Promenade SW, 5th Floor
Washington, DC 20447   202-401-5529
To demonstrate the effectiveness of assisting states and Indian Tribes in the prevention of family violence and to provide immediate shelter and related assistance for victims of family violence and their dependents. Types of assistance: grants. Estimate of annual funds available: $93,534,400.

* Independent Living 93.674

Michael Ambrose, Director
Children's Bureau
Administration for Children, Youth and Families
P.O. Box 1182
Washington, DC 20013   202-205-8740
To assist states and localities in establishing and carrying out programs designed to assist children, with respect to whom foster care maintenance payments are being made by the state and who have attained age 16, in making the transition from foster care to independent living. Types of assistance: grants. Estimate of annual funds available: $140,000,000.

* State Medicaid Fraud Control Units 93.775

James Wright, Director
State Fraud Branch, Office of the Secretary
U.S. Department of Health and Human Services (DHHS)
Room 5449, North Bldg.
330 Independence Ave., SW
Washington, DC 20201   202-619-3557
To control provider fraud in the states Medicaid program. Types of assistance: grants. Estimate of annual funds available: $103,500,000.

* State Survey and Certification of Health Care Providers and Suppliers 93.777

Wayne Smith, Ph.D., Director
Office of Survey and Certification
Health Standards and Quality Bureau

Health Care Financing Administration
6325 Security Blvd.
Baltimore, MD 21207   410-966-6810
To provide financial assistance to any state which is able and willing to determine through its state health agency or other appropriate state agency that providers and suppliers of health care services are in compliance with federal regulatory health and safety standards. Types of assistance: grants. Estimate of annual funds available: Title XVIII- $182,347,000; Title XIX - $192,000,000.

* Preventive Health Services - Sexually Transmitted Diseases Control Grants 93.977

Dr. Judith Wasserheit, Acting Director
Centers for Disease Control
Public Health Service
U.S. Department of Health and Human Services (DHHS)
1600 Clifton Road, NE
Atlanta, GA 30333   404-639-8258
To reduce morbidity and mortality by preventing cases and complications of sexually transmitted diseases (STD). Types of assistance: grants. Estimate of annual funds available: $100,000,000.

* Mental Health Disaster Assistance and Emergency Mental Health 93.982

Dr. Brian Flynn, Chief
Emergency Services and Disaster Relief Branch
National Institute of Mental Health
5600 Fishers Lane
Rockville, MD 20857   301-443-4735
Provision of supplemental emergency mental health counseling to individuals affected by major disasters, including the training of volunteers to provide such counseling. Types of assistance: grants. Estimate of annual funds available: $10,000,000.

* Cooperative Agreements for State-Based Diabetes Control Programs and Evaluation of Surveillance Systems 93.988

Chief, Grants Management Office
Procurement and Grants Office
Centers for Disease Control
Public Health Service
U.S. Department of Health and Human Services (DHHS)
255 E. Paces Ferry Rd.
Atlanta, GA 30305   404-842-6640
To implement comprehensive programs which will ensure that persons with diabetes who are at high risk for certain complications of diabetes are identified, entered into the health are system and receive on going state-of-the-art preventive care and treatment. Types of assistance: grants. Estimate of annual funds available: $21,930,000.

* National Health Promotion 93.990

Deputy Director
Office of Disease Prevention and Health Promotion
U.S. Department of Health and Human Services (DHHS)
330 C St, SW, Room 2132
Washington, DC 20201   202-205-8611
To engage national membership organizations from various sectors as a means of expanding and coordinating health promotion efforts. Types of assistance: grants. Estimate of annual funds available: $350,000.

* Preventive Health and Health Services Block Grant (PHS Block Grants) 93.991

Chief, Grants Management Branch
Centers for Disease Control
255 E. Paces Ferry Rd.
Atlanta, GA 30305   404-842-6508
To provide states with resources for comprehensive preventive health services including: emergency medical services, health incentive activities, hypertension programs, rodent control, etc. Types of assistance: grant. Estimate of annual funds available: $180,000,000.

* Maternal and Child Health Services Block Grant to the States 93.994

Maternal and Child Health Bureau

Health Resources and Services Administration
Public Health Service (PHS)
Room 18A-55, 5600 Fishers Lane
Rockville, MD 20857   301-443-3163
To enable states to maintain and strengthen their leadership in planning, promoting, coordinating and evaluating health care for mothers and children and in providing health services for mothers and children who do not have access to adequate health care. Types of assistance: grants. Estimate of annual funds available: $576,000,000.

* Adolescent Family Life-Demonstration Projects 93.995

Office of Adolescent Pregnancy Programs
Office of the Assistant Secretary for Health
U.S. Department of Health and Human Services (DHHS)
East West Tower S
Suite 200, West Tower
Rockville, MD 20857   301-594-4004
To promote adoption as an alternative for adolescent parents. Types of assistance: grants. Estimate of annual funds available: $34,500,000.

* Foster Grandparent Program (FGP) 94.011

Program Officer
Foster Grandparent Program
Corporation for National Service
1201 New York Ave., NW
Washington, DC 20525   202-606-5000
To provide part-time volunteer service opportunities for low income persons age 60 and over and to give supportive person-to-person service in health, education welfare and related settings to help alleviate the physical mental and emotional problems of infants, children or youth having special or exceptional needs. Types of assistance: grants. Estimate of annual funds available: $97,782,000.

* Retired and Senior Volunteer Program (RSVP) 94.002

Program Officer
Retired Senior Volunteer Program
Corporation for National Service
1201 New York Ave., NW
Washington, DC 20525   202-606-5000
To provide a variety of opportunities for retired persons, aged 60 or over to serve their community through significant volunteer service. Types of assistance: grants. Estimate of annual funds available: $50,565,000.

* Learn and Serve America-Higher Education 94.005

Student Community Service Programs
Corporation for National Service
1201 New York Ave., NW
Washington, DC 20525   202-606-5000
To encourage and enable students in secondary, vocational and post-secondary schools to participate in community service projects addressing poverty related problems. Types of assistance: grants. Estimate of annual funds available: $10,750,000.

* Senior Companion Program 94.016

Program Officer
Senior Companion Program (SCP)
Corporation for National Service
1201 New York Ave., NW
Washington, DC 20525   202-606-5000
To provide volunteer opportunities for low income people aged 60 and older which enhance their ability to remain active and provide critically needed community services. Types of assistance: grants. Estimate of annual funds available: $41,669,000.

"Vaclav Havel, the philosopher president of the Czech Republic, remarked recently on the paradox of our times: 'Experts can explain anything in the objective world to us, yet we understand our lives less and less. We live in a post-modern world, where anything is possible and almost nothing is certain.'"

Source: *New Passages*, Gail Sheehy, Random House. 1995

I Wanna New Career
And I'm a Woman

Matthew Lesko, Information USA, Inc., 12081 Nebel Street, Rockville, MD 20852 • 1-800-955-7693 • www.lesko.com

Money and Help For Women Entrepreneurs

Did you know that the recent surge in economic growth is actually being driven by small businesses that are in large part owned by women? That's right — women are starting businesses at **twice** the rate of men, and it's probably because women are finding that their dual careers as businesswomen and mothers are not being accommodated by big business very well at all. An increasing number of women are finding that rigid corporate structures fail to make allowances for their roles as executives, wives, and mothers. Because of this inflexibility, more and more women are striking out on their own or with a partner that shares a similar philosophy, and these women are finding success on their own terms. Corporate America has held women as a group back long enough, and for that reason, women are launching their own businesses in unprecedented numbers.

When someone mentions the word "entrepreneur", most people conjure up an image of someone like Donald Trump smiling on the cover of some glossy business trade magazine. But these days, chances are that smiling face will be decidedly more feminine looking than Donald's — it might be Donna's face, as in Donna Karan, who grew her apparel business into a million dollar money maker in just a few short years. As with men, hard work and commitment to make a business work are the ingredients women are using to create their own success, and not waiting for others to hand it to them. Just look at some of these incredible statistics that the U.S. Small Business Administration has gathered on women business owners:

-   Over the last 15 years, the number of women-owned businesses has almost **doubled**.

-   In that same amount of time, the percentage of women-owned businesses increased by 10%, while those owned by men decreased by as much.

-   Over one-third of all businesses are now owned by women.

-   Women-owned businesses were awarded over $2 billion in federal prime contracts last year, compared to only $180 million ten years ago, an increase of over ten fold.

-   75% of new businesses started by women succeed, compared to only 25% of those started by men.

Since most people in the U.S. actually work for small businesses, the government has been forced to take notice of this ever-increasing trend toward women-owned businesses. Chances are your new boss or CEO is going to be a woman, not someone like Lee Iacocca. Why else would the Small Business Administration (SBA) put a women's business ownership specialist at over 100 SBA offices across the country? You don't see the Small Business Administration bending over to help men out with special programs — anyone who reads the statistics can see who's going to be the most powerful group of emerging business owners over the next couple of decades.

As you'll see in this chapter, both the Federal and state governments have created special programs to help women business owners compete and succeed like never before.

* Small Business Administration Pilot Program

The Women's Pre-Qualified Loan Program is being tested in Charlotte, North Carolina, and other cities nationwide. This program will give the Small Business Administration greater influence on the number of loans extended to women.

This program began on June 1, 1994. Through the program, women business owners can go directly to the Small Business Administration (SBA) for a loan guarantee review, instead of being required to go to a bank first. If the woman business owner qualifies, the SBA will issue a commitment letter that she can present as part of her loan application to a bank. If the bank approves the loan, the application is returned to the SBA for final review. The SBA's decision will be based on the ability of the woman business owner to pay back the loan.

Businesses must be 51% owned and operated by women to qualify for the lending program. Only Mecklenburg County businesses qualify for Charlotte's pilot program. The pilot women's program backs loans up to $250,000. The women's program backs loans up to $250,000, and will guarantee 90% of loans up to $155,000. Bigger loans will be backed 85%. There is no cap on the number of loans that will be processed through the pilot program.

Following the guidelines for the pilot program, women applicants will go to a "facilitator", who will screen applications for the SBA for a small fee. These fees have not been established as of this printing. Pilot sites for the Women's Pre-qualification Pilot Loan Program are: Buffalo, New York; Chicago, Illinois; Columbus, Ohio; Louisville, Kentucky; New Orleans, Louisiana; Philadelphia, Pennsylvania; Portland, Oregon; St. Louis, Missouri; and San Francisco, California. The program is offered statewide in the following states: Colorado, Maine, Massachusetts, Montana, New Mexico and Utah. While there is no way to monitor the number of women applicants who are rejected at the bank level under the existing system, the pilot program will work to improve that situation.

For more information, contact the Charlotte SBA office during business hours at 6302 Fairview Road, Suite 300, Charlotte, NC 28210; 704-344-6563; Fax: 704-344-6769. You can also check the Small Business Administration website at {www.sba.gov}.

* Fight Suppliers Who Won't Give You Credit

Federal Trade Commission (FTC)
600 Pennsylvania Ave., NW
Washington, DC 20580   877-FTC-HELP
www.ftc.gov/bcp/conline/pubs/credit/ecoa.htm   202-326-2222

Often women who have been divorced have trouble establishing credit. And you need credit if you're going to run a business. The Federal Trade Commission (FTC) enforces the laws that prohibit creditors and credit bureaus from discriminating against women because of their sex or marital status, and they can send you the free publication, *Equal Credit Opportunity*. This pamphlet explains your credit rights under the law, how to get help in establishing your own credit, and what to do if you feel your credit application has been unfairly denied.

* Grants, Loans and Loan Guarantees for Women-Owned Businesses

Contact your state office of Economic Development located in your state capital.

All federal money programs aimed at small business do not discriminate between women and non-women-owned businesses. However, at the state level there are a number of specific money programs that are set aside only for women-owned businesses. The programs vary from state to state and are changing all the time so it is best to check with your State Office of Economic Development in your state capital to insure you have the latest available information. Here is a listing of what a few states offer specifically for women entrepreneurs:

- Illinois has low interest loans up to $50,000
- Iowa has grants up to $25,000 and loan guarantees up to $40,000
- Louisiana has loans and loan guarantee programs up to $250,000
- Minnesota offers low interest loans for up to 50% of your project
- New York offers low interest loans from $20,000 to $500,000
- Wisconsin offers low interest loans for women-owned businesses under $500,000 in sales

* Federal Government Set-Asides For Women Entrepreneurs

Contact your state office of Economic Development located in your state capital

or

Superintendent of Documents
Government Printing Office   866-512-1800
Washington, DC 20402   Fax: 202-512-2168
www.onlinewbc.gov/DOCS/procure/sellgov.doc

Many Federal government contracting offices are trying to insure that a certain percentage of their contracts go to women entrepreneurs. Most even have special offices that will help women entrepreneurs sell to their agencies. For help in selling your product or service to the government, contact your State Economic Development Office in your state capital and obtain a copy of *Equal Credit Opportunity*. It is available from the Government Printing Office or free online.

* 15% Set-Aside for Women Entrepreneurs

Contact your state office of Economic Development located in your state capital.

Not only is the Federal government active in insuring that women get a fair share of government contracts, but many state governments are becoming involved. Some states, like California for example, have passed laws that force their state agencies to give at least 15% of their contracts to women and minority-owned firms. Other states like Illinois, Iowa, Maine, Minnesota, Montana, New Jersey, Oregon, and Washington are among those who are active in insuring that women obtain a fair share of state government contracts. Contact your State Office of Economic Development to see how your business can take advantage of set-asides in your state.

* 28 States Offer Free Consulting To Women Only

Contact your state office of Economic Development located in your state capital.

Although every state offers free help to any person wishing to start or expand a business in their state, there are 28 states that have set up special offices just for women entrepreneurs. As an example, Colorado established a women's clearinghouse which provides hands-on assistance with business planning, marketing, financing, and government contracts. They also hold seminars at 16 locations throughout the state. Ohio offers a wide range of free services including loan packaging and marketing research. Contact your State Office of Economic Development to see what your state has to offer. If they don't have a "Women Only" office, don't let that stop you. It just means you'll have to share the help available with the men in your state.

* What To Do If You Suspect Your Bank Denied You Credit Because You Are a Woman or Divorced

Credit Practices Division
Federal Trade Commission
600 Pennsylvania Ave., NW   877-FTC-HELP
Washington, DC 20580   202-326-2222
www.ftc.gov/bcp/bcpcp.htm

Women looking for money to start up and run their businesses might run into lenders that discriminate against them simply because they are women or divorced. The Federal Trade Commission (FTC) enforces the Equal Credit Opportunity Act, which prohibits any creditor from denying credit to a consumer on the basis of sex or marital status. If you think you've been discriminated against by a lender, contact the Federal Trade Commission. While the Federal Trade Commission won't act on individual complaints, a number of complaints against the same lender may force them to investigate. If necessary, the Federal Trade Commission can take violators to court to get them to stop their illegal practices. If you want your complaint investigated and action taken immediately, contact one of the following agencies, depending on the type of lending institution involved:

National Banks
Comptroller of the Currency, Compliance Management, Mail Stop 7-5, U.S. Department of the Treasury, Washington, DC 20219, 202-874-5000.

Savings & Loans
Office of Thrift Supervision, U.S. Department of Treasury, 1700 G St., NW, Washington, DC 20552, 202-906-6000.

FDIC State-Chartered Bank (not member of Federal Reserve System)
Federal Deposit Insurance Corporation, Consumer Affairs Division, Washington, DC 20429

Federally-Chartered Credit Union
National Credit Union Administration, Consumer Affairs Division, Washington, DC 20456

Small Loan/Finance Company, Public Utility, Credit Card or Government Lending Program
Consumer Response Center, Federal Trade Commission, Washington, DC 20580

For all other complaints against creditors, contact: Department of Justice, Civil Rights Division, Washington, DC 20530

* How To Juggle The Stress of Your Business and Your Family

National Institute for Occupational Safety and Health
200 Independence Ave., SW, Room 715H   800-356-4674
Washington, DC 20201   202-401-6997

Trying to run a business can put a lot of added stress on you, your family, and your marriage, especially when business isn't going very well. The National Institute for Occupational Safety and Health offers a variety of information in the subject including: Stress...At Work booklet, Working with Stress video and a listing of other work stress resources. All of this information about stress and more is available at {www.cdc.gov/niosh/stresshp.html}.

* Free Publications For Women Business Owners

Women's Bureau
Office of the Secretary
U.S. Department of Labor
200 Constitution Ave., NW, Room S-3311   800-827-5355
Washington, DC 20210   202-693-6731

Are you interested in how many other women business owners there are in the U.S? How about what your chances are for climbing up through various management levels? If you're interested in finding out more about women in the workforce, including trends and future projections, you might find the following free publications informative:

Characteristics of Self-Employed Women
Developments in Women's Labor Force Participation
Employed Women About as Likely as Men to be Looking for Jobs
Marriage, Children and Women's Employment: What Do We Know
Married Women, Work and Values
Much Variation in Women's Employment Across Metropolitan Areas
'Second-Chance' Strategies for Women Who Drop Out of School
Twenty Facts on Women Workers
Women Business Owners
Women in High-Tech Jobs
Women in Jobs Recessions
Women in Jobs Recoveries
Women at the Millennium
Women's Share of Labor Force to Edge Higher by 2008
Differences in Women's and Men's Earnings by Age
Income and Spending Patterns for Working Women
Women in Managerial, Professional Occupations Earn More Than Others
Women's Earning's: An Overview
Job Absent Rate Higher for Women Than for Men
Women in the Construction Workplace: Providing Equitable Safety and Health Protection
Work Injuries and Illnesses Occurring to Women

These titles can also be accessed online at {www.dol.gov/dol/audience/aud-women.htm}.

* How To Get Start-Up Capital From Being Pregnant, Sexually Harassed, or From A Bad Shopping Experience

U.S. Customs Service
Fraud Division
1300 Pennsylvania Avenue, NW
Washington, DC 20229   800-BE-ALERT
www.customs.ustreas.gov

or

Equal Employment Opportunity Commission (EEOC)
1801 L St., NW   800-669-4000
Washington, DC 20570   202-663-4900
www.eeoc.gov   800-669-3362 (publications)

More people would quit what they're doing and start their own business if they had a small windfall of money to get them started. Here are two government programs that may turn a bad experience into the capital needed to begin a business.

As a business owner, there are times you may come across unscrupulous wholesalers who try to sell you some counterfeit products at cut-rate prices. Instead of risking your business by buying and reselling the bogus products, report the fraud to the U.S. Customs Service. If your complaint, which will be kept completely anonymous, leads to the seizure of counterfeit goods, you could receive a reward of up to $250,000, depending on the size of the case. What small business couldn't use some extra operating capital like that to keep it going?

So you want to start your own business because you've just been fired because you were pregnant, or wouldn't sleep with your boss to get a promotion? Before you go taking out any business loan, contact the Equal Employment Opportunity Commission (EEOC) and report how you think your former boss discriminated against you. The EEOC will investigate your complaint, and if they think there are grounds for prosecuting your former boss, they'll proceed with the case. If they prove the case, you could end up with enough money in back pay and other remedies to finance your own company.

* Health Insurance for Divorcees Who Start Their Own Business

Women Work
1625 K St. NW, #300   202-467-6346
Washington, DC 20006   Fax: 202-467-5366
www.womenwork.org

Under the new law, divorced and separated women and their children can continue to receive the same health insurance coverage they had before they were divorced or separated from their husbands at the group rate. The only difference is that they must pay the premium. This law applies to all private businesses that employ more than 20 people and to federal, state, and local government plans. Depending on the reason for displacement, you may be eligible to continue coverage for up to 36 months. You must contact the health plan within 60 days of the divorce or separation to indicate that you're electing to continue coverage. If the plan refuses to honor the law, contact your state's Insurance Commissioner, and they will investigate your complaint and get you the coverage to which you're entitled. For more information on this law, contact the Women Work at the above address.

* Meet Women Entrepreneurs In Your Neighborhood For Lunch

Office of Women's Business Ownership
U.S. Small Business Administration
409 3rd St., SW   800-8-ASK-SBA
Washington, DC 20416   202-205-6673
www.sba.gov/womeninbusiness/wnet.html

One of the biggest problems women entrepreneurs face is breaking into the "old boys" network of successful businessmen, and important opportunities can be lost without access to these kinds of connections. To help women interested in networking with other successful business people, the U.S. Small Business Administration has a new program that pairs up a woman who is just starting out with an experienced female Chief Executive Officer running the same kind of company. This business mentor can help the novice business-woman make connections that might otherwise take her years to make on her own. Those interested in networking should also think about joining relevant professional associations, such as the National Association of Women Business Owners at 800-55-NAWBO or the National Association for Female Executives at 212-351-6451 or 800-927-6233, or by contacting their local Chamber of Commerce.

* Seminars On How Women Can Sell to the Government

Office of Women's Business
U.S. Small Business Administration
409 3rd St., SW   800-8-ASK-SBA
Washington, DC 20416   202-205-6673
www.sba.gov/womeninbusiness/wnet.html

If you're not sure how to start doing business with the government, you might consider taking a seminar sponsored by the U.S. Small Business Administration on the procurement process. These seminars will give you a complete overview on what you'll need to know and do to get involved in bidding on and landing government business contracts. For information on when these seminars are scheduled in your area, contact the office above, or the Women's Business Ownership Representative nearest you listed elsewhere in this chapter.

* Creative Financing for Women Entrepreneurs

Office of Women's Business Ownership
U.S. Small Business Administration
409 3rd St., SW   800-8-ASK-SBA
Washington, DC 20416   202-205-6673
www.sba.gov/womeninbusiness/wnet.html

One of the toughest parts of running a business is finding the capital resources to do it: MONEY. The Women's Business Ownership Office runs seminars on how women can use creative ways to locate financing if they've been turned down for loans by regular banks. For more information about these seminars, contact the office above or the Women's Business Ownership Representative nearest you listed elsewhere in this chapter.

* Free Mentors for New Women Entrepreneurs

Office of Women's Business Ownership
U.S. Small Business Administration
409 3rd St., SW   800-8-ASK-SBA
Washington, DC 20416   202-205-6673
www.sba.gov/womeninbusiness/wnet.html

How valuable would it be to your business to find a successful role model who's already gone through what's facing you as a female entrepreneur and who's willing to share her expertise with you at no charge? Through the Small Business Administration's Women's Network for Entrepreneurial Training (WNET) you can be paired up with a successful mentor who will meet with you at least once a week for an entire year, allowing you to learn from her experience and begin networking with other successful business people. If you've had your business going for at least a year and have gross receipts of at least $50,000, you can qualify for the WNET program. For more information, contact the office above or the Women's Business Ownership Representative nearest you listed elsewhere in this chapter.

* Changing Laws to Help Women Business Owners

Congressional Caucus for Women's Issues
409 12th Street, SW, Suite 310   202-554-2323
Washington, DC 20024   Fax: 202-554-2346
www.womenspolicy.org/caucus

If you think that the climate for women business owners could be improved by passing a new law, you might think of sending your ideas to the Congressional Caucus for Women's Issues. This group keeps track of the issues most important to women across the country and introduces new legislation that can help meet those needs, including those of the community of women entrepreneurs. Recently, a new law was passed that allowed federal funding for U.S. Small Business Administration Demonstration Centers that specialize in offering counseling to women interested in starting and expanding businesses. Contact this office if you have any new ideas or would simply like them to send you information about the most recent legislation currently before Congress that concerns women business owners.

"More than twelve hundred women aged 50 to 64 are currently studying in the United States for their first professional degrees, seriously applying themselves to law, dentistry, pharmacy or social psychology, or increasingly, coming out of divinity schools."

Source: *New Passages*, Gail Sheehy, Random House, 1995

Women's Business
Ownership Representatives

Women entrepreneurs have special needs, and the U.S. Small Business Administration recognizes those needs. That's why they've added staff members who specialize in promoting women-owned businesses in the U.S. These Women's Business Ownership (WBO) reps can help solve your unique business problems, such as how to network with other women business owners, where to find financial assistance on the state level, or how to get in on the lucrative government procurement programs, especially the ones that offer preferences to women-owned businesses. The WBO rep serving your area is your best ally in helping you cut through the red tape and direct you to free counseling and other valuable information sources. Remember, these offices do not have grants to start a business, but they do have access to very low interest loans for women entrepreneurs, as well as hundreds of other resources to help you successfully start your business!

Alabama
Susan Baxter
U.S. Small Business Administration
801 Tom Martin Dr., Suite 201
Birmingham, AL 35211
205-290-7707
Fax: 202-481-5710
www.sbaonline.sba.gov/al/index.html

Alaska
Diana Storo
U.S. Small Business Administration
510 L Street, Suite 310
Anchorage, AK 99501
907-271-4537
Fax: 202-481-1640
www.sbaonline.sba.gov/ak/index.html

Arizona
Arlene Binkowski
U.S. Small Business Administration
2828 North Central, Suite 800
Phoenix, AZ 85004-1093
602-745-7233
Fax: 202-481-0318
www.sbaonline.sba.gov/az/index.html

Arkansas
Johnna Bach
U.S. Small Business Administration
2120 Riverfront, Suite 100
Little Rock, AR 72202
501-324-5871, ext. 297
Fax: 202-481-2679
www.sbaonline.sba.gov/ar/index.html

California
Lola Robinson
U.S. Small Business Administration
455 Market St., 6th Floor
San Francisco, CA 94105
415-744-8485
Fax: 202-481-4189
www.sbaonline.sba.gov/ca/sf/index.html

Gilda Perez
U.S. Small Business Administration
650 Capitol Mall, Suite 7-500
Sacramento, CA 95814-2413
916-930-3707
Fax: 916-930-3737
www.sbaonline.sba.gov/ca/sacr/index.html

Cynthia Harris
U.S. Small Business Administration
550 W. C St., Suite 550
San Diego, CA 92101
619-557-7250, ext. 1149

Fax: 202-481-0895
www.sbaonline.sba.gov/ca/sandiego/index.html

Vicki Reynolds
U.S. Small Business Administration
200 W. Santa Ana Blvd., Suite 700
Santa Ana, CA 92701-4134
714-550-7420, ext. 3711
Fax: 202-481-5975
www.sbaonline.sba.gov/ca/santa/index.html

Marchelle Bailey
U.S. Small Business Administration
330 N. Brand Blvd., Suite 1200
Glendale, CA 91203-2304
818-552-3334
Fax: 202-481-4293
www.sbaonline.sba.gov/ca/la/index.html

Bonnie Chadwick
U.S. Small Business Administration
2719 N. Air Fresno Dr., Suite 200
Fresno, CA 93727-1547
559-487-5785, ext. 135
Fax: 202-481-0512
www.sbaonline.sba.gov/ca/fresno/index.html

Colorado
Jeanette DeHerrera
U.S. Small Business Administration
721 19th St., Suite 426
Denver, CO 80202-2599
303-844-2607, ext. 226
Fax: 202-481-2452
www.sbaonline.sba.gov/co/index.html

Connecticut
Kathleen Duncan
U.S. Small Business Administration
330 Main St., 2nd Floor
Hartford, CT 06106
860-240-4700, ext. 236
Fax: 202-481-2879
www.sbaonline.sba.gov/ct/index.html

Delaware
Carlotta Catullo
U.S. Small Business Administration
824 Market St., Suite 610
Wilmington, DE 19801
302-573-6380
Fax: 202-481-0601
www.sbaonline.sba.gov/de/index.html

District of Columbia
Ms. Cynthia Pope
U.S. Small Business Administration

1110 Vermont Ave. NW, 9th Floor
Washington, DC 20005
(P.O. Box 34500
Washington, DC 20043-4500)
202-606-4000, ext. 345
Fax: 202-481-0884
www.sbaonline.sba.gov/dc/index.html

Florida
Donna Padgug
U.S. Small Business Administration
7825 Bay Meadows Way, Suite 100B
Jacksonville, FL 32256-7504
904-443-1971
Fax: 202-481-1719
www.sbaonline.sba.gov/fl/north/index.html

Althea Harris
U.S. Small Business Administration
100 S. Biscayne Blvd., 7th Floor
Miami, FL 33131
305-536-5521 ext. 152
Fax: 202-481-0178
www.sbaonline.sba.gov/fl/south/index.html

Georgia
Charlotte Johnson
U.S. Small Business Administration
233 Peachtree Street, NE, Suite 1900
Atlanta, GA 30303
404-331-0100 ext. 405
Fax: 202-481-0742
www.sbaonline.sba.gov/ga/index.html

Hawaii
Doreen Ezuka
U.S. Small Business Administration
300 Ala Moana, Room 2-235
Honolulu, HI 96850-4981
808-541-2971
Fax: 202-481-1733
www.sbaonline.sba.gov/hi/index.html

Idaho
Sherrie Sudgen
U.S. Small Business Administration
1020 Main St., Suite 290
Boise, ID 83702-5745
208-334-1696, ext. 234
Fax: 202-481-5581
www.sbaonline.sba.gov/id/index.html

Illinois
Carole Harris
U.S. Small Business Administration
500 W. Madison St., Suite 1240
Chicago, IL 60661-2511
312-353-4003

Fax: 202-481-0639
www.sbaonline.sba.gov/il/index.html

Valerie Ross
U.S. Small Business Administration
511 W. Capitol St., Suite 302
Springfield, IL 62704
217-492-4416, ext. 108
Fax: 202-481-5937

Indiana
Joyce Able
U.S. Small Business Administration
429 N. Pennsylvania St., Suite 100
Indianapolis, IN 46204
317-226-7272, ext. 243
Fax: 202-481-2753
www.sbaonline.sba.gov/in/index.html

Iowa
Carolyn Tonn
U.S. Small Business Administration
215 4th Ave. SE, Suite 200
Cedar Rapids, IA 52401
319-362-6405, ext. 207
Fax: 202-481-0649
www.sbaonline.sba.gov/ia/cedar/index.html

Jackie Blanchard
U.S. Small Business Administration
210 Walnut St., Room 749
Des Moines, IA 50309
515-284-4560
Fax: 202-481-2288
www.sbaonline.sba.gov/ia/desmo/index.html

Kansas
Iris Newton
U.S. Small Business Administration
271 W. 3rd St., North, Suite 2500
Wichita, KS 67202
316-269-6631, ext. 213
Fax: 202-481-2265
www.sbaonline.sba.gov/ks/index.html

Kentucky
Carol Halfield
U.S. Small Business Administration
600 Dr. Martin Luther King, Jr. Pl.
Room 188
Louisville, KY 40202
502-582-5971, ext. 238
Fax: 202-481-5961
www.sbaonline.sba.gov/ky/index.html

Louisiana
Loretta Poree
U.S. Small Business Administration
365 Canal St., Suite 2820
New Orleans, LA 70130
504-589-2853
Fax: 202-481-4197
www.sbaonline.sba.gov/la/index.html

Maine
Helen Brimigion
U.S. Small Business Administration
68 Sewall Street, Room 512
Augusta, ME 04330
207-622-8394
Fax: 202-481-2216
www.sbaonline.sba.gov/me/index.html

Maryland
Martha Brown
U.S. Small Business Administration
10 S. Howard St., Suite 6220
Baltimore, MD 21201
410-962-6195, ext. 339
Fax: 202-481-4429
www.sbaonline.sba.gov/md/index.html

Massachusetts
Lisa Gonzalez
U.S. Small Business Administration
10 Causeway St., Room 265
Boston, MA 02222-1093
617-565-5588
Fax: 202-481-4166
www.sbaonline.sba.gov/ma/index.html

Harry Webb
U.S. Small Business Administration
1441 Main St., Room 410
Springfield, MA 01103
413-785-0484
Fax: 202-481-2184

Michigan
Catherine Gase
U.S. Small Business Administration
477 Michigan Ave., Room 515
Detroit, MI 48226
313-226-6075, ext. 223
Fax: 202-481-0675
www.sbaonline.sba.gov/mi/index.html

Minnesota
Cynthia Collett
U.S. Small Business Administration
100 N. 6th St., Suite 610C
Minneapolis, MN 55403-1563
612-370-2312
Fax: 202-481-0889
www.sbaonline.sba.gov/mn/index.html

Missouri
Janice Bowman
U.S. Small Business Administration
830 East Primrose, #101
Springfield, MO 65807-5254
417-890-8501 ext. 203
Fax: 202-481-2422

Cassandra Parks
U.S. Small Business Administration
323 W 8th, Suite 307
Kansas City, MO 64105
816-374-6380
Fax: 202-481-0670
www.sbaonline.sba.gov/mo/kansas/index.html

Laverne Johnson
U.S. Small Business Administration
815 Olive St., Suite 242
St. Louis, MO 63101
314-539-6600, ext. 232
Fax: 202-481-0236
www.sbaonline.sba.gov/mo/stlouis/index.html

Mississippi
Judith Adcock
U.S. Small Business Administration
One Hancock Plaza, Suite 1001
Gulfport, MS 39501
601-863-4449
Fax: 202-481-2791

Valencia Jamila
U.S. Small Business Administration
Am South Polaza, Suite 900
210 East Capitol
Jackson, MS 39201
601-965-4378, ext. 234
Fax: 202-481-5930
www.sbaonline.sba.gov/ms/index.html

Montana
U.S. Small Business Administration
301 South Park Ave., Room 334
Helena, MT 59626
406-441-1081
Fax: 202-481-4195
www.sbaonline.sba.gov/mt/index.html

Nebraska
Barbara Foster
U.S. Small Business Administration
11145 Mill Valley Rd.
Omaha, NE 68154
402-221-7212
Fax: 202-481-0393
www.sbaonline.sba.gov/ne/index.html

Nevada
Donna Hopkins
U.S. Small Business Administration
400 S. Fourth St., Suite 250
Las Vegas, NV 89101
702-388-6684
Fax: 202-481-1729
www.sbaonline.sba.gov/nv/index.html

New Hampshire
Alice Zachs
U.S. Small Business Administration
143 N. Main St.
Concord, NH 03301
603-225-1400, ext. 122
Fax: 202-481-0159
www.sbaonline.sba.gov/nh/index.html

New Jersey
Karen D'Antico
U.S. Small Business Administration
2 Gateway Center, 15th Floor
Newark, NJ 07102
973-645-3683
Fax: 202-481-2837
www.sbaonline.sba.gov/nj/index.html

New Mexico
Susan Chavez
U.S. Small Business Administration
625 Silver SW, Room 320
Albuquerque, NM 87102
505-346-6759
Fax: 202-481-5723
www.sbaonline.sba.gov/nm/index.html

New York
Martha Soffer
U.S. Small Business Administration
26 Federal Plaza, Room 3100
New York, NY 10278
212-264-1472
Fax: 202-481-4649
www.sbaonline.sba.gov/ny/ny/index.html

U.S. Small Business Administration
100 S. Clinton St., Room 1073
P.O. Box 7317
Syracuse, NY 13261
315-448-0428
Fax: 315-448-0410

Patricia Estelle
U.S. Small Business Administration
333 E. Water St., 4th Floor
Elmira, NY 14901
607-734-8130, ext. 24
Fax: 202-481-4826

Donald Butzek
U.S. Small Business Administration
111 W. Huron St., Room 1311
Buffalo, NY 14202
716-551-5670
Fax: 202-481-1692
www.sbaonline.sba.gov/ny/buffalo/index.html

U.S. Small Business Administration
35 Pinelawn Rd., Room 207W
Melville, NY 11747
631-454-0766
Fax: 202-481-0376

Cathy Pokines
U.S. Small Business Administration
401 South Salina Street, 5th Floor
Syracuse, NY 13202
315-471-9393 ext. 241
Fax: 202-481-0688
www.sbaonline.sba.gov/ny/syracuse/index.html

Marcia Ketchum
U.S. Small Business Administration
100 State St., Room 410
Rochester, NY 14614
716-263-6700, ext. 103
Fax: 202-481-4295

North Carolina
April Gonzalez
U.S. Small Business Administration
6302 Fairview Road, Suite 300
Charlotte, NC 28210
704-344-6811
Fax: 202-481-0315
www.sbaonline.sba.gov/nc/index.html

North Dakota
Fay Behm
U.S. Small Business Administration
657 Second North Avenue, Room 219
Fargo, ND 58102
701-239-5131
Fax: 202-481-0413
www.sbaonline.sba.gov/nd/index.html

Ohio
Rosemary Darling
U.S. Small Business Administration
1111 Superior Ave., Suite 630
Cleveland, OH 44144
216-522-4180 ext. 228
Fax: 202-481-5388
www.sbaonline.sba.gov/oh/cleveland/index.html

Carole Dailey
U.S. Small Business Administration
2 Nationwide Plaza, Suite 1400
Columbus, OH 43215-2542
614-469-6860, ext. 232
Fax: 202-481-2776
www.sbaonline.sba.gov/oh/columbus/index.html

Bonnie Schenck
U.S. Small Business Administration
JWP Federal Building
550 Main St., Room 2522
Cincinnati, OH 45202
513-684-2814, ext. 207
Fax: 202-481-0514

Oklahoma
Cindy Anderson
U.S. Small Business Administration
Federal Building
301 NW 6th Street
Oklahoma City, OK 73102
905-609-8000
Fax: 202-481-5837
www.sbaonline.sba.gov/ok/index.html

Oregon
Sue Richardson
U.S. Small Business Administration
1515 SW 5th Ave., Suite 1050
Portland, OR 97201
503-326-7251
Fax: 202-481-5694
www.sbaonline.sba.gov/or/index.html

Pennsylvania
Ana Gallardo
U.S. Small Business Administration

Robert N.C. Nix Federal Building
900 Market St.
Philadelphia, PA 19107
215-580-2707
Fax: 202-481-0193
www.sbaonline.sba.gov/pa/phil/index.html

Linda Carey
U.S. Small Business Administration
1000 Liberty Ave.
Federal Bldg., #1128
Pittsburgh, PA 15222
412-395-6560, ext. 118
Fax: 202-481-4149
www.sbaonline.sba.gov/pa/pitt/index.html

Rhode Island
Patricia O'Rourke
U.S. Small Business Administration
380 Westminister St., 5th Floor
Providence, RI 02903
401-528-4592
Fax: 202-481-4811
www.sbaonline.sba.gov/ri/index.html

South Carolina
Teresa Singleton
U.S. Small Business Administration
1835 Assembly St., Room 358
Columbia, SC 29201
803-253-3121
Fax: 202-481-5809
www.sbaonline.sba.gov/sc/index.html

South Dakota
Darla Newborg
U.S. Small Business Administration
110 S. Phillips Ave., Suite 200
Sioux Falls, SD 57104-6727
605-330-4243, ext. 38
Fax: 202-481-0945
www.sbaonline.sba.gov/sd/index.html

Tennessee
Lisa Denson
U.S. Small Business Administration
50 Vantage Way, Suite 201
Nashville, TN 37228-1550
615-736-5881, ext. 247
Fax: 202-481-4175
www.sbaonline.sba.gov/tn/index.html

Texas
Suze Aguirre
U.S. Small Business Administration
10737 Gateway West
Suite 320
El Paso, TX 79925
915-633-7003
Fax: 202-481-4940
www.sbaonline.sba.gov/tx/elpaso/index.html

Wila Lewis
U.S. Small Business Administration
8701 S. Gessner Drive, Suite 1200
Houston, TX 77074
713-773-6500, ext. 222
Fax: 202-481-5224
www.sbaonline.sba.gov/tx/hous/index.html

Graciela Guillen
U.S. Small Business Administration
222 E. Van Buren St.
Suite 500
Harlingen, TX 78550
956-427-8533, ext. 225
Fax: 202-481-2143
www.sbaonline.sba.gov/tx/harlington/index.html

Joanna White
U.S. Small Business Administration
1205 Texas Ave., Suite 408

Lubbock, TX 79401
806-472-7462, ext. 245
Fax: 202-481-2690
www.sbaonline.sba.gov/tx/lubbock/index.html

U.S. Small Business Administration
17319 San Pedro, Suite 200
San Antonio, TX 78232-1411
210-403-5900
Fax: 202-403-5936
www.sbaonline.sba.gov/tx/sanantonio/index.html

Adrienne Hudson
U.S. Small Business Administration
4300 Amon Carter Blvd.
Suite 114
Ft. Worth, TX 76155
817-684-5500
Fax: 202-481-5516
www.sbaonline.sba.gov/tx/dallas/index.html

Debbie Fernandez
U.S. Small Business Administration
606 N. Caranchua
Corpus Christi, TX 78476
361-879-0017, ext. 30
Fax: 202-481-1545

Utah
Melinda Workman
U.S. Small Business Administration
125 S. State St., Room 2229
Salt Lake City, UT 84138-1195
801-524-3213
Fax: 202-481-4526
www.sbaonline.sba.gov/ut/index.html

Vermont
Brenda Fortier
U.S. Small Business Administration
87 State St., Room 205
Montpelier, VT 05602
802-828-4422, ext. 206
Fax: 202-481-0525
www.sbaonline.sba.gov/vt/index.html

Virginia
Emma Wilson
U.S. Small Business Administration
400 North 8th Street, Suite 1150
Richmond, VA 23240-0126
804-771-2400 x154
Fax: 202-481-1864
www.sbaonline.sba.gov/va/index.html

Washington
Carol McIntosh
U.S. Small Business Administration
1200 Sixth Ave., Suite 1700
Seattle, WA 98101
206-553-7315
Fax: 202-481-0633
www.sbaonline.sba.gov/wa/seattle/index.html

Coralie Myers
U.S. Small Business Administration
801 W. Riverside Ave., Suite 240
Spokane, WA 99201
509-353-2800
509-353-2630
Fax: 202-481-0861
www.sbaonline.sba.gov/wa/spokane/index.html

West Virginia
Sharon Weaver
U.S. Small Business Administration
Federal Center, Suite 330
320 West Pike
Clarksburg, WV 26301
304-623-5631, ext. 239
Fax: 202-481-5546
www.sbaonline.sba.gov/wv/index.html

Wisconsin

Becky Freund
U.S. Small Business Administration
740 Regent Street, Suite 100
Madison, WI 53715
608-441-5519
Fax: 202-481-0411
www.sbaonline.sba.gov/wi/index.html

Mary Trimmier
U.S. Small Business Administration
310 W. Wisconsin Ave., Suite 400
Milwaukee, WI 53203
414-297-1093
Fax: 202-481-4497
www.sbaonline.sba.gov/wi/index.html

Wyoming

Debra Farris
U.S. Small Business Administration
100 E. B St., Room 4001
Casper, WY 82602-2839
307-261-6509
Fax: 307-261-6535
www.sbaonline.sba.gov/wy/index.html

Matthew Lesko, Information USA, Inc., 12081 Nebel Street, Rockville, MD 20852 • 1-800-955-7693 • www.lesko.com

Local Woman-To-Woman Entrepreneur Help Centers

The U.S. Small Business Administration (SBA) has co-funded 60 Demonstration Centers across the country to assist women interested in starting up and expanding small businesses. What is unique about these programs is that most offer woman-to-woman, one-on-one counseling in all aspects of business, from employee relations, budgeting, and dealing with lenders, to legal, marketing, and accounting assistance. Unlike the help you might receive at an SBA office, these centers offer help by women exclusively for women. These nonprofit centers are public/private-funded ventures, which means they will charge nominal fees for their services, although much less than you'd expect to pay for your own private business advisor.

Alabama

Women's Business Center of Southern Alabama
Kathryn Cariglino, Director
1301 Azalea Road, Suite 201A
Mobile, AL 36693
251-660-2725
800-378-7461
Fax: 251-660-8854
Email: womenbiz@aol.com
http://ceebic.org/~whac

Central Alabama Women's Business Center
Trudy M. Phillips, President
110 12th Street North
Birmingham, AL 35203
866-252-5787
205-453-0249
Fax: 205-453-0253
Email: info@cawbc.org
www.cawbc.org

Alaska

WOMEN$ Finance
Jennifer Abbott, Program Director
245 West Fifth Avenue
P.O. Box 102059
Anchorage, AK 99510-2059
907-274-1524
Fax: 907-272-3146
Email: jabbott@wcaak.org
www.alaskabizbuilders.org/women$fund

Arizona

Self-Employment Loan Fund, Inc. (SELF)
1601 N. 7th Street, Suite 340
Phoenix, AZ 85340
602-340-8834
Fax: 602-340-8953
Email: milnerachel@hotmail.com
www.selfloanfund.org

Microbusiness Advancement Center of Southern Arizona
P. O. Box 42100
10 East Broadway Road, Suite 210
Tucson, AZ 85733-2108
520-620-1241
Fax: 520-622-2235
Email: admin@mac-sa.org
www.mac-sa.org

Arkansas

Arkansas Women's Business Development Center
Miriam Karanja, Program Director
2304 W. 29th Avenue
Pine Bluff, AR 71603
870-535-6233 ext. 14
888-323-6233

Fax: 870-535-0741
Email: mkaranja@ehlot.org
Email: info@goodfaithfund.org
www.goodfaithfund.org

California

Renaissance Entrepreneurship Center
Janet Lees, Program Director
275 Fifth Street
San Francisco, CA 94103-4120
415-541-8580, ext. 237
Fax: 415-541-8589
Email: janet@rencenter.org
www.rencenter.org

Women's Initiative for Self Employment (WI)
Laura Hoover, Microfinance and Business Development Manager
1390 Market Street, Suite 113
San Francisco, CA 94102
415-247-9473
Fax: 415-247-9471
Email: lhoover@womensinitiative.org
www.womensinitiative.org

WEST Company - Ukiah Office
367 North State Street, Suite 201
Ukiah, CA 95482
707-468-3553
Fax: 707-468-3555
Email: info@westcompany.org
www.westcompany.org

WEST Company - Fort Bragg Office
306 East Redwood Avenue, Suite 2
Fort Bragg, CA 95437
707-964-7571
Fax: 707-964-7576
Email: joy@westcompany.org
www.westcompany.org

Colorado

Mi Casa Resource Center for Women, Inc.
360 Acoma Street
Denver, CO 80223
303-573-1302
Fax: 303-595-0422
Email: info@micasadenver.org
www.micasadenver.org

Mi Casa Resource Center for Women, Inc.
505 West Abriendo Avenue
Pueblo, CO 81004
719-542-0091
Fax: 719-542-1006
Email: info@micasadenver.org
www.micasadenver.org

Connecticut

Women Business Development Center (WBDC)
Fran Pastore, Director of Training and Programs

400 Main Street, Suite 500
Stamford, CT 06901
203-353-1750
Fax: 203-353-1084
Email: fpastore@ctwbdc.org
www.ctwbdc.org

SBA and OWBO-CT at The Entrepreneurial Center of Hartford's College for Women
Jean Blake-Jackson, Director
50 Elizabeth Street
Hartford, CT 06105-2280
860-768-5681
Fax: 860-768-5622
Email: entrectr@hartford.edu
http://uhaweb.hartford.edu/entrectr

District of Columbia

Women's Business Center of the Capital Area
Susan Kuhn, Director of Program Services
1001 Connecticut Avenue NW, Suite 312
Washington, DC 20036
202-785-4922
Fax: 202-785-4110
Email: info@womensbusinesscenter.org
www.womensbusinesscenter.org

Florida

Women's Business Center of Northwest Florida
Rosemary Fraser, Director
6235 North David Hwy., Suite 111 B
Pensacola, FL 32504
850-484-2765
Fax: 850-484-3697
Email: womenbiz@womenbiz.biz

Georgia

Greater Atlanta Women's Business Project
241 Peachtree Street NW, Suite 200
Atlanta, GA 30303
404-965-3983, ext.108
404-659-5955
Fax: 404-880-9561
www.graspnet.org

Hawaii

Hawaii Women's Business Center
Beverly Cabrera, Executive Director
1041 Nuuanu Ave., Suite A
Honolulu, HI 96817
808-522-8136 ext. 227
Fax: 808-522-8135
Email: info@hwbc.org
www.Hawaiiwbc.org

Idaho

Entrepreneurial Resources, Inc.
Amy Davis, Executive Director
119 North 9th Street
P.O. Box 6700
Boise, ID 83707-0700
208-336-5464

Fax: 208-375-9333
Email: frontdesk@wcidaho.org
www.wbcidaho.org/index.asp

Illinois

*Women's Business Development Center
(WBDC)*
8 South Michigan Avenue
Suite 400
Chicago, IL 60603-3306
312-853-3477, ext. 517
Fax: 312-853-0145
Email: wdbc@wbdc.org
www.wbdc.org

Indiana

*Women's Enterprise, A Program of the Fort
Wayne's Women's Business Bureau*
Leslie Alford, Director
3521 Lake Ave., Suite 1
Fort Wayne, IN 46805-5533
260-424-7977
Fax: 260-426-7576
Email: info@womensenterprise.org
www.womensenterprise.org

Iowa

The Iowa Women's Enterprise Center
910 23rd Avenue
Coralville, IA 52241
888-849-9589
319-338-2331
Fax: 319-338-5824
Email: info@ised.org
www.ised.org/EconomicDevelopment/Women
EntCenter.asp

Kansas

Kansas Women's Business Center
Sandy Licata, Executive Director
8527 Bluejacket Street
Lenexa, KS 66214
913-492-5922
Fax: 913-888-6928
Email: slicata@kansaswbc.com
www.kansaswbc.com

Kentucky

Women's Enterprise Institute
Nicole Bryan, Interim Director
512 East Stephens Street
Midway College
Midway, KY 40347-1120
859-846-5800
Fax: 859-546-5872
Email: wei@midway.edu
www.weimidway.org

Louisiana

*Urban League of Greater New Orleans
Women's Business Resource Center*
2322 Canal Street, Suite 100
New Orleans, LA 70119
504-620-9650
Fax: 504-620-9659
www.urbanleagueneworleans.org/women'sbusi
nessresource.htm

Maine

Coastal Enterprises Inc. (CEI)
Women's Business Development Program
(WBDP)
Ellen Golden, Senior Project Manager
P.O. Box 268
36 Water Street
Wiscasset, ME 04578
207-882-7552
Fax: 207-882-7308
Email: cei@ceimaine.org
www.ceimaine.org

Maryland

*Women Entrepreneurs of Baltimore, Inc.
(WEB)*
Amanda Crook Zinn, Chief Executive Officer
1118 Light Street, Suite 202
Baltimore, MD 21230
410-727-4921
Fax: 410-727-4989
Email: services@webinc.org
www.webinc.org

Women's Business Institute, Inc.
Beatrice Checket, Chief Executive Officer
10 S. Howard St., 6th Floor
Baltimore, MD 21201
410-266-8746
Email: checket@juno.com

Massachusetts

Center for Women & Enterprise
Cheri Boegemann, Program Coordinator
150 Elm Street, 2nd Floor
Worcester, MA 01609
508-363-2300
Fax: 508-363-2323
Email: cboegemann@cweonline.org
www.cweboston.org

Center for Women & Enterprise
Alison Corwin, Program Manager
Renaissance Park
1135 Tremont Street, Suite 480
Boston, MA 02120
617-536-0700 ext. 223
Fax: 617-536-7373
Email: acorwin@cwconline.org
www.cweboston.org

Michigan

*Women's Initiative for Self-Employment
(WISE)*
Center for Empowerment and Economic
Development (CEED)
Michelle Richards, Executive Director
2002 Hogback Road, Suite 12
Ann Arbor, MI 48105
734-677-1400
Fax: 734-677-1465
Email: mrichards@miceed.org
www.miceed.org

*Grand Rapids Opportunities for Women
(GROW)*
Rita VenderVen, Executive Director
25 Sheldon SE, Suite 210
Grand Rapids, MI 49503
616-458-3404
Fax: 616-458-6557
Email: grow@voyager.net
www.growbusiness.org

Detroit Entrepreneurship Institute, Inc.
Cathy McClelland, President
455 W. Fort Street, 4th Floor
Detroit, MI 48226
313-961-8426
Fax: 313-961-8831
Email: cmcclelland@deibus.org
www.deibus.org

Minnesota

The People Connection
Michelle Landsverk, Operations Director
226 East 1st Street
Fosston, MN 56542
218-435-2134
Fax: 218-435-1347
Email: michelle@thepeopleconnection.org
www.thepeopleconnection.org

Women Venture
Tene Wells, President
2324 University Avenue West, Suite 200
St. Paul, MN 55114
651-646-3808
Fax: 651-641-7223
Email: twells@womenventure.org
www.womenventure.org

Mississippi

MACE Women's Business Center
Ruby Buck, President
119 South Theobald Street
Greenville, MS 38701
662-335-3523
Fax: 601-334-2939
Email: mace@tecinco.com
www.deltamace.org

Missouri

*Women's Business Center at Growth
Opportunity Connection, Inc.*
Alan Corbet, Executive Director
4747 Troost Avenue
Kansas City, MO 64110
816-235-6146
Fax: 816-235-6177
Email: acorbet@goconnection.org
www.goconnection.org

Grace Hill Neighborhood Services
Lynette Watson, Director
2600 Hadley Street
St. Louis, MO 63106
314-539-7500
Fax: 314-241-8938
Email: LynneS@gracehill.org
www.gracehill.org

Montana

Business Resource Center
Travis Brazill, Director
347 North Last Chance Gulch
Helena, MT 59601
800-254-6607
406-443-0800
Fax: 406-442-2745
Email: tbrazill@ctibrc.org
www.ctibrc.org

Nebraska

Rural Enterprise Assistance Project
P.O. Box 136
145 Main Street
Lyons, NE 68038
402-687-2100
Fax: 402-687-2200
Email: REAPinfo@cfra.org
www.cfra.org/reap/default.htm

New Hampshire

Women's Business Center, Inc.
Ellen Fineberg, Executive Director
150 Greenleaf Avenue, #8
Portsmouth, NH 03801
603-430-2892
Fax: 603-430-3706
Email: info@womenbiz.org
www.womenbiz.org

New Jersey

*New Jersey Association of Women Business
Owners, Women's Business Center*
Penni Nafus, Director
White Horse Commercial Park
127 US Highway 206 South, Suite 28
Hamilton, NJ 08610
609-581-2220
Fax: 609-581-6749
Email: wbcnj@njawbo.org
www.njawbo.org

New Mexico

*Women's Economic Self-Sufficiency Team
(WESST Corp.)*

Local Woman-to-Woman Entrepreneur Help Centers

414 Silver Southwest
Albuquerque, NM 87102
800-GO-WESST
505-241-4753
Fax: 505-241-4766
www.wesst.org

*Women's Economic Self-Sufficiency Team
Corp.*
4601 East Main Street, Suite 580
Farmington, NM 87401
800-GO-WESST
505-325-0678
Fax: 505-325-0695
www.wesst.org

New York
Women's Venture
240 West 35 Street, Suite 501
New York, NY 10001
212-563-0499
Fax: 212-868-9116
Email: info@wvf-ny.org
www.womensventurefund.org

*The Women's Business Resource Center (Hunts
Point)*
Josephine Infante, Executive Director
866B Hunts Point Avenue
Bronx, NY 10474
718-842-8888
Fax: 718-842-6592
Email: Jinfante@huntspointedc.org
www.hpwbrc.org

Queens Women's Business Center
Madeleine Gordillo, Program Officer
120-55 Queens Boulevard, Suite 309
Kew Gardens
Queens, NY 11424
718-263-0546
Fax: 718-263-0594
Email: services@queensny.org
www.queensny.org

*The Local Development Corporation of East
New York*
80 Jamaica Avenue
Brooklyn, NY 11207
718-385-6700
Fax: 718-385-7505
Email: ldceny@hotmail.org
www.ldceny.org

North Carolina
The Women's Center of Fayetteville
Sylvia Ray, Executive Director
230 Hay Street
Fayetteville, NC 28301
910-323-3377
Fax: 910-323-8828
Email: jsuperak@wcof.org
www.wcof.org

*North Carolina Institute of Minority Economic
Development*
Verona P. Edmond, Director
114 West Parrish Street, 4th Floor
P.O. Box 1331
Durham, NC 27701
919-956-8889
Fax: 919-688-4358
Email: info@ncimed.com
www.ncimed.com/wbc/index.cfm

North Dakota
The Center for Technology and Business
Tara Holt, Project Director
1022 East Divide Avenue
P.O. Box 2535
Bismarck, ND 58502
866-294-2136
701-223-0707
Fax: 701-223-2507

Email: holt@techwomen.org
www.techwomen.org

Ohio
*Ohio's Women's Business Development
Council, Inc.*
Linda Steward, Program Director
3360 E. Livingston Ave., Suite 213
Columbus, OH 43227
614-621-0881
Fax: 614-238-0168

Oklahoma
*Oklahomans for Indian Opportunity (OIO)
Women's Business Center*
Betty Olivas, Program Director
3001 South Berry Road, Suite B
Norman, OK 73072
800-375-3737
405-329-3737
Fax: 405-329-8488
Email: bolivas@oiooio.com
www.oiooio.com

*Rural Enterprise of Oklahoma, Inc. (REO)
Rural Women's Business Center*
Barbara Rackley, Program Director
P.O. Box 1335
2912 Enterprise Drive
Durant, OK 74702
800-658-2523
580-924-5094
Fax: 580-920-2745
Email: barbara@ruralenterprise.com
www.ruralenterprises.com/wbc.htm

Center for Entrepreneurial Excellence
Anne Coleman, Executive Director
2709 West I-44 Service Road
Oklahoma City, OK 73112
405-601-1930
Fax: 405-601-1935
Email: info@helpyourbiz.org
www.helpyourbiz.org

Oregon
*Southern Oregon Women's Access to Credit
(SOWAC)*
Helen Wallace, Director
33 North Central, Suite 209
Medford, OR 97501
866-608-6094
541-779-3992
Fax: 541-779-5195
Email: hwallace@sowac.org
www.sowac.org

Pennsylvania
*Women's Business Development Center
(WBDC)*
1315 Walnut Street
Suite 1116
Philadelphia, PA 19107-4711
215-790-9232
Fax: 215-790-9231
Email: info@womensbdc.org
www.womensbdc.org

Puerto Rico
Women's Business Institute (WBI)
Universidad Del Sagrado Corazon
(The University of the Sacred Heart)
Teresa Sotero, Director
Center for Women's Entrepreneurial
 Development
P.O. Box 12383
San Juan, PR 00914-0383
787-726-7045
Fax: 787-726-6550
Email: empresaria@sagrado.edu
www.wbipr.org

Rhode Island
Center for Women & Enterprise, Inc. (CWE)
Carol Malysz, Director
55 Claverick Street, Suite 102
Providence, RI 02903
401-277-0800
Fax: 401-277-1122
Email: cmalysz@cweonline.org
www.cweboston.org

South Carolina
*South Carolina Manufacturing Extension
Partnership/WBC*
Haidee Stith, Client Impact
817 Calhoun Street
Columbia, SC 29201
800-MEP-4MFG
803-252-6976, ext. 225
Email: hstith@scmep.org
www.scmep.org

South Dakota
Center for Women Business Institute
Tricia Cole, Interim Executive Director
1101 W. 22nd Street
Sioux Falls, SD 57105
866-556-6744
605-331-6697
Fax: 605-331-6615
Email: tricia.cole@usiouxfalls.edu
www.usiouxfalls.edu/als/bus_institute.htm

Tennessee
*The National Assn. for Women Business
Owners - Nashville Chapter (NAWBO)*
Janice S. Thomas, Executive Director
P.O. Box 292283
1112 8th Avenue South
Nashville, TN 37229-2283
615-746-5930
Fax: 615-256-2706
Email: info@nawbo.com
www.nashvillenawbo.com

Southeast Women's Business Center
Sandi Brock, Program Director
P.O. Box 4757
535 Chestnut Street
Chattanooga, TN 37405
423-266-5781
Fax: 423-267-7705
Email: sbrock@sedev.org
www.sewbc.com

Texas
Women's Empowerment Business Center
1201 University Drive
Edinburg, TX 78539-2999
956-292-7535
Fax: 956-292-7561
Email: webc@panam.edu
www.coserve.org/webc/

*Texas Center for Women's Business Enterprise
(CWBE)*
Dianne Olson, Project Director
4100 Ed Bluestein Boulevard, Building 5
Austin, TX 78721
888-352-2525
512-472-8522
Fax: 512-472-8513
Email: dianne@txcwbe.org
www.txcwbe.org

Women's Business Border Center
Terri Adams-Reed, Project Director
201 E. Main Street, Suite 100
El Paso, TX 79901
915-566-4066
Fax: 915-566-9714
Email: treed@ephcc.org
www.womenbordercenter.com

Fort Worth Women's Business Center
M. Tipper, Program Director
1150 South Freeway
Fort Worth, TX 76104
817-871-6001
Fax: 817-871-6031
Email: mtipper@fwbac.com
www.fwbac.com

Utah

Womens Business Center at the Chamber
Salt Lake Area Chamber of Commerce
Nancy Mitchell, Director
175 East 400 South, Suite 600
Salt Lake City, UT 84111
801-364-3631
Fax: 801-328-5098
Email: nmitchell@saltlakechamber.org
www.saltlakechamber.org

Vermont

Vermont Women's Business Center (CVCAC)
Linda Ingold, Project Director
660 Elm Street
Montpelier, VT 05602
800-266-4062
802-229-2181
Fax: 802-229-2141
Email: lmase@cvcac.org
www.vwbc.org

Virgin Islands

St. Croix Foundation for Community Development, Inc.
Virgin Islands Women's Business Center
Bernadette Richards, Program Director
72 Flag Drive, Gallows Bay
St. Croix, USVI 00820
340-773-4995
Fax: 340-773-8503
Email: staff@wbcvi.org
www.wbcvi.org

Virginia

Women's Business Center of Northern Virginia
Barbara Wrigley, Director
7001 Loisdale Road, Suite C

Springfield, VA 22150
703-778-9922
Fax: 703-768-0547
Email: bwrigley@wbcnova.org
www.wbcnova.org

Washington

Northwest Women's Business Center
728 134th Street, SW
Everett, WA 98204
425-787-9856
Fax: 425-745-5563
Email: info.nwwbc@seattleccd.com
www.seattleccd.com/wbc-nw/index.htm

Women's Business Center
P.O. Box 22283
1437 South Jackson Street
Seattle, WA 98144
206-324-4330
Fax: 206-324-4322
Email: info@seattleccd.com
www.seattleccd.com/wbc/index.htm

West Virginia

Women's Business Institute, Inc. (WBI)
Kathryn Johnston,
1000 Technology Drive
Allan B. Mollahan Technical Center
Fairmont, WV 26554
304-366-1400
Email: wbifairmontkj@hotmail.com
www.wbi-wv.org

Women's Business Institute
Beatrice Checket
Grand Central Business Ctr., #3050
One Grand Central Park
Keyser, WV 26726
301-786-4646
Fax: 304-788-1687
Email: keyserwbi@juno.com
www.wbi-wv.org

Wisconsin

Wisconsin Women's Business Initiative Corporation (WWBIC)

Wendy K. Baumer, President
2745 North Dr. Martin Luther King Jr. Drive
Milwaukee, WI 53212
414-263-5450
Fax: 414-263-5456
Email: info@wwbic.com
www.wwbic.com

Wisconsin Women's Business Initiative Corporation (WWBIC)
Jill French, Project Director
2300 South Park Street, Suite 4
Madison, WI 53713
608-257-5450
Fax: 608-257-5454
Email: info@wwbic.com
www.wwbic.com

Western Dairyland Women's Business Center (WDWBDC)
Renee Walz, Business Development Director
P.O. Box 125; 23122 Whitehall Road
Independence, WI 54747
715-985-2391, ext 210
800-782-1063, ext 210
Fax: 715-985-3239
Email: info@westerndairyland.org
www.westerndairyland.org

Wyoming

Wyoming Women's Business Center
Andrea Lewis, Program Coordinator
University of Wyoming
Education Annex/Business Technology Center
Rooms 155 & 158
13th and Lewis Streets
P.O. Box 764
Laramie, WY 82071
307-766-3084
888-524-1947
Fax: 307-766-3085
Email: wwbc@uwyo.edu
www.wyomingwomen.org

State Women Business Assistance Programs

The feds aren't the only ones noticing the emerging importance of female entrepreneurship in the U.S. business economy. Many states now have special programs to help new and expanding women-owned businesses get the special assistance they need to succeed. So far, almost half the states offer some kind of assistance to women business owners, from special set-aside programs to help women compete for lucrative government contracts, to nuts-and-bolts, one-on-one counseling, to special low interest loan programs, such as the ones offered by Iowa and Louisiana.

It's important to keep in mind that just because your state doesn't currently have any special programs for women entrepreneurs, that doesn't mean that they won't in the near future. In fact, many states, like Florida and Utah, now have special women's business advocates in the state capital to help bring the needs of women business owners to the attention of their legislators. We all know that many newly elected legislators happen to be women, too. This could mean new business programs for women offered in the future, so keep in touch with your state capital to keep informed on the current status of these programs.

Alabama

Office of Minority Business Enterprise (OMBE)
Alabama Development Office
401 Adams Ave.   334-242-0400
Montgomery, AL 36130   800-248-0033
http://www.ado.state.al.us

The Office of Minority Business Enterprise (OMBE) helps women and minority entrepreneurs interested in starting or expanding their businesses prepare business plans and applications for SBA loans, fill out applications for state and federal procurement opportunities, and certify women and minority-owned businesses to participate in the state purchasing programs.

Alaska

Minority Business Development Center
122 1st Avenue, Suite 600
Fairbanks, AK 99701   907-452-8251
http://akbiz.org

The Minority Business Development Center provides management and financial consulting services including loan packaging, development, marketing, investment decisions, accounting systems, and other valuable business advice.

Bureau of Indian Affairs
Alaska Area Office
P.O. Box 25520
Juneau, AK 99802-5520   907-586-7106

Indian Business Development Grants: This program provides grants to assist in the development of Native-owned enterprise that will create jobs and other economic benefits for Alaska Native communities. Priority is given to rural business development projects. For profit businesses are eligible if they are at least 51% owned and operated by individual natives. Grants to individual natives range up to $100,000 with a minimum 75% match from private and/or public sector. The applicant must demonstrate that sufficient funding is not available from other sources.

Indian Loans for Economic Development: The program provides business management, and technical and financial assistance to individual natives and Native organizations for starting, expanding, or purchasing a business enterprise whose enterprise will create jobs and have other economic benefits. Priority is given to rural business development projects. Financial assistance is in the form of guaranteed or direct loans. 20% equity is required on loans and businesses must demonstrate economic feasibility.

Arizona

Minority & Women Owned Businesses
Arizona Department of Commerce
Executive Tower, Suite 600
1700 W. Washington
Phoenix, AZ 85007   602-771-1100
http://www.commerce.state.az.us/SmallBus

This office serves as a clearinghouse of information to assist small businesses. One-on-one counseling is available.

Arkansas

Arkansas Economic Development Commission
One Capitol Mall
Little Rock, AR 72201   501-682-6105
www.1-800-arkansas.com/Small_Business

The Minority and Small Business Development Division provides business loan packaging, contract procurement assistance, bonding information, general business counseling, seminars, workshops, and referrals to other agencies.

California

California Small Business & DVBE
Department of General Services
707 Third Street
West Sacramento, CA 95605   916-375-4940
www.pd.dgs.ca.gov/smbus

This office helps minority businesses interested in participating in the state's purchasing/contracting system along with counseling and outreach programs.

Business Enterprise Program
Department of Transportation
1823 14th Street   866-810-6346
Sacramento, CA 95814   916-324-1700
http://www.dot.ca.gov/hq/bep

This office offers women-owned businesses information on the certification necessary to participate in the state procurement program.

Colorado

Women's Business Office
Office of Business Development
1625 Broadway, Suite 1710   303-892-3840
Denver, CO 80202   800-592-5920 (in CO)
http://www.state.co.us/gov_dir/wbo

The Women's Business Office acts as a resource clearinghouse for women business owners. They refer callers to the appropriate state and local offices that can provide them with the hands-on assistance they need, from business planning and marketing assistance to procurement programs and financing. The program also holds business planning seminars at 16 locations throughout the state.

Connecticut

Community Economic Development Fund
430 New Park Avenue, 2nd Floor
West Hartford, CT 06110-1142   860-249-3800
www.cedf.com

A loan guarantee program designed to help women and minority-owned businesses obtain financing. The funds are available for start-up as well as for the growth of an existing company.

Delaware

Minority Enterprise Office
800 French St., 6th Floor
Wilmington, DE 19801
www.ci.wilmington.de.us/mbeo.htm   302-571-4093

The agency assists minority businesses in the city of Wilmington by providing technical assistance, certificate of minority businesses, and workshops. They sponsor a Minority Business Trade Fair (the largest in the Northeast) once a year. The agency works with the Wilmington Economic Development Corporation to provide financing.

Department of Administrative Services
Office of Minority and Women Business Enterprise
Margaret O'Neill Building
410 Federal Street
Dover, DE 19901   302-739-7830
www2.state.de.us/omwdbe/

Florida

Florida Department of Transportation
Disadvantaged Business Enterprise
605 Suwannee St.
Tallahassee, FL 32399   850-414-4100
www.dot.state.fl.us

The office develops outreach programs to recruit and inform disadvantaged business enterprises about contracting opportunities with the Department of Transportation. It also has a business support component which assesses business needs for training and technical assistance. Specific programs include classroom training, on-the-job training, conferences, seminars, workshops, and proficiency standards attainment.

Office of Supplier Diversity
Florida Department Management Services
4050 Esplanade Way, Suite 360
Tallahassee, FL 32399-0950   850-487-0915
http://mbaao.fdles.state.fl.us/

This office is responsible for certifying minority businesses to do business with the state and for maintaining a directory of these certified businesses. The directory is available to all state agencies. They identify the concerns and unique needs of small and minority-owned businesses in Florida. It serves as a liaison between the business community, state agencies, and the legislature. It also serves as a review board for policies, procedures, and regulations as they relate to key issues of concern.

Florida Minority Business Opportunity Committee
6880 Lake Ellenor Drive, Suite 104G
Orlando, FL 32809   407-245-6493
www.mbocflorida.org/

The Florida MBOC provides opportunities for minority-owned companies to access capital, develop strategies for success through mentoring and to bring businesses and organizations together.

Georgia

Small and Minority Business Affairs
Georgia Department of Administrative Services
200 Piedmont Ave., SE
West Tower #1620
Atlanta, GA 30602   404-656-6315
http://www.doas.state.ga.us

The office assists small businesses in conducting business with state government, identification of coordinating offices in state agencies, and prerequisites. The Minority Subcontractors Tax Incentive is available to any company which subcontracts with a minority-owned firm to furnish goods, property, or services to the state of Georgia. The credit is for 10% of the total amount of qualified payments to minority subcontractors during the tax year, but may not exceed $100,000 per year.

Minority Business Development Agency
401 W. Peachtree, Suite 1715
Atlanta, GA 30308   404-730-3300
http://www.mbda.gov

At any of the regional offices of the Minority Business Development Agency (of the U.S. Department of Commerce), a minority owner can get help with preparing a business loan package, securing sales, or solving a management problem. The centers maintain networks of local business development organizations, assist business people in the commercialization of technologies, and coordinate other federal agency activities which assist minority entrepreneurs.

Hawaii

Honolulu Minority Business Development Center
1132 Bishop St.
1st Hawaiian Tower #1000
Honolulu, HI 96813   808-531-6232
www.hawaii.gov/dbedt

The center provides management and technical assistance to qualified ethnic minority individuals and firms in the areas of business and financial planning, contract procurement, marketing analyses, general management, bonding, office systems, and procedures.

Illinois

Illinois Women's Business Ownership Council
Illinois Department of Commerce and Community Affairs
State of Illinois Center
100 W. Randolph St.
Suite 3-400
Chicago, IL 60601   312-814-7179
www.illinoisbiz.biz/bus/IWBOChome.html

The Small Business Advocate specializes in helping women, minorities, startups, and home-based business owners cut through the bureaucratic red tape and get the answers they need by offering information and expertise in dealing with various state, federal, and local agencies.

Small Business Assistance Bureau
Illinois Department of Commerce and Community Affairs
State of Illinois Center
620 E. Adams   217-782-7500
Springfield, IL 62701   800-252-2923 (in IL)
http://www.commerce.state.il.us

The Women's Business Advocate offers programs to women entrepreneurs through a business calendar of events, which includes conferences at which business owners have an opportunity to network. The Advocate also maintains an extensive mailing list of women entrepreneurs. Through the Women's Business Development Center of The Neighborhood Institute, women business owners can get assistance in all phases of business development.

Under the Minority and Women Business Loan Program, women business owners can get long-term, fixed rate direct financing at below market rates for loans from $5,000 to $50,000. One job must be created or retained for each $5,000 borrowed. Business owners can use the money for leasing or purchasing land and buildings, construction or renovation of fixed assets, purchase and installation of machinery and equipment, and working capital.

Under the Minority and Female Business Enterprise Program, Matchmaker Conferences are held to connect women business owners interested in landing government contracts with state and local purchasing agents.

Indiana

Small Business Development Corporation
One North Capitol, Suite 900   888-ISBD-244
Indianapolis, IN 46204   317-234-2082
www.isbdcorp.org

This office helps women and minority-owned small businesses with all phases of development, from management and technical assistance, to contract bidding, procurement, educational seminars and training, and financial alternatives. As part of their Procurement Program, women and minority-owned businesses receive help in seeking government services contracts.

Iowa

Targeted Small Business Financial Assistance Program
Iowa Department of Economic Development
200 East Grand Avenue   515-242-4819
Des Moines. IA 50309   800-532-1215
www.iowasmart.com/services/entrepreneurial/programs.html

Under the Targeted Small Business Program, women and minority-owned businesses can receive direct loans of up to $25,000 and loan guarantees of up to $40,000. In limited cases, equity grants are available in amounts of up to $25,000.

Kansas

Office of Minority and Women Business
Kansas Department of Commerce
1000 SW Jackson Street, Suite 100
Topeka, KS 66603-3712   785-296-3425
http://kdoch.state.ks.us

This office helps women and minority-owned businesses with the bidding procedures for public and private procurement opportunities in Kansas. They also offer management assistance to these businesses and help identify financial resources for them.

Kentucky

Small and Minority Business
Kentucky Cabinet for Economic Development
500 Mero Street
Capital Plaza Tower
Frankfort, KY 40601   502-564-7670
www.thinkkentucky.com/SMBD/

The Small and Minority Business Division is a resource center for small and minority business owners/managers. It identifies construction contracts, procurement opportunities, and offers training programs that address the business needs of these enterprises. It focuses on new job creation and job retention by serving existing small and minority businesses in the roles of ombudsman and expediter for business growth and retention.

Louisiana

Louisiana Economic Development
Capital Annex
1051 N. 3rd Street
P.O. Box 94185
Baton Rouge, LA 70804-9185   225-342-3000
www.lded.state.la.us/businessresources/rules_matching.asp

The Louisiana Minority Venture Capital Matching Grant Program allows qualifying minority-owned businesses to invest $1 in their business and receive $2 of private capital.

Maine

Maine Department of Transportation
Division of Equal Opportunity
Disadvantaged & Women Business Enterprise
16 State Station House
Augusta, ME 04333   207-624-3061
www.maine.gov/mdot

Under the Disadvantaged/Minority/Women Business Enterprise Program, women-owned businesses can get certification to obtain government contracts. This office helps business owners with the procurement procedures used to obtain government contracts.

Maryland

Maryland Department of Business and Economic Development
Governor's Office of Minority Affairs
217 East Redwood Street
Baltimore, MD 21202   410-767-8232
www.oma.state.md.us

Assists minority firms in Maryland seeking contract and procurement opportunities with the State. OMA provides referral assistance and consultation to minority business owners on both public and private sector opportunities and resources, co-sponsors conferences and seminars that provide information to minority entrepreneurs regarding business opportunities and more.

Massachusetts

State Office of Minority and Women Business Assistance
Department of Commerce
10 Park Plaza, Suite 3740
Boston, MA 02116   617-973-8692
www.somwba.state.ma.us

This office helps women and minority-owned businesses get certified to participate in the state procurement programs.

Michigan

Michigan Economic Development Corporation
300 N Washington Square
Lansing, MI 48913   517-373-9808
http://medc.michigan.org

The Michigan Economic Development Corporation provides a number of general business start-up and expansion services, which include a Directory of minority and women-owned businesses.

Minnesota

Department of Administration
Materials Management Division
Administrative Building, Room 112
St. Paul, MN 55155   612-296-2600
http://www.mmd.admin.state.mn.us

This office certifies women-owned businesses to participate in the Small Business Program for procurement opportunities with the state. Once certified, a business earns a 6% preference on government contract bids.

Mississippi

Department of Economic and Community Development
P.O. Box 849
Jackson, MS 39205   601-359-3449
www.mississippi.org

Under the Minority Business Enterprise Loan Program, women-owned businesses that show that they are economically disadvantaged are eligible to receive low interest loans for up to 50% of a business project's cost.

Missouri

Missouri Women's Council
P.O. Box 1684
421 East Dunklin Street   573-751-0810
Jefferson City, MO 65102   877-426-9284
www.womenscouncil.org

The Council helps women small business owners through various programs, seminars, and conferences. The Missouri Council on Women's Economic Development and Training assists women in small business enterprises. The Council conducts programs, studies, seminars, and conferences. It promotes increased economic and employment opportunities through education, training, and greater participation in the labor force.

Missouri Department of Economic Development
P.O. Box 118
Jefferson City, MO 65102   573-751-3237
www.ded.state.mo.us/business/officeofminoritybusiness

The Minority Business Assistance Program is designed to promote and encourage the development of minority-owned businesses in Missouri. The program provides assistance in obtaining technical and financial assistance, education programs, minority advocacy, and networking with other programs and agencies.

Montana

DBE Program Specialist
Civil Rights Bureau
Montana Department of Transportation
2701 Prospect Ave.
P.O. 201001
Helena, MT 59620-1001   406-444-6337
www.mdt.state.mt.us

The Disadvantaged Business Enterprise and Women Business Enterprise program certifies women-owned businesses interested in bidding on and obtaining federal-aid highway construction contracts.

Nebraska

Office of Women's Business Ownership
Small Business Administration
11145 Mill Valley Rd.
Omaha, NE 68154   402-221-4691
www.sba.gov/ne

The office directs Small Business Administration (SBA) programs to women business owners through special women's groups, seminars, networks, and other activities for women in the private sector.

Disadvantaged Business Enterprise
Minority Business Office
Nebraska Department of Roads
P.O. Box 94759
Lincoln, NE 68509-4759   402-479-4531
www.dor.state.ne.us

New Hampshire

Office of Business and Industrial Development
Division of Economic Development
172 Pembroke Rd.
P.O. Box 856
Concord, NH 03302-0856   603-271-2411
www.nheconomy.com

This office serves as a clearinghouse and referral center of programs for women and minority-owned businesses.

New Jersey

Office of Small, Women & Minority-Owned Business
New Jersey Commerce and Economic Growth Commission
P.O. Box 820
Trenton, NJ 08625-0820   609-777-0885
www.state.nj.us/commerce/smallbiz.html

The Office of Business Services provides services to New Jersey's small businesses to succeed, from assisting firms with public procurement opportunities by registering eligible businesses for "set-aside" contracts, to certifying women and minority business enterprises for program participation.

New Mexico

Economic Development Department
State Purchasing Division
P.O. Drawer 26110
Santa Fe, NM 87502   505-827-0425
www.state.nm.us/clients/spd/spd.html

The Procurement Assistant Program educates business owners in all phases of government contracting, and provides comprehensive technical procurement counseling for obtaining defense, federal, state, and local government contracts. It offers training seminars (hands-on workshops), and offers small, minority, and women-owned businesses the opportunity to be entered into the annual New Mexico MSBPAP Business Directory.

New York

Division of Minority and Women's Business
Empire State Development
30 South Pearl Street
Albany, NY 12245   800-STATWE-NY
or
633 Third Ave.
New York, NY 10017   212-803-2410
www.nylovesbiz.com/Small_and_Growing_Businesses/mwbe.asp

This office gives women and minority-owned businesses consulting and technical assistance in obtaining benefits from state programs, with a focus on business financing. They also help these businesses get the proper certification to participate in the state procurement opportunities. Additionally, this office can help these business owners obtain Federal government contracts.

North Carolina

North Carolina Minority Business Development Agency
205 Fayetteville St. Mall
Raleigh, NC 27601   919-833-6122

The agency provides information, referral, and support assistance to minority businesses. It offers technical referral assistance, procurement opportunities referral, management workshops and seminars, and coordination with other state and federal agencies.

North Dakota

Center for Technology & Business/Women & Technology
P.O. Box 2535
Bismarck, ND 58502   701-223-0707
www.growingnd.com

These offices provide technical assistance in getting businesses started. Some of the services provided include location of funding and preparation of business plans. They also certify women businesses for federal and state contracting.

Ohio

Office of Small Business
Ohio Department of Development
P.O. Box 1001   800-848-1300
Columbus, OH 43266-0101   614-466-2711
www.odod.state.oh.us/edd/osb/sbdc/women.htm

Under the Women's Business Resource Program, women can get help for start-up, expansion and management of their businesses. The program seeks to provide women with equal access to assistance and lending programs, and helps businesswomen locate government procurement opportunities. This office also acts as a statewide center of workshops, conferences, and Women's Business Owners statistics. All of the program's services are free. This office also publishes *Ohio Women Business Leaders*, a directory of women-owned businesses in Ohio, along with other free publications.

Oklahoma

Oklahoma Department of Commerce
Small Business Division
P.O. Box 26980

Oklahoma City, OK 73126-0980   405-815-6552
http://www.odoc.state.ok.us

Under the Women Owned Business Assistance Program, businesswomen can get a variety of technical assistance, from business planning and marketing assistance, to financial information and government procurement practices.

The Minority Business Development Program provides support and assistance in the establishment, growth, and expansion of viable business enterprises. Counseling in the preparation of business plans and marketing strategies is available. The program also provides assistance for loan packaging, bid preparation, feasibility studies, and certification requirements.

Oregon

Office of Minority, Women & Emerging Small Businesses
P.O. Box 14480
Salem, OR 97309-0405   503-947-7922
http://www.cbs.state.or.us

This office certifies women-owned, disadvantaged, and emerging small businesses, allowing them to participate in the state's targeted purchasing programs.

Pennsylvania

Bureau of Minority & Women Business Opportunities
North Office Building, Room 502
Harrisburg, PA 17125   717-787-6708
www.dgs.state.pa.us/bcabd

The Bureau of Minority and Women Business Opportunities provides resources for minority and women business owners to compete for and participate in the state contracting process. Minority and women owned business can be certified and instructed on the statewide compliance program.

Rhode Island

Office of Minority Business Assistance
Department of Economic Development
One West Exchange St.
Providence, RI 02903   401-222-6670
www.rimbe.org

This office certifies women and minority-owned businesses under federal and state set-aside and goal programs and provides counseling assistance to these companies.

South Carolina

Governor's Office of Small and Minority Business Assistance
1205 Pendleton Street, Suite 329
Columbia, SC 29201   803-734-0657
www.govoepp.state.sc.us/osmba/

The goals of Office of Small and Minority Business Assistance are to promote the growth and development of small and minority owned businesses in South Carolina and to advocate that an equitable portion of State procurement contracts be awarded to small and minority owned businesses

South Dakota

Women's Business Center
University of Sioux Falls, Center for Women
Sioux Falls, SD 57104   605-331-6697
www.sdgreatprofits.com/start-up/resourcesba.htm

The center provides advice, planning and support for women starting their own business.

Tennessee

Office of Minority Business Enterprise
Department of Economic & Community Development
312 8th Avenue North   615-741-1888
Nashville, TN 37243   800-342-8470 (in TN)
http://www.state.tn.us/ecd/minority.htm

This office offers information, advocacy, referral, procurement, and other services to minority businesses in the state. They publish a directory of minority businesses, offer conferences and seminars on topics useful to business owners, and serve as a clearinghouse of important information to women and minorities. They also match vendors with potential clients and help women and minorities identify and obtain procurement opportunities.

Utah

Small Business Administration
Salt Lake District Office

125 S. State St.
Salt Lake City, UT 84138 801-524-3209
www.sba.gov/ut

The Women's Business Ownership Program offers a series of business training seminars and workshops for women business owners and for women who want to start their own small firms. This program provides a focus on business planning and development, credit, and procurement as it relates specifically to women and their businesses.

Vermont

Women's Small Business Program
Trinity College
208 Colchester Avenue
Burlington, VT 05401 802-846-7160
www.sdgreatprofits.com/start-up/resourcesba.htm

The Women's Small Business Program offers many to women seeking to identify, start, stabilize, and expand a small business. Services include: Getting Serious, a workshop to determine a business idea and whether business meets personal goals; Start-Up, a 15-week intensive course to develop a business plan and business management skills; and Working Solutions, a topic specific workshops for micro-business owners. Courses are offered statewide. Grants and scholarships for training are available to income eligible women.

Virginia

Women's Business Center of Northern Virginia
Department of Business Assistance
6521 Arlington Blvd., Suite 204
Falls Church, VA 22042 703-534-6220
www.dba.state.va.us

The Center provides women with the training, assistance and support need to start or expand a successful business.

Washington

Office of Minority and Women's Business Enterprises
P.O. Box 41160
Olympia, WA 98504-1160 360-753-9693
www.omwbe.wa.gov

This office helps women and minority-owned businesses interested in participating in state contracting opportunities by moving them through the certification process. Once certified, businesses are eligible to receive a 5% preference when bidding competitively on goods and services purchased by the state. Upon request, businesses can be placed on bid lists maintained by individual agencies, education institutions, or contractors by contacting them directly.

West Virginia

West Virginia Small Business Development Center
Women and Minority-Owned Business DataBase
Capitol Complex
1900 Kanawha Blvd., East
Building 6, Room 652
Charleston, WV 25305-0311 304-558-2960
www.sbdcwv.org/women-minority.php#pagetitle

The West Virginia Minority and Women-Owned Business Database provides companies with exposure to purchasing agents from all levels of government as well as the private sector.

Wisconsin

Department of Commerce
P.O. Box 7970 800-435-7287 (in WI)
Madison, WI 53707 608-266-1018
http://commerce.wi.gov

The Women's Business Services offers assistance in gaining information about the state's loan programs available to women business owners. The office keeps track of the top 50 fastest growing and top 10 women-owned businesses in Wisconsin. They also maintain a database of women-owned businesses in the state.

Wisconsin Housing and Economic Development Authority
One South Pinckney St., #500
P.O. Box 1728 800-334-6873
Madison, WI 53701-1728 608-266-7884
http://www.wheda.com

Under the Linked Deposit Loan Program, women or minority-owned businesses with gross annual sales of less than $500,000 can qualify for low rate loans. Loans are available under the prime lending rate for purchase or improvement of buildings, equipment, or land, but not for working capital. Business must be in manufacturing, retail trade, tourism, or agriculture packaging or processing.

Wyoming

Wyoming Business Council
214 West 15th Street 307-777-2800
Cheyenne, WY 82002 800-262-3425
www.wyomingbusiness.org

The Wyoming Women's Council provides business development and training opportunities along with other women's issues.

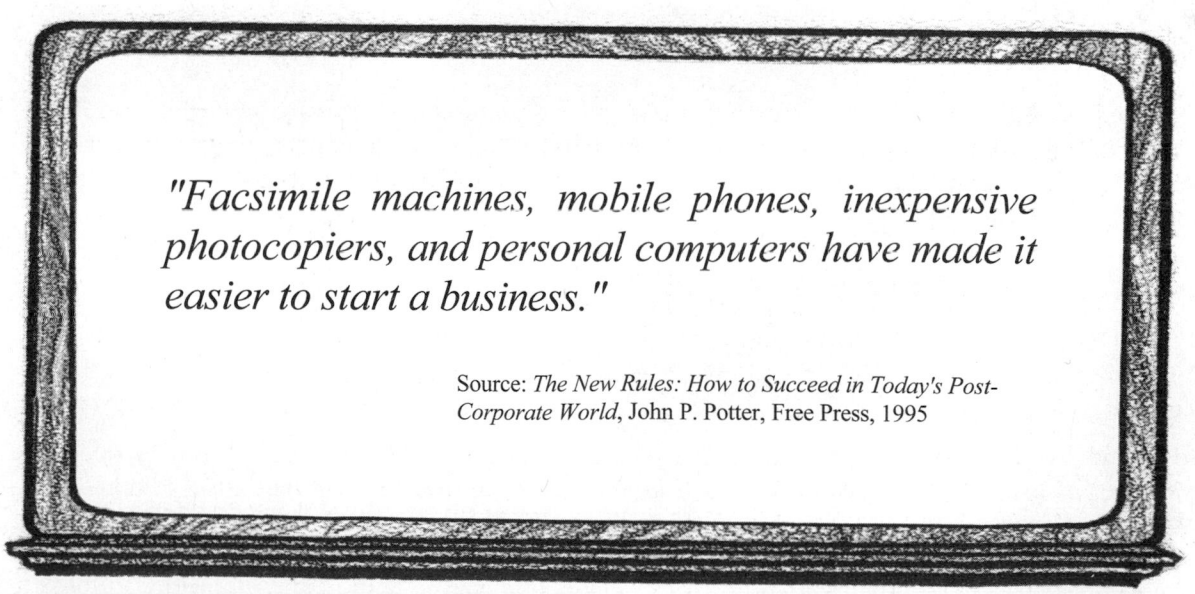

"Facsimile machines, mobile phones, inexpensive photocopiers, and personal computers have made it easier to start a business."

Source: *The New Rules: How to Succeed in Today's Post-Corporate World*, John P. Potter, Free Press, 1995

Separated, Divorced, Widowed Women
Get Free Help From 1200 Offices

Single mothers deserve respect, as does any woman who suddenly needs to become a principal breadwinner for her family. It's a leap of faith, but looking for career opportunities has never been easier for women than it is today. There are over 1,200 offices across the country that provide job training for single moms and other women who need to start making money because of dramatic changes in their lives due to:

- separation
- divorce
- widowhood
- loss of public assistance
- a husband's long term unemployment or disability

Women Work! is a national network of over 1500 programs sponsored by the National Network for Women's Employment. Services are available to all women, but especially those who are widowed, divorced, homeless, battered, or abandoned. Most programs provide career training, job search, and counseling services. What else? Other types of assistance include:

- safe havens
- support networks
- ways to become self-sufficient
- improved self esteem
- connections to employers
- financial management skills
- counseling
- workshops
- skills training
- job placement assistance
- internships
- tuition assistance

Funded by federal and state money, community resources, and private contributions, these programs are often located in women's centers, local YWCAs, community colleges, universities, and vocational education institutions. Women Work! maintains the most up-to-date catalog of programs in your area.

Some of the programs have included:

Learn Computers in New York City

In New York, the YWCA Reentry Employment Program — in Manhattan — is only one of a number of locations throughout the state where women can receive comprehensive computer and business training. Not just learning to finger a keyboard, but acquiring real marketable skills, such as accounting principles, Lotus 1 2 3, business English, problem solving, and job interviewing techniques. They also sponsor a number of seminars designed to help women find jobs in today's complex job market.

Matthew Lesko, Information USA, Inc., 12081 Nebel Street, Rockville, MD 20852 • 1-800-955-7693 • www.lesko.com

Project STAND
(Science and Technology Advancing Non-Traditional Student Dreams)

Women and ethnic minorities interested in science and technology can take advantage of the Project STAND program at Monroe Community College in Rochester New York. This program enhances the success rate for women and minorities. They provide a mentoring program to encourage academic achievement while establishing relationships with men and women currently working in the industry. They even have a free Survival Kit that has been developed for non-traditional students.

RITA
(Recruiting for the Information Technology Age)

Designed by Women Work!, this initiative aims to increase the number of women in the information technology sector. The project includes recruitment, training, hiring and retention strategies. RITA partners with local programs to recruit and train women for IT careers. Currently there are programs in the following states: New Jersey, North Carolina, West Virginia, Pennsylvania, Indiana, Oregon and South Dakota.

Truck Driving in Arizona

The Arizona Women Employment and Education (AWEE) Program {www.awee.org} trains women to develop job skills that emphasize and expand on their natural talents. Existing skills and personal interests are assessed, then women are placed in programs for which they are most suited. They are encouraged to explore non-traditional careers for women — such as truck driving — or to become electricians, plumbers, or construction workers. These jobs often pay four or more times what a woman might earn as a secretary, and that's an important consideration to women who are the sole wage earner in their family.

Not only can women receive employment and career training, but they can also attend "Fresh Start" days at the Sheraton Ritz Hair Consultants and learn how to look professional on a limited budget.

AWEE sponsors lectures by guest speakers, lunch, and hands-on sessions at the salon. One 19-year-old displaced mother of three young boys received a haircut, highlighting, and makeover through this program.

AWEE also helped a 42-year-old divorced mother of four children, two of which are still at home, pursue her lifelong ambition of becoming a nurse. She was awarded Scholar of the Year.

Women Work! has a number of publications to help displaced homemakers and other women seeking job training dollars. In addition to individual publications on such topics as career options for younger women and programs for displaced homemakers, members can order special discount packages on multiple books and booklets that explain various state and federal targeted employment programs for women.

For additional information, call toll free:

Women Work!
National Network for Women's Employment
1625 K St., Suite 300
Washington, DC 20006
800-235-2732
202-467-6346
Fax: 202-467-5366
www.womenwork.org

"The basic economic resource — 'the means of production' to use the economists's term — is no longer capital, nor natural resources nor labor. It is and will be knowledge."

Source: *Post-Capitalist Society*, Peter Drucker, Harper Business, 1993

Commissions, Committees, and Councils
On the Status of Women

Because women so often put the needs of others before their own, they are oftentimes reluctant to seek help for themselves. Feelings of guilt, low self esteem, depression, anger, and stress often accompany the changes that can occur during a woman's life — changes like divorce, separation, job termination or change, abuse, or sexual harassment. Never before have there been more options for women seeking help, whether it is in learning new career skills or finding a support group of other women coping with life's ups and downs that affect all of us at one time or another.

In almost every state, there are Women's Commissions and similar groups that provide direction or assistance to women. Missions and programs vary, but these groups all share the goal of working toward eliminating the inequities that affect women at home and in the workplace. Some commissions are simply advocacy groups, bringing attention to issues that affect women and working to bring about legislative changes that would improve situations that women face. Others provide information and referrals to help women get ahead — some even provide direct services to help women get the training, education, and financial help they need to succeed.

Through research, education, legislative action and special projects, the commissions are a strong voice for women's rights. Areas of interest and support include, but are not limited to:

- Child support laws
- Advancement in non-traditional jobs
- Sexual harassment
- Child care and dependent care programs
- Violence against women
- Housing
- Insurance
- Credit
- Legal rights
- Education
- Employment
- Economic equity
- Appointment of qualified women for all positions of government

Some also provide other services such as:

- Referrals and information on women's issues
- Seminars
- Workshops and/or workshop leaders
- Conferences
- Speakers bureaus
- Public forums
- Publications
- Audio-visual libraries
- Resource directories

Please don't hesitate to call your local commission. The people who work there are caring and very willing to help with just about any kind of problem. If you do not see a commission listed for your state, call the Governor's office to see if one has been established — or ask them for guidance with your problem.

Check the following list for the commission nearest you.

U.S. Department of Labor Women's Bureau
Women's Bureau
U.S. Department of Labor
200 Constitution Ave., NW
Room S-3002
Washington, DC 20210
800-827-5335
202-693-6710
Fax: 202-693-6725
www.dol.gov/wb/welcome.html

National Association of Commissions for Women (NACW)
Mary J. Watkins
President NACW
6667 Forest Ave.
Gary, IN 46403
312-353-6236
Fax: 312-353-9563

Carrolena M. Key
Executive Director
NACW National Office
8630 Fenton St., Suite 934
Silver Spring, MD 20910
800-338-9267
301-585-8101
Fax: 301-585-3445
E-mail: nacw2@nacw.org
www.nacw.org

Alabama
Alabama Women's Commission
200 S. Franklin Dr.
Troy, AL 36081-4508
205-566-8744
Jean Boutwell, elected Secretary
Bab F. Hart, Chair

Alaska
Anchorage Women's Commission
P.O. Box 196650
Anchorage, AK 99519-6650
907-343-6730
Fax: 907-343-6320
Norma Wilkerson
Email: wilkersonn@ci.anchorage.ak.us
www.ci.anchorage.ak.us

Juneau Women's Council
City and Borough of Juneau
155 South Seward
Juneau, AK 99801
907-586-5257

Arizona
Phoenix Women's Commission
Equal Opportunity Department
251 West Washington, 7th Floor
Phoenix, AZ 85003-6211
602-261-8242
Fax: 602-256-3389
LaVina Horne, Equal Opportunity Specialist

Pima County/Tucson Women's Commission
240 North Court Ave.
Tucson, AZ 85701

520-624-8318
Fax: 520-624-5599
E-mail: tctwc@starnet.com
Debra Ruffnes, Executive Director

Arkansas
Closed 96-99

California
California Commission on the Status of Women
1303 J St., Suite 400
Sacramento, CA 95814-2900
916-445-3173
Fax: 916-322-9466
E-mail: info@women.ca.gov
www.statusofwomen.ca.gov
Karmi Speece, Executive Director

Alameda County Commission on the Status of Women
24100 Amador St., 6th Floor
Hayward, CA 94544
510-259-3868
Fax: 510-259-3880
Lillian Litzsey, Contact Person

Berkeley Commission on the Status of Women
2180 Milvia Street, 2nd floor
Berkeley, CA 94704
510-981-6900

Compton Commission for Women
205 Willowbrook Avenue
Compton, CA 90220
310-605-5590
Fax: 310-605-5449

Concord Status of Women Committee
City of Concord
1950 Parkside Drive
Concord, CA 94519
925-671-3283
Fax: 925-671-3375
www.ci.concord.ca.us

Contra Costa County Women's Advisory Committee
20 Allen St.
Martinez, CA 94553
925-370-5149
Fax: 925-370-5098
Linda Douglas, Staff Person
www.womenscommission.com

El Dorado County Commission on the Status of Women
901 H Street, Suite 310
Sacramento, CA 95814
916-444-7486

Fresno City/County Commission on the Status of Women
c/o Human Resources Department
2600 Fresno Street
Fresno, CA 93721-3650
209-498-1680
Fax: 209-237-1914
Dodie Orndorf, Administration

Humboldt County Commission on the Status of Women
c/o County Courthouse

825 5th Street
Eureka, CA 95501
707-445-6395
Fax: 707-441-5777
Mary Ann Murphy, Contact Person

Los Angeles City Commission on the Status of Women
200 N. Spring Street, #2111
Los Angeles, CA 90012-3260
213-978-0300
Fax: 213-978-0309
Paula Petrotta, Exec. Dir.
www.cityofla.org/CSW

Los Angeles County Commission for Women
500 West Temple St., Rm. 383
Los Angeles, CA 90012
213-974-1455
Fax: 213-633-5102
Yvonne Hayes, Exec. Dir.

Lynwood Commission on the Status of Women
11330 Bullis Road
Lynwood, CA 90262
310-603-0220, ext. 203
Fax: 310-764-4908
Carol de Jesus, Staff
www.lynwood.ca.us

Marin County Commission on the Status of Women
3501 Civic Center Dr., Rm. 403
San Rafael, CA 94903
415-499-6195
Fax: 415-499-3669
Patricia A. Warren, Staff Coordinator
www.co.marin.ca.us

Mendocino County Commission on the Status of Women
150 N. McPherson Street
Ft. Bragg, CA 95437
707-961-0326
Fax: 707-961-6367

Monterey County Commission on the Status of Women
1000 So. Main St., Suite 208
Salinas, CA 93901
831-755-4499
Fax: 831-753-2678

Napa County Commission on the Status of Women
2261 Elm Street
Napa, CA 94559
707-253-4616
Fax: 707-253-6172

Pasadena Commission on the Status of Women
Jackie Robinson Center
1020 North Fair Oaks Ave., #200
Pasadena, CA 91107
626-744-6940
Fax: 626-744-3721
Yesceni Ramirez, Progm. Coord
E-mail: yramirez@ci.pasadena.ca.us

Commissions, Committees, and Councils on the Status of Women

Riverside County Commission for Women
4080 Lemon Street, 12th Floor
Riverside, CA 92501
909-955-1100
Fax: 909-955-1105
http://cfw.co.riverside.ca.us

San Bernardino County Commission on the
Status of Women
157 West 5th Street, 1st Floor
San Bernardino, CA 92415-0440
909-387-5543
Fax: 909-387-6075
Patricia Vargas, Staff
www.co.san-bernardino.ca.us/hrcsw

San Diego Commission on the Status of
Women
County of San Diego
1200 Pacific Highway, Room 207
San Diego, CA 92101-2942
619-469-9920
Fax: 619-469-3257

San Francisco Commission on the Status of
Women
25 Van Ness, Room 130
San Francisco, CA 94102
415-252-2570
Fax: 415-252-2575
Belle Taylor-McGhee, Ex. Dir.
E-mail: cosw@ci.sf.ca.us
www.sfgov.org/site/cosw_index.asp

San Joaquin Commission on the Status of
Women
P.O. Box 4633
Stockton, CA 95204
209-463-6957

San Luis Obispo County Commission on the
Status of Women
P.O. Box 104
Saint Margarita, CA 93453
805-434-2348
Fax: 805-438-4405

Commission on the Status of Women of San
Mateo County
County Office Building
455 County Center, 5th floor
Redwood City, CA 94063
650-363-4872
Fax: 650-363-4872
Lisa Lopez Coffey, Director
E-mail: lcoffey@co.sanmateo.ca.us
www.co.sanmateo.ca.us/smc/department/home
/0,,65178_65224,00.html

Santa Barbara County Commission for
Women
105 East Anapamu St., Rm. 104
Santa Barbara, CA 93101
805-568-3410
Fax: 805-568-3426
Pamela Polan, Staff

Santa Clara County Commission on the Status
of Women
70 West Hedding Street
Lower Level, West Wing
San Jose, CA 95110
408-299-3131
Fax: 408-297-2463
Mary Jane Solis, Contact Person
www.sccgov.org

Santa Cruz County Women's Commission
701 Ocean Street, Room 30
Santa Cruz, CA 95060
813-454-2772
Fax: 831-454-2433
Andres Smith, Coordinator

E-mail: commissions@co.santa-cruz.ca.us
www.sccwc.net

Santa Monica Commission on the Status of
Women
1685 Main Street, Room 212
Santa Monica, CA 90401
310-458-8701
Fax: 310-458-3380
Linda Ashman, Staff Liaison
http://pen.ci.santa-
monica.ca.us/cityclerk/boards/directory/bcv7.h
tml

Sonoma County Commission on the Status of
Women
2300 County Center Dr., #B-167
Santa Rosa, CA 95403
707-565-2693
Fax: 707-565-3166
Lorene Irizary, Exec. Dir.

Stanislaus County Commission on the Status
of Women
P.O. Box 4254
Modesto, CA 95352
209-524-3987
Fax: 209-521-4784

Ventura County Commission for Women
505 Poli Street, Code: 4400
Ventura, CA 93001
805-652-7611
805-384-9057

Colorado
Denver Women's Commission
303 West Colfax, Suite 1600
Denver, CO 80204
720-913-8450
Fax: 702-913-8470
www.denvergov.org/women
Keller Hayes, Chair
Chaer Robert, Director

Fort Collins City Commission on the Status of
Women
c/o Human Resources, City of Ft. Collins
P.O. Box 580
405 Canyon
Fort Collins, CO 80522-0580
970-221-6871
970-224-6050
www.ci.fort-collins.co.us
Barbara Spalding, Human Rights Officer

Connecticut
Connecticut Permanent Commission of the
Status of Women
18-20 Trinity St.
Hartford, CT 06106
860-240-8300
Fax: 860-240-8314
E-mail: pcsw@po.state.ct.us
www.cga.state.ct.us/pcsw
Leslie Brett, Ph.D, Executive Director
Barbara DeBaptiste, Commissioner

Bridgeport Permanent Commission on the
Status of Women
City of Bridgeport
Office of the Mayor
45 Lyon Terrace
Bridgeport, CT 06604
203-576-7201

Danbury Commission on the Status of Women
c/o City Hall
155 Deer Hill Avenue
Danbury, CT 06810
203-797-4511

Permanent Commission on the Status of
Hartford Women

c/o Human Relations Commission
550 Main Street, Rm. 5
Hartford, CT 06112
860-543-8595
Fax: 860-722-6486

Norwalk Commission on the Status of Women
62 William Street
Norwalk, CT 06851
203-226-1206 ext. 142 (daytime)
Kathleen F. Rorick, Treas.

Delaware
Delaware Commission for Women
4425 N. Market St., 4th Floor
Wilmington, DE 19802
302-761-8005
Fax: 302-761-6652
E-mail: cgomez@state.de.us
Romona S. Fullman, Esq., Director
www.delawareworks.com/divisions/dcw/welc
ome.htm

District of Columbia
Women's Bureau
U.S. Department of Labor
200 Constitution Ave., NW
Washington, DC 20210
800-827-5335
202-219-6631
Fax: 202-219-5529
www.dol.gov/dol.wb
Shinae Chun, Director

DC Commission for Women
1745 Portal Drive, NW
Washington, DC 20012
202-727-6624
Brenda Atkinson-Willoughby, Chair

Florida
Florida Commission on the Status of Women
Office of the Attorney General, The Capitol
Tallahassee, FL 32399-1050
850-414-3300
Fax: 850-921-4131
E-mail: webmaster@fcsw.net
www.fcsw.net
Kayty Pappas, Chair

Brevard County Commission on the Status of
Women
c/o Brenda H. Harris, Chair
3065 Rio Bonita Street
Indiatlantic, FL 32903
321-674-8962
Fax: 321-674-6150
E-mail: bharris@fit.edu

Broward County Commission on the Status of
Women
115 South Andrews Ave., Room 433
Fort Lauderdale, FL 33301
954-357-6375
Fax: 954-468-3592
Evodie Antoine, staff
E-mail: eantoine@broward.org

Gainesville Commission on the Status of
Women
P.O. Box 140055
Gainesville, FL 32614-0055
352-395-5047
Fax: 352-395-4122
www.afn.org/~gcosw

Jacksonville Mayor's Advisory Commission
on the Status of Women
117 West Duval St., Suite 310A
Jacksonville, FL 32202
904-630-1650
Fax: 904-630-7397
Lorrie DeFrank, Liaison

www.coj.net/Departments/Advisory+Boards+
and+Commissions/Commission+on+the+Statu
s+of+Women/default.htm.

Manatee County Commission on the Status of
Women
c/o Patrizia Arends, Chair
P.O. Box 217
Longboat Key, FL 34228
941-383-6235
E-mail: jparends@aol.com

Miami Beach Commission on the Status of
Women
c/o City Manager's Office
1700 Convention Center Dr.
Miami Beach, FL 33139
305-538-1997
Gail Harris, Chair

City of Miami Commission on the Status of
Women
c/o Office of Equal Opportunity/Diversity
Programs
Miami Riverside Center
444 SW 2nd Ave., 6th fl.
Miami, FL 33130
MAILING ADDRESS:
P.O. Box 330708
Miami, FL 33233-0708
305-416-1990
305-995-1492
Anita McGruder, Chair
E-mail; amcgruder@sbab.dade.k12.fl.us

Miami-Dade County Commission for Women
111 N.W. 1st Street, Suite 660
Miami, FL 33128-1989
305-375-4967
Fax: 305-375-5715
Laura Morilla, Exec. Dir.
E-mail: morilla@co.miami-dade.fl.us
www.co.miami-dade.fl.us/commwomen

Monroe County Commission on the Status of
Women
c/o Pam Martin, Pres.
217 Coral Road
Islamorada, FL 33036
305-853-0907
Fax: 305-853-0908

City of North Miami Beach Commission on
the Status of Women
c/o Councilwoman Jacquelyn Smith
City of North Miami Beach
17011 NE 19th Avenue
North Miami Beach, FL 33162-3100
305-948-2986
Fax: 305-957-3539

City of South Miami Commission on the
Status of Women
c/o Jena J. Staly, Chair
The Enrichment Group
7355 SW 87th Ave., Suite 300
Miami, FL 33173
305-274-1600
Fax: 305-274-5002
E-mail: jjmi65@aol.com

Okaloosa County Commission on the Status of
Women
c/o Jeanne Rief, Chair
810 Eglin Parkway NE, #7
Ft. Walton Beach, FL 32547
850-863-1111 ext. 1371
Fax: 850-863-7834

Palm Beach County Commission on the Status
of Women
c/o Libby Webb

420 Columbia Drive
West Palm Beach, FL 33401
407-684-6686

Sarasota County Advisory Commission on the
Status of Women
2448 Foster Lane
Sarasota, FL 34239
941-954-5092
Gini C. Hyman, office contact

City of South Miami Commission on the
Status of Women
1501 Venera, #213
Coral Gables, FL 33146
305-274-1600
Fax: 305-666-5328

University of South Florida
Status of Women Committee
4202 E. Fowler Ave., Bldg. SCA 110
Tampa, FL 33620
813-974-2327
Fax: 813-974-1614
Mary Jane Saunders, Assoc. Prof.

University of Miami Women's Commission
P.O. Box 248193
Coral Gables, FL 33124
Nancy Ryan, President
305-284-4922
Fax: 305-284-3749

Georgia
Georgia State Commission of Women
148 International Blvd., NE
Suite 600
Atlanta, GA 30303
404-657-9260
Fax: 404-657-2963
Email: gawomen@mindspring.com
Nellie D. Duke, Chair
Julianna McConnell, Vice Chair

Hawaii
Hawaii State Commission on the Status of
Women
235 S. Beretania St., Room 407
Honolulu, HI 96813
808-586-5757
Fax: 808-586-5756
E-mail: hscsw@pixi.net
www.state.hi.us/hscsw
Jeanne Ohta, Executive Director

Hawaii County Commission on the Status of
Women
Mayor's Office
25 Aupuni Street, Room 215
Hilo, HI 96720
808-961-8211
Fax: 808-961-6553

Honolulu County Committee on the Status of
Women
Dept. of Community Services
715 South King Street, Rm. 311
Honolulu, HI 96813
808-523-4073
Fax: 808-527-5237
Patti Cook, Staff

Kauai County Committee in the Status of
Women
444 Rice Street
Lihue, Kauai 96766
808-241-6300
Fax: 808-241-6877

Maui County Committee on the Status of
Women
Office of the Mayor
200 South High Street
Wailuku, HI 96793

808-270-7855
Fax: 808-270-7870

Idaho
Idaho Commission on the Women's Program
P.O. Box 8915
Moscow, ID 83843
208-885-3758
Fax: 208-885-3759
E-mail: cagidius@women.state.id.us
www.state.id.us/women
Cindy Agidius, Executive Director

Illinois
Governor's Commission on the Status of
Women
100 W. Randolph
Suite 16-100
Chicago, IL 60601
312-814-5743
Fax: 312-814-3823
Ellen Solomon, Executive Director
wwwa.illinois.gov/gov/women2

Chicago Advisory Council on Women
510 North Peshtigo Ct., Rm. 6B
Chicago, IL 60611
312-744-4113
Fax: 312-744-1081
Cece Lobin, Exec. Dir.

Cook County Commission on Women's Issues
69 W. Washington St., Ste. 3040
Chicago, IL 60602-3007
312-603-1100
Fax: 312-603-9988
Jennifer D. Vidis, Exec. Dir.
E-mail: jevidis@cookcountygov.com
http://co.cook.il.us

Indiana
Indiana Commission for Women
10 N. Senate Ave., SE 205
Indianapolis, IN 46204
317-233-6303
Fax: 317-232-7485
E-mail: icw@state.in.us
www.state.in.us/icw
Gazella A. Summitt, Chair
Annette Cray Craft, Executive Director

Bloomington City Commission on the Status
of Women
Human Resources Department
P.O. Box 100
Bloomington, IN 47402
812-331-6430
Jillina Kinzie, Contact Person
www.city.bloomington.in.us/cfrd/csw

Crawfordsville Commission on the Status of
Women
Mayor's Office, City Building
300 East Pike Street
Crawfordsville, IN 47933
317-364-5160

East Chicago Women's Commission
3901 Indianapolis Boulevard
East Chicago, IN 46312-3299
219-391-8467
Pat Dixon, Exec. Dir.,
Human Rights Commission 219-391-8477

Gary Commission on the Status of Women
475 Broadway, Suite 508
Gary, IN 46402
219-883-4155
Fax: 219-881-5287
Sharon Mark-Taylor, Exec. Dir.

Mishawaka City Commission on the Status of
Women

600 East Third Street, City Hall
Mishawaka, IN 46544
219-258-1601
Fax: 219-258-1728
Linda Benner, Pres.

South Bend Committee on the Status of
Women Human Rights Commission
227 West Jefferson Blvd.
1440 County Building
South Bend, IN 46601
219-284-9355
Catherine Hubbard, Exc. Dir.

Iowa

Iowa Commission on the Status of Women
Lucas State Office Building
Des Moines, IA 50319
515-281-4461
Fax: 515-242-6119
E-mail: dhr.icsw@dhr.state.ia.us
www.state.ia.us/government/dhr/sw/index.htm
l
Charlotte Nelson, Executive Director
Kathryn Burt, Chair

Kansas

Kentucky

Kentucky Commission on Women
312 W. Main St.
Frankfort, KY 40601
502-564-6643
Fax: 502-564-2315
E-mail: kcw@mail.state.ky.us
http://women.ky.gov
Betsy Nowland-Curry, Executive Director

University Commission on the Status of
Women
University of Louisville
Louisville, KY 40292
502-852-2029
Fax: 502-852-2154
www.louisville.edu/president/cosw

Jefferson County Office for Women
Jefferson County Courthouse
527 West Jefferson Street
Louisville, KY 40202
502-574-5360
Fax: 502-574-6888
Edwina Bell, Dir.
www.loukymetro.org

Louisiana

Louisiana Office of Women's Services
P.O. Box 94095
1885 Woodale Blvd., 9th Floor
Baton Rouge, LA 70804-9095
504-922-0960
Fax: 504-922-0959
E-mail: vera@ows.state.la.us
www.state.la.us/lawomen
Vera Clay, Executive Director

Bossier City Mayor's Commission for Women
1984 Airline Drive
Bossier City, LA 71112
318-742-6000
Vera Clay, Exec. Dir.

Lafayette Mayor's Commission on the Needs
of Women
P.O. Box 52082
Lafayette, LA 70505
337-291-8447
Fax: 337-291-5459

Lake Charles Mayor's Commission for
Women
P.O. Box 6712
Lake Charles, LA 70606-6712

Monroe Mayor's Commission on the Needs of
Women
P.O. Box 123
Monroe, LA 71210
318-329-2310

New Orleans Women's Office
City Hall, City of New Orleans
Room 2W02
New Orleans, LA 70122
504-586-3165

Ruston Mayor's Commission for Women
P.O. Box 576
Ruston, LA 71273-0576

Maine
Abolished

Maryland

Maryland Commission for Women
45 Calvert Street
Baltimore, MD 21401
410-260-6047
877-868-2196
Fax: 410-974-2307
E-mail: mcw@dhr.state.md.us
www.marylandwomen.org
Alyson Reed, Executive Dir.
Kathleen E. Schafer, Chair

Baltimore County Commission for Women
400 Washington Ave.
Court House - Suite 124
Towson, MD 21204
410-887-3448
Fax: 410-769-8914
Jackie Wilson, Liasion
E-mail: jwilson@co.ba.md.us
www.co.ba.md.us/Agencies/women

Calvert County Commission for Women
Courthouse
175 Main Street
Prince Frederick, MD 20678-3337
410-535-1600
Fax: 410-535-1787

Frederick County Commission for Women
Winchester Hall, 1st Floor
12 East Church Street
Frederick, MD 21701-5243
301-694-1066
Fax: 301-694-1636
www.co.frederick.md.us/fccfw
E-mail: fccfw_online@hotmail.com

Garrett County Commission for Women
P.O. Box 623
Oakland, MD 21550
301-387-2141
Sandy Flockhart, Pres.
E-mail: sflock@mindspring.com

Harford County Commission for Women
220 South Main Street
Bel Air, MD 21014
410-879-2000, ext. 373
Fax: 410-893-5987
Phyllis Martin, Contact Person

Howard County Commission for Women
P.O. Box 348
Simpsonville, MD 21150-0348
410-313-6400
Fax: 410-313-6424

Montgomery County Commission for Women
401 North Washington Street, Suite 100
Rockville, MD 20850-1703
240-777-8300
Fax: 301-279-1318
Judith Vaughn-Prather, Exec. Dir.

http://montgomerycountymd.gov
E-mail: Judith.Vaughn-Prather@co.mo.md.us

The Prince George's County Gov't
Department of Family Services
Commission for Women
5012 Rhode Island Ave., Room 226
Hyattsville, MD 20787
301-985-3532
Fax: 301-699-2845
Ebony Irving, Coordinator
E-mail: evirving@co.pg.md.us

St. Mary's County Commission for Women
Office of Community Services
P.O. Box 653
Leonardtown, MD 20650
301-475-4632
Fax: 301-475-4268
Cynthia Brown, staff

Washington County Commission for Women
100 W. Washington Street
Hagerstown, MD 21740
301-791-3090
Fax: 301-791-3336
www.washco-md.net
E-mail: mjbray@aol.com

Wicomico County Commission for Women
P.O. Box 1309
Salisbury, MD 21802
410-546-8033
Fax: 410-546-8035

Massachusetts

Massachusetts Governor's Advisory
Committee on Women's Issues
Statehouse Governor's Office
Room 111
Boston, MA 02133
617-973-8646
Fax: 617-973-8637
www.state.ma.us/womenissues
Joanne Thompson, Chair

MA Commission on the Status of Women
Hurley Building
19 Stanford Street, 6th Floor
Boston, MA 02114
617-626-6520
Fax: 617-626-6530
www.state.ma.us/women

Berkshire County Commission on the Status
of Women
c/o Berkshire Community College
Pittsfield, MA 01201
413-499-4660

Boston Women's Commission
City Hall, Room 716
1 City Hall Plaza
Boston, MA 02201
617-635-4427
Fax: 617-635-3031
Marie Turley, Exec. Dir.

Cambridge Commission on the Status of
Women
51 Inman Street
Cambridge, MA 02139
617-349-4697
Fax: 617-349-4766
Nancy Ryan, Dir.
E-mail: nryan@ci.cambridge.ma.us
www.ci.cambridge.ma.us/~Women

Quincy Mayor's Commission on the Status of
Women
1305 Hancock Street
Quincy, MA 02170
617-773-1380, ext. 301

Somerville Commission for Women
Mayor's Office of Human Services
167 Holland Street, Rm. 208
Somerville, MA 02144
617-625-6600 ext. 2400
Fax: 617-625-2519
Maya Hasegawa, Exec. Dir.

City Manager's Committee on the Status of
Women
9 Olive Street
Worchester, MA 01603
508-831-9721

Michigan

Michigan Women's Commission
110 W. Michigan Ave., Suite 800
Lansing, MI 48933
517-373-2884
Fax: 517-335-1649
www.michigan.gov/mdcr
Judy Karandjeff, Executive Director

Minnesota

Minnesota Commission on the Economic
Status of Women
G-22 State Capitol
St. Paul, MN 55155
800-657-3949
651-296-8590
Fax: 651-297-3697
E-mail: lcesw@commissions. leg.state.mn.us
www.commissions.leg.state. mn.us/cesw
Diane Cushman, Executive Director

Mississippi

Mississippi Commission on the Status of
Women
P.O. Box 13372
Jackson, MS 39236-3372
Onetta S. Whitley, Chair
601-359-4208
Fax: 601-359-4471
E-mail: owhit@ago.state.ms.us
www.geocities.com/mississippiwomen2002

Missouri

Missouri Women's Council
P.O. Box 1684
Jefferson City, MO 65102
573-751-0810
Fax: 573-751-8835
E-mail: wcouncil@mail. state.mo.us
www.womenscouncil.org
Cheryl Grazier, Executive Director
Katherine Emke, Chair

Montana

Interdepartmental Coordinating Committee for
Women (ICCW)
P.O. Box 1728
Helena, MT 59624
406-444-4521
E-mail: hkiedrowski@state.mt.us
www.mdt.state.mt.us/iccw
Heather Kiedrowski, Chair
Diane West, Vice Chair

Nebraska

Nebraska Commission on the Status of
Women
301 Centennial Mall South
Box 94985
Lincoln, NE 65809
402-471-2039
Fax: 402-471-5655
E-mail: ncswmail@mail.state.ne.us
www.women.state.ne.us
Carlene Bourn, Executive Director

Lincoln/Lancaster Women's Commission
440 So. 8th Street, #100

"K" Street Complex
Lincoln, NE 68502
402-441-7716
Fax: 402-441-6824
Bonnie Coffey, Exec. Dir.
www.ci.lincoln.ne.us/city/mayor/women/index

Nevada

Nevada Women's Fund
770 Smithridge Dr., Suite 300
Reno, NV 89502
775-786-2335
Fax: 775-786-8152
Email: info@nevadawomensfund.org
www.nevadawomensfund.org

Nevada Commission for Women
c/o Denise Dumenie
8615 Channell Way
Reno, NV 89506
702-972-1413 (home)

Reno City Commission on the Status of
Women
P.O. Box 1900
Reno, NV 89509

New Hampshire

New Hampshire Commission on the Status of
Women
State House Annex, Room 414
Concord, NH 03301-6312
603-271-2660
Fax: 603-271-4032
E-mail: tdelangis@admin.state.nh.us
www.state.nh.us/csw
Theresa deLangis, Executive Director
Molly Kelly, Chair

New Jersey

New Jersey Dept. of Community Affairs
Division of Women
101 South Broad St. CN 801
Trenton, NJ 08625-0801
609-292-8840
Fax: 609-633-6821
Email: t.daniels@dca.state.nj.us
www.nj.gov/dca/dow/adviscom.htm
Theresa Daniels, Legislative Coordinator

Bergen County Comm. on the Status of
Women
One Bergen County Plaza, 2nd Floor
Hackensack, NJ 07601
201-336-7474
Fax: 201-336-7450
Gina Meyers, Administrator
www.bergenonline.org/bergenwomen
E-mail: gRosewater@co.bergen.nj.us

Burlington County Commission on Women
Office of Human Rights
Burlington County Office Bldg.
49 Rancocas Road
Mount Holly, NJ 08060
609-265-5538
Suzanne Menges, Staff

Camden City Commission on the Status of
Women
Dept. of Administration - Suite 409
P.O. Box 95120
Camden, NJ 08101-5120
609-757-7211
Fax: 609-342-7728

Camden County Commission on Women
520 Market Street, 2nd floor
Camden, NJ 08102-1375
609-225-5454

Cape May County Advisory Commission on
the Status of Women

Freeholder's Off. Crest Haven Comp.
Cape May Court House
4 Moore Road
Cape May, NJ 08210
609-463-6695 (answering machine)

East Orange City Committee on the Status of
Women
44 City Hall Plaza
East Orange, NJ 07019
201-266-5120
Attention: Theresa Green

Essex County Advisory Board on the Status of
Women
c/o Office of Deputy County Administrator
Hall of Records
465 Dr. M.L. King, Jr. Blvd.
Newark, NJ 07102
201-621-4432

Gloucester County Commission on Women
County of Gloucester
P.O. Box 337
Woodbury, NJ 08096

Mercer County Advisory Comm. on the Status
of Women
McDade Administration Bldg.
640 South Broad Street, Box 8068
Trenton, NJ 08650-8068
609-989-6033
Fax: 609-989-6032
Kim Rogers, contact person

Monmouth County Commission on the Status
of Women
Human Services Bldg,
Box 3000 Kozloski Road
Freehold, NJ 07728
908-577-6681
Fax: 908-308-3700
Elaine Valentino, Director

Newark City Mayor's Commission on the
Status of Women
Office of the Mayor - Newark
920 Broad Street, Rm. 200
Newark, NJ 07102
201-733-6400
Dolores Henry-Mertz, Coordinator

Ocean County Commission on Women
1027 Hooper Ave., Bldg.2.
Toms River, NJ 08754
732-929-2136
Fax: 732-341-4539
Faith Liguori
E-mail: FLigouri@co.ocean.nj.us

Salem County Commission on Women
Courthouse - 92 Market Street
Salem, NJ 08079

Somerset County Commission for Women
P.O. Box 3000
County Administration Bldg.
Somerville, NJ 08812-0123
908-231-7036
Rose C. McConnell, Director

Union County Advisory Commission on the
Status of Women
c/o Freeholders' Office County
Administration Bldg.
Elizabethtown Plaza
Elizabeth, NJ 07207

Warren County Commission for Women
Freeholders' Office
Wayne Dumont Jr. Adm. Bldg.
165 County Road - 519 South
Belvidere, NJ 07823-1949

908-475-6500
908-475-6528

New Mexico

New Mexico Commission on the Status of
Women
4001 Indian School Rd., NE, Suite 300
Albuquerque, NM 87110
505-841-8920
Fax: 505-841-8926
E-mail: womenscommission@state.nm.us
www.state.nm.us/womenscommission
Rebecca Jo Dakota, Executive Director
Elizabeth McKinney-Brown, Chair

New York

New York State Division for Women
633 Third Ave., 38th Floor
New York, NY 10017
212-681-4547
Fax: 212-681-7626
E-mail: women@women.state.ny.us
www.state.ny.us/women
Betsy Robertson, Director

Erie County Commission on the Status of
Women
95 Franklin Street, Rm.1655
Buffalo, NY 14202
716-858-8307
Fax: 716-858-8464
Clotilde Dedecker, Exec. Dir.
http://csw.erie.gov
E-mail: dedecker@bflo.co.erie.ny.us

Town of Islip Women's Services
Division of Human Development
401 Main Street
Islip, NY 11751
516-224-5397

New York City Commission on Women Issues
100 Gold Street, 2nd floor
New York, NY 10038
212-788-2738
Fax: 212-788-3298
Carmen Rita Torrent, Exec. Dir.

Rockland County Commission on Women's
Issues
11 New Hempstead Road
New City, NY 10956
914-638-5100

Suffolk County Women's Services
P.O. Box 6100
Hauppauge, NY 11788-0099
516-853-3762
Fax: - same
Joan-Therese Hudson, contact

Syracuse Commission for Women
City Hall Commons
201 East Washington St., #612
Syracuse, NY 13202
315-448-8620
Fax: 315-448-8618
Maria de Lourdes Fallace, Exec. Dir.

Westchester County Office for Women
112 E. Post, Room 110B
White Plains, NY 10601
914-995-5972
Fax: 914-995-5054
Camille Failla Murphy, Director
http://www.westchestergov.com/women
E-mail: cfm2@westchestergov.com

North Carolina

North Carolina Council for Women
1320 Mail Service Center
Raleigh, NC 27699
919-733-2455

Fax: 919-733-2464
www.doa.state.nc.us/doa/ cfw/cfw.htm
Leslie Starsoneck, Executive Director
Jane Carver, Chair

North Carolina Council for Women
Asheville Regional Office
46 Haywood Street, Ste. 349
Asheville, NC 28801
828-251-6169
Fax: 828-251-6068
Charlotte Regional Office
500 West Trade Street, Rm. 349
Charlotte, NC 28202
704-342-6367
Fax: - same
Greensboro Regional Office
1400 Battleground Ave., Ste. 202
Greensboro, NC 27408
336-334-5094
Fax: 336-342-5922
Greenville Regional Office
404 Saint Andrews Dr.
Greenville, NC 27834-6850
252-830-6595
Fax: 336-830-6596
New Bern Regional Office
P.O. Box 595
New Bern, NC 28560
252-514-4869
Fax: - same

Brunswick County Council on the Status of
Women
P.O. Box 230
Supply, NC 28462
910-754-5726
Cheryl Francis

Burke County Council for Women
203 Shamrock Drive
Morganton, NC 28655
828-439-2326

Caldwell County Council on the Status of
Women
P.O. Box 213
Collettsville, NC 28611
828-758-9364

Carteret County Council for Women
711 Windy Trail
Newport, NC 28570
252-247-0177

Catawba Council for Women
Women's Resource Center
328 North Center Street
Hickory, NC 28601
704-328-6738

Cherokee County Council for Women
209 Ranger Hill
Murphy, NC 28906
828-644-5988

Cleveland County Commission for Women
Cleveland Co. DDS
130 S. Post Street
Shelby, NC 28150
704-484-0959

Columbus County Council for Women
P.O. Box 230
Supply, NC 28462
910-754-5726

Craven County Council on Women, Inc.
P.O. Box 1285
New Bern, NC 28563
252-638-3381

Durham County Women's Commission
15 Bonsell Place

P.O. Box 1642
Durham, NC 27702-1642

Gaston County Council on the Status of
Women
4109 Stoneleigh Place
Gastonia, NC 28056
704-865-7463

Greensboro Commission on the Status of
Women
P O Box 3136
Greensboro, NC 27402-3136
336-373-2390
Fax: 336-373-2505
Agnes W.H. Roseboro, Administrator
E-mail: agnes.roseboro@ci.greensboro.nc.us
www.ci.greensboro.nc.us/csw

Harnett County Council for Women
Rte 3, Leander Lee Farm
Lillington, NC 27546

Henderson County Council for Women
Rte. 3, Box 375
Hendersonville, NC 28742
828-891-3317

Hertford County Council for Women
Rt. 1, Box 434-B
Colerain, NC 27924
919-826-4513

Johnston County Council on the Status of
Women
400 Dogwood Street
Smithfield, NC 27577
919-934-0791

Lee County Council for Women
2420 Tramway Road
Sanford, NC 27330
919-775-5624
Fax: 919-775-1302
Susan Condlin

Martin County Council for Women
P.O. Box 37
Parmele, NC 27861

Mecklenburg County Women's Commission
700 North Tryon Street
Charlotte, NC 28202
704-336-3210
Fax: 704-336-4198
Pat E. Grigg, Exec. Dir.
www.charmeck.org/Departments/Womens+Co
mmission/Home.htm
E-mail: griggpe@co.mecklenburg.nc.us

Moore County Council for Women
205 Poplar Street
Carthage, NC 28327
910-947-2590

New Hanover County Council for Women
P.O. Box 15056
Wilmington, NC 28408
919-763-3524

Onslow County Council for Women
109 Howell Road
Hubert, NC 28539
910-326-6743

Orange County Commission for Women
P.O.Box 8181
Hillsborough, NC 27278
919-245-2250
Fax: 919-688-3048

Pearson County Council on the Status of
Women
7510 Durham Road

Timberlake, NC 27583
336-364-4151

Pitt County Council on the Status of Women
P.O. Box 3503
Greenville, NC 27836-3503
252-756-9750

Sampson County Council for Women
P.O. Box 36
Autryville, NC 28318
910-592-8081

Wake County Commission for Women
500 Buckingham Rd.
Garner, NC 27529
919-779-1110

Winston-Salem/Forsyth County Council on
the Status of Women
660 West 5th Street
Winston-Salem, NC 27106
336-727-8409
Fax: 336-727-2549

North Dakota
North Dakota Governor's Commission on the
Status of Women
P.O. Box 1913
Bismarck, ND 58502
701-530-2059
Fax: 701-530-2111
http://governor.state.nd.us/boards-
query.asp?Board_ID=144
Carol Reed, Chairman

Ohio
none

Oklahoma
Oklahoma Commission on the Status of
Women
c/o Office of Personnel Management
2101 North Lincoln Blvd.
Oklahoma City, OK 73105-4904
405-522-6897
Fax: 405-524-6942
Debbie Leftwich, Chair
Patricia Presley, Senior Vice Chair
www.opm.state.ok.us/ocsw

Lawton Mayor's Commission on the Status of
Women
102 SW 5th St.
Lawton, OK 73501
405-581-3260
Janet Childress, Chair
Emma Crowder, Vice Chair

Tulsa Mayor's Commission on the Status of
Women
c/o Department of Human Rights
200 Civic Center
Tulsa, OK 74103
918-582-0558
918-592-7818

Oregon
Oregon Commission for Women
P.O. Box 751-CW
Portland, OR 97207
503-725-5889
Fax: 503-725-8152
Jennifer Webber, Executive Director

Eugene City Women's Commission
777 Pearl Street
Eugene, OR 97401

Jackson County Women's Comm.
Jackson County Commissioners
Jackson County Courthouse
Medford, OR 97501

Pennsylvania
Pennsylvania Commission for Women
Finance Building, Room 205
Harrisburg, PA 17120
888-615-7477
717-787-8128
Fax: 717-772-0653
E-mail: ra-pcwwebemail@state.pa.us
www.pcw.state.pa.us
Leslie Stiles, Executive Director

Bucks County Commissioner's Advisory
Council for Women
Administration Bldg.
55 East Court Street
Doylestown, PA 18901
215-348-6676
Miriam Moyer, Contact Person

Delaware County Women's Commission
20 South 69th St., 4th fl.
Upper Darby, PA 19082
610-713-2308
Fax: 610-713-2254
Nancy R. Day, Director

Lackawanna County Commission for Women
200 Adams Avenue
Scranton, PA 18503-1607
570-963-6750
Fax: 570-963-6812
Beth Hopkins, Coordinator
E-mail:
womenscomm@countyoflackawanna.org

Luzerne County Commission for Women
93-95 State Street
Wilkes-Barre, PA 18701
570-970-9248
Fax: 570-970-9249
Dawn Seidel, Director

Mercer County Commission for Women
103 Courthouse
Mercer, PA 16137
724-662-3800
Fax: 724-662-1530
www.mcc.co.mercer.pa.us/women
E-mail: webmaster@mcc.co.mercer.pa.us

Montgomery County Commission on Women
and Families
Human Services Center
1430 DeKalb Street
Norristown, PA 19404-0311
610-292-5000
Fax: 610-278-3356

Mayor's Commission for Women
Attn: Lila Fox
City Hall, Room 214
Philadelphia, PA 19107
215-686-2171
Valerie Chestnut, Coordinator

Puerto Rico
Puerto Rico Commission for Women's Affairs
Office of the Governor
Commonwealth of Puerto Rico
P.O. Box 11382
Fernandez Juncos Station
Santurce, PR 00910
787-721-0606
787-724-7404
Fax: 787-723-3611
E-mail: egavilan@prtc.net
Enid M. Gavilan, Executive Director

Rhode Island
Rhode Island Commission on Women
One Capitol Hill
Providence, RI 02908
401-222-6105

Fax: 401-222-5638
E-mail: ricw@state.ri.us
www.ricw.state.ri.us
Toby Ayers, Ph.D., Director

South Carolina
Governor's Office Commission on Women
1205 Pendleton St., Suite 366
Columbia, SC 29201
803-734-1609
Fax: 803-734-0241
Email: rcollier@govoepp.state.sc.us
Rebecca Collier, Executive Director

City of Charleston Commission for Women
Attn: Clerk of Council
City Hall, 80 Broad Street
Charleston, SC 29401
803-577-6970

South Dakota
Abolished

Tennessee
TN Economic Council on Women
Snodgrass Tenn. Tower, 3rd fl.
312 - 8th Avenue North
Nashville, TN 37243
615-253-4264
Fax: 615-253-4263
Brenda Speer, Chair
www.state.tn.us/sos/ecw

Texas
Texas Governor's Commission for Women
P.O. Box 12428
Austin, TX 78711-2428
512-463-1782
512-475-2615
Fax: 512-463-1832
Email: Lguthrie@governor.state.tx.us
www.governor.state.tx.us/women/
Lesley Guthrie, Executive Director

Austin Commission for Women
c/o Jo Ann Cruz
City of Austin
P.O. Box 1088
Austin, TX 78767
512-974-3215
Fax: 512-974-6031
www.austinwomen.org

Corpus Christi Commission for Women
320 Laurel
Corpus Christi, TX 78404
512-888-0410, ext. 2567

Fort Worth Commission on the Status of
Women
City Manager's Office
1000 Throckmorton
Fort Worth, TX 76102
817-871-7525
Dee Stewart, Action Center Manager
www.fortworthgov.org/women

Longview Commission on the Status of
Women
Public Information Office
P.O. Box 1952
Longview, TX 75606
903-237-1096

Mayor's Commission on the Status of Women
City of San Antonio
P.O. Box 839966
San Antonio, TX 78283-3966
210-207-7067
Fax: 210-207-4168
E-mail: tvasquez-romero@ci.sat.tx.us
Teresa Vasquez-Romero, Ass't to the Mayor

San Marcos Commission for Women
111 West Holland
San Marcos, TX 78666
512-353-1111

Wichita Falls Mayor's Commission on Human
Needs
c/o City Manager's Office
P.O. Box 1431
Wichita Falls, TX 76307
940-761-7619
Fax: 940-761-8877
Rita Vokes, staff

Utah

Utah Governor's Commission for Women and
Families
111 State Capitol
Salt Lake City, UT 84114
801-538-1533
Fax: 801-538-1304
E-mail: mreese@utah.gov
www.families.utah.gov
Melanie Reese, Executive Director

Vermont

Vermont Governor's Commission on the
Status of Women
126 State St., Drawer 33
Montpelier, VT 05633-6801
802-828-2851
Fax: 802-828-2930
E-mail: info@women.state.vt.us
www.women.state.vt.us
Wendy Love, Executive Dir.

Women's Coalition of Burlington
PO Box 8324
Burlington, VT 05402-8324
802-862-0614
(walk-in: 111 St. Paul St.
upstairs from Pacific Rim)

Virgin Islands

Virgin Islands Commission for Women
P.O. Box 6334
St. Thomas, USVI 00804
340-693-1276
Fax: 340-693-1265

Virginia

Alexandria Office on Women
301 King St., Suite 400
Alexandria, VA 22314
703-838-4000
Fax: 703-838-4976
http://ci.alexandria.va.us/oow
Lisa Baker, Director

Arlington County Commission on the Status
of Women
2100 Clarendon Blvd., Suite 414
Arlington, VA 22201
703-228-3314
Fax: 703-228-7720
E-mail: publicaffairs@co.arlington.va.us
www.co.arlington.va.us/cbo/women
Jana Lynch, Chair

Fairfax City Commission for Women
10455 Armstrong St.
Fairfax, VA 22030
703-385-7894
Fax: 703-385-7811
Email: Larmitage@ci.fairfax.va.us
www.ci.fairfax.va.us/host/women/cfw.html
Louise Armitage, Director

Fairfax County Commission for Women
12000 Government Center Parkway, Suite 318
Fairfax, VA 22035
703-324-5730
Fax: 703-324-3959
TTY: 703-222-3504
Email: ofw@co.fairfax.va.us
Leia Francisco, Executive Director
www.co.fairfax.va.us/ofw

Richmond Mayor's Committee on the
Concerns of Women
City Hall
900 East Broad St., Suite 1603
Richmond, VA 23219
804-646-3997
Fax: 804-646-5145
Caprichia Smith, Staff

Virginia Council on the Status of Women
7805 Kahlua Drive
Richmond, VA 23227
804-786-7765

Falls Church City Commission for Women
300 Park Avenue
Falls Church, VA 22046
703-241-5005; 703-241-5123
Fax: 703-241-5184
Sarah Singer, Liaison

Loudoun County Commission on Women
1 Harrison Street, SE, 5th Floor
MAILING ADDRESS:
   P.O. Box 7000
   Leesburg, VA 20177
703-777-0204
Fax: 703-777-0421
Sally Keefer, staff
www.lccw.org
E-mail: lccw@aol.com

Prince William County Commission for
Women
4370 Ridgewood Center Dr., #D
Woodbridge, VA 22192
703-792-6611
Fax: 703-792-6893
Phyllis Aggrey, Director

Washington

Seattle Women's Commission
c/o Seattle Office for Civil Rights
700 Third Ave, Suite 250
Seattle WA 98104-1849
206-684-4537
TTY: 206-684-4503
Fax: 206-684-0332
E-mail: Kristin.Distelhorst@ci.seattle.wa.us
www.cityofseattle.net/womenscommission/def
ault.htm
Indra Trujillo, Chair

West Virginia

West Virginia Women's Commission
Building 6, Room 850
Capitol Complex
Charleston, WV 25305
304-558-0070
Fax: 304-558-5167
E-mail: wvwc@wvdhhr.org
www.wvdhhr.org/women
Cinda Lee Kinsey, Executive Director
Wendy D. Thomas, Chair

Wisconsin

Wisconsin Women's Council
14 W. Mifflin Street, Suite 212
Madison, WI 53702
608-266-2219
Fax: 608-261-2432
E-mail: info@wwc.state.wi.us
Katie Manuck, Executive Director

Wyoming

Wyoming State Government Commission for
Women
c/o Department of Employment
Herschler Building
122 West 25th St.
Cheyenne, WY 82002
307-777-7672
http://wydoe.state.wy.us
Beth Nelson, Director

Wyoming Council for Women's Issues
c/o Wyoming Business Council
214 West 15th Street
Cheyenne, WY 82002
307-332-9402

Special One-on-One Business Training
For Women Only

Are you a woman who wants to start your own business, expand an existing one or move up the corporate ladder? Consider joining AWED (American Woman's Economic Development). Since 1976, AWED has helped over 100,000 women get ahead through formal training, one-on-one business counseling, seminars, and peer support groups. Their volunteer staff of experts (entrepreneurs and professionals) is ready to serve you — no matter who you are, where you live, or what your background might be. Women of all ages, socioeconomic, and ethnic backgrounds and marital statuses have received assistance through the AWED programs.

In 1984, Ebony Kirkland, an African-American woman originally from Costa Rica, decided to start her own business. She had worked as the Assistant Director to the Dean at a local college and had also been a door-to-door interviewer on a part time basis. After knocking on several doors, she soon saw the need for an ethnic marketing research company. With no real training or educational background in this field, she formed Ebony Marketing Research, Inc.

After about a year of working on her own she felt as though she needed some guidance and assistance to help her business grow. She turned to the New York office of American Women's Economic Development (AWED) and enrolled in their business program. According to Ebony, this program "propelled me most to get to the level where I am today."

With their support she has been able to turn a "one person, kitchen table" business into one that generates over a million dollars in revenues each year.

Ebony says that "AWED allows you to build self confidence. Women know that they can be wives and mothers, but they don't know that they can be good businesswomen". At AWED, women are encouraged to take skills such as budgeting, scheduling, and time management that they have developed through running households and transfer them to their own businesses.

AWED offers:
- structured training and networking for beginners with ideas for home-based businesses to multi-million dollar business owners
- business counseling
- technical assistance and membership support services
- an annual conference that brings together 6,000 women in business
- coaching program

Course offerings include:
- Starting Your Own Business
- Managing Your Own Business
- Business Development Roundtable
- Chief Executive Roundtable and Finance
- Free "Brown Bag Lunch" Workshops

Entrepreneurial training is available to insure the success of your business at any stage of development. If you are unable to participate in these programs, assistance is available through telephone counseling and a hotline. Fees range from $10 for up to 15 minutes of quick answers to urgent questions, to $35 for an hour of counseling, whether it be in-house or over the telephone.

For members, course offerings range from $225 for a 10-session program on Starting Your Own Business to $400 for a 26-session course on Managing Your Own Business.

Over 23,000 women have received individual business counseling through AWED, including 90-minute telephone counseling by experts in whatever business they are starting. Almost 5,000 women planning to start or just starting a business have participated in AWED's 10-day, Starting Your Own Business training program.

For more information contact:
American Woman's Economic Development Corporation
Headquarters/New York Program Center
216 E 45th Street, 10th Floor
New York, NY 10017
917-368-6100
Fax: 212-986-7114
www.awed.org

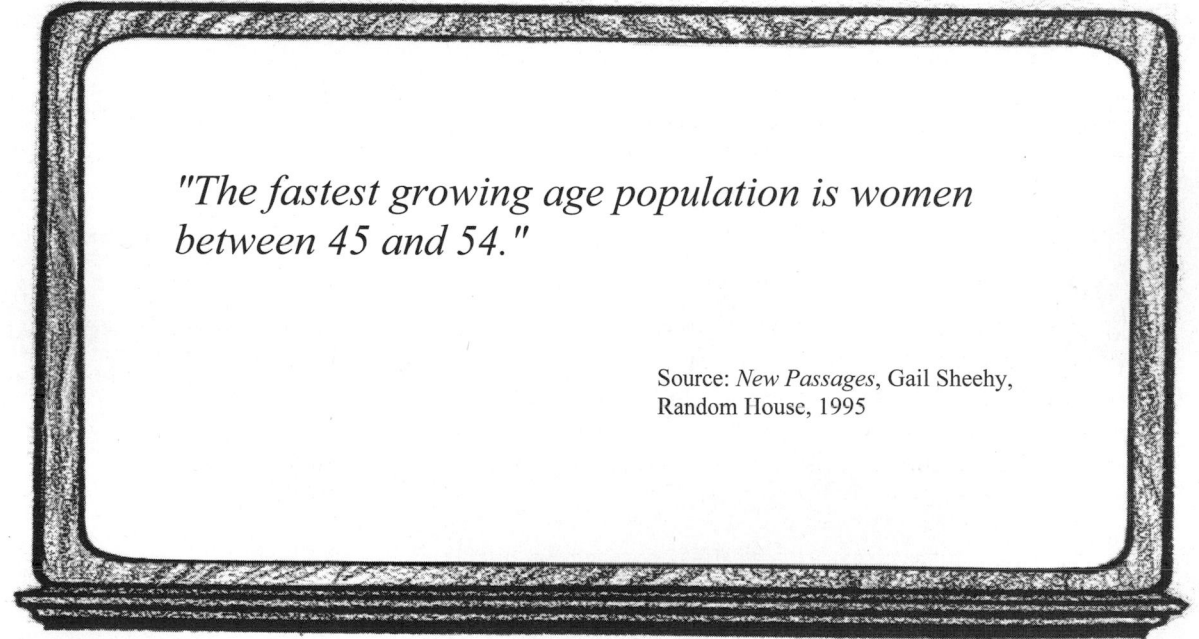

"The fastest growing age population is women between 45 and 54."

Source: *New Passages*, Gail Sheehy, Random House, 1995

$10 Million Available to Train Women
In the Construction Industry
(So why isn't it being used?)

Maybe you don't want to stop at just working in the construction field — you're thinking of owning your own construction company. First enroll in the Disadvantaged Business Enterprises (DBE) program. To make sure that your company is successful and well-run, the DBE program offers support services for women and minorities, such as training and consultants in business management. By participating in this program, you also get a big boost in becoming eligible for large federal contracts — its goal is to use 10% of woman-and minority-owned subcontractors on all highway construction projects.

To participate in the DBE program, you must be certified in each state in which your company will do business. Certification confirms that you are socially and economically disadvantaged, and that you own at least 51% of the business. You should apply for certification through the Office of Civil Rights within your State Department of Transportation. To learn more, contact the Department of Transportation, Office of Small and Disadvantaged Business Utilization, 400 7th Street, SW, Room 9414, Washington, DC 20590; 202-366-1930; 800-532-1169; Fax: 202-366-7538; {http://osdbuweb.dot.gov/about/index.html}.

Where to Go

Alabama
Alabama Department of Transportation
1409 Coliseum Boulevard
Montgomery, AL 36130-3050
334-242-6534
Fax: 334-263-7586
www.dot.state.al.us/

Alaska
State of Alaska Department of Transportation
2200 E. 42nd Ave.
P.O. Box 196900
Anchorage, AK 99508
907-269-0851
Fax: 907- 269-0847
www.dot.state.ak.us/

Arizona
Arizona Department of Transportation
1739 W. Jackson Street #127-A, MD 154-A
Phoenix, AZ 85007-3213
602-712-7761
Fax: 602-712-8429
www.dot.state.az.us/

Arkansas
Arkansas State Highway and Transportation
Department
P.O. Box 2261
Little Rock, AR 72203
501-569-2259/2288
Fax: 501-569-2664
www.ahtd.state.ar.us/

California
Civil Rights Program, MS -79
CALTRANS

1823 14th St,
Sacramento, CA 95814
866-810-6346
www.dot.ca.gov/

Colorado
Colorado Dept. of Transportation
4201 East Arkansas Avenue
Denver, CO 80222
303-757-9148
Fax: 303-757-9019
www.dot.state.co.us/

Connecticut
Connecticut Department of Transportation
2800 Berlin Turnpike
Newington, CT 06131-7546
860-594-2717
Fax: 860-594-3016
www.dot.state.ct.us/

Delaware
Delaware Department of Transportation
P.O. Box 778
Dover, DE 19903
302-760-2035
Fax: 302-739-2254
www.deldot.net/

District of Columbia
District of Columbia Department of Public
Works
Construction Contract Branch
2000 14th Street, NW, 6th Floor
Washington, DC 20009
202-671-2270 Ext. 12268
Fax: 202-939-3037
www.ddot.dc.gov/main.shtm

Florida
Florida Department of Transportation – Equal
Employment Office
605 Suwannee St
Tallahassee, FL 32399-0450
850-414-4747
Fax: 850-488-3914
www11.myflorida.com/publicinformationoffice/

Georgia
Georgia Department of Transportation
No. 2 Capitol Square, SW, Room 142
Atlanta, GA 30334-1002
404-656-5323
Fax: 404-656-5509
www.dot.state.ga.us/

Hawaii
Hawaii Department of Transportation
869 Punchbowl Street, Rm. 112
Honolulu, HI 96813
808-587-2135
Fax: 808-587-2025
www.state.hi.us/dot/

Idaho
Idaho Transportation Department
P.O. Box 7129
Boise, ID 83707 -1129
208-334-8567
Fax: 208-332-7812
www2.state.id.us/itd/

Illinois
Bureau of Small Business Enterprise
Illinois Department of Transportation
2300 South Dirksen Parkway, Room. 319
Springfield, IL 62764
217-785-5947

Matthew Lesko, Information USA, Inc., 12081 Nebel Street, Rockville, MD 20852 • 1-800-955-7693 • www.lesko.com

Fax: 217-785-1524
http://dot.state.il.us/

Indiana
Department of Administration
Minority Business Development
Indiana Government Center
South 402 W. Washington Street, Room 474
Indianapolis, IN 46204
317-232-3061
Fax: 317-233-6921
http://www.ai.org/dot/

Iowa
Iowa Department of Transportation
800 Lincoln Way
Ames, IA 50010
515-239-1414
Fax: 515-239-1325
www.dot.state.ia.us/

Kansas
Kansas Department of Transportation
Docking State Office Building
915 Harrison
Topeka, KS 66612
785-296-7940
Fax: 785-296-1095
www.ksdot.org/public/kdot/

Kentucky
Kentucky Transportation Cabinet
State Office Building, Room 904
501 High Street
Frankfort, KY 40622
502-564-3601
Fax: 502-564-2114
www.kytc.state.ky.us/

Louisiana
Louisiana Department of Transportation &
Development
P.O. Box 94245
Baton Rouge, LA 70804-9245
225-379-1382
Fax: 225-379-1865
www.dotd.state.la.us/

Maine
Maine Department of Transportation
State House Station #16- Child Street
Augusta, ME 04333
Phone: 207-624-3066
Fax: 207-624-3051
www.maine.gov/mdot-stage/

Maryland
Office of Minority Businesses Enterprises
Maryland Department of Transportation
7201 Corporate Center
P. O. Box 548
Hanover, MD 21706
410-865-1269
Fax: 410-850-9263
www.mdot.state.md.us/

Massachusetts
Massachusetts Highway Department
10 Park Plaza, Room 3190
Boston, MA 02116
617-973-7339
Fax: 617-973-7311
www.state.ma.us/mhd/home.htm

Michigan
Equal Employment Office
Michigan Department of Transportation
P.O. Box 30050
Lansing, MI 48909
517-373-2377

Fax: 517-335-0945
www.michigan.gov/mdot/

Minnesota
Office of Equal Employment Opportunity and
Contract Management
Minnesota Department of Transportation
395 John Ireland Blvd., M.S. 170
St. Paul, MN 55155
651-215-0446
Fax: 651-297-2158
www.dot.state.mn.us/

Mississippi
Mississippi Dept. of Transportation
Office of Civil Rights
P.O. Box 1850
Jackson, MS 39215-1850
601-359-7466
Fax: 601-359-7428
www.mdot.state.ms.us/

Missouri
Missouri Highway & Dept. of Transportation
P.O. Box 270
105 W. Capitol Ave.
Jefferson City, MO 65102
573-751-2859
Fax: 573-526-5640
www.modot.state.mo.us/

Montana
Department of Transportation
2701 Prospect Ave.
P.O. Box 201001
Helena, MT 59620-1001
406-444-6331
TTY: 406-444-7696
Fax: 406-444-7685
www.mdt.state.mt.us/

Nebraska
DBE Civil Rights Coordinator
P.O. Box 94759
Lincoln, NE 68509-4791
402-479-4531
Fax: 402-479-4854
www.dor.state.ne.us/

Nevada
DBE Program
Nevada Department of Transportation
1263 South Stewart Street
Carson City, NV 89712-0002
775-888-7497
Fax: 775-888-7235
www.nevadadot.com/

New Hampshire
New Hampshire Department of Transportation
P.O. Box 483
John O. Morton Building
Concord, NH 03302-0483
603-271-6611
Fax: 603-271-3102
www.state.nh.us/dot/

New Jersey
Disadvantaged Business Enterprise Unit
New Jersey Department of Transportation
P O Box 600
Trenton, NJ 08625-0600
609-530-2130
Fax: 609-530-4030
www.state.nj.us/transportation/

New Mexico
New Mexico State Highway & Transportation
Department
596 Pacheco Aspen Plaza
Santa Fe, NM 87501
505-827-1775

Fax: 505-827-1779
www.nmshtd.state.nm.us/

New York
Development & Compliance
New York State Department of Transportation
1220 Washington Avenue
Building 4-G-16
Albany, NY 12232-0444
518-457-1129
Fax: 518-457-9678
www.dot.state.ny.us/

North Carolina
North Carolina Department of Transportation
P.O. Box 25201
Raleigh, NC 27611
919-733-2300
Fax: 919-733-8649
www.ncdot.org/

North Dakota
North Dakota Department of Transportation
608 East Boulevard Avenue
Bismarck, ND 58505-0700
701-328-2576
Fax: 701-328-1965
www.state.nd.us/dot/

Ohio
Office of Contracts
Ohio Department of Transportation
1980 W. Broad Street
Columbus, OH 43223
614-728-8498
Fax: 614-728-5930
www.dot.state.oh.us/

Oklahoma
Regulatory Services Division
Oklahoma Department of Transportation
200 NE. 21st Street
Oklahoma City, OK 73105
405-521-6046
Fax: 405-522-2136
www.okladot.state.ok.us/

Oregon
Oregon Department of Transportation
800 Airport Road
Salem, OR 97301
503-986-4350
Fax: 503-986-6382
www.odot.state.or.us/home/

Pennsylvania
Pennsylvania Department of Transportation
Chief Counsel & Investigations Section
Commonwealth Keystone Bldg.
400 N Street, 9th Floor
Harrisburg, PA 17120-0096
717-787-7014
Fax: 717-772-2741
www.dot.state.pa.us/

Rhode Island
MBE Compliance Office
Department of Administration
c/o Economic Development Corporation
1 West Exchange Street, 5th Floor
Providence, RI 02903
401-222-6670
Fax: 401-222-2102
www.riedc.com/

South Carolina
Disadvantaged Business Enterprise Program
Development
South Carolina Department of Transportation
955 Park Street, Room 403
Columbia, SC 29202
803-737-1372

Fax: 803-737-2021
www.dot.state.sc.us/

South Dakota
South Dakota Disadvantaged Business
Enterprise Compliance Office
South Dakota Department of Transportation
700 East Broadway Ave.
Pierre, SD 57501
605-773-4906
Fax: 605-773-3921
www.sddot.com/

Tennessee
Tennessee Department of Transportation
James K. Polk Building, Suite 1800
Nashville, TN 37243
615-741-3681
Fax: 615-741-3169
www.tdot.state.tn.us/

Texas
Texas Department of Transportation
125 E. 11th St.
Austin, TX 78701-2483
512-486-5500
Fax: 512-486-5509
www.dot.state.tx.us/

Utah
Utah Department of Transportation - Civil
Rights Section

4501 South 2700 West
Salt Lake City, UT 84119-5998
801-965-4356
Fax: 801-965-4101
www.sr.ex.state.ut.us/

Vermont
Office of Civil Rights and Labor Compliance
Vermont Agency of Transportation
National Life Bldg., Drawer 33
Montpelier, VT 05633-5001
802-828-2715
Fax: 802-828-1047
www.aot.state.vt.us/

Virginia
Equal Employment Office
Virginia Department of Transportation
1401 East Broad Street, Room 1403
Richmond, VA 23219
804-786-3761
Fax: 804-371-8040
www.vdot.state.va.us/

Washington
Office of Equal Opportunity
Washington State Department of
Transportation
P.O. Box 47314
310 Maple Park
Olympia, WA 98504-7314

360-705-7090
Fax: 360-705-6801
www.wsdot.wa.gov/

West Virginia
West Virginia Division of Highways
1900 Kanawha Blvd. East
Bldg 5, Room 925
Charleston, WV 25305
304-558-3931
Fax: 304-558-4236
www.wvdot.com/

Wisconsin
Wisconsin Department of Transportation
DBE Program - Room 451
4802 Sheboygan Avenue,
P.O. Box 7965, Room 451
Madison, WI 53707-7965
608-266-0503
Fax: 608-267-3641
www.dot.state.wi.us/

Wyoming
Wyoming Department of Transportation
5300 Bishop Blvd.
Cheyenne, WY 82009-3340
307-777-4457
Fax: 307-777-4765
http://wydotweb.state.wy.us/

Free Training and Jobs for Women
Who Want to Work in a "Man's" World

Every day, women are entering the workforce in traditionally "male" jobs, such as welders, construction workers, plumbers, electricians — even garbage collectors. And they're making much more money than they would as secretaries, nurses, receptionists or teachers. How are they getting the training to do this? Many are using little known training programs funded by Uncle Sam.

Women are being trained to be firefighters in California, pipefitters in Massachusetts, and welders in Maine. The training is often free, especially for women who are displaced homemakers or economically disadvantaged in other ways. So why aren't more women taking advantage of these programs? Because most of these training opportunities just aren't advertised or widely publicized.

What you'll find in this section are scores of programs that are available to women who need the training, encouragement, and financial support to pursue a career in a "man's" world. Many programs even provide child care, tuition, and transportation expenses.

Find the programs in your state by using the following list and by contacting local employment and national women's groups — most have gotten money from Uncle Sam to help you compete with men. And many of the training services they offer are free. What's to lose except a low paying job and long hours?

Training Opportunities for Women

Arizona

Arizona Women's Education and Employment, Inc.
640 North 1st Avenue   602-223-4333
Phoenix, AZ 85003-1515   Fax: 602-223-4338
www.awee.org
Pre-employment job readiness training, job placement, vocational education, and support services are offered along with building self esteem, problem solving, goal setting, career exploration, interviewing techniques, resumes and cover letters, and communications skills. AWEE does a 2-year followup.

Eligibility: Primarily economically disadvantaged single parents, teen parents, displaced homemakers, homemakers, recipients of AFDC, unemployed and underemployed persons, and the homeless.

Arkansas

Arkansas Construction Industry Craft Training
Department of Workforce Education
No. 3 Capital Mall   501-682-1500
Little Rock, AR 72201   Fax: 501-682-1509
www.work-ed.state.ar.us
The Arkansas Construction Industry Craft Training Program provides for enhanced industry training education programs at the apprenticeship and postsecondary levels. The Department of Workforce Education implements other programs to help workers including: Dislocated Worker Program, Arkansas Adult Learning Resource Center, ESL and GED classes and Short-Term Adult Occupational Skill Training.

California

Women in the Skilled Trades
Oakland Private Industry Council
1212 Broadway, Suite 100-300   510-768-4498
Oakland, CA 94612   Fax: 510-839-3766
www.oaklandpic.org/Cypress_Mandela-WIST.htm

Women in the Skilled Trades (WIST) uses a classroom model to provide basic skills training in the major construction trades. Participants attend classes in carpentry, welding, electrical, plumbing and pipe fitting. They also complete course work in construction math and physical fitness (weight training). Another component of the curriculum addresses the "life skills" participants will need to succeed on the job. Topics covered include sexual harassment, communication and safety. In addition, the WIST curriculum includes certification by the American Red Cross in First Aid and CPR. Job search and placement are an integral and ongoing component of the WIST training program.

Women at Work
Gina Frierman-Hunt
Program Director
50 North Hill Ave., Suite 300   626-796-6870
Pasadena, CA 91106   Fax: 626-793-7396
www.womenatwork1.org
Women at Work is a career information and job resource center that assists women looking for jobs in all fields. The program offers thousands of job listings in Southern California area, career counseling, occupational testing, evening workshops, and special programs in a variety of fields including nontraditional areas. It also provides the services of the Women in the Trades support group.

Eligibility: These services are available to all women.

Women in Apprenticeship and Nontraditional Occupations Training
Century Housing Corporation
Equal Opportunity Division
1000 Corporate Pointe, Suite 200   310-258-0700
Culver City, CA 90230   Fax: 310-258-0701
http://centuryhousing.org/training.htm
This program provides, at no cost to qualified applicants, one-on-one counseling, training, construction on-the-job training, job placement assistance, union fee payment plan and an opportunity to be employed in a high-paying construction job. This program is open to all women, regardless of income level or background.

Tradeswomen Inc.
P.O. Box 882103

San Francisco, CA 34188-2103   510-891-8773 ext. 313
www.treadeswomen.org

Tradeswomen Inc. promotes and supports women in non-traditional jobs. They offer mentoring and some workshops. They are a valuable resource for many programs in the San Francisco Bay area.

Colorado

Northeast Women's Center
Hazel J. Whitset
Executive Director
4821 E. 38th Ave.   303-355-3486
Denver, CO 80207-1005   Fax: 303-355-3488
www.newomenscenter.com

Northeast Women's Center (NEWC) Program Services: Women train for jobs in construction, weatherization, landscaping, carpentry, electrical, and for other nontraditional positions. Job search and life skills are taught; counseling and math tutoring are provided. Women are placed directly into employment or apprenticeship positions or referred to voc-ed training programs. NEWC has coordinated efforts with the AFL/CIO and major area businesses as with major state development projects.

Eligibility: Single parents, displaced homemakers, dislocated workers are eligible.

Connecticut

Preliminary Awareness of Construction Trades Training
Jennifer DesJardins
Project Director
National Association of Women
  in Construction (NAWIC)
Hartford Chapter
125 Silas Deane Highway
Hartford, CT 06109   860-291-8917
www.nawic165.org

Sponsored by the NAWIC Connecticut chapters, Preliminary Awareness of Construction Trades Training (PACTT) offers 8 weeks of hands-on exploration of four construction trades: carpentry, electrical, masonry, plumbing. The curriculum covers industry and apprenticeship overview, construction vocabulary, how a job progresses from beginning to end, blueprint reading, math, tool care and safety, and how to dress for job-site conditions. Job interview skills are taught along with personal budgeting, how to recognize and handle sexual and racial harassment, physical stamina building, and health issues. PACTT assists in the job search, provides a mentor for each student, and tracks students through followup. NAWIC chapters plan to expand the program to other States and to Canada.

Eligibility: Women interested in exploring a career in the construction industry are eligible. (The average student is 32 years of age and a single parent on welfare or in a low paying job.)

District of Columbia

Wider Opportunities for Women, Inc.
Lina Dobs
Executive Director
1001 Connect5icut Avenue, NW, Suite 930   202-464-1596
Washington, DC 20036   Fax: 202-464-1660
www.wowonline.org

Wider Opportunities for Women, Inc. (WOW), a national organization, offers programs related to women in nontraditional jobs, including introducing low income mothers to computer skills. "Educational Equity Options Project" offers technical assistance to vocational education institutions to help overcome barriers to nontraditional programs; and "Nontraditional Employment Training Project" assists JTPA programs in recruiting and retaining women in nontraditional training.

Florida

When Entering New Directions
Meme Thomas
WENDI Coordinator
Brevard Community College
Room U12
1519 Clearlake Rd.
Cocoa, FL 32922   321-632-1111, ext. 65517

www.brevardcc.edu/cpe/pages/office_wendi.html

To assist persons going through life transitions and reentering training and jobs, When Entering New Directions (WENDI) offers career testing, decision making, goal setting, job finding, basic computer skills. Also provided are counseling for displaced homemakers, weekly Job Club for job seekers, and limited assistance with scholarships.

Eligibility: Persons age 16 and over seeking to return to school or work are eligible.

Resource Center for Women
Dolores K. Benjamin
Executive Director
1301 Seminole Blvd.
Suite 150, Plaza Center   727-586-1110
Largo, FL 53770   Fax: 727-585-4089
www.resourcecenterforwomen.org

This multipurpose center offers pre-employment training, career counseling, educational information, and classes to help individuals manage finances, build self esteem, cope with tension/stress, and gain skills in other areas of personal growth and career development.

Perkins Funding
Orange County Public Schools
Mid Florida Tech
2900 West Oak Ridge Rd.   407-855-5880, ext. 2294
Orlando, FL 32809   Fax: 407-251-6197
www.mft.ocps.net

Mid Florida Tech provides funding to qualifying women to assist them in entering nontraditional programs. Women may receive funding to help with childcare costs, books and tuition.

Illinois

Technical Opportunity Program
Lauren Sugerman
Director
Chicago Women in Trades
1657 West Adams Street, Suite 401   312-942-1444
Chicago, IL 60612   Fax: 312-942-0802
www.chicagowomenintrades.org

The curriculum covers math, mechanical aptitude and spatial relations, introduction to blueprint reading, and physical conditioning/strength building during the 12 weeks of training. The program incorporates apprenticeship orientation, job readiness and "survival" skills, and safety procedures to help women cope with obstacles they may encounter in the construction work setting and to help keep the workplace safe. The program also provides job placement assistance, a support group of tradeswomen, and scholarships. Evening and Saturday classes accommodate women who are employed regular hours.

Women Employment and Training Program
Debra Walker Johnson
Director
Southwest Women Working Together
4051 West 63rd St.   773-582-0550
Chicago, IL 60629   Fax: 773-582-9669

The Southwest Women Working Together Women Employment and Training Program provides education assistance and employment placement to displaced homemakers and single mothers. The program provides: job counselors, financial assistance, employment services, skills assessment, employment training and job support. In addition, they sponsor an annual non-traditional job fair to introduce women to careers in fields that provide higher earning potential than traditional fields.

Women Employed Institute
Sheila Rogers
Women Employed Institute
111 N. Wabash, 13th Floor   312-782-3902
Chicago, IL 60602   Fax: 312-782-5249
www.womenemployed.org

This is a three week pre-employment training and placement program that focuses on self-assessment, career decision making, job hunting and job retention. It includes a support group, individual counseling, and placement assistance for employment or referral to skills training that encourages participants to consider nontraditional jobs. The Women Employed Institute (WEI) has provided technical assistance on nontraditional jobs for women to the State of Illinois, to State funded job training providers, and to elementary and high school librarians. It also conducts research, education, and advocacy programs to improve women's economic status.

Eligibility: Low income displaced homemakers are eligible.

Indiana

New Directions Single Parent/Homemaker Program
C. Joanne Reid
Coordinator
Evansville-Vanderburgh School Corporation
Henry Reis Education Center
1900 Stringtown Rd.   812-435-8271
Evansville, IN 47711   Fax: 812-435-8601
www.evsc.k12.in.us/schoolzone/schools/henri/reis
Comprehensive life management skills training and vocational education are
offered to single parents and homemakers. Participants acquire marketable job
skills to help them achieve a greater sense of self-sufficiency.

Eligibility: All single parents qualify; there are no financial guidelines for
eligibility. Also, homemakers who have, without remuneration, cared for the
home and family and who are unemployed or underemployed are served.

Fort Wayne Women's Bureau
Ronnie Greenberg, CEO
3521 Lake Avenue, Suite 1   260-424-7977
Fort Wayne, IN 46805   Fax: 260-426-7576
www.womensbureau.com/index.html
Among the employment and training programs offered, some have a focus on
nontraditional careers and peer counseling. Services include workshops and
events for the community, such as rape awareness and drug and alcohol
education prevention programs. Networks which meet regularly include
Minority Women's Network, Women Business Owners Association, Career
Planners, Women Decision Makers, Minority Women's Teen Network.

Eligibility: Basic services are open to all women; specific projects may have
eligibility criteria.

Circle Seven Training Council. Inc.
Lance D. Ratliff
Executive Director
143 Green Meadows Dr.
Suite 2
Greenfield, IN 46140   317-467-0248, ext. 317
This program has a vocational training option, job search skills, and a
computerized service that matches job openings with applicants. Women are
helped individually to develop employability plans which may include
nontraditional training. Services are provided through seven county offices.

Eligibility: To receive funded training. persons must be eligible for JTPA or
IMPACT (JOBS or food stamps).

Iowa

Promise Jobs Program
Iowa Workforce Development
1000 East Grand Avenue   515-281-5387
Des Moines, IA 50319-0209   800-JOB-IOWA
www.iowaworkforce.org/region11/promisejobs.htm
Promise Jobs or "Promoting Independence and Self-Sufficiency through
Employment" is Iowa's welfare reform program. Designed to help families
become self-sufficient, it is a requirement for most Family Investment
Program (FIP) recipients. They provide vocational training to prepare the
participant for specific employment. The program offers these additional
services: Life Skills Workshops, Job Seeking and Skills Training, Job Search
Assistance, Basic Education, Parenting Skills, and Family Development
Services.

Program for Women in Science and Engineering
Mary Ann Evans
Program Director
Iowa State University
210 Lab of Mechanics
Ames, IA 50011-2131   515-294-0966
www.pwse.iastate.edu
Career conferences, summer internships, scholarships, videotapes, and a data
base directory are offered. The directory of Iowa women in science,
mathematics, and engineering identifies women who might serve as mentors
and role models; conferences feature women scientists and engineers as
speakers, career exploration workshops, and special sessions for parents and
educators; summer programs give high school girls and undergraduate women
opportunities to work with mentors in the university's science and engineering
research laboratories; videotapes feature Iowa women working in
nontraditional fields.

New Choices
Jackie Davis, Coordinator
Iowa Western Community College
2700 College Rd., Box C0214
Council Bluffs, IA 51503   712-325-3269 x 269
Presentations are given on nontraditional careers at high schools in southwest
Iowa, and a brochure on nontraditional careers was developed for distribution
at Career Days during visits to the high schools.

Speakers Bureau
Charlotte Nelson
Commissions on the Status of Women
Iowa Department of Human Rights
Lucas State Office Building   515-281-4461
Des Moines, IA 50319   Fax: 515-242-6119
The Iowa Commission on the Status of Women is an advocacy agency for
Iowa women. They even have a division for advocating equitable services for
girls. This division offers a speakers bureau for the community. In addition,
the Commission has wealth of information for women trying to make it in
non-traditional occupations.

Indian Hills Community College
Vicki Brown
Equal Employment Opportunity
525 Grandview   641-683-5111
Ottumwa, IA 52501   800-726-2585, ext. 231
www.ihcc.cc.ia.us
The recruitment program encourages women and men to enroll in
nontraditional occupations training. The program recruits through career
conferences, the media, brochures, and group presentations. It determines
readiness for specific college programs through assessment; offers assistance
with tuition, child care, and transportation; provides tutors, peer support
networks, and workshops on job seeking skills, stress, and single parenting;
and assists in job placement.

Eligibility: No requirements.

Kansas

Career Assistance Network
Women and Minorities in Highway Construction Program
Nancy Ochoa, Outreach Coordinator
225 SW 12th Street   785-233-1750 ext. 260
Topeka, KS 66612-1392   Fax: 785-233-4867
www.ywcatopeka.org/jobtraining/
The YWCA Women and Minorities Highway Construction Program is a free,
eight-week program open to all women and minorities. The program involves
intensive physical training and classroom instruction. Self-awareness training
includes: communication skills, workplace issues, problem solving,
assertiveness, and mathematical instruction. They provide the student with
class work in vocational math, mechanical concepts and terminology,
spelling, grammar and usage. They then will get your body ready for
construction work with rigorous physical training to increase strength,
endurance and cardiovascular fitness. When the student is ready the YWCA
will provide orientation for apprenticeship opportunities and job placement
assistance.

Butler County Community College
901 S. Haverhill Road
El Dorado, KS 67042   316-321-BCCC
www.butlercc.edu
Economically and academically disadvantaged women are offered training for
entry level nontraditional jobs, reentry into educational institutions, or referral
for further training. Preparation includes diagnostic testing, intake interviews,
and individualized planning and counseling regarding education, training, and
financial aid opportunities. Instruction covers career exploration and
development, GED preparation and testing, pre-employment skills training,
and life/job search skills.

Eligibility: Varies according to special grants or project guidelines. Generally,
the age ranges are 14 and older. Primary target populations are the
economically and academically disadvantaged, unemployed or
underemployed, women first offenders or ex-offenders on probation or parole
referred by court services or community corrections, and referrals by social
service and other agencies.

Southeast Kansas Non-Traditional Center
Coffeyville Community College
400 W. 11th St.   620-252-7180
Coffeyville, KS 67337   Fax: 620-252-7098
www.ccc.cc.ks.us/mtc
Through assessment, counseling, training, and job search assistance, women

learn about nontraditional job opportunities and acquire skills to enter the job market. The program provides training for effective communication; interview skills such as preparing a resume, job application, and cover letter; and gaining an understanding of the responsibilities of employment. Preparation may include enrollment in vocational training at Coffeyville Community College.

Project Re-Entry
Monica Kane, Director
Colby Community College
1255 S. Range
Colby, KS 67701   785-462-3784, ext. 314
www.colbycc.edu

Individuals are tested, counseled, and assisted with course planning and enrollment for certificate, 2-year degree, vocational, or 4-year transfer programs. Workshops and seminars are offered on assertiveness, job searching and interviewing, single parenting, stress management, life planning, career exploration, and financial aid application process.

Eligibility: Any adults 24 years of age or older who are seeking job, career, or educational alternatives are eligible.

Single Parent/Homemaker Program
Randy Kettler, Coordinator
Allen County Community College
1801 N. Cottonwood
Iola, KS 66749   620-365-5116
www.allen.cc.ks.us

Testing, job skills training, and help with basic reading, English, and math enable women to find jobs in nontraditional and other fields. Also, counseling, emotional support, and financial aid for tuition, child care, and transportation are provided.

Eligibility: Participants must be single parents, displaced homemakers, or under or unemployed.

Pratt Community College/Area Vocational School
Jerry Burkhart
Highway 61
Pratt, KS 67124   620-672-9800
www.prattcc.edu

The Career Development Center helps women learn about benefits of nontraditional jobs. Self-assessment and interest inventories direct students into areas of increasing employment opportunities. The Vocational School offers 1- and 2-year degree programs to students with a GED or high school diploma. Nontraditional areas for women include agriculture, aircraft maintenance, automotive/diesel mechanics, building trades, medical and manufacturing technology, among others. Financial aid and scholarships are available for most economically disadvantaged students. The program is located in rural south-central Kansas.

Eligibility: The program targets women living in a rural environment. Women aged 16-24, including high school students, single parents, displaced homemakers, and pregnant women are eligible for admission.

Community Outreach Counseling Program/WRC
Women's Resource Center
Kansas City Kansas Community College
7250 State Ave.
Kansas City, KS 66112   913-288-7270
www.kckcc.edu

Career and academic counseling is provided to women in transition, particularly single parents, displaced homemakers, and career changers. Emphasis of presentations, workshops, and conferences is on nontraditional careers. Tuition assistance is available. The center is a clearinghouse for information and referral to community agencies.

Kentucky

Community Education
Virginia Dever
Center for Women and Families
226 West Breckinridge St.
P.O. Box 2048   502-581-7200
Louisville, KY 40201-2048   Fax: 502-581-7204
www.thecenteronline.org

Employment and career counseling, vocational and on-the-job training prepare women to enter or reenter the job market. Preparation occurs through job readiness skills and career exploration workshops; job development and placement assistance are provided also. Motivational peer/support group meetings are held monthly.

Louisiana

Louisiana Technical College
150 3rd Street
Baton Rouge, LA 70801   225-219-8778
http://theltc.net

The College provides occupational training in areas including carpentry, welding, automotive technician, electrical, computer electronics, and air conditioning and refrigeration.

Eligibility: Residents of Louisiana 16 years of age or older who receive acceptable test scores are eligible.

Maine

ASPIRE--JOBS and JET Programs
Stephen Telow
Maine Department of Human Services
Bureau of Family Independence
221 State Street   207-287-3309
Augusta, ME 04333-0011   Fax: 202-287-2637
www.state.me.us/dhs/bfi/Services.htm

ASPIRE operates two federally mandated employment and training programs--JOBS for TANF (Temporary Assistance for Needy Families) recipients and JET for food stamp recipients. Both programs provide case management, assessment, employment plan development, employment counseling, education, training, job search assistance, child care, and transportation to enable participants to reduce or eliminate their dependency on welfare and improve their quality of life. Nontraditional employment is encouraged and supported when appropriate to meet a participant's needs.

Eligibility: Persons who receive TANF or food stamps are eligible.

Maryland

Starting Over
Maryland New Directions
611 Park Avenue   410-230-0630
Baltimore, MD 21201   Fax: 410-230-0270
www.mdnewdirections.org

Maryland New Direction is a career counseling and job placement agency sponsored by the Department of Human Resources, helping citizens become part of the contributing community. Their Starting Over Program helps those over 30 who have been impacted by divorce, widowhood or separation to become employed or upgrade their underemployed status.

Massachusetts

Apprenticeship Preparedness Program
Wesley J. Lee
Program Director
Building and Construction Trades Council
of the Metropolitan District
12A Everclean St.
Boston, MA 02122   617-282-2242

A Building Opportunities Project, the Apprenticeship Preparedness Program (APP) prepares individuals for construction careers and to enter State registered apprenticeship programs. Training covers the jobs of carpenter, electrician, iron worker, pile driver, pipefitter, and plumber, among others. The Building Opportunities Project opens opportunities for people outside the economic mainstream--women, minorities, residents of neighborhoods impacted by construction, economically disadvantaged, and disabled persons. It offers training in offsite jobs in engineering and design and on-site jobs in building trades--the focus of APP. This is a 130 hour training program. Their motto is,"We provide a career, not just a job."

Eligibility: Applicants must be at least 18 years of age and physically able to do work of the trades, have no prior building trades affiliations, have a high school diploma or GED certificate, and low to moderate HUD income level. There is drug and alcohol pre-employ testing.

Minnesota

Minnesota Women in the Trades
Terry Clements
Coordinator
550 Rice St.

Women's Building
St. Paul, MN 55103
www.mnwomenintrades.org

612-228-9955
Fax: 612-292-9417

Women in the Trades is a support network for women to help other women in becoming tradeswomen. They offer a free, monthly orientation session designed to answer questions and concerns for women interested in entering non-traditional occupation. They also offer a Speakers Bureau to reach organizations throughout the community. When you decide that a non-traditional career is for you, they produce a Building Trades Resource Book listing career opportunities in the construction trades. You can even meet informally with women from non-traditional fields at their monthly social.

Missouri

New Traditions
Diana Reynolds
Regional Coordinator
Kirksville Area Vocational Technical Center
1103 South Cottage Grove
Kirksville, MO 63501
www.kirksville.k12.mo.us

660-665-2865

Through career counseling, decision making seminars, and vocational assessment, this program helps individuals interested in nontraditional careers to choose a best career. It assists prospective students in finding and financing job skills training, schedules support activities to ease the transition from home to school, and provides job seeking information to help individuals find and keep employment in their chosen field.

Eligibility: Individuals who fall under the definition of single parents, displaced homemakers, nontraditional students, or young women ages 14-25; who are seeking a marketable skill; and who want to enter a vocational education/training program are eligible.

Outreach/Reentry Programs
Janet Weaver
Counselor
Maple Woods Community College
2601 NE. Barry Rd.
Kansas City, MO 64156
http://kcmetro.edu/maplewoods/development

816-437-3007

The "Outreach Program" is for individuals with special needs such as the disabled, financially or economically disadvantaged, single parents, homemakers, or persons with limited English proficiency. The "Reentry Program" is for individuals returning to school after time spent working or establishing a family. Both programs offer vocational and personal counseling, academic and interest assessment, and referral to campus or community services.

Eligibility: Individuals who are disabled, financially or academically disadvantaged, single parents, homemakers, adults age 25 and older are eligible.

New Traditions
Peggy Ropelle
Coordinator
Missouri Department of Elementary
 and Secondary Education
Special Vocational Services
Mineral Area College
P.O. Box 1000
Park Hills, MO 63601
www.mineralarea.org

573-431-4593

The Consortium program, which serves four community colleges and seven area vocational-technical schools in 15 counties, helps individuals learn about nontraditional careers for consideration in choosing careers. The program also focuses on new and emerging jobs in high tech areas. It offers seminars, career counseling, help in locating financial aid, and support groups. Financial assistance is available for students entering a nontraditional training program; support is provided from outreach and orientation through training and job placement.

Nebraska

New Beginnings
Trudy Jones
Coordinator
Northeast Community College
801 East Benjamin
P.O. Box 469
Norfolk, NE 68702-0469
www.northeastcollege.com

800-348-9033
402-644-7275

Involvement in the program may include any combination of: classes and workshops designed especially for single parents and displaced homemakers; individual vocational counseling related to career planning, career exploration, and referral to training programs; and personal support such as individual consultation, advocacy, and referral to existing agencies. Participants may be involved in self esteem and confidence building, career exploration, and job seeking skills.

Eligibility: Individuals who are displaced homemakers, who have experienced a layoff, or who have farm related financial needs are eligible. Unemployed or underemployed single parents with full or part-time custody of their children and single pregnant women are also eligible. Applicants must reside in the college's 20-county area.

Women in Transition
Director
Mid-Plains Community College
Voc-Tech Campus
1101 Halligan Dr.
North Platte, NE 69101

308-532-8740, ext. 3621

Activities assist women in goal setting and removing barriers to a positive change. Training covers such options as auto mechanics, building construction and maintenance, diesel mechanics, drafting, electrical, electronics, and welding. Accompanying services are career assessment; basic skills review; workshops on building self esteem, coping with divorce, and seeking a job; support such as assistance with child care and transportation; and referral to community resources.

Eligibility: Single parents, single pregnant women, displaced homemakers are eligible.

New Jersey

Training for Trades and Technology
Denise DiMicelli
Program Manager
Bergen County Technical Institute
Career and Life Counseling Center
540 Hudson St.
Hackensack, NJ 07601
www.onestopbwc.org

201-329-9600, ext. 4041

Over a six week period, instruction is provided in basic technical skills covering math, blueprint reading, and tool awareness and safety; trade skills including hands-on experience in a variety of trades as well as a construction project; job preparation focusing on skills and knowledge necessary to make a nontraditional career choice and succeed in it; and physical conditioning offering weight training and aerobic conditioning. Support services assist with child care and transportation, and provide financial aid. Placement is typically in an entry level job in a skilled trade, an apprenticeship, on-the-job training program, or enrollment in a technical school.

Eligibility: Entrance requires an aptitude test and interview. A high school diploma is not required, but those without a diploma of GED are encouraged to attain it.

Training, Recruiting, Educating and Employing, Inc.
Pete Martiak
Coordinator
Middlesex County Vocational School System
256 Easton Ave.
New Brunswick, NJ 08901
www.mc-votech.org

732-257-3300

The 16 weeks of pre-apprenticeship training encompasses orientation, hands-on experience, and placement assistance in the electrical, plumbing, taping, and painting trades. Electrical training covers basic house wiring and troubleshooting methods; plumbing includes venting and draining, installation of pipes and venting systems; taping includes preparation of walls and ceilings and proper use of other tools and taping compounds; painting covers outside and inside work and includes preparation of buildings, walls, and ceilings.

Eligibility: Applicants must be eligible under JTPA and must reside in Middlesex, Somerset, or Hunterdon Counties.

The PACT Program
Career and Life Counseling Center
Bergen County Technical Institute
540 Hudson St.
Hackensack, NJ 07601
www.onestopbwc.org

201-343-9600

The PACT Program (People Access Construction Trades) provides free education, job training, tools, and job placement assistance to women and minorities who wish to enter construction careers. The career options are: electrical/electronic, plumbing, carpentry, heating/air conditioning, sheet metal and welding.

New Mexico

New Mexico State Department of Education
Vocational-Technical and
Adult Education Unit
Education Building
300 Don Gaspar
Santa Fe, NM 87501-2786 505-827-6571
http://sde.state.nm.us

This program is structured to address the traditional barriers that have inhibited school success of the targeted groups, facilitate enrollment in marketable skills training, and provide job placement and follow-up. Participants receive assistance with payment of child care, books, tuition, fees, and transportation.

Eligibility: Single parents, displaced homemakers and single, pregnant women are eligible.

New York

Nontraditional Employment for Women
Susan Hayes
Director
243 West 20th St. 212-627-6252
New York, NY 10011 Fax: 212-255-8021
www.new-nyc.org

Initiatives help women train for and find work in construction and other blue-collar trades. "Apprenticeship Prep" prepares women academically, physically, and psychologically for construction work. Courses include math and reading, spatial relations and mechanical reasoning, job readiness, interview skills, career exploration. Counseling is provided. A videotape, "New Choices: Women in Nontraditional Careers," was developed for the New York City Board of Education to promote this effort.

"Blue Collar Prep" prepares women to enter non-construction blue-collar jobs as service technicians, utility workers, mechanics and in many similar jobs. Nontraditional Employment for Women (NEW) has developed a publication, "Creating a Harassment-Free Work Environment," for use in training. The program includes issues of *NEW's Letter*, provides technical assistance to institutions and groups in Northeastern States, and provides legal advocacy to eliminate gender gap in blue-collar industries.

Eligibility: Disadvantaged women including displaced homemakers, dislocated workers, welfare recipients, single heads of households and AFDC recipients are eligible.

Access for Women
Linda Silverman
Program Director
New York City Technical College
300 Jay St., M 407
Brooklyn, NY 11201 718-552-1131
www.nyctc.cuny.edu

The Access for Women program supports women who are interested in nontraditional careers in trades and engineering technologies. It includes pre-vocational training consisting of basic math, mechanical skills, career counseling, and job readiness; pre-college math review; outreach to community based programs and schools, including junior and senior high schools, to emphasize sex equity and career counseling, math, and technical skills; building maintenance training program; job placement; and GED instruction for teen mothers. Support services include driver's education, counseling, case management, and referral to training and education programs.

Eligibility: Economically disadvantaged female single heads of households age 16-21, unemployed, underemployed, or career changers are eligible.

Everywoman Opportunity Center, Inc.
Myrna F. Young
Executive Director
237 Main St.
Suite 330
Buffalo, NY 14203 877-847-1121
www.everywoman.org 716-847-1120

Designed to help women move toward personal and economic self-sufficiency, the program provides both individual and group assessment, career counseling, career readiness training, career-life planning, and creative

job search techniques to help women enter, reenter, upgrade or change careers in the paid work force. Math brush-up and math anxiety classes enhance opportunities for entry into nontraditional areas. The center has strong linkages with area vocational training facilities and provides follow-up placement upon completion of the training process.

Eligibility: Homemakers, displaced homemakers, single parents, incarcerated women, women at risk of family violence, young women/girls, non-English speaking women, and women already in the paid work force are eligible.

North Carolina

North Carolina Apprenticeship and Training Bureau
Vonna Viglione
Assistant Director
Division for Training Initiative
North Carolina Department of Labor
1101 Mall Service Center
Raleigh, NC 27699-1101 919-733-7533

This program includes a short term, intensive training program which serves both women and men. Training is provided for jobs in model, pilot, and demonstration programs for targeted populations or selected business or industry sectors.

Eligibility: Dependent on individual job programs.

Ohio

Hard Hatted Women
Kathy Augustine
Director of Development
3043 Superior Ave. 216-861-6500
Cleveland, OH 44114 Fax: 216-961-0927
www.hardhattedwomen.org

Hard Hatted Women (HHW) is a Cleveland based nonprofit organization that facilitates a woman's entry into a nontraditional, blue collar occupation. HHW offers education, training, support, and assistance with job placement to women seeking or holding a nontraditional job. HHW focuses on nontraditional employment because it offers wages that are 20-30% higher than wages earned in traditional jobs. HHW's clientele are adult women seeking to establish a career in blue collar, nontraditional occupations.

Eligibility: Adult women seeking to establish a career in blue collar, nontraditional occupations.

Preparation, Recruitment, Employment Program, Inc.
Lucy Green
Executive Director
2261 Francis Lane
P.O. Box 68018
Cincinnati, OH 45206 513-221-4700

Preparation, Recruitment, Employment Program, Inc. (PREP, Inc.), recruits, prepares, and places women in nontraditional employment. The program offers vocational testing, guidance, labor market information, and preparation for placement in occupations. In operation since 1968, PREP, Inc., was among the first U.S. Department of Labor funded outreach programs to place minorities in apprenticeships. Later it expanded its focus to include women, and now operates at two Ohio sites.

Eligibility: Varies in accordance with funding source guidelines. Some sites serve primarily dislocated workers, displaced homemakers, and long tern unemployed; other sites serve women regardless of economic or employment status.

Oklahoma

Nontraditional/Careers Unlimited Program
Barbara J. Miller
Nontraditional Advisor
Francis Tuttle Vo-Tech Center
12777 N. Rockwell 405-717-4300
Oklahoma City, OK 73142-2789 405-717-4252
www.francistuttle.com/cu

Skills training prepares women for jobs in auto body work, carpentry, machining, electronics, welding, and other traditionally male jobs. The program helps participants improve their self-image, learn to cope with stresses of work and home, and develop a strong support system. The program provides job readiness training and assistance with child care and transportation.

Eligibility: Individuals 18-25 years of age.

Single Parent/Homemaker Program
    Fern Green
    Oklahoma Department of Career
    and Technology Education   403-793-6162
    1500 West Seventh Ave.   405-377-2000
    Stillwater, OK 74074-4364   Fax: 405-743-5541
    www.okcareertech.org

Assistance is provided through assessment of needs and skills, job readiness classes, job training, and information on entry or reentry into employment. Job placement assistance. Personal and emotional independence is promoted through counseling and referral to community and State agencies.

Eligibility: Single parents, displaced homemakers and single, pregnant women are eligible.

Oregon

Building Futures in Industry and Trades (BFIT)
    Spencer Hinkle
    Director
    P.O. Box 19000
    Portland, OR 97280-0880   503-614-7255, ext. 7449
    www.pcc.edu

Training takes place at Portland Community College. The program focuses on construction, electrical, and mechanical trades; incorporates trades math, physical strength building, first aid and safety in the workplace, cooperative education or worksite training, and job search skills. Reading and math basic skills and tutoring are offered. If reading and math levels are below those needed for the training and apprenticeship programs, the college's Alternative Learning Center helps participants improve skills. The program assists with job placement, provides follow-up, and has a support group of women working in the trades.

Pennsylvania

Tradeswomen of Purpose/ Women in Non-Traditional Work, Inc. (TOP/WIN)
    Dawn Moody
    2300 Alter St.   215-545-3700
    Philadelphia, PA 19146   Fax: 215-545-8713

Over a 41-week period, women train for jobs in construction and related trades. Math component is geared to trades; literacy classes focus on reading and writing, helping trainees to increase their comprehension of communications and to attain GED's if they are without a high school diploma; "survival" skills cover assertiveness training, consciousness raising, communication skills, and proper work behavior to give potential tradeswomen the psychological tools needed to deal with obstacles they may face on the job. Job development helps with preparation of resumes and job applications, job hunting, and interviews; physical conditioning improves strength/muscle endurance and cardiovascular conditioning. Shop classes include theory and hands-on experience related to carpentry, electrical, and plumbing basics; forklift operation; engine maintenance; and housing rehabilitation; they encompass hand and power tool identification and operation; safety; and mock construction projects. Support services include an emergency fund, counseling, case management, encouragement from veteran tradeswomen, and a mentoring system. TOP/ WIN also offers information and technical assistance such as seminars and workshops, and a speaker's bureau.

Eligibility: Women served under JTPA are eligible; other women are also eligible.

Tennessee

Women in Trades
    La Sherrie Bates
    YWCA of Greater Memphis
    1044 Mississippi Blvd.   901-948-8899
    Memphis, TN 38126   Fax: 901-942-9383

Nontraditional career orientation and workshops, tool and safety courses, math refresher classes, physical fitness, aptitude testing, counseling, and follow-up comprise major components. Support services include assistance with child care, transportation, union dues, tuition, books, supplies, and tools. Participants move directly into employment or on-the-job training, or enroll in nontraditional skills training or apprenticeship programs. Women in Trades (WIT) pays one-half of salary for participants who are placed in nontraditional on-the-job training and also provides after school care for program participants, if needed.

Eligibility: Age 18 or older; female (preferably displaced homemakers, single parents); male if minority and less than 25% of trade is minority or occupations predominantly held by women; high school education preferred; economically disadvantaged preferred; physically fit.

Texas

South Central Texas Regional Training Center
    Career Advancement Programs and Training
    Texas Engineering Extension Service
    9350 S. Presa
    San Antonio, TX 78223   210-633-1000
or
    Texas Engineering Extension Service
    P.O. Box 40
    San Antonio, TX 78291   210-208-9300
    http://teexweb.tamu.edu

Through a broad range of vocational and technical programs, training is offered to Texas residents. An example is the training conducted by the San Antonio Training Division in basic skills, safety, technical knowledge, and related skills. Beginning with orientation and progressing through a competency based curriculum. students train in job seeking/job keeping skills, and in on-the-job situations in laboratories and shops with tools, equipment, and materials comparable to those in industry. Counseling and placement assistance are available.

Eligibility: Applicants must meet physical requirements, JTPA eligibility, Carl Perkins scholarships, financial aid requirements, or have funds to pay tuition.

Women in Technology
    Vicki Di Benedetto, Coordinator
    P.O. Box 20500
    El Paso, TX 79998   915-831-5085

The Center recruits women to attend classes at the community college in four fields: auto mechanics, drafting and electrical, heating/air conditioning, and environmental technology. They attempt to arrange day care and financial aid to support program participants who need assistance.

Jobs NOW
    Women's Center of Tarrant County, Inc.
    P.O. Box 11860
    1723 Hemphill
    Fort Worth, TX 76110   817-927-4050
    www.womenscenter.info

The Club, a one-week course (M-F, 8:30 - 12:30) group activity, helps unemployed and underemployed individuals find jobs or upgrade employment. A trainer skilled in job search strategies and group training/ motivation trains clients to find the best possible job in the shortest possible time and teaches them permanently enabling job finding and job retention skills. The program is supported by social service referrals, employment counseling, and job development, and includes a skills assessment test and a self-inventory.

Eligibility: Tarrant County residents who are ready, willing, and able to work when they enter the program are eligible.

National Association of Women in Construction
    P.O. Box 162898   800-552-3506
    Fort Worth, TX 76161-9712   817-877-5551
    www.nawic-fw.org

An association of women in construction industry, the National Association of Women in Construction (NAWIC) enhances members' careers. With more than 204 chapters in the United States and Canada and over 6200 members employed in all phases of the industry, NAWIC committees provide resources for continuing education, legislative awareness, employment referral, business ownership, and networking with others who share the same interests and goals. The organization publishes a membership directory and publications, and sponsors regional conferences and annual conventions. The NAWIC Education Foundation offers three construction education programs.

Eligibility: Membership is open to women employed in diverse aspects of the construction industry and women students pursuing a degree of certification related to the construction industry.

Washington

Apprenticeship and Nontraditional Employment for Women
    P.O. Box 2490   425-235-2212
    Renton, WA 98056   Fax: 425-235-7864

In cooperation with the Renton Vocational Technical Institute, Apprenticeship and Nontraditional Employment for Women (ANEW) offers five months of training in trades, math, blueprint reading and drawing, mechanical and electrical theory and practice, basic carpentry, and construction techniques. The program introduces students to welding, pipefitting, cement masonry, and other trades. Training in weightlifting and endurance is built into the curriculum, along with career planning, building good work attitudes, and assertiveness training. The program provides career counseling; job search assistance; and personal counseling to help trainees with issues affecting their program participation and job readiness; child care, tuition, books, and work equipment; and a support system of women in nontraditional jobs.

Eligibility: Applicants must be at least 18 years of age.

Women in Transition: Strategies and Displaced Homemakers

Julia Armstrong
Coordinator
Lower Columbia College
P.O. Box 3010
Longview, WA 98632-0310   360-442-2370
www.lcc.ctc.edu/programs/wit-dh

Classes explore career and educational options and opportunities for women in nontraditional jobs; cover self-assessment and values, career search skills, risk taking, decision making, assertiveness techniques, and improving self esteem.

West Virginia

Technical Schools

Putnam County Technical School
P.O. Box 640
Eleanor, WV 25070   304-586-3494

Cabell County Vocational School
1035 Norway Ave.
Huntington, WV 25705   304-528-5172

Monongalia County Technical Education Center
1000 Mississippi St.   304-291-9240
Morgantown, WV 26501   Fax: 304-291-9247
http://boe.mono.k12.wv.us/montec

These technical schools have programs which provide training to women in nontraditional jobs.

Center for Economic Options

214 Capitol Street, Suite 200   304-345-1298
Charleston, WV 25301   Fax: 304-312-0641
www.centerforeconomicoptions.org

The program provides information about employment options and access to job training, support for women in self-employment, and advocacy for women's legal rights in employment training and education. The Center is working to develop programs for training women in housing rehabilitation, and developing an "entrepreneurial" curriculum to provide displaced homemakers with self-employment training. The main goal is to help women set up microbusinesses.

State Department of Education

Sex Equity
Building 6, Room 230
1900 Kanawha Blvd. East   304-558-7881
Charleston, WV 25305   Fax: 304-558-2584
http://wvde.state.wv.us

This program provides referral to area programs in nontraditional training for women.

Sex Equity Program

Education Outreach Counselor
Bluefield State College
219 Rock Street
Bluefield, WV 24701   304-327-4000
www.bluefield.wvnet.edu

The goals of the program are to educate women about the opportunities in non-traditional career fields and to attract them to two-year non-traditional academic programs that have been traditionally male dominated. Participants of the Sex Equity Program may receive the following: assistance with admissions and financial paperwork, scholarship information, seminars and workshops, and support and encouragement.

Wisconsin

Wing Span

Blackhawk Technical College
6004 Prairie Rd.
P.O. Box 5009   800-498-1282
Janesville, WI 53547   608-757-7752
www.blackhawk.edu/eo

The Wingspan program provides career education for single parents and displaced homemakers, those widowed, divorced, separated, or who have a disabled spouse. Workshops and individualized services help to prepare potential students for successful entry or re-entry into vocational training programs. They offer a Non-Traditional Options Workshop that helps students explore non-traditional careers through hands-on experiences as well as shadowing experiences.

The Opportunity Center

Western Wisconsin Technical College
Coleman Building, Room 129-S   800-322-99982
304 N. 6th St.   608-785-9436
La Crosse, WI 54601   Fax: 608-785-9148
www.wwtc.edu/opcenter

The Opportunity Center is committed to assisting individuals, particularly special populations, to become economically self-sufficient and successful in their personal, education and career goals. Services are provided through case management, workshops, career counseling and planning, educational planning, skills identification activities, job seeking assistance, career interests and personality preference assessments, support groups, limited financial assistance for tuition, financial assistance while attending workshops, and job student success skills training.

Eligibility: Teen parents, single parents, separated, divorced or widowed people, those with disabled spouses and those interested in occupations nontraditional to their gender are eligible.

Center for Nontraditional Students

Waukesha County Technical College
800 Main Street   262-691-5400
Pewaukee, WI 53072   Fax: 262-691-7869
http://web.waukesha.tec.wi.us/home/student/wdc/wdc.htm

The Center assists individuals in becoming self-sufficient by accessing technical training and continuing education. The Center for Nontraditional Students offers career assessment programs, personal and professional development cases. The center is located in the College Center Building and offers a variety of free services. The Center's programs include: PACT (Planning and Accessing Careers in Technology, Displaced Homemakers, Nontraditional Program for Women, a Women's Development Center and a Men's Development Center.

Millions Set Aside For Welfare Moms
To Start Their Own Businesses

If you are on public assistance, you're in luck. Uncle Sam wants to give you the start-up capital necessary to get your business off the ground and keep it flying. The Job Opportunities for Low Income Individuals (JOLI) program can turn any good idea into a money making powerhouse, and it won't cost you a cent. Of all the business startup programs the government offers, this has got to be one of the best.

Under the JOLI program, grants are awarded each year to nonprofit organizations that, in turn, work to create permanent jobs for people who are interested in running their own successful small businesses. As a collaborative partnership, the JOLI projects bring together community support services to lend a hand to those who want to climb that tough ladder of success.

Depending on your state, you can receive:
- loan guarantees
- help getting restrictive asset rules waived
- free child care and transportation
- business skills training
- help with business plans and loan applications
- personal and family development assistance
- ongoing technical advice and feedback

For federal information on grants in your area, contact the federal JOLI office at the Department of Health and Human Services, Office of Community Services, 370 L'Enfant Promenade, SW, Fifth Floor, Washington, DC 20447; 202-401-9346, Fax: 202-401-4687; {www.acf.hhs.gov/programs/joli/welcome.htm}. They have a complete list.

What follows is a listing of the community development organizations that have received federal grant money over the last three years to run JOLI self-employment programs for low-income people. Call the one nearest you for more information on what services are available.

Alaska
Fairbanks Native Association
201 First Avenue, Suite 200
Fairbanks, AK 99701-4892
907-452-1648
Fax: 907-456-4148
www.fairbanksnative.org

Arkansas
Arkansas Enterprise Group
Mr. William Brandon, President
605 Main Street, Suite 202
Arkadelphia, AR 71923
870-246-9736
Fax: 870-246-2182

California
Jobs for Homeless Consortium, Inc.
436 14th Street, Suite 716
Oakland, CA 94612
510-587-7394

Silicon Valley Economic Development
Ms. Consuelo Santos-Killins, President
1155 N. First Street, Suite 107
San Jose, CA 95112

408-298-8455
www.sved.org

Stitches Technology Sewn Products Training
Centers, Inc.
Ms. Clotee McAfee , Executive Director
5609 McKinley Avenue
Los Angeles, CA 90011
323-846-5110
www.dreams.20m.com/about.html

Valley Economic Development Center, Inc.
5121 Van Nuys Boulevard, 3rd Floor
Van Nuys, CA 91403
818-907-9977
Fax: 818-907-9720
Email: info@vedc.org
www.vedc.org

District of Columbia
United Planning Organization
301 Rhode Island Avenue, NW
Washington, DC 20001-1826
202-238-4600
Email: info@upo.org
www.upo.org

Georgia
GRASP Enterprises, Inc.
241 Peachtree St., NE, Suite 200
Atlanta, GA 30303
404-659-5955
Fax: 404-880-9561
www.graspnet.org

Hawaii
Parents and Children Together
1505 Dillingham Boulevard - Suite 208
Honolulu, HI 96819
808-841-2245
Fax: 808-842-9604
http://pacthawaii.org

Illinois
Bethel New Life, Inc.
4950 W. Thomas
Chicago, IL 60651
773-473-7870
Fax: 773-473-7871
www.bethelnewlife.org

Community & Economic Development
Association of Cook County, Inc.

208 S. LaSalle - Suite 1900
Chicago, IL 60604
312-795-8983
Fax: 312-795-0240

Gateway East Metropolitan Ministry
Mr. Frank Childress
Executive Director
575 N. 14th Street
East St. Louis, IL 62205
618-482-5733

Women's Self-Employment Project
11 South LaSalle - Suite 1850
Chicago, IL 60603
312-606-8255
Fax: 312-606-9215
www.wsep.net

Iowa

Institute for Social and Economic Development
910 23 rd Avenue
Coralville, IA 52241
319-338-2331
Fax: 319-338-5824
www.ised.org

Kentucky

Kentucky River Foothills Development
Council, Inc.
1623 Foxhaven Drive
P.O. Box 743
Richmond, KY 40476
606-624-2046
www.kyriverfoothills.org

Massachusetts

Jewish Vocational Service
105 Chauncy Street
Boston, MA 02111
617-451-8147
Fax: 617-451-9973
www.jvs-boston.org

Minnesota

St. Paul Urban League
Ms. Willie Mae Wilson, President
401 Selby Avenue
St. Paul, MN 55102
651-224-5771

Missouri

George Washington Carver House
3035 Bell Avenue
St. Louis, MO 63106
314-652-8485

Nebraska

Lincoln Action Program, Inc.
210 O Street
Lincoln, NE 68502
402-471-4515
www.lincoln-action.org/

Omaha Opportunities Industrialization Center,
Inc.
2724 North 24th Street
Omaha, NE 68110
302-457-4222
Fax: 402-457-6635
www.oicofamerica.org

New York

Centros Sor Isolina Ferre, Inc.
P.O. Box 34360
Ponce, PR 00734-4360
787-844-7743/7720 or 7745
Fax: 787-843-2347

Massachusetts Avenue Project
382 Massachusetts Avenue
Buffalo, NY 14213
716-882-9239

Northern Manhattan Improvement Corporation
Ms. Barbara Lowry
Executive Director
76 Wadsworth Avenue
New York, NY 10033
212-822-8300 Ext. 336
www.nmic.org

North Dakota

Turtle Mountain Community College
P. O. Box 340
Belcourt, ND 58316
701-477-5605
www.turtle-mountain.cc.nd.us/

Ohio

The Neighborhood House, Inc.
1000 Atcheson Street
Columbus, OH 43203
614-252-4941 ext. 41

WSOS Community Action Commission, Inc.
109 S. Front Street
P. O. Box 590
Fremont, OH 43420
419-334-8911
www.wsos.org/viewpage/

Oklahoma

Housing Partners of Tulsa, Inc.
P. O. Box 6369
415 E. Independence
Tulsa, OK 74148-0369
918-581-5777
www.tulsahousing.org/

Pennsylvania

Northside Leadership Conference
415 East Ohio Street - Suite 300
Pittsburgh, PA 15212
412-231-4714
Fax: 415-231-5306
www.pittsburghnorthside.com

South Carolina

Innovative Alternative for Education, Inc.
Ms. Jennifer A. Sgro, Chairperson
MSC Box 1002
701 East Bay Street - Suite 3A-100
Charleston, SC 29403
843-577-2103

Tennessee

UMCA of Greater Memphis
766 S. Highland
Memphis, TN 38111
901-323-323-2211
Fax: 901-458-3784

Texas

Business Invest In Growth, Inc.
1009 East 11th Street, Suite 216
Austin, TX 78702
512-494-8044

George Gervin Youth Center, Inc.
6903 Sunbelt Drive South
San Antonio, TX 78218
210-804-1786
Fax: 210-804-1469

Vermont

Central Vermont Community Action Council,
Inc.
195 US Route 302 -- Berlin
Barre, VT 05641
802-479-1053
www.eveac.org/default.aspx

Virginia

Arlington Community Action Program, Inc.
P. O. Box 6250
Arlington, VA 22206
703-241-2040 ext. 25
www.arlingtoncap.org/

Washington

Metropolitan Development Council
J. Lindsey Hinand, President
622 Tacoma Avenue South
Tacoma, WA 98402
253-597-6703

Wisconsin

Western Dairyland Economic Opportunity
Council, Inc.
Mr. James W. Schwartz, Executive Director
23122 Whitehall Road
P.O. Box 45
Independence, WI 54747
715-985-2391
www.westerndairyland.org/

Free Help For Girls and Women Interested in Math and Science

Traditionally, from the time they are in elementary school, and then all the way through college, women have been subtly discouraged from pursuing careers in math, science, and technical fields. Young women were directed to the fields of nursing, teaching, and office management and encouraged to pursue limited careers in these areas. Well, finally the government has taken notice of this bias and started to do something about it.

Under the Women's Educational Equity Act Program, each year the U.S. Department of Education awards a number of local school districts and other nonprofit groups and individuals money to study this problem and develop programs that will help change the climate to be more female friendly in math and science classes across the country.

Many of these projects offer kids and adults alike free training in school and out of school — in math, science, and vocational and technical fields. Check the project in your state for what's going on to change the way math and science are taught in your schools.

Listed below are the current projects that are now receiving funding. To learn more, contact School Improvement Programs, U.S. Department of Education, 400 Maryland Ave., SW, Washington, DC 20202; 202-260-1280; {www.ed.gov/programs/equity}.

Women's Educational Equity Act Program
2002 Grantees and Project Directors

US Department of Education
Parental Options and Information
400 Maryland Ave., SW, Room 5C149, FB-6
Washington, DC 20202-6140
202-260-1280
Fax: 202-205-5630
www.ed.gov/programs/equity/awards.html

Arizona
Aurora Foundation
P.O. Box 85623
Tucson, AZ 85623
520-370-7594

California
San Mateo County Office of Education
101 Twin Dolphin Drive
Redwood, CA 94065
605-802-5619

ETR Associates
P.O. Box 1830
Santa Cruz, CA 95061
931-438-4060

District of Columbia
Howard University School of Social Work
2400 6th Street, NW
P.O. Box 1071
Washington, DC 20059
202-806-8321

Illinois
Chicago Public Schools
125 S. Clark Street
Chicago, IL 60603
773-553-2055

Massachusetts
Children's Hospital
300 Longwood Avenue
Boston, MA 02115
617-355-6506

Boston Public Schools
20 Court Street
Boston, MA 02108
617-635-9857

Minnesota
Tyler Public School
100 Strong Street
Tyler, MN 56178
507-247-5911

Mississippi
Hinds County Sheriff's Department
409 Pacagoula Street
Jackson, MS 39215
601-974-2934

Alcorn State University
Department of Education and Psychology
1000 ASU Drive, Suite #210
Alcorn, MS 39096
601-877-6141

Montana
Montana State University
Montana Center on Disabilities
1500 North 30th Street
Billings, MT 59101
406-657-2312

Puerto Rico
University of Puerto Rico/
Humacao University College
CUH Station
100 908th Road
Humacao, PR 00791
787-850-9343

South Dakota
Southeast Technical Institute
2301 Career Place
Sioux Falls, SD 57107
605-224-3189

Aberdeen Area Career Planning Center
420 S. Roosevelt
Aberdeen, SD 57402
605-626-2301

Texas
University of Texas
500 West University Avenue
El Paso, TX 799686
915-747-5552

I Wanna New Career And I'm Over 50

Matthew Lesko, Information USA, Inc., 12081 Nebel Street, Rockville, MD 20852 • 1-800-955-7693 • www.lesko.com

Special Programs to Help the Elderly Get Jobs

America's population is aging and aging fast. Americans over the age of 65 is the fastest growing age group today. Upon retirement, many of these people will discover that their Social Security benefits and pension income just aren't enough to make ends meet.

All across the country there are free job training programs set up just for the elderly who need help in getting the job skills they need even if they:

- haven't worked in a long time
- have never worked outside the home
- have limitations on their ability to work
- live in a small town or in the country
- receive Social Security income
- do not have a high school education

In most states free training and employment services are offered through the Senior Community Service Employment Program and the Job Training Partnership Act Program. This is how the programs work:

Senior Community Service Employment
(Title V - 17.235)

Title V of the Older Americans Act offers a special program for the elderly who are in search of employment. This program offers part-time training and employment opportunities for low-income persons 55 years of age and older in a variety of public or private nonprofit community service settings, such as senior centers, nutrition programs, social service agencies, libraries, environmental projects, and many others.

The program provides older persons with minimum wage income and with the opportunity to acquire new skills or upgrade the ones they already have. The program also helps enrollees make an easier transition to the private job market through training, job finding, support, and counseling.

Typical program participants work at jobs such as:

activities coordinator	janitor
bookkeeper	mechanic
cashier	museum guard
clerk typist	park ranger
custodian	receptionist
data entry clerk	salesperson
day care worker	school aide
driver	security guard
food service worker	teacher's aide
grounds keeper	

For more information about the Senior Community Service Employment Program, look at the state listings below or contact Office of Special Targeted Programs, Employment and Training Administration, U.S. Department of Labor, Room N4641, 200 Constitution Ave., NW, Washington, DC 20210; 202-693-3842; {http://wdsc.doleta.gov/seniors}.

Workforce Investment Act

On August 7, 1998, the President signed the Workforce Investment Act of 1998 (WIA), comprehensive reform legislation that supersedes the Job Training Partnership Act (JTPA). WIA reforms Federal job training programs and creates a new, comprehensive workforce investment system. The Workforce Investment Act program trains and places workers with private businesses.

Program participants not only receive experience on a job, but also an opportunity to develop valuable employment skills and good work habits. The reformed system is intended to be customer-focused, to help Americans access the tools they need to manage their careers through information and high quality services, and to help U.S. companies find skilled workers.

Additional services available to older workers in this program include employment counseling, resume writing help, job searches, and classroom training. To be eligible for employment assistance, you just need to be facing some obstacles in finding adequate employment

To learn more about WIA, contact your state office listed below or contact the Office of Job Training Programs, Employment and Training Administration, U.S. Department of Labor, 200 Constitution Ave., NW, Washington, DC 20210; 202-219-6236.

State Listings

The offices listed below will help direct you to job training programs for older workers in your area. They are also great sources for information about general assistance programs for the elderly.

Alabama
Alabama Commission on Aging
RSA Plaza, Suite 470
770 Washington Avenue
Montgomery, AL 36130-1851
334-242-5743
www.coa.state.al.us
This office can refer you to Senior Community Service Employment Program (Title V) sites in your area and general programs and benefits available to older Americans. Call the Alliance for Retired Americans, 888 16th Street NW, Washington, D.C., 20006; 888-373-6497 for help with Senior Aides Program. The National Black Caucus on Black Aging, 908 South Hull, Suite 115, Montgomery, AL 36104; 334-265-1451 can give you regional assistance with Title V in nine counties, including Montgomery.

Alabama Department of Economic and Community Affairs
401 Adams Avenue
P.O. Box 5690
Montgomery, AL 66103-5690
334-242-5100
www.adeca.state.al.us/
This office will refer you to Workforce Investment Act (WIA) sites in your area.

Alaska
Alaska Commission on Aging
Division of Senior Services
Department of Administration
P.O. Box 110209
Juneau, AK 99811-0209
907-465-3250
www.alaskaaging.org/
This office can refer you to Senior Community Service Employment Program (Title V) sites in your area, and give you information on other programs and benefits to older Americans.

AHRIC
3601 C Street, Suite 380
Anchorage, AK 99503
907-269-7485
www.gov.state.ak.us/ahric/ahric.htm
This office will refer you to Workforce Investment Act (WIA) sites in your area.

Arizona
Aging and Adult Administration
Department of Economic Security
1789 West Jefferson Street, #950A-2SW
Phoenix, AZ 85007
602-542-4446
www.de.state.az.us/links/aaa/
This office will refer you to Senior Service Employment Program (Title V) sites in your area.

AZ Department of Commerce
3800 North Central Ave.
Building D
Phoenix, AZ 85012
602-280-1300
www.commerce.state.az.us/
This office will refer you to Workforce Investment Act sites in your area.

Arkansas
Division Aging and Adult Services
Arkansas Dept of Human Services
P.O. Box 1437, Slot 1412
1417 Donaghey Plaza South
Little Rock, AR 72203-1437
501-682-2441
www.state.ar.us/dhs/aging/
This office can refer you to Senior Community Service Employment Program (Title V) sites in your area.

Arkansas Workforce Investment Board
320 Executive Court, Suite 302
Little Rock, AR 72205
501-371-1020
www.arworks.org/
This office will refer you to Workforce Investment Act sites in your area.

California
California Department of Aging
1600 K Street
Sacramento, CA 95814
916-322-3887
www.aging.state.ca.us/

This office can refer you to Senior Community Service Employment Program (Title V) sites in your area.

CA Health and Human Services Agency
1600 Ninth Street, Room 460
Sacramento, CA 95814
916-654-3454
www.chhs.ca.gov
This office will refer you to Workforce Investment Act (WIA) sites in your area.

Colorado

Aging and Adult Services
Department of Social Services
110 16th Street, Suite 200
Denver, CO 80202-4147
303-866-2800
www.cdhs.state.co.us/oss/aas/index1.html
This office can refer you to Senior Community Service Employment Program (Title V) sites in your area.

Colorado Workforce Coordinating Council
Office of the Governor
1580 Logan, Suite 410
Denver, CO 80203
303-894-2077
www.coworkforce.com/emp/WFCs.asp
This office will refer you to Workforce Investment Act (WIA) sites in your area.

Connecticut

Division of Elderly Services
25 Sigourney Street, 10th Floor
Hartford, CT 06106-5033
800-994-9422
www.ctelderlyservices.state.ct.us
This office can refer you to Senior Community Service Employment Program (Title V) sites in your area.

Connecticut Labor Department
200 Folly Brook Blvd.
Wethersfield, CT 06109
860-263-6515
www.ctdol.state.ct.us/
This office will refer you to Workforce Investment Act (WIA) sites in your area. They can also give you information on the Older Worker Support Network.

Delaware

Delaware Division of Services for Aging and
   Adults with Physical Disabilities
Department of Health and Social Services
1901 North DuPont Highway
New Castle, DE 19720
302-577-4791
800-223-9074
www.dsaapd.com
This office can refer you to Senior Community Service Employment Program (Title V) sites in your area.

Policy Advisor for Family Services
820 French Street
Wilmington, DE 19801
302-577-3210
This office will refer you to Workforce Investment Act sites in your area.

District of Columbia

District of Columbia Office on Aging
One Judiciary Square, 9th Floor
441 Fourth Street, N.W., Suite 900 South
Washington, DC 20001
202-724-5622
www.dc.gov
This office can refer you to Senior Community Service Employment Program (Title V) sites in your area.

DC Department of Employment Services
500 C Street, NW
Washington, DC 20001

202-724-7185
This office will refer you to Workforce Investment Act (WIA) sites in your area.

Florida

Department of Elder Affairs
Building B, Suite 152
4040 Esplanade Way
Tallahassee, FL 32399-7000
850-414-2000
http://elderaffairs.state.fl.us/
This office can refer you to Senior Community Service Employment Program (Title V) sites in your area.

Agency for Workforce Innovation
1320 Executive Center Drive Room
300 Atkins Bldg
Tallahassee, FL 32399-0667
850-921-5421
www2.myflorida.com/awi/
This office will refer you to Workforce Investment Act sites in your area.

Georgia

Division of Aging Services
Department of Human Resources
2 Peachtree Street N.E., 36th Floor
Atlanta, GA 30303-3176
404-657-5258
www2.state.ga.us/Departments/DHR/aging.html
This office can refer you to Senior Community Service Employment Program (Title V) sites in your area.

Georgia Department of Labor
148 Andrew Young International Blvd. NE
Suite 600, Sussex Place
Atlanta, GA 30303
404-656-3011
www.dol.state.ga.us
This office will refer you to Workforce Investment Act sites in your area.

Hawaii

Hawaii Executive Office on Aging
250 South Hotel Street, Suite 109
Honolulu, HI 96813-2831
808-586-0100
www2.state.hi.us/eoa
This office can refer you to Senior Community Service Employment Program (Title V) sites in your area.

Department of Labor and Industrial Relations
830 Punchbowl Street, Room 321
Honolulu, HI 96813
808-586-8844
www.dlir.state.hi.us
This office will refer you to Workforce Investment Act (WIA) sites in your area.

Idaho

Idaho Commission on Aging
3380 Americana Terrace, Suite 120
Boise, ID 83706
208-334-3833
www.idahoaging.com/abouticoa/
This office can refer you to Senior Community Service Employment Program (Title V) sites in your area.

Office of the Governor
PO Box 83740
Boise, ID 83720-0034
208-334-2100
www.gov.state.id.us
This office will refer you to Workforce Investment Act sites in your area.

Illinois

Illinois Department on Aging
421 East Capitol Avenue, Suite 100
Springfield, IL 62701-1789
217-785-2870

800-252-8966
www.state.il.us/aging
This office can refer you to Senior Community Service Employment Program (Title V) sites in your area.

Department of Commerce and Community Affairs
620 East Adams, 4th Floor
Springfield, IL 62701
217-785-6006
www.commerce.state.il.us
This office will refer you to Workforce Investment Act (WIA) sites in your area.

Indiana
Bureau of Aging and In-Home Services
Division of Disability, Aging and Rehabilitative Services
Family and Social Services Administration
402 W. Washington Street, #W454
P.O. Box 7083
Indianapolis, IN 46207-7083
317-232-7020
www.state.in.us/fssa/elderly/aaa/
This office can refer you to Senior Community Service Employment Program (Title V) sites in your area.

Department of Workforce Development
10 North Senate Avenue
Indiana Government Center
Indianapolis, IN 46204
317-233-5661
www.dwd.state.in.us
This office will refer you to Workforce Investment Act (WIA) sites in your area.

Iowa
Iowa Department of Elder Affairs
Clemens Building, 3rd Floor
200 Tenth Street, Suite 300
Des Moines, IA 50309-3609
515-281-5187
www.state.ia.us/elderaffairs
This office can refer you to Senior Community Service Employment Program (Title V) sites in your area.

Iowa Workforce Development
1000 East Grand Ave.
Des Moines, IA 50319
515-281-5365
www.iwd.state.ia.us
This office will refer you to Workforce Investment Act (WIA) sites in your area.

Kansas
Department on Aging
New England Building
503 S. Kansas Ave.
Topeka, KS 66603-3404
785-296-4986
800-432-3535
www.k4s.org/kdoa/
This office can refer you to Senior Community Service Employment Program (Title V) sites in your area.

Division of Employment and Training
Kansas Department of Human Resources
512 SW 6th Avenue
Topeka, KS 66603-3174
785-296-7874
www.hr.state.ks.us
This office will refer you to Workforce Investment Act (WIA) sites in your area.

Kentucky
Office of Aging Services
Cabinet for Families and Children
Commonwealth of Kentucky
275 East Main Street
Frankfort, KY 40621
502-564-6930

www.chs.state.ky.us/aging
This office can refer you to Senior Community Service Employment Program (Title V) sites in your area.

Commissioner
Department for Training and Re-Employment
Cabinet for Workforce Development
209 St. Clair Street, 4th Floor
Frankfort, KY 40601
502-564-5360
www.kycwd.org/
This office will refer you to Workforce Investment Act (WIA) sites in your area.

Louisiana
Governor's Office of Elderly Affairs
P.O. Box 80374
Baton Rouge, LA 70898-0374
225-342-7100
www.gov.state.la.us/depts/elderly.htm
This office can refer you to Senior Community Service Employment Program (Title V) sites in your area.

State Department of Labor
1001 North 23rd Street
PO Box 94094
Baton Rouge, LA 70804-9094
225-342-7693
www.ldol.state.la.us
This office will refer you to Workforce Investment Act (WIA) sites in your area.

Maine
Bureau of Elder and Adult Services
Department of Human Services
35 Anthony Avenue
State House, Station #11
Augusta, ME 04333
207-624-5335
800-262-2232
www.state.me.us/dhs/beas
This office can refer you to Senior Community Service Employment Program (Title V) sites in your area.

Workforce Investment Commissioner
20 Union Street
PO Box 309
Augusta, ME 04332-0309
207-287-3788
www.state.me.us
This office will refer you to Workforce Investment Act (WIA) sites in your area.

Maryland
Maryland Department of Aging
State Office Building, Room 1007
301 West Preston Street
Baltimore, MD 21201-2374
800-AGE-DIAL
www.mdoa.state.md.us/information
This office can refer you to Senior Community Service Employment Program (Title V) sites in your area.

Governor's Workforce Investment Board
1414 Key Highway, 2nd Floor
Baltimore, MD 21230
410-333-4454
www.gwib.state.md.us
This office will refer you to Workforce Investment Act (WIA) sites in your area.

Massachusetts
Massachusetts Executive Office of Elder Affairs
One Ashburton Place, 5th Floor
Boston, MA 02108
617-727-7750
www.state.ma.us/elder
This office can refer you to Senior Community Service Employment Program (Title V) sites in your area.

Matthew Lesko, Information USA, Inc., 12081 Nebel Street, Rockville, MD 20852 • 1-800-955-7693 • www.lesko.com

Massachusetts Department of Labor & Workforce Development
One Ashburton Place, Room 1402
Boston, MA 02108
617-727-6573
www.detma.org
This office will refer you to Workforce Investment Act (WIA) sites in your area.

Michigan

Michigan Office of Services to the Aging
611 W. Ottawa
N. Ottawa Tower, 3rd Floor
P.O. Box 30676
Lansing, MI 48909
517-373-8230
www.mdch.state.mi.us/mass/masshome.html
This office can refer you to Senior Community Service Employment Program (Title V) sites in your area

Office of Workforce Development
Michigan Department of Career Development
201 N. Washington Square
Victor Office Center, 5th Floor
Lansing, MI 48913
517-335-5858
www.mdcd.org/Core/pdfactsheet/OWD-201.html
This office will refer you to Workforce Investment Act (WIA) sites in your area.

Minnesota

Aging and Adult Services
444 Lafayette Road
St. Paul, MN 55155-3843
651-296-2544
www.dhs.state.mn.us/Agingint/Services/aasdiv.htm
This office will refer you to general programs and services for older Americans in your area.

Department of Economic Security
390 North Robert Street
St Paul, MN 55101
651-297-4336
www.mnwfo.org
This office will refer you to Workforce Investment Act (WIA) sites in your area.

Mississippi

Division of Aging and Adult Services
750 N. State Street
Jackson, MS 39202
601-359-4929
800-346-6347
www.mdhs.state.ms.us/aas.html
This office can refer you to Senior Community Service Employment Program (Title V) sites in your area.

Employment Training Division
Mississippi Development Authority
P.O. Box 849
Jackson, MS 39225
601-359-9250
www.wininmississippi.org
This office will refer you to Workforce Investment Act (WIA) sites in your area.

Missouri

Division of Aging
Department of Social Services
P.O. Box 1337
615 Howerton Court
Jefferson City, MO 65102-1337
573-751-3082
800-235-5503
www.dss.state.mo.us/da/index.htm
This office can refer you to Senior Community Service Employment Program (Title V) sites in your area.

Department of Economic Development
P.O. Box 1087
Jefferson City, MO 65101
573-751-3349
www.ecodev.state.mo.us
This office will refer you to Workforce Investment Act (WIA) sites in your area.

Montana

Senior and Long Term Care Division
Department of Public Health & Human Services
P.O. Box 4210
111 Sanders, Room 211
Helena, MT 59620
406-444-7788
800-332-2272
www.dphhs.state.mt.us/sltc/
This office can refer you to Senior Community Service Employment Program (Title V) sites in your area.

Department of Labor and Industry
1327 Lockey
Helena, MT 59624-1728
406-444-9091
www.dl.state.mt.us
This office will refer you to Workforce Investment Act in your area.

Nebraska

Department of Health and Human Services
Division on Aging
P.O. Box 95044
1343 M Street
Lincoln, NE 68509-5044
402-471-2307
www.hhs.state.ne.us/ags/agsindex.htm
This office can refer you to Senior Community Service Employment Program (Title V) sites in your area.

Nebraska Department of Labor
550 South 16th Street
P.O. Box 94600
Lincoln, NE 68509-4600
402-471-9000
www.dol.state.ne.us
This office will refer you to Workforce Investment Act (WIA) sites in your area.

Nevada

Nevada Division of Aging Services
Department of Human Resources
State Mail Room Complex
3416 Goni Road, Building D
Carson City, NV 89706
775-687-4210
http://aging.state.nv.us/
This office can refer you to Senior Community Service Employment Program (Title V) sites in your area.

Department of Employment Training & Rehabilitation
1830 East Sahara Ave, Suite 201
Las Vegas, NV 89104
702-486-7923
http://detr.state.nv.us/
This office will refer you to Workforce Investment Act (WIA) sites in your area.

New Hampshire

Division of Elderly and Adult Services
State Office Park South
129 Pleasant Street, Brown Bldg. #1
Concord, NH 03301
603-271-4680
www.state.nh.us/
This office can refer you to Senior Community Service Employment Program (Title V) sites in your area.

New Hampshire Job Training Council
64 Old Suncook Road
Concord, NH 03301
603-228-9500, ext. 307
This office will refer you to Workforce Investment Act sites in your area.

New Jersey

Department of Health and Senior Services
New Jersey Division of Senior Affairs
P.O. Box 807
Trenton, New Jersey 08625-0807
609-588-3141
800-792-8820
www.state.nj.us./health/senior/sraffair.htm
This office can refer you to Senior Community Service Employment
Program (Title V) sites in your area.

New Jersey Department of Labor
P.O. Box 110
Trenton, NJ 08625-0110
609-292-1906
www.dol.state.nj.us
This office will refer you to Workforce Investment Act (WIA) sites in your
area.

New Mexico

State Agency on Aging
La Villa Rivera Building
228 East Palace Avenue, Ground Floor
Santa Fe, NM 87501
505-827-7640
www.nmaging.state.nm.us/
This office can refer you to Senior Community Service Employment
Program (Title V) sites in your area.

Department of Labor
P.O. Box 1928
Albuquerque, NM 87103
505-841-8409
www3.state.nm.us/dol/dol_home.html
This office will refer you to Workforce Investment Act (WIA) sites in your
area.

New York

New York State Office for The Aging
2 Empire State Plaza
Albany, NY 12223-1251
518-474-5731
800-342-9871
http://aging.state.ny.us/index.htm
This office can refer you to Senior Community Service Employment
Program (Title V) sites in your area.

New York State Department of Labor
Building 12, State Office Campus
Albany, NY 12240
518-457-0380
www.labor.state.ny.us
This office will refer you to Workforce Investment Act (WIA) sites in your
area.

North Carolina

Department of Health and Human Services
Division of Aging
2101 Mail Service Center
Raleigh, NC 27699-2101
919-733-3983
www.dhhs.state.nc.us/aging/home.htm
This office can refer you to Senior Community Service Employment Program
(Title V) sites in your area.

North Carolina Department of Commerce
301 North Wilmington Street
Raleigh, NC 27601
919-715-3300
www.nccommerce.com
This office will refer you to Workforce Investment Act (WIA) sites in your
area.

North Dakota

Department of Human Services
Aging Services Division
600 South 2nd Street, Suite 1C
Bismarck, ND 58504
701-328-8910

http://lnotes.state.nd.us/dhs/dhsweb.nsf
This office can refer you to Senior Community Service Employment
Program (Title V) sites in your area.

Department of Commerce
400 E. Broadway, Suite 50
P.O. Box 2057
Bismarck, ND 58502-2057
701-328-5345
www.growingnd.com
This office will refer you to Workforce Investment Act (WIA) sites in your
area.

Ohio

Ohio Department of Aging
50 West Broad Street, 9th Floor
Columbus, OH 43215-5928
614-466-5500
www.state.oh.us/age/
This office can refer you to Senior Community Service Employment
Program (Title V) sites in your area.

Ohio Bureau of Employment Services
145 South Front Street
Columbus, OH 43215
614-466-2100
www.obes.state.oh.us
This office will refer you to Workforce Investment Act (WIA) sites in your
area.

Oklahoma

Aging Services Division
Department of Human Services
P.O. Box 25352
312 N.E. 28th Street
Oklahoma City, OK 73125
405-521-2281
405-521-2327
www.okdhs.org/aging/
This office can refer you to Senior Community Service Employment
Program (Title V) sites in your area.

State Employment Security Commission
Will Rogers Memorial Office Bldg.
2401 N. Lincoln
Okalahoma City, OK 73152
405-557-5329
www.oesc.state.ok.us
This office will refer you to Workforce Investment Act (WIA) sites in your
area.

Oregon

Senior and Disabled Services Division
500 Summer Street, N.E., 2nd Floor
Salem, OR 97310-1015
503-945-5811
www.sdsd.hr.state.or.us/
This office can refer you to Senior Community Service Employment
Program (Title V) sites in your area.

Governor's Office of Education and Workforce Policy
255 Capital Street NE, Suite 126
Salem, OR 97310
503-378-3921
www.governor.state.or.us/gol_workforce.htm
This office will refer you to Workforce Investment Act (WIA) sites in your
area.

Pennsylvania

Pennsylvania Department of Aging
Commonwealth of Pennsylvania
555 Walnut Street, 5th Floor
Harrisburg, PA 17101-1919
717-783-1550
www.aging.state.pa.us/aging/site/
This office can refer you to Senior Community Service Employment
Program (Title V) sites in your area.

Matthew Lesko, Information USA, Inc., 12081 Nebel Street, Rockville, MD 20852 • 1-800-955-7693 • www.lesko.com

Team Pennsylvania Human Resources Investment Council
518 Forum Bldg
Harrisburg, PA 17120
717-772-4966
www.dced.state.pa.us
This office will refer you to Workforce Investment Act (WIA) sites in your area.

Rhode Island

Department of Elderly Affairs
160 Pine Street
Providence, RI 02903-3708
401-222-2858
This office can refer you to Senior Community Service Employment Program (Title V) sites in your area.

Rhode Island Department of Labor and Training
101 Friendship Street
Providence, RI 02903
401-222-3648
www.dlt.state.ri.us
This office will refer you to Workforce Investment Act (WIA) sites in your area.

South Carolina

Office of Senior and Long Term Care Services
Department of Health and Human Services
P.O. Box 8206
Columbia, SC 29202-8206
803-898-2501
www.dea.state.ri.us/
This office can refer you to Senior Community Service Employment Program (Title V) sites in your area.

South Carolina Employment Security Commission
P.O. Box 995
Columbia, SC 29202
803-737-2617
www.sces.org
This office will refer you to Workforce Investment Act (WIA) sites in your area.

South Dakota

Office of Adult Services and Aging
Richard F. Kneip Building
700 Governors Drive
Pierre, SD 57501-2291
605-773-3656
www.state.sd.us/asa/
This office can refer you to Senior Community Service Employment Program (Title V) sites in your area.

South Dakota Department of Labor
Kneip Bldg
700 Governors Drive
Pierre, SD 57501-2291
605-773-3101
www.state.sd.us/dol/dol.asp
This office will refer you to Workforce Investment Act (WIA) sites in your area.

Tennessee

Commission on Aging
Andrew Jackson Building. 9th floor
500 Deaderick Street
Nashville, Tennessee 37243-0860
615-741-2056
www.state.tn.us/comaging/
This office can refer you to Senior Community Service Employment Program (Title V) sites in your area.

Tennessee Department of Labor and Workforce Development
Andrew Johnson Tower, 8th Floor
710 James Robertson Parkway
Nashville, TN 37243
615-741-6642
www.state.tn.us/labor-wfd
This office will refer you to Workforce Investment Act (WIA) sites in your area.

Texas

Texas Department on Aging
4900 North Lamar, 4th Floor
Austin, TX 78751-2316
512-424-6840
www.tdoa.state.tx.us/
This office can refer you to Senior Community Service Employment Program (Title V) sites in your area.

Texas Workforce Commission
101 E. 15th Street
Austin, TX 78778-0001
512-463-2800
www.twc.state.tx.us
This office will refer you to Workforce Investment Act (WIA) sites in your area.

Utah

Division of Aging & Adult Services
Box 45500
120 North 200 West
Salt Lake City, UT 84145-0500
801-538-3910
www.hsdaas.state.ut.us/SrvAge.htm
This office can refer you to Senior Community Service Employment Program (Title V) sites in your area.

Department of Workforce Services
140 East 300 South
Salt Lake City, UT 84111
801-526-9210
www.dws.state.ut.us
This office will refer you to Workforce Investment Act sites in your area.

Vermont

Vermont Department of Aging and Disabilities
Waterbury Complex
103 South Main Street
Waterbury, VT 05671-2301
802-241-2400
www.dad.state.vt.us/
This office can refer you to Senior Community Service Employment Program (Title V) sites in your area.

Vermont Department of Employment and Training
5 Green Mountain Drive
P.O. Box 488
Montpelier, VT 05601-0488
802-828-4000
www.det.state.vt.us
This office will refer you to Workforce Investment Act (WIA) sites in your area.

Virginia

Virginia Department for the Aging
1600 Forest Avenue, Suite 102
Richmond, VA 23229
804-662-9333
800-662-9354
www.aging.state.va.us/
This office can refer you to Senior Community Service Employment Program (Title V) sites in your area.

Virginia Employment Commission
703 East Main Street, Room 300
Richmond, VA 23219
804-786-3001
www.vec.state.va.us
This office will refer you to Workforce Investment Act sites in your area.

Washington

Aging and Adult Services Administration
Department of Social and Health Services
P.O. Box 45050
Olympia, WA 98504-5050
360-493-2500
www.aasa.dshs.wn.gov/
This office can refer you to Senior Community Service Employment Program (Title V) sites in your area.

Executive Policy Advisor
P.O. Box 43113
Olympia, WA 98504-3113
360-902-0664
www.ofm.wa.gov
This office will refer you to Workforce Investment Act (WIA) sites in your area.

West Virginia

West Virginia Bureau of Senior Services
Holly Grove, Building 10
1900 Kanawha Boulevard East
Charleston, WV 25305
304-558-3317
www.state.wv.us/seniorservices/
This office can refer you to Senior Community Service Employment Program (Title V) sites in your area.

West Virginia Human Resource Investment Council
McJunkin Corporation
835 Hillcrest Drive
Charleston, WV 25311
304-348-4962
www.state.wv.us/HRIC
This office will refer you to Workforce Investment Act sites in your area.

Wisconsin

Department of Health and Family Services
P.O. Box 7851
Madison, WI 53707
608-266-1865

www.dhfs.state.wi.us/Aging/
This office can refer you to Senior Community Service Employment Program (Title V) sites in your area.

WI Department of Workforce Development
201 East Washington Ave., Room 400X
P.O. Box 7946
Madison, WI 53707
608-266-7552
www.dwd.state.wi.us
This office will refer you to Workforce Investment Act (WIA) sites in your area.

Wyoming

Office on Aging
Department of Health
6101 Yellowstone Road, Room 259B
Cheyenne, WY 82002
307-777-7996
800-442-2766
http://wdhfs.state.wy.us/aging/
This office can refer you to Senior Community Service Employment Program (Title V) sites in your area.

Department of Employment
PO Box 2760
Casper, WY 82602
307-235-3254
http://wydoe.state.wy.us
This office will refer you to Workforce Investment Act (WIA) sites in your area.

"As recently as 1900, about one half of the men and women who reached the age of twenty did not live to be sixty-five; now four out of five reach sixty-five."

Source: *Ambition: How We Manage Success and Failure Throughout Our Lives,* Gilbert Brim, Basic Books, 1992

Jobs With the Federal Government

The Federal government is obviously an equal employment opportunity employer, but two agencies make a special effort to employ seniors 55 and over in part time to full time positions. These jobs are not only in Washington, DC, but throughout the United States at Environmental Protection Agency (EPA) and Forest Service regional offices. There are a couple of differences between the programs. The EPA hires people at all skill and professional levels and recruits people through six senior citizen organizations. The Forest Service takes part in the Senior Community Service Employment Program described earlier in this chapter. Seniors must be 55 or older and meet income eligibility guidelines. This program is designed to help seniors receive training or skill upgrading, and pays at least minimum wage. Read on to learn more about these important programs for seniors.

* JOBS With The EPA

(Senior Environmental Employment Program (SEE) - 66.508)
Senior Environmental Employment Program (SEE)
U.S. Environmental Protection Agency MC 3650
1200 Pennsylvania Ave., NW
Washington, DC 20460   202-260-2574
The Environmental Protection Agency (EPA) has a special program for hiring senior citizens 55 years and over. When an EPA regional office has a shortage of workers, they notify one of the organizations listed below, which in turn recruit workers. Senior citizens get involved in all kinds of activities from conducting national surveys to fulfilling general administrative tasks. The jobs carry national unemployment, workmen's compensation, Social Security, and health benefits. There are four levels of pay:

Level 1- Xerox operators, messengers, telephone assistants, etc.: $6-8/hour
Level 2- secretaries, administrative assistance, etc.; $7.25-10/hour
Level 3- writers and editors, etc.: $8.50-11/hour
Level 4- professionals with relevant degrees, etc.: $10.50-15/hour

For general information, contact the Senior Environmental Employment Program office at the address listed above.

For recruitment information contact:
National Older Worker Career Center, 1615 L St., NW, Suite 750, Washington, DC 20036; 202-331-5017; {www.nowcc.org/}.

National Association for Hispanic Elderly, 234 E. Colorado Blvd., Suite 300, Pasadena, CA 91101; 213-487-1922.

National Caucus and Center on Black Aged, Suite 800, 1200 L St., NW, Washington, DC 20005; 202-637-8400; {www.ncba-blackaged.org/}.

National Senior Citizens Education and Research Center, 8403 Colesville Rd., Suite 1200, Silver Spring, MD 20910; 301-578-8900; {www.ncscinc.org/about/nscerc.htm}.

National Council on the Aging, 409 Third St., SW, Washington, DC 20024; 202-479-1200; {www.ncoa.org/}.

National Pacific/Asian Resource Center on Aging, Suite 914, 1511 3rd Ave., Seattle, WA 98121; 206-624-0313; {www.napca.org/}.

* Get A Job With The Forest Service

U.S. Forest Service
U.S. Department of Agriculture
Human Resource Programs
P.O. Box 96090
Washington, DC 20090   703-235-8855
If you are over 55 years of age and meet some income eligibility guidelines, you may be a candidate for the Senior Community Service Employment Program (SCSEP).

This program provides part-time outdoor and indoor employment and training opportunities, while providing community services to the general public. Employees work an average of 20 hours per week at a nearby Forest Service Office in their local community. They are paid at least the federal or state minimum wage, receive training and skill upgrading, health programs, and more.

SCSEP supplements the permanent Forest Service workforce. You can be assigned a variety of jobs including visitor information, receptionist, computer aide, carpenter, researcher, or more.

Over 5,600 seniors are employed through this program with $26,100,000 set aside for their salaries. To learn about the program, contact your local Forest Service office or the office listed above.

Senior Volunteer Opportunities

Shuffleboard, dominoes, bridge, and golf...Excited yet? Wouldn't you rather improve your neighborhood, lead nature walks or teach children to read? Being retired doesn't have to mean spending your afternoons idling chasing a little white ball. And just because now you might find yourself on a fixed income, it doesn't mean that you can't take that trip to Africa that you've always dreamed about. The government has hundreds of ways to help you get excited about your new found free time. Some of these can even pay you a small stipend. Read on to learn more about these opportunities to give a part of yourself to help others. What a satisfying way to spend some of your retirement time and give something back to your community?

* Keep A Fellow Senior Out Of A Nursing Home

(Senior Companion Program - 94.016)
National Senior Service Corps
1201 New York Ave., NW
Washington, DC 20525   800-424-8867
www.seniorcorps.org

Nursing homes have got to be one of the last places people want to spend the remaining years of their lives. Through the Senior Companion Program, you can be matched up with someone who needs just a little help to stay in the comfortable surroundings of their own home, and you can gain a friend in the bargain. As a participant, you will give individual care to other seniors who need help with transportation and shopping, or just sharing their reminiscences with someone that shows interest.

Volunteers must be 60 years of age or older and have a low income. Volunteers usually provide 20 hours a week of service and receive a small paycheck and other benefits. Nearly 14,000 Senior Companions provide 13 million hours of service annually to help more than 36,000 frail elderly stay independent. The federal budget for the program is $43,090,000. For more information, contact the office listed above.

* $3,000 To Help The Kids

(Foster Grandparent Program - 94.011)
National Senior Service Corps
1201 New York Ave., NW
Washington, DC 20525   800-424-8867
www.seniorcorps.org/joining/fgp/

The Foster Grandparent Program matches low income seniors with young people who need various kinds of special help. Volunteers serve as mentors, tutors, and caregivers for children and young kids with special needs, and can also work in schools, hospitals, and recreation centers in their communities.

To be eligible, Foster Grandparents must be 60 years of age or over, with a low income, and interested in serving infants, children, and youth with special or exceptional needs. Volunteers work twenty hours per week, and receive a small paycheck and other benefits such as transportation costs or uniforms. 80,000 children, teenagers and their families are supported by the services of nearly 24,000 Foster Grandparents each year. The funds allocated from the federal budget for this program is $78,810,000. For more information, contact the office listed above.

* Share Your Know-How

(Retired Senior Volunteer Program (RSVP) - 94.002)
National Senior Service Corps
1201 New York Ave., NW
Washington, DC 20525   800-424-8867
www.seniorcorps.org/joining/rsvp

You've got 40 years of business experience out there with you on the golf course during your retirement. There are hundreds of businesses and even nonprofit groups starting up each day, run by people who have the energy, but not the experience that you possess. You can lend your expertise to those who need your help the most.

The Retired Senior Volunteer Program (RSVP) gives retired people a chance to continue using their professional experience by working with local service organizations doing such things as conducting employment workshops and acting as consultants to nonprofit organizations. You can even work in schools, libraries, hospitals, and other community service centers. RSVP participants can serve from one to forty hours a week, providing assistance to hundreds of services and organizations. Participants are not restricted in income and are not compensated for their service.

450,000 RSVP members serve through more than 60,000 public and nonprofit community agencies. RSVP's annual budget is $44,500,000. For more information, contact the office listed above.

* Be A Big Shot Executive

(Service Corps of Retired Executives - 59.026)
SCORE
409 Third St., SW, Fourth Floor
Washington, DC 20024   800-634-0245
www.score.org

Your spouse may want you to slow down now that you're retired, but every time you walk into a business, you have this sudden urge to help. Instead of getting kicked out of every place you shop, try volunteering with SCORE, Service Corps of Retired Executives. SCORE volunteers are usually retired business professionals who want to share their expertise with the next generation of business owners. You won't get paid as a volunteer, although you may get reimbursed for certain out-of-pocket expenses. SCORE even conducts seminars and workshops covering major considerations for running a business.

Since it began, SCORE has responded to over 3 million requests for assistance and has an annual budget of $3,250,000. If you are interested in becoming one of over 13,000 SCORE members nationwide, contact SCORE at the office listed above.

* Travel The World At Government Expense

(Peace Corps)
Peace Corps
1111 20th Street, NW
Washington, DC 20526   800-424-8580
www.peacecorps.gov

The average roundtrip ticket to Nepal will cost you $2,800, Poland is $1,800, and Sudan is $2,100. Who can afford those prices on a fixed income? Become one of the senior Peace Corps volunteers and see the world.

As a volunteer, you will serve for two years, living among the native people, and becoming part of the local community. The Peace Corps sends volunteers throughout Latin America, Africa, the Near East, Asia, the Pacific, and Eastern Europe to share their expertise in education, agriculture, health, economic development, urban development, and the environment. Volunteers receive a stipend and health benefits. Currently over 6,500 volunteers are serving with an annual budget of $231,300,000. For more information, contact the office listed above.

Free or Cheap College Tuition For Seniors

You are never too old if you choose to be young and your education is never finished if you choose to continue. Don't let the inflated cost of a higher education discourage your thirst for greater knowledge. Here is a list of more than 350 colleges and universities that offer big savings to qualified senior citizens. Make sure to check colleges near you to see if they offer similar programs. So why not go to college with your grandchildren, earn a certificate, diploma or a degree, graduate magna cum laude, start a new business, or...

On the other hand if homework is not for you, why not take an art appreciation class, learn to swim, weave a basket, or cook a gourmet meal? You can study just about anything your heart desires for little or no cost. **It's never too late to learn!!!** After all, a mind <u>is</u> a terrible thing to waste.

Alabama

Gadsden State Community College
Admissions
P.O. Box 227
Gadsden, AL 35902-0227
205-549-8201
Minimum Age: 60
Tuition: free
Basic Fees: none
Credit: yes

Jefferson State Community College
Admissions
2601 Carson Rd.
Birmingham, AL 35215-3098
205-853-1200
Minimum Age: 60
Tuition: free
Basic Fees: $4 per credit hour
Credit: yes

Livingston University
Station 2
Livingston, AL 35470
205-652-3400
Minimum Age: 55
Tuition: free
Basic Fees: $15 one time application fee
Credit: no

University of Montevallo
Station 6030
Montevallo, AL 35115
205-665-6065
800-292-4349
Minimum Age: 65
Tuition: free
Basic Fees: $15 per class
Credit: no

Alaska

Prince William Sound Community College
P.O. Box 97
Valdez, AK 99686
907-835-2678
Minimum Age: 60
Tuition: free
Basic Fees: $2.50 for 1-3 credit hours; $5 for 4-5 credit hours; $25 for 7+ credit hours
Credit: yes

University of Alaska/ Anchorage
Enrollment Services
3211 Providence Dr.
Anchorage, AK 99508
907-786-1525
Minimum Age: 60
Tuition: free

Basic Fees: $45 for 3 credit hours; $57 for 6 credit hours
Credit: yes

University of Alaska/ Fairbanks
Admissions and Records
P.O. Box 757640
Fairbanks, AK 99775-0060
907-474-7821
Minimum Age: 60
Tuition: free
Basic Fees: $25 for 3 credit hours; $155 for 12 credit hours; parking and health insurance can be waived if not needed
Credit: yes

University of Alaska/ Southeast
11120 Glacier Hwy.
Juneau, AK 99801
907-465-6457
Minimum Age: 60
Tuition: free
Basic Fees: $5 for 1 credit hour; $8 for 2 credit hours; $17 for 3+ credit hours
Credit: yes

Arizona

Arizona Western College
P.O. Box 929
Yuma, AZ 85366-0929
602-726-1050
Minimum Age: 60
Tuition: $16 per credit hour
Basic Fees: none
Credit: yes

Central Arizona College
Student Records
8470 North Overfield Rd.
Coolidge, AZ 85228
520-426-4444
Minimum Age: 60
Tuition: $18 per credit hour with the 6th, 16th, 17th and 18th free
Basic Fees: none
Credit: yes

Arkansas

Arkansas State University
Admissions
P.O. Box 1630
State University
Jonesboro, AR 72467-1630
800-382-3030
Minimum Age: 60
Tuition: free

Basic Fees: $4 per credit hour
Credit: yes

Arkansas State University: Beebe Branch
P.O. Drawer H
Beebe, AR 72012
501-882-6452
Minimum Age: 60
Tuition: free
Basic Fees: none (auto sticker $5)
Credit: yes

Arkansas Tech University
Admissions
Russelville, AR 72801-2222
501-968-0343
Minimum Age: 60
Tuition: free
Basic Fees: none
Credit: yes

East Arkansas Community College
1700 Newcastle Rd.
Forest City, AR 72335-9598
501-633-4480
Minimum Age: 62
Tuition: free
Basic Fees: $3 per credit hour
Credit: yes

Garland County Community College
101 College Dr.
Hot Springs, AR 71913
501-767-9371
Minimum Age: 60
Tuition: free
Basic Fees: $10 per session
Credit: yes

Henderson State University
Registrar
P.O. Box 7534
Arkadelphia, AR 71999-7534
501-203-5000
Minimum Age: 60
Tuition: free
Basic Fees: $36 for 3 credit hours
Credit: yes

Northern Arkansas Community College
Pioneer Ridge
Harrison, AR 72601
501-743-3000
Minimum Age: 60
Tuition: free
Basic Fees: none
Credit: yes

Phillips County Community College
Campus Dr.

P.O. Box 785
Helena, AR 72342
501-338-6474
Minimum Age: 60
Tuition: free
Basic Fees: none
Credit: yes

California

California State University - Sacramento
Re-Entry Services
6000 J St.
Sacramento, CA 95819-6048
916-278-6750
Minimum Age: 60
Tuition: $3 per session
Basic Fees: none (students receive free public
transportation in the Sacramento area)
Credit: yes

Colorado

Adams State College
Alamosa, CO 81102
719-589-7712
Minimum Age: 65
Tuition: free
Basic Fees: none
Credit: no

Colorado Moutain College: Alpine Campus
1330 Bob Adams Dr.
Steamboat Springs, CO 80487
970-870-4444
Minimum Age: 62
Tuition: 50% off (regular tuition $32 per credit
hour)
Basic Fees: $50 for 0-9 credit hours; $65 for
12+ credit hours
Credit: yes

Colorado State University
Admissions
Ft. Collins, CO 80523
970-491-6909
Minimum Age: 62
Tuition: free
Basic Fees: none
Credit: no

Metropolitan State College of Denver
Adult Learning Services
P.O. Box 173362
Denver, CO 80217
303-556-8342
Minimum Age: 62
Tuition: free
Basic Fees: none
Credit: no

University of Colorado, Boulder
Regent Administrative Center 125
Office of Admissions
Campus Box 6
Boulder, CO 80309
303-492-6301
Minimum Age: 55
Tuition: member of alumni $5 per session;
non-alumni member $15 per session
Basic Fees: none
Credit: no

University of Colorado at Denver
P.O. Box 173364
Campus Box 146
Denver, CO 80217-3364
303-556-2400
Minimum Age: 60
Tuition: free
Basic Fees: none
Credit: no

University of Northern Colorado
Admissions
Greeley, CO 80639
970-351-2881
Minimum Age: 60
Tuition: free
Basic Fees: none
Credit: no

Connecticut

Asnuntuck Community College
Admissions
170 Elm St.
Enfield, CT 06082
203-253-3043
Minimum Age: 62
Tuition: free
Basic Fees: none (lab fee also waived)
Credit: yes

Central Connecticut State University
Admissions Office
1615 Stanley St.
New Britain, CT 06050
860-832-3200
Minimum Age: 62
Tuition: free
Basic Fees: $37 per semester
Credit: yes

Eastern Connecticut State University
Registrar
83 Windham St.
Willimantic, CT 06226
203-465-5389
Minimum Age: 62
Tuition: free
Basic Fees: $12 per credit hour for part-time
Credit: yes

University of Connecticut, Storrs
2131 Hillside Rd.
Storrs, CT 06269-3088
203-486-3137
Minimum Age: 62
Tuition: free
Basic Fees: $222 full-time per semester
Credit: yes

University of Hartford
Adult Services
200 Bloomfield Ave.
West Hartford, CT 06117-0395
203-768-4457
Minimum Age: 70
Tuition: free
Basic Fees: $30 per semester (1 class limit)
Credit: no

Western Connecticut State University
Office of Continuing Education
181 White St.
Danbury, CT 006810
203-837-8230
Minimum Age: 62
Tuition: $10 per semester (non-credit $10 per
class)
Basic Fees: Part-time none (full-time varies)
Credit: yes

Delaware

Delaware State College
Admissions
1200 N. Dupont Hwy.
Dover, DE 19901-2277
302-739-4917
Minimum Age: 62
Tuition: free
Basic Fees: $25 per semester
Credit: yes

Delaware Technical and Community College:
Jack F. Owens Campus
P.O. Box 610
Georgetown, DE 19947
302-856-5400
Minimum Age: 60
Tuition: free
Basic Fees: none
Credit: yes

Delware Technical and Community College:
Stanton/Wilmington Campus
333 Shipley St.
Wilmington, DE 19801
302-571-5343
Minimum Age: 60
Tuition: free
Basic Fees: none
Credit: yes

Deleware Technical and Community College:
Terry Campus
1832 North Dupont Parkway
Dover, DE 19901
302-741-2700
Minimum Age: 60
Tuition: free
Basic Fees: none
Credit: yes

District of Columbia

University of the District of Columbia
1100 Harvard St., Room 114
Washington, DC 20008
202-274-5010
Minimum Age: 65
Tuition: free (50% off if going for a degree)
Basic Fees: $20 per semester
Credit: yes

Florida

Broward Community College, Ft. Lauderdale
Registration
225 E. Lasolas Blvd.
Ft. Lauderdale, FL 33301
305-761-7465
Minimum Age: 65
Tuition: free
Basic Fees: the school will cover up to
$181.50 of basic fees
Credit: yes

Florida Atlantic University
500 Northwest 20th St.
Boca Raton, FL 33431-0991
407-367-3294
Minimum Age: 60
Tuition: free
Basic Fees: none
Credit: no

Florida International University
University Park
Miami, FL 33199
305-348-2363
Minimum Age: 60
Tuition: free
Basic Fees: none
Credit: no

Florida State University
2249 University Ct.
Tallahassee, FL 32306-1009
904-644-6200
Minimum Age: 62
Tuition: free
Basic Fees: none
Credit: no

Santa Fe Community College
P.O. Box 1530
3000 NW 83rd St.

Gainesville, FL 32602
352-395-5443
Minimum Age: 60
Tuition: free
Basic Fees: none
Credit: yes

University of Central Florida
P.O. Box 160111
Orlando, FL 32816-0111
407-823-3000
Minimum Age: 60
Tuition: free
Basic Fees: none
Credit: no

Georgia

Albany State College
504 College Dr.
Albany, GA 31705
912-430-4650
Minimum Age: 62
Tuition: free
Basic Fees: $10 per session
Credit: yes

Armstrong State College
11935 Abercorn St.
Savannah, GA 31419
800-633-2349
Minimum Age: 62
Tuition: free
Basic Fees: $10 per session
Credit: yes

Athens Area Technical Institute
US Highway 29 North
Athens, GA 30610-3099
706-542-8050
Minimum Age: 62
Tuition: free
Basic Fees: $12.50 per quarter
Credit: yes

Bainbridge College
2500 E. Shotwell St.
Bainbridge, GA 31717
912-248-2500
Minimum Age: 62
Tuition: free
Basic Fees: none
Credit: yes

Brunswick College
Admissions
3700 Altama Ave.
Brunswick, GA 31520-3644
912-264-7253
Minimum Age: 62
Tuition: free
Basic Fees: none
Credit: yes

Clayton State College
Admissions/Registrar
P.O. Box 285
Morrow, GA 30260
770-961-3400
Minimum Age: 62
Tuition: free
Basic Fees: none
Credit: yes

Columbus College
4225 University Ave.
Columbus, GA 31907-5645
706-568-2035
Minimum Age: 62
Tuition: free
Basic Fees: none
Credit: yes

Georgia College
Admissions and Records
Campus Box 023
Milledgeville, GA 31061
912-453-5004
Minimum Age: 62
Tuition: free
Basic Fees: none
Credit: yes

Georgia Southern University
Admissions
Landrum Box 8024
Statesboro, GA 30460-8024
912-681-5531
Minimum Age: 62
Tuition: free
Basic Fees: none
Credit: yes

Georgia Southwestern College
800 Wheatly St.
Americus, GA 31709-4693
912-928-1273
Minimum Age: 62
Tuition: free
Basic Fees: none
Credit: yes

Georgia State University
P.O. Box 4009
Atlanta, GA 30302-4009
404-651-2365
Minimum Age: 62
Tuition: free
Basic Fees: $82 per quarter
Credit: yes

Hawaii

University of Hawaii: Hawaii Community
College
200 West Kawili St.
Hilo, HI 96720
808-933-3611
Minimum Age: 60
Tuition: free (no summer classes)
Basic Fees: none
Credit: yes

University of Hawaii: Honolulu Community
College
874 Dillingham Blvd.
Honolulu, HI 96817
808-845-9129
Minimum Age: 60
Tuition: free
Basic Fees: $10 per semester
Credit: yes

University of Hawaii: Kapiolani Community
College
4303 Diamond Head Rd.
Honolulu, HI 96816
808-734-9559
Minimum Age: 60
Tuition: free
Basic Fees: $10 per semester
Credit: yes

University of Hawaii: Kauai Community
College
3-1901 Kaomualii Hwy.
Lihue, HI 96766
808-245-8212
Minimum Age: 60
Tuition: free
Basic Fees: none
Credit: yes

University of Hawaii: Leeward Community
College
96-045 Ala Ike
Pearl City, HI 96782

808-455-0217
Minimum Age: 60
Tuition: free
Basic Fees: none
Credit: yes

University of Hawaii at Manoa
2600 Campus Rd.
Honolulu, HI 96822
808-956-8975
Minimum Age: 60
Tuition: free
Basic Fees: none
Credit: yes

University of Hawaii: Maui Community
College
310 Kaahumanu Ave.
Kahului, HI 96732
808-244-9181
Minimum Age: 60
Tuition: free
Basic Fees: $4 per session plus .50 cents per
credit hour
Credit: yes

University of Hawaii: Windward Community
College
45-720 Keaahala Rd.
Kaneohe, HI 96744
808-235-7432
Minimum Age: 60
Tuition: free
Basic Fees: none
Credit: yes

Idaho

Boise State University
1910 University Dr.
Boise, ID 83725
800-824-7017
Minimum Age: 60
Tuition: $5 per credit hour
Basic Fees: $20 per semester
Credit: yes

College of Southern Idaho
Admissions
P.O. Box 1238
Twin Falls, ID 83303-1238
208-733-9554
Minimum Age: 60
Tuition: free
Basic Fees: none
Credit: yes

Idaho State University
Enrollment Planning
Campus Box 8054
Pocatello, ID 83209
208-236-2123
Minimum Age: 60
Tuition: $5 per credit hour
Basic Fees: $20 per semester
Credit: yes

Lewis Clark State College
500 Eighth Ave.
Lewiston, ID 83501
208-799-5272
Minimum Age: 60
Tuition: $5 per credit hour
Basic Fees: $20 per semester
Credit: yes

North Idaho College
Business Office
1000 West Garden Ave.
Coeur d'Alene, ID 83814
208-769-3311
Minimum Age: 60
Tuition: 50% off (regular tuition $50 per credit
hour)

Basic Fees: $130 full-time
Credit: yes

Illinois

Belleville Area College
2500 Carlyle Rd.
Belleville, IL 62221
618-235-2700
Minimum Age: 60
Tuition: $35 per credit hour
Basic Fees: $10 one time application fee
Credit: yes

Chicago State University
95th St. and King Dr.
Chicago, IL 60628
312-995-2513
Minimum Age: 65
Tuition: free (income limitaiton of $12,000 annually)
Basic Fees: none (lab also waived)
Credit: yes

College of Du Page
22nd St. and Lambert Rd.
Glen Ellyn, IL 60137
708-858-2800 ext. 2482
Minimum Age: 65
Tuition: $3.45 per credit hour
Basic Fees: none
Credit: yes

Illinois State University
Adult Services
Campus Box 2200
Normal, IL 61790-2200
309-438-2181
Minimum Age: 65
Tuition: free
Basic Fees: none
Credit: no

Northern Illinois University
Office of Admissions
101 Williston Hall
Dekalb, IL 60115-2857
815-753-0446
Minimum Age: 65
Tuition: free (income limitation of $14,000 annually)
Basic Fees: $20-$40 per session
Credit: yes

Indiana

Ball State University
Office of Admission
Lucina Hall
Muncie, IN 47306
317-285-8300
Minimum Age: 60
Tuition: 50% off (regular tuition $478 for 0-3 credit hours; $638 for 4-5 credit hours; $1008 for 6-8 credit hours)
Basic Fees: none
Credit: yes

Indiana University at Kokomo
P.O. Box 9003
Kokomo, IN 46904-9003
317-453-2000
Minimum Age: 60
Tuition: 50% off up to 9 hours (regular tuition $83.30-87.05 per credit hour)
Basic Fees: $15 maximum activity fee plus $2 per credit hour
Credit: yes

Indiana University-Purdue University at Fort Wayne
Financial Aid
2101 Coliseum Blvd., East
Fort Wayne, IN 46805

219-481-6820
Minimum Age: 60
Tuition: 50% off (regular tuition $80.25 per credit hour)
Basic Fees: none
Credit: yes

Indiana University Southeast
4201 Grant Line Rd.
New Albany, IN 47150
812-941-2212 ext. 2335
Minimum Age: 60
Tuition: 50% off up to 9 hours (regular tuition $87.05 per credit hour)
Basic Fees: none
Credit: yes

University of Southern Indiana
8600 University Blvd.
Evansville, IN 47712
812-464-1765
Minimum Age: 60
Tuition: $5 per class
Basic Fees: $10 ID fee per session
Credit: yes

Iowa

Clinton Community College
Enrollment Services
1000 Lincoln Blvd.
Clinton, IA 52732-6299
319-242-6841
Minimum Age: 62
Tuition: $3.65 per semester hour
Basic Fees: $5.50 per hour
Credit: yes

Des Moines Area Community College
Records and Services
2006 South Ankeny Blvd.
Ankeny, IA 50021
515-964-6241
Minimum Age: 65
Tuition: free
Basic Fees: none
Credit: yes

Indian Hills Community College
Admissions
525 Grandview St.
Ottumwa, IA 52501
515-683-5111
Minimum Age: 62
Tuition: 50% off (regular tuition $40 per credit hour)
Basic Fees: $4.50 per credit hour
Credit: yes

Iowa Western Community College
Business
923 East Washington St.
Clarinda, IA 51632
712-542-5117
Minimum Age: 55
Tuition: $22 per credit hour (3 credit hour limit per semester)
Basic Fees: $15 one time application fee plus $6 per credit hour
Credit: yes

Kansas

Allen County Community College
1801 North Cottonwood St.
Iola, KS 66749
316-365-5116
Minimum Age: 60
Tuition: $28 per credit hour (book rental and fees are free)
Basic Fees: none
Credit: yes

Barton County Community College
Registrar
Rt. 3, Box 1362

Great Bend, KS 67530-9283
316-792-2701 ext. 215
Minimum Age: 65
Tuition: free (must be resident of Colorado)
Basic Fees: $10 per credit hour
Credit: yes

Butler County Community College
901 South Haverhill Rd.
Eldorado, KS 67042
316-321-2222
Minimum Age: 60
Tuition: free
Basic Fees: $10 per credit hour
Credit: yes

Cloud County Community College
221 Campus Dr.
P.O. Box 1002
Concordia, KS 66901-1002
913-234-1435
Minimum Age: 55
Tuition: $24 per credit hour (fee will increase this fall)
Basic Fees: none
Credit: yes

Coffeyville Community College
400 West 11th
Coffeyville, KS 67337
316-251-7700
Minimum Age: 60
Tuition: free
Basic Fees: $10 per credit hour
Credit: yes

Emporia State University
Admissions
1200 Commercial
Emporia, KS 66801-5087
316-341-5465
Minimum Age: 60
Tuition: free
Basic Fees: none
Credit: no

Fort Hays State University
600 Park St.
Hays, KS 67601-4099
913-628-4222
Minimum Age: 60
Tuition: free
Basic Fees: none
Credit: no

Garden City Community College
Dean of Admissions
801 Campus Dr.
Garden City, KS 67846
316-276-7611
Minimum Age: 65
Tuition: free
Basic Fees: $7 per credit hour
Credit: yes

Hutchinson Community College
1300 North Plum St.
Hutchinson, KS 67501
316-665-3535
Minimum Age: 60
Tuition: $21 per credit hour
Basic Fees: none
Credit: yes

Kentucky

Ashland Community College
1400 College Dr.
Ashland, KY 41101
606-329-2999
Minimum Age: 65
Tuition: free
Basic Fees: none
Credit: yes

Eastern Kentucky University
Coates Box 2A
203 Jones Building
Richmond, KY 40475-3101
606-622-2106
Minimum Age: 65
Tuition: free
Basic Fees: none
Credit: yes

Elizabethtown Community College
600 College Street Rd.
Elizabethtown, KY 42701
502-769-1632
Minimum Age: 65
Tuition: free
Basic Fees: none
Credit: yes

Lexington Community College
203 Oswald Building
Cooper Dr.
Lexington, KY 40506-0235
606-257-4872
Minimum Age: 65
Tuition: free
Basic Fees: none
Credit: yes

Madisonville Community College
2000 College Dr.
Madisonville, KY 42431
502-821-2250
Minimum Age: 65
Tuition: free
Basic Fees: none
Credit: yes

Maysville Community College
1755 US 68
Maysville, KY 41056
606-759-7141
Minimum Age: 65
Tuition: free
Basic Fees: none
Credit: yes

Morehead State University
306 Howell McDowell
Morehead, KY 40351
606-783-2000
Minimum Age: 65
Tuition: free
Basic Fees: none
Credit: yes

Murray State University
Bursars Office
P.O. Box 9
Murray, KY 42071-0009
502-762-3741
800-272-4678
Minimum Age: 65
Tuition: free
Basic Fees: none
Credit: yes

Northern Kentucky University
Office of Admissions
Highland Heights, KY 41099-7010
606-572-5220
800-637-9948
Minimum Age: 65
Tuition: free
Basic Fees: none
Credit: yes

University of Kentucky
100 Funkhouser Bldg.
Lexington, KY 40506-0054
606-257-2000
Minimum Age: 65
Tuition: free
Basic Fees: none
Credit: yes

University of Louisville
Admission AO
University of Louisville
Louisville, KY 40292
502-852-6531
Minimum Age: 65
Tuition: free (10% off non-academic)
Basic Fees: none
Credit: yes

Louisiana

Delgado Community College
615 City Park Ave.
New Orleans, LA 70119
504-483-4114
Minimum Age: 60
Tuition: 3 credit hours free per semester
Basic Fees: $15 per semester
Credit: yes

Grambling State University
P.O. Box 864
Grambling, LA 71245
318-274-2435
Minimum Age: 65
Tuition: free
Basic Fees: $15 per semester
Credit: yes

Louisiana State University and Agricultural
and Mechanical College
Records and Registration
112 Thomas Boyd Hall
Baton Rouge, LA 70803
504-388-1175
Minimum Age: 65
Tuition: free
Basic Fees: none
Credit: yes

Louisiana State University at Alexandria
Financial Aid
8100 Highway 71 South
Alexandria, LA 71302-9633
318-473-6423
Minimum Age: 65
Tuition: free
Basic Fees: none
Credit: yes

Louisiana State University - Baton Rouge
Office of Admissions
Room 110 Thomas Boyd Hall
Baton Rouge, LA 70803
504-388-1175
Minimum Age: 65
Tuition: free
Basic Fees: none
Credit: yes

Louisiana State University at Eunice
P.O. Box 1129
Eunice, LA 70535
318-457-7311
Minimum Age: 65
Tuition: free
Basic Fees: $10 per semester
Credit: yes

Louisiana State University in Shreveport
Admissions and Records
One University Place
Shreveport, LA 71115
318-797-5207
Minimum Age: 65
Tuition: free; one time application fee of $5
Basic Fees: $50 for part-time; $65 for full-time
Credit: yes

Louisiana Tech University
P.O. Box 3178
Tech Station
Ruston, LA 71272

318-257-3036
Minimum Age: 65
Tuition: 1 class per quarter free
Basic Fees: $35 per quarter
Credit: yes

McNeese State University
P.O. Box 92495
Lake Charles, LA 70609
318-475-5000
Minimum Age: 60
Tuition: 3 credit hours free per semester
Basic Fees: $10 per semester
Credit: yes

Nicholls State University
P.O. Box 2004
College Station
Thibodaux, LA 70310
504-448-4139
Minimum Age: 60
Tuition: 3 credit hours free per semester
Basic Fees: $10 per semester
Credit: yes

Northeast Louisiana University
Student Affairs
Office of the Registrar
Monroe, LA 71209-1110
318-342-5252
Minimum Age: 60
Tuition: 3 credit hours free per semester
Basic Fees: $15 per semester
Credit: yes

Northwestern State University
Fiscal Affairs
Cashier Section
Natchitoches, LA 71497
318-357-4503
Minimum Age: 60
Tuition: 3 credit hours free per semester
Basic Fees: $5 one time application fee
Credit: yes

Southeastern Louisiana University
Enrollment Services
P.O. Drawer 752
Hammond, LA 70402-0752
504-549-2123
Minimum Age: 60
Tuition: 3 credit hours free per semester
Basic Fees: $10 per semester
Credit: yes

Maine

University of Maine
Admissions
7513 W. Chadbourne Hall
Orono, ME 04469
207-581-1561
Minimum Age: 65
Tuition: free
Basic Fees: $9 for 3 credit hours; $246.50 for
12 credit hours
Credit: yes

University of Maine at Augusta
Admissions
46 University Dr.
Augusta, ME 04330
207-621-3000
Minimum Age: 65
Tuition: free
Basic Fees: $4.50 per credit hour
Credit: yes

University of Maine at Farmington
102 Main St.
Farmington, ME 04938
207-778-7052
Minimum Age: 65
Tuition: no reduced rate; case by case basis

Basic Fees: case by case basis
Credit: yes

University of Maine at Fort Kent
Admissions
25 Pleasant St.
Fort Kent, ME 04743
207-834-7500
Minimum Age: 65
Tuition: free (2 course limit)
Basic Fees: $20 for 6 credit hours
Credit: yes

Maryland

Alleghany Community College
Continuing Education
Willow Brook Rd.
Cumberland, MD 21502
301-724-7700
Minimum Age: 60
Tuition: free (non-academic only)
Basic Fees: up to $3 per course
Credit: no

Baltimore City Community College
Registration
2901 Liberty Heights Ave.
Baltimore, MD 21215
410-462-8300
Minimum Age: 60
Tuition: free
Basic Fees: $20 per credit hour (non-credit
$10 per course)
Credit: yes

Bowie State University
Human Resources
14000 Jericho Park Rd.
Bowie, MD 20715
301-464-6515
Minimum Age: 62
Tuition: free
Basic Fees: $83.50 for 0-11 credit hours; $369
for 12+ credit hours
Credit: yes

Coppin State College
Human Resources
2500 W. North Ave.
Baltimore, MD 21216
410-383-5990
Minimum Age: 60
Tuition: free
Basic Fees: part-time $47 plus $8 per credit
hour; $333 for 12 credit hours
Credit: yes

Frostburg State University
Admissions
Frostburg, MD 21532-1099
687-680-4201
Minimum Age: 60
Tuition: free (3 course limit)
Basic Fees: 9 credit hours approximately $115
Credit: yes

Salisbury State University
Human Resourses
Camden and College Avenues
Salisbury, MD 21801-6862
410-543-6035
Minimum Age: 60
Tuition: free (2 course limit)
Basic Fees: 6 credit hours approximately $18
Credit: yes

St. Mary's College of Maryland
Admission
St. Mary's City, MD 20686
301-862-0292
Minimum Age: 60
Tuition: free; apply for waiver
Basic Fees: $230 for 9-11 credit hours if space
available
Credit: yes

University of Maryland - College Park
Golden ID Program
College Park, MD 20742
301-314-8237
Minimum Age: 65 (60 if employed less than
20 hours per week)
Tuition: $103.50 per semester (3 class limit
per semester)
Basic Fees: $30 one time application fee
Credit: yes

Massachusetts

Berkshire Community College
1350 West St.
Pittsfield, MA 01201
413-499-4660
Minimum Age: 60
Tuition: free
Basic Fees: $25 per credit hour
Credit: yes

Boston University
881 Commonwealth Ave., 6th Floor
Boston, MA 02215
617-353-2300
Minimum Age: 60
Tuition: $20 per course
Basic Fees: none
Credit: no

Bridgewater State College
Gates House
Bridgewater, MA 02325
508-697-1237
Minimum Age: 60
Tuition: 50% off regular fee
Basic Fees: $201.42 for 3 credit hours;
$491.25 for 12 credit hours
Credit: yes

Briston Community College
777 Elsbree St.
Fall River, MA 02720
508-678-2811
Minimum Age: 60
Tuition: $42 for 3 credit hours, $55 for 4 credit
hours
Basic Fees: none
Credit: yes

Bunker Hill Community College
250 New Rutherford Ave.
Boston, MA 02129-2991
617-228-2000
Minimum Age: 60
Tuition: free
Basic Fees: $35 per credit hour
Credit: yes

Cape Cod Community College
Rt. 132
West Barnstable, MA 02668-1599
508-362-2131
Minimum Age: 60
Tuition: 50% off fees; apply for waiver
Basic Fees: $138 for 3 credit hours
Credit: yes

Salem State College
352 Lafayette St.
Salem, MA 01970
508-741-6200
Minimum Age: 60
Tuition: $41-60 per credit
Basic Fees: $61 per credit hour; full-time
$743.50
Credit: yes

North Adams State College
Admissions
Church St.
North Adams, MA 01247
413-662-5000

Minimum Age: 65
Tuition: free
Basic Fees: none
Credit: yes

Michigan

Alpena Community College
666 Johnson St.
Alpena, MI 49707
517-356-9021
Minimum Age: 60
Basic Fees: $10 per session plus $6 per credit
hour
Tuition: free
Credit: yes

Central Michigan University
Admissions
105 Warriner Hall
Mount Pleasant, MI 48859
517-774-3076
Minimum Age: 60
Tuition: free
Basic Fees: none
Credit: no

Charles Stewart Mott Community College
4503 East Court St.
Flint, MI 48503
810-762-0200
Minimum Age: 60
Tuition: free (50% off non-academic)
Basic Fees: none
Credit: yes

Delta College
Admissions
University Center, MI 48710
517-686-9092
Minimum Age: 60
Tuition: 50% off (regular tuition $65 per credit
hour)
Basic Fees: $25 per session
Credit: yes

Glen Oaks Community College
62249 Shimmel Rd.
Centreville, MI 49032
616-467-9945
Minimum Age: 60
Tuition: based on context hours
Basic Fees: none
Credit: yes

Macomb Community College
2800 College Dr., SW
Sidney, MI 48885-0300
517-328-2111 ext. 215
Minimum Age: 60
Tuition: in-district 50% off tuition; out-of-
district $22 per credit hour
Basic Fees: $1.50 per credit hour
Credit: yes

Oakland Community College
District Office
George AB
Administration Center
2480 Opdyke Rd.
Bloomfield Hills, MI 48304-2266
810-540-1567
Minimum Age: 60
Tuition: 20% off (regular tuition $47 per credit
hour)
Basic Fees: $35 per session
Credit: yes

Wayne State University
Office of Undergraduate Admission
Detroit, MI 48202
313-577-3577
Minimum Age: 60
Tuition: 50% off (regular tuition $98 per credit
hour)

Basic Fees: $70 per semester
Credit: yes

Western Michigan University
Office of Admission and Orientation
Kalamazoo, MI 49008-5120
616-387-2000
Minimum Age: 62
Tuition: free
Basic Fees: none
Credit: no

University of Michigan - Ann Arbor
515 East Jefferson
1220 Student Activities
Ann Arbor, MI 48109-1316
313-764-7433
Minimum Age: 65
Tuition: 50% off (regular tuition full-time $2,500)
Basic Fees: $87 per term
Credit: yes

Minnesota

Anoka-Ramsey Community College
11200 Mississippi Blvd., NW
Coon Rapids, MN 55433
612-427-2600
Minimum Age: 62
Tuition: $10 per credit hour
Basic Fees: $15 per session plus $1 per credit hour
Credit: yes

Austin Community College
1600 Eighth Ave., NW
Austin, MN 55912
507-433-0535
Minimum Age: 62
Tuition: $6 per credit hour
Basic Fees: 0-7 credit hours free; 8+ credit hours $15 plus $2 per credit hour
Credit: yes

Bemidji State University
1500 Birchmont Dr., NE
Bemidji, MN 56601
218-755-2040
Minimum Age: 62
Tuition: $10 per credit hour
Basic Fees: $15 per session
Credit: yes

Brainerd Community College
501 West College Dr.
Brainerd, MN 56401
218-828-2508
Minimum Age: 62
Tuition: $10 per credit hour
Basic Fees: $15 per session plus $2 per credit hour
Credit: yes

Fergus Falls Community College
1414 College Way
Fergus Falls, MN 56537
218-739-7501
Minimum Age: 62
Tuition: $6 per credit hour
Basic Fees: 0-7 credit hours free; 8+ credit hours $15 plus $3 per credit hour
Credit: yes

Hibbing Community College
1515 East 25th St.
Hibbing, MN 55746
218-262-6700
Minimum Age: 62
Tuition: $6 per credit hour
Basic Fees: 0-7 credit hours free; 8+ credit hours $15 plus $2 per credit hour
Credit: yes

Minnesota Universities - Twin Cities
Room 240, Pillsbury Dr., SE
Minneapolis, MN 55455
800-752-1000
Minimum Age: 62
Tuition: $6 per credit hour
Basic Fees: none
Credit: yes

Mississippi

Copiah-Lincoln Community College
Financial Aid Office
P.O. Box 649
Wesson, MS 39191
601-643-8307
Minimum Age: 65
Tuition: free
Basic Fees: none
Credit: yes

Delta State University
Registrar
Cleveland, MS 38733
601-846-4656
Minimum Age: 60
Tuition: $10 for 1 course up to 3 credit hours
Basic Fees: none
Credit: yes

East Central Community College
Admissions
Decatur, MS 39327
601-635-2111
Minimum Age: 65
Tuition: free
Basic Fees: none
Credit: yes

Holmes Community College
P.O. Box 369
Goodman, MS 39079
601-472-2312
Minimum Age: 65
Tuition: free
Basic Fees: none
Credit: yes

Itawamba Community College
Admissions
602 W. Hill St.
Fulton, MS 38843
601-862-3101
Minimum Age: 65
Tuition: free
Basic Fees: none
Credit: yes

Jones County Junior College
Guidance Office
900 South Court St.
Ellisville, MS 39437
601-477-4025
Minimum Age: 65
Tuition: free
Basic Fees: none
Credit: yes

Meridian Community College
910 Highway 19 North
Meridian, MS 39307
601-483-8241
Minimum Age: 65
Tuition: $2.50 per class
Basic Fees: none
Credit: yes

Mississippi Gulf Coast Community College:
Jackson County Campus
Business Services
P.O. Box 100
Gautier, MS 39553
601-497-9602
Minimum Age: 65 (62-64 also qualify if retired)

Tuition: free
Basic Fees: none
Credit: yes

Missouri

Crowder College
601 LaClede Ave.
Neosho, MO 64850
417-451-3223
Minimum Age: 60
Tuition: free
Basic Fees: $12 per credit hour
Credit: yes

East Central College
Registration
P.O. Box 529
Union, MO 63048
314-583-5193
Minimum Age: 60
Tuition: free
Basic Fees: none
Credit: yes

Jefferson College
Continuing Education
1000 Viking Dr.
Hillsboro, MO 63050
314-789-3951
Minimum Age: 60
Tuition: 50% off (regular tuition $38 per credit hour)
Basic Fees: $1 for a Lifetime Card
Credit: no

Lincoln University
820 Chestnut St.
Jefferson City, MO 65102-0029
314-681-5000
Minimum Age: 60
Tuition: $12 per course
Basic Fees: $17 per session
Credit: no

Longview Community College
500 Longview Rd., SW
Lee's Summit, MO 64081
816-672-2000
Minimum Age: 65
Tuition: free
Basic Fees: none
Credit: yes

Maple Woods Community College
Development Center
2601 Northeast Barry Rd.
Kansas City, MO 64156
816-437-3050
Minimum Age: 65
Tuition: free
Basic Fees: none
Credit: yes

Missouri Southern State College
Business Office
3950 East Newman Rd.
Joplin, MO 64801-1595
417-625-9300
Minimum Age: 60
Tuition: free
Basic Fees: none
Credit: yes

Missouri Western State College
4525 Downs Dr.
St. Joseph, MO 64507
816-271-4200
Minimum Age: 60
Tuition: free
Basic Fees: none
Credit: yes

Moberly Area Community College
Financial Aid Office
College Ave. and Rollins St.
Moberly, MO 65270
816-263-4110
Minimum Age: 60
Tuition: free
Basic Fees: none
Credit: yes

St. Louis Community College
Office of Admission
11333 Big Bend Blvd.
Kirkwood, MO 63122
314-984-7601
Minimum Age: 62
Tuition: 50% off (regular tuition $40 per credit hour)
Basic Fees: none
Credit: yes

Montana

Dawson Community College
Business Office
300 College Dr.
Glendive, MT 59330
406-365-3396
Minimum Age: 60
Tuition: free
Basic Fees: none (most books can be borrowed)
Credit: yes

Flathead Valley Community College
777 Grandview Dr.
Kalispell, MT 59901
406-756-3846
Minimum Age: 62
Tuition: $30.25 per credit hour
Basic Fees: none
Credit: yes

Fort Belknap College
P.O. Box 159
Harlem, MT 59526
406-353-2607
Minimum Age: 55 (must be a member of a federally recognized tribe)
Tuition: free
Basic Fees: none
Credit: yes

Fort Peck Community College
P.O. Box 398
Poplar, MT 59255
406-768-5551
Minimum Age: 60
Tuition: free
Basic Fees: $12 per credit hour
Credit: yes

Miles Community College
2715 Dickinson St.
Miles City, MT 59301
406-232-3031
Minimum Age: 62
Tuition: free
Basic Fees: none
Credit: yes

Montana College of Mineral Science and Technology
1300 West Park St.
Butte, MT 59701
406-496-4178
800-445-8324
Minimum Age: 62
Tuition: apply for waiver
Basic Fees: $26.25 for 3 credit hours; $171 for 12 credit hours Credit: yes

Northern Montana College
P.O. Box 7751

Havre, MT 59501
406-265-3700
Minimum Age: 62
Tuition: free
Basic Fees: $80.25 for 3 credit hours
Credit: yes

Western Montana College at the University of Montana
Continuing Education
710 South Atlantic
Dillon, MT 59725
406-683-7537
Minimum Age: 62
Tuition: 1 credit hour $20 and $3 for each additional credit hour
Basic Fees: $30
Credit: yes

University of Montana
Missoula, MT 59812
406-243-0211
Minimum Age: 62
Tuition: all state supported costs waived; no discount on tuition
Basic Fees: $30 one time fee
Credit: yes

Nebraska

Chadron State College
Admissions
1000 Main St.
Chadron, NE 69337
308-432-6263
Minimum Age: 62
Tuition: no discount on tuition
Basic Fees: $35 for 3 credit hours
Credit: yes

McNook Community College
Registrar
1205 East Third St.
McNook, NE 69001
308-345-6303
800-348-5343
Minimum Age: 62
Tuition: free
Basic Fees: none
Credit: no

Metropolita Community College
Student Accounts
P.O. Box 3777
Omaha, NE 68103
402-449-8418
Minimum Age: 62
Tuition: 50% off (regular tuition $23 per credit hour)
Basic Fees: none
Credit: yes

Mid-Plains Community College
Accounting
1101 Halligan Dr.
North Platte, NE 69101
308-532-8740
Minimum Age: 60
Tuition: free
Basic Fees: $1.50 per credit hour
Credit: yes

Nebraska Indian Community College
Financial Aid Office
Mayce, NE 42837
402-878-2414
Minimum Age: 55
Tuition: free
Basic Fees: $10 one time application fee
Credit: yes

Southeast Community College: Beatrice Campus
Adult Education

Rt. 2, Box 35A
Beatrice, NE 68310
402-228-3468
Minimum Age: 62
Tuition: no discount on tuition (regular tuition $35.25 per credit hour)
Basic Fees: none
Credit: no

Southeast Community College: Lincoln Campus
Cashier
8800 O St.
Lincoln, NE 68520
402-437-2600
Minimum Age: 62
Tuition: no discount on tuition; cashier: 402-437-2558
Basic Fees: varies by class
Credit: no

Southeast Community College: Milford Campus
Student Accounts
Rt. 2, Box D
Milford, NE 68405
402-761-2131
800-999-7223
Minimum Age: 65
Tuition: no discount on tuition
Basic Fees: varies by class
Credit: no

Nevada

Community College of Southern Nevada
3200 East Cheyenne Ave.
North Las Vegas, NV 89030
702-651-4060
Minimum Age: 62
Tuition: free
Basic Fees: none
Credit: yes

Northern Nevada Community College
1500 College Parkway
Elko, NV 89801
702-738-8493
Minimum Age: 62
Tuition: free
Basic Fees: none
Credit: yes

Truckee Meadows Community College
7000 Dandini Blvd.
Reno, NV 89512
702-673-7000
Minimum Age: 62
Tuition: free
Basic Fees: none
Credit: yes

University of Nevada: Las Vegas
4505 Maryland Pkwy.
Las Vegas, NV 89154-1021
702-895-3011
Minimum Age: 62
Tuition: free
Basic Fees: none
Credit: yes

University of Nevada: Reno
Records and Enrollment Services
Reno, NV 89557
702-784-6865
Minimum Age: 62
Tuition: tuition waiver fall-spring, 50% off during summer
Basic Fees: none
Credit: yes

Western Nevada Community College
2201 West College Pkwy.
Carson City, NV 89703

702-887-3138
Minimum Age: 62
Tuition: free spring and fall only
Basic Fees: none
Credit: yes

New Hampshire

New Hampshire Technical College: Berlin
2020 Riverside Dr.
Berlin, NH 03570
603-752-1113
800-445-4525
Minimum Age: 65
Tuition: free
Basic Fees: $16 for 3 credit hours
Credit: yes

New Hampshire Technical College: Claremont
One College Dr.
Claremont, NH 03743
603-542-7744
Minimum Age: 65
Tuition: free
Basic Fees: $10 per course
Credit: yes

New Hampshire Technical College: Manchester
1066 Front St.
Manchester, NH 03102
603-668-6706
Minimum Age: 65
Tuition: free
Basic Fees: none
Credit: yes

New Hampshire Technical College: Nashua
505 Amherst St.
Nashua, NH 03063
603-882-6923
Minimum Age: 65
Tuition: free
Basic Fees: none
Credit: no

New Hampshire Technical College: Stratham
Tech Dr. and Rt. 101
277 Portsmouth Ave.
Stratham, NH 03885
603-772-1194
Minimum Age: 65
Tuition: free
Basic Fees: none
Credit: yes

New Hampshire Technical Institute
Institute Dr.
Concord, NH 03301-7412
603-225-1800
Minimum Age: 65
Tuition: free
Basic Fees: none
Credit: yes

Notre Dame College
2321 Elm St.
Manchester, NH 03104
603-669-4298
Minimum Age: 65
Tuition: free (2 course per semester limit - 6 courses per year)
Basic Fees: $60 per semester
Credit: yes

Plymouth State College of the University System of New Hampshire
Bursars
17 High St.
Plymouth, NH 03264-1600
603-535-2237
Minimum Age: 65
Tuition: free

Basic Fees: $35 per credit hour
Credit: yes

School for Lifelong Learning
Learner Services
NSNH
125 N. State St.
Concord, NH 03301
603-228-8300
Minimum Age: 65
Tuition: free
Basic Fees: $15 per session
Credit: yes

University of New Hampshire at Manchester
220 Hackett Hill Rd.
Manchester, NH 03102
603-668-0700
Minimum Age: 65
Tuition: free up to 8 credit hours, 8 credit hours or 2 non-credit courses; no discount if courses are being taken for economic gain; space available basis
Basic Fees: none
Credit: yes

New Jersey

Atlantic Community College
5100 Black Horse Pike
Mays Landing, NJ 08330
609-343-4922
Minimum Age: 62
Tuition: free
Basic Fees: $20 per session
Credit: yes

Bergen Community College
Admissions and Registration
400 Paramus Rd.
Paramus, NJ 07652
201-447-7857
Minimum Age: 65
Tuition: $9.50 per credit hour
Basic Fees: $8.60 per credit hour
Credit: yes

Brookdale Community College
765 Newman Springs Rd.
Lincroft, NJ 07738
908-842-1900
Minimum Age: 65
Tuition: free
Basic Fees: $28 for 3 credit hours
Credit: yes

Burlington County College
Admission
County Rt. 530
Pemberton, NJ 08068
609-894-9311
Minimum Age: 62
Tuition: $65 for 3 credit hours
Basic Fees: none
Credit: yes

Camden County College
P.O. Box 200
Blackwood, NJ 08012
609-227-7200
Minimum Age: 62 (55 if unemployed)
Tuition: free
Basic Fees: none
Credit: yes

County College of Morris
214 Center Grove Rd.
Randolf, NJ 07869
201-328-5000
Minimum Age: 65
Tuition: $5 per credit hour
Basic Fees: none
Credit: yes

Essex County College
303 University Ave.
Newark, NJ 07102
201-877-3100
Minimum Age: 60
Tuition: free
Basic Fees: none
Credit: yes

Rowan State College
Oak Hall
Glassboro, NJ 08028
609-256-4200
Minimum Age: 55
Tuition: free; space available basis
Basic Fees: none
Credit: no

Gloucester County College
Business Office
Tanyard Rd.
Deptford Township
RR #4, Box 203
Sewell Post Office, NJ 08080
609-468-5000
Minimum Age: 60
Tuition: $5 per credit hour
Basic Fees: $10 per credit hour
Credit: yes

Jersey City State College
2039 Kennedy Blvd.
Bursars Office
Jersey City, NJ 07305
201-200-3234
Minimum Age: 62
Tuition: free
Basic Fees: $73.50 for 3 credit hours
Credit: yes

Kean College of New Jersey
1000 Morris Ave.
Union, NJ 07083
908-527-2195
Minimum Age: 62
Tuition: free; space available basis
Basic Fees: $60 for 3 credit hours
Credit: yes

Mercer County Community College
1200 Old Trenton Rd.
Trenton, NJ 08690-1099
609-586-0505
Minimum Age: 65
Tuition: free; must be resident of Mercer County
Basic Fees: none
Credit: yes

Middlesex County College
155 Mill Rd.
P.O. Box 3050
Edison, NJ 08818
808-906-2510
Minimum Age: 65
Tuition: apply for waiver
Basic Fees: $20 per semester plus $6 per credit hour
Credit: yes

Montclair State College
Normal Ave. and Valley Rd.
Upper Montclair, NJ 07043
201-655-4136
Minimum Age: 65
Tuition: free
Basic Fees: $25 per session
Credit: yes

Ocean County College
College Dr.
P.O. Box 2001
Toms River, NJ 08754
908-255-0304

Minimum Age: 65
Tuition: $24 per credit hour
Basic Fees: $15 per semester
Credit: yes

Ramapo College of New Jersey
505 Ramapo Valley Rd.
Mahwah, NJ 07430
201-529-7700
Minimum Age: 65
Tuition: free
Basic Fees: none
Credit: no

State University of New Jersey - Rutgers
Office of University Undergraduate
Admissions
Administrative Services Bldg.
P.O. Box 2101
New Brunswick, NJ 08903-2101
908-445-3770
Minimum Age: 62
Tuition: free
Basic Fees: none
Credit: no

New Mexico

Clovis Community College
417 Schepps Blvd.
Clovis, NM 88101
505-769-4025
Minimum Age: 65
Tuition: $13 first credit hour, $5 for each
additional credit hour
Basic Fees: none
Credit: yes

New Mexico State College at Carlsbad
1500 University Dr.
Calrsbad, NM 88220
505-885-8831
Minimum Age: 65
Tuition: $6 per credit hour
Basic Fees: $10 one time admission fee
Credit: yes

New Mexico State University
Registrars Office
Las Cruces, NM 88003
505-646-3121
Minimum Age: 65
Tuition: $25 per hour; NM residents only (6
credit hour limit in the fall)
Basic Fees: $15 per semester for part-time
(full-time free)
Credit: yes

New Mexico State University at Alamogordo
Admissions
P.O. Box 477
Alamogordo, NM 88311
505-439-3600
Minimum Age: 65
Tuition: $8 per credit hour for in-district, $13
per credit hour out-of-district
Basic Fees: $10 one time admission fee (6
credit hour limit)
Credit: yes

New Mexico State University at Grants
1500 North Third St.
Grants, NM 87020
505-287-7981
Minimum Age: 65
Tuition: $8 per credit hour
Basic Fees: $10 one time application fee
Credit: yes

University of New Mexico
Cashier
Student Services Center
Room 140
Albuquerque, NM 87131
505-277-5363

800-225-5866
Minimum Age: 65
Tuition: $5 per credit hour (6 credit hour limit)
Basic Fees: none
Credit: yes

New York

Adirondack Community College
Registrar
Bay Rd.
Queensbury, NY 12804
518-743-2264
Minimum Age: 60
Tuition: free
Basic Fees: none
Credit: no

Broome Community College
Student Accounts
P.O. Box 1017
Binghamton, NY 13902
607-778-5000
Minimum Age: 60
Tuition: free
Basic Fees: none
Credit: no

Cayuga County Community College
Records Office
197 Franklin St.
Auburn, NY 13021
315-255-1743
Minimum Age: 60
Tuition: free; space available basis
Basic Fees: none
Credit: no

City University of New York: Baruch College
P.O. Box 279
17 Lexington Ave.
New York, NY 10010
212-802-2222
Minimum Age: 62
Tuition: free
Basic Fees: $52 per session
Credit: yes

City University of New York: Bronx
Community College
Bursars Office
West 181st and University Ave.
New York, NY 10453
718-289-5100
Minimum Age: 65
Tuition: free
Basic Fees: $52 per session
Credit: yes

City University of New York: Brooklyn
College
1602 William James Hall
2900 Bedford Ave.
Brooklyn, NY 11210
718-951-5000
Minimum Age: 65
Tuition: $50 per session
Basic Fees: $50 per session
Credit: yes

City University of New York: City College
Convent Ave. at 138th St.
New York, NY 10031
212-650-6977
Minimum Age: 65
Tuition: free
Basic Fees: $52 per session
Credit: yes

City University of New York: College of
Staten Island
Registrar
2800 Victory Blvd.

Bldg. 2A-110
Staten Island, NY 10314
718-982-2000
Minimum Age: 65
Tuition: free
Basic Fees: $52 per session
Credit: yes

City University of New York: Hostos
Community College
Admissions
500 Grand Concourse
Bronx, NY 10451
718-518-4444
Minimum Age: 65
Tuition: $75 per semester
Basic Fees: $52 per session
Credit: yes

City University of New York: Hunter College
Admissions
695 Park Ave.
Room 203, North Bldg.
New York, NY 10021
212-772-4490
Minimum Age: 65
Tuition: free
Basic Fees: $52 per session
Credit: yes

City University of New York: Kingsborough
Community College
2001 Oriental Blvd.
Brooklyn, NY 11235
718-368-5079
Minimum Age: 65
Tuition: free
Basic Fees: no registration fee
Credit: yes

North Carolina

Alamance Community College
Student Services
P.O. Box 8000
Graham, NC 27253
910-578-2002
Minimum Age: 65
Tuition: free
Basic Fees: none
Credit: yes

Anson Community College
P.O. Box 126
Polkton, NC 28135
704-272-7635
Minimum Age: 65
Tuition: free
Basic Fees: $2 per quarter plus $5 per credit
hour
Credit: yes

Appalachian State University
Cashier's Office
Administration Bldg.
Boone, NC 28608
704-262-2120
Minimum Age: 65
Tuition: free plus fees (lab, etc.)
Basic Fees: $117.50 for 3 credit hours; $235
for 6 credit hours
Credit: yes

Beaufort County Community College
P.O. Box 1069
Washington, NC 27889
919-946-6194
Minimum Age: 65
Tuition: free
Basic Fees: maximum $6 activity fee per
semester
Credit: yes

Bladen Community College
P.O. Box 266
Dublin, NC 28332
910-862-2164
Minimum Age: 65
Tuition: free
Basic Fees: none
Credit: yes

Blue Ridge Community College
College Dr.
Flat Rock, NC 28731
704-692-3572
Minimum Age: 65
Tuition: free
Basic Fees: $1.25 per quarter
Credit: yes

Brunswick Community College
P.O. Box 30
Supply, NC 28462
910-754-6900
Minimum Age: 65
Tuition: free
Basic Fees: $1.05 per quarter
Credit: yes

Cape Fear Community College
411 North Front St.
Wilmington, NC 28401-3993
910-343-0481
Minimum Age: 65
Tuition: free
Basic Fees: $1 ID fee per semester, maximum
$6 activity fee per semester
Credit: yes

Carteret Community College
3505 Arendell St.
Morehead City, NC 28557
919-247-4142
Minimum Age: 65
Tuition: free
Basic Fees: $3.25 for 3 credit hours
Credit: yes

Catawba Valley Community College
2550 Highway 70, SE
Hickory, NC 28602
704-327-7009
Minimum Age: 65
Tuition: free
Basic Fees: $1.75 per quarter
Credit: yes

North Carolina University - Raleigh
Adult Credit Program
Box 7401
Raleigh, NC 27695-7401
919 515-2434
Minimum Age: 65
Tuition: free
Basic Fees: none
Credit: yes

University of North Carolina - Chapel Hill
CB# 2200, Jackson Hall
Chapel Hill, NC 27599
919-966-3621
Minimum Age: 65
Tuition: free
Basic Fees: $10 per semester
Credit: yes

North Dakota

North Dakota State University
P.O. Box 5454
Admissions
Fargo, ND 58105
701-231-8643
Minimum Age: 65
Tuition: free
Basic Fees: $20 per session
Credit: no

North Dakota State University: Bottineau and
Institute of Forestry
First and Simrall Blvd.
Bottineau, ND 58318
Minimum Age: 65
701-228-2277
Minimum Age: 55
Tuition: free
Basic Fees: none
Credit: no

Standing Rock College
HCI Box 4
Fort Yates, ND 58538
701-854-3861
Tuition: free (tuition, books and fees all
waived if you don't qualify for Pell Grant)
Basic Fees: none (see above)
Credit: yes

University of North Dakota: Lake Region
1801 College Dr., North
Devils Lake, ND 58301-1598
701-662-1600
Minimum Age: 65
Tuition: free
Basic Fees: none
Credit: no

University of North Dakota: Williston
1410 University Ave.
Williston, ND 58801
701-774-4210
Minimum Age: 65
Tuition: free
Basic Fees: $10 per credit hour
Credit: no

Valley City State University
101 College St., SE
Valley City, ND 58072
701-845-7990
Minimum Age: 65
Tuition: free
Basic Fees: none
Credit: no

Ohio

Belmont Technical College
120 Fox Shannon Pl.
St. Clarisville, OH 43950
614-695-9500
Minimum Age: 60
Tuition: free
Basic Fees: none
Credit: yes

Bowling Green State University
Department of Continuing Education
McFall Center
40 College Park
Bowling Green, OH 43403
419-372-2086
Minimum Age: 60
Tuition: free; space available basis
Basic Fees: none
Credit: no

Bowling Green State University - Firelands
College
901 Rye Beach Rd.
Huron, OH 44839
419-433-5560
Minimum Age: 60
Tuition: free; $10 registry fee
Basic Fees: $5 per semester
Credit: no

Central Ohio Technical College
1179 University Dr.
Newark, OH 43055
614-366-9222
Minimum Age: 60

Tuition: free
Basic Fees: $5 per credit hour
Credit: no

Central State University
Registrar
1400 Brush Row Rd.
Wilberforce, OH 45384
513-376-6231
Minimum Age: 60
Tuition: free
Basic Fees: none
Credit: no

Cuyahoga Community College District
Downtown Campus
Office of Admissions
2900 Community College Ave.
Cleveland, OH 44115
216-987-4200
Minimum Age: 60
Tuition: free
Basic Fees: none
Credit: yes

Kent State University
P.O. Box 5190
Kent, OH 44242-0001
216-672-2444
Minimum Age: 5O and retired or 60
Tuition: free
Basic Fees: none
Credit: no

Ohio State University
Continuing Education
152 Mount Hall
Columbus, OH 43210
614-292-8860
Minimum Age: 60
Tuition: free
Basic Fees: none
Credit: no

University of Akron
381 Buchtel Common
Akron, OH 44325-2001
216-972-7100
Minimum Age: 60
Tuition: free (3 course limit)
Basic Fees: none
Credit: no

University of Cincinnati
Office of Admission
P.O. Box 210091
Cincinnati, OH 45221-0091
513-556-1100
Minimum Age: 60
Tuition: free
Basic Fees: none
Credit: no

University of Toledo
Evening Session
University of Toledo
Toledo, OH 43606-3398
419-530-4137
Minimum Age: 60
Tuition: free (income limitation of $50,000
annually)
Basic Fees: none
Credit: yes

Oklahoma

Cameron University
Business Office
2800 West Fore Blvd.
Lawton, OK 73505
405-581-2230
Minimum Age: 65
Tuition: free
Basic Fees: none
Credit: no

Carl Albert State College
P.O. Box 1507 South McLenna
Poteau, OK 74953-5208
918-647-1200
Minimum Age: 65
Tuition: free
Basic Fees: none
Credit: no

Connors State College
Business Office
Rt. 1, Box 1000
Warner, OK 74469
918-463-6250
Minimum Age: 65
Tuition: free
Basic Fees: none
Credit: no

Oklahoma Panhandle State University
P.O. Box 430
Goodwell, OK 73939
405-349-2611
Minimum Age: 65
Tuition: free; space available basis only
Basic Fees: none
Credit: no

Oklahoma State University
104 Whitehurse
Stillwater, OK 74078
405-744-6858
Minimum Age: 65
Tuition: free
Basic Fees: none
Credit: no

University of Oklahoma
Office of Admissions
1000 Asp Ave.
Room 127
Norman, OK 73019
405-325-2251
Minimum Age: 65
Tuition: free
Basic Fees: none
Credit: no

Oregon
Blue Mountain Community College
Continuing Education
P.O. Box 100
Pendleton, OR 97801
503-276-1260
Minimum Age: 60
Tuition: $10 per credit hour
Basic Fees: none
Credit: yes

Central Oregon Community College
Admissions
2600 Northwest College Way
Bend, OR 97701
541-382-6112
Minimum Age: 62
Tuition: 25% off (regular tuition $32 per credit hour)
Basic Fees: $1.50 per credit hour
Credit: yes

Chemeketa Community College
Business Office
P.O. Box 14007
4000 Lancaster Dr., NE
Salem, OR 97305
503-399-5006
Minimum Age: 62
Tuition: 35% off (regular tuition $32 per credit hour)
Basic Fees: none
Credit: yes

Clackamas Community College
19600 South Molalla Ave.

Oregon City, OR 97045
503-657-6958
Minimum Age: 62
Tuition: free
Basic Fees: none
Credit: yes

Clatsop Community College
Extended Learning
1653 Jerome Ave.
Astoria, OR 97103
503-325-0910
Minimum Age: 62
Tuition: 50% off (another 10% for early payment-regular tuition $30 per credit hour
Basic Fees: none
Credit: yes

Lane Community College
Admissions
4000 East 30th Ave.
Eugene, OR 97405
541-726-2207
Minimum Age: 62
Tuition: 50% off (regular tuition $30 per credit hour)
Basic Fees: none
Credit: yes

Linn-Benton Community College
Registration
6500 Pacific Blvd., Southwest
Albany, OR 97321-3779
541-917-4999
Minimum Age: 62
Tuition: 50% off (regular tuition $32 per credit hour)
Basic Fees: none
Credit: yes

Mount Hood Community College
Business Office
26000 Southeast Stark St.
Gresham, OR 97030
503-667-6422
Minimum Age: 62
Tuition: free
Basic Fees: none (self-enrichment classes are usually $5 each plus materials)
Credit: yes

Oregon Institute of Technology
Registrar
3201 Campus Dr.
Klamath Falls, OR 97601-8801
541-885-1150
800-343-6653
Minimum Age: 65
Tuition: free
Basic Fees: none to audit
Credit: no

Oregon State University
Corvallis, OR 97331
503-737-4411
Minimum Age: 65
Tuition: free to audit
Basic Fees: none
Credit: no

Portland Community College
Admissions
P.O. Box 19000
Portland, OR 97280-0990
503-244-6111 ext. 4724
Minimum Age: 62
Tuition: 50% off (regular tuition $30 per credit hour)
Basic Fees: $7 for full-time per quarter; $2 for part-time per quarter
Credit: yes

Portland State University
Senior Adult Learning Center

P.O. Box 751
Portland, OR 97207-0751
503-725-3511
800-547-8887
Minimum Age: 65
Tuition: free to audit
Basic Fees: none
Credit: no

Pennsylvania
Bloomsburg University of Pennsylvania
Extended Learning
700 West Main St.
Bloomsburg, PA 17815
717-389-4420
Minimum Age: 60
Tuition: free; space available basis
Basic Fees: $42.50 for 3 credit hours; $304 for 12 credit hours
Credit: yes

Bucks County Community College
Swamp Rd.
Newtown, PA 18940
215-968-8100
Minimum Age: 65
Tuition: free
Basic Fees: $48-$57 per semester
Credit: yes

Butler County Community College
Registrar
P.O. Box 1203
Butler, PA 16003-1203
412-287-8711
Minimum Age: 60
Tuition: free
Basic Fees: none
Credit: no

California University of Pennsylvania
COPE Program
250 University Ave.
California, PA 15419
412-938-5930
Minimum Age: 60
Tuition: free
Basic Fees: $135 for 3 credit hours; $408 for 12 credit hours
Credit: yes

Clarion University of Pennsylvania
Admissions
B-16 Carrier Hall
Clarion, PA 16214
814-226-2306
Minimum Age: 65
Tuition: free
Basic Fees: none
Credit: no

Community College of Beaver County
One Campus Dr.
Monaca, PA 15061
412-775-8561
Minimum Age: 65
Tuition: free
Basic Fees: $20 per session
Credit: yes

Pennsylvania State University
201 Shields
University Park, PA 16802
814-865-6528
Minimum Age: 60
Tuition: free
Basic Fees: none
Credit: yes (evening classes)

University of Pennsylvania
3440 Market St., Suite 100
Philadelphia, PA 19104
215-898-7326

Minimum Age: 65
Tuition: $50 donation for 1 class; $75 donation for 2 classes
Basic Fees: none
Credit: no

University of Pittsburgh
407 CL
Pittsburgh, PA 15260
412-624-7308
Minimum Age: 60
Tuition: $15 per class
Basic Fees: none
Credit: no

Rhode Island

Community College of Rhode Island
Admissions
400 East Ave.
Warwick, RI 02886
401-825-2285
Minimum Age: 62
Tuition: free; apply for waiver
Basic Fees: $15 per session
Credit: yes

Rhode Island College
Records Office
600 Mt. Pleasant Ave.
Providence, RI 02908
401-456-8234
Minimum Age: 65
Tuition: free plus registration fee
Basic Fees: $135 full-time per semester
Credit: yes

University of Rhode Island
Financial Aid
Kingston, RI 02881-0806
401-792-2314
Minimum Age: 60
Tuition: free (income limitation); apply for waiver; space available basis
Basic Fees: $96 for 3 credit hours; $619 for 12 credit hours plus $480 for insurance, which can be waived if they have comprable coverage
Credit: yes

South Carolina

Aiken Technical College
P.O. Drawer 696
Aiken, SC 29802-0696
803-593-9231
Minimum Age: 60
Tuition: free
Basic Fees: none
Credit: yes

Chesterfield-Marlboro Technical College
Student Development
P.O. Drawer 1007
Cheraw, SC 29520
803-921-6900
Minimum Age: 60
Tuition: free
Basic Fees: $14.50 per semester
Credit: yes

The Citadel
171 Moultri St.
Charleston, SC 29409
803-953-5000
Minimum Age: 60
Tuition: free; $15 registration fee
Basic Fees: $40 per semester
Credit: yes

Clemson University
Business Affairs
G-08 Sikes Hall
P.O. Box 345307

Clemson, SC 29634-5307
864-656-2287
Minimum Age: 65
Tuition: free
Basic Fees: none
Credit: yes

College of Charleston
Treasurers Office
Charleston, SC 29424
803-953-5592
Minimum Age: 60
Tuition: $25 per semester
Basic Fees: none
Credit: yes

Denmark Technical College
Business Office
P.O. Box 327
Solomon Blatt Blvd.
Denmark, SC 29042
803-793-3301
Minimum Age: 62
Tuition: free
Basic Fees: none
Credit: yes

Florence-Darlington Technical College
Admissions
P.O. Box 100548
Florence, SC 29501-0548
803-661-8151
Minimum Age: 60
Tuition: free
Basic Fees: none
Credit: yes

Francis Marion College
Financial Aid
P.O. Box 100547
Florence, SC 29501-0547
803-661-1231
Minimum Age: 65
Tuition: free
Basic Fees: none
Credit: yes

Greenville Technical College
Admissions
P.O. Box 5616
Station B
Greenville, SC 29606-5616
803-250-8109
Minimum Age: 60
Tuition: free
Basic Fees: $23 per semester
Credit: yes

Horry-Georgetown Technical College
Financial Aid
P.O. Box 1966
Conway, SC 29526
803-347-3186
Minimum Age: 60
Tuition: $10 per class; $45 for computer classes
Basic Fees: $15 per session
Credit: yes

Lander College
Admissions
P.O. Box 6007
320 Stanley Ave.
Greenwood, SC 29649
864-229-8307
800-768-3600
Minimum Age: 60
Tuition: free
Basic Fees: none
Credit: yes

Midlands Technical College
Admissions
P.O. Box 2408

Columbia, SC 29202
803-738-7764
Minimum Age: 60
Tuition: free
Basic Fees: none
Credit: yes

South Dakota

Black Hills State University
Records and Admissions
USB 9502
Spearfish, SD 57799-9502
605-642-6343
800-255-2478
Minimum Age: 65
Tuition: $12.86 per credit hour
Basic Fees: none
Credit: yes

Dakota State University
Cashier
Heston Hall
Madison, SD 57042
605-256-5139
Minimum Age: 65
Tuition: $12.86 per credit hour
Basic Fees: $147.33 for 3 credit hours
Credit: yes

Northern State University
Finance Office
1200 South Jay St.
Aberdeen, SD 57401
605-626-2544
Minimum Age: 65
Tuition: 75% off (regular tuition $45.78 per credit hour)
Basic Fees: $29.05 per credit hour
Credit: yes

South Dakota School of Mines and Technology
Registrars Office
501 East St. Joseph St.
Rapid City, SD 57701-3995
605-394-2400
Minimum Age: 65
Tuition: $13.25 per credit hour
Basic Fees: $15 per session
Credit: yes

University of South Dakota
Admissions
414 East Clark
Vermillion, SD 57069-2390
605-677-5434
Minimum Age: 65
Tuition: 75% off (regular tuition $47.18 per credit hour)
Basic Fees: $15 per session
Credit: yes

Tennessee

Austin Peay State University
Admissions
P.O. Box 4548
Clarksville, TN 37044
615-648-7661
800-426-2604
Minimum Age: 65
Tuition: $33 per credit hour not to exceed $75 per session
Basic Fees: none
Credit: yes

Chattanooga State Technical Community College
Records Office
4501 Amnicola Hwy.
Chattanooga, TN 37406
423-634-7702
Minimum Age: 65 (60 to audit free)

Tuition: 50% of not to exceed $45 per session
Basic Fees: $12 per session
Credit: yes

Cleveland State Community College
P.O. Box 3570
Cleveland, TN 37320
423-472-7141
Minimum Age: 65 (60 for audit)
Tuition: $16 per credit hour not to exceed $45
per session; audit free
Basic Fees: $5 per semester
Credit: yes

Columbia State Community College
Admissions
P.O. Box 1315
Columbia, TN 38402-1315
615-540-2722
Minimum Age: 65 (60 for audit)
Tuition: $20 per session
Basic Fees: $5 one time application fee and $5
per session
Credit: yes

Dyersburg State Community College
P.O. Box 648
Dyersburg, TN 38025-0648
901-286-3200
Minimum Age: 65
Tuition: 50% off not to exceed $50 per session
Basic Fees: $10-$28 per session
Credit: yes

East Tennessee State University
Admissions
P.O. Box 70731
Johnson City, TN 37614
423-929-4213
Minimum Age: 65 (60 for audit)
Tuition: free
Basic Fees: $75 per semester
Credit: yes

Jackson State Community College
Business Office
2046 North Pkwy.
Jackson, TN 38301
901-424-3520
Minimum Age: 65
Tuition: 50% off (regular tuition $43 per credit
hour)
Basic Fees: $5 per session
Credit: yes

Memphis State University
Admissions Office, Room 167
Memphis, TN 38152
901-678-2101
800-669-9678
Minimum Age: 65 (60 audit)
Tuition: $75 per semester; audit free
Basic Fees: none
Credit: yes

Middle Tennessee State University
Accounting and Records
Murfreesboro, TN 37132
615-898-2111
Minimum Age: 65
Tuition: 50% off regular tuition
Basic Fees: $20 per session
Credit: yes

Motlow State Community College
P.O. Box 88100
Tullahoma, TN 37388-8100
615-393-1500
Minimum Age: 65 (60 to audit)
Tuition: $20 per credit hour not to exceed $45
per session
Basic Fees: $5 per session
Credit: yes

University of Tennessee
451 Communication Bldg.
Knoxville, TN 37996-0341
423-974-5361
Minimum Age: 65 (60 can audit free)
Tuition: $7 per credit hour not to exceed $75
per session
Basic Fees: $15 one time application fee
Credit: yes

Texas

Alvin Community College
Records
3110 Mustang Rd.
Alvin, TX 77511-4898
713-388-4636
Minimum Age: 65
Tuition: no discount
Basic Fees: none
Credit: no

Amarillo College
Business Office
P.O. Box 447
Amarillo, TX 79176
806-371-5000
Minimum Age: 65 or belong to senior citizen
association
Tuition: free (some courses excluded)
Basic Fees: $3 per semester
Credit: yes

Angelina College
P.O. Box 1768
Lufkin, TX 75902
409-639-1301
Minimum Age: 65
Tuition: free
Basic Fees: none
Credit: no

Bee County College
Business Office
3800 Charco Rd.
Beeville, TX 78102
512-358-3130
Minimum Age: 65
Tuition: free
Basic Fees: none
Credit: yes

Southwest Texas State University
SWT General Accounting
601 University Dr.
San Marcos, TX 78666-4603
512-245-2541
Minimum Age: 65
Tuition: free; space available basis
Basic Fees: none
Credit: no

University of Houston - Central Campus
Bursars Office
Houston, TX 77204-2160
713-743-1096
Minimum Age: 65
Tuition: free
Basic Fees: none
Credit: no

University of North Texas
P.O. Box 13797
Denton, TX 76203
817-565-2681
Minimum Age: senior citizen
Tuition: free
Basic Fees: none
Credit: no

University of Texas - Austin
Office of the Registrar
Main Bldg., Room 1
Austin, TX 78712-1157

512-471-7701
Minimum Age: 65
Tuition: free
Basic Fees: none
Credit: no

Utah

Brigham Young University
BYU Evening Classes
120 Harman Bldg.
Provo, UT 84602
801-378-2872
Minimum Age: 55
Tuition: $10 per class
Basic Fees: none
Credit: no

College of Eastern Utah
451 East 400 North
Price, UT 84501
801-637-2120
Minimum Age: 65
Tuition: $10 per class
Basic Fees: none
Credit: no

Dixie College
The Office of the Registrar
225 South 700 East
St. George, UT 84770
801-673-4811 ext. 348
Minimum Age: 62
Tuition: $10 quarter (some classes are
excluded)
Basic Fees: none
Credit: no

Salt Lake Community College
Admissions
4600 South Redwood Rd.
Salt Lake City, UT 84130
801-957-4297
Minimum Age: 63
Tuition: $10 per class
Basic Fees: none
Credit: yes

Snow College
150 East College Ave.
Ephraim, UT 84627
801-283-4021
Minimum Age: 62
Tuition: $10 per quarter
Basic Fees: none
Credit: no

Southern Utah University
Cashiers Office
351 West Center
Cedar City, UT 84720
801-586-7740
Minimum Age: 62
Tuition: $10 per quarter
Basic Fees: none
Credit: yes

University of Utah
DCE
1185 Annex
Salt Lake City, UT 84112
801-581-8113
Minimum Age: 60
Tuition: $10 per quarter
Basic Fees: none
Credit: no

Utah State University
Registrar
Logan, UT 84322-1600
801-797-1107
800-662-3950
Minimum Age: 62
Tuition: $10 per class to audit

Basic Fees: none
Credit: no

Utah Valley State College
Registrar
800 West 1200 South
Orem, UT 84058
801-222-8000
Minimum Age: 65
Tuition: $20 per class
Basic Fees: $20 one time admission fee
Credit: no

Weber State University
3750 Harrison
Ogden, UT 84408-1015
801-626-6050
Minimum Age: 62
Tuition: $10 per quarter
Basic Fees: none
Credit: no

Vermont

Castleton State College
Admissions
Castleton, VT 05735
802-468-5611
Minimum Age: 62
Tuition: free
Basic Fees: $19 per credit hour
Credit: yes

Community College of Vermont
Registrar
P.O. Box 120
Waterbuty, VT 05676
802-241-3535
Minimum Age: 62
Tuition: 50% off (regular tuition $88 per credit
hour)
Basic Fees: $42 per semester
Credit: yes

Johnson State College
Student Accounts
Stowe Rd.
Johnson, VT 05656
802-635-2356
800-635-2356
Minimum Age: 62
Tuition: 50% off (regular tuition $138 per
credit hour)
Basic Fees: $292 per semester plus $125 in
one time fees
Credit: yes

Lyndon State College
Business Office
Lyndonville, VT 05851
802-626-9371 ext. 163
800-225-1998
Minimum Age: 60
Tuition: 50% off (regular tuition $138 per
credit hour)
Basic Fees: $58.50 for 3 credit hours ($19.50
per credit hour)
Credit: yes

University of Vermont
194 South Prospect
Burlington, VT 05401
802-656-3170
Minimum Age: 62
Tuition: free
Basic Fees: none
Credit: yes

Virginia

In the State of Virginia the following rule
applies: If annual federal taxable income is
less than $10,000, tuition and application fees
are waived (audit only).

Blue Ridge Community College
P.O. Box 80
Weyers Cave, VA 24486-9989
540-234-9261
Minimum Age: 60
Tuition: free
Basic Fees: none
Credit: yes

Central Virginia Community College
Student Services
3506 Wards Rd.
Lynchburg, VA 24502
804-386-4500
Minimum Age: 60
Tuition: free
Basic Fees: none
Credit: yes

Clinch Valley College of the University of
Virginia
Admissions
College Ave.
Wise, VA 24293
540-328-0116
Minimum Age: 60
Tuition: free
Basic Fees: none
Credit: yes

College of William and Mary
Bursars Office
P.O. Box 8795
Williamsburg, VA 23187-8795
804-221-4000
Minimum Age: 60
Tuition: free
Basic Fees: none
Credit: yes

Dabney S. Lancaster Community College
Continuing Education
P.O. Box 1000
Clifton Forge, VA 24422
540-862-4246
Minimum Age: 60
Tuition: free
Basic Fees: none
Credit: yes

Danville Community College
1008 S. Main St.
Danville, VA 24541
804-797-3553
Minimum Age: 60
Tuition: free
Basic Fees: none
Credit: yes

Eastern Shore Community College
Student Services
Rt. 1, Box 6
Melfa, VA 23410-9755
804-787-5912
Minimum Age: 60
Tuition: free
Basic Fees: none
Credit: no

George Mason University
Office of Admissions
GMU
4400 University Dr.
Fairfax, VA 22030
703-993-2400
Minimum Age: 60
Tuition: free
Basic Fees: none
Credit: no

Germanna Community College
Admissions
P.O. Box 339
Locust Grove, VA 22508

540-727-3000
Minimum Age: 60
Tuition: free
Basic Fees: none
Credit: yes

James Madison University
Student Accounts
Harrisonburg, VA 22807
540-568-6147
Minimum Age: 60
Tuition: free
Basic Fees: none
Credit: yes

Northern Virginia Community College
Admissions Office
8333 Little River Turnpike
Annandale, VA 22003
703-323-3400
Minimum Age: 60
Tuition: free
Basic Fees: none
Credit: no

University of Virginia
Charlottesville Regional Programs
Division of Continuing Education
P.O. Box 3697
Charlottesville, VA 22903
804-982-3200
Minimum Age: 60
Tuition: free
Basic Fees: none
Credit: no

Washington

Bellevue Community College
3000 Landerholm Circle, SE
Bellevue, WA 98007
206-641-2222
Minimum Age: 60
Tuition: free (2 class limit)
Basic Fees: $2.50 per class
Credit: yes

Big Bend Community College
7662 Chanute St.
Moses Lake, WA 98837
509-762-6226
Minimum Age: 60
Tuition: $10 per course (2 course limit)
Basic Fees: none
Credit: yes

Central Washington University
400 E. 8th Ave.
Ellensburg, WA 98926
509-963-1211
Minimum Age: 60
Tuition: $5 per credit hour up to 6 credit hours
Basic Fees: $25 per session
Credit: no

Centralia College
600 West Locust
Centralia, WA 98531
360-736-9391
Minimum Age: 60
Tuition: $20 (2 class limit)
Basic Fees: none
Credit: no

Clark College
1800 East McLaughlin Blvd.
Vancouver, WA 98663
360-992-2000
Minimum Age: 60
Tuition: $5 per class (2 class limit)
Basic Fees: none
Credit: no

University of Washington
Access Program
Undergraduate Extension Office
5001 25th Ave., NE
Seattle, WA 98195
206-543-2320
Minimum Age: 60
Tuition: free plus $5 registration fee per quarter
Basic Fees: $5 per session
Credit: no

West Virginia

Apparently, Legislature has been proposed several times to no avail. We were unable to find any schools who offered a discount to senior citizens.

Wisconsin

Chippewa Valley Technical College
620 West Clarmont Ave.
Eau Claire, WI 54701
715-833-6244
Minimum Age: 62
Tuition: free
Basic Fees: none
Credit: no

Madison Area Technical College
3350 Anderson St.
Madison, WI 53704-2599
608-246-6205
Minimum Age: 62
Tuition: varies ($3.50 and up non-credit only); inquire on course number
Basic Fees: varies
Credit: no

Mid-State Technical College
500 - 32nd St., North
Wisconsin Rapids, WI 54494-5599
715-422-5500
Minimum Age: 62
Tuition: free

Basic Fees: none
Credit: no

Milwaukee Area Technical College
Downtown Campus
700 West State St.
Milwaukee, WI 53233
414-297-6600
Minimum Age: 62
Tuition: free
Basic Fees: none
Credit: no

Northcentral Technical College
Registrar
1000 W. Campus Dr.
Wausau, WI 54401
715-675-3331
Minimum Age: 62
Tuition: reduced rate (varies)
Basic Fees: none
Credit: no

Northeast Wisconsin Technical College
Registrar's Office
P.O. Box 19043
Green Bay, WI 54307-9042
414-498-5703
800-272-2740
Minimum Age: 62
Tuition: up to 50% off (non-credit only)
Basic Fees: none
Credit: no

Wyoming

Casper College
125 College Dr.
Casper, WY 82601
307-268-2110 ext. 2491
Minimum Age: 60
Tuition: free; must be resident of Wyoming
Basic Fees: none
Credit: yes with Golden Age card

Central Wyoming College
Continuing Education

2660 Peck Ave.
Riverton, WY 82501
307-856-9291 ext. 181
Minimum Age: 60
Tuition: free
Basic Fees: $11.50 per credit hour
Credit: yes

Eastern Wyoming College
Records
3200 West C St.
Torrington, WY 82240
307-532-8334
800-658-3195
Minimum Age: 60
Tuition: free
Basic Fees: $9 per credit hour
Credit: yes

Laramie County Community College
Admissions
1400 East College Dr.
Cheyenne, WY 82007
307-778-1212
Minimum Age: 65
Tuition: $5 per credit hour
Basic Fees: $10 one time application fee
Credit: yes

University of Wyoming
Admissions
P.O. Box 3435
Laramie, WY 82071
307-766-5160
Minimum Age: 65
Tuition: free
Basic Fees: none
Credit: yes

Western Wyoming Community College
P.O. Box 428
Rock Springs, WY 82901
307-382-1600
Minimum Age: 60
Tuition: free
Basic Fees: none
Credit: yes

Tuition and basic fees are based on the lowest fees (in-state, in-district, in-county, non-degree seeking, undergraduate etc.). Special fees may apply to some classes. Generally, lab, books and materials are additional, and vary depending upon class. Some other additional fees include parking, health insurance, and a fee for degree seeking and graduate students.

An interested individual should contact the school they wish to attend to find out how to apply for a discount or waiver. Qualifications vary from school to school. Some limitations and restrictions apply such as an income limit, residency, and space availability.

I Wanna New Career And I'm Disabled

Matthew Lesko, Information USA, Inc., 12081 Nebel Street, Rockville, MD 20852 • 1-800-955-7693 • www.lesko.com

Free Job Training, Help and Money for the Disabled

Over 43 million Americans have disabilities of one kind or another. Many of them dream of supporting themselves with good paying jobs but can't make this dream come true because of their disabilities or because their lack of job skills stand in the way of leading independent lives. It's the kind of discouragement felt by many, regardless of their age, ambition, or economic status.

The Federal Government has stepped in and funded programs across the country to help the disabled and handicapped reach their goals by providing them with all kinds of services to get them on their way. The help available ranges from free information services, self help groups (for specific disabilities and disabilities in general), free legal aid, and independent living programs, to free money for education, job training, living expenses, transportation, equipment, and mobility aids. You can even get money to have your home retrofitted to make it more accessible to you, given your specific handicap. And if you're denied any of these programs or services, there are several free sources of legal help that can get you what you're legally entitled to.

Typical of the free services available in your state:

- medical examinations and treatment
- vocational evaluation, training, and placement
- disability counseling
- assistive devices
- transportation
- occupational equipment
- rehabilitation engineering
- postemployment services
- independent living training
- student services
- financial assistance
- supported employment
- deaf services

Your state Vocational Rehabilitation office will evaluate your skills, needs, and goals, and work with you to keep you a productive member of society. As their client, they will assist you in getting the equipment you need to do your job, and sometimes even help you with transportation to work. College is also an option. We know of a massage therapist who developed carpal tunnel syndrome and got a four year college degree paid for so she could be trained for a new profession.

Want to start a business? The Office of Disability Employment Policy {www.dol.gov/odep} knows that people with disabilities have a strong interest in working for themselves. In fact statistics show that people with disabilities have a higher rate of self-employment than people without disabilities (12.2% versus 7.8%). But there are barriers that people with disabilities must face:

- possible loss of cash benefits for Social Security or Supplemental Security disability programs
- possible loss of health care benefits associated with cash programs
- possible loss of housing and other subsidies
- inability to access capital needed to start a business.

Despite these barriers, many enterprising people with disabilities do run successful business. The U.S. Department of Labor has developed a new office call Small Business Self-Employment Service that links to other entrepreneurship sites, provides information on a variety of technical assistance resources, as well as resources for writing business plans, financing, and other issues. These services are provided at no cost. Contact:

Small Business and Self-Employment Service
Job Accommodation Network
P.O. Box 6080
Morgantown, WV 26506
800-526-6234
Fax: 304-293-5407
www.jan.wvu.edu/SBSES

You can also learn about programs and activities in your state for people with disabilities who want to work by checking out {www.ssa.gov/work}. Also don't forget to check out the federal government's website {www.disability.gov} that lists all the government programs relating to disabilities.

You can be like Jim Bell:

Jim Bell was classified as disabled the same year he was downsized out of his job. He always dreamed of starting a home-based business, and began looking through Matthew's Free Money To Change Your Life book. He found the VESID (Vocational Educational Services for Individuals with Disabilities) program, which is part of the New York State Education Department. This is a special program to help disabled individuals start a business. After working with someone from VESID for a couple of months, Jim was awarded an $11,000 grant to help buy inventory, a computer, fax machine, and office supplies. He now sells golf equipment online at www.bellmerchandise.com and www.golferscaddy.com. This past year Jim was awarded the honor of being "Disabled Entrepreneur of the Year."

Terri Handshoe was the youngest member of her family, and was the only one who was deaf. In 1977, she dropped out of high school with no plans for the future. Sitting at home soon grew old, so she decided to work on getting her GED. She studied and passed, and a friend suggested that she contact the vocational rehabilitation office to see about furthering her education or vocational training. After working with her counselor, Terri attended a local college for a quarter. Her counselor was able to persuade Terri to transfer to Gallaudet University in Washington, DC, the world renowned school for students who are deaf. During school, vocational rehabilitation provided a much needed interpreter and books. "It was great! I had to study hard, but I didn't have to worry about those things," said Terri, referring to the assistance that she was provided that made getting her education so much easier. Terri went on to complete a graduate degree and is now a program coordinator for the deaf.

Sandy Smith lost her sight in high school because of an operation to treat a brain tumor. She worked with vocational rehabilitation upon her return to school. She liked office work and was very motivated to find a job that would put her new skills to good use. Sandy was hired as a switchboard operator for a major hotel. Because she couldn't see the blinking lights on the multi-line telephone keypad, Sandy couldn't determine which line was ringing. Vocational rehabilitation was able to custom design a plastic overlay which allows pins to pop out wherever a line is ringing. The device cost $3,000 which vocational rehabilitation paid for. They were also able to supply Sandy with a computer so she could put through calls on her own. Sandy is very satisfied with her job, and says, "If you don't try, you'll never know if you can do it."

The three best places where you should begin your search for information about services and money programs for the disabled and handicapped are:

- The Social Security Administration
- your State Office of Vocational Rehabilitation
- Client Assistance Programs

In this section, you'll find descriptions and listings of contacts for these three programs, along with several additional best places for self help and aid for handicapped or disabled individuals.

General Information Sources

* Clearinghouse on Disability Information

Office of Special Education
and Rehabilitation Services
U.S. Department of Education
Room 3132 Switzer Building
Washington, DC 20202-2524   202-205 8241
http://www.ed.gov/about/offices/list/osers/index.html

The clearinghouse responds to inquiries, provides referrals, and gives out information about services for individuals with disabilities at the national, state, and local levels. Free publications include:

- *Pocket Guide to Federal Help for Individuals with Disabilities*
- Brochure: *America needs us all, people with disabilities learning and earning.*
- *Clearinghouse on Disability Information* fact sheet

* National Association of Rehabilitation Agencies

National Association of Rehabilitation Agencies
11250 Roger Baron Dr., Suite 8   703-437-4377
Reston, VA 20190-5202   Fax: 703-435-4390
http://www.naranet.org/

A private membership organization of rehabilitation agencies and professionals. Refer inquiries to members.

* National Dissemination Center for Children with Disabilities

P.O. Box 1492   800-695-0285
Washington, DC 20013-1492   202-884-8200 (Voice/TDD)
http://www.nichcy.org/

The Clearinghouse is an information and referral center that provides information on disabilities and disability related issues, as well as referrals to a wide network of specialists from agencies and organizations across the nation. They focus on children and youth ages birth to 22. There is a great state resources section to help you find the right office.

* National Rehabilitation Association

633 South Washington St.   703-836-0849 (TDD)
Alexandria, VA 22314   703-836-0850
http://www.nationalrehab.org

A private membership organization of professionals, vendors and suppliers of rehabilitation services, consumers and family members, students and professors. Refer inquiries to members.

* ABLEDATA

ABLEDATA
8630 Fenton St., Suite 930   800-227-0216
Silver Spring, MD 20910   TTY: 301-608-8912
www.abledata.com

National database containing information on assistive technology and rehabilitation equipment for persons with disabilities. Contains more than 25,000 products from over 2,700 manufacturers and distributors. Publications include the *Assistive Technology Directory*; *ABLEDATA thesaurus*; *ADA Source book*; Fact sheets and computer guides.

* Rehabilitation Information Hotline

National Rehabilitation Information
Center (NARIC)   800-346-2742
4200 Forbes Blvd.   301-459-5900
Suite 202   TTY: 301-495-5626
Lanham MD 20706   Fax: 301-562-2401
http://www.naric.com

The National Rehabilitation Information Center, a library and information center on disability and rehabilitation, collects and disseminates the results of federally funded research projects. NARIC also maintains a vertical file of pamphlets and fact sheets published by other organizations. NARIC has documents on all aspects of disability and rehabilitation including, physical disabilities, mental retardation, psychiatric disabilities, independent living, employment, law and public policy and assistive technology.

Their user services include the ABLEDATA database which describes thousands of assistive devices from eating utensils to wheelchairs. A printed listing of fewer than 50 products is $5; NARIC charges $10 for 51 to 100 products, and $5 for each additional hundred products. ABLEDATA also provides an information specialist to answer simple information requests and provide referrals immediately at no cost. 800-227-0216.

* Free Money for Education and Job Training

If your disability stops you from being able to keep a full time job or from being able to competitively look for a job, your state's Office of Vocational Rehabilitation (OVR) can help. OVR can give you up to $6,000 each year for job training or education. You can use this grant money, which you do not have to repay, to cover any expenses related to your training or education, including tuition and fees, travel expenses, books, supplies, equipment (computers, motorized wheelchairs, etc.), food allowances, tutoring fees, photocopies, and so on. For more information, contact your state's Office of Vocational Rehabilitation listed at the end of this section.

* Technical Assistance Project

Rehabilitation Engineering and Assertive Technology
Society of North America (RESNA)
1700 North Moore Street, #1540   703-524-6686
Arlington, VA 22209   TTY: 703-524-6639
www.resna.org   Fax: 703-524-6630

This project, funded by the U.S. Department of Education, has established an office in each state that provides information about how the latest technology can improve the lives of disabled persons. They also have an equipment loan program, which allows people to borrow new technology devices before purchasing them. They provide information on sources of funding for equipment and special loans. For more information contact your state office listed at the end of this section.

* What To Do When OVR Benefits Are Denied

The first place to start when your state Office of Vocational Rehabilitation denies you handicap or disability benefits is your nearest state Client Assistance Program (CAP) office. CAP is a free information, referral, and legal service that helps disabled or handicapped individuals appeal a denial by OVR (or another agency). For a variety of reasons, it is not uncommon for a disabled individual to be turned down for services by OVR even when he/she is in fact eligible to receive them. It is often helpful to get a photocopy of section 103 of Chapter 34 of the *Code of Federal Regulations of the U.S. Department of Education* from your local or county library. These are the federal guidelines that each state OVR must follow when determining eligibility. This part of the code is only a few pages in length and can help you explain to the Client Assistance Program officer why you believe you are eligible even though you've been denied. CAP can take your appeal process from the first stages all the way to the U.S. Supreme Court if necessary — and it won't cost you a penny.

It is also sometimes helpful to contact the state Office of Vocational Rehabilitation (OVR) itself and make the executive director aware of your circumstances. When it appears that progress via CAP is stalled or has been dragging on for months, it can also be very helpful to contact the regional commissioner of the Rehabilitation Services Administration (RSA), a branch of the Office of Special Education Programs of the U.S. Department of Education. RSA is responsible for overseeing and funding the state OVR agencies and is generally receptive to a short explanatory phone call and letter from those who believe they can clearly show that they have been wrongly denied OVR services. If they think you've got a case, they'll contact the OVR in question and make sure that they review your application more favorably.

To get in touch with a Rehabilitation Services Administration official, contact the U.S. Department of Education, Office of Special Education and Rehabilitative Services, RSA, Washington, DC 20202: 202-205-5465, and ask for the address and phone number of the regional commissioner for the ED-OSERS-RSA office serving your area, or check the website {http://www.ed.gov/about/offices/list/osers/index.html}.

* Three Important Tips When Appealing an OVR Denial Of Services

1. If your state Office of Vocational Rehabilitation (OVR) denies you services based on other similar cases in which they have denied other prospective clients, it is important and effective to argue that such reasons for denial are not allowable under federal regulations. The 34 Code of Federal Regulations Chapter III section 361.31(b)(1) states clearly that the barriers faced by a disabled individual are unique to each individual and to each individual set of circumstances.

2. If you have previously been accepted by your state Office of Vocational Rehabilitation (OVR) as a client and you have gained employment but your disability has not improved and you lose employment due to no fault of your own, then OVR can again provide you with their services to help you regain employment. For more specifics, consult again the 34 Code of Federal Regulations, Chapter III and check under the *Post-Employment Services* sections and *Supported Employment* sections.

3. If you're currently receiving Social Security Disability (SSD), make sure that your state Office of Vocational Rehabilitation (OVR) and Client Assistance Program (CAP) are aware of this fact. Because of the more restrictive SSD definition of what it means to be disabled (compared to OVR), being on SSD almost always automatically qualifies an SSD recipient for OVR services. It is very difficult for OVR to argue otherwise.

* More Free Legal Help for the Disabled

A national nonprofit law and policy center, the Disability Rights Education and Defense Fund (DREDF) can provide you with direct legal representation and act as co-counsel in cases of disability based discrimination. They also seek to educate legislators and policy makers on issues affecting the rights of people with disabilities. Contact: Disability Rights Education and Defense Fund (DREDF), 2212 Sixth St., Berkeley, CA 94710; 510-644-2555 (Voice/TDD); http://www.dredf.org.

* Plan for Achieving Self- Support (PASS)

Many people with disabilities want to work, and you're probably one of them. But maybe you need to go back to school before you can get a job. Or, maybe you'd like to start your own business, but you don't have the money. Whatever your work goal may be, a PASS can help you reach it. A PASS lets you set aside money and/or other things you own to help you reach your goal. For example, you could set aside money to start a business or to go to school or to get training for a job.

Your goal must be a job that will produce sufficient earnings to reduce your dependency on Supplemental Security Income (SSI) payments. A PASS is meant to help you acquire those items, services or skills you need so that you can compete with able-bodied persons for an entry level job in a professional, business or trade environment. If you have graduated from college or a trade/technical school, we usually consider you capable of obtaining such a

position without the assistance of a PASS. You can contact your local Social Security office to find out whether a PASS is appropriate for you.

* How Will A Plan Affect My SSI Benefit?

Under regular SSI rules, your SSI benefit is reduced by the other income you have. But the income you set aside for a PASS doesn't reduce your SSI benefit. This means you can get a higher SSI benefit when you have a PASS. But you can't get more than the maximum SSI benefit for the state where you live.

Money you save or things you own, such as property or equipment, that you set aside for a PASS won't count against the resource limit of $2,000 (or $3,000 for a couple). Under regular SSI rules, you wouldn't be eligible for SSI if your resources are above $2,000. But with a plan, you may set aside some resources so you would be eligible.

* Who Can Have A PASS?

You can, if:
- you want to work;
- you get SSI (or can qualify for SSI) because of blindness or a disability; or
- you have or expect to receive income (other than SSI) and/or resources to set aside toward a work goal.

* What Kinds Of Expenses Can A Plan Help Pay For?

A plan may be used to pay for a variety of expenses that are necessary to help you reach your work goal.
For example, your plan may help you save for:
- supplies to start a business;
- tuition, fees, books and supplies that are needed for school or training;
- employment services, such as payments for a job coach;
- attendant care or child care expenses;
- equipment and tools to do the job;
- transportation to and from work; or
- uniforms, special clothing and safety equipment.

These are only examples. Not all of these will apply to every plan. You might have other expenses depending on your goal.

* How Will A Plan Affect Other Benefits I Get?

You should check with the agency that is responsible for those benefits to find out if the plan (and the extra SSI) might affect those benefits.
In many cases, income and resources set aside under a plan will not be counted for food stamps and housing assistance provided through the U.S. Department of Housing and Urban Development. But, it's important that you contact the particular agency to find out how your benefits will be affected.
For more information, ask Social Security for the booklet, *Working While Disabled — How We Can Help* (Publication No. 05--10095); {www.ssa.gov}.

* Ticket To Work

Maximus Inc.
866-968-7842 (toll-free 866-YOUR-TICKET)
866-833-2967 (TTY)
www.ssa.gov/work

Ticket to Work is part of the new Work Incentives Improvement Act which increases your choice in obtaining rehabilitation and vocational services. It removes the barriers that require people with disabilities to choose between health care coverage and work. Most Social Security and Supplemental Security Income (SSI) disability beneficiaries will receive a "ticket" they may use to obtain vocational rehabilitation, employment or other support services from an approved provider of their choice to help them go to work and achieve their employment goals. This is voluntary program. Medicare coverage is extended for a period of time and states have the option of extending Medicaid coverage. Maximus Inc. is managing the program for Social Security.

State Vocational Rehabilitation Offices

Alabama

Steven Shivers, Commissioner, Alabama Department of Rehabilitation Services, 2129 East South Boulevard, P.O. Box 11586, Montgomery, AL 36111-0586; 334-281-8780, 800-441-7607, TDD: 334-613-2249, Fax: 334-281-1973; {www. rehab.state.al.us}. Assistance offered:

- medical examinations and treatment
- psychological evaluation
- vocational evaluation, training and placement
- disability counseling
- assistive devices
- transportation
- occupational equipment
- rehabilitation engineering
- postemployment services
- independent living training
- student services
- Hemophilia Program
- OASIS Project (Older Alabamians System of Information and Services)
- in home care
- financial assistance
- Business Enterprise Program (BEP)
- supported employment
- deaf services

Alaska

Duane French, Director, Division of Vocational Rehabilitation, 801 West 10th St., Suite A, Juneau, AK 99801-1894; 907-465-2814, 800-478-2815; Email: {stevie.raleigh@educ.state.ak.us}, {http://www.labor.state.ak.us/dvr/home.htm}. Assistance offered:

- medical and psychiatric examinations
- vocational evaluation, training, and placement
- medical treatment
- adaptive equipment
- transportation
- postemployment counseling

American Samoa

Peter P. Galea'i, Director, Division of Vocational Rehabilitation, Dept. Of Human Resources, American Samoa Government, Pago Pago, AS 96799, 011684-699-1371, {www.ipacific.com/samoa/samoa.html}

Arizona

Fred "Skip" Bingham, Administrator, Arizona Rehabilitation Services Administration, 1789 West Jefferson 2, NW, Phoenix, AZ 85007; 602-542-3651, 800-563-1221, TDD: 602-542-6049, Fax: 602-542-3778, Email: {mepps@mail.de.state.az.us}, {http://www.de.state.az.us/rsa}. Assistance offered:

- vocational evaluation, training, and evaluation
- independent living counseling
- Business Enterprise Program (BEP)
- deaf and Blind services
- communication devices
- adaptive equipment

Arkansas

John Wyvill, Director, Division of Vocational Rehabilitation, 1616 Brookwood Drive, Little Rock, AR 72203;, 501-296-1661, 800-285-7192, TDD: 501-296-1669, Fax: 501-296-1655, Email: {jcwyvill@ars.state.ar.us}, {http://www.arsinfo.org}. Assistance offered:

- individual and family counseling
- adaptive equipment
- in home care services
- vocational evaluation, training, and placement
- rehabilitation facilities

James C. Hudson, Director, Division of Services for the Blind, Dept. of Human Services, 522 Main Street, Little Rock, AR 72203; 501-682-0198, 800-960-9270, TTY: 501-682-0093, Fax: 501-682-0366; http://www.state.ar.us/dhs/dsb/index.html. Assistance offered:

- vocational training and placement
- medical diagnosis and treatment
- counseling on independent living
- personal adjustment counseling for family and children
- Vending Facility Program
- library materials
- radio reading service
- information referrals

California

Catherine Campisi, Director, Department of Rehabilitation, P.O. Box 944222, Sacramento, CA 95815; 916-263-8981, TTY: 916-263-7477, {http://www.doc.ca.gov/}. Assistance offered:

- medical and vocational evaluation
- medical treatment
- job training and placement
- transportation
- occupational licenses and equipment
- family services
- reader and interpreter services
- communication devices
- rehabilitation engineering
- adaptive equipment
- supported employment
- small business incentives
- postemployment services

Colorado

Diana Huerta, Director, Division of Vocational Rehabilitation, Dept. Of Social Services, 2211 West Evans, Bldg. B, Denver, Co 80223; 720-884-1234 (V/TDD), Fax: 720-884-1213, Email: {debbiepowell@state.co.us}, {http://www.cdhs.state.co.us/ods/dvr}. Assistance offered:

- vocational evaluation, training, and placement
- employer services
- rehabilitation engineering
- personal adjustment counseling
- Client Assistance Program (CAP)

Connecticut

Bureau of Rehabilitation Services, Department of Social Services, 25 Sigourney St., Hartford, CT 06106-5033, 800-842-4848, 860-424-4848; TDD: 860-424-4839, Fax: 860-424-4850, Email: {john.halliday@po.state.ct.us}, {http://www.brs.state.ct.us/}. Assistance offered:

- vocational counseling, training, and placement
- physical therapy
- adaptive technology
- psychotherapy
- academic training
- occupational tools and licenses
- architectural modifications to home and workplace
- rehabilitation employment
- supported employment
- transportation

Donna Balaski, Director, Board of Education and Services for the Blind, Vocational Rehabilitation Division, 184 Windsor Avenue, Windsor, CT 06095; 800-842-4510 (in CT), 860-602-4000, TTY: 860-602-4002, Fax: 860-602-4020, Email: {besb@po.state.ct.us}, {http://www.besb.state.ct.us}. Assistance offered:

- Radio Information Service
- individual and family counseling
- mobility instruction
- vocational training and placement
- industries opportunities
- financial counseling
- legal benefits
- recreation

- follow up services
- low vision exams and treatment
- home management training
- communication devices
- information and referral

Delaware

Andrea Guest, Director, Division of Vocational Rehabilitation, P.O. Box 9969, 4425 N. Market Street, Wilmington, DE 19809-0969; 302-761-8275, TDD: 302-761-8336, Fax: 302-761-6611, Email: {director@dvr.state.de.us}, {http://www.delawareworks.com/dvr/welcome.htm}. Assistance offered:

- vocational training and placement
- independent living counseling
- adaptive equipment
- family counseling
- home management training
- transportation
- financial assistance
- physical therapy
- occupational tools and licenses

Harry B. Hill, Director, Division for the Visually Impaired, Biggs Building, Health & Social Services Campus, 1901 N. Dupont Highway, New Castle, DE 19720; 302-255-9800, Fax: 302-255-4441, {http://www.state.de.us/dhss/dvi/dvihome.htm}. Assistance offered:

- low vision services
- counseling
- education
- mobility instruction
- job training and placement
- deaf/blind services
- independent living training
- personal adjustment counseling
- optical aids
- preventive examinations
- information and referral
- communication devices

District of Columbia

D.C. Rehabilitation Services Administration, Dept. of Human Services, 801 East Building, 2700 Martin Luther King Ave., SE, Washington, DC 20032; 202-279-6002, 202-729-6014, http://dhs.dc.gov. Assistance offered:

- vocational evaluation, training, and placement
- adaptive equipment
- personal adjustment counseling
- physical therapy
- transportation
- postemployment services
- occupational tools and licenses
- small business assistance

Florida

Tamira Bibb Allen, Director, Division of Vocational Rehabilitation, Dept. Of Labor and Employment, Security, Building A, 2002 Old St. Augustine Road, Tallahassee, FL 32399-0696; 850-245-3399, Information & Referral line: 800-451-4327, {http://www.rehabworks.org/}. Assistance offered:

- vocational and medical evaluation
- financial assistance
- job training and placement
- work adjustment training
- in home care
- postemployment counseling
- supported employment
- determination of benefit eligibility

Craig Kiser, Director, Division of Blind Services, Department of Education, 2551 Executive Center Circle, Tallahassee, FL 32399; 800-342-1330, 800-342-1828 (in FL), 850-488-1330, Fax: 850-487-1804, {http://www.state.fl.us/dbs/}. Assistance offered:

- medical, psychological, and vocational evaluation
- counseling
- medical services
- mobility instruction

- job training and placement
- rehabilitation facilities
- communication skills and equipment
- family and children services
- in home instruction
- Bureau of Business Enterprises
- library services

Georgia

Peggy Rosser, Director, Division of Rehabilitation Services, Georgia Department of Human Resources, Suite 510 Sussex Place, 148 Andrew Young International Blvd., NE, Atlanta, GA 30303; 404-232-3910; Email: {Gradye@gomail.doas.state.ga.us}, {http://www.vocrehabga.org/}. Assistance offered:

- vocational rehabilitation programs for competitive employment and sheltered employment
- independent living counseling
- evaluate clients to determine eligibility for health care and disability benefits
- refer clients to appropriate nearby facilities for rehabilitation services

Guam

Nobert Ungacto, Director, Dept. Of Vocational Rehabilitation, Government of Guam, 122 Harmon Plaza, Room B201, Harmon Industrial Park, Guam 96911; 011-671-475-4646, {www.gov.gu/}.

Hawaii

Neil Shim, Administrator, Division of Vocational Rehabilitation & Services for the Blind, Dept. Of Human Services, Bishop Trust Bldg., 1000 Bishop St., Room 615, Honolulu, HI 96813; 808-586-5366, Fax: 808-586-5377, {http://www.state.hi.us/dhs/}. Assistance offered:

- optical aids
- personal adjustment counseling
- independent living training
- communication devices
- low vision services
- preventive eye care
- vocational evaluation, training and placement
- job site modification

Idaho

Barry J. Thompson, Administrator, Division of Vocational Rehabilitation, P.O. Box 83720, 650 West State Street, Room 150, Boise, ID 83720-0096; 208-334-3390, TDD: 208-327-7040, Fax: 208-334-5305, E-mail: {pyoung@idvr.state.id.us}, {http://www2.state.id.us/idvr/idvrhome.htm}. Assistance offered:

- vocational evaluation, training, and placement
- medical treatment
- assistive devices
- occupational tools and licenses
- Business and Industry Program
- specialized rehabilitation
- personal adjustment counseling
- independent living training
- kidney program
- transportation
- recreation programs
- attendant care
- communication aids
- family services
- information and referral
- housing
- health maintenance

Michael Graham, Director, Idaho Commission for the Blind, Division of Vocational Rehabilitation, P.O. Box 83720, 341 West Washington, Boise, ID 83720, 208-334-3220, 800-542-8688 (in ID), Fax: 208-334-2963, Email: {mstarkov@icbvi.state.id.us}, {http://www.icbvi.state.id.us}. Assistance offered:

- Business Enterprise Program
- radio reading and taping
- independent living counseling
- information and referral
- job training and placement
- financial assistance
- orientation and adjustment center
- adaptive equipment

- prevention programs
- academic training
- home instruction

Illinois

Robert E. Davis, State Director, Illinois Office Rehabilitation Services, 100 South Grand Ave., E, 3rd Floor, Springfield, IL 62762, 217-785-0234, 800-843-6154, Fax: 217-558-4270, Email: {ors@dhs.state.il.us}, {http://www.state.il.us/agency/ dhs}. Assistance offered:

- job training and placement
- educational assistance
- transportation
- independent living training
- in home care
- Illinois Children's School and Rehabilitation Center
- supported employment
- information and referral
- interpreter services
- personal adjustment counseling
- vending Facility Program
- Disability Determination Services

Indiana

Deputy Director, Department of Human Services, Vocational Rehabilitation Services, Room W453, 402 West Washington St., P.O. Box 7083, Indianapolis, IN 46207-7083; 800-545-7763 (IN only), 317-232-1319, TDD: 317-232-1427, {http://www.in.gov/fssa/}. Assistance offered:

- vocational evaluation, training and placement
- assistive devices
- rehabilitation engineering
- physical therapy
- information referral
- financial assistance
- transportation
- communication devices
- personal adjustment counseling
- independent living training

Linda Quarles, Deputy Director, Division of the Blind and Visually Impaired, Room W453, 402 W. Washington St., P.O. Box 7083, Indianapolis, IN 46207-7083; 317-232-1438; 877-241-8144; {www.state.in.us/fssa/servicedisabl/blind/index.html}.

Iowa

R. Creig Slayton, Director, Department for the Blind, 524 4th Street, Des Moines, IA 50309-2364; 515-281-1333, 800-362-2587 (IA only), TTY: 515-281-1355, {www.blind.state.ia.us}. Assistance offered:

- library services
- vocational evaluation, training and placement
- orientation and adjustment center
- independent living counseling
- Business Enterprises Program (BEP)
- adaptive equipment
- occupational tools
- registry of the blind
- information and referral
- communication training and equipment

Iowa Division of Vocational Rehabilitation Services, 510 East 12th Street, Des Moines, IA 50319, 515-281-4211 (V/TTY), 800-532-1486 (V/TTY); Email: {webmaster@dvrs.state.ia.us}, {http://www.dvrs.state.ia.us}.

Kansas

Vocational Rehabilitation, Department of Social and Rehabilitation Services, 915 Harrison Street, 6th Floor, Docking State Office Building, Topeka, Kansas 66612; 785-296-5301, Fax: 785-296-2173, {http://www.srskansas. org}.

Kentucky

Mr. Sam Serraglio, Commissioner, Kentucky Department of Vocational Rehabilitation, 209 St. Clair St., Frankfort, KY 40601; 800-372-7172 (KY), 502-564-4440, Fax: 502-564-6742, {http://kydvr.state.ky.us}. Assistance offered:

- Assessment for determining eligibility and vocational rehabilitation needs

- Counseling and guidance
- Information and referral to other agencies
- Physical and mental restoration services
- Vocational and other training services
- Supported employment
- Transportation and other services necessary to participate fully in your rehabilitation program
- Personal assistance services
- Interpreter and note taking services
- Telecommunications, sensory, and other technological aids and devices
- Rehabilitation technology
- Job Placement and Job Retention Services
- Employment follow-up and postemployment services

Department for the Blind, P.O. Box 757, 209 St. Clair Street, Frankfort, KY 40602; 502-564-4754, 800-321-6668, TDD: 502-564-2929, Fax: 502-564-2951, {http://www.kyblind.state.ky.us}. Assistance offered:

- diagnosis and evaluation
- counseling
- medical treatment
- vocational training and placement
- room and board
- transportation
- reader services
- orientation and mobility training
- optical aids
- communication technology
- occupational licenses, tools and equipment
- postemployment services
- Business Enterprises Program (BEP)
- Industries for the Blind

Louisiana

Mary Nelson, Director, Rehabilitation Services, Department of Social Services, 8225 Florida Blvd., Baton Rouge, LA 70806; 225-925-4131, 800-737-2958, Fax: 225-925-4481, {www.dss.state.la.us/}. Assistance offered:

- vocational evaluation, training and placement
- assistive devices
- personal adjustment counseling
- independent living training
- in home care services
- deaf and blind services
- communication training
- transportation
- financial assistance
- occupational licenses and tools

Maine

Maine Bureau of Rehabilitation Services, 150 State House Station, Augusta, ME 04333, 207-624-5950, 800-698-4440, TTY: 888-755-0023, 207-624-5980, {www.state.me.us/rehab}.

Maryland

Division of Vocational Rehabilitation, State Department of Education, 2301 Argonne Drive, Baltimore, MD 21218-1696; 410/554-9385, 888/554-0334, TTY: 410/554-9411, Fax: 410/554-9412, E-mail: {dors@msde.state.lib. md.us}, {www.dors.state.md.us/voc_rehab.html}. Assistance offered:

- physical therapy
- vocational evaluation, training, and rehabilitation
- personal adjustment counseling
- transportation
- financial assistance
- occupational licenses and equipment
- assistive devices
- psychological evaluations
- independent living training

Massachusetts

Rehabilitation Commission, Fort Point Place, 27-43 Wormwood Street, Boston, MA 02210-1616; 800-245-6543, 617-204-3600, Fax: 617-727-1354, {http://www.mass,gov/mrc}. Assistance offered:

- head injury program
- home based employment
- adaptive housing

- injured workers program
- supported employment
- deaf services
- bilingual specialty services
- independent living center
- transportation
- home care assistance program
- personal care assistance
- disability determination
- library services
- job training and placement
- job site modification
- information and referral

Commission for the Blind, 88 Kingston St., Boston, MA 02111-2227; 617-727-5550, 800-392-6450 (in MA), TDD: 617-727-9063, {http://www.mass.gov.gov/mcb}. Assistance offered:

- talking book and radio reading services
- administer Medicaid
- low vision and hearing aids
- information referral
- individual and family counseling
- homemaker services
- mobility instruction
- home management training
- protective services, including arranging guardianship
- interpreter services
- elder blind services
- recreation, housing assistance, and advocacy
- services for multi-handicapped individuals
- vocational training and placement
- Ferguson Industries program

Michigan

Patrick Cannon, Director, Commission for the Blind, 201 N. Washington Square, P.O. Box 30652, Lansing, MI 48909; 517-373-3390, TDD: 517-373-4025, Fax: 517-355-5140, {http://www.michigan.gov/mdcd}. Assistance offered:

- vocational evaluation
- financial aid
- academic instruction
- postemployment services
- medical treatment
- transportation
- reader services
- occupational licenses and equipment
- interpreter services
- daily living costs assistance
- disability determination

Michigan Rehabilitation Services, Michigan Department of Career Development, P.O. Box 30010, Lansing, MI 48909, 517-241-0377, 800-605-6722, Fax: 513-373-0565, {http://www.michigan.gov/mdcd}.

Minnesota

Paul Bridges, Ed.D., Department of Employment and Economic Development, Rehabilitation Services Branch, 390 North Robert Street, St. Paul, MN 55101; 651-296-9981, 800-328-9095, 888-GET-JOBS, TTY: 651-296-3900, {http://www.dccd.state.mn.us}. Assistance offered:

- vocational evaluation, training, and placement
- personal adjustment counseling
- independent living training
- assistive devices
- transportation
- information referral
- postemployment services
- physical therapy

Richard C. Davis, Minnesota Department of Economic Security, State Services for the Blind, 2200 University Ave. W. #240, St. Paul, MN 55114-1840; 651-642-0500, TTY: 651-642-0506, 800-652-9000, Email: {Richard.Davis@state.mn.us}, {http://www.mnssb.org}. Assistance offered:

- personal adjustment counseling
- training in independent living
- job training, placement and retention
- assistive technologies
- rehabilitation engineering
- low vision services

- blind vendor program
- child development
- parent support
- communication equipment and aids, including transcription to tape or braille

Mississippi

Mississippi Department of Rehabilitation Services, 1281 Highway 51 North, Madison, MS 39110, P.O. Box 1698, Jackson, MS 39215, 601-853-5100, 800-443-1000, {www.mdrs.state.ms.us}.

Missouri

Ronald Vessell, Director, Missouri Division of Vocational Rehabilitation, 3024 Dupont Circle, Jefferson City, MO 65109; 573-751-3251, 573-751-0881, TTY: 877-222-8963, {http://vr.dese.mo.gov}. Assistance offered:

- medical examinations
- vocational evaluation, training, and placement
- health care
- assistive devices
- living expenses and transportation assistance
- occupational tools and licenses
- counseling in independent living
- Personal Care Assistance Program

Missouri Rehabilitation Services for the Blind, P.O. Box 88, Jefferson City, MO 65103-0088; 573-751-4249, 800-592-6004, Fax: 573-751-4984, Email: {mgiboney@mail.state.mo.us}, {http://www.dss.mo.gov/dfs/rehab/index.htm}. Assistance offered:

- diagnosis and evaluation
- physical restoration
- instruction in daily living
- vocational training, including college
- job placement
- adaptive technology
- rehabilitation facilities
- Business Enterprise Program (BEP)
- counseling for children, adults, and families
- vision screening
- resource referrals

Montana

Joe Matthews, Administrator, Dept. Of Social and Rehabilitation Services, Rehabilitation/Visual Services, 111 North Sanders, Helena, MT 59620; P.O. Box 4210, Helena, MT 59604-4210; 406-444-2590, 877-296-1197, TDD: 406-444-2590, Fax: 406-444-3632, {http://www.dphhs.state.mt.us/dsd/index.htm}. Assistance offered:

- vocational evaluation, training and placement
- work adjustment training
- supported and sheltered employment
- counseling and training in independent living
- resource referrals
- adaptive equipment
- housing assistance
- Native American Vocational Rehabilitation Projects
- low vision treatment
- financial assistance

Nebraska

Director, Frank C. Lloyd, Vocational Rehabilitation Services, 301 Centennial Mall South, P.O. Box 94987, Lincoln, NE 68509; 402-471-3644, 877-637-3422, Fax: 402-471-0788, {http://www.vocrehab.state.ne.us}. Assistance offered:

- vocational evaluation, training, and placement
- transportation
- medical treatment
- personal adjustment counseling
- financial assistance
- postemployment services

Cheryl Puff, Director, Services for Visually Impaired, Dept. Of Public Institutions, 4600 Valley Road, Suite 420, Lincoln, NE 68510-4844; 402-471-2891, 877-809-2419; {www.ncbvi.state.ne.us/}. Assistance offered:

- training for independent living
- educational assistance
- vocational evaluation, training and placement

- occupational equipment
- small business enterprises program
- medical services
- advocacy services
- individual and family counseling
- consultation services for employers
- computer training
- peer support groups

Nevada

Maynard Yasmer, Administrator, Department of Employment, Training and Rehabilitation, Rehabilitation Division, Bureau of Vocational Rehabilitation, 505 E. King St., #501, Carson City, NV 89701-3704; 775-684-4040, Fax: 775-684-4186, {http://detr.state.nv.us/rehab/reh_index.htm}. Assistance offered:

- adaptive equipment
- physical and occupational therapy
- vocational training and placement
- occupational tools and licenses
- communication services and technology
- education for employers
- transportation
- counseling in independent living
- rehabilitation engineering
- resource referrals

New Hampshire

Paul K. Leather, Director, Division of Vocational Rehabilitation, 78 Regional Drive, Concord, NH 03301-9686; 603-271-3471, 800-299-1647, Email: {cfairneny@ed.state.nh.us}, {www.ed.state.nh.us/}, Assistance offered:

- vocational evaluation, training, and placement
- independent living counseling
- physical and mental restoration
- assistive devices
- supported employment
- financial assistance
- postemployment services
- information and referral

New Jersey

Thomas G. Jennings, Director, 135 East State Street, P.O. Box 398, Trenton, NJ 08625-0398; 609-292-5987, TTY: 609-292-2919, Fax: 609-292-8347, Email: {dvradmin@dol.state.nj.us}, {http://www.state.nj.us/labor/}. Assistance offered:

- medical and psychological evaluation
- vocational counseling, training, and placement
- adaptive equipment
- financial assistance with equipment and transportation

Jamie Casabianca-Hilton, Director, Commission for the Blind and Visually Impaired, Dept. of Human Services, 153 Halsey Street, 6th Floor, P.O. Box 47017, Newark, NJ 07102; 973-648-2324, Email: {ddaniels@dhs. state. nj.us}, {http://www.state.nj.us/humanservices/cbvi/index.html}. Assistance offered:

- childcare
- individual and family counseling
- tutoring
- vocational evaluation, training, and placement
- high school and college counseling
- business enterprise programs
- instruction in independent living, including housing assistance
- eye health screenings and education
- community benefits for the disabled

New Mexico

Terry Brigance, Director, Division of Vocational Rehabilitation, 435 St. Michael's Drive, Building D, Santa Fe, NM 87505; 505-954-8500, 800-224-7005, Fax: 505-954-8562, E-mail: {SKelley@state.nm.us}, {http://www.dvrgetsjobs.com}. Assistance offered:

- vocational evaluation, training, and placement
- academic training
- work adjustment training
- adaptive equipment
- job site modification
- counseling
- postemployment services

- physical and psychological examination
- independent living counseling
- medical services
- occupational supplies
- meal allowance and transportation
- job coach assistance
- supported employment
- job seeking skills training
- postemployment counseling

New York

New York State Education Department, Vocational and Educational Services for Individuals with Disabilities, One Commerce Plaza, Room 1624, Albany, NY 12234; 800-222-JOBS; {www.vesid.nysed.gov}.

John A. Johnson, Commissioner, Dept. Of Social Services, Commission for the Blind and Visually Handicapped, 40 North Pearl Street, Albany, NY 11243--0001; 518-473-1675, TDD: 518-473-1698, Fax: 518-473-9255, Email: {CBVH@dfa.state.ny.us}, {http://www.ocfs.state.ny.us/main/cbvh}. Assistance offered:

- children services
- independent living training
- communications training and equipment
- mobility instruction
- vocational evaluation, training, and placement
- low vision aids
- medical exams
- counseling
- vending facility program
- academic instruction
- information and referral

North Carolina

George McCoy, Director, Division of Vocational Rehabilitation Services, 2801 Mail Service Center, Raleigh, NC 27699; 919-855-3500, Fax: 919-733-7968, {http://dvr.dhhs.state.nc.us}. Assistance offered:

- vocational evaluation, training, and placement
- assistive devices
- personal adjustment counseling
- independent living training
- financial assistance
- transportation

John DeLuca, Director, Division of Services for the Blind, 309 Ashe Ave., Raleigh, NC 27606; 919-733-9822, Fax: 919-733-9769, Email: {johndeluca@ncmail.net}, {http://www.dhhs.state.nc/dsb}. Assistance offered:

- vision screening
- eye health education
- low vision services
- job evaluation, training, and placement
- small business assistance
- individual and family adjustment counseling
- housing and home improvement services
- home management training
- consultation and training for preschool visually impaired children and their families
- communication resources
- financial assistance

North Dakota

Gene Hysjulien, Director, N.D. Disability Services Division, Vocational Rehabilitation, 600 South 2nd Street, Suite 1B, Bismarck, ND 58504; 701-328-8950, 800-472-2622, TDD: 701-328-8968, Fax: 701-328-8969, Email: {dhsds@state.nd.us}, {http://www.state.nd.us/humanservices/services/disabilities/vr/}. Assistance offered:

- diagnosis and evaluation
- vocational training and placement, including resume writing and interviewing workshops
- physical and mental retardation
- trade school/college training
- transportation
- rehabilitation engineering services
- postemployment services
- adaptive equipment

Ohio

John M. Connelly, Administrator, Ohio Rehabilitation Services Commission, 400 E. Campus View Blvd., Columbus, OH 43235-4604; 800-282-4536 (OH only), 614-438-1200, Fax: 614-438-1257, {http://www.state.oh.us/rsc/}. Assistance offered:

- determination of benefit eligibility
- vocational evaluation, training, and placement
- rehabilitation engineering
- medical and psychological evaluation
- personal care assistance
- independent living counseling
- community centers for the deaf
- peer counseling
- supported employment
- business enterprise programs
- head injury program
- communication technology and resources

Oklahoma

Linda Parker, Director, Dept. of Rehabilitation Services, 3535 NW 58th St., Suite 500, Oklahoma City, OK 73112-4815; 405-951-3400, 800-845-8476, Fax: 405-951-3529, Email: {drspiowm@onenet.net}, {http://www.okrehab.org}. Assistance offered:

- medical examinations and treatment
- assistive devices
- job training and placement
- interpreter services
- maintenance and transportation
- occupational licenses and equipment
- initial inventory for small businesses
- rehabilitation engineering
- library services
- communication equipment
- independent living training
- supported employment
- work-study program
- school for the deaf
- school for the blind

Oregon

Gary K. Weeks, Director, Vocational Rehabilitation Division, Administration Office, 500 Summer Street NE, Salem, OR 97310-1012; 503-945-5880, TTY: 503-945-5894, Fax: 503-945-8991, E-mail: {dhr.info@state.or.us}, {http://www.dhs.state.ir.us/vr}. Assistance offered:

- vocational evaluation, training (including on-the-job), and placement
- education
- books, supplies, or tools
- transportation
- medical treatment
- adaptive equipment
- postemployment services
- independent living counseling
- Disability Determination Services (DDS)

Charles Young, Administrator, Commission for the Blind, 535 SE 12th Avenue, Portland, OR 97214; 503-731-3221, 888-202-5463, E-mail: {ocbmail@state.or.us}, {www.cfb.state.or.us}. Assistance offered:

- mobility instruction
- alternative communication skills and technology
- counseling on independent living
- optical and environmental aids
- individual, group, and family counseling
- employment counseling, training, and placement

Pennsylvania

Susan L. Aldrete, Executive Director, Office of Vocational Rehabilitation, Labor & Industry Building, 1521 N. 6th St., Harrisburg, PA 17102; 717-787-5244, 800-257-4232, TTY: 800-233-3008, Email: {ovr@dli.state.pa.us}, {www.dli. state.pa.us/}. Assistance offered:

- medical, psychological, and audiological exams
- vocational evaluation, training, and placement
- academic instruction
- counseling
- adaptive equipment
- occupational and physical therapy

- independent living training
- transportation
- occupational licenses and tools
- home and auto modifications
- attendant care
- communication devices

Rose Putric, Acting Director, Bureau of Blindness & Visual Services, Dept. of Labor and Industry, 1521 N. 6th St., Harrisburg, PA 17102; 717-787-6176, {http://www.dli.state.pa.us/}. Assistance offered:

- optical aids
- low vision services
- communication devices and training
- transportation
- personal adjustment counseling
- vocational evaluation, training and placement

Rhode Island

Raymond A. Carroll, Administrator, Office of Vocational Rehabilitation Services, Department of Human Services, 40 Fountain St., Providence, RI 02908; 800-752-8088, ext. 2300, 401-421-7005, TDD: 401-421-7016, Fax: 401-421-9259, E-mail: {rcarroll@ors.state.ri.us}, {www.ors.ri.gov}. Assistance offered:

- optical aids
- low vision services
- transportation
- personal adjustment counseling
- communication training
- vocational and medical evaluation
- job training and placement
- information referral

South Carolina

South Carolina Vocational Rehabilitation Department, 1410 Boston Ave., P.O. Box 15, West Columbia, SC 29171-0015, 803-896-6500, TDD: 803-896-6635, Fax: 803-896-6529, Email: {scvrd@rehabnet.work.org}, {http://www.scvrd.net}.

South Dakota

Grady Kickul, Director, Division of Rehabilitation Services, East Highway 34, Hillsview Plaza, c/o 500 East Capitol Avenue, Pierre, SD 57501; 605-773-3195, Fax: 605-773-5483, E-mail: {infors@dhs.state.sd.us}, {http://www.state.sd.us/dhs/drs/}. Assistance offered:

- vocational and medical diagnosis
- family and individual personal adjustment counseling
- physical restoration through treatment and/or hospitalization
- orthotic and prosthetic devices
- job training and placement
- occupational licenses, tools, and equipment
- postemployment services
- transportation and financial assistance

Gaye Mattke, Director, Division of Service to the Blind and Visually Impaired, Hillsview Plaza, E. Hwy 34, c/o 500 East Capitol, Pierre, SD 57501-5070; 605-773-4644, Fax: 605-773-5483, E-mail: {infosbvi@dhs.state.sd.us}, {http://www.state.sd.us/dhs/sbvi}. Assistance offered:

- orientation and mobility counseling
- home management training and equipment
- communication skills training
- specialized library and radio reading services
- optical aids
- training for health care professionals and employers

Tennessee

Tennessee Division of Rehabilitation Services, 400 Deadrick St., Nashville, TN 78248, 615-313-4700, TTY: 800-270-1349, Fax: 615-741-4165, {http://www.state.tn.us/humanserv/}

Texas

Vernon M. Arrell, Commissioner, Texas Rehabilitation Commission, 4900 North Lamar Blvd, Austin, TX 78751; 800-628-5115, 512-424-4410, TDD: 512-424-4417, {www.rehab.state.tx.us/}. Assistance offered:

- vocational evaluation, training, and placement
- personal adjustment counseling
- independent living training
- physical therapy
- information referral

Terry Murphy, Executive Director, Texas Commission for the Blind, 4800 North Lamar, Austin, TX 78756-3175; 512-459-2500, Voice/TDD: 800-252-5204, Fax: 512-459-2685, {www.tcb.state.tx.us/}. Assistance offered:

- orientation and mobility instruction
- home management training
- communication skills and equipment
- occupational therapy
- low vision services
- college prep
- therapeutic recreation
- independent living counseling
- medical/health management
- optical aids
- vocational evaluation, training, and placement
- Business Enterprises Program (BEP)
- bilingual services

Utah

Blaine Petersen, Executive Director, Vocational Rehabilitation Services, 250 East 500 South, Salt Lake City, UT 84111; 801-538-7530, 800-473-7530, Fax: 801-538-7522, {http://www.usor.utah.gov}. Assistance offered:

- vocational evaluation, training, and placement
- personal adjustment counseling
- medical treatment
- psychotherapy
- physical and occupational therapy
- assistive devices
- academic instruction
- transportation
- occupational tools and licenses
- interpreter services
- postemployment services
  - information and referral

Vermont

Diane P. Dalmasse, Director, Division of Vocational Rehabilitation, 103 South Main Street, Waterbury, VT 05671-2303; 802-241-2186, 866-879-6757; {http://www.vocrehabvermont.org}. Assistance offered:

- vocational evaluation and placement
- transportation
- interpreter services
- adaptive equipment
- books, supplies, and tools
- financial support
- occupational and personal adjustment services
- upported employment

Division for the Blind and Visually Impaired, 103 S. Main St., Waterbury, VT 05671-2304; 802-241-2210, Fax: 802-241-3359, E-mail: {fred@dad. state.vt.us}, {www.dad.state.vt.us/dbvi}. Assistance offered:

- physical restoration
- adaptive aids
- vocational aassessment and training
- optical aids
- education
- personal adjustment through counseling
- job placement
- researching available financial benefits

Virgin Islands

Caterine Mall, Administrator, Division of Disabilities & Rehabilitation Services, Dept. Of Human Services, 1303 Hospital Road, St. Thomas, VI 00802; 340-774-0930, Email: {humanservices@usvi.org}, {http://www.usvi. org/humanservices}.

Virginia

Joseph Ashley, Director, Virginia Department of Rehabilitation Services, 8004 Franklin Farms Drive, P.O. Box K-300, Richmond, VA 23288; 800-

552-5019, 804-662-7000, TTY: 800-464-9950, Fax: 804-662-9533, Email: {DRS@drs.state.va.us}, {http://www.vadrs.org/}. Assistance offered:

- physical, psychological, and vocational evaluation
- counseling
- restoration services
- job training and placement
- transportation
- interpreter services
- telecommunication aids
- occupational licenses and equipment
- supported employment
- postemployment services
- Long-Term Mentally Ill Program
- school-to-work transition programs
- personal assistance
- assistive devices
- independent living services
- Transitional Living Center

W. Roy Grizzard, Jr., Commissioner, Dept. For the Visually Handicapped, Commonwealth of Virginia, 397 Azalea Avenue, Richmond, VA 23227; 804-371-3140, 800-622-2155, {http://www.vdbvi.org}. Assistance offered:

- deaf-blind services
- independent living counseling
- information and referral
- low vision examinations and training
- determine eligibility for financial assistance
- youth programs
- instructional material center
- transportation
- medical, psychological, and vocational evaluation
- job training and placement
- medical treatment
- library services
- rehabilitation center
- small business assistance

Washington

Jeanne Munro, Director, Division of Vocational Rehabilitation, Dept. Of Social & Health Services, P.O. Box 45340, Olympia WA 98504; 612 Woodland Sq. Loop SE, Lacey, WA 98503-1044;, 800-637-5627, 360-438-8000, Fax: 360-438-8007, {http://www1.dshs.wa.gov/dvr}. Assistance offered:

- school-to-work transition program
- on-the-job training
- job placement
- supported employment
- independent living counseling
- attendant care
- assistive technology
- family counseling
- transportation
- medical treatment
- occupational supplies
- postemployment services

Bill Palmer, Acting Director, Dept. Of Services for the Blind, 402 Legion Way, SE, Suite 100, P.O. Box 40933, Olympia, WA 98504-0933; 360-586-1224, 800-552-7103, TDD: 360-586-6437, Fax: 360-586-7627, {www.dsb.wa.gov}.

- vocational evaluation, training and placement
- Business Enterprise Program (BEP)
- training center for independent living
- coordination of community and educational resources for adults and children
- in home training for the elderly
- recreation program

West Virginia

Janice Holland, Director, West Virginia Department of Education and the Arts, Division of Rehabilitation Services, State Capitol, P. O. Box 50890, Charleston, WV 25305-0890; 800-642-8207, 304-766-4600, Fax: 304-766-4690, E-mail: {penneyh@mail.drs.state.wv.us}, {http://www.wvdrs.org}. Assistance offered:

- vocational evaluation, training, and placement
- personal adjustment counseling
- communication devices

- physical, occupational, speech, and hearing therapy
- rehabilitation hospital
- low vision services
- medical treatment
- remedial education
- driver education
- counseling
- information and referral
- crisis intervention
- student financial aid

Wisconsin

Tom Dixon, Administrator, Division of Vocational Rehabilitation, 2917 International Lane, Suite 300, P.O. Box 7852, Madison, WI 53707-7852; 800-442-3477, 608-243-5600, TTY: 608-243-5601, Fax: 608-243-5680 or 608-243-5681, {http://www.dwd.state.wi.us/dvr}. Assistance offered:

- medical, psychological and vocational evaluation
- counseling
- job placement
- job training
- transportation
- job seeking skills
- job site modification
- technological aids and devices
- small business opportunities

- home based business development and marketing assistance
- occupational licenses and equipment
- independent living services
- training and education in approved schools
- cost of living benefits

Wyoming

Gary W. Child, Administrator, Division of Vocational Rehabilitation, Department of Employment, 1100 Herschler Building, Cheyenne, WY 82002; 307-777-7389, {http://wyomingworkforce.org}. Assistance offered:

- evaluation of rehabilitation potential
- individual and family personal adjustment counseling
- information referrals
- physical and mental restoration
- job training and placement
- financial assistance
- communication aids and training
- transportation
- occupational licenses, tools, and equipment
- Business Enterprise Program (BEP)
- attendant services
- postemployment services

State Client Assistance Program (CAP)

The first place to start when your state Office of Vocational Rehabilitation denies your handicap or disability benefits is your nearest state Client Assistance Program (CAP) office. CAP is a free information, referral, and legal service that helps disabled or handicapped individuals appeal a denial by OVR (or other agency). CAP can take your appeal process from the first stages all the way to the U.S. Supreme Court if necessary — and it won't cost you a penny.

A CAP Specialist can help in many ways by:

- Providing assistance and advocacy services to help you resolve any problems you may have in applying for or receiving rehabilitation services;
- Explaining your rights and your responsibilities throughout the rehabilitation process;
- Helping you to communicate your concerns to DORS staff;
- Giving you accurate information on rehabilitation programs and services;
- Explaining DORS policies and procedures to you;
- Helping you when a service has been denied or when you are not satisfied with a service provided;
- Providing legal services when necessary to represent you in a formal hearing; and
- Providing information about your employment rights under the Americans With Disabilities Act.

Alabama
Jerry Norsworthy, Director
Client Assistance Program
2125 East South Boulevard
Montgomery, AL 361116-2454
334-281-2276
In-State Toll Free: 800-228-3231
E-mail: sacap@hotmail.com
http://www.clik.to/SACAP

Alaska
Pam Stratton, Director
Client Assistance Program
2900 Boniface Parkway, #100
Anchorage, AK 99504-3195
907-333-2211
800-478-0047
Fax: 907-333-1186
Email: akcap@alaska.com
http://home.gci.net/~alaskacap/

American Samoa
Hellene F. Stanley, Director
Client Assistance Program
P. O. Box 3937
Pago Pago, American Samoa 96799
011-684-633-2441
Fax: 011-684-633-7286
E-Mail: opad@samoatelco.com

Arizona
Arizona Center for Disability Law
100 N. Stone Ave., Suite 305
Tucson, AZ 85701
520-327-9547 (V/TTY)
800-922-1447 (V/TTY)
Fax: 520-884-0992
Emaiol: center@acdl.com
http://www.acdl.com

Arkansas
Eddie Miller, Director
Client Assistance Program

Disability Rights Center, Inc.
Evergreen Place, Suite 201
1100 North University
Little Rock, AR 72207
501-296-1775
800-482-1174
Fax: 501-296-1779
E-mail: panda@advocacyservices.org
www.arkdisabilityrights.org

California
Sheila Conlen-Mentkowski, Director
Client Assistance Program
2000 Evergreen Street, 2nd Floor
Sacramento, CA 95815
916-263-8981
TTY: 916-263-7477
800-952-5544
Fax: 916-263-7464
E-mail: smentkow@rehab.cahwnet.gov
www.dor.ca.gov

Colorado
Jeff Peterson, Director
Client Assistance Program
The Legal Center
455 Sherman Street, Suite 130
Denver, CO 80203
303-722-0300
800-288-1376
Fax: 303-722-0720
E-mail: tlcmail@thelegalcenter.org
http://www.thelegalcenter.org

Connecticut
Susan Werboff, Director
Client Assistance Program
Office of P&A for Persons with Disabilities
60B Weston Street
Hartford, CT 06120-1551
860-297-4300
860-566-2102 (TDD)
800-842-7303 (statewide)

Fax: 860-566-8714
E-mail: hn2571@handsnet.org
www.state.ct.us/opapd

Delaware
Theresa Gallagher, Director
Client Assistance Program
United Cerebral Palsy, Inc.
254 East Camden-Wyoming Avenue
Camden, DE 19934
302-698-9336
800-640-9336
Fax: 302-698-9338
E-mail: capucp@magpage.com

District of Columbia
Joseph Cooney, Director
Client Assistance Program
University Legal Services
220 I Street, NE, Suite 130
Washington, DC 20002
202-547-0198
Fax: 202-547-2662
E-mail: jcooney@uls-dc.com
www.depanda.org

Florida
Ann Robinson, CAP Program
Advocacy Center for Persons with Disabilities
2671 Executive Center, Circle West
Webster Building, Suite 100
Tallahassee, FL 32301-5092
Phone: 850-488-9071
800-342-0823
800-346-4127 (TDD)
Fax: 850-488-8640
www.advocacycenter.org

Georgia
Charles Martin, Director
Client Assistance Program
123 N. McDonough
Decartur, GA 30030

404-373-2040
800-822-9727
Fax: 404-373-4110
E-mail: GaCAPDirector@
theOmbudsman.com
www.theOmbudsman.com/CAP/

Guam

Fidela Limtiacho
President of the Board
Client Assistance Program
Parent Agencies Network
P.O. Box 23474
GMF, Guam 96921
671-649-1948
Fax: 671-472-2568

Hawaii

Executive Director
Client Assistance Program
Protection & Advocacy Agency
900 Fort St. Mall, Suite 1040
Honolulu, HI 96814
808-949-2922
800-882-1057
Fax: 808-949-2928
E-mail: pahi@pixi.com
www.hawaiidisabilityrights.org

Idaho

Shawn DeLoyola, Director
Client Assistance Program
Co-Ad, Inc.
4477 Emerald, Suite B-100
Boise, ID 83706
208-336-5353
866-262-3462
Fax: 208-336-5396
E-mail: coadinc@mcleodusa.net
http://users.moscow.com/co-ad

Illinois

Cynthia Grothaus, Director
Client Assistance Program
100 N. First Street, 1st Floor
Springfield, IL 62702
217-782-5374
800-641-3929
Fax: 217-524-1790
www.dhs.state.il.us/ors/cap/

Indiana

Amy Ames
Client Assistance Program
Indiana Protection and Advocacy Services
4701 N. Keystone Ave., Suite 222
Indianapolis, IN 46204
317-722-5555
800-622-4845
Fax: 317-722-5564
E-mail: tgallagher@ipas.state.in.us
http://www.in.gov/ipas/

Iowa

Harlietta Helland, Director
Client Assistance Program
Division on Persons with Disabilities
Lucas State Office Building
Des Moines, IA 50319
515-281-3957
800-652-4298
Fax: 515-242-6119
Email: dhr.disabilities@dhr.state.ia.us
http://www.state.ia.us/government/dhr/pd/
pdfs/DisabilityRightsGuide.pdf

Kansas

Mary Reyer, Director
Client Assistance Program
3640 SW Topeka Blvd., Suite 150
Topeka, KS 66611
785-266-8193

800-432-2326
Fax: 785-266-8574
Email: mreyer5175@aol.com
http://www.srskansas.org/rehab/text/CAP.htm

Kentucky

Gerry Gordon-Brown, Consumer Advocate
Client Assistance Program
209 St. Clair, 5th Floor
Frankfort, KY 40601
Phone: 502-564-8035 \ 800-633-6283
Fax: 502-564-2951
E-mail: dianehigh@uky.campus.mci.net
http://kydvr.state.ky.us/index.htm

Louisiana

Susan Howard, CAP Director
Client Assistance Program
Advocacy Center for the Elderly and Disabled
225 Baronne, Suite 2112
New Orleans, LA 70112-1724
Phone: 504-522-2337
800-960-7705
Fax: 504-522-5507
E-mail: simplo@advocacyLA.org
http://www.advocacyla.org

Maine

Steve Beam, Director
Client Assistance Program
CARES, Inc.
4-C Winter Street
August, ME 04330
Phone: 207-622-7055
800-773-7055
Fax: 207-621-1869
E-mail: capsite@aol.com
http://www.caresinc.org

Maryland

Peggy Dew, Director
Client Assistance Program
Maryland Rehabilitation Center
Division of Rehabilitation Services
2301 Argonne Drive
Baltimore, MD 21208
410-554-9361
800-638-6243
Fax: 410-554-9362
Email: cap@dors.state.md.us
http://www.dors.state.md.us/services/
client_assist.htm

Massachusetts

Barbara Lybarger
Client Assistance Program
Massachusetts Office on Disability
One Ashburton Place, Room 1305
Boston, MA 02108
617-727-7440
800-322-2020
Fax: 617-727-0965
E-mail: blybarger@modi.state.ma.us
www.mass.gov/mof

Michigan

Amy Maes, Director
Client Assistance Program
Michigan P&A Service
106 West Allegan, Suite 300
Lansing, MI 48933
517-487-1755
CAP only: 800-288-5923
Fax: 517-487-0827
E-mail: ebauer@mpas.org
www.mpas.org

Minnesota

Pamela Hoopes, Director
Client Assistance Program
Minnesota Disability Law Center
430 First Avenue North, Suite 300

Minneapolis, MN 55401-1780
612-332-1441
800-292-4150
Fax: 612-334-5755
E-mail hn0518@handsnet.org
http://www.mnlegalservices.org/

Mississippi

Presley Posey, Director
Client Assistance Program
3226 N. State Street
P.O. Box 4958
Jackson, MS 39296
601-362-2585
E-mail: pposey8803@aol.com

Missouri

Cecilia Callahan, Director of Advocacy
Client Assistance Project
Missouri P&A Services
925 S. Country Club Drive, Unit B-1
Jefferson City, MO 65109
573-893-3333
800-392-8667
Fax: 573-893-4231
E-mail: mopasjc@socket.net
www.moadvocacy.org

Montana

Lynn Wislow, Director
Client Assistance Project
Montana Advocacy Program
316 N. Park, Room 211
P.O. Box 1680
Helena, MT 59624
406-449-2344
800-245-4743
800-245-4743
Fax: 406-444-0261
E-mail: advocate@mt.net
http://www.mtadv.org

Nebraska

Victoria L. Rasmussen, Director
Client Assistance Program
Division of Rehabilitation Services
Nebraska Department of Education
301 Centennial Mall South
Lincoln, NE 68509
402-471-3656
800-742-7594
Fax: 402-471-0117
E-mail: Vicki_r@nde4.nde.state.ne.us
http://www.cap.state.ne.us/

Nevada

William E. Bauer, Director
Client Assistance Program
505 East King St.
Carson City, NV 89701-3705
775-688-1440
800-633-9879
Fax: 775-688-1627
Email: detrcap@nvdetr.org
http://www.detr.state.nv.us/rehab/reh_cap.htm

New Hampshire

Michael D. Jenkins
Executive Director
Client Assistance Program
Governor's Commission on Disability
57 Regional Drive
Concord, NH 03301-9686
603-271-4175
800-852-3405
Fax: 603-271-2837
E-mail: bhagy@gov.state.nh.us
www.state.nh.us/disability/caphomepage.html

New Jersey

Ellen Lence, Director
Client Assistance Program
New Jersey P&A, Inc.
210 S. Broad Street, 3rd Floor

Trenton, NJ 08608
609-292-9742
800-922-7233
Fax: 609-777-0187
E-mail: advoca@njpanda.org
www.njpanda.org

New Mexico

Barna Dean, CAP Coordinator
Protection & Advocacy, Inc
1720 Louisiana Blvd., NE, Suite 204
Albuquerque, NM 87106
505-256-3100
800-432-4682
Fax: 505-256-3184
E-mail: nmpanda@nmprotection-
advocacy.com
www.nmpanda.org

New York

Gary O'Brien, Director
Client Assistance Program
NY Commission on Quality of Care for the
Mentally Disabled
401 State Street
Schenectody, NY 12305-2397
518-381-7098
800-624-4143 (TDD)
Fax: 518-381-7095
www.cqc.state.ny.us
michealp@cqc.state.ny.us

North Carolina

Kathy Brack, Director
Client Assistance Program
North Carolina Division of Vocational
Rehabilitation Services
2801 Mail Service Center
Raleigh, NC 27699-2801
919-855-3600
800-215-7227
Fax: 919-715-2456
E-mail: kbrack@dhr.state.nc.us
http://dvr.dhhs.state.nc.us/DVR/CAP/
caphome.htm

North Dakota

Teresa Larsen, Director
Client Assistance Program
600 South 2nd Street, Suite 1B
Bismarck, ND 58504-5729
701-328-8964
800-207-6122
Fax: 701-328-8969
E-mail: panda@state.nd.us
http://www.state.nd.us/cap/

N. Marianas Islands

Client Assistance Program
Northern Marianas
Protection and Advocacy System, Inc.
P.O. Box 3529 C.K.
Saipan, MP 96950
011-670-235-7274/3
Fax: 011-670-235-7275
E-mail: lbarcinasp&a@saipan.com
http://www.saipan.com/gov/branches/ovr/
service.htm

Ohio

Caroline Knight, Director
Client Assistance Program
Ohio Legal Rights Service
8 East Long Street, 5th Floor
Columbus, OH 43215
614-466-7264
800-282-9181
Fax: 614-644-1888
E-mail: cknight@mail.olrs.ohio.gov
http://drs.ohio.gov

Oklahoma

Helen Kutz, Director
Client Assistance Program
Oklahoma Office of Handicapped Concerns
2712 Villa Prom
Oklahoma City, OK 73107
405-521-3756
800-522-8224
Fax: 405-943-7550
Email: cap@ohc.state.ok.us
www.ohc.state.ok.us/cap

Oregon

Barbara Fields, Director
Client Assistance Program
Oregon Advocacy Center
620 W. Fifth Ave., 5th Floor
Portland, OR 97204-1428
503-243-2081
TTY: 503-323-9161
800-452-1694
TTY: 800-556-5351
Email: welcome@oradvocacy.org
http://www.oradvocacy.org

Pennsylvania

Stephen Pennington
Executive Director
Client Assistance Program
Center for Disability Law & Policy
1617 J.F.K. Blvd.
Suite 800
Philadelphia, PA 19103
215-557-7112
888-745-2357
Fax: 215-557-7602
E-mail: capcdkt@trfn.clpgh.org
http://www.equalemployment.org/cap.html

Puerto Rico

Enrique Rodriguez Otero, Director
Client Assistance Program
Office of the Governor
Ombudsman for the Disabled
P. O. Box 41309
San Juan, PR 00902-4234
787-725-2333
TTY: 787-725-4014
800-981-4125
Fax: 787-721-2455
E-mail: erodriguez@oppi.gobierno.pr
http://www.oppi.prstar.net

Republic of Palau

Client Assistance Program
Bureau of Public Health
Ministry of Health
P.O. Box 6027
Koror, Republic of Palau 96940
011-680-488-2813
Fax: 011-680-488-1211
E-mail phpa@palaunet.com

Rhode Island

Raymond Bandusky, Director
Client Assistance Program
Rhode Island Disability Law Center Inc.
151 Broadway
Providence, RI 02903
401-831-3150
401-831-5335 (TDD)
800-733-5332
Fax: 401-274-5568
E-mail: hn7384@handsnet.org
http://ridlc.org/RIDLC/ridlc.html

South Carolina

Larry Barker, Director
Client Assistance Program
Office of the Governor
Division of Ombudsman and Citizen Services
1205 Pendleton St.

Columbia, SC 29205
803-734-0285
800-868-0040
TDD: 803-734-1147
Fax: 803-734-0546
E-mail: mbutler@govoepp.state.sc.us
http://www.govoepp.state.sc.us/cap

South Dakota

Nancy Schade, Director
Client Assistance Program
South Dakota Advocacy Services
221 South Central Avenue
Pierre, SD 57501
605-224-8294
800-658-4782
Fax: 605-224-5125
E-mail:sdas@sdadvocacy.com
www.sdadvocacy.com

Tennessee

Dann Suggs, Director
Client Assistance Program
Tennessee P&A, Inc.
P. O. Box 121257
Nashville, TN 37212
615-298-1080
TTY: 615-298-2471
800-342-1660
Fax: 615-298-2046
E-mail: shirleys@tpainc.org
www.tpainc.org

Texas

Judy Sokolow, Coordinator
Client Assistance Program
Advocacy, Inc.
7800 Shoal Creek Blvd.
Suite 171-E
Austin, TX 78757
512-454-4816
800-252-9108
Fax: 512-323-0902
E-mail: hn2414@handsnet.org
www.advocacyinc.org

Utah

Nancy Friel, Director
Client Assistance Program
Disability Law Center
455 East 400 South
Suite 410
Salt Lake City, UT 84111
801-363-1347
800-662-9080
Fax: 801-363-1437
E-mail: info@disabilitylawcenter.org
www.disabilitylawcenter.org

Vermont

Laura Phillips, Director
Client Assistance Program
57 North Main St., Suite 2
Rutland, VT 05401
802-775-0021
800-769-7459
Email: nbrieden@vtlegalaid.org
http://www.vtlegalaid.org

Virginia

Client Assistance Program
Virginia Office for Protection and Advocacy
1910 Byrd St., Suite 5
Richmond, VA 23230
804-225-2042
800-552-3962
Fax: 804-662-7057
www.vopa.state.va.us

Virgin Islands

Amelia Headley LeMont
Client Assistance Program

Virgin Islands Advocacy Agency
63 Estate Cane Carlton
Frederiksted
St. Croix, USVI 00840
340-772-1200
340-776-4303
340-772-4641 (TDD)
Fax: 340-772-0609
E-mail: info@viadvocacy.org
http://www.viadvocacy.org

Washington

Jerry Johnsen, Director
Client Assistance Program
2531 Ranier Ave. South
Seattle, WA 98144
Phone: 206-721-5999
800-544-2121
Fax: 206-721-4537
E-mail: capseattle@att.net
http://www.wata.org/resource/legal/
agencies/cap.htm

West Virginia

Susan Edwards, Director
Client Assistance Program
West Virginia Advocates, Inc.
Litton Bldg, 4th Floor
1207 Quarrier Street
Charleston, WV 25301
304-346-0847
800-950-5250
Fax: 304-346-0867
E-mail: wvadvocates@newwave.net
www.wvadvocates.org

Wisconsin

Linda Vegoe
Department of Health and
Family Services
Client Assistance Program
2811 Agriculture Dr.
P.O. Box 8911

Madison, WI 53708-8911
608-224-5070
800-362-1290
Fax: 608-224-5069
E-mail: linda.vegoe@datcp.state.wi.us
http://www.dwd.state.wi.us/dvr/cap.htm

Wyoming

Jeanne Thobro, Director
Client Assistance Program
Wyoming P&A System
320 West 25th St., 2nd Floor
Cheyenne, WY 82001
307-632-3496
800-821-3091 (Voice/TDD)
800-624-7648
Fax: 307-638-0815
E-mail: wypanda@vcn.com
http://wypanda.vcn.com

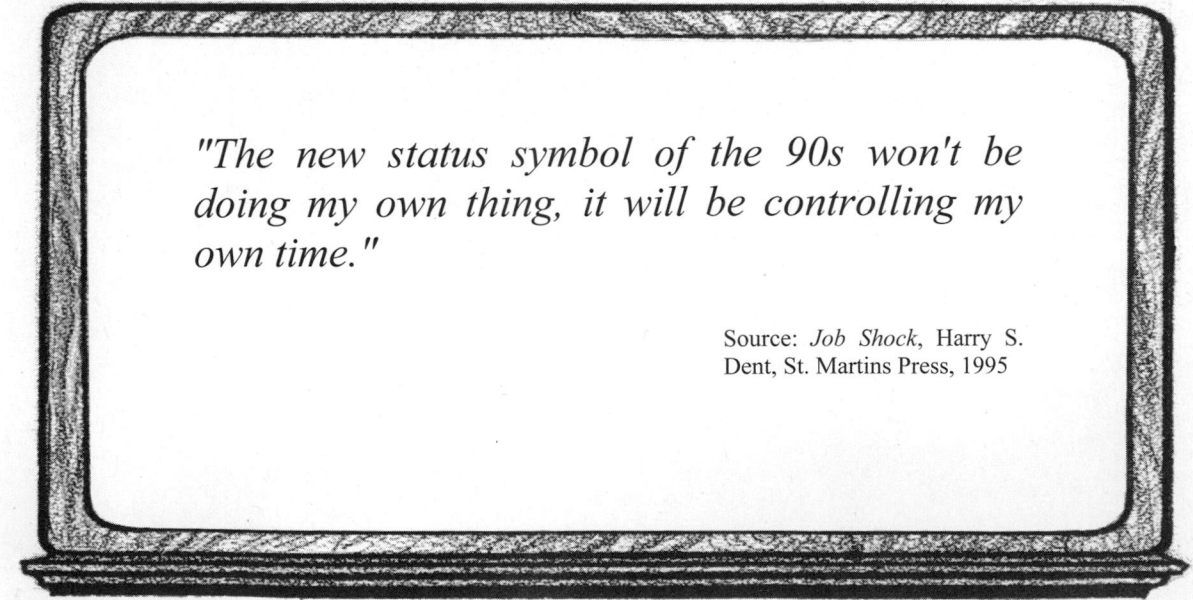

"The new status symbol of the 90s won't be doing my own thing, it will be controlling my own time."

Source: *Job Shock*, Harry S. Dent, St. Martins Press, 1995

I Wanna New Career
And I'm a Veteran

Matthew Lesko, Information USA, Inc., 12081 Nebel Street, Rockville, MD 20852 • 1-800-955-7693 • www.lesko.com

I Wanna New Career And I'm a Veteran

Veterans have completed their service to our country. It's a service that benefits all of us as a country. Now it is our turn to provide needed services to them. Whether it's help in returning to school, starting a business, or finding a job, the government has programs to give veterans a hand in building a rewarding career and stable future.

Most people have heard of the GI Bill where veterans can receive help obtaining a college education. But did you know that disabled vets can receive up to four years of vocational training? There is a program to help homeless vets find and retain jobs, and veterans can get help returning to their old jobs, even if they have been in the service for five years.

Special consideration is given to veterans who wish to start a business and learn how to run it successfully. The Small Business Administration has Veteran Affairs Officers in most offices to help vets become their own boss. Also, don't forget to check out the "I Wanna Start My Own Business" chapter for other great programs.

* Free Help with Veterans Benefits

The Department of Veterans Affairs has toll-free numbers for the convenience of veterans and their dependents. In addition, the Veterans Affairs Federal Benefits booklet and other VA information is available to the public by computer.

Dept. of Veterans Affairs	888-442-4551 (888-GIBILL)
VA Benefits	800-827-1000
Life Insurance	800-669-8477
Health Care Benefits	877-222-8387
Telecommunications Device for the Deaf (TDD)	800-829-4833
Headstones and Markers	800-697-6947
Persian Gulf Helpline	800-PGW-VETS
Persian Gulf (TDD)	800-829-4833
WWW	www.va.gov
Transaction Bulletin Board	http://dod.jobsearch.org
VA online	telnet://vaonline.va.gov
Or via data line	800-USA-VETS
Income Verification and Means Testing	800-929-8387
Mammography Helpline	888-492-7488

* College Money For Service Time After 1985

Contact your nearest Department of Veterans Affairs Regional Office or Vets Center listed at the end of this chapter.

It's called the Montgomery GI Bill (Active Duty) Program and it's for individuals who enter active duty after June 30, 1985, serve at least two years of continuous duty, and have a high school diploma or an equivalency before the first period of active duty ends. Participants elect to have $100 deducted from their pay for twelve months and the government contributes up to $536 a month for three years (or $19,296), which all goes into a savings account to be used for education upon discharge. Benefits under this program end 10 years after discharge. Also eligible for this program are those who had remaining entitlement under the Vietnam Era GI Bill on December 31, 1989, and served on active duty sometime during the period October 19, 1984 and June 30, 1985 and continued to serve on active duty to July 1, 1988 or to June 30, 1987, followed by four years in the Selected Reserve after release from active duty.

* College Money To Join The Reserves

Contact your nearest Department of Veterans Affairs Regional Office or Vets Center listed at the end of this chapter.

Individuals who sign up for a six-year reserve commitment that begins after July 1, 1985 are eligible for the Montgomery GI Bill (Selected Reserve) Program. It's basically the same as the Active Duty Program described above, but Uncle Sam contributes only $255 per month (full-time education) for 36 months, and participants are not required to contribute $100 per month. Veterans must maintain selected reserve status, and benefits must be used within 10 years from your eligibility date.

* College Money For Service Time Before 1985

Contact your nearest Department of Veterans Affairs Regional Office or Vets Center listed at the end of this chapter.

If you entered active duty for the first time after December 31, 1976 and before July 1, 1985 you are eligible for the Veterans Educational Assistance Program (VEAP). Under this program, the government contributes $2 for every $1 the participant contributes into a fund to be used for education. Service members may volunteer to contribute between $25 and $100 a month. You may be eligible to receive up to a maximum of 36 months. The maximum individual contribution is $3,600 with the government contributing a maximum of $7,200 for a total of $10,800.

Benefits are available up to ten years from the date of discharge or release from active duty. In certain instances extensions are permitted for reasons such as disability and hardship. You are also permitted to attend part time at a lesser rate if you are unable to go full time.

There are a wide variety of educational options available including earning a high school diploma or equivalent, undergraduate or graduate degree programs, cooperative training programs, a correspondence course, flight training, and even studying abroad provided the program will lead to a degree. A state agency or VA must approve the program.

* Vocational and Educational Counseling For All Vets

Contact your nearest Department of Veterans Affairs Regional Office or Vets Center listed at the end of this chapter.

Servicemembers, veterans, and dependents of deceased or totally disabled veterans may receive a full range of educational and vocational counseling and testing. This program aids in selecting an educational or vocational goal, and providing facilities that may help satisfy that goal. To locate your nearest counseling center, contact your nearest Department of Veterans Affairs Regional Office or Vets Center listed below.

* Vocational Rehabilitation For Vets With Disabilities

Contact your nearest Department of Veterans Affairs Regional Office or Vets Center listed at the end of this chapter.

Veterans and servicemembers who served in the Armed Forces on or after September 16, 1940, were discharged under honorable conditions, and have a disability rating of at least 20%, may be eligible for up to four years of rehabilitation services. Most veterans participate on a full time basis, but less than full time is possible. Veterans may: 1) enroll in a trade, business, or technical school or in college level institutions; 2) train on the job or in an apprenticeship program; 3) take on-farm training; 4) enter programs which combine school and on-the-job training; 5) train in special rehabilitation facilities or at home when this is necessary because of serious disability; or, self employment. The government pays for all the costs for tuition, fees, books, supplies and equipment □ and may also pay for special services like tutorial assistance to gain additional work skills. The eligibility period for this benefit is 48 months to be used with 12 years from the award date, with certain exceptions.

* Help For Homeless Vets

VA Homeless Grant and Per Diem Program Office
Department of Veterans Affairs   877-332-0334
810 Vermont Avenue NW   202-273-8966
Washington, DC 20420   202-693-4701
Contact: Roger Casey
Email: roger.casey@mail.va.gov

The Homeless Veterans' Reintegration Projects (HVRP) Program was created to assist homeless veterans in obtaining and retaining jobs. HVRP staff develop job openings for veterans. The program also helps to link veterans with other providers including Veterans' Affairs offices and medical facilities, Job Training Partnership Act and social service agencies. These providers can help stabilize the homeless veteran and remove barriers to employment such as lack of skills, clothing, medical care, and job skills. They provide treatment for substance abuse and support long-term housing.

HVRP uses veterans who have experienced homelessness themselves to reach out to homeless veterans. They go into the streets, shelters, soup kitchens, and other places where veterans might be to encourage them to take advantage of the available services. HVRP's goal is to get homeless veterans off the street and into gainful employment with an emphasis on long-term job retention.

* Vocational Training For Retired Veterans

Contact your nearest Department of Veterans Affairs Regional Office or Vets Center listed at the end of this chapter.

Veterans who were awarded a pension prior to December 31, 1995 may be eligible for up to 24 months □ or more under certain circumstances □ of vocational training. This includes trade school, college, apprenticeships, and even self-employment assistance. Program participants may also receive up to 18 months of employment-counseling, job search assistance and work adjustment services.

* College Money And Training For Surviving Spouse And Children

Contact your nearest Department of Veterans Affairs Regional Office or Vets Center listed at the end of this chapter.

Under the Dependents Educational Assistance Program (DEA), educational assistance and training benefits are available to spouses and children of:

1. Veterans who died as a result of a disability arising from active service.
2. Veterans who died from any cause while rated permanently and totally disabled form service-connected disability.
3. Service members currently missing in action or captured in the line of duty.
4. Servicepersons detained or interred in line of duty by a foreign government.

Benefits include $485 per month for attending school full time with lesser amounts for part time education. Individuals may be entitled to receive up to 45 months of education benefits.

Children generally have 8 years in which they can use their benefits. A son or daughter must be between the age of 18 and 26 to receive benefits however there are some exceptions. The extension cannot go beyond one's 31st birthday. There are a wide variety of opportunities. A few of the many options include pursuing a degree at a college or university (this would include associate, bachelor, master, or doctorate degrees). You may also take independent study or cooperative training programs.

Spouses may receive benefits for up to 10 years from the date the VA finds you eligible or from the date of the death of the veteran. Opportunities are extensive and include but are not limited to the following: pursing an undergraduate or graduate degree, taking a correspondence course, studying abroad (provided the program leads to a college degree), cooperative training programs, or apprenticeship and job training. A spouse's remarriage blocks further benefits.

* Job Finding Assistance

Contact the State Employment Office or
Job Service Office nearest you

Local Veterans Employment Representatives (LVER) are available at state job service offices around the country. The LVER contact employers to develop job openings for veterans, and monitor job listings from federal contractors. They provide free job counseling, testing, training, referral, and placement services to veterans. Priority in referral to job openings and training opportunities is given to eligible veterans. The highest priority is given to disabled veterans. LVER also work with the Department of Veterans Affairs to identify and aid veterans who need work-specific prosthetic devices, sensory aids, or other special equipment to improve their employability. They also provide information about unemployment compensation, job marts and on-the-job and apprenticeship training opportunities. Contact the Job Service Office nearest you and ask for the Local Veterans Employment Representative. The number would be listed under State Government in the blue pages.

* Get Your Old Job Back With A Raise After 5 Years In The Military

Contact your nearest Veterans' Employment and Training Service (VETS) office (see page 970)

The Uniformed Services Employment and Reemployment Rights Act of 1994 (USERRA) clarifies and strengthens the Veterans' Reemployment Rights (VRR) Act of 1940. USERRA continues the protection of civilian job rights and benefits for veterans and members of Reserve components. However, USERRA makes major improvements in protecting servicemember rights and benefits by clarifying the law, improving enforcement mechanisms, and providing Federal Government employees with Department of Labor assistance in providing claims.

USERRA expands the cumulative length of time that an individual may be absent from work for military duty and retain reemployment rights for five years (the previous law provided four years of active duty, plus an additional year if it was for the convenience of the government). There are important exceptions to the five year limit, including initial enlistments lasting more than five years, periodic training duty, and involuntary active duty extension and recalls, especially during a time of national emergency. USERRA clearly establishes that reemployment protection does not depend on the timing, frequency, duration, or nature of an individual's service.

The program also provides enhanced protection for disabled veterans, requiring employers to make reasonable efforts to accommodate the disability. Servicemembers convalescing from injures received during service of training may have up to two years to return to their jobs (as opposed to the one year provided by the old law).

As under the previous law, USERRA provides that returning servicemembers be reemployed in the job that they would have attained had they not been absent for military service (the long-standing "escalator" principle), with the same seniority, status, and pay as well as other rights and benefits determined by seniority. USERRA also requires that reasonable efforts (such as training or retraining) be made to enable returning servicemembers to refresh or upgrade their skills in order to help qualify them for reemployment. The law clearly provides for alternative reemployment positions if the servicemembers cannot qualify for the "escalator" position. USERRA also reaffirms and clarifies that while an individual is performing military service, he or she is deemed to be on furlough or leave of absence and is entitled to the non-seniority rights accorded other individuals on non-military leave of absence.

The period an individual has to make application for reemployment or report back to work after military service is now based on time spent on military duty; not the category of service performed. For service of less than 31 days, the servicemember must return at the beginning of the next regularly scheduled work period on the first full day after release from service, taking into account safe travel home, plus an eight hour rest period. For service of more than 30 days but less than 181 days, the servicemember must submit an application for reemployment within 14 days of release from service. For service of more than 180 days, an application for reemployment must be submitted within 90 days of release from service.

USERRA also requires than servicemembers provide advance written or verbal notice to their employers for all military duty unless giving notice is impossible, unreasonable, or precluded by military necessity. In addition, servicemembers are able to use accrued vacation or annual leave while performing military duty.

The Department of Labor, through the Veterans' Employment and training Service (VETS) provides assistance to all persons having claims under USERRA. If you have questions about the program, please contact your nearest VETS office. There is an electronic advisor online that may be able to answer questions regarding your rights and responsibilities. The address is {http://www.elaws.dol.gov/userra/wren/userra.htm}. It is called the USERRA Expert System.

* Job Protection For Reservists And Members Of The National Guard

Contact your nearest Veterans' Employment and Training Service (VETS) office (see page 970)

Congress has provided certain protection for reservists and members of the National Guard with respect to their civilian employers. The Uniformed Services Employment and Reemployment Rights Act of 1994 (USERRA) provides that a reservist or member of the National Guard will be granted a leave of absence to perform active duty training or inactive duty training and will not be denied benefits due to this obligation. Written orders are not required before leaving your job, but reservists and National Guard members are encouraged to inform their employers that they will need a leave of absence. The leave of absence applies to active duty for training (ADT) and to inactive duty (IDT) which includes drills. Reservists and National Guard members are also encouraged to submit written requests to their employers in order to avoid any misunderstanding. The employer regardless of the format cannot deny the request, and the service member must submit the written request upon re-application.

There is no limitation on either the frequency or duration of a military leave of absence to perform ADT or IDT so long as the individual has been ordered to perform military training. In this case, his or her job is protected. It is also unlawful to make a reservist or national Guard member use his or her vacation to perform military training.

Upon completion of training, reservists or National Guard members must report back to their civilian job at their first regularly scheduled shift after their arrival home. Upon reporting back they must be allowed to return with seniority, status pay, and vacation as though they had not been gone.

The Department of Labor, through the Veterans' Employment and Training Service (VETS) provides assistance to all persons having claims under USERRA. If you have any questions about the program, please contact your nearest VETS office.

* Unemployment Compensation When Leaving The Military

Contact your nearest State Employment Office

Ex-service members are eligible for a weekly income for a limited period of time to help meet basic needs while searching for employment. The amount and duration of payments are governed by state laws, which vary considerably. Be sure to bring a copy of military discharge form DD-214 when you are applying. Contact your nearest state employment office listed in the blue pages of your telephone book under State Government.

* Government Contractors Who Have To Hire Vets

Office of the Assistant Secretary for
Veterans' Employment and Training
U.S. Department of Labor
400 Constitution Ave., NW
Washington, DC 20210   202-693-4700

Contractors or subcontractors with at least $10,000 of work with the Federal government must take affirmative action to hire and promote qualified Vietnam-era and "special disabled" veterans (who are also covered under the Americans with Disabilities Act). Special disabled veterans are veterans who have a disability rating of 30 percent or more, or veterans who are rated at 10% to 20% and have a serious employment handicap, or those veterans who were discharged due to a service connected disability. Job openings must be listed with the nearest state job-service or employment service office. Qualified Vietnam and special disabled veterans are then given priority referral for openings. Companies are not required to hire all those referred but must have affirmative action plans when applicable. Companies must file a VETS 100 report, which shows veteran hiring information. Previous reporting has shown that in one year there were new hires of 112,027 of Vietnam-era veterans and 22,905 of special disabled veterans.

For additional information about the VETS 100 report, contact the office listed above.

You may also get copies of written information regarding the Obligations of Contractors and Subcontractors for Disabled Veterans and Veterans by contacting the U.S. Department of Labor at the number listed above.

* Troops To Teachers

DANTES (Defense Activity for Non-Traditional Education Support)
6490 Saufley Field Rd.   850-452-1320
Pensacola, FL 32509-5243   Fax: 850-452-1096
Email: ttt@voled.doded.mil
http://voled.doded.mil

Troops to Teachers is a Department of Defense program that provides departing Service members, military personnel planning a career change, and civilian personnel assistance in obtaining teacher certification and employment opportunities through placement in schools. The emphasis of the program is relieving shortages of teachers and teachers aides in schools with students of low income families. Priority subjects are math and science.

Qualified schools that employ participants may also receive an incentive grant to offset a portion of the individual's salary.

To get additional information, contact the office listed above.

* Job Training Partnership Act For Vets

Office of the Assistant Secretary for
Veterans Employment and Training Service
U.S. Department of Labor
200 Constitution Ave., NW
Washington, DC 20210   202-693-4700

Veterans are entitled to receive training and other help to find suitable employment under the Federal Job Training Partnership Act (JTPA). Programs are primarily designed to meet the needs of service connected disabled veterans, Vietnam-era veterans, and veterans that have recently been separated (within the last 48 months).

In addition to classroom, vocational, skills-based, and on the job training, JTPA can include:

-     counseling, vocational and aptitude testing and career assessment
-     remedial education
-     on-site industry specific training
-     supportive services and other training related assistance.

Veterans are also eligible for other JTPA-funded programs that help economically disadvantaged or dislocated workers find jobs and relocate to other areas or occupations.

To get additional information, contact your nearest Veterans' Employment and Training Service listed on page 970 or the main office listed above.

* Establishment of Veterans Programs

Assistant Secretary for Veterans' Employment and Training
U.S. Department of Labor
200 Constitution Ave., NW
Washington, DC 20210   202-693-4700

The Assistant Secretary for Veterans Employment and Training at the Department of Labor is in charge of establishing programs under the Job Training Partnership Act especially for disabled, Vietnam era, and recently separated veterans.

In addition to these programs, the Assistant Secretary also assures proper emphasis on veterans' employment and advancement by employers with federal contracts, carries out all other Department of Labor employment, unemployment and training programs that affect veterans and provides grants to states to fund veterans programs.

For information about available programs in your area, contact your regional or state Veterans' Employment and Training Service listed on page 970 or the main office listed above.

* Special Job Counseling For Disabled Vets

Assistant Secretary for Veterans' Employment and Training Service
U.S. Department of Labor
200 Constitution Ave., NW
Washington, DC 20210   202-693-4700

States receive funding from the Federal government to locate disabled veterans and help them find jobs, especially veterans of the Vietnam era. Disabled Veterans Outreach Program (DVOP) Specialists work with employers, veterans' organizations, the Departments of Veterans' Affairs and Defense, and community based organizations to match qualified disabled veterans with jobs and training opportunities. DVOP specialists receive lists of all veterans with service-connected disabilities in each state from the Department of Veterans Affairs. They then contact veterans to inform them of available employment and training programs, vocational guidance and employment counseling. Specialists serve as case managers for veterans enrolled in federally funded job training programs and state services. DVOP's maintain monthly contact with veterans and their employers to make sure that training is completed and that there are no problems. Most staff members are located in offices of the state employment service (job service offices) but some may be stationed in Veterans Affairs regional office and readjustment counseling centers (Vet Centers). Your nearest job service office is located under State Government in the blue pages of your phone book or contact the main office listed above.

* Free Workshop For Vets Leaving The Military

Veterans' Employment and Training Service
U.S. Department of Labor
200 Constitution Ave., NW (S-1316)   202-693-4700
Washington, DC 20210   Fax: 202-693-4754
www.dol.gov/dol/vets/public/aboutvets/contacts/main.htm

The Transition Assistance Program (TAP) established a partnership with the Department of Defense, Veterans Employment and Training Service, Department of Veterans Affairs and the Labor Department to meet the needs of separating service members by offering job search assistance and related services within 180 days of separation or retirement.

TAP consists of comprehensive three day workshops at selected military installations throughout the nation. Workshop attendees learn how to conduct successful job searches, decisions in careers, current occupational and labor market conditions, resume and cover letter preparation, and a realistic evaluation of their employability.

Service members leaving the military with a service connected disability are offered the Disabled Transition Assistance Program (DTAP) which includes the three day TAP workshop and four hours of instruction to help determine job readiness and address the special needs of disabled veterans.

For additional information, contact the main office listed above or your nearest Veterans Affairs Center listed on page 977.

* Get National Employment Information

Transaction Bulletin Board   http://dod.jobsearch.org

The military services provide civilian transition counseling at least 90 days prior to each servicemembers's discharge in a program called Operation Transition. A Defense Department document (DD Form 2586) is prepared to verify information valuable for civilian jobs and education, including military experience, training history, associated civilian equivalent job titles, and recommended educational credit information. The document is delivered to servicemembers 90 to 180 days before they are scheduled for separation.

The Defense Outplacement Referral System (DORS) refers mini-resumes to potential employers through 350 transition offices worldwide. Resumes are provided to employers by Email, fax or mail, based on the geographic and occupational preferences of each individual. Employers may place job ads on the electronic Transaction Bulletin Board (TBB) kept by transition offices.

Those employers having the proper computer equipment are able to place their ads electronically; others may mail or fax their ads to TBB. Service members are encouraged to respond to employers with their resumes. In addition, the bulletin board contains information on seminars, events, and other helpful information.

Two special registries have been developed to help separating servicemembers obtain public community service jobs. The "Registry of Public and Community Service Organizations" contains information on organizations desiring to hire servicemembers who are seeking employment in public and community service occupations. Defense matches people and employers on the two registries, and counsels separating servicemembers on how to apply for positions with public and community service organizations. Contact TBB for more information.

* Veterans Readjustment Appointment (VRA)

The VRA is a special authority by which agencies can employ an eligible veteran without competition. The candidate does not have to be on a list of eligibles, but must meet basic requirements. You must have served on active duty for more than 180 days, except if you were released due to a service connected disability. For more information, contact the Federal agency personnel office where you are interested in working. Agencies recruit candidates and make VRA appointments directly. You may also use the Department of labor and VETS "expert system" on the Internet to find out which preferences you are entitled to. The address is www.dol.gov/dol/vets/public/programs/programs/preference/main.htm.

* Operation Allied Force

Under provisions of the Soldiers' and Sailors' Relief Act of 1940, a service member called to active duty in support of Operation Allied Force or any other operation, may qualify for any or all of the following:

- Reduced interest rate on mortgage payments.
- Reduced interest rate on credit cards
- Protection from eviction if your rent is $1,200 or less.
- Delay of all civil court actions

Most provisions of the act are automatic, and are based on "material effect", which refers to how military service affects one's life and their inability to meet their obligations.

Free Tutoring and Counseling for Veterans Interested in a College Education

(Upward Bound - 84.047)

Are you a veteran with a high school diploma or GED? Want to go to college? Then take advantage of a great program called Upward Bound. This FREE program can help you prepare for admission to the college of your choice.

Upward Bound assesses your strengths and weaknesses and provides one-on-one training in math, reading, study skills, and more to prepare you for the rigors of college. They will help you complete financial aid forms, help you study for entrance exams, and even coach you on interview skills. They will do whatever it takes to help make you a success in college.

Veterans Upward Bound is open to veterans who are economically or educationally disadvantaged, with two-thirds of enrollees being first generation college graduates. Veterans' Upward Bound programs are currently located at 36 colleges across the U.S, and 50 Veterans Upward Bound Projects are now being funded. You do not have to be admitted or enrolled in these colleges, nor do you have to enroll in them after you complete the program.

Approximately 4,200 participants are served annually. Contact the program nearest you for more information, or contact the main office at the Division of Student Services, Education Outreach Branch, Office of Post-secondary Education, U.S. Department of Education, Federal Trio Program, 600 Maryland Ave., SW, Portals Bldg., Suite 600D, Washington, DC 20202; 202-708-4804.

Veterans Upward Bound State Offices

Alabama
Valerie Richardson
Gadsden State Community College
Arledge Center for Adult Learners
P.O. Box 227
Gadsden, AL 35902-0227
256-549-8396
Fax: 256-549-8404

Arizona
William C. Weir, Director
Arizona State University
1000 East Apache Blvd.
Tempe, AZ 85281
408-894-8451
Fax: 408-894-9538

Jake Lindsay
Yavapai College
1100 East Sheldon Street
Box 6043
Prescott, AZ 86301
520-776-2309
Fax: 520-771-9097
Email: jake_lindsay@yavapai.cc.az.us

Arkansas
Gerald Hudder
University of Arkansas/Fayetteville
725 Hotz Hall
Fayetteville, AR 72701
501-575-2821
Fax: 501-575-5748
Email: ghudder@comp.uark.edu

California
Cai Williams, Director
Humboldt State University
University Annex, Room 158
Arcata, CA 95521-2400
707-826-4971/4974
Fax: 707-826-5237
Email: cwl@axe.humboldt.edu
www.humboldt.edu

Frank Alderete, Coordinator
Telacau Education Foundation
5400 East Olympic Blvd., Suite 100
Los Angeles, CA 90022
323-838-8955
Fax: 323-838-8960

Colorado
Glenn A. Morris
Metropolitan State College
Campus Box 89
P.O. Box 173362
Denver, CO 80217-3362
303-556-3947
Fax: 303-556-6245
Email: morrisg@mscd.edu

Delaware
Mariko Tapper-Taylor
Delaware State University
1200 North DuPont Highway
Dover, De 19901
302-857-6130
Fax: 302-857-6131
Email: mtaylor@dsc.edu

Florida
Bernice Belcher, Director
Miami-Dade Community College
11011 SW 104th Street
Miami, FL 33176
305-237-0940
Fax: 305-237-0868
www.kendall.mdcc.edu/studsvc/veterans.htm
Email: bbelcher@kendall.mdcc.edu

Ned Couey
Okaloosa-Walton Community College
100 College Boulevard
Niceville, FL 32578
850-729-5366
Fax: 850-729-5278
Email: coueyn@owcc.net

Georgia
Arthur Barham, Executive Director
Veterans Opportunity and Resource Center, Inc.
2001 Martin Luther King Drive, NW
Suite 503
Atlanta, GA 30310
P.O. Box 92425
Atlanta, GA 30314
404-755-7675
Fax: 404-775-5225
Email: vorci@bellsouth.net

Illinois
Christopher Chalko
Roosevelt University
430 S. Michigan Ave., Room 321 HCC

Chicago, IL 60605
312-341-6382
Fax: 312-341-6382
www.veterans-ru.org
Email: cchalko@roosevelt.edu

Indiana

Lim Kaiser, Director
Vincennes University
1002 North First Street
Vincennes, IN 47591
317-927-5373
Fax: 812-888-5958
Email: lkaiser@vunet.vinu.edu

Kansas

Ngondi Kamatuka
University of Kansas
301 Pearson Hall
Lawrence, KS 66045
785-272-582/
Fax: 785-272-4408
Email: kamatuka@falcon.cc.ukans.edu

Kentucky

Randy Wilson, Director
Western Kentucky University
Jones-Jaggers Hall Room 114
1 Big Red Way
Bowling Green, KY 42101-3576
270-745-5008
Fax: 270-745-3487
Email: randal.d.wilson@wku.edu
www2.wku.edu/www/veterans/vub.html

Louisiana

Claudia Sophie
Delgado Community College
City Park Avenue, Bldg., 2615
New Orleans, LA 70119-4399
504-483-4114
Fax: 504-483-4386
Email: csauci@pop3.dcc.edu

Kim Barker, Director
Southeastern Louisiana University
548 West Stadium Room 28, SLU 10571
Hammond, LA 70402
504-549-2955
800-616-2316
Fax: 504-549-3389
Email: kbarker@selu.edu
www.selu.edu/Academics/contEd/VUB.html

Robert Carmouche
University of Southwestern Louisiana
106 Declouet Hall
P.O. Box 43452
Lafayette, LA 70504
337-482-6831
Fax: 337-482-6833

Massachusetts

Charles Diggs
University of Massachusetts - Boston
100 Morrisey Blvd.
Chancellor's Office
Boston, MA 02125-3393
617-287-5870
Fax: 617-265-7173
Email: diggs@umbsky.cc.umb.edu

Michigan

Paul Rease
Wayne State University
3127 East Canfield
Detroit, MI 48207
313-571-9500
Fax: 313-993-9727
www.es.wayne.edu/access/veop/index.html

Minnesota

Jim Kilps
Minneapolis Community and Technical College
1501 Hennepin Avenue
Minneapolis, MN 55403
612-341-7076
Fax: 612-373-2797
Email: kilpsji@mctc.mnscu.edu

Montana

Luke L. Petriccione, Director
Veterans Upward Bound
Montana State University Northern
1500 N. 30th Street
Billings, MT 59101-0298
406-657-2075
800-356-8387
877-356-8387
Fax: 406-657-4077
Email: lukevets@hotmail.com
www.msubillings.edu/vub/index.htm

Nevada

Robert Hernandez, Director
Truckee Meadows Community College
7000 Dandini Blvd.
Reno, NV 89512
775-829-9007
Fax: 775-829-9048
www.scs.unr.edu/~mela-ken/veteran.html
Email: r_h@unv.edu

New Jersey

Betty Foster
Essex County College
303 University Avenue, Room 3310
Newark, NJ 07102
201-973-3196
Fax: 201-973-3044
Email: foster@essex.edu

North Dakota

Bruce Steele, Director
North Dakota State University
Veterans Reentry Program
319 Ceres Hall
Box 5625, University Station
Fargo, ND 58105-5625
701-231-8543
800-570-5719
Fax: 701-231-9669
Email: Bruce_Steele @ndsu.nodak.edu
www.ndsu.nodak.edu/trio/vrp/vrp.html

Ohio

Eric Weimer
Cuyahoga Community College
3740 Carnegie Ave., Suite 200
Cleveland, OH 44115-2716
216-987-4196
Fax: 216-987-4941
www.tri-c.cc.oh.us/eop/docs/vubs.htm

Rose Nelson
University of Cincinnati
P.O. Box 210119
Cincinnati, OH 45221
513-556-8387
Fax: 513-556-2089
Email: rosana.nelson@uc.edu
www.oz.uc.edu/vub

Oklahoma

Mary Huckleberry
East Central University
ECU Box S-36
Ada, OK 74820
580-310-5541
Fax: 580-436-4563
Email: mhuckleb@mailclerk.ecok.edu

Darren Wise
Seminole Junior College
P.O. Box 351
Seminole, OK 74868-0351
405-382-0059
Fax: 405-382-0167

James E. Wydeman Sanders
Connors State College
1000 College Road
Route 1, Box 1000
Warner, OK 74469
918-463-2931
Fax: 918-463-2233

Pennsylvania

Annette Hampton, Director
University of Pennsylvania
3933 Walnut Street
Philadelphia, PA 19104-6184
215-898-6892
Fax: 215-764-2084
Email: hampton@pobox.upenn.edu

Puerto Rico

Francisco Feliciano
Aspira Inc. de Puerto Rico
P.O. Box 21509
UPR Station
San Juan, PR 00931
787-768-1985 ext. 232
Fax: 787-257-2725
Email: ffelicia@rrpac.upr.clu.edu

Tennessee

Arthur Neal
Austin Peay State University
P.O. Box 4455
Clarksville, TN 37044
931-221-6235
Fax: 931-503-1526
Email: neala@apsu02.apsu.edu

Ronnie Gross
East Tennessee State University
1227 Volunteer Parkway
Bristol, TN 37620
423-844-6304
Fax: 423-844-6303
Email: grossrd@etsu.edu

Joel Coates
University of Tennessee/Knoxville
1914 Andy Holt Ave.
HPER Bldg. Room 25
Knoxville, TN 37996-2745
865-974-4466
Fax: 865-974-3961
http://web.uk.edu/~utkvub/veterans.html

Utah

Jim Kopecky
Weber State University
1308 University Circle
Ogden, UT 84408-1308
801-626-7173
Fax: 801-626-6826
Email: jkopecky@weber.edu

Virginia

Ms. Lucy Hawkins
Norfolk State University
700 Park Ave.
Norfolk, VA 23504
757-823-2471
Fax: 757-823-8803
Email: lhawkins@vger.nsu.edu

West Virginia

Michael Fisher
Davis & Elkins College

100 Campus Drive
Elkins, WV 26241-3996
304-624-3157
Fax: 304-637-1428
Email: vub@euclid.dne.wvnet.edu

Ron Holt
Bluefield State University
219 Rock Street
Bluefield, WV 24701

304-327-4030
Fax: 304-327-4427
Email: rholt@aol.com

Wisconsin
Alan Caldwell
College of Menominee Nation
P.O. Box 1179
Keshena, WI 54135
715-799-5602

Fax: 715-799-1326
Email: acaldwell@menominee.com

Ketmani Kouanchao
University of Wisconsin-Milwaukee
324 Johnston Hall
P.O. Box 413
Milwaukee, WI 53201
414-229-6799
Fax: 414-229-2859
Email: ketmani@uwm.edu

Non-Competitive Government Jobs

The Veterans Employment Opportunity Act of 1998 allows preference eligibles or veterans who have been separated under honorable conditions from the armed forces, with three or more years of continuous active service, to compete for vacancies under merit promotion procedures when an agency accepts applications from outside its own workforce. Under the Office of Personnel Management's Disabled Veterans Affirmative Action Program, all federal agencies are required to establish action plans to facilitate the recruitment, employment, and advancement of disabled veterans. These appointments may lead to conversion to career or career-conditional employment upon satisfactory work for two years.

Veterans also receive additional preferences including extra point to employment examinations, first consideration for certain jobs, and preferences for retention in reductions in force. Preference is also provided for: 1) unremarried widows and widowers of deceased veterans and mothers of military personnel who died in service; 2) spouses of service-connected disabled veterans who are no longer able to work in their usual occupations; and 3) mothers of veterans who have permanent and total service-connected disabilities. Individuals interested in federal employment should contact the personnel offices of the agencies of interest. There is also a manual available through the Office of Personnel Management, which is designed to assist veterans with employment in the Federal government. Additional information is available by contacting the U.S. Office of Personnel Management through USA Jobs online or USA Jobs by Phone. Their Internet address is www.usajobs.opm.gov. The USA Jobs by Phone telephone numbers for each state are listed below.

A formal complaint may be filed with the US Department of Labor if a veteran believes that an agency has violated his or her veterans preference entitlements.

USA Jobs by Phone

California
415-744-5627

Colorado
303-969-7050

District of Columbia
202-606-2700

Georgia
404-331-4315
912-757-3000

Hawaii
808-541-2791

Iowa
816-426-7820

Louisiana
210-805-2402

Massachusetts
617-565-5900

Michigan
313-226-6950

Minnesota
612-725-3430

Missouri
816-426-5702

Nebraska
816-426-7819

North Carolina
919-790-2822

Texas
210-805-2402

Wisconsin
612-725-3430

Matthew Lesko, Information USA, Inc., 12081 Nebel Street, Rockville, MD 20852 • 1-800-955-7693 • www.lesko.com

Small Business Administration

In each local Small Business Administration office, there is a person who is designated as the Veterans Affairs Officer (VAO). This person should be your initial contact and resource person for SBA programs. You can contact the VAO by calling the applicable number listed below.

The following are among the programs by the Small Business Administration specifically targeted for veterans.

* Loans To Veterans To Start A Business

Director
Loan Policy and Procedures Branch
Small Business Administration
409 Third St., SW   202-205-6570
Washington, DC 20416   800-827-5722
www.sba.gov

The United States Congress has authorized the Small Business Administration to make loans for business purposes. However, before SBA can consider a loan application, the applicant must show that funding is not otherwise available on reasonable terms.

A letter of declination from the bank is required. These are loans, not grants, and the applicant must demonstrate that the loan can be repaid from the earnings of the business. There are no grants available for starting and maintaining a small business. Veterans who meet SBA loan criteria are placed ahead of non-veterans who apply on the same day (see Special Consideration below). There is a pre-qualification program available in most states to veterans, that pre-approves a loan between $15,000 to $200,000 before you even go to the bank.

All veterans must meet the same SBA standard loan criteria as any other applicant. If you are a veteran who is a farmer or from a rural community, contact the United States Department of Agriculture Rural Business - Cooperative Service. For those eligible, SBA offers a broad range of loan programs. Many of these loans are made by financial institutions and are guaranteed by SBA. Regular business loans are available to veterans on a special consideration basis. Loans range from $500 to $750,000, with approximately $16 million worth of loans made per year. Contact the Veterans Affairs Officer at your local U.S. Small Business Administration Field office listed below or you can call the national toll free number, 800-827-5722 (800-U-ASK-SBA), or online at {www.sba.gov}.

* "Special Consideration" To Start A Business

Office of Veterans Affairs
U.S. Small Business Administration
409 Third St., SW, Suite 6500   800-U-ASK-SBA
Washington, DC 20416   TDD: 202-205-7333

The Small Business Administration (SBA) wants veterans to receive the benefits of all programs the agency provides. To ensure that this happens, a policy was adopted giving veterans "special consideration" in agency programs. Special Consideration involves designing unique management training programs specifically for veterans, processing veterans loan applications before non-veteran applications submitted the same day, monitoring loan and procurement activities to measure veteran participation, coordinating training and counseling activities for veterans with other agency departments and allocating a portion of direct loan funds for veterans. To get additional information on SBA services, contact the main office listed above or the VAO (Veterans Affairs Officer) in your nearest SBA office listed below.

* Veteran's Guide To Entrepreneurship

Small Business Administration
409 Third St., SW, Suite 6500
Washington, DC 20416   800-U-ASK-SBA

A Veteran's Guide to Entrepreneurship is a publication that was developed by the Office of Veterans Affairs and will assist those servicemembers who choose to start a business. Many servicemembers choose self-employment for various reasons.

This publication will help provide the needed information on starting a business. The information is very comprehensive and will assist with all aspects of having your own business. In addition, there is a Veteran's Handbook which also may be very helpful. To get both publications, contact the main office listed above or the VAO in your nearest SBA office listed below.

Small Business Administration Field Offices and Phone Numbers

Region I
John Gardner
Veterans Affairs Officer
68 Sewall St., Room 512
Augusta, ME 04330
207-622-8555
Fax: 207-622-8277

Donna Harper
Veterans Affairs Officer
Stewart Nelson Plaza
143 North Main Street, Suite 202
Concord, NH 03301
603-225-1400

Thomas Schroeder
Veterans Affairs Officer
87 State St. Room 205
Montpelier, VT 05602
802-828-4422, ext. 204
Fax: 802-828-4485

Horace Cammack
Veterans Affairs Officer
10 Causeway Street, Room 265
Boston, MA 02222-1093

617-565-5597
Fax: 617-565-5597

Paul Bouchard
Veterans Affairs Officer
380 Westminister St., Room 511
Providence, RI 02903
401-528-4691

Harvey Morrison
Veterans Affairs Officer
330 Main St. 2nd Floor
Hartford, CT 06106-1800
860-240-4700, ext. 232

Region II
Ana Maria Vera
Veterans Affairs Officer
252 Ponce De Leon Ave., Suite 201
San Juan, PR 00918
787-766-5309

Frank Dito
Veterans Affairs Officer
26 Federal Plaza, Room 3100
New York, NY 10278

212-264-7752
Fax: 212-264-4963

David Laveck
Veterans Affairs Officer
401 South Salina, 5th Floor
Syracuse, NY 13260-2413
315-471-9393, ext. 247

Richard Keffer
Veterans Affairs Officer
111 West Huron St. Room 1311
Buffalo, NY 14202
716-551-5664

Howard Garrity
Veterans Affairs Officer
333 East Water Street, 4th Floor
Elmira, NY 14901
607-734-8130, ext. 30

Dan O'Connel
Veterans Affairs Office
1 Computer Drive South
Albany, NY 12205
518-446-1118, ext. 231

Martin McHenry
Veterans Affairs Officer
Two Gateway Center, 15th Floor
Newark, NJ 07102
973-645-2427

Region III

Stanley Karwacki
Veterans Affairs Officer
10 S. Howard Street, Suite 6220
Baltimore, MD 21202
410-962-6195, ext. 340

Joyce Howard
Veterans Affairs Officer
1110 Vermont Avenue, 9th Floor
Washington, DC 20005
202-606-4000, ext. 204

Jane Armstrong
Veterans Affairs Officer
1824 Market Street, Suite 610
Wilmington, DE 19801
302-573-6294

William Durham
Veterans Affairs Officer
405 Capital Street, Room 412
Charleston, WV 25301
304-347-5350

Leroy Harris
Veterans Affairs Officer
400 North 8th Street, Suite 1150
Richmond, VA 23240
804-771-2400, ext. 132

Donald Nemchick
Veterans Affairs Officer
700 River Ave., Suite 510
Pittsburgh, PA 15212
412-322-6441
Fax: 412-322-3513

William Dougherty
Veterans Affairs Officer
Stegmaier Bldg., Suite 407
Wilkes-Barre, PA 18702
570-826-6497

Joe McDevitt
Veterans Affairs Officer
Robert N.C. Nix Federal Building
900 Market St., 5th Floor
Philadelphia, PA 19107
215-580-2706

Region IV

Charles Atwood
Veterans Affairs Officer
7825 Baymeadows Way
Suite 100-B
Jacksonville, FL 32256-7504
904-443-1951

Robert Chavarria
Veterans Affairs Officer
1045 16th St. South
St. Petersburg, FL 33705
727-893-9683
Fax: 727-893-9688

Tommie Causey
Veterans Affairs Officer
188 Federal Office Bldg.
600 Martin Luther King Place
Louisville, KY 40211
502-571-1144, ext. 245

Don Winters
Veterans Affairs Officer
50 Vantage Way, Suite 201
Nashville, TN 37228-1500
615-736-5881, ext. 248

Edgar Fleetwood
Veterans Affairs Officer
6302 Fairview Rd., Suite 300
Charlotte, NC 28210-2227
704-344-6587, ext. 1134

Susan Chavis
Veterans Affairs Officer
1835 Assembly St., Room 358
Columbia, SC 29201
803-765-5378

Charlotte Johnson
Veterans Affairs Officer
233 Peachtree St., Suite 1900
Atlanta, GA 30309
404-331-0100, ext. 405
Fax: 404-331-0244

Raymond Hembree
Veterans Affairs Officer
801 Tom Martin Dr., Suite 201
Birmingham, AL 35211
205-290-7340, ext. 226
Fax: 205-290-7404

Tommy Traxler
Veterans Affairs Officer
210 E. Capitol St., Suite 900
Jackson, MS 39201
601-965-4378, ext. 241

Gary Reed
Veterans Affairs Officer
2909 13th Street, Suite 203
Gulfport, MS 39501-1949
228-863-4449, ext. 14
Fax: 228-864-0179

Region V

George Saumweber
Veterans Affairs Officer
100 North 6th St., Suite 210-C
Minneapolis, MN 55403-1525
612-370-2322

Jon Lonsdale
Veterans Affairs Officer
Henry Russ Federal Plaza
310 West Wisconsin Avenue
Suite 400
Milwaukee, WI 53203
414-297-1231
Fax: 414-297-1377

Charles T. Davis
Veterans Affairs Officer
477 Michigan Avenue, Room 515
Detroit, MI 48226
313-226-6075, ext. 245

Steve Konkle
Veterans Affairs Officer
500 W. Madison St., Room 1250
Chicago, IL 60661
312-886-4208

Jim Ryan
Veterans Affairs Officer
511 West Capitol Street, Suite 302
Illinois Financial Center
Springfield, IL 62704
217-492-4416, ext. 109

Paul Wyatt
Veterans Affairs Officer
429 N. Pennsylvania Street
Suite 100
Indianapolis, IN 46204-1873
317-226-7272, ext. 240

Russell Miller
Veterans Affairs Officer
1111 Superior St., Room 630
Cleveland, OH 44114
216-522-4996

Douglas Sweazy
Veterans Affairs Officer
2 Nationwide Plaza, Suite 1400
Columbus, OH 43215-2542
614-469-6860, ext. 276

Ronald Carlson
Veterans Affairs Officer
550 Main St., Room 2-522
Cincinnati, OH 45202
513-684-2814, ext. 205

Region VI

Willie Williams
Veterans Affairs Officer
365 Canal Street., Suite 2820
New Orleans, LA 70130
504-589-2706

Andy Lamonica
Veterans Affairs Officer
2120 River Front Drive #100
Little Rock, AR 72202
501-324-5871, ext. 239

Sandra Ransome
Veterans Affairs Officer
210 Park Avenue, Suite 130
Oklahoma City, OK 73102
405-231-5521, ext. 247
Fax: 405-231-4876

Alonzo Garcia
Veterans Affairs Officer
2412 S. Closner
Edinburg, TX 78539
956-316-2610, ext. 226
Fax: 956-316-2612

Stephen Curry
Veterans Affairs Officer
8701 South Gessner Dr.
Houston, TX 77054
713-773-6500, ext. 242
Fax: 713-773-6550

Armando Garcia
Veterans Affairs Officer
1205 Texas Ave., Room 408
Lubbock, TX 79401-2693
806-472-7462, ext. 244
Fax: 806-472-7487

Henry Cardenas
Veterans Affairs Officer
727 E. Durango Blvd., Room A-527
San Antonio, TX 78206-1204
210-472-5928
Fax: 210-472-5942

Daniel Chacon
Veterans Affairs Officer
10737 Gateway West., Suite 320
El Paso, TX 79935
915-633-7031
Fax: 915-633-7005

Matthew Lesko, Information USA, Inc., 12081 Nebel Street, Rockville, MD 20852 • 1-800-955-7693 • www.lesko.com

Small Business Administration Field Offices

Bill Medina
Veterans Affairs Officer
4300 Amon Carter Blvd., Suite 114
Ft. Worth, TX 76155
817-684-5517
Fax: 817-684-5516

John Tillotson
Veterans Affairs Officer
625 Silver SW, Suite 320
Albuquerque, NM 87102
505-346-6736
Fax: 505-346-6711

Region VII

Dennis Larkin
Veterans Affairs Officer
11145 Mill Valley Road
Omaha, NE 68154-3949
402-221-7208
Fax: 402-221-3680

Tom Harbison
Veterans Affairs Officer
210 Walnut St., Room 749
Des Moines, IA 50309
515-284-4653
Fax: 515-284-4572

Roger Hoffman
Veterans Affairs Officer
Small Business Administration
215 4th Avenue, SE, Suite 200
Cedar Rapids, IA 52401-1806
319-362-6405, ext. 218
Fax: 319-362-7861

Patrick Carney
Veterans Affairs Officer
217 W. 3rd St., N, Suite 2500
Wichita, KS 67202-1212
316-269-6273, ext. 225
Fax: 316-269-6618

F. Steven Parker
Veterans Affairs Officer
323 W. 8th Street, Suite 501
Kansas City, MO 64105
816-374-6708, ext. 226
Fax: 816-374-6759

Garry Ayers
Veterans Affairs Officer
7062 N. Jefferson Ave.
St. Louis, MO 63103
314-436-2202, ext. 324
Fax: 314-436-2627

Brent Jones
Veterans Affairs Officer
830 E. Primrose St.
Springfield, MO 65807-5254
417-890-8501, ext. 209
Fax: 417-889-0074

Region VIII

Donald Dahlseide
Veterans Affairs Officer
10 West 15th St., Suite 1100

Helena, MT 59626
406-441-1081, ext. 134
Fax: 406-441-1090

Dave Denke
Veterans Affairs Officer
100 East B. St., Suite 400
P.O. Box 2839
Casper, WY 82602
307-261-6523
Fax: 307-261-6535

Eric Giltner
Veterans Affairs Officer
202 N. 3rd St., Suite 300
Grand Forks, ND 58203
701-746-5160
Fax: 701-746-5748

E. Chuck Schroder
Veterans Affairs Officer
110 S. Phillips Ave., Suite 200
Sioux Falls, SD 57104
605-330-4243, ext. 15
Fax: 605-330-4215

Loy Rasmuson
Veterans Affairs Officer
125 South State St., Room 2231
Salt Lake City, UT 84138
801-524-3207
Fax: 801-524-4410

Jeannette Deherrera
Veterans Affairs Officer
721 19th Street, Suite 426
Denver, CO 80202
303-844-2607, ext. 266
Fax: 303-844-6539

Region IX

Chuck Stewart
Veterans Affairs Officer
455 Market Street, 6th Floor
San Francisco, CA 94105
415-744-6791
Fax: 415-744-9062

Alan Converse
Veterans Affairs Officer
550 West "C" Street, Suite 550
San Diego, CA 92101
619-557-7250 ext. 1116
Fax: 619-557-5894

Reynold Johnson
Veterans Affairs Officer
2719 North Air Fresno Drive, Suite 200
Fresno, CA 93727-1547
559-487-5785, ext. 114
Fax: 559-487-5636

David Casteneda
Veterans Affairs Officer
650 Capitol Mall, Suite 7-500
Sacramento, CA 65814
916-930-3709
Fax: 916-930-3737

Sami Marcos
Veterans Affairs Officer

200 West Santa Ana Blvd.
Suite 700
Santa Ana, CA 92701
714-550-7420, ext. 3702
Fax: 714-550-7409

Gabriel Cartwright
Veterans Affairs Officer
330 N. Brand Blvd., Suite 1200
Glendale, CA 91203
818-552-3314
Fax: 818-552-3620

Pete Peterson
Veterans Affairs Officer
300 Las Vegas Blvd. South, Suite 1100
Las Vegas, NV 89101
702-388-6800
Fax: 702-388-6469

Jerry Dukauskas
Veterans Affairs Officer
2828 North Central Avenue, Suite 800
Phoenix, AZ 85004-1093
602-745-7221
Fax: 602-745-7210

Albert Sampson
Veterans Affairs Officer
First Hawaiian Bank Bldg., Suite 302
Mongnong, GU 96927
671-472-7277
Fax: 671-472-7365

Kimberly Hite
Veterans Affairs Officer
300 Ala Moana, Room 2-235
Honolulu, HI 96850-4981
808-541-3024
Fax: 808-541-2976

Region X

Tom Ewbank
Veterans Affairs Officer
Small Business Administration
1200 6th Ave., Suite 1700
Seattle, WA 98101-1128
206-553-0961
Fax: 206-553-6259

Dennis Lloyd
Veterans Affairs Officer
1515 SW Fifth Avenue
Suite 1050
Portland, OR 97201-5494
503-326-5205
Fax: 503-326-2808

Rod Grzadzieleski
Veterans Affairs Officer
1020 Main Street, Suite 290
Boise, ID 83702-5745
208-334-1696, ext. 233

Terrence Moore
Veterans Affairs Officer
510 L Street, Suite 310
Anchorage, AK 99501
907-271-4854
Fax: 907-271-4545

Veterans' Employment and Training Service and Regional Administrators

The Veterans' Employment and Training Service has 10 regional offices as well as at least one office in every state. The regional offices are administered by Regional Administrators (RAVET), and the state offices are administered by a Director for Veterans' Employment and Training. These offices can give you information about veterans employment and training programs, and reemployment rights for veterans reservists and members of the National Guard.

Veterans Employment and Training Services Offices

Region I
(Connecticut, Maine, Massachusetts, New Hampshire, Rhode Island, Vermont)
David Houle, Regional Administrator
Barbara Thompson, Management Services Assistant
Christine Beech, Secretary
Veterans' Employment and Training Service
U.S. Department of Labor
J.F. Kennedy Federal Building
Room E-315, Government Center
Boston, MA 02203
617-565-2080
Fax: 617-565-2082
Email: houle-david@dol.gov
Email: thompson-barbara@dol.gov
Email: beech-christine@dol.gov

Region II
(New Jersey, New York, Puerto Rico, Virgin Islands)
Vacant, Regional Administrator
Tim Hays, Veterans' Program Specialist
Sonia J. Sanchez, Management Services Assistant
Veterans' Employment and Training Service
U.S. Department of Labor
201 Varick Street, Room 766
New York, NY 10014
212-337-2211
Fax: 212-337-2634
Email: sanchez-sonia@dol.gov
Email: hays-timothy@dol.gov

Region III
(Delaware, District of Columbia, Maryland, Pennsylvania, Virginia, West Virginia)
Joseph W. Hortiz. Jr., Regional Administrator
Raymond Minor, Veterans Program Specialist
Rosie Baker, Veterans Program Specialist
Cheryl Grigsby Thomas, Management Services Assistant
Veterans' Employment and Training Service
U.S. Department of Labor
The Curtis Center
VETS/770 West
170 S. Independence Mall
Philadelphia, PA 19106-3310
215-861-5390
Fax: 215-861-5389
Email: hortiz-joseph@dol.gov

Region IV
(Alabama, Florida, Georgia, Kentucky, Mississippi, North Carolina, South Carolina, Tennessee)
William J. Bolls, Jr., Regional Administrator
Harry Bean, Jr., Assistant Regional Administrator

Janice W. Lane, Senior Investigator, VPS
Joseph J. Miles, Senior Investigator, VPS
Vivian D. Blair, Secretary
Veterans' Employment and Training Service
U.S. Department of Labor
Atlanta Federal Center
61 Forsyth Street, SW, Room 6-T85
Atlanta, GA 30303
404-562-2305
Fax: 404-562-2313
Email: bolls-william@dol.gov
Email: lane-janice@dol.gov
Email: miles-jospeh@dol.gov
Email: blair-vivian@dol.gov
Email: beam-henry@dol.gov

Region V
(Illinois, Indiana, Michigan, Minnesota, Ohio, Wisconsin)
Ronald G. Bachman, Regional Administrator
Cheryl Santilli, Senior Investigator
Kristine Alvarez, Veterans' Program Specialist
Shirley Skoien, Veterans' Program Specialist
Caroline Neal, Administrative Officer
Calvin Lane, Secretary
Veterans' Employment and Training Service
U.S. Department of Labor
230 South Dearborn, Room 1064
Chicago, IL 60604
312-353-4942
312-353-0970 (ans. machine)
Fax: 312-886-1184
Email: bachman-ronald@dol.gov
Email: santilli-cheryl@dol.gov
Email: alvarez-kristine@dol.gov

Region VI
(Arkansas, Louisiana, New Mexico, Oklahoma, Texas)
Lester L. Williams, Jr., Regional Administrator
Bernadette Clay, Administrative Office
Ramona C. Lopez, Secretary
Veterans' Employment and Training Service
U.S. Department of Labor
525 Griffin Street, Room 858
Dallas, TX 75202
214-767-4987
Fax: 214-767-2734
Email: williams-lester@dol.gov
Email: clay-bernadette@dol.gov
Email: lopez-ramona@dol.gov

Region VII
(Iowa, Kansas, Missouri, Nebraska)
Lester L. Williams, Jr, Regional Administrator
Sharon Harrison, Assistant Regional Administrator
Ricardo L. Martinez, Veterans' Program Specialist

Veterans Employment and Training Service
U.S. Department of Labor
City Center Square Building
1100 Main Street, Suite 850
Kansas City, MO 64105-2112
816-426-7151
Fax: 816-426-7259
Email: williams-lester@dol.gov
Email: harrison-sharon@dol.gov
Email: martinez-ricardo@dol.gov

Region VIII
(Colorado, Montana, North Dakota, South Dakota, Utah, Wyoming)
Ronald G. Bachman, Regional Administrator
Veterans' Employment and Training Service
U.S. Department of Labor
1999 Broadway, Suite 1730
Denver, CO 80202
303-844-1175
303-844-1176
303-844-1178
Fax: 303-844-1179
Email: bachman-ronald@dol.gov

Region IX
(Arizona, California, Hawaii, Nevada)
Vacant, Regional Administrator
Vincent Rios, Assistant Regional Administrator
Joleen Sherrill-Irish, Veterans' Program Specialist
Nelia Bedia Nacor, Management Services Assistant
Veterans' Employment and Training Service
U.S. Department of Labor
71 Stevenson Street, Suite 705
San Francisco, CA 94105
415-975-4700 (ans. machine)
415-975-4701
415-975-4702
415-975-4754
415-975-4703
Fax: 415-975-4704
Email: Rios-Vincent@dol.gov
Email: irish-joleen@dol.gov
Email: nacor-canosa-nelia@dol.gov

Region X
(Alaska, Idaho, Oregon, Washington)
Regional Administrator Vacant
Senior Investigator Karen Marin
Veterans' Employment and Training Service
U.S. Department of Labor
1111 Third Avenue, Suite 800
Seattle, WA 98101-3212
206-553-4831
Fax: 206-553-6853
Email: marin-karen@dol.gov

Matthew Lesko, Information USA, Inc., 12081 Nebel Street, Rockville, MD 20852 • 1-800-955-7693 • www.lesko.com

Veterans' Employment And Reemployment Rights Assistance And Information

Alabama
Thomas M. Karrh, Director
Robert D. Franks, Assistant Director
Gay Coughlin, Veterans' Program Assistant
Veterans' Employment and Training Service
U.S. Department of Labor
649 Monroe Street, Room 2218
Montgomery, AL 36131-6300
334-223-7677
334-242-8115
Fax: 334-242-8927
Email: franks-robert@dol.gov
Email: karrh-Thomas@dol.gov
Email: coughlin-gay@dol.gov

Alaska
Dan Travis, Director
Arnold Lauri, Veterans' Program Assistant
Veterans' Employment and Training Service
U.S. Department of Labor
P.O. Box 25509
1111 West 8th Street
Juneau, AK 99802-5509
907-465-2723
Fax: 907-465-5528
Email: travis-dan@dol.gov
Email: lauri-arnold@dol.gov

Arizona
Michael Espinosa, Director
Alfredo Mendoza, Assistant Director
Veterans' Employment and Training Service
U.S. Department of Labor
P.O. Box 6123-SC760E
1400 West Washington
Phoenix, AZ 85005
602-379-4961
Fax: 602-542-4103
Email: espinosa-michael@dol.gov
Email: mendoza-alfredo@dol.gov

Arkansas
Billy R. Threlkeld, Director
Olga "Gene" Richards, Veterans' Program Assistant
Veterans' Employment and Training Service
U.S. Department of Labor
Employment Security Building #2
State Capitol Mall, Room G-12
Little Rock, AK 72201
P.O. Box 128
Little Rock, AK 72203
501-324-5502
501-682-3786
Fax: 501-682-3752
Email: threlkeld-billy@dol.gov
Email: richards-olga@dol.gov

California
Rosendo A. "Alex" Cuevas, Director
Leonard Dobish, Assistant Director
John E. Giannelli, Jr., Assistant Director
Tracy V. Tooley, Veterans' Program Assistant
Veterans' Employment and Training Service
U.S. Department of Labor
800 Capitol Mall, Room W1142
P.O. Box 826880
Sacramento, CA 94280-0001
916-654-8178
Fax: 916-654-9469
Email: cuevas-rosendo@dol.gov
Email: dobish-leonard@dol.gov

Email: giannelli-john@dol.gov
Email: tooley-tracy@dol.gov

Steven L. Bragman, Assistant Director
Veterans' Employment and Training Service
U.S. Department of Labor
2550 Mariposa Mall, Room 1080
Fresno, CA 93721-2296
559-445-5193
Fax: 559-445-5023
Email: bragman-steven@dol.gov

Christopher Still, Assistant Director
Veterans' Employment and Training Service
U.S. Department of Labor
363 Civic Drive
Pleasant Hills, CA 94523-1987
925-602-1541
Fax: 925-602-5023
Email: still-christopher@dol.gov

Kevin D. Nagel, Veterans' Program Specialist
EDD, Redlands Field Office
814 W. Colton Avenue
Redlands, CA 92374-2930
909-335-6763
Fax: 909-335-8303
Email: nagel-kevin@dol.gov

Linda Jacobe, Assistant Director
Veterans' Employment and Training Service
U.S. Department of Labor
320 Campus Lane
Suisun, CA 94583
707-863-3583
Fax: 707-864-3216
Email: jacobe-linda@dol.gov

Carolyn C. McMillan, Assistant Director
Veterans' Employment and Training Service
U.S. Department of Labor
1501 East Arrow Hwy.
Pomona, CA 91767-2198
909-392-2675
Fax: 909-593-8913
Email: mcmillan-carolyn@dol.gov

Michael S. Beadle, Assistant Director
Veterans' Employment and Training Service
U.S. Department of Labor
932 Broadway
Santa Monica, CA 90401-2383
310-576-6444
Fax: 310-395-4819
Email: beadle-michael@dol.gov

Nancy Ise, Assistant Director
Veterans' Employment and Training Service
U.S. Department of Labor
2450 E. Lincoln Avenue
Anaheim, CA 92806-4175
714-687-4845
Fax: 714-518-2391
Email: ise-nancy@dol.gov

Edward J. Scheer, Assistant Director
Veterans' Employment and Training Service
U.S. Department of Labor
8977 Activity Road
San Diego, CA 92126-4427
619-689-6008
Fax: 619-689-6012
Email: scheer-edward@dol.gov

Colorado
Mark A. McGinty, Director
Milton Gonzales, Assistant Director
Thresa Kitzmiller, Veterans' Program Assistant
Veterans' Employment and Training Service
U.S. Department of Labor
Tower #2, Suite 400
1515 Arapahoe Street

P.O. Box 46550
Denver, CO 80202-2117
303-844-2151
303-844-2152
Fax: 303-620-4257
Email: mcginty-mark@dol.gov
Email: gonzales-milton@dol.gov
Email: kitzmiller-thresa@dol.gov

Donald Rincon, Assistant Director
Veterans' Employment and Training Service
U.S. Department of Labor
2555 Airport Road
Colorado Springs, CO 80910-3176
719-475-3750
Fax: 719-636-1682
Email: rincon-donald@dol.gov

Connecticut
William Mason, Jr., Director
Lisa Jones, Assistant Director
Karen King, Veterans' Program Assistant
Veterans' Employment and Training Service
U.S. Department of Labor
Connecticut Department of Labor Building
200 Folly Brook Boulevard
Wethersfield, CT 06109
860-263-6490
Fax: 860-263-6498
Email: mason-william@dol.gov
Email: jones-lisa@dol.gov
Email: king-karen@dol.gov

Delaware
David White, Director
Virginia M. Youst, Veterans' Program Assistant
U.S. Department of Labor
Veterans' Employment and Training Service
4425 North Market Street, Room 420
Wilmington, DE 19809-0828
302-761-8138/9
Fax: 302-761-6621 (temp)
Email: white-david@dol.gov
Email: youst-virginia@dol.gov

District of Columbia
Stanley K. Williams, Director
Veterans' Employment and Training Service
U.S. Department of Labor
1500 Franklin St., NE
Washington, DC 20018
202-576-3082
Fax: 202-576-3113
Email: williams-stanley@dol.gov

Florida
Derek W. Taylor, Director
Ursula Lemme, Assistant Director
Bernadette Walsh, Veterans Program Assistant
Veterans' Employment and Training Service
U.S. Department of Labor
P.O. Box 1527
Tallahassee, FL 32301-5006
Marathon Building, Suite 205
2574 Seagate Drive
Tallahassee, FL 32399-0676
904-942-8800
904-877-4164
904-488-2967
Fax: 904-922-2690
Email: lemme-ursula@dol.gov
Email: taylor-derek@dol.gov
Email: walsh-bernadette@dol.gov

Richard Bate, Assistant Director
Veterans' Employment and Training Service
U.S. Department of Labor
P.O. Box 17747

Jacksonville, FL 32245-7747
904-359-6080, ext. 2191
Fax: 904-359-6154
Email: bate-richard@dol.gov

Ronnie L. Carter, Assistant Director
Veterans' Employment and Training Service
U.S. Department of Labor
P.O. Box 149084
1001 Executive Drive
2nd Floor, Room 26
Orlando, FL 32803-2999
954-677-5818
Fax: 954-677-5820 (call ahead)
Email: carter-ronnie@dol.gov

Craig Spry, Assistant Director
Veterans' Employment and Training Service
U.S. Department of Labor
P.O. Box 12528
St. Petersburg, FL 33731-0084
3160 - 5th Avenue North, Suite 200
St. Petersburg, FL 33713
727-893-2415
Fax: 727-893-2378 (call ahead)
Email: spry-craig@dol.gov

Oscar G. Fuentes, Assistant Director
Veterans' Employment and Training Service
U.S. Department of Labor
c/o Ft. Lauderdale Jobs & Benefits Office
2660 West Oakland Park Boulevard
Ft. Lauderdale, FL 33311-1347
P.O. Box 5124
Ft. Lauderdale, FL .32814-9084
954-677-5400
Fax: 954-457-2889
Email: fuentes-oscar@dol.gov

Georgia
Ed Gresham, Director
June Scott, Assistant Director
Stephen Dewer, Assistant Director
Tina Frett, Veterans' Program Assistant
Veterans' Employment and Training Service
U.S. Department of Labor
Georgia State Employment Service
Sussex Place, Suite 504
148 International Boulevard, NE
Atlanta, GA 30303-1751
404-656-3127
404-656-3138
404-331-3893
Fax: 404-657-7403
Email: gresham-ed@dol.gov
Email: scott-june@dol.gov
Email: dewey-stephen@dol.gov
Email: frett-tinorah@dol.gov

Hawaii
Gilbert N. Hough, Director
Sharon N. Muraki, Veterans' Program
Assistant
Veterans' Employment and Training Service
U.S. Department of Labor
P.O. Box 3680
Honolulu, HI 96811
830 Punchbowl Street, Room 315
Honolulu, HI 96813
808-522-8216 (ans. service)
Fax: 808-586-9258
Email: hough-gilbert@dol.gov
Email: muraki-sharon@dol.gov

Idaho
Director (vacant)
Pam Langley, Assistant Director
Karla Draper, Veterans' Program Assistant
Veterans' Employment and Training Service
U.S. Department of Labor

P.O. Box 2697
Boise, ID 83701
317 Main Street, Room 303
Boise, ID 83735
208-334-6163
Fax: 208-334-6389
208-334-6430
Email: langley-pamela@dol.gov
Email: draper-karla@dol.gov

Illinois
Samuel Parks, Director
Dottress Reeres, Assistant Director
Carol Motley, Assistant Director
Randall Hori, Assistant Director
Bianca Elmore, Veterans' Program Assistant
Veterans' Employment and Training Service
U.S. Department of Labor
401 South State Street, Room 744 North
Chicago, IL 60605
312-793-3433
Fax: 312-793-4795
Email: parks-samuel@dol.gov
Email: curry-dottress@dol.gov
Email: Motley-Carol@dol.gov
Email: elmore-bianca@dol.gov
Email: hori-randall@dol.gov

David Lyles, Assistant Director
Veterans' Employment and Training Service
U.S. Department of Labor
555 S. Pasfield
Springfield, IL 62704
217-524-7769
Fax: 217-785-9715
Email: lyles-david@dol.gov

James R. Harris, Assistant Director
Veterans' Employment and Training Service
U.S. Department of Labor
221 N. Genesee Street
Waukegan, IL
847-543-7400, ext. 273
Fax: 847-543-7465
Email: harris-james@dol.gov

Indiana
Bruce Redman, Director
George Patrick, Assistant Director
Harry "Jack" Hale, Assistant Director
Velma Brock, Veterans' Program Assistant
Veterans' Employment and Training Service
U.S. Department of Labor
10 North Senate Ave., Room SE 103
Indianapolis, IN 46204
317-232-6804
COM 317-232-6805
Fax: 317-233-4262
Email: redman-david@dol.gov
Email: patrick-george@dol.gov
Email: hale-harry@dol.gov
Email: brock-velma@dol.gov

Iowa
Anthony J. Smithhart, Director
Vacant, Assistant Director
Aurea Neal, Veterans' Program Assistant
Veterans' Employment and Training Service
U.S. Department of Labor
150 Des Moines Street
Des Moines, IA 50309-5563
515-281-9061
Fax: 515-281-9063
Email: smithhart-anthony@dol.gov
Email: neal-aurea@dol.gov

Kansas
Gayle A. Gibson, Director
Juan A. Talavera, Jr., Assistant Director
Shawn Johnson, Veterans' Program Assistant

Veterans' Employment and Training Service
U.S. Department of Labor
401 Topeka Boulevard
Topeka, KS 66603-3182
785-296-5032
Fax: 785-296-0264
Email: gibson-gayle@dol.gov
Email: talavera-juan@dol.gov
Email: johnson-shawn@dol.gov

Kentucky
Charles R. "Rick" Netherton, Director
Bonnie J. Kunkle, Veterans' Program Asst.
Veterans' Employment and Training Service
U.S. Department of Labor
c/o Department for Employment Services
275 East Main Street
(CHR Building), 2nd Floor West. 2WD
Frankfort, KY 40621-2339
502-564-7062
Fax: 502-564-1476
Email: kunkle-bonnie@dol.gov
Email: netherton-charles@dol.gov

Robert Kuenzli, Veterans' Program Specialist
Veterans' Employment and Training service
U.S. Department of Labor
320 Garrard Street
Covington, KY 41011
859-292-6666, ext. 253
Fax: 859-292-6708
Email: kuenzle-robert@dol.gov

Louisiana
Lester L. Parmenter, Director
Woody S. Lambert, Senior Investigator
Ramona M. Hand, Assistant Director
Dorothy Vaughan, Veterans' Program
Assistant
Veterans' Employment and Training Service
U.S. Department of Labor
Louisiana Department of Labor
Administration Building, Room 184
1001 North 23rd Street
Baton Rouge, LA 70802
P.O. Box 94094, Room 184
Baton Rouge, LA 70804-9094
225-389-0440
Fax: 225-342-3066
Email: parmenter-lester@dol.gov
Email: lambert-woody@dol.gov
Email: hand-ramona@dol.gov
Email: vaughan-dorothy@dol.gov

Maine
Jon Guay, Director
Edwina Bagley, Veterans' Program Assistant
Veterans' Employment and Training Service
U.S. Department of Labor
5 Mollison Way
P.O. Box 3106
Lewiston, ME 04243
207-753-9090
Fax: 207-783-5304
Email: guay-jon@dol.gov
Email: bagley-edwina@dol.gov

Maryland
Gary Lobdell, Director
Janet L. Boyd, Veterans' Program Assistant
U.S. Department of Labor
Veterans' Employment and Training Service
1100 North Eutaw Street, Room 210
Baltimore, MD 21201
410-767-2110
410-767-2111
Fax: 410-333-5136
Email: labdell-gary@dol.gov
Email: boyd-janet@dol.gov

Larry Mettert, Assistant Director
U.S. Department of Labor
Veterans' Employment and Training Service
201 Baptist Street
Salisbury, MD 21801
410-334-6897
Email: mettert-larry@dol.gov

James Theriault, Assistant Director
Charles "Nick" Dawson, Senior Investigator
U.S. Department of Labor
Veterans' Employment and Training Service
P.O. Box 1317
Wheaton, MD 20915
301-929-4379
Fax: 301-929-4383
Email: theriault-james@dol.gov

Massachusetts

Paul Desmond, Director
George Kincannon, Assistant Director
Patricia Newsom, Veterans' Program Assistant
Veterans' Employment and Training Service
U.S. Department of Labor
C.F. Hurley Building, 2nd Floor
19 Staniford Street
Boston, MA 02114-2502
617-626-6690
Fax: 617-727-2330
Email: kincannon-george@dol.gov
Email: desmond-paul@dol.gov
Email: newsom-patricia@dol.gov

Reginald E. Dupuis, Assistant Director
Veterans' Employment and Training Service
U.S. Department of Labor
Division of Employment Security
72 School Street
Taunton, MA 02780
508-977-4414
Fax: 617-727-2112
Email: dupuis-reginald@dol.gov

Michigan

Kim Fulton, Director
Robert Castillo, Assistant Director
Dennis Opoka, Veterans' Program Specialist
Mary Bivens, Veterans' Program Assistant
Veterans' Employment and Training Service
U.S. Department of Labor
3032 W. Grand Blvd., Suite 48202
Detroit, MI 48202
313-456-3180
Fax: 313-456-3181
Email: fulton-kim@dol.gov
Email: bivens-mary@dol.gov

Edgar J. Hekman, Assistant Director
Veterans' Employment and Training Service
U.S. Department of Labor
Employment Security Commission
3391 Plainfield, NE
Grand Rapids, MI 49505
616-361-3254
Email: hekman-edgar@dol.gov

Minnesota

Michael Graham, Director
Dennis Dahlien, Assistant Director
Vacant, Veterans' Program Assistant
Veterans' Employment and Training Service
U.S. Department of Labor
390 Robert St. North, 1st Floor
St. Paul, MN 55101-1812
651-296-3665
Fax: 651-282-2711
Email: graham-michael@dol.gov
Email: dahlien-dennis@dol.gov

Vacant, Assistant Director
Veterans' Employment and Training Service
U.S. Department of Labor
Job Service
320 West 2nd Street, Room 205
Duluth, MN 55802
218-723-4766

Mississippi

Angelo Terrell, Director
Melanie Jackson, Veterans Program Assistant
Veterans' Employment and Training Service
U.S. Department of Labor
P.O. Box 1699
1520 West Capitol Street
Jackson, MS 39215-1699
601-965-4204
601-961-7588
Fax: 601-961-7717
Email: terrell-angelo@dol.gov
Email: jackson-melanie@dol.gov

Missouri

Mick Jones, Director
Dennis R. McElroy, Assistant Director
Patricia A. Baughman, Veterans' Program
Assistant
Veterans' Employment and Training Service
U.S. Department of Labor
421 East Dunklin Street
Jefferson City, MO 65104-3138
P.O. Box 1087
Jefferson City, MO 65104-1087
573-751-3921
Fax: 573-751-6710
Email: jones-mickey@dol.gov
Email: mcelroy-dennis@dol.gov
Email: baughman-patricia@dol.gov

Montana

H. Polly LaTray-Holmes, Director
Alvy Chapman, Veterans' Program Assistant
Veterans' Employment and Training Service
U.S. Department of Labor
1215 8th Avenue
Helena, MT 59601
406-449-5431
406-442-2541
Fax: 406-444-3365
Email: latray-holmes-hazel@dol.gov
Email: chapman-alvy@dol.gov

Nebraska

Richard "Rick" Nelson, Director
Greg Wiltshire, Veterans' Program Assistant
Veterans' Employment and Training Service
U.S. Department of Labor
550 South 16th Street
Lincoln, NE 68508
P.O. Box 94600
Lincoln, NE 68509-4600
402-471-9833
Fax: 402-471-2092
Email: nelson-richard@dol.gov
Email: henson-brenda@dol.gov

Nevada

Judy A. Carlisle, Director
Veterans' Program Assistant (Vacant)
Veterans' Employment and Training Service
U.S. Department of Labor
1923 North Carson Street, Room 205
Carson City, NV 89702
702-687-4632
Fax: 702-687-3976
Email: carlisle-judy@dol.gov

New Hampshire

John Gagne, Director
Eileen Woods, Veterans' Program Assistant
Veterans' Employment and Training Service
U.S. Department of Labor
143 North Main Street, Room 208
Concord, NH 03301
603-225-1424
Fax: 603-225-1545
Email: gagne-john@dol.gov
Email: woods-eileen@dol.gov

New Jersey

Alan E. Grohs, Director
Robert F. Ranger, Assistant Director
Coleen Warren, Veterans' Program Assistant
U.S. Department of Labor
Veterans' Employment and Training Service
Labor Building, 11th Floor, CN-058
Trenton, NJ 08625
609-292-2930
609-989-2305
609-989-2396
Fax: 609-292-9070
Email: grohs-alan@dol.gov
Email: ranger-robert@dol.gov
Email: warren-coleen@dol.gov

James J. Curcio, Assistant Director
U.S. Department of Labor
Veterans' Employment and Training Service
2600 Mr. Ephraim Ave.
Camden, NJ 08104
856-614-3163
Fax: 856-614-3156
Email: curcio-james@dol.gov

New Mexico

Sharon Mitchell, Acting Director
Dolores M. "Monica" Martinez, Veterans'
Program Assistant
Veterans' Employment and Training Service
U.S. Department of Labor
501 Mountain Road, NE
Albuquerque, NM 87102
P.O. Box 25085
Albuquerque, NM 87125-5085
505-346-7502
Fax: 505-346-7503
Email: mitchell-sharon@dol.gov
Email: martinez-dolores@dol.gov

New York

James H. Hartman, Director
J. Frank Merges, Assistant Director
Joan M. Cramer, Veterans' Program Assistant
U.S. Department of Labor
Veterans' Employment and Training Service
Harriman State Campus Bldg. 12, Room 518
Albany, NY 12240-0099
518-457-7465
518-435-0831
Fax: 518-435-0833
Email: hartman-james@dol.gov
Email: merges-frank@dol.gov
Email: cramer-joan@dol.gov

Alice F. Jones, Assistant Director
Daniel A. Friedman, Assistant Director
Veterans' Employment and Training Service
U.S. Department of Labor
345 Hudson Street, Room 8209
P.O. Box 668, Mail Stop 8C
New York, NY 10014-0668
212-227-5213
212-352-6184
Fax: 212-352-6185
Email: jones-alice@dol.gov
Email: friedman-daniel@dol.gov

Vacant, Assistant Director
U.S. Department of Labor
Veterans' Employment and Training Service
State Office Building, Room 702
207 Genesee Street
Utica, NY 13501
315-793-2323
Fax: 315-793-2303

James C. Donahue, Assistant Director
U.S. Department of Labor
Veterans' Employment and Training Service
290 Main Street, Room 231
Buffalo, NY 14202-4076
716-851-2748
Fax: 716-851-2792
Email: donahue-james@dol.gov

Frank J. Policastri, Assistant Director
U.S. Department of Labor
Veterans' Employment and Training Service
450 South Salina St., 2nd Floor, Room 200
Syracuse, NY 13202-2402
315-479-3381
Fax: 315-479-3421
Email: policastri-frank@dol.gov

North Carolina
Steven W. Guess, Director
Angel H. Alvarez, Assistant Director
Evon Digregorio, Assistant Director
Lela Norman, Veterans' Program Assistant
Veterans' Employment and Training Service
U.S. Department of Labor
P.O. Box 27625
Raleigh, NC 27611-7625
700 Wade Avenue, Building M
Raleigh, NC 27605-1154
828-466-5535
919-856-4792
919-733-7402
Fax: 919-733-1508
Email: norman-lela@dol.gov
Email: alvarez-angel@dol.gov
Email: guess-steven@dol.gov
Email: digregorio-evon@dol.gov

Thomas West, Assistant Director
Veterans' Employment and Training Service
U.S. Department of Labor c/o NCESC
3301 Highway US 70 SE
Newton, NC 28658
828-466-5535
Fax: 828-466-5545
Email: west-tom@dol.gov

North Dakota
Gerald Meske, Director
Noreen Bartlett, Veterans' Program Assistant
Veterans' Employment and Training Service
U.S. Department of Labor
P.O. Box 1632
1000 E. Divide Avenue
Bismarck, ND 58502-1632
701-250-4337
701-328-2865
Fax: 701-328-2890
Email: meske-gerald@dol.gov
Email: bartlett-noreen@dol.gov

Ohio
Carl Price, Director
Cloudy Williams, Assistant Director
Roy Davis, Veterans' Program Specialist
Dorinda Johnston, Veterans' Program Assistant
Veterans' Employment and Training Service
U.S. Department of Labor
P.O. Box 1618
Columbus, OH 43216
145 South Front Street, Room 523

Columbus, OH 43215
Com 614-466-2768/2769
Fax: 614-752-5007
Email: price-carl@dol.gov
Email: williams-cloudy@dol.gov
Email: davis-roy@dol.gov
Email: johnston-dorinda@dol.gov

Kevin Patterson, Assistant Director n
Veterans' Employment and Training Service
U.S. Department of Labor
684 N. Park Avenue
P.O. Box 1188
Warren, OH 44482-1188
330-399-8114
Fax: 330-399-1957
Email: patterson-kevin@dol.gov

William Forester, Assistant Director
Veterans' Employment and Training Service
U.S. Department of Labor
1841 Prospect Ave.
Cleveland, OH 44115
216-787-5660
Fax: 216-787-5213
Email: forester-william@dol.gov

Oklahoma
Darrell H. Hill, Director
Joseph "Joe" Dyer, Assistant Director
Carolyn S. Clark, Veterans' Program Assistant
Veterans' Employment and Training Service
U.S. Department of Labor
2401 N. Lincoln Blvd., Room 304-2
Oklahoma City, OK 73105
P. O. Box 52003
Oklahoma City, OK 73152-2003
405-231-5088
405-557-7189
Fax: 405-557-7123
Email: hill-darrell@dol.gov
Email: dyer-joseph@dol.gov
Email: clark-carolyn@dol.gov

Oregon
Ron Cannon, Director
Vacant, Veterans' Program Assistant
Veterans' Employment and Training Service
U.S. Department of Labor
Employment Division Building, Room 108
875 Union Street, NE
Salem, OR 97311-0100
503-947-1490
Fax: 503-947-1492
Email: cannon-ron@dol.gov

Ronja Pardo, Assistant Director
Veterans' Employment and Training Service
U.S. Department of Labor
1433 Southwest 6th Avenue
Portland, OR 97201
503-731-3478
Fax: 503-229-5829
Email: pardo-tonja@dol.gov

Pennsylvania
Larry Babitts, Director
Phillip Potter, Veterans' Program Assistant
U.S. Department of Labor
Veterans' Employment and Training Service
Labor and Industry Bldg., Room 1108
Seventh and Forster Streets
Harrisburg, PA 17121
717-787-5834
717-787-5835
Fax: 717-783-2631
Email: babitts-larry@dol.gov
Email: potter-phillip@dol.gov

Darrell R. Fritzinger, Assistant Director
U.S. Department of Labor
Veterans' Employment and Training Service
10th Floor, 640 Hamilton Street
Allentown, PA 18103
610-821-6571
Email: fritzinger-darrell@dol.gov

Denise M. Adair, Veterans' Program Specialist
U.S. Department of Labor
Veterans' Employment and Training Service
State Office Building
300 Liberty Avenue, Room 1307
Pittsburgh, PA 15222
412-565-2469
Fax: 412-565-2518
Email: adair-denise@dol.gov

Wayne E. Faith, Assistant Director
U.S. Department of Labor
Veterans' Employment and Training Service
Job Service Office
135 Franklin Avenue
Scranton, PA 18503
717-963-4735
Email: faith-wayne@dol.gov

Richard P. Schaffer, Assistant Director
Veterans' Employment and Training Service
U.S. Department of Labor
71 South Union Avenue
Lansdowne, PA 19050
610-284-7588
Email: schaffer-richard@dol.gov

Puerto Rico
Angel Mojica, Director
Miguel Gonzales, Veterans' Program Assistant
U.S. Department of Labor
Veterans' Employment and Training Service
Puerto Rico Department of Labor and Human Resources
#198 Calle Guayama
Hato Rey, PR 00917
787-754-5391
787-751-0731
Fax: 787-754-2983
Email: gonzales-miguel@dol.gov
Email: mojica-angel@dol.gov

Rhode Island
John F. Dunn, Director
Agnes Entwistle, Veterans' Program Assistant
U.S. Department of Labor
Veterans' Employment and Training Service
4808 Tower Hill Road
Wakefield, Ri 02879
401-528-5134
Fax: 401-528-5106
Email: dunn-john@dol.gov
Email: entwistle-agnes@dol.gov

South Carolina
William C. Plowden, Jr., Director
Willie J. Perry, Assistant Director
Rebecca L. Baston, Veterans' Program Assistant
Veterans' Employment and Training Service
U.S. Department of Labor
P.O. Box 1755
Columbia, SC 29202-1755
Lem Harper Building
631 Hampton Street, Suite 141
Columbia, SC 29201
803-765-5195
803-253-7649
Fax: 803-253-4153
Email: plowden-william@dol.gov
Email: perry-willie@dol.gov
Email: baston-rebecca@dol.gov

South Dakota

Earl R. Schultz, Director
Shirley H. Moffenbier, Veterans' Program
Assistant
Veterans' Employment and Training Service
U.S. Department of Labor
P.O. Box 4730
420 South Roosevelt Street
Aberdeen, SD 57402-4730
605-626-2325
Fax: 605-626-2322
Email: schultz-earl@dol.gov
Email: moffenbier-shirley@dol.gov

Tennessee

Richard E. Ritchie, Director
Deann Schloesser, Veterans' Program
Assistant
Cynthia (Cindy) M. Morrison, Assistant
Director
Veterans' Employment and Training Service
U.S. Department of Labor
P.O. Box 280656
Nashville, TN 37228-0656
615-736-7680
615-741-2135
Fax: 615-741-4241
615-736-5037
Email: ritchie-richard@dol.gov
Email: morrison-cynthia@dol.gov
Email: schloesser-deann@dol.gov

Jim George Pearson, Assistant Director
Veterans' Employment and Training Service
U.S. Department of Labor
1309 Poplar Avenue
Memphis, TN 38104-2006
901-543-7853
Fax: 901-543-7882
Email: pearson-jim@dol.gov

Texas

John D. McKinny, Director
Donald L. Watson, Assistant Director
Denise D. Mayfield, Veterans' Program
Assistant
Veterans' Employment and Training Service
U.S. Department of Labor
TWC Building, Room 516-T
1117 Trinity Street
Austin, TX 78701
P.O. Box 1468
Austin, TX 78767
512-463-2207
512-463-2815
512-463-2814
Fax: 512-475-2999
Email: mckinny-john@dol.gov
Email: watson-donald@dol.gov
Email: mayfield-denise@dol.gov

Ronny J. Hays, Assistant Director
Veterans' Employment and Training Service
U.S. Department of Labor
1602 16th Street
Lubbock, TX 79401
P.O. Box 2858
Lubbock, TX 79408-2858
806-763-6416
Fax: 806-747-8629
Email: hays-ronny@dol.gov

Randy Walker, Assistant Director
Veterans' Employment and Training Service
U.S. Department of Labor
8323 Culebra Road, Suite #103
San Antonio, TX 78251
Mailing Address:
P.O. Box 830277
San Antonio, TX 78283-0277
210-684-1051, ext. 241
Fax: 210-684-1822
Email: walker-randolph@dol.gov

Alberto Navarro, Assistant Director
Veterans' Employment and Training Service
U.S. Department of Labor
5425 Polk St., G-20
Houston, TX 77023
713-767-2022
Fax: 713-767-2489

Albert L. Arredondo, Assistant Director
Veterans' Employment and Training Service
U.S. Department of Labor
412 South High Street
Longview, TX 75606
P.O. Box 2152
Longview, TX 75606-2152
903-758-1783 Ext 211
Fax: 903-757-7835
Email: arredondo-albert@dol.gov

Vacant, Assistant Director
Veterans' Employment and Training Service
U.S. Department of Labor
3649 Leopard Street, Suite 600
Corpus Christi, TX 78408
512-882-3994
Fax: 512-882-1621

Robert A. Marterella, Assistant Director
Veterans' Employment and Training Service
U.S. Department of Labor
301 W. 13th Street, Room 407
FT. Worth, TX 76102-4699
P.O. Box 591
Ft. Worth, TX 76101-0591
817-335-5111, ext 404
Fax: 817-336-8723
Email: marterella-robert@dol.gov

Utah

Dale Brockbank, Director
Nancy Bailey, Veterans' Program Asst.
Veterans' Employment and Training Service
U.S. Department of Labor
Suite 209, 140 East 300 South
Salt Lake City, UT 84111-2333
801-524-5703
Fax: 801-524-3099
Email: brockbank-howard@dol.gov
Email: bailey-nancy@dol.gov

Vermont

Richard Gray, Director
Geri Orton, Veterans' Program Assistant
Veterans' Employment and Training Service
U.S. Department of Labor
P.O. Box 603
Post Office Building
87 State Street, Room 303
Montpelier, VT 05601
802-828-4441
Fax: 802-828-4445
Email: gray-richard@dol.gov
Email: orton-geraldine@dol.gov

Virginia

Roberto L. Pineda, Director
Heather Higgins, Assistant Director
Veterans' Employment Commission
13370 Minnieville Road
Woodbridge, VA 22192
703-897-0433
Fax: 703-897-0440
Email: pineda-roberto@dol.gov
Email: higgins-heather@dol.gov

Patricia Sykes, Veterans' Program Assistant
U.S. Department of Labor
Veterans' Employment and Training Service
703 East Main Street, Room 118

Richmond, VA 23219
804-786-7270
804-786-7269
804-786-6599
Fax: 804-786-4548
Email: sykes-patricia@dol.gov

Michael T. Skidmore, Assistant Director
U.S. Department of Labor
Veterans' Employment and Training Service
Virginia Employment Commission
P.O. Box 40008
Roanoke, VA 24022
5060 Valleyview Boulevard, N.W.
Roanoke, VA 24012
540-561-7494
Fax: 540-561-7510
Email: skidmore-michael@dol.gov

Virgin Islands
Vacant, RAVET
Tim Hays, Veterans Program Specialist
Sonia Sanchez, MSA
Veterans' Employment and Training Service
U.S. Department of Labor
201 Varick Street, Room 766
New York, NY 10014
Email: hays-timothy@dol.gov
Email: sanchez-sonia@dol.gov

Washington

Tom Pearson, Director
James Arrington, Assistant Director
Gregory Mercer, Assistant Director
Kathy Smith, Veterans Program Assistant
Veterans' Employment and Training Service
U.S. Department of Labor
P.O. Box 165
Olympia, WA 98507-0165
605 Woodview Square Loop, SE, 3rd Floor
Lacey, WA 98503-1040
360-438-4600
Fax: 360-438-3160
Email: pearson-thomas@dol.gov
Email: arrington-james@dol.gov
Email: mercer-gregory@dol.gov
Email: smith-kathy@dol.gov

West Virginia

Charles Stores, Jr., Director
Cynthia Collins, Veterans' Program Assistant
U.S. Department of Labor
Veterans' Employment and Training Service
Capitol Complex, Room 204
112 California Avenue
Charleston, WV 25305-0112
304-558-4001
Fax: 304-344-4591
Email: stores-charles@dol.gov
Email: collins-cynthia@dol.gov

Wisconsin

James Gutowski, Director
Daniel Schmitz, Assistant Director
Thomas R. Stehlik, Veterans' Program
Assistant
Veterans' Employment and Training Service
U.S. Department of Labor
P.O. Box 8310
Madison, WI 53708-8310
201 East Washington Ave., Room G201A
Madison, WI 53703
FTS 8-608-264-5371
COM 608-266-3110
Fax: 608-261-6710
Email: gutowski-james@dol.gov
Email: schmitz-daniel@dol.gov
Email: stehlik-thomas@dol.gov

Wyoming

David McNulty, Director
Teri Muller, Veterans' Program Assistant
Veterans' Employment and Training Service
U.S. Department of Labor
P.O. Box 2760
100 West Midwest Avenue
Casper, WY 82602-2760
307--261-5454
307-235-3281
307-235-3282
Fax: 307-473-2642
Email: mcnulty-david@dol.gov
Email: muller-teri@dol.gov

"Thoughts about being self-employed...You're not so much taking a risky chance as you are simply getting ahead of the crowd."

Source: *Job Shift: How to Prosper in a Workplace Without Jobs*, William Bridges, Addison Wesley, 1993

U.S. Department of Veterans Affairs Regional Offices and Vet Centers

Department of Veterans Affairs Headquarters
810 Vermont Ave. NW
Washington, D.C. 20420
202-273-5400
www.va.gov

Alabama
Regional Office:
Montgomery Regional Office
345 Perry Hill Rd.
Montgomery, AL 36109
800-827-1000
334-213-3400
Fax: 334-213-3407

Vet Centers:
Birmingham Vet Center
1500 5th Avenue South
Birmingham, AL 35205
205-731-0550
Fax: 205-731-0564

Mobile Vet Center
Festival Center
3725 Airport Blvd. Suite 143
Mobile, AL 36608
205-304-0108

Alaska
Regional Office:
Anchorage Regional Office
2925 DeBarr Road
Anchorage, AK 99508-2989
800-827-1000

Vet Centers:
Anchorage Vet Center
4201 Tudor Center Drive Suite 115
Anchorage, AK 99508
907-563-6966
Fax: 907-561-7183

Fairbanks Vet Center
540 4th Avenue, Suite 100
Fairbanks, AK 99701
907-456-4238
Fax: 907-456-0475

Kenai Vet Center
43335 K-Beach Rd.
Building F, Suite 4
Soldotna, AK 99669
907-260-7640
Fax: 907-260-7642

Wasila Vet Center
851 E. Westpoint Ave.
Suite 111
Wasila, AK 99654
907-376-4318
Fax: 907-373-1883

Arizona
Regional Office:
Phoenix Regional Office
3225 N. Central Ave.
Phoenix, AZ 85012
800-827-1000

Vet Centers:
Phoenix Vet Center
77 E. Weldon, Suite 100

Phoenix, AZ 85012
602-640-2981
Fax: 602-640-2967

Prescott Vet Center
161 S. Granite St., Suite B
Prescott, AZ 86303
520-778-3469
Fax: 520-776-6042

Tucson Vet Center
3055 North 1st Avenue
Tucson, AZ 85719
520-882-0333
Fax: 520-670-5862

Arkansas
Regional Office:
North Little Rock Regional Office
Building 65, Fort Roots
P.O. Box 1280
Little Rock, AR 72115
800-827-1000

Vet Centers:
North Little Rock Vet Center
201 W. Broadway, Suite A
Little Rock, AR 72114
501-324-6395

California
Regional Offices:
Los Angeles Regional Office
Federal Building
11000 Wilshire Boulevard
Los Angeles, CA 90024
800-827-1000

Oakland Regional Office
1301 Clay Street
Room 1300 North
Oakland, CA 94612
800-827-1000

San Diego Regional Office
8810 Rio San Diego Drive
San Diego, CA 92108
800-827-1000

Vet Centers:
Anaheim Vet Center
859 S. Harbor Blvd.
Anaheim, CA 92805
714-776-0161

Santa Cruz County Vet Center
1350 41st Ave., Suite 102
Capitola, CA 95010-3906
831-464-4575

Chico Vet Center
25 Main St., Suite 100
Chico, CA 95928
530-899-8549

Commerce Vet Center
VA East L A. Clinic
5400 E. Olympic Blvd., # 140
Commerce, CA 90022
213-728-9966

Concord Vet Center
1899 Clayton Rd.
Suite 140

Concord, CA 94520
925-680-4526

Culver City Vet Center
5730 Uplander Way, Suite 100
Culver City, CA 90230
310-641-0326

Eureka Vet Center
2839 G St., Suite A
Eureka, CA 95501
707-444-8271

Fresno Vet Center
3636 N. 1st. St. Suite 112
Fresno, CA 93726
559-487-5660

Los Angeles Vet Center
S. Central LA
251 W. 85th Pl.
Los Angeles, CA 90003
310-215-2380

Peninsula Vet Center
2946 Broadway St.
Redwood City, CA 94062-1594
650-299-0672

Oakland Vet Center
1540 Franklin St., Suite 200
Oakland, CA 94612
510-763-3904

Riverside Vet Center
4954 Arlington Ave., Suite A
Riverside, CA 92571
909-359-6342

Rohnert Park Vet Center
6225 State Farm Dr., Suite 101
Rohnert Park, CA 94928
707-586-3295

Sacramento Vet Center
1111 Howe Ave., Suite 390
Sacramento, CA 95825
916-566-7430

San Diego Vet Center
2900 6th Ave.
San Diego, CA 92103
858-294-2040

San Francisco Vet Center
505 Polk St.
San Francisco, CA 94102
415-441-5051

San Jose Vet Center
278 N. 2nd St.
San Jose, CA 95112-4017
408-993-0729

Colorado
Regional Office
Denver Regional Office
155 Van Gordon St.
Lakewood, CO 80228
800-827-1000

Vet Centers:
Boulder Vet Center
2336 Canyon Blvd., Suite 130

Boulder, CO 80302
303-440-7306

Colorado Springs Vet Center
416 E. Colorado Avenue
Colorado Springs, CO 80903
719-471-9992

Denver Vet Center
7465 E. First Avenue, Suite B
Denver, CO 80220
303-326-0645
303-433-7123

Connecticut
Regional Office:
Hartford Regional Office
450 Main Street
Hartford, CT 06103
800-827-1000

Vet Centers:
Hartford Vet Center
30 Jordan Lane
Wethersfield, CT 06109
860-240-3543

New Haven Vet Center
141 Captain Thomas Blvd.
New Haven, CT 06516
203-932-9899

Norwich Vet Center
100 Main Street
Norwich, CT 06360
203-887-1755

Delaware
Regional Office:
Wilmington Regional Office
1601 Kirkwood Hwy.
Wilmington, DE 19805
800-827-1000

Vet Centers:
Wilmington Vet Center
VAMROC Bldg. 2
1601 Kirkwood Hwy.
Wilmington, DE 19805
302-994-1660

District of Columbia
Regional Office:
Washington DC Regional Office
1120 Vermont Avenue N.W.
Washington DC, DC 20421
800-827-1000

Vet Center:
Washington DC Vet Center
911 Second St., NE
Washington, DC 20002
202-543-8821
Fax: 202-745-8648

Florida
Regional Office:
St. Petersburg Regional Office
9500 Bay Pines Blvd.
Bay Pines, FL 33708
800-827-1000

Vet Centers:
Ft. Lauderdale Vet Center
713 NE 3rd Ave.
Ft. Lauderdale, FL 33304
954-356-7926
Fax: 954-356-7609

Jacksonville Vet Center
1833 Boulevard St.
Jacksonville, FL 32206
904-232-3621

Miami Vet Center
2700 SW 3rd Ave., Suite 1A
Miami, FL 33129
305-859-8387
Fax: 305-530-7870

Orlando Vet Center
5001 Orange Ave., Suite A
Orlando, FL 32809
407-857-2800

Palm Beach Vet Center
2311 10th Ave., North #13
Palm Beach, FL 33461
561-585-0441

Pensacola Vet Center
4501 Twin Oaks Dr., Suite 104
Pensacola, FL 32506
850-456-9403

Sarasota Vet Center
4801 Swift Road
Sarasota, FL 34231
941-927-8285

St. Petersburg Vet Center
2880 1st Ave., N.
St. Petersburg, FL 33713
727-893-3791

Tallahassee Vet Center
249 E. 6th Ave.
Tallahassee, FL 32303
850-942-8810

Tampa Vet Center
1507 W. Sligh Ave.
Tampa, FL 33604
813-228-2621

Georgia
Regional Office:
1700 Clairmont Rd.
Decatur, GA 30033
800-827-1000

Vet Centers:
Atlanta Vet Center
77 Peachtree Pl., NW
Atlanta, GA 30309
404-347-7264

Savannah Vet Center
8110 White Bluff Road
Savannah, GA 31406
912-652-4097

Guam
Vet Centers:
Guam Vet Center
222 Chalan Santo Papast
Reflection Center, Suite 102
Agana, GU 96910
705-472-7161

Hawaii
Regional Office:
Honolulu Regional Office
459 Patterson Rd., E-Wing
Honolulu, HI 96819-1522
800-827-1000
Fax: 808-433-0390
Toll Free From:
Neighboring Islands: 800-827-1000
Guam: 475-8387
American Samoa: 800-844-7928

Vet Centers:
Hilo Vet Center
120 Keawe St. Suite 201
Hilo, HI 96720
808-969-3833

Honolulu Vet Center
1680 Kapiolani Blvd, Suite F
Honolulu, HI 96814
808-566-1764

Kallua-Kona Vet Center
Pottery Terrace, Fern Bldg.
75-5995 Kuakini Hwy. #415
Kallua-Kona, HI 96740
808-329-0574

Kauai Vet Center
3367 Kuhio Hwy., Suite 101
Lihue, HI 96766-1061
808-246-1163

Maui Vet Center
35 Lunaliho St., Suite 101
Wailuku, HI 96793-2523
808-242-8557

Idaho
Regional Office:
Boise Regional Office
805 W. Franklin Street
Boise, ID 83702
800-827-1000

Vet Centers:
Boise Vet Center
5440 Franklin Rd., Suite 100
Boise, ID 83705
208-342-3612
Fax: 208-342-0327

Pocatello Vet Center
1800 Garrett Way
Pocatello, ID 86303
208-232-0316

Illinois
Regional Office:
Chicago Regional Office
436 S. Clark St.
Chicago, IL 60605-1523
800-827-1000
Fax: 312-353-2907

Vet Centers:
Chicago Vet Center
1514 E. 63rd Street
Chicago, IL 60637
774-684-5500

Chicago Heights Vet Center
1600 Halsted Street
Chicago Heights, IL 60411
708-754-0340
Fax: 708-754-0373

Evanston Vet Center
565 Howard Street
Evanston, IL 60202
847-332-1019
Fax: 847-332-1024

Oak Park Vet Center
155 S. Oak Park Avenue
Oak Park, IL 60302
708-383-3325
Fax: 708-383-3247

Peoria Vet Center
3310 N. Prospect Street
Peoria, IL 61603
309-671-7300

Springfield Vet Center
624 S. 4th Street
Springfield, IL 62701
217-492-4955

East St. Louis Vet Center
1269 N. 89th Street, Suite 1

St. Louis, IL 62203
618-397-6602

Indiana
Regional Office:
Indianapolis Regional Office
575 N. Pennsylvania St.
Indianapolis, IN 46202
800-827-1000

Vet Centers:
Fort Wayne Vet Center
528 West Berry St.
Fort Wayne, IN 46802
219-460-1456

Indianapolis Vet Center
3833 Meridian
Indianapolis, IN 46208
317-927-6440

Merillville Vet Center
6505 Broadway
Merillville, IN 46410-3009
219-736-5633
Fax: 219-736-5936

Iowa
Regional Office:
Des Moines VA Regional Office
210 Walnut Street
Des Moines, IA 50309
800-827-1000
Fax: 515-284-4149
Cedar Rapids 319-378-0016

Kansas
Regional Office:
Wichita Regional Office
5500 E. Kellogg
Wichita, KS 67211
800-827-1000

Vet Centers:
Wichita Vet Center
413 S. Pattie
Wichita, KS 67211
800-478-3381
316-265-3260

Kentucky
Regional Office:
Louisville Regional Office
545 S 3rd St.
Louisville, KY 40202
800-827-1000

Vet Centers:
Lexington Vet Center
301 East Vine St., Suite C
Lexington, KY 40503
606-253-0717

Louisville Vet Center
1347 South 3rd St.
Louisville, KY 40208
502-634-1916

Louisiana
Regional Office:
New Orleans Regional Office
701 Loyola Avenue
New Orleans, LA 70113
800-827-1000

Vet Centers:
New Orleans Vet Center
1529 N. Claiborne Avenue
New Orleans, LA 70116
504-943-8386

Shreveport Vet Center
2800 Youree Drive

LA Suite l-105
Shreveport, LA 71104
318-861-1776

Maine
Medical and Regional Office:
Togus VA Medical/Regional Office Center
1 VA Center
Togus, ME 04330
207-623-8411

Maryland
Regional Office:
Baltimore Regional Office
31 Hopkins Plaza federal Building
Baltimore, MD 21201
800-827-1000

Vet Centers:
Baltimore Vet Center
6666 Security Blvd., Suite 2
Baltimore, MD 21207
410-277-3600
Fax: 410-277-3601

Cambridge Vet Center
5510 West Shore Drive
Cambridge, MD 21613
410-228-6305, ext. 4123

Elkton Vet Center
103 Chesapeake Blvd., Suite A
South Bridge Street
Elkton, MD 21921
410-392-4485
Fax: 410-392-6381

Silver Spring Vet Center
1015 Spring Street, Suite 101
Silver Spring, MD 20910
301-589-1073
Fax: 301-588-4882

Massachusetts
Regional Office:
Boston VA Regional Office
JFK Federal Building
Government Center
Boston, MA 02114
800-827-1000

Vet Centers:
Boston Vet Center
665 Beacon Street, Suite 100
Boston, MA 02215
617-424-0665

Brockton Vet Center
1041-L Pearl Street
Brockton, MA 02401
508-580-2730

Lowell Vet Center
Community Care Center
81 Bridge Street
Lowell, MA 01852
508-934-9124

Springfield Vet Center
1985 Main Street
Springfield, MA 01103
508-737-5167

Winchendon Vet Center
Town Hall
Winchendon, MA1475
508-297-3028

Worcester Vet Center
605 Lincoln Street
Worcester, MA 01605
508-856-7046

Michigan
Regional Office:
Detroit Regional Office
Patrick V. McNamara Federal Bldg.
477 Michigan Ave.
Detroit, MI 48226
800-827-1000

Vet Centers:
Detroit Vet Center
4161 Cass Ave.
Detroit, MI 48201
313-831-6509

Grand Rapids Vet Center
1940 Eastern Ave. SE
Grand Rapids, MI 49507
616-243-0385

Lincoln Park Vet Center
1766 Fort St.
Lincoln Park, MI 48146
313-381-1370

Minnesota
Regional Office:
St. Paul Regional Office
1 Federal Drive, Fort Snelling
St. Paul, MN 55111-4050
800-827-1000

Vet Centers:
Duluth Vet Center
405 East Superior St.
Duluth, MN 55802
218-722-8654

St. Paul Vet Center
2480 University Ave.
St. Paul, MN 55114
612-644-4022

Mississippi
Regional Office:
Jackson Regional Office
1600 E. Woodrow Wilson Avenue
Jackson, MS 39216
800-827-1000
601-364-7000
Fax: 601-364-7007

Vet Centers:
Biloxi Vet Center
313 Abbey Court
Biloxi, MS 39531
228-388-9938

Jackson Vet Center
4436 N. State St., Suite A3
Jackson, MS 39206
601-965-5727

Missouri
Regional Office:
St. Louis Regional Office
Federal Building
400 South, 18th Street
St. Louis, MO 63103
800 827 1000

Vet Centers:
Kansas City Vet Center
3931 Main Street
Kansas, MO 64111
816-753-1866
FTS: 816-753-2328

St. Louis Vet Center
2345 Pine Street
St. Louis, MO 63103
314-231-1260
Fax: 314-289-6539

Montana
Regional Office:
Fort Harrison Medical and Regional Office
William Street off Highway
Fort Harrison, MT 59636
800-827-1000

Vet Centers:
Billings Vet Center
1234 Ave. C
Billings, MT 59102
406-657-6071

Missoula Vet Center
500 N. Higgins Avenue
Missoula, MT 59802
406-721-4918

Nebraska
Regional Office:
Lincoln Regional Office
5631 South 48th Street
Lincoln, NE 68516
800-827-1000

Vet Centers:
Lincoln Vet Center
920 L. St.
Lincoln, NE 68508
402-476-9736

Omaha Vet Center
2428 Cuming St.
Omaha, NE 68131-1600
402-346-6735

Nevada
Regional Office:
Reno Regional Office
1201 Terminal Way
Reno, NV 89520
800-827-1000

Vet Centers:
Las Vegas Vet Center
704 S 6th St.
Las Vegas, NV 89101
702-388-6368

Reno Vet Center
1155 W. 4th St.
Suite 101
Reno, NV 89503
702-323-1294

New Hampshire
Regional Office:
Manchester Regional Office
Norris Cotton Federal Bldg.
275 Chestnut St.
Manchester, NH 03101
800-827-1000

Vet Centers:
Manchester Vet Center
103 Liberty St.
Manchester, NH 03104
603-668-7060

New Jersey
Regional Office:
Newark Regional Office
20 Washington Place
Newark, NJ 07102
800-827-1000

Vet Centers:
Jersey City Vet Center
115 Christopher Columbus Dr.
Room 200
Jersey, NJ 07302
201-645-2038

Newark Vet Center
157 Washington St.
Newark, NJ 07102
201-645-5954
Fax: 201-645-5932

Trenton Vet Center
171 Jersey St., Bldg. 36
Trenton, NJ 08611
609-989-2260

Ventnor Vet Center
6601 Ventnor Ave., Suite 401
Ventnor, NJ 08406
609-927-8387

New Mexico
Regional Office:
Albuquerque Regional Office
Danis Chavez Federal Building
500 Gold Avenue, SW
Albuquerque, NM 87102
800-827-1000

Vet Centers:
Albuquerque Vet Center
1600 Mountain Road NW
Albuquerque, NM 87104
505-346-6562
Fax: 505-346-6572

Farmington Vet Center
4251 E. Main, Suite B
Farmington, NM 87402
505-327-9684
Fax: 505-327-9519

Santa Fe Vet Center
2209 Brothers Rd., Suite 110
Santa Fe, NM 87505
505-988-6562
Fax: 505-988-6564

New York
Regional Offices:
Buffalo Regional Office
Federal Building
111 W Huron St.
Buffalo, NY 14202
800-827-1000
(Serves Counties not served by the New York, NY Regional Office).

New York Regional Office
245 W Houston St.
New York, NY 10014
800-827-1000
Fax: 212-807-4024
(Serves the Counties of Albany, Bronx, Clinton, Columbia, Delaware, Dutchess, Essex, Franklin, Fulton, Greene, Hamilton, Kings, Montgomery, Nassau, New York, Orange, Otsego Putnam, Queens, Rensselaer, Richmond, Rockland, Saratoga, Schenectady, Schoharie, Suffolk, Sullivan, Ulster, Warren, Washington, and Westchester).

Vet Centers:
Albany Vet Center
875 Central Ave.
Albany, NY 12206
518-438-2505

Babylon Vet Center
116 West Main Street
Babylon, NY 11702
516-661-3930

Bronx Vet Center
226 East Fordham Road
Room 220
Bronx, NY 10458
718-367-3500

Brooklyn Vet Center
25 Chapel St., Suite 604
Brooklyn, NY 11201
718-330-2825

Buffalo Vet Center
564 Franklin Street
Buffalo, NY 14202
716-882-0505
Fax: 716-882-0525

Harlem Vet Center
55 West 125th Street, 7th Floor
New York, NY 10027
212-870-8126

Manhattan Vet Center
201 Varick St., Room 707
New York, NY 10014
212-620-3306

Rochester Vet Center
134 South Fitzhugh St.
Rochester, NY 14614
716-263-5710

Staten Island Vet Center
150 Richmond Terrace
Staten Island, NY 10301
718-816-4499

Syracuse Vet Center
716 East Washington St.
Syracuse, NY 13203
315-478-7127

White Plains Vet Center
300 Hamilton Avenue
White Plains, NY 10601
914-682-6250

Queens Vet Center
75-108 91st Avenue
Woodhaven, NY 11421
718-296-2871

North Carolina
Regional Office:
Winston-Salem Regional Office
Federal Building
251 N. Main Street
Winston-Salem, NC 27155
800 827 1000

Vet Centers:
Charlotte Vet Center
223 S. Brevard St., Suite 103
Charlotte, NC 28202
704-333-6107

Fayetteville Vet Center
4140 Ramsey Street, Suite 110
Fayetteville, NC 28311
910-488-6252

Greensboro Vet Center
2009 Elm-Eugene St.
Greensboro, NC 27406
910-333-5366

Greenville Vet Center
150 Arlington Blvd., Suite B
Greenville, NC 27858
919-355-7920

North Dakota
Medical and Regional Office:
Fargo VA Medical/Regional Office Center
2101 Elm Street
Fargo, ND 58102
800-827-1000
701-232-3241
Fax: 701-239-3705

Matthew Lesko, Information USA, Inc., 12081 Nebel Street, Rockville, MD 20852 • 1-800-955-7693 • www.lesko.com

Vet Centers:
Fargo Vet Center
3310 Feichtner Dr., Suite 100
Fargo, ND 58102
701-237-0942
Fax: 701-237-5734

Minot Vet Center
3041 3rd St., NW
Minot, ND 58703
701-852-0177
Fax: 701-862-5225

Ohio
Regional Office:
Cleveland Regional Office
A.J. Celebrezze Federal Building
1240 East 9th Street
Cleveland, OH 44199
800-827-1000

Vet Centers:
Cincinnati Vet Center #204
801 B. West 8th Street
Suite 126
Cincinnati, OH 45203
513-763-3500
Fax: 513-763-3505

Cleveland Vet Center #206
11511 Lorain Ave.
Cleveland, OH 44111
440-845-5023
Fax: 440-845-5024

Cleveland Heights Vet Center #205
2134 Lee Rd.
Cleveland Heights, OH 44118
216-932-8476

Columbus Vet Center #221
30 Spruce St.
Columbus, OH 43215
614-257-5550
Fax: 614-257-5551

Dayton Vet Center #225
111 W. 1st Street
Dayton, OH 45402
937-461-9150
937-461-9151

Oklahoma
Regional Office:
Muskogee Regional Office
125 South Main Street
Muskogee, OK 74401
800-827-1000
Oklahoma City: 405-270-5184
Tulsa: 918-748-5105

Oregon
Regional Office:
Portland Regional Office
1220 SW 3rd Avenue
Portland, OR 97204
800-827-1000

Vet Centers:
Eugene Vet Center
1255 Pearl St., Suite 200
Eugene, OR 97401
541-465-6918
Fax: 541-465-6656

Grants Pass Vet Center
211 SE 10th Street
Grants Pass, OR 97526
541-479-6912
Fax: 541-474-4589

Portland Vet Center
8383 N.E. Sandy Blvd.

Suite 110
Portland, OR 97220
503-273-5370
Fax: 503-273-5377

Salem Vet Center
617 Chemeketa St., NE
Salem, OR 97301
503-362-9911
Fax: 503-364-2534

Pennsylvania
Regional Offices:
Philadelphia Regional Office and Insurance
Center
5000 Wissahickon Avenue
Philadelphia, PA 19101
800-827-1000

Pittsburgh Regional Office
1000 Liberty Avenue
Pittsburgh, PA 15222
800-827-1000

Vet Centers:
Erie Vet Center
1000 State Street
Suite 1-2
Erie, PA 16501
814-453-7955

Harrisburg Vet Center
1007 N. Front Street
Harrisburg, PA 17102
717-782-3954

McKeesport Vet Center
2001 Lincoln Way
McKeesport, PA 15131
412-678-7704

Philadelphia Vet Center
801 Arch Street
Philadelphia, PA 19107
215-627-0238

Philadelphia Vet Center
101 E. Olney Ave.
Box C-7
Philadelphia, PA 19120
215-924-4670

Pittsburgh Vet Center
954 Penn Ave.
Pittsburgh, PA 15222
412-765-1193

Scranton Vet Center
959 Wyoming Ave.
Scranton, PA 18509
570-344-2676

Philippines
Regional Office:
Manila Regional Office
1131 Roxas Blvd., Ermita
Manila, PI 96440
800-827-1000
011-632-528-2500
FTS: 011-632-528-2500

Puerto Rico
Regional Office:
San Juan Regional Office
150 Carlos Chardon Avenue
Hato Rey, PR 00918
800-827-1000
Fax: 787-772-7458

Vet Centers:
Arecibo Vet Center
52 Gonzalo Marin St.
Arecibo, PR 00612

809-879-4510
FTS: 809-879-4581

Ponce Vet Center
35 Mayor Street
Ponce, PR 00731
809-841-3260

San Juan / Rio Piedros Vet Center
Condomino Medical Center Plaza, Suite
LCBA, LC9, La Riviera
San Juan, PR 00921
787-783-8794

Rhode Island
Regional Office:
Providence Regional Office
380 Westminister Mall
Providence, RI 02903
800-827-1000

Vet Centers:
Cranston Vet Center
789 Park Avenue
Cranston, RI 02910
401-528-5271

Providence Vet Center
909 N. Main St.
Providence, RI 02904
401-528-5271

South Carolina
Regional Office:
Columbia Regional Office
1801 Assembly Street
Columbia, SC 29201
800-827-1000

Vet Centers:
Columbia Vet Center
1513 Pickens St.
Columbia, SC 29201
803-765-9944

Greenville Vet Center
14 Lavinia St.
Greenville, SC 29601
803-271-2711

North Charleston Vet Center
5603A Rivers Ave.
North Charleston, SC 29418
803-747-8387

South Dakota
Regional Office:
Sioux Falls Regional Office
P.O. Box 5046, 2501 W 22nd St.
Sioux Falls, SD 57117
800-827-1000

Vet Centers:
Rapid City Vet Center
610 Kansas City St.
Rapid City, SD 57701
605-348-0077

Sioux Falls Vet Center
601 South Cliff Ave. Suite C
Sioux Falls, SD 57102
605-332-0856

Tennessee
Regional Office:
Nashville Regional Office
110 9th Avenue South
Nashville, TN 37203
800-827-1000

Vet Centers:
Chattanooga Vet Center
425 Cumberland St.

Suite 140
Chattanooga, TN 37404
423-855-6570

Johnson City Vet Center
1615A Market St.
Johnson City, TN 37604
615-928-8387

Knoxville Vet Center
2817 E. Magnolia Ave.
Knoxville, TN 37914
423-545-4680

Memphis Vet Center
1835 Union, Suite 100
Memphis, TN 38104
901-722-2510

Texas
Regional Offices:
Houston Regional Office
6900 Almeda Road
Houston, TX 77030
800 827 1000

Waco Regional Office
1 Veterans Plaza
701 Clay Ave.
Waco, TX 76799
800-827-1000

Vet Centers:
Amarillo Vet Center
3414 E. Olsen Blvd.
Suite E.
Amarillo, TX 79109
806-354-9779
Fax: 806-351-1104

Austin Vet Center
1110 W. William Canon Dr.
Suite 301
Austin, TX 78723
512-416-1314

Corpus Christi Vet Center
3166 Reid Dr., Suite 1
Corpus Christi, TX 78404
512-854-9961

Dallas Vet Center
5232 Forest Lane, Suite 111
Dallas, TX 75244
214-361-5896

El Paso Vet Center
Sky Park II
6500 Boeing
Suite L-112
El Paso, TX 79925
915-772-0013
Fax: 915-772-3983

Fort Worth Vet Center
1305 W. Magnolia, Suite B
Fort Worth, TX 76104
817-921-9095

Houston Vet Center
503 Westheimer
Houston, TX 77006
713-523-0884

Houston Vet Center
701 N. Post Oak Road
Houston, TX 77024
713-682-2288

Laredo Vet Center
6020 Mcpherson Road
Laredo, TX 78041
956-723-4680

Lubbock Vet Center
3208 34 St.
Lubbock, TX 79410
806-792-9782
Fax: 806-792-9785

McAllen Vet Center
1317 E. Hackberry Street
McAllen, TX 78501
956-631-2147

Midland Vet Center
3404 W. Illinois, Suite 1
Midland, TX 79703
915-697-8222
Fax: 915-697-0561

San Antonio Vet Center
231 W. Cypress Street
San Antonio, TX 78212
210-229-4025

Utah
Regional Office:
Salt Lake City Regional Office
125 South State Street
Salt Lake City, UT 84147
800-827-1000

Vet Centers:
Provo Vet Center
750 North 200 West
Suite 105
Provo, UT 84601
801-377-1117

Salt Lake City Vet Center
1354 East 3300, South
Salt Lake City, UT 84106
801-584-1294

Vermont
Regional Office:
White River Junction Regional Office
N. Hartland Road
White River Junction, VT 05009
800 827 1000

Vet Centers:
South Burlington Vet Center
359 Dorset St.
Burlington, VT 05403
802-862-1806

White River Junction Vet Center
2 Holiday Dr.
Gilman Office Building # 2
White River Junction, VT 05001
802-295-2908

Virginia
Regional Office:
Roanoke Regional Office
210 Franklin Rd. SW
Roanoke, VA 24011
800-827-1000

Vet Centers:
Alexandria Vet Center
8796 D Sacramento Dr.
Alexandria, VA 22309
703-360-8633
Fax: 703-360-6143

Norfolk Vet Center
2200 Colonial Ave. Suite 3
Norfolk, VA 23517
804-623-7584

Richmond Vet Center
3022 West Clay St.
Richmond, VA 23230
804-353-8958

Roanoke Vet Center
320 Mountain Ave SW
Roanoke, VA 24016
703-342-9726

Virgin Islands
Vet Centers:
St. Croix Vet Center
Box 12, R.R. 02
Village Mall, #113
St. Croix, VI 00850
809-778-5553

St. Thomas Vet Center
Buccaneer Mall
St. Thomas, VI 00801
809-774-6674

Washington
Regional Office:
Seattle Regional Office
Federal Building
915 2nd Avenue
Seattle, WA 98174
800-827-1000

Vet Centers:
Bellingham Vet Center
3800 Byron, Suite 124
Bellingham, WA 98226
360-733-9226
Fax: 360-733-9117

Seattle Vet Center
2030 9th Ave.
Suite 210
Seattle, WA 98121
206-553-2706
Fax: 206-553-0380

Spokane Vet Center
100 N. Mullan Rd.
Suite 102
Spokane, WA 99206
509-444-8387
Fax: 509-444-8388

Tacoma Vet Center
4916 Center St., Suite E
Tacoma, WA 98409
206-565-7038
Fax: 253-589-4026

West Virginia
Regional Office:
Huntington Regional Office
640 Fourth Ave.
Huntington, WV 25701
800-827-1000
Fax: 304-529-5776

Vet Centers:
Beckley Vet Center
101 Ellison Ave.
Beckley, WV 25801
304-252-8220

Charleston Vet Center
512 Washington St. West.
Charleston, WV 25302
304-343-3825

Huntington Vet Center
1005 6th Ave.
Huntington, WV 25701
304-523-8387

Martinsburg Vet Center
900 Winchester Ave.
Martinsburg, WV 25401
304-263-6776
Fax: 304-262-7448

Matthew Lesko, Information USA, Inc., 12081 Nebel Street, Rockville, MD 20852 • 1-800-955-7693 • www.lesko.com

Morgantown Vet Center
1083 Greenbag Road
Morgantown, WV 26508
304-285-4303

Mt. Gay Vet Center
Mt. Gay, WV 25637
304-752-4453

Princeton Vet Center
905 Mercer St.
Princeton, WV 24740
304-425-5653

Wheeling Vet Center
1070 Market St.
Wheeling, WV 26003
304-232-0587

Wisconsin

Regional Office:
Milwaukee Regional Office
5000 West National Avenue
Milwaukee, WI 53295
800 827 1000

Vet Centers:
Madison Vet Center
147 S. Butler Street
Madison, WI 53703
608-264-5342

Milwaukee Vet Center
3400 Wisconsin
Milwaukee, WI 53208
414-344-5504

Wyoming

Medical and Regional Office:
Cheyenne VA Medical/Regional Office Center
2360 E. Pershing Blvd.
Cheyenne, WY 82001
800-827-1000

Vet Centers:
Casper Vet Center
111 S. Jefferson, Suite 100
Casper, WY 82601
307-261-5355

Cheyenne Vet Center
2424 Pioneer Ave., Suite 103
Cheyenne, WY 82001
307-778-7370
Fax: 307-638-8923

I Wanna New Career And I'm an Ex-Offender

Matthew Lesko, Information USA, Inc., 12081 Nebel Street, Rockville, MD 20852 • 1-800-955-7693 • www.lesko.com

I Wanna New Career And I'm an Ex-Offender

Since 1990 the nation's prison and jail population has nearly doubled. In 1990, there were 773, 919 prison inmates as compared to 1,302,019 in 1998. At about $15,000 per prisoner, the nation's tab for corrections is now approximately $25 billion a year, and the price tag continues to grow each year.

From 1980 to 1993, the number of U.S. ex-offenders released yearly from state or federal prison has more than tripled, jumping from 122,952 to 456,408. If this trend continues, the community of ex-offenders will continue to grow, and at an exponential rate.

Here are some more worrisome statistics. According to recent Justice Department figures, an estimated 63 percent of released state prisoners are rearrested for a felony or serious misdemeanor within three years, 43 percent are re-convicted, and 41 percent are returned to prison or jail; an estimated 21 percent are rearrested for a violent offense -- such as robbery, rape, kidnapping and homicide. Those are frightening statistics but true, nonetheless.

It's not difficult to understand why most ex-offenders end up back behind bars. Once on the street, they face an almost endless series of obstacles such as lack of food, shelter, employment, clothes, start-up money, transportation, and medical services. To add to the problem, most ex-offenders don't possess a marketable skill, are semi-literate, and have no knowledge of community resources available to them. Statistics from the Division of Criminal Justice show that 83% of ex-offenders that violated parole were unemployed at the time of violation. Despite these odds, here are some examples of ex-offenders who have used programs to start a new career:

* After 22 Years In Prison A Masters Degree And His Own Nonprofit

Thomas R. Sims, an ex-offender who spent 22 years in county, state, and federal institutions, is now the executive director of People United Together (P.U.T.), an organization that offers services and programs to offenders, ex-offenders and the community. In 1988, while incarcerated in Holmesburg Prison for theft, he and two other inmates teamed up and developed a community partnership with a Pastor and his congregation in North Central Philadelphia. This led to the development of P.U.T., which was started the following year. Sims credits the Pennsylvania Prison Society for providing help during and after his incarceration. "They were the only organization around that really fought for the rights of offenders. They provided opportunities such as vocational training and educational guidance for guys like me just getting out of prison." Mr. Sims is now completing his Masters Degree in Human Services at Lincoln University.

* Ex-Drug Dealer Becomes Foster Mom And Counselor

Rose Marie Tappa, a former cocaine and heroin addict, has turned her life around with the help of Project Return, an ex-offender support agency located in Milwaukee, WI. After serving nine months in prison for drug dealing, Ms. Tappa turned to Project Return for help. "I was afraid of the future and ashamed of my past. Project Return gave me an opportunity to build my self-esteem and learn how to deal with difficult situations instead of running away from them." In addition to being a full time mother and foster parent, Ms. Tappa works part time for Project Return, is involved in a neighborhood watch program, and speaks of her experiences to halfway houses, prisons, and schools. "I'm here to say that it can work. If I can plant just one seed of that idea in someone's mind, I've succeeded."

* New York Prisoner Gets Help In Nebraska

Glenn Thomas, a former inmate, read about Nebraska's CEGA Offender Referral Service while still in prison in New York and sent for a referral form. He said the New York prison system didn't offer any pre-release services while he was incarcerated and he didn't get any significant help from parole officers. Within five days, Glenn got the form from CEGA, filled it out, and two months later received his list. Within two weeks of his release, he was working full time. Glenn added that the agencies CEGA referred him to also taught him how to interview and got him involved in CURE-SORT, an advocacy group for sex offenders. "CEGA is looking out for the best interest of the inmate...These people are for real and inmates need to trust them," he said.

* Ex-Offender In California Gets Help To Get A Degree And Help Others

Derrick Jones, 38, was serving time for grand theft in California's Donovan State Prison when he heard about the pre-release planning program offered through the Community Connection Resource Center. "They helped me with job referrals, taught me how to write a resume, and helped me find my first job," he said. Now completing his B.A. in human behavior from National University, he works full time at Community Connection counseling ex-gang members and other ex-offenders.

* Chicago Alderman Convicted Of Bribery Gets Help To Re-enter Society

Lou Farina, a former Chicago alderman, served one year in prison, after being indicted on charges of election bribery. Now Director of Public Affairs at Chicago's Safer Foundation, he considers himself a "man with a mission" and acts as a "semi-lobbyist" for ex-offenders. "I work toward getting ex-offenders to become successful taxpaying citizens, help them to go straight, and get a job," he said. "Only after being in prison for a year did I realize what we have to do to get ex-offenders back in the mainstream of society." Mr. Farina first became involved with the Safer Foundation in 1985 during his trial and has worked with them ever since, first as a volunteer and later as a paid staff member.

Federal Program To Help Employers Hire Ex-Offenders

* Federal Bonding Program

Federal Bonding Program
1725 De Sales St., NW, Suite 900
Washington, DC 20036

202-293-5566
800-233-2258

The Federal Bonding program provides insurance (coverage that protects the employer from employee theft or destruction up to $10,000) for people that the employer's bonding company will not insure. The government provides bonding coverage at no cost to the employer or the applicant. The only standards for qualification are that the applicant be qualified for the job position, not be commercially bondable, and have a firm offer for full time work. Application is made through any one of the 1,700 local offices of the state employment service (or Job Service). All ex-offenders are automatically eligible.

Between 1966 and Oct. 1990, 25,000 persons who otherwise would not have received bonding did; during this period there was a default rate of only 1.57%. Research shows that those who received bonding assistance could not have obtained the job without this coverage.

Public and Private Agencies That Help

There are, however, public and private agencies that work to help ex-offenders find another way of life and remain out of prison. Some agencies are funded by state or local governments. Others are supported by charities, religious, and business groups. The organizations listed on page 990 offer after care services such as education/training programs, social services, and job development assistance.

According to our research, Kentucky, Nebraska, Oklahoma, Oregon, and Wyoming offer no after care programs specifically geared toward ex-offenders. These states do have charitable organizations such as the YMCA and YWCA, Goodwill Industries, Salvation Army, and United Way's First Call for Help Program. They can be found in the white business pages of the phone book. These organizations are always good places to contact and may provide other referrals that are useful.

Although most of the organizations listed do not provide legal services, a few like the National Legal Aid and Defender Association (NLADA), listed under National Organizations, provides assistance to legal aid and public defender offices. Although it doesn't provide direct services to individual clients, it does act as a referral service, providing the names of local programs that can provide inmates or ex-offenders with representation.

There are also several national advocacy groups that work to achieve reforms in the criminal justice system. Organizations such as the American Civil Liberties Union, American Friends Service Committee and CURE (Citizens United for the Rehabilitation of Errants) have state programs that offer information on education, policy development, and advocacy organization tactics. Check the white business pages of your phone book for local listings or contact the national office listed on page 990 under National Organizations.

Employment Rights For Ex-Offenders

Ex-offenders may encounter certain discrimination in their efforts to change their lives. Here are some laws and sources that can help overcome these obstacles.

* Misuse of Information

U.S. Department of Justice
Civil Rights Employment Litigation
601 O St., NW
Washington, DC 20004   202-514-3831

American Civil Liberties Union (ACLU)
125 Broad St.
New York, NY 10004-2400   212-549-2500
www.aclu.org/

According to state and federal laws, a potential employer can ask about an ex-offender's arrest or conviction only if it is related to job duties. Federal and state laws largely limit a potential employer inquiring about arrests and convictions or using any information about arrests or convictions in making employment decisions. Without such laws, an employer's use of these records could have a discriminatory impact on minority groups.

For example, someone convicted of tax fraud who applies for a bank teller's position could be denied employment since the required job-related duties involve the handling of money.

Arrest records and conviction records may be treated slightly differently since an arrest does not always mean that charges were filed. Even if charged, a person may have been acquitted.

If a company is collecting the information because it is job-related, some state laws limit the availability of an applicant's history within the company, itself. Access to that information may be restricted to one focal point such as the personnel office. Such restrictions help maintain the applicant's privacy.

* Garnishment and Credit History

American Civil Liberties Union (ACLU)
125 Broad St.
New York, NY 10004-2400   212-549-2500
www.aclu.org

An employer cannot inquire about credit history or financial history without substantiating that it is job-related. If you have a history of bad credit, you can receive a copy of your credit report from the credit bureau in your home town or from a national credit reporting agency. A national CRA will send you a free copy of your credit report if you have been denied credit, employment or insurance within the last 60 days. Otherwise, they may charge up to $8 for a report.

Trans Union Corporation
P.O. Box 390
Springfield, PA 19064   800-888-4213
www.trw.com

Experian Information Solutions, Inc.
P.O. Box 2104
Allen, TX 75013   888-397-3742
www.experian.com

Equifax Credit Info
P.O. Box 740241
Atlanta, GA 30374   800-685-1111
www.equifax.com

Once you have received a copy of your report, check it for errors. You can challenge the mistakes by explaining the error in writing to the credit reporting agency. Valid debts can be postponed or cleared by writing to the creditor and explaining your circumstances. Many creditors will accept small payments as long as they are sent on a regular basis. Credit agencies don't keep criminal records or release that information.

Another way to improve your credit rating is to apply for a secured credit card. Some major banks are now offering this service to people with troubled credit histories.

Your first step is to mail in a cash deposit. The bank will then issue you a credit card with a charge limit equal to your deposit. In other words, if you don't pay your bill, the bank will seize your deposit to cover losses.

Requirements vary from bank to bank. Some banks accept any applicant who can come up with the cash deposit. Others will reward you by converting your card to a regular account if you make reliable payments on a regular basis. Signet Bank offers cards ranging from $300 to $5,000. If you don't have $300, they will open a savings account with any amount you can afford to send, and then issue the card when your deposit reaches $300. Be sure to ask questions to discover any hidden costs or penalties. And, remember, the reason for obtaining a credit card is to re-establish good credit, not dig yourself further into debt.

* Employment Opportunities

In some states, the parole board can restore to ex-offenders certain legal rights. If an ex-offender has only one felony conviction and completes parole without another felony conviction, the parole board can issue a Certificate of Relief from Disability. Those with more than one felony conviction can get a Certificate of Good Conduct if they stay out of trouble for a specified time. However, this depends upon how severe the crime was. Contact your parole office for details.

Getting one of these certificates shows that an individual is serious about obtaining work. They may also make it easier to get some jobs or occupational licenses.

Other Sources Of Help And Info For Ex-Offenders

* Starting A Business With Government Money

Small Business Administration
Small Business Answer Desk
P.O. Box 34500   800-UASK-SBA
Washington, DC 20043-4500   202-606-4000
www.sba.gov

If you are interested in going into business for yourself, you can call the U.S. Small Business Administrations (SBA) Small Business Answer Desk or your local SBA office.. SBA can provide you with information on starting and financing your own business, and counseling and training programs such as SCORE (Service Corps of Retired Executives) and state Small Business Development Centers. Ex-offenders are eligible to apply for the same loan programs as anyone else if not on parole or probation. See the chapter entitled, "I Wanna Start My Own Business."

* Public Employment Service

U.S. Department of Labor
Employment and Training
200 Constitution Ave., NW
Washington, DC 20210   202-219-6871

The local public One Stop Career Center was established to help unemployed workers, including ex-offenders, find jobs. Services include job counseling and guidance, job-search training, help with preparing a resume or job application, and evaluation of workers' job skills. Offices generally do not have specific programs for ex-offenders, but serve all unemployed or underemployed persons. Some, however, do have special programs for ex-offenders, so be sure to ask when you call. See the chapter entitled, "I Wanna Get A Government Job."

* JTPA Programs

U.S. Department of Labor
Employment and Training
200 Constitution Ave., NW, Room N4469
Washington, DC 20210   202-219-6871

State and local governments and businesses work together to provide free job training and retraining programs under the Job Training Partnership Act (JTPA). To qualify, individuals must have a low income, so ex-offenders should apply as soon as they are released from prison. The program can provide job counseling, classroom and on-the-job training, and help with job searches, work experience, counseling, basic skills training and support services.

Ex-offenders can ask their case worker or job counselor for information about JTPA programs. Also, look in the white pages of the telephone book for Private Industry Council or under the city or county government listings for Employment and Training or Human Resources or Job Service. Individuals can also call the Mayor's office or the national office of the Employment and Training Programs of the U.S. Department of Labor at 202-219-5580. Jobs Bank Joint project of Federal and Local employment service: Call local employment service office or http://www.ajb.dnt.us

* Social Security Information

Social Security Administration
Office of Public Inquiries
6401 Security Blvd.   800-772-1213
Baltimore, MD 21235-6401   TTY: 800-325-0778

Social Security is a benefits package of protection for you and your family upon retirement, disability, or survivorship. It is an insurance program and is based on earnings you had while working. Supplemental Security Income (SSI) is an income maintenance program for poor people who are elderly (age 65), blind, or disabled.

Social Security and SSI are not offender/ex-offender programs, as such. They are programs for all citizens of the United States (also, legally admitted refugees and sponsored aliens) if you quality under the eligibility guidelines. While in prison, benefits are forfeited and will not be paid by SSI or Social Security. However, if any family member was receiving Social Security payments on your entitlement prior to your incarceration, they may still be eligible. If they think they qualify they should contact their nearest local Social Security Office or call the Social Security toll-free information line at 800-772-1213.

* Your Social Security Card

Social Security Administration
Office of Public Inquiries
6401 Security Blvd.   800-772-1213
Baltimore, MD 21235-6401   TTY: 800-325-0778

Upon release from prison, you may be required to furnish your Social Security card in order to obtain some services or get a job. In may cases, you will be asked to show your Social Security card as evidence of the number assigned to you. If you are age 18 or older and never had a Social Security Number before, you will need to apply for one in person. If you already have a Social Security Number but no longer have your card, you can apply for a card by writing any Social Security office and requesting an Application Form SS-5. Complete the application and mail it back to the Social Security office with the required evidence. The application explains what documents are required, depending on whether you are applying for an original or a replacement card.

* Educational Opportunities

Contact a case worker, job counselor

or

Distance Education and Training Council
1601 18th St., NW
Washington, DC 20009   202-234-5100
www.detc.org

At least seven of every ten inmates have not completed high school. Prison inmates and ex-offenders who don't have a high school diploma can work toward their G.E.D. (General Equivalency Diploma) by participating in home study (correspondence) courses. Individuals enroll with an accredited educational institution which provides lesson materials for study by students on their own. When each lesson is completed, the student mails the assigned work to the school for correction and grading. Corrected assignments are returned to the student. Many courses provide complete vocational training. Emphasis is on learning what you need to know.

A number of schools offer full four-year high school diploma programs and academic degree programs. The National Home Study Council offers a directory of member schools. The following publications also provide information on educational opportunities:

Bear's Guide to Earning College Degrees Non-Traditionally by Ten Speed Press. Send $27.95 to Dr. John Bear, 6923 Stockton Ave., El Cerrito, CA 94530.

Campus-free College Degrees, 5th Edition by Marcie Kisner Thorson, M.A., Adams Media Corp., P.O. Box 470886, Tulsa, OK 74147; 800-741-7771.

The Independent Study Catalog, Peterson's Guides, P.O. Box 2123, Princeton, NJ 08543-2123; 800-338-3282.

Ex-offenders can also earn educational credits by taking standardized exams. Tests generally cost less than $70 each. For more information about credit by examination contact:

ACT/PEP Candidate Registration Guide
American College Testing
P.O. Box 4014
Iowa City, IA 52243
319-337-1000

The Official Handbook for the CLEP Examination
College Entrance Examination Board
45 Columbus Ave.
New York, NY 10023-6992
212-713-8000

To Order Book:
College Board Publications
P.O. Box 286
New York, NY 10101-0886

TECEP Test Description Booklets
Office of Test Development and Research
Thomas Edison State College
101 W. State St.
Trenton, NJ 08608-1176
609-984-1140

The U.S. Department of Education publishes booklets entitled *The Student Guide* and *Funding Your Education* which outlines major sources of federal educational assistance for post-secondary education. For a free copy, write to: Financial Aid, U.S. Department of Education, P.O. Box 84, Washington, DC 20044, or call: 800-4-FED-AID.

Publications

There are many different kinds of materials that can help ex-offenders find work. The U.S. Department of Labor produces the *Occupational Outlook Handbook* which is published every two years by the Bureau of Labor Statistics. It presents information about the nature of the work, working conditions, employment, training requirements, job outlook, earnings, and places to find more information. The Employment and Training Administration publishes *Tips for Finding the Right Job* that may make the job search easier. These books are available in most public libraries, or contact the Employment and Training Administration, U.S. Department of Labor, 200 Constitution Ave., NE, Washington, DC 20002-0730; 202-219-6871.

The organizations listed below offer free catalogues of publications that include employment information for ex-offenders:

OPEN, INC. - Offender Preparation and Education Network, Inc.
Ned Rollo, Executive Director
P.O. Box 566025
Dallas, TX 75356-6025   972-271-1971
This publishing house develops educational materials for offenders and their families and for criminal justice agents. They publish an employment manual, *Man, I Need a Job* (English and Spanish) for $5.95.

Hazelden Educational Materials
15251 Pleasant Valley Rd.
P.O. Box 176
Center City, MN 55012   800-328-9000
www.hazelden.org

The Safer Foundation
571 West Jackson St.
Chicago, IL 60661   312-922-2200

The National Prison Project of the ACLU
  (American Civil Liberties Union)
1875 Connecticut Ave., NW, Suite 410   202-234-4830
Washington, DC 20009   Fax: 202-234-4890
The National Prison Project publishes the following materials for inmates and ex-offenders:

The Prisoners' Assistance Directory. Identifies and describes various organizations and agencies that provide assistance to prisoners. Lists national, state, and local organizations and sources of assistance including legal, AIDS, family support, and ex-offender aid. 10th edition. Published August 1996, Paperback. $30 prepaid from NPP.

National Prison Project Journal. $30/yr. $2/yr to prisoners.

Bibliography of Material on Women in Prison. Lists information on this subject available from the National Prison Project and other sources concerning health care, drug treatment, incarcerated mothers, juveniles, legislation, parole, the death penalty, sex discrimination, race and more. 35 pages. $5 prepaid from NPP.

A Primer for Jail Litigators. Detailed manual with practical suggestions for jail litigations. Includes chapter on legal analysis, use of expert witnesses, class actions, attorneys' fees, enforcement, defenses' proof. 1st Edition. February 1984. 180 pages. (Note: This is not a "jailhouse lawyers" manual.) $20 prepaid from NPP.

1996 AIDS in Prison Bibliography. Lists resources on AIDS in prison that are available from the National Prison Project and other sources, including corrections policies on AIDS, educational materials, medical and legal articles, and recent AIDS studies. $10 prepaid from NPP.

Additional Publications from Other Presses:

Post-Release Assistance Programs for Prisoners: A National Directory. Anthony J. Bosoni, 176 pp., ISBN 0-7864-0025-0, $34.50, 1995 2nd Edition or call McFarland Publishing 800-253-2187. Directed at parolees and those working with them, lists agencies and private assistance organizations. Organized by state, lists agencies that provide housing, and emergency shelter, employment referrals, job training, food, clothing, and counseling services. Each entry provides agency name, location, phone number, and services offered. Separate sections list organizations specifically targeted at women and those aimed at veterans.

The Ex-Inmates Complete Guide to Successful Employment. Errol Craig Sull, 400 pp., 370 Franklin St., Buffalo, NY 14202, 716-882-3456. Covers aspects of the job search for the inmate soon-to-be released or newly released ex-inmate. Special emphasis on problems encountered by the inmate and ex-inmate in his/her career search.

From Freedom to Felon. Vietnam Veterans of America, Inc., 1224 M St., NW, Washington, DC 20005, 202-628-2700; {www.vva.org}. VVA publishes a free guidebook for incarcerated veterans which details information on loss of benefits on incarceration, government programs and assistance after release, and restoration of benefits.

National Organizations

* American Civil Liberties Union (ACLU)
125 Broad St.   212-549-2500
New York, NY 10004-2400   800-775-ACLU
This is the national headquarters of the ACLU. Their main function is organizational, and to oversee litigation. Those interested in becoming members of the ACLU should contact this office.

* CEGA Services
Darrell Bryan, Director
P.O. Box 81826
Lincoln, NE 68501   402-464-0602
This is a national for-profit information and referral service that provides assistance to inmates, ex-offenders and their families. Individuals can ask for help in locating the addresses, phone numbers, and criteria of agencies that will help them with employment, shelter, financial advice, educational programs, alcohol/drug counseling, legal or medical advice. There is a $10 fee. Write for a referral form.

* CURE (Citizens United for the Rehabilitation of Errants)
P.O. Box 2310
National Capitol Station
Washington, DC 20013-2310   202-789-2126
www.curenational.org
CURE organizes prisoners, their families and other concerned citizens to achieve reforms in the criminal justice system. They are an advocacy, not an after care organization. However, various state chapters can provide prisoners and their families with information about rehabilitative programs.

* The National Legal Aid and Defender Association (NLADA)
1625 K St., Suite 800   202-452-0620
Washington, DC 20006   Fax: 202-872-1031
www.nlada.org
E-mail: info@nlada.org
This organization provides assistance to legal aid and public defender offices. The NLADA does not provide direct services to individual clients. However, NLADA will act as a referral service, providing the names of local programs that do provide representation to individual clients.

* Prison Fellowship Ministries
P.O. Box 17500
Washington, DC 20041-0500   703-478-0100
www.prisonfellowship.org/
Prison Fellowship works toward getting churches involved in ministering directly to ex-prisoners, in referring ex-prisoners to other organizations when beneficial, and in being an after care resource to other community organizations.

State and Local Organizations

Alabama
Re-Entry Ministries, Inc.
Hank or Jackie Gray
2224 3rd Ave., N
Birmingham, AL 35210
205-320-2101
Works with ex-offenders and offers limited services to prisoners. Numerous programs include support groups for ex-offenders and families of prisoners, church services, job assistance, and AA meetings. Provides Christian literature free of charge.

Arizona
Middle Ground Prison Reform
Donna Leone Hamm/James Hamm
139 East Encanto Dr.
Tempe, AZ 85281
480-966-8116
Fax: 480-966-3885
www.mgprisonreform.com
E-mail: donna@mgprisonreform.com
Offers counseling, education/training programs and referrals to social service agencies. Advocacy and public education performed on state and national levels. Direct services are provided statewide in Arizona.

Arkansas
Women's Project
Janet Perkins
2224 Main St.
Little Rock, AR 72206
501-372-5113
Although all services are provided at the state women's prison, the Women's Project does maintain a job notebook at their office headquarters with information on potential employment opportunities.

Second Genesis
4823 Woodlawn Dr.
Little Rock, AR 72205-0375
501-666-6831
Transitional House with space for seven women. Length of stay varies with individual need (up to 18 months). Offers job counseling, substance abuse recovery, aids prevention, parenting skills, and family enrichment.

California

Community Connection Resource Center
4080 Centre St.
Suite 202
San Diego, CA 92103
619-294-3900
Comprehensive services for prisoners and ex-offenders. Re-entry services include pre-release planning in local, state and federal correctional institutions, vocational assistance, assistance with emergency needs such as shelter, food and clothing, and job development and placement. Also provides residential recovery/re-entry for women on parole.

Jewish Committee for Personal Service
216 S. Lake St.
Los Angeles, CA 90057
323-644-2026
The Jewish Committee for Personal Service (JCPS) is a social service agency that works with Jewish offenders and their families, mostly in the Los Angeles County jail system, but also in some state and federal institutions. JCPS offers counseling and referrals for housing and jobs in the Los Angeles area. It has a 20-bed re-entry facility at the address listed above.

Northern California Service League
28 Boardman Place
San Francisco, CA 94103
415-863-2323
Fax: 415-863-1882
www.jps.net/ncsl/index.htm
This organization offers after care counseling and referral services for prisoners and their families. They also offer job development assistance to state/county ex-offenders. San Francisco County Jail caseworkers act as liaisons between prisoners and public agencies.

Office for Prisoner-Community Justice
Catholic Charities
433 Jefferson St.
Oakland, CA 94607
510-834-5656
Catholic Charities offers counseling and emergency assistance referrals to ex-offenders. They provide religious, pastoral services in the jails and juvenile halls of Alameda and Contra Costa Counties and victim/offender mediation services.

VOA Elizabeth Fry Center for Women
1251 Second Ave.
San Francisco, CA 94122
415-681-0430
Services are provided for state prisoners and their children only including housing, meals, preschool program, AA counseling, computer classes, tutoring, basic literacy skills training and parenting classes, self-esteem counseling, and NA.

Colorado

Colorado CURE
3470 S. Poplar, Suite 406
Denver, CO 80224
303-758-3390
Prison Advocacy works through legislative channels to reduce crime through reform of the criminal justice system. Provides prisoners and families with information about rehabilitative programs.

Colorado Ex-Offender Employment
Colorado Division of Employment Services
639 E. 18th Ave.
Denver, CO 80203
303-830-3002
http://employsvcs.cdle.state.co.us
Provides job placement and referral for ex-offenders.

Connecticut

Community Partners in Action
Deanne Scaringe
Parkville Business Center
110 Bartholomew Ave., Suite 3010
Hartford, CT 06106

860-566-2030
Fax: 860-566-8089
www.hartnet.org/~ctpas
They offer pre-trial, community and volunteer sponsor services. Also, Coalition Employment Services and a Resettlement Program. Contact the following branch office for employment services to ex-offenders: 9-11 Willis St., Hartford, CT 06106, 203-525-6691.

Families in Crisis, Inc.
30 Arbor St., North Wing
Hartford, CT 06106
860-236-3593
Offers a wide range of counseling and support services to offenders and their families. Services include individual and family counseling, crisis intervention, child care programs, and training programs. Serves Greater Hartford, New Haven, Waterbury, and Bridgeport areas.

Delaware

Career Exploration Program
2516 W. 4th St.
Wilmington, DE 19805
302-573-2474
Helps juvenile offenders (ages 16-21) who have dropped out of high school obtain GED equivalency training and part-time employment.

Limon House for Women
624 N. Broom St.
Wilmington, DE 19805
302-571-1216
Halfway house for women who have completed a 21-28 drug or alcohol rehabilitation program.

Limon House for Men
903 N. Madison
Wilmington, DE 19801
302-652-7969
Halfway house for men who have been drug or alcohol free for at least 10 days.

District of Columbia

Education and Training
Education, GED, Vocational Training
Adult Education Services
Lemuel Ten Center
1709 3rd St., NE
Washington, DC 20002
202-576-6308
The Adult Continuing and Community Education Branch sponsors day and evening adult basic education, GED preparation, high school alternative or completion programs, and vocational courses. Counseling and referral services are available at major centers and schools are near public transportation. Tuition-free, open enrollment programs are available for residents 18 and older.

Housing
Coalition for the Homeless
1234 Massachusetts Ave., NW
Washington, DC 20005
202-347-8870
Provides emergency shelter and support services, and referrals.

Community for Creative Non-Violence
425 2nd St., NW
Washington, DC 20001
202-393-4409
This is the central clearinghouse for CCNV information and referrals. This is the largest homeless shelter in the U.S. that provides all appropriate services. Provides information on food, shelters, and clothing distribution.

Department of Social Services
25 M St., SW
Washington, DC 20024
202-399-7093 - Shelter Hotline
or call:
202-724-3932 - Family Shelter
The Department of Social Services has emergency shelters for single adults on a walk-in basis from 7 p.m. to 7 a.m. at sites around the city. When a site is full, individuals may receive transportation to another.

EFEC (Efforts for Ex-Convicts)
1514 8th St., NW
Washington, DC 20001
202-232-1932
This halfway house for men provides transitional shelter for up to six months.

Extended House
81 14th St., NE
Washington, DC 20002
202-396-2272
Fax: 202-399-8637
This halfway house for men offers transitional shelter and counseling. Lengths of stay vary according to the situation. They have substance abuse and danger management counseling.

Gospel Mission
810 5th St., NW
Washington, DC 20001
202-842-1731
Overnight dormitory-style rooms, with capacity for 60 male residents. Offers dinner, breakfast, drug rehabilitation program, and employment counseling. Accepts walk-ins. Operates from 3pm to 9am.

Hope Village
2840 Langston Place, SE
Washington, DC 20020
202-678-1077
This halfway house for men offers transitional shelter and counseling.

Irving St. Shelter (La Casa)
1436 Irving St., NW
Washington, DC 20010
202-673-3592
La Casa is an emergency shelter that accepts people on a first come, first serve basis. It provides temporary shelter, and employment, housing and English and Spanish speaking social service counselors. There are open Alcoholics Anonymous and Return from Addiction meetings, showers, and recreational activities. There is a soup dinner at 7 p.m.

Luther Place Night Shelter
1226 Vermont Ave., NW
Washington, DC 20005
202-387-5464
Overnight facility with space from 32 women. Offers breakfast and dinner. Social services include mental and physical health resources. Does not take walk-ins, so call to get on waiting list.

New Endeavors for Women
611 N St., NW
Washington, DC 20001
202-682-5825
This is a structured transitional housing program with residents staying an average of 5 months. Offers case management, employment and job training services, educational tutoring and housing. Residents must be drug-free for 30 days and must save 75% of income, which is returned upon program completion. Referrals through agency or person having strong knowledge of candidate.

Emergency Food/Soup Kitchens
Interfaith Conference of Metropolitan Washington
1419 V St., NW
Washington, DC 20009
202-234-6300
The Interfaith Conference publishes a free Emergency Food and Shelter Directory that can be obtained from this address.

Proof of residence is typically required for the following agencies. Always call to verify food availability.

Northwest
Associated Catholic Charities
1438 Rhode Island Ave., NE
Washington, DC 20018
202-526-4100
Fax: 202-526-1829
www.catholiccharitiesdc.org
Full social service agency. Call for 65 locations in Metro area.

Community Family Life Services
500 3rd St.
(temporarily until 305 E. St., NW is rebuilt)
Washington, DC 20001
202-347-0511
Serves residents for 4 blocks each direction. Food for families monthly; social services, counseling, job placement and training with transportation, emergency utility and financial assistance.

Southeast
Allen Community Outreach Center (ACOC)
2443 Ainger Place, SE

Washington, DC 20020
202-889-5607
Emergency food and clothing, employment counseling and job placement; advocacy counseling and referral. Tutoring services.

Friendship House
619 D St., SE
Washington, DC 20003
202-675-9050
Emergency food for SE residents, and clothing.

Paramount Baptist Church
3924 4th St., SE
Washington, DC 20032
202-562-6339
Emergency food and clothing to anyone in need. Referrals preferred.

Southwest
Southwest Community House
156 Q St., SW
Washington, DC 20024
202-488-7210
Budgeting, clothes and food bank. Low-income housing assistance and tutoring for seniors and young adults. Employment counseling and referrals.

Florida
James E. Scott Community Associates (JESCA)
2322 NE 4th Ave.
Miami, FL 33137
305-573-0691
Job program to assist ex-offenders in finding employment.

Coconut Grove Cares
Barnyard Community Center
3870 Washington Ave.
Miami, FL 33133
305-446-6216
Only provides services to juveniles at high risk.

PRIDE (Prison Rehabilitative Industries and Diversified Enterprises, Inc.)
12425 28th St. North, Suite 103
St. Petersburg, FL 33716
727-572-1987
Fax: 727-570-3374
www.pridefl.com/index.htm
PRIDE is a nonprofit private corporation that manages the state prison industries. It functions in partnership with private industry, the state government, public agencies and community organizations. In addition to operating 53 industries in 21 state prisons, PRIDE offers job placement assistance upon release and support in transition back to the community for PRIDE workers only.

Georgia
Habitat for Humanity
121 Habitat St.
Americus, GA 31709
912-924-6935
Habitat for Humanity welcomes applications from ex-prisoners. Habitat's work (building homes for the poor) is done by close to 400 different local projects scattered across the country. A person wanting to apply to one of those affiliate projects is best off contacting that project directly. A second way to be involved with Habitat in the U.S. is to work at the Americus headquarters. Most of the work is not building, but office and administration. Habitat uses mostly "volunteers" but can provide furnished housing with utilities and a subsistence stipend for them. Habitat for Humanity also welcomes applications from prisoners who will soon be released.

Reach Ministry, Inc.
Rev. Joe Cobb
P.O. Box 299
Atlanta, GA 30301
404-344-4572
The Reach Ministry operates a transitional shelter which offers a 12-step drug counseling program, Christian counseling and evangelism, clothing and food assistance.

Hawaii
John Howard Association of Hawaii
Gerald Reardon
Executive Director
200 N. Vineyard Blvd., #330
Honolulu, HI 96817
808-537-2917

This is a private nonprofit criminal justice agency. Its programs include delinquency intervention efforts, transition housing for youth, sex offender programs, juvenile anger management, and counseling and employment assistance for ex-offenders.

Illinois

Gateway Foundation, Inc.
Chuck Schwartz, Senior Vice-President
819 S. Wabash, Suite 300
Chicago, IL 60605
312-663-1130
Agency provides after care treatment, addiction assessment and referrals, family support services and incarcerative treatment to inmates at Sheridan, Graham and Dwight state prisons, and Cook County Jail and Juvenile Detention Center.

Institute of Women Today
Sister Margaret Ellen Traxler
7315 S. Yale Ave.
Chicago, IL 60621
312-651-8372
Offers employment and vocational guidance, counseling, skills training. Operates two shelters for women and children.

Jewish Prisoners Assistance Foundation
Rabbi Binyomin Scheiman
2833 West Howard
Chicago, IL 60645
847-296-1770
Works to protect the rights of Jewish prisoners in Illinois. Offers support programs to obtain housing and employment for ex-offenders. Although the foundation does not operate a halfway house, it can refer ex-offenders to other rehabilitation centers and service organizations. The foundation also provides pre- and post-release counseling with prisoners and their families. The rabbi visits with the prisoners.

John Howard Association
59 E. Van Buren St., Suite 1600
Chicago, IL 60605
312-554-1901
Fax: 312-554-1905
www.bni-net.com/jha
Offers no direct after care services to ex-prisoners but can provide referrals to rehabilitation and social agencies within Illinois.

Prisoner Release Ministry, Inc.
37 E. Cass St.
P.O. Box 69
Joliet, IL 60432
815-723-8998
Numerous services include job preparation, counseling and placement for people on probation, parole, and work release in Cook, Grundy, Kendall, DuPage, Kane, Kankakee and Will Counties. Provides emergency assistance after obtaining employment by providing work tools and transportation. Offers state computerized job bank.

Private Industry Council for Job Training Partnership Act (JTPA)
510 N. Peshdigo
Chicago, IL 60611
312-744-5734
Offers various job training programs for income-eligible individuals under the federal job program.

Safer Foundation
Diane Williams, Executive Director
571 West Jackson
Chicago, IL 60661-5701
312-922-2200
Fax: 312-922-7640
www.safer-fnd.org
E-mail: saferDG@aol.com
Offers ex-offenders job counseling and placement, drug abuse counseling, car fare to a temporary shelter and referral to those services other agencies provide. Services are open to ex-offenders released from prison to the Chicago, Rock Island, IL and Davenport, IA areas.

St. Leonard's House
2100 W. Warren Blvd.
Chicago, IL 60612
312-738-1414
Transitional residence for ex-offenders. Offers housing, counseling work and social services programs. Outpatient programs for alcohol, narcotics, mental health and sexual counseling. One hour in-house counseling (meditation, spirituality, etc) as well as an outreach program.

Strive/Chicago Employment Service
4910 S. King Dr., Room 35
Chicago, IL 60615
312-624-9700
This nonprofit organization provides job training, placement, and counseling services to people who have not worked for six months or witness work history, or have problems finding employment. There are no fees to clients since STRIVE is funded by foundations, corporations, and individuals. It also serves as a referral service for day care and GED programs, and assists in getting entitlements from Public Aid and other programs. Priority is given to public aid recipients and public housing residents.

Indiana

PACT, Inc.
254 S. Morgan Blvd.
Valparaiso, IN 46383
219-462-1127
This community-based corrections organization offers residential centers for adult males, community service restitution, employment referrals, short term emergency housing, counseling, and a domestic violence program.

Iowa

Safer Foundation
605 Main St., Room 215
Davenport, IA 52803
319-322-7974
Fax: 319-322-1086
Offers ex-offenders job counseling and placement, drug abuse counseling, car fare to a temporary shelter, and referral to those services other agencies provide. Services are open to ex-offenders released from prison.

Kentucky

This state does not have any local programs at the time of publication. For assistance, contact one of the offices listed under National Organizations.

Louisiana

Community Service Center
Octavia Edinburg
4000 Magazine St.
New Orleans, LA 70115
504-897-6277
Provides counseling, job placement assistance, follow-up and referral services to ex-offenders in the greater metro New Orleans area. Also provides emergency assistance on a limited basis.

Southwest Louisiana Education and Referral Center, Inc.
439 Heyman Blvd.
Lafayette, LA 70503
318-232-4357
Provides ex-offenders with referrals to community and state agencies and organizations. Offers free brochures on health informational, drug testing, developmental disabilities, and dental programs.

Maine

Preble Street Resource Center
252 Oxford St. and 5 Portland
P.O. Box 1459
Portland, ME 04104
207-775-0026
This program provides assistance to homeless and low income persons at risk for homelessness by locating housing or providing transitional support. It acts as a clearinghouse for information on housing programs and related health and human services. They offer a breakfast program and a day shelter which provides free clothes, telephones, showers, laundry and condoms, plus a mailing address for homeless and low income persons. Their Homelessness Prevention Program provides intensive one-on-one case management and survival services to clients after an apartment has been secured to avoid future episodes of homelessness.

York County Shelters, Inc.
Shaker Hill Rd.
P.O. Box 820
Alfred, ME 04002
207-324-1137
Hotline: 800-639-3770
Fax: 207-324-5290
This residential treatment facility serves York County. Its services include a co-ed adult emergency shelter, halfway house, extended care, referral to social services, and on-site training in baking, institutional cooking, and building trades. It also functions as a family emergency shelter and transitional facility offering on-site child care services. The staff includes a registered substance abuse counselor, social worker, medical director, and dietician.

Soup Kitchens

There are numerous soup kitchens throughout Maine. Some serve noontime meals, others evening dinners. Most serve on weekdays, while a few are weekend only. Call the soup kitchen or look in a local newspaper to check on meal schedules.

Augusta
Bread of Life Kitchen
157 Water St.
Augusta, ME 04330
207-626-3434

Bangor
Dorothy Day Soup Kitchen
c/o Salvation Army
65 South Park St.
Bangor, ME 04401
207-941-2990

Brunswick
Brunswick Area Council of Churches Soup Kitchen
c/o St. Paul's
P.O. Box 195
27 Pleasant St.
Brunswick, ME 04001
207-725-5342

Portland
St. Luke's Soup Kitchen
Preble Street Resource Center
252 Oxford St. and 5 Portland
Portland, ME 04104
207-775-0026

St. Bernard's Soup Kitchen
150 Broadway
Rockland, ME 04841
207-594-5204

Waterville
Notre Dame Soup Kitchen
112 Silver St.
Waterville, ME 04901
207-872-8061

Winthrop
Soup Kitchen
10 Lake St.
Winthrop, ME 04364
207-377-8404

Maryland

Prisoners Aid Association of Maryland
2000 N. Calvert St.
Baltimore, MD 21218
410-727-8130
http://jewel.morgan.edu/~nmiles/index.htm
Offers a wide range of services to inmates and ex-offenders through community involvement and professional programs. Services include employment and housing placement and counseling. There is a residential facility for homeless and jobless ex-offenders.

Massachusetts

Aid to Incarcerated Mothers (AIM)
32 Rutland St., 4th Floor
Boston, MA 02118
617-536-0058
Provides services to incarcerated mothers and their children in Massachusetts. The organization's main focus is to help the inmate mother meet her parental responsibilities with the final goal of reuniting her family. Their RENEW program, Reentry for New Emerging Women, counsels women and develops housing, education, parenting and employment resources.

SPAN, Inc.
110 Arlington St.
Boston, MA 02116
617-423-0750
SPAN is a re-integration counseling program for offenders and ex-offenders. They offer individual and group counseling and referrals to employment and social services.

COERS (Comprehensive Offender Employment Resource System)
79 Chandler St.
Boston, MA 02116

617-338-1096
This state-wide organization provides a number of programs for recently released ex-offenders. Their main focus is job placement, although they also offer counseling and GED tutoring.

Michigan

CURE-SORT (Sex Offenders Restored Through Treatment)
Wayne Bowers
P.O. Box 1191
Okemos, MI 48805-1191
Chapter of a National Prison Reform Organization, emphasizing the need for proper treatment of sex offenders.

Minnesota

AMICUS
100 N. Sixth St., Suite 347-B
Minneapolis, MN 55403
612-348-8570
This nonprofit private organization offers a Community Resource Outreach Project which assists ex-offenders with housing, clothing, and job seeking resources. Assists in ex-offenders families seeking resources. Offers a transition program at Lino Lakes (a reformatory).

Women's Shelter, Inc.
P.O. Box 457
Rochester, MN 55903
507-285-1010
24 hour Hotline: 507-285-0527
www.womens-shelter.org
E-mail: wsi5@ll.net
The shelter operates a work release program for women in Shakopee Women's Prison and a jail diversion program for women from Olmsted County, MN.

Mississippi

Beginning Again in Christ After Care Center
P.O. Box 26
Brandon, MS 39043
601-825-0535
This privately funded Christian ministry provides residential housing for ex-offenders who have accepted Christianity while in prison. Services include educational training, job placement referrals, and individual counseling.

Missouri

COPE (Congregation and Offender Partnership Enterprise)
3529 Marcus Ave.
St. Louis, MO 63115
314-389-4804
COPE is an ecumenical local nonprofit organization that engages St. Louis congregations in supportive partnerships with selected ex-offenders for a year as they re-enter the community. Volunteers work with inmates while in prison and then continue to give assistance after release. Services vary depending upon individual needs, but may include temporary shelter and job placement assistance.

Montana

U.M. Women's Center
University of Montana
UC 210
Missoula, MT 59812
406-243-4153
This Referral Center helps to refer male and female ex-offenders to legal aid and medical assistance.

Nebraska

This state does not have any local programs at the time of publication. For assistance, contact one of the offices listed under National Organizations.

Nevada

Center St. Mission
650 N. Center St.
Reno, NV 89502
775-348-2619
Halfway house for males provides transitional housing.

Ridge House, Inc.
275 Hill St.
Suite 281
Reno, NV 89501
775-322-8941
Halfway house for ex-felons and parolees recently released from prison with substance abuse problems. Offers room and board, individual, career and drug/alcohol counseling, and financial planning. Flat fee of $114/wk.

New Jersey

American Friends Service Committee
972 Broad St., 6th Floor
Newark, NJ 07102
973-643-3079
Fax: 973-643-8924
www.afsc.org/afscnyhp.htm
AFSC provides counseling workshops and re-entry services to inmates, ex-offenders, and members of their families.

H.O.P.E. for Ex-Offenders, Inc.
106 Central Ave.
Hackensack, NJ 07601
201-646-1995
Offers employment referral, temporary emergency housing, food, clothing, emergency utilities assistance, and medication for inmates of Bergen and Passaic counties in New Jersey.

Jericho Ministries
35 Garden St.
Mt. Holly, NJ 08060
609-261-2045
Services include individual Bible studies, and aftercare, help ministries. Primarily support group for families: one-on-one, envelope visitation, fellowship night for ex-offenders.

Sanford Bates House
33 Remsen Ave.
New Brunswick, NJ 08901
732-846-7220
This residential program is open to female state pre-release inmates. Services include individual, group and family counseling, job assistance, and counseling in the areas of substance abuse and financial management. The program assists inmates in the transition from incarceration to living in the community. Residents pay house fees on a sliding scale.

Clinton House
21 N. Clinton Ave.
Trenton, NJ 08609
609-396-9186
This residential program is open to male state pre-release inmates. Services include individual, group and family counseling, job assistance, and counseling in the areas of substance abuse and financial management. The program assists inmates in the transition from incarceration to living in the community. Residents pay house fees on a sliding scale. The program also provides drug aftercare services to federal probationers through a contract.

Middlesex Resource Center
5 Elm Row, Suite 306
New Brunswick, NJ 08901
732-247-2770
Provides services on an out-client basis to adults 18 years or older with an offense record. The program accepts referrals from probation or parole programs, L.S.P. or county jail. Walk-in clients also accepted. The center provides referrals for mental health, substance abuse and long term counseling. It also offers crisis intervention in the form of emergency food, clothing, and housing assistance. Project Reunion provides counseling to women incarcerated at Middlesex Adult Correction Center. Children are brought to visit their mothers on a weekly basis. A similar group is available on an outpatient basis.

Offender Aid and Restoration of Essex County
Essex Community College
303 University Ave., Room 3271
Newark, NJ 07102
973-624-6610
OAR provides transitional services for inmates in Essex County Jail and some services for inmates returning to Essex County from federal and state institutions. They provide counseling, referrals, and visitation to prisoners. OAR has also developed an inmate literacy program and uses community volunteers for inmate services.

New Mexico

This state does not have any local programs at the time of publication. For assistance, contact one of the offices listed under National Organizations.

New York

Cephas Attica, Inc.
258 Monroe Ave.
Rochester, NY 14614
716-546-7472
Fax: 716-546-8579
http://freenet.buffalo.edu/~cpm/home.html

Offers post-release services that include housing for parolees with a commitment to Cephas Attica's 90-day program. They also offer counseling and assistance with educational, housing, and job opportunities.

Fortune Society
39 W. 19th St.
New York, NY 10011
212-206-7070
Fax: 212-633-6845
www.fortunesociety.org
This ex-offender self help organization works with ex-offenders in the New York area. Services include ex-offender to ex-offender counseling, one-on-one tutoring, job training placement, GED preparation and out-patient substance abuse services. The society also acts as a referral agency for drug or alcohol addiction programs, halfway houses and other social services.

Justice Works Community
1012 Eighth Ave.
Brooklyn, NY 11215
718-499-6704
The Community Justice Resource Center provides referrals for housing, job training, employment, drug and alcohol programs for women prisoners, ex-prisoners and their families.

The Osborne Association
135 East 15th St.
New York, NY 10003
212-673-6633
The Osborne Association operates model programs and provides direct services to defendants, prisoners, ex-offenders and their families.

PROBE, Inc.
229 State St.
Binghamton, NY 13901-2711
607-772-8912
PROBE provides community development, 16 development and community services, mandated volunteer services in juvenile court, transitional services for those in local jails, D.E.P. Program (GED and Life skills, pre-employment skills), pre-trial diversions (professional counseling), employment services, and agencies referral help.

Project Greenhope SFW, Inc.
448 E. 119th St.
New York, NY 10031
212-369-5100
This halfway house for ex-offenders is the only residential facility in New York City which services both parolees and women referred by the courts. It provides educational and vocational training and job and housing referrals.

Reality House, Inc.
637 West 125th St.
New York, NY 10027
212-666-8000
Reality House offers counseling services and group therapy to recently released ex-offenders with a history of addiction. After care services include medical assistance, counseling, and educational and vocational guidance. It also provides recently released ex-offenders of the New York City Department of Correction at Rikers Island with community based substance abuse treatment (ages 18 and older) and HIV care such as counseling, HIV testing, medical evaluation, monitoring and case management.

South Forty Corporation
500 8th Ave., Suite 1203
New York, NY 10018
212-563-2288
South Forty Corporation provides vocational counseling to prisoners at Bayview Correctional Facility and job placement assistance for ex-offenders who are residents of New York City.

Stay'N Out Criminal Justice Program
500 8th Ave., Suite 801
New York, NY 10018
212-971-6033
This program provides a wide variety of services for incarcerated men and women with drug-related offenses. It has established segregated units in the Arthur Kill and Bayview Correctional Facilities. Inmates participating in this voluntary program receive group, family, individual and vocational counseling and remedial education. Upon release or parole, it assists ex-offenders into one of the member agencies of New York Therapeutic Communities, Inc. Inmates of all New York State facilities are eligible for this program after meeting specified criteria.

Women's Prison Association
110 Second Ave.

New York, NY 10003
212-674-1163
This agency provides counseling for women ex-offenders in the form of direct referrals and housing placement assistance. They also provide alternatives to incarceration programs for women in the Department of Correction at Rikers Island. The services are aimed at women with HIV and AIDS.

North Carolina

Alcohol/Drug Council of North Carolina
3500 Westgate Dr., Suite 204
Durham, NC 27707
800-688-4232
919-493-0003
Information/Referral service for individuals with a history of drug or alcohol problems, and also has a service for families and agencies. Operates a county by county database that includes information on halfway housing, counseling, and related services.

Guilford County Community Action Program, Inc.
201 S. Elm St., Suite 101
Greensboro, NC 27401
336-274-4673
Offers job development and assistance counseling to ex-offenders.

North Dakota

CENTRE (Center for Extended Nuclear Transitional Residence for Ex-Offenders)
123 15th St., N.
Fargo, ND 58102
701-237-9340
This is a transitional residence which offers a structured, supervised program of assistance to ex-offenders. CENTRE provides job counseling and assistance with recovering addicts who have been through treatment. The average stay at CENTRE is between three and six months. Residents are court-ordered to this program.

Ohio

Justice Watch/Garden Street Transitional House
1120 Garden St.
Cincinnati, OH 45214
513-241-0490
Provides shelter and recovery services to homeless men released from prison who are at a high risk of reincarceration due to chemical dependency and poverty.

Talbert House Cornerstone
2216 Vine St.
Cincinnati, OH 45219
513-684-7965
Talbert House is a halfway house for ex-offenders and homeless individuals. Services include individual vocational, and substance abuse counseling. Those who complete a 97-day program are eligible for employment referral.

Oklahoma

This state does not have any local programs at the time of publication. For assistance, contact one of the offices listed under National Organizations.

Oregon

This state does not have any local programs at the time of publication. For assistance, contact one of the offices listed under National Organizations.

Pennsylvania

Concerned Seniors/Gray Panthers of Graterford
Dr. Julia Hall
Dept. PSA
327 and Chestnut Sts.
Drexel University
Philadelphia, PA 19104
215-895-2472
Advocacy, support, and information group for inmates and parolees 50 years and older. Specializes in services including health care/medical needs, employment, housing, and socialization for both institutional and community elderly offenders and parolees. Provides pre-release counseling and community resource information.

Offender Aid and Restoration of Philadelphia
2000 Spring Garden St.
Philadelphia, PA 19130
215-557-8131
OAR offers job development assistance to ex-offenders as well as volunteer services and visitation to prisoners.

Pennsylvania Prison Society
2000 Spring Garden St.
Philadelphia, PA 19130-3805
215-564-6005
800-227-2307
Fax: 215-564-7926
www.prisonsociety.org
Provides educational and informational link to the state legislature, community organizations, prisoners, and prisoners families in areas including alternatives to incarceration, parole eligibility for lifers, need for earned/good time legislation, and effects of mandatory sentencing laws. Staff also serve as an information, referral, and counseling service for newly released prisoners.

Thomas R. Sims
People United Together
1209 W. Lehigh Ave.
Philadelphia, PA 19133-1115
215-226-5890
This organization offers services and programs to offenders, ex-offenders in the areas of parole planning, housing, public assistance, employment and vocational training referrals, substance abuse counseling, and other referrals. They also run a "Youth Self-Empowerment Project" that addresses the social and economic conditions of at-risk youth and their families.

Pre-Release Counseling
Program for Female Offenders
1520 Penn Ave.
Pittsburgh, PA 15222
412-281-7380
Program works with women who are or have been in trouble with the law and who have a history of substance abuse. Services include employment, counseling, career education, parole planning, workshops, referrals and job placement, remedial education, and pre-release counseling. Operates two centers: The Program Center at 3342 5th Ave., and the Allegheny County Treatment Alternative (ACTA) at 2410 5th Ave. These centers function as an alternative program to serving time in the Allegheny County Jail. There are three affiliate offices:

The Program for Female Offenders of S. Central PA, Inc.
22 S. 3rd St., 2nd Floor
Harrisburg, PA 17101
717-238-9950

Woodside Family Center
451 Mall Rd.
Harrisburg, PA 17111
717-558-9871

Lehigh Valley Office
1031 Linden St.
Allentown, PA 18102
215-433-6556

Victim/Offender Reconciliation Program
Dr. Julia Hall
Dept. PSA
32nd and Chestnut St.
Philadelphia, PA 19104
215-895-2472
This program operates on principles of restorative justice, which allows both victims and offenders a chance to heal from the trauma of crime. Offenders can take responsibility for their offenses and make amends to victims. Victims can tell stories, get answers to questions, and receive actual or symbolic restoration.

Step Program (Services to Elder Prisoners)
Pennsylvania Prison Society
2000 Spring Garden St.
Philadelphia, PA 19130-3805
215-564-6005, ext. 7916
www.prisonsociety.org
Services to elderly prisoners and ex-offenders. Prisoners housed in eight Pennsylvania State institutions, focused on institutional adjustment and pre-release training for release back into the community includes: parole planning, home plans, and individual goal plans. Clients are referred by the PA Dept. of Corrections. Re-entry and referral services are given to assist ex-offenders in re-establishing a community life.

Re-Entry Services Project
Pennsylvania Prison Society
2000 Spring Garden St.
Philadelphia, PA 19130-3805
215-564-6005
www.prisonsociety.org

Life skills and job preparation programs for prisoners coming out of the Philadelphia prison programs. 30-60 days pre-release, plus six months ex-offender assistance. Program is for offenders 34 years or older or for parents with dependent children.

Rhode Island

This state does not have any local programs at the time of publication. For assistance, contact one of the offices listed under National Organizations.

South Carolina

Alston Wilkes Society
3519 Medical Dr.
Columbia, SC 29203
803-748-7489
This statewide social service organization provides a wide variety of services to adult and juvenile offenders, ex-offenders, former offenders, homeless veterans, emotionally disturbed youth, and their immediate families. Assistance includes employment, mediation, life skills, rehabilitation, prevention, volunteering, and transitional housing, (halfway houses including two youth homes). It accepts out-of-state referrals of residents of South Carolina and of probationers under jurisdiction of the Federal Bureau of Prisons.

South Dakota

Glory House
4000 South West Ave.
Sioux Falls, SD 57109-1001
605-332-3273
Glory House is a transitional residential facility for ex-offenders. Services include individual and group counseling, as well as job placement assistance.

ARCH Halfway House
333 South Spring Ave.
Sioux Falls, SD 57104
605-332-6730
ARCH offers a transitional residential facility for people that have a chemical dependency. Completion of, or participation in, a formal treatment program is required. Chemical dependency counseling is available. Residents are expected to find employment during their stay.

Texas

Dallas County Jail Inmates Program Division
899 Stemmons Freeway
Dallas, TX 75207
214-761-9025
Although the program's main focus is to coordinate education and substance abuse programs for inmates within the Dallas County Jail System, this program also assists in referrals to outside community agencies for released inmates.

Utah

Department of Corrections
6100 South Fashion Blvd.
Murray, UT 84107
801-265-5500
Fax: 801-265-5670
www.cr.ex.state.ut.us
Utah's Department of Corrections has several Community Correctional Centers located throughout the state. Those in need of continued treatment and counseling are referred to a halfway house. They have a new 150 bed facility in Ogden, as well as three facilities in Salt Lake City. During their stay, residents are employed and receive counseling and referrals.

Vermont

Vermont Catholic Charities
Deacon Steve Ratte Diocesan Director of Prison Ministry
351 North Ave.
Burlington, VT 05401
802-658-6110, ext. 312
Fax: 802-860-0451
Provides one-on-one pastoral counseling, family visitation, inmate supervised passes, and referral services. Services are limited to Vermont offenders, ex-offenders and their families.

Virginia

Offender Aid and Restoration of Arlington County
1400 N. Uhle St., Suite 704
Arlington, VA 22201
703-228-7030
Offers employment and vocational guidance, skills training, and direct referrals. Also provides counseling and limited job placement.

Offender Aid and Restoration of Charlottesville/Albemarle
750 Harris St., Suite 207
Charlottesville, VA 22903
804-296-2441
OAR offers job assistance and emergency assistance for offenders and their families. Also provides pretrial services and supervision of community service and restitution. Volunteer services for inmates are also available.

Offender Aid and Restoration of Fairfax
10640 Page Ave., Suite 250
Fairfax, VA 22030
703-246-3033
This private, nonprofit agency provides services for inmates, ex-prisoners, and their families who are Fairfax County residents. It provides referrals to community resources, employment and vocational guidance, and scholarships for inmates to take college level correspondence courses. It also offers emergency financial loans to ex-offenders to obtain food, clothes, and temporary housing. Has support groups for families of offenders and children of offenders.

Offender Aid and Restoration of Richmond, Inc.
1 N. 3rd St., Suite 200
Richmond, VA 23219
804-643-2746
This OAR branch provides post-release services for inmates in local jails. Services are limited to offenders in Richmond and Petersburg, and Henrico, Chesterfield, and Hanover counties only. Services include job placement/search, housing referrals and basic social services (clothing, work tools, etc) and volunteer counseling.

STEP-UP, Inc.
7510 Grandy St., Suite 203
Norfolk, VA 23502
757-588-3151
Step-up works with all ex-offenders and offenders (federal, state, local and military). It offers parole preparation and pre-release services. Upon release, Step-Up provides ex-offenders with job development and placement, resume/application services, local transportation funds, and job skills training. Housing support services are provided on an availability basis.

Washington

Friendship, Inc. - Spokane County
P.O. Box 11215
Olympia, WA 98508
360-357-8021
Post charge diversion program for first time felony offenders (adults only, work with prosecutors office).

Interaction/Transition
935 - 16th Ave.
Seattle, WA 98122-4529
206-324-3924
Provides re-entry support for ex-felons returning to the community from Washington State penal institutions. Support includes emergency housing, comprehensive employment services, counseling, and referral.

United Indians of All Tribes Foundation
1945 Yale Place E.
Seattle, WA 98102
206-325-6381
Offers employment counseling, job referrals, and placement assistance.

West Virginia

Shawnee Hills, Inc.
P.O. Box 3694
Charleston, WV 25336-3698
304-341-0199
This private, nonprofit organization offers mental health, mental retardation, and substance abuse programs. It works with the Charleston Work Release Center and provides counseling to ex-convicts to help them readjust back into family life and the community.

Wisconsin

Horizon House
2511 W. Vine St.
Milwaukee, WI 53205
414-342-3237
Horizon House offers employment and vocational guidance, counseling, direct referrals for women on probation and women being released from federal and state institutions in Wisconsin. It offers room and board to ex-offenders referred from the state Department of Corrections. Services also include a parent education/children's program and an alcohol and drug treatment program.

Project Return
Tom Schaffer
1821 N. 16th St.
Milwaukee, WI 53205
414-344-5013
Provides support groups and housing and job locating services for ex-offenders.

Wisconsin Correctional Service
230 W. Wells St., Suite 500
Milwaukee, WI 53203
414-271-2512

Operates alternative and community programs for offenders including drug residential treatment programs, adult halfway houses, community service options programs, and pretrial release programs. Job program is also included.

Project Return
1821 N. 16th St.
Milwaukee, WI 53205
414-344-5013
Provides support groups which include AODA and At-Risk-Youth. They also assist in locating drug-free housing and employment for ex-offenders. Assistance for other material needs, as well as all other services, are on a "for-need" basis.

Free Help to Write a Resume

Matthew Lesko, Information USA, Inc., 12081 Nebel Street, Rockville, MD 20852 • 1-800-955-7693 • www.lesko.com

Free Help to Write a Resume

You need a job and you need it now. Somewhere, an employer has the job you want. But, how do you two connect? By marketing your job talents, and showing prospective employers you have the skills they need, that's how.

Do you have job talents? Of course you do! Homemakers, disabled individuals, veterans, students just out of school, people already working — they all have skills and experience suited for many good jobs.

What you need to learn is how to market your talents effectively to find the right place for you. Writing a good resume is the best way to let a prospective employer learn about your individual interests and skills.

Developing a Resume

The two main types of resumes are the chronological and the functional. A chronological resume is used when you have had a fairly direct path of development from one position to another within the same field. A functional resume emphasizes your skills and is used by people who change jobs or careers frequently. A good resume will be no more than one page long and will capture the highlights of your career goals, education, and work history.

A resume should include the following information: name, address, telephone number; job objective or career goal; educational history (degrees, certificates, courses, accomplishments); work history including military service (skills, experience); and memberships related to your job objective. Depending on the position for which you are applying, it might also include work related honors or achievements, knowledge of foreign languages, ability to travel or relocate, and security clearance information.

Job Application Forms

Some jobs do not require a formal resume but may call for a written application. Most application forms require basic information such as your name, address, and telephone number; social security number; dates of previous jobs; names and addresses of former employers; and dates of schooling and training. Before you fill out the application, read it through to be sure that you have all of the required information. It is very important that you print the information neatly and legibly. If your application makes a poor first impression, you are unlikely to get any further with that employer.

Although not every job calls for letters of reference, you should ask people if they would be willing to write one for you. Do not list someone as a reference unless you have their permission to do so. Candidates for reference include former employers, teachers, volunteer supervisors, and other people who can accurately assess your character.

Locating Employers

There are several methods of locating potential employers:
-   Cold Calls — visit employers to see if there are any openings in their organization. You may find yourself in the right place at the right time, but this is a difficult and time consuming method of job hunting.

- Networking — learning about openings through friends, relatives, or co-workers is probably the most successful way to get a job, and referrals of this kind often guarantee an interview.

- Newspaper Ads — classified ads list specific openings, but there is often intense competition for those jobs. Want ads list just a small proportion of available jobs.

- Employment Agencies — public employment agencies provide job hunt services at no cost, but are usually looking for unskilled labor. Private agencies will, for a fee, try to match employers and employees. Some agencies specialize in a particular field, but the main disadvantage is the fee, often paid for by the job seeker. Be sure to check on an agency's policy regarding fees before you begin to work with them.

Applying and Interviewing for Jobs

Once you have found a job that sounds good to you, you must apply for it. This involves writing to the company offering the job and including your resume or a job application. In either case, your cover letter is very important — it is the first thing that your prospective employer will see, and it will say a lot about you. The letter should be personalized and contain information such as where you heard about the job, an indication of your interest, why you are suited for the position, and your interest in interviewing. It should include your name, address, and phone number.

The next step in the job search is the job interview, which involves an exchange between people trying to find out whether they can work together. Before you go to the interview, learn as much as you can about a prospective employer by reading brochures, talking to present employees, calling the local Chamber of Commerce in that area, or visiting the public library. Some important interviewing techniques: Do be honest, be prompt; use a firm handshake; dress appropriately; make eye contact; address interviewer by name; prepare to ask and answer intelligent and thoughtful questions; ask for the job.

After the interview, it is important to maintain contact with the prospective employer. Write a short thank you letter, indicating that you will call at a specific time to find out the status of the position. Call when you said you would. If the answer is no, ask why without being a pest. Knowing why you did not get a job may help you get the next one.

There are several resources where you can turn for help in writing your resume:

- Your State Employment Service Office will help you pull together your work history into effective categories. Look in the blue pages for the office nearest you, or page 655 for a listing of state offices.

- Your County Cooperative Extension Service offers a variety of services to assist you in writing your resume. Some offices offer classes, while others have pamphlets. Most of these services are usually free. Since services vary from one area to the next, contact your County Cooperative Extension Service to learn what is available near you. To locate this office, look in the blue pages of your phone book, or call Cooperative State Research, Education, and Extension Service, U.S. Department of Agriculture, 1400 Independence Ave., SW, Stop 2201, Washington, DC 20250; 202-720-7441 {www.reeusda.gov} for a referral to your local office.

- Tap the government for tips on finding the best work opportunities. *Tips For Finding The Right Job* is a free publication that can help you evaluate your interests and skills, and provide information on resumes, application letters, job interviews, and more. Contact Employment and Training Administration, U.S. Department of Labor, 200 Constitution Ave., NW, Room N4700, Washington, DC 20210; 202-219-6871 {www.doleta.gov}.

Free Help to Write a Resume

- Many companies offer job hunting and resume writing assistance for a fee. Before you sign on the dotted line, read two free publications offered by the Federal Trade Commission. *Job Ads, Job Scams* explains things you need to look out for when looking for a new job. *Job Hunting: Should You Pay* explains about head hunter services and things you need to consider before you sign on with an agency. To receive your copies, contact the Federal Trade Commission, Public Reference, Room 130, 6th and Pennsylvania Ave., NW, Washington, DC 20580; 202-326-2222 {www.ftc.gov}.

- The ERIC Clearinghouse for Adult, Careers, and Vocational Education covers all areas of career and vocational/technical education from basic literacy training through professional skill upgrading. Although they do not have publications specific to writing a resume, they do have a series of free ERIC Digests to help you look at the job market in a variety of ways. Some of the titles include: *Job Search Methods for the 21st Century*; *Changing Career Patterns*; *Wired: The Electronic Job Search*. For your copies, contact ERIC Clearinghouse for Adult, Career, and Vocational Education, The Ohio State University, 1900 Kenny Rd., Columbus, OH 43210; 800-848-4815 {http://ericacve.org/textonly/index.html}.

Matthew Lesko, Information USA, Inc., 12081 Nebel Street, Rockville, MD 20852 • 1-800-955-7693 • www.lesko.com

Job Hunt on the Internet

Job Hunt on the Internet

The Internet provides a variety of services to let job seekers and employers contact each other without playing the typical phone tag game, and you can learn all about them in this chapter, dedicated to job seekers like you. For your convenience, the sites have been divided into two sections — general and specific job sites — with appropriate subcategories.

The general employment sites section features websites that can be helpful to any job seeker, regardless of occupation or location. The kind of sites you will find will nevertheless vary. Sites such as America's Help Wanted! (http://www.jobquest.com/), Career Network (http://www.careernetwork.com/), IntelliMatch (http://www.intellimatch.com/) and a number of others for example, are sites primarily concerned with resumes. The sites have resume banks where you can submit your resume and wait for an employer to contact you, or they provide services that will compare your resume with posted job openings and notify you of matches. Some resume focused sites even specialize in helping you create a well organized and effective resume. There are also sites that are focused mainly around a search engine — that is, sites that require you to enter an occupation or location of your choice into their search engine which in turn provide you with names and contact information of hiring companies that match your request. The Career Search Launch Pad (http://www.anet-dfw.com/~tsull/career/cslp.html), The Job Exchange (http://www.jobexchange.com/) and The Job Zone (http://www.thezones.com/jobzone/) are best examples of such search engine based sites. If it's straight job listings you are looking for, the Internet offers that as well. Hotflash Jobs (http://iquest.com/~ntes/jobslist.html), Jobs & Careers Online (http://www.servonet.com/temp_jc/jchome.html), 123 Careers (http://www.webplaza.com/pages/Careers/123Careers/123Careers.html) and USA Jobz (http://www.adgrafix.com/jobz/index.html) and several other sites provide just that — straightforward job listings complete with career descriptions and contact information.

Many of the sites that you will find listed below, however, are not limited to one specific service and often combine features such as resume banks and search engines with other helpful services. Of these multi-service sites, some stand out as particularly well organized, powered by exhaustive databases or using new and innovative methods. America Job Bank (http://www.ajb.dni.us/), for instance, has been recognized by *PC magazine* as one of the top 100 sites and can perform a nationwide job opportunity search, link to state search engines, or provide you with employer maintained job listings. Similarly, Career Mosaic (http://www.careermosaic.com/cm/), has succeeded in accumulating an exhaustive database of numerous employment opportunities and features a search engine as well as a resume posting service. Sites such as The Virtual Job Fair (http://www.vjf.com/) and The Monster Board (http://www3.monster.com:80/) also stand out as one of the fastest growing collections of links to over 55,000 job opportunities worldwide.

The section of specific employment sites has several subdivisions, such as international and regional employment, and sections where employment related websites are listed under occupational headings. In the international and regional employment sections, the sites are categorized by country and/or state, and provide information concerning available job opportunities in various parts of the world, with a focus on the United States. The other specific employment related sites, are divided into sections such as entertainment industry, finance market, sciences, careers for minorities and women, computers and technology and several others. The kinds of websites you can find in these categories can also vary: in the Entry Level Jobs category, for example, you may find sites such as the Job Source (http://www.jobsource.com/) that offers information about internships, tips for interviewing and connections to other sites along with a listing of entry level and part time job openings as well. Included in this listing would be encounter sites similar to the Student Center, (http://www.studentcenter.com) that includes a 35,000 company searchable database and a self-diagnostic test to determine the best career opportunities for you. Similarly, in the Environmental Careers section, the sites vary from those that provide you with listings of environmental sources, and career opportunities such as GreenBeat! (http://earth.tec.org/greenbeat/mar96) and more specifically oriented sites such as UWIN (http://www.uwin.siu.edu/announce/jobs/) that serves as a clearinghouse of jobs and related opportunities in various water resources fields.

In addition to the general and specific job websites, the following listings also include a section of online classifieds that function as electronic versions of regular newspaper classified advertisements. Generally, however, these sites offer much wider databases and quicker ways to find what you're looking for than the regular newspaper help wanted sections.

Still confused about where to begin? Check out these sites that are dedicated to helping the beginning Internet job searcher find her/his way through the multitude of options: JobHunt: OnLine Job Meta-List (http://rescomp.stanford.edu/jobs/jobs-all.shtml), Career Planning Process (http://www.bgsu.edu/offices/careers/process/process.html), Occupational Outlook Handbook (http://stats.bls.gov:80/ocohome.htm) and Sources of Information on Career Preparation and Training (http://www.espan.com/docs/sources.html) offer a variety of services that range from listings of accessible job search resources to self assessment tools and occupational reading archives.

Below you will find a listing of services which have taken the first step in revolutionizing the job market through the Internet. Visit these sites often, because the information on many of them changes almost daily. New sites are added frequently, as well.

The sites below are categorized as follows:

1: General Career Sites:
   Describes those sites that offer help in more than one area of expertise and are more general in nature when identifying a new job. Some of these sites also offer help in career planning and resume preparation.

2: Career Planning:
   These sites typically will not offer you specific job opportunities, but will help you develop strategies for finding the right job or in resume preparation.

3: Career Specific:
   Describes those sites that offer job opportunities in specific career areas.

4: Area Specific:
   These sites offers opportunities for those looking for jobs only in specific areas of the country or overseas.

Matthew Lesko, Information USA, Inc., 12081 Nebel Street, Rockville, MD 20852 • 1-800-955-7693 • www.lesko.com

General Career Sites

* Adams Jobbank Online
Website: http://www.careercity.com
Explore current career possibilities in the fields of computer, finance, management, healthcare, sales, and lots more. Adams Jobbank Online offers an excellent job search engine to facilitate your research. Corporations will be glad to discover that this service offers free job posting. The Career Center offers links dedicated especially to graduating students.

* Adguide
www.adguide.com
Even though they call themselves a "College Recruiter Employment Site," these job listings are for entry level or experienced employees. Each job has a link to the potential employer through e-mail and/or a company web page. Check out a prospective employer before even submitting your resume. By entering your e-mail address, you will be notified of the new help wanted ads immediately. They also have an expansive list of articles and links to free information on financial aid if you want to further your education.

* Allied Technology International, Inc. (ATI)
Website: http://www.mindspring.com/~mcafee/ATI/index.html
Allied Technology International, Inc., provides a multitude of services related to employment of personnel and submission of proposals for work. Their database contains a wide variety of positions that range from medical, engineering and technician fields in a number of locations. It is an excellent place to begin your job search.

* America Job Bank
Website: http://www.ajb.dni.us/
Quite likely the most successful job search site on the Net, America Job Bank has been recognized by *PC Magazine* as one of the top 100 sites. In other words, this is a great place to start your search for employment. Three options are available: you can perform a nationwide search, link to state search engines, or link to employer maintained job listings. The nationwide listings include opportunities for people looking for federal or military employment. Be forewarned that not all states have developed a web site to go along with its other employment services. According to the Job Bank however, most states are in the process of putting up a site.

* American Federal Jobs Digest
www.jobsfed.com
Working in the Federal Government offers paid training, tuition reimbursement, accrued sick days, job security and a host of other benefits. This site offers you a place to look for those jobs. You can either search the Live Jobs section or use the Job Matching service to find the job right for you. These sections have detailed information on what type of person they want to hire and how you can advance to a higher level. Also, check out the Federal Hiring News that has information on job leads.

* America's Employers
Website: http://www.americasemployers.com/
Developed by professional career consultants to help you complete an easy and successful electronic job search, America's Employers is at your service. New employment opportunities are added continually and company databases are updated weekly to help job seekers tap into the "hidden" job market, and the site also offers a discreet and confidential resume bank for hundreds of hiring employers to see. With America's Employers, you have nothing to lose.

* America's Employers Company Databases
Website: http://americasemployers.com/database.html
This site concentrates on the "hidden job market" and lets the job seeker contact potential employers directly. According to the site, "the hidden job market is responsible for the bulk of hiring that goes on in companies." You may search for companies in several states and industries of your choice. Once you submit your criteria, the search engine returns the names, addresses, and phone numbers of companies that match your request. This site is updated almost daily, so it pays to check in often!

* America's Help Wanted!
Website: http://www.jobquest.com/
This diversified site has a lot of tools to help you with your job hunt. After you create your free personal account, you will create an online resume which potential employers will be able to browse. Once the profile forms are filled out, you will be able to access the job search tools and try to find the perfect job. This service takes the job seeker very seriously, so stop by!

* Best Jobs In The USA Today
Website: http://www.bestjobsusa.com/
Through this outstanding site, you can search employment ads from USA TODAY and have access to a free resume depository that's searched by thousands of companies worldwide. In addition to providing lists of national career events and a career store that features books, audio tapes and videos designed to maximize the effectiveness of your job search, Best Jobs In The USA Today also allows you to keep up with new positions and new employment trends through the online employment review magazine. Best Jobs In The USA Today surely has something for anyone seeking a career.

* Brave New Work World
Website: http://www.newwork.com:80/
There are those who prophesy the coming of a great revolution. And then there are those who claim that the revolution is already here. This site would agree with the latter ▯ at least as far as world economics and employment are concerned. Brave New Work World, a site that represents many academic, professional fields and practical experience fields, conducts daily surveys of worldwide press reports and is committed to informing you about what you can do to succeed in the revolutionary new world economy. As the site itself claims, it consists of "information, ideas, opinion, advice, continuing work education, and a range of interesting, entertaining content through a variety of media, helping you prepare for the new millennium. " Along with links to many other resources and archives of articles, this interesting and empowering site is a must to check out.

* Bridgepath.com
www.bridgepath.com
At Bridgepath, you receive job announcements by e-mail. After filling out a questionnaire about your skills, job preferences and background, employers will contact you directly. This is all confidential too. If you use Resume Review, your resume will be critiqued by professionals and colleagues when it is posted. There also is a newsletter published weekly which you can view. You will find suggested publications, links to the hottest sites and some fun ones too!

* Business Job Finder
www.cob.ohio-state.edu/-fin/osufobs.htm
This site is a great place to visit to identify which business career is right for you. It will help to determine how to start in a career, what it takes to do the job, and what skills are needed for the work. They also include recommendations on books with topics such as Self-Exploration and Careers, and Jobs in Business. It has information on an array of business career areas and other reference material. This is an excellent site for those wanting a career in the business world.

* Candidate Pool
www.candidatepool.com
Although they specialize in the areas of technology, they also offer a broad range of job listings. They have over 2,000 jobs to search listed through 500 hiring companies. Your resume will be sent to companies looking for an employee with your skills once it posted. The potential employer will contact you personally to set up an interview. You can also check out the company profiles so that you know who it is you will be dealing with.

* Career and Resume Management for the 21st Century
Website: http://crm21.com/
Through Career and Resume Management for the 21st Century, job seekers can post their resumes electronically onto a listing of resume databases on the

net, browse through available job opportunities and have access to other free employment related resources such as resume review and evaluation, articles on interviewing, resumes, networking, hot tips on interviewing and listing of career-advancement books. Check it out.

* Career Avenue
www.careeravenue.com

With this free service, job-seekers can search for all types of positions. All it takes is a job description and a location to begin! After that, you can receive help to create a resume before posting it. The Human Resource Team is available for questions concerning employment issues. They also have advice and job columns available that contain additional information.

* Career Builder
www.careerbuilder.com

Career Builder has a Personal Search Agent! With this free service you will be e-mailed when your "dream" job is located. You can also research any company in their database or use the links provided to search other companies. Also included are guides titled, Getting Hired, How to Succeed at Work and Managing Your Career. This site offers a lot of information!

* CareerCast
www.careercast.com

This easy to search site offers numerous jobs to review. You can search all of the jobs posted in UseNet Groups, or directly from the employer's web site. It can even be narrowed down as far as the specific city you would like to work in! You will also be able to link to different career sites that contain information that will aid you in finding a great job and how to get it.

* Career Expo
www.careerexpo.com

Career Expo calls themselves a "Virtual Job Fair." They have a job search, company directory and company search just to start. There are over 300,000 jobs listed that are updated daily. Career Index allows you to search specific job databases such as High-Tech Employment, Company Pages, and Business/Financial. Through the Human Resource Center you can submit your resume and use the Salary Calculator. Be sure to check the Job Fair Schedule for an event in your area.

* CareerFile
Website: http://www.careerfile.com/

CareerFile is a free and confidential resume referral service for executive, managerial and technical talent, specifically designed for busy professionals like you seeking a new step in your career. The services are simple, efficient and free. When there is a job match to your credentials and interest, one of CareerFile's recruiters will let you know and you can decide where your resume will go and who will see it. What could be better?

* Career Information Access
www.jobservices.com

This free service will link you to employment agencies and recruiters nationwide. Instead of a resume, you will fill out a job search profile containing the most important information needed as an initial qualifier for a job. It includes career objectives, qualifications and other information. To keep your information private, your profile will only be accessed by agencies and recruiters that specialize in your job area.

* CareerMart
Website: http://www.careermart.com/

CareerMart offers a wide variety of employment information and resources, including an extensive jobs database, information on recruitment specialists, and general career reference materials. By entering "the one stop Internet marketplace for worldwide employment information" the job shoppers can browse through a variety of job listings, learn about employers, view company home pages, and have access to a myriad of pertinent formation useful to a job seeker.

* CareerMosaic
Website: http://www.careermosaic.com/cm/

A job search site that has been recognized by many Internet ratings as one of the best of its kind, CareerMosaic has a lot to offer. The CareerMosaic J.O.B.S. database offers "thousands of up-to-date opportunities from hundreds of employers." Here you'll find a search engine that covers all regional and national job listings on the Usenet. You may want to take advantage of the

CareerMosaic ResumeCM service and post your resume online for employers to browse. Also available here are entry-level job opportunities, as well as detailed profiles of potential employers.

* Career Park
www.careerpark.com

Use the quick links to featured jobs or search the databases by job category. Also, check Hot Jobs to see what the most popular career is, and who is offering work at this time. The employer list shows a little about a specific company and if there are any current job openings. There are also updates on the time and place of current job fairs being put on. Connect to Professional organizations, employers and career information sites through the Resource Center for help with your career. You can submit a resume either by using the available form or follow the guidelines for your own scannable or electronic resume.

* CareerPath.com
Website: http://www.careerpath.com/infoseek/index3.html

If you live anywhere in the vicinity of Boston, Chicago, Los Angeles, New York, San Jose, or Washington, DC, or simply would like to find out what jobs are available in these areas, visit CareerPath.com. This site lets you search for job classifieds from major newspapers in those cities. The search engine is very well designed, letting your browse through one or all of the newspapers, and as many job categories as you wish. If you wish to take advantage of all the features at CareerPath.com, you may register online and gain instant access. The service is completely free.

* Career Planning Process
Website: http://www.bgsu.edu/offices/careers/process/process.html

This site, providing you with self assessment tools necessary to execute a successful career search, "encourages individuals to explore and gather information which enables them to synthesize, gain competencies, make decisions, set goals and take action." Career Planning Process, offering the job seeker many interesting exercises, definition and informative resources along with information concerning internships and employment, is a truly wonderful site that you shouldn't pass by.

* Career Search Launch Pad
Website: http://www.pantos.org/cslp

The Career Search Launch Pad is a comprehensive guide to keyword searchable career databases on the 'Net. Use the help of this service and the job of your dreams may be only a click away.

* Career Shop's Resume, Job and Employment Site
Website: http://www.careershop.com

Designed for professionals seeking careers in fields of their choosing, this online database for resume profiles and employment opportunities is designed to assist job seekers just like you. Free of any charge, you can post resume profiles on the resume database and perform job searches of the online database by city, state, company name, category or any combination. The Career Shop also features tips for conducting a successful interview and links to other career related sites.

* careers.wsj.com
www.careers.wsj.com

This site is from the Wall Street Journal Interactive Edition. There is so much information to check out at this site! The question and answer, career columnists, salaries and profiles sections are just the beginning of what is available. Of course, there is a job seeker section. You can look for jobs by category and area, or check out a specific company for a job. Read up on what the experts have to say about sending out a resume after locating the job you want. So, whether you are just starting your career search, or are ready to get that job, this is the site to look at!

* CareerWEB
Website: http://www.cweb.com/

CareerWeb is much more than a simple collection of job opportunities. Visiting this site will enable you to get on track for a new career, or enhance your current one. A number of tools are available. The Resource Center offer`s sure-fire ways to present yourself or discover the perfect career. Also here is a listing of advertising agencies, books, and publications, that might help you along the way. A monthly newspaper is released by CareerWeb with some of the latest information from this agency. Of course, those who are looking for a job will be happy to know that CareerWeb offers a premier job search service.

* The Catapult on JobWeb

Website: http://www.jobweb.org/catapult/catapult.htm

The Catapult lives up to its name: it is among the choice places on the Net to launch your new career. The Catapult does not list job openings, it is rather a site that organizes links to over 200 career sites on the Web into categories. Plenty of resources are available for career practitioners, as well as novices in the labor force. Other sites are listed under Help Guides and Career Library Resources and Professional Development Opportunities. The Catapult is updated very often, so its a must site for your bookmark file!

* Center on Education and Work

Website: http://www.cew.wisc.edu/

Maintained by the University of Wisconsin-Madison, this site " conducts, research, development and capacity building technical assistance designed to improve the connections for youth and adults between places of education and places of work." In other words, the Center on Education and Work is concerned with improving the links between education and work to help people engage in meaningful and productive careers. The site provides information concerning education related publications and software, conferences, seminars and workshops and consulting and technical assistance. It can be a useful resource to help keep you at the top of the job market.

* Cool Jobs

www.cooljobs.com

Have you ever wanted a career in the rescue field, electronic game design, or a space job? Well, you can find all of them and many other "cool" jobs at this site. You will be connected to many different companies that have these job openings and are just waiting for the right person to fill them!

* Direct Marketing World

Website: http://www.dmworld.com/

Direct Marketing World is a site that can prove to be useful both to the employer and the employee, and the best part is that most of the services offered here are free! The job hunter will be delighted to find a sophisticated search engine that allows searches by region and nature of the job. Also, DM World allows its visitors to post their resume, discover information on mailing lists and databases available on the Net, and even browse the library which contains helpful online documents designed to help anyone in the job market.

* Eagleview

www.eagleview.com

Whether you are looking for your first job or are a seasoned employee, Eagleview has numerous opportunities for the jobseeker. After the brief registration process, your resume will be posted. After that, hiring managers from leading companies will be able to view you credentials. Take advantage of the opportunities that are available at this free site.

* E-SPAN

Website: http://www.espan.com/

E-SPAN claims to be your online employment connection, and it really does offer many tools to help you find a job. Two databases are available for the job seeker, as well as a variety of "job tools", which include tips on how to create a resume, how to conduct yourself in your next interview, and even help you get job ads in your virtual mailbox! You can also check out profiles of several employers featured at E-SPAN, and read some useful related articles.

* 4Work.Com

Website: http://www.4work.com/

A simple and concise job search site, 4Work.Com lets seekers across the country look for openings in their area. It is also possible to search for internship and volunteer openings here, and employers may find out how to post on this server.

* Go Jobs

www.gojob.com

Start your job search off at the Career Center. Besides having great advice, it also has links to major jobs boards by region or occupation. You will be able to pinpoint what it is you want! You can conduct a job search locally or nationwide with the parameters that you choose. They offer a lot of resources for someone looking for employment.

* HeadHunter.NET

www.HeadHunter.NET

This site boasts that thousands of professionals have found new careers using its services. You can search professional categories such as computer jobs, engineering jobs, accounting, work from home and so many more. Your resume will be posted for free, or upgraded for a small fee so that it is at the top of a search. You also have the option to keep it private at VIP resume services, where only the most serious employers will view it.

* HEART/Career Connections

Website: http://www.career.com/HCC/hcc.html

Would you like to find out about the hottest job openings in over 35 companies? How about joining a CyberFair hosted by an employer in your area? If these prospects interest you, or you simply want to explore other features offered by this service, than point your browser HEARTs way. This site is under development at the moment, but has big plans for the future, so check in often to see what's new.

* Hot Jobs

www.hotjobs.com

Have the Personal Search find the job you want and e-mail it to you. Submit your resume and control which of the member companies can see it. You will also be able to track how many times it has been accessed! The Message Board can be used to contact staff for assistance or to talk to fellow job seekers. Check out all this site has to offer!

* InPursuit's Employment Network

Website: http://www.inpursuit.com/e-network/

InPursuit's Employment Network offers a wide range of products and services that could help you, the job seeker. The site's best features include a resume center, career related articles and a professional career center. To find out about their other superb ways to assist you in finding the career of your dreams, simply check out their site.

* Integro Temporary Staffing Services

Website: http://www.integrostaffing.com

This temporary and permanent placement service specializes in strategic staffing solutions. Integro places professionals in four areas: office, legal, scientific and accounting and financial services. Unlike many other staffing service providers, Integro offers professional personnel through its special services divisions so that it can provide the personal attention necessary to fully understand and work in specific markets. If you are interested in working in one of the fields mentioned above, check out this site ⬜ you won't regret it.

* Internet Professional Association

Website: http://www.ipa.com/

This site is a successful virtual employment association with over 1800 members. Through Internet Professional Association, you can search exhaustive job banks featuring numerous available job openings, post your resume or consult the career center for career advice. It is the purpose of this site to help employment professionals and those looking for contacts to find each other and pave ways to successful and long lasting careers.

* IPA, Recruiter Online Network

Website: http://www.ipa.com/

The Internet Professional Association offers the job seeker career advice, a facility for resume postings and valuable connections to employment professionals, including recruiting firms. With over 1,800 members and associate firms linked together, IPA claims to be the world's largest virtual association of employment professionals. All you have to do is apply for free membership, browse through the current job listings and find the one that suits you best. Nothing could be easier.

* JobCenter

Website: http://www.mindspring.com/~cultech/jobc.htm

Tired of searching through thousands of job ads, day after day, week after week? Tired of constantly wondering which ads are new and which ones you've seen before? Have you asked yourself if there's an easier way? There is. Finding a job has never been simpler than through this site. Post your resume on the Employment Services Section of JobCenter and let them conduct your job search for you! JobCenter maintains a database of resumes from prospective employees and compares them with job descriptions from hiring employers. When a match is found, the copy of your resume is sent directly to the employer. You also receive a message to inform you of the status of your resume, and copy of the job description so that you know exactly what the employers are seeking. Instead of searching for new job ads in papers, through JobCenter, you'll receive new matching ads right in your electronic mail box each day! In addition, this site includes a special feature for the recent graduates to ensure that they'll have positions immediately after their graduation and an online search engine to browse through the job ads posted in JobCenter's databases.

* The JobExchange

Website: http://www.jobexchange.com/
The JobExchange claims to match the talents of individuals seeking employment opportunities with the specific requirements of companies wishing to fill available positions. It offers two different searchable databases – one for part and full time employment and one for work on a contract basis. Accessible 24 hours a day, seven days a week, the site is updated daily and operates in an efficient, easy to use manner.

* JobHunt: OnLine Job Meta-List

Website: http://www.job-hunt.org
If you're not certain where to begin your job search, check out this extensive, well maintained and current site. It is the purpose of JobHunt to provide you with a listing of useful accessible job-search resources and services on the Internet and it's sure to include something for everyone.

* JobNet: Human Resources Online

Website: http://www.jobnet.com/
This is far from being a passive Internet resume listing service. JobNet is, on the contrary, an active database linking employers with prospective employees through lists of available opportunities and a resume service. It guarantees that you will receive the best services to aid and empower you in finding the job of your dreams, so you should definitely give their services a shot.

* Job Resources by U.S. Region

www.wm.edu/csrv/career/stualum/jregion.html
This site links the job-seeker to regional sites where they then choose a specific state. From that, pick from local sites that offer work in their area. Besides connecting to local communities, Job Resources, also offers Help Guides. The information can be used to help to create better resumes and interview skills. Access to national sites and short-term work is also included.

* Jobs on the Web

www.jobontheweb.com
This is an excellent site with precise job listings. Each field is broken down into separate occupational categories. After you have made your job choice you pick which state that you would like to work in. Each listing has job requirements, descriptions and salary ranges. They are updated a couple of times a week. After visiting the Help/Writing section, submit your resume for free by e-mail, fax, or mail. There are job hunting and interviewing tips, as well as links to many professional organizations. There is an enormous amount of information here!

* JobSAT

Website: http://www.jobsat.com/
This free site, designated to help you better execute your job search, features thousands of currently available job opportunities from across Canada and United States. Their database is easy to use and can quickly help you find the career that you've always desired.

* JobWeb

Website: http://www.jobweb.org/
JobWeb is very likely America's most effective and efficient link to assist students, recent graduates and experienced professionals in their career search. Owned and maintained by the National Association of Colleges and Employers, this site is an up-to-date info source of salaries, legal issues, diversity recruitment, internships, college relations and general employment/labor statistics relating to professional staffing and college-educated work force. JobWeb has 40 years of experience, an established reputation and a solid brand image as the leading publisher of career information for graduating college students and experienced alumni. Most importantly, it's here to help you find a career and you shouldn't miss out on its excellent services.

* The JobZone

Website: http://www.thezones.com/jobzone/
Are you frustrated with seeking employment through newspapers and bulletin boards? If so, there are sites on the Internet that can make your job search a whole lot easier. This free search engine, for example, is devoted to helping those seeking employment by providing thousands of job listings from private sector and government employers. You can simply search through their database and find a job that suits you best. The JobZone is updated weekly so keep checking back for updates.

* MBA Placement Program

Website: http://phoenix.placement.oakland.edu/career/emplist.htm
This direct and comprehensive site offers an alphabetical list of employers currently hiring MBA's and other professional disciplines. All you have to do is browse through the categories, find the ones that suit your interests and you will have already taken the first step toward a successful career.

* The Monster Board

Website: http://www.monster.com
This is by far the best place the place to begin your search for a fulfilling career. The Monster Board offers free access to over 55,000 job opportunities worldwide in all levels and fields. Whether you hunt for a job, post your resume to their national database or conduct extensive research on employers worldwide, you won't be disappointed with the results from this superb site.

* Nation Job Network

www.nationjob.com
Search for a job or a company that meets your wants. Their flagship service, PJ Scout, sends the job seeker any new jobs that fall into the category that they are looking in. The Specialty Pages list a variety of job types available and links to the job openings in that field. Check out the Community Sponsorship Program that has up-to-date openings and profiles of selected communities.

* National Business Employment Weekly

Website: http://www.nbew.com
Maintained by the National Business Employment Weekly, this site claims to be the nation's preeminent career guidance and job-search publication. The page's best features include profitable tips related to self-employment, job interviews and resumes, truths about job hunting and a savvy buyers guide to advance-fee job search to help you choose among career marketing firms.

* National Employment Job Bank

Website: http://www.nlbbs.com/~najoban/
This great site offers the browser lists of current career opportunities that range from accounting to human resources. All offers come from some of the finest employers and employment services in the country and what's more, the service is completely free to you.

* NetJobs

Website: http://www.netjobs.com/index.html
This informative sight is a job seeker's dream. In addition to browsing through the employment listings, resume online services, job related newsgroups, resume writing tips from the experts, job interview tactics, unemployment insurance information and a training resource inventory, you can initiate your own search by company name and job location or find links to complimenting employment searches. This site also has bonuses for the recent graduate and the self-employed: NetJobs maintains a special service designed for the college graduate's first job hunt and a consultant's corner through which individuals working for themselves can utilize the Internet to improve their businesses.

* Net-Temps

Website: http://www.net-temps.com/
Whether you're seeking temporary or permanent work, this in an ideal location to begin your quest. Through this free service, your resume information is taken via an online form and placed directly into the resume bank to be accessed by hiring employers looking for qualified candidates. You can also access Net-Temps' powerful job search engine that links you to a career magazine downloading and indexing all of the job postings from the major Internet job newsgroups and making them searchable by location, job title and/or skills required. Or you can browse through Net-Temps' archive of articles about job fairs, interviewing and personal networking. As if that

wasn't enough, this comprehensive site also maintains access to a directory of employer profiles where you will find detailed information on employers of your interest around the world.

* NCS Career Magazine

Website: http://www.careermag.com/

This site is bound to be useful to anyone who is currently in the job market. The most impressive feature of this service is the job search engine, which uses data from all the Usenet job announcement groups. You may also want to browse the numerous employer profiles, discover the products and services available from Career Magazine, and even catch up on the latest news in the labor market! Also available here is a career links section and a World Wide Web resume bank.

* 123 Careers

Website: http://www.123Careers.com

123 Careers features sections of new available job listings in various fields of employment and offers a free and effective way to forward your resume online to major companies and leading recruiters. Whatever you are looking for, this site will surely answer your needs in job search.

* Opportunity Knocks

www.oppknocks.com

At this site they will walk you through creating a multimedia resume. They believe adding an audio or video presentation will set you apart from a paper only resume. It will be active for as long as you want it accessed by employers. After finishing that, start your search for jobs using the custom keyword, position and salary range options. They also have a great list of links to sites that include maps, moving calculators, labor statistics and a lot more.

* Passport Access Employment Network

Website: http://www.passportaccess.com/

Whether you have a current job and are looking for a better one or seeking a brand new opportunity , by placing your resume on this site, you can easily keep your options open. In addition to free resume posting, The Passport Access Employment Network also offers links to recruiting services and additional employment information. When you utilize their services, you have easily obtained the passport to a new, successful career.

* PROFESSIONS

Website: http://www.jobsarus.com/

Take advantage of this site's no fee, no obligation services that include information concerning specific career fields and hot resume tips and networking tips. What better way to find a way to the profession of your choice than through PROFESSIONS?

* Recruiting-links.com

Website: http://www.recruiting-links.com/job_search.asp

Recruiting-links.com is a free, comprehensive search engine with links to employers' recruiting pages. The database can be searched, for free, through over 700 combinations of geographic, industry and occupational employment preferences. If simplicity, accuracy, swiftness and good results is what you desire in your job search, recruiting-links.com can provide all of that and more.

* SearchEase

www.searchease.com

SearchEase advertises that they have much more to offer in a search for a career. They have a job search where you can apply immediately or use the Job Search Agent to look for you. They also offer a Jobs In-Box in which you can keep job postings that are appealing, view interview requests submitted to you and even enter notes of previous interviews. You will be able to post a resume and add pictures, hyperlinks, and more creative features. All of this is free too!

* USA Jobz

Website: http://www.adgrafix.com/jobz/index.html

USA Jobz is a free, comprehensive database of vacant job opportunities offered across the United States. You can search by categories ▢ whether it be professional, medical, sales, retail, business or general information you require ▢ as well as by location. USA Jobz has got you covered all across the nation.

* Usenet Jobs List

Website: http://www.careermosaic.com/cm/usenet.html

This site is a well designed, free search engine that can easily locate your dream job for you. All you have to do is type in a job description, and the search begins. You can also narrow the search by specifying a particular field, company, city etc, that suits your interests best. In addition, Usenet Jobs List has an index of thousands of postings from newsgroups with career opportunities that can match the ones appropriate for you. Try it, it's simple to use and produces immediate results.

* Virtual Job Fair

Website: http://www.vjf.com/

The Virtual Job Fair claims to be the fastest growing career site on the Web. An easy-to-follow and direct place to begin your job search, this site has links to bulletin boards that provide information about the job of your choice, helpful ways to search for employers and career opportunities by title, technology, location or company and chances to send your resume directly to employers online. It claims to have connections throughout America and with such an exhaustive database, it is hard to doubt. This site offers a quick and easy way to begin your job search and the effective results are bound to follow.

* WinWay

Website: http://www.winway.com/

Utilize this site and you'll surely win your way into a new successful career. WinWay is most helpful in assisting you to discover strategies for resume writing, interviewing and salary negotiations. In addition, it offers connections to online job finding resources, places to post your resume, and links to seek out hiring employers on the Web. WinWay also has an added bonus ▢ if you're bored from your job hunt and need a refresher break, WinWay offers links to cool sites on the Web that range from helpful to humorous. This site is a friendly and empowering place to start your job search.

* Work-Web

Website: http://www.work-web.com/

This educational and informative site provides a database of jobs and resume banks to assist people who need to brush up on classroom and/or job skills, or who otherwise need assistance in gaining employment. If you are looking for a job or just want to change your current position, this site is for you. You can search through available job openings and create your own resume and display it at no charge ▢ either way, your dream job could be only a click away through Work-Web.

Career Planning

* Equal Opportunity Publications
Website: http://www.eop.com/

This empowering Website specializes in affirmative action and workforce diversity recruitment for minorities, women and people with disabilities. Equal Opportunity Publications is dedicated to connecting employers committed to the recruitment of a diversified work force with qualified career seekers. The site links to five career magazines to help you land the job you want, a career center with a listing of career opportunities offered by leading companies, government agencies, schools and hospitals, information on upcoming career fairs and a fact center with tips for a better career search. What more could you ask for?

* 1st Steps In The Hunt
Website: http://www.interbiznet.com/hunt/

This newsletter for the job seeker is updated almost daily, and contains a lot of useful information. Discover great online points to start your job hunt, design and distribute your resume, and lots more! The best starting point for your hunt, this site has been named "Hot Site" by USA Today.

* Good Thinking Co.
Website: http://www.dnai.com/g-think/

This is without a doubt one of the more interesting career related sites the 'Net has to offer. The Good Thinking Co. features articles on college success, career planning, and personal development, a list of web sites with similar foci, success stories about profitable career moves and inspiring people, and a list of hot success books and inspirational movies. As a bonus, the site also features a collection of cool, interesting quotes. The best thing to demonstrate your good thinking power would be to sign on to this list for free and receive the frequently updated list of hot tips, success suggestions, and inspirational quotes directly in your e-mail box.

* Job Options
Website: ttp://www.joboptions.com/esp/plsql/espan_enter.sepan_home

Job Options is a job database, private resume builder and recruitment resource for anyone looking for employment. You can search a job by category, location in the country, or by a keyword. You can send your resume e-mail with a single click of a button.

* Outsource 2000 Handbook
Website: http://www.outsource2000.com/?id+917364159

The Outsource 2000 Handbook offers a listing of sources that provide specific career information, an archive of articles about finding jobs and evaluating a job offer, and other occupational information valuable to any job seeker. The site also links to other occupational publications that can help you during your search for a better career.

* Relocation Salary Calculator
Website: http://www.homefair.com/homefair/cmr/salcalc.html

Are you planning to relocate but are unsure about what you are getting yourself into? The Relocation Salary Calculator can at least help you out in some aspects — it provides a living index for over 450 cities in the US which allows you to figure out the income you will need to maintain your current living standard when you move to a new city. Maintained by the Center For Mobility Resources, this effective tool thus allows you to determine the salary you would need to make in a new city, based on cost of living differences with your current location. This is a truly useful and necessary sight for anyone planning a move.

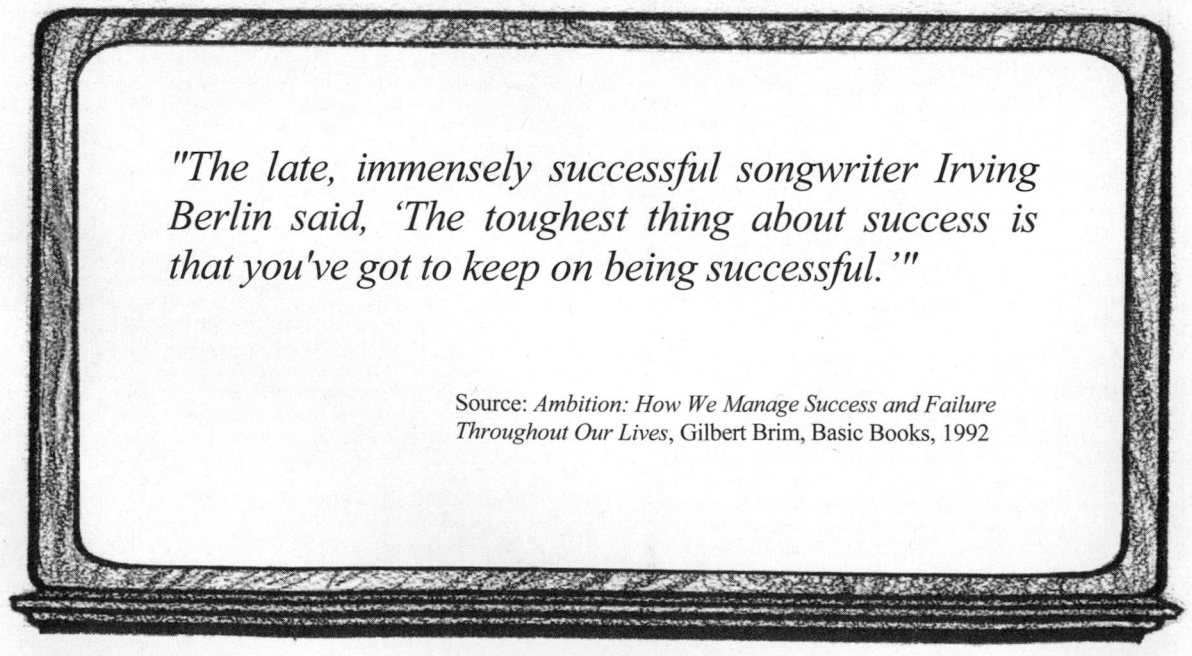

"The late, immensely successful songwriter Irving Berlin said, 'The toughest thing about success is that you've got to keep on being successful.'"

Source: *Ambition: How We Manage Success and Failure Throughout Our Lives*, Gilbert Brim, Basic Books, 1992

Specialized Career Sites

Academic Career Sites

* Academic Employment Network
Website: http://www.academploy.com/

If you're looking for a job in teaching or seeking other academic positions, this is an educational must. AEN contains a comprehensive listing of educational employment opportunities for teachers and other school-related positions at all academic levels, categorized in alphabetical order by state, educational institutions and positions. All position listings include info about inquiries, resume submissions, contact person, and best ways to submit your application. The Academic Employment Network also provides relocation services that present data concerning salary differentials, rental rates, demographic comparisons and various other statistics.

* Academic Physician and Scientist
Website: www.acphysci.com

"Academic Physician and Scientist is the centralized resource for positions in academic medicine," claim the founders of this site. Indeed this site has listings of current administrative, basic science, and clinical science openings. Also here you will find job announcements from the National Institute of Health, and the FDA.

* The Academic Position Network
Location (via gopher): wcni.cis.umn.edu:11111/

This gopher site is dedicated to posting job announcements from colleges and universities throughout the world. From Alabama to Sri Lanka to Wyoming, this site covers more ground that most WWW sites of the same nature. You don't need to have a Ph.D. to find a job at the Academic Position Network plenty of administrative and research positions are available for the taking all around the globe.

* Agora Employment Listings
Website: http://agoralang.com:2410/agora/employment.html

If you are interested in teaching a language, check out this site. Agora Employment Listings provides current nationwide job listings in the field of language instruction. The openings range from administrative positions to jobs as ESL and specific foreign language teachers.

* American Mathematical Society
Website: http://www.ams.org

Is your job search in the field of mathematics not adding up to success? Let The American Mathematical Society help you find the job that you've been seeking. Their informative and daily updated site presents an impressive list of employment opportunities for those with an advanced degree in mathematics. Included are many positions in academia as well as in business and nonprofit organizations. Employing this site to help you can equal success in your career search.

* EDUCAUSE Job Posting Service
Website: http://www.educause.edu/

Maintained by the association for managing and using information resources in higher education, EDUCAUSE Job Posting Service is dedicated to providing a career searching service for professionals interested in the field of information resources. The site lists a number of information resource related positions, available for your search as well as links to other informative and helpful sites on the 'Net. Furthermore, EDUCAUSE is completely free to you.

* Job Openings In Academy (from Academe This Week publication)
Website: http://chronicle.com/jobs/

This site is dedicated wholly to the job opportunities in Academia. Listings are usually available in the fields of humanities, social sciences, science and technology, and professional fields. A section of this site has been apportioned for administrative and executive openings. The ads are updated very often, so this is a good site to bookmark.

* Job Openings for Economists (JOE)
Website: gopher://vuinfo.vanderbilt.edu:70/11/employment/joe

This site is right on the money in assisting the job seeker in his job search. JOE features a large collection of employment postings, most of which are faculty positions in academe, but also carries information about job opportunities in businesses and nonprofit organizations. Featuring both browsable and searchable listings, JOE makes the job search easy and economical.

* National Information on Software and Services (NISS)
Website: http://www.niss.ac.uk/noticeboard/index.html#jobs

This career related site features available job vacancies in the worldwide academic community. Arranged by discipline, the listings are easy to choose from and browse. NISS' overseas job vacancies contain career opportunities in universities in the UK and Associations Of Commonwealth Universities in Africa, the Caribbean, Australia, Hong Kong, New Zealand and Canada.

* Telejob
Website: http://www.telejob.ethz.ch/

Telejob is an electronic job exchange board, maintained by the associations of assistants and doctoral students from the technological institutes of Zurich and Lausanne. If you've always wished to work in Europe, this site contains plenty of interesting jobs for young professionals from the academic or business worlds. Through an easily accessible directory, all that you have to do is choose the area of interest and read all the erudite offers that range from positions in architecture to law.

Arts and Design

* ARTJOB
Website: http://www.webart.com/artjob/

Are you having difficulty finding employment as an artist? This bi-monthly newsletter can come to your rescue. ARTJOB, an elegantly created site, presents comprehensive, up-to-date national and international listings of arts employment, including information regarding academic agencies, internships, presenting and producing organizations and publications. It also features areas of specific interest concerning artistic performances, conferences and related opportunities. Any way you view it, ARTJOB is your source of opportunities in the arts.

* DesignSphere Online Job Hunt
Website: http://www.dsphere.net/comm/jobs.html

Are you looking for a new position in the field of art and design? Here is a place to let the community know that you're available as well as conduct a search of your own. DesignSphere provides job opportunities and jobs wanted listings for everyone involved in the communication arts, including designers, illustrators, photographers and software and print experts!

* Internet Fashion Exchange
Website: http://www.fashionexch.com/

Has it always been your dream to work as a designer or be involved in the fashion industry? Let this site help you find a position that you're looking for. Internet Fashion Exchange claims to be the only Website exclusively dedicated to providing centralized employment marketplace for the fashion and retail industry. Here is your opportunity to make your unique qualifications known to thousands of companies by utilizing IFE's resume bank where they can be accessed by people who are seriously looking for qualified industry professionals. Confidentiality is assured, and moreover, the services provided by this site are absolutely free.

Careers For Minorities and Women

* Saludos: National Job Listings
Website: http://www.saludos.com/

As part of their service to the Hispanic community, this web site is a home to job listings from employers who are actively recruiting qualified Hispanics for positions in their companies. Whether you are seeking a career in administration, computers, engineering, finance, human resources, management, marketing, entertainment industry, sales, telecommunications or therapy, Saludos can offer you a helping hand. You can browse a list of all current job openings, arranged by state, view their tips on creating effective resumes or visit other career and employment sites on the "Net, all for no charge whatsoever. This is a truly empowering and informative site.

* Women's Studies Employment Opportunities
Website: http://www.inform.umd.edu/WomensStudies/Employment/
Designed as a straightforward bulletin board, this site presents connections to job-offers specifically for women and concerning women, along with direct contacts and dates the offers expire. The selection of opportunities is wide and ranges from careers in teaching and leadership to legal studies, counseling and research. In addition, this site offers excellent information about grants aimed to help those interested in the field of women's studies. No woman searching for employment should let this site pass by.

* Women's Wear Daily
Website: http://www.wwd.com/classified/classified.htm
Looking for a more attractive career move? Let this site help you. If you are a woman interested in working in the field of fashion, apparel, cosmetics or retail, Women's Wear Daily lists many vogue opportunities that range from sales to management and could get you the job of your dreams. Check it out.

Computers and Technology

* AD&A Software Jobs Home Page
Website: http://www.softwarejobs.com/
With a network of over 600 recruiting affiliates, in almost every state, AD&A has access to career opportunities from coast to coast and you shouldn't miss out on their services. Their Software Jobs Home Page lists over 100 software job openings featuring many permanent, full time positions offering full benefits. You can search this database, access information on how to apply for the positions that interest you as well as link to other useful career related resources. In addition to providing general recruitment and placement services, AD&D also provides guidance on the job market for candidates in specialized areas. This is an excellent free and up to date service.

* Computer Consultant Job Board and Resource Center
Website: http://computerwork.com/
Computer Consultant Job Board and Resource Center, a NACBB sponsored site, displays a broad job board for computer consultants in search of their next contracting opportunity. If you choose this site to search for current opportunities and submit your resume to the resume bank for companies to see, you can pick your dream career from the best technical job and contract employment opportunities currently available.

* Computer Software/Systems Job Openings
Website: http://www.nationjob.com/computers
This virtual bulletin board is updated almost as often as a real one (once a week), and holds even more information. Services obtainable from this location include P. J. Scout, a search engine that will e-mail any new openings that fit criteria you specify (its free!), a list of featured employers and links to their Web sites, and, of course, job announcements from all over the country! This is a five-star site and a definite must for your bookmark file if you are in the computer industry.

* Computerworld
Website: http://careers.computerworld.com/jobs/jobs.html
Are you seeking employment in the world of computers? Check out this site. Computerworld can help you search current jobs through the automated career system called CareerMail, a special agent that enables the careers you desire find you. All you have to do is register for free and have relevant career opportunities automatically arrive at your electronic mail box. Through this service, you can also skim through the corporate profiles and review descriptions of the employers who have posted their career opportunities on Computerworld.

* Contract Employment Weekly Online
Website: http://www.ceweekly.wa.com/
Contract Employment Weekly claims to have "more job listings for contract technical employment than any other publication in the world." Unfortunately, the full database is only accessible to subscribers, who pay a

moderate fee. The non-subscribers can also access this site and even browse some job announcements. There are plenty of other resources this site offers, such as a list of other related career sites, and interesting online articles. But to get the full benefit from Contract Employment Weekly, make sure you have a recent browser that supports Java, and be prepared to dish out a little money.

* Cyberspace Jobs
Website: http://www.careersbest.com
If you've ever wondered what kinds of jobs are out there in cyberspace, this is the place to check out all the various opportunities. Each of the 17 job descriptions that range from interactive actor to online researcher and cyberjournalist link to related web sites, and news groups to provide you with more info if you are interested. Check it out ⬚ you won't regret it.

* Data Processing Independent Consultants Exchange (DICE)
Website: http://www.dice.dlinc.com
This site offers a high-tech job search engine for high-tech professionals. Free of charge, you may browse the index of companies currently offering jobs. You may also perform a search by keyword, state, area code, job type, and term. At the time of this review, the site had 4,802 job announcements. DICE claims that they renew the site every week, so this one is a must for your bookmark file!

* Get A Job!
Website: http://sensemedia.net/getajob
Get A Job will post your HTML format resume for no charge and will then promote their site as a place to find hypermedia professionals so that hiring companies may hire you directly. Get A Job also offers links to other job search engines that you shouldn't miss in your career search.

* Hummer Winblad Venture Partners
Website: http://www.humwin.com/
Looking for a new job or a more exciting career? This site is ready to assist people from programmers to vice presidents win positions in the software industry's fastest growing companies. If you're searching for a cool job in a hot company, this site is for you.

* IndustryNET
Website: http://www.industry.net/
Along with bringing you the latest in engineering design, automation and manufacturing news that includes information concerning new products and online tradeshows, the IndustryNET also provides job postings from nearly 3000 top technological companies. Search their vast database and discover the ultimate business connections through this impressive site.

* Job Marketplace
Website: http://www.scrip.org/jobmrkt.html
This straightforward bulletin board of job listings can be of help to those seeking employment in the field of computers and technology. The Job Marketplace provides list of browsable job descriptions complete with contact info and job requirements. This may well be the place through which you will find the perfect career for you.

* Job.Net
Website: http://www.vnu.co.uk
There are a lot of solutions to job hunting, and a lot of answers as well. This site provides all of the good aspects of job searching in one location to help you find exactly what you're looking for. If you are searching for a career in computer technology, Job.Net features listings of the latest contract opportunities to computing professionals as well as an inventory of companies looking for employees. If you are a newcomer into the field, let this site offer you a helping hand through the informative guide for first time contractors.

* Pencom Career Center
Website: http://www.pencomsi.com/careerhome.html
If you're seeking new career opportunities and possess technical or managerial expertise in today's computer technology, this is the right place for you to begin your search. PCC's well organized site's features include an interactive salary guide, nationwide job listings and in-depth articles covering both career and technology issues in the field of your choice. Check it out today and find a hiring company in need of your skills.

* Training and Development Job Mart

Website: http://www.tcm.com/ht-careers/career/

This is a job market site designed especially for training and development and multimedia positions. It offers a listing of the top US and Canadian companies in the field, access to full information of the available positions, and an opportunity to e-mail your resume directly to the hiring organizations. If after browsing through their data, you still haven't found what you're looking for and are open to a career in a foreign country, the site also offers a link to the Hong Kong job market.

* Unixis Solutions

Website: http://www.it-connect.com/

This UK based Recruitment Consultancy focuses on employment in the client server, open systems, and technical computing arenas. Providing information about permanent, contract and graduate vacancies as well as opportunities for computing researchers, Unixis Solutions' quick and simple listings make it easy to find the job you're looking for in the United Kingdom.

* Virtual Search

Website: http://www.vsearch.com/

Virtual Search provides listings of positions in the interactive multimedia and game development field. It focuses on the Interactive Multimedia talent pool that specializes in highly qualified technical, creative and marketing professionals for companies involved in advanced technology and next generation applications and products.

* Westech Career Expos

Website: http://www.vjf.com/jobsearch.html

In addition to Westech's specialty ☐ career expos, where companies and their potential employees can get acquainted ☐ this site also offers a multitude of other free services. Along with listing the participating exhibitors and locations for the expos (complete with directions and maps), Westech has links to employer homepages, chances to post your resume and an online job search for those interested in a technological profession. A bulletin board is available, boasting over 15,000 possible high-tech career opportunities. This site has links to archived articles that enable you to research companies and technologies that match your interest. This site is a must see, packed tightly with helpful, high quality information.

* ZDNet Job Database

Website: http://www.jobengine.com/

ZDNet Job Database is a comprehensive, nationwide listing of employment opportunities for professionals in the high technology field. Whether you wish to search for a job or post your resume, this is a site that can help you in an efficient and orderly manner.

Education Related Career Sites

* USJOBNET

Website: http://WWW.USJOBNET.COM/

The creators of this site have succeeded in centralizing all the US school districts' employment opportunities into one Internet location. It offers a list of jobs available in K-12 that range from administration to teaching and counseling, as well as links to other education related jobs, individual schools and school districts with a homepage on the Internet, education related associations and lists of upcoming job fairs for educators. Through this masterfully organized site, anyone looking for a career in the field of education can place an ad on the Internet and be on the way to a challenging and rewarding job.

Entertainment, Sports and Recreation Industries

* Carbonate Your Brain: Job Pool

Website: http://www.7up.com/html/nonflash/sindex.html

This 7UP sponsored site is a truly cool spot, particularly for students interested in the music industry. Carbonate Your Brain: Job Pool is serving up a new world of music and fun, fizzling job opportunities (some of which include additional information concerning salary, housing allotment and travel costs) and political expressions. Drink up!

* CPB Jobline

Website: http://www.cpb.org/jobline/index.html

If it's always been your dream to work either in the radio or television industry, this site offers a perfect opportunity. Provided by the Corporation for Public Broadcasting, job announcements from all over the country are posted on this Web server. Each job opening post includes the requirements to qualify for the position, the starting salary, the address to direct your resume, and the deadline for the application.

* EMAP Media Web

Website: http://www.emap.co.uk/jobs/

This straightforward bulletin board features jobs in the fields of advertising and journalism as well as the radio and television industries. Clearly organized listings make it easy to browse through the available opportunities to search for the job of your choice and directly contact the hiring employers. If it has always been your dream to work in the entertainment industry, visiting this site is a definite must.

* Online Sports Career Center

Website: http://www.onlinesports.com/pages/CareerCenter.html

If you've always wished for a career in the sports or recreation industry, you can begin scoring points in your job search by checking out this site. Maintained by Sports Management Enterprises, a professional search firm for the sporting goods industry, the site is complete with resources on sports-related career opportunities, and a resume bank where potential employers within the many segments of the sports and recreation industries can have access to your qualifications. The online career center also provides links to other invaluable job search resources on the net. Surely, this site can put you ahead of the game in your pursuit for employment.

Entry Level Jobs

* College Grad Job Hunter

Website: http://www.collegegrad.com/

The one thing that is on the mind of most recent college graduates is getting a good job. This site offers numerous tips and strategies to find that job. Look into the step-by-step guide on how to look for the job, write your resume, plan for interviewing success, behave during the negotiation period, and even prepare for the first day on the job!

* JobDirect

Website: http://www.jobdirect.com/

Whether you are a graduating senior worried about what's awaiting you after college or a motivated undergrad trying to find internships, you have come to the right place to find assistance. JobDirect specializes in entry level positions for students and recent grads, especially non-technical jobs. JobDirect is the most effective way to obtain current information on entry level job market, internship opportunities, student related nonprofit organizations and international employment. Once you've registered, the site's services conduct a constant job hunting process which notifies you of any new posted jobs which match your interests. JobDirect is free, fast, and easy to use.

* JOBTRAK

Website: http://www.jobtrak.com/

Yes, there is indeed life after college, and this site is proof of it. JOBTRACK, a college recruiting database, maintains partnerships with over 300 college and university career centers to provide a resume bank, list of top recruiters and a search engine for job listings to assist recent college graduates to look for their first jobs. This comprehensive and organized site also includes job search and resume writing tips and a guide to graduate.

* Seacnet

Website: http://www.seacnet.org

Seacnet, also known as the Southeastern-Atlantic Coast Career Network, is dedicated to helping students find their way in the "real world" of employment opportunities. The job seeker can search hundreds of job postings at participating universities in southeast United States, visit the links to employment centers, graduate and professional schools and potential employers. Though still in development, Seacnet already provides promising services for the college job seeker, and will surely have more to offer in the near future.

* Student Center

Website: http://www.studentcenter.com/
Are you a recent graduate in search of a job and having a little trouble out there in the "real world"? Visit the Student Center and all your troubles may be over. This site offers the latest in career-related information for entry-level job seekers just like you, including a 35,000 company searchable database and resume, interview, and job hunting tips. The Student Center is here to help you identify your personal strengths, define your career goals, and learn about the companies that best match your interests. Among other useful tools, their services enable you to take a self-diagnostic test to determine the right career for you and explore employment opportunities in major cities in all 50 states, as well as familiarize yourself with the international career market. In every way, this excellent site truly aspires to "help job seekers develop the sophisticated job search skills they need in today's competitive environment."

Environmental Careers

* The Environmental Careers Organization

Website: http://www.eco.org/
The Environmental Careers Organization is a national nonprofit company dedicated to promoting careers in the environment. Their homepage specializes in services related to environmental internships, career counseling, employment resources, conferences, and job listings. By supporting "the development of environmental professionals and citizens who will make effective, balanced, and responsible decisions", this site can assist you in making environmentally responsible and successful career moves. The site also offers a link to a hot list of other ecological employment related Web Sites to assist you in your search for an environmental career.

* Environmental Careers World Online

Website: http://www.infi.net/
To check out this semi-monthly listing of job opportunities and career information published in Hampton, Va. is the best way to start your environmental job search. Environmental Careers World Online helps people work for the environment by improving access to and awareness of environmental career information. Their consolidated and comprehensive information exchange fosters greater environmental workforce diversity and offers available employment listings in the fields of ecology, biology, forestry, natural resources, environmental education, policy, advocacy, law, science and engineering. Don't miss out on this great opportunity to start your job search.

* JobBoard

Website: http://wfscnet.tamu.edu/jobs.htm
There are many ways to search for jobs and the Internet can prove an effective tool in this quest. This site, maintained by the Department of Wildlife and Fisheries Sciences of Texas A&M University, includes job postings that range from entry-level to professional, in the field of natural resources. Along with info on internships, seasonal employment and volunteer opportunities, this site also features links to other mechanisms to search for employment via Internet. Don't miss out.

* UWIN

Website: http://www.uwin.siu.edu/announce/jobs/
UWIN is designated to serve as a clearinghouse of jobs and related opportunities in various water resources fields. The positions categorized into academic and student opportunities and are complete with contact information. If you think this is a field of your interest, check it out to begin in a winning career.

The Finance Market

* Accounting Net

Website: http://www.accountingnet.com/index.html
The Accounting Net features a job search database for accountants and auditors along with an area designed for the posting of resumes. It is user-friendly and free of charge, an excellent utility to the accounting professional seeking a new career move.

* The Business Job Finder

Website: http://www.cob.ohio-state.edu/dept/fin/osujobs.htm
Want to get into the business industry? Check this site for the current job opportunities in the areas of finance, accounting, and management. You may

also browse the list of sites maintained by individual employers, find information on several MBA programs, and link to other career sites on the Net.

* Financial/Accounting/Insurance Job Openings

Website: http://www.nationjob.com/financial
If your expertise lies in the field of finance, accounting, or insurance, this site will help you find a way to apply your knowledge. New job announcements from all over the country are added every week to an already extensive database of openings. Companies from all over the country post on this site, although most of the job openings seem to center around the mid-US region. Nevertheless, this is a good site to visit regularly regardless of your current location.

* Marketing Classifieds

Website: http://www.marketingjobs.com/
This is a carefully designed site dedicated to helping professionals find a career in their chosen field of marketing, sales or advertising. The featured online resume database is divided into two sections: the executive resumes division for professionals with over 10 years of marketing, sales or advertising experience, and a general marketing resume division for job seekers with less exposure in these fields. Both sections are password protected and confidential. The site also features a list of current employment opportunities from across the United States, links to company web pages, a resume shop where you can tune up your resume, an address book where you can find addresses, phone and fax numbers for companies of your interest and links to other employment related sites on the Internet. And, of course, the best feature of all ⬤ these services are absolutely free to you, the job seeker.

* Marketing and Sales Jobs Page

Website: http://www.nationjob.com/marketing
This weekly updated site features hundreds of marketing and sales jobs. All you have to do is click on the job you would like to view and the information you need to begin a new career is at your fingertips. Moreover, you can just enter your job preferences and your e-mail address, and they'll send you any new jobs that match your choices each week, all through a free and confidential service. What more could you ask for?

* Top Jobs on the Net

Website: http://www.topjobs.co.uk
If you are looking for a job in IT, sales, finance, marketing or consulting, Top Jobs on the Net is the best place for you to begin your search. This sophisticated site provides services to some of the most prestigious companies in the world and is dedicated to match the best candidates with the best companies. Complete with a career index of available positions listings and links to companies that range from Lotus to Kellogg, this display might ensure you either a contract or permanent career opportunity in the UK or the rest of Europe. Check it out.

* 100 Careers in Wall Street

Website: http://www.globalvillager.com/villager/wsc.html
If you've been searching for a profitable career in the investment business, this Web site is well worth your time. You may browse job opening ads placed by the most prestigious companies all around the U.S. You may also submit a "job wanted" ad of your own and read the online pamphlet *Career Guide To Wall Street*. This site is aimed at the novice as well as the Wall Street shark.

Government/Federal Jobs

* Department of the Interior Automated Vacancy Announcement System (AVAILS)

Website: http://www.doi.gov/doi_empl.html
This authoritative and direct site announces job announcements with the US Department of the Interior. You can limit your search to different bureaus of the department and begin searching for a career that fits your interest best. Job search through this site is easy ⬤ specific contact addresses needed for you to take the necessary measures toward advancing your career included in each announcement.

* Federal Jobs Central

Website: http://www.fedjobs.com/
Dedicated to matching people with jobs in the Federal government, Federal Job Central has put together a toolbox specifically targeted for federal job hunters, helpful to both first time applicants as well as those already employed

in the field. Their listings include various types of federal employment — white or blue collar, full-time or temporary — in every possible location throughout the United States, and their services give job seekers the advice and how-to information they need to land the jobs they want and tips on how to make the most of their career investment. Updated every work day, the listings provide all the information needed to apply for the jobs, including a contact person and a telephone number. Current, comprehensive and accurate, this site is an authoritative database for federal job openings.

* U.S. Office of Personnel Management

Website: http://usajobs.opm.gov/

This is the complete listing of all government jobs available. You can search from A to Z or by agency. You can also look at the types of jobs available. Online applications are accessable with the click of the mouse.

Health Care Industry

* MedSearch America

Website: http://medsearch.com/

It is the purpose of this site to assist professionals in the field of health care search for employment. MedSearch can aid you whether you are seeking permanent, temporary, internship, contract, or volunteer positions and the fields range from pharmaceuticals to sports medicine and health insurance. You can search for opportunities by job category, organization, title, or location and there are never any fees for the services.

* NursingNet

Website: http://nationjob.com/nursingnet

If you are a nurse seeking employment, the NursingNet can put you on the right track in your search for successful employment. The site can attend to your concerns regarding domestic, foreign, and overseas careers and also in resume preparation and offer you a helping hand in any other employment related issue you may have.

Military Positions

* Navy Jobs

Website: http://www.navyjobs.com/

The United States Navy is in need of a few good men and women. Whether you're a high school or a college graduate, the Navy has great opportunities for your career moves by offering employment in fleet or in the medical field and you can find out all about it through this site. If you're a recent college-bound high school graduate, be sure to check out the details of the Navy's many programs which could help you pay for your college education.

* U.S.Army

Website: http://www.goarmy.com/

Be all that you can be and check out this site. The U.S.Army homepage informs you of the opportunities in the United States Army for high school graduates as well as those with college experience. There are nearly 250 military occupational specialties that range from positions in accounting to medical services, and if you are interested, it is easy to find a fitting place in the Army through this site.

Sciences

* AAS Job Register - American Astronomical Society

Website: http://www.aas.org/JobRegister/aasjobs.html

This site is a straightforward bulletin board for those with careers in the field of astronomy. Available positions range from astrophysicists to research associates and are complete with a brief job description and contact information.

* Academic Chemistry Employment Clearinghouse

Website: http://hackberry.chem.niu.edu:70/1/ChemJob

Academic Chemistry Employment Clearinghouse provides information concerning vacancies in the fields of analytical, inorganic, organic, physical and biochemistry. Positions are supplied from universities and other academic institutions across United States and can be searched by location or job description.

* American Institute of Physics

Website: http://www.aip.org/aip/careers/careers.html

Have you ever asked yourself what to do with your physics major now that you're out of college or wondered what the next step in your physics vocation should be? With a weekly updated database of over 200 physics related job listings in academia, government and industry, this site can come to your rescue. The American Institute of Physics' services inform students about various careers in physical sciences as well as assist individuals with experience in the field search for new chances.

* American Physiologist Society

Website: gopher://oac.hsc.uth.tmc.edu:3300/00/employ/list

If you are looking for employment in the field of physiology, this site, maintained by the American Physiologist Society can help you search for new career options. The frequently updated entries are listed with the recently submitted options on top for your convenience, and the positions range from postdoctoral research to avial physiologists and department chairs in America's universities. Without a doubt, a good place to begin your job search.

* Biomedical Positions

Website: http://www.informatik.uni-rostock.de/HUM-MOLGEN/ positions/

This server contains job opening announcements for research associates, professors, as well as clinical, higher academic, and non-academic positions. Interested parties may post an ad of their own for free.

* BIO Online Career Center

Website: http://www.bio.com/hr/hr_index.html

The BIO Online Career Center lists a number of resources related to careers in the biological sciences. Their listing of job opportunities includes positions from companies such as Genetech, Cell Therapeutics and Icos and the site contains links to other field related sites as well as an archive of biology related articles. It is a comprehensive and orderly site created for your convenience when searching for a job in the field of biology.

* BioSpace Career Center

Website: http://www.biospace.com/b2/job_index.cfm

Are you seeking a job in the field of biosciences? By checking out this frequently updated site, you can materialize in the best place to begin your job search. The BioSpace Career Center features a vast body of information concerning employment in the bioscience industries. The positions are grouped by region, category, and company and include employment in companies such as Bio-Rad Laboratories and Roche Molecular Systems. The site also links to other biotechnology resources that can assist you during your job search.

* Biotechnology Job Bank

Website: http://www.labmart.com/employ

Maintained by Delco Scientific, this site "helps individuals seek high quality employment in sales, management, administration and technology in the fields of biotechnology, biopharmaceutical and laboratory products." If interested in any ad posted here, you will have the opportunity to e-mail the employer your resume right away.

* Career Connection

Website: http://www.ebi.ac.uk/htbin/biojobs.pl

Maintained by the European Bioinformatics Institute, this straightforward classifieds site lists numerous job opportunities in the fields of bioinformation, biochemistry, and molecular biology. You can execute your search by entering keywords or categories and find positions that suit you best in the category of your choice, whether it be in government, academia, or industry related occupations.

* Cell Positions Available

Website: http://jobs.cell.com/

If you are a professional in the life sciences, you might want to point your browser to this address. Job announcements are listed in a very straightforward fashion, and there are plenty of them. Hyperlinks are available to classifieds from Neuron and Immunity publications. The site is updated regularly.

* Employment Links for the Biomedical Scientist
Website: http://www.his.com/~graeme/employ.html
As we all know, it is difficult to gain access to favorable positions in the field of sciences. The Internet can offer a particularly useful medium for exchange of employment related information, but not everybody has the time to sort through the wide variety of material out there. This site makes the search a whole lot simpler by offering links to employment related sites in the fields of biomedics, as well as other sciences.

* Experimental Medicine: Job Listings
Website: http://www.medcor.mcgill.ca/EXPMED/DOCS/jobs.html
If you are interested in experimental medicine, this site can help you find the perfect job. Experimental Medicine: Job Listings offers a bulletin board of post doctorate and university placement job listings in United States and Canada, along with links to many other field related resources. It's efficient and resourceful.

* FASEB Careers OnLine
Website: http://www.faseb.org/careers/
Maintained by the Federation of American Societies for Experimental Biology, this career resources site specializes in biomedical career advancement services. FASEB Careers OnLine confidentially matches applicants at all career levels with employers who need biomedical scientists and technicians. The site also provides information regarding national and international job fairs.

* Franklin Search Group
Website: http://www.medmarket.com/employ/empall.html
This free online career service is particularly helpful to those with interest in employment in the bio-technical and medical industries. You can post your resume, search for jobs or check out salary surveys and articles about employment ▢ all at no charge whatsoever.

* FSG Online Jobs in Biotechnology, Pharmaceuticals and Medicine
Website: http://www.medzilla.com
This site provides a forum where employers and candidates can easily find each other and explore new job opportunities. Through FSG, you can easily find a new job in the field of biotechnology, pharmaceuticals, and medicine through their accessible database. Among other services, this site also allows you to post your resume, browse articles concerning employment, and current salaries in the field of science, and access an online book store featuring books and publications about working and finding jobs.

* Job Opportunities in Entomology
Website: http://www.colostate.edu/Depts/Entomology/jobs/jobs.html
Are you getting bogged down by the job search that seems to get you nowhere? This site may hold the answer for you. Stop the rest of your search now and browse through Job Opportunities in Entomology ▢ a comprehensive listing of hiring research centers, universities and colleges around the country that could make your career search fly faster than before. You won't regret it.

* Jobs in physics, astronomy and other fields
Website: http://yorty.sonoma.edu/people/faculty/tenn/Jobs.html
This comprehensive site provides useful links to any young scientist looking for a job. It features a career planning center for beginning scientists and engineers, a student planning guide to grad school and beyond as well as a listing of part-time, temporary and summer jobs for students and a complete collection of links to other field related job pages. If you are just beginning your career in the field of science, this is a site you shouldn't miss.

* Journal of Minerals, Metals, and Materials Classifieds
Website: http://www.tms.org/
This site lists all the ads that appeared in the last three issues of JOM. The JOM page is a perfect place to visit whether you are looking to start a new career in the metallurgy and minerals field or are a bona-fide specialist in those areas.

* Medical Ad Mart
Website: http://www.medical-admart.com/
Medical Ad Mart is a compilation of current classified advertising of positions from widely read medical journals. It includes a listing of over 330 positions intended for physicians, pharmacists, laboratorians, life scientists, veterinarians, physician assistants, and nurses and provides messages from companies that specialize in servicing the medical community's needs for products, equipment, supplies, and continuing educational opportunities.

* MedSearch America
Website: http://www.medsearch.com/
This site is a database of jobs in the medical and healthcare industries. You can either submit your resume into their database via an online form, execute an individual job search, or browse through health career forums and employers profiles. All the services are free and offer a complete coverage of the medical and healthcare fields that can help you during your job search.

* National Physician Job Listing - EMBBS
Website: http://www.embbs.com
The National Physician Job Listing - EMBBS contributes practice opportunities through North America for all medical specialties with a focus on emergency, internal and family medicine and pediatrics. This is the place to find the ideal practice opportunity for you and the site also offers a variety of other information related to the field, such as radiology, library, and clinical photos.

* NIH Senior Job Opportunities
Website: http://helix.nih.gov:8001/jobs/
The NIH Senior Job Opportunities site offers a comprehensive listing of senior scientific, medical, and administrative job openings at the National Institutes of Health. As the foremost biomedical research organization in the world, they constantly seek candidates of the highest caliber to fill these senior leadership positions. To find the opportunity that suits you best, you can browse through the hypertext job announcements, submit your resume online or jump to related sites.

* Physics Jobs online
Website: http://physicsweb.org/TIPTOP/
This is a dynamic job list for physicists, through which one can both search for and submit jobs in the physics field. The services are absolutely free of charge and up-to-date, since the. old announcements are removed automatically after a week from the application deadline. Though the site offers mostly Ph.D. studentships, there are plenty of other opportunities as well for the job seeker in the field of physics.

* Physics World Jobs Online
Website: http://www.iop.org
If you are looking for a job in physics, you need to look no further. There is no more need to scan other different publications ▢ you can see the latest opportunities directly on Physics World Jobs Online. Here, new job vacancies in the physics field as published in the Physics World magazine or if you prefer, you can receive notification of new vacancies by e-mail directly to your mailbox. It is an efficient and wonderful site.

* Poly-Links
Website: http://www.polymers.com/polylink/jobank.html
Poly-Links presents job listings in the plastic and polymers industries. Whether you wish to browse the help wanted ads, create and post a resume or view the other field related sites, Poly-Links is flexible and can fit all of your job seeking needs.

* R.Ph On The Go
Website: http://www.rphonthego.com
R Ph On The Go is an efficient pharmacy employment service placing pharmacists in pharmacies both as relief and full-time placements. On this site, the new job postings are updated regularly and the creators of the site are "committed to making a significant contribution with the rapidly changing health care industry". They also offer a growing menu of products and services designed to meet the changing needs of pharmacies and pharmacists.

* Science's Next Wave
Website: http://www.edoc.com/
Science's Next Wave, "an electronic network for the next generation of scientists" displays a series of forums on science careers, a section focused on alternative scientific careers, a network of correspondents and data on the latest trends in science related careers. If you still haven't found what you are looking for, the site also offers hot links to other science related fields in funding, academia and other similar topics.

* Sonus Technical Search
Website: http://www.starnetinc.com/
Sonus Technical Search provides engineers and scientists with listings of outstanding jobs in the fields of electronics, acoustics, physics, mechanical and electrical engineering and computer science. The listings are complete with a location, brief job description, summary of qualifications and contact information. In addition, Sonus allows you to submit your resume directly to the company of your choice. This is a thorough and excellent service. Check it out.

* YSN Jobs Page
Website: http://www.physics.uiuc.edu/
Are you a scientist looking for a job? YSN Jobs Page offers a listing of jobs posted to the Young Scientists' Network. In addition to a number of links to other related resources, the site also provides hints of interviews, tips on interviewing in industry, job hotlines of various sorts and information about job fairs and regional meetings of the scientific community.

Transportation Industry

* Airline Employee Placement Service
Website: http://www.aeps.com/aeps/aepshm.html
This site is the online source for professionals looking for employment in the aviation industry. You may browse the latest job postings, add your resume to the listing of available employees, and even ask a question in the Aviation Information Exchange forum. Employers can post a job opening without paying a penny. Also available here is a site newsletter, and a hot link to the main aviation site on the Internet. Happy flying!

* Direct Transit Job Openings
Website: http://www.nationjob.com/
This weekly updated site is a list of current job openings with Direct Transit. Whether you are looking for a job as a long haul driver, operator or team driver, this site provides you with a list of nationwide and regional opportunities. All you have to do is simply click on the job title to view a more detailed description of the offered opportunity and you can be steering directly toward the job you've been searching for.

* Flight Instructor
Website: http://www.cogweb.com/chode/
You have just landed on a site dedicated to finding employment for pilots and flight instructors around the world. If you're seeking employment in the aviation industry, this is the place to launch your new career. Flight Instructor provides lists of commercial pilots around the world as well as aviation classifieds and links to other cool, aviation related sites. With a little help from this site, your career could soar to new heights.

Working At Home

* National Home Workers Association
Website: http://www.homeworkers.com/
As this site claims, "if you work at home, you are one of more than 30,000 million home employees, united by a common need for comprehensive insurance, technology assistance, and practical services for the home work place." And if, as home worker, you are in need of a new job or simply considering the possibility of home employment, check out this highly comprehensive site. The National Home Workers Association lists more than 125,000 work-from-home positions open across North America ▯ positions that range from typing, jewelry making and sewing, proofreading, writing, and much, much more. Their broad listings allow you to pick from thousands of legitimate home income opportunities and save time and money by doing so. Check it out and you won't regret it.

Miscellaneous

Au Pair
* Aupair JobMatch
Website: http://www.aupairs.co.uk/
Located in the United Kingdom, this service matches nannies and families from all over the world. If you think you have what it takes to be a professional au pair, visit this site and find the perfect job/travel opportunity! If you are looking for an au pair, you may find out how to advertise on this server.

Building Industry
* Building Industry Exchange
Website: http://www.building.org/index.html
If you are currently seeking a career in the building industry, let this site help you with your search. Building Industry Exchange is a lofty resource for career info, job listings and other services for building industry professionals. Complete with an online database, lists of upcoming events, building industry related newsgroups and services, this site is a great place to begin assembling the career of your dreams.

Journalism
* National Diversity Journalism Job Bank
Website: http://www.newsjobs.com/
This comprehensive list of job openings in the field of journalism should be an essential source for any journalist. Not an employment agency or a representative of any one newspaper, this ample job bank helps newspapers link up with potential applicants and encourages the participation of minorities and women. Complete with a list of job openings and a place to post your resumes, the site also links to other job banks and journalism related sites. Check back often for updates and new career opportunities hot off the press!

Landscaping
* Landnet Job Listing
Website: http://www.asla.org/
Maintained by American Society for Landscape Architects, this site is allotted especially for the benefit of those who seek employment in the field of landscaping. The site features numerous postings of positions in landscape architecture and ecology and in other related fields along with a resume bank. It is an easy to access, resourceful, and well maintained spot on the 'Net.

Law
* Law Employment Center
Website: http://www.lawjobs.com/
Finding a job that's just right for you may be a hard case to crack, but there's no need to lose hope. The Law Employment Center is here to assist you. If you're an attorney seeking employment, this is an excellent place to check out some new opportunities. The Law Employment Center's site contains hundreds of legal employment listings from the National Law Journal, New York Law Journal, and the Law Technology Product News along with an index of legal recruiting firms in states all over America, answers to your questions regarding the law employment marketplace and national salary survey. This is a truly superb site.

Library and Informational Sciences
* Library and Information Science JobSearch
Website: http://carousel.lis.uiuc.edu/~jobs/
Are you interested in library and information services related employment? Maintained by the University of Illinois, this site may have just what you're looking for. With as many as 180 new records added each month, Library and Information Science JobSearch allows you to view notices by experience level, employer, keywords, library type or region, and links to library jobs from other online sources. Let your search begin here.

Seasonal Employment
* Summer Jobs Web
Website: http://www.summerjobs.com/
Out of school for the summer and looking for a job? Let this site clue you in to the hottest summer opportunities around the country and abroad. The opportunities are organized by country, state or province, region, city or town and encompass all fields possible from retail to childcare. While the primary focus is summer employment for students and educational professionals, other jobs may be posted here as well, so it's worth a look.

Senior Citizens
* The Senior Staff Home Page
Website: http://www.srstaff.com/
Designed exclusively for the job seeker over 50 years of age, The Senior Staff Home Page collects, categorizes, and markets current job information reserved particularly for that age group. If this category applies to you, you're in luck, for this site offers some of the best information around.

* Popjobs

Website: http://www.popjobs.com/

This career site is designed specifically for the point of purchase advertising industry and is thus particularly useful for P-O-P professionals seeking careers in account management, merchandising, design, engineering or production. Popjob's page also offers details on the latest technological developments and applications in the field, along with profiles of merchandising professionals and departments at leading consumer product companies.

Regional Employment in the United States

Alaska

* Alaska Jobs Center
Website: http://www.ilovealaska.com/alaskajobs

The Alaska Job Center, job seekers resource page from the Alaska Department of Labor, is well equipped in providing the best resources to assist Alaskans seeking employment. The site's services include Alaska's economic indicators, relocation information and listings of government, seasonal employment, and volunteer positions. If you are seeking employment in Alaska, this site is a helpful tool.

Arizona

* Arizona Careers Online
Website: http://www.arizonajobs.com/

If you are seeking employment or relocation in the state of Arizona, check out this site. With diverse and up-to-date resources, ACO provides access to community, academic, and professional links, over 10,000 weekly updated position announcements, and comprehensive lists of job hotlines. Your resume is simply forwarded to employers and recruiters for no charge and you will be personally contacted if there are matches for your qualifications. What could be more convenient?

Arkansas

* Arkansas Careers Online
Website: http://www.arkansas.com/relocation/index.html

Arkansas Careers Online is the premier, cost free location for local employment information in Arkansas, dedicated to electronically linking employers to employees. As the site itself claims, it is" a valuable resource center for people seeking a wide range of information concerning employment, entrepreneurial, career and education related issues". For best results, you can execute a keyword search for a position of your choice or electronically post your resume to their database. Check it out □ you won't regret it.

Atlanta and the Southwest

* Atlanta's ComputerJobs Store
Website: http://www.computerjobs.com/

This is the premier site, updated and validated every day, for available high tech and computer related job openings in Atlanta and the Southwest. Designed to inform professionals seeking contracting, consulting, or permanent jobs, the ComputerJobs store offers a variety of available job opportunities, links to other job centers in the Southwest and Dallas area, a list of 100+ Atlanta computer firms, along with brief descriptions and information on high tech careers fairs in Atlanta and the Southwest. All you have to do to make your job search even more effective is enter your resume online and wait for recruiters to contact you when appropriate jobs become available. Through this site, you can also learn more about Atlanta's computer market and advance your career with training and certification.

Baltimore and Washington

* Global Commerce and Information
Website: http://www.globalci.com/

Global Commerce provides permanent and contracting employment information located in the Baltimore and Washington area. Updated weekly, this well maintained site seeks top individuals in a variety of technical areas, from client server to mainframe to multi platform environments, and aspires to help them find the jobs for which they are best suited.

California, Northern

* Opportunity NOCs
Website: http://www.tmcenter.org/

This weekly updated listing of paid positions in Northern California nonprofit agencies can be of help to everybody seeking employment in the area. The job opportunities range from entry level to executive positions and are categorized conveniently for your benefit. Most positions are located primarily in the SF Bay Area and Sacramento. If this is what you are looking for, your dream career could be only a click away.

California, Southern

* Job Search
Website: http://www.ventura.com/jsearch/jshome1.html

The so called "hidden job market" comes from successful, dynamic and growing companies that seldom publicize their job openings. In such a case, relying on help wanted ads, computer postings, agencies, recruiters, or even networking contacts gets you nowhere. There is hope, however, through Job Search. It is the aim of this site to help you get your foot in the door of the hidden job market. With exclusive databases of 40,000 companies and over 100,000 continually updated news stories that identify the "hidden job market" in Southern California, Job Search is a job seeker's dream. Through their services, you can target companies for potential employment, prepare job winning resumes and cover letters and even mail them to decision makers of companies of your choice so that you can be directly contacted by the company for an interview. In addition, Job Search's powerful search engine allows quick access to over 100,000 revealing and continually updated news stories and editorials regarding the job market in Southern California.

Colorado

* Colorado Online Job Connection
Website: http://www.peakweb.com/index.html

If you are ready for an office with a Rocky Mountain view, check out the current job openings through this site. The Colorado Online Job Connection is the best access to the Rocky Mountain region's job market, providing you with a listing of job openings, salary info and other useful resources that can help you locate a career in Colorado. In fact, you can even send them your resume and let their database search for the perfect job match for you.

District of Columbia (Washington, DC)

* CareerBuilder
Website: http://www.careerbuilder.com/

CareerBuilder allows you to search for jobs in a number of companies in the Washington, DC area. You can immediately launch your search by selecting from a variety of limitations including location, job category and salary, or register with a free personal search agent who will search the site each day and e-mail you new positions that meet your search criteria. Either way, CareerBuilder can be your path to a new successful career in Washington, DC.

Florida, Southern

* Career Spot, The
Website: http://www.careerspot.com/

If you live in Southern Florida or are planning to move there and are in need of employment, this is the site for you. The Career Spot, an easy to use job search database, provides current job listings, industry profiles and insightful articles that can assist you in executing a successful job search. Through their services, you can learn about top companies, search for a specific job or browse through all the available opportunities. This is a great place to begin the search that will lead to that perfect job.

Nebraska

* Omaha Career Link
Website: http://www.omaha.org/careerlink.html

If you are interested in employment in Nebraska, you need to look no further. The Cornhusker state needs workers, especially in the information technology, telecommunication and engineering sectors and the Omaha Career Link is your "one-stop shopping center for professional staff opportunities in Nebraska." Maintained by the Applied Information Management Institute, this site provides efficient career search facilities to match qualified professionals with available opportunities. You can explore the available job and internship positions, as well as search through company profiles and be on the way to the career of your dreams in Nebraska.

New England and New York

* ADEPT, Inc.
Website: http://www.adeptinc.com/

ADEPT, Inc. is an Information Services consulting firm located in Massachusetts with many openings in the New England and the New York area. It claims to be "the absolute choice in information technology consulting" and assists you by enabling you to submit your resume for employers to view and to view corporate job openings. If you're looking for a job in the field of information technology consulting, this site can offer excellent help.

New Jersey

* Workforce New Jersey Public Information Network
Website: http://www.wnjpin.state.nj.us/

Are you interested in being employed in New Jersey? If the answer is yes, check out this superb site. The goal of Workforce New Jersey Public Information Network is to enable workers, students and those seeking employment to access a rich variety of information including education, employment and training opportunities, labor market info, job search tools and social services. It certainly lives up to its promise, providing job listings, demographic and economic information about New Jersey and its counties and information about services available from the NJ Departments of Labor, Human Services and Commerce and Economic Development. What more do you need?

* NYWorks
Website: http://www.nyworks.com/

Through this fascinating web site, you can find information and links to nearly anything that concerns employment in the Big Apple. NYWorks can help you define your professional skills and help you search for customers, people or companies that will pay you for your product, service, or ability. In addition, it provides lists of available offers, links to job search and networking resources, a resume bank, tips and tactics of a successful job search as well as lists of alternative job opportunities in freelance, temp or telecommute. In short, this is everything you could ever ask for and more. Don't miss out!

North Carolina

* Charlotte's Web JobPage
Website: http://www.charweb.org/job/jobpage.html

This North Carolina based site features listings of available job opportunities, job banks, government agencies, educational institutions and nonprofit organizations in North and South Carolina. Charlotte's Web, a community network, also offers a link to a job hunters support group that may be of help to the frustrated career seeker.

Northwest United States

* JobsNorthwest
Website: http://www.jobsnorthwest.com/

Serving software companies, consulting firms, and MIS departments all over the northwestern United States, JobsNorthwest guarantees to match quality people with the quality positions they deserve. If you're a high tech specialist from the Northwest in need of a new job, check out this site for the job openings in your area of interest and you won't be disappointed.

Oregon

* Oregon Employment Department
Website: http://www.emp.state.or.us/

Are you seeking employment in Oregon? Check out this site maintained by the Oregon Employment Department. Their homepage features information concerning jobs available throughout Oregon, resources concerning quality child care, and lists of local entities that can provide you with the career information that you need. Research and labor market statistics along with recent news releases and fact sheets on the Oregon economy are also included. And if that weren't enough, the site also provides links to local unemployment insurance services and other employment related state agencies.

Seattle

* Seattle Employment Opportunities
Website: http://www.pan.ci.seattle.wa.us/

Are you seeking employment in the rainy city? Close your umbrella and look no further the Seattle Employment Opportunities website can offer you all the information you need. Whether you need to browse through current city jobs and internships or are inquiring about information regarding women's employment and employment related newsgroups, this site provides everything you need to find a great job.

Texas

* Texas Parks and Wildlife Department
Website: http://www.tpwd.state.tx.us/involved/jobvac/job.htm

This site is a statewide listing of jobs available at the Texas Parks and Wildlife Department. The job info is sorted conveniently into departments such as human resources, wildlife, fisheries, public lands, law enforcement, conservation communications and resource protection. If this is the field you've always wished to work in, there is no better place to begin your search for employment.

Vermont

* Vermont Department of Employment and Training
Website: http://www.det.state.vt.us

If you're seeking employment information about the State of Vermont, this site can really help you. The Vermont Department of Employment and Training provides ample info concerning Vermont's labor market, job listings for both full and part time employment, resumes, and the latest unemployment rates. If you're thinking about working in Vermont, this site can find you the job that you desire.

International Employment

Asia

* Daedal International
Website: http://www.ozemail.com.au/~daedal/
If you are an international student returning home to Asia and need a job, Daedal can help you locate a career in an easy and quick manner. They specialize in assisting overseas trained graduates just like you, and the employment offers can range from engineering to teaching located in a wide variety of countries from Thailand to Vietnam.

Australia

* The Age Classified Ads
Website: http://www.theage.com.au:80/class/
Interested in a career Down Under? This site brings you classified ads from The Age, the biggest daily newspaper in Melbourne, Australia. The Age Classified Ads, updated weekly, lists top jobs in information technology, higher education, health, and hospitals. Whether you wish to execute a specific job search or browse through all the ads, you can benefit from The Age.

* JOBNET Australia
Website: http://www.jobnet.com.au/index.html
If you are seeking employment in the field of computers and technology and would be interested in working in Australia or Asia, this site is a must to check out. JOBNET Australia, updated daily, enables you to browse through a list of current job vacancies that include skills specification and contact details, or use the JOBNet Daily Email service to receive announcements of suitable job opportunities directly in your e-mail box. This site claims to be the best source of IT employment opportunities in Australia and Asia.

Canada

* Resume Canada
Website: http://www.bconnex.net/~resume/
If you are seeking employment in Canada, Resume Canada can help you both post your resume and search through available career opportunities. This service is simple to use and free to the jobseeker.

Central America

* Green Arrow's Guide to Volunteer Work
Website: http://www.greenarrow.com/nature/work.htm
If you're looking for information on voluntary work, research opportunities and courses in tropical agriculture, forestry and sustainable development, this is the site for you. Green Arrow's Guide to Volunteer Work, the largest Central American website in the world, provides information on tourism and conservation to an international market of over 40 million and works closely with environmental organizations, universities and ecotourism projects which enable it to develop and maintain a comprehensive database of opportunities in the field. Their site offers access to a large database and can help applicants find jobs in the areas of ecotourism, forestry, conservation, tropical agriculture and others. It is well maintained, informative and fascinating – a definite must for any job seeker.

Japan

* O-Hayo Sensei, English Teaching Jobs in Japan
Website: http://www.wco.com/~ohayo/
Have you always wanted to teach English abroad but didn't know how to go about scoring a job overseas? Have you considered a teaching position in Japan? If so, O-Hayo Sensei can help you find suitable employment anywhere in Japan. Its extensive lists feature teaching positions at conversation and public schools, colleges and universities as well as survival tips, articles and information about contacting schools by phone or mail. This excellent site will also inform you in detail about the qualifications that will get you hired, current salaries, benefits, specific schools, housing, transportation, and contracts; help you search for jobs by city or region and network by mail, e-mail or fax. O-Hayo Sensei can save you time and money by allowing you to place your job search in their hands and helping you find the job that you really want.

New Zealand

* CV-Web
Website: http://www.stimulus.co.nz/
Has it always been your dream to be employed in New Zealand? This site may help make your dream come true. CV-Web is a New Zealand based job site through which you can write about yourself and your qualifications and submit it into the database or search for a suitable position from the classified ads. Either way, after checking out this site, you may be on your way to an exciting new career in New Zealand.

United Kingdom and Europe

* JobServe - The Job Server
Website: http://www.jobserve.com/
Updated every weekday, JobServe features thousands of contract and permanent vacancies from hundreds of IT recruitment agencies in the United Kingdom and Europe. If you specify your needs and skills, JobServe will send you information from the wide range of job openings that apply specifically to your needs. Their services are fast, reliable, friendly, and free, and aimed to help you find the career that you desire.

Matthew Lesko, Information USA, Inc., 12081 Nebel Street, Rockville, MD 20852 • 1-800-955-7693 • www.lesko.com

Help With Choosing a Career

Matthew Lesko, Information USA, Inc., 12081 Nebel Street, Rockville, MD 20852 • 1-800-955-7693 • www.lesko.com

Help With Choosing a Career

To assist you with some career choices and directions, the Federal government has published a variety of reference materials. You can purchase any of these documents through the U.S. Government Printing Office at Superintendent of Documents, U.S. Government Printing Office, Washington, DC 20402; 202-512-1800, or you can contact your library to see if they have these publications available.

U.S. Industrial Outlook: widely used resource features analyses of more than 350 U.S. industries and predictions of how they will perform in the short-term and through the 1990s. Industries discussed range from energy, to communications, to industrial materials, to health care. (s/n 003-009-00635-0; $37)

Occupational Outlook Handbook: easy-to-use, comprehensive, and fully illustrated encyclopedia of today's occupations and tomorrow's hiring trends. Use it to find detailed descriptions of more than 200 occupations, matching your skills and interests with a broad range of opportunities. The index is useful for answering questions about specific jobs. (s/n 029-001-03158-1; $32)

Dictionary of Occupational Titles: an essential resource for job placement research, employment counseling, occupational and career guidance, wage restructuring, and labor market information, this dictionary defines and indexes over 20,000 job titles. The current edition covers the professional, technical and managerial fields; clerical and sales; services; agriculture, fisheries; forestry and related areas; processing; machine trades; and more. (s/n 029-013-00094-2; $50)

Occupational Outlook Handbook CD-ROM: an ideal companion to the printed version with the added attraction of research capabilities and on-site demand printing. Describes in detail jobs in approximately 250 occupational categories, with summaries of additional occupations. (s/n 029-001-01393-9; $28)

Job Search Guide: Strategies for Professionals: An overview of important aspects of the job search. Subjects include handling job loss, managing personal resources, career self-assessment, researching the job market, conducting the job search, networking, resume preparation, and interviewing. Contains tips on employment testing and job protection, and includes listings of additional information sources and state employment service offices. (s/n 029-014-00247-0; $5.50)

Career Guide to Industries: Career counselors and job seekers can compare occupational opportunities across a spectrum of U.S. industries with this companion publication to the *Occupational Outlook Handbook*. Surveys occupations in more than 40 industries, from transportation and communications to health care and the computer and data processing fields. The text and tables describe the nature of each industry and detail employment, working conditions, occupations, training and advancement, earnings, benefits, and outlook. (s/n 029-001-03127-1; $14)

Government Resources

The Federal government spends a great deal of time examining the current labor market, projecting the future market, analyzing wage and benefit data and more. The following offices can answer your questions or direct you to bulletins and other publications for more information as you search for your ideal employment opportunity.

* Current Employment Analyses

Office of Employment and Unemployment Statistics
Bureau of Labor Statistics
U.S. Department of Labor
Postal Square Bldg.
2 Massachusetts Ave. NE
Washington, DC 20212   202-606-6378

Labor force statistics from the Current Population Survey provide a comprehensive body of information on the employment and unemployment experience of the nation's population, classified by age, sex, race, and a variety of other characteristics. The data is published in a variety of sources, including the monthly news release, *The Employment Situation*, and the monthly periodical, *Employment and Earnings*. Data uses include economic indicators, measure of potential labor supply, and evaluation of wage rates and earnings trends for specific demographic groups.

* Employment and Unemployment: Monthly Data and Estimates

Office of Employment and Unemployment Statistics
Bureau of Labor Statistics
Postal Square Bldg.
2 Massachusetts Ave. NE, Room 4675
Washington, DC 20212   202-606-6378

This office collects, analyzes, and publishes detailed industry data on employment, wages, hours, and earnings of workers on payrolls of non-agricultural business establishments. In addition, the office provides current data on occupational employment for more industries for economic analysis and for vocational guidance and education planning.

* Employment Projections: 650 Occupations and 300 Industries

Office of Economic Growth and Employment Projections
U.S. Department of Labor
Postal Square Bldg.
2 Massachusetts Ave. NW, Room 2135
Washington, DC 20212   202-606-5720

This office produces national occupational employment projections for over 650 detailed occupations for all industries combined, within more than 300 detailed industries.

* Employment Statistics for 800 Occupations and 400 Industries

Office of Employment and Unemployment
Bureau of Labor Statistics
U.S. Department of Labor
Postal Square Bldg.
2 Massachusetts Ave. NE
Washington, DC 20212   202-606-6515

Available occupational employment statistics include data on employment by occupation and industry for about 800 occupations and 400 industries. Published in bulletins, such as *Occupational Employment*, data are used for evaluation of current and historical employment by industry and occupation and vocational planning.

* Industry-Occupation Employment Matrix

Office of Economic Growth and Employment Projections
Bureau of Labor Statistics
U.S. Department of Labor
Postal Square Bldg.
2 Massachusetts Ave. NE
Washington, DC 20212   202-606-5730

The national Industry-Occupation Employment Matrix provides detailed information on the distribution of occupational employment by industry. Coverage is for over 650 detailed occupations--wage and salary, self-employed, and unpaid family workers, and wage and salary workers for over 300 detailed occupations.

* Wage Surveys: Area, Industry and White Collar Earnings

Office of Compensation and Working Conditions
Bureau of Labor Statistics
U.S. Department of Labor
Postal Square Bldg.
2 Massachusetts Ave. NE
Washington, DC 20210   202-606-6220

This office conducts three different types of wage surveys. The area and industry surveys provide annual data on averages and distributions of earnings for selected occupations in major industry groups in metropolitan areas. The white-collar salary survey is the annual Professional, Administrative, Technical, and Clerical Survey which is used in the federal pay setting process and provides data on salaries in white-collar occupations from a national sample of establishments.

* White-Collar Salaries

Benefit Levels Division
Office of Compensation Levels and Trends
Bureau of Labor Statistics
U.S. Department of Labor
Washington, DC 20210   202-606-6225

The annual white-collar salary survey provides data on salaries in white-collar occupations from a national sample of establishments. The data available includes averages and distributions of salary rates for about 50 blue collar and 100 professional, administrative, technical, and clerical work levels. The results are published in the annual news release, *White-Collar Salaries*, and the annual bulletin, *National Survey of Occupational Pay*.

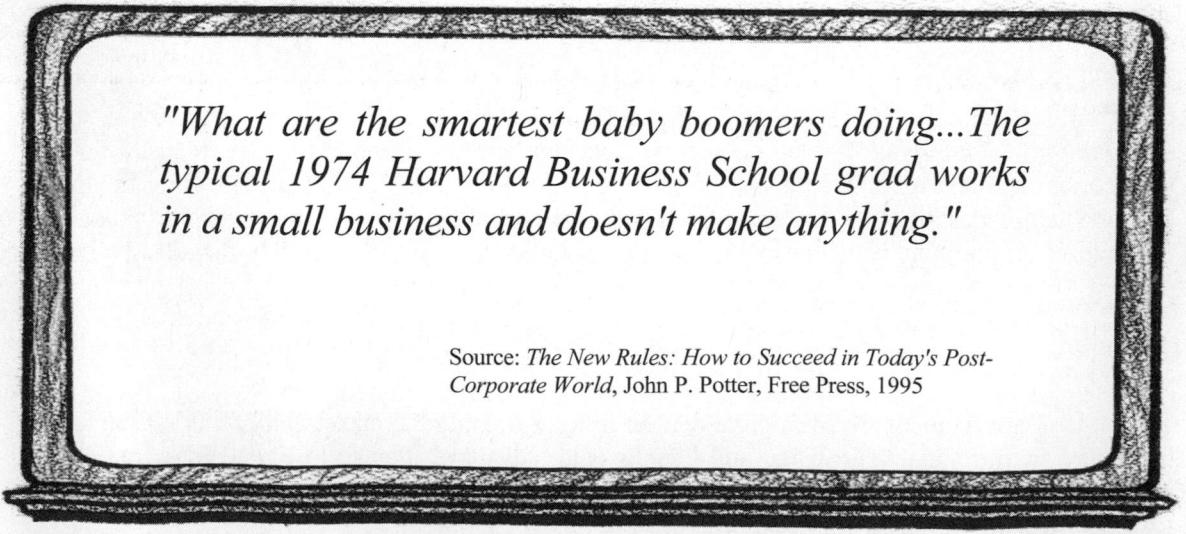

"What are the smartest baby boomers doing...The typical 1974 Harvard Business School grad works in a small business and doesn't make anything."

Source: *The New Rules: How to Succeed in Today's Post-Corporate World*, John P. Potter, Free Press, 1995

State Labor Offices

Want to know if teachers are going to be needed in your state in four years? What about nurses? Manicurists? Computer programmers? By contacting your state labor office, you can learn the answers to these questions and more. You can find out which counties offer the highest salaries, and have the fastest growing population of managerial positions. The primary function of each state labor information office is to collect data in conjunction with the Federal government in order to produce employment, unemployment, occupational, and wage information. In addition, each state compiles data showing future manpower needs within the state. By studying labor trends, economic conditions and school enrollments, these agencies can project the future supply and demand for up to 1,000 different occupations. Isn't that incredible? No need to spend four years worrying about whether you will find a job after you graduate from college. You can choose a profession that will have the greatest demand and amaze your friends and family with your ability to predict the future.

An important function of each of these offices is to provide career and job counseling information. If you are looking for a job, each office has access to a state database which identifies available job openings throughout the state. They project which jobs will be in demand in the next 10 to 20 years. Moreover, you can obtain the starting salaries and median wages for occupations. Many states give out free books designed for job seekers, as well as information on how to participate in training programs and vocational education opportunities.

Don't overlook the marketing and business information these offices can also provide. The data can cover both the consumer and industrial markets. You can find five to ten year projections of industries by city and county, how many hotels with fewer than 100 employees operate in a given city, what the fastest growing industries in any county are, and much more. Whether you are establishing a new plant, a real estate business, or a fast food franchise, these offices can help you find the best location with regard to labor availability, customer availability, and competition. You can even discover what wages are being paid by your competitors in the area for similar jobs.

You must remember that no two states operate in the same manner or generate identical data. Contact the state you live in, as well as other potential new locations to find out more about their predictions for the future.

Alabama

Department of Industrial Relations, Research and Statistics Division, 649 Monroe St., Room 427, Montgomery, AL 36130, 334-242-8855; {www2.dir.state.al.us/}; Selected Publications: *Monthly Labor Market, Annual Average Labor Force, Occupational Trends.* Computer Readable Formats; Custom Research: Limited amount available free.

Alaska

Department of Labor, Research and Analysis, P.O. Box 25501, Juneau, AK 99802-5501, 907-465-4500; {www.labor.state.ak.us/research}; Selected Publications: *Economic Trends, Akcens Quarterly Newsletter, Career Guide, Industry-Occupation Outlook to 1994, Micro-Computer Occupational Information System (Micro-OIS), Wage Rates, Occupational Injury and Illness Information, Population Overview, Special Demographic Reports, Directory of Licensed Occupations, Residency Analysis of Alaska's Workers by Firm, Employment Insurance, Actuarial Study and Financial Handbook, State Salary Survey.* Computer Readable Formats; Custom Research: Limited amount available free.

Arizona

Department of Economic Security West, Research Administration, 1789 West Jefferson, Site Code 733A, Phoenix, AZ 85005, 602-542-3871; {www.de.state.az.us/oscc/LMI.htm}; Selected Publications: *Arizona Economic Trends, Job Searchers Guide, Metro, Non-Metro Affirmative Action Planning Information, Applying for Government Jobs, Arizona Labor Market Newsletter, Arizona Occupational Employment Forecasts, Arizona Occupational Profiles, Employer Wage Survey, Helpful Hints for Job Seekers, Map of Major Employers.* Charge for special projects; all shelf publications are free.

Arkansas

Employment Security Department, Labor Market Information Section, P.O. Box 2981, Little Rock, AR 72203, 501-682-5227; {www.state.ar.us/esd/labormarketinformation.htm}; Selected Publications: *Annual Planning Information, Annual Report, Annual Report of the Employment Security Division, Arkansas Labor Force Statistics, Covered Employment and Earnings, Interface Supply and Demand, Statistical Review, Current Employment Developments, Monthly Employment Trends, Monthly County Labor Market Information, Directory of Licensed Occupations, Job Hunters Guide to AR, Occupational Trends, Staffing Patterns.* Computer Readable Formats: Occupational trends on disk; Custom Research: A limited amount is available free.

California

Employment Development Department, Labor Market Information Division, 7000 Franklin Blvd., #100, Sacramento, CA 95823, 916-262-2162; {www.calmis.cahwnet.gov}; Selected Publications: *Annual Planning Information, California Labor Market Bulletin, Labor Market Information for Affirmative Action Programs, Labor Market Conditions in California, California Occupational Guides, Projections of Employment By Industry and*

Occupation. Computer Readable Formats: Limited; Custom Research: Most everything is free.

Colorado

Department of Labor and Employment, Labor Market Information Section, 1515 Arapahoe Street, Tower II, Suite 300, Denver, CO 80202; 303-620-4856; {www.coworkforce.com/lmi}; Selected Publications: *Affirmative Action Packets, Annual Planning Information Report, Colorado Springs Labor Force, Employment and Wages Quarterly, Occupational Employment Outlook Projection, Job Bank Wage Listing, Occupational Employment in Selected Industries, Quarterly Occupational Supply/Demand Outlook, Pueblo Labor Force, Occupational Supply and Demand, Denver, Boulder, Front Range, Western Slope, Occupational Employment Survey Publishing, Employment Projections.* Computer Readable Formats: No; Custom Research: Free on a limited basis.

Connecticut

Department of Labor, Office of Research and Information, 200 Folly Brook Blvd, Wethersfield, CT 06109-1114, 860-263-6255; {www.ctdol.state.ct.us/lim/index.htm}; Selected Publications: *Annual Report of the Commission of the Labor in Economy Work Force and Training Needs in Connecticut, Planning for the Future Publishing, Work Place 2000, Labor Situation, Labor Force Data, Annual Planning Information, The Occupational Outlook, New Manufacturing Firms* ($7 per year fee), *Occupations in Demand, Labor Market Review, Occupational Projections and Training Data.* Computer Readable Formats; No: Custom Research: Free.

Delaware

Labor Department, Occupational and Labor Market Information Office, Occupational and Labor Market Information, Department of Labor, 4425 N. Market Street, P.O. Box 9965, Wilmington, DE 19809-0965; 302-761-8069; {http://www.oolmi.net/}; Selected Publications: *Delaware Annual Brief, Delaware Monthly Digest, Delaware Jobs to 2005* $7.50, *Delaware Career Compass, Career Guidance-High School Information on Job Growth, ES202 Series, Occupational Wage Data-Government and Educational Services* (three year cycle), *Delaware Labor Supply and Demand: Occupational and Industrial Projections.* Computer Readable Formats: Inquire requested; Custom Research: Limited amount available free.

District of Columbia

Department of Employment Services, Labor Market Information and Research Division, 77 P Street, NE, Room 3302, Washington, DC 20002; 202-671-1633; {http://does.ci.washington.dc.us/info/labor_mkt.shtm}; Selected Publications: *Area Labor Summary, Labor Market Information for Affirmative Action Programs, Directory of 200 Major Employers, Annual Population Estimates By Census Tract*; Computer Readable Formats: No; All shelf publications are free.

Florida

Department of Labor and Employment Security, Bureau of Labor Market Information, Suite 200, Hartman Building, 2012 Capital Circle, S.E., Tallahassee, FL 32399-0674, 904-488-6037; {http://www2.myflorida.com/les/}; Selected Publications: *Affirmative Action Statistical Packets, Florida Employment Statistics, Florida Industry and Occupational Employment 1995, Florida Occupational Employment in Hospitals, Labor Force Summary, Labor Market Trends, Occupational Employment in Federal Government, Occupations Employment in the Finance, Insurance and Real Estate Industry, Occupational Employment in the Services Industry, Occupational Wage Surveys.* Computer Readable Formats: Bulletin board system for direct downloading.

Georgia

Department of Labor, Labor Information Systems, 148 International Blvd., NE, Atlanta, GA 30303, 404-656-3177; {http://www.dol.state.ga.us/lmi/}; Selected Publications: *Area Labor Profiles, Civilian Labor Force Estimates, GA Employment and Earnings, GA Employment and Wages, GA Labor Market Trends, GA Occupational Employment, Civilian Labor Force Estimates, Data on Occupational Supply and Demand, Earnings by Industry and Area.* Computer Readable Formats: No; Custom Research: Charge for Large projects, all others free.

Hawaii

Labor Market and Employment Services Branch, Labor and Industrial Relations Dept., 830 Punchbowl St., Research Division, Honolulu, HI 96813, 808-586-8999; {http://www.state.hi.us/dlir/rs/loihi/}; Selected Publications: *Labor Shortages in Agriculture, Demand Occupations, Occupations in Communication Industry, Job Hunters's Guide, Selected Wage Information, Unemployment Insurance Fact Book, Licensed Occupations, Occupational Employment Statistics, Occupational Illness and Injuries, Wage Rate, Workers Compensation, Characteristics of the Insured Unemployed, Employment and Payrolls, Labor Area News, Labor Force Information for Affirmative Action Programs.* Computer Readable Formats: No; Custom Research: Free.

Idaho

Department of Employment, Research and Analysis Bureau, 317 Main St., Boise, ID 83735, 208-334-6169; {http://www.labor.state.id.us/lmi/id-lmi.htm#menu}; Selected Publications: *LMI Directory, Idaho Monthly Employment Newsletter, Labor Forces in Idaho, Basic Economic Data, Annual Demographics Report, Affirmative Action Statistics, Area Employment Newsletter, Employment and Wages by Industry in Idaho.* Most everything is free, Fee for larger projects.

Illinois

Employment Security Bureau, Research and Analysis, 401 South State St., Room 25, Chicago, IL 60605, 312-793-2316; {http://lmi.ides.state.il.us/}; Selected Publications: *Country Labor Force Summary-2000, Labor Market Review, Illinois at Work, Affirmative Action Information, Occupational Employment Statistics, Occupational Projections, Wage Survey, Where Workers Work, Illinois Employment Industrial Summary.* Computer Readable Formats: No; Custom Research: Nominal fee.

Indiana

Employment Security Division, Labor Market Information, 10 N. Senate Ave., Indianapolis, IN 46204, 317-233-5724; {http://www.in.gov/dwd/}; Selected Publications: *Annual County Employment Patterns, Indiana Employment Review, Labor Force Estimates, Quarterly Covered Employment and Payrolls, Regional Economic Profiles, Occupational Employment Projections, Occupational Wage Surveys, Occupations In Demand, Hours and Earnings of Production Workers.* Computer Readable Formats: No; All shelf publications are free.

Iowa

Department of Employment Services, Labor Market Information Unit, 1000 E. Grand Ave., Des Moines, IA 50319, 515-281-8182; {http://www.iowaworkforce.org/ris/lmi/index.html}; Selected Publications: *Condition of Employment Report/Analysis of the Iowa Market, Labor Market Information for Service Delivery Areas, State-Wide Wage Surveys, Labor Market Information for Affirmative Action Programs, Industry/Occupational Projections, Job Insurance Benefits, Iowa Occupational Planning Guide, Licensed Occupations, Labor Market Information Directory, Wages and Employment Covered by Employment Security, Affirmative Action Data for Iowa, Condition of Employment.* Computer Readable Formats: Electronic bulletin board; Custom Research: Free, nominal fee for larger projects.

Kansas

Department of Human Resources, Division of Employment and Training, Research and Analysis Section, 401 S.W. Topeka Blvd., Topeka, KS 66603, 913-296-5058; {http://laborstats.hr.state.ks.us/}; Selected Publications: *Occupational Staffing Patterns, Kansas Unemployment Insurance Claims, Monthly Labor Market Summary, Kansas Wage Survey, Affirmative Action Packet, Labor Market Review, Report on Employment-Hours and Earnings, Labor Force Estimates.* Computer Readable Formats: Limited; Custom Research: Charge for large projects, all others free.

Kentucky

Department for Employment Services, Research and Statistics, 275 E. Main St., CHR Bldg and Fl., Frankfort, KY 40621, 502-564-7976; {http://www.kycwd.org/des/lmi/lmi.htm}; Selected Publications: *Non-Agricultural Wage and Salary Employment, Kentucky Labor Market Newsletter, Estimate of Production Workers and Average Hours and Earnings, Labor Force Estimates, Occupational Outlook, Labor Area Summary, Labor Area Profile, Annual Planning Information, Affirmative Action, Labor Supply Estimates, Characteristics of Insured Unemployed, Average Covered Monthly Workers in Manufacturing by Industry Division and County, Total Wages by Industrial Division and County, Average Weekly Wages by Industrial Division and County.* Computer Readable Formats: No; Custom Research: Limited.

Louisiana

Department of Employment Security, Research and Statistics Unit, P.O. 94094, Baton Rouge, LA 70804-4094, 504-342-3141; {http://www.ldol.state.la.us/LMIQM.asp}; Selected Publications: *Occupational Projections-1999-2000, Quarterly Employment and Wages, Annual Employment and Wages, Monthly Labor Market Information, Manpower for Affirmative Action, Annual Planning Report, Occupational Employment Statistics, Average Weekly Wage, LA Occupational Injuries and Illnesses.* Computer Readable Formats: Limited; Custom Research: Limited amount available free.

Maine

Bureau of Employment Security, Division of Economic Analysis and Research, 20 Union St., Augusta, ME 04330-6826, 207-287-2271; {http://www.state.me.us/labor/lmis/frdef.htm}; Selected Publications: *Labor Market Digest Monthly, Maine Occupational Staffing Patterns in Hospitals-Government-Manufacturing/ Nonmanufacturing-Trade, Careers In Maine Woods.* Computer Readable Formats: Yes; Custom Research: Charge for larger projects, all others free.

Maryland

Department of Human Resources, Research and Analysis, Employment and Training, 1100 N. Eutaw St., Baltimore, MD 21201, 410-767-2250; {http://www.dllr.state.md.us/lmi/index.htm}; Selected Publications: *Affirmative Action Data, Maryland Occupational Industrial Outlook, Civilian Labor Force Employment and Unemployment by Place of Residence, Claims Processed for Unemployment Insurance Benefits, Occupations in Maryland, Current Employment Statistics, Employment and Payrolls Covered by the Unemployment Insurance Law of Maryland, Zoned Employment and Unemployment Statistics, Industries in Maryland, Highlights of Maryland's Population Projections, Maryland Rural Manpower Report, Occupational Wage Information, Year in Review, Population and Labor Force in Maryland, A Profile: Services Industry in Maryland 1980-Present.* Computer Readable Formats: No. Customer Research: Limited amount available free.

Massachusetts

Division of Employment Security, Massachusetts Employment and Training Center, 19 Stanford Street, Charles F. Hurley Building, Boston, MA 02114, 617-626-6556; {http://www.detma.org/lmi/lmi.htm}; Selected Publications: *Planning Data: Massachusetts, Employment and Wages, Massachusetts Employment Review* (monthly), *Careers and Training in Allied Health, Career Choices in a Changing Economy.* Computer Readable Formats: Limited amount available free; Publications free when available.

Michigan

Michigan Department of Career Development, 201 N. Washington Square, Victor Office Center, 7th Floor, Lansing, MI 48913; 517-241-0592, 866-MY-GOALS (694-6257); {http://www.michigan.gov/mdcd}; Selected Publications: *Affirmative Action Information Report, Annual Planning Information, Claims Counter, Covered Employment Statistics, Monthly Labor Market Review, Occupational Employment Statistics Survey Publications, Occupations in Education, Occupational Wage Information, Michigan Regulated and Trade Industries, Occupational Projections and Training Data, Occupational Projections and Training Information for Michigan-OPTIM, Civilian Labor Force, Employment and Unemployment Estimates, Employment Hours and Earnings Estimates, Unemployment Insurance Program Statistics, Employment Trends, Hours and Earnings Trends, Production Worker Employee Trends 1982 to Present.* Computer Readable Formats: Limited, electronic bulletin board; Custom Research: Limited amount available free.

Minnesota

Department of Jobs and Training, Research Office, 390 North Robert St., St. Paul MN 55101, 612-296-6546; {http://www.mnworkforcecenter.org/lmi/}; Selected Publications: *Consumer Price Index, Career Bulletin, Employment Outlook by Region, Minnesota Wage Data by Industry and Area, Minnesota Employment Outlook to 1996, Minnesota Careers, MN Wage Data By Industry and Size of Firm, Employment and Wage Data By County, Minnesota Labor Market Review.* Computer Readable Format: Some data available; Custom Research: Charge for large projects, all others free.

Mississippi

Employment Security Commission, Labor Market Information Department, P.O. Box 1699, Jackson, MS 39215-1699, 601-961-7424; {http://www.mesc.state.ms.us/lmi/}; Selected .PA Publications: *Guide to Labor Market Information, Annual Labor Force Averages, Annual Report, Employment and Job Openings 2005, Farm Income and Expenditures, Affirmative Action Programs, Monthly Labor Market Data, Labor Market Trends for Jackson Metro Area, Mississippi's Business Population, Occupational Employment and Job Openings by Unit of Analysis, Personal Income by Major Sources, Quarterly Labor Market Summary, Transfer Payments by Major Sources.* Computer Readable Formats: Yes, some publications available online; Customer Research: Limited amount available free.

Missouri

Division of Employment Security, Research and Analysis, P.O. Box 59, Jefferson City, MO 65104, 314-751-3595; {http://www.works.state.mo.us/lmi/index.html}; Selected Publications: *Monthly Area Labor Trends, Labor Market Information for Affirmative Action Programs, Wages Paid in Selected Occupations, Employment Outlook.* Custom Research: Limited research available.

Montana

Department of Labor and Industry, Research and Analysis Bureau, P.O. Box 1728, Helena, MT 59624, 406-444-2430; {http://rad.dli.state.mt.us/}; Selected Publications: *Wage Surveys of the Private Sector, Wage Surveys of the Public Sector, Wage Surveys of Public Education, Quarterly Employment and Labor Force, Monthly Statistics in Brief, Annual Planning Information.* Computer Readable Formats: Yes; Custom Research: Limited Amount available free.

Nebraska

Department of Labor, Labor Market Information, 550 South 16th St., Lincoln, NE 68509, 402-471-9964; {http://www.dol.state.ne.us/nwd/center.cfm?PRICAT=4&SUBCAT=4C}; Selected Publications: *Prairie/Farm and Ranch Profile, NE Labor Market Information Quarterly, Careers and Education in Nebraska, Monthly Labor Area Summary, Occupational Employment Statistics by Industry, Monthly Labor Force, Affirmative Action, Survey of Average Hourly Wage Rates, Occupational Newsletter.* Computer Readable Formats: Yes; Custom Research: Limited amount available for free.

Nevada

Employment Security Department, Employment Security Research Section, 500 E Third St., Carson City, NV 89713, 775-684-0450; {http://detr.state.nv.us/lmi/index.htm}; Selected Publications: *Area Labor Review, Directory of Labor Market Information, Quarterly and Monthly Economic Update, Nevada Wage Survey, Occupational Projections, Job Finding Techniques.* Computer Readable Formats: Yes; Custom Research: Limited amount available free.

New Hampshire

Employment Security Department, Economic Analysis and Reports and Labor Market Information Bureau, 32 South Main St., Concord, NH 03301, 603-228-4123; {http://www.nhes.state.nh.us/elmi/index.html}; Selected Publications: *Wage Survey, Vital Signs, Staffing Patterns in NH, Annual Report, Annual Planning Information, Annual Planning Information MSAs, Community Patterns NH, Economic Conditions, Employment and Wages by County, Employment and Wages MSAs, Employment and Wages by Planning Region, Fact Book: Cities and Towns, Firms By Size, Local Area Unemployment Statistics, NH Affirmative Action Data, NH Occupational Outlook 2005, Users Guide to Labor Market Information.* Computer Readable Formats: Yes; Custom Research: Free.

New Jersey

Labor Department, Labor Market Information Office, John Fitch Plaza CN 056, Trenton, NJ 08625, 609-292-2643; {http://www.wnjpin.state.nj.us/OneStopCareerCenter/LaborMarketInformation/lmilist.htm}; Selected Publications: *Regional Labor Market Reviews, Regional Labor Market Newsletters, Compendium of New Jersey Wage Surveys, Employment and Economy Newsletter, Employment Trends, Economic Indicators Monthly.* Computer Readable Formats: Limited electronic bulletin board usage; Custom Research: Limited amount available free.

New Mexico

Department of Employment Security, Economic Research and Analysis, P.O. Box 1928, Albuquerque, NM 87103, 505-841-8645; {http://www3.state.nm.us/dol/dol_lmif.html}; Selected Publications: *Covered Employment and Wages, Basic Concepts, Monthly Labor Market Review, Nonagricultural Wage and Salary Employment, Facts and Figures about New Mexico, Hours and Earnings Estimates, Albuquerque Small Employer Wage Survey, Area Job Market Flyers, Large Employers in New Mexico by County.* Computer Readable Formats: Limited; Customer Research: Limited amount available for free.

New York

Department of Labor, Division of Research and Statistics, State Office Bldg. Campus #12, Albany, NY 12240, 518-457-6369; {http://www.labor.state.ny.us/labor_market/labor_market_info.html}; Selected Publications: *Statistics on Operations, Occupational Outlooks, Civilian Labor Force by Occupation, Selected Demographic Groups, Regular and Extended Benefits, State Unemployment Insurance, Collective Bargaining Settlements, Directory of Labor Unions and Employee Organizations in New York State Employment Review, Current Population Survey Data, Earnings and Hours in Selected Industries, The Job Seeker, Labor Area Summary Monthly Statistical Report, Labor Area Summary Quarterly Analytical Report, Labor Market Assessment: Occupational Supply and Demand, Occupational Brief, Occupational Projections, Occupational Employment Statistics, Occupational Guide, Occupational Needs, Occupation Licensed or Certified by New York State, Operations, Resident Employment Status of the Civilian Labor Force, Careers Exploration and Job Seeking, Total and Civilian Labor Force Summary, Selected Demographic Groups - NYS, Counties and SMSAs, Selected Labor Research Reports, Apprentice Training Hours and Earnings, Insured Employment and Payrolls, Local Area Unemployment Statistics, Non-Agricultural Wage and Salary Employment, Unemployment Insurance Operating Statistics.* Custom Research: Charge for large projects, all others free.

North Carolina

Employment Security Commission, Labor Market Information Division, P.O. Box 25903, Raleigh, NC 27611, 919-733-2936; {http://www.ncesc.com/lmi/default.asp}; Selected Publications: *Employment and Wages in NC Quarterly, Market Areas Newsletter, Past High School Intentions of NC Graduates by*

County, Occupational Trends: Year 2000: NC, NC Metro State Planning Regions A-F; G-L; M-R, NC Preliminary Civilian Labor Force Estimates, Active Job Applicants by County, Registered Applicants and Job Openings, Follow-Up Survey of NC High School Graduates by County, Wage Rates in Selected Occupations. Computer Readable Formats: Yes; Custom Research: Free, charge for larger projects.

North Dakota

Job Service, Research and Statistics, P.O. Box 5507, Bismarck, ND 58506, 701-328-2868; {http://www.state.nd.us/jsnd/publications.htm?database=main}; Selected Publications: *Occupational Supply/Demand Report, Employment and Wages, Monthly Labor Market Advisor, Occupations Wage Surveys and Benefits for Major Cities, Employment Surveys by Major City, Annual Planning Report.* Computer Readable Formats: Yes; Custom Research: Charge for large amounts, all others free.

Ohio

Bureau of Employment Services, Labor Market Information Division, 145 South Front St., Columbus, OH 43216, 614-752-9494; {http://lmi.state.oh.us/}; Selected Publications: *Employment and Unemployment Estimates, Covered Employment and Payroll, Trend Tables, Monthly Labor Market Review, County Labor Force Reports, Labor Force Estimates, Metropolitan Profile, Occupational Projections, Composition of Job Placements, Summary of Ohio Worker Training Program Activities.* Computer Readable Formats: Yes; Custom Research: Charge for large projects, all others free.

Oklahoma

Oklahoma Labor Market Information, Economic Research & Analysis Division, Oklahoma Employment Security Commission, PO Box 52003, Oklahoma City, OK 73152-2003; 405-557-7261; {http://www.oesc.state.ok.us/lmi/default.htm}; Selected Publications: *Labor Market Information, Manpower Information for Affirmative Action, Annual Report to the Governor, Handbook of Employment Statistics, County Employment and Wage Data, Occupational Wage Surveys.* Computer Readable Formats: Yes; Custom Research: Charge for large projects, all other free.

Oregon

Employment Division, Research and Statistics, 875 Union NE, Salem, OR 97311, 503-378-8656; {http://www.emp.state.or.us/}; Selected Publications: *Oregon Work Force at Risk, Dislocated Workers, Oregon Works, Affirmative Action Programs, Agricultural Employment, Average Weekly Earnings-Hours, Business and Employment Outlook, Monthly Local Labor Trends, Occupational Program Planning System, Oregon Wage Information.* Computer Readable Formats: Yes; Custom Research: Charge for large projects, all others free.

Pennsylvania

Center for Workforce Information and Analysis, Department of Labor and Industry, Commonwealth of Pennsylvania, Harrisburg, PA 17121; 717-787-2114; Information Line: 1-877-4WF-DATA; {http://www.lmi.state.pa.us/}, Selected Publications: *Civilian Work Force Data by Labor Market Area of Residence, Annual Average Labor Force Data, Civilian Labor Force Series by Labor Market Area, PA Labor Market Areas Ranked on Basis of Rate of Unemployment, PA Unemployment Fact Sheet, Occupational Wage Surveys, Employment and Wages of Workers Covered by the PA Unemployment Compensation Law, Occupations Employment in Hospital Occupational Staffing Patterns for Selected Non-Manufacturing Industries, Affirmative Action Report, Labor Market Job Guides, Current Trends in Employment and Wages in PA Industries, PA Labor Force, Annual Planning Information Report, Hours and Earnings in Manufacturing and Selected Non-manufacturing Industries.* Computer Readable Formats: Yes; Custom Research: Charge for large projects, all others free.

Rhode Island

Department of Employment Security, Research and Statistics, 107 Friendship St., Providence, RI 02903, 401-462-8766; {http://www.det.state.ri.us/webdev/lmi/lmihome.html}; Selected Publications: *Occupational Projections 2000, Characteristics of Insured Unemployed, RI Employment Newsletter, Quarterly Labor Supply and Demand Report, Employment and Wages by City and Industry, Annual Planning Information, Manpower Information for Affirmative Action Programs, Employment In RI Hospitals.* Computer Readable Format: Yes; Custom Research: Free.

South Carolina

Employment Security Commission, Labor Market Information Division, P.O. Box 995, Columbia, SC 29202, 803-737-2660; {http://www.sces.org/lmi/}; Selected Publications: *Industrial Monographs, Wage Survey, Labor Market Review, Employment Trends, Occupational Projections 2005, Labor Force in Industry, Covered Employment and Wages in SC.* Computer Readable Formats: Limited; Custom Research: Charge for large projects, all others free.

South Dakota

Department of Labor, Labor Market Information Center, P.O. Box 4730, Aberdeen, SD 57402-4730, 605-626-2314; {http://www.state.sd.us/dol/lmic/}; Selected Publications: *Labor Availability Studies, Labor Bulletin, Occupational Wage Information, Occupational Outlook Handbook, Employment and Earnings, Affirmative Action Package, Statewide Job Listings.* Computer Readable Formats: Yes; Custom Research: Limited amount available free.

Tennessee

Department of Employment Security, Research and Statistics Division, 11th Floor, James Robertson Parkway, Nashville, TN 37245-1040, 615-741-2284; {http://www.state.tn.us/labor-wfd/}; Selected Publications: *Occupational Wage and Benefit Information, Minorities in Tennessee, Occupations in Demand, Licensed Occupations in Tennessee, Monthly Available Labor, Monthly Labor Force Summary, Commuting Patterns, Tennessee Employment Projections 2005, Tennessee Youth Report, Veterans in Tennessee, Women in the Labor Force, Tennessee High School Graduates.* Computer Readable Formats: Yes; Custom Research: Limited amount available free.

Texas

Texas Employment Commission, Economic Research and Analysis Dept., 101 E. 15th St., Room 208-T, TEC Building, Austin, TX 78778, 512-463-2616; {http://www. twc.state.tx.us/customers/rpm/rpmsub3.html}; Selected Publications: *Labor Force Estimates, Current Population Survey, Nonagricultural Wage and Salary Employment Estimates, Average Hours and Earnings Data, Employment and Wages by Industry and County, Affirmative Action Packets, Characteristics of the Insured Unemployed, Regional Reports, Occupational Employment Statistics.* Computer Readable Formats: Yes; Custom Research: Charge for large projects, all others free.

Utah

Utah Department of Employment Security, Labor Market Information Services, P.O. Box 45249, Salt Lake City, UT 84145, 801-526-9675; {http://jobs.utah.gov/}; Selected Publications: *Annual Labor Market Report, Licensed Occupations in Utah, Utah Directory of Business and Industry.* Computer Readable Formats: Yes. Custom Research: Free.

Vermont

Department of Employment and Training, Labor Market Information, P.O. Box 488, Montpelier, VT 05601, 802-828-4202; {http://www.det.state.vt.us/}; Selected Publications: *Occupation, Wage and Employment Survey, Job Openings, Affirmative Action Planning Data, Annual Planning Information, Combined Annual Report of DET and JTPA, Directory of Labor Market Information Employment and Earnings, Labor Market Area Bulletins, Vermont Labor Market, Employment and Wages Covered by Unemployment Insurance, Licensed Occupations in Vermont Mining and Quarrying, Construction, Unemployment Compensation Statistical Table, Vermont Economic and Demographic Profile Series.* Computer Readable Formats: Yes; Custom Research: Upon request, limited time available.

Virginia

Economic Information Service, Employment Commission, 703 E. Main Street, Richmond, VA 23219; 804-786-7496; {http://www.vec.state.va.us/index.cfm?loc=lbrmkt&info=lmi; Selected Publications: *Guide to Establishing a Business, LMI Directory, Business Registration Guide, Work Force 2000, Labor Force by Sex and Minority Status, Commuting Patterns, Data on Public Schools, Economic Assumptions for the U.S. and VA, Economically Disadvantaged Data, Employment and Training Indicators, Employment and Wages in Establishments, Employment and Wages in VA, Monthly Labor Market Review, Wage Survey Selected Manufacturers Occupation, Licensed Occupations in VA, List of Employers By Size, State and County Veteran Population, Trends in Employment-Hours and Earnings, Quarterly Virginia Economic Indicators, Virginia Business Resource Directory.* Computer Readable Formats: ALICE (Virginia based only); Custom Research: Limited for nominal fee.

Washington

Employment Security Group, Labor Market and Economic Analysis Branch, 605 Woodland Square Loop S.E., Lacey, WA 98503, mailing address P.O. Box 9046, Olympia, WA 98507-9046, 206-438-4804; [http://www.wa.gov/esd/lmea/}; Selected Publications: *Washington Labor Market, LMI Review, Annual Demographic Information, Area Wage Survey, Employment and Payrolls in Washington, Occupational Profiles and Projections.* Computer Readable Formats: Some; Custom Research: Large projects are charged on a contract basis.

West Virginia

Employment Security Department, Labor and Economic Research, 112 California Ave., Charleston, WV 25305, 304-558-2660; {http://www.state.wv.us/bep/lmi/}; Selected Publications: *Affirmative Action, West Virginia Women in* the Labor Force, Annual Planning Information, Metropolitan Statistical Areas Annual Planning Information, Job Training Partnership Act, West Virginia County Profiles, WV Economic Summary, Employment and Earnings Trends, Insured Workers Summary, Occupational Projections, Veterans Report, Wage Survey, Directory of Publications, Licensed Occupations in West Virginia. Computer Readable Formats: Yes; Custom Research: Limited amount available free.

Wisconsin

Department of Industry, Labor and Human Relations, Employment and Training Library, P.O. Box 7944, Madison, WI 53707, 608-266-5843; {http://www.dwd.state.wi.us/lmi/}; Selected Publications: *LMI: A Reference Guide of WI Publications, Labor Market Planning Information, Taxes Due Covered by Wisconsin U.C. Law, Affirmative Action Data, Career Connection, Monthly Wisconsin Economic Indicators, Civilian Labor Force Estimates, Consumer Price Index, Employment and Wages, Wage Survey, Covered Employment By Size of Industry and County, Wisconsin Employment Picture, Wisconsin Works, Inform Bi-Monthly*. Computer Readable Formats: Some; Custom Research: Charge for large projects.

Wyoming

Employment Security Commission, Research and Analysis, P.O. Box 2760, Casper, WY 82602, 307-473-3801; {http://lmi.state.wy.us/}; Selected Publications: *Manufacturing and Hospitals, Wyoming's Annual Planning Report, Wyoming's Covered Employment and Wage Data, Labor Force Trends, Affirmative Action Package*. Computer Readable Format: yes; Custom Research: Limited amount available.

Matthew Lesko, Information USA, Inc., 12081 Nebel Street, Rockville, MD 20852 • 1-800-955-7693 • www.lesko.com

How Do I
Check Out a Move?

Matthew Lesko, Information USA, Inc., 12081 Nebel Street, Rockville, MD 20852 • 1-800-955-7693 • www.lesko.com

How Do I Check Out A Move?

Finding a new home can be a nightmare anytime. But what if you don't know the first thing about the area where you are relocating? A bank account and the local real estate ads aren't enough anymore to make the right decisions on a move. You need help. Uncle Sam has sympathy for those who have learned to hate cardboard boxes and unreal-estate agents.

When you move to a new town, there are things you should know before you settle on your dream house. Are some neighborhoods safer than others? What about the schools? Are they as good or better than the schools your children now attend? Are they asking too much for a house in this area? What about the mortgage options? Know the score for yourself. Don't depend on the real estate agent interested in seeing her commission for telling you everything.

A house selling in Washington, DC for $125,000 would only go for $62,000 in Columbus, Ohio. Know the value of homes in your potential city, so you don't pay an arm and a leg for something not worth a foot. There are many government resources to help you on your way to a successful move.

Here are some best kept secrets to make any transition easier:

* Moving Expenses As A Tax Deduction

Contact Your Local IRS Office

or

IRS Forms Line   800-829-3676
www.irs.ustreas.gov

You can write off many moving expenses if certain conditions are met. You can even deduct expenses of moving back to the United States if you retire while living and working overseas. Just call the IRS and ask for Publication 521, *Moving Expenses*, which outlines expenses you can and cannot deduct, explains what happens when your company pays for part of the move, details issues such as gas, food, and lodging during the move, and more. You can also download this publication from the web.

* Get Your Moving Expenses Paid

Employment Training Administration
U.S. Department of Labor
Office of Worker Retraining and Adjustment Programs
200 Constitution Ave., NW, Room N-5426
Washington, DC 20210   202-219-5577
www.doleta.gov/programs/factsht/edwaa.htm

If you have been laid off from work and are not likely to return to the same employer, you may be considered a dislocated worker. Dislocated workers are those who have been laid off from a job due to factory downsizing, reorganization, trade issues, military downsizing, and more. There are many services available to dislocated workers through the Title III Program which provides for retraining and readjustment assistance for dislocated workers. In many cases, funds are available to assist the dislocated worker in moving to a new location where the worker has a job offer. To become eligible for these services, you must contact your local State Employment Services office, your state's Dislocated Worker Unit, or the Job Training Partnership Act office (look in the blue pages of your phone book). Each local office has funds that they can disperse for a variety of services to the worker, including training, child care, job search services, and education.

* Eliminate High Crime Cities

Criminal Justice Inf. Service Division
Federal Bureau of Investigation
935 Pennsylvania Ave., NW
Washington, DC 20535-0001   202-324-3000
www.fbi.gov/ucr/ucr.htm

To find a safe little hamlet to raise Junior, you better do some research before you move. *Crime In The U.S.*, the Federal Bureau of Investigation's (FBI) annual report of violent and property crime, contains statistics for many towns with over 10,000 people, and can provide you with information such as the number of murders, robberies, assaults, burglaries, auto thefts, and more, but they do not rank cities. Many libraries carry this publication, or you can call the FBI for information on your city.

* When Weather's Important

National Climatic Data Center
National Oceanic and Atmospheric Administration
Federal Bldg.
151 Patton Ave., #120   828-271-4800
Asheville, NC 28801-5001   Fax: 282-271-4876
www.ncdc.noaa.gov/nedc.html

Weatherheads can take the chill out of moving by contacting Uncle Sam's Climatic Data Center, which can help you move to a sunny location through their book, *Comparative Climate Data* ($5, free online), covering weather data for 270 major locations. Pick a city and find out if it's warmer, colder, sunnier, or snowier than other cities.

* Move To A City With Lots Of Single Men

Marriage and Family Statistics Branch
Population Division
Bureau of the Census
Bldg. 3, Room 2353
Washington, DC 20233   301-457-2465
www.census.gov/population/www/

You can check out the singles scene anywhere in the country by contacting the Bureau of the Census. They keep some interesting figures regarding the population, such as the ratio of total number of single men to single women in metro areas. Give them a call to find out what areas of the country will improve your chances of finding that special someone...if that's what you're interested in.

* A Library Of Information

Your local library

Check the blue pages of your telephone directory.

A wonderful resource for information about a town is its local library. Library workers, familiar with the area can answer questions such as the population change of the town over time, how the city operates, the city budget, and demographics. The library can also provide information on the history of a town, city parks and recreation facilities, school board information, community resources, and even election results. You can locate the local library by looking in the blue pages of the town's telephone directory, or take a look at nearly 700 public libraries online at <www.yahoo.com/reference/libraries/public_libraries/>.

* Check Out The Town Business Scene

Your local Chamber of Commerce

Check the blue pages of your telephone directory.

Local Chambers of Commerce can provide you with a wealth of information regarding a new town. They usually offer a map of the town, parks and recreation directories, walking tours, information about the type of government and the town's annual report, along with information on schools, real estate, and industry. You can also look through the Chamber's membership directory to see the types of industry located in the town to get a sense of the business climate. You can locate the Chamber of Commerce by looking in the blue pages of the local phone directory, or by contacting the city hall. To look for chambers on the web, try <www.worldchambers.com/ >.

* Salaries, Unemployment, And The Job Market

Office of Publications
Bureau of Labor Statistics
U.S. Department of Labor
2 Massachusetts Ave., NE, Room 2863
Washington, DC 20212   202-691-5200
www.bls.gov/

If you are looking for an overview of labor information, then the Bureau of Labor Statistics (BLS) is for you. The Bureau collects, processes, analyzes, and disseminates data relating to employment, unemployment, and other characteristics of the labor force; wages, other worker compensation; economic growth and employment projections; and more. BLS can refer you to experts within the Bureau who can answer your specific questions, provide you with historical information, and refer you to tables and charts for data. They can answer questions such as:
- What is the employment statistics and the outlook for a particular occupation?
- What is the unemployment rate for a state?
- What is the current wage for a word processor in Seattle, and what are the average benefits likely to be?
- What is the employment projection for a specific job?

* Highway Looking Like A Parking Lot?

Office of Highway Information Management
Federal Highway Administration
U.S. Department of Transportation
400 7th St., SW
Washington, DC 20590   202-366-0650
www.fhwa.dot.gov/ohim/

Want to know how many people own cars in your state? What about fatal and injury accident rates for the Nation's highways? Want to know the number of licensed women drivers or the ratio of licensed drivers to the population? What about highway finance or highway usage? An extensive list of publications is maintained by the Office of Highway Information Management. For information about your state or for ordering information, contact the office listed above.

* Don't Get Washed Out In A Flood

Federal Emergency Management Agency
500 C St., SW
Washington, DC 20472   202-646-4600
www.fema.gov/

Know the law of the land before you sign on the dotted line. The Federal Emergency Management Agency publishes the *Flood Boundary Way Map* which shows the flood-prone areas within the community. Each map accompanies a study which shows directions in which flooding may occur. To obtain this map for your area of interest, call 1-800-358-9616. The *Flood Insurance Manual* has many useful sections for homeowners, including "How To Read A Flood Insurance Rate Map," which is a guide to help identify and understand key features of the Flood Insurance Rate Map. For this free publication, call 1-800-FEMA-MAP.

* Flood Insurance Made Simple

National Flood Insurance Program
451 Hungerford Dr.
Rockford, MD 20850   800-611-6125
www.fema.gov/diz98/98059.htm

Some victims of the recent flood were covered under the government's National Flood Insurance Program (NFIP), but many were not. To find out if you qualify, get the free brochure, *Answers to Questions About The National Flood Insurance Program* which explains NFIP, and the type of assistance it provides. For information on rules, regulations, claims, and publications, contact National Flood Insurance Program at 800-480-2520.

* How Not To Buy Swamp Land In Florida

Interstate Land Sales
Registration Division
U.S. Department of Housing and Urban Development (HUD)
451 7th St., SW, Room 9160
Washington, DC 20410   202-708-1112
www.hud.gov/fha/ils/ilshome.html

Thinking about buying lakefront property in Arizona or a condo on a golf course in Florida? Before you send a dime to a land developer in another state, find out before you buy what your rights are from the following free publications: *Buying Lots from Developers* and *Before Buying Land....Get The Facts*. There are several things a developer must do before a lot can be sold or leased. They must file a Statement of Record with the U.S. Department of Housing and Urban Development (HUD), containing full and current disclosure about ownership and more, and a printed Property Report must be delivered to each purchaser or lessee in advance of signing the contract or agreement.

* Make Sure Your Kid Learns The 3 R's

ERIC Clearinghouse on Elementary and Early Childhood Education
University of Illinois at Urbana-Champaign
Children's Research Center
51 Gerty Drive   217-333-1386
Champaign, IL 61820-7469   Voice/TTY: 800-583-4135
http://ericeece.org or http://npin.org

How do you choose the best schools for your child? What role do grandparents have in education today? Should you delay starting kindergarten if your child has a summer birthday? How do you motivate your middle school student? The ERIC Clearinghouse on Elementary and Early Childhood Education and the National Parent Information Network both are wonderful resources for all kinds of education questions. You can find the answers to these questions and many more at the websites.

* Rural Housing Help

Administrator
Rural Housing Service
U.S. Department of Agriculture
14th and Independence Ave., Room 5037
Washington, DC 20250   202-720+-4323
www.rurdev.usda.gov.rhs/index.html

For those who live or are considering moving to a rural area, the Rural Housing Service offers a variety of housing assistance. Direct loans are available to assist lower-income rural families obtain decent, safe homes, loan guarantees, home repair loans and grants, and rural rental assistance payments to name only a few of the programs. Contact the office listed above for more information.

* Housing Finance Statistics

Program Evaluation Division
Mortgage Survey Information Center
Assistant Secretary for Housing
U.S. Department of Housing and Urban Development (HUD)
451 7th St., SW
Washington, DC 20410   202-755-7470, ext. 145
www.hud.gov/

Monthly reports are compiled by the Program Evaluation Division of the U.S. Department of Housing and Urban Development (HUD) in areas relating to the mortgage market, securities, taxation, market trends, interest rates, among others. You can receive a free survey of mortgage lending activity and a survey of FHA and conventional mortgage rates. If you are interested in receiving information about these subjects or want to be placed on the mailing list, contact this office.

* How Much Did A House Sell For?

County Recorder of Deeds
Check the blue pages of your telephone directory.

If you know when the current owner bought the house and how much they paid, you will be a better prepared negotiator. All this information is available at the county Recorder of Deeds. Other information available includes the legal description of the property located at the address, and the bank or company who financed the purchase. Also available at the county level is information on the property's assessed value, which is different from the appraised value, and the amount of taxes charged for the property. To locate the County Recorder of Deeds, look in the blue pages of the local telephone directory.

* What's The Housing Market Like?

HUD USER
P.O. Box 6091   800-245-2691
Rockville, MD 20850   301-251-5154 (DC metro area)
www.huduser.org/

If you are planning on moving, it might be helpful to know some general information about the housing situation of a prospective area. The U.S. Department of Housing and Urban Development (HUD) and the Bureau of the Census have released the results of the American Housing Survey for the

United States in 2000, the largest and most detailed survey of the Nation's housing stock. It provides information on national or regional housing conditions, markets, or policies. It presents detailed data on the characteristics of occupied and vacant housing units, including size, structural condition, housing costs and values, and indicators of neighborhood quality. It also provides basic demographic data on the age, sex, race, income, and mobility of householders. In addition to the Survey available for $5, results from 11 metropolitan areas have also been released ($5 each). Contact HUD USER for more information.

* Veterans Home Ownership

Veterans Assistance Office
Department of Veterans Affairs
810 Vermont Ave., NW
Washington, DC 20420   800-827-1000
www.va.gov/

If you are a veteran or an unmarried surviving spouse, you can obtain VA-guaranteed loans for the purchase and refinancing of homes, condominiums and manufactured homes. You can usually do so without a down payment (except for manufactured homes). For eligibility and more information on VA loan guaranties, contact your regional VA office. The following publications are available to veterans:

Pointers for the Veteran Homeowner - a guide for veterans whose home mortgage is guaranteed or insured under the GI Bill. (26-5)
To the Home-Buying Veteran - a guide for veterans planning to buy or build homes with a VA loan. (26-6)
VA-Guaranteed Home Loans for Veterans - helps you understand what the VA can and cannot do for the home purchaser. (26-4)
VA Direct Home Loans for Native Americans Living on Trust Lands. (27-93-1)
Veterans Benefits for Older Americans. (27-80-2)

* Counseling for Homebuyers, Homeowners, and Tenants

National Servicing Center
U.S. Department of Housing and Urban Development
500 W. Main St., Suite 400
Oklahoma City, OK 73102   888-297-8685
www.hud.gov/offices/hsg/sth/hcc/hccprof14.cfm

To help reduce delinquencies, defaults, and foreclosures, the U.S. Department of Housing and Urban Development (HUD) provides free counseling to homeowners and tenants under its programs through HUD-approved counseling agencies. The counselors advise and assist homeowners with budgeting, money management, and buying and maintaining their homes. This is not just for HUD homes, but for all home buyers and owners. The amount of service available does vary for each counseling agency. Contact this office or your local HUD office of information for the counseling agency nearest you.

* Housing Discrimination

Fair Housing Enforcement Division
Office of Fair Housing and Equal Opportunity
U.S. Department of Housing and Urban Development
Washington, DC 20410-2000   800-669-9777
www.hud.gov/offices/fheo/index.cfm

The U.S. Department of Housing and Urban Development (HUD) administers the law that prohibits discrimination in housing on the basis of race, color, religion, sex, and national origin; investigates complaints of housing discrimination; and attempts to resolve them through conciliation. Two common forms of discrimination are redlining and steering. Redlining is the illegal practice of refusing to originate mortgage loans in certain neighborhoods on the basis of race or ethnic origin. Steering is the illegal act of limiting the housing shown by a real estate agent to a certain ethnic group. If you have experienced housing discrimination, you should file a complaint with any HUD office in person, by mail, or by telephone at the numbers listed here. HUD refers complaints to state and local fair housing agencies. To receive a copy of the free publication *Fair Housing Act Regulations*, contact the Housing Discrimination Hotline at 1-800-669-9777.

* Mortgage Manuals

Federal Trade Commission
6th and Pennsylvania Ave., NW
Washington, DC 20580   202-326-2222
www.ftc.gov   877-FTC-HELP

There are tons of houses out there begging for your attention, but getting your foot in the door shouldn't cost you an arm and a leg. Before you carry your cash across the threshold, check out the latest on mortgages, real estate brokers, and home financing through publications available at the Federal Trade Commission. Some of the titles include:

Getting a Loan: Your Home as Security
Home Equity Credit Lines
Home Equity Scams: Borrowers Beware!
Home Financing Primer
Lawn Service Contracts
Mortgage Discrimination
Mortgage Servicing
Refinancing Your Home
Reverse Mortgages
Second Mortgage Financing
Timeshare Resales
Timeshare Tips
Using Ads to Shop for Home Financing

Crime In Your Neighborhood

The crime rate for a neighborhood can be a whole lot different than the rate for the entire city. You don't want to put your kid in a day care center near an outdoor drug market or buy a fast food franchise in an area where the crime rate is ten times the national average. Real estate agents can brag all they want about how a certain area has a low crime rate, but if you want the facts and not the opinion of a biased salesperson, you have to get local crime statistics. Your State Crime Statistics Office collects information or can tell you where to locate information like:

- The rate of auto thefts in your town
- The rate of robberies in your town
- Crime and arrest data by county

Before drawing conclusions from state crime data, a number of factors should be considered, including strength of local police departments, economic profile of the town, and attitudes of residents toward police and crime. Most states have publications that report crime and can produce computer printouts of specific topics.

State Crime Statistics

Alabama
Criminal Justice Information Center
770 Washington Ave., Suite 350
Montgomery, AL 36130-0660   334-242-4900
http://acjic.state.al.us/alacrime.htm
This division publishes the *Crime in Alabama Annual Report*. Computer printouts of selected data are provided if the information is readily available. Special statistical analysis of data not found in the annual report is also provided. There is no cost for these services.

Alaska
Department of Public Safety
Information Systems
Uniform Crime Reporting Section
5700 E. Tudor Rd.
Anchorage, AK 99507   907-465-4322
www.dps.state.ak.us/
The *Crime in Alaska Annual Report* is free. Computer printouts are not provided at this time.

Arizona
Department of Public Safety
Uniform Crime Reporting Section
P.O. Box 6638
Phoenix, AZ 85005   602-223-2000
www.dps.state.az.us/
The department publishes the *Arizona Uniform Crime Annual Report*. Computer printouts of selected data are provided at no charge.

Arkansas
Crime Information Center
Uniform Crime Reporting Section
1 Capitol Mall, Room 4D 200
Little Rock, AR 72201   501-682-2222
www.acic.org/statistics/stats.htm
The Crime Information Center publishes an annual report on crime rates in Arkansas. Call or write for a free copy.

California
Department of Justice
Law Enforcement Information Center
Box 944255
Sacramento, CA 94244-2550   916-302-3360
http://caag.state.ca.us/cjsc/
Publications include the *Crime and Delinquency in California Report* and *Annual Criminal Justice Profile*, which are free upon request. Other publications, customized statistical reports, and statistical information on California are also available.

Colorado
Department of Public Safety
Division of Criminal Justice
700 Kipling St., Suite 1000
Denver, CO 80215   303-239-4442
www.state.co.us/gov_dir/edps/dcj/dcj.htm
Publications include *Community Corrections Annual Report*. The office does not provide crime statistics printouts upon request.

Connecticut
Department of Public Safety
Department of State Police
Uniform Crime Reporting Program
Crimes Analysis Division
P.O. Box 2794
Middletown, CT 06457-9294   860-685-8030
www.state.ct.us/dps/
Publications include the *Annual Uniform Crime Report*, *Crime in Connecticut Quarterly Report*, and the *Family Violence Report*.

Delaware
Delaware State Police
State Bureau of Identification
Statistical Services
P.O. Box 430
Dover, DE 19903-0430   302-739-5900
www.state.de.us/dsp/
This bureau publishes the *Crime in Delaware Annual Report*. Selected data runs are also available. Fees vary according to the complexity of the request.

District of Columbia
Metropolitan Police Department
Planning and Research Section (CRAS)
300 Indiana Ave., NW, Room 3125
Washington, DC 20001   202-724-4100
http://mpdc.dc.gov/info/districts/crstats.shtm
Computer printouts of selected data are provided with a Freedom of Information request. Information can be faxed right to you or mailed.

Florida
Department of Law Enforcement
Uniform Crime Reporting Section
Attn: FDL/FSAC
P.O. Box 1489
Tallahassee, FL 32302   850-410-7140
www.fdle.state.fl.us/index.html
This department publishes a four-page summary pamphlet of Florida crime statistics which is available at no cost. Computer printouts of selected data are

available at no charge. Information that was included in previous annual reports is also available upon request.

Georgia
Georgia Bureau of Investigation
Georgia Crime Information Center
P.O. Box 370748
Decatur, GA 30037-0748   404-244-2840
www.ganet.org/gbi/
The Crime Information Center publishes an annual four-page summary of the *Georgia Criminal Justice Data Report*. Computer printouts of selected data are also provided upon request, generally at no cost.

Hawaii
Department of the Attorney General
Statistical Analysis Center
235 S. Beretania St., Suite 401
Honolulu, HI 96813   808-586-1150
www.cpja.ag.state.hi.us/rs/
A *Crime in Hawaii Annual Report* is published. Computer printouts of selected data are available depending upon the complexity of the request.

Idaho
Criminal Identification Bureau
P.O. Box 700
Meridian, ID 83680-0700   208-884-7000
www.isp.state.id.us/
The Crime Identification Bureau publishes an annual *Uniform Crime Reporting Program Report*. Computer printouts of selected data are provided free upon request. Some information is available on diskette or magnetic tape if you supply your own software.

Illinois
Department of State Police
Division of Forensic Services and Identification
Bureau of Identification
125 E. Monroe St., Room 103
P.O. Box 19461
Springfield, IL 62794-9461   217-782-7263
www.isp.state.il.us
Publications include the *Crime in Illinois Annual Report*. The office will re-run monthly special reports for individuals upon request. There is no charge for this service.

Indiana
Indiana State Police
Data Division
100 Indiana Government Center North
100 N. Senate, Room N340
Indianapolis, IN 46204-2259   317-232-8200
www.ai.org/isp/index.html
Although this office does not publish an annual report, it will provide individuals with computer printouts or copies of crime statistics. There is no charge involved in these instances. Data is also available on diskette or magnetic tape. Charges vary according to the complexity of the request. Detailed requests should be made in writing.

Iowa
Department of Public Safety
Field Services Bureau
Wallace State Office Bldg.
Des Moines, IA 50319   515-281-8494
www.state.ia.us/government/dps/index.html
This department publishes the *Iowa Uniform Crime Annual Report*.

Kansas
Statistical Analysis Center
Kansas Bureau of Investigation
1620 SW Tyler
Topeka, KS 66612   785-296-8200
www.ink.org/public/kbi/
The Statistical Analysis Center publishes the *Crime in Kansas Annual Report*. Computer printouts of selected data is free upon request if the data is available. If you provide your own magnetic tapes or diskettes the staff will transfer the data on to them at no extra cost.

Kentucky
State Police
Information Section
1250 Louisville Rd.
Frankfort, KY 40601   502-227-8700, ext. 359
www.state.ky.us/agencies/ksp/ksphome.htm

Publications include the *Crime in Kentucky Annual Report* and *Traffic Accident Facts Report*. Computer printouts of selected data are available in special circumstances, depending upon the request. Most printouts are free. Some accident data requires an additional charge.

Louisiana
Louisiana Commission on Law Enforcement
1885 Wooddale Blvd., Room 708
Baton Rouge, LA 70806-1511   225-925-4418
www.cole.state.la.us
This office provides statistics on crime to the general public such as basic index crimes and arrest information.

Maine
Department of Public Safety
Uniform Crime Reporting Division
18 Meadow Rd.
104 State House Station
Augusta, ME 04333-0104   207-287-3619
www.state.me.us/dps
Publications include the *Crime in Maine Annual Report*. Computer printouts of selected data is available on a limited basis, usually at no charge.

Maryland
Maryland State Police
Uniform Crime Reporting Unit
1201 Reistertown Rd.
Pikesville, MD 21208
Attn. UCR   410-486-3101
www.inform.umd.edu/ums+state/md_resources/mdsp/index.html
Publications include the annual *Crime in Maryland Report*. Computer printouts are not generally provided, but can be done upon special request.

Massachusetts
Executive Office of Public Safety
1 Ashburton Place, Room 2133
Boston, MA 02108   617-727-7775
www.state.ma.us/eops/
Publications include a *Hate Crime Statistics Report* and yearly crime comparison reports. Computer services are available.

Michigan
Department of State Police
7145 Harrison Rd..
Uniform Crime Reporting
Lansing, MI 48823   517-332-2521
www.msp.state.mi.us/index.html
The Uniform Crime Reporting Division publishes an annual *Michigan Crime Report*, which is free upon request. Computer printouts of selected data are also free.

Minnesota
Department of Public Safety
Bureau of Criminal Apprehension
1246 University Ave.
St. Paul, MN 55104-4197   651-642-0670
www.dps.state.mn.us/bca/bca.html
Publications include an *Annual Report* and the *Uniform Crime Report Summaries*.

Mississippi
Department of Public Safety
City of Jackson Police Department
P.O. Box 958
Jackson, MS 39205   601-987-1212
www.dps.state.ms.us/
Mississippi does not have a central agency for collecting crime statistics. Each county or city has a department of safety that keeps individual records of criminal data. Computer printouts are not available.

Missouri
State Highway Patrol
Technical Service Bureau
Criminal Records Division
P.O. Box 749
Truman State Office Bldg., Room 870
Jefferson City, MO 65102   573-526-6153
www.dps.state.mo.us/dps/mshp/hp.htm
The Criminal Records Division publishes an annual *Missouri Crime Index Report*.

Montana

Montana Board of Crime Control
3075 N. Montana Ave.
P.O. Box 201408
Helena, MT 59620-1408   406-444-3604
http://bccdoj.doj.state.mt.us
Free publications include the *Crimes of Montana Annual Report*. Computer printouts of selected data are provided upon written request.

Nebraska

Commission on Law Enforcement and Criminal Justice
301 Centennial Mall South
P.O. Box 94946
Lincoln, NE 68509-4946   402-471-2194
www.state.ne.us/home/crime.com
The Commission publishes a *Crime In Nebraska Annual Report* which is free upon request.

Nevada

Nevada Highway Patrol
Uniform Crime Report Division
555 Wrightway
Carson City, NV 89711-0585   775-687-5300
http://nhp.state.nv.us/index.htm
Nevada began compiling crime statistics in a computer database in 1993. They publish an annual report, which is available for $4.

New Hampshire

Department of Safety
Division of State Police
Uniform Crime Reports
10 Hazen Dr.
Concord, NH 03305   603-271-2575
www.state.nh.us/nhsp/contents.html
Publications include the *Crime In New Hampshire* report. Computer printouts of selected data are provided at no charge upon written request.

New Jersey

Department of Law and Public Safety
Division of State Police
Uniform Crime Reporting Unit
Box 7068
West Trenton, NJ 08628-0068   609-882-2000, ext. 2392
www.njsp.org/front.html
The *Crime In New Jersey Report* is published annually. The office can supply computer printouts of selected data.

New York

Division of Criminal Justice Services
4 Tower Place, 8th Floor
Albany, NY 12203-3702   518-485-7675
http://criminaljustice.state.ny.us/
This division publishes the *Crime and Justice Annual Report* which is free upon request. Computer printouts are available at no cost.

North Carolina

Division of Criminal Information
P.O. Box 629
Raleigh, NC 27602   919-716-6400
www.jus.state.nc.us/cleframe.htm
The *Crime in North Carolina Annual Statistics Report* is available for a fee. Printouts of statistics already collected in their annual report are provided at no cost, if requests are reasonable. Individualized computer runs can also be performed but may become expensive. Costs vary according to the complexity of the request.

North Dakota

State Crime Bureau
Bureau of Criminal Investigation
P.O. Box 1054
Bismarck, ND 58502-1054   701-328-5500
www.ag.state.nd.us
Publications include an *Annual Report* which is free upon request. Computerized printouts of crime data are available. In most cases the cost is minimal. Detailed requests should be placed in writing. Information can also be transferred to computer diskette or magnetic tape if you supply the software.

Ohio

Governor's Office of Criminal Justice Services
Capitol Square
400 E. Town St., Suite 300

Columbus, OH 43215-4242   614-466-7782
www.ocjs.state.oh.us/
This office publishes a report entitled *Crime and Arrest Data by County* which is free upon request. The office does not provide computer printouts of selected data.

Oklahoma

Oklahoma State Bureau of Investigation
6600 N. Harvey, Building 6
Oklahoma City, OK 73116   405-879-2528
www.osbi.state.ok.us
The statistics unit publishes the *Crime in Oklahoma Annual Report*. Computer printouts of selected data are provided at no cost.

Oregon

State Executive
Law Enforcement Data System
955 Center St., NE, US20
Salem, OR 97301   503-378-3055
www.leds.state.or.us/
This division publishes the *Criminal Offenses and Arrests Annual Report*. Computer services are not available, but standard output reports can be obtained upon request.

Pennsylvania

Pennsylvania State Police
Commission on Crime and Delinquency
1800 Elmerton Ave.
Harrisburg, PA 17110   866-782-7711
http://ucr.psp.state.pa.us/UCR/ComMain.asp
The *Commission on Crime and Delinquency Annual Report* is free upon request. Computer printouts of annual data are also provided at no charge.

Rhode Island

Justice Commission
1 Capitol Hill
Providence, RI 02908   401-222-2620
www.rijustice.state.ri.us/sac/sac.htm
This department publishes the *Serious Crime in Rhode Island Annual Report*, which is free.

South Carolina

South Carolina Law Enforcement Division
Uniform Crime Reporting
P.O. Box 21398
Columbia, SC 29221-1398   803-896-7216
www.sled.state.sc.us
This division publishes *Crime in South Carolina* which is available for a fee. Free copies may be obtained from the Freedom of Information Office at 803-896-7013.

South Dakota

Division of Criminal Investigation
Statistical Analysis Center
500 E. Capitol St.
Pierre, SD 57501-5070   605-773-3331
www.sddci.com
Publications include a newsletter and annual and quarterly reports which are free upon request. Computerized printouts of selected crime data are available at no cost. Detailed requests should be made in writing. Information can also be transferred to computer diskette or magnetic tape if you supply the software.

Texas

Department of Public Safety
Uniform Crime Reporting Section
5805 N. Lamar Blvd.
P.O. Box 4087
Austin, TX 78773424-2000
www.txdps.state.tx.us/
Publications include the *Crime In Texas Annual Report*. Computer printouts of selected data are provided free, upon request.

Utah

Department of Public Safety
Bureau of Criminal Identification
4501 South, 2700 West
Salt Lake City, UT 84114   801-965-4461
http://publicsafety.utah.gov
Publications include the *Crime in Utah Annual Report* which is free upon request. Computer printouts of selected data are available, usually at no cost.

Vermont

Department of Public Safety
Vermont Criminal Information Center
103 S. Main St.
Waterbury VT 05671-2101   802-244-8786
www.dps.state.vt.us/cjs
The Criminal Information Center publishes the *Vermont Annual Crime Report* which is free upon request.

Virginia

Department of State Police
Uniform Crime Reporting Section
Records Management
P.O. Box 27472
Richmond, VA 23261-7472   804-674-2000
www.vsp.state.va.us/index.htm
The *Crime in Virginia Annual Report* is available for $5. Computer printouts of selected data are provided on a cost recovery basis.

Washington

Washington Association of Sheriffs and Police Chiefs
P.O. Box 826
2629 12th Court SW
Olympia, WA 98507   360-586-3221
www.waspc.org/
This organization produces the *Crime in Washington State Annual Report*, which is free upon request. Information that is not included in the annual report but readily accessible in their data banks is available to the public upon request.

West Virginia

Department of Public Safety
Uniform Crime Reporting Division
725 Jefferson Rd.
South Charleston, WV 25306   304-558-2930
www.state.wv.us
The UCR Division publishes a *Crime in West Virginia Annual Report*. No computer services are available, but data can be retrieved manually and the staff will fill requests as needed.

Wisconsin

Office of Justice Assistance
Wisconsin Statistical Analysis Center
131 W. Wilson St., Suite 202
Madison, WI 53702-0001   608-266-3323
www.oja.state.wi.us/static
The Statistical Analysis Center publishes a free *Crime and Arrests Annual Report* which is available upon request. Computer printouts of selected data provided at no charge.

Wyoming

Criminal Justice Information Section
316 W. 22nd St.
Cheyenne, WY 82002   307-777-7181
http://attorneygeneral.state.wy.us/dci/index.html
Publications include the *Uniform Crime Annual Report*. Computer printouts of selected data are provided at no charge. The office will furnish special reports if the data requested is of the type they usually collect. These reports are usually in table or letter form. Services are free, unless there is significant computer programming involved. Complex requests should be made in writing.

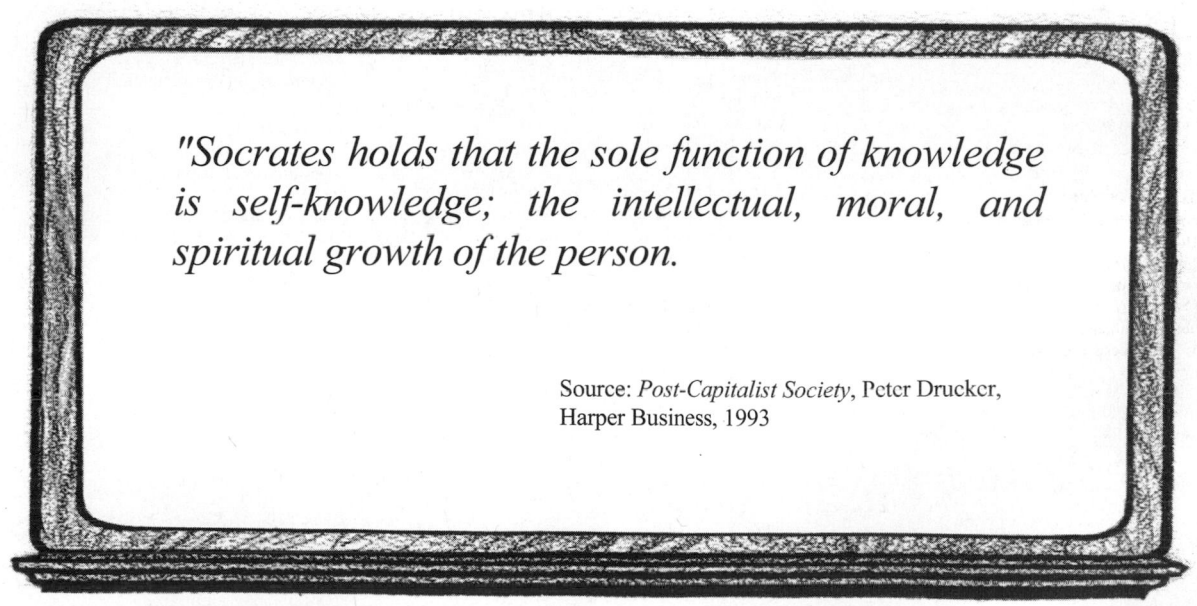

"Socrates holds that the sole function of knowledge is self-knowledge; the intellectual, moral, and spiritual growth of the person.

Source: *Post-Capitalist Society*, Peter Drucker, Harper Business, 1993

Sample The State Statistics

Every ten years, we all fill out the Census form and then what happens with all of that information? Approximately 1,300 organizations nationwide receive data from the U.S. Bureau of the Census and then disseminate that information to the public free of charge or on a cost recovery basis. These organizations are called state data centers and can provide you with specific information on your state or town. Want to move to a town full of twenty-somethings? Want to know the area with the most 20-year old houses which will need new roofs for your roofing business? Want to stay away from teenagers? Want to know the number of churches, hospitals, or recreational facilities in a town? You can sometimes even get information for a particular zip code. The data centers can provide you with information on specific reports they have available, customized searches that they can perform, and their free and fee schedules for particular information.

State Data Centers

Below is a roster of data centers in all 50 states as well as the District of Columbia, Puerto Rico and the Virgin Islands. Some of these Census Bureau information providers are based in state departments and agencies, universities, business colleges, and libraries.

Alabama

Center for Business and Economic Research
University of Alabama
P.O. Box 870221
Tuscaloosa, AL 34587-0221
205-348-6191
Fax: 205-348-2951
http://cber.cba.ua.edu/asdc.html

Alabama Department of Economic and
Community Affairs
Communication and Information Division
P.O. Box 5690
401 Adams Ave.
Montgomery, AL 36103-5690
334-242-5525
www.adeca.state.al.us

Alabama Public Library Service
6030 Monticello Dr.
Montgomery, AL 36130
334-213-3900
800-723-8459
www.apls.state.al.us/

Alaska

Alaska State Data Center
Research and Analysis Section
Department of Labor
P.O. Box 25501
Juneau, AK 99802-5501
907-465-4500
Fax: 907-465-2101
http://146.63.75.50/research

Alaska State Library
Government Publications
P.O. Box 110571
Juneau, AK 99811-0571
907-465-2927
Fax: 907-465-2665
www.library.state.ak.us/asp/asp.html

Dept. of Community and Regional Affairs
Community and Business Development
P.O. Box 110809
Juneau, AK 99811-0809
907-269-4521
Fax: 907-269-4539
www.dced.state.ak.us/cdb/home.htm

Institute for Social and Economic Research
University of Alaska

3211 Providence Dr.
Anchorage, AK 99508
907-786-7710
Fax: 907-786-7739
www.iser.uaa.alaska.edu/home.htm

Arizona

Arizona Department of Economic Security
Site Code 045Z
P.O. Box 6123
1789 W. Jefferson St., NE
Phoenix, AZ 85005
602-542-5984
www.de.state.az.us/links/economic/webpage/
page2.html

Center for Business Research
College of Business Administration
Arizona State University
Box 874011
Tempe, AZ, 85287-4011
480-965-3961
Fax: 480-965-5458
www.cob.asu.edu/seid/cbr/

Bureau of Business and Economic Research
Bank One Center for Business Outreach
College of Business Administration
Northern Arizona University
Box 15066
Flagstaff, AZ 86011-5066
928-523-7313
Fax: 928-523-1612
www.cba.nau.edu/bber

Research Library
Dept. of Library Archives and Public Records
1700 W. Washington, 3rd Floor
Phoenix, AZ 85007
602-542-4035
800-255-5841 (AZ)
www.dlapr.lib.az.us/

Economic and Business Research Program
College of Business and Public Administration
University of Arizona
McClelland Hall 204
Tucson, AZ 85721-0108
520-621-2155
Fax: 520-621-2150
http://ebr.eller.arizona.edu/Library/sdc.htm

Arkansas

State Data Center
UALR Institute for Economic Advancement
2801 S. University Ave.
Little Rock, AR 72204
501-569-8530
Fax: 501-569-8538
www.aiea.ualr.edu/csdc/default.html

Arkansas State Library
1 Capitol Mall
Little Rock, AR 72201
501-682-2864
www.asl.lib.ar.us

Research and Analysis Section
Arkansas Employment Security Division
P.O. Box 2981
Little Rock, AR 72203
501-682-3159
www.accessarkansas.org/esd/
labormarketinformation.htm

California

State Census Data Center
Department of Finance
915 L St.
Sacramento, CA 95814
www.dof.ca.gov/html/Demograp/druhpar.htm
916-445-3878

Sacramento Area COG
3000 S Street, Suite 300
Sacramento, CA 95816
916-457-2264
www.sacog.org/

Association of Bay Area Governments
P.O. Box 2050
Oakland, CA 94604-2050
510-464-7957
Fax: 510-433-5557
www.abag.ca.gov

Southern California Association of Govts.
818 W. 7th St., 12th Floor
Los Angeles, CA 90017-3435
213-236-1800
Fax: 213-236-1825
www.scag.ca.gov/census

San Diego Association of Governments
Wells Fargo

Matthew Lesko, Information USA, Inc., 12081 Nebel Street, Rockville, MD 20852 • 1-800-955-7693 • www.lesko.com

401 B St., Suite 800
San Diego, CA 92101
619-595-5300
Fax: 619-595-5305
www.sandag.cog.ca.us/

State Data Center Program
University of California-Berkeley
2538 Channing Way, #5100
Berkeley, CA 94720-5100
510-642-6571
Fax: 510-643-8292
http://ucdata.berkeley.edu

Colorado

Division of Local Government
Colorado Department of Local Affairs
1313 Sherman St., Room 521
Denver, CO 80203
303-866-4147
Fax: 303-866-2660
www.dlg.oem2.state.co.us/demog/ demog.htm

Business Research Division
Graduate School of Business Administration
420 UCB
University of Colorado-Boulder
Boulder, CO 80309-0420
303-492-8227
Fax: 303-492-3620
http://leeds.colorado.edu/brd/index.cfin

Agriculture and Resource Economics
Colorado State University
Clark B-320
Fort Collins, CO 80523-1172
907-491-6325
Fax: 970-491-2067
http://dare.agsci.colostate.edu

Documents and Department of the Libraries
Colorado State University
Fort Collins, CO 80523-1172
303-491-1880
http://lib.colostate.edu/research/colorado

Connecticut

Policy Development and Planning Division
Connecticut Office of Policy and Management
450 Capitol Ave.
MS#52ASP
Hartford, CT 06106-1308
860-418-6230
www.opm.state.ct.us

Government Information Services
Connecticut State Library
231 Capitol Ave.
Hartford, CT 06106
860-757-6570
www.cslib.org/gis.htm

Connecticut Department of Economic and
Community Development
Research Division
505 Hudson St.
Hartford, CT 06106
860-270-8165
www.state.ct.us/ecd/research/index.html

Center for Population Research
University of Connecticut
344 Mansfield Road, Unit 2068
Storrs, CT 06269-2068
860-486-9269

Delaware

Delaware Economic Development Office
99 Kings Highway
P.O. Box 1401
Dover, DE 19901
302-739-4271
Fax: 302-739-2028

www.state.de.us/dedo/new_web_site/
frame_data_center.html

College of Urban Affairs and Public Policy
University of Delaware
Graham Hall, Room 286
Academy St.
Newark, DE 19716
302-831-8406
www.udel.edu/suapp

District of Columbia

Data Services Division
Mayor's Office of Planning
801 N. Capitol St., NE
Suite 4000
Washington, DC 20002
202-442-7600
www.planning.dc.gov/main.shtm

Metropolitan Washington Council of
Governments
777 N. Capitol St., NE, Suite 300
Washington, DC 20002-4239
202-962-3293
www.mwcog.org/hspps/censusreports.html

Center for Neighborhood Information Services
1825 K Street, Suite 710
Washington, DC 20006-1202
202-223-2598
Fax: 202-223-2604
www.dcagenda.org/pages/nis

Florida

Center for the Study of Population
Institute for Social Research
654 Bellemy Bldg., R-93
Florida State University
Tallahassee, FL 32306-4063
850-644-7101
www.fsu.edu/~popctr

State Library of Florida
500 S. Bronough St.
Tallahassee, FL 32399-0250
850-245-6600
http://dlis.dos.state.fl.us/stlib/

State Data Center
Agency for Workforce Innovation
Office of Workforce Information Services
Labor Market Statistics
C&M Industrial Center
Building B
4972 Woodville Highway
Tallahassee, FL 32311-0902
850-488-1048
Fax: 850-921-0776
http://lmi.floridajobs.org/census2000/
index.htm

Georgia

Div. of Demographic and Statistical Services
Georgia Office of Planning and Budget
270 Washington St., SW
Atlanta, GA 30334
404-656-3820
Fax: 404-656-3828
www.opb.state.ga.us/

University of Georgia Libraries
Government Documents, 2nd Floor
Athens, GA 30602
706-542-0662
www.libs.uga.edu/govdocs/govdocs.html

State Data and Research Center
101 Marietta St., Suite 2550
Atlanta, GA 30303
404-463-1100
Fax: 404-463-1137
www.gadata.org

Gilbert Memorial Library
Government Information Department
Georgia Institute of Technology
Atlanta, GA 30332-0900
404-894-4519
http://ibid.library.gatech.edu/%7Egovweb

Hawaii

Hawaii State Data Center
Department of Business, Economic
Development, and Tourism
Research and Economic Analysis Division
#1 Capitol District Bldg.
250 S. Hotel St., 4th Floor
Honolulu, HI 96813
Mailing Address: P.O. Box 2359
Honolulu, HI 96804
808-586-2423
www.hawaii.gov/dbedt/sdcrpt.html

Information and Communication Services
Division
State Department of Accounting and General
Services
P.O. Box 0150
1151 Punchbowl St.
Honolulu, HI 96813
808-586-1800
olepe.icsd.hawaii.gov/dags/icsd

University of Hawaii at Manoa
Information Technology Services
265 McCarthy Mall, Keller Hall
Honolulu, HI 96822-2302
808-956-2387
Fax: 808-956-2412

Idaho

Idaho Department of Commerce
700 W. State St.
P.O. Box 83720
Boise, ID 83720-0093
208-334-2470
800-842-5858
www.idoc.state.id.us/

Institutional Research
Room 319, Business Bldg.
Boise State University
1910 University Drive
Boise, ID 83725
208-385-1613
www.idbsu.edu/

The Idaho State Library
325 W. State St.
Boise, ID 83702
208-334-2150
Fax: 208-334-4016
www.lili.org/isl/

Center for Business Research and Services
Campus Box 8044
Idaho State University
Pocatello, ID 83209
208 236-3049
Fax: 208-236-5960
www.isu.edu/departments/cbr/

Illinois

Census and Data Users Services
Department 4690
Campus Box 4950
6 Research Services Bldg.
Beauford and Fell St.
Normal, IL 61790-4950
309-438-5946
Fax: 309-438-2898
www.cadus.ilstu.edu/population.htm

Center for Governmental Studies
Northern Illinois University
Social Science Research Bldg.

138 N. 3rd St.
DeKalb, IL 60115
815-753-0934
www.nibidc.com/index.html

Chicago Area Geographic Information Study
Department of Geography (M/C 092)
1007 W. Harrison St., Room 2102
University of Illinois at Chicago
Chicago, IL 60607-7138
312-996-5274
Fax: 312-996-6343
www.cagis.uic.edu/

Northeastern Illinois Planning Commission
Research Services Department
222 S. Riverside Plaza, Suite 1800
Chicago, IL 60606-6097
312-454-0400
Fax: 312-454-0411
www.nipc.cog.il.us/

State Data Center
Division of Policy Development/Planning &
Research
Department of Commerce & Community
Affairs
620 East Adams Street
Springfield, IL 62701
217-782-1381
Fax: 217-524-3701
www.commerce.state.il.us/
doingbusiness/research/factsand.htm

Indiana

Indiana State Library
Indiana State Data Center
140 N. Senate Ave.
Indianapolis, IN 46204
317-232-3733
Fax: 317-232-3728
www.statelib.lib.in.us/www/ rl/sdcmenu.html

Indiana Business Research Center
Indiana University
Research Park 110
Kelly School of Business
501 N. Morton St.
Bloomington, IN 47404
812-855-5507
Fax: 812-855-7763
www.ibrc.indiana.edu

Indiana Business Research Center
Kelley School of Business
Indiana University
Suite 210, 777 Indiana Avenue
Indianapolis, IN 46202
317-274-2979
Fax: 317-615-0031
www.ibrc.indiana.edu

Office of Research and Technology
Indiana Department of Commerce
1 N. Capitol, Suite 700
Indianapolis, IN 46204
317-232-8959
www.ai.org/doc/index.html

Indiana Business Research Center
Kelley School of Business
Indiana University
Suite 210, 777 Indiana Avenue
Indianapolis, IN 46202
317-274-2979
Fax: 317-615-0031
www.ibrc.indiana.edu

Iowa

State Library of Iowa
E. 12th and Grand
Des Moines, IA 50319
515-281-4350
800-248-4483

Fax: 515-242-6543
www.silo.lib.ia.us/datacenter

Center for Social and Behavioral Research
221 Sabin Hall
University of Northern Iowa
Cedar Falls, IA 50614-0402
319-273-2105
Fax: 219-273-3104
http://csbsnt.csbs.uni.edu/dept/csbr

Census Services
Iowa State University
303 East Hall
Ames, IA 50011-1070
515-294-8337
Fax: 515-294-0592
http://socserver.soc.iastate.edu/census

Department of Sociology
University of Iowa
W140 Seashore Hall
Iowa City, IA 52242
319-335-2887
www.uiowa.edu/~soc/icpsr_frm.htm

Kansas

State Library
300 SW. 10th St., Room 343-N
Topeka, KS 66612-1593
785-296-3296
800-432-3919 (KS)
http://skyways.lib.ks.us/kansas/ksl/
ref/cen01.htm

Division of the Budget
Room 152-E, Statehouse
Topeka, KS 66612-1504
785-296-2436
Fax: 785-296-0231
http://da.state.ks.us/budget

Research Institute
1541 Lilac Ln.
607 Blake Hall
The University of Kansas
Lawrence, KS 66044-3177
785-864-3701
Fax: 785-864-3683
www.ku.edu/pri/ab_ippbr/pri.shtml

Center for Economic Development and
Business Research
1845 Fairmont
2nd Floor, Devlin Hall
Wichita State University
Wichita, KS 67260-0121
316-978-3225
Fax: 316-978-3950
www.webs.wichita.edu/cedbr

Population and Research Laboratory
Department of Sociology
204 Waters Hall
Kansas State University
Manhattan, KS 66506
785-532-6865
www.ksu.edu/sasw/

Kentucky

Urban Studies Institute
College of Business and Public Administration
University of Louisville
426 W. Bloom St.
Louisville, KY 40208
502-852-7990
Fax: 502-852-7386
www.louisville.edu/ksdc

Governor's Office of Policy and Management
Capitol Annex, 700 Capitol Ave.
Frankfort, KY 40601
502-564-7300
www.osbd.state.ky.us

State Library Division
Department for Libraries and Archives
300 Coffeetree Rd.
P.O. Box 537
Frankfort, KY 40602-0537
502-564-8300
Fax: 502-564-5773
www.kdla.state.ky.us/

Louisiana

State Census Data Center
Office of Electronic Services
P.O. Box 94095
1051 N. 3rd St.
Baton Rouge, LA 70804
225-219-4025
www.state.la.us/demo.htm

Division of Business and Economic Research
University of New Orleans
Lake Front
New Orleans, LA 70148
504-280-6240
Fax: 504-280-6094
www.uno.edu/~coba/dber/index.html

Economic Research Division
Louisiana Tech University
College of Business and Administration
P.O. Box 10318
Ruston, LA 71272
318-257-3701
www.cab.latech.edu/public/centers/
research/index.htm

Louisiana State Library
Referenced Bibliography Section
P.O. Box 131
Baton Rouge, LA 70821-0131
225-342-4913
www.state.lib.la.us/

Louisiana Population Data Center
Department of Sociology
126 Stubbs Hall
Louisiana State University
Baton Rouge, LA 70803-5411
Mr. Charles Tolbert
225-578-5360
www.lapop.lsu.edu/

Louisiana Economic Assistance Program
(LEAP)
Center for Business and Economic Research
(CBER)
University of Louisiana at Monroe
Monroe, LA 71209-6277
318-342-1215/1219
Fax: 318-342-1209
http://leap.ulm.edu

Maine

Maine State Planning Office
Census Data Center Program & Maine Census
Consortium
184 State Street
Augusta, ME 04330
MAILING ADDRESS:
c/o 38 State House Station
Augusta, ME 04333
207-287-2989
Fax: 207-287-6489
www.state.me.us/spo/census.htm

Maryland

Maryland Department of Planning
State Data Center
301 W. Preston St.
Baltimore, MD 21201
Ms. Jane Traynham
410-767-4450
Fax: 410-767-4480
www.mdp.state.md.us/msdc

University of Maryland
UMCP McKeldin Library
4th Floor, Government Documents
College Park, MD 20742
301-405-9165
Fax: 301-314-5651
www.lib.umd.edu/gov/govt_docs.html

Enoch Pratt Free Library
Resource Center
Maryland Room
400 Cathedral St.
Baltimore, MD 21201-4484
410-396-1789
www.epfl.net/sirc/md

Small Business Development Center
7100 Baltimore Ave., Suite 401
College Park, MD 20740
301-403-8300

Massachusetts
Massachusetts Institute for Social and
Economic Research
128 Thompson Hall, Box 37515
University of Massachusetts
Amherst, MA 01003-7515
413-545-3460
Fax: 413-545-3686
www.umass.edu/miser/

Massachusetts Institute for Social and
Economic Research, McCormack Bldg.
1 Ashburton Place, Room 1004
Boston, MA 02108
617-727-4537
Fax: 617-727-4660
www.umass.edu/miser

Michigan
Michigan Information Center
Department of Management and Budget
Census Data
George W. Romney Bldg.
10th Floor, 111 S. Capitol
Lansing, MI 48933
517-373-7910
www.state.mi.us/dmb/mic/

MIMIC/Center for Urban Studies
Wayne State University
656 W. Kirby, Room 3057
Detroit, MI 48202
313-577-8996
Fax: 313-577-1274
www.cus.wayne.edu/mimic/

The Library of Michigan
Government Documents Service
P.O. Box 30007
717 W. Allegan St.
Lansing, MI 48909
517-373-1580
www.libofmich.lib.mi.us/

Minnesota
State Demographer's Office
Minnesota Planning
658 Cedar St., Room 300
St. Paul, MN 55155
612-296-2557
www.mnplan.state.mn.us/demography/
index.html

Minnesota Population Center
Minnesota Data Center
University of Minnesota
271 19th Ave., South
537 Heller Hall
Minneapolis, MN 54555
612-624-4389
Fax: 612-626-8375
www.pop.umn.edu/index.html

Educational Resources Center
Department of Education
1500 Hwy. 36 West
Roseville, MN 55113
651-582-8719
http://cfl.state.mn.us/library/edures.htm

Metropolitan Council
Mears Park Center
230 East 5th Street
St. Paul, MN 55101
651-602-1000
www.metrocouncil.org/resources/
resources.htm

Mississippi
Center for Population Studies
The University of Mississippi
Leavell Hall, Room 102
University, MS 38677
662-915-7288
Fax: 662-915-7736
www.olemiss.edu/depts/sdc

Div. of Research and Information Systems
Department of Economic and Community
Development
1200 Walter Sillas Bldg.
P.O. Box 849
Jackson, MS 39205
601-359-3449
www.decd.state.ms.us/

Southern Mississippi Planning and
Development District
9229 Highway 49
Gulfport, MS 39503-4317
228-868-2311
Fax: 228-868-7094
www.smpdd.com

Missouri
Missouri State Census Data Center
Missouri State Library
600 W. Main St.
P.O. Box 387
Jefferson City, MO 65102
573-526-7648
Fax: 573-751-3612
www.oseda.missouri.edu/mscdc/

Office of Administration
124 Capitol Bldg.
P.O. Box 809
Jefferson City, MO 65102
573-751-2345
www.oa.state.md.us

Office of Social and Economic Data Analysis
University of Missouri-Columbia
602 Clark Hall
Columbia, MO 65211
573-882-7396
Fax: 573-884-4635
www.oseda.missouri.edu/index.html

Geographic Resources Center
University of Missouri-Columbia
Stewart Hall
Columbia, MO 65211
573-882-1404
Fax: 573-884-4095
www.msdis.missouri.edu/

Small Business Research Information Center
University of Montana-Rolla
104 Nagogami Teerrace
Rolla, MO 65409-1340
573-341-4559
Fax: 573-341-6495
www.umr.edu/~tscsbdc

Center for Economic Information
207 Haag Hall

University of Missouri-Kansas City
5100 Rockhill Road
Kansas City, MO 641110
816-235-2832
Fax: 816-235-5263
http://cei.haag.umkc.edu

Montana
Census and Economic Information Center
Montana Department of Commerce
P.O. Box 200501
1424 9th Ave.
Helena, MT 59620-0505
406-444-2896
Fax: 406-444-1518
http://ceic.commerce.state.mt.us

Montana State Library
1515 E. 6th Ave.
P.O. Box 201800
Helena, MT 59620-1800
406-444-3115
800-338-5087
http://msl.state.mt.us

Bureau of Business and Economic Research
University of Montana
Gallagher Business Bldg.
32 Campus Dr., #6840
Missoula, MT 59812
406-243-5113
www.bber.umt.edu

Research and Analysis Bureau
Workforce Services Division
Montana Department of Labor and Industry
P.O. Box 1728
Helena, MT 59624
406-444-2430
800-633-0229 (MT)
http://rad.dli.state.mt.us

Natural Resource Information System
1515 East 6th Avenue
Helena, MT 59620-1800
406-444-5354
http://nris.state.mt.us/index.html

Nebraska
Center for Public Affairs Research
Nebraska State Data Center
Peter Kiewit Conference Center, #232
University of Nebraska at Omaha
Omaha, NE 68182
402-554-2134/2132
www.unomaha.edu/~cpar

Governor's Policy Research Office
P.O. Box 94601
State Capitol, Room 1319
Lincoln, NE 68509-4601
402-471-2414

Federal Documents Librarian
Nebraska Library Commission
The Atrium, 1200 N. St., Suite 120
Lincoln, NE 68508-2023
402-471-2045
800-307-2665 (NE)
www.nlc.state.ne.us/

The Central Data Processing Division
Department of Administration Services
Nebraska Department of Economic
Development
301 Centennial Mall S., Lower Level
P.O. Box 95045
Lincoln, NE 68509-5045
402-471-4855
www.info.neded.org

Nebraska Department of Labor
550 S. 16th St.
P.O. Box 94600

Lincoln, NE 68509-4600
402-471-2518
www.dol.state.ne.us/

Department of Natural Resources
301 Centennial Mall South
P.O. Box 94876
Lincoln, NE 68509-4676
402-471-3964
www.dnr.state.ne.us

Nevada
Nevada State Data Center
Nevada State Library and Archives
Capitol Complex
100 N. Stewart St.
Carson City, NV 89701
775-684-3326
800-922-2880 (NV)
http://dmla.clan.lib.nv.us/docs/nsla/sdc

New Hampshire
Office of State Planning
2-1/2 Beacon St.
Concord, NH 03301-4497
603-271-2155
Fax: 603-271-1728
www.state.nh.us/osp/sdc/sdc.html

New Hampshire State Library
20 Park St.
Concord, NH 03301-6303
603-271-2060
www.state.nh.us/nhsl/index.html

New Jersey
New Jersey Department of Labor
Labor Planning and Analysis
P.O. Box 388
Trenton, NJ 08625-0388
609-984-2595
Fax: 609-984-6833
www.state.nj.us/labor/lra/njsdc.htm

New Jersey State Library
U.S. Documents Office
185 W. State St.
P.O. Box 520
Trenton, NJ 08625-0520
609-292-6259
Fax: 609-984-7900
www.njstatelib.org/aboutus/SGIS/
libusdoc.htm/

Data and Statistical Services
Social Science Reference Center
Princeton University
One Washington Rd.
Princeton, NJ 08544
609-258-6052
www.princeton.edu/~sbwhite/ssrcwebb.html

Edward J. Bloustein School of Planning and
Public Policy
Rutgers, The State University of New Jersey
Civic Square Building
33 Livingston Avenue, Suite 300
New Brunswick, NJ 08901-1981
732-932-5475
http://policy.rutgers.edu'

Rutgers University Computing Services
CCIS-Hill Center, Busch Campus
258A Hill Center, Box 879
Piscataway, NJ 08854-0879
732-445-3137

New Mexico
Economic Development Department
P.O. Box 20003
Santa Fe, NM 87504-5003
505-827-0264
www.edd.state.nm.us/

New Mexico State Library
Federal Documents
1209 Camino Carlos Rey
Santa Fe, NM 87507
505-476-97
www.stlib.state.nm.us/libraryservices/
statepubs/sg6.html

Bureau of Business and Economic Research
University of New Mexico
1920 Lomas NE
Albuquerque, NM 87131-6021
505-277-6626
Fax: 505-277-7066
www.unm.edu/~bber

State Data Center
Department of Economics and International
Business
New Mexico State University
Box 30001, Dept. 3CQ
Las Cruces, NM 88003-8001
Dr. Kathleen Brook
505-646-2113
http://cbae.nmsu.edu/MainPage/
Pub_Centers/Data_Center

New York
Cornell University
CISER Data Archive
201 Caldwell Hall
Ithaca, NY 14850
607-255-4801
Fax: 607-255-9353
www.ciser.cornell.edu/

Nelson A. Rockefeller Institute of Government
411 State St.
Albany, NY 12203-1003
518-443-5522
Fax: 518-443-5788
http://rockinst.org

New York State Library
6th Floor, Cultural Education Center
Empire State Plaza
Albany, NY 12230
518-474-3940
www.nysl.nysed.gov/

Office of Real Property Services
16 Sheridan Ave.
Albany, NY 12210-2714
518-486-5446
www.orps.state.ny.us/

State Data Center
Empire State Development
30 South Pearl Street
Albany, NY 12245
518-292-5300
Fax: 518-292-5806
www.empire.state.ny.us/data_home.html

North Carolina
Division of State Library
109 E. Jones St.
Raleigh, NC 27699-4641
919-733-3270
Fax: 919-733-5679
http://statelibrary.dcr.state.nc.us

Institute for Research in Social Science
University of North Carolina-Chapel Hill
Manning Hall CB 3355
Chapel Hill, NC 27599-3355
919-962-0512
Fax: 919-962-4777
www.irss.unc.edu

Center for Geographic Information
Office of State Planning
301 N. Wilmington St., Suite 700
Raleigh, NC 27601

919-733-2090
Fax: 919-715-0725
www.cgia.state.nc.us/

Office of State Budget and Management
Data Service Unit
State Data Center
20321 Mail Service Center
Raleigh, NC 27699-0321
LOCATION:
  5050 Administration Building
  116 West Jones
919-733-7061
Fax: 919-715-3562
http://sdc.state.nc.us

North Dakota
North Dakota State Data Center
North Dakota State University
Agribusiness and Applied Economics
Room 424, IACC
P.O. Box 5636
Fargo, ND 58105-5636
701-231-7980
www.ndsu.nodak.edu/sdc

Division of Community Service
400 E. Broadway, Suite 50
Bismarck, ND 58502
701-328-2676
www.state.nd.us/dcs/tahome.html

Department of Geography
University of North Dakota
Box 9020
Grand Forks, ND 58202
701-777-4246
Fax: 701-777-6195
www.und.nodak.edu/dept/Geog/
mainpage.html

North Dakota State Library
Liberty Memorial Bldg.
604 East Boulevard Ave.
Department 250
Bismarck, ND 58505-0800
701-328-4622
800-472-2104
ndsl.lib.state.nd.us

Ohio
Office of Strategic Research
Ohio Department of Development
P.O. Box 1001
77 High St., 27th Floor
Columbus, OH 43215
614-466-2115
Fax: 614-466-9697
www.odod.state.oh.us/osr/data.htm

State Library of Ohio
274 E. First Ave.
Columbus, OH 43201
614-644-1971
http://winslo.state.oh.us/govinfo/stgvtop.html

Cleveland State University
Northern Ohio Data and Information Service
The Urban Center
Maxine Goodman Levin College of Urban
Affairs
Cleveland, OH 44115-2440
216-687-2209
http://nodisnet1.csuohio.edu/nodis/index.html

Data Center
Department of Human and Community
Resource Development
248 Agricultural Administration
2120 Fyffe Road
Columbus, OH 43210
614-688-8760
www.osuedc.org/current

Buckeye Hills-Hocking Valley Regional
Development District
Route 1, County Road 9
Box 299D
Marietta, OH 45750-9286
740-374-9436
Fax: 740-374-8038
www.seovirtual.com

Ohio Occupational Information
Division of Labor Market Information
Ohio Department of Job and Family Services
145 South Front Street
P.O. Box 1618
Columbus, OH 43216-1618
614-752-6865
http://lmi.state.oh.us/Index.htm

Oklahoma

Oklahoma State Data Center
Oklahoma Department of Commerce
900 N. Stiles
MAILING ADDRESS:
    P.O. Box 26980
    Oklahoma City, OK 73126-0980
405-815-5184
800-652-8779
www.odoc.state.ok.us/osdc.htm

Oklahoma Department of Libraries
200 NE 18th St.
Oklahoma City, OK 73105
405-522-3335
www.odl.state.ok.us/usinfo

Center for Economic and Management
Research
The University of Oklahoma
Michael F. Price College of Business
307 W. Brooks, Room 4
Norman, OK 73019-0450
405-325-2931
http://cemr.ou.edu/

Oregon

Oregon State Library
250 Winter St., NE
Salem, OR 97301
503-378-4277
Fax: 503-588-7119
www.osl.state.or.us/

Population Research Center
School of Urban and Public Affairs
Portland State University
506 SW Mill-URBN 570J
Portland, OR 97207-0751
503-725-5159
Fax: 503-725-5162
www.upa.pdx.edu/CPRC

Office of Economic Analysis
155 Cottage St., NE, U20
Salem, OR 97301
503-378-4967
www.oea.das.state.or.us/population.htm

Documents Center
Main Floor Knight Library
1501 Kincaid Street
1299 University of Oregon
Eugene, OR 97403-1299
503-346-3070
Fax: 503-346-3094
http://libweb.uoregon.edu/govdocs

Pennsylvania

Pennsylvania State Data Center
Institute of State and Regional Affairs
Pennsylvania State University at Harrisburg
777 W. Harrisburg Pike
Middletown, PA 17057
717-948-6336

Fax: 717-948-6754
http://pasdc.hbg.psu.edu/index.html

Penn State University
Social Sciences Library
201 Paterno
University Park, PA 16801
814-865-4861
Fax: 814-865-1403
www.libraries.psu.edu/crsweb/docs/
govmain.htm

Rhode Island

Rhode Island Department of Administration
Statewide Planning Program
One Capitol Hill
Providence, RI 02908-5873
401-222-7901
www.planning.state.ri.us

Office of Health Statistics
Rhode Island Department of Health
3 Capitol Hill, Room 407
Providence, RI 02908-5097
401-222-2550
Fax: 401-273-4350
www.healthri.org/chic/statistics/home.htm

Rhode Island Economic Development
Corporation
One West Exchange St.
Providence, RI 02903
401-222-2601
Fax: 401-222-2102
www.riedc.com/

Office of Library and Information Services
Department of Administration
One Capitol Hill
Providence, RI 02908
401-222-2726
Fax: 401-222-4195
www.lori.state.ri.us/lori

Population Studies and Training Center
Brown University
P.O. Box 1916
112 George Street
Providence, RI 02912
401-863-2278
Fax: 401-863-3351
www.pstc.brown.edu

United Way of Southeastern New England
229 Waterman Street
Providence, RI 02906
401-444-0600
Fax: 401-444-0635
www.unitedwaysene.org

South Carolina

South Carolina State Library
1500 Senate St.
P.O. Box 11469
Columbia, SC 29211
803-734-8026
www.state.sc.us/scsl/den

Office of Research and Statistics
South Carolina Budget and Control Board
Rembert Dennis Building
Room 425
Columbia, SC 29201
803-734-3793
www.ors.state.sc.us

South Dakota

Business Research Bureau
School of Business
University of South Dakota
414 E. Clark
Vermillion, SD 57069
605-677-5287

605-677-5427
www.usd.edu/brbinfo/

Government Publication
South Dakota State Library
800 Governors Dr.
Pierre, SD 57501-2294
605-773-5241
800-423-6665
www.sdstatelibrary.com

Labor Market Information Center
South Dakota Department of Labor
420 S. Roosevelt, Box 4730
Aberdeen, SD 57401
605-626-2314
Fax: 605-626-2322
www.sdjobs.org/lmic

Office of Administration Services
South Dakota Department of Health
600 E. Capitol Ave.
Pierre, SD 57501-2536
605-773-5303
Fax: 605-773-5683
800-738-2301
www.state.sd.us/index.htm

South Dakota State University
Rural Sociology Department
Scobey Hall, Box 504
Brookings, SD 57007-1296
605-688-4899
Fax: 605-688-6354
www.abs.sdstate.edu:81/sociology/census_dat

Tennessee

Center for Business and Economic Research
College of Business Administration
University of Tennessee
Glocker Bldg., Suite 100
Knoxville, TN 37996-4170
865-974-5441
Fax: 865-974-3100
http://cber.bus.utk.edu/

Texas

Business and Industry Data Center
Department of Economic Development
P.O. Box 12728
1700 N. Congress Ave.
Austin, TX 78701
512-936-0292
www.bidc.state.tx.us

State Data Center
Department of Rural Sociology
Texas A & M University
2125 TAMU
College Station, TX 77843-2125
979-845-5115
Fax: 979-862-3061
http://txsdc.tamu.edu/

Texas State Library and Archive Commission
P.O. Box 12927
Austin, TX 78711
512-463-5455
www.tsl.state.tx.us/

Texas Natural Resources Information System
P.O. Box 13231
Austin, TX 78711-3231
512-463-8337
Fax: 512-463-7274
www.tnris.state.tx.us

Utah

Office of Planning and Budget
116 State Capitol
Salt Lake City, UT 84114
801-538-1027

Fax: 801-538-1547
www.governor.state.ut.us/dea/

University of Utah
Bureau of Economic and Business Research
1645 E. Campus Center Dr., Room 401
Salt Lake City, UT 84112
801-581-6333
Fax: 801-581-3354
www.business.utah.edu/BEBR/

Department of Community and Economic
Development
324 S. State St., Suite 500
Salt Lake City, UT 84111
801-538-8700
877-4UTDCED (488-3233)
www.dced.state.ut.us/

Department of Workforce Services
140 E. 300 S.
P.O. Box 45249
Salt Lake City, UT 84145-0249
801-536-9786
Fax: 801-526-9238
http://wi.dws.state.ut.us

Vermont

Center for Rural Studies
University of Vermont
207 Morrill Hall
Burlington, VT 05405-0106
802-656-3021
http://crs.uvm.edu/

Vermont Department of Libraries
109 State St.
Montpelier, VT 05609-0601
802-828-3261
http://dol.state.vt.us/

Virginia

Virginia Employment Commission
Labor Market information
703 E. Main St.
Richmond, VA 23219
804-786-7496
www.vec.state.va.us/

Wheldon Cooper Center for Public Service
University of Virginia
918 Emmet St. N., Suite 300
Charlottesville, VA 22903-4832
434-982-5582
www.ccps.virginia.edu/demographics

Virginia State Library
Documents Section
800 E. Broad St.
Richmond, VA 23219-8000
804-692-3562
www.lva.lib.va/us/

Washington

Forecasting Division
Office of Financial Management
450 Insurance Bldg.
Box 43113
Olympia, WA 98504-3113
360-902-0599
www.ofm.wa.gov/demographics.htm

Puget Sound Regional Council
1011 Western Ave., Suite 500
Seattle, WA 98104-1035
206-464-7532
www.psrc.org/

Social Research Center
Department of Rural Sociology
Washington State University
P.O. Box 644006
Pullman, WA 99164-4006
509-335-8623
www.ruralsoc.wsu.edu/

Department of Sociology
Demographic Research Laboratory
Amtzen Hall 501A
Western Washington University
Bellingham, WA 98225-9081
360-650-3176
Fax: 360-650-7295
www.ac.wwu.edu/~drl/

Department of Employment Security
LMEA
P.O. Box 9046
Olympia, WA 98507-9046
360-438-4804
800-215-1617
www.wa.gov/esd/lmea

CSSCR
University of Washington
145 Savery Hall, DK 45
Seattle, WA 98195
206-543-8110
Fax: 206-543-8670
http://julius.csscr.washington.edu/

Department of Sociology
Applied Social Data Center
Central Washington University
Ellensburg, WA 98926-7545
509-963-1300
Fax: 509-963-1308
www.cwu.edu/~asdc/home.html

West Virginia

West Virginia Development Office
Research and Strategic Planning Division
Capitol Complex
Bldg. 6, Room 553
Charleston, WV 25305

304-558-4010
Fax: 304-558-0362
www.wvdo.org/business/research.htm

Reference Library
West Virginia State Library Commission
1900 Kanawha Blvd. East
Cultural Center
Charleston, WV 25305
304-558-2045
800-642-9021, #1
http://129.71.160.4

Office of Health Services Research
WVU Health Science Center
Medical Center Dr.
P.O. Box 9140
Morgantown, WV 26506-9145
304-293-1080
www.hsc.wvu.edu/som/cmed/ohsr

Bureau of Business and Economic Research
College of Business and Economics
West Virginia University
P.O. Box 6025
Morgantown, WV 26506-6025
304-293-7832
www.be.wvu.edu/serve/bureau/data.htm

Wisconsin

Department of Administration
Demographic Services Center
101 E. Wilson St.
Madison, WI 53702
608-266-1927
www.doa.state.wi.us/dhir/boir/demographic

Applied Population Laboratory
Department of Rural Sociology
University of Wisconsin
1450 Linden Dr., Room 316
Madison, WI 53706
608-262-1515
Fax: 608-262-6022
www.ssc.wisc.edu/poplab/

Wyoming

Survey Research Center
University of Wyoming
P.O. Box 3925
College of Business Building
Laramie, WY 82071-3925
307-766-2030
www.uwyo.edu/src/

Department of Administration and Information
Economic Analysis Division
1807 Capitol Ave., Suite 206
Cheyenne, WY 82002-0060
307-777-7504
Fax: 307-632-1819
http://eadiv.state.wy.us/

Highway Information Closer To Home

You can get more specific information on the roadways in your town by contacting your state Highway Department. Want to know how safe your corner is for kids? How many accidents occur on the beltway and when? How safe are the bike paths? Where are accidents most likely to occur? Every state highway department has a database made up of reports completed by all law enforcement agencies which investigate accidents. In most instances, the computerized system can be searched and printouts provided by a number of variables including accident type, county, month of year, alcohol involvement, driver sex, age, and more. Some states provide these printouts free of charge, while others charge up to $150 per hour or require a Freedom of Information act request. Many states also publish an annual report, which is usually free.

Highway Department Offices

Alabama
Alabama Highway Department
Accident Identification and Surveillance Section
Traffic Engineering
1409 Coliseum Blvd.
Montgomery, AL 36130
334-242-6128
www.dot.state.al.us/default.asp
A report, *Alabama Traffic Accident Facts*, is available to individuals at no cost. The accident database can be searched, sorted, and a printout produced.

Alabama Department of Public Safety
500 Dexter Avenue
Montgomery, AL 36130
To view the reports, visit the Critical Analysis Reporting Environment at http://care.cs.ua.edu.

Alaska
Department of Transportation and Public Facilities
3132 Channel Dr.
Juneau, AK 99801-7908
907-465-3900
888-PLAN-DOT
www.dot.state.ak.us/
Publications include a free annual report. Accident database printouts are provided. You can download the information at their website.

Arizona
Arizona Department of Transportation
Traffic Records Section
2828 N. Central Ave., Suite 880
Phoenix, AZ 85004
602-712-7437
www.dot.state.az.us/
Publications include the *Arizona Motor Vehicle Crash Facts*. The accident database can be searched, sorted, and a printout provided at no charge. Their website has data that covers the past four years.

Arkansas
Arkansas State Highway and Transportation Department
Attn: Traffic Safety Section
P.O. Box 2261
Little Rock, AR 72203
501-569-2648
www.ahtd.state.ar.us/
Publications include an annual *State Accident Data Report*. Information from accident databases is not released on a routine basis.

California
Department of Transportation
Caltrans
Publications Unit
1900 Royal Oaks Dr.
Sacramento, CA 95815-3800
916-445-3520
http://caltrans-opac.ca.gov/publicat.htm
Publications include the annual *California Accident Data*. The accident database can be searched, sorted, and a printout provided on a cost recovery basis.

Colorado
Department of Highways
Staff Traffic Division
4201 E. Arkansas Ave., Room 172
Denver, CO 80222
303-757-9271
www.dot.state.co.us/Programs/Safety
This department's publications include: *Accidents by County*, and *Accidents by City*. Both are free. A report entitled, *Accidents by Rates*, is $5. The Department of Revenue issues standard summaries of motor vehicle reports for a nominal fee. Information from accident databases is not released as a general policy.

Connecticut
Department of Transportation
Bureau of Policy and Planning
Office of Inventory and Forecasting
2800 Berlin Turnpike
Newington, CT 06131-7546
860-594-2022
www.dot.state.ct.us/bureau/pp/pp.html
The accident database can be searched, sorted, and a printout provided at no cost. Requests should be in writing. Go to the website listed above to view the information online.

Delaware
State Police Headquarters
Delaware State Traffic Control Section
P.O. Box 430
Dover, DE 19903-0430
302-739-5969
www.state.de.us/
Publications include monthly and annual reports. The database can be searched, sorted, and a printout provided at no cost. Delaware's *Annual Traffic Statistical Report* can be viewed at their website.

District of Columbia
Traffic Studies
Department of Public Works
2000 14th St., NW, 6th Floor
Washington, DC 20009
202-727-1000
No listings are provided on a regular basis. General questions are answered over the telephone.

Florida
Department of Transportation
Safety Engineer Office
605 Suwannee St., MS 53
Tallahassee, FL 32399-0450
850-458-3546
www11.myflorida.com/safety/default.htm
To view reports, see www.hsmv.state.fl.us/html/safety.html
Publications include the *Florida Traffic Accident Facts Report* which is free upon request. The accident database can be searched, sorted, and a printout provided, usually free of charge. If the department must perform a mainframe computer search, there is an additional charge.

Georgia

Department of Public Safety
Accident Reporting Section
P.O. Box 1456
Atlanta, GA 30371
404-624-7660
www.ganet.org/dps/index.html
Standard accident summaries and an annual report is free upon request. Copies of individual accident reports are also provided. The agency does not routinely provide computer printouts of accident data. You can view the *Georgia Traffic Accidents Report* at their website.

Hawaii

Department of Transportation
Public Affairs Office
869 Punchbowl St., Room 120
Honolulu, HI 96813
808-587-2160
www.state.hi.us/dot
General questions are answered over the phone. A publication entitled *Major Traffic Accidents in Hawaii* is available free of charge.

Idaho

Office of Highway Safety
Idaho Transportation Department
P.O. Box 7129
Boise, ID 83707-1129
208-334-8100
www2.state.id.us/itd/index.htm
Publications include the *Idaho Traffic Collisions* report, which is free upon request and is available for online searching. The accident database can be searched, sorted, and a printout provided. A broad search of the database is usually under $10, but fees vary depending upon the complexity of the request. A specific accident report is $4 plus tax and shipping.

Illinois

Department of Transportation
Division on Traffic Safety
3215 Executive Park Dr.
Springfield, IL 62794-9245
217-782-2575
http://dot.state.il.us/
Publications include an *Aggressive Driver/Smooth Operator*. The accident database can be searched, sorted, and a printout provided at no cost. The *Illinois Crash Facts and Statistics* report is available online and covers statistics from 1998 to the present.

Indiana

Governor's Council on Impaired and Dangerous Driving
Indiana Criminal Justice Institute
One North Capitol Avenue, Suite 1000
Indianapolis, IN 46204
www.in.gov/cji/research/traffic_data.htm
Publications include annual summaries of motor vehicle traffic accidents entitled *Crash Facts*. The report plus others on traffic safety are available at their website. The accident database can be searched, sorted, and a printout provided on a cost recovery basis

Iowa

Iowa Department of Transportation
Driver Services
Park Fair Mall
100 Euclid Avenue
P.O. Box 9204
Des Moines, IA 50306-9204
515-237-3153
800-532-1121
www.dot.state.ia.us/mvd/ods/index.htm
Publications include the *Iowa Crash Facts*. The accident database can be searched, sorted, and a printout provided for a cost recovery fee. It can also be searched online.

Kansas

Department of Transportation
Bureau of Traffic Safety
7th Floor DSOB
915 Harrison
Topeka, KS 66612
785-296-3756
www.ink.org/public/kdot/safety/index.html
Publications include the *Annual Kansas Accident Facts*, and an *Alcohol*

Related Accidents and Accidents by Driver Age Group Report. These reports can be downloaded from their website.

Kentucky

State Police
Statistics Division
Records Branch
1250 Louisville Rd.
Frankfort, KY 40601
502-226-2169
www.state.ky.us/agencies/ksp/traffic.htm
Publications include a *Kentucky Traffic Accident Facts Annual Report*. The accident database can be searched for records dating back five years. A written request for information is required. These reports can also be viewed at the website listed above.

Louisiana

Department of Public Safety and Corrections
Highway Safety Commission
P.O. Box 66336
265 S. Foster Dr.
Baton Rouge, LA 70896
225-925-6991
www.dps.state.la.us/hwswww.nsf
The accident database can be searched, sorted, and a printout provided upon written request. It can also be downloaded from their website.

Maine

Department of Public Safety
Bureau of Highway Safety
164 State House Station
Augusta, ME 04333-0164
207-624-8756
www.state.me.us/dps/Bhs/homepage.htm
The accident database can be searched, sorted, and a printout provided at no cost upon request. A publication entitled *Maine Highway Crash Facts* is available.

Maryland

State Highway Administration
Traffic Safety Analysis Division
7491 Connelly Dr.
Hannover, MD 21076
410-787-5822
www.sha.state.md.us/
The staff will supply data and selected excerpts from publications for reasonable requests. There is normally no charge, but fees are based on the amount of data requested and staff time involved.

Massachusetts

Governor's Highway Safety Bureau
10 Park Plaza, Suite 5220
Boston, MA 02116
617-973-8900
www.massghsb.com/safety_data.html
The Highway Safety Data report is available on-line for review and searching.

Michigan

Michigan State Police
Office of Highway Safety Planning
4000 Collins Rd.
P.O. Box 30633
Lansing, MI 48909-8133
517-322-6025
www.michigan.gov/msp/1,1607,7-123-1645_3501_4626---,00.html
Publications include *Michigan Traffic Crash Statistics*, and *Fatal and Serious Injury Traffic Crash Trends in Michigan*.

Minnesota

Department of Public Safety
Office of Traffic Safety
444 Cedar St., Suite 150
St. Paul, MN 55101-5150
651-296-3804
www.dps.state.mn.us/trafsafe/trafsafe.asp
Publications include *Crash Facts Report*. The report is available at the website listed above. This department does not provide accident database searches.

Mississippi

Department of Public Safety
Highway Safety

P.O. Box 958
Jackson, MS 39205
601-987-1212
www.dps.state.ms.us/
This department does not provide accident database searches. General questions are handled over the phone.

Missouri

State Highway Patrol
Division of Highway Safety
P.O. Box 104808
Jefferson City, MO 65110
573-751-4161
800-800-BELT
www.dps.state.mo.us/dps/mshs/hs.htm
Publications include the annual *Missouri Traffic Safety Compendium*. The accident database can be searched, sorted, and a printout provided upon special request. Fees vary and are based on a cost recovery basis.

Montana

Montana Department of Transportation
Traffic Safety Bureau
P.O. Box 201001
Helena, MT 59620-1001
406-444-7301
www.mdt.state.mt.us
Publications include their free *Problem Identification Paper*. The accident database can be searched, sorted, and a printout provided at no cost. It is also available online.

Nebraska

Department of Roads
Highway Safety Bureau
Accident Records
P.O. Box 94669
Lincoln, NE 68509
402-479-4645
www.dor.state.ne.us/highway_safety
Publications include the annual *Traffic Accident Facts Report*. The report is available online. The accident database can be searched, sorted, and a printout provided, usually at no cost.

Nevada

Department of Transportation
Safety Engineering
1263 S. Stewart St.
Carson City, NV 89712
702-888-7000
www.nevadadot.com
Publications include the annual *Nevada Crashes*. The accident database can be searched, sorted, and a table provided. This can be researched at their website.

New Hampshire

Department of Transportation
John O. Mortin Bldg.
P.O. Box 483
Concord, NH 03302-0483
603-271-3734
www.state.nh.us/dot
A *Fatal Accident Summary* is free to the public. The accident database can be searched, sorted, and a printout provided.

New Jersey

Department of Law and Public Safety
Division of Highway Traffic Safety
P.O. Box 048
Trenton, NJ 08625
609-633-9300
800-422-3750
www.state.nj.us/lps/hts
Publications include *Traffic Safety Facts Annual Report*. The department has a link to the Fatality Analysis Reporting System (FARS) where you can look up a report based on a set of data or create your own report.

New Mexico

Highway and Transportation Department
Traffic Safety Bureau
P.O. Box 1149
Santa Fe, NM 87504-1149
505-827-0427
www.unm.edu/~dgrint/tsb.html

Publications include the annual *New Mexico Traffic Crash Data Report*. The accident database can be searched, sorted, and a printout provided at no cost. Requests for data not found in the annual report should be placed in writing. Go to their website to view the data yourself.

New York

State Department of Motor Vehicles
Accident Safety Division
Research Bureau, Room 420
6 Empire State Plaza
Albany, NY 12228
518-473-5595
800-CALL-DMV
www.nydmv.state.ny.us/stats.htm
Publications include an annual *Accident Facts*, and the *Ten Year Accident Summary*. The accident database can be searched, sorted, and a printout provided. Fees vary according to the complexity of the request. Visit their website to view those and other reports.

North Carolina

Division of Motor Vehicles
Traffic Records Section
1100 New Bern Ave.
Annex Bldg., Room 101
Raleigh, NC 27697
919-715-7000
www.dmv.dot.state.nc.us/
Publications include a free report entitled *North Carolina Traffic Crash Facts Book*. To obtain a copy of the book, call 919-861-3062. A summary of the data is available at the DOT website. You will find traffic safety information at the Highway Safety Research Center website. The accident database can be searched, sorted, and a printout provided for a fee from: Highway Safety Research Center, CB 3430, UNC Campus, Chapel Hill, NC 27599; 919-962-2202; or online at <www.hrsc.unc.edu/>.

North Dakota

Department of Transportation
Drivers License and Traffic Safety Division
608 E. Boulevard Ave.
Bismarck, ND 58505-0700
701-328-2600
www.state.nd.us/dot/dl&ts.html
Publications include the *Vehicle Crash Facts*. This report is available at their website. The accident database can be searched, sorted, and a printout provided.

Ohio

Department of Public Safety
Public Information Office
P.O. Box 182081
Columbus, OH 43218-2081
614-466-4344
www.state.oh.us/odps/
Ohio publishes a number of safety-related publications, including *Traffic Crash Facts*, and *Facts and Figures*. You can view these at the website listed above.

Oklahoma

Department of Public Safety
Highway Safety Division
3223 N. Lincoln Blvd.
Oklahoma City, OK 73105
405-523-1571
www.dps.state.ok.us/ohso
Publications include the annual *Oklahoma Crash Facts Report*, which is free. You can download this report at their website. Computer printouts are available upon written request. Fees vary according to the complexity of the data search.

Oregon

Department of Transportation
Crash Analysis and Reporting Unit
Accident Data
Transportation Development Division
355 Capitol St., NE, Room 135
Salem OR, 97301
503-986-4232
888-275-6368
www.odot.state.or.us/tdb/accident_data/
Publications include an *Oregon Accident Rate Table*. This report can be downloaded at their website. The accident database can be searched, sorted, and a printout provided at no cost.

Pennsylvania

Department of Transportation
Department of Highway Safety and Traffic Engineering
Keystone Building
400 North Street
Harrisburg, PA 17120
717-783-0352
www.dot.state.pa.us
This office publishes a free report entitled *Crash Facts and Statistics*. The report will soon be available online. The accident database can be searched, sorted, and a printout provided. Fees vary according to the scope of the request. All requests should be made in writing.

Rhode Island

Department of Transportation
State Office Bldg., Room 251
Two Capitol Hill
Providence, RI 02903
401-222-3025 (Governor's Office on Highway Safety)
800-354-9595 (General Department of Transportation)
www.dot.state.ri.us
Standard tables of accident reports are published yearly and are available upon request. The accident database can be searched, sorted, and a printout provided upon special, written request. Individuals must first complete an open records request. Costs vary according to the actual research and computer time involved.

South Carolina

Department of Pubic Safety
Office of Highway Safety
Statistical Services Section
5400 Broad River Road
Columbia, SC 29212
803-896-9963
877-349-7187
www.scdps.org/ohs
Publications include the *South Carolina Traffic Collision Fact Book*. It can be viewed at their website. The accident database can be searched, sorted, and a printout provided.

South Dakota

Department of Transportation
Accident Records
Becker-Hansen Building
700 E. Broadway Ave.
Pierre, SD 57501-2586
605-773-3868
www.sddot.com/pe/data/accident.asp
Publications include an annual *South Dakota Accident Report*. This and other reports can be found at their website. Be sure to look at all of their publications. Individual computer runs of selected data are provided generally at no cost.

Tennessee

Governor's Highway Safety Office
505 Deaderick Street, Suite 1800
Nashville, TN 37243
615-741-2589
www.tdot.state.tn.us
This office is responsible for collecting and analyzing traffic accident data. The accident database can be searched, sorted, and a printout provided.

Texas

Department of Public Safety
Accident Records Bureau
Box 15999
Austin, TX 78761-1599
512-465-2600
www.txdps.state.tx.us/administration/driver_licensing_control/arb.html
Publications include the *Motor Vehicle Traffic Accidents Report*. The accident database can be searched, sorted, and a printout provided for a cost recovery fee. This information is available online.

Utah

Department of Transportation
Division of Traffic Safety
4501 S. Constitution Blvd.
Salt Lake City, UT 84114-3200
801-965-4284
www.dot.utah.gov/ops/traff_saf/traff_saf.htm
Publications include *Utah Annual Safety Report* and *Accident Statistics*. These reports can be downloaded from the website. The accident database can be searched and printouts provided. Requests should be in writing and individuals must first complete a request form. Fees for computer printouts vary. Individuals may receive data within the last five years. Fees vary.

Vermont

Governor's Highway Safety Program
103 S. Main St.
Waterbury, VT 05671-2101
802-244-1317
www.dps.state.vt.us/cjs/ghsp.htm
Publications include an annual report entitled *Vermont Crash Data Book*. This report is also available online. The accident database can be searched, sorted, and printouts provided. Costs for individual searches vary depending upon the scope of the request. Requests should be made in writing.

Virginia

Department of Motor Vehicles
P.O. Box 27412
Richmond, VA 23269
866-DMVLINE (368-5463)
800-435-5137
www.dmv.state.va.us/webdoc/citizen/drivers/crash_facts.asp
Publications include an *Virginia Traffic Crash Facts Report*. The accident database can be searched, sorted, and printouts provided upon special, written request. There may be a charge depending upon the complexity of the information requested. You can search the report online at the website listed above.

Washington

Department of Transportation
Transportation Data Office
310 Maple Park Ave., SE
Olympia, WA 98504
360-705-7932
www.wsdot.wa.gov/ppsc/TDO/default.htm
Publications include the *Washington State Annual Collision Data Report*. Go to the website to view the report yourself. The accident database can be searched, sorted, and a printout provided. Most requests usually require only one hour of staff time.

West Virginia

Department of Highways
Traffic Engineering Division, Building 5
1900 Kanawah Blvd. E.
Charleston, WV 25305
304-558-3063
www.wvdot.com
Publications include the *West Virginia Crash Data Report* which is free. The accident database is not available to the general public.

Wisconsin

Department of Transportation
Traffic Accidents Section
P.O. Box 7919
Madison, WI 53707-7919
608-267-1847
608-266-2265
www.dot.state.wi.us/dmv/accident.html
Publications include a report entitled *Wisconsin Traffic Crash Statistics* which is free to the public. Computer printouts not normally available. Go to their website to view the above report.

Wyoming

Highway Safety Branch
Department of Transportation
5300 Bishop Blvd.
Cheyenne, WY 82009
307-777-4450
http://dot.state.wy.us
Publications include the *Wyoming Comprehensive Report on Traffic Accidents*. The accident database can be searched and printouts provided at no cost.

Go To School Before Your Kid Does

The difference between school districts and individual schools can be staggering. It's an important consideration that's bound to affect where you decide to live. Should you count on the information that you get from a real estate agent interested in selling you a house? No! If you are house hunting and have children in school, you can find all the answers to all of your questions simply by contacting both the State Department of Education and the local school district. The amount spent per child, student-teacher ratio, tests scores, experience, and more are only some of the data available from these offices. Once you have compiled the information, you can make an informed choice on what school is best for your kids.

State Department of Education Offices

Alabama

Alabama Department of Education
50 N. Ripley
P.O. Box 302101
Montgomery, AL 36104
334-242-9700
www.alsde.edu/html/home.asp
The department produces the *School Report Cards*, *System Report Cards*, and the *State Report Card*. You can view the documents individually, or download the entire set from the website. The monthly newsletter, *Alabama Education News*, is also available.

Alaska

Alaska Department of Education and Early Development
Public Information
801 W. 10th St., Suite 200
Juneau, AK 99801-1894
907-465-2851
www.eed.state.ak.us/home.html
This office provides computer searches and printouts. Specialized requests should be placed in writing. Due to budget cuts, the *Annual Report* is no longer being published. Information such as the enrollment or dropout rates can be found, however, in the *Alaska Public School District's Report Card to the Public*. The report can be viewed and downloaded from the website.

Arizona

Arizona Department of Education
Academic Standards and Accountability Division
1535 W. Jefferson
Phoenix, AZ 85007
602-542-5022
800-352-4558
www.ade.state.az.us/
The office publishes the *Arizona School Report Cards*, a detailed collection of information about each Arizona public school.

Arkansas

Arkansas Department of Education
IT-Information and Reporting
#4 Capitol Mall
Little Rock, AR 72201
501-682-1189
http://arkedu.state.ar.us
This office provides computer searches and information via printouts and diskettes to non-profit organizations, only. Requests may be made directly over the telephone, but those of a complex nature should be placed in writing. There is no fee for services. Publications include *Report Card of Arkansas Schools*. This and other reports can be viewed online.

California

California Department of Education
721 Capitol Mall
P.O. Box 944272
Sacramento, CA 95814
916-657-2451
http://goldmine.cde.ca.gov/
or
Demographics Office
428 J Street, 2nd Floor
Sacramento, CA 95814
916-327-0219
http://goldmine.cde.ca.gov/demographics
The Educational Demographics Unit provides searches and printouts free of charge. The office's publications include: *School Profiles*, *Demographic Reports*, *California School District Data*, and *DataQuest*. All these reports are available online.

Colorado

Colorado Department of Education
Education Statistics and Data
201 E. Colfax
Denver, CO 80203
303-866-6600
www.cde.state.co.us/
This office provides computer searches on staff and student enrollment. The office publishes *Graduation Statistics*, and *Statewide Education Facts*. All this information can be found at their website.

Connecticut

Connecticut Department of Education
Public Information Office
165 Capitol Ave.
P.O. Box 2219
Hartford, CT 06145
860-713-6548
www.state.ct.us/sde/
This office provides information through computer analyses, printouts, and magnetic tapes, or it can be viewed online. The publication office publishes *Strategic School Profiles*, and comprehensive surveys of each Connecticut public school.

Delaware

Delaware Department of Education
Federal and Lockerman Sts.
P.O. Box 1402
Dover, DE 19903-1402
302-739-4601
www.doe.state.de.us/
The office provides board approved reports listing statistics on school enrollments, number of teachers, educational statistics, and teacher personnel reports. Titles include *Summary of Public Schools*, *Statistics for Delaware School Districts*, and *Delaware Education at a Glance*. Check out their website for a wealth of information.

Florida

Florida Department of Education
Education Information and Accountability Services
325 W. Gaines St., Room 852
Tallahassee, FL 32399-0400
850-487-2280
www.firn.edu/doe/eias/home0050.htm
Publications include *Statistical Briefs*, *Florida School Indicator Reports*, and *Graduation Rates;* all of which are available online.

Georgia

Georgia Department of Education
205 Jennie Hill, Jr. SE
Atlanta, GA 30334

404-656-2800
800-311-3627
www.doe.k12.ga.us/
The Administrative Technology Department provides information such as basic attendance and enrollment data, some financial information, types of enrollment, and the expenditure and cost per child. The publication *Georgia Public Education Report Card* is free and has a wealth of information on Georgia schools. All this information can be found at their website, and downloaded for free.

Hawaii
Hawaii Department of Education
Information Branch
P.O. Box 2360
Honolulu, HI 96804
808-586-3230
http://doe.k12.hi.us
Enrollment data can be obtained free of charge from this office. At present, computer diskettes and magnetic tapes are not available. Specialized requests should be placed in writing. Publications include the *Annual Financial Report* which may be obtained by calling 808-586-3230. There are many reports available for viewing at their website.

Idaho
Idaho Department of Education
P.O. Box 83720
Boise, ID 83720-0027
208-332-6800
www.sde.state.id.us/Dept
Their publications include financial summaries, an *Annual Statistical Report*, and *Accreditation Summary Report of Idaho Schools*. They also provide an *Educational Directory* and school profiles. These are all available online.

Illinois
Illinois State Board of Education
100 N. First St.
Springfield, IL 62777-0001
217-782-3950
www.isbe.state.il.us/research/Default.htm
The Research Division has compiled a variety of reports and publications. Their publications include *Annual Statistical Report of Illinois Public School Districts, School Directories,* and *School Report Cards*. Download them from their website, or call the number above.

Indiana
Indiana Department of Education
Accountability System for Academic Progress (ASAP)
Room 229, State House
Indianapolis, IN 46204-2798
317-232-0808
www.doe.state.in.us/
This office provides computer searches and printouts. Types of information available include enrollment figures, graduation rates, and teacher to pupil ratios. Their publications include the *Annual Performance Report, Expulsion Reports,* and *School Directory*. At their website you can choose the data you are interested in and create your own personal report.

Iowa
Iowa Department of Education
Bureau of Planning, Research and Evaluation
Grimes State Office Bldg.
Des Moines, IA 50319-0146
515-281-4837
www.state.ia.us/educate/
This office gathers and posts data and reports for viewing. Teachers' names and school addresses are released. Publications include the *Annual Condition of Education Report* and the *Basic Educational Data Survey (BEDS)*.

Kansas
Kansas State Department of Education
120 SE 10th Ave.
Topeka, KS 66612
785-296-3201
www.ksde.org/welcome_main.shtml
A variety of information can be looked up at their website for each school. This office provides computer searches and, on occasion, printouts. The office publishes the *Kansas Educational Directory, Education Matters,* and *School Building Report Card*. Most of these are available online.

Kentucky
Kentucky Department of Education
Division of Data Policy Management and Research

500 Mero Street
Frankfort, KY 40601
502-564-5279
www.kde.state.ky.us/
This office provides computer searches, printouts, and bulletins. Information such as *School Report Cards, School and District Profiles,* and the *Kentucky Schools Directory*. Check ou their website for that and much more information.

Louisiana
Louisiana Department of Education
P.O. Box 94064
626 North 4th Street
Baton Rouge, LA 70804
225-342-4411
877-4LEAP21
www.doe.state.la.us/
The Division of Planning, Analysis & Information Resources produces the *School Report Card* which is posted at their website. They also have an Interact with the Data feature where you can choose information to compare schools. Publications include the *Annual Financial* and *Statistical Report*.

Maine
Maine Department of Education
Station House 23
Augusta, ME 04333
207-624-6616
www.state.me.us/education/homepage.htm
Access reports such as the *Maine Educational Assessment* and *Graduates On To Post-Secondary Schools* from the Data Center to help make the best school choice. Publications include *Students Educated at Public Expense,* and *Maine Educational Staff*. All publications are available on the website only.

Maryland
Maryland Department of Education
Office of Planning
Results and Information Management
200 W. Baltimore St.
Baltimore, MD 21201
410-767-0100
888-246-0016
www.msde.state.md.us/
This office produces the Maryland School Performance Report that can be search by school, system, or state data. Information is in categories such as , Student Performance and Participation with more detailed subcategories.

Massachusetts
Massachusetts Department of Education
350 Main St.
Malden, MA 02148
781-388-3000
800-439-0183
www.doe.mass.edu
They produce and post the results of the MCAS assessment test for each school. The School Performance Ratings let you look at each school to see how they fared in the state. Other statistical reports are also available on-line. Enrollment figures, attendance data, and drop-out reports are available. Publications include: *School Facts, Children First,* and *Per Pupil Expenditures by Program*.

Michigan
Michigan Department of Education
Information Center Data Services
608 W. Allegan St., Hannah Bldg.
P.O. Box 30008
Lansing, MI 48933
517-373-3324
www.mde.state.mi.us/
You can do in depth research at this website, MEAP scores, analysis of financial data, and more. They even have a link to Standards & Poor for the School Evaluation Service. This office provides computer searches and printouts on a limited basis. Diskettes are available. At present, there is no base charge for services, but this would depend upon the extent of the request. Publications include *Michigan School Report, School District Data Book,* and *Michigan K12 Database*.

Minnesota
Minnesota Department of Education
Information and Technology Unit
1500 Highway 36 West
Roseville, MN 55113
651-582-8200

http://children.state.mn.us/
This office provides computer searches, printouts, and diskettes, free of charge. Teachers' names and school addresses are available on labels from the Documents Division. *School District Profiles* can be viewed online.

Mississippi

Mississippi Department of Education
P.O. Box 771
Jackson, MS 39205-0771
601-359-5615
www.mde.k12.ms.us
The office provides computer searches, printouts, and magnetic tapes. The Office of Accountability Reporting provides the *Mississippi Report Card* and the *Superintendents Annual Report* which has data such as Promotions and Non-Promotion, Dropouts, and Public School Personnel. This and other publications can be reviewed at their website.

Missouri

Missouri Department of Education School Data Section
P.O. Box 480
Jefferson City, MO 65102-0480
573-751-4212
http://services.dese.state.mo.us/
The Division of Improvement supplies *School Data*, *School Improvement Planning Profiles* which lists information concerning demographics, educational performance and more. Also, check the results of the Missouri Assessment Program to see the top 10 schools. Other publications include *At School Manuals* and MAP Assessments, which can also be downloaded from their site. Computer searches and printout requests are available.

Montana

Montana Office of Public Instruction
Capitol Station
Helena, MT 59620-2501
406-444-3656
www.opi.mt.gov/index.html
This office does not provide individual computer searches. However, information on grades kindergarten through twelfth is available in their *Montana School Directory. Database Files of Montana Schools* are available on the website for downloading and searching. Other information at their site includes *Education Profiles and Services* and MontCAs results.

Nebraska

Nebraska Department of Education
Data Center
P.O. Box 94987
Lincoln, NE 68509
402-471-2295
www.nde.state.ne.us/
This office's services include computer searches, printouts, and magnetic tapes. Fees vary depending upon the scope of the project. The office prefers that requests be in writing. The office publishes the *Nebraska Education Directory*, and *Nebraska Public School District Statistical Facts*. The office provides the *State of Schools Report* that can be downloaded from their website. All of these informative reports will give you what is needed to choose the school that is right for you.

Nevada

Nevada Department of Education
Office of Finance Accountability and Audit
400 W. King St.
Carson City, NV 89710
702-687-9200
www.nde.state.nv.us
This office provides computer searches and printouts based upon aggregated student demographic data. Requests should be placed in writing. Their publications include the *School Accountability Data*.

New Hampshire

New Hampshire Department of Education
Office of Information Services
State Office Park South
101 Pleasant St.
Concord, NH 03301-3860
603-271-3494
www.ed.state.nh.us
The Office provides computer searches and printouts. Information is also available on diskette or magnetic tape, depending upon the data requested. Teachers' names and school addresses are released under certain circumstances. The office has numerous Reports and Statistics available at their website. You can access information on enrollment, financial data, and student-teacher ratios.

New Jersey

New Jersey Department of Education
Office of Public Information
CN 500, 100 River View Executive Plaza
Trenton, NJ 08625
609-292-4041
www.state.nj.us/education/
Services include computer searches, printouts, and magnetic tapes upon individual request. There is no set fee for services, since it varies according to the scope of the request. This website has all of the information you need to compare schools. You can view the *School Report Cards*, compare school in other states, and use their Data Search and Analysis. You will also be able to look-up the *Statewide Assessment Reports*.

New Mexico

New Mexico Department of Education
Education Bldg.
Data Collection and Reporting Unit
300 Don Gaspar Ave.
Santa Fe, NM 87501-2786
505-827-6526
http://sde.state.nm.us/
This office provides computer searches and printouts free of charge. The office publishes the *Accountability Report*, *Dropout Report*, and the *New Mexico Educational Personnel Directory*. There are many reports and publications available to the public detailing information on the schools. The *District Report Card* and *School Fact Sheets* are just a few. They also maintain a rating of each school.

New York

New York Department of Education
Fiscal Analysis and Research Unit
Room 301, State Education Bldg.
Albany, NY 12234
518-474-5213
www.nysed.gov/
This office provides computer searches, printouts, and magnetic tapes. Recent Reports on school statistical data is available at this website. Not only will you find a report on each school, but also individual reports of *Most Improved Schools at Grade 4 and Grade 8*, *Middle Math Results*, and more. Some of the publications are *School District Fiscal Profiles* and *Statistical Profiles of Public School Districts*.

North Carolina

North Carolina Department of Public Instruction
301 N. Wilmington St.
Raleigh, NC 27601-2825
919-807-3300
800-663-1250
www.dpi.state.nc.us/
The Publication Office has an abundance of information online for you. The reports are on *Student Testing Results Evaluation and Analysis*, and *About North Carolina Schools*. Some of the Reports and Statistics can be downloaded such as the *ABCs School Report Card*. Other publications on topics like *Education Initiatives* and *Education Directory* can be obtained online or ordered from the above phone number.

North Dakota

North Dakota Department of Education
Department of Public Instruction
600 E. Boulevard Ave.
Dept. 201, Floors 9, 10, and 11
Bismarck, ND 58505-0440
701-328-2260
www.dpi.state.nd.us/
This office provides computer searches and printouts. The *North Dakota Educational Directory* is available for $8, or it can be downloaded at their website. There are also eight different files from the directory that can be viewed separately; Statistical Summary and Directory Guide, Educational Directory, and more. Other publications include *School District Profiles* and *School Finance Facts*.

Ohio

Ohio Department of Education
25 S. Front St.
Columbus, OH 43215-4183
614-995-1545
877-644-6338
www.ode.state.oh.us
This office provides computer searches and printouts. Publications include *School District Profiles*, *State Composite Profiles*, and *Proficiency Test Data*. Not only can you view the Ohio Local Report Cards for the District, Buildings, and Community Schools, but they also have the Interactive Local

Report Card. With this you can create your own report based upon the criteria you choose. Check out the enrollment and discipline data too.

Oklahoma

Oklahoma State Department of Education
Documents
2500 N. Lincoln Blvd.
Oklahoma City, OK 73105-4599
405-521-2293
www.sde.state.ok.us/home/default.html
This office provides computer searches and printouts. The department makes the *Report Cards for the State, District, and Sites* available to the public on-line. Some other publications they have available are the *Oklahoma Directory of Education*, *Test Scores*, and *School District Database*.

Oregon

Oregon Department of Education
School Finance, Data and Analysis
Public Service Bldg.
255 Capitol St., NE
Salem, OR 97310-0230
503-378-0203
www.ode.state.or.us/
This office provides computer searches and printouts. Fees vary, depending upon the scope of the project. Requests should be made in writing. This office provides the *District Profile Reports* which you can use to compare districts or similar schools. The *School Report Card* is available with information covering the past 3 years. Other publications include *District and School Mailing Labels* and the *School Directory*.

Pennsylvania

Pennsylvania Department of Education
Office of Data Services
333 Market St.
Harrisburg, PA 17126-0333
717-787-2644
www.pde.state.pa.us
This office provides computer searches and printouts. Requests should be placed in writing for complex data. The office publishes the *Status Report On Education In Pennsylvania, Public, Private and Non-Public School High School Graduates*, and *School Profiles*. School profiles will help you to evaluate a specific school or district in Pennsylvania. Data on available programs, enrollment, technology and resource, and test results are available. Some of the Statistical Reports they offer are, *Status Report on Education in Pennsylvania, Public, Private and Nonpublic Schools*.

Rhode Island

Information Works!
Rhode Island Department of Elementary and Secondary Education
255 Westminster St.
Providence, RI 02903-3400
401-222-4600, ext. 2231
www.ridoe.net
Information Works! lists all of the data on a school that you would hope to find. The *School Performance Grouping* lists schools by their performance and improvement over a 3 year period. For those and other reports on demographics and financial information, check out their website.

South Carolina

South Carolina Department of Education
1429 Senate St.
Columbia, SC 29201
803-734-8500
www.sde.state.sc.us
This office provides computer searches and printouts. Fees vary for the use of computer time, and are dependent upon the complexity of the request. Their list of publications includes: *Pupils in South Carolina Schools*, *School Crime Incident Report* and *Quick Facts about South Carolina Public Schools*. Their website posts *Report Cards* for each school in the state. It also has a list of high achieving schools. The Publications Office has test results for each school and district of up to 7 different assessment tests.

South Dakota

South Dakota Department of Education and Cultural Affairs
Office of Finance and Management
700 Governors Dr.
Pierre, SD 57501-2291
605-773-3248
605-773-4748
www.state.sd.us/
This office provides computer searches and printouts. Special requests should be placed in writing. The office publishes *Education in South Dakota: A Statistical Profile* and *An Educational Directory*. These are available online.

Tennessee

Tennessee Department of Education
Office of Accountability
6th Floor, Andrew Jackson Tower
710 James Robertson Parkway
Nashville, TN 37243-0375
615-532-4703
www.state.tn.us/education
This office does not normally provide computer searches, but will provide you with a free copy of their *Annual Statistical Report*, *School Directory*, or *21st Century Schools Report Card*. These are available at their website.

Texas

Texas Education Agency
Division of Public Information
1701 N. Congress
Austin, TX 78701-1494
(Mail: P.O. Box 13817
Austin, TX 78711-3817)
512-463-9734
www.tea.state.tx.us/
Publications include *Texas Education Directory and Snapshot: School District Profiles*. The *Comprehensive Annual Report on Texas Public Schools* provides information on the overall state of education in Texas. The *Accountability Data Tables* will give you a more in depth picture of each school or district. There is also a link to the *Comparable Improvement Report*.

Utah

Utah Board of Education
School Finance and Statistics Section
250 E. 500 S.
Salt Lake City, UT 84111
801-538-7660
www.usoe.k12.ut.us/
Publications available include the free *Superintendent's Annual Report*. All of the information is available from their website, including numerous statistical spreadsheets.

Vermont

Vermont Department of Education
Communications Department
State Office Bldg.
120 State St.
Montpelier, VT 05620-2501
802-828-3154
www.state.vt.us/educ/
This office provides information via printouts to profit and non-profit organizations. The department publishes *Vermont School Report*, *Education Facts and Ratios*, *Standards for Vermont Educators* and *Student Performance Data*. These can be examined at their website.

Virginia

Virginia Department of Education
Office of Information Technology
101 N. 14th St., 22nd Floor
Richmond, VA 23219
804-225-2951
800-292-3820
www.pen.k12.va.us/Anthology/VDOE/
The office provides information via printouts and booklets. Requests for specialized information must be placed in writing. The office publishes the free *Superintendent's Annual Report*, *The DOE Directory*, and *The Literacy Program Testing Data*, which are available online. This office makes available the *School Report* and results of the state's Assessment Tests at this website.

Washington

Washington Superintendent of Public Instruction
Data Administration
Old Capitol Bldg.
P.O. Box 47200
Olympia, WA 98504-7200
360-725-6370
www.wednet.k12.wa.us
This office provides information via printouts, diskettes, and computer tapes. Special requests should be placed in writing. Publications include *Dropout and Graduation Statistics*, *Minority Enrollment Report*, *Enrollment Facts in Washington State*, and *Enrollment by Grade Level by County*, which are available at their website. From the Washington State Education Profile, you can download WASL scores by district or school, demographic information, and more.

West Virginia

West Virginia Department of Education
WV Education Information System
Bldg. 6, 1900 Kanawha Blvd. E., Room 346
Charleston, WV 25305-0330
304-558-3927
http://wvde.state.wv.us/

This office provides computer searches and printouts. Although the staff does not normally provide information on diskette or magnetic tape, they can do so if you specify your required format. The office publishes an *Annual Educational Summary* and *West Virginia Report Cards*. From the *Washington State Education Profile*, you can download WASL scores by district or school, demographic information, and more.

Wisconsin

Wisconsin Department of Public Instruction
Statistical Information Center
125 S. Webster
P.O. Box 7841
Madison, WI 53707-7841
608-266-3390

800-441-4563
www.dpi.state.wi.us/

The *School Performance Report* contains in depth information by school or district. Each category; academics, attendance and behavior, staff and money, demographics, has a number of sub-categories. That along with other reports such as *School Financial Data* and *SAGE Evaluation Reports* provides all of the information needed for parents. All of these are available from their website.

Wyoming

Wyoming Department of Education
Statistical Department
Hathaway Bldg., 2nd Floor
2300 Capitol Ave.
Cheyenne, WY 82002-0050
307-777-5252
www.k12.wy.us/wdehome.html

This office provides free statistical which are available online. Publications include *Enrollment History, Wyoming CAS Student Assessment Results,* and *School Directory.*

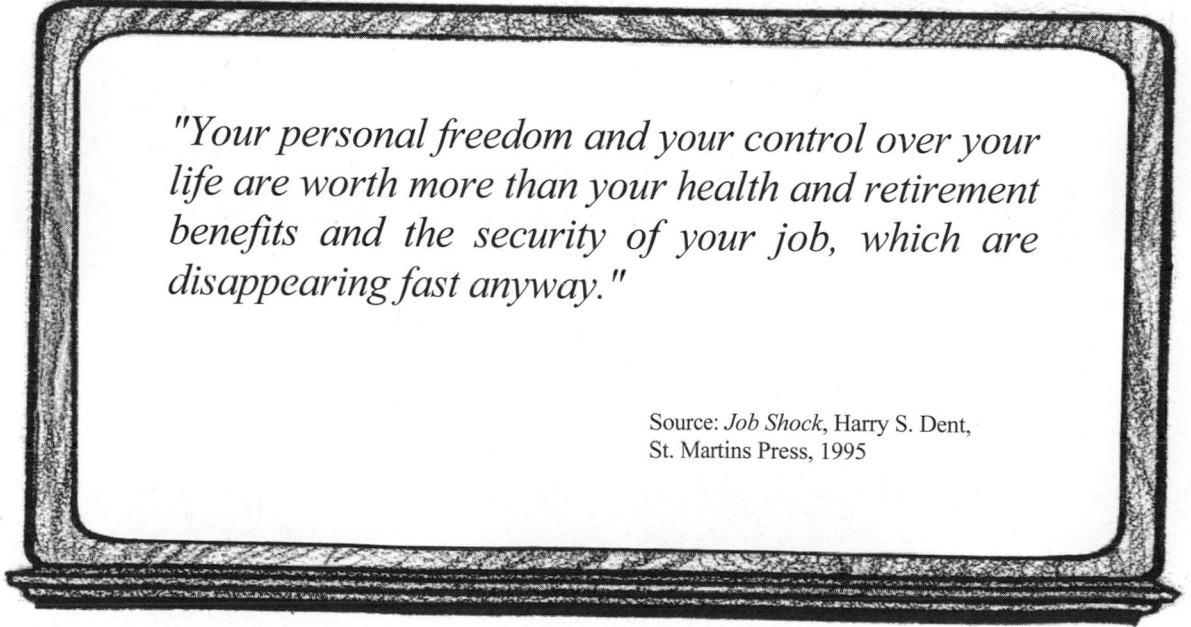

"Your personal freedom and your control over your life are worth more than your health and retirement benefits and the security of your job, which are disappearing fast anyway."

Source: *Job Shock*, Harry S. Dent, St. Martins Press, 1995

Housing Made Affordable

The U.S. Department of Housing and Urban Development (HUD) has several different programs available to help people become first time homebuyers, assist with the housing needs of the elderly and disabled, help people who are having trouble paying their mortgage, mortgage insurance for those deemed ineligible for FHA mortgage insurance, and even find subsidized rent for people who are struggling with their finances. In some cases, housing funds are made available through local community organizations. HUD also offers properties for sale through real estate brokers, and these homes can often be purchased for less than the going rate. Contact the HUD regional office near you for more information about HUD programs, or look at the HUD field office website at <http://www.hud.gov/directory/ascdir3.cfm>.

HUD Regional Offices

Regional Director
Office for New England
10 Causeway Street
Room 301
Boston, MA 0222-1092
617-994-8200

Regional Director
Office for Mid West
Ralph Metcalfe Federal Building
77 West Jackson Boulevard
Chicago, IL 60604-3507
312-353-5680

Regional Director
Office for Rocky Mountain Area
633 17th Street, 14th Floor
Denver, CO 80202-3607
303-672-5440

Regional Director
Office for New York/New Jersey

26 Federal Plaza, Suite 3541
New York, NY 10278-0068
212-264-1161

Regional Director
Office for Southwest
801 Cherry Street
Fort Worth, TX 76113-2905
817-978-5980

Regional Director
Office for Pacific/Hawaii
450 Golden Gate Avenue
San Francisco, CA 94102-3448
415-436-6550

Regional Director
Office for Mid-Atlantic
100 Penn Square East
Wanamaker Building
Philadelphia, PA 19107-3380
215-656-0600

Regional Director
Office for Great Plains
400 State Avenue
Room 200
Kansas City, KS 66101-2406
913-551-5462

Regional Director
Office for Southeast/Caribbean
40 Marietta Street
Five Points Plaza
Atlanta, GA 30303-2806
404-331-4111

Regional Director
Office for Northwest and Alaska
909 1st Avenue
Suite 200
Seattle, WA 98104-1000
206-220-5108

Matthew Lesko, Information USA, Inc., 12081 Nebel Street, Rockville, MD 20852 • 1-800-955-7693 • www.lesko.com

State Housing Assistance

Every state has a variety of programs to help with the construction and purchase of homes. Housing finance agencies (HFAs) have been created by states to issue tax-exempt bonds to finance mortgages for lower-income first-time home buyers and to build multi-family housing. Funds are also available for persons who take steps to make their homes more energy efficient, for home owners and landlords who remove lead paint from dwelling units, for houses without plumbing or those with plumbing that is dysfunctional, for handicapped persons, and to help landlords defray the costs of bringing low-income housing into compliance. In many states, elderly home owners can look to the HFA to obtain financing and/or support services they need to remain in their homes and avoid institutionalization. Some of the states have more than one agency dedicated to housing, and many cities and counties have quasi-federal/quasi-local housing authorities with addition programs.

State Housing Offices

Alabama
Alabama Housing Finance Authority
P.O. Box 230909
Montgomery, AL 36123-0909
334-244-9200
800-325-AHFA
www.ahfa.com

Alaska
Alaska Housing Finance Corporation
P.O. Box 101020
4300 Boniface Parkway
Anchorage, AK 99510
907-338-6100
800-478-2432 (AK)
www.ahfc.state.ak.us

Arizona
Arizona Department of Commerce
Governor's Office of Housing Development
3800 N. Central, Suite 1200
Phoenix, AZ 85012
602-280-8165
www.housingaz.com

Arkansas
Arkansas Development Finance Authority
100 Main St., Suite 200
Little Rock, AR 72203
501-682-5900
www.accessarkansas.org/adfa

California
California Housing Finance Agency
1121 L St., 7th Floor
Sacramento, CA 95814
916-322-3991
www.chfa.ca.gov

California Department of Housing and
Community Development
P.O. Box 952050
Sacramento, CA 94252-2050
916-445-4782
http://housing.hcd.ca.gov

Colorado
Colorado Housing and Finance Authority
1981 Blake St.
Denver, CO 80202-1272
303-297-2432
www.colohfa.org

Connecticut
Connecticut Housing Finance Authority
999 West St.

Rocky Hill, CT 06067
860-721-9501
www.chfa.org/MainPages

Delaware
Delaware State Housing Authority
Division of Housing and Community
Development
18 the Green
Dover, DE 19901
302-739-4263
www2.state.de.us/dsha

District of Columbia
DC Department of Housing and Community
Development
801 North Capitol Street, NE, Suite 8000
Washington, DC 20002
202-442-7200
www.dhcd.dcgov.org/main.shtm

DC Housing Finance Agency
815 Florida Avenue, NW
Washington, DC 20001
202-777-1600
www.dchfa.org

Florida
Florida Housing Finance Corp.
227 N. Bronough St., Suite 5000
Tallahassee, FL 32301-1329
850-488-4197
www.floridahousing.org

Georgia
Georgia Housing Finance Division
60 Executive Park NE
Atlanta, GA 30329
404-679-4840
800-359-4663
www.dca.state.ga.us/housing/index.html

Hawaii
Housing & Community Development
Corporation of Hawaii
677 Queen Street, Suite 300
Honolulu, HI 96813
808-587-0597
www.hcdch.state.hi.us

Idaho
Idaho Housing & Finance Association
565 W. Myrtle
P.O. Box 7899
Boise, ID 83707-1899

208-331-4882
www.ihfa.org

Illinois
Illinois Housing Development Authority
401 N. Michigan Ave., Suite 900
Chicago, IL 60611
312-836-5200
800-942-8439
www.ihda.org

Indiana
Indiana Housing Finance Authority
115 W. Washington
South Tower, Suite 1350
Indianapolis, IN 46204-3413
317-232-7778
800-872-0371 (IN)
www.in.gov/ihfa

Iowa
Iowa Finance Authority
100 E. Grand Ave., Suite 250
Des Moines, IA 50309
515-242-4990
800-432-7230
www.ifahome.com

Kansas
Kansas Housing Development
1000 SW Jackson Street, Suite 100
Topeka, KS 66612-1354
785-296-5865
http://kdoch.state.ks.us/ProgramApp/
index_mm.jsp

Kentucky
Kentucky Housing Corporation
1231 Louisville Rd.
Frankfort, KY 40601
502-564-7630
800-633-8896
www.kentuckyhousing.org

Louisiana
Louisiana Housing Finance Agency
200 Lafayette St.
Baton Rouge, LA 70801
504-342-1310
www.lhfa.state.la.us

Maine
Maine State Housing Authority
353 Water St.

Augusta, ME 04330-4633
207-626-4600
800-452-4668
www.mainehousing.org

Maryland
Department of Housing and Community
Development
100 Community Place
Crownsville, MD 21032
410-514-7000
800-756-0119 (MD)
www.dhcd.state.md.us

Massachusetts
Massachusetts Housing Finance Agency
1 Beacon St.
Boston, MA 02108
617-854-1000
www.mhfa.com/

Department of Housing & Community
Development
One Congress Street
Boston, MA 02114-2010
617-727-7765
www.state.ma.us/dhcd

Michigan
Michigan State Housing Development
Authority
735 East Michigan Avenue
P.O. Box 30044
Lansing, MI 48912
517-373-8370
800-327-9158
www.mshda.org

Minnesota
Minnesota Housing Finance Agency
400 Sibley St., Suite 300
St. Paul, MN 55101
612-296-7608
800-657-3769
www.mhfa.state.mn.us

Mississippi
Mississippi Home Corporation
P.O. Box 23369
Jackson, MS 39225-3369
601-718-4642
www.mshomecorp.com

Missouri
Missouri Housing Development Commission
3435 Broadway
Kansas City, MO 64111-2415
816-759-6600
www.mhdc.com

Montana
Montana Board of Housing
836 Front St.
Helena, MT 59601
406-444-3040
800-761-6264
http://commerce.state.mt.us/housing/
hous_home.html

Nebraska
Nebraska Investment Finance Authority
1230 O St., Commerce Court
Lincoln, NE 68508
402-434-3900
800-204-NIFA
www.nifa.org

Nevada
Department of Business & Industry
Housing Division
Evergreen Center
1802 N. Carson St., Suite 154

Carson City, NV 89701-1229
775-687-4258
800-227-4960
www.state.nv.us/busi_industry/hd

Nevada Rural Housing Authority
2100 California St.
Carson City, NV 89701
775-887-1795

New Hampshire
Housing Finance Authority
P.O. Box 5087
Manchester, NH 03108
603-472-8623
800-640-7239 (NH)
www.nhhfa.org

New Jersey
New Jersey Housing and Mortgage Finance
Agency
637 S. Clinton Ave.
P.O. Box 18550
Trenton, NJ 08650-2085
609-278-7400
800-NJ-HOUSE
www.state.nj.us/dca/hmfa

New Mexico
Mortgage Finance Authority
344 4th Street, SW
Albuquerque, NM 87102
505-843-6880
800-444-6880
www.housingnm.org/default.htm

New York
New York Division of Housing and
Community Renewal
Albany:
Hampton Plaza
38-40 State Street
Albany, NY 12207
518-473-2517
New York:
25 Beaver Street
New York, NY 10004
212-480-6700
866-ASK-DHCR (both locations)
www.dhcr.state.ny.us

North Carolina
North Carolina Housing Finance Agency
3508 Bush St.
Raleigh, NC 27609
919-877-5700
www.nchfa.com

North Dakota
Housing Finance Agency
P.O. Box 1535
Bismarck, ND 58502-1535
701-328-8080
800-292-8621
www.ndhfa.org

Ohio
Ohio Housing Finance Agency
57 E. Main St.
Columbus, OH 43215-5135
614-466-7970
www.odod.state.oh.us/OHFA.htm

Oklahoma
Oklahoma Housing Finance Agency
P.O. Box 26720
Oklahoma City, OK 73126-0720
405-848-1144
800-256-1489
www.state.ok.us/~ohfa

Oregon
Oregon Housing & Community Services
Housing Division
1600 State St.
Salem, OR 97309-0409
503-986-2106
www.hcs.state.or.us

Pennsylvania
Pennsylvania Housing Finance Agency
2101 North Front St.
P.O. Box 8029
Harrisburg, PA 17105-8029
717-780-3800
www.phfa.org

Rhode Island
Rhode Island Housing and Mortgage Finance
Corporation
44 Washington St.
Providence, RI 02903
401-751-5566
800-427-5560
www.rihousing.com

South Carolina
South Carolina State Housing Financing and
Development Authority
919 Bluff Rd.
Columbia, SC 29201
803-734-2000
www.sha.state.sc.us

South Dakota
South Dakota Housing Development
Authority
P.O. Box 1237
Pierre, SD 57501-1237
605-773-3181
www.sdhda.org

Tennessee
Tennessee Housing Development Agency
404 James Robertson Pkwy, Suite 1114
Nashville, TN 37243-0900
615-741-2400
www.state.tn.us/thda

Texas
Texas Department of Housing & Community
Affairs
Waller Creek Office Building
507 Sabine Street
P.O. Box 13941
Austin, TX 78711-3941
512-475-3800
www.tdhca.state.tx.us

Utah
Utah Housing Corporation
554 South, 300 East
Salt Lake City, UT 84111
801-521-6950
800-344-0452
800-284-6950 (UT)
www.utahhousingcorp.org

Vermont
Vermont Housing Finance Agency
One Burlington Sq.
164 St. Paul St.
Burlington, VT 05401-4364
802-864-5743
800-287-8432
www.vhfa.org

Vermont State Housing Authority
1 Prospect St.
Montpelier, VT 05602-3556
802-828-3295
www.vsha.org

Virginia

Virginia Housing Development Authority
601 S. Belvidere St.
Richmond, VA 23220-6504
804-782-1986
800-968-7837
www.vhda.com

Washington

Washington State Housing Finance
Commission
1000 Second Ave., Suite 2700
Seattle, WA 98104-1046
206-464-7139

800-767-4663
www.wshfc.org

West Virginia

West Virginia Housing Development Fund
814 Virginia St., East
Charleston, WV 25301
304-345-6475
800-933-9843
www.wvhdf.com/

Wisconsin

Wisconsin Housing and Economic
Development Authority

P.O. Box 1728
Madison, WI 53701-1728
608-266-7884
800-334-6873
www.wheda.com

Wyoming

Wyoming Community Development Authority
155 North Beech
Casper, WY 82602
307-265-0603
www.wyomingcda.com

Insurance: Car, Homeowner, and Health

Each state has its own laws and regulations for all types of insurance, including car, homeowner, and health insurance. The officials listed below enforce these laws. Many of these offices can provide you with information to help you make informed insurance buying decisions. If you have a question or complaint about your insurance company's policies, contact the company in question first. If you do not receive a satisfactory response, then contact the state insurance regulator. They can answer many questions, including:

- What are some tips on how to choose an insurance policy?
- Are there consumer guides to different policies?
- What should you do if you have been unfairly treated by an insurance company?

State Insurance Commissioners

Alabama
Insurance Commissioner
201 Monroe St., Suite 1700
Montgomery, AL 36104
www.aldoi.org
334-269-3550

Alaska
Director of Insurance
P.O. Box 110805
Juneau, AK 99811-0805
907-465-2515
800-INSUR-AK
www.dced.state.ak.us/insurance

Arizona
Director of Insurance
2910 N. 44th St., Suite 210
Phoenix, AZ 85018
602-912-8400
800-325-2548
www.state.az.us/id/

Arkansas
Insurance Commissioner
1200 W. 3rd St.
Little Rock, AR 72201
501-371-2600
800-282-9134
www.accessarkansas.org/insurance

California
Commissioner of Insurance
300 S. Spring St., 13th Floor
Los Angeles, CA 90013
916-492-3500 (Sacramento)
213-897-8921 (Los Angeles)
800-927-HELP
www.insurance.ca.gov/docs/index.html

Colorado
Commissioner of Insurance
1560 Broadway, Suite 850
Denver, CO 80202
303-894-7499
800-930-3745
www.dora.state.co.us/insurance

Connecticut
Insurance Commissioner
P.O. Box 816
Hartford, CT 06142-0816
860-297-3800
800-203-3447
www.state.ct.us/cid/

Delaware
Insurance Commissioner
841 Silver Lake Blvd.
Dover, DE 19904
302-739-4251
800-282-8611
www.state.de.us/inscom

District of Columbia
Director of Insurance
810 First St., NE, Suite 701
Washington, DC 20002
202-727-8000
www.disr.washingtondc.gov/main.shtm

Florida
Insurance Commissioner
200 E. Gaines St.
Tallahassee, FL 32399-0300
850-413-3100
800-342-2762
www.doi.state.fl.us/

Georgia
Insurance Commissioner
West Tower, Suite 704
2 Martin Luther King, Jr. Dr.
Atlanta, GA 30334
404-656-2070
800-656-2298
www.inscomm.state.ga.us

Hawaii
Insurance Commissioner
250 S. King St., 5th Floor
P.O. Box 3614
Honolulu, HI 96811
808-586-2790
www.state.hi.us/dcca/ins

Idaho
Director of Insurance
P.O. Box 83720
Boise, ID 83720-0043
208-334-4250
800-721-3272 (complaints)
www.doi.state.id.us/

Illinois
Director of Insurance
320 W. Washington St.
Springfield, IL 62767-0001
217-782-4515
877-527-9431 (health)
866-445-5364 (toll-free)
www.state.il.us/ins/

Indiana
Commissioner of Insurance
311 W. Washington St.
Suite 300
Indianapolis, IN 46204-2787
317-232-2385
800-622-4461
www.ai.org/idoi/index.html

Iowa
Insurance Commissioner
330 Maple St.
Des Moines, IA 50319
515-281-5705
877-955-1212
www.iid.state.ia.us/

Kansas
Commissioner of Insurance
420 SW 9th St.
Topeka, KS 66612-1678
785-296-5865
800-432-2484
www.ksinsurance.org

Kentucky
Insurance Commissioner
215 W. Main St.
P.O. Box 517
Frankfort, KY 40602
502-564-3630
800-595-6053
www.doi.state.ky.us/kentucky

Louisiana
Commissioner of Insurance
P.O. Box 94214
Baton Rouge, LA 70804-9214
225-342-5900
800-259-5300
www.ldi.state.la.us/

Maine
Superintendent of Insurance
#34 State House Station
Augusta, ME 04333
207-624-8475
800-300-5000 (ME)
www.state.me.us/pfr/ins/ins_index.htm

Maryland
Insurance Commissioner
525 St. Paul Place
Baltimore, MD 21202
410-486-2000

Matthew Lesko, Information USA, Inc., 12081 Nebel Street, Rockville, MD 20852 • 1-800-955-7693 • www.lesko.com

800-492-6116
www.mdinsurance.state.md.us

Massachusetts
Commissioner of Insurance
One South Station
Boston, MA 02210-2208
617-521-7794
www.state.ma.us/doi

Michigan
Commissioner of Insurance
Insurance Bureau
P.O. Box 30220
Lansing, MI 48909-7720
517-373-0220
877-999-6442
www.cis.state.mi.us/ofis

Minnesota
Commissioner of Commerce
85 7th Place E, Suite 500
St. Paul, MN 55101
612-297-7161
800-657-3602 (complaints)
800-657-3978 (license status)
www.commerce.state.mn.us/pages/
InsuranceMain.htm

Mississippi
Commissioner of Insurance
1001 Woolfolk State Office Building
501 N. Main St.
P.O. Box 79
Jackson, MS 39205
601-359-3569
800-562-2957
www.doi.state.ms.us

Missouri
Director of Insurance
301 W. High St.
P.O. Box 690
Jefferson City, MO 65102-0690
573-751-4126
800-726-7390
www.insurance.state.mo.us

Montana
Commissioner of Insurance
P.O. Box 4009
Helena, MT 59604-4009
406-444-2040
800-332-6148 (MT)
www.discoveringmontana.com/sao/
default.htm

Nebraska
Director of Insurance
941 O St., Suite 400
Lincoln, NE 68508-3639
402-471-2201
www.nol.org/home/ndoi/

Nevada
Commissioner of Insurance
788 Fairview Dr., Suite 300
Carson City, NV 89701-5491
775-687-4270
800-992-0900
http://doi.state.nv.us

New Hampshire
Insurance Commissioner
56 Old Suncook Rd.
Concord, NH 03301
603-271-2261
800-852-3416
http://webster.state.nh.us/insurance

New Jersey
Commissioner
Department of Insurance
20 W. State St.
P.O. Box 325
Trenton, NJ 08625-0325
609-292-5360
www.state.nj.us/dobi/index.html

New Mexico
Superintendent of Insurance
P.O. Drawer 1269
Santa Fe, NM 87504-1269
505-827-4601
800-947-4722
www.nmprc.state.nm.us

New York
Superintendent of Insurance
25 Beaver St.
New York, NY 10004
212-480-6400
800-342-3736 (in NY)
www.ins.state.ny.us/njins.htm

North Carolina
Commissioner of Insurance
P.O. Box 26387
Raleigh, NC 27611
919-733-2032
800-546-5664
www.ncdoi.com

North Dakota
Commissioner of Insurance
600 E. Boulevard Ave., Dept. 401
Bismarck, ND 58505-0320
701-328-2440
800-247-0560 (in ND)
www.state.nd.us/ndins

Ohio
Director of Insurance
2100 Stella Court
Columbus, OH 43215-1067
614-644-2658
800-686-1526 (consumer)
800-686-1527 (fraud)
800-686-1578 (senior health)
www.ohioinsurance.gov

Oklahoma
Insurance Commissioner
P.O. Box 53408
Oklahoma City, OK 73152-3408
405-521-2828
800-522-0071
www.oid.state.ok.us

Oregon
Insurance Commissioner
350 Winter St., NE, Room 440
Salem, OR 97301
503-947-7980
800-722-4134
www.cbs.state.or.us/external/ins

Pennsylvania
Insurance Commissioner
1326 Strawberry Square
Harrisburg, PA 17120
717-787-2317
877-881-6388
www.insurance.state.pa.us

Rhode Island
Insurance Commissioner
233 Richmond St., Suite 233
Providence, RI 02903
401-222-2223
www.dbr.state.ri.us/insurance.html

South Carolina
Chief Insurance Commissioner
P.O. Box 100105
Columbia, SC 29202-3105
803-737-6150
800-768-3467
www.state.sc.us/doi/

South Dakota
Director of Insurance
Insurance Bldg.
118 W. Capitol St.
Pierre, SD 57501
605-773-3563
www.state.sd.us/dcr/insurance/

Tennessee
Commissioner of Insurance
500 James Robertson Parkway, 4th Floor
Nashville, TN 37243-0565
615-741-2218
800-342-4029
www.state.tn.us/commerce/insurdiv.html

Texas
Insurance Commissioner
P.O. Box 149104
Austin, TX 78701
512-463-6169
800-578-4677
www.tdi.state.tx.us

Utah
Commissioner of Insurance
State Office Bldg., Room 3110
Salt Lake City, UT 84114
801-538-3800
800-439-3805
www.insurance.utah.gov

Vermont
Commissioner of Banking and Insurance
89 Main St., Drawer 20
Montpelier, VT 05620-3101
802-828-3301
800-964-1784
www.bishca.state.vt.us/InsurDiv/
Insur_index.htm

Virginia
Commissioner of Insurance
Tyler Bldg.
1300 E. Main St.
P.O. Box 1157
Richmond, VA 23218
804-371-9741
800-552-7945
www.state.va.us/scc/division/voi/
webpages/homepageb.htm

Washington
Insurance Commissioner
P.O. Box 40255
Olympia, WA 98504-0255
360-753-7300
800-562-6900 (WA)
www.insurance.wa.gov

West Virginia
Insurance Commissioner
1124 Smith St.
P.O. Box 50540
Charleston, WV 25305-0540
304-558-3386
800-642-9004
www.state.wv.us/insurance

Wisconsin
Commissioner of Insurance
121 E. Wilson St.
Madison, WI 53702

608-266-3585
800-236-8517 (WI)
http://oci.wi.gov/oci_home.htm

Wyoming
Commissioner of Insurance
Herschler Building

3rd Floor, East
122 W. 25th St
Cheyenne, WY 82002
307-777-7401
800-438-5768 (WY)
http://insurance.state.wy.us/index.htm

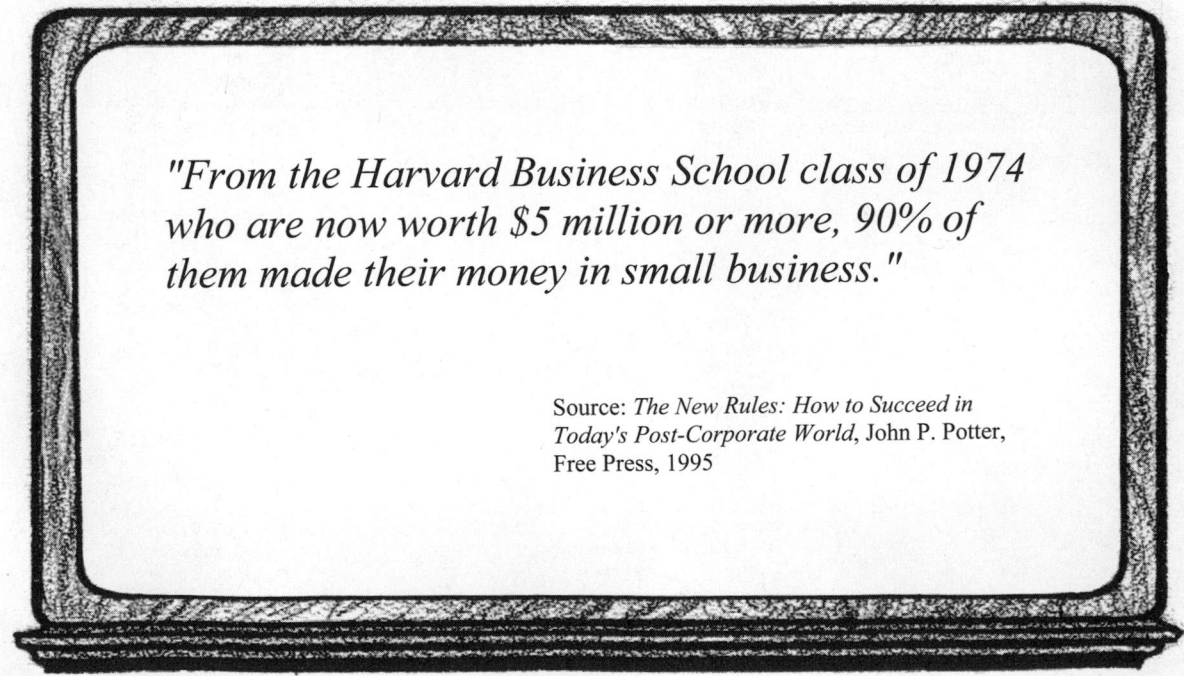

"From the Harvard Business School class of 1974 who are now worth $5 million or more, 90% of them made their money in small business."

Source: *The New Rules: How to Succeed in Today's Post-Corporate World*, John P. Potter, Free Press, 1995

Put Your Money In A Safe (Place, That Is)

Finding the right bank, savings and loan, or credit union means figuring out your own needs first. How much money can you keep on deposit and how many checks will you write? Examine your future loans and savings needs, as well as look at the convenience of the financial institution, its service charges, fees, and deposit and loan interest rates. Before making your final choice, make sure the institutions you're considering are federally insured. The offices listed below can answer such questions as:

- what is a bank's asset size?
- what are all the banks in a state that are covered by their office?
- where is a particular bank located and where are its branches?

For information about a particular financial institution, contact one of the following offices:

National Banks (banks that have the word "National" in their names or the initials "N.A." after their names)
Comptroller of the Currency, Compliance Management, Department of the Treasury, 250 E St., SW, Washington, DC 20219, 202-874-5000; {www.occ.treas.gov}.

FDIC-Insured Banks
Division of Compliance and Consumer Affairs, FDIC, 550 17th St., NW, Washington, DC 20429, 877-ASK-FDIC, 202-942-3080, 800-934-3342; {www.fdic.gov}.

Savings and Loans
Office of Thrift Supervision, Department of Treasury, 1700 G St., NW, Washington, DC 20552, 202-906-6237, 800-842-6929; {www.ots.treas.gov}.

State Banks
Contact your State Government Banking Commissioner located in your state capital (see state by state listing below).

State Government Banking Commissioners

Alabama
Superintendent of Banks
401 Adams Ave., Suite 680
Montgomery, AL 36130
334-242-3452
www.bank.state.al.us

Alaska
Department of Community and Economic
Development
Division of Banking, Securities, and
Corporations
150 Third Street
Suite 217
Juneau, AK 99801
MAILING ADDRESS:
   P.O. Box 110807
   Juneau, AK 99811-0807
907-465-2521
www.dced.state.ak.us/bsc/home.htm

Arizona
Superintendent of Banks
2910 N. 44th St., Suite 310
Phoenix, AZ 85018
602-255-4421

800-544-0708 (toll free in AZ)
www.azbanking.com

Arkansas
Bank Commissioner
The Sedgwick Center
400 Hardin Road, Suite 100
Little Rock, AR 72211
501-324-9019
www.accessarkansas.org/bank

California
Commissioner of Financial Institutions
State Banking Department
111 Pine St., Suite 1100
San Francisco, CA 94111-5613
415-263-8500
800-622-0620 (toll free in CA)
www.dfi.ca.gov

Colorado
State Bank Commissioner
Division of Banking
Denver Post Bldg.
1560 Broadway, Suite 1175
Denver, CO 80202

303-894-7575
www.dora.state.co.us/banking

Connecticut
Banking Commissioner
260 Constitution Plaza
Hartford, CT 06103
860-240-8200
800-831-7225 (toll free in CT)
www.state.ct.us/dob/

Delaware
State Bank Commissioner
555 E. Lockerman St.
Suite 210
Dover, DE 19901
302-739-4235
800-638-3376 (toll free in DE for complaints only)
www.state.de.us/bank/index.htm

District of Columbia
Commissioner of Banking and Financial
Institutions
1400 L Street, NW, Suite 400
Washington, DC 20005

202-727-1563
http://dbfi.dc.gov/main.shtm

Florida

Florida Department of Banking & Finance
State Comptroller
101 East Gaines Street
Tallahassee, FL 32399-0350
850-410-9286
800-848-3792
www.dbf.state.fl.us

Georgia

Commissioner of Banking and Finance
2990 Brandywine Rd., Suite 200
Atlanta, GA 30341-5565
770-986-1633
www.ganet.org/dbf/dbf.html

Hawaii

Commissioner of Financial Institutions
Department of Commerce and Consumer
Affairs
P.O. Box 2054
1010 Richards St., Room 602A
Honolulu, HI 96805
808-586-2820
www.state.hi.us/dcca/dfi

Idaho

Department of Finance
P.O. Box 83720
700 W. State St., 2nd Floor
Boise, ID 83720-0031
208-332-8000
888-346-3378 (ID)
www.finance.state.id.us/home.asp

Illinois

Commissioner of Banks and Real Estate
500 E. Monroe St.
Springfield, IL 62701
217-782-3000
877-793-3470
www.obre.state.il.us

Indiana

Department of Financial Institutions
402 W. Washington, Room W066
Indianapolis, IN 46204
317-232-3955
800-382-4880 (toll free in IN)
www.dfi.state.in.us/

Iowa

Superintendent of Banking
200 E. Grand, Suite 300
Des Moines, IA 50309
515-281-4014
www.idob.state.ia.us

Kansas

State Bank Commissioner
700 Jackson St., Suite 300
Topeka, KS 66603-3714
785-296-2266
www.osbckansas.org

Kentucky

Commissioner
Department of Financial Institutions
1025 Capital Center Dr., Suite 200
Frankfort, KY 40601
502-573-3390
800-223-2579
www.dfi.state.ky.us/

Louisiana

Commissioner of Financial Institutions
8660 United Plaza Blvd., 2nd Floor
P.O. Box 94095

Baton Rouge, LA 70804-9095
225-925-4660
www.ofi.state.la.us

Maine

Superintendent of Banking
#36 State House Station
Augusta, ME 04333-0036
207-624-8570
800-965-5235
www.state.me.us/pfr/bkg/bkg_index.htm

Maryland

Commissioner of Financial Regulation
500 North Calvert St., Room 402
Baltimore, MD 21202-2272
410-230-6100
www.dllr.state.md.us/finance

Massachusetts

Commissioner of Banks
One South Station
Boston, MA 02110
617-956-1500
800-495-2265
www.state.ma.us/dob/

Michigan

Commissioner of Financial & Insurance
Services
P.O. Box 30220
Lansing, MI 48909-7720
517-373-0220
877-999-6442
www.cis.state.mi.us/ofis

Minnesota

Department of Commerce
Division of Financial Examinations
85 7th Place East, Suite 500
St. Paul, MN 55101-2198
651-296-2135
www.commerce.state.mn.us/pages/
FinancialServicesMain.htm

Mississippi

Commissioner of Banking and Consumer
Finance
P.O. Box 23729
Jackson, MS 39225-3729
601-359-1031
800-844-2499
www.dbcf.state.ms.us/

Missouri

Commissioner of Finance
P.O. Box 716
Jefferson City, MO 65102
573-751-3242
800-722-3321
www.ecodev.state.mo.us/finance/
finhome.htm

Montana

Commissioner of Banking and Financial
Institutions
P.O. Box 200546
Helena, MT 59620-0546
406-444-2091
http://discoveringmontana.com/doa/banking

Nebraska

Director of Banking and Finance
P.O. Box 95006
1200 N. Street
The Atrium, Suite 311
Lincoln, NE 68509-5006
402-471-2171
www.ndbf.org

Nevada

Commissioner of Financial Institutions
406 E. Second St., Suite 3
Carson City, NV 89701-4758
775-684-1830
http://fid.state.nv.us

New Hampshire

Bank Commissioner
64B Old Suncook Road
Concord, NH 03301
603-271-3561
http://webster.state.nh.us/banking

New Jersey

Commissioner of Banking
P.O. Box 040
Trenton, NJ 08625
609-292-5360
www.state.nj.us/dobi/index.html

New Mexico

Financial Institutions Division
722 St. Michael's Drive
Santa Fe, NM 87501
505-827-7100
www.rld.state.nm.us/fid/index.htm

New York

Superintendent of Banks
Two Rector St., 118th Floor
New York, NY 10006-1894
212-618-6553
800-522-3330 (consumer)
800-832-1838 (small business)
www.banking.state.ny.us/

North Carolina

Commissioner of Banks
316 W. Edenton St.
Raleigh, NC 27603
MAILING ADDRESS:
    4309 Mail Service Center
    Raleigh, NC 27699-4309
919-733-3016
www.banking.state.nc.us/

North Dakota

Commissioner of Banking and Financial
Institutions
2000 Schafer St., Suite G
Bismarck, ND 58501-1204
701-328-9933
www.state.nd.us/dfi

Ohio

Superintendent of Financial Institutions
77 S. High St., 21st Floor
Columbus, OH 43215-0121
614-728-8400
www.com.state.oh.us/odoc/dfi

Oklahoma

Bank Commissioner
4545 N. Lincoln Blvd., Suite 164
Oklahoma City, OK 73105-3427
405-521-2782
www.state.ok.us/~osbd/

Oregon

Administrator
Division of Finance and Corporate Securities
350 Winter St., NE, Room 410
Salem, OR 97301-3881
503-378-4140
800-722-4134
www.cbs.state.or.us/dfcs/

Pennsylvania

Secretary of Banking
333 Market St., 16th Floor
Harrisburg, PA 17101-2290

717-787-2665
800-PA-BANKS (toll free in PA)
www.banking.state.pa.us/

Rhode Island
Director and Superintendent of Banking
Department of Business Regulation
Division of Banking
233 Richmond St., Suite 231
Providence, RI 02903-4231
401-222-2405
www.dbr.state.ri.us

South Carolina
Commissioner of Banking
Calhoun Office Bldg.
Columbia, SC 29211
803-734-2001
www.lpitr.state.sc.us/gvtdir97/p225.htm

South Dakota
Director of Banking
Division of Banking
217 1/2 West Missouri
Pierre, SD 57501-4590
605-773-3421
www.state.sd.us/dcr/bank/BANK-HOM.htm

Tennessee
Commissioner of Financial Institutions
500 Charlotte Ave.
John Sevier Bldg., 4th Floor
Nashville, TN 37243-0705
615-741-2236
www.state.tn.us/financialinst/

Texas
Banking Commissioner
2601 N. Lamar Blvd.
Austin, TX 78705
512-475-1300
877-276-5554 (consumer hotline)
www.banking.state.tx.us

Utah
Commissioner of Financial Institutions
P.O. Box 89
Salt Lake City, UT 84110-0089
801-538-8830
www.dfi.utah.gov

Vermont
Deputy Commissioner of Banking
89 Main St., Drawer 20
Montpelier, VT 05620-3101
802-828-3307
www.bishca.state.vt.us

Virginia
Bureau of Financial Institutions
1300 E. Main St.
Suite 800
P.O. Box 640
Richmond, VA 23218-0640
804-371-9657
800-552-7945 (toll free in VA)
www.state.va.us/scc/division/banking

Washington
Department of Financial Institutions
Division of Banking

210 11th Ave., SW, Room 300
P.O. Box 41200
Olympia, WA 98504-1200
360-902-8700
800-372-8303
www.dfi.wa.gov

West Virginia
Commissioner of Banking
1900 Kanawha Blvd. East
Bldg. 3, Room 311
Charleston, WV 25305-0240
304-558-2294
800-642-9056
www.wvdob.org

Wisconsin
Secretary of Financial Institutions
345 W. Washington Ave., 4th Floor
P.O. Box 7876
Madison, WI 53707
608-261-7578
800-452-3328
www.wdfi.org

Wyoming
Banking Commissioner
Division of Banking
Department of Audit
Herschler Bldg.
3 East, 122 W. 25th St.
Cheyenne, WY 82002
307-777-7797
http://audit.state.wy.us/banking/banking.htm

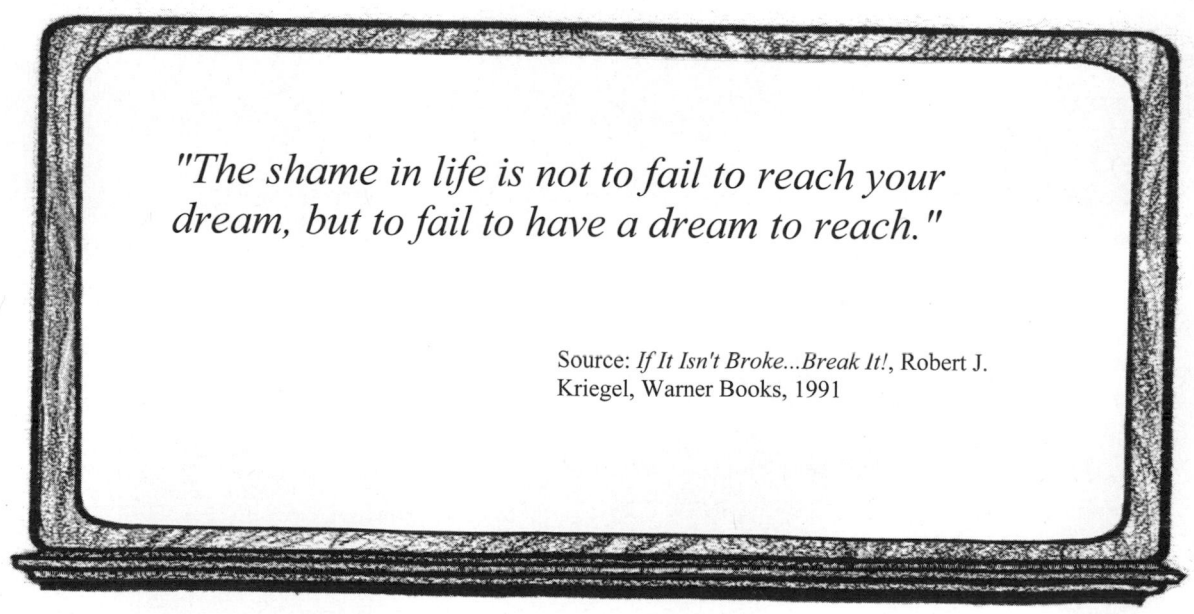

"The shame in life is not to fail to reach your dream, but to fail to have a dream to reach."

Source: *If It Isn't Broke...Break It!*, Robert J. Kriegel, Warner Books, 1991

How Do I
Take Care Of The Kids?

How Do I Take Care Of The Kids?

Families all over the country are taking advantage of government programs to help parents find affordable day care for their little ones. States get money to fund grants, contracts, and certificates for these day care centers. Many also provide money for after- and before-school programs. But they also spend the money on people who want to start a day care center. Each state is given a great deal of latitude as to how the child care money is distributed, so it is important that you ask about child care assistance when you apply for JOB CORPS, other training or education programs, Temporary Assistance for Needy Families (TANF), or if you are just making ends meet. If you are a parent wondering if there are programs to help you pay for day care, or if you want to start a day care center and want to know which major programs support families who use day care...here they are.

Former AFDC Recipient

Robvato Gray, a 27-year old mother of four children, had been on welfare since the age of 18 and had lived in government housing for eight years. She received food stamps and $184 per month from AFDC.

Wanting to improve herself, she started to provide child care for mothers at $25 per week. Soon she began to realize that she was providing the same quality care that centers in her area were providing, but she was charging only about one-third of the money that the centers were receiving.

She began checking into government programs and started to participate in a program where the government paid Day Care Home Providers weekly to watch the children of welfare recipients, while the mothers worked. The program also gives the day care provider money on a monthly basis to provide food for the children in her care. Additionally, she got a government grant through a neighborhood center to purchase $1000 worth of toys for the children she watched.

By increasing her weekly fee to about $75, Robvato not only increased her income from $104 per month to $4000 per month, but also increased her self esteem, and it was a welcome benefit. She has been off welfare for a year and a half, has two homes, and two vehicles. The inspiration of this success has led her to start a janitorial business, as well as to give speeches and to train other women on AFDC to become self-sufficient as she was able to do.

* Let Every Child Get A Head Start

Administration For Children and Families
U.S. Department of Health and Human Services
Head Start Bureau
330 C Street, SW
Washington, DC 20447
MAILING ADDRESS:
P.O. Box 1182
Washington, DC 20013   202-205-8572
www2.acf.dhhs.gov/programs/hsb/

Each year, almost one million children from low-income families enter school for the first time, and many have health problems and a lack of self confidence. The Head Start Program addresses the needs of low-income preschool children, and provides educational, social, medical, dental, nutrition, and mental health services. In 1996, Head Start had 1,440 grantees offering services to nearly 800,000 children. In order to qualify to enroll a child in a Head Start program, a parent must meet certain income guidelines (in 2001 a family of 3 could earn $14,630), and parent involvement is encouraged. The U.S. Department of Health and Human Services awards grants to local public agencies, private nonprofit organizations and school systems for the purpose of operating Head Start programs at the community level. To locate a Head Start Program near you, contact your local board of education or Department of Social Services (look in the blue pages of your phone book), or contact the office listed above. For a complete list of grantees in your state, check out this website: {www2.acf.dhhs.gov/programs/hsb/grantees/index.htm}

* Ease Some Of Your Employees Concerns

Women's Bureau Clearinghouse
Women's Bureau
U.S. Department of Labor
200 Constitution Ave., NW, Room S-3311   202-219-6652
Washington, DC 20210   800-827-5335
www.dol.gov/dol/wb/

The Women's Bureau is in the process of updating publications. They are concentrating on new issues with the new administration; retirement benefits, family leave, etc. For more information, contact the office listed above.

* Get Up To $3,556 In Credits Or Refunds

Internal Revenue Service
Information Line   800-829-1040
www.irs.gov

Take advantage of some of the perks the IRS gives to those who have children. If you have a job, earn less than $32,121 (2001 figure), and have 2 or more qualifying children, or earn less than $28,281 with one qualifying child living with you, you could be eligible for the Earned Income Credit (EIC). This Credit reduces the amount of tax you owe, and is intended to offset some of the increases in living expenses and social security taxes. The EIC is comprised of three different credits: basic, health insurance, and extra credit for a child born in the tax year. You could qualify for up to $2,428 for one qualifying child, and $4,008 for 2 or more qualifying children. Get a copy of Publication 596 which explains the form you need to file and eligibility guidelines.

* Get A Kid, Get A Credit

Internal Revenue Service
Information Line   800-829-1040
www.irs.gov/

You may be able to take a credit if you pay someone to care for your dependent who is under age 13, your disabled dependent, or your disabled spouse, so that you can work. For purposes of the credit, "disabled" refers to a person physically or mentally not capable of self-care. Request Publication 503 Child and Dependent Care Expenses which outlines the credit, as well as explains the tax rules covering benefits paid under an employer-provided dependent care assistance plan.

* Child Care While You Train

Employment and Training Administration
U.S. Department of Labor
Office of Worker Retraining and
   Adjustment Programs
200 Constitution Ave., NW
Room N-4469
Washington, DC 20210   202-219-5577
www.doleta.gov/layoff

If you have been laid off from work and are not likely to return to the same employer, you may be considered a dislocated worker. Dislocated workers are those who have been laid off from a job due to factory downsizing, reorganization, trade issues, military downsizing, and more. There are many services available to dislocated workers through the Title III Program which provides for retraining and readjustments for these workers. Some local providers cover the cost of child care while you retrain for another job. To become eligible for these services, you must contact your local State Dislocated Worker Unit at 877-US-2JOBS or check out the website for a state listing. If you are part of any government training program, make sure to ask if child care or transportation costs are covered. In many instances, there are some funds available. The following programs also may offer child care:

Job Corps
U.S. Department of Labor
200 Constitution Ave., NW
Room N4507
Washington, DC 20210   202-219-5556
www.jobcorps.doleta.gov

Workforce Investment Act
U.S. Department of Labor
200 Constitution Ave., NW
Room S4231
Washington, DC 20210   202-693-3045
www.usworkforce.org

* Indian and Native American Job Training Program

U.S. Department of Labor
200 Constitution Ave., NW, Room N4641
Washington, DC 20210   202-219-8502
http://wdsc.doleta.gov/dinap/

* Workplace Literacy

U.S. Department of Education
Office of Vocational and Adult Education
4090 MES
400 Maryland Avenue, SW
Washington, DC 20202   202-205-5451
www.ed.gov/offices/OVAE/AdultEd/index.html

In order to improve the literacy rate for adults, many literacy programs are being started in the workplace. These programs teach basic skills that can result in new or continued employment, career advancement, or increased productivity for workers. Money is available for projects to improve literacy skills, adult secondary education services, and even to provide education counseling, transportation, and non-working hours child care services to adult workers while they participate in the program. To learn more about the grant application process or to learn what programs exist in your state, contact the office listed above.

* Money To Let You Hit The Books

Contact: Your College Admissions Office

In a survey of colleges around the country, it was discovered that over a thousand community colleges and four year colleges and universities provide child care for free or reduced costs. Most operate on a sliding fee scale, and offer a variety of services with some offering hot lunches and infant care. These child care centers are frequently staffed with preschool and early education students to provide them training while taking care of your child. Talk to the admission officer at schools which you are considering attending to learn if they offer this benefit, the cost of service with your income, and even if there is a waiting list.

* Give Everyone An Even Start

Compensatory Education Programs
U.S. Department of Education
Office of Elementary and Secondary Education
400 Maryland Ave., SW, Room 2043
Washington, DC 20202-6132   202-401-0113
www.evenstart.org/
or   www.ed.gov/offices/OESE/CEP/evenstrtquick.html

If someone you know is in need of training to learn to read and they also have a child under seven years of age, they may be able to participate in the Even Start Program. Even Start is designed to provide family centered education programs that involve parents and children. It includes instructional programs that promote adult literacy, train parents to support the educational growth of their children, and help children to succeed in school. Transportation to the program is offered, as is child care for the periods when parents are in the program. To be eligible, parents must reside in an elementary school area served by Chapter 1, which is for areas with a predominance of lower-income residents. Even Start is often offered by community based organizations, local education agencies, and others. The Office listed above can provide you with information on Even Start Programs near you, as well as provide you with information on Even Start Programs for Migrant Education and Indian Tribes.

Money For Child Care Or Even To Start
A Day Care Center

Child care issues should not be a stumbling block for people who want to start a training program or continue their education. This program emphasizes the role of parents in choosing the care that best meets their family's child care needs. Parents may choose from a variety of child care providers, including center-based, family child care and in-home care, care provided by relatives, and sectarian child care providers. You can even **get money to start a day care center.** Federal funds are available to states, Indian tribes, and territories to provide grants, contracts, and certificates for child care services for low income families with a parent who is working or attending a training or education program. Funding is also provided to improve the availability and quality of child care and for early childhood development and before- and after-school services. For information on how to take advantage of this program in your state and to find out about eligibility requirements, contact your state agency listed below or the main office at Division of Child Care, Administration for Children, Youth, and Families, U.S. Department of Health and Human Services, 200 Independence Ave., SW, Room 352G, Washington, DC 20201; 202-690-6782. You may also contact the National Child Care Information Center at 1-800-616-2242 <www.nccic.org/>.

Child Care and Development Block Grant State Lead Agencies

Alabama
Alabama Department of Human Resources
Family Services Division
50 N. Ripley St.
Montgomery, AL 36130
334-242-1773
Fax: 334-242-0513
www.dhr.state.al.us/fsd

Alaska
Alaska Department of Education and Early
Development
333 West 4th Avenue, Suite 320
Anchorage, AK 99501-2341
907-269-4500
Fax: 907-269-4520
www.eed.state.ak.us

Arizona
Arizona Department of Economic Security
Child Care Administrator
Box 6123
Phoenix, AZ 85005-6123
602-542-4248
Fax: 602-542-4197
www.dc.state.az.us/links/chdcare/fund.htm

Arkansas
Arkansas Department of Human Services
Division of Child Care and Early Childhood
Education
P.O. Box 1437, Slot S14-
Little Rock, AR 72203
501-682-4891
Fax: 501-682-4897/2317
www.state.ar.us/childcare

California
Child Development Division
California State Department of Education
560 J St., Suite 220
Sacramento, CA 95814-4785
916-322-6233
Fax: 916-323-6853
www.cde.ca.gov/cyfsbranch/
child development

Colorado
Office of Child Care Services
Colorado Department of Human Services
1575 Sherman St.
Denver, CO 80203-1714
303-866-5958
800-799-5876
Fax: 303-866-4453
www.cdhs.state.ca.us/childcare/home.html

Connecticut
Family Services Division
Child Care Team
Connecticut Department of Social Services
25 Sigourney St., 10th Floor
Hartford, CT 06106-5033
860-424-5006
Fax: 860-951-2996
www.dss.state.ct.us/ccare.htm

Delaware
Social Services Administrator
Delaware Dept. of Health and Social Services
1901 N. DuPont Hwy.
Lewis Bldg.
New Castle, DE 19720
302-577-4400
Fax: 302-577-4557
www.state.de.us/dss/dsshome.html

District of Columbia
Office of Early Childhood Development
717 14th St., NW, Suite 730
Washington, DC 20005
202-727-1839
Fax: 202-727-8166

Florida
Florida Partnership for School Readiness
600 South Calhoun Street
Holland Building, Room 251
Tallahassee, FL 32399
850-488-0337
Fax: 850-922-0337
www.myflorida.com/myflorida/government/
governmentinintives/schoolreadiness

Georgia
Child Care and Parent Services
Division of Family and Children Services
Georgia Department of Human Resources
Two Peachtree St., NW
Suite 21-293
Atlanta, GA 30303-3142
404-657-3438
Fax: 404-657-3489
www.div.dhr.state.ga.us/dfcs_caps/

Guam
Guam Department of Public Health and Social
Services
P.O. Box 2816
Agana, GU 96910
671-735-7102
Fax: 671-734-5910

Hawaii
Hawaii Department of Human Services
Benefits, Employment and Support Services
Division
820 Mililani St., Suite 600
Honolulu, HI 96813
808-586-7050
Fax: 808-586-5229

Idaho
Department of Health and Welfare Policy
Division of Welfare, 6th Floor
P.O. Box 83720
Boise, ID 83720-0036
208-334-5815
Fax: 208-334-5817
www2.state.id.us/dhw/ICCP/index_iccp.htm

Illinois
Office of Child Care and Family Services
Illinois Department of Human Services
300 Iles Park Place, Suite 270
Springfield, IL 62762
217-785-2559
877-20-CHILD
Fax: 217-524-6030
www.state.il.us/agency/dhs/childcnp.html

Indiana

Indiana Family and Social Services
Administration
Bureau of Child Development
402 W. Washington St., Room W386
P.O. Box 7083
Indianapolis, IN 46204-7083
317-232-1144
800-441-STEP (in IN)
Fax: 317-232-7948
www.ai.org/fssa/children/bcd/index.html

Iowa

Federal Day Care Program Manager
Iowa Department of Human Services
Division of ACFS
Hoover State Office Building, 5th Floor
Des Moines, IA 50319-0114
515-281-4357
Fax: 515-281-4597
www.dhs.state.ia.us/

Kansas

Integrated Service Delivery Division
Kansas Department of Social and
Rehabilitation Services
915 SW Harrison, Room 681W
Topeka, KS 66612
785-296-3349
Fax: 785-296-0146
www.srskansas.org/srseesco.nm.html

Kentucky

DCBS, Division of Policy Development
Cabinet for Families and Children
275 E. Main St., 3WB
Frankfort, KY 40621
502-564-7536
Fax: 502-564-0328
http://cfc.state.ky.agencies/
Comm-Base/Child_care

Louisiana

Child Care Assistance Program
Louisiana Department of Social Services
P.O. Box 91193
Baton Rouge, LA 70802
225-342-9108
Fax: 225-342-9111
www.dss.state.la.us/offofs/html/
child_care_assistance.html

Maine

Bureau of Child Care and Family Services
Maine Dept. of Human Services
221 State St.
Augusta, ME 04333-0011
207-287-5060
Fax: 207-287-5031
www.state.me.us/dhs/bcfs/index.htm

Maryland

Child Care Administration
Maryland Department of Human Resources
311 W. Saratoga St., 1st Floor
Baltimore, MD 21201
410-767-7128
Fax: 410-333-8699
www.dhr.state.md.us/cca-home.htm

Massachusetts

Office of Child Care Services
Massachusetts Executive Office of Health and
Human Services
One Ashburton Place, Room 1105
Boston, MA 02108
617-626-2000
Fax: 617-626-2028
www.qualitychildcare.org

Michigan

Office of Day Care
Michigan Family Independence Agency
235 S. Grand Ave., Suite 131502
P.O. Box 30037
Lansing, MI 48909
517-373-2035
Fax: 517-335-6101
www.michigan.gov/fia/1,1607,7-124-
5453_5529---,00.html

Minnesota

Child Care Program Administrator
Minnesota Children
Familiees and Learning
500 Hwy 36 West
Roseville, MN 55113
651-582-8390

Mississippi

Office for Children and Youth
Mississippi Department of Human Services
750 N. State St.
Jackson, MS 39202
601-359-4544
Fax: 601-359-4422
www.mdhs.state.ms.us/ocy.html

Missouri

Division of Family Services
Missouri Department of Social Services
P.O. Box 88
Jefferson City, MO 65103
573-751-3221
800-735-2466
Fax: 573-751-0507
www.dss.state.mo.us/dfs/index.htm

Montana

Human and Community Services Division
Montana Department of Public Health and
Human Services
P.O. Box 202952
Helena, MT 59620-2952
406-444-1828
Fax: 406-444-2547
www.dphhs.state.mt.us/divisions/ hcs/hcs.htm

Nebraska

Child Care
Nebraska Department of Health and Human
Services
P.O. Box 95044
Lincoln, NE 68509-5044
402-471-9235
Fax: 402-471-9455
www.hhs.state.ne.us/chc

Nevada

CCDBG Coordinator
Nevada Department of Human Resources
1470 E. College Pkwy.
Carson City, NV 89710
775-687-1172
Fax: 775-687-1079
http://welfare.state.nv.us/childcare.htm

New Hampshire

Child Development Bureau
Division for Children Youth and Families
Department of Health and Human Services
129 Pleasant Street
Brown Building
Concord, NH 03301
800-852-3345
603-271-8153
Fax: 603-271-7982
www.dhhs.state.nh.us

New Jersey

Division of Family Development
New Jersey Department of Human Services
P.O. Box 716
Trenton, NJ 08625
609-588-2401
Fax: 609-588-3369
www.state.nj.us/humanservices/
dfd/index.html

New Mexico

Bureau Chief, Child Care Bureau
Department of Children, Youth and Families
P.O. Drawer 5160
Santa Fe, NM 87502
505-827-4033
Fax: 505-827-9978
www.newmexicokids.org

New York

Bureau of Early Childhood Services
Office of Children and Family Services
Riverview Center, 6th Floor
52 Washington Street, 3N
Rensselaer, NY 12144
518-474-2445
www.ocf.state.ny.us/main

North Carolina

Division of Child Development
North Carolina Department of Human
Resources
2201 Mail Service Center
Raleigh, NC 27699-2201
919-662-4543
Fax: 919-662-4568
www.dhhs.state.nc.us/dcd/

North Dakota

Public Assistance Division
North Dakota Department of Human Services
600 E. Boulevard Ave.
Department 325
Bismarck, ND 58505
701-328-4603
Fax: 701-328-1544
http://lnotes.state.nd.us/dhs/dhsweb.nsf

Northern Mariana Islands

Northern Mariana Islands State Board of
Education
P.O. Box 1370 CK
Saipan, MP 96950
670-664-3714
Fax: 670-664-3717

Ohio

Bureau of Child Care
Ohio Department of Jobs and Family Services
30 E. Broad St., 32nd Floor
Columbus, OH 43215
614-466-1043
Fax: 614-728-6803
www.state.oh.us/odhs/cdc

Oklahoma

Division of Child Care
Oklahoma Department of Human Services
Sequoyah Memorial Office Building
2400 North Lincoln Boulevard
P.O. Box 25352
Oklahoma City, OK 73125
405-521-3561
800-347-2276
www.okdhs.org/childcare

Oregon

Child Care Division
Department of Employment
875 Union St., NE
P.O. Box 14050
Salem, OR 97309-4050
503-947-1409
Fax: 503-947-1428
http://findit.emp.state.or.us/childcare

Palau

Child Care Program Developer

Matthew Lesko, Information USA, Inc., 12081 Nebel Street, Rockville, MD 20852 • 1-800-955-7693 • www.lesko.com

Palau Community Action Agency
P.O. Box 3000
Koror, Palau 96940
690-488-1170/2514
Fax: 680-488-1169

Pennsylvania

CCDBG Administrator
Office of Children, Youth and Families
Pennsylvania Dept. of Public Welfare
Box 2675
Harrisburg, PA 17105-2675
717-787-8691
Fax: 717-787-1529
www.dpw.state.pa.us/ocyf/dpwocyf.asp

Puerto Rico

Puerto Rico Department of the Family
Administration for Families and Children
Avenida Ponce de Leon PDA.2
San Juan, Apartado 15091
San Juan, PR 00902
787-722-8157
Fax: 787-721-6366

Rhode Island

Rhode Island Department of Human Services
Individual and Family Support Services
Louis Pasteur Bldg.
600 New London Ave.
Cranston, RI 02920
401-462-3415
Fax: 401-464-1881
www.dhs.state.ri.us/index.htm

South Carolina

South Carolina Health and Human Services
Bureau of Community Services
P.O. Box 8206
Columbia, SC 29202-8206
803-476-0199
Fax: 803-898-4510
www.dhhs.state.sc.us/Programs/
programsindex.html

South Dakota

Child Care Services
South Dakota Department of Social Services
700 Governors Dr.
Pierre, SD 57501-2291
605-773-4766

800-227-3020
Fax: 605-773-6834
www.state.sd.us/social/ccs/ccshome.htm

Tennessee

Child Care Services
Tennessee Department of Human Services
Citizens Plaza - 14th Floor
400 Deaderick St.
Nashville, TN 37248
615-313-4778
Fax: 615-532-9956
www.state.tn.us/humanserv/childcare.htm

Texas

Texas Workforce Commission
Child Care Services
Work and Family Clearinghouse
101 E. 15th St., Suite 434-T
Austin, TX 78778-0001
512-936-0474
Fax: 512-936-3255
www.twc.state.tx.us/

Utah

Utah Department of Workforce Services
Office of Child Care
140 East 300 South
Salt Lake City, UT 84111
801-526-4341
Fax: 801-526-4349
http://occ.dws.state.ut.us

Vermont

Child Care Services Division
Vermont Department of Social and
Rehabilitation Services
103 S. Main St.
Waterbury, VT 05671-2401
802-241-3110
Fax: 802-241-1220
www.state.vt.us/childcare/index.htm

Virginia

Virginia Department of Social Services
Child Day Care
730 E. Broad St.
Richmond, VA 23219-1849
804-692-1210
Fax: 804-692-2209
www.dss.state.va.us/family/cdcplan.html

Virgin Islands

Virgin Islands Department of Human Services
Knud Hansen Complex, Building A
1303 Hospital Ground
Charlotte Amalie, VI 00802
340-774-0930, ext. 4189
Fax: 340-774-3466

Washington

Division of Child Care and Early Learning
Washington Department of Social and Health
Services
P.O. Box 45480
Olympia, WA 98504-5480
360-413-3209
Fax: 360-413-3482
www.va.gov/dshs/occp/ccfund.html

West Virginia

Bureau for Children and Families
Office of Social Services
350 Capitol St., Room 691
Charleston, WV 25301
304-558-7980
Fax: 304-558-8800
www.wvdhhr.org/oss/childcare/
stateplan01-03.htm

Wisconsin

Wisconsin Department of Workforce
Development
Child Care Planner
201 E. Washington, Room G160
P.O. Box 7935
Madison, WI 53707-7935
608-266-7001
Fax: 608-267-3240
www.dwd.state.wi.us/dws/programs/
childcare/default.htm

Wyoming

CCDBG Administrator
Wyoming Department of Family Services
Hathaway Building, Room 344
2300 Capitol Ave.
Cheyenne, WY 82002-0490
307-777-6848
Fax: 307-777-3659
http://dfsweb.state.wy.us/

More Child Care Help Close To Home

The Federal government gives money to the states, who then in turn give money to local organizations to provide child care services. Sometimes it is difficult to track the money, but one way is to contact your local Department of Human Services. They can let you know what programs are available to you in your area, as well as direct you to other programs and resources you can use. Many have established special programs, such as Child Care Management Services or Child Care Resource Centers to help you locate appropriate services. Look for the Department of Human Services in the blue pages of your phone book under your county's listings. If you have trouble locating the number, contact your state office which is listed below.

State Day Care Offices

Alabama
State Department of Human Resources
Family Services Division
Office of Child Care
50 N. Ripley St.
Montgomery, AL 36130
334-242-9500
www.dhr.state.al.us/fsd/Child_Care.asp

Alaska
Department of Health and Social Services
Division of Public Assistance
P.O. Box 110640
Juneau, AK 99811-0640
907-465-2680
www.hss.state.ak.us/dpa

Arizona
Department of Economic Security
Child Care Administration
Box 6123
Phoenix, AZ 85005
602-542-4248
www.de.state.az.us/links/chdcare.html

Arkansas
State Department of Human Services
Division of Child Care
P.O. Box 1437, Slot 5140
Little Rock, AR 72203
501-682-4891
www.state.ar.us/childcare

California
Department of Education
Child Development Division
560 J Street, Room 220
Sacramento, CA 95814
916-322-6233
www.cde.ca.gov/cyfsbranch/
child_development

Colorado
State Department of Human Services
Division of Child Care
1575 Sherman St.
Denver, CO 80203
303-866-5958
www.cdhs.state.co.us/childcare/home.html

Connecticut
Child Care Info
25 Sigourney St.
Hartford, CT 06106
860-424-5598
888-214-KIDS
www.dss.state.ct.us/ccare/ccare.htm

Delaware
Child Care
Division of Social Services
1901 North DuPont Highway
Lewis Building
New Castle, DE 19720
302-577-4400
www.state.de.us/dhss/dss/childcare.html

District of Columbia
Early Childhood Development
Department of Human Services
801 East Building
2700 MLK Jr. Avenue, SE
Washington, DC 20032
202-727-1839
http://dhs.dc.gov/info/earlychildhood.shtm

Florida
Department of Children and Families
Child Care
1317 Winewood Boulevard
Building 1, Room 202
Tallahassee, FL 32399-0700
850-487-1111
www5.myflorida.com/cf_web/
myflorida2/healthhuman

Georgia
Department of Human Resources
Family Support Unit
2 Peach Tree St., NW, Suite 19-490
Atlanta, GA 30303-3142
404-657-7660
www.dir.dhr.state.ga.us/dfcs_caps

Hawaii
Department of Human Services
Benefit, Employment and Support Services
Division
810 Richards Street, 5th Floor
Honolulu, HI 96813
808-586-5230
www.state.hi.us/dhs

Idaho
Department of Health and Welfare
Division of Welfare
Child Care Program
450 West State Street, 10th Floor
P.O. Box 83720
Boise, ID 83720-0036
208-334-5815
www2.state.id.us/dhw/ICCP/index_iccp.htm

Illinois
Office of Child Care and Family Services
Department of Human Services
300 Iles Park Place
Springfield, IL 62762
217-785-2559
www.state.il.us/agency/dhs/childcnp.html

Indiana
Division of Family and Children Services
Bureau of Child Development
402 W. Washington, St., Room W. 386
Indianapolis, IN 46204-2739
317-232-1144
www.state.in.us/fssa/children/bcd/index.html

Iowa
State Department of Human Services
Adult, Children and Family Services
Hoover State Office Bldg., 5th Floor
Des Moines, IA 50319-0114
515-281-6212
www.dhs.state.ia.us/acfs/acfs.asp

Kansas
Dept. of Social and Rehabilitative Services
Child Care Services
915 SW Harrison, 6th Floor
Topeka, KS 66612
785-296-6750
www.srskansas.org/ees/child_care.htm

Kentucky
Cabinet for Families and Children
Child Care Services Branch
275 E. Main St., 6 West
Frankfort, KY 40621
502-564-2524
800-421-1903
http://cfc.state.ky.us/help/child_care.asp

Louisiana
Department of Social Services
Childcare Assistance Program
438 Main St., Room 201
P.O. Box 91193
Baton Rouge, LA 70821
225-342-9108
www.dss.state.la.us/offofs/html/
child_care_assistance.html

Maine
Bureau of Child and Family Services
221 State St.
Augusta, ME 04333
207-287-5060
www.state.me.us/dhs/bcfs/index.htm

Maryland
Department of Human Resources
Child Care Administration

Matthew Lesko, Information USA, Inc., 12081 Nebel Street, Rockville, MD 20852 • 1-800-955-7693 • www.lesko.com

Licensing Division
311 W. Saratoga St., 1st Floor
Baltimore, MD 21201
410-767-7805
www.dhr.state.md.us/cca-home.htm

Massachusetts
Office of Child Care Services
1 Ashburton Pl., Room 1105
Boston, MA 02108
617-626-2000
www.qualitychildcare.org

Michigan
Michigan Child Development and Care
Program
P.O. Box 30037
Lansing, MI 48909
517-373-2035
www.mfia.state.mi.us/ChldDevCare/cdc1.htm

Minnesota
Children, Families and Learning Office
Division of Early Childhood and Family
Support
1500 Highway 36 West
Roseville, MN 55113-4266
651-582-8392
http://cfl.state.mn.us/cfldirectory/
section_d.html

Mississippi
Mississippi Department of Human Services
Office for Children and Youth
750 North State Street
Jackson, MS 39202
601-359-4544
800-877-7882
www.mdhs.state.ms.us/ocy.html

Missouri
Department of Social Services
Division of Family Services
Income Maintenance and Self-Sufficiency
Programs
P.O. Box 88
Jefferson City, MO 65103
573-751-3221
800-735-2466
www.dss.state.mo.us/dfs/ccs.htm

Montana
Human and Community Services Division
1400 Broadway
P.O. Box 202952
Helena, MT 59620
406-444-5901
www.dphhs.state.mt.us/divisions/hcs/hcs.htm

Nebraska
Department of Health and Human Services
Children's Services
P.O. Box 95044
Lincoln, NE 68509
402-471-2306
www.hhs.state.ne.us/chc/chcindex.htm

Nevada
Division of Welfare
Child Care
1470 East College Parkway
Carson City, NV 89706
775-684-0500
www.welfare.state.nv.us/childcare.htm

New Hampshire
Department of Health and Human Services
Division for Children, Youth and Families
129 Pleasant St.
Concord, NH 03301
603-271-4714
www.dhhs.state.nh.us

New Jersey
Department of Human Services
Division of Youth and Family Services
Child Care
P.O. Box 717
Trenton, NJ 08625-0717
609-292-6920
800-332-9227
www.state.nj.us/humanservices/
dfd/chldca.html

New Mexico
Department of Children, Youth and Families
Child Care Services Bureau
P.O. Drawer 5160
PERA Building, Room 111
Santa Fe, NM 87502
505-827-9932
800-244-6615
www.newmexicokids.org/EarlyCareBureaus/
ChildCare/default.htm

New York
State Office of Children and Family Services
52 Washington St.
Rensselaer, NY 12144
518-474-9454
www.ocfs.state.ny.us/main/becs/default.htm

North Carolina
State Department of Health and Human
Services
Division of Child Development
2201 Mail Service Center
Raleigh, NC 27626
919-662-4499
800-859-0829 (in NC)
www.dhhs.state.nc.us/dcd/index.htm

North Dakota
State Department of Human Services
Child and Family Services Division
600 E. Boulevard Ave.
Bismarck, ND 58505
701-328-2316
http://lnotes.state.nd.us/dhs/dhsweb.nsf/
ServicePages/ChildrenandFamilyServices

Ohio
Department of Job and Family Services
Bureau of Child Care Services
65 E. State St., 5th Floor
Columbus, OH 43215
614-466-1043
www.state.oh.us/odhs/cdc/

Oklahoma
State Department of Human Services
Division of Child Care
P.O. Box 25352
Oklahoma City, OK 73125
405-521-3561
800-347-2276
www.okds.org/childcare

Oregon
State Department of Employment
Child Care Division
875 Union St., NE
Salem, OR 97311
503-947-1400
http://findit.emp.state.or.us/childcare

Pennsylvania
State Department of Public Welfare
Office of Children, Youth and Families
P.O. Box 2675
Harrisburg, PA 17105
717-783-3856
877-4PA-KIDS

Central Region: 800-222-2117
Western Region: 800-222-2149

Northeast Region: 800-222-2108
Southeast Region: 800-346-2929.

Rhode Island
Department of Human Services
Center for Children & Families
Louis Pasteur Building
600 New London Avenue
Cranston, RI 02920
401-462-2423
www.dhs.state.ri.us/dhs/famchild/dcspgm.htm

South Carolina
To obtain a listing of day care centers contact:
State Department of Social Services, Child
Care Licensing Division, P.O. Box 1520,
Room 520, Columbia, SC 29202-1520; 803-
898-7345; <www.state.sc.us/dss/cdclrs/
index.html/>. To find out whether or not you
qualify for assistance, contact the ABC
Voucher Program at 800-476-0199; <www.
dhhs.state.sc.us/faq/child_care.htm>.

South Dakota
Department of Social Services
Child Care Services
700 Governor's Dr.
Pierre, SD 57501-2291
605-773-4766
800-227-3020
www.state.sd.us/state/ccs.ccshome.htm

Tennessee
State Department of Human Services
Adult and Family Services Division
400 Deaderick St.
Nashville, TN 37243
615-313-4778
www.state.tn.us/humanserv/childcare.htm

Texas
Dept. of Protective and Regulatory Services
Child Care Services
P.O. Box 149030
Austin, TX 78714-9030
512-438-3267
800-862-5252
www.tdprs.state.tx.us/child_care

Utah
Department of Workforce Services
Office of Child Care
140 East 300 South
Salt Lake City, UT 84111
801-526-4341
800-622-7390
http://occ.dws.state.ut.us

Vermont
Department of Social and Rehabilitative
Services
Childcare Services Division
103 S. Main St.
Waterbury, VT 05761-2901
802-241-3110
800-649-2642
www.state.vt.us/srs/childcare/index.htm

Virginia
Department of Social Services
Division of Family Services
730 East Broad Street
Richmond, VA 23219
804-692-1900
www.dss.state.va.us/family

Washington
Department of Social and Health Services
Division of Child Care and Early Learning
P.O. Box 45480
Olympia, WA 98504-5480
800-737-0614

West Virginia
Department of Health and Human Resources
Office of Social Services
Bldg. 6, Room 850, State Capitol
Charleston, WV 25305
304-558-0938
www.wvdhhr.org/oss/childcare

Wisconsin
State Department of Workforce Development
Office of Child Care
201 E. Washington Ave., (GEF-1)
Madison, WI 53702
MAILING ADDRESS:
  P.O. Box 7946
  Madison, WI 53707-7946
608-266-6946
www.dwd.state.wi.us/dws/programs/
childcare/default.htm

Wyoming
State Department of Family Services
Office of Child Care Licensing
Hathaway Bldg.
2300 Capitol Ave.
Cheyenne, WY 82002-0490
307-777-6848
http://dfsweb.state.wy.us/childcare.html

"Manpower Inc., a temporary help firm, now employs twice as many people as General Motors."

Source: *The New Rules: How to Succeed in Today's Post-Corporate World*, John P. Potter, Free Press, 1995

Check Out Day Care Before You Sign Up Junior

We don't trust our kids with just anyone, so how do you check out a day care before you enroll your child? Each state has a different type of licensing procedure and requirements, so you can contact your state office listed below to learn more about what is required of day care facilities (many states require that facilities which operate out of individual homes also be licensed). In addition, some states have special offices where you can register a complaint concerning a day care establishment, as well as learn whether complaints are already on file regarding a particular facility.

There are several national organizations which have excellent websites containing the child care licensing regulations for each state, plus other helpful information. Some of these are:

National Resource Center for Health and Safety in Child Care (NRC) - {http://nrc.uchsc.edu/states.html}

National Network for Child Care (NNCC) – {www.nncc.org/states/stateindex.html}

National Child Care Information Center – {www.nccic.org/statepro.html}
This website does not have the regulations, but does give demographic information and staff-to-child ratios and requirements for each state as well as state agencies. There is also an excellent list of child care resources on the Internet.

Day Care Licensing Offices

The following offices are starting places for finding out what agency within a state government licenses day care centers:

Alabama
State Department of Human Resources
Office of Child Care
50 N. Ripley St.
Montgomery, AL 36130
334-242-1425
www.dhr.state.al.us/fsd/child_case.asp

Alaska
Department of Education & Early Development
333 West 4th Avenue, Suite 320
Anchorage, AK 99501
907-269-4600
800-764-9466(message)
Fax: 907-269-1064
www.eed.state.ak.us/EarlyDev/licensing.html

Arizona
State Department of Health Services
Office of Child Care licensure
1647 E. Morton St.
Phoenix, AZ 85020
602-674-4340
www.hs.state.az.us/als/childcare/ index.html

Arkansas
State Department of Human Services
Division of Child Care and Early Childhood Education
P.O. Box 1437, Slot 720
Little Rock, AR 72203-1437
501-682-8590
www.state.ar.us/childcare

California
Department of Social Services
Community Care Licensing Division
744 P St., Mail Station 19-50
Sacramento, CA 95814
916-324-4031
http://ccld.ca.gov

Colorado
State Department of Human Services
Division of Child Care
1575 Sherman St.
Denver, CO 80203-1714
303-866-5958
800-799-5876
www.state.co.us/gov_dir/
human_services_dir/hs_home.html

Connecticut
State of Connecticut Department of Public Health
Division of Community Based Regulation
410 Capital Ave.
MS #12DAC
P.O. Box 340308
Hartford, CT 06134-3038
860-509-8045
800-282-6063
www.dph.state.ct.us/BRS/Day_Care/
day_care.htm

Delaware
Department of Health and Social Services
Office of Child Care Licensing
DSCYF, 1825 Falkland Rd.
Wilmington, DE 19805
302-892-5800
www.state.de.us/kids/occ/home.htm

District of Columbia
Department of Health
Health Regulation Administration
825 North Capitol Street, NE, 2nd Floor
Washington, DC 20002
202-442-5888
http://dchealth.dc.gov/index.asp

Florida
Florida Department of Children and Families/Child Care

1317 Windwood Blvd.
Building 1, Room 202
Tallahassee, FL 32399-0700
850-487-1111
www.state.fl.us/cf_web

Georgia
Department of Human Resources
Office of Regulatory Services
2 Peachtree St., NW, Suite 32.458
Atlanta, GA 30303-3142
404-657-5562
www2.state.ga.us/Departments/DHR/
ORS/orsmaintarget.htm

Hawaii
Department of Human Services
Employment/Child Care Program Office
820 Miliani St., Suite 606
Honolulu, HI 96813
808-586-7058

Idaho
Department of Health and Welfare
Bureau of Family and Children's Services
450 W. State St., 5th Floor
Boise, ID 83720-0036
208-334-2475
www2.state.id.us/dhw

Illinois
Department of Children and Family Services
406 E. Monroe St.
Springfield, IL 62701-1498
217-524-1983
877-746-0829
www.state.il.us/dcfs/inday.htm

Indiana
Indiana Family and Social Services Administration
Division of Family and Children

Bureau of Child Development
402 W. Washington St., Room 386
Indianapolis, IN 46204
317-232-4740
877-511-1144
www.carefinderindiana.org

Iowa
Department of Human Services
Child Care Licensing Department
Hoover State Office Building, 5th Floor
Des Moines, IA 50319
515-281-4357
www.dhs.state.ia.us/

Kansas
Kansas Dept. of Health and Environment
Child Care Licensing and Regulation
1000 SW Jackson, Suite 200
Topeka, KS 66612-1274
785-296-1270
www.kdhe.state.ks.us/kidsnet/index.html

Kentucky
Kentucky Cabinet for Health Services
Division of Licensed Child Care
275 E. Main St., 5E-A
Frankfort, KY 40621
502-564-2800
http://chs.state.ky.us/oig/childcare

Louisiana
Department of Social Services
Bureau of Licensing
P.O. Box 3078
Baton Rouge, LA 70821
225-922-0015
www.dss.state.la.us/offos/html/licensing.html

Maine
Day Care Licensing Bureau
Maine DHS
221 State St., Station 11
Augusta, ME 04333
207-287-5060
www.state.me.us/dhs/

Maryland
Department of Human Resources
Child Care Administration
Office of Licensing
311 W. Saratoga St., 1st Floor
Baltimore, MD 21201
410-767-7805
www.dhr.state.md.us/cca-homt.htm

Massachusetts
Department of Health
Office of Child Care Services
Day Care Licensing Division
1 Ashburton Place, Room 1105
Boston, MA 02108
617-626-2000
www.qualitychildcare.org/licensing.shtml

Michigan
Division of Child Day Care Licensing
Bureau of Regulatory Services
7109 W. Saginaw, 2nd Floor
P.O. Box 30650
Lansing, MI 48917-8150
517-373-8300
www.cis.state.mi.us/brs/cdc/home.htm

Minnesota
Department of Human Services
Division of Licensing
444 Lafayette Rd., North
St. Paul, MN 55155-3842
651-296-3971
www.dhs.state.mn.us/Licensing/ default.htm

Mississippi
Mississippi State Department of Health
Child Care Division
750 N. State St.
Jackson, MS 39202
601-576-7613
800-877-7882
www.mdhs.state.ms.us/ocy_cclicens.html

Missouri
State Department of Social Services
Bureau of Child Care and Safety Licensure
P.O. Box 570
Jefferson City, MO 65101
573-751-2450
www.dss.state.mo.us/cclic.htm

Montana
Department of Health and Human Services
Licensing Bureau
Child Care Licensing Program
P.O. Box 202953
Helena, MT 59620-2953
406-444-2012
www.dphhs.state.mt.us/ccrd/ caretype.htm

Nebraska
Nebraska Health and Human Services System
Credentialing Division
P.O. Box 94986
Lincoln, NE 68509
402-471-9278
800-600-1289
www.hhs.state.ne.us/crl/childcare.htm

Nevada
Division of Child & Family Services
Bureau of Services for Child Care
711 East 5th Street
Carson City, NV 89701
775-684-4400
http://dcfs.state.nv.us/page23.html

New Hampshire
State Department of Health and Human
Service
Child Care Licensing Bureau
129 Pleasant Street
Concord, NH 03301
603-271-4624
800-852-3345
http://webster.state.nh.us/dhhs/

New Jersey
Division of Youth and Family Services
Bureau of Licensing
P.O. Box 717
Trenton, NJ 08625-0717
609-292-1018
www.state.nj.us/humanservices/dyfs/
licensing.html

New Mexico
Children, Youth & Families Department
Office of Child Development
P.O. Drawer 5160
Santa Fe, NM 87502-5160
505-827-7946
www.newmexicokids.org

New York
Office of Children & Family Services
Bureau of Early Childhood Services
Riverview Center, 6th Floor
52 Washington Street, 3N
Rensselaer, NY 12144
518-474-2445
www.ocf.state.ny.us/main

North Carolina
North Carolina Division of Child development
2201 Mail Service Center

Raleigh, NC 27626-2201
919-662-4499
800-859-0829
www.dhhs.state.nc.us/dcd

North Dakota
Department of Human Services
Children and Family Services Division
600 E. Blvd., Dept. 325
Bismarck, ND 58505-0250
701-328-2316
800-245-3736
http://lnotes.state.nd.us/dhs/dhsweb.nsf

Ohio
Child Care Licensing Section
Ohio Department of Job and Family Services
30 East Broad Street, 332nd Floor
Columbus, OH 43266-0401
614-466-1043
www.state.oh.us/odhs/cdc

Oklahoma
Department of Human Services
Office of Child Care
P.O. Box 25352
Oklahoma City, OK 73125
405-521-3561
800-347-2276 (in OK)
www.okdhs.org/childcare

Oregon
Employment Department
Child Care Division
875 Union Street, NE
Salem, OR 97311
503-947-1400
800-566-6616
http://findit.emp.state.or.us/childcare

Pennsylvania
Child Care Works
Office of Children, Youth and Families
P.O. Box 2675
Harrisburg, PA 17105-2675
717-783-3856
877-4-PA-KIDS
www.dpw.state.pa.us/ocyf/dpwocyf.asp

Rhode Island
Department of Children, Youth and Families
Day Care Licensing Division
101 Friendship St.
Providence, RI 02903
401-528-3624
www.dcyf.state.ri.us/licensing.htm

South Carolina
Department of Social Services
Division of Child Day Care Licensing and
Regulatory Services
P.O. Box 1520
Columbia, SC 29202-1520
803-898-7345
877-886-2384
www.state.sc.us/dss/cdclrs/index.html

South Dakota
Department of Social Services
Child Care Services
Child Care Licensing Division
700 Governor's Dr.
Pierre, SD 57501-2291
605-773-4766
www.state.sd.us/social/ccs/ ccshome.htm

Tennessee
Department of Human Services
Child Care Services
400 Deaderick St.
Nashville, TN 37248-9800
615-313-4778
www.state.tn.us/humanserv/ childcare.htm

Texas

Dept. of Protective and Regulatory Services
Child Care Licensing
P.O. Box 149030
Austin, TX 78714-9030
512-438-4800
800-862-5252
www.tdprs.state.tx.us/child_care

Utah

Bureau of Licensing
Child Care Unit
288 N. 1460 West
P.O. Box 142003
Salt Lake City, UT 84114-2003
801-538-9299
www.health.utah.gov/html/
licensing_certifying.html

Vermont

Dept. of Social and Rehabilitation Services
Child Care Licensing Unit
103 S. Main St.
Montpelier, VT 05761
802-241-3110
www.state.vt.us/srs/childcare/
licensing/license.htm

Virginia

Department of Social Services
Child Care Licensing Division
730 Broad St., 7th Floor
Richmond, VA 23219-1849
804-692-1787
800-543-7545
www.dss.state.va.us/family/childcare.html

Washington

Division of Child Care and Early Learning
Child Care Licensing Division
P.O. Box 45480
Olympia, WA 98504-5480
360-902-0239
866-482-4325
www.wa.gov/dshs/occp/license.html

West Virginia

Department of Health and Human Resources
Office of Social Services
350 Capitol St., Room 691
P.O. Box 2590
Charleston, WV 25301
304-558-7980
www.wvdhhr.org/oss/childcare/licensing.htm

Wisconsin

Department of Health and Social Services
Bureauo f Regulation and Licensing
1 Wilson St.
Madison, WI 53702
608-266-9314
www.dhfs.state.wi.us/rl_dcfs/index.htm

Wyoming

Department of Family Services
Office of Child Care Licensing
Hathaway Building, Room 323
2300 Capitol Ave.
Cheyenne, WY 82002-0490
307-777-6285
http://dfsweb.state.wy.us/

TANF For You

Are you on public assistance, but would like to be working? TANF (Temporary Assistance for Needy Families) is a state and federally funded program which provides education and training for public assistance recipients along with the necessary support services to help you find quality jobs. TANF became effective July 1, 1997, and replaced what was then commonly known as welfare: Aid to Families with Dependent Children (ADFC) and the Job Opportunities and Basic Skills Training (JOBS) programs. You can take part in basic math and reading skills classes, job training programs, and even on-the-job training. TANF is required to provide or reimburse you for transportation and other work related expenses, as well as offer child care for those who need it. Child care is subsidized for parents, so that they may choose the best child care provider for the child. Payment rates are set by the state, and the care must meet certain standards. Contact your local Public Assistance office, or contact the State TANF Coordinator for information on the TANF program nearest you. For more information, contact Office of Family Assistance, Administration for Children and Families, 370 L'Enfant Promenade, SW, Washington, DC 20447; 202-401-9289; <www.acf.dhhs.gov/programs/ofa>.

TANF Program Directory

Alabama
Department of Human Resources
Family Asst. Division
S. Gordon Persons Building
50 N. Ripley St.
Montgomery, AL 36130
334-242-1773/1950
www.dhr.state.ak.us/fad/default.asp

Alaska
Division of Public Assistance
Department of Health and Social Service
P.O. Box 110601
Juneau, AK 99811-0601
907-465-3030
www.hss.state.ak.us/dpa/programs/dtap.html

Arizona
Department of Economic Security
P.O. Box 6123-010A
Phoenix, AZ 85005
602-542-4791
www.de.state.az.us

Arkansas
Department of Human Services
P.O. Box 1437
Mail Slot 1230
Little Rock, AR 72203-1437
501-682-8650
www.state.ar.us/dhs/webpolicy/
TEA%20Policy/TEA-TOC.htm

California
Department of Social Services
744 P St., M/S 6-700
Sacramento, CA 95814
916-657-3661
www.dss.cahwnet.gov/calworks/default.htm

Colorado
Department of Human Services
Office of Self-Sufficiency
1575 Sherman St., 3rd Floor
Denver, CO 80203-1714
303-866-5981
www.cdhs.state.ci.us/oss/tanfplan.html

Connecticut
Family Support Team
Department of Social Services
25 Sigourney St.
Hartford, CT 06106
860-424-4908
800-842-1508
www.dss.state.ct.us/dss.htm

Delaware
Division of Social Services
1901 N. DuPont Hwy
Lewis Building
New Castle, DE 19720
302-577-4408
www.state.de.us/dss/welfaretowork.html

District of Columbia
Department of Human Services
801 East Building
2700 M.L.K. Ave., SE
Washington, DC 20032
202-279-6002
www.dhs.dc.gov/main.shtm

Florida
Department of Children and Families
Building 1, Room 202
1317 Winewood Blvd.
Tallahassee, FL 32399-0700
850-487-1111
www5.myflorida.com/cf_web/myflorida2/
healthhuman/ess/index.html

Georgia
Department of Human Resources
Division of Family and Children Services
2 Peachtree St., NW, Suite 19-490
Atlanta, GA 30303
404-657-7660
www2.state.ga.us/Departments/DHR/
dfcs.html

Hawaii
Department of Human Services
Benefit Employment and Support Services
Division

810 Richards Street, 5th Floor
Honolulu, HI 96813
808-586-5230
www.state.hi.us/dhs

Idaho
Department of Health and Welfare
P.O. Box 83720
450 W. State St., 10th Floor
Boise, ID 83720-0036
208-334-5500
www2.state.id.us/dhw/welfare

Illinois
Department of Human Services
100 S. Grand East, 2nd Floor
Springfield, IL 62762
217-785-9657
800-252-8635
www.state.il.us/agency/dhs/tanfnp.html

Indiana
Family Social Service Administration
Division of Family and Children
402 W. Washington, Room W363
Indianapolis, IN 46204
317-233-4903
800-622-4932
www.in.gov/fssa/families/tanf/index.html

Iowa
Department of Human Services
Economic Assistance
Hoover State Office Building, 5th Floor
Des Moines, IA 50319
515-281-3131
800-972-2017
www.dhs.state.ia.us/homepages/dhs/TANF/
tanf.asp

Kansas
Department of Social and Rehabilitation
Services
Economic and Employment Support
915 Harrison, 6th Floor
Topeka, KS 66612
785-296-6750
www.srskansas.org/ees/taf_ga.htm

Matthew Lesko, Information USA, Inc., 12081 Nebel Street, Rockville, MD 20852 • 1-800-955-7693 • www.lesko.com

Kentucky

Department of Social Insurance
Cabinet for Families and Children
275 E. Main St.
Frankfurt, KY 40621
502-564-7130
http://cfc.state.ky.us/help/aboutKTAP_2.asp

Louisiana

Department of Social Services
Office of Family Support
P.O. Box 94065
Baton Rouge, LA 70804
225-342-4054
www.dss.state.la.us/offofs/html/
tanf_state_plan.html

Maine

Maine Department of Human Services
Bureau of Family Independence
11 Statehouse Station
221 State St.
Augusta, ME 04333
207-287-5089
www.state.me.us/dhs/bfi/tanfmenu.htm

Maryland

Department of Human Resources
311 W. Saratoga St., Room 714
Baltimore, MD 21201
410-767-7242
800-332-6347
www.dhr.state.md.us/fia/

Massachusetts

Department of Transitional Assistance
600 Washington St.
Boston, MA 02111
617-348-8400
800-249-2007
www.state.ma.us/dta/index.htm

Michigan

Family Independence Agency
P.O. Box 30037
Lansing, MI 48909
517-373-2035
www.mfia.state.mi.us/

Minnesota

Department of Human Services
Economic and Community Supports
444 Lafayette Rd.
St. Paul, MN 55155
612-296-4476
www.dhs.state.mn.us/ecs/Welfare/
tanfplan.htm

Mississippi

Department of Human Services
Division of Economic Analysis
750 N. State St., 5th Floor
Jackson, MS 29202
601-359-4800
www.mdhs.state.ms.us/ea_tanf.html

Missouri

Department of Social Services
Division of Family Services
P.O. Box 88
Jefferson City, MO 65103
573-751-3221
800-735-2466
www.dss.state.mo.us/dfs/tempa.htm

Montana

Dept. of Public Health and Human Services
Human and Community Services Division
P.O. Box 2952
Helena, MT 59620-2952
406-444-5901
www.dphhs.state.mt.us/division/hcs/hcs.htm

Nebraska

Department of Health and Human Services
Office of Economic and Family Support
Services
P.O. Box 95044
Lincoln, NE 68509
402-471-9325
www.hhs.state.ne.us/wer/werindex.htm

Nevada

Nevada Department of Human Resources
1470 East College Parkway
Carson City, NV 89706
775-684-0500
www.welfare.state.nv.us/elig_pay/
tanf_home.htm

New Hampshire

New Hampshire Department of Health and
Human Services
Family Assistance Division
129 Pleasant St.
Concord, NH 03301
603-271-4580
www.dhhs.state.nh.us

New Jersey

Department of Human Services
Division of Family Development
P.O. Box 716
Quakerbridge Plaza, Building 6
Trenton, NJ 08625
609-588-2400
www.state.nj.us/humanservices/dfd

New Mexico

New Mexico Human Services Department
P.O. Box 2348
Santa Fe, NM 87504-2348
505-827-7250
888-473-3676
www.state.nm.us/hsd/isd.html

New York

New York Office of Temporary and Disability
Assistance
40 North Pearl St.
Albany, NY 12243
518-474-9475
800-343-8859
www.otda.state.ny.us/ltda/ta/default.htm

North Carolina

Department of Human Resources
Division of Social Services
325 North Salisbury St.
Raleigh, NC 27611
919-733-3055
www.dhhs.state.nc.us/dss/ei/ei_hm.htm

North Dakota

Department of Human Services
Public Assistance
600 E. Boulevard, Dept. 325
Bismarck, ND 58505
701-328-3513
800-755-2716 (IN ND)
http://state.nd.us/dhs/dhsweb.nsf

Ohio

Department of Job and Family Services
30 East Broad St., 32nd Floor
Columbus, OH 43215-3414
614-466-9274
www.state.oh.us/odhs/factsheets/
ICOOowf.stm

Oklahoma

Department of Human Services
Family Support Services Division
P.O. Box 25352

Oklahoma City, OK 73125
405-521-3076
www.okdhs.org/fssd

Oregon

Department of Human Services
Children, Adults and Family Services
500 Summer St., E46
Salem, OR 97301
503-945-5600
www.afs.hr.state.or.us

Pennsylvania

Department of Public Welfare
Office Income Maintenance
Health and Welfare Bldg., Room 432
P.O. Box 2675
Harrisburg, PA 17105-2675
717-787-1894
www.dpw.state.pa.us/oim/dpwoim.asp

Puerto Rico

Puerto Rico Department of the Family
P.O. Box 11398
San Juan, PR 00910-1398
787-725-4511

Rhode Island

Department of Human Services
600 New London Ave.
Cranston, RI 02920
401-462-5300
www.dhs.state.ri.us/dhs/dfipref.htm

South Carolina

Department of Social Services
Division of Family Independence
P.O. Box 1520
Room 605
Columbia, SC 29202-1520
803-898-7825
www.state.sc.us/dss.fi/index.html

South Dakota

Department of Social Services
Pierre, SD 57501-2291
605-773-4678
www.state.sd.us/TANF/index.htm

Tennessee

Department of Human Services
400 Deadericks, 12th Floor
Nashville, TN 37248
615-313-5790
888-863-6178
www.state.tn.us/humanserv/famfir.htm

Texas

Texas Workforce Commission
101 E. 15th St.
Austin, TX 78778-0001
512-463-2678
www.twc.state.tx.us/welref/
welrefinfo.html#choices

Utah

Department of Workforce Services
Family Employment Program
P.O. Box 45249
Salt Lake City, UT 84145-0249
801-526-9675
http://jobs.utah.gov/services/financial/fep.asp

Vermont

Department of Social Welfare
State Office Building
103 South Main St.
Waterbury, VT 05671
802-241-2889
www.dsw.state.vt.us/wrp/wrp.htm

Virgin Islands
Department of Human Services
Knud Hansen Complex
Building A
1303 Hospital Ground
St. Thomas, VI 00802
304-774-0930

Virginia
Department of Social Services
730 E. Broad St, 9th Floor
Richmond, VA 23219-1849
804-692-1900
www.dss.state.va.us/benefit/tanf.html

Washington
Department of Social and Health Services
P.O. Box 45010
Olympia, WA 98504-5010
360-902-7800
800-865-7801
www.wa.gov/WORKFIRST/index.htm/

West Virginia
Department of Health and Human Services
Bureau for Children and Families
350 Capitol St., Room 730
Charleston, WV 25305-3711
304-558-0684
www.wvdhhr.org/bcf

Wisconsin
Department of Workforce Development
P.O. Box 7946
Madison, WI 53707-7946
608-266-9663
www.dwd.state.wi.us/wtw

Wyoming
Department of Family Services
Hathaway Building, 3rd Floor
2300 Capitol Ave.
Cheyenne, WY 82002-0490
307-777-7564
http://dfsweb.state.wy.us/

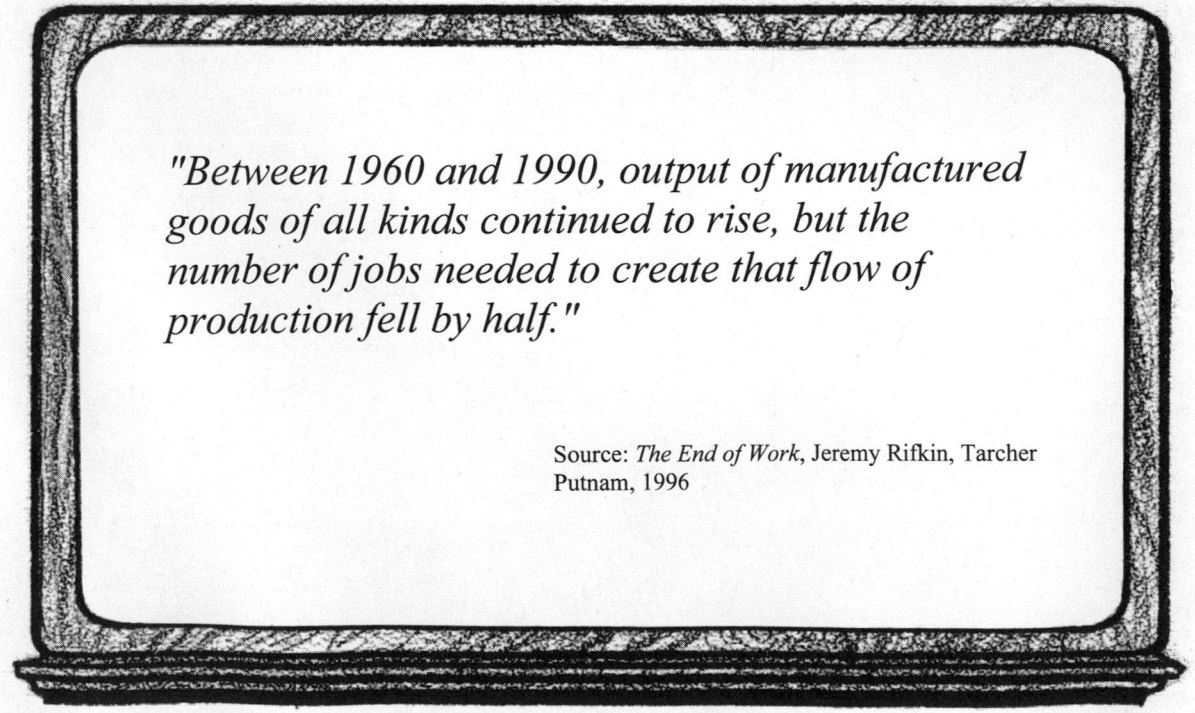

"Between 1960 and 1990, output of manufactured goods of all kinds continued to rise, but the number of jobs needed to create that flow of production fell by half."

Source: *The End of Work*, Jeremy Rifkin, Tarcher Putnam, 1996

Child Care Help From Your State

In order to give states the freedom to choose what particular services they need, the Federal government provides the Social Services Block Grant (Title XX). This allows each state to provide social services which best suit the needs of the individuals residing in the state. Examples of funded services include child day care, protective and emergency services for children and adults, homemaker and chore services, information and referral, adoption, foster care, counseling, and transportation. To find out what services are provided in your state, contact your state Department of Social Services. For more information, contact Office of Community Services, Division of State Assistance, 370 L'Enfant Promenade, SW, Washington, DC 20447; 202-401-5284; <www.acf.dhhs.gov/programs/ocs/>.

Social Services Block Grant State Contacts

Alabama
Bill Fuller, Commissioner
Department of Human Resources
Gordon Persons Bldg.
50 N. Ripley Street
Montgomery, AL 36130
334-242-1160
www.dhr.state.al.us

Alaska
Jay Livey, Commissioner
Department of Health and Social Services
P.O. Box 110601
Juneau, AK 99811-0601
907-465-3030
www.hss.state.ak.us

Arizona
John L. Clayton, Director
Department of Economic Security
1789 West Jefferson
Phoenix, AZ 85007
602-542-5678
www.de.state.az.us

Arkansas
Kurt Knickrehm, Director
Arkansas Department of Human Services
Donaghey Plaza
7th and Maine Street
P.O. Box 1437
Little Rock, AR 72203-1437
501-682-8650
www.state.ar.us/dhs

California
Rita Saenz, Director
California Department of Social Services
744 P Street
Mail Station 17-ll
Sacramento, CA 95814
916-657-2598
www.dss.cahwnet.gov/cdssweb/default.htm

Colorado
Marva Hammons, Executive Director
Department of Human Services
1575 Sherman Street
Denver, CO 80203-1714
303-866-5096
www.cdhs.state.co.us/default.htm

Connecticut
Patricia A. Wilson-Coker, Commissioner
Department of Social Services
25 Sigourney Street

Hartford, CT 06106-5033
860-424-5008
www.dss.state.co.us

Delaware
Gregg C. Sylvester, M.D., Acting Secretary
Delaware Department of Health and Social Services
1901-N. Dupont Highway
New Castle, DE 19720
302-577-4502
www.state.de.us/dhss/dhss.htm

District of Columbia
Ricardo Lyles, Commissioner
Commission on Social Services
2416 24th Place, NE
Washington, DC 20018
202-727-5930
http://dhs.dc.gov/main.shtm

Florida
Kathleen Kearney, Secretary
Department of Children and Families
Office of Financial Management
1323 Winewood Boulevard
Tallahassee, FL 32399-0700
850-487-0834
www.state.fl.us/cf_web

Georgia
Audrey Home, Commissioner
Georgia Department of Human Resources
2 Peachtree Street, NW
29th Floor, Suite 250
Atlanta, GA 30303-3180
404-651-6314
www.legis.state.ga.us/Departments/OHR

Hawaii
Susan M. Chandler, M.S.W., Ph.D, Director
Hawaii Department of Human Services
P. O. Box 339
Honolulu, HI 96809
808-548-6260
www.state.hi.us/dhs

Idaho
Karl Kurtz, Director
Idaho Department of Health and Welfare
State House
450 West State Street
Boise, ID 83720-5450
208-334-5546
www2.state.id.us/dhw

Illinois
Mr. Howard A. Peters III, Secretary
Department of Human Services
Harris Bldg. II, 3rd Floor
100 South Grand Avenue East
Springfield, IL 62762-0001
217-557-1601
www.state.il.us/agency/dhs

Indiana
Peter A. Sybinsky, Secretary
Family & Social Services Administration
402 W. Washington St., Room W461
P.O. Box 7083
Indianapolis, IN 46207-7083
317-233-4454
800-545-7763
www.state.in.us/fssa

Iowa
Jessie K. Rasmusser, Director
Department of Human Services
Hoover State Office Building
E. 13th and Walnut
Des Moines, IA 50319
515-281-5452
www.dhs.state.ia.us/

Kansas
Janet Schalansky, Secretary
Department of Social and Rehabilitation Services
Docking State Office Building
915 Harrison Street, Room 603-N
Topeka, KS 66612
785-296-3271
www.srskansas.org

Kentucky
Diedra Paris, Commissioner
Department for Community Based Services
275 E. Main Street, 3WA Floor
Frankfort, KY 40621
502-564-3703
http://cfc.state.ky.us/agencies/comm_base/index.asp

Louisiana
Mrs. Madlyn B. Bagneris, Secretary
Department of Social Services
P. O. Box 3776
755 Third St., Room 228
Baton Rouge, LA 70821
504-342-0286
www.dss.state.la.us

Maine
Mr. Kevin W. Concannon, Commissioner
Department of Human Services
221 State Street
Augusta, ME 04333-0011
207-287-2736
www.state.me.us/dhs/welcome_to_dhs.htm

Maryland
Lynda Fox, Secretary
Department of Human Resources
311 West Saratoga Street
Baltimore, MD 21202
410-767-7109
www.dhr.state.md.us

Massachusetts
Jeffrey Locke, Commissioner
Department of Social Services
24 Farnsworth Street
Boston, MA 02110
617-727-0900
www.state.ma.us/dss

Michigan
Lynda Crandall, Director
Michigan Family Independence Agency
235 South Grand Avenue
P.O. Box 30037
Lansing, MI 48809
517-335-3094
www.michigan.gov/fia

Minnesota
Michael O'Keefe, Commissioner
Minnesota Department of Human Services
444 Lafayette Road
St. Paul, MN 55155-3815
651-296-2701
www.dhs.state.mn.us

Mississippi
Mr. Donald R. Taylor, Executive Director
Department of Human Services
750 North State Street
Jackson, MS 39202
601-359-4500
www.mdhs.state.ms.us

Missouri
Mr. Gary J. Stangler, Director
Department of Social Services
Broadway State Office Building
P. O. Box 1527
Jefferson City, MO 65102-1527
573-751-4815
www.dss.state.mo.us

Montana
Ms. Laurie Ekanger, Director
Dept. of Public Health and Human Services
P. O. Box 4210
Helena, MT 59604
406-444-5622
www.dphhs.state.mt.us

Nebraska
Ron Ross, Director
Department of Health and Human Services
P. O. Box 95004
Lincoln, NE 68509-5044
402-471-9106
www.hhs.state.ne.us

Nevada
Charlotte Crawford, Director
Department of Human Resources
505 E. King Street, Room 660
Carson City, NV 89701
775-684-4000
www.hr.state.nv.us

New Hampshire
Donald Shumway, Commissioner
Department of Health and Human Services
129 Pleasant Street
Concord, NH 03301
603-271-4688
www.dhhs.state.nh.us

New Jersey
Michael Guhl, Commissioner
New Jersey Department of Human Services
Capital Place 1 CN-700
P.O. Box 700
Trenton, NJ 08625
609-292-3717
www.state.nj.us/humanservices

New Mexico
Ms. Deborah D. Hartz, Cabinet Secretary
Department of Children, Youth and Families
P. O. Drawer 5160
Santa Fe, NM 87502
505-827-7602
www.cyfd.org

New York
Mr. John A. Johnson, Commissioner
New York Office of Children and Family
Services
52 Washington St.
Capital View Office Park
Rensselaer, NY 12144
518-473-9131
www.ocfs.state.ny.us

North Carolina
EC Modlin, Director
Division of Social Services
Department of Human Resources
325 North Salisbury Street
Raleigh, NC 27603
919-733-3055
www.dhhs.state.nc.us/dss

North Dakota
Ms. Yvonne M Smith, Associate Director
Office of Field Services and Program
Development
North Dakota Department of Human Services
600 E. Boulevard Avenue
Bismarck, ND 58505-0265
701-328-2310
http://lnotes.state.nd.us/dhs/dhsweb.nsf

Ohio
Jacqui Romer-Sensky, Director
Ohio Department of Job and Family Services
30 East Broad Street, 32nd Floor
Columbus, OH 43215-3414
614-466-6282
www.state.oh.us/odjfs

Oklahoma
Howard Hendrick, Director
Department of Human Services
P. O. Box 25352
Oklahoma City, OK 73125
405-521-3646
www.okdhs.org

Oregon
Mr. Gary K. Weeks, Director
Oregon Department of Human Services
500 Summer Street, NE, E25
Salem, OR 97310
503-945-5944
www.hr.state.or.us

Pennsylvania
Ms. Feather O. Houstoun, Secretary
Pennsylvania Department of Public Welfare
Room 333, Health and Welfare Building
Harrisburg, PA 17120
717-787-2600
www.dpw.state.pa.us/default.htm

Rhode Island
Ms. Christine C. Ferguson, Director
Department of Human Services
600 New London Avenue
Cranston, RI 02920
401-464-6856
www.dhs.state.ri.us

South Carolina
Samuel Griswold, Director
Department of Health & Human Services
P.O. Box 8206
Columbia, SC 29202-8206
803-253-6100
www.dhhs.state.sc.us

South Dakota
Mr. James Ellenbecker, Secretary
Department of Social Services
Richard Kneip Building
700 Governor's Drive
Pierre, SD 57501
605-773-3165
www.state.sd.us/social/social.html

Tennessee
Natasha Metcalf, Commissioner
Department of Human Services
Citizens Plaza Building
400 Deaderick Street
Nashville, TN 37248
615-741-4710
www.state.tn.us/humanserv

Texas
Mr. Eric Bost, Commissioner
Texas Department of Human Services
701 W. 51st Street
P. O. Box 149030
Austin, TX 78714-9030
512-438-4220
www.dhs.state.tx.us

Utah
Robin Arnold-Williams, D.S.W., Executive
Director
Department of Human Services
120 North 200 West #319
Salt Lake City, UT 84103
801-538-4001
www.dhs.utah.gov

Vermont
Jane Kitchel, Secretary
Agency of Human Services
103 South Main Street
Waterbury, VT 05671
802-241-2220
www.ahs.state.vt.us

Virginia
Sonia Rivero, Commissioner
Department of Social Services
Theater Row Building
730 East Broad Street
Richmond, VA 23219-1849
804-692-1900
www.dss.state.va.us

Washington
Dennis Braddock, Secretary
Washington Department of Social and Health
Services
P.O. Box 45010
Olympia, WA 98504-5010
360-902-8400
www.wa.gov/dshs

West Virginia

Ann Byrd, Director
Office Of Social Services
350 Capitol St., Room 591
State Capitol Complex
Charleston, WV 25301
304-558-7980
www.wvdhhr.org/oss

Wisconsin

Susan Dreyfus, Administrator
Wisconsin Department of Health and Family
Services
P.O. Box 7850
Madison, WI 53707
608-266-3728
www.dhfs.state.wi.us

Wyoming

Kari Jo Gray, Executive Director
Department of Family Services
2300 Capital Ave, 3rd Floor
Cheyenne, WY 82002-0490
307-777-7561
http://dfsweb.state.wy.us

Matthew Lesko, Information USA, Inc., 12081 Nebel Street, Rockville, MD 20852 • 1-800-955-7693 • www.lesko.com

How Do I
Get Free Research Help?

Animals and Agriculture

* Agriculture Exports Clearinghouse

Foreign Agricultural Service
U.S. Department of Agriculture
Room 5074   202-720-7115
Washington, DC 20050   Fax: 202-720-1727
Email: fasinfo@fas.usda.gov
www.fas.usda.gov

The Foreign Agricultural Service compiles and disseminates agricultural trade and commodity production information to agribusinesses and the general public. They offer private companies and cooperatives assistance in marketing their products overseas by collecting and publicizing information on foreign buyers and advertising U.S. export availability. They have a monthly magazine, commodity and trade reports, publications, and fact sheets (many of which are free). They can answer such questions as:

1) What are the market prospects for U.S. food and farm products in Japan?
2) What are some overseas markets and buying trends for a particular product?
3) What are some overseas promotional activities?
4) How do I begin an export business?
5) How do I advertise my product directly to buyers overseas?

* Economic Research Service (Agriculture)

U.S. Department of Agriculture
1800 M St., NW   202-694-5110
ERS, Room 3100   Fax: 202-694-5641
Washington, DC 20036-5831   Fax on Demand: 202-694-5700
Email: service@econ.ag.gov
www.ers.usda.gov

The Economic Research Service conducts research on the economic and socio-demographic issues of rural America; the marketing, trade, and consumption of farm commodities; U.S. and foreign economic policies and their effects on trade; and more. They produce monographs and journal articles ranging from very technical research reports to easy-to-read leaflets. They offer situation and outlook reports providing a mixture of outlook and in-depth analysis of current commodity, trade, resource, and policy issues. Most of the information is available free of charge. They can answer such questions as:

1) What are the links between development and world trade?
2) What information exists on the U.S. and world markets for agricultural products?
3) How can farmers better conserve water resources?
4) What are the benefits of organic farming?
5) How can farmers adjust their techniques to keep pace with global market trends?

* National Agricultural Statistics Service

NASS-USDA   800-727-9540
Room 5805, South   202-720-3896
Washington, DC 20250   Fax: 202-690-1311
Email: nass@nass.usda.gov
www.usda.gov/nass/

The National Agricultural Statistics Service collects data on crops, livestock, poultry, dairy, chemical use, prices, and labor, and publishes the official USDA State and national estimates through its Agricultural Statistics Board. There are nearly 400 reports annually covering domestic agriculture, such as estimates of production, stocks, inventories, prices, disposition, utilization, farm numbers and land, and other factors. They provide national profiles from regular surveys of thousands of farmers, ranchers, and agribusinesses that voluntarily provide data on a confidential basis. Publications are available and range from free to $12. They can answer such questions as:

1) How has the use of a specific chemical for crop growth changed over the past five years?
2) Has the size of farms increased or decreased over the past ten years?
3) What statistics exist on wildlife damage to crops?
4) How has the weekly crop weather effected crop growth?
5) What data is there on livestock slaughter?

* Alternative Farming Systems Information Center

U.S. Department of Agriculture
National Agricultural Library
10301 Baltimore Blvd., Room 304   301-504-6559
Beltsville, MD 20705-2351   Fax: 301-504-6409
Email: afsic@nal.usda.gov
www.nal.usda.gov/afsic

The Alternative Farming Systems Information Center encourages research, education, and information delivery about farming systems that preserve the natural resource base while maintaining economic viability. The Center is the focal point for information on all types of alternative farming practices. They can refer you to organizations or experts, identify current research, furnish you with bibliographies, and more. Brief data base searches are free, while exhaustive searches are conducted on a cost recovery basis. They can answer such questions as:

1) How do you establish and maintain an organic garden?
2) What is involved in building a compost pile?
3) What are the effects of herbicide and fertilizer run off?
4) How can I avoid ground water contamination?
5) What are some solar energy alternatives for agriculture?

* Animal Welfare Information Center

National Agricultural Library
U.S. Department of Agriculture
10301 Baltimore Blvd., 5th Floor   301-504-6212
Beltsville, MD 20705-2351   Fax: 301-504-7125
Email: awic@nal.usda.gov
www.nal.usda.gov/awic

The Animal Welfare Information Center is the focal point for all aspects of animal welfare. They have information on the care, handling, and management of animals used in research; training guides and manuals for animal care personnel; ethical issues; animal behavior; and pain control. They have a publications list of free fact sheets, bibliographies, and other resources. They can answer such questions as:

1) What information is there on the ethical and moral issues relating to animals and the philosophy of animal rights?
2) What alternatives are there to the use of live animals in research?
3) What videos exist on the care of animals?
4) What are some of the legislation regarding animal welfare?
5) What are some of the resources available regarding the raising of poultry?

* Aquaculture Information Center

National Agricultural Library
U.S. Department of Agriculture
10301 Baltimore Blvd.   301-504-5724
Beltsville, MD 20705-2351   Fax: 301-504-6409
Email: afsaqua@nal.usda.gov
www.nal.usda.gov/afsic/afsaqua.htm

The Aquaculture Information Center collects information on the culture of aquatic plants and animals in freshwater, brackish, and marine environments. Examples include: catfish farming, oyster culture, salmon ranching, and trout farming. They have a publications list of free fact sheets, bibliographies, and other resources. They can answer such questions as:

1) How do you start a catfish farm?
2) What are the effects of sodium, cadmium, and lead on aquatic plants?
3) What types of algae are edible?
4) What is involved in raising snails?
5) What can be done to stop the pollution of freshwater environments?

* Food and Nutrition Information Center

Agriculture Research Services
National Agriculture Library, Room 304   301-504-5719
10301 Baltimore Blvd.   Fax: 301-504-6409
Beltsville, MD 20705-2351   TTY: 301-504-6856
Email: fnic@nal.usda.gov
www.nal.usda.gov/fnic

The Food and Nutrition Information Center serves many types of users including educators, students, researchers, and consumers. Reference services are provided. Subjects covered include human nutrition research and education, diet and diet-related diseases, food habits, food composition, nutrition education, and more. The Center offers a variety of services which include answers to specific questions, lending books and audiovisuals, and providing computerized literature searches. A publications list is available, many of which are free. They can answer such questions as:

1) What studies exist on the effects of the school breakfast program?
2) What information can you provide to parents concerned about their overweight children?
3) Do you have information on anorexia nervosa?
4) Is it dangerous to consume caffeine while pregnant?
5) Are canned peaches as nutritious as fresh?

* Alternative Farming Systems Information Center (Horticulture)

AFSIC
U.S. Department of Agriculture
10301 Baltimore Blvd., Room 304   301-504-6559
Beltsville, MD 20705-2351   Fax: 301-504-6409
www.nal.usda.gov/afsic

The Alternative Farming Systems Information Center covers technical horticultural or botanical questions, economic botany, wild plants of possible use, herbs, bonsai, and floriculture. They can answer such questions as:

1) How can you grow lavender commercially as a source of essential oils?
2) How do you grow and dry herbs?
3) How much would landscaping improve the value of a home?
4) Which plants can be used for medicinal purposes?
5) How can I control garden insects without using chemical sprays?

* Meat and Poultry Hotline

Food Safety and Inspection Service
U.S. Department of Agriculture   800-535-4555
Washington, DC 20250-3700   Fax: 202-690-2859
www.fsis.usda.gov

The Meat and Poultry Hotline takes calls from consumers regarding cases of meat or poultry food poisoning or complaints about meat or poultry spoilage due to improper packaging or processing. They can also provide you with health-oriented information on safe handling and storage of meats and poultry. They can answer such questions as:

1) What should be done during a power outage?
2) What is salmonella and how can people be protected?
3) What are the different type of foodborne illnesses?
4) How long should you cook poultry?
5) What information should be included on meat and poultry labels and what does it mean?

* Organic Gardening

Public Information Center, 3404
U.S. Environmental Protection Agency
401 M St., SW   202-260-7751
Washington, DC 20460-0003   Fax: 202-260-6257
Email: public-access@epamail.epa.gov
www.epa.gov

The Public Information Center has free information sheets on organic gardening, composting, and recycling. They can answer such questions as:

1) What plants should be planted near each other to deter pests?
2) What are the dangers of pesticides?
3) Who can I talk to regarding composting and recycling?
4) What are the advantages of organic fertilizers?
5) What is required to maintain a lawn?

* Plant Information Service

U.S. Botanic Garden
245 1st St., SW   202-225-8333
Washington, DC 20024   Fax: 202-225-1561
www.aoc.gov/pages/usbgpage.htm

The U.S. Botanic Garden serves as a center for plant information offering a telephone information service as well as responding to written inquiries, Monday through Friday from 9:00 to 11:30 a.m. They can answer such questions as:

1) What are the benefits of organic gardening?
2) How can I use insects to control garden pests?
3) Which house plants are poisonous?
4) What are the dangers of chemical fertilizers?
5) Which herbs grow best indoors?

* Rural Information Center

National Agricultural Library
U.S. Department of Agriculture (USDA)   301-504-5547
10301 Baltimore Blvd., Room 304   800-633-7701
Beltsville, MD 20705-2351   Fax: 301-504-5181
Email: ric@nal.usda.gov
www.nal.usda.gov/ric

The Rural Information Center is designed to provide information and referral services to local government officials, businesses, community organizations, and rural citizens working to maintain the vitality of America's rural areas. The Center provides: customized information products to specific inquiries; refers users to organizations or experts in the field; performs database searches; furnishes bibliographies; identifies current USDA research and Cooperative Extension System programs; and assists users in accessing the National Agricultural Libraries' extensive collection. There is a cost recovery fee for photocopying articles and searches. They can answer such questions as:

1) Which organizations focus on rural health issues?
2) What resources for the historic preservation of farmland are available in rural areas?
3) How can tourism be promoted in small towns?
4) What are examples of the more innovative economic development projects in rural communities?
5) What rural organizations focus specifically on research and development?

* Seafood Hotline

Office of Seafood
Food and Drug Administration
200 C St., SW   800-SAFEFOOD
Washington, DC 20204   Fax: 202-401-3532
Email: oco@fdacf.sw.dhhs.gov
http://vm.cfsan.fda.gov/seafood1.html

The Seafood Hotline can provide consumers with information on how to buy and use seafood products, including storing and handling of seafood, and questions on seafood labeling and nutrition. The Hotline has many free publications on a variety of seafood issues. They can answer such questions as:

1) Can fish be kept frozen for a year?
2) How do you know if a seafood vendor is reputable?
3) What are the dangers of eating raw shellfish?
4) What information is available on canned tuna?
5) What are some seafood safety concerns for people with particular medical conditions?

Business and Industry

* Advertising Practices

Federal Trade Commission (FTC)
6th and Pennsylvania Ave., NW
Washington, DC 20580
Email: consumerline@ftc.gov
www.ftc.gov/bcp/menu-ads.htm

202-326-2222
Fax: 202-326-3259

This division of the Federal Trade Commission promotes the distribution of truthful information to the public through law enforcement and oversight activities in the following areas: general advertising for deceptive claims; advertising claims for food and over-the-counter drugs, particularly claims relating to safety or effectiveness; tobacco advertising; and performance and energy-savings claims for solar products, furnaces, window coverings, wood burning products, and more. They can answer such questions as:

1) How do you file a complaint with the FTC?
2) When and where is the advertising of tobacco products legal, and what are the reasons behind this?
3) How long are over-the-counter drugs tested before they are released on the market?
4) What penalties are levied against a company that has been charged with deceptive advertising?
5) How effective are over-the-counter diet pills?

* Federal Aviation Administration

Office of Public Affairs
800 Independence Ave., SW
Washington, DC 20591
Email: gramick@postmaster2.dot.gov
www.faa.gov

202-267-3883

The Federal Aviation Administration (FAA) is the starting place for any information on airlines, airports, and aircraft. The FAA regulates air commerce, develops civil aeronautics, installs and operates airports, conducts aeronautic research and provides guidance and policy on accident prevention in general aviation. They keep statistics on air travel, accidents, and more. There are free publications on airline careers, aviation, and airplanes, as well as videos and curriculum guides. They can answer such questions as:

1) Which airlines had penalties of $50,000 or more for safety and security issues?
2) What videos are available on aviation?
3) What historical information is available on women in aviation?
4) What are the current statistics on air traffic accidents?
5) What methods are used to reduce the noise level of new aircraft?

* Board of Governors of the Federal Reserve System (Banking)

Publications Services, MS-127
20th and C Sts., NW
Washington, DC 20551
www.federalreserve.gov

202-452-3244
Fax: 202-728-5886

The Federal Reserve System, the central bank of the United States, is charged with administering and making policy for the Nation's credit and monetary affairs. The Federal Reserve helps to maintain the banking industry in sound condition, capable of responding to the Nation's domestic and international financial needs and objectives. It has publications and audiovisual materials prepared which are designed to increase public understanding of the functions and operations of the Federal Reserve System, monetary policy, financial markets and institutions, consumer finance, and the economy. They can answer such questions as:

1) How did the Federal Reserve begin and how does it function today?
2) What is the history of the U.S. monetary policy and how is it formulated?
3) Is there a brief overview available on banking regulation?
4) What is the evolution of money?
5) How are checks used, processed, and collected?

* Business Assistance Service

Office of Business Liaison
U.S. Department of Commerce
Room 5062
Washington, DC 20230
www.doc.gov/obl

202-482-1360
Fax: 202-482-4054

The Office of Business Liaison is responsible for keeping the Department of Energy Secretary informed of issues affecting the business community. The Office provides information and guidance on programs throughout the Federal government. Although it cannot provide legal advice or intervene on an inquirer's behalf with a federal agency, it can alleviate the necessity of making numerous attempts to locate or obtain federal information, programs, and services. Most requests are for information having to do with government procurement, exporting, marketing, statistical sources, and regulatory matters. They can answer such questions as:

1) Where can someone get information on what the government is buying and what steps are required to sell to the government?
2) Who can advise a business on unfair trade practices?
3) Where are the statistics on a specific type of business?
4) Where is there information on federal databases?
5) Is there U.S. tariff information available?

* Central and Eastern Europe Business Information Center

U.S. Department of Commerce
International Trade Administration
14th and Constitution Ave., NW
Room 7414
Washington, DC 20230
www.ita.doc.gov

202-482-2645
Fax: 202-482-4473

The Central and Eastern Europe Business Information Center serves as a clearinghouse for information on business conditions in Eastern European countries, and on emerging trade and investment opportunities in those countries. It also serves as a source of information on U.S. government programs supporting private enterprise, trade, and investment in Eastern Europe. The Center also serves as a referral point for voluntary assistance programs. A variety of printed materials are available directly from the Center, as are bibliographies on data available from other sources. Most of the services are free of charge. They can answer such questions as:

1) What are the export procedures for a particular product to Poland?
2) What are the population, economic, commercial, and trade statistics on Romania?
3) Is there a list of contacts for export information in Bulgaria?
4) What political and economic issues should be considered when investing in businesses in Eastern Europe?
5) How can I advertise directly in Eastern European countries?

* Commodity Futures Trading Commission

Office of Public Affairs
Commodity Futures Trading Commission
3 Lafayette Center
1155 21st St., NW
Washington, DC 20581
www.cftc.gov/

202-418-5080
Fax: 202-418-5525

The Commodity Futures Trading Commission (CFTC) promotes economic growth, protects the rights of customers, and ensures fairness of the marketplace through regulation of futures trading. CFTC regulates the activities of numerous commodity exchange members, public brokerage houses, commodity trading advisers, and others, as well as approves the rules under which an exchange operates. They have free publications and can refer you to other offices within CFTC for specific information. They can answer such questions as:

1) What is the purpose of futures trading?
2) How do you read a commodity futures price table?
3) Do brokers have to be registered, and if so, how does one check on a broker?
4) What are some of the important issues that people should be aware of before entering the futures market?
5) What do I do if I suspect my broker of dishonest or unethical behavior?

* Federal Communications Commission

Federal Communications Commission
Public Service Commission
445 12th St., SW
Washington, DC 20554
Email: psd@fcc.gov
www.fcc.gov

888-225-5322
202-418-0190
Fax: 202-418-0232
TTY: 202-418-2555

The Federal Communications Commission regulates interstate and foreign communications by radio, television, wire, satellite, and cable. It is responsible for the development and operation of broadcast services and the provision of rapid, efficient nationwide and worldwide telephone and telegraph services at reasonable rates. They take complaints and have free information on all areas falling within their responsibility. They can answer questions such as:

1) What can be done if someone is having trouble with their cable company?
2) Where do you complain if you find the local D.J.'s show to be offensive?
3) What are the rules regarding pay per call services?
4) Where can you learn more about cellular radio regulations?
5) What happens when radio signals are picked up by consumer electronic products?

* Export Country Experts

U.S. Foreign and Commercial Services
Export Promotion Services
U.S. Department of Commerce, Room 2810   202-482-3809
Washington, DC 20230   Fax: 202-482-5819
www.doc.gov

The Country Desk Officers at the U.S. Department of Commerce can provide businesses with information on a market, company, or most any other aspect of commercial life in a particular country. These specialists can look at the needs of an individual U.S. firm wishing to sell in a particular country in the full context of that country's overall economy, trade policies, and political situation, and also in light of U.S. policies toward that country. Desk officers keep up to date on the economic and commercial conditions in their assigned countries. Each desk officer collects information on the country's regulations, tariffs, business practices, economic and political developments, trade data and trends, market size, and growth. They have free reports and other information available or they can refer callers to other country specialists. They can answer such questions as:

1) How can I expand my business through a foreign franchise?
2) How can I reduce my company's distribution and transportation costs overseas?
3) What type of export opportunities exist for computer manufacturing companies who want to expand to Germany?
4) What are some recent foreign labor trends in Japan?
5) Which markets are growing the fastest overseas?

* Economic Research Service

U.S. Department of Agriculture
1800 M St., NW   202-694-5050
Washington, DC 20036-5831   AutoFax: 202-694-5700
Email: service@econ.ag.gov
www.ers.usda.gov

The Economic Research Service conducts research on the economic and socio-demographic issues of rural America; the marketing, trade, and consumption of farm commodities; U.S. and foreign economic policies and their effects on trade; and more. They produce monographs and journal articles ranging from very technical research reports to easy-to-read leaflets. Situation and outlook reports providing a mixture of outlook and in-depth analysis of current commodity, trade, resource, and policy issues are also available. Most of the information is free of charge. They can answer such questions as:

1) What are the links between development and world trade?
2) What information exists on the U.S. and world markets for agricultural products?
3) How can farmers better conserve water resources?
4) What are the benefits of organic farming?
5) How can farmers adjust their techniques to keep pace with global market trends?

* Economics: National, Regional, and International

Bureau of Economic Analysis
U.S. Department of Commerce
1441 L St., NW   202-606-9900
Washington, DC 20230   Fax: 202-606-5310
www.bea.doc.gov

The Bureau of Economic Analysis (BEA) provides information on national and regional economics. BEA collects basic information on such key issues as economic growth, inflation, regional development, and the Nation's role in the world economy. It distributes a number of publications that measure, analyze and forecast economic trends, and are available on recorded messages, online through the Economic Bulletin Board, and in BEA reports. They can answer such questions as:

1) What is the average per capita income in the United States?
2) Will the rate of inflation increase or decrease over the next five years, and by what percent?
3) What percentage of the Gross National Product (GNP) does the government spend on health care?
4) How does the United States' national unemployment rate compare to other industrialized countries?
5) What was the unemployment rate in Pennsylvania from 1989-1993?

* Exporter's Hotline

Trade Information Center
U.S. Department of Commerce   800-USA-TRADE
Washington, DC 20230   Fax: 202-482-4473
www.ita.doc.gov/   TDD: 800-TDD-TRADE

The Trade Information Center is a comprehensive one-stop shop for information on U.S. government programs and activities that support exporting efforts. This hotline is staffed by trade specialists who can provide information on seminars and conferences, overseas buyers and representatives, overseas events, export financing, technical assistance, and export counseling. They also have access to the National Trade Data Bank, which provides basic export information, country-specific information, and industry-specific information. They can provide a great deal of free assistance, but there is a fee charged for data bank searches and other technical assistance. They can answer such questions as:

1) What countries are increasing or decreasing imports of a particular product, and at what rates?
2) What 10 countries are the top importers of a specific product?
3) How can a businessman meet prescreened prospects who are interested in a product or service?
4) How can a business assess their export potential?
5) How can a businessman obtain background data on potential foreign partners?

* Fishery Statistics and Economics Division

Office of Research and Environmental Information
National Marine Fisheries Service
National Oceanic and Atmospheric Administration
U.S. Department of Commerce
1315 East-West Highway, SSMC3   301-713-2328
Silver Spring, MD 20910   Fax: 301-713-4137
www.noaa.gov/fisheries.html

The Fisheries Statistics and Economics Division publishes statistical bulletins on marine recreational fishing and commercial fishing, and on the manufacture and commerce of fishery products. This Division has several annual and biannual reports available. They can answer such questions as:

1) How many fish were imported in a year, and what kind?
2) What is the most popular fish to export?
3) What kinds of fish are frozen?
4) What statistics exist on processed fish?
5) How many fish were caught by weekend fishermen?

* Office of Industries

United States International Trade Commission
500 E St., SW   202-205-3296
Washington, DC 20436   Fax: 202-205-3161
Email: cunningham@usitc.gov
www.usitc.gov

The Office of Industries at the U.S. International Trade Commission has experts assigned to every commodity imported into the U.S. These experts are responsible for investigation of the customs laws of the United States and foreign countries; the volume of imports in comparison with domestic production; the effects relating to competition of foreign industries; and all other factors affecting competition between articles of the U.S. and imported articles. They are knowledgeable about the domestic and foreign industry, and have statistical and factual information. They also have information regarding the tariff schedules. There is no charge for this information. They can answer such questions as:

1) What is the rate of duty for a product from a particular country?
2) What is the rate of import-export, the size of the market and the major producers of women's sweaters?
3) How much of a product is exported and what is the size of the potential market?
4) What happens if someone suspects an imported article is being subsidized or sold at less then fair value?
5) What can a company do if they feel they are being unfairly effected by import trade?

* Technical Data Center (Job Safety)

Technical Data Center
Occupational Safety and Health Administration
U.S. Department of Labor
200 Constitution Ave., NW, Room N2625   202-693-2350
Washington, DC 20210   Fax: 202-219-5046
www.osha.gov

The Technical Data Center compiles technical information on all industries covered by the Occupational Safety and Health Administration (OSHA). The Center maintains a library of 6,000 volumes and 200 journals, as well as an extensive microfilm collection of industry standards and OSHA rule-making records. The Center is also the docket office and holds the hearing records on

standards, the comments, and final rules. Literature searches are conducted free of charge. They can answer such questions as:
1) What are some hazard training programs that can be implemented in the workplace to teach employees to work safely in a variety of situations?
2) When was a particular company inspected and what violations were found?
3) What are the health hazards of a particular chemical?
4) What are some dangers of working around chemicals while pregnant?
5) Have there been similar reports of spinal cord injuries in a particular job?

* Federal Mediation and Conciliation Service (Labor-Management)

Federal Mediation and Conciliation Service (FMCS)
2100 K St., NW   202-606-8100
Washington, DC 20427   Fax: 202-606-4216
Email: publicinformation@fmcs.gov
www.fmcs.gov

The Federal Mediation and Conciliation Service represents the public interest by promoting the development of sound and stable labor-management relationships; preventing or minimizing work stoppages by assisting labor and management in settling their disputes through mediation; advocating collective bargaining, and much more. They can answer such questions as:
1) What is "alternative dispute resolution", and how can it by used?
2) How can companies work to develop effective labor-management committees?
3) What statistics exist on dispute mediation, preventive medication, work stoppages, and contract mediation?
4) What are some steps that companies can take to improve communication between labor and management?
5) What happens when a Federal agency and employee representative reach a negotiation impasse?

* Federal Labor Relations Authority

Federal Labor Relations Authority
607 14th St., NW   202-482-6550
Washington, DC 20424-0001   Fax: 202-482-6636
Bulletin Board: 202-512-1387
www.flra.gov

The Federal Labor Relations Authority oversees the Federal service labor-management relations program. It administers the law that protects the right of employees of the Federal Government to organize, bargain collectively, and participate through labor organizations of their own choosing. They can answer such questions as:
1) What laws protect Federal employees?
2) What steps can be taken when labor and management have reached an impasse?
3) How does an employee file a union grievance procedure?
4) How do I get a copy of my local union's collective bargaining agreement?
5) Is an agency permitted to negotiate a particular bargaining proposal?

* Labor Statistics Clearinghouse

Division of Information Services
Bureau of Labor Statistics   202-606-5886
U.S. Department of Labor   Fax: 202-606-7890
2 Massachusetts Ave., NE, Room 2860   TDD: 202-606-5897
Washington, DC 20212   Fax on Demand: 202-606-6325
Email: blsdatastaff@bls.gov
http://stats.bls.gov/opbinfo.htm

The Bureau of Labor Statistics (BLS) is the principal data-gathering agency of the Federal Government in the field of labor economics. The Bureau collects, processes, analyzes, and disseminates data relating to employment, unemployment, and other characteristics of the labor force; prices and consumer expenditures; wages, other worker compensation, and industrial relations; productivity; economic growth and employment projections; and occupational safety and health. This office can also provide you with a release schedule for BLS major economic indicators and the recorded message number. BLS can refer you to experts within the Bureau who can answer your specific question, provide you with historical information, and refer you to tables and charts for data. The BLS has publications, periodicals, magnetic tapes, diskettes, and more for sale. They can answer questions such as:
1) What are the employment statistics and the outlook for a particular occupation?
2) What is the unemployment rate for a particular state?
3) What is the current wage for a word processor in Seattle, and what are the usual benefits associated with that position?
4) What is the employment projection for a specific job?
5) What is the consumer/producer price index and how has it changed over time?

* Mine Safety Clearinghouse

Office of Information and Public Affairs
Mine Safety and Health Administration
U.S. Department of Labor
4015 Wilson Blvd.   703-235-1452
Arlington, VA 22203   Fax: 703-235-4323
Email: ksnyder@msha.gov
www.msha.gov

The Mine Safety and Health Administration develops mandatory safety and health standards, ensures compliance with such standards, assesses civil penalties for violations, and investigates accidents. It cooperates with and provides assistance to states in the development of effective state mine safety and health programs and improves and expands training programs. The Clearinghouse can provide general information regarding the Mine Safety and Health Administration, as well as free brochures, manuals, and other publications regarding mine safety and health. They can answer such questions as:
1) How can mine operators train miners effectively to prevent accidents and to avoid unsafe conditions?
2) What are the inspection procedures for a mine?
3) What is the latest information on the treatment and prevention of black lung and other respiratory diseases that are common to miners?
4) What is the latest research on robotics and automation in the mining industry?
5) What mines have been ordered to close because of safety concerns?

* Mineral Commodity Statistics Information

Minerals Information
U.S. Geological Survey   888-ASK-USGS
983 National Center   703-648-6100
Reston, VA 20192   Fax: 703-648-6057
Email: minerals@usgs.gov
http://minerals.usgs.gov

The U.S. Geological Survey (USGS) Minerals Resources Program is staffed by mineral experts who distribute a wide variety of mineral-related information and publications to meet and support the needs of the public, as well as government agencies and the scientific and industrial sectors. The staff provides information on the most current as well as past published reports pertaining to minerals, mining, processing, and research. They have statistics on import sources, uses, government stockpile, reserves, world resources, and substitutes. Dozens of commodity specialists are also available to assist you. They can answer such questions as:
1) What will the price of silver be over the next five years?
2) What is the role of gold in the international monetary system?
3) How can industries improve the quality of domestic steel?
4) How many tons of coal did U.S. industries produce last year?
5) What methods are used to recycle scrap metal?

* Minority Energy Information Clearinghouse

Office of Minority Economic Impact
U.S. Department of Energy
Forrestal Building, Room 5B-110
1000 Independence Ave., SW   202-586-5876
Washington, DC 20585   Fax: 202-586-3075
Email: ann.young@hq.doe.gov
www.hr.doe.gov/cd/index.html

The Minority Energy Information Clearinghouse develops and disseminates information related to energy programs that have an impact upon minorities, minority business enterprises, minority educational institutions, and other minority organizations. They can direct callers to government programs that will assist minority businesses in entering the energy field, as well as giving information about educational programs for minority students who are energy majors. They can answer such questions as:
1) What type of fellowships are available to minority college students attending Historically Black Colleges and Universities who want to pursue energy-related careers?
2) What types of energy-related loans are available to minority businesses?
3) Can I receive a listing of minority energy conferences or workshops?
4) How does the Clearinghouse's electronic bulletin board work?
5) How has recent energy legislation had an impact upon minority businesses?

* Overseas Private Investment Corporation

Investor Information Service
1100 New York Ave., NW
MS 7412   202-336-8663
Washington, DC 20527   Fax: 202-408-5155
www.opic.gov

Investor Information Service assists U.S. firms in gathering information on foreign countries and their business environments, as well as facilitating the flow of information about developing countries to potential U.S. investors. OPIC created the Investor Information Service (IIS). Country-specific information is available in kit form on more than 100 countries, as well as on 16 regions. Kits include materials covering the economies, trade laws, business regulations, political conditions and investment incentives of developing countries and regions. Kit costs range from $10-$420. They can answer such questions as:

1) What information exists for someone who wants to set up a fast food business in Greece?
2) What is the latest information on the foreign economic trends and their implications for the U.S. in Hungary?
3) What issues should be considered in purchasing an overseas venture?
4) Is it possible to meet with local business representatives, and experienced U.S. investors, and to attend briefings by the U.S. Ambassador in a foreign country?
5) What is the current investment climate in France? Is it favorable to new U.S. businesses?

* Pension Benefit Guaranty Corporation

Communications and Public Affairs Department
1200 K St., NW, Suite 240   202-326-4040
Washington, DC 20005-4026   Fax: 202-326-4042
www.pbgc.gov

The Pension Benefit Guaranty Corporation works to ensure the solvency and viability of company-sponsored pension plans. They can provide you with information and publications on pension plans, as well as information pertaining to laws and regulations on pensions. They can answer questions such as:

1) What is the federal pension law?
2) What are pensions plans and how do they operate?
3) What information on plans is a company required to give to members?
4) What are the rights and options of participants?
5) What is the employer's responsibilities regarding pension plans?

* Pension and Welfare Benefits Administration

U.S. Department of Labor
200 Constitution Ave., NW, N5619   202-219-8776
Washington, DC 20210   Fax: 202-219-5362
www.dol.gov/dol/pwba/welcome.html

The Pension and Welfare Benefits Administration (PWBA) helps to protect the economic future and retirement security of working Americans. It requires administrators of private pension and welfare plans to provide plan participants with easily understandable summaries; to file those summaries with the agency; and to report annually on the financial operation of the plans. PWBA has publications and other information available. They can answer questions such as:

1) What is the effect of job mobility on pension plans?
2) What is the Employee Retirement Income Security Act (ERISA)?
3) What studies have been done on the investment performance of ERISA plans?
4) What information are pension plans required to provide to participants?
5) What employee benefit documents are available from the Department of Labor?

* Federal Procurement Data Division

General Services Administration
7th and D St., SW, Room 5652   202-401-1529
Washington, DC 20407   Fax: 202-401-1546
Email: linda.hornsby@gsa.gov
www.fpds.gsa.gov

The Federal Procurement Data Center stores information about federal procurement actions, from 1978 to present, that totaled $25,000 or more. The systems contain information on purchasing or contracting office; date of award; dollars obligated; principal product or service; name and address of contractor; and more. Searches and printouts are available on a cost recovery basis. They can answer such questions as:

1) How many contracts did a particular company receive in a given year?
2) Who in the government is buying winter parkas?
3) What types of contracts are being awarded in Franklin county?
4) What has the National Park Service purchased in the last month?
5) Who do I need to talk to in order to sell my particular product?

* Science, Technology and Business Division

Library of Congress
101 Independence Ave., SE
Washington, DC 20540   202-707-5639
www.loc.gov

The Science, Technology and Business Division's collection numbers 3.5

million books, nearly 60,000 journals, and 4.4 million technical reports. The collections include such treasures as first editions of Copernicus and Newton and the personal papers of the Wright Brothers and Alexander Graham Bell. The Division has primary responsibility for providing reference and bibliographic services and for recommending acquisitions in the broad areas of science and technology. Reference services are provided to users in person, by telephone, and by correspondence. Indirect reference service is provided through bibliographic guides (Tracer Bullets) and research reports prepared by Division subject specialists and reference librarians. Copies of reference guides are available at no charge. They can answer such questions as:

1) Where can someone begin looking for information on lasers and their applications?
2) What are good sources of information on volcanoes?
3) What resources exist on extraterrestrial life?
4) Where could someone find sources for information on medicinal plants?
5) How would someone go about creating a hologram?

* U.S. Securities and Exchange Commission

Office of Public Affairs
450 5th St., NW   202-942-0020
Washington, DC 20549   Fax: 202-942-9654
www.sec.gov   TTY: 202-628-9039

The Securities and Exchange Commission (SEC) administers federal securities laws that seek to provide protection for investors; to ensure that securities markets are fair and honest; and to provide the means to enforce securities laws through sanctions. They have free publications, a public reference room, disclosure reports, and information on how individuals can protect themselves. They can answer such questions as:

1) What are pyramid schemes and how do they work?
2) Where can someone find out if there have been complaints about a particular broker or adviser?
3) How does someone choose investments safely?
4) Who needs to register with the SEC and what is required?
5) What is the SEC and how does it operate?

* U.S. Small Business Administration

Answer Desk
409 3rd St., SW   800-827-5722
Washington, DC 20416   202-205-6400
www.sbaonline.sba.gov/helpdesk   Fax: 202-205-7064

The Small Business Administration (SBA) aids, counsels, assists, and protects the interests of small business, and ensures that small business concerns receive a fair portion of government purchases, contracts, and subcontracts. SBA also makes loans and licenses, and regulates small business investment companies. The Small Business Answer Desk helps callers with questions on how to start and manage a business, where to get financing, and other information needed to operate and expand a business. They have a publications catalogue, with most items available for under $5.00. They can answer such questions as:

1) What programs or forms of assistance are available to women entrepreneurs?
2) What help exists for a business interested in developing an export market?
3) Is there a way a business can receive free management consulting?
4) Are there programs designed specifically for businesses in small towns?
5) How does a company enter the federal procurement market?

* National Center for Standards and Certification

National Institute of Standards and Technology
Building 820, Room 164   301-975-4040
Gaithersburg, MD 20899   Fax: 301-926-1559
Email: ncsci@nist.gov
http://ts.nist.gov/ts/htdocs/210/217/bro.htm

The National Center for Standards and Certification Information provides a free service which will identify standards for selling any product to any country in the world. This federal agency will tell you what the standard is for a given product or suggest where you can obtain an official copy of the standard. They can answer such questions as:

1) What U.S. industry standards pertain to certain products?
2) What foreign standards apply to a product?
3) What is the latest GATT information on proposed foreign regulations?
4) Where can I locate the organizations that have standards information?
5) How are military standards different for U.S. standards?

* Transportation Research Information Services

Transportation Research Board
2101 Constitution Ave., NW   202-334-2934

Washington, DC 20418
Fax: 202-334-2003
www.nas.edu/trb

The Transportation Research Information Services (TRIS) is the prime source of transportation research information in the United States. TRIS is an information clearinghouse designed to identify worldwide sources of transportation research information. TRIS contains more than 250,000 abstracts of completed research and summaries of research projects in progress. TRIS is regularly used by transportation administrators, operators, academics, planners, designers, engineers, and managers. TRIS contains information on various modes and aspects of transportation including planning, design, finance, construction, maintenance, traffic operations, management, marketing, and other topics. Publications are available for a fee. They can answer such questions as:

1) What is the latest research on airport capacity?
2) What information exists on the privatization of toll roads?
3) What data should be considered when building a bypass?
4) What studies have been conducted on land traffic getting to and from airports?
5) What technology exists to weigh trucks in motion rather than at weigh stations?

* Women's Bureau Clearinghouse

U.S. Department of Labor
200 Constitution Ave., NW, Room S3306   800-827-5335
Washington, DC 20210   202-219-4486
Email: wb-wwc@dol.gov   Fax: 202-219-5529
www.dol.gov/dol/wb/welcome.html

The Women's Bureau Clearinghouse was designed and established to assist employers in identifying the most appropriate policies for responding to the dependent care needs of employees seeking to balance their dual responsibilities. They can also provide information on women's issues, as well as work force issues that affect women. They offer information and guidance in areas such as women-owned businesses, women workers, alternative work schedules, dependent care issues, and much more. They also have publications and other information available, much of which is free. They can answer such questions as:

1) What are some elder care program options?
2) What is the earning difference between men and women?
3) How does flex time work in companies similar to mine?
4) What are some examples of alternate work schedules and how do they work?
5) What literature and other resources are available on employer-supported child care?

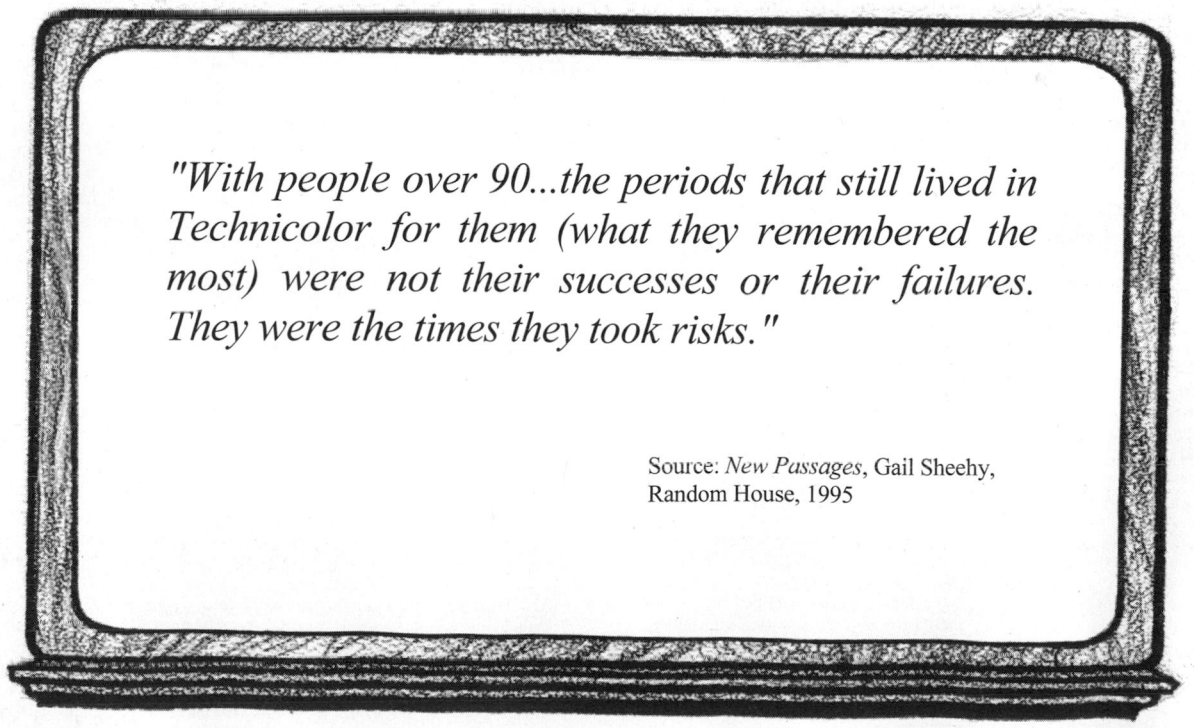

"With people over 90...the periods that still lived in Technicolor for them (what they remembered the most) were not their successes or their failures. They were the times they took risks."

Source: *New Passages*, Gail Sheehy, Random House, 1995

Consumer and Housing

* Animal Welfare Information Center
National Agricultural Library
U.S. Department of Agriculture
10301 Baltimore Blvd., 5th Floor   301-504-6212
Beltsville, MD 20705-2351   Fax: 301-504-7125
Email: awic@nal.usda.gov
www.nal.usda.gov/awic

The Animal Welfare Information Center is the focal point for all aspects of animal welfare. They have information on the care, handling, and management of animals used in research; training guides and manuals for animal care personnel; ethical issues; animal behavior; and pain control. They have a publications list of free fact sheets, bibliographies, and other resources. They can answer such questions as:
1) What information is there on the ethical and moral issues relating to animals and the philosophy of animal rights?
2) What alternatives are there to the use of live animals in research?
3) What videos exist on the care of animals?
4) What are some of the legislation regarding animal welfare?
5) Are there resources available regarding the raising of poultry?

* Auto Safety Hotline
Office of Defects Investigation (NEF-10)
National Highway Traffic Safety Administration
U.S. Department of Transportation
400 7th St., SW   800-424-9393
Washington, DC 20590   Fax: 202-366-7882
Email: hotline@nhtsa.dot.gov
www.nhtsa.dot.gov

The Auto Safety Hotline can provide information on recalls, defects, investigations, child safety seats, tires, drunk driving, crash test results, seat belts, air bags, odometer tampering, and other related topics. They also accept reports of automobile safety problems. The Hotline publishes the New Car Assessment Program, which provides comparable data on the frontal crashworthiness of selected new vehicles. They have free fact sheets and publications on these topics and more. They can answer such questions as:
1) What is the safest new car?
2) Which child car seats have been recalled?
3) What should you do if you suspect an odometer has been tampered with?
4) How many states have seat belt laws, and what are the statistics regarding their use and benefits?
5) What are the statistics for drunk driving, and what information exists for alcohol's involvement in fatalities?
6) What is the fuel efficiency of a particular car?

* Federal Communications Commission
Federal Communications Commission
445 12th St., SW   202-418-0190
Washington, DC 20554   Fax: 202-418-0232
Email: fccinfo@fcc.gov
www.fcc.gov

The Federal Communications Commission regulates interstate and foreign communications by radio, television, wire, satellite, and cable. It is responsible for the development and operation of broadcast services and the provision of rapid, efficient nationwide and worldwide telephone and telegraph services at reasonable rates. They take complaints and have free information on all areas falling within their responsibility. They can answer questions such as:
1) What can be done if someone is having trouble with their cable company or does not understand their cable bill?
2) Where do you complain if you find the local D.J.'s show to be offensive?
3) What are the rules regarding pay per call services?
4) Where can you learn more about cellular radio regulations?
5) What happens when radio signals are picked up by consumer electronic products?

* Consumer Product Safety Commission
Office of Information and Public Affairs
U.S. Consumer Product Safety Commission   800-638-2772
Washington, DC 20207   Fax: 301-504-0862
Email: info@cpsc.gov
www.cpsc.gov

The Consumer Product Safety Commission (CPSC) protects the public against unreasonable risks of injury from consumer products; assists consumers in evaluating the consumer products and minimizes conflicting state and local regulations; and promotes research and investigation into the causes and prevention of product-related deaths, illnesses, and injuries. The CPSC Hotline can provide you with information on product recalls and will take reports of hazardous products or product-related injuries. You can write to the CPSC for a complete list of publications which describe some of the common hazards associated with the use of consumer products, recommending ways to avoid these hazards. They can answer such questions as:
1) What toys are currently being recalled?
2) What types of consumer products are the most dangerous?
3) What safety information exists for the school playground?
4) Are there special precautions you should take for the elderly?
5) What is some current information regarding poisons?

* Credit Information
Office of Consumer Affairs
Federal Deposit Insurance Corporation
550 17th St., NW, Room F-130   202-942-3100
Washington, DC 20429   800-934-3342
Email: consumer@fdic.gov
www.fdic.gov

The Federal Deposit Insurance Corporation (FDIC) was established to promote and preserve public confidence in banks, protecting the money supply through provision of insurance coverage for bank deposits and periodic examinations of insured state-chartered banks that are not members of the Federal Reserve System. The FDIC can provide you with information and an overview of the FDIC, and the major consumer and civil rights laws and regulations that protect bank customers. They can answer questions on such topics as:
1) Equal Credit Opportunity and Age
2) Equal Credit Opportunity and Women
3) Fair Credit Billing
4) Fair Credit Reporting Act
5) Truth in Lending

* National Credit Union Administration
Public Information
1775 Duke St.   703-518-6330
Alexandria, VA 22314-3428   Fax: 703-518-6429
Email: pacamail@ncua.gov
www.ncua.gov

The National Credit Union Administration is responsible for chartering, insuring, supervising, and examining federal credit unions and administering the National Credit Union Share Insurance Fund. They have free publications and can refer you to the correct office for more information on credit unions. They can answer such questions as:
1) How are credit unions chartered?
2) What are the rules and regulations regarding the organization of credit unions?
3) Is there a master list of all federally insured credit unions?
4) How are credit unions liquidated?
5) How are credit unions insured?

* Food and Nutrition Information Center
National Agricultural Library
U.S. Department of Agriculture
10301 Baltimore Blvd., Room 304   301-504-5719
Beltsville, MD 20705   Fax: 301-504-6409
Email: fnic@nal.usda.gov   TTY: 301-504-6856
www.nal.usda.gov/fnic

The Food and Nutrition Information Center serves many types of users including educators, students, researchers, and consumers. Reference services are provided. Subjects covered include human nutrition research and education, diet and diet-related diseases, food habits, food composition, nutrition education, and more. The Center offers a variety of services which includes answers to specific questions, lending books and audiovisuals, and providing computerized literature searches. A publications list is available, many of which are free. They can answer such questions as:
1) What studies exist on the effects of the school breakfast program?
2) What information can you provide to parents concerned about their overweight children?
3) Do you have information on anorexia nervosa?

4) Is it dangerous to consume caffeine while pregnant?
5) Are canned peaches as nutritious as fresh?

* Federal Trade Commission (Fraud)

Public Reference Branch, Room 130	877-FTC-HELP
Pennsylvania Ave. at 6th St., NW	202-326-2222
Washington, DC 20580	Fax: 202-326-2050
www.ftc.gov	TTY: 202-326-2502

The Federal Trade Commission (FTC) protects consumers against unfair, deceptive, or fraudulent practices. The FTC enforces a variety of consumer protection laws enacted by Congress, as well as trade regulation rules issued by the Commission. Its actions include individual company and industry-wide investigations, administrative and federal court litigation, rulemaking proceedings, and consumer and business education. The FTC has a wealth of information and free publications on a variety of topics. They can answer such questions as:

1) What are the laws regarding shopping by mail or phone?
2) What are some things people should know before looking for a job with a head hunter?
3) What information exists for people checking out mortgages or refinancing?
4) What should someone do if their lifetime membership in a health club expires?
5) What can be done to protect against credit card fraud?

* Horticulture Clearinghouse

U.S. Department of Agriculture	
10301 Baltimore Blvd.	301-504-5204
Beltsville, MD 20705	Fax: 301-504-6927
www.nal.usda.gov	

The Horticulture Clearinghouse covers technical horticultural or botanical questions, economic botany, wild plants of possible use, herbs, bonsai, and floriculture. They can answer such questions as:

1) How can you grow lavender commercially as a source of essential oils?
2) How do you grow and dry herbs?
3) How much might landscaping improve the worth of a home?
4) Which plants can be used for medicinal purposes?
5) How can I control garden insects without using chemical sprays?

* HUD USER (Housing)

P.O. Box 6091	800-245-2691
Rockville, MD 20849	Fax: 301-519-5767
Email: huduser@aspensys.com	TDD: 800-483-2209
www.huduser.org	

HUD USER, a service of the U.S. Department of Housing and Urban Development, is an information source for housing and community development researchers and policymakers that collects, creates, and distributes a wide variety of materials. You can find information on low-income housing, community development strategies, environmental hazards, land development regulations, population shifts, and housing for elderly and disabled people. A free monthly newsletter and a publications catalogue is available. They can answer such questions as:

1) What information is there on housing for people with special needs?
2) How does one remove lead-based paint from their home?
3) What are "enterprise zones" and what are their goals?
4) What are some federal programs and other sources of assistance for homelessness?
5) What video programs are there on housing issues?

* Housing Discrimination

Fair Housing Enforcement Division
Office of Fair Housing and Equal Opportunity
U.S. Department of Housing and Urban Development (HUD)
Washington, DC 20410-2000   800-669-9777
www.hud.gov/fhe

The U.S. Department of Housing and Urban Development administers the law that prohibits discrimination in housing on the basis of race, color, religion, sex, and national origin; investigates complaints of housing discrimination; and attempts to resolve them through conciliation. Two common forms of discrimination are redlining and steering. Redlining is the illegal practice of refusing to originate mortgage loans in certain neighborhoods on the basis of race or ethnic origin. Steering is the illegal act of limiting the housing shown by a real estate agent to a certain ethnic group. HUD refers complaints to state and local fair housing agencies. They can answer such questions as:

1) How do I file a discrimination complaint?
2) What are the regulations regarding housing discrimination?
3) Is sexual harassment a violation of the Fair Housing Act?
4) Can someone be denied housing because of a mental disability?

5) Do landlords have to pay for physical changes to your apartment if you need them, such as grab bars in the bathroom or wider doors?

* Public Housing Drug Strategy Clearinghouse

Drug Information and Strategy Clearinghouse	
U.S. Department of Housing and Urban Development (HUD)	
P.O. Box 6424	800-578-3472
Rockville, MD 20850	Fax: 301-251-5767

Sponsored by the Department of Housing and Urban Development, the Drug Information and Strategy Clearinghouse provides housing officials, residents, and community leaders with information and assistance on drug abuse prevention and drug trafficking control techniques. They have created a database containing information on improving resident screening procedures, strengthening eviction policies, increasing cooperation with local law enforcement, implementing drug tip hotlines, forming resident patrols, starting child care centers, and organizing drug education/prevention activities. The clearinghouse also provides information packages, resource lists, HUD regulations, referrals, and a newsletter. There is no charge for most information. They can answer such questions as:

1) How can housing authorities apply for government grants?
2) What are some anti-drug strategies that have been successfully carried out in public housing units?
3) What are the latest drug abuse prevention theories and have there been demonstration projects based on these models?
4) What resident patrols and related programs have been successful in building drug-free neighborhoods?
5) How can there be an increase in cooperation with local law enforcement and other agencies?

* National Injury Information Clearinghouse

U.S. Consumer Product Safety Commission	
4330 East-West Highway	301-504-0424
Washington, DC 20207	Fax: 301-504-0025
Email: info@cpsc.gov	
www.cpsc.gov/about/clrnghse.html	

The National Injury Information Clearinghouse maintains thousands of detailed investigative reports of injuries associated with consumer products. It has access to automated databases with several million incidents of injuries that have been reported by a nationwide network of hospital emergency departments. You can find the victim's background, including age, race, injury diagnosis, consumer product involved, and more. The Clearinghouse distributes documents and will fulfill search requests, usually at no charge. They can answer such questions as:

1) How many children under the age of five are injured each year while playing with toys?
2) Are all-terrain vehicles considered dangerous?
3) How many injuries/deaths have been reported within the last five years for all-terrain vehicles?
4) How many fires are caused each year by range/ovens?
5) Which children's clothing manufacturers produce flame retardant materials and how effective are they?

* U.S. Postal Service (Mailing)

Office of Consumer Affairs	
475 L'Enfant Plaza, SW	
Room 5821	202-268-2281
Washington, DC 20260-2200	Fax: 202-268-2304
www.usps.gov	

The Postal Service provides mail processing and delivery services to individuals and businesses and protects the mail from loss or theft. They can answer all your postal service questions and provide you with publications and referrals to other postal service departments. They can answer such questions as:

1) How can a business protect itself against mail fraud?
2) What services does the Postal Service offer?
3) How does a business set up a mail room?
4) What international mail services are offered?
5) How can a person stop undesirable material from being delivered to their home?

* Meat and Poultry Hotline

Food Safety and Inspection Service	
U.S. Department of Agriculture	800-535-4555
Washington, DC 20250-3700	Fax: 202-690-2859
Email: fsis.webmaster@usda.gov	TDD/TTY: 800-256-7072
www.fsis.usda.gov	

The Meat and Poultry Hotline takes calls from consumers on cases of meat or poultry food poisoning or complaints about meat or poultry spoilage due to improper packaging or processing. They can also provide you with health-

oriented information on safe handling and storage of meats and poultry. They can answer such questions as:
1) What should be done during a power outage?
2) What is salmonella and how can people be protected?
3) What are the different type of foodborne illnesses?
4) How long should you cook poultry?
5) What information should be included on meat and poultry labels and what does it mean?

* Mortgage Information Center

Program Evaluation Division
Assistant Secretary for Housing
U.S. Department of Housing and Urban Development (HUD)
451 7th St., SW
Attn: B133   202-755-7470, ext. 145
Washington, DC 20410   Fax: 202-755-7455
Bulletin Board: 202-708-3563

Monthly reports are compiled by the Program Evaluation Division of HUD in areas relating to the mortgage market, securities, taxation, market trends, interest rates, among others. You can receive a free survey of mortgage lending activity and a survey of FHA and conventional mortgage rates. They can answer such questions as:
1) What are the average mortgage rates for different parts of the country?
2) What is the difference in mortgage rates over the past 10 years?
3) What is the average interest rate on new home loans versus existing home loans?
4) What is the number of unsold new houses in a given month?
5) What is the current FHA rate?

* Organic Gardening

Public Information Center, 3404
U.S. Environmental Protection Agency
401 M St., SW   202-260-7751
Washington, DC 20460   Fax: 202-260-6257
Email: access@epamail.epa.gov
www.epa.gov

The Public Information Center has free information sheets on organic gardening, composting, and recycling. They can answer such questions as:
1) What plants should be planted near each other to deter pests?
2) What are the dangers of pesticides?
3) Who can I talk to regarding composting and recycling?
4) What are the advantages of organic fertilizers?
5) What is required to maintain a lawn?

* Pension Benefit Guaranty Corporation

Public Affairs
1200 K St., NW   202-326-4040
Washington, DC 20005-4026   Fax: 202-326-4042
www.pbgc.gov

The Pension Benefit Guaranty Corporation works to ensure the solvency and viability of company-sponsored pension plans. They can provide you with information and publications on pension plans, as well as laws and regulations on pensions. They can answer questions such as:
1) What is the federal pension law?
2) What are pensions plans and how do they operate?
3) What information on plans is a company required to give to members?
4) What are the rights and options of participants?
5) What is the employer's responsibilities regarding pension plans?

* Pension and Welfare Benefits Administration

U.S. Department of Labor
200 Constitution Ave., NW
N5656   202-219-8921
Washington, DC 20210   Fax: 202-219-5362
www.dol.gov/dol/pwba

The Pension and Welfare Benefits Administration (PWBA) helps to protect the economic future and retirement security of working Americans. It requires administrators of private pension and welfare plans to provide plan participants with easily understandable summaries; to file those summaries with the agency; and to report annually on the financial operation of the plans. PWBA has publications and other information available. They can answer questions such as:
1) What is the effect of job mobility on pension plans?
2) What is the Employee Retirement Income Security Act (ERISA)?
3) What studies have been done on the investment performance of ERISA plans?
4) What information are pension plans required to provide to participants?
5) What employee benefit documents are available from the Department of Labor?

* Plant Information Service

U.S. Botanic Garden
245 1st St., SW   202-225-8333
Washington, DC 20024   Fax: 202-225-1561
www.aoc.gov/

The U.S. Botanic Garden serves as a center for plant information offering a telephone information service, as well as responding to written inquiries from Monday through Friday, from 9:00 to 11:30 a.m. They can answer such questions as:
1) What are the benefits of organic gardening?
2) How can I use insects to control garden pests?
3) Which house plants are poisonous?
4) What are the dangers of chemical fertilizers?
5) Which herbs grow best indoors?

* Seafood Hotline

Office of Seafood
Food and Drug Administration
200 C St., SW   800-SAFEFOOD
Washington, DC 20201   Fax: 202-401-3532
Email: oco@fdacf.sw.dhhs.gov
http://vm.cfsan.fda.gov/seafood1.html

The Seafood Hotline can provide consumers with information on how to buy and use seafood products, including storing and handling of seafood, and questions on seafood labeling and nutrition. The Hotline has many free publications on a variety of seafood issues. They can answer such questions as:
1) Can fish be kept frozen for a year?
2) How do you know if a seafood vendor is reputable?
3) What are the dangers of eating raw shellfish?
4) What information is available on canned tuna?
5) What are some seafood safety concerns for people with particular medical conditions?

* Social Security Administration

Social Security Administration
Office of Public Inquiries
6401 Security Blvd.   800-772-1213
Room 4-C-5 Annex   410-965-7700
Baltimore, MD 21235-6401   TTY: 800-325-0778
www.ssa.gov

The Social Security Administration administers the Social Security and Medicare programs. They can assist certain beneficiaries in claiming reimbursement and developing and adjudicating claims. They can answer such questions as:
1) If you were to retire today, how much would you receive in benefits?
2) What should be done once you turn 65?
3) What is supplemental security income and how do you apply for it?
4) What disability insurance benefits do you qualify for?
5) What survivor benefits are available to children?

* Internal Revenue Service (Taxes)

U.S. Department of Treasury
1111 Constitution Ave., NW
Washington, DC 20224   800-829-1040
Fax on Demand: 703-487-4160
www.irs.ustreas.gov

The Internal Revenue Service is responsible for administering and enforcing the internal revenue laws and related statutes. Its mission is to collect the proper amount of tax revenue at the least cost to the public. They can answer such questions as:
1) How do you get copies of your back tax forms?
2) What is required when you deduct your home office?
3) What are the rules about writing off a vacation/work trip?
4) What happens if you can't pay your taxes?
5) Can you deduct your mother as a dependent if she lives with you?

* Women's Bureau Clearinghouse

U.S. Department of Labor
200 Constitution Ave., NW
Room S3306   800-827-5335
Washington, DC 20210   202-219-4486
Email: wb-wwc@dol.gov   Fax: 202-219-5529
www.dol.gov/dol/wb/welcome.html

The Women's Bureau Clearinghouse was established to assist employers in identifying the most appropriate policies for responding to the dependent care needs of employees seeking to balance their dual responsibilities. They can also provide information on women's issues, as well as work force issues that affect women. They can offer information and guidance in areas such as women-owned businesses, women workers, alternative work schedules, dependent care issues, and much more. They also have many free publications and other information available. They can answer such questions as:

1) What are some elder care program options?
2) What is the earning difference between men and women?
3) How does flex time work in companies similar to mine?
4) What are some examples of alternate work schedules and how do they work?
5) What literature and other resources are available on employer-supported child care?

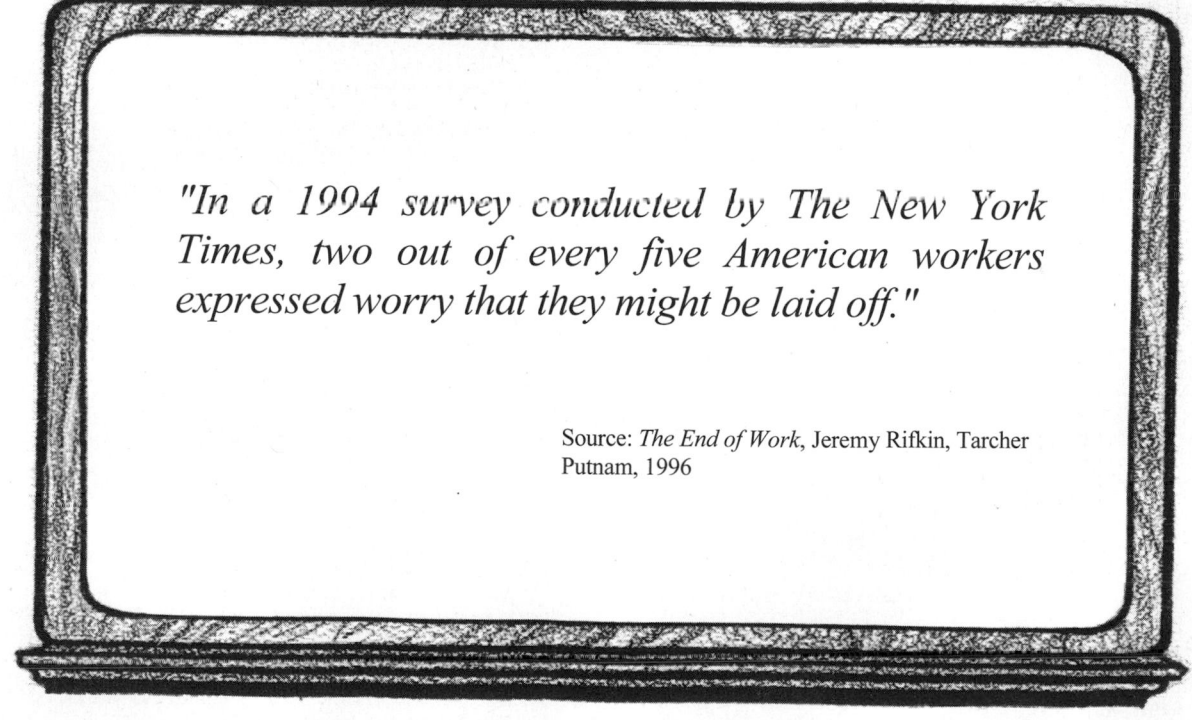

"In a 1994 survey conducted by The New York Times, two out of every five American workers expressed worry that they might be laid off."

Source: *The End of Work*, Jeremy Rifkin, Tarcher Putnam, 1996

Criminal Justice

* Bureau of Alcohol, Tobacco, and Firearms

Distribution Center
U.S. Department of Treasury
P.O. Box 5950
Springfield, VA 22150-5950   703-455-7801
www.atf.treas.gov

The Bureau of Alcohol, Tobacco, and Firearms (ATF) is responsible for enforcing and administering firearms and explosives laws, as well as those laws covering the production, use, and distribution of alcohol and tobacco products. ATF can provide you with a wealth of information, statistics, and publications. They can answer such questions as:
1)   What explosive incidents and stolen explosives occurred in a year by state and by type of explosives?
2)   What are the different types of firearms available?
3)   What are the license requirements for a given state to carry a weapon?
4)   How do law enforcement officials trace firearms?

* National Criminal Justice Reference Service

National Institute of Justice/NCJRS
Box 6000   800-851-3420
Rockville, MD 20849   301-519-5500
Email: askncjrs@ncjrs.org   Fax: 301-251-5212
www.ncjrs.org/

The National Criminal Justice Reference Service brings the latest criminal justice research findings to criminal justice policymakers, practitioners, and researchers from around the world. Their database features summaries of books, reports, articles, and audiovisual materials. They have a free bi-monthly catalogue which lists new publications (many of which are free), upcoming conferences, and more. They can answer such questions as:
1)   What videotapes are there on criminal justice topics?
2)   What information exists on community safety issues?
3)   How effective is parole and probation?
4)   What drug abuse programs are in place for offenders?
5)   What is date rape?

* Drug and Crime Data Center and Clearinghouse

1600 Research Boulevard
Rockville, MD 20850   800-666-3332
Email: ondc@ncjrs.org
http://virlib.ncjrs.org/DrugsAndCrime.asp

The Data Center and Clearinghouse serves the drugs-and-crime information needs of federal, state, and local policy makers, criminal justice and public health practitioners, researchers and universities, private corporations, the media, and the general public. The most current data is available on illegal drugs, drug law violations, drug-related crime, drug-using offenders in the criminal justice system, and the impact of drugs on criminal justice administration. The Clearinghouse maintains a database of some 1,500 annotated bibliographies of statistical and research reports, books, and journal articles on drugs and crime. All documents are free. They can answer such questions as:
1)   What are the economic costs of drug-related crime?
2)   What data exists on the quantity and flow of illicit drugs from cultivation to consequences?
3)   What percentage of high school seniors used cocaine last year?
4)   What tactics have been used to build integrity and reduce drug corruption in police departments?
5)   What percentage of rapists report that their victims were well known to them?

* National Clearinghouse on Election Administration

Federal Election Commission   202-694-1100
999 E St., NW   800-424-9530
Washington, DC 20463   Fax: 202-219-8500
www.fec.gov

The National Clearinghouse on Election Administration is an agency of the Federal Election Commission. Its overall objective is to enhance the honesty, integrity, and efficiency of the federal election process by providing information and assistance to state and local election officials, to state legislatures and legislative reference bureaus, and to other interested organizations regarding the conduct of Federal elections. They can answer such questions as:
1)   What research reports are available on state campaign finance laws?
2)   Where can I obtain advice and assistance in making polling places more accessible to the elderly and handicapped?
3)   What statistics exist that could summarize state and national voting age populations, the number of registered voters, turnout, and results in

presidential elections for 1960 through 1988?
4)   What landmark judicial decisions have been made involving elections over the past twenty years?
5)   What are the registration techniques and procedures in a particular state?

* Equal Employment Opportunity Commission (EEOC)

Publications and Information Center
P.O. Box 12549   800-669-EEOC
Cincinnati, OH 45212-0549   Fax: 513-489-8695
www.eeoc.gov

The purpose of the Equal Employment Opportunity Commission is to eliminate discrimination based on race, color, religion, sex, national origin, or age in hiring, promoting, firing, setting wages, testing, training, and all other terms and conditions of employment. The Commission conducts investigations of alleged discrimination, and provides voluntary assistance programs for employers, unions, and others. They have free publications and information available. They can answer such questions as:
1)   What questions cannot be asked in an employment interview?
2)   What constitutes sexual harassment?
3)   What federal law prohibits employers from discriminating between men and women in the payment of wages, and to whom does the law apply?
4)   What can be done if you feel you have been unfairly discriminated against?
5)   What information exists to train personnel officers on the prevailing laws and regulations?

* Bureau of Justice Assistance Clearinghouse

P.O. Box 6000
U.S. Department of Justice   800-688-4252
Rockville, MD 20849   Fax: 301-251-5212
Email: askncjrs@ncjrs.org
www.ncjrs.org

The Bureau of Justice Assistance Clearinghouse (BJA) informs state and local criminal justice practitioners about BJA products and programs. They provide federal funding and technical assistance to state and local units of government to improve the criminal justice system. They can answer such questions as:
1)   What information is available regarding a variety of anti-drug programs?
2)   What programs are in place to improve the efficiency of the criminal justice system?
3)   What are the estimated costs of drug testing for a pretrial service program?
4)   What training programs exist for narcotics enforcement?
5)   What are the treatment alternatives to street crimes?

* Justice Statistics Clearinghouse

Bureau of Justice Statistics
U.S. Department of Justice
Box 6000   800-732-3277
Rockville, MD 20849   301-519-5500
Email: askncjrs@ncjrs.org
http://virlib.ncjrs.org/Statistics.asp

The Bureau of Justice Statistics (BJS) supports this clearinghouse for those seeking crime and criminal justice data. In addition to distributing BJS publications, the Clearinghouse responds to statistics requests by offering document database searches, statistics information packages, referrals, and other related products and services. They can answer such questions as:
1)   What is the annual national estimate of the amount of crime against persons and households?
2)   What are some of the characteristics of victims?
3)   How differently are juveniles handled from adults?
4)   How prevalent is organized crime?
5)   What is the recidivism rate, and when criminals are rearrested, with what crimes are they normally charged?

* Juvenile Justice Clearinghouse

National Criminal Justice Reference Service
U.S. Department of Justice
Box 6000
Rockville, MD 20849   800-638-8736
Email: askncjrs@ncjrs.org
http://virlib.ncjrs.org/JuvenileJustice.asp

The Juvenile Justice Clearinghouse disseminates publications, research findings, and program evaluations supported by the Office of Juvenile Justice and Delinquency Prevention. In addition, the staff can prepare customized responses to information requests. They can answer such questions as:

1) How do juvenile courts vary in handling drug and alcohol cases?
2) What can a community do in response to youth gangs?
3) What methods have been successful in dealing with juvenile reinstitution?
4) How many juveniles were arrested last year for possession of illegal drugs?
5) What methods are effective in reducing violence in the schools?

* National Clearinghouse for Poverty Law (Legal Services)

205 W. Monroe, 2nd Floor   312-263-3830
Chicago, IL 60606   Fax: 312-263-3846

The National Clearinghouse for Poverty Law is the most comprehensive source for information concerning civil poverty law. Also, the Clearinghouse has many publications dealing with issues of vital interest to the non poverty lawyer. Problems with health care, housing, and social security strike people in all economic situations. These are just some of the 20 major areas of law that Clearinghouse publications cover, providing practical information useful to people in all economic and social strata. The Clearinghouse, as a resource center and a legal research system, offers the most complete source of civil poverty law publications that can be found. They have a free publications list. They can answer such questions as:

1) What information exists on the eligibility requirements for Medicare home health care?
2) What models exist on establishing pro bono programs?
3) What are the various issues concerning the tax burden on the poor?
4) What are the litigation issues concerning homeless persons and emergency shelter?
5) Where can information be obtained on child custody cases?

* National Center for Missing and Exploited Children

699 Prince St.   800-843-5678
Alexandria, VA 22314   703-274-3900

www.missingkids.org   Fax: 703-274-2220

The National Center for Missing and Exploited Children serves as a clearinghouse of information on missing and exploited children; provides technical assistance to citizens and law-enforcement agencies; offers training programs to law-enforcement and social service professionals; distributes photos and descriptions of missing children nationwide; coordinates child protection efforts with the private sector; networks with nonprofit service providers and state clearinghouses on missing persons; and provides information on effective state legislation to ensure the protection of children. They can answer such questions as:

1) How can a parent work through the civil and criminal justice systems in order to regain custody of the child her ex-husband stole from her?
2) How can a parent protect children against day care abuse?
3) What are some of the warning signs of child sexual exploitation?
4) What is the profile of a runaway and the patterns of runaway behavior?
5) What information is available to help a child testify in court?

* Office for Victims of Crime Resource Center

U.S. Department of Justice
Box 6000   800-627-6872
Rockville, MD 20849   Fax: 301-251-5212
Email: askncjrs@ncjrs.org
http://virlib.ncjrs.org/VictimsOfCrime.asp

The Office for Victims of Crime Resource Center is sponsored by the Office of Victims of Crime. It can provide access to resources, such as more than 7,000 victim-related books and articles, national victimization statistics, federally sponsored victim-related research studies, and information on state victim compensation programs. From the Clearinghouse, you can get free publications, borrow hard-to-find publications, and buy selected videotapes. Information specialists can also conduct database searches. They can answer such questions as:

1) What is the relationship between child abuse and delinquency?
2) What information is there for police when confronting a domestic violence incident?
3) What are some of the programs which compensate victims of crime?
4) What is the criminal justice response to victim harm?
5) How can one improve the use and effectiveness of the Neighborhood Watch program?

Education And The Arts

* ERIC Clearinghouse on <u>Adult, Career, and Vocational</u> Learning

Ohio State University Center on Education and
  Training for Employment   800-848-4815
1900 Kenny Rd.   614-292-7069
Columbus, OH 43210   Fax: 614-292-1260
Email: ericacve@magnus.acs.ohio_state.edu
http://ericacve.org

The Clearinghouse on Adult, Career, and Vocational Learning provides materials covering all levels of adult and continuing education from: basic literacy training through professional skill upgrading; vocational and technical education covering all service areas for secondary, postsecondary, and adult populations; and career education and career development programs for all ages and populations. A publications list and price sheet are available. They can answer questions such as:

1) What research exists on the effectiveness of flex time and job share programs?
2) What is the job placement rate of graduates from vocational schools?
3) What are the statistics on job satisfaction and wage earnings?
4) What are the benefits of vocational education?
5) What information exists on how people can find a job and make effective career choices?

* ERIC Clearinghouse on Educational <u>Assessment and Evaluation</u>

College of Library and Information Services
University of Maryland   800-464-3742
1129 Shriver Laboratory   301-405-7449
College Park, MD 20742-5701   Fax: 202-319-6692
Email: feedback@ericae.net
http://ericae.net

The Clearinghouse on Assessment and Evaluation provides information on the assessment and evaluation of education projects or programs, tests and other measurement devices, methodology of measurement and evaluation, and more. A publications list and price sheet are available. They can answer such questions as:

1) Do statistics show that tests discriminate against certain minority groups?
2) What tests are given to handicapped children and what is the research behind these tests?
3) Is the Scholastic Aptitude Test (SAT) an effective tool of measurement?
4) What is computer-assisted testing?
5) How often are SAT tests updated and who designs the questions?

* <u>Bilingual Education</u> Clearinghouse

National Clearinghouse for Bilingual Education
George Washington University
Center for the Study of Language and Education
2011 Eye St., NW, Suite 2001   202-467-0867
Washington, DC 20006   Fax: 202-467-0867
Email: askncbe@ncbe.gwu.edu
www.ncbe.gwu.edu

The Bilingual Education Clearinghouse provides information to practitioners in the field on curriculum materials, program models, methodologies, and research findings on the education of limited English proficient (LEP) individuals. They also offer an electronic information system, free to users, where access is available to a database of curriculum materials and literature related to the education of LEP persons. An electronic bulletin board is also available which contains news from federal, state, and local education agencies, conference announcements, and other current information. Their newsletter and other publications are available, many of which are free of charge. They can answer such questions as:

1) How do you mainstream language minority students?
2) What computer programs exist to assist in teaching limited English proficient students?
3) What are some of the issues and practices involved in meeting the needs of gifted and talented minority language students?
4) How can parents become involved in the education of limited English students?
5) How can teachers integrate multi-cultural materials in instructional programs?

* ERIC Clearinghouse on <u>Counseling and Student Services</u>

School of Education
101 Park Building   800-414-9769
University of North Carolina at Greensboro   910-334-4114
Greensboro, NC 27412-5001   Fax: 910-334-4116
Email: ericcass@iris.uncg.edu
http://ericcass.uncg.edu

The Clearinghouse on Counseling and Student Services provides documents relating to all levels of counseling and personnel services including preparation, practice, and supervision of counselors at all education levels and in all settings; personnel procedures such as testing and interviewing; group work and case work; career planning; and more. They have free publications, and will conduct searches for a fee. They can answer such questions as:

1) How can counselors enhance a student's self-esteem through counseling?
2) What are the emerging priorities for the counseling field?
3) What dropout prevention programs have been effective?
4) What is the current high school dropout rate?
5) What tests are available to students who are undecided on a choice of career?

* ERIC Clearinghouse on <u>Disabilities and Gifted Education</u>

The Council for Exceptional Children
1920 Association Dr.
Reston, VA 22091   800-328-0272
Email: ericec@cec.sped.org
http://ericec.org

The Clearinghouse on Disabilities and Gifted Education provides information on all aspects of education and development of handicapped persons, including prevention of handicaps, identification and assessment of handicaps, and intervention and enrichment programs. All aspects of the education and development of gifted persons are covered as well. A publications list and price sheet are available. They can answer such questions as:

1) What are the issues concerning the mainstreaming of a handicapped student?
2) How do you "home school" a gifted child?
3) What is the research concerning the post-school status of learning disabled students?
4) What preschool services are available for children with handicaps?
5) Under what criteria is a child considered gifted?

* ERIC Clearinghouse on <u>Educational Management</u>

College of Education
5207 University of Oregon   541-346-5043
Eugene, OR 97403-5207   800-438-8841
Email: eric@eric.oregon.edu   Fax: 541-346-2334
http://eric.uoregon.edu

The Clearinghouse on Educational Management distributes information on the following subjects: the leadership, management, and structure of public and private educational organizations; practice and theory of administration; preservice and inservice preparation of administrators; and tasks and processes of administration. The Clearinghouse also provides information on sites, buildings, and equipment for education, and planning, financing, construction, renovating, and evaluating educational facilities. They can answer such questions as:

1) What are "mentor teachers" and how do you prepare them to assist new teachers?
2) How do you best confront racism in schools?
3) How do you recruit, select, and retain good teachers?
4) What research has been done on the various methods of school discipline?
5) What elements must be considered in the design of a new school?

* <u>Educational Research</u>

Office of Educational Research and Improvement's Information Service
U.S. Department of Education
Education Information Branch
Capitol Plaza Building, Suite 300
555 New Jersey Ave., NW
Washington, DC 20208-5641   800-424-1616

www.ed.gov/offices/OERI

The Education Information Branch staff specialists can provide information on topics such as early childhood education, elementary and secondary education, higher education, adult and vocational education, education finance, longitudinal statistical studies, and special education. They have publications and reports, many of which are free. They can answer such questions as:

1) What statistics are there on the number of students who receive loans, grants, and work-study assistance from state sources?
2) What are the statistics on private postsecondary education, such as enrollment, earned degrees conferred, full and part-time faculty members and their salaries, and more?
3) What information is available on how to choose a school for a child and what makes a school good?
4) How can parents help their children become better readers?
5) What are the enrollment outcomes for recent master's and bachelor's degree recipients?

* Educational Resources Information Center

ACCESS ERIC
Aspen Systems Corporation
2277 Research Blvd.   800-LET-ERIC
Rockville, MD 20850   Fax: 301-309-2084
Email: accesseric@access.eric.org
www.accesseric.org

Educational Resources Information Center (ERIC) is a nationwide information service set up to collect materials about current developments in education and make them available to the public. The system includes 16 clearinghouses, each of which is responsible for acquiring, processing, and disseminating information about a particular aspect of education. The ERIC database contains bibliographic information, including key descriptors and abstracts, on over 950,000 research documents, journal articles, curricular materials, and resource guides. The Clearinghouses offer a wide variety of services and products, and can answer questions about: subject fields, run computer searches, develop short bibliographies, newsletters, and other free or inexpensive materials; publish monographs; publish handbooks; and develop materials to help you use ERIC.

ACCESS ERIC is the main center for the ERIC clearinghouses. It answers all questions on how to use ERIC and helps anyone stay up-to-date on the latest developments in the education field. They can answer such questions as:

1) How can I use ERIC to answer my education question?
2) What is required to have a database search run on a topic?
3) How can I have something that I have written entered into the ERIC system?
4) Where can I find the latest statistics on an education topic?
5) How can school administrators develop new management tools and practices?

* ERIC Clearinghouse on Elementary and Early Childhood Education

University of Illinois at Urbana-Champaign
Children's Resource Center
51 Gerty Dr.   800-583-4135
Champaign, IL 61820   217-333-1386
Email: ericeece@uiuc.edu   Fax: 217-333-3767
http://ericeece.org

The Clearinghouse on Elementary and Early Childhood Education provides information covering all aspects of the cognitive, emotional, social and physical development, and education of children from birth through early adolescence, excluding specific elementary school curriculum areas. Among the topics covered are: prenatal and infant development and care; child care programs and community services for children at local, state, and federal levels; parent, child, and family relationships; home and school relationships; foster care and adoption; and more. A publications list and price sheet are available. They can answer such questions as:

1) How do you start a day care center?
2) How do you choose a day care center and how do you assess a preschooler's development?
3) How can parents become involved in the education of their children?
4) How do you meet the needs of homeless children?
5) How do you help children with their social development?

* ERIC Clearinghouse on Higher Education

George Washington University   800-773-ERIC
One Dupont Circle, Suite 630   202-296-2597
Washington, DC 20036-1183   Fax: 202-452-1844
Email: mkozi@eric-hc.edu
www.eriche.org

The Clearinghouse on Higher Education provides information covering

education beyond the secondary level that leads to a four-year, masters, doctoral or professional degree and that includes courses and programs designed to enhance or update skills obtained in these degree programs. Areas include: academic advising, faculty, continuing education, legal issues, curriculum development, and more. They can answer such questions as:

1) What research and assessments are available on the trends and issues in higher education today?
2) What percentage of staff of higher education facilities are minorities and women?
3) What information is available on the issue of student stress?
4) How do we raise academic standards as a country?
5) What techniques are useful in improving a student's organizational skills?

* ERIC Clearinghouse on Information and Technology

Syracuse University School of Education   800-464-9107
621 Skytop Rd., Suite 160   315-443-3640
Syracuse, NY 13244-5290   Fax: 315-443-5448
Email: eric@ericir.syr.edu
http://ericir.syr.edu/ithome

The Clearinghouse on Information and Technology provides information covering educational technology and library and information science at all levels. Instructional design, development, and evaluation with emphasis on educational technology; computers, audio and video recordings, and more. They can answer such questions as:

1) What is the latest research on the value of using computers and applying video technology to enhance learning?
2) What are the various studies comparing the different types of computer based media?
3) Is there an overview of instructional television and its effectiveness for teaching children?
4) At what grade level are computers introduced in the classroom, on average?
5) Are audio recordings an effective tool for teaching foreign languages?

* ERIC Clearinghouse on Community Colleges

University of California at Los Angeles
3051 Moore Hall   800-832-8256
Box 951521   310-825-3931
Los Angeles, CA 90095   Fax: 310-206-8095
www.gseis.ucla.edu/ERIC/eric.html

The Clearinghouse on Community Colleges provides information covering the development, administration, and evaluation of two-year public and private community and junior colleges, technical institutes, and two-year branch university campuses. They have free publications and will conduct database searches for a fee. They can answer such questions as:

1) What are the main problems involved with transfer students?
2) How many students working on A.A. degrees in nursing are mothers and other women returning to further their education?
3) How do you implement a cultural exchange or study abroad program?
4) How do you recruit and retain minorities and women at junior colleges?
5) What percentage of students attending two-year programs receive financial assistance?

* ERIC Clearinghouse on Languages and Linguistics

Center for Applied Linguistics   800-276-9834
4646 40th St., NW   202-362-0700
Washington, DC 20016-1859   Fax: 202-362-3740
Email: eric@cal.org
www.cal.org/ericcll

The Clearinghouse on Languages and Linguistics provides information on languages and language sciences; all areas of foreign language, second language, and linguistics instruction; cultural and intercultural context of languages; international exchanges; teacher training; and more. Mini-bibliographies and fact sheets are available free of charge. Ready-made search printouts are available for a fee, and prices vary for specific searches. They can answer such questions as:

1) How do you institute teaching English as a second language in the workplace?
2) How do you develop a curriculum and training program for volunteer tutors for limited-English proficient adults?
3) What are the pros and cons of language immersion programs in schools?
4) What are the issues regarding the foreign language requirement?
5) What are some available opportunities abroad for teaching English as a foreign language?

How Do I Get Free Research Help?

* National Clearinghouse on <u>Literacy Education</u>

Center for Applied Linguistics
4646 40th St., NW   202-362-0700
Washington, DC 20016-1859   Fax: 202-362-3740
Email: ncle@cal.org
www.cal.org/ncle

The National Clearinghouse on Literacy Education produces and disseminates materials summarizing current research and information available on selected topics; develops a directory of effective adult literacy programs and projects; and supports a user services program to respond to information requests. They have a publications list available, and many of the items are free. They can answer such questions as:

1) What organizations offer programs for senior citizens interested in learning to read and write?
2) How can workplaces promote English as a second language?
3) What free resources are available to adult literacy instructors?
4) What percentage of U.S. immigrants are illiterate? What programs exist to help them?
5) What type of educational materials and programs are available to teach English to out-of-school youth?

* <u>Museum</u> Reference Center

Smithsonian Institution
Office of Museum Programs
900 Jefferson Dr., SW   202-786-2271
Washington, DC 20560   Fax: 202-357-2311
Email: libmail@sil.si.edu
http://museumstudiese.si.edu

The Museum Reference Center serves as a clearinghouse for museum programs providing professional development training, advisory assistance, and research services to the national and international museum community and the Smithsonian staff. The Center participates through the sponsorship of workshops, internships, and professional visitor programs, an audiovisual production loan program, publications, and more. They can answer such questions as:

1) Where can information be obtained regarding internship programs for museum careers?
2) What is the latest research on climate control and security for museums?
3) What information exists on how to train docents and volunteers?
4) Where can examples of exhibit designs be found?
5) Where can information be found on collection sharing?

* <u>Performing Arts</u> Library

John F. Kennedy Center for the Performing Arts
2700 F St., NW
Washington, DC 20566   202-416-8780

The Performing Arts Library is a joint project of the Library of Congress and the Kennedy Center, and offers information and reference assistance on dance, theater, opera, music, film, and broadcasting. The Performing Arts Library serves the research and information needs of the public, artists, and staff of the Center. The Library also identifies and locates the creative and resource materials necessary to develop new works and productions in the performing arts. Reference service is available by phone, in person, or by mail. They can answer such questions as:

1) How can an orchestral program of Irish composers be tailored for a young audience?
2) What information exists on different dance companies based in New York?
3) Is there information on what is required to start a record company?
4) Are their recordings of interviews or videotapes of famous actresses discussing their works?
5) Where can recordings be located on poetry readings?

* ERIC Clearinghouse on <u>Reading, English and Communication Skills</u>

Indiana University
Smith Research Center
Suite 150   800-855-5847
2805 East Tenth St.   812-855-5847
Bloomington, IN 47408-2698   Fax: 812-855-4220
Email: ericcs@indiana.edu
www.indiana.edu/~eric_rec

The Clearinghouse on Reading, English and Communication Skills provides information on reading, English, communication skills, identification, diagnosis and remediation of reading problems, and more. A catalogue of publications including prices is available. The Clearinghouse will also conduct custom database searches for a fee. They can answer such questions as:

1) How do you teach elementary students listening skills?
2) How can parents help their child to read?
3) How do you help a quiet student communicate in the classroom?
4) Where can teachers obtain written activities for junior high social studies classes?
5) Is there information on sex stereotypes in children's literature?

* ERIC Clearinghouse for <u>Science, Mathematics, and Environmental Education</u>

Ohio State University   800-276-0462
1929 Kenny Rd.   614-292-6717
Columbus, OH 43210   Fax: 614-292-0263
Email: ericse@osu.edu
www.ericse.org

The Clearinghouse for Science, Mathematics, and Environmental Education acquires educational literature on the following topics: development of curriculum and instructional materials; teachers and teacher education; learning theory; educational programs; and computer applications. They can answer such questions as:

1) Is there information on how to teach a lesson on environmental education?
2) What can be done to boost students' enthusiasm for math?
3) What are some of the common safety hazards in science classrooms?
4) Where can teachers obtain free science instructional materials?
5) Are there financial aid programs available to teachers interested in continuing education?

* ERIC Clearinghouse for <u>Social Studies/Social Science Education</u>

Social Studies Development Center
Indiana University   800-266-3815
2805 East Tenth St., Suite 120   812-855-3838
Bloomington, IN 47408   Fax: 812-855-0455
Email: ericso@indiana.edu
www.indiana.edu/%7Essdc/eric_chess.htm

The Clearinghouse for Social Studies/Social Science Education acquires journal articles and documents at all levels of social studies and social science education, including anthropology, economics, geography, sociology, social psychology, civics, and political science, as well as on history and social topics. A publications catalogue is available, including prices. They can answer such questions as:

1) What are some interesting learning activities designed to teach social studies?
2) What resources exist to supplement teachers' lessons on Africa and African Culture?
3) How do you teach geography at home?
4) How can you teach the law incorporating Supreme Court cases?
5) How can teachers stimulate children's interest in anthropology?

* ERIC Clearinghouse on <u>Teaching and Teacher Education</u>

American Association of Colleges for Teacher Education
1307 New York Ave., NW   800-822-9229
Suite 300   202-293-2450
Washington, DC 20005   Fax: 202-457-8095
Email: query@aacte.edu
www.ericsp.org

The ERIC Clearinghouse on Teacher Education acquires, publishes, and disseminates documents conveying research, theory, and practice in teacher education and in all aspects of health education, physical education, recreation education, nutrition education, and more. They can answer such questions as:

1) What are the teacher certification requirements?
2) How effective are student teachers in the classroom?
3) What computer games are there to help kids learn math?
4) What techniques can a teacher use to improve classroom productivity?
5) What are "at risk" students and how can they best be served?

* ERIC Clearinghouse on <u>Urban Education</u>

Teachers College
Columbia University Institute for Urban and Minority Education
Main Hall   800-601-4868
Room 303, Box 40   212-678-3433
New York, NY 10027   Fax: 212-678-4012
Email: eric-cue@columbia.edu
http://eric-web.tc.columbia.edu

The Clearinghouse on Urban Education provides information on the programs and practices in schools in urban areas. In addition, the education of racial/ethnic minority children and youth in various settings is studied: on the

Matthew Leško, Information USA, Inc., 12081 Nebel Street, Rockville, MD 20852 • 1-800-955-7693 • www.lesko.com

local, national, and international level; theory and practice of education equity; and urban and minority experiences. A publications list and price sheet are available. They can answer such questions as:

1) What is the current research on effective programs for reducing the dropout rates among inner city high school students?

2) What research is available on the number of pregnant, minority teenagers who obtain their high school diplomas in inner city schools?

3) What information is there on mentoring programs?

4) What issues are involved in linking schools with human service agencies?

5) Are urban schools financed equitably?

Energy and Environment

* EPA Control Technology Center Hotline (<u>Air Pollution</u>)

U.S. Environmental Protection Agency (EPA)
AEERL
Research Triangle Park, NC 27711   919-541-0800

The EPA Control Technology Center Hotline provides technical support to state and local agencies and to EPA regional offices in implementing air pollution control programs. They can answer such questions as:

1) What type of computer software can my company use to assess pollution control problems and evaluate potential solutions?
2) What impacts have control technologies had on air pollution?
3) What type of air pollution permits does my company need to operate in my state?
4) How can my company reduce its air pollution control costs?
5) What are the best cost-effective methods to maintain my company's air pollution control equipment?

* BACT/LAER Clearinghouse (MD-13) (<u>Air Pollution</u>)

U.S. Environmental Protection Agency (EPA)
Clean Air Technology Center   919-541-0800
Research Triangle Park, NC 27711   Fax: 919-541-5742
www.epa.gov/ttn/cact

The BACT/LAER Clearinghouse assists state and local air pollution control agencies in selecting the best available control technology (BACT) and the lowest achievable emission rate (LAER). It controls new or modified sources in a nationally consistent manner. They can answer such questions as:

1) How can my agency get assistance in compiling inventories of air toxic emissions?
2) How does the EPA estimate air toxic emissions?
3) Where can I get a listing of national emissions estimates and factors for air that is made toxic from motor vehicles?
4) Where can I find out about the toxic emissions for a particular consumer product?
5) How can my company achieve the lowest achievable emission rate for our product?

* <u>Asbestos</u> and Small Business Ombudsman Clearinghouse

U.S. Environmental Protection Agency (EPA)
401 M St., SW   800-368-5888
Washington, DC 20460   703-305-5938
www.epa.gov   Fax: 703-305-6462

The assigned mission of the Asbestos Ombudsman Clearinghouse is to provide to the public sector, including individual citizens and community services, information on the handling and abatement of asbestos in schools, the workplace, and the home. In addition, interpretation of the asbestos-in-school requirements and publications are provided to explain recent legislation. The EPA Asbestos Ombudsman receives complaints and requests for information and provides assistance with regard to them. They can answer such questions as:

1) What is asbestos, and in what era was it used?
2) How do I know if I have asbestos in my home or at work and how do I find help to contain or eliminate it?
3) What do I do if I have been exposed to asbestos?
4) How can I safe-proof my house from asbestos?
5) Are the schools in my particular neighborhood safe from asbestos?

* <u>Boating Safety</u> Hotline

Office of Boat Safety
U.S. Coast Guard
U.S. Department of Transportation
2100 2nd St., SW   800-368-5647
Washington, DC 20593   202-267-1077
Email: BoatWeb@mail.rmit.com   Fax: 202-267-4285
www.uscgboating.org/

The Boating Safety Hotline can provide you with information on such topics of interest to boaters as safety recalls, publications, Coast Guard department contacts and addresses, public education courses, and free Coast Guard Services. They have a wealth of free information and publications to share. They can answer such questions as:

1) What statistics exist on boating accidents?
2) How can parents teach children about water safety?
3) What things do people need to consider in evaluating floatation devices?
4) What licenses or regulations should boaters be aware of before they hit the water?
5) Where can people receive information on water charts and other navigational aids?

* National <u>Climatic</u> Data Center

National Oceanic and Atmospheric Administration
U.S. Department of Commerce
Federal Building
151 Patton Ave., Room 120   704-271-4800
Asheville, NC 28801   Fax: 704-271-4876
Email: orders@ncdc.noaa.gov
www.ncdc.noaa.gov

The National Climatic Data Center (NCDC) provides an important historical perspective on climate. Through the use of over a hundred years of weather observations, reference databases are generated. NCDC's data and information are available to everyone including the general public, the legal profession, engineering, industry, agriculture, and government policy makers. They can answer such questions as:

1) What were the weather conditions like in a particular part of a state on a specific day, and can this information be used for a court case?
2) In what parts of the country is the climate moderate allowing energy bills to be held to a minimum?
3) What information is available on severe storms, such as the occurrences of storms, data on the paths of individual storms, deaths, injuries, and estimated property damage?
4) Are droughts becoming more widespread?
5) Is the greenhouse theory becoming a reality?

* <u>Energy Efficiency</u> and Renewable Energy Clearinghouse

P.O. Box 3048   800-363-3732
Merrifield, VA 22116   Fax: 703-893-0400
Bulletin Board: 800-273-2955
www.eren.doe.gov

The Energy Efficiency and Renewable Energy Clearinghouse can provide information on how to save energy, as well as information on solar, wind, or any other aspect of renewable energy. They have the latest research on renewable energy technologies and energy conservation, and can refer you to other valuable resources. A list of free publications is available. They can answer questions such as:

1) How can you convert a home to solar heat?
2) How do heat pumps work and are they efficient?
3) What should you look for in a wood-burning appliance?
4) What can be done to improve the energy efficiency of a home?
5) Is the wind a practical source of energy?

* Safe <u>Drinking Water</u> Hotline

U.S. Environmental Protection Agency (EPA)
401 M St., SW   800-426-4791
Washington, DC 20460   Fax: 202-260-8072
Email: hotline_sdwa@epamail.epa.gov
www.epa.gov/safewater

The Safe Drinking Water Hotline responds to questions concerning the Safe Drinking Water Act, water standards, regulations, and the Underground Injection Program. It will also provide selected free publications. They can answer such questions as:

1) How do I find out if there is lead in my drinking water?
2) What is the Underground Injection Program?
3) What are some of the newer techniques for removing and disposing of water pollutants?
4) What research is being done to develop safer drinking water?
5) What can I do if there is too much fluoride in my drinking water?

* EROS Data Center (<u>Earth Resources</u>)

U.S. Geological Survey
Mundt Federal Bldg.   605-594-6511
Sioux Falls, SD 57198   Fax: 605-594-6589
http://edcwww.cr.usgs.gov

The Earth Resources Observation Systems (EROS) Data Center is a national archive, production, and research facility for remotely sensed data and other forms of geographic information. It receives, processes, and distributes data from the U.S.' Landsat satellite sensors and from airborne mapping cameras.

The Center houses over 2,000,000 worldwide scenes of Earth acquired by Landsat satellites and nearly 6,000,000 aerial photographs of U.S. sites. Maps and photographs range from $6 to $65 and can be obtained from the Center's customer service department. The staff can answer such questions as:

1) How can I receive a listing of aerial photographs of a particular hurricane that I am studying?
2) How do the Landsat satellite sensors work?
3) How can EROS help my company's geologic exploration projects?
4) How can EROS help my company form a geochemical assessment of a potential land site that we are interested in developing?
5) Can the Center furnish me with a printout of land ownership lists in my particular county?

* Earth Science Information Centers

U.S. Geological Survey
508 National Center   703-648-6892
Reston, VA 20192   888-ASK-USGS
Email: esicmail@usgs.gov   Fax: 703-648-4888
http://mapping.usgs.gov/

Earth Science Information Centers (ESIC) offer nationwide information and sales service for U.S. Geological Survey map products and earth science publications. This network of ESICs provides information about: geologic, hydrologic, and land use maps, books, and reports; aerial, satellite, and radar images and related products; earth science and map data in digital format and related applications software; and geodetic data. ESICs can fill orders for custom products and provide information about earth science materials from many public and private producers. They can answer such questions as:

1) Where can maps of Indian lands be located?
2) What earth-science teaching aids are available?
3) Where can accurate topographic maps be found which show the location and measurable elevation of natural and man made features?
4) Where can out-of-print maps be located?
5) Where can wetlands be found in the state of Ohio?

* National Earthquake Information Center

U.S. Geological Survey
Box 25046, DFS, MS967   303-273-8500
Denver, CO 80225   Fax: 303-273-8450
Email: sedas@gldfs.cr.usgs.gov
wwwneic.cr.usgs.gov

National Earthquake Information Center compiles, computes, and distributes digital and analog data on earthquakes that have occurred around the world. They have information on seismograms, earthquake magnitudes, intensities, and epicenter locations. They can answer such questions as:

1) What information exists on the most recent earthquake in California?
2) How many fault lines are known in California and where are they located?
3) What should people do in the event of an earthquake?
4) Where has there been seismic activity around the world in a given month?
5) What is the largest earthquake on record?

* Emergency Planning and Community-Right-To-Know Information Hotline

Booz, Allen & Hamilton, Inc.
401 M St., SW   800-535-0202
Washington, DC 20466   Fax: 703-412-3333
www.epa.gov/swercepp/crtk.html

The Emergency Planning and Community-Right-To-Know Information Hotline (EPCRA) provides information on what types of waste may be hazardous to the public's health. All information is open to local agencies, citizens, attorneys, consultants, and communities. EPCRA helps answer questions on the best ways to remove and store hazardous and solid waste. They can answer such questions as:

1) What constitutes a hazardous chemical release?
2) Which releases are especially dangerous?
3) What type of emergency planning is available for those working around or in contact with hazardous waste?
4) How are companies and communities regulated?
5) What documents are available to the average citizen concerned about waste?

* Emissions Clearinghouse

Emission Factor Clearinghouse, MD-14
U.S. Environmental Protection Agency (EPA)
Research Triangle Park, NC 27711   919-541-5285
www.epa.gov/ttn/chief/index.html

The Emissions Clearinghouse is a means of exchanging information on air pollution control matters. It addresses the criteria pollutants and toxic

substances from stationary and area sources, as well as mobile sources. The *Emission Factor Clearinghouse Newsletter* is issued quarterly, and contains information on recent publications, inquiries about EPA emission inventory policy, newly developed emission factors, and requests for assistance in dealing with general or specific air pollution emissions. The Clearinghouse does have a database for which there is a user fee. They can answer such questions as:

1) How can I get a FAX Chief system?
2) What information exists on the underground storage of fuel tanks?
3) How can I find an engineer to assist me with my emissions questions?
4) What are atmospheric tanks and how are they used?

* National Energy Information Center

U.S. Department of Energy
1F048 Forrestal Building
1000 Independence Ave., SW   202-586-8800
Washington, DC 20585   Fax: 202-586-0727
Email: infoctr@eia.doe.gov
www.eia.doe.gov

The National Energy Information Center provides general reference services on U.S. Department of Energy data. It can provide statistical and analytical data, information, and referral assistance on a wide variety of energy-related issues. A publications directory, including many free publications, is available. They can answer such questions as:

1) What energy-related educational materials exist for elementary and secondary students?
2) What are some of the issues surrounding the Clean Air Act Amendments?
3) What is the short-term energy outlook?
4) What companies have purchased uranium and how much?
5) What is the petroleum supply statistics for a particular month?

* National Environmental Data Referral Service

NEDRES Office
National Oceanic and Atmospheric Administration
U.S. Department of Commerce
Environmental Information Services
1305 East-West Highway   301-713-0575
Silver Spring, MD 20910   Fax: 301-713-1249
Email: barton@esdim.noaa.gov
www.esdim.noaa.gov/

The National Environmental Data Referral Service (NEDRES) is designed to provide convenient, economical, and efficient access to widely scattered environmental data. NEDRES is a publicly available service which identifies the existence, location, characteristics, and availability conditions of environmental data sets. NEDRES database contains only descriptions, and not the actual data. Major subject categories include climatology and meteorology, oceanography, geophysics and geology, geography, hydrology and limnology, terrestrial resources, toxic and regulated substances, and satellite remotely sensed data. For more information on the NEDRES database, contact the office listed above. They can provide the information and pointers to data on such questions as:

1) What data exists on the air quality in the U.S.?
2) Where can information be found on the Chesapeake Bay?
3) Where can data be located on the estuarine water of California?
4) How has acid rain affected the environment?
5) How has pollution affected the ocean environment?

* Environmental Financing Information Network

Labat-Anderson, Inc.
401 M St., SW, 2731R
Washington, DC 20460   202-564-4994
Email: efin@epa.gov
www.epa.gov/efinpage

The Environmental Financing Information Network is an online database service. They help state and local officials find different ways to finance and improve the environment in which we live. They assist towns in locating funds to update wastewater treatment plants and other environmental projects all the way down to the sewage system. Information on State Revolving Funds and Public-Private Partnerships is included. They can answer such questions as:

1) How can we get financial funding for a nonprofit organization?
2) What are the pros and cons of forming a public or private partnership?
3) What other cities have revamped their waste management system?
4) How can towns or cities find technical assistance to help with new waste technology?
5) What ways can a state economically enhance their waste treatment systems?

* U.S. Environmental Protection Agency (EPA)

Public Information Center
401 M St., SW   202-260-2080
Washington, DC 20460   Fax: 202-260-6257
Email: public_access@epamail.epa.gov
www.epa.gov

The Public Information Center of the Environmental Protection Agency should be the first point of contact for all environmental issues. They have free publications on a variety of environmental topics, and can refer you to other experts within the EPA for more specific responses to your inquiries. They can answer such questions as:

1) What cars have the best gas mileage?
2) What are the current pesticide regulations?
3) What environmental education materials exist for teachers?
4) What can be done to reduce pollution?
5) What is radon, and how can it be removed from a home?

* Center for Environmental Research Information

Technology Transfer
U.S. Environmental Protection Agency (EPA)
26 W. Martin Luther King Dr.
Cincinnati, OH 45268   513-569-7369
To order publications   513-569-7562
Email: mailto:ord.ceri@epamail.epa.gov   Fax: 513-569-7566
www.epa.gov/docs/ord/

The Office of Research and Development (ORD) has centralized most of its information distribution and technology transfer activities in the Center for Environmental Research Information (CERI). CERI also serves as a central point of distribution for ORD research results and reports. They have statistics, regulations, and publications available at no charge. They can answer such questions as:

1) How can I protect my home from pesticides and pollution?
2) What types of pollution can cause harm to my family?
3) What safety guidelines must a company or lab follow?
4) How can a business get grant money to do research?
5) What certifications must companies meet in regulating their pollution?

* National Marine Fisheries Service

Public Affairs
National Oceanic and Atmospheric Administration
U.S. Department of Commerce
1315 East-West Highway
Room 9272
Silver Spring, MD 20910   301-713-2370
www.nmfs.noaa.gov   Fax: 202-501-2953 (constituent services)

The National Marine Fisheries Service (NMFS) manages the country's stocks of saltwater fish and shellfish for both commercial and recreational interests. NMFS enforces the Magnuson Fishery Conservation and Management Act to assure that fishing stays within sound biological limits. Scientists conduct research relating to these management responsibilities in science and research centers and have special knowledge of the fish in their geographical area. They can answer such questions as:

1) What is currently being done to protect whales and what statistics exist regarding these mammals?
2) What are some issues currently under discussion regarding fishing on an international level?
3) What is the Habitat Conservation Program and where can someone find out more information about it?
4) What information exists on seafood inspection?
5) What is currently being done to restore the marine habitat in the Chesapeake Bay?

* Forest Service

U.S. Department of Agriculture
Public Affairs
201 14th and Independence Ave., SW   202-205-1760
Washington, DC 20250   Fax: 202-205-0885
Email: mailroom@fs.fed.us
www.fs.fed.us

This country's national forests offer more than 114,300 miles of trails, a Scenic Byway System consisting of nearly 5,000 miles of highways in 32 states, 70 wild and scenic rivers covering nearly 3,500 miles and much more. *A Guide to Your National Forest* lists regional offices, several private and one Forest Service Interpretative Association, and a list of State Boards of Tourism where camping information may be obtained. They can answer such questions as:

1) What state forests in Maryland offer good sailing opportunities?
2) How far in advance must I reserve a campsite?

3) What is the best time of year to plan a camping trip in Tennessee?
4) Which rivers in North Carolina are recommended for canoeing or rafting?
5) How do I receive a listing of national scenic and historic trails?

* Geologic Inquiries Group

U.S. Geological Survey (USGS)
907 National Center   703-648-4383
Reston, VA 22092   Fax: 703-648-4888
http://geology.usgs.gov

The Geologic Inquiries Group is the primary information group of the Geologic Division of the USGS. The Group can provide information and answers to questions concerning all aspects of geology, such as the geology of specific areas, energy and mineral resources, earthquakes, volcanoes, geochemistry, geophysics, and other geoscience disciplines, and geologic map coverage. They have publications available, some of which are free. They can answer such questions as:

1) Where can information be obtained on a particular volcano?
2) Where can geologic maps for a specific area of a state be located?
3) What educational materials exist for teachers who want to teach their students about geology?
4) What geologic information is available on earthquakes?
5) What help is available for someone doing a science project on volcanoes?

* National Geophysical Data Center

National Oceanic and Atmospheric Administration
Mail Code E/GC
325 Broadway, Dept. NGB   303-497-6826
Boulder, CO 80303   Fax: 303-497-6513
Email: info@ngdc.noaa.gov
www.noaa.gov

The National Geophysical Data Center (NGDC) combines in a single center all data activities in the fields of solid earth geophysics, marine geology and geophysics, and solar-terrestrial physics. NGDC fills thousands of requests each year for data services and publications. Typical specialized data services may include digitization of analog charts, derivation of geomagnetic indexes, and customized computer graphics. They can answer such questions as:

1) Where can historical earthquake data be obtained?
2) Where can data on solar flare activity be located?
3) What causes avalanches, and what methods are used to ensure the safety of skiers in areas where avalanches typically occur?
4) Where are thermal springs and thermal wells located in Nevada?
5) Where can information on earthquake damage to transportation systems be obtained so that new systems can better withstand the effects of an earthquake?

* National Response Center (Hazardous Chemicals)

U.S. Coast Guard Headquarters
2100 2nd St., SW, Room 2611
Washington, DC 20593   800-424-8802

The National Response Center receives notification and calls reporting oil spills, hazardous chemical releases, biological and radiological releases that have spilled into the environment. They pass the accidents on to a Federal On-Scene Coordinator, who coordinates and begins the clean-up efforts. The Hotline is open to the general public and to companies to call with sightings. Most of the information available from the Center is free. They can answer such questions as:

1) Has there ever been a report of hazardous waste spilled in a specific neighborhood or location?
2) How can I get a report released about a company regarding hazardous waste?
3) What is hazardous waste?
4) How does the Environmental Protection Agency enforce hazardous waste storage?

* RCRA Hotline (Hazardous Waste)

U.S. Environmental Protection Agency (EPA)
401 M St., SW   800-424-9346
Washington, DC 20460   703-412-9810
www.epa.gov/oswer   Fax on Demand: 202-651-2060

RCRA stands for the Resource Conservation and Recovery Act which has the goals of: protecting human health and the environment from the potential hazards of waste disposal; conserving energy and natural resources; reducing the amount of waste generated, including hazardous waste; and ensuring that wastes are managed in an environmentally sound manner. They can answer questions regarding recycling, hazardous waste, solid waste issues, and much more. They have a catalogue of publications, as well as a publication, *Solving the Hazardous Waste Problem: EPA's RCRA Program*, which provides an

overview of RCRA. They can answer such questions as:
1) What are the hazardous waste disposal regulations in my state?
2) Which plant pesticides are considered safe?
3) What are the laws and regulations concerning hazardous waste transportation?
4) How can I begin a recycling program in my community?
5) What are some of the most recent technologies and management strategies for hazardous waste control?

* National Water Information Center

U.S. Geological Survey
501 National Center
Reston, VA 20192   888-ASK-USGS
Email: h2info@usgs.gov
http://water.usgs.gov/

The National Water Information Center answers general questions on hydrology, water as a resource, and hydrologic mapping, as well as providing information on the products, projects, and services of the Water Services Division. The Center also provides information and materials for specific needs and is a reference office for Water-Resources Investigation reports released before 1982. The Information Center has maps showing a wide range of water-resources information. The staff can answer such questions as:
1) How can my company improve its waste disposal practices?
2) Where can I receive information on water resource conditions in my state?
3) What can people do to help reduce the problem of acid rain?
4) How can my company prevent ground water contamination?
5) Where can I receive introductory information on ground water hydraulics?

* Indoor Air Quality Information Clearinghouse

P.O. Box 37133   800-438-4318
Washington, DC 20013   Fax: 202-484-1510
Email: iaqinfo@aol.com

The Indoor Air Quality Information Clearinghouse of the Environmental Protection Agency can provide information and assistance on indoor air quality problems. It brings together information on more than 17 issues (from asbestos to wood preservatives), for the range of agencies involved in addressing those issues, from health agencies to energy departments. This office also has information on home humidifiers, residential air cleaners, Sick Building Syndrome, indoor air quality, new carpet, and more. They can answer such questions as:
1) What is Sick Building Syndrome, and what agency do I contact if I suspect my building is unsafe?
2) How do I identify and eliminate radon gas from my home?
3) How do I determine if the paint in my home is lead based?
4) What is the most recent legislation concerning asbestos-in-school requirements?
5) What is the Toxic Substance Control Act?

* Bureau of Land Management

Office of Public Affairs
U.S. Department of the Interior
1849 C St., NW
Room 406-CS   202-452-5125
Washington, DC 20240   Fax: 202-452-5124
www.blm.gov/nhp/index.htm

There are close to 270 million acres of public lands located primarily, but not exclusively, in the West and in Alaska comprising one-eighth of our nation's land area. It is the charge of the Bureau of Land Management (BLM) to administer and care for these lands. To accomplish this task, the BLM has a variety of programs and activities, from the very new Heritage Education program aimed at involving and educating young people about America's cultural heritage to finding out about the availability of public lands for sale. They have free publications and can direct you to other resources within the BLM. They can answer such questions as:
1) Where are campgrounds located on BLM lands and what facilities or recreational areas do they have?
2) What videos are available concerning rivers?
3) How can I find out which public lands are for sale in my state?
4) How do I stake a mining claim on federal lands?
5) How can I receive a listing of wildlife habitats on public lands?

* U.S. Nuclear Regulatory Commission

Public Document Room   202-634-3273
Washington, DC 20555   Fax: 202-634-3343
www.nrc.gov

The Nuclear Regulatory Commission (NRC) licenses and regulates civilian use of nuclear energy to protect public health and safety and the environment.

The NRC licenses persons and companies to build and operate nuclear reactors and other facilities, and to own and use nuclear materials. The Commission makes rules, sets standards, and carefully inspects companies to ensure that they do not violate existing safety rules. They can answer such questions as:
1) What information exists on abnormal occurrences in nuclear facilities?
2) What is the construction permit process for nuclear facilities?
3) What specific operational information must nuclear facilities submit to the NRC?
4) What statistics are available related to nuclear power?
5) How are radioactive materials packaged for transport?

* National Oceanic and Atmospheric Administration

14th St. and Constitution Ave.   202-482-6090
Washington, DC 20230   Fax: 202-482-3154
www.noaa.gov

The National Oceanic and Atmospheric Administration gathers data, conducts research, and makes predictions about the state of the environment in which we live. NOAA charts the seas and skies, and enriches our understanding of the oceans, atmosphere, space, and sun. They can refer you to other offices and experts for specific questions, and they also offer a variety of publications and films. They can answer such questions as:
1) What research is being conducted on tropical weather and how can we better predict hurricanes?
2) How has the greenhouse effect changed the environment?
3) What are the physical and chemical processes that occur within the Earth's atmosphere?
4) What is being done to protect marine mammals?
5) What research exists on the solar activity in the upper atmosphere?

* Oceanographic Information

National Oceanographic Data Center (NODC)
National Environmental Satellite, Data, and
  Information Service
National Oceanic and Atmospheric Administration
U.S. Department of Commerce
1315 East West Highway   301-713-3277
Silver Spring, MD 20910   Fax: 301-713-3302
Email: services@nodc.noaa.gov
www.nodc.noaa.gov

The National Oceanographic Data Center (NODC) provides global coverage of oceanographic data and services. NODC's databases cover physical and chemical properties of the world's oceans, seas, and estuaries, plus information on selected continental shelf and coastal waters. Simple questions usually can be answered without charge by telephone or mail, but more complicated ones requiring research or computer processing normally carry a fee. They can answer such questions as:
1) How does the Pacific Ocean temperature vary over a year?
2) How has the Atlantic Ocean been effected by pollution and what data exists on this topic?
3) What are the responsibilities of the NODC and what directories of information do they maintain?
4) Is there any bottom current data on the South China Sea?
5) Is the water warmer in Miami Beach or Myrtle Beach?

* National Park Service

Office of Public Inquiries
1849 C St., NW
Washington, DC 20240   202-208-6843
www.nps.gov

Along with other responsibilities, the Park Service administers 350 maintained areas in the National Park System, collects the National Register of Historic Places and a registry of natural sites, and manages the Urban Park and Recreation Recovery Program. It provides technical assistance in planning, acquisition and development of recreation resources, conducts surveys of historic buildings and engineering works, has available programs and resources for teachers, and administers a program in interagency archeological services. Information, including brochures, maps, and a publications catalogue can be ordered from the Government Printing Office. The Office of Public Inquiries can refer you to other Park Service offices and can answer such questions as:
1) What archeological digs are currently in progress and where are they located?
2) What statistics are available on Park Service use, such as total visits, visits by region and state, and overnight stays?
3) Where can I locate videos on historic people or national landmarks?
4) How do I find out whether or not my home is eligible for listing on the National Historic Register?
5) How can I receive a listing of the lesser known National Parks?

How Do I Get Free Research Help?

* National <u>Pesticide</u> Telecommunication Network

Oregon State University
NPTN Ag Chem Extension
333 Weniger   800-858-PEST (7378)
Corvallis, OR 97331-6502   Fax: 541-737-0761

The National Pesticide Telecommunication Network (NPTN) is a toll-free telephone service that provides a wide variety of health information on pesticides. Phones are staffed by pesticide specialists with agricultural, environmental, and public health backgrounds. Inquiries are also answered by graduate students in such fields as biology, anatomy, biochemistry, and entomology. They can answer such questions as:

1) Where can I get information on pesticides that might be found in drinking water wells?
2) What are some guidelines for the safe use of pesticides by farmers?
3) What plants have a natural ability to repel insects?
4) How do I make the transition from pesticide lawn control to natural pest control?
5) What is the toxicity and proper use of the pesticide R-11? How can I dispose of it safely?

* <u>Pollution Prevention</u> Information Clearinghouse

Labat-Anderson, Inc.
401 M St., SW   202-260-1023
Washington, DC 20460   Fax: 202-260-0178
Email: ppic@epamail.epa.gov

The Pollution Prevention Information Clearinghouse is designed to help national and international industries reduce pollutants that are released into our environment. They specialize in using education and public awareness to prevent excessive pollution. The Clearinghouse has four information exchange directories that can be ordered. There is no charge for any service. They can answer such questions as:

1) How can pollution prevention benefit businesses?
2) How do you implement a pollution prevention program?
3) Are there training opportunities for pollution control/waste management?
4) How do you get technical assistance for pollution control?
5) What are the differences between large and small waste generators?

* EPA <u>Radon</u> Information Hotline

U.S. Environment Protection Agency (EPA), OAR
401 M St., SW (MS6604J)
Washington, DC 20460   800-767-7236
www.epa.gov/iaq/radon

The EPA Radon Information Hotline can answer all your questions concerning radon. The staff can answer such questions as:

1) What is radon? How does it affect people?
2) How do I determine whether or not my home has a radon problem?
3) How can I obtain a radon detector for my home? How does it work?
4) What are some effective radon prevention methods?
5) What are some control methods for eliminating radon in well water?

* National <u>Sea</u> Grant Depository

Pell Library Building
The University of Rhode Island
Bay Campus   401-874-6114
Narragansett, RI 02882   Fax: 401-874-6160
Email: nsgd@gso.uri.edu
http://nsgd.gso.uri.edu

The National Sea Grant Depository provides a wide variety of information on America's oceans, Great Lakes, and coastal zones. It maintains the only complete collection of publications generated by the National Sea Grant College Program. Publications include information on: oceanography, marine education, fisheries, coastal zone management, aquaculture, marine recreation and law. The collection includes journal reprints, technical and advisory reports, handbooks, charts, maps, manuals, directories, books, audiovisual materials, computer programs, annual reports, conference proceedings, and newsletters produced by Sea Grant funded researchers. The staff can answer such questions as:

1) What are some of the most common fish found in Alaska?
2) How do I begin a fish culture enterprise?
3) What is the impact of pollution on the marine environment?
4) What can people do to prevent the pollution of coastal waters?
5) What are some of the potential risks to coastal investment?

* <u>Small Business</u> Ombudsman Clearinghouse

U.S. Environmental Protection Agency (EPA)
Small Business Ombudsman, 1230C   800-368-5888
401 M St., SW   703-305-5938

Washington, DC 20460   Fax: 703-305-6462
www.epa.gov

The Small Business Ombudsman Clearinghouse helps your business comply with all environmental regulations. They provide information on current policies, safety precautions, and general information on keeping the air you breathe healthy. They are available to assist private citizens, small communities, enterprises, trade associations, technical consultants, and laboratories. Listings on all aspects of current EPA regulatory developments are available at no charge. Over 200 EPA publications are maintained for distribution. They can answer such questions as:

1) Am I covered under the new Clear Air Act requirements?
2) How do I get an I.D. number for hazardous waste disposal?
3) What are the requirements for any underground storage waste?
4) How do I know if my community is following proper safety guidelines?
5) What type of waste material could be hazardous to my community?

* National <u>Snow and Ice</u> Data Center

World Data Center-A For Glaciology
CIRES, Box 449
University of Colorado   303-492-5171
Boulder, CO 80309   Fax: 303-492-2468
Email: nsidc@kyros.colorado.edu
http://nsidc.org/index.html

The National Snow and Ice Data Center provides a national and international focus for snow and ice data information services. The Center provides: broad user access to snow and ice data through specialized data reports and inventories in Glaciological Data; through special data sets maintained in the Center; through tailored bibliographies; and through access to the Snow and Ice Library. There is a small fee for some services. They can answer such questions as:

1) How does exhaust from jet aircraft affect cloud cover?
2) Where can data be accessed on glacier fluctuations?
3) How has snow cover varied over time in North America?
4) What current research is being undertaken regarding avalanches?
5) What is the difference between fresh water ice and sea ice?

* <u>Solid Waste</u> Information Clearinghouse

P.O. Box 7219   800-67-SWICH
1100 Wayne Ave., Suite 700   301-585-2898
Silver Spring, MD 20910   Fax: 301-589-7068
Email: info@swana.org
www.swana.org

The Solid Waste Information Clearinghouse (SWICH) is concerned with how state and local offices and industries get rid of solid waste. The general public is also welcome to request information. SWICH can show how to economically and ecologically get rid of waste by source reduction, recycling, composting, planning, education, public training, public participation, legislation and regulation, waste combustion, and collection. They can answer such questions as:

1) How can I implement a recycling program in my community?
2) What is the most economical way to dispose of a waste product?
3) How have other communities started and benefitted from recycling?
4) What types of disposal is available to my community or business?

* National <u>Space Science</u> Data Center

National Aeronautics and Space Administration
Goddard Space Flight Center   301-286-7354
Greenbelt, MD 20771   Data Request: 301-286-6695
Email: request@nssdca.gsfca.nasa.gov   Fax: 301-286-1771
http://nssdc.gsfc.nasa.gov/

The National Space Science Data Center (NSSDC) is an organization that provides a variety of valuable services for scientists throughout the world. The Center furthers the use of data obtained from space and earth science investigations, maintains an active data repository, and supports scientific research. The data are contained on more than 120,000 magnetic tapes, tens of thousands of film products, and optical, video, and magnetic disks. NSSDC works with individual users to address their specific requirements. There is a charge for most data, but it is only on a cost recovery basis. They can answer such questions as:

1) What satellites are currently operating in space and which ones are planned for future launch?
2) What data from space can provide estimates of marine phytoplankton in the ocean?
3) Where can photographs taken from APOLLO be located?
4) What data is available to researchers studying the ozone?
5) What information exists on a particular rocket launch?

* Technology Transfer Competitiveness

Administrator
Federal Laboratory Consortium
P.O. Box 545   360-683-1005
Sequim, WA 98382   Fax: 360-683-6654
www.federallabs.org/

The mission of the Federal Laboratory Consortium is to facilitate technology transfer among government, business, and academic entities in order to promote American economic and technological competitiveness. It sponsors conferences and seminars and publishes a free monthly newsletter. For very specific questions from researchers who find themselves at an impasse, the Consortium will conduct a database search to refer the inquirer to an appropriate lab. Write or call for a free general information packet explaining the organization, how to access its services, facilities available for testing, and examples of technology transfers. They can answer such questions as:

1) How can the heat pipes used to cool satellites be converted for use in a business?
2) How can toothpaste used by astronauts benefit those that are used on Earth?
3) What research is being conducted on electric cars?
4) Where can a business locate information on humidity control for a warehouse?

* Technology Transfer Program

NASA Scientific and Technical Information Facility
Technology Transfer Office
NASA-CASI
800 Elkridge Landing Rd.   410-859-5300, ext. 242
Linthicum Heights, MD 21090-2934   Fax: 301-621-0134
www.sti.nasa.gov/

Technology Transfer is an ideal way to apply the National Aeronautics and Space Administration's (NASA) experience and discoveries to your research or business. The transfer of aerospace technology which embraces virtually every scientific and technical discipline is paying off in a broad spectrum of practical applications in industry. The Technology Transfer System is a network of specialized organizations dedicated to helping industry access, apply, and utilize NASA's pool of innovations and technical resources. This allows you to access a wide range of information, products, services and technical expertise. A staff of experts assists you in pinpointing problems, identifying needs, and exchanging ideas. They can answer such questions as:

1) How can ultra-sensitive measuring devices used to measure space dust be put to use measuring environmental pollutants?
2) How can standard doorknobs be replaced with electronic openers?
3) Is it possible to convert spacesuits for use by firefighters or workers in industrial situations?
4) What lunar tool technology can be used in designing cordless power tools?

* Toxic Substance Control Act

U.S. Environmental Protection Agency (EPA)
Environmental Assistance Division
401 M St., SW   202-554-1404
Washington, DC 20460   Fax: 202-554-5603
Email: tsca_hotline@epamail.epa.gov

The Toxic Substance Control Act (TSCA) regulates the storage and removal of toxic substances and spills. They are concerned with safely containing toxic substances that may be harmful to our environment. TSCA is open to the general public as well as to industries and environmental groups. They can answer such questions as:

1) What chemicals can a manufacturer produce, and are they on the toxic inventory list?
2) What can I do if a toxic substance was spilled or contained on my property?
3) What are the latest regulations regarding production and handling of toxic substances?
4) How can I get a listing of places where toxic waste is stored?

* Undersea Research

National Undersea Research Program
National Oceanic and Atmospheric Administration (NOAA)
U.S. Department of Commerce
R/OR2, Room 11853, Building SSMC-3
1315 East-West Highway   301-713-2427
Silver Spring, MD 20910   Fax: 301-713-1967
www.nurp.noaa.gov

The National Undersea Research Program (NURP) develops programs and provides support to scientists and engineers to accomplish research underwater for the study of biological, chemical, geological, and physical processes in the world's oceans and lakes. NURP provides investigators with modern undersea facilities including submersibles, habitats, air and mixed gas SCUBA, and remotely operated vehicles. They can answer such questions as:

1) How do I get a grant from NURP?
2) What is the appropriate undersea center for me to contact in my region?
3) How deep in the sea does NURP support scientists work?
4) What kind of research expenses will be covered under a NURP grant?
5) Does NURP support coral reef research?

* EPA National Small Flows Clearinghouse (Wastewater)

West Virginia University
P.O. Box 6064   800-624-8301
Morgantown, WV 26506   Fax: 304-293-3161

The National Small Flows Clearinghouse is the center for small systems wastewater technology transfer. The Clearinghouse provides training resources and expertise in management and maintenance of small wastewater systems. It assists small communities in meeting environmental goals and water quality requirements. The Clearinghouse offers products and services to aid consultants, local officials, and developers in designing, constructing, operating, and managing small wastewater systems. Its products and services include databases, publications, video programs, workshops, and seminars. The staff can answer such questions as:

1) How can I find out more about the use of constructed wetlands that are used to treat domestic wastewater?
2) How can I find out more about sequencing batch reactors? How do they compare with conventional continuous waste treatment systems?
3) What should I look for when hiring qualified wastewater personnel?
4) How can our community get the most out of our existing wastewater resources and facilities?
5) What are some current technologies for cleansing polluted water?

* Watershed Resource Information System

Terrene Institute
U.S. Environmental Protection Agency (EPA)
4 Herbert St.
Alexandria, VA 22305   800-726-LAKE (5253)
www.epa.gov

The Watershed Resource Information System is an information resource on lake restoration, protection, and management. Its Watershed Information Resource Database contains abstracts and citations of technical materials and information and bibliographies. A specialist will conduct a database search for you for a fee of $25, plus $.10 per page per reference. You may purchase the system for $250 or a demo disk for $20. The staff can answer such questions as:

1) What information exists on different methods for restoring polluted lakes?
2) How can I find out about a particular lake's water quality?
3) What are some effective watershed management techniques?
4) What techniques can be used to reduce the incidence of acidification in lakes?
5) What are some effective methods of reducing toxic substances in lakes?

* National Weather Service

National Oceanic and Atmospheric Administration
1325 East-West Highway
Silver Spring, MD 20910   301-713-0622
www.nws.noaa.gov

The National Weather Service, through a network of field offices, predicts the nation's weather and issues storm and flood warnings. They also publish a weekly series of daily weather maps which include the highest and lowest temperatures chart and the precipitation areas. They can send anyone interested a sample copy or subscription information on this material. They also have publications on a variety of weather conditions, as well as films, videos, and slides. They can answer such questions as:

1) What should be done in the event of a hurricane?
2) What is a tornado?
3) How are severe storms forecast and where can more information be obtained about them?
4) Is there information available on monthly and seasonal predictions of temperature and precipitation?
5) What is a flash flood?

* Wetlands Protection Hotline

Labat-Anderson, Inc.
401 M St.
MC4502F   800-832-7828
Washington, DC 20460   Fax: 703-525-0201
www.epa.gov/owoc/wetlands/

The Wetlands Protection Hotline is a toll-free telephone service that responds to questions about the value and function of wetlands in our world. The staff is interested in protecting our wetlands and showing how wetlands play an important role in our changing environment. They have free publications and fact sheets available. They can answer such questions as:

1) Where can I get the *1987 Corps of Engineers Wetlands Delineation Manual*?
2) Is there any information available on constructed wetlands?
3) Is it legal to dig out a wetlands area?
4) What is the White House's policy on the protection of wetlands?
5) What regulations must farmers comply with when they have wetlands on their property?

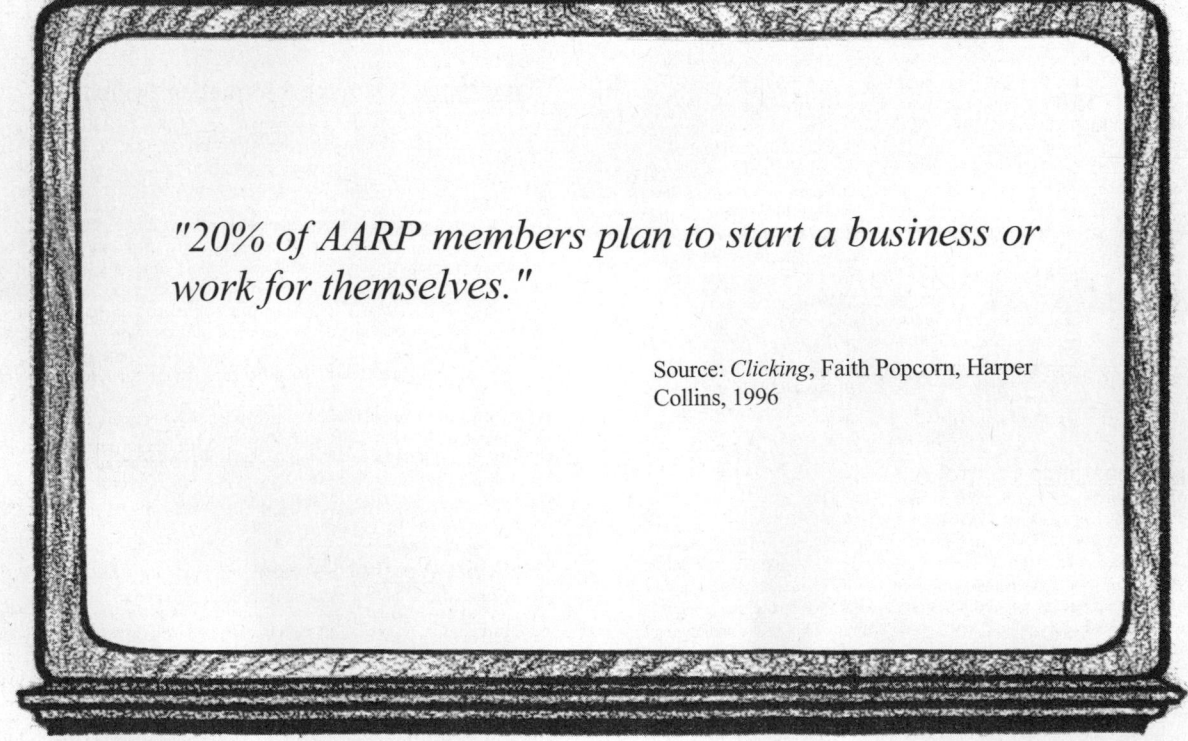

"20% of AARP members plan to start a business or work for themselves."

Source: *Clicking*, Faith Popcorn, Harper Collins, 1996

Health

* National Institute on Aging

Public Information Office
Building 31, Room 5C27
31 Center Dr., MSC 2292
Bethesda, MD 20892-2292   800-222-2225
www.nih.gov/nia   Fax: 301-496-1752

The National Institute on Aging conducts research related to the aging process and looks at diseases and other special problems related to the needs of the aged. They have a publications list of free items dealing with a variety of consumer issues. They can answer such questions as:

1) What is a good exercise program for an elderly person?
2) What information exists on menopause and how can symptoms be treated?
3) How can the elderly improve their diet?
4) What is osteoporosis and what can be done to minimize its effects?
5) What factors should people be aware of when taking certain medications?

* National AIDS Information Clearinghouse

P.O. Box 6003   800-458-5231
Rockville, MD 20849   Fax: 301-251-5343
Email: hivmail@cdc.gov
www.cdc.gov/hiv/dhap.htm

The National AIDS Hotline offers 24-hour service seven days a week to respond to any question about HIV infection and AIDS. Information specialists can refer you to groups in your area, and can direct you to local counseling and testing centers. The Clearinghouse can also connect people with the Clinical Trials Information Center, where they can learn what trials are currently taking place and what the requirements are for participants. They have free resources and publications on AIDS and HIV infection. They can answer such questions as:

1) What videos are available on AIDS that are appropriate for kids?
2) What are the signs and symptoms of infection?
3) How can parents most effectively discuss AIDS with their children?
4) What information exists on AIDS clinical trials?
5) Where can someone get information on caring for an AIDS patient at home?

* National Clearinghouse for Alcohol and Drug Information

P.O. Box 2345   800-729-6686
11426 Rockville Pike, Suite 200   Fax: 301-468-6433
Rockville, MD 20852   TDD: 800-487-4889
www.health.org

The National Clearinghouse for Alcohol and Drug Information (NCADI) gathers and disseminates current information on alcohol and drug-related subjects, and can make referrals to other alcohol, tobacco, and drug resource experts. The Clearinghouse is the national resource center for information on the latest research results, popular press and scholarly journal articles, videos, prevention curricula, print materials, and program descriptions. Services include subject searches on an in-house database and response to inquiries for statistics and other information. NCADI can make referrals to self-help organizations, and can provide information on drug and alcohol abuse treatment. They have a publications catalogue listing, booklets, videos, and posters which range in price from free to $25. They can answer such questions as:

1) How do you implement a drug-free workplace program, and what are the laws regarding drug testing at the workplace?
2) How do you teach kids about the dangers of drugs and alcohol, and what are the warning signs parents should know?
3) What are the effects of Fetal Alcohol Syndrome and where can people turn for more information about it?
4) What are some statistics on drug abuse among college students and what prevention programs exist?
5) What research is being done on children of alcoholics and are there support groups in place for them?

* National Institute of Allergy and Infectious Diseases

NIAID Office of Communications and Public Liaison
Building 31, Room 7A50
31 Center Dr., MSC 2520
Bethesda, MD 20892-2520   301-496-5717
    Fax: 301-402-0120

www.niaid.nih.gov/

The National Institute of Allergy and Infectious Diseases (NIAID) conducts and supports research to study the causes of allergic, immunologic, and infectious diseases, and to develop better means of preventing, diagnosing, and treating these illnesses. Some studies look at the role of the immune system in chronic diseases, such as arthritis, and at disorders of the immune system, as in asthma. NIAID has become the lead component at the National Institutes of Health for coordinating and conducting AIDS research. They have publications, journal articles, and more. They can answer such questions as:

1) What research is currently being done on allergies to pollen?
2) What is the current research being undertaken on AIDS?
3) How can I help my child handle asthma?
4) What is Chronic Fatigue Syndrome and what are the options for treating it?
5) What research exists on problems associated with the immune system?

* Alzheimer's Disease Education and Referral Center

P.O. Box 8250   800-438-4380
Silver Spring, MD 20907-8250   Fax: 301-495-3334
Email: adear@alzheimers.org
www.alzheimers.org/adear

The Alzheimer's Disease Education and Referral Center distributes information about Alzheimer's disease to health professionals, patients and their families, and the general public. The Center provides information about the diagnosis and treatment of Alzheimer's disease, research, and services available to patients and family members. The bibliographic references of the Center are included in a computerized index that includes references to patient and professional education materials, including information about health promotion programs. A list is available of free publications, in addition to a free newsletter. They can answer such questions as:

1) What are the symptoms of Alzheimer's disease and what are the causes?
2) What research has been done to evaluate special long-term care units for Alzheimer patients?
3) Where are research centers located which deal with Alzheimer's?
4) What are some statistics on Alzheimer's?
5) What help is available for families caring for an Alzheimer's patient at home?

* National Arthritis and Musculoskeletal and Skin Diseases Information Clearinghouse

National Institute of Health
1 AMS Circle   301-495-4484
Bethesda, MD 20892-3675   Fax: 301-718-6366
Email: NIAMSWEB-L@mail.nih.gov   TTY: 301-565-2966
www.nih.gov/niams

The National Institute of Arthritis and Musculoskeletal and Skin Diseases handles inquiries on arthritis, bone diseases, and skin diseases. They conduct and support basic and clinical research concerning the causes, prevention, diagnosis, and treatment of these diseases. They serve as an information exchange for individuals and organizations involved in public, professional, and patient education. The Clearinghouse has free publications on a variety of topics and can search their database for other information that might be needed. They can answer questions such as:

1) What can be done to prevent osteoporosis and who is most at risk for acquiring this disease?
2) Does chocolate cause acne and how can acne be treated?
3) What information exists on joint replacement for people who suffer from severe arthritis?
4) What are some different types of birth marks, and how can they be removed?
5) What educational materials are there for a continuing education forum on arthritis?

* Asthma Clearinghouse

National Asthma Education Program
P.O. Box 30105   301-592-8573
Bethesda, MD 20824-0105   Fax: 301-592-8563
www.nhlbisupport.com/asthma/index.html

The Asthma Clearinghouse is a new clearinghouse providing publications, reports, resources, and referrals to experts in the field of asthma. One report, *The Executive Summary: Guidelines for the Diagnosis and Management of*

Asthma, explains the diagnosis, therapy, and other important considerations for those that suffer from asthma. They can answer such questions as:
1) What materials are available for kids that explain the causes and treatment of asthma?
2) What conditions trigger an asthma attack?
3) Are there different types of asthma?
4) What are some forms of treatment for asthma sufferers?
5) What are the guidelines for treatment of asthma?

* Blood Resources

National Blood Resource Education Program
P.O. Box 30105   301-592-8573
Bethesda, MD 20824-0105   Fax: 301-592-8563
www.nhlbi.nih.gov/

The National Blood Resource Education Program was established to ensure an adequate supply of safe blood and blood components to meet our country's needs, ensuring that blood and blood components are transfused only when therapeutically appropriate. The Program helps health professionals understand the risks and benefits of blood transfusions, and ensures that patients receive appropriate information regarding transfusions. They also work to increase public awareness that donating blood is a safe process. They can answer such questions as:
1) What should people should be aware of when donating blood?
2) Is it still possible to get AIDS from blood transfusions?
3) Can you donate your own blood before you undergo surgery in the event you might require a transfusion?
4) How long can blood be kept before it is no longer usable?
5) What are some of the problems that people encounter when they have unusual blood types?

* The Cancer Information Service

National Cancer Institute
Building 31, Room 10A03
31 Center Dr.   800-4-CANCER
Bethesda, MD 20892-2580   800-435-3848
www.nci.nih.gov/   Fax: 301-402-0894
TTY: 800-332-8615

The toll-free Cancer Information Service can provide accurate, up-to-date information about cancer and cancer-related resources in local areas. A wide variety of free publications on specific types of cancer, treatment methods, coping methods, and other cancer-related subjects are distributed. A database is available, that can access information on clinical trials and treatment options. The Cancer Information Service can help you locate materials and research on a specific type of cancer. They can answer such questions as:
1) Is the new prostate cancer test accurate, and to what degree?
2) How often should you get a mammogram and at what age should you begin?
3) What are the side effects of a particular anti-cancer drug?
4) What are the different stages of breast cancer?
5) What are clinical trials and where can I participate in them?

* National Clearinghouse on Child Abuse and Neglect Information

330 C St., SW   800-FYI-3366
P.O. Box 1182   703-385-7565
Washington, DC 20447   Fax: 703-385-3206
Email: nccanch@calib.com
www.calib.com/nccanch

The Clearinghouse on Child Abuse and Neglect Information was established to help professionals and concerned citizens locate information on child abuse and neglect. They collect and disseminate a wide variety of information including publications, audiovisuals, public awareness materials, and more, and can refer you to other resources. Stock publications and many other services are provided at no cost to the user. User fees are required however, for services such as custom database searches and bibliographies. They can answer such questions as:
1) What statistics exist on the incidence of child abuse and neglect?
2) What laws exist that protect children against child abuse?
3) What is the role of the courts in child protection?
4) What funding sources are there for child abuse and neglect programs?
5) What role do teachers play in the prevention and treatment of child abuse?

* National Institute of Child Health and Human Development

P.O. Box 3006   301-496-5133
Rockville, MD 20847   Fax: 301-496-7101
www.nichd.nih.gov

The National Institute of Child Health and Human Development conducts and supports research in maternal and child health and the population sciences. They will respond to individual inquiries on related topics such as studies on reproductive biology and contraception, fertility, mental retardation, and developmental issues. They have free publications and can refer you elsewhere for additional information. They can answer such questions as:
1) Is reversing letters a sign of a reading disability?
2) What are the possible causes of Down Syndrome?
3) What are some important issues to think about when considering a vasectomy?
4) Where is there research being conducted on mental retardation?
5) What are the newest forms of birth control being used?

* National Information Center for Children and Youth with Disabilities

P.O. Box 1492   800-695-0285
Washington, DC 20013-1492   202-884-8200
Email: nichcy@aed.org   Fax: 202-884-8441
www.nichcy.org

The National Information Center for Children and Youth with Disabilities operates a national clearinghouse providing free information to assist parents, educators, caregivers, advocates, and others in helping children and youth with disabilities to become active members of the community. The staff provides personal responses to specific questions, as well as information on local, state, or national disability groups for parents, prepared information packets, publications on current issues, and technical assistance to parent and professional groups. They can answer such questions as:
1) How can I help my hyperactive child?
2) At what age do public schools begin mainstreaming students?
3) Can the Center provide a listing of national Down Syndrome support groups?
4) Where can I obtain captioned films for the deaf?
5) How do I make my home more wheelchair accessible? Are there any financial assistance programs available to help me accomplish this?

* Cholesterol Information

National Cholesterol Education Program
 Information Center
National Heart, Lung, and Blood Institute
P.O. Box 30105   301-592-8573
Bethesda, MD 20824-0105   Fax: 301-592-8563
www.nhlbi.nih.gov/

Do you know your cholesterol number or has your doctor advised you to change your diet? The National Cholesterol Education Program (NCEP) is for you. NCEP aims to raise awareness and understanding about high blood cholesterol as a risk factor for coronary heart disease and the benefits of lowering cholesterol levels as a means of preventing coronary heart disease. They have specialists on staff to answer questions and they provide printed information on cholesterol, diet, and high blood pressure to the public and health professionals. They can answer such questions as:
1) Is it possible to eat bacon on a low cholesterol diet?
2) Are medications required when trying to lower cholesterol levels?
3) How does exercise affect cholesterol levels?
4) What are the different types of home cholesterol test kits available?
5) What do the cholesterol numbers mean and what is meant by good and bad cholesterol?

* National Institute on Deafness and Other Communication Disorders Clearinghouse

31 Center Dr., MSC 2320   301-496-7243
Bethesda, MD 20892-3456   Fax: 301-402-0018
Email: nidcd@aeric.com   TTY: 301-402-0252

The National Institute on Deafness and Other Communication Disorders disseminates information on normal and disordered processes of human communication. They have information about hearing, balance, smell, taste, voice, speech, and language for health professionals, patients, and the general public. They have fact sheets, bibliographies, information packets, and directories. They can answer such questions as:
1) What are the treatment options for someone who has aphasia?
2) What can be done for children with frequent ear infections?
3) Are all hearing aids created equal?
4) What can be done to help someone who stutters?
5) What are the current statistics on deafness and hearing disorders?

* National Institute of Dental and Craniofacial Research

Information Office
Building 31, Room 2C35
31 Center Dr., MSC-2290   301-496-4261
Bethesda, MD 20892   Fax: 301-496-9988
Email: nidrinso@od31.nidr.nih.gov

www.nidr.nih.gov

The National Institute of Dental Research conducts research on the causes, prevention, diagnosis, and treatment of diseases and conditions of the mouth and teeth. They have free publications and posters on a variety of topics, and can refer people to experts for further information. They can answer such questions as:
1) What are the oral problems related to AIDS?
2) What information exists on fever blisters and canker sores?
3) What are the causes of periodontal disease and what are some effective treatment options?
4) Are fluoride treatments safe and when should they be started?
5) What are dental sealants and how effective are they in preventing cavities?

* National Diabetes Information Clearinghouse

1 Information Way   301-654-3327
Bethesda, MD 20892   Fax: 301-907-8906
Email: ndic@info.niddk.nih.gov
www.niddk.nih.gov/

The National Diabetes Information Clearinghouse was established to increase the knowledge and understanding of diabetes among patients, health professionals, and the general public. The Clearinghouse has a publications list available, with items ranging in price from free to $25, and a free quarterly newsletter featuring news about diabetes. They can also search their database for information on a specific topic. They can answer such questions as:
1) What is the latest research on the ways to manage diabetes, along with nutrition and diet information?
2) What are the issues and reports regarding diabetes and athletics?
3) What is gestational diabetes and the special risks and dangers it presents?
4) What are the types of insulins currently available, along with the time action of the insulin preparations?
5) What are some common foot care problems frequently experienced by diabetics?

* National Digestive Diseases Information Clearinghouse

2 Information Way   301-496-3583
Bethesda, MD 20892-3570   Fax: 301-496-7422
Email: nddic@info.niddk.nih.gov
www.niddk.nih.gov/

The Digestive Diseases Information Clearinghouse provides information about digestive diseases to educate the public, patients and their families, as well as physicians and other health care providers. The Clearinghouse provides information products and services such as factsheets, as well as an inquiry and referral service, information about research developments, and organizational and governmental activities related to digestive diseases. The Clearinghouse also maintains a database containing references to literature, products, programs, and services. A list of free publications is available. They can answer such questions as:
1) What are the surgical procedures involved in having a gall bladder removed and are there options to surgery?
2) What are the symptoms, causes, and treatments of ulcers?
3) How do you prevent heartburn?
4) What is a hiatal hernia and does it always require surgery?
5) What is pancreatitis?

* Disabilities Information Clearinghouse

Clearinghouse on Disability Information Programs
U.S. Department of Education
330 C St., SW, Room 3132
Mary Switzer Building   202-205-8241
Washington, DC 20202   Fax: 202-401-2608
www.ed.gov/offices/

The Clearinghouse on Disability Information responds to inquiries on a wide range of topics. Information is especially strong in the areas of Federal funding for programs serving individuals with disabilities, Federal legislation affecting the disability community, and Federal programs benefiting people with disabilities. A publications list is available, many of which are free. The Clearinghouse also maintains a database of sources for equipment to assist disabled people. They can answer such questions as:
1) What information exists about housing disabled people?
2) What handicapped assistance loans are available?
3) What is the law regarding Equal Employment Opportunities for handicapped persons?
4) What are the requirements for public education of students with handicaps?
5) How can businesses best accommodate workers with disabilities?

* Disease Information

Centers for Disease Control
Information Resources Management Office
Mail Stop C-15
1600 Clifton Rd., NE   404-332-4555
Atlanta, GA 30333   Fax on Demand: 404-332-4565

The Centers for Disease Control (CDC) has developed a Voice Information System that allows anyone using a touch tone telephone to obtain prerecorded information on particular health issues. The materials include information about certain diseases or health areas, symptoms and prevention methods, immunization requirements, current statistics, recent disease outbreaks, and other available printed materials. Currently information is available on AIDS, Chronic Fatigue Syndrome, encephalitis, hepatitis, Lyme disease, malaria, and more. They can answer such questions as:
1) What are the current statistics on AIDS?
2) Have there been recent disease outbreaks and where have they occurred?
3) Are vaccines required for travel to Africa?
4) When should children be immunized?
5) What is Chronic Fatigue Syndrome and where can I learn more about this condition?

* Drug Evaluation Clearinghouse

Center for Drug Evaluation and Research
Food and Drug Administration (FDA)
5600 Fishers Lane
Rockville, MD 20857   301-594-1012
www.fda.gov/cder

The Center for Drug Evaluation and Research responds to inquiries covering a wide spectrum of drug issues. They develop policy with regard to the safety, effectiveness, and labeling of all drug products, as well as evaluate new drug applications. The Center conducts research and develops scientific standards on the composition, quality, safety, and effectiveness of drugs. A list of guidelines is available to help manufacturers comply with the requirements of the regulations. The staff will respond to requests for information regarding the laws, regulations, policies, and functions of the FDA as it pertains to drugs. Materials are available on pharmaceuticals, drug labeling, and consumer education. They can answer such questions as:
1) What are the pros and cons of estrogen?
2) What information exists on the different forms of The Pill?
3) Do over-the-counter hair growth products really work?
4) What research has been done on Norplant?
5) What information is required on drug package labels?

* National Eye Institute

Office of Health, Education and Communication
Building 31, Room 6A32
31 Center Dr.   301-496-5248
Bethesda, MD 20892-2510   Fax: 301-402-1065
Email: 2020@b31.nei.nih.gov
www.nei.nih.gov/

The National Eye Institute (NEI) conducts and supports research related to the cause, natural history, prevention, diagnosis, and treatment of disorders of the eye and visual system. NEI distributes information on eye disorders, and can refer people to other organizations. They have free publications on a variety of topics. They can answer such questions as:
1) What is the latest information about cataracts and how can they safely be removed?
2) Are disposable contact lenses safe?
3) What are the causes of blindness?
4) How can glaucoma be detected early and are there treatment options to be considered?
5) What is Age-Related Macular Degeneration?

* Food and Drug Information

Office of Consumer Affairs, HFE-88
Food and Drug Administration
5600 Fishers Lane
Room 16-85   301-827-4422
Rockville, MD 20857   Fax: 301-443-9767
www.fda.gov/oca/oca.htm

The Food and Drug Administration (FDA) is charged with ensuring that food is safe and wholesome; that drugs, biological products, medical devices are safe and effective; that cosmetics are safe; that the use of radiological products does not result in unnecessary exposure to radiation; and that all of these products are honestly and informatively labeled. The Office of Consumer Affairs of the FDA handles consumer inquiries on issues under the FDA's responsibility, and serves as a clearinghouse for FDA publications (most of which are free). They can also refer callers to the appropriate office for more information. Topics covered include foods, nutrition, federal regulations, cosmetics, drug labeling, medical devices, pharmaceuticals, and more. They can answer such questions as:

1) What nutritional information is available for pregnant women?
2) Are extended wear lenses safe?
3) What information is required on food labels, and what does it mean?
4) What are the different forms of birth control and how effective are they?
5) What is the status of breast implants and where can someone turn for more information on the subject?

* National Health Information Center

Referral Specialist
Office of Disease Prevention and Health Promotion
P.O. Box 1133   301-565-4167
Washington, DC 20013   800-336-4797
Email: nhicinfo@health.org   Fax: 301-984-4256
www.health.gov/nhic

The National Health Information Center is a health information referral organization that puts people with health questions in touch with those organizations that are best able to answer them. The Center's main objectives are to identify health information resources, channel requests for information to these resources, and develop publications on health-related topics of interest to health professionals, the health media, and the general public. The Center meets these objectives by using a variety of information resource materials, a database of health-related organizations, and an information referral system. There is a publications catalogue available, with prices ranging from free to $5, and the Center covers topics such as community health, school health, worksite health, nutrition, and more. They can answer such questions as:

1) What health education program materials exist for employers and how can they be implemented at the worksite?
2) What organizations and support groups exist for people suffering from cerebral palsy?
3) What toll-free numbers are available for various health information?
4) What is the latest information about a specific rare disease and where can people turn for support?
5) How physically fit are America's six-year-olds and what statistics exist on this topic?

* Health Care Delivery

Bureau of Primary Health Care
Health Resources and Services Administration
5600 Fishers Lane, Room 7-05
Rockville, MD 29857   301-594-4110

The Bureau of Primary Health Care helps assure that health care services are provided to medically underserved populations and to persons with special health care needs. The Bureau serves as a national focus for the development of primary health care delivery capacity, and for placement of health care professionals in Health Professional Shortage Areas to promote sustained sources of health services. Support for primary health care is provided primarily through Community Health Centers, Migrant Health Centers, Services for Special Populations, Services for Residents of Public Housing, and the National Health Service Corps. They can answer such questions as:

1) How can nurses or doctors get their college loans repaid through service?
2) What programs exist for migrant health care?
3) What programs deal with the special health care needs of the homeless?
4) What research is being undertaken on meeting the health care needs of the elderly in this country?
5) What areas of the country are currently designated as health professional shortage areas?

* Health Care Policy Clearinghouse

Agency for Health Care Policy and Research
P.O. Box 8547   800-358-9295
Silver Spring, MD 20907-8547   TDD: 888-586-6340
Email: info@ahcpr.gov   Fax on Demand: 301-594-2800
www.ahcpr.gov

The Agency for Health Care Policy and Research (AHCPR) is the primary source of Federal support for research on problems related to the quality and delivery of health services. AHCPR programs evaluate health services, assess technologies, and improve access to new scientific and technical information for research users. Research findings are disseminated through publications, conferences, and workshops. Materials are available on medical treatment effectiveness, health care costs and utilizations, health care expenditures, health information systems, health technology assessment, and funding opportunities for grants and contracts. They can answer such questions as:

1) What are clinical practice guidelines for the treatment of cataracts?
2) What statistics exist on medical expenditures?
3) How effective is a specific treatment strategy for ulcers?

4) What type of person uses a nursing home and what is their average medical condition upon entering such a facility?
5) What are some treatment options for depression and how effective are they?

* Clearinghouse on Health Indexes

National Center for Health Statistics
U.S. Department of Health and Human Services
Public Health Service
6525 Belcrest Rd.
Hyattsville, MD 20782   301-436-8500
www.cdc.gov/nchs/

The National Center for Health Statistics provides information assistance in the development of health measures to health researchers, administrators, and planners. The Clearinghouse's definition of a health index is a measure that summarizes data from two or more components and purports to reflect the health status of an individual or defined group. Services provided to users include annotated bibliographies and a reference and referral service. A publications catalogue is available, with items ranging in price from free to $20. They can answer such questions as:

1) What are the typical characteristics of persons with and without health care coverage?
2) What type of health care is provided to adolescents?
3) What method of contraception is used most frequently in the U.S.?
4) What data exists on the current living arrangements of women of childbearing ages in the U.S.?
5) What survey data exists on the firearm mortality among children?

* National Heart, Lung, and Blood Institute Information Center

P.O. Box 30105   301-592-8573
Bethesda, MD 20824-0105   Fax: 301-592-8563
Email: NHLBIinfo@rover.nhlbi.nih.gov
www.nhlbi.nih.gov/

The National Heart, Lung, and Blood Institute is responsible for the scientific investigation of heart, blood vessel, lung, and blood diseases. The Information Center can provide the most current information on cholesterol, high blood pressure, asthma, blood products, and more. Subject specialists can provide information in response to inquiries, which may include publications, bibliographies, program descriptions, referrals to other agencies or organizations free of charge. They can answer such questions as:

1) What are the treatment options for someone suffering from emphysema?
2) What should the level of cholesterol be in blood, and how can it be lowered?
3) What information exists on high blood pressure and is medication the only real option to lowering blood pressure?
4) What is the current research on angioplasty?
5) What help is there for children who have asthma?

* High Blood Pressure Information

National High Blood Pressure Education Program
P.O. Box 30105   301-592-8573
Bethesda, MD 20824-0105   Fax: 301-592-8563
www.nhlbi.nih.gov/

The National High Blood Pressure Education Program is a source of information on educational materials for consumers, providers, and planners of high blood pressure control services. The goal of the Center is to reduce death and disability related to high blood pressure through programs of professional, patient, and public education. Print and audiovisual materials, as well as research reports are available. A free newsletter, InfoMemo, covers topics of interest concerning blood pressure. They can answer such questions as:

1) Is there a way to lower your high blood pressure through diet and exercise?
2) What is the effect of alcohol on blood pressure?
3) What research exists on alternative therapies such as biofeedback in reducing blood pressure?
4) How can a blood pressure education program be instituted in the workplace?
5) What resources exist for health educators who work with patients with high blood pressure?

* Homelessness

National Resource Center on Homelessness and Mental Illness
Policy Research Associates, Inc.
262 Delaware Ave.   800-444-7415
Delmar, NY 12054   Fax: 518-439-7612
Email: nrc@pranic.com

www.prainc.com/nrc

Under contract with the National Institute of Mental Illness, Policy Research Associates develops and disseminates new knowledge about the coordination of housing and services for homeless mentally ill persons. The Center publishes a newsletter, and has free information packets and can conduct database searches. They can refer you to organizations concerned with homelessness and mental illness, as well as Federal programs in the field. They can answer such questions as:

1) What are some of the health issues particularly related to homeless people?
2) What are grant programs currently available to homeless organizations to improve services?
3) What self-help programs exist for homeless people?
4) What are some of the issues organizations need to consider when dealing with homeless children?
5) What housing demonstration programs have succeeded with the homeless population?

* Public Housing Drug Strategy Clearinghouse

Drug Information and Strategy Clearinghouse
U.S. Department of Housing and
Urban Development (HUD)
P.O. Box 8577   800-955-2232
Silver Spring, MD 20907   Fax: 301-251-5767

Sponsored by the Department of Housing and Urban Development, the Drug Information and Strategy Clearinghouse provides housing officials, residents, and community leaders with information and assistance on drug abuse prevention and drug trafficking control techniques. They have created a database containing information on improving resident screening procedures, strengthening eviction policies, increasing cooperation with local law enforcement, implementing drug tip hotlines, forming resident patrols, starting child care centers, and organizing drug education/prevention activities. The Clearinghouse also provides information packages, resource lists, HUD regulations, referrals, and a newsletter. There is no charge for most of this information. They can answer such questions as:

1) How can housing authorities apply for government grants?
2) What are some anti-drug strategies that have been successfully carried out in public housing units?
3) What are the latest drug abuse prevention theories and have there been demonstration projects conducted that are based on these models?
4) What resident patrols and related programs have been particularly successful in building drug-free neighborhoods?
5) How can there be an increase in cooperation with local law enforcement and other agencies in preventing drug abuse?

* Indian Health Clearinghouse

Indian Health Service
5600 Fishers Lane, Room 635   301-443-3593
Rockville, MD 20857   Fax: 301-443-0507
www.ihs.gov

The Indian Health Services provides comprehensive health services through IHS facilities, tribally contracted hospitals, health centers, school health centers, and health stations. Reports, directories, brochures, and pamphlets are available. They can answer such questions as:

1) How can doctors get their student loans repaid by working for the Indian Health Service?
2) Where are there health professional shortages within the Indian Health Service?
3) Where are health service facilities currently located?
4) What are some of the health care needs specific to Native Americans?
5) What research is being conducted on substance abuse programs for Native Americans?

* National Kidney and Urologic Diseases Information Clearinghouse

3 Information Way   301-654-4415
Bethesda, MD 20892   Fax: 301-907-8906
Email: nkudic@aerie.com
www.niddk.nih.gov/

The National Kidney and Urologic Disease Information Clearinghouse (NKUDIC) is an information resource and referral organization seeking to increase the knowledge and understanding of kidney and urologic diseases. They can provide education and information on kidney and urologic diseases to patients, professionals, and the public, as well as make referrals to other appropriate organizations. The Clearinghouse provides products and services such as publications, a computerized database of educational materials, and annotated bibliographies and topical literature searches on selected topics. A publications sheet is available, with most items being free. They can answer such questions as:

1) What are the symptoms, diagnosis, and treatment of kidney stones?
2) What are the different types of urinary incontinence that some elderly people experience?
3) What information exists about the success rate of kidney transplant operations?
4) What professionals deal with kidney and urologic diseases in my area and what services do they provide?
5) What help is there for men who suffer from impotence?

* National Maternal and Child Health Clearinghouse

8201 Greensboro Dr., Suite 600   703-821-8955
McLean, VA 22102   888-434-4MCH
www.nmchc.org

The National Maternal and Child Health Clearinghouse provides education and information services in maternal and child health. The Clearinghouse provides current information through the collection and dissemination of publications on maternal and child health topics, and provides technical assistance in educational resource development, program planning, and topical research. They can also refer individuals to other organizations for further information. A publications catalogue is available, with most items free. They can answer such questions as:

1) What are the dangers of lead poisoning, and how can I protect my children?
2) What are the special nutrition needs of pregnant adolescents?
3) What are some of the concerns and issues pregnant women need to know about to ensure a healthy pregnancy?
4) How can parents be sure they are feeding their children nutritious foods?
5) Where can one go for more information on breastfeeding?

* Medical Devices Clearinghouse

Center for Devices and Radiological Health
Food and Drug Administration
Consumer Staff   888-463-6332
1350 Piccard Dr.   301-827-3990
Rockville, MD 20850   Fax: 301-443-9535
Email: dsma@cdrh.fda.gov
www.fda.gov/cdrh/index.html

The Center for Devices and Radiological Health is responsible for analyzing factors affecting the safe and effective use of medical devices and radiation-emitting products by lay users and on patients. They answer consumer inquiries by telephone or mail on general issues relating to medical devices or radiation-emitting products. Inquiries can be answered on such products as thermometers, hearing aids, contact lenses, condoms, magnetic resonance imaging devices, hemodialysis equipment, tampons, medical x-rays, pacemakers, and artificial hearts. Publications cover topics such as pregnancy test kits, IUDs, eyeglass lenses, ultraviolet radiation, including general information on medical devices and radiological health products. They can answer such questions as:

1) How effective are condoms and what standards are they required to meet?
2) Are breast implants still considered unsafe?
3) Is it safe to make your own sterile fluids to wash your contacts?
4) What should people be aware of before they undergo an x-ray?
5) Are ultrasounds safe?

* National Library of Medicine

8600 Rockville Pike   888-346-3656
Bethesda, MD 20894   301-496-6095
www.nim.nih.gov   Fax: 301-496-2809
Regional Library   800-338-7657

The National Library of Medicine (NLM) is the world's largest research library in a single scientific and professional field. The collection today stands at four million books, journals, technical reports, manuscripts, microfilms, and pictorial materials. The Library's computer-based Medical Literature Analysis and Retrieval System MEDLARS) has bibliographic access to NLM's vast store of biomedical information. All of the MEDLARS databases are available through NLM's online network of more than 20,000 institutions and individuals. NLM charges a user fee for access to the system. They can answer such questions as:

1) What videos are available on a specific health topic?
2) How can a researcher access NLM's database from home?
3) How can a search be conducted for a specific health topic?
4) What reference guides exist to help researchers locate materials?
5) Where can information on ethics in health care be found?

* Mental Health Clearinghouse

National Institute of Mental Health
6001 Executive Blvd.   301-443-4513
Room 8184, MSC 9663   Fax: 301-443-4279

Bethesda, MD 20892
Email: nimhinfo@nih.gov
www.nimh.nih.gov/

Fax on Demand: 301-443-5158

The National Institute of Mental Health conducts and supports research to learn more about the causes, prevention, and treatment of mental and emotional illnesses. The Institute collects and distributes scientific and technical information related to mental illness, as well as educational materials for the general public. A publications list is available, with items ranging from free to $25. They can answer such questions as:

1) What are the latest statistics and information on bipolar disorder?
2) What are the various treatment options for someone suffering from depression?
3) What current research is available on the causes and treatment of schizophrenia?
4) What information should you be aware of when looking for a mental health professional?
5) What help exists for people who experience panic attacks?

* Minority Health Clearinghouse

Office of Minority Health Resource Center
P.O. Box 37337
Washington, DC 20013
www.omhrc.gov

800-444-6472
Fax: 301-589-0884
TT: 301-589-0951

The Office of Minority Health Resource Center's mission is to improve the health status of Asians, Pacific Islanders, Blacks, Hispanics, and Native Americans. Major activities include: the dissemination of accurate and timely information regarding health care issues and status through conferences and workshops; the awarding of grants for innovative community health strategies developed by minority coalitions; and research on risk factors affecting minority health. The Resource Center has information on minority health-related data and information resources available at the federal, state, and local levels and provides assistance and information to people interested in minority health and minority health programs. They have a database of minority health-related publications, as well as organizations and programs that concentrate on minority health. They can answer such questions as:

1) How can minority health goals be achieved?
2) What research is being conducted regarding African Americans and their particular risk for high blood pressure?
3) What are health issues particular to Alaskan Natives?
4) What programs are effective in encouraging pregnant Mexican Americans to seek prenatal care?
5) Are there programs specific to Native Americans with substance abuse problems?

* National Institute of Neurological Disorders and Stroke

Office of Communications and Public Liaison
P.O. Box 5801
Bethesda, MD 20824
www.ninds.nih.gov

800-352-9424
Fax: 301-402-2186

The National Institute of Neurological Disorders and Stroke conducts and supports research on the causes, prevention, diagnosis, and treatment of neurological disorders and stroke. They have free publications on a wide variety of consumer materials and can refer people to other organizations for further information. They can answer such questions as:

1) What is Bell's Palsy and what are the ways in which it is treated?
2) What are the different forms of multiple sclerosis?
3) What current research is being conducted on strokes?
4) What can be done to minimize or reverse the effects of Parkinson's?
5) Is there relief available for chronic pain sufferers?

* Center for Nutrition Policy and Promotion

Center for Nutrition Policy and Promotion
U.S. Department of Agriculture
1120 20th St., NW, Suite 200 North
Washington, DC 20036
www.usda.gov/cnpp

202-418-2312
Fax: 202-208-2321

The Center for Nutrition Policy and Promotion conducts applied research in food consumption, nutrition knowledge and attitudes, dietary survey methodology, food composition, and dietary guidance and nutrition education techniques. The Center uses the research data to monitor the food and nutrient content of diets of the American population, assess dietary status and trends in food consumption, further understand the factors that influence consumer food choices, maintain the National Nutrient Data Bank of the nutrient content of foods, provide dietary guidance in food selection and preparation and in food money management. The Center reports results of research in both technical and popular publications, and a publications list is available. They can answer such questions as:

1) What are the dietary guidelines for Americans?

2) What is the composition of specific foods?
3) What data exists on what people eat?
4) What factors influence consumer food choices?
5) How aware are people of the relationship between diet and health?

* National Institute for Occupational Safety and Health

Division of Standard Development and Technology Transfer
Technology Information Branch
4676 Columbia Parkway, Mail Stop C-13
Cincinnati, OH 45226-1998
Email: pubstaff@cdc.gov
www.cdc.gov/niosh

800-35-NIOSH
Fax: 513-533-8573

The National Institute for Occupational Safety and Health provides technical information on programs and issues dealing with occupational safety and health. The Clearinghouse maintains a database through which they can search for journal articles and other materials on a specific topic. They have publications, reports, and bibliographies, many of which are free. They can answer such questions as:

1) Are video display terminals dangerous to the average individual?
2) What is Carpal Tunnel Syndrome and what can be done to treat it?
3) What are some of the dangers of working in a dry cleaning store?
4) How many deaths occurred on a particular job site?
5) What do I do if I suspect a health problem in my workplace?

* National Clearinghouse For Primary Care Information

8201 Greensboro Dr., Suite 600
McLean, VA 22102

703-821-8955

The National Clearinghouse For Primary Care provides information services to support the planning, development, and delivery of ambulatory health care to urban and rural areas that have shortages of medical personnel and services. They distribute publications focusing on ambulatory care, financial management, primary health care, and health services administration. The Clearinghouse provides information on federal guidances and policies affecting primary care delivery. A list is available of free publications on community health centers, migrant health centers, childhood injury prevention efforts, clinical care, and many other health concerns. They can answer such questions as:

1) What information should be considered when establishing a rural medical practice?
2) What are some of the ways older adults can improve their nutrition and is there information that can be distributed to these clients?
3) What are particular health problems of the migrant population and how can these be addressed?
4) What are some of the characteristics of successful dental programs in community and migrant health centers?
5) What is the status of medical personnel shortages in inner city hospitals and what is being done to alleviate this crisis?

* National Rehabilitation Information Center

8455 Colesville Rd., Suite 935
Silver Spring, MD 20910
Email: naric@capaccess.org
www.naric.com/naric

800-34-NARIC
800-346-2742
Fax: 301-587-1967

The National Rehabilitation Information Center (NARIC) is a library and information center on disability and rehabilitation. The Center is funded by the National Institute for Disability and Rehabilitation Research to collect and disseminate the results of federally-funded research projects. In addition, the Center includes commercially-published books and journal articles in its collection. They also maintain a database of disability and rehabilitation materials which they will search for a small fee. NARIC provides quick reference and referral services, database searches, and photocopies of documents in the collection. They publish a newsletter and other directories and provide information specialists to field the many questions on various topics of concern to people. A list of publications is available, with items ranging in price from free to $25. They can answer such questions as:

1) What resources, support, and information are available for people suffering from traumatic brain injury?
2) Where can you buy a computer keyboard which responds correctly to your patterns of movement if you have cerebral palsy?
3) How effective have supported employment programs been in improving employment opportunities for people with severe disabilities?
4) What are the different education methods available to educate a deaf child, and what are some of the factors to consider when making this choice?
5) What information exists on helping someone who has suffered a spinal cord injury?

* Office on <u>Smoking</u> and Health

Centers for Disease Control
4770 Buford Highway, NE
Mail Stop K-50   770-488-5705
Atlanta, GA 30341   800-CDC-1311
www.cdc.gov/tobacco   Fax: 301-986-5001

The Smoking Hotline can answer all your questions regarding cigarettes and stop smoking methods. They can provide fact sheets, pamphlets, posters and other publications, as well as information in response to inquiries. The Center can access information on the Combined Health Information Database, and their library and reading room are open to the public. The Infomemo newsletter contains information on disease prevention, education, and control. They can answer such questions as:

1) What are the pros and cons of various stop smoking methods?
2) What is the current status report on smoking?
3) How does smoking affect a person's health?
4) What are the ways in which a person over 50 might stop smoking?
5) What are the rules or regulations regarding smoking in an office or other public place?

* National Clearinghouse for Professions In <u>Special Education</u>

The Council for Exceptional Children   800-641-7824
1920 Association Dr.   703-264-9476
Reston, VA 22091   Fax: 703-264-1637
www.cec.sped.org/cl/ncpseabo.htm

The National Clearinghouse for Professions in Special Education provides information that will help people in making a career choice. They have information about the demand for special educators in the U.S., about college and university programs that prepare people for these careers, about financial assistance available, and more. They can answer such questions as:

1) What fellowships are available to work with the deaf?
2) How is music therapy used to work with individuals with disabilities?
3) What different sorts of careers are possible in special education?
4) What type of training is required to work with autistic children?
5) How has mainstreaming affected the special education job market?

* <u>Sudden Infant Death</u> Hotline

National Sudden Infant Death Syndrome Resource Center
2070 Chainbridge Rd., Suite 450   703-821-8955
Vienna, VA 22182   Fax: 703-821-2098
Email: sids@cirsol.com
www.circsol.com/SIDS/

The Sudden Infant Death Clearinghouse was established to provide information and educational materials on Sudden Infant Death Syndrome (SIDS), apnea, and other related issues. The staff responds to information requests from professionals, families with SIDS-related deaths, and the general public by sending written materials and making referrals. The Clearinghouse maintains a library of reference materials and mailing lists of state programs, groups, and individuals concerned with SIDS. Their publications include bibliographies on SIDS and self-help support groups, a publications catalogue, and a newsletter. They can answer such questions as:

1) What is crib death?
2) What are the current views on home monitoring to prevent SIDS?
3) How can parents help the grieving process in children after the death of a sibling?
4) How many children died of SIDS in a given state last year?
5) How can SIDS be distinguished from child abuse and neglect?

* Family <u>Violence and Sexual Assault</u> Institute

1310 Clinic Dr.   903-595-6600
Tyler, TX 75701   Fax: 903-595-6799

The goal of the Family Violence and Sexual Assault Institute is to provide information services to practitioners and researchers who are working to prevent family violence and provide assistance for victims. A publications list and price sheet are available. They can answer such questions as:

1) What journal articles and bibliographies are there on elder abuse, as well as what statistics, copies of legislation, and organizations concerned with elder abuse issues exist?
2) What are some of the signs of sexual abuse?
3) What are some centers and organizations concerned with child maltreatment?
4) What bibliographies are there on the characteristics of abusive and neglecting parents?
5) What agency should a person contact first if abuse is suspected?

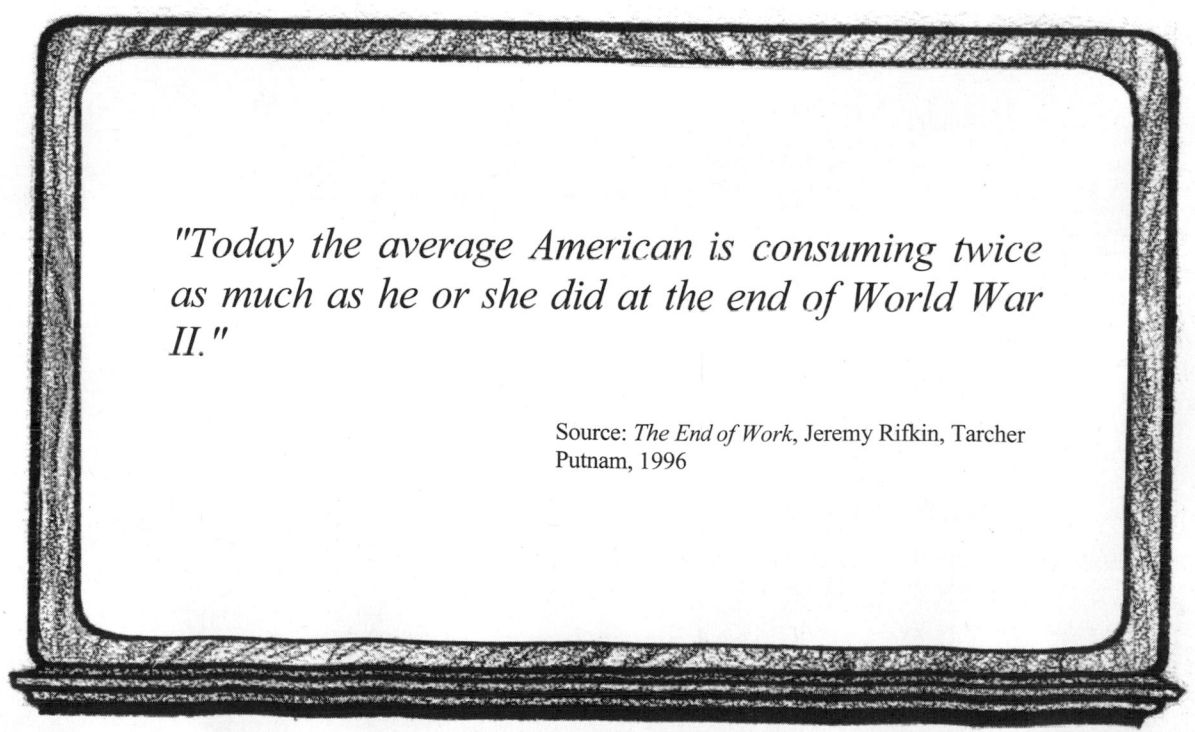

"Today the average American is consuming twice as much as he or she did at the end of World War II."

Source: *The End of Work*, Jeremy Rifkin, Tarcher Putnam, 1996

National and World Affairs

* <u>Agriculture Exports</u> Clearinghouse

Foreign Agricultural Service
U.S. Department of Agriculture, Room 5074   202-720-7115
Washington, DC 20250   Fax: 202-720-1727
Email: fasinfo@fas.usda.gov
www.fas.usda.gov

The Foreign Agricultural Service disseminates agricultural trade and commodity production information to agribusinesses and the general public. They offer private companies and cooperatives assistance in marketing their products overseas by collecting and publicizing information on foreign buyers and advertising U.S. export availability. They have a monthly magazine, commodity and trade reports, publications, and fact sheets (many of which are free). They can answer such questions as:
1) What are the market prospects for U.S. food and farm products in Japan?
2) What are some overseas markets and buying trends for a particular product?
3) What are some overseas promotional activities?
4) How do I begin an export business?
5) How do I advertise my product directly to buyers overseas?

* <u>Arms Control and Disarmament</u> Agency

Office of Public Information
2201 C St., NW   800-581-ACDA
Washington, DC 20451   202-647-6575
Bulletin Board   202-736-4436
www.state.gov/www/global/arms/bureauac.html

The Arms Control and Disarmament Agency (ACDA) coordinates the ongoing negotiations between the United States and other nuclear powers to reduce their arsenals. This federal agency also takes the lead in other efforts to reduce the risk of war by, for example, verifying other countries' compliance with the Nuclear Non-Proliferation Treaty and other international agreements. Weapons sales to foreign governments, technology transfer, and treaties are also important elements of arms control. The Agency can answer such questions as:
1) What details exist on certain weapons systems and what analyses have been done on the impact that such systems have on arms control agreements, treaties, and negotiations?
2) What are some of the economic issues related to defense strategies?
3) What is the INF Treaty?
4) What is the current status of arms control and disarmament goals?
5) What is the current arms control policy of the U.S.?

* <u>Central Intelligence Agency</u>

Public Affairs   703-482-0623
Washington, DC 20505   Fax: 703-482-1739
www.cia.gov

The Central Intelligence Agency (CIA) is strictly a foreign intelligence organization and has no domestic or law enforcement duties. The CIA occasionally issues unclassified publications which provide additional research aids to the academic and business communities. The majority of these reports contain foreign or international economic and political information or are directories of foreign officials. They are available for sale. They can answer such questions as:
1) What is the history of the CIA?
2) What are the steps involved in the intelligence cycle?
3) What agencies or departments are involved with the intelligence community?
4) What involvement does the White House have in intelligence activities?
5) Who oversees the CIA?

* <u>Export Country</u> Experts

U.S. Foreign and Commercial Services
Export Promotion Services
U.S. Department of Commerce   800-872-8723
Room 2810   202-482-6220
Washington, DC 20230   Fax: 202-482-4473
www.ita.doc.gov

The Country Desk Officers at the U.S. Department of Commerce can provide businesses with information on a market, company, and any other aspect of commercial life in a particular country. These specialists can look at the needs of an individual U.S. firm wishing to sell in a particular country in the full context of that country's overall economy, trade policies, and political situation, bearing in mind current U.S. policies toward that country. Desk officers keep up-to-date on the economic and commercial conditions in their assigned countries. Each officer collects information on the country's regulations, tariffs, business practices, economic and political developments, trade data and trends, market size, and growth. They have free reports and other information at their fingertips or they can refer callers to other country specialists. They can answer such questions as:
1) How can I expand my business through a foreign franchise?
2) How can I reduce my company's distribution and transportation costs overseas?
3) What type of export opportunities exist for computer manufacturing companies who want to expand to Germany?
4) What are some recent foreign labor trends in Japan?
5) Which markets are growing the fastest overseas?

* <u>Country</u> Officers

U.S. Department of State
2201 C St., NW
Washington, DC 20520   202-647-4000
www.state.gov

Hundreds of country experts at the U.S. Department of State are responsible for following all activities in their assigned countries, from a political, economic, and social perspective. These officers are in constant contact with embassies, deliver and receive documents from those embassies, and write reports on the current activities in the country. They have several publications they can send, plus up-to-date information on each country's population, culture, geography, political condition, and more. Call to ask for the number of a specific country officer. They can answer such questions as:
1) What is the current political situation of a particular country?
2) What is the current population, as well as the health situation of a country?
3) Are there any travel advisories for a particular country?
4) Is there a brief overview of a specific country available?
5) What is the status of human rights in a particular country?

* U.S. <u>Customs</u> Service

Public Information Office
U.S. Department of the Treasury
P.O. Box 7407
Washington, DC 20044   202-927-6724
www.customs.ustreas.gov

The U.S. Customs Service collects the revenue from imports and enforces customs and related laws. It assists in the administration and enforcement of over 400 provisions of law on behalf of more than 40 government agencies. They have many free publications and information on customs rules and travel tips. They can answer such questions as:
1) What are the rules regarding the bringing of pets into the U.S.?
2) Is there a limit to the amount of a particular item one can bring into the country?
3) What are duty-free exemptions, and restricted or prohibited articles?
4) What is required when a traveler declares articles?
5) What is the current duty rate for a particular item?

* <u>Defense</u> Technical Information Center

8725 John J. Kingman Rd., Suite 0944   800-225-3842
Ft. Belvoir, VA 22060-6218   703-767-8274
Email: help@dtic.mil
www.dtic.mil

The Defense Technical Information Center (DTIC) is the clearinghouse within the Department of Defense (DOD) for acquiring, storing, retrieving, and disseminating scientific and technical information to support the management and conduct of DOD research, development, engineering, and studies programs. DTIC services are available to DOD and its contractors and to other U.S. Government organizations and their contractors. Organizations may also become eligible for service under certain programs. DTIC also responds indirectly to the general public's information requests. Most products and services are free, but, there are some fees for technical reports and on-line access. *A DTIC Handbook for Users* is available. They can answer such questions as:
1) What technical reports exist concerning aeronautics?
2) Is there a listing of defense contractors and/or potential contractors?
3) How does a company obtain defense contract work?
4) What type of security clearance procedures are used for defense contractors?

* Defense Clearinghouse

Directorate for Public Communication
U.S. Department of Defense
1400 Defense Pentagon, Room 1E757
Washington, DC 20301-1400   703-697-5737
www.defenselink.mil

The Department of Defense is responsible for providing the military forces needed to deter war and protect the security of our country. The Directorate for Public Communication is a good starting point for Defense Department information. They have publications available, some of which are free, and they can direct you to other sources within the Department. They can answer such questions as:

1) What is the current Department of Defense budget, and how has it changed since the previous year?
2) What is the status of our troops overseas?
3) What is the federal government's security strategies?
4) What Department of Defense bases have closed within the last year?
5) How can I sell my company's products or services to the Army?

* Federal Emergency Management Agency

500 C St., SW   800-480-2520
Washington, DC 20472   202-646-4600
www.fema.gov   Fax: 202-646-4086

Federal Emergency Management Agency (FEMA) is the part of our government which deals with planning for and/or coordinating relief in various national emergencies. FEMA plans for nuclear attacks, security emergencies, disaster recovery aid, and helps to coordinate food, shelter, and financial aid in the event of any natural or man made disasters. FEMA has a publications catalogue which lists free publications on subjects such as civil defense, earthquakes, floods, hurricanes, tornadoes, and more. They can answer such questions as:

1) How can people best prepare for an earthquake?
2) What information exists on emergency medical services needed during a time of crisis?
3) How can homeowners repair their home after a flood?
4) Are there plans available on how to build an effective fallout shelter?
5) What are some safety tips for winter storms?

* American Foreign Policy Information Clearinghouse

Bureau of Public Affairs
U.S. Department of State
2201 C St., NW, Room 6808   202-647-6575
Washington, DC 20520-6810   Fax: 202-647-7120
Email: publicaffairs@panet.us-state.gov
www.state.gov

The Department of State receives thousands of reports daily, and produces hundreds of publications, speeches, and conferences on foreign policy issues. The Bureau of Public Affairs informs the American people on foreign policy and advises the Secretary of State on public opinion. If unable to answer an inquiry directly, the staff will direct you to the appropriate source. This bureau issues various publications covering U.S. foreign relations, some of which are free. They can answer such questions as:

1) Where can someone get a copy of the PLO-Israel Peace Treaty and what information does it contain?
2) Are there resource materials available that would allow a business to learn more about the relationship between the U.S. and a foreign country before they invest in that country?
3) What information exists on global terrorism?
4) Where could one find out more information on human rights practices in a particular country?
5) How can one access the U.S.'s or a foreign country's diplomatic records?

* Immigration and Naturalization Service

Central Office
425 Eye St., NW
Washington, DC 20536   202-514-4316
www.usdoj.gov/ins

The Immigration and Naturalization Service (INS) facilitates the entry of persons legally admissible as visitors or as immigrants to the United States, provides assistance to those seeking permanent resident status, and apprehends those who attempt illegal entry into this country. They have established a telephone service system that provides pre-recorded information on immigration and citizenship-related topics. They can answer such questions as:

1) Where is the local INS office located for a particular community?
2) What are the rules regarding the marriage of a foreign citizen to a U.S. citizen?
3) What are the citizenship requirements for children born outside the U.S.?
4) What constitutes political asylum?
5) What are some visa requirements for travel overseas?

* Agency for International Development (AID)

Document Information Services Clearinghouse
1500 Wilson Blvd., Suite 1010   703-351-4006
Arlington, VA 22209   Fax: 703-351-4039
www.usaid.gov

AID's Center for Development Information and Evaluation (CDIE) produces an evaluation publications series which includes a broad range of subjects of interest to those working in international development. The series comprises project impact evaluations, program evaluations, special studies, program design and evaluation methodology reports, and discussion papers. The CDIE Evaluation Publications List is arranged by general subject category and by type of report within each category. Each document is available for $3. They can answer such questions as:

1) What research has been conducted on family planning issues?
2) How do private volunteer organizations assist in the development of a country?
3) How has the emergency food program operated in a particular country?
4) How have health programs been successfully initiated in developing countries and how can they be sustained?
5) What types of agriculture programs have been attempted and what are the results of those programs?

* National Clearinghouse for U.S.-Japan Studies

Indiana University   800-266-3815
2805 East Tenth St., Suite 120   812-855-3838
Bloomington, IN 47408   Fax: 812-855-0455
Email: japan@indiana.edu
www.indiana.edu/~japan

The National Clearinghouse for U.S.- Japan Studies is a database system providing timely and comprehensive information about educational resources available to teach about Japan. The Clearinghouse collects, analyzes, abstracts, and creates a database of materials and resources that can assist school systems and individual teachers in developing and implementing curricula and lessons on broad areas of Japanese culture and society, and on U.S.-Japan relationships. The Clearinghouse also includes items such as videos, films, some simulations, artifact kits, and the like, and teacher-developed materials. They can answer such questions as:

1) What information exists on the Japanese educational system?
2) Where can I obtain copies of Japanese War relocation records?
3) What information is available on the Japanese stock market?
4) What are current U.S. trade policies toward Japan?
5) How can I locate programs that offer study abroad opportunities in Japan?

* Boating Safety Hotline

Office of Boating Safety
U.S. Coast Guard
U.S. Department of Transportation   800-368-5647
2100 2nd St., SW   202-267-1077
Washington, DC 20593   Fax: 202-267-4285
Email: BoatWeb@mail.rmit.com
www.uscgboating.org

The Boating Safety Hotline can provide you with information on such topics of interest to boaters as safety recalls, publications, Coast Guard department contacts and addresses, public education courses, and free Coast Guard Services. They have a wealth of free information and publications to share. They can answer such questions as:
1) What statistics exist on boating accidents?
2) How can parents teach children about water safety?
3) What things do people need to consider regarding floatation devices?
4) What licenses or regulations should boaters be aware of?
5) Where can people receive information on water charts and other navigational aids?

* Children's Literature Center

Library of Congress   202-707-5535
Washington, DC 20540   Fax: 202-707-4632
www.loc.gov/rr/child

The Children's Center prepares lists and scholarly bibliographies and provides other reference services for individuals and organizations who study, produce, collect, interpret, and disseminate children's books, films, television programs, or other forms of materials destined for children's information and recreational use, usually outside of the classroom. The Library holds approximately 200,000 children's books and related items, such as boxed and board games, sound recordings, maps, and illustrations. The Center also provides many publisher's catalogues that list titles to be published in the upcoming year, a wide range of periodicals about children's literature, and lists from rare and used book sellers. They can answer such questions as:
1) How can literature be used in the classroom to teach history to 7th graders?
2) What information sources exist for Japanese children's books published after World War II?
3) How can children learn about people with disabilities through literature?
4) Are there books specific to helping children deal with the issues of death and dying?
5) Where could a writer locate materials to help with a book on teaching children to be aware of strangers?

* Congressional Research Service

Library of Congress   202-707-5700
Washington, DC 20540   Fax: 202-707-6745
www.loc.gov/rr

The Congressional Research Service (CRS) at the Library of Congress prepares hundreds of non-partisan background reports each year on current issues large and small, domestic and foreign, social and political. CRS also publishes hundreds of major Issue Briefs each year designed to keep members of Congress informed on timely issues. Written in simple and direct language, these briefs provide background information and are updated daily. These studies generated by CRS cover almost any topic imaginable and are a fantastic resource for students, researchers, and anyone else who needs statistics or an analysis of a subject. You must request free copies of these reports through your U.S. Representative or Senator (202-224-3121 Congress Switchboard). The CRS Reports can answer such questions as:
1) What is the history of abortion rights in the U.S. and what legislation is currently before Congress regarding abortion?
2) What information exists on the protection of endangered sea turtles?
3) What is the current status of nuclear missile proliferation in the world?
4) What reports have been done on obscenity on television and radio?
5) What programs are there for working in a foreign country?

* Federal Assistance Programs Retrieval System

Federal Domestic Assistance Catalog Staff
General Services Administration
300 7th St., SW, Suite 101   202-708-5126
Washington, DC 20407   800-669-8331
www.cfda.gov

The Federal Assistance Programs Retrieval System (FAPRS) is your online link to the Catalog of Federal Domestic Assistance. It contains federal domestic assistance programs, including federal grants, loans, loan guarantees, and technical assistance. Their database contains more than 1,000 assistance programs administered by 51 federal agencies, with summaries of agency functions, descriptions of assistance programs, eligibility criteria, and contact information. Users include state and local governments, small businesses, researchers, and libraries. Fees are on a cost-recovery basis, with no initiation or monthly fees. Contact FAPRS for telephone and data processing charges. They can answer such questions as:
1) What assistance programs would help a rural hospital obtain needed medical equipment?
2) How can a student obtain a doctorate in housing policy at no cost?
3) How can schools obtain science equipment from the government?
4) How can a choreographer receive funds to create a dance?
5) Where can a business turn for assistance in the field of energy?

* American Folklife Center

Library of Congress   202-707-5510
Washington, DC 20540   Fax: 202-707-2076
www.loc.gov/folklife

The American Folklife Center at the Library of Congress has been a national advocate for the preservation and presentation of American folklife. The Center serves a varied constituency (state and local organizations, scholars, researchers, students, and the general public), maintains relations and coordinates programs with other federal agencies, and offers a wide range of programs and services. The Folklife Center has conducted or assisted with surveys or major field projects in many states. It conducts research projects based on the documentary collections of the Library of Congress. It sponsors a variety of conferences, workshops, concerts, and other events at the Library and elsewhere. The Archive houses more that 35,000 hours of audio recordings, controls more than 100,000 pages of manuscript materials, and maintains over 4,000 books, directories, and periodicals dealing with folk music and folklore. They can answer such questions as:
1) What information or recordings exist regarding early jazz?
2) Where can someone locate information on Native American architecture?
3) Where are recordings on Australian folk songs?
4) What data is there on the native crafts of Hawaii?
5) Are there videos available to educate students about various cultures?

* Forest Service

U.S. Department of Agriculture
Public Affairs Office
Mailing:
    P.O. Box 96090
    Washington, DC 20090
201 14th and Independence Ave., SW   202-205-1760
Washington, DC 20250   Fax: 202-205-0885
Email: mailroom@fs.fed.gov
www.fs.fed.us

The nation's National Forests offer more than 114,300 miles of trails, a Scenic Byway System consisting of nearly 5,000 miles of highways in 32 states, 70 wild and scenic rivers covering nearly 3,500 miles and much more. *A Guide to Your National Forest* lists regional offices, several private and one Forest Service Interpretative Association, and a list of State Boards of Tourism where camping information may be obtained. They can answer such questions as:
1) What state forests in Maryland offer good sailing opportunities?
2) How far in advance must I reserve a campsite?
3) What is the best time of year to plan a camping trip in Tennessee?
4) Which rivers in North Carolina are recommended for canoeing or rafting?
5) How do I receive a listing of national scenic and historic trails?

* Genealogy Research

Reference Services Branch
700 Pennsylvania Ave., NW   202-501-5400
Washington, DC 20408   Fax: 202-501-7154
Email: inquire@nara.gov
www.nara.gov/research

The National Archives maintains the historically valuable records of the U.S. Government dating from the Revolutionary War era to the recent past. They preserve records and prepare finding aids to facilitate their use and makes records available for use in research rooms. They can provide assistance and

training aids to help you with your research. They can answer such questions as:
1) Where can information be located regarding ship passenger arrival records?
2) What ship plans are available on World War II navy vessels?
3) How can military service and pension records be accessed?
4) How can people most easily trace their family history?
5) Where are prisoner-of-war records of the Civil War maintained?

* Geographic Names Information

Branch of Geographic Names
U.S. Geological Survey (USGS)   888-ASK-USGS
523 National Center   703-648-4544
Reston, VA 20192   Fax: 703-648-5644
http://mapping.usgs.gov

The USGS Branch of Geographic Names maintains a national research, coordinating, and information center to which all problems and inquiries concerning domestic geographic names can be directed. This office compiles name information, manages a names data repository, maintains information files, and publishes materials on domestic geographic names. The Branch works on standardizing names within the Federal government by keeping track of all the names put on maps that the various government agencies publish. They also assist the Board of Geographic Names in resolving name problems, such as if a name is derogatory or the usage is conflicting. The USGS, in cooperation with the Board of Geographic Names, maintains the National Geographic Names Data Base and compiles The National Gazetteer of the United States of American on a state-by-state basis. They can answer such questions as:
1) Where are islands located referred to as "No Man's Island"?
2) Where can a researcher find the location of a town that no longer exists?
3) What background information exists on the name of a town?
4) What is a variant name for the town of Rocky Gap, Colorado?
5) What are the geographic coordinates for a particular location?

* Geography and Map Division

Library of Congress   202-707-6277
Washington, DC 20540   Fax: 202-707-8531
Email: maps@loc.gov
www.loc.gov/rr/geogmap

The Geography and Map Division of the Library of Congress provides cartographic and geographic information for all parts of the world to the Congress, federal and local governments, the scholarly community, and to the general public. It is the largest and most comprehensive cartographic collection in the world, numbering almost 4.5 million maps, 60,000 atlases, and 6,000 reference works. The Division also has custody of over 350 globes, 2,000 three-dimensional plastic relief models, and a large number of cartographic materials in other formats. They can answer such questions as:
1) What maps are available for genealogists tracing a family history in Virginia?
2) What maps exist on colonial America?
3) Where can aerial photos be located in order to assess erosion and flood damage in a particular area?
4) Are there maps of old railroad lines available?
5) Where can information be located on Revolutionary War battlefields?

* Bureau of Indian Affairs

Office of Public Affairs
U.S. Department of the Interior
1849 C St., NW   202-208-3711
Washington, DC 20240   Fax: 202-501-1516
www.doi.gov/bureau-indian-affairs.html

The Bureau of Indian Affairs principal objectives are to encourage and assist Indian and Alaska Native people to manage their own affairs under the trust relationship with the federal government; to facilitate the full development of their human and natural resource potential; and to mobilize all aids for their advancement. The Bureau can provide you with a wide variety of information on Native Americans, the history of the Bureau and more. They have publications and fact sheets, and can refer you to other resources for more information. They can answer such questions as:
1) What tribes are currently recognized by the U.S.?
2) What are the demographics of American Indians?
3) Which state has the largest percentage of American Indians?
4) What are the labor force estimates by states for Native Americans?
5) How do Indian Tribes govern themselves?

* Library of Congress

101 Independence Ave., SE
Washington, DC 20540   202-707-5000
Email: lcweb@loc.gov

www.loc.gov

The Library of Congress is the national library of the United States, offering diverse materials for research including the world's most extensive collections in many areas such as American history, music, and law. They not only have books and periodicals, but also prints, photographs, films, music, and more. This office can direct you to the correct division within the Library. If your question requires extensive research and you cannot come to the Library, they have lists of freelance researchers to assist you for a fee. Many Divisions have their own databases to search citations or bibliographies or literature guides to help readers locate published materials on a particular subject. There may be a charge involved for some services, although many are free. To begin a search, researchers should first contact their local library, and then, proceed to the Library of Congress if they are unable to find adequate information. The Library can answer such questions as:
1) Where can one find information about medicinal plants?
2) What are some good reference sources for children's literature?
3) Where can information be found on medieval law?
4) How can books in braille be accessed?
5) Where can literature guides on a variety of science topics be found?

* Manuscript Division

Library of Congress   202-287-5387
Washington, DC 20540   Fax: 202-707-6336
www.loc.gov/rr/mss

The Manuscript Division holds nearly 50 million items, including some of the greatest manuscript treasures of American history and culture. Among these are Jefferson's rough draft of the Declaration of Independence, James Madison's notes on the Federal Convention, George Washington's first inaugural address, the paper tape of the first telegraphic message, Abraham Lincoln's Gettysburg Address and second inaugural address, Alexander Graham Bell's first drawing of the telephone, and many more. The holdings encompass approximately 11,000 separate collections. The Reading Room is open only to qualified researchers. Only under exceptional circumstances are undergraduates permitted to consult manuscripts. The staff at the Division can answer such questions as:
1) Where can copies of George Washington's speeches be located for a biography of Washington?
2) Are records kept of nongovernmental organizations which have significantly affected American life, such as the NAACP?
3) Where is information held on the first Supreme Court justices?
4) How did the Declaration of Independence change from the rough draft version to the final copy?
5) What resources exist for a researcher studying the generals active in World War II?

* Motion Picture Broadcasting and Recorded Sound Division

Library of Congress   202-707-8572
Washington, DC 20540   Fax: 202-707-2371
www.loc.gov/rr/mopic

The Motion Picture Broadcasting and Recorded Sound Division has responsibility for the acquisition, cataloging, preservation, and service of the motion picture and television collections, including items on film, videotape, and videodisc. The Division has similar responsibilities for the Library's collections of sound recordings and radio programs. Viewing facilities are provided for those doing research of a specific nature, and must be scheduled well in advance. The reference staff answers written and telephone inquiries about its holdings. They can answer such questions as:
1) What World War II newsreels were produced in Germany?
2) What collections exist for films produced prior to 1915?
3) Where can a researcher look for information on silent films and their music?
4) Where can Afro-American folk music be found?
5) Are their recordings of authors, poets, and other artists reading their own works, such as Robert Frost?

* National Park Service

Office of Public Affairs
U.S. Department of the Interior
P.O. Box 37127   202-208-6843
Washington, DC 20013-7127   Fax: 202-219-0916
www.nps.gov

Along with other responsibilities, the Park Service administers 350 maintained areas in the National Park System, collects the National Register of Historic Places and a registry of natural sites, and manages the Urban Park and Recreation Recovery Program. It provides technical assistance in planning, acquisition and development of recreation resources, conducts surveys of historic buildings and engineering works, has available programs and resources for teachers, and administers a program in interagency archeological services. Information including brochures, maps, and a publications catalogue listing items ranging in price from $1 to $30 can be ordered from the Government Printing Office. The Office of Public Inquiries can refer you to other Park Service offices and can answer such questions as:

1) What archeological digs are currently in progress and where are they located?
2) What statistics are available on Park Service use, such as: total visits, visits by region and state, and overnight stays?
3) Where can I locate videos on historic people or national landmarks?
4) How do I find out whether or not my home is eligible for listing on the National Historic Register?
5) How can I receive a listing of the lesser known National Parks?

* Performing Arts Division

Library of Congress
Thomas Jefferson Bldg.
Washington, DC 20540   202-707-5507
www.loc.gov/rr/perform

The Performing Arts Library is a joint project of the Library of Congress and the Kennedy Center, and offers information and reference assistance on dance, theater, opera, music, film, and broadcasting. The Performing Arts Library serves the research and information needs of the public, artists, and staff of the Center. The Library also identifies and locates the creative and resource materials necessary to develop new works and productions in the performing arts. Reference service is available by phone, in person, or by mail. They can answer such questions as:

1) How can an orchestral program of Irish composers be tailored for a young audience?
2) What information exists on different dance companies based in New York?
3) Is there information on what is required to start a record company?
4) Are there recordings of interviews or videotapes of famous actresses discussing their works?
5) Where can recordings of poetry readings be located?

* Prints and Photographs Division

Library of Congress
James Madison Memorial Building, Room LM 337
First St. and Independence Ave., SW   202-707-6394
Washington, DC 20540   Fax: 202-707-6647
www.loc.gov/rr/print/

The visual collections of the Library of Congress provide a record of people, places, and events in the United States and throughout the world. The Prints and Photographs Division has custody of more than 10 million images in a variety of forms and media: Architecture, Design, and Engineering collections, Documentary Photographs, Fine Prints, Master Photographs, Popular and Applied Graphic Art, and Posters. Researchers may consult the collections in the Prints and Photographs Reading Room. The Reading Room houses the general and special card catalogues, files of photoprint reference copies, and a limited collection of reference books. Reference specialists are available for assistance. The division will accept limited requests by letter, but the staff cannot make lengthy searches. They can answer such questions as:

1) How can someone obtain a print of the Wright Brothers first flight?
2) What photos taken by Brady exist on the Civil War?
3) Where can someone locate photos of various housing projects undertaken by the Work Projects Administration under President Roosevelt?
4) What material is available to study the architecture of Frank Lloyd Wright?
5) What references are there chronicling the history of political cartooning?

* Rare Books and Special Collections

Library of Congress
Thomas Jefferson Building
Washington, DC 20540   202-707-5434
www.loc.gov/rr/rarebook/

The Rare Book and Special Collections Division contains more than 650,000 volumes and broadsides, pamphlets, theater playbills, title pages, prints, manuscripts, posters, and photographs acquired with various collections. The materials the Division houses have come into its custody for a variety of reasons: monetary value, importance in the history of printing, binding, association interest, or fragility. Reference assistance is offered by telephone, in person, and by mail. They can answer such questions as:

1) What information exists on the history of ballooning?
2) What books do you have that contain the Confederate States imprint?
3) What references do you have on the history of print making?

4) Do you have information researchers can study regarding Columbus' discovery of America?
5) Do you have 15th century illuminated manuscripts for art history research?

* Rural Information Center

National Agricultural Library
U.S. Department of Agriculture (USDA)   301-504-5547
10301 Baltimore Blvd.   800-633-7701
Beltsville, MD 20705   Fax: 301-504-5181
Email: ric@nal.usda.gov
www.nal.usda.gov/ric

The Rural Information Center is designed to provide information and referral services to local government officials, businesses, community organizations, and rural citizens working to maintain the vitality of America's rural areas. The Center provides customized information products to specific inquiries, refers users to organizations or experts in the field, performs database searches, furnishes bibliographies, identifies current USDA research and Cooperative Extension System programs, and assists users in accessing the National Agricultural Libraries' extensive collection. There is a cost recovery fee for photocopying articles and searches. They can answer such questions as:

1) Which organizations focus on rural health issues?
2) What resources for the historic preservation of farmland are available in rural areas?
3) How can tourism be promoted in small towns?
4) What are some examples of the more innovative economic development projects in rural communities?
5) What rural organizations focus specifically on research and development?

* Science and Technology Division

Library of Congress
John Adams Building
Washington, DC 20540   202-707-5639
www.loc.gov/rr/scitech

The Science and Technology Division's collection contains 3.5 million books, nearly 60,000 journals, and 3.7 million technical reports. The collections include such treasures as first editions of Copernicus and Newton and the personal papers of the Wright Brothers and Alexander Graham Bell. The Division has primary responsibility for providing reference and bibliographic services and for recommending acquisitions in the broad areas of science and technology. Reference services are provided to users in person, by telephone, and by mail. Indirect reference service is provided through bibliographic guides (Tracer Bullets) and research reports prepared by Division subject specialists and reference librarians. Copies of reference guides are available at no charge. They can answer such questions as:

1) Where can one begin looking for information on lasers and their applications?
2) What are some good sources of information on volcanoes?
3) What resources exist on extraterrestrial life?
4) Where could someone find sources for information on medicinal plants?
5) How would one go about creating a hologram?

* Women's Bureau Clearinghouse

U.S. Department of Labor
200 Constitution Ave., NW
Room S3002   800-827-5335
Washington, DC 20210   202-219-4486
Email: wb_wwc@dol.gov   Fax: 202-219-5529
www.dol.gov/dol/wb/

The Women's Bureau Clearinghouse was designed and established to assist employers in identifying the most appropriate policies for responding to the dependent care needs of employees seeking to balance their dual responsibilities. They can also provide information on women's issues, as well as work force issues that affect women. They can offer information and guidance in areas such as women-owned businesses, women workers, alternative work schedules, dependent care issues, and much more. They also have publications and other information available, much of which is free. They can answer such questions as:

1) What are some elder care program options?
2) What is the earning difference between men and women?
3) How does flex time work in companies similar to mine?
4) What are some alternate work schedules and how do they work?
5) What literature and other resources are available on employer-supported child care?

Statistics

* National <u>Agricultural</u> Statistics Service

USDA South Bldg., Room 5805   800-727-9540
U.S. Department of Agriculture (USDA)   202-720-3896
Washington, DC 20250   Fax: 202-690-1311
Email: nass@nass.usda.gov
www.usda.gov/nass/

The National Agricultural Statistics Service collects data on crops, livestock, poultry, dairy, chemical use, prices, and labor, and publishes the official USDA state and national estimates through its Agricultural Statistics Board. There are nearly 400 reports annually covering domestic agriculture, such as estimates of production, stocks, inventories, prices, disposition, utilization, farm numbers and land, and other factors. They provide national profiles gathered from regular surveys of thousands of farmers, ranchers, and agribusinesses that voluntarily provide data on a confidential basis. Publications are available and range from free to $12. They can answer such questions as:

1) How has the use of a specific chemical for crop growth changed over the past five years?
2) Has the size of farms increased or decreased over the past ten years?
3) What statistics exist on wildlife damage to crops?
4) How has the weekly crop weather affected crop growth?
5) What data is there on livestock slaughter?

* Federal <u>Aviation</u> Administration

Office of Public Affairs
800 Independence Ave., SW
Washington, DC 20591
Email: gramick@postmaster2.dot.gov   202-366-4000
www.faa.gov

The Federal Aviation Administration (FAA) is the starting place for any information on airlines, airports, and aircraft. The FAA regulates air commerce, develops civil aeronautics, installs and operates airports, conducts aeronautic research, and provides guidance and policy on accident prevention in general aviation. They keep statistics on air travel, accidents, and more. There are free publications on airline careers, aviation, and airplanes, as well as videos and curriculum guides. They can answer such questions as:

1) Which airlines had the worst on time rate for a given month?
2) What videos are available on aviation?
3) What is some historical information on women in aviation?
4) What are some statistics on air traffic accidents?
5) What methods are used to reduce the noise level of new aircraft?

* National Clearinghouse for <u>Census</u> Data Services

Administrative Customer Service Division
Bureau of the Census   301-457-4100
Washington, DC 20233   Fax: 301-457-4714
www.census.gov

The National Clearinghouse for Census Data Services provides a referral service for persons who need assistance in obtaining Census Bureau data or in using Census Bureau products. This assistance ranges from market research using census data to tape copying or microcomputer services. The Clearinghouse includes organizations that provide services for accessing and using economic data and information from the Census Bureau's 2000 Census TIGER geographic database. They can answer such questions as:

1) How can I update my business's mailing list using 2000 census statistics?
2) How can the census help me trace my genealogical history?
3) What is the TIGER geographic database, and how can I use it?
4) Which products are available on CD-ROM?
5) Does the Bureau have an on-line data service?

* <u>Census</u> Information on Business

Bureau of the Census
U.S. Department of Commerce   301-457-4100
Washington, DC 20233   Fax: 301-457-4714
www.census.gov

The Bureau of the Census is a statistical agency that collects, tabulates, and publishes a wide variety of statistical data about the people and the economy of our nation. The Bureau makes available statistical results of its censuses, surveys, and other programs to the public through printed reports, computer tape, CD-ROMs, microfiche, and more. It also produces statistical compendia, catalogues, guides, and directories that are useful in locating information on specific subjects. A fee is charged for some of the information and searches.

They can answer such questions as:
1) What is the percentage of people who have a bachelor's degree in a particular state?
2) What percent of women in the U.S. had a child last year?
3) What is the total amount of water area in a given state?
4) What are some statistics available on city government expenditures?
5) What are the 10 fastest growing occupations?

* <u>Crime</u> Statistics

Law Enforcement Support Section
Federal Bureau of Investigation
J. Edgar Hoover Bldg.
935 Pennsylvania Ave.
Washington, DC 20535   202-324-3000
www.fbi.gov

The Law Enforcement Support Section of the Federal Bureau of Investigation collects statistics for many towns with over 10,000 people, and can provide you with information such as the number of murders, robberies, assaults, burglaries, auto thefts, and more, although they do not rank cities. Many libraries carry their annual report, *Crime In The U.S.*, for which there is a cost. They can run a search on their database for specific information, although there is a fee assessed for this service. They can answer questions such as:

1) When weapons are involved in a crime, which ones are most frequently used?
2) How has the rate of auto theft in the U.S. changed over the past five years?
3) Is Washington, DC still the murder capitol of the U.S.?
4) Have the number of murders committed changed since the death penalty was reinstituted?
5) What is the difference in the rate of burglaries from small towns to major metropolitan areas?

* <u>Economics</u>: National and Regional

Bureau of Economic Analysis
U.S. Department of Commerce   202-606-9900
Washington, DC 20230   Fax: 202-606-5310
www.bea.doc.gov

The Bureau of Economic Analysis (BEA) provides information on national and regional economics. BEA collects basic information on such key issues as economic growth, inflation, regional development, and the nation's role in the world economy. It distributes a number of publications that measure, analyze, and forecast economic trends, which are available on recorded messages, online through the Economic Bulletin Board, and in BEA reports. They can answer such questions as:

1) What is the average per capita income in the United States?
2) Will the rate of inflation increase or decrease over the next five years, and by what percent?
3) What percentage of the Gross National Product (GNP) does the government spend on health care?
4) How does the United States' national unemployment rate compare to that of other industrialized countries?
5) What was the unemployment rate in Pennsylvania from 1989 to 1993?

* <u>Educational Research</u>

U.S. Department of Education, OERI   800-424-1616
555 New Jersey Ave., NW   202-219-1556
Washington, DC 20208-5641   Fax: 202-219-1321
www.ed.gov/offices/OERI

The Education Information Branch staff specialists can provide information on topics such as early childhood education, elementary and secondary education, higher education, adult and vocational education, education finance, longitudinal statistical studies, and special education. They have publications and reports, many of which are free. They can answer such questions as:

1) What statistics are there on the number of students who receive loans, grants, and work/study assistance from state sources?
2) What are the statistics on private postsecondary education, such as enrollment, earned degrees conferred, and full and part-time faculty members and their salaries?
3) What information is available on how to choose a school for a child and what factors make a school a good one?
4) How can parents help their children become better readers?
5) What are the enrollment outcomes for recent master's and bachelor's degree recipients?

* Fishery Statistics Division

NOAA Fisheries Headquarters
1335 East-West Highway, SSMC3   301-713-2328
Silver Spring, MD 20910   Fax: 301-713-4137
www.nmfs.noaa.gov

The Fisheries Statistics Division publishes statistical bulletins on marine recreational fishing and commercial fishing, and on the manufacture and commerce of fishery products. This Division has several annual and biannual reports available. They can answer such questions as:
1) How many fish were imported in a year, and what kind?
2) What is the most popular fish to export?
3) What kinds of fish are frozen?
4) What statistics exist on processed fish?
5) How many fish were caught by weekend fishermen?

* Clearinghouse on Health Indexes

National Center for Health Statistics
U.S. Department of Health and Human Services
Public Health Service
6525 Belcrest Rd.
Hyattsville, MD 20782   301-436-8500
www.cdc.gov/nchs/

The National Center for Health Statistics provides information assistance in the development of health measures to health researchers, administrators, and planners. The Clearinghouse's definition of a health index is a measure that summarizes data from two or more components and purports to reflect the health status of an individual or defined group. Services provided to users include annotated bibliographies and reference and referral service. A publications catalogue is available, with items ranging in price from free to $20. They can answer such questions as:
1) What are the characteristics of persons with and without health care coverage?
2) What type of health care is generally provided to adolescents?
3) What method of contraception is used most frequently in the U.S.?
4) What data exists on the current living arrangements of women of childbearing ages in the U.S.?
5) What survey data exists on the firearm mortality rate among children?

* United States International Trade Commission

Office of Industries
500 E St., SW   202-205-3296
Washington, DC 20436   Fax: 202-205-3161
www.usitc.gov/

The Office of Industries at the U.S. International Trade Commission has experts assigned to every commodity imported into the U.S. These experts are responsible for investigation of the customs laws of the United States and foreign countries, the volume of imports in comparison with domestic production, the effects relating to competition of foreign industries, and all other factors affecting competition between articles of the U.S. and imported articles. They are knowledgeable about the domestic and foreign industry, and have statistical and factual information. They also have information regarding the tariff schedules. There is no charge for this information. They can answer such questions as:
1) What is the rate of duty for a product from a particular country?
2) What is the rate of import-export, the size of the market, and the major producers of women's sweaters?
3) How much of a product is exported and what is the size of the potential market for that product?
4) What happens if someone suspects an imported article is being subsidized or sold at less then fair value?
5) What can a company do if they feel they are being unfairly affected by import trade?

* Justice Statistics Clearinghouse

Bureau of Justice Statistics
U.S. Department of Justice
Box 6000   800-732-3277
Rockville, MD 20849   Fax: 301-251-5212
Email: askncjrs@ncjrs.org
www.ncjrs.org

The Bureau of Justice Statistics (BJS) supports this Clearinghouse for those seeking crime and criminal justice data. In addition to distributing BJS publications, the Clearinghouse responds to statistics requests by offering document database searches, statistics information packages, referrals, and other related products and services. They can answer such questions as:
1) What is the annual national estimate of crime against persons and households?
2) What are the characteristics of victims?
3) In what ways are juveniles handled differently from adults in the criminal justice system?
4) How prevalent is organized crime?
5) What is the recidivism rate, and when criminals are rearrested, with what crimes are they normally charged?

* Labor Statistics Clearinghouse

Office of Publications
Bureau of Labor Statistics
U.S. Department of Labor
2 Massachusetts Ave., NE, Room 2863   202-606-7828
Washington, DC 20212   Fax: 202-606-7890
Email: labstat.helpdesk@ bls.gov
http://stats.bls.gov

The Bureau of Labor Statistics (BLS) is the principal data-gathering agency of the federal government in the field of labor economics. The Bureau collects, processes, analyzes, and disseminates data relating to employment, unemployment, and other characteristics of the labor force; prices and consumer expenditures; wages, other worker compensation, and industrial relations; productivity; economic growth and employment projections; and occupational safety and health. This office can also provide you with a release schedule for BLS major economic indicators and the recorded message number. BLS can refer you to experts within the Bureau who can answer your specific question, provide you with historical information, and refer you to tables and charts for data. The BLS has publications, periodicals, magnetic tapes, diskettes, and more for sale. They can answer questions such as:
1) What are the employment statistics and the outlook for a particular occupation?
2) What is the unemployment rate for a state?
3) What is the current wage for a word processor in Seattle, and what benefits are normally offered with such a position?
4) What is the employment projection for a specific job?
5) What is the consumer/producer price index, and how has it changed over time?

I Wanna Change My Name

Matthew Lesko, Information USA, Inc., 12081 Nebel Street, Rockville, MD 20852 • 1-800-955-7693 • www.lesko.com

I Wanna Change My Name

What's in a name anyway? A lot for many people. If you are saddled with Michael Michael or Kelly Kelly, or your rotten ex-husband's name, don't feel like it's got to be yours forever. You can become James, Brandon, Tiffany, or even Countess Regina. Name changes are often for religious purposes, or to have a name which reflects a person's personal beliefs or interests. Many naturalized citizens may change their names to help make English pronunciations easier.

All you need to do is fill out a simple form and pay a fee, usually ranging from $35-$200. This is all done through your county probate court, where you must be a resident of the county for at least one year. The form asks for your current name, address, and other identifying information, as well as the name you would like to have and the reason for the change. The exact rules vary from county to county, but basically the courts all follow the same pattern. Some require that you attend a hearing in front of a magistrate to explain your reasons for changing your name. Your name change needs to be posted locally for four to six weeks to see if anyone objects. You must also prove that the name change is not to dodge creditors or to run from your criminal history, or for other questionable purposes. Denial for name changes are rare. Most frequently a denial is when one parent tries to change the name of a child and the ex-spouse objects. If you have met all the requirements, then the court will legally change your name. For those going through a divorce, you can easily add your name change request in conjunction with your divorce proceedings.

The next order of business for you is to get all your legal records in order. You must let the Social Security Administration know about your new name so they can keep your earning records in order. You can go to the local Social Security Administration office to complete the form, or you can call the Social Security hotline at 800-772-1213. Make sure your credit cards and bank accounts are changed to your new name. Even your employer needs to know, so your paycheck and retirement accounts can be changed. If you have a will, this may be a good time to update it as well. All that is left is for you to get your friends and family to start calling you by your new legal name.

Matthew Lesko, Information USA, Inc., 12081 Nebel Street, Rockville, MD 20852 • 1-800-955-7693 • www.lesko.com

Index

Index

Index

Index

M

Index

O

Index

Index

Index

Writer's organizations, 108